Merriam-Webster's French-English Dictionary

Merriam-Webster's French-English Dictionary

MERRIAM-WEBSTER, INCORPORATED
Springfield, Massachusetts, U.S.A.

A GENUINE MERRIAM-WEBSTER

The name *Webster* alone is no guarantee of excellence. It is used by a number of publishers and may serve mainly to mislead an unwary buyer.

Merriam-Webster™ is the name you should look for when you consider the purchase of dictionaries or other fine reference books. It carries the reputation of a company that has been publishing since 1831 and is your assurance of quality and authority.

ISBN- 978-0-87779-917-7

MADE IN THE UNITED STATES OF AMERICA

19TH PRINTING QUAD GRAPHICS MARTINSBURG WV SEPTEMBER

Contents

Preface	7a
Explanatory Notes	9a
French Grammar	22a
Conjugation of French Verbs	40a
Abbreviations in this Work	59a
Pronunciation Symbols	60a
French–English Dictionary	1
English–French Dictionary	367
Common French Abbreviations	799
French Numbers	803

Preface

MERRIAM-WEBSTER'S FRENCH-ENGLISH DICTIONARY is a completely new dictionary designed to meet the needs of English and French speakers throughout the world. It is intended for language learners, teachers, office workers, tourists, business travelers—anyone who needs to communicate effectively in the French and English languages as they are spoken and written today.

This dictionary provides up-to-date coverage of French words and phrases as they are spoken in France and in other European countries, and special care has been taken to include the unique terminology of French-speaking Canada as well. The English vocabulary and spellings included here reflect North American usage and are primarily those of American English, but British terms and spellings commonly used in Canada are also included.

All of this material is presented in a format that is based firmly upon, and in many ways is similar to, the traditional styling found in other Merriam-Webster dictionaries. The reader who is familiar with Merriam-Webster dictionaries will immediately recognize the style, with its emphasis on clarity and concision of the information, precise discrimination of senses, and the frequent inclusion of example phrases to illustrate idiomatic usage. Also included are pronunciations (in the International Phonetic Alphabet) of the entered words in both languages, extensive coverage of French irregular verbs, a section on basic French grammar, a table of the most common French abbreviations, and a detailed Explanatory Notes section designed to assist readers in the use of this book.

Merriam-Webster's French-English Dictionary represents the combined efforts of many members of the Merriam-Webster Editorial Department, along with the help of consultants outside the company. The primary defining work was done by Anne Eason and Peter A. Sokolowski, with the assistance of Jocelyn Woods; early contributions to the text were also submitted by Jonathan Brook, Ronald Giguère, Lynn A. Prince, and Anna K. Sandström. Anne Eason, Seán O'Mannion-Espejo, and Peter A.

Sokolowski were responsible for preparing the front and back matter in the book. Joanne M. Despres, Ph.D. provided the pronunciations, assisted by Emily B. Arsenault, Deanna M. Chiasson, Kory L. Stamper, and Karen L. Wilkinson. The coordination of typesetting and other production steps was done by Thomas F. Pitoniak, Ph.D., who also offered many helpful suggestions regarding content and format. Proofreading was carried out by Joanne M. Despres, Anne Eason, Seán O'Mannion-Espejo, Thomas F. Pitoniak, Peter A. Sokolowski, Karen L. Wilkinson, and Jocelyn D. Woods. Georgette B. Boucher provided invaluable typing assistance. Madeline L. Novak provided guidance on typographic matters. John M. Morse was responsible for the conception of this book as well as for numerous ideas and continued support along the way.

Eileen M. Haraty
Editor

Explanatory Notes

Entries

1. Main Entries

A boldface letter, word, or phrase appearing flush with the left-hand margin of each column of type is a main entry or entry word. The main entry may consist of letters set solid, of letters joined by a punctuation mark (as a hyphen), or of letters separated by a space:

collant[1], **-lante** . . . *adj* . . .

eye–opener . . . *n* . . .

walk out *vi* . . .

The main entry, together with the material that follows it on the same line and succeeding indented lines, constitutes a dictionary entry.

2. Order of Main Entries

The main entries follow one another in alphabetical order letter by letter without regard to intervening spaces or hyphens; for example, *shake-up* follows *shaker.*

Homographs (words with the same spelling) having different parts of speech are given separate dictionary entries. These entries are distinguished by superscript numerals following the entry word:

mauvais[1] . . . *adv* . . .

mauvais[2], **-vaise** *adj* . . .

salt[1] . . . *vt* . . .

salt[2] *adj* . . .

salt[3] *n* . . .

Numbered homograph entries are listed in the following order: verb, adverb, adjective, noun, conjunction, preposition, pronoun, interjection, article.

Homographs having the same part of speech are normally included at the same dictionary entry, without regard to their different semantic origins. On the English-to-French side, however, separate entries are made if the homographs have distinct pronunciations or if homographic verbs have distinct inflected forms.

3. Guide Words

A pair of guide words is printed at the top of each page, indicating the first and last main entries that appear on that page:

velours • vérifiable

4. Variants

When a main entry is followed by the word *or* and another spelling, the two spellings are variants. Both are standard, and either one may be used according to personal inclination:

jailer *or* **jailor** . . . *n* . . .

lis *or* **lys** . . . *nms & pl* . . .

Occasionally, a variant spelling is used only for a particular sense of a word. In these cases, the variant spelling is listed after the sense number of the sense to which it pertains:

flier . . . *n* . . . **2** *or* **flyer** . . .

Sometimes the entry word is used interchangeably with a longer phrase containing the entry word. For the purposes of this dictionary, such phrases are considered variants of the headword:

bunk[2] *n* **1** *or* **bunk bed** . . .

risée . . . *nf or* **objet de risée** . . .

ward[1] . . . *vt or* **to ward off** . . .

Variant wordings of boldface phrases may also be shown:

table . . . *nf* . . . **4 table de chevet** *or* **table de nuit** . . .

abattre . . . *vt* . . . **5 abattre ses cartes** *or* **abattre son jeu** . . .

5. Run-On Entries

A main entry may be followed by a derivative word in a different part of speech. This is a run-on entry. It is introduced by a boldface dash and has a functional label. It is not defined, however, since its equivalent can be readily derived by adding the corresponding foreign-language suffix to the term or terms used to define the entry word:

illegal . . . *adj* : illégal **— illegally** *adv*

(the French adverb is *illégalement*)

bureaucratie . . . *nf* : bureaucracy **— bureaucratique** . . . *adj*

(the English adjective is *bureaucratic*)

On the French-to-English side of the book, reflexive verbs are sometimes run on undefined:

appauvrir . . . *vt* : to impoverish **— s'appauvrir** *vr*

The absence of a definition indicates that *s'appauvrir* has the simple reflexive meaning "to become impoverished" or "to impoverish oneself."

6. Bold Notes

A main entry may be followed by one or more phrases containing the entry word or an inflected form of it. These are bold notes. Each bold note is defined at its own numbered sense:

abeille . . . *nf* **1** : bee, honeybee **2 abeille mâle** : drone

hold¹ . . . *vi* . . . **3 to hold forth** : . . . **4 to hold to** : . . .

If the bold note consists only of the entry word and a single preposition, the entry word is represented by a boldface swung dash **~**.

> **pente** . . . *nf* **1** : slope **2 en ~** : sloping

The same bold note phrase may appear at two or more senses if it has more than one distinct meaning:

> **affaire** . . . *nf* . . . **5 affaires** *nfpl* : possessions, belongings **6 affaires** *nfpl* : business <homme d'affaires : businessman> . . .

Pronunciation

Pronunciation of Entry Words

The matter between a pair of brackets [ ] following the entry word indicates the pronunciation. The symbols used are from the International Phonetic Alphabet and are explained in the Pronunciation Symbols chart on page 60a.

The presence of variant pronunciations indicates that not all educated speakers pronounce words the same way. A second-place variant is not to be regarded as less acceptable than the pronunciation that is given first. It may, in fact, be used by as many educated speakers as the first variant, but the requirements of the printed page are such that one must precede the other:

> **often** ['ɔfən, 'ɔftən] . . .

When a compound word has less than a full pronunciation, the missing part is to be supplied from the pronunciation at the entry for the unpronounced element of the compound:

> **gamma ray** ['gæmə] . . .
>
> **ray** ['reɪ] . . .

In general, no pronunciation is indicated for open compounds consisting of two or more English words that are main entries at their own alphabetical place:

> **smoke detector** . . .
>
> **smoke**[1] ['smok] . . .
>
> **detector** [dɪ'tɛktər] . . .

Only the first entry in a series of numbered homographs is given a pronunciation if their pronunciations are the same:

dab[1] ['dæb] *vt* . . .

dab[2] *n* . . .

On the English-to-French side, no pronunciation is shown for principal parts of verbs that are formed by regular suffixation, nor for most derivative adverbs formed by the suffix *-ly*.

The aspirate pronunciation of the letter *h* in French is indicated by a symbol ['] preceding the pronunciation of the headword:

habile [abil]

hasard ['azar]

Functional Labels

An italic label indicating a part of speech or some other functional classification follows the pronunciation or, if no pronunciation is given, the main entry. The parts of speech are indicated as follows:

mendier . . . *v* . . .

maintenant . . . *adv* . . .

daily[2] *adj* . . .

jackal . . . *n* . . .

and . . . *conj* . . .

par . . . *prep* . . .

neither[3] *pron* . . .

allô . . . *interj* . . .

le . . . *art*

Verbs that are intransitive are labelled *vi;* verbs that are transitive are labelled *vt.* Entries for verbs that are both transitive and intransitive are labelled *v,* with the labels *vi* and *vt* serving to introduce any transitive and intransitive subdivisions:

necessitate . . . *vt* **-tated; -tating** : nécessiter, exiger

déborder . . . *vi* : to overflow

satisfy . . . *v* **-fied; -fying** *vt* . . . — *vi* . . .

Two other labels are used to indicate functional classifications of verbs: *v aux* (auxiliary verb) and *v impers* (impersonal verb).

may . . . *v aux, past* **might** . . .

aller[1] . . . *vi* . . . — *v aux* : to be going to, to be about to . . . — *v impers* **1** **en ~** : to happen, to go . . .

Gender Labels

In French-to-English noun entries, the gender of the entry word is indicated by an italic *m* (masculine), *f* (feminine), or *mf* (masculine or feminine), immediately following the functional label:

magnésium . . . *nm* . . .

galaxie . . . *nf* . . .

touriste . . . *nmf* . . .

If both the masculine and feminine forms are shown for a noun referring to a person, the label is simply *n*:

directeur[2], **-trice** *n* . . .

French noun equivalents of English entry words are also labeled for gender:

amnesia . . . *n* : amnésie *f*
earache . . . *n* : mal *m* d'oreille

gamekeeper . . . *n* : garde-chasse *m*

Inflected Forms

1. Nouns

The plurals of nouns are shown in this dictionary when they are irregular, when plural suffixation brings about a change in the spelling of the root word, when an English noun ends in a consonant plus *-o* or in *-ey,* when an English noun ends in *-oo,* when an English noun is a compound that pluralizes any element but the last, when a French noun is a hyphenated compound, when a noun has variant plurals, or whenever the dictionary user might have reasonable doubts regarding the spelling of a plural:

tooth . . . *n, pl* **teeth** . . .

madame . . . *nf, pl* **mesdames** . . .

adieu . . . *nm, pl* **adieux** . . .

potato . . . *n, pl* **-toes** . . .

abbey . . . *n, pl* **-beys** . . .

cuckoo[2] *n, pl* **-oos** . . .

brother–in–law . . . *n, pl* **brothers–in–law** . . .

court–circuit . . . *nm, pl* **courts–circuits** . . .

quail[2] *n, pl* **quail** *or* **quails** . . .

récital . . . *nm, pl* **-tals** . . .

Cutback inflected forms are used for most multisyllabic nouns on the English-to-French side, regardless of the number of syllables. On the French-to-English side, cutback inflections are given for nouns that have three or more syllables; plurals for shorter words are written out in full:

shampoo[2] *n, pl* **-poos** . . .

calamity . . . *n, pl* **-ties** . . .

mouse . . . *n, pl* **mice** . . .

terminal[2] *nm, pl* **-naux** . . .

caillou . . . *nm, pl* **cailloux** . . .

If only the masculine gender form has a plural which is irregular, that plural form will be given with the appropriate label:

jumeau, -melle . . . *adj & n, mpl* **jumeaux** : twin

The plurals of nouns are usually not shown when the base word is unchanged by the addition of the regular *-s* plural or when the noun is unlikely to occur in the plural:

apple . . . *n* : pomme *f*

anglais[2] *nm* : English (language)

Nouns that are plural in form and that regularly occur in plural constructions are labeled *npl* (for English nouns), *nmpl* (for French masculine nouns), or *nfpl* (for French feminine nouns):

knickers . . . *npl* . . .

parages . . . *nmpl* . . .

tenailles . . . *nfpl* . . .

Entry words that are unchanged in the plural are labeled *ns & pl* (for English nouns), *nms & pl* (for French masculine nouns), *nfs & pl* (for French feminine nouns), and *nmfs & pl* (for French gender-variable nouns):

deer . . . *ns & pl* . . .

perdrix . . . *nfs & pl* . . .

débours . . . *nms & pl* . . .

après-midi . . . *nmfs & pl* . . .

2. Verbs

ENGLISH VERBS

The principal parts of verbs are shown in English-to-French entries when they are irregular, when suffixation brings about a change in spelling of the root word, when the verb ends in *-ey,* or when there are variant inflected forms:

break[1] . . . *v* **broke** . . . ; **broken** . . . ; **breaking** . . .

drag[1] . . . *v* **dragged; dragging** . . .

imagine . . . *vt* **-ined; -ining** . . .

monkey[1] . . . *vi* **-keyed; -keying** . . .

label[1] . . . *vt* **-beled** *or* **-belled; -beling** *or* **-belling** . . .

Cutback inflected forms are usually used when the verb has two or more syllables:

multiply . . . *v* **-plied; -plying** . . .

bevel[1]. . . *vt* **-eled** *or* **-elled; -eling** *or* **-elling** . . .

forgo *or* **forego** . . . *vt* **-went** . . . ; **-gone** . . . ; **-going** . . .

commit . . . *vt* **-mitted; -mitting** . . .

The principal parts of an English verb are usually not shown when they are regular and the root word is unchanged by suffixation.

delay[1] . . . *vt*

pack[1] . . . *vt*

FRENCH VERBS

The conjugations of French verbs are not shown at the entry but are included in the Conjugation of French Verbs section beginning on page 40a. Regular verbs ending in *-er* or *-ir* have no cross-reference number at their entries, and their conjugations are shown at the beginning of that section. Entries for irregular French verbs are cross-referenced by number to the model conjugations appearing in the Conjugation of French Verbs section:

arranger {17} *vt* . . .

joindre {50} *vt* . . .

Entries for frequently used irregular forms of French verbs are cross-referenced to the corresponding infinitive:

tenu[1] . . . *pp* → **tenir**

joigne . . . , *etc.* → **joindre**

Irregular composite verbs, such as *retenir* and *rejoindre*, do not have cross-referenced forms entered in the dictionary, since their conjugations are based upon the corresponding verbal root.

Adverbs and Adjectives

The comparative and superlative forms of English adjective and adverb main entries are shown when suffixation brings about a change in spelling of the root word, when the inflection is irregular, and when there are variant inflected forms:

fat . . . *adj* **fatter; fattest** . . .

well[2] *adv* **better** . . . ; **best** . . .

evil[1] . . . *adj* **eviler** *or* **eviller; evilest** *or* **evillest** . . .

The superlative forms of adjectives and adverbs of two or more syllables are usually cut back; the superlative is shown in full, however, when it is desirable to indicate the pronunciation of the inflected form:

gaudy . . . *adj* **gaudier; -est** . . .

early[1] . . . *adv* **earlier; -est** . . .

secure[1] . . . *adj* **securer; -est** . . .

but

young[1] . . . *adj* **younger** [ˈjəŋgər;]; **youngest** [ˈjəŋgəst] . . .

The absence of the comparative form at an adjective entry indicates that there is no evidence of its use:

mere . . . *adj, superlative* **merest** . . .

The comparative and superlative forms of adjectives and adverbs are usually not shown when the base word is unchanged by suffixation.

quiet[2] *adj* **1** . . .

Usage

1. Usage Labels

The two types of usage labels in this dictionary address a word's regional derivation and register. Words that are limited in use to France, French-speaking Canada, Belgium, Switzerland, or English-speaking Canada are given labels indicating the countries in which they are most commonly used:

bachoter . . . *vi France* : to cram . . .

cocotte . . . *nf* . . . **2** *Can* : pinecone . . .

auditoire . . . *nm* . . . **2** *Bel & Switz* : auditorium

furnace . . . *n* : fourneau *m,* fournaise *f Can*

bloke . . . *n Brit* : type *m*

The following regional labels are used in this book: *Bel* (Belgium), *Brit* (Great Britain and English-speaking Canada), *Can* (French-speaking Canada), *France, Switz* (Switzerland).

A number of French words are given a *fam* (familiar) label as well, indicating that these words are suitable for informal contexts but would not normally be used in formal writing or speaking. The stylistic labels *sometimes offensive* or *usu vulgar* are added for a word which is thought to be vulgar or offensive in many contexts but whose widespread use justifies its inclusion in this book. These labels are intended to warn the reader that the word in question may be inappropriate in polite conversation.

2. Usage Notes

Definitions are sometimes preceded by parenthetical usage notes that give supplementary semantic information:

> **not** . . . *adv* **1** (*used to form a negative*) **:** . . .
>
> **when**[2] *conj* **1** (*referring to a particular time*)**:** . . .
>
> **se** . . . *pron* **1** (*used with reflexive verbs*) **:** . . . **2** (*used to indicate reciprocity*) **:** . . .
>
> **si**[1] . . . *adv* . . . **2** (*used to contradict a negative statement or question*) **:** . . .

Additional semantic orientation is also occasionally given in the form of parenthetical notes appearing within the definition:

> **calibrate** . . . *vt* . . . **:** calibrer (une arme, etc.), étalonner (une balance)
>
> **paille** . . . *nf* . . . **2 :** (drinking) straw

Occasionally a usage note is used in place of a definition. This is usually done when the entry word has no single foreign-language equivalent. Usage notes of this type will be accompanied by an example or examples of common use:

> **shall** . . . *v aux* . . . **1** (*used to express a command*) <you shall do as I say : vous ferez comme je vous dis> . . .

3. Illustrations of Usage

Definitions are sometimes followed by verbal illustrations that show a typical use of the word in context or a common idiomatic usage. These verbal illustrations include a translation and are enclosed in angle brackets:

> **ici** . . . *adv* **1 :** here <ici et là : here and there> <par ici : this way> . . .
>
> **make**[1] . . . *vt* . . . **8** EARN **:** gagner <to make a living : gagner sa vie> . . .

Sense Division

A boldface colon is used to introduce a definition:

> **failing**[1] . . . *n* **:** défaut *m*

Boldface Arabic numerals separate the senses of a word that has more than one sense:

> **maîtriser** . . . *vt* **1** : to master **2** : to control, to restrain . . .

Whenever some information (such as a synonym, a boldface word or phrase, a usage note, a cross-reference, or a label) follows a sense number, it applies only to that specific numbered sense and not to any other boldface numbered senses:

> **abord** . . . *nm* **1** ACCÈS : . . .
>
> **pile**[1] . . . *vi* **1** *or* **to pile up** : . . .
>
> **caoutchouc** . . . *nm* . . . **2 caoutchoucs** *nmpl* : . . .
>
> **extension** . . . *n* . . . **5 extension cord** : . . .
>
> **myself** . . . *pron* **1** (*used reflexively*) : . . .
>
> **pike** . . . *n* . . . **3** → **turnpike**
>
> **ambitionner** . . . *vt* . . . **2** *Can* : . . .

Cross-References

Three different kinds of cross-references are used in this dictionary: synonymous, cognate, and inflectional. In each instance the cross-reference is readily recognized by the boldface arrow following the entry word.

Synonymous and cognate cross-references indicate that a definition at the entry cross-referred to can be substituted for the entry word:

> **cable**[2] . . . **2** → **cablegram**
>
> **sceptic** . . . → **skeptic**

An inflectional cross-reference is used to identify the entry word as an inflected form of another word (as a noun or verb):

> **aura**[1] . . . , etc. → **avoir**
>
> **mice** → **mouse**

Synonyms

At many entries or senses in this book, a synonym in small capital letters is provided before the boldface colon and the following defining text. These synonyms are all main entries or bold notes elsewhere in the book. They serve as a helpful guide to the meaning of the entry or sense and also give the reader an additional term that might be substituted in a similar context. On the English-to-French side synonyms are particularly abundant, since special care has been taken to guide the English speaker—by means of synonyms, verbal illustrations, or usage notes—to the meaning of the French terms at each sense of a multisense entry.

croiser . . . **3** RENCONTRER **:** . . .

demand[2] . . . **2** CLAIM **:** . . .

French Grammar

Accents and Diacritics

French makes use of accents and diacritics to indicate either the phonetic value of a given letter, or to distinguish one word from another which has the same pronunciation and would otherwise share the same spelling. There are three types of accents:

> ***The acute accent*** /´/ ordinarily indicates closed pronunciation.
>
> ***The grave accent*** /`/ ordinarily indicates open pronunciation.
>
> ***The circumflex*** /ˆ/ ordinarily indicates open pronunciation.

In addition to accents, French makes use of the ***diaeresis*** /¨/ which, as in English, indicates that the vowel preceding the marked letter is pronounced separately: *maïs* [mais] (corn) is thus pronounced differently from *mais* [mɛ] (but, however).

> The ***cedilla*** /¸/ indicates soft pronunciation of a *c* /s/ which precedes an *a, o,* or *u* (*ça, rançon, aperçu*).

Diacritics in the French language do not affect word stress.

Capitalization

In French, unlike English, the following words are usually not capitalized:

- Names of days, months, languages, and most religions (*jeudi, octobre, français, judaïsme*).
- Names of holidays composed of two or more words. Unlike English, in French only the distinguishing word and any preceding adjectives are capitalized (*la fête du Travail,* Labor Day; *mercredi des Cendres,* Ash Wednesday).

- French adjectives or nouns derived from proper nouns (*l'équipe sénégalaise, le marxisme*), except for nouns of geographic or national identity, which are usually capitalized (*les Antillais, une Vietnamienne*).

Articles

1. Definite Article

French has three forms of the definite article: *le* (masculine singular), *la* (feminine singular), and the plural article, *les,* which does not distinguish for gender. *Le* and *la* contract to *l'* when they precede a word beginning with a vowel sound (*l'arbre, l'heure*). In some instances an initial *h,* although mute, is considered to be aspirate, in which case the article does not contract (*le héros*). The definite article agrees in gender and number with the noun that follows it (*le bâtiment,* the building; *la rue,* the street; *les bâtiments,* the buildings; *les rues,* the streets).

Whenever the plural article *les* or the singular masculine article *le* immediately follows either *de* or *à,* the two combine to form the contractions *des, aux, du,* and *au* respectively (*les jouets des enfants,* the children's toys; *la maison aux fenêtres larges,* the house with the wide windows; *le cabinet du médecin,* the doctor's office; *elles sont allées au café,* they went to the café). However, if a singular article of either gender is preceded by *de* or *à* and followed by a word with an initial vowel sound, the article becomes *l'* (*le nom de l'église,* the name of the church; *arriver à l'heure,* to arrive on time). The use of *le, la,* and *les* in French corresponds largely to the use of *the* in English; some exceptions are noted below.

The definite article is used:

- With certain geographical regions, including countries and continents (*l'Afrique,* Africa; *le Canada,* Canada; *la Nouvelle-Écosse,* Nova Scotia).
- With languages, except when the language is preceded by *en* or *parler* (*Patti comprend le français,* Patti understands French; *Joseph parle hongrois,* Joseph speaks Hungarian; *c'est en japonais,* it's in Japanese).

- With abstract nouns (*il adore les chiens,* he loves dogs; *l'hiver est long,* winter is long; *le petit déjeuner est inclus,* breakfast is included).
- With body parts (*j'ai mal au bras,* my arm hurts; *elle se brosse les dents,* she's brushing her teeth).

2. Indefinite Article

French has three forms of the indefinite article: *un* (masculine singular), *une* (feminine singular), and the plural article *des,* which is used for both genders. The indefinite article agrees in number and gender with the noun it precedes (*une table,* a table; *un couteau,* a knife; *des verres,* some glasses).

- The use of *un, une,* and *des* in French corresponds largely to the use of *a, an,* and *some* in English (*un oiseau,* a bird; *une poupée,* a doll; *des oranges,* oranges, some oranges). The plural article *des* becomes *de* or *d'* when immediately followed by an adjective (*des amis,* friends; *de bons amis,* good friends). When the adjective begins with a vowel sound, then the article becomes *d'* (*d'énormes quantités,* enormous quantities).
- In a negative statement, the indefinite article is replaced with *de* or, when preceding a word with an initial vowel sound, *d'* (*Marc n'a pas de voiture,* Marc doesn't have a car; *il n'y a plus d'eau,* there is no more water). This rule does not apply to negative statements with the verb *être* (*ce livre n'est pas un roman,* this book is not a novel).

3. Partitive Article

French makes use of the partitive article to indicate that the following noun represents part of an implied, and uncountable, whole. The partitive is formed by *de* plus the definite article, contracting where applicable to *du, de la, de l',* or *des* (*elle écoute de la musique,* she listens to music; *pomper de l'essence,* to pump gas).

Nouns

1. Gender

Nouns in French are either masculine or feminine. Although a noun's gender can be arbitrary and must be learned as one acquires vocabulary, it can often be determined according to the following guidelines:

- Nouns ending in *-age, -èle, -exe, -isme, -oir, -phone,* and *-scope* are usually masculine (*un visage, un modèle, le sexe, le mysticisme, le miroir, un téléphone, un magnétoscope*).
- Nouns deriving from verbs will often signal masculine gender with the ending *-eur* or *-ant*, or feminine gender with the ending *-euse* or *-ante* (*un chanteur, la gagnante*).
- Nouns ending in *-ade, -ance, -ence, -esse, -ette, -ie, -ise, -sion, -té, -tion, -trice, -tude* or *-ure* are usually feminine (*une croisade, la chance, une essence, la jeunesse, une vedette, la patrie, une crise, une décision, l'université, une abstraction, l'empératrice, la similitude, une aventure*).

Most nouns referring to people or animals agree in gender with the subject (*un homme, une femme; le frère, la sœur; le cheval, la jument*). However, some nouns referring to people, including those ending in *-ique* and *-iste,* use the same form for both sexes (*un artiste, une artiste; un diabétique, une diabétique*).

Many names of animals exist in only one gender form (*la souris, le crapaud,* etc.). In these instances, the adjectives *mâle* and *femelle* are sometimes used to distinguish between males and females (*une souris mâle,* a male mouse).

2. Pluralization

Plurals of French nouns are formed as follows:

- As in English, most French nouns are pluralized by adding *-s* (*un médecin, des médecins; l'arbre, les arbres*).
- Nouns ending in *-au* or *-eu* are ordinarily pluralized by adding a final *-x* (*un tuyau, des tuyaux; le feu, les feux*).

- Nouns ending in *-al* are often pluralized by changing the ending to *-aux* (*un animal, des animaux*).
- Singular nouns which end in *-s, -x,* or *-z* do not change in the plural (*un matelas, deux matelas; la croix, les croix; un gaz, des gaz*).

Adjectives

1. Gender and Number

Most adjectives agree in gender and number with the nouns or pronouns they modify (*un poète espagnol, des poètes espagnols; elle est espagnole, elles sont espagnoles*). Many adjectives ending in *-e* (*riche*) and most of those ending in *-ble, -ique,* and *-iste* (*probable, fantastique, altruiste*) vary only for number.

Many masculine adjectives add a final *-e* to form the feminine (*petit* → *petite, français* → *française*). In some cases, the feminine is formed by modifying the final syllable, according to the following patterns:

-anc → *-anche* (*franc* → *franche*)

-el → *-elle* (*actuel* → *actuelle*)

-en → *-enne* (*moyen* → *moyenne*)

-er → *-ère* (*passager* → *passagère*)

-eur → *-euse* (*frondeur* → *frondeuse*)

-eux → *-euse* (*respectueux* → *respectueuse*)

-if → *-ive* (*tardif* → *tardive*)

-il → *-ille* (*gentil* → *gentille*)

Some masculine adjectives, including *beau, fou, nouveau,* and *vieux,* modify their ending when immediately followed by a word which begins with a vowel sound:

beau → *bel* (*un bel arbre,* a beautiful tree)

fou → *fol* (*un fol appétit,* a tremendous appetite)

nouveau → *nouvel* (*un nouvel album,* a new album)

vieux → *vieil* (*un vieil ami,* an old friend)

Adjectives of this type ordinarily form the feminine by adding *-le* to these modified masculine forms:

beau → *bel* → *belle*

vieux → *vieil* → *vieille*

2. Pluralization

Plurals of French adjectives are formed as follows:

- Most adjectives are pluralized by adding *-s* (*de bons livres,* some good books; *des yeux bleus,* blue eyes).
- Masculine adjectives ending in *-au* are ordinarily pluralized by adding a final *-x* (*les beaux arts,* the fine arts; *des mots nouveaux,* new words).
- Masculine adjectives ending in *-al* are often pluralized by changing the ending to *-aux* (*les moyens normaux,* the normal means).

3. Position

Unlike English, most descriptive adjectives in French follow the nouns they modify (*une chose utile, un écrivain célèbre*). Common exceptions include *autre, beau, bon, chaque, faux, gros, jeune, joli, nouveau, petit,* and *vieux,* which usually appear before the noun (*une belle maison, une vieille dame*).

Some adjectives change meaning depending on whether they occur before or after the noun: *un pauvre enfant,* a poor (pitiable) child, *un enfant pauvre,* a poor (not rich) child; *un grand homme,* a great man, *un homme grand,* a tall man; *mes chers amis,* my dear friends; *un ordinateur cher,* an expensive computer.

4. Comparative and Superlative Forms

The comparative of French adjectives is generally rendered as *plus . . . que* (more . . . than) or *moins . . . que* (less . . . than): *je suis plus grande que lui,* I'm taller than he; *ils sont moins intelligents que toi,* they're less intelligent than you.

The superlative of French adjectives usually follows the formula: (definite article + noun) + definite article + *plus/moins* + adjective (*elle est l'étudiante la plus travailleuse,* she is the hardest-working student; *il est le moins connu,* he's the least well-known; *les voitures les plus rapides,* the fastest cars).

Like their English counterparts *good* and *bad,* the adjectives *bon* and *mauvais* have irregular comparative and superlative forms:

Positive	**Comparative**	**Superlative**
c'est **bon,** it is good	*c'est* ***meilleur*** *que les autres,* it is better than the rest	*c'est* ***le meilleur*** *de tous,* it is the best (one) of all
c'est ***mauvais,*** it is bad	*c'est* ***pire*** *que les autres,* it is worse than the rest	*c'est* ***le pire*** *de tous,* it is the worst (one) of all

The absolute superlative is most often formed by placing *très,* or other adverbs such as *fort, extrêmement,* etc., before the adjective (*elle est très sympathique,* she is very nice; *c'est fort probable,* it is quite likely).

Adverbs

French adverbs are often formed by adding the adverbial suffix *-ment* to an adjective (*facile → facilement, prétendu → prétendument*). If the masculine form of an adjective ends with a consonant, the suffix is normally added to the feminine form (*ouvert → ouverte → ouvertement*). Adjectives whose masculine form ends in *-ant* or *-ent* will usually form the adverb by replacing this ending with *-amment* or *-emment* (*indépendant → indépendamment, prudent → prudemment*). A few adjectives add the acute accent to the final *e* to form the adverb (*énorme → énormément, expresse → expressément*).

As in English, there are many French adverbs that do not stem from an adjective (*assez,* enough; *bien,* well; *déjà,* already; *très,* very, etc.).

Pronouns

1. Personal (Subject) Pronouns

The personal pronouns in French are:

Person	Singular		Plural	
FIRST	**je**	I	**nous**	we
SECOND	**tu**	you (familiar)	**vous**	you[1]
	vous	you (formal)	**vous**	you[1]
THIRD	**il**	he	**ils,**	they
	elle	she	**elles**	
	on	one (*also* they, someone, you, we, people)		

[1] The pronoun *vous* acts as the plural for both the familiar *tu* and the formal *vous.*

FAMILIAR VS. FORMAL

The second person personal pronouns exist in both familiar and formal forms. The familiar forms are generally used when addressing relatives, friends, and children; the formal forms are ordinarily used to show courtesy, respect, or emotional distance.

USAGE OF *ON*

The third person pronoun *on* is an impersonal subject pronoun and is an approximate equivalent of the impersonal *you* or *they* in English (*comment dit-on ça en russe?,* how do you say it in Russian?; *on a fermé la pharmacie,* they've closed the drugstore).

2. Disjunctive Pronouns

The disjunctive pronouns in French are:

Singular		Plural	
moi	I, me	**nous**	us, we
toi	you	**vous**	you
vous	you (formal)	**vous**	you
lui	him	**eux**	them, they (masculine or mixed)
elle	her	**elles**	them, they (feminine)
soi[1]	oneself		

[1] Used in impersonal constructions (*travailler chez soi,* to work out of one's home)

Disjunctive pronouns are used:

- as the objects of prepositions (*est-ce pour moi?,* is it for me?; *il le leur a donné,* he gave it to them).
- after *c'est* or *ce sont* (*c'est moi,* it is I, it's me; *ce sont elles,* it is they, it's them).
- to add emphasis to, or merely to complement, the subject of a sentence (*c'est elle qui les a achetés,* she's the one who bought them; *il arrive toujours en retard, lui,* he always arrives late).
- in comparisons (*Danielle est plus sportive qu'eux,* Danielle is more athletic than they).
- in compound subjects (*Louis et moi, nous travaillons ensemble,* Louis and I work together).

3. Object Pronouns

DIRECT OBJECT PRONOUNS

Direct object pronouns represent the goal or result of the action of a verb (*Corinne va appeler Charlotte,* Corinne is going to call Charlotte → *Corinne va l'appeler,* Corinne is going to call her; *Jean-Luc a vu Michel et Isabelle,* Jean-Luc saw Michel and Isabelle → *Jean-Luc les a vus,* Jean-Luc saw them). The direct object pronouns in French are:

Singular		Plural	
me, m'[1]	me	**nous**	us
te, t'[1]	you (informal)	**vous**	you (informal and formal)
vous	you (formal)		
le, l'	him, it	**les**	them (masculine, feminine, or mixed)
la, l'	her, it		

[1] These become *moi* or *toi* in affirmative commands: *ne me regarde pas!,* don't look at me!; *regarde-moi!,* look at me!

INDIRECT OBJECT PRONOUNS

Indirect object pronouns represent the secondary goal of the action of a verb (*il m'a donné le cadeau,* he gave me the gift; *je leur ai dit non,* I told them no; *ils lui ont téléphoné hier,* they phoned her yesterday). The indirect object pronouns in French are:

Singular		Plural	
me, m'	(to, for, from) me	**nous**	(to, for, from) us
te, t'	(to, for, from) you	**vous**	(to, for, from) you
lui	(to, for, from) him, her	**leur**	(to, for, from) them

Position of Object Pronouns

The position of the object pronoun in French syntax differs from its English counterpart. The object pronoun can be found before the verb of which it is the object (*je ne peux pas la voir,* I can't see her; *Alice le lit,* Alice is reading it). In affirmative commands, the object pronoun follows the imperative and is linked to it by a hyphen (*écoutez-moi!,* listen to me!). In negative commands, the object pronoun precedes the verb (*ne les achète pas,* don't buy them).

Adverbial Pronouns *y* and *en*

The adverbial pronoun *y* is used to replace many prepositional phrases introduced by *à/dans/en* (+ article and/or adjective) + noun (but not the name of a person). *Y* is ordinarily placed immediately before the verb of which it is the object:

> *il faut répondre à leurs questions,* you have to answer their questions → *il faut y répondre,* you have to answer
>
> *je consens à l'examination,* I consent to the examination → *j'y consens,* I consent, I consent to it

In affirmative commands, *y* appears after the verb and is joined to it by a hyphen:

> *n'y pense pas!* don't think about it! → *penses-y!* think about it!

The pronoun *en* is frequently used to replace phrases consisting of *de* (+ article and/or adjective) + noun. Like *y, en* is placed immediately before the verb of which it is the object:

> *nous aurons besoin d'argent,* we'll need money → *nous en aurons besoin,* we'll need some
>
> *ils parlaient des impôts,* they were talking about taxes → *ils en parlaient,* they were talking about it
>
> *combien de pages as-tu lues?* how many pages have you read? → *j'en ai lu une centaine,* I've read about a hundred
>
> *Jean leur a donné de la nourriture,* Jean gave them some food → *Jean leur en a donné,* Jean gave them some

Word Order of Object Pronouns

When several object pronouns precede the verb, the following order applies:

me	→	*le*	→	*lui*	→	*y*	→	*en*	→	*verb*
te		*la*		*leur*						
nous		*les*								
vous										

For example:

ne le lui donne pas, don't give it to him

ne lui en donne pas, don't give any to him, don't give him any

je ne m'y fie plus, I no longer rely on it

When several object pronouns follow the verb (as in affirmative commands), the order is:

verb →	*le* →	*moi* →	*y* →	*en*
	la	*toi*		
	les	*lui*		
		nous		
		vous		
		leur		

For example:

donnez-leur en!, give them some!

envoie-le moi, send it to me

4. Reflexive Pronouns

Reflexive pronouns are used to refer back to the subject of the verb (*je m'habille,* I'm getting dressed, I'm dressing myself; *ils se préparent,* they're getting ready, they're preparing themselves). The reflexive pronouns in French are:

Singular		Plural	
me[1]	myself	**nous**	ourselves
te[1]	yourself	**vous**	yourselves
se[1]	yourself, himself, herself, itself	**se**[1]	yourselves, themselves

[1] These pronouns drop the final *e* when followed by words beginning with a vowel sound: *s'accoutumer, je m'y défends, ils s'habillent,* etc.

Reflexive pronouns normally appear before the verb (*ne t'en fais pas,* don't worry about it; *il faut que tu te dépêches,* you must hurry), but they are placed immediately after the verb in affirmative commands (*dépêchez-vous!* hurry!, hurry up!).

In the plural, reflexive pronouns can indicate reciprocal action (*nous nous voyons fréquemment,* we see each other frequently; *ils ne se parlent plus,* they no longer speak to each other).

It should be noted that many verbs which take reflexive pronouns in French have intransitive equivalents in English (*se coucher,* to lie down; *se réveiller,* to wake up; *s'en aller,* to leave, etc.).

5. Relative Pronouns

Relative pronouns introduce subordinate clauses or modifiers (*les fleurs que nous avons cueillies,* the flowers that we gathered; *les filles dont tu as fait la connaissance,* the girls whom you met). In French, the relative pronouns are:

que[1] (that, which, who, whom)

qui (that, which, who)

quoi (what)

où (where)

lequel, laquelle, lesquels, lesquelles (which)

dont (of which, of whom, whose)

[1]Contracts to *qu'* when followed by a word beginning with a vowel sound

The relative pronoun *qui* refers to the subject of the relative clause, regardless of whether it is a person or thing, while the pronoun *que* refers to its object:

le livre qui est sur le bureau	the book that/ which is on the desk	(*livre* is the subject)
le livre que j'aime	the book (that) I like	(*livre* is the object)

Quoi refers to things only and is used after prepositions:

> *on aura de quoi causer,* people will have plenty to talk about
>
> *quelque chose sur quoi s'appuyer,* something to lean on

Où also refers exclusively to things and can be used to refer to time as well as place:

> *le pays d'où tu viens,* the country you come from
>
> *le jour où nous sommes partis,* the day (on which) we left

The pronoun *lequel* varies for gender and number: *lequel* (masculine singular), *laquelle* (feminine singular), *lesquels* (masculine plural), *lesquelles* (feminine plural). Because the first component of this pronoun is the definite article *le,* it observes the same rules of contraction that apply to the masculine singular article *le* and the plural article *les* (see the section Definite Article on page 23a) and combines with the prepositions *à* and *de* to form the following:

à	+	*lequel*	→	*auquel*
à	+	*lesquels*	→	*auxquels*
à	+	*lesquelles*	→	*auxquelles*
de	+	*lequel*	→	*duquel*
de	+	*lesquels*	→	*desquels*
de	+	*lesquelles*	→	*desquelles*

> *des amis auxquels j'écris souvent,* friends to whom I often write
>
> *un dîner au cours duquel un prix sera décerné,* a dinner in the course of which a prize will be awarded
>
> *l'adresse à laquelle vous recevez votre courrier,* the address at which you receive your mail

The relative pronoun *dont* can often be used in place of *de qui, de laquelle, duquel, desquels,* and *desquelles,* except after a preposition:

> *l'organisation dont il est le chef,* the organization of which he is the head
>
> *tout ce dont elle a envie,* all that she desires
>
> *les choses dont nous avons parlé,* the things we talked about

Possessives

1. Possessive Adjectives

French possessive adjectives precede the nouns they modify. Unlike their English counterparts, they agree in both gender and number with the noun they precede, and not with their possessor (*il a mis sa chemise,* he put on his shirt; *mes chaussures,* my shoes; *notre voiture,* our car; *nos voitures,* our cars). Plural possessive adjectives do not vary for gender (*mes cousins, mes cousines*).

Singular Masculine	Singular Feminine	Plural	English Equivalent
mon	**ma**	**mes**	my
ton	**ta**	**tes**	your (informal)
son	**sa**	**ses**	his, her
notre	**notre**	**nos**	our
votre	**votre**	**vos**	your (formal and/or plural)
leur	**leur**	**leurs**	their

The feminine adjectives *ma, ta,* and *sa* change to the masculine forms *mon, ton,* and *son* when immediately followed by a word with an initial vowel sound (*mon amie, son histoire*).

2. Possessive Pronouns

French possessive pronouns are always preceded by the definite article, and they agree in number and gender with the nouns they replace (*mes clefs,* my keys → *les miennes,* mine; *nos gants,* our gloves → *les nôtres,* ours).

Sing. Masc.	Sing. Fem.	English Equivalent
le mien	**la mienne**	mine
le tien	**la tienne**	yours (informal)

continued

Sing. Masc.	Sing. Fem.	English Equivalent
le sien	**la sienne**	his, hers
le nôtre	**la nôtre**	ours
le vôtre	**la vôtre**	yours (formal and/or plural)
le leur	**la leur**	theirs

Plural Masc.	Plural Fem.	English Equivalent
les miens	**les miennes**	mine
les tiens	**les tiennes**	yours (informal)
les siens	**les siennes**	his, hers
les nôtres	**les nôtres**	ours
les vôtres	**les vôtres**	yours (formal)
les leurs	**les leurs**	theirs

Demonstratives

1. Demonstrative Adjectives

French demonstrative adjectives agree with the nouns they modify in gender and number, and precede them in a sentence. The demonstrative adjectives in French are:

ce masculine singular: *ce mur,* this wall

cet masculine singular, used when the following word begins with a vowel sound: *cet homme,* that man

cette feminine singular: *cette femme,* this woman

ces plural, does not vary for gender: *ces hommes,* these men; *ces femmes,* those women

When the difference between "this" and "that" or "these" and "those" cannot be ascertained from context, or if one wishes to stress the difference, the suffixes *-ci* and *-là* are added to the noun: *cet homme-ci,* this (particular) man; *ces hommes-là,* those (particular) men.

2. Demonstrative Pronouns

Demonstrative pronouns are used in place of a noun modified by *ce, cette,* or *ces* as outlined below:

CELUI AND VARIANTS

Pronouns belonging to the *celui* group always agree in gender and number with the noun which they replace. The pronouns are:

celui	masculine singular
ceux	masculine plural
celle	feminine singular
celles	feminine plural

j'ai reçu deux colis: le tien, et celui de ma sœur, I received two packages: yours, and my sister's

ceux qu'elle préfère sont plus chers, the ones she prefers are more costly

celles qui ont travaillé le plus sont Rose et Marie, the ones who worked the most are Rose and Marie

te souviens-tu de ce qu'elle t'a dit?, do you remember what she told you?

The suffixes *-ci* and *-là* are attached to the pronouns *celui, ceux, celle,* or *celles* for emphasis:

celui-ci est plus important que celui-là, this one is more important than that one

emporte-moi ceux-là, bring me those

CE

Ce does not change for gender and combines with *être* to form a rough equivalent of the English "it is" or "they are," but it differs somewhat in usage and application from its English counterpart. Note that *ce* contracts to *c'* when immediately followed by a vowel sound:

ce sont mes amis, they are my friends

ce sont eux qui me l'ont acheté, they're the ones who bought it for me

c'est chouette!, that's great!

c'est un médecin, he's a doctor, she's a doctor

est-ce vrai?, is it true?

ÇA, CECI, AND *CELA*

The demonstrative pronouns *ça, ceci,* and *cela* act as rough equivalents of the English "this" or "that," with some differences in usage and application:

ça m'est égal, it's all the same to me, it doesn't matter to me

oui, c'est ça!, yes, that's it!

ceci n'est qu'un test, this is only a test

ceci et cela, this and that

Although *cela* and *ça* are often interchangeable, *ça* tends to be used more frequently in spoken French.

Conjugation of French Verbs

Simple Tenses

Tense	Regular verbs ending in -ER	
	PARLER	
PRESENT INDICATIVE	je parle tu parles il parle	nous parlons vous parlez ils parlent
PRESENT SUBJUNCTIVE	je parle tu parles il parle	nous parlions vous parliez ils parlent
PRETERIT INDICATIVE	je parlai tu parlas il parla	nous parlâmes vous parlâtes ils parlèrent
IMPERFECT INDICATIVE	je parlais tu parlais il parlait	nous parlions vous parliez ils parlaient
IMPERFECT SUBJUNCTIVE	je parlasse tu parlasses il parlât	nous parlassions vous parlassiez ils parlassent
FUTURE INDICATIVE	je parlerai tu parleras il parlera	nous parlerons vous parlerez ils parleront
CONDITIONAL	je parlerais tu parlerais il parlerait	nous parlerions vous parleriez ils parleraient
IMPERATIVE	 parle, parlez	parlons parlez
PRESENT PARTICIPLE (GERUND)	parlant	
PAST PARTICIPLE	parlé	

Tense	Regular verbs ending in -IR GRANDIR	
PRESENT INDICATIVE	je grandis tu grandis il grandit	nous grandissons vous grandissez ils grandissent
PRESENT SUBJUNCTIVE	je grandisse tu grandisses il grandisse	nous grandissions vous grandissiez ils grandissent
PRETERIT INDICATIVE	je grandis tu grandis il grandit	nous grandîmes vous grandîtes ils grandirent
IMPERFECT INDICATIVE	je grandissais tu grandissais il grandissait	nous grandissions vous grandissiez ils grandissaient
IMPERFECT SUBJUNCTIVE	je grandisse tu grandisses il grandît	nous grandissions vous grandissiez ils grandissent
FUTURE INDICATIVE	je grandirai tu grandiras il grandira	nous grandirons vous grandirez ils grandiront
CONDITIONAL	je grandirais tu grandirais il grandirait	nous grandirions vous grandiriez ils grandiraient
IMPERATIVE	grandis, grandissez	grandissons grandissez
PRESENT PARTICIPLE (GERUND)	grandissant	
PAST PARTICIPLE	grandi	

Perfect Tenses

The perfect tenses are formed with *avoir* and the past participle:

PRESENT PERFECT

j'ai parlé, nous avons parlé, etc. (*indicative*)
j'aie parlé, nous ayons parlé, etc. (*subjunctive*)

PAST PERFECT

j'avais parlé, nous avions parlé, etc. (*indicative*)
j'eusse parlé, nous eussions parlé, etc. (*subjunctive*)

PRETERIT PERFECT

j'eus parlé, nous eûmes parlé, etc.

FUTURE PERFECT

j'aurai parlé, nous aurons parlé, etc.

CONDITIONAL PERFECT

j'aurais parlé, nous aurions parlé, etc.
or
j'eusse parlé, nous eussions parlé, etc.

PAST IMPERATIVE

aie parlé, ayons parlé, ayez parlé

The perfect tenses of the following verbs are formed with *être*:

aller, arriver, décéder, devenir, échoir, éclore, entrer, mourir, naître, partir, repartir, rentrer, rester, retourner, sortir, tomber, venir, revenir, parvenir, survenir

For example, the present perfect of *arriver* would be as follows:

je suis arrivé, nous sommes arrivés, etc. (*indicative*)

Irregular Verbs

The *imperfect subjunctive*, the *conditional*, and the first and second person plural of the *imperative* are not included in the model conjugations list but can be derived from other verb forms:

The *imperfect subjunctive* is formed by using the second person singular of the preterit indicative, removing the final *s*, and adding the following suffixes: *-sse, -sses, -t* (and adding a circumflex accent on the preceding vowel), *-ssions, -ssiez, -ssent*. *Servir* is conjugated as follows:

PRETERIT INDICATIVE, SECOND PERSON SINGULAR	servis – *s* = servi
IMPERFECT SUBJUNCTIVE	je servisse, tu servisses, il servît, nous servissions, vous servissiez, ils servissent

The conditional is formed by using the stem of the future indicative and adding the following suffixes : *-ais, -ais, -ait, -ions, -iez,- aient*. *Prendre* is conjugated as follows:

FUTURE INDICATIVE	je prendrai – *ai* = prendr
CONDITIONAL	je prendrais, tu prendrais, il prendrait, nous prendrions, vous prendriez, ils prendraient

The first and second person plural of the *imperative* are the same as the corresponding forms of the present indicative.

Model Conjugations of Irregular Verbs

The model conjugations below include the following simple tenses : the *present indicative* (IND), the *present subjunctive* (SUBJ), the *preterit indicative* (PRET), the *imperfect indicative* (IMPF), the *future indicative* (FUT), the second person singular form of the *imperative* (IMPER), the *present participle* or *gerund* (PRP), and the *past participle* (PP). Each set of conjugations is preceded by the corresponding infinitive form of the verb, shown in bold type. Only tenses containing irregularities are listed, and the irregular verb forms within each tense are displayed in bold type.

Also note that some conjugated verbs are labeled *defective verb*. This refers to a verb lacking one or more of the usual forms of grammatical inflection (tense, mood, etc.), for example, in French, the verbs *bruire* and *ouïr*.

Each irregular verb entry in the French-English section of this dictionary is cross-referred by number to one of the following model conjugations. These cross-reference numbers are shown in curly braces { } immediately preceding the entry's functional label.

The three main categories of verbs are:

1) Verbs ending in -ER

2) Verbs ending in -IR

Present indicative endings for verbs in these categories are:

-is, -is, -it, -issons, -issez, -issent

For example, *j'arrondis, nous arrondissons,* etc. for infinitive *arrondir*

3) Verbs ending in -IR/-OIR/-RE

Present indicative endings for verbs in these categories are:

-e, -es, -e, -ons, -ez, -ent

For example, *j'accueille, nous accueillons,* etc. for infinitive *accueillir*

or

-s(x), -s(x), -t(d), -ons, -ez, -ent

For example, *je rends, nous rendons,* etc. for infinitive *rendre*

Note that in the third group there are two different sets of endings for both the present indicative and preterit indicative depending on the verb in question, as shown above for the present indicative. For clarity, these forms are included in the model conjugations in an attempt to prevent the reader from inadvertently choosing the wrong endings.

1 **absoudre :** *IND* **j'absous, tu absous, il absout, nous absolvons, vous absolvez, ils absolvent;** *SUBJ* **j'absolve, tu absolves, il absolve, nous absolvions, vous absolviez, ils absolvent;** *PRET* (*not used*); *IMPF* **j'absolvais, tu absolvais, il absolvait, nous absolvions, vous absolviez, ils absolvaient;** *IMPER* **absous;** *PRP* **absolvant;** *PP* **absous**

2 **accroire** (*defective verb*) *Used only in the infinitive*

3 **accueillir** : *IND* **j'accueille, tu accueilles, il accueille,** nous accueillons, vous accueillez, ils accueillent; *PRET* **j'accueillis, tu accueillis, il accueillit, nous accueillîmes, vous accueillîtes, ils accueillirent;** *FUT* **j'accueillerai, tu accueilleras, il accueillera, nous accueillerons, vous accueillerez, ils accueilleront;** *IMPER* **accueille**

4 **advenir** (*defective verb) Used only in the infinitive and in the following tenses* : *IND* **il advient;** *SUBJ* **il advienne;** *PRET* **il advint;** *IMPF* **il advenait;** *FUT* **il adviendra;** *PRP* **advenant;** *PP* **advenu**

5 **aller** : *IND* **je vais, tu vas, il va, nous allons, vous allez, ils vont;** *SUBJ* **j'aille, tu ailles, il aille, nous allions, vous alliez, ils aillent;** *FUT* **j'irai, tu iras, il ira, nous irons, vous irez, ils iront;** *IMPER* **va**

6 **annoncer** : *IND* j'annonce, tu annonces, il annonce, **nous annonçons,** vous annoncez, ils annoncent; *PRET* **j'annonçai, tu annonças, il annonça, nous annonçâmes, vous annonçâtes, ils annoncèrent;** *IMPF* **j'annonçais, tu annonçais, il annonçait,** nous annoncions, vous annonciez, **ils annonçaient;** *PRP* **annonçant**

7 **apparaître** : *IND* **j'apparais, tu apparais, il apparaît, nous apparaissons, vous apparaissez, ils apparaissent;** *SUBJ* **j'apparaisse, tu apparaisses, il apparaisse, nous apparaissions, vous appparaissiez, ils apparaissent;** *PRET* **j'apparus, tu apparus, il apparut, nous apparûmes, vous apparûtes, ils apparurent;** *IMPF* **j'apparaissais, tu apparaissais, il apparaissait, nous apparaissions, vous apparaissiez, ils apparaissaient;** *IMPER* **apparais;** *PRP* **apparaissant;** *PP* **apparu**

8 **appeler** : *IND* **j'appelle, tu appelles, il appelle,** nous appelons, vous appelez, **ils appellent;** *SUBJ* **j'appelle, tu appelles, il appelle,** nous appelions, vous appeliez, **ils appellent;** *FUT* **j'appellerai, tu appelleras, il appellera, nous appellerons, vous appellerez, ils appelleront;** *IMPER* **appelle**

9 **asseoir** : *IND* **j'assieds** *or* **j'assois, tu assieds** *or* **tu assois, il assied** *or* **il assoit, nous asseyons** *or* **nous assoyons, vous asseyez** *or* **vous assoyez, ils asseyent** *or* **ils assoient;** *SUBJ* **j'asseye** *or* **j'assoie, tu asseyes** *or* **tu assoies, il asseye** *or* **il assoie, nous asseyions** *or* **nous assoyions, vous asseyiez** *or*

vous assoyiez, ils asseyent *or* **ils assoient;** *PRET* **j'assis, tu assis, il assit, nous assîmes, vous assîtes, ils assirent;** *IMPF* **j'asseyais** *or* **j'assoyais, tu asseyais** *or* **tu assoyais, il asseyait** *or* **il assoyait, nous asseyions** *or* **nous assoyions, vous asseyiez** *or* **vous assoyiez, ils asseyaient** *or* **ils assoyaient;** *FUT* (*not used*); *IMPER* **assieds** *or* **assois;** *PRP* **asseyant** *or* **assoyant;** *PP* **assis**

10 **avoir :** *IND* **j'ai, tu as, il a, nous avons, vous avez, ils ont;** *SUBJ* **j'aie, tu aies, il ait, nous ayons, vous ayez, ils aient;** *PRET* **j'eus, tu eus, il eut, nous eûmes, vous eûtes, ils eurent;** *IMPF* **j'avais, tu avais, il avait, nous avions, vous aviez, ils avaient;** *FUT* **j'aurai, tu auras, il aura, nous aurons, vous aurez, ils auront;** *IMPER* **aie, ayons ayez;** *PRP* **ayant;** *PP* **eu**

11 **balayer :** *IND* **je balaie** *or* je balaye, **tu balaies** *or* tu balayes, **il balaie** *or* il balaye, nous balayons, vous balayez, **ils balaient** *or* ils balayent; *SUBJ* **je balaie** *or* je balaye, **tu balaies** *or* tu balayes, **il balaie** *or* il balaye, nous balayions, vous balayiez, **ils balaient** *or* ils balayent; *FUT* **je balaierai** *or* je balayerai, **tu balaieras** *or* tu balayeras, **il balaiera** *or* il balayera, **nous balaierons** *or* nous balayerons, **vous balaierez** *or* vous balayerez, **ils balaieront** *or* ils balayeront; *IMPER* **balaie** *or* balaye

12 **battre :** *IND* **je bats, tu bats, il bat,** nous battons, vous battez, ils battent; *PRET* **je battis, tu battis, il battit, nous battîmes, vous battîtes, ils battirent;** *IMPER* **bats;** *PP* **battu**

13 **boire :** *IND* je bois, tu bois, il boit, **nous buvons, vous buvez, ils boivent;** *SUBJ* **je boive, tu boives, il boive, nous buvions, vous buviez, ils boivent;** *PRET* **je bus, tu bus, il but, nous bûmes, vous bûtes, ils burent;** *IMPF* **je buvais, tu buvais, il buvait, nous buvions, vous buviez, ils buvaient;** *PRP* **buvant;** *PP* **bu**

14 **bouillir :** *IND* **je bous, tu bous, il bout,** nous bouillons, vous bouillez, ils bouillent; *PRET* **je bouillis, tu bouillis, il bouillit, nous bouillîmes, vous bouillîtes, ils bouillirent;** *IMPER* **bous**

15 **braire** (*defective verb*) *Used only in the infinitive and in the following tenses :* *IND* **il brait, ils braient;** *IMPF* **brayait, brayaient;** *FUT* **il braira, ils brairont**

16 **bruire** (*defective verb*) *Used only in the infinitive and in the following tenses* : *IND* **il bruit, ils bruissent;** *SUBJ* (*not used*); *PRET* (*not used*); *IMPF* **il bruissait, ils bruissaient;** *PRP* **bruissant;** *PP* **bruit**

17 **changer** : *IND* je change, tu changes, il change, **nous changeons**, vous changez, ils changent; *PRET* **je changeai, tu changeas, il changea, nous changeâmes, vous changeâtes, ils changèrent;** *IMPF* **je changeais, tu changeais, il changeait**, nous changions, vous changiez, **ils changeaient;** *PRP* **changeant**

18 **choir** (*defective verb*) *Used only in the following tenses* : *IND* **je chois, tu chois, il choit, ils choient;** *SUBJ* (*not used*); *PRET* **il chut;** *IMPF* (*not used*); *FUT* il choira; *IMPER* (*not used*); *PRP* (*not used*); *PP* **chu**

19 **clore** (*defective verb*) *Used only in the following tenses* : *IND* je clos, tu clos, **il clôt, ils closent;** *SUBJ* **je close, tu closes, il close, nous closions, vous closiez, ils closent;** *PRET* (*not used*); *IMPF* (*not used*); *FUT* (*used but regularly formed*); *PRP* **closant;** *PP* **clos**

20 **congeler** : *IND* **je congèle, tu congèles, il congèle,** nous congelons, vous congelez, **ils congèlent;** *SUBJ* **je congèle, tu congèles, il congèle,** nous congelions, vous congeliez, **ils congèlent;** *FUT* **je congèlerai, tu congèleras, il congèlera, nous congèlerons, vous congèlerez, ils congèleront;** *IMPER* **congèle**

21 **conquérir** : *IND* **je conquiers, tu conquiers, il conquiert,** nous conquérons, vous conquérez, **ils conquièrent;** *SUBJ* **je conquière, tu conquières, il conquière,** nous conquérions, vous conquériez, **ils conquièrent;** *PRET* **je conquis, tu conquis, il conquit, nous conquîmes, vous conquîtes, ils conquirent;** *FUT* **je conquerrai, tu conquerras, il conquerra, nous conquerrons, vous conquerrez, ils conquerront;** *IMPER* **conquiers;** *PP* **conquis**

22 **coudre** : *IND* je couds, tu couds, il coud, **nous cousons, vous cousez, ils cousent;** *SUBJ* **je couse, tu couses, il couse, nous cousions, vous cousiez, ils cousent;** *PRET* **je cousis, tu cousis, il cousit, nous cousîmes, vous cousîtes, ils cousirent;** *IMPF* **je cousais, tu cousais, il cousait, nous cousions, vous cousiez, ils cousaient;** *PRP* **cousant;** *PP* **cousu**

23 **courir** : *IND* **je cours, tu cours, il court**, nous courons, vous courez, ils courent; *PRET* **je courus, tu courus, il courut, nous courûmes, vous courûtes, ils coururent**; *FUT* **je courrai, tu courras, il courra, nous courrons, vous courrez, ils courront**; *IMPER* **cours**; *PP* **couru**

24 **croire** : *IND* je crois, tu crois, il croit, **nous croyons, vous croyez**, ils croient; *SUBJ* je croie, tu croies, il croie, **nous croyions, vous croyiez**, ils croient; *PRET* **je crus, tu crus, il crut, nous crûmes, vous crûtes, il crurent**; *IMPF* **je croyais, tu croyais, il croyait, nous croyions, vous croyiez, ils croyaient**; *PRP* **croyant**; *PP* **cru**

25 **croître** : *IND* **je croîs, tu croîs, il croît, nous croissons, vous croissez, ils croissent**; *SUBJ* **je croisse, tu croisses, il croisse, nous croissions, vous croissiez, ils croissent**; *PRET* **je crûs, tu crûs, il crût, nous crûmes, vous crûtes, ils crûrent**; *IMPF* **je croissais, tu croissais, il croissait, nous croissions, vous croissiez, ils croissaient**; *IMPER* **croîs**; *PRP* **croissant**; *PP* **crû**

26 **décevoir** : *IND* **je déçois, tu déçois, il déçoit**, nous décevons, vous décevez, **ils déçoivent**; *SUBJ* **je déçoive, tu déçoives, il déçoive**, nous décevions, vous déceviez, **ils déçoivent**; *PRET* **je déçus, tu déçus, il déçut, nous déçûmes, vous déçûtes, ils déçurent**; *IMPER* **déçois**; *PP* **déçu**

27 **déchoir** (*defective verb*) *Used only in the following tenses* : *IND* je déchois, tu déchois, il déchoit *or* **il déchet, nous déchoyons, vous déchoyez, ils déchoient**; *SUBJ* je déchoie, tu déchoies, il déchoie, **nous déchoyions, vous déchoyiez, ils déchoient**; *PRET* **je déchus, tu déchus, il déchut, nous déchûmes, vous déchûtes, ils déchurent**; *IMPF* (*not used*); *FUT* (*used but regularly formed*); *IMPER* (*not used*); *PRP* (*not used*); *PP* **déchu**

28 **devoir** : *IND* **je dois, tu dois, il doit**, nous devons, vous devez, **ils doivent**; *SUBJ* **je doive, tu doives, il doive**, nous devions, vous deviez, **ils doivent**; *PRET* **je dus, tu dus, il dut, nous dûmes, vous dûtes, ils durent**; *IMPER* **dois**; *PRP* **dû**

29 **dire** : *IND* je dis, tu dis, il dit, **nous disons, vous dites, ils disent**; *SUBJ* **je dise, tu dises, il dise, nous disions, vous disiez, ils disent**; *PRET* **je dis, tu dis, il dit, nous dîmes,**

vous dîtes, ils dirent; *IMPF* **je disais, tu disais, il disait, nous disions, vous disiez, ils disent;** *PRP* **disant;** *PP* **dit**

30 **dormir** : *IND* **je dors, tu dors, il dort,** nous dormons, vous dormez, ils dorment; *PRET* **je dormis, tu dormis, il dormit, nous dormîmes, vous dormîtes, ils dormirent;** *IMPER* **dors**

31 **échoir** (*defective verb*) *Used only in the following tenses* : *IND* **il échoit, ils échoient;** *SUBJ* **il échoie;** *PRET* **il échut, ils échurent;** *IMPF* (not used); *FUT* il échoira *or* **il écherra;** ils échoiront *or* **ils écherront;** *IMPER* (not used); *PRP* **échéant;** *PP* **échu**

32 **éclore** (*defective verb*) *Used only in the following tenses* : *IND* **il éclot;** *PP* **éclos**

33 **écrire** : *IND* j'écris, tu écris, il écrit, **nous écrivons, vous écrivez, ils écrivent;** *SUBJ* **j'écrive, tu écrives, il écrive, nous écrivions, vous écriviez, ils écrivent;** *PRET* **j'écrivis, tu écrivis, il écrivit, nous écrivîmes, vous écrivîtes, ils écrivirent;** *IMPF* **j'écrivais, tu écrivais, il écrivait, nous écrivions, vous écriviez, ils écrivaient;** *PRP* **écrivant;** *PP* **écrit**

34 **enclore** (*defective verb*) *Used only in the following tenses* : *IND* j'enclos, tu enclos, il enclot, **nous enclosons, vous enclosez, ils enclosent**; *SUBJ* **j'enclose, tu encloses, il enclose, nous enclosions, vous enclosiez, ils enclosent**; *PRET* (*not used*); *IMPF* (*not used*); *FUT* (*used but regularly formed*); *IMPER* enclos; *PRP* **enclosant;** *PP* **enclos**

35 **ensuivre (s')** (*defective verb*) *Used only in the following tenses* : *IND* **il s'ensuit;** *SUBJ* **il s'ensuive;** *PRET* **il s'ensuivit**; *IMPF* **il s'ensuivait**; *FUT* **il s'ensuivra;** *PP* **s'ensuivi**

36 **envoyer** : *IND* **j'envoie, tu envoies, il envoie**, nous envoyons, vous envoyez, **ils envoient;** *SUBJ* **j'envoie, tu envoies, il envoie**, nous envoyions, vous envoyiez, **ils envoient;** *FUT* **j'enverrai, tu enverras, il enverra, nous enverrons, vous enverrez, ils enverront;** *IMPER* **envoie**

37 **éteindre** : *IND* **j'éteins, tu éteins, il éteint, nous éteignons, vous éteignez, ils éteignent;** *SUBJ* **j'éteigne, tu éteignes, il éteigne, nous éteignions, vous éteigniez, ils éteignent;** *PRET* **j'éteignis, tu éteignis, il éteignit, nous éteignîmes, vous éteignîtes, ils éteignirent;** *IMPF* **j'éteignais, tu éteignais, il**

éteignait, nous éteignions, vous éteigniez, ils éteignaient; *IMPER* **éteins;** *PRP* **éteignant;** *PP* **éteint**

38 **être :** *IND* **je suis, tu es, il est, nous sommes, vous êtes, ils sont;** *SUBJ* **je sois, tu sois, il soit, nous soyons, vous soyez, ils soient;** *PRET* **je fus, tu fus, il fut, nous fûmes, vous fûtes, ils furent;** *IMPF* **j'étais, tu étais, il était, nous étions, vous étiez, ils étaient;** *FUT* **je serai, tu seras, il sera, nous serons, vous serez, ils seront;** *IMPER* **sois;** *PRP* **étant;** *PP* **été**

39 **exclure :** *IND* **j'exclus, tu exclus, il exclut, nous excluons, vous excluez, ils excluent;** *PRET* **j'exclus, tu exclus, il exclut, nous exclûmes, vous exclûtes, ils exclurent;** *IMPER* **exclus;** *PP* **exclu**

40 **extraire :** *IND* j'extrais, tu extrais, il extrait, **nous extrayons, vous extrayez,** ils extraient; *SUBJ* j'extraie, tu extraies, il extraie, **nous extrayions, vous extrayiez,** ils extraient; *PRET* (not used); *IMPF* **j'extrayais, tu extrayais, il extrayait, nous extrayions, vous extrayiez, ils extrayaient;** *PRP* **extrayant;** *PP* **extrait**

41 **faillir** (*defective verb) Used only in the infinitive and as a PP* **failli**

42 **faire :** *IND* je fais, tu fais, il fait, **nous faisons, vous faites, ils font;** *SUBJ* **je fasse, tu fasses, il fasse, nous fassions, vous fassiez, ils fassent;** *PRET* **je fis, tu fis, il fit, nous fîmes, vous fîtes, ils firent;** *IMPF* **je faisais, tu faisais, il faisait, nous faisions, vous faisiez, ils faisaient;** *FUT* **je ferai, tu feras, il fera, nous ferons, vous ferez, ils feront;** *PRP* **faisant;** *PP* **fait**

43 **falloir** (*defective verb*) *Used only in the following tenses* **:** *IND* **il faut;** *SUBJ* **il faille;** *PRET* **il fallut;** *IMPF* **il fallait;** *FUT* **il faudra;** *IMPER* (not used); *PRP* (*not used*); *PP* **fallu**

44 **forfaire** (*defective verb) Used only in the infinitive and in the following tenses* **:** *IND* **il forfait;** *PP* **forfait**

45 **frire** (*defective verb*) *Used only in the following tenses* **:** *IND* **je fris, tu fris, il frit;** *FUT* je frirai, tu friras, il frira, nous frirons, vous frirez, ils friront; *IMPER* **fris;** *PP* **frit**

46 **fuir :** *IND* je fuis, tu fuis, il fuit, **nous fuyons, vous fuyez, ils fuient;** *SUBJ* je fuie, tu fuies, il fuie, **nous fuyions, vous**

fuyiez, ils fuient; *PRET* je fuis, tu fuis, il fuit, **nous fuîmes, vous fuîtes, ils fuirent;** *IMPF* **je fuyais, tu fuyais, il fuyait, nous fuyions, vous fuyiez, ils fuyaient;** *PRP* **fuyant;** *PP* **fui**

47 **gésir** (*defective verb*) *Used only in the following tenses* : *IND* **je gis, tu gis, il gît, nous gisons, vous gisez, ils gisent;** *IMPF* **je gisais, tu gisais, il gisait, nous gisions, vous gisiez, ils gisaient;** *PRP* **gisant**

48 **haïr** : *IND* **je hais, tu hais, il hait, nous haïssons, vous haïssez, ils haïssent;** *SUBJ* **je haïsse, tu haïsses, il haïsse, nous haïssions, vous haïssiez, ils haïssent;** *PRET* **je haïs, tu haïs, il haït, nous haïmes, vous haïtes, ils haïrent;** *IMPF* **je haïssais, tu haïssais, il haïssait, nous haïssions, vous haïsssiez, ils haïssaient;** *IMPER* **hais;** *PRP* **haïssant;** *PP* **haï**

49 **instruire** : *IND* j'instruis, tu instruis, il instruit, **nous instruisons, vous instruisez, ils instruisent;** *SUBJ* **j'instruise, tu instruises, il instruise, nous instruisions, vous instruisiez, ils instruisent;** *PRET* **j'instruisis, tu instruisis, il instruisit, nous instruisîmes, vous instruisîtes, ils instruisirent;** *IMPF* **j'instruisais, tu instruisais, il instruisait, nous instruisions, vous instruisiez, ils instruisaient;** *PRP* **instruisant;** *PP* **instruit**

50 **joindre** : *IND* **je joins, tu joins, il joint, nous joignons, vous joignez, ils joignent;** *SUBJ* **je joigne, tu joignes, il joigne, nous joignions, vous joigniez, ils joignent;** *PRET* **je joignis, tu joignis, il joignit, nous joignîmes, vous joignîtes, ils joignirent;** *IMPF* **je joignais, tu joignais, il joignait, nous joignions, vous joigniez, ils joignaient;** *IMPERF* **joins;** *PRP* **joignant;** *PP* **joint**

51 **lire** : *IND* je lis, tu lis, il lit, **nous lisons, vous lisez, ils lisent;** *SUBJ* **je lise, tu lises, il lise, nous lisions, vous lisiez, ils lisent;** *PRET* **je lus, tu lus, il lut, nous lûmes, vous lûtes, ils lurent;** *IMPF* **je lisais, tu lisais, il lisait, nous lisions, vous lisiez, ils lisaient;** *PRP* **lisant;** *PP* **lu**

52 **mener** : *IND* **je mène, tu mènes, il mène,** nous menons, vous menez, **ils mènent;** *SUBJ* **je mène, tu mènes, il mène,** nous menions, vous meniez, **ils mènent;** *FUT* **je mènerai, tu mèneras, il mènera, nous mènerons, vous mènerez, ils mèneront;** *IMPER* **mène**

53 **mettre** : *IND* **je mets, tu mets, il met**, nous mettons, vous mettez, ils mettent; *PRET* **je mis, tu mis, il mit, nous mîmes, vous mîtes, il mirent**; *IMPER* **mets**; *PP* **mis**

54 **moudre** : *IND* je mouds, tu mouds, il moud, **nous moulons, vous moulez, ils moulent**; *SUBJ* **je moule, tu moules, il moule, nous moulions, vous mouliez, ils moulent**; *PRET* **je moulus, tu moulus, il moulut, nous moulûmes, vous moulûtes, ils moulurent**; *IMPF* **je moulais, tu moulais, il moulait, nous moulions, vous mouliez, ils moulaient**; *PRP* **moulant**; *PP* **moulu**

55 **mourir** : *IND* **je meurs, tu meurs, il meurt**, nous mourons, vous mourez, **ils meurent**; *SUBJ* **je meure, tu meures, il meure**, nous mourions, vous mouriez, **ils meurent**; *PRET* **je mourus, tu mourus, il mourut, nous mourûmes, vous mourûtes, ils moururent**; *FUT* **je mourrai, tu mourras, il mourra, nous mourrons, vous mourrez, ils mourront**; *IMPER* **meurs**; *PRP* **mourant**; *PP* **mort**

56 **mouvoir** : *IND* **je meus, tu meus, il meut**, nous mouvons, vous mouvez, **ils meuvent**; *SUBJ* **je meuve, tu meuves, il meuve**, nous mouvions, vous mouviez, **ils meuvent**; *PRET* **je mus, tu mus, il mut, nous mûmes, vous mûtes, ils murent**; *IMPER* **meus**; *PP* **mû**

57 **naître** : *IND* **je nais, tu nais, il naît, nous naissons, vous naissez, ils naissent**; *SUBJ* **je naisse, tu naisses, il naisse, nous naissions, vous naissiez, ils naissent**; *PRET* **je naquis, tu naquis, il naquit, nous naquîmes, vous naquîtes, ils naquirent**; *IMPF* **je naissais, tu naissais, il naissait, nous naissions, vous naissiez, ils naissaient**; *IMPER* **nais**; *PRP* **naissant**; *PP* **né**

58 **nettoyer** : *IND* **je nettoie, tu nettoies, il nettoie**, nous nettoyons, vous nettoyez, **ils nettoient**; *SUBJ* **je nettoie, tu nettoies, il nettoie**, nous nettoyions, vous nettoyiez, **ils nettoient**; *FUT* **je nettoierai, tu nettoieras, il nettoiera, nous nettoierons, vous nettoierez, ils nettoieront**; *IMPER* **nettoie**

59 **oindre** (*defective verb*) *Used only in the infinitive and as a* PP **oint**

60 **ouïr** (*defective verb*) *Used only in the infinitive and as a* PP **ouï**

61 **paître** (*defective verb*) *Used only in the following tenses* : *IND* **je pais, tu pais, il paît, nous paissons, vous paissez, ils paissent**; *SUBJ* **je paisse, tu paisses, il paisse, nous paissions, vous paissiez, ils paissent**; *PRET* (*not used*); *IMPF* **je paissais, tu paissais, il paissait, nous paissions, vous paissiez, ils paissaient**; *FUT* (*used but regular*); *IMPER* **pais**; *PRP* **paissant**; *PP* (*not used*)

62 **parfaire** (*defective verb*) *Used only in the infinitive and in the following tenses IND* **il parfait**; *PP* **parfait**

63 **perdre** : *IND* je perds, tu perds, **il perd**, nous perdons, vous perdez, ils perdent; *PRET* **je perdis, tu perdis, il perdit, nous perdîmes, vous perdîtes, ils perdirent**; *PP* **perdu**

64 **piéger** : *IND* **je piège, tu pièges, il piège, nous piégeons,** vous piégez, **ils piègent**; *SUBJ* **je piège, tu pièges, il piège**, nous piégions, vous piégiez, **ils piègent**; *PRET* **je piégeai, tu piégeas, il piégea, nous piégeâmes, vous piégeâtes, ils piégèrent**; *IMPF* **je piégeais, tu piégeais, il piégeait**, nous piégions, vous piégiez, **ils piégeaient**; *IMPER* **piège**; *PRP* **piégeant**; *PP* **piégé**

65 **plaindre** : *IND* je plains, tu plains, il plaint, **nous plaignons, vous plaignez, ils plaignent**; *SUBJ* **je plaigne, tu plaignes, il plaigne, nous plagnions, vous plagniez, ils plaignent**; *PRET* **je plaignis, tu plaignis, il plaignit, nous plaignîmes, vous plaignîtes, ils plaignirent**; *IMPF* **je plaignais, tu plaignais, il plaignait, nous plaignions, vous plaigniez, ils plaignaient**; *PRP* **plaignant**; *PP* **plaint**

66 **plaire** : *IND* je plais, tu plais, **il plaît, nous plaisons, vous plaisez, ils plaisent**; *SUBJ* **je plaise, tu plaises, il plaise, nous plaisions, vous plaisiez, ils plaisent**; *PRET* **je plus, tu plus, il plut, nous plûmes, vous plûtes, ils plurent**; *IMPF* **je plaisais, tu plaisais, il plaisait, nous plaisions, vous plaisiez, ils plaisaient**; *PRP* **plaisant**; *PP* **plu**

67 **pleuvoir** (*defective verb*) *Used in the infinitive and in the following tenses IND* **il pleut, ils pleuvent** (*only in the figurative*); *SUBJ* **il pleuve, ils pleuvent** (*only in the figurative*); *PRET* **il plut**; *IMPF* **il pleuvait, ils pleuvaient** (*only in the figurative*); *FUT* **il pleuvra**; *IMPER* (not used); *PRP* **pleuvant**; *PP* **plu**

68 **pourvoir** : *IND* **je pourvois, tu pourvois, il pourvoit, nous**

pourvoyons, vous pourvoyez, ils pourvoient; *SUBJ* **je pourvoie, tu pourvoies, il pourvoie, nous pourvoyions, vous pourvoyiez, ils pourvoient;** *PRET* **je pourvus, tu pourvus, il pourvut, nous pourvûmes, vous pourvûtes, ils pourvurent;** *IMPF* **je pourvoyais, tu pourvoyais, il pourvoyait, nous pourvoyions, vous pourvoyiez, ils pourvoyaient;** *FUT* **je pourvoirai, tu pourvoiras, il pourvoira, nous pourvoirons, vous pourvoirez, ils pourvoiront;** *IMPER* **pourvois;** *PRP* **pourvoyant;** *PP* **pourvu**

69 **pouvoir** : *IND* **je peux** *or* **je puis, tu peux, il peut,** nous pouvons, vous pouvez, **ils peuvent;** *SUBJ* **je puisse, tu puisses, il puisse, nous puissions, vous puissiez, ils puissent;** *PRET* **je pus, tu pus, il put, nous pûmes, vous pûtes, ils purent;** *FUT* **je pourrai, tu pourras, il pourra, nous pourrons, vous pourrez, ils pourront;** *IMPER* (*not used*); *PP* **pu**

70 **prendre** : *IND* je prends, tu prends, **il prend, nous prenons, vous prenez, ils prennent;** *SUBJ* **je prenne, tu prennes, il prenne, nous prenions, vous preniez, ils prennent;** *PRET* **je pris, tu pris, il prit, nous prîmes, vous prîtes, ils prirent;** *IMPF* **je prenais, tu prenais, il prenait, nous prenions, vous preniez, ils prenaient;** *PRP* **prenant;** *PP* **pris**

71 **prévaloir** : *IND* **je prévaux, tu prévaux, il prévaut,** nous prévalons, vous prévalez, ils prévalent; *PRET* **je prévalus, tu prévalus, il prévalut, nous prévalûmes, vous prévalûtes, ils prévalurent;** *FUT* **je prévaudrai, tu prévaudras, il prévaudra, nous prévaudrons, vous prévaudrez, ils prévaudront;** *IMPER* **prévaux;** *PP* **prévalu**

72 **rassir** (*defective verb*) *Used only in the infinitive and as a PP* **rassis**

73 **ravoir** (*defective verb*) *Used only in the infinitive*

74 **résoudre** : *INF* **je résous, tu résous, il résout, nous résolvons, vous résolvez, ils résolvent;** *SUBJ* **je résolve, tu résolves, il résolve, nous résolvions, vous résolviez, ils résolvent;** *PRET* **je résolus, tu résolus, il résolut, nous résolûmes, vous résolûtes, ils résolurent;** *IMPF* **je résolvais, tu résolvais, il résolvait, nous résolvions, vous résolviez, ils résolvaient;** *IMPER* **résous;** *PRP* **résolvant;** *PP* **résolu**

75 **résulter** (*defective verb) Used only in the infinitive and in the following tenses* : IND **il résulte;** PRP **résultant**

76 **rire** : IND **je ris, tu ris, il rit, nous rions, vous riez, ils rient;** SUBJ je rie, tu ries, il rie, **nous riions, vous riiez,** ils rient; PRET **je ris, tu ris, il rit, nous rîmes, vous rîtes, ils rirent;** IMPER **ris;** PP **ri**

77 **rompre** : IND je romps, tu romps, **il rompt**, nous rompons, vous rompez, ils rompent; PRET **je rompis, tu rompis, il rompit, nous rompîmes, vous rompîtes, ils rompirent;** PP **rompu**

78 **saillir** : IND **je saille, tu sailles, il saille,** nous saillons, vous saillez, ils saillent; PRET **je saillis, tu sallis, il saillit, nous saillîmes, vous saillîtes, ils saillirent;** FUT **je saillerai, tu sailleras, il saillera, nous saillerons, vous saillerez, ils sailleront;** IMPER **saille**

79 **savoir** : IND **je sais, tu sais, il sait,** nous savons, vous savez, ils savent; SUBJ **je sache, tu saches, il sache, nous sachions, vous sachiez, ils sachent;** PRET **je sus, tu sus, il sut, nous sûmes, vous sûtes, ils surent;** FUT **je saurai, tu sauras, il saura, nous saurons, vous saurez, ils sauront;** IMPER **sache, sachons, sachez;** PRP **sachant;** PP **su**

80 **seoir** (*defective verb*) *Used in the following tenses* : IND **il sied, il siéent;** SUBJ **il siée, ils siéent;** PRET (*not used*); IMPF **il seyait, ils seyaient;** FUT **il siéra, ils siéront;** IMPER (*not used*); PRP **séant** *or* **seyant;** PP (*not used*)

81 **servir** : IND **je sers, tu sers, il sert,** nous servons, vous servez, ils servent; PRET **je servis, tu servis, il servit, nous servîmes, vous servîtes, ils servirent;** FUT **je servirai, tu serviras, il servira, nous servirons, vous servirez, ils serviront;** IMPER **sers;** PP **servi**

82 **sortir** : IND **je sors, tu sors, il sort,** nous sortons, vous sortez, ils sortent; PRET **je sortis, tu sortis, il sortit, nous sortîmes, vous sortîtes, ils sortirent;** FUT **je sortirai, tu sortiras, il sortira, nous sortirons, vous sortirez, ils sortiront;** IMPER **sors;** PRP **sortant;** PP **sorti**

83 **souffrir** : IND **je souffre, tu souffres, il souffre,** nous souffrons, vous souffrez, ils souffrent; PRET **je souffris, tu souf-**

fris, il souffrit, nous souffrîmes, vous souffrîtes, ils souffrirent; *FUT* **je souffrirai, tu souffriras, il souffrira, nous souffrirons, vous souffrirez, ils souffriront;** *IMPER* **souffre;** *PP* **souffert**

84 **sourdre** (*defective verb*) *Used only in the infinitive and in the following tenses* : *IND* **il sourd, ils sourdent;** *IMPF* **il sourdait, ils sourdaient**

85 **stupéfaire** (*defective verb*) *Used only in the following tense* *PP* **stupéfié**

86 **suffire** : *IND* je suffis, tu suffis, il suffit, **nous suffisons, vous suffisez, ils suffisent;** *SUBJ* **je suffise, tu suffises, il suffise, nous suffisions, vous suffisiez, ils suffisent;** *PRET* **je suffis, tu suffis, il suffit, nous suffîmes, vous suffîtes, ils suffirent;** *IMPF* **je suffisais, tu suffisais, il suffisait, nous suffisions, vous suffisiez, ils suffisaient;** *PRP* **suffisant;** *PP* **suffi**

87 **suggérer** : *IND* **je suggère, tu suggères, il suggère,** nous suggérons, vous suggérez, **ils suggèrent;** *SUBJ* **je suggère, tu suggères, il suggère,** nous suggérions, vous suggériez, **ils suggèrent;** *IMPER* **suggère**

88 **suivre** : *IND* **je suis, tu suis, il suit,** nous suivons, vous suivez, ils suivent; *PRET* **je suivis, tu suivis, il suivit, nous suivîmes, vous suivîtes, ils suivirent;** *IMPER* **suis;** *PP* **suivi**

89 **suppléer** : *IND* **je supplée, tu supplées, il supplée, nous suppléons, vous suppléez, ils suppléent;** *SUBJ* **je supplée, tu supplées, il supplée, nous suppléions, vous suppléiez, ils suppléent;** *PRET* **je suppléai, tu suppléas, il suppléa, nous suppléâmes, vous suppléâtes, ils suppléèrent;** *FUT* **je suppléerai, tu suppléeras, il suppléera, nous suppléerons, vous suppléerez, ils suppléeront;** *IMPER* **supplée;** *PP* **suppléé**

90 **surseoir** : *IND* **je sursois, tu sursois, il sursoit, nous sursoyons, vous sursoyez, ils sursoient;** *SUBJ* **je sursoie, tu sursoies, il sursoie, nous sursoyions, vous sursoyiez, ils sursoient;** *PRET* **je sursis, tu sursis, il sursit, nous sursîmes, vous sursîtes, ils sursirent;** *IMPF* **je sursoyais, tu sursoyais, il sursoyait, nous sursoyions, vous sursoyiez, ils sursoyaient;** *FUT* **je surseoirai, tu surseoiras, il surseoira, nous surseoirons, vous surseoirez, ils surseoiront;** *IMPER* **sursois;** *PRP* **sursoyant;** *PP* **sursis**

91 **taire** : *IND* je tais, tu tais, **il tait, nous taisons, vous taisez, ils taisent;** *SUBJ* **je taise, tu taises, il taise, nous taisions, vous taisiez, ils taisent;** *PRET* **je tus, tu tus, il tut, nous tûmes, vous tûtes, ils turent;** *IMPF* **je taisais, tu taisais, il taisait, nous taisions, vous taisiez, ils taisaient;** *PRP* **taisant;** *PP* **tu**

92 **tenir** : *IND* **je tiens, tu tiens, il tient**, nous tenons, vous tenez, **ils tiennent;** *SUBJ* **je tienne, tu tiennes, il tienne**, nous tenions, vous teniez, **ils tiennent;** *PRET* **je tins, tu tins, il tint, nous tînmes, vous tîntes, ils tinrent;** *FUT* **je tiendrai, tu tiendras, il tiendra, nous tiendrons, vous tiendrez, ils tiendront;** *IMPER* **tiens;** *PP* **tenu**

93 **tressaillir** : *IND* **je tressaille, tu tressailles, il tressaille,** nous tressaillons, vous tressaillez, ils tressaillent; *PRET* **je tressaillis, tu tressaillis, il tressaillit, nous tressaillîmes, vous tressaîllites, ils tressaillirent;** *FUT* **je tressaillirai, tu tressailliras, il tressaillira, nous tressaillirons, vous tressaillirez, ils tressailliront;** *IMPF* **tressaille;** *PP* **tressailli**

94 **vaincre** : *IND* **je vaincs, tu vaincs, il vainc, nous vainquons, vous vainquez, ils vainquent;** *SUBJ* **je vainque, tu vainques, il vainque, nous vainquions, vous vainquiez, ils vainquent;** *PRET* **je vainquis, tu vainquis, il vainquit, nous vainquîmes, vous vainquîtes, ils vainquirent;** *IMPF* **je vainquais, tu vainquais, il vainquait, nous vainquions, vous vainquiez, ils vainquaient;** *IMPER* **vaincs;** *PRP* **vainquant;** *PP* **vaincu**

95 **valoir** : *IND* **je vaux, tu vaux, il vaut,** nous valons, vous valez, ils valent; *SUBJ* **je vaille, tu vailles, il vaille,** nous valions, vous valiez, **ils vaillent;** *PRET* **je valus, tu valus, il valut, nous valûmes, vous valûtes, ils valurent;** *FUT* **je vaudrai, tu vaudras, il vaudra, nous vaudrons, vous vaudrez, ils vaudront;** *IMPER* **vaux;** *PP* **valu**

96 **vérifier** : *SUBJ* je vérifie, tu vérifies, il vérifie, **nous vérifiions, vous vérifiiez,** ils vérifient; *IMPF* je vérifiais, tu vérifiais, il vérifiait, **nous vérifiions, vous vérifiiez,** ils vérifiaient

97 **vêtir** : *IND* **je vêts, tu vêts, il vêt,** nous vêtons, vous vêtez, ils vêtent; *PRET* **je vêtis, tu vêtis, il vêtit, nous vêtîmes, vous vêtîtes, ils vêtirent;** *FUT* **je vêtirai, tu vêtiras, il vêtira, nous vêtirons, vous vêtirez, ils vêtiront;** *IMPER* **vêts;** *PP* **vêtu**

98 **vivre :** *IND* **je vis, tu vis, il vit,** nous vivons, vous vivez, ils vivent; *PRET* **je vécus, tu vécus, il vécut, nous vécûmes, vous vécûtes, ils vécurent**; *IMPER* **vis;** *PP* **vécu**

99 **voir :** *IND* je vois, tu vois, il voit, **nous voyons, vous voyez,** ils voient; *SUBJ* je voie, tu voies, il voie, **nous voyions, vous voyiez,** ils voient; *PRET* **je vis, tu vis, il vit, nous vîmes, vous vîtes, ils virent;** *IMPF* **je voyais, tu voyais, il voyait, nous voyions, vous voyiez, ils voyaient;** *FUT* **je verrai, tu verras, il verra, nous verrons, vous verrez, ils verront;** *PRP* **voyant;** *PP* **vu**

100 **vouloir :** *IND* **je veux, tu veux, il veut,** nous voulons, vous voulez, **ils veulent;** *SUBJ* **je veuille, tu veuilles, il veuille,** nous voulions, vous vouliez; **ils veuillent;** *PRET* **je voulus, tu voulus, il voulut, nous voulûmes, vous voulûtes, ils voulurent;** *FUT* **je voudrai, tu voudras, il voudra, nous voudrons, vous voudrez, ils voudront;** *IMPER* **veux** *or* **veuille;** *PP* **voulu**

Abbreviations in this Work

adj	adjective
adv	adverb
art	article
Bel	Belgium
Brit	Great Britain
Can	Canada
conj	conjunction
esp	especially
f	feminine
fam	familiar or colloquial
fpl	feminine plural
France	France
interj	interjection
m	masculine
mf	masculine or feminine
mpl	masculine plural
n	noun
nf	feminine noun
nfpl	feminine plural noun
nfs & pl	invariable singular or plural feminine noun
nm	masculine noun
nmf	masculine or feminine noun
nmfpl	plural noun invariable for gender
nmfs & pl	noun invariable for both gender and number
nmpl	masculine plural noun
nms & pl	invariable singular or plural masculine noun
npl	plural noun
ns & pl	noun invariable for plural
pl	plural
pp	past participle
prep	preposition
pron	pronoun
qqch	quelque chose (something)
qqn	quelqu'un (someone)
s	singular
s.o.	someone
sth	something
Switz	Switzerland
usu	usually
v	verb (transitive and intransitive)
v aux	auxiliary verb
vi	intransitive verb
vi impers	impersonal verb
vr	reflexive verb
vt	transitive verb

Pronunciation Symbols

VOWELS

æ **ask**, **bat**, **glad**
ɑ **cot**, **bomb**
ɑ̃ *French* ch**an**t, **en**nui
a *New England* **au**nt, *British* **a**sk, gl**a**ss
ɛ **e**gg, b**e**t, f**e**d
ɛ̃ *French* lap**in**, m**ain**
ə **a**bout, jav**e**lin, Al**a**bam**a**
ə when italicized as in əl, əm, ən, indicates a syllabic pronunciation of the consonant as in bot**tle**, pri**sm**, butt**on**
i ver**y**, an**y**, thirt**y**
iː **ea**t, b**ea**d, b**ee**
ɪ **i**d, b**i**d, p**i**t
o **O**hio, yell**o**wer, potat**o**
oː **oa**ts, **ow**n, z**o**ne, bl**ow**
ɔ **aw**l, m**au**l, c**au**ght, p**aw**
ɔ̃ **om**bre, m**on**
ʊ s**u**re, sh**ou**ld, c**ou**ld
uː b**oo**t, tw**o**, c**oo**
ʌ **u**nder, p**u**tt, b**u**d
y *French* p**u**r, *German* f**ü**hlen
eɪ **ei**ght, w**a**de, b**ay**
aɪ **i**ce, b**i**te, t**ie**
aʊ **ou**t, g**ow**n, pl**ow**
ɔɪ **oy**ster, c**oi**l, b**oy**
ɸ *French* d**eu**x, *German* H**ö**he
œ *French* b**œu**f, *German* G**ö**tt
œ̃ *French* l**un**di, parf**um**

CONSONANTS

b **b**a**b**y, la**b**or, ca**b**
d **d**ay, rea**d**y, ki**d**
dʒ **j**ust, ba**dg**er, fu**dg**e
ð **th**en, ei**th**er, ba**th**e
f **f**oe, tou**gh**, bu**ff**
g **g**o, bi**gg**er, ba**g**
h **h**ot, a**h**a
j **y**es, vine**y**ard
k **c**at, **k**eep, la**cqu**er, flo**ck**
l **l**aw, ho**ll**ow, boi**l**
m **m**at, he**m**p, ha**mm**er, ri**m**
n **n**ew, te**n**t, te**n**or, ru**n**
ŋ ru**ng**, ha**ng**, swi**ng**er
ɲ *French* di**gn**e, a**gn**eau
p **p**ay, la**p**se, to**p**
r **r**ope, bu**r**n, ta**r**
s **s**ad, mi**s**t, ki**ss**
ʃ **sh**oe, mi**ss**ion, slu**sh**
t **t**oe, bu**tt**on, ma**t**
ṱ indicates that some speakers of English pronounce this sound as a voiced alveolar flap, as in later, catty, battle
tʃ **ch**oose, ba**tch**
θ **th**in, e**th**er, ba**th**
v **v**at, ne**v**er, ca**v**e
w **w**et, soft**w**are
ɥ *French* c**u**ir, app**u**i
x *German* Ba**ch**, *Scottish* lo**ch**
z **z**oo, ea**s**y, bu**zz**
ʒ a**z**ure, bei**g**e
h, k, p, t when italicized indicate sounds which are present in the pronunciation of some speakers of English but absent in the pronunciation of others, so that *whence* ['*h*wɛn*t*s] can be pronounced as ['hwɛns], ['hwɛnts], ['wɛnts], or ['wɛns].

OTHER SYMBOLS

ˈ high stress **pen**manship
ˌ low stress penman**ship**
ʼ aspiration; when used before French words in *h-*, indicates absence of liaison, as in *le héros* [lə 'ero]
( ) indicate sounds that are present in the pronunciation of some speakers of French but absent in that of others, as in *cenellier* [s(ə)nɛlje], *but* [by(t)]

French–English Dictionary

A

a [a] *nm* : a, the first letter of the alphabet

à [a] *prep* **1** : to <je vais à Montréal : I am going to Montreal> <as-tu téléphoné à ton père? : did you call your dad?> <il a donné la clé à son frère : he gave the key to his brother> **2** : at <à deux heures : at two o'clock> <nous sommes à l'aéroport : we are at the airport> **3** : on <à pied : on foot, by foot> <à temps : on time> **4** : with <la fille aux cheveux blonds : the girl with blond hair> **5** (*with infinitive*) : to <ils ont appris à lire : they learned how to read> <problèmes à résoudre : problems to be solved> **6** : from <voler aux riches : to steal from the rich> **7** : per <60 kilomètres à l'heure : 60 kilometers per hour> **8** : in, according to <à leur avis : in their opinion>

abaissement [abɛsmɑ̃] *nm* **1** : lowering **2** DIMINUTION : reduction, drop, fall **3** : abasement, humbling

abaisser [abese] *vt* **1** BAISSER : to lower **2** DIMINUER : to reduce **3** : to humble, to abase — **s'abaisser** *vr* **1** : to go down, to slope (down) **2** : to demean oneself, to grovel **3** ~ **à** : to stoop to

abandon [abɑ̃dɔ̃] *nm* **1** : state of neglect **2** : desertion, abandonment **3** : abandon, freedom **4** : surrender, renunciation **5** : withdrawal, retirement (in sports) **6 laisser à l'abandon** : to neglect, to abandon

abandonner [abɑ̃dɔne] *vt* **1** : to abandon **2** : to surrender, to renounce — *vi* : to give up — **s'abandonner** *vr* **1** : to let oneself go, to neglect oneself **2** ~ **à** : to give oneself up to (pleasures, etc.)

abaque [abak] *nm* : abacus

abasourdir [abazurdir] *vt* **1** : to stun **2** : to deafen

abâtardir [abatardir] *vt* : to debase, to degrade — **s'abâtardir** *vr* : to degenerate, to deteriorate

abat–jour [abaʒur] *nm* : lampshade

abats [aba] *nmpl* **1** : entrails, offal **2 abats de volaille** : giblets

abattage [abataʒ] *nm* **1** : felling (of trees) **2** : slaughtering (of animals) **3** : extraction (of metals) **4 avoir de l'abattage** : to be full of vim and vigor

abattant [abatɑ̃] *nm* : flap, leaf (of furniture)

abattement [abatmɑ̃] *nm* **1** : reduction, allowance <abattement à la base : income-tax deduction> **2** : despondency, sadness **3** : weakness, exhaustion

abattis [abati] *nmpl* : giblets

abattoir [abatwar] *nm* : abattoir, slaughterhouse

abattre [abatr] {12} *vt* **1** : to knock down, to cut down, to bring down **2** ÉPUISER : to wear out, to exhaust **3** DÉMORALISER : to demoralize <ne te laisse pas abattre : don't let things get you down> **4** : to slaughter, to kill **5 abattre ses cartes** *or* **abattre son jeu** : to lay one's cards on the table — **s'abattre** *vr* **1** : to come down, to fall, to crash **2** ~ **sur** : to pounce on, to descend on

abattu, -tue [abaty] *adj* : despondent, downcast, dejected

abbaye [abei] *nf* : abbey

abbé [abe] *nm* **1** : abbot **2** PRÊTRE : priest

abbesse [abɛs] *nf* : abbess

abcès [apsɛ] *nm* : abscess

abdication [abdikasjɔ̃] *nf* : abdication, renunciation

abdiquer [abdike] *vt* **1** : to abdicate **2** : to renounce — *vi* **1** : to abdicate **2** : to surrender, to give up

abdomen [abdɔmɛn] *nm* : abdomen

abdominal, -nale [abdɔminal] *adj, mpl* **-naux** [-no] : abdominal

abdominaux *nmpl* **les abdominaux** : stomach muscles, abs

abécédaire [abesedɛr] *nm* : speller, primer

abeille [abɛj] *nf* **1** : bee, honeybee **2 abeille mâle** : drone

aberrant, -rante [abɛrɑ̃, -rɑ̃t] *adj* **1** : aberrant, abnormal **2** : absurd

aberration [abɛrasjɔ̃] *nf* : aberration

abêtir [abetir] *vt* : to make stupid — *vi* : to become stupid — **s'abêtir** *vr*

abhorrer [abɔre] *vt* : to abhor, to abominate

abîme [abim] *nm* **1** : abyss, gulf **2 au bord de l'abîme** : on the brink of ruin **3 au fond de l'abîme** : in the depths of despair

abîmer [abime] *vt* DÉTÉRIORER : to damage, to spoil — **s'abîmer** *vr* **1** : to spoil, to become damaged **2** : to sink, to founder <s'abîmer dans la réflexion : to be lost in thought>

abject, -jecte [abʒɛkt] *adj* **1** : despicable, contemptible **2** : abject — **abjectement** [-ʒɛktəmɑ̃] *adv*

abjurer [abʒyre] *vt* : to abjure, to renounce

ablation [ablasjɔ̃] *nf* : removal, excision (in medicine)

ablution [ablysjɔ̃] *nf* : ablution

abnégation [abnegasjɔ̃] *nf* : selflessness, self-denial

aboie [abwa], **aboiera** [abwara], *etc.* → **aboyer**

aboiement [abwamɑ̃] *nm* : barking, baying

abois [abwa] *nmpl* **être aux abois** : to be at bay, to be desperate

abolir [abɔlir] *vt* : to abolish

abolition [abɔlisjɔ̃] *nf* : abolition

abominable [abɔminabl] *adj* : abominable — **abominablement** [-nabləmɑ̃] *adv*
abomination [abɔminasjɔ̃] *nf* : abomination
abominer [abɔmine] *vt* : to abominate, to loathe
abondamment [abɔ̃damɑ̃] *adv* : abundantly
abondance [abɔ̃dɑ̃s] *nf* **1** : abundance **2 en ~** : in plenty, galore
abondant, -dante [abɔ̃dɑ̃, -dɑ̃t] *adj* : abundant
abonder [abɔ̃de] *vi* **1** : to abound, to be plentiful <abonder en bonheur : to be full of happiness> **2 abonder dans le sens de** : to agree wholeheartedly with
abonné, -née [abɔne] *n* : subscriber
abonnement [abɔnmɑ̃] *nm* : subscription
abonner [abɔne] *vt* : to take out a subscription for — **s'abonner** *vr* : to subscribe
abord [abɔr] *nm* **1** ACCÈS : access, approach **2** : manner <il est d'un abord facile : he's very approachable> **3 abords** *nmpl* : surroundings **4 d' ~** : at first, firstly **5 de prime abord** *or* **au premier abord** : at first glance
abordable [abɔrdabl] *adj* **1** ACCESSIBLE : accessible **2** : affordable **3** : approachable
abordage [abɔrdaʒ] *nm* **1** : boarding (of a ship) **2** : collision
aborder [abɔrde] *vt* **1** : to approach **2** : to tackle, to deal with **3** : to board (an enemy ship) — *vi* : to land, to berth <aborder à port : to reach port>
aborigène[1] [abɔriʒɛn] *adj* : aboriginal, indigenous
aborigène[2] *nmf* : aborigine, native
abortif, -tive [abɔrtif, -tiv] *adj* : abortive
aboucher [abuʃe] *vt* : to join (things) end to end — **s'aboucher** *vr* : to get in touch
aboutir [abutir] *vi* **1** RÉUSSIR : to succeed **2 ~ à** *or* **~ dans** : to result in, to end up in
aboutissants [abutisɑ̃] *nmpl* → **tenant**
aboutissement [abutismɑ̃] *nm* : outcome, result
aboyer [abwaje] {58} *vi* : to bark, to bay — *vt* : to bark (out), to shout (an order, etc.)
aboyeur, -yeuse [abwajœr, -jøz] *adj* : barking
abraser [abraze] *vt* : to abrade
abrasif[1], -sive [abrazif, -ziv] *adj* : abrasive
abrasif[2] *nm* : abrasive
abrasion [abrazjɔ̃] *nf* : abrasion
abrégé [abreʒe] *nm* : summary, abstract, abridgment <en abrégé : in summary, in brief>
abrègement [abrɛʒmɑ̃] *nm* : summarizing, abridgment
abréger [abreʒe] {64} *vt* : to shorten, to abridge, to abbreviate
abreuver [abrœve] *vt* **1** : to water (an animal) **2** : to soak, to irrigate **3** ACCABLER : to shower, to heap <abreuver qqn de : to overwhelm s.o. with> — **s'abreuver** *vr* : to drink
abreuvoir [abrœvwar] *nm* : watering place (in a river, etc.), drinking trough
abréviation [abrevjasjɔ̃] *nf* : abbreviation
abri [abri] *nm* **1** : shelter, shed <à l'abri : under cover> **2 les sans abri** : the homeless
abricot [abriko] *nm* : apricot
abrier [abrije] {96} *vt Can* : to cover (with a blanket, etc.)
abriter [abrite] *vt* **1** : to shelter, to protect **2** HÉBERGER : to house, to accommodate
abrogation [abrɔgasjɔ̃] *nf* : repeal, abrogation
abroger [abrɔʒe] {17} *vt* : to abrogate, to repeal, to annul
abrupt, -brupte [abrypt] *adj* **1** ESCARPÉ : sheer, steep **2** BRUSQUE : abrupt
abruti, -tie [abryti] *n fam* : fool, idiot
abrutir [abrytir] *vt* **1** ÉTOURDIR : to daze, to stupefy **2** : to wear out, to exhaust **3** ABÊTIR : to make stupid
abrutissant, -sante [abrytisɑ̃, -sɑ̃t] *adj* : exhausting, numbing, stupefying
absence [apsɑ̃s] *nf* : absence
absent[1], -sente [apsɑ̃, -sɑ̃t] *adj* : absent
absent[2], -sente *n* : absentee
absentéisme [apsɑ̃teism] *nm* : absenteeism
absenter [apsɑ̃te] *v* **s'absenter** *vr* : to leave, to stay away
absinthe [apsɛ̃t] *nf* **1** : absinthe **2** : wormwood
absolu[1], -lue [apsɔly] *adj* : absolute — **absolument** [-lymɑ̃] *adv*
absolu[2] *nm* : absolute
absolution [apsɔlysjɔ̃] *nf* : absolution
absorbant, -bante [apsɔrbɑ̃, -bɑ̃t] *adj* **1** : absorbent **2** : absorbing, engrossing
absorber [apsɔrbe] *vt* **1** : to absorb, to engross **2** : to consume, to take up, to absorb — **s'absorber** *vr* **~ dans** : to become engrossed in
absorption [apsɔrpsjɔ̃] *nf* : absorption
absoudre [apsudr] {1} *vt* : to absolve
abstenir [apstənir] {92} *v* **s'abstenir** *vr* **1** : to abstain **2 s'abstenir de faire** : to refrain from doing
abstention [apstɑ̃sjɔ̃] *nf* : abstention
abstinence [apstinɑ̃s] *nf* : abstinence
abstraction [apstraksjɔ̃] *nf* **1** : abstraction **2 faire abstraction de** : to disregard, to set aside
abstraire [apstrɛr] {40} *vt* : to abstract — **s'abstraire** *vr* : to isolate oneself
abstrait[1], -traite [apstrɛ, -trɛt] *adj* : abstract — **abstraitement** [-trɛtmɑ̃] *adv*
abstrait[2] *nm* : abstract <dans l'abstrait : in the abstract>

abstrus, -struse [apstry, -stryz] *adj* : abstruse

absurde [apsyrd] *adj* : absurd

absurdité [apsyrdite] *nf* : absurdity

abus [aby] *nm* : abuse, misuse <abus de confiance : breach of trust>

abuser [abyze] *vt* : to deceive, to mislead — *vi* **1** ~ **de** : to misuse **2** ~ **de** : to take advantage of, to exploit — **s'abuser** *vr* : to be mistaken

abuseur [abyzœr] *nm Can* : abuser

abusif, -sive [abyzif, -ziv] *adj* **1** EXAGÉRÉ : excessive <parents abusifs : overprotective parents> **2** IMPROPRE : incorrect, improper — **abusivement** [-zivmɑ̃] *adv*

abyssal, -sale [abisal] *adj, mpl* **-saux** [-so] : abyssal, unfathomable

acabit [akabi] *nm* : sort, type <de tout acabit : of every kind>

acacia [akasja] *nm* : acacia

académicien, -cienne [akademisjɛ̃, -sjɛn] *n* : academician

académie [akademi] *nf* **1** : academy **2** : school district **3** : learned society **4** : nude (in a work of art)

académique [akademik] *adj* : academic

acadien, -dienne [akadjɛ̃, -djɛn] *adj* **1** : Acadian **2** : Cajun

Acadien, -dienne *n* **1** : Acadian **2** : Cajun

acajou [akaʒu] *nm* : mahogany

acariâtre [akarjatr] *adj* : cantankerous

accablant, -blante [akablɑ̃, -blɑ̃t] *adj* : overwhelming, oppressive

accablement [akabləmɑ̃] *nm* : despondency, dejection

accabler [akable] *vt* **1** ÉCRASER : to overwhelm **2** : to condemn

accalmie [akalmi] *nf* : lull, respite

accaparement [akaparmɑ̃] *nm* : monopolizing, hoarding

accaparer [akapare] *vt* **1** MONOPOLISER : to monopolize **2** : to buy up, to hoard

accéder [aksede] {87} *vi* **1** : to gain access, to reach, to obtain **2** : to accede

accélérateur[1], -trice [akseleratœr, -tris] *adj* : accelerating

accélérateur[2] *nm* : accelerator

accélération [akselerasjɔ̃] *nf* : acceleration

accélérer [akselere] {87} *v* : to accelerate — **s'accélérer** *vr*

accent [aksɑ̃] *nm* **1** : accent <un accent allemand : a German accent> **2** : stress, emphasis **3** : accent mark <accent aigu : acute accent> **4** NUANCE : hint, tone <un accent plaintif : a plaintive tone>

accentuer [aksɑ̃tɥe] *vt* **1** : to mark with an accent **2** : to stress (a syllable) **3** : to emphasize, to highlight — **s'accentuer** *vr* : to become more pronounced

acceptabilité [aksɛptabilite] *nf* : acceptability

acceptable [aksɛptabl] *adj* : acceptable, passable

acceptation [aksɛptasjɔ̃] *nf* : acceptance

accepter [aksɛpte] *vt* : to accept, to agree to

acception [aksɛpsjɔ̃] *nf* **1** : sense, meaning **2 sans acception de** : regardless of

accès [aksɛ] *nm* **1** : access **2** : entry, entrance <accès interdit : no entry> **3** CRISE : fit, attack <accès de fièvre : bout of fever> <accès d'excitation : fit of excitement>

accessibilité [aksɛsibilite] *nf* : accessibility

accessible [aksɛsibl] *adj* **1** ABORDABLE : accessible **2 accessible au public** : open to the public

accession [aksɛsjɔ̃] *nf* AVÈNEMENT : accession, attainment

accessoire[1] [aksɛswar] *adj* : accessory, incidental

accessoire[2] *nm* **1** : accessory **2 accessoires** *nmpl* : props

accessoirement [aksɛswarmɑ̃] *adv* **1** : secondarily, incidentally **2** : if necessary, if need be

accident [aksidɑ̃] *nm* : accident <par accident : by accident, accidentally>

accidenté[1], -tée [aksidɑ̃te] *adj* **1** BLESSÉ : injured **2** ENDOMMAGÉ : damaged **3** INÉGAL : uneven, broken <terrain accidenté : uneven ground>

accidenté[2], -tée *n* : victim (of an accident), injured person

accidentel, -telle [aksidɑ̃tɛl] *adj* : accidental — **accidentellement** [-tɛlmɑ̃] *adv*

accise [aksiz] *nf Bel, Can* : excise tax

acclamation [aklamasjɔ̃] *nf* : acclamation, cheering

acclamer [aklame] *vt* : to acclaim, to cheer

acclimatation [aklimatasjɔ̃] *nf* : acclimatization

acclimater [aklimate] *vt* : to acclimatize — **s'acclimater** *vr*

accolade [akɔlad] *nf* **1** : accolade **2** EMBRASSADE : embrace **3** : brace, bracket (in printing)

accoler [akɔle] *vt* **1** : to join side by side **2** : to bracket together (in printing)

accommodant, -dante [akɔmɔdɑ̃, -dɑ̃t] *adj* : accommodating, flexible

accommodation [akɔmɔdasjɔ̃] *nf* : accommodation, adaptation

accommodement [akɔmɔdmɑ̃] *nm* : arrangement, compromise, terms

accommoder [akɔmɔde] *vt* : to accommodate, to adapt — **s'accommoder** *vr* ~ **de** : to make do, to put up with

accompagnateur, -trice [akɔ̃paɲatœr, -tris] *n* **1** : accompanist **2** GUIDE : chaperone, guide

accompagnement [akɔ̃paɲmɑ̃] *nm* : accompaniment

accompagner [akɔ̃paɲe] *vt* : to accompany
accompli, -lie [akɔ̃pli] *adj* **1** ACHEVÉ : finished, accomplished **2** CONSOMMÉ : consummate, expert
accomplir [akɔ̃plir] *vt* : to accomplish, to perform, to realize — **s'accomplir** *vr* **1** : to take place **2** : to be fulfilled
accomplissement [akɔ̃plismɑ̃] *nm* : accomplishment, performance
accord [akɔr] *nm* **1** : agreement, understanding <d'accord : in agreement, agreed> <en accord avec : in harmony with> **2** PACTE : pact, agreement, accord (in politics, etc.) **3** : approval, consent **4** : chord (in music)
accordéon [akɔrdeɔ̃] *nm* : accordion
accorder [akɔrde] *vt* **1** : to make agree, to reconcile, to match **2** OCTROYER : to grant, to give **3** : to tune (a musical instrument) — **s'accorder** *vr* : to be in agreement
accordeur [akɔrdœr] *nm* : tuner (of musical instruments)
accoster [akɔste] *vt* **1** ABORDER : to approach, to accost **2** : to come alongside — *vi* : to dock, to land
accotement [akɔtmɑ̃] *nm* : shoulder (of a road)
accoter [akɔte] *vt* : to lean, to rest — **s'accoter** *vr* **~ à** *or* **~ contre** : to lean against
accouchement [akuʃmɑ̃] *nm* : childbirth
accoucher [akuʃe] *vt* : to deliver (a child) — *vi* **1** : to be in labor **2 ~ de** : to give birth to
accoucheur, -cheuse [akuʃœr, -ʃøz] *n* : obstetrician
accoucheuse *nf* SAGE-FEMME : midwife
accouder [akude] *v* **s'accouder** *vr* **1** : to lean on one's elbows **2 ~ à** *or* **~ sur** : to lean (one's elbows) on
accoudoir [akudwar] *nm* : armrest
accouplement [akupləmɑ̃] *nm* **1** : coupling **2** : mating
accoupler [akuple] *vt* **1** : to couple, to link **2** : to mate (of animals) **3** : to yoke (draft animals) — **s'accoupler** *vr* : to mate
accourir [akurir] {23} *vi* : to come running, to run up
accoutrement [akutrəmɑ̃] *nm* : outfit, getup
accoutumance [akutymɑ̃s] *nf* **1** ACCLIMATATION : acclimatization, habituation **2** DÉPENDANCE : dependency, addiction
accoutumé, -mée [akutyme] *adj* : usual, customary
accoutumer [akutyme] *vt* HABITUER : to accustom — **s'accoutumer** *vr* **~ à** : to get accustomed to, to get used to
accréditation [akreditasjɔ̃] *nf* : accreditation
accréditer [akredite] *vt* **1** : to accredit (a person) **2** : to substantiate (a rumor, etc.) —**s'accréditer** *vr* : to gain credibility
accroc [akro] *nm* **1** DÉCHIRURE : rip, tear **2** OBSTACLE : obstacle, hitch, snag
accrochage [akrɔʃaʒ] *nm* **1** : hanging (for display) **2** : hooking, hitching **3** : (military) skirmish **4** : clash, dispute **5** : minor collision (of an automobile)
accroche [akrɔʃ] *nf* : slogan, catch phrase
accrocher [akrɔʃe] *vt* **1** : to hang up **2** : to hook, to hitch **3** : to get hold of (a person), to catch <accrocher le regard : to catch the eye> <accrocher un client : to buttonhole a client> **4** : to bump into, to hit — *vi* **1** : to catch, to stick, to snag **2** : to attract attention, to catch on — **s'accrocher** *vr* **1** : to hang on, to persevere **2** SE DISPUTER : to quarrel **3 ~ à** : to hold on to, to cling to
accrocheur, -cheuse [akrɔʃœr, -ʃøz] *adj* **1** TENACE : tenacious **2** : catchy, eye-catching
accroire [akrwar] {2} *vt* **en faire accroire à** : to take in, to dupe
accroissement [akrwasmɑ̃] *nm* AUGMENTATION : growth, increase
accroître [akrwatr] {25} *vt* : to increase — **s'accroître** *vr*
accroupir [akrupir] *v* **s'accroupir** *vr* : to squat, to crouch
accueil [akœj] *nm* RÉCEPTION : welcome, reception <faire bon accueil à : to welcome>
accueillant, -lante [akœjɑ̃, -jɑ̃t] *adj* HOSPITALIER : welcoming, hospitable
accueillir [akœjir] {3} *vt* : to greet, to welcome
acculer [akyle] *vt* **1** : to drive, to force **2 ~ à** *or* **~ contre** : to drive (someone) back against **3 ~ dans** : to corner (someone) in
accumulateur [akymylatœr] *nm* : storage battery
accumulation [akymylasjɔ̃] *nf* : accumulation
accumuler [akymyle] *vt* : to accumulate, to amass — **s'accumuler** *vr*
accusateur[1], -trice [akyzatœr, -tris] *adj* : accusatory, incriminating
accusateur[2], -trice *n* : accuser
accusatif [akyzatif] *nm* : accusative (case)
accusation [akyzasjɔ̃] *nf* **1** : accusation **2 l'accusation** : the prosecution **3 mise en accusation** : indictment **4 mettre en accusation** : to indict
accusé[1], -sée [akyze] *adj* : marked, pronounced, prominent
accusé[2], -sée *n* : defendant, accused
accusé[3] *nm* **accusé de réception** : acknowledgment of receipt
accuser [akyze] *vt* **1** : to accuse, to blame **2** : to show (up), to emphasize, to accentuate **3 accuser réception de** : to acknowledge receipt of
acerbe [asɛrb] *adj* : acerbic, harsh

acéré, -rée [asere] *adj* : sharp

acétate[1] [asetat] *nm* : acetate

acétate[2] *nf Can* : transparency

acétylène [asetilɛn] *nm* : acetylene

achalandage [aʃalɑ̃daʒ] *nm* : clientele

achalandé, -dée [aʃalɑ̃de] *adj* **bien achalandé** : well-stocked

achaler [aʃale] *vt Can fam* : to annoy — **achalant, -lante** [aʃalɑ̃, -lɑ̃t] *adj*

acharné, -née [aʃarne] *adj* : fierce, unremitting, relentless

acharnement [aʃarnəmɑ] *nm* : determination, relentlessness

acharner [aʃarne] *v* **s'acharner** *vr* **1** : to persevere, to persist **2 ~ sur** : to persecute, to hound

achat [aʃa] *nm* **1** : purchasing, buying <faire des achats : to do some shopping> **2** EMPLETTE : purchase

acheminement [aʃminmɑ̃] *nm* : transporting, dispatch (of goods)

acheminer [aʃmine] *vt* : to transport, to convey — **s'acheminer** *vr* **~ vers** : to move toward, to head for

acheter [aʃte] {20} *vt* : to buy, to purchase

acheteur, -teuse [aʃtœr, -tøz] *n* ACQUÉREUR : buyer

achèvement [aʃɛvmɑ̃] *nm* : completion

achever [aʃve] {52} *vt* TERMINER : to complete, to finish — **s'achever** *vr* **1** : to reach completion, to end **2** : to draw to a close

achigan [aʃigɑ̃] *nm Can* : black bass

achoppement [aʃɔpmɑ̃] *nm* **pierre d'achoppement** : obstacle, stumbling block

achopper [aʃɔpe] *vi* : to stumble — **s'achopper** *vr*

acide[1] [asid] *adj* : acid, acidic

acide[2] *nm* : acid

acidité [asidite] *nf* : acidity, tartness, sourness

acidulé, -lée [asidyle] *adj* : somewhat acid, tangy

acier [asje] *nm* : steel <acier inoxydable : stainless steel>

aciérie [asjeri] *nf* : steelworks

acné [akne] *nf* : acne

acolyte [akɔlit] *nm* **1** : acolyte (in religion) **2** : accomplice, confederate

acompte [akɔ̃t] *nm* **1** : deposit, down payment **2** : installment

aconit [akɔnit] *nm* : monkshood

acoquiner [akɔkine] *v* **s'acoquiner** *vr* **~ avec** : to team up with, to gang up with

à–côté [akote] *nm, pl* **à–côtés 1** : side issue **2** : extra money, perk

à–coup [aku] *nm, pl* **à–coups** : jerk, jolt <par à-coups : in fits and starts>

acoustique[1] [akustik] *adj* : acoustic

acoustique[2] *nf* : acoustics

acquéreur, -reuse [akerœr, -røz] *n* ACHETEUR : buyer

acquérir [akerir] {21} *vt* **1** : to acquire, to obtain **2** : to purchase — **s'acquérir** *vr* : to gain, to win (approval, etc.)

acquière [akjɛr], **acquiert** [akjɛr], *etc.* → **acquérir**

acquiescement [akjɛsmɑ̃] *nm* : acquiescence

acquiescer [akjese] {6} *vi* : to aquiesce, to agree

acquis[1] [aki] *pp* → **acquérir**

acquis[2], **-quise** [aki, -kiz] *adj* **1** : acquired **2** : established, accepted <fait acquis : accepted fact> <tenir pour acquis : to take for granted>

acquis[3] *nms & pl* **1** : knowledge, experience **2** : benefit, gain

acquisition [akizisjɔ̃] *nf* **1** : acquisition **2** : purchase

acquit [aki] *nm* **1** : receipt <par acquit : received> **2 par acquit de conscience** : to put one's mind at ease

acquittement [akitmɑ̃] *nm* **1** : payment (of a debt), fulfillment (of a promise, etc.) **2** : acquittal

acquitter [akite] *vt* **1** : to acquit **2** PAYER : to settle, to pay (off) — **s'acquitter** *vr* **~ de** : to pay (a debt), to fulfill (an obligation, etc.)

acre [akr] *nf* : acre

âcre [akr] *adj* : acrid, bitter, pungent

âcreté [akrəte] *nf* : bitterness, pungency

acrimonie [akrimɔni] *nf* : acrimony

acrimonieux, -nieuse [akrimɔnjø, -njøz] *adj* : acrimonious — **acrimonieusement** [-njøzmɑ̃] *adv*

acrobate [akrɔbat] *nmf* : acrobat

acrobatie [akrɔbasi] *nf* : acrobatics

acrobatique [akrɔbatik] *adj* : acrobatic

acronyme [akrɔnim] *nm* : acronym

acrylique [akrilik] *adj & nm* : acrylic

acte [akt] *nm* **1** : action, deed <acte gratuit : gratuitous act> <faire acte de présence : to put in an appearance> **2** : act (in a play) **3** : certificate, document <acte de naissance : birth certificate> <acte de vente : bill of sale> **4 actes** *nmpl* : proceedings

acteur, -trice [aktœr, -tris] *n* COMÉDIEN : actor, actress *f*

actif[1], **-tive** [aktif, -tiv] *adj* **1** : active **2** : working <les mères actives : working mothers>

actif[2] *nm* **1** : assets *pl*, credits *pl* **2** : active voice (in grammar)

action [aksjɔ̃] *nf* **1** : action, act <une bonne action : a good deed> <passer à l'action : to go into action> **2** : effect <sous l'action de : due to the effect of, because of> **3** : share (of a security) **4** : lawsuit **5 action de grâce(s)** : thanksgiving (in religion)

actionnaire [aksjɔnɛr] *nmf* : stockholder, shareholder

actionner [aksjɔne] *vt* **1** : to engage, to put into motion, to turn on **2** : to sue

activement [aktivmɑ̃] *adv* : actively, busily

activer [aktive] *vt* **1** : to activate **2** : to speed up — **s'activer** *vr* **1** : to bustle

about, to be busy **2** *fam* : to get a move on
activisme [aktivism] *nm* : activism
activiste [aktivist] *adj & nmf* : activist
activité [aktivite] *nf* : activity <être en activité : to be active, to be in operation>
actrice → **acteur**
actuaire [aktɥɛr] *nmf* : actuary
actualisation [aktɥalizasjɔ̃] *nf* : updating, modernization
actualiser [aktɥalize] *vt* : to update, to modernize
actualité [aktɥalite] *nf* **1** : current events *pl* **2** : relevance **3 les actualités** : the news
actuel, -tuelle [aktɥɛl] *adj* : current, present — **actuellement** [-tɥɛlmɑ̃] *adv*
acuité [akɥite] *nf* : acuteness
acupuncture [akypɔ̃ktyr] *nf* : acupuncture
adage [adaʒ] *nm* MAXIME : adage
adaptabilité [adaptabilite] *nf* : adaptability
adaptable [adaptabl] *adj* : adaptable, adjustable
adaptateur [adaptatœr] *nm* : adapter
adaptation [adaptasjɔ̃] *nf* : adaptation
adapter [adapte] *vt* : to adapt, to fit — **s'adapter** *vr* **1** : to adapt **2** : to suit, to be appropriate
additif [aditif] *nm* : additive
addition [adisjɔ̃] *nf* **1** : addition **2** NOTE : bill, check (in a restaurant)
additionnel, -nelle [adisjɔnɛl] *adj* : additional
additionner [adisjɔne] *vt* : to add, to add up
adepte [adɛpt] *nmf* : follower, enthusiast
adéquat, -quate [adekwa, -kwat] *adj* **1** SUFFISANT : adequate **2** CONVENABLE : appropriate — **adéquatement** [-kwatmɑ̃] *adv*
adéquation [adekwasjɔ̃] *nf* : appropriateness, suitability
adhérence [aderɑ̃s] *nf* : adhesion
adhérent[1], **-rente** [aderɑ̃, -rɑ̃t] *adj* : adhering, sticking
adhérent[2], **-rente** *n* MEMBRE : member
adhérer [adere] {87} *vi* **1** : to adhere, to stick <adhérer à la route : to stick to the road> **2 ~ à** : to join
adhésif[1], **-sive** [adezif, -ziv] *adj* : adhesive
adhésif[2] *nm* : adhesive
adhésion [adezjɔ̃] *nf* **1** : adhesion, sticking **2** : adherence, support **3** : joining, membership
adieu [adjø] *nm, pl* **adieux** : farewell, good-bye <faire ses adieux à : to say good-bye to> <un discours d'adieu : a farewell address>
adjacent, -cente [adʒasɑ̃, -sɑ̃t] *adj* : adjacent
adjectif[1], **-tive** *adj* [adʒɛktif, -tiv] : adjectival
adjectif[2] *nm* : adjective
adjectival, -vale [adʒɛktival] *adj, mpl* **-vaux** [-vo] : adjectival
adjoindre [adʒwɛ̃dr] {50} *vt* **1** : to appoint (as an assistant) **2** : to add, to attach — **s'adjoindre** *vr* **s'adjoindre qqn** : to take s.o. on, to hire s.o.
adjoint, -jointe [adʒwɛ̃, -ʒwɛ̃t] *adj & n* : assistant
adjonction [adʒɔ̃ksjɔ̃] *nf* : addition
adjudant [adʒydɑ̃] *nm* : warrant officer, adjutant
adjudication [adʒydikasjɔ̃] *nf* **1** : auctioning, sale by auction **2** : awarding (of a contract)
adjuger [adʒyʒe] {17} *vt* **1** DÉCERNER : to award **2** : to auction — **s'adjuger** *vr* : to claim, to take for oneself
adjurer [adʒyre] *vt* SUPPLIER : to implore, to beseech
admettre [admɛtr] {53} *vt* **1** : to admit, to let in **2** : to acknowledge, to concede **3** : to permit, to accept
administrateur, -trice [administratœr, -tris] *n* : director, administrator
administratif, -tive [administratif, -tiv] *adj* : administrative — **administrativement** [-tivmɑ̃] *adv*
administration [administrasjɔ̃] *nf* : administration <administration commerciale : business administration>
administrer [administre] *vt* **1** GÉRER : to administer, to manage **2** : to dispense <administrer un médicament : to administer a drug>
admirable [admirabl] *adj* : admirable — **admirablement** [-rabləmɑ̃] *adv*
admirateur, -trice [admiratœr, -tris] *n* : admirer
admiratif, -tive [admiratif, -tiv] *adj* : admiring — **admirativement** [-tivmɑ̃] *adv*
admiration [admirasjɔ̃] *nf* : admiration
admirer [admire] *vt* : to admire
admissible [admisibl] *adj* : admissible, eligible
admission [admisjɔ̃] *nf* **1** : admission **2** : intake, induction
admonester [admɔnɛste] *vt* : to admonish
admonition [admɔnisjɔ̃] *nf* : admonition
ADN [adeɛn] *nm* : DNA
ado [ado] *nmf fam* : adolescent, teenager
adolescence [adɔlesɑ̃s] *nf* : adolescence — **adolescent, -cente** [-lesɑ̃, -sɑ̃t] *adj & n*
adon [adɔ̃] *nm Can* : lucky break
adonner [adɔne] *vi Can fam* : to be convenient <viens me voir si ça adonne : drop by if you get a chance> — **s'adonner** *vr* **1 ~ à** : to devote oneself to **2 ~ avec** *Can* : to get along well with
adopter [adɔpte] *vt* : to adopt
adoptif, -tive [adɔptif, -tiv] *adj* : adoptive, adopted

adoption [adɔpsjɔ̃] *nf* : adoption

adorable [adɔrabl] *adj* : adorable — **adorablement** [-rabləmɑ̃] *adv*

adoration [adɔrasjɔ̃] *nf* : adoration

adorer [adɔre] *vt* **1** : to adore, to worship **2** : to love

adosser [adose] *vt* **1** : to place back to back **2** **~ à** *or* **~ contre** : to lean against — **s'adosser** *vr*

adoucir [adusir] *vt* **1** : to soften, to tone down, to subdue **2** : to sweeten **3** : to alleviate, to ease — **s'adoucir** *vr*

adoucissement [adusismɑ̃] *nm* **1** : softening **2** : sweetening **3** : alleviation, easing, mitigation

adrénaline [adrenalin] *nf* : adrenalin

adresse [adrɛs] *nf* **1** : address **2** HABILETÉ : skill, dexterity <adresse au tir : marksmanship>

adresser [adrese] *vt* **1** : to address (correspondence) **2** : to direct, to aim (remarks, etc.) — **s'adresser** *vr*

adroit, -droite [adrwa, -drwat] *adj* **1** HABILE : skillful **2** : clever, shrewd — **adroitement** [-drwatmɑ̃] *adv*

aduler [adyle] *vt* : to adulate — **adulation** [adylasjɔ̃] *nf*

adulte [adylt] *adj & nmf* : adult, grown-up

adultère[1] [adyltɛr] *adj* : adulterous

adultère[2] *nm* : adultery

adultère[3] *nmf* : adulterer *m*, adulteress *f*

advenir [advənir] {4} *v impers* **1** : to occur, to happen <advienne que pourra : whatever happens, come what may> **2** **~ de** : to become of <qu'est-il advenu de Jeanne? : what(ever) became of Jeanne?>

adverbe [advɛrb] *nm* : adverb — **adverbial, -biale** [-vɛrbjal] *adj*

adversaire [advɛrsɛr] *nmf* : adversary, opponent

adverse [advɛrs] *adj* **1** : opposing **2** : adverse, unfavorable <circonstances adverses : adverse circumstances>

adversité [advɛrsite] *nf* : adversity

aération [aerasjɔ̃] *nf* **1** : ventilation **2** : aeration

aérer [aere] {87} *vt* **1** VENTILER : to ventilate, to air out **2** : to aerate (soil, etc.) **3** : to lighten, to thin out (a written text) — **s'aérer** *vr* : to get some fresh air

aérien, -rienne [aerjɛ̃, -rjɛn] *adj* **1** : aerial, air <transport aérien : air transport> **2** : overhead, aerial **3** : ethereal, airy

aérobic [aerɔbik] *nm* : aerobics

aérobie [aerɔbi] *adj* : aerobic

aérobique [aerɔbik] *adj Can* : aerobic <danse aérobique : aerobics>

aérodrome [aerɔdrom] *nm* : airfield

aérodynamique[1] [aerɔdinamik] *adj* : aerodynamic — **aérodynamiquement** [-mikmɑ̃] *adv*

aérodynamique[2] *nf* : aerodynamics

aérogare [aerɔgar] *nf* : air terminal

aéroglisseur [aerɔglisœr] *nm* : hovercraft

aérogramme [aerɔgram] *nm* : air letter, aerogram

aéronaute [aerɔnot] *nmf* : balloonist

aéronautique[1] [aerɔnotik] *adj* : aeronautical

aéronautique[2] *nf* : aeronautics

aéronaval, -vale [aerɔnaval] *adj, pl* **-vals** : air and sea

aéronef [aerɔnɛf] *nm* : aircraft

aéroport [aerɔpɔr] *nm* : airport

aéroporté, -tée [aerɔpɔrte] *adj* : airborne

aéropostal, -tale [aerɔpɔstal] *adj, mpl* **-taux** [-to] : airmail

aérosol [aerɔsɔl] *nm* : aerosol

aérospatial, -tiale [aerɔspasjal] *adj, mpl* **-tiaux** [-sjo] : aerospace

affabilité [afabilite] *nf* : affability

affable [afabl] *adj* : affable — **affablement** [afabləmɑ̃] *adv*

affadir [afadir] *vt* **1** : to make bland **2** : to cause to fade — **s'affadir** *vr*

affaiblir [afeblir] *vt* : to weaken — **s'affaiblir** *vr* **1** : to become weak **2** : to diminish, to fade

affaire [afɛr] *nf* **1** : affair, matter, business <ce n'est pas mon affaire : that's none of my business> <affaire de cœur : love affair> **2** : business, enterprise **3** : deal <une (bonne) affaire : a bargain, a good deal> **4** PROCÈS : case, lawsuit **5** **affaires** *nfpl* : possessions, belongings **6** **affaires** *nfpl* : business <homme d'affaires : businessman> **7** **avoir affaire à** : to be faced with, to be dealing with

affairé, -rée [afere] *adj* OCCUPÉ : busy

affairer [afere] *v* **s'affairer** *vr* : to be busy, to bustle about

affaissement [afɛsmɑ̃] *nm* **1** EFFONDREMENT : subsidence (of the earth), caving in **2** : sagging, sinking

affaisser [afese] *v* **s'affaisser** *vr* **1** : to collapse **2** : to sag, to sink, to subside

affaler [afale] *v* **s'affaler** *vr* : to collapse, to fall, to slump

affamé, -mée [afame] *adj* : famished, starving

affamer [afame] *vt* : to starve

affectation [afɛktasjɔ̃] *nf* **1** : assignment, appointment **2** : allocation, allotment <affectation des fonds : allocation of funds> **3** : affectation

affecté, -tée [afɛkte] *adj* : mannered, affected

affecter [afɛkte] *vt* **1** : to affect **2** : to assign **3** : to allocate, to allot **4** FEINDRE : to feign

affectif, -tive [afɛktif, -tiv] *adj* : affective, emotional

affection [afɛksjɔ̃] *nf* **1** : affection, caring **2** : ailment, condition <affection respiratoire : respiratory complaint>

affectionner [afɛksjɔne] *vt* AIMER : to like, to be fond of

affectueux, -tueuse [afɛktɥø, -tɥøz] *adj* : affectionate — **affectueusement** [-tɥøzmɑ̃] *adv*
afférent, -rente [aferɑ̃, -rɑ̃t] *adj* ~ **à** : pertaining to, relating to
affermir [afɛrmir] *vt* **1** : to strengthen, to firm up (muscles, etc.) **2** : to reinforce, to consolidate
affermissement [afɛrmismɑ̃] *nm* : strengthening
affichage [afiʃaʒ] *nm* **1** : publicizing, posting **2** : display <affichage numérique : digital display> **3 panneau d'affichage** : bulletin board **4 tableau d'affichage** : scoreboard
affiche [afiʃ] *nf* **1** : poster, notice **2 tenir l'affiche** : to open (of a play, etc.)
afficher [afiʃe] *vt* **1** : to post <défense d'afficher : post no bills> **2** : to show, to display — **s'afficher** *vr*
affidavit [afidavit] *nm* : affidavit
affilé, -lée [afile] *adj* : sharp, keen
affilée [afile] *adv* **d'**~ : in a row
affiler [afile] *vt* : to sharpen
affiliation [afiljasjɔ̃] *nf* : affiliation
affilier [afilje] {96} *vt* : to affiliate — **s'affilier** *vr* ~ **à** : to become affiliated with, to join
affiner [afine] *vt* **1** : to refine **2** : to ripen (cheese) — **s'affiner** *vr*
affinité [afinite] *nf* : affinity
affirmatif, -tive [afirmatif, -tiv] *adj* : affirmative — **affirmativement** [-tivmɑ̃] *adv*
affirmation [afirmasjɔ̃] *nf* : affirmation, assertion
affirmative *nf* : affirmative <répondre par l'affirmative : to answer in the affirmative>
affirmer [afirme] *vt* **1** : to maintain, to contend, to affirm **2** : to assert (authority, etc.) — **s'affirmer** *vr* : to assert oneself
affleurement [aflœrmɑ̃] *nm* : outcrop
affleurer [aflœre] *vt* : to make even or flush — *vi* : to come to the surface
affliction [afliksjɔ̃] *nf* : affliction
affligeant, -geante [afliʒɑ̃, -ʒɑ̃t] *adj* : distressing, sorrowful
affliger [afliʒe] {17} *vt* : to afflict, to distress — **s'affliger** *vr*
affluence [aflyɑ̃s] *nf* **1** : crowd **2** ABONDANCE : abundance **3 heure d'affluence** : rush hour
affluent [aflyɑ̃] *nm* : tributary
affluer [aflye] *vi* **1** COULER : to flow, to roll in (of money) **2** : to flock, to surge
afflux [afly] *nm* : influx, rush
affolé, -lée [afɔle] *adj* : panicked, frightened
affolement [afɔlmɑ̃] *nm* : panic
affoler [afɔle] *vt* **1** : to drive crazy **2** EFFRAYER : to frighten — **s'affoler** *vr* : to panic
affranchir [afrɑ̃ʃir] *vt* **1** LIBÉRER : to liberate, to free **2** TIMBRER : to stamp, to postmark
affranchissement [afrɑ̃ʃismɑ̃] *nm* **1** LIBÉRATION : liberation, emancipation **2** : franking, stamping **3** : postage (of a letter, etc.)
affres [afr] *nfpl* : agony, pangs, throes
affrètement [afrɛtmɑ̃] *nm* : renting, chartering
affréter [afrete] {87} *vt* : to charter <vols affrétés : chartered flights>
affreux, -freuse [afrø, -frøz] *adj* : awful, dreadful — **affreusement** [afrøzmɑ̃] *adv*
affrioler [afrijɔle] *vt* : to tempt, to entice — **affriolant, -lante** [-jɔlɑ̃, -lɑ̃t] *adj*
affront [afrɔ̃] *nm* INSULTE : affront
affrontement [afrɔ̃tmɑ̃] *nm* : confrontation, clash
affronter [afrɔ̃te] *vt* : to confront, to brave, to face — **s'affronter** *vr*
affubler [afyble] *vt fam* : to dress up, to deck out — **s'affubler** *vr*
affût [afy] *nm* **1** : carriage (for heavy artillery) **2** : hiding place, blind <être à l'affût de : to lie in wait for, to be on the lookout for>
affûter [afyte] *vt* AIGUISER : to sharpen, to hone
afghan, -ghane [afgɑ̃, -gan] *adj* : Afghan
Afghan, -ghane *n* : Afghan
afin [afɛ̃] *adv* **1** ~ **de** : in order to <afin de trouver une solution : in order to find a solution> **2** ~ **que** : so that <afin que le public comprenne : so that the public understands>
africain, -caine [afrikɛ̃, -kɛn] *adj* : African
Africain, -caine *n* : African
agaçant, -çante [agasɑ̃, -sɑ̃t] *adj* : annoying, irritating
agacement [agasmɑ̃] *nm* IRRITATION : irritation, annoyance
agacer [agase] {6} *vt* ÉNERVER : to annoy, to irritate
agate [agat] *nf* : agate
âge [aʒ] *nm* **1** : age <quel âge avez-vous? : how old are you?> <les gens du troisième âge : senior citizens> **2** : age, era <le Moyen Âge : the Middle Ages>
âgé, -gée [aʒe] *adj* **1** : old, aged, of age <âgé de seize ans : sixteen years old> **2** VIEUX : elderly, old <les personnes âgées : elderly persons>
agence [aʒɑ̃s] *nf* BUREAU : agency, office <agence de voyage : travel agency> <agence immobilière : real estate agency>
agencement [aʒɑ̃smɑ̃] *nm* : layout, arrangement
agencer [aʒɑ̃se] {6} *vt* **1** : to arrange, to lay out **2** : to put together, to construct
agenda [aʒɛ̃da] *nm* **1** : agenda **2** CARNET : appointment book
agenouiller [aʒnuje] *v* **s'agenouiller** *vr* : to kneel

agent[1], **-gente** [aʒɑ̃, -ʒɑ̃t] *n* **1** : agent <agent d'assurances : insurance agent> <agent de change : stockbroker> **2** : officer <agent de police : police officer>

agent[2] *nm* **1** : agent, factor <agents économiques : economic factors> **2** : agent (in chemistry, medicine, etc.)

agglomération [aglɔmerasjɔ̃] *nf* **1** AMAS, ASSEMBLAGE : conglomeration, agglomeration **2** : city, town **3** : urban area

aggloméré [aglɔmere] *nm* **1** : particleboard, fiberboard **2** : briquette, charcoal

agglomérer [aglɔmere] {87} *vt* : to agglomerate, to pile up — **s'agglomérer** *vr* : to aggregate, to gather together

agglutiner [aglytine] *vt* : to stick together — **s'agglutiner** *vr* : to gather

aggravation [agravasjɔ̃] *nf* : aggravation, worsening

aggraver [agrave] *vt* : to aggravate, to make worse — **s'aggraver** *vr* EMPIRER : to worsen, to get worse

agile [aʒil] *adj* : agile — **agilement** [aʒilmɑ̃] *adv*

agilité [aʒilite] *nf* : agility

agir [aʒir] *vi* **1** : to act, to take action **2** : to behave <elle agit comme une sainte : she acts like a saint> **3** : to operate, to take effect <la drogue agira vite : the drug will take effect quickly> — **s'agir** *vr* **1 ~ de** : to concern, to be a question of <de quoi s'agit-il? : what is it about?> **2 ~ de** : to be necessary <pour vivre, il s'agit de manger : one must eat to live>

agissements [aʒismɑ̃] *nmpl* : dealings, schemes, machinations

agitation [aʒitasjɔ̃] *nf* **1** : agitation, restlessness **2** : hustle and bustle, activity **3** : (social) unrest **4** : choppiness (of the sea)

agité, -tée [aʒite] *adj* **1** : restless, agitated **2** : rough <eaux agitées : rough waters>

agiter [aʒite] *vt* **1** SECOUER : to agitate, to shake **2** TROUBLER : to disturb **3** DÉBATTRE : to debate — **s'agiter** *vr* **1** : to bustle about **2** : to fidget **3** : to become agitated

agneau [aɲo] *nm, pl* **agneaux 1** : lamb **2** : lambskin

agnelle [aɲɛl] *nf* : young ewe

agnostique [agnɔstik] *adj & nmf* : agnostic

agonie [agɔni] *nf* : death throes *pl*

agoniser [agɔnize] *vi* : to be dying

agrafe [agraf] *nf* **1** : hook, fastener **2** : staple **3** : clamp, clip (in medicine)

agrafer [agrafe] *vt* **1** : to fasten **2** : staple **3** *fam* : to catch, to nab

agrafeuse [agraføz] *nf* : stapler

agraire [agrɛr] *adj* : agrarian <réforme agraire : land reform>

agrandir [agrɑ̃dir] *vt* : to enlarge, to expand — **s'agrandir** *vr* : to grow, to be enlarged

agrandissement [agrɑ̃dismɑ̃] *nm* : enlargement, expansion

agréable [agreabl] *adj* : pleasant, agreeable — **agréablement** [-abləmɑ̃] *adv*

agréé, agréée [agree] *adj* : accepted, certified <expert-comptable agréé : certified public accountant>

agréer [agree] *vt* {89} **1** ACCEPTER : to accept, to approve <veuillez agréer, l'expression de mes sentiments les meilleurs : yours sincerely> **2 ~ à** : to suit, to agree with

agrégat [agrega] *nm* : aggregate, mass

agrégation [agregasjɔ̃] *nf* **1** *France* : qualifying exam for a teacher or professor **2** : aggregation

agrégé, -gée [agreʒe] *n France* : certified teacher or professor

agréger [agreʒe] *vt* {64} **1** : to aggregate **2** INTÉGRER : to incorporate, to accept (into a group)

agrément [agremɑ̃] *nm* **1** CONSENTEMENT : consent, authorization **2** : pleasure <voyage d'agrément : pleasure trip> **3** : charm, attractiveness

agrémenter [agremɑ̃te] *vt* ORNER : to decorate, to trim, to embellish

agrès [agrɛ] *nmpl* : apparatus (for gymnastics)

agresser [agrese] *vt* ASSAILLIR : to attack, to assault

agresseur [agrɛsœr] *nm* : attacker, assailant, aggressor

agressif, -sive [agrɛsif, -siv] *adj* : aggressive — **agressivement** [-sivmɑ̃] *adv*

agression [agrɛsjɔ̃] *nf* **1** : attack, assault **2** : aggression

agressivité [agrɛsivite] *nf* : aggressiveness

agricole [agrikɔl] *adj* : agricultural

agriculteur, -trice [agrikyltœr, -tris] *n* : farmer

agriculture [agricyltyr] *nf* : agriculture, farming

agripper [agripe] *vt* : to clutch, to grab — **s'agripper** *vr* : to cling

agrumes [agrym] *nmpl* : citrus fruits

aguets [agɛ] *nmpl* **aux aguets** : on the lookout

aguicher [agiʃe] *vt* : to entice, to allure

ah [a] *interj* : oh <ah oui? : is that so?>

ahuri, -rie [ayri] *adj* **1** : amazed, dumbfounded **2** : dazed, stupefied

ahurir [ayrir] *vt* : to astound, to stun, to daze

ahurissant, -sante [ayrisɑ̃, -sɑ̃t] *adj* : astounding, amazing

ahurissement [ayrismɑ̃] *nm* STUPÉFACTION : amazement, stupefaction

aide[1] [ɛd] *nmf* : assistant

aide[2] *nf* **1** : help, aid <à l'aide! : help!> <à l'aide de : with the help of> **2** *Can* : assist (in sports)

aider [ede] *vt* ASSISTER : to help, to assist

aïe [aj] *interj* : ouch!

aïeul, aïeule [ajœl] *n* : grandfather *m*, grandmother *f*

aïeux [ajø] *nmpl* : ancestors, forefathers

aigle [ɛgl] *nm* **1** : eagle **2 aigle d'Amérique** *or* **aigle à tête blanche** : bald eagle

aiglefin [ɛgləfɛ̃] *nm* → **églefin**

aigre [ɛgr] *adj* **1** : sour, tart **2** : sharp, bitter <un vent aigre : a bitter wind>

aigre–doux, -douce [ɛgrədu, -dus] *adj* **1** : bittersweet **2** : sweet and sour

aigrette [ɛgrɛt] *nf* **1** : egret **2** : tuft, spray (of feathers)

aigreur [ɛgrœr] *nf* **1** : sourness, tartness **2** : bitterness

aigrir [egrir] *vt* **1** : to turn sour **2** : to embitter — *vi* : to sour, to become sour — **s'aigrir** *vr*

aigu, -guë [egy] *adj* **1** : sharp, keen **2** : acute, intense <une douleur aiguë : an acute pain> **3** STRIDENT : strident, high-pitched **4** → **accent**

aiguille [egɥij] *nf* **1** : needle **2** : hand (of a clock) <l'aiguille des minutes : the minute hand> **3** PIC : mountain peak **4 aiguille de glace** : icicle **5 travail à l'aiguille** : needlework

aiguiller [egɥije] *vt* **1** : to switch (in railroading) **2** : to steer, to direct

aiguilleur [egɥijœr] *nm* **1** : switchman **2 aiguilleur du ciel** : air traffic controller

aiguillon [egɥijɔ̃] *nm* **1** : goad **2** : stinger **3** : incentive, spur

aiguillonner [egɥijɔne] *vt* **1** : to goad, to prod **2** : to stimulate, to spur

aiguise–crayon [egizkrɛjɔ̃] *nm, pl* **aiguise–crayons** *Can* : pencil sharpener

aiguiser [egize] *vt* **1** AFFÛTER : to sharpen, to hone **2** : to stimulate, to whet

aiguisoir [egizwar] *nm* : (knife) sharpener

ail [aj] *nm, pl* **ails** *or* **aulx** [o] : garlic

aile [ɛl] *nf* **1** : wing **2** : fender (of an automobile) **3** : **voler de ses propres ailes** : to stand on one's own two feet

aileron [ɛlrɔ̃] *nm* **1** : flap, aileron **2** : fin (of a shark, etc.), wing tip (of a bird)

ailier [elje] *nm* : wing, winger (in sports)

aille [aj], *etc.* → **aller**

ailleurs [ajœr] *adv* **1** : elsewhere **2 d'~** : besides, moreover, by the way **3 par ~** : in addition, what's more

aimable [ɛmabl] *adj* GENTIL : kind, likeable — **aimablement** [ɛmabləmɑ̃] *adv*

aimant[1], **-mante** [ɛmɑ̃, -mɑ̃t] *adj* : loving, caring

aimant[2] *nm* : magnet

aimanter [ɛmɑ̃te] *vt* : to magnetize

aimer [eme] *vt* **1** : to love **2** *or* **aimer bien** : to like **3 aimer mieux** : to prefer

aine [ɛn] *nf* : groin

aîné[1], **-née** [ene] *adj* **1** : elder, older **2** : eldest, oldest **3** : senior

aîné[2], **-née** *n* **1** : elder child, elder son *m*, elder daughter *f* **2** : eldest child, eldest son *m*, eldest daughter *f* **3** : older person, oldest person <il est mon aîné de cinq ans : he's five years older than me>

ainsi [ɛ̃si] *adv* **1** : thus, in this way, in that way <il m'a regardé ainsi : he looked at me like that> **2 ainsi que** : just as <elle l'a fait ainsi que tu disais : she did it just as you said she would> **3 ainsi que** : as well as <mes mains ainsi que mes pieds : my hands as well as my feet> **4 et ainsi de suite** : and so on **5 ainsi soit-il** : so be it, amen **6 pour ainsi dire** : so to speak

air [ɛr] *nm* **1** : air <en plein air : outside, in the open air> <courant d'air : draft> <air conditionné : air-conditioning> **2** MÉLODIE : tune, melody <air d'opéra : aria> **3** : appearance, look <avoir un air distingué : to look distinguished> **4** AMBIANCE : atmosphere, ambience **5 être en air** *Can* : to be ready and willing

aire [ɛr] *nf* **1** : area <aire de repos : rest area> **2** SURFACE : surface, area **3** DOMAINE : field, sphere <aire d'influence : sphere of influence> **4** : aerie

airelle [ɛrɛl] *nf* : blueberry

aisance [ezɑ̃s] *nf* **1** : ease, facility, fluency **2** : affluence, wealth <vivre dans l'aisance : to be well-off>

aise[1] [ɛz] *adj* : pleased

aise[2] *nf* **1** : ease <être mal à l'aise : to be ill at ease> **2** : pleasure **3 aises** *nfpl* : creature comforts

aisé, -sée [eze] *adj* **1** FACILE : easy **2** RICHE : wealthy, well-off **3** : graceful, fluent

aisément [ezemɑ̃] *adv* FACILEMENT : easily

aisselle [ɛsɛl] *nf* : armpit

ajouré, -rée [aʒure] *adj* : openworked, perforated

ajournement [aʒurnəmɑ̃] *nm* **1** : postponement **2** : adjournment, continuance (of a trial)

ajourner [aʒurne] *vt* **1** : to adjourn **2** : to postpone, to defer

ajout [aʒu] *nm* : addition (to a house, etc.)

ajouter [aʒute] *vt* ADDITIONNER : to add

ajustement [aʒystəmɑ̃] *nm* : adjustment

ajuster [aʒyste] *vt* **1** : to adjust, to adapt, to fit **2** : to arrange (hair, etc.) **3** VISER : to aim at <ajuster son tir : to aim, to adjust one's aim>

ajutage [aʒytaʒ] *nm* : nozzle (of a hose)

alambic [alɑ̃bik] *nm* : still

alambiqué, -quée [alɑ̃bike] *adj* : overcomplicated, convoluted

alangui, -guie [alɑ̃gi] *adj* : languid, listless

alanguir [alɑ̃gir] *vt* : to make languid

alarmant, -mante [alarmɑ̃, -mɑ̃t] *adj* : alarming

alarme [alarm] *nf* **1** ALERTE : alarm <donner l'alarme : to raise the alarm> **2** PEUR : alarm, fear <un état d'alarme : a state of alarm>

alarmer [alarme] *vt* : to alarm, to frighten — **s'alarmer** *vr*

albanais[1], -naise [albanɛ, -nɛz] *adj* : Albanian

albanais[2] *nm* : Albanian (language)

Albanais, -naise *n* : Albanian

albâtre [albatr] *nm* : alabaster

albatros [albatros] *nm* : albatross

albinos [albinos] *adj & nmfs & pl* : albino

album [albɔm] *nm* : album

albumen [albymɛn] *nm* : albumen

albumine [albymin] *nf* : albumin

alcali [alkali] *nm* **1** : alkali **2** AMMONIAQUE : ammonia

alcalin, -line [alkalɛ̃, -lin] *adj* : alkaline <pile alcaline : alkaline battery>

alchimie [alʃimi] *nf* : alchemy — **alchimiste** [-ʃimist] *nmf*

alcool [alkɔl] *nm* : alcohol

alcoolique [alkɔlik] *adj & nmf* : alcoholic — **alcoolisme** [-kɔlism] *nm*

alcoolisé, -sée [alkɔlize] *adj* : alcoholic <boisson non-alcoolisée : nonalcoholic beverage>

alcôve [alkov] *nf* **1** : alcove **2 secrets d'alcôve** : intimate secrets, pillow talk

alcyon [alsjɔ̃] *nm* : kingfisher

aléa [alea] *nm* : hazard, risk

aléatoire [aleatwar] *adj* **1** : uncertain, risky **2** : random

alêne [alɛn] *nf* : awl

alentour [alɑ̃tur] *adv* : around, about, surrounding <dans la forêt alentour : in the surrounding forest>

alentours [alɑ̃tur] *nmpl* **1** ENVIRONS : surrounding area, region **2 aux alentours de** : around, in the vicinity of

alerte[1] [alɛrt] *adj* **1** : alert **2** : lively, brisk — **alertement** [alɛrtəmɑ̃] *adv*

alerte[2] *nf* ALARME : alert, warning, alarm

alerter [alɛrte] *vt* PRÉVENIR : to alert, to warn

alésage [alezaʒ] *nm* : bore (of a pipe or tube)

aléser [aleze] {87} *vt* : to bore, to ream

alevin [alvɛ̃] *nm* : young fish, fry

alevinage [alvinaʒ] *nm* : fish farming <station d'alevinage : fish hatchery>

algarade [algarad] *nf* : altercation, quarrel

algèbre [alʒɛbr] *nf* : algebra

algébrique [alʒebrik] *adj* : algebraic — **algébriquement** [-brikmɑ̃] *adv*

algérien, -rienne [alʒerjɛ̃, -rjɛn] *adj* : Algerian

Algérien, -rienne *n* : Algerian

algue [alg] *nf* : alga, seaweed

alias [aljas] *adv* : alias

alibi [alibi] *nm* : alibi

aliénation [aljenasjɔ̃] *nf* **1** : alienation **2** *or* **aliénation mentale** : insanity

aliéné, -née [aljene] *n* : insane person <être reconnu aliéné : to be declared insane>

aliéner [aljene] {87} *vt* **1** : to transfer, to give over **2** : to alienate — **s'aliéner** *vr* : to lose support, esteem, etc.

alignement [aliɲmɑ̃] *nm* **1** : row, line <ne pas être à l'alignement : to be out of line> **2** : alignment

aligner [aliɲe] *vt* : to align, to line up — **s'aligner** *vr* : to fall into line

aliment [alimɑ̃] *nm* **1** : food **2 aliments** *nmpl* : alimony

alimentaire [alimɑ̃tɛr] *adj* **1** : alimentary, food <la chaîne alimentaire : the food chain> **2** : money-making <œuvre alimentaire : potboiler>

alimentation [alimɑ̃tasjɔ̃] *nf* **1** : feeding **2** : nourishment, diet **3** : food <magasin d'alimentation : grocery store, food store> **4** : provision, supply <l'alimentation en eau : the water supply>

alimenter [alimɑ̃te] *vt* **1** NOURRIR : to feed, to nourish **2** APPROVISIONNER : to supply

alinéa [alinea] *nm* **1** : indentation <à l'alinéa : indented> **2** : paragraph

alité, -tée [alite] *adj* : bedridden

alizé [alize] *nm* : trade wind

Allah [ala] *nm* : Allah

allaitement [alɛtmɑ̃] *nm* : feeding, nursing <allaitement maternel : breast-feeding>

allaiter [alete] *vt* : to nurse, to breast-feed

allant[1], -lante [alɑ̃, -lɑ̃t] *adj* : active

allant[2] *nm* : drive, spirit

alléchant, -chante [aleʃɑ̃, -ʃɑ̃t] *adj* : tempting, enticing

allécher [aleʃe] {87} *vt* : to allure, to tempt

allée [ale] *nf* **1** : path, passage **2** : road **3** : drive, driveway **4** : aisle **5** *or* **allée de quilles** *Can* : bowling alley **6 allées et venues** : comings and goings

allégation [alegasjɔ̃] *nf* : allegation

allégeance [aleʒɑ̃s] *nf* : allegiance

allègement [alɛʒmɑ̃] *nm* : lightening (up), easing

alléger [aleʒe] {64} *vt* **1** : to lighten **2** RÉDUIRE : to reduce **3** : to soothe, to relieve

allégorie [alegɔri] *nf* : allegory

allégorique [alegɔrik] *adj* : allegorical

allègre [alɛgr] *adj* : lively, cheerful — **allègrement** [alɛgrəmɑ̃] *adv*

allégresse [alegrɛs] *nf* : exuberance, joy

alléguer [alege] {87} *vt* **1** : to allege, to put forward **2** : to quote, to cite

alléluia [aleluja] *nm & interj* : hallelujah

allemand[1], -mande [almɑ̃, -mɑ̃d] *adj* : German

allemand[2] *nm* : German (language)

Allemand, -mande *n* : German

aller[1] [ale] {5} *vi* **1** : to go, to move, to travel <nous allons au cinéma : we're going to the movies> <aller à pied : to go by foot> <allons-y! : let's go!> **2** MARCHER : to work, to run <sa montre ne va pas : his watch isn't working> **3** : to proceed, to get along, to come along <ses études vont mal : her studies are going badly> <comment allez-vous? ça va : how are you? OK, fine> **4 ~ à** : to fit <cette robe me va bien : this dress fits me well> — *v aux* : to be going to, to be about to <il va terminer de bonne heure : he's going to finish early, he'll finish early> <nous allions partir : we were just leaving> — *v impers* **1 en ~** : to happen, to go <il en ira mieux demain : things will go better tomorrow> **2 y aller de** : to be a matter of <il y va de ton bonheur : you're risking your happiness> — **s'en aller** *vr* : to leave, to go <va-t'en! : go away!>

aller[2] *nm* **1** : outward journey **2** *or* **aller simple** : one-way, one-way ticket **3 aller–retour** : round-trip, round-trip ticket

allergène [alɛrʒɛn] *nm* : allergen

allergie [alɛrʒi] *nf* : allergy

allergique [alɛrʒik] *adj* : allergic

alliage [aljaʒ] *nm* : alloy

alliance [aljɑ̃s] *nf* **1** : alliance **2** : wedding ring **3** : marriage, union <tante par alliance : aunt by marriage> **4** : mixture, combination

allié[1], **-liée** [alje] *adj* : allied

allié[2], **-liée** *n* **1** : ally, supporter **2** : relative (by marriage)

allier [alje] {96} *vt* **1** : to mix, to combine **2** : to ally, to unite — **s'allier** *vr*

alligator [aligatɔr] *nm* : alligator

allitération [aliterasjɔ̃] *nf* : alliteration — **allitératif, -tive** [-ratif, -tiv] *adj*

allô [alo] *interj* : hello

allocation [alɔkasjɔ̃] *nf* **1** : allocation, allotment **2** : allowance, benefit <allocation de chômage : unemployment benefit>

allocution [alɔkysjɔ̃] *nf* : short speech, address

allongé, -gée [alɔ̃ʒe] *adj* **1** : elongated <un visage allongé : a long face> **2** : lying down

allongement [alɔ̃ʒmɑ̃] *nm* : lengthening, extension

allonger [alɔ̃ʒe] {17} *vt* **1** : to lengthen, to elongate **2** : to stretch (out) **3** : to thin (a sauce, etc.) **4** : to lay down **5** *fam* : to hand over, to fork over — *vi* : to get longer — **s'allonger** *vr* **1** : to lengthen **2** : to lie down

allouer [alwe] *vt* **1** : to allocate, to allot **2** : to allow, to grant

allumage [alymaʒ] *nm* **1** : lighting (of a fire), switching on (of a lamp, etc.) **2** : ignition (of a motor)

allumer [alyme] *vt* **1** : to light, to ignite **2** : to turn on, to switch on **3** : to excite — **s'allumer** *vr*

allumette [alymɛt] *nf* : match

allure [alyr] *nf* **1** : pace, speed <à toute allure : at full speed> **2** : look, appearance <avoir bonne allure : to look good> **3** : style <avoir de l'allure : to have style, to look stylish>

allusion [alyzjɔ̃] *nf* **1** : allusion **2 faire allusion à** : to allude to

almanach [almana] *nm* : almanac

aloès [alɔɛs] *nms & pl* : aloe

alors [alɔr] *adv* **1** : then, at that time **2** : then, in that case **3** : so, therefore <et alors? : so?, so what?> **4 alors même que** : even if, even though **5 alors que** : while, when, whereas **6 ou alors** : or else

alose [aloz] *nf* : shad

alouette [alwɛt] *nf* **1** : lark **2 alouette des champs** : skylark

alourdir [alurdir] *vt* **1** : to make heavy, to weigh down **2** : to increase — **s'alourdir** *vr* : to grow heavy

alourdissement [alurdismɑ̃] *nm* **1** : heaviness **2** : increase

aloyau [alwajo] *nm, pl* **aloyaux** : sirloin

alpaga [alpaga] *nm* : alpaca

alphabet [alfabɛ] *nm* : alphabet

alphabétique [alfabetik] *adj* : alphabetic, alphabetical — **alphabétiquement** [-tikmɑ̃] *adv*

alphabétisation [alfabetizasjɔ̃] *nf* **1** : alphabetizing **2** : literacy teaching

alphabétiser [alfabetize] *vt* **1** : to alphabetize **2** : to teach to read and write

alpin, -pine [alpɛ̃, -pin] *adj* : alpine

alpinisme [alpinism] *nm* : mountain climbing

alpiniste [alpinist] *nmf* : mountain climber, mountaineer

altération [alterasjɔ̃] *nf* **1** FALSIFICATION : falsification, distortion **2** DÉTÉRIORATION : deterioration **3** : extreme thirst

altercation [altɛrkasjɔ̃] *nf* : altercation, quarrel

altérer [altere] {87} *vt* **1** FALSIFIER : to falsify, to distort **2** CORROMPRE : to spoil, to impair **3** : to make thirsty — **s'altérer** *vr* : to deteriorate

alternance [altɛrnɑ̃s] *nf* **1** : alternation, rotation **2 en ~** : alternately

alternateur [altɛrnatœr] *nm* : alternator

alternatif, -tive [altɛrnatif, -tiv] *adj* **1** : alternative, alternate **2** : alternating

alternative [altɛrnativ] *nf* : alternative

alternativement [altɛrnativmɑ̃] *adv* : in turn, alternately

alterner [altɛrne] *v* : to alternate

altesse [altɛs] *nf* : highness <Son Altesse : His Highness, Her Highness>

altier, -tière [altje, -tjɛr] *adj* : haughty

altimètre [altimɛtr] *nm* : altimeter

altitude [altityd] *nf* : altitude <en altitude : at high altitude(s)> <à 2 000 mètres d'altitude : at a height of 2,000 meters>

alto [alto] *nm* **1** : viola **2** : alto (instrument)

altruisme [altrɥism] *nm* : altruism

altruiste[1] [altrɥist] *adj* : altruistic

altruiste[2] *nmf* : altruist

aluminium [alyminjɔm] *nm* : aluminum

alun [alœ̃] *nm* : alum

alunir [alynir] *vi* : to land on the moon

alvéole [alveɔl] *nmf* **1** : alveolus, cell <alvéole dentaire : tooth socket> **2** : pit, cavity (in geology)

alvéolé, -lée [alveɔle] *adj* : honeycombed

amabilité [amabilite] *nf* **1** : kindness <avoir l'amabilité de : to be so kind as to> **2** : politeness <avec amabilité : courteously> **3 amabilités** *nfpl* : civilities, polite remarks

amadou [amadu] *nm* : tinder

amadouer [amadwe] *vt* **1** : to coax, to cajole **2** : to mollify

amaigrir [amegrir] *vt* : to make thin

amaigrissement [amegrismɑ̃] *nm* **1** : reducing, slimming **2** : weight loss, emaciation

amalgame [amalgam] *nm* **1** : amalgam **2** MÉLANGE : mixture

amalgamer [amalgame] *vt* **1** : to amalgamate **2** : to mix, to combine — **s'amalgamer** *vr*

amande [amɑ̃d] *nf* **1** : almond **2** : kernel (of a fruit or nut)

amant, -mante [amɑ̃, -mɑ̃t] *n* : lover

amarrage [amaraʒ] *nm* : mooring <poste d'amarrage : anchorage, berth>

amarrer [amare] *vt* **1** : to moor **2** : to tie (up), to secure — **s'amarrer** *vr*

amaryllis [amarilis] *nf* : amaryllis

amas [ama] *nm* **1** : pile, heap **2** : cluster (in astronomy), mass (in mineralogy)

amasser [amase] *vt* ACCUMULER : to amass, to pile up — **s'amasser** *vr* : to build up

amateur[1] [amatœr] *adj* : amateur

amateur[2] *nm* **1** : connoisseur, enthusiast **2** : amateur

amazone [amazon] *nf* **1** : horsewoman **2 monter en amazone** : to ride sidesaddle

ambages [ɑ̃baʒ] *nfpl* **sans ~** : plainly, unambiguously

ambassade [ɑ̃basad] *nf* : embassy

ambassadeur, -drice [ɑ̃basadœr, -dris] *n* : ambassador

ambiance [ɑ̃bjɑ̃s] *nf* : ambience, atmosphere

ambiant, -biante [ɑ̃bjɑ̃, -bjɑ̃t] *adj* : ambient, surrounding

ambidextre [ɑ̃bidɛkstr] *adj* : ambidextrous

ambigu, -guë [ɑ̃bigy] *adj* : ambiguous — **ambiguïté** [ɑ̃bigɥite] *nf*

ambitieux, -tieuse [ɑ̃bisjø, -sjøz] *adj* : ambitious — **ambitieusement** [-sjøzmɑ̃] *adv*

ambition [ɑ̃bisjɔ̃] *nf* **1** : ambition **2** : claim, pretension

ambitionner [ɑ̃bisjɔne] *vt* **1** : to aim for, to aspire to **2** *Can* : to exaggerate, to go overboard

ambivalence [ɑ̃bivalɑ̃s] *nf* : ambivalence — **ambivalent, -lente** [-valɑ̃, -lɑ̃t] *adj*

ambler [ɑ̃ble] *vi* : to amble — **amble** [ɑ̃bl] *nm*

ambre [ɑ̃br] *nm* **1** : amber **2 ambre gris** : ambergris

ambroisie [ɑ̃brwazi] *nf* : ragweed

ambulance [ɑ̃bylɑ̃s] *nf* : ambulance

ambulancier, -cière [ɑ̃bylɑ̃sje, -sjɛr] *n* : ambulance driver

ambulant, -lante [ɑ̃bylɑ̃, -lɑ̃t] *adj* : traveling, itinerant <cirque ambulant : traveling circus>

ambulatoire [ɑ̃bylatwar] *adj* : ambulatory

âme [am] *nf* **1** : soul, spirit <rendre l'âme : to breathe one's last, to give up the ghost> <âme sœur : soul mate, kindred spirit> **2 état d'âme** : state of mind

amélioration [ameljɔrasjɔ̃] *nf* : amelioration, improvement

améliorer [ameljɔre] *vt* : to ameliorate, to improve — **s'améliorer** *vr*

amen [amɛn] *interj* : amen

aménagement [amenaʒmɑ̃] *nm* **1** : development, planning <l'aménagement urbain : urban development> **2** : conversion (of rooms, buildings, etc.) **3** : equipping, fitting out <aménagements intérieurs : fittings, fixtures> **4** : adjustment (of taxes, schedules, etc.)

aménager [amenaʒe] {17} *vt* **1** : to plan, to lay out **2** : to convert <une grange aménagée : a converted barn> **3** : to equip, to fit out **4** : to adjust, to arrange

amende [amɑ̃d] *nf* **1** : fine, penalty **2 faire amende honorable** : to make amends

amendement [amɑ̃dmɑ̃] *nm* : amendment

amender [amɑ̃de] *vt* **1** : to amend **2** AMÉLIORER : to improve — **s'amender** *vr* : to mend one's ways

amener [amne] {52} *vt* **1** : to bring, to take **2** : to bring about, to cause **3** : to bring up — **s'amener** *vr fam* : to show up, to turn up

amenuiser [amənɥize] *vt* : to reduce — **s'amenuiser** *vr* : to diminish, to dwindle

amer, -mère [amɛr] *adj* : bitter — **amèrement** [amɛrmɑ̃] *adv*

américain, -caine [amerikɛ̃, -kɛn] *adj* : American

Américain, -caine *n* : American

américanisme [amerikanism] *nm* : Americanism

amertume [amɛrtym] *nf* : bitterness

améthyste [ametist] *nf* : amethyst

ameublement [amœbləmɑ̃] *nm* **1** : furnishing **2** MEUBLES : furniture

ameuter [amœte] *vt* : to stir up, to rouse — **s'ameuter** *vr* : to form a mob

ami[1], -mie [ami] *adj* : friendly

ami[2], -mie *n* **1** : friend <ami intime : close friend> <ami des bêtes : animal lover> <ami des arts : patron of the arts> **2** *or* **petit ami** : boyfriend **3** *or* **petite amie** : girlfriend

amiable [amjabl] *adj* **à l'amiable** : amicable, private <un accord à l'amiable : a settlement out of court>

amiante [amjɑ̃t] *nm* : asbestos

amibe [amib] *nf* : amoeba

amibien, -bienne [amibjɛ̃, -bjɛn] *adj* : amoebic

amical, -cale [amikal] *adj, mpl* **-caux** [-ko] : friendly

amicalement [amikalmɑ̃] *adv* **1** : amicably, in a friendly manner **2** (*used in correspondence*) : yours (truly), best wishes

amidon [amidɔ̃] *nm* : starch

amidonner [amidɔne] *vt* : to starch

amincir [amɛ̃sir] *vt* : to make thinner — **s'amincir** *vr*

aminé [amine] *adj* **acide aminé** : amino acid

amiral [amiral] *nm, pl* **-raux** [-ro] : admiral

amitié [amitje] *nf* **1** : friendship <prendre en amitié : to befriend, to take a liking to> **2** : kindness, favor **3 amitiés** *nfpl* : best wishes, best regards

ammoniac [amɔnjak] *nm* : ammonia (gas)

ammoniaque [amɔnjak] *nf* : ammonia, ammonia water

amnésie [amnezi] *nf* : amnesia

amnésique [amnezik] *adj & nmf* : amnesiac, amnesic

amnistie [amnisti] *nf* : amnesty

amocher [amɔʃe] *vt fam* : to bash

amoindrir [amwɛ̃drir] *vt* RÉDUIRE : to reduce, to diminish, to undermine — **s'amoindrir** *vr* : to lessen, to diminish

amoindrissement [amwɛ̃drismɑ̃] *nm* : reduction

amollir [amɔlir] *vt* : to soften — **s'amollir** *vr* **1** : to become soft **2** : to weaken

amonceler [amɔ̃sle] {8} *vt* : to pile up, to accumulate — **s'amonceler** *vr*

amoncellement [amɔ̃sɛlmɑ̃] *nm* : pile, heap, mass

amont [amɔ̃] *nm* **en ~** : upstream, uphill

amoral, -rale [amɔral] *adj, mpl* **-raux** [-ro] : amoral

amorce [amɔrs] *nf* **1** : beginning(s), start <l'amorce de récession : the beginnings of recession> **2** APPÂT : bait **3** : detonator, cap

amorcer [amɔrse] {6} *vt* **1** : to begin **2** APPÂTER : to bait, to entice **3** : to prime **4** : to boot (a computer)— **s'amorcer** *vr* : to begin

amorphe [amɔrf] *adj* **1** APATHIQUE : apathetic, passive **2** : amorphous

amorti [amɔrti] *nm Can* : bunt (in baseball) <amorti-sacrifice : sacrifice bunt>

amortir [amɔrtir] *vt* **1** : to absorb, to cushion (a blow, etc.), to deaden (sound) **2** : to make (something) pay for itself **3** : to pay off, to amortize

amortissement [amɔrtismɑ̃] *nm* **1** : absorption, cushioning **2** : amortization

amortisseur [amɔrtisœr] *nm* : shock absorber

amour [amur] *nm* **1** : love, affection, passion <l'amour du prochain : love of one's neighbor> <faire l'amour : to make love> **2** : romance, love affair

amoureusement [amurøzmɑ̃] *adv* : lovingly, amorously

amoureux[1], -reuse [amurø, -røz] *adj* **1** : in love, amorous **2** : loving

amoureux[2], -reuse *n* : lover

amour–propre [amurprɔpr] *nm* : self-esteem

amovible [amɔvibl] *adj* : removable, detachable

ampère [ɑ̃pɛr] *nm* : ampere

ampèremètre [ɑ̃pɛrmɛtr] *nm* : ammeter

amphétamine [ɑ̃fetamin] *nf* : amphetamine

amphibie [ɑ̃fibi] *adj* : amphibious

amphibien [ɑ̃fibjɛ̃] *nm* : amphibian

amphithéâtre [ɑ̃fiteatr] *nm* **1** : amphitheater **2** : lecture hall, auditorium

ample [ɑ̃pl] *adj* : ample, full, generous — **amplement** [ɑ̃pləmɑ̃] *adv*

ampleur [ɑ̃plœr] *nf* **1** : size, scale, extent **2** : fullness (of clothing)

amplificateur [ɑ̃plifikatœr] *nm* : amplifier

amplification [ɑ̃plifikasjɔ̃] *nf* **1** : amplification **2** : development, expansion

amplifier [ɑ̃plifje] {96} *vt* **1** : to amplify, to enlarge, to magnify **2** : to expand, to increase — **s'amplifier** *vr*

amplitude [ɑ̃plityd] *nf* : amplitude

ampoule [ɑ̃pul] *nf* **1** : lightbulb **2** : blister **3** : vial

ampoulé, -lée [ɑ̃pule] *adj* : pompous, bombastic

amputation [ɑ̃pytasjɔ̃] *nf* : amputation

amputer [ɑ̃pyte] *vt* **1** : to amputate **2** : to cut drastically

amulette [amylɛt] *nf* : amulet

amusant, -sante [amyzɑ̃, -zɑ̃t] *adj* : amusing

amuse–gueule [amyzgøl] *nms & pl* : appetizer, canapé

amusement [amyzmɑ̃] *nm* **1** : amusement **2** : diversion, pastime

amuser [amyze] *vt* DIVERTIR : to amuse — **s'amuser** *vr* **1** : to play **2** : to enjoy oneself, to have fun
amuseur, -seuse [amyzœr, -zøz] *n* : entertainer
amygdale [amidal] *nf* : tonsil
amygdalite [amidalit] *nf* : tonsilitis
an [ɑ̃] *nm* **1** : year <elle a treize ans : she is thirteen years old> <l'an prochain : next year> **2 bon an, mal an** : year in, year out **3 le Jour de l'an** *or* **le Nouvel An** : New Year's Day
anachronique [anakrɔnik] *adj* : anachronistic
anachronisme [anakrɔnism] *nm* : anachronism
anaconda [anakɔ̃da] *nm* : anaconda
anagramme [anagram] *nf* : anagram
anal, -nale [anal] *adj, mpl* **anaux** [ano] : anal
analgésique [analʒezik] *adj & nm* : analgesic
analogie [analɔʒi] *nf* : analogy
analogique [analɔʒik] *adj* : analog
analogue [analɔg] *adj* : analogous, similar
analphabète [analfabɛt] *adj & nmf* : illiterate
analphabétisme [analfabetism] *nm* : illiteracy
analyse [analiz] *nf* **1** : analysis **2** : test <analyse du sang : blood test>
analyser [analize] *vt* **1** : to analyze **2** : to test (in medicine)
analyste [analist] *nmf* : analyst
analytique [analitik] *adj* : analytic, analytical — **analytiquement** [-tikmɑ̃] *adv*
ananas [anana(s)] *nms & pl* : pineapple
anarchie [anarʃi] *nf* : anarchy — **anarchique** [anarʃik] *adj*
anarchiste[1] [anarʃist] *adj* : anarchist, anarchistic
anarchiste[2] *nmf* : anarchist
anathème [anatɛm] *nm* : anathema
anatife [anatif] *nm* : barnacle
anatomie [anatɔmi] *nf* : anatomy
anatomique [anatɔmik] *adj* : anatomic, anatomical — **anatomiquement** [-mikmɑ̃] *adv*
ancestral, -trale [ɑ̃sɛstral] *adj, mpl* **-traux** [-tro] : ancestral
ancêtre [ɑ̃sɛtr] *nmf* : ancestor
anche [ɑ̃ʃ] *nf* : reed (of a musical instrument)
anchois [ɑ̃ʃwa] *nms & pl* : anchovy
ancien[1]**, -cienne** [ɑ̃sjɛ̃, -sjɛn] *adj* **1** : former <anciens combattants : veterans> **2** VIEUX : ancient, old **3 ancien elève, ancienne elève** : alumnus *m*, alumna *f*
ancien[2] *nm* **1** : elder, old man **2 l'ancien** : antiques *pl* **3 les anciens** *nmpl* : the ancients
anciennement [ɑ̃sjɛnmɑ̃] *adv* : formerly
ancienneté [ɑ̃sjɛnte] *nf* **1** : seniority **2** : antiquity **3** : oldness, age
ancrage [ɑ̃kraʒ] *nm* : anchorage
ancre [ɑ̃kr] *nf* : anchor <jeter l'ancre : to drop anchor>
ancrer [ɑ̃kre] *vt* **1** : to anchor **2** : to fix firmly, to root — **s'ancrer** *vr*
andorran, -rane [ɑ̃dɔrɑ̃, -ran] *adj* : Andorran
Andorran, -rane *n* : Andorran
andouille [ɑ̃duj] *nf* **1** : andouille (sausage made from chitterlings) **2** *fam* : fool
androgyne [ɑ̃drɔʒin] *adj* : androgynous
âne [an] *nm* **1** : ass, donkey **2** IMBÉCILE : fool, idiot
anéantir [aneɑ̃tir] *vt* **1** DÉTRUIRE : to destroy, to wipe out **2** : to overwhelm, to exhaust — **s'anéantir** *vr* : to be dashed, to be shattered
anéantissement [aneɑ̃tismɑ̃] *nm* : annihilation, destruction
anecdote [anɛkdɔt] *nf* : anecdote
anecdotique [anɛkdɔtik] *adj* : anecdotal
anémie [anemi] *nf* : anemia — **anémique** [anemik] *adj*
anémone [anemɔn] *nf* : anemone
ânerie [anri] *nf* **1** BÊTISE : blunder, stupid mistake **2** : stupidity **3** : stupid remark, nonsense
anesthésie [anɛstezi] *nf* : anesthesia
anesthésier [anɛstezje] {96} *vt* : to anesthetize
anesthésique [anɛstezik] *adj & nm* : anesthetic
anesthésiste [anɛstezist] *nmf* : anesthetist
aneth [anɛt] *nm* : dill
anfractuosité [ɑ̃fraktɥɔzite] *nf* : crevice
ange [ɑ̃ʒ] *nm* : angel <ange gardien : guardian angel>
angélique [ɑ̃ʒelik] *adj* : angelic, angelical — **angéliquement** [-likmɑ̃] *adv*
angelot [ɑ̃ʒlo] *nm* : cherub
angine [ɑ̃ʒin] *nf* **1** : sore throat, throat infection **2** *or* **angine rouge** : tonsillitis **3** *or* **angine de poitrine** : angina
anglais[1]**, -glaise** [ɑ̃glɛ, -glɛz] *adj* : English
anglais[2] *nm* : English (language)
Anglais, -glaise *n* : Englishman *m*, Englishwoman *f*
angle [ɑ̃gl] *nm* **1** : angle <angle droit : right angle> <angle aigu : acute angle> **2** COIN : corner
anglicisme [ɑ̃glisism] *nm* : anglicism
anglophone[1] [ɑ̃glɔfɔn] *adj* : English-speaking
anglophone[2] *nmf* : English speaker
anglo–saxon[1]**, -saxonne** [ɑ̃glɔsaksɔ̃, -saksɔn] *adj* : Anglo-Saxon
anglo–saxon[2] *nm* : Anglo-Saxon (language)
Anglo–Saxon, -Saxonne *n* : Anglo-Saxon
angoissant, -sante [ɑ̃gwasɑ̃, -sɑ̃t] *adj* : agonizing
angoisse [ɑ̃gwas] *nf* : anguish

angoisser [ɑ̃gwase] *vt* : to distress, to worry
angolais, -laise [ɑ̃gɔlɛ, -lɛz] *adj* : Angolan
Angolais, -laise *n* : Angolan
angora [ɑ̃gɔra] *nm* : angora
anguille [ɑ̃gij] *nf* **1** : eel **2 il y a anguille sous roche** : there's something fishy going on
angulaire [ɑ̃gylɛr] *adj* : angular
anguleux, -leuse [ɑ̃gylø, -løz] *adj* : angular, sharp
anicroche [anikrɔʃ] *nf* ACCROC : snag, small problem
animal[1], **-male** [animal] *adj, mpl* **-maux** [-mo] : animal <le règne animal : the animal kingdom>
animal[2] *nm, pl* **-maux** : animal
animalier, -lière [animalje, -ljɛr] *adj* : animal <un peintre animalier : a wildlife painter>
animateur, -trice [animatœr, -tris] *n* **1** : leader, organizer **2** : host <animateur d'une émission de télévision : television show host> **3** : (cartoon) animator
animation [animasjɔ̃] *nf* **1** : organizing, coordinating **2** : liveliness, vivacity **3** : animation (in movies)
animé, -mée [anime] *adj* **1** : lively, animated **2** : living, animate
animer [anime] *vt* **1** : to enliven, to brighten up **2** : to drive, to impel **3** : to host, to present **4** : to animate, to bring to life — **s'animer** *vr* **1** : to become lively **2** : to come to life
animosité [animɔzite] *nf* : animosity
anis [ani(s)] *nm* : anise
ankyloser [ɑ̃kiloze] *v* **s'ankyloser** *vr* : to stiffen (up)
ankylostome [ɑ̃kilɔstɔm] *nm* : hookworm
annales [anal] *nfpl* : annals
anneau [ano] *nm, pl* **anneaux** : ring
année [ane] *nf* : year <année bissextile : leap year> <souhaiter la bonne année à qqn : to wish s.o. a happy New Year>
année–lumière [anelymjɛr] *nf, pl* **années–lumière** : light-year
annexe[1] [anɛks] *adj* **1** : related, associated **2** : appended, attached
annexe[2] *nf* **1** : annex (of a building) **2** : appendix, annex (of a document)
annexer [anɛkse] *vt* **1** : to annex **2** : to append
annexion [anɛksjɔ̃] *nf* : annexation
annihilation [aniilasjɔ̃] *nf* : destruction, annihilation
annihiler [aniile] *vt* : to destroy, to annihilate
anniversaire [anivɛrsɛr] *nm* **1** : anniversary **2** : birthday
annonce [anɔ̃s] *nf* **1** : announcement, notice **2** : advertisement <petite annonce : classified ad> <annonce publicitaire : commercial>
annoncer [anɔ̃se] {6} *vt* **1** DÉCLARER : to announce **2** PRÉDIRE : to predict — **s'annoncer** *vr* **1** : to be looming **2** : to look (to be) <les négociations s'annoncent difficiles : the negotiations promise to be difficult>
annonceur, -ceuse [anɔ̃sœr, -søz] *n* **1** : advertiser **2** *Can* : announcer (on radio, television, etc.)
annonciateur, -trice [anɔ̃sjatœr, -tris] *adj* : heralding, presaging
annoter [anɔte] *vt* : to annotate — **annotation** [anɔtasjɔ̃] *nf*
annuaire [anɥɛr] *nm* **1** : directory <annuaire téléphonique : telephone directory> **2** : yearbook
annuel, -nuelle [anɥɛl] *adj* : annual — **annuellement** [anɥɛlmɑ̃] *adv*
annulaire [anylɛr] *nm* : ring finger
annulation [anylasjɔ̃] *nf* **1** : cancellation **2** : annulment
annuler [anyle] *vt* **1** : to cancel, to call off **2** : to revoke, to annul
anode [anɔd] *nf* : anode
anodin, -dine [anɔdɛ̃, -din] *adj* **1** INSIGNIFIANT : insignificant **2** : harmless, innocuous
anomalie [anɔmali] *nf* : anomaly
ânonner [anɔne] *vt* : to stumble through (a speech) — *vi* : to hem and haw, to drone on
anonymat [anɔnima] *nm* : anonymity, obscurity
anonyme [anɔnim] *adj* : anonymous — **anonymement** [-nimmɑ̃] *adv*
anorexie [anɔrɛksi] *nf* : anorexia — **anorexique** [-rɛksik] *adj*
anormal, -male [anɔrmal] *adj, mpl* **–maux** [-mo] : abnormal — **anormalement** [-malmɑ̃] *adv*
anormalité [anɔrmalite] *nf* : abnormality
anse [ɑ̃s] *nf* **1** : handle **2** : cove
antagonisme [ɑ̃tagɔnism] *nm* : antagonism
antagoniste[1] [ɑ̃tagɔnist] *adj* : antagonistic
antagoniste[2] *nmf* : antagonist
antan [ɑ̃tɑ̃] *nm* **d'~** : of old, of yesteryear
antarctique [ɑ̃tarktik] *adj* : antarctic
antécédent[1], **-dente** [ɑ̃tesedɑ̃, -dɑ̃t] *adj* : previous
antécédent[2] *nm* **1** : antecedent **2** : history, record <antécédents médicaux : medical history>
antenne [ɑ̃tɛn] *nf* **1** : antenna <antenne parabolique : satellite dish> **2** : antenna, feeler (of an insect)
antérieur, -rieure [ɑ̃terjœr] *adj* **1** PRÉCÉDENT : prior, previous <engagements antérieurs : previous engagements> **2** : front
antérieurement [ɑ̃terjœrmɑ̃] *adv* : previously <antérieurement à : prior to>
anthère [ɑ̃tɛr] *nf* : anther
anthologie [ɑ̃tɔlɔʒi] *nf* FLORILÈGE : anthology

anthracite [ɑ̃trasit] *nm* : anthracite
anthropoïde[1] [ɑ̃trapɔid] *adj* : anthropoid
anthropoïde[2] *nm* : anthropoid, large ape
anthropologie [ɑ̃trɔpɔlɔʒi] *nf* : anthropology
anthropologique [ɑ̃trɔpɔlɔʒik] *adj* : anthropological
anthropologiste [ɑ̃trɔpɔlɔʒist] *or* **anthropologue** [-pɔlɔg] *nmf* : anthropologist
anthropophage[1] [ɑ̃trɔpɔfaʒ] *adj* : cannibalistic
anthropophage[2] *nmf* CANNIBALE : cannibal
anthropophagie [ɑ̃trɔpɔfaʒi] *nf* : cannibalism
antiadhésif, -sive [ɑ̃tiadesif, -siv] *adj* : antiadhesive, nonstick
antiaérien, -rienne [ɑ̃tiaerjɛn] *adj* : antiaircraft
antibiotique [antibiɔtik] *adj & nm* : antibiotic
antiblocage [ɑ̃tiblɔkaʒ] *adj* : antilock
antichambre [ɑ̃tiʃɑ̃br] *nf* : anteroom
anticipation [ɑ̃tisipasjɔ̃] *nf* **1** : anticipation **2 par ~** : in advance
anticiper [ɑ̃tisipe] *vt* **1** PRÉVOIR : to anticipate, to foresee **2** : to do or pay in advance — *vi* : to think ahead
anticlérical, -cale [ɑ̃tiklerikal] *adj, mpl* **-caux** [-ko] : anticlerical
anticommuniste [ɑ̃tikɔmynist] *adj & nmf* : anticommunist
anticonceptionnel, -nelle [ɑ̃tikɔ̃sɛpsjɔnɛl] *adj* CONTRACEPTIF : contraceptive
anticorps [ɑ̃tikɔr] *nms & pl* : antibody
antidater [ɑ̃tidate] *vt* : to antedate, to predate
antidémocratique [ɑ̃tidemɔkratik] *adj* : antidemocratic, undemocratic
antidépresseur [ɑ̃tidepresœr] *adj & nm* : antidepressant
antidérapant, -pante [ɑ̃tiderapɑ̃, -pɑ̃t] *adj* : nonskid
antidote [ɑ̃tidɔt] *nm* : antidote
antidrogue [ɑ̃tidrɔg] *adj* : antidrug
antifasciste [ɑ̃tifaʃist] *adj* : antifascist
antigel [ɑ̃tiʒɛl] *nm* : antifreeze
antihistaminique [ɑ̃tiistaminik] *nm* : antihistamine
anti–inflammatoire [ɑ̃tiɛ̃flamatwar] *adj* : anti-inflammatory
antillais, -laise [ɑ̃tijɛ, -jɛz] *adj* : West Indian
Antillais, -laise *n* : West Indian
antilope [ɑ̃tilɔp] *nf* : antelope
antimite [ɑ̃timit] *adj* **boules antimites** : mothballs
antimoine [ɑ̃timwan] *nm* : antimony
antinucléaire [ɑ̃tinykleɛr] *adj* : antinuclear
antioxydant [antiɔksidɑ̃] *nm* : antioxidant — **antioxydant, -dante** [-sidɑ̃, -dɑ̃t] *adj*
antipathie [ɑ̃tipati] *nf* AVERSION : antipathy
antipode [ɑ̃tipɔd] *nm* **1** : antipode **2 être aux antipodes de** : to be diametrically opposed to
antiquaire [ɑ̃tikɛr] *nmf* : antique dealer
antique [ɑ̃tik] *adj* **1** : ancient **2** : antique **3** : old-fashioned, antiquated
antiquité [ɑ̃tikite] *nf* **1** : antiquity **2** : antique
antirabique [ɑ̃tirabik] *adj* : rabies <vaccin antirabique : rabies vaccine>
antirévolutionnaire [ɑ̃tirevɔlysjɔnɛr] *adj* : antirevolutionary
antisémite [ɑ̃tisemit] *adj* : anti-Semitic
antisémitisme [ɑ̃tisemitism] *nm* : anti-Semitism
antiseptique [ɑ̃tisɛptik] *adj & nm* : antiseptic
antisocial, -ciale [ɑ̃tisɔsjal] *adj, mpl* **-ciaux** [-sjo] : antisocial
antitabac [ɑ̃titaba] *adj* : antismoking
antithèse [ɑ̃titɛz] *nf* : antithesis
antitoxine [ɑ̃titɔksin] *nf* : antitoxin
antitrust [ɑ̃titrœst] *adj* : antitrust
antitussif, -sive [ɑ̃titysif, -siv] *adj* : cough <sirop antitussif : cough syrup>
antivol [ɑ̃tivɔl] *adj* : antitheft
antonyme [ɑ̃tɔnim] *nm* : antonym
antre [ɑ̃tr] *nm* **1** : den, lair **2** : cave
anus [anys] *nms & pl* : anus
anxiété [ɑ̃ksjete] *nf* : anxiety
anxieux, anxieuse [ɑ̃ksjø, -sjøz] *adj* : anxious — **anxieusement** [-sjøzmɑ̃] *adv*
aorte [aɔrt] *nf* : aorta
août [u(t)] *nm* : August
apaisement [apɛzmɑ̃] *nm* **1** : calming (down), soothing **2** : appeasement (in politics) **3 apaisements** *nmpl* : reassurances
apaiser [apeze] *vt* **1** : to pacify, to appease **2** : to assuage (hunger, thirst, etc.) **3** : to soothe, to calm, to mollify — **s'apaiser** *vr* : to die down, to calm down, to abate
apanage [apanaʒ] *nm* : prerogative
aparté [aparte] *nm* **1** : aside (in theater) **2** : private conversation
apartheid [apartɛd] *nm* : apartheid
apathie [apati] *nf* : apathy
apathique [apatik] *adj* : apathetic
apercevoir [apɛrsəvwar] {26} *vt* : to perceive, to see — **s'apercevoir** *vr* **1** : to catch sight of each other **2 ~ de** : to notice, to become aware of **3 ~ que** : to notice that, to realize that
aperçu [apɛrsy] *nm* **1** : glimpse **2** : outline, general idea <avoir des aperçus sur : to have some insight into>
apéritif [aperitif] *nm* : aperitif
apesanteur [apəzɑ̃tœr] *nf* : weightlessness
à–peu–près [apøprɛ] *nms & pl* : approximation

apeuré, -rée [apœre] *adj* : frightened, scared
apex [apɛks] *nms & pl* : apex
aphorisme [afɔrism] *nm* : aphorism
aphrodisiaque [afrɔdizjak] *adj & nm* : aphrodisiac
apiculteur, -trice [apikyltœr, -tris] *n* : beekeeper
apitoiement [apitwamɑ̃] *nm* : pity, compassion
apitoyer [apitwaje] {58} *vt* : to move (someone) to pity — **s'apitoyer** *vr* **~ sur** : to feel sorry for
aplanir [aplanir] *vt* **1** : to plane, to level **2** : to iron out, to resolve (a problem) — **s'aplanir** *vr*
aplatir [aplatir] *vt* : to flatten — **s'aplatir** *vr*
aplomb [aplɔ̃] *nm* **1** : aplomb, composure <perdre son aplomb : to lose one's nerve> **2** : perpendicularity **3 d'aplomb** : steady, balanced, upright
apocalypse [apɔkalips] *nf* : apocalypse
apocalyptique [apɔkaliptik] *adj* : apocalyptic
apocryphe [apɔkrif] *nm* **les Apocryphes** : the Apocrypha
apogée [apɔʒe] *nm* **1** : peak, culmination **2** : apogee (in astronomy)
apolitique [apɔlitik] *adj* : apolitical
apologie [apɔlɔʒi] *nf* : defense, justification
apoplexie [apɔplɛksi] *nf* : apoplexy — **apoplectique** [-plɛktik] *adj*
apostolique [apɔstɔlik] *adj* : apostolic
apostrophe [apɔstrɔf] *nf* **1** : direct address (in grammar) **2** : invective, rude remark **3** : apostrophe (sign of punctuation)
apostropher [apɔstrɔfe] *vt* : to shout at, to address rudely
apothéose [apɔteoz] *nf* **1** : highlight, crowning moment, grand finale **2** : apotheosis
apôtre [apotr] *nm* : apostle
apparaître [aparɛtr] {7} *vi* : to appear — *v impers* : to appear, to seem <il apparaît que : it seems that>
apparat [apara] *nm* **1** CÉRÉMONIE : pomp **2 d'~** : ceremonial
appareil [aparɛj] *nm* **1** : apparatus, device, appliance <appareil de télévision : television set> <appareil photo : camera> <appareil auditif : hearing aid> <appareil de chauffage : heater> **2** : telephone **3** : system <appareil digestif : digestive system>
appareillage [aparɛjaʒ] *nm* **1** : outfitting, equipment **2** : casting off (of a ship)
appareiller [aparɛje] *vt* **1** : to fit out (a ship, etc.) **2** : to match up, to pair — *vi* : to get under way
apparemment [aparamɑ̃] *adv* : apparently
apparence [aparɑ̃s] *nf* **1** ASPECT : appearance, appearing, guise **2 en ~** : apparently
apparent, -rente [aparɑ̃, -rɑ̃t] *adj* : apparent
apparenté, -tée [aparɑ̃te] *adj* : related
apparier [aparje] {96} *vt* : to pair, to match (up)
apparition [aparisjɔ̃] *nf* **1** : appearance **2** : apparition, ghost
appartement [apartəmɑ̃] *nm* : apartment
appartenance [apartənɑ̃s] *nf* : membership, affiliation, belonging
appartenir [apartənir] {92} *vi* **1 ~ à** : to belong to <ça m'appartient : that belongs to me> **2 ~ à** : to be a member of — *v impers* : to be up to <il appartient à vous de le faire : it's up to you to do it>
appât [apa] *nm* : bait, lure <mordre à l'appât : to take the bait>
appâter [apate] *vt* **1** : to bait **2** : to lure, to entice
appauvrir [apovrir] *vt* : to impoverish — **s'appauvrir** *vr*
appauvrissement [apovrismɑ̃] *nm* : impoverishment
appeau [apo] *nm, pl* **appeaux** : decoy
appel [apɛl] *nm* **1** : call <un appel téléphonique : a telephone call> <cri d'appel : call for help> **2** : appeal
appelé [aple] *nm* : draftee
appeler [aple] {8} *vt* **1** : to call <appeler au secours : to call for help> <tu m'appelleras au téléphone ce soir? : you'll phone me tonight?> **2** : to summon <faire appeler le médecin : to send for the doctor> **3** EXIGER : to require, to call for **4** NOMMER : to name **5 en appeler à** : to appeal to **6 en appeler de** : to appeal against, to dispute — **s'appeler** *vr* : to be named, to be called <je m'appelle Isabelle : my name is Isabelle>
appellation [apelasjɔ̃] *nf* **1** : name, designation **2 appellation contrôlée** : guaranteed vintage (of wine)
appelle [apɛl], **appellera** [apɛləra], *etc.* → **appeler**
appendice [apɑ̃dis] *nm* **1** : appendix (of a book) **2** : appendix (in anatomy) **3** : appendage, annex
appendicectomie [apɛ̃disɛktɔmi] *nf* : appendectomy
appendicite [apɑ̃disit] *nf* : appendicitis
appentis [apɑ̃ti] *nm* : lean-to, shed
appesantir [apəzɑ̃tir] *vt* : to weigh down, to slow down, to dull <les sens appesantis par l'épuisement : senses dulled by fatigue> — **s'appesantir** *vr* **1** : to grow heavier **2 ~ sur** : to dwell upon
appétissant, -sante [apetisɑ̃, -sɑ̃t] *adj* : appetizing
appétit [apeti] *nm* : appetite <bon appétit! : enjoy your meal!> <ouvrir l'appétit de qqn : to whet s.o.'s appetite>
applaudir [aplodir] *vt* : to applaud <applaudir une décision : to applaud a

decision> — *vi* : to applaud, to clap — **s'applaudir** *vr* : to congratulate oneself

applaudissements [aplodismɑ̃] *nmpl* : applause

applicable [aplikabl] *adj* : applicable — **applicabilité** [-kabilite] *nf*

applicateur [aplikatœr] *nm* : applicator

application [aplikasjɔ̃] *nf* **1** : applying (of paint, etc.) **2** : application, practicing <mettre en application : to put into practice> **3** : care <avec application : diligently, industriously>

applique [aplik] *nf* : appliqué

appliqué, -quée [aplike] *adj* : careful, industrious, diligent

appliquer [aplike] *vt* : to apply — **s'appliquer** *vr* **1** : to apply oneself, to take pains **2 ~ à** : to apply to <la loi s'applique à tous : the law applies to all>

appoint [apwɛ̃] *nm* **1** : change <faire l'appoint : to make exact change> **2** : contribution, support **3 d'~** : supplementary, extra

appointements [apwɛ̃təmɑ̃] *nmpl* : salary

appointer [apwɛ̃te] *vt* **1** : to pay a salary to **2** : to sharpen

apport [apɔr] *nm* **1** : contribution **2** : intake, supply

apporter [apɔrte] *vt* **1** AMENER : to bring **2** : to provide, to supply

apposer [apoze] *vt* : to put, to affix <apposez votre signature ici : sign here>

appréciable [apresjabl] *adj* : appreciable, considerable

appréciatif, -tive [apresjatif, -tiv] *adj* : appreciative

appréciation [apresjasjɔ̃] *nf* **1** : assessment, judgment **2** : appraisal, estimate **3** : appreciation (in value)

apprécier [apresje] {96} *vt* **1** : to appreciate, to value **2** ESTIMER : to appraise, to estimate — **s'apprécier** *vr* : to appreciate in value

appréhender [apreɑ̃de] *vt* **1** ARRÊTER : to apprehend, to arrest **2** : to dread

appréhension [apreɑ̃sjɔ̃] *nf* **1** : arrest **2** : dread

apprenait [aprənɛ] *etc.* → **apprendre**

apprendre [aprɑ̃dr] {70} *vt* **1** : to learn <j'apprends à parler l'anglais : I am learning to speak English> **2** : to hear, to learn of **3** : to teach <il m'a appris à jouer : he taught me how to play> **4** : to inform of, to tell — *vi* : to apprehend — **s'apprendre** *vr* : to be learned

apprenne [aprɛn] *etc.* → **apprendre**

apprenti, -tie [aprɑ̃ti] *n* : apprentice

apprentissage [aprɑ̃tisaʒ] *nm* **1** : apprenticeship <mettre en apprentissage : to apprentice> **2** : learning <faire l'apprentissage de : to learn about>

apprêt [aprɛ] *nm* **1** : finish, sizing, primer **2** : affectation <sans apprêt : unaffectedly> **3 apprêts** *nmpl* : preparations

apprêté, -tée [aprɛte] *adj* : affected, mannered

apprêter [aprɛte] *vt* **1** : to finish, to size, to dress **2** PRÉPARER : to prepare — **s'apprêter** *vr* : to get ready

appris [apri] *pp* → **apprendre**

apprivoiser [aprivwaze] *vt* : to tame — **s'apprivoiser** *vr* : to become tame, to become more sociable

approbateur, -trice [aprɔbatœr, -tris] *adj* : approving

approbation [aprɔbasjɔ̃] *nf* : approbation, approval

approchant, -chante [aprɔʃɑ̃, -ʃɑ̃t] *adj* : similar <qqch d'approchant : sth like that>

approche [aprɔʃ] *nf* **1** : approach <à l'approche du printemps : at the coming of spring> **2 approches** *nfpl* : surrounding area, vicinity

approcher [aprɔʃe] *vt* : to approach, to draw near to — *vi* **1** : to come near, to get nearer **2 ~ de** : to approach, to near <nous approchons de la fin : we're nearing the end> — **s'approcher** *vr* : to approach <il s'est approché de moi : he came up to me, he approached me>

approfondi, -die [aprɔfɔ̃di] *adj* : thorough, detailed

approfondir [aprɔfɔ̃dir] *vt* **1** : to deepen **2** : to enter deeply into, to delve into

approfondissement [aprɔfɔ̃dismɑ̃] *nm* : deepening

appropriation [aprɔprijasjɔ̃] *nf* : appropriation (of property, etc.)

approprié, -priée [aprɔprije] *adj* : appropriate, suitable

approprier [aprɔprije] {96} *vt* : to adapt — **s'approprier** *vr* **1** : to appropriate **2** S'ADAPTER : to be appropriate, to be suited

approuver [apruve] *vt* **1** : to approve, to pass **2** : to approve of

approvisionnement [aprɔvizjɔnmɑ̃] *nm* : provision, supply

approvisionner [aprɔvizjɔne] *vt* **1** : to supply, to stock **2** : to pay money into (an account, etc.) — **s'approvisionner** *vr* : to stock up

approximatif, -tive [aprɔksimatif, -tiv] *adj* : approximate — **approximativement** [-tivmɑ̃] *adv*

approximation [aprɔksimasjɔ̃] *nf* : approximation

appui [apɥi] *nm* **1** SOUTIEN : support <à l'appui de : in support of> <prendre appui sur : to lean on> **2 appui de fenêtre** : windowsill

appui-bras [apɥibra] *nm, pl* **appuis-bras** : armrest

appuie [apɥi], **appuiera** [apɥira], *etc.* → **appuyer**

appui-livres [apɥilivr] *nm, pl* **appuis-livres** *Can* : bookend

appuyer [apɥije] {58} *vt* **1** : to rest, to lean **2** : to support, to back up — *vi* **1** ~ **sur** : to push, to press **2** ~ **sur** : to emphasize, to stress **3** ~ **sur** : to bear <appuyer sur la droite : to bear right> — **s'appuyer** *vr* **1** : to lean **2** ~ **à** *or* ~ **contre** : to rest against **3** ~ **sur** : to depend on, to rely on

âpre [apr] *adj* **1** : sour, acrid **2** : harsh, bitter <après un âpre débat : following a bitter debate> **3 âpre au gain** AVIDE : acquisitive, greedy

après[1] [aprɛ] *adv* **1** : afterwards, later **2** : after, farther on (in space) **3** : next <qui est après? : who's next?>

après[2] *prep* **1** : after <jour après jour : day after day> <tournez après le pont : turn after the bridge> **2** : at, with <crier après qqn : to shout at s.o.> <je suis furieux après toi : I'm angry with you> **3 après coup** : afterwards **4 après que** : after <après qu'il a parlé : after he spoke> **5 après tout** : after all **6 d'**~ : according to, from <d'après lui : in his opinion>

après–demain [aprɛdmɛ̃] *adv* : the day after tomorrow

après–guerre [aprɛgɛr] *nm* : postwar period

après–midi [aprɛmidi] *nmfs & pl* : afternoon

âpreté [aprəte] *nf* **1** : bitterness, harshness **2** : tartness, pungency

à–propos [apropo] *nm* : appropriateness, aptness <faire preuve d'à-propos : to show presence of mind> <avec à-propos : aptly, suitably>

apte [apt] *adj* : capable, fit

aptitude [aptityd] *nf* : aptitude

aquarelle [akwarɛl] *nf* : watercolor

aquarium [akwarjɔm] *nm* : aquarium

aquatique [akwatik] *adj* : aquatic <plantes aquatiques : aquatic plants>

aqueduc [akdyk] *nm* : aqueduct

aquilin [akilɛ̃] *adj m* : aquiline

ara [ara] *nm* : macaw

arabe[1] [arab] *adj* : Arab, Arabian, Arabic

arabe[2] *nm* : Arabic (language)

Arabe *nmf* : Arab, Arabian

arabesque [arabɛsk] *nf* : arabesque

arable [arabl] *adj* : arable

arachide [araʃid] *nf* : peanut

araignée [areɲe] *nf* **1** : spider **2 araignée de mer** : spider crab

arbalète [arbalɛt] *nf* : crossbow

arbitrage [arbitraʒ] *nm* **1** : arbitration **2** : refereeing, umpiring

arbitraire [arbitrɛr] *adj* : arbitrary — **arbitrairement** [-trɛrmɑ̃] *adv*

arbitre [arbitr] *nm* **1** : arbitrator **2** : umpire, referee **3** : arbiter <un arbitre du goût : an arbiter of taste> **4 libre arbitre** : free will

arbitrer [arbitre] *vt* **1** : to arbitrate **2** : to referee, to umpire — *vi* ~ **entre** : to arbitrate between

arborer [arbɔre] *vt* **1** PORTER : to wear, to sport **2** : to bear, to display (a flag, etc.)

arboricole [arbɔrikɔl] *adj* : arboreal

arbre [arbr] *nm* **1** : tree <arbre de Noël : Christmas tree> <arbre généalogique : family tree> **2** : shaft

arbrisseau [arbriso] *nm* : shrub

arbuste [arbyst] *nm* : small shrub, bush

arc [ark] *nm* **1** : arc, curve **2** ARCHE : arch **3** : bow (in archery)

arcade [arkad] *nf* **1** : arch <arcade dentaire : dental arch> **2** : arcade

arcanes [arkan] *nmpl* : mysteries

arc–boutant [arkbutɑ̃] *nm, pl* **arcs–boutants** : flying buttress

arc–en–ciel [arkɑ̃sjɛl] *nm, pl* **arcs–en–ciel** : rainbow

archaïque [arkaik] *adj* : archaic

archange [arkɑ̃ʒ] *nm* : archangel

arche [arʃ] *nf* **1** : arch **2** : ark <l'arche de Noé : Noah's ark>

archéologie [arkeɔlɔʒi] *nf* : archaeology

archéologique [arkeɔlɔʒik] *adj* : archaeological

archéologue [arkeɔlɔg] *nmf* : archaeologist

archer [arʃe] *nm* : archer

archet [arʃɛ] *nm* : bow <archet de violon : violin bow>

archétype [arketip] *nm* : archetype

archevêque [arʃəvɛk] *nm* : archbishop

archidiocèse [arʃidjɔsɛz] *nm* : archdiocese

archipel [arʃipɛl] *nm* : archipelago

architecte [arʃitɛkt] *nmf* : architect

architecture [arʃitɛktyr] *nf* : architecture — **architectural, -rale** [-tyral] *adj, mpl* **-raux** [-ro]

archives [arʃiv] *nfpl* : archives

archiviste [arʃivist] *nmf* : archivist

arctique [arktik] *adj* : arctic <cercle arctique : arctic circle>

ardemment [ardamɑ̃] *adv* : ardently, passionately

ardent, -dente [ardɑ̃, -dɑ̃t] *adj* **1** : burning, glowing, blazing **2** : ardent, passionate

ardeur [ardœr] *nf* **1** : heat **2** : ardor, fervor

ardillon [ardijɔ̃] *nm* **1** : prong (of a buckle) **2** : barb (of a fishhook, etc.)

ardoise [ardwaz] *nf* : slate

ardu, -due [ardy] *adj* **1** : arduous, difficult **2** : steep

aréna [arena] *nm Can* : arena

arène [arɛn] *nf* **1** : arena **2 arènes** *nfpl* : amphitheater, bullring

arête [arɛt] *nf* **1** : fish bone **2** : edge, ridge **3 l'arête du nez** : the bridge of the nose

argent [arʒɑ̃] *nm* **1** : money <payer en argent comptant : to pay in cash> **2** : silver

argenté, -tée [arʒɑ̃te] *adj* **1** : silver-plated **2** : silvery **3** *fam* : loaded, well-heeled

argenterie [arʒɑ̃tri] *nf* : silverware
argentin, -tine [arʒɑ̃tɛ̃, -tin] *adj* **1** : silvery **2** : Argentine, Argentinean, Argentinian
Argentin, -tine *n* : Argentine, Argentinean, Argentinian
argile [arʒil] *nf* : clay
argileux, -leuse [arʒilø, -løz] *adj* : clayey
argon [argɔ̃] *nm* : argon
argot [argo] *nm* : argot, slang
argotique [argɔtik] *adj* : slang, slangy
arguer [argɥe] *vt* **1** : to deduce, to infer **2** ~ **de** : to use as a pretext **3** ~ **que** : to argue that, to protest that
argument [argymɑ̃] *nm* : argument
argumentation [argymɑ̃tasjɔ̃] *nf* : argumentation, rationale
argumenter [argymɑ̃te] *vi* : to argue, to debate
argutie [argysi] *nf* : quibble
aria [arja] *nf* : aria
aride [arid] *adj* **1** : arid, dry **2** : dull, uninteresting
aridité [aridite] *nf* : aridity
aristocrate [aristɔkrat] *nmf* : aristocrat — **aristocratique** [-kratik] *adj*
aristocratie [aristɔkrasi] *nf* : aristocracy
arithmétique[1] [aritmetik] *adj* : arithmetic, arithmetical
arithmétique[2] *nf* : arithmetic
arithmétiquement [aritmetikmɑ̃] *adv* : arithmetically
arlequin [arləkɛ̃] *nm* : harlequin
armada [armada] *nf* : armada
armature [armatyr] *nf* : frame, framework, reinforcement
arme [arm] *nf* **1** : weapon, arm <arme à feu : firearm> <prendre les armes : to take up arms> **2 armes** *nfpl* : coat of arms
armée [arme] *nf* : army
armement [armәmɑ̃] *nm* **1** : arming, equipping (of a military force) **2** : armament, weaponry, arms *pl* <la course aux armements : the arms race>
arménien[1], **-nienne** [armenjɛ̃, -njɛn] *adj* : Armenian
arménien[2] *nm* : Armenian (language)
Arménien, -nienne *n* : Armenian
armer [arme] *vt* **1** : to arm **2** : to cock (a gun) **3** : to reinforce
armistice [armistis] *nm* : armistice
armoire [armwar] *nf* : cupboard, cabinet, wardrobe <armoire à pharmacie : medicine cabinet>
armoiries [armwari] *nfpl* : coat of arms
armoise [armwaz] *nf* : sagebrush
armure [armyr] *nf* : armor
arnaque [arnak] *nf fam* : swindle, gyp
arnaquer [arnake] *vt fam* : to rip off, to swindle, to gyp
arnaqueur, -queuse [arnakœr, -køz] *n fam* : swindler
aromate [arɔmat] *nm* : spice, herb
aromatique [arɔmatik] *adj* : aromatic
aromatiser [arɔmatize] *vt* : to flavor
arôme [arom] *nm* **1** : aroma, fragrance **2** : flavor, flavoring
arpège [arpɛʒ] *nm* : arpeggio
arpentage [arpɑ̃taʒ] *nm* : surveying
arpenter [arpɑ̃te] *vt* **1** : to pace, to stride along **2** : to survey
arpenteur, -teuse [arpɑ̃tœr, -tøz] *n* : surveyor
arqué, -quée [arke] *adj* : arched, curved <jambes arquées : bandy legs>
arrache-pied [araʃpje] *adv* **d'arrache-pied** : nonstop, relentlessly
arracher [araʃe] *vt* **1** : to uproot, to tear out **2** : to extract, to pull out <arracher une dent : to extract a tooth> **3** : to snatch, to grab — *vi* **en** ~ *Can* : to have difficulty, to have problems — **s'arracher** *vr* **1** : to pull out, to pluck <s'arracher les cheveux : to tear one's hair> **2** : to fight over **3** ~ **de** : to tear oneself away from
arraisonner [arezɔne] *vt* : to board and inspect (a ship, plane, etc.)
arrangeant, -geante [arɑ̃ʒɑ̃, -ʒɑ̃t] *adj* : accommodating, obliging
arrangement [arɑ̃ʒmɑ̃] *nm* : arrangement
arranger [arɑ̃ʒe] {17} *vt* **1** : to arrange **2** RÉPARER : to repair, to fix **3** CONVENIR : to suit, to please <cette idée arrangera tout le monde : that idea will please everyone> **4** : to settle, to sort out — **s'arranger** *vr* **1** : to come to an agreement **2** : to get better, to improve <cela va s'arranger : things will turn out all right> **3 s'arranger pour faire** : to make sure something gets done
arrérages [areraʒ] *nmpl* : arrears
arrestation [arɛstasjɔ̃] *nf* : arrest
arrêt [arɛ] *nm* **1** : stopping, halt <sans arrêt : nonstop> **2** : stop <arrêt d'autobus : bus stop> **3** : ruling, decree **4** : save (in sports) **5 arrêts** *nmpl* : arrest (in the military) **6 arrêt du cœur** : heart failure, cardiac arrest
arrêt-court [arɛkur] *nm* : shortstop
arrêté[1], **-tée** [arete] *adj* : fixed, decided
arrêté[2] *nm* **1** : order, decree **2 arrêté de comptes** : settlement of accounts
arrêter [arete] *vt* **1** : to stop, to halt **2** : to switch off <arrêtez la radio : turn off the radio> **3** : to give up, to discontinue **4** : to arrest **5** : to decide upon, to fix — *vi* : to stop — **s'arrêter** *vr* **1** : to stop, to come to a halt **2** ~ **à** : to dwell on **3** ~ **de** : to give up <s'arrêter de fumer : to give up smoking>
arrhes [ar] *nfpl France* : deposit, down payment
arrière[1] [arjɛr] *adj* : back, rear <siège arrière : back seat>
arrière[2] *nm* **1** : back, rear <à l'arrière : in the back, at the rear, astern> <en arrière : backwards, back> <en arrière de : behind> **2** : fullback, back (in sports) **3 arrières** *nmpl* : rear (in

the military) **4 prendre de l'arrière** *Can* : to be slow <ma montre prend de l'arrière : my watch is slow>
arriéré[1], **-rée** [arjere] *adj* **1** : late, overdue **2** : backward <être arriéré : to be behind the times> **3** : (mentally) retarded
arriéré[2] *nm* **1** : arrears *pl* **2** : backlog
arrière–cours [arjɛrkur] *nf* : backyard
arrière–garde [arjɛrgard] *nf* : rear guard
arrière–goût [arjɛrgu] *nm* : aftertaste
arrière–grand–mère [arjɛrgrɑ̃mɛr] *nf, pl* **arrière–grands–mères** : great-grandmother
arrière–grand–père [arjɛrgrɑ̃pɛr] *nm, pl* **arrière–grands–pères** : great-grandfather
arrière–grands–parents [arjɛrgrɑ̃parɑ̃] *nmpl* : great-grandparents
arrière–pays [arjɛrpei] *nms & pl* : hinterland
arrière–pensée [arjɛrpɑ̃se] *nf* : ulterior motive
arrière–petite–enfante *f* : great-granddaughter
arrière–petit–enfant *m* : great-grandson
arrière–plan [arjɛrplɑ̃] *nm* : background
arrière–saison [arjɛrsɛzɔ̃] *nf* : late autumn
arrière–train [arjɛrtrɛ̃] *nm* **1** : hindquarters **2** *fam* : buttocks, bottom
arrimer [arime] *vt* **1** : to stow **2** : to secure, to fix
arrivage [arivaʒ] *nm* **1** : delivery **2** : arrival, influx (of persons)
arrivant, -vante [arivɑ̃, -vɑ̃t] *n* : newcomer, new arrival
arrivée [arive] *nf* **1** : arrival **2** : finish <ligne d'arrivée : finish line> **3** : inlet, intake (for air, gas, etc.)
arriver [arive] *vi* **1** : to arrive, to come <j'arrive! : I'm coming!> <arriver en retard : to be late> **2** : to succeed <arriver à sa fin : to achieve one's goal> <arriver à faire : to succeed in doing> **3** : to happen, to occur <cela m'est arrivé : that happened to me> <il arrive que : it happens that> **4 ~ à** ATTEINDRE : to reach
arriviste[1] [arivist] *adj* : (overly) ambitious, pushy
arriviste[2] *nmf* : upstart, go-getter
arrogance [arɔgɑ̃s] *nf* : arrogance
arrogant, -gante [arɔgɑ̃, -gɑ̃t] *adj* : arrogant
arroger [arɔʒe] {17} *v* **s'arroger** *vr* : to assume, to take upon oneself
arrondi [arɔ̃di] *nm* **1** : roundness **2** : hemline
arrondir [arɔ̃dir] *vt* **1** : to round, to make round **2** : to round off **3** AUGMENTER : to increase — **s'arrondir** *vr*
arrondissement [arɔ̃dismɑ̃] *nm* : district, subdivision
arrosage [arozaʒ] *nm* : watering, spraying
arroser [aroze] *vt* **1** : to water, to sprinkle, to spray **2** : to wash down (with wine), to drink to (a success, etc.) **3** : to baste (in cooking)
arroseur [arozœr] *nm* : sprinkler
arrosoir [arozwar] *nm* : watering can
arsenal [arsənal] *nm, pl* **-naux** [-no] **1** : arsenal, armory **2** : (naval) shipyard **3** : gear, equipment
arsenic [arsənik] *nm* : arsenic
art [ar] *nm* **1** : art <musée des beaux arts : museum of fine arts> <un œuvre d'art : a work of art> **2** : technique, skill
artère [artɛr] *nf* **1** : artery <durcissement des artères : hardening of the arteries> **2** : main road, thoroughfare
artériel, -rielle [arterjɛl] *adj* : arterial
artériosclérose [arterjɔskleroz] *nf* : arteriosclerosis
arthrite [artrit] *nf* : arthritis
arthritique [artritik] *adj* : arthritic
arthropode [artrɔpɔd] *nm* : arthropod
artichaut [artiʃo] *nm* : artichoke
article [artikl] *nm* **1** : article (in a publication) <article de fond : feature (article)> **2** : clause, section, article **3** : item (in commerce) <articles de toilette : toiletries> **4** : dictionary entry **5** : article (in grammar) <l'article indéfini : the indefinite article>
articulation [artikylasjɔ̃] *nf* **1** : articulation **2** JOINTURE : joint (in anatomy)
articuler [artikyle] *vt* **1** PRONONCER : to articulate, to state, to pronounce **2** : to join, to hinge — **s'articuler** *vr* : to connect <s'articuler autour de : to be based on, to hinge on>
artifice [artifis] *nm* **1** : trick, ruse **2** : artifice, device
artificiel, -cielle [artifisjɛl] *adj* : artificial, false — **artificiellement** [-sjɛlmɑ̃] *adv*
artificieux, -cieuse [artifisjø, -sjøz] *adj* : deceitful, cunning
artillerie [artijri] *nf* : artillery, gunnery
artilleur [artijœr] *nm* **1** : artilleryman, gunner **2** *Can* : pitcher (in baseball)
artisan, -sane [artizɑ̃, -zan] *n* **1** : artisan, craftsman *m*, craftswoman *f* **2** : maker, architect <artisan de la paix : peacemaker>
artisanat [artizana] *nm* **1** : artisans **2** : craft industry
artiste [artist] *nmf* : artist
artistique [artistik] *adj* : artistic — **artistiquement** [-tikmɑ̃] *adv*
as [as] *nm* **1** : ace <l'as de pique : the ace of spades> **2** : champion, ace (in sports)
ascaride [askarid] *nm* : roundworm
ascendance [asɑ̃dɑ̃s] *nf* **1** : descent, ancestry <d'ascendance égyptienne : of Egyptian descent> **2** : ascent, rising (in astronomy)

ascendant[1], -dante [asɑ̃dɑ̃, -dɑ̃t] *adj* : rising, ascending

ascendant[2] *nm* **1** : ascendancy, influence **2** : ascendant (in astronomy) **3 ascendants** *nmpl* : ancestors

ascenseur [asɑ̃sœr] *nm* : elevator

ascension [asɑ̃sjɔ̃] *nf* : ascent, climb

ascensionnel, -nelle [asɑ̃sjɔnɛl] *adj* : upward

ascète [asɛt] *nmf* : ascetic

ascétique [asetik] *adj* : ascetic

ascétisme [asetism] *nm* : asceticism

aseptique [asɛptik] *adj* : aseptic

aseptiser [asɛptize] *vt* : to sterilize, to disinfect

asiatique [azjatik] *adj* : Asian

Asiatique *nmf* : Asian

asile [azil] *nm* **1** : asylum, refuge <asile politique : political asylum> **2** : retreat, shelter <un asile de paix : a peaceful retreat> <asile pour la nuit : shelter for the night>

aspect [aspɛ] *nm* **1** : aspect, side **2** APPARENCE : appearance, look

asperge [aspɛrʒ] *nf* : asparagus (spear)

asperger [aspɛrʒe] *vt* {17} : to spray, to sprinkle, to splash

aspérité [asperite] *nf* **1** : bump, protrusion **2** : harshness, asperity

asphalte [asfalt] *nm* : asphalt

asphyxie [asfiksi] *nf* : asphyxiation

asphyxier [asfiksje] {96} *vt* **1** : to asphyxiate, to suffocate **2** : to stifle — **s'asphyxier** *vr*

aspic [aspik] *nm* **1** : asp **2** : aspic

aspirant, -rante [aspirɑ̃, -rɑ̃t] *n* : aspirant

aspirateur [aspiratœr] *nm* **1** : vacuum cleaner **2 passer l'aspirateur** : to vacuum

aspiration [aspirasjɔ̃] *nf* **1** : aspiration, hope **2** : suction **3** : inhaling

aspirer [aspire] *vt* **1** : to aspirate, to suck up **2** : to inhale — *vi* : to aspire <aspirer à une carrière politique : to aspire to a political career>

aspirine [aspirin] *nf* : aspirin

assagir [asaʒir] *vt* **1** : to make wiser **2** : to calm, to quiet down — **s'assagir** *vr* : to settle down

assaillant, -lante [asajɑ̃, -jɑ̃t] *n* : assailant, attacker

assaillir [asajir] {93} *vt* ATTAQUER : to assail, to attack

assainir [asenir] *vt* **1** : to clean, to purify **2** : to stabilize (an economy, etc.) — **s'assainir** *vr*

assainissement [asenismɑ̃] *nm* **1** : cleaning up, purification **2** : stabilization

assaisonnement [ɑsɛzɔnmɑ̃] *nm* : seasoning

assaisonner [asɛzɔne] *vt* : to season

assassin[1], -sine [asasɛ̃, -sin] *adj* **1** : murderous **2** : provocative

assassin[2] *nm* : murderer, assassin

assassinat [asasina] *nm* : murder, assassination

assassiner [asasine] *vt* : to murder, to assassinate

assaut [aso] *nm* **1** : assault, attack <prendre d'assaut : to storm, to take by storm> **2** : match (in fencing)

assécher [aseʃe] {87} *vt* **1** : to drain **2** : to dry (up)

assemblage [asɑ̃blaʒ] *nm* **1** : assembling, combining **2** : assembly, collection **3** : joint

assemblée [asɑ̃ble] *nf* **1** RÉUNION : meeting **2** : gathering <assemblée des fidèles : congregation> **3** : assembly, parliament

assembler [asɑ̃ble] *vt* : to assemble, to bring together, to put together — **s'assembler** *vr* : to gather <s'assembler en troupeau : to herd together>

asséner [asene] {87} *vt* : to strike <asséner un coup : to deal a blow>

assentiment [asɑ̃timɑ̃] *nm* : assent, consent

asseoir [aswar] {9} *vt* **1** : to seat, to sit (someone) up, to sit (someone) down **2** : to set up, to establish — **s'asseoir** *vr* : to sit down

assermentation [asɛrmɑ̃tasjɔ̃] *nf Can* : swearing in

assermenté, -tée [asɛrmɑ̃te] *adj* : sworn

assertion [asɛrsjɔ̃] *nf* : assertion

asservir [asɛrvir] *vt* **1** : to enslave **2** : to control

asservissement [asɛrvismɑ̃] *nm* **1** : enslavement **2** : subservience

assez [ase] *adv* **1** SUFFISAMMENT : enough, sufficiently <il ne rit pas assez : he doesn't laugh enough> **2** : rather, quite <elle le fait assez bien : she does it fairly well> **3 ~ de** : enough of, sufficient

assidu, -due [asidy] *adj* **1** ZÉLÉ : diligent, zealous **2** FRÉQUENT : constant, regular — **assidûment** [-dymɑ̃] *adv*

assiduité [asidɥite] *nf* **1** APPLICATION : assiduousness, diligence **2** FRÉQUENTATION : regular attendance **3 assiduités** *nfpl* : attentions

assiéger [asjeʒe] {64} *vt* ASSAILLIR : to besiege, to assail

assiette [asjɛt] *nf* **1** : plate, dish **2** : seat (on a horse) **3** : tax base **4 ne pas être dans son assiette** : to feel unwell

assiettée [asjete] *nf* : plateful

assignation [asiɲasjɔ̃] *nf* **1** : assignment, allocation **2** : summons, subpoena

assigner [asiɲe] *vt* **1** : to assign, to allot **2** : to summon, to subpoena

assimilation [asimilasjɔ̃] *nf* : assimilation

assimiler [asimile] *vt* **1** INTÉGRER : to assimilate, to integrate **2** APPRENDRE : to learn **3** IDENTIFIER : to liken, to compare, to consider the equivalent of — **s'assimiler** *vr* : to become assimilated

assis[1] [asi] *pp* → **asseoir**

assis[2], -sise [asiz] *adj* : seated, sitting down

assise *nf* **1** BASE : foundation, base **2** COUCHE : layer, stratum **3 assises** *nfpl* RÉUNION : meeting, conference **4 assises** *nfpl* : court <assises criminelles : criminal court>

assistance [asistɑ̃s] *nf* **1** AIDE : assistance, aid **2** : attendance **3** : audience

assistant, -tante [asistɑ̃, -tɑ̃t] *n* **1** ADJOINT : assistant <assistante sociale : social worker> **2** : spectator, audience member

assister [asiste] *vt* AIDER : to assist — *vi* **~ à** : to attend, to be present at

association [asɔsjasjɔ̃] *nf* **1** : association **2** : partnership

associé, -ciée [asɔsje] *n* : associate, partner

associer [asɔsje] {96} *vt* **1** : to associate, to bring together, to join <associer des idées : to associate ideas> **2 associer qqn à** : to include s.o. in — **s'associer** *vr* **1** : to join together, to be combined **2 ~ à** : to share in

assoie [aswa], **assoit** [aswa], *etc.* → **asseoir**

assoiffé, -fée [aswafe] *adj* : thirsty

assombrir [asɔ̃brir] *vt* **1** : to darken **2** : to cast a shadow over, to make gloomy — **s'assombrir** *vr*

assommant, -mante [asɔmɑ̃, -mɑ̃t] *adj* : boring, tiresome

assommer [asɔme] *vt* **1** : to stun, to knock out **2** *fam* : to bore stiff

assommoir [asɔmwar] *nm* : bludgeon, blackjack

assorti, -tie [asɔrti] *adj* : assorted

assortiment [asɔrtimɑ̃] *nm* **1** : assortment, collection, set **2** : matching, harmony (of colors, etc.) **3** : stock, inventory

assortir [asɔrtir] *vt* **1** : to match **2** APPROVISIONNER : to stock **3 ~ de** : to combine with, to add to — **s'assortir** *vr*

assoupir [asupir] *vt* **1** ENDORMIR : to make drowsy **2** ENGOURDIR : to dull, to numb — **s'assoupir** *vr* **1** : to doze off **2** : to wane, to die down

assoupissement [asupismɑ̃] *nm* : drowsiness

assouplir [asuplir] *vt* **1** : to make supple, to soften **2** : to ease, to relax, to limber up — **s'assouplir** *vr*

assouplisseur [asuplisœr] *nm* : fabric softener

assourdir [asurdir] *vt* **1** : to deafen **2** : to deaden, to muffle

assouvir [asuvir] *vt* : to appease, to satisfy, to satiate

assoyait [aswajɛ], *etc.* → **asseoir**

assujettir [asyʒetir] *vt* **1** : to subjugate **2** FIXER : to fix, to fasten **3 ~ à** : to subject to — **s'assujettir** *vr* : to submit

assujettissement [asyʒetismɑ̃] *nm* : subjugation

assumer [asyme] *vt* **1** : to assume, to take on **2** : to accept, to endure <le diagnostic était difficile à assumer : the diagnosis was difficult to accept>

assurance [asyrɑ̃s] *nf* **1** : insurance **2** PROMESSE : assurance, promise **3** CONFIANCE : confidence, self-confidence

assurance-vie *nf, pl* **assurances-vie** [asyrɑ̃svi] : life insurance

assuré[1], -rée [asyre] *adj* **1** : certain, sure **2** : assured, self-confident

assuré[2], -rée *n* : insured person

assurément [asyremɑ̃] *adv* : certainly, definitely, assuredly

assurer [asyre] *vt* **1** GARANTIR : to assure, to guarantee **2** POURVOIR : to provide, to supply **3** : to insure **4** : to secure, to steady — **s'assurer** *vr* **1** : to make sure **2** : to secure, to get

assureur [asyrœr] *nm* : insurance agent

aster [astɛr] *nm* : aster

astérisque [asterisk] *nm* : asterisk

astéroïde [asterɔid] *nm* : asteroid

asthmatique [asmatik] *adj & nmf* : asthmatic

asthme [asm] *nm* : asthma

asticot [astiko] *nm* : maggot

astigmate [astigmat] *adj* : astigmatic

astigmatisme [astigmatism] *nm* : astigmatism

astiquer [astike] *vt* : to polish

astral, -trale [astral] *adj, mpl* **astraux** [astro] : astral

astre [astr] *nm* : star

astreignant, -gnante [astrɛɲɑ̃, -ɲɑ̃t] *adj* : demanding, exacting

astreindre [astrɛ̃dr] {37} *vt* : to oblige, to compel, to force — **s'astreindre** *vr*

astringent, -gente [astrɛ̃ʒɑ̃, -ʒɑ̃t] *adj* : astringent

astrologie [astrɔlɔʒi] *nf* : astrology

astrologique [astrɔlɔʒik] *adj* : astrological

astrologue [astrɔlɔg] *nmf* : astrologer

astronaute [astrɔnot] *nmf* : astronaut

astronautique [astrɔnotik] *nf* : astronautics

astronome [astrɔnɔm] *nmf* : astronomer

astronomie [astrɔnɔmi] *nf* : astronomy

astronomique [astrɔnɔmik] *adj* : astronomical — **astronomiquement** [-mikmɑ̃] *adv*

astuce [astys] *nf* **1** : astuteness, cleverness **2** TRUC : trick, maneuver **3** PLAISANTERIE : joke, pun

astucieux, -cieuse [astysjø, -sjøz] *adj* : astute, clever — **astucieusement** [-sjøzmɑ̃] *adv*

asymétrie [asimetri] *nf* : asymmetry

asymétrique [asimetrik] *adj* : asymmetrical, asymmetric

asymptomatique [asɛ̃ptomatik] *adj* : asymptomatic

atavique [atavik] *adj* : atavistic

atelier [atəlje] *nm* **1** : studio **2** : workshop

atermoiements [atɛrmwamɑ̃] *nmpl* : procrastination

atermoyer [atɛrmwaje] {58} *vi* : to procrastinate
athée[1] [ate] *adj* : atheistic
athée[2] *nmf* : atheist
athéisme [ateism] *nm* : atheism
athlète [atlɛt] *nmf* : athlete
athlétique [atletik] *adj* : athletic
athlétisme [atletism] *nm* : athletics
atlantique [atlɑ̃tik] *adj* : Atlantic
atlas [atlas] *nm* : atlas
atmosphère [atmɔsfɛr] *nf* : atmosphere
atmosphérique [atmɔsferik] *adj* : atmospheric
atoca *or* **atocas** [atɔka] *nm Can* : cranberry
atoll [atɔl] *nm* : atoll
atome [atom] *nm* **1** : atom **2 avoir des atomes crochus avec qqn** : to hit it off with s.o.
atomique [atɔmik] *adj* : atomic
atomiseur [atɔmizœr] *nm* BOMBE : spray bottle, atomizer
atone [atɔn] *adj* **1** : dull, lifeless **2** : expressionless **3** : unaccented
atours [atur] *nmpl* : finery
atout [atu] *nm* **1** : trump (card) **2** AVANTAGE : advantage, asset
âtre [atr] *nm* : hearth
atroce [atrɔs] *adj* HORRIBLE : atrocious, horrible — **atrocement** [atrɔsmɑ̃] *adv*
atrocité [atrɔsite] *nf* : atrocity
atrophie [atrɔfi] *nf* : atrophy
atrophier [atrɔfje] {96} *vt* : to atrophy — **s'atrophier** *vr*
attabler [atable] *v* **s'attabler** *vr* : to sit down at the table
attachant, -chante [ataʃɑ̃, -ʃɑ̃t] *adj* : appealing, likeable
attache [ataʃ] *nf* **1** : fastener, string, strap **2** LIEN : tie, bond
attaché, -chée [ataʃe] *n* : attaché
attaché–case [ataʃekɛz] *nm, pl* **attachés–cases** : attaché case
attachement [ataʃmɑ̃] *nm* : attachment, close tie
attacher [ataʃe] *vt* **1** : to tie, to attach, to fasten **2** : to tie up — *vi* : to stick — **s'attacher** *vr* **1** : to fasten (up), to be buttoned **2** : to adhere, to cling **3 s'attacher à faire** : to apply oneself to doing
attaquant, -quante [atakɑ̃, -kɑ̃t] *n* **1** : attacker **2** : forward (in sports)
attaque [atak] *nf* **1** : attack **2** : stroke, fit, attack (in medicine)
attaquer [atake] *vt* **1** : to attack, to assault **2** : to tackle, to get started on — **s'attaquer** *vr* **~ à** : to attack
attardé [atarde] *adj* **1** : late **2** : retarded **3** ARRIÉRÉ : backward, old-fashioned
attarder [atarde] *vt* : to delay, to slow down — **s'attarder** : to linger
atteignait [ateɲɛ], **atteignions** [ateɲiɔ̃], *etc.* → **atteindre**
atteigne [ateɲə], *etc.* → **atteindre**
atteindre [atɛ̃dr] {37} *vt* **1** : to reach, to attain, to achieve **2** : to strike, to hit **3** : to affect **4** : to contact, to get in touch with
atteinte [atɛ̃t] *nf* **1** : attack <porter atteinte à : to undermine> **2 hors d'atteinte** : out of reach
attelage [atlaʒ] *nm* : team (of animals)
atteler [atle] {8} *vt* : to harness, to yoke — **s'atteler** *vr* **~ à** : to apply oneself to
attelle [atɛl] *nf* : splint
attenant, -nante [atnɑ̃, -nɑ̃t] *adj* : adjacent, adjoining
attendre [atɑ̃dr] {63} *vt* **1** : to wait for, to await <je l'attends : I'm waiting for him> <attendez voir : let's wait and see> **2** : to expect, to anticipate <attendre un bébé : to be expecting (a baby)> **3** : to be ready for <le dîner t'attend : your dinner's ready> **4** : to be in store for — *vi* **1** : to wait <faire attendre qqn : to keep s.o. waiting> **2 ~ après** : to be in a hurry for **3 en attendant** : in the meantime — **s'attendre** *vr* **~ à** : to expect
attendri, -drie [atɑ̃dri] *adj* : tender
attendrir [atɑ̃drir] *vt* **1** ÉMOUVOIR : to move, to touch **2** : to tenderize, to soften — **s'attendrir** *vr*
attendrissant, -sante [atɑ̃drisɑ̃, -sɑ̃t] *adj* ÉMOUVANT : moving, touching
attendrissement [atɑ̃drismɑ̃] *nm* **1** : compassion **2** : tenderness
attendu[1], **-due** [atɑ̃dy] *adj* **1** : expected **2** : long-awaited
attendu[2] *prep* **1** : considering, given <attendu sa pauvreté, il s'habille bien : considering his poverty, he dresses well> **2 attendu que** : considering that, seeing that
attentat [atɑ̃ta] *nm* **1** : attack, assault <attentat à la pudeur : indecent assault> **2** : murder attempt, assassination attempt
attente [atɑ̃t] *nf* **1** : wait, waiting <dix minutes d'attente : a ten-minute wait> **2** : expectation, hope
attenter [atɑ̃te] *vi* **~ à** : to make an attempt on (someone's life), to violate (rights, etc.)
attentif, -tive [atɑ̃tif, -tiv] *adj* **1** : attentive <être attentif à : to pay attention to> **2** : careful, scrupulous — **attentivement** [-tivmɑ̃] *adv*
attention [atɑ̃sjɔ̃] *nf* **1** : attention <faire attention : to pay attention> **2 attention!** : look out!, beware!
attentionné, -née [atɑ̃sjɔne] *adj* : considerate, attentive
atténuant, -nuante [atenɥɑ̃, -nɥɑ̃t] *adj* : extenuating, mitigating <circonstances atténuantes : extenuating circumstances>
atténuation [atenɥasjɔ̃] *nf* : reduction, easing, mitigation
atténuer [atenɥe] *vt* : to ease, to tone down, to reduce — **s'atténuer** *vr*
atterrer [atere] *vt* : to dismay, to appall

atterrir [aterir] *vi* : to land, to make a landing

atterrissage [aterisaʒ] *nm* : landing <atterrissage d'urgence : emergency landing>

attestation [atɛstasjɔ̃] *nf* **1** : affidavit, attestation **2** : certificate

attester [atɛste] *vt* : to attest, to vouch for, to testify to

attiédir [atjedir] *vt* : to make lukewarm, to cool down

attifer [atife] *vt fam* : to deck out, to doll up

attirail [atiraj] *nm* **1** : gear, equipment **2** *fam* : paraphernalia

attirance [atirɑ̃s] *nf* : attraction

attirant, -rante [atirɑ̃, -rɑ̃t] *adj* ATTRAYANT : attractive

attirer [atire] *vt* **1** : to attract **2** : to lure, to entice **3 attirer des ennuis à** : to make trouble for

attiser [atize] *vt* : to stir up, to fuel <attiser le feu : to fan the flames>

attitré, -trée [atitre] *adj* **1** OFFICIEL : official, authorized **2** HABITUEL : regular

attitude [atityd] *nf* **1** : attitude **2** : posture, bearing

attouchement [atuʃmɑ̃] *nm* : touching, fondling

attraction [atraksjɔ̃] *nf* **1** : attraction <l'attraction magnétique : magnetic force> **2 attractions** *nfpl* : attractions, amusements

attrait [atrɛ] *nm* **1** : appeal, attraction **2 attraits** *nmpl* : charms

attrape [atrap] *nm* : trick, joke, catch

attrape-nigaud [atrapnigo] *nm fam* : con, con game

attraper [atrape] *vt* : to capture, to catch <attraper un rhume : to catch a cold> — **s'attraper** *vr*

attrayant, -trayante [atrɛjɑ̃, -trɛjɑ̃t] *adj* ATTIRANT : attractive <peu attrayant : unappealing, unattractive>

attribuable [atribɥabl] *adj* : attributable, ascribable

attribuer [atribɥe] *vt* **1** : to attribute, to ascribe **2** : to assign — **s'attribuer** *vr* : to claim, to appropriate

attribut [atriby] *nm* : attribute

attribution [atribysjɔ̃] *nf* **1** : attribution **2** : awarding, allotment, allocation

attrister [atriste] *vt* : to sadden

attroupement [atrupmɑ̃] *nm* : crowd

attrouper [atrupe] *v* **s'attrouper** *vr* : to gather (together)

au [o] → **à, le**

aubaine [obɛn] *nf* **1** : godsend, windfall **2** : good deal, bargain

aube [ob] *nf* **1** AURORE : dawn **2** : paddle, blade <bateaux à aubes : paddle boat>

aubépine [obepin] *nf* : hawthorn

auberge [obɛrʒ] *nf* : inn <auberge de jeunesse : youth hostel>

aubergine [obɛrʒin] *nf* : eggplant

aubergiste [obɛrʒist] *nmf* : innkeeper

aucun¹, -cune [okœ̃, -kyn] *adj* **1** (*in negative constructions*) : no, none, not any <il n'y a aucun doute : there is no doubt> **2** : any <plus qu'aucun autre : more than any other>

aucun², -cune *pron* **1** : none, not any <aucune de ses idées n'est bonne : none of his ideas is good> **2** : any, anyone <il travaille plus qu'aucun de ses amis : he works more than any of his friends> **3 d'aucuns** : some, some people

aucunement [okynmɑ̃] *adv* NULLEMENT : not at all, in no way

audace [odas] *nf* **1** : audacity, nerve **2** COURAGE : boldness, daring

audacieux, -cieuse [odasjø, -jøz] *adj* **1** : audacious **2** HARDI : bold, daring — **audacieusement** [odasjøzmɑ̃] *adv*

au-dedans [odədɑ̃] *adv* **1** : inside **2 ~ de** : inside (of), within <au-dedans du bâtiment : inside the building>

au-dehors [odəɔr] *adv* **1** : outside **2 ~ de** : outside (of) <au-dehors de la ville : outside the city>

au-delà¹ [odəla] *adv* **1** : beyond **2 ~ de** : beyond <au-delà de l'horizon : beyond the horizon>

au-delà² *nm* **l'au-delà** : eternity, the afterlife

au-dessous [odsu] *adv* **1** : below **2 ~ de** : beneath, below, under <au-dessous de la table : under the table>

au-dessus [odsy] *adv* **1** : above **2 ~ de** : above, over <au-dessus de la terre : above ground>

au-devant [odvɑ̃] *adv* : ahead <aller au-devant de qqn : to go to meet s.o.> <aller au-devant des demandes : to anticipate requests> <aller au-devant du danger : to court danger>

audible [odibl] *adj* : audible — **audibilité** [-bilite] *nf*

audience [odjɑ̃s] *nf* **1** PUBLIC : audience **2** : hearing, session <audiences publiques : public hearings>

audio [odjo] *adj* : audio

audiovisuel, -suelle [odjɔvizɥɛl] *adj* : audiovisual

audit [odit] *nm* : audit

auditer [odite] *vt* : to audit

auditeur, -trice [oditœr, -tris] *n* **1** : listener <les auditeurs : the audience> **2** : auditor

auditif, -tive [oditif, -tiv] *adj* : auditory, hearing

audition [odisjɔ̃] *nf* **1** : hearing (sense) **2** : audition **3** : examination, (judicial) hearing

auditionner [odisjɔne] *v* : to audition

auditoire [oditwar] *nm* **1** PUBLIC : audience **2** *Bel & Switz* : auditorium

auditorium [oditɔrjɔm] *nm* : auditorium

auge [oʒ] *nf* : trough

augmentation [ogmɑ̃tasjɔ̃] *nf* **1** ACCROISSEMENT : augmentation, increase **2** : raise (in salary, prices, etc.)

augmenter [ogmɑ̃te] *vt* : to augment, to increase, to raise — *vi* : to increase, to rise
augure [ogyr] *nm* **1** : omen <c'est de bon augure : that's a good omen> **2** : oracle, soothsayer
augurer [ogyre] *vt* : to augur, to bode <cela augure mal pour lui : that doesn't bode well for him>
auguste [ogyst] *adj* : august, noble, majestic
aujourd'hui [oʒurdɥi] *adv & nm* : today <il y a aujourd'hui un mois : a month ago today>
aulne [on] *nm* : alder
aulx → **ail**
aumône [omon] *nf* : alms *pl* <faire l'aumône à : to give alms to>
aumônier [omonje] *nm* : chaplain
auparavant [oparavɑ̃] *adv* **1** AVANT : before, previously **2** : beforehand, first
auprès [oprɛ] *adv* **~ de 1** : beside, near, next to **2** : with, on, over <avoir de l'influence auprès de qqn : to have influence over s.o.> **3** : to <ambassadeur auprès des Nations Unies : ambassador to the United Nations> **4** : compared with **5** : in the opinion of
auquel [okɛl] → **lequel**
aura[1] [ɔra] *pp* → **avoir**
aura[2] [ora] *nf* : aura
auréole [oreɔl] *nf* **1** : halo **2** TACHE : spot, ring
auriculaire *nm* [orikylɛr] : little finger, pinkie
aurique [orik] *adj* : fore-and-aft
aurore [ɔrɔr] *nf* **1** : aurora <aurore boréale : aurora borealis, northern lights> **2** AUBE : dawn
ausculter [oskylte] *vt* : to examine (with a stethoscope), to sound
auspices [ospis] *nmpl* : auspices <sous les auspices de : under the auspices of>
aussi[1] [osi] *adv* **1** : too, also, as well **2** TELLEMENT : so <je ne savais pas qu'elle était aussi occupée : I didn't know she was so busy> **3** : as <il est aussi grand que moi : he is as tall as me> <aussi difficile qu'il soit : however difficult it may be> **4 aussi bien que** : as well as
aussi[2] *conj* **1** : so, therefore **2** D'AILLEURS : but, in any case
aussitôt [osito] *adv* **1** : immediately **2 aussitôt que** : as soon as
austère [ostɛr] *adj* : austere — **austèrement** [ostɛrmɑ̃] *adv*
austérité [osterite] *nf* : austerity
austral, -trale [ostral] *adj, mpl* **australs** : southern
australien, -lienne [ostraljɛ̃, -jɛn] *adj* : Australian
Australien, -lienne *n* : Australian
autant [otɑ̃] *adv* **1** : as much, as many, so much, so many <il n'en a jamais vu autant : he never saw so much of it> **2 ~ de** : as much, as many, so much, so many <autant d'enfants que d'adultes : as many children as adults> **3 ~ que** : as much as, as many as, as far as <j'en ai autant que vous : I have as much as you do> <(pour) autant que je sache : as far as I know> **4 autant comme autant** *Can* : time and time again **5 d'autant plus** : all the more **6 pour autant** : for all that **7 pour autant que** : insofar as, as far as
autel [otɛl] *nm* : altar
auteur [otœr] *nm* **1** : author, composer, artist <auteur dramatique : playwright> **2** : originator, inventor **3** : perpetrator
auteure [otœr] *nf Can* : author
authenticité [otɑ̃tisite] *nf* : authenticity
authentifier [otɑ̃tifje] {96} *vt* : to authenticate
authentique [otɑ̃tik] *adj* : authentic — **authentiquement** [-tikmɑ̃] *adv*
autisme [otism] *nm* : autism
autiste [otist] *or* **autistique** [otistik] *adj* : autistic
auto [oto] *nf* : car, automobile
autobiographie [otɔbjɔgrafi] *nf* : autobiography
autobiographique [otɔbjɔgrafik] *adj* : autobiographical
autobus [otɔbys] *nm* BUS : bus
autocar [otɔkar] *nm* : bus, coach
autochtone [otɔktɔn] *adj & nmf* : native
autocollant[1], **-lante** [otɔkɔlɑ̃, -lɑ̃t] *adj* : self-adhesive
autocollant[2] *nm* : sticker, bumper sticker
autocrate [otɔkrat] *nmf* : autocrat — **autocratique** [-kratik] *adj*
autocratie [otɔkrasi] *nf* : autocracy
autocritique [otɔkritik] *nf* : self-criticism
autocuiseur [otɔkɥizœr] *nm* : pressure cooker
autodéfense [otɔdefɑ̃s] *nf* : self-defense
autodestructeur, -trice [otɔdɛstryktœr, -tris] *adj* : self-destructive
autodétermination [otɔdetɛrminasjɔ̃] *nf* : self-determination
autodidacte[1] [otɔdidakt] *adj* : self-taught
autodidacte[2] *nmf* : autodidact, self-taught person
autodiscipline [otɔdisiplin] *nf* : self-discipline
autographe [otɔgraf] *nm* : autograph
auto–infligé, -gée [otɔɛ̃fliʒe] *adj* : self-inflicted
automate [otɔmat] *nm* : automaton
automation [otɔmasjɔ̃] *nf* : automation
automatique [otɔmatik] *adj* : automatic — **automatiquement** [-tikmɑ̃] *adv*
automatisation [otɔmatizasjɔ̃] *nf* : automation, automating
automatiser [otɔmatize] *vt* : to automate

automnal, -nale [otɔnal] *adj, mpl* **-naux** [-no] : autumnal
automne [otɔn] *nm* : autumn, fall
automobile[1] [otɔmɔbil] *adj* : automotive, motor <l'industrie automobile : the motor industry>
automobile[2] *nf* : automobile, car
automobiliste [otɔmɔbilist] *nmf* : motorist, driver
autonome [otɔnɔm] *adj* : autonomous
autonomie [otɔnɔmi] *nf* : autonomy
autoportrait [otɔpɔrtrɛ] *nm* : self-portrait
autopropulsé, -sée [otɔprɔpylsi] *adj* : self-propelled
autopsie [otɔpsi] *nf* : autopsy — **autopsier** [-sje] *vt*
autoradio [otɔradjo] *nm* : car radio
autorisation [otɔrizasjɔ̃] *nf* **1** : authorization, permission **2** : license, permit
autorisé, -sée [otɔrize] *adj* **1** : permitted, allowed **2** : authoritative
autoriser [otɔrize] *vt* : to authorize, to give permission for, to empower
autoritaire [otɔritɛr] *adj* : authoritative — **autoritairement** [-tɛrmɑ̃] *adv*
autorité [otɔrite] *nf* : authority <faire autorité : to be authoritative>
autoroute [otɔrut] *nf* : (interstate) highway, freeway <autoroute à péage : turnpike>
auto-stop [otɔstɔp] *nm* **1** : hitchhiking **2 faire de l'auto-stop** : to hitchhike
auto-stoppeur, -peuse [otɔstɔpœr, -pøz] *n* : hitchhiker
autosuffisance [otɔsyfizɑ̃s] *nf* : self-sufficiency, self-reliance
autosuffisant, -sante [otɔsyfizɑ̃, -zɑ̃t] *adj* : self-sufficient
autour [otur] *adv* **1** : around, about <tout autour : all around> **2 ~ de** : around, about <autour de la table : around the table> <autour de six heures : about six o'clock>
autre[1] [otr] *adj* **1** : other, different <l'autre jour : the other day> <un autre problème : another problem> <se sentir autre : to feel different> **2 autre chose** : something else, something different **3 autre part** : somewhere else
autre[2] *pron* : other, another <suivons les autres : let's follow the others> <prenez-en un autre : take another one>
autrefois [otrəfwa] *adv* **1** JADIS : formerly, in the past **2 d'~** : of old, of the past <ma vie d'autrefois : my past life>
autrement [otrəmɑ̃] *adv* **1** : otherwise, differently <elle ne pouvait pas faire autrement : she couldn't act differently> <autrement dit : in other words> **2** : otherwise, if not <autrement vous le regretterez : otherwise you will be sorry> **3** : far (more) <c'est autrement moins sérieux : it's much less serious> **4 pas autrement** : not especially
autrichien, -chienne [otriʃjɛ̃, -ʃjɛn] *adj* : Austrian
Autrichien, -chienne *n* : Austrian
autruche [otryʃ] *nf* : ostrich
autrui [otrɥi] *pron* : others, other people
auvent [ovɑ̃] *nm* : canopy, awning
aux [o] → **à, les**
auxiliaire[1] [oksiljɛr] *adj* : auxiliary
auxiliaire[2] *nmf* : auxiliary
auxiliaire[3] *nm* : auxiliary (verb)
auxquels, auxquelles [okɛl] → **lequel**
avachi, -chie [avaʃi] *adj* **1** : shapeless, misshapen **2** : limp, flabby
aval [aval] *nm* **1** : endorsement (in law and finance) **2** : SOUTIEN : support, backing **3** : **en ~** : downstream, lower down
avalanche [avalɑ̃ʃ] *nf* : avalanche
avaler [avale] *vt* **1** : to swallow **2** : to inhale
avaliser [avalize] *vt* : to endorse, to support
avance [avɑ̃s] *nf* **1** : advance **2** : lead **3 à l'avance** : in advance, ahead of schedule **4 d'avance** *or* **par ~** : in advance, already **5 en ~** : early **6 avances** *nfpl* : advances, overtures
avancé, -cée [avɑ̃se] *adj* **1** : advanced **2** : progressive
avancée *nf* : overhang, projection
avancement [avɑ̃smɑ̃] *nm* **1** : advancement, progress **2** : promotion
avancer [avɑ̃se] {6} *vt* **1** : to advance, to put forward **2** : to promote, to further — *vi* **1** : to advance, to go forward **2** : to be ahead of time <ma montre avance de trois minutes : my watch is three minutes fast> — **s'avancer** *vr* **1** : to advance, to move forward **2** : to progress, to get ahead **3** : to project, to protrude
avanie [avani] *nf* : snub
avant[1] [avɑ̃] *adv* **1** : before <quelques semaines avant : a few weeks before> <la page d'avant : the preceding page> **2** : first <tu devrais manger avant : you should eat first> **3** : far, deep <avant dans la forêt : deep within the forest> **4** : in front <elle marchait avant : she was walking in front> **5 ~ de** : before <avant de partir : before leaving> **6 avant que** : before, until <ne parlez pas avant qu'il ne le fasse : don't speak until he does>
avant[2] *adj* : front <la roue avant : the front wheel>
avant[3] *nm* **1** : front **2** : forward (in sports) **3 en ~** : forward, ahead **4 en avant de** : ahead of
avant[4] *prep* **1** : before, by <avant la fin : before the end> <avant huit heures : by eight o'clock> <avant peu : shortly> **2 avant tout** : first and foremost, above all

avantage [avɑ̃taʒ] *nm* **1** : advantage <tirer avantage de : to take advantage of> **2** : benefit <avantages sociaux : fringe benefits> **3 être à son avantage** : to look one's best

avantager [avɑ̃taʒe] {17} *vt* **1** FAVORISER : to favor, to give an advantage to **2** : to flatter, to show to advantage

avantageux, -geuse [avɑ̃taʒø, -ʒøz] *adj* **1** : advantageous, attractive <prix avantageux : attractive prices> **2** : flattering — **avantageusement** [-ʒøzmɑ̃] *adv*

avant–bras [avɑ̃bra] *nm* : forearm

avant–coureur [avɑ̃kurœr] *adj* : precursory, early

avant–dernier, -nière [avɑ̃dɛrnje, -njɛr] *adj* : next to last

avant–garde [avɑ̃gard] *nf* **1** : vanguard **2** : avant-garde

avant–goût [avɑ̃gu] *nm* : foretaste

avant–hier [avɑ̃tjɛr] *adv* : the day before yesterday

avant–midi [avɑ̃midi] *nf & pl Can nms & pl Belg* : morning

avant–poste [avɑ̃pɔst] *nm* : outpost

avant–première [avɑ̃prəmjɛr] *nf* : preview

avant–projet [avɑ̃prɔʒe] *nm* : (rough) draft

avant–propos [avɑ̃prɔpo] *nms & pl* : foreword

avant–toit [avɑ̃twa] *nm* : eaves *pl*

avare[1] [avar] *adj* : miserly, greedy

avare[2] *nmf* : miser

avarice [avaris] *nf* : avarice, miserliness

avaricieux, -cieuse [avarisjø, -sjøz] *adj* : miserly, stingy

avarie [avari] *nf* : damage (in shipping)

avatar [avatar] *nm* **1** : mishap **2** : metamorphosis, transformation **3** : avatar

avec[1] [avɛk] *adv fam* : with it, with that, with them <voulez-vous du vin avec? : would you like wine with that?>

avec[2] *prep* : with

aveline [avlin] *nf* : filbert (nut)

avenant[1], **-nante** [avnɑ̃, -nɑ̃t] *adj* : pleasant, attractive

avenant[2] *nm* **1** : endorsement **2** : codicil **3 à l'avenant** : in keeping, in conformity

avènement [avɛnmɑ̃] *nm* **1** : accession (to a throne) **2** : coming, advent

avenir [avnir] *nm* : future <à l'avenir : in the future>

avent [avɑ̃] *nm* **l'avent** : Advent

aventure [avɑ̃tyr] *nf* **1** : adventure **2** : venture **3** LIAISON : love affair **4 d'**~ : by chance

aventurer [avɑ̃tyre] *vt* : to risk — **s'aventurer** *vr* : to venture

aventureux, -reuse [avɑ̃tyrø, -røz] *adj* **1** : adventurous, venturesome **2** : risky

aventurier, -rière [avɑ̃tyrje, -rjɛr] *n* : adventurer

avenu, -nue [avny] *adj* **nul et non avenu** : null and void

avenue *nf* : avenue

avéré, -rée [avere] *adj* : acknowledged, recognized

avérer [avere] {87} *v* **s'avérer** *vr* : to prove to be, to turn out to be

averse [avɛrs] *nf* : shower, storm

aversion [avɛrsjɔ̃] *nf* : aversion, dislike

avertir [avɛrtir] *vt* **1** : to warn **2** AVISER : to advise, to inform

avertissement [avɛrtismɑ̃] *nm* **1** : warning **2** : official notice, reprimand **3** : foreword (of a book)

avertisseur [avɛrtisœr] *nm* **1** : (car) horn **2** : alarm <avertisseur de fumée : smoke alarm>

aveu [avø] *nm, pl* **aveux** : confession, admission <passer aux aveux : to confess>

aveuglant, -glante [avœglɑ̃, -glɑ̃t] *adj* : blinding, glaring

aveugle[1] [avœgl] *adj* : blind

aveugle[2] *nmf* : blind person

aveuglement [avœgləmɑ̃] *nm* : blindness

aveuglément [avœglemɑ̃] *adv* : blindly

aveugler [avœgle] *vt* **1** : to blind, to dazzle **2** : to block, to stop up — **s'aveugler** *vr* ~ **sur** : to turn a blind eye to

aveuglette [avœglɛt] *adv* **à l'aveuglette** : blindly <avancer à l'aveuglette : to grope one's way>

aviateur, -trice [avjatœr, -tris] *n* : aviator, pilot

aviation [avjasjɔ̃] *nf* : aviation

aviculture [avikyltyr] *nf* : poultry farming

avide [avid] *adj* **1** : greedy **2** : eager — **avidement** [avidmɑ̃] *adv*

avidité [avidite] *nf* **1** : greed **2** : eagerness

avilir [avilir] *vt* : to degrade, to debase — **s'avilir** *vr*

avilissement [avilismɑ̃] *nm* : degradation, debasement

aviné, -née [avine] *adj* : inebriated

avion [avjɔ̃] *nm* : airplane <avion à réaction : jet plane> <avion de ligne : airliner> <avion de chasse : fighter plane>

avion–cargo [avjɔ̃kargo] *nm, pl* **avions–cargos** : cargo plane, freighter

aviron [avirɔ̃] *nm* **1** RAME : oar **2** *Can* : paddle **3** : rowing

avis [avis] *nm* **1** : opinion <à mon avis : in my opinion> <changer d'avis : to change one's mind> **2** ANNONCE : notice, notification **3** CONSEIL : advice

avisé, -sée [avize] *adj* : prudent, sensible

aviser [avize] *vt* INFORMER : to advise, to inform, to notify — *vi* RÉFLÉCHIR : to think things over, to decide — **s'aviser** *vr* : to realize, to take notice

aviver [avive] *vt* **1** : to revive, to stir up **2** : to brighten, to liven up

avocat[1], **-cate** [avɔka, -kat] *n* **1** : lawyer, attorney **2** : advocate

avocat[2] *nm* : avocado

avoine [avwan] *nf* : oats *pl*

avoir[1] [avwar] {10} *vt* **1** : to have <il a de l'argent : he has money> <elle va avoir un enfant : she's going to have a baby> **2** : to get <j'ai eu mes billets hier : I got my tickets yesterday> **3** : to be (a particular age) <j'ai seize ans : I'm sixteen years old> **4** : to suffer, to feel <qu'est-ce que tu as? : what's wrong?> <j'ai mal : I'm hurt> **5 ~ à** : to have to <j'ai à vous parler : I must speak to you> **6 se faire avoir** *fam* : to be had, to be conned — *v impers* **il y a** : there is, there are — *v aux* : to have <je l'ai écrit : I wrote it, I have written it, I did write it> <elle y avait été : she had been there> <ils auront fini demain : they will have finished tomorrow>

avoir[2] *nm* **1** : assets *pl*, property **2** : credit

avoirdupoids [avwardypwa] *nm* : avoirdupois

avoisiner [avwazine] *vt* : to neighbor, to be near

avortement [avɔrtəmɑ̃] *nm* **1** : abortion <avortement spontané : miscarriage> **2** : failure, collapse

avorter [avɔrte] *vi* **1** : to abort, to miscarry **2** : to fail, to abort

avorton [avɔrtɔ̃] *nm* : runt

avoué[1], **-vouée** [avwe] *adj* : avowed, declared

avoué[2] *nm* : attorney

avouer [avwe] *vt* : to admit, to confess to — *vi* : to own up — **s'avouer** *vr* : to admit <s'avouer coupable : to admit one's guilt>

avril [avril] *nm* : April

axe [aks] *nm* **1** : axis **2** : axle **3** : major road, highway **4** : main line, mainstream (in politics, etc.)

axer [akse] *vt* : to center, to focus

axiomatique [aksjɔmatik] *adj* : axiomatic

axiome [aksjom] *nm* : axiom

axis [aksis] *nms & pl* : axis

ayoye *or* **ayoille** [ajɔj] *interj Can* : ouch!

azalée [azale] *nf* : azalea

azimut [azimyt] *nm* **1** : azimuth **2 tous azimuts** : all out, total **3 dans tous les azimuts** : all over the place

azote [azɔt] *nm* : nitrogen

azur [azyr] *nm* : azure

azyme [azim] *adj* : unleavened

B

b [be] *nm* : b, the second letter of the alphabet

babeurre [babœr] *nm* : buttermilk

babiche [babiʃ] *nf Can* : leather lacing (for moccasins, snowshoes, etc.)

babillage [babijaʒ] *nm* : babbling, prattle

babillard [babijar] *nm Can* : bulletin board

babiller [babije] *vi* : to babble, to chatter

babines [babin] *nfpl* : chops <se lécher les babines : to lick one's chops>

babiole [babjɔl] *nf* : bauble, trinket

bâbord [babɔr] *nm* : port (side), larboard

babouin [babwɛ̃] *nm* : baboon

baboune [babun] *nf Can fam* **faire la baboune** : to sulk

baby-sitter [bebisitœr] *nmf, pl* **baby-sitters** *France* : baby-sitter

baby-sitting [bebisitiŋ] *nm France* : baby-sitting

bac [bak] *nm* **1** : ferry **2** : tub, vat <bac à glace : ice tray> **3** *fam* → **baccalauréat**

baccalauréat [bakalɔrea] *nm* **1** *France* : school-leaving certificate **2** *Can* : bachelor's degree

bâche [baʃ] *nf* : tarpaulin

bachelier, -lière [baʃəlje, -ljɛr] *n* : person who holds a *baccalauréat*

bachot [baʃo] *nm France fam* → **baccalauréat**

bachoter [baʃɔte] *vi France* : to cram (for an exam)

bacille [basil] *nm* : bacillus

bâcler [bakle] *vt* : to rush through, to dash off <travail bâclé : slapdash job, botched-up work>

bacon [bekɔn] *nm* : bacon

bactérie [bakteri] *nf* : bacterium

bactérien, -rienne [bakterjɛ̃, -rjɛn] *adj* : bacterial

bactériologie [bakterjɔlɔʒi] *nf* : bacteriology — **bactériologiste** [-lɔʒist] *nmf*

badaud, -daude [bado, -dod] *n* **1** : stroller, passerby **2** : (curious) onlooker

badge [badʒ] *nm* : badge

badigeonner [badiʒɔne] *vt* **1** : to daub, to smear **2** : to whitewash **3** : to paint (in medicine)

badin, -dine [badɛ̃, -din] *adj* : playful, jocular

badinage [badinaʒ] *nm* : banter, joking

badine [badin] *nf* : switch, cane

badiner [badine] *vi* **1** : to joke, to jest **2 ~ avec** : to trifle with, to toy with

badminton [badmintɔn] *nm* : badminton

bâdrer [badre] *vt Can fam* : to bother, to annoy

baffe [baf] *nf fam* : slap, smack
bafouer [bafwe] *vt* RIDICULISER : to ridicule, to scorn
bafouillage [bafujaʒ] *nm* **1** : mumbling, stammering **2** : gibberish
bafouiller [bafuje] *v* : to mumble, to stammer
bâfrer [bafre] *vt fam* : to gobble, to guzzle — *vi fam* : to stuff oneself
bagage [bagaʒ] *nm* **1** : baggage, luggage <bagages à main : hand luggage> <plier bagage : to pack up and leave> **2** : knowledge, background
bagarre [bagar] *nf* : fight, brawl
bagarrer [bagare] *vi* : to fight, to brawl — **se bagarrer** *vr*
bagarreur, -reuse [bagarœr, -røz] *n* : fighter, brawler
bagatelle [bagatɛl] *nf* **1** : trifle, trinket **2** : trifling sum
bagnard [baɲar] *nm* : convict
bagne [baɲ] *nm* **1** : penal colony **2** : hard labor
bagnole [baɲɔl] *nf fam* : jalopy, car
bague [bag] *nf* **1** : ring <bague de fiançailles : engagement ring> **2** : band, circlet
baguette [bagɛt] *nf* **1** : stick, rod, baton <baguette à fusil : ramrod> <baguette de tambour : drumstick> <baguette magique : magic wand> **2** : baguette (loaf of French bread) **3 baguettes** *nfpl* : chopsticks
bahreïni, -nie [barejni] *adj* : Bahraini
Bahreïni, -nie *n* : Bahraini
baie [bɛ] *nf* **1** : bay **2** : berry **3** *or* **baie vitrée** : picture window
baignade [bɛɲad] *nf* : swimming, bathing
baigner [beɲe] *vt* : to bathe, to wash — *vi* : to soak, to steep — **se baigner** *vr* **1** : to take a bath **2** : to go swimming
baigneur, -gneuse [bɛɲœr, -ɲøz] *n* : swimmer, bather
baignoire [beɲwar] *nf* : bathtub
bail [baj] *nm, pl* **baux** [bo] : lease
bâillement [bajmɑ̃] *nm* : yawn
bâiller [baje] *vi* **1** : to yawn **2** : to gape (open)
bailleur, -leresse [bajœr, -jrɛs] *n* **1** : lessor **2 bailleur de fonds** : financial backer
bâillon [bajɔ̃] *nm* : gag
bâillonner [bajɔne] *vt* **1** : to gag **2** : to silence
bain [bɛ̃] *nm* **1** : bath <bain de bouche : mouthwash> <bain de sang : bloodbath> <bain de soleil : sunbath> <prendre un bain : to take a bath> **2** : swim **3 se mettre dans le bain** : to get into the swing of things
bain–marie [bɛ̃mari] *nm, pl* **bains–marie** : double boiler
baïonnette [bajɔnɛt] *nf* : bayonet
baiser[1] [beze] *vt* : to kiss
baiser[2] *nm* : kiss
baisse [bɛs] *nf* **1** : fall, drop, decline **2 à la baisse** : downward
baisser [bese] *vt* **1** : to let down, to lower <baisser les yeux : to look down> <baisser les bras : to give up> **2** : to reduce (volume, light) — *vi* : to go down, to drop, to decline — **se baisser** : to bend down, to stoop, to duck
bajoues [baʒu] *nfpl* : chops, jowls
bal [bal] *nm* : ball, dance
balade [balad] *nf* PROMENADE : stroll, walk
balader [balade] *vt* : to take for a walk — *vi* : to stroll, to saunter — **se balader** *vr* : to go for a walk, to stroll about, to gallivant (around)
baladeur [baladœr] *nm* : portable radio–cassette player
balafre [balafr] *nf* **1** : gash, slash **2** CICATRICE : scar
balai [balɛ] *nm* **1** : broom, brush <passer le balai : to sweep the floor> **2** : windshield-wiper blade
balaie [bale], **balaiera** [balera], *etc.* → **balayer**
balance [balɑ̃s] *nf* **1** : scale, scales *pl* <faire pencher la balance : to tip the scales> **2** : balance <balance de commerce : balance of trade> **3** *Can* : difference, remainder <la balance de : the rest of>
Balance *nf* : Libra
balancement [balɑ̃smɑ̃] *nm* : swaying, swinging
balancer [balɑ̃se] {6} *vt* **1** : to sway, to swing, to rock **2** *fam* : to fling, to chuck, to junk — *vi* **1** : to sway **2** : to waver, to hesitate — **se balancer** *vr* : to rock, to swing, to sway
balancier [balɑ̃sje] *nm* : pendulum
balançoire [balɑ̃swar] *nf* **1** : swing **2** BASCULE : seesaw
balayage [balɛjaʒ] *nm* : sweeping
balayer [baleje] {11} *vt* **1** : to sweep, to sweep away **2** : to scan
balayeur, balayeuse [balɛjœr, balɛjøz] *n* : street sweeper
balayeuse [balɛjøz] *nf* **1** : street-cleaning truck **2** *Can* : vacuum cleaner
balbutiement [balbysimɑ̃] *nm* **1** : stammering, stuttering **2 balbutiements** *nmpl* : early stages, beginnings
balbutier [balbysje] {96} *v* : to stammer, to stutter
balbuzard [balbyzar] *nm or* **balbuzard pêcheur** : osprey
balcon [balkɔ̃] *nm* : balcony
baldaquin [baldakɛ̃] *nm* : canopy
baleine [balɛn] *nf* **1** : whale **2** : rib (of an umbrella)
baleinier [balenje] *nm* : whaler (ship or person)
baleinière [balenjɛr] *nf* : whaleboat
balise [baliz] *nf* **1** : buoy, beacon **2** : signpost, marker
baliser [balize] *vt* : to mark (with beacons or signs)
balistique[1] [balistik] *adj* : ballistic
balistique[2] *nf* : ballistics

balivernes [balivɛrn] *nfpl* SORNETTES : nonsense, humbug

ballade [balad] *nf* : ballad

ballant[1], -lante [balɑ̃, -lɑ̃t] *adj* : dangling

ballant[2] *nm* : slack, looseness

ballast [balast] *nm* : ballast

balle [bal] *nf* **1** : ball <balle de tennis : tennis ball> <renvoyer la balle : to pass the buck> **2** : bullet **3** : bale, bundle **4** : husk, chaff **5** *France fam* : franc

balle–molle [balmɔl] *nf Can* : softball

ballerine [balrin] *nf* : ballerina

ballet [balɛ] *nm* : ballet

ballon [balɔ̃] *nm* **1** : ball <ballon de football : football, soccer ball> **2** : balloon **3** : wine glass, brandy glass **4 ballon d'oxygène** : oxygen tank

ballonner [balɔne] *vt* : to bloat, to distend (the stomach)

ballon–panier [balɔ̃panje] *nm Can* : basketball (game)

ballot [balo] *nm* **1** BALUCHON : pack, bundle **2** *fam* : chump, fool

ballottage [balɔtaʒ] *nm* : second ballot

ballotter [balɔte] *vt* SECOUER : to shake, to toss about — *vi* : to toss, to roll around

balloune [balun] *nf Can* **1** : balloon **2** : bubble <gomme balloune : bubble gum>

balluchon [balyʃɔ̃] → **baluchon**

balnéaire [balneɛr] *adj* : seaside <station balnéaire : seaside resort>

balourd[1], -lourde [balur, -lurd] *adj* : awkward, clumsy, stupid

balourd[2], -lourde *n* : clumsy oaf, dolt

balourdise [balurdiz] *nf* **1** : awkwardness, clumsiness **2** : gaffe, blunder

balsa [balza] *nm* : balsa

balsamine [balzamin] *nf* : balsam fir

balte [balt] *adj* : Baltic

baluchon [balyʃɔ̃] *nm* BALLOT : pack, bundle <faire son baluchon : to pack one's bag>

balustrade [balystrad] *nf* **1** : balustrade **2** : railing, bannister

balustre [balystr] *nf* : baluster

bambin, -bine [bɑ̃bɛ̃, -bin] *n* : child, toddler

bambou [bɑ̃bu] *nm* : bamboo

ban [bɑ̃] *nm* **1** : round of applause **2 bans** *nmpl* : banns **3 mettre au ban** : to banish, to ostracize

banal, -nale [banal] *adj, mpl* **banals 1** ORDINAIRE : commonplace, ordinary **2** : banal, trite

banaliser [banalize] *vt* **1** : to make commonplace **2 voiture banalisée** : unmarked car

banalité [banalite] *nf* **1** : banality, triteness **2** : platitude, cliché

banane [banan] *nf* : banana

bananier [bananje] *nm* : banana tree

banc [bɑ̃] *nm* **1** : bench <banc des accusés : dock (in court)> <banc d'église : pew> **2** : shoal, school (of fish) **3** : bank <banc de sable : sandbank> <banc de neige *Can* : snowbank>

bancaire [bɑ̃kɛr] *adj* : banking, bank <compte bancaire : bank account>

bancal, -cale [bɑ̃kal] *adj, mpl* **bancals** : shaky, wobbly

bandage [bɑ̃daʒ] *nm* **1** : bandaging **2** PANSEMENT : bandage, dressing

bande [bɑ̃d] *nf* **1** : gang, group, troop **2** : pack (of animals) **3** : band, strip <bande dessinée : comic strip> **4** : tape, (reel of) film <bande vidéo : videotape> <bande sonore : soundtrack> **5 donner de la bande** : to list (of a ship)

bandeau [bɑ̃do] *nm, pl* **bandeaux 1** : blindfold **2** : headband

bandelette [bɑ̃dlɛt] *nf* : narrow strip (of cloth, etc.)

bander [bɑ̃de] *vt* **1** : to bandage **2** : to bend (a bow) **3** : to flex, to tense **4 bander les yeux à** : to blindfold

banderole [bɑ̃drɔl] *nf* : banner, pennant

bandit [bɑ̃di] *nm* **1** VOLEUR : bandit, robber **2** : scoundrel **3** *or* **petit bandit** : rascal

banditisme [bɑ̃ditism] *nm* : banditry

bandoulière [bɑ̃duljɛr] *nf* : shoulder strap <en bandoulière : slung over one's shoulder>

bangladais, -daise [bɑ̃gladɛ, -dɛz] *adj* : Bangladeshi

Bangladais, -daise *n* : Bangladeshi

banjo [bɑ̃(d)ʒo] *nm* : banjo

banlieue [bɑ̃ljø] *nf* : suburb(s) <de banlieue : suburban>

banlieusard[1], -sarde [bɑ̃ljøzar, -zard] *adj* : suburban

banlieusard[2], -sarde *n* : suburbanite, suburban commuter

banni[1], -nie [bani] *adj* : exiled, banished

banni[2], -nie *n* : exile

bannière [banjɛr] *nf* : banner

bannir [banir] *vt* : to banish, to exile

bannissement [banismɑ̃] *nm* : banishment

banque [bɑ̃k] *nf* **1** : bank <banque commerciale : commercial bank> <banque du sang : blood bank> **2** : banking

banqueroute [bɑ̃krut] *nf* **1** : bankruptcy **2 faire banqueroute** : to go bankrupt

banquet [bɑ̃kɛ] *nm* FESTIN : banquet, feast

banquette [bɑ̃kɛt] *nf* : bench, seat (in a booth or vehicle) <banquette arrière : back seat>

banquier, -quière [bɑ̃kje, -kjɛr] *n* : banker

banquise [bɑ̃kiz] *nf* : ice floe

bans [bɑ̃] *nmpl* : banns (of marriage)

baptême [batɛm] *nm* : baptism, christening

baptiser [batize] *vt* : to baptize, to christen

baptismal, -male [batismal] *adj, mpl* **-maux** [-mo] : baptismal

baptistaire [batistɛr] *nm Can* : certificate of baptism

bar [bar] *nm* **1** : bar **2** : sea bass

baragouin [baragwɛ̃] *nm* : gibberish, gobbledegook

baragouiner [baragwine] *vi* : to talk gibberish — *vt* : to speak (a language) badly <baragouiner l'anglais : to speak broken English>

baraque [barak] *nf* **1** BICOQUE : hut, shack **2** : stall, stand (at a fair, etc.)

baraquement [barakmɑ̃] *nm* : group of shacks

baratin [baratɛ̃] *nm* : smooth talk, sales patter

baratte [barat] *nf* : churn

baratter [barate] *vt* : to churn

barauder [barode] *vt Can* : to move back and forth, to skid (on ice, etc.)

barbant, -bante [barbɑ̃, -bɑ̃t] *adj fam* RASANT : boring

barbare[1] [barbar] *adj* : barbarous, barbaric

barbare[2] *nmf* : barbarian

barbarie [barbari] *nf* : barbarity, barbarism

barbarisme [barbarism] *nm* : barbarism (in language, manners, etc.)

barbe [barb] *nf* **1** : beard **2** : barb (of a feather, of metal) **3** : tuft, awn (of a plant) **4** *fam* : bore <quelle barbe! : what a bore!>

barbecue [barbəkju] *nm* : barbecue

barbelé[1], -lée [barbəle] *adj* : barbed

barbelé[2] *nm* : barbed wire

barber [barbe] *vt fam* : to bore — **se barber** *vr*

barbiche [barbiʃ] *nf* **1** : goatee **2** : beard (of a goat)

barbier [barbje] *nm Can* : barber

barbiturique [barbityrik] *nm* : barbiturate

barboter [barbɔte] *vi* : to paddle, to splash around — *vt fam* : to filch

barboteuse [barbɔtøz] *nf Can* : wading pool

barbouillage [barbujaʒ] *nm* : daub, smear

barbouiller [barbuje] *vt* **1** : to smear, to daub **2** : to scribble **3** : to nauseate, to make sick <ça me barbouille le coeur : it turns my stomach>

barbu, -bue [barby] *adj* : bearded

barda [barda] *nm fam* : gear, stuff

bardane [bardan] *nf* : bur, burr (in botany)

barde [bard] *nm* : bard

bardeau [bardo] *nm, pl* **bardeaux 1** : shingle **2 manquer un bardeau** *Can fam* : to be a little crazy

barder [barde] *vt* : to bard (in cooking) — *v impers* **ça va barder!** *fam* : there's going to be trouble!, sparks will fly!

barème [barɛm] *nm* : scale, table <barème de salaires : salary scale>

baril [baril] *nm* TONNELET : barrel, keg

barillet [barijɛ] *nm* **1** : small barrel **2** : cylinder (of a revolver)

bariolé, -lée [barjɔle] *adj* MULTICOLORE : multicolored

barman [barman] *nm, pl* **barmans** *or* **barmen** : bartender

baromètre [barɔmɛtr] *nm* : barometer — **barométrique** [-metrik] *adj*

baron, -ronne [barɔ̃, -rɔn] *n* : baron *m*, baroness *f*

baroque [barɔk] *adj* **1** : baroque **2** BIZARRE : weird, odd

baroud [barud] *nm fam* : fight, set-to <baroud d'honneur : last stand>

barque [bark] *nf* : small boat

barracuda [barakyda] *nm* : barracuda

barrage [baraʒ] *nm* **1** : dam **2** : roadblock, barricade

barre [bar] *nf* **1** : bar, rod **2** : (written) line, stroke **3** : mark <sous la barre des deux pour cent : below the two percent mark> **4** : helm <prendre la barre : to take the helm, to take charge> **5** : bar (in law) **6** : sandbar **7 ~ d'outils** : toolbar

barreau [baro] *nm, pl* **barreaux 1** : bar <derrière les barreaux : behind bars> **2** : rung (of a ladder, etc.) **3 le barreau** : the bar, the legal profession

barrer [bare] *vt* **1** : to bar, to block **2** : to mark, to cross, to cross out **3** : to steer (a boat) **4** *Can* : to lock (a door) — **se barrer** *vr fam* : to clear out <barrez-vous! : get out of here!>

barrette [barɛt] *nf* **1** : barrette **2** : biretta

barricade [barikad] *nf* : barricade

barricader [barikade] *vt* : to barricade — **se barricader** *vr* : to barricade oneself, to shut oneself away

barrière [barjɛr] *nf* **1** OBSTACLE : barrier <barrières douanières : trade barriers> **2** : fence, gate

barrique [barik] *nf* TONNEAU : barrel, cask

barrir [barir] *vi* : to trumpet (of an elephant)

baryton [baritɔ̃] *nm* : baritone

baryum [barjɔm] *nm* : barium

bas[1] [ba] *adv* **1** : low <tomber bas : to sink low> **2** : softly, quietly

bas[2], basse [ba, baz (*before a vowel or mute h*), bas] *adj* **1** : low **2** : base, vile **3** : bass

bas[3] *nms & pl* **1** : bottom, lower part <de haut en bas : from top to bottom> <à bas : down with> <en bas : downstairs, below, at the bottom> <en bas de : at the bottom of, beneath> **2** : stocking **3** : bass (part)

basalte [bazalt] *nm* : basalt

basané, -née [bazane] *adj* **1** : tanned, sunburned **2** : swarthy

bascule [baskyl] *nf* **1** : balance, scales *pl* **2** : rocker <fauteuil à bascule : rocking chair> **3** BALANÇOIRE : seesaw

basculer [baskyle] *vi* **1** : to tip, to topple over **2** : to rock, to swing
base [baz] *nf* **1** : base <à la base de : at the root of> <base de lancement : launching site> **2** : basis **3** **base de données** : database
baseball *or* **base–ball** [bɛzbol] *nm* : baseball
baseballeur, -leuse [bɛzbolœr, -løz] *n Can* : baseball player
baser [baze] *vt* FONDER : to base, to found
bas–fond [bafɔ̃] *nm* **1** : shallows *pl* **2** : lowland **3** **bas–fonds** *nmpl* : dregs (of society), slums
basilic [bazilik] *nm* : basil
basilique [bazilik] *nf* : basilica
basique [bazik] *adj* : basic (in chemistry)
basket [baskɛt] *or* **basket-ball** *or* **basketball** [baskɛtbol] *nm* : basketball
basketteur, -teuse [baskɛtœr, -tøz] *n* : basketball player
basque[1] [bask] *adj* : Basque
basque[2] *nm* : Basque (language)
Basque *nmf* : Basque
bas–relief [barəljɛf] *nm, pl* **bas–reliefs** : bas-relief
basse [bas] *nf* **1** → **bas**[2] **2** : bass (in music)
basse–cour [baskur] *nf, pl* **basses–cours** **1** : farmyard, barnyard **2** : poultry
bassesse [basɛs] *nf* : baseness, meanness
basset [basɛ] *nm* : basset hound
bassin [basɛ̃] *nm* **1** : basin (of a river) **2** : lake, pond, pool **3** : pelvis
bassine [basin] *nf* **1** : large bowl, basin **2** *Can* : bedpan **3** : bowlful
basson [basɔ̃] *nm* : bassoon
bastion [bastjɔ̃] *nm* : bastion
bas–ventre [bavɑ̃tr] *nm, pl* **bas–ventres** : lower abdomen
bât [ba] *nm* **1** : packsaddle **2** **c'est là où le bât blesse** : that's where the shoe pinches
bataclan [bataklɑ̃] *nm fam* **1** : stuff, gear **2** **tout le bataclan** : the whole kit and caboodle
bataille [bataj] *nf* **1** : battle, fight **2** **en ~** : in disarray, disheveled
batailler [bataje] *vi* : to fight
batailleur[1], **-leuse** [batajœr, -jøz] *adj* : quarrelsome, belligerent
batailleur[2], **-leuse** *n* : fighter
bataillon [batajɔ̃] *nm* : battalion
bâtard[1], **-tarde** [batar, -tard] *adj* **1** : hybrid, crossbred **2** : bastard
bâtard[2], **-tarde** *n* : bastard
bâtard[3] *nm France* : small loaf of bread
bateau[1] [bato] *adj, s & pl* **bateau** : hackneyed
bateau[2] *nm, pl* **bateaux** **1** : boat, ship <bateau de pêche : fishing boat> <bateau amiral : flagship> <bateau de guerre : warship> <bateau de plaisance : launch> <bateau à voile : sailboat> **2** **faire du bateau** : to go sailing
bateau–mouche [batomuʃ] *nm, pl* **bateaux–mouches** : sightseeing boat
bateleur, -leuse [batlœr, -løz] *n* **1** : juggler, tumbler **2** : fool, buffoon
batelier, -lière [batəlje, -ljɛr] *n* : boatman
bâti [bati] *nm* **1** : framework, support **2** : tacking, basting (in sewing)
batifoler [batifɔle] *vi* : to frolic, to romp
bâtiment [batimɑ̃] *nm* **1** : building **2** : building trade **3** : ship <bâtiment de guerre : man-of-war>
bâtir [batir] *vt* **1** CONSTRUIRE : to build, to erect **2** : to build up, to develop **3** : to baste, to tack
bâtisseur, -seuse [batisœr, -søz] *n* : builder
bâton [batɔ̃] *nm* **1** : rod, pole <bâton de ski : ski pole> **2** : piece, stick <bâton de rouge (à lèvres) : lipstick> **3** : nightstick **4** : baton **5** *Can* : bat <bâton de baseball : baseball bat>
bâtonnet [batɔnɛ] *nm* : short stick, rod
battage [bataʒ] *nm* **1** : beating, threshing **2** : hype **3** : shuffle, shuffling (of playing cards)
battant[1], **-tante** [batɑ̃, -tɑ̃t] *adj* : beating, driving, banging <pluie battante : driving rain> <le cœur battant : with a pounding heart>
battant[2] *nm* **1** : flap, section (of a door, window, etc.) **2** : clapper (of a bell)
battant[3], **-tante** [batɑ̃, -tɑ̃t] *nmf* : fighter, go-getter
batte [bat] *nf* : bat (in sports)
battement [batmɑ̃] *nm* **1** : beating, fluttering, blinking **2** : clapping, tapping, banging **3** : interval, wait
batterie [batri] *nf* **1** : set, group, battery <une batterie de tests : a string of tests> **2** : battery (of artillery) **3** : drums, drum set **4** : battery (of a motor vehicle)
batteur [batœr, -tøz] *nm* **1** : (egg) whisk, eggbeater <batteur électrique : electric mixer> **2** : drummer **3** : batter (in sports)
batteuse [batøz] *nf* : thresher, threshing machine
battre [batr] {12} *vt* **1** FRAPPER : to hit, to strike, to beat **2** VAINCRE : to defeat <battre à plates coutures : to defeat soundly, to wallop> **3** : to shuffle (playing cards) — *vi* : to beat — **se battre** *vr* : to fight
batture [batyr] *nf Can* : sandbar
baudet [bodɛ] *nm fam* : jackass
baudrier [bodrije] *nm* BANDOULIÈRE : shoulder strap
bauge [boʒ] *nf* : wallow (for animals)
baume [bom] *nm* **1** : balm, balsam **2** **mettre du baume au cœur** : to be of comfort
baux → **bail**

bavard[1], **-varde** [bavar, -vard] *adj* : talkative

bavard[2], **-varde** *n* : talkative person, chatterbox

bavardage [bavardaʒ] *nm* : idle talk, chatter

bavarder [bavarde] *vi* **1** : to chatter **2** : to gossip

bavarois, -roise [bavarwa, -rwaz] *adj* : Bavarian

Bavarois, -roise *n* : Bavarian

bave [bav] *nf* : dribble, drool, spittle

baver [bave] *vi* **1** : to dribble, to drool **2** : to run, to leak **3 ~ en** : to have a hard time of it **4 ~ sur** : to slander

bavette [bavɛt] *nf* **1** : bib **2** : flank (of beef) **3** : mudguard

baveux[1], **-veuse** [bavø, -vøz] *adj* **1** : dribbling, drooling **2** : runny (of an omelette, etc.)

baveux[2], **-veuse** *n Can fam* : pain in the neck, annoying person

bavoir [bavwar] *nm* : bib (for babies)

bavure [bavyr] *nf* **1** : smudge, blur **2** : error, blunder

bayer [baje] {11} *vi* **bayer aux corneilles** : to gape, to gaze into space

bayou [baju] *nm* : bayou

bazar [bazar] *nm* **1** : bazaar **2** : general store **3** : clutter, mess

bazou [bazu] *nm Can fam* : jalopy

beagle [bigœl] *nm* : beagle

béant, béante [beɑ̃, beɑ̃t] *adj* : gaping

béat, béate [bea, beat] *adj* **1** : blissful **2** : self-satisfied, smug

béatement [beatmɑ̃] *adv* : blissfully

béatitude [beatityd] *nf* **1** : bliss **2** : beatitude

beau[1] [bo] *adv* **1 avoir beau** : to do (something) in vain <j'ai beau essayer : it's useless for me to try> **2 faire beau** : to be fine, to be fair <il fait beau : it's nice outside>

beau[2] **(bel** [bɛl] *before vowel or mute h*), **belle** [bɛl] *adj, mpl* **beaux** [bo] **1** : beautiful, handsome **2** : good, noble **3** : fine, fair <beau temps : nice weather> **4** : excellent, desirable <belle santé : good health> **5** : considerable, great (in quantity) <un bel âge : a ripe old age> <une belle somme : a tidy sum> **6 bel et bien** : for sure, truly

beau[3] *nm* **1 le beau** : the beautiful, beauty **2 faire le beau** : to sit up and beg (of a dog)

beaucoup [boku] *adv* **1** : much, a lot <je t'aime beaucoup : I love you very much> **2 ~ de** : much, many, a lot of <beaucoup de livres : a lot of books> **3 de ~** : by far

beau-fils [bofis] *nm, pl* **beaux-fils 1** : son-in-law **2** : stepson

beau-frère [bofrɛr] *nm, pl* **beaux-frères 1** : brother-in-law **2** : stepbrother

beau-père [bopɛr] *nm, pl* **beaux-pères 1** : father-in-law **2** : stepfather

beauté [bote] *nf* : beauty

beaux-arts [bozar] *nmpl* : fine arts

beaux-parents [boparɑ̃] *nmpl* : in-laws

bébé [bebe] *nm* : baby, infant

bebelle [bəbɛl] *nf Can fam* **1** : gadget **2 bebelles** *nfpl* : things <tes bebelles puis dans ta cour : pack your things and go>

bébête [bebɛt] *adj* : silly, babyish

bébite [bebit] *nf Can fam* : bug, insect

bec [bɛk] *nm* **1** : beak, bill **2** *fam* : mouth, nose, face **3** EMBOUCHURE : mouthpiece **4** : burner <bec à gaz : gas burner> **5** : point, nib **6** : spout, lip (of a jug, etc.) 7 *Belg, Can, Switz fam* : kiss **8 bec fin** : gourmet **9 tomber sur un bec** : to run into a snag

bécane [bekan] *nf fam* : bike

bécasse [bekas] *nf* **1** : woodcock **2** *fam* : featherbrain, silly goose

bécasseau [bekaso] *nm* : sandpiper

bécassine [bekasiːn] *nf* : snipe

bec-de-lièvre [bɛkdəljɛvr] *nm, pl* **becs-de-lièvre** : harelip

bêche [bɛʃ] *nf* : spade

bêcher [beʃe] *vt* **1** : to dig (up) **2** : to criticize

bêcheur[1], **-cheuse** [bɛʃœr, -ʃøz] *adj* : stuck-up

bêcheur[2], **-cheuse** *n* : stuck-up person, snob

becqueter [bɛkte] {8} *vt* **1** : to peck at **2** *fam* : to eat

bedaine [bədɛn] *nf* : paunch, potbelly

bedonnant, -nante [bədɔnɑ̃, -nɑ̃t] *adj* : paunchy, portly, potbellied

bédouin, -douine [bedwɛ̃, -dwin] *n* : bedouin

bée [be] *adj* **bouche bée** : openmouthed <être bouche bée devant : to gape at>

beffroi [befrwa] *nm* : belfry

bégaie [bege], **bégaiera** [begera], *etc.* → **bégayer**

bégaiement [begɛmɑ̃] *nm* : stuttering, stammering

bégayer [begeje] {11} *v* : to stutter, to stammer

bégonia [begɔnja] *nm* : begonia

bégueule [begœl] *nmf* : prude

béguin [begɛ̃] *nm fam* : crush, infatuation

beige [bɛʒ] *adj & nm* : beige

beigne[1] [bɛɲ] *nf fam* : smack, sock, punch

beigne[2] *nm Can* : doughnut

beignet [bɛɲɛ] *nm* **1** : doughnut **2** : fritter

bel → **beau**

bêlement [bɛlmɑ̃] *nm* : bleat

bêler [bele] *vi* : to bleat

belette [bəlɛt] *nf* : weasel

belge [bɛlʒ] *adj* : Belgian

Belge *nmf* : Belgian

bélier [belje] *nm* **1** : ram **2** : battering ram

Bélier *nm* : Aries

bélizien, -zienne [belizjɛ̃] *adj* : Belizean
Bélizien, -zienne *n* : Belizean
belladone [beladɔn] *nf* : belladonna
belle[1] → **beau**
belle[2] *nf* : beauty, belle
belle–famille [bɛlfamij] *nf, pl* **belles–familles** : in-laws *pl*
belle–fille [bɛlfij] *nf, pl* **belles–filles 1** : daughter-in-law **2** : stepdaughter
belle–mère [bɛlmɛr] *nf, pl* **belles–mères 1** : mother-in-law **2** : stepmother
belle–sœur [bɛlsœr] *nf, pl* **belles–sœurs** : sister-in-law
bellicisme [bɛlisism] *nm* : bellicosity, warmongering
belliciste[1] [bɛlisist] *adj* : bellicose, warmongering
belliciste[2] *nmf* : warmonger
belligérant, -rante [beliʒerɑ̃, -rɑ̃t] *adj & n* : belligerent — **belligérance** [-ʒerɑ̃s] *nf*
belliqueux, -queuse [bɛlikø, -køz] *adj* GUERRIER : warlike
bémol [bemɔl] *adj & nm* : flat (in music)
bénédicité [benedisite] *nm* : grace <dire le bénédicité : to say grace>
bénédictin, -tine [benediktɛ̃, -tin] *adj & n* : Benedictine
bénédiction [benediksjɔ̃] *nf* **1** : blessing, benediction **2** AUBAINE : godsend
bénéfice [benefis] *nm* **1** AVANTAGE : benefit, advantage **2** : profit <faire du bénéfice : to make a profit>
bénéficiaire[1] [benefisjɛr] *adj* : profitable <marge bénéficiaire : profit margin>
bénéficiaire[2] *nmf* : beneficiary, payee
bénéficier [benefisje] {96} *vi* **∼ de** : to profit from, to receive the benefits of
bénéfique [benefik] *adj* : beneficial, advantageous
benêt[1] [bənɛ] *adj* : simpleminded, silly
benêt[2] *nm* : simpleton
bénévolat [benevɔla] *nm* : volunteer work
bénévole[1] [benevɔl] *adj* : voluntary, volunteer
bénévole[2] *nmf* : volunteer
bengali[1] [bɛ̃gali] *adj* : Bengali
bengali[2] *nm* : Bengali (language)
Bengali *nmf* : Bengali
bénin, -nigne [benɛ̃, beniɲ] *adj* **1** : slight, minor **2** : benign
béninois, -noise [beninwa, -nwaz] *adj* : Beninese
Béninois, -noise *n* : Beninese
bénir [benir] *vt* : to bless
bénit, -nite [beni, -nit] *adj* : blessed, consecrated <eau bénite : holy water>
bénitier [benitje] *nm* : holy water font
benjamin, -mine [bɛ̃ʒamɛ̃, -min] *n* CADET : youngest child
benzène [bɛ̃zɛn] *nm* : benzene
béotien, -tienne [beɔsjɛ̃, -sjɛn] *adj & n* : philistine
béquille [bekij] *nf* **1** : crutch **2** : kickstand
bercail [bɛrkaj] *nm* : fold <rentrer au bercail : to return to the fold>
berçante [bɛrsɑ̃t] *nf or* **chaise berçante** *Can* : rocking chair
berceau [bɛrso] *nm, pl* **berceaux** : cradle
bercer [bɛrse] {6} *vt* **1** : to rock (a baby) **2** : to soothe, to lull — **se bercer** *vr* **1** : to rock, to swing **2** : to delude oneself
berceuse [bɛrsøz] *nf* **1** : lullaby **2** : rocking chair
béret [berɛ] *nm* : beret
berge [bɛrʒ] *nf* RIVE : bank (of a river, etc.)
berger[1], **-gère** [bɛrʒe, -ʒɛr] *n* : shepherd, shepherdess *f*
berger[2] *nm* : sheepdog <berger allemand : German shepherd>
bergerie [bɛrʒəri] *nf* : sheepfold
berline [bɛrlin] *nf* : sedan
berlingot [bɛrlɛ̃go] *nm* **1** : carton (for milk, etc.) **2** : hard candy
berlue [bɛrly] *nf* **avoir la berlue** : to be seeing things, to delude oneself
berne [bɛrn] *nf* **en ∼** : at half mast
berner [bɛrne] *vt* : to fool, to deceive
besogne [bəzɔɲ] *nf* : task, job
besogner [bəzɔɲe] *vi* : to drudge, to slave away
besogneux, -gneuse [bəzɔɲø, -ɲøz] *adj* **1** : poor, needy **2** : plodding, hardworking
besoin [bəzwɛ̃] *nm* **1** : need, requirement <besoins essentiels : basic needs> **2** : neediness, want <enfants dans le besoin : needy children> **3 au ∼** *or* **si besoin est** : if necessary, if need be **4 avoir besoin de** : to need
bestial, -tiale [bɛstjal] *adj, mpl* **bestiaux** [bɛstjo] : brutish, bestial — **bestialement** [bɛstjalmɑ̃] *adv*
bestialité [bɛstjalite] *nf* : brutishness
bestiaux [bɛstjo] *nmpl* BÉTAIL : livestock, cattle
bestiole [bɛstjɔl] *nf* : bug, tiny creature
bétail [betaj] *nm* : livestock, cattle *pl*
bête[1] [bɛt] *adj* **1** STUPIDE : stupid, foolish **2** : simple <c'est tout bête! : there's nothing to it!> — **bêtement** [bɛtmɑ̃] *adv*
bête[2] *nf* **1** ANIMAL : animal <bête de somme : beast of burden> <bête sauvage : wild animal> **2** BESTIOLE : insect, creature <bête à bon Dieu : ladybug> **3** : fool, idiot **4 bête noire** : pet peeve **5 bête puante** *Can* : skunk
bêtise [betiz] *nf* **1** : stupidity, foolishness **2** : nonsense **3** : stupid mistake
béton [betɔ̃] *nm* : concrete
bétonnière [betɔnjɛr] *nf* : cement mixer

bette [bɛt] *nf* **1** : Swiss chard **2** *Can fam* : face <se montrer la bette : to show one's face>
betterave [bɛtrav] *nf* : beet
beuglement [bøgləmɑ̃] *nm* **1** : bellow **2** : blare (of a radio, etc.)
beugler [bøgle] *vi* : to low, to moo, to bellow — *vt* : to bellow out <beugler une chanson : to bellow out a song>
beurre [bœr] *nm* : butter
beurrée [bœre] *nf Can* : slice of bread and butter topped with jam or maple sugar
beurrer [bœre] *vt* : to butter
beurrier [bœrje] *nm* : butter dish
beuverie [bœvri] *nf* : drinking bout, binge
bévue [bevy] *nf* BOURDE : blunder
biais [bjɛ, bjɛz] *nm* **1** : means, way <par le biais de : by means of, via> **2** : bias, slant
biaiser [bjeze] *vi* : to hedge, to dodge the issue
bibelot [biblo] *nm* : trinket, curio
biberon [bibrɔ̃] *nm* : bottle (for a baby)
bible [bibl] *nf* **1** : bible **2 la Bible** : the Bible
bibliobus [biblijɔbys] *nm* : bookmobile
bibliographe [biblijɔgraf] *nmf* : bibliographer
bibliographie [biblijɔgrafi] *nf* : bibliography
bibliographique [biblijɔgrafik] *adj* : bibliographic
bibliothécaire [biblijɔtekɛr] *nmf* : librarian
bibliothèque [biblijɔtɛk] *nf* **1** : library **2** : bookcase
biblique [biblik] *adj* : biblical, scriptural
bicaméral, -rale [bikameral] *adj, mpl* **-raux** [-ro] : bicameral
bicarbonate [bikarbɔnat] *nm* : bicarbonate <bicarbonate de soude : baking soda>
bicentenaire [bisɑ̃tnɛr] *nm* : bicentennial
biceps [bisɛps] *nms & pl* : biceps
biche [biʃ] *nf* **1** : doe **2 ma biche** *fam* : my darling
bicher [biʃe] *vi France fam* : to get on well <ça biche? : how's it going?>
bichonner [biʃɔne] *vt* **1** : to pamper **2** : to spruce up, to doll up — **se bichonner** *vr* : to preen oneself
bicolore [bikɔlɔr] *adj* : two-colored, two-tone
bicoque [bikɔk] *nf* BARAQUE : shack, hut
bicorne [bikɔrn] *nm* : cocked hat
bicyclette [bisiklɛt] *nf* : bicycle <faire de la bicyclette : to ride a bicycle>
bidet [bidɛ] *nm* : bidet
bidon[1] [bidɔ̃] *adj fam* : bogus, phoney
bidon[2] *nm* **1** : can, (oil) drum **2** : flask, canteen **3** *fam* : belly, gut **4** *fam* : nonsense, hot air <c'est du bidon! : that's baloney!>
bidonner [bidɔne] *v* **se bidonner** *vr fam* : to laugh one's head off
bidonville [bidɔ̃vil] *nm* : shantytown
bidule [bidyl] *nm fam* MACHIN : thingamajig
bien[1] [bjɛ̃] *adv* **1** : well, satisfactorily **2** : very, quite <bien souvent : quite often> **3** : definitely, really **4** : readily, happily <j'aimerais bien un café : I could go for a coffee> **5** : at least <il y avait bien dix personnes : there were at least ten people> **6 ~ de** : a good many, many <bien des fois : many times> **7 bien que** : although <bien que malade, elle travaille : though ill, she is working> **8 bien sûr** : of course
bien[2] *adj* **1** : good, fine, satisfactory **2** : well, in good health <je me sens bien : I feel good> **3** : good-looking **4** : nice, decent, respectable <un voisinage bien : a nice neighborhood> **5** : comfortable
bien[3] *nm* **1** : good <faire le bien : to do good> **2 biens** *nmpl* : possessions, property <biens de consommation : consumer goods> <biens immobiliers : real estate>
bien[4] *interj* : OK, all right, good, very well <bien, allons-nous-en : OK, let's go> <bien! bien! j'entends : all right! all right! I understand> <bien, je le prendrai : good! I'll take it>
bien–aimé, -aimée [bjɛ̃neme] *adj & n* : beloved
bien–être [bjɛ̃nɛtr] *nm* **1** : well-being **2** : comfort **3 bien–être social** *Can* : (public) welfare
bienfaisance [bjɛ̃fəzɑ̃s] *nf* : charity, beneficence
bienfaisant, -sante [bjɛ̃fəzɑ̃, -zɑ̃t] *adj* **1** : charitable, beneficent **2** : beneficial
bienfait [bjɛ̃fɛ] *nm* **1** : act of kindness **2** AVANTAGE : benefit, advantage
bienfaiteur, -trice [bjɛ̃fɛtœr, -tris] *n* : benefactor, benefactress *f*
bien–fondé [bjɛ̃fɔ̃de] *nm* **1** : validity, soundness **2** LÉGITIMITÉ : legitimacy (in law)
bienheureux, -reuse [bjɛ̃nørø, -røz] *adj* **1** : happy, joyful **2** : blessed
biennal, -nale [bjenal] *adj, mpl* **-naux** [-no] : biennial — **biennalement** [-nalmɑ̃] *adv*
bien–pensant, -sante [bjɛ̃pɑ̃sɑ̃, -sɑ̃t] *adj* : right-minded, conformist
bienséance [bjɛ̃seɑ̃s] *nf* : propriety, decorum
bienséant, -séante [bjɛ̃seɑ̃, -seɑ̃t] *adj* : proper, seemly
bientôt [bjɛ̃to] *adv* **1** : soon <à bientôt! : see you soon!> **2** : nearly <il est bientôt trois heures : it's nearly three o'clock>
bienveillance [bjɛ̃vejɑ̃s] *nf* : kindness, benevolence
bienveillant, -lante [bjɛ̃vejɑ̃, -jɑ̃t] *adj* : kind, benevolent

bienvenu[1], **-nue** [bjɛ̃vny] *adj* : welcome, opportune
bienvenu[2], **-nue** *n* **être le bienvenu** : to be welcome
bienvenue *nf* **1** : welcome <souhaiter la bienvenue à : to welcome> **2 bienvenue** *Can fam* : you're welcome!
bière [bjɛr] *nf* **1** : beer <bière pression : draft beer> <bière blonde : lager> **2** : casket, coffin
biffer [bife] *vt* : to cross out
bifteck [biftɛk] *nm* : steak
bifurcation [bifyrkasjɔ̃] *nf* : fork, junction
bifurquer [bifyrke] *vi* : to fork, to branch off
bigame[1] [bigam] *adj* : bigamous — **bigamie** [-gami] *nf*
bigame[2] *nmf* : bigamist
bigarré [bigare] *adj* MULTICOLORE : multicolored, variegated
bigot[1], **-gote** [bigo, -gɔt] *adj* : overly devout, sanctimonious
bigot[2], **-gote** *n* : zealot, (religious) bigot
bigoterie [bigɔtri] *nf* : (religious) bigotry
bigoudi [bigudi] *nm* : hair curler, roller
bijou [biʒu] *nm, pl* **bijoux 1** : jewel, piece of jewelry **2** : gem, marvel
bijouterie [biʒutri] *nf* **1** BIJOUX : jewelry, jewels *pl* **2** : jewelry store
bijoutier, -tière [biʒutje, -tjɛr] *n* JOAILLIER : jeweler
bikini [bikini] *nm* : bikini
bilan [bilɑ̃] *nm* **1** : assessment, appraisal <faire le bilan de : to take stock of> **2** : balance sheet <déposer son bilan : to declare bankruptcy> **3** *or* **bilan de santé** : (medical) check-up
bilatéral, -rale [bilateral] *adj, mpl* **-raux** [-ro] : bilateral — **bilatéralement** [-ralmɑ̃] *adv*
bile [bil] *nf* **1** : bile **2 se faire de la bile** : to worry, to fret
biliaire [biljɛr] *adj* → **vésicule**
bilieux, -lieuse [biljø, -ljøz] *adj* : bilious, irritable
bilingue [bilɛ̃g] *adj* : bilingual
billard [bijar] *nm* : billiards *pl*
bille [bij] *nf* **1** : marble <jouer aux billes : to play marbles> **2** : billiard ball **3** : log **4** → **roulement**
billet [bijɛ] *nm* **1** : bill, banknote <un billet de vingt dollars : a twenty-dollar bill> **2** TICKET : ticket **3 billet doux** : love letter
billetterie [bijɛtri] *nf* **1** : ticket office, ticket agency **2** : automatic teller machine
billion [biljɔ̃] *nm* : trillion (United States), billion (Great Britain)
billot [bijo] *nm* **1** : block **2** *Can* : log
bimensuel, -suelle [bimɑ̃sɥɛl] *adj* : semimonthly, twice a month
binaire [binɛr] *adj* : binary
bine [bin] *nf Can* : white bean, broad bean
biner [bine] *vt* : to hoe, to harrow
binette [binɛt] *nf* : hoe
bingo [bingo] *nm Can* : bingo
binoculaire [binɔkylɛr] *adj* : binocular
biochimie [bjɔʃimi] *nf* : biochemistry — **biochimiste** [-ʃimist] *nmf*
biochimique [bjɔʃimik] *adj* : biochemical
biodégradable [bjɔdegradabl] *adj* : biodegradable
biographe [bjɔgraf] *nmf* : biographer
biographie [bjɔgrafi] *nf* : biography
biographique [bjɔgrafik] *adj* : biographical
biologie [bjɔlɔʒi] *nf* : biology — **biologiste** [-lɔʒist] *nmf*
biologique [bjɔlɔʒik] *adj* : biological
biophysicien, -cienne [bjɔfizisjɛ̃, -sjɛn] *n* : biophysicist
biophysique [bjɔfizik] *nf* : biophysics
biopsie [bjɔpsi] *nf* : biopsy
biosphère [bjɔsfɛr] *nf* : biosphere
biotechnologie [bjɔtɛknɔlɔʒi] *nf* : biotechnology
bip [bip] *nm* **1** : beep **2** *fam* : beeper
bipartite [bipartit] *adj* : bipartite, bipartisan
bipède [bipɛd] *adj & nm* : biped
bipolaire [bipɔlɛr] *adj* : bipolar
birman, -mane [birmɑ̃, -man] *adj* : Burmese
Birman, -mane *n* : Burmese
bis[1] [bis] *adv* **1** : twice, repeat (in music) **2** : A (in an address) <14 bis : 14A>
bis[2], **bise** [bi, biz] *adj* : grayish brown
bis[3] [bis] *nm & interj* : encore
bisannuel, -nuelle [bizanɥɛl] *adj & nf* : biannual, biennial — **bisannuellement** [-nɥɛlmɑ̃] *adv*
bisbille [bizbij] *nf fam* : squabble, tiff
biscornu, -nue [biskɔrny] *adj* **1** : misshapen, crooked **2** : quirky, bizarre
biscotte [biskɔt] *nf* : zwieback
biscuit [biskɥi] *nm* **1** : cookie **2** : sponge cake
bise [biz] *nf* **1** : north wind **2** *fam* : kiss, smack <faire la bise : to kiss on the cheeks>
biseau [bizo] *nm* **1** : bevel **2 en ~** : beveled
biseauter [bizote] *vt* : to bevel
bisexuel, -sexuelle [bisɛksɥɛl] *adj* : bisexual — **bisexualité** [-sɛksɥalite] *nf*
bismuth [bismyt] *nm* : bismuth
bison [bizɔ̃] *nm* : bison, buffalo
bisser [bise] *vt* : to encore
bissextile [bisɛkstil] *adj* **année bissextile** : leap year
bistouri [bisturi] *nm* : lancet
bistro *or* **bistrot** [bistro] *nm* : bistro, café
bit [bit] *nm* : bit (unit of information)
bitume [bitym] *nm* **1** : bitumen **2** : blacktop, asphalt
bitumineux, -neuse [bityminø, -nøz] *adj* : bituminous
bivalve [bivalv] *adj & nm* : bivalve

bivouac [bivwak] *nm* : bivouac

bivouaquer [bivwake] *vi* : to bivouac

bizarre [bizar] *adj* : bizarre, strange, odd — **bizarrement** [-zarmɑ̃] *adv*

bizarrerie [bizarri] *nf* **1** : strangeness **2** : eccentricity, peculiarity

blackbouler [blakbule] *vt* : to blackball

blafard, -farde [blafar, -fard] *adj* : pale, pallid

blague [blag] *nf* PLAISANTERIE : joke, trick, fib <sans blague! : no kidding!>

blaguer [blage] *vi* PLAISANTER : to joke, to kid, to fib

blagueur, -gueuse [blagœr, -gøz] *n fam* : joker, prankster

blaireau [blɛro] *nm, pl* **blaireaux** **1** : badger **2** : shaving brush

blairer [blɛre] *vt fam* : to stand, to stomach <personne ne peut la blairer : no one can stand her>

blamable [blamabl] *adj* : blameworthy

blâme [blam] *nm* **1** : blame, censure **2** : reprimand

blâmer [blame] *vt* **1** : to blame, to censure **2** : to reprimand

blanc[1], **blanche** [blɑ̃, blɑ̃ʃ] *adj* **1** : white **2** PÂLE : light-colored, pale **3** : blank **4** : pure, innocent

blanc[2] *nm* **1** : white **2** INTERVALLE : gap, blank space **3 blanc d'œuf** : egg white

blanc-bec [blɑ̃bɛk] *nm, pl* **blancs-becs** : greenhorn

blanchâtre [blɑ̃ʃatr] *adj* : whitish, off-white

blancheur [blɑ̃ʃœr] *nf* : whiteness

blanchiment [blɑ̃ʃimɑ̃] *nm* **1** : whitening, bleaching **2** : money laundering

blanchir [blɑ̃ʃir] *vt* **1** : to whiten, to bleach **2** : to launder **3** : to blanch, to parboil (vegetables) **4** : to clear (someone's name) **5** *Can* : to shut out (in sports) — *vi* : to turn white — **se blanchir** *vr* : to clear one's name

blanchissage [blɑ̃ʃisaʒ] *nm* **1** : washing, laundering **2** : refining (of sugar, etc.) **3** *Can* : shutout (in sports)

blanchisserie [blɑ̃ʃisri] *nf* : laundry

blanchisseur, -seuse [blɑ̃ʃisœr, -søz] *n* : laundry worker

blasé, -sée [blaze] *adj* : blasé, jaded

blason [blazɔ̃] *nm* **1** : coat of arms **2 redorer son blason** : to restore one's good name

blasphématoire [blasfematwar] *adj* : blasphemous

blasphème [blasfɛm] *nm* : blasphemy

blasphémer [blasfeme] {87} *v* : to blaspheme

blatte [blat] *nf France* : cockroach

blazer [blazɛr] *nm* : blazer (jacket)

blé [ble] *nm* **1** : wheat **2 blé d'Inde** *Can* : Indian corn, maize **3 blé noir** SARRASIN : buckwheat

bled [blɛd] *nm fam* : small village, boondocks *pl*

blême [blɛm] *adj* : pale, wan, pallid

blennorragie [blenɔraʒi] *nf* : gonorrhea

bléser [bleze] {87} *vi* : to lisp

blessé, -sée [blese] *n* : casualty, injured person

blesser [blese] *vt* : to injure, to wound, to hurt

blessure [blesyr] *nf* : injury, wound

bleu[1], **bleue** [blø] *adj* **1** : blue <des yeux bleus : blue eyes> **2** : very rare (of steak, etc.)

bleu[2] *nm* **1** : blue **2** : bruise <se faire un bleu : to bruise oneself> <couvert de bleus : black-and-blue> **3** *or* **fromage bleu** : blue cheese **4** : blueprint

bleuâtre [bløatr] *adj* : bluish

bleuet [bløɛ] *nm* **1** : cornflower **2** *Can* : blueberry

bleuir [bløir] *v* : to turn blue

bleuté, -tée [bløte] *adj* : bluish

blindage [blɛ̃daʒ] *nm* : armor (plating)

blindé[1], **-dée** [blɛ̃de] *adj* : armored

blindé[2] *nm* : armored vehicle

bloc [blɔk] *nm* **1** : block (of wood) **2** : bloc (in politics) **3** : pad (of paper) **4** *Can* : block <faire le tour du bloc en courant : to run around the block> **5 en ~** : as a whole, outright

blocage [blɔkaʒ] *nm* **1** : locking, jamming (of mechanisms) **2** : mental block **3** : freezing (of prices, wages, etc.)

blocus [blɔkys] *nm* : blockade

blond, blonde [blɔ̃, blɔ̃d] *adj & n* : blond

blonde *nf Can fam* : girlfriend

blondeur [blɔ̃dœr] *nf* : blondness, fairness

bloquer [blɔke] *vt* **1** : to block **2** : to freeze (a bank account), to stop (a check) **3** : to jam, to lock — **se bloquer** *vr*

bloquiste [blɔkist] *nmf Can* : member of the Bloc québécois party

blottir [blɔtir] *v* **se blottir** *vr* : to nestle, to cuddle, to snuggle up

blouse [bluz] *nf* **1** CHEMISIER : blouse **2** SARRAU : smock **3** : pocket (in billiards)

blouson [bluzɔ̃] *nm* : jacket <blouson d'aviateur : bomber jacket>

blue-jean [bludʒin] *nm, pl* **blue-jeans** : jeans *pl*, blue jeans *pl*

bluff [blœf] *nm* : bluff <c'est du bluff : he's just bluffing>

bluffer [blœfe] *v* : to bluff

boa [bɔa] *nm* : boa

bob [bɔb] *nm* → **bobsleigh**

bobard [bɔbar] *nm fam* : fib, tall tale

bobine [bɔbin] *nf* **1** : spool, reel, bobbin <bobine de pellicule : roll of film> **2** : electric coil

bobo [bobo] *nm fam* : boo-boo, scratch

bobsleigh [bɔbslɛg] *nm* : bobsled

bocal [bɔkal] *nm, pl* **bocaux** [bɔko] : jar

bock [bɔk] *nm* **1** CHOPE : beer glass **2** : glass of beer

bœuf [bœf] *nm, pl* **bœufs** [bø] **1** : beef **2** : steer, ox

bohème [bɔɛm] *adj & nmf* : bohemian

bohémien, -mienne [bɔemjɛ̃, -mjɛn] *n* : Bohemian, gypsy

boire[1] [bwar] {13} *vt* **1** : to drink <boire un coup : to have a drink> **2** : to absorb, to soak up — *vi* **1** : to drink **2** **~ à** : to toast

boire[2] *nm* : drink <le boire et le manger : food and drink>

bois [bwa] *nms & pl* **1** : wood <bois à brûler : firewood> <bois dur : hardwood> <petit bois : kindling> **2** FORÊT : woods *pl* **3** : woodcut **4 bois** *nmpl* : antlers **5 bois** *nmpl* : woodwinds

boisé[1], **-sée** [bwaze] *adj* : wooded

boisé[2] *nm Can* : woods *pl*, wooded area

boisement [bwazmɑ̃] *nm* : afforestation

boiserie [bwazri] *nf* **1** : woodwork **2 boiseries** *nfpl* : paneling

boisseau [bwaso] *nm* : bushel

boisson [bwasɔ̃] *nf* **1** : drink, beverage <boisson gazeuse : pop, soda> **2 en ~** *Can* : drunk

boîte [bwat] *nf* **1** : (tin) can <mettre en boîte : to can> **2** : box <boîte à gantes : glove compartment> <boîte aux lettres : mailbox> **3** *fam* : nightclub **4 boîte de vitesses** : transmission (of a motor vehicle)

boiter [bwate] *vi* **1** : to limp **2** : to wobble

boiterie [bwatri] *nf* : limp

boiteux, -teuse [bwatø, -tøz] *adj* **1** : lame **2** : wobbly, shaky

boîtier [bwatje] *nm* : casing, housing

boitillement [bwatijmɑ̃] *nm* : hobble, (slight) limp

boitiller [bwatije] *vi* : to limp slightly

bol [bɔl] *nm* **1** : bowl **2** : bowlful <un bol d'air : a breath of fresh air> **3 coup de bol** : stroke of luck

boléro [bɔlero] *nm* : bolero

bolide [bɔlid] *nm* **1** : meteorite **2** : racing car

bolivien, -vienne [bɔlivjɛ̃, -vjɛn] *adj* : Bolivian

Bolivien, -vienne *n* : Bolivian

bombarde [bɔ̃bard] *nf* : Jew's harp

bombardement [bɔ̃bardəmɑ̃] *nm* : bombing, bombardment

bombarder [bɔ̃barde] *vt* **1** : to bomb **2** : to bombard, to pelt

bombardier [bɔ̃bardje] *nm* **1** : bomber **2** : bombardier

bombe [bɔ̃b] *nf* **1** : bomb **2** ATOMISEUR : aerosol spray, atomiser **3 faire la bombe** *fam* : to live it up, to go on a spree

bomber [bɔ̃be] *vt* **1** GONFLER : to puff up, to stick out <bomber le torse : to swell with pride> **2** : to spray (paint) — *vi* : to bulge out

bon[1] [bɔ̃, bɔn *before a vowel or mute h*] *adv* **1 faire bon** : to be nice, to be good, to be acceptable <il fait bon ici : it's nice here> <il ne ferait pas bon l'arrêter : it would be unwise to stop him> **2 tenir bon** : to hold firm, to stand fast

bon[2], **bonne** [bɔ̃ (bɔn *before a vowel or mute h*), bɔn] *adj* **1** : good, honest, upright **2** : sound, high-quality **3** : pleasant, desirable <bonne chance! : good luck!> <ça sent bon : that smells good> **4** : correct, proper **5** : capable, knowledgeable <bon en science : good at science> **6** : good, profitable <être bon à faire : to be worth doing> **7** : effective <bon contre la douleur : good for pain> **8** (*used as an intensive*) <un bon nombre : a good many> <trois bonnes heures : three solid hours> **9 bon enfant** : easygoing **10 bon marché** : cheap, inexpensive **11 bon mot** : witticism **12 bonne femme** *fam* : woman, old lady **13 bonne sœur** : nun **14 bon sens** : common sense **15 de bonne heure** : early **16 pour de bon** : really, for good <il est parti pour de bon : he's gone for good>

bon[3] *nm* **1** : good thing, good person <les bons : the good> <avoir du bon : to have (some) good points> **2** : voucher, coupon **3** : bond <bon du Trésor : treasury bond> <bon de commande : purchase order>

bon[4] *interj* **1** : right, OK, fine <bon, mangeons : OK, let's eat> **2** : so, now, well <bon, où en étions-nous? : now, where were we?>

bonasse [bɔnas] *adj* : meek

bonbon [bɔ̃bɔ̃] *nm* : candy

bonbonnière [bɔ̃bɔnjɛr] *nf* : candy box

bond [bɔ̃] *nm* **1** : bound, jump, leap <faire un bond : to leap> <bond en avant : leap forward, breakthrough> **2** : bounce

bondé, -dée [bɔ̃de] *adj* : crammed, jampacked

bondir [bɔ̃dir] *vi* **1** SAUTER : to jump, to leap **2** : to rush, to dash

bonheur [bɔnœr] *nm* **1** : happiness **2** : pleasure **3** : luck, good fortune <par bonheur : fortunately>

bonhomie [bɔnɔmi] *nf* : good-naturedness, cordiality

bonhomme[1] [bɔnɔm] *adj, pl* **bonshommes** : affable, good-natured

bonhomme[2] *nm, pl* **bonshommes 1** *fam* : fellow, guy **2 bonhomme de neige** : snowman

boni [bɔni] *nm* **1** : bonus **2** : surplus

bonification [bɔnifikasjɔ̃] *nf* **1** : improvement (of land, etc.) **2** : bonus points *pl* (in sports)

bonifier [bɔnifje] {96} *vt* : to improve — **se bonifier** *vr*

boniment [bɔnimɑ̃] *nm* **1** : sales pitch **2** *fam* : tall story **3** *Can* : short speech

bonimenteur [bɔnimɑ̃tœr] *nm* : barker (at a fair)

bonjour [bɔ̃ʒur] *nm* **1** : hello, good morning, good afternoon **2** *Can* : good-bye

bonne [bɔn] *nf* **1** DOMESTIQUE : maid **2 bonne d'enfants** : nanny

bonnement [bɔnmɑ̃] *adv* **tout bonnement** : quite simply

bonnet [bɔnɛ] *nm* **1** : cap, bonnet **2** : cup (of a brassiere) **3 c'est blanc bonnet et bonnet blanc** : it's six of one, half dozen of the other **4 gros bonnet** *fam* : bigwig, big shot

bonneterie [bɔnɛtri] *nf* : hosiery

bonsoir [bɔ̃swar] *nm* : good evening, good night

bonté [bɔ̃te] *nf* : goodness, kindness

bookmaker [bukmɛkœr] *nm* : bookmaker

boom [bum] *nm* : boom (in economics)

boomerang [bumrɑ̃g] *nm* : boomerang

bord [bɔr] *nm* **1** : edge **2** : bank, shore **3** : border (of fabric, etc.) **4** : rim, brim **5** CÔTÉ : side **6 à ~** : on board, aboard **7 au bord de** : on the verge of, on the brink of **8 par–dessus ~** : overboard

bordeaux [bɔrdo] *nm* **1** : Bordeaux (wine) **2** : maroon

bordée [bɔrde] *nf* **1** : broadside, volley <une bordée d'injures : a volley of abuse> **2** : tack (of a ship) <faire une bordée : to tack> **3 bordée de neige** *Can* : snowstorm

bordel [bɔrdɛl] *nm fam* **1** : brothel **2** : mess, shambles

bordelais, -laise [bɔrdəlɛ, -lɛz] *adj* : of or from Bordeaux

border [bɔrde] *vt* **1** : to border, to line, to ring **2** : to tuck in

bordereau [bɔrdəro] *nm, pl* **-reaux** [-ro] : statement (of an account), note, slip <bordereau de dépôt : deposit slip>

bordure [bɔrdyr] *nf* **1** BORD : border, edge **2** : side (of a road), curb

bore [bɔr] *nm* : boron

boréal, boréale [bɔreal] *adj, mpl* **boréaux** [bɔreo] **1** : boreal, northern **2 → aurore**

borgne [bɔrɲ] *adj* : one-eyed

borique [bɔrik] *adj* : **acide borique** : boric acid

borne [bɔrn] *nf* **1** : milestone, landmark **2** *France fam* : kilometer **3** : terminal (in electricity) **4 bornes** *nfpl* : limits, boundaries **5 borne d'incendie** : fire hydrant

borné, -née [bɔrne] *adj* : narrow-minded

borne–fontaine [bɔrnfɔ̃tɛn] *nf Can* : fire hydrant

borner [bɔrne] *vt* **1** : to mark out the boundaries of **2** LIMITER : to limit, to restrict **— se borner** *vr*

bosniaque [bɔsnjak] *adj* : Bosnian

Bosniaque *nmf* : Bosnian

bosquet [bɔske] *nm* : grove, copse

bosse [bɔs] *nf* **1** : hump (of a person or animal) **2** : lump, bump, dent **3 avoir la bosse de** : to have a flair for

bosseler [bɔsle] {8} *vt* **1** : to emboss **2** : to dent

bosser [bɔse] *vi France fam* : to work, to slave away

bossu[1], -sue [bɔsy] *adj* : hunchbacked

bossu[2], -sue *n* : hunchback (person)

botanique[1] [bɔtanik] *adj* : botanical

botanique[2] *nf* : botany **— botaniste** [-tanist] *nmf*

botte [bɔt] *nf* **1** : boot **2** : bunch, sheaf, bale **3** : thrust, lunge (in fencing)

botter [bɔte] *vt* **1** : to put boots on **2** : to kick (in sports)

botteur, -teuse [bɔtœr, -tøz] *n* : kicker (in sports)

bottillon [bɔtijɔ̃] *nm* : bootee

bottin [bɔtɛ̃] *nm* : telephone directory

bottine [bɔtin] *nf* : ankle boot

botulisme [bɔtylism] *nm* : botulism

bouc [buk] *nm* **1** : goat, billy goat **2** : goatee **3 bouc émissaire** : scapegoat

boucan [bukɑ̃] *nm fam* : din, racket

boucane [bukan] *nf Can* : smoke

boucanier [bukanje] *nm* : buccaneer

bouche [buʃ] *nf* **1** : mouth <de bouche à l'oreille : confidentially> **2** : opening, entrance <bouche d'égout : manhole> **3 le bouche à bouche** : mouth-to-mouth resuscitation **4 bouche d'incendie** : fire hydrant **5 faire la fine bouche** : to turn up one's nose **6 → bée**

bouchée [buʃe] *nf* : mouthful

boucher[1] [buʃe] *vt* : to stop up, to plug, to block **— se boucher** *vr* **1** : to get blocked **2 se boucher le nez** : to hold one's nose

boucher[2], -chère [buʃe, -ʃɛr] *n* : butcher

boucherie [buʃri] *nf* **1** : butcher's shop **2** MASSACRE : butchery, slaughter

bouche–trou [buʃtru] *nm, pl* **bouche–trous** : stand-in, stopgap

bouchon [buʃɔ̃] *nm* **1** : cork, stopper **2** : float (in fishing) **3** : traffic jam, gridlock

boucle [bukl] *nf* **1** : buckle, loop **2** : curl, loop **3 boucle d'oreille** : earring

boucler [bukle] *vt* **1** : to buckle, to fasten **2** : to complete, to finish off <boucler la boucle : to come full circle> **3** *fam* : to lock up, to imprison **—** *vi* : to curl

bouclier [buklije] *nm* : shield

bouddhisme [budism] *nm* : Buddhism **— bouddhiste** [budist] *adj & nmf*

bouder [bude] *vt* : to avoid, to be cool towards **—** *vi* : to sulk, to pout

bouderie [budri] *nf* : sulking, sulkiness

boudeur, -deuse [budœr, -døz] *adj* : sulky

boudin [budɛ̃] *nm* **1** : blood sausage **2** : flange (on a wheel)

boudiné, -née [budine] *adj* **1** : pudgy (of fingers, etc.) **2 ~ dans** : squeezed into, bulging out of
boue [bu] *nf* : mud
bouée [bwe] *nf* **1** : buoy **2 bouée de sauvetage** : life preserver
bouette [bwɛt] *nf Can fam* : mud
boueux, boueuse [buø, buøz] *adj* : muddy
bouffant, -fante [bufɑ̃, -fɑ̃t] *adj* **1** : puffed out, baggy **2** : bouffant
bouffe [buf] *nf fam* : grub, chow
bouffée [bufe] *nf* **1** : puff, gust **2** : surge, fit (of pride, etc.)
bouffer [bufe] *vt fam* : to eat, to gobble up
bouffi, -fie [bufi] *adj* : puffy, swollen
bouffir [bufir] *v* : to puff up
bouffisure [bufisyr] *nf* : puffiness (of the face, etc.)
bouffon[1], -fonne [bufɔ̃, bufɔn] *adj* : farcical, comical
bouffon[2] *nm* : clown, buffoon, jester
bouffonnerie [bufɔnri] *nf* : buffoonery, antics *pl*
bouge *nm* [buʒ] **1** : hovel, dump **2** : dive, seedy café
bougeoir [buʒwar] *nm* : candlestick
bougeotte [buʒɔt] *nf* : fidgets *pl* <avoir la bougeotte : to be fidgety>
bouger [buʒe] {17} *vt* : to move — *vi* : to budge, to stir — **se bouger** *vr*
bougie [buʒi] *nf* **1** : candle **2** : spark plug
bougonner [bugɔne] *vi* : to grumble, to complain
bougre [bugr] *nm fam* : guy, fellow
bougrement [bugrəmɑ̃] *adv fam* : awfully, damned
bouillabaisse [bujabɛs] *nf* : bouillabaisse, fish soup
bouillie [buji] *nf* : baby cereal, gruel
bouillir [bujir] {14} *vi* **1** : to boil **2** : to seethe (with anger, etc.)
bouilloire [bujwar] *nf* : kettle, teakettle
bouillon [bujɔ̃] *nm* **1** : broth, stock **2** : bubble
bouillonnant, -nante [bujɔnɑ̃, -nɑ̃t] *adj* **1** : bubbling, foaming **2** : lively
bouillonnement [bujɔnmɑ̃] *nm* **1** : bubbling, foaming **2** : agitation, ferment
bouillonner [bujɔne] *vi* **1** : to bubble, to foam **2** : to seethe
boulanger, -gère [bulɑ̃ʒe, -ʒɛr] *n* : baker
boulangerie [bulɑ̃ʒri] *nf* : bakery
boule [bul] *nf* **1** : ball <boule de neige : snowball> **2 se mettre en boule** *fam* : to blow one's top
bouleau [bulo] *nm, pl* **bouleaux** : birch
bouledogue [buldɔg] *nm* : bulldog
boulet [bulɛ] *nm* **1** : cannonball **2** : ball and chain **3** : fetlock (of a horse)
boulette [bulɛt] *nf* **1** : pellet **2** *fam* : blunder **3 boulette de pâte** : dumpling **4 boulette de viande** : meatball
boulevard [bulvar] *nm* : boulevard
bouleversant, -sante [bulvɛrsɑ̃, -sɑ̃t] *adj* : distressing, upsetting
bouleversement [bulvɛrsəmɑ̃] *nm* : upheaval, upset
bouleverser [bulvɛrse] *vt* **1** : to overwhelm, to upset **2** : to disrupt, to turn upside down
boulier [bulje] *nm* : abacus
boulimie [bulimi] *nf* : bulimia — **boulimique** [-limik] *adj*
boulon [bulɔ̃] *nm* : bolt
boulot[1], -lotte [bulo, -lɔt] *adj* : plump, chubby
boulot[2] *nm fam* **1** : work, task **2** : job <petit boulot : odd job>
boum[1] [bum] *nm* **1** : bang **2** : boom (of business, births, etc.)
boum[2] *nf France* : party
bouquet [bukɛ] *nm* **1** : bouquet, bunch (of flowers, etc.) **2** : clump (of trees) **3** : bouquet (of wine) **4** : crowning event <ça, c'est le bouquet! : that takes the cake!>
bouquetin [buktɛ̃] *nm* : ibex
bouquin [bukɛ̃] *nm fam* : book
bouquiner [bukine] *v fam* : to read
bouquiniste [bukinist] *nmf* : second-hand bookseller
bourbeux, -beuse [burbø, -bøz] *adj* : muddy, swampy
bourbier [burbje] *nm* : swamp, quagmire
bourbon [burbɔ̃] *nm* : bourbon
bourde [burd] *nf* BÉVUE : blunder
bourdon [burdɔ̃] *nm* **1** : bumblebee **2 avoir le bourdon** *fam* : to have the blues
bourdonnement [burdɔnmɑ̃] *nm* **1** : buzzing, droning **2 bourdonnement d'oreilles** : ringing in the ears
bourdonner [burdɔne] *vi* : to buzz, to hum, to drone
bourg [bur] *nm* : market town
bourgade [burgad] *nf* : small town, village
bourgeois, -geoise [burʒwa, -ʒwaz] *adj & n* : bourgeois
bourgeoisie [burʒwazi] *nf* : bourgeoisie, middle class
bourgeon [burʒɔ̃] *nm* : bud
bourgeonner [burʒɔne] *vi* : to bud
bourgogne [burgɔɲ] *nm* : Burgundy (wine)
bourguignon, -gnonne [burgiɲɔ̃, -ɲɔn] *adj* **1** : Burgundian **2 bœuf bourguignon** : beef bourguignon
bourrage [buraʒ] *nm* **1** : filling, stuffing **2** : cramming (for an exam) **3 bourrage de crâne** : brainwashing
bourrasque [burask] *nf* : squall, gust (of wind), flurry (of snow)
bourrasser [burase] *vt Can fam* : to be rough with, to push around
bourre [bur] *nf* : stuffing, padding, wad
bourreau [buro] *nm, pl* **bourreaux 1** : executioner, hangman **2** : torturer, tormentor **3 bourreau de travail** : workaholic

bourrée [bure] *nf Can* : spurt <travailler par bourrées : to work in spurts>

bourrelet [burlɛ] *nm* **1** : weather strip **2** : roll (of fat)

bourrer [bure] *vt* : to fill, to stuff, to cram — *vi* : to be filling — **se bourrer** *vr* : to stuff oneself

bourrique [burik] *nf* **1** ÂNE : ass, donkey **2** *fam* : stubborn fool

bourru, -rue [bury] *adj* : gruff

bourrure [buryr] *nf Can* : stuffing, padding

bourse [burs] *nf* **1** PORTE-MONNAIE : change purse **2** : scholarship, grant **3 la Bourse** : the stock market

boursier[1], -sière [bursje, -sjɛr] *adj* : stock, stock-market

boursier[2], -sière *n* **1** : scholarship holder, scholar **2** : stock-market trader

boursouflé, -flée [bursufle] *adj* **1** : puffy, bloated **2** : bombastic

boursoufler [bursufle] *vt* : to puff up, to cause to swell — **se boursoufler** *vr* **1** : to swell (up) **2** : to blister (of paint)

boursouflure [bursuflyr] *nf* **1** : swelling, puffiness **2** : pomposity **3** : blister (on paint, etc.)

bousculade [buskylad] *nf* **1** : crush, jostling **2** : rush, scramble

bousculer [buskyle] *vt* **1** : to bump into, to jostle, to shove **2** : to rush, to hurry — **se bousculer** *vr* : to bump into each other

bouse [buz] *nf* : cow dung, cowpat

bousiller [buzije] *vt fam* **1** : to bungle, to botch **2** : to wreck **3** : to bump off, to kill

bousilleur, -leuse [busijœr, -jøz] *n fam* : bungler

boussole [busɔl] *nf* : compass

bout[1] [bu], *etc.* → **bouillir**

bout[2] [bu] *nm* **1** EXTRÉMITÉ : end, tip <bout de doigt : fingertip> <bout de la table : head of the table> **2** : bit, piece **3 à bout portant** : point-blank **4 au bout de** : after <au bout de cinq minutes : after five minutes> **5 au bout du compte** : in the end, ultimately **6 être à bout** : to be exhausted <ma patience est à bout : my patience has run out>

boutade [butad] *nf* PLAISANTERIE : joke, witticism

bouteille [butɛj] *nf* : bottle

boutique [butik] *nf* : store, shop, boutique

boutiquier, -quière [butikje, -kjɛr] *n* : shopkeeper

bouton [butɔ̃] *nm* **1** : button **2** BOURGEON : bud **3** : pimple **4 bouton de porte** : doorknob

bouton–d'or [butɔ̃dɔr] *nm, pl* **boutons–d'or** : buttercup

boutonner [butɔne] *vt* : to button — **se boutonner** *vr* : to button up

boutonneux, -neuse [butɔnø, -nøz] *adj* : pimply

boutonnière [butɔnjɛr] *nf* : buttonhole

bouton–pression [butɔ̃presjɔ̃] *nm, pl* **boutons–pression** : snap (fastener)

bouture [butyr] *nf* : cutting (from a plant)

bouvier, -vière [buvje, -vjɛr] *n* : cowherd

bovin, -vine [bɔvɛ̃, -vin] *adj* : bovine

bovins [bɔvɛ̃] *nmpl* : cattle

bowling [buliŋ] *nm* **1** : bowling **2** : bowling alley

box [bɔks] *nm, pl* **boxes 1** : stall, alcove, cubicle **2 box des accusés** : dock (in court)

boxe [bɔks] *nf* : boxing

boxer[1] [bɔkse] *vi* : to box — *vt fam* : to strike, to punch

boxer[2] [bɔksɛr] *nm* : boxer (dog)

boxeur [bɔksœr] *nm* : boxer, fighter

box–office [bɔksɔfis] *nm, pl* **box–offices** : box office

boyau [bwajo] *nm, pl* **boyaux 1** TUYAU : hose, tube **2** INTESTIN : intestine, gut **3** : narrow passageway **4 boyau d'arrosage** *Can* : hose

boycott [bɔjkɔt] *or* **boycottage** [bɔjkɔtaʒ] *nm* : boycott

boycotter [bɔjkɔte] *vt* : to boycott

bozo [bozo] *nm Can fam* : idiot, fool

bracelet [braslɛ] *nm* **1** : bracelet **2** *or* **bracelet de montre** : watchband

bracelet–montre [braslɛmɔ̃tr] *nm, pl* **bracelets–montres** : wristwatch

braconner [brakɔne] *vi* : to poach

braconnier, -nière [brakɔnje, -njɛr] *n* : poacher

brader [brade] *vt* : to sell (off) cheaply

braderie [bradri] *nf* : clearance sale

braguette [bragɛt] *nf* : fly (of pants, etc.)

braille [braj] *nm* : braille

brailler [braje] *vi fam* : to bawl, to yell, to howl — *vt fam* : to bellow out

braiment [brɛmɑ̃] *nm* : bray, braying

braire [brɛr] {15} *vi* : to bray

braise [brɛz] *nf* : embers *pl*, coals *pl*

braiser [breze] *vt* : to braise

bran [brɑ̃] *nm* **1** : bran **2 bran de scie** : sawdust

brancard [brɑ̃kar] *nm* **1** CIVIÈRE : stretcher **2** : shaft (of a carriage, etc.)

branche [brɑ̃ʃ] *nf* **1** : branch, bough (of a tree) **2** : branch (of a family, a river, etc.) **3** : field (of activity) **4** : sidepiece (of eyeglasses)

branché, -chée [brɑ̃ʃe] *adj fam* : fashionable, trendy, in

brancher [brɑ̃ʃe] *vt* **1** : to connect up (a utility) **2** : to plug in **3** *fam* : to interest, to turn on <le rock, ça ne me branche pas : I'm not into rock music>

branchie [brɑ̃ʃi] *nf* : gill (of a fish, etc.)

brandir [brɑ̃dir] *vt* : to brandish, to wave about

branlant, -lante [brɑ̃lɑ̃, -lɑ̃t] *adj* : shaky, wobbly, unsteady

branle [brɑ̃l] *nm* **1** : oscillation, swing **2** : impetus, momentum <mettre en branle : to set in motion>

branle–bas [brɑ̃lba] *nms & pl* : commotion, bustle

branler [brɑ̃le] *vi* : to wobble, to be loose

branleux, -leuse [brɑ̃lø, -løz] *adj Can fam* **1** : lazy **2** : indecisive

braquer [brake] *vt* **1** : to aim, to point, to fix on **2** : to turn (a steering wheel) **3** : to antagonize — *vi* : to turn the steering wheel

bras [bra] *nms & pl* **1** : arm **2 bras** *nmpl* : workers, manpower **3 bras de mer** : inlet **4 bras droit** : right-hand man

brasero [brazero] *nm* : brazier

brasier [brazje] *nm* : blaze, inferno

bras–le–corps [bralkɔr] **à bras–le–corps** *adv* **1** : bodily **2** : head-on

brassage [brasaʒ] *nm* **1** : mixing, intermingling **2** : brewing

brasse [bras] *nf* **1** : breaststroke **2** : fathom

brassée [brase] *nf* **1** : armful **2** *Can* : load (of laundry)

brasser [brase] *vt* **1** : to mix, to toss, to shuffle **2** : to brew (beer)

brasserie [brasri] *nf* **1** : large café, restaurant **2** : brewery

brasseur, -seuse [brasœr, -søz] *n* **1** : brewer **2 brasseur d'affaires** : tycoon, financier

brassière [brasjɛr] *nf Can* : bra, brassiere

bravade [bravad] *nf* : bravado

brave[1] [brav] *adj* **1** GENTIL : good, decent, nice <c'est un brave homme : he's a good man> **2** : brave, courageous <c'est une femme brave : she's a brave woman>

brave[2] *nmf* : brave person, hero

bravement [bravmɑ̃] *adv* : bravely, boldly

braver [brave] *vt* : to defy, to challenge

bravo [bravo] *nm & interj* : bravo

bravoure [bravur] *nf* : bravery

break [brɛk] *nm* **1** *France* : station wagon **2** : break (in music, sports, etc.) **3 prendre un break** *Can* : to take a break

brebis [brəbi] *nf* **1** : ewe **2 brebis** *nfpl* : flock (in religion) **3 brebis galeuse** : black sheep

brèche [brɛʃ] *nf* **1** : hole, gap **2** : breach

bréchet [breʃɛ] *nm* : wishbone

bredouille [brəduj] *adj* : empty-handed

bredouiller [brəduje] *v* : to mumble, to mutter

bref[1] [brɛf] *adv* or **en bref** : briefly, in short

bref[2], **brève** [brɛf, brɛv] *adj* : brief, short

breloque [brəlɔk] *nf* : charm (on a bracelet)

brésilien, -lienne [breziljɛ̃, -ljɛn] *adj* : Brazilian

Brésilien, -lienne *n* : Brazilian

bretelle [brətɛl] *nf* **1** : strap, shoulder strap **2** : ramp <bretelle de sortie : exit ramp> **3 bretelles** *nfpl* : suspenders

breton, -tonne [brətɔ̃, brətɔn] *adj* : Breton

bretzel [brɛtzɛl] *nm* : pretzel

breuvage [brœvaʒ] *nm* : beverage, drink

brevet [brəvɛ] *nm* **1** : patent **2** : diploma, certificate **3** : commission (in the armed forces)

breveté, -tée [brəvte] *adj* **1** : patented **2** : qualified, certified

breveter [brəvte] {8} *vt* : to patent

bréviaire [brevjɛr] *nm* : breviary

bribes [brib] *nfpl* : bits, pieces <bribes de conversation : snatches of conversation>

bric–à–brac [brikabrak] *nms & pl* : bric-a-brac, odds and ends

brick [brik] *nm* : brig (ship)

bricolage [brikɔlaʒ] *nm* **1** : do-it-yourself work **2** : makeshift repairs

bricole [brikɔl] *nf* **1** : trifle, trinket **2 bricoles** *nfpl* : bits and pieces

bricoler [brikɔle] *vi* **1** : to fix things up **2** : to do odd jobs, to putter — *vt* **1** : to fix up, to mend **2** : to tinker with

bricoleur, -leuse [brikɔlœr, -løz] *n* **1** : handyman **2** : do-it-yourselfer

bride [brid] *nf* **1** : bridle <tenir en bride : to keep a tight rein on> **2** : flange (of a pipe, etc.)

brider [bride] *vt* **1** : to bridle (a horse) **2** : to keep in check

bridge [bridʒ] *nm* **1** : bridge (card game) **2** or **bridge dentaire** : denture, bridgework

brièvement [brijɛvmɑ̃] *adv* : briefly

brièveté [brijɛvte] *nf* : brevity

brigade [brigad] *nf* **1** : brigade **2** : squad, team

brigadier[1] [brigadje] *nm* **1** : corporal (in the military) **2** : police sergeant

brigadier[2], **-dière** [brigadje, -djɛr] *n Can* : crossing guard

brigand [brigɑ̃] *nm* : robber, thief

brigandage [brigɑ̃daʒ] *nm* : armed robbery

briguer [brige] *vt* **1** : to aspire to **2** : to solicit, to seek

brillamment [brijamɑ̃] *adv* : brilliantly

brillant, -lante [brijɑ̃, -jɑ̃t] *adj* **1** : brilliant, outstanding **2** : bright, sparkling, shiny

briller [brije] *vi* : to shine, to sparkle

brimade [brimad] *nf* : bullying, harassment, hazing

brimer [brime] *vt* : to bully, to haze

brin [brɛ̃] *nm* **1** : blade (of grass), sprig, twig **2** : touch, little bit <il est un brin ennuyeux : he's rather boring> **3** : iota **4** : strand (of wool, thread, etc.)

brindille [brɛ̃dij] *nf* : twig

bringue [brɛ̃g] *nf fam* : binge <faire la bringue : to go on a binge>
brio [brijo] *nm* **1** : brilliance, panache **2 avec ~** : brilliantly
brioche [brijɔʃ] *nf* **1** : brioche **2** *fam* : paunch
brique [brik] *nf* : brick
briquet [brikɛ] *nm* **1** : (cigarette) lighter **2** : beagle
bris [bri] *nms & pl* : breaking, breakage
brise [briz] *nf* : breeze
brise–glace [brizglas] *nms & pl* : icebreaker
brise–lames [brizlam] *nms & pl* : breakwater
briser [brize] *vt* **1** : to break, to smash **2** : to ruin, to wreck, to crush <des faux bruits ont brisé sa carrière : false rumors wrecked his career> — *vi* : to break <briser avec la tradition : to break with tradition> — **se briser** *vr* **1** : to shatter, to break up, to break down **2** : to break <son cœur se brisait : her heart was breaking>
briseur, -seuse [brizœr, -zøz] *n* **1** : wrecker **2 briseur de grève** : strikebreaker
brise–vent [brizvɑ̃] *nms & pl* : windbreak
brisure [brizyr] *nf* : break, crack
britannique [britanik] *adj* : British
Britannique *nmf* : British person, Briton
broc [bro] *nm* : jug, pitcher
brocante [brɔkɑ̃t] *nf* **1** : secondhand trade **2** : flea market
brocanteur, -teuse [brɔkɑ̃tœr, -tøz] *n* : secondhand dealer
brocart [brɔkar] *nm* : brocade
broche [brɔʃ] *nf* **1** : brooch **2** : spit, skewer **3** : spindle (on a spinning machine) **4** *Can* : wire <broche piquante : barbed wire>
broché, -chée [brɔʃe] *adj* : paperbound
brochet [brɔʃɛ] *nm* : pike (fish)
brochette [brɔʃɛt] *nf* **1** : skewer **2** : shish kebab
brochure [brɔʃyr] *nf* : brochure, pamphlet, booklet
brocoli [brɔkɔli] *nm* : broccoli
broder [brɔde] *vt* : to embroider — *vi* **~ sur** : to elaborate on, to embellish
broderie [brɔdri] *nf* : embroidery
broie [brwa], **broiera** [brwara], *etc.* → **broyer**
brome [brom] *nm* : bromine
broncher [brɔ̃ʃe] *vi* **1** : to flinch **2** : to stumble (of a horse)
bronches [brɔ̃ʃ] *nfpl* : bronchial tubes
bronchite [brɔ̃ʃit] *nf* : bronchitis
bronzage [brɔ̃zaʒ] *nm* : suntan
bronze [brɔ̃z] *nm* : bronze
bronzé, -zée [brɔ̃ze] *adj* : tanned, suntanned
bronzer [brɔ̃ze] *vt* **1** : to tan **2** : to bronze (metals) — *vi* : to get a suntan
brossage [brɔsaʒ] *nm* : brushing
brosse [brɔs] *nf* **1** : brush <brosse à cheveux : hairbrush> <brosse à dents : toothbrush>
brosser [brɔse] *vt* **1** : to brush **2** : to paint (a picture) — **se brosser** *vr* : to brush oneself <se brosser les cheveux : to brush one's hair>
broue [bru] *nf Can* **1** : froth **2 péter de la broue** *fam* : to show off
brouette [bruɛt] *nf* : wheelbarrow
brouhaha [bruaa] *nm* : brouhaha, hubbub
brouillard [brujar] *nm* **1** : fog, mist **2 être dans un brouillard** : to be in a fog
brouille [bruj] *nf* **1** : quarrel, misunderstanding **2** : discord
brouiller [bruje] *vt* **1** : to mix up, to shuffle (cards), to scramble (eggs, etc.) **2** : to blur, to cloud **3** : to interfere with (radio transmission, etc.) **4** : to turn against, to fall out with — **se brouiller** *vr* **1** : to quarrel, to fall out **2** : to become confused **3** : to cloud over
brouillon[1], -lonne [brujɔ̃, -jɔn] *adj* **1** DÉSORGANISÉ : disorganized **2** DÉSORDONNÉ : untidy
brouillon[2] *nm* : rough draft
broussaille [brusaj] *nf* : undergrowth
broussailleux, -leuse [brusajø, -jøz] *adj* : bushy, scrubby
brousse [brus] *nf* **1** : brush (vegetation) **2** *fam* : boondocks <en pleine brousse : in the middle of nowhere>
brouter [brute] *vt* : to graze on, to nibble on — *vi* : to graze
broutille [brutij] *nf* : trifle
broyer [brwaje] {58} *vt* **1** : to grind, to crush **2 broyer du noir** : to be in the doldrums, to brood, to mope
broyeur *nm* [brwajœr] **1** : grinder, crusher **2 broyeur à ordures** : garbage disposal unit
bru [bry] *nf* : daughter-in-law
bruant [bryɑ̃] *nm* : bunting, small finch
brucelles [brysɛl] *nfpl* : tweezers
brugnon *nm* [bryɲɔ̃] : nectarine
bruine [brɥin] *nf* : drizzle — **bruiner** [brɥine] *vi*
bruire [brɥir] {16} *vi* **1** : to rustle (of leaves, etc.) **2** : to murmur, to hum, to drone, to buzz
bruissement [brɥismɑ̃] *nm* : rustling, murmuring, humming
bruit [brɥi] *nm* **1** : noise, sound <faire du bruit : to make noise, to be noisy> <bruit de fond : background noise> **2** : commotion, fuss, uproar **3** : rumor, gossip
bruitage [brɥitaʒ] *nm* : sound effects *pl*
brûlant, -lante [brylɑ̃, -lɑ̃t] *adj* **1** : burning hot **2** : passionate, fervent **3** : urgent <un sujet brûlant : a burning issue>
brûlé, -lée [bryle] *adj Can fam* : worn-out, beat

brûler [bryle] *vt* **1** : to burn, to scald **2** : to run (a red light) — *vi* **1** : to burn (up), to be on fire **2** ~ **de** : to long for, to be consumed with — **se bruler** *vr* : to burn oneself
brûleur [brylœr] *nm* : burner (of a stove)
brulôt [brylo] *nm Can* : gnat
brûlure [brylyr] *nf* **1** : burn **2** : burning <brûlures d'estomac : heartburn>
brume [brym] *nf* : mist, haze
brumeux, -meuse [brymø, -møz] *adj* : misty, foggy, hazy
brun[1], brune [brœ̃, bryn] *adj* : brown
brun[2], brune *n* : brown-haired person, brunet
brun[3] *nm* : brown
brunante [brynɑ̃t] *nf Can* : dusk
brunâtre [brynatr] *adj* : brownish
brunch [brœnʃ] *nm* : brunch
brunette [brynɛt] *nf* : brunette
brunir [brynir] *vt* **1** : to burnish **2** BRONZER : to tan — *vi* **1** : to get tan **2** : to darken, to brown
brusque [brysk] *adj* : brusque, abrupt, curt — **brusquement** [bryskəmɑ̃] *adv*
brusquer [bryske] *vt* **1** : to be brusque with **2** : to rush, to hurry
brusquerie [bryskəri] *nf* **1** : brusqueness **2** : suddenness
brut, brute [bryt] *adj* **1** : raw, crude, rough **2** : dry (of wine) **3** : total, gross <poids brut : gross weight>
brutal, -tale [brytal] *adj, mpl* **brutaux** [bryto] **1** : brutal, violent **2** : sudden, sharp **3** : blunt, stark — **brutalement** [-talmɑ̃] *adv*
brutaliser [brytalize] *vt* : to abuse, to mistreat
brutalité [brytalite] *nf* **1** : brutality **2** : suddenness
brute [bryt] *nf* : brute, beast
bruxellois, -loise [brysɛlwa, -lwaz] *adj* : of or from Brussels
Bruxellois, -loise *n* : person from Brussels
bruyamment [brɥijamɑ̃] *adv* : loudly, noisily
bruyant, bruyante [brɥijɑ̃, -jɑ̃t] *adj* : noisy
bruyère [bryjɛr] *nf* **1** : heather **2** : heath, moor
bu [by] *pp* → **boire**
buanderie [byɑ̃dri] *nf* **1** : laundry room **2** *Can* : self-service laundry
buandier, -dière [byɑ̃dje, -djɛr] *n Can* : laundry worker
buccal, -cale [bykal] *adj, mpl* **buccaux** [byko] : oral
buccin [byksɛ̃] *nm* : whelk
bûche [byʃ] *nf* : log
bûcher[1] [byʃe] *vt* **1** *fam* : to plod away at **2** *Can* : to chop down (trees) — *vi* **1** *fam* : to keep working, to slave away **2** *Can* : to fell trees
bûcher[2] *nm* **1** : stake, pyre **2** : woodshed
bûcheron, -ronne [byʃrɔ̃, -rɔn] *n* : logger, lumberjack
bûcheur[1], -cheuse [byʃœr, -ʃøz] *adj fam* : hardworking
bûcheur[2], -cheuse *n fam* : grind, hard worker
bucolique [bykɔlik] *adj* : bucolic
budget [bydʒɛ] *nm* : budget
budgétaire [bydʒetɛr] *adj* : budgetary
budgétiser [bydʒetize] *vt* : to budget
buée [bɥe] *nf* : steam, mist, condensation
buffet [byfɛ] *nm* **1** : sideboard **2** : buffet-style meal or restaurant
buffle [byfl] *nm* : Cape buffalo, water buffalo
buis [bɥi] *nm* : box (plant), boxwood
buisson [bɥisɔ̃] *nm* : bush, shrub
buissonnière [bɥisɔnjɛr] *adj* **faire l'école buissonnière** : to skip school
bulbe [bylb] *nm* : bulb (of a plant)
bulbeux, -beuse [bylbø, -bøz] *adj* : bulbous
bulgare[1] [bylgar] *adj* : Bulgarian
bulgare[2] *nm* : Bulgarian (language)
Bulgare *nmf* : Bulgarian
bulldozer [byldozɛr] *nm* : bulldozer
bulle [byl] *nf* **1** : bubble **2** : balloon (in a comic strip) **3** : papal bull
bulletin [byltɛ̃] *nm* **1** : report, bulletin, newsletter <bulletin météorologique : weather forecast> <bulletin scolaire : report card> **2** : certificate <bulletin de naissance : birth certificate> **3** : form, slip, ticket <bulletin de commande : order form> **4** *or* **bulletin de vote** : ballot (form)
bureau [byro] *nm, pl* **bureaux** **1** : office, study **2** : desk **3** : department, agency, bureau <bureau de poste : post office> <bureau de placement : employment agency> **4** : board, committee
bureaucrate [byrokrat] *nmf* : bureaucrat
bureaucratie [byrokrasi] *nf* : bureaucracy — **bureaucratique** [-kratik] *adj*
bureautique [byrotik] *nf* : office automation
burette [byrɛt] *nf* **1** : cruet **2** : oilcan
buriné, -née [byrine] *adj* : furrowed, deeply lined <un visage buriné : a craggy face>
burlesque[1] [byrlɛsk] *adj* : farcical, ludicrous
burlesque[2] *nm* : burlesque
burundais, -daise [burundɛ, -dɛz] *adj* : Burundian
Burundais, -daise *n* : Burundian
bus [bys] *nm* AUTOBUS : bus
buse [byz] *nf* : buzzard
buste [byst] *nm* **1** : chest **2** : bust (in sculpture) **3** : bust, bosom (of a woman)
but [by(t)] *nm* **1** : aim, objective <aller droit au but : to go straight to the point> <sans but : aimlessly> **2** : goal,

target, touchdown **3** *Can* : base (in baseball) <but sur balles : base on balls, walk> **4 de but en blanc** : point-blank, bluntly
butane [bytan] *nm* : butane
buté, -tée [byte] *adj* : obstinate, stubborn
butée [byte] *nf* : abutment
buter [byte] *vi* **1 ~ contre** *or* **~ sur** : to stumble on, to trip over **2 ~ contre** : to rest on, to abut — *vt* **1** : to prop up **2** : to antagonize, to make (someone) stubborn **3** *fam* : to kill, to bump off
butin [bytɛ̃] *nm* : booty, loot, spoils *pl*
butiner [bytine] *vt* **1** : to gather (nectar) **2** : to glean, to pick up (ideas, information)
butoir [bytwar] *nm* **1** : buffer, stop <butoir de porte : doorstop> **2** *or* **date butoir** : deadline
butor [bytɔr] *nm* : bittern
butte [byt] *nf* **1** : small hill, mound **2 être en butte à** : to come up against
buvable [byvabl] *adj* POTABLE : drinkable, potable
buvard [byvar] *nm* : blotter
buveur, -veuse [byvœr, -vøz] *n* : drinker
buvons [byvɔ̃], *etc.* → **boire**
byzantin, -tine [bizɑ̃tɛ̃, -tin] *adj* : Byzantine

C

c [se] *nm* : c, the third letter of the alphabet
ça[1] [sa] *pron* **1** : that, this <je n'aime pas ça : I don't like that> <ça coûte combien? : how much does this cost?> **2** : it, that <ça va? : how's it going?> <c'est ça : that's it, that's right> **3 ça alors!** : well!, really! **4 ça y est** : there, that's it **5 et avec ça?** : anything else?
ça[2] *nm* **le ça** : the id
çà [sa] *adv* **çà et là** : here and there
cabale [kabal] *nf* : cabal
cabane [kaban] *nf* **1** HUTTE : cabin, hut **2** ABRI : shelter <cabane à lapins : rabbit hutch> **3** *or* **cabane à sucre** *Can* : sugarhouse **4 en ~** *fam* : in jail, in the clink
cabanon [kabanɔ̃] *nm* **1** ABRI : shed **2** : country cottage (in Provence)
cabaret [kabarɛ] *nm* : cabaret, nightclub
cabas [kaba] *nms & pl France* : shopping bag
cabestan [kabɛstɑ̃] *nm* : capstan
cabillaud [kabijo] *nm* : cod
cabine [kabin] *nf* : cabin, cubicle, cab (of a truck, etc.), booth <cabine téléphonique : telephone booth> <cabine de pilotage : cockpit>
cabinet [kabinɛ] *nm* **1** *or* **cabinet de travail** BUREAU : office **2** *or* **cabinet médical** : doctor's office **3** : cabinet (in government) **4 cabinet de toilette** *France* : toilet, bathroom
câblage [kablaʒ] *nm* : wiring
câble [kabl] *nm* **1** : cable, line, rope **2** : cable television **3** : cablegram
câbler [kable] *vt* : to cable
câblodistribution [kablɔdistribysjɔ̃] *nf* : cable television
câblogramme [kablɔgram] *nm* : cablegram
cabochard, -charde [kabɔʃar, -ʃard] *adj fam* : stubborn, pigheaded
caboche [kabɔʃ] *nf* **1** : hobnail **2** *fam* : head, nut
cabosser [kabɔse] *vt* : to dent <un chapeau cabossé : a battered hat>
cabotin, -tine [kabɔtɛ̃, -tin] *n* : ham actor, show-off
cabrer [kabre] *v* **se cabrer** *vr* **1** : to rear up (of a horse), to climb steeply (of a plane) **2** : to rebel, to protest
cabriole [kabrijɔl] *nf* **1** : capering (about) **2 faire des cabrioles** : to caper, to gambol, to cavort, to prance
cabriolet [kabrijɔlɛ] *nm* DÉCAPOTABLE : convertible
caca [kaka] *nm fam* : excrement
cacahuète [kakaɥɛt] *nf* : peanut
cacao [kakao] *nm* **1** : cocoa **2** : cocoa bean
cacarder [kakarde] *vi* : to honk (of a goose)
cacatoès [kakatɔɛs] *nm* : cockatoo
cache [kaʃ] *nf* : hiding place, cache
cache–cache [kaʃkaʃ] *nms & pl* : hide-and-seek <jouer à cache-cache : to play hide-and-seek>
cache–col [kaʃkɔl] *nms & pl* : scarf
cachemire [kaʃmir] *nm* : cashmere
cache–nez [kaʃne] *nms & pl* : scarf, muffler
cache–pot [kaʃpo] *nm* : planter, container for a flowerpot
cacher [kaʃe] *vt* **1** : to hide, to conceal **2** : to cover up, to mask — **se cacher** *vr*
cachet [kaʃɛ] *nm* **1** COMPRIMÉ : tablet, pill **2** : seal, stamp <cachet de la poste : postmark> **3** : fee **4** : style, character, charm
cacheter [kaʃte] {8} *vt* SCELLER : to seal
cachette [kaʃɛt] *nf* **1** CACHE : hiding place, hideout **2** *Can* : hide-and-seek <jouer à la cachette : to play hide-and-seek> **3 en ~** : secretly
cachot [kaʃo] *nm* **1** : prison, dungeon **2** *Can* : penalty box (in hockey)
cachotterie [kaʃɔtri] *nf* : little secret
cachottier, -tière [kaʃɔtje, -tjɛr] *adj* : secretive

cacophonie [kakɔfɔni] *nf* : cacophony
cactus [kaktys] *nms & pl* : cactus
cadastre [kadastr] *nm* : land office
cadavérique [kadaverik] *adj* : deathly (pale)
cadavre [kadavr] *nm* : corpse, cadaver
caddie *or* **caddy** [kadi] *nm* : caddie, caddy
cadeau [kado] *nm, pl* **cadeaux** : gift, present <cadeau de Noël : Christmas present> <faire un cadeau à : to give a gift to>
cadenas [kadna] *nm* : padlock — **cadenasser** [-nase] *vt*
cadence [kadɑ̃s] *nf* **1** RYTHME : cadence, rhythm **2** : rate, pace
cadet[1], **-dette** [kadɛ, -dɛt] *adj* : younger, youngest
cadet[2], **-dette** *n* **1** : younger (son, daughter, child), youngest (son, daughter, child) **2** : junior <elle est son cadet de quatre ans : she is four years his junior> **3** : cadet **4 c'est le cadet de mes soucis** : that's the least of my worries
cadmium [kadmjɔm] *nm* : cadmium
cadran [kadrɑ̃] *nm* **1** : dial, face **2** *Can fam* : alarm clock **3 cadran solaire** : sundial
cadre [kadr] *nm* **1** : frame **2** : setting, surroundings *pl* **3** : framework, structure **4** : manager, executive
cadrer [kadre] *vt* : to center (an image, etc.) — *vi* : to fit, to correspond
caduc, -duque [kadyk] *adj* **1** : obsolete, outmoded **2** : null and void **3** : deciduous **4** : mute, silent <e caduc : silent e>
cafard[1] [kafar] *nm* **1** BLATTE : cockroach **2** : melancholy, blues <avoir le cafard : to be down in the dumps>
cafard[2], **-farde** [kafar, -fard] *n fam* : sneaky person, squealer
café [kafe] *nm* **1** : coffee <café en poudre : instant coffee> **2** : café, bar
caféine [kafein] *nf* : caffeine
cafétéria [kafeterja] *nf* : cafeteria
cafetière [kaftjɛr] *nf* **1** : coffeepot, coffeemaker **2 cafetière à pression** : percolator
cafouillage [kafujaʒ] *nm fam* : mess, confusion
cafouiller [kafuje] *vi fam* : to get into a mess, to flounder around
cage [kaʒ] *nf* **1** : cage <cage à oiseaux : birdcage> <cage thoracique : rib cage> **2 cage d'ascenseur** : elevator shaft **3 cage d'escalier** : stairwell
cageot [kaʒo] *nm* : crate
cagibi [kaʒibi] *nm* : storeroom
cagneux, -gneuse [kaɲø, -ɲøz] *adj* : knock-kneed
cagnotte [kaɲɔt] *nf* : pool, kitty
cagoulard, -larde [kagular, -lard] *n Can* : masked robber
cagoule [kagul] *nf* : hood, cowl
cahier [kaje] *nm* **1** : notebook **2** : section, supplement (of a periodical) **3 cahiers** *nmpl* : journal
cahin–caha [kaɛ̃kaa] *adv* **aller cahin-caha** : to struggle along
cahot [kao] *nm* SECOUSSE : bump, jolt
cahoter [kaɔte] *vi* : to bump around, to jolt along
cahoteux, -teuse [kaɔtø, -tøz] *adj* : rough, bumpy
cahute [kayt] *nf* : shack, hut
caïd [kaid] *nm fam* : ring leader, big shot
caille [kaj] *nf* : quail
caillé [kaje] *nm* : curds *pl*
cailler [kaje] *vt* : to curdle — *vi* **1** : to curdle, to congeal **2 ça caille** *fam* : it's freezing — **se cailler** *vr*
caillot [kajo] *nm* : clot
caillou [kaju] *nm, pl* **cailloux** : pebble, stone
caillouteux, -teuse [kajutø, -tøz] *adj* : pebbly, stony
cailloutis [kajuti] *nm* : gravel, crushed stone
caisse [kɛs] *nf* **1** BOÎTE : box, crate **2** : case, casing, body (of a vehicle) **3** *or* **caisse enregistreuse** : till, cash register **4** : fund, funding organization <caisse de retraite : pension fund> <caisse populaire *Can* : cooperative bank> **5** : drum <caisse claire : snare drum>
caissier, -sière [kesje, -sjɛr] *n* **1** : cashier, sales clerk **2** : (bank) teller
caisson [kɛsɔ̃] *nm* **1** : caisson **2 la maladie des caissons** : caisson disease, the bends
cajoler [kaʒɔle] *vt* **1** : to fuss over, to cuddle **2** : to cajole, to wheedle
cajolerie [kaʒɔlri] *nf* : cuddling
cajou [kaʒu] *nm* **noix de cajou** : cashew nut
cajun [kaʒœ̃] *adj* : Cajun
Cajun *nmf* : Cajun
cake [kɛk] *nm* : fruitcake
cal [kal] *nm, pl* **cals** : callus
calamine [kalamin] *nf* : calamine
calamité [kalamite] *nf* DÉSASTRE : calamity
calandre [kalɑ̃dr] *nf* : radiator grill (of an automobile)
calcaire[1] [kalkɛr] *adj* : chalky, hard (of water)
calcaire[2] *nm* : limestone
calciner [kalsine] *vt* : to char, to burn to a crisp
calcium [kalsjɔm] *nm* : calcium
calcul [kalkyl] *nm* **1** : calculation, sum (in mathematics) **2** : arithmetic **3** : calculus **4** : stone <calcul rénal : kidney stone> <calcul bilaire : gallstone>
calculateur, -trice [kalkylatœr, -tris] *adj* : calculating
calculatrice *nf* : calculator
calculer [kalkyle] *vt* : to calculate, to compute

cale [kal] *nf* **1** : wedge, chock **2** : hold (of a ship) **3 cale sèche** : dry dock
calé, -lée [kale] *adj fam* **1** : brainy, clever **2** : tough (of a problem, etc.)
calebasse [kalbas] *nf* : calabash
calèche [kalɛʃ] *nf* : (horse-drawn) carriage
caleçon [kalsɔ̃] *nm* **1** : boxer shorts *pl* **2** *or* **caleçons de bain** : swimming trunks **3** : leggings
calembour [kalɑ̃bur] *nm* : pun
calendes [kalɑ̃d] *nfpl* **renvoyer aux calendes grecques** : to put something off indefinitely
calendrier [kalɑ̃drije] *nm* : calendar
calepin [kalpɛ̃] *nm* : notebook
caler [kale] *vt* **1** : to wedge **2** : to prop up **3** *fam* : to fill up (one's stomach) **4** *Can fam* : to gulp down — *vi* **1** : to stall out **2** : to give up **3** *Can* : to sink (in snow, etc.)
calfeutrer [kalføtre] *vt* : to seal, to make draftproof — **se calfeutrer** *vr* : to make oneself snug
calibre [kalibr] *nm* **1** : caliber, bore **2** : grade, size **3** : class, stature
calibrer [kalibre] *vt* : to calibrate, to grade
calice [kalis] *nm* **1** : chalice **2** : calyx
calicot [kaliko] *nm* : calico
calife [kalif] *nm* : caliph
califourchon [kalifurʃɔ̃] **à califourchons** : astride, astraddle
câlin, -line [kalɛ̃, -lin] *adj* : tender, affectionate
câliner [kaline] *vt* : to cuddle — **se câliner** *vr*
calleux, -leuse [kalø, -løz] *adj* : calloused, hard
calligraphie [kaligrafi] *nf* : calligraphy — **calligraphique** [-grafik] *adj*
callosité [kalɔzite] *nf* : callus
calmant[1], -mante [kalmɑ̃, -mɑ̃t] *adj* : soothing
calmant[2] *nm* : sedative
calmar [kalmar] *nm* : squid, calamari
calme[1] [kalm] *adj* TRANQUILLE : calm — **calmement** [kalməmɑ̃] *adv*
calme[2] *nm* **1** : calm, peace <calme plat : dead calm> **2 garder son calme** : to keep one's head
calmer [kalme] *vt* **1** APAISER : to calm **2** : to ease, to soothe — **se calmer** *vr* : to calm down
calomnie [kalɔmni] *nf* DIFFAMATION : slander, libel
calomnier [kalɔmnje] {96} *vt* : to slander, to libel
calomnieux, -nieuse [kalɔmnjø, -njøz] *adj* : slanderous, libelous
calorie [kalɔri] *nf* : calorie
calorifère[1] [kalɔrifɛr] *adj* : heating, heat-carrying
calorifère[2] *nm* **1** : heater, stove **2** *Can* : room radiator
calorique [kalɔrik] *adj* : caloric
calotte [kalɔt] *nf* **1** : skullcap **2** *Can* : cap **3 calotte glaciaire** : ice cap
calque [kalk] *nm* **1** DESSIN : tracing <papier calque : tracing paper> **2** : exact copy, replica
calquer [kalke] *vt* **1** : to trace **2** IMITER : to copy exactly, to imitate
calumet [kalymɛ] *nm* : peace pipe
calvaire [kalvɛr] *nm* **1** : wayside cross **2** : ordeal, suffering
calvitie [kalvisi] *nf* : baldness
calypso [kalipso] *nm* : calypso
camarade [kamarad] *nmf* : comrade, friend <camarade de classe : classmate>
camaraderie [kamaradri] *nf* : camaraderie, friendship
cambiste [kɑ̃bist] *nm* : exchange broker, money changer
cambodgien[1], -dgienne [kɑ̃bɔdʒjɛ̃, -dʒjɛn] *adj* : Cambodian
cambodgien[2] *nm* : Cambodian (language)
Cambodgien, -dgienne *n* : Cambodian
cambrer [kɑ̃bre] *vt* : to bend, to arch <cambrer les reins : to arch one's back> — **se cambrer** *vr* : to arch one's back
cambriolage [kɑ̃brijɔlaʒ] *nm* : burglary
cambrioler [kɑ̃brjɔle] *vt* : to burglarize
cambrioleur, -leuse [kɑ̃brijɔlør, -løz] *n* : burglar
cambrure [kɑ̃bryr] *nf* **1** : arch, curve **2 cambrure des pieds** : instep
came [kam] *nf* : cam <arbre à cames : camshaft>
camée [kame] *nm* : cameo
caméléon [kameleɔ̃] *nm* : chameleon
camélia [kamelja] *nf* : camelia
camelot [kamlo] *nm* **1** : street vendor **2** *Can* : paperboy
camelote [kamlɔt] *nf fam* : trash, junk
camembert [kamɑ̃bɛr] *nm* : Camembert
caméra [kamera] *nf* : movie camera, television camera
camerounais, -naise [kamrunɛ, -nɛz] *adj* : Cameroonian
Camerounais, -naise *n* : Cameroonian
caméscope [kameskɔp] *nm* : camcorder
camion [kamjɔ̃] *nm* : truck
camionnage [kamjɔnaʒ] *nm* : trucking
camionner [kamjne] *vt* : to transport (by truck)
camionnette [kamjɔnɛt] *nf* : van, pickup truck
camionneur, -neuse [kamjɔnœr, -nøz] *n* ROUTIER : truck driver, trucker
camisole [kamizɔl] *nf* **1** : camisole **2 camisole de force** : straitjacket
camomille [kamɔmij] *nf* : camomile
camouflage [kamuflaʒ] *nm* : camouflage
camoufler [kamufle] *vt* : to camouflage
camp [kɑ̃] *nm* **1** CAMPEMENT : camp <lever le camp : to strike camp> <camp de concentration : concentra-

tion camp> 2 PARTI : side, team, faction
campagnard[1], **-gnarde** [kɑ̃paɲar, -ɲard] *adj* : country, rustic
campagnard[2], **-gnarde** *n* : countryman *m*, countrywoman *f*
campagne [kɑ̃paɲ] *nf* **1** : country, countryside **2** : campaign <faire campagne contre : to agitate against>
campagnol [kɑ̃paɲɔl] *nm* : vole
campement [kɑ̃pmɑ̃] *nm* : camp, encampment
camper [kɑ̃pe] *vt* **1** : to encamp **2** POSER : to place firmly **3** : to portray (a character) — *vi* : to camp — **se camper** *vr* : to stand firmly
campeur, -peuse [kɑ̃pœr, -pøz] *n* : camper
camphre [kɑ̃fr] *nm* : camphor
camping [kɑ̃piŋ] *nm* **1** : camping <faire du camping : to go camping> **2** : campground, campsite
campus [kɑ̃pys] *nm* : campus
camus, -muse [kamy, -myz] *adj* **nez camus** : pug nose
canadien, -dienne [kanadjɛ̃, -djɛn] *adj* : Canadian
Canadien, -dienne *n* : Canadian
canadien–français, canadienne–française *adj*, *pl* **canadiens–français, canadiennes–françaises** : French-Canadian
canaille [kanaj] *nf* **1** : rabble, riffraff **2** : scoundrel, rascal
canal [kanal] *nm*, *pl* **canaux** [kano] **1** : canal **2** : channel
canaliser [kanalize] *vt* : to channel
canapé [kanape] *nm* **1** : sofa, couch **2** : canapé
canapé–lit [kanapeli] *n*, *pl* **canapés–lits** : sofa bed
canard [kanar] *nm* **1** : duck **2** : false note (in music) **3** *fam* : rag, newspaper
canari [kanari] *nm* : canary
canasson [kanasɔ̃] *nm fam* : nag (horse)
cancan [kɑ̃kɑ̃] *nm* **1** : cancan **2** : rumor, gossip
cancaner [kɑ̃kane] *vi* **1** : to quack **2** : to spread gossip
cancanier, -nière [kɑ̃kanje, -njɛr] *n* : gossip
cancer [kɑ̃sɛr] *nm* : cancer
Cancer *nm* : Cancer
cancéreux[1], **-reuse** [kɑ̃serø, -røz] *adj* : cancerous
cancéreux[2], **-reuse** *n* : cancer patient
cancérigène [kɑ̃seriʒɛn] *adj* : carcinogenic
cancre [kɑ̃kr] *nm fam* : dunce
candélabre [kɑ̃delabr] *nm* : candelabrum
candeur [kɑ̃dœr] *nf* INGÉNUITÉ : ingenuousness
candidat, -date [kɑ̃dida, -dat] *n* : candidate
candidature [kɑ̃didatyr] *nf* : candidacy
candide [kɑ̃did] *adj* : ingenuous, naïve
cane [kan] *nf* : (female) duck
caneton [kantɔ̃] *nm* : duckling
canette [kanɛt] *nf* **1** BOUTEILLE : (small) bottle **2** BOÎTE : can (of a beverage) **3** : spool **4** : (female) duckling
canevas [kanva] *nms & pl* **1** : canvas **2** : framework
caniche [kaniʃ] *nm* : poodle
canicule [kanikyl] *nf* : heat wave
canidé [kanide] *nm* : canine
canif [kanif] *nm* : jackknife, pocketknife
canin, -nine [kanɛ̃, -nin] *adj* : canine
canine *nf* : canine (tooth)
caniveau [kanivo] *nm*, *pl* **-veaux** : (street) gutter
cannabis [kanabis] *nm* : cannabis
canne [kan] *nf* **1** : cane, walking stick **2** : cane (in botany) <canne à sucre : sugarcane> **3** **canne à pêche** : fishing rod
canneberge [kanbɛrʒ] *nf* : cranberry
cannelé, -lée [kanle] *adj* : fluted, grooved
canneler [kanle] {8} *vt* : to groove
cannelle [kanɛl] *nf* : cinnamon
cannette [kanɛt] *nf* → **canette**
cannibale [kanibal] *nmf* : cannibal — **cannibalisme** [-balism] *nm*
canoë [kanɔe] *nm* : canoe
canon [kanɔ̃] *nm* **1** : cannon **2** : barrel, muzzle (of a gun) **3** : canon, rule **4** : shank (of a horse)
canoniser [kanɔnize] *vt* : to canonize — **canonisation** [-nizasjɔ̃] *nf*
canonnière [kanɔnjɛr] *nf* : gunboat
canot [kano] *nm* **1** *France* : boat, dinghy **2** *Can* : canoe **3** **canot de sauvetage** : lifeboat
canotage [kanɔtaʒ] *nm* **1** *France* : boating **2** *Can* : canoeing
cantaloup [kɑ̃talu] *nm* : cantaloupe
cantate [kɑ̃tat] *nf* : cantata
cantatrice [kɑ̃tatris] *nf* : opera singer
cantilever [kɑ̃tilevœr] *adj & nm* : cantilever
cantine [kɑ̃tin] *nf* : canteen, cafeteria
cantique [kɑ̃tik] *nm* HYMNE : canticle, hymn
canton [kɑ̃tɔ̃] *nm* **1** *Can* : township <les cantons de l'Est : the Eastern Townships> **2** *France* : district
cantonnement [kantɔnmɑ̃] *nm* : billet, billeting
cantonner [kɑ̃tɔne] *v* **1** : to confine, to limit **2** : to station, to billet — **se cantonner** *vr* SE CONFINER : to confine oneself, to lock oneself away
cantonnière [kɑ̃tɔnjɛr] *nf* : valance
canular [kanylar] *nm* : hoax, practical joke
canyon [kaɲɔ̃] *nm* : canyon
caoutchouc [kautʃu] *nm* **1** : rubber **2** **caoutchoucs** *nmpl* : galoshes
caoutchouteux, -teuse [kautʃutø, -tøz] *adj* : rubbery

cap [kap] *nm* **1** PROMONTOIRE : cape, headland **2** : mark, milestone **3** DIRECTION : course, direction
capable [kapabl] *adj* **1** : capable, able **2** : likely **3** *Can* : strong, robust
capacité [kapasite] *nf* **1** : capacity **2** APTITUDE : ability
cape [kap] *nf* : cape, cloak
capillaire[1] [kapilɛr] *adj* **1** : capillary **2** : hair <lotion capillaire : hair lotion>
capillaire[2] *nm* : capillary
capitaine [kapitɛn] *nm* **1** : captain **2** **capitaine de corvette** : lieutenant commander
capital[1], **-tale** [kapital] *adj, mpl* **-taux** [-to] **1** : major, crucial **2** : capital <peine capitale : capital punishment>
capital[2] *nm, pl* **-taux** : capital, assets *pl*
capitale *nf* : capital (city)
capitaliser [kapitalize] *vt* : to capitalize (in finance) — *vi* : to save
capitalisme [kapitalism] *nm* : capitalism
capitaliste[1] [kapitalist] *adj* : capitalist, capitalistic
capitaliste[2] *nmf* : capitalist
capiteux, -teuse [kapitø, -tøz] *adj* : heady, intoxicating
capitole [kapitɔl] *nm* : capitol
capitonner [kapitɔne] *vt* : to pad
capitulation [kapitylasjɔ̃] *nf* : capitulation, surrender
capituler [kapityle] *vi* : to capitulate, to surrender
caporal–chef [kapɔralʃɛf] *nm, pl* **caporaux–chefs** [-ro] : corporal
capot [kapo] *nm* **1** : cover, casing **2** : hood (of an automobile)
capote [kapɔt] *nf* **1** : greatcoat **2** : top (of a convertible)
capoter [kapɔte] *vi* **1** CHAVIRER : to capsize, to overturn **2** *fam* : to fall through, to come to nothing **3** *Can fam* : to lose one's head
câpre [kapr] *nf* : caper
caprice [kapris] *nm* **1** : caprice, whim **2** : tantrum <faire un caprice : to throw a tantrum>
capricieux, -cieuse [kaprisjø, -sjøz] *adj* : capricious, temperamental — **capricieusement** [-sjøzmɑ̃] *adv*
Capricorne [kaprikɔrn] *nm* : Capricorn
capsule [kapsyl] *nf* **1** : capsule <capsule spatiale : space capsule> **2** : top, cap **3** : capsule (in pharmacy)
capter [kapte] *vt* **1** RECEVOIR : to receive, to pick up (radio or television signals) **2** : to capture, to catch <capter l'attention de : to capture the attention of>
capteur [kaptœr] *nm* : sensor
captieux, -tieuse [kapsjø, -sjøz] *adj* FALLACIEUX : fallacious, misleading
captif, -tive [kaptif, -tiv] *adj & n* : captive
captivant, -vante [kaptivɑ̃, -vɑ̃t] *adj* FASCINANT : fascinating, captivating
captiver [kaptive] *vt* : to captivate, to fascinate
captivité [kaptivite] *nf* : captivity
capture [kaptyr] *nf* **1** : capture, seizure **2** PRISE : catch
capturer [kaptyre] *vt* : to capture, to catch
capuche [kapyʃ] *nf* : hood
capuchon [kapyʃɔ̃] *nm* **1** : hood **2** : cap, top (of a pen, etc.)
capucine [kapysin] *nf* : nasturtium
cap–verdien, -dienne [kapvɛrdjɛ̃, -djɛn] *adj* : Cape Verdean
Cap–verdien, -dienne *n* : Cape Verdean
caquet [kakɛ] *nm* **1** : cackle, cackling **2** BAVARDAGE : chatter, prattle
caqueter [kakte] {8} *vi* **1** : to cackle **2** BAVARDER : to chatter, to prattle
car[1] [kar] *nm* AUTOCAR : bus, coach
car[2] *conj* : for, because
carabine [karabin] *nf* : carbine, rifle
caracoler [karakɔle] *vt* **1** : to prance (of a horse) **2** : to gambol, to skip
caractère [karaktɛr] *nm* **1** : letter, character, graphic sign <en gros caractères : in large print> **2** : character, nature, disposition <avoir mauvais caractère : to be ill-tempered> **3** : characteristic, feature
caractériser [karakterize] *vt* : to characterize, to describe — **caractérisation** [-rizasjɔ̃] *nf*
caractéristique [karakteristik] *adj & nf* : characteristic
carafe [karaf] *nf* : carafe, decanter
caraïbe[1] [karaib] *adj* : Caribbean
caraïbe[2] *nm* : Carib (language)
carambolage [karɑ̃bɔlaʒ] *nm* **1** : pileup, multicar accident **2** : carom (in billiards, etc.)
caramboler [karɑ̃bɔle] *vi* : to carom (in billiards) — *vt* : to collide with, to crash into (an automobile)
caramel [karamɛl] *nm* : caramel
carapace [karapas] *nf* : shell
carat [kara] *nm* : carat
caravane [karavan] *nf* **1** : caravan **2** : trailer
carbone [karbɔn] *nm* **1** : carbon **2** *or* **papier carbone** : carbon paper
carbonique [karbɔnik] *adj* **1** **gaz carbonique** : carbon dioxide **2** **neige carbonique** : dry ice
carboniser [karbɔnize] *vt* : to char
carburant [karbyrɑ̃] *nm* : fuel
carburateur [karbyratœr] *nm* : carburetor
carcan [karkɑ̃] *nm* **1** : constraint, yoke **2** : iron collar
carcasse [karkas] *nf* **1** : carcass **2** : frame (of a building, vehicle, etc.)
carcéral, -rale [karseral] *adj, mpl* **-raux** [-ro] : prison
carcinogène [karsinɔʒɛn] *adj* : carcinogenic
carcinome [karsinɔm] *nm* : carcinoma
carder [karde] *vt* : to card (fibers)

cardiaque [kardjak] *adj* : cardiac

cardigan [kardigɑ̃] *nm* : cardigan

cardinal[1], -nale [kardinal] *adj, mpl* **-naux** [-no] : cardinal, chief

cardinal[2] *nm, pl* **-naux 1** : cardinal (in religion) **2** : cardinal number **3** : cardinal, redbird

cardiologie [kardjolɔʒi] *nf* : cardiology

cardiologue [kardjolɔg] *nmf* : cardiologist

cardio–vasculaire [kardjovaskylɛr] *adj* : cardiovascular

carême [karɛm] *nm* : Lent

carence [karɑ̃s] *nf* **1** ABSENCE : lack, deficiency **2** : shortcomings *pl* **3** : insolvency

carène [karɛn] *nf* : hull (of a ship)

caréner [karene] {87} *vt* **1** : to careen (a ship) **2** : to streamline

caressant, -sante [karɛsɑ̃, -sɑ̃t] *adj* : affectionate, tender

caresse [karɛs] *nf* : caress

caresser [karese] *vt* **1** : to caress **2** : to cherish, to entertain (hopes, etc.)

cargaison [kargɛzɔ̃] *nf* : cargo, freight

cargo [kargo] *nm* : freighter

cari [kari] *nm* → **curry**

caribou [karibu] *nm* : caribou

caricature [karikatyr] *nf* : caricature, cartoon

caricaturer [karikatyre] *vt* : to caricature — **caricaturiste** [-tyrist] *nmf*

carie [kari] *nf* **1** : blight (in botany) **2** *or* **carie dentaire** : caries, tooth decay <une carie : a cavity>

carier [karje] {96} *vt* : to rot, to decay — **se carier** *vr*

carillon [karijɔ̃] *nm* : bell, chime

carillonnement [karijɔnmɑ̃] *nm* : peal

carillonner [karijɔne] *v* : to chime, to peal

caritatif, -tive [karitatif, -tiv] *adj* : charitable

carlin [karlɛ̃] *nm* : pug (dog)

carlingue [karlɛ̃g] *nf* : cabin (of an airplane)

carmin [karmɛ̃] *adj & nm* : carmine (red)

carnage [karnaʒ] *nm* TUERIE : carnage, slaughter

carnassier[1], -sière [karnasje, -sjɛr] *adj* : carnivorous

carnassier[2] *nm* : carnivore

carnaval [karnaval] *nm, pl* **-vals** : carnival

carnet [karnɛ] *nm* **1** : notebook **2** : book (of stamps, tickets, etc.) <carnet de chèques : checkbook>

carnivore[1] [karnivɔr] *adj* : carnivorous

carnivore[2] *nm* : carnivore

carotte [karɔt] *nf* : carrot

carotter [karɔte] *vt fam* : to swindle, to chisel, to cheat

caroubier [karubje] *nm* : locust (tree)

carpe [karp] *nf* : carp

carpelle [karpɛl] *nm* : carpel

carpette [karpɛt] *nf* : rug

carquois [karkwa] *nm* : quiver

carré[1], -rée [kare] *adj* **1** : square **2** : straightforward, forthright

carré[2] *nm* **1** : square **2** : plot, patch (of land) **3** : (square) scarf **4** : four of a kind <un carré d'as : four aces>

carreau [karo] *nm, pl* **carreaux 1** : tile **2** VITRE : windowpane **3** : square, check <à carreaux : checkered> **4** : diamond (in playing cards)

carreauté, -tée [karote] *adj Can* : checkered, checked

carrefour [karfur] *nm* : intersection, crossroads

carrelage [karlaʒ] *nm* : tile, tiled floor

carreler [karle] {8} *vt* : to tile

carrément [karemɑ̃] *adv* **1** : squarely, firmly **2** : bluntly, straight out

carrer [kare] *v* **se carrer** *vr* : to settle oneself

carrière [karjɛr] *nf* **1** : career **2** : stone quarry

carriole [karjɔl] *nf* **1** : cart **2** *Can* : sleigh

carrossable [karɔsabl] *adj* : suitable for motor vehicles

carrosse [karɔs] *nm* **1** : carriage, coach **2** *Can* : baby carriage

carrosserie [karɔsri] *nf* **1** : body (of a car) **2** : (automobile) bodywork

carrousel [karuzɛl] *nm* : carousel

carrure [karyr] *nf* **1** : build, shoulder width **2** STATURE : stature, caliber

carry [kari] *nm* → **curry**

carte [kart] *nf* **1** : card <carte postale : postcard> <carte de crédit : credit card> <carte d'identité : identification card> **2** : map <carte routière : road map> **3** : menu <carte de vins : wine list> **4** *or* **carte à jouer** : playing card <jouer cartes sur table : to lay one's cards on the table>

cartel [kartɛl] *nm* : cartel

cartilage [kartilaʒ] *nm* : cartilage, gristle

cartilagineux, -neuse [kartilaʒinø, -nøz] *adj* : gristly, cartilaginous

cartographe [kartɔgraf] *nmf* : cartographer

cartographie [kartɔgrafi] *nf* : cartography

cartomancie [kartɔmɑ̃si] *nf* : fortune-telling (with cards)

cartomancien, -cienne [kartɔmɑ̃sjɛ̃, -sjɛn] *n* : fortune-teller (with cards)

carton [kartɔ̃] *nm* **1** : cardboard **2** : cardboard box, carton

carton–pâte [kartɔ̃pat] *nm* : pasteboard

cartouche [kartuʃ] *nf* **1** : cartridge <cartouche d'encre : fountain-pen refill> **2** : carton (of cigarettes, etc.)

carvi [karvi] *nm* : caraway

cas [ka] *nms & pl* **1** : case **2 en cas de** : in case of <en cas de bien : if need be> **3 en tout cas** : in any case **4** → **limite**

casanier, -nière [kazanje, -njɛr] *n* : homebody

cascade [kaskad] *nf* **1** : stream, cascade, torrent **2** CHUTE : waterfall **3** : stunt (in movies)

case [kaz] *nf* **1** : box (on a form or questionnaire) **2** : compartment **3** CABANE : hut **4** : square (in a board game) <retourner à la case départ : to go back to square one> **5 case postale** : post office box

caser [kaze] *vt* **1** PLACER : to put **2** *fam* : to put up, to lodge **3** *fam* : to marry off **4** *fam* : to find a job for

caserne [kazɛrn] *nf France* **1** : barracks *pl* **2 caserne de pompiers** : fire station

casher [kaʃɛr] → **kascher**

casier [kazje] *nm* **1** : compartment, pigeonhole **2** : rack (for bottles, etc.) **3 casier judiciaire** : police record

casino [kazino] *nm* : casino

casque [kask] *nm* **1** : helmet **2** : headphones *pl* **3** *Can* : fur cap

casquette [kaskɛt] *nf* : cap

cassable [kasabl] *adj* : breakable

cassant, -sante [kasɑ̃, -sɑ̃t] *adj* **1** : brittle **2** : abrupt, curt

casse [kas] *nf* **1** : breakage, damage **2** : scrap yard **3** : case (in printing) <haut de casse : uppercase>

cassé, -sée [kase] *adj fam* : out of money, broke

casse–cou [kasku] *nms & pl* **1** : danger spot **2** : daredevil

casse–croûte [kaskrut] *nms & pl* **1** : snack, lunch **2** *Can* : restaurant, snack bar

casse–noisettes [kasnwazɛt] *nms & pl* : nutcracker

casse–noix [kasnwa] *nms & pl* : nutcracker

casse–pieds [kaspje] *nmfs & pl fam* : pain in the neck, bore

casser [kase] *vt* **1** BRISER : to break **2** DÉGRADER : to demote **3** ANNULER : to quash, to annul — *vi* : to break — **se casser** *vr* **1** : to break <se casser le cou : to break one's neck> **2** *fam* : to go away <casse-toi! : get out of here!>

casserole [kasrɔl] *nf* : saucepan

casse–tête [kastɛt] *nms & pl* **1** : puzzle **2** : problem, headache

cassette [kasɛt] *nf* : cassette

cassonade [kasɔnad] *nf* : brown sugar

cassure [kasyr] *nf* **1** : break **2** : crack, fissure

castagnettes [kastaɲɛt] *nfpl* : castanets

caste [kast] *nf* : caste

castor [kastɔr] *nm* : beaver

castration [kastrasjɔ̃] *nf* : castration

castrer [kastre] *vt* : to castrate, to neuter

cataclysme [kataklism] *nm* : cataclysm

catacombes [katakɔ̃b] *nfpl* : catacombs

catafalque [katafalk] *nm* : bier (stand)

catalogue [katalɔg] *nm* : catalog

cataloguer [katalɔge] *vt* **1** : to catalog **2** : to categorize, to label (as)

catalyseur [katalizœr] *nm* : catalyst

catalytique [katalitik] *adj* : catalytic

catamaran [katamarɑ̃] *nm* : catamaran

cataplasme [kataplasm] *nm* : poultice

catapulte [katapylt] *nf* : catapult

catapulter [katapylte] *vt* : to catapult

cataracte [katarakt] *nf* **1** : cataract, falls **2** : cataract (in medicine)

catarrhe [katar] *nm* : catarrh

catastrophe [katastrɔf] *nf* : disaster, catastrophe

catastrophique [katastrɔfik] *adj* : disastrous, catastrophic

catch [katʃ] *nm* **1** : wrestling **2 faire du catch** : to wrestle

catéchisme [kateʃism] *nm* : catechism

catégorie [kategɔri] *nf* **1** : category **2** : grade, quality (of meat, etc.)

catégorique [kategɔrik] *adj* : categorical — **catégoriquement** [-rikmɑ̃] *adv*

catharsis [katarsis] *nf* : catharsis — **cathartique** [-tartik] *adj*

cathédrale [katedral] *nf* : cathedral

cathéter [katetɛr] *nm* : catheter

cathode [katɔd] *nf* : cathode

catholicisme [katɔlisism] *nm* : Catholicism

catholique[1] [katɔlik] *adj* **1** : Roman Catholic **2** : **pas (très) catholique** : dubious, questionable

catholique[2] *nmf* : Roman Catholic

catimini [katimini] **en ~** : stealthily, on the sly

caucasien, -sienne [kokazjɛ̃, -zjɛn] *adj* : Caucasian

cauchemar [kɔʃmar] *nm* : nightmare

cauchemardesque [kɔʃmardɛsk] *adj* : nightmarish

cause [koz] *nf* **1** : cause, reason <à cause de : because, on account of> <pour cause de : owing to> **2** AFFAIRE : case, lawsuit <être en cause : to be at issue, to be involved>

causer [koze] *vt* PROVOQUER : to cause — *vi* : to chat <causer de : to talk about>

causerie [kozri] *nf* : talk, chat

causette [kozɛt] *nf fam* : chat, chitchat <faire la causette à : to have a chat with>

causeur[1], **-seuse** [kozœr, -zøz] *adj* : talkative, chatty

causeur[2], **-seuse** *n* : conversationalist, talker

causeuse *nf* : love seat

caustique [kostik] *adj* : caustic

cauteleux, -leuse [kotlø, -løz] *adj* : sly, wily

cautériser [koterize] *vt* : to cauterize — **cautérisation** [-rizasjɔ̃] *nf*

caution [kosjɔ̃] *nf* **1** : security, guarantee **2 libérer sous caution** : to release on bail

cautionnement [kosjɔnmɑ̃] *nm* : bail, guarantee

cautionner [kosjɔne] *vt* **1** : to guarantee **2** : to support, to sanction

cavalcade [kavalkad] *nf* **1** : cavalcade **2** : stampede, rush
cavale [kaval] *nf fam* **en ~** : on the run
cavalerie [kavalri] *nf* : cavalry
cavalier[1], **-lière** [kavalje, -ljɛr] *adj* : cavalier, offhand
cavalier[2], **-lière** *n* **1** : rider, horseman *m*, horsewoman *f* **2** : dance partner, escort <faire cavalier seul : to go it alone>
cavalier[3] *nm* **1** : cavalryman **2** : knight (in chess)
cave[1] [kav] *adj* : hollow, sunken
cave[2] *nf* **1** : cellar **2 de la cave au grenier** : from top to bottom, high and low
caveau [kavo] *nm, pl* **caveaux 1** : small cellar **2** : burial vault
caverne [kavɛrn] *nf* GROTTE : cave, cavern
caverneux, -neuse [kavɛrnø, -nøz] *adj* : cavernous
caviar [kavjar] *nm* : caviar
cavité [kavite] *nf* : cavity
CD [sede] *nm* : CD (compact disc)
ce[1] [sə] **(cet** [sɛt] *before a vowel or mute h*), **cette** [sɛt] *adj, pl* **ces** [se] **1** : this, that, these, those <un de ces jours : one of these days> <cette fois-ci : this time> <cet homme-là : that man> <ces livres sur la table : those books on the table> **2** (*used for emphasis*) <cette idée! : what an idea!>
ce[2] **(c'** [s] *before a vowel*) *pron* **1** : it, that, these, those <c'est lui : it's him, that's him> <qui est-ce? : who is it?, who's that?> <ce sont mes amis : these are my friends, they are my friends> <c'est cela : that's right> **2 ce que, ce qui, ce dont** : what, which <il comprend ce que je lui dis : he understands what I'm telling him> <montrez-moi ce que vous avez fait : show me what you did> <ce dont on parle : what they're talking about> <il faut être patient, ce que je ne suis pas : you have to be patient, which I'm not> **3 ce faisant** : in so doing **4 pour ce faire** : to this end
ceci [səsi] *pron* **1** : this <écoutez ceci : listen to this> **2 à ceci près que** : except that
cécité [sesite] *nf* : blindness
céder [sede] {87} *vt* : to give up, to yield, to cede — *vi* : to give in
cédille [sedij] *nf* : cedilla
cédrat [sedra] *nm* : citron (fruit)
cèdre [sɛdr] *nm* : cedar
cégep [seʒɛp] **(collège d'enseignement général et professionnel)** *nm Can* : junior college
cégépien, -pienne [seʒepjɛ̃, -pjɛn] *n Can* : junior college student
ceindre [sɛ̃dr] {37} *vt* : to gird, to put on
ceinture [sɛ̃tyr] *nf* **1** : belt <ceinture de sauvetage : life belt> <ceinture de sécurité : safety belt> **2** : waist (in anatomy) **3** : waistband **4** : ring, belt, circle
ceinturer [sɛ̃tyre] *vt* ENTOURER : to surround
cela [səla] *pron* **1** : that <cela dit : that said> <malgré cela : in spite of that, nonetheless> **2** : it <cela ne fait rien : it doesn't matter>
célébration [selebrasjɔ̃] *nf* : celebration
célèbre [selɛbr] *adj* FAMEUX : famous
célébrer [selebre] {87} *vt* **1** : to celebrate **2** : to extol, to praise
célébrité [selebrite] *nf* **1** RENOMMÉE : fame, renown **2** : celebrity, famous person
celer [səle] {20} *vt* : to conceal
céleri [sɛlri] *nm* : celery
célérité [selerite] *nf* VITESSE : swiftness, speed
céleste [selɛst] *adj* : celestial, heavenly
célibat [seliba] *nm* **1** : unmarried life **2** : celibacy
célibataire[1] [selibatɛr] *adj* : single, unmarried
célibataire[2] *nmf* : single person, bachelor *m*, spinster *f*
celle, celles → **celui**
cellier [selje] *nm* : storeroom
cellophane [selɔfan] *nf* : cellophane
cellulaire [selylɛr] *adj* : cellular
cellule [selyl] *nf* : cell
cellulose [selyloz] *nf* : cellulose
Celsius [sɛlsjys] *adj s & pl* : Celsius
celte [sɛlt] *adj* : Celtic
Celte *nmf* : Celt
celtique [sɛltik] *adj* : Celtic
celui [səlɥi], **celle** [sɛl] *pron, pl* **ceux** [sø], **celles** [sɛl] **1** : the one(s), those <mon livre et celui de Jean : my book and John's> <les récipients en acier et ceux en plastique : steel containers and plastic ones> **2** : he, she, those <celui qui danse : he who dances> <ceux d'entre vous : those among you>
celui–ci [səlɥisi], **celle–ci** [sɛlsi] *pron, pl* **ceux–ci** [søsi], **celles–ci** [sɛlsi] **1** : this (one), these **2** : the latter **3** : one <celle-ci chante, celle-là joue de la guitare : one sings, another plays the guitar>
celui–là [səlɥila], **celle–là** [sɛlla] *pron, pl* **ceux–là** [søla], **celles–là** [sɛlla] **1** : that (one), those **2** : the former **3** : another <celui-ci fait la cuisine, celui-là fait la vaisselle : one cooks, another washes the dishes>
cénacle [senakl] *nm* : circle, (literary) club
cendre [sɑ̃dr] *nf* **1** : ashes *pl*, cinders *pl* **2 cendres** *nfpl* : ashes, remains (of the dead)
cendreux, -dreuse [sɑ̃drø, -drøz] *adj* **1** : ashen, pale **2** : ashy
cendrier [sɑ̃drije] *nm* : ashtray
cène [sɛn] *nf* **la Cène** : the Last Supper

cenellier [s(ə)nɛlje] *nm Can* : hawthorn (tree)
censé, -sée [sɑ̃se] *adj* : supposed <elle est censée arriver lundi : she is supposed to arrive on Monday>
censément [sɑ̃semɑ̃] *adv* : supposedly
censeur [sɑ̃sœr] *nm* **1** : censor **2** : critic
censure [sɑ̃syr] *nf* **1** : censorship **2** : censure
censurer [sɑ̃syre] *vt* **1** : to censor, to ban **2** : to censure
cent[1] [sɑ̃] *adj* : a hundred, one hundred <trois cents hommes : three hundred men>
cent[2] *nm* **1** : hundred <un cent de livres : one hundred books> **2** : cent, 1/100 of a dollar **3 pour ~** : percent
centaine [sɑ̃tɛn] *nf* : hundred <une centaine de chaises : about a hundred chairs> <des centaines de fleurs : hundreds of flowers>
centaure [sɑ̃tɔr] *nm* : centaur
centenaire[1] [sɑ̃tnɛr] *adj* : hundred-year-old
centenaire[2] *nm* : centennial
centenaire[3] *nmf* : centenarian
centième[1] [sɑ̃tjɛm] *adj & nmf & nm* : hundredth
centième[2] *nf* : hundredth performance
centigrade [sɑ̃tigrad] *adj* : centigrade, Celsius
centigramme [sɑ̃tigram] *nm* : centigram
centime [sɑ̃tim] *nm* : centime <il n'a pas un centime : he hasn't got a cent>
centimètre [sɑ̃timɛtr] *nm* **1** : centimeter **2** : tape measure
central[1], **-trale** [sɑ̃tral] *adj, mpl* **centraux** [sɑ̃tro] **1** : central **2** : main
central[2] *nm* **central téléphonique** : telephone exchange
centrale *nf* **1** : generating station <centrale électrique : electric power plant> **2** : confederation <centrales syndicales : labor unions>
centraliser [sɑ̃tralize] *vt* : to centralize — **centralisation** [-zasjɔ̃] *nf*
centraméricain, -caine [sɑ̃tramerikɛ̃, -kɛn] *adj* : Central American
Centraméricain, -caine *n* : Central American
centre [sɑ̃tr] *nm* **1** : center <centre de gravité : center of gravity> **2 centre commercial** : shopping center, shopping mall **3 centre communautaire** *Can* : community center **4 centre d'accueil** *Can* : nursing home **5 centres vitaux** : vital organs
centrer [sɑ̃tre] *vt* : to center
centre–ville [sɑ̃trəvil] *nm, pl* **centres–villes** : downtown
centrifuge [sɑ̃trifyʒ] *adj* : centrifugal
centripète [sɑ̃tripɛt] *adj* : centripetal
centuple [sɑ̃typl] *nm* **1 au ~** : a hundredfold **2 être le centuple de** : to be a hundred times (a number)
centupler [sɑ̃typle] *v* : to increase a hundredfold
cépage [sepaʒ] *nm* : vine
cependant [səpɑ̃dɑ̃] *conj* **1** : however, yet **2 cependant que** : while, whereas
céramique[1] [seramik] *adj* : ceramic
céramique[2] *nf* : ceramics
cerbère [sɛrbɛr] *nm* **1** : strict doorkeeper, watchdog **2** *Can* : goalkeeper, goalie
cerceau [sɛrso] *nm, pl* **cerceaux** : hoop
cercle [sɛrkl] *nm* **1** : circle <cercle vicieux : vicious circle> **2** : group, set (of friends, etc.) **3** : club **4** : range, scope **5** : hoop
cercueil [sɛrkœj] *nm* : coffin, casket
céréale [sereal] *nf* : cereal
céréalier, -lière [serealje, -ljɛr] *adj* : cereal
cérébral, -brale [serebral] *adj, mpl* **-braux** [-bro] : cerebral
cérémonial [seremɔnjal] *nm, pl* **-nials** : ceremonial
cérémonie [seremɔni] *nf* : ceremony
cérémoniel, -nielle [seremɔnjɛl] *adj* : ceremonial, ceremonious
cérémonieux, -nieuse [seremɔnjø, -njøz] *adj* : ceremonious, formal — **cérémonieusement** [-njøzmɑ̃] *adv*
cerf [sɛr] *nm* **1** : stag, red dear **2 cerf de Virginie** *Can* → **chevreuil**
cerf–volant [sɛrvɔlɑ̃] *nm* : kite <faire voler un cerf-volant : to fly a kite>
cerise[1] [səriz] *adj or* **rouge cerise** : cerise, cherry-colored
cerise[2] *nf* : cherry
cerisier [sərizje] *nm* : cherry tree
cerne [sɛrn] *nm* : ring <avoir des cernes : to have rings under one's eyes>
cerner [sɛrne] *vt* **1** : to surround **2** : to define, to determine
certain, -taine [sɛrtɛ̃, -tɛn] *adj* **1** : certain, sure, definite <c'est une chose certaine : there's no doubt about it> **2** : certain <une certaine aptitude : a certain aptitude, some aptitude> <dans un certain sens : in a way> <à certains moments : at certain times, sometimes>
certainement [sɛrtɛnmɑ̃] *adv* : certainly, surely
certains, certaines [sɛrtɛ̃, -tɛn] *pron pl* : some (people), certain (ones)
certes [sɛrt] *adv* : of course, indeed
certificat [sɛrtifika] *nm* : certificate <certificat de naissance : birth certificate>
certifier [sɛrtifje] {96} *vt* : to certify, to attest to, to notarize
certitude [sɛrtityd] *nf* : certainty, certitude
cérumen [serymɛn] *nm* : earwax
cerveau [sɛrvo] *nm, pl* **cerveaux 1** : brain, cerebrum **2** : mind, intellect
cervelet [sɛrvəlɛ] *nm* : cerebellum

cervelle [sɛrvɛl] *nf* **1** : brain (in anatomy) **2** : brains *pl* <se creuser la cervelle : to rack one's brains>

cervical, -cale [sɛrvikal] *adj, mpl* **-caux** [-ko] : cervical

ces → **ce**[1]

césarienne [sezarjɛn] *nf* : caesarean section

césium [sezjɔm] *nm* : cesium

cessation [sɛsasjɔ̃] *nf* : cessation, suspension

cesse [sɛs] *nf* **sans ~** : unceasingly, incessantly, constantly

cesser [sese] *v* : to cease, to stop

cessez-le-feu [seselfø] *nms & pl* : cease-fire

cession [sɛsjɔ̃] *nf* : transfer

c'est-à-dire [sɛtadir] *conj* **1** : that is (to say) **2 c'est-à-dire que** : which means (that) <il s'est endormi tard hier soir, c'est-à-dire qu'il sera fatigué aujourd'hui : he went to bed late last night, which means he'll be tired today>

cet, cette → **ce**

ceux → **celui**

ceux-ci → **celui-ci**

ceux-là → **celui-là**

chacal [ʃakal] *nm, pl* **chacals** : jackal

chacun, chacune [ʃakœ̃, -kyn] *pron* **1** : each (one) **2** : everybody, everyone <chacun pour soi : everybody for himself>

chagrin[1], **-grine** [ʃagrɛ̃, -grin] *adj* **1** : sorrowful, doleful **2** : peevish, ill-humored

chagrin[2] *nm* PEINE : grief, sorrow

chagriner [ʃagrine] *vt* **1** PEINER : to grieve, to distress **2** CONTRARIER : to annoy, to bother

chahut [ʃay] *nm* : uproar, racket, rumpus

chahuter [ʃayte] *vi* : to create an uproar — *vt* : to heckle

chaîne [ʃɛn] *nf* **1** : chain **2** : series, range <chaîne de montagnes : mountain range> <chaîne d'idées : train of thought> **3** : (television) channel **4** : audio system <chaîne hi-fi : hi-fi (system)> **5** : warp (in weaving)

chaînon [ʃɛnɔ̃] *nm* : link <chaînon manquant : missing link>

chair [ʃɛr] *nf* **1** : flesh **2** : meat **3 chair de poule** : goose bumps

chaire [ʃɛr] *nf* **1** : (university) chair **2** : pulpit

chaise [ʃɛz] *nf* **1** : chair, seat **2 chaise roulante** : wheelchair

chaland [ʃalɑ̃] *nm* : barge, scow

châle [ʃal] *nm* : shawl

chalet [ʃalɛ] *nm* **1** : chalet **2** *Can* : cottage

chaleur [ʃalœr] *nf* **1** : heat **2** : warmth, fervor

chaleureux, -reuse [ʃalœrø, -røz] *adj* : warm, cordial — **chaleureusement** [-røzmɑ̃] *adv*

challenge [ʃalɑ̃ʒ] *nm* **1** DÉFI : challenge **2** : tournament

chaloupe [ʃalup] *nf* **1** : launch <chaloupe de sauvetage : lifeboat> **2** : rowboat

chalumeau [ʃalymo] *nm, pl* **-meaux 1** : blowtorch **2** *Can* : tap (for collecting sap from a tree)

chalut [ʃaly] *nm* : trawl

chalutier [ʃalytje] *nm* : trawler

chamade [ʃamad] *nf* **battre la chamade** : to beat wildly, to pound

chamailler [ʃamaje] *v* **se chamailler** *vr* : to squabble, to bicker

chamarrer [ʃamare] *vt* : to adorn

chambardement [ʃɑ̃bardəmɑ̃] *nm fam* **1** : upheaval, shake-up **2** : mess

chambarder [ʃɑ̃barde] *vt fam* **1** : to mess up, to turn upside down **2** : to shake up

chambouler [ʃɑ̃bule] *vt fam* : to mess up, to turn upside down

chambranle [ʃɑ̃brɑ̃l] *nm* **1** : frame (of a door or window) **2** : mantelpiece

chambre [ʃɑ̃br] *nf* **1** : room, bedroom **2** : chamber (of a gun, etc.) **3** : (legislative) chamber, house **4 musique de chambre** : chamber music

chambrée [ʃɑ̃bre] *nf* : barracks

chambreur, -breuse [ʃɑ̃brœr, -brøz] *n Can* : roomer

chameau [ʃamo] *nm, pl* **chameaux** : camel

chamois[1] [ʃamwa] *adj s & pl* : buff(-colored)

chamois[2] *nms & pl* **1** : chamois (animal) **2** : buff (color)

champ [ʃɑ̃] *nm* **1** : field, land area <champ de maïs : cornfield> <champ de courses : racecourse, racetrack> <champ de bataille : battlefield> <petit champ : infield> **2** : area, domain <champ d'action : sphere of activity> **3** : field (in physics, physiology, mathematics) <champ magnétique : magnetic field> <champ visuel : visual field> **4 champs** *nmpl* : countryside, country **5** → **sur-le-champ**

champagne [ʃɑ̃paɲ] *nm* : champagne

champêtre [ʃɑ̃pɛtr] *adj* : rustic, rural

champignon [ʃɑ̃piɲɔ̃] *nm* : mushroom

champion[1], **-pionne** [ʃɑ̃pjɔ̃, -pjɔn] *adj fam* : great, terrific

champion[2], **-pionne** *n* : champion

championnat [ʃɑ̃pjɔna] *nm* : championship

champlure [ʃɑ̃plyr] *nf Can* : faucet

chance [ʃɑ̃s] *nf* **1** : luck, fortune <coup de chance : stroke of luck> <par chance : fortunately, luckily> **2** : chance, opportunity **3** : possibility, likelihood

chancelant, -lante [ʃɑ̃slɑ̃, -lɑ̃t] *adj* **1** : unsteady, groggy **2** : flagging, faltering

chanceler [ʃɑ̃sle] {8} *vi* **1** : to totter **2** : to waver, to falter

chancelier [ʃɑ̃səlje] *nm* : chancellor

chanceux, -ceuse [ʃɑ̃sø, -søz] *adj* : lucky, fortunate
chancre [ʃɑ̃kr] *nm* : chancre (in medicine)
chandail [ʃɑ̃daj] *nm* : sweater, pullover
chandelier [ʃɑ̃dəlje] *nm* **1** : candlestick **2** : candelabrum
chandelle [ʃɑ̃dɛl] *nf* : candle
change [ʃɑ̃ʒ] *nm* **1** : exchange, exchange rate **2 donner le change à qqn** : to throw s.o. off the trail
changeant, -geante [ʃɑ̃ʒɑ̃, -ʒɑ̃t] *adj* **1** : changing **2** : fickle, changeable
changement [ʃɑ̃ʒmɑ̃] *nm* **1** : change **2 changement de vitesse** : gears *pl* (of an automobile)
changer [ʃɑ̃ʒe] {17} *vt* **1** : to change, to exchange, to replace **2** : to alter, to transform — *vi* **1** : to undergo change **2 ~ de** : to change <changer d'avis : to change one's mind> <changer de vitesse : to change gears> — **se changer** *vr* **1** : to change (one's clothes) **2** : to be transformed
changeur, -geuse [ʃɑ̃ʒœr, -ʒøz] *n* : money changer
chanoine [ʃanwan] *nm* : canon (in religion)
chanson [ʃɑ̃sɔ̃] *nf* : song
chansonnette [ʃɑ̃sɔnɛt] *nf* : simple song, ditty
chansonnier, -nière [ʃɑ̃sɔnje, -njɛr] *n Can* : songwriter
chant [ʃɑ̃] *nm* **1** : song <chant de Noël : Christmas carol> **2** : singing **3** : canto, ode **4** : edge <de chant, sur chant : edgewise, on edge>
chantage [ʃɑ̃taʒ] *nm* : blackmail
chantant, -tante [ʃɑ̃tɑ̃, -tɑ̃t] *adj* **1** : singsong, lilting **2** : tuneful, catchy
chanter [ʃɑ̃te] *vt* **1** : to sing **2** : to relate, to tell of — *vi* **1** : to sing **2** : to chirp, to crow **3 ~ à** *fam* : to appeal to, to catch the fancy of **4 faire chanter** : to blackmail
chanteur, -teuse [ʃɑ̃tœr, -tøz] *n* : singer
chantier [ʃɑ̃tje] *nm* **1** : (construction) site **2** : depot, yard <chantier naval : shipyard> **3 mettre en chantier** : to start work on, to undertake
chantonner [ʃɑ̃tɔne] *v* : to croon, to hum
chantre [ʃɑ̃tr] *nm* : cantor
chanvre [ʃɑ̃vr] *nm* : hemp
chaos [kao] *nm* : chaos
chaotique [kaɔtik] *adj* : chaotic
chaparder [ʃaparde] *vt fam* PIQUER : to pilfer, to swipe
chapeau [ʃapo] *nm, pl* **chapeaux 1** : hat, cap <tirer son chapeau à : to take one's hat off to> **2 chapeau!** : well done!
chapeauter [ʃapote] *vt* : to head, to lead
chapelain [ʃaplɛ̃] *nm* : chaplain
chapelet [ʃaplɛ] *nm* **1** : rosary **2** : series, string <un chapelet d'îlots : a chain of small islands>
chapelier, -lière [ʃapəlje, -ljɛr] *n* : hatter
chapelle [ʃapɛl] *nf* : chapel
chapelure [ʃaplyr] *nf* : bread crumbs *pl*
chaperon [ʃaprɔ̃] *nm* : chaperon, chaperone
chaperonner [ʃaprɔne] *vt* : to chaperon
chapiteau [ʃapito] *nm, pl* **-teaux 1** : capital (of a column) **2** : big top, circus tent
chapitre [ʃapitr] *nm* **1** : chapter (of a book) **2** : topic, subject matter **3** : item, heading (in a budget)
chapon [ʃapɔ̃] *nm* : capon
chaque [ʃak] *adj* : each, every <chaque personne : each person, everyone> <cent dollars chaque : a hundred dollars each>
char [ʃar] *nm* **1** : cart, wagon **2** : chariot **3** *Can fam* : car **4** *or* **char d'assaut** : tank
charabia [ʃarabja] *nm fam* : gibberish, gobbledegook
charade [ʃarad] *nf* **1** : riddle **2** : charades (game)
charançon [ʃarɑ̃sɔ̃] *nm* : weevil
charbon [ʃarbɔ̃] *nm* **1** : coal **2** : smut (of grains) **3 charbon ardent** : ember **4 charbon de bois** : charcoal
charcuterie [ʃarkytri] *nf* **1** : delicatessen, pork butcher's shop **2** : cooked pork products
charcutier, -tière [ʃarkytje, -tjɛr] *n* : pork butcher
chardon [ʃardɔ̃] *nm* : thistle
chardonneret [ʃardɔnrɛ] *nm* : goldfinch
charge [ʃarʒ] *nf* **1** : load, weight <charge limite : maximum load> **2** : responsibility, job <à charge de : dependent on> <charge de travail : workload> **3** : office <charge élective : elective office> **4** : charge (of explosives or electricity) **5** : assault, (military) charge **6** : cost, expense <charges de l'état : government expenditures> **7** : accusation, indictment **8** : emotional burden **9** : caricature
chargé[1], -gée [ʃarʒe] *adj* **1** : full, loaded, heavy **2** : busy, full
chargé[2], -gée *n* **1 chargé d'affaires** : chargé d'affaires **2 chargé de cours** : (university) lecturer
chargement [ʃarʒəmɑ̃] *nm* **1** : loading **2** : load, cargo
charger [ʃarʒe] {17} *vt* **1** : to load, to fill (up), to overload **2** : to load (a gun, etc.), to charge (with electricity) **3** : to charge at, to attack **4 ~ de** : to put in charge of, to give responsibility for, to command — *vi* : to charge, to attack — **se charger** *vr* **~ de** : to take responsibility for
chargeur [ʃarʒœr] *nm* **1** : magazine, clip (of a firearm) **2** : shipper, shipping agent

chariot [ʃarjo] *nm* **1** : cart, wagon <chariot de supermarché : shopping cart> **2** : truck <chariot élévateur : forklift truck> **3** : carriage (of a typewriter)

charisme [karism] *nm* : charisma — **charismatique** [-rismatik] *adj*

charitable [ʃaritabl] *adj* : charitable — **charitablement** [-bləmɑ̃] *adv*

charité [ʃarite] *nf* : charity

charivari [ʃarivari] *nm* : racket, hullabaloo

charlatan [ʃarlatɑ̃] *nm* : charlatan, quack

charmant, -mante [ʃarmɑ̃, -mɑ̃t] *adj* : charming, delightful

charme [ʃarm] *nm* **1** : charm, attraction **2** : spell

charmer [ʃarme] *vt* : to charm

charmeur[1], -meuse [ʃarmœr, -møz] *adj* : charming

charmeur[2], -meuse *n* : charmer

charnel, -nelle [ʃarnɛl] *adj* : carnal

charnier [ʃarnje] *nm* : mass grave

charnière[1] [ʃarnjɛr] *adj* : transitional, pivotal

charnière[2] *nf* **1** : hinge **2** : turning point

charnu, -nue [ʃarny] *adj* : fleshy, plump

charognard [ʃarɔɲar] *nm* : scavenger (animal)

charogne [ʃarɔɲ] *nf* **1** : carrion **2** *fam* : bastard

charpente [ʃarpɑ̃t] *nf* **1** : framework, structure **2** : frame, build (of the body)

charpenté, -tée [ʃarpɑ̃te] *adj* : built, constructed

charpenterie [ʃarpɑ̃tri] *nf* : carpentry

charpentier [ʃarpɑ̃tje] *nm* : carpenter

charpie [ʃarpi] *nf* **1** : lint **2 en ~** : in shreds

charrette [ʃarɛt] *nf* : cart <charrette à bras : pushcart>

charrier [ʃarje] {96} *vt* **1** : to cart, to carry along **2** *fam* : to poke fun at — *vi* : to exaggerate, to go too far

charrue [ʃary] *nf* : plow

charte [ʃart] *nf* : charter

charter [ʃarte] *nm* **1** : charter flight **2** : chartered plane

chas [ʃa] *nm* : eye (of a needle)

chasse [ʃas] *nf* **1** : hunting <aller à la chasse : to go hunting> **2** POURSUITE : chase <donner chasse à : to chase> <chasse à l'homme : manhunt> **3** *or* **chasse d'eau** : flush (of a toilet) <actionner la chasse d'eau : to flush the toilet>

chassé–croisé [ʃasekrwaze] *nm, pl* **chassés–croisés** : coming and going, moving back and forth

chasse–neige [ʃasnɛʒ] *nms & pl* : snowplow

chasser [ʃase] *vt* **1** : to hunt, to chase **2** : to chase away, to drive away **3** : to dispel — *vi* **1** : to go hunting, to hunt **2** : to skid

chasseur[1], -seuse [ʃasœr, -søz] *n* **1** : hunter **2 chasseur de têtes** : headhunter

chasseur[2] *nm* **1** : fighter <chasseur-bombardier : fighter-bomber> **2** : bellhop, bellboy

châssis [ʃasi] *nm* **1** : frame (of a window, etc.) **2** : chassis

chaste [ʃast] *adj* : chaste — **chastement** [ʃastmɑ̃] *adv*

chasteté [ʃastəte] *nf* : chastity

chasuble [ʃazybl] *nf or* **robe chasuble** : pinafore (dress)

chat, chatte [ʃa, ʃat] *n* **1** : cat **2 chat sauvage** : wildcat **3 chat sauvage** *Can* : raccoon

châtaigne [ʃatɛɲ] *nf* : chestnut

châtaignier [ʃateɲe] *nm* : chestnut tree

châtain [ʃatɛ̃] *adj* : chestnut brown

château [ʃato] *nm, pl* **châteaux 1** : castle **2 château fort** : fortified castle, stronghold

châtier [ʃatje] {96} *vt* **1** : to chastise, to punish **2** : to polish, to refine (style, etc.)

châtiment [ʃatimɑ̃] *nm* PUNITION : punishment

chaton [ʃatɔ̃] *nm* **1** : kitten **2** : catkin (in botany) **3** : setting (of a ring)

chatouillement [ʃatujmɑ̃] *nm* : tickle, tickling

chatouiller [ʃatuje] *vt* **1** : to tickle **2** : to titillate (the senses), to pique (curiosity, pride, etc.)

chatouilleux, -leuse [ʃatujø, -jøz] *adj* **1** : ticklish **2** : sensitive, touchy

chatoyant, -yante [ʃatwajɑ̃, -jɑ̃t] *adj* : iridescent, shimmering

chatoyer [ʃatwaje] {58} *vi* : to shimmer

châtrer [ʃatre] *vt* : to castrate, to neuter

chaud[1] [ʃo] *adv* **1 avoir chaud** : to feel warm, to feel hot **2 boire chaud** : to drink something hot **3 il fait chaud** : it's warm, it's hot **4 manger chaud** : to eat hot food

chaud[2], chaude [ʃo, ʃod] *adj* **1** : warm, hot **2** : enthusiastic, keen **3** : heated, tense

chaud[3] *nm* : heat, warmth

chaudement [ʃodmɑ̃] *adv* **1** : warmly **2** : heartily

chaudière [ʃodjɛr] *nf* : boiler

chaudron [ʃodrɔ̃] *nm* : cauldron

chauffage [ʃofaʒ] *nm* : heating <chauffage central : central heating>

chauffard [ʃofar] *nm* : reckless driver

chauffe–eau [ʃofo] *nms & pl* : water heater

chauffer [ʃofe] *vt* : to heat, to warm — *vi* : to become warm, to warm up — **se chauffer** *vr*

chaufferette [ʃofrɛt] *nf Can* **1** : space heater **2** : heater (in a car)

chaufferie [ʃofri] *nf* : boiler room

chauffeur [ʃofœr] *nm* **1** CONDUCTEUR : driver **2** : chauffeur **3** : stoker, fireman

chaume [ʃom] *nm* **1** : thatch **2** : stubble (of grain)

chaumière [ʃomjɛr] *nf* : (thatched) cottage

chaussée [ʃose] *nf* : roadway, causeway

chausser [ʃose] *vt* **1** : to put on (boots, skis, etc.) **2** : to put shoes on (s.o.) **3** : to fit (with shoes) — *vi* ~ **de** : to take (a shoe size) — **se chausser** *vr* : to put on shoes

chausse–trape *or* **chausse–trappe** [ʃostrap] *nf* : trap, pitfall

chaussette [ʃosɛt] *nf* : sock

chausseur [ʃosœr] *nm* : shoemaker

chausson [ʃosɔ̃] *nm* **1** : slipper **2** : turnover <chausson aux pommes : apple turnover>

chaussure [ʃosyr] *nf* **1** : shoe **2** : footwear industry

chauve [ʃov] *adj* : bald

chauve–souris [ʃovsuri] *nf, pl* **chauves–souris** : bat (animal)

chauvin[1], **-vine** [ʃovɛ̃, -vin] *adj* : chauvinistic — **chauvinisme** [ʃovinism] *nm*

chauvin[2], **-vine** *n* : chauvinist

chaux [ʃo] *nf* **1** : lime **2 lait de chaux** : whitewash

chavirer [ʃavire] *vt* **1** CAPOTER : to capsize, to overturn, to keel over **2** ÉMOUVOIR : to upset, to overwhelm — *vi* : to capsize

cheddar [ʃedar] *nm* : cheddar

chef [ʃɛf] *nm* **1** : leader, boss, head **2** *or* **chef cuisinier** : chef **3 au premier chef** : above all, primarily **4 chef d'accusation** : charge, count (in law) **5 chef d'orchestre** : conductor **6 en chef** : chief, head

chef–d'oeuvre [ʃɛdœvr] *nm, pl* **chefs–d'oeuvre** : masterpiece

chefferie [ʃɛfri] *nf Can* : leadership (of a political party)

cheikh *or* **cheik** [ʃɛk] *nm* : sheikh

chemin [ʃəmɛ̃] *nm* **1** : way, road, path **2 chemin de fer** : railroad

cheminée [ʃəmine] *nf* **1** : fireplace **2** : chimney **3** : mantel, mantelpiece

cheminement [ʃəminmɑ̃] *nm* **1** AVANCE : advance, progress **2** : development

cheminer [ʃəmine] *vi* **1** : to walk along **2** : to advance, to progress

cheminot [ʃəmino] *nm* : railroad worker, railroader

chemise [ʃəmiz] *nf* **1** : shirt **2** : folder **3 chemise de nuit** : nightgown

chemisier [ʃəmizje] *nm* CORSAGE : blouse

chenal [ʃənal] *nm, pl* **chenaux** [ʃəno] : channel (in a river, harbor, etc.)

chêne [ʃɛn] *nm* : oak

chéneau [ʃeno] *nm, pl* **chéneaux** : gutter (of a roof)

chenet [ʃənɛ] *nm* : andiron

chenil [ʃənil] *nm* : kennel

chenille [ʃənij] *nf* **1** : caterpillar **2** : chenille (fabric)

chenu, -nue [ʃəny] *adj* : white-haired, hoary

cheptel [ʃɛptɛl] *nm* : livestock

chèque [ʃɛk] *nm* : check <chèque en blanc : blank check> <chèque de voyage : traveler's check>

chèque–cadeau [ʃɛkkado] *nm, pl* **chèques–cadeaux** : gift certificate

cher[1] [ʃɛr] *adv* **1 coûter cher** : to cost a lot **2 payer cher** : to pay dearly

cher[2], **chère** [ʃɛr] *adj* **1** : dear, beloved **2** COÛTEUX : expensive

cher[3], **chère** *n* : dear <ma chère : my dear>

chercher [ʃɛrʃe] *vt* **1** : to look for, to seek **2 chercher à faire** : to try to do **3 aller chercher** : to go and get

chercheur[1], **-cheuse** [ʃɛrʃœr, -ʃøz] *adj* : inquiring

chercheur[2], **-cheuse** *n* : researcher

chercheur[3] *nm* : finder (of a telescope, etc.)

chère [ʃɛr] *nf* : food, fare

chèrement *adv* [ʃɛrmɑ̃] : dearly, at great cost

chéri, -rie [ʃeri] *adj & n* : darling, dear

chérir [ʃerir] *vt* : to cherish

cherté [ʃɛrte] *nf* : expensiveness, high cost

chérubin [ʃerybɛ̃] *nm* : cherub

chétif, -tive [ʃetif, -tiv] *adj* **1** : sickly, weak **2** MALINGRE : puny

cheval [ʃəval] *nm, pl* **chevaux** [ʃəvo] **1** : horse <à cheval : on horseback> **2** *or* **cheval–vapeur** : horsepower

chevaleresque [ʃəvalrɛsk] *adj* : chivalrous, knightly

chevalerie [ʃəvalri] *nf* **1** : chivalry **2** : knighthood

chevalet [ʃəvalɛ] *nm* **1** : easel **2** : rack (instrument of torture) **3** : stand, trestle, sawhorse

chevalier [ʃəvalje] *nm* : knight

chevalin, -line [ʃəvalɛ̃, -lin] *adj* **1** : equine **2** : horsey

cheval–vapeur [ʃəvalvapœr] *nm, pl* **chevaux–vapeur** → **cheval**

chevauchée [ʃəvoʃe] *nf* : ride

chevauchement [ʃəvoʃmɑ̃] *nm* : overlap

chevaucher [ʃəvoʃe] *vt* **1** : to straddle **2** : to overlap — *vi* : to overlap

chevelu, -lue [ʃəvly] *adj* : hairy

chevelure [ʃəvlyr] *nf* CHEVEUX : hair

chevet [ʃəvɛ] *nm* : bedside, head (of a bed) <rester au chevet de qqn : to stay at s.o.'s bedside>

cheveu [ʃəvø] *nm, pl* **cheveux 1** POIL : hair <être à un cheveu de : to be within a hair's breadth of> **2 cheveux** *nmpl* : hair, head of hair

cheville [ʃəvij] *nf* **1** : ankle **2** : pin, peg **3 cheville ouvrière** : kingpin

chèvre [ʃɛvr] *nf* : goat

chevreau [ʃəvro] *nm, pl* **chevreaux** : kid, young goat (male)

chèvrefeuille [ʃɛvrəfœj] *nm* : honeysuckle

chevrette [ʃəvrɛt] *nf* : kid, young goat (female)
chevreuil [ʃəvrœj] *nm* **1** : roe deer **2** : venison **3** *Can* : white-tailed deer
chevron [ʃəvrɔ̃] *nm* **1** : rafter **2** : chevron
chevronné, -née [ʃəvrɔne] *adj* : seasoned, experienced
chevrotement [ʃəvrɔtmɑ̃] *nm* : quavering
chevroter [ʃəvrɔte] *vi* : to quaver
chevrotine [ʃəvrɔtin] *nf* : buckshot
chewing–gum [ʃwiŋgɔm] *nm France* : chewing gum
chez [ʃe] *prep* **1** : at the home, business, or practice of <chez elle : at her house> <chez le dentiste : at the dentist's office> **2** : among, in <chez les Suisses : among the Swiss> <chez les Québécois : in Quebec> **3** : in the works of <chez Victor Hugo : in Victor Hugo's writing> **4** : in (a person) <le meilleur trait chez lui, c'est sa gentillesse : his best trait is his kindness>
chez–soi [ʃeswa] *nm* : place of one's own, home
chialer [ʃiale] *vi* **1** *fam* : to blubber, to snivel **2** *Can fam* : to whine, to complain
chic[1] [ʃik] *adj s & pl* **1** : chic, stylish **2** : nice
chic[2] *nm* **1** : stylishness, elegance **2** **avoir le chic pour** : to have a knack for
chicane [ʃikan] *nf* : bickering, squabble, quibble
chicaner [ʃikane] *vt* : to quibble with — *vi* : to bicker, to squabble <chicaner sur : to quibble over>
chiche [ʃiʃ] *adj* **1** AVARE : stingy, mean **2** : meager, scanty — **chichement** [ʃiʃmɑ̃] *adv*
chichi [ʃiʃi] *nm fam* **1** : affectation, airs **2** **faire des chichis** : to make a fuss
chicorée [ʃikɔre] *nf* **1** : endive **2** : chicory (for coffee)
chicoter [ʃikɔte] *vt Can fam* : to worry, to bother
chien[1], **chienne** [ʃjɛ̃, -ʃjɛn] *n* **1** : dog, bitch *f* **2** **chien d'arrêt** : bird dog, pointer, retriever **3** **chien de berger** : sheepdog **4** **chien de chasse** : retriever, hunting dog **5** **chien courant** : hound **6** **chien esquimau** : husky **7** **chien de garde** : watchdog **8** **chien de meute** : hound **9** **chien de prairie** : prairie dog
chien[2] *nm* : hammer (of a firearm)
chien–loup [ʃjɛ̃lu] *nm, pl* **chiens–loups** : German shepherd
chiffe [ʃif] *nf* : spineless person
chiffon [ʃifɔ̃] *nm* : rag, dustcloth
chiffonner [ʃifɔne] *vt* **1** : to crease, to crumple **2** : to bother
chiffre [ʃifr] *nm* **1** : numeral <chiffre romain : Roman numeral> **2** : amount, sum <chiffre d'affaires : turnover> **3** : cipher, code **4** : monogram
chiffrer [ʃifre] *vt* **1** : to number (pages, etc.) **2** : to calculate, to assess **3** : to encode **4** : to mark, to monogram — **se chiffrer** *vr* ~ **à** : to amount to
chignon [ʃiɲɔ̃] *nm* : chignon, (hair) bun
chilien, -lienne [ʃiljɛ̃, -jɛn] *adj* : Chilean
Chilien, -lienne *n* : Chilean
chimère [ʃimɛr] *nf* **1** : Chimera (in mythology) **2** : illusion, pipe dream
chimérique [ʃimerik] *adj* : illusory, fanciful
chimie [ʃimi] *nf* : chemistry
chimique [ʃimik] *adj* : chemical — **chimiquement** [-mikmɑ̃] *adv*
chimiste [ʃimist] *nmf* : chemist
chimpanzé [ʃɛ̃pɑ̃ze] *nm* : chimpanzee
chinchilla [ʃɛ̃ʃila] *nm* : chinchilla
chine [ʃin] *nm* **1** : china, porcelain ware **2** : rice paper
chinois[1], **-noise** [ʃinwa, -nwaz] *adj* : Chinese
chinois[2] *nm* : Chinese (language)
Chinois, -noise *n* : Chinese
chinoiserie [ʃinwazri] *nf* **1** : chinoiserie, Chinese curio **2** **chinoiseries administratives** : red tape
chintz [ʃints] *nm* : chintz
chiot [ʃjo] *nm* : puppy
chiper [ʃipe] *vt fam* : to pinch, to swipe
chipie [ʃipi] *nf* : shrew, vixen
chipoter [ʃipɔte] *vi* **1** : to haggle, to quibble **2** : to pick at one's food
chips [ʃips] *nfpl* : potato chips
chiquenaude [ʃiknod] *nf* : flick (with the finger)
chiquer [ʃike] *vt* : to chew (tobacco) — *vi* : to chew tobacco
chiropraticien, -cienne [kirɔpratisjɛ̃, -sjɛn] *n* : chiropractor
chiropratique [kiropratik] *nf Can* : chiropractic
chiropraxie [kirɔpraksi] *or* **chiropractie** [kirɔprakti] *nf* : chiropractic
chirurgical, -cale [ʃiryrʒikal] *adj, mpl* **-caux** [-ko] : surgical
chirurgie [ʃiryrʒi] *nf* : surgery <chirurgie plastique *or* chirurgie esthétique : plastic surgery>
chirurgien, -gienne [ʃiryrʒjɛ̃, -ʒjɛn] *n* : surgeon
chirurgien–dentiste [ʃiryrʒjɛ̃dɑ̃tist] *nm, pl* **chirurgiens–dentistes** : oral surgeon
chlore [klɔr] *nm* : chlorine
chloroforme [klɔrɔfɔrm] *nm* : chloroform
chloroformer [klɔrɔfɔrme] *vt* : to chloroform
chlorophylle [klɔrɔfil] *nf* : chlorophyll
chlorure [klɔryr] *nm* : chloride
choc [ʃɔk] *nm* **1** : shock **2** : impact, crash **3** : clash (of opinions, etc.)
chocolat [ʃɔkɔla] *nm* : chocolate
chœur [kœr] *nm* **1** : choir **2** : chorus (song)

choir [ʃwar] {18} *vi* : to drop, to fall
choisi [ʃwazi] *adj* **1** : selected **2** : select, choice
choisir [ʃwazir] *vt* : to choose, to select
choix [ʃwa] *nm* **1** : choice, selection **2 de (premier) choix** : select, choice, first-rate
choléra [kɔlera] *nm* : cholera
cholestérol [kɔlɛsterɔl] *nm* : cholesterol
chômage [ʃomaʒ] *nm* : unemployment
chômer [ʃome] *vi* : to be unemployed, to be idle
chômeur, -meuse [ʃomœr, -møz] *n* : unemployed person
chope [ʃɔp] *nf* : (beer) mug, tankard
choquant, -quante [ʃɔkɑ̃, -kɑ̃t] *adj* : shocking
choquer [ʃɔke] *vt* **1** HEURTER : to knock, to bump **2** OFFUSQUER : to shock, to offend **3** : to shake up, to devastate — **se choquer** *vr* **1** : to be shocked **2** *Can* : to get angry
choral[1], **-rale** [kɔral] *adj, mpl* **chorals** or **choraux** [kɔro] : choral
choral[2] *nm, pl* **chorals** : chorale
chorale *nf* : choir
chorégraphe [kɔregraf] *nmf* : choreographer — **chorégraphique** [-grafik] *adj*
chorégraphie [kɔregrafi] *nf* : choreography — **chorégraphier** [-grafie] *vt*
choriste [kɔrist] *n* : choir member, chorus member
chose[1] [ʃoz] *adj fam* : peculiar, funny <se sentir tout chose : to feel out of sorts>
chose[2] *nf* **1** : thing <choses à faire : things to do> **2** : matter, affair <avant toute chose : above all, before all else>
chose[3] *nm fam* **1** : thingamajig **2** : what's-his-name, what's-her-name
chou[1] [ʃu] *adj fam* : sweet, nice, cute
chou[2], **choute** *n fam* : darling, dear
chou[3] *nm, pl* **choux 1** : cabbage **2 chou frisé** : kale
chouchou, -choute [ʃuʃu, -ʃut] *n fam* : pet, favorite <chouchou du prof : teacher's pet>
choucroute [ʃukrut] *nf* : sauerkraut
chouette[1] [ʃwɛt] *adj fam* : great, terrific, neat
chouette[2] *nf* **1** : owl **2** *fam* : goody, neat thing **3 ma chouette** *Can* : sweetheart, darling
chou-fleur [ʃuflœr] *nm, pl* **choux-fleurs** : cauliflower
chou-rave [ʃurav] *nm* : kohlrabi
chow-chow [ʃoʃo] *nm, pl* **chows-chows** : chow (dog)
choyer [ʃwaje] {58} *vt* : to pamper, to coddle
chrétien, -tienne [kretjɛ̃, -tjɛn] *adj & n* : Christian
chrétienté [kretjɛ̃te] *nf* : Christendom
christianisme [kristjanism] *nm* : Christianity
chromatique [krɔmatik] *adj* : chromatic
chrome [krom] *nm* **1** : chromium **2 chromes** *nmpl* : chrome (of an automobile)
chromé, -mée [krome] *adj* : chrome-plated
chromosome [krɔmɔzom] *nm* : chromosome
chronique[1] [krɔnik] *adj* : chronic
chronique[2] *nf* **1** : chronicle **2** : column (in a newspaper), report (in radio or television)
chroniqueur, -queuse [krɔnikœr, -køz] *n* **1** : chronicler **2** : columnist, commentator
chronologie [krɔnɔlɔʒi] *nf* : chronology
chronologique [krɔnɔlɔʒik] *adj* : chronological — **chronologiquement** [-ʒikmɑ̃] *adv*
chronomètre [krɔnɔmɛtr] *nm* **1** : chronometer **2** : stopwatch
chronométrer [krɔnɔmetre] {87} *vt* : to time
chronométreur, -treuse [krɔnɔmetrœr, -trøz] *n* : timekeeper
chrysalide [krizalid] *nf* : chrysalis
chrysanthème [krizɑ̃tɛm] *nm* : chrysanthemum
chu [ʃy] *pp* → **choir**
chuchotement [ʃyʃɔtmɑ̃] *nm* : whisper, murmur
chuchoter [ʃyʃɔte] *v* : to whisper, to murmur
chuintement [ʃɥɛ̃tmɑ̃] *nm* : hiss
chuinter [ʃɥɛ̃te] *vi* **1** : to hoot **2** : to hiss
chum[1] [tʃɔm] *nmf Can fam* : friend, pal
chum[2] *nm Can fam* : boyfriend
chut [ʃyt] *interj* : sh!, hush!
chute [ʃyt] *nf* **1** : fall <faire une chute : to take a fall> <chute de cheveux : hair loss> <chute du jour : nightfall> <chute de neige : snowfall> <chute de pluie : rainfall> **2** *or* **chute d'eau** CASCADE : waterfall **3 chute des reins** : small of the back
chuter [ʃyte] *vi fam* **1** : to fall down **2** : to fail, to flop
chypriote [ʃiprijɔt] *adj* : Cypriot
Chypriote *nmf* : Cypriot
ci[1] [si] *adv* **1** (*used with* **ce, cette, ces, celui, celle, ceux**) <ce livre-ci : this book> <ceux-ci : these ones> **2** : here <par-ci par-là : here and there>
ci[2] *pron* **1** : this <ci et ça : this and that> **2** → **comme**
ci-après [siaprɛ] *adv* : below, hereafter, herein
ci-bas [siba] *adv* : below
cible [sibl] *nf* : target, mark
cibler [sible] *vt* : to target
ciboule [sibul] *nf* : scallion
ciboulette [sibulɛt] *nf* : chive
cicatrice [sikatris] *nf* : scar
cicatriser [sikatrize] *v* : to heal, to scar over — **se cicatriser** *vr* : to scar
ci-contre [sikɔ̃tr] *adv* : opposite

ci–dessous [sidəsu] *adv* : below <voir ci-dessous : see below>
ci–dessus [sidəsy] *adv* : above <voir ci-dessus : see above>
ci–devant [sidəvɑ̃] *adv* : formerly, previously
cidre [sidr] *nm* : cider
cidrerie [sidrəri] *nf* **1** : cider house **2** : cidermaking
ciel [sjɛl] *nm* **1** *pl* **ciels** : sky (in meteorology) **2** *pl* **cieux** [sjø] : sky <à ciel ouvert : open-air> **3** *pl* **cieux** : heaven **4 en plein ciel** : midair
cierge [sjɛrʒ] *nm* **1** : candle (in a church) **2 cierge magique** : sparkler
cigale [sigal] *nf* : cicada
cigare [sigar] *nm* : cigar
cigarette [sigarɛt] *nf* : cigarette
ci–gît [siʒi] *adv* : here lies
cigogne [sigɔɲ] *nf* : stork
ciguë [sigy] *nf* : hemlock (plant)
ci–inclus[1] [siɛ̃kly] *adv* : enclosed
ci–inclus[2], **-cluse** [siɛ̃kly, -klyz] *adj* : enclosed, included
ci–joint[1] [siʒwɛ̃] *adv* : enclosed, attached
ci–joint[2], **-jointe** [siʒwɛ̃, -ʒwɛ̃t] *adj* : enclosed, attached
cil [sil] *nm* : eyelash
ciller [sije] *vi* : to blink
cime [sim] *nf* SOMMET : summit, top, peak
ciment [simɑ̃] *nm* : cement
cimenter [simɑ̃te] *vt* : to cement
cimetière [simtjɛr] *nm* **1** : cemetery, graveyard **2** : churchyard
cinéaste [sineast] *nmf* : film director, filmmaker
cinéma [sinema] *nm* **1** : movie theater <aller au cinéma : to go to the movies> **2** : cinema, filmmaking
cinémathèque [sinematɛk] *nf* : film library
cinématographie [sinematɔgrafi] *nf* : cinematography
cinématographique [sinematɔgrafik] *adj* : film, movie, cinematic <œuvres cinématographiques : films, movies>
ciné–parc [sinepark] *nm Can, pl* **ciné–parcs** : drive-in theater
cinéphile [sinefil] *nmf* : movie buff
cinglant, -glante [sɛ̃glɑ̃, -glɑ̃t] *adj* : cutting, biting, scathing
cinglé, -glée [sɛ̃gle] *adj fam* : crazy, nuts
cingler [sɛ̃gle] *vt* : to whip, to lash — *vi* **~ vers** : to head for
cinq[1] [sɛ̃k] *adj* **1** : five **2** : fifth <le cinq juin : the fifth of June>
cinq[2] *nms & pl* : five
cinquantaine [sɛ̃kɑ̃tɛn] *nf* **une cinquantaine de** : about fifty
cinquante [sɛ̃kɑ̃t] *adj & nms & pl* : fifty
cinquantenaire [sɛ̃kɑ̃tnɛr] *nm* : fiftieth anniversary
cinquantième [sɛ̃kɑ̃tjɛm] *adj & nmf & nm* : fiftieth
cinquième[1] [sɛ̃kjɛm] *adj & nmf* : fifth
cinquième[2] *nm* **1** : fifth floor **2** : fifth (in mathematics)
cintre [sɛ̃tr] *nm* **1** : curve, bend **2** : arch <arc en plein cintre : semicircular arch> **3** : coat hanger
cintré, -trée [sɛ̃tre] *adj* **1** : arched, vaulted **2** : fitted, tailored
cirage [siraʒ] *nm* **1** : waxing, polishing **2** : shoe polish **3 être dans le cirage** *fam* : to be in a daze
circoncire [sirkɔ̃sir] {86} *vt* : to circumcise
circoncision [sirkɔ̃sizjɔ̃] *nf* : circumcision
circonférence [sirkɔ̃ferɑ̃s] *nf* : circumference
circonflexe [sirkɔ̃flɛks] *adj* **accent circonflexe** : circumflex (accent)
circonlocution [sirkɔ̃lɔkysjɔ̃] *nf* : circumlocution
circonscription [sirkɔ̃skripsjɔ̃] *nf* : district, ward <circonscription électorale : electoral district>
circonscrire [sirkɔ̃skrir] {33} *vt* **1** DÉLIMITER : to define, to mark out **2** : to contain (a fire, etc.)
circonspect, -specte [sirkɔ̃spɛ, -spɛkt] *adj* : circumspect, cautious, wary
circonspection [sirkɔ̃spɛksjɔ̃] *nf* : circumspection, caution
circonstance [sirkɔ̃stɑ̃s] *nf* : circumstance <circonstances atténuantes : mitigating circumstances> <être de circonstance : to be fitting>
circonstancié, -ciée [sirkɔ̃stɑ̃sje] *adj* : detailed
circonstanciel, -cielle [sirkɔ̃stɑ̃sjɛl] *adj* **complément circonstanciel** : adverbial phrase
circonvenir [sirkɔ̃vnir] {92} *vt* : to circumvent
circuit [sirkɥi] *nm* **1** : circuit <circuit intégré : integrated circuit> **2** : tour, trip **3** *or* **coup de circuit** *Can* : home run (in baseball)
circulaire [sirkylɛr] *adj & nf* : circular
circulation [sirkylasjɔ̃] *nf* **1** : circulation **2** : traffic
circulatoire [sirkylatwar] *adj* : circulatory
circuler [sirkyle] *vi* **1** : to circulate (of air, blood, etc.) **2** : to move along, to get around **3** : to run (of buses, etc.) **4 faire circuler** : to circulate, to spread (rumors, etc.)
cire [sir] *nf* **1** : wax **2 cire d'abeille** : beeswax
ciré [sire] *nm* : oilskin
cirer [sire] *vt* : to wax, to polish
cireux, -reuse [sirø, -røz] *adj* **1** : waxen, pale **2** : waxy
cirque [sirk] *nm* **1** : circus **2** *fam* : disorder, shambles
cirrhose [siroz] *nf* : cirrhosis
cirrus [sirys] *nms & pl* : cirrus
cisailler [sizaje] *vt* **1** : to cut, to snip **2** : to prune
cisailles [sizaj] *nfpl* : shears

ciseau [sizo] *nm, pl* **ciseaux 1** : chisel **2 ciseaux** *nmpl* : scissors

ciseler [sizle] {20} *vt* : to engrave, to carve

ciselure [sizlyr] *nf* **1** : engraving **2** : carving

citadelle [sitadɛl] *nf* : citadel, stronghold

citadin, -dine [sitadɛ̃, -din] *n* : city dweller

citation [sitasjɔ̃] *nf* **1** : citation, quotation **2** : summons (to court), subpoena **3** : (military) citation

cité [site] *nf* **1** : city **2 cité universitaire** *France* : college dormitories *pl* **3 cité universitaire** *Can* : college campus

citer [site] *vt* **1** : to quote **2** : to cite, to mention **3** : to summon, to subpoena

citerne [sitɛrn] *nf* : cistern, tank, reservoir

cithare [sitar] *nf* : zither

citoyen, citoyenne [sitwajɛ̃, -jɛn] *n* : citizen

citoyenneté [sitwajɛnte] *nf* : citizenship

citron[1] [sitrɔ̃] *adj* : lemon, lemon yellow

citron[2] *nm* **1** : lemon **2 citron vert** : lime

citronnade [sitrɔnad] *nf* : lemonade

citronné, -née [sitrɔne] *adj* : lemon-flavored, lemony

citronnier [sitrɔnje] *nm* : lemon tree

citrouille [sitruj] *nf* **1** : pumpkin **2** *fam* : head

cive [siv] *nf* : chive

civet [sivɛ] *nm* : stew <civet de lapin : rabbit stew>

civière [sivjɛr] *nf* : stretcher

civil[1], -vile [sivil] *adj* **1** : civil <droit civil : civil law> **2** : civilian, secular **3** : polite, civil

civil[2], -vile *n* : civilian

civilement [sivilmɑ̃] *adv* **1** : civilly, politely **2 se marier civilement** : to have a civil marriage

civilisation [sivilizasjɔ̃] *nf* : civilization

civiliser [sivilize] *vt* : to civilize

civilité [sivilite] *nf* : civility

civique [sivik] *adj* **1** : civic **2 instruction civique** *or* **éducation civique** : civics

civisme [sivism] *nm* : good citizenship

clair[1] [klɛr] *adv* **1** : clearly <voir clair : to see clearly> **2 il fait clair** : it's light, it's getting light (outside)

clair[2], claire [klɛr] *adj* **1** : clear **2** : light, bright **3** : light-colored

clair[3] *nm* **1** : light <clair de lune : moonlight> **2** : light color **3 mettre au clair** : to make clear, to shed light on

clairement [klɛrmɑ̃] *adv* : clearly

claire–voie [klɛrvwa] *nf, pl* **claires–voies** : openwork fence <à claire-voie : openwork, open-worked>

clairière [klɛrjɛr] *nf* : clearing, glade

clair–obscur [klɛropskyr] *nm, pl* **clairs–obscurs** : twilight

clairon [klɛrɔ̃] *nm* **1** : bugle **2** : bugler

claironnant [klɛrɔnɑ̃] *adj* : resonant, strident

claironner [klɛrɔne] *vt* : to trumpet, to broadcast (news, etc.)

clairsemé, -mée [klɛrsəme] *adj* : scattered, sparse

clairvoyant, -voyante [klɛrvwajɑ̃, -jɑ̃t] *adj* : clairvoyant — **clairvoyance** [-vwajɑ̃s] *nf*

clamer [klame] *vt* : to shout out, to proclaim

clameur [klamœr] *nf* : clamor, outcry

clan [klɑ̃] *nm* : clan, clique

clandestin[1], -tine [klɑ̃dɛstɛ̃, -tin] *adj* **1** : clandestine, covert, underground **2 passager clandestin** : stowaway

clandestin[2], -tine *n* : illegal alien

clapoter [klapɔte] *vi* : to lap (of waves)

clapotis [klapɔti] *nm* : lapping (of the waves)

claque [klak] *nf* **1** : slap, smack **2 claques** *nfpl Can* : rubbers, galoshes

claqué, -quée [klake] *adj fam* : dog-tired, exhausted

claquement [klakmɑ̃] *nm* : slamming, slapping, snapping, flapping

claquemurer [klakmyre] *v* **se claquemurer** *vr* : to shut oneself away

claquer [klake] *vt* **1** GIFLER : to slap **2** : to slam **3** *fam* : to spend, to squander **4** *fam* : to exhaust **5** : to strain (a muscle) — *vi* **1** : to make a clicking sound <ses dents claquent : his teeth are chattering> <faire claquer ses doigts : to snap one's fingers> **2** : to slam, to bang **3** *fam* : to wear out, to conk out, to fall through

claquettes [klakɛt] *nfpl* : tap dancing

clarifier [klarifje] {96} *vt* : to clarify — **clarification** [-rifikasjɔ̃] *nf*

clarinette [klarinɛt] *nf* : clarinet — **clarinettiste** [-nɛtist] *nf*

clarté [klarte] *nf* **1** : clearness **2** : clarity, lucidity **3** : brightness, light (of the moon, etc.)

classe [klas] *nf* **1** : class, category, rank <première classe : first class> <classe moyenne : middle class> **2** : class, classroom (in a school) <aller en classe : to go to school>

classement [klasmɑ̃] *nm* **1** : classification **2** : place, ranking

classer [klase] *vt* : to class, to classify, to rate — **se classer** *vr* : to be classified, to rank

classeur [klasœr] *nm* **1** : binder, loose-leaf file **2** : filing cabinet

classicisme [klasisism] *nm* : classicism

classification [klasifikasjɔ̃] *nf* : classification

classifier [klasifje] {96} *vt* : to classify

classique[1] [klasik] *adj* : classic, classical

classique[2] *nm* **1** : classic **2** : classical author **3** : classical art, music, etc.

claudication [klodikasjɔ̃] *nf* : lameness

clause [kloz] *nf* : clause

claustrophobe [klostrɔfɔb] *adj* : claustrophobic
claustrophobie [klostrɔfɔbi] *nf* : claustrophobia
clavecin [klavsɛ̃] *nm* : harpsichord
clavicule [klavikyl] *nf* : collarbone, clavicle
clavier [klavje] *nm* **1** : keyboard **2** : range, gamut
clé *or* **clef**[1] [kle] *adj* : key, important
clé *or* **clef**[2] *nf* **1** : key <clé de contact : ignition key> <sous clé : under lock and key> **2** : clue, means, solution <la clé du bonheur : the key to happiness> **3** : clef <clé de sol : treble clef> **4 clé à molette** : monkey wrench **5 clé de voûte** : keystone
clémence [klemɑ̃s] *nf* : clemency, leniency
clément, -mente [klemɑ̃, -mɑ̃t] *adj* **1** : lenient **2** : mild, clement
clémentine [klemɑ̃tin] *nf* : tangerine
clenche [klɑ̃ʃ] *nf* : latch
clencher [klɑ̃ʃe] *vt Can* : to latch
cleptomanie [klɛptɔmani] *nf* → **kleptomanie**
clerc [klɛr] *nm* **1** : clerk **2** : cleric
clergé [klɛrʒe] *nm* : clergy
clérical, -cale [klerikal] *adj, mpl* **-caux** [-ko] : clerical
clic [klik] *nm* : click, clicking
cliché [kliʃe] *nm* **1** : negative (in photography) **2** : cliché
client, cliente [kliɑ̃, kliɑ̃t] *n* **1** : customer, client **2** : patient **3** : guest (in a hotel)
clientèle [kliɑ̃tɛl] *nf* **1** : clientele, customers *pl* **2** : practice (of a doctor)
cligner [kliɲe] *vi* **1** : to squint, to blink **2 cligner de l'œil** : to wink
clignotant *nm* [kliɲɔtɑ̃] : blinker, turn signal
clignoter [kliɲɔte] *vi* **1** : to flash, to twinkle, to flicker **2** : to blink
climat [klima] *nm* : climate
climatique [klimatik] *adj* : climatic
climatisation [klimatizasjɔ̃] *nf* : air-conditioning
climatisé, -sée [klimatize] *adj* : air-conditioned
climatiseur [klimatizœr] *nm* : air conditioner
clin [klɛ̃] *nm* **1 clin d'œil** : wink **2 en un clin d'œil** : in a flash
clinique[1] [klinik] *adj* : clinical — **cliniquement** [-nikmɑ̃] *adv*
clinique[2] *nf* : clinic, private hospital
clinquant[1], **-quante** [klɛ̃kɑ̃, -kɑ̃t] *adj* : flashy
clinquant[2] *nm* **1** : tinsel **2** : flashiness
clip [klip] *nm* **1** : (music) video **2** : brooch
clique [klik] *nf* **1** : clique **2** : (military) band **3 prendre ses cliques et ses claques** : to pack up and go
cliquer [klike] *vi* : to click (on a computer)
cliqueter [klikte] {8} *vi* : to clink, to clack, to rattle, to jingle
cliquetis [klikti] *nm* : clink, clack, rattle, jingle
clitoris [klitɔris] *nm* : clitoris
clivage [klivaʒ] *nm* **1** : cleaving, split **2** : cleavage
cloaque [klɔak] *nm* : cesspool
clochard, -charde [klɔʃar, -ʃard] *n* : tramp, hobo
cloche [klɔʃ] *nf* **1** : bell **2** *fam* : dope, idiot
cloche–pied [klɔʃpje] **sauter à cloche–pied** : to hop
clocher[1] [klɔʃe] *vi fam* : to go wrong
clocher[2] *nm* **1** : belfry, bell tower **2 de ~** : parochial, small-town
clochette [klɔʃɛt] *nf* : small bell
cloison [klwazɔ̃] *nf* **1** : partition, divider <mur de cloison : dividing wall> **2** : bulkhead **3** : septum
cloisonner [klwazɔne] *vt* : to partition (off)
cloître [klwatr] *nm* : cloister — **cloîtrer** [klwatre] *vt*
clone [klon] *nm* : clone
cloner [klone] *vt* : to clone
clopin–clopant [klɔpɛ̃klɔpɑ̃] *adv* **aller clopin–clopant** *fam* : to hobble along
clopiner [klɔpine] *vi* : to hobble (along)
cloquer [klɔke] *vi* : to blister
clore [klor] {19} *vt* : to close, to conclude
clos[1], **close** [klo, -kloz] *adj* **1** : closed, shut **2** : concluded
clos[2] *nm* **1** : enclosure, enclosed field **2** *or* **clos de vigne** : vineyard
clôture [klotyr] *nf* **1** BARRIÈRE : enclosure, fence **2** : closure
clôturer [klotyre] *vt* **1** : to enclose **2** : to bring to a close
clou [klu] *nm, pl* **clous 1** : nail **2** : feature, attraction **3** FURONCLE : boil **4 clou de girofle** : clove **5 clous** *nmpl France fam* : crosswalk **6 au clou** *fam* : in hock **7 cogner des clous** *Can* : to nod off
clouer [klue] *vt* **1** : to nail **2** : to pin down <être cloué au lit : to be bedridden> **3 clouer le bec à qqn** *fam* : to shut s.o. up
clouté, -tée [klute] *adj* **1** : studded **2 passage clouté** *France* : crosswalk
clown [klun] *nm* : clown <faire le clown : to clown around, to play the fool>
club [klœb] *nm* : club
coaguler [kɔagyle] *vt* : to coagulate — **se coaguler** *vr* : to coagulate, to clot — **coagulation** [-gylasjɔ̃] *nf*
coaliser [kɔalize] *v* **se coaliser** *vr* : to unite, to form a coalition
coalition [kɔalisjɔ̃] *nf* : coalition
coassement [kɔasmɑ̃] *nm* : croaking
coasser [kɔase] *vi* : to croak
cobalt [kɔbalt] *nm* **1** : cobalt **2 bleu de cobalt** : cobalt blue
cobaye [kɔbaj] *nm* : guinea pig
cobra [kɔbra] *nm* : cobra

cocagne [kɔkaɲ] *nf* **pays de cocagne** : land of plenty

cocaïne [kɔkain] *nf* : cocaine

cocarde [kɔkard] *nf* : rosette

cocasse [kɔkas] *adj* : comical

coccinelle [kɔksinɛl] *nf* : ladybug

coche [kɔʃ] *nf* **1** : notch, mark **2 être à côté de la coche** *Can* : to be wrong, to be mistaken

cocher[1] [kɔʃe] *vt* **1** ENTAILLER : to notch **2** POINTER : to check (off)

cocher[2] *nm* : coachman

cochon[1], **-chonne** [kɔʃɔ̃, -ʃɔn] *adj fam* **1** : smutty, indecent **2** : dirty, messy

cochon[2], **-chonne** *n fam* : slob, dirty pig

cochon[3] *nm* **1** : pig **2 cochon d'Inde** : guinea pig **3 cochon de mer** : porpoise

cochonnerie [kɔʃɔnri] *nf* **1** : junk, trash **2** : filthiness, mess **3** : smut **4** : dirty trick

cockpit [kɔkpit] *nm* : cockpit

cocktail [kɔktɛl] *nm* : cocktail

coco [kɔkɔ] *nm or* **noix de coco** : coconut

cocon [kɔkɔ̃] *nm* : cocoon

cocotier [kɔkɔtje] *nm* : coconut palm

cocotte [kɔkɔt] *nf* **1** : casserole dish **2** *Can* : pinecone **3** *fam* : chicken (in baby talk) **4 ma cocotte** *fam* : my sweetie

code [kɔd] *nm* : code <code à barres : bar code> <code postal : zip code> <code d'honneur : code of honor>

codéine [kɔdein] *nf* : codeine

coder [kɔde] *vt* : to code, to encode

codicille [kɔdisil] *nm* : codicil

codifier [kɔdifje] {96} *vt* : to codify

coefficient [kɔefisjɑ̃] *nm* : coefficient <coefficient d'erreur : margin of error>

coéquipier, -pière [kɔekipje, -jɛr] *n* : teammate

coercitif, -tive [kɔɛrsitif, -tiv] *adj* : coercive

coercition [kɔɛrsisjɔ̃] *nf* : coercion

cœur [kœr] *nm* **1** : heart <maladie de cœur : heart disease> **2** : stomach <mal au cœur : upset stomach, nausea> **3** : spirit, courage <de bon cœur : with good spirits, willingly> **4** : heart, feelings *pl*, mind <avoir bon cœur : to be kindhearted> <à cœur joie : to one's heart's content> <apprendre par cœur : to learn by heart> **5** : center, middle <au cœur de la nuit : in the dead of night> <le cœur de l'été : the height of summer> **6** : core (of a fruit) **7** : hearts *pl* (in playing cards)

coexister [kɔɛgziste] *vi* : to coexist — **coexistence** [-zistɑ̃s] *nf*

coffre [kɔfr] *nm* **1** : chest, bin <coffre à jouets : toy chest> **2** : safe, strongbox **3** : trunk (of a car)

coffre–fort [kɔfrəfɔr] *nm, pl* **coffres–forts** : safe

coffrer [kɔfre] *vi Can* : to warp (of wood)

coffret [kɔfrɛ] *nm* : small box, case <coffret à bijoux : jewelry box>

cogiter [kɔʒite] *vi* RÉFLÉCHIR : to cogitate, to reflect

cognac [kɔɲak] *nm* : cognac

cogner [kɔɲe] *vt* : to knock, to bang — *vi* **cogner contre** : to bump against — **se cogner** *vr* : to bump oneself <se cogner la tête : to hit one's head>

cohabiter [kɔabite] *vi* : to live together

cohérent, -rente [kɔerɑ̃, -rɑ̃t] *adj* : coherent — **cohérence** [-erɑ̃s] *nf*

cohésion [kɔezjɔ̃] *nf* : cohesion, cohesiveness

cohorte [kɔɔrt] *nf fam* : band, troop

cohue [kɔy] *nf* **1** FOULE : crowd **2** BOUSCULADE : crush

coi, coite [kwa, kwat] *adj* SILENCIEUX : silent, speechless <se tenir coi : to keep quiet>

coiffe [kwaf] *nf* : headdress

coiffer [kwafe] *vt* **1** : to top, to cover **2** : to head **3 coiffer qqn** : to do s.o's hair — **se coiffer** *vr* : to do one's hair

coiffeur, -feuse [kwafœr, -føz] *n* : hairdresser, barber

coiffeuse [kwaføz] *nf* : vanity, dressing table

coiffure [kwafyr] *nf* **1** : hat, headdress **2** : hairdo **3** : hairdressing

coin [kwɛ̃] *nm* **1** : corner <au coin du feu : by the fireside> <regard en coin : sidelong glance> **2** : place, spot <un coin de ciel : a patch of sky> **3** : wedge

coincé, -cée [kwɛ̃se] *adj fam* : repressed, uptight

coincer [kwɛ̃se] {6} *vt* **1** : to wedge, to jam **2** : to catch (out), to get someone stuck — *vi* : to jam, to get stuck — **se coincer** *vr*

coïncidence [kɔɛ̃sidɑ̃s] *nf* : coincidence

coïncider [kɔɛ̃side] *vi* : to coincide, to tally

coin–coin [kwɛ̃kwɛ̃] *nm* : quack

coing [kwɛ̃] *nm* : quince

coït [kɔit] *nm* : coitus

coke [kɔk] *nm* : coke

col [kɔl] *nm* **1** : collar <col roulé : turtleneck> **2** : neck (of bottle) **3** : mountain pass, gap **4** *or* **col de l'utérus** : cervix

coléoptère [kɔleɔptɛr] *nm* : beetle

colère [kɔlɛr] *nf* **1** : anger **2 en ~** : angry <se mettre en colère : to get angry>

coléreux, -reuse [kɔlerø, -røz] *adj* : bad-tempered, irritable

colérique [kɔlerik] → **coléreux**

colibri [kɔlibri] *nm* : hummingbird

colifichet [kɔlifiʃɛ] *nm* : trinket

colimaçon [kɔlimasɔ̃] *nm* **1** : snail **2 en ~** : spiral

colin [kɔlɛ̃] *nm* : hake (for cooking)

colique [kɔlik] *nf* **1** : diarrhea **2** *or* **coliques** *nfpl* : colic, stomachache **3** *fam* : hassle, pain in the neck

colis [kɔli] *nm* PAQUET : parcel, package <colis postal : parcel post>

collaborateur, -trice [kɔlabɔratœr, -tris] *n* **1** COLLÈGUE : colleague, coworker **2** : contributor **3** : collaborator

collaborer [kɔlabɔre] *vi* : to collaborate — **collaboration** [-bɔrasjɔ̃] *nf*

collage [kɔlaʒ] *nm* : collage

collant[1], -lante [kɔlɑ̃, -lɑ̃t] *adj* **1** : sticky, tacky **2** : tight-fitting

collant[2] *nm* **1** : panty hose *pl* **2** *or* **collants** *mpl* : leotard, leggings *pl*, tights *pl* **3** *Can* : sticker

collation [kɔlasjɔ̃] *nf* : snack

collationner [kɔlasjɔne] *vt* : to collate

colle [kɔl] *nf* **1** : paste, glue **2 poser une colle** *fam* : to ask a trick question (on an exam)

collecte [kɔlɛkt] *nf* : collection

collecter [kɔlɛkte] *vt* : to collect

collecteur[1], -trice [kɔlɛktœr, -tris] *n* : collector

collecteur[2] *nm* **1** : main sewer **2** : manifold (of an automobile)

collectif, -tive [kɔlɛktif, -tiv] *adj* : collective, joint — **collectivement** [-tivmɑ̃] *adv*

collection [kɔlɛksjɔ̃] *nf* : collection

collectionner [kɔlɛksjɔne] *vt* : to collect <collectionner les timbres : to collect stamps>

collectionneur, -neuse [kɔlɛksjɔnœr, -nøz] *n* : collector

collectivité [kɔlɛktivite] *nf* : community

collège [kɔlɛʒ] *nm* **1** *France* : junior high school **2** *Can* : junior college, vocational college **3** : college <collège électoral : electoral college>

collégial, -giale [kɔleʒjal] *adj, mpl* **-giaux** [-ʒjo] : collegiate

collégien, -gienne [kɔleʒjɛ̃, -ʒjɛn] *n* **1** *France* : schoolboy *m*, schoolgirl *f* **2** *Can* CÉGÉPIEN : junior-college student

collègue [kɔlɛg] *nmf* : colleague

coller [kɔle] *vt* **1** : to stick, to glue **2** APPUYER : to press <coller son visage contre la fenêtre : to press one's face against the window> — *vi* **1** : to adhere, to cling **2 ~ à** : to stick close to — **se coller** *vr* **~ à** : to press oneself (up) against

collet [kɔlɛ] *nm* **1** : snare, noose **2** : collar, neck <être collet monté : to be prim, to be straight-laced>

colleter [kɔlte] {8} *vt* : to collar — **se colleter** *vr* **~ avec** : to fight with, to grapple with

colley [kɔlɛ] *nm* : collie

collier [kɔlje] *nm* **1** : necklace **2** : collar (of an animal, a machine, etc.) **3** *or* **collier de barbe** : short close beard

collimateur [kɔlimatœr] *nm* **avoir qqn dans le collimateur** : to have s.o. in one's sights

colline [kɔlin] *nf* : hill

collision [kɔlizjɔ̃] *nf* : collision <entrer en collision avec : to collide with>

colloque [kɔlɔk] *nm* : colloquium, symposium

collusion [kɔlyzjɔ̃] *nf* : collusion

collyre [kɔlir] *nm* : eye drops *pl*

colmater [kɔlmate] *vt* : to fill in, to seal up, to plug

colombe [kɔlɔ̃b] *nf* : dove

colombien, -bienne [kɔlɔ̃bjɛ̃, -bjɛn] *adj* : Colombian

Colombien, -bienne *n* : Colombian

colon [kɔlɔ̃] *nm* : colonist, settler

côlon [kolɔ̃] *nm* : colon

colonel [kɔlɔnɛl] *nm* : colonel

colonial[1], -niale [kɔlɔnjal] *adj, mpl* **-niaux** [-njo] : colonial — **colonialisme** [-njalism] *nm*

colonial[2], -niale *n, mpl* **-niaux** [-njo] : colonial (person)

colonie [kɔlɔni] *nf* : colony

colonisateur, -trice [kɔlɔnizatœr, -tris] *n* : colonist, settler

colonisation [kɔlɔnizasjɔ̃] *nf* : colonization

coloniser [kɔlɔnize] *vt* : to colonize, to settle

colonnade [kɔlɔnad] *nf* : colonnade

colonne [kɔlɔn] *nf* **1** : column <en colonne par quatre : four abreast> **2** : pillar, column (in architecture) **3 colonne vertébrale** : spinal column, backbone

colophane [kɔlɔfan] *nf* : rosin

colorant[1], -rante [kɔlɔrɑ̃, -rɑ̃t] *adj* : coloring

colorant[2] *nm* : dye, stain

coloration [cɔlɔrasjɔ̃] *nf* : coloring

coloré, -rée [kɔlɔre] *adj* **1** : colored **2** : colorful, lively

colorer [kɔlɔre] *vt* : to color, to tint — **se colorer** *vr* : to flush, to blush

colorier [kɔlɔrje] {96} *vt* : to color

coloris [kɔlɔri] *nm* **1** : color, shade **2** : colors *pl*, color scheme

colossal, -sale [kɔlɔsal] *adj, mpl* **-saux** [-so] ÉNORME : colossal, enormous

colosse [kɔlɔs] *nm* GÉANT : colossus, giant

colporter [kɔlpɔrte] *vt* : to hawk, to peddle

colporteur, -teuse [kɔlpɔrtœr, -tøz] *n* : peddler

coltiner [kɔltine] *vt* : to carry, to lug — **se coltiner** *vr* **1** : to lug around **2** : to get stuck with

colvert [kɔlvɛr] *nm* : mallard (duck)

colza [kɔlza] *nm* : rapeseed, rape (plant)

coma [kɔma] *nm* : coma

comateux, -teuse [kɔmatø, -tøz] *adj* : comatose

combat [kɔ̃ba] *nm* **1** : combat, fighting <combat de boxe : boxing match> **2** : conflict, struggle

combatif, -tive [kɔ̃batif, -tiv] *adj* : combative, aggressive

combattant, -tante [kɔ̃batɑ̃, -tɑ̃t] *n* : combatant, fighter
combattre [kɔ̃batr] {12} *v* : to fight
combien [kɔ̃bjɛ̃] *adv* **1** : how much, how many <combien coûte cela : how much does that cost?> <combien sont-ils? : how many (of them) are there?> **2 ~ de** : how much, how many <combien de temps : how long> <combien de livres : how many books>
combinaison [kɔ̃binɛzɔ̃] *nf* **1** : combination **2** : (full-length) slip **3** : suit, overalls <combinaison spatiale : space suit> **4** : plan, scheme
combine [kɔ̃bin] *nf fam* : scheme, trick
combiné [kɔ̃bine] *nm* : (telephone) receiver
combiner [kɔ̃bine] *vt* **1** : to combine **2** : to contrive, to work out (a plan, etc.) — **se combiner** *vr* : to combine
comble[1] [kɔ̃bl] *adj* : packed, filled up
comble[2] *nm* **1** : extreme point <le comble de la joie : the height of joy> <c'est le comble! : that takes the cake!> **2 combles** *nmpl* : attic **3 de fond en comble** : from top to bottom
combler [kɔ̃ble] *vt* **1** : to fill in, to fill up **2** : to fulfill, to satisfy
combustible[1] [kɔ̃bystibl] *adj* : combustible, inflammable
combustible[2] *nm* : fuel
combustion [kɔ̃bystjɔ̃] *nf* : combustion
comédie [kɔmedi] *nf* **1** : comedy <comédie musicale : musical> **2** : playacting, pretense
comédien, -dienne [kɔmedjɛ̃, -djɛn] *n* **1** ACTEUR : actor *m*, actress *f* **2** : comedian **3** HYPOCRITE : sham
comestible [kɔmɛstibl] *adj* : edible
comestibles *nmpl* : food
comète [kɔmɛt] *nf* : comet
comique[1] [kɔmik] *adj* **1** : comic **2** : comical, funny
comique[2] *nmf* : comedian, comic
comique[3] *nm* **1** : comedy **2** : funny thing, funny part
comité [kɔmite] *nm* : committee
commandant [kɔmɑ̃dɑ̃] *nm* **1** : commandant, commander **2** : major (in the army) **3 commandant de bord** : captain (in the navy or air force)
commande [kɔmɑ̃d] *nf* **1** : order <passer une commande : to place an order> **2 commande à distance** : remote control **3 fait sur commande** : made-to-order
commandement [kɔmɑ̃dmɑ̃] *nm* **1** ORDRE : command, order **2** AUTORITÉ : authority, control **3** : commandment (in religion)
commander [kɔmɑ̃de] *vt* **1** : to command **2** : to commission, to order (a meal, etc.) — *vi* : to be in command
commanditaire [kɔmɑ̃ditɛr] *nm* : sponsor, backer
commandite [kɔmɑ̃dit] *nf* : limited partnership
commanditer [kɔmɑ̃dite] *vt* : to finance, to back
commando [kɔmɑ̃do] *nm* : commando
comme[1] [kɔm] *adv* **1** : how <comme c'est beau! : how beautiful it is!> **2 comme de bonne** *Can* : naturally, as one might expect **3 comme du monde** *Can fam* : properly
comme[2] *conj* **1** : as, like <faites comme moi : do as I do> <blanc comme la neige : white as snow> **2** : since <comme elle se sentait malade, elle est partie : since she felt ill, she left> **3** : when, as <comme il disait au revoir, elle pleurait : as he said goodbye, she cried> **4 comme ci, comme ça** : so-so **5 comme il faut** : properly **6 comme si** : as if, as though
comme[3] *prep* **1** : like <un visage comme un masque : a face like a mask> **2** : as, in the capacity of <il travaille comme rédacteur : he works as an editor>
commémoration [kɔmemɔrasjɔ̃] *nf* : commemoration
commémorer [kɔmemɔre] *vt* : to commemorate — **commémoratif, -tive** [-mɔratif, -tiv] *adj*
commencement [kɔmɑ̃smɑ̃] *nm* **1** : beginning, start **2 au commencement** : in the beginning, at first
commencer [kɔmɑ̃se] {6} *v* : to begin, to start
comment[1] [kɔmɑ̃] *adv* **1** : how <comment ça va? : how is it going?> <je me demande comment elle va en finir : I wonder how she'll end up> **2** : what <comment! tu n'as pas d'argent? : what! you have no money?> **3** : sorry, who, what <Anne comment? : Anne who?> **4 comment donc** : of course, by all means
comment[2] *nm inv* **1 le comment** : the how **2** → **pourquoi**
commentaire [kɔmɑ̃tɛr] *nm* **1** REMARQUE : comment, remark **2** : commentary
commentateur, -trice [kɔmɑ̃tatœr, -tris] *n* : commentator
commenter [kɔmɑ̃te] *vt* : to comment on
commérage [kɔmeraʒ] *nm fam* : gossip
commerçant[1], **-çante** [kɔmɛrsɑ̃, -sɑ̃t] *adj* : commercial, shopping
commerçant[2], **-çante** *n* : merchant, storekeeper
commerce [kɔmɛrs] *nm* : business, commerce, trade <faire du commerce : to be in business> <commerce en gros : wholesale trade>
commercer [kɔmɛrse] {6} *vi* : to trade, to deal
commercial [kɔmɛrsjal] *adj, mpl* **-ciaux** [-sjo] : commercial — **commercialement** [-sjalmɑ̃] *adv*
commercialisation [kɔmɛrsjalizasjɔ̃] *nf* : marketing

commercialiser [kɔmɛrsjalize] *vt* : to market

commère [kɔmɛr] *nf fam* : gossip (person)

commettre [kɔmɛtr] {53} *vt* **1** : to commit (a crime, etc.), to make (an error) **2** : to appoint, to nominate

commis [kɔmi] *nm* **1** : clerk **2 commis voyageur** : traveling salesman

commisération [kɔmizerasjɔ̃] *nf* : commiseration

commissaire [kɔmisɛr] *nm* : superintendent, commissioner

commissaire–priseur [kɔmisɛrprizœr] *nm, pl* **commissaires–priseurs** : auctioneer

commissariat [kɔmisarja] *nm* **commissariat de police** : police station

commission [kɔmisjɔ̃] *nf* **1** : commission, committee **2** : commission, percentage **3** MESSAGE : message **4** COURSE : errand **5 commissions** *nfpl* : shopping

commissionnaire [kɔmisjɔnɛr] *nm* **1** : agent, broker **2** : messenger

commissionner [kɔmisjɔne] *vt* : to commission

commode[1] [kɔmɔd] *adj* **1** : convenient, handy, useful **2** FACILE : easy <ce n'est pas commode! : it's not easy!> **3** AIMABLE : easy to get along with

commode[2] *nf* : chest of drawers

commodément [kɔmɔdemɑ̃] *adv* : comfortably, conveniently

commodité [kɔmɔdite] *nf* : comfort, convenience

commotion [kɔmɔsjɔ̃] *nf* **1** : shock **2 commotion cérébrale** : concussion

commuer [kɔmɥe] *vt* : to commute, to reduce (a legal penalty)

commun[1], **-mune** [kɔmœ̃, -myn] *adj* **1** : common, joint **2** : mutual, shared **3** : usual, ordinary

commun[2] *nm* **1** : ordinary (one), average person or thing <le commun des lecteurs : the average reader> <hors du commun : out of the ordinary> **2 en ~** : in common, jointly

communautaire [kɔmynotɛr] *adj* : community, communal

communauté [kɔmynote] *nf* **1** : community **2** : commune

commune [kɔmyn] *nf* **1** : village, town **2** *Can* : rural area used in common

communément [kɔmynemɑ̃] *adv* : commonly, generally

communicable [kɔmynikabl] *adj* : communicable

communicatif, -tive [kɔmynikatif, -tiv] *adj* **1** : communicative, talkative **2** CONTAGIEUX : contagious, infectious

communication [kɔmynikasjɔ̃] *nf* **1** : communication, report **2** : communication(s), communicating <la communication de masse : mass media> **3 communication téléphonique** : telephone call

communier [kɔmynje] {96} *vi* **1** : to receive Communion **2 ~ avec** : to commune with

communion [kɔmynjɔ̃] *nf* **1** : Communion **2 être en communion avec** : to be in communion with, to be of the same mind as

communiqué [kɔmynike] *nm* : communiqué, press release

communiquer [kɔmynike] *vt* : to communicate, to pass on, to transmit — *vi* **~ avec** : to communicate with

communisme [kɔmynism] *nm* : communism, Communism

communiste [kɔmynist] *adj & nmf* : communist, Communist

commutateur [kɔmytatœr] *nm* : switch

commutation [kɔmytasjɔ̃] *nf* **1** : commutation (in law) **2** : switching

compact[1], **-pacte** [kɔ̃pakt] *adj* : compact, dense

compact[2] *nm* : compact disc

compacte *nf* : compact (car)

compacter [kɔ̃pakte] *vt* : to compact

compagne [kɔ̃paɲ] *nf* : (female) companion, partner

compagnie [kɔ̃paɲi] *nf* **1** : company, companionship <tenir compagnie à qqn : to keep s.o. company> **2** : company, firm <compagnie d'assurances : insurance company> **3** : company (in the military, in theater) **4 en compagnie de** : with, accompanied by

compagnon [kɔ̃paɲɔ̃] *nm* **1** CAMARADE : companion, comrade **2** : journeyman, apprentice

comparable [kɔ̃parabl] *adj* : comparable

comparaison [kɔ̃parɛzɔ̃] *nf* **1** : comparison **2** : simile

comparaître [kɔ̃parɛtr] {7} *vi* : to appear (before a court)

comparatif[1], **-tive** [kɔ̃paratif, -tiv] *adj* : comparative — **comparativement** [-tivmɑ̃] *adv*

comparatif[2] *nm* : comparative (case)

comparer [kɔ̃pare] *vt* : to compare

comparse [kɔ̃pars] *nmf* **1** : sidekick **2** FIGURANT : extra, bit player

compartiment [kɔ̃partimɑ̃] *nm* : compartment

compartimenter [kɔ̃partimɑ̃te] *vt* **1** : to partition **2** : to compartmentalize

comparution [kɔ̃parysjɔ̃] *nf* : appearance (in court)

compas [kɔ̃pa] *nms & pl* : compass

compassion [kɔ̃pasjɔ̃] *nf* : compassion

compatibilité [kɔ̃patibilite] *nf* : compatibility

compatible [kɔ̃patibl] *adj* : compatible

compatir [kɔ̃patir] *vi* **~ à** : to sympathize with

compatissant, -sante [kɔ̃patisɑ̃, -sɑ̃t] *adj* : compassionate, sympathetic

compatriote [kɔ̃patrijɔt] *nmf* : compatriot, fellow countryman, fellow countrywoman *f*

compensateur, -trice [kɔ̃pɑ̃satœr, -tris] *adj* : compensatory
compensation [kɔ̃pɑ̃sasjɔ̃] *nf* : compensation
compensatoire [kɔ̃pɑ̃satwar] *adj* : compensatory
compenser [kɔ̃pɑ̃se] *vt* : to compensate for, to make up for
compère [kɔ̃pɛr] *nm* : accomplice
compétent, -tente [kɔ̃petɑ̃, -tɑ̃t] *adj* : competent — **compétence** [-petɑ̃s] *nf*
compétiteur, -trice [kɔ̃petitœr, -tris] *n* : competitor, rival
compétitif, -tive [kɔ̃petitif, -tiv] *adj* : competitive
compétition [kɔ̃petisjɔ̃] *nf* **1** RIVALITÉ : rivalry **2** CONCOURS : competition, competitive event
compétitivité [kɔ̃petitivite] *nf* : competitiveness
compilateur, -trice [kɔ̃pilatœr] *n* : compiler
compilation [kɔ̃pilasjɔ̃] *nf* : compilation
compiler [kɔ̃pile] *vt* : to compile
complainte [kɔ̃plɛ̃t] *nf* : lament
complaire [kɔ̃plɛr] {66} *vi* **~ à** : to please — **se complaire** *vr* **1 ~ dans** : to delight in (something) **2 ~ à faire** : to delight in doing
complaisance [kɔ̃plɛzɑ̃s] *nf* **1** : obligingness, kindness **2** : complacency **3** : indulgence, leniency
complaisant, -sante [kɔ̃plɛzɑ̃, -zɑ̃t] *adj* **1** : obliging, kind **2** : complacent, smug **3** : indulgent — **complaisamment** [-zamɑ̃] *adv*
complément [kɔ̃plemɑ̃] *nm* : complement
complémentaire [kɔ̃plemɑ̃tɛr] *adj* **1** : complementary **2** ADDITIONNEL : supplementary
complet[1], **-plète** [kɔ̃plɛ, -plɛt] *adj* **1** : complete **2** PLEIN : full (of a hotel, theater, etc.)
complet[2] *nm* : suit
complètement [kɔ̃plɛtmɑ̃] *adv* **1** : completely, totally **2** : fully, thoroughly
compléter [kɔ̃plete] {87} *vt* **1** : to complete **2** : to complement, to supplement — **se compléter** *vr* : to complement one another
complexe [kɔ̃plɛks] *adj & nm* : complex
complexé, -plexée [kɔ̃plɛkse] *adj* : full of complexes, neurotic
complexité [kɔ̃plɛksite] *nf* : complexity, intricacy
complication [kɔ̃plikasjɔ̃] *nf* : complication
complice[1] [kɔ̃plis] *adj* **1** : knowing (of a look, etc.) **2** : accessory
complice[2] *nmf* : accomplice
complicité [kɔ̃plisite] *nf* : complicity
compliment [kɔ̃plimɑ̃] *nm* **1** : compliment **2 compliments** *nmpl* FÉLICITATIONS : compliments, congratulations
complimenter [kɔ̃plimɑ̃te] *vt* : to compliment, to congratulate
compliqué, -quée [kɔ̃plike] *adj* : complicated, complex
compliquer [kɔ̃plike] *vt* : to complicate — **se compliquer** *vr*
complot [kɔ̃plo] *nm* MACHINATION : plot, conspiracy
comploter [kɔ̃plɔte] *v* : to plot, to conspire
comploteur, -teuse [kɔ̃plɔtœr, -tøz] *n* : plotter, schemer
comportement [kɔ̃pɔrtəmɑ̃] *nm* **1** : behavior, conduct **2** : performance
comporter [kɔ̃pɔrte] *vt* **1** : to include **2** : to comprise, to consist of **3** : to entail (risks, etc.) — **se comporter** *vr* : to behave, to perform
composant[1], **-sante** [kɔ̃pozɑ̃, -zɑ̃t] *adj* : component, constituent
composant[2] *nm* ÉLÉMENT : component, constituent
composante *nf* : (mathematical) component, constituent
composé[1], **-sée** [kɔ̃poze] *adj* : compound
composé[2] *nm* : compound
composer [kɔ̃poze] *vt* **1** : to compose (music, writings, etc.) **2** : to constitute, to make up **3** : to dial (a number) **4** : to typeset — *vi* : to compromise — **se composer** *vr* : to be made up of
composite[1] [kɔ̃pozit] *adj* **1** : composite **2** : varied, heterogeneous
composite[2] *nm* : composite
compositeur, -trice [kɔ̃pozitœr, -tris] *n* **1** : composer **2** : typesetter
composition [kɔ̃pozisjɔ̃] *nf* **1** : composition **2** : typesetting **3 de bonne composition** : good-natured, accommodating
compost [kɔ̃pɔst] *nm* : compost
composter [kɔ̃pɔste] *vt* **1** : to compost **2** : to stamp, to validate (a ticket, etc.)
compote [kɔ̃pɔt] *nf* **1** : stewed fruit **2 compote de pommes** : apple sauce
compréhensible [kɔ̃preɑ̃sibl] *adj* : comprehensible
compréhensif, -sive [kɔ̃preɑ̃sif, -siv] *adj* **1** : comprehensive **2** : understanding
compréhension [kɔ̃preɑ̃sjɔ̃] *nf* : understanding
comprenait [kɔ̃prənɛ], *etc.* → **comprendre**
comprendre [kɔ̃prɑ̃dr] {70} *vt* **1** : to comprise, to consist of **2** : to include **3** : to understand <mal comprendre : to misunderstand> — **se comprendre** *vr* **1** : to understand each other **2** : to be understandable
comprenne [kɔ̃prɛn], *etc.* → **comprendre**
compresse [kɔ̃prɛs] *nf* : compress

compresseur [kɔ̃prɛsœr] *nm* : compressor

compression [kɔ̃prɛsjɔ̃] *nf* **1** : compression **2** : reduction

comprimé[1] [kɔ̃prime] *adj* : compressed <air comprimé : compressed air>

comprimé[2] *nm* : tablet, pill

comprimer [kɔ̃prime] *vt* **1** : to compress **2** : to reduce, to cut **3** : to repress

compris[1] [kɔ̃pri] *pp* → **comprendre**

compris[2], **-prise** [kɔ̃pri, -priz] *adj* **1** : understood **2** INCLUS : included <tout compris : inclusive, in total> <y compris : including>

compromettant, -tante [kɔ̃prɔmetɑ̃, -tɑ̃t] *adj* : compromising, incriminating

compromettre [kɔ̃prɔmɛtr] {53} *vt* **1** : to compromise, to implicate, to involve **2** : to endanger — **se compromettre** *vr* : to compromise oneself

compromis [kɔ̃prɔmi] *nm* : compromise

compromission [kɔ̃prɔmisjɔ̃] *nf* : compromising, (shady) deal

comptabiliser [kɔ̃tabilize] *vt* **1** : to count **2** : to enter into the books

comptabilité [kɔ̃tabilite] *nf* : accounting, bookkeeping

comptable[1] [kɔ̃tabl] *adj* **1** : accounting **2** : accountable

comptable[2] *nmf* : accountant, bookkeeper

comptant [kɔ̃tɑ̃] *adv & adj* **1** : cash <payer comptant : to pay cash> <500 francs comptant : 500 francs cash> **2** **au comptant** : in cash, for cash

compte [kɔ̃t] *nm* **1** : account <compte bancaire : bank account> **2 à bon compte** : cheap, cheaply **3 au bout du compte** : when all is said and done **4 compte à rebours** : countdown **5 compte rendu** : report, review **6 en fin de compte** : all things considered **7 se rendre compte de** : to notice, to realize **8 tenir compte de** : to take into account, to allow for <sans tenir compte de : irrespective of>

compte-gouttes [kɔ̃tgut] *nms & pl* : dropper

compter [kɔ̃te] *vt* **1** : to count **2** : to allow (for) **3** INCLURE : to include, to count **4** : to have **5** : to charge (for) **6** : to intend **7** : to expect — *vi* **1** : to count **2** : to matter **3 à compter de** : as from, as of **4 compter sur** : to count on

compte-rendu [kɔ̃trɑ̃dy] *nm, pl* **comptes-rendus** → **compte**

compteur[1] [kɔ̃tœr] *nm* **1** : meter **2 compteur de vitesse** : speedometer **3 compteur Geiger** : Geiger counter

compteur[2], **-teuse** [kɔ̃tœr, -tøz] *n Can* : scorer

comptoir [kɔ̃twar] *nm* **1** : counter, bar **2** : trading post **3** SUCCURSALE : branch (of a bank)

compulsion [kɔ̃pylsjɔ̃] *nf* : compulsion — **compulsif, -sive** [-pylsif, -siv] *adj*

comte, -tesse [kɔ̃t, -tɛs] *n* : count *m*, countess *f*

comté [kɔ̃te] *nm* : county

con[1], **conne** [kɔ̃, kɔn] *adj, usu vulgar* : stupid, idiotic

con[2], **conne** *n, usu vulgar* : stupid idiot, fool

concasser [kɔ̃kase] *vt* : to crush, to grind

concave [kɔ̃kav] *adj* : concave

concéder [kɔ̃sede] {87} *vt* : to concede, to grant

concentration [kɔ̃sɑ̃trasjɔ̃] *nf* : concentration

concentré[1], **-trée** [kɔ̃sɑ̃tre] *adj* **1** : concentrated, condensed **2** ATTENTIF : concentrating

concentré[2] *nm* : concentrate <concentré de tomate : tomato paste>

concentrer [kɔ̃sɑ̃tre] *vt* : to concentrate — **se concentrer** *vr*

concentrique [kɔ̃sɑ̃trik] *adj* : concentric

concept [kɔ̃sɛpt] *nm* : concept

concepteur, -trice [kɔ̃sɛptœr, -tris] *n* : designer

conception [kɔ̃sɛpsjɔ̃] *nf* : conception

concernant [kɔ̃sɛrnɑ̃] *prep* : concerning, regarding

concerner [kɔ̃sɛrne] *vt* : to concern, to affect <en ce qui me concerne : as far as I'm concerned>

concert [kɔ̃sɛr] *nm* **1** : concert **2 de ~** : together, jointly, in unison

concertation [kɔ̃sɛrtasjɔ̃] *nf* : dialogue, consultation

concerté, -tée [kɔ̃sɛrte] *adj* : concerted

concerter [kɔ̃sɛrte] *vt* : to devise, to plan (out) — **se concerter** *vr* : to consult (each other)

concerto [kɔ̃sɛrto] *nm* : concerto

concession [kɔ̃sesjɔ̃] *nf* **1** COMPROMIS : concession, compromise **2** : dealership **3** : plot (in a cemetery)

concessionnaire [kɔ̃sesjɔnɛr] *nmf* : dealer, agent

concevoir [kɔ̃səvwar] {26} *vt* **1** : to conceive (a child) **2** : to conceive of, to design, to imagine **3** : to understand — **se concevoir** *vr* **1** : to be imagined **2** : to be understandable

concierge [kɔ̃sjɛrʒ] *nmf* : concierge, superintendent

conciliant, -liante [kɔ̃siljɑ̃, -ljɑ̃t] *adj* : conciliatory

conciliateur, -trice [kɔ̃siljatœr, -tris] *adj* : conciliatory (of a person)

conciliation [kɔ̃siljasjɔ̃] *nf* **1** : conciliation **2** : reconciliation

concilier [kɔ̃silje] {96} *vt* : to reconcile — **se concilier** *vr* : to gain, to win (over)

concis, -cise [kɔ̃si, -siz] *adj* : concise

conclave [kɔ̃klav] *nm* : conclave

concluant, -cluante [kɔ̃klyɑ̃, -klyɑ̃t] *adj* : conclusive

conclure [kɔ̃klyr] {39} *vt* **1** : to conclude, to decide **2** : to conclude, to end **3** : to finish up, to settle <conclure un marché : to clinch a deal>

conclusion [kɔ̃klyzjɔ̃] *nf* : conclusion

concocter [kɔ̃kɔkte] *vt* : to concoct

conçoit [kɔ̃swa], **conçoive** [kɔ̃swav], *etc.* → **concevoir**

concombre [kɔ̃kɔ̃br] *nm* : cucumber

concomitant, -tante [kɔ̃kɔmitɑ̃, -tɑ̃t] *adj* : concomitant

concordance [kɔ̃kɔrdɑ̃s] *nf* **1** : similarity, agreement **2** : index, concordance

concordant, -dante [kɔ̃kɔrdɑ̃, -dɑ̃t] *adj* : conforming, corresponding

concorde [kɔ̃kɔrd] *nf* : concord, harmony

concorder [kɔ̃kɔrde] *vi* : to agree, to tally

concourir [kɔ̃kurir] {23} *vi* **1** : to compete **2 ~ à** : to work toward

concours [kɔ̃kur] *nm* **1** COMPÉTITION : competition, contest **2** AIDE : assistance, aid **3 concours de circonstances** : combination of circumstances

concret, -crète [kɔ̃krɛ, -krɛt] *adj* : concrete

concrètement [kɔ̃krɛtmɑ̃] *adv* : in concrete terms

concrétiser [kɔ̃kretize] *vt* : to put in concrete form, to realize

conçu [kɔ̃sy] *pp* → **concevoir**

concubin, -bine [kɔ̃kybɛ̃, -bin] *n* : common-law spouse, partner

concupiscent, -cente [kɔ̃kypisɑ̃, -sɑ̃t] *adj* : lustful

concurremment [kɔ̃kyramɑ̃] *adv* : jointly, concurrently

concurrence [kɔ̃kyrɑ̃s] *nf* **1** RIVALITÉ : competition, rivalry <concurrence déloyale : unfair competition> <faire concurrence à : to compete with> **2 jusqu'à concurrence de** : up to, not exceeding

concurrencer [kɔ̃kyrɑ̃se] {6} *vt* : to rival, to compete with

concurrent[1], **-rente** [kɔ̃kyrɑ̃, -rɑ̃t] *adj* : competing, rival

concurrent[2], **-rente** *n* : competitor

concurrentiel, -tielle [kɔ̃kyrɑ̃sjɛl] *adj* : competitive

condamnable [kɔ̃danabl] *adj* RÉPRÉHENSIBLE : reprehensible

condamnation [kɔ̃danasjɔ̃] *nf* **1** : condemnation **2** PEINE : conviction, sentence

condamné, -née [kɔ̃dane] *n* : convict

condamner [kɔ̃dane] *vt* **1** : to condemn **2** : to sentence <condamner qqn à une amende : to fine s.o.> **3** : to block up, to seal off

condensation [kɔ̃dɑ̃sasjɔ̃] *nf* : condensation

condensé [kɔ̃dɑ̃se] *nm* : digest, summary

condenser [kɔ̃dɑ̃se] *vt* : to condense — **se condenser** *vr*

condescendance [kɔ̃desɑ̃dɑ̃s] *nf* : condescension

condescendant, -dante [kɔ̃desɑ̃dɑ̃, -dɑ̃t] *adj* : condescending

condescendre [kɔ̃desɑ̃dr] {63} *vi* **~ à** : to condescend to

condiment [kɔ̃dimɑ̃] *nm* : condiment, seasoning

condisciple [kɔ̃disipl] *nmf* : schoolmate, fellow student

condition [kɔ̃disjɔ̃] *nf* **1** : condition, stipulation <sans conditions : unconditionally> <sous condition que : on the condition that> **2** FORME : condition, shape <se mettre en condition : to get in shape> **3** : social status, background, walk of life **4 conditions** *nfpl* : conditions, circumstances <conditions de vie : living conditions>

conditionné, -née [kɔ̃disjɔne] *adj* **1** : conditioned **2** : packaged <conditionné sous vide : vacuum-packed>

conditionnel, -nelle [kɔ̃disjɔnɛl] *adj* : conditional — **conditionnellement** [-nɛlmɑ̃] *adv*

conditionner [kɔ̃disjɔne] *vt* **1** : to condition **2** : to determine, to govern **3** EMBALLER : to package

condoléances [kɔ̃dɔleɑ̃s] *nfpl* : condolences

condom [kɔ̃dɔm] *nm* PRÉSERVATIF : condom

condominium [kɔ̃dɔminjɔm] *nm* : condominium

conducteur[1], **-trice** [kɔ̃dyktœr, -tris] *n* **1** : driver **2** : operator (of a machine, etc.)

conducteur[2] *nm* : conductor (of electricity)

conduction [kɔ̃dyksjɔ̃] *nf* : conduction

conductivité [kɔ̃dyktivite] *nf* : conductivity

conduire [kɔ̃dɥir] {49} *vt* **1** : to drive **2** MENER : to lead **3** DIRIGER : to run, to manage — **se conduire** *vr* : to behave

conduisait [kɔ̃dɥizɛ], **conduisions** [kɔ̃dɥizjɔ̃], *etc.* → **conduire**

conduise [kɔ̃dɥiz], *etc.* → **conduire**

conduit [kɔ̃dɥi] *nm* **1** : conduit, duct <conduit de fumée : flue> **2** : canal (in anatomy)

conduite [kɔ̃dɥit] *nf* **1** : conduct, behavior **2** : conducting, leading **3** : driving <conduite à droite : right-hand drive> **4** : pipe <conduite d'eau : water main>

cône [kon] *nm* : cone

confection [kɔ̃fɛksjɔ̃] *nf* **1** ÉLABORATION : making, preparation **2 la confection** : the clothing industry

confectionner [kɔ̃fɛksjɔne] *vt* : to make, to prepare

confédération [kɔ̃federasjɔ̃] *nf* : confederation, confederacy

confédérer [kɔ̃federe] {87} *vt* : to confederate — **se confédérer** *vr*

conférence [kɔ̃ferɑ̃s] *nf* **1** : conference <conférence de presse : press conference> **2** : lecture

conférencier, -cière [kɔ̃ferɑ̃sje, -sjɛr] *n* : lecturer

conférer [kɔ̃fere] {87} *v* : to confer

confesser [kɔ̃fese] *vt* : to confess

confession [kɔ̃fesjɔ̃] *nf* **1** : confession **2** : faith, denomination

confessionnal [kɔ̃fesjɔnal] *nm, pl* **-naux** [-no] : confessional

confessionnel, -nelle [kɔ̃fesjɔnɛl] *adj* : denominational

confetti [kɔ̃feti] *nm* : (piece of) confetti <des confettis : confetti>

confiance [kɔ̃fjɑ̃s] *nf* **1** : confidence, trust, faith <avoir confiance en : to have confidence in> <faire confiance à : to trust> **2 confiance en soi** : self-confidence **3 de confiance** : trustworthy, reliable

confiant, -fiante [kɔ̃nfjɑ̃, -fjɑ̃t] *adj* **1** : confident **2** : trusting, trustful **3** ASSURÉ : self-confident

confidence [kɔ̃fidɑ̃s] *nf* : confidence, secret <être dans la confidence : to be in the know> <faire des confidences à qqn : to confide in s.o.>

confident, -dente [kɔ̃fidɑ̃, -dɑ̃t] *n* : confidant, confidante *f*

confidentiel, -tielle [kɔ̃fidɑ̃sjɛl] *adj* SECRET : confidential, secret — **confidentiellement** [-sjɛlmɑ̃] *adv*

confier [kɔ̃fje] {96} *vt* **1 confier (qqch) à qqn** : to entrust (sth) to s.o. **2 confier à qqn** : to confide to s.o. — **se confier** *vr* **se confier à qqn** : to confide in s.o.

configuration [kɔ̃figyrasjɔ̃] *nf* : configuration

configurer [kɔ̃figyre] *vt* : to configure

confiner [kɔ̃fine] *vt* **1** : to confine **2 confiner qqn à** : to restrict s.o. to — *vi* **~ à** : to border on — **se confiner** *vr* **1** : to shut oneself away **2 ~ à** *or* **dans** : to confine oneself to

confins [kɔ̃fɛ̃] *nmpl* : borders, confines

confire [kɔ̃fir] {86} *vt* : to preserve, to candy, to pickle

confirmation [kɔ̃firmasjɔ̃] *nf* : confirmation

confirmer [kɔ̃firme] *vt* : to confirm

confiscation [kɔ̃fiskasjɔ̃] *nf* : confiscation, seizure

confiserie [kɔ̃fizri] *nf* **1** : candy store **2** : candy, confection

confisquer [kɔ̃fiske] *vt* : to confiscate

confit, -fite [kɔ̃fi, -fit] *adj* : candied, crystallized

confiture [kɔ̃fityr] *nf* : jam, preserves

conflagration [kɔ̃flagrasjɔ̃] *nf* : conflagration

conflictuel, -tuelle [kɔ̃fliktɥɛl] *adj* : conflicting

conflit [kɔ̃fli] *nm* : conflict, struggle

confluence [kɔ̃flyɑ̃s] *nf* : confluence, convergence

confluer [kɔ̃flye] *vi* : to meet, to converge

confondre [kɔ̃fɔ̃dr] {63} *vt* **1** : to confuse **2** MÉLANGER : to merge, to intermingle **3** ÉTONNER : to astound **4** DÉMASQUER : to expose — **se confondre** *vr* **1** : to merge **2 se confondre en excuses** : to apologize profusely

conforme [kɔ̃fɔrm] *adj* **1 ~ à** : corresponding to, in keeping with **2 ~ à** : true to <une copie conforme à l'original : an exact copy>

conformé, -mée [kɔ̃fɔrme] *adj* : formed, shaped <bien conformé : well-formed> <mal conformé : misshapen>

conformément [kɔ̃fɔrmemɑ̃] *adv* **~ à** : in accordance with, in compliance with

conformer [kɔ̃fɔrme] *vt* : to conform, to shape — **se conformer** *vr* **~ à** : to conform to

conformiste [kɔ̃fɔrmist] *nmf* : conformist

conformité [kɔ̃fɔrmite] *nf* **1** : conformity, conventionality **2** RESSEMBLANCE : similarity

confort [kɔ̃fɔr] *nm* **1** : comfort **2 tout confort** : with all (modern) conveniences

confortable [kɔ̃fɔrtabl] *adj* : comfortable — **confortablement** [-tabləmɑ̃] *adv*

conforter [kɔ̃fɔrte] *vt* : to strengthen, to reinforce

confrère [kɔ̃frɛr] *nm* : colleague

confrérie [kɔ̃freri] *nf* : brotherhood, association

confrontation [kɔ̃frɔ̃tasjɔ̃] *nf* **1** : confrontation **2** : comparison

confronter [kɔ̃frɔ̃te] *vt* **1** : to confront **2** : to compare

confus [kɔ̃fy] *adj* **1** : confused **2** : embarrassed <je suis vraiment confus : I'm truly sorry>

confusément [kɔ̃fyzemɑ̃] *adv* **1** : indistinctly, vaguely **2** : confusedly

confusion [kɔ̃fyzjɔ̃] *nf* **1** DÉSORDRE : confusion, disarray **2** GÊNE : embarrassment **3** MÉPRISE: confusion, mix-up

congé [kɔ̃ʒe] *nm* **1** VACANCES : vacation **2** : leave <congé de maladie : sick leave> **3** : notice <donner son congé à : give (one's) notice to> **4 prendre congé de** : to take leave of

congédier [kɔ̃ʒedje] {96} *vt* : to dismiss, to give notice to

congélateur [kɔ̃ʒelatœr] *nm* : freezer

congeler [kɔ̃ʒle] {20} *vt* : to freeze — **se congeler** *vr*

congénère [kɔ̃ʒenɛr] *nmf* : fellow creature

congénital, -tale [kɔ̃ʒenital] *adj, mpl* **-taux** [-to] : congenital

congère [kɔ̃ʒɛr] *nf France* : snowdrift, snowbank

congestion [kɔ̃ʒɛstjɔ̃] *nf* : congestion

congestionner [kɔ̃ʒɛstjɔne] *vt* **1** : to congest **2** : to make (one's face) flushed — **se congestionner** *vr* : to flush

conglomérat [kɔ̃glɔmera] *nm* : conglomerate, conglomeration

congloméré, -rée [kɔ̃glɔmere] *adj* : conglomerate

congolais, -laise [kɔ̃gɔlɛ, -lɛz] *adj* : Congolese

Congolais, -laise *n* : Congolese

congratuler [kɔ̃gratyle] *vt* : to congratulate

congrès [kɔ̃grɛ] *nm* CONFÉRENCE : congress, conference, convention

congru, -grue [kɔ̃gry] *adj* : congruent (in mathematics)

conifère[1] [kɔnifɛr] *adj* : coniferous

conifère[2] *nm* : conifer

conique [kɔnik] *adj* : conic, conical

conjecture [kɔ̃ʒɛktyr] *nf* SUPPOSITION : conjecture, guess

conjecturer [kɔ̃ʒɛktyre] *vt* PRÉSUMER : to conjecture, to presume

conjoint[1], **-jointe** [kɔ̃ʒwɛ̃, -ʒwɛ̃t] *adj* : joint, conjoint — **conjointement** [-ʒwɛ̃tmɑ̃] *adv*

conjoint[2], **-jointe** *n* ÉPOUX : spouse

conjonctif, -tive [kɔ̃ʒɔ̃ktif, -tiv] *adj* **1** : conjunctive **2** → **tissu**

conjonction [kɔ̃ʒɔ̃ksjɔ̃] *nf* : conjunction

conjonctivite [kɔ̃ʒɔ̃ktivit] *nf or* **conjonctivite aiguë contagieuse** : pinkeye

conjoncture [kɔ̃ʒɔ̃ktyr] *nf* : circumstances *pl*, situation

conjugaison [kɔ̃ʒygɛzɔ̃] *nf* **1** : conjugation **2** : combination, uniting

conjugal, -gale [kɔ̃ʒygal] *adj, mpl* **-gaux** [-go] : conjugal, marital

conjuguer [kɔ̃ʒyge] *vt* **1** : to conjugate (a verb) **2** COMBINER, UNIR : to combine, to unite — **se conjuguer** *vr*

conjuration [kɔ̃ʒyrasjɔ̃] *nf* COMPLOT : conspiracy

conjuré, -rée [kɔ̃ʒyre] *n* : conspirator

conjurer [kɔ̃ʒyre] *vt* **1** : to avert, to ward off **2** IMPLORER : to beseech, to implore — **se conjurer** *vr* : to conspire

connaissable [kɔnɛsabl] *adj* : knowable

connaissait [kɔnɛsɛ], *etc.* → **connaître**

connaissance [kɔnɛsɑ̃s] *nf* **1** : knowledge, understanding <à ma connaissance : to the best of my knowledge> <connaissance anticipée : foreknowledge> **2** : acquaintance <faire connaissance avec qqn : to meet s.o.> **3** CONSCIENCE : consciousness <avoir connaissance de : to be aware of> **4 connaissances** *nfpl* : knowledge, learning

connaisse [kɔnɛs], *etc.* → **connaître**

connaisseur[1], **-seuse** [kɔnɛsœr, -søz] *adj* : knowledgeable, expert

connaisseur[2], **-seuse** *n* : connoisseur, expert

connaître [kɔnɛtr] {7} *vt* **1** : to know <il faut connaître la vérité : we need to know the truth> <faire connaître : to make known> **2** : to be acquainted with, to know <je connais bien cette ville : I know this city well> **3** : to experience (sensation, emotion), to enjoy (success), to have (problems) — **se connaître** *vr* **1** : to know each other **2** : to know oneself **3 s'y connaître en** : to know about, to be an expert in

connecter [kɔnɛkte] *vt* : to connect

connerie [kɔnri] *nf fam* : blunder, stupid remark

connexe [kɔnɛks] *adj* : connected, related

connivence [kɔnivɑ̃s] *nf* COMPLICITÉ : connivance, complicity

connu[1] [kɔny] *pp* → **connaître**

connu[2], **-nue** [kɔny] *adj* : well-known

conque [kɔ̃k] *nf* : conch

conquérant, -rante [kɔ̃kerɑ̃, -rɑ̃t] *n* : conqueror

conquérir [kɔ̃kerir] {21} *vt* **1** : to conquer, to capture **2** : to win, to win over

conquête [kɔ̃kɛt] *nf* : conquest

conquière [kɔ̃kjɛr], **conquiert** [kɔ̃kjɛr], *etc.* → **conquérir**

conquis [kɔ̃ki] *pp* → **conquérir**

consacrer [kɔ̃sakre] *vt* **1** : to consecrate **2** : to sanction **3 ~ à** : to devote to — **se consacrer** *vr* **~ à** : to dedicate oneself to

consciemment [kɔ̃sjamɑ̃] *adv* : consciously

conscience [kɔ̃sjɑ̃s] *nf* **1** : conscience **2** : consciousness, awareness <avoir conscience de : to become aware of>

consciencieux, -cieuse [kɔ̃sjɑ̃sjø, -sjøz] *adj* : conscientious — **consciencieusement** [-sjøzmɑ̃] *adv*

conscient, -ciente [kɔ̃sjɑ̃, -sjɑ̃t] *adj* : conscious, aware

conscrit [kɔ̃skri] *nm* : conscript, draftee

consécration [kɔ̃sekrasjɔ̃] *nf* **1** : sanctioning, recognition **2** : consecration (in religion)

consécutif, -tive [kɔ̃sekytif, -tiv] *adj* : consecutive — **consécutivement** [-tivmɑ̃] *adv*

conseil [kɔ̃sɛj] *nm* **1** : counsel, (piece of) advice <donner un conseil à qqn : to give s.o. advice> <des conseils : advice> **2** : council <conseil d'administration : board of directors>

conseiller[1] [kɔ̃seje] *vt* **1** : to counsel, to give advice to **2** : to recommend, to advise

conseiller[2], **-lère** [kɔ̃seje, -jɛr] *n* **1** : counselor, advisor **2** : councillor

consensus [kɔ̃sɛ̃sys] *nm* : consensus

consentant, -tante [kɔ̃sɑ̃tɑ̃, -tɑ̃t] *adj* : consenting, willing
consentement [kɔ̃sɑ̃tmɑ̃] *nm* : consent
consentir [kɔ̃sɑ̃tir] {82} *vi* : to consent, to agree — *vt* : to grant
conséquence [kɔ̃sekɑ̃s] *nf* **1** : consequence, outcome **2 agir en conséquence** : to act accordingly
conséquent[1], -quente [kɔ̃sekɑ̃, -kɑ̃t] *adj* **1** : consistent, logical **2** *fam* : substantial, important
conséquent[2] *nm* **par ~** : consequently, therefore
conservateur[1], -trice [kɔ̃sɛrvatœr, -tris] *adj* : conservative
conservateur[2], -trice *n* **1** : conservative **2** : curator
conservation [kɔ̃sɛrvasjɔ̃] *nf* PRÉSERVATION : preservation, conservation
conservatisme [kɔ̃sɛrvatism] *nm* : conservatism
conservatoire [kɔ̃sɛrvatwar] *nm* : academy, conservatory
conserve [kɔ̃sɛrv] *nf* **1** : canned food <en conserve : canned> **2 de ~** : in concert, together
conserver [kɔ̃sɛrve] *vt* **1** GARDER : to keep **2** : to preserve, to conserve (food) — **se conserver** *vr* : to keep, to store
conserverie [kɔ̃sɛrvəri] *nf* : cannery
considérable [kɔ̃siderabl] *adj* : considerable — **considérablement** [-rabləmɑ̃] *adv*
considération [kɔ̃siderasjɔ̃] *nf* **1** : consideration <en considération de : because of, in view of> **2** : respect, consideration
considérer [kɔ̃sidere] {87} *vt* **1** : to consider <tout bien considéré : all things considered> **2** : to think highly of, to regard
consigne [kɔ̃siɲ] *nf* **1** : instructions *pl*, orders *pl* **2** : checkroom **3** : deposit
consigner [kɔ̃siɲe] *vt* **1** : to record, to write down **2** : to check (luggage, etc.) **3** : to deposit
consistance [kɔ̃sistɑ̃s] *nf* **1** : consistency <prendre consistance : to thicken> **2** : substance, strength <sans consistance : unfounded, groundless>
consistant, -tante [kɔ̃sistɑ̃, -tɑ̃t] *adj* **1** : thick (of sauce, paint, etc.) **2** : substantial, nourishing **3** : solid, well-founded (of an argument, etc.)
consister [kɔ̃siste] *vi* **1 ~ dans** *or* **~ à** : to lie in, to consist in <le bonheur consiste dans la modération : happiness lies in moderation> <son devoir consiste à partir : it is her duty to leave> **2 ~ en** : to be composed of, to consist of
consolation [kɔ̃sɔlasjɔ̃] *nf* : consolation
console [kɔ̃sɔl] *nf* : console
consoler [kɔ̃sɔle] *vt* : to console, to comfort, to soothe — **se consoler** *vr*
consolidation [kɔ̃sɔlidasjɔ̃] *nf* : consolidation
consolider [kɔ̃sɔlide] *vt* : to consolidate, to strengthen — **se consolider** *vr* : to grow stronger
consommateur, -trice [kɔ̃sɔmatœr, -tris] *n* **1** : consumer **2** : customer (in a café, etc.)
consommation [kɔ̃sɔmasjɔ̃] *nf* **1** : consumption **2** BOISSON : drink **3** : consummation (of a marriage) **4** PERPÉTRATION : perpetration (of a crime)
consommé[1], -mée [kɔ̃sɔme] *adj* : consummate
consommé[2] *nm* : consommé, clear soup
consommer [kɔ̃sɔme] *vt* **1** : to consume **2** : to consummate — *vi* : to have a drink
consonance [kɔ̃sɔnɑ̃s] *nf* : consonance (in music or poetry)
consonne [kɔ̃sɔn] *nf* : consonant
corsortium [kɔ̃sɔrsjɔm] *nm* : consortium, syndicate
conspirateur, -trice [kɔ̃spiratœr, -tris] *n* : conspirator, plotter
conspiration [kɔ̃spirasjɔ̃] *nf* : conspiracy
conspirer [kɔ̃spire] *vi* : to conspire, to plot
constant, -tante [kɔ̃stɑ̃, -tɑ̃t] *adj* **1** : constant, unchanging **2** : continual **3** : firm, steadfast — **constamment** [kɔ̃stamɑ̃] *adv*
constante [kɔ̃stɑ̃t] *nf* : constant
constat [kɔ̃sta] *nm* **1** : affidavit, official report **2** : acknowledgment
constatation [kɔ̃statasjɔ̃] *nf* OBSERVATION : observation, noticing
constater [kɔ̃state] *v* **1** : to notice, to observe **2** : to certify, to state
constellation [kɔ̃stelasjɔ̃] *nf* : constellation
consternation [kɔ̃stɛrnasjɔ̃] *nf* : consternation, dismay
consterner [kɔ̃stɛrne] *vt* : to dismay, to distress
constiper [kɔ̃stipe] *vt* : to constipate — **constipation** [-stipasjɔ̃] *nf*
constituant, -tuante [kɔ̃stitɥɑ̃, -tɥɑ̃t] *adj* : constituent
constituer [kɔ̃stitɥe] *vt* **1** : to constitute, to make up, to impanel (a jury) **2** : to set up, to form **3** : to settle (in law)
constitutif, -tive [kɔ̃stitytif, -tiv] *adj* : constituent
constitution [kɔ̃stitysjɔ̃] *nf* **1** : establishment, setting up **2** : constitution (in politics or physiology) **3** : composition, makeup
constitutionnel, -nelle [kɔ̃stitysjɔnɛl] *adj* : constitutional
constructeur, -trice [kɔ̃stryktœr, -tris] *n* **1** : builder **2** : manufacturer (of automobiles, etc.)
constructif, -tive [kɔ̃stryktif, -tiv] *adj* : constructive
construction [kɔ̃stryksjɔ̃] *nf* : building, construction

construire [kɔ̃strɥir] {49} *vt* : to construct, to build — **se construire** *vr Can* : to build <il se construit à Québec : he's building in Quebec>

consul [kɔ̃syl] *nm* : consul

consulat [kɔ̃syla] *nm* : consulate

consultant, -tante [kɔ̃syltɑ̃, -tɑ̃t] *n* : consultant

consultatif, -tive [kɔ̃syltatif, -tiv] *adj* : advisory

consultation [kɔ̃syltasjɔ̃] *nf* **1** : consulting, checking **2** : consultation (with an expert, a doctor, etc.) <heures de consultation : office hours> <aller à la consultation : to go to the doctor's> <entrer en consultation avec : to consult with> **3 consultation électorale** : election, voting

consulter [kɔ̃sylte] *vt* **1** : to consult, to seek advice from **2** : to refer to — *vi France* : to see patients — **se consulter** *vr* : to confer

consumer [kɔ̃syme] *vt* **1** : to consume **2** : to burn, to destroy — **se consumer** *vr* **1** : to burn (up, out) **2** : to waste away

contact [kɔ̃takt] *nm* **1** : contact, touch <rester en contact : to keep in touch> **2** : electrical contact, switch <couper le contact : to switch off the ignition> **3** : contact, connection (person)

contacter [kɔ̃takte] *vt* : to contact <j'ai contacté ma sœur : I got in touch with my sister>

contagion [kɔ̃taʒjɔ̃] *nf* : contagion — **contagieux, -gieuse** [-taʒjœ, -ʒjøz] *adj*

contaminer [kɔ̃tamine] *vt* **1** POLLUER : to contaminate, to pollute **2** INFECTER : to infect — **contamination** [-minasjɔ̃] *nf*

conte [kɔ̃t] *nm* **1** HISTOIRE : tale, story **2 conte de fées** : fairy tale

contempler [kɔ̃tɑ̃ple] *vt* **1** : to contemplate, to gaze at **2** : to reflect upon — **contemplation** [-tɑ̃plasjɔ̃] *nf*

contemporain, -raine [kɔ̃tɑ̃pɔrɛ̃, -rɛn] *adj & n* : contemporary

contenance [kɔ̃tnɑ̃s] *nf* **1** CAPACITÉ : capacity (of a container) **2** AIR : bearing, attitude <perdre contenance : to lose (one's) composure>

contenant [kɔ̃tnɑ̃] *nm* RÉCIPIENT : container

contenir [kɔ̃tnir] {92} *vt* **1** : to contain, to hold **2** : to restrain — **se contenir** *vr* : to control oneself

content, -tente [kɔ̃tɑ̃, -tɑ̃t] *adj* HEUREUX : content, pleased, happy

contentable [kɔ̃tɑ̃tabl] *adj* **il n'est pas contentable** *Can* : he can't be satisfied

contentement [kɔ̃tɑ̃tmɑ̃] *nm* SATISFACTION : contentment, satisfaction

contenter [kɔ̃tɑ̃te] *vt* SATISFAIRE : to satisfy, to please — **se contenter** *vr* **~ de** : to be contented with

contentieux[1], -tieuse [kɔ̃tɑ̃sjø, -sjøz] *adj* : contentious

contentieux[2] *nm* **1** : dispute **2** : legal department **3** : litigation

contenu [kɔ̃tny] *nm* : contents *pl*

conter [kɔ̃te] *vt* **1** RELATER : to tell, to relate **2 s'en laisser conter** : to be fooled, to be taken in

contestable [kɔ̃tɛstabl] *adj* : contestable, debatable

contestation [kɔ̃tɛstasjɔ̃] *nf* **1** : challenging, questioning **2** DISPUTE : dispute **3** : (political) protest

contester [kɔ̃tɛste] *vt* : to contest, to dispute — *vi* : to protest

conteur, -teuse [kɔ̃tœr, -tøz] *n* : storyteller, narrator

contexte [kɔ̃tɛkst] *nm* : context

contigu, -guë [kɔ̃tigy] *adj* : adjacent

continence [kɔ̃tinɑ̃s] *nf* : self-restraint, continence — **continent, -nente** [-tinɑ̃, -nɑ̃t] *adj*

continent [kɔ̃tinɑ̃] *nm* **1** : continent **2 le continent** : the mainland — **continental, -tale** [-nɑ̃tal] *adj, mpl* **-taux** [-to]

contingence [kɔ̃tɛ̃ʒɑ̃s] *nf* : contingency

contingent [kɔ̃tɛ̃ʒɑ̃] *nm* : contingent

continu, -nue [kɔ̃tiny] *adj* : continuous, ongoing

continuation [kɔ̃tinɥasjɔ̃] *nf* **1** : continuation **2 bonne continuation!** : carry on!

continuel, -nuelle [kɔ̃tinɥɛl] *adj* **1** : continuous **2** : continual, constant — **continuellement** [kɔ̃tinɥɛlmɑ̃] *adv*

continuer [kɔ̃tinɥe] **1** : to continue, to keep up **2** PROLONGER : to extend — *vi* : to continue, to carry on — **se continuer** *vr*

continuité [kɔ̃tinɥite] *nf* : continuity

contorsion [kɔ̃tɔrsjɔ̃] *nf* : contortion, twisting

contorsionner [kɔ̃tɔrsjɔne] *v* **se contorsionner** *vr* : to contort oneself, to writhe

contour [kɔ̃tur] *nm* : contour, outline

contourner [kɔ̃turne] *vt* **1** : to skirt, to bypass **2** : to get around (a difficulty, a law, etc.)

contraceptif[1], -tive [kɔ̃trasɛptif, -tiv] *adj* : contraceptive

contraceptif[2] *nm* : contraceptive

contraception [kɔ̃trasɛpsjɔ̃] *nf* : contraception

contracter [kɔ̃trakte] *vt* **1** : to contract, to tense **2** : to incur (a debt) **3** : to contract, to catch (a cold, etc.) **4** : to shorten, to contract (a word)

contracteur, -teuse [kɔ̃traktœr, -tøz] *nm Can* : contractor

contraction [kɔ̃traksjɔ̃] *nf* **1** CRISPATION : contraction, tensing **2** : contraction, shortening (of a word) **3 contraction de texte** : summary, précis

contractuel, -tuelle [kɔ̃traktɥɛl] *adj* : contractual — **contractuellement** [-tɥɛlmɑ̃] *adv*

contradiction [kɔ̃tradiksjɔ̃] *nf* : contradiction

contradictoire [kɔ̃tradiktwar] *adj* : conflicting, contradictory

contraignait [kɔ̃trɛɲɛ], **contraignions** [kɔ̃trɛɲɔ̃], *etc.* → **contraindre**

contraigne, *etc.* → **contraindre**

contraindre [kɔ̃trɛ̃dr] {65} *vt* **1** : to compel, to constrain <elle l'a contraint à agir : she compelled him to act> <j'étais contraint de parler : I was forced to speak> **2** : to restrain — **se contraindre** *vr*

contraint, -trainte [kɔ̃trɛ̃, -trɛ̃t] *adj* **1** : strained, forced **2 contraint et forcé** : under duress

contrainte *nf* **1** : constraint, restraint <sans contrainte : freely> **2** : pressure, coercion

contraire [kɔ̃trɛr] *adj & nm* : contrary, opposite <au contraire : on the contrary>

contrairement [kɔ̃trɛrmɑ̃] *adv* **~ à** : contrary to

contralto[1] [kɔ̃tralto] *nmf* : alto, contralto (singer)

contralto[2] *nm* : alto, contralto (voice)

contrariant, -riante [kɔ̃trarjɑ̃, -rjɑ̃t] *adj* **1** : contrary, balky **2** : annoying

contrarier [kɔ̃trarje] {96} *vt* **1** : to annoy, to vex **2** : to thwart

contrariété [kɔ̃trarjete] *nf* : annoyance, vexation

contraste [kɔ̃trast] *nm* : contrast

contraster [kɔ̃traste] *v* : to contrast

contrat [kɔ̃tra] *nm* **1** : contract, agreement **2 passer un contrat avec** : to enter into a contract with

contravention [kɔ̃travɑ̃sjɔ̃] *nf* **1** : infraction **2** : ticket, violation notice

contre[1] [kɔ̃tr] *adv* : being against <je m'appuyais contre : I was leaning against it> <parler contre : to speak in opposition>

contre[2] *nm* **1** : opposition <le pour et le contre : the pros and cons> **2** : counterattack (in sports) **3 par contre** : on the other hand

contre[3] *prep* **1** : against <contre le mur : against the wall> <contre la guerre : against the war> **2** : (in exchange) for <envoi contre remboursement : cash on delivery> **3** : (in proportion) to <trois contre un : three to one> **4** : from <se protéger contre le danger : to protect oneself from danger> **5** : in spite of

contre-amiral [kɔ̃tramiral] *nm, pl* **-raux** [-ro] : rear admiral

contre-attaque [kɔ̃tratak] *nf, pl* **-attaques** : counterattack — **contre-attaquer** [kɔ̃tratake] *vi*

contrebalancer [kɔ̃trəbalɑ̃se] {6} *vt* : to counterbalance, to offset — **se contrebalancer** *vr* **1** : to offset each other **2** *fam* : not to give a damn <je m'en contrebalance : I couldn't care less>

contrebande [kɔ̃trəbɑ̃d] *nf* **1** : smuggling **2** : contraband, smuggled goods

contrebandier, -dière [kɔ̃trəbɑ̃dje, -djɛr] *n* : smuggler

contrebas [kɔ̃trəba] **en contrebas** : (down) below

contrebasse [kɔ̃trəbas] *nf* : double bass

contrecarrer [kɔ̃trəkare] *vt* : to thwart

contrecœur [kɔ̃trəkœr] **à ~** : unwillingly, grudgingly

contrecoup [kɔ̃trəku] *nm* : repercussion, consequence

contre-courant [kɔ̃trəkurɑ̃] *nm, pl* **-courants 1** : countercurrent **2 à ~** : upstream, against the current

contredire [kɔ̃trədir] {29} *vt* : to contradict — **se contredire** *vr*

contredit [kɔ̃trədi] **sans ~** : indisputably, without question

contrée [kɔ̃tre] *nf* : country, land, region

contre-espionnage [kɔ̃trɛspjɔnaʒ] *nm* : counterespionage

contrefaçon [kɔ̃trəfasɔ̃] *nf* **1** : counterfeiting **2** : forgery

contrefaire [kɔ̃trəfɛr] {42} *vt* **1** : to imitate, to mimic **2** : to counterfeit **3** : to disguise (one's voice, etc.)

contrefait, -faite [kɔ̃trəfɛ, -fɛt] *adj* **1** : counterfeit, forged **2** DIFFORME : deformed

contrefort [kɔ̃trəfɔr] *nm* **1** : buttress, abutment **2 contreforts** *nmpl* : foothills

contre-indiqué, -quée [kɔ̃trɛ̃dike] *adj* : inadvisable, unwise

contre-interrogatoire [kɔ̃trɛ̃terɔgatwar] *nm, pl* **-toires** : cross-examination

contremaître, -maîtresse [kɔ̃trəmɛtr, -mɛtrɛs] *n* : foreman *m*, forewoman *f*

contrepartie [kɔ̃trəparti] *nf* **1** : compensation <en contrepartie : in compensation, in return> **2** : opposing view

contre-performance [kɔ̃trəpɛrfɔrmɑ̃s] *nf, pl* **-mances** : poor performance

contre-pied [kɔ̃trəpje] *nm, pl* **-pieds 1** : opposite opinion **2 prendre qqn à contre-pied** : to catch s.o. off balance

contre-plaqué [kɔ̃trəplake] *nm, pl* **-plaqués** : plywood

contrepoids [kɔ̃trəpwa] *nm* : counterweight, counterbalance

contrepoint [kɔ̃trəpwɛ̃] *nm* : counterpoint

contrepoison [kɔ̃trəpwazɔ̃] *nm* : antidote

contrer [kɔ̃tre] *vt* : to counter, to block

contre-révolution [kɔ̃trərevɔlysjɔ̃] *nf* : counterrevolution — **contre-révolutionnaire** [-sjɔnɛr] *adj & nmf*

contresens [kɔ̃trəsɑ̃s] *nm* **1** : misinterpretation, mistranslation **2 à ~** : the wrong way, in the opposite direction

contresigner [kɔ̃trəsiɲe] *vt* : to countersign
contretemps [kɔ̃trətɑ̃] *nm* **1** : mishap, hitch **2** : offbeat (in music) **3 à ~** : inopportunely
contre–torpilleur [kɔ̃trətɔrpijœr] *nm* : destroyer (ship)
contrevenant[1], **-nante** [kɔ̃trəvnɑ̃, -vnɑ̃t] *adj* : contravening, offending
contrevenant[2], **-nante** *n* : offender, lawbreaker
contrevenir [kɔ̃trəvnir] {92} *vi* **~ à** : to contravene, to infringe
contrevent [kɔ̃trəvɑ̃] *nm* : window shutter
contribuable [kɔ̃tribɥabl] *nmf* : taxpayer
contribuer [kɔ̃tribɥe] *vi* : to contribute
contribution [kɔ̃tribysjɔ̃] *nf* **1** : contribution **2 contributions** *nfpl* IMPÔTS : taxes, taxation
contrit, -trite [kɔ̃tri, -trit] *adj* : contrite
contrôle [kɔ̃trol] *nm* **1** : control <contrôle des naissances : birth control> <contrôle de soi-même : self-control> **2** : checking, monitoring, auditing <contrôle de sécurité : security check>
contrôler [kɔ̃trole] *vt* **1** : to control **2** : to check, to inspect **3** SUPERVISER : to supervise, to monitor
contrôleur, -leuse [kɔ̃trolœr, -løz] *n* **1** : inspector, assessor **2** : controller <contrôleur aérien : air-traffic controller>
controverse [kɔ̃trɔvɛrs] *nf* : controversy
controversé, -sée [kɔ̃trɔvɛrse] *adj* : controversial
contusion [kɔ̃tyzjɔ̃] *nf* : contusion, bruise
convaincant, -cante [kɔ̃vɛ̃kɑ̃, -kɑ̃t] *adj* : persuasive, convincing
convaincre [kɔ̃vɛ̃kr] {94} *vt* **1** PERSUADER : to convince, to persuade **2** : to convict
convalescence [kɔ̃valesɑ̃s] *nf* : convalescence
convalescent, -cente [kɔ̃valesɑ̃, -sɑ̃t] *adj & n* : convalescent
convenable [kɔ̃vnabl] *adj* **1** APPROPRIÉ : suitable, appropriate **2** ACCEPTABLE : acceptable, adequate **3** : proper, decent — **convenablement** [-vnabləmɑ̃] *adv*
convenance [kɔ̃vnɑ̃s] *nf* **1** : suitability **2 convenances** *nfpl* : conventions, proprieties
convenir [kɔ̃vnir] {92} *vt* : to agree, to admit <je conviens que j'ai eu tort : I admit that I was wrong> — *vi* **1 ~ à** : to suit, to fit **2 ~ de** : to acknowledge, to admit — *v impers* **il convient de** : it is advisable to <il convient de partir maintenant : we should leave now>
convention [kɔ̃vɑ̃sjɔ̃] *nf* **1** : convention, norm <de convention : conventional> **2** : agreement <convention collective : collective (labor) agreement> **3** : (political) convention
conventionnel, -nelle [kɔ̃vɑ̃sjɔnɛl] *adj* : conventional — **conventionnellement** [-nɛlmɑ̃] *adv*
convenu, -nue [kɔ̃vny] *adj* **1** : agreed **2** : conventional
converger [kɔ̃vɛrʒe] {17} *vi* **1** : to converge **2** : to meet, to agree <nos avis convergent : our opinions tend in the same direction>
conversation [kɔ̃vɛrsasjɔ̃] *nf* : conversation, talk
converser [kɔ̃vɛrse] *vi* : to converse, to talk
conversion [kɔ̃vɛrsjɔ̃] *nf* : conversion
convertible [kɔ̃vɛrtibl] *adj* : convertible
converti, -tie [kɔ̃vɛrti] *n* : convert (to a religion)
convertir [kɔ̃vɛrtir] *vt* **1** : to convert **2 ~ en** : to transform into — **se convertir** *vr*
convertisseur [kɔ̃vɛrtisœr] *nm* : converter
convexe [kɔ̃vɛks] *adj* : convex
conviction [kɔ̃viksjɔ̃] *nf* CERTITUDE : conviction
convier [kɔ̃vje] {96} *vt* **1** INVITER : to invite **2** : to urge
convive [kɔ̃viv] *nmf* : guest (at a meal)
convivial, -viale [kɔ̃vivjal] *adj, mpl* **-viaux** [-vjo] **1** : convivial **2** : user-friendly — **convivialité** [-vjalite] *nf*
convocation [kɔ̃vɔkasjɔ̃] *nf* **1** : inviting, summoning **2** : notification (to attend), summons
convoi [kɔ̃vwa] *nm* **1** : convoy **2** *or* **convoi funèbre** : funeral procession
convoiter [kɔ̃vwate] *vt* : to covet
convoitise [kɔ̃vwatiz] *nf* **1** : covetousness, greed **2** : lust
convoluté, -tée [kɔ̃vɔlyte] *adj* : coiled, convoluted
convoquer [kɔ̃vɔke] *vt* **1** : to convoke, to convene **2** : to summon
convoyer [kɔ̃vwaje] {58} *vt* : to escort
convoyeur [kɔ̃vwajœr] *nm* **1** : convoy, escort (ship) **2** : conveyor
convulser [kɔ̃vylse] *vt* : to convulse, to distort (one's face, etc.)
convulsif, -sive [kɔvylsif, -siv] *adj* : convulsive
convulsion [kɔ̃vylsjɔ̃] *nf* : convulsion
coopératif, -tive [kɔɔperatif, -tiv] *adj* : cooperative
coopérative *nf* : cooperative
coopérer [kɔɔpere] {87} *vi* : to cooperate — **coopération** [-perasjɔ̃] *nf*
coopter [kɔɔpte] *vt* : to co-opt
coordination [kɔɔrdinasjɔ̃] *nf* : coordination
coordonnateur[1], **-trice** [kɔɔrdɔnatœr, -tris] *adj* : coordinating
coordonnateur[2], **-trice** *n* : coordinator
coordonné, -née [kɔɔrdɔne] *adj* **1** : coordinated **2** : coordinate <prop-

osition coordonnée : coordinate clause>

coordonnées [kɔɔrdɔne] *nfpl* **1** : (mathematical) coordinates *pl* **2** *fam* : address and telephone number

coordonner [kɔɔrdɔne] *vt* : to coordinate

copain, -pine [kɔpɛ̃, -pin] *n* **1** : friend, pal, buddy **2** *or* **petit copain, petite copine** : boyfriend *m*, girlfriend *f*

copeau [kɔpo] *nm* : chip, flake (of wood, metal, etc.)

copie [kɔpi] *nf* **1** : copy, duplicate **2** IMITATION : imitation **3** : manuscript, printer's copy **4** : paper, schoolwork

copier [kɔpje] {96} *vt* **1** : to copy, to transcribe **2** REPRODUIRE : to reproduce **3** : to copy (s.o.'s schoolwork)

copieux, -pieuse [kɔpjø, -pjøz] *adj* : copious — **copieusement** [-pjøzmɑ̃] *adv*

copilote [kɔpilɔt] *nmf* : copilot

copine → **copain**

copiste [kɔpist] *nmf* : copyist

copropriété [kɔprɔprijete] *nf* : joint ownership

copuler [kɔpyle] *vi* : to copulate — **copulation** [-pylasjɔ̃] *nf*

copyright [kɔpirajt] *nm* : copyright

coq [kɔk] *nm* : rooster

coq–à–l'âne [kɔkalan] *nm, pl* **coqs–à–l'âne** : abrupt change of subject

coq–l'oeil[1] [kɔklœj] *adj Can* **1** : one-eyed **2** : cross-eyed

coq–l'oeil[2] *nmf Can* **1** : one-eyed person **2** : cross-eyed person

coque [kɔk] *nf* **1** : cockle **2** : shell (of a nut) **3** : bow, loop, curl (of hair) **4** : hull (of a boat) **5** **œuf à la coque** : soft-boiled egg

coquelicot [kɔkliko] *nm* : poppy

coqueluche [kɔklyʃ] *nf* **1** : whooping cough **2** *fam* : idol (in entertainment, sports, etc.)

coquerelle [kɔkrɛl] *nf Can* : cockroach

coquet, -quette [kɔke, -kɛt] *adj* **1** : stylish **2** : charming, pretty **3** *fam* : considerable <une coquette somme : a substantial sum>

coquette *nf* : coquette, flirt

coquetterie [kɔkɛtri] *nf* **1** : affectation **2** : flirtatiousness **3** : clothes-consciousness, stylishness

coquillage [kɔkijaʒ] *nm* **1** : shellfish **2** COQUILLE : shell

coquille [kɔkij] *nf* **1** : shell <coquille de noix : nutshell> **2** FAUTE : misprint **3** **coquille Saint–Jacques** : scallop

coquin[1], **-quine** [kɔkɛ̃, -kin] *adj* ESPIÈGLE : mischievous, naughty

coquin[2], **-quine** *n* : little rascal, scamp

cor [kɔr] *nm* **1** : horn <cor anglais : English horn> **2** : corn (on one's foot)

corail [kɔraj] *nm, pl* **coraux** [kɔro] : coral

Coran [kɔrɑ̃] *nm* **le Coran** : the Koran

corbeau [kɔrbo] *nm, pl* **corbeaux** **1** : crow **2** *or* **grand corbeau** : raven

corbeille [kɔrbɛj] *nf* **1** : basket <corbeille à papier : wastepaper basket> **2** **corbeille de mariage** : wedding presents *pl*

corbillard [kɔrbijar] *nm* : hearse

cordage [kɔrdaʒ] *nm* **1** : rope **2** **cordages** *nmpl* : rigging

corde [kɔrd] *nf* **1** : rope, cord <corde raide : tightrope> **2** : string <instrument à cordes : stringed instrument> **3** **corde dorsal** : spinal cord **4** **cordes vocales** : vocal cords **5** **usé jusqu'à la corde** : threadbare

cordée [kɔrde] *nf* **1** : cord (of wood) **2** : roped party (of climbers)

cordial[1], **-diale** [kɔrdjal] *adj, mpl* **-diaux** [-djo] : cordial — **cordialement** [-djalmɑ̃] *adv*

cordial[2] *nm, pl* **cordiaux** : cordial

cordialité [kɔrdjalite] *nf* : cordiality, geniality

cordon [kɔrdɔ̃] *nm* **1** : cord, string, lace <cordon ombilical : umbilical cord> <cordon de soulier : shoelace> **2** : cordon (of police, etc.)

cordon–bleu [kɔrdɔ̃blø] *nm, pl* **cordons–bleus** : cordon-bleu chef

cordonnerie [kɔrdɔnri] *nf* **1** : cobbler's shop **2** : shoemaking, shoe repair

cordonnier, -nière [kɔrdɔnje, -njɛr] *n* : shoemaker, cobbler

coréen[1], **-réenne** [kɔreɛ̃, -reɛn] *adj* : Korean

coréen[2] *nm* : Korean (language)

Coréen, -réenne *n* : Korean

coriace [kɔrjas] *adj* DUR : tough

coriandre [kɔrjɑ̃dr] *nf* : coriander

cormoran [kɔrmɔrɑ̃] *nm* : cormorant

corne [kɔrn] *nf* **1** : antler, horn **2** : horny substance, tortoiseshell **3** : callus **4** : horn (instrument) <corne de brume : foghorn> **5** **corne d'abondance** : cornucopia, horn of plenty

corned–beef [kɔrnbif] *nms & pl* : corned beef

cornée [kɔrne] *nf* : cornea

corneille [kɔrnɛj] *nf* : crow, rook

cornemuse [kɔrnəmyz] *nf* : bagpipes *pl*

corner [kɔrne] *vt* : to turn down (the corner of a page) — *vi* KLAXONNER : to honk, to toot

cornet [kɔrnɛ] *nm* **1** : cone <cornet de crème glacée : ice-cream cone> **2** **cornet à pistons** : cornet

corniche [kɔrniʃ] *nf* **1** : cornice **2** : ledge, cliff road

cornichon [kɔrniʃɔ̃] *nm* **1** : gherkin **2** *fam* : idiot, dope

cornouiller [kɔrnuje] *nm* : dogwood

cornu, -nue [kɔrny] *adj* : horned

corollaire [kɔrɔlɛr] *nm* : corollary

corolle [kɔrɔl] *nf* : corolla

coronaire [kɔrɔnɛr] *adj* : coronary <artère coronaire : coronary artery>

coroner [kɔrɔnɛr] *nm* : coroner

corporatif, -tive [kɔrpɔratif, -tiv] *adj* : corporate

corporation [kɔrpɔrasjɔ̃] *nf* : corporation

corporel, -relle [kɔrpɔrɛl] *adj* : bodily, corporeal

corps [kɔr] *nm* **1** : body <corps à corps : hand to hand> **2** : corps (in the army, etc.), professional body <corps médical : medical profession> **3** : substance, body <corps étranger : foreign body> <prendre corps : to take shape> **4** *Can* : undershirt **5 à corps perdu** : headlong, with all one's might **6 à son corps défendant** : unwillingly, despite oneself **7 corps à corps** : hand-to-hand combat, clinch (in boxing)

corpulence [kɔrpylɑ̃s] *nf* : corpulence, stoutness — **corpulent, -lente** [kɔrpylɑ̃, -lɑ̃t] *adj*

corpuscule [kɔrpyskyl] *nm* : corpuscle

correct, -recte [kɔrɛkt] *adj* : correct — **correctement** [-rɛktəmɑ̃] *adv*

correcteur[1], -trice [kɔrɛktœr, -tris] *adj* : corrective

correcteur[2], -trice *n* **1** : corrector, grader **2** : proofreader

correctif, -tive [kɔrɛktif, -tiv] *adj* : corrective

correction [kɔrɛksjɔ̃] *nf* **1** : correction **2** : grading, marking **3** : thrashing, punishment **4** : correctness **5** : proofreading

correctionnel, -nelle [kɔrɛksjɔnɛl] *adj* : correctional

corrélation [kɔrelasjɔ̃] *nf* **1** : correlation **2 mettre en corrélation** : to interrelate

correspondance [kɔrɛspɔ̃dɑ̃s] *nf* **1** : correspondence **2** : connection (of a plane, bus, etc.)

correspondant, -dante [kɔrɛspɔ̃dɑ̃, -dɑ̃t] *n* **1** : correspondent, letter writer **2** : person being called (on the telephone) **3** : press correspondent

correspondre [kɔrɛspɔ̃dr] {63} *vi* **1** : to correspond, to write <elle correspond avec lui : she writes to him> **2** : to communicate (by telephone, etc.) **3 ~ à** : to correspond to, to match

corrida [kɔrida] *nf* : bullfight

corridor [kɔridɔr] *nm* : corridor, passageway

corrigé [kɔriʒe] *nm* : correct version

corriger [kɔriʒe] {17} *vt* **1** : to correct, to mark, to proofread **2** : to alleviate, to remedy **3** : to thrash — **se corriger** *vr* **~ de** : to cure oneself of

corroborer [kɔrɔbɔre] *vt* : to corroborate — **corroboration** [-bɔrasjɔ̃] *nf*

corroder [kɔrɔde] *vt* : to corrode

corrompre [kɔrɔ̃pr] {77} *vt* **1** PERVERTIR : to corrupt **2** SOUDOYER : to bribe

corrompu, -pue [kɔrɔ̃py] *adj* : corrupt

corrosif, -sive [kɔrɔzif, -ziv] *adj* : corrosive

corrosion [kɔrɔzjɔ̃] *nf* : corrosion

corruption [kɔrypsjɔ̃] *nf* **1** : corruption **2** : bribery

corsage [kɔrsaʒ] *nm* **1** CHEMISIER : blouse **2** : bodice (of a dress)

corsaire [kɔrsɛr] *nm* : privateer

corse [kɔrs] *adj* : Corsican

Corse *nmf* : Corsican

corsé, -sée [kɔrse] *adj* **1** ÉPICÉ : spicy **2** DIFFICILE : tough, tricky **3** : full-bodied (of wine), strong (of coffee, etc.)

corser [kɔrse] *vt* **1** : to add spice to **2** : to aggravate <pour corser l'affaire : to complicate matters> **3** : to liven up **4** : to spike (a drink) — **se corser** *vr* : to get more complicated <l'affaire se corse : the plot thickens>

corset [kɔrsɛ] *nm* : corset

cortège [kɔrtɛʒ] *nm* : procession, cortege

cortex [kɔrtɛks] *nm* : cortex

cortisone [kɔrtizɔn] *nf* : cortisone

corvée [kɔrve] *nf* **1** : chore **2** : duty (in the military)

cosignataire [kɔsiɲatɛr] *nmf* : cosigner, cosignatory

cosigner [kɔsiɲe] *vt* : to cosign

cosmétique [kɔsmetik] *adj* : cosmetic

cosmétiques *nmpl* : cosmetics, beauty products

cosmique [kɔsmik] *adj* : cosmic

cosmonaute [kɔsmɔnot] *nmf* : cosmonaut

cosmopolite [kɔsmɔpɔlit] *adj* : cosmopolitan

cosmos [kɔsmos] *nm* : cosmos

cosse [kɔs] *nf* : pod, husk

cossins [kɔsɛ̃] *nmpl Can fam* : things, stuff <ramasse tes cossins : pick up your things>

cossu, -sue [kɔsy] *adj* **1** : well-to-do, affluent **2** : opulent, posh

costaricain, -caine [kɔstarikɛ̃, -kɛn] *adj* : Costa Rican

Costaricain, -caine *n* : Costa Rican

costaud, -taude [kɔsto, -tod] *adj fam* : strong, sturdy, robust

costume [kɔstym] *nm* **1** : suit **2** : costume, dress

costumer [kɔstyme] *vt* : to dress up — **se costumer** *vr* **~ en** : to get dressed up as

cotation [kɔtasjɔ̃] *nf* : quotation (in finance)

cote [kɔt] *nf* **1** : quotation, quoted value **2** : rating, standing <cote de popularité : popularity rating> **3** : odds **4** : dimension (in construction) **5** : height <cote d'alerte : flood level> **6** : call number (of a library book)

côte [kot] *nf* **1** : coast, shore **2** : rib **3** : side <côte à côte : side by side> **4** : chop, cutlet **5** : hill, slope

côté [kote] *nm* **1** : side <se coucher sur le côté : to lie on one's side> **2** ASPECT : aspect, point of view <d'un autre côté : on the other hand> <de mon côté : for my part> **3** : way,

direction <de quel côté? : which way?> **4 à ~** : nearby **5 à côté de** : next to **6 de côté** : sideways, sidelong **7 de ~** : aside, to one side <mettre de côté : to put aside> **8 du côté de** : toward <allons du côté de la plage : let's head for the beach>
coteau [kɔto] *nm, pl* **coteaux 1** PENTE, VERSANT : slope, hillside **2** COLLINE : hill
côtelé, -lée [kotle] *adj* **1** : ribbed **2 velours côtelé** : corduroy
côtelette [kotlɛt] *nf* : chop
coter [kɔte] *vt* **1** : to classify (books) **2** : to quote, to value (in finance)
coterie [kɔtri] *nf* : clique, set (of cronies)
côteux, -teuse [kotø, -tøz] *adj Can* : hilly
côtier, -tière [kotje, -tjɛr] *adj* : coastal
cotisation [kɔtizasjɔ̃] *nf* : dues *pl*, fee
cotiser [kɔtize] *vi* **1** : to subscribe, to pay one's dues **2** : to contribute (to a fund)
coton [kɔtɔ̃] *nm* : cotton
cotonnade [kɔtɔnad] *nf* : cotton fabric
cotonneux, -neuse [kɔtɔnø, -nøz] *adj* : fleecy, fluffy
côtoyer [kotwaje] {58} *vt* **1** : to skirt, to run alongside **2** : to be close to, to mix with
cotre [kɔtr] *nm* : cutter (boat)
cottage [kɔtaʒ] *nm* **1** *France* : cottage **2 → fromage**
cotte [kɔt] *nf* **1** *France* : overalls *pl* **2 cotte de mailles** : coat of mail
cou [ku] *nm* : neck
couard[1], couarde [kwar, kward] *adj* POLTRON : cowardly
couard[2], couarde *n* : coward
couardise [kwardiz] *nf* : cowardice
couchage [kuʃaʒ] *nm* **1** : bed, sleeping arrangements **2 → sac**
couchant[1], -chante [kuʃɑ̃, -ʃɑ̃t] *adj* : setting <le soleil couchant : the setting sun>
couchant[2] *nm* **1** : sunset **2** : west
couche [kuʃ] *nf* **1** : layer, stratum <couche d'ozone : ozone layer> <couche sociale : social stratum> **2** : coat (of paint) **3** : diaper **4 couches** *nfpl* : childbirth **5 → faux**
coucher[1] [kuʃe] *vt* **1** : to put up, to provide a bed for **2** : to put to bed **3** : to lay down flat, to flatten **4** : to put in writing — *vi* **1** : to sleep, to spend the night **2 ~ avec** : to sleep with — **se coucher** *vr* : to lie down, to go to bed
coucher[2] *nm* **1** : bedtime **2 coucher du soleil** : sunset
couchette [kuʃɛt] *nf* **1** : cot (for a child) **2** : berth, bunk (in a train or ship)
coucou [kuku] *nm* **1** : cuckoo <coucou terrestre : roadrunner> **2** : cuckoo clock **3** : cowslip
coude [kud] *nm* **1** : elbow **2** : bend, angle **3 coude à coude** : side by side, shoulder to shoulder
coudée [kude] *nf* **avoir les coudées franches** : to have elbow room
cou-de-pied [kudpje] *nm, pl* **cous-de-pied** : instep
coudon [kudɔ̃] *interj Can fam* : come on! <coudon, que'est-ce qu'ils font? : what on earth are they doing?>
coudoyer [kudwaje] {58} *vt* : to rub shoulders with
coudre [kudr] {22} *v* : to sew
coudrier [kudrije] *nm* : hazel (tree)
couenne [kwan] *nf* **1** : pork rind **2 avoir la couenne dure** *Can* : to be resilient, to be hard-shelled
couette [kwɛt] *nf* **1** : comforter, duvet **2 couettes** *nfpl* : pigtails
couguar [kug(w)ar] *nm* PUMA : cougar, puma
couinement [kwinmɑ̃] *nm* : squeaking, squealing
couiner [kwine] *vt* : to squeak, to squeal
coulant[1], -lante [kulɑ̃, -lɑ̃t] *adj* **1** : flowing (of style, etc.) **2** : runny <fromage coulant : runny cheese> **3** : easygoing
coulant[2] *nm* : runner (of a plant)
coulée [kule] *nf* **1** : flow, slide <coulée de lave : lava flow> **2** : casting (of metal) **3** *Can* : ravine, gully
couler [kule] *vt* **1** : to sink (a ship) **2** : to pour, to cast **3** : to ruin, to cause to fail **4** : to spend, to pass (time) — *vi* **1** : to flow, to run **2** : to slide, to slip **3** : to leak **4** : to sink — **se couler** *vr* **1 ~ dans** : to slip into **2 se la couler douce** *fam* : to have an easy time of it
couleur [kulœr] *nf* **1** : color **2** : suit (of cards)
couleuvre [kulœvr] *nf* : grass snake
coulisse [kulis] *nf* **1** : groove, slot **2** : slide (of a trombone) **3** *Can* : trickle, drip (of paint, sap, water, etc.) **4 coulisses** *nfpl* : backstage, wings (in a theater)
coulisser [kulise] *vi* : to slide, to run (in a groove)
couloir [kulwar] *nm* **1** : corridor, passage **2** : lane (in sports or transportation) **3** : gully
coup [ku] *nm* **1** : knock, blow <coup de pied : kick> <coup de poing : punch> **2** : shock <ça lui a donné un coup : that gave him a shock> **3** : shot <coup de feu : gunshot> **4** : movement <un coup d'œil : a glance> **5** : stroke, shot (in sports) <coup droit : forehand (drive)> **6** : action, effect <coup de soleil : sunburn> <coup de téléphone : telephone call> <coup de foudre : love at first sight> **7** : (political) coup <coup d'État : coup d'état> **8 à coup sûr** : definitely, for sure **9 après coup** : afterwards **10 coups et blessures** : assault and battery **11 coup sûr** *Can* : base hit **12 coup sur coup** : one af-

ter another **13 du coup** : as a result **14 tout à coup** : suddenly
coupable[1] [kupabl] *adj* : guilty
coupable[2] *nmf* : culprit
coupant, -pante [kupɑ̃, -pɑ̃t] *adj* **1** : sharp **2** TRANCHANT : cutting, curt (of a remark, etc.)
coupe [kup] *nf* **1** : goblet, fruit dish **2** : cup (in sports) **3** : cut, cutting <coupe (de cheveux) : haircut> **4** : section (in biology)
coupé [kupe] *nm* : coupé, coupe
coupe–circuit [kupsirkɥi] *nms & pl* : circuit breaker
coupée [kupe] *nf* : gangway
coupe–feu [kupfø] *nms & pl* : firebreak
coupe–ongles [kupɔ̃gl] *nms & pl* : nail clippers
coupe–papier [kuppapje] *nms & pl* : letter opener
couper [kupe] *vt* **1** : to cut, to cut up, to cut down **2** : to cut off, to break off, to block off **3** : to cut across, to intersect **4** : to dilute (wine, etc.) — *vi* **1** : to cut **2** : to take a shortcut **3 couper à court** : to cut short, to curtail — **se couper** *vr* **1** : to cut oneself <il s'est coupé le doigt : he cut his finger> <se couper les cheveux : to cut one's hair> **2** : to intersect **3 ~ de** : to cut oneself off from
couperet [kuprɛ] *nm* **1** : cleaver **2** : blade (of a guillotine)
couperosé, -sée [kuproze] *adj* : blotchy
coupe–vent [kupvɑ̃] *nms & pl* : windbreaker
couplage [kuplaʒ] *nm* : (mechanical) coupling
couple [kupl] *nm* : couple, pair
coupler [kuple] *vt* : to couple, to pair (up)
couplet [kuplɛ] *nm* : verse
coupoir [kupwar] *nm* : cutter (tool)
coupole [kupɔl] *nf* : cupola, dome
coupon [kupɔ̃] *nm* **1** : coupon **2** : remnant (of cloth) **3** : ticket, pass
coupure [kupyr] *nf* **1** : cut <coupure profonde : deep cut> <coupure du salaire : salary cut> **2** : gap **3** : break <coupure publicitaire : commercial break> **4** BILLET : banknote **5 coupure de presse** : newspaper clipping
cour [kur] *nf* **1** : court <Cour suprême : Supreme Court> **2** : courtyard <cour de récréation : playground> **3** : courtship **4 cour martiale** : court-martial
courage [kuraʒ] *nm* **1** : courage **2** : will, spirit <bon courage! : stick to it!, good luck!>
courageux, -geuse [kuraʒø, -ʒøz] *adj* **1** : courageous, brave **2** : energetic — **courageusement** [-ʒøzmɑ̃] *adv*
courailler [kuraje] *vi Can fam* : to run around from one place to another
couramment [kuramɑ̃] *adv* **1** : fluently **2** : commonly
courant[1], **-rante** [kurɑ̃, -rɑ̃t] *adj* **1** : current **2** : common, frequent **3** COMMUN : usual, ordinary
courant[2] *nm* **1** : current <courant continu : direct current> <courant alternatif : alternating current> <courant d'air : draft> <contre le courant : against the tide> **2** : trend **3** : movement (of populations, etc.) **4** : course <dans le courant de l'année : in the course of the year> **5 au courant** : up-to-date, in the know
courbature [kurbatyr] *nf* : stiffness, ache, charley horse
courbaturé, -rée [kurbatyre] *adj* : aching
courbe[1] [kurb] *adj* : curved
courbe[2] *nf* **1** : (graphic) curve **2** : bend, curve
courber [kurbe] *vt* **1** : to bend, to curve **2** : to bow — *vi* : to bend (over), to bow — **se courber** *vr*
courbette [kurbɛt] *nf* : low bow <faire des courbettes à : to kowtow to>
courbure [kurbyr] *nf* : curvature
coureur[1], **-reuse** [kurœr, -røz] *n* **1** : runner **2** : racer <coureur cycliste : bicycle racer> <coureur automobile : race car driver>
coureur[2] *nm or* **oiseau coureur** : flightless bird
courge [kurʒ] *nf* : gourd, squash
courgette [kurʒɛt] *nf* : zucchini
courir [kurir] {23} *vt* **1** : to run <courir le risque : to run the risk> **2** : to go around, to roam **3** FRÉQUENTER : to frequent **4** POURSUIVRE : to run after, to pursue — *vi* **1** : to run **2** : to race **3** : to rush **4 le bruit court** : rumor has it **5 par les temps qui courent** : nowadays, at the present time
courlis [kurli] *nm* : curlew
couronne [kurɔn] *nf* **1** : crown **2** : wreath **3** : corona
couronnement [kurɔnmɑ̃] *nm* **1** : coronation, crowning **2** : crowning achievement
couronner [kurɔne] *vt* : to crown
courra [kura], *etc.* → **courir**
courriel [kurjɛl] *nm* : e-mail, electronic mail
courrier [kurje] *nm* : mail, correspondence <courrier des lecteurs : letters to the editor> <courrier électronique : electronic mail>
courroie [kurwa] *nf* **1** : strap **2** : belt <courroie de ventilateur : fan belt>
courroucé, -cée [kuruse] *adj* : wrathful, infuriated
courroux [kuru] *nm* COLÈRE : anger, wrath
cours [kur] *nm* **1** : course <au cours de : in the course of, during> **2** : course, class, lesson <suivre un cours : to take a class> **3** : school <cours du soir : night school> **4** MANUEL : textbook **5** : flow, current <cours d'eau : riv-

er, stream> **6** : rate, price <cours des devises : foreign exchange rate> <avoir cours : to be legal tender, to be current, to be used> **7 en ~** : current, in progress

course [kurs] *nf* **1** : run, running **2** : race <course cycliste : bicycle race> <course contre la montre : race against time> **3** : errand <faire des courses : to go shopping> **4** : course, path **5** : journey, ride (in a taxi)

coursier[1], -sière [kursje, -sjɛr] *n* : messenger

coursier[2] *nm* : steed

court[1] [kur] *adv* **1** : short <s'arrêter court : to stop short> **2 à court de** : short of **3 tout court** : simply

court[2], courte [kur, kurt] *adj* **1** : short (in height), narrow **2** : brief, quick

court[3] *nm* : court <court de tennis : tennis court> <tenir court : to hold court>

courtage [kurtaʒ] *nm* : brokerage

court–circuit [kursirkɥi] *nm, pl* **courts–circuits** : short circuit

court–circuiter [kursirkɥite] *vt* **1** : to short-circuit **2** : to bypass

courtepointe [kurtəpwɛ̃t] *nf* : duvet, quilt

courtesane [kurtizan] *nf* : courtesan

courtier, -tière [kurtje, -tjɛr] *n* : broker, agent

courtisan [kurtizɑ̃] *nm* **1** : sycophant, flatterer **2** : courtier

courtiser [kurtize] *vt* : to court, to woo

court–métrage [kurmetraʒ] *nm* : short (film)

courtois, -toise [kurtwa, -twaz] *adj* : courteous — **courtoisement** [-twazmɑ̃] *adv*

courtoisie [kurtwazi] *nf* : courtesy

cousait [kuzɛ], *etc.* → **coudre**

couse [kuz], *etc.* → **coudre**

cousin[1], -sine [kuzɛ̃, -zin] *n* : cousin <cousin germain : first cousin>

cousin[2] *nm* : mosquito

coussin [kusɛ̃] *nm* **1** : cushion **2** *Can* : base (in baseball)

cousu [kuzy] *pp* → **coudre**

coût [ku] *nm* : cost <le coût de la vie : the cost of living>

coûtant [kutɑ̃] *adj* **à prix coûtant** : at cost

couteau [kuto] *nm, pl* **couteaux** : knife <couteau de poche : pocketknife, jacknife>

coutelas [kutla] *nm* **1** : cutlass **2** : butcher knife

coutellerie [kutɛlri] *nf* **1** : cutlery, knives **2** *Can* : silverware (set)

coûter [kute] *vt* : to cost <coûter cher : to be expensive> <ça coûte combien? : how much is it?> — *vi* : to cost

coûteux, -teuse [kutø, -tøz] *adj* : costly

coutume [kutym] *nf* **1** : custom **2 de coutume** : usual, customary

coutumier, -mière [kutymje, -mjɛr] *adj* : customary

couture [kutyr] *nf* **1** : sewing, needlework **2** : dressmaking **3** : seam

couturier [kutyrje] *nm* : fashion designer

couturière [kutyrjɛr] *nf* : dressmaker

couvée [kuve] *nf* : brood

couvent [kuvɑ̃] *nm* : convent, monastery

couver [kuve] *vt* **1** : to brood, to hatch **2** : to overprotect — *vi* **1** : to smolder, to be brewing **2** : to brood

couvercle [kuvɛrkl] *nm* **1** : lid, cover **2** : top, cap (of a spray can, etc.)

couvert[1] [kuvɛr] *pp* → **couvrir**

couvert[2], -verte [kuvɛr, -vɛrt] *adj* **1** : covered, indoor <piscine couverte : indoor swimming pool> **2** : overcast, cloudy

couvert[3] *nm* **1** : place setting (at a table) <couverts : eating utensils, flatware> **2** ABRI : shelter, cover **3** : cover charge

couverture [kuvɛrtyr] *nf* **1** : cover (of a book, etc.) **2** : blanket **3** : coverage **4** : roofing

couveuse [kuvøz] *nf* **1** : brood hen **2** : incubator

couvoir [kuvwar] *nm* : hatchery (for chickens, etc.)

couvre–chef [kuvrəʃɛf] *nm, pl* **couvre–chefs** : headgear

couvre–feu [kuvrəfø] *nm, pl* **couvre–feux** : curfew

couvre–lit [kuvrəli] *nm, pl* **couvre–lits** : bedspread

couvre–pieds [kuvrəpje] *nms & pl* : quilt, coverlet

couvre–plancher [kuvrəplɑ̃ʃe] *nm, pl* **couvre–planchers** *Can* : flooring

couvrir [kuvrir] {83} *vt* **1** : to cover **2** : to cover up for, to shield **3** : to drown out (sound) — **se couvrir** *vr* **1** : to wrap (oneself) up **2** : to cover oneself **3** : to cloud over **4 ~ de** : to be covered with

covoiturage [kovwatyraʒ] *nm Can* : car pool(ing)

cow–boy [kɔbɔj] *nm, pl* **cow–boys** : cowboy

coyote [kɔjɔt] *nm* : coyote

crabe [krab] *nm* : crab

crachat [kraʃa] *nm* : spittle

craché, -chée [kraʃe] *adj fam* **être (qqn) tout craché** : to be the spitting image (of s.o.)

cracher [kraʃe] *vt* **1** : to spit (out) **2** : to belch out (smoke, lava, etc.) **3** *fam* : to cough up (money, etc.) — *vi* : to spit

crachin [kraʃɛ̃] *nm* : drizzle — **crachiner** [kraʃine] *vi*

crachoir [kraʃwar] *nm* : spittoon

crack [krak] *nm* **1** : crack (cocaine) **2** *fam* : whiz, ace <c'est un crack aux échecs : he's a whiz at chess>

craie [krɛ] *nf* : chalk

craignait [krɛɲɛ], **craignions** [krɛɲiɔ̃], *etc.* → **craindre**

craigne [krɛɲ], *etc.* → **craindre**

craindre [krɛ̃dr] {65} *vt* **1** REDOUTER : to fear, to be afraid of **2 ~ que** : to regret that, to fear that **3** : to be susceptible to

crainte [krɛ̃t] *nf* : fear, dread <de crainte que : lest>

craintif, -tive [krɛ̃tif, -tiv] *adj* : fearful, timid — **craintivement** [-tivmɑ̃] *adv*

cramoisi [kramwazi] *nm* : crimson

crampe [krɑ̃p] *nf* : cramp, spasm

crampon [krɑ̃pɔ̃] *nm* **1** : clamp **2** : cleat

cramponner [krɑ̃pɔne] *vt* **1** : to clamp together **2** *fam* : to pester — **se cramponner** *vr* **~ à** : to hold on to, to cling to

cran [krɑ̃] *nm* **1** : notch, hole (in a belt) **2** *fam* : courage <avoir du cran : to have guts>

crâne [kran] *nm* **1** : cranium, skull **2 bourrer le crâne à qqn** *fam* : to brainwash s.o.

crâner [krane] *vi fam* : to show off

crâneur[1], **-neuse** [kranœr, -nøz] *adj fam* : boastful

crâneur[2], **-neuse** *n fam* : show-off

crânien, -nienne [kranjɛ̃, -njɛn] *adj* **1** : cranial **2 boîte crânienne** : cranium, skull

crapaud [krapo] *nm* : toad

crapule [krapyl] *nf* : scoundrel, crook

crapuleux, -leuse [krapylø, -løz] *adj* : crooked, villainous

craque [krak] *nf Can* : crack, crevasse

craquement [krakmɑ̃] *nm* : crack, crunch, creak

craquer [krake] *vi* **1** : to crack, to crunch, to creak **2** SE DÉCHIRER : to burst apart, to tear **3** *fam* : to collapse, to break down — *vt* **1** : to tear, to rip **2** : to strike (a match)

crasse[1] [kras] *adj* : crass, gross — **crassement** [krasmɑ̃] *adv*

crasse[2] *nf* **1** : filth, grime **2** : dross, slag **3 faire une crasse** : to play a dirty trick

crasseux, -seuse [krasø, -søz] *adj* : filthy, grimy

cratère [kratɛr] *nm* : crater

cravache [kravaʃ] *nf* : whip, crop

cravacher [kravaʃe] *vt* : to horsewhip

cravate [kravat] *nf* : necktie, cravat

crayeux, crayeuse [krɛjø, -jøz] *adj* : chalky (of the complexion)

crayon [krɛjɔ̃] *nm* **1** : pencil <crayon de couleur : colored pencil> **2 crayon à bille** : ballpoint pen **3 crayon de cire** : crayon

crayonner [krɛjɔne] *vt* **1** : to scribble, to jot down (in pencil) **2** : to sketch

créance [kreɑ̃s] *nf* **1** : debt **2** : letter of credit **3** : credence, credibility

créancier, -cière [kreɑ̃sje, -sjɛr] *n* : creditor

créateur[1], **-trice** [kreatœr, -tris] *adj* : creative

créateur[2], **-trice** *n* : creator, originator

création [kreasjɔ̃] *nf* : creation

créativité [kreativite] *nf* : creativity

créature [kreatyr] *nf* : creature

crécelle [kresɛl] *nf* : noisemaker

crèche [krɛʃ] *nf* **1** : crèche, Nativity scene **2** *France* : day-care center, nursery

crédible [kredibl] *adj* : credible — **crédibilité** [-dibilite] *nf*

crédit [kredi] *nm* **1** : credit <acheter à crédit : to buy on credit> **2** : credence, credibility **3 crédits** *nmpl* : funds

crédit–bail [kredibaj] *nm, pl* **crédits–bails** : leasing

créditer [kredite] *vt* : to credit

créditeur, -trice [kreditœr, -tris] *n* **1** : creditor **2 être crediteur** : to be in the black

crédo [kredo] *nm* : creed

crédule [kredyl] *adj* NAIF : credulous, gullible — **crédulité** [-dylite] *nf*

créer [kree] {89} *vt* **1** : to create **2** : to set up, to establish

crémage [krɛ(e)maʒ] *nm Can* : icing (on a cake)

crème [krɛm] *nf* **1** : cream <crème hydratante : moisturizer> **2 crème glacée** *Can* : ice cream

crémerie [krɛmri] *nf France* : dairy shop

crémeux, -meuse [kremø, -møz] *adj* : creamy

créneau [kreno] *nm, pl* **créneaux** **1** : slot, gap, window (of time) **2** : niche, share <créneau du marché : market share> **3** : crenellation, battlement **4 faire un créneau** : to back into a parking space

créole[1] [kreɔl] *adj* : creole

créole[2] *nm* : Creole (language)

Créole *nmf* : Creole

créosote [kreɔzɔt] *nf* : creosote

crêpe[1] [krɛp] *nf* : pancake, crepe

crêpe[2] *nm* : crepe (fabric)

crépitement [krepitmɑ̃] *nm* : crackling, clacking, patter (of rain)

crépiter [krepite] *vi* : to crackle, to splutter, to patter

crépuscule [krepyskyl] *nm* : twilight, dusk

crescendo [krɛʃɛndo, krɛʃɛ̃do] *nms & pl* : crescendo

cresson [krɛsɔ̃] *nm* : cress, watercress

crête [krɛt] *nf* **1** : crest, peak **2** : comb, crest

crétin, -tine [kretɛ̃, -tin] *n* IDIOT : idiot, moron

cretons [krətɔ̃] *nmpl Can* : pâté made with pork and veal

creusement [krøzmɑ̃] *nm* : digging, excavation

creuser [krøze] *vt* **1** : to dig, to hollow out, to furrow **2** : to study in depth **3** : to flex, to bend <creuser le dos : to arch one's back> **4 ça creuse!** *fam* : that gives one an appetite! — *vi* : to dig, to excavate — **se creuser**

vr **se creuser la tête** *fam* : to rack one's brains

creuset [krøzɛ] *nm* **1** : crucible **2** : melting pot

creux[1], **creuse** [krø, krøz] *adj* **1** VIDE : hollow, empty **2** CONCAVE : concave, sunken **3** : shallow, superficial

creux[2] *nm* : hollow, hole, cavity <le creux de l'estomac : the pit of the stomach>

crevaison [krəvɛzɔ̃] *nf* : flat tire, puncture

crevasse [krəvas] *nf* **1** : crevasse **2** : crack, crevice **3 avoir des crevasses aux mains** : to have chapped hands

crevé, -vée [krəve] *adj* **1** : punctured, flat (of a tire) **2** : dead **3** *fam* : exhausted, dead tired

crève–cœur [krɛvkœr] *nms & pl* : heartbreak

crever [krəve] {52} *vt* **1** : to burst, to puncture **2** *fam* : to wear out **3 crever de faim** : to be starving — *vi* **1** : to burst **2** *fam* : to die — **se crever** *vr fam* : to wear oneself out

crevette [krəvɛt] *nf* : shrimp, prawn

cri [kri] *nm* **1** : cry, shout <à grands cris : at the top of one's lungs> **2 le dernier cri** : the latest thing

criaillement [kriajmɑ̃] *nm* : squawking, screeching, honking

criailler [kriaje] *vi* **1** : to squawk, to screech, to honk **2** : to complain, to grumble

criant, criante [krijɑ̃, krijɑ̃t] *adj* : obvious, flagrant, striking

criard, criarde [krijar, krijard] *adj* **1** : shrill **2** : loud, garish

crible [kribl] *nm* **1** : sieve, screen **2 passer au crible** : to screen, to examine closely

cribler [krible] *vt* **1** : to sift, to screen **2** : to riddle, to fill with holes

cric [krik] *nm* VÉRIN : jack

cricket [krikɛt] *nm* : cricket (sport)

criée [krije] *nf* : auction

crier [krije] {96} *vi* **1** : to shout, to cry out **2** : to squeal, to squeak — *vt* **1** : to shout **2** : to proclaim, to protest

crieur, crieuse [krijœr, krijøz] *n* : hawker, peddler

crime [krim] *nm* **1** : crime **2** : murder

criminel[1], **-nelle** [kriminɛl] *adj* : criminal — **criminellement** [-nɛlmɑ̃] *adv*

criminel[2], **-nelle** *n* **1** : criminal **2** MEURTRIER : murderer

crin [krɛ̃] *nm* **1** : horsehair **2 à tout crin** : die-hard, fanatical

crinière [krinjɛr] *nf* : mane

crique[1] [krik] *nf* : cove, inlet

crique[2] *nm Can* : creek

criquet [krikɛ] *nm* **1** *or* **criquet migrateur** : locust (insect) **2** *Can* : cricket (insect)

crise [kriz] *nf* **1** : crisis **2** ACCÈS : fit, outburst <crise de désespoir : fit of despair> **3** ATTAQUE : attack (in medicine) <crise cardiaque : heart attack>

crispant, -pante [krispɑ̃, -pɑ̃t] *adj* AGAÇANT : aggravating, annoying

crispation [krispasjɔ̃] *nf* CONTRACTION : tension, contraction

crispé, -pée [krispe] *adj* : tense, strained, nervous

crisper [krispe] *vt* **1** CONTRACTER : to tense, to contract **2** *fam* : to irritate <sa voix me crispe : her voice gets on my nerves>

crissement [krismɑ̃] *nm* **1** : screeching, squealing **2** : grating, grinding **3** : crunching

crisser [krise] *vi* **1** : to screech, to squeal **2** : to grate, to grind **3** : to crunch

cristal [kristal] *nm, pl* **cristaux** [kristo] : crystal — **cristallin, -line** [-stalɛ̃, -lin] *adj*

cristallin [kristalɛ̃] *nm* : lens (of the eye)

cristalliser [kristalize] *v* : to crystallize — **se cristalliser** *vr*

critère [kritɛr] *nm* : criterion

critérium [kriterjɔm] *nm* : heat (in sports)

critiquable [kritikabl] *adj* : open to criticism, questionable

critique[1] [kritik] *adj* : critical

critique[2] *nmf* : critic

critique[3] *nf* **1** : criticism, reproach **2** : critique, review

critiquer [kritike] *vt* : to criticize

critiqueur, -queuse [kritikœr, -køz] *n* : faultfinder

croassement [krɔasmɑ̃] *nm* : caw, croak

croasser [krɔase] *vi* : to croak, to caw

croate [krɔat] *adj* : Croatian

Croate *nmf* : Croat, Croatian

croc [kro] *nm* **1** CROCHET : hook **2** : fang

croc–en–jambe [krɔkɑ̃ʒɑ̃b] *nm, pl* **crocs–en–jambe** : tripping <faire un croc-en-jambe à qqn : to trip s.o. up>

croche[1] [krɔʃ] *adj Can* **1** : bent, crooked **2** : dishonest

croche[2] *nf* : eighth note

croche–pied [krɔʃpje] *nm fam* → **croc–en–jambe**

crochet [krɔʃɛ] *nm* **1** : hook **2** : crochet, crocheting <faire du crochet : to crochet> **3** : crochet hook **4** : square bracket **5** : detour <faire un crochet : to make a detour> **6** : fang (of a snake) **7 vivre aux crochets de qqn** : to scrounge off s.o.

crocheter [krɔʃte] {20} *vt* **1** : to pick (a lock) **2** : to crochet

crochir [krɔʃir] *vt Can* : to bend (out of shape), to distort

crochu, -chue [krɔʃy] *adj* : hooked, bent, crooked

crocodile [krɔkɔdil] *nm* : crocodile

crocus [krɔkys] *nm* : crocus

croire [krwar] {24} *v* **1** : to believe, to trust **2** PENSER : to think <tu crois?

: do you think so?> — *vi* **1** : to believe (in religion) **2 ~ à** *or* **~ en** : to believe in, to have confidence in — **se croire** *vr* : to consider oneself
croisade [krwazad] *nf* : crusade
croisé[1], **-sée** [krwaze] *adj* **1** : crossed **2** : double-breasted
croisé[2] *nm* **1** : crusader **2** : twill
croisée *nf* **1** : crossroads, crossing **2** : casement (window)
croisement [krwazmɑ̃] *nm* **1** : crossing, intersection <croisement en trèfle : cloverleaf> **2** : crossbreeding
croiser [krwaze] *vt* **1** : to cross <croiser les bras : to fold one's arms> **2** : to intersect **3** RENCONTRER : to pass, to meet **4** : to crossbreed — *vi* : to cruise (of a ship) — **se croiser** *vr* **1** : to intersect **2** : to pass each other
croiseur [krwazœr] *nm* : cruiser (ship)
croisière [krwazjɛr] *nf* **1** : cruise **2 vitesse de croisière** : cruising speed
croissait [krwasɛ], *etc.* → **croître**
croissance [krwasɑ̃s] *nf* : growth
croissant[1], **-sante** [krwasɑ̃, -sɑ̃t] *adj* : growing, increasing
croissant[2] *nm* **1** : crescent **2** : croissant
croître [krwatr] {25} *vi* : to grow, to increase
croix [krwa] *nf* : cross
croquant, -quante [krɔkɑ̃, -kɑ̃t] *adj* : crisp, crunchy
croque–mitaine [krɔkmitɛn] *nm, pl* **croque–mitaines** : bogey, bogeyman
croque–monsieur [krɔkməsjø] *nms & pl* : grilled ham and cheese sandwich
croque–mort [krɔkmɔr] *nm, pl* **croque–morts** *fam* : undertaker
croquer [krɔke] *vt* **1** : to crunch, to munch **2** ESQUISSER : to sketch **3** *fam* : to squander — *vi* **1** : to be crunchy **2 ~ dans** : to bite into (an apple, etc.)
croquet [krɔkɛ] *nm* : croquet
croquette [krɔkɛt] *nf* : croquette
croquis [krɔki] *nm* ESQUISSE : sketch, drawing
cross [krɔs] *or* **cross–country** [krɔskuntri] *nm* : cross-country run, cross-country race
crosse [krɔs] *nf* **1** : butt, grip (of a gun) **2** : stick, lacrosse stick <crosse de hockey : hockey stick> **3** LACROSSE : lacrosse **4** : crosier, crook
crotale [krɔtal] *nm* : rattlesnake
crotte [krɔt] *nf* : droppings *pl,* dung
crotté, -tée [krɔte] *adj* : muddy
crottin [krɔtɛ̃] *nm* : (horse) manure
crouler [krule] *vi* : to collapse, to crumble
croupe [krup] *nf* **1** : rump (of a horse) **2** : crest, summit
croupir [krupir] *vi* **1** : to stagnate **2** : to wallow <croupir dans l'ignorance : to wallow in ignorance>
croustillant, -lante [krustijɑ̃, -jɑ̃t] *adj* **1** : crisp, crunchy **2** : spicy, bawdy
croustiller [krustije] *vi* : to crunch, to be crispy
croûte [krut] *nf* **1** : crust **2** : scab **3 casser la croûte** : to have a snack
croûteux, -teuse [krutø, -tøz] *adj* : scabby
croûton [krutɔ̃] *nm* **1** : crust, heel (of bread) **2** : crouton
croyable [krwajabl] *adj* : credible, believable
croyait [krwajɛ], *etc.* → **croire**
croyance [krwajɑ̃s] *nf* : belief
croyant[1], **croyante** [krwajɑ̃, -jɑ̃t] *adj* : believing <être croyant : to be a believer>
croyant[2], **croyante** *n* : believer
cru[1] [kry] *pp* → **croire**
cru[2], **crue** [kry] *adj* **1** : raw, uncooked **2** : crude, harsh **3 à ~** : bareback, barebacked
cru[3] *nm* **1** VIGNOBLE : vineyard **2** : vintage (of wine) **3 du ~** : local
crû [kry] *pp* → **croître**
cruauté [kryote] *nf* : cruelty
cruche [kryʃ] *nf* **1** : jug, pitcher **2** *fam* : nitwit, dumbell
crucial, -ciale [krysjal] *adj, pl* **-ciaux** [-sjo] : crucial
crucifier [krysifje] {96} *vt* : to crucify
crucifix [krysifi] *nms & pl* : crucifix
crucifixion [krysifiksjɔ̃] *nf* : crucifixion
crudité [krydite] *nf* **1** : crudeness **2 crudités** *nfpl* : raw vegetables (as hors d'oeuvres)
crue [kry] *nf* : rising (of waters), flood
cruel, cruelle [kryɛl] *adj* : cruel — **cruellement** [-ɛlmɑ̃] *adv*
crûment [krymɑ̃] *adv* **1** : crudely, coarsely **2** : bluntly
crustacé [krystase] *nm* **1** : crustacean **2 crustacés** *npl* : shellfish
crypte [kript] *nf* : crypt
cryptographie [kriptɔgrafi] *nf* : cryptography
cubain, -baine [kybɛ̃, -bɛn] *adj* : Cuban
Cubain, -baine *n* : Cuban
cube[1] [kyb] *adj* : cubic <mètre cube : cubic meter>
cube[2] *nm* : cube
cubique [kybik] *adj* : cubic
cubitus [kybitys] *nm* : ulna
cueillette [kœjɛt] *nf* : gathering, picking
cueillir [kœjir] {3} *vt* **1** : to pick, to gather **2** *fam* : to catch, to nab **3 être cueilli à froid** : to be caught off guard
cuillère *or* **cuiller** [kɥijɛr] *nf* **1** : spoon **2** : spoonful **3 cuillère à thé** *or* **cuillère à café** : teaspoon
cuillerée [kɥijere] *nf* **1** : spoonful **2 cuillerée à café** : teaspoonful
cuir [kɥir] *nm* **1** : leather **2** : hide <cuir brut : rawhide> **3 cuir chevelu** : scalp
cuirasse [kɥiras] *nf* **1** : breastplate **2** : armor (of a tank, etc.)
cuirassé [kɥirase] *nm* : battleship
cuirasser [kɥirase] *vt* **1** : to armor **2** : to harden — **se cuirasser** *vr* : to harden oneself

cuire [kɥir] {49} *vt* **1** : to cook, to bake **2** : to fire (pottery) — *vi* **1** : to cook **2** : to sting, to burn

cuisait [kɥizɛ], **cuisions** [kɥizjɔ̃], *etc.* → **cuire**

cuisant, -sante [kɥizɑ̃, -zɑ̃t] *adj* **1** : stinging, smarting **2** : bitter

cuise [kɥiz], *etc.* → **cuire**

cuisine [kɥizin] *nf* **1** : kitchen **2** : cooking, cuisine **3 faire la cuisine** : to cook

cuisiné, -née [kɥizine] *adj* **plat cuisiné** : prepared food

cuisiner [kɥizine] *vt* **1** : to cook **2** *fam* : to grill, to interrogate — *vi* : to cook

cuisinette [kɥizinɛt] *nf* : kitchenette

cuisinier, -nière [kɥizinje, -njɛr] *n* : chef, cook

cuisinière *nf* : stove

cuisse [kɥis] *nf* **1** : thigh **2** : leg <cuisses de grenouilles : frogs' legs>

cuisson [kɥisɔ̃] *nf* : cooking, baking

cuit, cuite [kɥi, kɥit] *adj* **1** : cooked <bien cuit : well-done> **2 être cuit** *fam* : to be done for, to have had it

cuite *nf* **prendre une cuite** *fam* : to get drunk

cuivre [kɥivr] *nm* **1** *or* **cuivre rouge** : copper **2** *or* **cuivre jaune** : brass **3 cuivres** *nmpl* : brass (musical instruments)

cuivré, -vrée [kɥivre] *adj* **1** : copper-colored, bronzed **2** : resonant

culbute [kylbyt] *nf* **1** : somersault **2** CHUTE : tumble, fall

culbuter [kylbyte] *vt* **1** : to knock over **2** : to overthrow — *vi* **1** : to somersault **2** TOMBER : to tumble, to fall

cul–de–sac [kydsak] *nm, pl* **culs–de–sac** : dead end, cul-de-sac

culinaire [kylinɛr] *adj* : culinary

culminant, -nante [kylminɑ̃, -nɑ̃t] *adj* **point culminant** : high point, peak

culminer [kylmine] *vi* **1** : to culminate, to peak **2** DOMINER : to dominate, to tower

culot [kylo] *nm fam* : impudence, cheek <avoire du culot : to have a lot of nerve>

culotte [kylɔt] *nf* **1** PANTALON : pants *pl*, trousers *pl* **2** : panties *pl*

culotté, -tée [kylɔte] *adj fam* : sassy, cheeky

culpabiliser [kylpabilize] *vt* **~ qqn** : to make someone feel guilty — *vi* : to feel guilty

culpabilité [kylpabilite] *nf* : guilt

culte [kylt] *nm* **1** : worship, cult <liberté de culte : freedom of worship> <le culte de personalité : the cult of personality> **2** : religion, creed **3** : (Protestant) service

cultivateur, -trice [kyltivatœr, -tris] *n* AGRICULTEUR : farmer

cultivé, -vée [kyltive] *adj* **1** : cultivated **2** : cultured

cultiver [kyltive] *vt* : to cultivate — **se cultiver** *vr*

culture [kyltyr] *nf* **1** : culture **2** : cultivation, growing **3 culture physique** : physical education

culturel, -relle [kyltyrɛl] *adj* : cultural — **culturellement** [-rɛlmɑ̃] *adv*

culturisme [kyltyrism] *nm* : bodybuilding

cumin [kymɛ̃] *nm* : cumin

cumul [kymyl] *nm* **1** : holding concurrently <cumul de fonctions : holding several offices at the same time> **2** : accumulation

cumulatif, -tive [kymylatif, -tiv] *adj* : cumulative

cumuler [kymyle] *vt* **1** : to hold concurrently **2** ACCUMULER : to accumulate, to pile up — **se cumuler** *vr* : to accrue

cumulus [kymylys] *nms & pl* : cumulus

cupide [kypid] *adj* : greedy

cupidité [kypidite] *nf* : greed

curatif, -tive [kyratif, -tiv] *adj* : curative

cure [kyr] *nf* **1** : treatment, cure **2** : parish, vicarage **3 n'avoir cure de** : to have little concern for <elle n'en a cure : she doesn't care about it>

curé [kyre] *nm* : pastor, parish priest

cure–dent *or* **cure–dents** [kyrdɑ̃] *nm, pl* **cure–dents** : toothpick

curer [kyre] *vt* : to clean out, to scrape out — **se curer** *vr* : to clean (one's nails, etc.)

curieusement [kyrjøzmɑ̃] *adv* : curiously, strangely

curieux[1], -rieuse [kyrjø, -rjøz] *adj* **1** : curious, inquisitive **2** : strange, odd

curieux[2], -rieuse *n* **1** : onlooker **2** : busybody

curieux[3] *nm* : curious thing, oddity <le curieux dans tout ça : the strange thing in all that>

curiosité [kyrjɔzite] *nf* : curiosity

curry [kyri] *nm* : curry

curseur [kyrsœr] *nm* : cursor

cuspide [kyspid] *nf* : cusp

cutané, -née [kytane] *adj* : cutaneous, skin

cuve [kyv] *nf* : tub, tank, vat

cuvée [kyve] *nf* : vintage

cuver [kyve] *vi* : to ferment

cuvette [kyvɛt] *nf* **1** : bowl, washbasin **2** : basin (in geology)

cyanure [sjanyr] *nm* : cyanide

cyberespace [sibɛrɛspas] *nm* : cyberspace

cyclable [siklabl] *adj* **piste cyclable** : bicycle path

cycle [sikl] *nm* : cycle

cyclique [siklik] *adj* : cyclic, cyclical

cyclisme [siklism] *nm* : cycling, bicycling

cycliste[1] [siklist] *adj* : cycle, bicycle <course cycliste : bicycle race>

cycliste[2] *nmf* : cyclist, bicyclist

cyclomoteur [siklɔmɔtœr] *nm* : moped

cyclone [siklon] *nm* : cyclone

cygne [siɲ] *nm* : swan

cylindre [silɛ̃dr] *nm* : cylinder
cylindrée [silɛ̃dre] *nf* : capacity (of an engine)
cylindrique [silɛ̃drik] *adj* : cylindrical
cymbale [sɛ̃bal] *nf* : cymbal
cynique[1] [sinik] *adj* : cynical — **cyniquement** [-nikmɑ̃] *adv*
cynique[2] *nmf* : cynic
cynisme [sinism] *nm* : cynicism
cyprès [siprɛ] *nm* : cypress
cypriote [siprijɔt] *adj* : Cypriot
Cypriote *nmf* : Cypriot
cytoplasme [sitɔplasm] *nm* : cytoplasm

D

d [de] *nm* : d, the fourth letter of the alphabet
d'abord [dabɔr] → **abord**
d'accord [dakɔr] → **accord**
dactylo[1] [daktilo] *or* **dactylographe** [daktilɔgraf] *nmf* : typist
dactylo[2] *nf* **1** → **dactylographie 2** *Can* : typewriter
dactylographie [daktilɔgrafi] *nf* : typing
dactylographier [daktilɔgrafje] {96} *vt* : to type
dada [dada] *nm* **1** *fam* : hobbyhorse, pet subject **2** : Dada
dadais [dadɛ] *nms & pl* : silly fool, oaf
dague [dag] *nf* : dagger
dahlia [dalja] *nm* : dahlia
daigner [deɲe] *vt* : to deign, to condescend <il n'a pas daigné répondre : he didn't deign to reply>
daim [dɛ̃] *nm* **1** : fallow deer **2** : suede
dais [dɛ] *nms & pl* : canopy
dallage [dalaʒ] *nm* **1** : paving **2** : pavement
dalle [dal] *nf* **1** : paving stone, flagstone **2** : slab (of stone or concrete)
daller [dale] *vt* : to pave
dalmatien [dalmasjɛ̃] *nm* : dalmatian (dog)
daltonien, -nienne [daltɔnjɛ̃, -njɛn] *adj* : color-blind
dam [dam] *nm* **au grand dam de** : much to the detriment of, to the great displeasure of
damas [damås] *nms & pl* : damask
dame [dam] *nf* **1** : lady **2** : queen (in chess or card games) **3 dames** *nfpl or* **jeu de dames** : checkers
damer [dame] *vt* **1** : to pack down **2** : to crown (in checkers) **3 damer le pion à** : to get the better of
damier [damje] *nm* : checkerboard
damnation [danasjɔ̃] *nf* : damnation
damné[1], **-née** [dane] *adj* : damned, cursed
damné[2], **-née** *n* : damned person
damner [dane] *vt* : to damn
dandinement [dɑ̃dinmɑ̃] *nm* : waddling, waddle
dandiner [dɑ̃dine] *v* **se dandiner** *vr* : to waddle
dandy [dɑ̃di] *nm* : dandy
danger [dɑ̃ʒe] *nm* : danger
dangereux, -reuse [dɑ̃ʒrø, -røz] *adj* : dangerous — **dangereusement** [-røzmɑ̃] *adv*
danois[1], **-noise** [danwa, -waz] *adj* : Danish
danois[2] *nm* **1** : Danish (language) **2** : Great Dane
Danois, -noise *n* : Dane
dans [dɑ̃] *prep* **1** : in <dans la boîte : in the box> <dans dix jours : in ten days> **2** : into <monter dans l'auto : to get into the car> **3** : from, out of <elle buvait dans une tasse : she was drinking from a cup>
dansant, -sante [dɑ̃sɑ̃, -sɑ̃t] *adj* : dancing <soirée dansante : dance (party)>
danse [dɑ̃s] *nf* : dance, dancing
danser [dɑ̃se] *v* : to dance
danseur, -seuse [dɑ̃sœr, -søz] *n* : dancer
dard [dar] *nm* **1** AIGUILLON : stinger **2** : spear, javelin **3** *Can* : dart <jouer aux dards : to play darts>
darder [darde] *vt* : to shoot forth, to hurl
date [dat] *nf* **1** : date <date de naissance : date of birth> **2** : time <de longue date : long-standing> **3** → **limite**
dater [date] *vt* : to date — *vi* **1** : to be dated, to be old-fashioned **2 ~ de** : to date from, to date back to
datte [dat] *nf* : date (fruit)
daube [dob] *nf* : casserole, stew
dauphin [dofɛ̃] *nm* **1** : dolphin **2** : dauphin, heir apparent
davantage [davɑ̃taʒ] *adv* **1** : more <elle ne se souvient pas davantage : she doesn't remember more> **2** : longer, any longer <je voudrais rester davantage : I'd like to stay longer>
DDT [dedete] *nm* : DDT
de [də] (**d'** *before vowels and mute h*) *prep* **1** : from <de Québec à Montréal : from Quebec to Montreal> **2** : by <de nuit : by night> <une comédie de Molière : a play by Molière> **3** : of <au bout du monde : at the ends of the earth> **4** : with <je tombe de fatigue : I'm completely worn out> **5** (*before infinitive*) : to, of <il craint d'être en retard : he's afraid of being late> **6 de la, du, des** : some, any <voulez-vous des haricots? : would you like some beans?>
dé [de] *nm* **1** : die, dice *pl* **2** *or* **dé à coudre** : thimble

déambuler [deɑ̃byle] *vi* : to stroll, to wander about
débâcle [debakl] *nf* : debacle, fiasco
déballer [debale] *vt* **1** : to unpack, to unwrap **2** : to display (merchandise)
débandade [debɑ̃dad] *nf* **1** : rout, stampede **2 à la débandade** : in disarray
débarbouiller [debarbuje] *v* **se débarbouiller** *vr* : to wash one's face
débarbouillette [debarbujɛt] *nf Can* : washcloth, facecloth
débarcadère [debarkadɛr] *nm* : wharf, dock
débardeur [debardœr] *nm* : longshoreman
débarquement [debarkəmɑ̃] *nm* **1** : unloading **2** : landing, disembarcation
débarquer [debarke] *vt* **1** : to unload (goods) **2** : to land (troops, etc.) — *vi* : to disembark
débarrasser [debarase] *vt* **1** : to clear **2 ~ de** : to relieve of, to free from — **se débarrasser** *vr* **~ de** : to get rid of
débarrer [debare] *vt Can* : to unlock
débat [deba] *nm* **1** : debate, discussion **2 débats** *nmpl* : proceedings
débattre [debatr] {12} *vt* : to debate, to discuss — *vi Can* : to pound, to race (of the heart) — **se débattre** *vr* : to struggle, to thrash about
débauche [deboʃ] *nf* : debauchery, vice
débauché[1], **-chée** [deboʃe] *adj* : debauched
débauché[2], **-chée** *n* : debauched person, libertine
débaucher [deboʃe] *vt* **1** CORROMPRE : to corrupt **2** LICENCIER : to lay off **3** : to cause to go on strike
débile [debil] *adj* **1** : weak, feeble **2** *fam* : stupid, idiotic
débilité [debilite] *nf* **1** : debility **2** *fam* : silliness, stupidity
débiliter [debilite] *vt* **1** : to debilitate **2** : to demoralize
débiner [debine] *vt Can fam* : to disconcert
débit [debi] *nm* **1** : debit **2** : turnover (of merchandise, etc.) **3** : (rate of) flow, discharge **4** ÉLOCUTION : delivery, speech **5** *France* : shop <débit de boissons : bar>
débiter [debite] *vt* **1** : to debit **2** : to sell, to retail **3** : to produce, to yield **4** : to cut up **5** : to discharge, to flow (out) **6** : to drone, to reel off
débiteur[1], **-trice** [debitœr, -tris] *adj* : debit <compte débiteur : debit account>
débiteur[2], **-trice** *n* : debtor
déblai [deblɛ] *nm* **1** : excavation **2 déblais** *nmpl* DÉCOMBRES : rubble, debris
déblaiement [deblɛmɑ̃] *nm* : clearing (of earth)
déblatérer [deblatere] {87} *vi* **~ contre** : to rant against
déblayer [debleje] {11} *vt* **1** : to clear (away) **2** : to prepare, to sort out
débloquer [deblɔke] *vt* **1** : to free, to release **2** : to unfreeze (funds), to release — *vi fam* **1** : to talk nonsense **2** : to be out of one's mind
déboguer [debɔge] *vt* : to debug
déboires [debwar] *nmpl* **1** DÉCEPTIONS : disappointments **2** ENNUIS : difficulties, tribulations
déboiser [debwaze] *vt* : to deforest
déboîtement [debwatmɑ̃] *nm* : dislocation
déboîter [debwate] *vt* **1** : to dislocate (in medicine) **2** : to disconnect, to unfasten — *vi* : to pull out, to change lanes (in an automobile) — **se déboîter** *vr* : to dislocate (one's shoulder, etc.)
débonnaire [debɔnɛr] *adj* : easygoing, good-natured
débordant, -dante [debɔrdɑ̃, -dɑ̃t] *adj* : overflowing, brimming <débordant d'énergie : bursting with energy>
débordé, -dée [debɔrde] *adj* : overwhelmed, overloaded (with work, etc.)
débordement [debɔrdəmɑ̃] *nm* : overflow, excess
déborder [debɔrde] *vi* : to overflow — *vt* **1** : to jut out from, to extend beyond **2** : to overwhelm **3** : to overflow
débouché [debuʃe] *nm* **1** : outlet, market **2** : opportunity, prospect
déboucher [debuʃe] *vt* **1** : to clear, to unblock **2** : to uncork, to open — *vi* **1 ~ de** : to emerge from, to come out of **2 ~ sur** : to open onto, to lead to — **se déboucher** : to become unblocked
déboucler [debukle] *vt* : to unbuckle, to undo
débouler [debule] *vi* **1** *fam* : to tumble down **2** : to bolt, to shoot out — *vt* : to charge down (a stairway, etc.)
débours [debur] *nms & pl* : expense, outlay
débourser [deburse] *vt* : to pay out, to spend <sans rien débourser : without paying a penny>
déboussolé, -lée [debusɔle] *adj fam* : disoriented, confused
debout [dəbu] *adv* **1** : standing up **2** : upright, on end **3** : up, out of bed **4 tenir debout** : to stand up to examination, to hold water
déboutonner [debutɔne] *vt* : to unbutton, to undo — **se déboutonner** *vr*
débraillé, -lée [debraje] *adj* : disheveled, slovenly
débrancher [debrɑ̃ʃe] *vt* : to unplug, to disconnect
débrayage [debrɛjaʒ] *nm* **1** : disengaging the clutch **2** : strike, walkout
débrayer [debreje] {11} *vi* **1** : to disengage the clutch **2** : to go on strike
débridé, -dée [debride] *adj* : unbridled, unrestrained

débris [debri] *nms & pl* **1** : fragment **2** **débris** *nmpl* : rubbish, scraps, remains

débrouillard, -larde [debrujar, -jard] *adj fam* : resourceful

débrouillardise [debrujardiz] *nf fam* : resourcefulness

débrouiller [debruje] *vt* **1** DÉMÊLER : to disentangle **2** : to unravel, to solve — **se débrouiller** *vr* **1** : to manage <se débrouiller pour obtenir : to wangle, to finagle> **2** : to get by <il se débrouille bien : he's getting along all right>

débroussailler [debrusaje] *vt* **1** : to clear (land) **2** : to lay the groundwork for

débusquer [debyske] *vt* : to flush, to drive out (from hiding)

début [deby] *nm* **1** : beginning, start <au début : at the beginning> <dès le début : from the start> **2** (*used in expressions of time*) <début juin : in early June> **3** **débuts** *nmpl* : debut, early stages <faire ses débuts : to make one's debut> **4** **au début** : to begin with, at first

débutant, -tante [debytɑ̃, -tɑ̃t] *n* : beginner, novice, learner

débutante *nf* : debutante

débuter [debyte] *v* : to begin, to start

deçà [dəsa] *adv* **1** **deçà, delà** : here and there **2** **en deçà de** : on this side of **3** **en deçà de** : short of, below

décacheter [dekaʃte] {8} *vt* : to unseal (an envelope)

décade [dekad] *nf* **1** : period of ten days **2** : decade

décadence [dekadɑ̃s] *nf* : decadence

décadent, -dente [dekadɑ̃, -dɑ̃t] *adj* : decadent

décaféiné, -née [dekafeine] *adj* : decaffeinated

décalage [dekalaʒ] *nm* **1** : discrepancy **2** : gap, space **3** : interval <décalage horaire : time difference>

décalcomanie [dekalkɔmani] *nf* : decal

décaler [dekale] *vt* **1** : to move forward or back (a time, a date) **2** : to move, to shift (an object)

décamper [dekɑ̃pe] *vi* : to clear out, to decamp

décanter [dekɑ̃te] *vt* **1** : to allow (a liquid) to settle **2** : to clarify (ideas, etc.) — **se décanter** *vr*

décapant[1]**, -pante** [dekapɑ̃, -pɑ̃t] *adj* : caustic, abrasive

décapant[2] *nm* **1** : scouring agent **2** : paint stripper

décaper [dekape] *vt* **1** : to clean, to scour **2** : to strip (paint, etc.)

décapiter [dekapite] *vt* : to decapitate, to behead

décapotable [dekapɔtabl] *adj & nf* : convertible

décapsuleur [dekapsylœr] *nm* : bottle opener

décati, -tie [dekati] *adj* : decrepit

décédé, -dée [desede] *adj* : deceased

décéder [desede] {87} *vi* : to die, to pass away

déceler [desle] {20} *vt* **1** DÉCOUVRIR : to detect, to uncover **2** RÉVÉLER : to indicate, to reveal

décélération [deselerasjɔ̃] *nf* : deceleration

décembre [desɑ̃br] *nm* : December

décemment [desamɑ̃] *adv* : decently

décence [desɑ̃s] *nf* : decency

décennie [deseni] *nf* : decade

décent, -cente [desɑ̃, -sɑ̃t] *adj* : decent

décentraliser [desɑ̃tralize] *vt* : to decentralize — **décentralisation** [-lizasjɔ̃] *nf*

déception [desɛpsjɔ̃] *nf* : disappointment

décerner [desɛrne] *vt* **1** : to award **2** : to issue (a writ)

décès [desɛ] *nm* : death

décevant, -vante [desəvɑ̃, -vɑ̃t] *adj* : disappointing

décevoir [desəvwar] {26} *vt* : to disappoint

déchaîné, -née [deʃene] *adj* : raging, unbridled

déchaînement [deʃɛnmɑ̃] *nm* **1** : fury, raging (of the elements) **2** EXPLOSION : outburst (of emotion)

déchaîner [deʃene] *vt* : to unleash, to arouse — **se déchaîner** *vr* : to erupt, to burst out

déchanter [deʃɑ̃te] *vi* : to become disillusioned

décharge [deʃarʒ] *nf* **1** : discharge (of a firearm) **2** : garbage dump **3** **décharge électrique** : electric shock

déchargement [deʃarʒəmɑ̃] *nm* : unloading

décharger [deʃarʒe] {17} *vt* **1** : to unload **2** : to discharge (a firearm, etc.) **3** : to relieve, to unburden **4** : to exonerate, to clear **5** : to give vent to

décharné, -née [deʃarne] *adj* : emaciated, bony

déchausser [deʃose] *v* **se déchausser** *vr* : to take off one's shoes

déchéance [deʃeɑ̃s] *nf* : decay, decline

déchet [deʃɛ] *nm* **1** : scrap **2** : waste, wastage **3** **déchets** *nmpl* : refuse, waste (materials) <déchets toxiques : toxic waste>

déchiffrer [deʃifre] *vt* **1** : to decipher **2** : to sight-read (music)

déchiqueté, -tée [deʃikte] *adj* : jagged, ragged

déchiqueter [deʃikte] {8} *vt* : to tear into pieces

déchirant, -rante [deʃirɑ̃, -rɑ̃t] *adj* : heartbreaking, heartrending

déchirement [deʃirmɑ̃] *nm* **1** : tearing **2** : heartbreak **3** : rift, split

déchirer [deʃire] *vt* **1** : to tear up, to rip **2** : to tear apart, to split — **se déchirer** *vr*

déchirure [deʃiryr] *nf* : tear <déchirure ligamentaire : torn ligament>

déchoir |deʃwar| {27} *vi* **1** : to demean oneself **2** : to fall, to decline (in prestige)

déchu[1] |deʃy| *pp* → **décevoir**

déchu[2], **-chue** |deʃy| *adj* **1** : fallen (from grace or favor) **2** : deposed

décibel |desibɛl| *nm* : decibel

décidé, -dée |deside| *adj* **1** : decided, settled **2** DÉTERMINÉ : determined, resolved

décidément |desidemɑ̃| *adv* : definitely, really

décider |deside| *vt* **1** : to decide <j'ai décidé de partir : I decided to leave> **2** CONVAINCRE : to persuade **3 ~ de** : to decide on, to determine <nous avons décidé d'une date : we've set a date> — **se décider** *vr* : to make up one's mind

décimal, -male |desimal| *adj, mpl* **-maux** |-mo| : decimal

décimale *nf* : decimal

décimer |desime| *vt* : to decimate

décisif, -sive |desizif, -ziv| *adj* : decisive — **décisivement** |-zivmɑ̃| *adv*

décision |desizjɔ̃| *nf* **1** : decision <prendre une decision : to make a decision> **2** : decisiveness

déclamer |deklame| *vi* : to declaim

déclaratif, -tive |deklaratif, -tiv| *adj* : declarative

déclaration |deklarasjɔ̃| *nf* **1** : declaration, statement <déclaration de guerre : declaration of war> <faire sa déclaration : to declare one's love> **2** : (official) notification <déclaration d'impôts : income tax return> **3** : testimony, statement (in court)

déclarer |deklare| *vt* **1** : to declare, to announce **2** : to claim, to register (births, deaths, etc.) <déclarer qqch à la douane : to declare sth at customs> — **se déclarer** *vr* **1** : to declare oneself **2** : to declare one's love **3** : to break out, to show itself (of a disease, a fire, etc.)

déclassement |deklasmɑ̃| *nm* : downgrading, demotion

déclasser |deklase| *vt* **1** : to demote, to downgrade **2** : to get out of order, to disarrange **3** : to demean

déclenchement |deklɑ̃ʃmɑ̃| *nm* : start, launching

déclencher |deklɑ̃ʃe| *vt* **1** : to release, to set off **2** PROVOQUER : to trigger, to prompt **3** : to launch, to begin

déclencheur |deklɑ̃ʃœr| *nm* **1** : release mechanism **2** : trigger

déclic |deklik| *nm* **1** : trigger (mechanism) **2** : click

déclin |deklɛ̃| *nm* **1** : decline, waning **2** : close <le déclin du jour : the close of day>

déclinaison |deklinɛzɔ̃| *nf* : declension

décliner |dekline| *vi* : to decline, to wane — *vt* **1** : to refuse **2** : to decline (a noun) **3** : to state, to give (one's name, address, etc.)

déclivité |deklivite| *nf* : slope, incline

décloisonner |deklwazɔne| *vt* : to open up, to decompartmentalize

décocher |dekɔʃe| *vt* **1** : to shoot, to hurl **2** : to flash, to dart <il a décoché un sourire : he flashed a smile>

décoder |dekɔde| *vt* : to decode

décoiffer |dekwafe| *vt* **décoiffer qqn** : to mess up s.o.'s hair — *vi* **ça décoiffe** *fam* : it takes your breath away

décoincer |dekwɛ̃se| {6} *vt* **1** : to loosen, to unjam **2** *fam* : to loosen (someone) up — **se décoincer** *vr*

déçoit |deswa|, **déçoive** |deswav|, *etc.* → **décevoir**

décolérer |dekɔlere| {87} *vi* : to calm down, to cool off

décollage |dekɔlaʒ| *nm* : takeoff

décoller |dekɔle| *vt* : to unstick, to remove — *vi* : to take off (of an airplane, a project, etc.)

décolleté[1], **-tée** |dekɔlte| *adj* : low-cut

décolleté[2] *nm* **1** : low neckline **2** : cleavage

décolorant |dekɔlɔrɑ̃, -rɑ̃t| *nm* : bleach

décoloration |dekɔlɔrasjɔ̃| *nf* **1** : fading, discoloration **2** : bleaching

décolorer |dekɔlɔre| *vt* : to bleach, to cause to fade — **se décolorer** *vr* **1** : to fade **2** : to bleach one's hair

décombres |decɔ̃br| *nmpl* : rubble, debris

décommander |dekɔmɑ̃de| *vt* : to cancel — **se décommander** *vr* : to cancel one's appointment

décomposer |dekɔ̃poze| *vt* **1** : to break down, to break up **2** POURRIR : to rot, to cause to decompose **3** : to contort, to distort (one's face) — **se décomposer** *vr*

décomposition |dekɔ̃pozisjɔ̃| *nf* : decomposition, rotting

décompresser |dekɔ̃prese| *vt* : to decompress — *vi* : to relax, to unwind

décompte |dekɔ̃t| *nm* **1** : account, statement **2** : breakdown, count **3** : deduction, discount

décompter |dekɔ̃te| *vt* **1** : to deduct **2** : to calculate, to count — *vi* : to strike the wrong hour

déconcentration |dekɔ̃sɑ̃trasjɔ̃| *nf* **1** : decentralization **2** : distraction, loss of concentration

déconcentrer |dekɔ̃sɑ̃tre| *vt* **1** : to decentralize **2** : to distract — **se déconcentrer** *vr* : to lose one's concentration

déconcerter |dekɔ̃sɛrte| *vt* : to disconcert

déconfit, -fite |dekɔ̃fi, -fit| *adj* : downcast, crestfallen

déconfiture |dekɔ̃fityr| *nf* **1** : failure, collapse, defeat **2** : insolvency, bankruptcy

décongeler |dekɔ̃ʒle| {20} *v* : to thaw, to defrost

décongestif |dekɔ̃ʒɛstif, -tiv| *nm* : decongestant

décongestionnant[1], **-nante** [dekɔ̃ʒɛstjɔnɑ̃, -nɑ̃t] *adj* : decongestant
décongestionnant[2] *nm* : decongestant
décongestionner [dekɔ̃ʒɛstjɔne] *vt* : to relieve congestion in, to decongest
déconnecter [dekɔnɛkte] *vt* : to disconnect
déconner [dekɔne] *vi fam* **1** : to talk nonsense **2** : to mess around **3** : to be on the blink
déconseiller [dekɔ̃seje] *vt* : to dissuade, to advise against <elle m'a déconseillé d'y aller : she advised me not to go>
déconsidération [dekɔ̃siderasjɔ̃] *nf* : discredit
déconsidérer [dekɔ̃sidere] {87} *vt* : to discredit — **se déconsidérer** *vr*
décontaminer [dekɔ̃tamine] *vt* : to decontaminate
décontenancer [dekɔ̃tnɑ̃se] {6} *vt* : to disconcert — **se décontenancer** *vr* : to lose one's composure
décontracté, -tée [dekɔ̃trakte] *adj* **1** : relaxed **2** : casual, laid-back
décontracter [dekɔ̃trakte] *vt* : to relax — **se décontracter** *vr*
déconvenue [dekɔ̃vny] *nf* DÉCEPTION : disappointment
décor [dekɔr] *nm* **1** : decor **2** : scenery **3** : set, scenery (of movies or theater) **4 dans le décor** : off the road <il est rentré dans le décor : he drove off the road>
décorateur, -trice [dekɔratœr, -tris] *n* **1** : interior decorator **2** : set designer
décoratif, -tive [dekɔratif, -tiv] *adj* : decorative, ornamental
décorer [dekɔre] *vt* ORNER : to decorate — **décoration** [-kɔrasjɔ̃] *nf*
décortiquer [dekɔrtike] *vt* **1** : to shell, to hull **2** : to dissect, to analyze
décorum [dekɔrɔm] *nm* : decorum, propriety
découcher [dekuʃe] *vi* : to stay out all night
découdre [dekudr] {22} *vt* : to unstitch, to rip — *vi* **en ~** : to fight
découler [dekule] *vi* : to result, to follow, to ensue
découpage [dekupaʒ] *nm* **1** : cutting up, carving **2** : cutout **3** : shooting script (of a film) **4 découpage électoral** : districting
découper [dekupe] *vt* **1** : to cut up, to carve **2** : to cut out **3** : to indent (landforms, etc.) — **se découper** *vr* : to stand out
découplé, -plée [dekuple] *adj* **bien découplé** : well-built, well-proportioned
découpure [dekupyr] *nf* **1** : cutting **2** : indented outline
découragement [dekuraʒmɑ̃] *nm* : discouragement, despondency
décourager [dekuraʒe] {17} *vt* **1** : to discourage, to dishearten **2** : to deter, to put off
décousu, -sue [dekusy] *adj* **1** : unstitched **2** : disjointed, disconnected
découvert[1], **-verte** [dekuvɛr, -vɛrt] *adj* : bare, uncovered, exposed
découvert[2] *nm* : overdraft <être à découvert : to be overdrawn>
découverte *nf* : discovery, find
découvreur, -vreuse [dekuvrœr, -vrøz] *n* : discoverer, finder
découvrir [dekuvrir] {83} *vt* **1** : to discover **2** : to uncover **3** : to disclose, to reveal **4** : to catch sight of, to see — **se découvrir** *vr* **1** : to doff one's hat **2** : to undress, to uncover oneself **3** : to understand oneself **4** : to expose oneself to attack **5** : to clear up (of weather)
décrasser [dekrase] *vt* **1** : to clean, to scrub **2** : to polish, to remove the rough edges from (a person) — **se décrasser** *vr*
décrépit, -pite [dekrepi, -pit] *adj* : decrepit
décrépitude [dekrepityd] *nf* : decrepitude
décret [dekrɛ] *nm* : decree, edict
décréter [dekrete] {87} *vt* : to decree, to order
décrier [dekrije] {96} *vt* : to decry, to disparage
décrire [dekrir] {33} *vt* : to describe
décrocher [dekrɔʃe] *vt* **1** : to unhook, to take down, to undo <décrocher le téléphone : to pick up the telephone> **2** *fam* : to get, to land <décrocher une bonne situation : to land a good job> — *vi* **1** *fam* : to drop out, to give up **2** *fam* : to tune out, to stop paying attention **3** : to fall behind
décrocheur, -cheuse [dekrɔʃœr, -ʃøz] *n Can* : high school dropout
décroissance [dekrwasɑ̃s] *nf* : decrease, decline
décroître [dekrwatr] {25} *vi* : to decrease, to decline
décrotter [dekrɔte] *vt* : to scrape mud off
décrue [dekry] *nf* : drop in the water level
décrypter [dekripte] *vt* : to decipher
déçu[1] [desy] *pp* → **décevoir**
déçu[2], **-çue** [desy] *adj* : disappointed
décupler [dekyple] *v* : to increase tenfold
dédaigner [dedeɲe] *vt* : to disdain, to scorn
dédaigneux, -neuse [dedɛɲø, -ɲøz] *adj* : disdainful, scornful — **dédaigneusement** [-ɲøzmɑ̃] *adv*
dédain [dedɛ̃] *nm* MÉPRIS : disdain, scorn
dédale [dedal] *nm* : maze, labyrinth
dedans[1] [dədɑ̃] *adv* **1** : inside, in **2 de ~** : from within **3 en ~** : on the inside, inwardly, within
dedans[2] *nm* : inside, interior <du dehors vers le dedans : from the outside in>

dédicace [dedikas] *nf* : dedication, inscription (in a book, etc.)

dédicacer [dedikase] {6} *vt* : to inscribe, to autograph, to dedicate

dédier [dedje] {96} *vt* **1** : to dedicate (a work of art, etc.) **2** : to devote, to dedicate

dédire [dedir] {29} *v* **se dédire** *vr* **1** : to retract (a statement) **2 ~ de** : to go back on, to fail to honor

dédit [dedi] *nm* **1** : retraction **2** : penalty (for breach of contract)

dédommagement [dedɔmaʒmɑ̃] *nm* INDEMNITÉ : compensation

dédommager [dedɔmaʒe] {17} *vt* **1** : to compensate **2** : to repay, to make up for

dédouaner [dedwane] *vt* **1** : to clear through customs **2** : to clear (one's name), to rehabilitate

dédoubler [deduble] *vt* **1** : to divide, to split in two **2** : to remove the lining of (a garment) — **se dédoubler** *vr* **1** : to split (up), to come apart **2** : to be in two places at once

déductible [dedyktibl] *adj* : deductible

déduction [dedyksjɔ̃] *nf* **1** : deduction **2** : conclusion, inference

déduire [dedɥir] {49} *vt* **1** : to deduct **2** : to deduce, to infer

déesse [deɛs] *nf* : goddess

défaillance [defajɑ̃s] *nf* **1** : failure, fault **2** : failing, weakness **3** ÉVANOUISSEMENT : blackout, fainting fit

défaillant, -lante [defajɑ̃, -jɑ̃t] *adj* **1** : failing, unsteady **2** : weak, faint

défaillir [defajir] {93} *vi* **1** : to faint **2** : to weaken, to falter

défaire [defɛr] {42} *vt* **1** : to undo, to untie, to unravel **2** : to unpack **3** DÉMONTER : to dismantle, to take down, to break up **4 défaire le lit** : to strip the bed — **se défaire** *vr* **1** : to come undone, to come apart **2 ~ de** : to part with

défait, -faite [defɛ, -fɛt] *adj* **1** : undone **2** : defeated **3** : haggard

défaite *nf* : defeat

défaitisme [defetism] *nm* : defeatism — **défaitiste** [-fetist] *adj & nmf*

défalquer [defalke] *vt* : to deduct — **défalcation** [-falkasjɔ̃] *nf*

défausser [defose] *vt* : to straighten — **se défausser** *vr* : to discard (in card games)

défaut [defo] *nm* **1** IMPERFECTION : flaw, defect <défaut d'élocution : speech impediment> **2** FAIBLESSE : fault, shortcoming **3** MANQUE : lack, shortage <faire défaut : to be lacking> **4 à défaut de** : for lack of

défaveur [defavœr] *nf* : disfavor

défavorable [defavɔrabl] *adj* : unfavorable — **défavorablement** [-rabləmɑ̃] *adv*

défavoriser [defavɔrize] *vt* DÉSAVANTAGER : to put at a disadvantage

défection [defɛksjɔ̃] *nf* **1** : defection, desertion **2 faire défection** : to defect

défectueux, -tueuse [defɛktɥø, -tɥøz] *adj* : defective, faulty

défectuosité [defɛktɥozite] *nf* **1** : defectiveness **2** : defect, fault

défendable [defɑ̃dabl] *adj* : defensible, justifiable

défendeur, -deresse [defɑ̃dœr, -drɛs] *n* : defendant

défendre [defɑ̃dr] {63} *vt* **1** SOUTENIR : to defend, to champion **2** PROTÉGER : to protect, to safeguard **3** INTERDIRE : to forbid, to prohibit <il est défendu de fumer : smoking is prohibited> — **se défendre** *vr* **1** : to defend oneself **2** : to make sense <ses raisons se défendent : he's got a point> **3** *fam* : to get by, to manage **4 ~ de** : to refrain from **5 ~ de** : to deny

défense [defɑ̃s] *nf* **1** : defense **2** INTERDICTION : prohibition <défense d'entrer : no admittance> **3** : tusk

défenseur [defɑ̃sœr] *nm* **1** : defender, advocate **2** : defender (in sports) **3** : defense attorney

défensif, -sive [defɑ̃sif, -siv] *adj* : defensive — **défensivement** [-sivmɑ̃] *adv*

défensive *nf* : defensive <se tenir sur la défensive : to be on the defensive>

déféquer [defeke] {87} *vi* : to defecate

déférence [deferɑ̃s] *nf* : deference

déférent, -rente [deferɑ̃, -rɑ̃t] *adj* RESPECTUEUX : deferential, respectful

déférer [defere] {87} *vt* : to refer (a case) to a court — *vi* **~ à** : to defer to

déferlement [defɛrləmɑ̃] *nm* **1** : surge, breaking (of waves) **2** : surge, wave (of emotion)

déferler [defɛrle] *vt* : to unfurl — *vi* **1** : to break (of waves) **2** : to flood in <les spectateurs déferlent dans le théâtre : the audience is streaming into the theater>

défi [defi] *nm* **1** : challenge, dare **2** : (act of) defiance

défiance [defjɑ̃s] *nf* : distrust

défiant, -fiante [defjɑ̃, -fjɑ̃t] *adj* : distrustful

déficeler [defisle] {8} *vt* : to untie (a package) — **se déficeler** *vr*

déficience [defisjɑ̃s] *nf* : deficiency

déficient, -ciente [defisjɑ̃, -sjɑ̃t] *adj* : deficient

déficit [defisit] *nm* **1** : deficit **2** MANQUE : deficiency, lack

déficitaire [defisitɛr] *adj* **1** : in deficit **2** : meager, poor <une récolte déficitaire : a poor harvest>

défier [defje] {96} *vt* **1** : to challenge **2** : to defy — **se défier** *vr* **~ de** : to distrust

défigurement [defigyrmɑ̃] *n* : disfigurement

défigurer [defigyre] *vt* **1** : to disfigure **2** : to distort <défigurer les faits : to distort the facts>

défilé [defile] *nm* **1** : parade **2** : stream <défilé de pensées : stream of thoughts> **3** : gorge, pass

défiler [defile] *vi* **1** : to march, to parade **2** : to succeed one another <les heures défilent : the hours pass one after the other> **3** : to stream past **4** : to scroll (on a computer) — **se défiler** *vr* : to sneak off, to slip away

défini, -nie [defini] *adj* **1** : defined <bien défini : well-defined> **2** : definite <article défini : definite article>

définir [definir] *vt* : to define — **se définir** *vr*

définitif, -tive [definitif, -tiv] *adj* : definitive, final

définition [definisjɔ̃] *nf* **1** : definition **2** : clue (in a crossword puzzle) **3** : resolution (of a televised image)

définitive *nf* **en ~** : finally, in the final analysis

définitivement [definitivmɑ̃] *adv* **1** : definitively, permanently **2** : definitely

déflagration [deflagrasjɔ̃] *nf* : explosion, combustion

déflation [deflasjɔ̃] *nf* : deflation

déflorer [deflɔre] *vt* **1** : to deflower **2** : to spoil <la répétition a défloré la plaisanterie : repetition made the joke stale>

défoncer [defɔ̃se] {6} *vt* **1** : to smash, to demolish, to break **2** : to knock the bottom out of — **se défoncer** *vr fam* **1** : to give it one's all **2** : to get high (on drugs)

déforestation [defɔrɛstasjɔ̃] *nf* : deforestation

déformation [defɔrmasjɔ̃] *nf* **1** : deformation, distortion **2 déformation professionnelle** : conditioning by one's job, force of habit

déformer [defɔrme] *vt* **1** : to bend (out of shape) **2** : to deform, to distort — **se déformer** *vr* : to lose its shape

défoulement [defulmɑ̃] *nm* : release, letting off of steam

défouler [defule] *v* **se défouler** *vr* **1** : to unwind, to relax **2** : to vent (one's anger, etc.)

défraîchi, -chie [defreʃi] *adj* : faded, dingy, shopworn

défrayer [defreje] {11} *vt* **1** : to defray, to pay **2 défrayer la chronique** : to be in the news

défricher [defriʃe] *vt* **1** : to clear, to reclaim (land) **2** : to do the spadework for

défriser [defrize] *vt* **1** : to straighten (hair) **2** *fam* : to annoy, to bug

défroisser [defrwase] *vt* : to smooth out

défunt, -funte [defœ̃, -fœ̃t] *adj & n* : deceased

dégagé, -gée [degaʒe] *adj* **1** : clear, open, bare **2** LIBRE : casual, free and easy

dégager [degaʒe] {17} *vt* **1** DÉLIVRER : to release, to free **2** : to clear <dégagez la voie! : clear the way!> **3** : to make (funds) available <dégager des profits : to show a profit> **4** EXTRAIRE : to bring out, to extract **5** ÉMETTRE : to emit, to give off — **se dégager** *vr* **1** : to emanate **2** : to clear (up) **3 ~ de** : to get free of, to extricate oneself from

dégaine [degɛn] *nf* : odd gait, gawky appearance

dégainer [degene] *vt* : to draw (a weapon)

dégarnir [degarnir] *vt* **1** VIDER : to empty, to clear **2** : to withdraw (troops) — **se dégarnir** *vr* **1** : to empty, to be cleared out **2** : to go bald **3** : to lose its leaves

dégâts [dega] *nmpl* : damage <dégâts des eaux : flood damage>

dégel [deʒɛl] *nm* : thaw

dégeler [deʒle] {20} *vt* **1** : to thaw out, to defrost **2** : to unfreeze (assets) **3** *fam* : to relax, to loosen up — *vi* : to thaw

dégêner [deʒɛne] *vt Can* : to put at ease — **se dégêner** *vr* : to come out of one's shell

dégénéré, -rée [deʒenere] *adj* : degenerate

dégénérer [deʒenere] {87} *vi* : to degenerate

dégénérescence [deʒeneresɑ̃s] *nf* : degeneration

dégingandé, -dée [deʒɛ̃gɑ̃de] *adj* : lanky, gangling

dégivrer [deʒivre] *vt* : to defrost, to deice

dégivreur [deʒivrœr] *nm* : defroster, deicer

déglinguer [deglɛ̃ge] *vt fam* : to bust, to break — **se déglinguer** *vr fam* : to break down, to go on the blink

déglutir [deglytir] *vi* : to swallow

déglutition [deglytisjɔ̃] *nf* : swallowing

dégommer [degɔme] *vt fam* : to sack, to fire

dégonflement [degɔ̃fləmɑ̃] *nm* : deflation (of a tire, etc.)

dégonfler [degɔ̃fle] *vt* **1** : to deflate **2** : to reduce (swelling) **3** *fam* : to debunk — **se dégonfler** *vr* **1** : to deflate, to go flat **2** : to go down **3** *fam* : to chicken out, to lose one's nerve

dégorger [degɔrʒe] {17} *vt* **1** : to disgorge (liquid) **2** : to unblock, to clear **3** : to soak clean — *vi* **1** : to run (of fabric) **2 faire dégorger** : to soak

dégouliner [deguline] *vi* **1** : to trickle **2** : to drip

dégourdi, -die [degurdi] *adj* : smart, clever

dégourdir [degurdir] *vt* **1** : to warm up, to loosen up (one's legs, etc.) **2** *fam* : to bring (s.o.) out, to make less timid — **se dégourdir** *vr* **1** : to move about

<se dégourdir les jambes : to stretch one's legs> **2** *fam* : to wise up

dégoût [degu] *nm* **1** : disgust, repugnance **2 dégoût de la vie** : world-weariness

dégoûtant, -tante [degutɑ̃, -tɑ̃t] *adj* : disgusting, revolting

dégoûté, -tée [degute] *adj* **1** : disgusted **2** DIFFICILE : fastidious <il n'est pas dégoûté : he's not fussy>

dégoûter [degute] *vt* : to disgust — **se dégoûter** *vr* ~ **de** : to get sick of

dégoutter [degute] *vi* : to drip

dégradation [degradasjɔ̃] *nf* **1** : degradation, deterioration **2** : decline (of conditions, morals, etc.) **3** : damage **4 dégradation civique** : loss of civil rights

dégradé [degrade] *nm* : gradation, shading (of colors)

dégrader [degrade] *vt* **1** : to degrade **2** ABÎMER : to damage, to spoil — **se dégrader** *vr*

dégrafer [degrafe] *vt* : to unhook, to unclasp

dégraissage [degrɛsaʒ] *nm* **1** : downsizing, cutbacks *pl* **2** : removal of grease stains **3** : trimming (of meat)

dégraisser [degrese] *vt* **1** : to downsize **2** : to remove grease marks from **3** : to trim the fat from

degré [dəgre] *nm* **1** : degree <un angle de 90 degrés : a 90-degree angle> **2** : proof (of alcohol) **3** : level, extent <une brûlure du premier degré : a first-degree burn> <cousins au second degré : second cousins> **4** : step <les degrés de l'échelle sociale : the rungs of the social ladder> **5 par degrés** : gradually

dégressif, -sive [degrɛsif, -siv] *adj* : graduated (of taxes, etc.)

dégrèvement [degrɛvmɑ̃] *nm* : tax relief

dégringolade [degrɛ̃gɔlad] *nf fam* : tumble, collapse

dégringoler [degrɛ̃gɔle] *fam vt* : to tumble down, to rush down — *vi* : to fall, to tumble

déguerpir [degɛrpir] *vi* **1** : to clear out **2 faire déguerpir** : to drive away

dégueulasse [degœlas] *adj fam* : disgusting

déguisement [degizmɑ̃] *nm* : disguise

déguiser [degize] *vt* : to disguise — **se déguiser** *vr* ~ **en** : to dress up as, to masquerade as

dégustateur, -trice [degystatœr, -tris] *n* : taster

déguster [degyste] *vt* **1** : to taste, to sample **2** : to savor, to enjoy

dehors¹ [dəɔr] *adv* **1** : outside, outdoors **2** : out <allons dehors ce soir : let's go out tonight> **3 en** ~ : (toward the) outside **4 en dehors de** : outside of, apart from

dehors² *nms & pl* **1** : outside, exterior **2 les dehors** : appearances

déifier [deifje] {96} *vt* : to deify

déjà [deʒa] *adv* **1** : already **2** : before, previously **3** *fam* : again <tu viens quand, déjà? : tell me again when you're coming?> **4** (*used for reinforcement*) <ce n'est déjà pas si mal : it's not all that bad>

déjeté, -tée [deʒte] *adj* : warped, lopsided

déjeuner¹ [deʒœne] *vi* **1** : to have lunch **2** *Bel, Can, Switz* : to have breakfast

déjeuner² *nm* **1** : lunch **2** *Bel, Can, Switz* : breakfast

déjouer [deʒwe] *vt* : to thwart, to outsmart

delà [dəla] *adv* **1** → **deçà 2** → **au–delà, par–delà**

délabré, -rée [delabre] *adj* : dilapidated

délabrement [delabrəmɑ̃] *nm* **1** : dilapidation, deterioration **2** : ruin (of reputation, health, etc.)

délabrer [delabre] *vt* : to ruin — **se délabrer** *vr* : to deteriorate

délai [delɛ] *nm* **1** : time limit, deadline **2** : extension (of time) **3** : waiting period <sans délai : immediately, without delay>

délaissement [delɛsmɑ̃] *nm* : abandonment, desertion, neglect

délaisser [delese] *vt* **1** ABANDONNER : to abandon, to desert **2** : to neglect

délassement [delasmɑ̃] *nm* : relaxation

délasser [delase] *vt* : to relax — **se délasser** *vr*

délateur, -trice [delatœr, -tris] *n* : informer

délation [delasjɔ̃] *nf* : informing, denunciation

délavé, -vée [delave] *adj* : faded

délayage [delɛjaʒ] *nm* **1** : mixing **2** : dragging out (of a speech, etc.)

délayer [deleje] {11} *vt* **1** : to dilute, to mix **2** : to pad out, to drag out (a speech, etc.)

délectable [delɛktabl] *adj* : delectable, delicious

délectation [delɛktasjɔ̃] *nf* : delight

délecter [delɛkte] *v* **se délecter** *vr* ~ **de** : to delight in

délégation [delegasjɔ̃] *nf* **1** : delegation, assignment **2** : group of delegates

délégué, -guée [delege] *n* : delegate, representative

déléguer [delege] {87} *vt* : to delegate

délester [delɛste] *vt* **1** : to remove ballast from, to unload **2** : to relieve, to unburden **3** : to divert traffic away from **4** *fam* : to rob

délibération [deliberasjɔ̃] *nf* : deliberation

délibéré, -rée [delibere] *adj* **1** INTENTIONNEL : deliberate **2** DÉCIDÉ : resolute, determined — **délibérément** [-remɑ̃] *adv*

délibérer [delibere] {87} *vi* : to deliberate

délicat, -cate [delika, -kat] *adj* **1** : delicate, sensitive, tender **2** : dainty, refined, delicious **3** : considerate, tactful **4** : awkward, tricky **5** : scrupulous **6** : fussy, difficult

délicatement [delikatmɑ̃] *adv* **1** : delicately, gently, daintily **2** : thoughtfully, tactfully

délicatesse [delikatɛs] *nf* **1** : delicacy, tenderness **2** : fineness **3** : tactfulness **4** : awkwardness, difficulty **5** : scrupulousness

délice [delis] *nm* : delight

délicieux, -cieuse [delisjø, -sjøz] *adj* : delicious, delightful — **délicieusement** [-sjøzmɑ̃] *adv*

délictueux, -tueuse [deliktɥø, -tɥøz] *adj* : criminal

délié, -liée [delje] *adj* **1** : slender, fine **2** : nimble

délier [delje] {96} *vt* **1** : to untie **2** : to loosen (up) <l'alcool a délié sa langue : alcohol loosened his tongue> **3 ~ de** : to release from — **se délier** *vr*

délimitation [delimitasjɔ̃] *nf* : delimitation, boundary

délimiter [delimite] *vt* **1** : to delimit, to demarcate **2** : to define, to determine

délinquance [delɛ̃kɑ̃s] *nf* : crime, delinquency <délinquance juvenile : juvenile delinquency>

délinquant, -quante [delɛ̃kɑ̃, -kɑ̃t] *adj & n* : delinquent, offender

délirant, -rante [delirɑ̃, -rɑ̃t] *adj* **1** : delirious **2** : frenzied, wild

délire [delir] *nm* **1** : delirium **2 en ~** : delirious, frenzied

délirer [delire] *vi* **1** : to be delirious **2** : to rave, to be out of one's mind

délit [deli] *nm* : crime, offense

délivrance [delivrɑ̃s] *nf* **1** : freeing, release **2** : delivery, issue **3** : relief

délivrer [delivre] *vt* **1** : to set free **2** : to issue, to award, to hand over **3 ~ de** : to relieve of — **se délivrer** *vr* **~ de** : to rid oneself of

déloger [delɔʒe] {17} *vt* **1** : to evict, to throw out **2** : to remove, to dislodge — *vi* : to leave home, to move out

déloyal, déloyale [delwajal] *adj, mpl* **déloyaux** [-jo] **1** : disloyal **2** : unfair, dishonest — **déloyalement** [-mɑ̃] *adv*

déloyauté [delwajote] *nf* : disloyalty

delta [dɛlta] *nm* : delta

déluge [delyʒ] *nm* **1** : deluge, flood **2** : downpour

déluré, -rée [delyre] *adj* **1** : sharp, smart **2** : forward, brazen

démagogie [demagɔʒi] *nf* : demagogy — **démagogique** [-gɔʒik] *adj*

démagogue [demagɔg] *nmf* : demagogue

demain[1] [dəmɛ̃] *adv* **1** : tomorrow <demain soir : tomorrow evening> **2** : in the future

demain[2] *nm* **1** : tomorrow <à demain : see you tomorrow!> **2** : the future <le monde de demain : the world of the future, tomorrow's world>

démancher [demɑ̃ʃe] *vt Can* : to take apart, to dismantle

demande [dəmɑ̃d] *nf* **1** : request <demande en mariage : marriage proposal> **2** : application <demande d'emploi : job application> **3** : demand <l'offre et la demande : supply and demand> **4** : claim (in law)

demander [dəmɑ̃de] *vt* **1** : to ask for, to request **2** : to call for <on vous demande au téléphone : you are wanted on the telephone> **3** : to ask (about) <demander son chemin : to ask directions> **4** EXIGER : to demand, to ask <il m'en demande trop : he asks too much of me> **5** NÉCESSITER : to require, to need **6** : to send for (a doctor, etc.) — *vi* **~ à** : to ask to — **se demander** *vr* : to wonder

demandeur[1], **-deuse** [dəmɑ̃dœr, -døz] *n* : applicant <demandeur d'emploi : job applicant>

demandeur[2], **-deresse** [dəmɑ̃dœr, -drɛs] *n* : plaintiff

démangeaison [demɑ̃ʒɛzɔ̃] *nf* **1** : itch, itching **2** : urge

démanger [demɑ̃ʒe] {17} *vt* : to itch, to make itchy

démanteler [demɑ̃tle] {20} *vt* **1** : to demolish **2** : to break up, to dismantle

démaquillant [demakijɑ̃, -jɑ̃t] *nm* : makeup remover, cleansing cream

démaquiller [demakije] *v* **se démaquiller** *vr* : to remove one's makeup

démarcation [demarkasjɔ̃] *nf* : demarcation

démarchage [demarʃaʒ] *nm* : door-to-door solicitation <démarchage électoral : canvassing>

démarche [demarʃ] *nf* **1** : gait, walk **2** : step, action <faire des démarches : to take steps> **3** : approach, thought process

démarquer [demarke] *vt* **1** : to mark down (merchandise) **2** : to plagiarize — **se démarquer** *vr* : to distance oneself

démarrage [demaraʒ] *nm* : starting up

démarrer [demare] *vt* **1** : to start up (an automobile) **2** : to start, to launch (a project) — *vi* **1** : to start up (of an automobile) **2** : to drive off (of a driver) **3** : to get under way

démarreur [demarœr] *nm* : starter (of an automobile)

démasquer [demaske] *vt* : to unmask — **se démasquer** *vr* : to drop one's mask

démêlé [demele] *nm* **1** : quarrel **2 démêlés** *nmpl* : problems <avoir des démêlés avec la justice : to get in trouble with the law>

démêler [demele] *vt* **1** : to disentangle, to untangle **2** : to clear up, to sort out — **se démêler** *vr* **~ de** : to extricate oneself from (a problem, etc.)

démembrer [demɑ̃bre] *vt* **1** : to dismember, to cut up **2** : to divide up
déménagement [demenaʒmɑ̃] *nm* : moving, relocation
déménager [demenaʒe] {17} *v* : to move, to relocate
déménageur, -geuse [demenaʒœr, -ʒøz] *n* : (furniture) mover
démence [demɑ̃s] *nf* : madness, insanity
démener [demne] {52} *v* **se démener** *vr* **1** : to thrash about, to struggle **2** : to exert oneself
dément[1], -mente [demɑ̃, -mɑ̃t] *adj* **1** : demented, insane **2** *fam* : incredible, fantastic
dément[2], -mente *n* : demented person
démenti [demɑ̃ti] *nm* : denial
démentiel, -tielle [demɑ̃sjɛl] *adj* : insane
démentir [demɑ̃tir] {82} *vt* **1** : to deny **2** CONTREDIRE : to refute, to contradict
démérite [demerit] *nm* : demerit
démériter [demerite] *vi* **1** : to show oneself unworthy **2 démériter auprès de qqn** : to lose s.o.'s esteem
démesuré, -rée [deməzyre] *adj* : excessive, immoderate — **démesurément** [-remɑ̃] *adv*
démettre [demɛtr] {53} *vt* **1** DESTITUER : to dismiss, to fire **2** : to dislocate (in medicine) — **se démettre** *vr* **1** : to resign **2 se démettre l'épaule** : to dislocate one's shoulder
demeurant [dəmœrɑ̃] *adv* **au ~** : after all, for all that
demeure [dəmœr] *nf* **1** : residence, abode **2 à ~** : permanently **3 mettre en demeure** : to require **4 mise en demeure** : summons, demand
demeurer [dəmœre] *vi* **1** (*with auxiliary verb* **être**) : to remain **2** (*with auxiliary verb* **avoir**) : to reside **3 il n'en demeure pas moins** : the fact remains, nonetheless
demi[1] [dəmi] *adv* **1** : half <demi-cuit : half-cooked> **2 à ~** : halfway <faire les choses à demi : to do things by halves>
demi[2], -mie *adj* **1** : half <un demi pain : half a loaf> **2 et ~** : and a half <sept litres et demi : seven and a half liters> <à cinq heures et demie : at five-thirty>
demi[3], -mie *n* : half <voulez-vous une bouteille? non, une demie : do you want a bottle? no, (just) a half>
demi[4] *nm* **1** : half <trois demis : three halves> **2** *France* : half-pint (of beer) **2** : halfback
demi–bas [dəmiba] *nms & pl* : kneesock
demi–bouteille [dəmibutɛj] *nf, pl* **demi–bouteilles** : half-bottle
demi–cercle [dəmisɛrkl] *nm, pl* **demi–cercles** : semicircle — **demi–circulaire** [-sirkylɛr] *adj*
demi–dieu [dəmidjø] *nm, pl* **demi–dieux** : demigod
demi–douzaine [dəmiduzɛn] *nf, pl* **demi–douzaines** : half a dozen
demie *nf* : half hour <la cloche a sonné la demie : the bell rang the half hour> <à la demie : at half past>
demi–finale [dəmifinal] *nf, pl* **demi–finales** : semifinal — **demi–finaliste** [-nalist] *nmf*
demi–frère [dəmifrɛr] *nm, pl* **demi–frères** : half brother
demi–heure [dəmijœr] *nf, pl* **demi–heures** : half hour
demi–jour [dəmiʒur] *nm, pl* **demi–jours** : half-light
demi–journée [dəmiʒurne] *nf, pl* **demi–journées** : half a day, half day
demi–litre [dəmilitr] *nm, pl* **demi–litres** : half-liter
demi–lune [dəmilyn] *nf, pl* **demi–lunes** **1** : half-moon **2 en ~** : semicircular
demi–mal [dəmimal] *nm* **il n'y a que demi–mal** : things could be worse
demi–mesure [dəmiməzyr] *nf, pl* **demi–mesures** : half measure
demi–mot [dəmimo] **à ~** : without having to spell things out
demi–pension [dəmipɑ̃sjɔ̃] *nf, pl* **demi–pensions** : half board (one meal furnished daily)
demi–place [dəmiplas] *nf, pl* **demi–places** **1** : half-price seat (at the theater) **2** : half-price fare (on a train, etc.)
demi–saison [dəmisɛzɔ̃] *nf* **vêtements de demi–saison** : spring or fall clothing
demi–sel [dəmisɛl] *nms & pl* : slightly salted (cheese, butter, etc.)
demi–sœur [dəmisœr] *nf, pl* **demi–sœurs** : half sister
démission [demisjɔ̃] *nf* **1** : resignation **2** : abdication of responsibility
démissionnaire [demisjɔnɛr] *adj* : outgoing, resigning
démissionner [demisjɔne] *vi* **1** : to resign **2** : to give up <je démissionne après cet essai : I'm giving up after this try> — *vt fam* : to oust
demi–tarif [dəmitarif] *nm, pl* **demi–tarifs** : half-price ticket
demi–teinte [dəmitɛ̃t] *nf, pl* **demi–teintes** : halftone
demi–tour [dəmitur] *nm, pl* **demi–tours** **1** : half turn <faire un demi-tour : to turn back> **2** : about-face **3** : U-turn
demi–vie [dəmivi] *nf, pl* **demi–vies** : half-life
démobiliser [demɔbilize] *vt* : to demobilize — **démobilisation** [-lizasjɔ̃] *nf*
démocrate[1] [demɔkrat] *adj* : democratic
démocrate[2] *nmf* : democrat
démocratie [demɔkrasi] *nf* : democracy

démocratique [demɔkratik] *adj* : democratic — **démocratiquement** [-tikmɑ̃] *adv*

démodé, -dée [demɔde] *adj* : old-fashioned, out-of-date

démographie [demɔgrafi] *nf* : demography — **démographique** [-grafik] *adj*

demoiselle [demwazɛl] *nf* **1** : young lady **2 demoiselle d'honneur** : bridesmaid

démolir [demɔlir] *vt* **1** : to demolish, to tear down **2** : to destroy, to ruin

démolition [demɔlisjɔ̃] *nf* **1** : demolition **2** : destruction, ruin

démon [demɔ̃] *nm* **1 le démon** : the devil **2** : demon, evil spirit **3 être en démon** *Can fam* : to be furious

démoniaque [demɔnjak] *adj* : fiendish, diabolical

démonstrateur, -trice [demɔ̃stratœr, -tris] *n* : demonstrator

démonstratif, -tive [demɔ̃stratif, -tiv] *adj* : demonstrative

démonstration [demɔ̃strasjɔ̃] *nf* **1** MANIFESTATION : demonstration, show <une démonstration de force : a show of strength> **2** PREUVE : proof

démontable [demɔ̃tabl] *adj* : collapsible, able to be dismantled

démonter [demɔ̃te] *vt* **1** : to dismantle **2** : to remove, to take down **3** : to disconcert — **se démonter** *vr*

démontrer [demɔ̃tre] *vt* : to demonstrate, to show, to prove

démoralisant, -sante [demɔralizɑ̃, -zɑ̃t] *adj* : demoralizing

démoraliser [demɔralize] *vt* : to demoralize — **se démoraliser** *vr*

démordre [demɔrdr] {63} *vt* **ne pas démordre de** : to stick to, to refuse to give up

démuni, -nie [demyni] *adj* **1** : poor, impoverished **2** : powerless

démunir [demynir] *vt* : to deprive — **se démunir** *vr* **~ de** : to part with

démystifier [demistifje] {96} *vt* **1** : to demystify **2** : to disabuse

dénaturé, -rée [denatyre] *adj* **1** : denatured **2** : unnatural

dénaturer [denatyre] *vt* **1** : to distort, to misrepresent **2** : to denature, to alter completely

dénégation [denegasjɔ̃] *nf* : denial

déneigement [denɛʒmɑ̃] *nm* : snow removal

déneiger [deneʒe] {17} *vt* : to clear snow from

déni [deni] *nm* : denial

dénicher [deniʃe] *vt* **1** : to unearth, to discover **2** : to take (a bird) from the nest — *vi* : to leave the nest

denier [dənje] *nm* **deniers publics** : public funds

dénier [denje] {96} *vt* : to deny

dénigrement [denigrəmɑ̃] *nm* : disparagement

dénigrer [denigre] *vt* : to denigrate, to disparage

denim [dənim] *nm* : denim

dénivellation [denivɛlasjɔ̃] *nf* **1** : difference in altitude or level **2** : gradient, slope

dénivellement [denivɛlmɑ̃] *nm* → **dénivellation**

dénombrement [denɔ̃brəmɑ̃] *nm* : counting, count

dénombrer [denɔ̃bre] *vt* : to count

dénominateur [denɔminatœr] *nm* : denominator <dénominateur commun : common denominator>

dénomination [denɔminasjɔ̃] *nf* **1** : naming **2** : name, designation

dénommé, -mée [denɔme] *n* **un dénommé** : a person by the name of <une dénommée Marie : a certain Marie>

dénommer [denɔme] *vt* : to name, to call

dénoncer [denɔ̃se] {6} *vt* : to denounce, to inform on — **se dénoncer** *vr* : to give oneself up

dénonciation [denɔ̃sjasjɔ̃] *nf* : denunciation

dénoter [denɔte] *vt* : to denote, to indicate

dénouement [denumɑ̃] *nm* **1** : denouement (in theater) **2** : outcome

dénouer [denwe] *vt* **1** : to untie **2** : to unravel, to resolve — **se dénouer** *vr*

dénoyauter [denwajote] *vt* : to pit (a fruit)

denrée [dɑ̃re] *nf* : commodity <denrées alimentaires : foods> <une denrée rare : a rare commodity>

dense [dɑ̃s] *adj* : dense — **densément** [dɑ̃semɑ̃] *adv*

densité [dɑ̃site] *nf* : density, denseness

dent [dɑ̃] *nf* **1** : tooth <dents de sagesse : wisdom teeth> <dents de lait : baby teeth> **2** : cog (of a wheel, etc.) **3** : prong, tine (of a fork) **4 avoir une dent contre** : to hold a grudge against **5 en dents de scie** : serrated **6 faire ses dents** : to teethe

dentaire [dɑ̃tɛr] *adj* : dental

dent–de–lion [dɑ̃dəljɔ̃] *nf, pl* **dents–de–lion** : dandelion

denté, -tée [dɑ̃te] *adj* : toothed

dentelé, -lée [dɑ̃tle] *adj* : serrated, jagged, indented

dentelle [dɑ̃tɛl] *nf* : lace

dentier [dɑ̃tje] *nm* : dentures *pl*

dentifrice [dɑ̃tifris] *nm* : toothpaste

dentiste [dɑ̃tist] *nmf* : dentist

dentisterie [dɑ̃tistəri] *nf* : dentistry

dentition [dɑ̃tisjɔ̃] *nf* : teeth *pl*, dentition <avoir une belle dentition : to have nice teeth>

dénudé, -dée [denyde] *adj* **1** : bare **2** : bald

dénuder [denyde] *vt* **1** : to bare **2** : to strip (off) — **se dénuder** *vr* **1** : to strip **2** : to go bald

dénué, -nuée [denɥe] *adj* **~ de** : devoid of, lacking in

dénuement [denymɑ̃] *nm* : destitution
déodorant [deɔdɔrɑ̃] *adj & nm* : deodorant
dépanner [depane] *vt* **1** : to fix, to repair **2** : to help out
dépanneur[1], **-neuse** [depanœr, -nøz] *n* : repairman, repairwoman
dépanneur[2] *nm Can* : convenience store
dépanneuse *nf* : tow truck, wrecker
dépareillé, -lée [depareje] *adj* **1** : incomplete **2** : odd, unpaired
déparer [depare] *vt* : to spoil, to mar
déparler [deparle] *vi Can fam* : to rave, to talk nonsense
départ [depar] *nm* **1** : departure **2** : start (in sports) <ligne de départ : starting line> **3 au départ** : at first, initially **4 être sur le départ** : to be about to leave
départager [departaʒe] {17} *vt* : to decide between
département [departəmɑ̃] *nm* **1** : department **2** : territorial division in France — **départemental, -tale** [-mɑ̃tal] *adj*
départir [departir] {82} *vt* : to assign, to allot — **se départir** *vr* : to abandon, to give up
dépassé, -sée [depase] *adj* : outdated, outmoded
dépassement [depasmɑ̃] *nm* **1** : passing (with an automobile) **2** : excess, overrun
dépasser [depase] *vt* **1** : to pass, to go past **2** EXCÉDER : to exceed, to go beyond <l'addition a depassé la somme prévue : the bill exceeded the expected amount> **3** : to outshine, to surpass **4 cela me dépasse!** : that's beyond me! — *vi* : to show, to stick out <ton jupon dépasse : your slip is showing>
dépaysement [depeizmɑ̃] *nm* **1** : disorientation **2** : change of scenery
dépayser [depeize] *vt* **1** : to disorient **2** : to provide with a change of scenery
dépecer [depəse] {6} *and* {52} *vt* : to carve up, to cut up
dépêche [depɛʃ] *nf* **1** : dispatch **2** *or* **dépêche télégraphique** : telegram
dépêcher [depeʃe] *vt* : to dispatch — **se dépêcher** *vr* SE HÂTER : to hurry
dépeindre [depɛ̃dr] {37} *vt* : to depict, to describe
dépendamment [depɑ̃damɑ̃] *adv* **~ de** *Can* : depending on
dépendance [depɑ̃dɑ̃s] *nf* **1** : dependence **2** : dependency (on drugs, etc.) **3** : outbuilding
dépendant, -dante [depɑ̃dɑ̃, -dɑ̃t] *adj* : dependent
dépendre [depɑ̃dr] {63} *vi* **1 ~ de** : to depend on **2 ~ de** : to belong to — *vt* : to take down
dépens [depɑ̃] *nmpl* **aux dépens de** : at the expense of
dépense [depɑ̃s] *nf* **1** : spending, expenditure **2** : expense **3** : consumption
dépenser [depɑ̃se] *vt* **1** : to spend **2** : to use up, to expend <j'ai dépensé toute mon énergie : I've used up all my energy> — **se dépenser** *vr* : to exert oneself
dépensier[1], **-sière** [depɑ̃sje, -sjɛr] *adj* : extravagant, wasteful
dépensier[2], **-sière** *n* : spendthrift
déperdition [depɛrdisjɔ̃] *nf* : loss
dépérir [deperir] *vi* **1** : to wither (of a plant) **2** : to waste away (of persons) **3** : to be on the decline
dépêtrer [depetre] *v* **se dépêtrer** *vr* **~ de** : to extricate oneself from
dépeupler [depœple] *vt* : to depopulate
déphasé, -sée [defaze] *adj* : out of touch (with reality), out of it
dépilatoire [depilatwar] *adj* : depilatory
dépiler [depile] *vt* : to remove hair from
dépistage [depistaʒ] *nm* : screening, testing <dépistage précoce : early detection>
dépister [depiste] *vt* **1** : to detect (a disease) **2** : to track down
dépit [depi] *nm* **1** : pique, vexation **2 en dépit de** MALGRÉ : in spite of, despite <en dépit de sa bonne volonté : despite his good will>
déplacé, -cée [deplase] *adj* **1** MALVENU : out of place, uncalled-for **2** : displaced <personnes déplacées : displaced persons>
déplacement [deplasmɑ̃] *nm* **1** : displacement **2** : moving, shifting **3** : trip, traveling <frais de déplacement : travel expenses> <être en déplacement : to be away on business>
déplacer [deplase] {6} *vt* **1** : to move, to shift, to change **2** : to displace — **se déplacer** *vr*
déplaire [deplɛr] {66} *vi* **1** : to be disliked **2 ~ à** : to put off, to repel <cela me déplaît : I don't like it> **3 ~ à** : to annoy, to offend <ne t'en déplaise : whether you like it or not>
déplaisant, -sante [deplɛzɑ̃, -zɑ̃t] *adj* : unpleasant, disagreeable
déplaisir [deplezir] *nm* : annoyance, displeasure
déplantoir [deplɑ̃twar] *nm* : (garden) trowel
dépliant [deplijɑ̃, -jɑ̃t] *nm* : brochure, pamphlet
déplier [deplije] {96} *vt* : to unfold — **se déplier** *vr*
déplisser [deplise] *vt* : to smooth out, to remove the pleats from
déploiement [deplwamɑ̃] *nm* **1** : deployment **2** : unfolding, spreading **3** : display
déplorable [deplɔrabl] *adj* : deplorable — **déplorablement** [-rabləmɑ̃] *adv*
déplorer [deplɔre] *vt* : to deplore, to lament

déployer [deplwaje] {58} *vt* **1** : to deploy **2** : to unfold, to spread out **3** : to display, to exhibit

déplumer [deplyme] *vt* : to pluck (a bird) — **se déplumer** *vr* **1** : to molt **2** *fam* : to go bald

dépoli, -lie [depɔli] *adj* **verre dépoli** : frosted glass

déporter [depɔrte] *vt* **1** : to inter in a concentration camp **2** DÉVIER : to divert, to carry off course — **se déporter** *vr* : to swerve

déposant, -sante [depozɑ̃, -zɑ̃t] *n* **1** : depositor **2** : witness (in law)

déposé, -sée [depoze] *adj* : registered <marque déposée : registered trademark>

déposer [depoze] *vt* **1** : to lay down, to put down **2** : to deposit **3** : to drop off, to leave **4** : to register, to file **5** : to depose **6** : to remove, to take down — *vi* **1** : to settle, to form a sediment **2** : to give evidence (in court) — **se déposer** *vr* : to settle

dépositaire [depɔzitɛr] *nmf* **1** : agent, dealer **2** : trustee **3** : repository (of a secret, etc.)

déposition [depozisjɔ̃] *nf* : evidence, testimony (in court)

déposséder [depɔsede] {87} *vt* : to dispossess

dépôt [depo] *nm* **1** : deposit, depository <dépôt en coffre-fort : safe deposit> **2** ENTREPÔT : warehouse, depot **3** : (retail) outlet **4** : registration, filing (of documents) **5** : sediment, (geological) deposit

dépotoir [depɔtwar] *nm* : dump

dépouille [depuj] *nf* **1** : hide, skin **2** *or* **dépouille mortelle** : mortal remains *pl* **3 dépouilles** *nfpl* : spoils

dépouillement [depujmɑ̃] *nm* **1** : austerity, soberness **2** : counting, perusal <dépouillement du scrutin : tally of votes>

dépouiller [depuje] *vt* **1** : to strip (off) **2** : to dispossess, to despoil **3** : to peruse, to scrutinize <dépouiller le scrutin : to tally the votes> **4** : to skin — **se dépouiller** *vr* **~ de** : to divest oneself of

dépourvu, -vue [depurvy] *adj* **1 ~ de** : lacking in, devoid of, without **2 au ~** : by surprise

dépravation [depravasjɔ̃] *nf* : depravity

dépraver [deprave] *vt* : to deprave — **dépravé, -vée** [-ve] *adj*

dépréciation [depresjasjɔ̃] *nf* : depreciation

déprécier [depresje] {96} *vt* **1** : to depreciate **2** : to disparage, to belittle — **se déprécier** *vr* **1** : to depreciate **2** : to put oneself down

déprédations [depredasjɔ̃] *nfpl* : damage

dépresseur [depresœr] *nm* : depressant

dépressif, -sive [depresif, -siv] *adj & n* : depressive

dépression [depresjɔ̃] *nf* **1** : depression **2 dépression nerveuse** : nervous breakdown

déprimant, -mante [deprimɑ̃, -mɑ̃t] *adj* : depressing

déprimé, -mée [deprime] *adj* : depressed, dejected

déprimer [deprime] *vt* **1** : to depress, to demoralize **2** : to press in, to indent — *vi fam* : to be depressed

depuis[1] [dəpɥi] *adv* **1** : since (then) <nous ne les avons pas revus depuis : we've never seen them since> **2 depuis que** : (ever) since <depuis qu'ils sont partis : ever since they left>

depuis[2] *prep* **1** : since <depuis 1831 : since 1831> **2** : from <depuis le matin jusqu'au soir : from morning till night> <depuis Londres à New York : from London to New York> **3** : for <en fonction depuis deux ans : in office for two years>

députation [depytasjɔ̃] *nf* **1** : deputation **2** : position of deputy

député, -tée [depyte] *n* **1** : deputy, representative (in government) **2** : delegate

députer [depyte] *vt* : to delegate, to appoint as representative, to deputize

déraciner [derasine] *vt* **1** ARRACHER : to uproot **2** : to eradicate

déraillement [derajmɑ̃] *nm* : derailment

dérailler [deraje] *vi* : to derail

déraisonnable [derɛzɔnabl] *adj* : unreasonable — **déraisonnablement** [-nabləmɑ̃] *adv*

déraisonner [derɛzɔne] *vi* : to talk nonsense

dérangement [derɑ̃ʒmɑ̃] *nm* **1** : trouble **2** : disorder, breakdown <en dérangement : out of order>

déranger [derɑ̃ʒe] {17} *vt* **1** : to bother, to disturb <ne vous dérangez pas : don't bother> **2** : to disrupt, to upset — **se déranger** *vr* **1** : to get up, to go out **2** : to put oneself out

dérapage [derapaʒ] *nm* **1** : skid, slip **2** : blunder **3** : loss of control

déraper [derape] *vi* **1** : to skid, to slip **2** : to get out of hand

derby [dɛrbi] *nm, pl* **derbys** *or* **derbies** : derby (horse race)

déréglé, -lée [deregle] *adj* **1** : out of order **2** : dissolute

déréglementer [derɛgləmɑ̃te] *vt* : to deregulate — **déréglementation** [-mɑ̃tasjɔ̃] *nf*

dérégler [deregle] {87} *vt* **1** : to put out of order **2** : to upset, to disturb — **se dérégler** *vr* : to go wrong

dérhumer *v* **se dérhumer** *vr Can fam* : to clear one's throat

dérider [deride] *vt* : to cheer up

dérision [derizjɔ̃] *nf* MÉPRIS : derision

dérisoire [derizwar] *adj* **1** : ridiculous, laughable **2** : trivial, pathetic

dérivation |derivasjɔ̃| *nf* : derivation

dérivatif[1], **-tive** |derivatif, -tiv| *adj* : derivative

dérivatif[2] *nm* : distraction, diversion

dérive |deriv| *nf* **1** : drift **2 à la dérive** : adrift

dérivé |derive| *nm* **1** : derivation (of a word) **2** SOUS-PRODUIT : by-product

dériver |derive| *vt* **1** : to divert **2 ~ de** : to derive from — *vi* : to drift, to be adrift

dermatologie |dɛrmatɔlɔʒi| *nf* : dermatology

dermatologique |dɛrmatɔlɔʒik| *adj* : dermatologic, dermatological

dermatologue |dɛrmatɔlɔg| *nmf* : dermatologist

dernier[1], **-nière** |dɛrnje, -njɛr| *adj* **1** : last, previous <l'année dernière : last year> **2** : latest **3** : final, last **4** : highest <le dernier degré de : the height of> **5** : lowest <la dernière marche : the bottom step>

dernier[2], **-nière** *n* **1** : last (one) **2 ce dernier, cette dernière** : the latter

dernier[3] *nm* **en ~** : last <il est arrivé en dernier : he arrived last>

dernièrement |dɛrnjɛrmɑ̃| *adv* : recently, lately

dernier–né, dernière–née |dɛrnjene, dɛrnjɛrne| *n* : last-born child

dérobade |derɔbad| *nf* : evasion

dérobé, -bée |derɔbe| *adj* **1** : concealed, hidden **2 à la dérobée** : surreptitiously

dérober |derɔbe| *vt* **1** : to steal **2** MASQUER : to conceal, to hide — **se dérober** *vr* **1** : to shy away, to be evasive **2** : to give way, to collapse **3 ~ à** : to avoid, to shirk

dérogation |derɔgasjɔ̃| *nf* : dispensation, exemption

déroger |derɔʒe| {17} *vi* **~ à** : to depart from

dérougir |deruʒir| *vi Can fam* **ne pas dérougir** : to continue without interruption <le téléphone n'a pas dérougi : the phone rang off the hook>

dérouiller |deruje| *vt fam* : to beat up — *vi France fam* : to have a hard time — **se dérouiller** *vr* SE DÉGOURDIR : to limber up, to stretch (one's legs, etc.)

déroulement |derulmɑ̃| *nm* **1** : unwinding, unrolling **2** : development, progress

dérouler |derule| *vt* : to unwind, to unroll — **se dérouler** *vr* **1** : to take place **2** : to develop, to progress **3** : to unwind

déroute |derut| *nf* **1** : rout **2 en ~** : routed, in full flight

dérouter |derute| *vt* **1** : to reroute, to divert **2** : to disconcert, to confuse

derrière[1] |dɛrjɛr| *adv & prep* : behind

derrière[2] *nm* **1** : back, rear <le derrière de l'édifice : the back of the building> **2** : rump, haunches *pl* (of an animal) **3** *fam* : buttocks *pl*, bottom

des[1] |de| → **de, le**

des[2] → **un**

dès |dɛ| *prep* **1** : from <dès le début : from the start> <dès Boston jusqu'à Portland : from Boston to Portland> <dès son arrivée : as soon as he arrived> **2 dès lors** : from then on **3 dès lors que** : from the moment that, since **4 dès que** : as soon as

désabusé, -sée |dezabyze| *adj* : disillusioned, disenchanted

désaccord |dezakɔr| *nm* **1** DIFFÉREND : disagreement **2** : discrepancy

désaccoutumer |dezakutyme| *vt* **désaccoutumer qqn de** : to cure s.o. of the habit of — **se désaccoutumer** *vr* **~ de** : to get out of the habit of

désaffecté, -tée |dezafɛkte| *adj* : disused

désaffection |dezafɛksjɔ̃| *nf* : disaffection

désagréable |dezagreabl| *adj* DÉPLAISANT : disagreeable, unpleasant — **désagréablement** |-abləmɑ̃| *adv*

désagrégation |dezagregasjɔ̃| *nf* : disintegration, breakup

désagréger |dezagreʒe| {64} *vt* : to break up — **se désagréger** *vr* : to disintegrate

désagrément |dezagremɑ̃| *nm* : inconvenience, annoyance

désaligné, -née |dezaliɲe| *adj* : out of alignment

désaltérant, -rante |dezalterɑ̃, -rɑ̃t| *adj* : thirst-quenching

désaltérer |dezaltere| {87} *vt* : to quench the thirst of — **se désaltérer** *vr* : to quench one's thirst

désamorcer |dezamɔrse| {6} *vt* : to defuse

désappointer |dezapwɛ̃te| *vt* : to disappoint — **désappointement** |-pwɛ̃tmɑ̃| *nm*

désapprobateur, -trice |dezaprɔbatœr, -tris| *adj* : disapproving

désapprobation |dezaprɔbasjɔ̃| *nf* : disapproval

désapprouver |dezapruve| *vt* : to disapprove of

désarçonner |dezarsɔne| *vt* **1** : to throw (a rider), to unseat **2** : to nonplus

désargenté, -tée |dezarʒɑ̃te| *adj fam* : short of cash, broke

désarmant, -mante |dezarmɑ̃, -mɑ̃t| *adj* : disarming

désarmement |dezarməmɑ̃| *nm* : disarmament

désarmer |dezarme| *vt* : to disarm — *vi* **1** : to disarm **2** : to relent, to abate

désarroi |dezarwa| *nm* : confusion, distress, dismay

désassembler |dezasɑ̃ble| *vt* : to disassemble

désastre |dezastr| *nm* : disaster

désastreux, -treuse |dezastrø, -trøz| *adj* : disastrous

désavantage [dezavɑ̃taʒ] *nm* : disadvantage, drawback

désavantager [dezavɑ̃taʒe] {17} *vt* : to put at a disadvantage

désavantageux, -geuse [dezavɑ̃taʒø, -ʒøz] *adj* : disadvantageous, unfavorable

désaveu [dezavø] *nm, pl* **-veux 1** : repudiation **2** : disavowal, denial

désavouer [dezavwe] *vt* **1** : to deny **2** : to disown

désaxé, désaxée [dezakse] *adj* : (mentally) unbalanced

descendance [desɑ̃dɑ̃s] *nf* **1** : lineage, descent <de descendance irlandaise : of Irish descent> **2** PROGÉNITURE : offspring, descendants *pl*

descendant[1], **-dante** [desɑ̃dɑ̃, -dɑ̃t] *adj* : descending, downward

descendant[2], **-dante** *n* : descendant

descendre [dəsɑ̃dr] {63} *vt* **1** : to descend, to go down **2** : to take down, to bring down **3** : to lower — *vi* **1** : to descend, to go down, to come down **2** : to get off, to get out, to disembark, to dismount **3** ~ **à** : to stay at (a hotel, etc.) **4** ~ **de** : to be descended from

descente [desɑ̃t] *nf* **1** : descent **2** : (police) raid **3** : slope

descriptif, -tive [dɛskriptif, -tiv] *adj* : descriptive

description [dɛskripsjɔ̃] *nf* : description

désemparé, -rée [dezɑ̃pare] *adj* **1** : distraught, at a loss **2** : disabled (of a plane, ship, etc.)

désemparer [dezɑ̃pare] *vi* **sans** ~ : without interruption, continuously

désenchanter [dezɑ̃ʃɑ̃te] *vt* : to disenchant, to disillusion — **désenchantement** [-ʃɑ̃tmɑ̃] *nm*

désencombrer [dezɑ̃kɔ̃bre] *vt* : to unblock, to clear

désenfler [dezɑ̃fle] *vi* : to become less swollen, to go down

désengagement [dezɑ̃gaʒmɑ̃] *nm* : disengagement, withdrawal

désengager [dezɑ̃gaʒe] {17} *vt* : to disengage, to release — **se désengager** *vr* : to withdraw

désenivrer [dezɑ̃nivre] *vt* : to sober up — **se désenivrer** *vr*

déséquilibre [dezekilibr] *nm* **1** : lack of balance, instability **2** : imbalance

déséquilibrer [dezekilibre] *vt* : to unbalance — **déséquilibré, -brée** [dezekilibre] *adj*

désert[1], **-serte** [dezɛr, -zɛrt] *adj* : uninhabited, deserted <île déserte : desert island>

désert[2] *nm* : desert

déserter [dezɛrte] *v* : to desert

déserteur [dezɛrtœr] *nm* : deserter

désertion [dezɛrsjɔ̃] *nf* : desertion

désertique [dezɛrtik] *adj* **1** : desert **2** : barren

désespérance [dezɛsperɑ̃s] *nf* : despair

désespérant, -rante [dezɛsperɑ̃, -rɑ̃t] *adj* **1** : hopeless, despairing **2** : appalling, terrible

désespéré, -rée [dezɛspere] *adj* **1** : desperate **2** : hopeless

désespérément [dezɛsperemɑ̃] *adv* : desperately, hopelessly, helplessly

désespérer [dezɛspere] {87} *vi* : to despair <elle désespère d'une carrière : she has given up hope for a career> — *vt* : to drive to despair

désespoir [dezɛspwar] *nm* **1** : despair, desperation **2 en désespoir de cause** : as a last resort, in sheer desperation

déshabillé [dezabije] *nm* : negligee

déshabiller [dezabije] *vt* : to undress — **se déshabiller** *vr*

déshabituer [dezabitɥe] *vt* **déshabituer qqn de** : to break s.o. of the habit of — **se déshabituer** *vr* ~ **de** : to get out of the habit of

désherber [dezɛrbe] *v* : to weed

déshérité[1], **-tée** [dezerite] *adj* **1** : disinherited **2** : deprived, underprivileged

déshérité[2], **-tée** *n* **les déshérités** : the underprivileged

déshériter [dezerite] *vt* : to disinherit

déshonneur [dezɔnœr] *nm* : disgrace

déshonorant, -rante [dezɔnɔrɑ̃, -rɑ̃t] *adj* : dishonorable

déshonorer [dezɔnɔre] *vt* : to dishonor, to disgrace — **se déshonorer** *vr* : to disgrace oneself

déshumaniser [dezymanize] *vt* : to dehumanize

déshydratation [dezidratasjɔ̃] *nf* : dehydration

déshydrater [dezidrate] *vt* : to dehydrate — **se déshydrater** *vr*

design [dizajn] *nm* : design

désignation [deziɲasjɔ̃] *nf* **1** : designation, name **2** NOMINATION : appointment, nomination

designer [dizajnœr] *nmf* : designer

désigner [deziɲe] *vt* **1** : to designate, to indicate **2** NOMMER : to name, to appoint

désillusion [dezilyzjɔ̃] *nf* : disillusionment

désillusionner [dezilyzjɔne] *vt* : to disillusion

désincarné, -née [dezɛ̃karne] *adj* : disembodied

désinfectant[1], **-tante** [dezɛ̃fɛktɑ̃, -tɑ̃t] *adj* : disinfectant

désinfectant[2] *nm* : disinfectant

désinfecter [dezɛ̃fɛkte] *vt* : to disinfect

désinformation [dezɛ̃fɔrmasjɔ̃] *nf* : disinformation

désinstaller [dezɛ̃stale] *vt* : uninstall

désintégrer [dezɛ̃tegre] {87} *vt* : to disintegrate, to break up — **se désintégrer** *vr* — **désintégration** [-tegrasjɔ̃] *nf*

désintéressé, -sée [dezɛ̃terese] *adj* : disinterested, impartial

désintéressement [dezɛ̃terɛsmɑ̃] *nm* : disinterestedness
désintérêt [dezɛ̃terɛ] *nm* : lack of interest
désinvolte [dezɛ̃vɔlt] *adj* **1** : casual, unself-conscious **2** : offhand, flippant, glib
désinvolture [dezɛ̃vɔltyr] *nf* **1** : casualness, nonchalance **2** : offhand manner, flippancy, glibness
désir [dezir] *nm* : desire
désirable [dezirabl] *adj* : desirable
désirer [dezire] *vt* **1** : to want, to wish for **2** : to desire (sexually) **3 laisser à désirer** : to leave something to be desired
désireux, -reuse [dezirø, -røz] *adj* : anxious, desirous
désistement [dezistəmɑ̃] *nm* : withdrawal
désister [deziste] *v* **se désister** *vr* : to withdraw
désobéir [dezɔbeir] *vi* : to disobey <désobéir à ses parents : to disobey one's parents>
désobéissance [dezɔbeisɑ̃s] *nf* : disobedience
désobéissant, -sante [dezɔbeisɑ̃, -sɑ̃t] *adj* : disobedient
désobligeant, -geante [dezɔbliʒɑ̃, -ʒɑ̃t] *adj* : disagreeable, unpleasant
désobliger [dezɔbliʒe] {17} *vt* : to offend
désodorisant [dezɔdɔrizɑ̃] *nm* : air freshener, deodorizer
désodoriser [dezɔdɔrize] *vt* : to deodorize
désœuvré, -vrée [dezœvre] *adj* : idle
désœuvrement [dezœvrəmɑ̃] *nm* : idleness
désolant, -lante [dezɔlɑ̃, -lɑ̃t] *adj* : distressing
désolation [dezɔlasjɔ̃] *nf* **1** : desolation, devastation **2** : distress, grief
désolé, -lée [dezɔle] *adj* **1** : bleak, desolate **2** : contrite <je suis désolé : I'm sorry>
désoler [dezɔle] *vt* : to upset, to distress — **se désoler** *vr*
désolidariser [desɔlidarize] *v* **se désolidariser** *vr* **~ de** : to dissociate oneself from
désopilant, -lante [dezɔpilɑ̃, -lɑ̃t] *adj* : hilarious
désordonné, -née [dezɔrdɔne] *adj* **1** : disorganized **2** : untidy
désordre [dezɔrdr] *nm* **1** : confusion, disorder **2** : untidiness <en désordre : in a mess>
désorganiser [dezɔrganize] *vt* : to disorganize — **désorganisation** [-nizasjɔ̃] *nf*
désorienter [dezɔrjɑ̃te] *vt* **1** : to disorient **2** : to bewilder, to confuse
désormais [dezɔrmɛ] *adv* : henceforth, from now on
désosser [dezɔse] *vt* : to bone (meat)
despote [dɛspɔt] *nm* : despot — **despotisme** [-pɔtism] *nm*
despotique [dɛspɔtik] *adj* : despotic
desquels, desquelles [dekɛl] → **lequel**
dessécher [deseʃe] {87} *vt* **1** : to dry up, to desiccate, to parch **2** : to harden (one's heart)
dessein [desɛ̃] *nm* **1** : design, plan, intention **2 à ~** : intentionally, on purpose
desserrer [desere] *vt* **1** : to loosen **2** : to release (a brake) **3** RELÂCHER : to relax, to unclench
dessert [desɛr] *nm* : dessert
desserte [desɛrt] *nf* **1** : (transportation) service <desserte par bus : bus service> **2** : sideboard, serving table
desservir [desɛrvir] {81} *vt* **1** : to serve **2** : to lead into <deux portes desservent la salle de bain : two doors lead into the bathroom> **3** : to clear (the table) **4** : to do a disservice to
dessin [desɛ̃] *nm* **1** : drawing **2** : design, pattern **3** : outline **4 dessin animé** : (animated) cartoon
dessinateur, -trice [desinatœr, -tris] *n* **1** : artist, draftsman **2** : designer **3 dessinateur humoristique** : cartoonist
dessiner [desine] *vt* **1** : to draw **2** : to design **3** : to outline — *vi* : to draw, to sketch— **se dessiner** *vr* **1** : to stand out **2** : to take shape
dessoûler [desule] *v* : to sober up
dessous[1] [dəsu] *adv* : underneath
dessous[2] *nms & pl* **1** : underneath, underside **2 dessous** *nmpl* : underwear, lingerie **3 de ~** : from underneath **4 en ~** : underneath, down below **5 en dessous de** : below, beneath **6** → **au–dessous, par–dessous**
dessous–de–verre [d(ə)sudvɛr] *nms & pl* : coaster
dessus[1] [dəsy] *adv* : on top, on
dessus[2] *nms & pl* **1** : top **2** : upper (of a shoe) **3** : upper floor, upstairs **4 de ~** : off, from **5 en ~** : on top, above **6 avoir le dessus** : to have the upper hand **7** → **au–dessus, par–dessus**
déstabiliser [destabilize] *vt* : to destabilize
destin [dɛstɛ̃] *nm* : fate, destiny
destinataire [dɛstinatɛr] *nmf* **1** : addressee **2** : payee, beneficiary
destination [dɛstinasjɔ̃] *nf* **1** : destination **2 à destination de** : bound for
destinée [dɛstine] *nf* : fate, destiny
destiner [dɛstine] *vt* **1** : to intend **2** : to destine — **se destiner** *vr* **~ à** : to intend to become
destituer [dɛstitɥe] *vt* **1** DÉMETTRE : to dismiss, to discharge **2** : to depose
destructeur[1], **-trice** [dɛstryktœr, -tris] *adj* : destructive
destructeur[2], **-trice** *n* : destroyer, wrecker
destructible [dɛstryktibl] *adj* : destructible

destructif, -tive [dɛstryktif, -tiv] *adj* : destructive

destruction [dɛstryksjɔ̃] *nf* : destruction

désuet, -suète [dezɥɛ, -zɥɛt] *adj* : outdated, obsolete

désuétude [dezɥetyd] *nf* : obsolescence <tomber en désuétude : to fall into disuse>

désuni, -nie [dezyni] *adj* : disunited, divided

désunion [dezynjɔ̃] *nf* : disunity, dissension

désunir [dezynir] *vt* : to separate, to divide

détaché, -chée [detaʃe] *adj* **1** : detached **2** : transferred

détachement [detaʃmɑ̃] *nm* : detachment

détacher [detaʃe] *vt* **1** : to detach, to tear off **2** : to untie, to unfasten **3** DÉTOURNER : to turn (one's eyes, attention, etc.) away from **4** : to transfer **5** : to make stand out — **se détacher** *vr* **1** : to come undone **2 ~ de** : to grow away from, to lose interest in **3 ~ sur** : to stand out against

détail [detaj] *nm* **1** : detail <entrer dans les détails : to go into detail> **2** : retail <ventes au détail : retail sales>

détaillant, -lante [detajɑ̃, -jɑ̃t] *n* : retailer

détaillé, -lée [detaje] *adj* : detailed

détailler [detaje] *vt* **1** : to retail **2** ÉNUMÉRER : to detail, to itemize **3** : to scrutinize

détecter [detɛkte] *vt* : to detect

détecteur [detɛktœr] *nm* : detector, sensor <détecteur de mensonges : lie detector>

détection [detɛksjɔ̃] *nf* : detection

détective [detɛktiv] *nm* : detective <détective privé : private detective>

déteindre [detɛ̃dr] {37} *vt* : to make fade — *vi* **1** : to fade **2** : to run (of colors) **3 ~ sur** : to rub off on

détendre [detɑ̃dr] {63} *vt* **1** : to slacken, to loosen **2** : to relax, to ease — **se détendre** *vr* : to relax, to ease up

détendu, -due [detɑ̃dy] *adj* : relaxed

détenir [detnir] {92} *vt* **1** POSSÉDER : to hold, to be in possession of <détenir un secret : to have a secret> **2** : to detain, to hold (a prisoner)

détente [detɑ̃t] *nf* **1** : relaxation **2** : détente **3** : trigger

détenteur, -trice [detɑ̃tœr, -tris] *n* : holder <détenteur du record : record holder>

détention [detɑ̃sjɔ̃] *nf* **1** : possession, holding <détention de stupéfiants : drug possession> **2** EMPRISONNEMENT : detention, imprisonment

détenu, -nue [detny] *n* : prisoner

détergent [detɛrʒɑ̃] *nm* : detergent

détérioration [deterjɔrasjɔ̃] *nf* : deterioration

détériorer [deterjɔre] *vt* : to damage, to harm — **se détériorer** *vr* : to deteriorate

déterminant, -nante [detɛrminɑ̃, -nɑ̃t] *adj* : decisive, determining <un facteur déterminant : a determining factor>

détermination [detɛrminasjɔ̃] *nf* **1** : determination, resoluteness **2** RÉSOLUTION : decision

déterminé, -née [detɛrmine] *adj* **1** : determined, resolute **2** : specified, definite

déterminer [detɛrmine] *vt* **1** : to determine, to specify **2** : to encourage, to incite **3** : to cause — **se déterminer** *vr* : to decide, to make up one's mind

déterrer [detere] *vt* : to dig up, to unearth

détersif [detɛrsif, -siv] *nm* DÉTERGENT : detergent

détestable [detɛstabl] *adj* : detestable, foul, hateful — **détestablement** [-bləmɑ̃] *adv*

détester [detɛste] *vt* : to detest, to hate — **se détester** *vr*

détonant, -nante [detɔnɑ̃, -nɑ̃t] *adj* : explosive

détonateur [detɔnatœr] *nm* : detonator

détonation [detɔnasjɔ̃] *nf* : detonation, explosion

détoner [detɔne] *vi* : to detonate, to explode

détonner [detɔne] *vi* **1** : to be out of tune **2** : to clash

détordre [detɔrdr] {63} *vt* : to untwist, to unbend

détour [detur] *nm* **1** : curve, bend **2** DÉVIATION : detour **3 sans ~** : directly, frankly

détourné, -née [deturne] *adj* : indirect, roundabout, circuitous

détournement [deturnəmɑ̃] *nm* **1** : diversion, rerouting **2** : hijacking **3 détournement de fonds** : embezzlement, misappropriation of funds **4 détournement de mineur** : corruption of a minor

détourner [deturne] *vt* **1** : to divert, to reroute **2** : to turn aside <détourner les soupçons : to avert suspicion> <détourner la conversation : to change the subject> **3** : to hijack **4** : to misappropriate, to embezzle **5** : to twist, to distort, to corrupt

détracteur, -trice [detraktœr, -tris] *n* : detractor, faultfinder

détraqué, -quée [detrake] *adj* **1** : broken-down, out of order **2** *fam* : deranged, crazy

détraquer [detrake] *vt* **1** : to put out of order, to make go wrong **2** *fam* : to upset (one's stomach, etc.), to unhinge (mentally) — **se détraquer** *vr* : to break down, to go wrong

détremper [detrɑ̃pe] *vt* **1** : to soak, to saturate **2** : to dilute

détresse [detrɛs] *nf* : distress

détriment [detrimɑ̃] *nm* **au détriment de** : to the detriment of

détritus [detrity̆s] *nmpl* : waste, garbage, litter

détroit [detrwa] *nm* : strait <le détroit de Gibraltar : the strait of Gibraltar>

détromper [detrɔ̃pe] *vt* : to set straight, to disabuse — **se détromper** *vr* : to set oneself straight <détrompez-vous! : think again!>

détrôner [detrone] *vt* **1** : to depose, to dethrone **2** : to oust

détruire [detrɥir] {49} *vt* : to destroy — **se détruire** *vr*

dette [dɛt] *nf* : debt

deuil [dœj] *nm* : bereavement, mourning <porter le deuil : to be in mourning>

deux[1] [dø] *adj* **1** : two <deux cents : two hundred> <les deux côtés : both sides> **2** : second <le deux mai : May second> **3 à deux pas** : nearby, close **4 deux fois** : twice **5 tous les deux jours** : every other day

deux[2] *nm* **1** : two <couper en deux : to cut in two> **2 tous les deux** : both (of them)

deuxième [døzjɛm] *adj & nmf* : second

deuxièmement [døzjɛmmɑ̃] *adv* : secondly, second

deux–pièces [døpjɛs] *nms & pl* **1** : two-piece suit, two-piece swimsuit **2** : two-room apartment

deux–points [døpwɛ̃] *nms & pl* : colon

deux–roues [døru] *nms & pl* : two-wheeled vehicle

dévaler [devale] *vt* : to hurtle down

dévaliser [devalize] *vt* : to rob

dévalorisation [devalɔrizasjɔ̃] *nf* : depreciation

dévaloriser [devalɔrize] *vt* **1** : to devalue **2** : to belittle

dévaluation [devalɥasjɔ̃] *nf* : devaluation

dévaluer [devalɥe] *vt* : to devalue

devancer [dəvɑ̃se] {6} *vt* **1** : to be ahead of <devancer ses rivaux : to be ahead of one's rivals> **2** PRÉCÉDER : to arrive before **3** : to anticipate

devant[1] [dəvɑ̃] *adv* : in front, ahead, before <il marche devant : he is walking ahead>

devant[2] *nm* **1** : front <le devant de la maison : the front of the house> **2 prendre les devants** : to take the initiative

devant[3] *prep* **1** : in front of <devant chez toi : in front of your house> <jurer devant témoins : to swear before witnesses> **2** : ahead of <avoir du temps devant soi : to have time to spare> **3** : in the face of <sans peur devant le danger : fearless in the face of danger>

devanture [dəvɑ̃tyr] *nf* **1** : storefront **2** : shopwindow **3 en ~** : on display

dévastateur, -trice [devastatœr, -tris] *adj* : devastating, destructive

dévastation [devastasjɔ̃] *nf* : devastation

dévaster [devaste] *vt* : to devastate, to ravage

développement [devlɔpmɑ̃] *nm* **1** : development **2** CROISSANCE : growth, expansion **3** : developing (of photographic film)

développer [devlɔpe] *vt* : to develop — **se développer** *vr*

devenir [dəvnir] {92} *vi* : to become <je deviens vieux : I'm growing old> <qu'est-il devenu? : what has become of him?> <qu'est-ce que tu deviens? : what are you up to?>

déverrouiller [devɛruje] *vt* : to unbolt

déverser [devɛrse] *vt* : to pour (out), to dump — **se déverser** *vr* **~ dans** : to flow into

dévêtir [devetir] {97} *vt* : to undress — **se dévêtir** *vr*

déviation [devjasjɔ̃] *nf* **1** : deviation **2** DÉTOUR : detour

dévider [devide] *vt* : to unwind

dévier [devje] {96} *vi* **1** : to veer, to swerve **2 ~ de** : to deviate from — *vt* : to deflect, to divert <dévier la circulation : to divert traffic>

devin, -vineresse [dəvɛ̃,-vinrɛs] *n* : soothsayer, fortune-teller

deviner [dəvine] *vt* **1** : to guess **2** APERCEVOIR : to perceive, to sense **3** PRÉDIRE : to foretell

devinette [dəvinɛt] *nf* : riddle

devis [dəvi] *nms & pl* : estimate

dévisager [devizaʒe] {17} *vt* : to stare at

devise [dəviz] *nf* **1** : motto, slogan **2** : currency (money)

deviser [dəvize] *vi* : to converse

dévisser [devise] *vt* : to unscrew

dévoiler [devwale] *vt* : to unveil, to reveal

devoir[1] [dəvwar] {28} *vt* : to owe — *v aux* **1** : to have to, to be compelled to <il doit le faire : he must do it> **2** : to be advised to <tu dois lire les instructions : you should read the instructions> <elle doit répondre : she ought to reply> **3** : to be presumed to <il a dû payer : he must have paid> **4** : to be expected to <elles devaient se rencontrer plus tard : they were supposed to meet later> — **se devoir** *vr* **1** : to be obligated to each other **2 se devoir de faire** : to be duty bound to do (sth)> **3 comme il se doit** : as is proper, as might be expected

devoir[2] *nm* **1** : duty **2 devoirs** *nmpl* : homework

dévolu[1], **-lue** [devɔly] *adj* **~ à** : allotted to

dévolu[2] *nm* **jeter son dévolu sur** : to set one's sights on

dévorer [devɔre] *vt* **1** : to devour <être dévoré de : to be eaten up by> **2** CONSUMER : to consume

dévot, -vote [devo, -vɔt] *adj* : devout, pious

dévotion [devosjɔ̃] *nf* **1** : devotion <avec dévotion : devotedly> **2** : devoutness

dévoué, -vouée [devwe] *adj* : devoted

dévouement [devumɑ̃] *nm* : dedication, devotion

dévouer [devwe] *vt* : to devote — **se dévouer** *vr* **1** : to devote oneself **2** : to sacrifice oneself

dévoyé, -yée [devwaje] *adj & n* : delinquent

devra [dəvra], *etc.* → **devoir**

dextérité [dɛksterite] *nf* : dexterity, skill

diabète [djabɛt] *nm* : diabetes

diabétique [djabetik] *adj & nmf* : diabetic

diable [djabl] *nm* **1** : devil <avoir le diable au corps : to be the very devil> <ce n'est pas le diable : it's not all that bad> **2 à la diable** : any old way **3 au ~** : to hell with **4 en ~** : devilishly, terribly **5 mener le diable** *Can fam* : to make a racket **6 où (quand, qui, pourquoi) diable** : where (when, who, why) the devil

diablement [djabləmɑ̃] *adv fam* : very, extremely, awfully

diablerie [djabləri] *nf* : mischief

diablotin [djablɔtɛ̃] *nm* : little demon, imp

diabolique [djabɔlik] *adj* : diabolical, diabolic, devilish — **diaboliquement** [-likmɑ̃] *adv*

diachylon [djaʃilɔ̃] *nm Can* : adhesive bandage

diacre [djakr] *nm* : deacon

diadème [djadɛm] *nm* : diadem

diagnostic [djagnɔstik] *nm* : diagnosis — **diagnostique** [-nɔstik] *adj*

diagnostiquer [djagnɔstike] *vt* : to diagnose

diagonal, -nale [djagɔnal] *adj, mpl* **-naux** [-no] : diagonal

diagonale *nf* **1** : diagonal **2 en ~** : diagonally

diagramme [djagram] *nm* : graph, chart

dialecte [djalɛkt] *nm* : dialect

dialogue [djalɔg] *nm* : dialogue

dialoguer [djalɔge] *vi* **1** : to converse **2** : to engage in dialogue, to have talks

dialyse [djaliz] *nf* : dialysis

diamant [djamɑ̃] *nm* : diamond

diamétralement [djametralmɑ̃] *adv* : diametrically

diamètre [djamɛtr] *nm* : diameter

diapason [djapazɔ̃] *nm* **1** : tuning fork **2 être au même diapason** : to be on the same wavelength

diaphane [djafan] *adj* : diaphanous

diaphragme [djafragm] *nm* : diaphragm

diapositive [djapɔzitiv] *nf* : slide, transparency

diarrhée [djare] *nf* : diarrhea

diatribe [djatrib] *nf* : diatribe

dichotomie [dikɔtɔmi] *nf* : dichotomy

dictateur [diktatœr] *nm* : dictator

dictatorial, -riale [diktatɔrjal] *adj, mpl* **-riaux** [-rjo] : dictatorial

dictature [diktatyr] *nf* : dictatorship

dictée [dikte] *nf* : dictation

dicter [dikte] *vt* : to dictate

diction [diksjɔ̃] *nf* : diction

dictionnaire [diksjɔnɛr] *nm* : dictionary

dicton [diktɔ̃] *nm* : saying

didactique [didaktik] *adj* : didactic

dièse [djɛz] *adj & nm* : sharp (in music)

diesel [djezɛl] *adj & nm* : diesel

diète [djɛt] *nf* RÉGIME : diet — **diététique** [djɛtetik] *adj*

diététicien, -cienne [djetetisjɛ̃, -sjɛn] *n* : dietician

dieu [djø] *nm, pl* **dieux** : god

Dieu *nm* : God

diffamation [difamasjɔ̃] *nf* CALOMNIE : slander, libel

diffamatoire [difamatwar] *adj* : slanderous, defamatory

diffamer [difame] *vt* CALOMNIER : to defame, to slander, to libel

différé, -rée [difere] *adj* **1** : postponed, deferred **2 en ~** : prerecorded

différemment [diferamɑ̃] *adv* : differently

différence [diferɑ̃s] *nf* **1** : difference <faire la différence : to tell the difference> **2 à la différence de** : unlike

différencier [diferɑ̃sje] {96} *vt* DISTINGUER : to differentiate — **se différencier** *vr* **~ de** : to differ from

différend [diferɑ̃] *nm* : disagreement, difference (of opinion)

différent, -rente [diferɑ̃, -rɑ̃t] *adj* **1** : different, various **2 ~ de** : different from, unlike

différentiel, -tielle [diferɑ̃sjɛl] *adj* : differential

différer [difere] {87} *vt* : to defer, to postpone — *vi* **1** : to differ, to vary **2 ~ de** : to differ from

difficile [difisil] *adj* **1** : difficult, hard **2** : choosy, hard to please

difficilement [difisilmɑ̃] *adv* : with difficulty

difficulté [difikylte] *nf* **1** : difficulty **2** : problem <en difficulté : in trouble>

difforme [difɔrm] *adj* : deformed, misshapen

difformité [difɔrmite] *nf* : deformity

diffus, -fuse [dify, -fyz] *adj* : diffuse

diffuser [difyze] *vt* **1** : to broadcast **2** : to spread, to distribute **3** : to diffuse (light, etc.) — **se diffuser** *vr*

diffuseur [difyzœr] *nm* **1** : distributor **2** : broadcaster

diffusion [difyzjɔ̃] *nf* **1** : distribution **2** : diffusion **3** RADIODIFFUSION : broadcasting

digérer [diʒere] {87} *vt* **1** : to digest **2** : to assimilate **3** : to accept, to put up with

digeste [diʒɛst] *adj* : (easily) digestible

digestible [diʒɛstibl] *adj* : digestible

digestif, -tive [diʒɛstif, -tiv] *adj* : digestive

digestion [diʒɛstjɔ̃] *nf* : digestion

digital, -tale [diʒital] *adj, mpl* **-taux** [-to] **1** : digital **2** → **empreinte**

digitale [diʒital] *nf* **1** : digitalis **2** *or* **digitale pourprée** : foxglove

digne [diɲ] *adj* **1** : worthy <digne de foi : trustworthy> **2** : dignified

dignement [diɲmɑ̃] *adv* **1** : with dignity **2** : suitably, justly

dignitaire [diɲitɛr] *nm* : dignitary

dignité [diɲite] *nf* : dignity

digression [digresjɔ̃] *nf* : digression

digue [dig] *nf* **1** : dike, seawall **2** : barrier

dilapider [dilapide] *vt* : to squander, to waste

dilater [dilate] *vt* : to dilate, to expand — **se dilater** *vr*

dilatoire [dilatwar] *adj* : dilatory, delaying

dilemme [dilɛm] *nm* : dilemma

dilettante [diletɑ̃t] *nmf* : dilettante, amateur

diligence [diliʒɑ̃s] *nf* **1** : dispatch <faire diligence : to make haste> **2** : stagecoach

diligent, -gente [diliʒɑ̃, -ʒɑ̃t] *adj* : prompt, speedy

diluant [dilɥɑ̃] *nm* : thinner

diluer [dilɥe] *vt* : to dilute — **dilution** [dilysjɔ̃] *nf*

dimanche [dimɑ̃ʃ] *nm* : Sunday

dîme [dim] *nf* : tithe

dimension [dimɑ̃sjɔ̃] *nf* **1** : dimension, measurement **2** : aspect **3 dimensions** *nfpl* : dimensions, size

diminuer [diminɥe] *vt* RÉDUIRE : to lower, to reduce — *vi* : to diminish, to decrease, to drop

diminution [diminysjɔ̃] *nf* : reduction, decreasing

dinde [dɛ̃d] *nf* **1** : (female) turkey **2** : stupid woman

dindon [dɛ̃dɔ̃] *nm* **1** : (male) turkey **2 être le dindon de la farce** : to be made a fool of

dîner[1] [dine] *vi* **1** : to dine, to have dinner **2** *Bel, Can, Switz* : to have lunch

dîner[2] *nm* **1** : dinner **2** *Bel, Can, Switz* : lunch

dîneur, -neuse [dinœr, -nøz] *n* : diner (person)

dingue [dɛ̃g] *adj fam* **1** : crazy, nuts, goofy **2** : incredible

dinosaure [dinozɔr] *nm* : dinosaur

diocèse [djɔsɛz] *nm* : diocese

diphtérie [difteri] *nf* : diphtheria

diphtongue [diftɔ̃g] *nf* : diphthong

diplomate[1] [diplɔmat] *adj* : diplomatic

diplomate[2] *nmf* : diplomat

diplomatie [diplɔmasi] *nf* : diplomacy

diplomatique [diplɔmatik] *adj* : diplomatic — **diplomatiquement** [-tikmɑ̃] *adv*

diplôme [diplom] *nm* **1** : diploma, certificate, degree **2** : (qualifying) exam

diplômé[1], **-mée** [diplome] *adj* **1** : qualified, certified **2 être diplômé de** : to be a graduate of

diplômé[2], **-mée** *n* : graduate

dire[1] [dir] {29} *vt* **1** : to say <comme on dit : as they say> <cela va sans dire : that goes without saying> <sans dire mot : without saying a word> **2** : to tell <dire la vérité : to tell the truth> <c'est ce qu'on m'a dit : so I've been told> **3** : to think <qu'en dis-tu? : what do you think?> <on dirait qu'il est perdu : he seems lost> **4** : to show, to indicate <dire l'heure : to tell the time> **5** : to appeal to <cela vous dit d'aller dehors? : do you feel like going outside?> **6 pour ainsi dire** : so to speak **7 vouloir dire** : to mean <que veut dire ce mot? : what does this word mean?> — **se dire** *vr* **1** : to tell oneself **2** : to say to each other <se dire au revoir : to say good-bye (to each other)> **3** : to claim to be <elle se dit malade : she says she's sick> **4** : to say (in another language) <comment se dit *chien* en russe? : how do you say *dog* in Russian?> **5** : to be said <cela ne se dit pas : we shouldn't say that>

dire[2] *nm* **1 au dire de** : according to **2 avoir pour son dire** *Can* : to be in the habit of saying **3 dires** *nmpl* : statements

direct[1], **-recte** [dirɛkt] *adj* : direct — **directement** [-təmɑ̃] *adv*

direct[2] *nm* **1** : express train **2** : jab (in boxing) **3 en ~** : live, in person

directeur[1], **-trice** [dirɛktœr, -tris] *adj* **1** : directing, guiding <ligne directrice : guideline> **2** : main <idée directrice : main idea>

directeur[2], **-trice** *n* **1** : manager, director **2 directeur général** : general manager, chief executive officer **3 directeur d'école** : principal

direction [dirɛksjɔ̃] *nf* **1** : direction **2** GESTION : management, supervision, leadership <la direction du parti : party management> **3** : steering <direction assistée : power steering>

directive [dirɛktiv] *nf* ORDRE : order, directive

directorial, -riale [dirɛktɔrjal] *adj, pl* **-riaux** [-rjo] : managerial, directorial

dirigeable [diriʒabl] *nm* : airship, dirigible

dirigeant[1], **-geante** [diriʒɑ̃, -ʒɑ̃t] *adj* : ruling <la classe dirigeante : the ruling class>

dirigeant[2], **-geante** *n* **1** : leader (of a country, etc.) **2** : manager

diriger [diriʒe] {17} *vt* **1** : to direct, to manage <diriger une entreprise : to run a company> **2** : to aim, to direct (one's attention, efforts, etc.) **3** : to steer **4** : to conduct (an orchestra) — **se diriger** *vr* **1** : to find one's way **2** **~ vers** : to head toward

disait [dizɛ], **disions** [dizjɔ̃], *etc.* → **dire**

discernement [disɛrnəmɑ̃] *nm* : discernment, judgment

discerner [disɛrne] *vt* : to discern, to distinguish

disciple [disipl] *nm* : follower, disciple

disciplinaire [disiplinɛr] *adj* : disciplinary

discipline [disiplin] *nf* : discipline

discipliner [disipline] *vt* : to discipline — **se discipliner** *vr*

disc–jockey [diskʒɔkɛ] *nmf, pl* **disc–jockeys** : disc jockey

discontinu, -nue [diskɔ̃tiny] *adj* **1** : broken, dotted **2** : intermittent

discontinuer [diskɔ̃tinɥe] *vi* **sans ~** : without interruption

discordance [diskɔrdɑ̃s] *nf* **1** : clash, conflict **2** : dissonance

discordant, -dante [diskɔrdɑ̃, -dɑ̃t] *adj* **1** : conflicting, clashing **2** : dissonant

discorde [diskɔrd] *nf* **1** : discord, dissension **2** **pomme de discorde** : bone of contention

discothèque [diskɔtɛk] *nf* **1** : disco, nightclub **2** : record library

discourir [diskurir] {23} *vi* **1** : to discourse, to talk at length **2** **~ sur** : to hold forth on

discours [diskur] *nms & pl* **1** : speech, address **2** : discourse, speech (in grammar) <discours indirect : indirect discourse>

discourtois, -toise [diskurtwa, -twaz] *adj* : discourteous — **discourtoisement** [-twazmɑ̃] *adv*

discrédit [diskredi] *nm* : discredit

discréditer [diskredite] *vt* : to discredit, to disparage — **se discréditer** *vr*

discret, -crète [diskrɛ, -krɛt] *adj* **1** : discreet **2** : unassuming, unobtrusive

discrètement [diskrɛtmɑ̃] *adv* : discreetly

discrétion [diskresjɔ̃] *nf* **1** : discretion **2** **à ~** : unlimited, as much as one wants

discrétionnaire [diskresjɔnɛr] *adj* : discretionary

discrimination [diskriminasjɔ̃] *nf* **1** : discrimination **2** **sans ~** : indiscriminately

discriminatoire [diskriminatwar] *adj* : discriminatory

disculper [diskylpe] *vt* : to exonerate — **se disculper** *vr* : to vindicate oneself

discussion [diskysjɔ̃] *nf* **1** : discussion **2** : argument, debate

discutable [diskytabl] *adj* **1** : debatable, arguable **2** : questionable, doubtful

discuté, -tée [diskyte] *adj* : controversial

discuter [diskyte] *vt* **1** : to discuss, to debate **2** : to question — *vi* **1** : to talk **2** : to argue **3** **~ de** : to discuss

dise [diz], *etc.* → **dire**

disette [dizɛt] *nf* : shortage of food

diseur, -seuse [dizœr, -zøz] *n* **diseur de bonne aventure** : fortune-teller

disgrâce [disgras] *nf* **1** : disgrace, disfavor **2** : misfortune

disgracieux, -cieuse [disgrasjø, -sjøz] *adj* **1** : awkward, ungainly **2** : ugly

disjoindre [disʒwɛ̃dr] {50} *vt* **1** : to take apart **2** : to separate (out) — **se disjoindre** *vr* : to come apart

disjoncteur [disʒɔ̃ktœr] *nm* : circuit breaker

dislocation [dislɔkasjɔ̃] *nf* **1** : dislocation (in medicine) **2** : breaking up

disloquer [dislɔke] *vt* **1** LUXER : to dislocate (in medicine) **2** : to break up, to dismantle

disparaître [disparɛtr] {7} *vi* **1** : to disappear **2** MOURIR : to die (out) **3** **faire disparaître** : to get rid of

disparate [disparat] *adj* **1** : disparate, dissimilar **2** : clashing

disparité [diparite] *nf* : disparity

disparition [disparisjɔ̃] *nf* **1** : disappearance **2** : extinction, death

disparu[1], **-rue** [dispary] *adj* **1** : missing **2** : lost, vanished, extinct

disparu[2], **-rue** *n* **1** : missing person **2** : dead person <notre cher disparu : our dear departed>

dispendieux, -dieuse [dispɑ̃djø, -djøz] *adj* COÛTEUX : expensive, costly

dispensaire [dispɑ̃sɛr] *nm* : dispensary, free clinic

dispense [dispɑ̃s] *nf* : exemption, dispensation

dispenser [dispɑ̃se] *vt* **1** : to exempt, to excuse **2** : to dispense, to bestow — **se dispenser** *vr* **~ de** : to avoid, to get out of

disperser [dispɛrse] *vt* ÉPARPILLER : to disperse, to scatter — **se disperser** *vr*

dispersion [dispɛrsjɔ̃] *nf* : scattering, dispersal

disponibilité [dispɔnibilite] *nf* **1** : availability **2** **en ~** : on leave of absence **3** **disponibilités** *nfpl* : liquid assets

disponible [dispɔnibl] *adj* : available

dispos, -pose [dispo, -poz] *adj* **1** : refreshed **2** **frais et dispos** : as fresh as a daisy

disposé, -sée [dispoze] *adj* **1** : arranged **2** **~ à** : disposed to, willing to **3** **bien disposé envers** : well-disposed toward

disposer [dispoze] *vt* **1** PLACER : to arrange, to place **2** : to incline, to dispose — *vi* **1** : to leave <ils peuvent disposer : they may leave> **2** **~ de** : to have at one's disposal — **se disposer** *vr* **se disposer à faire** : to be about to do

dispositif [dispɔzitif] *nm* **1** : device, mechanism <dispositif de sûreté : safeguard> **2** : plan of action

disposition [dispozisjɔ̃] *nf* **1** : arrangement, layout **2** : aptitude **3** : tendency

4 **à la disposition de** : at the disposal of 5 **dispositions** *nfpl* : mood, state of mind 6 **dispositions** *nfpl* : steps, measures

disproportion [disprɔpɔrsjɔ̃] *nf* : disproportion

disproportionné, -née [disprɔpɔrsjɔne] *adj* : disproportionate

dispute [dispyt] *nf* : argument, quarrel

disputer [dispyte] *vt* **1** : to compete in, to play **2** : to contend with, to fight **3** *fam* : to tell off **4** *Can* : to scold, to chide — **se disputer** *vr* : to quarrel, to fight

disqualifier [diskalifje] {96} *vt* : to disqualify — **disqualification** [-lifikasjɔ̃] *nf*

disque [disk] *nm* **1** : record, disc <disque compact : compact disc> <disque vidéo : videodisc> **2** : disk (in anatomy, astronomy, etc.) **3** : discus

disquette [diskɛt] *nf* : diskette, floppy disk

dissection [disɛksjɔ̃] *nf* : dissection

dissemblable [disɑ̃babl] *adj* : dissimilar

dissemblance [disɑ̃blɑ̃s] *nf* : dissimilarity, difference

dissémination [diseminasjɔ̃] *nf* **1** : scattering, dispersal **2** : dissemination, spread (of ideas, etc.)

disséminer [disemine] *vt* **1** : to scatter **2** : to disseminate, to spread

dissension [disɑ̃sjɔ̃] *nf* : dissension, disagreement

dissentiment [disɑ̃timɑ̃] *nm* : dissent

disséquer [diseke] {87} *vt* : to dissect

dissertation [disɛrtasjɔ̃] *nf* : essay (in school)

dissident, -dente [disidɑ̃, -dɑ̃t] *adj & n* : dissident — **dissidence** [-sidɑ̃s] *nf*

dissimulation [disimylasjɔ̃] *nf* **1** : dissimulation, dissembling **2** : concealment

dissimulé, -lée [disimyle] *adj* **1** : hidden, concealed **2** : secretive

dissimuler [disimyle] *vt* CACHER : to conceal, to hide — **se dissimuler** *vr*

dissipation [disipasjɔ̃] *nf* **1** : dissipation **2** : squandering, wasting

dissipé, -pée [disipe] *adj* **1** : undisciplined, unruly **2** : dissipated, dissolute

dissiper [disipe] *vt* **1** : to disperse, to clear, to dispel **2** : to squander — **se dissiper** *vr* **1** : to clear (up), to vanish **2** : to become unruly

dissocier [disɔsje] {96} *vt* : to dissociate, to separate — **se dissocier** *vr*

dissolu, -lue [disɔly] *adj* : dissolute

dissolution [disɔlysjɔ̃] *nf* **1** : dissolution, breakup **2** : dissolving

dissolvant [disɔlvɑ̃] *nm* **1** : solvent **2** : nail polish remover

dissonant, -nante [disɔnɑ̃, -nɑ̃t] *adj* : dissonant, discordant — **dissonance** [-sɔnɑ̃s] *nf*

dissoudre [disudr] {1} *vt* : to dissolve — **se dissoudre** *vr*

dissuader [disɥade] *vt* : to dissuade

dissuasif, -sive [disɥazif, -ziv] *adj* : deterrent, dissuasive

dissuasion [disɥazjɔ̃] *nf* : dissuasion, deterrence

distance [distɑ̃s] *nf* **1** : distance <à distance : at a distance> <garder ses distances : to keep one's distance> **2** : gap, interval **3** **distance focale** : focal length

distancer [distɑ̃se] {6} *vt* : to outdistance, to outrun, to outstrip

distancier [distɑ̃sje] {96} *v* **se distancier** *vr* **~ de** : to distance oneself from

distant, -tante [distɑ̃, -tɑt] *adj* **1** : distant <une ville distante de deux kilomètres : a town two kilometers away> **2** : distant, aloof

distendre [distɑ̃dr] {63} *vt* : to distend, to stretch, to strain — **se distendre** *vr* **1** : to distend **2** : to slacken

distillation [distilasjɔ̃] *nf* : distillation

distiller [distile] *vt* **1** : to distill **2** : to secrete, to exude

distillerie [distilri] *nf* : distillery

distinct, -tincte [distɛ̃, -tɛ̃kt] *adj* : distinct — **distinctement** [-tɛ̃ktəmɑ̃] *adv*

distinctif, -tive [distɛ̃ktif, -tiv] *adj* : distinctive, distinguishing

distinction [distɛ̃ksjɔ̃] *nf* **1** : distinction **2** **distinction honorifique** : award

distingué, -guée [distɛ̃ge] *adj* : distinguished

distinguer [distɛ̃ge] *vt* **1** : to distinguish, to differentiate **2** : to discern **3** : to set apart — *vi* : to distinguish, to make a distinction — **se distinguer** *vr* **1** : to stand out **2** : to distinguish oneself

distorsion [distɔrsjɔ̃] *nf* : distortion

distraction [distraksjɔ̃] *nf* **1** : distraction, absentmindedness **2** : recreation, amusement

distraire [distrɛr] {40} *vt* **1** : to distract **2** DIVERTIR : to amuse, to entertain — **se distraire** *vr* : to amuse oneself

distrait, -traite [distrɛ, -trɛt] *adj* : absentminded — **distraitement** [-trɛtmɑ̃] *adv*

distrayant, -trayante [distrɛjɑ̃, -trɛjɑ̃t] *adj* : entertaining

distribuer [distribɥe] *vt* **1** : to distribute, to deal out **2** : to assign, to allocate **3** : to supply (water, etc.)

distributeur[1]**, -trice** [distribytœr, -tris] *n* : distributor

distributeur[2] *nm* **1** : distributor (of an automobile) **2** *or* **distributeur automatique** : dispenser, vending machine

distribution [distribysjɔ̃] *nf* **1** : distribution **2** : supplying (of utilities, etc.) **3** : casting (of a movie or play)

district [distrikt] *nm* : district

dit, dite [di, dit] *adj* **1** : agreed upon, stated <à l'heure dite : at the appointed time> **2** : called, known as

dites [dit] → **dire**

diurétique [djyretik] *adj & nm* : diuretic

diurne [djyrn] *adj* : diurnal, daytime

divagation [divagasjɔ̃] *nf* : rambling, raving

divaguer [divage] *vi* **1** : to ramble (on) **2** : to rave

divan [divɑ̃] *nm* : divan, couch

divergent, -gente [divɛrʒɑ̃, -ʒɑ̃t] *adj* : divergent — **divergence** [-vɛrʒɑ̃s] *nf*

diverger [divɛrʒe] {17} *vi* : to diverge

divers, -verse [divɛr, -vɛrs] *adj* **1** VARIÉ : diverse, varied **2** PLUSIEURS : various, sundry <en diverses occasions : on various occasions> **3** : miscellaneous

diversification [divɛrsifikasjɔ̃] *nf* : diversification

diversifier [divɛrsifje] {96} *vt* : to diversify, to vary — **se diversifier** *vr*

diversion [divɛrsjɔ̃] *nf* : diversion

diversité [divɛrsite] *nf* : diversity, variety

divertir [divɛrtir] *vt* : to amuse, to entertain — **se divertir** *vr*

divertissement [divɛrtismɑ̃] *nm* : entertainment, pastime

dividende [dividɑ̃d] *nm* : dividend

divin, -vine [divɛ̃, -vin] *adj* : divine — **divinement** [-vinmɑ̃] *adv*

divinité [divinite] *nf* : divinity

diviser [divize] *vt* **1** : to divide (in mathematics) <diviser 10 par 2 : to divide 10 by 2> **2** : to divide, to split up — **se diviser** *vr*

diviseur [divizœr] *nm* : divisor

divisible [divizibl] *adj* : divisible

division [divizjɔ̃] *nf* : division

divorce [divɔrs] *nm* : divorce

divorcé, -cée [divɔrse] *n* : divorced person, divorcé *m*, divorcée *f*

divorcer [divɔrse] {6} *vi* **1** : to get a divorce **2** ~ **avec** *or* ~ **d'avec** *or* ~ **de** : to divorce (s.o.)

divulgation [divylgasjɔ̃] *nf* : disclosure

divulguer [divylge] *vt* : to divulge, to disclose

dix[1] [dis, *bef. consonant* di, *bef. vowel or mute h* diz] *adj* **1** : ten **2** : tenth <le dix avril : April tenth>

dix[2] *nms & pl* : ten

dix–huit[1] [dizɥit] *adj* **1** : eighteen **2** : eighteenth <le dix-huit juin : June eighteenth>

dix–huit[2] *nms & pl* : eighteen

dix–huitième [dizɥitjɛm] *adj & nmf & nm* : eighteenth

dixième [dizjɛm] *adj & nmf & nm* : tenth

dix–neuf[1] [diznœf] *adj* **1** : nineteen **2** : nineteenth <le dix-neuf mai : May nineteenth>

dix–neuf[2] *nms & pl* : nineteen

dix–neuvième [diznœvjɛm] *adj & nmf & nm* : nineteenth

dix–sept[1] [disɛt] *adj* **1** : seventeen **2** : seventeenth <le dix-sept avril : April seventeenth>

dix–sept[2] *nms & pl* : seventeen

dix–septième [disɛtjɛm] *adj & nmf & nm* : seventeenth

dizaine [dizɛn] *nf* **1** : ten **2** : about ten, ten or so

docile [dɔsil] *adj* : docile, obedient — **docilement** [-silmɑ̃] *adv*

dock [dɔk] *nm* : dock, berth (for a ship)

docker [dɔkɛr] *nm* : longshoreman, stevedore

docteur [dɔktœr] *nm* : doctor

doctorat [dɔktɔra] *nm* : doctorate

doctrine [dɔktrin] *nf* : doctrine

document [dɔkymɑ̃] *nm* : document

documentaire[1] [dɔkymɑ̃tɛr] *adj* **1** : documentary **2 à titre documentaire** : for your information

documentaire[2] *nm* : documentary (film)

documentation [dɔkymɑ̃tasjɔ̃] *nf* **1** : documentation, information **2** : research

documenter [dɔkymɑ̃te] *vt* : to inform, to provide with evidence — **se documenter** *vr* ~ **sur** : to research

dodo [dodo] *nm* **1** : dodo (bird) **2 faire dodo** : to go to bed (in baby talk)

dodu, -due [dɔdy] *adj* : plump, chubby

dogmatique [dɔgmatik] *adj* : dogmatic

dogmatisme [dɔgmatism] *nm* : dogmatism

dogme [dɔgm] *nm* : dogma

dogue [dɔg] *nm* : mastiff

doigt [dwa] *nm* **1** : finger <bout du doigt : fingertip> **2 doigt de pied** : toe **3 montrer du doigt** : to point at **4 se mordre les doigts** : to regret

doigté [dwate] *nm* **1** TACT : diplomacy, tact **2** : fingering (in music)

doit [dwa], **doive** [dwav], *etc.* → **devoir**

doléance [dɔleɑ̃s] *nf* : grievance, complaint

dolent, -lente [dɔlɑ̃, -lɑ̃t] *adj* : doleful, plaintive

dollar [dɔlar] *nm* : dollar

domaine [dɔmɛn] *nm* **1** PROPRIÉTÉ : estate, property **2** SPÉCIALITÉ : field, domain **3 domaine public** : public domain

dôme [dom] *nm* : dome

domestique[1] [dɔmɛstik] *adj* **1** : domestic, home **2** : domesticated

domestique[2] *nmf* : domestic, servant

domestiquer [dɔmɛstike] *vt* **1** APPRIVOISER : to domesticate **2** : to harness (energy)

domicile [dɔmisil] *nm* : residence, home

domicilié, -liée [dɔmisilje] *adj* **être domicilié à** : to be a resident in

dominance [dɔminɑ̃s] *nf* : dominance

dominant, -nante [dɔminɑ̃, -nɑ̃t] *adj* **1** : dominant, ruling **2** : predominant

dominateur, -trice [dɔminatœr, -tris] *adj* : domineering, overbearing

domination [dɔminasjɔ̃] *nf* : domination

dominer [dɔmine] *vt* **1** : to dominate **2** MAÎTRISER : to master, to control **3** : to outclass, to surpass **4** : to tower over — *vi* **1** : to be in a dominant position **2** : to prevail — **se dominer** *vr* : to control oneself

dominicain, -caine [dɔminikɛ̃, -kɛn] *adj* : Dominican

Dominican, -caine *n* : Dominican

domino [dɔmino] *nm* : domino

dommage [dɔmaʒ] *nm* **1** PRÉJUDICE : harm, injury **2** DÉGÂTS : damage **3** **c'est dommage** : that's a pity, that's too bad

dommageable [dɔmaʒabl] *adj* : detrimental, harmful

dompter [dɔ̃te] *vt* : to tame, to subdue

dompteur, -teuse [dɔ̃tœr, -tøz] *n* : trainer, (wild-animal) tamer

don [dɔ̃] *nm* **1** CADEAU : gift **2** : donation **3** : talent **4** **don de soi** : self-sacrifice

donateur, -trice [dɔnatœr, -tris] *n* : donor, giver

donation [dɔnasjɔ̃] *nf* : donation

donc [dɔ̃k] *conj* **1** : so, therefore, consequently <je pense, donc je suis : I think, therefore I am> **2** : so, then <vous venez donc? : so you're coming?> **3** (*used for emphasis*) <écoutemoi donc! : would you listen to me!> <quoi donc? : what was that?>

donjon [dɔ̃ʒɔ̃] *nm* : keep (of a castle)

donne [dɔn] *nf* : deal (in card games)

donné, -née [dɔne] *adj* **1** : given <étant donné que : given that, considering that> **2** **c'est donné** : it's a bargain

donnée *nf* **1** : fact, piece of information **2** **données** *nfpl* : data <les données informatiques : computer data>

donner [dɔne] *vt* **1** : to give, to hand out, to donate **2** ATTRIBUER : to attribute to, to assign <quel âge lui donnez-vous? : how old would you say he is?> **3** : to provide, to transmit <donner un bon exemple : to set a good example> <donner un rhume à : to give a cold to> **4** CAUSER : to cause <donner du souci : to cause concern> <ça me donne froid : that makes me cold> **5** : to show, to put on (a film, play, etc.) **6** : to deal (cards) — *vi* **1** : to produce, to yield a crop **2** **~ contre** : to hit, to run into **3** **~ dans** : to lead toward (a place), to fall into (a trap), to tend toward (an opinion, etc.) — **se donner** *vr* **1** : to give to oneself, to have <se donner du bon temps : to have a good time> **2** **~ à** : to devote oneself to **3** **~ pour** : to pretend to be

donneur, -neuse [dɔnœr, -nøz] *n* **1** : donor **2** : dealer (in card games)

dont [dɔ̃] *pron* : of which, of whom, whose <la famille dont je sors : the family I come from> <ce dont il s'agit : what it's all about> <la fille dont la chevelure est bouclée : the girl whose hair is curly>

doper [dɔpe] *vt* : to dope

doré, -rée[1] [dɔre] *adj* **1** : gilded, gilt **2** : golden

dorénavant [dɔrenavɑ̃] *adv* : henceforth

dorer [dɔre] *vt* **1** : to gild **2** : to turn golden, to tan **3** : to glaze — *vi* : to brown (in cooking) — **se dorer** *vr* **se dorer au soleil** : to sunbathe, to tan

doris [dɔris] *nm* : dory (boat)

dorloter [dɔrlɔte] *vt* : to pamper, to baby

dormant, -mante [dɔrmɑ̃, -mɑ̃t] *adj* **1** : still, unmoving **2** : dormant (in botany)

dormeur, -meuse [dɔrmœr, -møz] *n* : sleeper

dormir [dɔrmir] {30} *vi* **1** : to sleep, to be asleep **2** : to be dormant, to be still, to lie idle

dorsal, -sale [dɔrsal, -sal] *adj, mpl* **dorsaux** [dɔrso] : dorsal

dort [dɔr], *etc.* → **dormir**

dortoir [dɔrtwar] *nm* : dormitory

dorure [dɔryr] *nf* **1** : gilt **2** : gilding

dos [do] *nms & pl* **1** : back <dos à dos : back to back> **2** : spine (of a book) **3** **de ~** : from behind

dos–d'âne [dodan] *nm* : speed bump

dose [doz] *nf* : dose

doser [doze] *vt* : to measure out (a dose of medicine, etc.), to apportion

doseur [dozœr] *nm* **1** : measure **2** *or* **bouchon doseur** : measuring cup

dossard [dosar] *nm* : number (worn by an athlete)

dossier [dosje] *nm* **1** : file, dossier <dossier criminel : criminal record> **2** : back (of a chair, etc.)

dot [dɔt] *nf* : dowry

dotation [dɔtasjɔ̃] *nf* : endowment

doter [dɔte] *vt* **1** : to endow **2** ÉQUIPER : to equip **3** : to allocate

douane [dwan] *nf* **1** : customs **2** : (import) duty

douanier[1], **-nière** [dwanje, -njɛr] *adj* : customs <tarif douanier : customs tariff>

douanier[2] *nm* : customs officer

doublage [dublaʒ] *nm* **1** : acting as an understudy **2** : lining **3** : dubbing

double[1] [dubl] *adv & adj* : double

double[2] *nm* **1** : double <le double de : twice as much as> <plus du double : more than double> **2** : copy, duplicate <un double de clés : a spare set of keys>

doublement[1] [dubləmɑ̃] *adv* : doubly

doublement[2] *nm* : doubling

doubler [duble] *vt* **1** : to double **2** : to line **3** : to dub (a film, etc.) **4** : to pass, to overtake **5** : *fam* : to double–cross — *vi* : to double, to increase twofold

doublure [dublyr] *nf* **1** : lining **2** : understudy, stand-in

doucement [dusmɑ̃] *adv* **1 :** gently, softly **2 :** slowly **3 :** meekly
doucereux, -reuse [dusrø, -røz] *adj* **1** MIELLEUX : smooth, unctuous **2** : sugary, saccharine
douceur [dusœr] *nf* **1 :** softness, smoothness **2 :** gentleness, mildness, meekness **3 douceurs** *nfpl* : candy, sweets **4 en ~ :** gently, smoothly
douche [duʃ] *nf* **1 :** shower <prendre une douche : to take a shower> **2** : douche (in medicine) **3 douche froide :** letdown
doucher [duʃe] *vt* **1 :** to give a shower to **2 :** to soak, to drench **— se doucher** *vr* : to take a shower
doué, douée [dwe] *adj* **1 :** gifted, talented **2 ~ de :** endowed with
douille [duj] *nf* **1 :** cartridge case **2** : electric socket
douillet, -lette [dujɛ, -jɛt] *adj* **1 :** cozy **2 :** oversensitive
douillette *nf Can* : comforter (for a bed)
douleur [dulœr] *nf* **1 :** pain, ache **2** CHAGRIN : sorrow, grief
douloureusement [dulurøzmɑ̃] *adv* **1** : grievously, terribly **2 :** painfully
douloureux, -reuse [dulurø, -røz] *adj* **1** : painful, sore **2 :** distressing **3 :** sorrowful, sad
doute [dut] *nm* : doubt
douter [dute] *vt* **1 :** to doubt **2 ~ de** : to question <douter de l'honnêteté de : to question the honesty of> **— se douter** *vr* **~ de :** to suspect <je ne me doutais de rien : I didn't suspect a thing>
douteux, -teuse [dutø, -tøz] *adj* **1** INCERTAIN : doubtful, uncertain **2** : questionable, dubious **3 :** ambiguous
douve [duv] *nf* **1 :** moat **2 :** stave (of a barrel)
doux, douce [du, dus] *adj* **1 :** sweet **2** : soft <une peau douce : soft skin> **3** : mild, gentle <un hiver doux : a mild winter> **4 :** meek **5 en ~ :** quietly, secretly
douzaine [duzɛn] *nf* **1 :** dozen **2 une douzaine de :** about twelve
douze[1] [duz] *adj* **1 :** twelve **2 :** twelfth <le douze avril : April twelfth>
douze[2] *nms & pl* : twelve
douzième [duzjɛm] *adj & nmf & nm* : twelfth
doyen, doyenne [dwajɛ̃, -jɛn] *n* **1 :** dean **2 doyen d'âge :** oldest person
draconien, -nienne [drakɔnjɛ̃, -njɛn] *adj* : draconian, harsh
dragage [dragaʒ] *nm* : dredging
dragée [draʒe] *nf* **1** *France* : sugar-coated almond **2 :** pill
dragon [dragɔ̃] *nm* : dragon
drague [drag] *nf* : dredge
draguer [drage] *vt* **1 :** to dredge **2** *fam* : to cruise, to try to pick up <il drague les filles : he's trying to pick up girls>
drainage [drɛnaʒ] *nm* : drainage, draining
drainer [drene] *vt* : to drain
dramatique [dramatik] *adj* **1 :** dramatic **2 :** tragic
dramatiquement [dramatikmɑ̃] *adv* : tragically
dramatisation [dramatizasjɔ̃] *nf* : dramatization
dramatiser [dramatize] *v* : to dramatize
dramaturge [dramatyrʒ] *nmf* : playwright, dramatist
drame [dram] *nm* **1 :** drama **2 :** tragedy
drap [dra] *nm* **1 :** woolen fabric **2** *or* **drap de lit :** bed sheet **3 drap fin** : broadcloth **4 drap mortuaire :** pall
drapé [drape] *nm* : drape, hang (of fabric)
drapeau [drapo] *nm, pl* **drapeaux :** flag
draper [drape] *vt* : to drape **— se draper** *vr* **~ dans :** to drape oneself in
draperie [drapri] *nf* **1 :** drapery, wall hanging **2 :** cloth industry
drastique [drastik] *adj* : drastic
drave [drav] *nf Can* : drive (of logs)
draver [drave] *vt Can* : to drive (logs down a stream)
dressage [drɛsaʒ] *nm* : (animal) training
dresser [drese] *vt* **1** LEVER : to raise **2** ÉRIGER : to put up, to erect **3 :** to lay out, to set (up) **4 :** to draft, to draw up <dresser une liste : to draw up a list> **5 :** to train <dresser un chien : to train a dog> **6 dresser qqn contre :** to set s.o. against **— se dresser** *vr* **1 :** to stand up **2 :** to rise up, to tower **3 ~ contre :** to rebel against
dresseur, -seuse [drɛsœr, -søz] *n* : trainer, tamer <dresseur de lions : lion tamer>
dressoir [drɛswar] *nm* : cupboard, sideboard
dribble [dribl] *nm* : dribble (in basketball)
dribbler [drible] *vi* : to dribble (in basketball)
drille [drij] *nm* **un joyeux drille :** a cheerful fellow
drogue [drɔg] *nf* : drug
drogué, -guée [drɔge] *n* : drug addict
droguer [drɔge] *vt* : to drug **— se droguer** *vr* : to take drugs
droit[1] [drwa] *adv* : straight, directly <droit au but : straight to the point>
droit[2]**, droite** [drwa, drwat] *adj* **1 :** right, right-hand **2 :** straight, direct **3 :** upright, vertical **4 :** honest, upright
droit[3] *nm* **1 :** right <les droits de l'homme : human rights> <avoir droit à : to have the right to, to be eligible for> **2 :** fee <droit d'entrée : entrance fee> **3 :** law <droit pénal : criminal law> **4 droits d'auteur** : copyright, royalties **5 à qui de droit** : to whom it may concern
droite *nf* **1 :** right, right-hand side **2 la droite :** the right, the right wing

droitier[1], **-tière** [drwatje, -tjɛr] *adj* : right-handed

droitier[2], **-tière** *n* : right-handed person

droiture [drwatyr] *nf* : uprightness, integrity

drôle [drol] *adj* **1** COMIQUE : funny, droll **2** BIZARRE : strange, odd **3 ~ de** : funny, strange <un drôle de chapeau : a strange hat> <une drôle d'idée : a funny idea>

drôlement [drolmɑ̃] *adv* **1** : amusingly, comically **2** : strangely, oddly **3** *fam* : really, awfully <les prix sont drôlement élevés : prices are terribly high>

drôlerie [drolri] *nf* **1** : drollness **2** : funny remark

dromadaire [drɔmadɛr] *nm* : dromedary

dru[1] [dry] *adv* : thickly, heavily

dru[2], **drue** [dry] *adj* **1** : thick, dense, bushy <avoir la barbe drue : to have a thick beard> **2** : heavy <une pluie drue : heavy rain>

du [dy] → **de, le**

dû[1] [dy] *pp* → **devoir**

dû[2], **due** [dy] *adj* **1** : due, owing **2** : proper, appropriate **3 ~ à** : due to

dû[3] *nm* : due <réclamer son dû : to claim one's due>

dubitatif, -tive [dybitatif, -tiv] *adj* : dubious, skeptical

duc [dyk] *nm* : duke

duchesse [dyʃɛs] *nf* : duchess

duel [dɥɛl] *nm* : duel

dûment [dymɑ̃] *adv* : duly

dune [dyn] *nf* : dune

duo [dyo] *nm* **1** : duet **2** : duo, pair

dupe [dyp] *nf* : dupe

duper [dype] *vt* : to dupe, to deceive

duplex [dyplɛks] *nm* **1** : duplex apartment **2** : (radio or television) linkup

duplicata [dyplikata] *nms & pl* : duplicate

duplicité [dyplisite] *nf* : duplicity

duquel → **lequel**

dur[1] [dyr] *adv* : hard <travailler dur : to work hard>

dur[2], **dure** [dyr] *adj* **1** : hard, stiff **2** : difficult **3** : harsh

dur[3] *nm* **1** : solid structure <construire en dur : to build with permanent materials> **2** *fam* : toughie, roughneck

durabilité [dyrabilite] *nf* : durability

durable [dyrabl] *adj* : durable, lasting

durant [dyrɑ̃] *prep* **1** : for <durant dix jours : for ten days> **2** : during

durcir [dyrsir] *v* : to harden — **se durcir** *vr*

durcissement [dyrsismɑ̃] *nm* : hardening

dure *nf* **1 à la dure** : the hard way **2 coucher sur la dure** : to sleep on the ground

durée [dyre] *nf* **1** : duration, length **2 de longue durée** : long-term, long-lasting

durement [dyrmɑ̃] *adv* : harshly, severely

durer [dyre] *vi* : to last, to go on

dureté [dyrte] *nf* **1** : hardness, arduousness **2** : harshness

durillon [dyrijɔ̃] *nm* CAL : callus

duvet [dyvɛ] *nm* **1** : down (feathers) **2** : sleeping bag

duveteux, -teuse [dyvtø, -tøz] *adj* : downy, fluffy, fuzzy

DVD [devede] *nm* : DVD (digital video disc)

dynamique[1] [dinamik] *adj* : dynamic — **dynamiquement** [-mikmɑ̃] *adv*

dynamique[2] *nf* : dynamics *pl*

dynamisme [dinamism] *nm* : dynamism

dynamite [dinamit] *nf* : dynamite

dynamiter [dinamite] *vt* : to dynamite, to blast

dynamo [dinamo] *nf* : dynamo

dynastie [dinasti] *nf* : dynasty — **dynastique** [-nastik] *adj*

dysenterie [disɑ̃tri] *nf* : dysentery

dyslexie [dislɛksi] *nf* : dyslexia — **dyslexique** [-lɛksik] *adj*

dyspepsie [dispɛpsi] *nf* : dyspepsia — **dyspepsique** [-pɛpsik] *or* **dyspeptique** [-pɛptik] *adj*

dystrophie [distrɔfi] *nf* **1** : dystrophy **2 dystrophie musculaire** : muscular dystrophy

E

e [ø] *nm* : e, fifth letter of the alphabet

eau [o] *nf, pl* **eaux 1** : water <eau douce : freshwater> <eau de pluie : rainwater> <eau bénite : holy water> <les eaux territoriales : territorial waters> **2 eau de Cologne** : cologne **3** → **Javel 4 eau oxygénée** : hydrogen peroxide **5 faire eau** : to leak **6 mettre l'eau à la bouche** : to make one's mouth water

eau-de-vie [odvi] *nf, pl* **eaux-de-vie** : brandy

eau-forte [ofɔrt] *nf, pl* **eaux-fortes** : etching

ébahi, -hie [ebai] *adj* : flabbergasted, dumbfounded

ébahir [ebair] *vt* ÉBERLUER : to astound, to dumbfound — **s'ébahir** *vr*

ébahissement [ebaismɑ̃] *nm* : astonishment

ébats [eba] *nmpl* GAMBADES : frolicking

ébattre [ebatr] {12} *v* **s'ébattre** *vr* : to frolic

ébauche [eboʃ] *nf* : outline, rough draft, sketch

ébaucher [eboʃe] *vt* : to sketch out, to outline — **s'ébaucher** *vr* : to form, to take shape

ébène [ebɛn] *nf* : ebony

ébéniste [ebenist] *nmf* : cabinetmaker

ébénisterie [ebenistəri] *nf* : cabinetmaking

éberluer [ebɛrlɥe] ÉBAHIR *vt* : to astonish, to astound

éblouir [ebluir] *vt* **1** : to dazzle **2** : to stun, to amaze — **éblouissant, -sante** [-isɑ̃, -sɑ̃t] *adj*

éblouissement [ebluismɑ̃] *nm* **1** ÉMERVEILLEMENT : amazement, wonder **2** VERTIGE : dizzy spell

éborgner [ebɔrɲe] *vt* **1** : to blind (in one eye) **2** *Can* : to chip (a glass, plate, etc.)

éboueur [ebwœr] *nm* : garbage collector, garbageman

ébouillanter [ebujɑ̃te] *vt* **1** : to scald, to burn (one's hands, etc.) **2** : to blanch (in cooking) — **s'ébouillanter** *vr*

éboulement [ebulmɑ̃] *nm* **1** : crumbling, collapse **2** : heap of fallen rocks or earth <éboulement de terre : landslide>

ébouler [ebule] *v* **s'ébouler** *vr* : to cave in, to collapse

éboulis [ebuli] *nms & pl* : heap of rocks or earth, debris

ébouriffer [eburife] *vt* **1** : to tousle, to ruffle **2** *fam* : to amaze, to stun

ébrancher [ebrɑ̃ʃe] *vt* ÉLAGUER : to prune

ébranlement [ebrɑ̃lmɑ̃] *nm* **1** : shaking, rattling **2** : shock

ébranler [ebrɑ̃le] *vt* **1** : to shake, to rattle **2** : to weaken, to undermine — **s'ébranler** *vr* : to move off

ébrécher [ebreʃe] {87} *vt* : to chip, to nick — **s'ébrécher** *vr*

ébréchure [ebreʃyr] *nf* : nick, chip, flaw

ébriété [ebrijete] *nf* : inebriation, drunkenness

ébrouer [ebrue] *v* **s'ébrouer** *vr* **1** : to snort **2** : to shake oneself

ébruiter [ebrɥite] *vt* : to spread, to divulge — **s'ébruiter** *vr* : to become known

ébullition [ebylisjɔ̃] *nf* **1** : boil, boiling <point d'ébullition : boiling point> **2** **en état d'ébullition** : in a fever of excitement, in turmoil

écaille [ekaj] *nf* **1** : scale (of fish, reptiles, etc.) **2** : oyster shell **3** : tortoiseshell **4** : flake, chip

écailler [ekaje] *vt* **1** : to scale (fish) **2** : to open (a shell) **3** : to chip (paint) — **s'écailler** *vr* : to flake off

écailleux, -leuse [ekajø, -jøz] *adj* : scaly, flaky

écale [ekal] *nf* : husk, hull

écaler [ekale] *vt* : to husk, to hull (nuts, etc.)

écarlate [ekarlat] *adj & nf* : scarlet

écarquiller [ekarkije] *vt* **écarquiller les yeux** : to open one's eyes wide

écart [ekar] *nm* **1** DISTANCE : distance, gap, interval **2** DIFFÉRENCE : difference, disparity, deviation **3** : lapse (in behavior, etc.) **4** : swerving <faire un écart : to swerve, to shy, to step aside> **5** **à l'écart** : apart, away <se tenir à l'écart : to stand apart, to keep to oneself> **6** **faire le grand écart** : to do the split (in gymnastics)

écarté, -tée [ekarte] *adj* **1** ISOLÉ : remote, secluded **2** : wide apart <avec les bras écartés : with arms outstretched>

écarteler [ekartəle] {20} *vt* **1** : to tear apart **2** **être écartelé entre** : to be torn between

écartement [ekartəmɑ̃] *nm* ESPACE : space, gap

écarter [ekarte] *vt* **1** : to spread, to open **2** ÉLOIGNER : to move aside, to push away **3** EXCLURE : to dismiss, to rule out **4** DÉTOURNER : to divert, to distract **5** *Can* : to lose **6** *France* : to discard (in card games) — **s'écarter** *vr* **1** : to move away, to deviate, to digress **2** : to part, to separate **3** **~ de** : to stray from

écartiller [ekartije] *vt Can fam* : to open, to spread <il a écartillé les bras pour les accueillir : he opened his arms to welcome them>

ecchymose [ekimoz] *nf* : bruise

ecclésiastique[1] [eklezjastik] *adj* : ecclesiastical

ecclésiastique[2] *nm* : clergyman

écervelé, -lée [esɛrvəle] *adj* ÉTOURDI : scatterbrained, empty-headed

échafaud [eʃafo] *nm* : scaffold

échafaudage [eʃafodaʒ] *nm* **1** : scaffolding **2** AMAS : heap, pile

échafauder [eʃafode] *vi* : to erect scaffolding — *vt* **1** : to stack, to pile up **2** : to construct, to build up (plans, theories, etc.)

échalier [eʃalje] *nm* **1** : gate **2** : stile

échalote [eʃalɔt] *nf* **1** : shallot **2** *Can* : scallion

échancré, -crée [eʃɑ̃kre] *adj* **1** : low-cut (of clothing) **2** : indented <un littoral échancré : a jagged coastline>

échancrure [eʃɑ̃kryr] *nf* **1** : low neckline **2** : indentation (of a coastline)

échange [eʃɑ̃ʒ] *nm* **1** : exchange <en échange de : in return for> **2** : trade <échange libre : free trade> <échanges internationaux : international trade>

échanger [eʃɑ̃ʒe] {17} *vt* : to exchange, to trade

échangeur [eʃɑ̃ʒœr] *nm* : interchange, junction (of highways)

échantillon [eʃɑ̃tijɔ̃] *nm* : sample, specimen

échantillonnage [eʃɑ̃tijɔnaʒ] *nm* **1** : sampling **2** : selection (of samples)

échappatoire [eʃapatwar] *nf* : way out, loophole

échappée [eʃape] *nf* **1** : breakaway (in sports) **2** VUE : vista, view **3** : brief period, break **4** : space, gap

échappement [eʃapmɑ̃] *nm* **1** : escapement (of a watch) **2** : exhaust (of an automobile) **3** → **pot**

échapper [eʃape] *vi* **1** ∼ **à** : to escape from (a person, a situation), to escape (danger, etc.) **2** ∼ **à** : to elude, to evade <rien ne lui échappe : nothing gets by him> **3 échapper à qqn** : to slip out (of s.o.'s hands) <le stylo lui a échappé des mains : the pen slipped out of his hands> <son nom m'échappe : her name escapes me> **4 laisser échapper** : to let out (a cry, a sigh, etc.) **5 échapper belle** : to have a narrow escape — *vt Can* : to drop <échapper un colis : to drop a parcel> — **s'échapper** *vr* : to escape

écharde [eʃard] *nf* : splinter

écharpe [eʃarp] *nf* **1** : scarf **2** : sash (of office) **3** : sling **4 prendre en écharpe** : to sideswipe

échasse [eʃas] *nf* : stilt

échassier [eʃasje] *nm* : wading

échauder [eʃode] *vt* **1** : to scald **2** : to teach a lesson, to make wary <échaudé par expérience : burned by experience>

échauffement [eʃofmɑ̃] *nm* **1** : heating up **2** : warm-up (in sports) **3** : overexcitement

échauffer [eʃofe] *vt* **1** : to make hot, to overheat **2** : to warm up (in sports) **3** EXCITER : to excite, to stimulate — **s'échauffer** *vr* : to warm up

échauffourée [eʃofure] *nf* **1** ESCARMOUCHE : skirmish **2** BAGARRE : brawl

échéance [eʃeɑ̃s] *nf* **1** : due date, expiration (date) <venir à échéance : to fall due> **2** : financial obligation, payment **3** : term <à longue échéance : in the long run>

échéancier [eʃeɑ̃sje] *nm* **1** : payment schedule **2** : schedule, calendar

échéant [eʃeɑ̃] *adv* **le cas échéant** : if need be

échec [eʃɛk] *nm* **1** : failure, setback **2 échecs** *nmpl* : chess **3 échec et mat** : checkmate **4 mise en échec** *Can* : check (in hockey) **5 tenir en échec** : to hold in check, to thwart

échelle [eʃɛl] *nf* **1** : ladder **2** : scale <carte à grande échelle : large-scale map> <échelle de salaires : pay scale> **3** GAMME : scale (in music) **4** : run, ladder (in stockings)

échelon [eʃlɔ̃] *nm* **1** : rung (of a ladder) **2** : step, grade, level **3** : echelon

échelonner [eʃlɔne] *vt* : to space out, to spread out — **s'échelonner** *vr*

écheveau [eʃvo] *nm, pl* **-veaux 1** : skein, hank **2** ENCHEVÊTREMENT : tangle

échevelé, -lée [eʃəvle] *adj* **1** : disheveled **2** : wild, disorderly

échine [eʃin] *nf* : backbone, spine

échiner [eʃine] *v* **s'échiner** *vr* : to work oneself to the bone

échiquier [eʃikje] *nm* : chessboard

écho [eko] *nm* **1** : echo **2** : repeating <se faire l'écho de : to repeat, to spread> **3** : response <recevoir un écho : to get a response> **4 échos** *nmpl* : gossip, rumors *pl*

échographie [ekografi] *nf* : ultrasound

échoir [eʃwar] {31} *vi* **1** : to expire **2** : to fall due **3** ∼ **à** : to fall to <le travail qui m'est échu : the task that fell to me>

échoppe [eʃɔp] *nf* : booth, stall

échouer [eʃwe] *vi* **1** : to run (a ship) aground **2** : to fail, to fall through — *vt* : to beach — **s'échouer** *vr* : to run aground

éclabousser [eklabuse] *vt* **1** : to splash, to spatter **2** : to stain, to smear (a reputation)

éclaboussure [eklabusyr] *nf* **1** : splash, spattering **2** : smear, blemish (on a reputation)

éclair [eklɛr] *nm* **1** : flash of lightning **2** : flash **3** : éclair

éclairage [eklɛraʒ] *nm* : lighting, illumination

éclaircie [eklɛrsi] *nf* **1** EMBELLIE : sunny spell **2** : clearing, glade

éclaircir [eklɛrsir] *vt* **1** : to lighten **2** CLARIFIER : to clarify, to shed light on **3** : to thin (in cooking) — **s'éclaircir** *vr* **1** : to clear <le temps s'éclaircit : the weather is clearing up> <s'éclaircir la gorge : to clear one's throat> **2** : to thin out **3** : to become clearer (of a situation, etc.)

éclaircissement [eklɛrsismɑ̃] *nm* : explanation, clarification

éclairer [eklere] *vt* **1** : to light, to light up **2** : to enlighten **3** CLARIFIER, EXPLIQUER : to shed light on, to clarify — *vi* : to give light — *v impers* **il éclaire** *Can* : it's thundering and lightening — **s'éclairer** *vr* **1** : to light up **2** : to become clearer

éclaireur[1], **-reuse** [eklɛrœr, -røz] *n* : boy scout *m*, girl scout *f*

éclaireur[2] *nm* : scout (in the military)

éclat [ekla] *nm* **1** : splinter, chip <voler en éclats : to fly into pieces> **2** : brilliance, radiance **3** : splendor, magnificence <coup d'éclat : remarkable feat> **4** : outburst, uproar <éclat de rire : burst of laughter> <éclats de voix : shouts, cries>

éclatant, -tante [eklatɑ̃, -tɑ̃t] *adj* **1** BRILLANT : bright, brilliant **2** RETENTISSANT : resounding <un succès écla-

tant : a resounding success> **3** : loud, piercing

éclatement [eklatmɑ̃] *nm* **1** EXPLOSION : explosion, bursting **2** : blowout (of a tire) **3** : rupture, split

éclater [eklate] *vi* **1** EXPLOSER : to burst, to explode **2** : to break up, to splinter **3** : to break out <la guerre a éclaté : war broke out> — **s'éclater** *vr fam* : to have a great time

éclectique [eklɛktik] *adj* : eclectic

éclipse [eklips] *nf* : eclipse

éclipser [eklipse] *vt* : to eclipse, to outshine — **s'éclipser** *vr* S'ESQUIVER : to slip away

éclopé, -pée [eklɔpe] *adj* : lame

éclore [eklɔr] {32} *vi* **1** : to hatch **2** : to open out, to blossom

éclosion [eklozjɔ̃] *nf* **1** : hatching **2** : blossoming

écluse [eklyz] *nf* : lock (of a canal)

écluser [eklyze] *vt* **1** : to provide with locks **2** *fam* : to swill down

écœurant, -rante [ekœrɑ̃, -rɑ̃t] *adj* **1** NAUSÉABOND : sickening, nauseating **2** : disgusting

écœuranterie [ekœrɑ̃tri] *nf Can fam* : dirty trick

écœurement [ekœrmɑ̃] *nm* **1** NAUSÉE : nausea **2** : disgust, distaste **3** DÉCOURAGEMENT : discouragement

écœurer [ekœre] *vt* **1** : to nauseate, to sicken **2** : to disgust **3** DÉCOURAGER : to discourage

école [ekɔl] *nf* **1** : school <école maternelle *France* : nursery school> <école maternelle *Can* : kindergarten> <école primaire : grade school> <école secondaire *Can* : high school> **2** : schooling, education **3** : training, experience <être à bonne école : to be in good hands> <être à rude école : to learn the hard way> **4** : movement, school (of artists, etc.)

écolier, -lière [ekɔlje, -ljɛr] *n* : schoolboy *m*, schoolgirl *f*

écologie [ekɔlɔʒi] *nf* : ecology

écologique [ekɔlɔʒik] *adj* : ecological — **écologiquement** [-ʒikmɑ̃] *adv*

écologiste [ekɔlɔʒist] *nmf* : ecologist, environmentalist

éconduire [ekɔ̃dɥir] {49} *vt* : to reject, to dismiss

économe[1] [ekɔnɔm] *adj* : thrifty, economical

économe[2] *nmf* : bursar

économie [ekɔnɔmi] *nf* **1** : economy **2** : economics **3** : saving, thrift <faire une économie de temps : to save time> **4 économies** *nfpl* : savings

économique [ekɔnɔmik] *adj* **1** : economic **2** : economical, inexpensive — **économiquement** [-mikmɑ̃] *adv*

économiser [ekɔnɔmize] *vt* : to economize, to save, to conserve — *vi* : to economize, to save money

économiste [ekɔnɔmist] *nmf* : economist

écoper [ekɔpe] *vt* : to bail out (a boat) — *vi fam* **~ de** : to get <écoper de trois ans de prison : to get a three-year sentence>

écorce [ekɔrs] *nf* **1** : bark **2** : peel, rind **3 l'écorce terrestre** : the earth's crust

écorcher [ekɔrʃe] *vt* **1** DÉPOUILLER : to skin **2** ÉRAFLER : to scratch, to graze, to chafe **3** : to mispronounce

écorchure [ekɔrʃyr] *nf* : graze, scratch, chafing

écorner [ekɔrne] *vt* **1** : to chip the corner off (furniture), to dog-ear (a page) **2** : to make a dent in (one's fortune, etc.) — **s'écorner** *vr*

écornifler [ekɔrnifle] *vt Can fam* : to spy on — *vi Can fam* : to snoop around

écossais[1], **-saise** [ekɔsɛ, -sɛz] *adj* **1** : Scottish **2 tissu écossais** : tartan, plaid **3 whisky écossais** : Scotch (whiskey)

écossais[2] *nm* **1** : Scots (language) **2** : tartan

Écossais, -saise *n* : Scot, Scottish person

écosser [ekɔse] *vt* : to shell

écosystème [ekɔsistɛm] *nm* : ecosystem

écot [eko] *nm* **payer son écot** : to pay one's share

écoulement [ekulmɑ̃] *nm* **1** : flowing, streaming **2** : discharge <écoulement sanguin : bleeding> **3** : dispersal (of a crowd) **4** : selling (of merchandise)

écouler [ekule] *vt* **1** : to sell **2** : to pass (into circulation) — **s'écouler** *vr* **1** : to flow (out) **2** : to drift away, to disperse **3** : to pass, to elapse <les minutes s'écoulent : the minutes pass by>

écourter [ekurte] *vt* : to cut short, to curtail

écoute [ekut] *nf* **1** : listening (in radio and television) <être aux écoutes : to be listening, to be tuned in> <les heures de grande écoute : prime time> **2** : listening (in) <écoutes téléphoniques : phone tapping> <poste d'écoute : listening post>

écouter [ekute] *vt* : to listen to — *vi* **1** : to listen **2 écouter aux portes** : to eavesdrop — **s'écouter** *vr*

écouteur [ekutœr] *nm* **1** : receiver (of a telephone) **2 écouteurs** *nmpl* : headphones, earphones

écoutille [ekutij] *nf* : hatchway

écrabouiller [ekrabuje] *vt fam* : to crush, to squash

écran [ekrɑ̃] *nm* : screen <le petit écran : television>

écrasant, -sante [ekrazɑ̃, -zɑ̃t] *adj* : crushing, overwhelming

écraser [ekraze] *vt* **1** : to crush, to squash, to mash **2** : to run over **3** ACCABLER : to overwhelm — **s'écraser** *vr* **1** : to get crushed **2** : to crash **3** *Can fam* : to collapse, to sink <elle s'est

écrasée sur le divan : she collapsed onto the sofa>
écrémer |ekreme| {87} *vt* : to skim (milk)
écrevisse |ekrəvis| *nf* : crayfish
écrier |ekrije| {96} *v* **s'écrier** *vr* : to exclaim
écrin |ekrɛ̃| *nm* : case, box
écrire |ekrir| {33} *vt* **1** : to write **2** ÉPELER : to spell <comment écrivez-vous ce mot? : how do you spell this word?> — *vi* : to write — **s'écrire** *vr* **1** : to be written, to be spelled **2** : to write to each other
écrit |ekri| *nm* **1** : writing, written work **2** : written exam **3 écrits** *nmpl* : writings, works **4 par ~** : in writing
écriteau |ekrito| *nm, pl* **-teaux** : notice, sign
écriture |ekrityr| *nf* **1** : handwriting, penmanship **2** : writing, script **3 écritures** *nfpl* : accounts, books **4 les Écritures** : the Scriptures
écrivaillon |ekrivajɔ̃| *nm fam* : hack (writer)
écrivain |ekrivɛ̃| *nm* : writer
écrivaine |ekrivɛn| *nf Can* : (female) writer
écrivait |ekrivɛ|, **écrivions** |ekrivjɔ̃|, *etc.* → **écrire**
écrive |ekriv|, *etc.* → **écrire**
écrou |ekru| *nm* : nut <écrou à ailettes : wing nut>
écrouer |ekrue| *vt* : to imprison
écroulement |ekrulmɑ̃| *nm* : collapse
écrouler |ekrule| *v* **s'écrouler** *vr* : to collapse, to fail, to fold
écru, -crue |ekry| *adj* **1** : raw, unbleached, natural <soie écrue : raw silk> **2** : ecru (color)
écu |eky| *nm* **1** BOUCLIER : shield **2** : crown (monetary unit)
écueil |ekœj| *nm* **1** RÉCIF : reef **2** : pitfall
écuelle |ekɥɛl| *nf* **1** : bowl **2** : bowlful
éculé, -lée |ekyle| *adj* **1** : worn at the heel **2** : hackneyed
écume |ekym| *nf* **1** : foam, froth **2** : scum
écumer |ekyme| *vt* **1** : to skim **2** PILLER : to plunder **3** : to search through, to scour — *vi* : to foam, to froth
écumeur, -meuse |ekymœr, -møz| *adj* : foamy, frothy
écureuil |ekyrœj| *nm* : squirrel
écurie |ekyri| *nf* : stable
écusson |ekysɔ̃| *nm* : badge
écuyer, -yère |ekɥije, -jɛr| *n* : horseman *m*, horsewoman *f*, rider
eczéma |ɛgzema| *nm* : eczema
éden |edɛn| *nm* : Eden, paradise
édenté, -tée |edɑ̃te| *adj* : toothless
édicter |edikte| *vt* : to decree
édifiant, -fiante |edifjɑ̃, -fjɑ̃t| *adj* : edifying
édification |edifikasjɔ̃| *nf* **1** : edification **2** : construction, building
édifice |edifis| *nm* : edifice, building
édifier |edifje| {96} *vt* **1** CONSTRUIRE : to erect, to build **2** : to edify
édit |edi| *nm* : edict
éditer |edite| *vt* **1** : to publish **2** : to edit
éditeur[1], **-trice** |editœr, -tris| *n* **1** : publisher **2** : editor
éditeur[2] *nm* **éditeur de textes** : text editing program
édition |edisjɔ̃| *nf* **1** : publishing <maison d'édition : publishing house> **2** : edition <nouvelle édition : new edition> **3** : editing
éditorial[1], **-riale** |editɔrjal| *adj, mpl* **-riaux** |-rjo| : editorial
éditorial[2] *nm, pl* **-riaux** : editorial
éditorialiste |editɔrjalist| *nmf* : editorial writer
édredon |edrədɔ̃| *nm* : comforter, eiderdown
éducateur[1], **-trice** |edykatœr, -tris| *adj* : educational
éducateur[2], **-trice** *n* : teacher, educator
éducatif, -tive |edykatif, -tiv| *adj* : educational
éducation |edykasjɔ̃| *nf* **1** ENSEIGNEMENT : education **2** : upbringing, breeding <avoir de l'éducation : to have good manners> **3** : training
édulcorant |edylkɔrɑ̃| *nm* : sweetener
édulcorer |edylkɔre| *vt* **1** SUCRER : to sweeten **2** ATTÉNUER : to tone down
éduquer |edyke| *vt* **1** : to educate **2** ÉLEVER : to bring up, to raise **3** : to train
efface *nf Can* |efas| : eraser
effacé, -cée |efase| *adj* **1** : faded **2** : retiring, self-effacing
effacement |efasmɑ̃| *nm* : erasing, obliteration
effacer |efase| {6} *vt* **1** : to erase, to delete **2** : to wipe out, to obliterate **3** : to outshine — **s'effacer** *vr* **1** : to wear off **2** : to fade, to diminish **3** : to stand aside
effarant, -rante |efarɑ̃, -rɑ̃t| *adj* : startling, alarming
effarement |efarmɑ̃| *nm* : alarm
effarer |efare| *vt* : to alarm
effaroucher |efaruʃe| *vt* **1** : to frighten, to scare away **2** : to alarm — **s'effaroucher** *vr*
effectif[1], **-tive** |efɛktif, -tiv| *adj* : effective, real
effectif[2] *nm* : size, strength, total number <un effectif de 160 personnes : a total of 160 people>
effectivement |efɛktivmɑ̃| *adv* **1** RÉELLEMENT : actually, really **2** : indeed, in fact
effectuer |efɛktɥe| *vt* EXÉCUTER : to carry out, to make <effectuer une enquête : to carry out an investigation>
efféminé, -née |efemine| *adj* : effeminate

effervescence [efɛrvesɑ̃s] *nf* **1** : effervescence **2** : agitation, turmoil <être en effervescence : to be all excited>

effervescent, -cente [efɛrvesɑ, -sɑ̃t] *adj* : effervescent

effet [efɛ] *nm* **1** : effect, result <faire de l'effet : to have an effect, to be effective> **2** : impression <il fait bon effet : he makes a good impression> **3** : operation, action <mettre à effet : to put into action> **4 à cet effet** : for that purpose **5 en ~** : indeed, actually **6 effets** *nmpl* : things, belongings

efficace [efikas] *adj* **1** : efficient **2** : efficacious, effective — **efficacement** [-kasmɑ̃] *adv*

efficacité [efikasite] *nf* **1** : efficiency **2** : effectiveness

efficience [efisjɑ̃s] *nf* : efficiency

effigie [efiʒi] *nf* : effigy

effilé, -lée [efile] *adj* **1** : sharp **2** : slim, slender **3** : frayed

effiler [efile] *vt* **1** : to make pointed, to taper **2** : to fray, to unravel — **s'effiler** *vr* : to fray

effiloche [efilɔʃ] *nf* : fraying, ravel

effilocher [efilɔʃe] *vt* : to shred, to fray — **s'effilocher** *vr* : to fray, to unravel

efflanqué, -quée [eflɑ̃ke] *adj* : emaciated

effleurement [eflœrmɑ̃] *nm* : light touch, caress

effleurer [eflœre] *vt* **1** FRÔLER : to touch lightly, to brush against **2** : to touch on (an idea, etc.) <ça m'a effleuré l'esprit : it crossed my mind>

effluve [eflyv] *nm* ÉMANATION : emanation, odor

effondrement [efɔ̃drəmɑ̃] *nm* : collapse

effondrer [efɔ̃dre] *v* **s'effondrer** *vr* : to sink, to collapse

efforcer [efɔrse] {6} *v* **s'efforcer** *vr* : to strive, to endeavor

effort [efɔr] *nm* **1** : effort <sans effort : effortless> **2** : stress (in engineering)

effraction [efraksjɔ̃] *nf* : housebreaking, breaking and entering

effraie [efrɛ], **effraiera** [efrɛra], *etc.* → **effrayer**

effranger [efrɑ̃ʒe] {17} *vt* : to fray — **s'effranger** *vr*

effrayant, -yante [efrɛjɑ̃, -jɑ̃t] *adj* **1** : frightening, scary **2** *fam* : terrible, frightful

effrayer [efreje] {11} *vt* **1** : to frighten, to scare **2** REBUTER : to put off, to scare away — **s'effrayer** *vr*

effréné, -née [efrene] *adj* **1** DÉCHAÎNÉ : unbridled, unrestrained **2** : frantic

effritement [efritmɑ̃] *nm* : crumbling, disintegration

effriter [efrite] *vt* : to crumble — **s'effriter** *vr* : to crumble away, to disintegrate

effroi [efrwa] *nm* TERREUR : terror, dread

effronté, -tée [efrɔ̃te] *adj* INSOLENT : insolent, impudent — **effrontément** [-temɑ̃] *adv*

effronterie [efrɔ̃tri] *nf* INSOLENCE : insolence, impudence

effroyable [efrwajabl] *adj* AFFREUX : dreadful, appalling

effroyablement [efrwajabləmɑ̃] *adv* **1** : appallingly **2** : extremely, terribly

effusion [efyzjɔ̃] *nf* **1** : effusion **2 effusion de sang** : bloodshed

égailler [egaje] *v* **s'égailler** *vr* : to disperse, to scatter

égal[1], -gale [egal] *adj, mpl* **égaux** [ego] **1** : equal **2** RÉGULIER : steady, regular <un pouls égal : a steady heartbeat> **3** : level, even **4 ça m'est égal** : it makes no difference to me

égal[2], -gale *n* **1** : equal **2 sans égal** : unequaled, matchless

également [egalmɑ̃] *adv* **1** : equally **2** AUSSI : also, as well, too

égaler [egale] *vt* **1** : to equal, to be equal to <deux plus deux égalent quatre : two plus two equals four> **2** : to match, to rival <personne ne l'égale : no one can match him>

égalisateur, -trice [egalizatœr, -tris] *adj* **1** : equalizing **2** : tying <le but égalisateur : the tying goal>

égaliser [egalize] *vt* **1** : to equalize **2** : to level (out), to even up — *vi* : to tie (in sports)

égalitaire [egalitɛr] *adj* : egalitarian

égalitarisme [egalitarism] *nm* : egalitarianism

égalité [egalite] *nf* **1** : equality **2** : evenness **3 à ~** : tied (in sports)

égard [egar] *nm* **1** : regard, consideration <sans égard pour les autres : without considering others> <par égard pour : out of deference to> **2 à l'égard de** : toward, with regard to **3 à cet égard** : in this respect **4 eu égard à** : in view of **5 égards** *nmpl* : consideration, respect

égaré, -rée [egare] *adj* **1** : lost, stray **2** : distraught

égarement [egarmɑ̃] *nm* **1** : distraction **2** : derangement, folly

égarer [egare] *vt* **1** : to lead astray **2** : to lose, to misplace — **s'égarer** *vr* **1** : to lose one's way **2** : to be misplaced **3** : to ramble, to digress

égayer [egeje] {11} *vt* : to cheer up, to brighten — **s'égayer** *vr*

égide [eʒid] *nf* : aegis <sous l'égide de : under the aegis of>

églantier [eglɑ̃tje] *nm* : wild rose (bush)

églantine [eglɑ̃tin] *nf* : wild rose

églefin [egləfɛ̃] *nm* : haddock

église [egliz] *nf* : church

ego [ego] *nm* : ego

égocentrique [egɔsɑ̃trik] *adj* : egocentric, self-centered

égoïsme [egɔism] *nm* : selfishness, egoism

égoïste[1] [egɔist] *adj* : selfish, egoistic — **égoïstement** [-istəmɑ̃] *adv*
égoïste[2] *nmf* : selfish person, egoist
égorger [egɔrʒe] {17} *vt* : to cut the throat of
égosiller [egɔzije] *v* **s'égosiller** *vr* **1** : to shout oneself hoarse **2** : to sing at the top of one's lungs
égotisme [egɔtism] *nm* : egotism
égotiste[1] [egɔtist] *adj* : egotistic, egotistical
égotiste[2] *nmf* : egotist
égout [egu] *nm* **1** : sewer **2 eaux d'égout** : sewage
égoutter [egute] *vt* : to allow to drip, to drain — **s'égoutter** *vr*
égouttoir [egutwar] *nm* **1** : dish drainer **2** : strainer, colander
égratigner [egratiɲe] *vt* ÉRAFLER : to scratch, to graze — **s'égratigner** *vr*
égratignure [egratiɲyr] *nf* : scratch
égrener [egrəne] {52} *vt* **1** : to shell (peas, etc.), to seed (grains, fruit), to gin (cottton) **2 égrener son chapelet** : to say one's rosary **3 égrener les heures** : to mark the hours
égreneuse [egrənøz] *nf* : cotton gin
égrillard, -larde [egrijar, -jard] *adj* : ribald, bawdy
égyptien, -tienne [eʒipsjɛ̃, -sjɛn] *adj* : Egyptian
Égyptien, -tienne *n* : Egyptian
eh [e] *interj* **1** : hey! **2 eh bien** : well <eh bien, allons-y : well, let's go>
éhonté, -tée [eɔ̃te] *adj* : shameless, brazen
éjaculation [eʒakylasjɔ̃] *nf* : ejaculation
éjaculer [eʒakyle] *vt* : to ejaculate
éjecter [eʒɛkte] *vt* **1** : to eject **2** *fam* : to kick out
éjection [eʒɛksjɔ̃] *nf* : ejection
élaboration [elabɔrasjɔ̃] *nf* : development, making, drawing up
élaborer [elabɔre] *vt* : to develop, to put together
élagage [elagaʒ] *nm* : pruning
élaguer [elage] *vt* ÉMONDER : to prune, to lop
élan [elɑ̃] *nm* **1** : momentum **2** : burst, rush, surge <un élan de colère : a burst of anger> <avec élan : enthusiastically> **3** : (European) elk **4** *Can* : swing (in baseball) **5 élan d'Amérique** *Can* → **orignal**
élancé, -cée [elɑ̃se] *adj* : slender
élancement [elɑ̃smɑ̃] *nm* : shooting pain
élancer [elɑ̃se] {6} *vi* : to give shooting pains — **s'élancer** *vr* **1** SE PRÉCIPITER : to dash forward, to rush **2** : to soar **3** *Can* : to swing (in baseball)
élargir [elarʒir] *vt* **1** : to widen, to broaden, to extend **2** LIBÉRER : to release, to discharge — **s'élargir** *vr* : to broaden, to expand
élargissement [elarʒismɑ̃] *nm* **1** : widening, broadening **2** LIBÉRATION : release, discharge
élasticité [elastisite] *nf* **1** : elasticity **2** : flexibility
élastique[1] [elastik] *adj* FLEXIBLE : elastic, flexible
élastique[2] *nm* **1** : elastic **2** : rubber band **3** : bungee cord
électeur, -trice [elɛktœr, -tris] *n* : voter, elector
électif, -tive [elɛktif, -tiv] *adj* : elective
élection [elɛksjɔ̃] *nf* **1** : election **2** CHOIX : choice
électoral, -rale [elɛktɔral] *adj, mpl* **-raux** [-ro] : electoral, election
électorat [elɛktɔra] *nm* : electorate
électricien, -cienne [elɛktrisjɛ̃, -sjɛn] *n* : electrician
électricité [elɛktrisite] *nf* : electricity
électrifier [elɛktrifje] {96} *vt* : to electrify — **électrification** [-trifikasjɔ̃] *nf*
électrique [elɛktrik] *adj* : electric, electrical — **électriquement** [-trikmɑ̃] *adv*
électrisant, -sante [elɛktrizɑ̃, -zɑ̃t] *adj* : electrifying, thrilling
électriser [elɛktrize] *vt* : to electrify
électroaimant [elɛktrɔɛmɑ̃] *nm* : electromagnet
électrocardiogramme [elɛktrɔkardjɔgram] *nm* : electrocardiogram
électrocardiographe [elɛktrɔkardjɔgraf] *nm* : electrocardiograph
électrocuter [elɛktrɔkyte] *vt* : to electrocute — **électrocution** [-trɔkysjɔ̃] *nf*
électrode [elɛktrɔd] *nf* : electrode
électrolyse [elɛktrɔliz] *nf* : electrolysis
électrolyte [elɛktrɔlit] *nm* : electrolyte
électromagnétisme [elɛktrɔmaɲetism] *nm* : electromagnetism — **électromagnétique** [-ɲetik] *adj*
électroménager[1] [elɛktrɔmenaʒe] *adj* **appareil électroménager** : household (electrical) appliance
électroménager[2] *nm* **l'électroménager** : household (electrical) appliances
électron [elɛktrɔ̃] *nm* : electron
électronicien, -cienne [elɛktrɔnisjɛ̃, -sjɛn] *n* : electronics engineer
électronique[1] [elɛktrɔnik] *adj* : electronic — **électroniquement** [-nikmɑ̃] *adv*
électronique[2] *nf* : electronics
élégamment [elegamɑ̃] *adv* : elegantly
élégance [elegɑ̃s] *nf* : elegance
élégant, -gante [elegɑ̃, -gɑ̃t] *adj* : elegant
élégiaque [eleʒjak] *adj* : elegiac
élégie [eleʒi] *nf* : elegy
élément [elemɑ̃] *nm* **1** : element **2** COMPOSANT : component, ingredient, part **3** : cell (of a battery) **4 éléments** *nmpl* : rudiments, basics
élémentaire [elemɑ̃tɛr] *adj* : elementary, basic
éléphant [elefɑ̃] *nm* : elephant

éléphantesque |elefɑ̃tɛsk| *adj* : elephantine, gigantic

élevage |ɛlvaʒ| *nm* **1** : breeding, raising <l'élevage de chevaux : horse breeding> **2** : ranch, livestock farm

élévateur |elevatœr| *nm* : (grain) elevator

élévation |elevasjɔ̃| *nf* **1** : elevation **2** : rise, increase **3** : raising

élève |elɛv| *nmf* : pupil, student

élevé, -vée |elve| *adj* **1** : high **2** : elevated, noble **3 bien élevé** : well-mannered, well brought up

élever |elve| {52} *vt* **1** : to raise, to increase **2** ÉRIGER : to erect, to build **3** : to elevate (mind, spirit, etc.) **4** : to bring up, to raise <élever un enfant : to raise a child> — **s'élever** *vr* **1** : to rise, to go up **2** : to be built, to stand **3** : to arise, to come up **4 ~ à** : to amount to, to come to **5 ~ contre** : to rise (up) against, to protest

éleveur, -veuse |ɛlvœr, -vøz| *n* : rancher, breeder

elfe |ɛlf| *nm* : elf

élider |elide| *vt* : to elide

éligibilité |eliʒibilite| *nf* : eligibility

éligible |eliʒibl| *adj* : eligible

élimé, -mée |elime| *adj* : threadbare, worn

élimination |eliminasjɔ̃| *nf* : elimination

éliminatoire[1] |eliminatwar| *adj* : qualifying

éliminatoire[2] *nf* : heat (in sports)

éliminer |elimine| *vt* : to eliminate

élire |elir| {51} *vt* **1** : to elect **2 élire domicile** : to take up residence

élision |elizjɔ̃| *nf* : elision

élite |elit| *nf* : elite

élixir |eliksir| *nm* : elixir

elle |ɛl| *pron* **1** : she, it <elle est heureuse : she's happy> <elle est toute neuve : it is brand new> **2** : her <c'était son idée à elle : it was her idea> **3 elles** *pron pl* : they, them <elles se trompent : they're mistaken> <selon elles : according to them>

elle–même |ɛlmɛm| *pron* **1** : herself, itself **2 elles–mêmes** *pron pl* : themselves

ellipse |elips| *nf* **1** OVALE : ellipse, oval **2** : ellipsis

elliptique |eliptik| *adj* : elliptical, elliptic

élocution |elɔkysjɔ̃| *nf* : elocution, diction

éloge |elɔʒ| *nm* **1** : eulogy **2** LOUANGE : praise

élogieux, -gieuse |elɔʒjø, -ʒjøz| *adj* : full of praise, laudatory

éloigné, -gnée |elwaɲe| *adj* : distant, remote

éloignement |elwaɲmɑ̃| *nm* **1** DISTANCE : remoteness, distance (in space or time) **2** : removal **3** : absence

éloigner |elwaɲe| *vt* **1** ÉCARTER : to push aside, to move away **2** DÉTOURNER : to divert, to turn away **3** : to postpone, to put off — **s'éloigner** *vr* : to move away, to go away

éloquence |elɔkɑ̃s| *nf* : eloquence

éloquent, -quente |elɔkɑ̃, -kɑ̃t| *adj* : eloquent — **éloquemment** |elɔkamɑ̃| *adv*

élu[1], **-lue** |ely| *adj* **1** : elect, future **2** : elected

élu[2], **-lue** *n* **1** : elected representative **2** : chosen one <l'élu de mon cœur : my beloved> <les élus : the elect>

élucider |elyside| *vt* CLARIFIER : to clarify, to elucidate — **élucidation** |-sidasjɔ̃| *nf*

élucubrations |elykybrasjɔ̃| *nfpl* : rantings, wild imaginings

éluder |elyde| *vt* : to elude, to evade

élusif, -sive |elyzif, -ziv| *adj* : elusive, evasive

émaciation |emasjasjɔ̃| *nf* : emaciation

émacié, -ciée |emasje| *adj* : emaciated

émail |emaj| *nm, pl* **émaux** |emo| **1** : enamel **2** *Can* : latex (paint)

émailler |emaje| *vt* **1** : to enamel **2** PARSEMER : to scatter, to sprinkle

émanation |emanasjɔ̃| *nf* **1** : emanation <émanations toxiques : toxic fumes> **2** : expression, manifestation

émancipation |emɑ̃sipasjɔ̃| *nf* : emancipation

émanciper |emɑ̃sipe| *vt* AFFRANCHIR : to emancipate, to liberate — **s'émanciper** *vr*

émaner |emane| *vi* **~ de** : to emanate from

émarger |emarʒe| {17} *vt* **1** : to sign, to initial **2** : to trim the margins of — *vi* **~ à** : to be paid from

émasculer |emaskyle| *vt* CASTRER : to emasculate

emballage |ɑ̃balaʒ| *nm* : packing, wrapping <papier d'emballage : wrapping paper>

emballement |ɑ̃balmɑ̃| *nm* **1** : surge, burst <un emballement d'enthousiasme : a burst of enthusiasm> **2** : racing (of an engine)

emballer |ɑ̃bale| *vt* **1** EMPAQUETER : to pack, to wrap **2** *fam* : to thrill <ça ne m'emballe pas : it doesn't thrill me> — **s'emballer** *vr* **1** : to surge **2** : to race (of an engine), to bolt (of a horse) **3** *fam* : to get carried away

embarcadère |ɑ̃barkadɛr| *nm* : wharf, pier

embarcation |ɑ̃barkasjɔ̃| *nf* BARQUE : small boat

embardée |ɑ̃barde| *nf* : swerve, lurch <faire une embardée : to swerve>

embargo |ɑ̃bargo| *nm* **1** : embargo **2 mettre l'embargo sur** : to embargo

embarquement |ɑ̃barkəmɑ̃| *nm* **1** : boarding, embarkation <carte d'embarquement : boarding pass> **2** CHARGEMENT : loading (on board)

embarquer |ɑ̃barke| *vt* **1** : to embark **2** : to load **3** *fam* : to start on, to get involved with — *vi* **1** : to board **2** **~ dans** *Can* : to get in, to climb in <embarque dans la voiture : get in the car> **3** **~ sur** *Can fam* : to climb (up) on — **s'embarquer** *vr* **1** : to board **2** **~ dans** *fam* : to get involved in, to launch into

embarras |ɑ̃bara| *nms & pl* **1** DIFFICULTÉ : difficulty, trouble <embarras financiers : financial problems> **2** GÊNE : embarrassment **3** : awkward situation, predicament <un embarras de choix : too much to choose from> **4** **embarras gastrique** : stomach upset

embarrassant, -sante |ɑ̃barasɑ̃, -sɑ̃t| *adj* **1** : embarrassing, awkward **2** ENCOMBRANT : cumbersome

embarrasser |ɑ̃barase| *vt* **1** ENCOMBRER : to clutter **2** : to hinder, to hamper **3** GÊNER : to embarrass — **s'embarrasser** *vr* **1** **~ dans** : to get tangled up in (lies, etc.) **2** **~ de** : to burden oneself with, to worry over

embarrer |ɑ̃bare| *vt Can* : to lock <ils l'ont embarré dans la chambre : they locked him in the room> — **s'embarrer** *vr Can* **~ dans** : to lock oneself in

embauche |ɑ̃boʃ| *nf* : hiring, employment

embaucher |ɑ̃boʃe| *vt* ENGAGER : to hire

embaumer |ɑ̃bome| *vt* **1** : to embalm **2** PARFUMER : to make fragrant, to scent — *vi* : to smell good

embellie |ɑ̃beli| *nf* **1** ÉCLAIRCIE : clear spell, bright spell **2** ACCALMIE : lull

embellir |ɑ̃belir| *vt* **1** ENJOLIVER : to make more attractive, to beautify **2** : to embellish (a story, etc.) — *vi* : to become more attractive

embellissement |ɑ̃bɛlismɑ̃| *nm* **1** : embellishment **2** : improvement

embêtant, -tante |ɑ̃bɛtɑ̃, -tɑ̃t| *adj* **1** : annoying **2** : awkward, tricky

embêtement |ɑ̃bɛtmɑ̃| *nm* : hassle, trouble, bother

embêter |ɑ̃bɛte| *vt* **1** : to annoy, to bother **2** : to bore — **s'embêter** *vr* : to be bored

emblée |ɑ̃ble| **d'~** : right away

emblématique |ɑ̃blemat'k| *adj* : emblematic

emblème |ɑ̃blɛm| *nm* : emblem

embobiner |ɑ̃bɔbine| *vt fam* : to bamboozle, to trick

emboîter |ɑ̃bwate| *vt* **1** : to fit together **2** **~ dans** : to fit into **3** **emboîter le pas à qqn** : to follow close behind s.o. — **s'emboîter** *vr*

embolie |ɑ̃bɔli| *nf* : embolism

embonpoint |ɑ̃bɔ̃pwɛ̃| *nm* CORPULENCE : stoutness, corpulence

embouchure |ɑ̃buʃyr| *nf* **1** : mouth (of a river) **2** : mouthpiece

embourber |ɑ̃burbe| *v* **s'embourber** *vr* **1** : to get stuck in the mud **2** S'EMPÊTRER : to get bogged down

embourgeoiser |ɑ̃burʒwaze| *v* **s'embourgeoiser** *vr* : to become middle-class

embouteillage |ɑ̃butɛjaʒ| *nm* **1** : bottling **2** : bottleneck, traffic jam

embouteiller |ɑ̃buteje| *vt* **1** : to bottle **2** : to block, to jam <la circulation est très embouteillée : traffic is very congested>

emboutir |ɑ̃butir| *vt* **1** : to stamp, to press (metal) **2** : to crash into, to ram

embranchement |ɑ̃brɑ̃ʃmɑ̃| *nm* **1** CARREFOUR : junction, fork <à l'embranchement des deux routes : at the fork in the road> **2** : branching **3** : branch (in botany and zoology) **4** : side street

embraser |ɑ̃braze| *vt* **1** : to set ablaze **2** ILLUMINER : to illuminate **3** : to inflame, to fire up (passion, enthusiasm, etc.) — **s'embraser** *vr* **1** : to catch fire **2** : to flare up

embrassade |ɑ̃brasad| *nf* : embrace, hugging and kissing

embrasser |ɑ̃brase| *vt* **1** : to kiss **2** ÉTREINDRE : to embrace, to hug **3** : to adopt, to take up (a cause, etc.) — **s'embrasser** *vr* : to kiss (each other)

embrasure |ɑ̃brazyr| *nf* OUVERTURE : opening <embrasure de la porte : doorway>

embrayage |ɑ̃brɛjaʒ| *nm* : clutch (of an automobile)

embrayer |ɑ̃breje| {11} *vi* **1** : to engage the clutch **2** **~ sur** *fam* : to get going on, to launch oneself into **3** **embraye** *Can fam* : get a move on!, hurry up!

embrigader |ɑ̃brigade| *vt* ENRÔLER : to recruit, to enlist

embrocher |ɑ̃brɔʃe| *vt* : to skewer, to put on a spit

embrouillamini |ɑ̃brujamini| *nm fam* : muddle, confusion

embrouillé, -lée |ɑ̃bruje| *adj* : confused, muddled

embrouiller |ɑ̃bruje| *vt* **1** : to tangle up **2** : to confuse, to mix up — **s'embrouiller** *vr*

embroussaillé, -lée |ɑ̃brusaje| *adj* **1** : overgrown (with plants) **2** : shaggy, bushy

embrumé, -mée |ɑ̃bryme| *adj* : misty

embruns |ɑ̃brœ̃| *nmpl* : sea spray

embryologie |ɑ̃brijɔlɔʒi| *nf* : embryology

embryon |ɑ̃brijɔ̃| *nm* : embryo

embryonnaire |ɑ̃brijɔnɛr| *adj* : embryonic

embûche |ɑ̃byʃ| *nf* : trap, pitfall

embuer |ɑ̃bɥe| *vt* : to mist up, to fog up <les yeux embués de larmes : eyes misty with tears> — **s'embuer** *vr*

embuscade |ɑ̃byskad| *nf* : ambush

embusquer |ɑ̃byske| *v* **s'embusquer** *vr* : to lie in ambush
éméché, -chée |emeʃe| *adj fam* : tipsy
émeraude[1] |emrod| *adj* : emerald green
émeraude[2] *nf* : emerald (stone)
émeraude[3] *nm* : emerald (color)
émergence |emɛrʒɑ̃s| *nf* : emergence
émerger |emɛrʒe| {17} *vi* **1** : to emerge **2** : to come to the fore, to stand out
émeri |emri| *nm* : emery
émérite |emerit| *adj* : eminent, outstanding
émerveillement |emɛrvɛjmɑ̃| *nm* ÉBLOUISSEMENT : amazement, wonder
émerveiller |emɛrveje| *vt* ÉBLOUIR : to amaze — **s'émerveiller** *vr* **~ de** : to marvel at, to be amazed at
émétique |emetik| *adj & nm* : emetic
émetteur[1], **-trice** |emetœr, -tris| *adj* **1** : transmitting **2** : issuing <banque émettrice : issuing bank>
émetteur[2], **-trice** *nm* **1** : transmitter **2** : issuer
émetteur[3] *n* : (radio or television) transmitter
émettre |emɛtr| {53} *vt* **1** PRODUIRE : to produce, to give off **2** DISTRIBUER : to issue **3** TRANSMETTRE : to transmit, to broadcast **4** EXPRIMER : to express
émeu |emø| *nm* : emu
émeute |emøt| *nf* : riot
émeutier, -tière |emøtje| *n* : rioter
émietter |emjete| *vt* **1** : to crumble, to flake **2** MORCELER : to break up, to disperse — **s'émietter** *vr*
émigrant, -grante |emigrɑ̃, -grɑ̃t| *n* : emigrant
émigration |emigrasjɔ̃| *nf* : emigration
émigré, -grée |emigre| *n* : emigrant, émigré
émigrer |emigre| *vi* **1** : to emigrate **2** : to migrate
éminemment |eminamɑ̃| *adv* : eminently
éminence |eminɑ̃s| *nf* **1** : eminence <Votre Éminence : Your Eminence> **2** COLLINE : hill **3** PROTUBÉRANCE : protuberance (in anatomy)
éminent, -nente |eminɑ̃, -nɑ̃t| *adj* : eminent, distinguished
émir |emir| *nm* : emir
émirat |emira| *nm* : emirate
émissaire |emisɛr| *nm* : emissary
émission |emisjɔ̃| *nf* **1** : emission **2** : transmission, broadcasting **3** : program, broadcast **4** : issue, issuing
emmagasinage |ɑ̃magazinaʒ| *nm* : storage
emmagasiner |ɑ̃magazine| *vt* **1** ENGRANGER : to store **2** ACCUMULER : to store up, to stockpile
emmailloter |ɑ̃majɔte| *vt* : to wrap up
emmêler |ɑ̃mele| *vt* **1** : to tangle up, to mat **2** : to muddle, to mix up — **s'emmêler** *vr*
emménager |ɑ̃menaʒe| {17} *vi* : to move in
emmener |ɑ̃mne| {52} *vt* **1** AMENER : to take <ils l'ont emmené au poste de police : they took him to the police station> **2** TRANSPORTER : to carry, to transport
emmitoufler |ɑ̃mitufle| *vt* : to wrap up, to bundle up — **s'emmitoufler** *vr*
emmurer |ɑ̃myre| *vt* : to wall in, to immure
émoi |emwa| *nm* **1** : agitation, strong emotion <en émoi : in a state, all agog> **2** : commotion, turmoil
émoluments |emɔlymɑ̃| *nmpl* : remuneration, salary
émonder |emɔ̃de| *vt* ÉLAGUER : to prune, to trim
émotif, -tive |emɔtif, -tiv| *adj* : emotional
émotion |emosjɔ̃| *nf* **1** : emotion, feeling **2 donner des émotions à qqn** *fam* : to give s.o. a fright
émotionnel, -nelle |emosjɔnɛl| *adj* : emotional
émousser |emuse| *vt* : to blunt, to dull — **s'émousser** *vr*
émoustiller |emustije| *vt* **1** : to exhilarate **2** : to titillate, to arouse
émouvant, -vante |emuvɑ̃, -vɑ̃t| *adj* TOUCHANT : moving, touching
émouvoir |emuvwar| {56} *vt* **1** TOUCHER : to move, to touch, to stir **2** TROUBLER : to disturb, to upset — **s'émouvoir** *vr*
empailler |ɑ̃paje| *vt* : to stuff
empaler |ɑ̃pale| *vt* : to impale
empaquetage |ɑ̃paktaʒ| *nm* EMBALLAGE : packaging, wrapping
empaqueter |ɑ̃pakte| {8} *vt* EMBALLER : to package, to wrap up
emparer |ɑ̃pare| *v* **s'emparer** *vr* **~ de** : to seize, to take hold of <s'emparer du pouvoir : to seize power>
empâté, -tée |ɑ̃pate| *adj Can* : spineless, weak
empâter |ɑ̃pate| *vt* **1** : to fatten out (the body) **2** : to thicken, to coat (the tongue) — **s'empâter** : to put on weight
empathie |ɑ̃pati| *nf* : empathy
empattement |ɑ̃patmɑ̃| *nm* **1** : footing, base (of a wall, etc.) **2** : wheelbase
empêchement |ɑ̃pɛʃmɑ̃| *nm* : unexpected obstacle, hitch, holdup
empêcher |ɑ̃peʃe| *vt* **1** : to prevent, to stop **2 il n'empêche que** : nevertheless, still — **s'empêcher** *vr* : to refrain, to stop oneself <il ne pouvait s'empêcher de rire : he couldn't keep from laughing>
empêcheur, -cheuse |ɑ̃pɛʃœr, -ʃøz| *n* **empêcheur de tourner en rond** : spoilsport, killjoy
empeigne |ɑ̃pɛɲ| *nf* : upper (of a shoe)
empereur |ɑ̃prœr| *nm* : emperor
empesé, -sée |ɑ̃pəze| *adj* **1** : starched **2** : stiff, affected
empeser |ɑ̃pəze| {52} *vt* AMIDONNER : to starch

empester [ɑ̃pɛste] *vt* **1** EMPUANTIR : to stink up **2** : to reek of — *vi* : to stink, to reek

empêtrer [ɑ̃petre] *vt* : to entangle, to involve — **s'empêtrer** *vr* **1** : to become entangled **2** ~ **dans** : to get bogged down in

emphase [ɑ̃faz] *nf* GRANDILOQUENCE : pomposity, bombast

emphatique [ɑ̃fatik] *adj* **1** : pompous **2** : emphatic — **emphatiquement** [-tikmɑ̃] *adv*

empiècement [ɑ̃pjɛsmɑ̃] *nm* : yoke (of a garment)

empiéter [ɑ̃pjete] {87} *vi* ~ **sur** : to encroach upon, to infringe on

empiffrer [ɑ̃pifre] *v* **s'empiffrer** *vr fam* : to stuff oneself

empilade [ɑ̃pilad] *nf Can* : pileup

empiler [ɑ̃pile] *vt* : to pile up, to stack — **s'empiler** *vr*

empire [ɑ̃pir] *nm* **1** : empire **2 sous l'empire de** : under the influence of

empirer [ɑ̃pire] *vt* AGGRAVER : to worsen, to make worse — *vi* : to worsen, to deteriorate

empirique [ɑ̃pirik] *adj* : empirical — **empiriquement** [-rikmɑ̃] *adv*

emplacement [ɑ̃plasmɑ̃] *nm* : site, location

emplâtre [ɑ̃platr] *nm* **1** : (medical) plaster **2** : patch (for a tire) **3** *fam* : clumsy oaf, clod

emplette [ɑ̃plɛt] *nf* **1** ACHAT : purchase **2 faire ses emplettes** : to go shopping

emplir [ɑ̃plir] *vt* **1** : REMPLIR : to fill **2 faire emplir** *Can* : to bamboozle, to trick — **s'emplir** *vr* : to fill up

emploi [ɑ̃plwa] *nm* **1** UTILISATION : use <mode d'emploi : instructions, directions> **2** TRAVAIL : employment, job **3** USAGE : usage (of language) **4 emploi du temps** : schedule, timetable

emploie [ɑ̃plwa], **emploiera** [ɑ̃plwara], *etc.* → **employer**

employé, -yée [ɑ̃plwaje] *n* : employee

employer [ɑ̃plwaje] {58} *vt* **1** UTILISER : to use **2** : to employ, to provide jobs for — **s'employer** *vr* **1** : to be used **2** : to apply oneself

employeur, -ployeuse [ɑ̃plwajœr, -plwajøz] *n* : employer

empocher [ɑ̃pɔʃe] *vt* : to pocket

empoignade [ɑ̃pwaɲad] *nf* : altercation, row

empoigner [ɑ̃pwaɲe] *vt* **1** SAISIR : to seize, to grasp **2** ÉMOUVOIR : to thrill, to grip — **s'empoigner** *vr* : to quarrel, to come to blows

empois [ɑ̃pwa] *nms & pl* : (laundry) starch

empoisonnement [ɑ̃pwazɔnmɑ̃] *nm* **1** : poisoning **2** *fam* : nuisance, trouble

empoisonner [ɑ̃pwazɔne] *vt* **1** : to poison **2** EMPUANTIR : to stink up **3** *fam* : to annoy, to bug — **s'empoisonner** *vr* **1** : to poison oneself **2** *fam* : to be bored stiff

emporté, -tée [ɑ̃pɔrte] *adj* : quick-tempered

emportement [ɑ̃pɔrtəmɑ̃] *nm* **1** : fit of anger, rage **2** : ardor, fervor

emporter [ɑ̃pɔrte] *vt* **1** : to take, to take away <plats à emporter : food to go> **2** : to carry away, to sweep away **3** : to carry off, to cause (a sick person) to die **4** : to carry, to win <l'emporter sur : to get the better of> — **s'emporter** *vr* : to lose one's temper

empoté, -tée [ɑ̃pɔte] *adj fam* : clumsy, awkward

empoter [ɑ̃pɔte] *vt* : to pot (a plant)

empourprer [ɑ̃purpre] *vt* : to turn crimson — **s'empourprer** *vr*

empreint, -preinte [ɑ̃prɛ̃, -prɛ̃t] *adj* ~ **de** : marked with, stamped with <empreint de douleur : imbued with sadness>

empreinte *nf* **1** : print, track <empreinte de pied : footprint> <empreinte digitale : fingerprint> **2** IMPRESSION : impression, stamp, imprint

empressé, -sée [ɑ̃prese] *adj* : attentive, eager (to please)

empressement [ɑ̃prɛsmɑ̃] *nm* **1** : attentiveness **2** ENTHOUSIASME : eagerness, enthusiasm, haste

empresser [ɑ̃prese] *v* **s'empresser** *vr* **1 s'empresser auprès de** : to be attentive toward **2** ~ **de** : to be in a hurry to <elle s'est empressée de partir : she hastened to leave>

emprise [ɑ̃priz] *nf* : influence, hold <sous l'emprise de : under the influence of>

emprisonnement [ɑ̃prizɔnmɑ̃] *nm* : imprisonment

emprisonner [ɑ̃prizɔne] *vt* **1** : to imprison **2** : to hold tightly, to grip

emprunt [ɑ̃prœ̃] *nm* **1** : loan **2** : borrowing **3** : word <un emprunt à l'allemand : a borrowing from the German> **4 d'**~ : borrowed <nom d'emprunt : assumed name>

emprunté, -tée [ɑ̃prœ̃te] *adj* **1** : awkward, self-conscious **2** : sham, feigned

emprunter [ɑ̃prœ̃te] *vt* **1** : to borrow **2** PRENDRE : to take, to follow <empruntez la nouvelle route : take the new road> **3** : to assume, to take on <emprunter un nom : to assume a name>

empuantir [ɑ̃pɥɑ̃tir] *vt* : to stink up

ému, -mue [emy] *adj* : moved, touched

émulation [emylasjɔ̃] *nf* : competition, emulation

émule [emyl] *nmf* : imitator, emulator

émulsion [emylsjɔ̃] *nf* : emulsion

émulsionner [emylsjɔne] *vt* : to emulsify

en[1] [ɑ̃] *prep* **1** : in <j'habite en ville : I live in town> <en français : in

French> <en 1847 : in 1847> **2** : to <elle va en Belgique : she's going to Belgium> <de mal en pis : from bad to worse> **3** : by <elle va en voiture : she's going by car> **4** : of <fait en plastique : made of plastic> **5** : at <en guerre : at war> **6** : as <je te parle en ami : I'm speaking to you as a friend> <il est habillé en militaire : he is dressed as a soldier> **7** : into <traduit en français : translated into French>

en[2] *pron* **1** (*representing a noun governed by* de) <je m'en souviens : I remember it> <qu'est-ce que tu en sais? : what do you know about it?> **2** (*used with expressions of quantity*) <j'en ai plusieurs : I have several> **3** (*used to replace the possessive*) <j'en ai perdu la clef : I lost its key> **4** (*used to replace a phrase*) <il n'a pas joué mais il en est capable : he didn't play but he can> **5** (*used in partitive constructions*) <en avez-vous? : do you have some?> <j'en connais : I know a few>

enamourer [ãnamure] *v* **s'enamourer** *vr* : to fall in love, to become enamored

encadrement [ãkadrəmã] *nm* **1** : frame **2** : staff <l'encadrement administratif : the administrative staff> **3** : supervision <les étudiants manquent d'encadrement : the students lack supervision> **4** : restriction, control (of prices, credit, etc.)

encadrer [ãkadre] *vt* **1** : to frame **2** : to surround, to flank **3** : to supervise, to train

encaisse [ãkɛs] *nf* : cash in hand

encaissé, -sée [ãkese] *adj* : steep-sided

encaisser [ãkese] *vt* **1** : to cash (a check), to collect (money) **2** *fam* : to take, to tolerate <encaisser un coup : to take a beating> <je ne peux pas l'encaisser! : I can't take it!>

encan [ãkã] *nm* : auction <vendre à l'encan : to auction off, to sell at auction>

encanailler [ãkanaje] *v* **s'encanailler** *vr* : to slum, to keep bad company

encanter [ãkãte] *vt Can* : to auction

encanteur, -teuse [ãkãtœr] *n Can* : auctioneer

encart [ãkar] *nm* : insert, pamphlet <encart publicitaire : advertising insert>

en–cas [ãka] *nms & pl* : snack

encastré, -trée [ãkastre] *adj* : built-in <un four encastré : a built-in oven>

encastrer [ãkastre] *vt* : to fit, to embed, to build in — **s'encastrer** *vr*

encaustique [ãkostik] *nf* CIRE : polish, wax — **encaustiquer** [-stike] *vt*

enceinte[1] [ãsɛ̃t] *adj* : pregnant

enceinte[2] *nf* **1** : surrounding wall, fence **2** ESPACE : interior, enclosure <dans l'enceinte du tribunal : inside the courtroom> **3 enceinte acoustique** : speaker

encens [ãsã] *nm* : incense

encenser [ãsãse] *vt* **1** : to perfume (with incense) **2** FLATTER : to flatter

encensoir [ãsãswar] *nm* : censer

encercler [ãsɛrkle] *vt* ENTOURER : to surround, to encircle

enchaînement [ãʃɛnmã] *nm* **1** SÉRIE : series, sequence **2** LIAISON : link, connection

enchaîner [ãʃene] *vt* **1** : to chain (up) **2** LIER : to link, to connect — *vi* : to continue, to move on — **s'enchaîner** *vr* : to link up, to be connected

enchanté, -tée [ãʃãte] *adj* **1** MAGIQUE : magic, enchanted **2** RAVI : delighted, pleased <enchanté de faire votre connaissance : pleased to meet you>

enchantement [ãʃãtmã] *nm* **1** : enchantment **2** : delight

enchanter [ãʃãte] *vt* **1** ENSORCELER : to enchant, to bewitch **2** RAVIR : to delight

enchanteur[1], **-teresse** [ɑʃãtœr, -trɛs] *adj* CHARMANT : enchanting, charming

enchanteur[2], **-teresse** *n* : enchanter *m*, enchantress *f*

enchâssement [ãʃasmã] *nm* : setting, mounting (of gems)

enchâsser [ãʃase] *vt* **1** : to mount, to set **2** INSÉRER : to insert (a word, etc.)

enchère [ãʃɛr] *nf* **1** : bid, bidding **2 vente aux enchères** : auction

enchérisseur, -seuse [ãʃɛrisœr, -søz] *n* : bidder

enchevêtrement [ãʃəvɛtrəmã] *nm* **1** : tangle **2** : confusion

enchevêtrer [ãʃəvɛtre] *vt* **1** : to tangle up **2** : to muddle, to confuse — **s'enchevêtrer** *vr*

enclave [ãklav] *nf* : enclave

enclaver [ãklave] *vt* **1** ENTOURER : to enclose, to surround **2** : to fit together, to interlock

enclencher [ãklãʃe] *vt* **1** : to engage (a mechanism) **2** : to set in motion, to get under way — **s'enclencher** *vr*

enclin, -cline [ãklɛ̃, -klin] *adj* ~ **à** : inclined to, prone to

enclore [ãklɔr] {34} *vt* : to enclose

enclos [ãklo] *nm* : enclosure

enclume [ãklym] *nf* : anvil

encoche [ãkɔʃ] *nf* : notch

encocher [ãkɔʃe] *vt* : to notch

encoder [ãkɔde] *vt* : to encode

encoignure [ãkwaɲyr] *nf* : corner (of a room)

encoller [ãkɔle] *vt* : to paste, to glue

encolure [ãkɔlyr] *nf* **1** COU : neck **2** : collar (size)

encombrant, -brante [ãkɔ̃brã, -brãt] *adj* : cumbersome

encombre [ãkɔ̃br] *adv* **sans** ~ : without mishap, without a hitch

encombrement [ãkɔ̃brəmã] *nm* **1** : clutter **2** : overall size, bulk **3** : blocking, jamming **4** : traffic jam **5** : congestion (in medicine)

encombrer [ɑ̃kɔ̃bre] *vt* **1** : to clutter up, to congest **2** : to block, to jam **3** : to burden, to encumber — **s'encombrer** *vr* **~ de** : to burden oneself with

encontre [ɑ̃kɔ̃tr] **à l'encontre de** : against, counter to, contrary to

encore [ɑ̃kɔr] *adv* **1** TOUJOURS : still <je travaille encore ici : I'm still working here> **2** DAVANTAGE : more, again <encore une fois : once more, once again> <il m'a encore parlé : he spoke to me again> **3** : yet <pas encore : not yet> <encore mieux : better yet> **4** : another <pendant encore trois mois : for another three months> **5 encore que** : although **6 si encore** *or* **encore si** : if only

encorner [ɑ̃kɔrne] *vt* : to gore

encornet [ɑ̃kɔrnɛ] *nm* : squid

encouragement [ɑ̃kuraʒmɑ̃] *nm* : encouragement

encourager [ɑ̃kuraʒe] {17} *vt* : to encourage

encourir [ɑ̃kurir] {23} *vt* : to incur

encrasser [ɑ̃krase] *vt* **1** SALIR : to dirty **2** OBSTRUER : to clog up — **s'encrasser** *vr*

encre [ɑ̃kr] *nf* : ink

encrer [ɑ̃kre] *vt* : to ink

encrier [ɑ̃krije] *nm* : inkwell

encroûter [ɑ̃krute] *v* **s'encroûter** *vr* : to get in a rut <encroûté dans ses habitudes : set in one's ways>

encyclique [ɑ̃siklik] *nf* : encyclical

encyclopédie [ɑ̃siklɔpedi] *nf* : encyclopedia — **encyclopédique** [-pedik] *adj*

endémique [ɑ̃demik] *adj* : endemic

endetté, -tée [ɑ̃dete] *adj* : in debt

endettement [ɑ̃dɛtmɑ̃] *nm* : debt

endetter [ɑ̃dete] *v* **s'endetter** *vr* : to get into debt

endeuiller [ɑ̃dœje] *vt* **1** : to plunge into mourning **2** : to cast gloom over (an event, etc.)

endiablé, -blée [ɑ̃djable] *adj* **1** : wild, furious **2** : boisterous

endiguer [ɑ̃dige] *vt* **1** : to dam up **2** RETENIR : to check, to hold back, to contain

endimanché, -chée [ɑ̃dimɑ̃ʃe] *adj* : in one's Sunday best

endisquer [ɑ̃diske] *vt Can* : to record (a CD)

endive [ɑ̃div] *nf* : endive, chickory

endocrine [ɑ̃dɔkrin] *adj* : endocrine

endoctrinement [ɑ̃dɔktrinmɑ̃] *nm* : indoctrination

endoctriner [ɑ̃dɔktrine] *vt* : to indoctrinate

endolori, -rie [ɑ̃dɔlɔri] *adj* : painful, sore

endommager [ɑ̃dɔmaʒe] {17} *vt* : to damage

endormant, -mante [ɑ̃dɔrmɑ̃, -mɑ̃t] *adj* ENNUYEUX : boring

endormi, -mie [ɑ̃dɔrmi] *adj* **1** : asleep, sleeping **2** LÉTHARGIQUE : sluggish, lethargic

endormir [ɑ̃dɔrmir] {30} *vt* **1** : to put to sleep **2** ANESTHÉSIER : to anesthetize, to numb **3** : to allay, to calm — **s'endormir** *vr* **1** : to fall asleep **2** : to slack off **3** : to subside, to die down **4** : to pass away, to die

endossement [ɑ̃dɔsmɑ̃] *nm* : endorsement

endosser [ɑ̃dose] *vt* **1** : to take on, to shoulder **2** : to endorse, to sign **3** : to don, to put on (clothes)

endroit [ɑ̃drwa] *nm* **1** : place, spot, locale **2** : right side (of a garment, etc.) <à l'endroit : right side up> **3 à l'endroit de** : toward, with regard to **4 par endroits** : here and there, in places

enduire [ɑ̃dɥir] {49} *vt* : to coat, to cover — **s'enduire** *vr*

enduit [ɑ̃dɥi] *nm* : coating

endurance [ɑ̃dyrɑ̃s] *nf* : endurance

endurant, -rante [ɑ̃dyrɑ̃, -rɑ̃t] *adj* : hardy, tough

endurci, -cie [ɑ̃dyrsi] *adj* **1** DUR : hard **2** INVÉTÉRÉ : hardened, inveterate

endurcir [ɑ̃dyrsir] *vt* **1** : to toughen, to strengthen **2** : to harden — **s'endurcir** *vr*

endurer [ɑ̃dyre] *vt* SUPPORTER : to endure

énergétique [enɛrʒetik] *adj* **1** : energy <ressources énergétiques : energy resources> **2** : energizing

énergie [enɛrʒi] *nf* : energy

énergique [enɛrʒik] *adj* **1** : energetic **2** : vigorous, forceful, emphatic — **énergiquement** [-ʒikmɑ̃] *adv*

énervant, -vante [enɛrvɑ̃, -vɑ̃t] *adj* AGAÇANT : irritating, annoying

énervement [enɛrvəmɑ̃] *nm* **1** AGACEMENT : irritation **2** : agitation, edginess

énerver [enɛrve] *vt* AGACER : to irritate, to annoy — **s'énerver** *vr* **1** : to become annoyed **2** : to get worked up

enfance [ɑ̃fɑ̃s] *nf* **1** : childhood **2** DÉBUT : infancy, beginning **3** : children *pl*

enfant[1] [ɑ̃fɑ̃] *adj* : childish, childlike <il est resté très enfant : he's still very childlike>

enfant[2] *nmf* **1** : child <faire l'enfant : to act childishly> <enfant prodige : child prodigy> <enfant trouvé : foundling> **2** : offspring, child <un enfant unique : an only child> **3 bon enfant** : good-natured **4 enfant de chœur** : altar boy

enfantement [ɑ̃fɑ̃tmɑ̃] *nm* : childbirth

enfanter [ɑ̃fɑ̃te] *vt* : to give birth to

enfantillage [ɑ̃fɑ̃tijaʒ] *nm* : childishness

enfantin, -tine [ɑ̃fɑ̃tɛ̃, -tin] *adj* **1** : childlike **2** : simple <c'est enfantin : it's child's play> **3** PUÉRIL : childish

enfarger [ɑ̃farʒe] {17} *vt Can* : to make (someone) trip — **s'enfarger** *vr* : to trip, to stumble

enfer [ɑ̃fɛr] *nm* **1** : hell **2 d'~** : infernal, hellish

enfermer [ɑ̃fɛrme] *vt* **1** : to shut up, to lock up **2** ENTOURER : to enclose, to surround — **s'enfermer** *vr* **1** : to shut oneself away **2 ~ dans** : to retreat into

enferrer [ɑ̃fere] *v* **s'enferrer** *vr* **~ dans** : to get tangled up in

enfilade [ɑ̃filad] *nf* : row, succession

enfiler [ɑ̃file] *vt* **1** METTRE : to slip on, to put on <enfiler un chandail : to put on a sweater> **2** : to thread, to string **3** : to take, to go down (a street, corridor, etc.) — **s'enfiler** *vr* **1** *fam* : to guzzle, to devour **2 ~ dans** : to disappear into (a doorway, etc.)

enfin [ɑ̃fɛ̃] *adv* **1** : finally, at last <enfin seuls! : alone at last!> **2** : lastly <enfin et surtout : last but not least> **3** : in short, in a word **4** : well, at least <enfin, je crois : at least I think so> **5** : anyhow, after all **6** (*used to show impatience*) <mais enfin, donne-le-moi! : come on, give it to me!>

enflammé, -mée [ɑ̃flame] *adj* **1** BRÛLANT : burning **2** PASSIONNÉ : passionate **3** : inflamed (in medicine)

enflammer [ɑ̃flame] *vt* **1** ALLUMER : to ignite, to set fire to **2** : to inflame — **s'enflammer** *vr* : to catch fire

enfler [ɑ̃fle] *vt* **1** : to cause to swell **2** : to increase the volume of (a sound, one's voice) — *vi* : to swell (up) — **s'enfler** *vr*

enflure [ɑ̃flyr] *nf* : swelling

enfoncé, -cée [ɑ̃fɔ̃se] *adj* : sunken, deep-set

enfoncer [ɑ̃fɔ̃se] {6} *vt* **1** : to drive in (a nail, etc.) **2** : to push in, to insert <enfoncer ses mains dans ses poches : to thrust one's hands in one's pockets> **3** : to break open, to break down — *vi* : to sink — **s'enfoncer** *vr* **1** CÉDER : to yield, to give way **2** PÉNÉTRER : to penetrate, to sink in **3 ~ dans** : to disappear into

enfouir [ɑ̃fwir] *vt* **1** : to bury **2** CACHER : to hide, to tuck away — **s'enfouir** *vr* **~ dans** : to bury oneself in

enfouissement [ɑ̃fwismɑ̃] *nm* : burying

enfourcher [ɑ̃furʃe] *vt* : to mount, to get on, to straddle

enfourner [ɑ̃furne] *vt* **1** : to put in the oven **2** *fam* : to gobble up

enfreindre [ɑ̃frɛ̃dr] {37} *vt* : to infringe, to violate <enfreindre la loi : to break the law>

enfuir [ɑ̃fɥir] {46} *v* **s'enfuir** *vr* S'ÉCHAPPER : to run away, to escape, to flee

enfumer [ɑ̃fyme] *vt* : to fill with smoke

engagé, -gée [ɑ̃gaʒe] *adj* **1** : committed, involved **2** *Can fam* : busy <la ligne est engagée : the line is busy>

engageant, -geante [ɑ̃gaʒɑ̃, -ʒɑ̃t] *adj* : engaging, attractive

engagement [ɑ̃gaʒmɑ̃] *nm* **1** PROMESSE : commitment, promise **2** : engagement, contract, enlistment (in the military) **3** DÉBUT : start **4** : involvement, participation **5** : (military) engagement

engager [ɑ̃gaʒe] {17} *vt* **1** : to bind, to commit **2** RECRUTER : to hire, to take on **3** IMPLIQUER : to involve **4** : to invest, to lay out (capital, etc.) **5** EXHORTER : to urge **6** COMMENCER : to start, to begin **7** INTRODUIRE : to insert — **s'engager** *vr* **1** : to commit oneself, to undertake **2** : to enlist, to join up **3** : to begin, to start up **4 ~ dans** : to enter, to turn into (a street, etc.)

engelure [ɑ̃ʒlyr] *nf* : chilblain

engendrer [ɑ̃ʒɑ̃dre] *vt* **1** : to engender, to generate **2** : to father, to beget

engin [ɑ̃ʒɛ̃] *nm* **1** APPAREIL : machine, device <engin explosif : explosive device> **2** VÉHICULE : vehicle <engin blindé : armored vehicle> **3** MISSILE : missile **4** *fam* MACHIN : gadget, contraption

englober [ɑ̃glɔbe] *vt* : to include

engloutir [ɑ̃glutir] *vt* **1** : to gobble up, to devour **2** : to engulf, to swallow up **3** : to squander

engoncé, -cée [ɑ̃gɔ̃se] *adj* **~ dans** : squeezed into

engorgement [ɑ̃gɔrʒəmɑ̃] *nm* : blocking (up), congestion

engorger [ɑ̃gɔrʒe] {17} *vt* **1** : to block, to jam up **2** : to congest (in medicine)

engouement [ɑ̃gumɑ̃] *nm* : infatuation

engouer [ɑ̃gwe] *v* **s'engouer** *vr* **~ de** : to become infatuated with

engouffrer [ɑ̃gufre] *vt* **1** : to engulf, to swallow up **2** : to gobble up, to devour — **s'engouffrer** *vr* **~ dans** : to rush into

engourdi, -die [ɑ̃gurdi] *adj* **1** : numb **2** : dulled, lethargic

engourdir [ɑ̃gurdir] *vt* **1** : to numb **2** : to dull — **s'engourdir** *vr*

engourdissement [ɑ̃gurdismɑ̃] *nm* **1** : numbness **2** : dullness, torpor

engrais [ɑ̃grɛ] *nm* **1** : fertilizer, manure **2 mettre à l'engrais** : to fatten

engraisser [ɑ̃grese] *vt* **1** : to fatten **2** : to fertilize — *vi* GROSSIR : to get fat, to put on weight — **s'engraisser** *vr*

engranger [ɑ̃grɑ̃ʒe] {17} *vt* **1** : to garner, to gather **2** EMMAGASINER : to store

engrenage [ɑ̃grənaʒ] *nm* **1** : gears *pl* **2 être pris dans l'engrenage** : to be caught up in the system

engrener [ɑ̃grəne] {52} *vt* : to engage, to mesh (gears) — **s'engrener** *vr*

engueulade [ɑ̃gœlad] *nf fam* : argument, shouting match

engueuler [ɑ̃gœle] *vt fam* : to yell at, to bawl out — **s'engueuler** *vr*

enguirlander [ɑ̃girlɑ̃de] *vt* : to garland, to adorn with garlands

énième [enjɛm] *adj* : nth, umpteenth <pour l'énième fois : for the umpteenth time>

énigmatique [enigmatik] *adj* : enigmatic — **énigmatiquement** [-tikmɑ̃] *adv*

énigme [enigm] *nf* : enigma, riddle

enivrant, -vrante [ɑ̃nivrɑ̃, -vrɑ̃t] *adj* : intoxicating

enivrement [ɑ̃nivrəmɑ̃] *nm* : intoxication

enivrer [ɑ̃nivre] *vr* **1** : to intoxicate, to make drunk **2** : to elate, to exhilarate — **s'enivrer** *vr*

enjambée [ɑ̃ʒɑ̃be] *nf* : stride

enjamber [ɑ̃ʒɑ̃be] *vt* **1** : to step over **2** : to span, to straddle

enjeu [ɑ̃ʒø] *nm, pl* **enjeux 1** : issue <les enjeux politiques : political issues> **2** : stake <son emploi est à l'enjeu : his job is at stake>

enjoindre [ɑ̃ʒwɛ̃dr] {50} *vt* : to enjoin, to order <enjoindre à qqn de faire qqch : to enjoin s.o. to do sth>

enjôler [ɑ̃ʒole] *vt* : to cajole, to wheedle

enjoliver [ɑ̃ʒɔlive] *vt* : to embellish

enjoliveur [ɑ̃ʒɔlivœr] *nm* : hubcap

enjoué, -jouée [ɑ̃ʒwe] *adj* : cheerful, light-hearted

enjouement [ɑ̃ʒumɑ̃] *nm* : playfulness, gaiety

enlacement [ɑ̃lasmɑ̃] *nm* **1** : embrace **2** : intertwining

enlacer [ɑ̃lase] {6} *vt* **1** ÉTREINDRE : to embrace, to hug **2** ENTRELACER : to entwine, to enlace — **s'enlacer** *vr*

enlaidir [ɑ̃ledir] *vt* : to make ugly — *vi* : to grow ugly — **s'enlaidir** *vr*

enlevant, -vante [ɑ̃lvɑ̃, -vɑ̃t] *adj Can* : lively, spirited

enlevé, -vée [ɑ̃lve] *adj* : lively, spirited

enlèvement [ɑ̃lɛvmɑ̃] *nm* **1** : kidnapping, abduction **2** : removal <enlèvement des ordures ménagères : garbage collection>

enlever [ɑ̃lve] {52} *vt* **1** : to remove, to take off, to take away **2** LEVER : to raise, to lift **3** KIDNAPPER : to abduct, to kidnap **4** GAGNER : to carry off, to win — **s'enlever** *vr* : to come off, to come out

enlisement [ɑ̃lizmɑ̃] *nm* : sinking, bogging down

enliser [ɑ̃lize] *v* **s'enliser** *vr* **1** : to sink, to get stuck **2** : to get bogged down

enneigé, -gée [ɑ̃neʒe] *adj* : snow-covered

enneigement [ɑ̃nɛʒmɑ̃] *nm* : snow accumulation, snow cover

ennemi[1]**, -mie** [ɛnmi] *adj* : enemy, hostile <en pays ennemi : in enemy territory>

ennemi[2]**, -mie** *n* : enemy

ennoblir [ɑ̃nɔblir] *vt* : to ennoble

ennui [ɑ̃nɥi] *nm* **1** PROBLÈME : trouble, problem <avoir des ennuis : to have problems> **2** : boredom, ennui

ennuie [ɑ̃nwi], **ennuiera** [ɑ̃nwira], *etc.* → **ennuyer**

ennuyant, ennuyante [ɑ̃nɥijɑ̃, ɑ̃nɥijɑ̃t] *adj Can* **1** : annoying, irritating **2** : boring

ennuyer [ɑ̃nɥije] {58} *vt* **1** AGACER : to annoy **2** : to bore — **s'ennuyer** *vr* : to be bored

ennuyeux, ennuyeuse [ɑ̃nɥijø, ɑ̃nɥijøz] *adj* **1** AGAÇANT : annoying, irritating **2** LASSANT : boring, tedious

énoncé [enɔ̃se] *nm* **1** : statement, declaration **2** : terms *pl*, wording **3** : utterance

énoncer [enɔ̃se] {6} *vt* : to express, to state — **s'énoncer** *vr*

énonciation [enɔ̃sjasjɔ̃] *nf* : stating, statement

enorgueillir [ɑ̃nɔrgœjir] *vt* : to make proud — **s'enorgueillir** *vr* : to pride oneself

énorme [enɔrm] *adj* : enormous, huge

énormément [enɔrmemɑ̃] *adv* **1** : enormously, tremendously **2 ~ de** : a great number of

énormité [enɔrmite] *nf* **1** : enormity, hugeness **2** : outrageous remark

enquérir [ɑ̃kerir] {21} *v* **s'enquérir** *vr* **~ de** : to inquire about

enquête [ɑ̃kɛt] *nf* **1** INVESTIGATION : investigation, inquiry, inquest **2** SONDAGE : poll, survey

enquêter [ɑ̃kete] *vi* : to investigate, to hold an inquiry

enquiquiner [ɑ̃kikine] *vt fam* : to irritate, to pester, to nag at

enraciner [ɑ̃rasine] *vt* **1** : to root **2** : to entrench, to establish — **s'enraciner** *vr* : to take root

enragé, -gée [ɑ̃raʒe] *adj* **1** : rabid **2** : furious

enrageant, -geante [ɑ̃raʒɑ̃, -ʒɑ̃t] *adj* : infuriating

enrager [ɑ̃raʒe] {17} *vi* **1** : to be furious, to be in a rage **2 faire enrager** : to enrage

enrayer [ɑ̃reje] {11} *vt* **1** : to check, to stop, to curb <enrayer une maladie : to bring a disease under control> **2** BLOQUER : to jam — **s'enrayer** *vr*

enrégimenter [ɑ̃reʒimɑ̃te] *vt* : to regiment

enregistrement [ɑ̃rəʒistrəmɑ̃] *nm* **1** : registration **2** : recording <enregistrement magnétique : tape recording> **3** : checking in <enregistrement des bagages : luggage check-in>

enregistrer [ɑ̃rəʒistre] *vt* **1** INSCRIRE : to register **2** : to record, to tape **3** : to check in

enregistreur[1], **-treuse** |ɑ̃rəʒistrœr, -trøz| *adj* **1** : recording **2 caisse enregistreuse** : cash register

enregistreur[2] *nm* : recorder <enregistreur de vol : flight recorder>

enrhumé, -mée |ɑ̃ryme| *adj* **être enrhumé** : to have a cold

enrhumer |ɑ̃ryme| *v* **s'enrhumer** *vr* : to catch a cold

enrichi, -chie |ɑ̃riʃi| *adj* : enriched, fortified <farine enrichie : enriched flour>

enrichir |ɑ̃riʃir| *vt* **1** : to make rich **2** : to enrich — **s'enrichir** *vr*

enrichissant, -sante |ɑ̃riʃisɑ̃, -sɑ̃t| *adj* : enriching, rewarding

enrichissement |ɑ̃riʃismɑ̃| *nm* : enrichment

enrobage |ɑ̃rɔbaʒ| *nm* : coating

enrober |ɑ̃rɔbe| *vt* **1** RECOUVRIR : to coat **2** : to wrap up, to dress up (words, etc.)

enrôlement |ɑ̃rolmɑ̃| *nm* : enrollment, enlistment

enrôler |ɑ̃role| *vt* : to enroll, to enlist — **s'enrôler** *vr*

enroué, -rouée |ɑ̃rwe| *adj* : hoarse, husky

enrouer |ɑ̃rwe| *vt* : to make hoarse — **s'enrouer** *vr*

enrouler |ɑ̃rule| *vt* : to wind, to coil, to roll up — **s'enrouler** *vr* **1 ~ dans** : to wrap oneself up in **2 ~ sur** : to wind around

ensabler |ɑ̃sable| *v* **s'ensabler** *vr* **1** : to get stuck in the sand **2** : to silt up

ensacher |ɑ̃saʃe| *vt* : to bag (merchandise)

ensanglanté, -tée |ɑ̃sɑ̃glɑ̃te| *adj* : covered with blood, bloodstained

enseignant[1], **-gnante** |ɑ̃sɛɲɑ̃, -ɲɑ̃t| *adj* : teaching

enseignant[2], **-gnante** *n* : teacher

enseigne[1] |ɑ̃sɛɲ| *nf* **1** : sign <enseigne lumineuse : neon sign> **2** DRAPEAU : flag, ensign **3 être logé à la même enseigne** : to be in the same boat

enseigne[2] *nm* **1** : ensign **2 enseigne de vaisseau** : midshipman

enseignement |ɑ̃sɛɲmɑ̃| *nm* **1** : teaching **2** : education **3** LEÇON : lesson, lecture

enseigner |ɑ̃seɲe| *v* : to teach

ensemble[1] |ɑ̃sɑ̃bl| *adv* : together

ensemble[2] *nm* **1** : group (of persons), set (of objects), series (of ideas, etc.) **2** : whole <dans l'ensemble : on the whole> **3** : unity <avec un ensemble parfait : simultaneously, in perfect unison> **4** : ensemble (in music) **5** : suit (of clothing), outfit **6** : set (in mathematics) **7 d'~** : overall, general **8 dans l'ensemble** : on the whole **9 grand ensemble** : housing development

ensemblier |ɑ̃sɑ̃blije| *nm* : interior decorator

ensemencer |ɑ̃səmɑ̃se| {6} *vt* : to sow, to seed

enserrer |ɑ̃sere| *vt* **1** : to fit tightly around, to encircle **2** SERRER : to clasp, to grip

ensevelir |ɑ̃səvlir| *vt* ENTERRER : to bury

ensoleillé, -lée |ɑ̃sɔleje| *adj* : sunny

ensoleillement |ɑ̃sɔlɛjmɑ̃| *nm* : (amount of) sunshine

ensommeillé, -lée |ɑ̃sɔmeje| *adj* : sleepy, drowsy

ensorceler |ɑ̃sɔrsəle| {8} *vt* : to bewitch, to charm

ensorcellement |ɑ̃sɔrsɛlmɑ̃| *nm* : bewitchment, enchantment

ensuite |ɑ̃sɥit| *adv* **1** : then, next **2** : afterwards, later

ensuivre |ɑ̃sɥivr| {35} *v* **s'ensuivre** *vr* : to ensue, to follow <il s'ensuit que . . . : it follows that . . . >

entacher |ɑ̃taʃe| *vt* **1** : to mar, to sully **2 entaché de nullité** : null and void

entaille |ɑ̃taj| *nf* **1** : cut, gash **2** ENCOCHE : notch

entailler |ɑ̃taje| *vt* : to gash, to slash, to cut (into) — **s'entailler** *vr* : to get a gash in

entamer |ɑ̃tame| *vt* **1** : to cut into, to make inroads into **2** : to start, to initiate **3** : to damage, to sully **4** : to shake, to undermine

entassement |ɑ̃tasmɑ̃| *nm* **1** : piling up **2** : pile, heap

entasser |ɑ̃tase| *vt* **1** : to pile up, to accumulate **2** : to cram, to pack together — **s'entasser** *vr* : to pile up

entendement |ɑ̃tɑ̃dmɑ̃| *nm* : understanding

entendeur |ɑ̃tɑ̃dœr| *nm* **à bon entendeur, salut!** : a word to the wise!

entendre |ɑ̃tɑ̃dr| {63} *vt* **1** : to hear **2** SIGNIFIER : to mean, to intend **3** COMPRENDRE : to understand <laisser entendre : to intimate> **4 entendre dire que** : to hear that **5 entendre parler de** : to hear of — *vi* **1** : to hear **2** : to understand — **s'entendre** *vr* **1** : to get along, to understand one another **2** : to agree **3** : to be understood <cela s'entend : it goes without saying> **4** : to be heard <cela s'entend à peine : it's barely audible> **5 ~ à** : to know about, to be good at

entendu, -due |ɑ̃tɑ̃dy| *adj* **1** : agreed, understood <entendu! : OK!> **2** : knowing, understanding <d'un air entendu : knowingly> **3 bien entendu** : of course

entente |ɑ̃tɑ̃t| *nf* **1** : harmony **2** : agreement, understanding **3 à double entente** : with a double meaning

entériner |ɑ̃terine| *vt* : to ratify, to confirm

enterrement |ɑ̃tɛrmɑ̃| *nm* **1** INHUMATION : burial, interment **2** FUNÉRAILLES : funeral **3** : funeral procession **4** : end, death <l'enterrement

de mon projet : the shelving of my project>

enterrer [ɑ̃tere] *vt* **1** : to bury, to inter **2** : to leave behind, to lay aside — **s'enterrer** *vr* : to bury oneself (away)

en–tête [ɑ̃tɛt] *nm, pl* **en–têtes 1** : letterhead **2** : heading

entêté[1], **-tée** [ɑ̃tete] *adj* : stubborn, obstinate

entêté[2], **-tée** *n* : stubborn person

entêtement [ɑ̃tɛtmɑ̃] *nm* : stubbornness, obstinacy

entêter [ɑ̃tete] *v* **s'entêter** *vr* : to persist

enthousiasmant, -mante [ɑ̃tuzjasmɑ̃, -mɑ̃t] *adj* : exciting

enthousiasme [ɑ̃tuzjasm] *nm* **1** : enthusiasm **2 avec ~** : enthusiastically

enthousiasmer [ɑ̃tuzjasme] *vt* : to fill with enthusiasm, to excite — **s'enthousiasmer** *vr* **~ pour** : to get enthusiastic about

enthousiaste[1] [ɑ̃tuzjast] *adj* : enthusiastic

enthousiaste[2] *nmf* : enthusiast

enticher [ɑ̃tiʃe] *v* **s'enticher** *vr* : to become infatuated <être entiché de : to be infatuated with>

entier[1], **-tière** [ɑ̃tje, -tjɛr] *adj* **1** : entire, whole <la ville entière : the whole town> <pendant des heures entières : for hours on end> **2** : complete, full <leur entière coopération : their full cooperation> **3** : intact, unaltered <rester entier : to remain unresolved> **4 tout entier** : completely, wholeheartedly <se donner tout entier : to devote oneself wholeheartedly>

entier[2] *nm* **1** : integer, whole number **2 en ~** : all of it, in its entirety

entièrement [ɑ̃tjɛrmɑ̃] *adv* : entirely, wholly, completely

entièreté [ɑ̃tjɛrte] *nf* : entirety, wholeness

entité [ɑ̃tite] *nf* : entity

entomologie [ɑ̃tɔmɔlɔʒi] *nf* : entomology — **entomologiste** [-lɔʒist] *nmf*

entomologique [ɑ̃tɔmɔlɔʒik] *adj* : entomological

entonner [ɑ̃tɔne] *vt* : to strike up (a song), to start singing

entonnoir [ɑ̃tɔnwar] *nm* **1** : funnel **2** : crater

entorse [ɑ̃tɔrs] *nf* **1** FOULURE : sprain <se faire une entorse à la cheville : to sprain one's ankle> **2** : infringement <faire une entorse à : to break (a law), to bend (a rule), to distort (the truth)>

entortiller [ɑ̃tɔrtije] *vt* **1** : to twist, to wind, to wrap (up) **2** : to tangle up, to complicate **3** *fam* : to hoodwink

entour [ɑ̃tur] *nm* **à l'entour** : in the vicinity, around

entourage [ɑ̃turaʒ] *nm* : circle, entourage

entouré, -rée [ɑ̃ture] *adj* **1** : popular **2 ~ de** : surrounded by

entourer [ɑ̃ture] *vt* **1** ENCERCLER : to surround, to encircle **2** : to rally around — **s'entourer** *vr* **~ de** : to surround oneself with <s'entourer de précautions : to take every possible precaution>

entourloupette [ɑ̃turlupɛt] *nf* : dirty trick

entournure [ɑ̃turnyr] *nf* **1** : armhole **2 être gêné aux entournures** : to be ill at ease, to be in awkward straits

entracte [ɑ̃trakt] *nm* : intermission

entraide [ɑ̃trɛd] *nf* : mutual aid

entraider [ɑ̃trede] *v* **s'entraider** *vr* : to help one another

entrailles [ɑ̃traj] *nfpl* **1** : entrails, guts **2** : womb **3** : depths, bowels, heart <les entrailles de la terre : the bowels of the earth> <sans entrailles : heartless>

entrain [ɑ̃trɛ̃] *nm* : liveliness, spirit

entraînant, -nante [ɑ̃trɛnɑ̃, -nɑ̃t] *adj* : lively

entraînement [ɑ̃trɛnmɑ̃] *nm* **1** : training <manquer d'entraînement : to be out of training> **2** : practice

entraîner [ɑ̃trene] *vt* **1** EMPORTER : to carry away <se laisser entraîner dans : to get carried away with> **2** PROVOQUER : to lead to, to provoke <cela pourrait entraîner des problèmes : that could lead to problems> **3** FORMER : to train, to coach — **s'entraîner** *vr* : to train, to practice

entraîneur, -neuse [ɑ̃trɛnœr, -nøz] *n* : trainer, coach

entrapercevoir *or* **entr'apercevoir** [ɑ̃trapɛrsəvwar] {26} *vt* : to catch a glimpse of

entrave [ɑ̃trav] *nf* **1** : hobble, shackle **2** : hindrance **3 sans entraves** : unfettered

entraver [ɑ̃trave] *vt* **1** : to shackle, to fetter **2** GÊNER : to hold up, to hinder

entre [ɑ̃tr] *prep* **1** : between <entre nous : between ourselves, between you and me> <entre les deux : in between> **2** PARMI : among <l'un d'entre eux : one of them> <entre autres : among others, among other things>

entrebâillement [ɑ̃trəbajmɑ̃] *nm* : gap, opening <par l'entrebâillement de la porte : through the half-open door>

entrebâiller [ɑ̃trəbaje] *vt* : to open halfway — **s'entrebâiller** *vr*

entrechoquer [ɑ̃trəʃɔke] *vt* : to bang together — **s'entrechoquer** *vr* **1** : to clink, to clatter, to chatter (of teeth) **2** : to clash (of ideas, etc.)

entrecôte [ɑ̃trəkot] *nf* : rib steak

entrecouper [ɑ̃trəkupe] *vt* **1** : to intersperse **2** : to interrupt — **s'entrecouper** *vr* : to intersect

entrecroiser [ɑ̃trəkrwaze] *vt* : to intertwine, to interlace — **s'entrecroiser** *vr* : to intersect

entre–deux [ɑ̃trədø] *nms & pl* : space, gap, interval

entrée [ɑ̃tre] *nf* **1** : entrance, entry **2** : admission, admittance <entrée libre : free admission> **3** PLACE : ticket, seat **4** : first course (of a meal) **5** VESTIBULE : hall, lobby **6** : entry (in a reference book), input (in a computer) **7** DÉBUT : beginning **8 d'∼ (de jeu)** : from the start, right off

entrefaite [ɑ̃trəfɛt] *nf* **sur ces entrefaites** : at the moment

entrefilet [ɑ̃trəfilɛ] *nm* : paragraph, news item

entregent [ɑ̃trəʒɑ̃] *nm* : tact, diplomacy

entre–jambes *or* **entrejambes** [ɑ̃trəʒɑ̃b] *nms & pl* : crotch

entrelacer [ɑ̃trəlase] {6} *vt* : to intertwine, to interlace — **s'entrelacer** *vr*

entremêler [ɑ̃trəmele] *vt* : to mix together, to intermingle — **s'entremêler** *vr*

entremets [ɑ̃trəmɛ] *nms & pl* : dessert

entremetteur, -teuse [ɑ̃trəmɛtœr, -tøz] *n* **1** : go-between **2** : procurer, pimp

entremettre [ɑ̃trəmɛtr] {53} *v* **s'entremettre** *vr* : to intervene

entremise [ɑ̃trəmiz] *nf* : intervention <par l'entremise de son avocat : through his lawyer>

entreposage [ɑ̃trəpozaʒ] *nm* : storage

entreposer [ɑ̃trəpoze] *vt* **1** : to store **2** : to bond (in commerce)

entrepôt [ɑ̃trəpo] *nm* : warehouse

entreprenant, -nante [ɑ̃trəprənɑ̃, -nɑ̃t] *adj* **1** : enterprising **2** : forward, brash

entreprendre [ɑ̃trəprɑ̃dr] {70} *vt* : to undertake, to start, to embark on

entrepreneur, -neuse [ɑ̃trəprənœr, -nøz] *n* **1** : contractor **2** : entrepreneur **3 entrepreneur de pompes funèbres** : undertaker, funeral director

entreprise [ɑ̃trəpriz] *nf* **1** : enterprise, undertaking, venture **2** FIRME : business, firm **3** CONTRAT : contract

entrer [ɑ̃tre] *vt* **1** : to take in, to bring in <entrer les meubles : to bring in the furniture> **2** ENFONCER : to push in, to stick **3** : to enter (in a computer) — *vi* **1** : to enter, to go in, to come in <il est entré dans la pièce : he entered the room> <entrer à l'hôpital : to go into the hospital> <entrez! : come in!> **2** : to fit <cette clé n'entre pas dans la serrure : this key doesn't fit in the lock> **3 ∼ dans** : to join, to go into <entrer dans l'armée : to join the army> **4 ∼ en** : to begin <entrer en ébullition : to start boiling>

entresol [ɑ̃trəsɔl] *nm* : mezzanine

entre–temps [ɑ̃trətɑ̃] *adv* : meanwhile, in the meantime

entretenir [ɑ̃trətnir] {92} *vt* **1** MAINTENIR : to maintain, to keep up **2** : to keep alive, to cherish, to harbor <entretenir des doutes : to entertain doubts> **3** : to support, to look after **4** : to speak to, to address — **s'entretenir** *vr*

entretenu, -nue [ɑ̃trətny] *adj* : kept, maintained <mal entretenu : poorly maintained>

entretien [ɑ̃trətjɛ̃] *nm* **1** : maintenance, upkeep **2** : discussion, talk, interview <entretien d'embauche : job interview> **3** : support, (financial) maintenance

entrevoir [ɑ̃trəvwar] {99} *vt* **1** APERCEVOIR : to glimpse, to perceive **2** PRÉVOIR : to foresee, to anticipate

entrevue [ɑ̃trəvy] *nf* : meeting, interview

entrouvert, -verte [ɑ̃truvɛr, -vɛrt] *adj & adv* : half open, ajar

entrouvrir [ɑ̃truvrir] {83} *vt* : to open halfway — **s'entrouvrir** *vr* : to be half open

énumérer [enymere] {87} *vt* : to enumerate — **énumération** [-merasjɔ̃] *nf*

envahir [ɑ̃vair] *vt* **1** : to invade **2** : to overcome <envahi par le chagrin : overcome by grief>

envahissant, -sante [ɑ̃vaisɑ̃, -sɑ̃t] *adj* **1** : intrusive, invasive **2** : pervasive

envahissement [ɑ̃vaismɑ̃] *nm* : invasion

envahisseur, -seuse [ɑ̃vaisœr, -søz] *n* : invader

enveloppe [ɑ̃vlɔp] *nf* **1** : envelope **2** : cover, casing, shell, husk (of corn, etc.) **3** : exterior **4** : sum of money, budget

envelopper [ɑ̃vlɔpe] *vt* **1** : to envelop, to shroud **2** RECOUVRIR : to wrap up, to cover — **s'envelopper** *vr*

envenimer [ɑ̃vnime] *vt* **1** INFECTER : to infect **2** : to inflame, to aggravate

envergure [ɑ̃vɛrgyr] *nf* **1** : wingspan **2** ÉTENDUE : breadth, scope, scale <de grande envergure : large-scale> **3** CALIBRE : caliber, stature

enverra [ɑ̃vera], *etc.* → **envoyer**

envers[1] [ɑ̃vɛr] *prep* **1** : toward, with regard to **2 envers et contre tout** : in spite of everything, against all opposition **3 être tout à l'envers** *Can* : to be very upset

envers[2] *nm* **1** REVERS : back, reverse **2 à l'envers** : inside out, upside down, backward

enviable [ɑ̃vjabl] *adj* : enviable

envie [ɑ̃vi] *nf* **1** JALOUSIE : envy, jealousy **2** DÉSIR : desire, wish, longing <avoir envie de : to feel like, to want> **3** : birthmark **4** : hangnail

envier [ɑ̃vje] {96} *vt* : to envy

envieux, -vieuse [ɑ̃vjø, -vjøz] *adj* : envious, jealous — **envieusement** [ɑ̃vjøzmɑ̃] *adv*

environ [ɑ̃virɔ̃] *adv* : about, around, approximately <viens dans environ une heure : come in an hour or so>

environnant, -nante [ɑ̃virɔnɑ̃, -nɑ̃t] *adj* : surrounding

environnement [ɑ̃virɔnmɑ̃] *nm* : environment

environnemental, -tale [ɑ̃virɔnmɑ̃tal] *adj, pl* **-taux** [-to] : environmental

environnementaliste [ɑ̃virɔnmɑ̃talist] *nmf* : environmentalist

environner [ɑ̃virɔne] *vt* : to surround

environs [ɑ̃virɔ̃] *nmpl* **1** : surroundings, vicinity **2 aux environs de** : around <aux environs de Pâques : around Easter>

envisager [ɑ̃vizaʒe] {17} *vt* **1** : to envisage, to contemplate **2 envisager de faire** : to plan to do, to consider doing

envoi [ɑ̃vwa] *nm* **1** : sending, dispatching <envoi contre remboursement : cash on delivery> **2** COLIS : parcel, package **3 coup d'envoi** : kickoff

envoie [ɑ̃vwa], *etc.* → **envoyer**

envol [ɑ̃vɔl] *nm* : takeoff

envolée [ɑ̃vɔle] *nf* **1** : takeoff, flight **2** *or* **envolée de l'imagination** : flight of fancy, inspired discourse **3** : rise, surge (in value, etc.)

envoler [ɑ̃vɔle] *v* **s'envoler** *vr* **1** : to take off **2** : to fly away **3** : to blow away **4** DISPARAÎTRE : to disappear, to vanish **5** : to surge (of prices, values, etc.)

envoûtement [ɑ̃vutmɑ̃] *nm* : spell, bewitchment

envoûter [ɑ̃vute] *vt* : to bewitch, to cast a spell over

envoyé, -voyée [ɑ̃vwaje] *n* **1** : messenger **2** : envoy **3 envoyé spécial** : special (press) correspondent

envoyer [ɑ̃vwaje] {36} *vt* **1** : to send, to send out <envoyer par la poste : to mail> **2** LANCER : to throw, to hurl **3 envoyer promener** *fam* : to send packing — **s'envoyer** *vr* **1** : to send to each other, to exchange **2** *fam* : to guzzle, to wolf down

envoyeur, -voyeuse [ɑ̃vwajœr, -vwajøz] *n* : sender

enzyme [ɑ̃zim] *nf* : enzyme

épagneul, -gneule [epaɲœl] *n* : spaniel

épais, épaisse [epɛ, -pɛs] *adj* : thick

épaisseur [epɛsœr] *nf* **1** : thickness **2** : layer

épaissir [epesir] *v* : to thicken — **s'épaissir** *vr* **1** : to thicken (up) **2** : to deepen <le mystère s'est épaissi : the mystery deepened>

épaississant [epesisɑ̃] *nm* : thickener

épaississement [epesismɑ̃] *nm* : thickening

épanchement [epɑ̃ʃmɑ̃] *nm* **1** : effusion, outpouring **2 épanchement de synovie** : water on the knee

épancher [epɑ̃ʃe] *vt* : to give vent to, to pour out (one's feelings, etc.) — **s'épancher** *vr* : to pour one's heart out

épandage [epɑ̃daʒ] *nm* : spreading

épandre [epɑ̃dr] {63} *vt* : to spread

épanoui, -nouie [epanwi] *adj* **1** : in full bloom **2** : radiant **3** : fully developed (of the body, etc.)

épanouir [epanwir] *vt* **1** : to make bloom **2** : to light up, to brighten — **s'épanouir** *vr* **1** : to bloom **2** : to light up **3** : to develop, to blossom, to flourish

épanouissement [epanwismɑ̃] *nm* **1** : blooming, flowering **2** : brightening, lighting up

épargnant, -gnante [eparɲɑ̃, -ɲɑ̃t] *n* : saver, investor

épargne [eparɲ] *nf* **1** ÉCONOMIE : saving, economy **2** : savings *pl*

épargner [eparɲe] *vt* **1** ÉCONOMISER : to save **2** : to spare — **s'épargner** *vr* : to spare oneself (trouble, etc.)

éparpillement [eparpijmɑ̃] *nm* : scattering, dispersal

éparpiller [eparpije] *vt* **1** : to scatter, to disperse **2** : to dissipate (efforts, etc.) — **s'éparpiller** *vr*

épars, éparse [epar, -pars] *adj* : scattered

épatant, -tante [epatɑ̃, -tɑ̃t] *adj fam* : great, fantastic

épater [epate] *vt fam* **1** ÉTONNER : to amaze **2** IMPRESSIONNER : to impress — **s'épater** *vr*

épaule [epol] *nf* : shoulder

épaulement [epolmɑ̃] *nm* **1** : retaining wall **2** : escarpment

épauler [epole] *vt* **1** AIDER : to back, to support **2** : to raise (a firearm), to take aim with — *vi* : to take aim

épaulette [epolɛt] *nf* **1** : epaulet **2** BRETELLE : shoulder strap **3** : shoulder pad

épave [epav] *nf* **1** : wreck (of a ship) **2 épave flottante** : flotsam

épée [epe] *nf* **1** : sword **2 coup d'épée dans l'eau** : wasted effort

épeler [eple] {8} *vt* : to spell — **s'épeler** *vr*

épelle [epɛl], **épellera** [epɛlra], *etc.* → **épeler**

épépiner [epepine] *vt* : to seed, to remove the seeds from

éperdu, -due [epɛrdy] *adj* **1** PASSIONNÉ : passionate, intense **2** : frantic, overwhelmed <éperdu de peur : overcome with fear>

éperdument [epɛrdymɑ̃] *adv* **1** : frantically, desperately <éperdument amoureux : madly in love> **2 je m'en moque éperdument** : I couldn't care less

éperlan [epɛrlɑ̃] *nm* : smelt

éperon [eprɔ̃] *nm* : spur

éperonner [eprɔne] *vt* : to spur (on)

épeurant, -rante [epørɑ̃, -rɑ̃t] *adj Can* : scary, frightening

éphémère[1] [efemɛr] *adj* : ephemeral, fleeting

éphémère[2] *nm* : mayfly

épi |epi| *nm* **1** : ear, cob <épi de maïs : corncob> **2** : tuft (of hair) **3 se garer en épi** : to park at an angle

épice |epis| *nf* : spice

épicé, -cée |epise| *adj* : highly spiced, spicy

épicéa |episea| *nm France* : spruce

épicentre |episɑ̃tr| *nm* : epicenter

épicer |epise| {6} *vt* : to spice

épicerie |episri| *nf* **1** : grocery store **2** : groceries *pl*

épicier, -cière |episje, -sjɛr| *n* : grocer

épicurien[1], **-rienne** |epikyrjɛ̃, -rjɛn| *adj* : epicurean

épicurien[2], **-rienne** *n* : epicure

épidémie |epidemi| *nf* : epidemic — **épidémique** |-demik| *adj*

épiderme |epidɛrm| *nm* : epidermis

épidermique |epidɛrmik| *adj* **1** : epidermal, skin **2 réaction épidermique** : automatic reaction, gut feeling

épier |epje| {96} *vt* **1** OBSERVER : to spy on, to watch closely **2** ATTENDRE : to watch out for

epigramme |epigram| *nf* : epigram

épilepsie |epilɛpsi| *nf* : epilepsy

épileptique |epilɛptik| *adj & nmf* : epileptic

épiler |epile| *vt* : to remove hair from, to pluck

épilogue |epilɔg| *nm* **1** : epilogue **2** : conclusion, outcome

épiloguer |epilɔge| *vt* ~ **sur** : to hold forth on, to go on and on about

épinard |epinar| *nm* **1** : spinach (plant) **2 épinards** *nmpl* : spinach (for eating)

épine |epin| *nf* **1** : thorn, prickle **2 épine dorsale** : spine, backbone

épinette |epinɛt| *nf* **1** : spinet **2** *Can* : spruce

épineux, -neuse |epinø, -nøz| *adj* : thorny, prickly

épingle |epɛ̃gl| *nf* **1** : pin <épingle de sûreté : safety pin> <épingle à linge : clothespin> <épingle à cheveux : hairpin> **2 tiré à quatre épingles** : impeccably dressed **3 tirer son épingle du jeu** : to extricate oneself, to pull out in time

épingler |epɛ̃gle| *vt* **1** : to pin **2** *fam* : to nab

épinglette |epɛ̃glɛt| *nf Can* **1** : brooch **2** : pin, button, badge

épinière |epinjɛr| *adj* → **moelle**

épique |epik| *adj* : epic

episcopal, -pale |episkɔpal| *adj, mpl* **-paux** |-po| : episcopal

épisode |epizɔd| *nm* : episode

épisodique |epizɔdik| *adj* : episodic — **épisodiquement** |-dikmɑ̃| *adv*

épisser |epise| *vt* : to splice

épissure |episyr| *nf* : splice

épistolaire |epistɔlɛr| *adj* : epistolary <avoir des relations épistolaires avec : to correspond with>

épitaphe |epitaf| *nf* : epitaph

épithète |epitɛt| *nf* : epithet

épître |epitr| *nf* : epistle

éploré, -rée |eplɔre| *adj* : tearful, in tears

éplucher |eplyʃe| *vt* **1** PELER : to peel **2** DÉCORTIQUER : to analyze, to scrutinize, to plow through (a text, etc.)

épluchure |eplyʃyr| *nf* : peel, peelings (of potatoes, etc.)

épointer |epwɛ̃te| *vt* : to blunt

éponge |epɔ̃ʒ| *nf* **1** : sponge **2 jeter l'éponge** : to throw in the towel **3 passer l'éponge** : to forget about it, to let bygones be bygones

éponger |epɔ̃ʒe| {17} *vt* **1** : to sponge up, to mop up **2** : to soak up, to absorb **3 éponger ses dettes** : to pay off one's debts — **s'éponger** *vr* **s'éponger le front** : to mop one's brow

épopée |epɔpe| *nf* : epic

époque |epɔk| *nf* **1** : epoch, era, age **2** : time, period <à cette époque : at that time>

épouse |epuz| *nf* → **époux**

épouser |epuze| *vt* **1** : to marry, to wed **2** : to espouse (an idea, etc.) **3** MOULER : to take the shape of, to fit closely

époussetage |epustaʒ| *nm* : dusting

épousseter |epuste| {8} *vt* : to dust

époustouflant, -flante |epustuflɑ̃, -flɑ̃t| *adj fam* : amazing, mind-boggling

époustoufler |epustufle| *vt* : to amaze, to flabbergast

épouvantable |epuvɑ̃tabl| *adj* : dreadful, horrible — **épouvantablement** |-tabləmɑ̃| *adv*

épouvantail |epuvɑ̃taj| *nm* **1** : scarecrow **2** : bogey(man)

épouvante |epuvɑ̃t| *nf* : terror, horror <roman d'épouvante : horror story>

épouvanter |epuvɑ̃te| *vt* TERRIFIER : to terrify, to fill with dread — **s'épouvanter** *vr* : to get frightened

époux, épouse |epu, epuz| *n* : spouse, husband *m*, wife *f*

éprendre |eprɑ̃dr| {70} *v* **s'éprendre** *vr* ~ **de** : to fall in love with, to be taken with

épreuve |eprœv| *nf* **1** : test <mettre à l'épreuve : to put to the test> <épreuve de force : test of strength, showdown> **2** : ordeal, trial **3** : examination, test <épreuve écrite : written exam> **4** : event (in sports) **5** : proof, print (in printing, photography, etc.) **6 à l'épreuve de** : proof against

épris, éprise |epri, epriz| *adj* ~ **de** : in love with

éprouvant, -vante |epruvɑ̃, -vɑ̃t| *adj* : trying, difficult to endure

éprouver |epruve| *vt* **1** TESTER : to test, to try (out) **2** RESSENTIR : to feel, to experience **3** : to suffer, to endure (a loss) **4** : to distress **5** : to try, to make suffer

éprouvette |epruvɛt| *nf* : test tube

épuisant, -sante [epɥizɑ̃, -zɑ̃t] *adj* : exhausting

épuisé, -sée [epɥize] *adj* **1** : exhausted **2** : out of stock

épuisement [epɥizmɑ̃] *nm* **1** : exhaustion, fatigue **2** : depletion (of stock, etc.)

épuiser [epɥize] *vt* **1** FATIGUER : to tire out, to wear out, to fatigue **2** : to exhaust, to use up — **s'épuiser** *vr*

épuration [epyrasjɔ̃] *nf* **1** : purification (of substances) **2** : refinement (of style, morals, etc.) **3** : purge (in politics)

épurer [epyre] *vt* **1** : to purify, to filter **2** : to refine (language, etc.) **3** : to purge (in politics)

équanimité [ekwanimite] *nf* : equanimity

équarrir [ekarir] *vt* **1** : to quarter (an animal) **2** : to square off

équateur [ekwatœr] *nm* : equator

équation [ekwasjɔ̃] *nf* : equation

équatorial, -riale [ekwatɔrjal] *adj, mpl* **-riaux** [-rjo] : equatorial

équatorien, -rienne [ekwatɔrjɛ̃, -rjɛn] *adj* : Ecuadoran, Ecuadorean, Ecuadorian

Équatorien, -rienne *n* : Ecuadoran, Ecuadorean, Ecuadorian

équerre [ekɛr] *nf* **1** : square <équerre en T : T square> **2 d'~** : square, straight **3 en ~** : at right angles **4 mettre d'équerre** : to square, to true

équestre [ekɛstr] *adj* : equestrian

équilatéral, -rale [ekɥilateral] *adj, mpl* **-raux** [-ro] : equilateral

équilibre [ekilibr] *nm* : equilibrium, balance <en équilibre : balanced, stable> <perdre l'équilibre : to lose one's balance> <équilibre sur les mains : handstand>

équilibré, -brée [ekilibre] *adj* : well-balanced, levelheaded

équilibrer [ekilibre] *vt* : to balance — **s'équilibrer** *vr*

équilibriste [ekilibrist] *nmf* **1** ACROBATE : acrobat **2** FUNAMBULE : tightrope walker

équinoxe [ekinɔks] *nm* : equinox

équipage [ekipaʒ] *nm* : crew

équipe [ekip] *nf* **1** : team <esprit d'équipe : team spirit> <faire équipe avec : to team up with> **2** : crew, gang, squad <équipe de nuit : night crew, night shift> <équipe de secours : rescue squad>

équipée [ekipe] *nf* **1** : escapade **2** : outing, jaunt

équipement [ekipmɑ̃] *nm* **1** MATÉRIEL : equipment **2 équipements** *nmpl* : facilities, installations <équipements sportifs : sports facilities>

équiper [ekipe] *vt* : to equip, to outfit — **s'équiper** *vr*

équipier, -pière [ekipje, -pjɛr] *n* : team member

équitable [ekitabl] *adj* : fair, equitable — **équitablement** [-tabləmɑ̃] *adv*

équitation [ekitasjɔ̃] *nf* : horseback riding, horsemanship

équité [ekite] *nf* : equity

équivalence [ekivalɑ̃s] *nf* : equivalence

équivalent[1], -lente [ekivalɑ̃, -lɑ̃t] *adj* : equivalent

équivalent[2] *nm* : equivalent

équivaloir [ekivalwar] {95} *vi* **~ à** : to be equivalent to, to be tantamount to

équivoque[1] [ekivɔk] *adj* **1** AMBIGU : equivocal, ambiguous **2** DOUTEUX : questionable, doubtful

équivoque[2] *nf* **1** AMBIGUÏTÉ : ambiguity, uncertainty **2** MALENTENDU : misunderstanding **3 sans ~** : unequivocal, unequivocally

érable [erabl] *nm* : maple <sirop d'érable : maple syrup>

éradication [eradikasjɔ̃] *nf* : eradication

éradiquer [eradike] *vt* : to eradicate

érafler [erafle] *vt* **1** : to graze, to scratch (the skin) **2** : to scrape (a surface)

éraflure [eraflyr] *nf* : scratch, scrape

éraillé, -lée [eraje] *adj* **1** : hoarse, rasping **2** : frayed **3 avoir les yeux éraillés** : to have bloodshot eyes

ère [ɛr] *nf* : era

érection [erɛksjɔ̃] *nf* : erection

éreintant, -tante [erɛ̃tɑ̃, -tɑ̃t] *adj* : backbreaking, exhausting

éreinter [erɛ̃te] *vt* **1** ÉPUISER : to exhaust, to wear out **2** CRITIQUER : to criticize, to pan — **s'éreinter** *vr* : to wear oneself out

ergonomie [ɛrgɔnɔmi] *nf* : ergonomics

ergonomique [ɛrgɔnɔmik] *adj* : ergonomic

ergot [ɛrgo] *nm* **1** : spur (of a rooster) **2 se dresser sur ses ergots** : to get up on one's high horse

ergoter [ɛrgote] *vi* : to quibble

ergoteur, -teuse [ɛrgɔtœr, -tøz] *adj* : quibbling, argumentative

ergothérapeute [ɛrgɔterapøt] *nmf* : occupational therapist

ergothérapie [ɛrgɔterapi] *nf* : occupational therapy

ériger [eriʒe] {17} *vt* **1** : to erect **2** : to establish, to set up — **s'ériger** *vr* **~ en** : to set oneself up as

ermitage [ɛrmitaʒ] *nm* **1** : hermitage **2** : retreat

ermite [ɛrmit] *nm* : hermit

éroder [erɔde] *vt* : to erode, to eat away — **s'éroder** *vr*

érogène [erɔʒɛn] *adj* : erogenous

érosion [erozjɔ̃] *nf* : erosion

érotique [erɔtik] *adj* : erotic — **érotiquement** [-tikmɑ̃] *adv*

érotisme [erɔtism] *nm* : eroticism

errant, -rante [ɛrɑ̃, -rɑ̃t] *adj* : wandering <un chien errant : a stray dog>

errata [erata] *nms & pl* : errata

erratique |eratik| *adj* : erratic (in geology or medicine)

errements |ɛrmɑ̃| *nmpl* : transgressions, bad habits

errer |ɛre| *vi* **1** : to wander, to stray, to roam **2** : to err

erreur |ɛrœr| *nf* : error, mistake <être dans l'erreur : to be wrong, to be mistaken> <par erreur : by mistake>

erroné, -née |ɛrɔne| *adj* : erroneous, wrong — **erronément** |-nemɑ̃| *adv*

éructer |erykte| *vi* : to belch

érudit[1], -dite |erydi, -dit| *adj* : erudite, learned

érudit[2], -dite *n* : scholar

érudition |erydisjɔ̃| *nf* : erudition

éruption |erypsjɔ̃| *nf* **1** : eruption (of a volcano) **2** : eruption, rash **3** : outburst <une éruption de colère : a fit of anger>

erythréen, -thréenne |eritreɛ̃, -treɛn| *adj* : Eritrean

Erythréen, -thréenne *n* : Eritrean

ès |ɛs| *prep* **docteur ès lettres** : doctor of letters, Ph.D.

esbroufe |ɛzbruf| *nf fam* : showing off, swagger

escabeau |ɛskabo| *nm, pl* **-beaux 1** TABOURET : stool **2** : stepladder

escadre |ɛskadr| *nf* : squadron

escadrille |ɛskadrij| *nf* : squadron

escadron |ɛskadrɔ̃| *nm* **1** : squad, squadron <escadron de la mort : death squad> **2** : crowd, bunch

escalade |ɛskalad| *nf* **1** : climbing, scaling **2** : escalation

escalader |ɛskalade| *vt* : to climb, to scale

escalator |ɛskalatɔr| *nm* : escalator

escale |ɛskal| *nf* **1** : port of call **2** : stopover

escalier |ɛskalje| *nm* : stairs, steps <escalier en colimaçon : spiral staircase> <escalier mécanique : escalator> <escalier de secours : fire escape>

escalope |ɛskalɔp| *nf* : cutlet <escalope de veau : veal cutlet>

escamotable |ɛskamɔtabl| *adj* **1** : retractable **2** : foldaway, collapsible

escamoter |ɛskamɔte| *vt* **1** : to cause to disappear **2** : to retract, to fold away **3** VOLER : to snatch, to filch **4** SAUTER : to leave out, to skip **5** ÉLUDER : to dodge, to evade

escampette |ɛskɑ̃pɛt| *nf* **prendre la poudre d'escampette** *fam* : to take to one's heels

escapade |ɛskapad| *nf* : escapade, jaunt <faire une escapade : to run away>

escarbille |ɛskarbij| *nf* : cinder

escargot |ɛskargo| *nm* : snail

escarmouche |ɛskarmuʃ| *nf* : skirmish

escarpé, -pée |ɛskarpe| *adj* : steep

escarpement |ɛskarpəmɑ̃| *nm* : escarpment, steep slope

escarpin |ɛskarpɛ̃| *nm* : pump (shoe)

escient |ɛsjɑ̃| *nm* **1 à bon escient** : judiciously, advisedly **2 à mauvais escient** : injudiciously, unwisely

esclaffer |ɛsklafe| *v* **s'esclaffer** *vr* : to burst out laughing, to guffaw

esclandre |ɛsklɑ̃dr| *nm* : scene, fracas

esclavage |ɛsklavaʒ| *nm* : slavery

esclave |ɛsklav| *adj & nmf* : slave

escompte |ɛskɔ̃t| *nm* : discount

escompter |ɛskɔ̃te| *vt* **1** : to discount **2** ANTICIPER : to expect, to anticipate

escopette |ɛskɔpɛt| *nf* : blunderbuss

escorte |ɛskɔrt| *nf* : escort

escorter |ɛskɔrte| *vt* : to escort

escorteur |ɛskɔrtœr| *nm* : escort ship

escouade |ɛskwad| *nf* **1** ESCADRON : squad **2** GROUPE : gang, group

escrime |ɛskrim| *nf* : fencing <faire de l'escrime : to fence>

escrimer |ɛskrime| *v* **s'escrimer** *vr* **1 s'escrimer à faire** : to wear oneself out doing **2 ~ sur** : to struggle with, to work away at

escrimeur, -meuse |ɛskrimœr, -møz| *n* : fencer

escroc |ɛskro| *nm* : swindler, crook

escroquer |ɛskrɔke| *vt* : to swindle, to defraud, to gyp

escroquerie |ɛskrɔkri| *nf* : swindle, fraud, gyp

eskimo |ɛskimo| → **esquimau**

ésotérique |ezɔterik| *adj* : esoteric

espace[1] |ɛspas| *nm* **1** : space, outer space **2** PLACE : area, room, space **3** : interval, gap <laissez un espace entre les deux : leave a space between the two> <en l'espace de dix minutes : within the space of ten minutes> **4 espaces verts** : parks, gardens

espace[2] *nf* : space (in printing)

espacer |ɛspase| {6} *vt* : to space (out)

espadon |ɛspadɔ̃| *nm* : swordfish

espadrille |ɛspadrij| *nf* **1** : espadrille **2 espadrilles** *nfpl Can* : sneakers

espagnol[1], -gnole |ɛspaɲɔl| *adj* : Spanish

espagnol[2] *nm* : Spanish (language)

Espagnol, -gnole *n* **1** : Spaniard **2 les Espagnols** : the Spanish

espar |ɛspar| *nm* : spar

espèce |ɛspɛs| *nf* **1** : species **2** SORTE : sort, kind <de toute espèce : of every kind> <espèce d'idiot! : you idiot!> **3 espèces** *nfpl* : cash <payer en espèces : to pay in cash>

espérance |ɛsperɑ̃s| *nf* **1** : hope, expectation **2** : expectancy <espérance de vie : life expectancy>

espérer |ɛspere| {87} *vt* **1** : to hope, to hope for <je l'espère bien : I hope so> **2** : to expect — *vi* **1** : to hope **2 ~ en** : to trust in

esperluette |ɛspɛrlɥɛt| *nf* : ampersand

espiègle |ɛspjɛgl| *adj* : mischievous, impish

espièglerie |ɛspjɛgləri| *nf* **1** : mischievousness, impishness **2** : prank, mischief

espion, -pionne [ɛspjɔ̃, -pjɔn] *n* : spy

espionnage [ɛspjɔnaʒ] *nm* : espionage

espionner [ɛspjɔne] *vt* : to spy on

espoir [ɛspwar] *nm* : hope <avoir bon espoir : to be confident, to have high hopes> <un cas sans espoir : a hopeless case>

esprit [ɛspri] *nm* **1** CERVEAU : mind, intellect <venir à l'esprit : to come to mind> **2** CARACTÈRE : character, mentality <avoir l'esprit étroit : to be narrow-minded> **3** HUMOUR : wit <avoir de l'esprit : to be witty> **4** HUMEUR : mood, disposition **5** PERSONNE : person **6** FANTÔME : spirit, ghost <esprit frappeur : poltergeist>

esquif [ɛskif] *nm* : skiff

esquimau[1], -maude [ɛskimo, -mod] *adj, mpl* **-maux** [-mo] : Eskimo

esquimau[2] *nm* : Eskimo (language)

Esquimau, -maude *n, mpl* **-maux** : Eskimo

esquinter [ɛskɛ̃te] *vt fam* **1** : to ruin, to mess up **2** : to pan — **s'esquinter** *vr* **s'esquinter à faire qqch** : to knock oneself out doing sth

esquisse [ɛskis] *nf* : sketch, outline, summary

esquisser [ɛskise] *vt* **1** : to sketch, to outline **2** : to give a hint of <esquisser un sourire : to give a slight smile>

esquive [ɛskiv] *nf* **1** : dodge (in sports) **2** : evasion, sidestepping

esquiver [ɛskive] *vt* : to avoid, to dodge, to evade — **s'esquiver** *vr* : to slip away

essai [esɛ] *nm* **1** TENTATIVE : attempt, try **2** : trial, test <essai nucléaire : nuclear test> <mettre à l'essai : to put to the test> **3** : essay

essaie [esɛ], **essaiera** [esɛra], *etc.* → **essayer**

essaim [esɛ̃] *nm* : swarm

essaimer [eseme] *vt* **1** : to swarm **2** : to spread (out), to expand

essayage [esɛjaʒ] *nm* : fitting, trying on <cabine d'essayage : fitting room>

essayer [eseje] {11} *vt* **1** TENTER : to try, to attempt **2** : to test, to try out **3** : to try on **4** : to assay (metals) — *vi* : to try — **s'essayer** *vr* **~ à** : to try one's hand at

essayeur, essayeuse [esɛjœr, esɛjøz] *n* : tester, fitter

essayiste [esejist] *nmf* : essayist

essence [ɛsɑ̃s] *nf* **1** : gasoline <essence sans plomb : unleaded gas> **2** : essence <par essence : in essence, essentially>

essentiel[1], -tielle [esɑ̃sjɛl] *adj* : essential — **essentiellement** [-sjɛlmɑ̃] *adv*

essentiel[2] *nm* **1** : main part, main thing, gist **2** : essentials *pl*, basics *pl*

esseulé, -lée [esœle] *adj* : forlorn

essieu [esjø] *nm, pl* **essieux** : axle

essor [esɔr] *nm* **1** : flight (of a bird) <prendre son essor : to take flight, to soar> **2** : expansion, growth, development <prendre son essor : to grow, to expand rapidly> <être en plein essor : to be booming>

essorer [esɔre] *vt* : to wring out, to spin dry

essoreuse [esɔrøz] *nf* : wringer

essoufflement [esufləmɑ̃] *nm* : breathlessness

essouffler [esufle] *vt* : to make breathless, to wind — **s'essouffler** *vr* **1** : to get out of breath **2** : to become exhausted, to run out of steam

essuie [esɥi], **essuiera** [esɥira], *etc.* → **essuyer**

essuie-glace [esɥiglas] *nm, pl* **essuie-glaces** : windshield wiper

essuie-mains [esɥimɛ̃] *nms & pl* : hand towel

essuie-tout [esɥitu] *nms & pl* : paper towel

essuyer [esɥije] {58} *vt* **1** : to wipe, to dry **2** SUBIR : to suffer, to endure — **s'essuyer** *vr* : to dry oneself

est[1] [ɛ], *etc.* → **être**

est[2] [ɛst] *adj* : east, eastern

est[3] *nm* **1** : east <le vent d'est : the east wind> <vers l'est : eastward> **2 l'Est** : the East

estafilade [ɛstafilad] *nf* : gash, slash

estampe [ɛstɑ̃p] *nf* : engraving, print

estamper [ɛstɑ̃pe] *vt* **1** : to stamp **2** *fam* : to swindle, to rip off

estampille [ɛstɑ̃pij] *nf* **1** : stamp (on a document) **2** : trademark, label (on merchandise)

est-ce que [ɛskə] *adv* (*used to introduce questions*) <est-ce qu'elle aime le café? : does she like coffee?> <est-ce qu'il y était? : was he there?> <pourquoi est-ce que tu pleures? : why are you crying?>

ester [ɛste] *nm* : ester

esthète [ɛstɛt] *nmf* : aesthete

esthéticien, -cienne [ɛstetisjɛ̃, -sjɛn] *n* : beautician

esthétique[1] [ɛstetik] *adj* **1** : aesthetic **2** : aesthetically pleasing, attractive — **esthétiquement** [-tikmɑ̃] *adv*

esthétique[2] *nf* : aesthetics

estimable [ɛstimabl] *adj* **1** : estimable, respected **2** : decent, sound

estimation [ɛstimasjɔ̃] *nf* **1** ÉVALUATION : valuation, appraisal **2** : estimate, reckoning

estime [ɛstim] *nf* : esteem, respect

estimer [ɛstime] *vt* **1** ÉVALUER : to assess, to appraise **2** : to estimate, to reckon **3** RESPECTER : to esteem, to respect **4 estimer que** : to consider that, to judge that — **s'estimer** *vr* SE JUGER : to consider oneself <je m'estime heureux : I consider myself fortunate>

estival, -vale [ɛstival] *adj, mpl* **-vaux** [-vo] : summer <la saison estivale : the summer season>

estivant, -vante [ɛstivɑ̃, -vɑ̃t] *n* : summer vacationer

estocade |ɛstɔkad| *nf* : deathblow, final thrust

estomac |ɛstɔma| *nm* **1** : stomach <mal à l'estomac : stomachache> **2 avoir de l'estomac** *fam* : to have guts **3 avoir l'estomac dans les talons** *fam* : to be famished

estomaqué, -quée |ɛstɔmake| *adj fam* : astounded, flabbergasted

estomper |ɛstɔ̃pe| *vt* : to blur, to dim — **s'estomper** *vr* : to fade away, to diminish

estonien[1], **-nienne** |ɛstɔnjɛ̃, -njɛn| *adj* : Estonian

estonien[2] *nm* : Estonian (language)

Estonien, -nienne *n* : Estonian

estrade |ɛstrad| *nf* : platform, dais

estragon |ɛstragɔ̃| *nm* : tarragon

estrogène |ɛstrɔʒɛn| *nm* : estrogen

estropié[1], **-piée** |ɛstrɔpje| *adj* : crippled, maimed

estropié[2], **-piée** *n* : cripple, disabled person

estropier |ɛstrɔpje| {96} *vt* **1** : to cripple, to maim **2** : to mispronounce, to misspell, to misquote

estuaire |ɛstɥɛr| *nm* : estuary

estudiantin, -tine |ɛstydjɑ̃tɛ̃, -tin| *adj* : student

esturgeon |ɛstyrʒɔ̃| *nm* : sturgeon

et |e| *conj* **1** : and <mon père et moi : my father and me> <et moi? : what about me?> **2 et . . . et . . .** : both . . . and . . . **3** (*used in numbers and fractions*) <vingt et un : twenty-one> <trois heures et demie : three-thirty, half past three>

étable |etabl| *nf* : cowshed

établi[1], **-blie** |etabli| *adj* : established

établi[2] *nm* : workbench

établir |etablir| *vt* **1** INSTITUER : to set up, to establish **2** : to draw up, to make out **3** PROUVER : to prove (guilt, innocence) **4** : to set (a record) — **s'établir** *vr* **1** : to get established, to set oneself up **2** : to settle

établissement |etablismɑ̃| *nm* **1** : establishment, setting up **2** : institution, establishment <établissement industriel : factory> <établissement scolaire : school>

étage |etaʒ| *nm* **1** : story, floor **2** : stage (of a rocket) **3** : tier, level

étager |etaʒe| {17} *vt* **1** : to lay out in tiers **2** : to stagger, to alternate — **s'étager** *vr*

étagère |etaʒɛr| *nf* **1** : shelf **2** : shelves *pl*, shelving unit

étai |etɛ| *nm* : prop, support

étain |etɛ̃| *nm* **1** : tin **2** : pewter

était |etɛ|, *etc.* → **être**

étal |etal| *nm, pl* **étals** |etal| *or* **étaux** |eto| **1** ÉVENTAIRE : stall (in a market) **2** : butcher's block

étalage |etalaʒ| *nm* **1** : display <faire étalage de : to show off, to flaunt> **2** DEVANTURE : window display

étaler |etale| *vt* **1** : to lay out, to spread out, to display **2** : to spread (on), to apply **3** ÉCHELONNER : to space out, to stagger **4** : to show off, to flaunt — **s'étaler** *vr* **1** : to spread <cette peinture s'étale mal : this paint doesn't spread well> **2** : to be spread, to extend (in time) **3** *fam* : to sprawl **4** *fam* : to fall on one's face

étalon |etalɔ̃| *nm* **1** : stallion **2** MODÈLE : standard, yardstick <l'étalon-or : the gold standard>

étalonner |etalɔne| *vt* **1** : to standardize **2** : to calibrate

étamine |etamin| *nf* **1** : stamen **2** : cheesecloth, muslin, bunting

étanche |etɑ̃ʃ| *adj* **1** : watertight, waterproof **2** *or* **étanche à l'air** : airtight

étancher |etɑ̃ʃe| *vt* **1** : to stem, to staunch **2** : to seal, to make watertight **3 étancher sa soif** : to quench one's thirst

étang |etɑ̃| *nm* : pond

étape |etap| *nf* **1** HALTE : stop, halt **2** : stage, leg (of a journey) **3** PHASE : step, stage, phase <les étapes de la vie : the stages of life>

état |eta| *nm* **1** : state, condition <en bon état : in good condition> <hors d'état : out of order> <état d'esprit : state of mind> <en état d'urgence : in a state of emergency> **2** : statement, inventory <états de comptes : financial statements> <faire état de : to give an account of> **3** : occupation, lot in life <de son état : by profession> **4 état civil** : civil status <bureau d'état civil : registry office>

État *nm* **1** : state, State <homme d'État : statesman> **2** : central government <monopole d'État : state monopoly>

étatique |etatik| *adj* : state, state-controlled

étatisation |etatizasjɔ̃| *nf* : state control, nationalization

étatiser |etatize| *vt* : to bring under state control

étatisme |etatism| *nm* : state control

état-major |etamaʒɔr| *nm, pl* **états-majors 1** : general staff (in the military) **2** : senior staff, management (in business, politics, etc.)

étau |eto| *nm, pl* **étaux** : vise

étayer |eteje| {11} *vt* **1** SOUTENIR : to prop up, to shore up **2** APPUYER : to support, to back up

et cætera *or* **et cetera** |ɛtsetera| : et cetera, and so on

été |ete| *nm* : summer

éteignait |etɛɲɛ|, **éteignions** |etɛɲiɔ̃|, *etc.* → **éteindre**

éteigne |etɛɲ|, *etc.* → **éteindre**

éteindre |etɛ̃dr| {37} *vt* **1** : to extinguish, to put out **2** : to turn off, to switch off — **s'éteindre** *vr* **1** : to go out, to die out **2** S'AFFAIBLIR : to subside, to fade **3** MOURIR : to die

étendard |etɑ̃dar| *nm* : standard, flag
étendre |etɑ̃dr| {63} *vt* **1** ÉTALER : to spread, to spread out **2** PENDRE : to hang up (laundry, etc.) **3** ALLONGER : to stretch (out) **4** ÉLARGIR : to extend, to expand, to widen **5** DILUER : to dilute, to thin — **s'étendre** *vr* **1** : to stretch **2** : to lie down **3** : to spread **4** ~ **sur** : to elaborate on
étendu, -due |etɑ̃dy| *adj* **1** VASTE : extensive, wide **2** ALLONGÉ : outstretched, spread
étendue *nf* **1** : area, expanse **2** : extent, range, scope
éternel, -nelle |etɛrnɛl| *adj* : eternal — **éternellement** |-nɛlmɑ̃| *adv*
éterniser |etɛrnize| *vt* **1** PERPÉTUER : to perpetuate **2** PROLONGER : to drag out, to prolong — **s'éterniser** *vr* : to go on and on
éternité |etɛrnite| *nf* : eternity <il y a une éternité que . . . : it's been ages since . . .> <de toute éternité : from time immemorial>
éternuement |etɛrnymɑ̃| *nm* : sneeze
éternuer |etɛrnɥe| *vi* : to sneeze
éthane |etan| *nm* : ethane
éther |etɛr| *nm* : ether
éthéré, -rée |etere| *adj* : ethereal
éthiopien, -pienne |etjɔpjɛ̃, -pjɛn| *adj* : Ethiopian
Éthiopien, -pienne *n* : Ethiopian
éthique[1] |etik| *adj* : ethical
éthique[2] *nf* : ethics
ethnie |ɛtni| *nf* : ethnic group
ethnique |ɛtnik| *adj* : ethnic
ethnologie |ɛtnɔlɔʒi| *nf* : ethnology
ethnologue |ɛtnɔlɔg| *nmf* : ethnologist
étincelant, -lante |etɛ̃slɑ̃, -lɑ̃t| *adj* : sparkling, glittering
étinceler |etɛ̃sle| {8} *vi* : to sparkle, to glitter
étincelle |etɛ̃sɛl| *nf* **1** : spark **2** : sparkle, flash
étioler |etjɔle| *v* **s'étioler** *vr* **1** : to wilt **2** : to weaken, to become sickly
étique |etik| *adj* : skinny, scrawny
étiqueter |etikte| {8} *vt* **1** : to label (merchandise) **2** ~ **comme** : to label as, to classify as
étiquette |etikɛt| *nf* **1** : label **2** : etiquette
étirer |etire| *vt* : to stretch — **s'étirer** *vr*
étoffe |etɔf| *nf* **1** TISSU : material, fabric **2** : substance, stuff <l'étoffe d'un héros : the stuff heroes are made of> <avoir l'étoffe de : to have the makings of>
étoffer |etɔfe| *vt* : to flesh out, to give substance to — **s'étoffer** *vr* : to fill out
étoile |etwal| *nf* **1** : star (in astronomy) <étoile filante : shooting star> <étoile polaire : North Star> **2** : star (of movies, sports, etc.) **3** : starlike object <général à quatre étoiles : four-star general> <en étoile : star-shaped> **4 à la belle étoile** : outdoors, under the stars **5 étoile de mer** : starfish
étoilé, -lée |etwale| *adj* : starry
étole |etɔl| *nf* : stole
étonnant, -nante |etɔnɑ̃, -nɑ̃t| *adj* : surprising, astonishing, amazing — **étonnamment** |-namɑ̃| *adv*
étonné, -née |etɔne| *adj* : surprised, astonished, amazed
étonnement |etɔnmɑ̃| *nm* : surprise, astonishment
étonner |etɔne| *vt* : to surprise, to astonish, to amaze — **s'étonner** *vr*
étouffant, -fante |etufɑ̃, -fɑ̃t| *adj* : stifling
étouffée |etufe| *nf* **à l'étouffée** : braised, steamed
étouffement |etufmɑ̃| *nm* **1** RÉPRESSION : suppression **2** ASPHYXIE : suffocation, asphyxiation
étouffer |etufe| *vt* **1** RÉPRIMER : to stifle, to suppress **2** ASPHYXIER : to suffocate, to smother **3** : to muffle <étouffer ses pas : to muffle one's footsteps> **4** : to hush up — **s'étouffer** *vr* **1** : to choke **2** : to suffocate
étourderie |eturdəri| *nf* **1** : careless mistake **2** : carelessness, thoughtlessness
étourdi[1], **-die** |eturdi| *adj* : absent-minded, scatterbrained
étourdi[2], **-die** *n* : scatterbrain
étourdir |eturdir| *vt* **1** ASSOMMER : to stun, to daze **2** GRISER : to make dizzy, to overpower <les louanges l'étourdissaient : the praise was going to his head> — **s'étourdir** *vr* : to lose oneself <s'étourdir de paroles : to get drunk on words>
étourdissant, -sante |eturdisɑ̃, -sɑ̃t| *adj* **1** : deafening **2** : stunning, exhilarating
étourdissement |eturdismɑ̃| *nm* **1** VERTIGE : dizziness **2** GRISERIE : exhilaration
étourneau |eturno| *nm, pl* **-neaux** |-no| : starling
étrange |etrɑ̃ʒ| *adj* : strange — **étrangement** |etrɑ̃ʒmɑ̃| *adv*
étranger[1], **-gère** |etrɑ̃ʒe, -ʒɛr| *adj* **1** : foreign **2** : strange, unfamiliar
étranger[2], **-gère** *n* **1** : foreigner **2** : stranger **3 à l'étranger** : abroad
étrangeté |etrɑ̃ʒte| *nf* : strangeness, oddity
étranglement |etrɑ̃gləmɑ̃| *nm* **1** : strangulation **2** : narrowing, constriction
étrangler |etrɑ̃gle| *vt* **1** : to strangle **2** : to constrict — **s'étrangler** *vr* : to choke
étrangleur, -gleuse |etrɑ̃glœr, -gløz| *n* : strangler
être[1] |ɛtr| {38} *vi* **1** : to be <il est mon frère : he is my brother> <Denise est belle : Denise is pretty> <sois sage! : be good!> <nous sommes à Paris : we're in Paris> **2** : to exist, to live <être ou ne pas être : to be or not to

be> **3** (*used with expressions of time, date, season*) <nous sommes le 15 mai : it is May 15th> <il est 10 heures : it is 10 o'clock> **4** (*used in formal expressions*) <il est des moments pareils : there are such moments> <il était une fois : once upon a time> **5 ~ à** : to belong to <ce livre est à moi : this book is mine> **6** (*indicating a state of action*) <j'étais à travailler : I was working> <tu es toujours à apprendre qqch : you're always learning sth> **7 soit . . . soit** : either . . . or — *v aux* **1** (*used in composite constructions*) <je serais partie : I would have left> <merci d'être venus! : thanks for coming!> **2** (*used in passive constructions*) <je suis passé te voir : I stopped by to see you> <elle a été blessée : she was injured> <il est né en 1938 : he was born in 1938> **3** (*used with an infinitive to indicate obligation*) <c'est un film à voir : it's a film you must see> <ses avis sont à entendre : her opinions should be heard>

être[2] *nm* **1** : organism, being <être humain : human being> **2** : person <un être cher : a loved one> **3** : soul, heart, being <au fond de mon être : deep in my heart>

étreindre |etrɛ̃dr| {37} *vt* **1** : to embrace, to hug **2** : to grip, to seize — **s'étreindre** *vr* : to embrace each other

étreinte |etrɛ̃t| *nf* **1** : embrace, hug **2** : grip, grasp <sous l'étreinte de la misère : in the grip of poverty>

étrenner |etrene| *vt* : to use for the first time

étrennes |etrɛn| *nfpl* : Christmas or New Year's present

étrier |etrije| *nm* : stirrup

étriller |etrije| *vt* **1** : to curry, to brush **2** : to criticize harshly, to pan

étriper |etripe| *vt* **1** : to gut, to disembowel **2** *fam* : to slaughter, to tear into (a person) — **s'étriper** *vr fam* : to tear each other to pieces

étriqué, -quée |etrike| *adj* **1** : skimpy, tight **2** : narrow, petty

étroit, étroite |etrwa, etrwat| *adj* **1** : narrow **2** ÉTRIQUÉ : tight **3** RIGOUREUX : strict **4** INTIME : close <étroite collaboration : close collaboration> **5 à l'étroit** : cramped

étroitement |etrwatmɑ̃| *adv* **1** : tightly, closely **2** : strictly

étroitesse |etrwatɛs| *nf* **1** : narrowness **2 étroitesse d'esprit** : narrow-mindedness

étude |etyd| *nf* **1** : study, studying <l'étude de la médecine : the study of medicine> <faire des études : to study> **2** : study, (research) paper **3** BUREAU : office **4** CLIENTÈLE : (professional) practice **5** : consideration <mettre à l'étude : to take under consideration> **6** : étude (in music)

étudiant, -diante |etydjɑ̃, -djɑ̃t| *adj & n* : student

étudié, -diée |etydje| *adj* **1** : carefully designed **2** AFFECTÉ : studied, affected

étudier |etydje| {96} *vt* **1** : to study, to learn **2** : to consider **3** : to devise, to design — *vi* : to study

étui |etɥi| *nm* : case <étui à lunettes : glasses case> <étui de révolver : holster>

étuve |etyv| *nf* **1** : steam room **2** : sterilizer

étymologie |etimɔlɔʒi| *nf* : etymology

étymologique |etimɔlɔʒik| *adj* : etymological — **étymologiquement** |-ʒikmɑ̃| *adv*

eu |ø| *pp* → **avoir**

eucalyptus |økaliptys| *nms & pl* : eucalyptus

Eucharistie |økaristi| *nf* : Eucharist

eunuque |ønyk| *nm* : eunuch

euphémique |øfemik| *adj* : euphemistic — **euphémiquement** |-mikmɑ̃| *adv*

euphémisme |øfemism| *nm* : euphemism

euphonie |øfɔni| *nf* : euphony

euphorie |øfɔri| *nf* : euphoria

euphorique |øfɔrik| *adj* : euphoric

eurasien, -sienne |ørazjɛ̃, -zjɛn| *adj* : Eurasian

Eurasien, -sienne *n* : Eurasian

euro |øro| *nm* : euro (monetary unit)

européen, -péenne |ørɔpeɛ̃, -peɛn| *adj* : European

Européen, -péenne *n* : European

eut |ø|, *etc.* → **avoir**

euthanasie |øtanazi| *nf* : euthanasia

eux |ø| *pron* : they, them <ce sont eux : they're the ones> <sans eux : without them> <eux deux : both of them>

eux–mêmes |ømɛm| *pron* : themselves

évacuation |evakɥasjɔ̃| *nf* **1** : evacuation **2** : draining, discharge

évacuer |evakɥe| *vt* **1** : to evacuate, to clear out **2** : to drain, to discharge

évadé, -dée |evade| *n* : fugitive, escapee

évader |evade| *v* **s'évader** *vr* : to escape

évaluateur, -trice |evalɥatœr, -tris| *n Can* : appraiser

évaluation |evalɥasjɔ̃| *nf* : evaluation, assessment, appraisal

évaluer |evalɥe| *vt* : to evaluate, to assess, to appraise

évangélique |evɑ̃ʒelik| *adj* : evangelical

évangéliste |evɑ̃ʒelist| *nm* **1** : Evangelist **2** : evangelist, preacher

évangile |evɑ̃ʒil| *nm* **1** : gospel **2 l'Évangile** : the Gospel

évanouir |evanwir| *v* **s'évanouir** *vr* **1** : to faint **2** DISPARAÎTRE : to vanish, to disappear

évanouissement |evanwismɑ̃| *nm* **1** : fainting, faint **2** DISPARITION : vanishing, disappearance

évaporation [evapɔrasjɔ̃] *nf* : evaporation
évaporé, -rée [evapɔre] *adj* : giddy, scatterbrained
évaporer [evapɔre] *v* **s'évaporer** *vr* **1** : to evaporate **2** *fam* : to vanish, to disappear
évasé, -sée [evaze] *adj* : flared, bell-shaped
évaser [evaze] *vt* : to widen, to flare — **s'évaser** *vr*
évasif, -sive [evazif, -ziv] *adj* : evasive — **évasivement** [-zivmɑ̃] *adv*
évasion [evazjɔ̃] *nf* **1** : escape **2 évasion fiscale** : tax evasion
évêché [eveʃe] *nm* : bishopric
éveil [evɛj] *nm* **1** : awakening **2 donner l'éveil** : to arouse suspicions **3 en ~** : on the alert
éveillé, -lée [eveje] *adj* **1** : awake **2** : bright, alert
éveiller [eveje] *vt* **1** RÉVEILLER : to awaken **2** STIMULER : to stimulate, to arouse (curiosity, suspicion, etc.) — **s'éveiller** *vr*
événement [evɛnmɑ̃] *nm* : event
éventail [evɑ̃taj] *nm* **1** : fan **2** : range, spread
éventaire [evɑ̃tɛr] *nm* : stall, stand
éventé, -tée [evɑ̃te] *adj* **1** : stale, flat **2** : exposed to the wind, breezy
éventer [evɑ̃te] *vt* **1** : to air (out) **2** : to fan **3** : to find out, to discover — **s'éventer** *vr* **1** : to fan oneself **2** : to go stale, to go flat
éventrer [evɑ̃tre] *vt* **1** : to disembowel **2** : to gore **3** : to tear open
éventualité [evɑ̃tɥalite] *nf* : eventuality, possibility
éventuel, -tuelle [evɑ̃tɥɛl] *adj* : possible — **éventuellement** [-tɥɛlmɑ̃] *adv*
évêque [evɛk] *nm* : bishop
évertuer [evɛrtɥe] *v* **s'évertuer** *vr* : to strive, to try one's best
éviction [eviksjɔ̃] *nf* **1** : eviction **2** : expulsion, ousting
évidemment [evidamɑ̃] *adv* : obviously, of course
évidence [evidɑ̃s] *nf* **1** : obviousness, clearness <de toute évidence : obviously> **2 mettre en évidence** : to display, to highlight **3 se mettre en évidence** : to come to the fore
évident, -dente [evidɑ̃, -dɑ̃t] *adj* : obvious, evident
évider [evide] *vt* : to hollow out, to scoop out
évier [evje] *nm* : (kitchen) sink
évincer [evɛ̃se] {6} *vt* **1** : to oust **2** : to evict
évitable [evitabl] *adj* : avoidable
éviter [evite] *vt* **1** : to avoid **2** : to dodge, to evade
évocateur, -trice [evɔkatœr, -tris] *adj* : evocative, suggestive
évocation [evɔkasjɔ̃] *nf* : evocation
évolué, -luée [evɔlɥe] *adj* : highly developed, advanced
évoluer [evɔlɥe] *vi* **1** : to evolve, to develop **2** : to maneuver, to move about
évolutif, -tive [evɔlytif, -tiv] *adj* : developing, progressive
évolution [evɔlysjɔ̃] *nf* **1** : evolution (in biology) **2** : development, advancement, change
évoquer [evɔke] *vt* **1** : to recall **2** : to mention **3** : to evoke, to conjure up
exacerber [ɛgzasɛrbe] *vt* : to exacerbate
exact, exacte [ɛgzakt] *adj* **1** PRÉCIS : exact, precise **2** JUSTE : accurate, correct <c'est exact : that's right> **3** PONCTUEL : punctual
exactement [ɛgzaktəmɑ̃] *adv* : exactly, precisely
exaction [ɛgzaksjɔ̃] *nf* : exaction, extortion
exactitude [ɛgzaktityd] *nf* **1** : exactness, accuracy **2** PONCTUALITÉ : punctuality
ex æquo [ɛgzeko] *adv* : equal, equally placed <ex æquo à la première place : tied for first place>
exagération [ɛgzaʒerasjɔ̃] *nf* : exaggeration
exagéré, -rée [ɛgzaʒere] *adj* : exaggerated, excessive — **exagérément** [-remɑ̃] *adv*
exagérer [ɛgzaʒere] {87} *vt* : to exaggerate — *vi* : to go too far, to overdo it
exaltant, -tante [ɛgzaltɑ̃, -tɑ̃t] *adj* : exciting, stirring
exaltation [ɛgzaltasjɔ̃] *nf* **1** GLORIFICATION : exalting, extolling **2** EXCITATION : excitement, enthusiasm
exalté, -tée [ɛgzalte] *adj* : excited, inflamed, hotheaded
exalter [ɛgzalte] *vt* **1** GLORIFIER : to exalt, to extol **2** EXCITER : to excite, to thrill — **s'exalter** *vr* : to get excited
examen [ɛgzamɛ̃] *nm* : examination <réussir à un examen : to pass an exam>
examinateur, -trice [ɛgzaminatœr, -tris] *n* : examiner
examiner [ɛgzamine] *vt* **1** : to examine **2** PESER : to consider — **s'examiner** *vr*
exaspération [ɛgzasperasjɔ̃] *nf* : exasperation
exaspérer [ɛgzaspere] {87} *vt* **1** IRRITER : to exasperate, to infuriate **2** AGGRAVER : to aggravate, to make worse — **s'exaspérer** *vr*
exaucer [ɛgzose] {6} *vt* : to fulfill, to grant
excavateur [ɛkskavatœr] *nm* : excavator, steam shovel
excavation [ɛkskavasjɔ̃] *nf* : excavation
excavatrice [ɛkskavatris] *nf* : excavator, steam shovel
excaver [ɛkskave] *vt* : to excavate
excédent [ɛksedɑ̃] *nm* : surplus, excess <excédent commercial : trade sur-

plus> <excédent de bagages : excess baggage>

excédentaire |ɛksedɑ̃tɛr| *adj* : surplus, excess

excéder |ɛksede| {87} *vt* **1** DÉPASSER : to exceed **2** EXASPÉRER : to exasperate, to infuriate

excellence |ɛkselɑ̃s| *nf* **1** : excellence **2** : excellency <Votre Excellence : Your Excellency>

excellent, -lente |ɛkselɑ̃, -lɑ̃t| *adj* : excellent

exceller |ɛksele| *vi* : to excel

excentricité |ɛksɑ̃trisite| *nf* **1** : eccentricity **2** : remoteness

excentrique[1] |ɛksɑ̃trik| *adj* **1** : eccentric, odd **2** : remote, outlying

excentrique[2] *nmf* : eccentric

excentriquement |ɛksɑ̃trikmɑ̃| *adv* : eccentrically

excepté |ɛksɛpte| *prep* SAUF : except, apart from

excepter |ɛksɛpte| *vt* : to except, to exclude

exception |ɛksɛpsjɔ̃| *nf* **1** : exception **2 à l'exception de** : except for, with the exception of **3 d'**∼ : exceptional, special

exceptionnel, -nelle |ɛksɛpsjɔnɛl| *adj* : exceptional, special

exceptionnellement |ɛksɛpsjɔnɛlmɑ̃| *adv* **1** : exceptionally, extremely **2** : by way of exception, in this instance

excès |ɛksɛ| *nm* **1** : excess <sans excès : in moderation> **2 à l'excès** : to excess, excessively **3 excès de vitesse** : speeding

excessif, -sive |ɛksɛsif, -siv| *adj* : excessive — **excessivement** |-sivmɑ̃| *adv*

exciser |ɛksize| *vt* : to excise, to cut out

excision |ɛksizjɔ̃| *nf* : excision

excitable |ɛksitabl| *adj* **1** : irritable, edgy **2** : excitable (in physiology)

excitant[1], **-tante** |ɛksitɑ̃, -tɑ̃t| *adj* : exciting, stimulating

excitant[2] *nm* : stimulant

excitation |ɛksitasjɔ̃| *nf* : excitement, arousal

excité[1], **-tée** |ɛksite| *adj* : excited

excité[2], **-tée** *n* : hothead

exciter |ɛksite| *vt* **1** ENTHOUSIASMER : to excite, to thrill **2** STIMULER : to stimulate, to arouse **3** INCITER : to incite, to stir up — **s'exciter** *vr* : to get excited

exclamatif, -tive |ɛksklamatif, -tiv| *adj* : exclamatory

exclamation |ɛksklamasjɔ̃| *nf* : exclamation

exclamer |ɛksklame| *v* **s'exclamer** *vr* : to exclaim

exclu, -clue |ɛkskly| *adj* **1** : excluded **2 il n'est pas exclu que** : it is not impossible that

exclure |ɛksklyr| {39} *vt* **1** EXPULSER : to expel **2** EXCEPTER : to exclude, to rule out — **s'exclure** *vr*

exclusif, -sive |ɛksklyzif, -ziv| *adj* **1** : exclusive **2** : sole — **exclusivement** |-sivmɑ̃| *adv*

exclusion |ɛksklyzjɔ̃| *nf* **1** : expulsion **2** : exclusion **3 à l'exclusion de** : with the exception of, except for

exclusivité |ɛksklyzivite| *nf* **1** : exclusive rights *pl* **2** : exclusive object, product, etc. **3 en** ∼ : exclusively

excommunier |ɛkskɔmynje| {96} *vt* : to excommunicate

excréments |ɛkskremɑ̃| *nmpl* : excrement, feces

excréter |ɛkskrete| {87} *vt* : to excrete

excrétion |ɛkskresjɔ̃| *nf* : excretion

excroissance |ɛkskrwasɑ̃s| *nf* : outgrowth, excrescence

excursion |ɛkskyrsjɔ̃| *nf* : excursion, trip <faire une excursion : to go on a trip>

excursionniste |ɛkskyrsjɔnist| *nmf* : vacationer, tourist

excusable |ɛkskyzabl| *adj* : excusable

excuse |ɛkskyz| *nf* **1** : excuse **2** : apology <présenter des excuses : to apologize>

excuser |ɛkskyze| *vt* **1** PARDONNER : to forgive, to pardon <excusez-moi : I'm sorry, forgive me> **2** JUSTIFIER : to justify **3** : to excuse <se faire excuser : to ask to be excused> — **s'excuser** *vr* : to apologize <je m'excuse : I apologize>

exécrable |ɛgzekrabl| *adj* : atrocious, awful

exécrer |ɛgzekre| {87} *vt* : to abhor, to loathe

exécutant, -tante |ɛgzekytɑ̃, -tɑ̃t| *n* : performer

exécuter |ɛgzekyte| *vt* **1** : to execute, to carry out **2** : to perform (music, etc.) **3** : to execute, to put to death — **s'exécuter** *vr* : to comply

exécuteur[1], **-trice** |ɛgzekytœr, -tris| *n* **exécuteur testamentaire** : executor (of a will)

exécuteur[2] *nm* : executioner

exécutif[1], **-tive** |ɛgzekytif, -tiv| *adj* : executive

exécutif[2] *nm* **l'exécutif** : executive power (of government)

exécution |ɛgzekysjɔ̃| *nf* **1** : execution, performance <mettre à exécution : to carry out> **2** : execution, putting to death

exécutoire |ɛgzekytwar| *adj* : enforceable, binding

exemplaire[1] |ɛgzɑ̃plɛr| *adj* : exemplary

exemplaire[2] *nm* **1** : copy **2** : specimen, example

exemple |ɛgzɑ̃pl| *nm* **1** : example <pour l'exemple : as an example> <donner l'exemple : to set an example> **2 par** ∼ : for example, for instance

exemplifier |ɛgzɑ̃plifje| {96} *vt* : to exemplify

exempt, exempte [ɛgzɑ̃, ɛgzɑ̃t] *adj* : exempt <exempt de taxes : tax-exempt>

exempter [ɛgzɑ̃te] *vt* : to exempt

exemption [ɛgzɑ̃psjɔ̃] *nf* : exemption

exercé, -cée [ɛgzɛrse] *adj* : trained, experienced

exercer [ɛgzɛrse] {6} *vt* **1** : to exercise, to train **2** : to exert (control, influence, etc.) **3** : to practice (a profession) — *vi* : to practice, to be in practice — **s'exercer** *vr*

exercice [ɛgzɛrsis] *nm* **1** : (physical or mental) exercise **2** : practice <en exercice : in office, in practice> **3** : exercising, carrying out **4 exercice budgétaire** : fiscal year

exerciseur [ɛgzɛrsizœr] *nm* : exercise machine

exergue [ɛgzɛrg] *nm* **1** : inscription, epigraph **2 mettre en exergue** : to highlight, to emphasize

exhalaison [ɛgzalɛzɔ̃] *nf* : odor, fume

exhaler [ɛgzale] *vt* **1** : to exhale (breath) **2** : to give off, to emit **3** : to utter, to give vent to

exhausser [ɛgzose] *vt* : to raise (up)

exhaustif, -tive [ɛgzostif, -tiv] *adj* : exhaustive

exhiber [ɛgzibe] *vt* **1** : to show, to exhibit **2** : to show off, to flaunt — **s'exhiber** *vr* : to make an exhibition of

exhibition [ɛgzibisjɔ̃] *nf* **1** : display, exhibition **2** : presentation **3** : flaunting

exhibitionnisme [ɛgzibisjɔnism] *nm* : exhibitionism

exhibitionniste [ɛgzibisjɔnist] *nmf* : exhibitionist

exhortation [ɛgzɔrtasjɔ̃] *nf* : exhortation

exhorter [ɛgzɔrte] *vt* : to exhort, to urge

exhumer [ɛgzyme] *vt* : to exhume, to dig up

exigeant, -geante [ɛgziʒɑ̃, -ʒɑ̃t] *adj* : demanding

exigence [ɛgziʒɑ̃s] *nf* : demand, requirement

exiger [ɛgziʒe] {17} *vt* : to demand, to require

exigu, -guë [ɛgzigy] *adj* : cramped, tiny

exiguïté [ɛgziguite] *nf* : smallness, narrowness

exil [ɛgzil] *nm* : exile <en exil : in exile>

exilé, -lée [ɛgzile] *n* : exile

exiler [ɛgzile] *vt* : to exile — **s'exiler** *vr* : to go into exile, to isolate oneself

existant, -tante [ɛgzistɑ̃, -tɑ̃t] *adj* : existing, extant

existence [ɛgzistɑ̃s] *nf* : existence

existentialisme [ɛgzistɑ̃sjalism] *nm* : existentialism

existentiel, -tielle [ɛgzistɑ̃sjɛl] *adj* : existential

exister [ɛgziste] *vi* : to exist

exode [ɛgzɔd] *nm* : exodus

exonération [ɛgzɔnerasjɔ̃] *nf* : exemption <exonération d'impôts : tax exemption>

exonérer [ɛgzɔnere] {87} *vt* EXEMPTER : to exempt

exorbitant, -tante [ɛgzɔrbitɑ̃, -tɑ̃t] *adj* : exorbitant

exorbité, -tée [ɛgzɔrbite] *adj* : bulging

exorciser [ɛgzɔrsize] *vt* : to exorcize — **exorcisme** [-zɔrsism] *nm*

exotique [ɛgzɔtik] *adj* : exotic

expansif, -sive [ɛkspɑ̃sif, -siv] *adj* : expansive, outgoing

expansion [ɛkspɑ̃sjɔ̃] *nf* : expansion

expansivité [ɛkspɑ̃sivite] *nf* : expansiveness

expatrié, -triée [ɛkspatrije] *adj & n* : expatriate

expatrier [ɛkspatrije] {96} *vt* : to expatriate, to deport — **s'expatrier** *vr* : to emigrate

expectative [ɛkspɛktativ] *nf* : expectation <être dans l'expectative : to be waiting to see>

expectorant[1], -rante [ɛkspɛktɔrɑ̃, -rɑ̃t] *adj* : expectorant <sirop expectorant : expectorant cough syrup>

expectorant[2] *nm* : expectorant

expédient[1], -diente [ɛkspedjɑ̃, -djɑ̃t] *adj* : expedient

expédient[2] *nm* : expedient <vivre d'expédients : to live by one's wits>

expédier [ɛkspedje] {96} *vt* **1** : to dispatch, to send **2** : to send (someone) off **3** : to deal with, to make short work of

expéditeur, -trice [ɛkspeditœr, -tris] *n* : sender, forwarder

expéditif, -tive [ɛkspeditif, -tiv] *adj* : expeditious, quick

expédition [ɛkspedisjɔ̃] *nf* **1** ENVOI : sending, dispatching **2** : shipment **3** : expedition

expérience [ɛksperjɑ̃s] *nf* **1** PRATIQUE : experience, practice **2** ESSAI : experiment

expérimental, -tale [ɛksperimɑ̃tal] *adj, mpl* **-taux** [-to] : experimental — **expérimentalement** [-talmɑ̃] *adv*

expérimentation [ɛksperimɑ̃tasjɔ̃] *nf* : experimentation

expérimenté, -tée [ɛksperimɑ̃te] *adj* : experienced

expérimenter [ɛksperimɑ̃te] *vt* **1** ESSAYER : to test **2** ÉPROUVER : to experience — *vi* : to experiment

expert, -perte [ɛkspɛr, -pɛrt] *adj & n* : expert — **expertement** [-pɛrtəmɑ̃] *adv*

expert–comptable [ɛkspɛrkɔ̃tabl] *nm, pl* **experts–comptables** : certified public accountant

expertise [ɛkspɛrtiz] *nf* **1** : expertise **2** : expert evaluation, appraisal

expertiser [ɛkspɛrtize] *vt* : to appraise, to assess

expiation [ɛkspjasjɔ̃] *nf* : atonement

expier |ɛkspje| {96} *vt* : to expiate, to atone for
expiration |ɛkspirasjɔ̃| *nf* **1** ÉCHÉANCE : expiration <venir à expiration : to expire> **2** : exhalation, breathing out
expirer |ɛkspire| *vi* **1** EXHALER : to exhale **2** : to expire <un bail qui expire le 30 juin : a lease which expires on June 30> — *vt* : to breathe out (air), to exhale
explicable |ɛksplikabl| *adj* : explicable
explicatif, -tive |ɛksplikatif, -tiv| *adj* : explanatory, illustrative
explication |ɛksplikasjɔ̃| *nf* **1** : explanation **2 explication de texte** : literary criticism
explicite |ɛksplisit| *adj* : explicit — **explicitement** |-sitmɑ̃| *adv*
expliciter |ɛksplisite| *vt* : to make explicit
expliquer |ɛksplike| *vt* : to explain — **s'expliquer** *vr* **1** : to explain oneself **2** : to understand <je m'explique mal sa réussite : I can't understand his success>
exploit |ɛksplwa| *nm* : exploit, feat
exploitable |ɛksplwatabl| *adj* : exploitable <exploitable par machine : machine-readable>
exploitant, -tante |ɛksplwatɑ̃, -tɑ̃t| *n* **1** : farmer **2** : manager of a movie theater
exploitation |ɛksplwatasjɔ̃| *nf* **1** : exploitation, utilizing **2** : running, operating, management **3 exploitation agricole** : farm
exploiter |ɛksplwate| *vt* **1** : to exploit **2** : to run, to operate, to manage
explorateur, -trice |ɛksplɔratœr, -tris| *n* : explorer
exploration |ɛksplɔrasjɔ̃| *nf* : exploration
exploratoire |ɛksplɔratwar| *adj* : exploratory
explorer |ɛksplɔre| *vt* : to explore
exploser |ɛksploze| *vi* **1** : to explode <faire exploser : to detonate, to blow up> **2** : to burst out, to flare up (with anger, etc.)
explosif[1], -sive |ɛksplozif, -ziv| *adj* : explosive
explosif[2] *nm* : explosive
explosion |ɛksplozjɔ̃| *nf* **1** : explosion **2** : outburst
exportateur[1], -trice |ɛkspɔrtatœr, -tris| *adj* : export, exporting
exportateur[2], -trice *n* : exporter
exportation |ɛkspɔrtasjɔ̃| *nf* : export, exportation
exporter |ɛkspɔrte| *vt* : to export
exposant[1], -sante |ɛkspozɑ̃, -zɑ̃t| *n* : exhibitor
exposant[2] *nm* : exponent
exposé[1], -sée |ɛkspoze| *adj* : exposed, oriented <exposé au nord : facing north>
exposé[2] *nm* **1** : lecture, talk **2** : account, report <un exposé des faits : an account of the facts>
exposer |ɛkspoze| *vt* **1** PRÉSENTER : to display, to exhibit **2** EXPLIQUER : to explain, to set out **3** ORIENTER : to orient, to set facing **4** : to endanger <exposer sa vie : to risk one's life> — **s'exposer** *vr* : to expose oneself (to the sun, to criticism, etc.)
exposition |ɛkspozisjɔ̃| *nf* **1** : display, exhibition <exposition d'art : art exhibition> **2** PRÉSENTATION : exposition, presentation (of facts, etc.) **3** : exposition (in literature or music) **4** : exposure **5** : orientation, aspect
exprès[1] |ɛksprɛ| *adv* **1** : on purpose, intentionally **2** SPÉCIALEMENT : specially, especially <une robe fabriquée exprès pour moi : a dress made specially for me>
exprès[2], -presse |ɛksprɛs| *adj* FORMEL : express, strict <défense expresse de nager : swimming strictly forbidden>
exprès[3] *adj* : special-delivery <lettre exprès : special-delivery letter> <envoyer en exprès : to send (as) special-delivery>
express[1] |ɛksprɛs| *adj* **1** : express <autobus express : express bus> **2** : espresso
express[2] *nms & pl* **1** : express **2** : espresso
expressément |ɛksprɛsemɑ̃| *adv* **1** : expressly, explicitly **2** : specially
expressif, -sive |ɛksprɛsif, -siv| *adj* : expressive
expression |ɛksprɛsjɔ̃| *nf* : expression <expression toute faite : set phrase, cliché> <sans expression : expressionless>
expressivité |ɛksprɛsivite| *nf* : expressiveness
exprimer |ɛksprime| *vt* **1** : to express **2** EXTRAIRE : to squeeze, to extract (juice, etc.) — **s'exprimer** *vr* : to express oneself
exproprier |ɛksprɔprije| {96} *vt* : to expropriate — **expropriation** |-prijasjɔ̃| *nf*
expulser |ɛkspylse| *vt* : to expel, to evict
expulsion |ɛkspylsjɔ̃| *nf* : expulsion, eviction, ouster
expurger |ɛkspyrʒe| {17} *vt* : to expurgate
exquis, -quise |ɛkski, -kiz| *adj* : exquisite, delightful
exsangue |ɛksɑ̃g| *adj* **1** : bloodless **2** : ashen, deathly pale
exsuder |ɛksyde| *v* : to exude
extase |ɛkstaz| *nf* : ecstasy
extasié, -siée |ɛkstazje| *adj* : rapturous, ecstatic
extasier |ɛkstazje| {96} *v* **s'extasier** *vr* : to be in ecstasy
extatique |ɛkstatik| *adj* : ecstatic, enraptured

extensible [ɛkstɑ̃sibl] *adj* : extendable, tensile

extensif, -sive [ɛkstɑ̃sif, -siv] *adj* **1** : extensive **2** : wider, extended <dans son sens extensif : in its extended sense>

extension [ɛkstɑ̃sjɔ̃] *nf* **1** : stretching (of a muscle, etc.) **2** : extension, expansion

exténuant, -ante [ɛkstenɥɑ, -ɥɑ̃t] *adj* : exhausting

exténuer [ɛkstenɥe] *vt* : to exhaust, to tire out

extérieur[1], **-rieure** [ɛksterjœr] *adj* **1** : exterior, external, outside <activités extérieures : outside activities> **2** : outward, apparent <signes extérieurs : outward signs> **3** : foreign <commerce extérieur : foreign trade>

extérieur[2] *nm* **1** : exterior, outside **2 à l'extérieur** : abroad **3 match à l'extérieur** : away game

extérieurement [ɛksterjœrmɑ̃] *adv* **1** : externally **2** : outwardly

extérioriser [ɛksterjɔrize] *vt* : to show, to express (one's feelings, etc.) — **s'extérioriser** *vr* : to express oneself

exterminateur, -trice [ɛkstɛrminatœr, -tris] *n* : exterminator

extermination [ɛkstɛrminasjɔ̃] *nf* : extermination

exterminer [ɛkstɛrmine] *vt* : to exterminate, to wipe out — **s'exterminer** *fam* : to knock oneself out (doing something)

externat [ɛkstɛrna] *nm* : day school

externe[1] [ɛkstɛrn] *adj* : external

externe[2] *nmf* : day student

extincteur [ɛkstɛ̃ktœr] *nm* : fire extinguisher

extinction [ɛkstɛ̃ksjɔ̃] *nf* **1** : extinction **2** : extinguishing **3 extinction de voix** : loss of voice

extirper [ɛkstirpe] *vt* **1** : to uproot (a plant) **2** : to root out, to eradicate

extorquer [ɛkstɔrke] *vt* : to extort

extorsion [ɛkstɔrsjɔ̃] *nf* : extortion

extra[1] [ɛkstra] *adj* **1** : first-rate, top-quality **2** *fam* : great, fantastic

extra[2] *nms & pl* **1** : extra person **2** : extra thing or amount **3 un petit extra** : a little extra, a treat

extraconjugal, -gale [ɛkstrakɔ̃ʒygal] *adj, pl* **-gaux** [-go] : extramarital

extraction [ɛstraksjɔ̃] *nf* : extraction

extrader [ɛkstrade] *vt* : to extradite — **extradition** [-stradisjɔ̃] *nf*

extraire [ɛkstrɛr] {40} *vt* **1** : to extract **2** : to excerpt — **s'extraire** *vr* : to extricate oneself

extrait [ɛkstrɛ] *nm* **1** : extract **2** : excerpt **3** : certificate, certified copy <extrait de naissance : birth certificate>

extraordinaire [ɛkstraɔrdinɛr] *adj* **1** : extraordinary **2 par ~** : by some unlikely chance

extraordinairement [ɛkstraɔrdinɛrmɑ̃] *adv* : extraordinarily, amazingly

extrapoler [ɛkstrapɔle] *vt* : to extrapolate — **extrapolation** [-pɔlasjɔ̃] *nf*

extrasensoriel, -rielle [ɛkstrasɑ̃sɔrjɛl] *adj* : extrasensory

extraterrestre [ɛkstratɛrɛstr] *adj & nmf* : extraterrestrial

extravagant, -gante [ɛkstravagɑ̃, -gɑ̃t] *adj* : extravagant — **extravagance** [-vagɑ̃s] *nf*

extraverti[1], **-tie** [ɛkstravɛrti] *adj* : extroverted

extraverti[2], **-tie** *n* : extrovert

extrême[1] [ɛkstrɛm] *adj* **1** : far, farthest, extreme <à l'extrême limite : to the farthest point> <l'extrême droite : the far right> **2** : extreme, great <avec extrême difficulté : with very great difficulty> **3** : extreme, excessive <il fait une chaleur extrême : it's extremely hot>

extrême[2] *nm* : extreme <pousser à l'extrême : to take to extremes> <passer d'un extrême à l'autre : to go from one extreme to the other>

extrêmement [ɛkstrɛmmɑ̃] *adv* : extremely

extrême–onction [ɛkstrɛmɔ̃ksjɔ̃] *nf, pl* **extrêmes–onctions** : extreme unction

Extrême–Orient [ɛkstrɛmɔrjɑ̃] *nm* : Far East

extrémisme [ɛkstremism] *nm* : extremism — **extrémiste** [-tremist] *adj & nmf*

extrémité [ɛkstremite] *nf* **1** : extremity, end **2** : extreme (act) <pousser à des extrémités : to drive to extremes> **3** : plight, straits *pl* <à la dernière extrémité : at the point of death> **4 extrémités** *nfpl* : extremities (in anatomy)

extruder [ɛkstryde] *vt* : extrude

exubérant, -rante [ɛgzyberɑ̃, -rɑ̃t] *adj* : exuberant — **exubérance** [-berɑ̃s] *nf*

exulter [ɛgzylte] *vi* : to exult — **exultation** [ɛgzyltasjɔ̃] *nf*

exutoire [ɛgzytwar] *nm* : outlet, release

ex–voto [ɛksvɔto] *nm* : commemorative plaque

F

f [ɛf] *nm* : f, the sixth letter of the alphabet

fable [fabl] *nf* **1** : fable **2** MENSONGE : story, lie

fabricant, -cante [fabrikɑ̃, -kɑ̃t] *n* : manufacturer

fabrication [fabrikasjɔ̃] *nf* : manufacture, making <de fabrication artisanale : handmade>

fabrique [fabrik] *nf* **1** USINE : factory, mill **2 marque de fabrique** : trademark

fabriquer [fabrike] *vt* **1** : to make, to manufacture **2** : to fabricate (a story), to forge (documents, money, etc.)

fabulation [fabylasjɔ̃] *nf* : fabrication, lie

fabuleusement [fabyløzmɑ̃] *adv* : fabulously

fabuleux, -leuse [fabylø, -løz] *adj* **1** EXTRAORDINAIRE : fabulous, extraordinary **2** : mythical

fac [fak] *nf France fam* : university

façade [fasad] *nf* **1** : facade, front **2** APPARENCE : appearance, pretense

face [fas] *nf* **1** VISAGE : face <face à face : face to face> **2** : side, facet <pile ou face : heads or tails> **3 de ∼** : from the front, head-on **4 d'en face** : facing, opposite **5 en ∼** : opposite, across the street, opposing **6 faire face à** : to face towards, to face up to **7 sauver la face** : to save face

facétie [fasesi] *nf* **1** : joke, witticism **2** FARCE : prank

facétieux, -tieuse [fasesjø, -sjøz] *adj* : mischievous, facetious — **facétieusement** [fasesjøzmɑ̃] *adv*

facette [fasɛt] *nf* : facet, aspect

fâché, -chée [faʃe] *adj* **1** : angry **2** DÉSOLÉ : sorry

fâcher [faʃe] *vt* : to anger — **se fâcher** *vr* : to get angry, to lose one's temper

fâcherie [faʃri] *nf* : quarrel, disagreement

fâcheux, -cheuse [faʃø, -ʃøz] *adj* **1** ENNUYEUX : annoying **2** REGRETTABLE : unfortunate — **fâcheusement** [-ʃøzmɑ̃] *adv*

facial, -ciale [fasjal] *adj, mpl* **faciaux** [fasjo] : facial

facile [fasil] *adj* **1** : easy **2** *or* **facile à vivre** : easygoing **3** : superficial, facile

facilement [fasilmɑ̃] *adv* : easily, readily

facilité [fasilite] *nf* **1** : easiness **2** MOYEN : means, opportunity **3** : aptitude **4 facilités de paiement** : easy terms (of payment)

faciliter [fasilite] *vt* : to facilitate, to make easier

façon [fasɔ̃] *nf* **1** : way, manner <de cette façon : in this way, thus> <façon de parler : manner of speaking> **2** : fashioning, making (of clothing, etc.) **3** : imitation <façon cuir : imitation leather> **4 façons** *nfpl* : behavior, manners <faire des façons : to put on airs> <sans façon : without a fuss, plain, simple> **5 de façon à** : so as to **6 de toute façon** : in any case **7 faire de la façon à qqn** *Can fam* : to be nice to s.o.

façonner [fasɔne] *vt* **1** : to shape, to fashion **2** FABRIQUER : to manufacture, to make

fac–similé [faksimile] *nm, pl* **fac–similés 1** REPRODUCTION : facsimile, copy **2** : fax

facteur[1], -trice [faktœr, -tris] *n* : letter carrier, mailman *m*

facteur[2] *nm* **1** : factor, element <le facteur chance : the element of chance> **2** : factor (in mathematics) **3** : builder, maker (of organs, pianos, etc.)

factice [faktis] *adj* : artificial, imitation, false

faction [faksjɔ̃] *nf* **1** : faction **2** : guard duty, watch

factionnaire [faksjɔnɛr] *nm* : sentry

factuel, -tuelle [faktɥɛl] *adj* : factual

facturation [faktyrasjɔ̃] *nf* : billing, invoicing

facture [faktyr] *nf* **1** : bill, invoice **2** : workmanship, technique

facturer [faktyre] *vt* : to bill, to invoice

facultatif, -tive [fakyltatif, -tiv] *adj* : optional

faculté [fakylte] *nf* **1** : faculty, ability **2** : right, option <la faculté de choisir : freedom of choice> **3** : faculty (of a college or university) **4** : department, school <faculté de droit : school of law>

fadaises [fadɛz] *nfpl* : drivel, nonsense

fade [fad] *adj* **1** : dull, drab **2** : tasteless, insipid

fadeur [fadœr] *nf* : blandness, dullness

fafiner [fafine] → **farfiner**

fagot [fago] *nm* : bundle of firewood

fagoté, -tée [fagɔte] *adj fam* : badly dressed, frumpy

Fahrenheit [farɛnajt] *adj* : Fahrenheit

faible[1] [fɛbl] *adj* **1** : weak, feeble <avoir la vue faible : to have weak eyes> <faible d'esprit : feebleminded> **2** : small, low <une faible quantité : a small quantity> <à faible revenu : low-income> **3** : faint, slight <un faible bruit : a faint sound> — **faiblement** [fɛbləmɑ̃] *adv*

faible[2] *nmf* : weak-willed person

faible[3] *nm* : weakness, partiality <avoir un faible pour : to have a soft spot for>

faiblesse [fɛblɛs] *nf* **1** : weakness, frailty **2** DÉFAUT : inadequacy, shortcoming **3** : faintness, dimness

faiblir [feblir] *vi* **1** : to weaken **2** DIMINUER : to diminish, to die down

faïence [fajɑ̃s] *nf* : earthenware

faille[1] [faj] → **falloir**

faille[2] [faj] *nf* **1** : fault (in geology) **2** : flaw, weakness

failli[1], **-lie** [faji] *adj* : bankrupt

failli[2], **-lie** *n* : bankrupt (person)

faillible [fajibl] *adj* : fallible

faillir [fajir] {41} *vi* : to fail <faillir à son devoir : to fail to do one's duty> — *vt* MANQUER : to barely escape, to narrowly miss <j'ai failli m'évanouir : I nearly fainted>

faillite [fajit] *nf* **1** ÉCHEC : failure **2** : bankruptcy <faire faillite : to go bankrupt>

faim [fɛ̃] *nf* : hunger <avoir faim : to be hungry> <mourir de faim : to be starving> <rester sur sa faim : to be disappointed>

fainéant[1], **fainéante** [feneɑ̃, -neɑ̃t] *adj* : lazy

fainéant[2], **fainéante** *n* : loafer, idler

fainéanter [feneɑ̃te] *vi* : to laze about, to bum around

faire [fɛr] {42} *vt* **1** : to do <que faites-vous comme métier? : what do you do for a living?> <elle fait ses études ici : she studies here> **2** : to make <tu fais une erreur : you're making a mistake> <faire savoir : to make known, to inform> **3** : to be <faire le difficile : to be fussy> <il fait soleil : it's sunny> **4** : to amount to, to measure <deux et deux font quatre : two plus two equals four> <la salle fait 7 mètres de long : the room is 7 meters long> **5** : to say <«eh bien,» fit-il : «well,» he said> **6 cela ne fait rien** : it doesn't matter **7 faire jeune** : to look young **8 faire mal à** : to hurt — **se faire** *vr* **1 ça ne se fait pas** : it's not done **2 s'en faire** : to worry, to be bothered **3 se faire à** : to get used to

faire–part [fɛrpar] *nms & pl* : announcement (of birth, death, marriage, etc.)

faire–valoir [fɛrvalwar] *nms & pl* : foil, straight man

faisable [fəzabl] *adj* : feasible — **faisabilité** [-zabilite] *nf*

faisait [fəzɛ], **faisions** [fəzjɔ̃], *etc.* → **faire**

faisan, -sane [fəzɑ̃] *n* : pheasant

faisandé, -dée [fəzɑ̃de] *adj* : gamy

faisceau [fɛso] *nm, pl* **faisceaux 1** : beam (of light) **2** : bundle

faiseur, -seuse [fəzœr, -zøz] *n* : maker, doer <faiseur d'intrigues : schemer>

fait[1], **faite** [fɛ, fɛt] *adj* **1** : made, done <bien fait : well done> **2** : ripe (of cheese) **3** : mature <un homme fait : a grown man> **4 tout fait** : ready-made

fait[2] *nm* **1** : fact **2** ACTE : act, deed **3** EXPLOIT : exploit, feat **4** ÉVÉNEMENT : event **5 au fait** : by the way, incidentally **6 au fait de** : informed about **7 comme de fait** *Can* : indeed **8 en fait de** : as regards

faîte [fɛt] *nm* **1** SOMMET : summit, top **2** APOGÉE : pinnacle <le faîte de la gloire : the height of glory>

fakir [fakir] *nm* : fakir

falaise [falɛz] *nf* : cliff

fallacieux, -cieuse [falasjø, -sjøz] *adj* CAPTIEUX : fallacious, misleading

falloir [falwar] {43} *v impers* **1** (*indicating a need*) <il faut partir : we must go> <il faut que je le fasse : I need to do it> **2** (*indicating an obligation*) <il fallait le faire : we had to do it> <j'y vais, il le faut : I'm going, I have to> <il fallait me le dire! : you should have said so!> **3** (*indicating a probability*) <il faut avoir été fou : he must have been out of his mind> **4 comme il faut** : proper, properly — **s'en falloir** *vr* **1 il s'en faut de peu** *or* **peu s'en faut** : very nearly, only just **2 il s'en faut de beaucoup** : (very) far from it

falot[1], **-lote** [falo, -lɔt] *adj* : colorless, insipid

falot[2] *nm* : lantern

falsification [falsifikasjɔ̃] *nf* : falsification, forgery, faking

falsifier [falsifje] {96} *vt* **1** : to falsify **2** : to adulterate

famé, -mée [fame] *adj* **mal famé** : disreputable

famélique [famelik] *adj* : half-starved, scrawny

fameusement [famøzmɑ̃] *adv fam* : really <c'est fameusement bien fait : it's really well done>

fameux, -meuse [famø, -møz] *adj* **1** CÉLÈBRE : famous **2** : excellent, first-rate **3** : real, remarkable <c'est un fameux mensonge : it's a whopping lie> **4 pas fameux** *fam* : not very good

familial, -liale [familjal] *adj, mpl* **-liaux** [-ljo] : family <revenu familial : family income>

familiale *nf* : station wagon

familiariser [familjarize] *vt* : to familiarize — **se familiariser** *vr*

familiarité [familjarite] *nf* **1** : familiarity **2 familiarités** *nfpl* : liberties, forwardness

familier, -lière [familje, -ljɛr] *adj* **1** : familiar, known **2** : informal, (overly) friendly **3** : colloquial, informal (of language) **4 animal familier** : pet

famille [famij] *nf* : family <c'est de famille : it runs in the family> <en famille : at home, with one's family>

famine [famin] *nf* : famine

fan [fan] *nmf* : fan, enthusiast

fana [fana] *nmf fam* : fanatic, freak

fanal [fanal] *nm, pl* **fanaux** [fano] : lantern

fanatique[1] [fanatik] *adj* : fanatic, fanatical

fanatique[2] *nmf* : fanatic — **fanatisme** [-natism] *nm*

faner [fane] *vt* **1** : to fade **2** : to wither — *vi* **1** : to fade **2** : to make hay (in agriculture) — **se faner** *vr* **1** : to wilt, to wither **2** : to fade (away)

fanfare [fɑ̃far] *nf* **1** : fanfare **2** : brass band

fanfaron[1], **-ronne** [fɑ̃farɔ̃, -rɔn] *adj* : boastful

fanfaron[2], **-ronne** *n* : braggart

fanfaronnade [fɑ̃farɔnad] *nf* : bragging, boasting

fanfaronner [fɑ̃farɔne] *vi* : to brag, to boast

fange [fɑ̃ʒ] *nf* : mire <traîner dans la fange : to drag through the mire>

fanion [fanjɔ̃] *nm* : pennant

fanon [fanɔ̃] *nm* **1** : whalebone **2** : wattle, dewlap **3** : fetlock (of a horse)

fantaisie [fɑ̃tezi] *nf* **1** : fantasy, imagination **2** CAPRICE : fancy, whim **3** : fantasia (in music)

fantaisiste [fɑ̃tezist] *adj* **1** : far-fetched, fanciful **2** : eccentric

fantasme [fɑ̃tasm] *nm* : fantasy

fantasmer [fɑ̃tasme] *vi* : to fantasize

fantasque [fɑ̃task] *adj* **1** : whimsical, capricious **2** BIZARRE : strange, weird

fantassin [fɑ̃tasɛ̃] *nm* : infantryman

fantastique [fɑ̃tastik] *adj* : fantastic — **fantastiquement** [-tikmɑ̃] *adv*

fantoche[1] [fɑ̃tɔʃ] *adj* : puppet <gouvernement fantoche : puppet government>

fantoche[2] *nm* MARIONNETTE : puppet

fantomatique [fɑ̃tɔmatik] *adj* : ghostly

fantôme [fɑ̃tom] *nm* SPECTRE : ghost, phantom

faon [fɑ̃] *nm* : fawn

faramineux, -neuse [faraminø, -nøz] *adj fam* : incredible, fantastic <une somme faramineuse : a staggering sum>

farce [fars] *nf* **1** : farce (in theater) **2** BLAGUE : practical joke, prank **3** : stuffing (in cooking)

farceur, -ceuse [farsœr, -søz] *n* : practical joker, prankster

farcir [farsir] *vt* **1** : to stuff (in cooking) **2 ~ de** *fam* : to cram with — **se farcir** *fam* : to have to put up with, to get stuck with

fard [far] *nm* **1** : makeup **2 sans ~** : plainly, openly

fardeau [fardo] *nm, pl* **fardeaux 1** : load **2** : burden, responsibility

farder [farde] *vt* **1** : to put makeup on **2** : to disguise, to conceal — **se farder** *vr* : to put on makeup

fardoches [fardɔʃ] *nfpl Can* : undergrowth, brush

farfelu, -lue [farfəly] *adj fam* : harebrained, wacky

farfiner [farfine] *vi Can fam* : to dawdle, to dillydally

farfouiller [farfuje] *vi fam* : to rummage (around)

farine [farin] *nf* : flour <farine d'avoine : oatmeal> <farine de maïs : cornmeal>

fariner [farine] *vt* : to flour

farineur, -neuse [farinœr, -nøz] *adj* **1** : covered with flour **2** : starchy, mealy

farouche [faruʃ] *adj* **1** SAUVAGE : wild, savage **2** TIMIDE : shy, timid **3** : fierce, unyielding

farouchement [faruʃmɑ̃] *adv* : fiercely

fart [far(t)] *nm* : (ski) wax

fascicule [fasikyl] *nm* **1** : installment, fascicle **2** : booklet

fascinant, -nante [fasinɑ̃, -nɑ̃t] *adj* : fascinating

fascination [fasinasjɔ̃] *nf* : fascination

fasciner [fasine] *vt* CAPTIVER : to fascinate

fascisme [faʃism] *nm* : fascism — **fasciste** [faʃist] *adj & nmf*

fasse [fas], *etc.* → **faire**

faste[1] [fast] *adj* : auspicious, lucky

faste[2] *nm* : pomp, splendor

fastidieux, -dieuse [fastidjø, -djøz] *adj* : tedious — **fastidieusement** [-djøzmɑ̃] *adv*

fastueux, -tueuse [fastɥø, -tɥøz] *adj* : luxurious, sumptuous

fatal, -tale [fatal] *adj, mpl* **fatals 1** MORTEL : fatal **2** INÉVITABLE : inevitable

fatalement [fatalmɑ̃] *adv* : inevitably

fatalisme [fatalism] *nm* : fatalism

fataliste[1] [fatalist] *adj* : fatalistic

fataliste[2] *nmf* : fatalist

fatalité [fatalite] *nf* **1** DESTIN : fate **2** : bad luck, misfortune **3** : inevitability

fatidique [fatidik] *adj* : fateful

fatigant, -gante [fatigɑ̃, -gɑ̃t] *adj* **1** : tiring **2** : tiresome

fatigue [fatig] *nf* : fatigue

fatigué, -guée [fatige] *adj* : tired, weary

fatiguer [fatige] *vt* **1** : to tire out **2** IMPORTUNER : to bother, to annoy **3** : to strain (an engine, a structure, etc.) — *vi* **1** : to labor (of an engine) **2** : to undergo strain — **se fatiguer** *vr* : to grow tired, to wear oneself out

fatras [fatra] *nm* : jumble

fatuité [fatɥite] *nf* : smugness, self-satisfaction

faubourg [fobur] *nm* BANLIEUE : suburb

fauché, -chée [foʃe] *adj fam* : broke <être complètement fauché : to be flat broke>

faucher [foʃe] *vt* **1** : to mow, to cut **2** : to mow down, to knock down **3** *fam* : to swipe, to pinch

faucheuse [foʃøz] *nf* : reaper, mowing machine

faucheux [foʃø] *nm* : harvestman, daddy longlegs

faucille [fosij] *nf* : sickle

faucon [fokɔ̃] *nm* : falcon, hawk

fauconnerie [fokɔnri] *nf* : falconry

faudra [fodra] → **falloir**

faufiler [fofile] *vt* : to baste (in sewing) — **se faufiler** *vr* : to thread one's way, to slip, to sneak

faune[1] [fon] *nf* : fauna, wildlife

faune[2] *nm* : faun

faunique [fonik] *adj* **réserve faunique** *Can* : wildlife reserve

faussaire [fosɛr] *nmf* : forger, counterfeiter

fausse → **faux**

faussement [fosmɑ̃] *adv* **1** : falsely **2** : wrongfully

fausser [fose] *vt* **1** : to falsify, to distort **2** DÉFORMER : to bend out of shape

fausset [fosɛ] *nm* **voix de fausset** : falsetto voice

fausseté [foste] *nf* **1** : falseness, falsity **2** : duplicity

faut [fo] → **falloir**

faute [fot] *nf* **1** : fault **2** : misdeed, transgression <faute professionnelle : malpractice> **3** ERREUR : mistake, error, foul (in sports) **4** MANQUE : lack, want <faute de mieux : for lack of anything better>

fauteuil [fotœj] *nm* **1** : armchair, easy chair **2** : seat (in a theater) **3** : chair, seat (in government or an organization) **4 fauteuil roulant** : wheelchair

fauteur, -trice [fotœr, -tris] *n* **fauteur de troubles** : troublemaker, agitator

fautif, -tive [fotif, -tiv] *adj* **1** : at fault **2** : faulty, inaccurate

fauve[1] [fov] *adj* : tawny, fawn

fauve[2] *nm* **1** : big cat **2** : fawn (color)

fauvette [fovɛt] *nf* : warbler

faux[1] [fo] *adv* **1** : out of tune **2** : false, wrong <ça sonne faux : that doesn't ring true>

faux[2], **fausse** [fo, fos] *adj* **1** : false, inaccurate **2** : wrong <faire un faux pas : to stumble> **3** : imitation, counterfeit, fake **4** : deceitful <un faux frère : a false friend> **5 fausse couche** : miscarriage **6 faux nom** : assumed name, alias **7 faux témoignage** : perjury

faux[3] *nm* **1** : forgery, fake **2 le faux** : the false, falsehood

faux[4] *nf* : scythe

faux-filet [fofilɛ] *nm, pl* **faux-filets** : sirloin

faux-fuyant [fofɥijɑ̃] *nm, pl* **faux-fuyants** : pretext, subterfuge

faux-monnayeur [fomɔnɛjœr] *nm, pl* **faux-monnayeurs** : counterfeiter, forger

faux-semblant [fosɑ̃blɑ̃] *nm, pl* **faux-semblants** : sham, pretense, pose

faux-sens [fosɑ̃s] *nms & pl* : mistranslation

faveur [favœr] *nf* **1** : favor **2 à la faveur de** : thanks to **3 en faveur de** : in favor of, on behalf of

favorable [favɔrabl] *adj* : favorable — **favorablement** [-rabləmɑ̃] *adv*

favori[1], **-rite** [favɔri, -rit] *adj* : favorite

favori[2], **-rite** *n* : favorite

favoris *nmpl* : sideburns

favoriser [favɔrize] *vt* **1** : to favor, to prefer **2** : to promote, to encourage

favoritisme [favɔritism] *nm* : favoritism

fax [faks] *nm* : fax

faxer [fakse] *vt* : to fax

fébrile [febril] *adj* : feverish, febrile — **fébrilement** [-brilmɑ̃] *adv*

fébrilité [febrilite] *nf* : feverishness

fécal, -cale [fekal] *adj, mpl* **fécaux** [-ko] : fecal

fèces [fɛs] *nfpl* : feces

fécond, -conde [fekɔ̃, -kɔ̃d] *adj* FERTILE : fecund, fertile — **fécondité** [fekɔ̃dite] *nf*

fécondation [fekɔ̃dasjɔ̃] *nf* **1** : fertilization **2 fécondation artificielle** : artificial insemination

féconder [fekɔ̃de] *vt* **1** : to fertilize **2** : to impregnate, to inseminate **3** : to pollinate

fécondité [fekɔ̃dite] *nf* FERTILITÉ : fecundity, fertility

fécule [fekyl] *nf* **1** : starch **2 fécule de maïs** : cornstarch

féculent[1], **-lente** [fekylɑ̃, -lɑ̃t] *adj* : starchy

féculent[2] *nm* : starchy food

fédéral, -rale [federal] *adj, mpl* **-raux** [-ro] : federal

fédéralisme [federalism] *nm* : federalism — **fédéraliste** [-ralist] *adj & nmf*

fédération [federasjɔ̃] *nf* : federation

fédérer [federe] {87} *vt* : to federate

fée [fe] *nf* : fairy

feed-back [fidbak] *nms & pl* : feedback

féerie [fe(e)ri] *nf* **1** : enchantment **2** : extravaganza, spectacular

féerique [fe(e)rik] *adj* : magical, enchanting

feignait [fɛɲɛ], **feignions** [fɛɲɔ̃], *etc.* → **feindre**

feigne [fɛɲ], *etc.* → **feindre**

feindre [fɛ̃dr] {37} *vt* : to feign — *vi* : to pretend, to dissemble

feinte [fɛ̃t] *nf* **1** : feint, fake (in sports) **2** PIÈGE : trick, ruse

feinter [fɛ̃te] *vt* : to fake, to feint at (in sports) — *vi* : to fake, to feint (in sports)

fêlé[1], **-lée** [fele] *adj* **1** : cracked **2 avoir la tête fêlée** *fam* : to be a little crazy

fêlé[2], **-lée** *n fam* : crackpot

fêler [fele] *vt* : to crack — **se fêler** *vr*

félicitations [felisitasjɔ̃] *nfpl* : congratulations

félicité [felisite] *nf* : bliss, happiness

féliciter [felisite] *vt* CONGRATULER : to congratulate — **se féliciter** *vr* **~ de** : to be very pleased about

félin[1], **-line** [felɛ̃, -lin] *adj* : feline

félin[2] *nm* : feline, cat

félon[1], **-lonne** [felɔ̃, -lɔn] *adj* : disloyal, treacherous

félon[2], **-lonne** *n* : traitor

félonie [felɔni] *nf* : treachery

fêlure [felyr] *nf* : crack

femelle [fəmɛl] *adj & nf* : female

féminin[1], **-nine** [feminɛ̃, -nin] *adj* : feminine

féminin[2] *nm* : feminine (in grammar)

féminisme [feminism] *nm* : feminism

féministe [feminist] *adj & nmf* : feminist

féminité [feminite] *nf* : femininity

femme [fam] *nf* **1** : woman **2** ÉPOUSE : wife **3 femme au foyer** : homemaker **4 femme d'affaires** : businesswoman **5 femme de chambre** : maid, chambermaid

fémoral, -rale [femɔral] *adj, mpl* **-raux** [-ro] : femoral

fémur [femyr] *nm* : femur, thighbone

fendant, -dante [fɑ̃dɑ̃, -dɑ̃t] *adj Can* : arrogant, pretentious

fendiller [fɑ̃dije] *vt* : to crack — **se fendiller** *vr* **1** SE GERCER : to chap **2** : to crack, to craze

fendre [fɑ̃dr] {63} *vt* **1** : to split <fendre le cœur : to break one's heart> **2** : to crack — **se fendre** *vr* : to crack, to split

fenêtre [fənɛtr] *nf* : window

fenouil [fənuj] *nm* : fennel

fente [fɑ̃t] *nf* **1** : slot, slit **2** : crack

féodal, -dale [feɔdal] *adj, mpl* **-daux** [-do] : feudal — **féodalisme** [-dalism] *nm*

fer [fɛr] *nm* **1** : iron <de fer : iron, strong> **2 fer à cheval** : horseshoe **3 fer à repasser** : iron (for pressing clothes) **4 fer de lance** : spearhead **5 fers** *nmpl* : irons, shackles

fera [fəra], *etc.* → **faire**

fer–blanc [fɛrblɑ̃] *nm, pl* **fers–blancs** : tinplate

férié, -riée [ferje] *adj* **jour férié** : holiday

ferme[1] [fɛrm] *adv* : firmly, hard <tiens ferme! : hold your ground!>

ferme[2] *adj* **1** : firm **2** : steady — **fermement** [fɛrməmɑ̃] *adv*

ferme[3] *nf* **1** : farm **2** *or* **maison de ferme** : farmhouse

fermé, -mée [fɛrme] *adj* **1** : closed **2** IMPÉNÉTRABLE : inscrutable, impassive **3** EXCLUSIF : exclusive

ferment [fɛrmɑ̃] *nm* : ferment

fermentation [fɛrmɑ̃tasjɔ̃] *nf* **1** : fermentation **2** AGITATION : agitation, ferment

fermenter [fɛrmɑ̃te] *vi* : to ferment

fermer [fɛrme] *vt* **1** : to close, to shut <fermer les rideaux : to draw the curtains> <fermer à clef : to lock up> <fermer au loquet : to latch> **2** : to close down, to shut down <fermer boutique : to close up shop> **3** : to close off, to block **4** ÉTEINDRE : to turn off, to switch off **5** CLORE : to conclude — *vi* : to close — **se fermer** *vr* **1** : to close up, to fasten **2 ~ à** : to be closed to

fermeté [fɛrməte] *nf* : firmness

fermeture [fɛrmətyr] *nf* **1** : closing, shutting **2** : latch, clasp, fastener **3 fermeture à glissière** : zipper

fermier[1], **-mière** [fɛrmje, -mjɛr] *adj* : farming, farm

fermier[2], **-mière** *n* : farmer

fermoir [fɛrmwar] *nm* : clasp

féroce [ferɔs] *adj* : ferocious — **férocement** [-rɔsmɑ̃] *adv*

férocité [ferɔsite] *nf* : ferocity, ferociousness

ferraille [fɛraj] *nf* **1** : scrap iron **2** : scrapheap, scrapyard **3** *fam* : small change

ferré, -rée [fɛre] *adj* **1** : ironclad, iron-tipped **2** : hobnailed **3** : shod (of a horse) **4 être ferré sur** *fam* : to be well up on, to be in the know about

ferrer [fɛre] *vt* **1** : to shoe (a horse) **2** : to tip with metal **3** : to catch (a fish on a hook)

ferreux, -reuse [fɛrø, -røz] *adj* : ferrous

ferrique [fɛrik] *adj* : ferric

ferronnerie [fɛrɔnri] *nf* **1** : ironworks **2** : metalwork, wrought iron

ferroviaire [fɛrɔvjɛr] *adj* : rail, railroad

ferry–boat [fɛribot] *nm, pl* **ferry–boats** : ferry

fertile [fɛrtil] *adj* **1** : fertile **2** : productive <fertile en événements : eventful>

fertilisant [fɛrtilizɑ̃] *nm* : fertilizer

fertiliser [fɛrtilize] *vt* : to fertilize — **fertilisation** [-lizasjɔ̃] *nf*

fertilité [fɛrtilite] *nf* : fertility

féru, -rue [fery] *adj* **être féru de** : to be passionately interested in

férule [feryl] *nf* **être sous la férule de qqn** : to be under s.o.'s authority

fervent[1], **-vente** [fɛrvɑ̃, -vɑ̃t] *adj* : fervent

fervent[2], **-vente** *n* : enthusiast, devotee

ferveur [fɛrvœr] *nf* : fervor

fesse [fɛs] *nf* **1** : buttock **2 fesses** *nfpl* : buttocks, bottom

fessée [fese] *nf* : spanking

fesser [fese] *vt* : to spank

festin [fɛstɛ̃] *nm* BANQUET : feast, banquet

festival [fɛstival] *nm, pl* **-vals** : festival

festivités [fɛstivite] *nfpl* : festivities

feston [fɛstɔ̃] *nm* : festoon

festonner [fɛstɔne] *vt* : to festoon

festoyer [fɛstwaje] {58} *vi* : to feast

fêtard, -tarde [fetar, -tard] *n fam* : merrymaker, reveler

fête [fɛt] *nf* **1** : party **2** : holiday <la fête des Mères : Mother's Day> **3** : festival <fête foraine : fair> **4 de ~** : festive **5 faire la fête** : to have a good time

fêter [fete] *vt* : to celebrate

fétiche [fetiʃ] *nm* : fetish

fétide [fetid] *adj* : foul, fetid

fétu [fety] *nm* **fétu de paille** : wisp of straw

feu[1], **feue** |fø| *adj* : late <feu la reine, la feue reine : the late queen>

feu[2] *nm, pl* **feux 1** : fire <prendre feu : to catch fire> <mettre le feu à : to set fire to> <feu de camp : campfire> <feu de joie : bonfire> **2** : light <feu de circulation : traffic light> <feux de la rampe : footlights> **3** : burner (of a stove) **4** : light (for a cigarette, etc.) <avez-vous du feu? : have you got a light?> **5** : fire, shooting <faire feu : to fire> <coup de feu : shot> **6** : passion, ardor <avec feu : passionately, heatedly> **7 feux d'artifice** : fireworks

feuillage |fœjaʒ| *nm* : foliage

feuille |fœj| *nf* **1** : leaf <feuille de nénuphar : lily pad> **2** : sheet (of paper or metal), foil **3** : form <feuille d'impôts : tax return>

feuillet |fœjɛ| *nm* : page, leaf

feuilleté[1], **-tée** |fœjte| *adj* **1** : laminated **2 pâte feuilletée** : puff pastry

feuilleté[2] *nm* : puff pastry

feuilleter |fœjte| {8} *vt* **1** : to leaf through (a book) **2** : to roll and fold (dough) **3** : to laminate (glass)

feuilleton |fœjtɔ̃| *nm* : series, serial

feuillu, -lue |fœjy| *adj* **1** : leafy **2** : broad-leaved

feutre |føtr| *nm* **1** : felt **2** → **stylo-feutre**

feutré, -trée |føtre| *adj* **1** : felt, feltlike **2** : muffled

fève |fɛv| *nf* : broad bean

février |fevrije| *nm* : February

fez |fɛz| *nm* : fez

fi |fi| *interj* **faire fi de** : to scorn, to turn up one's nose at

fiable |fjabl| *adj* : reliable — **fiabilité** |fjabilite| *nf*

fiacre |fjakr| *nm* : (horse-drawn) carriage, hackney

fiançailles |fijɑ̃saj| *nfpl* : engagement

fiancé, -cée |fijɑ̃se| *n* : fiancé *m*, fiancée *f*

fiancer |fijɑ̃se| {6} *v* **se fiancer** *vr* : to get engaged

fiasco |fjasko| *nm* : fiasco

fibre |fibr| *nf* **1** : fiber **2 fibre de verre** : fiberglass **3 fibres alimentaires** : roughage

fibreux, -breuse |fibrø, -brøz| *adj* : fibrous

ficeler |fisle| {8} *vt* : to tie up

ficelle |fisɛl| *nf* **1** : string, twine **2** : trick <les ficelles du métier : the tricks of the trade>

fiche |fiʃ| *nf* **1** : index card, slip (of paper) **2** FORMULAIRE : form **3** : (electric) plug

ficher |fiʃe| *vt* **1** ENFONCER : to drive in, to stick **2** : to put on file **3** *fam* : to do <qu'est-ce qu'elle fiche? : what's she doing?> **4** *fam* : to put, to push <fiche-le dehors! : kick him out!> **5** *fam* : to give <ficher une claque à qqn : to give s.o. a slap> — **se ficher** *vr* **1** **~ dans** : to stick into **2** **~ de** *fam* : to make fun of **3 je m'en fiche** *fam* : I don't give a damn

fichier |fiʃje| *nm* **1** : file, index **2** : index card box, filing cabinet

fichu[1] |fiʃy| *pp* → **ficher 3, 4, 5**

fichu[2], **-chue** *adj fam* **1** : rotten, awful <quelle fichue température! : what rotten weather!> **2** : done for, sunk **3** **~ de** : capable of

fichu[3] *nm* : scarf, shawl

fichument |fiʃymɑ̃| *adv Can fam* : really, extremely <fichument content : really pleased>

fictif, -tive |fiktif, -tiv| *adj* : fictional, fictitious — **fictivement** |-tivmɑ̃| *adv*

fiction |fiksjɔ̃| *nf* : fiction

fidèle[1] |fidɛl| *adj* **1** LOYAL : loyal **2** CONSTANT : faithful **3** : true, accurate — **fidèlement** |-dɛlmɑ̃| *adv*

fidèle[2] *nmf* **1** : believer <les fidèles : the faithful> **2** : supporter, follower **3** : regular (customer)

fidélité |fidelite| *nf* : fidelity, faithfulness

fidjien[1], **-jienne** |fidʒjɛ̃, -dʒjɛn| *adj* : Fijian

fidjien[2] *nm* : Fijian (language)

Fidjien, -jienne *n* : Fijian

fiduciaire[1] |fidysjɛr| *adj* : fiduciary

fiduciaire[2] *nmf* : trustee

fiducie |fidysi| *nf* : trust <société de fiducie : trust company>

fief |fjɛf| *nm* **1** : fief **2** : stronghold

fiel |fjɛl| *nm* **1** : gall, bile **2** : bitterness, acrimony

fier[1] |fje| *v* **se fier** *vr* **~ à** : to trust, to rely on

fier[2], **fière** |fjɛr| *adj* : proud — **fièrement** |fjɛrmɑ̃| *adv*

fierté |fjɛrte| *nf* : pride

fièvre |fjɛvr| *nf* : fever <avoir de la fièvre : to have a high fever> <fièvre jaune : yellow fever>

fiévreux, -vreuse |fjɛvrø, -vrøz| *adj* : feverish — **fiévreusement** |-vrøzmɑ̃| *adv*

fifre |fifr| *nm* : fife

figer |fiʒe| {17} *vt* **1** : to congeal, to coagulate **2** : to freeze, to paralyze <être figé sur place : to be rooted to the spot> — **se figer** *vr* **1** : to congeal **2** S'IMMOBILISER : to freeze <son sang se figea : his blood froze>

fignoler |fiɲɔle| *vt* : to refine, to put the finishing touch upon

figue |fig| *nf* : fig

figuier |figje| *nm* : fig tree

figurant, -rante |figyrɑ̃, -rɑ̃t| *n* COMPARSE : extra, bit player

figuratif, -tive |figyratif, -tiv| *adj* : figurative, representational

figuration |figyrasjɔ̃| *nf* **faire de la figuration** : to work as an extra

figurativement |figyrativmɑ̃| *adv* : figuratively

figure |figyr| *nf* **1** VISAGE : face **2** : appearance <faire bonne figure : to put

on a good show> **3** PERSONNAGE : figure, person **4** : illustration, figure (in a text) **5** : expression <figure de rhétorique : figure of speech>
figuré, -rée [figyre] *adj* : figurative
figurer [figyre] *vi* : to appear — *vt* REPRÉSENTER : to represent — **se figurer** *vr* : to imagine
figurine [figyrin] *nf* : figurine
fil [fil] *nm* **1** : thread, yarn <fil à coudre : sewing thread> <fil dentaire : dental floss> **2** : wire, cable <fil électrique : electric wire> <fil à pêche : fishing line> **3** : current, stream <le fil des événements : the chain of events> <au fil du temps : as time goes by> **4 coup de fil** *fam* : phone call
filament [filamɑ̃] *nm* : filament
filandreux, -dreuse [filɑ̃drø, -drøz] *adj* **1** : stringy **2** : rambling
filant, -lante [filɑ̃, -lɑ̃t] *adj* **1** : runny (in cooking) **2** → **étoile**
filature [filatyr] *nf* **1** FABRIQUE : mill **2** : spinning **3 prendre en filature** : to shadow, to tail
file [fil] *nf* **1** : line, file, row <prendre la file : to get in line> <file indienne : single file> **2** : lane (of a paved road) **3 en ~** *or* **à la file** : one after another
filée [file] *nf Can fam* : line, queue
filer [file] *vt* **1** : to spin (yarn) **2** : to shadow, to tail **3** *fam* : to give <je lui ai filé un billet de 100 francs : I slipped him a 100 franc note> — *vi* **1** : to trickle, to run **2** : to run (of stockings) **3** *fam* : to dash off, to rush away **4** *fam* : to fly by, to slip away <le temps filait : time was flying> **5 filer bien** *Can fam* : to be doing fine
filet [filɛ] *nm* **1** : net **2** : fillet **3** : trickle (of water)
filial, -liale [filjal] *adj, mpl* **-liaux** [-ljo] : filial
filiale *nf* : subsidiary (company)
filiation [filjasjɔ̃] *nf* **1** : line of descent **2** : relationship (of ideas, etc.)
filière [filjɛr] *nf* **1** : (official) channels *pl* **2** : field, line (of study or work) **3** : network, ring (of criminals)
filigrane [filigran] *nm* **1** : watermark **2** : filigree **3 lire en filigrane** : to read between the lines
fille [fij] *nf* **1** : girl **2** : daughter
fillette [fijɛt] *nf* : little girl
filleul, -leule [fijœl] *n* : godchild, godson *m*, goddaughter *f*
film [film] *nm* **1** : film, movie <film d'animation : cartoon> <film (pour projection) fixe : filmstrip> **2** PELLICULE : movie film **3** : film coating **4** : course, sequence (of events, etc.)
filmer [filme] *vt* : to film
filon [filɔ̃] *nm* **1** : vein, lode **2 trouver le filon** *fam* : to strike it rich
filou [filu] *nm* : crook, swindler
fils [fis] *nm* : son
filtrage [filtraʒ] *nm* **1** : filtering **2** : screening
filtration [filtrasjɔ̃] *nf* : filtration, filtering
filtre [filtr] *nm* : filter
filtrer [filtre] *vt* **1** : to filter **2** : to screen — *vi* : to filter through
fin[1] [fɛ̃] *adv* **1** : finely, thinly, sharply **2 être fin prêt** : to be ready, to be all set
fin[2]**, fine** *adj* **1** : fine, delicate <cheveux fins : fine hair> **2** : thin <tranches fines : thin slices> **3** : excellent, first-rate **4** : sharp, keen <avoir le nez fin : to have a keen sense of smell> **5** *Can* : nice **6** : ultimate, very <au fin fond : at the very bottom>
fin[3] *nf* **1** : end <mettre fin à : to put an end to> <prendre fin : to come to an end> <sans fin : endless, endlessly> **2** MORT : death, end <une fin prématurée : an untimely death> **3** BUT : aim, purpose, end **4 à la fin** : eventually, in the end **5 à toutes fins utiles** : for all practical purposes
final, -nale [final] *adj, mpl* **finals** *or* **finaux** [fino] : final, last
finale[1] *nm* : finale
finale[2] *nf* : final, finals *pl* (in sports)
finalement [finalmɑ̃] *adv* **1** : finally, at last **2** : after all, in fact
finaliser [finalize] *vt* : to finalize
finaliste [finalist] *nmf* : finalist
finance [finɑ̃s] *nf* **1** : finance **2 finances** *nfpl* : finances, resources
financement [finɑ̃smɑ̃] *nm* : financing
financer [finɑ̃se] {6} *vt* : to finance
financier[1]**, -cière** [finɑ̃sje,-sjɛr] *adj* : financial — **financièrement** [-sjɛrmɑ̃] *adv*
financier[2] *nm* : financier
finasser [finase] *vi* : to scheme, to wheel and deal
finaud, -naude [fino, -nod] *adj* : cunning, crafty
finement [finmɑ̃] *adv* **1** : finely **2** : shrewdly, subtly **3** : precisely
finesse [finɛs] *nf* **1** : finesse, delicacy **2** : fineness, thinness **3** : subtlety, shrewdness
fini[1]**, -nie** [fini] *adj* **1** : finished, ended, complete **2** : finite
fini[2] *nm Can* : finish (of a surface)
finir [finir] *vt* **1** : to finish, to end **2** : to use up — *vi* **1** : to finish, to come to an end **2 à n'en plus finir** : endless, never-ending **3 en finir avec** : to be done with **4 finir par faire** : to end up doing
finition [finisjɔ̃] *nf* : finish, finishing touches
finlandais[1]**, -daise** [fɛ̃lɑ̃dɛ, -dɛz] *adj* : Finnish
finlandais[2] *nm* : Finnish (language)
Finlandais, -daise *n* : Finn
finnois[1]**, -noise** [finwa, -nwaz] *adj* : Finnish
finnois[2] *nm* : Finnish (language)

fiole |fjɔl| *nf* : vial

fiord → **fjord**

fioriture |fjɔrityr| *nf* : ornament, embellishment

fioul |fjul| *nm* : fuel oil

firmament |firmamɑ̃| *nm* : firmament, heavens *pl*

firme |firm| *nf* : firm, company

fisc |fisk| *nm* : tax collection agency

fiscal, -cale |fiskal| *adj, mpl* **fiscaux** |fisko| : fiscal <fraude fiscale : tax evasion> — **fiscalement** |-kalmɑ̃| *adv*

fiscaliser |fiskalize| *vt* : to subject to tax

fiscalité |fiskalite| *nf* : tax system

fission |fisjɔ̃| *nf* : fission

fissure |fisyr| *nf* : fissure, crack

fiston |fistɔ̃| *nm fam* : son, youngster

fixatif |fiksatif| *nm* **1** : fixative **2** *Can* : hair spray

fixation |fiksasjɔ̃| *nf* **1** : fixing, fastening, attachment **2** : fixation (in psychology) **3** : ski binding

fixe |fiks| *adj* **1** IMMOBILE : fixed **2** : permanent, steady **3** : regular <à heure fixe : at a set time>

fixement |fiksəmɑ̃| *adv* : fixedly

fixer |fikse| *vt* **1** : to fix, to fasten **2** DÉTERMINER : to determine, to set **3** ÉTABLIR : to establish **4** : to focus <fixer son regard sur : to fix one's gaze on> **5** : to stare at — **se fixer** *vr* **1** : to settle down **2** : to decide (on something), to set (for) oneself

fjord *or* **fiord** |fjɔrd| *nm* : fjord

flaccidité |flaksidite| *nf* : flaccidity, flabbiness

flacon |flakɔ̃| *nm* : flask, small bottle

flagellation |flaʒɛlasjɔ̃| *nf* : flogging, whipping

flageller |flaʒɛle| *vt* FOUETTER : to flog, to whip — **se flageller** *vr*

flageoler |flaʒɔle| *vi* : to feel unsteady, to tremble <flageoler sur ses jambes : to be quaking in one's boots>

flageolet |flaʒɔlɛ| *nm* : flageolet, dwarf kidney bean

flagorneur, -neuse |flagɔrnœr, -nøz| *n* : toady, flatterer

flagrant |flagrɑ̃| *adj* **1** : flagrant, blatant **2 en flagrant délit** : red-handed

flair |flɛr| *nm* **1** ODORAT : sense of smell, nose **2** INTUITION : intuition

flairer |flɛre| *vt* **1** : to sniff, to smell **2** : to sniff out, to detect

flamand[1], **-mande** |flamɑ̃, -mɑ̃d| *adj* : Flemish

flamand[2] *nm* : Flemish (language)

Flamand, -mande *n* **1** : Fleming **2 les Flamands** : the Flemish

flamant |flamɑ̃| *nm* : flamingo

flambant, -bante |flɑ̃bɑ̃, -bɑ̃t| *adj* **1** : flaming **2 flambant neuf** : brand-new

flambeau |flɑ̃bo| *nm, pl* **flambeaux 1** TORCHE : torch **2** CHANDELIER : candlestick

flambée |flɑ̃be| *nf* **1** : blaze, fire **2** : outburst, explosion (of anger, etc.) **3** : sudden increase <une flambée des prix : skyrocketing prices>

flamber |flɑ̃be| *vt* **1** : to singe, to char **2** : to sterilize — *vi* **1** : to flame, to burn **2** : to soar, to skyrocket

flamboiement |flɑ̃bwamɑ̃| *nm* : blaze, flash

flamboyant, -boyante |flɑ̃bwajɑ̃, -bwajɑ̃t| *adj* **1** : blazing **2** : flamboyant (in architecture)

flamboyer |flɑ̃bwaje| {58} *vi* : to blaze, to flash

flamme |flam| *nf* **1** : flame <en flammes : in flames> **2** : passion, fervor **3** : pennant (of a ship)

flammèche |flamɛʃ| *nf* : spark

flan |flɑ̃| *nm* : baked custard

flanc |flɑ̃| *nm* : side, flank

flancher |flɑ̃ʃe| *vi fam* **1** : to flinch, to waver **2** : to fail, to give out

flanelle |flanɛl| *nf* : flannel

flanellette |flanɛlɛt| *nf Can* : brushed cotton, cotton flannel

flâner |flane| *vi* **1** SE BALADER : to stroll **2** PARESSER : to loaf around, to idle

flâneur, -neuse |flanœr, -nøz| *n* : idler, loiterer

flanquer |flɑ̃ke| *vt* **1** : to flank **2** *fam* : to fling **3** *fam* : to give <flanquer la frousse à qqn : to give s.o. a fright> <flanquer un coup de poing : to land a blow>

flanqueur |flɑ̃kœr| *nm Can* : wing (in sports)

flaque |flak| *nf* : puddle, pool

flash |flaʃ| *nm, pl* **flashes 1** : flash (in photography) **2** : news flash

flasque[1] |flask| *adj* : flabby, limp

flasque[2] *nf* FLACON : flask

flatter |flate| *vt* **1** : to flatter <flatter bassement qqn : to pander to s.o.> **2** : to please, to delight **3** : to pat, to stroke (an animal) — **se flatter** *vr* : to pride oneself

flatterie |flatri| *nf* : flattery

flatteur[1], **-teuse** |flatœr, -tøz| *adj* : flattering

flatteur[2], **-teuse** *n* : flatterer

flatulence |flatylɑ̃s| *nf* : flatulence

flatulent, -lente |flatylɑ̃, -lɑ̃t| *adj* : flatulent

fléau |fleo| *nm, pl* **fléaux 1** : calamity, scourge **2** : flail (in agriculture)

flèche |flɛʃ| *nf* **1** : arrow <monter en flèche : to shoot up, to soar> **2** : spire

fléchette |fleʃɛt| *nf* **1** : dart **2 fléchettes** *nfpl* : darts (game)

fléchir |fleʃir| *vt* **1** COURBER : to bend, to flex **2** : to sway, to move — *vi* **1** : to bend, to give way **2** : to diminish, to fall off **3** : to yield, to relent

fléchissement |fleʃismɑ̃| *nm* **1** : weakening, fall, drop **2** : yielding, bending

flegmatique |flɛgmatik| *adj* : phlegmatic

flegme [flɛgm] *nm* : composure <avec flegme : coolly, phlegmatically>
flemme [flɛm] *nf France fam* : laziness
flet [flɛt] *nm* : flounder
flétan [fletɑ̃] *nm* : halibut
flétrir [fletrir] *vt* **1** : to wither, to fade **2** : to blacken (a reputation, etc.), to condemn — **se flétrir** *vr* : to wither, to fade
fleur [flœr] *nf* **1** : flower, blossom **2 fleur bleue** : sentimental **3 faire une fleur à qqn** : to do s.o. a favor **4 fleur de lis** *or* **fleur de lys** : fleur-de-lis
fleurdelisé[1] [flœrdəlize] *adj* : adorned with the fleur-de-lis
fleurdelisé[2] *nm* : the provincial flag of Quebec
fleurer [flœre] *vt* : to smell of
fleuret [flœrɛ] *nm* : foil (in fencing)
fleuri, -rie [flœri] *adj* **1** : flowered, flowery **2** : florid, ruddy **3** : ornate
fleurir [flœrir] *vt* : to decorate with flowers — *vi* **1** : to flower, to blossom **2** : to flourish
fleuriste [flœrist] *nmf* : florist
fleuron [flœrɔ̃] *nm* **1** : floret **2** : jewel <le fleuron de ma collection : the jewel of my collection>
fleuve [flœv] *nm* : river
flexibilité [flɛksibilite] *nf* : flexibility
flexible [flɛksibl] *adj* : flexible
flexion [flɛksjɔ̃] *nf* **1** : bending, flexing **2** : inflection (in grammar)
flic [flik] *nm fam* : cop
flirt [flœrt] *nm* : flirtation, fling
flirter [flœrte] *vi* : to flirt
flo [flo] → **flot**
flocon [flɔkɔ̃] *nm* : flake <flocon de neige : snowflake> <flocons de maïs : cornflakes>
flopée [flɔpe] *nf fam* **une flopée de** : a whole bunch of
floraison [flɔrɛzɔ̃] *nf* : flowering, blossoming
floral, -rale [flɔral] *adj, mpl* **floraux** [flɔro] : floral
flore [flɔr] *nf* : flora
florilège [flɔrilɛʒ] *nm* : anthology
florissant, -sante [flɔrisɑ̃, -sɑ̃t] *adj* : flourishing
flot [flo] *nm* **1** : tide **2** : flood, stream, torrent <entrer à flots : to stream in> **3 à ~** : afloat <être à flot : to be on an even keel> **4** *or* **flo** *Can* : young boy, kid **5 flots** *nmpl* : waves (in the ocean)
flottabilité [flɔtabilite] *nf* : buoyancy
flottable [flɔtabl] *adj* : buoyant
flottaison [flɔtɛzɔ̃] *nf* **1** : floating **2 ligne de flottaison** : waterline
flottant, -tante [flɔtɑ̃, -tɑ̃t] *adj* **1** : floating **2** : flowing, loose **3** : indecisive
flotte [flɔt] *nf* **1** : fleet **2** *fam* : water, rain
flottement [flɔtmɑ̃] *nm* **1** INDÉCISION : hesitation, indecision **2** : fluttering, flapping **3** : fluctuation (in finance)
flotter [flɔte] *vi* **1** : to float **2** : to fly, to flutter, to drift **3** : to fluctuate
flotteur [flɔtœr] *nm* : float
flottille [flɔtij] *nf* : flotilla
flou[1], **floue** [flu] *adj* **1** : blurred, fuzzy **2** : loose, soft **3** : vague, hazy (of ideas, etc.)
flou[2] *nm* **1** IMPRÉCISION : vagueness **2** : fuzziness (of focus, outline, etc.)
fluctuer [flyktɥe] *vi* : to fluctuate — **fluctuation** [flyktɥasjɔ̃] *nf*
fluet, fluette [flyɛ, flyɛt] *adj* GRÊLE : thin, slender
fluide[1] [flɥid] *adj* **1** : fluid **2** : smooth, flowing freely
fluide[2] *nm* **1** : fluid **2** : (occult) force, psychic powers *pl*
fluidité [flɥidite] *nf* **1** : fluidity, (free) flow **2** : flexibility
fluor [flyɔr] *nm* : fluorine
fluoration [flyɔrasjɔ̃] *nf* : fluoridation
fluoré, -rée [flyɔre] *adj* : fluoridated
fluorescent, -cente [flyɔresɑ̃, -sɑ̃t] *adj* : fluorescent — **fluorescence** [-sɑ̃s] *nf*
fluorure [flyɔryr] *nm* : fluoride
flûte[1] [flyt] *nf* **1** : flute <flûte à bec : recorder> <petite flûte : piccolo> **2** : baguette **3** : tall champagne glass
flûte[2] *interj* **flûte alors**! : fiddlesticks!, nonsense!
flûtiste [flytist] *nmf* : flutist
fluvial, -viale [flyvjal] *adj, mpl* **-viaux** [-vjo] : river <eau fluviale : river water>
flux [fly] *nm* **1** : flow **2** FLOT : flood, influx <un flux d'appels : a flood of calls> **3** : flood tide <le flux et reflux : the ebb and flow> **4** : flux (in medicine and physics)
foc [fɔk] *nm* : jib
focal, -cale [fɔkal] *adj* : focal
focaliser [fɔkalize] *vt* : to focus
fœtal, -tale [fetal] *adj, mpl* **fœtaux** [feto] : fetal
fœtus [fetys] *nms & pl* : fetus
foi [fwa] *nf* **1** : faith **2** : trust, confidence <digne de foi : reliable, trustworthy> **3 bonne foi** : sincerity, honesty **4 mauvaise foi** : dishonesty, insincerity **5 faire foi de** : to be proof of **6 ma foi !** : well! **7 sous la foi du serment** : under oath
foie [fwa] *nm* **1** : liver <crise de foie : indigestion> **2** : liver (in cooking) <foies de volaille : chicken livers>
foin [fwɛ̃] *nm* **1** : hay **2** *Can fam* : money <avoir du foin : to be well off> **3** → **rhume**
foire [fwar] *nf* : fair, market
fois [fwa] *nf* **1** : time <cette fois-ci : this time> <à chaque fois : each time> **2 il était une fois** : once upon a time **3 maintes et maintes fois** : time and time again **4 une fois pour toutes** : once and for all
foison [fwazɔ̃] **à ~** : in abundance, aplenty
foisonnant, -nante [fwazɔnɑ̃, -nɑ̃t] *adj* : abundant, plentiful

foisonnement [fwazɔnmɑ̃] *nm* **1** : profusion, abundance **2** : swelling, expansion
foisonner [fwazɔne] *vi* **1** ABONDER : to abound **2** : to expand
fol → **fou**
folâtre [fɔlatr] *adj* : playful, frolicsome
folâtrer [fɔlatre] *vi* : to frolic, to gambol
folichon, -chonne [fɔliʃɔ̃, -ʃɔn] *adj* **ça n'est pas folichon** : it's not much fun
folie [fɔli] *nf* **1** : craziness, madness <la folie des grandeurs : delusions of grandeur> **2** : folly **3 à la folie** : madly, passionately <aimer à la folie : to be madly in love with>
folio [fɔljo] *nm* : folio
folk [fɔlk] *or* **folksong** [fɔlksɔ̃g] *nm* : folk music
folklore [fɔlklɔr] *nm* : folklore
folklorique [fɔlklɔrik] *adj* **1** : folk <danse folklorique : folk dancing> **2** *fam* : bizarre, eccentric
folle → **fou**
follement [fɔlmɑ̃] *adv* : madly, wildly
follicule [fɔlikyl] *nm* : follicle
fomenter [fɔmɑ̃te] *vt* : to foment, to stir up
foncé, -cée [fɔ̃se] *adj* : dark <un bleu foncé : a dark blue>
foncer [fɔ̃se] {6} *vt* ASSOMBRIR : to darken — *vi* **1** : to rush, to charge **2** *fam* : to tear along **3** S'ASSOMBRIR : to darken
fonceur[1], -ceuse [fɔ̃sœr, -søz] *adj fam* : dynamic, driven
fonceur[2], -ceuse *n fam* : dynamic person, go-getter
foncier, -cière [fɔ̃sje, -sjɛr] *adj* **1** : land <propriétaire foncier : landowner> <impôt foncier : property tax> **2** INNÉ : innate, inherent
foncièrement [fɔ̃sjɛrmɑ̃] *adv* : fundamentally, inherently
fonction [fɔ̃ksjɔ̃] *nf* **1** : function **2** : job, duties *pl,* position <faire fonction de : to serve as> **3 en fonction de** : according to **4 fonction publique** : civil service
fonctionnaire [fɔ̃ksjɔnɛr] *nmf* : official, civil servant
fonctionnel, -nelle [fɔ̃ksjɔnɛl] *adj* : functional — **fonctionnellement** [-nɛlmɑ̃] *adv*
fonctionnement [fɔ̃ksjɔnmɑ̃] *nm* : functioning, working <bon fonctionnement : good working order>
fonctionner [fɔ̃ksjɔne] *vi* : to function, to work
fond [fɔ̃] *nm* **1** : bottom, back <au fond de : at the bottom of, at the back of, in the depths of> <sans fond : bottomless> **2** : root, heart, essence **3** : background <sur fond bleu : on a blue background> <fond sonore : background music> **4 à ~** : completely, deeply **5 au fond** : in fact, basically **6 de fond en comble** : from top to bottom, thoroughly **7 fond de teint** : foundation (makeup)
fondamental, -tale [fɔ̃damɑ̃tal] *adj, mpl* **-taux** [-to] : fundamental — **fondamentalement** [-talmɑ̃] *adv*
fondamentalisme [fɔ̃damɑ̃talism] *nm* : fundamentalism
fondateur, -trice [fɔ̃datœr, -tris] *n* : founder
fondation [fɔ̃dasjɔ̃] *nf* **1** : founding, establishment **2** : foundation, endowment **3 fondations** *nfpl* : foundation(s) (in construction)
fondé, -dée [fɔ̃de] *adj* : well-founded, justified <mal fondé : groundless>
fondement [fɔ̃dmɑ̃] *nm* **1** : foundation, basis <sans fondement : unfounded, groundless> **2** *fam* : bottom, buttocks
fonder [fɔ̃de] *vt* **1** : to found, to establish **2** : to base — **se fonder** *vr* **~ sur** : to be based on
fonderie [fɔ̃dri] *nf* : foundry
fondre [fɔ̃dr] {63} *vt* **1** : to melt, to smelt **2** : to dissolve <fondre en larmes : to dissolve into tears> **3** : to cast (a statue, etc.) **4** : to merge, to blend — *vi* **1** : to melt **2** : to dissolve **3 ~ sur** : to swoop down on — **se fondre** *vr* : to merge, to blend
fondrière [fɔ̃drijɛr] *nf* : pothole
fonds [fɔ̃] *nms & pl* **1** : collection (in a museum, etc.) **2** : fund <Fonds Monétaire International : International Monetary Fund> **3** *or* **fonds de commerce** : business **4 fonds** *nmpl* : funds, capital
fondue [fɔ̃dy] *nf* : fondue
fongicide[1] [fɔ̃ʒisid] *adj* : fungicidal
fongicide[2] *nm* : fungicide
fontaine [fɔ̃tɛn] *nf* **1** : fountain **2** SOURCE : spring
fonte [fɔ̃t] *nf* **1** : melting, smelting **2** : casting **3** : cast iron **4** : font (in printing)
fonts [fɔ̃] *nmpl* **fonts baptismaux** : baptismal font
foot [fut] *nm fam* : soccer
football [futbol] *nm* **1** : soccer **2** *Can* : football **3 football américain** : football
footballeur, -leuse [futbolœr, -løz] *n* : soccer player, football player
footing [futiŋ] *nm France* : jogging
for [fɔr] *nm* **en son for intérieur** : in one's heart of hearts, inwardly
forage [fɔraʒ] *nm* : drilling, boring
forain, -raine [fɔrɛ̃, -rɛn] *adj* : fairground <marchand forain : fairground merchant>
forban [fɔrbɑ̃] *nm* **1** PIRATE : pirate, freebooter **2** ESCROC : crook
forçat [fɔrsa] *nm* **1** : convict, galley slave **2 travail de forçat** : drudgery, hard work
force [fɔrs] *nf* **1** : strength <reprendre des forces : to regain one's strength> <force de caractère : strength of

character> <force d'âme : fortitude> <force vitale : lifeblood> **2** : force <entrer de force dans : to force one's way into> <la force de l'habitude : the force of habit> **3** : force (in physics) <force électromagnétique : electromagnetic force> **4** : (military or security) force <les forces armées : the armed forces> <les forces de l'ordre : the police> **5 à force de** : as a result of, by dint of **6 à toute force** : at all costs **7 par la force des choses** : of necessity, inevitably

forcé, -cée [fɔrse] *adj* **1** : forced **2** : inevitable

forcément [fɔrsemɑ̃] *adv* : necessarily, inevitably

forcené[1], -née [fɔrsəne] *adj* : frantic, frenzied

forcené[2] *nm* : maniac

forceps [fɔrsɛps] *nms & pl* : forceps *pl*

forcer [fɔrse] {6} *vt* **1** : to force, to compel **2** : to force open, to force through **3** : to strain, to overtax — *vi* : to strain, to overdo it — **se forcer** *vr* : to force oneself, to make an effort

forclusion [fɔrklyzjɔ̃] *nf* : foreclosure

forer [fɔre] *vt* : to drill, to bore

foresterie [fɔrɛstəri] *nf* : forestry

forestier[1], -tière [fɔrɛstje, -tjɛr] *adj* : forest, forested

forestier[2], -tière *n* : forester

foret [fɔrɛ] *nm* : (manual) drill

forêt [fɔrɛ] *nf* : forest

foreuse [fɔrøz] *nf* : drill

forfaire [fɔrfɛr] {44} *vi* ~ **à** : to fail in, to be false to

forfait [fɔrfɛ] *nm* **1** : fixed price, package deal **2** : default <déclarer forfait : to withdraw, to give up> **3** : heinous crime

forfaitaire [fɔrfɛtɛr] *adj* : inclusive

forfanterie [fɔrfɑ̃tri] *nf* : bragging, boastfulness

forge [fɔrʒ] *nf* : forge

forgé, -gée [fɔrʒe] *adj* **1** : fabricated, made up **2 fer forgé** : wrought iron

forger [fɔrʒe] {16} *vt* **1** : to forge **2** : to form, to build (character, etc.) **3** : to concoct, to invent <c'est forgé de toutes pièces : it's a total fabrication>

forgeron [fɔrʒərɔ̃] *nm* : blacksmith

formaldéhyde [fɔrmaldeɪd] *nm* : formaldehyde

formaliser [fɔrmalize] *vt* : to formalize — **se formaliser** *vr* : to take offense

formalisme [fɔrmalism] *nm* : formalism

formalité [fɔrmalite] *nf* : formality

format [fɔrma] *nm* : format

formater [fɔrmate] *vt* : to format (a computer disk)

formateur[1], -trice [fɔrmatœr, -tris] *adj* : formative

formateur[2], -trice *n* : trainer

formation [fɔrmasjɔ̃] *nf* **1** : formation **2** : education, training <formation professionnelle : vocational training>

forme [fɔrm] *nf* **1** : form, shape <prendre forme : to take shape> <sans forme : formless, shapeless> **2** : method, way <forme de pensée : way of thinking> **3** : form, procedure <pour la forme : as a matter of form> **4** : form, fitness <être en pleine forme : to be in great shape> **5** : last (of shoes) **6 formes** *nfpl* : figure (of the human body), lines (of an object) **7 formes** *nfpl* : proprieties, conventions <y mettre les formes : to be tactful>

formel, -melle [fɔrmɛl] *adj* **1** : formal **2** CATÉGORIQUE : definitive, categorical, express — **formellement** [-mɛlmɑ̃] *adv*

former [fɔrme] *vt* **1** : to form, to shape **2** : to develop **3** : to constitute **4** : to train, to educate — **se former** *vr*

formidable [fɔrmidabl] *adj* **1** ÉNORME : tremendous <un formidable défi : a tremendous challenge> **2** *fam* : great, terrific **3** *fam* : incredible — **formidablement** [-dabləmɑ̃] *adv*

formulaire [fɔrmylɛr] *nm* : form, questionnaire

formulation [fɔrmylasjɔ̃] *nf* : formulation

formule [fɔrmyl] *nf* **1** : formula **2** : expression, phrase <formule de politesse : polite phrase, closing (of a letter)> **3** : method, way, option <formule de paiement : method of payment> **4** FORMULAIRE : (printed) form

formuler [fɔrmyle] *vt* **1** : to formulate, to express **2** : to draw up, to write out

fornication [fɔrnikasjɔ̃] *nf* : fornication

forniquer [fɔrnike] *vi* : to fornicate

fort[1] [fɔr] *adv* **1** TRÈS : very, extremely <vous savez fort bien : you know full well> **2** BEAUCOUP : greatly, very much <j'en doute fort : I doubt it very much> **3** : strongly, loudly, hard <frapper fort : to strike hard>

fort[2], forte [fɔr, fɔrt] *adj* **1** : strong, powerful <fort comme un bœuf : strong as an ox> <café fort : strong coffee> <c'est plus fort que moi : I can't help it> **2** : intense, loud, bright **3** : large, heavy, stout **4** : able, gifted <être fort de : to be good at> **5 c'est un peu fort!** *fam* : that's a bit much!

fort[3] *nm* **1** : strength, strong point **2** : strong person **3** : fort, fortress **4 au fort de** : at the height of, in the midst of, in the depths of

fortement [fɔrtəmɑ̃] *adv* : strongly, deeply, intensely

forteresse [fɔrtərɛs] *nf* : fortress

fortification [fɔrtifikasjɔ̃] *nf* : fortification

fortifier [fɔrtifje] {96} *vt* : to fortify, to strengthen — **se fortifier** *vr*

fortuit, -tuite [fɔrtɥi, -tɥit] *adj* : fortuitous, chance
fortuitement [fɔrtɥitmɑ̃] *adv* : fortuitously, by chance
fortune [fɔrtyn] *nf* **1** : fortune <faire fortune : to make one's fortune> **2** CHANCE : chance, luck **3 de ~** : makeshift
fortuné, -née [fɔrtyne] *adj* **1** : fortunate **2** RICHE : wealthy
forum [fɔrɔm] *nm* **1** : forum **2** : newsgroup (on the Internet)
fosse [fos] *nf* **1** : pit <fosse septique : septic tank> <fosse d'aisances : cesspool> <fosse d'orchestre : orchestra pit> **2** TOMBE : grave
fossé [fose] *nm* **1** : ditch, trench **2** : gulf, gap <fossé de générations : generation gap>
fossette [fosɛt] *nf* : dimple
fossile[1] [fosil] *adj* : fossil, fossilized
fossile[2] *nm* : fossil
fossiliser [fosilize] *vt* : to fossilize **— se fossiliser** *vr*
fossoyeur [foswajœr] *nm* : gravedigger
fou[1] [fu] (**fol** [fɔl] *before a vowel or mute h*), **folle** [fɔl] *adj* **1** : crazy, insane <devenir fou : to go mad> <il est fou d'elle : he's crazy about her> **2** : silly, ridiculous **3** : tremendous, extreme <avoir un talent fou : to be extremely talented> **4 ~ de** : crazy with <fou de joie : jumping for joy> <fou de jalousie : green with envy>
fou[2], **folle** *n* **1** : crazy person, lunatic **2 comme un fou** *fam* : like crazy
fou[3] *nm* **1** : bishop (in chess) **2** : fool, jester **3 fou de Bassan** : gannet
foudre [fudr] *nf* **1** : lightning **2 foudres** *nfpl* : wrath
foudroyant, foudroyante [fudrwajɑ̃, fudrwajɑ̃t] *adj* **1** : overwhelming, crushing **2** : violent (of an illness) <une mort foudroyante : a sudden death>
foudroyer [fudrwaje] {58} *vt* : to strike down
fouet [fwɛ] *nm* **1** : whip **2** : whisk <fouet à œufs : egg whisk> **3 de plein fouet** : full-force, head-on
fouetter [fwete] *vt* **1** : to whip, to lash **2** : to whisk <crème fouettée : whipped cream>
fougère [fuʒɛr] *nf* : fern, bracken
fougue [fug] *nf* : ardor, spirit, passion
fougueusement [fugøzmɑ̃] *adv* : with spirit, ardently
fougueux, -geuse [fugø, -gøz] *adj* : ardent, spirited
fouille [fuj] *nf* **1** : digging **2** : search **3 fouilles** *nfpl* : excavations, (archaeological) dig
fouiller [fuje] *vt* **1** : to search, to go through (baggage, pockets, etc.) **2** : to excavate, to dig **—** *vi* **1** : to dig, to root (of a pig) **2 ~ dans** : to rummage through, to delve into
fouillis [fuji] *nm* : jumble, mess
fouiner [fwine] *vi fam* : to be nosy, to snoop around
fouineur[1], **-neuse** [fwinœr, -nøz] *adj* : inquisitive, nosy
fouineur[2], **-neuse** *n* **1** : busybody **2** : bargain hunter
fouir [fwir] *vt* : to burrow, to dig
foulard [fular] *nm* : scarf, neckerchief
foule [ful] *nf* **1** : crowd, mob **2 une foule de** : masses of, lots of
foulée [fule] *nf* **1** : stride **2 dans la foulée** : while I was (he was, etc.) at it **3 dans la foulée de** : on the heels of, in the wake of
fouler [fule] *vt* **1** : to press **2** : to tread, to set foot on <fouler aux pieds : to trample on> **3** : to sprain **—** *vi Can* : to shrink <mes pantalons ont foulé : my pants shrank> **— se fouler** *vr* **1** : to sprain **2** *fam* : to strain oneself
foulure [fulyr] *nf* ENTORSE : sprain
four [fur] *nm* **1** : oven <four à micro-ondes : microwave (oven)> **2** : kiln **3** *fam* : flop (in theater, etc.)
fourbe [furb] *adj* : deceitful
fourberie [furbəri] *nf* : deceit
fourbir [furbir] *vt* **1** : to polish up **2 fourbir ses armes** : to prepare for battle
fourbu, -bue [furby] *adj* : exhausted
fourche [furʃ] *nf* **1** : pitchfork **2** : fork, branching
fourcher [furʃe] *vi* **1** : to fork **2 ma (sa) langue a fourché** : it was a slip of the tongue **—** *vt* : to fork (in agriculture)
fourchette [furʃɛt] *nf* **1** : fork **2** : range, bracket
fourchu, -chue [furʃy] *adj* forked, split
fourgon [furgɔ̃] *nm* **1** : van **2** : freight car, baggage car <fourgon de queue : caboose> **3** : poker (for a fireplace)
fourgonnette [furgɔnɛt] *nf* : minivan
fourmi [furmi] *nf* : ant
fourmilier [furmilje] *nm* : anteater
fourmilière [furmiljɛr] *nf* : anthill
fourmillement [furmijmɑ̃] *nm* **1** : swarming **2** : tingling, pins and needles *pl*
fourmiller [furmije] *vi* **1** : to swarm, to mill about **2** : to abound <fourmiller de : to be teeming with> **3** : to tingle, to have pins and needles
fournaise [furnɛz] *nf Can* : furnace
fourneau [furno] *nm, pl* **fourneaux** [furno] **1** : stove **2** : furnace
fournée [furne] *nf* : batch
fourni, -nie [furni] *adj* **1** : thick, bushy **2 bien fourni** : well-stocked
fournil [furnil] *nm* : bakery
fournir [furnir] *vt* **1** : to supply, to provide (with) **2** : to produce (wine, etc.) **3 fournir un effort** : to make an effort **—** *vi* **~ à** : to provide for **— se fournir** *vr* **~ chez** : to shop at
fournisseur, -seuse [furnisœr, -søz] *n* : supplier, dealer, purveyor
fourniture [furnityr] *nf* **1** : furnishing **2 fournitures** *nfpl* : equipment, sup-

plies <fournitures de bureaux : office supplies>

fourrage [furaʒ] *nm* : feed, fodder

fourrager [furaʒe] {17} *vi* : to rummage, to forage

fourré[1], **-rée** [fure] *adj* **1** : fur-lined **2** : filled (of candies)

fourré[2] *nm* : thicket

fourreau [furo] *nm, pl* **fourreaux 1** : sheath, case, scabbard **2** *or* **robe fourreau** : sheath dress

fourrer [fure] *vt* **1** : to line with fur **2** : to stuff, to fill **3** *fam* : to thrust, to stick — **se fourrer** *vr* **1** *fam* : to get, to put oneself <se fourrer sous les couvertures : to crawl under the covers> **2** *Can fam* : to mess up

fourre–tout [furtu] *nms & pl* : tote bag, carryall

fourreur, -reuse [furœr, -røz] *n* : furrier

fourrière [furjɛr] *nf* : pound (for animals or vehicles)

fourrure [furyr] *nf* **1** : fur **2** : coat (of an animal)

fourvoyer [furvwaje] {58} *vt* : to lead astray — **se fourvoyer** *vr* **1** : to make an error, to go astray **2 ~ dans** : to stray into, to get involved in

foyer [fwaje] *nm* **1** : hearth, fireplace **2** RÉSIDENCE : home <femme au foyer : housewife> <sans foyer : homeless> **3** : home (for the elderly, etc.) **4** : focus <lunettes à double foyer : bifocals> **5** : center, seat, source

fracas [fraka] *nms & pl* : crash, din

fracassant, -sante [frakasɑ̃, -sɑ̃t] *adj* **1** : deafening, thunderous **2** : sensational <un succès fracassant : a stunning success>

fracasser [frakase] *vt* : to shatter, to smash — **se fracasser** *vr*

fraction [fraksjɔ̃] *nf* : fraction

fractionnaire [fraksjɔnɛr] *adj* : fractional

fractionner [fraksjɔne] *vt* : to divide, to split (up) — **se fractionner** *vr*

fracture [fraktyr] *nf* : fracture <fracture du crâne : fractured skull>

fracturer [fraktyre] *vt* **1** : to fracture, to break **2** : to break open

fragile [fraʒil] *adj* **1** CASSABLE : fragile, breakable **2** FAIBLE : sensitive, weak, frail

fragiliser [fraʒilize] *vt* : to weaken, to make fragile

fragilité [fraʒilite] *nf* **1** : fragility **2** : frailty

fragment [fragmɑ̃] *nm* **1** : fragment, bit **2** : passage (from a book), snatch (of a conversation)

fragmentaire [fragmɑ̃tɛr] *adj* : fragmentary, sketchy

fragmenter [fragmɑ̃te] *vt* : to fragment, to break up — **se fragmenter** *vr*

fragmentation [fragmɑ̃tasjɔ̃] *nf* : fragmentation, splitting up

frai [frɛ] *nm* **1** : fry **2** : fish eggs, spawn

fraîchement [frɛʃmɑ̃] *adv* **1** : freshly, newly <fraises fraîchement cueillies : freshly picked strawberries> **2** : coolly <fraîchement reçu : coolly received>

fraîcheur [frɛʃœr] *nf* **1** : freshness **2** : coolness

fraîchir [frɛʃir] *vi* **1** : to cool off **2** : to freshen

frais[1] [frɛ] *adv* **1** : freshly, recently **2 il fait frais** : it's cool outside

frais[2], **fraîche** [frɛ, frɛʃ] *adj* **1** : fresh <fruits frais : fresh fruit> **2** RÉCENT : new, recent <nouvelles fraîches : recent news> **3** : cool <températures plus fraîches : cooler temperatures> **4 peinture fraîche** : wet paint

frais[3] *nm* **1 mettre au frais** : to put in a cool place **2 prendre le frais** : to take a breath of fresh air **3 frais** *nmpl* : expenses, fees, charges

fraise [frɛz] *nf* **1** : strawberry **2** : (dentist's) drill

fraiser [frɛze] *vt* : to ream

framboise [frɑ̃bwaz] *nf* : raspberry

franc[1] [frɑ̃] *adv* **à parler franc** : frankly, to be quite frank

franc[2], **franche** [frɑ̃, frɑ̃ʃ] *adj* **1** : frank, straightforward **2** : pure (of colors, etc.) **3** : absolute, downright **4** : free, exempt <port franc : duty-free port>

franc[3] *nm* : franc

français[1], **-çaise** [frɑ̃sɛ, -sɛz] *adj* : French

français[2] *nm* : French (language)

Français, -çaise *n* : Frenchman *m*, Frenchwoman *f*

franchement [frɑ̃ʃmɑ̃] *adv* **1** : frankly, candidly **2** : clearly, definitely **3** : boldly, firmly **4** : downright <c'est franchement ridicule! : it's really silly!>

franchir [frɑ̃ʃir] *vt* **1** : to cross over, to surmount, to clear **2** : to cover (a distance) **3** : to last through (a period of time)

franchise [frɑ̃ʃiz] *nf* **1** : frankness **2** : exemption <en franchise douanière : duty-free> <franchise postale : postage paid> **3** : deductible **4** : franchise

franchissement [frɑ̃ʃismɑ̃] *nm* : crossing, clearing

franciscain, -caine [frɑ̃siskɛ̃, -kɛn] *adj & n* : Franciscan

franciser [frɑ̃size] *vt* : to frenchify

franc–jeu [frɑ̃ʒø] *nm* : fair play

franc–maçon [frɑ̃masɔ̃] *nm* : Freemason — **franc–maçonnerie** [frɑ̃masɔnri] *nf*

franco–canadien[1], **-dienne** [frɑ̃kokanadjɛ̃, -djɛn] *adj* : French-Canadian

franco–canadien[2], **-dienne** *n* : Canadian French

francophile [frɑ̃kɔfil] *adj & nmf* : francophile

francophone[1] [frɑ̃kɔfɔn] *adj* : French-speaking
francophone[2] *nmf* : French speaker
francophonie [frɑ̃kɔfɔni] *nf* : French-speaking community
franc–parler [frɑ̃parle] *nm, pl* **franc–parlers** : frankness <avoir son franc-parler : to speak one's mind>
franc–tireur [frɑ̃tirœr] *nm, pl* **francs–tireurs 1** : irregular (soldier), guerrilla **2** : maverick <agir en franc-tireur : to act independently>
frange [frɑ̃ʒ] *nf* **1** : fringe **2** : bangs (of hair)
franger [frɑ̃ʒe] {17} *vt* : to fringe
frangin, -gine [frɑ̃ʒɛ̃, -ʒin] *n France fam* : brother *m*, sister *f*
franquette [frɑ̃kɛt] *nf* **à la bonne franquette** : without ceremony, informally
frappant, -pante [frapɑ̃, -pɑ̃t] *adj* : striking <un contraste frappant : a striking contrast>
frappe [frap] *nf* **1** : impression, stamp **2** : typing
frapper [frape] *vt* **1** : to strike, to hit **2** : to strike, to impress, to astonish **3** : to mint **4** : to ice, to chill **5 frapper d'ostracisme** : to ostracize — *vi* **1** : to hit, to knock, to bang **2** : to clap <frapper dans ses mains : to clap one's hands> — **se frapper** *vr* : to get all worked up
frappeur, -peuse [frapœr, -pøz] *n Can* : hitter, batter <frappeur désigné : designated hitter>
frasque [frask] *nf* : prank, escapade <faire des frasques : to get into mischief>
fraternel, -nelle [fratɛrnɛl] *adj* : fraternal — **fraternellement** [-nɛlmɑ̃] *adv*
fraterniser [fratɛrnize] *vi* : to fraternize — **fraternisation** [-nizasjɔ̃] *nf*
fraternité [fratɛrnite] *nf* : fraternity, brotherhood
fratricide[1] [fratrisid] *adj* : fratricidal
fratricide[2] *nm* : fratricide
fraude [frod] *nf* **1** : fraud <fraude fiscale : tax evasion> **2 passer en fraude** : to smuggle in
frauder [frode] *v* : to cheat
fraudeur, -deuse [frodœr, -døz] *n* : cheat, swindler
frauduleux, -leuse [frodylø, -løz] *adj* : fraudulent — **frauduleusement** [-løzmɑ̃] *adv*
frayer [frɛje] {11} *vt* : to open up, to clear — *vi* **1** : to spawn **2 ~ avec** : to associate with — **se frayer** *vr* **se frayer un chemin** : to make one's way
frayeur [frɛjœr] *nf* : fright
fredaine [frədɛn] *nf* : prank, escapade
fredonner [frədɔne] *vt* : to hum
freezer [frizœr] *nm* : freezer (of a refrigerator)
frégate [fregat] *nf* : frigate
frein [frɛ̃] *nm* **1** : brake **2** : check, restraint <mettre un frein à : to curb, to block> <sans frein : unrestrained, unbridled>
freinage [frɛnaʒ] *nm* : braking
freiner [frene] *vt* : to slow down, to check — *vi* : to brake
frelaté, -tée [frəlate] *adj* **1** : adulterated **2** : unnatural, artificial, corrupt
frêle [frɛl] *adj* **1** : weak, flimsy **2** : frail
frelon [frəlɔ̃] *nm* : hornet
frémir [fremir] *vi* **1** FRISSONNER : to tremble, to shiver, to shudder **2** : to quiver, to flutter **3** : to start to boil, to simmer
frémissant, -sante [fremisɑ̃, -sɑ̃t] *adj* : quivering, trembling
frémissement [fremismɑ̃] *nm* : trembling, shivering, shuddering
frêne [frɛn] *nm* : ash (tree or wood)
frénésie [frenezi] *nf* : frenzy
frénétique [frenetik] *adj* : frantic, frenetic — **frénétiquement** [-tikmɑ̃] *adv*
fréquemment [frekamɑ̃] *adv* : frequently
fréquence [frekɑ̃s] *nf* : frequency
fréquent, -quente [frekɑ̃, -kɑ̃t] *adj* : frequent
fréquentation [frekɑ̃tasjɔ̃] *nf* **1** : frequenting **2** : attendance <taux de fréquentation : attendance rate> **3** RELATION : acquaintance <mauvaises fréquentations : bad company> **4 fréquentations** *nfpl Can* : dating, courting
fréquenter [frekɑ̃te] *vt* **1** : to frequent **2** : to attend **3** : to associate with, to consort with — **se fréquenter** *vr* **1** : to see each other **2** : to go out (with each other), to date
frère [frɛr] *nm* **1** : brother **2** : friar, brother (in religion)
fresque [frɛsk] *nf* : fresco
fret [frɛ(t)] *nm* : freight
fréter [frete] {87} *vt* : to charter
frétillement [fretijmɑ̃] *nm* : wagging, wag (of a tail)
frétiller [fretije] *vi* **1** : to wriggle, to quiver <frétillant de joie : quivering with delight> **2** : to wag <sa queue frétille : its tail is wagging>
fretin [frətɛ̃] *nm* **menu fretin** : small fry
freux [frø] *nm* CORBEAU : rook
friable [frijabl] *adj* : crumbly
friand, friande [frijɑ̃, -jɑ̃d] *adj* **~ de** : partial to, fond of
friandise [frijɑ̃diz] *nf* **1** BONBON : candy **2** : delicacy
fric [frik] *nm fam* : dough, cash
fricassée [frikase] *nf* : fricassee — **fricasser** [frikase] *vt*
friche [friʃ] *nf* : fallow land, wasteland <en friche : fallow>
friction [friksjɔ̃] *nf* **1** : friction **2** MASSAGE : massage, rubdown
frictionner [friksjɔne] *vt* : to rub (down), to massage — **se frictionner** *vr*

frigide |friʒid| *adj* : frigid — **frigidité** |-ʒidite| *nf*
frigo |frigo| *nm fam* : fridge
frigorifier |frigɔrifje| {96} *vt* **1** : to refrigerate **2 être frigorifié** *fam* : to be frozen stiff
frigorifique |frigɔrifik| *adj* : refrigerated (of a truck, etc.)
frileux, -leuse |frilø, -løz| *adj* **1** : sensitive to cold **2** : cautious, timid
frimas |frima| *nms & pl* : hoarfrost
frime |frim| *nf fam* : sham, pretense <c'est pour la frime : it's just for show>
frimer |frime| *vi fam* : to put on an act
frimousse |frimus| *nf fam* : pretty little face
fringale |frɛ̃gal| *nf fam* **1 avoir la fringale** : to be starving **2 avoir une fringale de** : to have a craving for
fringant, -gante |frɛ̃gɑ̃, -gɑ̃t| *adj* **1** : dashing **2** : spirited (of a horse)
fringillidé |frɛ̃ʒilide| *nm* : finch
fringues |frɛ̃g| *nfpl fam* : gear, duds
friper |fripe| *vt* : to wrinkle, to crumple — **se friper** *vr*
friperie |fripri| *nf France* **1** : secondhand clothes shop **2** : secondhand clothes
fripon¹, -ponne |fripɔ̃, -pɔn| *adj* COQUIN : mischievous
fripon², -ponne *n* : rascal
fripouille |fripuj| *nf fam* : scoundrel, crook
frire |frir| {45} *v* : to fry
frise |friz| *nf* : frieze
friser |frize| *vt* **1** : to curl **2** : to graze, to skim (a surface) **3** : to border on <elle doit friser la quarantaine : she must be close to forty> — *vi* : to curl — **se friser** *vr* **se faire friser** : to have one's hair curled
frisette |frizɛt| *nf* : ringlet
frisquet, -quette |friskɛ, -kɛt| *adj* : chilly, nippy
frisson |frisɔ̃| *nm* **1** : shiver, shudder **2** : ripple (of water, etc.), rustle (of leaves)
frissonnement |frisɔnmɑ̃| *nm* **1** : shiver, shudder **2** : rippling, rustling
frissonner |frisɔne| *vi* **1** : to shiver, to shudder **2** : to rustle, to ripple
frites |frit| *nfpl* : french fries
friture |frityr| *nf* **1** : frying **2** : deep fat, oil **3** : fried food
frivole |frivɔl| *adj* : frivolous, trivial — **frivolement** |-vɔlmɑ̃| *adv*
frivolité |frivɔlite| *nf* : frivolity
froc |frɔk| *nm* **1** : (religious) habit **2** *fam* : pants *pl*, trousers *pl*
froid¹ |frwa| *adv* **il fait froid** : it's cold (outside)
froid², froide |frwa, frwad| *adj* **1** : cold **2** : unfeeling, insensitive
froid³ *nm* **1** : cold <un grand froid : intense cold> <avoir froid : to feel cold> <conservez au froid : keep in a cold place> **2** : cold (illness) <prendre froid : to catch cold> **3** : coolness, chill <être en froid avec : to be on bad terms with> **4 à ~** : calmly, cooly **5 à ~** : without preparation, spontaneous(ly)
froidement |frwadmɑ̃| *adv* : coldly, coolly
froideur |frwadœr| *nf* : coldness, coolness
froissement |frwasmɑ̃| *nm* **1** : crumpling, creasing **2** : rustle, rustling
froisser |frwase| *vt* **1** : to crumple, to crease, to muss up **2** BLESSER : to hurt, to offend, to upset — **se froisser** *vr* **1** : to crease, to crumple (up) **2 se froisser un muscle** : to strain a muscle
frôler |frole| *vt* EFFLEURER : to touch lightly, to brush, to graze
fromage |frɔmaʒ| *nm* **1** : cheese **2 fromage blanc** *or* **fromage cottage** : cottage cheese
fromager¹, -gère |frɔmaʒe, -ʒɛr| *adj* : cheese <l'industrie fromagère : the cheese industry>
fromager², -gère *n* : cheese maker, cheese merchant
fromagerie |frɔmaʒri| *nf* : cheese store
froment |frɔmɑ̃| *nm* : wheat
fronce |frɔ̃s| *nf* : gather (of fabric)
froncement |frɔ̃smɑ̃| *nm* **froncement de sourcils** : frown
froncer |frɔ̃se| {6} *vt* **1** : to gather (fabric) **2** : to wrinkle, to pucker <froncer les sourcils : to knit one's brow, to frown>
frondaison |frɔ̃dɛzɔ̃| *nf* : foliage
fronde |frɔ̃d| *nf* **1** : rebellion, revolt **2** : slingshot **3** : frond
frondeur, -deuse |frɔ̃dœr, -døz| *adj* : rebellious
front |frɔ̃| *nm* **1** : forehead, brow **2** : front (in meteorology, politics, war, etc.) **3** : audacity, effrontery <avoir le front de faire : to have the nerve to do> **4 de ~** : without hesitation, head-on **5 de ~** : abreast <à cinq de front : five abreast> **6 faire front à** : to confront, to face up to
frontal, -tale |frɔ̃tal| *adj, mpl* **frontaux** |frɔ̃to| : frontal
frontalier, -lière |frɔ̃talje, -ljɛr| *adj* : frontier, border
frontière |frɔ̃tjɛr| *nf* **1** : frontier, border **2** : boundary
frontispice |frɔ̃tispis| *nm* : frontispiece
fronton |frɔ̃tɔ̃| *nm* : pediment
frottement |frɔtmɑ̃| *nm* **1** : rubbing, scraping **2 frottements** *nmpl* : friction, disagreement
frotter |frɔte| *vt* **1** : to rub <frotter une allumette : to strike a match> **2** : to polish, to scrub — *vi* : to rub — **se frotter** *vr* **1** : to rub <ne te frotte pas les yeux : don't rub your eyes> **2** : to scrub oneself **3 ~ à** : to face up to, to take on

frou–frou *or* **froufrou** [frufru] *nm, pl* **frou–frous** *or* **froufrous** : rustle, swish
froufrouter [frufrute] *vi* : to rustle, to swish
frousse [frus] *nf fam* : scare, fright, jitters *pl*
fructifier [fryktifje] {96} *vi* **1** : to bear fruit **2** : to yield a profit
fructueux, -tueuse [fryktɥø, -tɥøz] *adj* **1** : fruitful, productive **2** RENTABLE : profitable
frugal, -gale [frygal] *adj, mpl* **frugaux** [frygo] : frugal — **frugalement** [-galmɑ̃] *adv*
frugalité [frygalite] *nf* : frugality
fruit [frɥi] *nm* **1** : fruit <jus de fruits : fruit juice> **2 fruits de mer** : seafood
fruité, -tée [frɥite] *adj* : fruity
fruitier[1], **-tière** [frɥitje, -tjɛr] *adj* : fruit <arbre fruitier : fruit tree>
fruitier[2], **-tière** *n* : fruit merchant
fruste [fryst] *adj* **1** : worn **2** GROSSIER : rough, uncouth
frustrant, -trante [frystrɑ̃, -trɑ̃t] *adj* : frustrating
frustration [frystrasjɔ̃] *nf* : frustration
frustrer [frystre] *vt* **1** DÉCEVOIR : to frustrate, to disappoint **2** PRIVER : to deprive
fuel [fjul] → **fioul**
fugace [fygas] *adj* ÉPHÉMÈRE : fleeting
fugitif[1], **-tive** [fyʒitif, -tiv] *adj* **1** : escaped, fugitive **2** : fleeting, elusive
fugitif[2], **-tive** *n* **1** : fugitive, escapee **2** : runaway
fugue [fyg] *nf* **1** : running away <faire une fugue : to run away (from home)> <fugue amoureuse : elopement> **2** : fugue
fuguer [fyge] *vi* : to run away
fugueur, -gueuse [fygœr, -gøz] *adj & n* : runaway
fuir [fɥir] {46} *vi* **1** : to flee **2** : to leak — *vt* **1** : to shun, to avoid **2** : to flee, to run away from
fuite [fɥit] *nf* **1** : flight, escape **2** : leak
fulgurant, -rante [fylgyrɑ̃, -rɑ̃t] *adj* **1** ÉBLOUISSANT : dazzling **2** : shooting, searing, intense
fulminant, -nante [fylminɑ̃, -nɑ̃t] *adj* : furious, enraged
fulminer [fylmine] *vt* : to bellow out (threats, etc.) — *vi* ENRAGER : to be enraged, to fulminate
fumé, -mée [fyme] *adj* **1** : smoked **2** : tinted
fumée *nf* **1** : smoke **2** : steam
fumer [fyme] *vt* **1** : to smoke **2** : to manure — *vi* **1** : to smoke **2** : to steam **3** : to fume (with anger)
fumet [fymɛ] *nm* : aroma (of food or wine)
fumier [fymje] *nm* : dung, manure
fumigation [fymigasjɔ̃] *nf* : fumigation
fumiste [fymist] *nmf fam* **1** : shirker **2** : phoney
fumisterie [fymistəri] *nf fam* **1** : joke, farce **2** : sham
fumoir [fymwar] *nm* **1** : smokehouse **2** : smoking room
fun [fœn] *nm Can fam* : fun <j'ai eu du fun : I had fun>
funambule [fynɑ̃byl] *nmf* ÉQUILIBRISTE : tightrope walker
funèbre [fynɛbr] *adj* **1** FUNÉRAIRE : funeral **2** LUGUBRE : funereal, gloomy
funérailles [fyneraj] *nfpl* : funeral
funéraire [fynerɛr] *adj* **1** : funeral, funerary **2 salon funéraire** *Can* : funeral home
funeste [fynɛst] *adj* **1** : fatal, deathly **2** CATASTROPHIQUE : disastrous, dire
fur [fyr] *nm* **au fur et à mesure** : little by little, as one goes along
furet [fyrɛ] *nm* : ferret
fureter [fyrte] {20} *vi* : to ferret around, to nose about
fureteur, -teuse [fyrtœr, -tøz] *adj* : inquisitive, prying
fureur [fyrœr] *nf* **1** RAGE : rage, fury **2 faire fureur** : to be all the rage
furibond, -bonde [fyribɔ̃, -bɔ̃d] *adj* : furious, livid
furie [fyri] *nf* **1** : fury, rage **2 avec ~** : furiously, violently
furieusement [fyrjøzmɑ̃] *adv* **1** : furiously **2** : extremely, tremendously
furieux, -rieuse [fyrjø, -jøz] *adj* **1** : furious, angry **2** : fierce, intense
furoncle [fyrɔ̃kl] *nm* : boil, carbuncle
furtif, -tive [fyrtif, -tiv] *adj* : furtive, sly — **furtivement** [-tivmɑ̃] *adv*
fusain [fyzɛ̃] *nm* **1** : spindle tree **2** : charcoal (for drawing) **3** : charcoal drawing
fuseau [fyzo] *nm, pl* **fuseaux 1** : spindle, bobbin **2 fuseau horaire** : time zone **3 pantalon fuseau** : ski pants
fusée [fyze] *nf* **1** : rocket **2 fusée éclairante** : flare
fuselage [fyzlaʒ] *nm* : fuselage
fuselé, -lée [fyzle] *adj* : slender, tapering
fuser [fyze] *vi* **1** : to stream out, to gush out **2** JAILLIR : to burst forth (of laughter, etc.)
fusible [fyzibl] *nm* : fuse <faire sauter un fusible : to blow a fuse>
fusil [fyzi] *nm* **1** : gun, rifle **2** : marksman
fusilier [fyzilje] *nm* **1** : rifleman **2 fusilier marin** : marine
fusillade [fyzijad] *nf* **1** : gunfire **2** : shooting
fusiller [fyzije] *vt* **1** : to shoot, to execute **2 fusiller du regard** : to look daggers at
fusil–mitrailleur [fyzimitrajœr] *nm, pl* **fusils–mitrailleurs** : automatic rifle, machine gun
fusion [fyzjɔ̃] *nf* **1** : fusion **2** : melting <roche en fusion : molten rock> **3** : merger
fusionner [fyzɔnje] *v* : to merge

fustiger [fystiʒe] {17} *vt* : to castigate, to censure
fut [fy], *etc.* → **être**
fût [fy] *nm* **1** TONNEAU : barrel, cask <bière en fût : draft beer> **2** : shaft (of a column) **3** : trunk (of a tree)
futaie [fytɛ] *nf* : forest (of tall trees)
futé, -tée [fyte] *adj* : cunning, crafty
futile [fytil] *adj* **1** : futile **2** FRIVOLE : trivial, frivolous
futilité [fytilite] *nf* : futility
futur[1], **-ture** [fytyr] *adj* : future
futur[2] *nm* **1** : future **2** : future tense
futuriste [fytyrist] *adj* : futuristic
fuyait [fɥijɛ], **fuyions** [fɥijɔ̃], *etc.* → **fuir**
fuyant, fuyante [fɥijɑ̃, fɥijɑ̃t] *adj* **1** INSAISISSABLE : elusive, shifty **2** : receding
fuyard, fuyarde [fɥijar, fɥijard] *n* **1** : runaway **2** : deserter (in the military)

G

g [ʒe] *nm* : g, the seventh letter of the alphabet
gabardine [gabardin] *nf* : gabardine
gabarit [gabari] *nm* **1** : template, gauge **2** : size, dimensions *pl* **3** *fam* : (physical) build **4** *fam* : caliber, sort <du même gabarit : of the same ilk>
gabonais, -naise [gabɔnɛ, -nɛz] *adj* : Gabonese
Gabonais, -naise *n* : Gabonese
gâcher [gaʃe] *vt* **1** : to spoil, to ruin **2** GASPILLER : to waste, to squander **3** : to mix (plaster, mortar, etc.)
gâchette [gaʃɛt] *nf* : trigger
gâchis [gaʃi] *nm* **1** DÉSORDRE : mess <faire du gâchis : to make a mess> **2** GASPILLAGE : waste
gadelle [gadɛl] *nf Can* : currant
gadget [gadʒɛt] *nm* **1** : gimmick, gadget **2 gadgets** *nmpl* : gadgetry
gadoue [gadu] *nf* **1** : mud, muck **2** *Can* : slush
gaélique[1] [gaelik] *adj* : Gaelic
gaélique[2] *nm* : Gaelic (language)
gaffe [gaf] *nf* **1** : boat hook **2** *fam* : blunder, stupidity, goof
gaffer [gafe] *vi fam* : to blunder, to goof (up)
gaffeur, -feuse [gafœr, -føz] *n fam* : blunderer
gag [gag] *nm* : gag, joke
gage [gaʒ] *nm* **1** : security <mettre en gage : to pawn> **2** : pledge, guarantee <en gage d'amitié : as a token of our friendship> **3** : forfeit (in games) **4 gages** *nmpl* : wages, pay
gager [gaʒe] {17} *vt* **1** : to bet, to wager **2** : to guarantee (a loan, etc.)
gageure [gaʒœr] *nf* **1** : challenge **2** *Can* : bet, wager
gagnant[1], **-gnante** [gaɲɑ̃, -ɲɑ̃t] *adj* : winning <billet gagnant : winning ticket>
gagnant[2], **-gnante** *n* : winner
gagne–pain [gaɲpɛ̃] *nms & pl* : job, livelihood
gagner [gaɲe] *vt* **1** : to win **2** : to earn <gagner sa vie : to earn one's living> **3** : to gain <gagner du terrain : to gain ground> <gagner de la vitesse : to pick up speed> **4** ÉCONOMISER : to save (time, space, etc.) **5** ATTEINDRE : to reach, to arrive at **6** : to win (someone) over **7** : to overcome — *vi* **1** : to win **2** : to gain, to advance, to encroach **3** : to increase <gagner en longueur : to grow longer> **4 ~ à** : to gain by <gagner à vieillir : to improve with age> **5 y gagner** : to be better off <ils y gagnent : it's to their advantage>
gai, gaie [gɛ] *adj* **1** JOYEUX : cheerful, happy, merry **2** HOMOSEXUEL : gay, homosexual
gaiement [gemɑ̃] *adv* : gaily, merrily
gaieté [gete] *nf* : cheerfulness, mirth
gaillard[1], **-larde** [gajar, -jard] *adj* **1** : lively, sprightly **2** GRIVOIS : ribald, bawdy
gaillard[2] , **-larde** *nmf* : sturdy fellow *m*, strapping individual
gaillard[3] *nm* **gaillard d'avant** : forecastle
gaillardement [gajardəmɑ̃] *adv* : cheerfully
gain [gɛ̃] *nm* **1** : earnings *pl* **2** : saving (of time, space, etc.) **3** : gain (in finance) **4** : winning <avoir gain de cause : to win the case>
gaine [gɛn] *nf* **1** : girdle, corset **2** : sheath
gainer [gene] *vt* : to cover, to sheathe
gala [gala] *nm* : gala, reception
galactique [galaktik] *adj* : galactic
galamment [galamɑ̃] *adv* : gallantly
galant[1], **-lante** [galɑ̃, -lɑ̃t] *adj* **1** : courteous, gallant **2 en galante compagnie** : with a person of the opposite sex **3 homme galant** : ladies' man
galant[2] *nm* : beau, suitor
galanterie [galɑ̃tri] *nf* : gallantry
galaxie [galaksi] *nf* : galaxy
galbe [galb] *nm* : curve, shapeliness
gale [gal] *nf* **1** : scabies **2** : mange **3** *Can* : scab
galéjade [galeʒad] *nf* : tall story
galère [galɛr] *nf* **1** : galley (ship) **2** *fam* : hard time, hassle
galerie [galri] *nf* **1** : gallery **2** : balcony (in a theater) **3** : roof rack (of an automobile) **4** *Can* : porch **5 galerie marchande** : shopping mall

galet |galɛ| *nm* CAILLOU : pebble
galette |galɛt| *nf* **1** : flat round cake **2** : pancake **3** *Can* : soft cookie <galette à la mélasse : molasses cookie> **4** *fam* : dough, cash
galeux, -leuse |galø, -løz| *adj* : mangy
galimatias |galimatja| *nm* : gibberish, nonsense
galion |galjɔ̃| *nm* : galleon
galipette |galipɛt| *nf fam* : somersault <faire des galipettes : to turn somersaults>
galipote |galipɔt| *nf* **courir la galipote** *Can* : to gallivant
galle |gal| *nf* : gall (in botany)
gallicisme |galisism| *nm* **1** : French idiom **2** : gallicism
gallium |galjɔm| *nm* : gallium
gallois[1], -loise |galwa, -lwaz| *adj* : Welsh
gallois[2] *nm* : Welsh (language)
Gallois, -loise *n* : Welshman *m*, Welshwoman *f*
gallon |galɔ̃| *nm* : gallon
galoche |galɔʃ| *nf* **1** SABOT : clog **2** : overshoe
galon |galɔ̃| *nm* **1** : braid (on fabric) **2** : stripe (in the military) <prendre du galon : to be promoted> **3** *Can* : measuring tape
galop |galo| *nm* : gallop <au galop : at a gallop>
galopant, -pante |galɔpɑ̃, -pɑ̃t| *adj* : runaway, galloping
galoper |galɔpe| *vi* **1** : to gallop **2** : to run about **3** : to run wild <son imagination galope : his imagination is running riot>
galopin |galɔpɛ̃| *nm* : rascal
galvaniser |galvanize| *vt* : to galvanize
galvauder |galvode| *vt* **1** : to tarnish, to sully **2** : to debase <une expression galvaudée : a hackneyed phrase> — **se galvauder** *vr*
gambade |gɑ̃bad| *nf* : leap, skip
gambader |gɑ̃bade| *vi* : to leap about, to gambol
gambien, -bienne |gɑ̃bjɛ̃, -bjɛn| *adj* : Gambian
Gambien, -bienne *n* : Gambian
gambit |gɑ̃bi| *nm* : gambit
gamelle |gamɛl| *nf* : mess kit
gamète *nm* |gamɛt|: gamete
gamin[1], -mine |gamɛ̃, -min| *adj* **1** ESPIÈGLE : mischievous, playful **2** PUÉRIL : childish
gamin[2], -mine *n fam* : kid, youngster
gaminerie |gaminri| *nf France* : childishness
gamme |gam| *nf* **1** : scale (in music) **2** SÉRIE : range (of colors, products, etc.), gamut (of emotions)
gang[1] |gɑ̃g| *nm France* : gang
gang[2] *nf Can fam* : gang, group <la gang du bureau : the gang in the office>
ganglion |gɑ̃glijɔ̃| *nm* **1** : ganglion **2 avoir des ganglions** *fam* : to have swollen glands
gangrène |gɑ̃grɛn| *nf* **1** : gangrene **2** : scourge, corrupting influence
gangreneux, -neuse |gɑ̃grənø, -nøz| *adj* : gangrenous
gangster |gɑ̃gstɛr| *nm* : gangster
gannet |ganɛ| *nm* : gannet
ganse |gɑ̃s| *nf* : braid (in sewing)
gant |gɑ̃| *nm* **1** : glove <gant de boxe : boxing glove> **2 gant de toilette** : washcloth **3 jeter le gant** : to throw down the gauntlet **4 prendre des gants pour** *or* **mettre des gants pour** : to handle with kid gloves
gantelet |gɑ̃tlɛ| *nm* : gauntlet
garage |garaʒ| *nm* **1** : garage <garage d'autobus : bus depot> <garage d'avions : hangar> **2** STATION-SERVICE : service station, repair shop
garagiste |garaʒist| *nmf* **1** : garage owner **2** : garage mechanic
garant[1], -rante |garɑ̃, -rɑ̃t| *n* **1** : guarantor, surety **2 se porter garant de** : to be answerable for, to vouch for
garant[2] *nm* : guarantee, assurance
garantie |garɑ̃ti| *nf* : guarantee, warranty
garantir |garɑ̃tir| *vt* **1** ASSURER : to guarantee, to assure **2 ~ de** : to protect from
garçon |garsɔ̃| *nm* **1** : boy, young man **2** SERVEUR : waiter **3** CÉLIBATAIRE : bachelor **4 garçon manqué** : tomboy
garçonnet |garsɔnɛ| *nm* : little boy
garde[1] |gard| *nm* **1** : guard, warden **2 garde côtière** *Can* : coast guard **3 garde du corps** : bodyguard **4 garde de nuit** : night watchman **5 garde forestier** : forest ranger
garde[2] *nf* **1** : nurse **2** : (military) guard, watch **3** : custody, care <avoir la garde des enfants : to have custody of the children> **4** : duty <être de garde : to be on duty> **5 chien de garde** : watchdog **6 mettre en garde** : to warn **7 prendre garde** : to be careful
garde–à–vous |gardavu| *nms & pl* : standing at attention
garde–boue |gardəbu| *nms & pl* : mudguard
garde–chasse |gardəʃas| *nm, pl* **gardes–chasse(s)** : gamekeeper, game warden
garde–feu |gardəfø| *nms & pl* **1** : fire screen **2** *Can* : fire warden
garde–fou |gardəfu| *nm, pl* **garde–fous** PARAPET : railing, parapet
garde–malade |gardəmalad| *nmf* **gardes–malade(s)** INFIRMIER : nurse
garde–manger |gardəmɑ̃ʒe| *nms & pl* : pantry
gardénia |gardenja| *nm* : gardenia
garde–pêche |gardəpɛʃ| *nm, pl* **gardes–pêche** : fish warden

garder [garde] *vt* **1** CONSERVER : to keep **2** : to keep on (clothing) **3** : to keep (oneself) in <garder le lit : to stay in bed> **4** SURVEILLER : to guard, to watch over <garder des enfants : to look after children, to baby-sit> **5 ~ de** : to protect from — **se garder** *vr* **1** SE CONSERVER : to keep **2 ~ de** : to be careful not to <gardez-vous de parler : be careful not to talk>

garderie [gardəri] *nf Can* : day-care center, nursery

garde-robe[1] [gardərɔb] *nf, pl* **garde-robes** : wardrobe, clothes

garde-robe[2] *nmf Can* : wardrobe, closet

gardien[1], **-dienne** [gardjɛ̃, -djɛn] *n* **1** : caretaker, attendant, custodian **2** : guardian, keeper <gardien des droits humains : guardian of human rights>

gardien[2] *nm* **1 gardien de but** : goalkeeper **2 gardien de la paix** *France* : police officer, policeman **3 gardien de troupeau** : herdsman

gardienne *nf* **gardienne d'enfants** : day-care worker, baby-sitter

gare[1] [gar] *nf* **1** : railroad station **2 gare d'autobus** *Can or* **gare routière** *France* : bus station

gare[2] *interj* **1 gare à vous!** : watch out! **2 sans crier gare** : without warning

garenne [garɛn] *nf* : (rabbit) warren

garer [gare] *vt* STATIONNER : to park — **se garer** *vr* **1** : to park **2** SE RANGER : to pull over

gargantuesque [gargɑ̃tɥɛsk] *adj* : gargantuan

gargariser [gargarize] *v* **se gargariser** *vr* **1** : to gargle **2 ~ de** *fam* : to revel in

gargarisme [gargarism] *nm* **1** : gargling **2** : gargle (product)

gargote [gargɔt] *nf* : cheap restaurant

gargouille [garguj] *nf* : gargoyle

gargouillement [gargujmɑ̃] *nm* : rumble, rumbling

gargouiller [garguje] *vi* : to gurgle (of water), to rumble (of one's stomach)

garnement [garnəmɑ̃] *nm* : rascal

garni, -nie [garni] *adj* : garnished (in cooking) <plat garni : meal with vegetables> <hamburger garni : hamburger with all the trimmings>

garnir [garnir] *vt* **1** REMPLIR : to fill **2** : to cover **3** : to decorate, to trim **4** : to garnish (a dish) — **se garnir** *vr* : to fill up

garnison [garnizɔ̃] *nf* : garrison

garniture [garnityr] *nf* **1** : filling, garnish (in cooking) <sans garniture : without vegetables> **2** : trimming **3 garniture de frein** : brake lining

garrocher [garɔʃe] *vt Can fam* : to throw

garrot [garo] *nm* **1** : tourniquet **2** : garrote **3** : withers (of a horse)

garrotter [garɔte] *vt* **1** LIGOTER : to tie up, to bind **2** BÂILLONNER : to gag, to stifle

gars [ga] *nm fam* **1** : boy, lad **2** TYPE : guy, fellow

gascon, -conne [gaskɔ̃, -skɔn] *adj* : Gascon

Gascon, -conne *n* : Gascon

gaspillage [gaspijaʒ] *nm* : waste

gaspiller [gaspije] *vt* : to waste, to squander

gaspilleur, -leuse [gaspijœr, -jøz] *adj* : wasteful

gastrique [gastrik] *adj* : gastric

gastronome [gastrɔnɔm] *nmf* : gourmet

gastronomie [gastrɔnɔmi] *nf* : gastronomy

gastronomique [gastrɔnɔmik] *adj* : gastronomic, gourmet

gâteau [gato] *nm, pl* **gâteaux 1** : cake <gâteau d'anniversaire : birthday cake> **2 gâteau sec** *France* : cookie **3 c'est du gâteau** *fam* : it's a piece of cake

gâter [gate] *vt* **1** CHOYER : to spoil, to pamper **2** : to spoil, to ruin — **se gâter** *vr* **1** : to go bad **2** : to deteriorate, to change for the worse

gâterie [gatri] *nf* : little treat, delicacy

gâteux, -teuse [gatø, -tøz] *adj* : senile

gâtisme [gatism] *nm* : senility

gauche[1] [goʃ] *adj* **1** : left <tourner à gauche : to make a left turn> <du côté gauche : on the left-hand side> **2** MALADROIT : awkward, clumsy **3** : warped

gauche[2] *nf* **1** : left <à gauche de : to the left of> **2 la gauche** : the Left, the left wing

gauchement [goʃmɑ̃] *adv* : awkwardly, clumsily

gaucher[1], **-chère** [goʃe, -ʃɛr] *adj* : left-handed

gaucher[2], **-chère** *n* : left-handed person

gaucherie [goʃri] *nf* : awkwardness, clumsiness

gauchir [goʃir] *vt* **1** : to warp **2** : to distort (facts, etc.) — *vi* : to warp

gauchissement [goʃismɑ̃] *nm* **1** : warp, warping **2** : distortion

gauchiste [goʃist] *adj & nmf* : leftist — **gauchisme** [goʃism] *nm*

gaufre[1] [gofr] *nm Can* : gopher

gaufre[2] *nf* **1** : waffle **2** : honeycomb

gaufrer [gofre] *vt* **1** : to emboss **2** : to crinkle

gaufrette [gofrɛt] *nf* : wafer

gaufrier [gofrije] *nm* : waffle iron

gaulois, -loise [golwa, -lwaz] *adj* **1** : Gallic **2** GRIVOIS : bawdy

gauloiserie [galwazri] *nf* **1** : bawdy joke **2** : bawdiness

gaulthérie [golteri] *nf* : wintergreen

gausser [gose] *v* **se gausser** *vr* SE MOQUER : to deride, to make fun of

gaver [gave] *vt* **1** : to force-feed **2** : to fill up — **se gaver** *vr* SE BOURRER : to stuff oneself

gay [gɛ] → **gai**

gaz [gaz] *nms & pl* **1** : gas <gaz carbonique : carbon dioxide> <gaz lacrymogène : tear gas> <gaz naturel : natural gas> **2** *Can fam* : gasoline **3** **mettre le gaz** *fam* : to step on the gas

gaze [gaz] *nf* : gauze

gazéifié, -fiée [gazeifje] *adj* : carbonated

gazelle [gazɛl] *nf* : gazelle

gazer [gaze] *vt* : to gas — *vi fam* : to be going well <ça gaze? : how are things going?>

gazette [gazɛt] *nf fam* : newspaper

gazeux, -zeuse [gazø, -zøz] *adj* **1** : gaseous **2** **eau gazeuse** : sparkling water **3** **boisson gazeuse** : soft drink

gazoduc [gazɔdyk] *nm* : gas pipeline

gazon [gazɔ̃] *nm* **1** : grass, turf, sod **2** PELOUSE : lawn

gazouillement [gazujmɑ̃] *nm* **1** : chirping, twittering **2** : babbling, gurgling

gazouiller [gazuje] *vi* **1** : to chirp **2** : to babble, to gurgle

gazouillis [gazuji] *nms & pl* **1** : chirp, twittering **2** : babbling

geai [ʒɛ] *nm* : jay

géant[1], **géante** [ʒeɑ̃, -ɑ̃t] *adj* : giant, gigantic

géant[2], **géante** *n* **1** : giant **2** **à pas de géant** : with giant strides, rapidly

geignard, -narde [ʒɛɲar, -ɲard] *adj fam* : whiny, whining

geignement [ʒɛɲəmɑ̃] *nm* : moaning, groaning

geindre [ʒɛ̃dr] {37} *vi* **1** : to groan, to moan **2** : to whine, to whimper

gel [ʒɛl] *nm* **1** : frost **2** : freeze, freezing **3** : gel <gel coiffant : hair gel>

gélatine [ʒelatin] *nf* : gelatine

gélatineux, -neuse [ʒelatinø, -nøz] *adj* : jelly-like, gelatinous

gelé, -lée [ʒəle] *adj* **1** : frozen **2** : frostbitten

gelée *nf* **1** : frost <gelée blanche : hoarfrost> **2** : jelly

geler [ʒəle] {20} *v* : to freeze — *v impers* : to freeze <il gèle! : it's freezing!> — **se geler** *vr*

gélifier [ʒelifje] {96} *vt* : to jell — **se gélifier** *vr* : to jell

gélule [ʒelyl] *nf* : capsule

gelure [ʒəlyr] *nf* : frostbite

Gémeaux [ʒemo] *nmpl* : Gemini

gémir [ʒemir] *vi* **1** : to groan, to moan **2** : to wail (of wind, etc.), to creak **3** **~ sur** : to bemoan

gémissement [ʒemismɑ̃] *nm* **1** : groan, moan **2** : creaking

gemme[1] [ʒɛm] *adj* **sel gemme** : rock salt

gemme[2] *nf* : gem, precious stone

gênant, -nante [ʒenɑ̃, -nɑ̃t] *adj* **1** EMBARRASSANT : embarrassing, awkward **2** ENCOMBRANT : cumbersome, in the way **3** ENNUYEUX : annoying, intrusive **4** *Can* : intimidating, imposing

gencives [ʒɑ̃siv] *nfpl* : gums

gendarme [ʒɑ̃darm] *nm* **1** *France* : gendarme, police officer **2** *Can* : federal police officer (member of the Royal Canadian Mounted Police)

gendarmerie [ʒɑ̃darməri] *nf* **1** *France* : police force **2** *France* : police station **3** *Can* : federal police force **3** **gendarmerie maritime** *France* : coast guard

gendre [ʒɑ̃dr] *nm* : son-in-law

gène [ʒɛn] *nm* : gene

gêne [ʒɛn] *nf* **1** NUISANCE : inconvenience, bother **2** CONFUSION : embarrassment **3** : difficulty, (physical) discomfort **4** PAUVRETÉ : poverty

gêné, -née [ʒene] *adj* **1** : embarrassed **2** : short of money **3** : uncomfortable **4** *Can* : shy

généalogie [ʒenealɔʒi] *nf* : genealogy

généalogique [ʒenealɔʒik] *adj* : genealogical

gêner [ʒene] *vt* **1** : to embarrass, to make uncomfortable **2** DÉRANGER : to bother **3** : to hamper, to restrict, to disrupt — **se gêner** *vr* **1** : to get in each other's way **2** : to put oneself out <ne te gêne pas! : don't mind me!>

général[1], **-rale** [ʒeneral] *adj, mpl* **-raux** [-ro]: general <en général : in general, for the most part> — **généralement** [-ralmɑ̃] *adv*

général[2] *nm, pl* **-raux** : general <général de brigade : brigadier general>

générale *nf* **1** : general's wife **2** : dress rehearsal

généralisation [ʒeneralizasjɔ̃] *nf* **1** : general application, spreading **2** : generalization

généraliser [ʒeneralize] *vt* : to make general, to put to general use — *vi* : to generalize — **se généraliser** *vr* : to become widespread

généraliste[1] [ʒeneralist] *adj* : general, nonspecialist

généraliste[2] *nmf* : general practitioner

généralité [ʒeneralite] *nf* : generality

générateur[1], **-trice** [ʒeneratœr, -tris] *adj* : generating, generative

générateur[2] *nm* : generator, producer

génération [ʒenerasjɔ̃] *nf* : generation

génératrice *nf* : generator (of electricity)

générer [ʒenere] {87} *vt* : to generate

généreux, -reuse [ʒenerø, -røz] *adj* : generous — **généreusement** [-røzmɑ̃] *adv*

générique[1] [ʒenerik] *adj* : generic

générique[2] *nm* : credits *pl* (in movies)

générosité [ʒenerɔzite] *nf* : generosity

genèse [ʒənɛz] *nf* : genesis

genêt [ʒənɛ] *nm* : broom (plant)

généticien, -cienne [ʒenetisjɛ̃] *n* : geneticist

génétique[1] [ʒenetik] *adj* : genetic — **génétiquement** [-tikmɑ̃] *adv*

génétique[2] *nf* : genetics

genévrier [ʒənevrije] *nm* : juniper

génial, -niale [ʒenjal] *adj, mpl* **-niaux** [-njo] **1** : of genius, brilliant **2** *fam* : fantastic, great

génie [ʒeni] *nm* **1** : genius **2** : genie **3** : engineering <génie civil : civil engineering>

génisse [ʒenis] *nf* **1** : heifer **2** *Can* : female calf

génital, -tale [ʒenital] *adj, mpl* **-taux** [-to] : genital

génitif [ʒenitif] *nm* : genitive (in grammar)

génocide [ʒenɔsid] *nm* : genocide

genou [ʒənu] *nm, pl* **genoux 1** : knee **2 se mettre à genoux** : to kneel down

genre [ʒɑ̃r] *nm* **1** SORTE : kind, sort, type **2** : style, manner **3** : gender **4** : genre (in art, etc.) **5** : genus

gens [ʒɑ̃] *nmfpl* **1** : people <la plupart des gens : most people> <vieilles gens : old folk> <jeunes gens : young people, teenagers> **2 gens d'affaires** : businessmen *m*, businesswomen *f* **3 gens de lettres** : writers, scholars

gentil[1], **-tille** [ʒɑ̃ti, -tij] *adj* **1** AIMABLE : kind, nice **2** SAGE : good, well-behaved **3** AGRÉABLE : pleasant **4** : fair <une gentille somme : a tidy sum>

gentil[2] [ʒɑ̃ti] *nm* : gentile

gentilhomme [ʒɑ̃tijɔm] *nm, pl* **gentilshommes** : gentleman

gentillesse [ʒɑ̃tijɛs] *nf* AMABILITÉ : kindness, niceness

gentiment [ʒɑ̃timɑ̃] *adv* : nicely, kindly

gentleman [dʒɛntləman] *nm, pl* **gentlemen** [-tləmɛn] : gentleman

génuflexion [ʒenyflɛksjɔ̃] *nf* : genuflexion

géochimie [ʒeɔʃimi] *nf* : geochemistry

géodésique [ʒeɔdezik] *adj* : geodesic

géographe [ʒeɔgraf] *nmf* : geographer

géographie [ʒeɔgrafi] *nf* : geography

géographique [ʒeɔgrafik] *adj* : geographic, geographical — **géographiquement** [-fikmɑ̃] *adv*

geôlier, -lière [ʒolje, -ljɛr] *n* : jailer

géologie [ʒeɔlɔʒi] *nf* : geology

géologique [ʒeɔlɔʒik] *adj* : geologic, geological — **géologiquement** [-ʒikmɑ̃] *adv*

géologue [ʒeɔlɔg] *nmf* : geologist

géomagnétique [ʒeɔmaɲetik] *adj* : geomagnetic

géomètre [ʒeɔmɛtr] *nmf or* **arpenteur géomètre** : surveyor

géométrie [ʒeɔmetri] *nf* : geometry

géométrique [ʒeɔmetrik] *adj* : geometrical

gérance [ʒerɑ̃s] *nf* : management

géranium [ʒeranjɔm] *nm* : geranium

gérant, -rante [ʒerɑ̃, -rɑ̃t] *n* : manager

gerbe [ʒɛrb] *nf* **1** : sheaf (of wheat) **2** : bunch (of flowers, etc.) **3** : spray, burst (of water, sparks, etc.)

gerbille [ʒɛrbij] *nf* : gerbil

gercer [ʒɛrse] {6} *vt* : to chap, to crack — **se gercer** *vr*

gerçure [ʒɛrsyr] *nf* : chapping, crack (in the skin)

gérer [ʒere] {87} *vt* : to manage, to run, to handle

gériatrie [ʒerjatri] *nf* : geriatrics

gériatrique [ʒerjatrik] *adj* : geriatric

germain, -maine [ʒɛrmɛ̃, -mɛn] *adj* **cousin germain** : first cousin

germanium [ʒermanjɔm] *nm* : germanium

germe [ʒɛrm] *nm* **1** : germ **2** : sprout **3** : seed (of an idea, etc.)

germer [ʒɛrme] *vi* **1** : to sprout, to germinate **2** : to form (of ideas, hopes, etc.)

germination [ʒɛrminasjɔ̃] *nf* : germination

gérondif [ʒerɔ̃dif] *nm* : gerund

gérontologie [ʒerɔ̃tɔlɔʒi] *nf* : gerontology

gérontologue [ʒerɔ̃tɔlɔg] *nmf* : gerontologist

gésier [ʒezje] *nm* : gizzard

gésir [ʒezir] {47} *vi* : to lie, to be lying

gestation [ʒɛstasjɔ̃] *nf* : gestation

geste [ʒɛst] *nm* : gesture, movement <ne faites pas un geste : don't move>

gestion [ʒɛstjɔ̃] *nf* : management <gestion de fichiers : file management>

gestionnaire [ʒɛstjɔnɛr] *nmf* : administrator

geyser [ʒezɛr] *nm* : geyser

ghanéen, -néenne [ganeɛ̃, -neɛn] *adj* : Ghanaian

Ghanéen, -néenne *n* : Ghanaian

ghetto [gɛto] *nm* : ghetto

gibbon [ʒibɔ̃] *nm* : gibbon

gibecière [ʒibsjɛr] *nf* **1** : game bag **2** : shoulder bag

gibet [ʒibɛ] *nm* : gallows

gibier [ʒibje] *nm* **1** : game (animals) **2** : prey <un gibier facile : an easy target>

giboulée [ʒibule] *nf* : sudden shower <les giboulées de mars : April showers>

giclée [ʒikle] *nf* : spurt, squirt

gicler [ʒikle] *vi* : to spurt, to squirt, to spatter

gicleur [ʒiklœr] *nm Can* : sprinkler (for fire)

gifle [ʒifl] *nf* : slap (in the face)

gifler [ʒifle] *vt* : to slap

gigantesque [ʒigɑ̃tɛsk] *adj* : gigantic, huge

gigogne [ʒigɔɲ] *adj* **1 lit gigogne** : trundle bed **2 tables gigognes** : nest of tables

gigot [ʒigo] *nm* : leg of lamb

gigoter [ʒigɔte] *vi fam* : to wriggle, to fidget

gigue [ʒig] *nf* : jig

gilet [ʒilɛ] *nm* **1** : vest <gilet pare-balles : bulletproof vest> <gilet de sauvetage : life jacket> **2** : cardigan (sweater)

gin [dʒin] *nm* : gin

gingembre [ʒɛ̃ʒɑ̃br] *nm* : ginger

ginseng [ʒinsɑ̃g] *nm* : ginseng

girafe [ʒiraf] *nf* : giraffe

giratoire [ʒiratwar] *adj* **sens giratoire** : rotary, traffic circle

girofle [ʒirɔfl] *nm* **clou de girofle** : clove

giroflée [ʒirɔfle] *nf* : wallflower

giron [ʒirɔ̃] *nm* **1** : lap **2** : bosom <dans le giron familial : in the bosom of one's family>

girouette [ʒirwɛt] *nf* : weather vane

gisement [ʒizmɑ̃] *nm* : deposit, bed (in geology)

gitan, -tane [ʒitɑ̃, -tan] *n* : Gypsy

gîte[1] [ʒit] *nm* **1** : shelter, lodging <le gîte et le couvert : room and board> **2** : shank (of beef, etc.)

gîte[2] *nf* : list, listing (of a boat)

gîter [ʒite] *vi* : to heel, to list (of a ship)

givre [ʒivr] *nm* : frost

givrer [ʒivre] *vt* : to cover with frost — *vi* : to ice up — **se givrer** *vr*

glabre [glabr] *adj* **1** : hairless **2** : clean-shaven

glaçage [glasaʒ] *nm* **1** : glazing (of fabric, etc.) **2** : icing (on cake)

glace [glas] *nf* **1** : ice **2** *France* : ice cream **3** VITRE : glass **4** MIROIR : mirror **5 glaces** *nfpl* : ice sheets **6 rester de glace** : to remain unmoved

glacé, -cée [glase] *adj* **1** GLACIAL : icy **2** : iced <thé glacé : iced tea> **3** GELÉ : frozen **4** : glossy (of paper, etc.)

glacer [glase] {6} *vt* **1** : to freeze, to chill **2** : to frost (a cake) **3** : to glaze, to give a shiny finish to **4** INTIMIDER : to intimidate

glacial, -ciale [glasjal] *adj, mpl* **-cials** *or* **-ciaux** [-sjo] : icy, frigid — **glacialement** [-sjalmɑ̃] *adv*

glaciaire [glasjɛr] *adj* : glacial (in geology)

glacier [glasje] *nm* : glacier

glacière [glasjɛr] *nf* : cooler, ice chest

glaçon [glasɔ̃] *nm* **1** : icicle **2** : ice cube

gladiateur [gladjatœr] *nm* : gladiator

glaïeul [glajœl] *nm* : gladiolus

glaire [glɛr] *nf* **1** : white of an egg **2** : mucus

glaise [glɛz] *nf* : clay

glaive [glɛv] *nm* : sword

gland [glɑ̃] *nm* **1** : acorn **2** : tassel

glande [glɑ̃d] *nf* : gland — **glandulaire** [-dylɛr] *adj*

glaner [glane] *v* : to glean

glapir [glapir] *vi* : to yelp

glapissement [glapismɑ̃] *nm* : yelp

glas [gla] *nm* **1** : toll, knell **2 sonner le glas de** : to sound the death knell for

glaucome [glokom] *nm* : glaucoma

glauque [glok] *adj* **1** : dull blue-green **2** LUGUBRE : gloomy, dreary

glissade [glisad] *nf* **1** : slide, sliding **2** CHUTE : fall, slip

glissant, -sante [glisɑ̃, -sɑ̃t] *adj* : slippery

glissement [glismɑ̃] *nm* **1** : sliding, gliding **2** : shift <glissement politique vers la droite : political shift to the right> **3 glissement de terrain** : landslide

glisser [glise] *vi* **1** : to slide **2** : to slip **3** DÉRAPER : to skid — *vt* **1** : to slip, to sneak <glissez la lettre sous la porte : slip the letter under the door> **2** : to drag <glisser-déposer : drag and drop> — **se glisser** *vr* : to slip, to creep

glissière [glisjɛr] *nf* **1** : slide, groove **2 porte à glissière** : sliding door

glissoire [gliswar] *nf* : slide

global, -bale [glɔbal] *adj, mpl* **globaux** [glɔbo] : overall, total

globalement [glɔbalmɑ̃] *adv* : as a whole

globe [glɔb] *nm* **1** : globe **2 globe oculaire** : eyeball **3 globe terrestre** : the earth

globulaire [glɔbylɛr] *adj* : globular

globule [glɔbyl] *nm* : corpuscle, blood cell <globules blancs : white blood cells>

globuleux, -leuse [glɔbylø, -løz] *adj* : protruding (of eyes)

gloire [glwar] *nf* **1** RENOMMÉE : glory, fame **2** MÉRITE : distinction, credit **3** HOMMAGE : praise, homage **4** : celebrity, star

glorieux, -rieuse [glɔrjø, -rjøz] *adj* : glorious — **glorieusement** [-jøzmɑ̃] *adv*

glorification [glɔrifikasjɔ̃] *nm* : glorification

glorifier [glɔrifje] {96} *vt* : to glorify, to extol — **se glorifier** *vr* **~ de** : to glory in

gloriole [glɔrjɔl] *nf* : vainglory

glose [gloz] *nf* : gloss, annotation

gloser [gloze] *vt* : to annotate, to gloss — *vi* **~ sur** : to ramble on about

glossaire [glɔsɛr] *nm* : glossary

glouglou [gluglu] *nm* **1** *fam* : gurgling **2** : gobbling (of a turkey)

glouglouter [gluglute] *vi* **1** *fam* : to gurgle **2** : to gobble (of a turkey)

gloussement [glusmɑ̃] *nm* : **1** clucking **2** : chuckling, chortling

glousser [gluse] *vi* **1** : to cluck **2** : to chuckle, to chortle

glouton[1], **-tonne** [glutɔ̃, -tɔn] *adj* : gluttonous, greedy

glouton[2], **-tonne** *n* : glutton

glouton[3] *nm* : wolverine

gloutonnerie [glutɔnri] *nf* : gluttony

gluant, gluante [glyɑ̃, -ɑ̃t] *adj* COLLANT : sticky, gummy, glutinous

glucose [glykoz] *nm* : glucose

gluten [glytɛn] *nm* : gluten

glutineux, -neuse [glytinø, -nøz] *adj* : glutinous

glycérine [gliserin] *nf* : glycerine

glycine |glisin| *nf* : wisteria
gnôle |ɲol| *nf France fam* : booze
gnome |gnom| *nm* : gnome
gnou |gnu| *nm* : gnu
go |go| *adv France fam* **tout de go** : straightaway, at once
gobelet |gɔblɛ| *nm* : tumbler, beaker
gober |gɔbe| *vt* **1** : to swallow whole **2** *fam* : to swallow, to fall for
godasse |gɔdas| *nf fam* : shoe
godet |gɔdɛ| *nm* **1** : jar, small pitcher **2** : pucker (in clothing)
godille |gɔdij| *nf* : scull, paddle
godiller |gɔdije| *vi* : to scull
goéland |gɔelɑ̃| *nm* : gull
goélette |gɔelɛt| *nf* : schooner
goglu |gɔgly| *nm Can* : bobolink
gogo |gogo| *nm fam* **à ~** : galore
goguenard, -narde |gognar, -nard| *adj* MOQUEUR : mocking
goinfre |gwɛ̃fr| *nm fam* : pig, glutton
goitre |gwatr| *nm* : goiter
golf |gɔlf| *nm* : golf
golfe |gɔlf| *nm* : gulf, bay
golfeur, -feuse |gɔlfœr, -føz| *n* : golfer
gombo |gɔ̃bo| *nm* : gumbo
gomme |gɔm| *nf* **1** : gum, resin **2** : eraser **3 gomme à mâcher** : chewing gum
gommer |gɔme| *vt* **1** : to gum <papier gommé : gummed paper> **2** EFFACER : to erase
gond |gɔ̃| *nm* **1** : hinge **2 sortir de ses gonds** *fam* : to fly off the handle
gondole |gɔ̃dɔl| *nf* : gondola
gondoler |gɔ̃dɔle| *v* **se gondoler** *vr* **1** : to warp, to buckle **2** *fam* : to laugh, to be in stitches
gonflable |gɔ̃flabl| *adj* : inflatable
gonflé, -flée |gɔ̃fle| *adj* **1** : swollen, bloated **2 être gonflé** *fam* : to have a nerve
gonflement |gɔ̃fləmɑ̃| *nm* **1** : inflation **2** : swelling
gonfler |gɔ̃fle| *vt* **1** : to blow up, to inflate (a balloon, a tire, etc.) **2** : to swell <avoir les yeux gonflés : to have swollen eyes> **3** : to inflate, to exaggerate <prix gonflés : inflated prices> — *vi* : to swell, to rise — **se gonfler** *vr* **1** : to swell **2 ~ de** : to swell up with, to be filled with
gonfleur |gɔ̃flœr| *nm* : (air) pump
gong |gɔ̃g| *nm* : gong
goret |gɔrɛ| *nm* : piglet
gorge |gɔrʒ| *nf* **1** : throat <mal de gorge : sore throat> <avoir la gorge serrée : to have a lump in one's throat> **2** : bosom, chest **3** : gorge (in geography) **4** : groove, channel
gorgée |gɔrʒe| *nf* : mouthful, sip, gulp
gorger |gɔrʒe| {17} *vt* : to fill, to stuff — **se gorger** *vr* **1** : to fill up **2** SE BOURRER : to stuff oneself
gorille |gɔrij| *nm* **1** : gorilla **2** *fam* : bodyguard
gosier |gozje| *nm* : throat
gosse |gɔs| *nmf France fam* : kid, youngster
gosser |gɔse| *vt Can fam* : to whittle
gothique |gɔtik| *adj* : Gothic
gouache |gwaʃ| *nf* : poster paint
gouaille |gwaj| *nf* : cocky humor, cheek
goudron |gudrɔ̃| *nm* : tar
goudronner |gudrɔne| *vt* : to tar (a road)
gouffre |gufr| *nm* **1** : gulf, abyss **2 au bord du gouffre** : on the brink of despair
gouge |guʒ| *nf* : gouge, chisel
goujat |guʒa| *nm* : boor
goujon |guʒɔ̃| *nm* : dowel
goulasch *or* **goulache** |gulaʃ| *nmf* : goulash
goule |gul| *nf* : ghoul
goulet |gulɛ| *nm* **1** : gully **2** : narrows **3 goulet d'étranglement** : bottleneck
goulot |gulo| *nm* **1** : neck (of a bottle) <boire au goulot : to drink from the bottle> **2 goulot d'étranglement** : bottleneck, obstacle
goulu[1], **-lue** |guly| *adj* : greedy, gluttonous — **goulûment** |-lymɑ̃| *adv*
goulu[2], **-lue** *n* : glutton
goupille |gupij| *nf* : pin
gourbi |gurbi| *nm* : foxhole
gourd, gourde |gur, gurd| *adj* : numb (with cold)
gourde |gurd| *nf* **1** : canteen, flask **2** : gourd **3** *fam* : dope, blockhead
gourdin |gurdɛ̃| *nm* : cudgel, club
gourmand[1], **-mande** |gurmɑ̃, -mɑ̃d| *adj* **1** : greedy **2** : fond of eating
gourmand[2], **-mande** *n* **1** : glutton **2** : gourmet, epicure
gourmandise |gurmɑ̃diz| *nf* **1** : greed **2** : gluttony **3 gourmandises** *nfpl* : sweets, delicacies
gourmet |gurmɛ| *nm* GASTRONOME : gourmet
gourmette |gurmɛt| *nf* : chain bracelet
gourou |guru| *nm* : guru
gousse |gus| *nf* **1** : pod **2 gousse d'ail** : clove of garlic
gousset |gusɛ| *nm* : vest pocket, watch pocket
goût |gu| *nm* **1** : taste (sense) **2** SAVEUR : flavor **3** : taste, discernment <avoir du goût : to have good taste> <de mauvais goût : tasteless, in bad taste> **4** : liking, fondness <prendre goût à : to develop a liking for>
goûter[1] |gute| *vt* **1** : to taste **2** : to relish, to enjoy — *vi* **1** : to have an afternoon snack **2 ~ à** *or* **~ de** : to try out, to sample **3 ~ à** *or* **~ de** : to get a taste of
goûter[2] *nm* : afternoon snack
goutte |gut| *nf* **1** : drop <une goutte de sang : a drop of blood> <tomber goutte à goutte : to drip> **2** : gout **3 gouttes** *nfpl* : drops (in medicine)
gouttelette |gutlɛt| *nf* : droplet, globule
goutter |gute| *vi* : to drip

gouttière [gutjɛr] *nf* **1** : gutter (on a roof) **2** : downspout **3** : cast, splint

gouvernail [guvɛrnaj] *nm* **1** : rudder **2** BARRE : helm <tenir le gouvernail : to take the helm>

gouvernante [guvɛrnɑ̃t] *nf* **1** : governess **2** : housekeeper

gouverne [guvɛrn] *nf* **1 gouverne de direction** : rudder (of an airplane) **2 pour votre gouverne** : for your information

gouvernement [guvɛrnəmɑ̃] *nm* : government — **gouvernemental, -tale** [-mɑ̃tal] *adj*

gouverner [guvɛrne] *vt* **1** DIRIGER : to steer (a ship) **2** : to govern, to rule **3** MAÎTRISER : to control (one's emotions, etc.) — *vi* : to steer

gouverneur [guvɛrnœr] *nm* **1** : governor **2 gouverneur général** *Can* : governor-general

goyave [gɔjav] *nf* : guava (fruit)

grabat [graba] *nm* : pallet (bed)

grabataire[1] [grabatɛr] *adj* : bedridden

grabataire[2] *n* : (bedridden) invalid

grabuge [grabyʒ] *nm fam* BAGARRE : brawl, fighting

grâce [gras] *nf* **1** : gracefulness, charm <avec grâce : gracefully> **2** : willingness <de bonne grâce : with good grace, willingly> **3** : favor <accorder une grâce : to grant a favor> **4** : mercy, pardon **5 ~ à** : thanks to **6 grâces** *nfpl* : grace <dire les grâces : to say grace>

gracier [grasje] {96} *vt* : to pardon

gracieuseté [grasjøzte] *nf* **1** : kindliness **2** : free gift

gracieux, -cieuse [grasjø, -sjøz] *adj* **1** : graceful **2** AIMABLE : gracious, kind **3** GRATUIT : free — **gracieusement** [-sjøzmɑ̃] *adv*

gracile [grasil] *adj* ÉLANCÉ : slender

gradation [gradasjɔ̃] *nf* : gradation

grade [grad] *nm* **1** : rank <monter en grade : to be promoted> **2** : university degree, title **3** : grade (of oil)

gradin [gradɛ̃] *nm* **1** : tier **2 gradins** *nmpl* : bleachers, stands

graduel, -duelle [gradɥɛl] *adj* : gradual, progressive — **graduellement** [-dɥɛlmɑ̃] *adv*

graduer [gradɥe] *vt* **1** : to graduate (a measuring instrument) **2** : to increase gradually

graffiti [grafiti] *nmpl* : graffiti

grafigne [grafiɲ] *or* **grafignure** [grafiɲyr] *nf Can* : scratch, scrape

grafigner [grafiɲe] *vt Can* : to scratch, to scrape

grain [grɛ̃] *nm* **1** : (cereal) grain **2** : seed, berry <grain de café : coffee bean> <grain de poivre : peppercorn> <grain de raisin : grape> **3** : bead **4** : speck, particle <grain de sable : grain of sand> <un grain d'originalité : a touch of originality> **5 grain de beauté** : mole

graine [grɛn] *nf* **1** : seed <monter en graine : to go to seed> **2 être de la mauvaise graine** : to be incorrigible, to be a bad lot

graisse [grɛs] *nf* **1** : grease **2** : fat **3 graisse de baleine** : blubber

graisser [grɛse] *vt* **1** : to lubricate, to grease, to oil **2** : to stain with grease

graisseux, -seuse [grɛsø, -søz] *adj* **1** : greasy **2** : fatty (in medicine)

grammaire [gramɛr] *nf* : grammar

grammatical, -cale [gramatikal] *adj, mpl* **-caux** [-ko] : grammatical — **grammaticalement** [-kalmɑ̃] *adv*

gramme [gram] *nm* : gram

granade [granad] *nf* : pomegranate

grand[1] [grɑ̃] *adv* **1** : wide <ouvrir grand : to open wide> **2 voir grand** : to think big **3 en ~** : on a large scale, in a big way

grand[2]**, grande** [grɑ̃, grɑ̃d] *adj* **1** : tall, long, wide **2** GROS : big, large **3** : abundant <un grand monde : many people> <au grand jour : in broad daylight> **4** : great <grandes distances : great distances> <c'est une grande travailleuse : she works very hard> **5** PRINCIPAL : main, principal **6** : important <un grand homme : a great man> **7** : elder, older, grown-up <ma grande sœur : my older sister> <les grandes personnes : grown-ups, adults> **8** : extreme, intense <avoir grand faim : to be very hungry> <il est grand temps que : it's high time that>

grand[3] *nm* : important person, leader, big power

grand–angle [grɑ̃tɑ̃gl] *or* **grand–angulaire** [-ɑ̃gylɛr] *nm, pl* **grands–angles** [grɑ̃zɑ̃gl] *or* **grands–angulaires** [grɑ̃zɑ̃gylɛr] : wide-angle lens

grand–chose [grɑ̃ʃoz] *pron* **pas grand–chose** : not much

grandement [grɑ̃dmɑ̃] *adv* **1** BEAUCOUP : greatly, a lot **2** : extremely

grandeur [grɑ̃dœr] *nf* **1** : size, scale, magnitude <grandeur nature : life-size> **2** NOBLESSE : greatness, nobility **3** SPLENDEUR : splendor, glory

grandiloquence [grɑ̃dilɔkɑ̃s] *nf* : pomposity, bombast

grandiloquent, -quente [grɑ̃dilɔkɑ̃, -kɑ̃t] *adj* : grandiloquent, pompous

grandiose [grɑ̃djoz] *adj* : grandiose

grandir [grɑ̃dir] *vt* **1** : to magnify, to make look taller **2** EXAGÉRER : to exaggerate **3** ENNOBLIR : to increase the stature of — *vi* **1** : to grow **2** AUGMENTER : to increase

grand–mère [grɑ̃mɛr] *nf, pl* **grands–mères** : grandmother

grand–oncle [grɑ̃tɔ̃kl] *nm, pl* **grands–oncles** [grɑ̃zɔ̃kl] : great-uncle

grand–peine [grɑ̃pɛn] *nf* **à ~** : with great difficulty

grand–père [grɑ̃pɛr] *nm, pl* **grands–pères** : grandfather

grands–parents [grɑ̃parɑ̃] *nmpl* : grandparents

grand–tante [grɑ̃tɑ̃t] *nf, pl* **grand(s)–tantes** : great-aunt

grand–voile [grɑ̃vwal] *nf, pl* **grand(s)–voiles** : mainsail

grange [grɑ̃ʒ] *nf* : barn

granit *or* **granite** [granit] *nm* : granite

granule [granyl] *nm* : small pill

granulé [granyle] *nm* : granule

granuleux, -leuse [granylø, -løz] *adj* : granular

graphique[1] [grafik] *adj* : graphic — **graphiquement** [-fikmɑ̃] *adv*

graphique[2] *nm* : graph

graphisme [grafism] *nm* **1** : writing, handwriting **2** : graphic arts *pl*

graphiste [grafist] *nmf* : graphic artist

graphite [grafit] *nm* : graphite

grappe [grap] *nf* : cluster <grappe de raisins : bunch of grapes>

grappiller [grapije] *vt* : to gather, to glean

grappin [grapɛ̃] *nm* **1** : grapnel **2 mettre le grappin sur** : to get one's hooks into

gras[1] [gra] *adv* **1 faire gras** : to eat meat (in religion) **2 manger gras** : to eat fatty foods **3 parler gras** : to talk coarsely

gras[2], **grasse** [gra, gras] *adj* **1** : fatty <matières grasses : fats> **2** GROS : fat (of persons) **3** HUILEUX : greasy, oily **4** : sticky, slimy **5** : throaty (of the voice), loose (of a cough) **6** VULGAIRE : crude, coarse **7** : lush, abundant **8** : bold (of type)

gras[3] *nm* **1** : fat **2** : grease **3** : fleshy part <gras de la jambe : calf>

grassement [grasmɑ̃] *adv* : highly, handsomely <grassement payé : well paid>

grassouillet, -lette [grasujɛ, -jɛt] *adj* POTELÉ : pudgy, plump

gratifiant, -fiante [gratifjɑ̃, -jɑ̃t] *adj* : gratifying, rewarding

gratification [gratifikasjɔ̃] *nf* **1** : bonus **2** : gratification

gratifier [gratifje] {96} *vt* **1** : to reward **2** : to gratify

gratin [gratɛ̃] *nm* **1** : dish baked with cheese or crumb topping **2** *fam* : upper crust (of society)

gratiné, -née [gratine] *adj* **1** : au gratin, browned **2** *fam* : extreme, difficult, weird

gratis [gratis] *adv* : free

gratitude [gratityd] *nf* : gratitude, gratefulness

gratte [grat] *nf Can* CHASSE-NEIGE : snowplow

gratte–ciel [gratsjɛl] *nms & pl* : skyscraper

grattement [gratmɑ̃] *n* : scratching (sound)

gratte–papier [gratpapje] *nms & pl* : pencil pusher, office drudge

gratte–pieds [gratpje] *nms & pl* : doormat

gratter [grate] *vt* **1** : to scratch **2** : to scrape (a surface) **3** *fam* : to scrape together **4** *fam* : to overtake **5 gratter (de) la guitare** : to strum a guitar — *vi* : to scratch — **se gratter** *vr* : to scratch oneself

gratteux, -teuse [gratø, -tøz] *adj Can fam* : stingy, cheap

grattoir [gratwar] *nm* : scraper

gratuit, -tuite [gratɥi, -tɥit] *adj* **1** : free **2** : gratuitous — **gratuitement** [-tɥitmɑ̃] *adv*

gratuité [gratɥite] *nf* **1** : exemption from payment **2** : gratuitousness

gravats [grava] *nmpl* : rubble

grave [grav] *adj* **1** SÉRIEUX : grave, serious **2** : solemn **3** : deep, low-pitched

graveleux, -leuse [gravlø, -løz] *adj* **1** : gravelly **2** : gritty **3** : indecent, smutty

gravelle [gravɛl] *nf Can* : fine gravel

gravement [gravmɑ̃] *adv* **1** : gravely, solemnly **2** : seriously

graver [grave] *vt* **1** : to engrave, to carve **2** : to fix, to etch <gravé dans ma mémoire : etched in my memory>

graveur, -veuse [gravœr, -vøz] *n* : engraver

gravier [gravje] *nm* : gravel, grit

gravillon [gravijɔ̃] *nm* : (fine) gravel

gravir [gravir] *vt* : to climb (up)

gravitation [gravitasjɔ̃] *nf* : gravitation

gravité [gravite] *nf* **1** : gravity **2** : seriousness, importance

graviter [gravite] *vi* : to gravitate, to revolve

gravure [gravyr] *nf* **1** : engraving <gravure sur bois : woodcutting> <gravure à l'eau forte : etching> **2** : print, plate

gré [gre] *nm* **1** VOLONTÉ : will <de plein gré : willingly> <contre son gré : unwillingly> **2** GOÛT : taste, liking <à votre gré : as you wish> **3 bon gré mal gré** : like it or not **4 savoir (bien) gré à** : to be grateful to

grèbe [grɛb] *nm* : grebe

grébiche [grebiʃ] *nf Can* : crone, hag

grec[1], **grecque** [grɛk] *adj* : Greek

grec[2] *nm* : Greek (language)

Grec, Grecque *n* : Greek

gréement [gremɑ̃] *nm* : rigging

gréer [gree] {89} *vt* : to rig (a ship)

greffe [grɛf] *nf* **1** : graft (in botany) **2** : graft, transplant (in medicine)

greffer [grɛfe] *vt* **1** : to graft **2** : to transplant (an organ) — **se greffer** *vr* : to come along, to arise

greffier, -fière [grɛfje, -fjɛr] *nm* : clerk of court

grégaire [gregɛr] *adj* : gregarious

grège [grɛʒ] *adj* : raw, unbleached

grêle[1] [grɛl] *adj* **1** : lanky, spindly **2** : high-pitched, shrill

grêle[2] *nf* : hail

grêlé, -lée [grele] *adj* : pockmarked

grêler |grele| *v impers* **il grêle** : it's hailing
grêlon |grɛlɔ̃| *nm* : hailstone
grelot |grəlo| *nm* : small bell, sleigh bell
grelotter |grəlɔte| *vi* **1** TREMBLER : to shiver **2** : to tinkle, to jingle
grenade |grənad| *nf* **1** : pomegranate **2** : grenade <grenade à main : hand grenade>
grenadin, -dine |grənadɛ̃, -din| *adj* : Grenadian
Grenadin, -dine *n* : Grenadian
grenadine |grənadin| *nf* : grenadine
grenat[1] |grəna| *adj* : dark red
grenat[2] *nm* : garnet
grenier |grənje| *nm* **1** : attic, loft <grenier à foin : hayloft> **2** *or* **grenier à blé** : breadbasket (region)
grenouille |grənuj| *nf* : frog
grès |grɛ| *nm* **1** : sandstone **2** : stoneware
grésil |grezil| *nm* : fine hail, sleet
grésillement |grezijmɑ̃| *nm* **1** : crackling (of a telephone, radio, etc.) **2** : sizzling
grésiller |grezije| *vi* : to crackle, to sizzle — *v impers* : to sleet, to hail
grève |grɛv| *nf* **1** PLAGE : shore **2** : strike <grève de la faim : hunger strike>
grever |grəve| {52} *vt* : to burden, to put a (financial) strain on
gréviste[1] |grevist| *adj* : striking
gréviste[2] *nmf* : striker
gribouillage |gribujaʒ| *nm* : scribble, scrawl
gribouiller |gribuje| *vt* : to scribble — *vi* : to doodle, to scribble
gricher |griʃe| *vt Can fam* : to grind (one's teeth)
grief |grijɛf| *nm* : grievance
grièvement |grijɛvmɑ̃| *adv* : seriously, severely
griffe |grif| *nf* **1** : claw <sortir ses griffes : to show one's claws> <les griffes de la mort : the jaws of death> **2** : signature, label (of a product)
griffer |grife| *vt* : to scratch — **se griffer** *vr*
griffonner |grifɔne| *vt* : to scribble, to jot down
griffure |grifyr| *nf* : scratch
grignoter |griɲɔte| *vt* **1** : to nibble **2** : to eat away at **3** : to gain, to acquire gradually — *vi* **1** : to gnaw **2** : to nibble
gril |gril| *nm* **1** : broiler **2** : grill (for cooking)
grill |gril| *nm* : grill (restaurant)
grillade |grijad| *nf* **1** : grilled meat, grill **2 faire des grillades** : to have a barbecue
grillage |grijaʒ| *nm* : wire fencing
grille |grij| *nf* **1** : metal fencing or gate **2** : bars *pl* **3** : grate **4** : grid, squares *pl* **5** : scale, table <grille des salaires : salary scale>
grille–pain |grijpɛ̃| *nms & pl* : toaster
griller |grije| *vt* **1** : to toast, to roast (nuts, etc.) **2** : to grill, to broil **3** : to burn out **4 griller un feu rouge** : to go through a red light — *vi* **1** : to broil **2 se faire griller** *Can fam* : to get a suntan
grillon |grijɔ̃| *nm* : cricket
grimace |grimas| *nf* : grimace, face <faire des grimaces : to make faces> <faire la grimace : to make a (long) face, to scowl>
grimacer |grimase| {6} *vi* : to grimace
grimper |grɛ̃pe| *vi* **1** : to climb **2** : to be steep **3** *fam* : to soar, to rocket — *vt* : to climb
grimpeur, -peuse |grɛ̃pœr, -pøz| *n* : climber
grinçant, -çante |grɛ̃sɑ̃, -sɑ̃t| *adj* **1** : creaking, grating **2** : caustic <humour grinçant : caustic wit>
grincement |grɛ̃smɑ̃| *nm* : creak, squeak
grincer |grɛ̃se| {6} *vi* **1** : to creak, to grate, to grind **2 grincer des dents** : to grind one's teeth
grincheux, -cheuse |grɛ̃ʃø, -ʃøz| *adj* GROGNON : grumpy
gringalet |grɛ̃galɛ| *nm* : puny person, weakling
grippe |grip| *nf* **1** : flu, influenza **2 prendre qqn en grippe** : to take a sudden dislike to s.o.
grippé, -pée |gripe| *adj* **être grippé** : to have the flu
gripper |gripe| *v* : to jam — **se gripper** *vr* : to seize up
grippe–sou |gripsu| *nm, pl* **grippe–sous** *fam* : tightwad, skinflint
gris[1], **grise** |gri, griz| *adj* **1** : gray **2** MORNE : dull, dreary <un temps gris : a gray day> **3** *fam* : tipsy
gris[2] *nm* : gray
grisaille |grizaj| *nf* **1** : grayness **2** MONOTONIE : dullness
grisant, -sante |grizɑ̃, -zɑ̃t| *adj* ENIVRANT : exhilarating, intoxicating
grisâtre |grizatr| *adj* : grayish
griser |grize| *vt* **1** ENIVRER : to intoxicate **2** : to exhilarate — **se griser** *vr*
griserie |grizri| *nf* : exhilaration
grisonnant |grizɔnɑ̃| *adj* : grizzled
grisonner |grizɔne| *vi* : to turn gray, to go gray
grive |griv| *nf* : thrush
grivois, -voise |grivwa, -waz| *adj* : bawdy, risqué
grizzli *or* **grizzly** |grizli| *nm* : grizzly bear
Groenlandais, -daise |grɔɛnlɑ̃dɛ, -dɛz| *n* : Greenlander
grog |grɔg| *nm* : grog
grogne |grɔɲ| *nf* : grumbling, discontent
grognement |grɔɲmɑ̃| *nm* **1** : growl, grunt **2** : grumble
grogner |grɔɲe| *vi* **1** : to growl, to grunt **2** : to grumble, to grouch

grognon, -gnonne [grɔɲɔ̃, -ɲɔn] *adj* : grumpy, grouchy

groin [grwɛ̃] *nm* : snout (of a pig)

grommeler [grɔmle] {8} *vt* : to mutter — *vi* **1** : to groan, to grumble **2** : to snort

grondement [grɔ̃dmɑ̃] *nm* **1** : rumble, roar **2** : growl

gronder [grɔ̃de] *vt* RÉPRIMANDER : to scold — *vi* **1** : to rumble, to roar **2** GROGNER : to growl **3** : to be brewing

gros[1] [gro] *adv* **1** BEAUCOUP : a great deal <coûter gros : to cost a lot> **2** **écrire gros** : to write in big letters

gros[2], **grosse** [gro, gros] *adj* **1** : big, large **2** : thick, bulky **3** : fat **4** : great, considerable <de gros dégâts : considerable damage> **5** : serious, major **6** : loud <une grosse voix : a booming voice> **7** : heavy <un gros fumeur : a heavy smoker> **8** : coarse, crude, rough **9** **gros lot** : jackpot **10** **gros plan** : close-up **11** **gros titre** : headline **12** **grosse caisse** : bass drum

gros[3], **grosse** *n* **1** : fat person **2** : rich person

gros[4] *nm* **1** : bulk, main part <le gros des étudiants : most of the students> **2** : wholesale business **3** **en ~** : roughly, in general

groseille [grozɛj] *nf* **1** : currant **2** **groseille à maquereau** : gooseberry

gros–porteur [gropɔrtœr] *nm, pl* **gros–porteurs** : jumbo jet, liner

grosse [gros] *nf* : gross, twelve dozen

grossesse [grosɛs] *nf* : pregnancy

grosseur [grosœr] *nf* **1** : fatness, corpulence **2** : size **3** : lump, tumor

grossier, -sière [grosje, -sjɛr] *adj* **1** : coarse, rough **2** : crude, vulgar **3** : flagrant, glaring (of an error, etc.)

grossièrement [grosjɛrmɑ̃] *adv* **1** IMPOLIMENT : rudely **2** LOURDEMENT : grossly <se tromper grossièrement : to be grossly mistaken> **3** : roughly, crudely, coarsely **4** : approximately

grossièreté [grosjɛrte] *nf* **1** : rudeness **2** : crudeness **3** : coarseness, vulgarity

grossir [grosir] *vt* **1** AUGMENTER : to increase **2** EXAGÉRER : to exaggerate **3** AGRANDIR : to magnify, to enlarge **4** : to make appear fatter — *vi* **1** ENGRAISSER : to put on weight **2** : to grow larger

grossissant, -sante [grosisɑ̃, -sɑ̃t] *adj* **1** : magnifying <verre grossissant : magnifying glass> **2** : swelling, growing

grossissement [grosismɑ̃] *nm* **1** : enlargement **2** : magnification

grossiste [grosist] *nmf* : wholesaler, jobber

grosso modo [grosomodo] *adv* : more or less, roughly

grotesque [grɔtɛsk] *adj* **1** : grotesque **2** : ridiculous — **grotesquement** [-tɛskmɑ̃] *adv*

grotte [grɔt] *nf* : cave, grotto

grouiller [gruje] *vi* **~ de** : to swarm with, to teem with — **se grouiller** *vr fam* : to hurry, to get a move on

groupe [grup] *nm* **1** : group (of persons or objects) <groupe ethnique : ethnic group> <groupe de pression : pressure group, lobby> <groupe d'arbres : clump of trees> **2** **groupe sanguin** : blood type

groupement [grupmɑ̃] *nm* **1** : grouping, group **2** : association

grouper [grupe] *vt* : to group, to pool (resources, etc.) — **se grouper** *vr* : to gather, to get together

groupuscule [grupyskyl] *nm* : faction, (political) clique

grouse [gruz] *nf* : grouse (bird)

gruau [gryo] *nm* **1** : (fine) wheat flour **2** : groats <gruau de maïs : grits> **3** *Can* : oatmeal, porridge

grue [gry] *nf* : crane

gruger [gryʒe] {17} *vt* **1** : to dupe, to swindle **2** *Can fam* : to eat away at

grumeau [grymo] *nm, pl* **grumeaux** : lump (in sauce, etc.)

grumeleux, -leuse [grymlø, -løz] *adj* : lumpy

gruyère [gryjɛr] *nm* : Gruyère (cheese)

guatémaltèque [gwatemaltɛk] *adj* : Guatemalan

Guatémaltèque *nmf* : Guatemalan

gué [ge] *nm* : ford, crossing <passer à gué : to ford>

guenille [gənij] *nf* **1** *Can* : rag **2** **guenilles** *nfpl* : rags and tatters (clothing)

guenon [gənɔ̃] *nf* : female monkey

guépard [gepar] *nm* : cheetah

guêpe [gɛp] *nf* : wasp

guêpier [gepje] *nm* **1** : wasps' nest **2** : sticky situation, trap

guère [gɛr] *adv* **1** **ne . . . guère** : hardly, scarcely <elle n'est guère aimable : she's not very kind> <il n'y a guère de voitures : there are hardly any cars> **2** **ne . . . guère** : not for long, not often <il ne vient guère me voir : he rarely comes to see me>

guérilla [gerija] *nf* : guerrilla warfare, guerrillas *pl* (fighters)

guérillero [gerijero] *nm* : guerrilla

guérir [gerir] *vt* : to cure, to heal — *vi* **1** SE RÉTABLIR : to get better, to recover **2** : to heal — **se guérir** *vr* **1** : to be cured **2** : to break oneself of, to get over

guérison [gerizɔ̃] *nf* **1** : cure, healing **2** RÉTABLISSEMENT : recovery

guérissable [gerisabl] *adj* : curable

guérisseur, -seuse [gerisœr, -søz] *n* : healer

guérite [gerit] *nf* **1** : sentry box **2** *France* : workman's hut

guerre |gɛr| *nf* : war <faire la guerre à : to wage war against> <guerre chimique : chemical warfare>
guerrier[1], **-rière** |gɛrje, -jɛr| *adj* : warlike, martial
guerrier[2], **-rière** *n* : warrior
guerroyer |gerwaje| {58} *vi* : to wage war
guet |gɛ| *nm* : watch, lookout <faire le guet : to be on the lookout>
guet–apens |gɛtapɑ̃| *nm, pl* **guets–apens** : ambush
guetter |gete| *vt* **1** ÉPIER : to watch intently **2** ATTENDRE : to watch out for, to lie in wait for
guetteur |getœr| *nm* : lookout
gueule |gœl| *nf* **1** : mouth (of an animal, a tunnel, etc.) **2** *fam* : mouth, trap <(ferme) ta gueule! : shut up!> **3** *fam* : face <faire la gueule : to pull a face, to look sulky> **4 gueule de bois** : hangover
gueule–de–loup |gœldəlu| *nf, pl* **gueules–de–loup** : snapdragon
gueuler |gœle| *v fam* : to bawl, to bellow
gueuleton |gœltɔ̃| *nm fam* : feast, spread
gui |gi| *nm* **1** : mistletoe **2** : boom (of a ship)
guichet |giʃɛ| *nm* **1** : window, counter **2** : box office <jouer à guichets fermés : to play to a full house> **3 guichet automatique** : automatic teller machine
guichetier, -tière |giʃtje, -tjɛr| *n* : counter clerk
guide[1] |gid| *nmf* **1** : guide <guide de montagne : mountain guide> **2** CONSEILLER : counselor, advisor
guide[2] *nm* **1** : guide **2** : guidebook <guide touristique : tourist guide>
guide[3] *nf* **1** : girl scout **2 guides** *nfpl* : reins
guider |gide| *vt* : to guide
guidon |gidɔ̃| *nm* : handlebars *pl*
guigne |giɲ| *nf fam* : bad luck <avoir la guigne : to be jinxed>
guigner |giɲe| *vt* : to eye, to take a look at
guignol |giɲɔl| *nm* **1** : puppet show <c'est du guignol : it's a complete farce> **2** : silly person, clown, fool
guillemets |gijmɛ| *nmpl* : quotation marks
guilleret, -rette |gijrɛ, -rɛt| *adj* : sprightly, perky
guillotine |gijɔtin| *nf* : guillotine — **guillotiner** *vt*
guimauve |gimov| *nf* **1** : marshmallow **2** *fam* : sentimentality, mush
guimbarde |gɛ̃bard| *nf* **1** : Jew's harp **2** *fam* : jalopy
guindé, -dée |gɛ̃de| *adj* : stiff, affected, prim
guindeau |gɛ̃d| *nm* : windlass
guinéen, -néenne |gineɛ̃, -neɛn| *adj* : Guinean
Guinéen, -néenne *n* : Guinean
guingois |gɛ̃gwa| **de ~** : askew <être de guingois : to be lopsided>
guinguette |gɛ̃gɛt| *nf France* : café featuring music and dancing
guirlande |girlɑ̃d| *nf* **1** : garland **2 guirlandes de Noël** : tinsel
guise |giz| *nf* **1 à ta guise** : as you wish **2 en guise de** : by way of
guitare |gitar| *nf* : guitar
guitariste |gitarist| *nmf* : guitarist
guppy |gypi| *nm* : guppy
gustatif, -tive |gystatif, -tiv| *adj* : gustatory, of taste
guttural, -rale |gytyral| *adj, mpl* **-raux** |-ro| : guttural
guyanais, -naise |gɥijanɛ, -nɛz| *adj* : Guyanese
Guyanais, -naise *n* : Guyanese
gymnase |ʒimnaz| *nm* : gymnasium
gymnaste |ʒimnast| *nmf* : gymnast
gymnastique[1] |ʒimnastik| *adj* : gymnastic
gymnastique[2] *nf* : gymnastics
gynécologie |ʒinekɔlɔʒi| *nf* : gynecology
gynécologique |ʒinekɔlɔʒik| *adj* : gynecologic, gynecological
gynécologue |ʒinekɔlɔg| *nmf* : gynecologist
gypse |ʒips| *nm* : gypsum
gyrophare |ʒirɔfar| *nm* : revolving flashing light (on a vehicle)
gyroscope |ʒirɔskɔp| *nm* : gyroscope

H

h |aʃ| *nm* : h, the eighth letter of the alphabet
ha |'a| *interj* **ha ha** : ha-ha, very funny
habile |abil| *adj* **1** ADROIT : skillful **2** : clever — **habilement** |abilmɑ̃| *adv*
habileté |abilte| *nf* **1** : skill, skillfulness **2** : cleverness
habilité, -tée |abilite| *adj* **~ à** : entitled to, authorized to
habiliter |abilite| *vt* : to entitle, to empower
habillage |abijaʒ| *nm* **1** : dressing, getting dressed **2** : packaging, covering, casing
habillé, -lée |abije| *adj* **1** : dressed <tout habillé : fully clothed> **2** CHIC : smart, stylish
habillement |abijmɑ̃| *nm* **1** : clothes *pl*, clothing **2** : clothing industry

habiller [abije] *vt* **1** : to dress, to clothe **2** : to fit, to suit <cette robe vous habille bien : that dress really suits you> **3** REVÊTIR : to cover — **s'habiller** *vr* **1** : to get dressed <comment vais-je m'habiller? : what will I wear?> **2 ~ chez** : to buy one's clothes from **3 ~ en** : to dress up as

habit [abi] *nm* **1** : outfit, costume **2** : (religious) habit **3** *or* **habit de soirée** : evening dress, tails *pl* **4 habits** *nmpl* : clothes

habitable [abitabl] *adj* : habitable, inhabitable

habitacle [abitakl] *nm* : cockpit

habitant[1], -tante [abitɑ̃, -tɑ̃t] *n* **1** : inhabitant, resident **2** : occupant, dweller

habitant[2] *nm Can* : farmer

habitat [abita] *nm* **1** : housing **2** : habitat

habitation [abitasjɔ̃] *nf* **1** : living <conditions d'habitation : living conditions> **2** : house, dwelling **3** : residence, home

habiter [abite] *vt* **1** : to live in, to inhabit **2** : to dwell in (one's heart, etc.) — *vi* DEMEURER : to live, to reside <habiter à l'étranger : to live abroad>

habitude [abityd] *nf* **1** : habit <j'ai l'habitude de travailler dur : I'm used to working hard> **2** COUTUME : custom **3 comme d'habitude** : as usual **4 d'~** : usually **5 par habitude** : out of habit

habitué[1], -tuée [abitɥe] *adj* **~ à** : used to, accustomed to

habitué[2], -tuée *n* : regular (customer)

habituel, -tuelle [abitɥɛl] *adj* : usual, regular — **habituellement** [-tɥɛlmɑ̃] *adv*

habituer [abitɥe] *vt* ACCOUTUMER : to accustom — **s'habituer** *vr* **~ à** : to get used to

hableur[1], -bleuse [ˈablœr, -bløz] *adj* : boastful

hableur[2], -bleuse *n* : braggart

hache [ˈaʃ] *nf* **1** : ax **2 hache d'armes** : battle-ax

haché, -chée [ˈaʃe] *adj* **1** : ground, chopped, minced <biftek haché : ground beef> **2** : jerky, disjointed

hacher [ˈaʃe] *vt* **1** : to chop, to mince **2** : to cut to pieces

hachette [aʃɛt] *nf* : hatchet

hache–viande [ˈaʃvjɑ̃d] *nms & pl* : meat grinder

hachis [ˈaʃi] *nms & pl* : ground or minced food, hash <hachis de viande : ground meat>

hachisch [ˈaʃiʃ] → **haschish**

hachoir [ˈaʃwar] *nm* **1** : meat grinder **2** : chopper, cleaver **3** : cutting board

hachure [ˈaʃyr] *nf* : shading, hatching

hachurer [aʃyre] *vt* : to shade in

hagard, -garde [ˈagar, -gard] *adj* : distraught, wild, frantic

haie [ˈɛ] *nf* **1** : hedge **2** : hurdle (in sports) **3** : row, line <haie d'honneur : honor guard>

haillons [ˈajɔ̃] *nmpl* : rags, tatters

haine [ˈɛn] *nf* : hatred, hate

haineux, -neuse [ˈɛnø, -nøz] *adj* : full of hatred

haïr [ˈair] {48} *vt* : to hate — **se haïr** *vr*

haïssable [ˈaisabl] *adj* : hateful, detestable

haïtien, -tienne [aisjɛ̃, -sjɛn] *adj* : Haitian

Haïtien, -tienne *n* : Haitian

hâle [ˈal] *nm* : suntan

hâlé, -lée [ˈale] *adj* : tanned, sunburned

haleine [alɛn] *nf* **1** : breath <avoir mauvaise haleine : to have bad breath> <hors d'haleine : out of breath> **2 de longue haleine** : long-term **3 tenir en haleine** : to hold spellbound

haler [ˈale] *vt* : to haul (in), to tow

haletant, -tante [ˈaltɑ̃, -tɑ̃t] *adj* : panting, breathless

halètement [ˈalɛtmɑ̃] *nm* : gasp

haleter [ˈalte] {20} *vi* **1** : to pant, to gasp for breath **2** : to puff, to chug (of an engine)

hall [ˈol] *nm* : (entrance) hall, lobby

halle [ˈal] *nf France* : (covered) market

hallier [ˈalje] *nm* : thicket, brush

Halloween [alowin] *nf* : Halloween

hallucinant, -nante [alysinɑ̃, -nɑ̃t] *adj* : extraordinary, astounding

hallucination [alysinasjɔ̃] *nf* : hallucination <avoir des hallucinations : to hallucinate>

hallucinogène[1] [alysinɔʒɛn] *adj* : hallucinogenic

hallucinogène[2] *nm* : hallucinogen

halo [ˈalo] *nm* : halo

halogène [alɔʒɛn] *nm* : halogen <lampe (à) halogène : halogen lamp>

halte [ˈalt] *nf* **1** ARRÊT : stop, halt **2** : stopping place **3 halte routière** *Can* : rest stop (on a highway)

haltère [altɛr] *nm* : dumbbell, barbell

haltérophilie [alterɔfili] *nf* : weightlifting

hamac [ˈamak] *nm* : hammock

hamamélis [amamelis] *nm* : witch hazel

hamburger [ˈɑ̃bœrgœr] *nm* : hamburger (cooked)

hameau [ˈamo] *nm, pl* **hameaux** : hamlet

hameçon [amsɔ̃] *nm* : fishhook

hampe [ˈampe] *nf* **1** : pole (for a flag, etc.) **2** : shaft **3** : flank (of beef)

hamster [ˈamstɛr] *nm* : hamster

hanche [ˈɑ̃ʃ] *nf* **1** : hip **2** : haunch (of a horse)

handball [ˈɑ̃dbal] *nm* : handball

handicap [ˈɑ̃dikap] *nm* : handicap

handicapé[1], -pée [ˈɑ̃dikape] *adj* : handicapped, disabled

handicapé[2], **-pée** *n* : handicapped person, disabled person
handicaper ['ɑ̃dikape] *vt* : to handicap
hangar ['ɑ̃gar] *nm* **1** : (large) shed **2** : hangar
hanter ['ɑ̃te] *vt* : to haunt
hantise ['ɑ̃tiz] *nf* : obsessive fear, dread
happer ['ape] *vt* **1** : to seize, to snatch **2 être happé par** : to be hit by (a car, train, etc.)
harangue ['arɑ̃g] *nf* : harangue — **haranguer** ['arɑ̃ge] *vt*
harasser ['arase] *vt* EXTÉNUER : to exhaust, to tire out
harcèlement ['arsɛlmɑ̃] *nm* : harassment
harceler ['arsəle] {8 *and* 20} *vt* **1** : to harass, to harry **2** : to pester
hardes ['ard] *nfpl* : rags, old clothes
hardi, -die ['ardi] *adj* : bold, daring — **hardiment** [-dimɑ̃] *adv*
hardiesse ['ardjɛs] *nf* : boldness, audacity
harem ['arɛm] *nm* : harem
hareng ['arɑ̃] *nm* **1** : herring **2 hareng saur** : smoked herring, kipper
hargne ['arɲ] *nf* : aggressiveness, bad temper
hargneux, -gneuse ['arɲø, -ɲøz] *adj* : quarrelsome, bad-tempered
haricot ['ariko] *nm* : bean <haricot de Lima : lima bean> <haricot rouge : kidney bean> <haricot vert : green bean, string bean>
harmonica [armɔnika] *nm* : harmonica
harmonie [armɔni] *nf* : harmony
harmonieux, -nieuse [armɔnjø, -njøz] *adj* : harmonious — **harmonieusement** [-njøzmɑ̃] *adv*
harmonique [armɔnik] *adj* : harmonic — **harmoniquement** [-nikmɑ̃] *adv*
harmoniser [armɔnize] *vt* **1** : to harmonize **2** : to bring into line, to reconcile — **s'harmoniser** *vr* : to coordinate, to go well together
harnachement ['arnaʃmɑ̃] *nm* **1** : harness, harnessing **2** *fam* : outfit, getup
harnacher ['arnaʃe] *vt* **1** : to harness (an animal) **2** *fam* : to rig out (a person)
harnais ['arnɛ] *nm* : harness
harpe ['arp] *nf* : harp — **harpiste** ['arpist] *nmf*
harpie ['arpi] *nf* : harpy
harpon ['arpɔ̃] *nm* : harpoon
harponner ['arpɔne] *vt* **1** : to harpoon **2** *fam* : to nab, to collar
hasard ['azar] *nm* **1** : chance, luck, coincidence <un heureux hasard : a stroke of luck> <à tout hasard : on the off chance, just in case> <au hasard : at random> **2** SORT : fate, destiny **3 hasards** *nmpl* : dangers, hazards
hasarder ['azarde] *vt* RISQUER : to risk, to venture — **se hasarder** *vr* **1 se hasarder à faire** : to risk doing **2 ~ dans** : to venture into
hasardeux, -deuse ['azardø, -døz] *adj* : hazardous, risky
haschisch ['aʃiʃ] *nm* : hashish
hâte ['at] *nf* **1** : haste, hurry **2 à la hâte** : hurriedly, hastily **3 avoir hâte de** : to be eager to
hâter ['ate] *vt* : to hasten, to hurry — **se hâter** *vr*
hâtif, -tive ['atif, -tiv] *adj* **1** : hurried **2** : hasty, rash **3** : early <une hâtive récolte : an early harvest>
hâtivement ['ativmɑ̃] *adv* : hurriedly, hastily
hausse ['os] *nf* **1** : rise, increase **2 à la hausse** *or* **en ~** : rising, up
haussement ['osmɑ̃] *nm* **1** : raising, increasing **2** : **haussement d'épaules** : shrug
hausser ['ose] *vt* : to raise <hausser la voix : to raise one's voice> <hausser les épaules : to shrug one's shoulders>
haut[1] ['o] *adv* **1** : high <voler haut : to fly high> <haut placé : in a high position, highly placed> **2** : loud, loudly <penser tout haut : to think out loud> **3 plus haut** : above, earlier (in a text)
haut[2], **haute** ['o, 'ot] *adj* **1** : high, tall <haut de cinq mètres : five meters high> <à mer haute : at high tide> **2** : high (up) <haut dans le ciel : high in the sky> <l'étagère la plus haute : the top shelf> **3** : high, advanced, increased <haute fréquence : high frequency> <haute pression : high blood pressure> <à haute voix : aloud, out loud> **4** : early <de la plus haute antiquité : from the earliest times> **5** : upper <le haut Nil : the Upper Nile>
haut[3] *nm* **1** HAUTEUR : height <un mètre de haut : one meter high> **2** : SOMMET : top <l'étage du haut : the top floor> <de haut en bas : from top to bottom> **3 avoir des hauts et des bas** : to have one's ups and downs **4 en ~** : upstairs **5 en ~** : on the top, atop
hautain, -taine ['otɛ̃, -tɛn] *adj* : haughty
hautbois ['obwa] *nms & pl* : oboe — **hautboïste** ['obɔist] *nmf*
haute–fidélité ['otfidelite] *nf, pl* **hautes–fidélités** : high fidelity
hautement ['otmɑ̃] *adv* **1** FORTEMENT : highly, extremely **2** OUVERTEMENT : openly
hauteur ['otœr] *nf* **1** : height <prendre de la hauteur : to take on height, to climb> <à la hauteur de : (on a) level with> **2** NOBLESSE : nobility, loftiness **3** : haughtiness **4** : hill, height (in geography)
haut–le–cœur ['olkœr] *nms & pl* : retching <avoir des haut-le-cœur : to retch, to gag>

haut–le–corps [ˈolkɔr] *nms & pl* : start, jump
haut–parleur [ˈoparlœr] *nm, pl* **haut–parleurs** : loudspeaker
hâve [ˈav] *adj* : gaunt
havre [ˈavr] *nm* : haven, refuge
hawaïen[1], **-waïenne** [awajɛ̃, -jɛn] *adj* : Hawaiian
hawaïen[2] *nm* : Hawaiian (language)
Hawaïen, -waïenne *n* : Hawaiian
hayon [ˈajɔ̃] *nm* : tailgate
hé [ˈe] *interj* **1** : hey **2 hé, hé!** : well! well!
hebdomadaire [ɛbdɔmadɛr] *adj & nm* : weekly
hébergement [ebɛrʒəmɑ̃] *nm* : accommodations *pl*, lodging
héberger [ebɛrʒe] {17} *vt* **1** : to accommodate, to put up **2** : to take in (a refugee, etc.)
hébété, -tée [ebete] *adj* AHURI : dazed, stupefied
hébéter [ebete] {87} *vt* : to daze, to stupefy
hébétude [ebetyd] *nf* : stupor
hébraïque [ebraik] *adj* : Hebrew, Hebraic
hébreu[1] (*masculine only*) [ebrø] *adj, pl* **hébreux** : Hebrew
hébreu[2] *nm* : Hebrew (language)
Hébreu *nm, pl* **Hébreux** : Hebrew
hédoniste [edɔnist] *adj* : hedonistic
hégémonie [eʒemɔni] *nf* : hegemony
hein [ˈɛ̃] *interj* : eh?, what?
hélas [ˈelas] *interj* : alas!
héler [ˈele] {87} *vt* : to hail, to summon
hélice [elis] *nf* **1** : helix **2** : propeller
hélicoptère [elikɔptɛr] *nm* : helicopter
héliotrope [eljɔtrɔp] *nm* : heliotrope
héliport [elipɔr] *nm* : heliport
hélium [eljɔm] *nm* : helium
hématologie [ematɔlɔʒi] *nf* : hematology
hémisphère [emisfɛr] *nm* : hemisphere
hémisphérique [emisferik] *adv* : hemispheric, hemispherical
hémoglobine [emɔglɔbin] *nf* : hemoglobin
hémophile [emɔfil] *adj & nmf* : hemophiliac
hémophilie [emɔfili] *nf* : hemophilia
hémorragie [emɔraʒi] *nf* : bleeding, hemorrhage <faire une hémorragie : to hemorrhage>
hémorroïdes [emɔrɔid] *nfpl* : hemorrhoids
henné [ˈene] *nm* : henna
hennir [ˈenir] *vi* : to neigh, to whinny
hennissement [ˈenismɑ̃] *nm* : neighing, whinny
hépatique [epatik] *adj* : hepatic, liver
hépatite [epatit] *nf* : hepatitis
héraldique[1] [eraldik] *adj* : heraldic
héraldique[2] *nf* : heraldry
héraut [ˈero] *nm* : herald, messenger
herbacé, -cée [ɛrbase] *adj* : herbaceous
herbage [ɛrbaʒ] *nm* : pasture
herbe [ɛrb] *nf* **1** : grass **2** : herb (in cooking) **3 en ~** : budding, in the making **4 herbe à (la) puce** *Can* : poison ivy, poison sumac **5 herbe aux chats** : catnip **6 mauvaise herbe** : weed
herbeux, -beuse [ɛrbø, -bøz] *adj* : grassy
herbicide [ɛrbisid] *nm* : herbicide, weed killer
herbivore[1] [ɛrbivɔr] *adj* : herbivorous
herbivore[2] *nm* : herbivore
herboriste [ɛrbɔrist] *nmf* : herbalist
herculéen, -léenne [ɛrkyleɛ̃, -ɛn] *adj* : herculean
hère [ˈɛr] *nm* **pauvre hère** : poor wretch
héréditaire [ereditɛr] *adj* : hereditary
hérédité [eredite] *nf* : heredity
hérésie [erezi] *nf* : heresy
hérétique[1] [eretik] *adj* : heretical
hérétique[2] *nmf* : heretic
hérissé, -sée [ˈerise] *adj* : standing on end, bristling
hérisser [ˈerise] *vt* **1** : to ruffle up (fur, feathers, etc.) **2 ~ de** : to spike with, to stud with <herissé de difficultés : fraught with problems> **3 hérisser qqn** *fam* : to ruffle s.o.'s feathers, to irritate s.o. — **se hérisser** *vr* **1** : to stand on end **2** *fam* : to bristle (with annoyance)
hérisson [ˈerisɔ̃] *nm* : hedgehog
héritage [eritaʒ] *nm* **1** : inheritance **2** : heritage, legacy
hériter [erite] *vi* **~ de** : to inherit <j'ai hérité de la maison : I inherited the house> — *vt* : to inherit
héritier, -tière [eritje, -tjɛr] *n* : heir, heiress *f*, inheritor
hermaphrodite [ɛrmafrɔdit] *nmf* : hermaphrodite
hermétique [ɛrmetik] *adj* **1** ÉTANCHE : airtight, watertight **2** OBSCUR : obscure, abstruse, hermetic
hermétiquement [ɛrmetikmɑ̃] *adv* : hermetically
hermine [ɛrmin] *nf* : ermine
herminette [ɛrminɛt] *nf* : adze
hernie [ˈɛrni] *nf* : hernia
héroïne [erɔin] *nf* **1** : heroine **2** : heroin
héroïque [erɔik] *adj* : heroic — **héroïquement** [-ikmɑ̃] *adv*
héroïsme [erɔism] *nm* : heroism
héron [ˈerɔ̃] *nm* : heron
héros [ˈero] *nm* : hero
herpès [ɛrpɛs] *nms & pl* : herpes
herpétologie [ɛrpetɔlɔʒi] *nf* : herpetology
herse [ˈɛrs] *nf* : harrow
herser [ˈɛrse] *vt* : to harrow
hertz [ˈɛrts] *nms & pl* : hertz
hésitant, -tante [ezitɑ̃, -tɑ̃t] *adj* **1** : hesitant **2** : faltering, wavering
hésitation [ezitasjɔ̃] *nf* **1** : hesitation <avec hésitation : hesitantly> **2** : indecision, hesitancy

hésiter [ezite] *vi* **1** : to hesitate **2** : to vacillate, to waver

hétéroclite [eterɔklit] *adj* : disparate, sundry

hétérogène [eterɔʒɛn] *adj* : heterogeneous

hétérosexuel, -sexuelle [eterɔsɛksyɛl] *adj & n* : heterosexual — **hétérosexualité** [-sɛksɥalite] *nf*

hêtre ['ɛtr] *nm* : beech

heure [œr] *nf* **1** : time <quelle heure est-il? : what time is it?> <avez-vous l'heure? : do you have the time?> **2** : hour <une demi-heure : half an hour> <cent kilomètres à l'heure : sixty miles per hour> **3 à l'~** : on time **4 de bonne heure** : early **5 heure avancée** *Can* : daylight saving time **6 heure d'été** : daylight saving time **7 heure de pointe** : rush hour **8 heure normale** *Can* : standard time **9 heures supplémentaires** : overtime **10 tout à l'heure** : later on

heureusement [œrøzmɑ̃] *adv* : fortunately, luckily

heureux, -reuse [œrø, -røz] *adj* **1** : happy, cheerful <vivre heureux : to live happily> **2** : glad, pleased <heureux de te revoir : glad to see you again> **3** : fortunate, lucky <heureux en amour : lucky in love> **4** : apt, pleasing

heurt ['œr] *nm* **1** : collision, crash **2** CONFLIT : clash, conflict **3 sans heurts** : smoothly, smooth

heurter ['œrte] *vt* **1** : to strike, to hit, to collide with **2** : to conflict with, to go against **3** : to offend — *vi* : to hit, to collide <heurter contre : to strike> — **se heurter** *vr* **1** : to collide **2 ~ à** : to come up against

heurtoir ['œrtwar] *nm* : (door) knocker

hexagonal, -nale [ɛgzagɔnal] *adj, mpl* **-naux** [-no] : hexagonal

hexagone [ɛgzagɔn] *nm* **1** : hexagon **2 l'Hexagone** : France

hiatus [jatys] *nms & pl* : hiatus

hiberner [ibɛrne] *vi* : to hibernate — **hibernation** [ibɛrnasjɔ̃] *nf*

hibou ['ibu] *nm, pl* **hiboux** [ibu] : owl

hic ['ik] *nm fam* : snag <voilà le hic! : that's the trouble!>

hickory ['ikɔri] *nm* : hickory

hideux, -deuse ['idø, -døz] *adj* : hideous — **hideusement** [-døzmɑ̃] *adv*

hier [ijɛr] *adv* : yesterday <hier matin : yesterday morning> <comme si s'était hier : as if it were yesterday>

hiérarchie ['jerarʃi] *nf* : hierarchy

hiérarchique ['jerarʃik] *adj* : hierarchical

hiéroglyphe [jerɔglif] *nm* : hieroglyph, hieroglyphic

hilarant, -rante [ilarɑ̃, -rɑ̃t] *adj* : hilarious

hilare [ilar] *adj* : merry, mirthful

hilarité [ilarite] *nf* : hilarity, mirth

hindou, -doue [ɛ̃du] *adj* : Hindu

Hindou, -doue *n* : Hindu

hindouisme [ɛ̃duism] *nm* : Hinduism

hippie *or* **hippy** ['ipi] *nmf, pl* **hippies** : hippie

hippique [ipik] *adj* : equestrian, horse <course hippique : horse race>

hippisme [ipism] *nm* : (horseback) riding

hippocampe [ipɔkɑ̃p] *nm* : sea horse

hippodrome [ipɔdrom] *nm* : racecourse

hippopotame [ipɔpɔtam] *nm* : hippopotamus

hirondelle [irɔ̃dɛl] *nf* **1** : swallow **2 hirondelle de mer** : STERNE : tern

hirsute [irsyt] *adj* **1** : tousled, disheveled **2** : hairy, shaggy

hispanique[1] [ispanik] *adj* : Hispanic

hispanique[2] *nmf* : Hispanic (person)

hispano-américain, -caine [ispanoamerikɛ̃, -kɛn] *adj* : Spanish-American

Hispano-Américain, -caine *n* : Spanish American

hisser ['ise] *vt* : to hoist, to haul up — **se hisser** *vr* : to raise oneself up <se hisser sur la pointe des pieds : to stand on tiptoe>

histogramme [istɔgram] *nm* : bar graph

histoire [istwar] *nf* **1** : history **2** : story **3** : affair, matter <c'est toujours la même histoire : it's always the same old story> **4 histoires** *nfpl* ENNUIS : trouble, problems <s'attirer des histoires : to be asking for trouble> **5 ~ de** : just <histoire de voir : just to see> **6 histoire naturelle** : natural history

historien, -rienne [istɔrjɛ̃, -rjɛn] *n* : historian

historique[1] [istɔrik] *adj* **1** : historical **2** : historic <champs de batailles historiques : historic battlefields> — **historiquement** [-rikmɑ̃] *adv*

historique[2] *nm* : account, story, history

hiver [ivɛr] *nm* : winter

hivernal, -nale [ivɛrnal] *adj, mpl* **-naux** [-no] : winter, wintry

hiverner [ivɛrne] *vi* : to winter

hochement ['ɔʃmɑ̃] *nm* **hochement de tête** : shake of the head, nod

hocher ['ɔʃe] *vt* **hocher la tête** : to nod, to shake one's head

hochet ['ɔʃɛ] *nm* : rattle

hockey ['ɔkɛ] *nm* : hockey

holà ['ɔla] *interj* **1** : stop!, whoa! **2** : hey! **3 mettre le holà à** : to put a stop to

hold-up ['ɔldœp] *nms & pl* : holdup, robbery

holistique [ɔlistik] *adj* : holistic

hollandais[1], **-daise** ['ɔlɑ̃dɛ, -dɛz] *adj* : Dutch

hollandais[2] *nm* : Dutch (language)

Hollandais, -daise *n* **1** : Dutchman *m*, Dutchwoman *f* **2 les Hollondais** : the Dutch

holocauste [ɔlɔkost] *nm* : holocaust

hologramme [ɔlɔgram] *nm* : hologram

homard ['ɔmar] *nm* : lobster

homélie [ɔmeli] *nf* : homily, sermon

homéopathie [ɔmeɔpati] *nf* : homeopathy — **homéopathique** [ɔmeɔpatik] *adj*

homicide[1] [ɔmisid] *adj* : homicidal

homicide[2] *nm* **1** : homicide **2 homicide involontaire** : manslaughter

hommage [ɔmaʒ] *nm* : homage, tribute <rendre hommage à : to pay tribute to>

hommasse [ɔmas] *adj* : mannish

homme [ɔm] *nm* **1** : man **2 l'homme** : man, mankind **3 homme d'affaires** : businessman **4 homme à tout faire** : handyman

homme–grenouille [ɔmgrənuj] *nm, pl* **hommes–grenouilles** : frogman

homogène [ɔmɔʒɛn] *adj* : homogeneous

homogénéiser [ɔmɔʒeneize] *vt* : to homogenize — **homogénéisé, -sée** [-ize] *adj*

homogénéité [ɔmɔʒeneite] *nf* : homogeneity

homographe [ɔmɔgraf] *nm* : homograph

homologation [ɔmɔlɔgasjɔ̃] *nf* : probate, ratification

homologue [ɔmɔlɔg] *nmf* : counterpart, opposite number

homologuer [ɔmɔlɔge] *vt* **1** : to ratify, to approve **2** : to probate (a will)

homonyme [ɔmɔnim] *nm* **1** : homonym **2** : namesake

homophone [ɔmɔfɔn] *nm* : homophone

homosexualité [ɔmɔsɛksyalite] *nf* : homosexuality

homosexuel, -sexuelle [ɔmɔsɛksyɛl] *adj & n* : homosexual

hondurien, -rienne ['ɔ̃dyrjɛ̃, -rjɛn] *adj* : Honduran

Hondurien, -rienne *n* : Honduran

hongrois[1], **-groise** ['ɔ̃grwa, -grwaz] *adj* : Hungarian

hongrois[2] *nm* : Hungarian (language)

Hongrois, -groise *n* : Hungarian

honnête [ɔnɛt] *adj* **1** INTÈGRE : honest, honorable **2** JUSTE : reasonable, fair **3** RESPECTABLE : decent, respectable — **honnêtement** [ɔnɛtmɑ̃] *adv*

honnêteté [ɔnɛtte] *nf* : honesty

honneur [ɔnœr] *nm* : honor <avoir l'honneur de : to have the honor of> <en l'honneur de : in honor of> <se faire l'honneur de : to pride oneself on>

honorable [ɔnɔrabl] *adj* **1** : honorable **2** : decent, satisfactory <un salaire honorable : a decent salary> **3** : creditable, worthy — **honorablement** [-rabləmɑ̃] *adv*

honoraire [ɔnɔrɛr] *adj* : honorary

honoraires *nmpl* : fees

honorer [ɔnɔre] *vt* **1** : to honor **2** : to be a credit to **3** : to honor (a debt), to pay — **s'honorer** *vr* **1** : to gain distinction **2 ~ de** : to pride oneself on

honorifique [ɔnɔrifik] *adj* : honorary

honte ['ɔ̃t] *nf* : shame, disgrace <avoir honte : to be ashamed> <faire honte à : to put to shame>

honteux, -teuse ['ɔ̃tø, -tøz] *adj* **1** : ashamed **2** : shameful — **honteusement** ['ɔ̃tøzmɑ̃] *adv*

hôpital [ɔpital] *nm, pl* **-taux** [-to] : hospital

hoquet ['ɔkɛ] *nm* : hiccup <avoir le hocquet : to have the hiccups>

hoqueter ['ɔkte] {8} *vi* : to hiccup

horaire[1] [ɔrɛr] *adj* : hourly

horaire[2] *nm* : timetable, schedule

horde ['ɔrd] *nf* : horde

horizon [ɔrizɔ̃] *nm* **1** : horizon <à l'horizon : on the horizon> **2** PAYSAGE : view, landscape **3** : outlook, prospect <horizons économiques : economic prospects> **4** : field of activity <ouvrir ses horizons : to broaden one's horizons>

horizontal, -tale [ɔrizɔ̃tal] *adj, mpl* **-taux** [-to] : horizontal — **horizontalement** [-talmɑ̃] *adv*

horizontale *nf* **à l' horizontale** : in a horizontal position

horloge [ɔrlɔʒ] *nf* : clock

horloger, -gère [ɔrlɔrʒe, -ʒɛr] *n* : watchmaker

hormis ['ɔrmi] *prep* : except, save

hormonal, -nale [ɔrmɔnal] *adj, mpl* **-naux** [-no] : hormonal

hormone [ɔrmɔn] *nf* : hormone

horoscope [ɔrɔskɔp] *nm* : horoscope

horreur [ɔrœr] *nf* **1** ÉPOUVANTE : horror, fear **2** ATROCITÉ : horror, atrocity **3** AVERSION : loathing, repugnance <avoir horreur de : to loathe, to detest> <quelle horreur! : how sickening!>

horrible [ɔribl] *adj* : horrible — **horriblement** [ɔribləmɑ̃] *adv*

horrifiant, -fiante [ɔrifjɑ̃, -fjɑ̃t] *adj* : horrifying

horrifier [ɔrifje] {96} *vt* : to horrify

horripiler [ɔripile] *vt* : to exasperate

hors ['ɔr] *prep* **1** : except for, save **2** : outside, beyond <hors normes : nonstandard> <hors pair : outstanding, exceptional> <hors service : out of service> <hors tout : overall> **3 ~ de** : out of <hors d'atteinte : out of reach> <hors de doute : beyond doubt> <hors de question : out of the question> <hors de la ville : outside of town> **4 être hors de soi** : to be beside oneself

hors–bord ['ɔrbɔr] *nms & pl* **1** : outboard motor **2** : speedboat

hors–concours ['ɔrkɔ̃kur] *nms & pl* : disqualification

hors–d'œuvre ['ɔrdœvr] *nms & pl* : hors d'oeuvre

hors–la–loi |ˈɔrlalwa| *nms & pl* : outlaw
hors–taxe |ˈɔrtaks| *nms & pl* : duty-free articles
hors–texte |ˈɔrtɛkst| *nms & pl* : plate (in a book)
horticole |ɔrtikɔl| *adj* : horticultural
horticulture |ɔrtikyltyr| *nf* : horticulture
hosanna |ozana| *nm & interj* : hosanna
hospice |ɔspis| *nm France* **1** : home (for the elderly, etc.) **2** : hospice
hospitalier, -lière |ɔspitalje, -jɛr| *adj* **1** : hospital <services hospitaliers : hospital services> **2** : hospitable
hospitalisation |ɔspitalizasjɔ̃| *nf* : hospitalization
hospitaliser |ɔspitalize| *vt* : to hospitalize
hospitalité |ɔspitalite| *nf* : hospitality
hostie |ɔsti| *nf* : host, eucharistic bread
hostile |ɔstil| *adj* : hostile — **hostilement** |ɔstilmɑ̃| *adv*
hostilité |ɔstilite| *nf* **1** : hostility **2 hostilités** *nfpl* : hostilities, war
hot–dog |ˈɔtdɔg| *nm, pl* **hot–dogs** : hot dog
hôte[1], hôtesse |ot, otɛs| *n* : host, hostess *f*
hôte[2] *nmf* **1** INVITÉ : guest **2** : occupant, guest (in a hotel, etc.)
hôte[3] *nm* : host (in biology)
hôtel |otɛl| *nm* **1** : hotel **2 hôtel de ville** : town hall **3 hôtel particulier** : mansion, townhouse
hôtelier[1], -lière |otəlje, -jɛr| *adj* : hotel
hôtelier[2], -lière *n* : hotelier, hotel manager
hôtellerie |otɛlri| *nf* : hotel business
hôtesse |otɛs| *nf* **1** → **hôte[1]** **2** *or* **hôtesse de l'air** : stewardess, flight attendant **3** *or* **hôtesse d'accueil** : receptionist
hotte |ˈɔt| *nf* **1** : basket (carried on the back) **2** : hood (of a chimney) **3** *or* **hotte aspirante** : range hood, ventilator
houblon |ˈublɔ̃| *nm* **1** : hop (plant) **2** : hops *pl*
houe |ˈu| *nf* : hoe
houille |ˈuj| *nf* **1** : coal **2 houille blanche** : hydroelectric power
houiller, -lère |ˈuje, -jɛr| *adj* : coal, coal-mining
houillère *nf* : coal mine
houle |ˈul| *nf* : swell, surge
houlette |ˈulɛt| *nf* **1** : crook, staff (of a shepherd) **2 sous la houlette de** : under the guidance of
houleux, -leuse |ˈulø, -løz| *adj* **1** : rough (of the sea) **2** : stormy, turbulent <débats houleux : stormy debates>
houppe |ˈup| *nf* **1** *or* **houppette** : powder puff **2** : tuft (of hair)
hourra |ˈura| *nm & interj* : hurrah
houspiller |ˈuspije| *vt* RÉPRIMANDER : to scold
housse |ˈus| *nf* : cover, slipcover, dust cover
houx |ˈu| *nms & pl* : holly
huard *or* **huart** |ˈyar| *nm Can* : loon
hublot |ˈyblo| *nm* : porthole
huche |ˈyʃ| *nf* **1** COFFRE : chest **2 huche à pain** : bread box
huées |ˈɥe| *nfpl* : boos
huer |ˈɥe| *vt* : to boo — *vi* : to hoot
huile |ɥil| *nf* **1** : (cooking) oil <huile d'olive : olive oil> **2** : oil, lubricant <huile moteur : motor oil> <huile de coude : elbow grease> **3** : oil (in pharmacy) <huile solaire : suntan lotion> **4** : oil (painting) **5 mer d'huile** : calm sea, sea of glass
huiler |ɥile| *vt* : to oil
huileux, -leuse |ɥilø, -løz| *adj* : oily
huilier |ɥilje| *nm* : cruet
huis |ɥi| *nm* **à huis clos** : behind closed doors
huissier |ɥisje| *nm* **1** : usher (in a court of law) **2** : bailiff
huit[1] |ˈɥit, *before consonant* ˈɥi| *adj* **1** : eight <huit jours : a week> **2** : eighth <le huit décembre : December eighth>
huit[2] *nms & pl* : eight
huitaine |ˈɥitɛn| *nf* **1** : about a week **2** : about eight
huitième |ˈɥitjɛm| *adj & nmf & nm* : eighth
huître |ɥitr| *nf* : oyster
hululement |ˈylylmɑ̃| *nm* : hoot
hululer |ˈylyle| *vi* : to hoot
humain[1], -maine |ymɛ̃, -mɛn| *adj* **1** : human <la nature humaine : human nature> **2** : humane — **humainement** |-mɛnmɑ̃| *adv*
humain[2] *nm* : human being
humaniser |ymanize| *vt* : to humanize
humanisme |ymanism| *nm* : humanism
humaniste[1] |ymanist| *adj* : humanist, humanistic
humaniste[2] *nmf* : humanist
humanitaire |ymanitɛr| *adj* : humanitarian
humanitarisme |ymanitarism| *nm* : humanitarianism
humanité |ymanite| *nf* : humanity
humanoïde |ymanɔid| *adj & nmf* : humanoid
humble |œ̃bl| *adj* : humble — **humblement** |œ̃bləmɑ̃| *adv*
humecter |ymɛkte| *vt* : to dampen, to moisten — **s'humecter** *vr*
humer |ˈyme| *vt* **1** : to breathe in, to inhale **2** : to smell
humérus |ymerys| *nms & pl* : humerus
humeur |ymœr| *nf* **1** : mood, humor <de bonne humeur : in a good mood> <sautes d'humeur : mood swings> **2** : temperament, temper <d'humeur égale : even-tempered> **3** : ill humor, bad temper <accès d'humeur : fit of bad temper>
humide |ymid| *adj* **1** : moist, damp **2** : humid, muggy
humidificateur |ymidifikatœr| *nm* : humidifier

humidifier [ymidifje] {96} *vt* : to humidify

humidité [ymidite] *nf* **1** : humidity **2** : dampness, moisture

humiliant, -liante [ymiljɑ̃, -jɑ̃t] *adj* : humiliating

humiliation [ymiljasjɔ̃] *nf* : humiliation

humilier [ymilje] {96} *vt* : to humiliate — **s'humilier** *vr* : to humble oneself

humilité [ymilite] *nf* : humility

humoriste [ymɔrist] *nmf* : humorist

humoristique [ymɔristik] *adj* : humorous

humour [ymur] *nm* : humor, wit <avoir de l'humour : to have a sense of humor>

humus [ymys] *nms & pl* : humus

huppé, -pée ['ype] *adj* **1** : tufted, crested **2** *fam* : posh, high-class

hurlement ['yrləmɑ̃] *nm* : howl, yell

hurler ['yrle] *vt* : to yell out — *vi* **1** : to howl, to roar **2** : to yell, to shout

hurluberlu, -lue [yrlybɛrly] *n* : oddball, crank

hurrah ['ura] → **hourra**

hutte ['yt] *nf* : hut

hyacinthe [jasɛ̃t] *nf* : hyacinth

hybride[1] [ibrid] *adj* : hybrid

hybride[2] *nm* : hybrid

hydratant[1], **-tante** [idratɑ̃, -tɑ̃t] *adj* : moisturizing

hydratant[2] *nm* : moisturizer

hydrate [idrat] *nm* **hydrate de carbon** : carbohydrate

hydraulique[1] [idrolik] *adj* : hydraulic

hydraulique[2] *nf* : hydraulics

hydravion [idravjɔ̃] *nm* : seaplane

hydrocarbure [idrɔkarbyr] *nm* : hydrocarbon

hydroélectrique *or* **hydro–électrique** [idrɔelɛktrik] *adj* : hydroelectric

hydrogène [idrɔʒɛn] *nm* : hydrogen

hydroglisseur [idrɔglisœr] *nm* : hydroplane (boat)

hyène [jɛn] *nf* : hyena

hygiène [iʒjɛn] *nf* : hygiene <hygiène publique : public health>

hygiénique [iʒjenik] *adj* : hygienic

hygiéniste [iʒjenist] *nmf* : hygienist

hygromètre [igrɔmɛtr] *nm* : hygrometer

hymne [imn] *nm* **1** : hymn **2** **hymne nationale** : national anthem

hyperactif, -tive *adj* : hyperactive

hyperbole [ipɛrbɔl] *nf* : hyberbole

hypermétrope [ipɛrmetrɔp] *adj* PRESBYTE : farsighted

hypermétropie [ipɛrmetrɔpi] *nf* PRESBYTIE : farsightedness

hypersensible [ipɛrsɑ̃sibl] *adj* : hypersensitive

hypertension [ipɛrtɑ̃sjɔ̃] *nf* : high blood pressure, hypertension

hypertexte [ipɛrtɛkst] *nm* : hypertext

hypnose [ipnoz] *nf* : hypnosis

hypnotique [ipnɔtik] *adj* : hypnotic

hypnotiser [ipnɔtize] *vt* : to hypnotize

hypnotiseur [ipnɔtizœr] *nm* : hypnotist

hypnotisme [ipnɔtism] *nm* : hypnotism

hypocondriaque[1] [ipɔkɔ̃drijak] *adj* : hypochondriacal, hypochondriac

hypocondriaque[2] *nmf* : hypochondriac

hypocondrie [ipɔkɔ̃dri] *nf* : hypochondria

hypocrisie [ipɔkrizi] *nf* : hypocrisy

hypocrite[1] [ipɔkrit] *adj* : hypocritical — **hypocritement** [-kritmɑ̃] *adv*

hypocrite[2] *nmf* : hypocrite

hypodermique [ipɔdɛrmik] *adj* : hypodermic <seringue hypodermique : hypodermic needle>

hypotension [ipɔtɑ̃sjɔ̃] *nf* : low blood pressure, hypotension

hypoténuse [ipɔtenyz] *nf* : hypotenuse

hypothécaire [ipɔtekɛr] *adj* : mortgage <prêt hypothécaire : mortgage loan>

hypothèque [ipɔtɛk] *nf* : mortgage

hypothéquer [ipɔteke] {87} *vt* : to mortgage

hypothermie [ipɔtɛrmi] *nf* : hypothermia

hypothèse [ipɔtɛz] *nf* : hypothesis

hypothétique [ipɔtetik] *adj* : hypothetical — **hypothétiquement** [-tikmɑ̃] *adv*

hystérectomie [isterɛktɔmi] *nf* : hysterectomy

hystérie [isteri] *nf* : hysteria

hystérique [isterik] *adj* : hysterical — **hystériquement** [-rikmɑ̃] *adj*

I

i [i] *nm* : i, the ninth letter of the alphabet

ibis [ibis] *nms & pl* : ibis

iceberg [ajsbɛrg] *nm* : iceberg

ichtyologie [iktjɔlɔʒi] *nf* : ichthyology

ici [isi] *adv* **1** : here <ici et là : here and there> <par ici : this way> **2** : now <jusqu'ici : up until now> <d'ici là : by then> **3** **d'ici** : hence, therefore <d'ici six ans : six years hence>

ici–bas [isiba] *adv* : here below, on earth

icône [ikon] *nf* : icon

iconoclasme |ikɔnɔklasm| *nm* : iconoclasm

iconoclaste[1] |ikɔnɔklast| *adj* : iconoclastic

iconoclaste[2] *nmf* : iconoclast

idéal[1], **idéale** |ideal| *adj, mpl* **idéals** *or* **idéaux** |ideo| : ideal — **idéalement** |-almɑ̃| *adv*

idéal[2] *nm* : ideal

idéaliser |idealize| *vt* : to idealize — **idéalisation** |-lizasjɔ̃| *nf*

idéalisme |idealism| *nm* : idealism

idéaliste[1] |idealist| *adj* : idealistic

idéaliste[2] *nmf* : idealist

idée |ide| *nf* **1** : idea <changer d'idée : to change one's mind> <se faire des idées : to imagine things> **2 idée de génie** : brainwave **3 idée fixe** : obsession **4 idée reçue** : accepted opinion, commonplace

idem |idɛm| *adv* : ditto, idem

identifiable |idɑ̃tifjabl| *adj* : identifiable

identification |idɑ̃tifikasjɔ̃| *nf* : identification

identifier |idɑ̃tifje| {96} *vt* **1** : to identify, to recognize **2** ASSIMILER : to liken, to consider equivalent — **s'identifier** *vr* **∼ avec** : to identify with

identique |idɑ̃tik| *adj* : identical — **identiquement** |-tikmɑ̃| *adv*

identité |idɑ̃tite| *nf* : identity

idéologie |ideɔlɔʒi| *nf* : ideology

idéologique |ideɔlɔʒik| *adj* : ideological

idiomatique |idjɔmatik| *adj* : idiomatic

idiome |idjom| *nm* : idiom

idiosyncrasie |idjɔsɛ̃krazi| *nf* : idiosyncrasy

idiot[1], **-diote** |idjo, -djɔt| *adj* : idiotic — **idiotement** |idjɔtmɑ̃| *adv*

idiot[2], **-diote** *n* : idiot, fool

idiotie |idjɔsi| *nf* **1** : idiocy **2** : idiotic action or remark

idiotisme |idjɔtism| *nm* : idiom, idiomatic expression

idoine |idwan| *adj* : suitable, fitting

idolâtrer |idɔlatre| *vt* : to idolize

idolâtrie |idɔlatri| *nf* : idolatry

idole |idɔl| *nf* : idol

idylle |idil| *nf* **1** : romance, love affair **2** : idyll (poem)

idyllique |idilik| *adj* : idyllic

if |if| *nm* : yew

igloo |iglu| *nm* : igloo

igname |iɲam| *nf* : yam

ignare[1] |iɲar| *adj* : ignorant

ignare[2] *nmf* : ignoramus

ignifuge |iɲifyʒ| *adj* : fireproof

ignifuger |iʒnifyʒe| {17} *vt* : to fireproof

ignoble |iɲɔbl| *adj* **1** INFÂME : base, vile **2** RÉPUGNANT : revolting, repugnant

ignominie |iɲɔmini| *nf* **1** : ignominy **2** : shameful act

ignominieux, -nieuse |iɲɔminjø, -njøz| *adj* : ignominious — **ignominieusement** |-njøzmɑ̃| *adv*

ignorance |iɲɔrɑ̃s| *nf* : ignorance

ignorant, -rante |iɲɔrɑ̃, -rɑ̃t| *adj* : ignorant

ignorer |iɲɔre| *vt* **1** : to be unaware of <je l'ignore : I don't know> **2** : to ignore

iguane |igwan| *nm* : iguana

il |il| *pron* **1** : he, it <il est en retard : he's late> <il se peut : it is possible> **2** (*as subject of an impersonal verb*) : it <il pleut : it's raining> **3 ils** *pron pl* : they **4 il y a** : there is, there are

île |il| *nf* : island, isle

illégal, -gale |ilegal| *adj, mpl* **-gaux** |-go| : illegal, unlawful — **illégalement** |-galmɑ̃| *adv*

illégalité |ilegalite| *nf* : illegality

illégitime |ileʒitim| *adj* **1** : illegitimate **2** : unwarranted, unjustified — **illégitimement** |-timmɑ̃| *adv*

illégitimité |ileʒitimite| *nf* : illegitimacy

illettré, -trée |iletre| *adj & n* ANALPHABÈTE : illiterate

illettrisme |iletrism| *nm* ANALPHABÉTISME : illiteracy

illicite |ilisit| *adj* : illicit — **illicitement** |-sitmɑ̃| *adv*

illico |iliko| *adv fam* : pronto, immediately

illimité, -tée |ilimite| *adj* **1** : unlimited, boundless **2** : indefinite

illisible |ilizibl| *adj* **1** : illegible **2** : unreadable

illisiblement |iliziblәmɑ̃| *adv* : illegibly

illogique |ilɔʒik| *adj* : illogical — **illogiquement** |-ʒikmɑ̃| *adv*

illumination |ilyminasjɔ̃| *nf* **1** : illumination, lighting **2** : inspiration **3 illuminations** *nfpl* : lights

illuminer |ilymine| *vt* ÉCLAIRER : to illuminate

illusion |ilyzjɔ̃| *nf* **1** : illusion <illusion d'optique : optical illusion> **2** : deception, delusion <se faire des illusions : to delude oneself>

illusionner |ilyzjɔne| *vt* : to delude, to deceive — **s'illusionner** *vr*

illusionniste |ilyzjɔnist| *nmf* : conjurer

illusoire |ilyzwar| *adj* : illusory

illustrateur, -trice |ilystratœr, -tris| *n* : illustrator

illustratif, -tive |ilystratif, -tiv| *adj* : illustrative

illustration |ilystrasjɔ̃| *nf* : illustration

illustre |ilystr| *adj* : illustrious, renowned

illustré[1], **-trée** |ilystre| *adj* : illustrated

illustré[2] *nm* : illustrated magazine

illustrer |ilystre| *vt* : to illustrate — **s'illustrer** *vr* : to distinguish oneself

îlot |ilo| *nm* **1** : small island **2** : block (of houses) **3** : pocket (of resistance, etc.)

ils |il| → **il**

image |imaʒ| *nf* **1** : image **2** DESSIN : picture **3 images** *nfpl* : imagery

imagé, -gée |imaʒe| *adj* : full of imagery, colorful

imagerie [imaʒri] *nf* **1** : images *pl* **2** : imaging
imaginable [imaʒinabl] *adj* : imaginable
imaginaire[1] [imaʒinɛr] *adj* : imaginary
imaginaire[2] *nm* : (world of the) imagination
imaginatif, -tive [imaʒinatif, -tiv] *adj* : imaginative
imagination [imaʒinasjɔ̃] *nf* : imagination
imaginer [imaʒine] *vt* **1** : to imagine, to suppose **2** : to devise, to think up — **s'imaginer** *vr* **1** : to imagine, to picture **2** : to picture oneself **3** : to believe, to delude oneself
imbattable [ɛ̃batabl] *adj* : invincible, unbeatable
imbécile[1] [ɛ̃besil] *adj* : stupid, idiotic
imbécile[2] *nmf* **1** : imbecile **2** : fool, idiot <faire l'imbécile : to goof off, to play the fool>
imbécillité [ɛ̃besilite] *nf* **1** : idiocy, stupidity **2** : stupid act or remark, nonsense
imbiber [ɛ̃bibe] *vt* TREMPER : to soak — **s'imbiber** *vr* **1** : to soak up, to get soaked **2** *fam* : to get drunk
imbrication [ɛ̃brikasjɔ̃] *nf* **1** : overlapping **2** : interweaving, interlocking
imbriquer [ɛ̃brike] *vt* **1** : to overlap **2** : to interweave — **s'imbriquer** *vr*
imbroglio [ɛ̃brɔljo] *nm* : imbroglio
imbu, -bue [ɛ̃by] *adj* ~ **de** : imbued with, full of
imbuvable [ɛ̃byvabl] *adj* **1** : undrinkable **2** *fam* : insufferable
imitateur[1], **-trice** [imitatœr, -tris] *adj* : imitative
imitateur[2], **-trice** *n* **1** : imitator **2** : mimic, impersonator
imitatif, -tive [imitatif, -tiv] *adj* : imitative
imitation [imitasjɔ̃] *nf* **1** : imitation, copy <imitation cuir : simulated leather> **2** : impersonation, mimicry
imiter [imite] *vt* **1** : to imitate **2** : to mimic **3** : to copy, to forge
immaculé, -lée [imakyle] *adj* : immaculate
immanent, -nente [imanɑ̃, -nɑ̃t] *adj* : immanent
immangeable [ɛ̃mɑ̃ʒabl] *adj* : inedible
immanquable [ɛ̃mɑ̃kabl] *adj* **1** INÉVITABLE : inevitable **2** : impossible to miss
immanquablement [ɛ̃mɑ̃kabləmɑ̃] *adv* : without fail, inevitably
immatériel, -rielle [imaterjɛl] *adj* **1** : immaterial **2** : intangible
immatriculation [imatrikylasjɔ̃] *nf* **1** : registration **2 plaque d'immatriculation** : license plate
immatriculer [imatrikyle] *vt* : to register (a motor vehicle)
immature [imatyr] *adj* : immature
immaturité [imatyrite] *nf* : immaturity
immédiat[1], **-diate** [imedja, -djat] *adj* : immediate — **immédiatement** [-djatmɑ̃] *adv*
immédiat[2] *nm* **dans l'immédiat** : for the time being
immémorial, -riale [imemɔrjal] *adj, mpl* **-riaux** [-rjo] : immemorial, ancient
immense [imɑ̃s] *adj* : immense — **immensément** [imɑ̃semɑ̃] *adv*
immensité [imɑ̃site] *nf* : immensity
immerger [imɛrʒe] {17} *vt* : to submerge, to immerse — **s'immerger** *vr* : to dive, to submerge oneself
immérité, -tée [imerite] *adj* : undeserved
immersion [imɛrsjɔ̃] *nf* : immersion
immeuble[1] [imœbl] *adj* **biens immeubles** : real estate
immeuble[2] *nm* : building, apartment building, office building
immigrant, -grante [imigrɑ̃, -grɑ̃t] *adj & n* : immigrant
immigration [imigrasjɔ̃] *nf* : immigration
immigré, -grée [imigre] *n* : immigrant
immigrer [imigre] *vi* : to immigrate
imminence [iminɑ̃s] *nf* : imminence
imminent, -nente [iminɑ̃, -nɑ̃t] *adj* : impending, imminent
immiscer [imise] {6} *v* **s'immiscer** *vr* ~ **dans** : to interfere with, to meddle in
immixtion [imiksjɔ̃] *nf* : interference
immobile [imɔbil] *adj* **1** : motionless, still **2** : fixed, unchanging
immobilier, -lière [imɔbilje, -jɛr] *adj* : real estate, property <agent immobilier : real estate agent>
immobilisation [imɔbilizasjɔ̃] *nf* **1** : immobilization **2 immobilisations** *nfpl* : fixed assets
immobiliser [imɔbilize] *vt* **1** : to immobilize **2** : to bring to a halt — **s'immobiliser** *vr* : to come to a halt
immobilisme [imɔbilism] *nm* : opposition to change, conservatism
immobilité [imɔbilite] *nf* : immobility, stillness
immodéré, -rée [imɔdere] *adj* : immoderate, excessive — **immodérément** [-remɑ̃] *adv*
immodeste [imɔdɛst] *adj* : immodest
immoler [imɔle] *vt* SACRIFIER : to immolate, to sacrifice
immonde [imɔ̃d] *adj* **1** : foul, filthy **2** : vile, sordid, revolting
immondices [imɔ̃dis] *nfpl* : waste, refuse
immoral, -rale [imɔral] *adj, mpl* **-raux** [-ro] : immoral — **immoralement** [-ralmɑ̃] *adv*
immoralité [imɔralite] *nf* : immorality
immortaliser [imɔrtalize] *vt* : to immortalize
immortalité [imɔrtalite] *nf* : immortality
immortel[1], **-telle** [imɔrtɛl] *adj* : immortal

immortel[2], **-telle** *n* : immortal

immuable [imɥabl] *adj* : immutable, unchanging — **immuablement** [imɥabləmɑ̃] *adv*

immuniser [imynize] *vt* : to immunize — **immunisation** [-nizasjɔ̃] *nf*

immunitaire [imynitɛr] *adj* : immune <système immunitaire : immune system>

immunité [imynite] *nf* : immunity

immunologie [imynɔlɔʒi] *nf* : immunology

impact [ɛ̃pakt] *nm* : impact

impair[1], **-paire** [ɛ̃pɛr] *adj* : odd <nombres impairs : odd numbers>

impair[2] *nm* : blunder, faux pas

impala [impala] *nm* : impala

imparable [ɛ̃parabl] *adj* : unstoppable

impardonnable [ɛ̃pardɔnabl] *adj* : unforgivable, unpardonable

imparfait[1], **-faite** [ɛ̃parfɛ, -fɛt] *adj* **1** : imperfect **2** : incomplete, unfinished — **imparfaitement** [-fɛtmɑ̃] *adv*

imparfait[2] *nm* : imperfect (tense)

impartial, -tiale [ɛ̃parsjal] *adj, mpl* **-tiaux** [-sjo] : unbiased, impartial — **impartialement** [-sjalmɑ̃] *adv*

impartialité [ɛ̃parsjalite] *nf* : impartiality

impartir [ɛ̃partir] *vt* : to grant, to bestow

impasse [ɛ̃pas] *nf* **1** : impasse, deadlock **2** CUL-DE-SAC : dead end

impassible [ɛ̃pasibl] *adj* : impassive — **impassiblement** [-sibləmɑ̃] *adv*

impatiemment [ɛ̃pasjamɑ̃] *adv* : impatiently

impatient, -tiente [ɛ̃pasjɑ̃, -sjɑ̃t] *adj* : impatient — **impatience** [-sjɑ̃s] *nf*

impatienter [ɛ̃pasjɑ̃te] *vt* : to irritate, to annoy — **s'impatienter** *vr* : to lose patience

impayable [ɛ̃pɛjabl] *adj fam* : priceless

impayé, -payée [ɛ̃pɛje] *adj* : unpaid, outstanding

impeccable [ɛ̃pekabl] *adj* : impeccable — **impeccablement** [-kabləmɑ̃] *adv*

impécunieux, -nieuse [ɛ̃pekynjø, -njøz] *adj* : impecunious

impénétrable [ɛ̃penetrabl] *adj* **1** : impenetrable **2** : inscrutable

impénitent, -tente [ɛ̃penitɑ̃, -tɑ̃t] *adj* : unrepentant

impensable [ɛ̃pɑ̃sabl] *adj* : unthinkable, inconceivable

imper [ɛ̃pɛr] *nm fam* → **imperméable**

impératif[1], **-tive** [ɛ̃peratif, -tiv] *adj* : imperative — **impérativement** [-tivmɑ̃] *adv*

impératif[2] *nm* **1** : requirement, necessity **2** : imperative (case)

impératrice [ɛ̃peratris] *nf* : empress

imperceptible [ɛ̃pɛ̃rseptibl] *adj* : imperceptible — **imperceptiblement** [-tibləmɑ̃] *adv*

imperfection [ɛ̃pɛrfɛksjɔ̃] *nf* : imperfection

impérial, -riale [ɛ̃perjal] *adj, mpl* **-riaux** [-rjo] : imperial

impérialisme [ɛ̃perjalism] *nm* : imperialism

impérialiste[1] [ɛ̃perjalist] *adj* : imperialist, imperialistic

impérialiste[2] *nmf* : imperialist

impérieusement [ɛ̃perjøzmɑ̃] *adv* **1** : imperiously **2** : urgently, absolutely

impérieux, -rieuse [ɛ̃perjø, -jøz] *adj* **1** : imperious **2** : pressing, urgent

impérissable [ɛ̃perisabl] *adj* : imperishable, undying

imperméabilisation [ɛ̃pɛrmeabilizasjɔ̃] *nf* : waterproofing

imperméabiliser [ɛ̃pɛrmeabilize] *vt* : to waterproof

imperméable[1] [ɛ̃pɛrmeabl] *adj* **1** : waterproof **2** ~ **à** : impervious to

imperméable[2] *nm* : raincoat

impersonnel, -nelle [ɛ̃pɛrsɔnɛl] *adj* : impersonal — **impersonnellement** [-nɛlmɑ̃] *adv*

impertinent, -nente [ɛ̃pɛrtinɑ̃, -nɑ̃t] *adj* : impertinent — **impertinence** [-tinɑ̃s] *nf*

imperturbable [ɛ̃pɛrtyrbabl] *adj* : imperturbable, unflappable

impétueux, -tueuse, [ɛ̃petɥø, -tɥøz] *adj* **1** : impetuous, rash **2** : raging, wild — **impétueusement** [-tɥøzmɑ̃] *adv*

impétuosité [ɛ̃petɥozite] *nf* : impetuosity

impie [ɛ̃pi] *adj* : impious, godless

impiété [ɛ̃pjete] *nf* : impiety

impitoyable [ɛ̃pitwajabl] *adj* : merciless, pitiless — **impitoyablement** [-jabləmɑ̃] *adv*

implacable [ɛ̃plakabl] *adj* **1** : implacable **2** : relentless — **implacablement** [-kabləmɑ̃] *adv*

implant [ɛ̃plɑ̃] *nm* : implant (in medicine)

implantation [ɛ̃plɑ̃tasjɔ̃] *nf* **1** : establishment, installation, setting up **2** : implantation

implanter [ɛ̃plɑ̃te] *vt* **1** : to establish, to set up **2** : to implant — **s'implanter** *vr* **1** : to be set up **2** : to settle (of persons)

implication [ɛ̃plikasjɔ̃] *nf* : implication

implicite [ɛ̃plisit] *adj* : implicit — **implicitement** [-sitmɑ̃] *adv*

impliquer [ɛ̃plike] *vt* **1** : to implicate, to involve **2** : to imply, to mean — **s'impliquer** *vr* : to become involved

implorer [ɛ̃plɔre] *vt* : to implore

imploser [ɛ̃ploze] *vi* : to implode — **implosion** [ɛ̃plozjɔ̃] *nf*

impoli, -lie [ɛ̃pɔli] *adj* : impolite, rude — **impoliment** [-limɑ̃] *adv*

impolitesse [ɛ̃pɔlitɛs] *nf* : impoliteness, rudeness

impondérable [ɛ̃pɔ̃derabl] *adj* : imponderable

impopulaire [ɛ̃pɔpylɛr] *adj* : unpopular — **impopularité** [-pylarite] *nf*

importance |ɛ̃pɔrtɑ̃s| *nf* **1** : importance **2** : size, extent, amount **3 d'importance** : important, considerable

important¹, -tante |ɛ̃pɔrtɑ̃, -tɑ̃t| *adj* **1** : important, significant **2** LARGE : considerable, sizable

important² *nm* : important point, main thing

importateur, -trice |ɛ̃pɔrtatœr, -tris| *n* : importer

importation |ɛ̃pɔrtasjɔ̃| *nf* **1** : importation **2** : import

importer |ɛ̃pɔrte| *vt* : to import — *vi* **1** : to matter, to be important <peu importe : no matter> **2 n'importe** : I don't mind, it doesn't matter **3 n'importe où** : anywhere **4 n'importe quand** : anytime **5 n'importe qui** : anyone, anybody **6 n'importe quoi** : anything

import–export |ɛ̃pɔrɛkspɔr| *nms & pl* : import-export (business)

importun¹, -tune |ɛ̃pɔrtœ̃, -tyn| *adj* **1** : troublesome, bothersome **2** : inopportune, untimely

importun², -tune *n* : nuisance, pest

importuner |ɛ̃pɔrtyne| *vt* : to pester, to annoy

imposable |ɛ̃pozabl| *adj* : taxable

imposant, -sante |ɛ̃pozɑ̃, -zɑ̃t| *adj* : imposing

imposé, -sée |ɛ̃poze| *adj* **1** : prescribed, compulsory (in sports) **2** : fixed (of prices, etc.)

imposer |ɛ̃poze| *vt* **1** : to impose **2** : to command (respect, etc.) **3** : to tax — **s'imposer** *vr* **1** : to be essential **2** : to impose (something) on oneself, to make it a rule **3** : to become known, to stand out **4** ~ **à** : to impose (oneself) on

imposition |ɛ̃pozisjɔ̃| *nf* : taxation, tax <taux d'imposition : tax rate>

impossibilité |ɛ̃pɔsibilite| *nf* : impossibility

impossible¹ |ɛ̃pɔsibl| *adj* : impossible

impossible² *nm* **l'impossible** : the impossible <faire l'impossible : to do one's utmost>

imposte |ɛ̃pɔst| *nf* : fanlight

imposteur |ɛ̃pɔstœr| *nm* : impostor

imposture |ɛ̃pɔstyr| *nf* : imposture, deception

impôt |ɛ̃po| *nm* : tax, duty <impôt sur le revenu : income tax>

impotence |ɛ̃pɔtɑ̃s| *nf* : infirmity, disability

impotent, -tente |ɛ̃pɔtɑ̃, -tɑ̃t| *adj* INFIRME : infirm, disabled

impraticable |ɛ̃pratikabl| *adj* **1** IRRÉALISABLE : impracticable, unworkable **2** : impassable

imprécis, -cise |ɛ̃presi, -siz| *adj* : imprecise, vague

imprécision |ɛ̃presizjɔ̃| *nf* : imprecision, vagueness

imprégner |ɛ̃preɲe| {87} *vt* **1** PÉNÉTRER : to impregnate, to soak **2** : to fill, to pervade — **s'imprégner** *vr* ~ **de** : to immerse oneself in

imprenable |ɛ̃prənabl| *adj* : impregnable

imprégnation |ɛ̃preɲasjɔ̃| *nf* : impregnation, saturation

imprésario |ɛ̃presarjo| *nm* : impresario

impression |ɛ̃presjɔ̃| *nf* **1** : impression <faire bonne impression : to make a good impression> **2** : mark, imprint **3** : printing <envoyer à l'impression : to send to the press>

impressionnable |ɛ̃presjɔnabl| *adj* : impressionable

impressionnant, -nante |ɛ̃presjɔnɑ̃, -nɑ̃t| *adj* **1** : impressive, imposing **2** : disturbing, upsetting

impressionner |ɛ̃presjɔne| *vt* **1** : to impress **2** : to disturb, to upset **3** : to expose (film)

impressionnisme |ɛ̃presjɔnism| *nm* : impressionism

impressionniste¹ |ɛ̃presjɔnist| *adj* : impressionistic

impressionniste² *nmf* : impressionist

imprévisible |ɛ̃previzibl| *adj* : unforeseeable, unpredictable

imprévoyance |ɛ̃prevwajɑ̃s| *nf* : lack of foresight, improvidence

imprévoyant, -voyante |ɛ̃prevwajɑ̃, -vwajɑ̃t| *adj* : improvident

imprévu, -vue |ɛ̃prevy| *adj* : unforeseen, unexpected

imprimante |ɛ̃primɑ̃t| *nf* : printer <imprimante à laser : laser printer>

imprimé¹, -mée |ɛ̃prime| *adj* : printed

imprimé² *nm* **1** : print, printed fabric **2** FORMULAIRE : form **3** : printed matter

imprimer |ɛ̃prime| *vt* **1** : to print, to stamp **2** : to imprint **3** : to publish **4** : to impart, to transmit

imprimerie |ɛ̃primri| *nf* **1** : printing **2** : print shop, printer's

imprimeur, -meuse |ɛ̃primœr, -møz| *n* : printer

improbable |ɛ̃prɔbabl| *adj* : improbable — **improbabilité** |-babilite| *nf*

improductif, -tive |ɛ̃prɔdyktif, -tiv| *adj* : unproductive

impromptu, -tue |ɛ̃prɔ̃pty| *adj* : impromptu

impropre |ɛ̃prɔpr| *adj* **1** : inappropriate, incorrect (of words, etc.) **2** ~ **à** : unsuited to, unfit for

improvisation |ɛ̃prɔvizasjɔ̃| *nf* : improvisation

improvisé, -sée |ɛ̃prɔvize| *adj* : improvised, makeshift

improviser |ɛ̃prɔvize| *v* : to improvise — **s'improviser** *vr* **1** : to be improvised **2** : to act as

improviste |ɛ̃prɔvist| **à l'improviste** : unexpectedly

imprudemment |ɛ̃prydamɑ̃| *adv* : carelessly, recklessly

imprudence |ɛ̃prydɑ̃s| *nf* : imprudence, carelessness

imprudent, -dente |ɛ̃prydɑ̃, -dɑ̃t| *adj* **1** : unwise, imprudent **2** : rash, foolhardy
impudence |ɛ̃pydɑ̃s| *nf* : impudence
impudent, -dente |ɛ̃pydɑ̃, -dɑ̃t| *adj* : impudent
impudeur |ɛ̃pydœr| *nf* : shamelessness, immodesty
impudique |ɛ̃pydik| *adj* : immodest, indecent — **impudiquement** |-dikmɑ̃| *adv*
impuissance |ɛ̃pɥisɑ̃s| *nf* **1** : helplessness, powerlessness **2** : (sexual) impotence
impuissant, -sante |ɛ̃pɥisɑ̃, -sɑ̃t| *adj* **1** : helpless, powerless **2** : impotent
impulsif, -sive |ɛ̃pylsif, -siv| *adj* : impulsive — **impulsivement** |-sivmɑ̃| *adv*
impulsion |ɛ̃pylsjɔ̃| *nf* **1** : impulse **2** : impetus
impulsivité |ɛ̃pylsivite| *nf* : impulsiveness
impunément |ɛ̃pynemɑ̃| *adv* : with impunity
impuni, -nie |ɛ̃pyni| *adj* : unpunished
impunité |ɛ̃pynite| *nf* : impunity
impur, -pure |ɛ̃pyr| *adj* : impure
impureté |ɛ̃pyrte| *nf* : impurity
imputable |ɛ̃pytabl| *adj* **1** : imputable, attributable **2 ~ sur** : chargeable to (an account, etc.)
imputer |ɛ̃pyte| *vt* **1** : to impute, to attribute **2** : to charge
inabordable |inabɔrdabl| *adj* **1** : unapproachable, inaccessible **2** : prohibitive (in price)
inacceptable |inaksɛptabl| *adj* : unacceptable
inaccessibilité |inaksesibilite| *nf* : inaccessibility
inaccessible |inaksesibl| *adj* **1** : inaccessible, unattainable **2 ~ à** : impervious to
inaccoutumé, -mée |inakutyme| *adj* : unaccustomed
inachevé, -vée |inaʃve| *adj* : unfinished
inactif, -tive |inaktif, -tiv| *adj* : inactive
inaction |inaksjɔ̃| *nf* : inaction, idleness
inactivité |inaktivite| *nf* : inactivity
inadaptation |inadaptasjɔ̃| *nf* **1** : maladjustment **2** : inappropriateness
inadapté[1], -tée |inadapte| *adj* **1** : maladjusted **2** INAPPROPRIÉ : unsuited, inappropriate
inadapté[2], -tée *n* : social misfit, maladjusted person
inadéquat, -quate |inadekwa, -kwat| *adj* : inadequate
inadéquation |inadekwasjɔ̃| *nf* : inadequacy
inadmissible |inadmisibl| *adj* : inadmissible, unacceptable
inadvertance |inadvɛrtɑ̃s| *nf* **par ~** : inadvertently
inaliénable |inaljenabl| *adj* : inalienable
inaltérable |inalterabl| *adj* **1** : stable, unchanging <inaltérable à : unaffected by> **2** : constant, unfailing
inamical, -cale |inamikal| *adj, mpl* **-caux** |-ko| : inimical, unfriendly
inamovible |inamɔvibl| *adj* : fixed, permanent
inanimé, -mée |inanime| *adj* **1** : inanimate **2** : unconscious, senseless
inanité |inanite| *nf* : futility, pointlessness
inanition |inanisjɔ̃| *nf* : starvation <tomber d'inanition : to faint with hunger>
inaperçu, -çue |inapɛrsy| *adj* : unseen, unnoticed <passer inaperçu : to go unnoticed>
inapplicable |inaplikabl| *adj* : inapplicable
inappliqué, -quée |inaplike| *adj* **1** : lacking in application **2** : not applied, unenforced
inappréciable |inapresjabl| *adj* **1** : invaluable **2** : inappreciable, imperceptible
inapproprié, -priée |inaprɔprije| *adj* : inappropriate
inapte |inapt| *adj* **1** : inept **2** : unfit, unsuited
inaptitude |inaptityd| *nf* : unfitness
inarticulé, -lée |inartikyle| *adj* : inarticulate
inassouvi, -vie |inasuvi| *adj* **1** : unsatisfied, unfulfilled **2** : insatiable
inattaquable |inatakabl| *adj* **1** IRRÉPROCHABLE : irreproachable **2** IRRÉFUTABLE : irrefutable **3** IMPRENABLE : impregnable
inattendu, -due |inatɑ̃dy| *adj* : unexpected
inattentif, -tive |inatɑ̃tif, -tiv| *adj* : inattentive, distracted <inattentif à l'avertissement : heedless of the warning>
inattention |inatɑ̃sjɔ̃| *nf* : inattention <faute d'inattention : careless mistake>
inaudible |inodibl| *adj* : inaudible
inaugural, -rale |inogyral| *adj, mpl* **-raux** |-ro| : inaugural <séance inaugurale : opening session>
inauguration |inogyrasjɔ̃| *nf* : inauguration
inaugurer |inogyre| *vt* **1** : to unveil, to open **2** : to inaugurate
inavouable |inavwabl| *adj* : shameful, unmentionable
inavoué, -vouée |inavwe| *adj* : unacknowledged, unavowed
incalculable |ɛ̃kalkylabl| *adj* : incalculable, countless
incandescent, -cente |ɛ̃kɑ̃desɑ̃, -sɑ̃t| *adj* : incandescent — **incandescence** |-desɑ̃s| *nf*
incantation |ɛ̃kɑ̃tasjɔ̃| *nf* : incantation
incapable |ɛ̃kapabl| *adj* : incapable, unable <incapable de chanter : unable to sing>

incapacité [ɛ̃kapasite] *nf* **1** : incapacity, inability <être dans l'incapacité de faire qqch : to be unable to do sth> **2** : incompetence **3** : (physical) disability

incarcérer [ɛ̃karsere] {87} *vt* : to incarcerate — **incarcération** [-serasjɔ̃] *nf*

incarnation [ɛ̃karnasjɔ̃] *nf* : incarnation

incarné, -née [ɛ̃karne] *adj* **1** : incarnate **2 ongle incarné** : ingrown toenail

incarner [ɛ̃karne] *vt* **1** : to incarnate, to embody **2** : to personify, to play

incartade [ɛ̃kartad] *nf* : escapade, prank

incassable [ɛ̃kasabl] *adj* : unbreakable

incendiaire[1] [ɛ̃sɑ̃djɛr] *adj* **1** : incendiary **2** : inflammatory

incendiaire[2] *nmf* : arsonist

incendie [ɛ̃sɑ̃di] *nm* **1** : fire **2 incendie criminel** : arson

incendier [ɛ̃sɑ̃dje] {96} *vt* **1** : to set on fire, to burn down **2** : to burn <ces piments incendient la gorge : these peppers burn my throat> **3** : to light up **4** : to stir up, to inflame

incertain, -taine [ɛ̃sɛrtɛ̃, -tɛn] *adj* **1** : uncertain, doubtful **2** : indistinct, blurred

incertitude [ɛ̃sɛrtityd] *nf* : uncertainty

incessant, -sante [ɛ̃sesɑ̃, -sɑ̃t] *adj* : incessant — **incessamment** [ɛ̃sesamɑ̃] *adv*

inceste [ɛ̃sɛst] *nm* : incest — **incestueux, -tueuse** [ɛ̃sɛstɥø, -tɥøz] *adj*

inchangé, -gée [ɛ̃ʃɑ̃ʒe] *adj* : unchanged

incidemment [ɛ̃sidamɑ̃] *adv* **1** : incidentally, in passing **2** : by chance

incidence [ɛ̃sidɑ̃s] *nf* **1** : effect, impact **2** : incidence (in physics)

incident[1], **-dente** [ɛ̃sidɑ̃, -dɑ̃t] *adj* : incidental

incident[2] *nm* **1** : incident, event **2** *or* **incident de parcours** : hitch, setback

incinérateur [ɛ̃sineratœr] *nm* : incinerator

incinération [ɛ̃sinerasjɔ̃] *nf* **1** : incineration **2** : cremation

incinérer [ɛ̃sinere] {87} *vt* **1** : to incinerate **2** : to cremate

inciser [ɛ̃size] *vt* **1** : to make an incision in, to incise **2** : to lance

incisif, -sive [ɛ̃sizif, -ziv] *adj* : incisive, cutting

incision [ɛ̃sizjɔ̃] *nf* : incision

incisive *nf* : incisor

incitatif, -tive [ɛ̃sitatif, -tiv] *adj* : motivating <mesure incitative : motivating factor, incentive>

incitation [ɛ̃sitasjɔ̃] *nf* **1** : incitement **2** : incentive

inciter [ɛ̃site] *vt* **1** : to incite (a riot, etc.) **2** : to encourage, to prompt

incivil, -vile [ɛ̃sivil] *adj* : uncivil, rude

inclassable [ɛ̃klasabl] *adj* : unclassifiable

inclinable [ɛ̃klinabl] *adj* : reclining, adjustable <fauteuil inclinable : recliner>

inclinaison [ɛ̃klinɛzɔ̃] *nf* : incline, slope, angle

inclination [ɛ̃klinasjɔ̃] *nf* **1** TENDANCE : inclination, tendency **2** : nod, bowing (of the head)

incliner [ɛ̃kline] *vt* **1** PENCHER : to tilt, to bend **2** : to incline, to prompt (s.o. to do sth) — *vi* **~ à** : to be inclined to, to tend toward — **s'incliner** *vr* **1** : to tilt, to lean **2 ~ devant** : to give in to **3 ~ devant** : to bow down before

inclure [ɛ̃klyr] {39} *vt* **1** : to include **2** : to enclose

inclus, -cluse [ɛ̃kly, -klyz] *adj* **1** COMPRIS : inclusive, including <de lundi à jeudi inclus : from Monday to Thursday inclusive> <samedi inclus : including Saturdays> **2** : impacted <dent incluse : impacted tooth> **3** → **ci–inclus**

inclusion [ɛ̃klyzjɔ̃] *nf* : inclusion

inclusivement [ɛ̃klyzivmɑ̃] *adv* : inclusive, inclusively

incognito [ɛ̃kɔɲito] *adv & adj* : incognito

incohérence [ɛ̃kɔerɑ̃s] *nf* **1** : incoherence **2** : inconsistency, discrepancy

incohérent, -rente [ɛ̃kɔerɑ̃, -rɑ̃t] *adj* **1** : incoherent **2** : inconsistent

incolore [ɛ̃kɔlɔr] *adj* : colorless

incomber [ɛ̃kɔ̃be] *vi* **~ à** : to be incumbent upon, to be the responsibility of

incombustible [ɛ̃kɔ̃bystibl] *adj* : incombustible

incommensurable [ɛ̃kɔmɑ̃syrabl] *adj* : immeasurable — **incommensurablement** [rabləmɑ̃] *adv*

incommodant, -dante [ɛ̃kɔmɔdɑ̃, -dɑ̃t] *adj* **1** : unpleasant **2** : annoying

incommode [ɛ̃kɔmɔd] *adj* **1** : inconvenient **2** : uncomfortable, awkward — **incommodément** [-demɑ̃] *adv*

incommoder [ɛ̃kɔmɔde] *vt* : to bother, to inconvenience

incommodité [ɛ̃kɔmɔdite] *nf* **1** : inconvenience **2** : discomfort

incomparable [ɛ̃kɔ̃parabl] *adj* : incomparable — **incomparablement** [-rabləmɑ̃] *adv*

incompatible [ɛ̃kɔ̃patibl] *adj* : incompatible — **incompatibilité** [-tibilite] *nf*

incompétence [ɛ̃kɔ̃petɑ̃s] *nf* **1** : incompetence **2** : lack of knowledge, ignorance

incompétent, -tente [ɛ̃kɔ̃petɑ̃, -tɑ̃t] *adj* **1** : incompetent **2** : ignorant

incomplet, -plète [ɛ̃kɔ̃plɛ, -plɛt] *adj* : incomplete — **incomplètement** [-plɛtmɑ̃] *adv*

incompréhensible [ɛ̃kɔ̃preɑ̃sibl] *adj* : incomprehensible

incompréhensif, -sive [ɛ̃kɔ̃preɑ̃sif, -siv] *adj* : unsympathetic
incompréhension [ɛ̃kɔ̃preɑ̃sjɔ̃] *nf* : lack of understanding
incompris, -prise [ɛ̃kɔ̃pri, -priz] *adj* : misunderstood
inconcevable [ɛ̃kɔ̃svabl] *adj* : inconceivable, unimaginable
inconciliable [ɛ̃kɔ̃siljabl] *adj* : irreconcilable
inconditionnel[1], -nelle [ɛ̃kɔ̃disjɔnɛl] *adj* : unconditional — **inconditionnellement** [-nɛlmɑ̃] *adv*
inconditionnel[2], -nelle *n* : enthusiast <un inconditionnel du jazz : a jazz enthusiast>
inconduite [ɛ̃kɔ̃dɥit] *nf* : misconduct
inconfort [ɛ̃kɔ̃fɔr] *nm* : discomfort
inconfortable [ɛ̃kɔ̃fɔrtabl] *adj* : uncomfortable — **inconfortablement** [-tabləmɑ̃] *adv*
incongru, -grue [ɛ̃kɔ̃gry] *adj* **1** : incongruous **2** : unseemly, inappropriate
incongruité [ɛ̃kɔ̃grɥite] *nf* **1** : incongruity **2** : unseemly remark
inconnu[1], -nue [ɛ̃kɔny] *adj* : unknown
inconnu[2], -nue *n* **1** : unknown (person) **2** : stranger
inconnue *nf* : unknown (in mathematics, etc.)
inconsciemment [ɛ̃kɔ̃sjamɑ̃] *adv* **1** : unconsciously **2** : thoughtlessly
inconscience [ɛ̃kɔ̃sjɑ̃s] *nf* **1** : unconsciousness **2** : thoughtlessness
inconscient[1], -ciente [ɛ̃kɔ̃sjɑ̃, -sjɑ̃t] *adj* **1** : unaware, oblivious **2** : unconscious
inconscient[2] *nm* **l'inconscient** : the unconscious
inconséquence [ɛ̃kɔ̃sekɑ̃s] *nf* **1** : inconsistency **2** : thoughtlessness
inconséquent, -quente [ɛ̃kɔ̃sekɑ̃, -kɑ̃t] *adj* **1** : inconsistent **2** : thoughtless
inconsidéré, -rée [ɛ̃kɔ̃sidere] *adj* : rash, thoughtless — **inconsidérément** [-remɑ̃] *adv*
inconsistant, -tante [ɛ̃kɔ̃sistɑ̃, -tɑ̃t] *adj* **1** : flimsy, weak **2** : watery, runny
inconsolable [ɛ̃kɔ̃sɔlabl] *adj* : inconsolable
inconstance [ɛ̃kɔ̃stɑ̃s] *nf* : inconstancy, fickleness
inconstant, -stante [ɛ̃kɔ̃stɑ̃, -stɑ̃t] *adj* : inconstant, fickle
inconstitutionnel, -nelle [ɛ̃kɔ̃stitysjɔnɛl] *adj* : unconstitutional
incontestable [ɛ̃kɔ̃tɛstabl] *adj* : unquestionable, indisputable — **incontestablement** [-stabləmɑ̃] *adv*
incontesté, -tée [ɛ̃kɔ̃tɛste] *adj* : uncontested, undisputed
incontinent, -nente [ɛ̃kɔ̃tinɑ̃, -nɑ̃t] *adj* : incontinent — **incontinence** [-tinɑ̃s] *nf*
incontournable [ɛ̃kɔ̃turnabl] *adj* : essential, that cannot be ignored
incontrôlable [ɛ̃kɔ̃trolabl] *adj* **1** : unverifiable **2** : uncontrollable
incontrôlé, -lée [ɛ̃kɔ̃trole] *adj* **1** : unchecked, unverified **2** : uncontrolled
inconvenance [ɛ̃kɔ̃vnɑ̃s] *nf* : impropriety, indecorousness
inconvenant, -nante [ɛ̃kɔ̃vnɑ̃, -nɑ̃t] *adj* INCONGRU : improper, indecorous, unseemly
inconvénient [ɛ̃kɔ̃venjɑ̃] *nm* : disadvantage, drawback
incorporation [ɛ̃kɔrpɔrasjɔ̃] *nf* **1** : incorporating, blending, mixing **2** : induction (into the military) **3** *Can* : incorporation (of a company)
incorporer [ɛ̃kɔrpɔre] *vt* **1** : to incorporate, to blend, to mix **2** : to induct (into the military) **3** *Can* : to incorporate (a company)
incorrect, -recte [ɛ̃kɔrɛkt] *adj* **1** IMPROPRE : incorrect **2** INCONVENANT : improper, unsuitable **3** DÉLOYAL : unfair, underhanded
incorrectement [ɛ̃kɔrɛktəmɑ̃] *adv* : incorrectly, wrongly
incorrigible [ɛ̃kɔriʒibl] *adj* : incorrigible
incorruptible [ɛ̃kɔryptibl] *adj* : incorruptible
incrédule [ɛ̃kredyl] *adj* : incredulous
incrédulité [ɛ̃kredylite] *nf* : incredulity
increvable [ɛ̃krəvabl] *adj* **1** : puncture-proof (of a tire) **2** *fam* : tireless
incriminer [ɛ̃krimine] *vt* : to incriminate — **incrimination** [ɛ̃kriminasjɔ̃] *nf*
incroyable [ɛ̃krwajabl] *adj* : unbelievable, incredible — **incroyablement** [-jabləmɑ̃] *adv*
incroyant, -croyante [ɛ̃krwajɑ̃, -jɑ̃t] *n* : unbeliever
incrustation [ɛ̃krystasjɔ̃] *nf* **1** : inlaying, inlay **2** : incrustation (in geology)
incruster [ɛ̃kryste] *vt* **1** : to encrust **2** : to inlay — **s'incruster** *vr* : to become embedded
incubateur [ɛ̃kybatœr] *nm* : incubator
incubation [ɛ̃kybasjɔ̃] *nf* : incubation
incuber [ɛ̃kybe] *vt* : to incubate
inculpation [ɛ̃kylpasjɔ̃] *nf* : indictment, charge
inculpé, -pée [ɛ̃kylpe] *n* : accused, defendant
inculper [ɛ̃kylpe] *vt* : to indict, to charge
inculquer [ɛ̃kylke] *vt* : to inculcate, to instill
inculte [ɛ̃kylt] *adj* **1** : uncultivated, wild **2** : unkempt **3** : uneducated, ignorant
inculture [ɛ̃kyltyr] *nf* : lack of culture
incurable [ɛ̃kyrabl] *adj* : incurable
incurie [ɛ̃kyri] *nf* NÉGLIGENCE : carelessness, negligence
incursion [ɛ̃kyrsjɔ̃] *nf* : foray, incursion, inroad
incurver [ɛ̃kyrve] *vt* : to bend, to curve — **s'incurver** *vr*
indécence [ɛ̃desɑ̃s] *nf* **1** : indecency **2** : indecent act or remark

indécent, -cente |ɛ̃desɑ̃, -sɑ̃t| *adj* : indecent — **indécemment** |-samɑ̃| *adv*

indéchiffrable |ɛ̃deʃifrabl| *adj* **1** : indecipherable **2** : incomprehensible

indécis, -cise |ɛ̃desi, -siz| *adj* **1** : indecisive **2** : undecided

indécision |ɛ̃desizjɔ̃| *nf* **1** : indecisiveness **2** : indecision

indécrottable |ɛ̃dekrɔtabl| *adj fam* : incorrigible

indéfectible |ɛ̃defɛktibl| *adj* : enduring, unfailing

indéfendable |ɛ̃defɑ̃dabl| *adj* : indefensible, untenable

indéfini, -nie |ɛ̃defini| *adj* **1** : indefinite **2** : undefined

indéfiniment |ɛ̃definimɑ̃| *adv* : indefinitely

indéfinissable |ɛ̃definisabl| *adj* : indefinable

indélébile |ɛ̃delebil| *adj* : indelible

indélicat, -cate |ɛ̃delika, -kat| *adj* **1** : coarse, indelicate **2** MALHONNÊTE : dishonest

indélicatesse |ɛ̃delikatɛs| *nf* : indelicacy

indemne |ɛ̃dɛmn| *adj* : undamaged, unharmed

indemnisation |ɛ̃dɛmnizasjɔ̃| *nf* : compensation, indemnity

indemniser |ɛ̃dɛmnize| *vt* **1** : to indemnify, to compensate **2** : to reimburse (for expenses)

indemnité |ɛ̃dɛmnite| *nf* **1** COMPENSATION : indemnity, compensation **2** ALLOCATION : allowance <indemnité de logement : housing allowance>

indéniable |ɛ̃denjabl| *adj* : undeniable — **indéniablement** |-njabləmɑ̃| *adv*

indépendamment |ɛ̃depɑ̃damɑ̃| *adv* **1** : independently **2 ~ de** : regardless of, apart from **3 ~ de** : in addition to

indépendant, -dante |ɛ̃depɑ̃dɑ̃, -dɑ̃t| *adj* : independent — **indépendance** |-pɑ̃dɑ̃s| *nf*

indescriptible |ɛ̃dɛskriptibl| *adj* : indescribable

indésirable |ɛ̃dezirabl| *adj* : undesirable

indestructible |ɛ̃dɛstryktibl| *adj* : indestructible — **indestructibilité** |-tibilite| *nf*

indéterminé, -née |ɛ̃detɛrmine| *adj* : indeterminate, unspecified

index |ɛ̃dɛks| *nm* **1** : index **2** : forefinger, index finger

indexation |ɛ̃dɛksasjɔ̃| *nf* **1** : indexing **2** : indexation (in economics)

indexer |ɛ̃dekse| *vt* : to index

indicateur¹, -trice |ɛ̃dikatœr, -tris| *adj* → **panneau, poteau**

indicateur² *nm* **1** INFORMATEUR : (police) informer **2** GUIDE : guide, directory **3** : gauge, meter <indicateur de vitesse : speedometer> **4** : economic indicator

indicatif¹, -tive |ɛ̃dikatif, -tiv| *adj* : indicative

indicatif² *nm* **1** : indicative (in grammar) **2** : theme (of a radio or television program) **3 indicatif de zone** : area code

indication |ɛ̃dikasjɔ̃| *nf* **1** APERÇU, SIGNE : indication **2** RENSEIGNEMENT : information **3 indications** *nfpl* : instructions, directions

indice |ɛ̃dis| *nm* **1** SIGNE : sign, indication **2** : clue, lead **3** : index <indice du coût de la vie : cost of living index> **4** : rating <indice d'écoute : audience ratings>

indicible |ɛ̃disibl| *adj* : unspeakable, inexpressible

indien, -dienne |ɛ̃djɛ̃, -djɛn| *adj* : Indian

Indien, -dienne *n* : Indian

indifféremment |ɛ̃diferamɑ̃| *adv* : indiscriminately, equally

indifférence |ɛ̃diferɑ̃s| *nf* : indifference

indifférent, -rente |ɛ̃diferɑ̃, -rɑ̃t| *adj* **1** : indifferent **2** : irrelevant, immaterial

indifférer |ɛ̃difere| {87} *vi* **~ à** : to be of no importance to <cela m'indiffère : it's all the same to me>

indigence |ɛ̃diʒɑ̃s| *nf* : indigence

indigène¹ |ɛ̃diʒɛn| *adj* : indigenous, native

indigène² *nmf* : native (of a country or region)

indigent¹, -gente |ɛ̃diʒɑ̃, -ʒɑ̃t| *adj* : indigent, destitute

indigent², -gente *n* **1** : pauper **2 les indigents** : the poor

indigeste |ɛ̃diʒɛst| *adj* : indigestible

indigestion |ɛ̃diʒɛstjɔ̃| *nf* : indigestion

indignation |ɛ̃diɲasjɔ̃| *nf* : indignation <avec indignation : indignantly>

indigne |ɛ̃diɲ| *adj* **1** : unworthy, undeserving **2** MÉPRISABLE : disgraceful

indigné, -gnée |ɛ̃diɲe| *adj* : indignant

indignement |ɛ̃diɲəmɑ̃| *adv* : disgracefully

indigner |ɛ̃diɲe| *vt* : to outrage — **s'indigner** *vr* : to be indignant

indignité |ɛ̃diɲite| *nf* **1** : unworthiness **2** : indignity, shameful act

indigo |ɛ̃digo| *adj & nm* : indigo

indiqué, -quée |ɛ̃dike| *adj* **1** : advisable, expedient **2** : appropriate

indiquer |ɛ̃dike| *vt* **1** : to indicate, to point out <ils m'ont indiqué le chemin : they showed me the way> **2** : to give, to name, to tell <indiquer l'heure : to give the time>

indirect, -recte |ɛ̃dirɛkt| *adj* : indirect — **indirectement** |-rɛktəmɑ̃| *adv*

indiscernable |ɛ̃disɛrnabl| *adj* : indiscernible

indiscipline |ɛ̃disiplin| *nf* : lack of discipline

indiscipliné, -née |ɛ̃disipline| *adj* : undisciplined, unruly

indiscret, -crète |ɛ̃diskrɛ, -krɛt| *adj* : indiscreet — **indiscrètement** |-krɛtmɑ̃| *adv*

indiscrétion [ɛ̃diskresjɔ̃] *nf* : indiscretion

indiscutable [ɛ̃diskytabl] *adj* : indisputable, unquestionable — **indiscutablement** [-tabləmɑ̃] *adv*

indispensable [ɛ̃dispɑ̃sabl] *adj* : indispensable, essential

indisponible [ɛ̃dispɔnibl] *adj* : unavailable

indisposé, -sée [ɛ̃dispoze] *adj* : unwell, indisposed

indisposer [ɛ̃dispoze] *vt* **1** : to annoy, to irritate **2** : to upset, to make ill

indisposition [ɛ̃dispozisjɔ̃] *nf* : indisposition, illness

indissociable [ɛ̃disɔsjabl] *adj* : inseparable

indistinct, -tincte [ɛ̃distɛ̃kt, -tɛ̃kt] *adj* : indistinct

indistinctement [ɛ̃distɛ̃ktəmɑ̃] *adv* **1** : indistinctly **2** : indiscriminately

individu [ɛ̃dividy] *nm* : individual

individualiser [ɛ̃dividɥalize] *vt* : to individualize

individualisme [ɛ̃dividɥalism] *nm* : individualism

individualiste[1] [ɛ̃dividɥalist] *adj* : individualistic

individualiste[2] *nmf* : individualist

individualité [ɛ̃dividɥalite] *nf* : individuality

individuel, -duelle [ɛ̃dividɥɛl] *adj* **1** : individual, particular **2** : personal, private

individuellement [ɛ̃dividɥɛlmɑ̃] *adv* : individually

indivis, -vise [ɛ̃divi, -viz] *adj* **1** : undivided **2 par ~** : jointly, in common

indivisible [ɛ̃divizibl] *adj* : indivisible

indolence [ɛ̃dɔlɑ̃s] *nf* **1** : indolence, laziness **2** : apathy

indolent, -lente [ɛ̃dɔlɑ̃, -lɑ̃t] *adj* **1** : indolent, lazy **2** : apathetic

indolore [ɛ̃dɔlɔr] *adj* : painless

indomptable [ɛ̃dɔ̃tabl] *adj* **1** : indomitable, invincible **2** : untamable

indonésien[1], **-sienne** [ɛ̃dɔnezjɛ̃, -zjɛn] *adj* : Indonesian

indonésien[2] *nm* : Indonesian (language)

Indonésien, -sienne *n* : Indonesian

indu, -due [ɛ̃dy] *adj* **1** : unseemly, ungodly <à des heures indues : at this ungodly hour> **2** : unwarranted, unjustified

indubitable [ɛ̃dybitabl] *adj* : indubitable — **indubitablement** [-tabləmɑ̃] *adv*

induction [ɛ̃dyksjɔ̃] *nf* : induction

inductif, -tive [ɛ̃dyktif, -tiv] *adj* : inductive

induire [ɛ̃dɥir] {49} *vt* **1** INCITER : to induce, to incite <induire en erreur : to mislead> **2** CONCLURE : to infer, to conclude

indulgence [ɛ̃dylʒɑ̃s] *nf* **1** : indulgence, leniency **2** : indulgence (in religion)

indulgent, -gente [ɛ̃dylʒɑ, -ʒɑ̃t] *adj* : indulgent, lenient

indûment [ɛ̃dymɑ̃] *adv* : unduly, unjustifiably

industrialiser [ɛ̃dystrijalize] *vt* : to industrialize — **industrialisation** [-lizasjɔ̃] *nf*

industrie [ɛ̃dystri] *nf* : industry

industriel[1], **-trielle** [ɛ̃dystrijɛl] *adj* : industrial

industriel[2], **-trielle** *n* : manufacturer, industrialist

industrieux, -trieuse [ɛ̃dystrijø, -trijøz] *adj* TRAVAILLEUR : industrious

inébranlable [inebrɑ̃labl] *adj* : unwavering, unshakeable

inédit, -dite [inedi, -dit] *adj* **1** : unpublished **2** ORIGINAL : novel, original

ineffable [inefabl] *adj* : ineffable, inexpressible — **ineffablement** [-fabləmɑ̃] *adv*

ineffaçable [inefasabl] *adj* : indelible

inefficace [inefikas] *adj* **1** : inefficient **2** : ineffective

inefficacité [inefikasite] *nf* **1** : inefficiency **2** : ineffectiveness

inégal, -gale [inegal] *adj, mpl* **-gaux** [-go] **1** : unequal **2** IRRÉGULIER : irregular, uneven — **inégalement** [-galmɑ̃] *adv*

inégalé, -lée [inegale] *adj* : unequaled

inégalité [inegalite] *nf* **1** : inequality **2** IRRÉGULARITÉ : unevenness, irregularity

inélégant, -gante [inelegɑ̃, -gɑ̃t] *adj* **1** : inelegant **2** : discourteous — **inélégance** [-gɑ̃s] *nf*

inéligible [inelizibl] *adj* : ineligible — **inéligibilité** [-ʒibilite] *nf*

inéluctable [inelyktabl] *adj* : inescapable — **inéluctablement** [-tabləmɑ̃] *adv*

inemployé, -ployée [inɑ̃plwaje] *adj* : unused

inénarrable [inenarabl] *adj* : hilarious, beyond words

inepte [inɛpt] *adj* : inept

ineptie [inɛpsi] *nf* **1** : ineptitude **2** : stupid action or remark

inépuisable [inepɥizabl] *adj* : inexhaustible

inéquitable [inekitabl] *adj* : inequitable

inerte [inɛrt] *adj* **1** : lifeless **2** : passive, apathetic **3** : inert

inertie [inɛrsi] *nf* : inertia

inespéré, -rée [inɛspere] *adj* : unhoped for, unexpected

inestimable [inɛstimabl] *adj* : inestimable, priceless

inévitable [inevitabl] *adj* : inevitable, unavoidable — **inévitablement** [-tabləmɑ̃] *adv*

inexact, inexacte [inɛgza(kt), -ɛgzakt] *adj* **1** : inaccurate **2** : unpunctual, late

inexactement [inɛgzaktəmɑ̃] *adv* : inaccurately, wrong

inexactitude [inɛgzaktityd] *nf* **1** : inaccuracy **2** : lateness, unpunctuality

inexcusable [inɛkskyzabl] *adj* : inexcusable
inexécutable [inɛgzekytabl] *adj* : impracticable, unworkable
inexercé, -cée [inɛgzɛrse] *adj* : untrained, inexperienced
inexistant, -tante [inɛgzistɑ̃, -tɑ̃t] *adj* : nonexistent — **inexistence** [-zistɑ̃s] *nf*
inexorable [inɛgzɔrabl] *adj* : inexorable — **inexorablement** [-rabləmɑ̃] *adv*
inexpérience [inɛksperjɑ̃s] *nf* : inexperience
inexpérimenté, -tée [inɛksperimɑ̃te] *adj* **1** : inexperienced **2** : untried, untested
inexplicable [inɛksplikabl] *adj* : inexplicable — **inexplicablement** [-kabləmɑ̃] *adv*
inexpliqué, -quée [inɛksplike] *adj* : unexplained
inexploité, -tée [inɛksplwate] *adj* : untapped, unexploited
inexpressif, -sive [inɛksprɛsif, -siv] *adj* : inexpressive, expressionless
inexprimable [inɛksprimabl] *adj* : inexpressible
inexprimé, -mée [inɛksprime] *adj* : unexpressed, unspoken
inextinguible [inɛkstɛ̃gibl] *adj* **1** : inextinguishable, unquenchable **2** : uncontrollable
in extremis [inɛkstremis] *adv* : at the last minute
inextricable [inɛkstrikabl] *adj* : inextricable — **inextricablement** [-kabləmɑ̃] *adv*
infaillibilité [ɛ̃fajibilite] *nf* : infallibility
infaillible [ɛ̃fajibl] *adj* **1** : infallible **2** : certain, reliable
infailliblement [ɛ̃fajibləmɑ̃] *adv* : without fail
infamant, -mante [ɛ̃famɑ̃, -mɑ̃t] *adj* **1** : defamatory **2** : dishonorable
infâme [ɛ̃fam] *adj* : vile, despicable
infamie [ɛ̃fami] *nf* **1** : infamy **2** CALOMNIE : calumny, slander
infanterie [ɛ̃fɑ̃tri] *nf* : infantry
infantile [ɛ̃fɑ̃til] *adj* : infantile, childish
infarctus [ɛ̃farktys] *nm or* **infarctus myocarde** : heart attack
infatigable [ɛ̃fatigabl] *adj* : indefatigable, tireless — **infatigablement** [-bləmɑ̃] *adv*
infatuation [ɛ̃fatɥasjɔ̃] *nf* : self-importance, conceit
infatué, -tuée [ɛ̃fatɥe] *adj* : conceited, self-important
infect, -fecte [ɛ̃fɛkt] *adj* **1** : foul, stinking **2** : horrible, vile
infecter [ɛ̃fɛkte] *vt* **1** : to infect **2** : to contaminate, to pollute, to poison — **s'infecter** *vr* : to become infected
infectieux, -tieuse [ɛ̃fɛksjø, -tjøz] *adj* : infectious
infection [ɛ̃fɛksjɔ̃] *nf* **1** : infection **2** PUANTEUR : stench
inférer [ɛ̃fere] {87} *vt* : to infer — **inférence** [ɛ̃ferɑ̃s] *nf*
inférieur[1], **-rieure** [ɛ̃ferjœr] *adj* **1** : inferior **2** : lower <lèvre inférieure : lower lip> **3** ~ **à** : less than
inférieur[2], **-rieure** *n* : inferior
infériorité [ɛ̃ferjɔrite] *nf* : inferiority
infernal, -nale [ɛ̃fɛrnal] *adj, mpl* **-naux** [-no] **1** : infernal **2** : fiendish, diabolical
infertile [ɛ̃fɛrtil] *adj* : infertile — **infertilité** [-tilite] *nf*
infester [ɛ̃fɛste] *vt* : to infest
infidèle[1] [ɛ̃fidɛl] *adj* **1** : unfaithful, disloyal **2** : inaccurate
infidèle[2] *nmf* **1** : infidel, unbeliever **2** : unfaithful spouse or lover
infidélité [ɛ̃fidelite] *nf* **1** : infidelity **2** : unfaithfulness, inaccuracy
infiltration [ɛ̃filtrasjɔ̃] *nf* : infiltration
infiltrer [ɛ̃filtre] *vt* : to infiltrate — **s'infiltrer** *vr* ~ **dans** : to penetrate, to seep into, to filter through
infime [ɛ̃fim] *adj* : minute, negligible
infini[1], **-nie** [ɛ̃fini] *adj* : infinite — **infiniment** [-nimɑ̃] *adv*
infini[2] *nm* **1** : infinity (in mathematics, etc.) **2 à l'infini** : endlessly, ad infinitum
infinité [ɛ̃finite] *nf* **1** : infinite number, lot **2** : infinity
infinitésimal, -male [ɛ̃finitezimal] *adj, mpl* **-maux** [-mo] : infinitesimal
infinitif [ɛ̃finitif] *nm* : infinitive
infirme[1] [ɛ̃firm] *adj* : disabled, infirm
infirme[2] *nmf* : disabled person, invalid
infirmer [ɛ̃firme] *vt* ANNULER : to invalidate, to annul
infirmerie [ɛ̃firməri] *nf* : infirmary
infirmier[1], **-mière** [ɛ̃firmje, -mjɛr] *adj* : nursing <personnel infirmier : nursing staff>
infirmier[2], **-mière** *n* GARDE-MALADE : nurse
infirmité [ɛ̃firmite] *nf* : disability, infirmity
inflammable [ɛ̃flamabl] *adj* : inflammable, flammable
inflammation [ɛ̃flamasjɔ̃] *nf* : inflammation
inflammatoire [ɛ̃flamatwar] *adj* : inflammatory
inflation [ɛ̃flasjɔ̃] *nf* : inflation
inflationniste [ɛ̃flasjɔnist] *adj* : inflationary
infléchir [ɛ̃fleʃir] *vt* **1** : to bend, to inflect **2** : to modify, to influence — **s'infléchir** *vr* **1** : to curve **2** : to deviate, to change course
inflexibilité [ɛ̃flɛksibilite] *nf* : inflexibility
inflexible [ɛ̃flɛksibl] *adj* : inflexible — **inflexiblement** [-sibləmɑ̃] *adv*
inflexion [ɛ̃flɛksjɔ̃] *nf* **1** CHANGEMENT : change, shift **2** COURBE : bend <inflexion de la tête : brief nod> **3** : inflection (of the voice)

infliger [ɛ̃fliʒe] {17} *vt* **1** : to inflict **2** : to impose (a penalty, etc.)
influence [ɛ̃flyɑ̃s] *nf* : influence
influencer [ɛ̃flyɑ̃se] {6} *vt* : to influence
influent, -fluente [ɛ̃flyɑ̃, -flyɑ̃t] *adj* : influential
influer [ɛ̃flye] *vi* **~ sur** : to have an influence on, to affect
infographie [ɛ̃fografi] *nf* : computer graphics *pl*
informateur, -trice [ɛ̃fɔrmatœr, -tris] *n* INDICATEUR : informant, informer
informaticien, -cienne [ɛ̃fɔrmatisjɛ̃, -sjɛn] *n* : computer programmer
informatif, -tive [ɛ̃fɔrmatif, -tiv] *adj* : informative
information [ɛ̃fɔrmasjɔ̃] *nf* **1** : information **2** : news item **3** *France* : (judicial) inquiry
informatique[1] [ɛ̃fɔrmatik] *adj* : computer <analyste informatique : computer analyst>
informatique[2] *nf* **1** : computer science, information technology **2** : data processing
informatiser [ɛ̃fɔrmatize] *vt* : to computerize — **informatisation** [-tizasjɔ̃] *nf*
informe [ɛ̃fɔrm] *adj* : formless, shapeless
informel, -melle [ɛ̃fɔrmɛl] *adj* : informal
informer [ɛ̃fɔrme] *vt* : to inform — **s'informer** *vr* **1** : to inquire **2** : to inform oneself, to find out
infortune [ɛ̃fɔrtyn] *nf* : misfortune
infortuné, -née [ɛ̃fɔrtyne] *adj* : unfortunate, luckless
infraction [ɛ̃fraksjɔ̃] *nf* : infraction <infraction à la loi : breach of the law>
infranchissable [ɛ̃frɑ̃ʃisabl] *adj* **1** : insurmountable **2** : impassable
infrarouge [ɛ̃fraruʒ] *adj & nm* : infrared
infrastructure [ɛ̃frastryktyr] *nf* : infrastructure
infructueux, -tueuse [ɛ̃fryktɥø, -tɥøz] *adj* : fruitless
infus, -fuse [ɛ̃fy, -fyz] *adj* : innate <avoir la science infuse : to know a lot without studying>
infuser [ɛ̃fyze] *v* **1** : to infuse **2** : to brew, to steep
infusion [ɛ̃fyzjɔ̃] *nf* : infusion
ingénier [ɛ̃ʒenje] {96} *v* **s'ingénier** *vr* : to strive, to do one's utmost
ingénierie [ɛ̃ʒeniri] *nf* : engineering
ingénieur, -nieure [ɛ̃ʒenjœr] *n* : engineer
ingénieux, -nieuse [ɛ̃ʒenjø, -njøz] *adj* : ingenious — **ingénieusement** [-njøzmɑ̃] *adv*
ingéniosité [ɛ̃ʒenjɔzite] *nf* : ingenuity
ingénu, -nue [ɛ̃ʒeny] *adj* : ingenuous, naive — **ingénuement** *adv*
ingénue *nf* : ingenue
ingénuité [ɛ̃ʒenɥite] *nf* : ingenuousness, naïveté
ingérence [ɛ̃ʒerɑ̃s] *nf* : interference
ingérer [ɛ̃ʒere] {87} *vt* : to ingest — **s'ingérer** *vr* : to interfere, to meddle
ingouvernable [ɛ̃guvɛrnabl] *adj* : ungovernable
ingrat[1], **-grate** [ɛ̃gra, -grat] *adj* **1** : ungrateful **2** : thankless, unrewarding **3** : barren **4** : unattractive
ingrat[2], **-grate** *n* : ingrate
ingratitude [ɛ̃gratityd] *nf* : ingratitude
ingrédient [ɛ̃gredjɑ̃] *nm* : ingredient
inguérissable [ɛ̃gerisabl] *adj* : incurable
ingurgiter [ɛ̃gyrʒite] *vt* **1** ENGLOUTIR : to gulp down **2** : to take in, to absorb (knowledge, etc.)
inhabile [inabil] *adj* : inept, clumsy
inhabitable [inabitabl] *adj* : uninhabitable
inhabité, -tée [inabite] *adj* : uninhabited
inhabituel, -tuelle [inabitɥɛl] *adj* : unusual
inhalant [inalɑ̃] *nm* : inhalant
inhalateur [inalatœr] *nm* : inhaler
inhaler [inale] *vt* : to inhale — **inhalation** [-alasjɔ̃] *nf*
inhérent, -rente [inerɑ̃, -rɑ̃t] *adj* : inherent
inhiber [inibe] *vt* : to inhibit
inhibition [inibisjɔ̃] *nf* : inhibition
inhospitalier, -lière [inɔspitalje, -ljɛr] *adj* : inhospitable
inhumain, -maine [inymɛ̃, -mɛn] *adj* : inhuman
inhumanité [inymanite] *nf* : inhumanity
inhumation [inymasjɔ̃] *nf* : burial, interment
inhumer [inyme] *vt* : to bury, to inter
ininflammable [inɛ̃flamabl] *adj* : nonflammable
inimaginable [inimaʒinabl] *adj* : unimaginable, incredible
inimitable [inimitabl] *adj* : inimitable
inimitié [inimitje] *nf* HOSTILITÉ : enmity, hostility
inintelligent, -gente [inɛ̃tɛliʒɑ̃, -ʒɑ̃t] *adj* : unintelligent
inintelligible [inɛ̃teliʒibl] *adj* : unintelligible
inintéressant, -sante [inɛ̃terɛsɑ̃, -sɑ̃t] *adj* : uninteresting
ininterrompu, -pue [inɛ̃tɛrɔ̃py] *adj* **1** : uninterrupted, non-stop **2** : unbroken **3** : continuous, unremitting
inique [inik] *adj* : iniquitous
iniquité [inikite] *nf* : iniquity
initial, -tiale [inisjal] *adj, mpl* **-tiaux** [-sjo] : initial — **initialement** [-sjalmɑ̃] *adv*
initiale *nf* : initial
initiateur, -trice [inisjatœr, -tris] *n* **1** : initiator **2** NOVATEUR : innovator, pioneer
initiation [inisjasjɔ̃] *nf* : initiation
initiatique [inisjatik] *adj* : initiatory

initiative |inisjativ| *nf* : initiative <prendre l'initiative : to take the initiative>

initié, -tiée |inisje| *n* : initiate, insider

initier |inisje| {96} *vt* **1 ~ à** : to initiate, to start **2 ~ à** : to introduce to — **s'initier** *vr* **~ à** : to learn

injecté, -tée |ɛ̃ʒɛkte| *adj* **yeux injectés (de sang)** : bloodshot eyes

injecter |ɛ̃ʒɛkte| *vt* : to inject

injection |ɛ̃ʒɛksjɔ̃| *nf* : injection

injonction |ɛ̃ʒɔ̃ksjɔ̃| *nf* : order, injunction

injure |ɛ̃ʒyr| *nf* : insult, abuse <faire injure à qqn : to insult s.o.>

injurier |ɛ̃ʒyrje| {96} *vt* : to insult

injurieux, -rieuse |ɛ̃ʒyrjø, -rjøz| *adj* : insulting, abusive

injuste |ɛ̃ʒyst| *adj* : unjust, unfair — **injustement** |ɛ̃ʒystəmɑ̃| *adv*

injustice |ɛ̃ʒystis| *nf* : injustice

injustifiable |ɛ̃ʒystifjabl| *adj* : unjustifiable, indefensible

injustifié, -fiée |ɛ̃jystifje| *adj* : unjustified

inlassable |ɛ̃lasabl| *adj* : tireless — **inlassablement** |-sabləmɑ̃| *adv*

inné, -née |ine| *adj* : innate, inborn

innocemment |inɔsamɑ̃| *adv* : innocently

innocence |inɔsɑ̃s| *nf* : innocence

innocent, -cente |inɔsɑ̃, -sɑ̃t| *adj & n* : innocent

innocenter |inɔsɑ̃te| *vt* **1** DISCULPER : to exonerate, to clear **2** EXCUSER : to excuse, to justify

innocuité |inɔkɥite| *nf* : innocuousness

innombrable |inɔ̃brabl| *adj* : innumerable

innommable |inɔmabl| *adj* : unspeakable, foul

innovateur[1], **-trice** |inɔvatœr, -tris| *adj* : innovative

innovateur[2], **-trice** *n* : innovator

innover |inɔve| *v* : to innovate — **innovation** |inɔvasjɔ̃| *nf*

inoccupation |inɔkypasjɔ̃| *nf* : inactivity

inoccupé, -pée |inɔkype| *adj* **1** : idle **2** : unoccupied, vacant

inoculer |inɔkyle| *vt* : to inoculate — **inoculation** |-kylasjɔ̃| *nf*

inodore |inɔdɔr| *adj* : odorless

inoffensif, -sive |inɔfɑ̃sif, -siv| *adj* : inoffensive, harmless

inondation |inɔ̃dasjɔ̃| *nf* : flood, inundation

inonder |inɔ̃de| *vt* **1** : to flood **2** : to inundate, to overrun

inopérable |inɔperabl| *adj* : inoperable

inopérant, -rante |inɔperɑ̃, -rɑ̃t| *adj* : ineffective, inoperative

inopiné, -née |inɔpine| *adj* : unexpected — **inopinément** |-nemɑ̃| *adv*

inopportun, -tune |inɔpɔrtœ̃, -tyn| *adj* INTEMPESTIF : inopportune, untimely — **inopportunément** |-tynemɑ̃| *adv*

inorganique |inɔrganik| *adj* : inorganic

inorganisé, -sée |inɔrganize| *adj* **1** : disorganized **2** : unorganized

inoubliable |inublijabl| *adj* : unforgettable — **inoubliablement** |inublijabləmɑ̃|

inouï, inouïe |inwi| *adj* : incredible, unheard of

inoxydable[1] |inɔksidabl| *adj* **1** : rustproof **2 acier inoxydable** : stainless steel

inoxydable[2] *nm* : stainless steel

inqualifiable |ɛ̃kalifjabl| *adj* : unspeakable

inquiet, -quiète |ɛ̃kjɛ, -kjɛt| *adj* **1** ANXIEUX : worried, anxious **2** AGITÉ : restless

inquiétant, -tante |ɛ̃kjetɑ̃, -tɑ̃t| *adj* : worrisome, ominous

inquiéter |ɛ̃kjete| {87} *vt* **1** : to worry **2** : to bother, to disturb — **s'inquiéter** *vr* **1** : to be worried **2 ~ de** : to bother about, to inquire about

inquiétude |ɛ̃kjetyd| *nf* : worry, anxiety, concern

inquisiteur, -trice |ɛ̃kizitœr, -tris| *adj* : inquisitive

inquisition |ɛ̃kizisjɔ̃| *nf* : inquisition

insaisissable |ɛ̃sezisabl| *adj* **1** FUYANT : elusive **2** IMPERCEPTIBLE : imperceptible

insalubre |ɛ̃salybr| *adj* : unhealthy, insalubrious

insanité |ɛ̃sanite| *nf* **1** : insanity **2** : nonsense, rubbish

insatiable |ɛ̃sasjabl| *adj* : insatiable

insatisfaction |ɛ̃satisfaksjɔ̃| *nf* : dissatisfaction

insatisfait, -faite |ɛ̃satisfɛ, -fɛt| *adj* **1** : unsatisfied **2** MÉCONTENT : dissatisfied

inscription |ɛ̃skripsjɔ̃| *nf* **1** : inscription **2** : registration, enrollment

inscrire |ɛ̃skrir| {33} *vt* **1** : to inscribe **2** : to register, to enroll **3** : to write, to note down — **s'inscrire** *vr* **1** : to register, to enroll **2 s'inscrire en faux contre** : to deny strongly

inscrivait |ɛ̃skrivɛ|, **inscrivions** |ɛ̃skrivjɔ̃|, *etc.* → **inscrire**

inscrive |ɛ̃skriv| *etc.* → **inscrire**

insecte |ɛ̃sɛkt| *nm* : insect

insecticide |ɛ̃sɛktisid| *nm* : insecticide

insectifuge |ɛ̃sɛktifyʒ| *nm* : insect repellent

insécurité |ɛ̃sekyrite| *nf* : insecurity

insémination |ɛ̃seminasjɔ̃| *nf* : insemination <insémination artificielle : artificial insemination>

inséminer |ɛ̃semine| *vt* : to inseminate

insensé, -sée |ɛ̃sɑ̃se| *adj* **1** : crazy, foolish, nonsensical **2** : considerable, phenomenal

insensibiliser |ɛ̃sɑ̃sibilize| *vt* ANESTHÉSIER : to anesthetize

insensibilité |ɛ̃sɑ̃sibilite| *nf* **1** : insensibility, numbnesss **2** : insensitivity, indifference

insensible [ɛ̃sɑ̃sibl] *adj* **1** : insensible, numb **2** : insensitive **3** : imperceptible
insensiblement [ɛ̃sɑ̃sibləmɑ̃] *adv* : gradually, imperceptibly
inséparable [ɛ̃separabl] *adj* : inseparable
insérer [ɛ̃sere] {87} *vt* INTRODUIRE : to insert — **s'insérer** *vr* **1 ~ dans** : to be part of, to be integrated into **2 ~ sur** : to be attached to (in anatomy)
insertion [ɛ̃sɛrsjɔ̃] *nf* **1** INTRODUCTION : insertion **2** : integration
insidieux, -dieuse [ɛ̃sidjø, -djøz] *adj* : insidious — **insidieusement** [-djøzmɑ̃] *adv*
insigne[1] [ɛ̃siɲ] *adj* : great, distinguished <insigne honneur : great honor>
insigne[2] *nm* **1** : badge, emblem **2** *or* **insignes** *nmpl* : insignia
insignifiant, -fiante [ɛ̃siɲifjɑ̃, -fjɑ̃t] *adj* **1** : insignificant, trivial **2** : meager, trifling — **insignifiance** [-ɲifjɑ̃s] *nf*
insinuant, -nuante [ɛ̃sinɥwɑ̃] *adj* : ingratiating
insinuation [ɛ̃sinɥasjɔ̃] *nf* : insinuation, innuendo
insinuer [ɛ̃sinɥe] *vt* : to insinuate, to imply — **s'insinuer** *vr* **1** : to insinuate oneself **2 s'insinuer dans les bonnes grâces de** : to ingratiate oneself with
insipide [ɛ̃sipid] *adj* : insipid
insistant, -tante [ɛ̃sistɑ̃, -tɑ̃t] *adj* : insistent — **insistance** [ɛ̃sistɑ̃s] *nf*
insister [ɛ̃siste] *vi* **1** : to insist **2 ~ sur** : to stress, to emphasize — *vt* : to insist
insociable [ɛ̃sɔsjabl] *adj* : unsociable
insolation [ɛ̃sɔlasjɔ̃] *nf* : sunstroke
insolence [ɛ̃sɔlɑ̃s] *nf* : insolence <avec insolence : insolently>
insolent, -lente [ɛ̃sɔlɑ̃, -lɑ̃t] *adj* **1** : insolent **2** : arrogant **3** : unabashed, outrageous
insolite [ɛ̃sɔlit] *adj* : unusual, bizarre
insoluble [ɛ̃sɔlybl] *adj* : insoluble
insolvabilité [ɛ̃sɔlvabilite] *nf* : insolvency
insolvable [ɛ̃sɔlvabl] *adj* : insolvent
insomniaque [ɛ̃sɔmnjak] *nmf* : insomniac
insomnie [ɛ̃sɔmni] *nf* : insomnia
insondable [ɛ̃sɔ̃dabl] *adj* : unfathomable
insonore [ɛ̃sɔnɔr] *adj* : soundproof
insonoriser [ɛ̃sɔnɔrize] *vt* : to soundproof
insouciance [ɛ̃susjɑ̃s] *nf* : insouciance, carefree attitude
insouciant, -ciante [ɛ̃susjɑ̃, -sjɑ̃t] *adj* **1** : carefree, happy-go-lucky **2 ~ de** : unconcerned about, heedless of
insoumis[1], **-mise** [ɛ̃sumi, -miz] *adj* **1** : rebellious, unsubdued **2 soldat insoumis** : deserter, draft dodger
insoumis[2] *nm* : deserter, draft dodger
insoumission [ɛ̃sumisjɔ̃] *nf* **1** : rebelliousness **2** : desertion (of one's military post)
insoutenable [ɛ̃sutnabl] *adj* **1** INDÉFENDABLE : untenable **2** INSUPPORTABLE : unbearable
inspecter [ɛ̃spɛkte] *vt* : to inspect
inspecteur, -trice [ɛ̃spɛktœr, -tris] *n* : inspector
inspection [ɛ̃spɛksjɔ̃] *nf* : inspection
inspirant, -rante [ɛ̃spirɑ̃, -rɑ̃t] *adj* : inspirational
inspiration [ɛ̃spirasjɔ̃] *nf* **1** : inspiration **2** : inhalation
inspiré, -rée [ɛ̃spire] *adj* **1** : inspired **2 bien inspiré** : well-advised **3 mal inspiré** : ill-advised
inspirer [ɛ̃spire] *vt* **1** : to inspire **2** : to breathe in, to inhale — *vi* : to inhale — **s'inspirer** *vr* **~ de** : to be inspired by
instabilité [ɛ̃stabilite] *nf* : instability
instable [ɛ̃stabl] *adj* **1** BRANLANT : unsteady, wobbly **2** : unsettled, unstable
installation [ɛ̃stalasjɔ̃] *nf* **1** : installation **2 installations** *nfpl* : installations, facilities, fittings <installations nucléaires : nuclear sites>
installer [ɛ̃stale] *vt* : to install, to put in, to set up — **s'installer** *vr* : to become established, to settle <ils se sont installés dans la maison : they have settled into the house>
instamment [ɛ̃stamɑ̃] *adv* : insistently
instance [ɛ̃stɑ̃s] *nf* **1** INSISTANCE : insistence, entreaty **2** AUTORITÉ : authority **3** : legal proceedings *pl*, lawsuit **4 en ~** : pending
instant[1], **-tante** [ɛ̃stɑ̃, -tɑ̃t] *adj* : urgent, pressing
instant[2] *nm* : instant, moment <à l'instant : just this minute, a moment ago> <dans un instant : in a minute, soon> <en un instant : in no time at all> <par instants : at times>
instantané[1], **-née** [ɛ̃stɑ̃tane] *adj* **1** : instantaneous **2** : instant <café instantané : instant coffee> **3** : candid <photo instantané : candid photo> — **instantanément** [-nemɑ̃] *adv*
instantané[2] *nm* : snapshot
instar [ɛ̃star] **à l'instar de** : following the example of, like
instauration [ɛ̃storasjɔ̃] *nf* : institution, establishing
instaurer [ɛ̃store] *vt* **1** : to establish, to institute **2** : to instill
instigateur, -trice [ɛ̃stigatœr, -tris] *n* : instigator
instigation [ɛ̃stigasjɔ̃] *nf* : instigation
instiller [ɛ̃stile] *vt* **1** : to apply drop by drop (as eyedrops) **2** : to instill
instinct [ɛ̃stɛ̃] *nm* : instinct <d'instinct : instinctively>
instinctif, -tive [ɛ̃stɛ̃ktif, -tiv] *adj* : instinctive, instinctual — **instinctivement** [-tivmɑ̃] *adv*

instituer [ɛ̃stitɥe] *vt* **1** : to institute **2** : to appoint (in law)

institut [ɛ̃stity] *nm* **1** : institute **2 institut de beauté** : beauty salon

instituteur, -trice [ɛ̃stitytœr, -tris] *n* : schoolteacher

institution [ɛ̃stitysjɔ̃] *nf* **1** : instituting, establishment **2** : institution <institution dotée : endowment, foundation>

institutionnaliser [ɛ̃stitysjɔnalize] *vt* : to institutionalize

institutionnel, -nelle [ɛ̃stitysjɔnɛl] *adj* : institutional

instructeur, -trice [ɛ̃stryktœr, -tris] *n* : instructor

instructif, -tive [ɛ̃stryktif, -tiv] *adj* : instructive

instruction [ɛ̃stryksjɔ̃] *nf* **1** FORMATION : training, instruction **2** : education <sans instruction : uneducated> **3** DIRECTIVE : order, directive **4 instructions** *nfpl* : instructions, directions

instruire [ɛ̃strɥir] {49} *vt* **1** ÉDUQUER, FORMER : to teach, to train, to instruct **2** : to inform <ils m'ont instruit des règlements : they informed me of the rules> **3 instruire une affaire** *France* : to prepare a case (in law) — **s'instruire** *vr* **1** : to educate oneself, to learn **2 ~ de** : to find out about

instruisait [ɛ̃strɥizɛ], **instruisions** [ɛ̃strɥizjɔ̃], *etc.* → **instruire**

instruit, -truite [ɛ̃strɥi, -trɥit] *adj* : learned, educated

instrument [ɛ̃strymɑ̃] *nm* **1** : instrument, tool **2 instrument de musique** : musical instrument

instrumental, -tale [ɛ̃strymɑ̃tal] *adj, mpl* **-taux** [-to] : instrumental

instrumentation [ɛ̃strymɑ̃tasjɔ̃] *nf* : instrumentation

instrumentiste [ɛ̃strymɑ̃tist] *nmf* : instrumentalist

insu [ɛ̃sy] **à l'insu de** : without the knowledge of, unknown to

insubmersible [ɛ̃submɛrsibl] *adj* : unsinkable

insubordination [ɛ̃sybɔrdinasjɔ̃] *nf* : insubordination

insubordonné, -née [ɛ̃sybɔrdɔne] *adj* : insubordinate

insuccès [ɛ̃syksɛ] *nm* : failure

insuffisance [ɛ̃syfizɑ̃s] *nf* **1** : insufficiency, lack **2** : insufficiency (in medicine) **3 insuffisances** *nfpl* : shortcomings, weaknesses

insuffisant, -sante [ɛ̃syfizɑ̃, -zɑ̃t] *adj* **1** : insufficient **2** : inadequate, unsatisfactory — **insuffisamment** [-zamɑ̃] *adv*

insuffler [ɛ̃syfle] *vt* : to instill, to infuse <insuffler une nouvelle énergie à : to infuse new energy into>

insulaire[1] [ɛ̃sylɛr] *adj* **1** : island <la population insulaire : the island population> **2** : insular

insulaire[2] *nmf* : islander

insularité [ɛ̃sylarite] *nf* : insularity

insuline [ɛ̃sylin] *nf* : insulin

insultant, -tante [ɛ̃syltɑ̃, -tɑ̃t] *adj* : insulting

insulte [ɛ̃sylt] *nf* : insult

insulter [ɛ̃sylte] *vt* : to insult

insupportable [ɛ̃sypɔrtabl] *adj* : unbearable — **insupportablement** [-bləmɑ̃] *adv*

insurgé[1], **-gée** [ɛ̃syrʒe] *adj* : insurgent

insurgé[2], **-gée** *n* : insurgent, rebel

insurger [ɛ̃syrʒe] {17} *v* **s'insurger** *vr* : to rebel, to rise up

insurmontable [ɛ̃syrmɔ̃tabl] *adj* **1** : insurmountable **2** : invincible, unconquerable

insurrection [ɛ̃syrɛksjɔ̃] *nf* : insurrection

intact, -tacte [ɛ̃takt] *adj* : intact

intangible [ɛ̃tɑ̃ʒibl] *adj* **1** : intangible **2** : inviolable

intarissable [ɛ̃tarisabl] *adj* : inexhaustible

intégral, -grale [ɛ̃tegral] *adj, mpl* **-graux** [-gro] **1** : complete <remboursement intégral : repayment in full> **2** : uncut, unabridged

intégrale [ɛ̃tegral] *nf* **1** : integral **2** : complete works <l'intégrale des symphonies de Brahms : the complete symphonies of Brahms>

intégralement [ɛ̃tegralmɑ̃] *adv* : completely, in full

intégralité [ɛ̃tegralite] *nf* : entirety, whole

intégrant, -grante [ɛ̃tegrɑ̃, -grɑ̃t] *adj* **partie intégrante** : integral part

intégration [ɛ̃tegrasjɔ̃] *nf* : integration

intègre [ɛ̃tɛgr] *adj* HONNÊTE : honest

intégrer [ɛ̃tegre] {87} *vt* **1** : to insert, to include **2** : to integrate, to assimilate — **s'intégrer** *vr* **1** : to become integrated, to fit in **2** : to fit together

intégrisme [ɛ̃tegrism] *nm* : fundamentalism

intégriste [ɛ̃tegrist] *adj & nmf* : fundamentalist

intégrité [ɛ̃tegrite] *nf* : integrity

intellect [ɛ̃telɛkt] *nm* : intellect

intellectualisme [ɛ̃telɛktɥalism] *nm* : intellectualism

intellectuel, -tuelle [ɛ̃telɛktɥɛl] *adj & n* : intellectual — **intellectuellement** [-tɥɛlmɑ̃] *adv*

intelligemment [ɛ̃teliʒamɑ̃] *adv* : intelligently

intelligence [ɛ̃teliʒɑ̃s] *nf* **1** : intelligence **2** COMPRÉHENSION : understanding <avoir l'intelligence de : to have a (good) grasp of> **3** : (secret) agreement <agir d'intelligence avec : to have an understanding with> **4** : **intelligences** *nfpl* : collusion, (secret) dealings <elle a des intelligences dans l'industrie : she has contacts in industry>

intelligent, -gente [ɛ̃teliʒɑ̃, -ʒɑ̃t] *adj* : intelligent

intelligentsia |ɛ̃teliʒɑ̃sja| *nf* : intelligentsia

intelligibilité |ɛ̃teliʒibilite| *nf* : intelligibility

intelligible |ɛ̃teliʒibl| *adj* : intelligible — **intelligiblement** |-ʒibləmɑ̃| *adv*

intempérant, -rante |ɛ̃tɑ̃perɑ̃, -rɑ̃t| *adj* : intemperate — **intempérance** |-perɑ̃s| *nf*

intempéries |ɛtɑ̃peri| *nfpl* : bad weather

intempestif, -tive |ɛ̃tɑ̃pɛstif, -tiv| *adj* : untimely, inopportune

intemporel, -relle |ɛ̃tɑ̃pɔrɛl| *adj* : timeless

intenable |ɛ̃tənabl| *adj* **1** : unbearable **2** : untenable, indefensible

intendant, -dante |ɛ̃tɑ̃dɑ̃, -dɑ̃t| *n* **1** : steward **2** : quartermaster **3** : bursar

intense |ɛ̃tɑ̃s| *adj* : intense

intensément |ɛ̃tɑ̃semɑ̃| *adv* : intensely

intensif, -sive |ɛ̃tɑ̃sif, -siv| *adj* : intensive

intensification |ɛ̃tɑ̃sifikasjɔ̃| *nf* : intensification

intensifier |ɛ̃tɑ̃sifje| {96} *vt* : to intensify — **s'intensifier** *vr*

intensité |ɛ̃tɑ̃site| *nf* : intensity

intenter |ɛ̃tɑ̃te| *vt* : to initiate, to pursue (legal action) <intenter un procès contre : to sue>

intention |ɛ̃tɑ̃sjɔ̃| *nf* : intention, intent <avoir l'intention de : to intend to> <à l'intention de : aimed at, for> <sans intention : unintentionally>

intentionné, -née |ɛ̃tɑ̃sjɔne| *adj* **1 bien intentionné** : well-meaning **2 mal intentionné** : ill-disposed

intentionnel, -nelle |ɛ̃tɑ̃sjɔnɛl| *adj* : intentional, deliberate — **intentionnellement** |-nɛlmɑ̃| *adv*

interactif, -tive |ɛ̃tɛraktif, -tiv| *adj* : interactive

interaction |ɛ̃tɛraksjɔ̃| *nf* : interaction

intercalaire[1] |ɛ̃tɛrkalɛr| *adj* **1 feuillet intercalaire** : insert **2 fiche intercalaire** : divider

intercalaire[2] *nm* : insert, inset, divider

intercaler |ɛ̃tɛrkale| *vt* INSÉRER : to insert

intercéder |ɛ̃tɛrsede| {87} *vi* : to intercede

intercepter |ɛ̃tɛrsɛpte| *vt* : to intercept

interception |ɛ̃tɛrsɛpsjɔ̃| *nf* : interception

intercession |ɛ̃tɛrsesjɔ̃| *nf* : intercession

interchangeable |ɛ̃tɛrʃɑ̃ʒabl| *adj* : interchangeable

interconfessionnel, -nelle |ɛ̃tɛrkɔ̃fesjɔnɛl| *adj* : interdenominational

interconnexion |ɛ̃tɛrkɔnɛksjɔ̃| *nf* : (electronic) networking

intercontinental, -tale |ɛ̃tɛrkɔ̃tinɑ̃tal| *adj, mpl* **-taux** |-to| : intercontinental

interdépartemental, -tale |ɛ̃tɛrdepartəmɑ̃tal| *adj, mpl* **-taux** |-to| : interdepartmental

interdépendant, -dante |ɛ̃tɛrdepɑ̃dɑ̃, -dɑ̃t| *adj* : interdependent — **interdépendance** |-dɑ̃s| *nf*

interdiction |ɛ̃tɛrdiksjɔ̃| *nf* : ban, prohibition

interdire |ɛ̃tɛrdir| {29} *vt* **1** : to ban, to prohibit **2** : to prevent, to block — **s'interdire** *vr* : to refrain from <je m'interdis d'y penser : I don't let myself think about it>

interdisciplinaire |ɛ̃tɛrdisipliner| *adj* : interdisciplinary

interdit, -dite |ɛ̃tɛrdi, -dit| *adj* **1** : forbidden, prohibited **2** STUPÉFAIT : taken aback, dumbfounded

intéressant[1], **-sante** |ɛ̃terɛsɑ̃, -sɑ̃t| *adj* **1** : interesting **2** AVANTAGEUX : attractive, worthwhile

intéressant[2], **-sante** *n* **faire l'intéressant** : to call attention to oneself, to show off

intéressé[1], **-sée** *adj* **1** : interested, attentive **2** : concerned, involved **3** : self-interested, self-involved

intéressé[2], **-sée** |ɛ̃terese| *n* : person involved <les intéressés : the interested parties>

intéresser |ɛ̃terese| *vt* **1** : to interest **2** CONCERNER : to concern, to affect **3 être intéressé dans** : to have a (financial) stake in — **s'intéresser** *vr* **~ à** : to take an interest in, to be interested in

intérêt |ɛ̃terɛ| *nm* **1** : interest <avoir de l'intérêt pour : to be interested in> <porter un intérêt à : to take an interest in> <elle a intérêt à refuser : she's well-advised to refuse> **2** : interest (in finance) <sans intérêt : interest-free> <intérêts composés : compound interest>

interface |ɛ̃tɛrfas| *nf* : interface (in computer science)

interférence |ɛ̃tɛrferɑ̃s| *nf* : interference

interférer |ɛ̃tɛrfere| {87} *vi* : to interfere

intergalactique |ɛ̃tɛrgalaktik| *adj* : intergalactic

intergouvernemental, -tale |ɛ̃tɛrguvɛrnəmɑ̃tal| *adj, mpl* **-taux** |-to| : intergovernmental

intérieur[1], **-rieure** |ɛ̃terjœr| *adj* **1** : interior, inner, inside **2** : internal, domestic

intérieur[2] *nm* **1** : inside <à l'intérieur : inside, indoors, within> <d'intérieur : indoor> **2** : interior (of a country, etc.)

intérieurement |ɛ̃terjœrmɑ̃| *adv* : inwardly, internally

intérim |ɛ̃terim| *nm* **1** : interim (period) **2** : temporary activity <faire des intérims : to work as a temp>

intérimaire[1] [ɛ̃terimɛr] *adj* : interim, temporary, acting
intérimaire[2] *nmf* : temporary employee, temp
interjection [ɛ̃tɛrʒɛksjɔ̃] *nf* : interjection
interjeter [ɛ̃tɛrʒəte] {8} *vt* **interjeter appel** : to file an appeal
interlocuteur, -trice [ɛ̃tɛrlɔkytœr, -tris] *n* **1** : speaker <mon interlocuteur : the person I am speaking to> **2** : representative, negotiator
interlope [ɛ̃tɛrlɔp] *adj* **1** LOUCHE : shady **2** ILLÉGAL : illegal
interloquer [ɛ̃tɛrlɔke] *vt* DÉCONTENANCER : to disconcert, to take aback
interlude [ɛ̃tɛrlyd] *nm* : (short) musical interlude
intermède [ɛ̃tɛrmɛd] *nm* : interlude
intermédiaire[1] [ɛ̃tɛrmedjɛr] *adj* : intermediate, intermediary
intermédiaire[2] *nmf* : intermediary, go-between, middleman
intermédiaire[3] *nm* : means, agency <sans intermédiaire : directly> <par l'intermédiaire de : by means of, through>
interminable [ɛ̃tɛrminabl] *adj* : interminable — **interminablement** [-nabləmɑ̃] *adv*
intermittence [ɛ̃tɛrmitɑ̃s] *nf* **par ~** : intermittently, off and on
intermittent, -tente [ɛ̃tɛrmitɑ̃, -tɑ̃t] *adj* : intermittent, sporadic
international, -nale [ɛ̃tɛrnasjɔnal] *adj, mpl* **-naux** [-no] : international — **internationalement** [-mɑ̃] *adv*
internaute [ɛ̃tɛrnot] *nmf* : Internet user
interne[1] [ɛ̃tɛrn] *adj* : internal, inner
interne[2] *nmf* **1** : boarder (at a school) **2** : intern
interné, -née [ɛ̃tɛrne] *n* : internee
internement [ɛ̃tɛrnəmɑ̃] *nm* **1** : (political) internment **2** : confinement (to a mental hospital, etc.)
interner [ɛ̃tɛrne] *vt* **1** : to intern **2** : to confine (to an institution)
Internet [ɛ̃tɛrnɛt] *nm* : Internet
interniste [ɛ̃tɛrnist] *nmf* : internist
interpellation [ɛ̃tɛrpelasjɔ̃] *nf* **1** : shouting out **2** : questioning
interpeller [ɛ̃tɛrpəle] *vt* **1** APOSTROPHER : to shout at, to call out to **2** INTERROGER : to question
interpersonnel, -nelle [ɛ̃tɛrpɛrsɔnɛl] *adj* : interpersonal
interphone [ɛ̃tɛrfɔn] *nm* : intercom
interplanétaire [ɛ̃tɛrplanetɛr] *adj* : interplanetary
interpoler [ɛ̃tɛrpɔle] *vt* : to interpolate
interposer [ɛ̃tɛrpoze] *vt* : to interpose — **s'interposer** *vr* : to intervene, to interpose
interprétation [ɛ̃tɛrpretasjɔ̃] *nf* : interpretation
interprète [ɛ̃tɛrprɛt] *nmf* **1** : interpreter **2** : spokesperson **3** : performer
interpréter [ɛ̃tɛrprete] {87} *vt* **1** : to interpret <mal interpreter : to misinterpret> **2** : to perform, to play (a role)
interprétif, -tive [ɛ̃tɛrpretif, -tiv] *adj* : interpretive, interpretative
interracial, -ciale [ɛ̃tɛrrasjal] *adj* : interracial
interrelation [ɛ̃terəlasjɔ̃] *nf* : interrelationship
interrogateur[1], **-trice** [ɛ̃terɔgatœr, -tris] *adj* : inquiring, questioning
interrogateur[2], **-trice** *n* : examiner, questioner
interrogatif[1], **-tive** [ɛ̃terɔgatif, -tiv] *adj* : interrogative
interrogatif[2] *nm* : interrogative (in grammar)
interrogation [ɛ̃terɔgasjɔ̃] *nf* **1** : questioning, interrogation **2** : test (in school) **3** : question <interrogation indirect : indirect question> **4** → **point**
interrogatoire [ɛ̃terɔgatwar] *nm* : interrogation, questioning, cross-examination
interroger [ɛ̃terɔʒe] {17} *vt* : to interrogate, to question — **s'interroger** *vr* **~ sur** : to wonder about
interrompre [ɛ̃terɔ̃pr] {77} *v* : to interrupt — **s'interrompre** *vr* : to break off, to come to a halt
interrupteur [ɛ̃teryptœr] *nm* : switch
interruption [ɛ̃terypsjɔ̃] *nf* **1** : interruption **2** : break <sans interruption : continuously>
intersection [ɛ̃tɛrsɛksjɔ̃] *nf* : intersection (in geometry)
interstellaire [ɛ̃tersteler] *adj* : interstellar
interstice [ɛ̃tɛrstis] *nm* : chink, crack
interuniversitaire [ɛ̃tɛryniversitɛr] *adj* : intercollegiate
interurbain[1], **-baine** [ɛ̃tɛryrbɛ̃, -bɛn] *adj* **1** : intercity **2** : long-distance
interurbain[2] *nm* **l'interurbain** : long-distance telephone service
intervalle [ɛ̃tɛrval] *nm* **1** : space, gap **2** : interval, period of time <dans l'intervalle : in the meantime>
intervenir [ɛ̃tɛrvənir] {92} *vi* **1** : to intervene **2** : to take place, to occur **3** OPÉRER : to operate (in medicine)
intervention [ɛ̃tɛrvɑ̃sjɔ̃] *nf* **1** : intervention **2** DISCOURS : speech **3** OPÉRATION : (medical) operation
interversion [ɛ̃tɛrvɛrzjɔ̃] *nf* INVERSION : inversion
intervertir [ɛ̃tɛrvɛrtir] *vt* INVERSER : to invert, to reverse
interview [ɛ̃tɛrvju] *nf* : interview
interviewer [ɛ̃tɛrvjuve] *vt* : to interview
intervieweur, -vieweuse [ɛ̃tɛrvjuvœr, -vjuvøz] *n* : interviewer
intestat [ɛ̃tɛsta] *adj* : intestate
intestin [ɛ̃tɛstɛ̃] *nm* **1** : intestine <gros intestin : large intestine> <intestin

grêle : small intestine> **2 intestins** *nmpl* : intestines, bowels

intestinal, -nale [ɛ̃tɛstinal] *adj, mpl* **-naux** [-no] : intestinal

intime[1] [ɛ̃tim] *adj* **1** : intimate, close **2** : private **3** : personal <hygiène intime : personal hygiene> **4** : innermost, profound <ma conviction intime : my deep conviction>

intime[2] *nmf* : close friend

intimement [ɛ̃timmɑ̃] *adv* : intimately

intimer [ɛ̃time] *vt* **1** : to tell, to instruct <intimer l'ordre : to order> **2** : to summon (to court)

intimidant, -dante [ɛ̃timidɑ̃, -dɑ̃t] *adj* : intimidating

intimider [ɛ̃timide] *vt* : to intimidate — **intimidation** [-midasjɔ̃] *nf*

intimité [ɛ̃timite] *nf* **1** : intimacy **2** : privacy <dans l'intimité : in private> **3** : depths *pl* <dans l'intimité de son âme : in the depths of one's soul>

intitulé [ɛ̃tityle] *nm* : title, heading

intituler [ɛ̃tityle] *vt* : to call, to title — **s'intituler** *vr* **1** : to be called, to be titled **2** : to call oneself

intolérable [ɛ̃tɔlerabl] *adj* : intolerable — **intolérablement** [-rabləmɑ̃] *adv*

intolérant, -rante [ɛ̃tɔlerɑ̃, -rɑ̃t] *adj* : intolerant — **intolérance** [-rɑ̃s] *nf*

intonation [ɛ̃tɔnasjɔ̃] *nf* : intonation

intouchable [ɛ̃tuʃabl] *adj & nmf* : untouchable

intoxication [ɛ̃tɔksikasjɔ̃] *nf* **1** EMPOISONNEMENT : poisoning <intoxication alimentaire : food poisoning> **2** : brainwashing

intoxiquer [ɛ̃tɔksike] *vt* **1** EMPOISONNER : to poison **2** : to brainwash

intraduisible [ɛ̃tradɥizibl] *adj* **1** : untranslatable **2** : inexpressible

intraitable [ɛ̃trɛtabl] *adj* : uncompromising, inflexible, intractable

intransigeance [ɛ̃trɑ̃ziʒɑ̃s] *nf* : intransigence

intransigeant, -geante [ɛ̃trɑ̃ziʒɑ, -ʒɑ̃t] *adj* : intransigent, uncompromising

intransitif, -tive [ɛ̃trɑ̃zitif, -tiv] *adj* : intransitive

intraveineux, -neuse [ɛ̃travɛnø, -nøz] *adj* : intravenous

intrépide [ɛ̃trepid] *adj* : intrepid, fearless

intrépidité [ɛ̃trepidite] *nf* : fearlessness, boldness

intrigant[1], -gante [ɛ̃trigɑ̃, -gɑ̃t] *adj* : scheming, conniving

intrigant[2], -gante *n* : schemer

intrigue [ɛ̃trig] *nf* **1** : intrigue **2** : plot (of a story)

intriguer [ɛ̃trige] *vt* : to intrigue, to puzzle — *vi* : to plot, to scheme

intrinsèque [ɛ̃trɛ̃sɛk] *adj* : intrinsic — **intrinsèquement** [-sɛkmɑ̃] *adv*

introduction [ɛ̃trɔdyksjɔ̃] *nf* **1** : introduction <lettre d'introduction : letter of introduction> **2** : introduction, adoption (of customs, products, etc.) **3** INSERTION : insertion

introduire [ɛ̃trɔdɥir] {49} *vt* **1** : to introduce **2** : to show in, to usher into **3** INSÉRER : to insert **4** : to enter, to input (data in a computer) — **s'introduire** *vr* **1** : to be introduced **2** : to penetrate, to get in

introniser [ɛ̃trɔnize] *vt* **1** : to enthrone **2** : to establish, to set up

introspectif, -tive [ɛ̃trɔspɛktif, -tiv] *adj* : introspective — **introspectivement** [-tivmɑ̃] *adv*

introspection [ɛ̃trɔspɛksjɔ̃] *nf* : introspection

introuvable [ɛ̃truvabl] *adj* : unobtainable, nowhere to be found

introverti[1], -tie [ɛ̃trɔvɛrti] *adj* : introverted

introverti[2], -tie *n* : introvert

intrus, -truse [ɛ̃try, -tryz] *n* : intruder

intrusion [ɛ̃tryzjɔ̃] *nf* : intrusion

intuitif, -tive [ɛ̃tɥitif, -tiv] *adj* : intuitive — **intuitivement** [-tivmɑ̃] *adv*

intuition [ɛ̃tɥisjɔ̃] *nf* : intuition <avoir l'intuition de : to have a feeling about>

inuit, inuite [inɥi, inɥit] *adj* : Inuit

Inuit, Inuite *n* : Inuit

inusable [inyzabl] *adj* : durable

inusité, -tée [inyzite] *adj* INHABITUEL : unusual, uncommon

inutile [inytil] *adj* **1** : useless **2** : pointless, unnecessary

inutilement [inytilmɑ̃] *adv* : needlessly, unnecessarily

inutilisable [inytilizabl] *adj* : unusable

inutilisé, -sée [inytilize] *adj* : unused

inutilité [inytilite] *nf* : uselessness

invaincu, -cue [ɛ̃vɛ̃ky] *adj* **1** : unbeaten, undefeated **2** : unconquered

invalide[1] [ɛ̃valid] *adj* **1** : disabled **2** : invalid

invalide[2] *nmf* : disabled person <les invalides : the disabled>

invalider [ɛ̃valide] *vt* : to invalidate

invalidité [ɛ̃validite] *nf* **1** : invalidity **2** : disability

invariable [ɛ̃varjabl] *adj* : invariable — **invariablement** [-bləmɑ̃] *adv*

invasif, -sive [ɛ̃vazif, -ziv] *adj* : invasive

invasion [ɛ̃vazjɔ̃] *nf* : invasion

invective [ɛ̃vɛktiv] *nf* : invective

invectiver [ɛ̃vɛktive] *vt* : to abuse verbally — *vi* **~ contre** : to inveigh against

inventaire [ɛ̃vɑ̃tɛr] *nm* : inventory <faire l'inventaire de : to take an inventory of>

inventer [ɛ̃vɑ̃te] *vt* **1** : to invent **2** : to make up (excuses, etc.)

inventeur, -trice [ɛ̃vɑ̃tœr, -tris] *n* : inventor

inventif, -tive [ɛ̃vɑ̃tif, -tiv] *adj* : inventive

invention [ɛ̃vɑ̃sjɔ̃] *nf* **1** : invention **2** CRÉATIVITÉ : inventiveness **3** MENSONGE : fabrication, lie

inventivité [ɛ̃vɑ̃tivite] *nf* : inventiveness
inventorier [ɛ̃vɑ̃tɔrje] {96} *vt* : to inventory
inverse[1] [ɛ̃vɛrs] *adj* **1** : inverse <rapport inverse : inverse relationship> **2** : opposite, reverse <en sens inverse : in the opposite direction>
inverse[2] *nm* **1 l'inverse** : the reverse, the opposite **2 à l'inverse** : conversely
inversement [ɛ̃vɛrsəmɑ̃] *adv* **1** : conversely <et inversement : and vice versa> **2** : inversely (in mathematics)
inverser [ɛ̃vɛrse] *vt* : to reverse, to invert
inversion [ɛ̃vɛrsjɔ̃] *nf* : inversion, reversal
invertébré, -brée [ɛ̃vɛrtebre] *adj & nm* : invertebrate
investigateur, -trice [ɛ̃vɛstigatœr, -tris] *n* : investigator, inquirer
investigation [ɛ̃vɛstigasjɔ̃] *nf* : investigation, inquiry
investir [ɛ̃vɛstir] *vt* **1** : to invest **2** : to induct, to inaugurate — *vi* : to invest (in stocks, etc.) — **s'investir** *vr* **~ dans** : to become involved in
investissement [ɛ̃vɛstismɑ̃] *nm* : investment
investisseur, -seuse [ɛ̃vɛstisœr, -søz] *n* : investor
investiture [ɛ̃vɛstityr] *nf* **1** : investiture, inauguration **2** : nomination
invétéré, -rée [ɛ̃vetere] *adj* : inveterate
invincibilité [ɛ̃vɛ̃sibilite] *nf* : invincibility
invincible [ɛ̃vɛ̃sibl] *adj* **1** : invincible, unbeatable **2** : insurmountable **3** : irresistible
inviolé, -lée [ɛ̃vjɔle] *adj* : inviolate
invisibilité [ɛ̃vizibilite] *nf* : invisibility
invisible [ɛ̃vizibl] *adj* **1** : invisible **2** : unseen <rester invisible : to stay out of sight>
invisiblement [ɛ̃viziblәmɑ̃] *adv* : invisibly
invitant, -tante [ɛ̃vitɑ̃, -tɑ̃t] *adj* : welcoming, hospitable
invitation [ɛ̃vitasjɔ̃] *nf* : invitation
invite [ɛ̃vit] *nf* : invitation, request
invité, -tée [ɛ̃vite] *n* : guest
inviter [ɛ̃vite] *vt* : to invite, to ask
invivable [ɛ̃vivabl] *adj* : unbearable
invocation [ɛ̃vɔkasjɔ̃] *nf* : invocation
involontaire [ɛ̃vɔlɔ̃tɛr] *adj* **1** : involuntary **2** : unintentional **3** : reluctant, unwilling
involontairement [ɛ̃vɔlɔ̃tɛrmɑ̃] *adv* : unintentionally, involuntarily
invoquer [ɛ̃vɔke] *vt* : to invoke
invraisemblable [ɛ̃vrɛsɑ̃blabl] *adj* **1** : improbable, unlikely **2** : incredible, fantastic, bizarre
invraisemblance [ɛ̃vrɛsɑ̃blɑ̃s] *nf* : improbability, unlikelihood
invulnérable [ɛ̃vylnerabl] *adj* : invulnerable
iode [jɔd] *nm* : iodine
iodé, -dée [jɔde] *adj* : iodized
iodler [jɔdle] *vi* : to yodel
iodure [jɔdyr] *nm* : iodide
ion [jɔ̃] *nm* : ion
ioniser [jɔnize] *vt* : to ionize
ionosphère [jɔnɔsfɛr] *nf* : ionosphere
iota [jɔta] *nm* : iota
ira [ira], *etc.* → **aller**
irakien, -kienne [irakjɛ̃, -kjɛn] *adj* : Iraqi
Irakien, -kienne *n* : Iraqi
iranien, -nienne [iranjɛ̃, -njɛn] *adj* : Iranian
Iranien, -nienne *n* : Iranian
iraquien, Iraquien [irakjɛ̃] → **irakien, Irakien**
irascible [irasibl] *adj* : irascible
iris [iris] *nm* **1** : iris (of the eye) **2** : iris (plant)
irisation [irizasjɔ̃] *nf* : iridescence
irisé, -sée [irize] *adj* : iridescent
irlandais[1], **-daise** [irlɑ̃dɛ, -dɛz] *adj* : Irish
irlandais[2] *nm* : Irish (language)
Irlandais, -daise *n* : Irishman *m*, Irishwoman *f*
ironie [irɔni] *nf* : irony
ironique [irɔnik] *adj* : ironic, ironical — **ironiquement** [-mɑ̃] *adv*
ironiser [irɔnize] *vi* : to speak ironically, to be ironic
irradiation [iradjasjɔ̃] *nf* **1** : radiation **2** : irradiation
irradier [iradje] {96} *vt* : to irradiate — *vi* : to radiate
irraisonné, -née [irɛzɔne] *adj* : unreasoning
irrationalité [irasjɔnalite] *nf* : irrationality
irrationnel, -nelle [irasjɔnɛl] *adj* : irrational — **irrationnellement** [-nɛlmɑ̃] *adv*
irréalisable [irealizabl] *adj* IMPRATICABLE : impracticable, unworkable
irréaliste [irealist] *adj* : unrealistic
irréalité [irealite] *nf* : unreality
irrecevable [irәsәvabl] *adj* : inadmissible
irréconciliable [irekɔ̃siljabl] *adj* : irreconcilable
irrécupérable [irekyperabl] **1** : irretrievable **2** : beyond repair **3** : irredeemable, beyond hope
irréductible [iredyktibl] *adj* **1** : irreducible **2** INDOMPTABLE : indomitable
irréel, -réelle [ireɛl] *adj* : unreal
irréfléchi, -chie [ireflefi] *adj* : thoughtless, rash
irréfutable [irefytabl] *adj* : irrefutable — **irréfutablement** [-tabləmɑ̃] *adv*
irrégularité [iregylarite] *nf* : irregularity
irrégulier, -lière [iregylje, -ljɛr] *adj* **1** : irregular, uneven **2** : erratic **3** : unauthorized, illegal
irrégulièrement [iregyljɛrmɑ̃] *adv* : irregularly

irréligieux, -gieuse [irelizjø, -zjøz] *adj* : irreligious
irrémédiable [iremedjabl] *adj* **1** : irreparable **2** : incurable — **irrémédiablement** [-djabləmɑ̃] *adv*
irremplaçable [irɑ̃plasabl] *adj* : irreplaceable
irréparable [ireparabl] *adj* : irreparable, beyond repair
irrépressible [irepresibl] *adj* : irrepressible
irréprochable [ireprɔʃabl] *adj* : irreproachable, beyond reproach
irrésistible [irezistibl] *adj* **1** : irresistible **2** : comical <elle est irrésistible : she's hilarious!>
irrésistiblement [irezistibləmɑ̃] *adv* : irresistibly
irrésolu, -lue [irezɔly] *adj* **1** : irresolute **2** : unresolved
irrespect [irɛspɛ] *nm* : disrespect
irrespectueux, -tueuse [irɛspɛktɥø, -tɥøz] *adj* : disrespectful
irrespirable [irɛspirabl] *adj* **1** : unbreathable **2** : stifling, oppressive
irresponsabilité [irɛspɔ̃sabilite] *nf* : irresponsibility
irresponsable [irɛspɔ̃sabl] *adj* : irresponsible
irrévérence [ireverɑ̃s] *nf* : irreverence
irrévérencieux, -cieuse [ireverɑ̃sjø, -sjøz] *adj* : irreverent
irréversible [ireversibl] *adj* : irreversible — **irréversibilité** [-sibilite] *nf*
irrévocabilité [irevɔkabilite] *nf* : irrevocability, finality
irrévocable [irevɔkabl] *adj* : irrevocable — **irrévocablement** [-kabləmɑ̃] *adv*
irrigation [irigasjɔ̃] *nf* : irrigation
irriguer [irige] *vt* : to irrigate
irritable [iritabl] *adj* : irritable — **irritabilité** [-tabilite] *nf*
irritant[1], -tante [iritɑ̃, -tɑ̃t] *adj* **1** : irritating, annoying **2** : irritant (in medicine)
irritant[2] *nm* : irritant (substance)
irritation [iritasjɔ̃] *nf* : irritation
irriter [irite] *vt* : to irritate — **s'irriter** *vr* : to get irritated
irruption [irypsjɔ̃] *nf* **1** : irruption **2** : inrush <faire irruption dans : to burst into>
islam [islam] *nm* : Islam
islamique [islamik] *adj* : Islamic
islandais[1], -daise [islɑ̃dɛ, -dɛz] *adj* : Icelandic
islandais[2] *nm* : Icelandic (language)
Islandais, -daise *n* : Icelander
isocèle [izɔsɛl] *adj* : isosceles
isolant[1], -lante [izɔlɑ̃, -lɑ̃t] *adj* : insulating
isolant[2] *nm* : insulating material, insulation
isolateur [izɔlatœr] *nm* : insulator
isolation [izɔlasjɔ̃] *nf* : insulation <isolation thermique : thermal insulation>
isolé, -lée [izɔle] *adj* **1** : isolated, separated **2** : remote, secluded
isolement [izɔlmɑ̃] *nm* **1** : isolation **2** ISOLATION : insulation
isolément [izɔlemɑ̃] *adv* : separately, individually
isoler [izɔle] *vt* **1** : to isolate **2** : to insulate — **s'isoler** *vr* : to isolate oneself, to withdraw
isoloir [izɔlwar] *nm* : voting booth
isométrique [izɔmetrik] *adj* : isometric
isotope [izɔtɔp] *nm* : isotope
israélien, -lienne [israeljɛ̃, -ljɛn] *adj* : Israeli
Israélien, -lienne *n* : Israeli
israélite [israelit] *adj* : Jewish
Israélite *nmf* **1** : Jew **2** : Israelite, Hebrew
issu, -sue [isy] *adj* **~ de 1** : descended from **2** : resulting from
issue *nf* **1** SORTIE : exit <rue sans issue : dead-end street> **2** SOLUTION : way out, solution **3** FIN : ending, outcome <à l'issue de : at the end of>
isthme [ism] *nm* : isthmus
italien[1], -lienne [italjɛ̃, -ljɛn] *adj* : Italian
italien[2] *nm* : Italian (language)
Italien, -lienne *n* : Italian
italique[1] [italik] *adj* : italic
italique[2] *nm* : italics *pl*
itinéraire [itinerɛr] *nm* : itinerary, route
itinérant[1], -rante [itinerɑ̃, -rɑ̃t] *adj* : itinerant, traveling
itinérant[2], -rante *n Can* : vagabond, tramp
ivoire [ivwar] *adj & nm* : ivory
ivoirien, -rienne [ivwarjɛ̃, -rjɛn] *adj* : of the Ivory Coast, Ivorian
Ivoirien, -rienne *n* : native or inhabitant of the Ivory Coast, Ivorian
ivre [ivr] *adj* **1** : drunk, intoxicated **2 ~ de** : drunk with <ivre de joie : delirious with joy>
ivresse [ivrɛs] *nf* : drunkenness, intoxication
ivrogne, ivrognesse [ivrɔɲ, -ɲɛs] *n* : drunkard

J

j [ʒi] *nm* : j, the 10th letter of the alphabet

jabot [ʒabo] *nm* **1** : crop (of a bird) **2** : jabot, ruffle

jacasser [ʒakase] *vi* BAVARDER : to chatter, to jabber

jachère [ʒaʃɛr] *nf* : fallow land <rester en jachère : to lie fallow>

jacinthe [ʒasɛ̃t] *nf* **1** : hyacinth **2** **jacinthe des bois** : bluebell

jack [dʒak] *nm* : jack, (telephone) socket

jackpot *or* **jack pot** [dʒakpɔt] *nm* : jackpot

jade [ʒad] *nm* : jade

jadis[1] [ʒadis] *adv* AUTREFOIS : in times past, formerly

jadis[2] *adj* : former, olden <au temps jadis : in days of old>

jaguar [ʒagwar] *nm* : jaguar

jaillir [ʒajir] *vi* **1** : to spurt out, to gush (out) **2** : to spring up, to shoot out, to burst out **3** : to arise, to emerge

jaillissement [ʒajismɑ̃] *nm* JET : spurt, gush

jais [ʒɛ] *nms & pl* **1** : jet (stone) **2** **de jais** *or* **d'un noir de jais** : jet-black

jalon [ʒalɔ̃] *nm* **1** : marker, milestone **2** **poser les (premiers) jalons** : to pave the way

jalonner [ʒalɔne] *vt* **1** : to mark out (a route, etc.) **2** LONGER : to line, to border **3** MARQUER : to mark, to punctuate <une histoire jalonnée de tragédie : a story marked by tragedy>

jalouser [ʒaluze] *vt* : to be jealous of

jalousie [ʒaluzi] *nf* **1** : jealousy **2** : slatted blind, venetian blind

jaloux, -louse [ʒalu, -luz] *adj* : jealous — **jalousement** [-luzmɑ̃] *adv*

jamaïquain, -quaine [ʒamaikɛ̃, -kɛn] *adj* : Jamaican

Jamaïquain, -quaine *n* : Jamaican

jamais [ʒamɛ] *adv* **1** : never <il ne pense jamais aux autres : he never thinks of others> **2** : ever <c'est pire que jamais : it's worse than ever> **3** **à (tout) jamais** *or* **pour ~** : forever

jambage [ʒɑ̃baʒ] *nm* **1** : downstroke (of a letter) **2** : jamb

jambe [ʒɑ̃b] *nf* **1** : leg **2** **à toutes jambes** : as fast as one's legs can carry one **3** **dans les jambes** *fam* : in the way, underfoot

jambon [ʒɑ̃bɔ̃] *nm* : ham

jamboree [ʒɑ̃bɔri] *nm* : jamboree

jante [ʒɑ̃t] *nf* : rim (of a wheel)

janvier [ʒɑ̃vje] *nm* : January

japonais[1], **-naise** [ʒapɔnɛ, -nɛz] *adj* : Japanese

japonais[2] *nm* : Japanese (language)

Japonais, -naise *n* : Japanese

jappement [ʒapmɑ̃] *nm* : yap, yelp

japper [ʒape] *vi* : to yap, to yelp

jaquette [ʒakɛt] *nf* **1** : dust jacket **2** : morning coat (for men), jacket (for women)

jardin [ʒardɛ̃] *nm* **1** : garden **2** : yard **3** **jardin d'enfants** *France* : kindergarten **4** **jardin zoologique** : zoo

jardinage [ʒardinaʒ] *nm* : gardening

jardiner [ʒardine] *vi* : to garden

jardinier[1], **-nière** [ʒardinje, -njɛr] *adj* : garden <plantes jardinières : garden plants>

jardinier[2], **-nière** *n* : gardener

jardinière *nf* **1** : window box **2** : mixed vegetables

jargon [ʒargɔ̃] *nm* **1** : jargon **2** : gibberish

jarre [ʒar] *nf* : (earthenware) jar

jarret [ʒarɛ] *nm* **1** : back of the knee, hamstring **2** : hock (of an animal) **3** : shank (in cooking)

jarretelle [ʒartɛl] *nf* : garter belt

jarretière [ʒartjɛr] *nf* : garter

jars [ʒar] *nms & pl* : gander (animal)

jaser [ʒaze] *vi* **1** BAVARDER : to chatter **2** MÉDIRE : to gossip

jasette [ʒazɛt] *or* **jase** [ʒaz] *nf* **avoir de la jasette** *Can fam* : to talk a mile a minute

jasmin [ʒasmɛ̃] *nm* : jasmine

jaspe [ʒasp] *nm* : jasper

jaspé, -pée [ʒaspe] *adj* : mottled, marbled

jatte [ʒat] *nf* : bowl, basin

jauge [ʒoʒ] *nf* **1** : capacity **2** : gauge <jauge d'essence : gas gauge> <jauge de niveau d'huile : dipstick>

jauger [ʒoʒe] {17} *vt* **1** : to gauge, to measure the capacity of **2** : to take the measure of, to size up

jaunâtre [ʒonatr] *adj* **1** : yellowish **2** **teint jaunâtre** : sallow complexion

jaune[1] [ʒon] *adv* **rire jaune** : to force a laugh

jaune[2] *adj* : yellow

jaune[3] *nm* **1** : yellow **2** *or* **jaune d'œuf** : egg yolk

jaune[4] *nmf* : strikebreaker

jaunir [ʒonir] *v* : to turn yellow

jaunisse [ʒonis] *nf* : jaundice

javanais[1], **-naise** [ʒavanɛ, -nɛz] *adj* : Javanese

javanais[2], **-naise** *n* : Javanese (language)

Javanais, -naise *n* : Javanese

Javel [ʒavɛl] *nf* **eau de Javel** : bleach

javelliser [ʒavelize] *vt* : to chlorinate — **javellisation** [ʒavelizasjɔ̃] *nf*

javelot [ʒavlo] *nm* : javelin

jazz [dʒaz] *nm* : jazz

je [ʒə] (**j'** *before vowel or mute h*) *pron* : I

jean [dʒin] *nm* **1** : denim **2** **jeans** *nmpl* : jeans, blue jeans

jeep [dʒip] *nf* : jeep

Jéhovah [ʒeɔva] *nm* : Jehovah

je–ne–sais–quoi [ʒənsekwa] *nms & pl* **un je–ne–sais–quoi** : a certain something

jérémiades [ʒeremjad] *nfpl fam* : whining, complaining

jersey [ʒɛrzɛ] *nm* : jersey (fabric)

je–sais–tout [ʒəsetu] *nmfs & pl* : know-it-all

Jésus [ʒezy] *nm* : Jesus

jet [ʒɛ] *nm* **1** : jet, spurt, flash (of light) <jet d'eau : fountain> **2** : throw, throwing <à un jet de pierre : a stone's throw away> **3** : jet (airplane) **4** : shoot (of a plant) **5 d'un seul jet** : in one try, at one go

jetable [ʒətabl] *adj* : disposable <rasoirs jetables : disposable razors>

jetée [ʒəte] *nm* **1** : pier, jetty **2** : breakwater

jeter [ʒəte] {8} *vt* **1** : to throw **2** : to throw away **3** ÉMETTRE : to cast, to give off, to let out <jeter un coup d'œil : to take a look> **4 jeter l'éponge** : to throw in the towel **5 jeter un sort** : to cast a spell — **se jeter** *vr* **1** : to throw oneself <se jeter sur : to pounce on> **2** : to be disposable **3** : to be discarded, to be disposed of **4 ~ dans** : to flow into

jeton [ʒətɔ̃] *nm* : token, counter

jette [ʒɛt], **jettera** [ʒɛra], *etc.* → **jeter**

jeu [ʒø] *nm, pl* **jeux 1** : play, playing <jeu d'enfant : child's play> <le jeu : gambling> <jeux de mains : horseplay> **2** : game <jeu d'equipe : team sport> **3** : hand (of playing cards) **4** : set <jeu d'échecs : chess set> <jeu de cartes : deck of cards> **5 en ~** : at stake **6 jeu de jambes** : footwork (in sports) **7 jeu de mots** : pun **8 jeu de sociéte** : board game

jeudi [ʒødi] *nm* : Thursday

jeun [ʒœ̃] *adv* **à ~** : on an empty stomach

jeune[1] [ʒœn] *adv* : youthfully <s'habiller jeune : to dress young>

jeune[2] *adj* **1** : young, youthful <jeune homme : young man> <jeunes gens : young people> <jeune fille : girl> **2** CADET : younger <ma jeune sœur : my younger sister> **3** : new, recent <jeunes mariés : newlyweds>

jeune[3] *nmf* : young person <les jeunes : young people>

jeûne [ʒøn] *nm* : fast <rompre le jeûne : to break one's fast>

jeûner [ʒøne] *vi* : to fast

jeunesse [ʒœnɛs] *nf* **1** : youth **2** : youthfulness **3** : young people

joaillerie [ʒɔajri] *nf* **1** : jewelry making, jewel trade **2** : jeweler's shop **3** : jewelry

joaillier, -lière [ʒɔaje, -jɛr] *n* BIJOUTIER : jeweler

job [dʒɔb] *nm fam* : job

jockey [ʒɔkɛ] *nm* : jockey

jodhpurs [ʒɔdpyr] *nmpl* : jodhpurs

jodler [jɔdle] → **iodler**

joggeur, -guese [dʒɔgœr, -gøz] *n* : jogger

jogging [dʒɔgiŋ] *nm* **1** : jogging **2** : sweatsuit

joie [ʒwa] *nf* **1** : joy <joie de vivre : joie de vivre, enjoyment of life> **2** PLAISIR : pleasure, delight <avec joie : with pleasure>

joignait [ʒwɛ̃ɲɛ], **joignions** [ʒwɛ̃ɲɔ̃], *etc.* → **joindre**

joigne [ʒwɛ̃ɲ], *etc.* → **joindre**

joindre [ʒwɛ̃dr] {50} *vt* **1** : to join, to link, to combine **2** : to enclose, to attach **3** : to reach, to get in touch with <joindre qqn par téléphone : to reach s.o. by phone> — **se joindre** *vr* **1** : to join together (of hands, etc.) **2 ~ à** : to join in with, to become a part of

joint[1], **jointe** [ʒwɛ̃, ʒwɛ̃t] *adj* **1** : joined <à mains jointes : with clasped hands> **2 ~ à** : attached to, enclosed with

joint[2] *nm* **1** : joint <joint universel : universal joint> **2** : seal, gasket <joint de robinet : washer (for a faucet)>

jointure [ʒwɛ̃tyr] *nf* : joint (in anatomy or technology)

joker [ʒɔkɛr] *nm* : joker (in playing cards)

joli, -lie [ʒɔli] *adj* **1** : pretty, attractive **2** : nice <une jolie somme d'argent : a nice sum of money>

joliment [ʒɔlimɑ̃] *adv* **1** : nicely, prettily **2** *fam* : really, awfully

jonc [ʒɔ̃] *nm* **1** : rush, bullrush **2** : plain band, ring <jonc de mariage : wedding band>

joncher [ʒɔ̃ʃe] *vt* : to strew, to litter

jonction [ʒɔ̃ksjɔ̃] *nf* : junction

jongler [ʒɔ̃gle] *vi* : to juggle

jongleur, -gleuse [ʒɔ̃glœr, -gløz] *n* : juggler

jonque [ʒɔ̃k] *nf* : junk (boat)

jonquille [ʒɔ̃kij] *nf* : daffodil, jonquil

jordanien, -nienne [ʒɔrdanjɛ̃, -njɛn] *adj* : Jordanian

Jordanien, -nienne *n* : Jordanian

jouable [ʒwabl] *adj* : playable

joue [ʒu] *nf* **1** : cheek **2 mettre en joue** : to take aim at

jouer [ʒwe] *vi* **1** S'AMUSER : to play <jouer avec des poupées : to play with dolls> <jouer aux cartes : to play cards> <jouer du piano : to play the piano> **2** : to play, to perform <elle a joué dans les plus grands théâtres : she played the leading theaters> **3** : to gamble, to speculate <il jouait aux courses : he was playing the horses> <jouer à la Bourse : to play the stock market> **4** : to come into play, to apply <la question d'argent ne joue pas entre nous : money is not an issue between us> **5 jouer sur les mots** : to play with words — *vt* **1** : to play (a card, etc.) **2** : to bet, to wager **3** : to perform <il jouera une sonate de

Mozart : he will play a Mozart sonata> <jouer la comédie : to put on an act> **4** : to feign, to affect <jouer les victimes : to play the victim> — **se jouer** *vr* **1** : to be played **2** : to be at stake **3 ~ de** : to make light work of **4 ~ de** : to defy

jouet [ʒwɛ] *nm* : toy, plaything

joueur, joueuse [ʒwœr, ʒwøz] *n* **1** : player <un beau joueur : a good sport> **2** : gambler

joufflu, -flue [ʒufly] *adj* : chubby-cheeked

joug [ʒu] *nm* : yoke

jouir [ʒwir] *vi* **1** : to have an orgasm **2 ~ de** : to enjoy, to make good use of, to benefit from

jouissance [ʒwisɑ̃s] *nf* **1** PLAISIR : pleasure, enjoyment **2** : orgasm, climax **3** : use, (legal) possession

jour [ʒur] *nm* **1** : day <tous les jours : every day> <huit jours : a week> <de nos jours : nowadays> <de jour en jour : day by day> <jour de l'An : New Year's Day> <jour férié : public holiday> **2** : daylight, daytime <il fait jour : it's (day)light> **3** : aspect <sous un jour favorable : in a favorable light> **4 donner le jour à** : to bring into the world, to give birth to **5 mettre à jour** : to bring up to date, to update

journal [ʒurnal] *nm, pl* **journaux 1** : diary, journal **2** : newspaper **3 journal télévisé** : television news

journalier[1], -lière [ʒurnalje, -ljɛr] *adj* : daily

journalier[2], -lière *n* : day worker, laborer

journalisme [ʒurnalism] *nm* : journalism

journaliste [ʒurnalist] *nmf* : journalist — **journalistique** [-listik] *adj*

journée [ʒurne] *nf* **1** : day <toute la journée : all day long> **2** : workday <journée de repos : day off>

joute [ʒut] *nf* **1** : joust **2** : sparring match, battle (of wits, etc.)

jouter [ʒute] *vi* : to joust

jovial, -viale [ʒɔvjal] *adj, mpl* **jovials** *or* **joviaux** [-vjo] : jovial, jolly — **jovialement** [-vjalmɑ̃] *adv*

jovialité [ʒɔvjalite] *nf* : cheerfulness, joviality

joyau [ʒwajo] *nm, pl* **joyaux** : jewel, gem

joyeux, joyeuse [ʒwajø, -jøz] *adj* : joyful, happy <Joyeux Noël! : Merry Christmas!> — **joyeusement** [-jøzmɑ̃] *adv*

jubilation [ʒybilasjɔ̃] *nf* : jubilation

jubilé [ʒybile] *nm* : jubilee

jubiler [ʒybile] *vi* : to rejoice, to exult

jucher [ʒyʃe] *vt* : to perch <elle a juché le bébé sur sa chaise : she perched the baby on his chair> — **se jucher** *vr* **~ sur** : to perch on

judaïque [ʒydaik] *adj* : Judaic

judaïsme [ʒydaism] *nm* : Judaism

judiciaire [ʒydisjɛr] *adj* : judicial — **judiciairement** [-sjɛrmɑ̃] *adv*

judicieux, -cieuse [ʒydisjø, -sjøz] *adj* : judicious — **judicieusement** [-sjøzmɑ̃] *adv*

judo [ʒydo] *nm* : judo

juge [ʒyʒ] *nm* **1** : judge <juge de paix : justice of the peace> <tu es seul juge : only you can judge> **2** *or* **juge–arbitre** : referee <juge de touche : linesman>

jugement [ʒyʒmɑ̃] *nm* **1** : decision, verdict, sentence **2** : judgment, opinion

jugeote [ʒyʒɔt] *nf fam* : common sense

juger [ʒyʒe] {17} *vt* **1** ÉVALUER : to judge, to form an opinion about **2** : to judge, to try **3** : to think, to consider **4 ~ de** : to assess, to judge <c'est vrai, autant que je puisse en juger : it's true, as far as I can tell> — **se juger** *vr* S'ESTIMER : to consider oneself

jugulaire [ʒygylɛr] *nf* : jugular vein

juguler [ʒygyle] *vt* **1** ENRAYER : to halt, to check, to curb **2** : to suppress, to put down

juif, juive [ʒɥif, ʒɥiv] *adj* : Jewish

Juif, Juive *n* : Jew

juillet [ʒɥijɛ] *nm* : July

juin [ʒɥɛ̃] *nm* : June

juke–box [dʒukbɔks] *nm, pl* **juke–box** *or* **juke–boxes** : jukebox

jumeau, -melle [ʒymo, -mɛl] *adj & n, mpl* **jumeaux** : twin

jumeler [ʒymle] {8} *vt* : to twin, to couple

jumelles [ʒymɛl] *nfpl* : binoculars, field glasses

jument [ʒymɑ̃] *nf* : mare

jungle [ʒœ̃gl] *nf* : jungle

junior [ʒynjɔr] *adj & nmf* : junior

junte [ʒœ̃t] *nf* : junta

jupe [ʒyp] *nf* : skirt

Jupiter [ʒypitɛr] *nf* : Jupiter (planet)

jupon [ʒypɔ̃] *nm* : slip, petticoat

juré, -rée [ʒyre] *n* : juror

jurer [ʒyre] *vt* : to swear, to vow — *vi* **1** SACRER : to swear, to curse **2 ~ avec** : to clash with **3 ~ de** : to swear to <j'en jurerais : I would swear to it, I'm sure of it>

juridiction [ʒyridiksjɔ̃] *nf* : jurisdiction — **juridictionel, -nelle** [-diksjɔnɛl] *adj*

juridique [ʒyridik] *adj* LÉGAL : legal — **juridiquement** [-dikmɑ̃] *adv*

jurisprudence [ʒyrisprydɑ̃s] *nf* **1** : jurisprudence **2 faire jurisprudence** : to set a precedent

juriste [ʒyrist] *nmf* : jurist, legal expert

juron [ʒyrɔ̃] *nm* : curse, oath, expletive

jury [ʒyri] *nm* : jury

jus [ʒy] *nms & pl* **1** : juice **2** : gravy **3** *fam* : juice, electricity

jusqu'au–boutiste [ʒyskobutist] *nmf fam, pl* **jusqu'au–boutistes** : hard-liner, extremist

jusque [ʒyskə] (**jusqu'** [ʒysk] *before a vowel*) *prep* **1** *or* **jusqu'à** : up to, as far as <jusque chez moi : all the way to my house> <avoir de la boue jusqu'aux genoux : to be knee-deep in mud> <jusqu'à présent : up to now> **2** : even, as far as <des délits jusque dans les banlieues : crime even in the suburbs> **3** **jusqu'à** : until, till <jusqu'à dix-sept heures : until five o'clock> **4** **jusqu'à** : up to, as much as <jusqu'à 50 kilogrammes : not exceeding 50 kilograms> **5** **jusqu'à** : up to, to the point of <méticuleux jusqu'au perfectionnisme : careful to the point of perfectionism> **6** **jusqu'à ce que** *or* **jusqu'au moment où** : until

jusque–là [ʒyskəla] *adv* **1** : up to here, up to there **2** : up until then

justaucorps [ʒystokɔr] *nms & pl* : leotard

juste[1] [ʒyst] *adv* **1** : just, exactly <c'est juste le contraire : it's just the opposite> **2** : in tune, on key <chanter juste : to sing in tune> **3** : only, just <après juste un an : after only a year> **4** *or* **tout juste** : only just <arriver tout juste à temps : to arrive barely on time>

juste[2] *adj* **1** ÉQUITABLE : just, fair **2** EXACT : correct, accurate <l'heure juste : the exact time> **3** SERRÉ : tight **4** **à juste titre** : justly, rightly **5** **au juste** : exactly, precisely

justement [ʒystəmɑ̃] *adv* **1** EXACTEMENT : exactly, precisely **2** : correctly **3** : justifiably, justly **4** : just <il est justement parti : he just left>

justesse [ʒystɛs] *nf* **1** : accuracy **2** : aptness, soundness <avec justesse : aptly> **3** **de** ~ : just barely

justice [ʒystis] *nf* **1** : fairness, justice **2** : law, justice <être traduit en justice : to be brought before the courts> **3** **se faire justice** : to take the law into one's own hands **4** **se faire justice** : to commit suicide

justiciable [ʒystisjabl] *adj* ~ **de** : subject to, answerable to

justifiable [ʒystifjabl] *adj* DÉFENDABLE : justifiable

justificatif[1], **-tive** [ʒystifikatif, -tiv] *adj* : supporting

justificatif[2] *nm* : supporting evidence

justification [ʒustifikasjɔ̃] *nf* **1** : justification, explanation **2** : proof

justifier [ʒystifje] {96} *vt* **1** : to justify **2** : to prove — *vi* ~ **de** : to give proof of — **se justifier** *vr* : to justify oneself <se justifier d'une accusation : to clear one's name>

jute [ʒyt] *nm* : jute

juteux, -teuse [ʒytø, -tøz] *adj* : juicy

juvénile [ʒyvenil] *adj* : juvenile, youthful

juxtaposer [ʒykstapoze] *vt* : to juxtapose — **juxtaposition** [-pozisjɔ̃] *nf*

K

k [ka] *nm* : the 11th letter of the alphabet

kaki[1] [kaki] *adj* : khaki

kaki[2] *nm* **1** : khaki **2** : persimmon

kaléidoscope [kaleidɔskɔp] *nm* : kaleidoscope

kangourou [kɑ̃guru] *nm* : kangaroo

kaolin [kaɔlɛ̃] *nm* : kaolin

karaté [karate] *nm* : karate

kascher [kaʃɛr] *adj* : kosher

kayak *or* **kayac** [kajak] *nm* : kayak

kenyan, kenyane [kenjɑ̃, -jan] *adj* : Kenyan

Kenyan, Kenyane *n* : Kenyan

kermesse [kɛrmɛs] *nf* : fair, bazaar

kérosène [kerɔzɛn] *nm* : kerosene

ketchup [kɛtʃœp] *nm* : ketchup

khan [kɑ̃] *nm* : khan

kibboutz [kibuts] *nm* : kibbutz

kidnapper [kidnape] *vt* : to kidnap

kidnappeur, -peuse [kidnapœr, -pøz] *n* : kidnapper

kif–kif [kifkif] *adj fam* **c'est kif–kif** : it's all the same

kilo [kilo] *nm* : kilo

kilogramme [kilɔgram] *nm* : kilogram

kilohertz [kilɔɛrts] *nms & pl* : kilohertz

kilométrage [kilɔmetraʒ] *nm* : distance in kilometers, mileage

kilomètre [kilɔmɛtr] *nm* : kilometer

kilo–octet [kilɔɔktɛ] *nm, pl* **kilo–octets** : kilobyte

kilowatt [kilɔwat] *nm* : kilowatt

kilt [kilt] *nm* : kilt

kimono [kimɔno] *nm* : kimono

kinésithérapeute [kinesiterapœt] *nmf* : physiotherapist, physical therapist

kinésithérapie [kineziterapi] *nf* : physical therapy

kiosque [kjɔsk] *nm* **1** : (garden) pavilion **2** : kiosk, stall <kiosque à journaux : newsstand> **3** **kiosque à musique** : bandstand

kipper [kipœr] *nm* : kipper

kirsch [kirʃ] *nm* : kirsch

kiwi [kiwi] *nm* : kiwi

klaxon [klaksɔn] *nm* : horn

klaxonner [klaksɔne] *vt* : to honk, to toot — *vi* : to honk one's horn

kleptomane [klɛptɔman] *nmf* : kleptomaniac

kleptomanie [klɛptɔmani] *nf* : kleptomania

knickers [knikərs] *nmpl* : knickers

koala |kɔala| *nm* : koala
koweïtien, -tienne *adj* |kɔwɛjtjɛ̃, -tjɛn| : Kuwaiti
Koweïtien, -tienne *n* : Kuwaiti
krach |krak| *nm* : crash <krach boursier : stock-market crash>
kraft |kraft| *nm or* **papier kraft** : brown (wrapping) paper
krypton |kriptɔ̃| *nm* : krypton
kumquat |kumkwat| *nm* : kumquat
kung-fu |kuŋfu| *nm* : kung fu
kurde[1] |kyrd| *adj* : Kurdish
kurde[2] *nm* : Kurdish (language)
Kurde *nmf* : Kurd
kyrielle |kirjɛl| *nf* : whole series, long list <une kyrielle de plaintes : a string of complaints>
kyste |kist| *nm* : cyst

L

l |ɛl| *nm* : l, the 12th letter of the alphabet
l' *pron & art* → **le**
la *pron & art* → **le**
là |la| *adv* **1** (*indicating a place*) : there, here <c'est là : there it is> <je suis là : I'm here> **2** : then <à partir de là : after that, from then on> **3** (*indicating a situation or a certain point*) <c'est bien là où je voulais en venir : that's just it, that's the point> <c'est là que j'ai compris : that's when I understood> **4** (*referring to a specified person or thing*) <cette femme-là : that woman (over there)> **5 de ~** : from there, hence **6 ~ où** : where **7 par ~** : over here, this way **8 tout est là** : that's most important <la santé, tout est là : health is everything>
là-bas |laba| *adv* : over there
label |labɛl| *nm* **1** : label, mark **2** : seal, stamp <label de qualité : stamp of quality>
labeur |labœr| *nm* : toil, work
labial, -biale |labjal| *adj, mpl* **labiaux** |labjo| : labial
laboratoire |labɔratwar| *nm* : laboratory
laborieusement |labɔrjøzmɑ̃| *adv* : laboriously
laborieux, -rieuse |labɔrjø, -rjøz| *adj* **1** PÉNIBLE : laborious, arduous **2** TRAVAILLEUR : hardworking, industrious <les classes laborieuses : the working classes> **3** : labored (in style)
labour |labur| *nm* **1** : plowing **2** : plowed field
labourage |laburaʒ| *nm* : plowing
labourer |labure| *vt* **1** : to plow **2** CREUSER : to furrow, to churn up **3** LACÉRER : to dig into, to lacerate
labyrinthe |labirɛ̃t| *nm* DÉDALE : labyrinth, maze
lac |lak| *nm* : lake
lacer |lase| {6} *vt* : to lace up, to tie
lacération |laserasjɔ̃| *nf* **1** : ripping, tearing up **2** : laceration
lacérer |lasere| {87} *vt* **1** DÉCHIRER : to tear up **2** : to lacerate
lacet |lasɛ| *nm* **1** : shoelace **2** : sharp bend, curve <une route en lacets : a winding road>
lâche[1] |lɑʃ| *adj* **1** : loose, slack **2** : lax, slipshod **3** : cowardly
lâche[2] *nmf* POLTRON : coward
lâchement |lɑʃmɑ̃| *adv* **1** : loosely **2** : in a cowardly way
lâcher |lɑʃe| *vt* **1** RELÂCHER : to slacken, to loosen **2** : to let go <lâche-moi! : let me go!> **3** : to let out, to come out with **4** *fam* : to drop out of (school) **5** *fam* : to leave, to drop (someone) — *vi* **1** : to give way **2** : to fail (of brakes)
lâcheté |lɑʃte| *nf* **1** COUARDISE : cowardice **2** BASSESSE : baseness **3** : cowardly act
lâcheur, -cheuse |lɑʃœr, -ʃøz| *n fam* : quitter, unreliable person
lacis |lasi| *nms & pl* **1** : maze, tangle **2** : network (of veins, etc.)
laconique |lakɔnik| *adj* : laconic, terse — **laconiquement** |-nikmɑ̃| *adv*
lacrymogène |lakrimɔʒɛn| *adj* : tear-inducing <gaz lacrymogène : tear gas>
lactation |laktasjɔ̃| *nf* : lactation
lacté, -tée |lakte| *adj* **1** : milk, milky **2** → **voie**
lactique |laktik| *adj* : lactic
lacune |lakyn| *nf* : lacuna, gap
lacustre |lakystr| *adj* : lake, lakeside
là-dedans |laddɑ̃| *adv* : in here, in there
là-dessous |ladsu| *adv* : under here, under there
là-dessus |ladsy| *adv* **1** : on here, on there **2** : about it, on it <il n'y a aucun doute là-dessus : there's no doubt about it> **3** : with that, at that point <il est parti là-dessus : with that, he left>
ladite |ladit| → **ledit**
ladre |ladr| *adj* : stingy, miserly
ladrerie |ladrəri| *nf* : miserliness, avarice
lagon |lagɔ̃| *nm* : (coral reef) lagoon
lagune |lagyn| *nf* : lagoon
là-haut |lao| *adv* **1** : up there **2** : upstairs
lai |lɛ| *nm* : lay, ballad
laïc |laik| *nm* **les laïcs** : the laity
laîche |lɛʃ| *nf* : sedge
laid, laide |lɛ, lɛd| *adj* **1** : ugly **2** : mean, rude

laideron [lɛdrɔ̃] *nm* : ugly girl

laideur [lɛdœr] *nf* **1** : ugliness **2** : meanness

lainage [lɛnaʒ] *nm* **1** : woolen fabric **2** : woolen garment

laine [lɛn] *nf* **1** : wool <laine peignée : worsted wool> **2 laine d'acier** *Can* : scouring pad, steel wool

laineux, -neuse [lɛnø, -nøz] *adj* : woolly

laïque[1] [laik] *adj* : lay, secular

laïque[2] *nmf* : layman, laywoman

laisse [lɛs] *nf* : lead, leash

laissé–pour–compte, laissée–pour–compte [lesepurkɔ̃t] *adj, pl* **laissés–pour–compte, laissées–pour–compte 1** : returned unsold **2** : rejected (of a person)

laisser [lɛse] *vt* **1** : to leave <laisser un pourboire : to leave a tip> <laissez la porte ouverte : leave the door open> **2** OUBLIER : to leave, to forget <j'ai laissé mes gants au bureau : I left my gloves at the office> **3** QUITTER : to leave, to abandon <elle a laissé son mari : she left her husband> **4** ACCORDER : to give <laisse-lui du temps : give him some time> — *v aux* **1** : to let, to allow <ne laissez rien voir : let nothing show> **2 laisse faire!** : never mind!, let it go! — **se laisser** *vr* **1** : to let oneself <il ne se laisse pas faire : he won't be pushed around> **2 se laisser aller** : to let oneself go

laisser–aller [lɛseale] *nms & pl* : carelessness, sloppiness

laisser–faire [lɛsefɛr] *nms & pl* : laissez-faire, noninterference

laissez–passer [lɛsepase] *nms & pl* : pass, permit

lait [lɛ] *nm* **1** : milk <lait concentré *or* lait condensé : condensed milk> <lait entier : whole milk> <lait écrémé : skim milk> <lait demi-écrémé : lowfat milk> **2 lait de poule** : eggnog

laiterie [lɛtri] *nf* **1** : dairy industry **2** : dairy

laiteux, -teuse [lɛtø, -tøz] *adj* : milky <peau laiteuse : milky skin>

laitier[1], **-tière** [lɛtje, -tjɛr] *adj* : dairy

laitier[2], **-tière** *n* **1** : milkman **2** : dairyman, dairymaid *f*

laiton [lɛtɔ̃] *nm* : brass

laitue [lety] *nf* : lettuce

laïus [lajys] *nms & pl fam* : spiel, speech

lama [lama] *nm* **1** : lama <le Grand Lama : the Dalai Lama> **2** : llama

lambeau [lɑ̃bo] *nm, pl* **lambeaux 1** GUENILLE : rag, scrap, shred <tomber en lambeaux : to fall to pieces> **2** : bit, fragment

lambiner [lɑ̃bine] *vi fam* : to dawdle

lambineux, -neuse [lɑ̃binœr, -nøz] *n Can fam* : slowpoke

lambrequin [lɑ̃brəkɛ̃] *nm* : valance (of a bed)

lambris [lɑ̃bri] *nms & pl* : paneling, wainscoting

lambrisser [lɑ̃brise] *vt* : to panel

lame [lam] *nf* **1** : strip, slat, lath **2** : blade <lame de rasoir : razor blade> **3** : sword **4** : wave <lame de fond : groundswell>

lamé [lame] *nm* : lamé

lamelle [lamɛl] *nf* **1** : small strip, sliver **2** : gill (of a mushroom) **3** : flake (of rock, etc.) **4** : slide (for a microscope)

lamentable [lamɑ̃tabl] *adj* **1** DÉPLORABLE : deplorable, lamentable **2** PITOYABLE : pitiful, pathetic — **lamentablement** [-tabləmɑ̃] *adv*

lamentation [lamɑ̃tasjɔ̃] *nf* **1** : lamentation, wailing **2** : whining, complaining

lamenter [lamɑ̃te] *v* **se lamenter** *vr* : to lament, to moan

laminer [lamine] *vt* **1** : to laminate **2** : to wipe out, to decimate

lampadaire [lɑ̃padɛr] *nm* **1** : floor lamp **2** : streetlight

lampe [lɑ̃p] *nf* **1** : lamp **2 lampe à souder** : blowtorch **3 lampe de poche** : flashlight

lampée [lɑ̃pe] *nf fam* : swig, gulp

lamper [lɑ̃pe] *vt* : to gulp down

lampion [lɑ̃pjɔ̃] *nm* : Chinese lantern

lamproie [lɑ̃prwa] *nf* : lamprey

lance [lɑ̃s] *nf* **1** : spear, lance **2** *or* **lance à eau** : hose <lance d'incendie : fire hose>

lancée [lɑ̃se] *nf* : momentum <continuer sur sa lancée : to keep on going, to forge ahead>

lance–flammes [lɑ̃sflam] *nms & pl* : flamethrower

lancement [lɑ̃smɑ̃] *nm* **1** : throwing **2** : launching, liftoff <base de lancement : launching site>

lance–missiles [lɑ̃smisil] *nms & pl* : missile launcher

lance–pierres [lɑ̃spjɛr] *nms & pl* : slingshot

lancer[1] [lɑ̃se] {6} *vt* **1** : to throw, to hurl **2** : to launch **3** : to issue, to put out <lancer un appel au calme : to issue an appeal for calm> **4** : to start up, to get going — **se lancer** *vr* **1** : to throw oneself, to jump **2** : to hurl at each other, to exchange (insults, etc.) **3 ~ dans** : to take up, to embark on

lancer[2] *nm* **1** : throw, toss <lancer de poids : shotput> **2** : casting, rod-and-reel fishing

lancette [lɑ̃sɛt] *nf* : lancet

lanceur, -ceuse [lɑ̃sœr, -søz] *n* **1** : thrower, pitcher (in baseball) **2** : promoter

lancinant, -nante [lɑ̃sinɑ̃, -nɑ̃t] *adj* **1** : shooting, throbbing **2** : haunting **3** : insistent, nagging

lanciner [lɑ̃sine] *vi* : to throb — *vt* **1** OBSÉDER : to haunt, to obsess **2** TOURMENTER : to torment

landau [lɑ̃do] *nm France* : baby carriage

lande [lɑ̃d] *nf* : moor

langage |lɑ̃gaʒ| *nm* : language <le langage des signes : sign language> <langage machine : machine language>
langagier, -gière |lɑ̃gaʒje, -ʒjɛr| *adj* LINGUISTIQUE : linguistic
lange |lɑ̃ʒ| *nm* **1** : baby blanket **2 être dans les langes** : to be in (its) infancy
langoureux, -reuse |lɑ̃gurø, -røz| *adj* : languorous — **langoureusement** |-røzmɑ̃| *adv*
langouste |lɑ̃gust| *nf* : crayfish, spiny lobster
langoustine |lɑ̃gustin| *nf* : langoustine, prawn
langue |lɑ̃g| *nf* **1** : tongue <tirer la langue : to stick out one's tongue> <donner sa langue au chat : to give up (guessing)> **2** : language <langue maternelle : native language, mother tongue> <de langue française : French-speaking> <langue vivante : modern language>
languette |lɑ̃gɛt| *nf* **1** : tongue (of a shoe) **2** : strip
langueur |lɑ̃gœr| *nf* : languor, languidness
languir |lɑ̃gir| *vi* **1** : to languish, to pine **2** : to flag, to wilt
languissant, -sante |lɑ̃gisɑ̃, -sɑ̃t| *adj* **1** : languid, listless **2** : dull, tiresome **3** : lovesick
lanière |lanjɛr| *nf* : strap, lash, thong
lanoline |lanɔlin| *nf* : lanolin
lanterne |lɑ̃tɛrn| *nf* **1** : lantern **2** : parking light **3 lanterne magique** : magic lantern
laotien, -tienne |laosjɛ̃, -sjɛn| *adj* : Laotian
Laotien, -tienne *n* : Laotian
laper |lape| *vt* : to lap up
lapidaire |lapidɛr| *adj* **1** : lapidary **2** : terse, pithy
lapider |lapide| *vt* : to stone
lapin, -pine |lapɛ̃, -pin| *n* **1** : rabbit **2 poser un lapin à qqn** : to stand s.o. up
lapon[1], -pone *or* **-ponne** |lapɔ̃, -pɔn| *adj* : Lappish
lapon[2] *nm* : Lapp, Lappish (language)
Lapon, -pone *or* **-ponne** *n* : Lapp
laps |laps| *nms & pl* : lapse (of time)
lapsus |lapsys| *nms & pl* : slip, error
laquais |lakɛ| *nms & pl* : lackey, footman
laque[1] |lak| *nm* : lacquer, lacquerware
laque[2] *nf* **1** VERNIS : lacquer, shellac **2** : hair spray
laquelle → **lequel**
laquer |lake| *vt* : to lacquer, to shellac
larbin |larbɛ̃| *nm fam* : flunkey, toady
larcin |larsɛ̃| *nm* **1** : petty theft **2** : booty, spoils *pl*
lard |lar| *nm* **1** : fat, lard **2** : bacon **3 faire du lard** *fam* : to put on weight
large[1] |larʒ| *adv* : on a large scale, generously <prévoir large : to allow a bit extra>
large[2] *adj* **1** : wide, broad **2** : considerable, extensive <dans une large mesure : to a large extent> **3** : loose-fitting **4** : generous **5 être large d'idées** : to be broad-minded
large[3] *nm* **1** LARGEUR : width, breadth <10 mètres de large : 10 meters wide> **2 le large** : the open sea
largement |larʒəmɑ̃| *adv* **1** : widely **2** : greatly, by far **3** : generously, lavishly **4** : easily, at least
largesse |larʒɛs| *nf* **1** GÉNÉROSITÉ : generosity **2 largesses** *nfpl* : gifts
largeur |larʒœr| *nf* **1** : width, breadth **2** OUVERTURE : openness <largeur d'esprit : broad-mindedness>
larguer |large| *vt* **1** : to release, to drop **2** *fam* PLAQUER : to ditch, to get rid of
larme |larm| *nf* **1** : tear <elle pleurait à chaudes larmes : she was crying her eyes out> **2** *fam* : small quantity, drop <une larme de vin : a drop of wine>
larmoyant, -moyante |larmwajɑ̃, -mwajɑ̃t| *adj* : tearful
larmoyer |larmwaje| {58} *vi* **1** : to water (of eyes) **2** : to whine, to whimper
larron |larɔ̃| *nm* : bandit, thief
larvaire |larvɛr| *adj* : larval
larve |larv| *nf* **1** : larva **2** *fam* : wimp, lazybones
larvé, -vée |larve| *adj* : latent
laryngite |larɛ̃ʒit| *nf* : laryngitis
larynx |larɛ̃ks| *nms & pl* : larynx
las, lasse |la, las| *adj* **1** FATIGUÉ : weary, tired **2 ~ de** : sick and tired of
lasagne |lazaɲ| *nf* : lasagna
lascif, -cive |lasif, -siv| *adj* : lascivious — **lascivement** |-sivmɑ̃| *adv*
lascivité |lasivite| *nf* : lasciviousness, lechery
laser |lazɛr| *nm* **1** : laser **2 disque laser** : laser disc, optical disc
lassant, -sante |lasɑ̃, -sɑ̃t| *adj* : wearisome, tiresome, tedious
lasser |lase| *vt* **1** : to weary, to tire out **2** ENNUYER : to bore, to try the patience of — **se lasser** *vr* **~ de** : to grow weary of
lassitude |lasityd| *nf* : weariness, lassitude
lasso |laso| *nm* : lasso, lariat
latence |latɑ̃s| *nf* : latency
latent, -tente |latɑ̃, -tɑ̃t| *adj* : latent
latéral, -rale |lateral| *adj, mpl* **-raux** |-ro| : side, lateral
latéralement |lateralmɑ̃| *adv* : laterally, sideways
latex |latɛks| *nms & pl* : latex
latin[1], -tine |latɛ̃, -tin| *adj* : Latin
latin[2] *nm* : Latin (language)
latino-américain, -caine |latinoamerikɛ̃, -kɛn| *adj* : Latin-American
Latino-Américain, -caine *n* : Latin American
latitude |latityd| *nf* **1** : latitude **2** : scope, freedom <je lui laissais toute latitude : I gave him all the room he needed>
latrines |latrin| *nfpl* : latrine

latte [lat] *nf* **1** : lath **2** : floorboard

lauréat, -réate [lɔrea, -reat] *n* : prizewinner

laurier [lɔrje] *nm* **1** : laurel <feuille de laurier : bay leaf> **2 lauriers** *nmpl* : laurels <reposer sur ses lauriers : to rest on one's laurels>

laurier–rose [lɔrjeroz] *nm, pl* **lauriers–roses** : oleander

lavable [lavabl] *adj* : washable

lavabo [lavabo] *nm* **1** : washbowl, (bathroom) sink **2 lavabos** *nmpl France* : toilets, washroom

lavage [lavaʒ] *nm* **1** : washing **2** : wash <mets tes chaussettes au lavage : put your socks in the wash> **3 lavage de cerveau** : brainwashing

lavande [lavɑ̃d] *nf* : lavender

lave [lav] *nf* : lava

lave–auto [lavɔto] *nm Can, pl* **lave–autos** : car wash

lave–glace [lavglas] *nm, pl* **lave–glaces** : windshield washer

lave–linge [lavlɛ̃ʒ] *nms & pl France* : washing machine

lavement [lavmɑ̃] *nm* : enema

laver [lave] *vt* **1** : to wash <laver la vaisselle : to do the dishes> <machine à laver : washing machine> **2** : to clear (one's conscience, someone's name, etc.) — **se laver** *vr* **1** : to wash oneself <se laver les mains : to wash one's hands> **2** SE DISCULPER : to vindicate oneself

laverie [lavri] *nf* : self-service laundry

lavette [lavɛt] *nf* **1** : dishcloth **2** *Can* : small mop or brush for washing dishes **3** *fam* : wimp, drip

laveur, -veuse [lavœr, -vøz] *n* : washer, cleaner <laveur de vitres : window washer>

laveuse *nf Can* : washing machine

lave–vaisselle [lavvesɛl] *nms & pl* : dishwasher

lavoir [lavwar] *nm Can* : self-service laundry

laxatif [laksatif] *nm* : laxative

laxisme [laksism] *nm* : laxity

le[1], **la** [lə, la] (**l'** [l] *before a vowel or mute h*) *pron, pl* **les** [le] **1** (*used as a direct object*) : him, her, it, them <je ne la connais pas : I don't know her> <il le mérite : he deserves it> <les voilà! : there they are!> **2** (*indicating a state or condition*) <elles le lui avaient bien dit : they told him so> <hier il n'était pas content, maintenant il l'est : he wasn't satisfied yesterday, (but) now he is>

le[2], **la** (**l'** *before a vowel or mute h*) *art, pl* **les 1** : the <le gateau est sur la table : the cake is on the table> <les enfants : the children> **2** (*used with abstract nouns and geographical names*) <la liberté : freedom> <le Canada : Canada> **3** (*used with parts of the body*) <avec un chapeau sur la tête : with a hat on his/her head> <se laver les dents : to brush one's teeth> **4** (*used with expressions of time*) <le 19 juin : June 19th> <je travaille le matin : I work mornings> **5** : a, an, per <trois fois la semaine : three times a week> <20 dollars l'once : 20 dollars an ounce> **6** (*used in exclamations*) <la belle fête! : (what) a lovely party!>

leader [lidœr] *nm* : leader

lécher [leʃe] {87} *vt* **1** : to lick **2** : to lap up **3** : to lick at, to wash up against **4** *fam* : to polish up (a text, etc.) — **se lécher** *vr* : to lick (one's fingers, etc.)

lèche–vitrines [lɛʃvitrin] *nms & pl* : window-shopping <faire du lèche-vitrines : to window-shop>

leçon [ləsɔ̃] *nf* **1** : schoolwork **2** COURS : lesson, class <prendre des leçons de piano : to take piano lessons> **3** ENSEIGNEMENT : lesson, lecture <il m'a fait la leçon : he gave me a lecture> <j'en ai tiré une leçon : I learned a lesson from it>

lecteur[1], **-trice** [lɛktœr, -tris] *n* : reader

lecteur[2] *nm* **1** : player <lecteur de CD : CD player> **2** : drive <lecteur de disquettes : disk drive> **3** : reader <lecteur de microfiches : microfiche reader>

lectorat [lɛktɔra] *nm* : readership

lecture [lɛktyr] *nf* **1** : reading **2 lecture sur les lèvres** : lipreading

ledit, ladite [lədi, ladit] *adj, pl* **lesdits, lesdites** [ledi, ledit] : the aforementioned, the aforesaid

légal, -gale [legal] *adj, mpl* **légaux** [lego] : legal, lawful — **légalement** [-galmɑ̃] *adv*

légaliser [legalize] *vt* **1** : to legalize **2** : to authenticate — **légalisation** [-lizasjɔ̃] *nf*

légalité [legalite] *nf* : legality, lawfulness

légat [lega] *nm* : legate

légation [legasjɔ̃] *nf* : legation

légendaire [leʒɑ̃dɛr] *adj* : legendary

légende [leʒɑ̃d] *nf* **1** : legend, story **2** : caption (of an illustration) **3** : key, legend (of a map, etc.)

léger, -gère [leʒe, -ʒɛr] *adj* **1** : light <légère comme une plume : light as a feather> <d'un cœur léger : with a light heart> <un repas léger : a light meal> **2** : slight, faint, weak <une légère augmentation : a slight increase> **3** : flimsy, superficial, frivolous <parler à la légère : to speak thoughtlessly> **4** : loose, lax, flighty <une femme légère : a loose woman>

légèrement [leʒɛrmɑ̃] *adv* **1** : lightly **2** : slightly **3** : thoughtlessly, rashly

légèreté [leʒɛrte] *nf* **1** : lightness **2** DÉSINVOLTURE : thoughtlessness, casualness

légiférer [leʒifere] {87} *vi* : to legislate

légion [leʒjɔ̃] *nf* : legion

légionnaire [leʒjɔnɛr] *nm* : legionary, legionnaire

législateur, -trice [leʒislatœr, -tris] *n* : legislator, lawmaker

législatif[1], -tive [leʒislatif, -tiv] *adj* : legislative

législatif[2] *nm* : legislature, legislative body

législation [leʒislasjɔ̃] *nf* : legislation

législature [leʒislatyr] *nf* **1** : term (of office) **2** : legislature

légiste[1] [leʒist] *adj* → **médecin**

légiste[2] *nm* : jurist

légitime [leʒitim] *adj* **1** LÉGAL : lawful **2** : legitimate, justifiable **3** : just, fair **4 légitime défense** : self-defense

légitimement [leʒitimmɑ̃] *adv* : legitimately

légitimer [leʒitime] *vt* **1** : to legitimize **2** JUSTIFIER : to justify

légitimité [leʒitimite] *nf* **1** : legitimacy **2** : fairness

legs [lɛg] *nms & pl* : legacy, bequest

léguer [lege] {87} *vt* **1** : to bequeath **2** TRANSMETTRE : to pass on

légume[1] [legym] *nm* : vegetable <légumes verts : green vegetables>

légume[2] *nf fam* **grosse légume** : bigwig

légumier [legymje] *nm* : vegetable dish

légumineuse [legyminøz] *nf* : legume, leguminous plant

lemming [lɛmiŋ] *nm* : lemming

lendemain [lɑ̃dmɛ̃] *nm* **1** : next day <le lendemain matin : the next morning> **2 au lendemain de** : just after, following **3 du jour au lendemain** : in a very short time, overnight **4 le lendemain** : the future <des lendemains heureux : happy days ahead> <sans lendemain : short-lived> **5 lendemains** *nmpl* : consequences, outcome

lénifiant, -fiante [lenifjɑ̃, -fjɑ̃t] *adj* : soothing

lent, lente [lɑ̃, lɑ̃t] *adj* : slow — **lentement** [lɑ̃tmɑ̃] *adv*

lente [lɑ̃t] *nm* : nit

lenteur [lɑ̃tœr] *nf* : slowness <avec lenteur : slowly> <lenteurs bureaucratiques : bureaucratic delays>

lentille [lɑ̃tij] *nf* **1** : lentil **2** : lens <lentilles cornéennes : contact lenses>

léonin, -nine [leɔnɛ̃, -nin] *adj* **1** : leonine **2** : one-sided, unfair, inequitable

léopard [leɔpar] *nm* : leopard

lèpre [lɛpr] *nf* : leprosy

lépreux[1], -preuse [leprø, -prøz] *adj* **1** : leprous **2** : flaking, peeling

lépreux[2], -preuse *n* : leper

lequel, laquelle [ləkɛl, lakɛl] *pron, pl* **lesquels, lesquelles** [lekɛl] (*with* **à** *and* **de** *contracted to* **auquel, auxquels, auxquelles; duquel, desquels, desquelles**) **1** : which <la réunion à laquelle il était convié : the meeting to which he was invited > <le compromis auquel il est parvenu : the compromise he reached> **2** : which one <lequel préférez-vous? : which one do you prefer?> **3** : who, whom <un de ses amis avec lequel il joue au tennis : one of his friends with whom he plays tennis>

les → **le**

lesbianisme [lɛsbjanism] *nm* : lesbianism

lesbienne [lɛsbjɛn] *nf* : lesbian

lesdits, lesdites → **ledit**

léser [leze] {87} *vt* **1** : to wrong **2** BLESSER : to injure

lésiner [lezine] *vi* **~ sur** : to skimp on, to be stingy with

lésion [lezjɔ̃] *nf* : lesion

lesquels, lesquelles → **lequel**

lessivage [lɛsivaʒ] *nm* : washing

lessive [lɛsiv] *nf* **1** LAVAGE : washing, wash <faire la lessive : to do the wash> **2** DÉTERGENT : detergent **3** : lye

lessiver [lɛsive] *vt* **1** : to wash, to scrub **2** : to leach **3 être lessivé** *fam* : to be washed out, to be exhausted **4 se faire lessiver** *fam* : to be cleaned out (in a card game, etc.)

lest [lɛst] *nm* **1** : ballast **2 lâcher du lest** : to make concessions

leste [lɛst] *adj* **1** AGILE : nimble, agile **2** : coarse, risqué

lestement [lɛstəmɑ̃] *adv* : nimbly, agilely

lester [lɛste] *vt* **1** : to ballast, to weight **2** *fam* : to stuff, to cram

létal, -tale [letal] *adj, mpl* **létaux** [-to] : lethal

léthargie [letarʒi] *nf* : lethargy <tomber en léthargie : to become lethargic>

léthargique [letarʒik] *adj* : sluggish, lethargic

letton[1], -tonne [lɛtɔ̃, -tɔn] *adj* : Latvian

letton[2] *nm* : Latvian (language)

Letton, -tonne *n* : Latvian

lettre [lɛtr] *nf* **1** : letter (of the alphabet) <en toutes lettres : in words, written out> **2** : letter <lettre d'amour : love letter> **3 lettres** *nfpl* : arts, humanities **4 à la lettre** : to the letter, exactly

lettré, -trée [lɛtre] *adj* : well-read

leucémie [løsemi] *nf* : leukemia

leur[1] [lœr] *adj, pl* **leurs** : their <leur mère et leur père : their mother and father>

leur[2] *pron, pl* **leurs 1** : to them <nous leur donnerons le livre : we will give them the book> **2 le leur, la leur, les leurs** : theirs

leurre [lœr] *nm* **1** APPÂT : lure, bait **2** ILLUSION, TROMPERIE : deception, delusion

leurrer [lœre] *vt* TROMPER : to deceive, to delude — **se leurrer** *vr*

levain [ləvɛ̃] *nm* : leaven <sans levain : unleavened>

levant [ləvɑ̃] *adj m* **au soleil levant** : at sunrise

levé, -vée [ləve] *adj* **1** : up <voilà trois heures que je suis levé : I've been up for three hours> **2** : raised <voter à main levée : to vote by a show of hands>

levée [ləve] *nf* **1** : lifting, suspension **2** : collection <levée du courrier : mail pickup> **3** : levying (of troops or taxes) **4** : levee

lever[1] [ləve] {52} *vt* **1** : to raise <lever la main : to put up one's hand> **2** : to lift, to raise (an object) <lever les fenêtres : to raise the windows> <lever les filets : to haul up nets> **3** : to suspend, to end <lever une interdiction : to lift a ban> <elle a levé la séance : she closed the meeting> **4** : to levy (taxes), to raise (funds) **5** : to get (someone) out of bed **6** : to flush (game) **7** : to levy (troops) — *vi* **1** : to come up (of plants) **2** : to rise (in cooking) — **se lever** *vr* **1** : to get up <se lever tôt : to get up early> **2** : to stand up **3** : to rise (of the sun), to become light <le soleil se lève : the sun is rising> <le jour se lève : day is breaking> **4** : to clear up <l'orage s'est levé : the storm lifted>

lever[2] [ləve] *nm* **1** : rising, rise <le lever du jour : daybreak> <au lever du soleil : at sunrise> **2** (*referring to persons*) <au lever : on getting up (from bed)> **3 lever de rideau** : curtain, curtain-raising (in theater)

levier [ləvje] *nm* **1** : lever **2 levier de vitesse** : gearshift

lèvre [lɛvr] *nf* **1** : lip <du bout des lèvres : reluctantly, half-heartedly> <être suspendu aux lèvres de qqn : to hang on s.o.'s every word> **2** : edge, rim, lip (in geology)

lévrier [levrije] *nm* : greyhound

levure [ləvyr] *nf* **1** : yeast **2 levure chimique** : baking powder

lexicographe [lɛksikɔgraf] *nmf* : lexicographer

lexicographie [lɛksikɔgrafi] *nf* : lexicography — **lexicographique** [-grafik] *adj*

lexique [lɛksik] *nm* **1** : vocabulary, glossary **2** : lexicon

lézard [lezar] *nm* : lizard

lézarde [lezard] *nf* FISSURE : crack

lézarder [lezarde] *vt* : to crack — *vi fam* : to bask in the sun — **se lézarder** *vr* : to crack

liaison [ljɛzɔ̃] *nf* **1** : (logical) connection **2** : link <liaison satellite : satellite link> **3** : contact <établir une liaison : to establish contact> **4** AVENTURE : love affair **5** : liaison (in linguistics)

liant, liante [ljɑ̃, ljɑ̃t] *adj* AFFABLE : sociable

liard [ljar] *nm Can* : cottonwood (tree)

liasse [ljas] *nf* : bundle, wad <liasse d'argent : roll of bills>

libanais, -naise [libanɛ, -nɛz] *adj* : Lebanese

Libanais, -naise *n* : Lebanese

libelle [libɛl] *nm* : lampoon

libellé [libele] *nm* : wording (of a document)

libeller [libele] *vt* **1** : to word **2** : to draw up **3** : to make out (a check or money order)

libellule [libelyl] *nf* : dragonfly

libéral, -rale [liberal] *adj & n, mpl* **-raux** [-ro] : liberal — **libéralement** [-ralmɑ̃] *adv*

libéraliser [liberalize] *vt* : to liberalize — **libéralisation** [-lizasjɔ̃] *nf*

libéralisme [liberalism] *nm* : liberalism

libéralité [liberalite] *nf* : liberality, generosity

libérateur[1], **-trice** [liberatœr, -tris] *adj* : liberating

libérateur[2], **-trice** *n* : liberator

libération [liberasjɔ̃] *nf* **1** : freeing, releasing <libération conditionnelle : release on parole> **2** : liberation <libération de la femme : women's liberation>

libéré, -rée [libere] *adj* **1** : liberated **2 ~ de** : free from

libérer [libere] {87} *vt* **1** : to free, to release **2** : to liberate (a country, etc.) **3** : to relieve **4** : to deregulate

libérien, -rienne [liberjɛ̃, -rjɛn] *adj* : Liberian

Libérien, -rienne *n* : Liberian

liberté [libɛrte] *nf* **1** : freedom, liberty <liberté de la presse : freedom of the press> <en liberté conditionnelle : on probation> <mettre en liberté : to set free> **2 libertés** *nfpl* : liberties <prendre des libertés : to take liberties>

libertin[1], **-tine** [libɛrtɛ̃, -tin] *adj* : dissolute, licentious

libertin[2], **-tine** *n* : libertine

libidineux, -neuse [libidinø, -nøz] *adj* : lustful, lewd

libido [libido] *nf* : libido

libraire [librɛr] *nmf* : bookseller

librairie [librɛri] *nf* : bookstore

libre [libr] *adj* **1** : free <un pays libre : a free country> <libre de soucis : free from care> **2** : free (and easy), open <une manière libre : an easygoing manner> **3** DISPONIBLE : available, unoccupied <il y a deux chambres libres : there are two rooms available> <avoir du temps libre : to have some spare time> **4** DÉGAGÉ : clear, free <avoir les mains libres : to have one's hands free> <la voie est libre : the coast is clear> **5 libre arbitre** : free will

libre–échange [libreʃɑ̃ʒ] *nm, pl* **libres–échanges** [librəzeʃɑ̃ʒ] : free trade

librement [librəmɑ̃] *adv* : freely

libre–service [librəsɛrvis] *nm, pl* **libres–services** **1** : self-service **2** : self-service store or restaurant

libyen, libyenne [libjɛ̃, libjɛn] *adj* : Libyan

Libyen, Libyenne *n* : Libyan

lice [lis] *nf* **entrer en lice** : to join in the fray, to be in the running

licence [lisɑ̃s] *nf* **1** : degree <licence ès lettres : bachelor of arts degree> **2** : license, permit **3** : license, freedom <licence poétique : poetic license>

licencié, -ciée [lisɑ̃sje] *n* **1** : (university) graduate <licencié de sciences : bachelor of science> **2** : permit holder, licensed vendor

licenciement [lisɑ̃simɑ̃] *nm* RENVOI : layoff, dismissal

licencier [lisɑ̃sje] {96} *vt* CONGÉDIER : to lay off, to dismiss

licencieux, -cieuse [lisɑ̃sjø, -sjøz] *adj* : licentious — **licencieusement** [-sjøzmɑ̃] *adv*

lichen [likɛn] *nm* : lichen

lichette [liʃɛt] *nf fam* : sliver, smidgin

licite [lisit] *adj* : lawful, licit

licorne [likɔrn] *nf* : unicorn

licou [liku] *nm* : halter (for an animal)

lie [li] *nf* **1** : sediment, lees *pl* **2 la lie de la société** : the dregs of society

lie–de–vin [lidvɛ̃] *adj s & pl* : wine-colored

liège [ljɛʒ] *nm* : cork (substance)

lien [ljɛ̃] *nm* **1** ATTACHE : bond, attachment **2** RAPPORT : link, connection **3** RELATION : tie, relationship <liens de parenté : family ties> <les liens d'amitié : the bonds of friendship>

lier [lje] {96} *vt* **1** : to bind, to tie up **2** RELIER : to link up, to join up **3** : to strike up (a friendship, etc.) **4** : to thicken (in cooking) — **se lier** *vr* **~ avec** : to become friends with

lierre [ljɛr] *nm* : ivy

liesse [ljɛs] *nf* : jubilation <être en liesse : to be jubilant>

lieu [ljø] *nm, pl* **lieux** **1** ENDROIT : place <lieu de naissance : birthplace> **2 au lieu de** : instead of **3 avoir lieu** : to take place <le spectacle aura lieu ce soir : the show is tonight> **4 avoir lieu de** : to have grounds to, to have every reason to **5 en premier lieu** : in the first place **6 lieu commun** : commonplace **7 tenir lieu de** : to serve as **8 lieux** *nmpl* : premises

lieu–dit *or* **lieudit** [ljødi] *nm, pl* **lieux–dits** *or* **lieudits** : locality

lieue [ljø] *nf* : league (measure of distance)

lieutenant [ljøtnɑ̃] *nm* : lieutenant

lieutenant–colonel [ljøtnɑ̃kɔlɔnɛl] *nm, pl* **lieutenants–colonels** : lieutenant colonel

lièvre [ljɛvr] *nm* : hare

lift [lift] *nm Can fam* : lift, ride

lifting [liftiŋ] *nm* : face-lift

ligament [ligamɑ̃] *nm* : ligament

ligature [ligatyr] *nf* : ligature

ligne [liɲ] *nf* **1** : line <ligne pointillée : dotted line> <en ligne droite : in a straight line> **2** : line, route <ligne de métro : subway line> <ligne d'autobus : bus route> **3** : telephone line, electric line, cable <la ligne est occupée : the line is busy> **4** : range, row <se mettre en ligne : to get into line, to line up> **5** : figure, shape <elle surveille sa ligne : she watches her weight> **6** : line, orientation <ligne de conduite : line of conduct> <grandes lignes : broad outlines> **7** : line (of products) **8 en ~** : online (in computers) **9 lignes** *nfpl Can* : border (between the United States and Canada)

lignée [liɲe] *nf* **1** POSTÉRITÉ : descendants *pl* **2** : line, lineage **3** : tradition

ligneux, -neuse [liɲø, -ɲøz] *adj* : woody (of plants)

lignite [liɲit] *nm* : lignite

ligoter [ligɔte] *vt* GARROTTER : to tie up

ligue [lig] *nf* : league, alliance

liguer [lige] *v* **se liguer** *vr* **1** : to join forces **2 ~ contre** : to conspire against, to gang up on

lilas [lila] *nms & pl* : lilac

limace [limas] *nf* : slug (mollusk)

limbes [lɛ̃b] *nmpl* **1** : limbo **2** : uncertainty <tout était dans les limbes : everything was up in the air>

lime [lim] *nf* : file <lime à ongles : nail file>

limer [lime] *vt* : to file — **se limer** *vr* **se limer les ongles** : to file one's nails

limier [limje] *nm* **1** : bloodhound **2** *or* **fin limier** *fam* : sleuth

limitatif, -tive [limitatif, -tiv] *adj* : restrictive, limiting

limitation [limitasjɔ̃] *nf* : limitation, restriction <limitation de temps : time limit> <limitation des naissances : birth control>

limite[1] [limit] *adj* **1 cas limite** : borderline case **2 date limite** : deadline **3 vitesse limite** : speed limit

limite[2] *nf* **1** : border, boundary **2** : limit <limite d'âge : age limit> <sans limites : limitless, boundless> <à la limite de : on the verge of> <dans les limites de : within the limits of> **3 limites** *nfpl* : limitations

limité, -tée [limite] *adj* : limited

limiter [limite] *vt* **1** BORNER : to bound **2** RESTREINDRE : to limit, to restrict — **se limiter** *vr* **1** : to limit oneself **2 ~ à** : to be limited to, to be restricted to

limitrophe [limitrɔf] *adj* : bordering, adjoining

limogeage [limɔʒaʒ] *nm* : dismissal

limoger [limɔʒe] {17} *vt* : to dismiss

limon [limɔ̃] *nm* : silt

limonade [limɔnad] *nf* : lemonade

limousine [limuzin] *nf* : limousine

limpide [lɛ̃pid] *adj* **1** : limpid **2** : lucid, clear

limpidité |lɛ̃pidite| *nf* **1** : limpidity **2** : lucidity, clearness
lin |lɛ̃| *nm* **1** : flax <huile de lin : linseed oil> **2** : linen
linceul |lɛ̃sœl| *nm* : shroud
linéaire |lineɛr| *adj* : linear
linéaments |lineamɑ̃| *nmpl* : lineaments
linge |lɛ̃ʒ| *nm* **1** : linen <linge de maison : household linen(s)> **2** : wash, washing **3** : cloth <un linge doux : a soft cloth> <linge à vaisselle *Can* : dishcloth> **4** : underwear **5** *Can fam* : clothes *pl*, clothing
lingerie |lɛ̃ʒri| *nf* **1** : lingerie **2** *Can* : linen closet
lingot |lɛ̃go| *nm* : ingot
linguiste |lɛ̃gɥist| *nmf* : linguist
linguistique[1] |lɛ̃gɥistik| *adj* : linguistic
linguistique[2] *nf* : linguistics
liniment |linimɑ̃| *nm* : liniment
linoléum |linɔleɔm| *nm* : linoleum
linteau |lɛ̃to| *nm, pl* **linteaux** : lintel
lion, lionne |ljɔ̃, ljɔn| *n* : lion, lioness *f*
Lion *nm* : Leo
lionceau |ljɔ̃so| *nm, pl* **lionceaux** : lion cub
lippu, -pue |lipy| *adj* : thick-lipped
liquéfier |likefje| {96} *vt* : to liquefy — **se liquéfier** *vr*
liqueur |likœr| *nf* **1** : liqueur **2** *Can* : soft drink, soda
liquidation |likidasjɔ̃| *nf* **1** : liquidation **2** : clearance sale **3** : settlement, payment
liquide[1] |likid| *adj* : liquid
liquide[2] *nm* **1** : liquid **2** ESPÈCES : cash
liquider |likide| *vt* **1** : to liquidate, to settle **2** : to sell off, to clear (an inventory)
liquidité |likidite| *nf* **1** : liquidity **2 liquidités** *nfpl* : liquid assets
liquoreux, -reuse |likɔrø, -røz| *adj* : syrupy (of wine)
lire |lir| {51} *vt* **1** : to read <lire à haute voix : to read aloud> **2** : to discern, to see <elle lisait la peur dans mes yeux : she saw the fear in my eyes> **3 lire les lignes de la main** : to read one's palm
lis *or* **lys** |lis| *nms & pl* **1** : lily **2** → **fleur**
lisait |lizɛ|, **lisions** |lizjɔ̃|, *etc.* → **lire**
lise |liz|, *etc.* → **lire**
lisible |lizibl| *adj* **1** : legible **2** : readable (of a novel, etc.) — **lisibilité** |-zibilite| *nf*
lisiblement |liziblәmɑ̃| *adv* : legibly
lisière |lizjɛr| *nf* **1** : selvage **2** : edge, outskirts *pl*
lisse |lis| *adj* : smooth, sleek
lisser |lise| *vt* **1** : to smooth out **2** : to preen (feathers)
liste |list| *nf* : list <liste d'attente : waiting list> <liste noire : blacklist> <liste électorale : electoral roll>
lit |li| *nm* **1** : bed <lit d'enfant : crib> <lit de mort : deathbed> <lits superposés : bunk (bed)> **2** : riverbed **3** : marriage <enfants du premier lit : children from the first marriage>
litanie |litani| *nf* : litany
literie |litri| *nf* : bedding
lithium |litjɔm| *nm* : lithium
lithographie |litɔgrafi| *nf* **1** : lithography **2** : lithograph
litière |litjɛr| *nf* **1** : litter, bedding (in a stable, etc.) **2 litière de chat** : kitty litter
litige |litiʒ| *nm* **1** : dispute <objet de litige : object of contention> **2** : litigation <parties en litige : litigants>
litigieux, -gieuse |litiʒjø, -ʒjøz| *adj* CONTENTIEUX : litigious, contentious
litote |litɔt| *nf* : understatement
litre |litr| *nm* : liter
littéraire |literɛr| *adj* : literary
littéral, -rale |literal| *adj, mpl* **-raux** |-ro| : literal — **littéralement** |-ralmɑ̃| *adv*
littérature |literatyr| *nf* : literature
littoral[1], **-rale** |litɔral| *adj, mpl* **-raux** |-ro| : littoral, coastal
littoral[2] *nm* : coast, coastline
lituanien[1], **-nienne** |litɥanjɛ̃, -njɛn| *adj* : Lithuanian
lituanien[2] *nm* : Lithuanian (language)
Lituanien, -nienne *n* : Lithuanian
liturgie |lityrʒi| *nf* : liturgy
liturgique |lityrʒik| *adj* : liturgical
livide |livid| *adj* **1** BLÊME : pallid, pale **2** BLEUÂTRE : livid, bluish
livraison |livrɛzɔ̃| *nf* : delivery <livraison à domicile : home delivery>
livre[1] |livr| *nm* **1** : book <livre de poche : paperback> <livre de recettes : cookbook> <grand livre : ledger> **2 le livre** : the book trade **3 livres de comptes** : accounts, (account) books
livre[2] *nf* **1** : pound <une livre de beurre : a pound of butter> **2** *or* **livre sterling** : pound (monetary unit)
livrée |livre| *nf* **1** : livery **2 en livrée** : liveried
livrer |livre| *vt* **1** : to deliver **2** : to hand over, to surrender **3 livré à soi-même** : left to one's own devices — **se livrer** *vr* ~ **à 1** : to engage in, to devote oneself to **2** : to indulge in, to surrender to **3** : to confide in
livresque |livrɛsk| *adj* : derived from books <savoir livresque : book learning>
livret |livrɛ| *nm* **1** : booklet <livret de banque : bankbook> **2** : libretto
livreur, -vreuse |livrœr, -vrøz| *n* : deliveryman *m*, delivery woman *f*
lob |lɔb| *nm* : lob (in sports)
lobe |lɔb| *nm* : lobe <lobe de l'oreille : earlobe>
lober |lɔbe| *v* : to lob
lobotomie |lɔbɔtɔmi| *nf* : lobotomy
local[1], **-cale** |lɔkal| *adj, mpl* **locaux** |lɔko| : local — **localement** |-kalmɑ̃| *adv*

local[2] *nm, pl* **locaux** : place, premises *pl* <locaux commerciaux : office space>

localisation [lɔkalizasjɔ̃] *nf* **1** : localizing, confining **2** : location, locating

localiser [lɔkalize] *vt* **1** SITUER : to locate **2** CIRCONSCRIRE : to localize, to confine

localité [lɔkalite] *nf* **1** : locality **2** : village, small town

locataire [lɔkatɛr] *nmf* : tenant

location [lɔkasjɔ̃] *nf* **1** : renting, leasing **2** : rental <contrat de location : rental agreement>

lock–out [lɔkaut] *nms & pl* : lockout

locomoteur, -trice [lɔkɔmɔtœr, -tris] *adj* : locomotive

locomotion [lɔkɔmɔsjɔ̃] *nf* : locomotion

locomotive [lɔkɔmɔtiv] *nf* **1** : locomotive, engine **2** *fam* : driving force, pacesetter

locuteur, -trice [lɔkytœr, -tris] *n* : speaker <locuteur natif : native speaker>

locution [lɔkysjɔ̃] *nf* : phrase, locution <locution figée : set phrase>

logarithme [lɔgaritm] *nm* : logarithm

loge [lɔʒ] *nf* **1** : dressing room **2** : box (at the theater) <être aux premières loges : to have a ringside seat> **3** : lodge

logement [lɔʒmɑ̃] *nm* **1** APPARTEMENT : apartment, accommodations *pl* **2** : housing

loger [lɔʒe] {17} *vt* **1** : to put up, to house **2** : to accommodate <une salle qui loge 700 personnes : a room which accommodates 700 people> **3** : to put, to lodge — *vi* : to lodge, to stay (at a hotel) — **se loger** *vr* **1** : to find accommodations **2** : to lodge <la balle s'est logée dans son bras : the bullet lodged itself in his arm>

logiciel [lɔʒisjɛl] *nm* : software

logique[1] [lɔʒik] *adj* : logical — **logiquement** [-ʒikmɑ̃] *adv*

logique[2] *nf* : logic

logis [lɔʒi] *nms & pl* : dwelling, abode

logistique[1] [lɔʒistik] *adj* : logistic

logistique[2] *nf* : logistics

logo [logo] *nm* : logo

loi [lwa] *nf* **1** : law <voter une loi : to pass a law> <faire la loi : to lay down the law> <loi de la gravitation : law of gravity> **2** : rule, convention <les lois de la mode : the dictates of fashion> <loi du silence : code of silence>

loin[1] [lwɛ̃] *adv* **1** : far, a long way (off) **2** : a long time ago **3 ~ de** : far from, distant from **4 d'aussi loin que** : as far back as **5 plus loin** : farther, further

loin[2] *n* **1 au ~** : in the distance, afar **2 de ~** : from a distance **3 de ~** : by far, far and away **4 de loin en loin** : here and there, from time to time

lointain[1], **-taine** [lwɛ̃tɛ̃, -tɛn] *adj* **1** ÉLOIGNÉ : distant, far-off **2** : remote, distant (in time)

lointain[2] *nm* : distance (in space or time) <dans le lointain : in the distance>

loir [lwar] *nm* : dormouse

loisible [lwazibl] *adj* : permissible, allowable <il est loisible de nager ici : you're allowed to swim here>

loisir [lwazir] *nm* **1** : leisure <heures de loisir : leisure time, spare time> **2** : time, opportunity **3 loisirs** *nmpl* : leisure activities, recreation

lombago [lɔ̃bago] → **lumbago**

lombes [lɔ̃b] *nmpl* : loins

lombric [lɔ̃brik] *nm France* : earthworm

long[1] [lɔ̃] *adv* **1** BEAUCOUP : much, a lot <il en disait trop long : he revealed too much> **2 s'habiller long** : to wear long skirts

long[2], **longue** [lɔ̃, lɔ̃g] *adj* **1** : long (in space) <une jupe longue : a long skirt> <long de six mètres : six meters long> **2** : long (in time) <un long silence : a lengthy silence> <une longue amitié : a long-standing friendship> <être long à faire : to be slow to do> **3 de long en large** : up and down, to and fro

long[3] *nm* **1** : length (of space) <deux pouces de long : two inches long> <tomber de tout son long : to fall flat> **2** : length (of time) <tout au long de la nuit : throughout the night> **3 le long de** : along <le long de la route : along the road>

longanimité [lɔ̃ganimite] *nf* : forbearance

longe [lɔ̃ʒ] *nf* **1** : tether **2** : loin (in cooking)

longer [lɔ̃ʒe] {17} *vt* **1** : to go along, to follow **2** : to run alongside, to border

longévité [lɔ̃ʒevite] *nf* : longevity

longhorn [lɔ̃gɔrn] *nmf* : longhorn

longitude [lɔ̃ʒityd] *nf* : longitude

longitudinal, -nale [lɔ̃ʒitydinal] *adj, mpl* **-naux** [-no] : longitudinal — **longitudinalement** [-nalmɑ̃] *adv*

longtemps [lɔ̃tɑ̃] *adv* : a long time <il y a longtemps qu'il n'a pas joué : he hasn't gambled in a long time> <je n'en ai pas pour longtemps : I won't be long>

longue[1] → **long**[2]

longue[2] [lɔ̃g] *nf* **à la longue** : in the long run

longuement [lɔ̃gmɑ̃] *adv* **1** : for a long time **2** : at length, in detail

longueur [lɔ̃gœr] *nf* **1** : length <à longueur de journée : all day long> <sur une longueur de deux mètres : over two meters long> <longueur d'onde : wavelength> **2 longueurs** *nfpl* : tedious parts (of a film, etc.)

longue–vue [lɔ̃gvy] *nf, pl* **longues–vues** : telescope

look [luk] *nm* : look, image <un nouveau look : a new look>

lopin [lɔpɛ̃] *nm* **lopin de terre** : plot of land

loquace [lɔkas] *adj* BAVARD : talkative, loquacious

loquacité [lɔkasite] *nf* : loquacity, garrulousness

loque [lɔk] *nf* **1** : wreck (person) **2 loques** *nfpl* : rags

loquet [lɔkɛ] *nm* : latch

loqueteux, -teuse [lɔktø] *adj* : in rags, in tatters

lord [lɔr(d)] *nm* : lord (in Great Britain) <la Chambre de lords : the House of Lords>

lorgner [lɔrɲe] *vt* : to eye, to ogle, to leer at

lorgnette [lɔrɲɛt] *nf* : opera glasses *pl*

loriot [lɔrjo] *nm* : oriole

lors [lɔr] *adv* **1 ~ de** : at the time of **2 ~ de** : during **3 lors même que** : even though

lorsque [lɔrskə] (**lorsqu'** [lɔrsk] *before a vowel or mute h*) *conj* : when

losange [lɔzɑ̃ʒ] *nm* **1** : lozenge, diamond <en losange : diamond-shaped> **2** *Can* : baseball diamond

lot [lo] *nm* **1** SORT : fate, lot **2** : prize (in a lottery) **3** PART : share **4** : lot, plot (of land)

loterie [lɔtri] *nf* : lottery

loti, -tie [lɔti] *adj* **bien loti** : well-off

lotion [lɔsjɔ̃] *nf* : lotion

lotir [lɔtir] *vt* : to divide into plots

lotissement [lɔtismɑ̃] *nm* **1** : housing development **2** : division (into plots)

lotus [lɔtys] *nm* : lotus

louable [lwabl] *adj* **1** : praiseworthy, commendable **2** : rentable

louage [lwaʒ] *nm* : renting <voiture de louage : rental car>

louange [lwɑ̃ʒ] *nf* : praise <à la louange de : in praise of> <chanter ses louanges : to sing one's praises>

louche[1] [luʃ] *adj* SUSPECT : shady, suspicious

louche[2] *nf* : ladle

loucher [luʃe] *vi* : to squint, to be cross-eyed

louer [lwe] *vt* **1** : to praise <Dieu soit loué! : praise be to God!> **2** : to rent (a car, etc.) **3** *or* **louer à bail** : to rent out, to lease (property) — **se louer** *vr* **1** : to be for rent **2** : to congratulate oneself

loufoque [lufɔk] *adj fam* : crazy, zany

loup [lu] *nm* **1** : wolf **2** *or* **loup de mer** : sea bass **3** : (eye) mask, domino

loup–cervier [lusɛrvje] *nm, pl* **loups–cerviers** : lynx

loupe [lup] *nf* : magnifying glass

louper [lupe] *vt fam* **1** : to bungle, to mess up **2** : to miss (a train, etc.)

loup–garou [lugaru] *nm, pl* **loups–garous** : werewolf

loup–marin [lumarɛ̃] *nm Can, pl* **loups–marins** : seal (animal)

lourd[1] [lur] *adv* **1 peser lourd** : to carry a lot of weight, to count heavily **2 il fait lourd** : it's hot and sticky (outside)

lourd[2], lourde [lur, lurd] *adj* **1** : heavy **2** : sultry, oppressive (of the weather) **3** : clumsy, ungainly **4** : weighty, serious **5** : dull, heavy-handed **6 ~ de** : fraught with

lourdaud[1], -daude [lurdo, -dod] *adj* : oafish

lourdaud[2], -daude *n* : oaf, clod

lourdement [lurdəmɑ̃] *adv* **1** PESAMMENT : heavily **2** MALADROITEMENT : clumsily **3** : GROSSIÈREMENT : greatly, grossly

lourdeur [lurdœr] *nf* **1** : heaviness <avoir des lourdeurs d'estomac : to feel bloated> **2** : clumsiness

lousse [lus] *adj Can fam* : loose, slack

loutre [lutr] *nf* : otter

louve [luv] *nf* : she-wolf

louveteau [luvto] *nm, pl* **louveteaux 1** : wolf cub **2** : Cub Scout

louvoyer [luvwaje] {58} *vi* **1** : to tack (in navigation) **2** : to hedge, to beat around the bush

lover [lɔve] *v* **se lover** *vr* : to coil up

loyal, loyale [lwajal] *adj, mpl* **loyaux** [lwajo] **1** FIDÈLE : loyal, faithful **2** HONNÊTE : honest, fair — **loyalement** [-jalmɑ̃] *adv*

loyauté [lwajote] *nf* **1** FIDÉLITÉ : loyalty, faithfulness **2** HONNÊTETÉ : honesty, fairness

loyer [lwaje] *nm* **1** : rent **2 loyer de l'argent** : interest rate

LSD [ɛlɛsde] *nm* : LSD

lu [ly] *pp* → **lire**

lubie [lybi] *nf* CAPRICE : whim, craze

lubricité [lybrisite] *nf* : lechery, lewdness

lubrifiant[1], -fiante [lybrifjɑ̃, -fjɑ̃t] *adj* : lubricating

lubrifiant[2] *nm* : lubricant

lubrifier [lybrifje] {96} *vt* : to lubricate — **lubrification** [lybrifikasjɔ̃] *nf*

lubrique [lybrik] *adj* **1** : lustful, lecherous **2** : lewd

lucarne [lykarn] *nf* **1** : skylight **2** : dormer window

lucide [lysid] *adj* **1** : lucid, clear-sighted **2** CONSCIENT : conscious, aware

lucidement [lysidmɑ̃] *adv* : clearly, lucidly

lucidité [lysidite] *nf* : lucidity, clear-sightedness

luciole [lysjɔl] *nf* : firefly

lucratif, -tive [lykratif, -tiv] *adj* : lucrative, profitable <organisation à but non lucratif : nonprofit organization>

ludique [lydik] *adj* : play, playing

luette [lɥɛt] *nf* : uvula

lueur [lɥœr] *nf* **1** : faint light **2** : glimmer, gleam <une lueur de colère dans les yeux : a gleam of anger in one's eyes> **3** : glow (of a fire, etc.)

luge |lyʒ| *nf* : sled
lugubre |lygybr| *adj* : gloomy, dismal — **lugubrement** |-gybrəmɑ̃| *adv*
lui |lɥi| *pron* **1** (*used as indirect object*) : (to) him, (to) her, (to) it <je le lui ai remis : I gave it back to her> **2** (*used as subject or for emphasis*) : he <elle va au théâtre, lui reste ici : she's going to the theater, he's staying here> **3** (*used as object of a preposition*) : him, it <ils vont chez lui : they're going to his house> <cette plume est à lui : this pen belongs to him> **4** (*used as a reflexive pronoun*) : himself <il ne pense qu'à lui : he only thinks of himself> **5 c'est tout lui!** : that's just like him!
lui–même |lɥimɛm| *pron* : himself, itself <c'est lui-même qui l'a dit : he said it himself>
luire |lɥir| {49} *vi* **1** : to shine, to gleam, to glisten **2** : to glow, to glimmer <l'espoir luit : there's a glimmer of hope>
luisant[1], -sante |lɥizɑ̃, -zɑ̃t| *adj* : shining, gleaming
luisant[2] *nm* : sheen
lumbago |lɛ̃bago, lœ̃-, lɔ̃-| *nm* : lumbago
lumière |lymjɛr| *nf* **1** : light <lumière du jour : daylight> <lumière du soleil : sunlight> <lumière des étoiles : starlight> <allumer la lumière : to turn on the light> **2** ÉCLAIRCISSEMENT : light, clarification <à la lumière de : in (the) light of> <mettre en lumière : to bring to light, to shed light on> **3** GÉNIE : luminary, shining light <elle n'est pas une lumière : she's hardly a genius> **4 lumières** *nfpl* : insight, understanding
luminaire |lyminɛr| *nm* : lamp, light
luminescent, -cente |luminɛsɑ̃, -sɑ̃t| *adj* : luminescent — **luminescence** |-nɛsɑ̃s| *nf*
lumineusement |lyminøzmɑ̃| *adv* **1** : luminously **2** : clearly, lucidly
lumineux, -neuse |lyminø, -nøz| *adj* **1** : luminous, of light **2** : radiant <son sourire lumineux : her radiant smile> **3** : bright, intense <un jaune lumineux : bright yellow> **4** : clear, lucid <une idée lumineuse : a brilliant idea>
luminosité |lyminozite| *nf* : luminosity, radiance
lunaire |lynɛr| *adj* : lunar, moon
lunatique |lynatik| *adj* CAPRICIEUX : whimsical, temperamental
lunch |lœʃ| *nm, pl* **lunchs** *or* **lunches 1** BUFFET : buffet **2** *Can* : lunch
lundi |lœ̃di| *nm* : Monday
lune |lyn| *nf* **1** : moon <pleine lune : full moon> **2 être dans la lune** : to have one's head in the clouds **3 lune de miel** : honeymoon <passer la lune de miel : to honeymoon>
luné, -née |lyne| *adj* **être bien (mal) luné** : to be in a good (bad) mood
lunette |lynɛt| *nf* **1** : opening, (round) window <lunette arrière : rear window (of an automobile)> **2** : toilet seat **3** : telescope <lunette d'approche : astronomical telescope> **4 lunettes** *nfpl* : glasses, spectacles, goggles <lunettes de soleil : sunglasses> <lunettes de ski : ski goggles>
lurette |lyrɛt| *nf* **belle lurette** : ages, a long time <il y a belle lurette : a long time ago> <ça fait belle lurette que : it's been ages since>
lustre |lystr| *nm* **1** : chandelier **2** : lustre, sheen **3 lustres** *nmpl* : ages <il y a des lustres : ages ago>
lustré, -trée |lystre| *adj* : shiny, glossy
lustrer |lystre| *vt* : to polish, to make shiny
luth |lyt| *nm* : lute
lutin |lytɛ̃| *nm* : imp, goblin, pixie
lutjanidé |lytjanide| *nm* : snapper
lutrin |lytrɛ̃| *nm* : lectern
lutte |lyt| *nf* **1** : fight, conflict <une lutte armée : an armed conflict> **2** : struggle, fight <la lutte contre la drogue : the fight against drugs> <lutte pour la vie : struggle for life> **3** : wrestling
lutter |lyte| *vi* **1** SE BATTRE : to fight, to contend **2** : to struggle **3** : to wrestle
lutteur, -teuse |lytœr, -tøz| *n* **1** : fighter **2** : wrestler
luxation |lyksasjɔ̃| *nf* : dislocation (of a joint)
luxe |lyks| *nm* : luxury <hôtel de luxe : luxury hotel>
luxembourgeois, -geoise |lyksɑ̃burʒwa, -ʒwaz| *adj* : Luxembourgian
Luxembourgeois, -geoise *n* : Luxembourger
luxer |lykse| *vt* : to dislocate (a joint) — **se luxer** *vr* : to dislocate <je me suis luxé l'épaule : I dislocated my shoulder>
luxueux, -xueuse |lyksɥø, -sɥøz| *adj* : luxurious — **luxueusement** |lyksɥøzmɑ̃| *adv*
luxure |lyksyr| *nf* : lust
luxuriant, -riante |lyksyrjɑ̃, -rjɑ̃t| *adj* : luxuriant, lush
luxurieux, -rieuse |lyksyrjø, -rjøz| *adj* : lascivious, lewd
luzerne |lyzɛrn| *nf* : alfalfa
lycée |lise| *nm France* : high school
lycéen, -céenne |liseɛ̃, -seɛn| *n France* : high school student
lymphatique |lɛ̃fatik| *adj* **1** : lymphatic **2** : lethargic, sluggish
lymphe |lɛ̃f| *nf* : lymph
lyncher |lɛ̃ʃe| *vt* : to lynch
lynx |lɛ̃ks| *nm* : lynx
lyophilisé, -sée |ljɔfilize| *adj* : freeze-dried
lyophiliser |ljɔfilize| *vt* : to freeze-dry

lyre |lir| *nf* : lyre
lyrique |lirik| *adj* **1** : lyrical **2** : lyric <poésie lyrique : lyric poetry> **3** : operatic, opera <chanteur lyrique : opera singer> <comédie lyrique : comic opera>
lyrisme |lirism| *nm* : lyricism
lys → **lis**

M

m |ɛm| *nm* : m, the 13th letter of the alphabet
ma → **mon**
maboul, -boule |mabul| *adj fam* CINGLÉ : loony, crazy
macabre |makabr| *adj* : macabre, gruesome
macadam |makadam| *nm* **1** : macadam **2** : (macadam) road
macareux |makarø| *nms & pl* : puffin
macaron |makarɔ̃| *nm* **1** : macaroon **2** : coil (of hair) **3** : (round) badge, sticker
macaronis |makarɔni| *nmpl* : macaroni <macaronis au gratin : macaroni and cheese>
macédoine |masedwan| *nf* : mixture (of fruits or vegetables) <macédoine de fruits : fruit salad> <macédoine de légumes : mixed vegetables>
macédonien, -nienne |masedɔnjɛ̃, -njɛn| *adj* : Macedonian
Macédonien, -nienne *n* : Macedonian
macérer |masere| {87} *vt* : to steep, to soak — *vi* : to soak <macérer dans une marinade : to marinate>
mâchefer |maʃfɛr| *nm* : clinker, slag
mâcher |maʃe| *vt* **1** MASTIQUER : to chew **2 ne pas mâcher ses mots** : not to mince one's words
machette |maʃɛt| *nf* : machete
machin |maʃɛ̃| *nm fam* : thingamajig, thing
Machin, -chine |maʃɛ̃, -ʃin| *n fam* : what's-his-name *m,* what's-her-name *f*
machinal, -nale |maʃinal| *adj, mpl* **-naux** |-no| AUTOMATIQUE : mechanical, automatic <une réaction machinale : an automatic reaction> — **machinalement** |-nalmɑ̃| *adv*
machination |maʃinasjɔ̃| *nf* COMPLOT : machination, plot
machine |maʃin| *nf* **1** : machine <machine à coudre : sewing machine> <machine à écrire : typewriter> <machine à laver : washing machine> **2** : engine <machine à vapeur : steam engine> **3** SYSTÈME : system, process <la machine administrative : bureaucratic machinery>
machine–outil |maʃinuti| *nf, pl* **machines–outils** : machine tool
machinerie |maʃinri| *nf* **1** : machinery, physical plant **2** : engine room
machinisme |maʃinism| *nm* : mechanization
machisme |matʃism| *nm* : machismo, male chauvinism
macho |matʃo| *adj fam* : macho
mâchoire |maʃwar| *nf* **1** : jaw <mâchoire supérieure : upper jaw> **2 mâchoire de frein** : brake shoe
mâchonner |maʃɔne| *vt* **1** : to chew **2** MARMONNER : to mumble
mâchouiller |maʃuje| *vt* : to chew (on), to nibble (at)
macis |masi| *nm* : mace (spice)
maçon |masɔ̃| *nm* **1** : bricklayer, mason **2** : builder
maçonner |masɔne| *vt* **1** : to construct (with masonry) **2** : to face (with stone), to brick up
maçonnerie |masɔnri| *nf* **1** : building, bricklaying **2** : masonry, stonework **3** : Freemasonry
maçonnique |masɔnik| *adj* : masonic
macramé |makrame| *nm* : macramé
macrocosme |makrɔkɔsm| *nm* : macrocosm
maculer |makyle| *vt* : to stain
madame |madam| *nf, pl* **mesdames** |medam| **1** : Mrs., Ms., Madam <bonjour, madame Dupont : good morning, Mrs. Dupont> **2** (*used as a polite form of address*) : lady <bonjour, mesdames : good morning, ladies> **3** (*used as a salutation*) <Madame : Dear Madam> <Mesdames, Mesdemoiselles, Messieurs! : Ladies and Gentlemen!>
mademoiselle |madmwazɛl| *nf, pl* **mesdemoiselles** |medmwazɛl| **1** : Miss, Ms. <bonjour, mademoiselle Dupont : good morning, Miss Dupont> **2** (*used as a polite form of address*) : Miss, Madam <merci, mademoiselle : thank you, Miss> **3** (*used as a salutation*) <Mademoiselle : Dear Madam> <Mesdames, Mesdemoiselles, Messieurs! : Ladies and Gentlemen!>
madère |madɛr| *nm* : Madeira (wine)
madone |madɔn| *nf* : Madonna
madrier |madrije| *nm* : beam (of wood)
madrigal |madrigal| *nm, pl* **-gaux** |-go| : madrigal
maelström |maɛlstrɔm| *nm* : maelstrom
maestria |maɛstrija| *nf* : mastery, skill, brilliance
mafia *or* **maffia** |mafja| *nf* : Mafia

magané, -née [magane] *adj Can fam* **1** : run-down, shabby **2** : weakened, tired

maganer [magane] *vt Can fam* : to ruin, to damage — **se maganer** *vr Can fam* : to tire out

magasin [magazɛ̃] *nm* **1** : shop, store <en magasin : in stock> <grand magasin : department store> **2** ENTREPÔT : warehouse **3** : magazine (of a gun or camera)

magasinage [magazinaʒ] *nm Can* : shopping

magasiner [magazine] *vi Can* : to shop, to go shopping

magazine [magazin] *nm* **1** REVUE : magazine **2** : program <un magazine d'actualités quotidiennes : a daily news program>

magenta [maʒɛ̃ta] *nm* : magenta

magicien, -cienne [maʒisjɛ̃, -sjɛn] *n* : magician

magie [maʒi] *nf* : magic

magique [maʒik] *adj* : magic, magical — **magiquement** [-ʒikmɑ̃] *adv*

magistral, -trale [maʒistral] *adj, mpl* **-traux** [-tro] **1** : brilliant, masterly **2** : authoritative **3 cours magistral** : lecture

magistralement [maʒistralmɑ̃] *adv* : masterfully

magistrat [maʒistra] *nm* : magistrate

magistrature [maʒistratyr] *nf* : magistracy

magma [magma] *nm* **1** : magma **2** : jumble

magnanime [maɲanim] *adj* : magnanimous

magnanimité [maɲanimite] *nf* : magnanimity

magnat [maɲa] *nm* : magnate, tycoon

magnésie [maɲezi] *nf* : magnesia

magnésium [maɲezjɔm] *nm* : magnesium

magnétique [maɲetik] *adj* : magnetic — **magnétiquement** [-tikmɑ̃] *adv*

magnétiser [maɲetize] *vt* : to magnetize — **magnétisme** [maɲetism] *nm*

magnétite [maɲetit] *nf* : magnetite, lodestone

magnétophone [maɲetɔfɔn] *nm* : tape recorder

magnétoscope [maɲetɔskɔp] *nm* : videocassette recorder, VCR

magnétoscoper [maɲetɔskɔpe] *vt* : to videotape

magnificence [maɲifisɑ̃s] *nf* **1** SPLENDEUR : magnificence, splendor **2** PRODIGALITÉ : lavishness, extravagance

magnifier [maɲifje] {96} *nf* **1** : to idealize **2** : to glorify

magnifique [maɲifik] *adj* SPLENDIDE : magnificent — **magnifiquement** [-fikmɑ̃] *adv*

magnitude [maɲityd] *nf* : magnitude

magnolia [maɲɔlja] *nm* : magnolia

magot [mago] *nm fam* : stash (of money), nest egg

magouille [maguj] *nf fam* : scheming, skulduggery

magouiller [maguje] *vi fam* : to scheme, to intrigue

mai [mɛ] *nm* : May

maigre[1] [mɛgr] *adj* **1** : thin, skinny **2** : meager, scanty **3** : lean, low-fat

maigre[2] *nm* **1** : lean (meat) **2 faire maigre** : to abstain from meat

maigrement [mɛgrəmɑ̃] *adv* : meagerly, poorly

maigreur [mɛgrœr] *nf* **1** : thinness **2** : scantiness, meagerness

maigrichon, -chonne [mɛgriʃɔ̃, -ʃɔn] *adj* : skinny, scrawny

maigrir [megrir] *vt* : to thin, to make look thinner — *vi* : to lose weight, to reduce

mail [maj] *nm* : mall, promenade

maille [maj] *nf* **1** : stitch (in knitting) **2** : mesh **3** : link (in a chain) **4** → **cotte**

maillet [majɛ] *nm* : mallet

maillon [majɔ̃] *nm* : link (in a chain)

maillot [majo] *nm* **1** : jersey, shirt (in sports) **2 maillot de bain** : bathing suit **3 maillot de corps** : undershirt

main [mɛ̃] *nf* **1** : hand <main droite : right hand> <la main dans la main : hand in hand> <serrer la main à : to shake hands with> <se tenir la main : to hold hands> **2** : skill <avoir la main : to have the knack> <se faire la main : to practice> **3** : style, touch <je reconnais la main d'un maître : I recognize the hand of a master> **4** : hand, deal (in card games) **5 de première main** : firsthand **6 de seconde main** : secondhand, used **7 donner un coup de main à** : to lend a helping hand to, to help **8 en mains propres** : in person **9 fait à la main** : handmade **10 main courante** : handrail **11 sous la main** : at hand, handy

main–d'œuvre [mɛ̃dœvr] *nf* : manpower, workforce

main–forte [mɛ̃fɔrt] *nf* : help, assistance <il m'a prêté main-forte : he came to my assistance>

mainmise [mɛ̃miz] *nf* : seizure, takeover

maint, mainte [mɛ̃, mɛ̃t] *adj* **1** : many a **2 maintes et maintes fois** : time and time again

maintenance [mɛ̃tnɑ̃s] *nf* : maintenance

maintenant [mɛ̃tnɑ̃] *adv* **1** : now <à partir de maintenant : from now on> **2** : nowadays

maintenir [mɛ̃tnir] {92} *vt* **1** ENTRETENIR : to maintain, to keep (up) **2** SOUTENIR : to hold up, to support **3** : to stand by (a decision, etc.) — **se maintenir** *vr* : to remain steady, to persist, to hold

maintien [mɛ̃tjɛ̃] *nm* **1** : maintaining, upholding <le maintien de l'ordre

: the maintenance of law and order> **2** : bearing, carriage

maire, mairesse [mɛr, merɛs] *n* : mayor

mairie [meri] *nf* **1** : town hall, city hall **2** : town or city council

mais[1] [mɛ] *adv* **1** (*used to reinforce an interjection*) <mais bien sûr! : but of course!, certainly!> <mais non! : of course not!> **2 n'en pouvoir mais** : to be able to do nothing, to be helpless

mais[2] *conj* : but <elle est petite mais forte : she is small but strong> <mais ce n'est pas vrai : but that's not true> <non seulement délicieux mais encore salutaire : not only tasty but healthful>

maïs [mais] *nm* **1** : Indian corn, maize **2 maïs explosé** : popcorn

maison[1] [mɛzɔ̃] *adj* **1** : homemade <spécialité maison : specialty of the house> **2** : in-house **3** *fam* : first-rate

maison[2] *nf* **1** : house, home <maison de campagne : country house> <rester à la maison : to stay home> **2** : institution, home <maison de retraite : retirement home> **3** FIRME : firm, company <maison d'édition : publishing company> **4 maison close** : brothel **5 maison de correction** : reformatory **6 maison des jeunes** : youth center **7 maison mobile** *Can* : mobile home

maisonnée [mɛzɔne] *nf* : household

maisonnette [mɛzɔnɛt] *nf* : small house

maître[1], **-tresse** [mɛtr, -trɛs] *adj* **1** : main, key <l'idée maîtresse : the main idea> **2** : master, expert <maître boulanger : master baker>

maître[2], **-tresse** *n* **1** : master, mistress <maître de maison : host> <maîtresse de maison : lady of the house, hostess> **2** : owner (of a pet) **3 être maître de soi** : to have self-control <elle est maîtresse de soi : she's her own woman>

maître[3] *nm* **1** : expert, master <être maître passé de : to be a past master at> **2** : master (of a pet) **3** : master (in the arts, etc.) <les vieux maîtres : the old masters> **4** (*used as a title for attorneys and other professionals*) : Mr., Mrs., Ms. **5 maître d'équipage** : boatswain **6 maître d'hôtel** : maître d'hôtel, headwaiter, butler

maître–chanteur [mɛtrəʃɑ̃tœr] *nm, pl* **maîtres–chanteurs** : blackmailer

maîtresse *nf* AMANTE : mistress

maîtrisable [metrizabl] *adj* : controllable

maîtrise [metriz] *nf* **1** : skill, mastery **2** : control <maîtrise de soi : self-control> **3** : master's degree

maîtriser [metrize] *vt* **1** : to master **2** : to control, to restrain — **se maîtriser** *vr*

majesté [maʒɛste] *nf* : majesty

majestueux, -tueuse [maʒɛstɥø, -tɥøz] *adj* : majestic — **majestueusement** [-tɥøzmɑ̃] *adv*

majeur[1], **-jeure** [maʒœr] *adj* **1** IMPORTANT : major, main <en majeure partie : for the most part> **2** : of age **3** : major (in music)

majeur[2] *nm* : middle finger

majoration [maʒɔrasjɔ̃] *nf* : increase

majorer [maʒɔre] *vt* : to increase

majoritaire [maʒɔritɛr] *adj* : majority <le parti majoritaire : the majority party>

majorité [maʒɔrite] *nf* : majority <en majorité : in the majority>

majuscule[1] [maʒyskyl] *adj* : capital, uppercase

majuscule[2] *nf* : capital letter

mal[1] [mal] *adv* **1** : poorly, badly <j'ai mal dormi : I didn't sleep well> <mal tourner : to turn out badly> **2** : with difficulty <il respire mal : it's hard for him to breathe> **3** : in poor health <se porter mal : to be unwell> **4** : wrongly <mal comprendre : to misunderstand> **5 mal à l'aise** : ill at ease **6 pas mal** : not bad(ly) **7 pas mal** : quite, quite a few <elle est pas mal sympathique : she's quite nice> <pas mal d'enfants : quite a lot of children>

mal[2] *adj* **1** : wrong <c'est mal de voler : it's wrong to steal> **2** : bad <pas mal du tout : not bad at all> **3** : sick, ill <se sentir mal : to feel sick>

mal[3] *nm, pl* **maux** [mo] **1** DOULEUR : pain <avoir mal à la gorge : to have a sore throat> **2** MALADIE : sickness <mal de mer : seasickness> **3** DOMMAGE : harm, hurt <le mal est fait : the damage is done> **4** : evil, ill <le bien et le mal : good and evil> **5** PEINE : trouble, difficulty <sans mal : easily>

malade[1] [malad] *adj* **1** : sick, ill <tomber malade : to get sick> <malade d'inquiétude : sick with worry> **2** : diseased (of an organ or a plant) **3** *fam* : crazy **4** : in a bad way <une économie malade : an ailing economy>

malade[2] *nmf* : sick person, patient

maladie [maladi] *nf* **1** : illness, disease <maladie mentale : mental illness> <maladie sexuellement transmissible : sexually transmitted disease> <maladie de Carré : distemper> **2** MANIE : mania, obsession

maladif, -dive [maladif, -div] *adj* **1** : sickly **2** MORBIDE : pathological <une jalousie maladive : pathological jealousy>

maladresse [maladrɛs] *nf* **1** : clumsiness, awkwardness **2** BÉVUE : blunder

maladroit, -droite [maladrwa, -drwat] *adj* MALHABILE : clumsy, awkward — **maladroitement** [-drwatmɑ̃] *adv*

malais[1], **-laise** [malɛ, -lɛz] *adj* : Malay, Malayan
malais[2] *nm* : Malay (language)
Malais, -laise *n* : Malay, Malayan
malaise [malɛz] *nm* **1** : faintness, dizziness <j'éprouvais un léger malaise : I was feeling faint> **2** : uneasiness, malaise
malaisé, -sée [maleze] *adj* PÉNIBLE : difficult
malaisément [malezemɑ̃] *adv* : with difficulty
malaisien, -sienne [malɛzjɛ̃, -zjɛn] *adj* : Malaysian
Malaisien, -sienne *n* : Malaysian
malard *or* **malart** [malar] *nm* **1** : drake **2** *Can* : mallard
malavenant, -nante [malavnɑ̃, -nɑ̃t] *adj Can* : disagreeable, unpleasant
malavisé, -sée [malvize] *adj* : ill-advised, unwise
malawien, -wienne [malawjɛ̃, -wjɛn] *adj* : Malawian
Malawien, -wienne *n* : Malawian
malaxer [malakse] *vt* : to blend, to mix
malaxeur [malaksœr] *nm* **1** : (cement) mixer **2** *Can* : (electric) beater, mixer **3** *Can* MÉLANGEUR : blender
malchance [malʃɑ̃s] *nf* : bad luck, misfortune
malchanceux, -ceuse [malʃɑ̃sø, -søz] *adj* : unlucky
malcommode [malkɔmɔd] *adj* **1** : impractical, uncomfortable, inconvenient **2** *Can* : ornery, cantankerous <un malade malcommode : a difficult patient>
mâle[1] [mal] *adj* **1** : male **2** : manly
mâle[2] *nm* : male
malédiction [malediksjɔ̃] *nf* : curse, malediction
maléfice [malefis] *nm* SORTILÈGE : evil spell
maléfique [malefik] *adj* : evil
malencontreusement [malɑ̃kɔ̃trøzmɑ̃] *adv* : inappropriately, ill-advisedly
malencontreux, -treuse [malɑ̃kɔ̃trø, -trøz] *adj* : unfortunate, untoward, inopportune
malendurant, -rante [malɑ̃dyrɑ̃, -rɑ̃t] *adj Can* : gruff, rough
malentendant[1], **-dante** [malɑ̃tɑ̃dɑ̃, -dɑ̃t] *adj* : hard of hearing
malentendant[2], **-dante** *n* **les malentendants** : the hearing impaired
malentendu [malɑ̃tɑ̃dy] *nm* : misunderstanding
mal–en–train [malɑ̃trɛ̃] *adj Can* : unwell, out of sorts
malfaçon [malfasɔ̃] *nf* DÉFAUT : fault, defect
malfaisant, -sante [malfəzɑ̃, -zɑ̃t] *adj* **1** NUISIBLE : harmful **2** : evil, wicked
malfaiteur [malfɛtœr] *nm* CRIMINEL : criminal, malefactor
malfamé, -mée [malfame] → **famé**
malformation [malfɔrmasjɔ̃] *nf* : malformation
malgache[1] [malgaʃ] *adj* : Madagascan, Malagasy
malgache[2] *nm* : Malagasy (language)
Malgache *nmf* : Madagascan, Malagasy
malgré [malgre] *prep* : in spite of, despite <malgré tout : in spite of everything, even so>
malhabile [malabil] *adj* MALADROIT : clumsy
malheur [malœr] *nm* **1** : misfortune, bad luck **2** CATASTROPHE : tragedy, calamity **3 faire un malheur** *fam* : to be very successful <le spectacle a fait un malheur : the show was a big hit>
malheureusement [malœrøzmɑ̃] *adv* : unfortunately
malheureux[1], **-reuse** [malœrø, -røz] *adj* **1** : unhappy, miserable **2** FÂCHEUX : unfortunate, regrettable <des suites malheureuses : unfortunate consequences> <c'est malheureux! : what a shame!>
malheureux[2], **-reuse** *n* **1** : unfortunate person, poor wretch **2** : poor person <les malheureux : the needy>
malhonnête [malɔnɛt] *adj* : dishonest — **malhonnêtement** [-nɛtmɑ̃] *adv*
malhonnêteté [malɔnɛtte] *nf* : dishonesty, uncleanliness
malice [malis] *nf* **1** : mischief, mischievousness <avec malice : mischievously> **2 sans ~** : innocent, guileless
malicieux, -cieuse [malisjø, -sjøz] *adj* ESPIÈGLE : mischievous — **malicieusement** [malisjøzmɑ̃] *adv*
malien, -lienne [maljɛ̃, -ljɛn] *adj* : Malian
Malien, -lienne *n* : Malian
malignité [maliɲite] *nf* **1** : malice, spite **2** : malignancy
malin, -ligne [malɛ̃, -liɲ] *adj* **1** FUTÉ : shrewd, clever **2** *fam* : tricky, difficult **3** : malicious **4** : malignant
malingre [malɛ̃gr] *adj* : puny
malintentionné, -née [malɛ̃tɑ̃sjɔne] *adj* : malicious, spiteful
malle [mal] *nf* **1** : trunk <faire ses malles : to pack one's bags> **2** *or* **malle arrière** : trunk (of a car)
malléable [maleabl] *adj* : malleable — **malléabilité** [-leabilite] *nf*
mallette [malɛt] *nf* **1** ATTACHÉ-CASE : attaché case, briefcase **2** : small suitcase, valise
malmener [malməne] {52} *vt* **1** MALTRAITER : to manhandle, to mistreat **2** : to give a rough time to
malnutrition [malnytrisjɔ̃] *nf* : malnutrition
malodorant, -rante [malɔdɔrɑ̃, -rɑ̃t] *adj* : foul-smelling, smelly
malotru, -true [malɔtry] *n* : boor
malpoli, -lie [malpɔli] *adj fam* : rude, impolite
malpropre [malprɔpr] *adj* **1** SALE : dirty, grubby **2** GROSSIER : vulgar,

smutty 3 MALHONNÊTE : dishonest, unsavory

malpropreté [malprɔprəte] *nf* : dirtiness

malsain, -saine [malsɛ̃, -sɛn] *adj* : unhealthy

malséant, -séante [malseɑ̃, -seɑ̃t] *adj* : unseemly, unbecoming

malsonnant, -nante [malsɔnɑ̃, -nɑ̃t] *adj* : offensive

malt [malt] *nm* : malt

maltais, -taise [maltɛ, -tɛz] *adj* : Maltese

Maltais, -taise *n* : Maltese

maltraiter [maltrete] *vt* **1** : to mistreat **2** : to criticize, to pan

malveillance [malvɛjɑ̃s] *nf* : spite, malevolence

malveillant, -lante [malvɛjɑ̃, -jɑ̃t] *adj* : spiteful, malicious

malvenu, -venue [malvəny] *adj* DÉPLACÉ : out of place <je suis malvenu de le critiquer : I'm in no position to criticize him>

malversation [malvɛrsasjɔ̃] *nf* : embezzlement

maman [mamɑ̃] *nf* : mom, mommy

mamelle [mamɛl] *nf* **1** : teat **2** PIS : udder

mamelon [mamɛlɔ̃] *nm* **1** : nipple **2** : hillock

mamie [mami] *nf France fam* : grandma, granny

mammaire [mamɛr] *adj* : mammary

mammifère [mamifɛr] *nm* : mammal

mammographie [mamɔgrafi] *nf* : mammogram

mammouth [mamut] *nm* : mammoth

management [manaʒmɑ̃, manadʒmɛnt] *nm* : management

manager [manadʒœr] *nm* : manager

manant [manɑ̃] *nm* : yokel, boor

manche[1] [mɑ̃ʃ] *nf* **1** : sleeve <sans manche : sleeveless> **2** : round, game, set **3** *Can* : inning (in baseball) **4** channel, strait(s)

manche[2] *nm* **1** : handle <manche à balai : broomstick> **2** : neck (of a musical instrument)

manchette [mɑ̃ʃɛt] *nf* **1** : cuff (of a shirt, etc.) **2** : headline

manchon [mɑ̃ʃɔ̃] *nm* : muff

manchot[1], **-chote** [mɑ̃ʃo, -ʃɔt] *adj* **1** : one-armed, one-handed **2** : armless, handless

manchot[2] *nm* : penguin

mandarin [mɑ̃darɛ̃] *nm* **1** : mandarin **2** : Mandarin (language)

mandarine [mɑ̃darin] *nf* : tangerine, mandarin orange

mandat [mɑ̃da] *nm* **1** : mandate **2** : term of office **3** : warrant <mandat d'arrêt : warrant for arrest> <mandat de perquisition : search warrant> **4** *or* **mandat postal** *or* **mandat–poste** : money order

mandataire [mɑ̃datɛr] *nmf* **1** REPRÉSENTANT : representative, agent **2** : proxy

mandater [mɑ̃date] *vt* : to appoint, to commission

mandibule [mɑ̃dibyl] *nf* : mandible

mandoline [mɑ̃dɔlin] *nf* : mandolin

manège [manɛʒ] *nm* **1** : riding school **2** : game, scheme, ploy **3** : merry-go-round, ride (in an amusement park)

manette [manɛt] *nf* : lever

manganèse [mɑ̃ganɛz] *nm* : manganese

mangeable [mɑ̃ʒabl] *adj* : edible

mangeoire [mɑ̃ʒwar] *nf* : feeding trough, manger

manger[1] [mɑ̃ʒe] {17} *vt* **1** : to eat **2** : to eat away, to devour **3** : to fill up, to cover up, to hide **4** : to consume, to use up **5 manger ses mots** : to mumble — *vi* : to eat

manger[2] *nm* : food <le boire et le manger : food and drink>

mange–tout [mɑ̃ʒtu] *nms & pl or* **pois mange–tout** : snow pea

mangeur, -geuse [mɑ̃ʒœr, -ʒøz] *n* : eater

manglier [mɑ̃glije] *nm* : mangrove

mangouste [mɑ̃gust] *nf* : mongoose

mangue [mɑ̃g] *nf* : mango

maniabilité [manjabilite] *nf* : maneuverability

maniable [manjabl] *adj* **1** COMMODE : handy **2** : easy to handle, maneuverable **3** : easily influenced

maniaque[1] [manjak] *adj* **1** : fussy, finicky **2** : maniacal

maniaque[2] *nmf* **1** : crank, fanatic **2** : maniac

manie [mani] *nf* **1** : quirk, odd habit **2** OBSESSION : mania, obsession

maniement [manimɑ̃] *nm* : handling, use, operation <maniement d'une langue : command of a language>

manier [manje] {96} *vt* **1** : to handle, to deal with **2** : to use, to operate — **se manier** *vr fam* : to get a move on

manière [manjɛr] *nf* **1** : manner, way <d'une certaine manière : in a way> <en aucune manière : in no way, under no circumstances> <de manière à : so as to> <de toute manière : in any case, anyway> **2** : way, personal style <sa manière de parler : his way of speaking> **3** : style <dans la manière romantique : in the romantic style> **4 manières** *nfpl* : manners

maniéré, -rée [manjere] *adj* : affected, mannered

manifestant, -tante [manifɛstɑ̃, -tɑ̃t] *n* : demonstrator, protestor

manifestation [manifɛstasjɔ̃] *nf* **1** : (political) demonstration, protest **2** : expression (of emotions) **3** : event <une manifestation sportive : a sporting event> **4** : symptom, sign

manifeste[1] [manifɛst] *adj* ÉVIDENT : manifest, obvious — **manifestement** [-fɛstmɑ̃] *adj*

manifeste[2] *nm* : manifesto

manifester |manifɛste| *vt* **1** : to express, to indicate **2** RÉVÉLER : to reveal, to show — *vi* : to demonstrate, to hold a demonstration — **se manifester** *vr* **1** : to manifest itself **2** : to appear
manigance |manigɑ̃s| *nf* : scheme, intrigue, trick
manigancer |manigɑ̃se| {6} *vt* : to plot, to scheme
manipulateur, -trice |manipylatœr, -tris| *n* **1** : technician **2** : conjurer **3** : manipulator
manipulation |manipylasjɔ̃| *n* **1** MANIEMENT : handling **2** : manipulation
manipuler |manipyle| *vt* **1** : to handle **2** : to manipulate
manivelle |manivɛl| *nf* : crank
manne |man| *nf* **1** : manna **2** : godsend
mannequin |mankɛ̃| *nm* **1** : dummy, mannequin **2** : model
manœuvrable |manœvrabl| *adj* : maneuverable
manœuvre |manœvr| *nf* **1** : maneuver **2 fausse manœuvre** : wrong move, error
manœuvrer |manœvre| *vt* **1** : to maneuver **2** : to work, to operate **3** MANIPULER : to manipulate — *vi* : to maneuver
manoir |manwar| *nm* : country estate, manor
manque |mɑ̃k| *nm* **1** INSUFFISANCE : lack, shortage <par manque d'imagination : for want of imagination> <manque de rapport : irrelevance> **2** LACUNE : gap <manque de crédit : credibility gap> **3 être en manque** : to be in withdrawal (from alcohol or drugs) **4 manque à gagner** : loss of earnings, shortfall
manqué, -quée |mɑ̃ke| *adj* **1** : failed <poète manqué : failed poet> **2** : missed <occasion manquée : missed opportunity **3** → **garçon**
manquement |mɑ̃kmɑ̃| *nm* : breach, lapse
manquer |mɑ̃ke| *vt* **1** : to miss <manquer une bonne occasion : to miss a good opportunity> **2** FAILLIR : to fall short of, to just miss <elle a manqué (de) tomber : she nearly fell> — *vi* **1** : to be lacking, to be missing <ce n'est pas l'envie qui me manque : it's not that I don't want to> <il manque deux tasses : two cups are missing> **2** ÉCHOUER : to fail <j'ai manqué à mon devoir : I failed to do my duty> **3** : to be absent <elle n'a jamais manqué : she's never been absent> **4 ~ de** : to be short of, to lack <il manque d'argent : he has no money>
mansarde |mɑ̃sard| *nf* : attic room, garret
mansuétude |mɑ̃sɥetyd| *nf* : leniency
mante |mɑ̃t| *nf or* **mante religieuse** : praying mantis
manteau |mɑ̃to| *nm, pl* **manteaux** |-to| **1** : coat **2** : blanket (of fog), mantle (of snow, etc.) **3 manteau de cheminée** : mantelpiece **4 sous le manteau** : undercover, clandestinely
manucure[1] |manykyr| *nmf* : manicurist
manucure[2] *nf* : manicure
manucurer |manykyre| *vt* : to manicure
manuel[1], **-elle** |manɥɛl| *adj* : manual — **manuellement** |-nɥɛlmɑ̃| *adv*
manuel[2] *nm* **1** : manual, handbook **2** *or* **manuel scolaire** : textbook
manuel[3], **-nuelle** *n* : manual worker
manufacture |manyfaktyr| *nf* **1** USINE : factory **2** : manufacture
manufacturer |manyfaktyre| *vt* : to manufacture
manufacturier, -rière |manyfaktyrje, -rjɛr| *n* : manufacturer, factory owner
manuscrit[1], **-scrite** |manyskri, -skrit| *adj* : handwritten
manuscrit[2] *nm* : manuscript
manutention |manytɑ̃sjɔ̃| *nf* **1** : handling <frais de manutention : handling charges> **2** ENTREPÔT : storehouse, warehouse
mappemonde |mapmɔ̃d| *nf* : map of the world
maquereau |makro| *nm, pl* **-reaux** |-ro| : mackerel
maquette |makɛt| *nf* : scale model
maquignon |makiɲɔ̃| *nm* **1** : horse dealer, cattle trader **2** *France* : shady operator
maquillage |makijaʒ| *nm* **1** : makeup **2** : doctoring, faking
maquiller |makije| *vt* **1** : to make up (one's face) **2** FALSIFIER : to falsify, to fake **3** DÉGUISER : to disguise, to hide <maquiller la vérité : to hide the truth> — **se maquiller** *vr* : to put on makeup
maquilleur, -leuse |makijœr, -jøz| *n* : makeup artist
maquis |maki| *nm* **1** *France* : scrubland, brush **2** : tangle, labyrinth
maraîcher[1], **-chère** |marɛʃe, -ʃɛr| *adj* : farming <culture maraîchère : truck farming>
maraîcher[2], **-chère** *n* : truck farmer
marais |marɛ| *nm* : marsh, swamp
marasme |marasm| *nm* **1** ACCABLEMENT : dejection, depression **2** : stagnation <marasme économique : economic stagnation>
marasquin |maraskɛ̃| *nm* : maraschino
marathon |maratɔ̃| *nm* : marathon
marâtre |maratr| *nf* : cruel mother
maraudage |marodaʒ| → **maraude**
maraude |marod| *nf* **1** : pilfering, thieving **2 en ~** : cruising <taxi en maraude : cruising taxi>
marauder |marode| *vi* **1** : to pilfer, to thieve **2** : to cruise (of a taxi), to prowl about

maraudeur, -deuse [marodœr, -døz] *n* **1** : prowler, pilferer **2** : marauder

marbre [marbr] *nm* **1** : marble **2** *Can* : home plate (in baseball) **3 rester de marbre** : to remain impassive, to be unmoved

marbrer [marbre] *vt* **1** : to marble <gateau marbré : marble cake> **2** : to mottle, to blotch

marbrure [marbryr] *nf* **1** : marbling (of paper, etc.) **2** : mottling, blotchiness

marc [mar] *nm* : (coffee) grounds

marchand[1], -chande [marʃɑ̃, -ʃɑ̃d] *adj* **1** : market, commercial <valeur marchande : market value> **2** → **marine**

marchand[2], -chande *n* **1** COMMERÇANT : storekeeper, merchant, dealer <marchand de vins : wine merchant> **2 marchand ambulant** : hawker, peddler **3 marchand en gros** GROSSISTE : wholesaler

marchandage [marʃɑ̃daʒ] *nm* : bargaining, haggling

marchander [marʃɑ̃de] *vt* **1** : to bargain over, to haggle over **2** : to spare <il n'a pas marchandé ses éloges : he wasn't sparing in his praise> — *vi* : to haggle, to bargain, to dicker

marchandeur, -deuse [marʃɑ̃dœr, -døz] *n* : haggler

marchandises [marʃɑ̃diz] *nfpl* : goods, merchandise

marche [marʃ] *nf* **1** : step, stair <attention à la marche : watch for the step!> **2** : walk, walking <faire une marche : to take a walk> **3** : moving, running <un véhicule en marche : a moving vehicle> <la marche du temps : the march of time> **4** : working, operating <en bon état de marche : in good working order> **5** : march, marching <marche de protestation : protest march> **6** : march (in music) <marche nuptiale : wedding march>

marché [marʃe] *nm* **1** : market <faire son marché : to do one's (grocery) shopping> <marché aux puces : flea market> **2** : market (in economics and finance) <le marché du travail : the labor market> <marché noir : black market> <étude de marché : market survey> **3** : deal <conclure un marché : to strike a deal> **4 bon marché** : cheap <à bon marché : at a good price, cheaply> **5 par-dessus le marché** : to top it all off

marchepied [marʃəpje] *nm* **1** : step, steps *pl* (of a vehicle) **2** : steppingstone

marcher [marʃe] *vi* **1** : to walk **2** : to step, to tread **3** FONCTIONNER : to work, to go, to run <ma montre ne marche pas : my watch isn't running> <cette auto marche trop vite : that car's going too fast> **4** : to be working, to be going well <si ça marche : if it works out> **5 faire marcher qqn** *fam* : to pull s.o.'s leg **6 marcher au pas** : to march

marchette [marʃɛt] *nf Can* : walker (for babies)

marcheur, -cheuse [marʃœr, -ʃøz] *n* : walker

mardi [mardi] *nm* **1** : Tuesday **2 mardi gras** : Mardi Gras

mare [mar] *nf* **1** : pond **2** : pool <une mare de sang : a pool of blood>

marécage [marekaʒ] *nm* : marsh, swamp

marécageux, -geuse [marekaʒø, -ʒøz] *adj* : marshy, swampy

maréchal [mareʃal] *nm, pl* **-chaux** [-ʃo] : marshal

maréchal-ferrant [mareʃalferɑ̃] *nm, pl* **maréchaux-ferrants** [mareʃoferɑ̃] : blacksmith

marée [mare] *nf* **1** : tide <à marée haute : at high tide> <marée descendante : ebb tide> **2** : flood, surge (of emotions, etc.) **3 marée noire** : oil slick

marelle [marɛl] *nf* : hopscotch

marémoteur, -trice [maremɔtœr, -tris] *adj* : tidal

margarine [margarin] *nf* : margarine

marge [marʒ] *nf* **1** : margin **2** : leeway, room <marge de manœuvre : room to maneuver> **3** *or* **marge bénéficiaire** : profit margin, markup **4 en marge de** : on the fringes of, outside <vivre en marge de la société : to live on the fringes of society> <en marge de la loi : outside the law>

marginal[1], -nale [marʒinal] *adj, mpl* **-naux** [-no] : marginal — **marginalement** [-nalmɑ̃] *adv*

marginal[2], -nale *n, mpl* **-naux** : dropout

marguerite [margərit] *nf* : daisy

mari [mari] *nm* : husband

mariage [marjaʒ] *nm* **1** : marriage <mariage mixte : intermarriage, mixed marriage> **2** : wedding **3** : blend, merger, alliance

marié[1], -riée [marje] *adj* : married

marié[2], -riée *n* **1** : groom *m*, bride *f* **2 les mariés** : the newlyweds

marier [marje] {96} *vt* **1** : to marry, to unite in marriage <le curé les a mariés : the priest married them> **2** *Can* ÉPOUSER : to marry, to get married to <il voulait la marier : he wanted to marry her> **3** : to combine, to blend — **se marier** *vr* **1** : to get married <se marier avec : to get married to> **2** : to go well together

marieur, -rieuse [marjœr, -jøz] *n* : matchmaker

marijuana [marirwana] *nf* : marijuana

marin[1], -rine [marɛ̃, -rin] *adj* **1** : sea, marine <paysage marin : seascape> **2** : offshore

marin[2] *nm* : sailor, mariner

marina [marina] *nf* : marina

marine[1] [marin] *adj or* **bleu marine** : navy blue

marine[2] *nf* **1** : navy <officier de marine : naval officer> **2 marine marchande** : merchant marine
marine[3] *nm* : navy blue
mariner [marine] *v* : to marinate
maringouin [marɛ̃gwɛ̃] *nm Can* : mosquito
marinière [marinjɛr] *nf* : smock
marionnette [marjɔnɛt] *nf* **1** : puppet **2 marionnette à fils** : marionette
marionnettiste [marjɔnɛtist] *nmf* : puppeteer
marital, -tale [marital] *adj, mpl* **-taux** [-to] : marital
maritime [maritim] *adj* **1** : maritime, coastal, seaboard **2** : naval, nautical **3** : shipping
marjolaine [marʒɔlɛn] *nf* : marjoram
marketing [markɛtiŋ] *nm* : marketing
marmaille [marmaj] *nf fam* : brats *pl*, noisy kids *pl*
marmelade [marməlad] *nf* **1** COMPOTE : stewed fruit **2** : marmalade
marmite [marmit] *nf* : cooking pot
marmonnement [marmɔnmɑ̃] *nm* : mumble, mutter
marmonner [marmɔne] *v* : to mutter, to mumble
marmot [marmo] *nm fam* : kid, brat
marmotte [marmɔt] *nf* **1** : marmot **2 marmotte d'Amérique** : groundhog, woodchuck
marmotter [marmɔte] *v* MARMONNER : to mutter, to mumble
marocain, -caine [marɔkɛ̃, -kɛn] *adj* : Moroccan
Marocain, -caine *nmf* : Moroccan
marotte [marɔt] *nf* : craze, fad
marquant, -quante [markɑ̃, -kɑ̃t] *adj* MÉMORABLE : memorable, outstanding
marque [mark] *nf* **1** : mark, trace, sign <marques de doigts : finger marks> <marques d'usure : signs of wear> **2** : brand, make <marque déposée : registered trademark> **3** : eminence, prominence <personnalité de marque : prominent figure> **4** : hallmark, stamp **5** : proof, sign <une marque de confiance : a sign of confidence> **6** : score (in sports, in games) **7 à vos marques! prêts! partez!** : on your marks! get set! go!
marqué, -quée [marke] *adj* **1** : marked **2** NET : distinct, decided
marquer [marke] *vt* **1** : to mark **2** INDIQUER : to show, to indicate **3** : to brand **4** : to score (in sports) **5** : to write down, to note **6 marquer le pas** : to mark time — *vi* **1** : to leave a mark **2** : to be significant, to stand out
marqueur[1], **-queuse** [markœr, -køz] *n* : scorekeeper
marqueur[2] *nm* : marker (pen), highlighter
marquis, -quise [marki, -kiz] *n* : marquess *m*, marquis *m*, marchioness *f*, marquise *f*
marquise *nf* **1** : canopy, marquee **2** AUVENT : awning
marraine [marɛn] *nf* : godmother
marrant, -rante [marɑ̃, -rɑ̃t] *adj fam* : amusing, funny
marre [mar] *adv fam* : enough <j'en ai marre : I'm fed up>
marron[1], **-ronne** [marɔ̃, -rɔn] *adj* **1** MALHONNÊTE : crooked, bogus <médecin marron : quack> **2** : brown
marron[2] *nm* **1** : chestnut **2** : brown
marronnier [marɔnje] *nm* : chestnut tree
mars [mars] *nm* : March
Mars *nf* : Mars (planet)
marsouin [marswɛ̃] *nm* : porpoise
marsupial, -piale [marsypjal] *adj & nm, pl* **-piaux** [-pjo] : marsupial
marteau [marto] *nm, pl* **marteaux** [marto] **1** : hammer **2** : gavel **3** : knocker **4 marteau pneumatique** : pneumatic drill
marteau-piqueur [martopikœr] *nm, pl* **marteaux-piqueurs** : jackhammer
martèlement [martɛlmɑ̃] *nm* : hammering
marteler [martəle] {20} *vt* **1** : to hammer, to pound **2** : to hammer out (words)
martial, -tiale [marsjal] *adj, mpl* **-tiaux** [-sjo] : martial
martinet [martinɛ] *nm* **1** : small whip **2** : swift, martin
martin-pêcheur [martɛ̃pɛʃœr] *nm, pl* **martins-pêcheurs** : kingfisher
martre [martr] *nf* **1** : marten **2** : sable (fur)
martyr[1], **-tyre** [martir] *adj* **1** : martyred **2 enfant martyr** : battered child
martyr[2], **-tyre** *n* : martyr
martyre *nm* **1** : martyrdom **2** : agony, torture <souffrir le martyre : to be in agony>
martyriser [martirize] *vt* **1** : to martyr **2** : to torment, to maltreat
marxisme [marksism] *nm* : Marxism — **marxiste** [marksist] *adj & nmf*
mascara [maskara] *nm* : mascara
mascarade [maskarad] *nf* : masquerade
mascotte [maskɔt] *nf* : mascot
masculin[1], **-line** [maskylɛ̃, -lin] *adj* **1** : male **2** : men's **3** : masculine, manly
masculin[2] *nm* : masculine (in grammar)
masculinité [maskylinite] *nf* : masculinity
maskinongé [maskinɔ̃ʒe] *nm* : muskellunge
masochisme [mazɔʃism] *nm* : masochism
masochiste[1] [mazɔʃist] *adj* : masochistic
masochiste[2] *nmf* : masochist

masque |mask| *nm* : mask <masque à gaz : gas mask> <masque de plongée : diving mask>
masqué, -quée |maske| *adj* **1** : masked **2** : concealed, disguised
masquer |maske| *vt* DISSIMULER : to mask, to conceal, to block from view
massacrant, -crante |masakrɑ̃, -krɑ̃t| *adj* **humeur massacrante** : foul mood
massacre |masakr| *nm* : massacre
massacrer |masakre| *vt* **1** : to massacre, to butcher **2** *fam* BOUSILLER : to botch
massage |masaʒ| *nm* : massage
masse |mas| *nf* **1** : mass, body <masse d'air froide : mass of cold air> <masse d'eau : body of water> **2** : great quantity <la (grande) masse : the majority> <une masse de renseignements : a mass of information> <en masse : en masse, in a body, in bulk> **3** : common people <l'art de masse : popular art> <les masses : the masses, the people> **4** : (electrical) ground <mettre à la masse : to ground> **5** : sledgehammer **6** : mass (in science) **7** *or* **masse d'armes** : mace
massepain |maspɛ̃| *nm* : marzipan
masser |mase| *vt* **1** : to massage **2** : to mass, to gather — **se masser** *vr* : to assemble, to gather together
massette |masɛt| *nf* : cattail
masseur, -seuse |masœr, -søz| *n* : massage therapist, masseur *m*, masseuse *f*
massif[1], -sive |masif, -siv| *adj* **1** : massive, solid, heavy <bois massif : solid wood> **2** : mass <migrations massives : mass migrations>
massif[2] *nm* **1** : clump, cluster <un massif d'arbres : a clump of trees> **2** : massif
massivement |masivmɑ̃| *adv* : massively
mass media |masmedja| *nmpl* : mass media
massue |masy| *nf* **1** : club, bludgeon **2** **coup de massue** : staggering blow
mastic |mastik| *nm* **1** : mastic **2** : putty, caulk
mastication |mastikasjɔ̃| *nf* : chewing, mastication
mastiff |mastif| *nm* : mastiff
mastiquer |mastike| *vt* **1** : to chew, to masticate **2** : to fill in, to putty
mastoc |mastɔk| *adj* : hefty
mastodonte |mastɔdɔ̃t| *nm* **1** : mastodon **2** : huge person, hulk
mastoïde |mastɔid| *nf* : mastoid
masturbation |mastyrbasjɔ̃| *nf* : masturbation
masturber |mastyrbe| *v* **se masturber** *vr* : to masturbate
m'as–tu–vu |matyvy| *nmfs & pl* : show-off
masure |mazyr| *nf* : hovel
mat, mate |mat| *adj* **1** : dull, unpolished, matte **2** : checkmated
mât |ma| *nm* **1** : mast **2** POTEAU : pole, post **3** *or* **mât de drapeau** : flagpole
matador |matadɔr| *nm* : matador, bullfighter
matamore |matamɔr| *nm* : braggart
match |matʃ| *nm* **1** : match, game **2** **match nul** : tie, draw
matelas |matla| *nm* : mattress <matelas pneumatique : air mattress> <matelas d'eau : waterbed>
matelasser |matlase| *vt* **1** : to pad **2** : to quilt
matelot |matlo| *nm* MARIN : sailor, seaman
mater |mate| *vt* **1** DOMPTER : to subdue, to curb **2** : to checkmate
matérialiser |materjalize| *vt* CONCRÉTISER : to realize, to make happen — **se matérialiser** *vr* : to materialize
matérialisme |materjalism| *nm* : materialism
matérialiste[1] |materjalist| *adj* : materialistic, materialist
matérialiste[2] *nmf* : materialist
matériau |materjo| *nm, pl* **-riaux** |-rjo| **1** : material, substance **2** **matériaux** *nmpl* : materials (for construction, etc.) **3** **matériaux** *nmpl* : material, documentation
matériel[1], -rielle |materjɛl| *adj* **1** : material, physical **2** : materialistic — **matériellement** |-rjɛlmɑ̃| *adv*
matériel[2] *nm* **1** : equipment, material(s) <matériel de pêche : fishing gear> **2** : computer hardware
maternel, -nelle |matɛrnɛl| *adj* **1** : maternal, motherly **2** **langue maternelle** : mother tongue — **maternellement** |-nɛlmɑ̃| *adv*
maternelle *nf or* **école maternelle** |ekɔlmatɛrnɛl| : nursery school
materner |matɛrne| *vt* : to mother
maternité |matɛrnite| *nf* **1** : maternity, motherhood **2** GROSSESSE : pregnancy **3** : maternity hospital
mathématicien, -cienne |matematisjɛ̃, -sjɛn| *n* : mathematician
mathématique |matematik| *adj* : mathematical — **mathématiquement** |-tikmɑ̃| *adv*
mathématiques |matematik| *nfpl* : mathematics
maths *or* **math** |mat| *nfpl fam* : math
matière |matjɛr| *nf* **1** : matter, substance <matière organique : organic matter> **2** : subject, subject matter <ma meilleure matière : my best subject> <matière à discussion : matter for discussion> **3** : material <matières premières : raw materials> **4** **donner matière à** : to give cause for **5** **en matière de** : as far as
matin[1] |matɛ̃| *adv* : early in the morning <elle déjeune très matin : she has breakfast very early>
matin[2] *nm* : morning <le matin : in the morning> <du matin au soir : from dawn to dusk>

matinal, -nale [matinal] *adj, mpl* **-naux** [-no] **1** : morning **2 être matinal** : to be up early, to be an early riser

matinée [matine] *nf* **1** : morning **2** : matinee

matois, -toise [matwa, -twaz] *adj* RUSÉ : sly, crafty

matou [matu] *nm* : tomcat

matraque [matrak] *nf* : (billy) club, nightstick

matraquer [matrake] *vt* **1** : to club, to bludgeon **2** : to plug (a product), to hype **3** *fam* : to rip off

matriarcal, -cale [matrijarkal] *adj, mpl* **-caux** [-ko] : matriarchal

matriarcat [matrijarka] *nm* : matriarchy

matrice [matris] *nf* **1** : womb **2** : matrix, mold

matricide [matrisid] *nm* : matricide

matricule[1] [matrikyl] *nm* : serial number

matricule[2] *nf* : register

matrimonial, -niale [matrimɔnjal] *adj, mpl* **-niaux** [-njo] : matrimonial, marriage

matrone [matrɔn] *nf* **1** : matron, matriarch **2** *Can* : female warden

maturation [matyrasjɔ̃] *nf* : maturing, maturation

mature [matyr] *adj* : mature

mâture [matyr] *nf* : masts *pl*

maturité [matyrite] *nf* : maturity

maudire [modir] *vt* : to curse, to damn

maudit, -dite [modi, -dit] *adj* : damned <cette maudite pluie! : this damned rain!>

maugréer [mogree] {89} *vi* GROGNER : to grumble

mauricien, -cienne [morisjɛ̃, -sjɛn] *adj* : Mauritian

Mauricien, -cienne *n* : Mauritian

mauritanien, -nienne [moritanjɛ̃, -njɛn] *adj* : Mauritanian

Mauritanien, -nienne *n* : Mauritanian

mausolée [mozɔle] *nm* : mausoleum

maussade [mosad] *adj* **1** MOROSE : sullen, morose **2** : dismal, gloomy

maussaderie [mosadri] *nf* : sullenness, moroseness

mauvais[1] [movɛ] *adv* : bad, poorly <il fait mauvais : the weather is bad>

mauvais[2], **-vaise** [movɛ, -vɛz] *adj* **1** : bad <ses mauvaises notes : his bad grades> **2** : wrong <un mauvais numéro : a wrong number> **3** : nasty, unpleasant **4** : rough <la mer est mauvaise : the sea is rough> **5** → **herbe 6 mauvaises rencontres** : bad company

mauve [mov] *adj & nm* : mauve

mauviette [movjɛt] *nf* : weakling

maxillaire [maksilɛr] *nm* : jawbone

maximal, -male [maksimal] *adj, mpl* **-maux** [-mo] : maximal, maximum

maxime [maksim] *nf* ADAGE : maxim, proverb

maximiser [maksimize] *vt* : to maximize

maximum[1] [maksimɔm] *adj, pl* **-mums** [-mɔm] *or* **-ma** [-ma] : maximum

maximum[2] *nm, pl* **-mums** *or* **-ma 1** : maximum **2 au ~** : as much as possible, at the very most

maya[1] [maja] *adj* : Mayan

maya[2] *nm* : Mayan (language)

Maya *nmf* : Maya

mayonnaise [majɔnɛz] *nf* : mayonnaise

mazout [mazut] *nm* : heating oil

me [mə] *pron* **1** (**m'** [m] *before a vowel or mute h*) : me, to me <elles m'ont aidé : they helped me> <il m'apparaît : it seems to me> **2** : myself, to myself <je me disais : I said to myself>

méandres [meɑ̃dr] *nmpl* : meandering, rambling

mec [mɛk] *nm fam* : guy

mécanicien, -cienne [mekanisjɛ̃, -sjɛn] *n* **1** : mechanic **2** : engineer (of a locomotive), flight engineer

mécanique[1] [mekanik] *adj* : mechanical — **mécaniquement** [-nikmɑ̃] *adv*

mécanique[2] *nf* **1** : mechanics **2** : mechanical engineering **3** : machine, mechanism

mécanisation [mekanizasjɔ̃] *nf* : mechanization

mécaniser [mekanize] *vt* : to mechanize

mécanisme [mekanism] *nm* : mechanism

mécano [mekano] *nm fam* : mechanic

mécénat [mesena] *nm* : patronage, sponsorship

mécène [mesɛn] *nm* : patron, sponsor

méchamment [meʃamɑ̃] *adv* : nastily, maliciously

méchanceté [meʃɑ̃ste] *nf* : nastiness, meanness, badness, malice

méchant[1], **-chante** [meʃɑ̃, -ʃɑ̃t] *adj* **1** : nasty, malicious **2** : naughty, bad **3** : vicious <attention chien méchant! : beware of the dog!> **4** : mediocre, second-rate **5** : bad, serious <ce n'est pas bien méchant : that's not too serious> **6** *fam* : remarkable, terrific <quelle méchante idée! : what a fantastic idea!>

méchant[2], **-chante** *n* : villain (in a book or film)

mèche [mɛʃ] *nf* **1** : wick **2** : fuse (of an explosive) **3** : lock (of hair) <mèche rebelle : cowlick> **4** : bit (of a drill)

mécompte [mekɔ̃t] *nm* DÉCEPTION : letdown, disappointment

méconnaissable [mekɔnɛsabl] *adj* : unrecognizable

méconnaissance [mekɔnɛsɑ̃s] *nf* : ignorance, lack of understanding

méconnaître [mekɔnɛtr] {7} *vt* **1** IGNORER : to be unaware of **2** MÉJUGER : to misjudge, to underestimate **3** : to disregard (rules, duties, etc.)

méconnu, -nue [mekɔny] *adj* : unrecognized
mécontent, -tente [mekɔ̃tɑ̃, -tɑ̃t] *adj* INSATISFAIT : discontented, dissatisfied
mécontentement [mekɔ̃tɑ̃tmɑ̃] *nm* INSATISFACTION : discontent, dissatisfaction
mécontenter [mekɔ̃tɑ̃te] *vt* : to annoy, to displease
mécréant[1], **-créante** [mekreɑ̃,-kreɑ̃t] *adj* : skeptical, unbelieving
mécréant[2], **-créante** *n* INFIDÈLE : unbeliever
médaille [medaj] *nf* : medal
médaillé, -lée [medaje] *n* : medalist
médaillon [medajɔ̃] *nm* **1** : medallion **2** : locket
médecin [medsɛ̃] *nm* : doctor, physician <médecin généraliste : general practitioner> <médecin légiste : medical examiner>
médecine [medsin] *nf* : medicine <médecine légale : forensic medicine>
média [medja] *nm* : medium <les médias : the (mass) media>
médian, -diane [medjɑ̃, -djan] *adj* : median
médiane *nf* : median (in mathematics)
médiateur, -trice [medjatœr, -tris] *n* : mediator, arbitrator, ombudsman
médiathèque [medjatɛk] *nf* : multimedia library
médiation [medjasjɔ̃] *nf* : mediation, arbitration
médiatique [medjatik] *adj* : media, newsworthy <geste médiatique : publicity stunt>
médiatisation [medjatizasjɔ̃] *nf* : media coverage
médiatiser [medjatize] *vt* : to cover in the media
médical, -cale [medikal] *adj, mpl* **-caux** [-ko] : medical — **médicalement** [-kalmɑ̃] *adv*
médicament [medikamɑ̃] *nm* : medicine, drug
médicamenteux, -teuse [medikamɑ̃tø, -tøz] *adj* : medicinal
médication [medikasjɔ̃] *nf* : medication, treatment
médicinal, -nale [medisinal] *adj, mpl* **-naux** [-no] : medicinal
médico–légal, -gale [medikɔlegal] *adj, mpl* **-gaux** [-go] : forensic
médiéval, -vale [medjeval] *adj, mpl* **-vaux** [-vo] : medieval
médiocre [medjɔkr] *adj* : mediocre, second-rate, ordinary
médiocrité [medjɔkrite] *nf* : mediocrity
médire [medir] {29} *vi* **~ de** : to speak ill of
médisance [medizɑ̃s] *nf* : malicious gossip
médisant, -sante [medizɑ̃, -zɑ̃t] *adj* : slanderous, malicious
méditatif, -tive [meditatif, -tiv] *adj* PENSIF : meditative, thoughtful
méditation [meditasjɔ̃] *nf* : meditation
méditer [medite] *vt* **1** : to reflect on, to think over **2** : to have in mind <méditer un projet : to plan a project> — *vi* : to meditate
médium [medjɔm] *nm* : medium, psychic, spiritualist
méduse [medyz] *nf* : jellyfish
méduser [medyze] *vt* : to dumbfound
meeting [mitiŋ] *nm* **1** : meeting, rally **2** : meet (in sports)
méfait [mefɛ] *nm* **1** : misdeed, misdemeanour **2 méfaits** *nmpl* : ravages (of time, etc.)
méfiance [mefjɑ̃s] *nf* : distrust, suspicion
méfiant, -fiante [mefjɑ̃, -fjɑ̃t] *adj* : distrustful, suspicious
méfier [mefje] {96} *v* **se méfier** *vr* **1** : to be careful, to beware <méfiez-vous dans cette rue : be careful on this street> **2 ~ de** : to distrust, to be wary of
mégahertz [megaɛrts] *nm* : megahertz
mégaoctet [megaɔktɛ] *nm* : megabyte
mégaphone [megafɔn] *nm* PORTE-VOIX : megaphone
mégarde [megard] *nf* **par ~** : inadvertently
mégot [mego] *nm* : cigarette butt
meilleur[1] [mɛjœr] *adv* : better <il fait meilleur cet hiver : the weather is better this winter>
meilleur[2], **-leure** *adj* **1** (*comparative of* **bon**) : better <le meilleur des deux : the better of the two> **2** (*superlative of* **bon**) : best <le meilleur choix : the best choice> <meilleurs vœux : best wishes> **3 meilleur marché** : cheaper
meilleur[3], **-leure** *n* : best person <que le meilleur gagne : may the best man win>
meilleur[4] *nm* : better part, best bit <pour le meilleur et pour le pire : for better or for worse>
méjuger [meʒyʒe] {17} *vt* : to misjudge — *vi* **~ de** : to underestimate — **se méjuger** *vr* : to underestimate oneself
mél [mel] *nm Bel, France* : e-mail, electronic mail
mélancolie [melɑ̃kɔli] *nf* : melancholy, gloom
mélancolique [melɑ̃kɔlik] *adj* : melancholy, gloomy
mélange [melɑ̃ʒ] *nm* **1** : mixing, blending **2** : mixture, blend
mélanger [melɑ̃ʒe] {17} *vt* **1** : to mix, to blend **2** : to mix up, to confuse — **se mélanger** *vr* : to mix, to intermingle
mélangeur [melɑ̃ʒœr] *nm Can* : blender
mélant, -lante [melɑ̃, -lɑ̃t] *adj Can* : complicated, difficult to understand
mélasse [melas] *nf* : molasses

melé, -lée |mele| *adj Can* **1** : mixed <des sentiments melés : mixed feelings> **2** *Can* : mixed-up, confused

mêlée |mele| *nf* **1** : battle, conflict, fray **2** : commotion, confusion <mêlée générale : free-for-all>

mêler |mele| *vt* : to mix — **se mêler** *vr* **1** : to mix, to mingle **2** : to meddle <mêlez-vous de vos affaires : mind your own business>

mélèze |melɛz| *nm* : larch

méli-mélo |melimelo| *nm, pl* **mélis-mélos** : hodgepodge, muddle

mélodie |melɔdi| *nf* : melody

mélodieux, -dieuse |melɔdjø, -djøz| *adj* : melodious — **mélodieusement** |-djøzmɑ̃| *adv*

mélodique |melɔdik| *adj* : melodic — **mélodiquement** |-dikmɑ̃| *adv*

mélodrame |melɔdram| *nm* : melodrama — **mélodramatique** |-dramatik| *adj*

mélomane |melɔman| *nmf* : music lover

melon |məlɔ̃| *nm* **1** : melon <melon d'eau : watermelon> **2** *or* **chapeau melon** : derby (hat)

membrane |mɑ̃bran| *nf* : membrane

membre |mɑ̃br| *nm* **1** : limb, member **2** : member (of a group)

mémé |meme| *nf France fam* : grandma, granny

même[1] |mɛm| *adv* **1** : even <personne n'y va, pas même Robert : nobody's going, not even Robert> <même si : even if, even though> **2 à ~** : directly on, straight from, right against <à même la bouteille : straight from the bottle> **3 de ~** : likewise, the same **4 de même que** : just as **5 tout de même** : even so, nonetheless

même[2] *adj* **1** : same, identical <le même jour : the same day> <en même temps : at the same time> **2** (*used as an intensifier*) : very, actual <ce sont ses paroles mêmes : those were his very words> **3** → **elle-même, lui-même, eux-mêmes**

même[3] *pron* **le même, la même, les mêmes** : the same (one, ones)

mémérage |memeraʒ| *nm Can* : gossip

mémère |memer| *nf* **1** *fam* : grandma **2** *Can fam* : gossip

mémérer |memere| *vi Can fam* : to gossip

mémoire[1] |memwar| *nm* **1** : dissertation, thesis **2 mémoires** *nmpl* : memoirs

mémoire[2] *nf* **1** : memory <avoir de la mémoire : to have a good memory> <de mémoire : from memory> **2 mémoire vive** : random-access memory, RAM

mémorable |memɔrabl| *adj* : memorable — **mémorablement** |-rabləmɑ̃| *adv*

mémorandum |memɔrɑ̃dɔm| *nm* **1** : (diplomatic) memorandum **2** : note, memo

mémorial |memɔrjal| *nm, pl* **-riaux** |-rjo| : memorial

mémoriser |memɔrize| *vt* **1** : to memorize **2** : to store (data)

menaçant, -çante |mənasɑ̃, -sɑ̃t| *adj* : threatening, menacing, ominous

menace |mənas| *nf* : threat <menaces en l'air : idle threats>

menacer |mənase| {6} *vt* **1** : to threaten **2** : to pose a threat to <être menacé : to be at risk> — *vi* : to threaten <la pluie menace : it looks like rain>

ménage |menaʒ| *nm* **1** : household, family <un ménage de quatre personnes : a household of four people> **2** : married couple <heureux en ménage : happily married> **3** : housework, housekeeping <faire le ménage : to do the housework> **4 faire bon ménage avec** : to get along well with

ménagement |menaʒmɑ̃| *nm* : consideration, thoughtfulness <avec ménagement : gently, tactfully> <sans ménagement : bluntly>

ménager[1] |menaʒe| {17} *vt* **1** ÉPARGNER : to save <ménager son argent : to save one's money> **2** : to use carefully, to handle with care **3** : to treat considerately **4** : to arrange, to organize — **se ménager** *vr* : to take it easy

ménager[2]**, -gère** |menaʒe, -ʒɛr| *adj* : household, domestic <travaux ménagers : housework>

ménagère |menaʒɛr| *nf* : housewife

ménagerie |menaʒri| *nf* : menagerie

mendiant, -diante |mɑ̃djɑ̃, -djɑ̃t| *n* : beggar, mendicant

mendicité |mɑ̃disite| *nf* : begging

mendier |mɑ̃dje| {96} *v* : to beg

mené |məne| *nm Can* : minnow

menées |məne| *nfpl* : scheming, intrigues

mener |məne| {52} *vt* **1** EMMENER : to take, to bring <mener promener un chien : to take a dog for a walk> **2** : to lead, to be at the head of **3** DIRIGER : to conduct, to run **4** : to carry out <mener à bien : to complete successfully, to see (something) through>

ménestrel |menɛstrɛl| *nm* : minstrel

meneur, -neuse |mənœr, -nøz| *n* **1** : leader <un meneur d'hommes : a born leader> **2** : ringleader **3 meneuse de claque** *Can* : cheerleader

méninges |menɛ̃ʒ| *nfpl fam* : brains <se creuser les méninges : to rack one's brains>

méningite |menɛ̃ʒit| *nf* : meningitis

ménopause |menɔpoz| *nf* : menopause

menotte |mənɔt| *nf* **1** : little hand **2 menottes** *nfpl* : handcuffs <passer les menottes à qqn : to handcuff s.o.>

mensonge [mɑ̃sɔ̃ʒ] *nm* **1** : lie **2 le mensonge** : lying
mensonger, -gère [mɑ̃sɔ̃ʒe, -ʒɛr] *adj* **1** FAUX : false **2** TROMPEUR : misleading
menstruation [mɑ̃stryasjɔ̃] *nf* RÈGLES : menstruation, period
menstruel, -struelle [mɑ̃stryɛl] *adj* : menstrual
mensualité [mɑ̃sɥalite] *nf* : monthly payment
mensuel[1]**, -suelle** [mɑ̃sɥɛl] *adj* : monthly — **mensuellement** [-sɥɛlmɑ̃] *adv*
mensuel[2] *nm* : monthly (magazine)
mensurations [mɑ̃syrasjɔ̃] *nfpl* : measurements
mental, -tale [mɑ̃tal] *adj, mpl* **mentaux** [-to] : mental — **mentalement** [-talmɑ̃] *adv*
mentalité [mɑ̃talite] *nf* : mentality
menterie [mɑ̃tri] *nf Can fam* : lie, fib
menteur[1]**, -teuse** [mɑ̃tœr, -tøz] *adj* : untruthful, false
menteur[2]**, -teuse** *n* : liar
menthe [mɑ̃t] *nf* **1** : mint **2 menthe poivrée** : peppermint **3 menthe verte** : spearmint
menthol [mɑ̃tɔl] *nm* : menthol
mentholé, -lée [mɑ̃tɔle] *adj* : mentholated
mention [mɑ̃sjɔ̃] *nf* **1** : mention <faire mention de : to mention> **2** : note, comment <porter la mention «secret» : to be labeled "secret">
mentionner [mɑ̃sjɔne] *vt* : to mention
mentir [mɑ̃tir] {82} *vi* : to lie
menton [mɑ̃tɔ̃] *nm* : chin
menu[1] [məny] *adv* : finely, small <oignons coupés menu : finely chopped onions>
menu[2]**, -nue** *adj* **1** PETIT : small, tiny, slender **2** : minor, trifling
menu[3] [məny] *nm* **1** : menu **2 par le menu** : in minute detail
menuet [mənɥɛ] *nm* : minuet
menuiserie [mənɥizri] *nf* : woodworking, carpentry
menuisier [mənɥizje] *nm* : woodworker, carpenter
méprendre [meprɑ̃dr] {70} *v* **se méprendre** *vr* **~ sur** : to be mistaken about
mépris [mepri] *nm* **1** DÉDAIN : contempt, scorn **2 au mépris de** : regardless of, in defiance of
méprisable [meprizabl] *adj* VIL : despicable, contemptible
méprisant, -sante [meprizɑ̃, -zɑ̃t] *adj* : contemptuous, scornful
méprise [mepriz] *nf* **1** ERREUR : mistake, error **2** MALENTENDU : misunderstanding
mépriser [meprize] *vt* : to despise, to scorn
mer [mɛr] *nf* **1** : sea <en mer : at sea> <niveau de la mer : sea level> <prendre la mer : to put to sea> **2** MARÉE : tide <mer haute : high tide> <mer basse : low tide>
mercantile [mɛrkɑ̃til] *adj* **1** : mercenary, greedy **2** : mercantile, commercial
mercenaire [mɛrsənɛr] *adj & nmf* : mercenary
mercerie [mɛrsəri] *nf* **1** : notions *pl* **2** : notions store
merci[1] [mɛrsi] *nm* : thank-you <mille mercis : thank you so much>
merci[2] *nf* **1** : mercy <à la merci de : at the mercy of> **2 sans ~** : merciless
merci[3] *interj* : thank you!, thanks! <merci beaucoup! *or* merci bien! : thank you very much!>
mercredi [mɛrkrədi] *nm* **1** : Wednesday **2 le mercredi des Cendres** : Ash Wednesday
mercure [mɛrkyr] *nm* : mercury
Mercure *nf* : Mercury (planet)
mère [mɛr] *nf* **1** : mother <mère célibataire : single mother> **2** : Mother (in religion)
méridien [meridjɛ̃] *nm* : meridian
méridional, -nale [meridjɔnal] *adj, mpl* **-naux** [-no] : southern
meringue [mərɛ̃g] *nf* : meringue
mérinos [merinos] *nm* : merino
merise [məriz] *nf* : wild cherry
méritant, -tante [meritɑ̃, -tɑ̃t] *adj* : deserving, meritorious
mérite [merit] *nm* **1** : merit, credit <le mérite lui revient : the credit goes to him> **2** VALEUR : merit, quality <ce film a ses mérites : this film has its merits>
mériter [merite] *vt* : to deserve, to merit
méritoire [meritwar] *adj* : commendable, praiseworthy
merlan [mɛrlɑ̃] *nm* : whiting
merle [mɛrl] *nm* : blackbird
merlu *or* **merlus** [mɛrly] *nm* : hake
mérou [meru] *nm* : grouper (fish)
merveille [mɛrvɛj] *nf* **1** : wonder, marvel **2 à ~** : wonderfully, excellently
merveilleux, -leuse [mɛrvɛjø, -jøz] *adj* : wonderful, marvelous — **merveilleusement** [-jøzmɑ̃] *adv*
mes → mon
mésange [mezɑ̃ʒ] *nf* : titmouse
mésaventure [mezavɑ̃tyr] *nf* : misfortune, mishap
mesdames → madame
mesdemoiselles → mademoiselle
mésentente [mezɑ̃tɑ̃t] *nf* DÉSACCORD : misunderstanding, disagreement
mésestimer [mezɛstime] *vt* SOUS-ESTIMER : to underestimate, to underrate
mesquin, -quine [mɛskɛ̃, -kin] *adj* **1** : mean, petty **2** : cheap, stingy — **mesquinement** [-kinmɑ̃] *adv*
mesquinerie [mɛskinri] *nf* **1** PETITESSE : pettiness **2** AVARICE : meanness, stinginess
mess [mɛs] *nm* : mess

message [mɛsaʒ] *nm* **1** : message **2 message publicitaire** : commercial
messager, -gère [mɛsaʒe, -ʒɛr] *n* : messenger
messagerie [mɛsaʒri] *nf* **1** : parcel delivery service **2 messagerie électronique** : electronic mail
messe [mɛs] *nf* : Mass (in religion)
messeigneurs [mesɛɲœr] → **monseigneur**
messie [mɛsi] *nm* **le Messie** : the Messiah
messieurs → **monsieur**
mesurable [məzyrabl] *adj* : measurable
mesurage [məzyraʒ] *nm* : measuring, measurement
mesure [məzyr] *nf* **1** : measurement, measuring **2** : measure <unité de mesure : unit of measure> <pour faire bonne mesure : for good measure> **3** : measure, step <mesures draconiennes : drastic measures> **4** RETENUE : moderation, restraint **5** : degree, limit <dans la mesure où : insofar as> **6 à la mesure de** : worthy of **7 à mesure que** : as **8 outre ~** : excessively **9 sur ~** : made-to-order
mesuré, -rée [məzyre] *adj* : measured, restrained
mesurer [məzyre] *vt* **1** : to measure, to take measurements of **2** : to weigh, to assess <mesurer ses paroles : to measure one's words> **3** : to limit <le temps lui est mesuré : his time is limited> **4** : to adapt, to gear — **se mesurer** *vr* **1** : to be measurable **2 ~ avec** : to pit oneself against
métabolique [metabɔlik] *adj* : metabolic
métaboliser [metabɔlize] *vt* : to metabolize
métabolisme [metabɔlism] *nm* : metabolism
métal [metal] *nm, pl* **métaux** [meto] : metal
métallique [metalik] *adj* : metallic
métallurgie [metalyrʒi] *nf* : metallurgy
métallurgique [metalyrʒik] *adj* : metallurgical
métallurgiste [metalyrʒist] *nm* : metallurgist, metalworker
métamorphose [metamɔrfoz] *nf* : metamorphosis
métaphore [metafɔr] *nf* : metaphor
métaphorique [metafɔrik] *adj* : metaphoric, metaphorical — **métaphoriquement** [-rikmɑ̃] *adv*
métaphysique[1] [metafizik] *adj* : metaphysical
métaphysique[2] *nf* : metaphysics
métayer, -tayère [meteje, -tejɛr] *n* : sharecropper
météo [meteo] *nf* : weather forecast
météore [meteɔr] *nm* : meteor
météorique [meteɔrik] *adj* : meteoric
météorite [meteɔrit] *nmf* : meteorite
météorologie [meteɔrɔlɔʒi] *nf* : meteorology
météorologique [meteɔrɔlɔʒik] *adj* : meteorological, weather <prévisions météorologiques : weather forecast>
météorologiste [meteɔrɔlɔʒist] *nmf* : meteorologist
méthane [metan] *nm* : methane
méthode [metɔd] *nf* **1** : method, system, way <avec méthode : methodically> **2** : manual, primer
méthodique [metɔdik] *adj* : methodical — **méthodiquement** [-dikmɑ̃] *adv*
méticuleux, -leuse [metikylø, -løz] *adj* : meticulous — **méticuleusement** [-løzmɑ̃] *adv*
métier [metje] *nm* **1** : job, profession, occupation <gens du métier : professionals, experts> **2** : experience, skill <manquer de métier : to lack experience> **3** *or* **métier à tisser** : loom
métis, -tisse [metis] *adj & n* : half-breed, half-caste
métrage [metraʒ] *nm* **1** : length (of an object) **2** : footage, length (of a film) <court métrage : short film> <long métrage : feature film>
mètre [mɛtr] *nm* **1** : meter <mètre carré : square meter> **2** : metric ruler <mètre ruban : tape measure>
métrer [metre] {87} *vt* : to measure (in meters)
métrique [metrik] *adj* : metric
métro [metro] *nm* : subway, metro
métronome [metrɔnɔm] *nm* : metronome
métropole [metrɔpɔl] *nf* : city, metropolis
métropolitain, -taine [metrɔpɔlitɛ̃, -tɛn] *adj* : metropolitan
mets [mɛ] *nm* PLAT : dish <c'est mon mets préféré : it's my favorite dish>
mettable [mɛtabl] *adj* PORTABLE : wearable
metteur [mɛtœr] *nm* **metteur en scène** : producer, director
mettre [mɛtr] {53} *vt* **1** PLACER : to put, to place <mets la plante par terre : put the plant on the floor> **2** : to put on, to wear <mets tes chaussures : put your shoes on> <elle met des jupes longues : she wears long skirts> **3** AJOUTER : to add (in), to put in **4** ÉCRIRE : to put down, to put in writing **5** INSTALLER : to put in, to install **6** : to prepare, to arrange <mettre la table : to set the table> **7** : to take (time) <elle a mis trois heures à le considérer : she took three hours to consider it> **8** : to turn on, to switch on **9** *fam* : to suppose <mettons qu'il n'était pas content : let's say he wasn't very happy> **10 mettre à la poste** : to mail **11 mettre au monde** : to give birth to **12 mettre au point** : to develop — **se mettre** *vr* **1** : to become, to get <il s'est mis en colère : he got angry> **2** : to put on, to wear <je n'ai

rien à me mettre : I have nothing to wear> **3 ~ à** : to start (doing something) <se mettre au travail : to get to work> **4 se mettre à table** : to sit down at the table

meuble[1] |mœbl| *adj* **1** : easily worked, friable **2 biens meubles** : movable goods, personal assets

meuble[2] *nm* **1** : piece of furniture **2 meubles** *nmpl* : furniture <meubles de bureau : office furniture>

meublé, -blée |mœble| *adj* : furnished

meubler |mœble| *vt* **1** : to furnish **2** REMPLIR : to occupy, to fill up <il meuble bien son temps : he fills up his time well> — **se meubler** *vr* : to acquire furniture, to furnish one's home

meuglement |møgləmɑ̃| *nm* : mooing, lowing

meugler |møgle| *vi* : to moo, to low

meule |møl| *nf* **1** : millstone, grindstone **2** : round (of cheese) **3 meule de foin** : haystack

meuler |møle| *vt* : to grind down

meunier, -nière |mønje, -njɛr| *n* : miller

meure |mør|, **meurt** |mœr|, *etc.* → **mourir**

meurtre |mœrtr| *nm* : murder

meurtrier[1], **-trière** |mœrtrije, -trijɛr| *adj* **1** : deadly, lethal **2** : murderous, dangerous

meurtrier[2], **-trière** *n* ASSASSIN : murderer, murderess *f*

meurtrir |mœrtrir| *vt* **1** : to bruise **2** BLESSER : to wound, to hurt (one's feelings, etc.)

meurtrissure |mœrtrisyr| *nf* : bruise

meut |mœ|, **meuve** |møv|, *etc.* → **mouvoir**

meute |møt| *nf* **1** : pack (of hounds) **2** : horde, crowd

mévente |mevɑ̃t| *nf* : slump, drop (in sales)

mexicain, -caine |meksikɛ̃, -kɛn| *adj* : Mexican

Mexicain, -caine *n* : Mexican

mezzanine |mɛdzanin| *nf* : mezzanine

miaou |mjau| *nm* : meow

miasme |mjasm| *nm* : miasma

miauler |mjole| *vi* : to meow

mi–bas |miba| *nms & pl* : kneesock

mica |mika| *nm* : mica

miche |miʃ| *nf* : round loaf of bread

mi–chemin |miʃmɛ̃| *adv* **à ~** : halfway, midway

mi–clos, -close |miklo, -kloz| *adj* : half-closed

mi–côte |mikot| *adv* **à ~** : halfway up (or down)

micro |mikro| *nm* : mike, microphone

microbe |mikrɔb| *nm* : germ, microbe

microbiologie |mikrɔbjɔlɔʒi| *nf* : microbiology

microcosme |mikrɔkɔsm| *nm* : microcosm

microfiche |mikrɔfiʃ| *nf* : microfiche

microfilm |mikrɔfilm| *nm* : microfilm

micromètre |mikrɔmɛtr| *nm* : micrometer

micro–onde |mikrɔɔ̃d| *nf* : microwave

micro–ondes |mikrɔɔ̃d| *nms & pl* : microwave oven

micro–ordinateur |mikrɔɔrdinatœr| *nm* : microcomputer

micro–organisme |mikrɔɔrganism| *nm* : microorganism

microphone |mikrɔfɔn| *nm* : microphone

microprocesseur |mikrɔprɔsesœr| *nm* : microprocessor

microscope |mikrɔskɔp| *nm* : microscope

microscopie |mikrɔskɔpi| *nf* : microscopy

microscopique |mikrɔskɔpik| *adj* : microscopic

microsillon |mikrɔsijɔ̃| *nm* : long-playing record, LP

midi |midi| *nm* **1** : midday, noon **2** : lunchtime **3** : south

mie |mi| *nf* : inside, soft part (of a loaf of bread)

miel |mjɛl| *nm* : honey

mielleux, -leuse |mjɛlø, -løz| *adj* DOUCEREUX : sugary, saccharine

mien,[1] **mienne** |mjɛ̃, mjɛn| *adj* : mine, my own <cette devise, que j'ai faite mienne : this motto that I have adopted> <une mienne amie : a friend of mine>

mien,[2] **mienne** *pron* **1 le mien, la mienne, les miens, les miennes** : mine <ce n'est pas le mien : it's not mine> **2 les miens** : my family

miette |mjɛt| *nf* **1** : crumb **2** : bit, scrap <en miettes : in pieces>

mieux[1] |mjø| *adv* **1** (*comparative of* **bien**) : better <il va mieux : he's feeling better> **2 le mieux, la mieux, les mieux** (*superlative of* **bien**) : the best <le mieux payé : the best paid> <c'est ici que je travaille le mieux : here's where I work best> **3 être mieux de** *Can* : to be better off to <vous seriez mieux de partir : it would be in your best interest to leave>

mieux[2] *adj* **1** (*comparative of* **bien**) : better <ses notes sont mieux cette année : her grades are better this year> **2 le mieux, la mieux, les mieux** (*superlative of* **bien**) : the best <le mieux de la ville : the best in town>

mieux[3] *nm* **1** : best <faire de son mieux : to do one's best> <pour le mieux : for the best> **2** : improvement <il y a du mieux : there's some improvement>

mieux–être |mjøzɛtr| *nm* : improved state, better quality of life

mièvre |mjɛvr| *adj* **1** : insipid **2** : mawkish, soppy

mièvrerie |mjɛvrəri| *nf* : sentimentality, mush

mignon, -gnonne |miɲɔ̃, -ɲɔn| *adj* **1** : sweet, cute **2** GENTIL : nice, kind

migraine |migrɛn| *nf* : headache, migraine
migrant, -grante |migrɑ̃, -grɑ̃t| *adj & n* : migrant
migrateur, -trice |migratœr, -tris| *adj* : migratory <oiseaux migrateurs : migratory birds>
migration |migrasjɔ̃| *nf* : migration
migrer |migre| *vi* : to migrate
mijoter |miʒɔte| *vt* **1** : to simmer **2** MANIGANCER : to plot, to cook up — *vi* : to simmer, to stew
mil |mil| → **mille**
milan |milɑ̃| *nm* : kite (bird)
mildiou |mildju| *nm* : mildew
mile |majl| *nm* MILLE : mile
milice |milis| *nf* : militia
milicien, -cienne |milisjɛ̃, -sjɛn| *n* : militiaman *m*, member of a militia
milieu |miljø| *nm, pl* **milieux 1** : middle <au beau milieu de la table : right in the middle of the table> <le milieu du jour : midday, noon> **2** : middle ground <un juste milieu : a happy medium> **3** : milieu, environment **4 au milieu de** : among, in the midst of **5 le milieu** : the underworld
militaire[1] |militɛr| *adj* : military — **militairement** |-tɛrmɑ̃| *adv*
militaire[2] *nm* SOLDAT : soldier, serviceman
militant,[1] **-tante** |militɑ̃, -tɑ̃t| *adj* : militant
militant,[2] **-tante** *n* : militant, activist
militarisme |militarism| *nm* : militarism
militariste |militarist| *adj* : militaristic
millage |milaʒ| *nm Can* : mileage (of a motor vehicle)
mille[1] |mil| *adj* : a thousand, one thousand <mille lumières : a thousand lights>
mille[2] *nm* **1** : mile **2 mille marin** : (nautical) knot
mille[3] *nms & pl* **1** : a thousand, one thousand **2** : bull's eye <taper dans le mille : to hit the bull's eye>
millénaire[1] |milenɛr| *adj* **1** : thousand-year-old **2** : age-old, ancient
millénaire[2] *nm* : millennium
mille–pattes |milpat| *nms & pl* **1** : centipede **2** : millipede
millésime |milezim| *nm* **1** : year of manufacture **2** : vintage year
millésimé, -mée |milezime| *adj* : vintage
millet |mijɛ| *nm* : millet
milliard |miljar| *nm* : billion
milliardaire |miljardɛr| *nmf* : billionaire
millième |miljɛm| *adj & nmf & nm* : thousandth
millier |milje| *nm* : thousand <par milliers : by the thousands>
milligramme |miligram| *nm* : milligram
millilitre |mililitr| *nm* : milliliter
millimètre |milimɛtr| *nm* : millimeter
million |miljɔ̃| *nm* : million
millionième |miljɔnjɛm| *adj & nmf & nm* : millionth
millionnaire |miljɔnɛr| *nmf* : millionaire
mime[1] |mim| *nmf* : mime (performer)
mime[2] *nm* : mime, miming
mimer |mime| *vt* **1** : to mime **2** : to mimic
mimétisme |mimetism| *nm* : mimicry (in biology)
mimique |mimik| *nf* **1** GRIMACE : facial expression, (funny) face **2** : gesticulations *pl*, sign language
minable |minabl| *adj* **1** MISÉRABLE : shabby, miserable **2** *fam* : pitiful, pathetic, measly <un film minable : a third-rate movie>
minaret |minarɛ| *nm* : minaret
minauder |minode| *vi* : to simper, to mince
mince |mɛ̃s| *adj* **1** : thin **2** : slim, slender **3** NÉGLIGEABLE : meager, scanty
minceur |mɛ̃sœr| *nf* : thinness, slenderness
mine |min| *nf* **1** : expression, appearance, demeanor <il avait bonne mine : he looked well> <je faisais mine de rien : I was acting as if nothing had happened> **2** : mine <mine de houille : coal mine> **3** : lead, graphite
miner |mine| *vt* **1** : to mine, to set mines in **2** : to erode, to eat away at **3** : to undermine
minerai |minrɛ| *nm* : ore
minéral[1], **-rale** |mineral| *adj, mpl* **-raux** |-ro| : mineral
minéral[2] *nm* : mineral
minéralogie |mineralɔʒi| *nf* : mineralogy — **minéralogiste** |-lɔʒist| *nmf*
minéralogique |mineralɔʒik| *adj* : mineralogical
minet, -nette |minɛ, -nɛt| *n* : kitty, pussy
mineur[1], **-neure** |minœr| *adj* : minor
mineur[2], **-neure** *nmf* : minor, underage person
mineur[3] *nm* : miner
miniature |minjatyr| *adj & nf* : miniature
minibus |minibys| *nm* : minibus
minier, -nière |minje, -njɛr| *adj* : mining
minijupe |miniʒyp| *nf* : miniskirt
minimal, -male |minimal| *adj, mpl* **-maux** |-mo| : minimal, minimum
minime |minim| *adj* : minimal, negligible, trifling
minimiser |minimize| *vt* : to minimize, to play down
minimum[1] |minimɔm| *adj, pl* **-mums** |-mɔm| *or* **-ma** |-ma| : minimum
minimum[2] *nm, pl* **-mums** *or* **-ma 1** : minimum <au minimum : at the least> **2 minimum vital** : living wage
mini–ordinateur |miniɔrdinatœr| *nm* : minicomputer

ministère [ministɛr] *nm* **1** : ministry, department (of government) <ministère des Relations extérieures : State Department> **2** : government, cabinet
ministériel, -rielle [ministerjɛl] *adj* : ministerial, governmental
ministre [ministr] *nm* : minister, secretary <premier ministre : prime minister> <le ministre du Commerce : the Secretary of Commerce>
minois [minwa] *nms & pl* : sweet little face
minoritaire [minɔritɛr] *adj* : minority
minorité [minɔrite] *nf* : minority
minoterie [minɔtri] *nf* : flour mill
minotier [minɔtje] *nm* MEUNIER : miller
minou [minu] *nm fam* **1** : kitty, pussy **2** : honey, sweetie
minoucher [minuʃe] *vt Can fam* : to caress, to pat
minoune [minun] *nf Can fam* **1** : (female) kitty **2** : honey, sweetie
minuit [minɥi] *nm* : midnight
minuscule[1] [minyskyl] *adj* : minute, tiny
minuscule[2] *nf* : small (lowercase) letter
minutage [minytaʒ] *nm* : timing
minute [minyt] *nf* **1** : minute **2 minute!** *fam* : just a minute!, hang on!
minuter [minyte] *vt* : to time
minuteur [minytœr] *nm* : timer
minuterie [minytri] *nf* : timer
minutie [minysi] *nf* : meticulousness <avec minutie : meticulously>
minutieux, -tieuse [minysjø, -sjøz] *adj* **1** MÉTICULEUX : meticulous **2** : detailed <travail minutieux : detailed work> — **minutieusement** [-sjøzmɑ̃] *adv*
miracle [mirakl] *nm* : miracle <par miracle : miraculously>
miraculeux, -leuse [mirakylø, -løz] *adj* : miraculous — **miraculeusement** [-løzmɑ̃] *adv*
mirador [miradɔr] *nm* : watchtower
mirage [miraʒ] *nm* : mirage
mire [mir] *nf* **1** : sight <ligne de mire : line of sight> **2 point de mire** : target, focal point <être le point de mire : to be the focus of attention>
mirifique [mirifik] *adj* : amazing, fabulous
mirobolant, -lante [mirɔbɔlɑ̃, -lɑ̃t] *adj fam* : fabulous, fantastic
miroir [mirwar] *nm* : mirror
miroitement [mirwatmɑ̃] *nm* : sparkling, shimmering
miroiter [mirwate] *vi* **1** BRILLER : to sparkle, to shimmer, to glint **2 faire miroiter** : to paint in glowing colors
mis[1] [mi] *pp* → **mettre**
mis[2]**, mise** [mi, miz] *adj* : clad <bien mis : well dressed>
misanthrope[1] [mizɑ̃trɔp] *adj* : misanthropic
misanthrope[2] *nmf* : misanthrope
misanthropie [mizɑ̃trɔpi] *nf* : misanthropy
mise [miz] *nf* **1** : putting, placing <mise en marche : starting up> <mise en scène : production (in theater)> <mise à jour : updating> **2** : stake (in games of chance) **3** : dress, attire **4 mise de fonds** : investment
miser [mize] *vt* : to bet — *vi* **1 ~ sur** : to bet on **2 ~ sur** : to count on
misérable[1] [mizerabl] *adj* **1** PITOYABLE : wretched, pitiful **2** INSIGNIFIANT : meager, paltry **3** PAUVRE : poverty-stricken
misérable[2] *nmf* **1** : wretch, pauper **2** : scoundrel
misérablement [mizerabləmɑ̃] *adv* **1** : miserably, wretchedly **2** : in poverty
misère [mizɛr] *nf* **1** : poverty, destitution **2** : misery, misfortune **3** : pittance, paltry sum
miséreux, -reuse [mizerø, -røz] *adj* : destitute, poverty-stricken
miséricorde [mizerikɔrd] *nf* : mercy, forgiveness
miséricordieux, -dieuse [mizerikɔrdjø, -djøz] *adj* : merciful, forgiving
misogyne [mizɔʒin] *nmf* : misogynist
missel [misɛl] *nm* : missal
missile [misil] *nm* : missile
mission [misjɔ̃] *nf* : mission
missionnaire [misjɔnɛr] *adj & nmf* : missionary
missive [misiv] *nf* : missive, letter
mitaine [mitɛn] *nf Can, Swiss* : mitten
mite [mit] *nf* : clothes moth
mi–temps[1] [mitɑ̃] *nms & pl* : part-time job <travailler à mi-temps : to work part-time>
mi–temps[2] *nfs & pl* : halftime (in sports)
miteux, -teuse [mitø, -tøz] *adj* : seedy, dingy, shabby
mitigation [mitigasjɔ̃] *nf* : mitigation
mitigé, -gée [mitiʒe] *adj* **1** : lukewarm, reserved **2** : mixed <sentiments mitigés : mixed feelings>
mitonner [mitɔne] *vt* **1** : to cook slowly, to simmer **2** : to prepare lovingly — **se mitonner** *vr* : to cook up for oneself
mitose [mitoz] *nf* : mitosis
mitoyen, mitoyenne [mitwajɛ̃, -jɛn] *adj* : common, dividing <mur mitoyen : dividing wall>
mitraille [mitraj] *nf* : hail of bullets
mitrailler [mitraje] *vt* : to machine-gun
mitraillette [mitrajɛt] *nf* : submachine gun
mitrailleuse [mitrajøz] *nf* : machine gun
mitre [mitr] *nf* : miter
mi–voix [mivwa] *nf* **à ~** : in a low voice
mixage [miksaʒ] *nm* : sound mixing
mixer [miksɛr] *or* **mixeur** [miksœr] *nm* : (food) mixer

mixette [miksɛt] *nf Can* : (small) mixer
mixité [miksite] *nf* : coeducation
mixte [mikst] *adj* **1** : mixed, joint **2** : coeducational
mixture [mikstyr] *nf* **1** : mixture **2** : concoction
mnémotechnique [mnemɔtɛknik] *adj* : mnemonic
mobile[1] [mɔbil] *adj* **1** : movable, removable <feuilles mobiles : loose-leaf paper> **2** : changeable <échelle mobile : sliding scale> **3** : mobile, moving (of populations, etc.) **4** : mobile, changing <un visage mobile : mobile features>
mobile[2] *nm* **1** : motive **2** : mobile
mobilier[1], **-lière** [mɔbilje, -ljɛr] *adj* **1** : movable <biens mobiliers : movable property> **2 valeurs mobilières** : securities, stocks and bonds
mobilier[2] *nm* MEUBLES : furniture
mobilisation [mɔbilizasjɔ̃] *nf* : mobilization
mobiliser [mɔbilize] *vt* : to mobilize
mobilité [mɔbilite] *nf* : mobility
mocassin [mɔkasɛ̃] *nm* : moccasin
moche [mɔʃ] *adj fam* **1** : ugly, awful **2** : rotten, despicable
modalité [mɔdalite] *nf* : form, mode <modalités de paiement : terms of payment>
mode[1] [mɔd] *nm* **1** : way, mode, method <mode de vie : way of life> <mode d'emploi : directions for use> **2** : mood (in grammar) **3** : mode (in computer science, music, philosophy)
mode[2] [mɔd] *nf* **1** : fashion <jupe à la mode : fashionable skirt> **2** : fashion industry
modèle[1] [mɔdɛl] *adj* : model, exemplary
modèle[2] *nm* **1** : model, pattern, example <prendre modèle sur : to take as a model> <servir de modèle : to serve as an example> <un modèle du bon élève : a model student> **2** : model, prototype <modèle réduit : small-scale model> **3** : (artist's) model, subject, sitter **4** : model, mannequin (in fashion) **5** : model (in commerce) <le dernier modèle : the latest model>
modeler [mɔdle] {20} *vt* **1** : to mold **2** : to model, to shape — **se modeler** *vr* **~ sur** : to model oneself on
modéliste [mɔdelist] *nmf* **1** : (clothing) designer **2** : model maker
modem [mɔdɛm] *nm* : modem
modérateur[1], **-trice** [mɔderatœr, -tris] *adj* : moderating, restraining
modérateur[2], **-trice** *n* : moderator, mediator
modération [mɔderasjɔ̃] *nf* MESURE : moderation, restraint
modéré, -rée [mɔdere] *adj* : moderate — **modérément** [-remɑ̃] *adv*
modérer [mɔdere] {87} *vt* : to moderate, to restrain, to curb — **se modérer** *vr* : to restrain oneself
moderne[1] [mɔdɛrn] *adj* : modern
moderne[2] *nm* : modern style
moderniser [mɔdɛrnize] *vt* : to modernize — **modernisation** [-nizasjɔ̃] *nf*
modernité [mɔdɛrnite] *nf* : modernity
modeste [mɔdɛst] *adj* **1** HUMBLE : modest, humble, simple <d'origine modeste : of humble origin> **2** MODIQUE : modest, small <un modeste salaire : a modest salary> **3** : modest, unpretentious, unassuming — **modestement** [-dɛstəmɑ̃] *adv*
modestie [mɔdɛsti] *nf* : modesty
modificateur [mɔdifikatœr, -tris] *nm* : modifier
modification [mɔdifikasjɔ̃] *nf* : modification
modifier [mɔdifje] {96} *vt* **1** : to modify, to alter **2** : to modify (in grammar) — **se modifier** *vr* : to change
modique [mɔdik] *adj* : modest <une somme modique : a modest sum> — **modiquement** [-dikmɑ̃] *adv*
modiste [mɔdist] *nmf* : milliner
modulaire [mɔdylɛr] *adj* : modular
modulation [mɔdylasjɔ̃] *nf* : modulation <modulation de fréquence : frequency modulation, FM>
module [mɔdyl] *nm* : module
moduler [mɔdyle] *vt* : to modulate
moelle [mwal] *nf* **1** : marrow (of bone), pith (of plants) **2 jusqu'à la moelle** : to the core **3 moelle épinière** : spinal cord
moelleux[1], **-leuse** [mwalø, -løz] *adj* **1** DOUX : soft <coussins moelleux : soft cushions> **2** : moist <gateau moelleux : moist cake> **3** : mellow, smooth
moelleux[2] *nm* : softness, mellowness
mœurs [mœr(s)] *nfpl* **1** CONDUITE : manners, morals **2** USAGES : customs, habits <c'est entré dans les mœurs : it's common practice> **3** : behavior (in zoology)
mohair [mɔɛr] *nm* : mohair
moi[1] [mwa] *nm* **le moi** : the self, the ego
moi[2] *pron* **1** : I <elle a depensé plus que moi : she spent more than I did> **2** : me <aide-moi : help me> <plus jeune que moi : younger than me> <moi, j'aime les chats : as for me, I like cats> **3 à ~** : mine <c'est à moi : it's mine> <c'est à moi de jouer : it's my turn to play>
moignon [mwaɲɔ̃] *nm* : stump (of a limb)
moi–même [mwamɛm] *pron* : myself
moindre [mwɛ̃dr] *adj* **1** : lesser, smaller, lower <à un moindre degré : to a lesser degree> **2 le moindre, la moindre** : the lesser, the least, the slightest <le moindre de deux maux : the lesser of two evils> <sans la moindre

hésitation : without a moment's hesitation>
moindrement \mwɛ̃drəmɑ̃\ *adv Can* : <s'ils sont le moindrement intéressés : if they are the least bit interested>
moine \mwan\ *nm* : monk
moineau \mwano\ *nm, pl* **moineaux** : sparrow
moins[1] \mwɛ̃\ *adv* **1** : less <moins grand que son frère : less tall than his brother> <moins je travaille, moins j'ai envie de travailler : the less I work, the less I feel like working> <de moins en moins : less and less> **2 le moins** : least, the least <le moins souvent : least often> <il est le moins fort : he's the least strong, he's the weakest (one)> **3 ~ de** : less than, fewer <moins de gens : fewer people> <pas moins de : no less than> **4 à moins de** : short of, barring **5 à moins que** : unless **6 en ~** : missing <une dent en moins : a missing tooth>
moins[2] *nm* **1** : minus (sign) **2 au ~** *or* **du ~** : at (the) least **3 pour le moins** *or* **tout le moins** : at (the very) least
moins[3] *prep* **1** : minus <sept moins deux font cinq : seven minus two equals five> **2** (*in expressions of time*) : to, of <il est cinq heures moins dix : it's ten to five> **3** (*in expressions of temperature*) : below <il fait moins cinq : it's five below zero, it's minus five>
mois \mwa\ *nm* **1** : month **2** *France* : monthly salary **3** *Can* : monthly payment
moisi[1], **-sie** \mwazi\ *adj* : moldy
moisi[2] *nm* : mold, mildew
moisir \mwazir\ *vi* **1** : to become moldy, to mildew **2** *fam* : to stagnate, to rot <moisir en prison : to rot in jail>
moisissure \mwazisyr\ *nf* : mold, mildew
moisson \mwasɔ̃\ *nf* **1** : harvest, crop **2** : abundance <une moisson de renseignements : a wealth of information>
moissonner \mwasɔne\ *vt* : to harvest, to reap
moissonneuse \mwasɔnøz\ *nf* : harvester (machine)
moissonneuse–batteuse \mwasɔnøzbatøz\ *nf, pl* **moissonneuses–batteuses** : combine (harvester)
moite \mwat\ *adj* **1** : sweaty, sticky **2** : muggy
moitié \mwatje\ *nf* **1** : half <la moitié du temps : half the time> <réduire de moitié : to reduce by half> **2 à ~** : half <à moitié rempli : half full> <faire à moitié : to do half-heartedly>
moitié–moitié *adv* : fifty-fifty
moka \moka\ *nm* : mocha
molaire \mɔlɛr\ *nf* : molar
moldave \mɔldav\ *adj* : Moldavian
Moldave *nmf* : Moldavian
moléculaire \mɔlekylɛr\ *adj* : molecular
molécule \mɔlekyl\ *nf* : molecule
molester \mɔlɛste\ *vt* : to maul, to manhandle
mollasse \mɔlas\ *adj* **1** APATHIQUE : apathetic, lethargic **2** FLASQUE : soft, flabby
mollasson \mɔlasɔ̃\ *adj fam* : sluggish
molle → **mou**
mollement \mɔlmɑ̃\ *adv* **1** DOUCEMENT : softly, gently **2** : weakly, feebly **3** : halfheartedly
mollesse \mɔlɛs\ *adj* **1** : softness **2** : limpness, flabbiness **3** INDOLENCE : indolence, apathy
mollet \mɔlɛ\ *nm* : calf (of the leg)
molleton \mɔltɔ̃\ *nm* : fleece, flannel
mollir \mɔlir\ *vi* **1** : to soften, to go soft **2** : to die down, to abate (of wind, etc.) **3** : to weaken, to give way **4** : to flag, to wane
mollusque \mɔlysk\ *nm* : mollusk
môme \mom\ *nmf France fam* GOSSE : kid, youngster
moment \mɔmɑ̃\ *nm* **1** : moment, while <prendre un moment : to take (quite) a while> <pour un bon moment : for a good while> **2** INSTANT : minute, instant <attends un moment! : just wait a minute!> **3** : moment, time, occasion <à tout moment : at any time> <au moment de sortir : just as she was leaving> <à ce moment : at this moment, now> **4** : present (time) <sujets du moment : issues of the day> **5 du moment que** PUISQUE : since **6 par moments** : at times, now and again
momentané, -née \mɔmɑ̃tane\ *adj* : momentary, temporary — **momentanément** \-nemɑ̃\ *adv*
momie \mɔmi\ *nf* : mummy
mon \mɔ̃\ , **ma** \ma\ (**mon** *before feminine nouns or adjectives beginning with a vowel or mute h*) *adj, pl* **mes** \mɛ\ : my
monarchie \mɔnarʃi\ *nf* : monarchy — **monarchiste** \mɔnarʃist\ *nmf*
monarque \mɔnark\ *nm* : monarch
monastère \mɔnastɛr\ *nm* : monastery
monastique \mɔnastik\ *adj* : monastic
monceau \mɔ̃so\ *nm, pl* **monceaux** \mɔ̃so\ : heap, pile
mondain, -daine \mɔ̃dɛ̃, -dɛn\ *adj* **1** : society, social <soirées mondaines : social gatherings> **2** : fashionable, refined **3** : wordly, mundane
mondanités \mɔ̃danite\ *nfpl* **1** : social events **2** : small talk
monde \mɔ̃d\ *nm* **1** TERRE : world, earth <au monde : in the world, on earth> **2** SOCIÉTÉ : world, society <le monde est petit : it's a small world> <le tiers monde : the third world> **3** COMMUNAUTÉ, DOMAINE : world, community <le monde des affaires : the business world> <le monde

végétal : the vegetable kingdom> 4 GENS : people *pl* <il y avait du monde partout : there were people everywhere> **5 comme du monde** *Can* : properly **6 tout le monde** : everyone **7 venir au monde** NAÎTRE : to be born

mondial, -diale [mɔ̃djal] *adj, mpl* **-diaux** [-djo] **1** : world <record mondial : world record> **2** : worldwide, global

mondialement [mɔ̃djalmɑ̃] *adv* : throughout the world, globally

monétaire [mɔnetɛr] *adj* : monetary

mongol[1], -gole [mɔ̃gɔl] *adj* : Mongolian, Mongol

mongol[2] *nm* : Mongolian (language)

Mongol, -gole *n* : Mongolian

moniteur[1], -trice [mɔnitœr, -tris] *n* **1** : instructor, coach **2** : counselor (in a camp)

moniteur[2] *nm* : monitor, screen

monitorat [mɔnitɔra] *nm* : instructorship

monnaie [mɔnɛ] *nf* **1** : money, currency <fausse monnaie : counterfeit money> **2** APPOINT : change <petite monnaie : small change> **3** PIÈCE : coin <monnaies d'or : gold coins> **4 monnaie courante** : commonplace

monnayer [mɔnɛje] {11} *vt* **1** : to convert into cash **2** : to capitalize on (experience, etc.)

monnayeur [mɔnɛjœr] *nm* → **faux–monnayeur**

monochrome [mɔnɔkrom] *adj & nm* : monochrome

monocle [mɔnɔkl] *nm* : monocle

monocorde [mɔnɔkɔrd] *adj* : droning, monotonous

monogame [mɔnɔgam] *adj* : monogamous

monogamie [mɔnɔgami] *nf* : monogamy

monogramme [mɔnɔgram] *nm* : monogram

monographie [mɔnɔgrafi] *nf* : monograph

monolingue [mɔnɔlɛ̃g] *adj* : monolingual

monolithe[1] [mɔnɔlit] *adj* : monolithic

monolithe[2] *nm* : monolith

monolithique [mɔnɔlitik] *adj* : monolithic

monologue [mɔnɔlɔg] *nm* : monologue, soliloquy

monopole [mɔnɔpɔl] *nm* : monopoly

monopoliser [mɔnɔpɔlize] *vt* : to monopolize — **monopolisation** [-lizasjɔ̃] *nf*

monopolistique [mɔnɔpɔlistik] *adj* : monopolistic

monosyllabe [mɔnɔsilab] *nm* : monosyllable

monosyllabique [mɔnɔsilabik] *adj* : monosyllabic

monothéisme [mɔnɔteism] *nm* : monotheism

monothéiste [mɔnɔteist] *adj* : monotheistic

monotone [mɔnɔtɔn] *adj* : monotonous, dull

monotonie [mɔnɔtɔni] *nf* : monotony, dullness

monseigneur [mɔ̃sɛɲœr] *nm, pl* **messeigneurs** [mesɛɲœr] **1** (*form of address*) : Your Royal Highness (for a prince), Your Eminence (for a cardinal) **2** (*title*) : His Grace (for a duke, an archbishop, etc.)

monsieur [məsjø] *nm, pl* **messieurs** [mɛsjø] **1** (*form of address*) : Mr., Sir <bonjour, monsieur : good morning, Sir; good morning, Mr. X> **2** (*used in correspondence*) <Monsieur : Dear Sir> **3** : man, gentleman <c'est un grand monsieur : he's a great man>

monstre[1] [mɔ̃str] *adj* : huge, colossal

monstre[2] *nm* : monster

monstrueusement [mɔ̃stryøzmɑ̃] *adv* : monstruously, hideously

monstrueux, -trueuse [mɔ̃stryø, -tryøz] *adj* **1** : monstrous **2** : hideous, ugly **3** : terrible <une monstrueuse erreur : an awful mistake>

monstruosité [mɔ̃stryozite] *nf* : monstrosity

mont [mɔ̃] *nm* : mount, mountain

montage [mɔ̃taʒ] *nm* **1** : assembly <chaîne de montage : assembly line> **2** : mounting, setting (of jewelry) **3** : editing (of a film)

montagnard[1], -gnarde [mɔ̃taɲar, -ɲard] *adj* : mountain

montagnard[2], -gnarde *n* : mountain dweller

montagne [mɔ̃taɲ] *nf* **1** : mountain **2 la montagne** : the mountains **3 montagnes russes** : roller coaster

montagneux, -gneuse [mɔ̃taɲø, -ɲøz] *adj* : mountainous, hilly

montant[1], -tante [mɔ̃tɑ̃, -tɑ̃t] *adj* : uphill, rising <chemin montant : uphill road>

montant[2] *nm* **1** : upright, post **2** SOMME : total, sum

mont–de–piété [mɔ̃dpjete] *nm, pl* **monts–de–piété** *France* : pawnshop

monte–charge [mɔ̃tʃarʒ] *nms & pl* : freight elevator

montée [mɔ̃te] *nf* **1** : rise, rising **2** : ascent, climb **3** PENTE : slope, upgrade

monter [mɔ̃te] *vi* **1** : to go up, to come up, to climb up <elle est montée : she went upstairs> **2** : to go uphill, to slope upward **3** : to rise (of rivers, temperature, prices, etc.) **4** : to well up <les larmes lui sont montées aux yeux : his eyes filled with tears> **5 ~ à** : to ride <monter à bicyclette : to ride a bicycle> **6 ~ dans** : to get into (a car or train), to board (a ship or plane) **7 ~ sur** : to get on (a horse) — *vt* (*with auxiliary verb* **avoir**) **1** : to take up, to bring up **2** : to put up, to raise (a curtain, etc.) **3** : to go up, to climb (up) **4** : to raise, to turn up (volume, etc.) **5** : to ride (a horse) **6** : to put together, to assemble (a machine, etc.), to edit (a film) **7** : to mount (an attack), to set up (a scheme, etc.), to put on (a show) — **se monter** *vr* **1 ~ à** : to amount to **2 ~ en** : to equip oneself with

monteur, -teuse [mɔ̃tœr, -tøz] *n* : film editor

montgolfière [mɔ̃gɔlfjɛr] *nf* : hot-air balloon

monticule [mɔ̃tikyl] *nm* **1** : hillock, mound **2** *Can* : pitcher's mound (in baseball)

montre [mɔ̃tr] *nf* **1** : watch <montre à quartz : quartz watch> **2** : show, display <en montre : on display> <faire montre de : to show, to display>

montréalais, -laise [mɔrealɛ, -lɛz] *adj* : of or from Montreal

Montréalais, -laise *n* : Montrealer

montre–bracelet [mɔ̃trəbraslɛ] *nf, pl* **montres–bracelets** : wristwatch

montrer [mɔ̃tre] *vt* **1** : to show **2** : to reveal, to display **3** : to point at, to point out <montrer qqn du doigt : to point the finger at s.o.> — **se montrer** *vr* **1** : to show oneself, to be seen **2** : to prove to be **3** : to appear, to come out

monture [mɔ̃tyr] *nf* **1** : mount (animal) **2** : setting (for jewelry) **3** : frames *pl* (for eyeglasses)

monument [mɔnymɑ̃] *nm* **1** : monument, memorial <monument aux morts : war memorial> **2** : (historic) building

monumental, -tale [mɔnymɑ̃tal] *adj, mpl* **-taux** [-to] : monumental

moquer [mɔke] *v* **se moquer ~ de** *vr* **1** : to make fun of, to mock <on se moque de toi : people are laughing at you> **2** : to be indifferent about <je m'en moque : I couldn't care less>

moquerie [mɔkri] *nf* : mockery

moquette [mɔkɛt] *nf* : wall-to-wall carpeting

moqueur[1], -queuse [mɔkœr, -køz] *adj* : mocking — **moqueusement** [-køzmɑ̃] *adv*

moqueur[2] *nm* : mockingbird

moraillon [mɔrɑjɔ̃] *nm* : hasp (for a door)

moraine [mɔrɛn] *nf* : moraine

moral[1], -rale [mɔral] *adj, mpl* **moraux** [mɔro] **1** : moral, ethical <sens moral : sense of right and wrong> **2** : mental <une victoire morale : a moral victory>

moral[2] *nm* : morale, spirits *pl* <je lui ai remonté le moral : I cheered him up>

morale *nf* **1** ÉTHIQUE : morals *pl*, ethics *pl* **2** : moral (of a story) **3 faire la morale à** SERMONNER : to lecture

moralement [mɔralmɑ̃] *adv* : morally, ethically

moralisateur, -trice [mɔralizatœr, -tris] *adj* : moralizing, sanctimonious

moraliser [mɔralize] *vi* : to moralize — *vt* SERMONNER : to lecture, to preach to

moraliste[1] [mɔralist] *adj* : moralistic

moraliste[2] *nmf* : moralist

moralité [mɔralite] *nf* **1** : morals *pl* **2** : morality **3** : moral, lesson

moratoire [mɔratwar] *nm* : moratorium

morbide [mɔrbid] *adj* : morbid — **morbidité** [-bidite] *nf*

morceau [mɔrso] *nm, pl* **morceaux** **1** : piece, bit <couper en morceaux : to cut into pieces> <manger un morceau : to have a bite to eat> **2** : extract, passage (of a text) **3** : piece (of music)

morceler [mɔrsəle] {8} *vt* : to break up, to divide

mordant[1], -dante [mɔrdɑ̃, -dɑ̃t] *adj* : biting, cutting, scathing

mordant[2] *nm* : keenness, bite, punch

mordicus [mɔrdikys] *adv fam* : obstinately, stubbornly

mordillement [mɔrdijmɑ̃] *nm* : nibbling

mordiller [mɔrdije] *vt* : to nibble at, to chew at

mordoré, -rée [mɔrdɔre] *adj* : bronze-colored

mordre [mɔrdr] {63} *vt* **1** : to bite **2** : to eat into (of acid, etc.) — *vi* **1** : to bite <ça mord : the fish are biting> **2 ~ dans** : to bite into, to take a bite out of **3 ~ sur** : to cross over (a line) — **se mordre** *vr* **1 se mordre la langue** : to bite one's tongue **2 se mordre les doigts** : to have bitter regrets

mordu[1] [mɔrdy] *pp* → **mordre**

mordu[2], -due *adj* : smitten (with love)

mordu[3], -due *n fam* : fan, buff <un mordu de sport : a sports buff>

morelle [mɔrɛl] *nf* : nightshade

morfondre [mɔrfɔ̃dr] {63} *v* **se morfondre** *vr* : to hang around, to mope <se morfondre à attendre : to wait around dejectedly> **2** *Can* : to exhaust oneself, to wear oneself out

morgue [mɔrg] *nf* **1** : morgue, mortuary **2** ARROGANCE : haughtiness, arrogance

moribond[1], -bonde [mɔribɔ̃, -bɔ̃d] *adj* : moribund, dying

moribond[2], -bonde *n* : dying person

morille [mɔrij] *nf* : morel

morne [mɔrn] *adj* **1** SOMBRE : dismal, gloomy **2** : glum, sullen

morose [mɔroz] *adj* : morose, sullen

morosité [mɔrozite] *nf* : moroseness, sullenness

morphine [mɔrfin] *nf* : morphine

mors [mɔr] *nm* : bit (of a bridle)

morse [mɔrs] *nm* **1** : walrus **2** : Morse code

morsure [mɔrsyr] *nf* : bite (of a dog, etc.)

mort[1] [mɔr] *pp* → **mourir**
mort[2], **morte** [mɔr, mɔrt] *adj* **1** : dead **2** : dying <être mort de faim : to be starving, to be dying of hunger> **3** : lifeless, stagnant <un temps mort : a slack period>
mort[3] *nf* **1** : death <mettre à mort : to put to death> <peine de mort : death penalty> <jusqu'à la mort : to the death, to the bitter end> **2** : great sorrow, agony <avoir la mort dans l'âme : to have a heavy heart>
mort[4], **morte** *n* **1** : dead person, corpse **2** VICTIME : fatality, casualty
mortalité [mɔrtalite] *nf* : mortality <taux de mortalité : death rate>
mortel[1], **-telle** [mɔrtɛl] *adj* **1** : mortal **2** FATAL : fatal, deadly, lethal <maladie mortelle : fatal disease>
mortel[2], **-telle** *n* : mortal
mortellement [mɔrtɛlmɑ̃] *adv* **1** : mortally, fatally **2** : deadly <mortellement ennuyeux : deadly boring>
mortier [mɔrtje] *nm* : mortar
mortifier [mɔrtifje] {96} *vt* : to mortify — **mortification** [-tifikasjɔ̃] *nf*
mort–né, -née [mɔrne] *adj, pl* **mort–nés, mort–nées** : stillborn
mortuaire [mɔrtɥɛr] *adj* **1** FUNÈBRE : funeral **2 salon mortuaire** *Can* : funeral home
morue [mɔry] *nf* : cod
morve [mɔrv] *nf* : nasal mucus
morveux, -veuse [mɔrvø, -vøz] *adj* : runny-nosed
mosaïque [mɔzaik] *adj & nf* : mosaic
mosquée [mɔske] *nf* : mosque
mot [mo] *nm* **1** : word (in language) <mot à mot : word for word> <peser ses mots : to weigh one's words> **2** PAROLE : word <avoir le dernier mot : to have the last word> <sans mot dire : without saying a word> **3** : note, line <écrire un mot à qqn : to drop a line to s.o.> **4 mot de passe** : password **5 mot d'ordre** : watchword, catchword **6 mots croisés** : crossword puzzle
motard [mɔtar] *nm* : motorcycle policeman
motel [mɔtɛl] *nm* : motel
moteur[1], **-trice** [mɔtœr, -tris] *adj* **1** : motor **2** : driving <force motrice : driving force> **3 à quatre roues motrices** : four-wheel drive
moteur[2] *nm* **1** : engine, motor **2 moteur à vapeur** : steam engine **3 moteur à combustion interne** *or* **moteur à explosion** : internal combustion engine **4 moteur à réaction** : jet engine
motif [mɔtif] *nm* **1** RAISON : motive, reason, grounds *pl* **2** DESSIN : pattern, design <nappe à motifs floraux : floral-design tablecloth> **3** : motif (in music)
motion [mɔsjɔ̃] *nf* **1** : motion <voter une motion : to pass a motion> **2 motion de censure** : vote of no confidence
motivant, -vante [mɔtivɑ̃, -vɑ̃t] *adj* : motivating
motivation [mɔtivasjɔ̃] *nf* : motivation
motivé, -vée [mɔtive] *adj* **1** : motivated <être peu motivé : to lack motivation> **2** : reasoned, justified
motiver [mɔtive] *vt* **1** : to motivate, to impel **2** : to justify, to explain
moto [mɔto] *nf* : motorbike
motocyclette [mɔtɔsiklɛt] *nf* : motorcycle
motocycliste [mɔtɔsiklist] *nmf* : motorcyclist
motoneige [mɔtɔnɛʒ] *nf* : snowmobile
motoriser [mɔtɔrize] *vt* : to motorize, to mechanize
motte [mɔt] *nf* : clod, lump (of earth, etc.), slab (of butter)
motton [mɔtɔ̃] *nm Can* : lump (of earth, of ice, etc.)
mou[1] [mu] (**mol** [mɔl] *before vowel or mute h*), **molle** [mɔl] *adj* **1** : soft **2** : weak, feeble <avoir les jambes molles : to be weak in the knees> **3** : limp, lifeless <une poignée de main molle : a limp handshake> **4** : sluggish, listless **5** : indulgent, lax
mou[2] *nm* : looseness, slack <donner du mou à : to loosen, to give some leeway to>
mouchard, -charde [muʃar, -ʃard] *n fam* : informer, stool pigeon
moucharder [muʃarde] *vt fam* : to spy on, to squeal on
mouche [muʃ] *nf* **1** : fly <mouche domestique : housefly> <mouche à miel : honeybee> **2** *or* **mouche artificielle** : fly (in fishing) **3** : beauty spot **4 faire mouche** : to hit the bull's eye
moucher [muʃe] *vt* **1** : to wipe the nose of (a child, etc.) **2** : to snuff out (a candle) — **se moucher** *vr* : to blow one's nose
moucheron [muʃrɔ̃] *nm* : gnat, midge
moucheter [muʃte] {8} *vt* TACHETER : to fleck, to speckle, to mottle
moucheture [muʃtyr] *nf* : spot, speck, speckle
mouchoir [muʃwar] *nm* **1** : handkerchief **2 mouchoir en papier** : tissue
moudre [mudr] {54} *vt* : to grind
moue [mu] *nf* **1** : pout **2 faire la moue** : to pout
mouette [mwɛt] *nf* : gull, seagull
mouffette *or* **moufette** [mufɛt] *nf* : skunk
moufle [mufl] *nf* : mitten
mouillage [mujaʒ] *nm* **1** : anchoring **2** : anchorage, moorings *pl*
mouillé, -lée [muje] *adj* : wet
mouiller [muje] *vt* **1** : to wet, to moisten **2** : to add liquid to, to dilute **3 mouiller l'ancre** : to drop anchor — **se mouiller** *vr* **1** : to get wet **2** *fam* : to become involved

moulage [mulaʒ] *nm* **1** : molding, casting **2** : cast
moulait [mulɛ], **moulions** [muljɔ̃], *etc.* → **moudre**
moulant, -lante [mulɑ̃, -lɑ̃t] *adj* : tight-fitting
moule[1] [mul], *etc.* → **moudre**
moule[2] [mul] *nm* **1** MATRICE : mold, matrix **2** : mold (in cooking) <moule à gâteau : cake pan>
moule[3] [mul] *nf* : mussel
mouler [mule] *vt* **1** : to mold **2** : to cast <moulé en bronze : cast in bronze> **3** : to hug (the body), to fit tightly
moulin [mulɛ̃] *nm* **1** : mill **2 moulin à café** : coffee grinder **3 moulin à paroles** *fam* : chatterbox **4 moulin à vent** : windmill
moulinet [mulinɛ] *nm* **1** : reel, winch **2** : waving (about)
moulu[1] [muly] *pp* → **moudre**
moulu[2], **-lue** *adj* **1** : ground <café moulu : ground coffee> **2** *fam* : worn-out, all in
moulure [mulyr] *nf* : molding
moumoute [mumut] *nf fam* : wig, toupee
mourant[1], **-rante** [murɑ̃, -rɑ̃t] *adj* : dying
mourant[2], **-rante** *n* : dying person
mourir [murir] {55} *vi* **1** : to die **2** : to die out, to die away **3 ~ de** : to be dying of <mourir d'ennui : to be bored to death> <mourir de faim : to be dying of hunger> <il l'aimait à en mourir : he was desperately in love with her>
mourra [mura], *etc.* → **mourir**
mousquet [muskɛ] *nm* : musket
mousquetaire [muskətɛr] *nm* : musketeer
mousqueton [muskətɔ̃] *nm* : carbine
moussant, -sante [musɑ̃, -sɑ̃t] *adj* **1** : foaming, lathering **2 bain moussant** : bubble bath
mousse [mus] *nf* **1** : moss **2** : froth, foam, lather **3** : mousse <mousse au chocolat : chocolate mousse> **4** *or* **caoutchouc mousse** : foam rubber
mousseline [muslin] *nf* **1** : muslin, chiffon **2 pommes mousseline** : pureed potatoes
mousser [muse] *vi* **1** : to foam, to froth, to lather **2 faire mousser** *fam* : to sing the praises of
mousseux[1], **-seuse** [musø, -søz] *adj* **1** : foaming, frothy **2 vin mousseux** : sparkling wine
mousseux[2] *nm* : sparkling wine
mousson [musɔ̃] *nf* : monsoon
moussu, -sue [musy] *adj* : mossy
moustache [mustaʃ] *nf* **1** : mustache **2 moustaches** *nfpl* : whiskers (of an animal)
moustachu, -chue [mustaʃy] *adj* : wearing a mustache
moustiquaire [mustikɛr] *nf* **1** : mosquito net **2** : screen (on windows and doors)
moustique [mustik] *nm* : mosquito
moutarde [mutard] *nf* : mustard
mouton [mutɔ̃] *nm* **1** : sheep, sheepskin **2** : mutton **3 moutons** *nmpl* : small fluffy clouds **4 moutons** *nmpl* : whitecaps
mouvement [muvmɑ̃] *nm* **1** : bodily movement, gesture **2** : movement, motion <mouvement perpétuel : perpetual motion> **3** : impulse, reaction **4** : activity, bustle **5** : trend, evolution <mouvement en hausse : upward trend> **6** : movement (in politics, etc.)
mouvementé, -tée [muvmɑ̃te] *adj* **1** VIVANT : animated, lively, hectic **2** ACCIDENTÉ : rough, uneven <terrain mouvementé : rough terrain>
mouvoir [muvwar] {56} *vt* **1** POUSSER : to move, to prompt **2** ACTIONNER : to drive <machine mue par l'électricité : electric-powered machine> **— se mouvoir** *vr* : to move
moyac [mɔjak] *nm Can* : eider (duck)
moyen[1], **-yenne** [mwajɛ̃, -jɛn] *adj* **1** : medium, medium-sized **2** : average, mean **3 la classe moyenne** : the middle class
moyen[2] *nm* **1** : way, means *pl* <par quel moyen? : how?> **2** : possibility <y a-t-il moyen de le voir? : is it possible to see him?> **3 moyens** *nmpl* : means, resources **4 au moyen de** : with, by means of
Moyen Âge [mwajɛnaʒ] *nm* : Middle Ages
moyennant [mwajɛnɑ̃] *prep* : for, in return for
moyenne [mwajɛn] *nf* : average <en moyenne : on an average>
moyennement [mwajɛnmɑ̃] *adv* MODÉRÉMENT : fairly, moderately
moyeu [mwajø] *nm, pl* **moyeux** : hub
mozambicain, -caine [mɔzɑ̃bikɛ̃, -kɛn] *adj* : Mozambican
Mozambicain, -caine *n* : Mozambican
mû [my] *pp* → **mouvoir**
mucilage [mysilaʒ] *nm* : mucilage
mucosité [mykozite] *nf* : mucus
mucus [mykys] *nm* : mucus
mue [my] *nf* : molting, shedding, sloughing
muer [mɥe] *vi* **1** : to molt, to shed, to slough **2** : to change, to break <sa voix mue : his voice is changing> **— se muer** *vr* : to transform oneself
muet[1], **muette** [mɥɛ, mɥɛt] *adj* **1** : dumb <sourd et muet : deaf and dumb> **2** : speechless, dumbfounded **3** SILENCIEUX : silent
muet[2], **-ette** *n* : mute, dumb person
muffin [mɔfœn] *nm Can* : muffin
mufle [myfl] *nm* **1** : muzzle **2** *fam* : boor, lout
muge [myʒ] *nm* : gray mullet

mugir [myʒir] *vi* **1** BEUGLER : to low, to moo, to bellow **2** : to howl, to wail, to roar

mugissement [myʒismɑ̃] *nm* **1** : lowing, bellowing, mooing **2** : howling (of the wind), roar (of the sea)

muguet [mygɛ] *nm* : lily of the valley

mulâtre, -tresse [mylatr, -trɛs] *n* : mulatto

mule [myl] *nf* **1** : female mule **2** PANTOUFLE : mule

mulet [mylɛ] *nm* **1** : male mule **2** : gray mullet

mulot [mylo] *nm* : field mouse

multicolore [myltikɔlɔr] *adj* : multicolored

multiculturel, -relle [myltikyltyrɛl] *adj* : multicultural

multiforme [myltifɔrm] *adj* : multiform, many-sided

multilatéral, -rale [myltilateral] *adj, mpl* **-raux** [-ro] : multilateral

multilingue [myltilɛ̃g] *adj* : multilingual — **multilinguisme** [-lɛ̃gɥism] *nm*

multimédia [myltimedja] *adj* : multimedia

multimillionnaire [myltimiljɔnɛr] *nmf* : multimillionaire

multinational, -nale [myltinasjɔnal] *adj, mpl* **-naux** [-no] : multinational

multiple[1] [myltipl] *adj* **1** NOMBREUX : multiple, numerous **2** DIVERS : many, various, diverse

multiple[2] *nm* : multiple

multiplication [myltiplikasjɔ̃] *nf* : multiplication

multiplicité [myltiplisite] *nf* : multiplicity

multiplier [myltiplije] {96} *vt* **1** ACCROÎTRE : to multiply, to increase **2** : to multiply (in mathematics) — **se multiplier** *vr* PROLIFÉRER : to increase, to proliferate

multitude [myltityd] *nf* : multitude, mass <une multitude de gens : a vast number of people>

municipal, -pale [mynisipal] *adj, mpl* **-paux** [-po] : municipal, local, town

municipalité [mynisipalite] *nf* **1** : municipality, town **2** : town council

munificent, -cente [mynifisɑ̃, -sɑ̃t] *adj* : munificent — **munificence** [-fisɑ̃s] *adj*

munir [mynir] *vt* : to equip, to provide <munir d'armes : to supply with arms> — **se munir** *vr* **~ de** : to equip oneself with

munitions [mynisjɔ̃] *nfpl* : ammunition, munitions

muqueuse *nf* : mucous membrane

muqueux, -queuse [mykø, -køz] *adj* : mucous

mur [myr] *nm* **1** : wall **2** OBSTACLE : obstacle, brick wall **3 mur du son** : sound barrier

mûr, mûre [myr] *adj* **1** : ripe **2** : mature <l'âge mûr : middle age> **3** : ready, prepared <mûr pour des responsabilités accrues : ready for increased responsibility>

muraille [myraj] *nf* : (high) wall

mural, -rale [myral] *adj, mpl* **muraux** [myro] : wall, mural

murale [myral] *nf* : mural

mûre [myr] *nf* **1** : blackberry **2** : mulberry

mûrement [myrmɑ̃] *adv* : carefully, with thought <ayant mûrement réfléchi : after much thought>

murène [myrɛn] *nf* : moray eel

murer [myre] *vt* : to wall in, to wall up — **se murer** *vr* : to shut oneself away

mûrier [myrje] *nm* : mulberry (tree)

mûrir [myrir] *vi* **1** : to ripen **2** : to mature, to develop — *vt* **1** : to ripen **2** : to develop, to nurture (a project, etc.)

murmure [myrmyr] *nm* **1** CHUCHOTEMENT : murmur **2 murmures** *nmpl* : mutterings, murmurings

murmurer [myrmyre] *vi* **1** CHUCHOTER : to murmur **2** SE PLAINDRE : to mutter, to complain — *vt* : to murmur

musaraigne [myzarɛɲ] *nf* : shrew

musarder [myzarde] *vi* FLÂNER : to idle around, to dawdle about

musc [mysk] *nm* : musk

muscade [myskad] *nf or* **noix muscade** : nutmeg

muscat [myska] *nm* : muscatel

muscle [myskl] *nm* : muscle

musclé, -clée [myskle] *adj* **1** : muscular **2** *fam* : powerful, strong <une politique musclée : a forceful stand>

musculaire [myskylɛr] *adj* : muscular

musculation [myskylasjɔ̃] *nf* : bodybuilding

musculature [mysklatyr] *nf* : musculature, muscles *pl*

muse [myz] *nf* : muse

museau [myzo] *nm, pl* **museaux** : muzzle, snout

musée [myze] *nm* : museum

museler [myzle] {8} *vt* : to muzzle

muselière [myzəljɛr] *nf* : muzzle (for a dog, etc.)

musette [myzɛt] *nf* : satchel, haversack

muséum [myzeɔm] *nm* : museum of natural history

musical, -cale [myzikal] *adj* **-caux** [-ko] : musical — **musicalement** [-kalmɑ̃] *adv*

musicien[1], **-cienne** [myzisjɛ̃, -sjɛn] *adj* : musical

musicien[2], **-cienne** *n* : musician

musique [myzik] *nf* **1** : music <musique d'ambiance : background music> <musique de chambre : chamber music> **2** : piece of music **3** : band <musique militaire : military band>

musqué, -quée [myske] *adj* **1** : musky **2 bœuf musqué** : musk ox **3 rat musqué** ONDATRA : muskrat

musulman, -mane [myzylmɑ̃, -man] *adj & n* : Muslim

mutable [mytabl] *adj* : mutable, changeable — **mutabilité** [-tabilite] *nf*

mutant[1], **-tante** |mytɑ̃, -tɑ̃t| *adj* : mutant
mutant[2], **-tante** *n* : mutant
mutation |mytasjɔ̃| *nf* **1** : transformation, change **2** : transfer (of an employee) **3** : mutation
muter |myte| *vt* : to transfer, to move — *vi* : to mutate
mutilation |mytilasjɔ̃| *nf* : mutilation
mutiler |mytile| *vt* : to mutilate, to maim
mutin[1], **-tine** |mytɛ̃, -tin| *adj* ESPIÈGLE : mischievous
mutin[2] *nm* : mutineer
mutiné[1], **-née** |mytine| *adj* : mutinous, rebellious
mutiné[2], **-née** *n* : mutineer
mutiner |mytine| *v* **se mutiner** *vr* : to mutiny, to rebel
mutinerie |mytinri| *nf* RÉBELLION : mutiny, rebellion
mutisme |mytism| *nm* **1** : dumbness, muteness **2** : silence
mutuel, -elle |mytɥɛl| *adj* : mutual — **mutuellement** |-tɥɛlmɑ̃| *adv*
myope |mjɔp| *adj* : shortsighted, nearsighted
myopie |mjɔpi| *nf* : myopia, shortsightedness, nearsightedness
myosotis |mjozɔtis| *nm* : forget-me-not
myriade |mirjad| *nf* : myriad
myrrhe |mir| *nf* : myrrh
myrte |mirt| *nf* : myrtle
myrtille |mirtil| *nf France* : blueberry
mystère |mistɛr| *nm* : mystery
mystérieux, -rieuse |misterjø, -rjøz| *adj* : mysterious — **mystérieusement** |-rjøzmɑ̃| *adv*
mysticisme |mistisism| *nm* : mysticism
mystification |mistifikasjɔ̃| *nf* **1** : hoax, practical joke **2** : myth, unfounded idea
mystifier |mistifje| {96} *vt* DUPER : to deceive, to dupe
mystique[1] |mistik| *adj* : mystical, mystic
mystique[2] *nmf* : mystic
mystique[3] *nf* **1** : mysticism **2** : mystique
mythe |mit| *nm* : myth
mythique |mitik| *adj* : mythical
mythologie |mitɔlɔʒi| *nf* : mythology
mythologique |mitɔlɔʒik| *adj* : mythological

N

n |ɛn| *nm* : n, the 14th letter of the alphabet
nacre |nakr| *nf* : mother-of-pearl
nacré, -crée |nakre| *adj* : pearly
nadir |nadir| *nm* : nadir
nage |naʒ| *nf* **1** : swimming **2** : stroke (in swimming) <nage libre : freestyle> **3 en ~** : dripping with sweat
nageoire |naʒwar| *nf* **1** : fin (of a fish) **2** : flipper
nager |naʒe| {17} *vi* **1** : to swim **2 ~ dans** : to be filled with <il nageait dans l'amour : he was brimming with love> — *vt* : to swim
nageur, -geuse |naʒœr, -ʒøz| *n* : swimmer
naguère |nagɛr| *adv* **1** RÉCEMMENT : recently, a short time ago **2** AUTREFOIS : formerly
naïade |najad| *nf* : naiad
naïf, naïve |naif, -iv| *adj* **1** INGÉNU : ingenuous, naive **2** CRÉDULE : credulous, gullible — **naïvement** |naivmɑ̃| *adv*
nain[1], **naine** |nɛ̃, nɛn| *adj* : dwarf, miniature <rosier nain : miniature rosebush>
nain[2], **naine** *n* : dwarf, midget
naissait |nɛsɛ|, **naissions** |nɛsjɔ̃|, *etc.* → **naître**
naissance |nɛsɑ̃s| *nf* **1** : birth **2** DÉBUT : origin, beginning <prendre naissance : to arise, to originate>
naissant, -sante |nɛsɑ̃, -sɑ̃t| *adj* : incipient
naisse |nɛs|, *etc.* → **naisse**
naître |nɛtr| {57} *vi* **1** : to be born <il est né en 1970 : he was born in 1970> **2** : to rise, to originate <faire naître : to give rise to>
naïveté |naivte| *nf* : naïveté
namibien, -bienne |namibjɛ̃, -bjɛn| *adj* : Namibian
Namibien, -bienne *n* : Namibian
nanti, -tie |nɑ̃ti| *adj* : affluent, well-to-do
nantir |nɑ̃tir| *vt* **~ de** : to provide with
nantissement |nɑ̃tismɑ̃| *nm* : collateral
naphtaline |naftalin| *nf or* **boules de naphtaline** : mothballs *pl*
naphte |naft| *nm* : naphtha
nappe |nap| *nf* **1** : tablecloth **2** : layer, sheet <nappe de brouillard : blanket of fog> <nappe d'eau : sheet of water> <nappe de mazout : oil slick>
napper |nape| *vt* : to coat, to cover <napper de sauce : to cover with sauce>
napperon |naprɔ̃| *nm* : mat, doily
narcisse |narsis| *nm* **1** : narcissus **2** : narcissist
narcissique |narsisik| *adj* : narcissistic — **narcissisme** |-sisism| *nm*
narcotique |narkɔtik| *adj & nm* : narcotic
narguer |narge| *vt* **1** : to mock, to taunt **2** : to flout (danger, etc.)
narine |narin| *nf* : nostril
narquois, -quoise |narkwa, -kwaz| *adj* RAILLEUR : sneering, derisive

narrateur, -trice [naratœr, -tris] *n* : narrator

narratif, -tive [naratif, -tiv] *adj* : narrative

narration [narasjɔ̃] *nf* : narration, narrative

narrer [nare] *vt* : to tell (a story), to relate (events, etc.)

narval [narval] *nm* : narwhal

nasal, -sale [nazal] *adj, mpl* **nasaux** [nazo] : nasal

naseau [nazo] *nm, pl* **naseaux** : nostril (of an animal)

nasillard, -larde [nazijar, -jard] *adj* : nasal <voix nasillarde : nasal voice>

nasiller [nazije] *vi* : to speak through one's nose, to have a nasal twang

natal, -tale [natal] *adj, mpl* **natals** : native, natal

natalité [natalite] *nf* : birthrate

natation [natasjɔ̃] *nf* : swimming

natif[1], -tive [natif, -tiv] *adj* : native

natif[2], -tive *n* : native

nation [nasjɔ̃] *nf* : nation

national, -nale [nasjɔnal] *adj, mpl* **-naux** [-no] : national — **nationalement** [-nalmɑ̃] *adv*

nationale *nf France* : highway

nationaliser [nasjɔnalize] *vt* : to nationalize — **nationalisation** [-lizasjɔ̃] *nf*

nationalisme [nasjɔnalism] *nm* : nationalism — **nationaliste** [-nalist] *adj & nmf*

nationalité [nasjɔnalite] *nf* : nationality

nativité [nativite] *nf* : nativity

natte [nat] *nf* **1** : mat **2** : braid, plait, pigtail

natter [nate] *vt* : to braid, to plait

naturaliser [natyralize] *vt* : to naturalize — **naturalisation** [-lizasjɔ̃] *nf*

naturalisme [natyralism] *nm* : naturalism

naturaliste[1] [natyralist] *adj* : naturalistic

naturaliste[2] *nmf* : naturalist

nature[1] [natyr] *nf* **1** : nature <les beautés de la nature : the beauties of nature> **2** CARACTÈRE : character, nature <une nature passive : a passive nature> **3 nature humaine** : human nature **4 nature morte** : still life

nature[2] *adj* : plain <yaourt nature : plain yogurt>

naturel[1], -relle [natyrɛl] *adj* : natural

naturel[2] *nm* **1** : nature, disposition **2** : naturalness **3 au naturel** : plain, unprocessed **4 au naturel** : in reality

naturellement [natyrɛlmɑ̃] *adv* **1** : naturally, by nature **2** : naturally, of course

naturisme [natyrism] *nm* : nudism — **naturiste** [-tyrist] *adj & nmf*

naufrage [nofraʒ] *nm* : shipwreck

naufragé, -gée [nofraʒe] *adj & n* : castaway

nauséabond, -bonde [nozeabɔ̃, -bɔnd] *adj* **1** : nauseating, revolting **2** : foul-smelling

nausée [noze] *nf* **1** : nausea **2 avoir la nausée** *or* **avoir des nausées** : to get sick to one's stomach

nautile [notil] *nm* : nautilus

nautique [notik] *adj* : nautical <ski nautique : water skiing>

nautisme [notism] *nm* : water sports

naval, -vale [naval] *adj, mpl* **navals** : naval

navet [navɛ] *nm* **1** : turnip **2** *fam* : third-rate film, novel, etc.

navette [navɛt] *nf* **1** : shuttle <navette spatiale : space shuttle> **2 faire la navette** : to commute

navigable [navigabl] *adj* : navigable — **navigabilité** [-gabilite] *nf*

navigant, -gante [navigɑ̃, -gɑ̃t] *adj* **1** : flying <personnel navigant : flight personnel, crew> **2** : seafaring

navigateur, -trice [navigatœr, -tris] *n* **1** : navigator **2** : sailor, seafarer **3** : browser (in computers)

navigation [navigasjɔ̃] *nf* **1** : navigation **2** : shipping

naviguer [navige] *vi* **1** : to sail **2** : to navigate **3** *fam* : to travel

navire [navir] *nm* **1** : ship, vessel **2 navire de guerre** : warship, man-of-war

navire–citerne [navirsitɛrn] *nm, pl* **navires–citernes** : tanker

navrant, -vrante [navrɑ̃, -vrɑ̃t] *adj* **1** : upsetting, distressing **2** : annoying

navrer [navre] *vt* **1** : to upset, to distress **2 être navré de** : to be sorry about

nazi, -zie [nazi] *adj & nmf* : Nazi — **nazisme** [nazism] *nm*

ne [nə] (**n'** *before a vowel or mute h*) *adv* **1** (*used with a negative word*) <il n'y a plus aucun espoir : there's no longer any hope> <elle ne sait pas : she doesn't know> <je ne lui parle guère : I almost never speak to him> **2** (*used with que*) : only, all that, not just <il n'y a pas que vous : you're not the only one> <il ne fait que se plaindre : all (that) he does is complain> **3** (*used alone*) <j'ai peur qu'elle n'oublie : I'm afraid she'll forget> <à moins qu'on ne t'appelle : unless they call you> <n'ayez crainte : don't worry, never fear>

né[1] [ne] *pp* → **naître**

né[2], née *adj* : born <un chanteur né : a born singer>

néanmoins [neɑ̃mwɛ̃] *adv* : nevertheless, yet

néant [neɑ̃] *nm* **1** : worthlessness, emptiness **2 le néant** : nothingness

nébuleuse [nebyløz] *nf* : nebula

nébuleux, -leuse [nebylø, -løz] *adj* **1** : cloudy <ciel nébuleux : cloudy sky> **2** : nebulous

nécessaire[1] [nesesɛr] *adj* : necessary

nécessaire[2] *nm* **1** : necessity <le strict nécessaire : the bare essentials> **2** : need <je ferai le nécessaire : I'll do

what's needed> **3** : bag, kit <nécessaire de toilette : toilet kit>

nécessairement [nesesɛrmɑ̃] *adv* **1** : necessarily **2** INÉVITABLEMENT : inevitably

nécessité [nesesite] *nf* **1** : necessity **2** : need <être dans la nécessité : to be in need>

nécessiter [nesesite] *vt* EXIGER : to require, to call for

nécessiteux, -teuse [nesesitø, -tøz] *adj* : needy

nécrologie [nekrɔlɔʒi] *nf* : obituary

nécromancie [nekrɔmɑ̃si] *nf* : necromancy

nectar [nɛktar] *nm* : nectar

nectarine [nɛktarin] *nf* : nectarine

néerlandais[1], **-daise** [neɛrlɑ̃dɛ, -dɛz] *adj* : Dutch

néerlandais[2] *nm* : Dutch (language)

Néerlandais, -daise *n* **1** : Dutch person, Dutchman *m* **2 les Néerlandais** : the Dutch

nef [nɛf] *nf* : nave

néfaste [nefast] *adj* **1** NUISIBLE : harmful **2** : ill-fated, unlucky

négatif[1], **-tive** [negatif, -tiv] *adj* : negative — **négativement** [-tivmɑ̃] *adv*

négatif[2] *nm* : negative (of a photograph)

négation [negasjɔ̃] *nf* **1** : denial, negation **2** : negative (in grammar)

négative *nf* : negative <répondre par la négative : to reply in the negative>

négativement [negativmɑ̃] *adv* : negatively

négligé[1], **-gée** [negliʒe] *adj* **1** : neglected **2** : slovenly, untidy

négligé[2] *nm* **1** LAISSER-ALLER : slovenliness **2** DÉSHABILLÉ : negligee

négligeable [negliʒabl] *adj* INSIGNIFIANT : negligible, insignificant

négligemment [negliʒamɑ̃] *adv* : negligently, carelessly

négligence [negliʒɑ̃s] *nf* : negligence, carelessness

négligent, -gente [negliʒɑ̃, -ʒɑ̃t] *adj* : negligent, neglectful

négliger [negliʒe] {17} *vt* **1** : to neglect **2** : to disregard, to ignore **3** OMETTRE : to omit, to forget <il a négligé de m'avertir : he forgot to let me know> — **se négliger** *vr* : to neglect oneself

négoce [negɔs] *nm* : business, trade

négociable [negɔsjabl] *adj* : negotiable

négociant, -ciante [negɔsjɑ̃, -sjɑ̃t] *n* : merchant

négociateur, -trice [negɔsjatœr, -tris] *n* : negotiator

négociation [negɔsjasjɔ̃] *nf* : negotiation

négocier [negɔsje] {96} *v* : to negotiate — **négociable** [negɔsjabl] *adj*

nègre, négresse [nɛgr, negrɛs] *adj & n sometimes offensive* : Negro

neige [nɛʒ] *nf* **1** : snow **2 neige carbonique** : dry ice **3 neige fondue** : slush

neiger [neʒe] {17} *v impers* : to snow <il neige : it's snowing>

neigeux, -geuse [nɛʒø, -ʒøz] *adj* : snowy

nénuphar [nenyfar] *nm* : water lily

néologisme [neɔlɔʒism] *nm* : neologism

néon [neɔ̃] *nm* : neon <éclairage au néon : neon lighting>

néophyte [neɔfit] *nmf* : neophyte, beginner

Néo-Zélandais, -daise [neɔelɑ̃dɛ, -dɛz] *n* : New Zealander

népalais[1], **-laise** [nepalɛ, -lɛz] *adj* : Nepali

népalais[2] *nm* : Nepali (language)

Népalais, -laise *n* : Nepali

népotisme [nepɔtism] *nm* : nepotism

Neptune [nɛptyn] *nf* : Neptune (planet)

nerf [nɛr] *nm* **1** : nerve **2** VIGUEUR : vigor, spirit **3 nerfs** *nmpl* : nerves <avoir les nerfs à vif : to be a bundle of nerves>

nerveux, -veuse [nɛrvø, -vøz] *adj* : nervous, tense — **nerveusement** [-vøzmɑ̃] *adv*

nervosité [nɛrvozite] *nf* : nervousness

nervure [nɛrvyr] *nf* **1** : vein (of a leaf, an insect's wing, etc.) **2** : rib (in architecture)

n'est-ce pas [nɛspa] *adv* : no?, isn't that right?, isn't it?, aren't you? <c'est bien ça, n'est-ce pas? : that's right, isn't it?> <tu viens, n'est-ce pas? : you're coming, aren't you?>

net[1] [nɛt] *adv* : plainly, flatly <j'ai refusé net : I flatly refused>

net[2], **nette** *adj* **1** PROPRE : clean, tidy **2** : net <salaire net : net earnings> **3** : clear <une nette amélioration : a clear improvement> **4** MARQUÉ : marked, distinct

nettement [nɛtmɑ̃] *adv* **1** : flatly, bluntly **2** DISTINCTEMENT : clearly, distinctly **3** : definitely

netteté [nɛtte] *nf* **1** : cleanness **2** : clearness, sharpness

nettoie [nɛtwa], **nettoiera** [nɛtwara], *etc.* → **nettoyer**

nettoyage [netwajaʒ] *nm* : cleaning

nettoyant [netwajɑ̃] *nm* : cleaning agent

nettoyer [nɛtwaje] {58} *vt* **1** : to clean, to clean off, to clean up **2** *fam* : to clean out, to rob

neuf[1] [nœf] *adj* **1** : nine **2** : ninth <le neuf juin : June ninth>

neuf[2] *nms & pl* : nine

neuf[3], **neuve** [nœf, nœv] *adj* : new <tout neuf : brand new>

neuf[4] *nm* : new thing <quoi de neuf? : what's new?>

neurologie [nørɔlɔʒi] *nf* : neurology

neurologique [nørɔlɔʒik] *adj* : neurological, neurologic

neurologue [nørɔlɔg] *nmf* : neurologist

neutraliser [nøtralize] *vt* : to neutralize — **neutralisation** [-lizasjɔ̃] *nf*

neutralité [nøtralite] *nf* : neutrality
neutre[1] [nøtr] *adj* **1** : neuter **2** : neutral
neutre[2] *nm* **1** : neuter (in grammar) **2** *Can* : neutral (gear position)
neutron [nøtrɔ̃] *nm* : neutron
neuvième [nœvjɛm] *adj & nmf & nm* : ninth
neveu [nəvø] *nm* : nephew
névralgie [nevralʒi] *nf* : neuralgia
névralgique [nevralʒik] *adj* **1** : neuralgic **2 point névralgique** : sensitive area, key point
névrite [nevrit] *nf* : neuritis
névrose [nevroz] *nf* : neurosis
névrosé, -sée [nevroze] *adj & n* : neurotic
névrotique [nevrɔtik] *adj* : neurotic
nez [ne] *nm* **1** : nose **2** : flair, good judgement **3 nez à nez** : face to face
ni [ni] *conj* **1 ni . . . ni** : neither . . . nor <ni l'un ni l'autre : neither one nor the other> **2 ni plus ni moins** : no more, no less
niais[1], **niaise** [njɛ, njɛz] *adj* : simple, foolish — **niaisement** [njɛzmɑ̃] *adv*
niais[2], **niaise** *n* : fool, simpleton
niaiser [njeze] *vi Can fam* **1** : to dillydally, to waste time **2 faire niaiser qqn** : to make s.o. wait — *vt Can fam* : to make (someone) look stupid
niaiserie [njɛzri] *nf* SOTTISE : silliness, foolishness, stupid remark <dire des niaiseries : to talk nonsense>
niaiseux, -seuse [njezø, -zøz] *n Can fam* : silly person, fool
nicaraguayen, -guayenne [nikaragwɛjɛ̃, -jɛn] *adj* : Nicaraguan
Nicaraguayen, -guayenne *n* : Nicaraguan
niche [niʃ] *nf* **1** : niche, recess **2** : kennel, doghouse
nicher [niʃe] *vi* : to nest, to brood — **se nicher** *vr* **1** : to nest **2** : to nestle **3** : to hide away
nickel [nikɛl] *nm* : nickel
nicotine [nikɔtin] *nf* : nicotine
nid [ni] *nm* **1** : nest **2** : den, lair <nid de brigands : den of thieves>
nid–de–poule *nm, pl* **nids–de–poule** : pothole
nièce [njɛs] *nf* : niece
nier [nje] {96} *vt* : to deny
nigaud, -gaude [nigo, nigod] *n* : simpleton, fool
nigérian, -rianne [niʒerjɑ̃, -rjan] *adj* : Nigerian
Nigérian, -rianne *n* : Nigerian
n'importe → **importer**
nirvana [nirvana] *nm* : nirvana
nitrate [nitrat] *nm* : nitrate
nitrique [nitrik] *adj* **acide nitrique** : nitric acid
nitrite [nitrik] *nm* : nitrite
nitroglycérine [nitrɔglisərin] *nf* : nitroglycerin, nitroglycerine
niveau [nivo] *nm, pl* **niveaux** [nivo] **1** : level <niveau de la mer : sea level> **2** : story <un bâtiment à trois niveaux : a three-story building> **3** : level, standard <niveau de vie : standard of living> **4** : stage, level, degree <négociations au plus haut niveau : top-level negotiations>
niveler [nivle] {8} *vt* : to level (off), to even out
nivellement [nivɛlmɑ̃] *nm* : leveling
noble[1] [nɔbl] *adj* **1** : noble **2 métaux nobles** : precious metals
noble[2] *nmf* : noble, nobleman *m*, noblewoman *f*
noblesse [nɔblɛs] *nf* : nobility
noce [nɔs] *nf* **1** : wedding, wedding party **2 noces** *nfpl* : wedding <noces d'or : golden wedding anniversary>
nocif, -cive [nɔsif, -siv] *adj* : noxious, harmful
noctambule [nɔktɑ̃byl] *nmf* : night owl
nocturne[1] [nɔktyrn] *adj* : nocturnal, night
nocturne[2] *nm* **1** : nocturne **2** : night hunter (bird)
nodule [nɔdyl] *nm* : nodule
Noël [nɔɛl] *nm* **1** : Christmas <joyeux Noël : Merry Christmas> **2 père Noël** : Santa Claus
noeud [nø] *nm* **1** : knot <noeud coulant : noose> **2** : bow <noeud papillon : bow tie> **3** : crux **4** : node **5** : knot (nautical speed)
noie [nwa], **noiera** [nwara], *etc.* → **noyer**
noir[1], **noire** [nwar] *adj* **1** : black **2** SALE : dirty, grimy **3** : dark <il fait noir : it's dark>
noir[2] *nm* **1** : black (color) **2** : darkness <peur du noir : fear of the dark> **3 au noir** : on the black market, on the side <travailler au noir : to moonlight> **4 noir à chaussures** *Can* : (black) shoe polish
Noir, Noire *n* : black man, black woman
noirâtre [nwaratr] *adj* : blackish
noirceur [nwarsœr] *nf* **1** : blackness **2** *Can* : darkness
noircir [nwarsir] *vi* : to darken, to turn black — *vt* : to black, to blacken <une réputation noircie : a tarnished reputation>
noircissure [nwarsisyr] *nf* : black mark
noise [nwaz] *nf* **chercher noise à qqn** : to pick a fight with s.o.
noisetier [nwaztje] *nm* : hazel (tree)
noisette [nwazɛt] *nf* **1** : hazelnut **2** : hazel (color)
noix [nwa] *nfs & pl* **1** : nut, walnut **2** : piece, lump <noix de beurre : round lump of butter> **3** → **cajou, coco, muscade**
noliser [nɔlize] *vt* : to charter, to rent out
nom [nɔ̃] *nm* **1** : name <nom de plume : pen name> <nom de famille : surname> <nom de jeune fille : maiden name> **2** : noun **3 au nom de** : in the name of, on behalf of

nomade[1] [nɔmad] *adj* : nomadic
nomade[2] *nmf* : nomad
nombre [nɔ̃br] *nm* **1** : number <nombre entier : whole number, integer> <nombre impair : odd number> **2** QUANTITÉ : quantity, number <un grand nombre de : a lot of, many> <sans nombre : countless> **3** MASSE : numbers *pl* <la loi du nombre : the sheer weight of numbers> **4 au nombre de** : among
nombreux, -breuse [nɔ̃brø, -brøz] *adj* **1** : large <une famille nombreuse : a large family> **2** : many, numerous
nombril [nɔ̃bril] *nm* : navel
nombrilisme [nɔ̃brilism] *nm fam* : self-centeredness
nomenclature [nɔmɑ̃klatyr] *nf* **1** : nomenclature **2** : word list
nominal, -nale [nɔminal] *adj, mpl* **-naux** [-no] : nominal <valeur nominale : face value> — **nominalement** [-nalmɑ̃] *adv*
nominatif [nɔminatif] *nm* : nominative
nomination [nɔminasjɔ̃] *nf* : appointment, nomination
nommément [nɔmemɑ̃] *adv* : by name, namely
nommer [nɔme] *vt* **1** PRÉNOMMER : to name, to call **2** : to appoint, to nominate **3** CITER : to name, to mention — **se nommer** *vr* **1** S'APPELER : to be named <elle se nomme Julie : her name is Julie> **2** : to introduce oneself
non[1] [nɔ̃] *adv* **1** : no <mais non! : no!, of course not!> **2** (*used to replace a clause*) <je pense que non : I don't think so> <c'est à ton goût, non? : you like it, don't you?> <moi non plus : me neither, neither do I, neither am I> **3** (*used to modify an adjective or adverb*) <non loin d'ici : not far from here> <non moins : no less> **4 non seulement . . . mais (encore)** : not only . . . but (also)
non[2] *nm* : no
non–aligné, -née [nɔnaliɲe] *adj* : nonaligned
nonante[1] [nɔnɑ̃t] *adj* : *Belg, Switz* : ninety
nonante[2] *n* : *Belg, Switz* : ninety
nonchalamment [nɔ̃ʃalamɑ̃] *adv* : nonchalantly
nonchalance [nɔ̃ʃalɑ̃s] *nf* : nonchalance, casualness
nonchalant, -lante [nɔ̃ʃalɑ̃, -lɑ̃t] *adj* : nonchalant, casual
non–combattant, -tante [nɔ̃kɔ̃batɑ̃, -tɑ̃t] *n* : noncombatant
non–conformité [nɔ̃kɔ̃fɔrmite] *nf* : nonconformity — **non–conformiste** [-fɔrmist] *nmf*
non–croyant, -croyante [nɔ̃krwajɑ̃, -jɑ̃t] *n* : nonbeliever
non–existence [nɔnɛgzistɑ̃s] *nf* : nonexistence — **non–existent** [nɔnɛgzistɑ̃] *adj*
non–fumeur, -meuse [nɔ̃fymœr, -møz] *n* : nonsmoker
nono, nonote [nɔno] *n Can fam* : fool, idiot
nonobstant [nɔnɔpstɑ̃] *adv & prep* : notwithstanding
nonoune [nɔnun] *adj Can fam* : stupid, thick
non–paiement [nɔ̃pɛmɑ̃] *nm* : nonpayment
non–prolifération [nɔ̃prɔliferasjɔ̃] *nf* : nonproliferation
non–sens [nɔsɑ̃s] *nms & pl* **1** ABSURDITÉ : absurdity, nonsense **2** : meaningless word or phrase
non–violence [nɔ̃vjɔlɑ̃s] *nf* : nonviolence
non–violent, -lente [nɔ̃vjɔlɑ̃, -lɑ̃t] *adj* : nonviolent
non–voyant, -voyante [nɔ̃vwajɑ̃, -jɑ̃t] *n* : blind person
nord[1] [nɔr] *adj* : north, northern
nord[2] *nm* **1** : north <exposé au nord : with a northerly aspect> <vent du nord : north wind> **2 le Nord** : the North **3 perdre le nord** *fam* : to become disoriented
nord–américain, -caine [nɔramerikɛ̃, -kɛn] *adj* : North American
Nord–Américain, -caine *n* : North American
nord–coréen, -réenne [nɔrkɔreɛ̃, -ɛn] *adj* : North Korean
Nord–Coréen, -réenne *n* : North Korean
nord–est[1] [nɔrɛst] *adj s & pl* **1** : northeast, northeastern **2** : northeasterly
nord–est[2] *nm* : northeast
nordique[1] [nɔrdik] *adj* : Nordic, Scandinavian
nordique[2] *nm* : Norse (language)
Nordique *nmf* : Scandinavian
nord–ouest[1] [nɔrwɛst] *adj s & pl* **1** : northwest, northwestern **2** : northwesterly
nord–ouest[2] *nm* : northwest
normal, -male [nɔrmal] *adj, mpl* **normaux** [nɔrmo] **1** : normal, standard, usual **2** : normal, natural <c'est bien normal : it's only natural>
normale *nf* **1** : average, normal <au-dessous de la normale : below normal> **2** NORME : norm, standard
normalement [nɔrmalmɑ̃] *adv* : normally, usually
normaliser [nɔrmalize] *vt* : to normalize, to standardize — **normalisation** [-lizasjɔ̃] *nf*
normalité [nɔrmalite] *nf* : normality, normalcy
norme [nɔrm] *nf* : norm, standard
norvégien[1], **-gienne** [nɔrveʒjɛ̃, -ʒjɛn] *adj* : Norwegian
norvégien[2] *nm* : Norwegian (language)

Norvégien, -gienne *n* : Norwegian

nos → **notre**

nostalgie [nɔstalʒi] *nf* : nostalgia — **nostalgique** [nɔstalʒik] *adj*

notable[1] [nɔtabl] *adj* : notable, noteworthy

notable[2] *nm* : notable

notablement [nɔtabləmɑ̃] *adv* : notably, considerably

notaire [nɔtɛr] *nm* : notary public

notamment [nɔtamɑ̃] *adv* PARTICULIÈREMENT : especially, particularly

notation [nɔtasjɔ̃] *nf* : notation

note [nɔt] *nf* **1** : note <prendre des notes : to take notes> **2** ADDITION : bill, check **3** : mark, grade (in school) **4** : note (in music) **5** : touch, hint <une note de tristesse : a note of sadness> **6 note de service** : memorandum **7 note en bas de la page** : footnote

noter [nɔte] *vt* **1** REMARQUER : to note, to take notice of **2** MARQUER : to mark <noter un passage important : to mark an important passage> **3** : to mark, to grade **4** INSCRIRE : to write, to note down

notice [nɔtis] *nf* **1** : note <notice bibliographique : bibliographical note> **2** : instructions *pl*

notifier [nɔtifje] {96} *vt* : to notify — **notification** [-tifikasjɔ̃] *nf*

notion [nɔsjɔ̃] *nf* **1** : notion, idea **2 notions** *nfpl* : rudiments, basic knowledge

notoire [nɔtwar] *adj* **1** CONNU : well-known **2** : notorious

notoirement [nɔtwarmɑ̃] *adv* : notoriously

notoriété [nɔtɔrjete] *nf* **1** : fame, renown **2** : celebrity (person) **3 de notoriété publique** : common knowledge

notre [nɔtr] *adj, pl* **nos** [no] : our

nôtre[1] [notr] *adj* : our own <nous avons fait nôtres ces idées : we have made these ideas ours>

nôtre[2] *pron* **le nôtre, la nôtre, les nôtres** : ours <nous avons les nôtres : we have ours>

nouer [nwe] *vt* **1** : to tie, to knot, to fasten **2** : to start up, to establish <nouer des relations avec : to begin a relationship with> **3 avoir la gorge nouée** : to have a lump in one's throat

noueux, noueuse [nwø, -øz] *adj* : knotty, knobby, gnarled

nougat [nuga] *nm* : nougat

nouille [nuj] *nf* **1** *fam* : nitwit, idiot **2 nouilles** *nfpl* : noodles, pasta

nourri, -rie [nuri] *adj* **1** : heavy (of gunfire) **2** : sustained, prolonged

nourrice [nuris] *nf* : wet nurse

nourrir [nurir] *vt* **1** ALIMENTER : to feed, to nourish **2** ALLAITER : to breast-feed **3** : to provide for (a family, etc.) **4** : to nurse, to harbor <nourrir des doutes : to entertain doubts> — **se nourrir** *vr* **1** : to eat **2** ~ **de** : to feed on

nourrissant, -sante [nurisɑ̃, -sɑ̃t] *adj* : nourishing, nutritious

nourrisson [nurisɔ̃] *nm* : infant

nourriture [nurityr] *nf* **1** : food **2** : diet **3** : (intellectual) nourishment

nous [nu] *pron* **1** : we **2** : us <il nous a dit de partir : he told us to go> **3** : ourselves <nous nous amusons : we're enjoying ourselves> **4 nous autres** *Can fam* : we <ils ne travaillent pas comme nous autres : they don't work as hard as we do>

nous–mêmes [numɛm] *pron* : ourselves

nouveau[1] [nuvo] **(-vel** [-vɛl] *before a vowel or mute h*), **-velle** [-vɛl] *adj, mpl* **nouveaux 1** : new **2** : novel, fresh <une nouvelle idée : an original idea> **3 de** ~ *or* **à** ~ : again, once again **4 nouveau venu** : newcomer

nouveau[2] *nm* **1 du nouveau** : something new **2 le nouveau** : the new

nouveau–né, -née [nuvone] *adj & n, mpl* **nouveau–nés** : newborn

nouveauté [nuvote] *nf* **1** : newness, novelty **2** : innovation

nouvelle [nuvɛl] *nf* **1** : piece of news <c'est une bonne nouvelle : that's good news> **2** : short story **3 nouvelles** *nfpl* : news <les nouvelles vont vite : news travels fast> <regarder les nouvelles : to watch the news>

nouvellement [nuvɛlmɑ̃] *adv* : newly, recently

novateur[1], **-trice** [nɔvatœr, -tris] *adj* : innovative

novateur[2], **-trice** *n* : innovator

novembre [nɔvɑ̃br] *nm* : November

novice[1] [nɔvis] *adj* : inexperienced

novice[2] *nmf* : novice, beginner

noviciat [nɔvisja] *nm* : novitiate

noyade [nwajad] *nf* : drowning

noyau [nwajo] *nm, pl* **noyaux 1** : pit, stone (of a fruit) **2** : nucleus, core (in science) **3** : group, core <un noyau de résistance : a pocket of resistance>

noyautage [nwajotaʒ] *nm* : infiltration

noyauter [nwajote] *vt* : to infiltrate

noyé[1], **noyée** [nwaje] *adj* **1** PERDU : lost, out of one's depth **2** : flooded <des yeux noyés de larmes : eyes brimming with tears>

noyé[2], **noyée** *n* : drowning victim

noyer[1] [nwaje] {58} *vt* **1** : to drown **2** : to flood <noyer le moteur : to flood the engine> **3** : to shroud, to blur, to drown out — **se noyer** *vr* **1** : to drown **2** : to be swamped, to be drowned (out) **3** ~ **dans** : to get bogged down in

noyer[2] *nm* **1** : walnut tree **2 noyer blanc d'Amérique** : hickory (tree)

nu[1], **nue** [ny] *adj* **1** : naked, nude **2** : uncovered <être pieds nus : to be barefoot(ed)> <à main nue : bare-handed> **3** : bare, plain, unadorned

nu[2] *nm* **1** : nude (in art) **2 à ~** : bare, exposed <mettre à nu : to expose, to lay bare>

nuage [nɥaʒ] *nm* **1** : cloud <sans nuages : cloudless, unclouded> <être dans les nuages : to have one's head in the clouds> **2** : cloud, mass (of dust, smoke, etc.) <un nuage de lait : a dash of milk>

nuageux, -geuse [nɥaʒø, -ʒøz] *adj* **1** COUVERT : cloudy, overcast **2** : hazy, obscure

nuance [nɥɑ̃s] *nf* **1** TON : hue, shade <nuance de vert : shade of green> **2** : subtlety, nuance **3 une nuance de** : a touch of, a trace of

nuancer [nɥɑ̃se] {6} *vt* : to qualify (thoughts, opinions, etc.)

nubile [nybil] *adj* : nubile

nucléaire[1] [nykleɛr] *adj* : nuclear

nucléaire[2] *nm* : nuclear energy

nudisme [nydism] *nm* : nudism — **nudiste** [nydist] *adj & nmf*

nudité [nydite] *nf* **1** : nudity, nakedness **2** : bareness

nuée [nɥe] *nf* : cloud, swarm

nues [ny] *nfpl* **1 porter qqn aux nues** : to praise s.o. to the skies **2 tomber des nues** : to be taken aback

nuire [nɥir] {49} *vi* **~ à** : to harm, to injure — **se nuire** *vr*

nuisait [nɥizɛ], **nuisions** [nɥizjɔ̃], *etc.* → **nuire**

nuisance [nɥizɑ̃s] *nf* : pollution <nuisance sonore : noise pollution>

nuise [nɥiz], *etc.* → **nuire**

nuisible [nɥizibl] *adj* : harmful, injurious

nuit [nɥi] *nf* **1** : night, nighttime **2** : darkness <il fait nuit : it's dark out> **3 de ~** : nocturnal, at night, by night

nul[1], **nulle** [nyl] *adj* **1** : no <je n'ai nul besoin de sortir : I have no need to go out> <sans nul doute : without a doubt, undoubtedly> <nulle part : nowhere> **2** : nil, nonexistent **3** : invalid, null and void **4** : hopeless, useless, worthless <il est nul en biologie : he is hopeless in biology>

nul[2] *pron* : no one, nobody

nullement [nylmɑ̃] *adv* : by no means

nullité [nylite] *nf* **1** : incompetence, worthlessness **2** : nonentity **3** : nullity (of a contract, etc.)

numéraire [nymerɛr] *nm* : cash

numéral[1], **-rale** [nymeral] *adj, mpl* **-raux** : numeral

numéral[2] *nm, pl* **-raux** : numeral

numérateur [nymeratœr] *nm* : numerator

numération [nymerasjɔ̃] *nf* **1** : notation <numération décimale : decimal notation> **2 numération globulaire** : blood count

numérique [nymerik] *adj* **1** : numerical **2** : digital — **numériquement** *adv*

numéro [nymero] *nm* **1** : number <le numéro deux : number two> <numéro de téléphone : telephone number> **2** : issue (of a periodical) **3 quel numéro!** *fam* : what a character!

numéroter [nymerɔte] *vt* : to number

numismate [nymismat] *nmf* : numismatist, coin collector

numismatique [nymismatik] *nf* : numismatics

nu–pieds [nypje] *adj* : barefoot(ed)

nuptial, -tiale [nypsjal] *adj, mpl* **-tiaux** [-sjo] : nuptial, wedding

nuque [nyk] *nf* : nape of the neck

nutritif, -tive [nytritif, -tiv] *adj* **1** : nourishing, nutritious **2** : nutritional

nutrition [nytrisjɔ̃] *nf* : nutrition — **nutritionnel, -nelle** [-sjɔnɛl] *adj*

nylon [nilɔ̃] *nm* **1** : nylon **2 bas de nylon** : nylon stockings, panty hose

nymphe [nɛ̃f] *nf* : nymph

O

o [o] *nm* : o, the 15th letter of the alphabet

oasis [ɔazis] *nf* : oasis

obédience [ɔbedjɑ̃s] *nf* : allegiance, persuasion <pays d'obédience communiste : Communist countries>

obéir [ɔbeir] *vi* **~ à 1** : to obey **2** SE CONFORMER : to follow, to comply with **3** : to respond to <les freins obéissent à la pression : the brakes respond to pressure>

obéissance [ɔbeisɑ̃s] *nf* : obedience

obéissant, -sante [ɔbeisɑ̃, -sɑ̃t] *adj* : obedient

obélisque [ɔbelisk] *nm* : obelisk

obèse [ɔbɛz] *adj* : obese

obésité [ɔbezite] *nf* : obesity

objecter [ɔbʒɛkte] *vt* **1** : to raise as an objection <il m'objecta que . . . : he objected (to me) that . . .> **2** PRÉTEXTER : to plead <objecter la fatigue : to plead tiredness>

objecteur [ɔbʒɛktœr] *nm* : objector <objecteur de conscience : conscientious objector>

objectif[1], **-tive** [ɔbʒɛktif, -tiv] *adj* : objective — **objectivement** [-tivmɑ̃] *adv*

objectif[2] *nm* **1** BUT : objective, goal **2** : lens (of an optical instrument)

objection [ɔbʒɛksjɔ̃] *nf* : objection

objectivité [ɔbʒɛktivite] *nf* : objectivity

objet [ɔbʒɛ] *nm* **1** : object, thing **2** : subject, topic **3** BUT : goal, purpose <sans objet : pointless, aimless> **4** : object (in grammar) **5 bureau des objets**

trouvés : lost-and-found department **6 objet de famille** : heirloom
obligation [ɔbligasjɔ̃] *nf* **1** : obligation, duty **2** : bond, debenture
obligatoire [ɔbligatwar] *adj* **1** : compulsory, obligatory, mandatory **2** *fam* : inevitable
obligatoirement [ɔbligatwarmɑ̃] *adv* **1** : necessarily, imperatively **2** *fam* : inevitably
obligé, -gée [ɔbliʒe] *adj* **1 être obligé à** : to be indebted to **2 c'est obligé** *fam* : it's bound to happen, it's inevitable
obligeamment [ɔbliʒamɑ̃] *adv* : obligingly
obligeance [ɔbliʒɑ̃s] *nf* AMABILITÉ : kindness, helpfulness
obligeant, -geante [ɔbliʒɑ̃, -ʒɑ̃t] *adj* COMPLAISANT : obliging, kind
obliger [ɔbliʒe] {17} *vt* **1** CONTRAINDRE : to force, to compel **2** : to oblige <vous m'obligez beaucoup : I am much obliged to you>
oblique [ɔblik] *adj* **1** : oblique **2 en ∼** : crosswise, diagonally — **obliquement** [ɔblikmɑ̃] *adv*
obliquer [ɔblike] *vi* : to bear, to turn (off) <obliquer à droite : to turn right>
oblitérer [ɔblitere] {87} *vt* : to cancel (a stamp) — **oblitération** [-terasjɔ̃] *nf*
oblong, oblongue [ɔblɔ̃, ɔblɔ̃g] *adj* : oblong
obnubiler [ɔbnybile] *vt* **1** OBSCURCIR : to cloud, to obscure **2** OBSÉDER : to obsess
obole [ɔbɔl] *nf* : small contribution
obscène [ɔpsɛn] *adj* : obscene
obscénité [ɔpsenite] *nf* : obscenity
obscur, -cure [ɔpskyr] *adj* **1** SOMBRE : dark **2** : obscure, vague **3** : abstruse, recondite — **obscurément** [-skyremɑ̃] *adv*
obscurcir [ɔpskyrsir] *vt* **1** ASSOMBRIR : to darken **2** : to obscure, to blur **3** : to make obscure, to confuse — **s'obscurcir** *vr* **1** : to become dark **2** : to become confused
obscurité [ɔpskyrite] *nf* **1** : darkness **2** ANONYMAT : obscurity
obsédant, -dante [ɔpsedɑ̃, -dɑ̃t] *adj* : obsessive, haunting
obsédé, -dée [ɔpsede] *n* : obsessive, fanatic
obséder [ɔpsede] {87} *vt* : to obsess, to haunt
obsèques [ɔpsɛk] *nfpl* : funeral
obséquieux, -quieuse [ɔpsekjø, -kjøz] *adj* : obsequious — **obséquieusement** [-kjøzmɑ̃] *adv*
obséquiosité [ɔpsekjozite] *nf* : obsequiousness
observance [ɔpsɛrvɑ̃s] *nf* : observance
observateur[1], **-trice** [ɔpsɛrvatœr, -tris] *adj* : observant, perceptive
observateur[2], **-trice** *n* : observer
observation [ɔpsɛrvasjɔ̃] *nf* **1** : observance **2** : observing, observation **3** REMARQUE : observation, remark
observatoire [ɔpsɛrvatwar] *nm* **1** : observatory **2** : observation post, vantage point
observer [ɔpsɛrve] *vt* **1** : to observe, to watch **2** : to note, to notice **3** : to keep, to maintain <observer sa position : to maintain one's position> <observer le silence : to keep quiet> — **s'observer** *vr*
obsession [ɔpsesjɔ̃] *nf* : obsession
obsessionnel, -nelle [ɔpsesjɔnɛl] *adj* : obsessive
obsolescent, -cente [ɔpsɔlɛsɑ̃, -sɑ̃t] *adj* : obsolescent — **obsolescence** [-lɛsɑ̃s] *nf*
obsolète [ɔpsɔlɛt] *adj* : obsolete
obstacle [ɔpstakl] *nm* **1** : obstacle <faire obstacle : to obstruct> **2** : fence, hurdle (in horseback riding)
obstétrical, -cale [ɔpstetrikal] *adj, mpl* **-caux** [-ko] : obstetric, obstetrical
obstétricien, -cienne [ɔpstetrisjɛ̃, -sjɛn] *n* : obstetrician
obstétrique [ɔpstetrik] *nf* : obstetrics
obstination [ɔpstinasjɔ̃] *nf* : obstinacy, stubbornness
obstiné, -née [ɔpstine] *adj* ENTÊTÉ : obstinate, stubborn — **obstinément** [-nemɑ̃] *adv*
obstiner [ɔpstine] *v* **s'obstiner** *vr* **1 s'obstiner à faire** : to insist on doing **2 ∼ dans** : to persist in, to cling to
obstruction [ɔpstryksjɔ̃] *nf* **1** : obstruction, blockage <faire de l'obstruction : to obstruct, to be obstructive> **2** : filibuster <faire de l'obstruction parlementaire : to filibuster>
obstructionniste [ɔpstryksjɔnist] *adj* : obstructive
obstruer [ɔpstrye] *vt* : to obstruct, to block — **s'obstruer** *vr*
obtempérer [ɔptɑ̃pere] {87} *vi* **∼ à** : to obey, to comply with
obtenir [ɔptənir] {92} *vt* : to obtain, to get, to secure — **s'obtenir** *vr*
obtention [ɔptɑ̃sjɔ̃] *nf* : obtaining
obtient [ɔptjɛ̃] *pp* → **obtenir**
obturateur [ɔptyratœr] *nm* : shutter (of a camera)
obturation [ɔptyrasjɔ̃] *nf* **1** : closing up, sealing **2** *or* **obturation dentaire** : filling
obturer [ɔptyre] *vt* **1** : to seal, to stop up **2** : to fill (a tooth)
obtus, -tuse [ɔpty, -tyz] *adj* **1** : obtuse (of an angle) **2** : slow-witted, dull
obus [ɔby] *nm* **1** : shell <obus de mortier : mortar shell> **2 éclats d'obus** : shrapnel
obusier [ɔbyzje] *nm* : howitzer
obvier [ɔbvje] {96} *vi* **∼ à** : to guard against, to obviate
occasion [ɔkazjɔ̃] *nf* **1** : opportunity, chance **2** : occasion <les grandes occasions : special occasions> **3** : bar-

gain **4 d'~** : secondhand <vêtements d'occasion : secondhand clothing>

occasionnel[1], **-nelle** [ɔkazjɔnɛl] *adj* **1** : occasional **2** FORTUIT : chance, fortuitous

occasionnel[2], **-nelle** *n Can* : temp, temporary employee

occasionnellement [ɔkazjɔnɛlmɑ̃] *adv* : occasionally

occasionner [ɔkazjɔne] *vt* CAUSER : to cause, to bring about

occident [ɔksidɑ̃] *nm* **1** : west **2 l'Occident** : the West

occidental, -tale [ɔksidɑ̃tal] *adj, mpl* **-taux** [-to] : western, Western

Occidental, -tale *n, mpl* **-taux** [-to] : Westerner

occidentaliser [ɔsidɑ̃talize] *vt* : to westernize

occulte [ɔkylt] *adj* : supernatural, occult

occulter [ɔkylte] *vt* **1** : to overshadow **2** : to cover up, to conceal

occupant[1], **-pante** [ɔkypɑ̃,-pɑ̃t] *adj* : occupying

occupant[2], **-pante** *n* : occupant, occupier

occupation [ɔkypasjɔ̃] *nf* **1** : occupation, job **2** : occupancy **3** : (military) occupation

occupé, -pée [ɔkype] *adj* **1** : busy **2** : taken, in use <cette place est occupée : this seat is taken> <la ligne est occupée : the line is busy> **3** : occupied <zone occupée : occupied zone>

occuper [ɔkype] *vt* **1** : to occupy, to hold **2** : to employ, to keep busy **3** REMPLIR : to take up, to fill **4** : to inhabit **— s'occuper** *vr* **1** : to keep busy **2 ~ de** : to handle, to deal with, to take care of

occurrence [ɔkyrɑ̃s] *nf* : instance, case <en l'occurrence : in this case>

océan [ɔseɑ̃] *nm* : ocean

océanien, -nienne [ɔseanjɛ̃, -njɛn] *adj* : Oceanian

Océanien, -nienne *n* : Oceanian

océanique [ɔseanik] *adj* : oceanic, ocean

océanographie [ɔseanɔgrafi] *nf* : oceanography **— océanographique** [-grafik] *adj*

ocelot [ɔslo] *nm* : ocelot

ocre [ɔkr] *nmf* : ocher

octave [ɔktav] *nf* : octave

octet [ɔktɛ] *nm* : byte

octobre [ɔktɔbr] *nm* : October

octogone [ɔktɔgɔn] *nm* : octagon **— octogonal, -nale** [-gɔnal] *adj*

octroi [ɔktrwa] *nm* : granting

octroyer [ɔktrwaje] {58} *vt* : to grant, to bestow

oculaire[1] [ɔkylɛr] *adj* : ocular, eye

oculaire[2] *nm* : eyepiece

oculiste [ɔkylist] *nmf* : oculist

ode [ɔd] *nf* : ode

odeur [ɔdœr] *nf* : odor, smell, scent

odieux, -dieuse [ɔdjø, -djøz] *adj* EXÉCRABLE : odious, hateful **— odieusement** [-djøzmɑ̃] *adv*

odorant, -rante [ɔdɔrɑ̃, -rɑ̃t] *adj* PARFUMÉ : fragrant, sweet-smelling, odorous

odorat [ɔdɔra] *nm* : sense of smell

odoriférant, -rante [ɔdɔriferɑ̃, -rɑ̃t] *adj* : fragrant

odyssée [ɔdise] *nf* : odyssey

œcuménique [ekymenik] *adj* : ecumenical, nondenominational

œdème [edɛm] *nm* : edema

œil [œj] *nm, pl* **yeux** [jø] **1** : eye <yeux verts : green eyes> <avoir à l'œil : to keep an eye on> <coup d'œil : glance> **2** : look, view <jeter un œil à : to have a quick look at> <d'un œil jaloux : jealously> <voir d'un mauvais œil : to take a dim view of> **3** : eye (of a needle, potato, storm, etc.) **4 → clin**

œillade [œjad] *nf* **1** : wink, glance **2 faire des œillades à** : to make eyes at

œillères [œjɛr] *nfpl* **1** : blinders, blinkers **2 avoir des œillères** : to be narrow-minded

œillet [œjɛ] *nm* **1** : eyelet, grommet **2** : carnation, pink

œsophage [ezɔfaʒ] *nm* : esophagus

œstrogène [ɛstrɔʒɛn] *nm* : estrogen

œuf [œf] *nm, pl* **œufs** [ø] **1** : egg <œufs pochés : poached eggs> **2 étouffer dans l'œuf** : to nip in the bud

œuvre[1] [œvr] *nm* : body of work <l'œuvre peint de Monet : Monet's paintings>

œuvre[2] *nf* **1** : work <œuvre d'art : work of art> **2** : undertaking, task, work <se mettre à l'œuvre : to get down to work> <mise en œuvre : implementation> **3** : effect, work <le médicament a fait son œuvre : the medicine has done its work> **4** *or* **œuvre de bienfaisance** : charitable organization

œuvrer [œvre] *vi* : to work

offensant, -sante [ɔfɑ̃sɑ̃, -sɑ̃t] *adj* INJURIEUX : offensive, insulting

offense [ɔfɑ̃s] *nf* **1** : offense, insult **2** : trespass, sin

offenser [ɔfɑ̃se] *vt* : to offend, to hurt **— s'offenser** *vr* : to take offense

offensif, -sive [ɔfɑ̃sif, -siv] *adj* : offensive, attacking **— offensivement** [-sivmɑ̃] *adv*

offensive *nf* **1** : offensive <passer à l'offensive : to go on the offensive> **2** : onset, onslaught

offert [ɔfɛr] *pp* **→ offrir**

offertoire [ɔfɛrtwar] *nm* : offertory

office [ɔfis] *nm* **1** : bureau, agency **2** : office, service (in religion) **3** : office, function <faire office de : to act as> **4 d'~** : automatically, as a matter of course <rejeter d'office : to dismiss out of hand>

officialiser [ɔfisjalize] *vt* : to make official

officiel[1], -cielle [ɔfisjɛl] *adj* : official — **officiellement** [-sjɛlmɑ̃] *adv*

officiel[2], -cielle *n* : official

officier[1] [ɔfisje] {96} *vi* : to officiate

officier[2] *nm* : officer

officieux, -cieuse [ɔfisjø, -sjøz] *adj* : unofficial, informal — **officieusement** [-sjøzmɑ̃] *adv*

officinal, -nale [ɔfisinal] *adj, mpl* **-naux** [-no] : medicinal <plantes officinales : medicinal plants>

officine [ɔfisin] *nf* **1** : pharmacy **2** : group, den (of conspirators, etc.)

offrande [ɔfrɑ̃d] *nf* : offering

offrant [ɔfrɑ̃] *nm* **vendre au plus offrant** : to sell to the highest bidder

offre [ɔfr] *nf* **1** : offer, bid <offre d'emploi : job opening> **2 l'offre et la demande** : supply and demand

offrir [ɔfrir] {83} *vt* : to give, to offer — **s'offrir** *vr* **1** : to offer oneself, to volunteer **2** : to treat oneself to <je me suis offerte des vacances : I gave myself a vacation> **3** SE PRÉSENTER : to present itself

offusquer [ɔfyske] *vt* : to offend — **s'offusquer** *vr* : to take offense

ogive [ɔʒiv] *nf* **1** : rib (in architecture) **2** : warhead <ogive nucléaire : nuclear warhead>

ogre, ogresse [ɔgr, ɔgrɛs] *n* **1** : ogre **2 manger comme un ogre** : to eat like a horse

oh[1] [o] *nm* **pousser des oh et des ah** : to ooh and ah

oh[2] *interj* : oh!

ohé [ɔe] *interj* **1** : hey there! **2 ohé du navire!** : ship ahoy!

ohm [om] *nm* : ohm

oie [wa] *nf* : goose

oignon [ɔɲɔ̃] *nm* **1** : onion **2** : bulb (of a flower) **3** : bunion **4 occupe–toi de tes oignons** *fam* : mind your own business

oindre [wɛ̃dr] {59} *vt* : to anoint

oiseau [wazo] *nm, pl* **oiseaux 1** : bird <oiseau chanteur : songbird> <oiseau de proie : bird of prey> <oiseau marin : seabird> **2** : hod (for bricks, etc.) **3** *fam* : character, oddball

oiseau–mouche [wazomuʃ] *nm, pl* **oiseaux–mouches** : hummingbird

oiseux, -seuse [wazø, -zøz] *adj* INUTILE : pointless, idle

oisif[1], -sive [wazif, -ziv] *adj* : idle — **oisivement** [-zivmɑ̃] *adv*

oisif[2], -sive *n* : idler

oisillon [wazijɔ̃] *nm* : fledgling

oisiveté [wazivte] *nf* : idleness

oison [wazɔ̃] *nm* : gosling

oléoduc [ɔleɔdyk] *nm* : (oil) pipeline

olfactif, -tive [ɔlfaktif, -tiv] *adj* : olfactory

oligarchie [ɔligarʃi] *nf* : oligarchy

olive[1] [ɔliv] *adj* : olive green

olive[2] *nf* : olive

olivier [ɔlivje] *nm* **1** : olive tree **2** : olive wood

olympiade [ɔlɛ̃pjad] *nf or* **olympiades** [-pjad] *nfpl* : Olympic Games, Olympics

olympique [ɔlɛ̃pik] *adj* : Olympic <les Jeux olympiques : the Olympic Games>

omanais, -naise [ɔmanɛ, -nɛz] *adj* : Omani

Omanais, -naise *n* : Omani

ombilical, -cale [ɔ̃bilikal] *adj, mpl* **-caux** [-ko] : umbilical

ombrage [ɔ̃braʒ] *nm* **1** : shade **2 porter ombrage à** : to offend **3 prendre ombrage de** : to take umbrage at

ombragé, -gée [ɔ̃braʒe] *adj* : shady, shaded

ombrager [ɔ̃braʒe] {17} *vt* : to shade, to darken

ombrageux, -geuse [ɔ̃braʒø, -ʒøz] *adj* **1** : skittish (of a horse) **2** : touchy, easily offended

ombre [ɔ̃br] *nf* **1** : shade <20 degrés à l'ombre : 20 degrees in the shade> **2** : shadow **3** : obscurity <sortir de l'ombre : to come out into the open> **4** : hint, trace <sans l'ombre d'un doute : without a shadow of a doubt> **5 ombre à paupières** : eyeshadow

ombrelle [ɔ̃brɛl] *nf* : parasol, sunshade

ombrer [ɔ̃bre] *vt* : to shade

omelette [ɔmlɛt] *nf* : omelet

omettre [ɔmɛtr] {53} *vt* : to omit, to leave out

omission [ɔmisjɔ̃] *nf* : omission

omnibus [ɔmnibys] *nm* : local train

omnipotent, -tente [ɔmnipɔtɑ̃, -tɑ̃t] *adj* : omnipotent — **omnipotence** [-tɑ̃s] *nf*

omniprésent, -sente [ɔmniprezɑ̃, -zɑ̃t] *adj* : omnipresent, ubiquitous

omniscient, -ciente [ɔmnisjɑ̃, -sjɑ̃t] *adj* : omniscient

omnivore [ɔmnivɔr] *adj* : omnivorous

omoplate [ɔmɔplat] *nf* : shoulder blade, scapula

on [ɔ̃] *pron* **1** : one, they, someone, you, we, people <on ne sait jamais : one never knows, you never know> <mon frère et moi, on va à Québec : my brother and I are going to Quebec> <on vous a appelé : someone called you> <comme on dit : as they say> <on jasait : people were talking> <ici on parle français : French is spoken here> **2** *fam* : we, you <alors, on est prêt? : well, are you (finally) ready?> <assez! on s'en va! : that's enough! we're leaving!>

once [ɔ̃s] *nf* : ounce

oncle [ɔ̃kl] *nm* : uncle

onction [ɔ̃ksjɔ̃] → **extrême–onction**

onctueux, -tueuse [ɔ̃ktɥø, -tɥøz] *adj* **1** : smooth, creamy **2** : unctuous

ondatra [ɔ̃datra] *nm* : muskrat

onde |ɔ̃d| *nf* **1** : wave <onde sonore : sound wave> <onde de choc : shock wave> <ondes courtes : shortwave> **2 sur les ondes** : on the radio, on the air

ondée |ɔ̃de| *nf* : (rain) shower

on–dit |ɔ̃di| *nms & pl* : rumor <ce ne sont que des on-dit : that's just hearsay>

ondoyer |ɔ̃dwaje| {58} *vi* : to ripple, to wave

ondulation |ɔ̃dylasjɔ̃| *nf* : undulation, wave

ondulé, -lée |ɔ̃dyle| *adj* **1** : wavy <cheveux ondulés : wavy hair> **2** : corrugated

onduler |ɔ̃dyle| *vi* **1** : to undulate, to wave **2 se faire onduler les cheveux** : to have one's hair waved, to get a permanent

onduleux, -leuse |ɔ̃dylø, -løz| *adj* : undulating, wavy

onéreux, -reuse |ɔnerø, -røz| *adj* COÛTEUX : costly — **onéreusement** |-røzmɑ̃| *adv*

ongle |ɔ̃gl| *nm* **1** : nail <ongles des mains : fingernails> <ongles des pieds : toenails> **2** : claw, talon

onglet |ɔ̃glɛ| *nm* **1** : thumbnail groove (on a knife, etc.) <assemblage à onglet : miter joint> **2** : thumb index

onguent |ɔ̃gɑ̃| *nm* : ointment

onirique |ɔnirik| *adj* : dreamlike, dreamy

onyx |ɔniks| *nm* : onyx

onze[1] |ɔ̃z| *adj* **1** : eleven **2** : eleventh <le onze mai : May eleventh>

onze[2] *nms & pl* : eleven

onzième |ɔ̃zjɛm| *adj & nmf & nm* : eleventh

opacité |ɔpasite| *nf* : opacity

opale |ɔpal| *nf* : opal

opaque |ɔpak| *adj* : opaque

opéra |ɔpera| *nm* **1** : opera <opéra bouffe : comic opera> **2** : opera house

opéra–comique |ɔperakɔmik| *nm, pl* **opéras–comiques** |-kɔmik| : light opera

opérateur, -trice |ɔperatœr, -tris| *n* **1** : operator (of a machine) **2 opérateur de saisie** : computer operator, keyboarder

opération |ɔperasjɔ̃| *nf* **1** : operation, process **2** : operation, surgery <salle d'opération : operating room> **3** CALCUL : calculation, (mathematical) operation **4** : transaction, dealing <opérations de bourse : stock transactions>

opérationnel, -nelle |ɔperasjɔnɛl| *adj* : operational

opératoire |ɔperatwar| *adj* **1** : operating, surgical **2** : operative

opérer |ɔpere| {87} *vt* **1** : to produce, to bring about **2** : to operate on **3** : to carry out, to implement — *vi* **1** : to take effect, to work **2** : to proceed, to operate — **s'opérer** *vr* SE PRODUIRE : to occur, to take place

opérette |ɔperɛt| *nf* : operetta, light opera

ophtalmologie |ɔftalmɔlɔʒi| *nf* : ophthalmology — **ophtalmologiste** |-lɔʒist| *or* **ophtalmologue** |-lɔg| *nmf*

opiacé |ɔpjase| *nm* : opiate

opiner |ɔpine| *vi* **1 ~ à** : to consent to **2 opiner du bonnet** : to nod in agreement

opiniâtre |ɔpinjatr| *adj* **1** OBSTINÉ : obstinate, stubborn **2** : dogged, persistent — **opiniâtrement** |-jatrəmɑ̃| *adv*

opiniâtreté |ɔpinjatrəte| *nf* **1** OBSTINATION : obstinacy, stubbornness **2** : doggedness, tenacity

opinion |ɔpinjɔ̃| *nf* : opinion, belief

opium |ɔpjɔm| *nm* : opium

opossum |ɔpɔsɔm| *nm* : opossum

opportun, -tune |ɔpɔrtœ̃, -tyn| *adj* : opportune, timely

opportunément |ɔpɔrtynemɑ̃| *adv* : at the right time, opportunely

opportunisme |ɔpɔrtynism| *nm* : opportunism

opportuniste[1] |ɔpɔrtynist| *adj* : opportunist, opportunistic

opportuniste[2] *nmf* : opportunist

opportunité |ɔpɔrtynite| *nf* : timeliness, appropriateness

opposant[1], **-sante** |ɔpozɑ̃, -zɑ̃t| *adj* : opposing

opposant[2], **-sante** *n* ADVERSAIRE : opponent

opposé[1], **-sée** |ɔpoze| *adj* **1** : opposing, conflicting <points de vues opposés : opposing views> **2** : opposite <le côté opposé : the opposite side> **3 ~ à** : opposed to

opposé[2] *nm* **1** : opposite **2 à l'opposé** : on the other hand **3 à l'opposé de** : contrary to

opposer |ɔpoze| *vt* **1** : to put forth (an objection, etc.) <il n'y a rien à opposer à celà : there's nothing to object to in that> **2** : to put up against <opposer nos troupes à l'ennemi : to pit our forces against the enemy> **3** : to set in opposition, to contrast (ideas, etc.) **4** : to divide, to bring into conflict — **s'opposer** *vr* **1** : to clash, to conflict, to be the opposite **2 ~ à** : to be opposed to

opposition |ɔpozisjɔ̃| *nf* **1** : opposition <en opposition avec : contrary to, against> <par opposition à : in contrast to> **2** : objection (in law, etc.) <faire opposition à un chèque : to stop a check>

oppressant, -sante |ɔpresɑ̃, -sɑ̃t| *adj* : oppressive

oppresser |ɔprese| *vt* : to oppress, to burden

oppresseur |ɔpresœr| *nm* : oppressor

oppressif, -sive |ɔpresif, -siv| *adj* : oppressive

oppression [ɔpresjɔ̃] *nf* **1** : oppression **2** : feeling of suffocation

opprimé, -mée [ɔprime] *n* : oppressed person, underdog

opprimer [ɔprime] *vt* **1** : to oppress **2** : to suppress, to stifle

opprobre [ɔprɔbr] *nm* : opprobrium, disgrace

opter [ɔpte] *vi* **~ pour** : to opt for, to choose

opticien, -cienne [ɔptisjɛ̃, -sjɛn] *n* : optician

optimal, -male [ɔptimal] *adj, mpl* **-maux** [-mo] : optimal, optimum

optimisme [ɔptimism] *nm* : optimism

optimiste[1] [ɔptimist] *adj* : optimistic

optimiste[2] *nmf* : optimist

optimum [ɔptimɔm] *adj & nm* : optimum

option [ɔpsjɔ̃] *nf* : option, choice

optionnel, -nelle [ɔpsjɔnɛl] *adj* FACULTATIF : optional

optique[1] [ɔptik] *adj* : optic, optical

optique[2] *nf* **1** : optics **2** : perspective, viewpoint

optométrie [ɔptɔmetri] *nf* : optometry — **optométriste** [-metrist] *nmf*

opulent, -lente [ɔpylɑ̃, -lɑ̃t] *adj* : opulent — **opulence** [-lɑ̃s] *nf*

opus [ɔpys] *nm* : opus

or[1] [ɔr] *nm* : gold

or[2] *conj* **1** : but, yet **2** : now

oracle [ɔrakl] *nm* : oracle

orage [ɔraʒ] *nm* **1** : storm, thunderstorm **2** : turmoil

orageux, -geuse [ɔraʒø, -ʒøz] *adj* : stormy

oraison [ɔrɛzɔ̃] *nf* **1** PRIÈRE : prayer **2 oraison funèbre** : funeral oration

oral, -rale [ɔral] *adj, mpl* **oraux** [ɔro] : oral — **oralement** [ɔralmɑ̃] *adv*

orange[1] [ɔrɑ̃ʒ] *adj* : orange

orange[2] *nf* : orange (fruit)

orange[3] *nm* : orange (color)

orangeade [ɔrɑ̃ʒad] *nf* : orangeade

oranger [ɔrɑ̃ʒe] *nm* : orange tree

orang–outan [ɔrɑ̃utɑ̃] *nm, pl* **orangs–outans** [-utɑ̃] : orangutan

orateur, -trice [ɔratœr, -tris] *n* : orator, speaker

oratoire[1] [ɔratwar] *adj* **1** : oratorical **2 l'art oratoire** : oratory, eloquence

oratoire[2] *nm* : chapel, oratory

oratorio [ɔratɔrjo] *nm* : oratorio

orbe [ɔrb] *nm* : orb

orbital, -tale [ɔrbital] *adj* **1** : orbital **2** : orbiting <station orbitale : space station>

orbite [ɔrbit] *nf* **1** : orbit <graviter dans l'orbite de : to orbit> **2** : eye socket

orchestre [ɔrkɛstr] *nm* : orchestra — **orchestral, -trale** [-kɛstral] *adj*

orchestrer [ɔrkɛstre] *vt* : to orchestrate — **orchestration** [-kɛstrasjɔ̃] *nf*

orchidée [ɔrkide] *nf* : orchid

ordinaire[1] [ɔrdinɛr] *adj* **1** : ordinary, common, standard **2** HABITUEL : habitual, usual — **ordinairement** [-nɛrmɑ̃] *adv*

ordinaire[2] *nm* **1** : ordinary <hors de l'ordinaire : out of the ordinary> **2** : regular (gas) **3 comme à l'ordinaire** : as usual **4 d'ordinaire** : usually, as a rule

ordinal[1], **-nale** [ɔrdinal] *adj, mpl* **-naux** [-no] : ordinal

ordinal[2] *nm* : ordinal number

ordinateur [ɔrdinatœr] *nm* **1** : computer **2 ordinateur personnel** *or* **ordinateur individuel** : personal computer, PC

ordination [ɔrdinasjɔ̃] *nf* : ordination

ordonnance [ɔrdɔnɑ̃s] *nf* **1** : order, organization **2** : ordinance, ruling **3** : (medical) prescription

ordonnateur, -trice [ɔrdɔnatœr, -tris] *n* **1** : organizer **2 ordonnateur des pompes funèbres** : funeral director

ordonné, -née [ɔrdɔne] *adj* : tidy, orderly

ordonner [ɔrdɔne] *vt* **1** ARRANGER : to put in order, to arrange **2** COMMANDER : to order, to decree **3** : to ordain (in religion)

ordre [ɔrdr] *nm* **1** : order <ordre alphabétique : alphabetical order> **2** : orderliness, tidiness **3** : order, command <à l'ordre de : payable to> **4** NATURE : nature, sort <d'ordre personnel : of a personal nature> **5** : order (in biology and architecture) **6** : order, society <l'ordre jésuite : the Jesuit order> **7** : (social) order <l'ordre publique : law and order> **8 ordre du jour** : agenda

ordure [ɔrdyr] *nf* **1** : filth **2 ordures** *nfpl* : trash, garbage

ordurier, -rière [ɔrdyrje] *adj* : filthy

oreille [ɔrej] *nf* **1** : ear <l'oreille interne : inner ear> <prêter l'oreille : to lend an ear, to listen> **2** OUÏE : hearing <avoir l'oreille fine : to have a keen sense of hearing> <dur d'oreille : hard of hearing> **3** : handle (of a bowl, etc.), wing (of furniture)

oreiller [ɔreje] *nm* : pillow

oreillette [ɔrɛjɛt] *nf* : auricle (of the heart)

oreillons [ɔrɛjɔ̃] *nmpl* : mumps

ores [ɔr] *adv* **d'ores et déjà** : already

orfèvre [ɔrfɛvr] *nm* : goldsmith

organe [ɔrgan] *nm* **1** : organ <organes génitaux : genitals> <organes des sens : sense organs> **2** : vehicle, instrument **3** VOIX : voice

organigramme [ɔrganigram] *nm* **1** : organizational chart **2** : diagram, flowchart

organique [ɔrganik] *adj* : organic — **organiquement** [-nikmɑ̃] *adv*

organisateur, -trice [ɔrganizatœr, -tris] *n* : organizer

organisation [ɔrganizasjɔ̃] *nf* : organization, organizing

organisationnel, -nelle [ɔrganizasjɔnɛl] *adj* : organizational

organisé, -sée [ɔrganize] *adj* : orderly, organized

organiser [ɔrganize] *vt* : to organize, to arrange, to structure — **s'organiser** *vr* : to get organized

organisme [ɔrganism] *nm* **1** : organism **2** : organization, body

organiste [ɔrganist] *nmf* : organist

orgasme [ɔrgasm] *nm* : orgasm, climax

orge[1] [ɔrʒ] *nm* : barley (grain)

orge[2] *nf* : barley (plant)

orgelet [ɔrʒəlɛ] *nm* : sty, stye (in the eye)

orgie [ɔrʒi] *nf* : orgy

orgue [ɔrg] *nm* : organ (musical instrument)

orgueil [ɔrgœj] *nm* : pride

orgueilleux, -leuse [ɔrgœjø, -jøz] *adj* : proud, haughty — **orgueilleusement** [-jøzmɑ̃] *adv*

orient [ɔrjɑ̃] *nm* **1** : east **2 l'Orient** : the Orient, the East

oriental, -tale [ɔrjɑ̃tal] *adj, mpl* **-taux** [-to] **1** : eastern **2** : oriental

Oriental, -tale *n, mpl* **-taux** : Oriental

orientation [ɔrjɑ̃tasjɔ̃] *nf* **1** POSITION : positioning, aspect (of a house, etc.) **2** : leanings *pl*, tendencies *pl* <orientation sexuelle : sexual orientation> **3** : guidance, counseling **4** : orientation, direction <sens de l'orientation : sense of direction>

orienter [ɔrjɑ̃te] *vt* **1** : to position, to orient **2** GUIDER : to guide, to direct — **s'orienter** *vr* : to find one's bearings

orifice [ɔrifis] *nm* : opening, orifice

oriflamme [ɔriflam] *nf* : banner

origan [ɔrigɑ̃] *nm* : oregano

originaire [ɔriʒinɛr] *adj* **être originaire de** : to be a native of

original[1], **-nale** [ɔriʒinal, -nal] *adj, mpl* **-naux** [-no] **1** : original **2** : eccentric

original[2], **-nale** *n, mpl* **-naux** : character, eccentric

original[3] *nm, pl* **-naux** : original (of a document, painting, etc.)

originalité [ɔriʒinalite] *nf* **1** : originality **2** : eccentricity

origine [ɔriʒin] *nf* **1** : origin **2 à l'origine** : originally

originel, -nelle [ɔriʒinɛl] *adj* : original <péché originel : original sin>

originellement [ɔriʒinɛlmɑ̃] *adv* **1** : originally **2** : from the beginning

orignal [ɔriɲal] *nm, pl* **-naux** [-ɲo] : moose

oripeaux [ɔripo] *nmpl* GUENILLES : rags, cheap finery

orme [ɔrm] *nm* : elm

ormeau [ɔrmo] *nm, pl* **ormeaux** [-mo] : abalone

orné, -née [ɔrne] *adj* : ornate, flowery

ornement [ɔrnəmɑ̃] *nm* **1** : ornament, adornment **2 ornements sacerdotaux** : (liturgical) vestments

ornemental, -tale [ɔrnəmɑ̃tal] *adj, mpl* **-taux** [-to] : ornamental

ornementation [ɔrnəmɑ̃tasjɔ̃] *nf* : ornamentation

orner [ɔrne] *vt* **1** DÉCORER : to decorate, to adorn **2** EMBELLIR : to embellish

ornière [ɔrnjɛr] *nf* **1** : rut (in a road) **2 sortir de l'ornière** : to get out of a rut, to get out of trouble

ornithologie [ɔrnitɔlɔʒi] *nf* : ornithology

ornithologiste [ɔrnitɔlɔʒist] *or* **ornithologue** [-tɔlɔg] *nmf* : ornithologist

ornithorynque [ɔrnitɔrɛ̃k] *nm* : platypus

orphelin, -line [ɔrfəlɛ̃, -lin] *n* : orphan

orphelinat [ɔrfəlina] *nm* : orphanage

orteil [ɔrtɛj] *nm* : toe <gros orteil : big toe>

orthodontie [ɔrtɔdɔ̃si] *nf* : orthodontics — **orthodondiste** [-dɔ̃tist] *nmf*

orthodoxe [ɔrtɔdɔks] *adj* : orthodox

orthodoxie [ɔrtɔdɔksi] *nf* : orthodoxy

orthographe [ɔrtɔgraf] *nf* : spelling, orthography

orthographier [ɔrtɔgrafje] {96} *vt* **1** : to spell **2 mal orthographier** : to misspell

orthographique [ɔrtɔgrafik] *adj* : orthographic

orthopédie [ɔrtɔpedi] *nf* : orthopedics — **orthopédiste** [-pedist] *nmf*

orthopédique [ɔrtɔpedi] *adj* : orthopedic

orthophonie [ɔrtɔfɔni] *nf* : speech therapy — **orthophoniste** [-fɔnist] *nmf*

ortie [ɔrti] *nf* : nettle

oryctérope [ɔrikterɔp] *nm* : aardvark

os [ɔs] *nm* **1** : bone **2 en chair et en os** : in the flesh, in person **3 jusqu'à l'os** *or* **jusqu'aux os** : to the core, completely <il était mouillé jusqu'aux os : he was soaked to the bone>

oscillation [ɔsilasjɔ̃] *nf* **1** : oscillation **2** VARIATION : fluctuation, variation **3** : rocking, swaying

osciller [ɔsile] *vi* **1** : to oscillate **2** HÉSITER : to vacillate, to waver **3** : to rock, to sway

osé, -sée [oze, -ze] *adj* **1** : daring, bold **2** : risqué

oseille [ozɛj] *nf* : sorrel (plant)

oser [oze] *vt* **1** : to dare **2 si j'ose dire** : if I may say so

osier [ozje] *nm* **1** : willow **2** : wicker <chaise en osier : wickerwork chair>

osmose [ɔsmoz] *nf* : osmosis

ossature [ɔsatyr] *nf* **1** : skeleton, bone structure **2** : framework

osselets [ɔslɛ] *nmpl* : jacks (game)

ossements [ɔsmɑ̃] *nmpl* : remains, bones

osseux, -seuse [ɔsø, -søz] *adj* : bony <tissu osseux : bone tissue>

ostensible [ɔstɑ̃sibl] *adj* : conspicuous, open — **ostensiblement** [-sibləmɑ̃] *adv*

ostentation |ɔstɑ̃tasjɔ̃| *nf* : ostentation, display

ostentatoire |ɔstɑ̃tatwar| *adj* : ostentatious, showy

ostéopathie |ɔsteɔpati| *nf* : osteopathy — **ostéopathe** |-pat| *nmf*

ostéoporose |ɔsteɔpɔroz| *nf* : osteoporosis

ostracisme |ɔstrasism| *nm* : ostracism

otage |ɔtaʒ| *nm* : hostage

otarie |ɔtari| *nf* : sea lion

ôter |ote| *vt* **1** RETIRER : to remove, to take away **2** : to take off <ôte tes bottes : take off your boots> **3** SOUSTRAIRE : to subtract <3 ôté de 10 égale 7 : 3 (subtracted) from 10 equals 7> — **s'ôter** *vr fam* **ôte–toi de là!** : get out of the way!

otite |ɔtit| *nf* : ear infection

oto–rhino–laryngologiste |ɔtɔrinɔlarɛ̃ʒɔlɔʒist| *nmf* : ear, nose, and throat specialist

ottomane |ɔtɔman| *nf* CANAPÉ : ottoman, sofa

ou |u| *conj* **1** : or **2 ou . . . ou . . .** : either . . . or . . . <ou bien en Grèce ou bien en Inde : either in Greece or India>

où[1] |u| *adv* **1** : where, wherever <où étiez-vous? : where were you?> <où que tu ailles : wherever you go> <par où passer? : which way should we go?> **2 d'~** : from which, from where, therefore

où[2] *pron* : where, that, in which, on which, to which <la ville où je suis né : the town where I was born> <le jour où il est parti : the day that he left>

ouailles |waj| *nfpl* : flock (in religion)

ouais |wɛ| *interj fam* : yeah!, oh sure!

ouate |wat| *nf* **1** : absorbent cotton **2** BOURRE : padding, wadding

ouaté, -tée |wate| *adj* : padded, quilted

oubli |ubli| *nm* **1** : forgetfulness **2** : omission, oversight **3 tomber dans l'oubli** : to sink into oblivion

oublier |ublije| {96} *vt* **1** : to forget, to forget about **2** OMETTRE : to leave out, to omit **3** NÉGLIGER : to forget, to neglect — **s'oublier** *vr* **1** : to be forgotten **2** : to forget oneself

oubliettes |ublijɛt| *nfpl* **1** : dungeon **2 jeter aux oubliettes** : to put completely out of mind

oublieux, -lieuse |ublijø, -jøz| *adj* : forgetful

ouest[1] |wɛst| *adj* : west, western

ouest[2] *nm* **1** : west <un vent d'ouest : west wind> <vers l'ouest : westward> **2 l'Ouest** : the West

ougandais, -daise |ugɑ̃dɛ, -dɛz| *adj* : Ugandan

Ougandais, -daise *n* : Ugandan

oui[1] |wi| *adv* : yes <mais oui! : yes!> <je pense que oui : I think so> <faut-il le prévenir, oui ou non? : do we have to warn him or not?> <tu viens, oui? : are you (really) coming?>

oui[2] *nms & pl* **1** : yes **2 pour un oui ou pour un non** : at the drop of a hat, for no apparent reason

ouï–dire |widir| *nms & pl* : hearsay

ouïe |wi| *nf* **1** : sense of hearing **2 ouïes** *nfpl* : gills (of a fish)

ouïr |wir| {60} *vt* : to hear

ouistiti |wistiti| *nm* : marmoset

ouragan |uragɑ̃| *nm* **1** : hurricane **2** : storm, tumult

ourdir |urdir| *vt* : to hatch (a plot, etc.)

ourler |urle| *vt* : to hem

ourlet |urlɛ| *nm* : hem

ours |urs| *nm* **1** : bear **2 ours polaire** : polar bear

ourse |urs| *nf* **1** : she-bear **2 la Grande Ourse** : the Big Dipper, Ursa Major **3 la Petite Ourse** : the Little Dipper, Ursa Minor

oursin |ursɛ̃| *nm* : sea urchin

ourson |ursɔ̃| *nm* : bear cub

ouste *or* **oust** |ust| *interj fam* : out!

outarde |utard| *nf Can* : Canada goose

outil |uti| *nm* : tool

outillage |utijaʒ| *nm* **1** : set of tools **2** : equipment <outillage agricole : agricultural equipment>

outiller |utije| *vt* ÉQUIPER : to equip — **s'outiller** *vr*

outrage |utraʒ| *nm* **1** : insult **2 outrage à la pudeur** : indecent behavior **3 outrage à magistrat** *France* : contempt of court **4 outrage au tribunal** *Can* : contempt of court

outragé, -gée |utraʒe| *adj* : gravely offended, outraged

outrageant, -geante |utraʒɑ̃, -ʒɑ̃t| *adj* INJURIEUX : insulting, abusive

outrager |utraʒe| {17} *vt* INSULTER : to offend, to insult

outrageusement |utraʒøzmɑ̃| *adv* : outrageously, excessively

outrance |utrɑ̃s| *nf* : excess <boire à outrance : to drink to excess>

outrancier, -cière |utrɑ̃sje, -sjɛr| *adj* : excessive, extreme

outre[1] |utr| *adv* **1 en ~** : in addition, besides **2 outre mesure** : overly, unduly **3 passer outre à** : to pay no heed to, to disregard

outre[2] *prep* : besides, in addition to <outre cela : in addition to that, furthermore>

outré, -trée |utre| *adj* **1** EXAGÉRÉ : exaggerated, excessive **2** INDIGNÉ : indignant, outraged

outre–Atlantique |utratlɑ̃tik| *adv* : across the Atlantic

outrecuidance |utrəkɥidɑ̃s| *nf* : presumptuousness

outrecuidant, -dante |utrəkɥidɑ̃, -dɑ̃t| *adj* : presumptuous, arrogant

outre–mer |utrəmɛr| *adv* : overseas

outrepasser |utrəpase| *vt* : to exceed, to overstep

outrer |utre| *vt* **1** EXAGÉRER : to exaggerate **2** INDIGNER : to outrage
ouvert[1] |uvɛr| *pp* → **ouvrir**
ouvert[2], **-verte** |uvɛr, -vɛrt| *adj* **1** : open <ouvert au public : open to the public> <grand ouvert : wide open> <à bras ouverts : with open arms> **2** : frank, open **3** : on, running <laissez la lumière ouverte : leave the light on>
ouvertement |uvɛrtəmɑ̃| *adv* : openly
ouverture |uvɛrtyr| *nf* **1** : opening, aperture **2** : openness <ouverture d'esprit : open-mindedness> **3** : overture (in music)
ouvrable |uvrabl| *adj* **1 jour ouvrable** : weekday, working day **2 heures ouvrables** : business hours
ouvrage |uvraʒ| *nm* **1** : work, working <se mettre à l'ouvrage : to get down to work> **2** : book **3** : piece of work <ouvrage d'art : construction work>
ouvragé, -gée |uvraʒe| *adj* : finely worked, elaborate
ouvrant, -vrante |uvrɑ̃, -vrɑ̃t| *adj* **toit ouvrant** : sunroof
ouvré, -vrée |uvre| *adj* : elaborate, finely worked
ouvre–boîtes |uvrəbwat| *nms & pl* : can opener
ouvre–bouteilles |uvrəbutɛj| *nms & pl* : bottle opener
ouvreur, -vreuse |uvrœr, -vrøz| *n* **1** : usher, usherette *f* (in a theater) **2** : opener (in games)
ouvrier[1], **-vrière** |uvrije, -vrijɛr| *adj* : working-class <la class ouvrière : the working class>
ouvrier[2], **-vrière** *n* : worker
ouvrir |uvrir| {83} *vt* **1** : to open **2** : to unlock, to undo **3** : to turn on (a light, radio, etc.) **4** : to start up, to begin <ouvrir le feu : to open fire> — *vi* : to open — **s'ouvrir** *vr* **1** : to open, to come open **2** : to open up, to confide **3** : to cut <s'ouvrir la main : to cut one's hand> **4 ~ à** : to become open to (opportunities, etc.)
ouzbek |uzbɛk| *adj* : Uzbek
Ouzbek *nmf* : Uzbek
ovaire |ɔvɛr| *nm* : ovary — **ovarien, -rienne** |ɔvarjɛ̃, -rjɛn| *adj*
ovale |ɔval| *adj & nm* : oval
ovation |ɔvasjɔ̃| *nf* : ovation
ovationner |ɔvasjɔne| *vt* : to applaud, to give an ovation to
overdose |ɔvœrdoz| *nf* SURDOSE : overdose
ovuler |ɔvyle| *vi* : to ovulate
ovulation |ɔvylasjɔ̃| *nf* : ovulation
ovule |ɔvyl| *nm* : ovum
oxydable |ɔksidabl| *adj* : liable to rust
oxyde |ɔksid| *nm* **1** : oxide **2 oxyde de carbone** : carbon monoxide
oxyder |ɔkside| *vt* : to oxidize — **oxydation** |-sidasjɔ̃| *nf*
oxygène |ɔksiʒɛn| *nm* : oxygen
oxyure |ɔksyr| *nm* : pinworm
ozone |ozɔn| *nm* : ozone <couche d'ozone : ozone layer>

P

p |pe| *nm* : p, the 16th letter of the alphabet
pacage |pakaʒ| *nm* **1** : grazing **2** : pasture
pacane |pakan| *nf Can or* **noix de pacane** : pecan
pacemaker |pɛsmekœr| *nm* : pacemaker
pachyderme |paʃidɛrm| *nm* : pachyderm, elephant
pacificateur[1], **-trice** |pasifikatœr, -tris| *adj* : pacifying, peacemaking
pacificateur[2], **-trice** *n* : peacemaker
pacification |pasifikasjɔ̃| *nf* : pacification
pacifier |pasifje| {96} *vt* APAISER : to pacify, to calm
pacifique |pasifik| *adj* **1** PAISIBLE : peaceful, pacific **2 l'océan Pacifique** : the Pacific Ocean — **pacifiquement** |-fikmɑ̃| *adv*
pacifisme |pasifism| *nm* : pacificism
pacifiste[1] |pasifist| *adj* : pacifist, pacifistic
pacifiste[2] *nmf* : pacifist
pack |pak| *nm* : pack
pacotille |pakɔtij| *nf* : shoddy goods <bijoux de pacotille : cheap jewelry>
pacte |pakt| *nm* ACCORD : pact, agreement
pactiser |paktize| *vi* : to come to an agreement, to come to terms
pactole |paktɔl| *nm* : gold mine, bonanza
paddock |padɔk| *nm* : paddock
pagaie |pagɛ| *nf* : paddle
pagaille *or* **pagaïe** |pagaj| *nf fam* **1** : mess, chaos **2 il y en a en pagaille** : there are loads of them
paganisme |paganism| *nm* : paganism
pagayer |pagaje| {11} *vi* : to paddle
page |paʒ| *nf* **1** : page <page blanche : blank page> **2** : passage (in a book or piece of music)
pagination |paʒinasjɔ̃| *nf* : pagination
paginer |paʒine| *vt* : to paginate
pagne |paɲ| *nm* : loincloth
pagode |pagɔd| *nf* : pagoda
paie[1] |pɛ|, **paiera** |pɛra|, *etc.* → **payer**
paie[2] |pɛ| *nf* : pay, wages *pl*
paiement |pɛmɑ̃| *nm* : payment
païen, païenne |pajɛ̃, -jɛn| *adj & n* : pagan, heathen

paillard, -larde [pajar, -jard] *adj* : bawdy

paillardise [pajardiz] *nf* : bawdiness

paillasse[1] [pajas] *nf* : straw mattress

paillasse[2] *nm* : clown

paillasson [pajasɔ̃] *nm* : doormat

paille [paj] *nf* **1** : straw, piece of straw <être sur la paille : to be penniless> **2** : (drinking) straw **3 paille de fer** : steel wool

pailler [paje] *vt* : to mulch

paillette [pajɛt] *nf* **1** : sequin <robe à paillettes : sequined dress> **2** : speck, flake <savon en paillettes : soap flakes>

paillis [paji] *nms & pl* : mulch

pain [pɛ̃] *nm* **1** : bread <pain grillé : toast> <pain d'épice : gingerbread> <pain doré *Can* : French toast> **2** : loaf **3** : cake, bar <pain de savon : bar of soap>

pair[1], **paire** [pɛr] *adj* : even <nombre pair : even number>

pair[2] *nm* **1** NOBLE : peer **2** ÉGAL : peer, equal <aller de pair : to go hand in hand> <hors pair : without equal, unrivaled> **3** : par (in finance) **4 travailler au pair** : to work as an au pair

paire [pɛr] *nf* : pair

paisible [pezibl] *adj* : peaceful, quiet — **paisiblement** [-zibləmɑ̃] *adv*

paître [pɛtr] {61} *vi* : to graze

paix [pɛ] *nf* **1** : peace <la paix mondiale : world peace> **2** CALME, TRANQUILLITÉ : peace, calm, tranquility

pakistanais, -naise [pakistanɛ, -nɛz] *adj* : Pakistani

Pakistanais, -naise *n* : Pakistani

palabrer [palabre] *vi* : to discuss endlessly

palabres [palabr] *nfpl* : endless discussions, palaver

palace [palas] *nm* : luxury hotel

palais [palɛ] *nms & pl* **1** : palace **2** : palate **3 palais de justice** : courthouse, courts of law

palan [palɑ̃] *nm* : hoist

pale [pal] *nf* **1** : blade (of a propeller, etc.) **2** : paddle

pâle [pal] *adj* **1** BLÊME : pale, pallid **2** CLAIR : light, pale <jaune pâle : pale yellow>

palefrenier, -nière [palfrənje] *n* : groom (in a stable)

paléontologie [paleɔ̃tɔlɔʒi] *nf* : paleontology — **paléontologiste** [-lɔʒist] *nmf*

paleron [palrɔ̃] *nm* : chuck (steak)

palestinien, -nienne [palestinjɛ̃, -njɛn] *adj* : Palestinian

Palestinien, -nienne *n* : Palestinian

palet [palɛ] *nm* : puck (in ice hockey)

paletot [palto] *nm* : short coat

palette [palɛt] *nf* **1** *Can* : wooden spatula (used in making maple products) **2** : palette **3** : shoulder <palette de porc : shoulder of pork> **4** : pallet, loading platform **5** : range (of colors, ideas, etc.)

palétuvier [paletyvje] *nm* : mangrove

pâleur [palœr] *nf* : paleness, pallor

palier [palje] *nm* **1** : landing (of a staircase), floor **2** NIVEAU : level, stage <par paliers : by stages>

pâlir [palir] *vi* **1** : to turn pale **2** : to fade, to dim

palissade [palisad] *nf* : fence, palisade

palissandre [palisɑ̃dr] *nm* : rosewood

palliatif[1], **-tive** [paljatif, -tiv] *adj* : palliative

palliatif[2] [paljatif] *nm* **1** : palliative **2** : stopgap, expedient

pallier [palje] {96} *vt* : to compensate for, to mitigate

palmarès [palmarɛs] *nms & pl* **1** : list of winners **2** : record of achievements

palme [palm] *nf* **1** : palm leaf **2** : palm, distinction <remporter la palme : to be victorious> **3** : flipper

palmé, -mée [palme] *adj* : webbed <patte palmée : webbed foot>

palmier [palmje] *nm* : palm tree

palmure [palmyr] *nf* : web (of a bird's foot)

pâlot, -lotte [palo, -lɔt] *adj* : pale, peaked

palourde [palurd] *nf* : clam

palpable [palpabl] *adj* : palpable, tangible

palper [palpe] *vt* **1** : to palpate (in medicine) **2** : to feel, to finger

palpitant, -tante [palpitɑ̃, -tɑ̃t] *adj* : thrilling, exciting

palpitation [palpitasjɔ̃] *nf* : palpitation

palpiter [palpite] *vi* **1** : to palpitate, to throb **2** : to quiver, to flutter

paludisme [palydism] *nm* : malaria

pâmer [pame] *v* **se pâmer** *vr* **1** : to be ecstatic, to swoon **2 ~ de** : to be overcome with

pâmoison [pamwazɔ̃] *nf* **tomber en pâmoison** : to swoon

pampa [pɑ̃pa] *nf* : pampas *pl*

pamphlet [pɑ̃flɛ] *nm* : lampoon

pamplemousse [pɑ̃pləmus] *nmf* : grapefruit

pan [pɑ̃] *nm* **1** : section, piece **2** : side, face **3** : tail (of a garment) <pan de chemise : shirttail>

panacée [panase] *nf* : panacea, nostrum

panache [panaʃ] *nm* **1** : plume <panache de fumée : trail of smoke> **2** : panache, verve

panaché, -chée [panaʃe] *adj* **1** : variegated, multicolored **2** : mixed <salade panachée : mixed salad>

panais [panɛ] *nms & pl* : parsnip

panaméen, -méenne [panameɛ̃, -meɛn] *adj* : Panamanian

Panaméen, -méenne *n* : Panamanian

pancarte [pɑ̃kart] *nf* **1** : sign, notice **2** : placard

pancréas [pɑ̃kreas] *nm* : pancreas — **pancréatique** [-kreatik] *adj*

panda |pɑ̃da| *nm* : panda
panégyrique |paneʒirik| *nm* : panegyric
paner |pane| *vt* : to coat with breadcrumbs, to bread
panier |panje| *nm* **1** : basket <panier à provisions : shopping basket> <panier de pêche : creel> **2 panier à salade** : lettuce spinner **3 panier percé** *fam* : spendthrift
panique[1] |panik| *adj* : panic <peur panique : terror>
panique[2] *nf* : panic <pris de panique : panic-stricken>
paniquer |panike| *vi fam* : to panic — *vt fam* : to throw into a panic
panne |pan| *nf* **1** : breakdown, failure <panne d'électricité : power failure, blackout> **2 en panne de** : out of <en panne d'essence : out of gas>
panneau |pano| *nm, pl* **panneaux 1** : panel **2** : sign, notice **3 panneau de signalisation** : road sign **4 panneau fibreux** : fiberboard **5 panneau indicateur** : signpost **6 panneau publicitaire** : billboard
panonceau |panɔ̃so| *nm, pl* **-ceaux 1** : plaque (at a professional office, etc.) **2** PANCARTE : sign
panoplie |panɔpli| *nf* **1** : display of arms **2** : array, range **3** : outfit, costume (for children)
panorama |panɔrama| *nm* **1** : panorama **2** : overview
panoramique |panɔramik| *adj* : panoramic
panse |pɑ̃s| *nf fam* : paunch, belly
pansement |pɑ̃smɑ̃| *nm* : dressing, bandage
panser |pɑ̃se| *vt* **1** : to groom (a horse) **2** : to dress, to bandage
pansu, -sue |pɑ̃sy| *adj* : potbellied
pantalon |pɑ̃talɔ̃| *nm* : pants *pl*, trousers *pl*
pantelant, -lante |pɑ̃tlɑ̃, -lɑ̃t| *adj* : panting, gasping for breath
panthère |pɑ̃tɛr| *nf* : panther
pantin |pɑ̃tɛ̃| *nm* **1** : jumping jack (toy) **2** FANTOCHE : puppet (person)
pantois, -toise |pɑ̃twa, -twaz| *adj* : flabbergasted
pantomime |pɑ̃tɔmim| *nf* **1** : mime **2** : pantomime show **3** : scene, fuss
pantouflard, -flarde |pɑ̃tuflar, -flard| *n fam* : homebody
pantoufle |pɑ̃tufl| *nf* : slipper
pantoute |pɑ̃tut| *adv Can fam* : no, not at all
panure |panyr| *nf* CHAPELURE : bread crumbs *pl*
paon |pɑ̃| *nm* : peacock
papa |papa| *nm fam* : dad, daddy
papal, -pale |papal| *adj, mpl* **papaux** |papo| : papal
papauté |papote| *nf* : papacy
papaye |papaj| *nf* : papaya
pape |pap| *nm* : pope
paperasserie |paprasri| *nf* : paperwork, red tape
papeterie |papɛtri| *nf* : stationery
papier |papje| *nm* **1** : paper **2** : document, paper **3** : article, review **4 papier d'aluminium** : aluminum foil, tinfoil **5 papier de verre** *France* : sandpaper **6 papier hygiénique** : toilet paper **7 papier journal** : newsprint **8 papier mouchoir** *Can* : tissue **9 papier peint** : wallpaper **10 papier sablé** *Can* : sandpaper **11 papier tue–mouches** : flypaper **12 papiers** *nmpl* : (identification) papers
papier–monnaie |papjemɔnɛ| *nm, pl* **papiers–monnaies** : paper money
papille |papij| *nf* **papilles gustatives** : taste buds
papillon |papijɔ̃| *nm* **1** : butterfly **2 papillon de nuit** : moth
papillonner |papijɔne| *vi* : to flit about, to flutter around
papillote |papijɔt| *nf* : aluminum foil, foil wrapping
papilloter |papijɔte| *vi* **1** : to flicker, to twinkle **2** : to blink, to flutter (of eyelids)
papotage |papɔtaʒ| *nm* : gabbing, chattering
papoter |papɔte| *vi* : to gab, to chatter
paprika |paprika| *nm* : paprika
papyrus |papirys| *nm* : papyrus
Pâque |pak| *nf* : Passover
paquebot |pakbo| *nm* : liner, ship
pâquerette |pakrɛt| *nf* : daisy
Pâques[1] |pak| *nm* : Easter <la semaine de Pâques : Easter week>
Pâques[2] *nfpl* : Easter <joyeuses Pâques! : Happy Easter!>
paquet |pakɛ| *nm* **1** : package, bundle **2** : packet, pack (of cigarettes, etc.) **3** : heap, pile, mass **4 mettre le paquet** *fam* : to go all out
paqueter |pakte| *vt Can fam* **1** : to pack (a suitcase) **2** : to pack, to fill to capacity
par |par| *prep* **1** : through <par la porte : through the door> **2** : by, by means of <par avion : by airmail> **3** : as, for <par exemple : for example> **4** : per <dix dollars par personne : ten dollars per person> **5** : around, near <il habite par ici : he lives around here> **6** : at, during <par moments : at times> **7** : from, out of, for the sake of <par amour : out of love> **8** : according to, by <classé par âge : ranked by age> **9 de ~** : throughout <de par le monde : all over the world> **10 de ~** : by virtue of **11** : **par–ci par–là** : here and there **12** : **par trop** : excessively
parabole |parabɔl| *nf* **1** : parable **2** : parabola
parabolique |parabɔlik| *adj* : parabolic
parachever |paraʃve| {52} *vt* PARFAIRE : to complete, to perfect

parachute [paraʃyt] *nm* : parachute — **parachuter** [-ʃyte] *vt*

parachutiste [paraʃytist] *nmf* **1** : parachutist **2** : paratrooper

parade [parad] *nf* **1** DÉFILÉ : parade **2** : parry (in sports) **3 de ~** : outward, superficial **4 faire parade de** : to display, to make a show of

parader [parade] *vi* : to strut about, to show off

paradigme [paradim] *nm* : paradigm

paradis [paradi] *nm* : paradise, heaven

paradisiaque [paradizjak] *adj* : heavenly

paradoxal, -xale [paradɔksal] *adj, mpl* **-xaux** [-kso] : paradoxical — **paradoxalement** [-ksalmɑ̃] *adv*

paradoxe [paradɔks] *nm* : paradox

parafe, parafer [paraf, parafe] → **paraphe, parapher**

paraffine [parafin] *nf* : paraffin

parafoudre [parafudr] *nm* : lightning rod

parages [paraʒ] *nmpl* **1** : waters <parages étrangers : foreign waters> **2 dans les parages** : in the vicinity, around

paragraphe [paragraf] *nm* : paragraph

paraguayen, -guayenne [paragwejɛ̃, -gwejɛn] *adj* : Paraguayan

Paraguayen, -guayenne *n* : Paraguayan

paraissait [parɛsɛ], *etc.* → **paraître**

paraisse [parɛs], *etc.* → **paraître**

paraître [parɛtr] {7} *vi* **1** : to appear <paraître en public : to appear in public> **2** : to be published <à paraître : forthcoming> **3** : to show, to be visible **4** SEMBLER : to seem, to look — *v impers* **1** : to seem, to appear <il paraît que tout s'est arrangé : everything seems to be all right> **2 paraît-il** *or* **à ce qu'il paraît** : apparently

parallèle[1] [paralɛl] *adj* **1** : parallel **2** SEMBLABLE : similar **3** : unofficial, alternative

parallèle[2] *nm* **1** : parallel **2** : comparison <mettre en parallèle : to compare>

parallèle[3] *nf* : parallel line

parallèlement [paralɛlmɑ̃] *adv* : at the same time, concurrently

parallélogramme [paralelɔgram] *nm* : parallelogram

paralyser [paralyze] *vt* **1** : to paralyze **2** : to bring to a standstill

paralysie [paralizi] *nf* **1** : paralysis **2 paralysie cérébrale** : cerebral palsy

paralytique [paralitik] *adj* : paralytic

paramètre [paramɛtr] *nm* : parameter

parangon [parɑ̃gɔ̃] *nm* MODÈLE : paragon

paranoïa [paranɔja] *nf* : paranoia

paranoïaque [paranɔjak] *adj & nmf* : paranoiac, paranoid

paranormal, -male [paranɔrmal] *adj, mpl* **-maux** [-mo] : paranormal

parapet [parapɛ] *nm* : parapet

paraphe [paraf] *nm* **1** : initials *pl* **2** : signature **3** : flourish, ornamental stroke (on a signature)

parapher [parafe] *vt* **1** : to initial **2** : to sign **3** : to add a flourish to (a signature)

paraphrase [parafraz] *nf* : paraphrase

paraphraser [parafraze] *vt* : to paraphrase

paraplégique [parapleʒik] *adj & nmf* : paraplegic

parapluie [paraplɥi] *nm* : umbrella

parascolaire [paraskɔlɛr] *adj* : extracurricular

parasitaire [parazitɛr] *adj* : parasitic

parasite[1] [parazit] *adj* : parasitic

parasite[2] *nm* **1** : parasite **2 parasites** *nmpl* : interference, static

parasol [parasɔl] *nm* : parasol, sunshade

paratonnerre [paratɔnɛr] *nm* : lightning rod

paravent [paravɑ̃] *nm* : screen, partition

parc [park] *nm* **1** : park <parc d'attractions : amusement park> <parc zoologique : zoological gardens> **2** : grounds *pl* **3** ENCLOS : playpen, pen, enclosure <parc à huîtres : oyster bed> <parc à moutons : sheepfold> <parc de stationnement : parking lot> **4** : total number, stock <parc de voitures : fleet of automobiles>

parcelle [parsɛl] *nf* **1** : fragment **2** : plot, parcel <parcelle de terre : plot of land>

parcelliser [parselize] *vt* : to divide, to split up

parce que [parskə] *conj* : because

parchemin [parʃəmɛ̃] *nm* : parchment

parcimonie [parsimɔni] *nf* : parsimony <avec parcimonie : sparingly>

parcimonieux, -nieuse [parsimɔnjø, -njøz] *adj* : parsimonious, sparing — **parcimonieusement** [-njøzmɑ̃] *adv*

par–ci, par–là [parsiparla] → **par**

parcmètre [parkmɛtr] *nm France* : parking meter

parcomètre [parkɔmɛtr] *nm Can* : parking meter

parcourir [parkurir] {23} *vt* **1** : to cover (a distance), to travel through **2** : to leaf through, to skim (a text)

parcours [parkur] *nm* **1** : course (of a river), route (of a bus, etc.) **2** : course (in sports) **3** : career, (professional) development

par–delà *or* **par delà** [pardəla] *prep* : beyond, across <par-delà les mers : beyond the seas> <par-delà les siècles : across the centuries>

par–dessous [pardəsu] *adv & prep* : underneath

pardessus [pardəsy] *nm* **1** : overcoat **2** *Can* CLAQUES : rubbers *pl*

par–dessus[1] [pardəsy] *adv* : over, above, on top <sauter par-dessus : to

jump over (it)> <mets-le par-dessus : put it up top>

par–dessus[2] *prep* **1** : over, above <par-dessus le mur : above the wall> <jeter qqch par-dessus bord : to throw sth overboard> **2 par–dessus tout** : above all

par–devant[1] |pardəvɑ̃| *adv* : in front, at the front

par–devant[2] *prep* : in front of, in the presence of

pardon |pardɔ̃| *nm* **1** : forgiveness, pardon **2 pardon?** : pardon?, what did you say? **3 pardon!** : pardon me!, sorry!

pardonnable |pardɔnabl| *adj* : forgivable, pardonable, excusable

pardonner |pardɔne| *vt* **1** : to forgive, to pardon **2 pardonnez–moi!** : excuse me! — *vi* **ne pas pardonner** : to be fatal <une maladie qui ne pardonne pas : a fatal illness>

paré, -rée |pare| *adj* : ready, prepared <vous voilà paré! : you're all set!>

pare–balles |parbal| *adj s & pl* : bulletproof

pare–brise |parbriz| *nms & pl* : windshield

pare–chocs |parʃɔk| *nms & pl* : bumper

pare–feu |parfø| *nms & pl* : firebreak

parégorique |paregɔrik| *nm or* **élixir parégorique** : paregoric

pareil[1] |parɛj| *adv fam* **1** : the same, in the same way <faire pareil : to do the same (thing)> **2** *Can fam* : all the same, anyhow <viens nous voir pareil : come see us anyway>

pareil[2], **-reille** |parɛj| *adj* **1** SEMBLABLE : similar, alike **2** TEL : such <une pareille maison : such a house, a house like this>

pareil[3], **-reille** *n* **1** : equal <il n'a pas son pareil : he's second to none> <son talent est sans pareil : her talent is unequaled> <une vue sans pareille : a view beyond compare> **2 ses pareils** : one's peers, one's fellows

pareil[4] *nm fam* **c'est du pareil au même** : it's all the same, six of one and a half dozen of the other

pareillement |parɛjmɑ̃| *adv* **1** ÉGALEMENT : in the same way <s'habiller pareillement : to dress alike> **2** AUSSI : also, too <et à vous pareillement : to you, too>

parement |parmɑ̃| *nm* : facing

parent[1], **-rente** |parɑ̃, -rɑ̃t| *adj* **1** : similar, related **2 ~ à** *or* **~ avec** : related to, kin to

parent[2], **-rente** *n* **1** : relative, relation **2 parent par alliance** : in-law

parental, -tale |parɑ̃tal| *adj, mpl* **-taux** |-to| : parental

parenté |parɑ̃te| *nf* **1** : relationship, kinship **2** : family, relations *pl*

parenthèse |parɑ̃tɛz| *nf* **1** : parenthesis, bracket **2** : digression <entre parenthèses *or* par parenthèse : incidentally, by the way>

parents |parɑ̃| *nmpl* **1** : parents **2** ANCÊTRES : ancestors, forebears

parer |pare| *vt* **1** : to adorn **2** : to dress, to trim (in cooking) **3** : to ward off, to parry — *vi* **~ à** : to guard against, to be prepared for, to deal with — **se parer** *vr* **1** : to dress oneself up **2 ~ contre** : to prepare oneself for

pare–soleil |parsɔlɛj| *nms & pl* : sun visor

paresse |parɛs| *nf* : laziness, idleness

paresser |parɛse| *vi* FAINÉANTER : to laze around

paresseux[1], **-seuse** |parəsø, -søz| *adj* : lazy — **paresseusement** |-søzmɑ̃| *adv*

paresseux[2] *nm* : sloth (animal)

parfaire |parfɛr| {62} *vt* PEAUFINER : to perfect, to complete, to refine (style, etc.)

parfait[1], **-faite** |parfɛ, -fɛt| *adj* **1** : perfect **2** : absolute, complete — **parfaitement** |-fɛtmɑ̃| *adv*

parfait[2] *nm* **1** : perfect (tense) **2** : parfait (dessert)

parfois |parfwa| *adv* QUELQUEFOIS : sometimes

parfum |parfœ̃| *nm* **1** : scent, fragrance **2** : flavor (of ice cream, tea, etc.) **3** : perfume

parfumé, -mée |parfyme| *adj* **1** ODORANT : fragrant, scented, sweet-smelling **2** : flavored <parfumé au citron : lemon-flavored>

parfumer |parfyme| *vt* **1** : to scent, to perfume **2** : to flavor — **se parfumer** *vr* : to wear perfume

parfumerie |parfymri| *nf* **1** : perfume shop **2** : perfume industry **3** : perfumes *pl*

pari |pari| *nm* : bet, wager

paria |parja| *nm* : pariah, outcast

parier |parje| {96} *vt* : to bet, to wager

parieur, -rieuse |parjœr, -rjøz| *n* : bettor, better

parisien, -sienne |parizjɛ̃, -zjɛn| *adj* : Parisian

Parisien, -sienne *n* : Parisian

paritaire |paritɛr| *adj* : joint <commission paritaire : joint commission>

parité |parite| *nf* : parity, equality

parjure[1] |parʒyr| *adj* : disloyal, faithless

parjure[2] *nm* : betrayal

parjure[3] *nmf* : traitor

parjurer |parʒyre| *v* **se parjurer** *vr* : to perjure oneself

parka |parka| *nm* : parka

parking |parkiŋ| *nm* **1** STATIONNEMENT : parking **2** : parking lot

parlant, -lante |parlɑ̃, -lɑ̃t| *adj* **1** : talking (of movies, etc.) **2** : vivid, eloquent, graphic **3** : talkative

parlement |parləmɑ̃| *nm* : parliament

parlementaire[1] |parləmɑ̃tɛr| *adj* : parliamentary

parlementaire[2] *nmf* : parliamentarian

parlementer |parləmɑ̃te| *vi* NÉGOCIER : to negotiate, to parley

parler[1] |parle| *vt* : to talk, to speak <parler (le) français : to speak French> <parler affaires : to talk business> — *vi* **1** : to talk, to speak **2 ~ à** : to talk to (someone) **3 ~ de** : to mention, to refer to <sans parler de son accent : not to mention his accent> **4 n'en parlons plus** : let's forget about it — **se parler** *vr* **1** : to speak to each other **2** : to be on speaking terms **3** : to be spoken

parler[2] *nm* **1** : speech, way of speaking **2** : dialect

parleur, -leuse |parlœr, -løz| *n* : talker, speaker <beau parleur : smooth talker>

parloir |parlwar| *nm* : parlor

parlote *or* **parlotte** |parlɔt| *nf fam* CAUSETTE : chat, chitchat

parmesan |parməzɑ̃| *nm* : Parmesan

parmi |parmi| *prep* **1** : among <une possibilité parmi d'autres : one possibility among others> **2** : in the midst of, with

parodie |parɔdi| *nf* : parody

parodier |parɔdje| {96} *vt* : to parody, to mimic

paroi |parwa| *nf* **1** CLOISON : partition **2** : wall (in anatomy and biology) **3** : inner surface, face <paroi rocheuse : rock face>

paroisse |parwas| *nf* : parish

paroissial, -siale |parwasjal| *adj, mpl* **-siaux** |-sjo| : parish, parochial

paroissien, -sienne |parwasjɛ̃, -sjɛn| *n* : parishioner

parole |parɔl| *nf* **1** : (spoken) word <prendre la parole : to speak> **2** PROMESSE : word, promise <parole d'honneur : word of honor> **3** : speech <elle a retrouvé la parole : she regained the power of speech> **4 paroles** *nfpl* : lyrics

paroxysme |parɔksism| *nm* : height, climax (of pain, enthusiasm, etc.)

parquer |parke| *vt* **1** : to pen <bétail parqué : penned cattle> **2** ENTASSER : to herd together **3** GARER : to park

parquet |parkɛ| *nm* **1** : parquet (floor) **2** *France* : public prosecutor's office **3 parquet de la bourse** : floor of the stock exchange

parrain |parɛ̃| *nm* **1** : godfather **2** : sponsor, patron

parrainage |parɛnaʒ| *nm* : sponsorship

parrainer |parɛne| *vt* : to sponsor

parsemer |parsəme| {52} *vt* **1** : to sprinkle **2 ~ de** : to scatter with, to strew with, to intersperse with

part |par| *nf* **1** : portion, share, piece **2** : proportion, element <une part de chance : an element of chance> **3** : part, share <faire sa part : to do one's share> <prendre part à : to take part in> **4** : side, position <de toutes parts : from all sides> <d'une part . . . : on (the) one hand . . .> <de la part de : on behalf of> **5 à ~** : apart from <à part ça : besides that> **6 à ~** : to one side, separate(ly) **7 à ~** : apart, unique <un cas à part : a special case> **8 → autre, nul, quelque**

partage |partaʒ| *nm* **1** : sharing, dividing <sans partage : total, undivided> **2** : share, lot

partagé, -gée |partaʒe| *adj* **1** : divided <opinions partagées : divided opinions> **2** : shared, mutual

partager |partaʒe| {17} *vt* **1** DIVISER : to divide up **2** : to share — **se partager** *vr*

partance |partɑ̃s| *nf* **1 en ~** : outbound, ready to depart **2 en partance pour** : bound for

partant[1] |partɑ̃| *adj* **être partant pour** : to be ready for, to be up to

partant[2], **-tante** |partɑ̃, -tɑ̃t| *n* : runner, starter (in sports)

partenaire |partənɛr| *nmf* : partner

partenariat |partənarja| *nm* : partnership

parterre |partɛr| *nm* **1** : flower bed **2** : orchestra section (in a theater)

parti[1], **-tie** |parti| *adj fam* : intoxicated, high

parti[2] *nm* **1** : group, camp, side **2** : political party **3** : course of action, option <prendre parti : to take a stand> <prendre son parti : to make up one's mind, to come to terms> **4** : advantage, profit <tirer parti de : to take advantage of> **5 parti pris** : bias

partial, -tiale |parsjal| *adj, mpl* **-tiaux** |-sjo| : biased, partial

partialement |parsjalmɑ̃| *adv* : in a biased manner

partialité |parsjalite| *nf* : bias, partiality

participant, -pante |partisipɑ̃, -pɑ̃t| *n* **1** : participant **2** : entrant (in a competition)

participation |partisipasjɔ̃| *nf* **1** : participation **2** : contribution **3** : share, interest (in a company, etc.)

participe |partisip| *nm* : participle

participer |partisipe| *vi* **~ à 1** : to participate in, to take part in **2** : to contribute to **3** : to share in

particulariser |partikylarize| *vt* : to distinguish, to characterize — **se particulariser** *vr*

particularité |partikylarite| *nf* : distinctive feature, characteristic, idiosyncrasy

particule |partikyl| *nf* : particle

particulier[1], **-lière** |partikylje, -ljɛr| *adj* **1** : particular, specific **2** : special, unique, idiosyncratic **3** SINGULIER : unusual **4** : private, personal <cours particuliers : private lessons> **5 en ~** : especially, in particular

particulier[2] *nm* : individual, private person

particulièrement |partikyljɛrmɑ̃| *adv* SPÉCIALEMENT : especially, particularly

partie |parti| *nf* **1** : part (of a whole) **2** : game, match **3** : party, participant **4** SORTIE : party, outing <partie de pêche : fishing party> **5** : field, line (of work) **6 en ～** : partly, in part **7 faire partie de** : to be a part of, to belong to

partiel, -tielle |parsjɛl| *adj* : partial — **partiellement** |-sjɛlmɑ̃| *adv*

partir |partir| {82} *vi* **1** : to leave, to depart **2** : to start up, to take off **3** COMMENCER : to start, to begin **4** S'ENLEVER : to come off, to come out (of a stain, etc.) **5 à partir de** : from <à partir de maintenant : from now on>

partisan¹, -sane |partizɑ̃, -zan| *adj* : partisan

partisan², -sane *n* : supporter, partisan

partition |partisjɔ̃| *nf* : score <partition de piano : piano score>

partout |partu| *adv* **1** : everywhere **2** : all (in sports) <trois partout : three all>

paru |pary| *pp* → **paraître**

parure |paryr| *nf* **1** : finery **2** ENSEMBLE : set (of jewelry, linens, etc.)

parution |parysjɔ̃| *nf* : publication, launch

parvenir |parvənir| {92} *vi* **1 ～ à** : to reach, to arrive at <elle est parvenue à une résolution : she arrived at a solution> **2 ～ à** : to manage to, to succeed in, to achieve

parvenu, -nue |parvəny| *n* : parvenu, upstart

parvis |parvi| *nm* : square (in front of a church)

party |parti| *nm Can fam* : party, gathering

pas¹ |pa| → **ne**

pas² *adv* (*without* **ne**) **1** : not <pas du tout : not at all> <pas vraiment : not really> <pas mal de : quite a lot of> <pas croyable! : incredible!> **2 pas un, pas une** : no one, none <il le fait comme pas un : he does it like nobody else>

pas³ *nms & pl* **1** : step, footstep **2** : footprint **3** : pace, gait **4** : move, progression <un pas en avant : a step forward> <faire le premier pas : to make the first move> **5** : step (in dancing) **6 de ce pas** : right away

pascal, -cale |paskal| *adj, mpl* **pascaux** |pasko| : Easter <congé pascal : Easter holiday>

passable |pasabl| *adj* **1** : passable, fair **2** *Can* : passable, negotiable <chemins passables : passable roads>

passablement |pasabləmɑ̃| *adv* **1** : quite, rather **2** : reasonably well

passade |pasad| *nf* : passing fancy

passage |pasaʒ| *nm* **1** : passing (by), crossing (through), traffic <être de passage : to be passing through> <au passage : in passing> **2** TARIF : fare, ticket **3** : transition, passage **4** CHEMIN : route, way **5** CORRIDOR : corridor, passageway <passage pour piétons : pedestrian crossing> **6** : entry <passage interdit : do not enter> **7** : passage (in a text)

passager¹, -gère |pasaʒe, -ʒɛr| *adj* **1** : passing, temporary **2** : busy <rue passagère : busy street>

passager², -gère *n* **1** : passenger **2 passager clandestin** : stowaway

passagèrement |pasaʒɛrmɑ̃| *adv* : temporarily

passant¹, -sante |pasɑ̃, -sɑ̃t| *adj* : busy <rue passante : busy street>

passant², -sante *n* : passerby

passe |pas| *nf* **1** : pass (in sports) **2** : period, time <j'ai traversé une mauvaise passe : I went through a difficult time> **3** : channel (in navigation)

passé¹, -sée |pase| *adj* **1** : last, past <l'an passé : last year> **2** : after, past <il est midi passé : it's after twelve> **3** : faded

passé² *nm* **1** : past <par le passé : in the past> **2** : past tense <passé composé : perfect tense>

passé³ *prep* : after, beyond <passé l'église il y a un parc : beyond the church is a park> <passé minuit : after midnight>

passe-droit |pasdrwa| *nm, pl* **passe-droits** : privilege, special treatment

passementerie |pasmɑ̃tri| *nf* : trimmings *pl* (for clothing, etc.)

passe-partout |paspartu| *nms & pl* : master key

passe-passe |paspas| *nms & pl* **tour de passe-passe** : conjuring trick, sleight of hand

passepoil |paspwal| *nm* : piping (in sewing)

passeport |paspɔr| *nm* : passport

passer |pase| *vt* **1** : to cross, to go over **2** : to pass, to go past **3** : to pass, to run <passer la main sur une surface : to pass one's hand over a surface> **4** : to pass, to hand over, to give <passer un ballon : to pass a ball> <passez-moi le poivre : pass me the pepper> <passer un rhume à qqn : to give s.o. a cold> **5** : to put through to (on the telephone) **6** : to take (an exam, etc.), to take on **7** : to spend (time) **8** : to excuse, to forgive **9** : to skip, to pass over **10** : to go over <passer l'aspirateur : to vacuum> **11** ENFILER : to slip on **12** : to show (a film), to play (a cassette, etc.) **13** : to shift into (a gear) — *vi* **1** : to pass, to go past, to run <le chemin passe devant ma maison : the road runs in front of my house> **2** : to drop by **3** : to go <où est-il passé? : where did he go?> **4** : to get through <laissez-moi passer : let me through> **5** : to be over, to pass, to go by **6** : to pass down, to be handed down **7 ~ par** : to go through <en passant par : including> **8 ~ pour** : to pass for, to appear to be **9 ~ sur** : to pass over, to overlook, to forget about **10 en passant** : incidentally **11 y passer** *fam* : to die — **se passer** *vr* **1** : to take place, to happen **2** : to go, to turn out **3** : to pass, to go by (of time) **4 ~ de** : to do without, to dispense with **5 se faire passer** : to masquerade, to disguise oneself

passereau [pasro] *nm, pl* **-reaux** : sparrow

passerelle [pasrɛl] *nf* **1** : footbridge **2** : gangplank, ramp (of an airplane) **3** : bridge (of a ship)

passe–temps [pastɑ̃] *nms & pl* : hobby, pastime

passeur, -seuse [pasœr, -søz] *n* : smuggler

passible [pasibl] *adj* **~ de** : liable to, punishable by <passible d'une amende : liable to a fine>

passif[1], -sive [pasif, -siv] *adj* : passive — **passivement** [-sivmɑ̃] *adv*

passif[2] *nm* **1** : passive case **2** : liabilities *pl*

passion [pasjɔ̃] *nf* : passion

passionnant, -nante [pasjɔnɑ̃, -nɑ̃t] *adj* CAPTIVANT : exciting, fascinating

passionné[1], -née [pasjɔne] *adj* : passionate, enthusiastic — **passionnément** [-nemɑ̃] *adv*

passionné[2], -née *n* : enthusiast

passionnel, -nelle [pasjɔnɛl] *adj* : passionate <crime passionnel : crime of passion>

passionner [pasjɔne] *vt* **1** CAPTIVER : to fascinate **2** : to impassion, to inflame — **se passionner** *vr* **~ pour** : to have a passion for

passivement [pasivmɑ̃] *adv* : passively

passivité [pasivite] *nf* : passivity

passoire [paswar] *nf* : sieve, strainer, colander

pastel [pastɛl] *adj & nm* : pastel

pastèque [pastɛk] *nf* : watermelon

pasteur [pastœr] *nm* : minister, pastor

pasteuriser [pastœrize] *vt* : to pasteurize — **pasteurisation** [-rizasjɔ̃] *nf*

pastiche [pastiʃ] *nm* : pastiche

pastille [pastij] *nf* : lozenge <pastilles contre la toux : cough drops>

pastoral, -rale [pastɔral] *adj, mpl* **-raux** [-ro] : pastoral

pastorat [pastɔra] *nm* : pastorate, (Protestant) ministry

pat [pat] *nm* : stalemate

patate [patat] *nf* **1** *fam* : potato **2** *fam* : blockhead **3** *or* **patate douce** : sweet potato

pataud, -taude [pato, -tod] *adj* : clumsy, lumbering

patauger [patoʒe] {17} *vi* **1** : to splash about, to paddle **2** S'EMBROUILLER : to flounder about, to get confused

patchwork [patʃwœrk] *nm* : patchwork

pâte [pat] *nf* **1** : dough, pastry, batter **2** : paste <pâte dentifrice : toothpaste> <pâte à modeler : modeling clay> **3** : pulp <pâte à papier : paper pulp> **4 être bonne pâte** : to be easygoing **5 pâtes** *nfpl* : pasta

pâté [pate] *nm* **1** : pâté **2** : inkblot **3** *or* **pâté de maisons** : block (of houses)

pâtée [pate] *nf* : mash, feed, slop

patelin [patlɛ̃] *nm fam* : little village

patent, -tente [patɑ̃, -tɑ̃t] *adj* : obvious, patent

patente [patɑ̃t] *nf Can fam* **1** : thing, thingamajig **2** : gadget, gizmo

patenté, -tée [patɑ̃te] *adj fam* : established, out-and-out

patère [patɛr] *nf* : peg, hook (for coats, etc.)

paternel, -nelle [patɛrnɛl] *adj* : fatherly, paternal — **paternellement** [-nɛlmɑ̃] *adv*

paternité [patɛrnite] *nf* **1** : fatherhood, paternity **2** : authorship

pâteux, -teuse [patø, -tøz] *adj* **1** : pasty, doughy **2** : thick <avoir la langue pâteuse : to have a coated tongue>

pathétique [patetik] *adj* : pathetic, moving — **pathétiquement** [-tikmɑ̃] *adv*

pathologie [patɔlɔʒi] *nf* : pathology

pathologique [patɔlɔʒik] *adj* : pathological

pathologiste [patɔlɔʒist] *nmf* : pathologist

pathos [patos] *nms & pl* : pathos

patibulaire [patibylɛr] *adj* : sinister-looking

patiemment [pasjamɑ̃] *adv* : patiently

patience [pasjɑ̃s] *nf* **1** : patience <j'ai perdu patience : I lost my patience> **2 jeu de patience** : solitaire

patient, -tiente [pasjɑ̃, -sjɑ̃t] *adj & n* : patient

patienter [pasjɑ̃te] *vi* : to wait

patin [patɛ̃] *nm* : skate <patins à glace : ice skates> <patins à roulettes : roller skates>

patinage [patinaʒ] *nm* : skating <patinage artistique : figure skating>

patine [patin] *nf* : patina

patiner [patine] *vi* **1** : to skate **2** : to spin, to slip (of wheels) **3** *Can* : to hedge, to shilly-shally

patinette [patinɛt] *nf* TROTTINETTE : scooter

patineur, -neuse [patinœr, -nøz] *n* : skater

patinoire [patinwar] *nf* : skating rink

patio [patjo, pasjo] *nm* : patio

pâtir [patir] *vi* **~ de** : to suffer because of

pâtisserie [patisri] *nf* **1** : cake, pastry **2** : pastry shop, bakery

pâtissier, -sière [patisje, -sjɛr] *n* : pastry chef

patois [patwa] *nms & pl* **1** : patois **2** *Can* : swearword, oath

patraque [patrak] *adj fam* : out of sorts

patriarcat |patrijarka| *nm* : patriarchy

patriarche |patrijarʃ| *nm* : patriarch — **patriarcal, -cale** |-jarkal| *adj*

patrie |patri| *nf* : mother country, homeland, fatherland

patrimoine |patrimwan| *nm* **1** : patrimony, legacy **2** HÉRITAGE : heritage

patriote[1] |patrijɔt| *adj* : patriotic

patriote[2] *nmf* : patriot — **patriotique** |patrijɔtik| *adj*

patriotisme |patrijɔtism| *nm* : patriotism

patron[1], **-tronne** |patrɔ̃, -trɔn| *n* **1** : patron saint **2** : owner **3** : boss, manager, employer

patron[2] *nm* : pattern (in sewing)

patronage |patrɔnaʒ| *nm* : patronage

patronal, -nale |patrɔnal| *adj, mpl* **-naux** |-no| : of employers <syndicat patronal : employers' union>

patronat |patrɔna| *nm* : management

patronner |patrɔne| *vt* : to support, to sponsor

patrouille |patruj| *nf* : patrol

patrouiller |patruje| *vi* : to patrol

patrouilleur[1], **-leuse** |patrujœr, -jøz| *n* **1** : soldier on patrol **2** *Can* : police officer (in a patrol car)

patrouilleur[2] *nm* : patrol boat, patrol plane

patte |pat| *nf* **1** : paw, hoof, foot (of a bird), leg (of an insect) <patte de devant : foreleg> **2** *fam* : leg, foot, hand <traîner la patte : to drag one's feet, to fall behind> **3** : tab, flap

pattes–d'oie |patdwa| *nfpl* : crow's feet

pâturage |patyraʒ| *nm* : pasture

pâture |patyr| *nf* **1** : feed, fodder **2** : pasture

paume |pom| *nf* : palm (of the hand)

paumer |pome| *v fam* : to lose — **se paumer** *vr fam* : to get lost

paupière |popjɛr| *nf* : eyelid

pause |poz| *nf* **1** : break <faire une pause : to pause, to take a break> **2** : pause **3** : rest (in music)

pauvre[1] |povr| *adj* **1** : poor, impoverished **2** : unfortunate **3** : poor, sparse

pauvre[2] *nm* : poor man, pauper <les pauvres : the poor>

pauvrement |povrəmɑ̃| *adv* : poorly

pauvreté |povrəte| *nf* : poverty

pavage |pavaʒ| *nm* : paving, cobblestones *pl*

pavaner |pavane| *v* **se pavaner** *vr* : to strut about

pavé |pave| *nm* **1** : pavement **2** : cobblestone, paving stone

paver |pave| *vt* : to pave

pavillon |pavijɔ̃| *nm* **1** : pavilion **2** *France* : (detached) house **3** : ward (in a hospital), (university) building **4** : auricle (of the ear) **5** : bell (of a wind instrument) **6** : flag (on a ship)

pavoiser |pavwaze| *vt* : to deck with flags — *vi* : to rejoice

pavot |pavo| *nm* : poppy

payable |pɛjabl| *adj* : payable

payant, payante |pɛjɑ̃, -jɑ̃t| *adj* **1** : paying **2** : for which one pays <télé payante : pay-TV>

paye |pɛj| → **paie**

payement |pɛmɑ̃| → **paiement**

payer |peje| {11} *vt* **1** : to pay, to pay for **2** *fam* : to buy <je lui ai payé un verre : I bought him a drink> **3** : to pay for, to suffer the consequences of **4** : to cover (one's expenses, etc.) — *vi* : to pay <un métier qui paie bien : a well-paying job> — **se payer** *vr* **1** : to have to be paid for **2** : to treat oneself

pays |pei| *nm* **1** : country **2** : region, area <du pays : local> **3** : village **4** : people (of a country) <s'adresser au pays : to address the nation>

paysage |peizaʒ| *nm* : scenery, landscape

paysagiste |peizaʒist| *nm* **1** : landscape painter **2** : landscape gardener

paysan[1], **-sanne** |peizɑ̃, -zan| *adj* **1** : agricultural, farming **2** : rural, rustic

paysan[2], **-sanne** *n* **1** : small farmer **2** : peasant

péage |peaʒ| *nm* **1** : toll **2** : tollbooth

peau |po| *nf, pl* **peaux 1** : (human) skin <être bien dans sa peau : to be at peace with oneself> **2** : hide, pelt <peau de mouton : sheepskin> <peau de daim : buckskin> <gants de peau : leather gloves> **3** : peel, rind, skin (of fruits or vegetables)

peaufiner |pofine| *vt* : to put the finishing touches on, to perfect

pécan *or* **pecan** |pekɑ̃| *nm France or* **noix de pécan** : pecan

peccadille |pɛkadij| *nf* : peccadillo

pêche |pɛʃ| *nf* **1** : peach **2** : fishing **3** : catch <une bonne pêche : a good catch of fish>

péché |peʃe| *nm* : sin

pécher |peʃe| {87} *vi* : to sin

pêcher[1] |pɛʃe| *vt* **1** : to fish for **2** *fam* : to get, to unearth — *vi* : to fish <pêcher à la ligne : to angle>

pêcher[2] |pɛʃœr| *nm* : peach tree

pêcherie |pɛʃri| *nf* **1** : fishery, fishing ground **2** : fish processing factory

pécheur, -cheresse |peʃœr, -ʃrɛs| *n* : sinner

pêcheur, -cheuse |pɛʃœr, -ʃøz| *n* **1** : fisherman **2 pêcheur à la ligne** : angler

pectine |pɛktin| *nf* : pectin

pectoral[1], **-rale** |pɛktɔral| *adj, mpl* **-raux** |-ro| **1** : pectoral **2** : cough <sirop pectoral : cough syrup>

pectoraux |pɛktɔro| *nmpl* : pectoral muscles

pécule |pekyl| *nm* ÉCONOMIES : savings *pl*

pécuniaire |pekynjɛr| *adj* FINANCIER : financial — **pécuniairement** |-njɛrmɑ̃| *adv*

pédagogie |pedagɔʒi| *nf* **1** : education, pedagogy **2** : teaching skill

pédagogique |pedagɔʒik| *adj* : educational, teaching <formation pédagogique : teacher training>

pédagogue |pedagɔg| *nmf* : educator, teacher

pédale |pedal| *nf* : pedal

pédaler |pedale| *vi* : to pedal

pédalier |pedalje| *nm* **1** : drive mechanism (of a bicycle) **2** : pedals *pl* (of an organ)

pédalo |pedalo| *nm* : pedal boat

pédant[1], **-dante** |pedɑ̃, -dɑ̃t| *adj* : pedantic

pédant[2], **-dante** *n* : pedant

pédantisme |pedɑ̃tism| *nm* : pedantry

pédestre |pedɛstr| *adj* : on foot <randonnée pédestre : hike>

pédiatre |pedjatr| *nmf* : pediatrician

pédiatrie |pedjatri| *nf* : pediatrics

pédiatrique |pedjatrik| *adj* : pediatric

pédicure |pedikyr| *nmf* : chiropodist

pedigree |pedigre| *nm* : pedigree

pègre |pɛgr| *nf* : (criminal) underworld

peignait |pɛɲɛ|, **peignions** |pɛɲɔ̃|, *etc.* → **peindre**

peigne[1] |pɛɲ|, *etc.* → **peindre**

peigne[2] |pɛɲ| *nm* : comb

peigner |peɲe| *vt* **1** : to comb **2** : to card (fibers) — **se peigner** *vr* : to comb one's hair

peignoir |pɛɲwar| *nm* : bathrobe, dressing gown

peignure |pɛɲyr| *nf Can fam* : hairdo, hairstyle

peindre |pɛ̃dr| {37} *vt* **1** : to paint **2** : to depict, to portray — *vi* : to paint — **se peindre** *vr* : to show, to manifest itself

peine |pɛn| *nf* **1** : sorrow, sadness **2** : trouble, effort <se donner la peine de : to take the trouble to> <ce n'est pas la peine : it's not worth the effort, never mind, forget it> **3** : difficulty <sans peine : easily> **4** : punishment, penalty <peine capitale : capital punishment> **5 à ~** : hardly, just, barely

peiner |pene| *vt* ATTRISTER : to distress, to sadden — *vi* **1** : to have trouble, to struggle **2** : to strain, to labor (of an engine, etc.)

peintre |pɛ̃tr| *nm* : painter

peinture |pɛ̃tyr| *nf* **1** : paint **2** : painting, picture **3** : painting <elle fait de la peinture à l'huile : she paints in oil>

peinturer |pɛ̃tyre| *vt Can* : to paint <peinturer la maison : to paint the house>

peinturlurer |pɛ̃tyrlure| *vt* : to daub (with paint)

péjoratif, -tive |peʒɔratif, -tiv| *adj* : pejorative, derogatory — **péjorativement** |-tivmɑ̃| *adv*

pelage |pəlaʒ| *nm* : coat, fur (of an animal)

pelé, -lée |pəle| *adj* **1** : hairless, bald **2** : bare, barren

pêle-mêle |pɛlmɛl| *adv* : every which way, pell-mell

peler |pəle| {20} *v* : to peel

pèlerin, -rine |pɛlrɛ̃| *n* : pilgrim

pèlerinage |pɛlrinaʒ| *nm* : pilgrimage

pèlerine |pɛlrin| *nf* : cape

pélican |pelikɑ̃| *nm* : pelican

pellagre |pɛlagr| *nf* : pellagra

pelle |pɛl| *nf* **1** : shovel **2 pelle à poussière** : dustpan

pelletée |pɛlte| *nf* : shovelful

pelleter |pɛlte| {8} *vt* : to shovel

pelleteuse |pɛltøz| *nf* : power shovel, excavator

pellicule |pelikyl| *nf* **1** : (photographic) film **2** : thin layer, film **3 pellicules** *nfpl* : dandruff

pelote |pəlɔt| *nf* **1** : ball (of string, thread, yarn, etc.) **2** : pincushion **3 pelote de neige** *Can* : snowball

peloter |pəlɔte| *vt fam* : to grope, to paw, to fondle — *vi fam* : to neck

peloton |plɔtɔ̃| *nm* **1** : group <peloton de tête : front runners, leaders of the pack> **2** : squad, platoon <peloton d'exécution : firing squad>

pelotonner |pəlɔtɔne| *v* **se pelotonner** *vr* : to curl up (into a ball), to snuggle

pelouse |pəluz| *nf* **1** : lawn, grass **2** : field (in sports)

peluche |pəlyʃ| *nf* **1** : plush **2** : (piece of) fluff, lint **3** *or* **animal en peluche** : stuffed animal, soft toy

pelucheux, -cheuse |pəlyʃø, -ʃøz| *adj* : fluffy

pelure |pəlyr| *nf* : peel, skin (of an apple, etc.)

pelvien, -vienne |pɛlvjɛ̃, -vjɛn| *adj* : pelvic

pelvis |pɛlvis| *nm* : pelvis

pénal, -nale |penal| *adj, mpl* **pénaux** |peno| : penal

pénalisation |penalizasjɔ̃| *nf* : penalty (in sports)

pénaliser |penalize| *vt* : to penalize

pénalité |penalite| *nf* : penalty (in sports)

penaud, -naude |pəno, -nod| *adj* : sheepish

penchant |pɑ̃ʃɑ̃| *nm* : tendency, inclination

pencher |pɑ̃ʃe| *vt* INCLINER : to tilt, to tip — *vi* **1** : to slant, to lean **2 ~ pour** : to incline towards, to favor — **se pencher** *vr* **1** : to hunch over, to bend (down) **2 ~ sur** : to look into, to examine

pendaison |pɑ̃dɛzɔ̃| *nf* **1** : hanging **2 pendaison de crémaillère** : housewarming

pendant[1], **-dante** |pɑ̃dɑ̃, -dɑ̃t| *adj* **1** : hanging, dangling **2** : pending

pendant[2] *nm* **1** *or* **pendant d'oreille** : drop earring **2** : counterpart, matching piece

pendant[3] *prep* **1** : during, for <pendant l'été : during the summer> <tra-

vailler pendant des heures : to work for hours> **2 pendant que** : while <pendant que vous y êtes : while you're at it>

pendentif [pɑ̃dɑ̃tif] *nm* : pendant

penderie [pɑ̃dri] *nf* : closet, wardrobe

pendre [pɑ̃dr] {63} *vt* **1** SUSPENDRE : to hang, to suspend **2** : to hang (someone) — *vi* **1** : to hang **2** : to hang down, to sag — **se pendre** *vr* : to hang oneself

pendule[1] [pɑ̃dyl] *nm* : pendulum

pendule[2] *nf* : clock

pêne [pɛn] *nm* : bolt (of a lock)

pénétrant, -trante [penetrɑ̃, -trɑ̃t] *adj* **1** : penetrating, piercing **2** : shrewd, perceptive

pénétration [penetrasjɔ̃] *nf* **1** : penetration **2** : perception, insight

pénétré, -trée [penetre] *adj* : earnest, intense <être pénétré de son importance : to be full of one's own importance>

pénétrer [penetre] {87} *vt* **1** IMPRÉGNER : to penetrate, to soak into **2** COMPRENDRE : to fathom, to understand — *vi* **1** S'ENFONCER : to penetrate, to sink in **2** S'INTRODUIRE : to enter, to penetrate

pénible [penibl] *adj* **1** : painful, distressing **2** ARDU : difficult, arduous

péniblement [penibləmɑ̃] *adv* **1** : with difficulty, laboriously **2** : barely, just about

péniche [peniʃ] *nf* **1** : barge **2 péniche aménagée** : houseboat

pénicilline [penisilin] *nf* : penicillin

péninsule [penɛ̃syl] *nf* : peninsula — **péninsulaire** [-sylɛr] *adj*

pénis [penis] *nm* : penis

pénitence [penitɑ̃s] *nf* **1** : penitence, repentance **2** : punishment

pénitencier [penitɑ̃sje] *nm* : penitentiary

pénitent[1], **-tente** [penitɑ̃, -tɑ̃t] *adj* : penitent, repentant

pénitent[2], **-tente** *n* : penitent

pénitentiaire [penitɑ̃sjɛr] *adj* : penal

penne [pɛn] *nf* : quill, quill pen

pénombre [penɔ̃br] *nf* : half-light

pense-bête [pɑ̃sbɛt] *nm, pl* **pense-bêtes** [-bɛt] : reminder

pensée [pɑ̃se] *nf* **1** : thought **2** : mind <en pensée : in one's mind> **3** : thinking <pensée claire : clear thinking> **4** : pansy

penser [pɑ̃se] *vt* **1** : to think <penser du bien de : to think well of> <qu'en pensez-vous? : what do you think about it?> **2** : to believe, to suppose <penser que oui : to think so> <je pense qu'elle a raison : I think she's right> **3** : to intend, to plan on <il pense sortir : he intends to go out> — *vi* **1** : to think **2 ~ à** : to think about <penser au passé : to think about the past>

penseur, -seuse [pɑ̃sœr, -søz] *n* : thinker

pensif, -sive [pɑ̃sif, -siv] *adj* MÉDITATIF : pensive, thoughtful

pension [pɑ̃sjɔ̃] *nf* **1** : pension <pension alimentaire : alimony> **2** : boardinghouse **3** : room and board

pensionnaire [pɑ̃sjɔnɛr] *nmf* : boarder, roomer

pensionnat [pɑ̃sjɔna] *nm* : boarding school

pensivement [pɑ̃sivmɑ̃] *adv* : pensively, thoughtfully

pentagone [pɛ̃tagɔn] *nm* : pentagon — **pentagonal** [-gɔnal] *adj*

pente [pɑ̃t] *nf* **1** : slope **2 en ~** : sloping

Pentecôte [pɑ̃tkot] *nf* : Pentecost

pénurie [penyri] *nf* : shortage, scarcity

péon [peɔ̃] *nm* : peon

pépé [pepe] *nm France fam* : grandpa

pépère[1] [pepɛr] *adj fam* : quiet, easy

pépère[2] *nm fam* **1** : chubby boy **2** : oldtimer **3** : grandpa

pépiement [pepimɑ̃] *nm* : peep, peeping

pépier [pepje] {96} *vi* : to chirp, to tweet, to peep

pépin [pepɛ̃] *nm* **1** : pip, seed **2** *fam* : snag, hitch

pépinière [pepinjɛr] *nf* **1** : (tree) nursery **2** : breeding ground

pépite [pepit] *nf* : nugget

péquenaud, -naude [pekno, -nod] *n France fam* : yokel, bumpkin

percale [pɛrkal] *nf* : percale

perçant, -çante [pɛrsɑ̃, -sɑ̃t] *adj* **1** : piercing, shrill **2** : sharp, keen <vue perçante : keen eyesight>

percée [pɛrse] *nf* **1** : opening, gap **2** : breakthrough, discovery

perce-neige [pɛrsənɛʒ] *nmfs & pl* : snowdrop

perce-oreille [pɛrsɔrɛj] *nm, pl* **perce-oreilles** [-ɔrɛj] : earwig

percepteur [pɛrsɛptœr] *nm* : tax collector

perceptible [pɛrsɛptibl] *adj* : perceptible, noticeable

perception [pɛrsɛpsjɔ̃] *nf* **1** : perception **2** RECOUVREMENT : collection (of taxes)

percer [pɛrse] {6} *vt* **1** : to pierce **2** : to open up, to build (a road, etc.) **3** PÉNÉTRER : to fathom, to penetrate **4 percer ses dents** : to be teething — *vi* **1** : to break through (of the sun) **2** : to come through (of a tooth)

perceuse [pɛrsøz] *nf* : drill

percevable [pɛrsəvabl] *adj* : collectable, payable

percevoir [pɛrsəvwar] {26} *vt* **1** : to perceive, to sense **2** RECOUVRER : to receive (money, etc.), to collect (taxes)

perche [pɛrʃ] *nf* **1** : pole **2** : perch, bass (fish)

percher [pɛrʃe] *vi* : to perch — **se percher** *vr* : to roost

perchoir [pɛrʃwar] *nm* : perch, roost
perclus, -cluse [pɛrkly, -klyz] *adj* **~ de** : crippled with
perçoit [pɛrswa], **perçoive** [pɛrswav], *etc.* → **percevoir**
percolateur [pɛrkɔlatœr] *nm* : percolator
perçu [pɛrsy] *pp* → **percevoir**
percussion [pɛrkysjɔ̃] *nf* : percussion — **percussionniste** [-kysjɔnist] *nmf*
percutant, -tante [pɛrkytɑ̃, -tɑ̃t] *adj* : forceful, striking
percuter [pɛrkyte] *vt* : to strike, to crash into — *vi* **1** : to explode **2 ~ contre** : to crash into
perdant[1], -dante [pɛrdɑ̃, -dɑ̃t] *adj* : losing
perdant[2], -dante *n* : loser
perdition [pɛrdisjɔ̃] *nf* **1** : perdition **2 en ~** : in distress
perdre [pɛrdr] {63} *vt* **1** : to lose **2** : to waste <perdre son temps : to waste one's time> **3** MANQUER : to miss **4** : to ruin (one's reputation, etc.) — *vi* : to lose — **se perdre** *vr* **1** : to get lost, to disappear **2** : to get lost, to lose one's way
perdreau [pɛrdro] *nm, pl* **perdreaux** : (young) partridge
perdrix [pɛrdri] *nfs & pl* : partridge
perdu, -due [pɛrdy] *adj* **1** : lost **2** : wasted **3** : ruined **4** : spare, free <à mes moments perdus : in my spare time> **5** : isolated, remote
père [pɛr] *nm* **1** : father **2 pères** *nmpl* : ancestors, forefathers
pérégrinations [peregrinasjɔ̃] *nfpl* : travels
péremptoire [perɑ̃ptwar] *adj* : peremptory
péréquation [perekwasjɔ̃] *nf* : equalization, adjustment (in finance)
perfectible [pɛrfɛktibl] *adj* : perfectible
perfection [pɛrfɛksjɔ̃] *nf* **1** : perfection **2 à la perfection** : to perfection, perfectly
perfectionné, -née [pɛrfɛksjɔne] *adj* : advanced, sophisticated
perfectionnement [pɛrfɛksjɔnmɑ̃] *nm* : perfecting, improvement
perfectionner [pɛrfɛksjɔne] *vt* : to perfect, to improve — **se perfectionner** *vr*
perfectionnisme [pɛrfɛksjɔnism] *nm* : perfectionism
perfectionniste[1] [pɛrfɛksjɔnist] *adj* : perfectionist, perfectionistic
perfectionniste[2] *nmf* : perfectionist
perfide [pɛrfid] *adj* : treacherous, perfidious — **perfidement** [-fidmɑ̃] *adv*
perfidie [pɛrfidi] *nf* : treachery
perforation [pɛrfɔrasjɔ̃] *nf* : perforation
perforer [pɛrfɔre] *vt* PERCER : to perforate, to pierce
performance [pɛrfɔrmɑ̃s] *nf* **1** : performance **2** : achievement
performant, -mante [pɛrfɔrmɑ̃, -mɑ̃t] *adj* **1** : high-performance (of machines, etc.) **2** : high-return (of investments)
péricliter [periklite] *vi* : to decline sharply
péril [peril] *nm* : peril, danger <au péril de sa vie : at the risk of one's life>
périlleux, -leuse [perijø, -jøz] *adj* : perilous — **périlleusement** [-jøzmɑ̃] *adv*
périmé, -mée [perime] *adj* **1** : outdated **2** : out-of-date, expired
périmètre [perimɛtr] *nm* : perimeter
période [perjɔd] *nf* **1** : period, time **2 par périodes** : periodically, from time to time
périodique[1] [perjɔdik] *adj* **1** : periodic (in science) **2** : periodical **3** : recurring
périodique[2] *nm* : periodical
périodiquement [perjɔdikmɑ̃] *adv* : periodically
péripétie [peripesi] *nf* : incident, event
périphérie [periferi] *nf* **1** : periphery, circumference **2** : outskirts *pl*
périphérique[1] [periferik] *adj* **1** : peripheral **2** : outlying
périphérique[2] *nm* : peripheral (in computer science)
périple [peripl] *nm* : journey
périr [perir] *vi* : to perish
périscope [periskɔp] *nm* : periscope
périssable [perisabl] *adj* : perishable
perle [pɛrl] *nf* **1** : pearl, bead **2** : gem, treasure, paragon **3** : drop <perle de sang : drop of blood> **4** *fam* : howler, blunder
perlé, -lée [pɛrle] *adj* **1** : pearly **2** : beaded
perler [pɛrle] *vi* : to form in droplets
permanence [pɛrmanɑ̃s] *nf* **1** : permanence **2 en ~** : permanently, without interruption **3 être de permanence** : to be on duty
permanent[1], -nente [pɛrmanɑ̃, -nɑ̃t] *adj* **1** : permanent **2** : constant
permanent[2], -nente *n* : permanent employee or member
permanente *nf* : permanent, perm
perméable [pɛrmeabl] *adj* **1** : permeable **2 ~ à** : receptive to
permettre [pɛrmɛtr] {53} *vt* **1** : to allow, to permit **2** : to enable, to make possible — **se permettre** *vr* **1** : to allow oneself **2 ~ de** : to take the liberty of
permis [pɛrmi] *nm* LICENCE : license, permit <permis de conduire : driver's license>
permissif, -sive [pɛrmisif, -siv] *adj* : permissive
permission [pɛrmisjɔ̃] *nf* **1** : permission **2** : leave (in the military)
permissivité [pɛrmisivite] *nf* : permissiveness
permutation [pɛrmytasjɔ̃] *nf* **1** : permutation **2** : exchange (of jobs)
permuter [pɛrmyte] *vt* : to exchange, to switch around — *vi* : to switch places

pernicieux, -cieuse [pɛrnisjø, -sjøz] *adj* : pernicious — **pernicieusement** [-sjøzmɑ̃] *adv*

péroné [perɔne] *nm* : fibula

pérorer [perɔre] *vi* : to declaim, to hold forth

peroxyde [pɛrɔksid] *nm* : peroxide <peroxyde d'hydrogène : hydrogen peroxide>

perpendiculaire [pɛrpɑ̃dikylɛr] *adj* : perpendicular — **perpendiculairement** [-lɛrmɑ̃] *adv*

perpétration [pɛrpetrasjɔ̃] *nf* : perpetration (of a crime, etc.)

perpétrer [pɛrpetre] {87} *vt* : to perpetrate

perpétuel, -tuelle [pɛrpetɥɛl] *adj* **1** : perpetual **2** : permanent, for life

perpétuellement [pɛrpetɥɛlmɑ̃] *adv* : constantly, perpetually

perpétuer [pɛrpetɥe] *vt* ÉTERNISER : to perpetuate

perpétuité [pɛrpetɥite] *nf* **à ~** : for life

perplexe [pɛrplɛks] *adj* : perplexed, puzzled

perplexité [pɛrplɛksite] *nf* : perplexity, bafflement

perquisition [pɛrkizisjɔ̃] *nf* : (police) search

perquisitionner [pɛrkizisjɔne] *vi* : to carry out a search

perron [perɔ̃] *nm* **1** : (front) steps **2** *Can* GALERIE : porch

perroquet [perɔkɛ] *nm* : parrot

perruche [peryʃ] *nf* : parakeet

perruque [peryk] *nf* : wig

pers [pɛr] *adj* : bluish green

persan[1], -sane [pɛrsɑ̃, -san] *adj* : Persian

persan[2] *nm* : Persian (language)

Persan, -sane *n* : Persian

persécuter [pɛrsekyte] *vt* **1** MARTYRISER : to persecute, to torment **2** HARCELER : to harass

persécuteur, -trice [pɛrsekytœr, -tris] *n* : persecutor, tormentor

persécution [pɛrsekysjɔ̃] *nf* : persecution

persévérance [pɛrseverɑ̃s] *nf* : perseverance

persévérant, -rante [pɛrseverɑ̃, -rɑ̃t] *adj* : persevering, persistent

persévérer [pɛrsevere] {87} *vi* : to persevere, to persist

persienne [pɛrsjɛn] *nf* : shutter

persiflage [pɛrsiflaʒ] *nm* : mockery

persil [pɛrsi] *nm* : parsley

persistance [pɛrsistɑ̃s] *nf* : persistence

persistant, -tante [pɛrsistɑ̃, -tɑ̃t] *adj* : persistent — **persistance** [-tɑ̃s] *nf*

persister [pɛrsiste] *vi* **1** PERSÉVÉRER : to persist, to persevere **2** : to continue, to last

personnage [pɛrsɔnaʒ] *nm* **1** : (fictional) character **2** : character, individual **3** : influential person, celebrity

personnaliser [pɛrsɔnalize] *vt* : to personalize

personnalité [pɛrsɔnalite] *nf* **1** : personality <une personnalité forte : a strong personality> **2** : celebrity

personne[1] [pɛrsɔn] *nf* **1** : person <quelques personnes : a few people> <la personne : the individual> **2** : self, (bodily) person <être bien de sa personne : to be good-looking> <content de sa (petite) personne : pleased with oneself> <en personne : in person> **3** : person (in grammar)

personne[2] *pron* **1** (*in negative constructions*) : no one, nobody <je n'ai vu personne : I didn't see anyone> <personne ne dit ça : nobody says that> **2** : anyone, anybody <mieux que personne : better than anybody> <presque personne : hardly anyone>

personnel[1], -nelle [pɛrsɔnɛl] *adj* **1** : personal, private **2** : selfish, self-centered **3** : personal (in grammar)

personnel[2] *nm* : personnel, staff

personnellement [pɛrsɔnɛlmɑ̃] *adv* : personally, in person

personne–ressource [pɛrsɔnrəsurs] *nf Can, pl* **personnes–ressources** : specialist, expert

personnifier [pɛrsɔnifje] {96} *vt* : to personify — **personnification** [-nifikasjɔ̃] *nf*

perspective [pɛrspɛktiv] *nf* **1** : perspective (in art) **2** : view **3** : point of view, viewpoint **4** : outlook, prospect <en perspective : in prospect, in the offing>

perspicace [pɛrspikas] *adj* : perspicacious, insightful, perceptive

perspicacité [pɛrspikasite] *nf* : insight, perspicacity

persuader [pɛrsɥade] *vt* CONVAINCRE : to persuade, to convince — **se persuader** *vr*

persuasif, -sive [pɛrswazif, -ziv] *adj* : persuasive

persuasion [pɛrsɥazjɔ̃] *nf* : persuasion

perte [pɛrt] *nf* **1** : loss **2** : waste **3** : disaster, ruin **4 à perte de vue** : as far as the eye can see **5 pertes** *nfpl* : losses

pertinemment [pɛrtinamɑ̃] *adv* : to the point <savoir pertinemment : to know full well>

pertinence [pɛrtinɑ̃s] *nf* : pertinence, relevance

pertinent, -nente [pɛrtinɑ̃, -nɑ̃t] *adj* : pertinent, relevant

perturbateur[1], -trice [pɛrtyrbatœr, -tris] *adj* : disruptive

perturbateur[2], -trice *n* : troublemaker

perturber [pɛrtyrbe] *vt* **1** : to disrupt **2** DÉRANGER : to disturb, to upset

péruvien, -vienne [peryvjɛ̃, -vjɛn] *adj* : Peruvian

Péruvien, -vienne *n* : Peruvian

pervenche [pɛrvɑ̃ʃ] *nf* : periwinkle (plant)

pervers[1], **-verse** [pɛrvɛr, -vɛrs] *adj* : perverted, depraved

pervers[2], **-verse** *n* : pervert

perversion [pɛrvɛrsjɔ̃] *nf* : perversion

perversité [pɛrvɛrsite] *nf* : perversity

pervertir [pɛrvɛrtir] *vt* CORROMPRE : to pervert, to corrupt

pesage [pəzaʒ] *nm* : weighing

pesamment [pəzamɑ̃] *adv* LOURDEMENT : heavily

pesant, -sante [pəzɑ̃, -zɑ̃t] *adj* **1** : heavy **2** : burdensome, oppressive **3** : unwieldy, ungainly

pesanteur [pəzɑ̃tœr] *nf* **1** : gravity **2** : heaviness, weight

pesée [pəze] *nf* **1** : weighing **2** : weight **3** : force

pèse–personne [pɛzpɛrsɔn] *nm, pl* **pèse–personnes** : (bathroom) scales *pl*

peser [pəze] {52} *vt* **1** : to weigh **2** EXAMINER : to consider — *vi* **1** : to weigh <combien pèses-tu? : how much do you weigh?> <peser lourd : to be heavy> **2** INFLUER : to carry weight, to have bearing **3 ~ sur** : to press, to pressure, to weigh on

pessimisme [pesimism] *nm* : pessimism

pessimiste[1] [pesimist] *adj* : pessimistic

pessimiste[2] *nmf* : pessimist

peso [pezo, peso] *nm* : peso

peste [pɛst] *nf* **1** : plague, pestilence **2** : pest, nuisance

pester [pɛste] *vi* **~ contre** : to curse

pesticide [pɛstisid] *nm* : pesticide

pestilence [pɛstilɑ̃s] *nf* : stench

pestilentiel, -tielle [pɛstilɑ̃sjɛl] *adj* FÉTIDE : foul, fetid

pétale [petal] *nm* : petal

pétanque [petɑ̃k] *nf* : petanque (game of bowls)

pétant, -tante [petɑ̃, -tɑ̃t] *adj fam* : sharp, on the dot <à neuf heures pétantes : at nine o'clock sharp>

pétarade [petarad] *nf* : backfiring

pétarader [petarade] *vi* : to backfire

pétard [petar] *nm* **1** : firecracker **2 être en pétard** *fam* : to be fuming

péter [pete] {87} *vi fam* **1** : to go off, to explode **2** : to bust, to break — *vt fam* **1** : to bust, to break **2 péter le feu** : to be full of energy

pétillant, -lante [petijɑ̃, -jɑ̃t] *adj* **1** : sparkling **2** : bubbly

pétillement [petijmɑ̃] *nm* **1** : fizziness, fizz **2** : crackling **3** : sparkle (of the eyes, etc.)

pétiller [petije] *vi* **1** : to sparkle **2** : to bubble, to fizz **3** : to crackle (of fire)

petit[1] [p(ə)ti] *adv* **1 tailler petit** : to run small **2 voir petit** : to underestimate **3 petit à petit** : gradually, little by little

petit[2], **-tite** [p(ə)ti, -tit] *adj* **1** : small, little **2** COURT : short **3** : young <ma petite sœur : my little sister> **4** (*used in terms of affection*) <mon petit chéri : my sweetie> **5** : minor, insignificant, slight **6 petit ami, petite amie** : boyfriend, girlfriend **7 petit déjeuner** : breakfast **8 petit doigt** : little finger **9 petite monnaie** : small change **10 petit pois** : (green) pea **11 petite vérole** : smallpox

petit[3], **-tite** *n* : child, little boy *m*, little girl *f*

petit[4] *nm* : cub (of an animal)

petitement [p(ə)titmɑ̃] *adv* **1** : poorly, humbly <petitement logé : living in cramped quarters> **2** : pettily

petitesse [p(ə)titɛs] *nf* **1** : smallness **2** MESQUINERIE : pettiness

petit–fils, petite–fille [p(ə)tifis, p(ə)titfij] *n* : grandson *m*, granddaughter *f*

pétition [petisjɔ̃] *nf* : petition

pétitionnaire [petisjɔnɛr] *nmf* : petitioner

pétitionner [petisjɔne] *vi* : to petition

petit–lait [p(ə)tilɛ] *nm, pl* **petits–laits** : whey

petits–enfants [p(ə)tizɑ̃fɑ̃] *nmpl* : grandchildren

pétrification [petrifikasjɔ̃] *nf* : petrification

pétrifier [petrifje] {96} *vt* : to petrify

pétrin [petrɛ̃] *nm fam* : fix, jam

pétrir [petrir] *vt* : to knead

pétrole [petrɔl] *nm* **1** : oil, petroleum **2** *or* **pétrole lampant** : kerosene

pétrolier[1], **-lière** [petrɔlje, -ljɛr] *adj* : oil, petroleum <industrie pétrolière : oil industry>

pétrolier[2] *nm* **1** : oil tanker **2** : oilman

pétulance [petylɑ̃s] *nf* EXUBÉRANCE : vivacity, exuberance

pétulant, -lante [petylɑ̃, -lɑ̃t] *adj* EXUBÉRANT : vivacious, exuberant

pétunia [petynja] *nm* : petunia

peu[1] [pø] *adv* **1** : little, not much <elle a dormi peu : she slept little> **2** : not very <peu connu : little known> **3** : shortly <peu après : not long after>

peu[2] *nm* **1** : lack <peu d'appétit : lack of appetite> **2** : little, bit <attends un peu : wait a little (longer)> <un peu moins de gens : somewhat fewer people> **3 le peu de** : the few, the little <le peu d'argent que j'ai mis de côté : the little money I've saved up> **4 peu à peu** : little by little **5 pour un peu** : almost, very nearly

peu[3] *pron* **1** : few (people) <peu lui font confiance : few trust him> **2 ~ de** : few, little <peu de mots : few words> <c'est peu de chose : it's just a little, it's not much>

peuplade [pøplad] *nf* : (small) tribe

peuple [pøpl] *nm* **1** : people *pl*, nation <le peuple anglais : the English people> **2** : common people *pl*, masses *pl* <un homme du peuple : a man of the people> **3** FOULE : crowd, multitude

peuplé, -lée [pœple] *adj* : populated

peuplement [pœpləmɑ̃] *nm* **1** : populating **2** : population

peupler [pœple] *vt* **1** : to populate, to stock, to plant **2** HABITER : to inhabit **3** : to occupy, to fill — **se peupler** *vr* : to become populated
peuplier [pøplije] *nm* : poplar
peur [pœr] *nf* **1** : fear **2 de peur que** : lest **3 faire peur à** : to frighten
peureusement [pœrøzmɑ̃] *adv* : fearfully
peureux, -reuse [pœrø, -røz] *adj* CRAINTIF : fearful, afraid
peut [pø], *etc.* → **pouvoir**
peut–être [pøtɛtr] *adv* : perhaps, maybe
phalange [falɑ̃ʒ] *nf* : phalanx
phallique [falik] *adj* : phallic
phallus [falys] *nms & pl* : phallus
pharaon [faraɔ̃] *nm* : pharaoh
phare [far] *nm* **1** : lighthouse **2** : headlight **3** : beacon
pharmaceutique [farmasøtik] *adj* : pharmaceutical
pharmacie [farmasi] *nf* : pharmacy, drugstore
pharmacien, -cienne [farmasjɛ̃, -sjɛn] *n* : pharmacist
pharmacologie [farmakɔlɔʒi] *nf* : pharmacology
pharynx [farɛ̃ks] *nm* : pharynx
phase [faz] *nf* : phase, stage
phénix [feniks] *nm* **1** : phoenix **2** : paragon
phénoménal, -nale [fenɔmenal] *adj, mpl* **-naux** [-no] : phenomenal — **phénoménalement** [-nalmɑ̃] *adv*
phénomène [fenɔmɛn] *nm* **1** : phenomenon **2** : freak (in a circus, etc.)
philanthrope [filɑ̃trɔp] *nmf* : philanthropist
philanthropie [filɑ̃trɔpi] *nf* : philanthropy — **philanthropique** [-trɔpik] *adj*
philatélie [filateli] *nf* : stamp collecting, philately
philippin, -pine [filipɛ̃, -pin] *adj* : Filipino, Philippine
Philippin, -pine *n* : Filipino
philistin[1], -tine [filistɛ̃, -tin] *adj* : philistine
philistin[2] *nm* : philistine
philodendron [filɔdɛ̃drɔ̃] *nm* : philodendron
philosophe[1] [filɔzɔf] *adj* : philosophical
philosophe[2] *nmf* : philosopher
philosopher [filɔzɔfe] *vi* : to philosophize
philosophie [filɔzɔfi] *nf* : philosophy
philosophique [filɔzɔfik] *adj* : philosophical — **philosophiquement** [-fikmɑ̃] *adv*
phlébite [flebit] *nf* : phlebitis
phlox [flɔks] *nms & pl* : phlox
phobie [fɔbi] *nf* : phobia
phonème [fɔnɛm] *nm* : phoneme
phonétique[1] [fɔnetik] *adj* : phonetic
phonétique[2] *nf* : phonetics
phonograph [fɔnɔgraf] *nm* : phonograph
phoque [fɔk] *nm* **1** : seal **2** : sealskin
phosphate [fɔsfat] *nm* : phosphate
phosphore [fɔsfɔr] *nm* : phosphorous
phosphorescence [fɔsfɔresɑ̃s] *nf* : phosphorescence — **phosphorescent, -cente** [-resɑ̃, -sɑ̃t] *adj*
photo [fɔto] *nf* : photo <photo d'identité : passport photo>
photocopie [fɔtɔkɔpi] *nf* **1** : photocopy **2** : photocopying
photocopier [fɔtɔkɔpje] {96} *vt* : to photocopy
photocopieur [fɔtɔkɔpjœr] *nm* : photocopier
photocopieuse [fɔtɔkɔpjøz] *nf* → **photocopieur**
photoélectrique [fɔtɔelɛktrik] *adj* : photoelectric
photogénique [fɔtɔʒenik] *adj* : photogenic
photographe [fɔtɔgraf] *nmf* : photographer
photographie [fɔtɔgrafi] *nf* **1** : photography **2** : photograph
photographier [fɔtɔgrafje] {96} *vt* : to photograph
photographique [fɔtɔgrafik] *adj* : photographic — **photographiquement** [-fikmɑ̃] *adv*
photosynthèse [fɔtosɛ̃tɛz] *nf* : photosynthesis
phrase [fraz] *nf* **1** : sentence **2** : phrase
phraséologie [frazeɔlɔʒi] *nf* **1** : phraseology **2** : verbiage, verbosity
phylum [filɔm] *nm* : phylum
physicien, -cienne [fizisjɛ̃, -sjɛn] *n* : physicist
physiologie [fizjɔlɔʒi] *nf* : physiology
physiologique [fizjɔlɔʒik] *adj* : physiological, physiologic
physiologiste [fizjɔlɔʒist] *nmf* : physiologist
physionomie [fizjɔnɔmi] *nf* : physiognomy
physiothérapie [fizjɔterapi] *nf* : physiotherapy, physical therapy
physique[1] [fizik] *adj* : physical — **physiquement** [-zikmɑ̃] *adv*
physique[2] *nm* : physique
physique[3] *nf* : physics
pi [pi] *nm* : pi
piaffer [pjafe] *vi* : to stamp one's feet, to tap one's foot
piailler [pjaje] *vi* : to squawk, to chirp
pianiste [pjanist] *nmf* : pianist
piano [pjano] *nm* : piano <piano à queue : grand piano>
pianoter [pjanɔte] *vi* **1** : to tinkle away (at the piano) **2** : to tap, to drum (one's fingers)
piastre [pjastr] *nf Can fam* : dollar, buck
piaule [pjol] *nf fam* : room, pad
piaulement [pjolmɑ̃] *nm* : cheep, peep
piauler [pjole] *vi* **1** : to cheep, to peep **2** *fam* : to whimper, to whine

pic [pik] *nm* **1** : woodpecker **2** CIME : peak <à pic : straight down, vertically> **3** : pick, pickax <pic à glace : ice pick>

pic–bois [pikbwa] *nm Can, pl* **pic–bois** : woodpecker

piccolo *or* **picolo** [pikɔlo] *nm* : piccolo

pichet [piʃɛ] *nm* **1** : pitcher **2** : pitcherful

pichou [piʃu] *nm Can fam* : slipper, (baby's) bootee

pickpocket [pikpɔkɛt] *nm* : pickpocket

pick–up [pikœp] *nm* : pickup (truck)

picoler [pikɔle] *vi fam* : to tipple, to drink

picorer [pikɔre] *v* : to peck

picot [piko] *nm Can* : polka dot

picotement [pikɔtmɑ̃] *nm* : prickling, stinging, tingling

picoter [pikɔte] *vt* **1** PICORER : to peck **2** : to sting — *vi* : to prickle, to sting

picotin [pikɔtɛ̃] *nm* : peck

pictural, -rale [piktyral] *adj, mpl* **-raux** [-ro] : pictorial

pie[1] [pi] *adj* : piebald, pied

pie[2] [pi] *nf* **1** : magpie **2** *fam* : chatterbox

pièce [pjɛs] *nf* **1** : piece, bit <mettre en pièces : to smash to pieces> **2** : piece, item <la pièce : apiece> <pièce de collection : collector's item> <pièce à conviction : exhibit (in a court of law)> **3** : room, bedroom **4** : paper, document <pièce jointe : enclosure> **5** : piece (in music or theater) <pièce de théâtre : play> **6** *or* **pièce de monnaie** : coin

pied [pje] *nm* **1** : foot <coup de pied : kick> <à pied : on foot> <pied à pied : inch by inch> **2** : base, bottom, leg (of a table, etc.) **3** : foot (in measurement) **4** : stalk, bunch, head <pied de salade : head of lettuce> **5 mettre sur pied** : to set up, to get off the ground

piédestal [pjedɛstal] *nm, pl* **-taux** [-to] : pedestal

piège [pjɛʒ] *nm* **1** : trap, snare **2** : snag, pitfall **3 prendre au piège** : to entrap

piéger [pjeʒe] {64} *vt* **1** : to trap **2** : to booby-trap

pie–grièche [pigrijɛʃ] *nf, pl* **pies–grièches** : shrike

pierre [pjɛr] *nf* **1** : stone **2 pierre à aiguiser** : whetstone **3 pierre angulaire** : cornerstone **4 pierre tombale** : tombstone, gravestone, headstone

pierreries [pjɛrri] *nfpl* : precious stones, gems

pierreux, -reuse [pjɛrø, -røz] *adj* : stony

piété [pjete] *nf* : piety

piétiner [pjetine] *vt* : to trample on, to crush underfoot — *vi* **1** : to stamp one's feet (with impatience, etc.) **2** STAGNER : to make no headway

piéton, -tonne [pjetɔ̃, -tɔn] *n* : pedestrian

piétonnier, -nière [pjetɔnje, -njɛr] *adj* : pedestrian

piètre [pjɛtr] *adj* : very poor, sorry <piètre consolation : cold comfort> <une piètre figure : a sorry figure>

pieu [pjø] *nm, pl* **pieux** : post, stake

pieuvre [pjøvr] *nf* POULPE : octopus

pieux, pieuse [pjø, pjøz] *adj* : pious — **pieusement** [pjøzmɑ̃] *adv*

pige [piʒ] *nf* **travailler à la pige** *or* **faire des piges** : to work freelance

pigeon [piʒɔ̃] *nm* : pigeon

pigeonneau [piʒɔno] *nm* : squab

pigeonnier [piʒɔnje] *nm* : pigeon house, dovecote

piger [piʒe] {17} *vt* **1** *fam* : to understand, to catch on to <tu piges? : get it?> **2** *Can* : to pick (a card, a number, etc.)

pigiste [piʒist] *nmf* : freelancer

pigment [pigmɑ̃] *nm* : pigment — **pigmentation** [-mɑ̃tasjɔ̃] *nf*

pignon [piɲɔ̃] *nm* **1** : gable **2** : cogwheel

pilaf [pilaf] *nm* : pilaf

pile[1] [pil] *adv fam* **1** : abruptly <arrêter pile : to stop dead> **2** : exactly <à dix heures pile : at ten o'clock sharp>

pile[2] *nf* **1** : pile, heap **2** : (storage) battery **3** : pier (of a bridge) **4** : reverse (of a coin) <pile ou face? : heads or tails?>

piler [pile] *vt* **1** BROYER : to crush, to pound **2** *fam* : to clobber, to defeat **3** *Can* : to mash (potatoes, etc.) — *vi* **1** *Can fam* : to walk, to step <j'ai pilé dans une flaque d'eau : I walked into a puddle> **2** *France fam* : to slam on the brakes

pilier [pilje] *nm* **1** : pillar, column **2** SOUTIEN : prop, mainstay

pillage [pijaʒ] *nm* : looting, pillaging

pillard, -larde [pijar, -jard] *n* : looter

piller [pije] *vt* : to loot, to pillage, to plunder

pilleur, -leuse [pilœr, -løz] *n* : pillager, looter

pilon [pilɔ̃] *nm* **1** : pestle **2** : wooden leg **3** : (chicken) drumstick

pilonner [pilɔne] *vt* **1** : to crush **2** : to bombard, to shell

pilori [pilɔri] *nm* : stocks *pl,* pillory

pilosité [pilozite] *nf* : hairiness

pilotage [pilɔtaʒ] *nm* : piloting, flying

pilote[1] [pilɔt] *adj* : pilot, test <projet pilote : pilot project>

pilote[2] *nm* **1** : pilot <pilote de ligne : airline pilot> **2** GUIDE : guide **3 pilote de course** : racing-car driver

piloter [pilɔte] *vt* **1** : to pilot, to fly, to drive **2** : to guide, to direct

pilotis [pilɔti] *nm* : stilts *pl,* piling

pilule [pilyl] *nf* : pill

piment [pimɑ̃] *nm* **1** : pepper <piment rouge : chili pepper> <piment de la Jamaïque : allspice> <piment doux : pimiento> **2** : piquancy, spice

pimenter [pimɑ̃te] *vt* **1** : to season with red pepper **2** : to spice up

pimpant, -pante [pɛ̃pɑ̃] *adj* : spruce, dapper
pin [pɛ̃] *nm* : pine (tree or wood)
pinacle [pinakl] *nm* **1** : pinnacle, summit **2 porter qqn au pinacle** : to praise s.o. to the skies
pinailler [pinaje] *vi fam* : to split hairs, to quibble
pinard [pinar] *nm fam* : (cheap) wine
pince [pɛ̃s] *nf* **1** : pliers *pl* **2** : tongs *pl* **3** : pincer, claw **4** : pleat, fold **5 pince à cheveux** : bobby pin **6 pince à épiler** : tweezers *pl* **7 pince à linge** : clothespin
pincé, -cée [pɛ̃se] *adj* : forced, stiff
pinceau [pɛ̃so] *nm, pl* **pinceaux** : paintbrush
pincée [pɛ̃se] *nf* : pinch <une pincée de sel : a pinch of salt>
pincement [pɛ̃smɑ̃] *nm* **1** : pinch **2** : twinge, pang
pince–monseigneur [pɛ̃smɔ̃sɛɲœr] *nf, pl* **pinces–monseigneur** : crowbar, jimmy
pincer [pɛ̃se] {6} *vt* **1** : to pinch **2** : to nip at, to sting (of wind, cold, etc.) **3** : to purse (one's lips) **4** : to pluck (a stringed instrument) **5** *fam* : to nab — *vi* : to be nippy (of weather) — **se pincer** *vr* **1** : to pinch oneself <se pincer le nez : to hold one's nose> **2** : to get caught, to be pinched <je me suis pincé le doigt dans la porte : I caught my finger in the door>
pince–sans–rire [pɛ̃ssɑ̃rir] *adj s & pl* : deadpan
pincettes [pɛ̃sɛt] *nfpl* **1** : small tweezers **2** : (fire) tongs
pinçon [pɛ̃sɔ̃] *nm* : pinch mark
pinède [pinɛd] *nf* : pine forest
pingouin [pɛ̃gwɛ̃] *nm* : auk
pingre [pɛ̃gr] *adj* AVARE : niggardly, stingy
pingrerie [pɛ̃grəri] *nf* : meanness, stinginess
pinotte [pinɔt] *nf Can fam* : peanut
pintade [pɛ̃tad] *nf* : guinea fowl
pinte [pɛ̃t] *nf* : pint
pioche [pjɔʃ] *nf* : pickax, pick
piocher [pjɔʃe] *vt* **1** CREUSER : to dig (up) **2** : to draw (a card) **3** *fam* : to cram for (an exam)
piolet [pjɔlɛ] *nm* : ice ax
pion[1], pionne [pjɔ̃, pjɔn] *n France fam* : student monitor
pion[2] *nm* **1** : pawn (in chess) **2** : piece (in checkers)
pionnier, -nière [pjɔnje, -njɛr] *n* : pioneer
pipe [pip] *nf* : pipe <fumer la pipe : to smoke a pipe>
pipeau [pipo] *nm, pl* **pipeaux** : (reed) pipe, flute
pipeline [pajplajn] *nm* : pipeline
piper [pipe] *vi* **ne pas piper (mot)** : to keep mum
piquant[1], -quante [pikɑ̃, -kɑ̃t] *adj* **1** : prickly, bristly **2** ÉPICÉ : hot, spicy **3** : sharp, biting **4** : racy, spicy
piquant[2] *nm* **1** : spiciness, piquancy **2** : prickle, thorn, barb **3** : spine, quill (of a porcupine, etc.)
pique[1] [pik] *nm* : spade (in playing cards)
pique[2] *nf* **1** : pike (weapon) **2** POINTE : cutting remark
piqué[1], -quée [pike] *adj* **1** : quilted **2** : sour, mildewed **3** : staccato (in music)
piqué[2] *nm* **1** : piqué (fabric) **2** : nosedive
pique–assiette [pikasjɛt] *nmfs & pl* : freeloader, sponger
pique–feu [pikfø] *nms & pl* TISONNIER : poker
pique–nique [piknik] *nm, pl* **pique–niques** : picnic
pique–niquer [piknike] *vi* : to have a picnic
piquer [pike] *vt* **1** : to prick, to puncture **2** : to give an injection to, to vaccinate **3** : to sting, to bite **4** : to stick (on), to pin (up) **5** : to make holes in **6** : to stitch **7** : to prickle, to tickle **8** : to needle, to irritate **9** ÉVEILLER : to arouse, to stimulate (interest, etc.) **10** *fam* : to pinch, to swipe **11** *fam* : to nab, to catch **12 piquer un somme** : to take a nap — *vi* **1** : to be prickly **2** : to sting, to burn **3** : to dive, to swoop down — **se piquer** *vr* **1** : to prick oneself, to inject oneself **2** : to get mildewed, to turn sour **3 ~ de** : to pride oneself on
piquet [pikɛ] *nm* **1** : post, stake **2** : peg **3 piquet de grève** : picket line
piqueter [pikte] {8} *vt* **1** : to stake out **2** : to mark, to dot — *vi Can* : to picket
piqueteur, -teuse [piktœr, -tøz] *n Can* : picketer, striker
piquette [pikɛt] *nf* : (cheap) wine
piqûre [pikyr] *nf* **1** : prick **2** : sting, bite **3** : injection, shot **4** : small hole, pitting **5** : stitch (in sewing)
piranha [pirana] *nm* : piranha
piratage [piratаʒ] *nm* : piracy (of software, etc.)
pirate [pirat] *nm* **1** : pirate **2** : crook, swindler **3 pirate de l'air** : hijacker
pirater [pirate] *vt* : to pirate
piraterie [piratri] *nf* **1** : piracy **2 piraterie aérienne** : hijacking
pire[1] [pir] *adj* **1** : worse <pire que jamais : worse than ever> **2 le pire, la pire, les pires** : the worst <le pire jour de ma vie : the worst day of my life> **3 pas tant pire** *Can* : not too bad, OK
pire[2] *nm* **1 le pire** : the worst **2 au pire** : at the worst
pirogue [pirɔg] *nf* : dugout (canoe)
pirouette [pirwɛt] *nf* : pirouette
pis[1] [pi] *adv* **1** : worse <de mal en pis : from bad to worse> **2 au pis aller**

: if worst comes to worst **3 tant pis** : too bad

pis[2] *adj* : worse

pis[3] *nms & pl* **1** : udder **2 le pis** : the worst

pis–aller |pizale| *nms & pl* : last resort, stopgap

piscine |pisin| *nf* : swimming pool

pissenlit |pisɑ̃li| *nm* : dandelion

pistache |pistaʃ| *nf* : pistachio

piste |pist| *nf* **1** TRACE : track, trail <sur la bonne piste : on the right track> **2** : trail, slope <piste de ski : ski slope> **3** : racetrack **4** INDICE : lead, clue **5** : path, route, course <piste cyclable : bike path> **6** *or* **piste d'atterrissage** : runway, airstrip **7 piste sonore** : soundtrack

pistil |pistil| *nm* : pistil

pistolet |pistɔlɛ| *nm* **1** : pistol, handgun **2** : spray gun

piston |pistɔ̃| *nm* **1** : piston **2** : valve (in a musical instrument)

pistonner |pistɔne| *vt fam* : to pull strings for

pitance |pitɑ̃s| *nf* : ration, sustenance

piteusement |pitøzmɑ̃| *adv* : pathetically, pitifully

piteux, -teuse |pitø, -tøz| *adj* : pitiful, miserable <un état piteux : a sorry state>

pitié |pitje| *nf* COMPASSION : pity, mercy

piton |pitɔ̃| *nm* **1** : hook **2** : piton **3** : peak (of a mountain) **4** *Can fam* : button, switch

pitonner |pitɔne| *vi Can fam* : to push a button, to flip a switch, to zap (with a remote control)

pitoyable |pitwajabl| *adj* : pitiful, pathetic — **pitoyablement** |-jabləmɑ̃| *adv*

pitre |pitr| *nm* CLOWN : clown, buffoon

pittoresque |pitɔrɛsk| *adj* : picturesque

pituitaire |pitɥitɛr| *adj* : pituitary <glande pituitaire : pituitary gland>

pivoine |pivwan| *nf* : peony

pivot |pivo| *nm* : pivot

pivoter |pivɔte| *vi* : to pivot, to revolve, to swivel

pizza |pidza| *nf* : pizza

pizzeria |pidzerja| *nf* : pizzeria

placage |plakaʒ| *nm* **1** : veneer **2** : (metal) plating **3** : tackle (in football)

placard |plakar| *nm* **1** : cupboard, closet **2** AFFICHE : poster, placard

placarder |plakarde| *vt* : to post, to put up (posters, notices, etc.)

place |plas| *nf* **1** : place, spot <chaque chose à sa place : everything in its place> <mets-les à leur place : put them where they belong> **2** : room, space <prendre de la place : to take up space> <il n'y a pas de place : there's no room> **3** : seat <louer des places au théâtre : to book seats at the theater> **4** : rank, position <prendre la première place : to take first place> **5** : placing, position, situation <à la place de : instead of, in place of> <se mettre en place : to be set up, to position oneself> **6** : (public) square **7** : job, position **8** : (financial) market **9 de place en place** : here and there

placebo |plasebo| *nm* : placebo

placement |plasmɑ̃| *nm* **1** : investment **2** : placement <bureau de placement : placement agency> **3** : field goal

placenta |plasɛ̃ta| *nm* : placenta

placer |plase| {6} *vt* **1** : to place, to set, to put **2** : to put in, to slip in, to interject <je n'ai pas pu placer un seul mot : I couldn't get a word in edgewise> **3** : to seat (someone) **4** : to sell, to place (a product) **5** : to invest **6** : to place, to find a job for — **se placer** *vr* **1** : to position oneself **2** : to rank **3** : to get a job

placeur, -ceuse |plasœr, -søz| *n* : usher (in a theater)

placide |plasid| *adj* : placid, calm — **placidement** |-sidmɑ̃| *adv*

placier, -cière |plasje, -sjɛr| *n* : traveling salesman

placoter |plakɔte| *vi Can fam* : to chat, to chitchat — *vt Can fam* : to divulge, to disclose

plafond |plafɔ̃| *nm* : ceiling

plafonner |plafɔne| *vt* : to put a ceiling in — *vi* : to reach a maximum

plafonnier |plafɔnje| *nm* : ceiling light

plage |plaʒ| *nf* **1** : beach, shore **2** : seaside resort **3 plage horaire** : time slot

plagiaire |plaʒjɛr| *nmf* : plagiarist

plagiat |plaʒja| *nm* : plagiarism

plagier |plaʒje| {96} *vt* : to plagiarize

plaider |plede| *vi* : to plead, to litigate — *vt* : to plead (a case)

plaideur, -deuse |plɛdœr, -døz| *n* : litigant

plaie |plɛ| *nf* **1** BLESSURE : wound, cut, sore **2** : scourge, plague **3** *fam* : pest

plaignait |plɛɲɛ|, *etc.* → **plaindre**

plaignard, -gnarde |plɛɲar, -ɲard| *n Can* : complainer, grouch

plaignant, -gnante |plɛɲɑ̃, -ɲɑ̃t| *n* : plaintiff

plaigne |plɛɲ|, *etc.* → **plaindre**

plain |plɛ̃| *nm* : high tide

plaindre |plɛ̃dr| {65} *vt* : to pity, to feel sorry for — **se plaindre** *vr* **1** : to complain, to moan **2** : to protest

plaine |plɛn| *nf* : plain, lowland

plain–pied |plɛ̃pje| *adj* **1 de ~** : on the same level <une maison de plain-pied : a single-story house> **2 être de plain–pied avec** : to be at ease with, to be on an equal footing with

plainte |plɛ̃t| *nf* **1** : complaint **2** : moan, groan

plaintif, -tive |plɛ̃tif, -tiv| *adj* : plaintive — **plaintivement** |-tivmɑ̃| *adv*

plaire |plɛr| {66} *vi* **1** : to be attractive, to be pleasing **2 ~ à** : to please, to suit — *v impers* : to please <ce qu'il

vous plaît : whatever you like> <s'il vous plaît : please> — **se plaire** *vr* **1** : to like oneself **2** : to like each other **3** ~ **à** : to enjoy

plaisait [plɛzɛ], **plaisions** [plɛzjɔ̃], *etc.* → **plaire**

plaisamment [plɛzamɑ̃] *adv* **1** : pleasantly **2** DRÔLEMENT : amusingly

plaisance [plɛzɑ̃s] *nf or* **navigation de plaisance** : sailing, boating

plaisancier, -cière [plɛzɑ̃sje, -sjɛr] *n* : amateur sailor, boating enthusiast

plaisant[1], **-sante** [plɛzɑ̃, -zɑ̃t] *adj* **1** AGRÉABLE : pleasant **2** AMUSANT : amusing, funny

plaisant[2] *nm* **mauvais plaisant** : practical joker

plaisanter [plɛzɑ̃te] *vi* : to joke, to jest — *vt* : to tease, to make fun of

plaisanterie [plɛzɑ̃tri] *nf* **1** BLAGUE : joke, jest **2** FARCE : prank

plaisantin [plɛzɑ̃tɛ̃] *nm* FARCEUR : practical joker

plaise [plɛz], *etc.* → **plaire**

plaisir [plezir] *nm* **1** : pleasure <avec plaisir! : with pleasure> <faire plaisir à : to please> **2 au plaisir** : see you soon **3 avec plaisir!** : of course!

plan[1], **plane** [plɑ̃, plan] *adj* PLAT : flat, level, plane

plan[2] *nm* **1** : plane **2** : plan, strategy, program **3** : map, diagram, blueprint **4** : outline, synopsis **5 laisser en plan** : to leave in the lurch **6 premier plan** : foreground

planche[1] [plɑ̃ʃ] *adj Can* : flat, even

planche[2] *nf* **1** : board, plank <planche à repasser : ironing board> **2** : plate (in engraving) **3** : plate, illustration (in a book) **4 planche à roulettes** : skateboard **5 les planches** : the stage

plancher [plɑ̃ʃe] *nm* **1** : floor **2** : minimum, lower limit

plancton [plɑ̃ktɔ̃] *nm* : plankton

planer [plane] *vi* **1** : to glide, to soar, to hover **2** ~ **sur** : to hang over, to hover over **3 avoir l'air de planer** : to be above it all, to appear distracted

planétaire [planetɛr] *adj* **1** : planetary **2** MONDIAL : global, worldwide

planétarium [planetarjɔm] *nm* : planetarium

planète [planɛt] *nf* : planet

planification [planifikasjɔ̃] *nf* : planning

planifier [planifje] {96} *vt* : to plan

planning [planiŋ] *nm* : planning <planning familial : family planning>

planque [plɑ̃k] *nf fam* **1** : hideout **2** : easy job

planquer [plɑ̃ke] *vt fam* : to hide away, to stash

plant [plɑ̃] *nm* **1** : patch, bed **2** : seedling, young plant

plantain [plɑ̃tɛ̃] *nm* : plantain

plantation [plɑ̃tasjɔ̃] *nf* **1** : planting **2** : plantation

plante [plɑ̃t] *nf* **1** : sole (of the foot) **2** : plant <plante grimpante : climbing plant>

planté, -tée [plɑ̃te] *adj* **1** : positioned, placed <dents mal plantées : uneven teeth> **2** *fam* : standing, rooted (to the spot) **3 bien planté** : sturdy, robust (of a child)

planter [plɑ̃te] *vt* **1** : to plant **2** : to stick in, to drive in **3** : to set, to set up **4** *fam* : to ditch, to drop — **se planter** *vr* **1** : to become embedded **2** *fam* : to stand, to plant oneself **3** *fam* : to crash, to smash **4** *fam* : to get it wrong, to mess up

planteur, -teuse [plɑ̃tœr, -tøz] *n* : planter

planton [plɑ̃tɔ̃] *nm* : orderly (in the military)

plantureux, -reuse [plɑ̃tyrø, -røz] *adj* **1** : copious, lavish <un repas plantureux : a lavish repast> **2** : buxom

plaque [plak] *nf* **1** : plate, sheet <plaques de glace : patches of ice> **2** : plaque, nameplate, badge (of a policeman) **3** : patch (of ice, etc.) **4 plaque chauffante** : hotplate, griddle **5 plaque d'immatriculation** : license plate **6 plaque dentaire** : dental plaque

plaqué, -quée [plake] *adj* : plated <plaqué or : gold-plated>

plaquer [plake] *vt* **1** : to veneer, to plate **2** : to stick, to plaster, to pin down **3** : to tackle (in football) **4** *fam* : to ditch, to get rid of

plaquette [plakɛt] *nf* **1** : small sheet <plaquette de beurre : pat of butter> **2** : booklet

plasma [plasma] *nm* : plasma

plastique[1] [plastik] *adj* **1** : plastic, malleable **2 chirurgie plastique** : plastic surgery

plastique[2] *nm* : plastic

plastique[3] *nf* **1** : plastic arts *pl*, modeling, sculpture **2** : beauty of form

plat[1], **plate** [pla, plat] *adj* **1** : flat, level **2** : shallow **3** : dull, bland, insipid **4** : obsequious **5** : lank <cheveux plats : lank hair> **6** *Can* : boring, dull

plat[2] *nm* **1** : plate **2** : dish <un plat méditerranéen : a Mediterranean dish> **3** : course <plat de résistance : main course, entrée> **4** : flat (part) <plat de la main : flat of the hand> **5 à** ~ : flat (down) <tomber à plat : to fall flat> **6 à** ~ : dead (of a battery)

platane [platan] *nm* : plane tree

plat-bord [plabɔr] *nm, pl* **plats-bords** : gunwale

plateau [plato] *nm, pl* **plateaux** **1** : tray, platter **2** : plateau <plateau continental : continental shelf> **3** : stage, set (in theater) **4** : pan (of a scale)

plate-bande [platbɑ̃d] *nf, pl* **plates-bandes** : flower bed

plate-forme [platfɔrm] *nf, pl* **plates-formes** : platform

platement [platmɑ̃] *adv* **1** : dully, uninterestingly **2** : abjectly

platine[1] [platin] *nm* : platinum

platine[2] *nf* **1** : turntable **2 platine cassette** : cassette deck **3 platine laser** : CD player

platitude [platityd] *nf* **1** BANALITÉ : banality, triteness **2** : platitude

platonique [platɔnik] *adj* : platonic

plâtre [platr] *nm* **1** : plaster **2** : plaster cast

plâtrer [platre] *vt* **1** : to plaster **2** : to put in a (plaster) cast

plâtrier [platrije] *nm* : plasterer

plausibilité [plozibilite] *nf* : plausibility

plausible [plozibl] *adj* VRAISEMBLABLE : plausible, likely

plèbe [plɛb] *nf* : common people *pl*, masses *pl*

plébéien, -béienne [plebejɛ̃, -bejɛn] *adj* : plebeian

plébiscite [plebisit] *nm* : plebiscite

plein[1], **pleine** [plɛ̃, plɛn] *adj* **1** REMPLI : full <une tasse pleine : a full cup> **2** : filled (up) <une salle pleine de monde : a roomful of people, a crowded room> <saisir à pleines mains : to grasp with both hands, to take a firm hold> <une journée pleine : a busy day> **3** : solid, rounded, full <la pleine lune : the full moon> **4** : pregnant (of an animal) **5** (*used as an intensifier*) <en pleine rue : in the middle of the street> <en plein jour : in broad daylight> **6 la pleine mer** : the open sea **7 le plein air** : the outdoors **8 plein d'entrain** : high-spirited **9 plein de soi-même** : conceited, self-centered

plein[2] *nm* **1** : fullest point, maximum <faire le plein de : to fill up on, to stock up with> <donner son plein : to give one's all> **2 à ~** *or* **en ~** : fully, totally, at full capacity

pleinement [plɛnmɑ̃] *adv* ENTIÈREMENT : fully, entirely

plénier, -nière [plenje, -njɛr] *adj* : plenary

plénipotentiaire [plenipɔtɑ̃sjɛr] *nmf* : plenipotentiary

plénitude [plenityd] *nf* **1** AMPLEUR : scale, extent **2** : fullness, peak

pléthore [pletɔr] *nf* : plethora, overabundance

pleumer [plə(œ)me] *vi Can fam* : to peel (of skin)

pleurer [plœre] *vt* **1** : to weep for, to lament **2** : to cry <pleurer des larmes de joie : to cry tears of joy> — *vi* **1** : to cry, to weep **2** : to water <il a les yeux qui pleurent : his eyes are watering> **3 ~ sur** : to shed tears over, to bemoan

pleurésie [plœrezi] *nf* : pleurisy

pleurnicher [plœrniʃe] *vi fam* : to whine, to snivel

pleurs [plœr] *nmpl* **être en pleurs** : to be in tears

pleut [plø] → **pleuvoir**

pleuvoir [pløvwar] {67} *v impers* : to rain <il pleut à verse : it's pouring> — *vi* : to rain down, to pour down <les invitations pleuvaient sur nous : invitations were pouring in on us>

pli [pli] *nm* **1** : fold, pleat **2** : crease **3** HABITUDE : habit <prendre un mauvais pli : to get into a bad habit> **4** : envelope, letter <sous ce pli : enclosed> **5** : trick (in card games)

pliable [plijabl] *adj* : pliable, flexible

pliant, pliante [plijɑ̃, plijɑ̃t] *adj* : folding <chaise pliante : folding chair>

plier [plije] {96} *vt* **1** : to fold, to fold up **2** : to bend **3 plié en deux** *fam* : doubled up with laughter — *vi* **1** : to bend, to sag **2** : to yield, to give in — **se plier** *vr* **1** : to bend over, to fold **2 ~ à** : to submit to

plinthe [plɛ̃t] *nf* **1** : plinth **2** : baseboard

plissé[1], **-sée** [plise] *adj* : pleated

plissé[2] *nm* : pleating, pleats *pl*

plisser [plise] *vt* **1** : to pleat, to fold **2** : to crease, to wrinkle (clothing) **3** FRONCER : to wrinkle (one's brow), to pucker (one's lips), to screw up (one's eyes) — **se plisser 1** : to get wrinkled **2** : to pucker up

pliure [plijyr] *nf* : fold, bend (of the arm or leg)

plomb [plɔ̃] *nm* **1** : lead <essence sans plomb : unleaded gas> **2** : shot, (lead) pellet **3** FUSIBLE : (electrical) fuse **4** : sinker (in fishing)

plombage [plɔ̃baʒ] *nm* : filling (of a tooth)

plomber [plɔ̃be] *vt* **1** : to weight with lead **2** : to fill (a tooth) **3** : to plumb

plomberie [plɔ̃bri] *nf* : plumbing

plombier [plɔ̃bje] *nm* : plumber

plonge [plɔ̃ʒ] *nf* **1** : dishwashing <faire la plonge : to wash dishes> **2 prendre une plonge** *Can fam* : to tumble down, to crash down

plongeant, -geante [plɔ̃ʒɑ̃, -ʒɑ̃t] *adj* **1** : plunging **2** : from above <vue plongeante : bird's-eye view>

plongée [plɔ̃ʒe] *nf* **1** : diving **2 plongée sous-marine** : skin diving, deep-sea diving

plongeoir [plɔ̃ʒwar] *nm* : diving board

plongeon [plɔ̃ʒɔ̃] *nm* **1** : dive **2** : loon (bird)

plonger [plɔ̃ʒe] {17} *vt* : to thrust, to plunge — *vi* **1** : to dive **2 ~ dans** : to plunge into — **se plonger** *vr* **~ dans** : to immerse oneself in, to sink into

plongeur, -geuse [plɔ̃ʒœr, -ʒøz] *n* **1** : diver **2** : dishwasher (person)

plot [plo] *nm* : (electrical) contact

plouc [pluk] *nm France fam* : bumpkin

plouf [pluf] *nm* : splash

ploutocratie [plutɔkrasi] *nf* : plutocracy

ployer [plwaje] {58} *vt* : to bow, to bend — *vi* **1** : to bend, to sag **2** CÉDER : to give in, to yield

plu[1] |ply| *pp* → **plaire**

plu[2] |ply| *pp* → **pleuvoir**

pluie |plɥi| *nf* **1** : rain, rainfall **2** : shower, hail, stream <une pluie de compliments : a shower of compliments>

plumage |plymaʒ| *nm* : plumage, feathers *pl*

plume |plym| *nf* **1** : feather **2** : quill pen, pen nib

plumeau |plymo| *nm, pl* **plumeaux** |plymo| : feather duster

plumer |plyme| *vt* : to pluck

plumet |plymɛ| *nm* : plume

plumitif |plymitif| *nm* : pencil pusher, hack writer

plupart |plypar| *nf* **1 la plupart des** : most, the majority of <dans la plupart des cas : in most cases> **2 pour la plupart** : mostly, for the most part

pluralité |plyralite| *nf* : plurality

pluriel[1], **-rielle** |plyrjɛl| *adj* : plural

pluriel[2] *nm* : plural

plus[1] |ply(s)| *adv* **1** : more <peux-tu aller plus vite? : can you go faster?> <plus je dors, plus j'ai envie de dormir : the more I sleep, the more I want to sleep> <plus que tout : more than anything> **2** (*used in negation*) : no more, no longer <il ne les voit plus : he doesn't see them anymore> <je n'ai plus soif : I'm no longer thirsty> **3 ~ de** : more, more than <plus de café : more coffee> <avoir plus de 50 ans : to be over 50> **4 le plus** : most, the most <le plus souvent : most often, most of the time> <le plus d'argent : the most money> <au plus : at the most> **5 de ~** : in addition, furthermore **6 en ~** : as well, extra **7 non plus** : neither, either <moi non plus : me neither> **8 plus ou moins** : more or less, approximately

plus[2] *nm* **1** : plus (sign) **2** *fam* : plus, advantage <son expérience est un vrai plus : his experience is a real plus>

plus[3] *conj* : plus <deux plus cinq font sept : two plus five equals seven>

plusieurs |plyzjœr| *adj & pron* : several

plutocracy |plytɔkrasi| *nf* : plutocracy

Pluton |plytɔ̃| *nf* : Pluto (planet)

plutonium |plytɔnjɔm| *nm* : plutonium

plutôt |plyto| *adv* : rather, instead <plutôt moins que trop : rather too little than too much> <plutôt du beurre que de l'huile : butter instead of oil> <plutôt que de les convaincre : rather than convincing them>

pluvial, -viale |plyvjal| *adj, mpl* **pluviaux** |plyvjo| : rain <eau pluviale : rainwater>

pluvier |plyvje| *nm* : plover

pluvieux, -vieuse |plyvjø, -vjøz| *adj* : rainy, wet

pneu |pnø| *nm, pl* **pneus** : tire

pneumatique |pnømatik| *adj* **1** : pneumatic **2** : inflatable <matelas pneumatique : inflatable mattress>

pneumonie |pnømɔni| *nf* : pneumonia

poche |pɔʃ| *nf* **1** : pocket (in clothing) **2** : pocket, cavity <une poche d'eau : a pocket of water> **3** SAC : bag, pouch **4 poches** *nfpl* CERNES : bags, circles <il a des poches sous les yeux : he has bags under his eyes>

pocher |pɔʃe| *vt* **1** : to poach (in cooking) **2 pocher l'œil à qqn** : to give s.o. a black eye — *vi* : to get baggy

pochette |pɔʃɛt| *nf* **1** : folder, case, (record) sleeve <pochette d'allumettes : book of matches> **2** : pocket handkerchief **3** : pouch, clutch bag

pochoir |pɔʃwar| *nm* : stencil

podium |pɔdjɔm| *nm* : podium

podologie |pɔdɔlɔʒi| *nf* : chiropody, podiatry

podologue |pɔdɔlɔg| *nmf* : podiatrist

poêle[1] |pwal| *nm* **1** FOURNEAU : stove <poêle à bois : wood-burning stove> **2** : pall, coffin cloth

poêle[2] *nf or* **poêle à frire** : frying pan

poêlon |pwalɔ̃| *nm* **1** : casserole dish **2** *Can* : frying pan

poème |pɔɛm| *nm* : poem

poésie |pɔezi| *nf* **1** : poetry **2** : poem

poète |pɔɛt| *nmf* : poet

poétique |pɔetik| *adj* : poetic

pogné, -gnée |pɔɲe| *adj Can fam* : uptight, tense

pogner |pɔɲe| *vt Can fam* **1** : to get, to catch <il l'a pognée à voler : he caught her stealing> **2 pogner les nerfs** : to have a fit — *vi Can fam* **1** : to be inhibited, to be hung up **2** : to be successful <artiste qui pogne : successful artist> — **se pogner** *vr Can fam* **~ avec** : to get into a fight with

pognon |pɔɲɔ̃| *nm France fam* : dough, money

pogrom |pɔgrɔm| *nm* : pogrom

poids |pwa| *nms & pl* **1** : weight, heaviness **2** FARDEAU : burden, responsibility **3** : weight <les poids et mesures : weights and mesures> <poids et haltères : weight lifting> **4** : meaning, importance <avoir du poids : to carry weight> **5 poids lourd** : heavyweight (in sports)

poignant, -gnante |pwaɲɑ̃, -ɲɑ̃t| *adj* ÉMOUVANT : moving, poignant

poignard |pwaɲar| *nm* : dagger

poignarder |pwaɲarde| *vt* : to stab

poigne |pwaɲ| *nf* **1** : grip, grasp **2 à ~** : firm, forceful

poignée |pwaɲe| *nf* **1** : handful **2** : handle **3 poignée de main** : handshake

poignet |pwaɲɛ| *nm* **1** : wrist **2** : cuff

poil |pwal| *nm* **1** : hair **2** : fur, coat <chat à poil long : long-haired cat> **3** : bristle (of a brush) **4** : nap (of fabric) **5 à ~** *fam* : stark naked

poilu, -lue |pwaly| *adj* : hairy

poinçon [pwɛ̃sɔ̃] *nm* **1** : awl, punch **2** MARQUE : hallmark, stamp
poinçonner [pwɛ̃sɔne] *vt* **1** : to hallmark, to stamp **2** : to punch, to perforate
poinçonneuse [pwɛ̃sɔnøz] *nf* : punch
poing [pwɛ̃] *nm* **1** : fist **2 coup de poing** : punch
point[1] [pwɛ̃] *adv* : not <je ne l'aime point : I do not like him> <point du tout : not at all>
point[2] *nm* **1** : point, position <point de départ : point of departure> <aller d'un point à un autre : to go from one place to the next> **2** DEGRÉ : degree, extent <à tel point que : to such an extent that, so much so that> **3** : period, dot (in punctuation) <point décimal : decimal point> <point d'exclamation : exclamation point> <point d'interrogation : question mark> <points de suspension : ellipsis> **4** QUESTION : question, matter, point <sur ce point, ils n'étaient pas d'accord : they couldn't agree on this matter> **5** : point (in sports) **6** : stitch (in sewing) **7 à ~** : just right <arriver à point : to arrive just in time> <faire cuire à point : to cook medium rare> **8 au point** : well designed, well done <mettre au point : to adjust, to perfect> **9 point culminant** : highlight **10 point de fusion** : melting point **11 point de vue** : point of view **12 point du jour** : daybreak **13 point mort** : blind spot (of an automobile) **14 point noir** : blackhead **15 points cardinaux** : points of the compass **16** → **deux–points**
pointage [pwɛ̃taʒ] *nm* **1** : checking off, marking off (on a list) **2** : aiming (of a firearm) **3** *Can* : points *pl*, score (in sports)
pointe [pwɛ̃t] *nf* **1** : point, tip <en pointe : pointed> <sur la pointe des pieds : on tiptoe> **2** : point, headland **3** : high (level), peak <vitesse de pointe : top speed> <heures de pointe : rush hour> <technologie de pointe : state-of-the-art technology> **4** SOUPÇON : touch, hint **5** PIQUE : cutting remark, dig **6** CLOU : nail **7 pointes** *nfpl* : spiked shoes (in sports)
pointer [pwɛ̃te] *vt* **1** COCHER : to check, to mark off **2** : to aim, to point <pointer un doigt sur : to point a finger at> <pointer un fusil vers : to aim a rifle at> — *vi* **1** : to clock in **2** : to stick out, to rise up **3** : to break, to dawn, to come up — **se pointer** *vr fam* : to show up
pointeur, -teuse [pwɛ̃tœr, -tøz] *n* **1** : timekeeper **2** *Can* : scorekeeper
pointillé[1], **-lée** [pwɛ̃tije] *adj* : dotted, stippled
pointillé[2] *nm* : dotted line
pointilleux, -leuse [pwɛ̃tijø, -jøz] *adj* : finicky, fussy
pointu, -tue [pwɛ̃ty] *adj* **1** : pointed, sharp **2** : sharp, querulous **3** : shrill **4** : precise, specialized
pointure [pwɛ̃tyr] *nf* : size (of clothing)
point–virgule [pwɛ̃virgyl] *nm, pl* **points–virgules** : semicolon
poire [pwar] *nf* : pear
poireau [pwaro] *nm, pl* **poireaux** : leek
poireauter [pwarote] *vi fam* : to hang around
poirier [pwarje] *nm* : pear tree
pois [pwa] *nms & pl* **1** : pea <petit pois : green peas> <pois chiche : chickpea> **2** : dot <à pois : spotted, polka-dot>
poison [pwazɔ̃] *nm* : poison
poisse [pwas] *nf fam* : bad luck
poisser [pwase] *vt* : to make sticky — *vi* : to be sticky
poisseux, -seuse [pwasø, -søz] *adj* GLUANT : sticky
poisson [pwasɔ̃] *nm* **1** : fish <poisson rouge : goldfish> <poisson plat : flatfish> **2 poisson d'avril!** : April fool!
poisson–chat [pwasɔ̃ʃa] *nm, pl* **poissons–chats** : catfish
poissonnerie [pwasɔnri] *nf* : fish market
poissonnier, -nière [pwasɔnje, -njɛr] *n* : fish merchant, fishmonger
Poissons [pwasɔ̃] *nmpl* : Pisces
poitrine [pwatrin] *nf* **1** : chest **2** : breasts *pl*, bust, bosom **3** : breast (in cooking)
poivre [pwavr] *nm* **1** : pepper **2 poivre de cayenne** : cayenne pepper
poivré, -vrée [pwavre] *adj* : peppery
poivrer [pwavre] *vt* : to pepper
poivrier [pwavrije] *nm* **1** : pepper plant **2** : pepper shaker
poivrière [pwavrijɛr] *nf* : pepper shaker
poivron [pwavrɔ̃] *nm* : pepper <poivron vert : green pepper>
poix [pwa] *nm* : pitch, tar
poker [pɔkɛr] *nm* : poker <partie de poker : game of poker>
polaire [pɔlɛr] *adj* : polar
polarisation [pɔlarizasjɔ̃] *nf* : polarization
polariser [pɔlarize] *vt* **1** : to polarize **2** : to concentrate, to focus **3** ATTIRER : to attract — **se polariser** *vr*
pôle [pol] *nm* : pole <le pôle Nord : the North Pole>
polémique[1] [pɔlemik] *adj* : controversial, polemical
polémique[2] *nf* : debate, controversy, polemics
poli[1], **-lie** [pɔli] *adj* **1** COURTOIS : polite **2** LISSE : polished, smooth
poli[2] *nm* : polish, shine
police [pɔlis] *nf* **1** : police, police force **2** : law enforcement, policing **3** : font (in printing) **4 police d'assurance** : insurance policy

policier[1], **-cière** [pɔlisje, -sjɛr] *adj* **1** : police **2** : detective <roman policier : detective novel>

policier[2], **-cière** *n* : police officer

policlinique [pɔliklinik] *nf* : outpatient clinic

poliment [pɔlimɑ̃] *adv* : politely

poliomyélite [pɔljɔmjelit] *nf* : poliomyelitis

polir [pɔlir] *vt* **1** : to polish, to shine **2** PARFAIRE : to refine, to perfect (style, etc.)

polisson, -sonne [pɔlisɔ̃, -sɔn] *n* : scamp, naughty child, brat

politesse [pɔlitɛs] *nf* **1** COURTOISIE : politeness, courtesy **2** : polite remark, pleasantry <échanger des politesses : to exchange courtesies>

politicien, -cienne [pɔlitisjɛ̃, -sjɛn] *n* : politician

politique[1] [pɔlitik] *adj* : political — **politiquement** [-tikmɑ̃] *adv*

politique[2] *nf* **1** : politics **2** TACTIQUE : policy, procedure

politique[3] *nm* : politician

polka [pɔlka] *nf* : polka

pollen [pɔlɛn] *nm* : pollen

pollinisation [pɔlinizasjɔ̃] *nf* : pollination

polliniser [pɔlinize] *vt* : to pollinate

polluant[1], **-luante** [pɔlɥɑ̃, -lɥɑ̃t] *adj* : polluting

polluant[2] *nm* : pollutant

polluer [pɔlɥe] *vt* : to pollute — **pollution** [pɔlysjɔ̃] *nf*

polo [pɔlo] *nm* **1** : polo **2** : polo shirt

polonais[1], **-naise** [pɔlɔnɛ, -nɛz] *adj* : Polish

polonais[2] *nm* : Polish (language)

Polonais, -naise *n* : Pole

poltron,[1] **-tronne** [pɔltrɔ̃, -trɔn] *adj* : cowardly

poltron,[2] **-tronne** *n* : coward

polycopie [pɔlikɔpi] *nf* : mimeograph

polyester [pɔliɛstɛr] *nm* : polyester

polygame[1] [pɔligam] *adj* : polygamous

polygame[2] *nmf* : polygamist

polygamie [pɔligami] *nf* : polygamy

polygone [pɔligɔn] *nm* **1** : polygon **2** *or* **polygone de tir** : firing range

polymère [pɔlimɛr] *nm* : polymer

polynésien[1], **-sienne** [pɔlinezjɛ̃, -zjɛn] *adj* : Polynesian

polynésien[2] *nm* : Polynesian (language)

Polynésien, -sienne *n* : Polynesian

polype [pɔlip] *nm* : polyp

polythéisme [pɔliteism] *nm* : polytheism

polythéiste [pɔliteist] *adj* : polytheist, polytheistic

polyvalent, -lente [pɔlivalɑ̃, -lɑ̃t] *adj* **1** : polyvalent **2** : versatile, multipurpose, all-around

polyvalente [pɔlivalɑ̃, -lɑ̃t] *nf or* **école polyvalente** *Can* : general and vocational high school

pommade [pɔmad] *nf* : ointment

pomme [pɔm] *nf* **1** : apple **2 pomme d'Adam** : Adam's apple **3 pomme de discorde** : bone of contention **4 pomme de pin** : pinecone **5 pomme de terre** : potato **6 pommes frites** : French fries

pommeau [pɔmo] *nm* : knob, pommel

pommelé, -lée [pɔmle] *adj* : dappled, mottled

pommette [pɔmɛt] *nf* : cheekbone

pommier [pɔmje] *nm* : apple tree

pompe [pɔ̃p] *nf* **1** : pump <pompe à essence : gas pump> **2** : pomp, ceremony **3 pompes funèbres** : funeral home, funeral parlor

pomper [pɔ̃pe] *vt* **1** : to pump **2** : to soak up

pompette [pɔ̃pɛt] *adj fam* : tipsy

pompeux, -peuse [pɔ̃pø, -pøz] *adj* : pompous — **pompeusement** [-pøzmɑ̃] *adv*

pompier[1], **-pière** [pɔ̃pje, -pjɛr] *adj* : pompous, pretentious

pompier[2] *nm* : firefighter, fireman

pompiste [pɔ̃pist] *nmf* : service station attendant

pompon [pɔ̃pɔ̃] *nm* : pompom

pomponner [pɔ̃pɔne] *vt* : to dress up — **se pomponner** *vr* : to get all dressed up, to preen oneself, to primp (up)

ponce [pɔ̃s] *nf* **pierre ponce** : pumice stone

ponceau [pɔ̃so] *nm, pl* **ponceaux** : small bridge

poncer [pɔ̃se] {6} *vt* : to sand (down)

poncho [pɔ̃tʃo] *nm* : poncho

poncif [pɔ̃sif] *nm* BANALITÉ : cliché, platitude

ponction [pɔ̃ksjɔ̃] *nf* : puncture (in medicine)

ponctualité [pɔ̃ktɥalite] *nf* : punctuality

ponctuation [pɔ̃ktɥasjɔ̃] *nf* : punctuation

ponctuel, -elle [pɔ̃ktɥɛl] *adj* **1** : prompt, punctual **2** : limited, selective

ponctuellement [pɔ̃ktɥɛlmɑ̃] *adv* : punctually

ponctuer [pɔ̃ktɥe] *vt* : to punctuate

pondération [pɔ̃derasjɔ̃] *nf* **1** : balancing **2** MESURE : levelheadedness

pondéré, -rée [pɔ̃dere] *adj* : levelheaded, sensible

pondérer [pɔ̃dere] {87} *vt* : to balance

pondeuse [pɔ̃døz] *nf* : laying hen, layer

pondre [pɔ̃dr] {63} *vt* **1** : to lay (eggs) **2** *fam* : to crank out, to produce

poney [pɔnɛ] *nm* : pony

pont [pɔ̃] *nm* **1** : bridge <pont suspendu : suspension bridge> **2** : deck (of a ship) **3** : axle (of an automobile) **4 pont aérien** : airlift

ponte [pɔ̃t] *nf* : laying (of eggs)

pontife [pɔ̃tif] *nm* : pontiff

pontifical, -cale [pɔ̃tifikal] *adj* : pontifical

pontifier |pɔ̃tifje| {96} *vi* : to pontificate

pont–levis |pɔ̃ləvi| *nm, pl* **ponts–levis** : drawbridge

ponton |pɔ̃tɔ̃| *nm* : pontoon

pop |pɔp| *adj s & pl* **pop** : pop <musique pop : pop music>

pop–corn |pɔpkɔrn| *nms & pl* : popcorn

popeline |pɔplin| *nf* : poplin

popote |pɔpɔt| *nf* **1** : mess (in the military) **2 faire la popote** *fam* : to do the cooking

populace |pɔpylas| *nf* : rabble

populaire |pɔpylɛr| *adj* **1** : popular **2** : working-class **3** : colloquial, vernacular

populariser |pɔpylarize| *vt* : to popularize

popularité |pɔpylarite| *nf* : popularity

population |pɔpylasjɔ̃| *nf* : population

populeux, -leuse |pɔpylø, -løz| *adj* : densely populated

populiste |pɔpylist| *adj & nmf* : populist — **populisme** |-pylism| *nm*

poque |pɔk| *nf Can fam* : bump, bruise

poquer |pɔke| *vt Can fam* : to dent (a car)

porc |pɔr| *nm* **1** : pig, hog **2** : pork **3** : pigskin

porcelaine |pɔrsəlɛn| *nf* **1** : porcelain **2** : china, chinaware

porcelet |pɔrsəlɛ| *nm* : piglet

porc–épic |pɔrkepik| *nm, pl* **porcs–épics** : porcupine

porche |pɔrʃ| *nm* : porch

porcherie |pɔrʃəri| *nf* : pigpen, pigsty

porcin, -cine |pɔrsɛ̃, -sin| *adj* **1** : pig, porcine **2** : piglike, piggy

pore |pɔr| *nm* : pore

poreux, -reuse |pɔrø, -røz| *adj* : porous

pornographie |pɔrnɔgrafi| *nf* : pornography — **pornographique** |-grafik| *adj*

porridge |pɔridʒ| *nm* : porridge

port |pɔr| *nm* **1** : port, harbor **2** : port city **3** HAVRE : haven, refuge **4** : wearing, carrying (a weapon, etc.) **5** MAINTIEN : carriage, bearing **6** : postage <port payé : postpaid>

portable |pɔrtabl| *adj* **1** METTABLE : wearable **2** PORTATIF : portable, laptop

portage |pɔrtaʒ| *nm* **1** : carrying, porterage **2** : portage

portail |pɔrtaj| *nm* : portal, gate

portant, -tante |pɔrtɑ̃, -tɑ̃t| *adj* **1 bien portant** : in good health **2 mal portant** : in poor health, ailing

portatif, -tive |pɔrtatif, -tiv| *adj* **1** : portable **2 ordinateur portatif** : laptop computer

porte |pɔrt| *nf* **1** : door, doorway <porte d'entrée : front door> <porte de sortie : exit, way out> <de porte à porte : door-to-door> **2** : gate <porte d'embarquement : departure gate> **3** : gateway, opening <ouvrir la porte à : to pave the way for>

porte–à–faux |pɔrtafo| *nms & pl* **1** : overhang, cantilever **2 être en porte à faux** : to be in an awkward position

porte–avions |pɔrtavjɔ̃| *nms & pl* : aircraft carrier

porte–bagages |pɔrtbagaʒ| *nms & pl* : luggage rack, roof rack

porte–bébé |pɔrtbebe| *nm, pl* **porte–bébés** : baby carrier

porte–bonheur |pɔrtbɔnœr| *nms & pl* : lucky charm

porte–clés *or* **porte–clefs** |pɔrtəkle| *nms & pl* : key ring

porte–documents |pɔrtdɔkymɑ̃| *nms & pl* ATTACHÉ-CASE : attaché case, briefcase

porte–drapeau |pɔrtdrapo| *nm, pl* **porte–drapeaux** : standard-bearer

portée |pɔrte| *nf* **1** : range <à longue portée : long-range> <portée de voix : earshot> <d'une grande portée : far-reaching> <à la portée de la main : within arm's reach, handy> **2** : impact, significance **3** : litter (of kittens) **4** : staff (in music)

portefeuille |pɔrtəfœj| *nm* **1** : wallet, billfold **2** : portfolio (in politics or finance)

porte–jarretelles |pɔrtʒartɛl| *nms & pl* : garter belt

portemanteau |pɔrtmɑ̃to| *nm, pl* **-teaux** |-to| : coat rack

porte–monnaie |pɔrtmɔnɛ| *nms & pl* : change purse

porte–parole |pɔrtparɔl| *nms & pl* : spokesperson, spokesman *m*, spokeswoman *f*

porte–poussière |pɔrt(ə)pusjɛr| *nms & pl Can* : dustpan

porter |pɔrte| *vt* **1** TRANSPORTER : to carry, to bear **2** : to wear **3** APPORTER : to bring **4** : to hold, to keep, to use <elle porte son nom de fille : she uses her maiden name> **5 être porté à** : to be inclined to — *vi* **1** : to carry <une voix qui porte : a voice that carries> **2 ~ sur** : to be about — **se porter** *vr* **1** : to be worn **2** : to be (in a certain state) <il se porte bien : he is doing well> **3 ~ à** : to carry out, to indulge in **4 se porter garant de** : to vouch for **5 ~ sur** : to turn to, to spread to

porte–savon |pɔrtsavɔ̃| *nms & pl* : soap dish

porte–serviettes |pɔrtsɛrvjɛt| *nms & pl* : towel rack

porteur[1], -teuse |pɔrtœr, -tøz| *adj* **1** : load-bearing, carrier (in technology) **2** : flourishing, booming (in commerce) **3 ~ de** : bringing, expressing <être porteur de : to be the bearer of> <être porteur de sens : to have meaning>

porteur[2], -teuse *n* **1** : porter **2** : holder, bearer **3** : carrier (of disease)

porte–voix |pɔrtəvwa| *nms & pl* : megaphone

portier, -tière |pɔrtje, -tjɛr| *n* : doorman *m*, attendant (at an entrance)

portière *nf* : door (of an automobile)

portillon |pɔrtijɔ̃| *nm* : gate

portion |pɔrsjɔ̃| *nf* **1** : portion, share **2** : helping (of food) **3** : part, section (of a road, etc.)

portique |pɔrtik| *nm* **1** : portico **2** *Can fam* : hall, lobby

porto |pɔrto| *nm* : port wine

portoricain, -caine |pɔrtɔrikɛ̃, -kɛn| *adj* : Puerto Rican

Portoricain, -caine *n* : Puerto Rican

portrait |pɔrtrɛ| *nm* **1** : portrait **2** : picture, description **3** : image, likeness <il est le portrait de son père : he looks just like his father>

portraitiste |pɔrtretist| *nmf* : portrait painter

portuaire |pɔrtɥɛr| *adj* : harbor, port

portugais[1], **-gaise** |pɔrtygɛ, -gɛz| *adj* : Portuguese

portugais[2] *nm* : Portuguese (language)

Portugais, -gaise *n* : Portuguese

pose |poz| *nf* **1** : installing, putting in, laying **2** : pose, posture <prendre la pose : to pose> **3** : pose, affectation **4** : exposure <film de 24 poses : 24-exposure film>

posé, -sée |poze| *adj* **1** : composed, calm **2** : steady, even

posément |pozemɑ̃| *adv* : calmly, coolly, thoughtfully

poser |poze| *vt* **1** : to put (down), to place **2** INSTALLER : to put up, to install **3** : to state, to assert **4** : to ask (a question) **5 poser sa candidature** : to apply for a job — *vi* **1** : to pose, to sit **2** : to put on airs — **se poser** *vr* **1** : to be installed <cette fenêtre se pose facilement : this window is easy to install> **2** : to land, to touch down, to alight **3** : to arise, to come up <la question ne se pose pas : it goes without saying> **4 ~ en** : to pose as, to claim to be

positif, -tive |pɔzitif, -tiv| *adj* : positive

position |pozisjɔ| *nf* **1** : position, place **2** : position, stance <prendre position : to take a stand> **3** SITUATION : position, situation <une position délicate : a difficult situation>

positionner |pozisjɔne| *vt* : to position, to place

positivement |pozitivmɑ̃| *adv* : positively

posologie |pozɔlɔʒi| *nf* : dosage

possédé, -dée |pɔsede| *adj* : possessed

posséder |pɔsede| {87} *vt* **1** AVOIR : to possess, to have **2** MAÎTRISER : to know thoroughly, to have mastered — **se posséder** *vr* : to control oneself

possesseur |pɔsesœr| *nm* : owner, possessor

possessif, -sive |pɔsesif, -siv| *adj* : possessive

possession |pɔsesjɔ̃| *nf* : possession, ownership

possibilité |pɔsibilite| *nf* **1** ÉVENTUALITÉ : possibility **2** OCCASION : opportunity, option **3 possibilités** *nfpl* : means, resources

possible[1] |pɔsibl| *adj* **1** : possible, feasible <dès que possible : as soon as possible> **2** PROBABLE : possible, probable <il est possible qu'il pleuve : it's likely to rain>

possible[2] *nm* **1 dans la mesure du possible** : as far as possible **2 faire son possible** : to do one's utmost

possiblement |pɔsibləmɑ̃| *adv Can* : possibly, perhaps

postal, -tale |pɔstal| *adj, mpl* **postaux** |pɔsto| : postal, mail

postdater |pɔstdate| *vt* : to postdate

poste[1] |pɔst| *nm* **1** : job, position **2** : post, station <poste d'essence : gas station, service station> <poste de travail : workstation> <poste de pilotage : cockpit> **3** : set <poste de télévision : television set> **4** : extension (of a phone system) **5 poste de pompiers** *Can* : fire station

poste[2] *nf* **1** : mail service <mettre à la poste : to put in the mail> **2** : post office

poster[1] |pɔste| *vt* **1** : to post, to station **2** : to mail

poster[2] |pɔstɛr| *nm* : poster

postérieur[1], **-rieure** |pɔsterjœr| *adj* **1** : later **2** : posterior, rear, back

postérieur[2] *nm fam* : bottom, buttocks *pl*

postérieurement |pɔsterjœrmɑ̃| *adv* : subsequently, later

postérité |pɔsterite| *nf* **1** : posterity **2** LIGNÉE : descendants *pl*

posthume |pɔstym| *adj* : posthumous

postiche[1] |pɔstiʃ| *adj* : false, fake

postiche[2] *nm* : hairpiece, toupee

postier, -tière |pɔstje, -tjɛr| *n* : postal worker

postnatal, -tale |pɔstnatal| *adj, mpl* **-tals** *or* **-taux** |-to| : postnatal

postopératoire |pɔstɔperatwar| *adj* : postoperative

postscolaire |pɔstskɔlɛr| *adj* **l'enseignement postscolaire** : continuing education

post–scriptum |pɔstskriptɔm| *nms & pl* : postscript

postulant, -lante |pɔstylɑ̃, -lɑ̃t| *n* **1** CANDIDAT : candidate, contestant **2** : postulant (in religion)

postulat |pɔstyla| *nm* : postulate

postuler |pɔstyle| *vt* **1** : to apply for **2** : to postulate

posture |pɔstyr| *nf* **1** POSITION : posture, position **2** SITUATION : situation

pot |po| *nm* **1** : pot, jar, container <pot de fleurs : flowerpot> **2** : potful **3** *fam* : drink, glass **4 pot d'échappement** : muffler (of an automobile)

potable |pɔtabl| *adj* **1** BUVABLE : drinkable <eau potable : drinking water> **2** *fam* : fair, passable
potage |pɔtaʒ| *nm* : soup
potager[1], **-gère** |pɔtaʒe, -ʒɛr| *adj* : edible <plantes potagères : edible plants>
potager[2] *nm or* **jardin potager** : vegetable garden
potasse |pɔtas| *nf* : potash
potassium |pɔtasjɔm| *nm* : potassium
pot–au–feu |pɔtofø| *nms & pl* : beef stew
pot–de–vin |podvɛ̃| *nm, pl* **pots–de–vin** : bribe
pote |pot| *nm fam* : pal, buddy
poteau |pɔto| *nm, pl* **poteaux 1** : post, stake, pole <poteau de téléphone : telephone pole> **2** : goalpost **3** **poteau indicateur** : signpost, guidepost
potelé, -lée |pɔtle| *adj* GRASSOUILLET : chubby, plump
potence |pɔtɑ̃s| *nf* : gallows
potentat |pɔtɑ̃ta| *nm* : potentate, ruler
potentiel[1], **-tielle** |pɔtɑ̃sjɛl| *adj* : potential — **potentiellement** |-sjɛlmɑ̃| *adv*
potentiel[2] *nm* : potential
poterie |pɔtri| *nf* : pottery
potiche |pɔtiʃ| *nf* **1** : large vase **2** : figurehead, puppet
potier, -tière |pɔtje, -tjɛr| *n* : potter
potin |pɔtɛ̃| *nm fam* **1** *France* : noise, racket **2 potins** *nmpl* : gossip
potion |pɔsjɔ̃| *nf* : potion
potiron |pɔtirɔ̃| *nm* : variety of large pumpkin
pot–pourri |popuri| *nm, pl* **pots–pourris** : potpourri
pou |pu| *nm, pl* **poux** : louse
poubelle |pubɛl| *nf* : garbage can, trash barrel
pouce |pus| *nm* **1** : thumb <se tourner les pouces : to twiddle one's thumbs> **2** : big toe **3** : inch **4 faire du pouce** *Can* : to hitchhike
pouding → **pudding**
poudre |pudr| *nf* **1** : powder <lait en poudre : powdered milk> **2** *or* **poudre à canon** : gunpowder **3** : face powder **4 poudre à pâte** *Can* : baking powder
poudrer |pudre| *vt* : to powder — *v impers Can* : to drift (of snow) — **se poudrer** *vr*
poudrerie |pudrəri| *nf Can* : (snow) flurries *pl*
poudreux, -dreuse |pudrø, -drøz| *adj* : powdery
poudrier |pudrije| *nm* : (face powder) compact
pouf |puf| *nm* : hassock
pouffer |pufe| *vi* **pouffer de rire** : to burst out laughing
pouilleux, -leuse |pujø, -jøz| *adj* **1** : lousy, flea-ridden **2** : seedy, shabby
pouillot |pujo| *nm* : warbler
poulailler |pulaje| *nm* : henhouse, chicken coop
poulain |pulɛ̃| *nm* **1** : colt, foal **2** PROTÉGÉ : protégé
poule |pul| *nf* **1** : hen **2** : (stewing) chicken **3 poule mouillée** *fam* : chicken, wimp
poulet |pulɛ| *nm* : chicken
poulette |pulɛt| *nf* : pullet, young hen
pouliche |puliʃ| *nf* : filly
poulie |puli| *nf* : pulley
pouliner |puline| *vi* : to foal
poulpe |pulp| *nm* PIEUVRE : octopus
pouls |pu| *nms & pl* : pulse
poumon |pumɔ̃| *nm* : lung
poupe |pup| *nf* : stern <en poupe : astern>
poupée |pupe| *nf* **1** : doll **2** : finger bandage
poupin, -pine |pupɛ̃, -pin| *adj* : chubby <visage poupin : baby face>
poupon |pupɔ̃| *nm* **1** : tiny baby **2** : baby doll
pouponner |pupɔne| *vi* : to dote (over a baby), to play mother
pouponnière |pupɔnjɛr| *nf* : nursery (for babies)
pour[1] |pur| *prep* **1** : for <en avance pour son âge : advanced for his age> <partir pour Québec : to leave for Quebec> **2** : to, in order to <on doit travailler dur pour réussir : you have to work hard to succeed> **3 pour cent** : percent **4 pour que** : in order that, so that
pour[2] *nm* **le pour et le contre** : the pros and cons
pourboire |purbwar| *nm* : tip
pourcentage |pursɑ̃taʒ| *nm* : percentage
pourchasser |purʃase| *vt* POURSUIVRE : to pursue, to hunt down
pourlécher |purleʃe| {87} *v* **se pourlécher** *vr* : to lick one's lips
pourparlers |purparle| *nmpl* : talks, negotiations, parley
pourpre[1] |purpr| *adj & nm* : crimson, reddish purple
pourpre[2] *nf* : purple (dye)
pourquoi[1] |purkwa| *adv & conj* : why
pourquoi[2] *nm* **1** : reason, cause **2 le pourquoi et le comment** : the whys and wherefores
pourra |pura|, *etc.* → **pouvoir**
pourri, -rie |puri| *adj* **1** : rotten, decayed **2** : coddled, spoiled **3** CORROMPU : corrupt, rotten **4** *fam* DÉGUEULASSE : lousy, abominable (of weather, etc.)
pourrir |purir| *vi* **1** SE DÉCOMPOSER : to rot **2** : to spoil, to go bad **3** SE DÉTÉRIORER : to deteriorate — *vt* **1** : to rot, to decay **2** GÂTER : to spoil, to pamper
pourrissement |purismɑ̃| *nm* : deterioration

pourriture |purityr| *nf* **1** : rot, rottenness **2** : corruption, (moral) decay **3** *fam* : rotten person, swine

poursuite |pursɥit| *nf* **1** : pursuit, chase **2 poursuites** *nfpl* : legal proceedings, lawsuit

poursuivant, -vante |pursɥivɑ̃, -vɑ̃t| *n* **1** : pursuer **2** : plaintiff

poursuivre |pursɥivr| {88} *vt* **1** : to pursue, to chase **2** : to carry on with, to continue **3** : to sue, to prosecute **4** HARCELER : to pester, to hound — *vi* : to continue, to go on

pourtant |purtɑ̃| *adv* : however, yet, nevertheless

pourtour |purtur| *nm* **1** CIRCONFÉRENCE : perimeter, circumference **2** : periphery, surrounding area

pourvoi |purvwa| *nm* : appeal (in law)

pourvoir |purvwar| {68} *vt* **1** : to fill (a position, etc.) **2 ~ de** : to provide with, to equip with **3 ~ de** : to endow with <pourvu d'un remarquable talent : gifted with an extraordinary talent> — *vi* **~ à** : to provide for — **se pourvoir** *vr* **1** : to appeal (in law) **2 ~ de** : to provide oneself with

pourvoyeur, -voyeuse |purvwajœr, -vwajøz| *n* : provider, supplier, purveyor

pourvu |purvy| *conj* **~ que 1** : provided that **2** : let's hope (that) <pourvu qu'il fasse beau! : let's hope the weather is good!>

pousse |pus| *nf* **1** : growth, sprouting **2** : shoot, sprout

poussé, -sée |puse| *adj* : elaborate, extensive, exhaustive <un argument poussé : an elaborate argument> <études poussées : advanced studies>

poussée |puse| *nf* **1** : pressure **2** : push, shove **3** : rise, upsurge **4** ACCÈS : fit, attack (in medicine)

pousse–pousse |puspus| *nms & pl* : rickshaw

pousser |puse| *vt* **1** : to push, to shove **2** INCITER : to encourage, to urge **3** POURSUIVRE : to pursue, to continue **4** : to let out, to emit <il a poussé un cri : he let out a scream> <pousser un soupir : to heave a sigh> — *vi* **1** : to push **2** CROÎTRE : to grow — **se pousser** *vr* **1** : to move along, to get out of the way **2** *fam* : to push ahead, to make one's way

poussette |pusɛt| *nf* : stroller

poussière |pusjɛr| *nf* : dust

poussiéreux, -reuse |pusjerø, -røz| *adj* : dusty

poussif, -sive |pusif, -siv| *adj* : wheezing, wheezy

poussin |pusɛ̃| *nm* : chick

poussoir |puswar| *nm* : push button

poutine |putin| *nf Can* : French fries served with cheese and gravy

poutre |putr| *nf* : beam, girder

pouvoir[1] |puvwar| {69} *v aux* **1** : to be able to, to have the capacity to <peux-tu m'aider? : can you help me?> <elle pourrait vous surprendre : she might surprise you> **2** : to be permitted to <est-ce que je peux m'en aller maintenant? : can I go now?> — *v impers* : to be possible <il pourrait y avoir un changement à l'horaire : there might be a change of plans> — *vt* **1** : to do something about, to cope with **2 je n'en peux plus!** : I can't take anymore! — **se pouvoir** *vr impers* : to be possible <ça ne se peut pas! : it can't be!>

pouvoir[2] *nm* **1** FACULTÉ : faculty, ability **2** : power, control **3** : authority

pragmatique |pragmatik| *adj* : pragmatic — **pragmatisme** |-matism| *nm*

praire |prɛr| *nf* : clam

prairie |preri| *nf* **1** PRÉ : meadow **2** *or* **prairies** *nfpl* : prairie, grassland, meadowland

praticable |pratikabl| *adj* **1** FAISABLE : practicable, feasible **2** ACCESSIBLE : accessible, passable (of roads, etc.)

praticien, -cienne |pratisjɛ̃, -sjɛn| *n* : practitioner

pratiquant[1], **-quante** |pratikɑ̃, -kɑ̃t| *adj* : practicing

pratiquant[2], **-quante** *n* : churchgoer, follower (of a religion)

pratique[1] |pratik| *adj* **1** : practical, useful **2** COMMODE : convenient, handy

pratique[2] *nf* **1** : practice <mettre en pratique : to put into practice> **2** : practicing, observance

pratiquer |pratike| *vt* **1** : to practice **2** : to play (a sport) **3** : to use, to apply **4** : to carry out, to execute — *vi* : to attend church regularly — **se pratiquer** *vr* : to be done, to be practiced

pré |pre| *nm* : meadow

préalable[1] |prealabl| *adj* **1** : preliminary **2** : previous, prior <sans avis préalable : without prior notice> **3 ~ à** : preceding

préalable[2] *nm* **1** : prerequisite, precondition **2 au préalable** : beforehand, in advance

préalablement |prealabləmɑ̃| *adv* **1** AUPARAVANT : beforehand **2 ~ à** : prior to

préambule |preɑ̃byl| *nm* **1** : preamble, prelude **2 sans ~** : without warning

préau |preo| *nm, pl* **préaux** |preo| : courtyard

préavis |preavi| *nm* : (prior) notice

précaire |prekɛr| *adj* : precarious, fragile, insecure

précarité |prekarite| *nf* : precariousness

précaution |prekosjɔ̃| *nf* **1** : precaution **2** PRUDENCE : caution, care <avec précaution : cautiously> <prends des précautions : be careful>

précautionneux, -neuse |prekosjɔnø, -nøz| *adj* : cautious, careful —

précautionneusement [-sjɔnøzmɑ̃] *adv*
précédemment [presedamɑ̃] *adv* : previously, before
précédent[1], **-dente** [presedɑ̃, -dɑ̃t] *adj* ANTÉRIEUR : previous, prior
précédent[2] *nm* : precedent
précéder [presede] {87} *vt* **1** : to precede **2** : to get ahead of
précepte [presɛpt] *nm* : precept
précepteur, -trice [presɛptœr, -tris] *n* : (private) tutor
préchauffer [preʃofe] *vt* : to preheat
prêcher [preʃe] *v* : to preach
prêcheur[1], **-cheuse** [prɛʃœr, -ʃøz] *adj* : preachy, moralizing
prêcheur[2], **-cheuse** *n* : preacher
précieusement [presjøzmɑ̃] *adv* SOIGNEUSEMENT : carefully
précieux, -cieuse [presjø, -sjøz] *adj* **1** : precious, valuable **2** : valued, invaluable, useful **3** : affected
préciosité [presjozite] *nf* : affectation, preciosity
précipice [presipis] *nm* **1** GOUFFRE : abyss, chasm **2 au bord du précipice** : on the brink of collapse
précipitamment [presipitamɑ̃] *adv* : hurriedly, hastily
précipitation [presipitasjɔ̃] *nf* **1** : hurry, haste **2 précipitations** *nfpl* : precipitation, rain, snow
précipité, -tée [presipite] *adj* **1** : hurried, rapid **2** : hasty, rash
précipiter [presipite] *vt* **1** : to hurl, to throw **2** : to hasten, to speed up — **se précipiter** *vr* **1** : to rush **2** : to act rashly **3** : to throw oneself <je me suis précipitée dans ses bras : I threw myself into his arms>
précis[1], **-cise** [presi, -siz] *adj* **1** EXACT : precise, exact, accurate **2** : clear, specific **3** : particular, very <à ce moment précis : at that very moment>
précis[2] *nms & pl* **1** ABRÉGÉ : abstract, summary **2** : handbook
précisément [presizemɑ̃] *adv* EXACTEMENT : precisely, exactly
préciser [presize] *vt* **1** DÉTERMINER : to specify, to state exactly **2** : to clarify — **se préciser** *vr* : to take shape, to become clearer
précision [presizjɔ̃] *nf* **1** EXACTITUDE : precision, accuracy **2** CLARTÉ : clarity
précoce [prekɔs] *adj* **1** : early <dépistage précoce : early detection> **2** : precocious <enfant précoce : precocious child>
précocement [prekɔsmɑ̃] *adv* : precociously
précocité [prekɔsite] *nf* : precocity
préconçu, -çue [prekɔ̃sy] *adj* : preconceived
préconiser [prekɔnize] *vt* PRÔNER : to recommend, to advocate
précurseur[1] [prekyrsœr] *adj* : precursory
précurseur[2] *nm* : forerunner, precursor
prédateur[1], **-trice** [predatœr, -tris] *adj* : predatory
prédateur[2] *nm* : predator
prédécesseur [predesɛsœr] *nm* : predecessor
prédestiner [predɛstine] *vt* : to predestine — **prédestination** [-stinasjɔ̃] *nf*
prédéterminer [predetɛrmine] *vt* : to predetermine
prédicateur, -trice [predikatœr, -tris] *n* : preacher
prédiction [prediksjɔ̃] *nf* : prediction
prédilection [predilɛksjɔ̃] *nf* **1** : predilection, partiality **2 de ~** : favorite <c'est mon lieu de prédilection : it's my favorite place>
prédire [predir] {29} *vt* : to foretell, to predict
prédisposer [predispoze] *vt* : to predispose — **prédisposition** [-pozisjɔ̃] *nf*
prédominance [predɔminɑ̃s] *nf* : predominance, prevalence
prédominer [predɔmine] *vi* : to predominate, to prevail
prééminence [preeminɑ̃s] *nf* : preeminence — **prééminent, -nente** [-minɑ̃, -nɑ̃t] *adj*
préexister [preɛgziste] *vi* : to preexist
préfabriqué, -quée [prefabrike] *adj* : prefabricated
préface [prefas] *nf* : preface — **préfacer** [-fase] *vt*
préfecture [prefɛktyr] *nf* **préfecture de police** *France* : police headquarters
préférable [preferabl] *adj* : preferable — **préférablement** [-rabləmɑ̃] *adv*
préféré[1], **-rée** [prefere] *adj* : favorite
préféré[2], **-rée** *n* : favorite (personal thing)
préférence [preferɑ̃s] *nf* **1** : preference **2 de ~** : preferably
préférentiel, -tielle [preferɑ̃sjɛl] *adj* : preferential
préférer [prefere] {87} *vt* : to prefer
préfet [prefɛ] *nm* **préfet de police** *France* : police commissioner
préfigurer [prefigyre] *vt* : to prefigure
préfixe [prefiks] *nm* : prefix
préhensile [preɑ̃sil] *adj* : prehensile
préhistorique [preistɔrik] *adj* : prehistoric
préjudice [preʒydis] *nm* : harm, damage <porter préjudice à : to harm, to cause harm to> <au préjudice de : to the detriment of>
préjudiciable [preʒydisjabl] *adj* **~ à** : detrimental to, harmful to
préjugé [preʒyʒe] *nm* : prejudice, bias
préjuger [preʒyʒe] {17} *vt* : to prejudge
prélart [prelar] *nm Can* : linoleum
prélasser [prelase] *v* **se prélasser** *vr* : to lounge (around)
prélat [prela] *nm* : prelate
prélèvement [prelɛvmɑ̃] *nm* **1** : withdrawal, deduction **2** : sample

<prélèvement de sang : blood sample>

prélever [prelǝve] {52} *vt* **1** : to withdraw, to deduct, to debit **2** : to take (a sample of), to remove (an organ)

préliminaire [preliminɛr] *adj* : preliminary

préliminaires [preliminɛr] *nmpl* : preliminaries

prélude [prelyd] *nm* : prelude

prématuré, -rée [prematyre] *adj* : premature — **prématurément** [-tyremɑ̃] *adv*

préméditation [premeditasjɔ̃] *nf* **1** : premeditation **2 avec préméditation** : with malice aforethought

préméditer [premedite] *vt* : to premeditate

prémenstruel, -struelle [premɑ̃stryɛl] *adj* : premenstrual

premier[1]**, -mière** [prǝmje, -mjɛr] *adj* **1** : first <à première vue : at first sight> **2** : top, leading **3** : primary, principal **4** : initial, original **5 premier ministre** : prime minister

premier[2]**, -mière** *n* : first (person or thing)

premier[3] *nm* **1** (*used in dates*) : first <le premier avril : the first of April> **2 en ~** : first of all, in the first place

première *nf* **1** : first class <billet de première : first-class ticket> **2** : premiere **3** : first gear, low gear

premièrement [prǝmjɛrmɑ̃] *adv* : in the first place, firstly

prémisse [premis] *nf* : premise

prémolaire [premɔlɛr] *nf* : premolar, bicuspid

prémonition [premɔnisjɔ̃] *nf* : premonition

prémunir [premynir] *vt* **~ contre** : to protect (someone) against — **se prémunir** *vr* **~ contre** : to protect oneself against

prenait [prǝnɛ], *etc.* → **prendre**

prendre [prɑ̃dr] {70} *vt* **1** : to take <prendre en main : to take in hand> **2** : to bring (along) <prends ton chapeau : take your hat> **3** : to get, to take out, to pick up **4** : to have (food or drink), to take (medicine) **5** : to take (a break, holiday, etc.) **6** : to take up (space or time) **7** : to take on (an employee, etc.) **8** : to catch (a thief, etc.) <se faire prendre : to get caught> **9** : to get (a warning, etc.), to catch (a cold) **10** : to take (a train, a road, etc.) **11** : to take on (responsibility), to tackle (a problem) **12** : to take down (notes, etc.) **13** : to assume, to take over (control) **14** : to seize, to capture — *vi* **1** : to set, to thicken (of cement, gelatin, etc.) **2** : to take hold, to catch on **3** : to break out (of fire) **4** : to go, to turn, to follow <prendre à droite : to bear right> **5 prendre sur soi** : to take upon oneself, to take responsibility — **se prendre** *vr* **1** : to be taken <ce médicament se prend avant les repas : this medicine is taken before meals> **2** : to get caught **3** : to catch <se prendre les doigts dans la porte : to catch one's fingers in the door> **4 ~ à** : to get caught up in **5 ~ pour** : to consider oneself <il se prend pour un autre : he thinks he's better than anyone else> **6 s'y prendre** : to go about it, to act <il faut s'y prendre à l'avance : it must be done in advance>

preneur, -neuse [prǝnœr, -nøz] *n* : buyer, taker <je suis preneur : I'll take it>

prenne [prɛn], *etc.* → **prendre**

prénom [prenɔ̃] *nm* : given name, first name

prénommer [prenɔme] *vt* : to name — **se prénommer** *vr* : to be called <elle se prénomme Anne : her first name is Anne>

prénuptial, -tiale [prenypsjal] *adj, mpl* **-tiaux** [-sjo] : prenuptial

préoccupant, -pante [preɔkypɑ̃, -pɑ̃t] *adj* INQUIÉTANT : worrisome

préoccupation [preɔkypasjɔ̃] *nf* INQUIÉTUDE : worry, concern

préoccuper [preɔkype] *vt* **1** INQUIÉTER : to worry, to concern **2** : to preoccupy — **se préoccuper** *vr*

préparateur, -trice [preparatœr, -tris] *n* : (laboratory) assistant

préparatifs [preparatif] *nmpl* : preparations

préparation [preparasjɔ̃] *nf* : preparation

préparatoire [preparatwar] *adj* : preparatory

préparer [prepare] *vt* **1** : to prepare, to make ready <préparer un repas : to prepare a meal> <préparer une prescription : to dispense a prescription> **2** : to prepare for (an exam, etc.) **3** : to prepare, to train — **se préparer** *vr* **1** : to prepare, to get ready **2** : to be in the offing

prépondérance [prepɔ̃derɑ̃s] *nf* : predominance

prépondérant, -rante [prepɔ̃derɑ̃, -rɑ̃t] *adj* : predominant, dominating

préposé, -sée [prepoze] *n* **1** : official, clerk, attendant **2** *France* : mailman

préposer [prepoze] *vt* : to appoint <être préposé à : to be (put) in charge of>

préposition [prepɔzisjɔ̃] *nf* : preposition — **prépositionnel, -nelle** [prepɔzisjɔnɛl] *adj*

prérequis [prereki] *nms & pl Can* : prerequisite (in college)

prérogative [prerɔgativ] *nf* : prerogative

près [prɛ] *adv* **1** : close, near <c'est tout près : it's close by> **2** : near, soon <lundi, c'est trop près : Monday's too soon> <les vacances sont tout près maintenant : it's almost time for vacation> **3 à . . . près** : more or less, close enough to, within about <à un centimètre près : within about a centimeter> <à cela près : except for that> **4 à peu près** PRESQUE : almost, just about, approximately **5 de ~** : closely <regarder de près : to take a close look at> **6 ~ de** : near, close to <près de partir : about to leave> <près d'ici : nearby>

présage |prezaʒ| *nm* : omen, sign, augur

présager |prezaʒe| {17} *vt* **1** PRÉVOIR : to foresee, to predict **2** : to portend, to bode

presbyte |prɛsbit| *adj* HYPERMÉTROPE : farsighted

presbytère |prɛsbitɛr| *nm* : rectory

presbytie |prɛsbisi| *nf* HYPERMÉTROPIE : farsightedness

prescience |presjɑ̃s| *nf* : foresight, prescience

préscolaire |preskɔlɛr| *adj* : preschool

prescription |prɛskripsjɔ̃| *nf* **1** : prescription **2** : limitation (in law)

prescrire |prɛskrir| {33} *vt* **1** : to prescribe **2** : to stipulate, to lay down

prescrivait |prɛskrivɛ|, **prescrivions** |prɛskrivjɔ̃|, *etc.* → **prescrire**

prescrive |prɛskriv|, *etc.* → **prescrire**

préséance |preseɑ̃s| *nf* : precedence

présence |prezɑ̃s| *nf* **1** : presence, attendance **2 en ~** : face to face **3 en présence de** : in the presence of, in front of **4 présence d'esprit** : presence of mind

présent[1], **-sente** |prezɑ̃, -zɑ̃t| *adj* **1** : present, in attendance **2** : existing, actual, current <le souvenir toujours présent : the ever-present memory> **3** : present, at hand <la présente lettre : the present letter, this letter>

présent[2] *nm* : present (time) <jusqu'à présent : until now>

présentateur, -trice |prezɑ̃tatœr, -tris| *n* : newscaster, anchor

présentation |prezɑ̃tasjɔ̃| *nf* **1** : presentation **2** ALLURE : appearance, look **3** : introduction <il a fait les présentations : he introduced us>

présente |prezɑ̃t| *nf* **1 par la présente** : hereby **2 des présentes** : hereof

présentement |prezɑ̃tmɑ̃| *adv* ACTUELLEMENT : at the moment, now

présenter |prezɑ̃te| *vt* **1** MONTRER : to present, to show, to display **2** : to introduce **3** : to offer, to give <présenter ses condoléances : to offer one's condolences> <présenter des excuses : to apologize> **4** : to submit (a proposal, etc.) **5** : to anchor (a television news program) — *vi* **présenter bien** : to have a pleasing appearance, to look well — **se présenter** *vr* **1** : to go, to come, to appear **2** : to introduce oneself **3 ~ à** : to run for (an office), to apply for (a job)

présentoir |prezɑ̃twar| *nm* : display shelf

préservatif |prezɛrvatif| *nm* CONDOM : condom

préservation |prezɛrvasjɔ̃| *nf* **1** : protection **2** CONSERVATION : preservation, conservation

préserver |prezɛrve| *vt* **1** : to protect **2** CONSERVER : to preserve, to conserve

présidence |prezidɑ̃s| *nf* **1** : presidency **2** : chairmanship

président, -dente |prezidɑ̃, -dɑ̃t| *n* **1** : president **2** : chair, chairperson **3 président de jury** : foreman (of a jury)

présidentiel, -tielle |prezidɑ̃sjɛl| *adj* : presidential

présidentielles |prezidɑ̃sjɛl| *nfpl France* : presidential election

présider |prezide| *vt* : to preside over, to chair — *vi* **~ à** : to rule over, to govern

présomption |prezɔ̃psjɔ̃| *nf* **1** : presumption, supposition **2** PRÉTENTION : pretentiousness

présomptueux, -tueuse |prezɔ̃ptɥø, -tɥøz| *adj* : presumptuous

presque |prɛsk| *adv* : almost, hardly, scarcely <presque jamais : hardly ever> <presque rien : next to nothing>

presqu'île |prɛskil| *nf* : peninsula

pressant, -sante |prɛsɑ̃, -sɑ̃t| *adj* : urgent, pressing

presse |prɛs| *nf* **1** : press (newspapers, magazines, etc.) <agence de presse : news agency> **2** : printing press **3 il n'y a pas de presse** *Can* : there's no hurry

pressé, -sée |prese| *adj* **1** : hurried **2** : urgent **3** : squeezed, pressed

presse–fruits |prɛsfrɥi| *nms & pl* : juicer

pressentiment |presɑ̃timɑ̃| *nm* : premonition, hunch

pressentir |presɑ̃tir| {82} *vt* **1** : to sense, to have a premonition about **2** : to contact, to approach

presse–papiers |prɛspapje| *nms & pl* : paperweight

presser |prese| *vt* **1** : to press, to squeeze **2** : to push **3** : to urge **4** : to hurry, to rush <presser le pas : to hurry up> **5 presser de questions** : to ply with questions — *vi* : to be pressing, to be urgent <le temps presse : time is running out> — **se presser** *vr* **1** : to crowd, to throng **2** SE HÂTER : to hurry up **3 ~ contre** *or* **~ sur** : to snuggle up against

pression |prɛsjɔ̃| *nf* **1** : pressure <pression artérielle : blood pressure> <faire pression sur : to put pressure on> **2** BOUTON-PRESSION : snap (fastener)

pressurer |presyre| *vt* : to press, to squeeze

pressuriser [presyrize] *vt* : to pressurize
prestance [prɛstɑ̃s] *nf* : (imposing) presence, bearing
prestataire [prɛstatɛr] *nm* **1** : recipient **2 prestataire de bien–être social** *Can* : welfare recipient
prestation [prɛstasjɔ̃] *nf* **1** : benefit, allowance **2** : performance **3 prestations d'assurance–chômage** *Can* : unemployment insurance benefits
preste [prɛst] *adj* : nimble — **prestement** [prɛstəmɑ̃] *adv*
prestidigitateur, -trice [prɛstidiʒitatœr, -tris] *n* : magician, conjurer
prestidigitation [prɛstidiʒitasjɔ̃] *nf* : sleight of hand, conjuring
prestige [prɛstiʒ] *nm* : prestige
prestigieux, -gieuse [prɛstiʒjø, -ʒjøz] *adj* : prestigious
presto [prɛsto] *interj* : presto!
présumément [prezymemɑ̃] *adv Can* : presumably, supposedly
présumer [prezyme] *vt* : to presume, to suppose — *vi* **~ de** : to overestimate, to overrate
présupposer [presypoze] *vt* : to presuppose — **présupposition** [-pozisjɔ̃] *nf*
prêt[1], **prête** [prɛ, prɛt] *adj* **1** PRÉPARÉ : ready, prepared <tout est prêt : everything's ready> **2** DISPOSÉ : willing <être tout prêt à : to be ready and willing to>
prêt[2] *nm* EMPRUNT : loan
prêt–à–porter [prɛtapɔrte] *nm, pl* **prêts–à–porter** : ready-to-wear (clothing)
prétendant[1], **-dante** [pretɑ̃dɑ̃, -dɑ̃t] *n* : pretender (to a throne)
prétendant[2] *nm* : suitor
prétendre [pretɑ̃dr] {63} *vt* **1** AFFIRMER : to claim, to maintain **2** : to expect <il ne prétend pas être récompensé : he doesn't expect to be rewarded> — *vi* **~ à** : to lay claim to, to aspire to
prétendu, -due [pretɑ̃dy] *adj* SOI-DISANT : so-called, alleged
prétendument [pretɑ̃dymɑ̃] *adv* : allegedly, supposedly
prétentieux, -tieuse [pretɑ̃sjø, -sjøz] *adj* : pretentious — **prétentieusement** [-sjøzmɑ̃] *adv*
prétention [pretɑ̃sjɔ̃] *nf* **1** : pretentiousness **2** AMBITION : claim, pretension, pretense
prêter [prete] *vt* **1** : to lend **2** ATTRIBUER : to attribute, to ascribe <prêter de l'importance à : to attach importance to> **3** ACCORDER : to offer, to give <prêter l'oreille : to listen, to lend an ear> <prêter attention : to pay attention> <prêter une main : to lend a hand> — *vi* **~ à** : to cause, to give rise to — **se prêter** *vr* **1 ~ à** : to lend oneself to **2 ~ à** : to be suitable for
prêteur, -teuse [prɛtœr, -tøz] *n* **1** : lender, moneylender **2 prêteur sur gages** : pawnbroker
prétexte [pretɛkst] *nm* : pretext, excuse
prétexter [pretɛkste] *vt* : to give as a pretext, to plead
prêtre [prɛtr] *nm* : priest
prêtresse [prɛtrɛs] *nf* : priestess
prêtrise [pretriz] *nf* : priesthood
preuve [prœv] *nf* **1** : proof, evidence **2 faire preuve de** : to show
prévale [preval], *etc.* → **prévaloir**
prévaloir [prevalwar] {71} *vi* PRÉDOMINER : to prevail — **se prévaloir** *vr* **1 ~ de** : to take advantage of **2 ~ de** : to claim, to boast of
prévaudra [prevodra], *etc.* → **prévaloir**
prévaut [prevo], *etc.* → **prévaloir**
prévenance [prevnɑ̃s] *nf* : consideration, thoughtfulness
prévenant, -nante [prevnɑ̃, -nɑ̃t] *adj* ATTENTIONNÉ : considerate, thoughtful
prévenir [prevnir] {92} *vt* **1** ÉVITER : to prevent, to avoid **2** AVISER, INFORMER : to inform **3** AVERTIR : to warn **4** ANTICIPER : to anticipate **5 ~ contre** : to prejudice (someone) against
préventif, -tive [prevɑ̃tif, -tiv] *adj* : preventive
prévention [prevɑ̃sjɔ̃] *nf* **1** : prevention <prévention routière : road safety> **2** : prejudice, bias
prévenu, -nue [prevny] *n* : defendant, accused
prévisible [previzibl] *adj* : predictable, foreseeable
prévision [previzjɔ̃] *nf* **1** : prediction, expectation **2 prévisions** *nfpl* : forecast <prévisions météorologiques : weather forecast>
prévoir [prevwar] {99} *vt* **1** : to predict, to anticipate, to forecast **2** : to plan (on), to schedule **3** : to provide for, to allow (for)
prévoyance [prevwajɑ̃s] *nf* : foresight
prévoyant, -voyante [prevwajɑ̃, -vwajɑ̃t] *adj* : provident, farsighted
prier [prije] {96} *vi* : to pray — *vt* **1** : to beg, to implore **2** : to ask, to request <vous êtes prié d'assister : you are requested to attend> **3 je vous en prie** : please, don't mention it, you're welcome
prière [prijɛr] *nf* **1** : prayer **2** : request, entreaty, plea
primaire [primɛr] *adj* **1** : primary, elementary **2** : limited, simplistic
primate [primat] *nm* : primate (in zoology)
prime[1] [prim] *adj* **1** : first <de prime abord : at first> <prime enfance : early childhood> **2** : prime (in mathematics) **3** *Can* : temperamental, irascible
prime[2] *nf* **1** INDEMNITÉ : premium, allowance **2** : bonus, gift
primer [prime] *vt* **1** : to take precedence over, to prevail over **2** : to award a

prize to — *vi* : to dominate, to be of primary importance
primesautier, -tière [primsotje, -tjɛr] *adj* : impulsive
primeur [primœr] *nf* **1 avoir la primeur de** : to be the first with, to be the first to hear **2 primeurs** *nfpl* : early fruit and vegetables
primevère [primvɛr] *nf* : primrose
primitif, -tive [primitif, -tiv] *adj* **1** : primitive **2** INITIAL : original, initial
primo [primo] *adv* : firstly, first (of all)
primordial, -diale [primɔrdjal] *adj, mpl* **-diaux** [-djo] **1** : essential, vital **2** : primordial
prince [prɛ̃s] *nm* : prince
princesse [prɛ̃sɛs] *nf* : princess
princier, -cière [prɛ̃sje, -sjɛr] *adj* : princely
principal[1], -pale [prɛ̃sipal] *adj, mpl* **-paux** [-po] : main, principal <plat principal : main course> <un rôle principal : a leading role>
principal[2] *nm* **1** ESSENTIEL : main thing **2** CAPITAL : principal (in finance)
principalement [prɛ̃sipalmɑ̃] *adv* : primarily, mainly
principauté [prɛ̃sipote] *nf* : principality
principe [prɛ̃sip] *nm* **1** : principle, rule <en principe : in principle, as a rule> **2** : assumption <partir du principe que : to work on the assumption that> **3** : concept, guiding principle **4** : origin, prime mover
printanier, -nière [prɛ̃tanje, -njɛr] *adj* : spring, springlike
printemps [prɛ̃tɑ̃] *nms & pl* : spring
priorité [prijɔrite] *nf* **1** : priority <en priorité : first> **2** : right-of-way
pris[1] [pri] *pp* → **prendre**
pris[2], prise [pri, priz] *adj* **1** : taken, full, sold (out) **2** : stricken, afflicted <pris de peur : panic-stricken> **3** : occupied, busy
prise [priz] *nf* **1** : taking, capture, catch **2** : hold, grip **3** *Can* : strike (in baseball) **4** *or* **prise de médicament** : dose (of medicine) **5 prise de bec** : squabble, spat **6 prise de courant** : (electrical) outlet **7 prise de sang** : blood specimen **8 prise d'eau** : hydrant **9 prise directe** : high gear
priser [prize] *vt* **1** : to take, to snort (drugs, snuff) **2** : to prize, to value
prisme [prism] *nm* : prism
prison [prizɔ̃] *nf* **1** : prison **2** : imprisonment <faire de la prison : to serve time>
prisonnier[1], -nière [prizɔnje, -njɛr] *adj* : captive, imprisoned
prisonnier[2], -nière *n* : prisoner
privation [privasjɔ̃] *nf* **1** : deprivation, loss **2** : privation, want <une vie de privations : a life of hardships>
privatisation [privatizasjɔ̃] *nf* : privatization — **privatiser** [-tize] *vt*
privautés [privote] *nfpl* : liberties <se permettre des privautés avec : to take liberties with>
privé[1], -vée [prive] *adj* : private
privé[2] *nm* **1** : private life <en privé : in private> **2** : private sector
priver [prive] *vt* : to deprive — **se priver** *vr* **1** ~ **de** : to go without, to do without **2 ne pas se priver de** : not to hesitate to
privilège [privilɛʒ] *nm* : privilege
privilégier [privileʒje] {96} *vt* FAVORISER : to privilege, to favor — **privilégié, -giée** [-leʒje] *adj*
prix [pri] *nms & pl* **1** : price, cost <hors de prix : exorbitantly expensive> <à tout prix : at all costs> <à prix coûtant : at cost> **2** : prize
probabilité [prɔbabilite] *nf* : probability, likelihood
probable [prɔbabl] *adj* : probable, likely <peu probable : unlikely>
probablement [prɔbabləmɑ̃] *adv* : probably
probant, -bante [prɔbɑ̃, -bɑ̃t] *adj* : convincing, conclusive
probité [prɔbite] *nf* : probity, integrity
problématique [prɔblematik] *adj* : problematic
problème [prɔblɛm] *nm* : problem
procédé [prɔsede] *nm* **1** : process, procedure **2** COMPORTEMENT : conduct, behavior
procéder [prɔsede] {87} *vi* **1** AVANCER : to proceed **2** : to act, to behave **3** ~ **à** : to carry out, to proceed with
procédure [prɔsedyr] *nf* **1** : procedure **2** : (legal) proceedings *pl*
procès [prɔsɛ] *nms & pl* **1** : lawsuit **2** : trial
procession [prɔsesjɔ̃] *nf* : procession
processus [prɔsesys] *nms & pl* : process, system
procès-verbal [prɔsɛvɛrbal] *nm, pl* **procès-verbaux** [-vɛrbo] **1** : minutes *pl* (of a meeting) **2** : (judicial) record, (police) report **3** *France* : (parking) ticket
prochain[1], -chaine [prɔʃɛ̃, -ʃɛn] *adj* **1** SUIVANT : next, following **2** : imminent, forthcoming **3 à la prochaine!** *fam* : see you!, until next time!
prochain[2] *nm* : fellowman
prochainement [prɔʃɛnmɑ̃] *adv* BIENTÔT : soon, shortly
proche [prɔʃ] *adj* **1** : near, nearby <proche de : close to, neighboring on> **2** : near, imminent <l'avenir proche : the near future> **3** : closely related <le plus proche parent : the next of kin> **4 de proche en proche** : step by step, gradually
proches [prɔʃ] *nmpl* : close relatives
proclamation [prɔklamasjɔ̃] *nf* : proclamation
proclamer [prɔklame] *vt* **1** : to proclaim **2** : to announce, to declare

procréer [prɔkree] {89} *vt* : to procreate — **procréation** [-kreasjɔ̃] *nf*

procuration [prɔkyrasjɔ̃] *nf* **1** : proxy (in an election) **2** : power of attorney

procurer [prɔkyre] *vt* **1** : to provide, to give <procurer un emploi à qqn : to give s.o. a job> **2** OCCASIONNER : to provide, to cause <le plaisir procuré par la musique : the pleasure provided by music> — **se procurer** *vr* : to get, to obtain

procureur [prɔkyrœr] *nm* **1** *or* **procureur général** : prosecutor **2 procureur de la République** *France* : attorney general **3 procureur de la Couronne** *Can* : Crown attorney (attorney general)

prodigalité [prɔdigalite] *nf* : lavishness, extravagance

prodige [prɔdiʒ] *nm* **1** : prodigy **2** : marvel, wonder

prodigieux, -gieuse [prɔdiʒjø, -ʒjøz] *adj* EXTRAORDINAIRE : prodigious, extraordinary — **prodigieusement** [-ʒjøzmɑ̃] *adv*

prodigue [prɔdig] *adj* **1** DÉPENSIER : prodigal, extravagant **2** GÉNÉREUX : generous, lavish

prodiguer [prɔdige] *vt* : to lavish

producteur[1], **-trice** [prɔdyktœr, -tris] *adj* : producing

producteur[2] *nm* : producer

productif, -tive [prɔdyktif, -tiv] *adj* **1** : productive **2** RENTABLE : profitable

production [prɔdyksjɔ̃] *nf* **1** : production, output **2** : produce, products *pl*

productivité [prɔdyktivite] *nf* : productivity

produire [prɔdɥir] {49} *vt* **1** : to produce, to generate, to yield **2** : to cause, to bring about — **se produire** *vr* **1** : to occur, to happen **2** : to perform, to appear (on stage)

produisait [prɔdɥizɛ], **produisions** [prɔdɥizjɔ̃], *etc.* → **produire**

produise [prɔdɥiz], *etc.* → **produire**

produit [prɔdɥi] *nm* **1** : product **2** : proceeds *pl*, yield

proéminence [prɔeminɑ̃s] *nf* : prominence, protuberance — **proéminent, -nente** [prɔeminɑ̃, -nɑ̃t] *adj*

profanation [prɔfanasjɔ̃] *nf* : desecration, defilement

profane[1] [prɔfan] *adj* **1** : secular **2** : ignorant, uninitiated

profane[2] *nmf* **1** : layperson **2** : beginner, tyro

profaner [prɔfane] *vt* : to defile, to desecrate

proférer [prɔfere] {87} *vt* : to utter <proférer des menaces : to make threats>

professer [prɔfese] *vt* : to profess, to declare

professeur [prɔfesœr] *nm* **1** : teacher, schoolteacher **2** : professor

profession [prɔfesjɔ̃] *nf* **1** OCCUPATION : occupation, trade **2** : profession, declaration

professionnel, -nelle [prɔfɛsjɔnɛl] *adj & n* : professional — **professionnellement** [-nɛlmɑ̃] *adv*

professoral, -rale [prɔfɛsɔral] *adj, mpl* **-raux** [-ro] : professorial

professorat [prɔfɛsɔra] *nm* : teaching

profil [prɔfil] *nm* **1** : profile **2 de ~** : in profile, from the side

profiler [prɔfile] *vt* : to profile, to outline — **se profiler** *vr* **1** : to emerge, to take shape **2** : to stand out

profit [prɔfi] *nm* **1** : profit **2** : benefit, advantage <tirer profit de : to benefit from, to take advantage of>

profitable [prɔfitabl] *adj* : profitable — **profitablement** [-tabləmɑ̃] *adv*

profiter [prɔfite] *vi* **1 ~ à** : to be of benefit to **2 ~ de** : to take advantage of

profiteur, -teuse [prɔfitœr, -tøz] *n* : profiteer

profond[1] [prɔfɔ̃] *adv* : deeply

profond[2], **-fonde** [prɔfɔ̃, -fɔ̃d] *adj* **1** : deep <profond de deux mètres : two meters deep> <une voix profonde : a deep voice> <au plus profond de : in the depths of> **2** : deep-seated, underlying **3** : profound, penetrating

profondément [prɔfɔ̃demɑ̃] *adv* : deeply, profoundly

profondeur [prɔfɔ̃dœr] *nf* : depth, profundity

profusion [prɔfyzjɔ̃] *nf* : profusion <à profusion : in abundance>

profusément [prɔfyzemɑ̃] *adv* : profusely

progéniture [prɔʒenityr] *nf* : offspring, progeny

programmable [prɔgramabl] *adj* : programmable

programmation [prɔgramasjɔ̃] *nf* : programming

programme [prɔgram] *nm* **1** : program **2** : plan, schedule **3** : curriculum, syllabus

programmer [prɔgrame] *vt* **1** : to program (a computer) **2** : to plan, to schedule

programmeur, -meuse [prɔgramœr, -møz] *n* : (computer) programmer

progrès [prɔgrɛ] *nm* : progress <faire des progrès : to make progress>

progresser [prɔgrese] *vi* **1** : to progress, to advance **2** : to make progress, to improve

progressif, -sive [prɔgresif, -siv] *adj* : progressive — **progressivement** [-sivmɑ̃] *adv*

progression [prɔgrɛsjɔ̃] *nf* **1** : progress, advance **2** : progression, spread, increase

prohiber [prɔibe] *vt* : to prohibit, to ban

prohibitif, -tive [prɔibitif, -tiv] *adj* : prohibitive

prohibition [prɔibisjɔ] *nf* : prohibition

proie [prwa] *nf* **1** : prey **2 en proie à** : prey to, beset with, suffering from
projecteur [prɔʒɛktœr] *nm* **1** : projector **2** : spotlight, floodlight
projectile [prɔʒɛktil] *nm* : missile, projectile
projection [prɔʒɛksjɔ̃] *nf* **1** : projection, showing <salle de projection : screening room> **2** : throwing (off), discharge, spattering **3** : projection (in mathematics or psychology)
projet [prɔʒɛ] *nm* **1** : plan, project **2** ÉBAUCHE : draft, outline
projeter [prɔʃte] {8} *vt* **1** LANCER : to throw **2** : to project, to show (a film, etc.) **3** : to cast, to project (light) **4** : to plan
prolétaire [prɔletɛr] *adj & nmf* : proletarian
prolétariat [prɔletarjat] *nm* : proletariat
prolétarien, -rienne [prɔletarjɛ̃, -rjɛn] *adj* : proletarian
proliférer [prɔlifere] {87} *vi* SE MULTIPLIER : to proliferate — **prolifération** [-ferasjɔ̃] *nf*
prolifique [prɔlifik] *adj* : prolific
prolixe [prɔliks] *adj* : verbose, wordy
prologue [prɔlɔg] *nm* : prologue
prolongation [prɔlɔ̃gasjɔ̃] *nf* **1** ALLONGEMENT : extension, prolongation **2** *or* **prolongations** *nfpl* : overtime (in sports)
prolongement [prɔlɔ̃ʒmɑ̃] *nm* **1** : extension (of a road, railway, etc.) **2** : outcome, consequence
prolonger [prɔlɔ̃ʒe] {17} *vt* : to prolong, to extend — **se prolonger** *vr* : to continue, to persist, to go on
promenade [prɔmnad] *nf* **1** : walk, stroll **2** : ride, trip **3** : walkway, promenade
promener [prɔmne] {52} *vt* **1** : to take (out) for a walk <promener son chien : to walk one's dog> **2** : to run over, to move across <promener son regard sur une foule : to cast one's eyes over a crowd> — **se promener** *vr* **1** SE BALADER : to go for a walk **2 ~ sur** : to wander over, to roam across (with one's eyes, fingers, etc.)
promeneur, -neuse [prɔmnœr, -nøz] *n* : walker, stroller
promesse [prɔmɛs] *nf* **1** : promise <manquer à sa promesse : to break one's word> **2** : (legal) commitment <promesse d'achat : commitment to buy> **3 être plein de promesses** : to be full of promise
prometteur, -teuse [prɔmɛtœr, -tøz] *adj* : promising
promettre [prɔmɛtr] {53} *vt* : to promise — *vi* : to promise, to show promise — **se promettre** *vr* **~ de** : to resolve to
promis, -mise [prɔmi, -miz] *adj* **1** : promised **2 ~ à** : destined for
promiscuité [prɔmiskɥite] *nf* : overcrowding, lack of privacy
promontoire [prɔmɔ̃twar] *nm* : promontory, headland
promoteur, -trice [prɔmɔtœr, -tris] *n* : promoter
promotion [prɔmɔsjɔ̃] *nf* **1** : promotion, advancement **2** : promotion, (special) offer (in advertising)
promotionnel, -nelle [prɔmɔsjɔnɛl] *adj* : promotional
promouvoir [prɔmuvwar] {56} *vt* : to promote
prompt, prompte [prɔ̃, prɔ̃t] *adj* : prompt, swift, rapid <être prompt à réagir : to be quick to react>
promptement [prɔ̃tmɑ̃] *adv* : promptly, swiftly
promptitude [prɔ̃tityd] *nf* : swiftness, rapidity
promulgation [prɔmylgasjɔ̃] *nf* : promulgation, enactment
promulguer [prɔmylge] *vt* : to promulgate
prôner [prone] *vt* : to extol, to advocate, to commend
pronom [prɔnɔ̃] *nm* : pronoun
pronominal, -nale [prɔnɔminal] *adj, mpl* **-naux** [-no] **1** : pronominal **2** : reflexive <verbe pronominal : reflexive verb>
prononcé, -cée [prɔnɔ̃se] *adj* : pronounced, marked
prononcer [prɔnɔ̃se] {6} *vt* **1** : to pronounce **2** : to state, to declare — *vi* : to hand down a decision (in law) — **se prononcer** *vr* **1** : to be pronounced **2** : to give one's opinion, to declare oneself
prononciation [prɔnɔ̃sjasjɔ̃] *nf* : pronunciation
pronostic [prɔnɔstik] *nm* **1** : prognosis **2** PRÉDICTION : forecast, prediction
pronostiquer [prɔnɔstike] *vt* : to forecast
propagande [prɔpagɑ̃d] *nf* : propaganda
propagation [prɔpagasjɔ̃] *nf* **1** : propagation **2** : spreading
propager [prɔpaʒe] {17} *vt* **1** : to propagate **2** : to spread — **se propager** *vr*
propane [prɔpan] *nm* : propane
propension [prɔpɑ̃sjɔ̃] *nf* TENDANCE : propensity
propergol [prɔpɛrgɔl] *nm* : (rocket) propellant
prophète, prophétesse [prɔfɛt, prɔfetɛs] *n* : prophet, prophetess *f*
prophétie [prɔfesi] *nf* : prophecy
prophétique [prɔfetik] *adj* : prophetic — **prophétiquement** [-tikmɑ̃] *adv*
prophétiser [prɔfetize] *vt* : to prophesy
propice [prɔpis] *adj* : favorable, propitious
proportion [prɔpɔrsjɔ̃] *nf* **1** : proportion, ratio, relation <hors de proportion : out of proportion> <une proportion de dix contre un : a ratio of ten to one> <à proportion de : proportional to> <en proportion

: proportionately> 2 **proportions** *nfpl* : dimensions, size

proportionné, -née [prɔpɔrsjɔne] *adj* **1** : proportioned <bien proportionné : well-proportioned> **2** ~ **à** : proportionate to

proportionnel, -nelle [prɔpɔrsjɔnɛl] *adj* : proportional — **proportionnellement** [-nɛlmɑ̃] *adv*

proportionner [prɔpɔrsjɔne] *vt* : to proportion

propos [prɔpo] *nms & pl* **1** : subject **2** : intention, point **3 propos** *nmpl* : comments, talk **4 à** ~ : appropriate, apropos **5 à propos de** : regarding, about

proposer [prɔpoze] *vt* **1** : to suggest, to propose **2** : to offer **3** : to nominate — **se proposer** *vr* ~ **de** : to intend to

proposition [prɔpozisjɔ̃] *nf* **1** : suggestion **2** : proposal, offer **3** : proposition (in logic) **4** : clause <proposition subordonnée : subordinate clause>

propre[1] [prɔpr] *adj* **1** NET : clean, neat **2** : toilet trained, housebroken **3** : own <par sa propre faute : through his own fault> **4** : correct, proper <le mot propre : the correct word> **5** ~ **à** : likely to <propre à lui faire plaisir : likely to please her> **6** ~ **à** : characteristic of **7** ~ **à** : suitable for

propre[2] *nm* **1** : cleanliness, neatness <cette maison sent le propre : this house smells clean> **2** : distinctive feature <être le propre de : to be peculiar to> **3 au propre** : literally

proprement [prɔprəmɑ̃] *adv* **1** : cleanly, neatly **2** : properly, correctly **3** : strictly, precisely <à proprement parler : strictly speaking> **4 proprement dit** : actual, as such <le débat proprement dit : the debate itself>

propret, -prette [prɔprɛ, -prɛt] *adj* : clean and neat

propreté [prɔprəte] *nf* : cleanliness, neatness

propriétaire [prɔprijetɛr] *nmf* **1** : owner, proprietor **2** : landlord, landlady *f*

propriété [prɔprijete] *nf* **1** : property <propriété privée : private property> **2** : ownership **3** CARACTÉRISTIQUE : property, characteristic **4** : appropriateness, suitability

propulser [prɔpylse] *vt* **1** : to propel **2** : to hurl, to fling

propulsif, -sive [prɔpylsif, -siv] *adj* : propellant, propulsive

propulsion [prɔpylsjɔ̃] *nf* : propulsion

prorata [prɔrata] *nms & pl* **au prorata de** : in proportion to

prorogation [prɔrɔgasjɔ̃] *nf* **1** : extension, deferment **2** : adjournment

proroger [prɔrɔʒe] {17} *vt* **1** : to extend, to defer **2** : to adjourn

prosaïque [prɔzaik] *adj* : prosaic, mundane

proscription [prɔskripsjɔ̃] *nf* **1** : ban, prohibition **2** : banishment

proscrire [prɔskrir] {33} *vt* **1** INTERDIRE : to ban, to prohibit **2** BANNIR : to banish

proscrit, -scrite [prɔskri, -skrit] *n* : outcast

prose [proz] *nf* : prose

prospecter [prɔspɛkte] *vt* **1** : to prospect (for oil, etc.) **2** : to canvass

prospecteur, -trice [prɔspɛktœr, -tris] *n* **1** : prospector **2** : canvasser

prospectus [prɔspɛktys] *nms & pl* : prospectus, leaflet

prospère [prɔspɛr] *adj* **1** : prosperous **2** : thriving, flourishing

prospérer [prɔspere] {87} *vi* : to flourish, to thrive

prospérité [prɔsperite] *nf* : prosperity

prostate [prɔstat] *nf* : prostate (gland)

prosterner [prɔstɛrne] *v* **se prosterner** *vr* : to bow down, to prostrate oneself

prostituée [prɔstitɥe] *nf* : prostitute

prostituer [prɔstitɥe] *vi* : to prostitute — **se prostituer** *vr* : to prostitute oneself

prostitution [prɔstitysjɔ̃] *nf* : prostitution

prostration [prɔstrasjɔ̃] *nf* : prostration

prostré, -trée [prɔstre] *adj* : prostrate

protagoniste [prɔtagɔnist] *nmf* : protagonist

protecteur[1], **-trice** [prɔtɛktœr, -tris] *adj* : protective

protecteur[2], **-trice** *n* **1** : protector, guardian **2** : patron **3 protecteur du citoyen** *Can* : ombudsman

protection [prɔtɛksjɔ̃] *nf* **1** : protection **2** : patronage, support

protectorat [prɔtɛktɔra] *nm* : protectorate

protégé, -gée [prɔteʒe] *n* : protégé

protéger [prɔteʒe] {64} *vt* **1** : to protect, to defend **2** PATRONNER : to support, to encourage — **se protéger** *vr* ~ **de** : to protect oneself from

protéine [prɔtein] *nf* : protein

protestant, -tante [prɔtɛstɑ̃, -tɑ̃t] *adj & n* : Protestant — **protestantisme** [-tɑ̃tism] *nm*

protestataire [prɔtɛstatɛr] *nmf* : protester

protestation [prɔtɛstasjɔ̃] *nf* **1** : protest **2** : protestation, declaration

protester [prɔtɛste] *vi* **1** : to protest **2** ~ **de** : to declare, to profess

prothèse [prɔtɛz] *nf* **1** : prosthesis **2 prothèse dentaire** : denture

protocolaire [prɔtɔkɔlɛr] *adj* : formal, conforming to protocol

protocole [prɔtɔkɔl] *nm* : protocol

proton [prɔtɔ̃] *nm* : proton

protoplasme [prɔtɔplasm] *nm* : protoplasm

prototype [prɔtɔtip] *nm* : prototype

protozoaire [prɔtɔzɔɛr] *nm* : protozoan

protubérance [prɔtyberɑ̃s] *nf* : protuberance
protubérant, -rante [prɔtyberɑ̃, -rɑ̃t] *adj* : protuberant, bulging, protruding
proue [pru] *nf* : prow, bow (of a ship)
prouesse [pruɛs] *nf* EXPLOIT : feat, exploit
prouver [pruve] *vt* **1** ÉTABLIR : to prove **2** MONTRER : to show, to demonstrate
provenance [prɔvnɑ̃s] *nf* **1** : source, origin **2 en provenance de** : from <train en provenance de Paris : train (arriving) from Paris>
provençal, -çale [prɔvɑ̃sal] *adj, mpl* **-çaux** [-so] : Provençal
Provençal, -çale *n* : Provençal
provenir [prɔvnir] {92} *vi* **1 ~ de** : to come from (a place) **2 ~ de** : to result from, to stem from
proverbe [prɔvɛrb] *nm* : proverb
proverbial, -biale [prɔvɛrbjal] *adj, mpl* **-biaux** [-bjo] : proverbial — **proverbialement** [-bjalmɑ̃] *adv*
providence [prɔvidɑ̃s] *nf* : providence — **providentiel, -tielle** [-dɑ̃sjɛl] *adj*
province [prɔvɛ̃s] *nf* : province — **provincial, -ciale** [-vɛ̃sjal] *adj, mpl* **-ciaux** [-sjo]
proviseur [prɔvizœr] *nm France* : principal (of a school)
provision [prɔvizjɔ̃] *nf* **1** : stock, supply <faire provision de : to stock up on> **2** : advance, retainer **3** : funds *pl* (in a bank) <un chèque sans provision : a bad check> **4 provisions** *nfpl* : provisions, food
provisoire [prɔvizwar] *adj* : provisional, temporary, interim — **provisoirement** [-zwarmɑ̃] *adv*
provocant, -cante [prɔvɔkɑ̃, -kɑ̃t] *adj* : provocative
provocateur[1], -trice [prɔvɔkatœr, -tris] *adj* : provocative, challenging
provocateur[2] *nm* : agitator, troublemaker
provocation [prɔvɔkasjɔ̃] *nf* : provocation
provoquer [prɔvɔke] *vt* **1** : to cause, to give rise to <provoquer des rires : to provoke laughter> **2** : to provoke, to stir up, to trigger
proximité [prɔksimite] *nf* : proximity, nearness, closeness
pruche [pryʃ] *nf Can* : hemlock (tree)
prude[1] [pryd] *adj* : prudish
prude[2] *nf* : prude
prudemment [prydamɑ̃] *adv* : carefully, cautiously
prudence [prydɑ̃s] *nf* **1** : care, caution **2 avec ~** : cautiously
prudent, -dente [prydɑ̃, -dɑ̃t] *adj* **1** AVISÉ : prudent, sensible **2** : careful, cautious <soyez prudents : be careful>
prune[1] [pryn] *adj* : plum-colored
prune[2] *nf* **1** : plum **2** *Can* : bruise
pruneau [pryno] *nm, pl* **pruneaux 1** : prune **2** *Can* : plum
prunelle [prynɛl] *nf* : pupil (of the eye)
prunier [prynje] *nm* : plum tree
psalmodie [psalmɔdi] *nf* : chanting, droning
psalmodier [psalmɔdje] {96} *v* **1** : to chant **2** : to drone
psaume [psom] *nm* : psalm
pseudonyme [psødɔnim] *nm* : pseudonym
psoriasis [psɔrjazis] *nm* : psoriasis
psychanalyse [psikanaliz] *nf* : psychoanalysis — **psychanalyste** [-list] *nmf*
psychanalyser [psikanalize] *vt* : to psychoanalyse
psychanalytique [psikanalitik] *adj* : psychoanalytic
psyché [psiʃe] *nf* : psyche
psychédélique [psikedelik] *adj* : psychedelic
psychiatre [psikjatr] *nmf* : psychiatrist
psychiatrie [psikjatri] *nf* : psychiatry
psychiatrique [psikjatrik] *adj* : psychiatric
psychique [psiʃik] *adj* : psychic, mental
psychisme [psiʃism] *nm* : psyche, mind
psychologie [psikɔlɔʒi] *nf* : psychology
psychologique [psikɔlɔʒik] *adj* : psychological — **psychologiquement** [-ʒikmɑ̃] *adv*
psychologue [psikɔlɔg] *nmf* : psychologist
psychopathe[1] [psikɔpat] *adj* : psychopathic
psychopathe[2] *nmf* : psychopath
psychose [psikoz] *nf* : psychosis
psychosomatique [psikɔsɔmatik] *adj* : psychosomatic
psychothérapeute [psikɔterapøt] *nmf* : psychotherapist
psychothérapie [psikɔterapi] *nf* : psychotherapy
psychotique [psikɔtik] *adj & nmf* : psychotic
pseudonyme[1] [psødɔnim] *adj* : pseudonymous
pseudonyme[2] *nm* : pseudonym
pu [py] *pp* → **pouvoir**
puant, puante [pɥɑ̃, -ɑ̃t] *adj* **1** : foul-smelling, stinking **2** *fam* : conceited, obnoxious
puanteur [pɥɑ̃tœr] *nf* : stink, stench
puberté [pybɛrte] *nf* : puberty
pubien, -bienne [pybjɛ̃, -bjɛn] *adj* : pubic
public[1], -blique [pyblik] *adj* : public
public[2] *nm* **1** : public <le grand public : the general public> **2** : audience, spectators *pl*
publication [pyblikasjɔ̃] *nf* : publication
publiciste [pyblisist] *nmf* : publicist, advertising executive
publicitaire [pyblisitɛr] *adj* : advertising, promotional

publicité |pyblisite| *nf* **1** : publicity **2** : advertisement, commercial
publier |pyblije| {96} *vt* : to publish
publiquement |pyblikmɑ̃| *adv* : publicly
puce |pys| *nf* **1** : flea **2** : computer chip
puceron |pysrɔ̃| *nm* : aphid
pudding *or* **pouding** |pudiŋ| *nm* : pudding
pudeur |pydœr| *nf* **1** : modesty, decency **2** : sense of propriety, tact
pudibond, -bonde |pydibɔ̃, -bɔ̃d| *adj* : prudish, prim
pudibonderie |pydibɔ̃dri| *nf* : prudishness
pudique |pydik| *adj* **1** : modest, decent **2** : restrained, discreet
pudiquement |pydikmɑ̃| *adv* **1** : modestly **2** : discreetly
puer |pɥe| *vi* : to smell, to stink — *vt* : to reek of
puéril, -rile |pɥeril| *adj* : childish, puerile
puérilité |pɥerilite| *nf* : childishness
pugilat |pyʒila| *nm* : fistfight
pugnace |pygnas| *adj* : pugnacious
puis |pɥi| *adv* **1** ENSUITE : then, afterwards, next **2 et puis** : and besides **3 et puis après?** *or* **et puis quoi?** *fam* : so?, so what?
puisard |pɥizar| *nm* : cesspool
puiser |pɥize| *vt* **~ dans** : to draw from, to dip into
puisque |pɥiskə| *conj* **1** : since, as, because <puisque vous insistez : since you insist> **2** (*used as an intensifier*) <puisque je te le dis! : because I'm telling you so!>
puissance |pɥisɑ̃s| *nf* : power
puissant, -sante |pɥisɑ̃, -sɑ̃t| *adj* : powerful
puisse |pɥis|, *etc.* → **pouvoir**
puits |pɥi| *nms & pl* **1** : well <puits artésien : artesian well> <puits de pétrole : oil well> **2** : shaft <puits de mine : mine shaft> **3 puits de science** : font of knowledge, learned person
pull *or* **pull-over** |pyl, pylɔvɛr| *nm France* : pullover sweater
pullulement |pylylmɑ̃| *nm* : proliferation
pulluler |pylyle| *vi* **1** SE MULTIPLIER : to proliferate **2** GROUILLER : to swarm, to teem
pulmonaire |pylmɔnɛr| *adj* : pulmonary, lung
pulpe |pylp| *nf* : pulp
pulpeux, -peuse |pylpø, -pøz| *adj* : pulpy
pulsation |pylsasjɔ̃| *nf* **1** : beat, pulsation **2** POULS : pulse
pulsion |pylsjɔ̃| *nf* : drive, urge
pulvérisateur |pylverizatœr| *nm* VAPORISATEUR : spray, atomizer
pulvériser |pylverize| *vt* **1** : to pulverize **2** : to spray **3** : to demolish (an argument, etc.)
puma |pyma| *nm* : puma, cougar
punaise |pynɛz| *nf* **1** : bug <punaise de lit : bedbug> **2** : thumbtack
punch |pɔ̃ʃ| *nm* **1** : punch (drink) **2** |pœnʃ| : punch, blow (of a boxer, etc.) **3** : drive, energy
punir |pynir| *vt* **1** : to punish **2** *Can* : to penalize (in sports)
punissable |pynisabl| *adj* : punishable
punitif, -tive |pynitif, -tiv| *adj* : punitive
punition |pynisjɔ̃| *nf* **1** : punishment **2** *Can* : penalty (in sports)
pupe |pyp| *nf* : pupa
pupille[1] |pypij| *nmf* : ward (of the court), orphan
pupille[2] *nf* : pupil (of the eye)
pupitre |pypitr| *nm* **1** BUREAU : desk **2** LUTRIN : lectern **3** : console, keyboard, control panel **4** : music stand
pur, pure |pyr| *adj* : pure — **purement** |pyrmɑ̃| *adv*
purée |pyre| *nf* **1** : puree <purée de pommes de terre : mashed potatoes> **2 purée de pois** : thick fog, pea soup
pureté |pyrte| *nf* : purity
purgatif[1]**, -tive** |pyrgatif, -tiv| *adj* : purgative
purgatif[2] *nm* : purgative, laxative
purgatoire |pyrgatwar| *nm* : purgatory
purge |pyrʒ| *nf* : purge, purging
purger |pyrʒe| {17} *vt* **1** : to drain (a radiator, etc.), to bleed (brakes) **2** : to rid of, to purge **3** : to purge, to give a laxative to **4** : to serve (a jail sentence)
purificateur |pyrifikatœr| *nm* : purifier <purificateur d'air : air purifier>
purification |pyrifikasjɔ̃| *nf* : purification
purifier |pyrifje| {96} *vt* : to purify — **se purifier** *vr*
purin |pyrɛ̃| *nm* : liquid manure
puritain[1]**, -taine** |pyritɛ̃, -tɛn| *adj* : puritanical
puritain[2]**, -taine** *n* : puritan
pur-sang |pyrsɑ̃| *nms & pl* : Thoroughbred
pus |py| *nm* : pus
pusillanime |pyzilanim| *adj* : pusillanimous
pustule |pystyl| *nf* : pustule
putain |pytɛ̃| *nf usu vulgar* : whore
putois |pytwa| *nms & pl* : polecat
putréfier |pytrefje| {96} *vt* : to putrefy — **se putréfier** *vr* : to putrefy, to rot
putride |pytrid| *adj* : putrid, rotten
puzzle |pœzl| *nm* : jigsaw puzzle
Pygmée |pigme| *nmf* : Pygmy
pyjama |piʒama| *nm* : pajamas *pl*
pylône |pilon| *nm* : pylon
pyramide |piramid| *nf* : pyramid
pyromane |pirɔman| *nmf* : pyromaniac
pyromanie |pirɔmani| *nf* : pyromania
pyrotechnie |pirɔtɛkni| *nf* : fireworks *pl*, pyrotechnics *pl*
python |pitɔ̃| *nm* : python

Q

q [ky] *nm* : q, the 17th letter of the alphabet
quadrant [kwadrɑ̃] *nm* : quadrant
quadrilatère [kwadrilatɛr] *nm* : quadrilateral, quadrangle (in geometry)
quadrillage [kadrijaʒ] *nm* : crisscross pattern, grid
quadrillé, -lée [kadrije] *adj* : squared <papier quadrillé : graph paper>
quadriller [kadrije] *vt* **1** : to mark into squares **2** : to surround, to control (an area)
quadrupède [k̊w̃adrypɛd] *nm* : quadruped
quadruple [k(w)adrypl] *adj* : quadruple
quadrupler [k(w)adryple] *v* : to quadruple
quadruplés, -plées [k(w)adryple] *npl* : quadruplets
quai [kɛ] *nm* **1** : quay, wharf **2** : platform (at a railway station)
qualification [kalifikasjɔ̃] *nf* : qualification
qualifié, -fiée [kalifje] *adj* : qualified, skilled
qualifier [kalifje] {96} *vt* **1** : to qualify **2** CARACTÉRISER : to describe, to call **— se qualifier** *vr*
qualité [kalite] *nf* **1** : quality, excellence **2** : quality, property, attribute **3** : capacity, role <en qualité d'observateur : in his role as an observer>
quand[1] [kɑ̃] *adv* : when <quand partez-vous? : when are you leaving?> <je sais quand ils arriveront : I know when they will arrive>
quand[2] *conj* **1** : when <quand je la verrai : when I see her> **2** (*used for emphasis*) <quand je vous le disais! : I told you so!> **3 quand même** : still, even so
quant [kɑ̃] **~ à** : as for, as to, regarding
quant–à–soi [kɑ̃taswa] *nm* : reserve, aloofness <rester sur son quant-à-soi : to keep one's distance>
quantifier [kɑ̃tifje] {96}*vt* : to quantify **— quantifiable** [-tifjabl] *adj*
quantitatif, -tive [kɑ̃titatif, -tiv] *adj* : quantitative **— quantitativement** [-tivmɑ̃] *adv*
quantité [kɑ̃tite] *nf* : quantity, amount, number <une quantité de : a lot of>
quantum [kwɑ̃tɔm] *nm, pl* **quanta** : quantum <théorie des quanta : quantum theory>
quarantaine [karɑ̃tɛn] *nf* **1** : quarantine **2 avoir la quarantaine** : to be in one's forties **3 une quarantaine de** : about forty
quarante [karɑ̃t] *adj & nms & pl* : forty
quarantième [karɑ̃tjɛm] *adj & nmf & nm* : fortieth
quart [kar] *nm* **1** : quarter, forth <un kilo et quart : a kilo and a quarter> **2** (*in expressions of time*) : quarter <deux heures et quart : a quarter after two> <un quart d'heure : fifteen minutes>
quarte–arrière [kartarjɛr] *nm Can* : quarterback (in football)
quartier [kartje] *nm* **1** : piece, segment, quarter <un quartier de pomme : a piece of apple> <quartier de devant : forequarter> **2** : area, district **3 quartier général** : headquarters (in the army, etc.)
quartz [kwarts] *nm* : quartz
quasi [kazi] *adv* : nearly, almost <quasi impossible : practically impossible>
quasiment [kazimɑ̃] *adv* : nearly, almost
quatorze[1] [katɔrz] *adj* **1** : fourteen **2** : fourteenth <le quatorze février : the fourteenth of February>
quatorze[2] *nms & pl* : fourteen
quatorzième [katɔrzjɛm] *adj & nmf & nm* : fourteenth
quatre[1] [katr] *adj* **1** : four **2** : fourth <le quatre avril : the fourth of April>
quatre[2] *nms & pl* **1** : four **2 à quatre pattes** : on all fours
quatre–vingt–dix [katrəvɛ̃dis] *adj & nms & pl* : ninety
quatre–vingt–dixième [katrəvɛ̃dizjɛm] *adj & nmf & nm* : ninetieth
quatre–vingtième [katrəvɛ̃tjɛm] *adj & nmf & nm* : eightieth
quatre–vingts [katrəvɛ̃] (**quatre-vingt** *with another numeral adjective*) *adj & nms & pl* : eighty <quatre-vingt-un : eighty-one> <quatre-vingts personnes : eighty people>
quatrième[1] [katrijɛm] *adj & nmf* **1** : fourth **2 en quatrième vitesse** : in a hurry
quatrième[2] *nmf* : fourth (in a series)
quatuor [kwatɥɔr] *nm* : quartet
que[1] [kə] *adv* **1** : how <que c'est beau! : how beautiful!> **2** : why <que n'est-il venu? : why didn't he come?>
que[2] *conj* **1** : that <il a avoué qu'il avait tort : he admitted that he was wrong> **2** : than <travailler plus que nécessaire : to work harder than necessary> **3** (*used in a subjunctive clause expressing an order or desire*) <qu'elle vienne! : tell her to come!> **4** : whether <qu'il fasse soleil ou non : whether it's sunny or not> **5** → **ne**
que[3] *pron* **1** : who, whom, that <l'homme que vous aimez : the man that you love> **2** : that, which <c'était la seule chose qu'il pouvait faire : it was the only thing that he could do> **3** : what <que faire? : what should we do?> <qu'est-ce que tu as? : what's wrong?> <qu'est-ce que c'est que ça? : what's that?>
québécois, -coise [kebekwa, -kwaz] *adj* : Quebec, from or of Quebec

Québécois, -coise *n* : Quebecer, person from Quebec
quel[1], **quelle** [kɛl] *adj* **1** : what, which <quelle heure est-il? : what time is it?> **2** (*used as an intensifier*) <quel dommage! : what a pity!> **3** : whatever, whichever, whoever <quelle que soit la raison : whatever the reason may be>
quel[2], **quelle** *pron* : who, which one <de quel s'agit-il? : which one are you talking about?>
quelconque [kɛlkɔ̃k] *adj* **1** : some sort of, any <une quelconque mesure : some sort of action> **2** : ordinary <un être quelconque : an ordinary person>
quelque[1] [kɛlkə] *adv* **1** : about, approximately <quelque 200 personnes : about 200 people> **2** : however <quelque important qu'il soit : however important he may be>
quelque[2] *adj* **1** : a few, several, some <il a dit quelques mots : he said a few words> **2 quelque chose** : something **3 quelque part** : somewhere **4 quelque peu** : somewhat <quelque peu déçu : somewhat disappointed>
quelquefois [kɛlkəfwa] *adv* : sometimes
quelques–uns, quelques–unes [kɛlkəzœ̃, kɛlkəzyn] *pron* : some, a few
quelqu'un [kɛlkœ̃] *pron* **1** : someone, somebody <quelqu'un d'autre : someone else> **2** : anyone, anybody <y a-t-il quelqu'un? : is anyone there?>
quémander [kemɑ̃de] *vt* : to beg for
qu'en–dira–t–on [kɑ̃diratɔ̃] *nms & pl* : gossip
quenouille [kənuj] *nf Can* : cattail (plant)
querelle [kərɛl] *nf* : quarrel
quereller [kərele] *v* **se quereller** *vr* : to quarrel
querelleur, -leuse [kərɛlœr, -løz] *adj* : quarrelsome
question [kɛstjɔ̃] *nf* **1** : question <poser une question : to ask a question> **2** : matter, issue
questionnaire [kɛstjɔnɛr] *nm* : questionnaire
questionner [kɛstjɔne] *vt* : to question **— se questionner** *vr*
quétaine [ketɛn] *adj Can fam* : hokey, corny
quête [kɛt] *nf* **1** : quest, search **2** : collection (of money)
quêter [kete] *vt* : to seek, to solicit (favors, money, etc.) **—** *vi* : to take a collection
quêteur, -teuse [kɛtœr, -tøz] *n* : collector
quêteux, -teuse [kɛtœ, -tøz] *n Can* : beggar
queue [kø] *nf* **1** : tail **2** : tail end, rear, bottom **3** : stem, stalk **4** : handle (of a pot) **5** : cue (in billiards) **6** : line <faire la queue : to stand in line> **7 queue d'aronde** : dovetail **8 queue de cheval** : ponytail
qui [ki] *pron* **1** : who, whom <qui est-ce? : who is it?> <à qui de droit : to whom it may concern> **2** : which, that <un livre qui est sur la table : a book which is on the table> **3 qui que** : whoever, whomever
quiconque [kikɔ̃k] *pron* **1** : whoever, whomever **2** : anyone, anybody
quiétude [kjetyd] *nf* : quiet, tranquility
quignon [kiɲɔ̃] *nm* : hunk, heel (of a loaf of bread)
quille [kij] *nf* **1** : keel **2 quilles** *nfpl or* **jeu de quilles** : ninepins
quincaillerie [kɛ̃kajri] *nf* **1** : hardware **2** : hardware store
quincaillier, -lière [kɛ̃kaje, -jɛr] *n* : hardware dealer
quinine [kinin] *nf* : quinine
quinquagénaire [kɛ̃kaʒenɛr] *nmf* : person in his or her fifties
quinquennal, -nale [kɛ̃kenal] *adj, mpl* **-naux** [-no] : five-year <plan quinquennal : five-year plan>
quintal [kɛ̃tal] *nm, pl* **quintaux** [kɛ̃to] : quintal
quinte [kɛ̃t] *nf or* **quinte de toux** : coughing fit
quintessence [kɛ̃tesɑ̃s] *nf* : quintessence **— quintessentiel, -tielle** [-sɑ̃sjɛl] *adv*
quintette [kɛ̃tɛt] *nm* : quintet
quintuple [kɛ̃typl] *adj* : quintuple, fivefold
quintupler [kɛ̃typle] *vt* : to quintuple
quintuplés, -plées [kɛ̃typle] *npl* : quintuplets
quinzaine [kɛ̃zɛn] *nf* **1 une quinzaine de** : about fifteen **2 une quinzaine de jours** : two weeks, a fortnight
quinze[1] [kɛ̃z] *adj* **1** : fifteen **2** : fifteenth <le quinze juin : June fifteenth>
quinze[2] *nms & pl* : fifteen
quinzième [kɛ̃zjɛm] *adj & nmf & nm* : fifteenth
quiproquo [kiprɔko] *nm* **1** : mistake, mistaken identity **2** MALENTENDU : misunderstanding
quiscale [kɥiskal] *nm* : grackle
quittance [kitɑ̃s] *nf* : receipt
quitte [kit] *adj* **1** : released from debt <être quitte envers : to be squared away with, to be quits with> <en être quitte pour : to get away with> **2 ~ à** : even if, at the risk of
quitter [kite] *vt* **1** : to leave, to abandon, to separate from **2** : to leave, to depart **3 ne quittez pas** : hold the (telephone) line **— se quitter** *vr* : to part, to separate
qui–vive [kiviv] *nms & pl* **être sur le qui–vive** : to be on the alert
quoi [kwa] *pron* **1** : what <à quoi bon? : what's the point?> <je sais à quoi tu penses : I know what you're thinking

about> **2** (*used as an interjection or interrogative*) : what!, what? **3 quoi que** : whatever <quoi qu'il arrive : whatever happens>
quoique [kwakə] *conj* : although, though, notwithstanding
quolibet [kɔlibɛ] *nm* : gibe, jeer
quorum [k(w)ɔrɔm] *nm* : quorum
quota [kɔta] *nm* **1** : quota **2 : avoir son quota** *Can fam* : to have had enough
quote–part [kɔtpar] *nf, pl* **quotes–parts** : share <payer sa quote-part : to pay one's share>
quotidien[1], **-dienne** [kɔtidjɛ̃, -djɛn] *adj* **1** : daily, every day **2** : everyday, routine
quotidien[2] *nm* **1** : daily (newspaper) <quotidien populaire : tabloid> **2 le quotidien** : everyday life
quotidiennement [kɔtidjɛnmɑ̃] *adv* : daily
quotient [kɔsjɑ̃] *nm* : quotient

R

r [ɛr] *nm* : r, the 18th letter of the alphabet
rabâcher [rabaʃe] *vt* : to repeat endlessly, to keep harping on — *vi* : to keep repeating oneself
rabais [rabɛ] *nms & pl* **1** RÉDUCTION : reduction, discount **2 au ~** : at a discount, cut-rate
rabaisser [rabɛse] *vt* **1** : to reduce, to lower, to lessen **2** DÉPRÉCIER : to belittle
rabat [raba] *nm* : flap
rabat–joie [rabaʒwa] *nmfs & pl* : killjoy, spoilsport
rabattre [rabatr] {12} *vt* **1** : to reduce, to diminish **2** : to bring down, to pull down **3** : to fold back — **se rabattre** *vr* **1** : to fold up, to go back (by itself) **2 ~ sur** : to fall back on, to make do with
rabbin [rabɛ̃] *nm* : rabbi
râblé, -blée [rable] *adj* : heavyset, stocky
rabot [rabo] *nm* : plane (tool)
raboter [rabɔte] *vt* : to plane (down)
raboteux, -teuse [rabɔtø, -tøz] *adj* INÉGAL : rough, uneven
rabougri, -grie [rabugri] *adj* **1** : stunted, puny **2** : wizened, shriveled (up)
rabrouer [rabrue] *vt* : to snub, to slight
racaille [rakaj] *nf* : riffraff, rabble
raccommoder [rakɔmɔde] *vt* RAPIÉCER : to mend, to patch up — **se raccommoder** *vr fam* : to make up (with someone)
raccompagner [rakɔ̃paɲe] *vt* : to take (someone) back, to see home
raccord [rakɔr] *nm* **1** : linkage, connection **2** : touch-up (in painting)
raccordement [rakɔrdəmɑ̃] *nm* : linking, connecting, joining (up)
raccorder [rakɔrde] *vt* : to connect, to link up — **se raccorder** *vr*
raccourci [rakursi] *nm* **1** : shortcut **2 en ~** : in short, briefly
raccourcir [rakursir] *vt* : to shorten — *vi* : to become shorter, to shrink
raccrocher [rakrɔʃe] *vt* **1** : to hang back up **2** : to rescue, to save at the last minute — *vi* : to hang up — **se raccrocher** *vr* : to hang on, to grab hold
race [ras] *nf* **1** : race <la race humaine : the human race> **2** : breed (of animals) **3** : line, descent **4 de ~** : Thoroughbred
racé, -cée [rase] *adj* **1** : Thoroughbred **2** DISTINGUÉ : distinguished
rachat [raʃa] *nm* **1** : repurchase **2** : atonement
racheter [raʃte] {20} *vt* **1** : to buy back **2** : to buy more of **3** : to redeem **4** : to atone for — **se racheter** *vr* : to redeem oneself
rachitisme [raʃitism] *nm* : rickets
racial, -ciale [rasjal] *adj, mpl* **raciaux** [rasjo] : racial, race — **racialement** [-sjalmɑ̃] *adv*
racine [rasin] *nf* **1** : root **2** : origin, source **3 racine carrée** : square root
racisme [rasism] *nm* : racism
raciste [rasist] *adj & nmf* : racist
racket [rakɛt] *nm* : racket, racketeering
racketteur [rakɛtœr] *nm* : racketeer
raclée [rakle] *nf fam* : beating, thrashing
racler [rakle] *vt* : to scrape (off), to scrape against
racloir [raklwar] *nm* GRATTOIR : scraper
racolage [rakɔlaʒ] *nm* : canvassing (in politics)
racoler [rakɔle] *vt* : to solicit (support, etc.), to canvass
racoleur, -leuse [rakɔlœr, -løz] *adj* : enticing, eye-catching
racontars [rakɔ̃tar] *nmpl* : gossip
raconter [rakɔ̃te] *vt* **1** CONTER : to tell, to relate **2** : to say, to talk about <qu'est-ce que tu racontes? : what are you talking about?>
raconteur, -teuse [rakɔ̃tœr, -tøz] *n* : raconteur, storyteller
racornir [rakɔrnir] *vt* : to toughen, to harden — **se racornir** *vr* **1** : to become hardened **2** SE RATATINER : to shrivel up
radar [radar] *nm* : radar

rade |rad| *nf* **1** : harbor **2 laisser en rade** : to leave stranded
radeau |rado| *nm, pl* **radeaux** : raft
radial, -diale |radjal| *adj, mpl* **radiaux** |radjo| : radial
radiant, -diante |radjɑ̃, -djɑ̃t| *adj* : radiant
radiateur |radjatœr| *nm* **1** : radiator **2** : heater <radiateur électrique : electric heater>
radiation |radjasjɔ̃| *nf* **1** : radiation **2** : crossing off (from a list)
radical[1], **-cale** |radikal| *adj, mpl* **-caux** |-ko| : radical — **radicalement** |-kalmɑ̃| *adv*
radical[2], **-cale** *n* : radical
radier |radje| {96} *vt* **1** : to radiate **2** RAYER : to cross off <radier un avocat : to disbar a lawyer>
radieux, -dieuse |radjø, -djøz| *adj* **1** : radiant, glowing (with joy, etc.) **2** : glorious, dazzling — **radieusement** |-djøzmɑ̃| *adv*
radin[1], **-dine** |radɛ̃, -din| *adj fam* : stingy
radin[2], **-dine** *n fam* : skinflint, cheapskate
radio[1] |radjo| *nf* **1** : radio **2** RADIOGRAPHIE : X ray
radio[2] *nm* : radio operator
radioactif, -tive |radjɔaktif, -tiv| *adj* : radioactive — **radioactivité** |-tivite| *nf*
radioamateur |radjɔamatœr| *nm* : ham (radio operator)
radiodiffuser |radjɔdifyze| *vt* : to broadcast
radiodiffusion |radjɔdifyzjɔ̃| *nf* : broadcasting
radiographie |radjɔgrafi| *nf* : radiography, X ray
radiographier |radjɔgrafje| {96} *vt* : to X-ray
radiologie |radjɔlɔʒi| *nf* : radiology
radiologique |radjɔlɔʒik| *adj* : radiological, radiologic
radiologiste |radjɔlɔʒist| *or* **radiologue** |radjɔlɔg| *nmf* : radiologist
radis |radi| *nm* : radish
radium |radjɔm| *nm* : radium
radja |radʒa| → **rajah**
radon |radɔ̃| *nm* : radon
radoter |radɔte| *vi* : to ramble on
radoucir |radusir| *vt* : to soften (up) — **se radoucir** *vr* **1** : to grow milder **2** : to calm down
rafale |rafal| *nf* **1** BOURRASQUE : gust (of wind, etc.) **2** : burst (of gunfire)
raffermir |rafɛrmir| *vt* **1** TONIFIER : to firm up, to tone up **2** : to strengthen, to reinforce
raffinage |rafinaʒ| *nm* : refining
raffiné, -née |rafine| *adj* : refined, sophisticated
raffinement |rafinmɑ̃| *nm* : refinement
raffiner |rafine| *vt* : to refine — *vi* ~ **sur** : to be meticulous about
raffinerie |rafinri| *nf* : refinery
raffoler |rafɔle| *vi* ~ **de** : to adore, to be crazy about
raffut |rafy| *nm fam* : din, racket
rafiot |rafjo| *nm fam* : old vessel, tub
rafistoler |rafistɔle| *vt fam* : to patch up, to fix up
rafle |rafl| *nf* DESCENTE : (police) raid
rafler |rafle| *vt fam* **1** : to swipe **2** : to walk off with <elle a raflé tous les prix : she walked off with all the prizes>
rafraîchir |rafrɛʃir| *vt* : to refresh, to cool, to chill — **se rafraîchir** *vr* **1** : to get cooler **2** : to freshen up **3 se rafraîchir la mémoire** : to refresh one's memory
rafraîchissant, -sante |rafrɛʃisɑ̃, -sɑ̃t| *adj* : refreshing
rafraîchissement |rafrɛʃismɑ̃| *nm* **1** : cooling **2 rafraîchissements** *nmpl* : cool drinks, refreshments
ragaillardir |ragajardir| *vt* REVIGORER : to perk up, to invigorate — **se ragaillardir** *vr* : to perk up
rage |raʒ| *nf* **1** : rage, fury <mettre en rage : to enrage> **2** : rabies **3 avoir la rage de** : to have a passion for **4 faire rage** : to rage (of storms, etc.)
rager |raʒe| {17} *vi* : to rage, to fume
rageur, -geuse |raʒœr, -ʒøz| *adj* **1** FURIEUX : furious **2** COLÉREUX : bad-tempered
rageusement |raʒøzmɑ̃| *adv* : furiously
ragot |rago| *nm fam* COMMÉRAGE : gossip, malicious rumor
ragoût |ragu| *nm* : ragout, stew
ragoûtant, -tante |ragutɑ̃, -tɑ̃t| *adj* **peu ragoûtant** : unappetizing, not very pleasant
ragtime |ragtajm| *nm* : ragtime
rai |rɛ| *nm* : ray, shaft (of light)
raid |rɛd| *nm* : raid <raid aérien : air raid>
raide[1] |rɛd| *adv* **1** : steeply **2 tomber raide** : to drop dead
raide[2] *adj* **1** : stiff, rigid **2** : taut, tight **3** : steep **4** : straight
raideur |rɛdœr| *nf* **1** : stiffness <avec raideur : stiffly> **2** : steepness
raidir |rɛdir| *vt* : to stiffen, to tighten, to tense (up) — **se raidir** *vr*
raie |rɛ| *nf* **1** : stripe **2** : part (in hair) **3** : ray, skate (fish)
raifort |rɛfɔr| *nm* : horseradish
rail |raj| *nm* **1** : rail, track **2 remettre sur les rails** : to put back on track
railler |raje| *vt* : to make fun of, to jeer at — **se railler** *vr* : to scoff
raillerie |rajri| *nf* : mockery
railleur, -leuse |rajœr, -jøz| *adj* MOQUEUR : mocking, derisive
rainer |rene| *vt* : to groove, to cut a groove in
rainure |rɛnyr| *nf* : groove, slot
raisin |rɛzɛ̃| *nm* **1** : grape **2 raisin sec** : raisin **3 raisin de Corinthe** : currant

raison |rɛzɔ̃| *nf* **1** : reason, rationality, good sense <as-tu perdu la raison? : are you out of your mind?> <comme de raison : as one might expect> <à juste raison : justifiably> **2** MOTIF : reason, motive, grounds *pl* **3** : rate, ratio <à raison de deux par semaine : at the rate of two a week> **4** **avoir raison** : to be right **5** **en raison de** : due to, because of

raisonnable |rɛzɔnabl| *adj* **1** SENSÉ : sensible, reasonable **2** : moderate, fair <à des prix raisonnables : moderately priced>

raisonnablement |rɛzɔnabləmɑ̃| *adv* **1** : reasonably **2** : moderately, fairly

raisonné, -née |rɛzɔne| *adj* : well thought-out, reasoned

raisonnement |rɛzɔnmɑ̃| *nm* **1** : reasoning **2** ARGUMENTATION : argument, rationale

raisonner |rɛzɔne| *vi* **1** PENSER : to reason, to think **2** : to argue, to reason <raisonner sur : to argue about> — *vt* : to reason with — **se raisonner** *vr* : to try to be reasonable, to reason with oneself

raja *or* **rajah** |raʒa| *nm* : rajah

rajeunir |raʒœnir| *vt* **1** : to rejuvenate, to make (someone) look younger **2** : to modernize, to update — *vi* : to look younger — **se rajeunir** *vr*

rajeunissement |raʒœnismɑ̃| *nm* : rejuvenation

rajout |raʒu| *nm* : addition

rajouter |raʒute| *vt* **1** : to add **2** **en ~** : to exaggerate

rajuster |raʒyste| *vt* **1** : to adjust, to straighten (clothing, etc.) **2** RÉAJUSTER : to readjust

râle |ral| *nm* **1** : groan **2** **râle de la mort** : death rattle

ralenti[1], -tie |ralɑ̃ti| *adj* : slow, idling

ralenti[2] *nm* **1** : slow motion **2** : idling speed (of an automobile)

ralentir |ralɑ̃tir| *v* : to slow down, to decelerate

ralentissement |ralɑ̃tismɑ̃| *nm* : slowing down, slowdown

râler |rale| *vi* **1** : to groan **2** *fam* : to moan, to grumble

ralliement |ralimɑ̃| *nm* : rallying

rallier |ralje| {96} *vt* **1** : to rally (troops, etc.) **2** : to win over **3** : to rejoin — **se rallier** *vr* **~ à** : to rally to, to join up with

rallonge |ralɔ̃ʒ| *nf* **1** : extension **2** : extension cord **3** : leaf (of a table)

rallonger |ralɔ̃ʒe| {17} *vt* : to lengthen, to extend — *vi fam* : to get longer

rallumer |ralyme| *vt* **1** : to relight, to turn back on **2** : to rekindle, to revive

ramage |ramaʒ| *nm* **1** : song (of a bird) **2** **ramages** *nmpl* : floral pattern (on cloth, etc.)

ramassage |ramasaʒ| *nm* **1** : collection **2** : picking, gathering **3** **ramassage scolaire** *France* : school bus service

ramassé, -sée |ramase| *adj* **1** : squat, stocky **2** : compact (of style, etc.)

ramasser |ramase| *vt* **1** : to pick up, to collect **2** CUEILLIR : to pick, to gather <ramasser des framboises : to pick raspberries> — **se ramasser** *vr* SE PELOTONNER : to huddle up, to crouch

ramassis |ramasi| *nm* : bunch, pile, jumble

rambarde |rɑ̃bard| *nf* : guardrail

rame |ram| *nf* **1** AVIRON : oar **2** : train <rame de métro : subway train> **3** : ream (of paper)

rameau |ramo| *nm, pl* **rameaux** **1** : branch, bough **2** **dimanche des Rameaux** : Palm Sunday

ramener |ramne| {52} *vt* **1** : to bring back, to take back **2** : to restore <ramener la semaine de travail à 32 heures : to restore the work week to 32 hours> **3** RÉDUIRE : to reduce **4** : to draw up, to pull back — **se ramener** *vr* **~ à** : to come down to, to be nothing more than

ramer |rame| *vi* : to row

rameur, -meuse |ramœr, -møz| *n* : rower

rami |rami| *nm* : rummy (card game)

ramification |ramifikasjɔ̃| *nf* : ramification

ramifier |ramifje| {96} *v* **se ramifier** *vr* : to branch out, to ramify

ramolli, -lie |ramɔli| *adj* **1** : soft, softened **2** *fam* : soft in the head

ramollir |ramɔlir| *vt* : to soften — **se ramollir** *vr*

ramoner |ramɔne| *vt* : to sweep (a chimney), to clean out (pipes, etc.)

ramoneur |ramɔnœr| *nm* : chimney sweep

rampe |rɑ̃p| *nf* **1** : ramp **2** : banister, handrail **3** : footlights *pl* **4** **rampe de lancement** : launching pad

ramper |rɑ̃pe| *vi* **1** : to crawl **2** : to creep (of a plant) **3** S'ABAISSER : to grovel, to lower oneself

ramure |ramyr| *nf* **1** : branches *pl* (of a tree) **2** : antlers *pl*

rancard |rɑ̃kar| *nm France fam* **1** : rendezvous, date **2** : lowdown, tip

rancart |rɑ̃kar| *nm* **mettre au rancart** *fam* : to discard, to scrap

rance |rɑ̃s| *adj* : rancid

ranch |rɑ̃tʃ| *nm* : ranch

rancir |rɑ̃sir| *vi* : to turn rancid

rancoeur |rɑ̃kœr| *nf* RESSENTIMENT : rancor, resentment

rançon |rɑ̃sɔ̃| *nf* : ransom

rançonner |rɑ̃sɔne| *vt* : to ransom

rancune |rɑ̃kyn| *nf* **1** : rancor, resentment **2** : grudge <garder rancune à : to hold a grudge against>

rancunier, -nière |rɑ̃kynje, -njɛr| *adj* : vindictive, spiteful

randonnée [rɑ̃dɔne] *nf* **1** : ride, trip **2** : walk, hike <faire de la randonnée : to backpack>
randonneur, -neuse [rɑ̃dɔnœr, -nøz] *n* : hiker, walker
rang [rɑ̃] *nm* **1** RANGÉE : row, line **2** : rank <de haut rang : high-ranking> **3** : standing, position (in society, etc.) **4** : ranks *pl* (in the military) <sortir du rang : to come up through the ranks>
rangé, -gée [rɑ̃ʒe] *adj* **1** : orderly, tidy **2** : well-behaved
rangée *nf* : row, line <une rangée d'arbres : a row of trees>
rangement [rɑ̃ʒmɑ̃] *nm* **1** : tidying up, putting away **2** AGENCEMENT : arrangement, layout **3** : storage space
ranger [rɑ̃ʒe] {17} *vt* **1** : to tidy up **2** : to put away, to store **3** CLASSER : to put in order — **se ranger** *vr* **1** : to line up **2** SE GARER : to pull over, to move aside **3** : to go along with, to side with **4** S'ASSAGIR : to settle down
ranimer [ranime] *vt* **1** : to revive, to resuscitate **2** : to renew, to rekindle — **se ranimer** *vr* **1** : to revive, to come to **2** : to flare up, to be rekindled
rapace[1] [rapas] *adj* : rapacious
rapace[2] *nm* : bird of prey
rapatriement [rapatrimɑ̃] *nm* : repatriation
rapatrier [rapatrije] {96} *vt* : to repatriate
râpe [rap] *nf* **1** : grater **2** : rasp
râpé, -pée [rape] *adj* **1** : grated **2** : threadbare
râper [rape] *vt* **1** : to grate **2** : to file down (with a rasp)
rapetasser [raptase] *vt fam* : to patch up
rapetisser [raptise] *vt* **1** : to shorten, to make smaller **2** : to belittle — *vi* **1** : to get shorter **2** : to shrink — **se rapetisser** *vr* : to get smaller, to shrink
râpeux, -peuse [rapø, -pøz] *adj* **1** : rough, harsh, grating **2** ÂPRE : bitter, harsh (of wine, etc.)
rapide[1] [rapid] *adj* **1** : quick, rapid **2** : steep
rapide[2] *nm* **1** : rapid **2** : express train
rapidement [rapidmɑ̃] *adv* : rapidly, quickly
rapidité [rapidite] *nf* : rapidity, speed
rapiécer [rapjese] {6} *vt* : to patch (up), to mend
rapière [rapjɛr] *nf* : rapier
rappel [rapɛl] *nm* **1** : reminder **2** : recall, return **3** : curtain call **4** ÉVOCATION : recall, remembrance **5** : repeat, repetition **6** : booster shot **7** **rappel à l'ordre** : call to order
rappeler [raple] {8} *vt* **1** : to remind **2** : to call back — **se rappeler** *vr* : to remember, to recall
rapport [rapɔr] *nm* **1** : report **2** : connection, association <sans rapport : irrelevant> **3** RENDEMENT : return, yield **4** : contact <en rapport avec : in touch with> **5** : ratio **6** **rapports** *nmpl* : dealings, affairs, relations <avoir de bons rapports avec : to have good relations with> <rapports avec l'étranger : foreign affairs> **7** **rapports** *nmpl* : sexual intercourse
rapporter [rapɔrte] *vt* **1** : to bring back, to take back **2** : to yield (in finance) **3** RELATER : to tell, to report **4** : to add, to insert **5** : to relate to — *vi* **1** : to yield a profit **2** *fam* : to tell tales — **se rapporter** *vr* ~ **à** : to relate to
rapporteur[1], -teuse [rapɔrtœr, -tøz] *n* : tattletale
rapporteur[2] *nm* : protractor
rapproché, -chée [raprɔʃe] *adj* **1** : close, nearby **2** frequent, at close intervals
rapprochement [raprɔʃmɑ̃] *nm* **1** : bringing together, coming together **2** : reconciliation **3** LIEN : link, connection
rapprocher [raprɔʃe] *vt* **1** : to bring closer, to move closer **2** COMPARER : to compare — **se rapprocher** *vr* **1** : to come closer **2** ~ **de** : to get closer to, to approximate **3** ~ **de** : to resemble
rapsodie [rapsɔdi] *nf* → **rhapsodie**
rapt [rapt] *nm* : abduction, kidnapping
raquette [rakɛt] *nf* **1** : racket <raquette de tennis : tennis racket> **2** : snowshoe
rare [rar] *adj* **1** : rare, uncommon, unusual **2** : rare, infrequent **3** : few, sparse, thin
raréfaction [rarefaksjɔ̃] *nf* **1** : rarefaction **2** : scarcity
raréfier [rarefje] {96} *vt* **1** : to rarefy **2** : to make scarce — **se raréfier** *vr*
rarement [rarmɑ̃] *adv* : seldom, rarely
rareté [rarte] *nf* : rarity, scarcity
ras[1] [ra] *adv* : short <couper ras : to cut short>
ras[2], rase [ra, raz] *adj* **1** : close-cropped <à poil ras : short-haired> <pelouse rase : closely-mown grass> **2** : level <cuillerée rase : level spoonful> <à ras bord : to the brim> **3** **en rase campagne** : in open country
rasage [razaʒ] *nm* : shaving
rasant, -sante [razɑ̃, -zɑ̃t] *adj fam* : boring
raser [raze] {87} *vt* **1** : to shave **2** : to raze **3** FRÔLER : to graze, to skim — **se raser** *vr* : to shave
raseur, -seuse [razœr, -zøz] *n fam* : bore <quelle raseuse! : what a bore she is!>
rasoir [razwar] *nm* : razor <rasoir électrique : electric razor>
rassasier [rasazje] {96} *vt* : to satisfy, to satiate — **se rassasier** *vr*
rassemblement [rasɑ̃bləmɑ̃] *nm* : gathering, assembly
rassembler [rasɑ̃ble] *vt* **1** RÉUNIR : to gather, to collect **2** **rassembler en**

troupeau : to herd — **se rassembler** *vr* : to gather together, to assemble
rasseoir [raswar] {9} *v* **se rasseoir** *vr* : to sit down again
rasséréner [raserene] {87} *vt* CALMER : to calm, to make serene — **se rasséréner** *vr* : to calm down
rassir [rasir] {72} *vi* : to go stale — **se rassir** *vr*
rassis, -sise [rasi, -siz] *adj* : stale
rassurant, -rante [rasyrɑ̃, -rɑ̃t] *adj* : reassuring
rassurer [rasyre] *vt* : to reassure
rat [ra] *nm* **1** : rat **2 rat musqué** : muskrat
ratatiner [ratatine] *v* **se ratatiner** *vr* **1** : to dry up, to shrivel **2** : to become wizened
rate [rat] *nf* : spleen
raté[1], -tée [rate] *n* : failure
raté[2] *nm* : backfiring
râteau [rato] *nm, pl* **râteaux** : rake
râteler [ratle] {8} *vt* : to rake up
râtelier [ratəlje] *nm* **1** : hayrack **2 manger à tous les râteliers** : to have a finger in every pie
rater [rate] *vt* **1** MANQUER : to miss (a chance, a train, etc.) **2** : to fail at — *vi* **1** ÉCHOUER : to fail, to miss **2** : to misfire
ratifier [ratifje] {96} *vt* : to ratify — **ratification** [-tifikasjɔ̃] *nf*
ratine [ratin] *nf Can* : terry cloth
ratio [rasjo] *nm* : ratio
ration [rasjɔ̃] *nf* **1** PORTION : share, ration **2** : rations *pl* (in the military)
rationaliser [rasjɔnalize] *vt* : to rationalize — **rationalisation** [-lizasjɔ̃] *nf*
rationnel, -nelle [rasjɔnɛl] *adj* : rational — **rationnellement** [-nɛlmɑ̃] *adv*
rationner [rasjɔne] *vt* : to ration
ratisser [ratise] *vt* **1** : to rake **2** : to search, to comb
raton [ratɔ̃] *nm* **raton laveur** : raccoon
ratoureur[1], -reuse [raturœr, -røz] *adj Can* : crafty, sly
ratoureur[2], -reuse *n* : crafty person
rattacher [rataʃe] *vt* **1** : to tie up again **2** RELIER : to link, to connect — **se rattacher** *vr* **~ à** : to be connected with, to relate to
rattrapage [ratrapaʒ] *nm* **1** : adjustment (of salaries, etc.) **2 cours de rattrapage** : remedial class(es)
rattraper [ratrape] *vt* **1** : to recapture **2** : to catch up with **3** : to make up for
raturer [ratyre] *vt* BIFFER : to cross out
rauque [rok] *adj* **1** : hoarse **2** : raucous
ravager [ravaʒe] {17} *vt* : to ravage, to devastate
ravages [ravaʒ] *nmpl* **1** : ravages, devastation **2 faire des ravages** : to wreak havoc
ravalement [ravalmɑ̃] *nm* : refacing (of a building), restoration
ravaler [ravale] *vt* **1** : to clean, to restore (a building, etc.) **2** : to choke back, to stifle, to swallow <ravaler ses larmes : to hold back tears>
ravauder [ravode] *vt Can* : to make a racket
ravi, -vie [ravi] *adj* ENCHANTÉ : delighted
ravigoter [ravigɔte] *vt fam* : to perk up, to invigorate
ravin [ravɛ̃] *nm* : ravine, gulch
raviner [ravine] *vt* : to furrow
ravir [ravir] *vt* **1** ENCHANTER : to delight **2 ~ à** : to rob of (a loved one, etc.) **3 à ~** : delightfully, beautifully
raviser [ravise] *v* **se raviser** *vr* : to change one's mind
ravissant, -sante [ravisɑ̃, -sɑ̃t] *adj* : delightful, beautiful
ravissement [ravismɑ̃] *nm* : rapture
ravisseur, -seuse [ravisœr, -søz] *n* KIDNAPPEUR : kidnapper, abductor
ravitaillement [ravitajmɑ̃] *nm* **1** : provision, supplying **2** : refueling
ravitailler [ravitaje] *vt* **1** : to supply (with food, etc.) **2** : to refuel
raviver [ravive] *vt* **1** RANIMER : to rekindle **2** : to brighten up
ravoir [ravwar] {73} *vt* : to get back
rayé, -yée [rɛje] *adj* **1** : striped, lined **2** : scratched
rayer [rɛje] {11} *vt* **1** ÉRAFLER : to scratch **2** : to cross out, to delete, to erase
rayon [rɛjɔ̃] *nm* **1** : ray, beam <rayon de soleil : sunbeam> <rayon de lune : moonbeam> **2** : radius **3** : range, scope **4** ÉTAGÈRE : shelf, bookshelf **5** : department (in a store) **6** : domain, concern **7 rayon de miel** : honeycomb **8 rayons** *nmpl* : rays, radiation <rayons gamma : gamma rays> <rayons X : X rays>
rayonnant, -nante [rɛjɔnɑ̃, -nɑ̃t] *adj* RADIEUX : radiant
rayonne [rɛjɔn] *nf* : rayon
rayonnement [rɛjɔnmɑ̃] *nm* **1** : radiation **2** : radiance **3** : influence (of art, culture, etc.)
rayonner [rɛjɔne] *vi* **1** : to radiate **2** : to shine, to glow **3** : to exert influence **4** : to tour around
rayure [rɛjyr] *nf* **1** : stripe <chemise à rayures : striped shirt> **2** ÉRAFLURE : scratch
raz–de–marée [radmare] *nms & pl* : tidal wave
razzia [razja] *nf* : raid, foray
réabonner [reabɔne] *v* **se réabonner** *vr* : to renew one's subscription
réaccoutumer [reakutyme] *v* **se réaccoutumer** *vr* SE RÉHABITUER : to get reaccustomed to
réacteur [reaktœr] *nm* **1** : jet engine **2** : reactor <réacteur nucléaire : nuclear reactor>
réaction [reaksjɔ̃] *nf* **1** : reaction <réaction en chaîne : chain reaction> **2 à ~** : jet-propelled **3 → avion, moteur**

réactionnaire |reaksjɔnɛr| *adj & nmf* : reactionary
réactiver |reaktive| *vt* : to reactivate
réadaptation |readaptasjɔ̃| *nf* **1** : readjustment **2** : (physical) rehabilitation
réadapter |readapte| *v* **se réadapter** *vr* : to readjust
réaffirmer |reafirme| *vt* : to reaffirm
réagir |reaʒir| *vi* : to react
réajuster |reaʒyste| *vt* : to readjust, to adjust — **réajustement** |-ʒystəmɑ̃| *nm*
réalisable |realizabl| *adj* FAISABLE : feasible
réalisateur, -trice |realizatœr, -tris| *n* : director (in movies, television, theater)
réalisation |realizasjɔ̃| *nf* **1** EXÉCUTION : execution, carrying out **2** : directory, production (of a film) **3** : achievement, accomplishment
réaliser |realize| *vt* **1** : to carry out, to execute **2** : to produce, to direct (a film) **3** : to achieve, to accomplish **4** : to realize (a profit) — **se réaliser** *vr* **1** : to materialize, to come true **2** : to fulfill oneself
réalisme |realism| *nm* : realism
réaliste[1] |realist| *adj* : realistic
réaliste[2] *nmf* : realist
réalité |realite| *nf* **1** : reality **2 en ~** : in fact, actually
réaménager |reamenaʒe| {17} *vt* : to refurbish
réanimer |reanime| *vt* : to resuscitate — **réanimation** |-nimasjɔ̃| *nf*
réapparaître |reaparɛtr| {7} *vi* : to reappear, to come back, to recur
réapparition |reaparisjɔ̃| *nf* : reappearance
réarranger |rearɑ̃ʒe| {17} *vt* : to rearrange
rebaptiser |rəbatize| *vt* : to rename
rébarbatif, -tive |rebarbatif, -tiv| *adj* **1** : forbidding, grim-looking **2** : daunting
rebattu, -tue |rəbaty| *adj* : hackneyed
rebelle[1] |rəbɛl| *adj* **1** : rebellious, unruly **2** : rebel <le camp rebelle : the rebel camp>
rebelle[2] *nmf* : rebel
rebeller |rəbɛle| *v* **se rebeller** *vr* : to rebel
rébellion |rebɛljɔ̃| *nf* : rebellion
rebiffer |rəbife| *v* **se rebiffer** *vr fam* : to rebel against, to strike back at
rebond |rəbɔ̃| *nm* : bounce, rebound
rebondi, -die |rəbɔ̃di| *adj* **1** : rounded **2** : plump, chubby
rebondir |rəbɔ̃dir| *vi* **1** : to bounce, to rebound **2** : to start (up) again
rebondissement |rəbɔ̃dismɑ̃| *nm* : new development
rebord |rəbɔr| *nm* : rim, edge, sill (of a window)
reboucher |rəbuʃe| *vt* **1** : to put the cork back in **2** : to plug, to stop up
rebours |rəbur| *nm* **1 à ~** : the wrong way **2** → **compte**
rebrousse–poil |rəbruspwal| **à rebrousse–poil** : the wrong way, against the grain
rebrousser |rəbruse| *vt* **1** : to brush back **2 rebrousser chemin** : to turn back
rebuffade |rəbyfad| *nf* : rebuff, snub
rébus |rebys| *nm* : rebus, riddle
rebut |rəby| *nm* **1** : trash, waste, scrap **2 de ~** : rejected, unwanted **3 mettre au rebut** : to discard, to throw away
rebutant, -tante |rəbytɑ̃, -tɑ̃t| *adj* : repellent, disagreeable
rebuter |rəbyte| *vt* **1** DÉCOURAGER : to dishearten, to discourage, to put off **2** : to disgust, to repel
récalcitrant, -trante |rekalsitrɑ̃, -trɑ̃t| *adj* : recalcitrant
recaler |rəkale| *vt France fam* : to fail (a student)
récapitulatif, -tive |rekapitylatif, -tiv| *adj* : summary
récapituler |rekapityle| *vt* RÉSUMER : to recapitulate, to sum up — **récapitulation** |-tylasjɔ̃| *nf*
recel |rəsɛl| *nm* : possession of stolen goods
receler |rəsəle| {20} *vt* : to receive (stolen goods), to conceal (a criminal)
récemment |resamɑ̃| *adv* DERNIÈREMENT : recently
recensement |rəsɑ̃smɑ̃| *nm* **1** : census (of populations) **2** : inventory
recenser |rəsɑ̃se| *vt* **1** : to take a census of **2** : to list, to inventory
récent, -cente |resɑ̃, -sɑ̃t| *adj* : recent
récépissé |resepise| *nm* : receipt
réceptacle |resɛptakl| *nm* : container, receptacle
récepteur[1], -trice |resɛptœr, -tris| *adj* : receiving
récepteur[2] *nm* : receiver <récepteur de téléphone : telephone receiver> <récepteur de radiomessagerie : beeper>
réceptif, -tive |resɛptif, -tiv| *adj* : receptive — **réceptivité** |-tivite| *nf*
réception |resɛpsjɔ̃| *nf* **1** : receiving, receipt **2** ACCUEIL : reception, welcome **3** : admission (into an organization, etc.) **4** FÊTE : reception, party **5** : registration desk **6** : reception (of radio, television, etc.)
réceptionner |resɛpsjɔne| *vt* : to receive, to take delivery of
réceptionniste |resɛpsjɔnist| *nmf* : receptionist
récession |resesjɔ̃| *nf* : recession
recette |rəsɛt| *nf* **1** : recipe **2** : formula, prescription **3** : take, receipts *pl*
recevable |rəsəvabl| *adj* : admissible, acceptable
recevant, -vante |rəsəvɑ̃, -vɑ̃t| *adj Can* : welcoming, hospitable
receveur, -veuse |rəsəvœr, -vøz| *n* **1** : recipient (of blood, transplants, etc.) **2** *Can* : catcher (in sports) **3 receveur**

des contributions : tax collector **4 receveur des postes** : postmaster

recevoir |rəsəvwar| {26} *vt* **1** : to receive, to get **2** ACCUEILLIR : to welcome, to be host to **3** : to see, to receive (patients, etc.) **4** ADMETTRE : to admit, to accept (into a society, school, etc.) <être reçu à l'université : to be accepted at the university> **5** : to accommodate, to hold **6** : to receive (radio or television signals) — **se recevoir** *vr* : to land (in sports, dance, etc.)

rechange |rəʃɑ̃ʒ| *nm* **1 de ~** : spare, extra <vêtements de rechange : change of clothes> **2 de ~** : alternative

réchapper |reʃape| *vi* **~ de** : to come through, to pull through

recharge |rəʃarʒ| *nf* **1** : refill, reload(ing) **2** : recharging (of a battery, etc.)

rechargeable |rəʃarʒabl| *adj* : rechargeable, refillable

recharger |rəʃarʒe| {17} *vt* **1** : to refill, to reload **2** : to recharge

réchaud |reʃo| *nm* **1** : (portable) stove **2 réchaud de table** : chafing dish

réchauffer |reʃofe| *vt* : to reheat, to warm up — **se réchauffer** *vr* **1** : to warm up, to get warmer **2** : to warm oneself up

rêche |rɛʃ| *adj* : rough, prickly, scratchy

recherche |rəʃɛrʃ| *nf* **1** : search <à la recherche de : in search of> **2** : research **3** : meticulousness, refinement **4** : affectation, pretentiousness **5 recherches** *nfpl* : investigations

recherché, -chée |rəʃɛrʃe| *adj* **1** : sought-after, in demand **2** : refined, studied, meticulous **3** : affected, pretentious

rechercher |rəʃɛrʃe| *vt* **1** : to search for, to seek **2** : to look into, to investigate

rechigner |rəʃiɲe| *vi* **1** : to grumble **2 ~ à** : to balk at

rechute |rəʃyt| *nf* : relapse <faire une rechute : to have a relapse>

rechuter |rəʃyte| *vi* : to relapse

récidive |residiv| *nf* **1** : second (or subsequent) offense **2** : recurrence (of an illness)

récidiver |residive| *vi* **1** : to relapse into crime **2** : to recur (of an illness)

récif |resif| *nm* : reef

récipiendaire |resipjɑ̃dɛr| *nmf* : recipient (of a diploma, a nomination, etc.)

récipient |resipjɑ̃| *nm* : container

réciprocité |resiprɔsite| *nf* : reciprocity

réciproque |resiprɔk| *adj* : reciprocal, mutual — **réciproquement** |-prɔkmɑ̃| *adv*

récit |resi| *nm* : account, story

récital |resital| *nm, pl* **-tals** : recital

récitation |resitasjɔ̃| *nf* **1** : recitation **2 apprendre une récitation** : to learn a text by heart

réciter |resite| *vt* : to recite

réclamation |reklamasjɔ̃| *nf* **1** PLAINTE : complaint **2** : claim (in law)

réclame |reklam| *nf* **1** : advertisement **2** : advertising, publicity **3 en ~** : on special (offer), on sale

réclamer |reklame| *vt* **1** : to ask for, to claim **2** : to demand, to call for — *vi* : to complain — **se réclamer** *vr* **~ de** : to claim an association with (a person or an organization)

reclasser |rəklase| *vt* : to reclassify

reclus, -cluse |rəkly, -klyz| *n* : recluse

réclusion |reklyzjɔ̃| *nf* DÉTENTION : imprisonment

recoin |rəkwɛ̃| *nm* : nook, corner <tous les coins et les recoins : every nook and cranny>

reçoit |rəswa|, **reçoive** |rəswav|, *etc.* → **recevoir**

recoller |rəkɔle| *vt* : to stick back together

récolte |rekɔlt| *nf* **1** : harvesting, gathering **2** : harvest, crop

récolter |rekɔlte| *vt* **1** : to harvest **2** : to gather, to collect

recommandable |rəkɔmɑ̃dabl| *adj* : commendable

recommandation |rəkɔmɑ̃dasjɔ̃| *nf* : recommendation

recommander |rəkɔmɑ̃de| *vt* **1** : to recommend **2** : to advise **3** : to register (a letter, etc.)

recommencement |rəkɔmɑ̃smɑ̃| *nm* : new beginning

recommencer |rəkɔmɑ̃se| {6} *v* : to begin again, to start anew

récompense |rekɔ̃pɑ̃s| *nf* : reward

récompenser |rekɔ̃pɑ̃se| *vt* : to reward

réconciliation |rekɔ̃siljasjɔ̃| *nf* : reconciliation

réconcilier |rekɔ̃silje| {96} *vt* : to reconcile — **se réconcilier** *vr*

reconduction |rəkɔ̃dyksjɔ̃| *nf* : renewal (of a budget, contract, etc.)

reconduire |rəkɔ̃dɥir| {49} *vt* **1** RACCOMPAGNER : to take home **2** : to show to the door **3** : to renew, to extend <reconduire qqn dans ses fonctions : to reelect s.o.>

réconfort |rekɔ̃fɔr| *nm* : comfort

réconfortant, -tante |rekɔ̃fɔrtɑ̃, -tɑ̃t| *adj* **1** : comforting **2** : fortifying, invigorating

réconforter |rekɔ̃fɔrte| *vt* **1** CONSOLER : to comfort **2** REVIGORER : to fortify, to invigorate

reconnaissable |rəkɔnɛsabl| *adj* : recognizable

reconnaissance |rɛkɔnɛsɑ̃s| *nf* **1** : recognition **2** GRATITUDE : gratitude **3** : admission, acknowledgment (of wrongs, debts, etc.) **4** : reconnaissance (in the military)

reconnaissant, -sante [rəkɔnɛsɑ̃, -sɑ̃t] *adj* : grateful

reconnaître [rəkɔnɛtr] {7} *vt* **1** : to recognize **2** : to admit, to acknowledge **3** : to reconnoiter — **se reconnaître** *vr* **1** : to see oneself (in someone) **2** : to recognize each other **3** : to be recognizable **4** : to orient oneself, to find one's way **5** S'AVOUER : to admit (to being), to own up

reconnu, -nue [rəkɔny] *adj* : recognized, well-known

reconquérir [rəkɔ̃kerir] {21} *vt* **1** : to reconquer **2** : to regain, to win back

reconsidérer [rəkɔ̃sidere] {87} *vt* : to reconsider

reconstituer [rəkɔ̃stitɥe] *vt* **1** : to piece together, to recreate, to rebuild **2** : to reconstruct (a crime)

reconstruction [rəkɔ̃stryksjɔ̃] *nf* : reconstruction, rebuilding

reconstruire [rəkɔ̃strɥir] {49} *vt* : to reconstruct, to rebuild

reconvertir [rəkɔ̃vɛrtir] *vt* **1** : to redeploy **2** : to convert, to restructure

recopier [rəkɔpje] {96} *vt* : to copy out (again), to transcribe

record [rəkɔr] *nm* : record

recoudre [rəkudr] {22} *vt* **1** : to sew back on **2** : to stitch up (in surgery)

recouper [rəkupe] *vt* **1** : to cut again **2** : to tally with — **se recouper** *vr* **1** : to tally, to add up **2** : to intersect

recourbé, -bée [rəkurbe] *adj* : curved, hooked <un nez recourbé : a hooked nose>

recourir [rəkurir] {23} *vi* **1** : to run again **2** : to appeal **3** ~ **à** : to resort to

recours [rəkur] *nm* **1** : recourse, resort <en dernier recours : as a last resort> <avoir recours à : to have recourse to, to fall back on> **2** : appeal (in law)

recouvert, -verte [rkuvɛr, -vɛrt] *adj* : overgrown

recouvrement [rəkuvrəmɑ̃] *nm* **1** : collection **2** : recovery **3** : covering, cover

recouvrer [rəkuvre] *vt* **1** : to recover, to regain **2** : to collect (taxes, etc.)

recouvrir [rəkuvrir] {83} *vt* **1** : to cover, to re-cover **2** MASQUER : to conceal, to hide — **se recouvrir** *vr* : to overlap

récréatif, -tive [rekreatif, -tiv] *adj* : recreational, entertaining

récréation [rekreasjɔ̃] *nf* **1** : recreation, entertainment **2** : recess, break

recréer [rəkree] {89} *vt* : to re-create

récrier [rekrije] {96} *v* **se récrier** *vr* : to exclaim

récrimination [rekriminasjɔ̃] *nf* : recrimination, reproach

récriminer [rekrimine] *vi* ~ **contre** : to recriminate against, to reproach

récrire [rekrir] {33} *vt* : to rewrite

recroqueviller [rəkrɔkvije] *v* **se recroqueviller** *vr* **1** : to huddle up, to curl up **2** : to shrivel up

recru, -crue [rəkry] *adj or* **recru de fatigue** : exhausted

recrudescence [rəkrydesɑ̃s] *nf* : new outbreak

recrue [rəkry] *nf* : recruit

recrutement [rəkrytmɑ̃] *nm* : recruitment

recruter [rəkryte] *vt* : to recruit, to appoint, to take on

rectal, -tale [rɛktal] *adj, mpl* **-taux** [-to] : rectal

rectangle [rɛktɑ̃gl] *nm* : rectangle — **rectangulaire** [-tɑ̃gylɛr] *adj*

recteur, -trice [rɛktœr, -tris] *nm* **1** *France* : superintendent (of schools) **2** : rector, administrator (of a university) **3** : rector (in religion)

rectificatif [rɛktifikatif] *nm* : correction <publier un rectificatif : to publish a correction>

rectification [rɛktifikasjɔ̃] *nf* : correcting, correction

rectifier [rɛktifje] {96} *vt* : to rectify, to correct

rectitude [rɛktityd] *nf* **1** : straightness (of a line) **2** DROITURE : uprightness, rectitude

recto [rɛkto] *nm* : recto

rectum [rɛktɔm] *nm* : rectum

reçu[1] [rəsy] *pp* → **recevoir**

reçu[2], **-cue** [rəsy] *adj* : accepted, approved

reçu[3] *nm* : receipt

recueil [rəkœj] *nm* : collection, compilation

recueillement [rəkœjmɑ̃] *nm* MÉDITATION : meditation, contemplation

recueillir [rəkœjir] {3} *vt* **1** : to collect, to gather **2** : to get, to obtain, to win **3** : to take in (a stray, etc.) — **se recueillir** *vr* **1** : to collect one's thoughts, to reflect **2** : to meditate

recuire [rəkɥir] {49} *vt* : to anneal

recul [rəkyl] *nm* **1** : recoil (of a firearm) **2** : retreat, backward movement <prendre du recul : to stand back> **3** : detachment <avec le recul : in retrospect, with hindsight> **4** : decline, drop (in production, prices, etc.)

reculer [rəkyle] *vt* **1** REPOUSSER : to move back, to push back **2** : to defer, to postpone — *vi* **1** : to move back **2** : to back up **3** : to be on the decline **4** ~ **devant** : to shrink from, to balk at

reculons [rəkylɔ̃] **à** ~ : backwards

récupérable [rekyperabl] *adj* **1** : recoverable **2** : salvageable, reusable

récupération [rekyperasjɔ̃] *nf* **1** : recovery, recuperation **2** : salvage, recycling

récupérer [rekypere] {87} *vt* **1** : to recover, to get back **2** : to salvage, to recycle **3** : to make up <récupérer des heures de travail : to make up the hours (at work)> **4** : to take over, to appropriate — *vi* SE RÉTABLIR : to recover, to recuperate

récurer |rekyre| *vt* : to scour <poudre à récurer : scouring powder>

récurrent, -rente |rekyrɑ̃, -rɑ̃t| *adj* : recurrent, recurring

récuser |rekyze| *vt* : to challenge, to object to (in law)

recyclable |rəsiklabl| *adj* : recyclable

recyclage |rəsiklaʒ| *nm* **1** : retraining **2** : recycling

recycler |rəsikle| *vt* **1** : to retrain **2** : to recycle — **se recycler** *vr* **1** : to update one's skills, to retrain **2** : to change jobs

rédacteur, -trice |redaktœr, -tris| *n* : editor

rédaction |redaksjɔ̃| *nf* **1** : writing, editing **2** : editorial staff

rédactionnel, -nelle |redaksjɔnɛl| *adj* : editorial

reddition |redisjɔ̃| *nf* : surrender

redécouvrir |rədekuvrir| *vt* : to rediscover

redéfinir |rədefinir| *vt* : to redefine

rédempteur[1], -trice |redɑ̃ptœr, -tris| *adj* : redeeming

rédempteur[2] *nm* : redeemer

rédemption |redɑ̃psjɔ̃| *nf* : redemption

redescendre |rədesɑ̃dr| {63} *vt* **1** : to take down again **2** : to go down (stairs, a hill, etc.) again — *vi* : to go down again

redevable |rədəvabl| *adj* **être redevable à** : to be indebted to

redevance |rədəvɑ̃s| *nf* : payments *pl,* fees *pl* (for services)

rediffusion |rədifyzjɔ̃| *nf* : rerun, rebroadcast, repeat

rédiger |rediʒe| {17} *vt* : to write, to draft

redire |rədir| {29} *vt* RÉPÉTER : to say again, to repeat

redistribuer |rədistribɥe| *vt* : to redistribute

redite |rədit| *nf* : (needless) repetition

redondant, -dante |rədɔ̃dɑ̃, -dɑ̃t| *adj* SUPERFLU : redundant — **redondance** |-dɔ̃dɑ̃s| *nf*

redonner |rədɔne| *vt* **1** RENDRE : to give back, to return **2** RÉTABLIR : to restore (confidence, etc.) **3** : to give again

redoubler |rəduble| *vt* **1** DOUBLER : to double **2** : to repeat (a class, etc.) **3** : to intensify <redoubler ses efforts : to redouble one's efforts> — *vi* **1** : to intensify **2 ~ de** : to increase in, to step up <redoubler de larmes : to cry even harder>

redoutable |rədutabl| *adj* : formidable, fearsome

redouter |rədute| *vt* : to fear, to dread

redressement |rədrɛsmɑ̃| *nm* **1** : recovery, upturn (of the economy) **2 maison de redressement** : reformatory

redresser |rədrɛse| *vt* **1** : to set upright, to straighten up, to straighten out **2** : to turn around, to set back on its feet **3** : to rectify, to redress (errors, wrongs, etc.) — **se redresser** *vr* **1** : to stand up, to sit up (straight) **2** : to recover, to pick up again

réduction |redyksjɔ̃| *nf* **1** : discount, rebate **2** : decrease, cut, reduction

réduire |redɥir| {49} *vt* **1** DIMINUER : to reduce, to decrease **2** : to scale down, to boil down **3** : to subdue (an enemy) **4 ~ à** : to reduce to, to constrain to <réduit au silence : reduced to silence> **5 ~ en** : to crush into <réduit en cendres : reduced to ashes>

réduit[1], -duite |redɥi, -dɥit| *adj* **1** : reduced, smaller, lower **2** : small, limited

réduit[2] *nm* : recess, nook

réédition |reedisjɔ̃| *nf* : new edition

rééducation |reedykasjɔ̃| *nf* **1** : rehabilitation (of criminals, etc.) **2** : physical therapy, (medical) rehabilitation

rééduquer |reedyke| *vt* : to rehabilitate (in law or medicine)

réel[1], -elle |reɛl| *adj* **1** : real **2** VÉRITABLE : true

réel[2] *nm* : reality

réélire |reelir| {51} *vt* : to reelect — **réélection** |-elɛksjɔ̃| *nf*

réellement |reɛlmɑ̃| *adv* : really, in fact

réemployer |reɑ̃plwaje| {58} *vt* **1** : to reuse **2** : to reinvest **3** : to reemploy, to take on again

rééquilibrer |reekilibre| *vt* : to readjust, to balance

réévaluer |reevalɥe| *vt* **1** : to revalue **2** : to reappraise, to reevaluate

réexamen |reɛgzamɛ̃| *nm* : reassessment, reconsideration

réexaminer |reɛgzamine| *vt* : to reexamine, to reassess

refaire |rəfɛr| {42} *vt* **1** : to do again **2** : to redo, to redecorate **3** : to change completely, to start all over again — **se refaire** *vr* **1** : to recoup one's losses **2** : to change (oneself) **3 se refaire une santé** : to regain one's health, to recuperate

réfection |refɛksjɔ̃| *nf* : repairing

référence |referɑ̃s| *nf* **1** : reference **2 faire référence à** : to refer to

référendum |referɛ̃dɔm| *nm* : referendum

référer |refere| {87} *vi* **en référer à** : to consult, to refer (a matter) to — **se référer** *vr* **~ à** : to refer to

refermer |rəfɛrme| *vt* : to close again

refiler |rəfile| *vt fam* : to palm off, to foist

réfléchi, -chie |refleʃi| *adj* **1** : reflective, thoughtful **2** : reflexive <verbe réfléchi : reflexive verb>

réfléchir |refleʃir| *vt* : to reflect — *vi* **1** PENSER : to reflect, to think things over **2 ~ à** : to think about, to reflect on

réfléchissant, -sante |refleʃisɑ̃, -sɑ̃t| *adj* : reflective (in physics)

réflecteur |reflɛktœr| *nm* : reflector

reflet |rəflɛ| *nm* **1** : reflection, image **2** : sheen, highlight

refléter |rəflete| {87} *vt* : to reflect — **se refléter** *vr*

réflexe |reflɛks| *adj & nm* : reflex

réflexion |reflɛksjɔ̃| *nf* **1** : reflection (of light, waves, etc.) **2** : reflection, thought **3** : comment, remark

refluer |rəflye| *vi* **1** : to ebb, to flow back **2** : to surge back (of crowds, etc.)

reflux |rəflys| *nm* **1** : ebb, flowing back **2** : backward surge

refondre |rəfɔ̃dr| {63} *vt* **1** : to recast **2** : to rewrite, to rework (a text)

réformateur[1], **-trice** |refɔrmatœr, -tris| *adj* : reforming

réformateur[2], **-trice** *n* : reformer

réforme |refɔrm| *nf* **1** : reform **2 la Réforme** : the Reformation

reformer |rəfɔrme| *vt* : re-form, to form again — **se reformer** *vr*

réformer |refɔrme| *vt* **1** AMÉLIORER : to reform, to improve <réformer les écoles : to reform the school system> **2** : to declare unfit for service, to discharge (a soldier) — **se réformer** *vr* : to reform, to turn over a new leaf

refoulement |rəfulmɑ̃| *nm* **1** : pushing back, holding back **2** : repression (in psychology)

refouler |rəfule| *vt* **1** : to drive back **2** : to hold back, to suppress **3** : to repress (in psychology)

réfractaire |refraktɛr| *adj* **1** : refractory **2 ~ à** : resistant to

réfracter |refrakte| *vt* : to refract — **réfraction** |-fraksjɔ̃| *nf*

refrain |rəfrɛ̃| *nm* : refrain, chorus

refréner |rəfrene| *or* **réfréner** |refrene| {87} *vt* : to curb, to check

réfrigérant, -rante |refriʒerɑ̃, -rɑ̃t| *adj* : cooling, refrigerating

réfrigérateur |refriʒeratœr| *nm* : refrigerator

réfrigérer |refriʒere| {87} *vt* : to refrigerate — **réfrigération** |-ʒerasjɔ̃| *nf*

refroidir |rəfrwadir| *vt* **1** : to cool, to chill **2** : to cool down, to dampen — *vi* : to cool down, to get cold — **se refroidir** *vr*

refroidissement |rəfrwadismɑ̃| *nm* **1** : cooling **2** RHUME : cold, chill <prendre un refroidissement : to catch a cold>

refuge |rəfyʒ| *nm* : refuge, shelter, haven

réfugié, -giée |refyʒje| *n* : refugee

réfugier |rəfyʒje| {96} *v* **se réfugier** *vr* : to take refuge

refus |rəfy| *nm* : refusal

refuser |rəfyze| *vt* **1** : to refuse, to turn down **2** : to deny (access, etc.) **3** : to reject, to turn away — **se refuser** *vr* **1** : to deny oneself **2 ~ à** : to refuse to

réfuter |refyte| *vt* : to refute — **réfutation** |-fytasjɔ̃| *nf*

regagner |rəgaɲe| *vt* **1** : to win back, to regain **2** : to return to

regain |rəgɛ̃| *nm* **1** : renewal, resurgence **2** : second crop (in agriculture)

régal |regal| *nm, pl* **régals** DÉLICE : delight, treat

régaler |regale| *vt* : to treat to a delicious meal — **se régaler** *vr* **1** : to eat something delicious **2** : to enjoy oneself thoroughly

regard |rəgar| *nm* **1** : look, glance, gaze **2** : look, expression **3 au regard de** : in regard to, concerning **4 en regard de** : in comparison with

regardant, -dante |rəgardɑ̃, -dɑ̃t| *adj* **1** : fussy, particular **2** AVARE : stingy

regarder |rəgarde| *vt* **1** : to look at, to watch **2** : to consider, to regard **3** : to concern, to involve <ça ne vous regarde pas : it's none of your business> — *vi* **1** : to look <regarder par la fenêtre : to look out the window> **2 ~ à** : to think about, to take into account — **se regarder** *vr* : to look at oneself

régate |regat| *nf* : regatta

régénération |reʒenerasjɔ̃| *nf* : regeneration

régénérer |reʒenere| {87} *vt* : to regenerate — **se régénérer** *vr*

régent, -gente |reʒɑ̃, -ʒɑ̃t| *n* : regent

régenter |reʒɑ̃te| *vt* : to dictate, to rule over

régie |reʒi| *nf* **1** *France or* **régie d'État** : state-owned corporation **2** *Can* : provincially controlled public-service agency

régime |reʒim| *nm* **1** : regime, government **2** : scheme, system, regulations *pl* <régime pénitentiaire : prison system> **3** : diet, regimen <être au régime : to be on a diet> **4** : cluster, bunch <régime de bananes : bunch of bananas>

régiment |reʒimɑ̃| *nm* : regiment

région |reʒjɔ̃| *nf* : region, area

régional, -nale |reʒjɔnal| *adj, mpl* **-naux** |-no| : regional — **régionalement** |-nalmɑ̃| *adv*

régir |reʒir| *vt* : to control, to govern

régisseur |reʒisœr| *nm* **1** : steward, manager **2** : stage manager

registre |rəʒistr| *nm* **1** : register, record **2** : range (of a voice or instrument) **3** : damper (in a chimney)

réglable |reglabl| *adj* **1** : adjustable **2** : payable

réglage |reglaʒ| *nm* **1** : regulating, setting, tuning (of a motor) **2** : adjustment

règle |rɛgl| *nf* **1** : ruler **2** : rule, regulation **3 règles** *nfpl* : menstrual period <avoir ses règles : to menstruate> **4 en ~** : in order, valid **5 en règle générale** : generally, as a rule

réglé, -glée |regle| *adj* **1** ORGANISÉ : orderly, organized **2** : settled, decided

<tout est réglé : everything has been taken care of> **3** : ruled, lined

règlement [rɛgləmɑ̃] *nm* **1** : rules *pl,* regulations *pl* **2** : settlement, resolution **3** : payment

réglementaire [rɛgləmɑ̃tɛr] *adj* **1** : prescribed, regulation **2** : regulatory

réglementation [rɛgləmɑ̃tasjɔ̃] *nf* **1** : regulation, control **2** : rules *pl*

réglementer [rɛgləmɑ̃te] *vt* : to regulate, to control

régler [regle] {87} *vt* **1** : to regulate, to adjust **2** : to resolve, to settle **3** : to rule (a page)

réglisse [reglis] *nf* : licorice

règne [rɛɲ] *nm* **1** : reign, rule **2** : kingdom <le règne animal : the animal kingdom>

régner [reɲe] {87} *vi* : to reign, to rule, to prevail

regorger [rəgɔrʒe] {17} *vi* **~ de** : to overflow with, to abound with

régresser [regrese] *vi* **1** : to diminish, to recede, to decline **2** : to regress

régressif, -sive [regresif, -siv] *adj* : regressive

régression [regresjɔ̃] *nf* **1** : decline **2** : regression

regret [rəgrɛ] *nm* : regret <avec regret : regretfully> — **regrettable** [-grɛtabl] *adj*

regretter [rəgrɛte] *vt* **1** : to regret, to be sorry about <je regrette de ne pas t'avoir écrit : I'm sorry I haven't written to you> **2** : to miss <nous la regrettons beaucoup : we miss her very much>

regroupement [rəgrupmɑ̃] *nm* **1** : grouping together **2** : merger **3** : rallying, rounding up

regrouper [rəgrupe] *vt* **1** : to group together, to pool **2** : to reassemble, to regroup

régulariser [regylarize] *vt* **1** : to put in order, to sort out **2** : to regulate

régularité [regylarite] *nf* : regularity

régulateur[1], -trice [regylatœr, -tris] *adj* : regulating

régulateur[2] *nm* : regulator, governor (of a machine)

régulation [regylasjɔ̃] *nf* : regulation

régulier, -lière [regylje, -ljɛr] *adj* **1** : regular, fixed, established <un programme régulier : a regular schedule> **2** : even, symmetrical <visage régulier : regular features> **3** : steady, consistent <à intervalles réguliers : with regularity, at regular intervals> **4** : legitimate, in order

régulièrement [regyljɛrmɑ̃] *adv* **1** : regularly **2** : evenly **3** : steadily

régurgiter [regyrʒite] *vt* : to regurgitate

réhabilitation [reabilitasjɔ̃] *nf* : rehabilitation

réhabiliter [reabilite] *vt* **1** : to rehabilitate **2** : to restore to favor **3** RÉNOVER : to renovate — **se réhabiliter** *vr* : to redeem oneself

réhabituer [reabitɥe] *vt* : to reaccustom — **se réhabituer** *vr* : to get reaccustomed to

rehausser [rəose] *vt* **1** SURÉLEVER : to heighten **2** : to set off, to enhance

réimpression [reɛ̃prɛsjɔ̃] *nf* **1** : reprinting **2** : reprint

réimprimer [reɛ̃prime] *vt* : to reprint

rein [rɛ̃] *nm* **1** : kidney **2 reins** *nmpl* : back <avoir mal aux reins : to have a backache>

réincarnation [reɛ̃karnasjɔ̃] *nf* : reincarnation

réincarner [reɛ̃karne] *vt* : to reincarnate

reine [rɛn] *nf* : queen

réinsérer [reɛ̃sere] {87} *vt* **1** : to reinsert **2** : to rehabilitate, to reintegrate (into society, etc.) — **réinsertion** [reɛ̃sɛrsjɔ̃] *nf*

réintégrer [reɛ̃tegre] {87} *vt* **1** : to return to (a place) **2** : to reinstate

réitérer [reitere] {87} *vt* : to reiterate, to repeat — **réitération** [-terasjɔ̃] *nf*

rejaillir [rəʒajir] *vi* **1** : to splash up **2 ~ sur** : to reflect on, to fall upon (someone)

rejet [rəʒɛ] *nm* **1** : rejection **2** : discharge, disposal **3** : shoot (from a tree stump)

rejeter [rəʒte] {8} *vt* **1** RELANCER : to throw back **2** : to reject (in medicine), to throw up **3** : to discharge, to eject **4** REFUSER : to decline, to turn down **5 rejeter la faute** : to shift the blame

rejeton [rəʒtɔ̃] *nm* : offshoot (in botany)

rejoindre [rəʒwɛ̃dr] {50} *vt* **1** RENCONTRER : to meet, to join **2** RATTRAPER : to catch up with **3** REGAGNER : to return to, to get back to **4** : to agree with — **se rejoindre** *vr* **1** SE RENCONTRER : to meet **2** : to be in agreement

réjouir [reʒwir] *vt* : to gladden, to delight — **se réjouir** *vr* : to be delighted, to exult, to rejoice

réjouissance [reʒwisɑ̃s] *nf* **1** : rejoicing **2 réjouissances** *nfpl* : festivities, merrymaking

réjouissant, -sante [reʒwisɑ̃, -sɑ̃t] *adj* : cheering, delightful

relâche [rəlaʃ] *nf* **1** RÉPIT : break, respite **2** : closure <le lundi est notre jour de relâche : we're closed on Mondays>

relâché, -chée [rəlaʃe] *adj* : loose, lax

relâcher [rəlaʃe] *vt* **1** DESSERRER : to relax, to loosen up (restraints, muscles, etc.) **2** LIBÉRER : to release, to let go **3** : to relax, to slacken (efforts, discipline, etc.) — **se relâcher** *vr* **1** : to loosen, to go slack **2** : to become lax

relais [rəlɛ] *nm* **1** : relay (in sports and telecommunications) <course de relais : relay race> <relais de télévision : television relay station> **2** : shift

<travailler par relais : to work shifts> **3 prendre le relais** : to take over

relance [rəlɑ̃s] *nf* : boost, revival, upsurge

relancer [rəlɑ̃se] {6} *vt* **1** REJETER : to throw back **2** : to restart (an engine) **3** : to revive, to boost

relater [rəlate] *vt* : to recount, to relate

relatif, -tive [rəlatif, -tiv] *adj* : relative — **relativement** [-tivmɑ̃] *adv*

relation [rəlasjɔ̃] *nf* **1** RAPPORT : relation, connection **2** : relationship <relations professionnelles : professional relationships> **3** CONNAISSANCE : acquaintance <avoir des relations : to have (personal) connections> **4 relations** *nfpl* : relations <relations extérieures : foreign relations> <relations sexuelles : sexual relations>

relativité [rəlativite] *nf* : relativity

relax, -laxe [rəlaks] *adj fam* : relaxed, easygoing

relaxation [rəlaksasjɔ̃] *nf* : relaxation

relaxer [rəlakse] *vt* **1** : to relax **2** : to release — **se relaxer** *vr*

relayer [rəlɛje] {11} *vt* **1** : to take over from, to relieve **2** : to relay (in telecommunications) — **se relayer** *vr* : to take turns

reléguer [rəlege] {87} *vt* : to relegate — **relégation** [-legasjɔ̃] *nf*

relent [rəlɑ̃] *nm* **1** : foul smell, stench **2** TRACE : hint, trace

relève [rəlɛv] *nf* **1** : relief, replacement **2 prendre la relève** : to take over

relevé[1], -vée [rəlɛve] *adj* **1** RETROUSSÉ : turned up, rolled up **2** : elevated, refined **3** : spicy, pungent

relevé[2] *nm* **1** : statement <relevé de compte : bank statement> **2** : reading (of electricity, gas, etc.)

relèvement [rəlɛvmɑ̃] *nm* **1** : rise, increase **2** : rebuilding, recovery (of the economy, etc.)

relever [rəlve] {52} *vt* **1** : to stand up again, to raise (up) **2** : to turn up, to roll up **3** AUGMENTER : to raise, to increase **4** : to rebuild **5** RAMASSER : to collect, to pick up **6** ASSAISONNER : to season, to spice up **7** : to relieve, to take over from **8** NOTER : to take notice of **9** : to enhance, to elevate — *vi* **1 ~ de** : to be a matter for, to concern **2 ~ de** : to recover from (an illness) — **se relever** *vr* **1** : to get up again **2 ~ de** : to get over (an illness)

relief [rəljɛf] *nm* **1** : relief (in art, geography, etc.) **2 mettre en relief** : to accentuate, to highlight

relier [rəlje] {96} *vt* **1** : to link, to join **2** : to bind (a book)

relieur, -lieuse [rəljœr, -ljøz] *n* : binder, bookbinder

religieusement [rəliʒjøzmɑ̃] *adv* : religiously, faithfully

religieux[1], -gieuse [rəliʒjø, -ʒjøz] *adj* **1** : religious **2** : reverent, conscientious

religieux[2], -gieuse *n* : monk *m*, friar *m*, nun *f*

religion [rəliʒjɔ̃] *nf* : religion

reliquat [rəlika] *nm* : remainder, balance

relique [rəlik] *nf* : relic

relire [rəlir] {51} *vt* : to reread

relish [rəliʃ] *nf Can* : relish (condiment)

reliure [rəljyr] *nf* : binding

reluire [rəlɥir] {49} *vi* BRILLER : to glisten, to gleam, to shine

reluisant, -sante [rəlɥizɑ̃, -zɑ̃t] *adj* **1** : gleaming **2 peu reluisant** : unpromising, far from brilliant

reluquer [rəlyke] *vt fam* : to ogle, to eye

remâcher [rəmaʃe] *vt* : to stew over, to brood about

remaniement [rəmanimɑ̃] *nm* : revision, modification

remanier [rəmanje] {96} *vt* : to revise, to redraft, to modify

remarier [rəmarje]{96} *v* **se remarier** *vr* : to remarry

remarquable [rəmarkabl] *adj* : remarkable — **remarquablement** [-kabləmɑ̃] *adv*

remarque [rəmark] *nf* : remark, comment

remarquer [rəmarke] *vt* **1** : to remark, to observe <faire remarquer : to point out> **2** : to notice **3 se faire remarquer** : to attract attention, to come to the fore

remballer [rɑ̃bale] *vt* : to repack, to pack up (again)

rembarrer [rɑ̃bare] *vt fam* : to rebuff, to put someone in his or her place

remblai [rɑ̃blɛ] *nm* : embankment

remblayer [rɑ̃bleje] {11} *vt* : to fill in, to bank up

rembobiner [rɑ̃bɔbine] *vt* : to rewind

rembourrage [rɑ̃buraʒ] *nm* : stuffing, padding

rembourrer [rɑ̃bure] *vt* : to stuff, to pad

remboursable [rɑ̃bursabl] *adj* : refundable

remboursement [rɑ̃bursəmɑ̃] *nm* : repayment, reimbursement

rembourser [rɑ̃burse] *vt* **1** : to repay **2** : to refund, to reimburse

rembrunir [rɑ̃brynir] *v* **se rembrunir** *vr* : to cloud over, to become gloomy

remède [rəmɛd] *nm* : remedy, cure

remédier [rəmedje] {96} *vi* **~ à** : to remedy, to cure, to put right

remémorer [rəmemɔre] *v* **se remémorer** *vr* SE RAPPELER : to remember, to recall

remerciement [rəmɛrsimɑ̃] *nm* **1** : thanking <lettre de remerciement : thank-you letter> **2 remerciements** *nmpl* : thanks

remercier [rəmɛrsje] {96} *vt* **1** : to thank **2** CONGÉDIER : to dismiss, to fire

remettre [rəmɛtr] {53} *vt* **1** REPLACER : to put back **2** : to put back on, to switch back on, to restart **3** RA-

JOUTER : to add, to put more in **4** REMPLACER : to replace (a button, etc.) **5** DONNER : to deliver, to hand over **6** REPORTER : to postpone, to put off **7** RECONNAÎTRE : to recognize, to place **8 : remettre à neuf** : to restore, to refurbish — **se remettre** *vr* **1** : to return, to get back **2** : to put on again **3** : to recover, to get better **4 ~ à** : to begin again <elle s'est remise à parler : she started to talk again> **5 ~ à** : to rely on **6 s'en remettre à** : to leave it up to, to defer to

réminiscence [reminisɑ̃s] *nf* : reminiscence

remise [rəmiz] *nf* **1** : putting off, postponement **2** LIVRAISON : handing over, delivery <remise des diplômes : commencement, graduation> **3** : remission (of a debt, etc.) **4** RABAIS : discount **5** : shed

remiser [rəmize] *vt* : to put away, to store

rémission [remisjɔ̃] *nf* : remission

remodeler [rəmɔdle] {20} *vt* **1** : to remodel **2** : to reorganize, to restructure

remontant [rəmɔ̃tɑ̃] *nm* TONIQUE : tonic

remontée [rəmɔ̃te] *nf* **1** : climb, ascent **2 remontée mécanique** : ski lift

remonte–pente [rəmɔ̃tpɑ̃t] *nm, pl* **remonte–pentes** : ski lift

remonter [rəmɔ̃te] *vt* **1** : to take back up, to bring back up, to raise up (again) **2** : to go back up **3** : to cheer up, to invigorate — *vi* **1** : to rise (again) **2 ~ à** : to date back to **3 remonter dans le temps** : to go back in time

remontrance [rəmɔ̃trɑ̃s] *nf* REPROCHE : reproach, reprimand

remords [rəmɔr] *nm* : remorse

remorquage [rəmɔrkaʒ] *nm* : towing, tow

remorque [rəmɔrk] *nf* **1** : trailer **2 être en remorque** : to be in tow

remorquer [rəmɔrke] *vt* : to tow

remorqueur [rəmɔrkœr] *nm* : tugboat

remorqueuse [rəmɔrkøz] *nf Can* : tow truck

remous [rəmu] *nm* **1** : eddy **2** : backwash

rempart [rɑ̃par] *nm* : rampart

rempirer [rɑ̃pire] *vi Can fam* : to worsen, to become worse

remplaçable [rɑ̃plasabl] *adj* : replaceable

remplaçant, -çante [rɑ̃plasɑ̃, -sɑ̃t] *n* SUPPLÉANT : substitute, stand-in, alternate

remplacement [rɑ̃plasmɑ̃] *nm* : replacement

remplacer [rɑ̃plase] {6} *vt* **1** : to replace **2** : to substitute for, to stand in for

remplir [rɑ̃plir] *vt* **1** : to fill (up) **2** : to fill out (a form, etc.) **3** : to carry out, to fulfill

remplissage [rɑ̃plisaʒ] *nm* : filling, filler

remporter [rɑ̃pɔrte] *vt* **1** REPRENDRE : to take back, to take away (again) **2** : to win, to achieve

remuant, -ante [rəmɥɑ̃, -ɑ̃t] *adj* : restless, fidgety

remue–ménage [rəmymenaʒ] *nms & pl* : commotion, upheaval

remue–méninges [rəmymenɛ̃ʒ] *nms & pl* : brainstorming

remuer [rəmɥe] *vt* **1** : to move <remuer les lèvres : to move one's lips> <remuer la queue : to wag its tail> **2** : to stir, to mix **3** ÉMOUVOIR : to stir, to touch, to move — *vi* **1** : to move **2** : to fidget, to squirm — **se remuer** *vr* **1** : to move (about) **2** *fam* : to get a move on

rémunérateur, -trice [remyneratœr, -tris] *adj* LUCRATIF : lucrative

rémunération [remynerasjɔ̃] *nf* : remuneration

rémunérer [remynere] {87} *vt* : to remunerate

renâcler [rənakle] *vi* **1** : to snort (of an animal) **2 ~ à** : to be reluctant to, to grumble about

renaissance [rənɛsɑ̃s] *nf* **1** : rebirth, revival **2 la Renaissance** : the Renaissance

renaître [rənɛtr] {57} *vi* **1** : to be reborn, to come back to life **2** : to revive, to return

rénal, -nale [renal] *adj, mpl* **rénaux** [reno] : renal

renard [rənar] *nm* : fox

renarde [rənard] *nf* : vixen

renchérir [rɑ̃ʃerir] *vi* **1** : to become more expensive **2 ~ sur** : to go (one step) further than

renchérissement [rɑ̃ʃerismɑ̃] *nm* : rise, increase (in price)

rencontre [rɑ̃kɔ̃tr] *nf* **1** : meeting <rencontre au sommet : summit meeting> **2** : encounter **3** : junction, intersection **4** : (military) engagement **5** : match, game, meet (in sports)

rencontrer [rɑ̃kɔ̃tre] *vt* **1** : to meet **2** : to come across, to encounter **3** : to join, to intersect **4** HEURTER : to strike **5** : to oppose, to play against (in sports) — **se rencontrer** *vr* **1** : to meet, to come together **2** : to be found

rendement [rɑ̃dmɑ̃] *nm* **1** : output, production **2** : yield, return

rendez–vous [rɑ̃devu] *nms & pl* **1** : appointment, meeting **2** : meeting place, rendezvous

rendre [rɑ̃dr] {63} *vt* **1** : to give back, to return **2** : to give, to render <rendre grâce : to give thanks> <rendre service : to render aid> **3** : to yield **4** : to pronounce (a verdict or decree) **5** : to express, to convey **6 rendre les larmes** : to give up **7 rendre la monnaie** : to make change — **se rendre** *vr* **1** : to surrender, to give in **2 ~ à**

: to go to, to travel to **3 se rendre compte de** : to realize, to be aware of
rêne |rɛn| *nf* : rein
renégat, -gate |rənega, -gat| *n* : renegade, turncoat
renégocier |rənegɔsje| {96} *vt* : to renegotiate
renfermé¹, -mée |rɑ̃fɛrme| *adj* : withdrawn
renfermé² *nm* : mustiness <sentir le renfermé : to smell musty>
renfermer |rɑ̃fɛrme| *vt* **1** : to contain, to hold **2** : to hold in, to hide — **se renfermer** *vr* : to withdraw (into oneself)
renflé, -flée |rɑ̃fle| *adj* : bulging, bulbous
renflement |rɑ̃fləmɑ̃| *nm* : bulge
renflouer |rɑ̃flue| *vt* **1** : to refloat **2** : to bail out (a person, business, etc.)
renfoncement |rɑ̃fɔ̃smɑ̃| *nm* : recess
renfoncer |rɑ̃fɔ̃se| {6} *vt* : to push further in
renforcement |rɑ̃fɔrsəmɑ̃| *nm* : reinforcement
renforcer |rɑ̃fɔrse| {6} *vt* : to reinforce, to strengthen — **se renforcer** *vr* : to increase, to become stronger
renfort |rɑ̃fɔr| *nm* **1** : reinforcement **2 à grand renfort de** : with a great deal of
renfrogné, -gnée |rɑ̃frɔɲe| *adj* : sullen, scowling
renfrogner |rɑ̃frɔɲe| *v* **se renfrogner** *vr* : to scowl
rengager |rɑ̃gaʒe| {17} *vt* : to rehire, to take on again — **se rengager** *vr* : to reenlist
rengaine |rɑ̃gɛn| *nf* : cliché, old story <c'est toujours la même rengaine : it's always the same old story>
rengainer |rɑ̃gɛne| *vt* : to sheathe, to put back in its holster
reniement |rɛnimɑ̃| *nm* : denial, disavowal
renier |rənje| {96} *vt* **1** : to deny, to disavow **2** : to renounce, to repudiate
reniflement |rənifləmɑ̃| *nm* : sniffing, sniffling, snorting
renifler |rənifle| *v* : to sniff, to sniffle, to snort
renne |rɛn| *nm* : reindeer
renom |rənɔ̃| *nm* **1** : renown, fame **2** : reputation
renommé, -mée |rənɔme| *adj* : famous, renowned
renommée *nf* : fame, renown
renoncement |rənɔ̃smɑ̃| *nm* : renouncing, renunciation
renoncer |rənɔ̃se| {6} *vi* **~ à** : to renounce, to give up
renonciation |rənɔ̃sjasjɔ̃| *nf* : renunciation
renouer |rənwe| *vt* **1** : to retie **2** : to renew, to revive — **se renouer** *vr* : to get together again
renouveau |rənuvo| *nm, pl* **-veaux** : revival
renouvelable |rənuvlabl| *adj* : renewable
renouveler |rənuvle| {8} *vt* **1** : to renew, to revive **2** : to repeat — **se renouveler** *vr* : to recur, to be repeated
renouvellement |rənuvɛlmɑ̃| *nm* **1** : renewal **2** : recurrence, repetition
rénovation |renɔvasjɔ̃| *nf* : renovation
rénover |renɔve| *vt* **1** : to renovate, to restore **2** : to reform
renseignement |rɑ̃sɛɲəmɑ̃| *nm* **1** : information <bureau des renseignements : information center> **2** : intelligence <agent de renseignements : intelligence agent>
renseigner |rɑ̃sɛɲe| *vt* : to inform <mal renseigner : to misinform> <bien renseigné : well-informed> — **se renseigner** *vr* **1** : to ask, to make inquiries <renseignez-vous auprès de la réceptionniste : please ask the receptionist> **2 ~ sur** : to inquire about
rentable |rɑ̃tabl| *adj* : profitable — **rentabilité** |-tabilite| *nf*
rente |rɑ̃t| *nf* **1** : annuity **2** : (private) income
rentrée |rɑ̃tre| *nf* **1** : start, beginning <la rentrée des classes : the start of the new school year> **2** : return **3** : comeback (in entertainment, politics, etc.) **4** : income, revenue
rentrer |rɑ̃tre| *vi* **1** : to go in, to get in **2** : to go back in **3** : to return <rentrer chez soi : to return home> **4** : to start (up) again, to reopen **5** : to come in <faire rentrer l'argent : to bring in money> **6** : to fit <rentrer dans la serrure : to fit into the lock> **7 ~ dans** : to be a part of, to be included in — *vt* **1** : to bring in, to take in **2** : to put in **3** : to hold back, to suppress
renversant, -sante |rɑ̃vɛrsɑ̃, -sɑ̃t| *adj* AHURISSANT : astounding, amazing
renverse |rɑ̃vɛrs| *nf* **tomber à la renverse** : to fall over backward
renversement |rɑ̃vɛrsəmɑ̃| *nm* **1** INVERSION : reversal, inversion **2** : shift, change (of direction) **3** : overthrow **4** : spilling, spillage
renverser |rɑ̃vɛrse| *vt* **1** : to knock down, to overturn **2** : to spill **3** : to turn over, to invert **4** : to reverse (sides, roles, etc.) **5** : to tilt (back) **6** : to overthrow **7** : to astound, to astonish — **se renverser** *vr* **1** : to fall over **2** : to bend over backwards
renvoi |rɑ̃vwa| *nm* **1** : return, sending back **2** : dismissal, discharge **3** : cross-reference **4** : postponement **5** : burp, belch <avoir des renvois : to burp>
renvoie |rɑ̃vwa|, *etc.* → **renvoyer**
renvoyer |rɑ̃vwaje| {36} *vt* **1** : to send back, to throw back **2** CONGÉDIER : to dismiss, to expel **3** REMETTRE : to put back, to postpone **4 ~ à** : to refer to, to relate back to **5** *Can fam* : to throw up

réorganiser |reɔrganize| *vt* : to reorganize — **réorganisation** |-nizasjɔ̃| *nf*

repaire |rəpɛr| *nm* : den, lair

répandre |repɑ̃dr| {63} *vt* **1** : to spread, to scatter, to spill **2** : to shed (blood, tears) **3** : to spread, to propagate (rumors, terror, etc.) **4** : to give off, to emit — **se répandre** *vr*

répandu, -due |repɑ̃dy| *adj* : widespread

réparable |reparabl| *adj* : reparable

reparaître |rəparɛtr| → **réapparaître**

réparation |reparasjɔ̃| *nf* **1** : repair, repairing **2** : **réparations** *nfpl* : reparations, damages

réparer |repare| *vt* **1** : to repair, to fix, to mend **2** : to make up for **3** : to restore (health, strength, etc.)

repartie |rəparti| *nf* : repartee, rejoinder

repartir |rəpartir| {82} *vt* : to retort — *vi* **1** : to leave again **2** : to start again <repartir à zero : to rebound>

répartir |repartir| *vt* **1** : to divide up, to distribute **2** : to spread (out) — **se répartir** *vr* : to divide, to split

répartition |repartisjɔ̃| *nf* : distribution, dividing up

repas |rəpa| *nm* **1** : meal **2 l'heure du repas** : mealtime

repassage |rəpasaʒ| *nm* : ironing

repasser |rəpase| *vt* **1** : to pass again, to take again, to show again **2** : to iron, to press **3** : to go (back) over <repasser ses leçons : to go over one's lessons> **4** : to hand over — *vi* : to pass by again, to come again

repentant, -tante |rəpɑ̃tɑ̃, -tɑ̃t| *adj* : repentant, penitent

repentir[1] |rəpɑ̃tir| {82} *v* **se repentir** *vr* **1** : to repent **2** : to regret

repentir[2] *nm* : repentance

répercussion |repɛrkysjɔ̃| *nf* : repercussion

répercuter |repɛrkyte| *vt* **1** : to reverberate, to echo **2** TRANSMETTRE : to reflect, to pass on — **se répercuter** *vr* **1** : to echo **2 ~ sur** : to affect, to have an effect on

repère |rəpɛr| *nm* **1** : line, mark **2** : point of reference, landmark (in space or time)

repérer |rəpere| {87} *vt* **1** : to mark **2** : to locate, to pinpoint **3** : to spot, to catch sight of — **se repérer** *vr fam* : to get one's bearings, to find one's way

répertoire |repɛrtwar| *nm* **1** : list, index **2** : notebook, directory <répertoire d'adresses : address book> **3** : repertory, repertoire

répertorier |repɛrtɔrje| {96} *vt* : to index, to list

répéter |repete| {87} *vt* **1** : to repeat **2** : to tell, to relate **3** : to go over, to rehearse — **se répéter** *vr* **1** : to repeat oneself **2** : to recur

répétitif, -tive |repetitif, -tiv| *adj* : repetitive

répétition |repetisjɔ̃| *nf* **1** : repetition **2** : rehearsal

répit |repi| *nm* : respite, break

replacer |rəplase| {6} *vt* **1** : to replace, to put back **2** : to reassign (to a new job) — **se replacer** *vr* : to find a new job

replanter |rəplɑ̃te| *vt* **1** : to transplant **2** : to replant

replâtrer |rəplatre| *vt* **1** : to replaster **2** *fam* : to patch up, to paper over

replet, -plète |rəplɛ, -plɛt| *adj* GRASSOUILLET : plump, chubby

repli |rəpli| *nm* **1** : fold, crease **2** : withdrawal (of troops, etc.) **3 replis** *nmpl* : inner recesses <les replis de l'âme : the depths of the soul>

replier |rəplije| {96} *vt* **1** : to fold up, to fold over **2** : to withdraw, to pull back — **se replier** *vr* **1** : to fold up **2** : to withdraw **3 se replier sur soi-même** : to withdraw into oneself

réplique |replik| *nf* **1** RIPOSTE : retort, reply **2** : line (in a play) **3** : replica

répliquer |replike| *vt* RÉPONDRE : to reply, to retort — *vi* **1** : to respond, to answer back <répliquer à la critique : to respond to criticism> **2** : to retaliate

répondant, -dante |repɔ̃dɑ̃, -dɑ̃t| *n* : guarantor

répondeur |repɔ̃dœr| *nm* : answering machine

répondre |repɔ̃dr| {63} *vt* : to answer, to reply — *vi* **1** : to answer, to reply, to respond **2** : to meet, to fulfill <répondre aux critères : to meet the criteria> **3** RÉPLIQUER : to answer back **4 ~ de** : to answer for, to vouch for

réponse |repɔ̃s| *nf* : answer, reply

report |rəpɔr| *nm* RENVOI : postponement

reportage |rəpɔrtaʒ| *nm* **1** : report **2** : reporting

reporter[1] |rəpɔrte| *vt* **1** : to take back **2** REMETTRE : to postpone, to put off **3** : to carry forward (a calculation, etc.), to transfer, to copy out **4** : to transfer, to shift <reporter ses affections : to shift one's affections>

reporter[2] |rəpɔrtɛr| *nm* : reporter

repos |rəpo| *nm* **1** : rest <jour de repos : day of rest> **2** TRANQUILLITÉ : peace, tranquillity <avoir l'esprit en repos : to put one's mind at rest> **3 à repos!** : at ease! **4 de tout repos** : safe, secure

reposant, -sante |rəpozɑ̃, -zɑ̃t| *nm* : restful, relaxing

reposé, -sée |rəpoze| *adj* : rested, refreshed

repose-pied |rəpozpje| *nm, pl* **repose-pieds** : footrest

reposer |rəpoze| *vt* **1** : to put (back) down, to put down again **2** : to ask again **3** : to rest (one's body or mind) — *vi* **1** : to rest, to lie **2** : to sleep, to be at rest <qu'il repose en paix : may he rest in peace> **3 ~ sur** : to be based on, to rest upon — **se reposer** *vr* **1** : to rest **2 ~ sur** : to rely on

repoussant, -sante [rəpusɑ̃, -sɑ̃t] *adj* DÉGOÛTANT : repulsive

repousser [rəpuse] *vi* : to grow back — *vt* **1** : to push back **2** : to disgust, to repel **3** REJETER : to refuse, to turn down **4** REPORTER : to put off, to postpone

repoussoir [rəpuswar] *nm* : foil, complement <servir de repoussoir : to act as a foil>

répréhensible [repreɑ̃sibl] *adj* : reprehensible

reprendre [rəprɑ̃dr] {70} *vt* **1** : to take (up) again **2** : to take back, to regain, to recapture **3** : to take over (a business, etc.) **4** : to take back (merchandise) <ça ne peut être ni repris ni échangé : it can't be returned or exchanged> **5** : to begin again, to continue <reprendre la parole : to resume speaking> **6** : to repair, to touch up, to correct — *vi* **1** : to pick up, to improve **2** RECOMMENCER : to start again — **se reprendre** *vr* **1** : to correct oneself **2** : to pull oneself together

représailles [rəprezaj] *nfpl* : reprisals, retaliation

représentant, -tante [rəprezɑ̃tɑ̃, -tɑ̃t] *n* **1** : representative **2** : salesman <représentant de commerce : traveling salesman>

représentatif, -tive [rəprezɑ̃tatif, -tiv] *adj* : representative

représentation [rəprezɑ̃tasjɔ̃] *nf* **1** : representation **2** : performance (in theater)

représenter [rəprezɑ̃te] *vt* **1** : to represent, to act for **2** JOUER : to perform **3** : to depict, to show **4** : to symbolize, to stand for **5** : to signify, to mean — **se représenter** *vr* **1** : to imagine, to picture **2** : to come up again

répressif, -sive [represif, -siv] *adj* : repressive

répression [represjɔ̃] *nf* : repression, suppression

réprimande [reprimɑ̃d] *nf* : reprimand

réprimander [reprimɑ̃de] *vt* : to reprimand, to scold

réprimé, -mée [reprime] *adj* : suppressed, held in

réprimer [reprime] *vt* : to repress, to suppress

reprise [rəpriz] *nf* **1** : recapture **2** : resumption **3** : rerun, repeat, revival (in movies, television, etc.) **4** : recovery <reprise économique : economic recovery> **5** : trade-in (of goods) **6** : round (in sports) **7** : acceleration (of an automobile) **8** : mend, darn (in sewing) **9 à maintes reprises** : on numerous occasions, repeatedly

repriser [rəprize] *vt* : to darn, to mend

réprobateur, -trice [reprɔbatœr, -tris] *adj* : reproving, reproachful

réprobation [reprɔbasjɔ̃] *nf* : disapproval

reproche [rəprɔʃ] *nm* : reproach <faire des reproches à : to reproach, to blame> <sans reproche : beyond reproach>

reprocher [rəprɔʃe] *vt* **~ à** : to reproach, to rebuke

reproducteur, -trice [rəprɔdyktœr, -tris] *adj* : reproductive

reproduction [rəprɔdyksjɔ̃] *nf* : reproduction

reproduire [rəprɔdɥir] {49} *vt* **1** : to reproduce **2** : to make a copy of **3** : to breed — **se reproduire** *vr* **1** : to reproduce, to breed **2** SE RÉPÉTER : to recur

réprouver [repruve] *vt* : to reprove, to condemn

reptile [rɛptil] *nm* : reptile

reptilien, -lienne [rɛptiljɛ̃, -ljɛn] *adj* : reptilian

repu, -pue [rəpy] *adj* : satiated, full

républicain, -caine [repyblikɛ̃, -kɛn] *adj & n* : republican

république [repyblik] *nf* : republic

répudier [repydje] {96} *vt* : to repudiate — **répudiation** [repydjasjɔ̃] *nf*

répugnance [repyɲɑ̃s] *nf* **1** : repugnance, aversion **2** : reluctance

répugnant, -nante [repyɲɑ̃, -ɲɑ̃t] *adj* : repugnant, disgusting

répugner [repyɲe] *vt* : to disgust, to be repugnant to — *vi* **~ à** : to be averse to <je ne répugne pas au travail : I'm not averse to work>

répulsion [repylsjɔ̃] *nf* : repulsion, repugnance

réputation [repytasjɔ̃] *nf* : reputation

réputé, -tée [repyte] *adj* : renowned, famous

requérir [rəkerir] {21} *vt* **1** NÉCESSITER : to call for, to require **2** : to request, to summon

requête [rəkɛt] *nf* **1** : request **2** : petition (in law)

requiem [rekɥijɛm] *nms & pl* : requiem

requière [rəkjɛr], **requiert** [rəkjɛr], *etc.* → **requérir**

requin [rəkɛ̃] *nm* : shark

requinquer [rəkɛ̃ke] *vt fam* : to pep up

requis[1] [rəki] *pp* → **requérir**

requis[2], **-quise** [rəki, -kiz] *adj* : requisite, required

réquisition [rekizisjɔ̃] *nf* : requisition

réquisitionner [rekizisjɔne] *vt* : to requisition

réquisitoire [rekizitwar] *nm* : indictment <un réquisitoire contre les moeurs contemporaines : an indictment against contemporary mores>

rescapé, -pée [rɛskape] *n* : survivor

rescousse |rɛskus| *nf* : rescue, aid <aller à la rescousse : to go to the rescue>
réseau |rezo| *nm, pl* **réseaux** : network
réservation |rezɛrvasjɔ̃| *nf* : reservation
réserve |rezɛrv| *nf* **1** : reserve, stock **2** RETENUE : reserve, restraint **3** : reservation <réserve indienne : Indian reservation> **4** : preserve, sanctuary **5** : storeroom **6** : reservation, hesitation <sous réserve de : subject to>
réservé, -vée |rezɛrve| *adj* **1** : private, reserved **2** : reserved, reticent
réserver |rezɛrve| *vt* **1** : to reserve, to book **2** : to reserve, to set aside — **se réserver** *vr* **1** : to save oneself **2** : to set aside for oneself
réservoir |rezɛrvwar| *nm* **1** : tank, cistern **2** : reservoir **3** : bulb (of a thermometer)
résidence |rezidɑ̃s| *nf* **1** : residence **2** **résidence universitaire** : dormitory
résident, -dente |rezidɑ̃, -dɑ̃t| *adj & n* : resident
résidentiel, -tielle |rezidɑ̃sjɛl| *adj* : residential
résider |rezide| *vi* **1** : to reside, to dwell **2** **~ en** : to lie in, to consist of
résidu |rezidy| *nm* **1** : residue **2** RESTE : remainder **3** **résidus** *nmpl* : waste <résidus industriels : industrial waste>
résiduel, -duelle |rezidɥɛl| *adj* : residual
résignation |reziɲasjɔ̃| *nf* : resignation
résigner |reziɲe| *vt* : to relinquish, to resign — **se résigner** *vr* **~ à** : to resign oneself to
résilier |rezilje| {96} *vt* : to terminate (a contract, etc.)
résille |rezij| *nf* : hair net
résine |rezin| *nf* : resin
résineux[1], **-neuse** |rezinø, -nøz| *adj* : resinous
résineux[2] *nmpl* : coniferous trees
résistance |rezistɑ̃s| *nf* **1** : resistance, opposition **2** : strength, endurance
résistant, -tante |rezistɑ̃, -tɑ̃t| *adj* **1** : resistant **2** : tough, hardy, durable
résister |reziste| *vi* **1** **~ à** : to resist, to oppose **2** **~ à** : to stand up to, to withstand **3** **~ à** : to bear, to tolerate
résolu[1] |rezɔly| *pp* → **résoudre**
résolu[2], **-lue** |rezɔly| *adj* : resolute, determined
résolument |rezɔlymɑ̃| *adj* : resolutely, firmly, adamantly
résolution |rezɔlysjɔ̃| *nf* **1** : resolution, decision **2** : determination, resolve **3** : solution
résonance |rezɔnɑ̃s| *nf* **1** : resonance **2** : echo, overtone
résonnant, -nante |rezɔnɑ̃, -nɑ̃t| *adj* : resonant
résonner |rezɔne| *vi* : to resound, to ring out
résorber |rezɔrbe| *vt* : to absorb, to reduce — **se résorber** *vr*
résoudre |rezudr| {74} *vt* : to solve, to resolve — **se résoudre** *vr* **1** **~ à** : to decide to **2** **~ à** : to reconcile oneself to
respect |rɛspɛ| *nm* **1** : respect, consideration **2** **respects** *nmpl* : respects, regards
respectabilité |rɛspɛktabilite| *nf* : respectability
respectable |rɛspɛktabl| *adj* : respectable
respecter |rɛspɛkte| *vt* **1** : to respect **2** **faire respecter** : to enforce
respectif, -tive |rɛspɛktif, -tiv| *adj* : respective — **respectivement** |-tivmɑ̃| *adv*
respectueux, -euse |rɛspɛktɥø, -øz| *adj* : respectful — **respectueusement** |-tɥøzmɑ̃| *adv*
respirateur |rɛspiratœr| *nm* : respirator
respiration |rɛspirasjɔ̃| *nf* : breathing, respiration
respiratoire |rɛspiratwar| *adj* : respiratory
respirer |rɛspire| *vi* : to breathe — *vt* **1** : to breathe in, to inhale **2** : to exude
resplendir |rɛsplɑ̃dir| *vi* **1** : to shine **2** **~ de** : to be radiant with (joy, etc.)
resplendissant, -sante |rɛsplɑ̃disɑ̃, -sɑ̃t| *adj* : radiant, resplendent
responsabilité |rɛspɔ̃sabilite| *nf* **1** : responsibility **2** : liability
responsable |rɛspɔ̃sabl| *adj* : responsible, answerable
resquiller |rɛskije| *vi fam* **1** : to sneak in without paying **2** : to cut in line
ressac |rəsak| *nm* : undertow, backwash
ressaisir |rəsezir| *v* **se ressaisir** *vr* : to pull oneself together, to rally
ressasser |rəsase| *vt* **1** RABÂCHER : to keep repeating **2** RUMINER : to brood over, to dwell on
ressemblance |rəsɑ̃blɑ̃s| *nf* **1** : resemblance, likeness <avoir une ressemblance avec qqn : to resemble s.o.> **2** : similarity
ressemblant, -blante |rəsɑ̃blɑ̃, -blɑ̃t| *adj* : lifelike
ressembler |rəsɑ̃ble| *vi* **~ à** : to look like, to resemble — **se ressembler** *vr* **1** : to look alike **2** : to be alike
ressentiment |rəsɑ̃timɑ̃| *nm* : resentment
ressentir |rəsɑ̃tir| {82} *vt* : to feel — **se ressentir** *vr* **~ de** : to feel the effects of
resserre |rəsɛr| *nf* REMISE : shed
resserrement |rəsɛrmɑ̃| *nm* **1** : tightening (up) **2** : narrowing, narrow part
resserrer |rəsere| *vt* **1** : to tighten **2** : to close up, to constrict — **se resserrer** *vr*
ressort |rəsɔr| *nm* **1** : spring (of a watch, mattress, etc.) **2** : impulse, drive, mo-

tivation **3** : recourse, appeal <en dernier ressort : as a last resort>
ressortir [rəsɔrtir] {82} *vt* **1** : to take out again, to bring out again **2** : to release again, to rerun — *vi* **1** : to go out again **2** : to stand out — *v impers* : to emerge, to be evident <il en ressort des faits intéressants : interesting facts are coming to light>
ressortissant, -sante [rəsɔrtisɑ̃, -sɑ̃t] *n* : national <ressortissants étrangers : foreign nationals>
ressource [rəsurs] *nf* **1** : recourse, option **2** : resourcefulness <avoir de la ressource : to be resourceful> **3 ressources** *nfpl* : resources, funds, reserves <ressources énergétiques : energy reserves> **4 ressources** *nfpl* : resources, possibilities <ressources de l'imaginaire : powers of the imagination>
ressusciter [resysite] *vt* **1** : to resuscitate, to bring back to life **2** : to revive, to rekindle — *vi* : to revive, to come back to life
restant[1], **-tante** [rɛstɑ̃, -tɑ̃t] *adj* : remaining
restant[2] *nm* : remainder, rest
restaurant [rɛstɔrɑ̃] *nm* : restaurant
restaurateur, -trice [rɛstɔratœr, -tris] *n* **1** : restaurant owner **2** : restorer (of artwork, etc.)
restauration [rɛstɔrasjɔ̃] *nf* **1** : restoration **2** : catering, food service <la restauration rapide : the fast-food industry>
restaurer [rɛstɔre] *vt* : to restore — **se restaurer** *vr* : to have something to eat
reste [rɛst] *nm* **1** : remainder, rest **2 au ~** *or* **du ~** : besides, moreover **3 restes** *nmpl* : leftovers, leavings **4 restes** *nmpl* : (last) remains
rester [rɛste] *vi* **1** DEMEURER : to stay, to remain <rester éveillé : to stay awake> <il ne peut pas rester en place : he can't sit still> **2** : to be left, to remain <il ne nous reste plus d'argent : we have no money left> **3** DURER : to last, to live on — *v impers* : to remain <il reste à savoir : it remains to be seen>
restituer [rɛstitɥe] *vt* **1** : to restore, to return **2** : to reconstruct **3** : to reproduce (sound, etc.) **4** *Can fam* : to throw up
restitution [rɛstitysjɔ̃] *nf* **1** : restitution, restoration **2** : reproduction
restreindre [rɛstrɛ̃dr] {37} *vt* : to restrict, to limit, to constrain — **se restreindre** *vr* **1** : to cut back **2** : to narrow, to become more limited
restreint, -treinte [rɛstrɛ̃, -trɛ̃t] *adj* : restricted, limited
restrictif, -tive [rɛstriktif, -tiv] *adj* : restrictive
restriction [rɛstriksjɔ̃] *nf* : restriction, limitation
restructuration [rəstryktyrasjɔ̃] *nf* : restructuring
restructurer [rəstryktyre] *vt* : to restructure
résultant, -tante [rezyltɑ̃, -tɑ̃t] *adj* : resultant
résultat [rezylta] *nm* **1** : result, outcome **2 résultats** *nmpl* : results (of an election, etc.), grades (of an exam) **3 résultats** *nmpl* : findings, results
résulter [rezylte] {75} *vi* **~ de** : to result from — *v impers* : to follow
résumé [rezyme] *nm* **1** : summary **2 en ~** : in short
résumer [rezyme] *vt* : to summarize, to sum up — **se résumer** *vr* **1** : to sum up **2 ~ à** : to come down to
résurgence [rezyrʒɑ̃s] *nf* : resurgence
résurrection [rezyrɛksjɔ̃] *nf* **1** : resurrection **2** : revival, rebirth
rétablir [retablir] *vt* **1** : to reestablish, to restore **2** : to reinstate (in a job, etc.) — **se rétablir** *vr* **1** : to get better, to recover **2** : to be restored, to return
rétablissement [retablismɑ̃] *nm* **1** : reestablishment, restoration **2** GUÉRISON : recovery
retaper [rətape] *vt* **1** : to retype **2** : to renovate **3** *fam* : to pep up — **se retaper** *vr fam* : to recover, to get back on one's feet
retard [rətar] *nm* **1** : lateness, delay <avoir du retard : to be late> <sans retard : without delay> <être en retard : to be behind schedule> <prendre du retard : to fall behind> **2** : backwardness <être en retard pour son âge : to be backward for one's age> <en retard sur son temps : behind the times>
retardataire[1] [rətardatɛr] *adj* **1** : late, delayed **2** : outdated
retardataire[2] *nmf* : latecomer
retardé, -dée [rətarde] *adj* : backward
retardement [rətardəmɑ̃] *nm* **1 à ~** : delayed-action **2 bombe à retardement** : time bomb
retarder [rətarde] *vt* **1** : to delay **2** : to put off, to postpone **3** : to set back (a clock, etc.) — *vi* **1** : to be slow, to lose time **2** : to be behind the times **3** *fam* : to be out of touch
retenir [rətənir] {92} *vt* **1** : to hold back, to stop, to check **2** : to keep, to detain **3** : to retain, to absorb **4** : to reserve, to book **5** : to remember **6** : to carry (in mathematics) — **se retenir** *vr* **1** : to restrain oneself **2 ~ à** : to hold onto, to grip
rétention [retɑ̃sjɔ̃] *nf* : retention, withholding
retentir [rətɑ̃tir] *vi* **1** : to ring, to resound, to boom **2 ~ sur** : to have an effect on
retentissant, -sante [rətɑ̃tisɑ̃, -sɑ̃t] *adj* : resounding <succès retentissant : resounding success>

retentissement [rətɑ̃tismɑ̃] *nm* **1** : resounding, ringing, booming **2** : effect, impact, repercussions *pl*
retenue [rətəny] *nf* **1** : deduction **2** : detention (in school) **3** RÉSERVE : reserve, self-restraint
réticent, -cente [retisɑ̃, -sɑ̃t] *adj* : reticent, reluctant — **réticence** [-tisɑ̃s] *nf*
rétif, -tive [retif, -tiv] *adj* **1** : restive **2** : rebellious
rétine [retin] *nf* : retina
retiré, -rée [rətire] *adj* **1** : remote, secluded **2** : isolated, withdrawn **3** : retired
retirer [rətire] *vt* **1** : to take off (clothing, etc.), to remove **2** : to withdraw, to move away **3** : to withdraw, to take back **4** : to collect (baggage, etc.), to withdraw (funds), to extract (minerals, etc.) **5** RECUEILLIR : to derive, to obtain <retirer un bénéfice : to make a profit> **6** *Can* : to retire, to put out (in baseball) — **se retirer** *vr* **1** : to withdraw, to retreat **2** : to retire
retombées [rətɔ̃be] *nfpl* **1** : repercussions, consequences **2 retombées radioactives** : radioactive fallout
retomber [rətɔ̃be] *vi* **1** : to come down, to land **2** : to fall again **3** : to subside, to die away **4** : to fall back, to relapse **5** : to fall, to go down (of temperature, value, etc.) **6 ~ sur** : to fall on <la responsabilité retombe toujours sur nous : the responsibility always falls on us>
rétorquer [retɔrke] *vt* : to retort
retors, -torse [rətɔr, -tɔrs] *adj* : wily, sly
rétorsion [retɔrsjɔ̃] *nf* : retaliation
retouche [rətuʃ] *nf* **1** : touching up **2** : alteration
retoucher [rətuʃe] *vt* **1** : to touch up **2** : to alter, to make alterations
retour [rətur] *nm* **1** : return <à mon retour : on my return> <être sur le chemin de retour : to be on the way back> <billet de retour : return ticket> **2 de ~** : back <de retour de la campagne : back (home) from the country> **3 retour de flamme** : backfire **4 retour en arrière** : flashback **5 sans ~** : irrevocably, forever
retournement [rəturnəmɑ̃] *nm* : reversal
retourner [rəturne] *vt* **1** : to turn over, to turn upside down, to turn around <retourner la situation : to reverse the situation> **2** : to turn inside out **3** : to return (a compliment, etc.) **4** : to return, to send back **5** *fam* : to shake up, to upset — *vi* REVENIR : to return, to go back — **se retourner** *vr* **1** : to turn around **2** : to turn over, to overturn **3** : to sort things out, to turn things around **4 ~ contre** : to turn against **5 s'en retourner** : to go back
retracer [rətrase] {6} *vt* **1** : to redraw, to trace over **2** : to recount (an event)
rétracter [retrakte] *v* **se rétracter** *vr* : to retract — **rétractable** [-traktabl] *adj* — **rétraction** [-traksjɔ̃] *nf*
retrait [rətrɛ] *nm* **1** : withdrawal (of funds, permission, etc.) **2 en ~** : set back <rester en retrait : to stand back, to stay in the background> **3** *Can* : out (in baseball) **4 retrait au bâton** : strikeout
retraite [rətrɛt] *nf* **1** : retreat (in religion, the military, etc.) **2** : pension <mettre à la retraite : to pension off> **3** : retirement <prendre sa retraite : to retire>
retraité[1], -tée [rətrɛte] *adj* : retired
retraité[2], -tée *n* : retiree
retrancher [rətrɑ̃ʃe] *vt* **1** ENLEVER : to take out, to remove **2** : to deduct **3** FORTIFIER : to entrench — **se retrancher** *vr* : to entrench oneself, to take refuge
retransmettre [rətrɑ̃smɛtr] {53} *vt* : to broadcast, to relay
retransmission [rətrɑ̃smisjɔ̃] *nf* : broadcast
rétrécir [retresir] *vt* **1** : to shrink **2** : to take in, to shorten (clothing) — *vi* : to shrink — **se rétrécir** *vr* **1** : to become narrower **2** : to contract, to shrink
rétrécissement [retresismɑ̃] *nm* **1** : narrowing (of a road, etc.) **2** : shrinkage (of clothing, etc.)
rétribuer [retribɥe] *vt* RÉMUNÉRER : to pay, to remunerate
rétribution [retribysjɔ̃] *nf* RÉMUNÉRATION : payment, remuneration
rétroactif, -tive [retrɔaktif, -tiv] *adj* : retroactive — **rétroactivement** [-tivmɑ̃] *adv*
rétrograde [retrɔgrad] *adj* **1** RÉACTIONNAIRE : reactionary, retrograde **2** : backward <un mouvement rétrograde : a backward movement>
rétrograder [retrɔgrade] *vt* : to demote — *vi* **1** : to regress **2** : to downshift
rétrospective [retrɔspɛktiv] *nf* : retrospective — **rétrospectif, -tive** [-tif, -tiv] *adj*
rétrospectivement [retrɔspɛktivmɑ̃] *adv* : retrospectively, in retrospect
retrousser [rətruse] *vt* : to turn up, to roll up <retrousser ses manches : to roll up one's sleeves>
retrouvailles [rətruvaj] *nfpl* : reunion
retrouver [rətruve] *vt* **1** : to find (again) **2** REDÉCOUVRIR : to rediscover **3** REVOIR : to see again, to be reunited with **4** SE RAPPELER : to recall, to remember **5** RECONNAÎTRE : to recognize — **se retrouver** *vr* **1** : to find oneself **2** : to meet again **3** : to find one's way
rétroviseur [retrɔvizœr] *nm* : rearview mirror
réunion [reynjɔ̃] *nf* **1** : meeting **2** : gathering, reunion **3** : uniting, merging
réunir [reynir] *vt* RASSEMBLER : to gather, to collect, to bring together

— se réunir *vr* : to meet, to get together
réussi, -sie [reysi] *adj* : successful
réussir [reysir] *vi* : to succeed — *vt* **1** : to make a success of, to bring off **2** : to pass (an exam)
réussite [reysit] *nf* : success
réutiliser [reytilize] *vt* : to reuse
revaloir [rəvalwar] {95} *vt* : to pay back <je te revaudrai cela! : I'll get even with you for that!>
revalorisation [rəvalɔrizasjɔ̃] *nf* : revaluation, raising (of salaries, fees, etc.)
revaloriser [rəvalɔrize] *vt* **1** : to revalue, to raise (salaries, etc.) **2** : to reassess, to upgrade
revanche [rəvɑ̃ʃ] *nf* **1** : revenge **2** : return match (in sports) **3 en ~** : on the other hand
rêvasser [rɛvase] *vi* : to daydream
rêve [rɛv] *nm* **1** : dream **2 de ~** *or* **de ses rêves** : ideal, of one's dreams <la maison de ses rêves : the house of his dreams> **3 rêve éveillé** : daydream
rêvé, -vée [rɛve] *adj* : ideal
revêche [rəvɛʃ] *adj* ACARIÂTRE : surly, crabby
réveil [revɛj] *nm* **1** : waking up **2** : awakening <un réveil brutal : a rude awakening> **3** : reawakening, recurrence **4** : alarm clock
réveille–matin [revɛjmatɛ̃] *nms & pl* : alarm clock
réveiller [reveje] *vt* **1** : to wake up **2** : to awaken, to revive, to arouse — **se réveiller** *vr*
réveillon [revɛjɔ̃] *nm* **1** : Christmas Eve supper or party **2** : New Year's Eve supper or party
réveillonner [revɛjɔne] *vi* : to celebrate Christmas Eve or New Year's Eve
révélateur, -trice [revelatœr, -tris] *adj* : revealing
révélation [revelasjɔ̃] *nf* : revelation
révéler [revele] {87} *vt* **1** DÉVOILER : to reveal, to disclose **2** INDIQUER : to show **3** : to develop (photographic film) — **se révéler** *vr* **1** : to show oneself as **2** : to turn out to be **3** : to be revealed
revenant, -nante [rəvnɑ̃, -nɑ̃t] *n* SPECTRE : ghost
revendeur, -deuse [rəvɑ̃dœr, -døz] *n* **1** DÉTAILLANT : retailer **2** : secondhand dealer
revendication [rəvɑ̃dikasjɔ̃] *nf* : claim, demand
revendiquer [rəvɑ̃dike] *vt* **1** : to claim **2** EXIGER : to demand
revendre [rəvɑ̃dr] {63} *vt* **1** : to sell (one's car, house, etc.) **2 à ~** : in abundance, to spare
revenir [rəvnir] {92} *vi* **1** : to come back, to return <je reviens tout de suite : I'll be right back> **2** : to recur, to reappear <un problème qui revient : a problem that comes up again> **3 ~ à** : to return to, to go back to <revenir à la barbarie : to revert to savagery> **4 ~ à** : to hark back to <ça me revient! : now it comes back to me!, now I remember!> **5 ~ à** : to come down to, to amount to **6 ~ de** : to get over (an illness, etc.), to abandon (ideas) **7 ~ sur** : to go back over, to review **8 faire revenir** : to brown (in cooking) **9 revenir à la vie** : to come back to life, to revive **10 revenir à soi** : to come to, to regain consciousness
revente [rəvɑ̃t] *nf* : resale
revenu [rəvəny] *nm* : revenue, income
rêver [rɛve] *vt* **1** : to dream **2** : to dream of, to imagine — *vi* **1** : to dream **2 ~ de** : to dream of, to aspire to
réverbération [revɛrberasjɔ̃] *nf* **1** : reflection **2** : reverberation
réverbère [revɛrbɛr] *nm* LAMPADAIRE : streetlight, streetlamp
réverbérer [revɛrbere] {87} *vt* : to reflect (light, heat, etc.) — **se réverbérer** *vr* **1** : to be reflected **2** : to reverberate
révérence [reverɑ̃s] *nf* **1** : reverence **2** : bow, curtsy <faire une révérence : to curtsy>
révérencieux, -cieuse [reverɑ̃sjø, -sjøz] *adj* : reverent
révérend, -rende [reverɑ̃, -rɑ̃d] *adj* : reverend <le Révérend Père Michel : Reverend Father Michel>
révérer [revere] {87} *vt* : to revere, to venerate
rêverie [rɛvri] *nf* : daydreaming, reverie
revers [rəvɛr] *nm* **1** ENVERS : back, reverse (side) **2** : lapel, cuff **3** : backhand (in tennis) **4** ÉCHEC : setback
réversible [reversibl] *adj* : reversible
revêtement [rəvɛtmɑ̃] *nm* **1** : coating, covering, facing (in construction) **2** : surface (of a road)
revêtir [rəvɛtir] {97} *vt* **1** : to put on, to don **2** : to assume, to take on (an appearance, etc.) **3** : to coat, to cover, to surface — **se revêtir** *vr* **1 ~ de** : to dress up in **2 ~ de** : to be covered with
rêveur[1], -veuse [rɛvœr, -vøz] *adj* : dreamy
rêveur[2], -veuse *n* : dreamer
revigorant, -rante [rəvigɔrɑ̃, -rɑ̃t] *adj* : invigorating
revigoration [rəvigɔrasjɔ̃] *nf* : invigoration
revigorer [rəvigɔre] *vt* : to invigorate, to revive
revirement [rəvirmɑ̃] *nm* : reversal, turnabout
revirer [rəvire] *vi Can fam* **revirer à l'envers** : to turn upside down and inside out — **se revirer** *vr Can fam* : to turn one's back
réviser [revize] *vt* **1** : to review, to reexamine **2** : to overhaul (a vehicle, etc.) **3** : to revise

révision [revizjɔ̃] *nf* **1** : review, reappraisal **2** : checkup, service (of a vehicle) **3** : revision (of a text)
revitaliser [rəvitalize] *vt* : to revitalize
revivre [rəvivr] {98} *vt* : to relive — *vi* : to come to life again
révocation [revɔkasjɔ̃] *nf* **1** : dismissal **2** : revocation, repeal
revoir[1] [rəvwar] {99} *vt* **1** : to see again **2** : to review, to reexamine — **se revoir** *vr* : to meet (each other) again
revoir[2] *nm* **1** : meeting again **2 au revoir** : goodbye
revoler [rəvɔle] *vi Can fam* **1** : to be flung into the air **2** : to spurt, to squirt
révoltant, -tante [revɔltɑ̃, -tɑ̃t] *adj* : revolting, appalling
révolte [revɔlt] *nf* **1** : revolt, rebellion **2** : outrage
révolter [revɔlte] *vt* : to outrage, to revolt — **se révolter** *vr* : to rebel
révolu, -lue [revɔly] *adj* : past, completed, over <en des temps révolus : in days gone by>
révolution [revɔlysjɔ̃] *nf* : revolution
révolutionnaire [revɔlysjɔnɛr] *adj & nmf* : revolutionary
révolutionner [revɔlysjɔne] *vt* **1** : to revolutionize **2** : to agitate, to stir up
revolver [revɔlvɛr] *nm* : revolver
révoquer [revɔke] *vt* **1** : to dismiss **2** : to revoke, to rescind
revue [rəvy] *nf* **1** : magazine, journal **2** : review, inspection (of troops) **3** : review, examination <passer en revue : to have a look at, to go over> **4** : revue
révulser [revylse] *vt* **1** : to revolt, to appall **2** : to contort — **se révulser** *vr* **1** : to be contorted **2** : to roll upward (of eyes)
révulsion [revylsjɔ̃] *nf* : revulsion
rez–de–chaussée [red∫ose] *nms & pl* : first floor, ground floor
rhabiller [rabije] *vt* : to dress again — **se rhabiller** *vr*
rhapsodie [rapsɔdi] *nf* : rhapsody
rhéostat [reɔsta] *nm* : dimmer (for lights)
rhétorique[1] [retɔrik] *adj* : rhetorical
rhétorique[2] *nf* : rhetoric
rhinocéros [rinɔserɔs] *nm* : rhinoceros
rhododendron [rɔdɔdɛ̃drɔ̃] *nm* : rhododendron
rhombe [rɔ̃b] *nm* : rhombus
rhubarbe [rybarb] *nf* : rhubarb
rhum [rɔm] *nm* : rum
rhumatismal, -male [rymatismal] *adj, mpl* **-maux** [-mo] : rheumatic
rhumatisme [rymatism] *nm* : rheumatism
rhume [rym] *nm* **1** : cold <rhume de cerveau : head cold> **2 rhume des foins** : hay fever
riant, riante [rijɑ̃, -jɑ̃t] *adj* **1** : smiling **2** : cheerful, pleasant
ribambelle [ribɑ̃bɛl] *nf* : flock, swarm, multitude
riboflavine [riboflavin] *nf* : riboflavin
ricanement [rikanmɑ̃] *nm* : snickering, sneering, giggling
ricaner [rikane] *vi* : to snicker, to giggle, to sneer
riche[1] [ri∫] *adj* **1** : rich, wealthy **2** : sumptuous, luxurious **3** : fertile (of soil), nutritious, rich (of foods) **4 ~ en** : rich in, full of
riche[2] *nmf* : rich person
richement [ri∫mɑ̃] *adv* : richly
richesse [ri∫ɛs] *nf* **1** : wealth **2** : richness, luxuriousness **3** : **richesses** *nfpl* : riches, wealth
ricin [risɛ̃] *nf* **huile de ricin** : castor oil
ricocher [rikɔ∫e] *vi* : to ricochet, to rebound
ricochet [rikɔ∫ɛ] *nm* : ricochet, rebound
ride [rid] *nf* **1** : wrinkle **2** : ripple (on water)
rideau [rido] *nm, pl* **rideaux** : curtain <rideau de douche : shower curtain>
rider [ride] *vt* **1** : to wrinkle **2** : to ripple (water) — **se rider** *vr*
ridicule[1] [ridikyl] *adj* : ridiculous — **ridiculement** [-kylmɑ̃] *adv*
ridicule[2] *nm* **1** : ridicule **2** : ridiculousness, absurdity
ridiculiser [ridikylize] *vt* : to ridicule — **se ridiculiser** *vr* : to make a fool of oneself
rien[1] [rjɛ̃] *nm* : trifle, little thing <perdre son temps à des riens : to waste one's time on trivia> <en un rien de temps : in no time at all>
rien[2] *pron* **1** : nothing <rien de nouveau : nothing new> <il n'y a plus rien : there's nothing left> <ça ne fait rien : it doesn't matter> **2** : anything <avant de ne rien faire : before doing anything> <rien d'autre : nothing else> **3 de ~** : don't mention it, you're welcome **4 rien que** : only, just <rien que pour elle : only for her>
rieur, rieuse [rijœr, -jøz] *adj* : cheerful
rigide [riʒid] *adj* **1** : rigid **2** : strict — **rigidement** [-ʒidmɑ̃] *adv*
rigidité [riʒidite] *nf* : rigidity, stiffness
rigolade [rigɔlad] *nf fam* **1** : fun <quelle rigolade! : what fun!, what a laugh!> **2** : joke, farce <la vie n'est qu'une rigolade : life is just a joke>
rigole [rigɔl] *nf* : trench, channel
rigoler [rigɔle] *vi fam* **1** : to have fun **2** : to laugh, to joke
rigolo[1], **-lote** [rigɔlɔ, -lɔt] *adj fam* : funny, comical
rigolo[2], **-lote** *n fam* : joker, card
rigoureux, -reuse [rigurø, -røz] *adj* **1** : rigorous, strict **2** : harsh, severe — **rigoureusement** [-røzmɑ̃] *adv*
rigueur [rigœr] *nf* **1** : rigor, harshness **2** : precision, meticulousness **3 à la rigueur** : if absolutely necessary **4 à la rigueur** : at the most **5 de ~** : essential, obligatory **6 rigueurs** *nfpl* : rigors, hardships

rime [rim] *nf* : rhyme
rimer [rime] *vi* : to rhyme
rinçage [rɛ̃saʒ] *nm* : rinsing, rinse
rince–doigts [rɛ̃sdwa] *nms & pl* : finger bowl
rincer [rɛ̃se] {6} *vt* : to rinse — **se rincer** *vr*
ring [riŋ] *nm* : boxing ring
ringard, -garde [rɛ̃gar, -gard] *adj France fam* : old-fashioned, corny
ripaille [ripaj] *nf fam* **faire ripaille** : to have a feast
riposte [ripɔst] *nf* **1** RÉPLIQUE : retort **2** CONTRE-ATTAQUE : counterattack, reprisal
riposter [ripɔste] *v* : to retort
rire[1] [rir] {76} *vi* **1** : to laugh **2** : to joke around, to have fun **3 ~ de** : to mock, to make fun of
rire[2] *nm* : laugh, laughter
risée [rize] *nf or* **objet de risée** : laughingstock
risible [rizibl] *adj* : ridiculous, laughable
risque [risk] *nm* **1** : risk **2 à vos risques et périls** : at your own risk
risqué, -quée [riske] *adj* **1** : risky **2** : risqué
risquer [riske] *vt* **1** : to risk **2 ~ de** : to be liable to, to have a chance of <il risque de s'ennuyer : he might be bored> <ça risque d'arriver : it may very well happen> — **se risquer** *vr* : to venture, to take a chance
rissoler [risɔle] *v* : to brown (in cooking)
ristourne [risturn] *nf* REMISE : discount, rebate
rite [rit] *nm* : rite, ritual
rituel[1], **-tuelle** [ritɥɛl] *adj* : ritual
rituel[2] *nm* : rite, ritual
rituellement [ritɥɛlmɑ̃] *adj* **1** : ritually **2** : religiously, unfailingly
rivage [rivaʒ] *nm* : shore
rival, -vale [rival] *adj & n, mpl* **rivaux** [rivo] : rival
rivaliser [rivalize] *vi* **~ avec** : to compete with, to rival
rivalité [rivalite] *nf* : rivalry
rive [riv] *nf* : bank (of a river)
river [rive] *vt* **1** : to rivet, to fasten **2** : to clinch (a nail)
riverain[1], **-raine** [rivrɛ̃, -rɛn] *adj* **1** : riverside, lakeside **2** : bordering the street, roadside
riverain[2], **-raine** *n* **1** : riverside or lakeside resident **2** : resident (along a street)
rivet [rivɛ] *nm* : rivet
riveter [rivte] {8} *vt* : to rivet
rivière [rivjɛr] *nf* : river
rixe [riks] *nf* BAGARRE : brawl, fight
riz [ri] *nm* : rice
rizière [rizjɛr] *nf* : (rice) paddy
robe [rɔb] *nf* **1** : dress, robe <robe de chambre : bathrobe> <robe d'intérieur : housecoat> <robe de mariée : wedding gown> **2** : gown (of a judge, etc.) **3** PELAGE : coat (of an animal) **4 robe de nuit** *Can* : nightgown
robinet [rɔbinɛ] *nm* : faucet
robot [rɔbo] *nm* **1** : robot **2 robot de cuisine** : food processor
robotique [rɔbɔtik] *nf* : robotics
robuste [rɔbyst] *adj* : robust, sturdy
robustesse [rɔbystɛs] *nf* : robustness, sturdiness
roc [rɔk] *nm* : rock
rocaille [rɔkaj] *nf* **1** : loose stones *pl* **2** : rock garden
rocailleux, -leuse [rɔkajø, -jøz] *adj* **1** : stony, rocky **2** : harsh, gravelly (of a voice)
rocambolesque [rɔkɑ̃bɔlɛsk] *adj* : incredible, extraordinary
roche [rɔʃ] *nf* : rock
rocher [rɔʃe] *nm* : rock
rochet [rɔʃɛ] *nm* : ratchet
rocheux, -cheuse [rɔʃø, -ʃøz] *adj* : rocky
rock [rɔk] *nm* : rock (music)
rodéo [rɔdeo] *nm* : rodeo
roder [rɔde] *vt* **1** : to break in (a vehicle) **2** *fam* : to polish up (a performance, etc.)
rôder [rode] *vi* **1** : to prowl **2** ERRER : to wander around, to roam about
rôdeur, -deuse [rodœr, -døz] *n* : prowler
rodomontades [rɔdɔmɔ̃tad] *nfpl* : bragging, boasting
rogne [rɔɲ] *nf fam* : anger, bad temper <être en rogne : to get mad, to see red>
rogner [rɔɲe] *vt* **1** : to trim, to clip **2** : to cut back on, to reduce (expenses, etc.)
rognon [rɔɲɔ̃] *nm* : kidney (in cooking)
rognures [rɔɲyr] *nfpl* **1** : trimmings, clippings **2** : scraps
rogue [rɔg] *adj* : arrogant, haughty
roi [rwa] *nm* : king
roitelet [rwatlɛ] *nm* : wren
rôle [rol] *nm* **1** : role, part **2** : list, roll **3 à tour de rôle** : one after the other, in turn
romain, -maine [rɔmɛ̃, -mɛn] *adj* : Roman
Romain, -maine *n* : Roman
romaine *nf* : romaine (lettuce)
roman[1], **-mane** [rɔmɑ̃, -man] *adj* **1** : Romance (in linguistics) **2** : Romanesque
roman[2] *nm* **1** : romance, chivalric tale **2** : novel
romance [rɔmɑ̃s] *nf* : ballad, love song
romancer [rɔmɑ̃se] {6} *vt* : to romanticize
romancier, -cière [rɔmɑ̃sje, -sjɛr] *n* : novelist
romanesque [rɔmanɛsk] *adj* **1** : fabulous, fantastic **2** : romantic **3** : fictional, novelistic
roman–feuilleton [rɔmɑ̃fœjtɔ̃] *nm, pl* **romans–feuilletons** → **feuilleton**

roman–savon [rɔmɑ̃savɔ̃] *nm Can, pl* **romans–savons** : soap opera
romantique [rɔmɑ̃tik] *adj* : romantic
romantisme [rɔmɑ̃tism] *nm* : romanticism
romarin [rɔmarɛ̃] *nm* : rosemary
rompre [rɔ̃pr] {77} *vt* **1** : to break (off) **2** : to break, to burst, to shatter **3** : to break (someone) in — *vi* : to break up
rompt [rɔ̃] → **rompre**
rompu, -pue [rɔ̃py] *adj* **1** FOURBU : worn-out, exhausted **2 ~ à** : well accustomed to
romsteck [rɔmstɛk] *nm* : rump steak
ronce [rɔ̃s] *nf* : bramble (bush)
ronchonnement [rɔ̃ʃɔnmɑ̃] *nm fam* : griping, grousing
ronchonner [rɔ̃ʃɔne] *vi fam* ROUSPÉTER : to grumble, to grouse
rond[1] [rɔ̃] *adv* **tourner rond** : to run smoothly, to go well <ça ne tourne pas rond : something's not quite right>
rond[2], ronde [rɔ̃, rɔ̃d] *adj* : round
rond[3] *nm* **1** : circle <en rond : in a circle> **2** : ring <rond de serviette : napkin ring> **3** : round slice **4** *Can* : burner (of a stove)
ronde *nf* **1** : rounds *pl,* patrol <faire sa ronde : to be on patrol> **2** : round dance **3** : whole note **4 à la ronde** : around <à des milles à la ronde : for miles around>
rondelet, -lette [rɔ̃dlɛ, -lɛt] *adj fam* **1** : plump **2 une somme rondelette** : a tidy sum
rondelle [rɔ̃dɛl] *nf* **1** : washer **2** : (round) slice **3** *Can* : (hockey) puck
rondement [rɔ̃dmɑ̃] *adv* **1** : briskly, promptly **2** : frankly, straight out
rondeur [rɔ̃dœr] *nf* **1** : roundness, curve (of the body) **2** : frankness
rondin [rɔ̃dɛ̃] *nm* : log <cabane en rondins : log cabin>
rond–point [rɔ̃pwɛ̃] *nm, pl* **ronds–points** : traffic circle, rotary
ronéo [rɔneɔ] *nf* : mimeograph
ronflement [rɔ̃fləmɑ̃] *nm* **1** : snore, snoring **2** : humming, drone, roar (of a fire, etc.)
ronfler [rɔ̃fle] *vi* **1** : to snore **2** : to hum, to drone, to roar
ronger [rɔ̃ʒe] {17} *vt* **1** : to gnaw, to nibble **2** : to corrode **3** : to eat away at, to wear down <rongé par le chagrin : grief-stricken> — **se ronger** *vr* **se ronger les ongles** : to bite one's nails
rongeur [rɔ̃ʒœr] *nm* : rodent
ronronnement [rɔ̃rɔnmɑ̃] *nm* : purring, humming
ronronner [rɔ̃rɔne] *vi* **1** : to purr **2** : to hum (of an engine, etc.)
roquette[1] [rɔkɛt] *nf* : rocket
roquette[2] *nf* : arugula
rosaire [rozɛr] *nm* : rosary
rosbif [rɔzbif] *nm* : roast beef
rose[1] [roz] *adj & nm* : rose, pink
rose[2] *nf* **1** : rose (flower) **2 rose trémière** : hollyhock
rosé, -sée [roze] *adj* : rose, pinkish
roseau [rozo] *nm, pl* **roseaux** : reed
rosée [roze] *nf* : dew <goutte de rosée : dewdrop>
rosette [rozɛt] *nf* : rosette
rosier [rozje] *nm* : rosebush
rosir [rozir] *v* : to turn pink
rosse[1] [rɔs] *adj fam* : nasty, horrid, mean
rosse[2] *nf fam* : nasty person, beast
rosser [rɔse] *vt* : to beat, to thrash
rossignol [rɔsiɲɔl] *nm* : nightingale
rostre [rɔstr] *nm* : rostrum
rot [ro] *nm fam* : belch, burp
rotatif, -tive [rɔtatif, -tiv] *adj* : rotary
rotation [rɔtasjɔ̃] *nf* : rotation
roter [rote] *vi fam* : to burp, to belch
rôti [roti] *nm* : roast (meat)
rôtie [roti] *nf* : toasted bread, toast
rotin [rɔtɛ̃] *nm* : rattan
rôtir [rotir] *v* : to roast
rôtissoire [rotiswar] *nf* : rotisserie, spit
rotonde [rɔtɔ̃d] *nf* : rotunda
rotondité [rɔtɔ̃dite] *nf* : roundness
rotor [rɔtɔr] *nm* : rotor
rotule [rɔtyl] *nf* : kneecap, patella
roturier, -rière [rɔtyrje, -rjɛr] *n* : commoner
rouage [rwaʒ] *nm* **1** : cogwheel <les rouages d'une montre : the movement of a watch> **2 rouages** *nmpl* : workings <les rouages de l'État : the wheels of state>
rouan[1], rouanne [rwɑ̃, rwan] *adj* : roan
rouan[2], rouanne *n* : roan (horse)
roublard, -blarde [rublar, -blard] *adj fam* : crafty, sly
rouble [rubl] *nm* : ruble
roucoulement [rukulmɑ̃] *nm* **1** : cooing **2** *fam* : billing and cooing
roucouler [rukule] *vi* : to coo
roue [ru] *nf* **1** : wheel (of a vehicle) <roue de secours : spare tire> **2** : (mechanical) wheel <roue dentée : cogwheel> <grande roue : Ferris wheel> **3** : cartwheel (in gymnastics)
roué, rouée [rwe] *adj* FUTÉ : slick, cunning
rouer [rwe] *vt* **rouer de coups** : to thrash, to beat
rouerie [ruri] *nf* : slyness, cunning
rouet [ruɛ] *nm* : spinning wheel
rouge[1] [ruʒ] *adj* : red
rouge[2] *n* : red <rouge à lèvres : lipstick> <être dans le rouge : to be in the red>
rougeâtre [ruʒatr] *adj* : reddish
rougeaud, -geaude [ruʒo, -ʒod] *adj* : red-faced, ruddy, florid
rouge–gorge [ruʒgɔrʒ] *nm, pl* **rouges–gorges** : robin
rougeoiement [ruʒwamɑ̃] *nm* : reddish glow
rougeole [ruʒɔl] *nf* : measles
rougeoyant, -geoyante [ruʒwajɑ̃, -ʒwajɑ̃t] *adj* : red, glowing

rougeoyer |ruʒwaje| {58} *vi* : to turn red, to glow

rouget |ruʒɛ| *nm* : red mullet

rougeur |ruʒœr| *nf* **1** : redness **2** : flushing **3** : red blotch, eruption (in medicine)

rougir |ruʒir| *vt* **1** : to make red **2** : to make red-hot — *vi* **1** : to redden, to turn red **2** : to blush **3** : to glow red

rouille |ruj| *nf* : rust

rouillé, -lée |ruje| *adj* : rusty

rouiller |ruje| *v* : to rust — **se rouiller** *vr*

roulant, -lante |rulɑ̃, -lɑ̃t| *adj* **1** : rolling **2** : on wheels

rouleau |rulo| *nm, pl* **rouleaux 1** : roller <rouleau à pâtisserie : rolling pin> <rouleau compresseur : steamroller> **2** : roll, scroll <rouleau de papier : roll of paper> **3** : roller, curler **4** : breaker (wave)

roulement |rulmɑ̃| *nm* **1** : rolling <avoir un roulement d'yeux : to roll one's eyes> **2** : rumble, roll <roulement de tonnerre : rumble of thunder> <roulement de tambour : drum roll> **3** : circulation, turnover (in finance) **4** : rotation, shift(s) <travailler par roulement : to work (in) shifts> **5 roulement à billes** : ball bearing

rouler |rule| *vt* **1** : to roll, to move along, to wheel **2** : to roll up **3** : to roll, to sway, to swing <rouler les yeux : to roll one's eyes> <rouler les hanches : to swing one's hips> — *vi* **1** : to roll <rouler en bas de la colline : to roll down the hill> **2** : to go, to run, to drive <roule moins vite! : slow down!> <ça roule bien : traffic is moving along well> **3** : to take turns, to rotate **4** : to circulate (of funds) **5** : to rumble, to roll **6 ~ sur** : to turn on, to be centered upon

roulette |rulɛt| *nf* **1** : caster (on furniture, etc.) **2** : roulette **3** : (dentist's) drill

roulis |ruli| *nm* : rolling (of a ship)

roulotte |rulɔt| *nf Can* : trailer, camper

roumain[1], **-maine** |rumɛ̃, -mɛn| *adj* : Romanian

roumain[2] *nm* : Romanian (language)

Roumain, -maine *n* : Romanian

roupie |rupi| *nf* : roupee

roupiller |rupije| *vi fam* : to snooze, to sleep

rouquin[1], **-quine** |rukɛ̃, -kin| *adj fam* : red-haired

rouquin,[2] **-quine** *n fam* : redhead

rouspétance |ruspetɑ̃s| *nf fam* : complaint, gripe

rouspéter |ruspete| {87} *vi fam* RONCHONNER : to fuss, to grumble

rouspéteur, -teuse |ruspetœr, -tøz| *n fam* : grumbler, grouch, nag

roussâtre |rusatr| *adj* **1** : reddish **2** : reddish brown, russet

rousseler |rusle| *vt Can* : to freckle

rousseur |rusœr| *nf* **1** : redness, russet color **2** → **tache**

roussir |rusir| *vt* **1** : to turn brown **2** : to scorch, to singe — *vi* **1** : to become brown **2 faire roussir** : to brown (in cooking)

route |rut| *nf* **1** : road <route de montagne : mountain road> <tenir la route : to hold the road> <par (la) route : by road> **2** : route, way, course <route aérienne : air route> <se mettre en route : to set out, to get going> <perdre sa route : to lose one's way> **3** : trip, journey <il y a deux heures de route : it's a two-hour journey> <bonne route! : have a good trip!>

routier[1], **-tière** |rutje, -tjɛr| *adj* : road <transport routier : road transportation>

routier[2] *nm* **1** : truck driver **2** : cyclist (in bicycle racing) **3** : truck stop

routine |rutin| *nf* : routine

routinier, -nière |rutinje, -njɛr| *adj* **1** : routine, humdrum **2** : set in one's ways

rouvrir |ruvrir| {83} *v* : to reopen, to open again — **se rouvrir** *vr*

roux[1], **rousse** |ru, rus| *adj* **1** : russet, red **2** : redheaded

roux[2], **rousse** *n* : redhead

royal, royale |rwajal| *adj, mpl* **royaux** |rwajo| : royal, regal — **royalement** |-jalmɑ̃| *adv*

royaume |rwajom| *nm* : kingdom, realm

royauté |rwajɔte| *nf* : royalty

ruade |ryad| *nf* : kick, bucking (of a horse)

ruban |rybɑ̃| *nm* **1** : ribbon **2 ruban adhésif** : adhesive tape

rubéole |rybeɔl| *nf* : German measles

rubicond, -conde |rybikɔ̃, -kɔ̃d| *adj* : ruddy, rosy-cheeked

rubis |rybi| *nms & pl* **1** : ruby **2** : jewel (of a watch)

rubrique |rybrik| *nf* **1** : column (in a newspaper) **2** : heading

ruche |ryʃ| *nf* : beehive

rucher |ryʃe| *nm* : apiary

rude |ryd| *adj* **1** : rough (to the touch) **2** PÉNIBLE : hard, tough, difficult **3** : harsh, severe <un rude hiver : a harsh winter>

rudement |rydmɑ̃| *adv* **1** : roughly, harshly **2** *fam* DRÔLEMENT : awfully, terribly

rudesse |rydɛs| *nf* **1** RUGOSITÉ : roughness **2** SÉVÉRITÉ : harshness, severity

rudimentaire |rydimɑ̃tɛr| *adj* ÉLÉMENTAIRE : rudimentary, basic

rudiments |rydimɑ̃| *nmpl* : rudiments

rudoyer |rydwaje| {58} *vt* : to treat harshly

rue |ry| *nf* : street <rue à sens unique : one-way street>

ruée |rɥe| *nf* : rush

ruelle |rɥɛl| *nf* : alley(way)

ruer |rɥe| *v* **se ruer** *vr* **1 ~ sur** : to fling oneself at **2 ~ vers** : to rush toward
rugir |ryʒir| *vt* : to bellow out — *vi* **1** : to roar (of lions, etc.) **2** : to howl
rugissement |ryʒismɑ̃| *nm* **1** : roar **2** : howling <rugissement du vent : howling of the wind>
rugosité |rygozite| *nf* : roughness
rugueux, -gueuse |rygø, -gøz| *adj* : rough, rugged
ruine |rɥin| *nf* **1** : ruin **2** : destruction, collapse **3 ruines** *nfpl* : ruins
ruiner |rɥine| *vt* **1** : to ruin **2** : to destroy, to wreck — **se ruiner** *vr*
ruineux, -neuse |rɥinø, -nøz| *adj* : extravagantly expensive, exorbitant
ruisseau |rɥiso| *nm, pl* **ruisseaux 1** : stream, brook **2** : flood, stream (of tears, etc.) **3** : gutter
ruisseler |rɥisle| {8} *vi* **1** : to stream, to flood
ruisselet |rɥislɛ| *nm* : small brook, stream
ruissellement |rɥisɛlmɑ̃| *nm* : streaming <le ruissellement de l'eau sur la rue : water streaming down the street>
rumeur |rymœr| *nf* **1** : rumor **2** : murmur, hum, rumble
ruminant[1], -nante |ryminɑ̃, -nɑ̃t| *adj* : ruminant
ruminant[2] *nm* : ruminant
ruminer |rymine| *vt* : to ruminate over — *vi* **1** : to ruminate, to chew the cud **2** : to brood
rupture |ryptyr| *nf* **1** : break, breaking **2** : breakup (of a relationship) **3** : breach (of contract)
rural, -rale |ryral| *adj, mpl* **ruraux** |ryro| : rural, country
ruse |ryz| *nf* **1** : ruse, trick **2** : cunning, cleverness
rusé, -sée |ryze| *adj* FUTÉ, MALIN : cunning, sly
russe[1] |rys| *adj* : Russian
russe[2] *nm* : Russian (language)
Russe *nmf* : Russian
rustaud, -taude |rysto, -tod| *n* : bumpkin, hick
rustique |rystik| *adj* : rural, rustic
rustre |rystr| *nmf* : boor, oaf, clod, bumpkin
rut |ryt| **être en rut** : to be in rut, to be in heat
rutilant, -lante |rytilɑ̃, -lɑ̃t| *adj* : gleaming
rutiler |rytile| *vi* BRILLER : to gleam, to shine
rwandais, -daise |rwɑ̃dɛ, -dɛz| *adj* : Rwandan
Rwandais, -daise *n* : Rwandan
rythme |ritm| *nm* **1** : rhythm, beat **2** : rate, pace, tempo
rythmé, -mée |ritme| *adj* : rhythmic, rhythmical
rythmer |ritme| *vt* : to give rhythm to
rythmique |ritmik| *adj* : rhythmic, rhythmical — **rythmiquement** |-mikmɑ̃| *adv*

S

s |ɛs| *nm* : s, the 19th letter of the alphabet
sabbat |saba| *nm* : Sabbath
sabbatique |sabatik| *adj* **congé sabbatique** : sabbatical
sable |sabl| *nm* **1** : sand **2 sables mouvants** : quicksand
sablé[1], -blée |sable| *adj* **1** : sandy **2** → **papier**
sablé[2] *nm* : shortbread (cookie)
sabler |sable| *vt* **1** : to sand **2 sabler le champagne** : to celebrate with champagne
sableux, -bleuse |sablø, -bløz| *adj* : sandy
sablier |sablije| *nm* : hourglass
sablonneux, -neuse |sablɔnø, -nøz| *adj* : sandy
saborder |sabɔrde| *vt* **1** : to scuttle (a ship) **2** : to put an end to, to scrap (a project, etc.)
sabot |sabo| *nm* **1** : clog, wooden shoe **2** : hoof **3 sabot de frein** : brake shoe **4 sabot de la Vierge** *or* **sabot de Vénus** : lady's slipper
sabotage |sabɔtaʒ| *nm* **1** : sabotage **2** : sabotaging, botching up
saboter |sabɔte| *vt* **1** : to sabotage **2** BÂCLER : to spoil, to botch up
saboteur, -teuse |sabɔtœr, -tøz| *n* : saboteur
sabre |sabr| *nm* : saber
sabrer |sabre| *vt* **1** : to cut down (an enemy) **2** : to cut, to slash <sabrer les dépenses : to cut spending> **3** *fam* : to tear to shreds, to pan
sac |sak| *nm* **1** : sack, bag <sac à dos : backpack, knapsack> <sac de couchage : sleeping bag> <sac à main : handbag, purse> <sac de voyage : traveling bag, valise> **2** : sac (in anatomy and botany) **3 mettre à sac** : to sack, to ransack
saccade |sakad| *nf* : jerk, jolt
saccadé, -dée |sakade| *adj* : jerky, abrupt
saccage |sakaʒ| *nm* : destruction, havoc
saccager |sakaʒe| {17} *vt* **1** PILLER : to sack, to pillage **2** DÉVASTER : to ravage, to vandalize, to wreck

saccharine [sakarin] *nf* : saccharin

saccharose [sakaroz] *nm* : sucrose

sacerdoce [sasɛrdɔs] *nm* **1** PRÊTRISE : priesthood **2** VOCATION : vocation

sacerdotal, -tale [sasɛrdɔtal] *adj, pl* **-taux** [-to] : sacerdotal, priestly

sache [saʃ], *etc.* → **savoir**

sachet [saʃɛ] *nm* **1** : packet, small bag <sachet de thé : tea bag> **2** : sachet

sacoche [sakɔʃ] *nf* **1** : bag, satchel **2** : saddlebag **3** *Bel, Can* : purse, pocketbook

sacramentel, -telle [sakramɑ̃tɛl] *adj* : sacramental

sacre [sakr] *nm* **1** COURONNEMENT : coronation **2** CONSÉCRATION : consecration

sacré, -crée [sakre] *adj* **1** : sacred, holy **2** *fam* : damned, hell of a <un sacré spectacle : a damned good show>

sacrement [sakrəmɑ̃] *nm* : sacrament

sacrer [sakre] *vt* **1** COURONNER : to crown **2** CONSACRER : to consecrate — *vi* : to swear

sacrifice [sakrifis] *nm* : sacrifice — **sacrificiel, -cielle** [-fisjɛl] *adj*

sacrifier [sakrifje] {96} *vt* : to sacrifice — *vi* ~ **à** : to conform to — **se sacrifier** *vr* : to sacrifice oneself

sacrilège[1] [sakrilɛʒ] *adj* : sacrilegious

sacrilège[2] *nm* : sacrilege

sacristain [sakristɛ̃] *nm* : sexton

sacristie [sakristi] *nf* : sacristy, vestry

sacro–saint, -sainte [sakrɔsɛ̃, sakrɔsɛ̃t] *adj* : sacrosanct

sadique[1] [sadik] *adj* : sadistic — **sadiquement** [-dikmɑ̃] *adv*

sadique[2] *nmf* : sadist

sadisme [sadism] *nm* : sadism

safari [safari] *nm* : safari

safran [safrɑ̃] *nm* : saffron

saga [saga] *nf* : saga

sagace [sagas] *adj* : shrewd, sagacious

sagacité [sagasite] *nf* : shrewdness, sagacity

sage[1] [saʒ] *adj* **1** SENSÉ : wise, sensible, sage **2** DOCILE : well-behaved, obedient **3** MODÉRÉ : moderate, restrained, sober

sage[2] *nm* : sage, wise person

sage–femme [saʒfam] *nf, pl* **sages–femmes** : midwife

sagement [saʒmɑ̃] *adv* **1** : wisely, sensibly **2** : quietly, properly

sagesse [saʒɛs] *nf* **1** : wisdom, good sense **2** : good behavior **3** MODÉRATION : moderation, restraint

Sagittaire [saʒitɛr] *nm* : Sagittarius

saignant, -gnante [sɛɲɑ̃, -ɲɑ̃t] *adj* **1** : bleeding **2** : rare, undercooked

saignée [seɲe] *nf* **1** : bleeding, bloodletting **2** *or* **saignée du bras** : bend of the arm **3** : drain (on finances) **4** : cut, groove, channel

saignement [seɲmɑ̃] *nm* **1** : bleeding **2 saignement de nez** : nosebleed

saigner [seɲe] *v* : to bleed

saillant, -lante [sajɑ̃, -jɑ̃t] *adj* **1** : prominent, projecting **2** : salient, notable

saillie [saji] *nf* **1** : projection, protuberance, ledge <en saillie : projecting> **2** : sally, witticism

saillir [sajir] {78} *vi* : to jut out, to project

sain, saine [sɛ̃, sɛn] *adj* **1** : healthy, sound <sain et sauf : safe and sound> <sain d'esprit : sane> **2** : wholesome, salutary

saindoux [sɛ̃du] *nm* : lard

sainement [sɛnmɑ̃] *adv* : healthily, soundly

saint[1], **sainte** [sɛ̃, sɛ̃t] *adj* **1** : holy <la Sainte Bible : the Holy Bible> **2** : godly, saintly **3 la Sainte Vierge** : the Blessed Virgin

saint[2], **sainte** *n* : saint

Saint–Esprit [sɛ̃tɛspri] *nm* : Holy Spirit

sainteté [sɛ̃tte] *nf* : holiness, sanctity, saintliness

saisie [sezi] *nf* **1** : seizure (of property) **2 saisie de données** : data entry

saisir [sezir] *vt* **1** : to seize, to grab, to impound **2** COMPRENDRE : to grasp, to understand **3** IMPRESSIONNER : to strike, to impress **4** : to keyboard, to enter (data) — **se saisir** *vr* ~ **de** : to take possession of, to capture

saisissant, -sante [sezisɑ̃, -sɑ̃t] *adj* **1** FRAPPANT : striking, gripping **2** : biting, piercing (of cold)

saison [sɛzɔ̃] *nf* : season

saisonnier, -nière [sɛzɔnje, -njɛr] *adj* : seasonal

salace [salas] *adj* : salacious

salade [salad] *nf* **1** : salad **2** LAITUE : lettuce **3** *fam* : muddle, mess **4 salades** *nfpl fam* : stories, tall tales

saladier [saladje] *nm* : salad bowl

salaire [salɛr] *nm* **1** : salary, wages **2** : reward

salamandre [salamɑ̃dr] *nf* : salamander

salami [salami] *nm* : salami

salarial, -riale [salarjal] *adj, mpl* **-riaux** [-rjo] : wage, pay <hausse salariale : wage increase>

salarié, -riée [salarje] *n* : salaried employee, wage earner

salaud [salo] *nm usu vulgar* : bastard

sale [sal] *adj* **1** : dirty, dingy, grimy **2** : nasty, foul <un sale tour : a dirty trick> <sale temps : nasty weather>

salé, -lée [sale] *adj* **1** : salty **2** : salted **3** *fam* : steep, stiff <condamnation salée : stiff sentence> **4** *fam* : risqué, spicy

saler [sale] *vt* : to salt

saleté [salte] *nf* **1** : dirt, filth **2** : dirtiness, filthiness, mess **3** OBSCÉNITÉ : obscenity **4** *fam* : dirty trick

salière [saljɛr] *nf* : saltshaker

salin, -line [salɛ̃, -lin] *adj* : saline

salir [salir] *vt* : to soil, to dirty — **se salir** *vr* : to get dirty

salissant, -sante |salisɑ̃, -sɑ̃t| *adj* **1** : easily soiled **2** : dirty, messy <travail salissant : dirty work>

salivaire |salivɛr| *adj* : salivary

saliver |salive| *vi* : to salivate

salive |saliv| *nf* : saliva

salle |sal| *nf* **1** : room <salle d'attente : waiting room> <salle de bains : bathroom> <salle à manger : dining room> <salle de séjour : living room> **2** : auditorium, hall <salle de concert : concert hall> <salles obscures : movie theaters> **3** : audience, house <faire salle comble : to play to a full house>

salmigondis |salmigɔ̃di| *nms & pl* : hodgepodge

salon |salɔ̃| *nm* **1** : living room, parlor, lounge **2** : salon <salon de beauté : beauty salon, beauty parlor> **3** EXPOSITION : exhibition, show **4 salon de thé** : tearoom **5 salon funéraire** *or* **salon mortuaire** *Can* : funeral parlor

salopette |salɔpɛt| *nf* : overalls *pl*

salsepareille |salsəparɛj| *nf* : sarsaparilla

saltimbanque |saltɛ̃bɑ̃k| *nmf* : acrobat

salubre |salybr| *adj* : salubrious, healthy

salubrité |salybrite| *nf* **1** : healthiness **2 salubrité publique** : public health

saluer |salɥe| *vt* **1** : to greet **2** : to say goodbye to **3** : to salute

salut |saly| *nm* **1** : greeting, wave, nod <salut! : hello!, hi!, good-bye!> **2** : salute **3** SAUVEGARDE : safety, security **4** : salvation (in religion)

salutaire |salytɛr| *adj* : salutary, beneficial

salutation |salytasjɔ̃| *nf* **1** : salutation, greeting **2 veuillez agréer mes salutations distinguées** : yours truly, yours sincerely

salvadorien, -rienne |salvadɔrjɛ̃, -rjɛn| *adj* : El Salvadoran

Salvadorien, -rienne *n* : El Salvadoran

salve |salv| *nf* : salvo, volley

samedi |samdi| *nm* : Saturday

samoan, -moane |samɔɑ̃, -mɔan| *adj* : Samoan

Samoan, -moane *n* : Samoan

sanatorium |sanatɔrjɔm| *nm* : sanitarium

sanctifier |sɑ̃ktifje| {96} *vt* : to sanctify

sanction |sɑ̃ksjɔ̃| *nf* **1** APPROBATION : sanction, approval **2** : sanction, penalty <prendre des sanctions contre : to take sanctions against>

sanctionner |sɑ̃ksjɔne| *vt* **1** CONSACRER : to sanction, to approve **2** PUNIR : to penalize

sanctuaire |sɑ̃ktɥɛr| *nm* **1** : sanctuary (in a church) **2** : shrine

sandale |sɑ̃dal| *nf* : sandal

sandwich |sɑ̃dwitʃ| *nm, pl* **sandwiches** *or* **sandwichs** |-witʃ| : sandwich

sang |sɑ̃| *nm* : blood

sang-froid |sɑ̃frwa| *nms & pl* **1** : composure, calm **2 de ~** : in cold blood

sanglant, -glante |sɑ̃glɑ̃, -glɑ̃t| *adj* **1** ENSANGLANTÉ : bloody **2** : cruel, savage <critique sanglante : scathing criticism>

sangle |sɑ̃gl| *nf* : strap, cinch

sangler |sɑ̃gle| *vt* : to girth, to cinch (a horse)

sanglier |sɑ̃glije| *nm* : wild boar

sanglot |sɑ̃glo| *nm* : sob

sangloter |sɑ̃glɔte| *vi* : to sob

sangsue |sɑ̃sy| *nf* : leech, bloodsucker

sanguin, -guine |sɑ̃gɛ̃, -gin| *adj* **1** : blood <groupe sanguin : blood type> **2** : sanguine

sanguinaire |sɑ̃ginɛr| *adj* **1** : bloodthirsty **2** : bloody

sanguinolent, -lente |sɑ̃ginɔlɑ̃, -lɑ̃t| *adj* : bloodstained

sanitaire |sanitɛr| *adj* **1** : sanitary **2** : health, medical <risques sanitaires : health risks> **3 appareils sanitaires** : bathroom plumbing fixtures

sans[1] |sɑ̃| *adv* : without <je ferai sans : I'll do without>

sans[2] *prep* **1** : without <sans doute : doubtless, no doubt> <sans plus tarder : without further ado> **2 sans que** : without <sans que vous le sachiez : without your knowing it>

sans-abri |sɑ̃zabri| *nmfs & pl* : homeless person

sans-emploi |sɑ̃zɑ̃plwa| *nmfs & pl* : unemployed person

sans-gêne[1] |sɑ̃ʒɛn| *adj* : inconsiderate

sans-gêne[2] *nm* : lack of consideration

santal |sɑ̃tal| *nm* : sandalwood

santé |sɑ̃te| *nf* **1** : health **2 à votre santé!** : to your health!, cheers!

saoudien, -dienne |saudjɛ̃, -djɛn| *adj* : Saudi, Saudi Arabian

Saoudien, -dienne *n* : Saudi, Saudi Arabian

saoul, saoule |su, sul| → **soûl**

saouler |sule| → **soûler**

saper |sape| *vt* MINER : to undermine

sapeur-pompier |sapœrpɔ̃pje| *nm, pl* **sapeurs-pompiers** *France* : firefighter

saphir |safir| *nm* **1** : sapphire **2** : needle (of a record player)

sapin |sapɛ̃| *nm* **1** : fir **2 sapin baumier** : balsam fir **3 sapin de Noël** : Christmas tree

sapinette |sapinɛt| *nf* : spruce

sarcasme |sarkasm| *nm* : sarcasm

sarcastique |sarkastik| *adj* : sarcastic — **sarcastiquement** |-tikmɑ̃| *adv*

sarcelle |sarsɛl| *nf* : teal (duck)

sarcler |sarkle| *vt* : to weed, to hoe

sarcophage |sarkɔfaʒ| *nm* : sarcophagus

sardine |sardin| *nf* : sardine

sardonique |sardɔnik| *adj* : sardonic — **sardoniquement** |-nikmɑ̃| *adv*

sari |sari| *nm* : sari

sarrasin [sarazɛ̃] *nm* : buckwheat
sarrau [saro] *nm, pl* **sarraus** : smock
sas [sas] *nm* **1** CRIBLE : sieve **2** : enclosure (in a canal lock) **3** : airlock
sassafras [sasafra] *nm* : sassafras
Satan [satɑ̃] *nm* : Satan
satanique [satanik] *adj* : satanic
satellite [satelit] *nm* : satellite
satiété [sasjete] *nf* : satiation, satiety <manger à satiété : to eat one's fill>
satin [satɛ̃] *nm* : satin
satire [satir] *nf* : satire
satirique [satirik] *adj* : satiric, satirical
satiriser [satirize] *vt* : to satirize
satisfaction [satisfaksjɔ̃] *nf* : satisfaction, gratification
satisfaire [satisfɛr] {42} *vt* CONTENTER : to satisfy — *vi* ~ **à** : to satisfy, to fulfill, to meet — **se satisfaire** *vr* ~ **de** : to be content with
satisfaisant, -sante [satisfəzɑ̃, -zɑ̃t] *adj* **1** : satisfactory, acceptable **2** : satisfying, pleasing
satisfait, -faite [satisfɛ, -fɛt] *adj* : satisfied, pleased
saturer [satyre] *vt* : to saturate — **saturation** [-tyrasjɔ̃] *nf*
Saturne [satyrn] *nf* : Saturn (planet)
satyre [satir] *nm* **1** : satyr **2** : lecher
sauce [sos] *nf* : sauce
saucisse [sosis] *nf* **1** : sausage (meat) **2 saucisse de Francfort** *or* **saucisse à hot-dog** *Can* : frankfurter, hot dog
saucisson [sosisɔ̃] *nm* : sausage, bologna, cold cut
sauf[1], **sauve** [sof, sov] *adj* **1** : safe, unharmed **2** : intact, saved
sauf[2] *prep* **1** : except (for), apart from **2 sauf si** : unless <sauf s'il neige : unless it snows>
sauge [soʒ] *nf* : sage (herb)
saugrenu, -nue [sogrəny] *adj* ABSURDE : preposterous, absurd
saule [sol] *nm* : willow <saule pleureur : weeping willow>
saumâtre [somatr] *adj* : brackish, briny
saumon[1] [somɔ̃] *adj* : salmon pink
saumon[2] *nm* : salmon
saumure [somyr] *nf* : brine
sauna [sona] *nm* : sauna
saupoudrer [sopudre] *vt* : to sprinkle
saura [sɔra], *etc.* → **savoir**
saut [so] *nm* **1** BOND : jump <saut en hauteur : high jump> <saut de main : handspring> <saut périlleux : somersault> <saut à skis : ski jump> **2** : leap, drop <faire le saut : to take the plunge> **3 faire faire un saut à qqn** *Can* : to scare s.o., to make s.o. jump **4 faire un saut chez qqn** : to drop in on s.o.
saute–mouton [sotmutɔ̃] *nms & pl* : leapfrog
sauter [sote] *vt* **1** FRANCHIR : to jump over, to clear **2** OMETTRE : to skip, to leave out — *vi* **1** BONDIR : to jump, to leap <sauter à cloche-pied : to hop> <sauter à la corde : to jump rope> **2** : to leap up, to jump <sauter aux yeux : to be glaringly obvious> **3** : to come off, to slip (of a gear, etc.) **4** EXPLOSER : to go off, to blow up **5 faire sauter** : to sauté
sauterelle [sotrɛl] *nf* : grasshopper
sauteur, -teuse [sotœr, -tøz] *n* : jumper (in sports)
sautillement [sotijmɑ̃] *nm* : hop, skip
sautiller [sotije] *vi* **1** : to hop, to skip **2** : to flit about
sautoir [sotwar] *nm* : long necklace, chain
sauvage[1] [sovaʒ] *adj* **1** : savage **2** : wild **3** FAROUCHE : unsociable, shy
sauvage[2] *nmf* **1** : savage **2** : unsociable person
sauvagerie [sovaʒri] *nf* **1** : savagery **2** : shyness, unsociability
sauvagine [sovaʒin] *nf* : waterfowl
sauve → **sauf**[1]
sauvegarde [sovgard] *nf* **1** : safeguard **2** : safety, security **3** : backup (of a computer file)
sauvegarder [sovgarde] *vt* **1** : to safeguard **2** : to save (a computer file)
sauve–qui–peut [sovkipø] *nms & pl* : stampede, panic
sauver [sove] *vt* **1** : to save, to rescue **2** : to salvage **3** : to redeem — **se sauver** *vr* **1** : to escape **2** *fam* FILER : to leave, to split, to rush off
sauvetage [sovtaʒ] *nm* **1** : rescue, lifesaving **2** : salvage
sauveteur [sovtœr] *nm* : rescuer, lifesaver
sauvette [sovɛt] **à la sauvette 1** : hastily, in a rush **2** : illegally, on the sly
sauveur [sovœr] *nm* : savior
savamment [savamɑ̃] *adv* **1** : learnedly **2** HABILEMENT : skillfully
savane [savan] *nf* **1** : savanna **2** *Can* : swamp
savant[1], **-vante** [savɑ̃, -vɑ̃t] *adj* **1** ÉRUDIT : learned, scholarly **2** HABILE : skillful, clever
savant[2], **-vante** *n* **1** ÉRUDIT : savant, scholar **2** SCIENTIFIQUE : scientist
saveur [savœr] *nf* GOÛT : flavor, savor
savoir[1] [savwar] {79} *vt* **1** : to know <savoir par coeur : to know by heart> <je le sais loyal : I know he's loyal> <en savoir long de : to know a great deal about> <sans le savoir : unknowingly> **2** POUVOIR : to know how to, to be able to <elle sait jouer du piano : she can play the piano> <je ne sais pas mentir : I cannot tell a lie> **3 à** ~ : that is to say, namely — **se savoir** *vr* : to become known
savoir[2] *nm* : learning, knowledge
savoir–faire [savwarfɛr] *nms & pl* : know-how, expertise
savoir–vivre [savwarvivr] *nms & pl* : good manners *pl*, tact
savon [savɔ̃] *nm* **1** : soap **2** *fam* **passer un savon à** : to reprimand

savonner [savɔne] *vt* : to soap (up), to lather
savonnette [savɔnɛt] *nf* : bar of soap
savonneux, -neuse [savɔnø, -nøz] *adj* : soapy
savourer [savure] *vt* : to savor
savoureux, -reuse [savurø, -røz] *adj* **1** DÉLECTABLE : savory, tasty **2** PIQUANT : racy, juicy <anecdote savoureuse : racy anecdote>
saxophone [saksɔfɔn] *nm* : saxophone — **saxophoniste** [-fɔnist] *nmf*
scabreux, -breuse [skabrø, -brøz] *adj* **1** INDÉCENT : indecent, risqué **2** : risky, tricky
scalpel [skalpɛl] *nm* : scalpel
scalper [skalpe] *vt* : to scalp
scandale [skɑ̃dal] *nf* **1** : scandal <faire scandale : to cause a scandal> **2** ÉCLAT : scene, uproar
scandaleux, -leuse [skɑ̃dalø, -løz] *adj* : scandalous, disgraceful — **scandaleusement** [-løzmɑ̃] *adv*
scandaliser [skɑ̃dalize] *vt* : to scandalize
scander [skɑ̃de] *vt* **1** : to scan (poetry) **2** : to chant **3** : to accentuate, to stress
scandinave [skɑ̃dinav] *adj* : Scandinavian
Scandinave *nmf* : Scandinavian
scanner [skanɛr] *nm* : scanner
scansion [skɑ̃sjɔ̃] *nf* : scan, scanning (in literature)
scaphandre [skafɑ̃dr] *nm* **1** : diving suit **2** : space suit
scaphandrier [skafɑ̃drije] *nm* : deep-sea diver
scarabée [skarabe] *nm* **1** : beetle **2** : scarab
scarlatine [skarlatin] *nf* : scarlet fever
scarole [skarɔl] *nf* : endive, escarole
sceau [so] *nm* **1** : seal **2** : hallmark, stamp
scélérat[1], -rate [selera, -rat] *adj* : villainous
scélérat[2], -rate *n* : villain, rogue
scellé [sele] *nm* : seal
sceller [sele] *vt* **1** : to seal **2** : to attach securely, to fix
scénario [senarjo] *nm* **1** : scenario **2** : screenplay
scène [sɛn] *nf* **1** : scene (in theater) **2** : stage <être en scène : to be on stage> **3** : scene, row <faire une scène : to make a scene> **4** → **metteur, mise**
scénique [senik] *adj* : theatrical
scepticisme [sɛptisism] *nm* : skepticism
sceptique[1] [sɛptik] *adj* : skeptical
sceptique[2] *nmf* : skeptic
sceptre [sɛptr] *nm* : scepter
scheik [ʃɛk] *nm* → **cheik**
schéma [ʃema] *nm* **1** : diagram **2** ESQUISSE : sketch, outline
schématique [ʃematik] *adj* **1** : schematic **2** : (over)simplified
schisme [ʃism] *nm* : schism
schiste [ʃist] *nm* **schiste argileux** : shale
schizophrène [skizɔfrɛn] *adj & nmf* : schizophrenic
schizophrénie [skizɔfreni] *nf* : schizophrenia
schooner [ʃunœr] *nm* GOÉLETTE : schooner
scie [si] *nf* **1** : saw <scie à métaux : hacksaw> <scie sauteuse : jigsaw> <scie à chaîne : chainsaw> **2** : catchphrase **3** *fam* : drag, bore
sciemment [sjamɑ̃] *adv* : knowingly
science [sjɑ̃s] *nf* **1** : science **2** SAVOIR : knowledge, learning
science-fiction [sjɑ̃sfiksjɔ̃] *nf* : science fiction
scientifique[1] [sjɑ̃tifik] *adj* : scientific — **scientifiquement** [-fikmɑ̃] *adv*
scientifique[2] *nmf* : scientist
scier [sje] {96} *vt* : to saw
scierie [siri] *nf* : sawmill
scinder [sɛ̃de] *vt* DIVISER : to split, to divide — **se scinder** *vr* : to be divided, to split up
scintillant, -lante [sɛ̃tijɑ̃, -jɑ̃t] *adj* : sparkling, twinkling
scintillement [sɛ̃tijmɑ̃] *nm* : sparkling, twinkling
scintiller [sɛ̃tije] *vi* : to scintillate, to twinkle, to sparkle
scission [sisjɔ̃] *nf* **1** : schism, split <faire scission : to secede, to break away> **2** : fission (in biology and physics)
sciure [sjyr] *nf* : sawdust
scolaire [skɔlɛr] *adj* : school, scholastic <l'année scolaire : the school year>
scolarité [skɔlarite] *nf* : schooling
scooter [skutœr] *nm* : motor scooter
scorbut [skɔrbyt] *nm* : scurvy
score [skɔr] *nm* : score
scorie [skɔri] *nf* **1** : slag **2** : dross, dregs
scorpion [skɔrpjɔ̃] *nm* : scorpion
Scorpion *nm* : Scorpio
scotch [skɔtʃ] *nm* : Scotch whiskey
scout[1], scoute [skut] *adj* : scout <camp scout : scout camp>
scout[2], scoute *n* : Boy Scout *m*, Girl Scout *f*
scribe [skrib] *nm* : scribe
script [skript] *nm* **1** : printing, lettering **2** : script (in movies, television, etc.)
scrotum [skrɔtɔm] *nm* : scrotum
scrupule [skrypyl] *nm* : scruple, qualm, compunction
scrupuleux, -leuse [skrypylø, -løz] *adj* : scrupulous — **scrupuleusement** [-løzmɑ̃] *adv*
scruter [skryte] *vt* : to scrutinize
scrutin [skrytɛ̃] *nm* **1** : ballot, voting **2** : polling, polls *pl*
sculpter [skylte] *vt* : to sculpt, to sculpture, to carve
sculpteur [skyltœr] *nm* : sculptor <elle est sculpteur : she's a sculptor>
sculpture [skyltyr] *nf* : sculpture — **sculptural, -rale** [-tyral] *adj*
se [sə] (**s'** *before a vowel or mute h*) *pron* **1** (*used with reflexive verbs*) : oneself,

himself, herself, themselves, itself <elle se regarde : she looks at herself> **2** (*used to indicate reciprocity*) : each other, one another <ils se sont parlés : they spoke to each other> **3** (*used in passive constructions*) <ça ne se fait pas : that is not done> **4** (*used when referring to parts of the body*) <il se lave les dents : he brushes his teeth> **5** (*used with impersonal verbs*) <il se peut qu'elle arrive demain : she may arrive tomorrow>

séance [seɑ̃s] *nf* **1** : session, meeting **2** : showing, performance **3 séance de spiritisme** : séance **4 séance tenante** : immediately, without delay

seau [so] *nm, pl* **seaux** : bucket, pail

sec[1] [sɛk] *adv* **1** : hard <frapper sec : to strike hard> **2** BRUSQUEMENT : abruptly, sharply

sec[2], **sèche** [sɛk, sɛʃ] *adj* **1** : dry **2** : dried <abricots secs : dried apricots> **3** MAIGRE : lean, gaunt **4** DUR : hard, harsh, sharp <une voix sèche : a harsh voice> <avec un bruit sec : with a snap>

sec[3] *nm* **1** : dryness **2 être à sec** *fam* : to be dried up, to go broke

sécateur [sekatœr] *nm* : clippers *pl*, (garden) shears

sécession [sesesjɔ̃] *nf* : secession <faire sécession : to secede>

sèche–cheveux [sɛʃʃəvø] *nms & pl* : hairdryer

sèchement [sɛʃmɑ̃] *adv* : dryly, curtly

sécher [seʃe] {87} *vt* **1** : to dry **2** *France fam* : to skip, to cut (a class, etc.) — *vi* **1** : to dry, to dry up, to dry out **2** *fam* : to be stumped, to draw a blank

sécheresse [sɛʃrɛs] *nf* **1** : drought **2** : dryness **3** : curtness

séchoir [seʃwar] *nm* : dryer

second[1], **-conde** [səgɔ̃, -gɔ̃d] *adj* **1** : second **2 de seconde main** : secondhand

second[2], **-conde** *nmf* : second

second[3] *nm* **1** : assistant, helper **2** : first mate **3** : second floor

secondaire [səgɔ̃dɛr] *adj* **1** : secondary **2** → **école**

seconde [səgɔ̃d] *nf* **1** : second <attends une seconde! : wait a second!> **2** : second class <voyager en seconde : to travel second class>

seconder [səgɔ̃de] *vt* : to assist, to back up

secouer [səkwe] *vt* **1** : to shake <secouer la tête : to shake one's head> **2** : to shake off **3** *fam* : to shake up, to rouse — **se secouer** *vr* : to pull oneself together, to get going

secourable [səkurabl] *adj* : helpful

secourir [səkurir] {23} *vt* **1** AIDER : to help, to aid **2** : to rescue

secourisme [səkurism] *nm* : first aid

secouriste [səkurist] *nmf* : first aid worker

secours [səkur] *nms & pl* **1** : help, aid <au secours! : help!> **2 de ~** : for emergency <pneu de secours : spare tire> <sortie de secours : emergency exit> **3 secours** *nmpl* : rescuers, reinforcements

secousse [səkus] *nf* **1** CAHOT : jolt, jerk **2** CHOC : shock, upset **3** *Can* : period of time **4** : tremor

secret[1], **-crète** [səkrɛ, -krɛt] *adj* **1** : secret **2** : secretive, reserved

secret[2] *nm* **1** : secret **2** : secrecy

secrétaire[1] [səkretɛr] *nmf* : secretary

secrétaire[2] *nm* : secretary (desk)

secrétariat [səkretarjat] *nm* **1** : secretariat **2** : secretarial work

secrètement [səkrɛtmɑ̃] *adv* : secretly

sécréter [sekrete] {87} *vt* : to secrete <sécréter du lait : to lactate> — **sécrétion** [-resjɔ̃] *nf*

sectaire [sɛktɛr] *adj* : sectarian

secte [sɛkt] *nm* : sect

secteur [sɛktœr] *nm* : sector, area, zone <le secteur privé : the private sector>

section [sɛksjɔ̃] *nf* **1** : section **2** : department, branch

sectionner [sɛksjɔne] *vt* **1** DIVISER : to section, to divide **2** TRANCHER : to sever

séculaire [sekylɛr] *adj* **1** : ancient, age-old, a hundred years old **2** : secular

séculier, -lière [sekylje, -ljɛr] *adj* LAÏQUE : secular

secundo [səgɔ̃do] *adv* : second, secondly

sécuriser [sekyrize] *vt* **1** RASSURER : to reassure **2** : to make (someone) feel secure

sécurité [sekyrite] *nf* **1** : security <sentiment de sécurité : sense of security> **2** : safety <sécurité publique : public safety>

sédatif[1], **-tive** [sedatif, -tiv] *adj* : sedative

sédatif[2] *nm* : sedative

sédation [sedasjɔ̃] *nf* : sedation

sédentaire [sedɑ̃tɛr] *adj* : sedentary

sédiment [sedimɑ̃] *nm* : sediment — **sédimentaire** [-mɑ̃tɛr] *adj*

séditieux, -tieuse [sedisjø, -sjøz] *adj* : seditious

sédition [sedisjɔ̃] *nf* : insurrection, revolt

séducteur[1], **-trice** [sedyktœr, -tris] *adj* : seductive

séducteur[2], **-trice** *n* : seducer

séduction [sedyksjɔ̃] *nf* **1** : seduction **2** : charm, appeal

séduire [sedɥir] {49} *vt* **1** : to seduce **2** : to charm **3** : to appeal to

séduisant, -sante [sedɥizɑ̃, -zɑ̃t] *adj* : seductive, attractive

segment [sɛgmɑ̃] *nm* : segment

segmentaire [sɛgmɑ̃tɛr] *adj* : segmented

ségrégation [segregasjɔ̃] *nf* : segregation

seiche [sɛʃ] *nf* : cuttlefish

seigle [sɛgl] *nm* : rye

seigneur |sɛɲœr| *nm* **1** : lord **2 le Seigneur** : the Lord

sein |sɛ̃| *nm* **1** : breast, bosom <donner le sein à : to breast-feed> **2** VENTRE : womb **3 au sein de** : within

séisme |seism| *nm* : earthquake

seize[1] |sɛz| *adj* **1** : sixteen **2** : sixteenth <le seize octobre : October sixteenth>

seize[2] *nms & pl* : sixteen

seizième |sɛzjɛm| *adj & nmf & nm* : sixteenth

séjour |seʒur| *nm* **1** : stay, sojourn **2** → **salle**

séjourner |seʒurne| *vi* **1** : to stay (at a hotel, etc.) **2** RESTER : to lie, to remain (of water, fog, etc.)

sel |sɛl| *nm* **1** : salt <sel gemme : rock salt> **2** : piquancy, wit

sélect, -lecte |selɛkt| *adj fam* : select, exclusive, posh

sélectif, -tive |selɛktif, -tiv| *adj* : selective

sélection |selɛksjɔ̃| *nf* **1** : selection **2 sélection naturelle** : natural selection

sélectionner |selɛksjɔne| *vt* : to select, to choose

self-made-man |sɛlfmedman| *nm* : self-made man

self-service |sɛlfsɛrvis| *nm, pl* **self-services** : self-service store or restaurant

selle |sɛl| *nf* **1** : saddle **2 aller à la selle** : to have a bowel movement

seller |sele| *vt* : to saddle

sellette |sɛlɛt| *nf* **être sur la sellette** : to be in the hot seat

selon |səlɔ̃| *prep* **1** : according to **2 ~ que** : depending on whether

semailles |səmaj| *nfpl* : sowing, seeding

semaine |səmɛn| *nf* **1** : week <une semaine de quarante heures : a forty-hour week> **2 vivre à la petite semaine** : to live day by day

sémantique[1] |semɑ̃tik| *adj* : semantic

sémantique[2] *nf* : semantics

sémaphore |semafɔr| *nm* : semaphore

semblable[1] |sɑ̃blabl| *adj* **1** : similar, like **2** TEL : such <il faut de semblables mesures : such measures are necessary>

semblable[2] *nmf* : fellow creature, like <vous et vos semblables : you and your kind>

semblant |sɑ̃blɑ̃| *nm* **1** : semblance, appearance **2 faire semblant** : to pretend

sembler |sɑ̃ble| *vi* : to seem <elle semble contente : she seems (to be) happy> — *v impers* **il semble que** : it seems that

semelle |səmɛl| *nf* **1** : sole **2** *or* **semelle intérieure** : insole

semence |səmɑ̃s| *nf* **1** GRAINE : seed **2** : tack, brad

semer |səme| {52} *vt* **1** : to sow, to seed **2** RÉPANDRE : to strew, to scatter **3** *fam* : to lose, to shake off (pursuers, etc.)

semestre |səmɛstr| *nm* : semester

semestriel, -trielle |səmɛstrijɛl| *adj* : biannual — **semestriellement** *adv*

semeur, -meuse |səmœr, -møz| *n* : sower

semi-circulaire |səmisirkylɛr| *adj* DEMI-CIRCULAIRE : semicircular

semi-conducteur |sɛmikɔ̃dyktœr| *nm, pl* **semi-conducteurs** : semiconductor

sémillant, -lante |semijɑ̃, -jɑ̃t| *adj* VIF : lively, spirited

séminaire |seminɛr| *nm* **1** : seminary **2** : seminar

séminal, -nale |seminal| *adj, mpl* **-naux** |-no| : seminal

semi-remorque |səmirəmɔrk| *nm, pl* **semi-remorques** : semitrailer

semis |səmi| *nm* **1** : seedling **2** : sowing **3** : seedbed **4** : small repeated pattern

semoir |səmwar| *nm* : drill (in agriculture)

semonce |səmɔ̃s| *nf* **1** RÉPRIMANDE : reprimand **2 coup de semonce** : warning shot

semoule |səmul| *nf* : semolina <semoule de maïs : cornflour>

sempiternel, -nelle |sɑ̃pitɛrnɛl| *adj* ÉTERNEL : eternal

sénat |sena| *nm* : senate

sénateur |senatœr| *nm* : senator

sénatrice |senatris| *nf Can* : (female) senator

sénégalais, -laise |senegalɛ, -lɛz| *adj* : Senegalese

Sénégalais, -laise *n* : Senegalese

sénile |senil| *adj* : senile

sénilité |senilite| *nf* : senility

sens |sɑ̃s| *nms & pl* **1** : sense (in physiology) <sens du toucher : sense of touch> **2** SIGNIFICATION : sense, meaning <dépourvu de sens : meaningless> **3** INSTINCT : sense, feeling <sens du rythme : sense of rhythm> **4** RAISON : sense <cela n'a pas de sens : that doesn't make any sense> **5** DIRECTION : direction, way <sens unique : one-way> **6** OPINION : opinion <à mon sens : in my opinion> **7 sens dessus dessous** : upside down

sensation |sɑ̃sasjɔ̃| *nf* **1** : sensation, feeling **2 faire sensation** : to cause a sensation

sensationnel, -nelle |sɑ̃sasjɔnɛl| *adj* : sensational

sensé, -sée |sɑ̃se| *adj* : sensible

sensibiliser |sɑ̃sibilize| *vt* : to sensitize

sensibilité |sɑ̃sibilite| *nf* : sensitivity, sensibility

sensible |sɑ̃sibl| *adj* **1** : sensitive **2** APPRÉCIABLE : appreciable, considerable **3** PERCEPTIBLE : perceptible

sensiblement [sɑ̃sibləmɑ̃] *adv* **1** : appreciably, noticeably **2** : roughly, approximately
sensiblerie [sɑ̃sibləri] *nf* : sentimentality
sensitif, -tive [sɑ̃sitif, -tiv] *adj* **1** : oversensitive **2** : sensory
sensoriel, -rielle [sɑ̃sɔrjɛl] *adj* : sensory
sensualité [sɑ̃sɥalite] *nf* : sensuality, sensuousness
sensuel, -suelle [sɑ̃sɥɛl] *adj* : sensual, sensuous — **sensuellement** [-sɥɛlmɑ̃] *adv*
sentence [sɑ̃tɑ̃s] *nf* **1** JUGEMENT : sentence **2** MAXIME : maxim, proverb
sentencieux, -cieuse [sɑ̃tɑ̃sjø, -sjøz] *adj* : sententious
senteur [sɑ̃tœr] *nf* : scent
senti, -tie [sɑ̃ti] *adj* **bien senti** : blunt, forthright <mots bien sentis : well-chosen words>
sentier [sɑ̃tje] *nm* : path <hors des sentiers battus : off the beaten track>
sentiment [sɑ̃timɑ̃] *nm* **1** : sentiment, feeling <avoir le sentiment de : to be aware of> <faire du sentiment : to be sentimental> **2** AVIS : opinion, feeling <c'est mon sentiment : that's my feeling, that's what I think> **3 recevez l'expression de mes sentiments respectueux** : yours truly
sentimental, -tale [sɑ̃timɑ̃tal] *adj, mpl* **-taux** [-to] : sentimental — **sentimentalité** [-talite] *nf*
sentinelle [sɑ̃tinɛl] *nf* : sentinel, sentry
sentir [sɑ̃tir] {82} *vt* **1** : to smell, to taste **2** : to smell like, to smell of <ça sent la rose : it smells like a rose> **3** : to feel <il n'a rien senti : he felt nothing> **4** : to have a feeling (for), to appreciate <je sens que c'est important : I have a feeling that it's important> <elle sent l'art moderne : she appreciates modern art> **5** : to smack of, to be indicative of — *vi* : to smell — **se sentir** *vr* **1** : to feel <il se sent malade : he feels sick> **2** : to be felt, to show
seoir [swar] {80} *vi* **~ à** : to suit, to be appropriate to — *v impers* **il sied** : it is fitting, it is appropriate
séparation [separasjɔ̃] *nf* : separation
séparé, -rée [separe] *adj* **1** : separate **2** : separated (from one's spouse)
séparément [separemɑ̃] *adv* : separately, apart
séparer [separe] *vt* **1** DÉTACHER : to separate, to detach **2** DISTINGUER : to distinguish (between) **3** : to divide — **se séparer** *vr* **1** : to separate, to part, to split up **2** : to divide **3 ~ de** : to part with, to be without
sépia [sepja] *nf* : sepia
sept[1] [sɛt] *adj* **1** : seven **2** : seventh <le sept mai : May seventh>
sept[2] *nms & pl* : seven
septante[1] [sɛptɑ̃t] *adj Bel, Switz* **1** : seventy **2** : seventieth
septante[2] *nms & pl Bel, Switz* : seventy
septembre [sɛptɑ̃br] *nm* : September
septentrional, -nale [sɛptɑ̃trijɔnal] *adj, mpl* **-naux** [-no] : northern
septième [sɛtjɛm] *adj & nmf & nm* : seventh
septique [sɛptik] *adj* **1** : septic **2** → **fosse**
sépulcre [sepylkr] *nm* : sepulchre, tomb
sépulture [sepyltyr] *nf* **1** TOMBE : grave **2** ENTERREMENT : burial
séquelle [sekɛl] *nf* **1** CONSÉQUENCE : consequence **2 séquelles** *nfpl* : aftereffects
séquence [sekɑ̃s] *nf* SUITE : sequence
séquentiel, -tielle [sekɑ̃sjɛl] *adj* : sequential
séquestre [sekɛstr] *nm* : escrow <en séquestre : in escrow>
séquestrer [sekɛstre] *vt* : to sequester
séquoia [sekɔja] *nm* : sequoia
sera [səra], *etc.* → **être**
sérail [seraj] *nm* : seraglio
séraphin, -phine [serafɛ̃, -fin] *adj Can fam* : stingy, miserly
serbe[1] [sɛrb] *adj* : Serb, Serbian
serbe[2] *nm* : Serbian (language)
Serbe *nmf* : Serb, Serbian
serein, -reine [sərɛ̃, -rɛn] *adj* **1** : clear, tranquil (of the sky, weather, etc.) **2** CALME : calm, serene — **sereinement** [-rɛnmɑ̃] *adv*
sérénade [serenad] *nf* : serenade
sérénité [serenite] *nf* : serenity
serf, serve [sɛrf, sɛrv] *n* : serf
serge [sɛrʒ] *nf* : serge
sergé [sɛrʒe] *nm* : twill
sergent [sɛrʒɑ̃] *nm* : sergeant
série [seri] *nf* **1** : series **2** : set, range, line **3 de ~** : mass-produced, standard, stock **4 fabrication en série** : mass production
sériel, -rielle [serjɛl] *adj* : serial
sérieusement [serjøzmɑ̃] *adv* : seriously
sérieux[1], **-rieuse** [serjø, -rjøz] *adj* **1** : serious, solemn **2** : important <une sérieuse argumentation : a weighty argument> **3** : reliable, dependable **4** : responsible, conscientious
sérieux[2] *nm* : seriousness, earnestness <se prendre au sérieux : to take oneself seriously>
serin [sərɛ̃] *nm* : canary
seringue [sərɛ̃g] *nf* : syringe
serment [sɛrmɑ̃] *nm* **1** : oath <prêter serment : to take the oath> **2** : vow, promise
sermon [sɛrmɔ̃] *nm* **1** : sermon **2** : lecture, talking-to
sermonner [sɛrmɔne] *vt* : to lecture
serpent [sɛrpɑ̃] *nm* **1** : snake, serpent **2 serpent à sonnettes** CROTALE : rattlesnake
serpenter [sɛrpɑ̃te] *vi* : to wind, to meander

serpentin [sɛrpɑ̃tɛ̃] *nm* : streamer

serrage [sɛraʒ] *nm* : tightening

serre [sɛr] *nf* **1** : greenhouse, hothouse <l'effet de serre : greenhouse effect> **2 serres** *nfpl* : claws, talons

serré, -rée [sere] *adj* **1** : tight **2** : thick, cramped, dense **3** : strict, tight, close <surveillance serrée : close supervision>

serre–livres [sɛrlivr] *nms & pl* : bookend

serrement [sɛrmɑ̃] *nm* : pressing, squeezing, constriction <serrement de main : handshake> <serrement de coeur : pang (of sorrow)>

serrer [sere] *vt* **1** : to press, to squeeze, to grip <serrer les poings : to clench one's fists> **2** : to tighten **3** : to squeeze tightly <ces chaussures me serrent : these shoes are too tight> **4** : to stay close to <serrer le trottoir : to hug the curb> **5** : to push (close) together, to pack together **6** : to cut (expenses, etc.) — **se serrer** *vr* **1** : to huddle up (together) **2** : to tighten up **3 se serrer la main** : to shake hands

serre–tête [sɛrtɛt] *nm, pl* **serre–têtes** : headband

serrure [sɛryr] *nf* : lock

serrurier [sɛryrje] *nm* : locksmith

sert [sɛr], *etc.* → **servir**

sertir [sɛrtir] *vt* : to set, to mount (gems)

sérum [serɔm] *nm* : serum

serveur[1], -veuse [sɛrvœr, -vøz] *n* : waiter *m*, waitress *f*

serveur[2] *nm* **1** : server (in sports) **2** : dealer (in card games) **3** : (computer) server

serviable [sɛrvjabl] *adj* OBLIGEANT : helpful, obliging

service [sɛrvis] *nm* **1** : service <mettre en service : to put in service, to set up> <hors service : out of order> <service de bus : bus service> **2** FAVEUR : favor <rendre un service à : to do a favor for> **3** : serving, course <repas à trois services : three-course meal> **4** : service, serving <être au service se son pays : to serve one's country> <à votre service! : not at all!, don't mention it!> <service militaire : military service> <faire le service : to serve a meal, to wait tables> **5** : department <service du personnel : personnel department> <services sociaux : social services> <service des urgences : emergency room> **6** : set <service de café : coffee service> **7** : service, serve (in sports)

serviette [sɛrvjɛt] *nf* **1** : napkin **2** : towel **3** : briefcase, portfolio **4 serviette hygiénique** : sanitary napkin

servile [sɛrvil] *adj* : servile — **servilité** [sɛrvilite] *nf*

servir [sɛrvir] {81} *vt* **1** : to serve **2** AIDER : to help, to assist **3** : to deal (cards) — *vi* **1** : to be useful <ça ne sert à rien : that is of no use> **2** : to serve (in the military) **3** : to deal (in card games) **4** ~ **de** : to serve as — **se servir** *vr* **1** : to serve oneself, to help oneself **2** ~ **de** : to make use of

serviteur [sɛrvitœr] *nm* : servant

servitude [sɛrvityd] *nf* **1** : servitude **2** : obligation, constraint

ses → **son**

sésame [sezam] *nm* : sesame (plant and seed)

session [sesjɔ̃] *nf* : session

set [sɛt] *nm* **1** : set (in tennis, etc.) **2** *or* **set de table** : placemat

seuil [sœj] *nm* **1** : threshold, doorstep **2 au seuil de** : on the threshold, on the brink of

seul[1], seule [sœl] *adv* **1** : alone, only <seule Marie répondit : only Marie replied> **2** : by oneself, singlehandedly <tout seul : all by oneself>

seul[2], seule *adj* **1** : alone <j'ai besoin d'être seul : I need to be alone> **2** : only, unique <le seul problème : the only problem> **3** SOLITAIRE : lonely, solitary

seul[3], seule *pron* : only one, single one <c'est le seul qui reste : it's the only one left>

seulement[1] [sœlmɑ̃] *adv* **1** : only <seulement trois fois : only three times> <pas seulement . . . , mais encore : not only . . . , but also> **2** MÊME : even <sans seulement dire un mot : without even saying a word>

seulement[2] *conj* CEPENDANT : however, but, only <je l'achèterais, seulement je n'ai pas d'argent : I'd buy it, only I don't have any money>

sève [sɛv] *nf* **1** : sap **2** VIGUEUR : vim, vigor

sévère [sevɛr] *adj* **1** : strict, severe, stern **2** : austere — **sévèrement** [-vɛrmɑ̃] *adv*

sévérité [severite] *nf* : severity

sévices [sevis] *nmpl* : cruelty, brutality, abuse

sévir [sevir] *vi* **1** : to clamp down, to impose restrictions <sévir contre la corruption : to clamp down on corruption> **2** : to be rampant, to rage

sevrage [səvraʒ] *nm* : weaning

sevrer [səvre] *vt* : to wean

sexe [sɛks] *nm* **1** : sex **2** : sex organs, genitals

sexisme [sɛksism] *nm* : sexism

sexiste [sɛksist] *adj & nmf* : sexist

sextant [sɛkstɑ̃] *nm* : sextant

sextuor [sɛkstɥɔr] *nm* : sextet

sexualité [sɛksɥalite] *nf* : sexuality

sexuel, sexuelle [sɛksɥɛl] *adj* : sexual — **sexuellement** [-sɥɛlmɑ̃] *adv*

sexy [sɛksi] *adj* : sexy

seyant, seyante [sɛjɑ̃, -jɑ̃t] *adj* : becoming, flattering

shampooing [ʃɑ̃pwɛ̃] *nm* : shampoo

shampouiner *or* **shampooiner** |ʃɑ̃pwine| *vt* : to shampoo
shérif |ʃerif| *nm* : sheriff
shopping |ʃɔpiŋ| *nm* : shopping <faire le shopping : to go shopping>
short |ʃɔrt| *nm* : shorts *pl*
si[1] |si| *adv* **1** TELLEMENT : so, such, as <elle est si intelligente : she is so intelligent> <un si grand pays : such a big country> <il n'est pas si célèbre que ça : he's not as famous as all that> **2** (*used to contradict a negative statement or question*) : yes <il n'est pas arrivé à l'heure? si : he didn't arrive on time? yes, he did> **3 si bien que** : with the result that, so **4 si . . . que** : however <si riche qu'elle soit : however wealthy she is>
si[2] *conj* : if, whether <si vous voulez : if you please> <je ne sais pas si elle vient ou pas : I don't know whether she's coming or not>
siamois, -moise |sjamwa, -waz| *adj* : Siamese
Siamois, -moise *n* : Siamese
sida |sida| *nm* : AIDS
sidérer |sidere| {87} *vt fam* : to stagger, to amaze
sidérurgie |sideryrʒi| *nf* : steel industry
sidérurgique |sideryrʒik| *adj* : steel <usine sidérurgique : ironworks, steelworks>
siècle |sjɛkl| *nm* : century
siège |sjɛʒ| *nm* **1** : seat <siège arrière : back seat (of an automobile)> **2** *or* **siège social** : headquarters **3** : siege
siéger |sjeʒe| {64} *vi* **1** : to sit, to serve <siéger à un comité : to sit on a committee> **2** : to be in session **3** : to be located, to have its headquarters
sien[1], **sienne** |sjɛ̃, sjɛn| *adj* : his, hers, its, one's
sien[2], **sienne** *pron* **le sien, la sienne, les siens, les siennes** : his, hers, its, one's, theirs
sieste |sjɛst| *nf* : siesta, nap
sifflement |siflәmɑ̃| *nm* **1** : whistle, whistling, hoot (of a train) **2** : hiss, hissing
siffler |sifle| *vt* **1** : to whistle **2** : to whistle for, to whistle at **3** : to boo **4** *fam* : to swill down, to swig — *vi* **1** : to whistle, to blow a whistle, to hoot (of a train) **2** : to hiss **3** : to wheeze
sifflet |siflɛ| *nm* **1** : whistle **2 sifflets** *nmpl* : boos, catcalls
siffloter |siflɔte| *v* : to whistle
sigle |sigl| *nm* : acronym
signal |siɲal| *nm, pl* **signaux** |siɲo| **1** : sign, signal (gesture) <donner le signal : to give the signal> **2** : signal <signal d'alarme : alarm (signal)>
signalement |siɲalmɑ̃| *nm* : description
signaler |siɲale| *vt* **1** : to signal **2** : to point out, to indicate **3** : to report — **se signaler** *vr* : to distinguish oneself, to stand out
signalisation |siɲalizasjɔ̃| *nf* : signals *pl*, signs *pl* <signalisation routière : road signs>
signataire |siɲatɛr| *nmf* : signatory
signature |siɲatyr| *nf* **1** : signature **2** : signing
signe |siɲ| *nm* **1** : sign, gesture <en signe d'estime : as a sign of respect> <faire signe que oui : to nod in agreement> **2** : sign, indication <signes de vie : signs of life> **3** : mark, symbol <signe de ponctuation : punctuation mark> <signe du zodiaque : sign of the zodiac> **4 signe avant–coureur** : herald, precursor
signer |siɲe| *vt* : to sign (one's name) — **se signer** *vr* : to cross oneself
signet |siɲɛ| *nm* : bookmark
significatif, -tive |siɲifikatif, -tiv| *adj* : significant
signification |siɲifikasjɔ̃| *nf* : significance, meaning
signifier |siɲifje| {96} *vt* : to signify, to mean
silence |silɑ̃s| *nm* **1** : silence <silence absolu : dead silence> <garder le silence : to keep quiet> **2** : rest (in music)
silencieux[1], **-cieuse** |silɑ̃sjø, -sjøz| *adj* : silent, quiet — **silencieusement** |-sjøzmɑ̃| *adv*
silencieux[2] *nm* **1** : silencer (of a firearm) **2** : muffler
silex |silɛks| *nm* : flint
silhouette |silwɛt| *nf* : silhouette, outline
silice |silis| *nf* : silica
silicium |silisjɔm| *nm* : silicon
sillage |sijaʒ| *nm* : wake (of a ship)
sillon |sijɔ̃| *nm* **1** : furrow **2** : groove (of a disc, etc.)
sillonner |sijɔne| *vt* **1** CREUSER : to furrow **2** PARCOURIR : to go all over, to crisscross
silo |silo| *nm* : silo
simagrée |simagre| *nf* **faire des simagrées** : to put on airs
similaire |similɛr| *adj* : similar — **similarité** |similarite| *nf*
simili |simili| *nm* : imitation (of leather, gems, etc.)
similitude |similityd| *nf* : similarity, resemblance
simple[1] |sɛ̃pl| *adj* **1** : simple, straightforward <directions simples : easy instructions> **2** : mere <une simple formalité : a mere formality> **3** : simple, plain, unaffected **4** *or* **simple d'esprit** : simpleminded **5** : single <lit simple : single bed> <un aller simple : a one-way ticket>
simple[2] *nm* **1** : singles (in tennis) **2** *Can* : single (in baseball)
simplement |sɛ̃plәmɑ̃| *adv* **1** : simply, merely, just **2** : simply, plainly **3** : easily
simplet, -plette |sɛ̃plɛ, -plɛt| *adj* **1** : simpleminded **2** SIMPLISTE : simplistic

simplicité [sɛ̃plisite] *nf* **1** : simplicity, informality **2** : simpleness
simplifier [sɛ̃plifje] {96} *vt* : to simplify — **simplification** [sɛ̃plifikasjɔ̃] *nf*
simpliste [sɛ̃plist] *adj* : simplistic, oversimplified
simulacre [simylakr] *nm* : sham, pretense
simuler [simyle] *vt* : to simulate — **simulation** [simylasjɔ̃] *nf*
simultané, -née [simyltane] *adj* : simultaneous — **simultanément** [-nemɑ̃] *adv*
sincère [sɛ̃sɛr] *adj* : sincere — **sincèrement** [-sɛrmɑ̃] *adv*
sincérité [sɛ̃serite] *nf* : sincerity
singapourien, -rienne [sɛ̃gapurjɛ̃, -rjɛn] *adj* : Singaporean
Singapourien, -rienne *n* : Singaporean
singe [sɛ̃ʒ] *nm* **1** : monkey <les grands singes : the great apes> **2 faire le singe** : to monkey about, to clown around
singer [sɛ̃ʒe] {17} *vt* **1** IMITER : to ape, to mimic **2** : to feign
singeries [sɛ̃ʒri] *nfpl* : antics
singulariser [sɛ̃gylarize] *vt* : to draw attention to (someone) — **se singulariser** *vr* : to call attention to oneself
singularité [sɛ̃gylarite] *nf* **1** : peculiarity, strangeness **2** : uniqueness
singulier[1], **-lière** [sɛ̃gylje, -ljɛr] *adj* **1** : uncommon, strange, remarkable **2** : singular (in grammar)
singulier[2] *nm* : singular (in grammar)
singulièrement [sɛ̃gyljɛrmɑ̃] *nm* **1** BEAUCOUP : very much, extremely **2** BIZARREMENT : oddly, strangely **3** PARTICULIÈREMENT : particularly
sinistre[1] [sinistr] *adj* **1** : sinister, eerie **2** : dismal, gloomy
sinistre[2] *nm* **1** DÉSASTRE : disaster **2** DOMMAGE : damage
sinistré[1], **-trée** [sinistre] *adj* : damaged, stricken
sinistré[2], **-trée** *n* : disaster victim
sinon [sinɔ̃] *conj* **1** : or else **2** : if not **3** **~ que** : except that
sinueux, -nueuse [sinɥø, -nɥøz] *adj* : sinuous, winding, meandering
sinus [sinys] *nms & pl* **1** : sinus **2** : sine (in mathematics)
sionisme [sjɔnism] *nm* : Zionism
sioniste [sjɔnist] *adj & nmf* : Zionist
siphon [sifɔ̃] *nm* **1** : siphon **2** : trap (in plumbing)
siphonner [sifɔne] *vt* : to siphon
sire [sir] *nm* **1** SEIGNEUR : lord **2 triste sire** : unsavory individual
sirène [sirɛn] *nf* **1** : siren, mermaid (in mythology) **2** : siren, alarm
sirop [siro] *nm* : syrup <sirop d'érable : maple syrup> <sirop contre la toux : cough syrup>
siroter [sirɔte] *vt fam* : to sip
sirupeux, -peuse [sirypø, -pøz] *adj* : syrupy
sis, sise [si, siz] *adj* : located (in law)
sisal [sizal] *nm* : sisal
sismique [sismik] *adj* : seismic
site [sit] *nm* **1** : site <site historique : historic site> <site Internet : Internet site> **2** : setting, locale
sitôt [sito] *adv* **1** (*used with a participle*) <sitôt arrivé : as soon as he arrives, immediately upon his arrival> <sitôt dit, sitôt fait : no sooner said than done> **2 sitôt après** : immediately after **3 sitôt que** : as soon as
sittelle [sitɛl] *nf* : nuthatch
situation [sitɥasjɔ̃] *nf* **1** : situation **2 situation de famille** : marital status
situer [sitɥe] *vt* : to situate, to locate — **se situer** *vr*
six[1] [sis, *before consonant* si, *before vowel* siz] *adj* **1** : six **2** : sixth <le six décembre : December sixth>
six[2] *nms & pl* : six
sixième [sizjɛm] *adj & nmf & nm* : sixth
ski [ski] *nm* **1** : ski **2** : skiing **3 ski nautique** : waterskiing
skier [skje] {96} *vi* : to ski
skieur, skieuse [skjœr, skjøz] *n* : skier
slave [slav] *adj* : Slavic
Slave *nmf* : Slav
slip [slip] *nm* **1** : briefs *pl*, men's underpants *pl* **2** : panties *pl*
slogan [slɔgɑ̃] *nm* : slogan
slovaque[1] [slɔvak] *adj* : Slovak, Slovakian
slovaque[2] *nm* : Slovakian (language)
Slovaque *nmf* : Slovak
slovène[1] [slɔvɛn] *adj* : Slovene, Slovenian
slovène[2] *nm* : Slovene (language)
Slovène *nmf* : Slovene, Slovenian
smoking [smɔkiŋ] *nm* : tuxedo
snob[1] [snɔb] *adj* : snobbish
snob[2] *nmf* : snob
snober [snɔbe] *vt* : to snub
snobisme [snɔbism] *nm* : snobbery, snobbishness
sobre [sɔbr] *adj* **1** : sober, abstemious **2** : restrained — **sobrement** [-brəmɑ̃] *adv*
sobriété [sɔbrijete] *nf* : sobriety
sobriquet [sɔbrikɛ] *nm* : nickname
soc [sɔk] *nm* : plowshare
soccer [sɔkɛr] *nm Can* : soccer
sociable [sɔsjabl] *adj* : sociable — **sociabilité** [sɔsjabilite] *nf*
social, -ciale [sɔsjal] *adj, mpl* **-ciaux** [-sjo] : social — **socialement** [-sjalmɑ̃] *adv*
socialiser [sksjalize] *vt* : to socialize
socialisme [sɔsjalism] *nm* : socialism — **socialiste** [-sjalist] *adj & nmf*
sociétaire [sɔsjetɛr] *nmf* : member
société [sɔsjete] *nf* **1** : society <la haute société : high society> <la société de ses semblables : the society of one's peers> **2** : colony (of bees, etc.) **3** COMPAGNIE : company, firm **4**

ASSOCIATION : society, association, club

sociologie [sɔsjɔlɔʒi] *nf* : sociology

sociologique [sɔsjɔlɔʒik] *adj* : sociological

sociologue [sɔsjɔlɔg] *nmf* : sociologist

socle [sɔkl] *nm* BASE : base, pedestal

socque [sɔk] *nm* SABOT : clog, wooden shoe

soda [sɔda] *nm* **1** : soda, soft drink **2** : soda water

sodium [sɔdjɔm] *nm* : sodium

soeur [sœr] *nf* **1** : sister **2** : nun, sister

sofa [sɔfa] *nm* : sofa

soi [swa] *pron* : oneself, himself, herself, itself <chacun pour soi : every man for himself> <en soi : in itself> <cela va de soi : it goes without saying>

soi–disant[1] [swadizɑ̃] *adv* : supposedly

soi–disant[2] *adj* : so-called

soie [swa] *nf* **1** : silk **2** : bristle

soif [swaf] *nf* : thirst <avoir soif : to be thirsty>

soigné, -gnée [swaɲe] *adj* **1** : carefully done, meticulous **2** : well-groomed, neat

soigner [swaɲe] *vt* **1** : to treat, to nurse **2** : to look after, to take care of **3** : to do with care, to take trouble over — **se soigner** *vr* **1** : to treat oneself (for an illness, etc.) **2** : to be treatable

soigneux, -gneuse [swaɲø, -ɲøz] *adj* **1** : careful, meticulous **2** : neat, tidy — **soigneusement** [swaɲøzmɑ̃] *adv*

soi–même [swamɛm] *pron* : oneself <par soi-même : (all) by oneself>

soin [swɛ̃] *nm* **1** ATTENTION : care, attention <prendre soin de : to take care of, to look after> **2** SOUCI : concern **3 soins** *nmpl* : (medical) attention, treatment <premiers soins : first aid> **4 soins** *nmpl* : care <confier aux bons soins de : to leave in the care of>

soir [swar] *nm* : evening, night <demain soir : tomorrow night>

soirée [sware] *nf* **1** : evening <pendant la soirée : during the evening> **2** FÊTE : party **3** : evening performance (of a show)

soit[1] [swa], *etc.* → **être**

soit[2] *adv* : so be it, very well

soit[3] *conj* **1** : that is, in other words, or <48 heures soit deux jours : 48 hours, that is, two days> **2** (*introducing an hypothesis*) <soit un triangle XYZ : let XYZ be a triangle> **3 soit . . . soit . . .** : either . . . or . . . <soit ceci soit cela : either this or that>

soixante[1] [swasɑ̃t] *adj* : sixty <les années soixantes : the sixties>

soixante[2] *nms & pl* : sixty

soixante–dix[1] [swasɑ̃tdis] *adj* : seventy

soixante–dix[2] *nms & pl* : seventy

soixante–dixième [swasɑ̃tdizjɛm] *adj & nmf & nm* : seventieth

soixantième [swasɑ̃tjɛm] *adj & nmf & nm* : sixtieth

soja [sɔʒa] *nm* : soybean <sauce de soja : soy sauce>

sol [sɔl] *nm* **1** : ground, floor, surface **2** PLANCHER : flooring **3** TERRE : soil (in agriculture, etc.) **4** TERRITOIRE : territory, soil <sol canadien : Canadian soil>

solage [sɔlaʒ] *nm Can* : foundation (of a house)

solaire [sɔlɛr] *adj* **1** : solar **2** : sun <crème solaire : suntan lotion>

soldat [sɔlda] *nm* : soldier

solde[1] [sɔld] *nf* : pay

solde[2] *nm* **1** : balance (in finance) **2** : sale <en solde : on sale> **3 soldes** *nmpl* : sale, bargains

solder [sɔlde] *vt* **1** : to settle (an account, etc.) **2** BRADER : to sell off, to put on sale — **se solder** *vr* **1 ~ par** : to end in **2 ~ par** : to show <se solder par un excédent : to show a surplus>

sole [sɔl] *nf* : sole (fish)

soleil [sɔlɛj] *nm* **1** : sun **2** : sunshine, sunlight **3** : sunflower

solennel, -nelle [sɔlanɛl] *adj* **1** : solemn **2** : formal — **solennellement** *adv*

solennité [sɔlanite] *nf* : solemnity

solfège [sɔlfɛʒ] *nm* : music theory

solidaire [sɔlidɛr] *adj* **1** : united, in solidarity <être solidaire de : to stand by, to back> **2** INTERDÉPENDANT : interdependent

solidariser [sɔlidarize] *v* **se solidariser avec** *vr* : to show solidarity with

solidarité [sɔlidarite] *nf* : solidarity

solide[1] [sɔlid] *adj & nm* **1** : solid **2** : sturdy, strong

solide[2] *nm* : solid

solidement [sɔlidmɑ̃] *adv* **1** : solidly **2** : firmly, securely

solidité [sɔlidite] *nf* : solidity

solidifier [sɔlidifje] {96} *vt* : to solidify — **se solidifier** *vr*

soliloque [sɔlilɔk] *nm* : soliloquy

soliste [sɔlist] *nmf* : soloist

solitaire[1] [sɔlitɛr] *adj* **1** SEUL : solitary, lonely **2** ISOLÉ : isolated

solitaire[2] *nmf* : loner, recluse

solitaire[3] *nm* : solitaire

solitude [sɔlityd] *nf* **1** : solitude **2** : loneliness

solive [sɔliv] *nf* : joist

sollicitation [sɔlisitasjɔ̃] *nf* : appeal, entreaty

solliciter [sɔlisite] *vt* **1** : to solicit, to seek (a favor, etc.) **2** : to appeal to, to approach

solliciteur, -teuse [sɔlisitœr] *nm* **1** : supplicant **2 solliciteur général** *Can* : attorney general

sollicitude [sɔlisityd] *nf* : solicitude, concern

solo[1] [sɔlo] *adj* : solo

solo[2] [sɔlo] *nm, pl* **solos** *or* **soli** : solo

solstice [sɔlstis] *nm* : solstice <solstice d'été : summer solstice>

soluble [sɔlybl] *adj* **1** : soluble **2** : solvable

solution [sɔlysjɔ̃] *nf* : solution

solutionner [sɔlysjɔne] *vt* : to solve

solvabilité [sɔlvabilite] *nf* : solvency

solvable [sɔlvabl] *adj* : solvent

solvant [sɔlvɑ̃] *nm* : solvent

somali, -lie [sɔmali] *adj* : somali

Somali, -lie *n* : Somali

somalien, -lienne [sɔmaljɛ̃, -ljɛn] *adj* : Somalian

Somalien, -lienne *n* : Somalian, Somali

sombre [sɔ̃br] *adj* **1** OBSCUR : dark **2** TRISTE : somber, gloomy — **sombrement** [sɔ̃brəmɑ̃] *adv*

sombrer [sɔ̃bre] *vi* **1** COULER : to sink **2** : to decline, to collapse, to fail

sommaire[1] [sɔmɛr] *adj* **1** COURT : brief **2** EXPÉDITIF : summary **3** RUDIMENTAIRE : rudimentary, superficial

sommaire[2] *nm* : summary

sommation [sɔmasjɔ̃] *nf* **1** : notice, summons (in law) **2** : warning <tirer sans sommation : to shoot without warning>

somme[1] [sɔm] *nf* **1** : sum **2 en somme** : on the whole, all in all

somme[2] *nm* : short nap, catnap

sommeil [sɔmɛj] *nm* : sleep <avoir sommeil : to be sleepy>

sommeiller [sɔmɛje] *vi* **1** SOMNOLER : to doze **2** : to lie dormant

sommelier, -lière [sɔməlje, -ljɛr] *n* : wine steward

sommer [sɔme] *vt* **1** : to summon **2** ENJOINDRE : to enjoin, to order <il m'a sommé de répondre : he commanded me to answer>

sommet [sɔmɛ] *nm* **1** CIME : summit, top, apex **2** : vertex (in geometry)

sommier [sɔmje] *nm* **1** : bed springs *pl*, box spring **2** : lintel, crossbar **3** *France* : register, (police) records *pl*

sommité [sɔmite] *nf* : leading figure, authority

somnambule [sɔmnɑ̃byl] *nmf* : sleepwalker

somnambulisme [sɔmnɑ̃bylism] *nm* : sleepwalking

somnifère [sɔmnifɛr] *nm* : sleeping pill

somnolence [sɔmnɔlɑ̃s] *nf* **1** : somnolence, drowsiness **2** LÉTHARGIE : lethargy

somnolent, -lente [sɔmnɔlɑ̃, -lɑ̃t] *adj* **1** : drowsy **2** LÉTHARGIQUE : lethargic

somnoler [sɔmnɔle] *vi* : to doze

somptueux, -tueuse [sɔ̃ptɥø, -tɥøz] *adj* : sumptuous, lavish

son[1], **sa** [sɔ̃, sa] *adj, pl* **ses** [se] : his, her, its, one's

son[2] *nm* **1** : sound <au son de : to the sound of> **2** : volume <monter le son : to turn up the volume> **3** : bran

sonar [sɔnar] *nm* : sonar

sonate [sɔnat] *nf* : sonata

sondage [sɔ̃daʒ] *nm* **1** ENQUÊTE : poll, survey **2** : probing, sounding

sonde [sɔ̃d] *nf* **1** : probe <sonde spatiale : space probe> **2** : sounding line **3** : catheter, probe (in medicine) **4** : drill (in geology, etc.)

sonder [sɔ̃de] *vt* **1** : to sound out, to survey, to poll **2** : to sound, to probe **3** : to drill (in geology)

songe [sɔ̃ʒ] *nm* RÊVE : dream

songer [sɔ̃ʒe] {17} *vt* : to consider, to imagine <avez-vous songé aux frais? : have you considered the costs?> — *vi* **1** : to dream **2 ~ à** : to think about, to contemplate, to consider

songeur, -geuse [sɔ̃ʒœr, -ʒøz] *adj* PENSIF : pensive

sonique [sɔnik] *adj* : sonic, sound

sonnant, -nante [sɔnɑ̃, -nɑ̃t] *adj* **à dix heures sonnantes** : at the stroke of ten

sonné, -née [sɔne] *adj* **1** : past <deux heures sonnées : past two o'clock> **2** *fam* : groggy **3** *fam* : crazy, nuts

sonner *v* **1** : to ring **2** : to strike, to sound

sonnerie [sɔnri] *nf* **1** : ringing, ring **2** : alarm (bell), chimes *pl* **3** : sounding, blare (of a trumpet, etc.)

sonnet [sɔnɛ] *nm* : sonnet

sonnette [sɔnɛt] *nf* : bell, doorbell, buzzer

sonore [sɔnɔr] *adj* **1** : sonorous, resonant **2** : sound <bande sonore : soundtrack> <effets sonores : sound effects> **3** : voiced (in linguistics)

sonorisation [sɔnɔrizasjɔ̃] *nf* : sound system, public address system

sonoriser [sɔnɔrize] *vt* **1** : to add sound to **2** : to install a sound system

sonorité [sɔnɔrite] *nf* **1** : sonority, tone **2** : resonance, acoustics

sophistication [sɔfistikasjɔ̃] *nf* : sophistication

sophistiqué, -quée [sɔfistike] *adj* : sophisticated

soporifique [sɔpɔrifik] *adj* : soporific

soprano [sɔprano] *nmf* : soprano

sorbet [sɔrbɛ] *nm* : sorbet, sherbet

sorcellerie [sɔrsɛlri] *nf* : sorcery, witchcraft

sorcier, -cière [sɔrsje, -sjɛr] *n* : sorcerer, wizard, witch

sordide [sɔrdid] *adj* **1** RÉPUGNANT : sordid **2** MISÉRABLE : squalid — **sordidement** [-didmɑ̃] *adv*

sorgho [sɔrgo] *nm* : sorghum

sornettes [sɔrnɛt] *nfpl* : nonsense

sort [sɔr] *nm* **1** : fate, lot, destiny **2** SORTILÈGE : spell, hex <jeter un sort à : to hex>

sortant, -tante [sɔrtɑ̃, -tɑ̃t] *adj* : outgoing, resigning <le président sortant : the outgoing president>

sorte [sɔrt] *nf* **1** ESPÈCE : sort, kind **2 de sorte à** : in order to **3 en aucune sorte** : not in the least **4 en quelque sorte** : somewhat, in a way

sortie [sɔrti] *nf* **1** : exit <sortie de secours : emergency exit> **2** DÉPART

: departure **3** : launch, release (of a film, book, etc.) **4** EXCURSION : outing **5** : sortie (of troops, etc.) **6** *fam* : quip, sally

sortilège [sɔrtilɛʒ] *nm* : spell, hex, enchantment

sortir[1] [sɔrtir] {82} *vt* **1** : to take out, to bring out **2** : to launch, to release, to issue — *vi* **1** : to go out, to come out, to open (of a film, etc.) **2** PARTIR : to leave, to exit **3 ~ de** : to come from, to come out of — **se sortir** *vr* **1 ~ de** : to get out of **2 s'en sortir** : to manage, to get by, to pull through (of an illness)

sortir[2] *nm* **au sortir de** : at the end of

sosie [sɔzi] *nm* : double

sot, sotte[1] [so, sɔt] *adj* RIDICULE : foolish, silly — **sottement** [sɔtmɑ̃] *adv*

sot, sotte[2] *n* : fool

sottise [sɔtiz] *nf* **1** : foolishness, stupidity **2** : foolish act or remark

sou [su] *nm* **1 sans le sou** : penniless **2 un sou de** : the least bit of <ils n'ont pas un sou de bon sens : they haven't an ounce of common sense>

soubassement [subasmɑ̃] *nm* : bedrock

soubresaut [subrəso] *nm* : jolt, start

souche [suʃ] *nf* **1** : stump (of a tree) **2** : stock, descent **3** : stub (of a check, etc.)

souci [susi] *nm* **1** INQUIÉTUDE : worry, care, concern **2** : marigold

soucier [susje] {96} *v* **se soucier** *vr* : to worry, to care

soucieux, -cieuse [susjø, -sjøz] *adj* : worried, concerned

soucoupe [sukup] *nf* **1** : saucer **2 soucoupe volante** : flying saucer

soudain[1] [sudɛ̃] *adv* SOUDAINEMENT : suddenly

soudain[2], **-daine** [sudɛ̃, -dɛn] *adj* : sudden — **soudainement** [-dɛnmɑ̃] *adv*

soudaineté [sudɛnte] *nf* : suddenness

soudanais, -naise [sudanɛ, -nɛz] *adj* : Sudanese

Soudanais, -naise *n* : Sudanese

soude [sud] *nf* : soda (in chemistry)

souder [sude] *vt* **1** : to weld, to solder **2** UNIR : to join, to bind

soudeur, -deuse [sudœr, -døz] *n* : welder

soudoyer [sudwaje] {58} *vt* : to bribe

soudure [sudyr] *nf* **1** : solder **2** : soldering, welding **3** : weld, joint

soue [su] *nf Can or* **soue à cochon** : sty, pigpen

souffert [sufɛr] *pp* → **souffrir**

souffle [sufl] *nm* **1** : breath <être à bout de souffle : to be out of breath> <second souffle : second wind> **2** RESPIRATION : breathing **3** : puff, gust, breath (of air) **4** INSPIRATION : inspiration

soufflé [sufle] *nm* : soufflé

souffler [sufle] *vt* **1** : to blow **2** : to blow out **3** CHUCHOTER : to whisper **4** : to blast, to blow down **5** *fam* : to take, to pinch **6 souffler son rôle à** : to prompt, to cue — *vi* **1** : to blow **2** : to pant, to puff

soufflet [suflɛ] *nm* **1** : bellows **2** GIFLE : slap **3** AFFRONT : insult, affront

souffleur, -fleuse [suflœr, -fløz] *n* **1** : glassblower **2** : prompter (in theater)

souffleuse *nf Can or* **souffleuse à neige** : snowblower

souffrance [sufrɑ̃s] *nf* **1** : suffering **2 en ~** : pending, awaiting

souffrant, -frante [sufrɑ̃, -frɑ̃t] *adj* **1** INDISPOSÉ : unwell **2** : suffering, miserable

souffreteux, -teuse [sufrətø, -tøz] *adj* : sickly

souffrir [sufrir] {83} *vt* **1** SUPPORTER : to tolerate, to stand, to put up with **2** PERMETTRE : to allow, to permit — *vi* : to suffer

soufre [sufr] *nm* : sulfur, brimstone

souhait [swɛ] *nm* **1** VOEU : wish **2 à vos souhaits!** : bless you!

souhaitable [swɛtabl] *adj* : desirable

souhaiter [swete] *vt* : to wish, to wish for, to hope for <souhaiter la bonne année à qqn : to wish s.o. Happy New Year>

souiller [suje] *vt* **1** SALIR : to soil **2** : to sully, to defile

souillure [sujyr] *nf* : stain, taint, blemish

soûl, soûle [su, sul] *adj fam* : drunk

soulagement [sulaʒmɑ̃] *nm* : relief

soulager [sulaʒe] {17} *vt* : to relieve — **se soulager** *vr*

soûler [sule] *vt* ENIVRER : to make drunk, to intoxicate — **se soûler** *vr* **1** : to get drunk **2 ~ de** : to be intoxicated with

soulèvement [sulɛvmɑ̃] *nm* **1** : uprising, upheaval (of the earth, etc.) **2** : insurrection, uprising

soulever [sulve] {52} *vt* **1** LEVER : to lift, to raise **2** PROVOQUER : to stir up, to arouse — **se soulever** *vr* **1** : to rise up **2** : to lift oneself up

soulier [sulje] *nm* : shoe

soulignement [suliɲmɑ̃] *nm* : underlining

souligner [suliɲe] *vt* **1** : to underline **2** : to emphasize

soumettre [sumɛtr] {53} *vt* **1** SUBJUGUER : to subjugate, to subdue **2** PRÉSENTER : to submit **3 ~ à** : to subject to — **se soumettre** *vr* : to submit, to give in

soumis, -mise [sumi, -miz] *adj* : submissive

soumission [sumisjɔ̃] *nf* **1** : submission, subjection **2** : bid

soumissionner [sumisjɔne] *vt* : to bid for

soupape [supap] *nf* : valve

soupçon [supsɔ̃] *nm* **1** : suspicion <au dessus de tout soupçon : above sus-

picion> 2 : drop, touch <un soupçon d'ironie : a hint of irony>
soupçonner [supsɔne] *vt* : to suspect
soupçonneux, -neuse [supsɔnø, -nøz] *adj* : suspicious — **soupçonneusement** [supsɔnøzmɑ̃] *adv*
soupe [sup] *nf* : soup <soupe à l'oignon : onion soup>
soupente [supɑ̃t] *nf* **1** : attic, garret **2** : closet (under the stairs)
souper[1] [supe] *vi Bel, Switz, Can* : to have supper
souper[2] *nm Bel, Switz, Can* : supper
soupeser [supəze] {52} *vt* **1** : to feel the weight of, to heft **2** PESER : to weigh, to consider
soupière [supjɛr] *nf* : tureen
soupir [supir] *nm* **1** : sigh **2** : quarter rest (in music)
soupirant [supirɑ̃] *nm* : suitor
soupirer [supire] *vi* **1** : to sigh **2 ~ après** *or* **~ pour** : to yearn for, to pine for
souple [supl] *adj* **1** : supple, flexible **2** : smooth, flowing — **souplement** [supləmɑ̃] *adv*
souplesse [suplɛs] *nf* : suppleness, flexibility
source [surs] *nf* **1** : source <tenir de bonne source : to have on good authority> **2** : spring, source (of waters) **3 sources** *nfpl* : headwaters
sourcil [sursi] *nm* **1** : eyebrow **2 froncer les sourcils** : to frown
sourciller [sursije] *vi* : to raise one's eyebrows, to react <sans sourciller : without batting an eye>
sourcilleux, -leuse [sursijø, -jøz] *adj* **1** HAUTAIN : haughty, supercilious **2** POINTILLEUX : finicky, fussy
sourd[1], **sourde** [sur, surd] *adj* **1** : deaf **2** : dull, muffled **3** : secret, clandestine **4** : voiceless <consonnes sourdes : voiceless consonants>
sourd[2], **sourde** *n* : deaf person
sourdine [surdin] *nf* **1** : mute (in music) <en sourdine : muted, quietly> **2 mettre une sourdine à** : to tone down
sourd–muet, sourde–muette [surmɥɛ, surdmɥɛt] *n* : deaf-mute
sourdre [surdr] {84} *vi* **1** : to rise, to seep up **2** MONTER : to well up
souriant, -riante [surjɑ̃, -rjɑ̃t] *adj* : smiling, cheerful
souricière [surisjɛr] *nf* : mousetrap
sourire[1] [surir] {76} *vi* **1** : to smile **2 ~ à** : to smile on, to be favorable to **3 ~ à** : to appeal to
sourire[2] *nm* : smile
souris [suri] *nf* : mouse
sournois[1], **-noise** [surnwa, -nwaz] *adj* **1** : sly, shifty **2** : underhanded, backhanded
sournois[2], **-noise** *n* : sly person, sneaky person
sournoisement [surnwazmɑ̃] *adv* : slyly, in an underhanded manner
sous [su] *prep* **1** : under, beneath **2** : within <sous huit jours : within a week> <sous peu : shortly> **3** : during <sous le règne de : during the reign of> **4** : under the effect of <sous anesthésie : under anesthesia> <sous la pression : under pressure>
sous–alimentation [suzalimɑ̃tasjɔ̃] *nf* : malnutrition
sous–alimenté, -tée [suzalimɑ̃te] *adj* : malnourished, undernourished
sous–bois [subwa] *nms & pl* : undergrowth, underbrush
sous–comité [sukɔmite] *nm, pl* **sous–comités** : subcommittee
souscripteur, -trice [suskriptœr] *n* : subscriber
souscription [suskripsjɔ̃] *nf* : subscription
souscrire [suskrir] {33} *vi* **~ à** : to subscribe to
sous–développé, -pée [sudevlɔpe] *adj* : underdeveloped
sous–développement [sudevlɔpmɑ̃] *nm, pl* **sous–développements** : underdevelopment
sous–entendre [suzɑ̃tɑ̃dr] {63} *vt* : to imply, to infer
sous–entendu [suzɑ̃tɑ̃dy] *nm, pl* **sous–entendus** : insinuation, innuendo
sous–estimer [suzɛstime] *vt* : to underestimate
sous–évaluer [suzevalɥe] *vt* : undervalue
sous–exposer [suzɛkspoze] *vt* : to underexpose (a photograph)
sous–jacent, -cente [suʒasɑ̃, -sɑ̃t] *adj* : underlying
sous–lieutenant [suljøtnɑ̃] *nm, pl* **sous–lieutenants** : second lieutenant
sous–louer [sulwe] *vt* : to sublet
sous–marin[1], **-rine** [sumarɛ̃, -rin] *adj* : underwater, submarine
sous–marin[2] *nm, pl* **sous–marins** : submarine
sous–officier [suzɔfisje] *nm, pl* **sous–officiers** : noncommissioned officer
sous–produit [suprɔdɥi] *nm, pl* **sous–produits** : by-product
sous–secrétaire [susəkretɛr] *nmf* : undersecretary
sous–sol [susɔl] *nm, pl* **sous–sols** : basement, cellar
sous–titre [sutitr] *nm, pl* **sous–titres** : subtitle
soustraction [sustraksjɔ̃] *nf* : subtraction
soustraire [sustrɛr] {40} *vt* **1** : to subtract **2** : to remove, to take away, to steal **3** : to shield, to hide (a person) — **se soustraire** *vr* **~ à** : to escape from, to evade
sous–traîter [sutrete] *vt* : to subcontract
sous–verre [suvɛr] *nms & pl Can* : coaster

sous–vêtement |suvɛtmɑ̃| *nm* **1** : undergarment **2 sous–vêtements** *nmpl* : underwear, underclothes

soutane |sutan| *nf* : cassock

soute |sut| *nf* : hold (of a ship)

soutenable |sutnabl| *adj* **1** DÉFENDABLE : defensible, supportable (of an argument, etc.) **2** SUPPORTABLE : bearable

soutènement |sutɛnmɑ̃| *nm* **mur de soutènement** : retaining wall

souteneur |sutnœr| *nm* : pimp

soutenir |sutnir| {92} *vt* **1** MAINTENIR : to support, to hold up **2** : to support, to back, to stand by **3** : to defend, to uphold <soutenir que : to maintain that> **4** : to sustain, to keep up **5** : to withstand, to bear — **se soutenir** *vr* **1** : to support each other **2** : to be defensible **3** : to hold oneself up

soutenu, -nue |sutny| *adj* **1** ÉLEVÉ : elevated, formal **2** : sustained, steady **3** VIF : bold, vivid (of colors)

souterrain[1], **-raine** |sutɛrɛ̃, -rɛn| *adj* **1** : underground, subterranean **2** : secret, hidden

souterrain[2] *nm* : underground passage

soutien |sutjɛ̃| *nm* **1** : support **2 soutien de famille** : breadwinner

soutien–gorge |sutjɛ̃gɔrʒ| *nm, pl* **soutiens–gorge** : bra, brassiere

soutirer |sutire| *vt* **∼ à** : to extract from, to squeeze out of

souvenir[1] |suvnir| {92} *v* **se souvenir** *vr* **1 ∼ de** : to remember **2 ∼ que** : to remember that — *v impers* **il me (lui, etc.) souvient** : I remember (he remembers, etc.)

souvenir[2] *nm* **1** : memory **2** : souvenir, memento **3** : regards, (good) wishes <mes meilleurs souvenirs à : my best regards to>

souvent |suvɑ̃| *adv* : often

souverain[1], **-raine** |suvrɛ̃, -rɛn| *adj* **1** SUPRÊME : supreme, superior <un remède souverain : an excellent remedy> **2** : sovereign <territoire souverain : sovereign territory>

souverain[2], **-raine** *n* : sovereign, monarch

souveraineté |suvrɛnte| *nf* : sovereignty

soviétique |sɔvjetik| *adj* : Soviet

soya |sɔja| → **soja**

soyeux, soyeuse |swajø, -jøz| *adj* : silky

spacieux, -cieuse |spasjø, -sjøz| *adj* : spacious

spaghetti |spagɛti| *nmpl* : spaghetti <boîte de spaghettis : box of spaghetti>

sparadrap |sparadra| *nm* : adhesive tape, adhesive bandage

spasme |spasm| *nm* : spasm — **spasmodique** |spasmɔdik| *adj*

spatial, -tiale |spasjal| *adj, mpl* **spatiaux 1** : spatial **2** : space <vaisseau spatial : spaceship>

spatule |spatyl| *nf* **1** : spatula **2** : tip (of a ski)

speaker[1], **-kerine** |spikœr, -krin| *n France* : announcer (on radio, TV, etc.)

speaker[2] *nm* **le Speaker** : the Speaker (of a legislative body)

spécial, -ciale |spesjal| *adj, mpl* **spéciaux** |-sjo| **1** : special **2** BIZARRE : odd, peculiar

spécialement |spesjalmɑ̃| *adv* **1** EXPRÈS : specially **2** TRÈS : especially, particularly

spécialiser |spesjalize| *v* **se spécialiser** *vr* : to specialize — **spécialisation** |-lizasjɔ̃| *nf*

spécialiste |spesjalist| *nmf* : specialist

spécialité |spesjalite| *nf* : specialty, field

spécieux, -cieuse |spesjø, -sjøz| *adj* : specious — **spécieusement** |-sjøzmɑ̃| *adv*

spécifier |spesifje| {96} *vt* : to specify — **spécification** |spesifikasjɔ̃| *nf*

spécifique |spesifik| *adj* : specific — **spécifiquement** |-fikmɑ̃| *adv*

spécimen |spesimɛn| *nm* **1** : specimen, example **2** : sample

spectacle |spɛktakl| *nm* **1** : spectacle, sight <se donner en spectacle : to make a spectacle of oneself> **2** REPRÉSENTATION : show, performance <spectacle somptueux : extravaganza> **3** : show businesss

spectaculaire |spɛktakylɛr| *adj* : spectacular

spectateur, -trice |spɛktatœr, -tris| *n* **1** : spectator, audience member **2** : observer, onlooker, bystander

spectre |spɛktr| *nm* **1** : specter, ghost **2** : spectrum

spéculateur, -trice |spekylatœr, -tris| *n* : speculator

spéculatif, -tive |spekylatif, -tiv| *adj* : speculative

spéculer |spekyle| *vi* : to speculate — **spéculation** |spekylasjɔ̃| *nf*

sperme |spɛrm| *nm* : sperm, semen

sphère |sfɛr| *nf* : sphere

sphérique |sferik| *adj* : spherical

spinal, -nale |spinal| *adj, mpl* **spinaux** |-no| : spinal

spiral, -rale |spiral| *adj, mpl* **spiraux** |-ro| : spiral

spirale *nf* : spiral

spire |spir| *nf* : whorl (of a shell)

spiritisme |spiritism| *nm* : spiritualism

spiritualité |spiritɥalite| *nf* : spirituality

spirituel, -tuelle |spiritɥɛl| *adj* **1** : spiritual **2** : witty — **spirituellement** |-tɥɛlmɑ̃| *adv*

spiritueux |spiritɥø| *nms & pl* : spirit <vins et spiritueux : wines and spirits>

spleen |splin| *nm* : spleen, melancholy

splendeur |splɑ̃dœr| *nf* MAGNIFICENCE : splendor, magnificence, glory

splendide [splɑ̃did] *adj* MAGNIFIQUE : splendid, magnificent — **splendidement** [-didmɑ̃] *adv*
spolier [spɔlje] {96} *vt* : to despoil
spongieux, -gieuse [spɔ̃ʒjø, -ʒjøz] *adj* : spongy
sponsor [spɔ̃sɔr] *nm* : sponsor
sponsoriser [spɔ̃sɔrize] *vt* : to sponsor
spontané, -née [spɔ̃tane] *adj* : spontaneous — **spontanément** [-nemɑ̃] *adv*
spontanéité [spɔ̃taneite] *nf* : spontaneity
sporadique [spɔradik] *adj* : sporadic — **sporadiquement** [-dikmɑ̃] *adv*
spore [spɔr] *nf* : spore
sport[1] [spɔr] *adj* **1** : sport, sports <vêtements sport : sport clothes> **2** SPORTIF : sporting
sport[2] *nm* : sport <sports d'équipe : team sports>
sportif[1], **-tive** [spɔrtif, -tiv] *adj* **1** : sport, sports <chroniqueur sportif : sportscaster> **2** : sporting, sportsmanlike **3** : athletic, sporty
sportif[2], **-tive** *n* : sportsman *m*, sportswoman *f*
sportivité [spɔrtivite] *nf* : sportsmanship
spot [spɔt] *nm* **1** : spotlight **2** PUBLICITÉ : spot, commercial
sprint [sprint] *nm* : sprint
sprinter [sprinte] *vi* : to sprint
square [skwar] *nm France* : small public garden
squash [skwaʃ] *nm* : squash (sport)
squatter[1] [skwate] *vt* : to squat in (land, a property, etc.)
squatter[2] [skwatœr] *nm* : squatter
squelette [skəlɛt] *nm* **1** : skeleton **2** : outline **3** : framework, skeleton (of a ship, etc.)
squelettique [skəletik] *adj* **1** : skeletal, scrawny **2** : sketchy, skimpy
sri lankais, -kaise [srilɑ̃kɛ, -kɛz] *adj* : Sri Lankan
Sri Lankais, -kaise *n* : Sri Lankan
stabilisateur[1], **-trice** [stabilizatœr, -tris] *adj* : stabilizing
stabilisateur[2] *nm* : stabilizer
stabiliser [stabilize] *vt* : to stabilize — **se stabiliser** *vr* **1** : to become stable **2** : to settle down
stabilité [stabilite] *nf* : stability
stable [stabl] *adj* : stable, steady
stade [stad] *nm* **1** : stadium **2** ÉTAPE : stage, phase
stage [staʒ] *nm* : training period, internship <faire un stage : to intern>
stagiaire [staʒjɛr] *nmf* : trainee, intern
stagnant, -nante [stagnɑ̃, -nɑ̃t] *adj* : stagnant
stagner [stagne] *vi* : to stagnate — **stagnation** [-gnasjɔ̃] *nf*
stalactite [stalaktit] *nf* : stalactite
stalagmite [stalagmit] *nf* : stalagmite
stalle [stal] *nf* : stall
stand [stɑ̃d] *nm* **1** : stand, stall **2 stand de tir** : shooting range
standard[1] [stɑ̃dar] *adj* : standard
standard[2] *nm* **1** : norm, standard **2** : (telephone) switchboard
standardiser [stɑ̃dardize] *vt* : to standardize
standardiste [stɑ̃dardist] *nmf* : switchboard operator, telephone operator
standing [stɑ̃diŋ] *nm* **1** : standing, status **2 de grand standing** : luxury
star [star] *nf* VEDETTE : star <star de cinéma : movie star>
starter [startɛr] *nm* **1** : choke (of an automobile) **2** : starter (in a race)
station [stasjɔ̃] *nf* **1** : station **2** : resort <station balnéaire : seaside resort> **3** : posture, position **4** : stop, pause
stationnaire [stasjɔnɛr] *adj* **1** : stationary **2** : stable (in medicine)
stationnement [stasjɔnmɑ̃] *nm* : parking <stationnement interdit : no parking>
stationner [stasjɔne] *vi* : to park
station–service [stasjɔ̃sɛrvis] *nf, pl* **stations–service** : gas station, service station
statique [statik] *adj* : static
statisticien, -cienne [statistisjɛ̃, -sjɛn] *n* : statistician
statistique[1] [statistik] *adj* : statistical
statistique[2] *nf* **1** : statistic **2** : statistics (field)
statue [staty] *nf* : statue
statuer [statɥe] *vi* : to decree, to ordain
statuette [statɥɛt] *nf* : statuette
statu quo [statykwo] *nm* : status quo
stature [statyr] *nf* : stature
statut [staty] *nm* **1** : statute **2** : status
statutaire [statytɛr] *adj* : statutory
steak [stɛk] *nm* : steak <steak haché : ground beef>
stellaire [stelɛr] *adj* : stellar
sténographe [stenɔgraf] *nmf* : stenographer
sténographie [stenɔgrafi] *nf* : stenography
steppe [stɛp] *nf* : steppe
stéréo [stereo] *adj & nf* : stereo
stéréophonique [stereɔfɔnik] *adj* : stereophonic
stéréotype [stereɔtip] *nm* **1** : stereotype **2** : cliché
stéréotypé, -pée [stereɔtipe] *adj* : stereotyped, stereotypical
stérile [steril] *adj* : sterile
stériliser [sterilize] *vt* : to sterilize — **stérilisation** [-lizasjɔ̃] *nf*
stérilité [sterilite] *nf* : sterility
sterne [stɛrn] *nf* : tern
sternum [stɛrnɔm] *nm* : sternum, breastbone
stéthoscope [stetɔskɔp] *nm* : stethoscope
stigmate [stigmat] *nm* : stigma
stigmatiser [stigmatize] *vt* : to stigmatize — **stigmatisation** [-tizasjɔ̃] *nf*
stimulant[1], **-lante** [stimylɑ̃, -lɑ̃t] *adj* : stimulating

stimulant[2] *nm* **1** : stimulant **2** : stimulus

stimulateur [stimylatœr] *nm* : stimulator (in medicine) <stimulateur cardiaque : pacemaker>

stimuler [stimyle] *vt* : to stimulate — **stimulation** [-mylasjɔ̃] *nf*

stipuler [stipyle] *vt* : to stipulate — **stipulation** [-pylasjɔ̃] *nf*

stock [stɔk] *nm* : stock (of merchandise) <en stock : in stock>

stockage [stɔkaʒ] *nm* : storage (of data)

stocker [stɔke] *vt* : to stock, to store

stoïcisme [stɔisizm] *nm* : stoicism

stoïque[1] [stɔik] *adj* : stoic, stoical — **stoïquement** [-ikmɑ̃] *adv*

stoïque[2] *nmf* : stoic

stolon [stɔlɔ̃] *nm* : runner (of a plant)

stop[1] [stɔp] *nm* **1** : stop sign **2** : brake light

stop[2] *interj* : stop

stopper [stɔpe] *vt* **1** ARRÊTER : to stop, to halt **2** RÉPARER : to mend — *vi* : to stop

store [stɔr] *nm* **1** : awning **2** : blind, window shade <store vénitien : venetian blind>

strabisme [strabism] *nm* : squint

strangulation [strɑ̃gylasjɔ̃] *nf* : strangulation

strapontin [strapɔ̃tɛ̃] *nm* : folding seat, jump seat

stratagème [strataʒɛm] *nm* : stratagem

strate [strat] *nf* : stratum

stratégie [strateʒi] *nf* : strategy

stratégique [strateʒik] *adj* : strategic — **stratégiquement** [-ʒikmɑ̃] *adv*

stratifié, -fiée [stratifje] *adj* : laminated, stratified

stratosphère [stratɔsfɛr] *nf* : stratosphere

stress [strɛs] *nms & pl* : stress

stressant, -sante [strɛsɑ̃, -sɑ̃t] *adj* : stressful

stresser [strɛse] *vt* : to put under stress

strict, stricte [strikt] *adj* **1** : strict **2** : austere, severe, plain — **strictement** [striktəmɑ̃] *adv*

strident, -dente [stridɑ̃, -dɑ̃t] *adj* : strident, shrill

strier [strije] {96} *vt* **1** : to streak **2** : to groove

strophe [strɔf] *nf* : stanza

structural, -rale [stryktyral] *adj, mpl* **-raux** [-ro] : structural — **structuralement** [-ralmɑ̃] *adv*

structure [stryktyr] *nf* : structure

structurer [stryktyre] *vt* : to structure, to organize — **se structurer** *vr* : to be structured, to take shape

stuc [styk] *nm* : stucco

studieux, -dieuse [stydjø, -djøz] *adj* : studious — **studieusement** [-djøzmɑ̃] *adv*

studio [stydjo] *nm* **1** : studio **2** : studio apartment

stupéfaction [stypefaksjɔ̃] *nf* ÉTONNEMENT : stupefaction, astonishment

stupéfaire [stypefɛr] {85} *vt* : to amaze, to astonish

stupéfait, -faite [stypefɛ, -fɛt] *adj* ÉTONNÉ : amazed, astounded

stupéfiant[1], **-fiante** [stypefjɑ̃, -fjɑ̃t] *adj* ÉTONNANT : amazing, astounding

stupéfiant[2] *nm* : drug, narcotic

stupéfié [stypefje] *pp* → **stupéfaire**

stupéfier [stypefje] {96} *vt* **1** : to astonish, to stun **2** : to stupefy (in medicine)

stupeur [stypœr] *nf* **1** ÉTONNEMENT : astonishment, amazement **2** HÉBÉTUDE : stupor

stupide [stypid] *adj* : stupid — **stupidement** [-pidmɑ̃] *adv*

stupidité [stypidite] *nf* : stupidity

style [stil] *nm* **1** : style <style de vie : lifestyle> <style gothique : Gothic style> **2** : speech form <style direct : direct speech> **3** : stylus

stylet [stilɛ] *nm* : stiletto

styliser [stilize] *vt* : to stylize

stylo [stilo] *nm* : pen <stylo à bille : ballpoint pen>

stylo–feutre [stiloføtr] *nm, pl* **stylos–feutres** : felt-tip pen, marker

su [sy] *pp* → **savoir**

suave [sɥav] *adj* **1** : sweet (of odors) **2** : smooth, mellow **3** : suave, sophisticated

suavement [sɥavmɑ̃] *adv* : sweetly

suavité [sɥavite] *nf* **1** : sweetness **2** : smoothness

subalterne [sybaltɛrn] *adj & nmf* : subordinate

subconscient[1], **-ciente** [sybkɔ̃sjɑ̃, -sjɑ̃t] *adj* : subconscious

subconscient[2] *nm* : subconscious

subdiviser [sybdivize] *vt* : to subdivide — **subdivision** [-vizjɔ̃] *nf*

subir [sybir] *vt* **1** : to undergo **2** : to suffer, to sustain <subir des pertes : to suffer losses> **3** : to be under, to come under <subir l'influence de : to come under the influence of> **4 faire subir à** : to inflict on

subit, -bite [sybi, -bit] *adj* : sudden — **subitement** [-bitmɑ̃] *adv*

subjectif, -tive [sybʒɛktif, -tiv] *adj* : subjective

subjectivité [sybʒɛktivite] *nf* : subjectivity

subjonctif [sybʒɔ̃ktif] *nm* : subjunctive

subjuguer [sybʒuge] *vt* **1** : to captivate **2** : to subjugate

sublime [syblim] *adj* : sublime

sublimer [syblime] *v* : to sublimate

submerger [sybmɛrʒe] {17} *vt* **1** : to submerge **2** : to overwhelm, to engulf, to swamp

submersible [sybmɛrsibl] *adj & nm* : submersible

submersion [sybmɛrsjɔ̃] *nf* : submersion

subordination [sybɔrdinasjɔ̃] *nf* : subordination

subordonné, -née [sybɔrdɔne] *adj & n* : subordinate

subordonner [sybɔrdɔne] *vt* : to subordinate

suborner [syborne] *vt* : to bribe (a witness)

subreptice [sybrɛptis] *adj* : surreptitious — **subrepticement** [-tismɑ̃] *adv*

subséquent, -quente [sybsekɑ̃, -kɑ̃t] *adj* : subsequent

subside [sypsid] *nm* : grant, subsidy

subsidiaire [sybzidjɛr] *adj* : subsidiary

subsistance [sybzistɑ̃s] *nf* : subsistence

subsister [sybziste] *vi* **1** SURVIVRE : to subsist, to survive (on) **2** RESTER : to remain

substance [sypstɑ̃s] *nf* : substance

substantiel, -tielle [sypstɑ̃sjɛl] *adj* : substantial

substantif [sypstɑ̃tif] *nm* : substantive, noun

substituer [sypstitɥe] *vt* : to substitute — **se substituer** *vr* **~ à** : to substitute for

substitut [sypstity] *nm* : substitute

substitution [sypstitysjɔ̃] *nf* : substitution

subterfuge [syptɛrfyʒ] *nm* : subterfuge, ploy

subtil, -tile [syptil] *adj* : subtle — **subtilement** [-tilmɑ̃] *adv*

subtiliser [syptilize] *vt fam* : to steal, to pinch

subtilité [syptilite] *nf* : subtlety

subvenir [sybvənir] {92} *vi* **~ à** : to provide for (a family), to meet (expenses, etc.)

subvention [sybvɑ̃sjɔ̃] *nf* SUBSIDE : subsidy

subventionner [sybvɑ̃sjɔne] *vt* : to subsidize

subversif, -sive [sybvɛrsif, -siv] *adj* : subversive

subversion [sybvɛrsjɔ̃] *nf* : subversion

suc [syk] *nm* **1** JUS : juice **2** SÈVE : sap **3** : pith, substance

succédané [syksedane] *nm* : substitute (for a medication, food product, etc.) <succédané de sucre : sugar substitute>

succéder [syksede] {87} *vi* **~ à** : to succeed, to follow — **se succéder** *vr*

succès [syksɛ] *nm* : success <avoir du succès : to be successful>

successeur [syksesœr] *nm* : successor

successif, -sive [syksesif, -siv] *adj* : successive — **successivement** [-sivmɑ̃] *adv*

succession [syksesjɔ̃] *nf* : succession

succinct, -cincte [syksɛ̃, -sɛ̃t] *adj* : succinct — **succinctement** [-sɛ̃tmɑ̃] *adv*

succion [syksjɔ̃, sysjɔ̃] *nf* : suction, sucking

succomber [sykɔ̃be] *vi* **1** : to die **2** : to collapse, to give way **3 ~ à** : to succumb to

succulent, -lente [sykylɑ̃, -lɑ̃t] *adj* : succulent

succursale [sykyrsal] *nf* : branch (of a bank, store, etc.)

sucer [syse] {6} *vt* : to suck

sucette [sysɛt] *nf* **1** : lollipop **2** : pacifier

suçon [sysɔ̃] *nm Can* : lollipop

sucre [sykr] *nm* : sugar <sucre en poudre : powdered sugar> <sucre d'érable : maple sugar>

sucré, -crée [sykre] *adj* **1** : sweet, sweetened **2** : sugary, honeyed (of speech, etc.)

sucrer [sykre] *vt* : to sweeten, to add sugar to

sucrerie [sykrəri] *nf* **1** : sugar refinery **2** *Can* : sugar-maple forest **3 sucreries** *nfpl* : sweets, candy

sucrier[1], -crière [sykrije, -krijɛr] *adj* : sugar <la production sucrière : sugar production>

sucrier[2] *nm* : sugar bowl

sud[1] [syd] *adj* : south, southern, southerly

sud[2] *nm* **1** : south <au sud de Montréal : south of Montreal> <exposé au sud : with a southerly aspect> <vent du sud : south wind> **2 le Sud** : the South

sud–africain, -caine [sydafrikɛ̃, -kɛn] *adj* : South African

Sud–Africain, -caine *n* : South African

sud–américain, -caine [sydamerikɛ̃, -kɛn] *adj* : South American

Sud–Américain, -caine *n* : South American

sud–est[1] [sydɛst] *adj s & pl* : southeast, southeastern

sud–est[2] *nm* : southeast

sud–ouest[1] [sydwɛst] *adj s & pl* : southwest, southwestern

sud–ouest[2] *nm* : southwest

suède [sɥɛd] *nm* : suede

suédois[1], -doise [sɥedwa, -dwaz] *adj* : Swedish

suédois[2] *nm* : Swedish (language)

Suédois, -doise *n* : Swede

suer [sɥe] *vi* : to sweat — *vt* **1** : to sweat, to ooze **2** : to exude

sueur [sɥœr] *nf* : sweat

suffire [syfir] {86} *vi* : to suffice, to be enough <ça suffit! : that's enough!> — **se suffire** *vr or* **se suffire à soi–même** : to be self-sufficient

suffisais [syfizɛ], **suffisions** [syfizjɔ̃], *etc.* → **suffire**

suffisamment [syfizamɑ̃] *adv* : sufficiently, enough

suffisance [syfizɑ̃s] *nf* **1** : self-importance, conceit **2 en ~** : sufficient

suffisant, -sante [syfizɑ̃, -zɑ̃t] *adj* **1** ADÉQUAT : sufficient, adequate **2** VANITEUX : self-important, conceited

suffise [syfiz], *etc.* → **suffire**

suffixe [syfiks] *nm* : suffix

suffocant, -cante [syfɔkɑ̃, -kɑ̃t] *adj* : suffocating
suffocation [syfɔkasjɔ̃] *nf* : suffocation
suffoquer [syfɔke] *vt* **1** ÉTOUFFER : to suffocate, to choke **2** : to stagger, to stun — *vi* S'ÉTOUFFER : to suffocate
suffrage [syfraʒ] *nm* : suffrage, vote
suggérer [sygʒere] {86} *vt* : to suggest
suggestible [sygʒɛstibl] *adj* : suggestible
suggestif, -tive [sygʒɛstif, -tiv] *adj* : suggestive
suggestion [sygʒɛstjɔ̃] *nf* : suggestion <faire une suggestion : to suggest>
suicidaire [sɥisidɛr] *adj* : suicidal
suicide [sɥisid] *nm* : suicide
suicidé, -dée [sɥiside] *n* : suicide
suicider *v* **se suicider** *vr* : to commit suicide
suie [sɥi] *nf* : soot
suif [sɥif] *nm* **1** : tallow **2** : suet
suintement [sɥɛ̃tmɑ̃] *nm* : seepage
suinter [sɥɛ̃te] *vi* : to ooze, to seep
suisse[1] [sɥis] *adj* : Swiss
suisse[2] *nm Can* : chipmunk
Suisse *nmf* : Swiss
suit [sɥi], *etc.* → **suivre**
suite [sɥit] *nf* **1** : suite **2** CONTINUATION : continuation, rest <sans suite : disconnected, discontinuous> **3** SÉRIE : series, sequence <à la suite : one after another> **4** CONSÉQUENCE : consequence, result <donner suite à : to follow up> **5 par la suite** : later, afterwards **6 par ~** : therefore, consequently **7 par suite de** : due to, as a result of
suivant[1], **-vante** [sɥivɑ̃, -vɑ̃t] *adj* : following, next
suivant[2], **-vante** *n* : next one, following one <au suite! : next!>
suivant[3] *prep* **1** SELON : according to **2** : along, in the direction of **3** : depending on
suivi[1], **-vie** [sɥivi] *adj* **1** RÉGULIER : regular, steady **2** COHÉRENT : coherent
suivi[2] *nm* : follow-up
suivre [sɥivr] {88} *vt* **1** : to follow **2** : to take (a course) **3** : to keep up with — *vi* **1** : to follow **2** : to pay attention, to keep up **3 faire suivre** : to forward (mail) — **se suivre** *vr* **1** : to follow one another **2** : to be in (the right) order **3** : to be coherent
sujet[1], **-jette** [syʒɛ, -ʒɛt] *adj* **~ à** : subject to, prone to
sujet[2], **-jette** *n* : subject (of a state or country)
sujet[3] *nm* **1** : subject, topic **2** RAISON : cause
sujétion [syʒesjɔ̃] *nf* **1** SOUMISSION : subjection **2** CONTRAINTE : constraint
sulfureux, -reuse [sylfyrø, -røz] *adj* : sulfurous
sulfurique [sylfyrik] *adj* **acide sulfurique** : sulfuric acid
sultan [syltɑ̃] *nm* : sultan
sumac [symak] *nm* **1** : sumac **2 sumac vénéneux** : poison ivy
summum [sɔmɔm] *nm* : height, peak, acme
sundae [sɔnde] *nm Can* : sundae
super [sypɛr] *adj s & pl fam* EXTRA : super, great
superbe[1] [sypɛrb] *adj* : superb — **superbement** [-pɛrbəmɑ̃] *adv*
superbe[2] *nm* : arrogance, pride
supercherie [sypɛrʃəri] *nf* : deception, fraud
superficialité [sypɛrfisjalite] *nf* : superficiality
superficie [sypɛrfisi] *nf* : area, surface
superficiel, -cielle [sypɛrfisjɛl] *adj* : superficial
superflu[1], **-flue** [sypɛrfly] *adj* : superfluous
superflu[2] *nm* : superfluity
supérieur[1], **-rieure** [syperjœr] *adj* **1** : superior **2** : upper <coin gauche supérieur : upper left-hand corner> **3** : higher <à un taux supérieur : at a higher rate>
supérieur[2], **-rieure** *n* : superior
supérieurement [syperjœrmɑ̃] *adv* : exceptionally
supériorité [syperjɔrite] *nf* : superiority
superlatif[1], **-tive** [sypɛrlatif, -tiv] *adj* : superlative
superlatif[2] *nm* : superlative
supermarché [sypɛrmarʃe] *nm* : supermarket
superposer [sypɛrpoze] *vt* **1** : to stack **2** : to superimpose
superpuissance [sypɛrpɥisɑ̃s] *nf* : superpower
supersonique [sypɛrsɔnik] *adj* : supersonic
superstitieux, -tieuse [sypɛrstisjø, -sjøz] *adj* : superstitious — **superstitieusement** [-sjøzmɑ̃] *adv*
superstition [sypɛrstisjɔ̃] *nf* : superstition
superstructure [sypɛrstryktyr] *nf* : superstructure
superviser [sypɛrvize] *vt* : to supervise — **supervision** [-vizjɔ̃] *nf*
superviseur [sypɛrvizœr] *nm* : supervisor
supplanter [syplɑ̃te] *vt* : to supplant
suppléant, -pléante [sypleɑ̃, -pleɑ̃t] *adj & n* : substitute, replacement, alternate
suppléer [syplee] {89} *vt* **1** REMPLACER : to replace, to fill in for **2** COMPENSER : to make up for, to compensate for — *vi* **~ à** : to make up for, to compensate for
supplément [syplemɑ̃] *nm* **1** : supplement **2** : extra charge, extra amount
supplémentaire [syplemɑ̃tɛr] *adj* **1** : additional, extra, supplementary **2** → **heure**
supplication [syplikasjɔ̃] *nf* : supplication, entreaty

supplice [syplis] *nm* **1** TORTURE : torture **2 être au supplice** : to be in agony
supplicier [syplisje] {96} *vt* TORTURER : to torture
supplier [syplije] {96} *vt* : to supplicate, to implore, to beg
support [sypɔr] *nm* **1** ÉTAI : support, stay, prop **2** : medium <support publicitaire : advertising medium>
supportable [sypɔrtabl] *adj* : bearable, tolerable
supporter[1] [sypɔrte] *vt* **1** SOUTENIR : to support, to hold up **2** ENDURER : to tolerate, to bear, to endure **3** : to stand up to, to withstand — **se supporter** *vr* **1** : to be bearable **2** : to stand each other
supporter[2] [sypɔrtɛr] *nm* : supporter, fan (in sports, etc.)
supposer [sypoze] *vt* **1** IMAGINER : to suppose, to assume **2** IMPLIQUER : to imply, to presuppose
supposition [sypozisjɔ̃] *nf* : supposition, assumption
suppositoire [sypozitwar] *nm* : suppository
suppôt [sypo] *nm* : henchman <suppôt de Satan : fiend>
suppression [sypresjɔ̃] *nf* **1** : abolition, elimination, suppression **2** : deletion (from a text)
supprimer [syprime] *vt* **1** : to abolish, to eliminate, to suppress **2** : to take out, to delete
suppurer [sypyre] *vi* : to suppurate, to fester
supputer [sypyte] *vt* : to compute, to calculate — **supputation** [-pytasjɔ̃] *nf*
suprématie [sypremasi] *nf* : supremacy
suprême [syprɛm] *adj* : supreme — **suprêmement** [-prɛmmɑ̃] *adv*
sur[1] [syr] *prep* **1** : on, upon, in <sur la table : on the table> <sur la photo : in the photo> **2** : over, above <sur les montagnes : over the mountains> **3** : about, on <un essai sur l'histoire : an essay about history> **4** VERS : towards <sur mon quatre-vingtième an : towards my eightieth year> **5** PARMI : out of <quatre sur cinq : four out of five> **6** : by <cinq mètres sur trois : five by three meters> **7 sur ce** : whereupon, upon which, hereon
sur[2], **sure** [syr] *adj* : sour
sûr, sûre [syr] *adj* **1** CERTAIN : sure, certain **2** FIABLE : reliable, trustworthy **3** : safe, secure **4** : sound <jugement sûr : sound judgment> — **sûrement** [syrmɑ̃] *adv*
surabondant, -dante [syrabɔ̃dɑ̃, -dɑ̃t] *adj* : overabundant — **surabondance** [-bɔ̃dɑ̃s] *nf*
suralimenter [syralimɑ̃te] *vt* : to overfeed
suranné, -née [syrane] *adj* : outdated, old-fashioned
surcharge [syrʃarʒe] *nf* **1** : extra load, overload **2** : correction, alteration **3** : surcharge
surcharger [syrʃarʒe] {17} *vt* **1** : to overload, to overburden **2** : to correct, to alter **3** : to impose a surcharge
surchauffer [syrʃofe] *vt* : to overheat
surclasser [syrklase] *vt* : to outclass
surcroît [syrkrwa] *nm* **1** : increase <un surcroît de travail : extra work> **2 de ～** *or* **par ～** : in addition, moreover **3 en ～** : in addition
surdité [syrdite] *nf* : deafness
surdose [syrdoz] *nf* : overdose
surdoué, -douée [syrdwe] *adj* : extremely intelligent, gifted
sureau [syro] *nm, pl* **sureaux** : elder (tree)
surélever [syrelve] {52} *vt* : to raise, to heighten
surenchère [syrɑ̃ʃɛr] *nf* **1** : higher bid **2** : exaggeration, overstatement
surenchérir [syrɑ̃ʃerir] *vi* **1** : to bid higher **2 ～ sur** : to outbid, to go one better than
surestimer [syrɛstime] *vt* : to overestimate, to overrate
sûreté [syrte] *nf* **1** SÉCURITÉ : safety, security **2** : soundness, steadiness, reliability **3** : surety, guarantee (in law) **4** : safety catch, safety lock
surexcité, -tée [syrɛksite] *adj* : overexcited
surexposer [syrɛkspoze] *vt* : to overexpose
surf [sœrf] *nm* : surfing, surfboarding
surface [syrfas] *nf* **1** : surface <faire surface : to surface> <en surface : on the surface, aboveground> **2 de ～** : superficial
surfait, -faite [syrfɛ, -fɛt] *adj* : overrated
surgelé [syrʒəle] *nm* : frozen food
surgeler [syrʒəle] {20} *vt* : to quick-freeze
surgir [syrʒir] *vi* **1** : to appear suddenly, to loom up **2** : to come up, to arise
surhumain, -maine [syrymɛ̃, -mɛn] *adj* : superhuman
surinamien, -mienne [syrinamjɛ̃, -mjɛn] *adj* : Surinamese
Surinamien, -mienne *n* : Surinamese
sur-le-champ [syrləʃɑ̃] *adv* : immediately, at once
surlendemain [syrlɑ̃dmɛ̃] *nm* **le surlendemain** : two days later
surmener [syrməne] {52} *vt* : to overwork — **se surmener** *vr* : to overwork, to work too hard
surmonter [syrmɔ̃te] *vt* **1** : to overcome, to surmount **2** : to top, to crown (a building, etc.)
surnager [syrnaʒe] {17} *vi* **1** FLOTTER : to float **2** PERSISTER : to persist, to linger on
surnaturel[1], **-relle** [syrnatyrɛl] *adj* : supernatural

surnaturel[2] *nm* **le surnaturel** : the supernatural

surnom [syrnɔ̃] *nm* SOBRIQUET : nickname

surnombre [syrnɔ̃br] *nm* **en ~** : excess, surplus <trois copies en surnombre : three too many copies>

surnommer [syrnɔme] *vt* : to nickname, to call

surpasser [syrpase] *vt* : to surpass, to outdo — **se surpasser** *vr*

surpeuplé, -plée [syrpœple] *adj* : overpopulated

surpeuplement [syrpœpləmɑ̃] *nm* : overpopulation

surplis [syrpli] *nm* : surplice

surplomb [syrplɔ̃] *nm* : overhang <en surplomb : overhanging>

surplomber [syrplɔ̃be] *v* : to overhang

surplus [syrply] *nm* **1** : surplus **2 au surplus** : moreover

surpopulation [syrpɔpylasjɔ̃] *nf* : overpopulation

surprenant, -nante [syrprənɑ̃, -nɑ̃t] *adj* : surprising, amazing

surprendre [syrprɑ̃dr] {70} *vt* **1** ÉTONNER : to surprise, to amaze **2** : to take by surprise, to catch in the act **3** : to overhear, to intercept

surprise [syrpriz] *nf* : surprise <avoir la bonne surprise : to be pleasantly surprised> <par surprise : by surprise>

surproduction [syrprɔdyksjɔ̃] *nf* : overproduction

surréalisme [syrrealism] *nm* : surrealism — **surréaliste** [-alist] *adj & nmf*

sursaut [syrso] *nm* **1** : start, jump <en sursaut : with a start> **2** : burst <un sursaut d'énergie : a burst of energy>

sursauter [syrsote] *vi* : to start, to jump

surseoir [syrswar] {90} *vi* **~ à** : to postpone, to defer

sursis[1] [syrsi] *pp* → **surseoir**

sursis[2] [syrsi] *nm* **1** : reprieve <condamné avec sursis : given a suspended sentence> **2** : respite, deferment, extension **3 être un mort en sursis** : to live on borrowed time

surtaxe [syrtaks] *nf* : surcharge

surtension [syrtɑ̃sjɔ̃] *nf* : surge (of electricity)

surtout[1] [syrtu] *adv* **1** : above all <surtout, pas de peur : above all, don't be afraid> **2** : especially, particularly <j'aime surtout la poésie : I especially like poetry>

surtout[2] *nm* : centerpiece

surveillance [syrvɛjɑ̃s] *nf* : surveillance, supervision <en surveillance médicale : under medical supervision>

surveillant, -lante [syrvɛjɑ̃, -jɑ̃t] *n* **1** : supervisor, overseer **2 surveillant de baignade** : lifeguard **3 surveillant de prison** : prison warden

surveiller [syrvɛje] *vt* **1** : to watch (over), to keep an eye on **2** : to supervise, to oversee

survenir [syrvənir] {92} *vi* **1** : to occur, to take place **2** : to arrive (unexpectedly)

survie [syrvi] *nf* **1** : survival (of a person) **2** : afterlife

survivance [syrvivɑ̃s] *nf* : survival

survivant, -vante [syrvivɑ̃, -vɑ̃t] *n* : survivor

survivre [syrvivr] {98} *vi* **1** : to survive **2 ~ à** : to survive, to outlive, to outlast

survol [syrvɔl] *nm* **1** : flying over **2** : quick look, overview

survoler [syrvɔle] *vi* **1** : to fly over **2** : to skim through

survolté, -tée [syrvɔlte] *adj* **1** : boosted (of an electronic circuit) **2** : overexcited

sus [sy(s)] *adv* **1 en ~** : extra **2 en sus de** : in addition to, on top of

susceptibilité [sysɛptibilite] *nf* : sensitivity, touchiness

susceptible [sysɛptibl] *adj* **1** : sensitive, touchy **2 ~ de** : likely to, capable of

susciter [sysite] *vt* **1** ÉVEILLER : to arouse (interest, feeling, etc.) **2** CRÉER : to create, to give rise to (problems, obstacles, etc.)

susmentionné, -née [sysmɑ̃sjɔne] *adj* : aforesaid, aforementioned

suspect[1]**, -pecte** [syspɛ, -pɛkt] *adj* : suspicious, suspect

suspect[2]**, -pecte** *n* : suspect

suspecter [syspɛkte] *vt* : to suspect

suspendre [syspɑ̃dr] {63} *vt* **1** : to suspend, to break off **2** PENDRE : to hang, to hang up — **se suspendre** *vr* **~ à** : to hang from

suspens [syspɑ̃] *nm* **1 en ~** : unresolved, uncertain **2 tenir en suspens** : to keep in suspense

suspense [syspɑ̃s] *nm* : suspense

suspension [syspɑ̃sjɔ̃] *nf* **1** : suspension **2 en ~** : suspended, hanging

suspicieux, -cieuse [syspisjø, -sjøz] *adj* : suspicious

suspicion [syspisjɔ̃] *nf* : suspicion

susurrer [sysyre] *v* CHUCHOTER : whisper

suture [sytyr] *nf* **1** : suture **2 point de suture** : stitch

suturer [sytyre] *vt* : to suture, to stitch

suzerain [syzrɛ̃] *nm* : liege, (feudal) lord

svelte [zvɛlt] *adj* : slender, svelte

sycomore [sikɔmɔr] *nm* : sycamore

syllabe [silab] *nf* : syllable — **syllabique** [-labik] *adj*

sylvestre [silvɛstr] *adj* : sylvan, forest

sylviculture [silvikyltyr] *nf* : forestry

symbole [sɛ̃bɔl] *nm* **1** : symbol **2** : creed <le Symbole des Apôtres : the Apostle's Creed>

symbolique [sɛ̃bɔlik] *adj* : symbolic — **symboliquement** [-likmɑ̃] *adv*

symboliser [sɛ̃bɔlize] *vt* : to symbolize

symbolisme [sɛ̃bɔlism] *nm* : symbolism

symétrie [simetri] *nf* : symmetry
symétrique [simetrik] *adj* : symmetrical, symmetric — **symétriquement** [-trikmɑ̃] *adv*
sympa [sɛ̃pa] *adj fam* : friendly, nice
sympathie [sɛ̃pati] *nf* **1** : liking, affection, fellow feeling **2** CONDOLÉANCES : condolences, sympathy
sympathique [sɛ̃patik] *adj* **1** AIMABLE : nice, likeable, pleasant **2** : sympathetic (in medicine)
sympathisant, -sante [sɛ̃patizɑ̃, -zɑ̃t] *n* : sympathizer
sympathiser [sɛ̃patize] *vi* : to get along <sympathiser avec qqn : to get on well with s.o.>
symphonie [sɛ̃fɔni] *nf* : symphony
symphonique [sɛ̃fɔnik] *adj* : symphonic
symptomatique [sɛ̃ptɔmatik] *adj* : symptomatic
symptôme [sɛ̃ptom] *nm* : symptom
synagogue [sinagɔg] *nf* : synagogue
synchroniser [sɛ̃krɔnize] *vt* : to synchronize
syncope [sɛ̃kɔp] *nf* **1** : faint, blackout **2** : syncopation
syncopé, -pée [sɛ̃kɔpe] *adj* : syncopated
syndicaliser [sɛ̃dikalize] *vt* : to unionize — **se syndicaliser** *vr*
syndicat [sɛ̃dika] *nm* : union, labor union
syndiquer [sɛ̃dike] *vt* : to unionize — **se syndiquer** *vr* : to join a union
syndrome [sɛ̃drom] *nm* : syndrome
synonyme[1] [sinɔnim] *adj* : synonymous
synonyme[2] *nm* : synonym
synopsis [sinɔpsis] *nf* : synopsis
syntaxe [sɛ̃taks] *nf* : syntax
synthèse [sɛ̃tɛz] *nf* : synthesis
synthétique [sɛ̃tetik] *adj* : synthetic — **synthétiquement** [-tikmɑ̃] *adv*
synthétiser [sɛ̃tetize] *vt* : to synthesize
syphilis [sifilis] *nf* : syphilis
syrien, -rienne [sirjɛ̃, -rjɛn] *adj* : Syrian
Syrien, -rienne *n* : Syrian
systématique [sistematik] *adj* : systematic — **systématiquement** [-tikmɑ̃] *adv*
systématiser [sistematize] *vt* : to systematize
système [sistɛm] *nm* : system <système métrique : metric system> <système solaire : solar system>
systémique [sistemik] *adj* : systemic

T

t [te] *nm* : t, the 20th letter of the alphabet
tabac [taba] *nm* **1** : tobacco **2 tabac à priser** : snuff **3** *France* : tobacco shop **4 c'est toujours le même tabac** *fam* : it's always the same old thing
tabagie [tabaʒi] *nf* **1** smoke-filled place **2** : *Can* : tobacco shop
tabasser [tabase] *vt fam* : to beat up, to clobber
tabatière [tabatjɛr] *nf* **1** : snuffbox **2** : skylight
tabernacle [tabɛrnakl] *nm* : tabernacle
table [tabl] *nf* **1** : table <mettre la table : to set the table> <se mettre à table : to sit down to eat> **2** : table, list <table des matières : table of contents> <table de multiplication : multiplication table> **3 table basse** : coffee table **4 table de chevet** *or* **table de nuit** : bedside table, night table **5 table ronde** : round table, roundtable
tableau [tablo] *nm, pl* **tableaux 1** PEINTURE : painting **2** : picture, scene **3** : table, chart **4 tableau d'affichage** : bulletin board **5 tableau de bord** : dashboard **6** *or* **tableau noir** : blackboard
tabler [table] *vt* **~ sur** : to count on, to rely on
tablette [tablɛt] *nf* **1** : shelf **2** : bar (of candy), stick (of gum) **3** : tablet (in pharmacy) **4** *Can* : notepad
tableur [tablœr] *nm* : spreadsheet
tablier [tablije] *nm* **1** : apron **2** : roadway, deck (on a bridge)
tabloïde *or* **tabloïd** [tablɔid] *nm* : tabloid
tabou[1], **-boue** [tabu] *adj* : taboo
tabou[2] *nm* : taboo
tabouret [taburɛ] *nm* : stool, footstool
tabulaire [tabylɛr] *adj* : tabular
tabulateur [tabylatœr] *nm* : tab, tabulator
tac [tak] *nm* **1** : tap, click **2 du tac au tac** : tit for tat
tache [taʃ] *nf* **1** : stain, spot **2 taches de rousseur** : freckles
tâche [taʃ] *nf* : task, job
tacher [taʃe] *vt* SALIR : to stain, to spot — **se tacher** *vr*
tâcher [taʃe] *vt* **tâcher que** : to try and be sure that <tâchez que ce soit correct : make sure that it's correct> — *vi* **~ de** : to try to <tâcher de réussir : to try to succeed>
tâcheron [taʃrɔ̃] *nm* **1** : hard worker, drudge **2** : jobber
tacheter [taʃte] {8} *vt* : to spot, to speckle
tacite [tasit] *adj* : tacit — **tacitement** [tasitmɑ̃] *adv*

taciturne |tasityrn| *adj* : taciturn

tacot |tako| *nm fam* : jalopy

tact |takt| *nm* DÉLICATESSE : tact <avec tact : tactfully>

tactile |taktil| *adj* : tactile

tactique[1] |taktik| *adj* : tactical — **tactiquement** |-tikmɑ̃| *adv*

tactique[2] *nf* STRATÉGIE : tactics *pl*, strategy, procedure

taffetas |tafta| *nms & pl* : taffeta

tahitien[1], **-tienne** |taisjɛ̃, -sjɛn| *adj* : Tahitian

tahitien[2] *nm* : Tahitian (language)

Tahitien, -tienne *n* : Tahitian

taie |tɛ| *nf or* **taie d'oreiller** : pillowcase

taillader |tajade| *vt* : to slash, to gash, to hack

taille |taj| *nf* **1** : cutting, pruning **2** : size <de taille moyenne : medium-sized> <de taille : sizable> **3** : height <une femme de haute taille : a tall woman> **4** : waist, waistline

taille–crayon |tajkrɛjɔ̃| *nm, pl* **taille–crayons** : pencil sharpener

tailler |taje| *vt* **1** : to cut, to prune, to trim **2** : to sharpen (a pencil) — *vi* **1 ~ dans** : to cut into **2 tailler grand/petit** : to run large/small (of clothes) — **se tailler** *vr* : to carve out (a way, a success, etc.) for oneself

tailleur |tajœr| *nm* **1** : woman's suit **2** : tailor

taillis |taji| *nms & pl* : coppice, copse

taire |tɛr| {91} *vt* : to hush up, to keep secret — **se taire** *vr* **1** : to be quiet <tais-toi! : be quiet!> **2** : to fall silent

taisait |tɛzɛ|, **taisions** |tɛzjɔ̃|, *etc.* → **taire**

taise |tɛz|, *etc.* → **taire**

taiwanais, -naise |tajwanɛ, -nɛz| *adj* : Taiwanese

Taiwanais, -naise *n* : Taiwanese

talc |talk| *nm* : talc, talcum powder

talent |talɑ̃| *nm* : talent, gift <avoir du talent : to be talented>

talentueux, -tueuse |talɑ̃tɥø, -tɥøz| *adj* : talented

taler |tale| *vt* : to bruise (fruit)

talion |taljɔ̃| *nm* **la loi du talion** : an eye for an eye

talisman |talismɑ̃| *nm* : talisman

taloche |talɔʃ| *nf fam* : slap, blow

talon |talɔ̃| *nm* **1** : heel **2** : stub (of a check)

talonner |talɔne| *vt* **1** : to follow closely **2** : to hound, to harass

talus |taly| *nms & pl* : embankment, slope

tambour |tɑ̃bur| *nm* **1** : drum **2** : drummer **3 sans tambour ni trompette** : without fanfare **4 tambour battant** : briskly

tambourin |tɑ̃burɛ̃| *nm* : tambourine

tambouriner |tɑ̃burine| *vt* : to drum, to tap (one's fingers, one's feet, etc.)

tamia |tamja| *nm* : chipmunk

tamis |tami| *nms & pl* : sieve, sifter

tamiser |tamize| *vt* **1** : to sift **2** : to filter <lumière tamisée : subdued lighting>

tampon |tɑ̃pɔ̃| *nm* **1** BOUCHON : plug, stopper **2** : pad <tampon à récurer : scouring pad> <tampon encreur : stamp pad, ink pad> **3** : buffer **4** : rubber stamp **5 tampon hygiénique** : tampon

tamponner |tɑ̃pɔne| *vt* **1** : to dab, to swab **2** HEURTER : to crash into, to collide with **3** : to stamp, to validate

tam–tam |tamtam| *nm, pl* **tam–tams** : tom-tom

tancer |tɑ̃se| {6} *vt* : to reprimand

tandem |tɑ̃dɛm| *nm* **1** : tandem (bicycle) **2 travailler en tandem** : to work in tandem

tandis |tɑ̃di| **tandis que 1** : while **2** : whereas

tangent, -gente |tɑ̃ʒɑ̃, -ʒɑ̃t| *adj* : tangential

tangente |tɑ̃ʒɑ̃t| *nf* : tangent

tangible |tɑ̃ʒibl| *adj* : tangible — **tangiblement** |-ʒibləmɑ̃| *adv*

tango |tɑ̃go| *nm* : tango

tanguer |tɑ̃ge| *vi* : to pitch, to toss about

tanière |tanjɛr| *nf* : lair, den

tanin |tanɛ̃| *nm* : tannin

tank |tɑ̃k| *nm* : tank

tanker |tɑ̃kœr| *nm* : tanker

tanné, -née |tane| *adj* : weathered, leathery (of skin)

tanner |tane| *vt* **1** : to tan (leather, skin) **2** *fam* : to pester, to annoy

tannerie |tanri| *nf* : tannery

tanneur, -neuse |tanœr, -nøz| *n* : tanner

tant |tɑ̃| *adv* **1** : so much, so many <tant de bruit : so much noise> <comme tant d'autres : like so many others> <il y a tant à faire : there's so much to do> **2** : so <tant il est déterminé : (since) he is so determined> **3 en tant que** : as, in so far as **4 en tant que tel** : as such **5 tant mieux!** : so much the better! **6 tant pis!** : too bad! **7 tant que** : as much as, so much as **8 tant que** : as long as

tante |tɑ̃t| *nf* : aunt

tantinet |tɑ̃tinɛ| *nm* : little bit

tantôt |tɑ̃to| *adv* **1** : sometimes <tantôt à bicyclette, tantôt à pied : sometimes by bicycle, sometimes on foot> **2** *Can* : later **3** *France* : this afternoon

tanzanien, -nienne |tɑ̃zanjɛ̃, -njɛn| *adj* : Tanzanian

Tanzanien, -nienne *n* : Tanzanian

taon |tɑ̃| *nm* : horsefly

tapage |tapaʒ| *nm* **1** VACARME : racket, uproar, din **2** SCANDALE : furor, scandal

tapageur, -geuse |tapaʒœr, -ʒøz| *adj* **1** : noisy, rowdy **2** VOYANT : flashy, ostentatious, garish

tapant, -pante |tapɑ̃, -pɑ̃t| *adj* : sharp, on the dot <à midi tapant : at twelve o'clock sharp>
tape |tap| *nf* : slap, tap, pat
tape-à-l'oeil[1] |tapalœj| *adj* : flashy, showy, gaudy
tape-à-l'oeil[2] *nms & pl* : flashiness, show
taper |tape| *vt* **1** : to hit, to slap, to beat **2** : to type **3 taper qqn de qqch** : to bum sth from s.o. — *vi* **1** : to hit, to knock, to bang <taper sur un clou : to hit (on) a nail> <taper à la porte : to knock on the door> **2** : to beat down (of the sun) **3** *or* **taper à la machine** : to type **4 taper des mains** : to clap one's hands **5 taper des pieds** : to stamp one's feet — **se taper** *vr* **1** *fam* : to knock each other down **2** *fam* : to put away, to eat, to drink **3** *fam* : to get stuck with (a chore)
tapette |tapɛt| *nf* **1** : light tap, pat **2 tapette à mouches** : flyswatter
tapinois |tapɛnwa| **en ~** : furtively
tapioca |tapjɔka| *nm* : tapioca
tapir |tapir| *v* **se tapir** *vr* **1** : to crouch (down) **2** : to hide away, to retreat
tapis |tapi| *nms & pl* **1** : carpet **2 tapis roulant** : moving walkway, (baggage) carousel, conveyor belt
tapisser |tapise| *vt* **1** : to wallpaper **2** : to upholster **3** : to cover, to carpet
tapisserie |tapisri| *nf* **1** : tapestry **2** : wallpaper **3 faire tapisserie** : to be a wallflower
taponner |tapɔne| *vt Can fam* : to touch, to handle <arrête de taponner mes choses : stop playing with my things>
tapotement |tapɔtmɑ̃| *nm* : tap, pat
tapoter |tapɔte| *vt* : to tap, to pat
taquin[1], **-quine** |takɛ̃, -kin| *adj* : teasing
taquin[2], **-quine** *n* : tease
taquiner |takine| *vt* : to tease
taquinerie |takinri| *nf* : teasing
tarabiscoté, -cotée |tarabiskɔte| *adj* : fussy, overelaborate
tarabuster |tarabyste| *vt* **1** : to pester **2** : to worry, to bother <ça me tarabuste : that's getting me down>
tard |tar| *adv* : late <plus tard : later> <au plus tard : at the latest>
tarder |tarde| *vi* **1** : to delay, to be a long time coming <ça ne devrait pas tarder : it shouldn't take long> **2 sans ~** : without delay
tardif, -dive |tardif, -div| *adj* : late <repas tardif : late meal>
tardivement |tardivmɑ̃| *adv* : late, belatedly
tare |tar| *nf* DÉFAUT : defect, flaw
tarentule |tarɑ̃tyl| *nf* : tarantula
targette |tarʒɛt| *nf* : bolt (on a door, etc.)
targuer |targe| *v* **se targuer** *vr* **~ de** : to boast about
tarif |tarif| *nm* **1** : rate, fare <payer plein tarif : to pay full fare> **2** : price, schedule of prices <tarif horaire : price per hour> **3 tarif douanier** : tariff, customs duty
tarir |tarir| *vt* : to dry up — *vi* **1** : to run dry, to dry up **2 ne pas tarir d'éloges** : to be full of praise
tartan |tartɛ̃| *nm* : tartan
tarte[1] |tart| *adj fam* : stupid, ridiculous
tarte[2] *nf* : pie
tartelette |tartəlɛt| *nf* : tart
tartine |tartin| *nf or* **tartine beurrée** : slice of bread and butter
tartiner |tartine| *vt* : to spread (with butter, etc.) <fromage à tartiner : cheese spread>
tartre |tartr| *nm* : tartar
tas |ta| *nms & pl* **1** : heap, pile **2 des tas de** : a lot of, piles of **3 formation sur le tas** : on-the-job training
tasse |tas| *nf* : cup <tasse à thé : teacup>
tasseau |taso| *nm, pl* **tasseaux** : brace, bracket
tasser |tase| *vt* **1** : to pack down **2** ENTASSER : to pack together, to cram **3** *Can* : to move over, to move aside — **se tasser** *vr* **1** : to shrink **2** : to squeeze together, to cram <elles sont tassées dans la voiture : they are crammed into the car>
tâter |tate| *vt* **1** PALPER : to feel **2** : to sound out <tâter le terrain : to check out the lay of the land> — *vi* **~ de** : to try one's hand at
tatillon[1], **-lonne** |tatijɔ̃, -jɔn| *adj* POINTILLEUX : fussy, finicky
tatillon[2], **-lonne** *n* : fussy person, fussbudget
tâtonner |tatɔne| *vi* : to grope one's way, to feel around
tâtons |tatɔ̃| **avancer à tâtons** : to feel one's way (along)
tatou |tatu| *nm* : armadillo
tatouage |tatwaʒ| *nm* **1** : tattoo **2** : tattooing
tatouer |tatwe| *vt* : to tattoo
taudis |todi| *nms & pl* : hovel, slum
taule |tol| *nf fam* : prison <faire de la taule : to do time>
taupe |top| *nf* **1** : mole **2 myope comme une taupe** : blind as a bat
taupinière |topinjɛr| *nf* : molehill
taureau |tɔro| *nm, pl* **taureaux** : bull
Taureau *nm* : Taurus
tauromachie |tɔrɔmaʃi| *nf* : bullfighting
taux |to| *nms & pl* **1** : rate <taux de change : exchange rate> <taux de natalité : birthrate> **2** : level <taux de cholestérol : cholesterol level>
tavelé, -lée |tavle| *adj* : marked, spotted
taverne |tavɛrn| *nf* : inn, tavern
taxe |taks| *nf* : tax — **taxation** |taksasjɔ̃| *nf*

taxer [takse] *vt* **1** IMPOSER : to tax **2** ACCUSER : to accuse <il m'a taxé de paresse : he accused me of laziness>
taxi [taksi] *nm* : taxi, taxicab
taxidermie [taksidɛrmi] *nf* : taxidermy — **taxidermiste** [-dɛrmist] *nmf*
tchadien, -dienne [tʃadjɛ̃, -djɛn] *adj* : Chadian
Tchadien, -dienne *n* : Chadian
tchécoslovaque [tʃekɔslɔvak] *adj* : Czechoslovak, Czechoslovakian
Tchécoslovaque *nmf* : Czechoslovak, Czechoslovakian
tchèque[1] [tʃɛk] *adj* : Czech
tchèque[2] *nm* : Czech (language)
Tchèque *nmf* : Czech
te [tə] (**t'** *before a vowel or mute h*) *pron* **1** : you, to you <je t'aime : I love you> <je te le donne : I'm giving it to you> **2** : yourself <tu vas te couper : you're going to cut yourself>
technicien, -cienne [tɛknisjɛ̃, -sjɛn] *n* : technician
technique[1] [tɛknik] *adj* : technical — **techniquement** [-nikmɑ̃] *adv*
technique[2] *nf* : technique
technologie [tɛknɔlɔʒi] *nf* : technology
technologique [tɛknɔlɔʒik] *adj* : technological
technologue [tɛknɔlɔg] *nmf* : technologist
teck [tɛk] *nm* : teak
teckel [tekɛl] *nm* : dachshund
tee–shirt [tiʃœrt] *nm, pl* **tee–shirts** : T-shirt
teigne [tɛɲ] *nf* **1** : ringworm **2** : moth **3** *fam* : nasty person, louse
teindre [tɛ̃dr] {37} *vt* : to dye — **se teindre** *vr* **se teindre les cheveux** : to dye one's hair
teint [tɛ̃] *nm* **1** : complexion, coloring **2 grand teint** *or* **bon teint** : colorfast
teinte [tɛ̃t] *nf* **1** TON : shade, hue **2** : tinge, hint
teinter [tɛ̃te] *vt* **1** : to tint, to stain **2 ~ de** : to tinge with <tristesse teintée de soulagement : sorrow tinged with relief>
teinture [tɛ̃tyr] *nf* **1** : dye **2** : dyeing **3** : tincture <teinture d'iode : tincture of iodine>
teinturerie [tɛ̃tyrri] *nf* : dry cleaner (shop)
teinturier, -rière [tɛ̃tyrje, -rjɛ] *n* : dry cleaner
tel[1], **telle** [tɛl] *adj* **1** : such <une telle femme : such a woman, a woman like that> <un tel bonheur! : such happiness!> <de telle manière que : in such a way that> **2** : such and such, a certain <je viens tel jour : I'm coming on such and such a day> **3 tel que** : such as, like <des livres tels que les dictionnaires : books such as dictionaries> **4 tel quel** : as (it) is <laissez-les tels quels : leave them as they are>
tel[2], **telle** *pron* **1** : a certain one, someone **2 un tel, une telle** : so-and-so, what's-his-name, what's-her-name
télé [tele] *nf fam* : TV
téléavertisseur [teleavɛrtisœr] *nm Can* : beeper
téléchargement [teleʃarʒmɑ̃] *nm* : download, downloading
télécharger [teleʃarʒe] {17} *vt* : to download (a computer file)
télécommande [telekɔmɑ̃d] *nf* : remote control
télécommunication [telekɔmynikasjɔ̃] *nf* : telecommunication
télécopie [telekɔpi] *nf* : fax, facsimile
télécopieur [telekɔpjœr] *nm* : fax machine
télédiffuser [teledifyze] *vt* : to broadcast (on television), to televise
téléfilm [telefilm] *nm* : film made for TV
télégramme [telegram] *nm* : telegram
télégraphe [telegraf] *nm* : telegraph — **télégraphique** [-grafik] *adj*
télégraphier [telegrafje] {96} *v* : to telegraph
télépathie [telepati] *nf* : telepathy
télépathique [telepatik] *adj* : telepathic
téléphone [telefɔn] *nm* : telephone, phone <donner un coup de téléphone : to make a phone call> <être au téléphone : to be (talking) on the telephone> <téléphone portable : cell phone *US*, mobile phone *Brit*>
téléphoner [telefɔne] *vt* **1** : to telephone, to call **2 téléphoner en PVC** *France* : to call collect **3 téléphoner à frais virés** *Can* : to call collect
téléphonique [telefɔnik] *adj* : telephone <cabine téléphonique : telephone booth>
téléphoniste [telefɔnist] *nmf* : telephone operator
télescope [teleskɔp] *nm* : telescope
télescoper [teleskɔpe] *vt* : to crash into, to collide with (a vehicle) — **se télescoper** *vr* **1** : to collide with each other **2** : to overlap, to intermingle (of ideas, etc.)
télescopique [teleskɔpik] *adj* : telescopic
télésiège [telesjɛʒ] *nm* : chairlift
téléski [teleski] *nm* : ski lift
téléspectateur, -trice [telespɛktatœr, -tris] *n* : television viewer
téléviser [televize] *vt* : to televise
téléviseur [televizœr] *nm* : television set
télévision [televizjɔ̃] *nf* **1** : television <à la télévision : on television> **2** TÉLÉVISEUR : television set
tellement [tɛlmɑ̃] *adv* **1** : so, so much <tellement vite : so fast> <c'est tellement mieux : it's so much better> **2 ~ de** : so many, so much <tellement de travail : so much work> **3 pas tellement** : not much, not really <il

n'a pas tellement changé : he hasn't really changed>
téméraire [temerɛr] *adj* : rash, reckless
témérité [temerite] *nf* : rashness, recklessness
témoignage [temwaɲaʒ] *nm* **1** RÉCIT : account, story **2** : testimony (in court) **3** PREUVE : evidence, sign <témoignage d'affection : token of affection>
témoigner [temwaɲe] *vt* **1** : to testify, to attest **2** MONTRER : to show, to evince — *vi* **1** : to testify, to give evidence **2 ~ de** : to show, to give evidence of
témoin [temwɛ̃] *nm* **1** : witness <témoin oculaire : eyewitness> **2** PREUVE : evidence, mark **3** : baton (in a relay)
tempe [tɑ̃p] *nf* : temple <tempes grisonnantes : graying temples>
tempérament [tɑ̃peramɑ̃] *nm* CARACTÈRE : temperament, disposition
tempérance [tɑ̃perɑ̃s] *nf* : temperance
tempérant, -rante [tɑ̃perɑ̃, -rɑ̃t] *adj* : temperate, sober
température [tɑ̃peratyr] *nf* : temperature
tempéré, -rée [tɑ̃pere] *adj* : temperate
tempérer [tɑ̃pere] {87} *vt* : to temper, to ease, to moderate
tempête [tɑ̃pɛt] *nf* : storm <tempête de neige : snowstorm, blizzard>
tempêter [tɑ̃pete] *vi* FULMINER : to rage, to rant
temple [tɑ̃pl] *nm* **1** : temple **2** : (protestant) church, meetinghouse
tempo [tɛmpo] *nm* : tempo
temporaire [tɑ̃pɔrɛr] *adj* : temporary — **temporairement** [-rɛrmɑ̃] *adv*
temporel, -relle [tɑ̃pɔrɛl] *adj* : temporal
temporiser [tɑ̃pɔrize] *vi* : to stall, to play for time
temps [tɑ̃] *nms & pl* **1** : time <à temps : in time, on time> <de temps à autre : from time to time> <pendant ce temps : meanwhile, in the meantime> <travailler à plein temps : to work full-time> <les temps ont changé : times have changed> **2** : weather <un temps pluvieux : rainy weather> <quel temps fait-il? : what's the weather like?, what's it like outside?> **3** : tense (in grammar)
tenable [tənabl] *adj* SUPPORTABLE : bearable <ce n'était pas tenable : it was unbearable>
tenace [tənas] *adj* : tenacious, persistent
tenacité [tənasite] *nf* : tenacity
tenailler [tenaje] *vt* TOURMENTER : to torture, to torment
tenailles [tənaj] *nfpl* **1** : pincers, nippers **2** : tongs
tenancier, -cière [tənɑ̃sje, -sjɛr] *n* : manager (of a hotel, etc.)
tenant, -nante [tənɑ̃, -nɑ̃t] *n* **1** PARTISAN : supporter **2 tenant d'un titre** : titleholder (in sports) **3 les tenants et les aboutissants** : the ins and outs
tendance [tɑ̃dɑ̃s] *nf* **1** : tendency **2** COURANT : trend
tendineux, -neuse [tɑ̃dinø, -nøz] *adj* **1** : tendinous, sinewy **2** : stringy (of meat)
tendon [tɑ̃dɔ̃] *nm* : tendon, sinew, hamstring
tendre[1] [tɑ̃dr] {63} *vt* **1** : to tense, to stretch (out), to draw tight **2** : to put up, to set up <tendre un piège à : to set a trap for> **3** : to spread out (cloth, etc.) **4** : to hold out, to extend <tendre la main : to hold out one's hand> <tendre le cou : to crane one's neck> <tendre l'oreille : to prick up one's ears> — *vi* **1 ~ à** : to tend to **2 ~ vers** : to strive for — **se tendre** *vr* **1** : to tighten, to become taut **2** : to become strained
tendre[2] *adj* **1** : tender, soft **2** : loving <un regard tendre : a tender glance>
tendrement [tɑ̃drəmɑ̃] *adv* : lovingly, tenderly
tendresse [tɑ̃drɛs] *nf* : tenderness, affection
tendu, -due [tɑ̃dy] *adj* **1** : tight, taut **2** : tense, strained
ténèbres [tenɛbr] *nfpl* : darkness
ténébreux, -breuse [tenebrø, -brøz] *adj* **1** OBSCUR : dark, gloomy **2** MYSTÉRIEUX : mysterious, obscure
teneur [tənœr] *nf* : content <teneur en gras : fat content>
ténia [tenja] *nm* : tapeworm
tenir [tənir] {92} *vt* **1** : to hold, to keep <tenir en position : to hold in place> <tenez la porte fermée : keep the door shut> **2** : to have, to catch <je te tiens! : I've got you!> <tenir les voleurs : to catch the thieves> **3** : to take hold of, to control <tenir les enfants : to keep the children under control> **4** : to run, to manage (a hotel, store, etc.) **5** : to hold down, to hold up, to keep up **6** : to hold (a quantity), to take up (a space) **7** : to regard, to consider <il me tient responsable : he holds me responsible> — *vi* **1** : to hold, to stay in place **2** : to hold up, to last **3** : to fit (into a space) **4** *or* **tenir bon** : to hang on, to hold out **5 ~ à** : to be fond of, to like **6 ~ à** : to be due to **7 ~ à** : to want to, to be anxious to **8 ~ de** : to be like (someone), to take after **9 ~ de** : to border on — *v impers* : to depend <il ne tient qu'à toi : it's up to you> — **se tenir** *vr* **1** : to hold, to hold up, to hold onto <se tenir par la main : to hold hands> **2** : to remain, to stay <se tenir prêt : to be ready> <se tenir debout : to stand still> **3** : to behave (oneself) **4** : to hold up, to make sense **5** : to consider oneself **6** : to hold to, to stand by <s'en tenir à : to confine oneself to>

tennis [tenis] *nm* **1** : tennis <tennis de table : table tennis> **2 tennis** *nmpl France* : sneakers

ténor [tenɔr] *nm* : tenor

tension [tɑ̃sjɔ̃] *nf* **1** : tension **2** *or* **tension artérielle** : blood pressure

tentacule [tɑ̃takyl] *nm* : tentacle

tentant, -tante [tɑ̃tɑ̃, -tɑ̃t] *adj* : tempting, tantalizing

tentateur, -trice [tɑ̃tatœr, -tris] *n* : tempter

tentation [tɑ̃tasjɔ̃] *nf* : temptation

tentative [tɑ̃tativ] *nf* : attempt <tentative d'homicide : attempted murder>

tente [tɑ̃t] *nf* : tent

tenter [tɑ̃te] *vt* **1** : to tempt <tenter le diable : to tempt fate> **2** ESSAYER : to attempt, to try <tenter la chance : to try one's luck>

tenture [tɑ̃tyr] *nf* : hanging, wall covering

tenu[1] [təny] *pp* → **tenir**

tenu[2], **-nue** [təny] *adj* **1** : obliged, bound **2** : controlled, kept in check **3 bien tenu** : well kept, tidy

ténu, -nue [teny] *adj* **1** : fine, slender **2** : thin (of voices, air, etc.) **3** : tenuous, subtle

tenue *nf* **1** : holding, running (of a meeting, etc.) **2** : organizing, keeping <tenue de livres : bookkeeping> **3** : conduct, manners *pl* **4** MAINTIEN : bearing, posture **5** : clothes *pl*, dress, outfit <tenue d'hiver : winter clothing> <tenue militaire : military dress, uniform> <tenue de soirée : formal dress>

térébenthine [terebɑ̃tin] *nf* : turpentine

tergiverser [tɛrʒivɛrse] *vi* : to shilly-shally, to beat around the bush

terme [tɛrm] *nm* **1** : term, word <en d'autres termes : in other words> **2** : end, termination <mettre un terme à : to put an end to> **3** ÉCHÉANCE : due date, deadline (for payment) **4 termes** *nmpl* : terms (of a contract) **5 termes** *nmpl* : relations <être en bons termes avec : to be on good terms with>

terminaison [tɛrminɛzɔ̃] *nf* : termination, ending

terminal[1], **-nale** [tɛrminal] *adj, mpl* **-naux** [-no] **1** : final, last **2** : terminal (in medicine)

terminal[2] *nm, pl* **-naux 1** : station, terminal **2** : computer terminal

terminer [tɛrmine] *v* FINIR : to end, to finish — **se terminer** *vr* : to end, to finish up

terminologie [tɛrminɔlɔʒi] *nf* : terminology

terminus [tɛrminys] *nms & pl* : terminus, end of the line (of a train, bus, etc.)

termite [tɛrmit] *nm* : termite

terne [tɛrn] *adj* **1** FADE : colorless, drab **2** ENNUYEUX : dull, dreary

ternir [tɛrnir] *vt* **1** : to tarnish, to dull **2** : to stain, to tarnish (one's reputation, etc.)

ternissure [tɛrnisyr] *nf* : tarnish

terrain [tɛrɛ̃] *nm* **1** : ground, soil **2** PARCELLE : plot (of land) **3** : land, terrain **4** : field <terrain de football : football field> <terrain de jeu : playground> <terrain de camping : campsite> <terrain d'aviation : airfield> **5** : field, sphere (of activity) <le terrain juridique : the field of law> **6** : area, ground, territory <perdre du terrain : to lose ground> <terrain d'entente : common ground> <être en terrain connu : to be on familiar territory>

terrasse [tɛras] *nf* : terrace

terrassement [tɛrasmɑ̃] *nm* : excavation

terrasser [tɛrase] *vt* **1** : to knock down, to floor **2** : to strike down <terrassé par une maladie : struck down by sickness>

terre [tɛr] *nf* **1** : ground <par terre : on the ground, on the floor> <sous terre : underground> **2** TERRAIN : land <basse terre : lowland> **3** : (dry) land <aller à terre : to go ashore> **4** : dirt, soil <chemin de terre : dirt road> **5** : earth, world <sur la terre : on earth, in the world> **6** : clay (for pottery), earthenware **7 terre à terre** : down-to-earth, matter-of-fact **8 terre cuite** : terra-cotta

Terre *nf* : Earth (planet)

terreau [tɛro] *nm, pl* **terreaux** : loam, compost

terre–plein [tɛrplɛ̃] *nm, pl* **terre–pleins** : median strip

terrer [tɛre] *v* **se terrer** *vr* : to hide, to go underground

terrestre [tɛrɛstr] *adj* **1** : earth, terrestrial **2** : earthly, worldly

terreur [tɛrœr] *nf* : terror

terreux, -reuse [tɛrø, -røz] *adj* **1** : muddy **2** BLAFARD : sallow, pallid **3** : earthy

terrible [tɛribl] *adj* **1** : terrible, dreadful **2** : intense, excessive **3** *fam* FORMIDABLE : terrific, great

terrien, -rienne [tɛrjɛ̃, -rjɛn] *adj* **propriétaire terrien** : landowner

terrier [tɛrje] *nm* **1** : hole, burrow **2** : terrier

terrifiant, -fiante [tɛrifjɑ̃, -fjɑ̃t] *adj* : terrifying

terrifier [tɛrifje] {96} *vt* ÉPOUVANTER : to terrify

territoire [tɛritwar] *nm* : territory

territorial, -riale [tɛritɔrjal] *adj, mpl* **-riaux** [-rjo] : territorial

terroir [tɛrwar] *nm* **1** : region, locality **2** : country, rural region

terroriser [tɛrɔrize] *vt* : to terrorize

terrorisme [tɛrɔrism] *nm* : terrorism — **terroriste** [-rɔrist] *adj & nmf*

tertiaire [tɛrsjɛr] *adj* : tertiary

tertre [tɛrtr] *nm* MONTICULE : hillock, mound
tes → **ton**[1]
tesson [tesɔ̃] *nm* : piece, fragment, shard <tesson de bouteille : piece of broken glass>
test [tɛst] *nm* : test
testament [tɛstamɑ̃] *nm* **1** : will, last will and testament **2** : legacy **3 Testament** *m* : Testament <Ancien Testament : Old Testament> <Nouveau Testament : New Testament>
tester [tɛste] *vt* : to test — *vi* : to make a will
testicule [tɛstikyl] *nm* : testicle
tétanos [tetanos] *nms & pl* : tetanus, lockjaw
têtard [tɛtar] *nm* : tadpole
tête [tɛt] *nf* **1** : head <être tête nue : to be bareheaded> <la tête haute : with head held high> **2** : (head of) hair <se laver la tête : to wash one's hair> **3** : face <faire la tête : to make a face, to sulk> **4** : mind, head <passer par la tête : to cross one's mind> <garder sa tête : to keep one's head> **5** : neck, life <risquer sa tête : to risk one's neck> **6** : head, leader **7** : head (of cattle, etc.) **8** : top, lead, head <tête d'un arbre : treetop> <à la tête de la classe : at the head of the class> **9** : header (in soccer) **10 tenir tête à** : to stand up to **11 tête brulée** : hothead **12 tête de mort** : skull **13 tête de pont** : beachhead
tête–à–queue [tɛtakø] *nms & pl* : spin (of an automobile)
tête–à–tête [tɛtatɛt] *nms & pl* **1** : tête-à-tête **2 être en tête–à–tête** : to be alone together
tétée [tete] *nf* : nursing, feeding (at the breast)
téter [tete] {87} *vt* : to suck at (the breast) — *vi* : to suckle, to nurse
tétine [tetin] *nf* **1** : teat **2** : nipple (of a baby bottle) **3** : pacifier
téton [tetɔ̃] *nm fam* : breast
têtu, -tue [tety] *adj* : stubborn
texte [tɛkst] *nm* : text
textile [tɛkstil] *nm* : textile
textuel, -elle [tɛkstɥɛl] *adj* : literal, word for word
textuellement [tɛkstɥɛlmɑ̃] *adv* : literally, verbatim
texture [tɛkstyr] *nf* : texture
thaï [taj] *nm* : Thai (language)
thaïlandais, -daise [tajlɑ̃dɛ, -dɛz] *adj* : Thai
Thaïlandais, -daise *n* : Thai
thé [te] *nm* : tea
théâtral, -trale [teatral] *adj, mpl* **-traux** [-tro] : theatrical
théâtre [teatr] *nm* **1** : theater (building, area) **2** : drama, theater **3 faire du théâtre** : to be an actor
théière [tejɛr] *nf* : teapot
théisme [teism] *nm* : theism
thème [tɛm] *nm* : theme
théologie [teɔlɔʒi] *nf* : theology
théologique [teɔlɔʒik] *adj* : theological
théologien, -gienne [teɔlɔʒjɛ̃, -ʒjɛn] *n* : theologian
théorème [teɔrɛm] *nm* : theorem
théorie [teɔri] *nf* : theory
théorique [teɔrik] *adj* : theoretical — **théoriquement** [-rikmɑ̃] *adv*
théoriser [teɔrize] *vi* : to theorize
thérapeute [terapøt] *nmf* : therapist
thérapeutique[1] [terapøtik] *adj* : therapeutic
thérapeutique[2] *nf* : therapy, treatment
thérapie [terapi] *nf* : therapy
thermal, -male [tɛrmal] *adj, mpl* **thermaux** [tɛrmo] : thermal <station thermale : spa>
thermique [tɛrmik] *adj* : thermal <centrale thermique : thermal power station>
thermodynamique [tɛrmɔdinamik] *nf* : thermodynamics
thermomètre [tɛrmɔmɛtr] *nm* : thermometer
thermos [tɛrmos] *nmfs & pl* : thermos
thermostat [tɛrmɔsta] *nm* : thermostat
thésauriser [tezɔrize] *vt* : to hoard — *vi* : to hoard money
thèse [tɛz] *nf* : thesis
thiamine [tjamin] *nf* : thiamine
thon [tɔ̃] *nm* : tuna
thorax [tɔraks] *nm* : thorax
thym [tɛ̃] *nm* : thyme
thyroïde [tirɔid] *nf* : thyroid (gland)
tiare [tjar] *nf* : tiara
tibétain[1], **-taine** [tibetɛ̃, -tɛn] *adj* : Tibetan
tibétain[2] *nm* : Tibetan (language)
Tibétain, -taine *n* : Tibetan
tibia [tibja] *nm* **1** : tibia, shinbone **2** : shin
tic [tik] *nm* **1** : tic, twitch **2** : mannerism
ticket [tikɛ] *nm* BILLET : ticket
tic–tac [tiktak] *nms & pl* : tick, ticking
tiède [tjɛd] *adj* **1** : lukewarm, tepid **2** : warm, mild (of weather, etc.)
tièdement [tjɛdmɑ̃] *adv* : halfheartedly
tiédir [tjedir] *vi* : to warm up, to cool down
tien[1], **tienne** [tjɛ̃, tjɛn] *adj* : yours, of yours <une tienne amie : a friend of yours> <je suis tien : I'm yours>
tien[2], **tienne** *pron* **le tien, la tienne, les tiens, les tiennes** : yours <le tien est plus joli : yours is prettier>
tiendra [tjɛ̃dra], *etc.* → **tenir**
tienne [tjɛn], *etc.* → **tenir**
tient [tjɛ̃], *etc.* → **tenir**
tiers[1], **tierce** [tjɛr, tjɛrs] *adj* : third <tierce personne : third person>
tiers[2] *nm* **1** : third <un tiers du livre : a third of the book> **2** : third party
tiers–monde [tjɛrmɔ̃d] *nm, pl* **tiers–mondes** : Third World
tige [tiʒ] *nf* **1** : stem, stalk **2** : (metal) rod
tignasse [tiɲas] *nf* : mop, shock (of hair)
tigre [tigr] *nm* : tiger

tigré, -grée [tigre] *adj* : striped

tigresse [tigrɛs] *nf* : tigress

tilleul [tijœl] *nm* : linden (tree)

timbale [tɛ̃bal] *nf* **1** : kettledrum **2 timbales** *nfpl* : timpani

timbre [tɛ̃br] *nm* **1** : (postage) stamp **2** : official stamp, postmark **3** SONNETTE : bell **4** TON : timbre, tone

timbré, -brée [tɛ̃bre] *adj* **1** : rich, mellow (of the voice) **2** *fam* : crazy, nuts

timbre–poste [tɛ̃brəpɔst] *nm, pl* **timbres–poste** : (postage) stamp

timbrer [tɛ̃bre] *vt* : to stamp, to postmark

timide [timid] *adj* : timid, shy — **timidement** [-midmɑ̃] *adv*

timidité [timidite] *nf* : timidity, shyness

timoré, -rée [timɔre] *adj* : timorous

tintamarre [tɛ̃tamar] *nm* : din, racket

tintement [tɛ̃tmɑ̃] *nm* : ringing, chiming, tinkling, clinking

tinter [tɛ̃te] *vt* : to ring, to toll — *vi* **1** : to ring, to chime **2** : to tinkle, to jingle, to clink **3** : to ring, to buzz (of ears)

tipi [tipi] *nm* : tepee

tique [tik] *nf* : tick (insect)

tiquer [tike] *vi* : to wince, to flinch

tir [tir] *nm* **1** : shooting, gunnery **2** : firing <déclencher le tir : to open fire> **3 tir à l'arc** : archery **4 tir antiaérien** : flak

tirade [tirad] *nf* : tirade

tirage [tiraʒ] *nm* **1** IMPRESSION : printing **2** : impression, run <second tirage : second printing> **3** : circulation (of a newspaper, etc.) **4** : (computer) printout **5** *or* **tirage au sort** : drawing (in a lottery) **6** : draft (of a chimney, etc.) **7** : pulling, hauling

tiraillement [tirajmɑ̃] *nm* **1** : tugging, pulling **2** : cramp, pang **3** : conflict <tiraillements internes : internal conflicts>

tirailler [tiraje] *vt* : to pull at, to tug at <être tiraillé entre le bien et le mal : to be torn between right and wrong>

tirant [tirɑ̃] *nm* **tirant d'eau** : draft (of a ship)

tire [tir] *nf Can* **1** : taffy **2** *or* **tire d'érable** : maple-sugar candy

tiré, -rée [tire] *adj* : drawn, haggard

tire–bouchon [tirbuʃɔ̃] *nm, pl* **tire–bouchons** : corkscrew

tire–d'aile [tirdɛl] **à ~** : in a flurry, hurriedly

tirelire [tirlir] *nf* : piggy bank

tirer [tire] *vt* **1** : to pull, to pull up, to pull back **2** : to draw (a curtain), to pull down (a blind, etc.) **3** : to fire, to shoot **4** : to take (in sports) <tirer un coup franc : to take a free kick> **5** : to draw (a card, a ticket, etc.) **6** : to withdraw **7** : to draw away, to pull out **8** : to derive (information) — *vi* **1** : to pull **2** : to fire, to shoot **3** : to take a shot (in sports) **4** *or* **tirer au sort** : to draw lots **5** : to draw (of a chimney) **6 ~ sur** : to draw from (an account, etc.) — **se tirer** *vr* **1 ~ de** : to get through, to extricate oneself from **2 se tirer une balle** : to shoot oneself **3 s'en tirer** *fam* : to cope, to pull through

tiret [tirɛ] *nm* **1** : dash **2** : hyphen

tireur, -reuse [tirœr, -røz] *n* **1** : gunman, marksman, markswoman *f* <tireur d'élite : sharpshooter> **2 tireur de cartes** : fortune-teller>

tiroir [tirwar] *nm* : drawer

tiroir–caisse [tirwarkɛs] *nm, pl* **tiroirs–caisses** : cash register, till

tisane [tizan] *nf* : herbal tea

tisonnier [tizɔnje] *nm* : poker

tissage [tisaʒ] *nm* **1** : weaving **2** : weave

tisser [tise] *vt* : to weave

tisserand, -rande [tisrɑ̃, -rɑ̃d] *n* : weaver

tissu [tisy] *nm* **1** : material, fabric **2** : tissue <tissu conjonctif : connective tissue> **3** : web, string (of lies, etc.) **4** : makeup, fabric <tissu social : social fabric>

titane [titan] *nm* : titanium

titanesque [titanɛsk] *adj* GIGANTESQUE : titanic, gigantic

titiller [titije] *vt* **1** : to titillate **2** : to tickle

titre [titr] *nm* **1** : title (of a book, song, etc.) **2** : title, rank, qualification <titre mondial : world title> **3** *or* **gros titre** : headline **4** : basis, respect, capacity <à titre d'exemple : as an example, for example> <à titre d'information : for your information> **5** : security (in the stock market) **6** : deed, title

titrer [titre] *vt* **1** : to run as a headline **2** : to subtitle (in movies) **3** : to titrate, to assay (in chemistry)

titubant, -bante [titybɑ̃, -bɑ̃t] *adj* : reeling, unsteady

tituber [titybe] *vi* : to reel, to stagger

titulaire[1] [titylɛr] *adj* : tenured, permanent

titulaire[2] *nmf* : officeholder, incumbent

titularisation [titylarizasjɔ̃] *nf* : tenure

toast [tost] *nm* **1** : toast <un toast aux nouveaux mariés : a toast to the newlyweds> **2** : (slice of) toast

toaster [toste] *vt Can* : to toast (bread)

toboggan [tɔbɔgɑ̃] *nm* : toboggan

toc[1] [tɔk] *adj fam* : trashy, tacky

toc[2] *nm* **en ~** : imitation, fake

tocsin [tɔksɛ̃] *nm* : alarm <sonner le tocsin : to sound the alarm>

toge [tɔʒ] *nf* **1** : gown, robe (of a judge, etc.) **2** : toga

togolais, -laise [tɔgɔlɛ, -lɛz] *adj* : Togolese

Togolais, -laise *n* : Togolese

tohu–bohu [tɔybɔy] *nms & pl* : noisy confusion, hubbub

toi [twa] *pron* **1** : you <je crois en toi : I believe in you> <occupe-toi! : keep

busy!> <toi, tu t'imagines des choses : you're imagining things> 2 TOI-MÊME : yourself <prends soin de toi : take care of yourself>

toile [twal] *nf* **1** : cloth, fabric <de la grosse toile : canvas> <toile à sac : burlap> <toile cirée : oilcloth> <toile goudronnée : tarpaulin> **2** TABLEAU : canvas, painting **3** WEB : Web **4 toile d'araignée** : spider's web **5 toile de fond** : backdrop

toilette [twalɛt] *nf* **1** : washing up, grooming <faire sa toilette : to get washed up> <produits de toilette : toiletries> **2** : grooming (of animals) **3** TENUE : clothing, outfit **4** *Can* : toilet, bathroom **5 toilettes** *nfpl* : toilet, bathroom <aller aux toilettes : to go to the bathroom>

toi–même [twamɛm] *pron* : yourself <tu l'as fait toi-même : you did it yourself>

toiser [twaze] *vt* : to look (a person) up and down

toison [twazɔ̃] *nf* **1** : fleece **2** : mane, mop (of hair)

toit [twa] *nm* : roof

toiture [twatyr] *nf* : roofing

tôle [tol] *nf* **1** : sheet metal **2 tôle ondulée** : corrugated iron

tolérable [tɔlerabl] *adj* : tolerable

tolérance [tɔlerɑ̃s] *nf* : tolerance — **tolérant, -rante** [tɔlerɑ̃, -rɑ̃t] *adj*

tolérer [tɔlere] {87} *vt* : to tolerate

tolet [tɔlɛ] *nm* : oarlock

tollé [tɔle] *nm* : outcry

tomate [tɔmat] *nf* : tomato

tombant, -bante [tɔ̃bɑ̃, -bɑ̃t] *adj* : sloping, drooping

tombe [tɔ̃b] *nf* **1** SÉPULTURE : grave, tomb **2** : gravestone, tombstone

tombeau [tɔ̃bo] *nm, pl* **tombeaux** : tomb, mausoleum

tombée [tɔ̃be] *nf* **à la tombée du jour** *or* **à la tombée de la nuit** : at nightfall, at the close of day

tomber [tɔ̃be] *vi* **1** : to fall (down), to fall off, to drop **2** : to come down, to fall <la pluie tombait : rain was falling> **3** : to go down (of prices, etc.), to die down, to subside **4** : to droop, to sag, to slope **5** : to hang, to fall (of hair, clothing, etc.) **6** : to come, to fall <tomber dans la désuétude : to fall into disuse> <tomber aux mains de : to fall into the hands of> **7** : to become <tomber amoureux : to fall in love> <elle est tombée malade : she fell ill> **8 ~ sur** : to run into, to come across **9 faire tomber** : to bring down, to break down **10 laisser tomber** : to give up, to drop (plans, etc.)

tombola [tɔ̃bɔla] *nf* : raffle

tome [tɔm] *nm* : volume (of a book)

ton[1] [tɔ̃[tɔn] *before a vowel or mute h*)], **ta** [ta] *adj, pl* **tes** [te] : your

ton[2] *nm* **1** : tone, pitch **2** : hue, shade **3 de bon ton** : in good taste, appropriate

tonalité [tɔnalite] *nf* **1** : tone (of voice, etc.) **2** : tonality, key (in music) **3** : dial tone

tondeuse [tɔ̃døz] *nf* **1** *or* **tondeuse à gazon** : lawn mower **2** : clippers *pl*, shears *pl*

tondre [tɔ̃dr] {63} *vt* **1** : to mow **2** : to clip, to shear

tongane, -ganne [tɔ̃gan] *adj* : Tongan

Tongane, -ganne *n* : Tongan

tonifiant, -fiante [tɔnifjɑ̃, -fjɑ̃t] *adj* : invigorating, bracing

tonifier [tɔnifje] {96} *vt* **1** REVIGORER : to invigorate **2** RAFFERMIR : to tone <muscles bien tonifiés : well-toned muscles>

tonique[1] [tɔnik] *adj* : fortifying, stimulating

tonique[2] *nm* : tonic (in medicine)

tonique[3] *nf* : tonic (in music)

tonitruant, -truante [tɔnitryɑ̃, -tryɑ̃t] *adj* : thundering, booming

tonnage [tɔnaʒ] *nm* : tonnage

tonne [tɔn] *nf* : ton

tonneau [tɔno] *nm, pl* **tonneaux** **1** BARRIQUE : barrel, cask **2** : rollover (of a motor vehicle)

tonnelet [tɔnlɛ] *nm* : keg

tonnelle [tɔnɛl] *nf* : arbor

tonner [tɔne] *vi* : to thunder

tonnerre [tɔnɛr] *nm* **1** : thunder <coup de tonnerre : thunderbolt> **2** : tumult, thundering <un tonnerre d'applaudissements : thundering applause> **3 du tonnerre** *fam* : great, terrific

tonte [tɔ̃t] *nf* : shearing

tonton [tɔ̃tɔ̃] *nm fam* : uncle

tonus [tɔnys] *nms & pl* **1** : tone <tonus musculaire : muscular tone> **2** : energy, vigor

topaze [tɔpaz] *nf* : topaz

topo [tɔpo] *nm fam* : spiel, story <c'est toujours le même topo : it's always the same old story>

topographie [tɔpɔgrafi] *nf* : topography

topographique [tɔpɔgrafik] *adj* : topographical, topographic

toquade [tɔkad] *nf fam* **1** : craze, fad **2** : crush, infatuation

toque [tɔk] *nf* : brimless hat <toque de fourrure : fur hat> <toque de cuisinier : toque, chef's hat>

toqué, -quée [tɔke] *adj fam* : crazy, touched

toquer [tɔke] *vi fam* : to rap, to knock <toquer à la porte : to knock on the door>

torche [tɔrʃ] *nf* : torch

torcher [tɔrʃe] *vt fam* : to wipe

torchon [tɔrʃɔ̃] *nm* CHIFFON : piece of cloth, rag

tordant, -dante [tɔrdɑ̃, -dɑ̃t] *adj fam* MARRANT : very funny, hilarious

tordre |tɔrdr| {63} *vt* : to twist, to wring **— se tordre** *vr* **1** : to twist <se tordre la cheville : to twist one's ankle> **2** : to writhe, to double up (with pain, laughter, etc.)

tordu, -due |tɔrdy| *adj* : twisted, warped

torero |tɔrero| *nm* : bullfighter, matador

tornade |tɔrnad| *nf* : tornado

toron |tɔrɔ̃| *nm* : strand (of rope)

torpeur |tɔrpœr| *nf* : torpor

torpide |tɔrpid| *adj* : torpid

torpille |tɔrpij| *nf* : torpedo

torréfier |tɔrefje| {96} *vt* : to roast (coffee, etc.)

torrent |tɔrɑ̃| *nm* **1** : torrent <pleuvoir à torrents : to be pouring> **2 un torrent de** : a flood of

torrentiel, -tielle |tɔrɑ̃sjɛl| *adj* : torrential

torride |tɔrid| *adj* : torrid, scorching hot

tors, torse |tɔr, tɔrs| *adj* **1** : twisted **2** : crooked, bent

torsade |tɔrsad| *nf* : twist, coil

torsader |tɔrsade| *vt* : to twist

torse |tɔrs| *nm* : torso, chest

torsion |tɔrsjɔ̃| *nf* **1** : twisting **2** : torsion

tort |tɔr| *nm* **1** : fault <reconnaître ses torts : to admit one's faults> **2** DÉFAUT : error, mistake **3** DOMMAGE : wrong, harm <faire du tort à qqn : to do harm to s.o.> **4 avoir tort** : to be wrong **5 à ~** : wrongly, unjustly **6 à tort et à travers** : senselessly

torticolis |tɔrtikɔli| *nms & pl* : stiff neck, crick in the neck

tortillement |tɔrtijmɑ̃| *nm* : wiggling, twisting

tortiller |tɔrtije| *vt* : to twist **—** *vi* : to wriggle **— se tortiller** *vr* : to squirm

tortillon |tɔrtijɔ̃| *nm* : twist

tortionnaire |tɔrsjɔnɛr| *nmf* : torturer

tortue |tɔrty| *nf* : turtle, tortoise

tortueux, -euse |tɔrtɥø, -øz| *adj* **1** : winding **2** : convoluted, tortuous

torture |tɔrtyr| *nf* : torture

torturer |tɔrtyre| *vt* : to torture

tôt |to| *adv* **1** : soon <le plus tôt possible : as soon as possible> **2** : early <se coucher tôt : to go to bed early> **3 tôt ou tard** : sooner or later

total[1], -tale |tɔtal| *adj, mpl* **totaux** |tɔto| : total **— totalement** |tɔtalmɑ̃| *adv*

total[2] *nm, mpl* **totaux** |tɔto| : total

totaliser |tɔtalize| *vt* : to total

totalitaire |tɔtalitɛr| *adj* : totalitarian

totalitarisme |tɔtalitarism| *nm* : totalitarianism

totalité |tɔtalite| *nf* **1** : total amount, totality **2 en ~** : completely, entirely

totem |tɔtɛm| *nm* : totem

touchant, -chante |tuʃɑ̃, -ʃɑ̃t| *adj* ÉMOUVANT : touching, moving

touche |tuʃ| *nf* **1** : key (on a keyboard), button **2** : stroke, touch (in art) **3** : trace, hint, touch **4** : touchline (in sports) **5** : bite (in fishing)

touché |tuʃe| *nm* : touchdown (in football)

toucher[1] |tuʃe| *vt* **1** : to touch, to handle **2** : to be in contact with, to hit **3** : to touch (in sports) **4** : to affect, to concern **5** ÉMOUVOIR : to move, to touch <toucher son coeur : to touch one's heart> **6** : to receive, to earn <toucher un bon salaire : to earn a good salary> **7** : to touch on, to be adjacent to **—** *vi* **1 ~ à** : to touch upon, to get into, to bring up **2 ~ à** : to relate to, to concern **3 ~ à** : to infringe on **— se toucher** *vr* : to touch, to be in contact

toucher[2] *nm* **1** : sense of touch **2** : feel

touffe |tuf| *nf* : tuft, clump

touffu, -fue |tufy| *adj* **1** : thick, dense, bushy <forêt touffue : dense forest> **2** : complex, dense (of style)

toujours |tuʒur| *adv* **1** : always, forever **2** ENCORE : still **3** : anyway, in any case

toundra |tundra| *nf* : tundra

toupet |tupɛ| *nm* **1** : forelock **2** *fam* : nerve, cheek

toupie |tupi| *nf* : top (toy)

tour[1] |tur| *nm* **1** : tour, circuit <faire le tour du monde : to go around the world> **2** : walk, ride <faire un tour : to go for a stroll> **3** : turn, revolution, rotation **4** : circumference, measurement (around) <tour de taille : girth (of a person)> **5** : turn, move <attendre son tour : to wait one's turn> **6** : trick <jouer un tour à qqn : to play a trick on s.o.> **7** : direction, aspect <prendre un mauvais tour : to take a bad turn, to go wrong> **8** : lathe **9 avoir le tour** *Can* : to be clever, to be skillful **10 tour de scrutin** : ballot, round of voting

tour[2] *nf* **1** : tower **2** : high-rise building **3** : castle (in chess)

tourbe |turb| *nf* : peat

tourbière |turbjɛr| *nf* : peat bog, peat marsh

tourbillon |turbijɔ̃| *nm* **1** : whirlwind, whirlpool **2** : whirl, bustle

tourbillonner |turbijɔne| *vi* : to whirl, to swirl (around)

tourelle |turɛl| *nf* : turret

tourisme |turism| *nm* : tourism

touriste |turist| *nmf* : tourist

touristique |turistik| *adj* : tourist <la saison touristique : the tourist season>

tourment |turmɑ̃| *nm* : torment

tourmente |turmɑ̃t| *nf* **1** : tempest, storm **2** : turmoil

tourmenter |turmɑ̃te| *vt* : to torment **— se tourmenter** *vr* S'INQUIÉTER : to worry

tournant[1], -nante |turnɑ̃, -nɑ̃t| *adj* : turning, revolving

tournant[2] *nm* **1** : bend (in a road, etc.) **2** : turning point

tourne–disque [turnədisk] *nm, pl* **tourne–disques** : record player

tournée [turne] *nf* **1** : tour **2** *fam* : round (of drinks)

tourner [turne] *vt* **1** : to turn, to rotate **2** : to stir, to toss **3** : to shoot (a film, scene, etc.) **4** : to get around, to circumvent **5** : to phrase, to present <une lettre bien tournée : a nicely phrased letter> **6 tourner en dérision** : to ridicule — *vi* **1** : to turn, to revolve, to spin <tourner autour de : to revolve around> <tourner en rond : to go around in circles> **2** : to turn, to change direction <tournez à droite : turn right> **3** : to run (of an engine, etc.) <tourner rond : to run smoothly> **4** : to turn out <bien tourner : to turn out well, to go well> **5** : to film, to make a film **6** : to go bad, to sour — **se tourner** *vr* : to turn around

tournesol [turnəsɔl] *nm* **1** : sunflower **2** : litmus <papier de tournesol : litmus paper>

tournevis [turnəvis] *nms & pl* : screwdriver

tourniquet [turnikɛ] *nm* **1** : turnstile **2** : tourniquet **3** : sprinkler

tournoi [turnwa] *nm* : tournament

tournoiement [turnwamɑ̃] *nm* : spinning, whirling

tournoyer [turnwaje] {58} *vi* **1** : to whirl, to spin, to gyrate **2** : to swirl around

tournure [turnyr] *nf* **1** : turn <tournure des événements : turn of events> **2** : turn of phrase, expression

tourte [turt] *nf France* : (meat or fish) pie

tourtereaux [turtəro] *nmpl* : lovebirds

tourterelle [turtərɛl] *nf* : turtledove

tourtière [turtjɛr] *nf* **1** *France* : pie pan **2** *Can* : meat pie

tousser [tuse] *vi* : to cough

tout[1] [tu] **(toute(s)** [tut] *before feminine adjectives beginning with a consonant or an aspirate h*) *adv* **1** COMPLÈTEMENT : completely <tout neuf : completely new> **2** : quite, very, all <tout dernièrement : very recently> <elle sont toutes seules : they are all alone> **3** : while <tout en travaillant : while working> **4** : already <tout prêt : ready-made> **5 tout à coup** : suddenly **6 tout à fait** : completely, entirely **7 tout de suite** : immediately, right away

tout[2], **toute** *adj, pl* **tous, toutes 1** : all <tout le monde : everyone, everybody> <tous les dix : all ten of them> <en toute franchise : in all honesty> **2** : each, every <toutes les fois : every time> <tous les jours : every day> <tous les trois ans : every three years> **3** : any <toute autre solution : any other solution> <à tout âge : at any age> **4** : utmost, full <à toute vitesse : at full speed>

tout[3] *nm* **1 le tout** : the main thing, the whole **2 du tout au tout** : completely, entirely **3 du tout** *or* **pas du tout** : not at all

tout[4] *pron, pl* **tous, toutes 1** : all, everything <tout change : everything changes> <nous sommes tous coupables : we are all guilty> **2** : anyone, everyone <oublié de tous : forgotten by everyone> **3 tout compte fait** : all in all

toutefois [tutfwa] *adv* : however

toute–puissance [tutpɥisɑ̃s] *nf, pl* **toutes–puissances** : omnipotence

tout–puissant, toute–puissante [tutpɥisɑ̃,-sɑ̃t] *adj, pl* **tout–puissants, toutes–puissantes** : all-powerful

toutou [tutu] *nm* **1** *fam* : doggie **2** *Can fam* : stuffed animal

toux [tu] *nfs & pl* : cough

toxicité [tɔksisite] *nf* : toxicity

toxicomane [tɔksikɔman] *nmf* : drug addict

toxicomanie [tɔksikɔmani] *nf* : drug addiction

toxine [tɔksin] *nf* : toxin

toxique [tɔksik] *adj* : toxic, poisonous

trac [trak] *nm* : stage fright, jitters *pl*

tracas [traka] *nms & pl* **1** : worry **2 tracas** *nmpl* ENNUIS : troubles, problems

tracasser [trakase] *vt* : to worry, to bother — **se tracasser** *vr*

trace [tras] *nf* **1** : track, trail <traces d'ours : bear tracks> <traces de pas : footprints> <suivre les traces de qqn : to follow in s.o.'s footsteps> **2** : mark <traces de doigts : finger marks> **3** : trace, vestige, sign <traces d'une ville disparue : traces of a lost city>

tracé [trase] *nm* **1** PLAN : plan, layout **2** : course (of a river, road, etc.) **3** : line, contour

tracer [trase] {6} *vt* **1** : to trace, to lay out **2** DESSINER : to draw <tracer une ligne : to draw a line> **3** : to map out, to plot <tracer le chemin : to pave the way>

trachée [traʃe] *nf* : trachea, windpipe

tract [trakt] *nm* : leaflet

tractations [traktasjɔ̃] *nfpl* : negotiations

tracter [trakte] *vt* : to tow

tracteur [traktœr] *nm* : tractor

traction [traksjɔ̃] *nf* **1** : traction **2** : pulling, haulage **3** : push-up, chin-up **4 traction avant** : front-wheel drive

tradition [tradisjɔ̃] *nf* : tradition

traditionnel, -nelle [tradisjɔnɛl] *adj* : traditional — **traditionnellement** [-nɛlmɑ̃] *adv*

traducteur, -trice [tradyktœr, -tris] *n* : translator

traduction [tradyksjɔ̃] *nf* : translation

traduire [tradɥir] {49} *vt* **1** : to translate **2 traduire en justice** : to arraign — **se traduire** *vr* **1** : to be translated **2 ~ par** : to result in

traduisait [tradɥizɛ], **traduisions** [tradɥizjɔ̃], *etc.* → **traduire**

traduise [tradɥiz], *etc.* → **traduire**

trafic [trafik] *nm* **1** : traffic **2** : trafficking <trafic de drogue : drug trafficking>

trafiquant, -quante [trafikɑ̃, -kɑ̃t] *n* : dealer, trafficker <trafiquant de drogue : drug dealer>

trafiquer [trafike] *vt* : to doctor, to tamper with — *vi* : to traffic, to trade (in the black market)

tragédie [traʒedi] *nf* : tragedy

tragique [traʒik] *adj* : tragic — **tragiquement** [-ʒikmɑ̃] *adv*

trahir [trair] *vt* **1** : to betray **2** RÉVÉLER : to reveal, to divulge **3** : to go against, to break <trahir sa promesse : to break one's word>

trahison [traizɔ̃] *nf* : betrayal

train [trɛ̃] *nm* **1** : train <train de voyageurs : passenger train> **2** : pace, rate <au train où vont les choses : at the rate things are going> **3** : series, set <train de réformes : series of reforms> **4 en train de** : in the process of **5 train de vie** : lifestyle

traînant, -nante [trɛnɑ̃, -nɑ̃t] *adj* : drawling <parler d'une voix traînante : to drawl>

traînard, -narde [trɛnar, -nard] *n* : slowpoke, laggard, straggler

traîne [trɛn] *nf* **1** : train (of a dress) **2** : dragnet, seine **3** *Can* : toboggan, sled **4 rester à la traîne** : to lag behind

traîneau [trɛno] *nm, pl* **traîneaux 1** : sled, sleigh **2** : dragnet

traînée [trene] *nf* **1** : streak (of blood, paint, etc.) **2** : trail (of light, of a comet, etc.) **3** : drag (of an airplane, etc.)

traîner [trene] *vt* **1** : to pull, to drag **2 traîner les pieds** : to drag one's feet — *vi* **1** : to drag along, to trail (on the ground) **2** : to dawdle, to lag behind **3** : to linger, to drag on **4** : to be lying around <elle laisse traîner son linge : she doesn't pick up after herself> **5** : to speak slowly, to drawl **6** : to wander about <traîner dans les rues : to roam the streets> — **se traîner** *vr* **1** : to drag oneself, to crawl (along) **2** : to drag on

train-train [trɛ̃trɛ̃] *nms & pl* ROUTINE : routine

traire [trɛr] {40} *vt* : to milk (an animal)

trait [trɛ] *nm* **1** : trait <trait de caractère : character trait> **2** : stroke <d'un trait de plume : with a stroke of the pen> **3 avoir trait à** : to relate to, to concern **4 tout d'un trait** : in one breath, in one gulp **5 trait d'esprit** : witticism, quip **6 trait d'union** : hyphen **7 traits** *nmpl* : features <traits fins : delicate features>

traitant, -tante [trɛtɑ̃, -tɑ̃t] *adj* **médecin traitant** : family doctor

traite [trɛt] *nf* **1** : trade (in human beings) <la traite des Noirs : the slave trade> **2** : milking **3 d'une traite** : in one go, without stopping **4 traite bancaire** : bank draft

traité [trete] *nm* **1** : treaty **2** : treatise

traitement [trɛtmɑ̃] *nm* **1** : treatment **2** : stipend, salary **3 traitement des données** *or* **traitement de l'information** : data processing **4 traitement de texte** : word processing

traiter [trete] *vt* **1** : to treat **2** : to process (data) **3** : to characterize as, to call <je l'ai traité d'imbécile : I called him a fool> **4** : to deal with, to handle — *vi* **~ de** : to deal with, to be concerned with

traiteur [trɛtœr] *nm* : caterer

traître[1], **-tresse** [trɛtr, -trɛs] *adj* **1** : treacherous, betraying **2 pas un traître mot** : not a single word

traître[2], **-tresse** *n* **1** : traitor **2 en ~** : in an underhanded way, treacherously

traîtreusement [trɛtrøzmɑ̃] *adv* : treacherously

traîtrise [trɛtriz] *nf* : treachery, betrayal

trajectoire [traʒɛktwar] *nf* : path, trajectory

trajet [traʒɛ] *nm* **1** CHEMIN : path, way, route <le trajet le plus direct : the quickest route> **2** : journey, trip

tralala [tralala] *nm fam* : fuss

trame [tram] *nf* **1** : weft (of fabric) **2** : framework

tramer [trame] *vt* **1** : to plot **2** : to weave

trampoline [trampɔlin] *nm* : trampoline

tramway [tramwɛ] *nm* : streetcar, trolley

tranchant[1], **-chante** [trɑ̃ʃɑ̃, -ʃɑ̃t] *adj* **1** : sharp, keen-edged **2** COUPANT : curt, sharp <une remarque tranchante : a cutting remark>

tranchant[2] *nm* **1** : cutting edge, sharpness **2 à double tranchant** : double-edged

tranche [trɑ̃ʃ] *nf* **1** : slice **2** : period, phase, stage <tranche horaire : time slot> <tranche d'âge : age bracket> **3** : edge (of a book, coin, etc.)

tranché, -chée [trɑ̃ʃe] *adj* **1** : sliced **2** : distinct, contrasting **3** : clear-cut, marked

tranchée *nf* : trench

trancher [trɑ̃ʃe] *vt* **1** COUPER : to cut (through), to slice, to sever **2** : to settle, to resolve **3** : to cut short — *vi* **1** : to contrast, to stand out **2** : to come to a decision

tranquille [trɑ̃kil] *adj* **1** : calm, quiet <tiens-toi tranquille! : sit still!> : untroubled, assured <avoir la con

science tranquille : to have a clear conscience> <soyez tranquille! : don't worry!>

tranquillement |trɑ̃kilmɑ̃| *adv* **1** CALMEMENT : quietly, calmly **2** LENTEMENT : unhurriedly, at a leisurely pace

tranquillisant¹, -sante |trɑ̃kilizɑ̃, -zɑ̃t| *adj* RASSURANT : reassuring

tranquillisant² *nm* : tranquilizer

tranquilliser |trɑ̃kilize| *vt* RASSURER : to reassure

tranquillité |trɑ̃kilite| *nf* **1** CALME : peacefulness, tranquillity **2 tranquillité d'esprit** : peace of mind

transaction |trɑ̃zaksjɔ̃| *nf* : transaction <transactions financières : financial transactions>

transatlantique |trɑ̃zatlɑ̃tik| *adj* : transatlantic

transcendant, -dante |trɑ̃sɑ̃dɑ̃, -dɑ̃t| *adj* **1** SUBLIME : sublime, transcendent **2** : transcendental

transcender |trɑ̃sɑ̃de| *vt* : to transcend — **se transcender** *vr* : to surpass oneself

transcontinental, -tale |trɑ̃skɔ̃tinɑ̃tal| *adj, mpl* **-taux** |-to| : transcontinental

transcription |trɑ̃skripsjɔ̃| *nf* : transcription, transcript

transcrire |trɑ̃skrir| {33} *vt* : to transcribe

transe |trɑ̃s| *nf* **1** : trance <entrer en transe : to go into a trance> **2 transes** *nfpl* : anxiety, upset <être dans les transes : to get all worked up>

transférer |trɑ̃sfere| *vt* : to transfer — **transférable** |trɑ̃sferabl| *adj*

transfert |trɑ̃sfɛr| *nm* : transfer <transfert de fonds : transfer of funds>

transfigurer |trɑ̃sfigyre| *vt* : to transfigure — **transfiguration** |-gyrasjɔ̃| *nf*

transformateur |trɑ̃sfɔrmatœr| *nm* : transformer

transformation |trɑ̃sfɔrmasjɔ̃| *nf* **1** : transformation **2** : conversion (in sports)

transformer |trɑ̃sfɔrme| *vt* **1** : to transform, to change, to alter **2** : to convert (in sports) **3 ~ en** : to convert (a building, etc.) into — **se transformer** *vr* **1** : to change, to be transformed **2 ~ en** : to turn into

transfuge |trɑ̃sfyʒ| *nmf* **1** : renegade, defector **2** : deserter (in the military)

transfuser |trɑ̃sfyze| *vt* : to transfuse

transfusion |trɑ̃sfyzjɔ̃| *nf* : transfusion

transgresser |trɑ̃sgrese| *vt* ENFREINDRE : to infringe, to violate, to disobey

transgression |trɑ̃sgrɛsjɔ̃| *nf* : infringement, transgression

transi, -sie |trɑ̃zi| *adj* **1** : numb (with cold) **2** : paralyzed (with fear)

transiger |trɑ̃ziʒe| {17} *vi* : to compromise

transir |trɑ̃zir| *vt* : to numb (with cold)

transistor |trɑ̃zistɔr| *nm* : transistor

transit |trɑ̃zit| *nm* : transit <en transit : in transit>

transitif, -tive |trɑ̃zitif, -tiv| *adj* : transitive

transition |trɑ̃zisjɔ̃| *nf* : transition

transitoire |trɑ̃zitwar| *adj* **1** : transitory, transient **2** : transitional

translucide |trɑ̃slysid| *adj* : translucent

transmetteur |trɑ̃smɛtœr| *nm* : transmitter

transmettre |trɑ̃smɛtr| {53} *vt* **1** : to transmit (signals, data, etc.) **2** : to pass on, to convey **3** : to broadcast **4** : to transfer (power, etc.) **5** : to transmit (a disease)

transmissible |trɑ̃smisibl| *adj* : transmittable, communicable

transmission |trɑ̃smisjɔ̃| *nf* : transmission

transparaître |trɑ̃sparɛtr| {7} *vi* **1** : to show through **2 laisser transparaître** : to manifest, to let show (of emotions, etc.)

transparence |trɑ̃sparɑ̃s| *nf* : transparency

transparent, -rente |trɑ̃sparɑ̃, -rɑ̃t| *adj* : transparent

transpercer |trɑ̃spɛrse| {6} *vt* : to go through, to pierce <la douleur me transperçait le dos : pain was shooting through my back>

transpiration |trɑ̃spirasjɔ̃| *nf* **1** SUEUR : perspiration, sweat **2** : transpiration (in botany)

transpirer |trɑ̃spire| *vt* **1** SUER : to perspire, to sweat **2** : to transpire (in botany) **3** : to come to light

transplantation |trɑ̃splɑ̃tasjɔ̃| *nm* : transplant

transplanter |trɑ̃splɑ̃te| *vt* : to transplant

transport |trɑ̃spɔr| *nm* **1** : transport (of goods, etc.) <transport aérien : air transport> **2 transports** *nmpl* : (system of) transportation <transports en commun : public transportation> **3 transports** *nmpl* : transports, strong emotions

transporter |trɑ̃spɔrte| *vt* **1** : to carry, to bear **2** : to transport, to convey (goods, etc.) **3** : to transport, to carry away <être transporté de joie : to be overjoyed>

transporteur |trɑ̃spɔrtœr| *nm* **1** : carrier, transporter (company) **2** : conveyor (machine)

transposer |trɑ̃spoze| *vt* : to transpose — **transposition** |-pozisjɔ̃| *nf*

transvaser |trɑ̃svaze| *vt* : to decant (a liquid)

transversal, -sale |trɑ̃svɛrsal| *adj, mpl* **-saux** |-so| : transverse, cross(ing) <coupe transversale : cross section> <rues transversales : cross streets>

transversalement |trɑ̃svɛrsalmɑ̃| *adv* : crosswise

trapèze |trapɛz| *nm* **1** : trapezoid **2** : trapeze
trappe |trap| *nf* **1** PIÈGE : trap, snare **2** : trapdoor
trappeur |trapœr| *nm* : trapper
trapu, -pue |trapy| *adj* : stocky, squat
traquenard |traknar| *nm* : trap
traquer |trake| *vt* POURSUIVRE : to pursue, to chase, to track down
traumatisant, -sante |tromatizɑ̃, -zɑ̃t| *adj* : traumatic
traumatiser |tromatize| *vt* : to traumatize
traumatisme |tromatism| *nm* : trauma
travail |travaj| *nm, pl* **travaux** |travo| **1** : work <travail scolaire : schoolwork> <se mettre au travail : to get down to work> **2** TÂCHE : task, job, work <avoir du travail : to have work to do> **3** EMPLOI : work, employment <travail à plein temps : full-time work> <sans travail : unemployed> <vivre de son travail : to work for one's living> **4** : labor <division de travail : division of labor> **5** : working, fashioning <travail du bois : woodworking> **6** : work (of art, literature, etc.) **7** : labor (in giving birth) **8 travaux** *nmpl* : works <travaux publics : public works> **9 travaux** *nmpl* : work, operations <travaux d'aiguille : needlework> <travaux de la ferme : farmwork>
travaillant, -lante |travajɑ̃, -jɑt| *adj Can* : hardworking, industrious
travaillé, -lée |travaje| *adj* : elaborate, finely made
travailler |travaje| *vt* **1** : to work, to treat <travailler la terre : to work the land> **2** : to mix together (in cooking) **3** : to work on, to practice, to polish up **4** : to bother, to worry <ça me travaille : it's preying on my mind> — *vi* **1** : to work <travailler beaucoup trop : to work too hard> **2** : to work (at a job) <travailler en indépendent : to be self-employed> <travailler au noir : to moonlight> **3** : to train, to work out **4 ~ à** : to work toward, to endeavor to
travailleur[1], **-leuse** |travajœr, -jøz| *adj* : hardworking, industrious
travailleur[2], **-leuse** *n* : worker
travée |trave| *nf* **1** : row (of seats) **2** : span (of a bridge)
travers |travɛr| *nms & pl* **1** : fault, failing **2 à ~** : across, through <à travers la chambre : across the room> <à travers les siècles : down through the centuries> **3 au travers** : through <passer au travers : to escape> **4 au travers de** : by means of **5 de ~** : askew, crooked, wrongly <comprendre de travers : to misunderstand> **6 en ~** : crosswise, sideways
traverse |travɛrs| *nf* **1** : railroad tie **2** : transom
traversée |travɛrse| *nf* : crossing
traverser |travɛrse| *vt* **1** : to cross <traverser la rue : to cross the road> **2** : to run through, to pass through, to flow through **3** : to penetrate, to soak through **4** : to go through, to experience (a crisis, etc.) **5 traverser l'esprit de qqn** : to cross s.o.'s mind
traversier |travɛrsje| *nm Can* : ferryboat
traversin |travɛrsɛ̃| *nm* : bolster
trayait |trɛjɛ|, **trayions** |trɛjɔ̃|, *etc.* → **traire**
trébuchement |trebyʃmɑ̃| *nm* : stumble, stumbling
trébucher |trebyʃe| *vi* : to stumble
trèfle |trɛfl| *nm* **1** : clover, shamrock **2** : clubs *pl* (in playing cards)
treillage |trɛjaʒ| *nm* : trellis, lattice
treille |trɛj| *nf* : climbing vine
treillis |trɛji| *nms & pl* : trellis, lattice
treize[1] |trɛz| *adj* **1** : thirteen **2** : thirteenth <le treize janvier : January thirteenth>
treize[2] *nms & pl* : thirteen
treizième |trɛzjɛm| *adj & nmf & nm* : thirteenth
tremblant, -blante |trɑ̃blɑ̃, -blɑ̃t| *adj* : shaking, trembling
tremble |trɑ̃bl| *nm* : aspen
tremblement |trɑ̃bləmɑ̃| *nm* **1** : shaking, trembling **2** : quavering, shakiness (of the voice, etc.) **3** : fluttering, flickering **4 tremblement de terre** : earthquake
trembler |trɑ̃ble| *vi* **1** : to shake, to tremble **2** : to quiver, to quaver **3** : to flutter, to flicker
trembloter |trɑ̃blɔte| *vi* : to tremble, to quiver, to shiver
trémie |tremi| *nf* : hopper
trémousser |tremuse| *v* **se trémousser** *vr* : to wriggle around
trempage |trɑ̃paʒ| *nm* : soak, soaking
trempe |trɑ̃p| *nf* **1** : temper (of metals) **2** : caliber, quality <un homme de sa trempe : a man of his caliber>
trempé, -pée |trɑ̃pe| *adj* **1** : soaked, drenched **2 acier trempé** : tempered steel
tremper |trɑ̃pe| *vt* **1** : to soak **2** : to dip, to dunk **3** : to temper (steel, etc.)
trempette |trɑ̃pɛt| *nf* **1** : dip (in swimming) <faire trempette : to take a quick dip> **2** *Can* : dip <trempette aux légumes : vegetable dip>
tremplin |trɑ̃plɛ̃| *nm* **1** : springboard **2** : stepping stone (in a career, etc.) **3** *or* **tremplin à ski** : ski jump
trémulation |tremylasjɔ̃| *nf* : tremor
trente[1] |trɑ̃t| *adj* **1** : thirty **2** : thirtieth <le trente septembre : September thirtieth>
trente[2] *nms & pl* : thirty
trente–sous |trɑ̃tsu| *nms & pl Can fam* : quarter (unit of currency)
trentième |trɑ̃tjɛm| *adj & nmf & nm* : thirtieth

trépasser [trepase] *vi* DÉCÉDER : to pass away

trépidant, -dante [trepidɑ̃, -dɑ̃t] *adj* **1** : vibrating **2** : hectic, frantic

trépidation [trepidasjɔ̃] *nf* **1** : vibration **2** : flurry, bustle

trépider [trepide] *vi* : to vibrate

trépied [trepje] *nm* : tripod

trépigner [trepiɲe] *vi* : to stamp one's feet

très [trɛ] *adv* : very <très heureux : very happy> <très bien : very well> <très à la mode : very fashionable> <elle a très soif : she's very thirsty>

trésor [trezɔr] *nm* **1** : treasure **2 le Trésor (public)** : public revenue **3 mon trésor** : my darling

trésorerie [trezɔrri] *nf* **1** : funds *pl*, accounts *pl* **2** : public revenue office

trésorier, -rière [trezɔrje, -rjɛr] *n* : treasurer

tressaillement [tresajmɑ̃] *nm* : wincing, flinching

tressaillir [trɛsajir] {93} *vi* **1** : to start, to flinch, to wince **2** : to quiver, to vibrate

tressauter [trɛsote] *vi* SURSAUTER : to start, to jump

tresse [trɛs] *nf* : braid, plait

tresser [trɛse] *vt* **1** : to braid, to plait **2** : to weave (a basket, etc.)

tréteau [treto] *nm, pl* **tréteaux** : trestle

treuil [trœj] *nm* : winch, windlass

trêve [trɛv] *nf* **1** : truce **2** : respite

tri [tri] *nm* : sorting (out)

triade [triad] *nf* : triad

triangle [trijɑ̃gl] *nm* : triangle

triangulaire [trijɑ̃gylɛr] *adj* : triangular

tribal, -bale [tribal] *adj, mpl* **tribaux** [tribo] : tribal

tribord [tribɔr] *nm* : starboard

tribu [triby] *nf* : tribe

tribulations [tribylasjɔ̃] *nfpl* : tribulations

tribunal [tribynal] *nm, pl* **-naux** [-no] **1** : courthouse, court <porter une affaire devant le tribunal : to take a matter to court> **2** : judgment, justice <le tribunal de l'histoire : the judgment of history>

tribune [tribyn] *nf* **1** : gallery, grandstand **2** : rostrum, platform **3** DÉBAT : forum

tribut [triby] *nm* : tribute

tributaire [tribytɛr] *adj* **être tributaire de** : to be dependent on

tricher [triʃe] *vi* **1** : to cheat **2 ~ sur** : to lie about

tricherie [triʃri] *nf* : cheating

tricheur, -cheuse [triʃœr, -ʃøz] *n* : cheat

tricolore [trikɔlɔr] *adj* : tricolor

tricot [triko] *nm* **1** : knitting **2** : knitted fabric **3** CHANDAIL : sweater, jersey

tricoter [trikɔte] *v* : to knit

tricoteur, -teuse [trikɔtœr, -tøz] *n* : knitter

trictrac [triktrak] *nm France* : backgammon

tricycle [trisikl] *nm* : tricycle

trident [tridɑ̃] *nm* : trident

tridimensionnel, -nelle [tridimɑ̃sjɔnɛl] *adj* : three-dimensional

triennal, -nale [trijenal] *adj, mpl* **-naux** [-no] : triennial

trier [trije] {96} *vt* **1** CLASSER : to sort (out) **2** : to pick out, to select

trigonométrie [trigɔnɔmetri] *nf* : trigonometry

trille [trij] *nf* : trill

triller [trije] *v* : to trill

trilogie [trilɔʒi] *nf* : trilogy

trimbaler *or* **trimballer** [trɛ̃bale] *vt fam* : to cart around, to drag along

trimer [trime] *vi fam* : to slave away

trimestre [trimɛstr] *nm* **1** : quarter (in economics, etc.) **2** : term (in school)

trimestriel, -trielle [trimɛstrijɛl] *adj* : quarterly

trimestriellement [trimɛstrijɛlmɑ̃] *adv* : quarterly

tringle [trɛ̃gl] *nf* : rod

trinidadien, -dienne [trinidadjɛ̃, -djɛn] *adj* : Trinidadian

Trinidadien, -dienne *n* : Trinidadian

trinité [trinite] *nf* **1** : trinity **2 la Trinité** : the (Holy) Trinity

trinquer [trɛ̃ke] *vi* **1** : to clink glasses, to toast **2** *fam* : to pay the price, to take the rap

trio [trijo] *nm* : trio

triomphal, -phale [trijɔ̃fal] *adj, mpl* **triomphaux** [-fo] : triumphal, triumphant

triomphalement [trijɔ̃falmɑ̃] *adv* : triumphantly

triomphant, -phante [trijɔ̃fɑ̃, -fɑ̃t] *adj* : triumphant

triomphateur, -trice [trijɔ̃fatœr, -tris] *n* : victor

triomphe [trijɔ̃f] *nm* : triumph, success

triompher [trijɔ̃fe] *vi* : to triumph, to prevail

tripartite [tripartit] *adj* : tripartite

tripe [trip] *nf* **1 tripes** *nfpl* : tripe **2 tripes** *nfpl fam* : guts <rendre tripes et boyaux : to vomit, to be sick as a dog>

triple [tripl] *adj & nm* : triple, treble

triplement [tripləmɑ̃] *adv* : triply, three times over

tripler [triple] *v* : to triple

triplés, -plées [triple] *npl* : triplets

tripoter [tripɔte] *vt* **1** : to fiddle with, to play around with **2** : to handle, to paw — *vi* **1** : to rummage about **2** : to dabble (in shady activities)

trique [trik] *nf* : cudgel

trisannuel, -nuelle [trizanɥɛl] *adj* : triennial

triste [trist] *adj* **1** : sad, sorrowful **2** : dismal, dreary <un paysage triste : a bleak landscape> **3** LAMENTABLE : deplorable, sorry <en un triste état : in a sorry state>

tristement [tristəmɑ̃] *adv* **1** : sadly, sorrowfully **2** : regrettably <c'est tristement vrai : it's all too true>
tristesse [tristɛs] *nf* : sadness, sorrow
triton [tritɔ̃] *nm* : newt
triturer [trityre] *vt* **1** BROYER : to grind **2** PÉTRIR : to knead **3** MANIPULER : to manipulate
trivial, -viale [trivjal] *adj, mpl* **triviaux** [-vjo] **1** GROSSIER : coarse, crude **2** BANAL : mundane, trivial
trivialité [trivjalite] *nf* **1** : coarseness, crudeness **2** : banality, triteness
troc [trɔk] *nm* **1** ÉCHANGE : exchange, swap **2** : barter
troène [trɔɛn] *nm* : privet (hedge)
trognon [trɔɲɔ̃] *nm* : core (of an apple, etc.), stalk (of cabbage, etc.)
trois[1] [trwa] *adj* **1** : three **2** : third <le trois juin : June third>
trois[2] *nms & pl* : three
troisième[1] [trwazjɛm] *adj & nmf* : third
troisième[2] *nm* : third floor
troisièmement [trwazjɛmmɑ̃] *adv* : thirdly
trolley [trɔlɛ] *nm* : trolley
trombe [trɔ̃b] *nf* **1** : waterspout **2** : whirlwind <en trombe : in a flurry> **3 trombes d'eau** : downpour, cloudburst
tromblon [trɔ̃blɔ̃] *nm* : blunderbuss
trombone [trɔ̃bɔn] *nm* **1** : trombone **2** : paper clip
tromboniste [trɔ̃bɔnist] *nmf* : trombonist
trompe [trɔ̃p] *nf* **1** : horn **2** : trunk, proboscis
trompe–l'oeil [trɔ̃plœj] *nms & pl* : trompe l'oeil
tromper [trɔ̃pe] *vt* **1** DUPER : to deceive, to mislead **2** : to be unfaithful to **3** : to elude, to outwit **4** : to fool, to trick <c'est ce qui m'a trompé : that's what fooled me> **5** : to stave off — **se tromper** *vr* : to make a mistake <se tromper de route : to take the wrong road>
tromperie [trɔ̃pri] *nf* : deception, deceit
trompette [trɔ̃pɛt] *nf* : trumpet
trompettiste [trɔ̃petist] *nmf* : trumpet player
trompeur[1], **-peuse** [trɔ̃pœr, -pøz] *adj* **1** : deceitful **2** : deceptive, misleading
trompeur[2], **-peuse** *n* : deceiver
trompeusement [trɔ̃pøzmɑ̃] *adv* : deceitfully, deceptively
tronc [trɔ̃] *nm* **1** : trunk (of a tree) **2** : collection box (in a church) **3** TORSE : torso **4 tronc commun** : common origin
tronçon [trɔ̃sɔ̃] *nm* : section
tronçonner [trɔ̃sɔne] *vt* : to cut into sections, to saw up
tronçonneuse [trɔ̃sɔnøz] *nf* : chain saw
trône [tron] *nm* : throne
trôner [trone] *vi* : to have the place of honor
tronquer [trɔ̃ke] *vt* **1** : to truncate **2** : to curtail, to shorten
trop [tro] *adv* **1** : too <trop difficile : too hard> <j'ai beaucoup trop dit : I've said far too much> **2 ~ de** : too many, too much <trop de livres : too many books> <il a bu trop de café : he's had too much coffee> **3 de ~** *or* **en ~** : too many, extra <une personne de trop : one person too many>
trophée [trɔfe] *nm* : trophy
tropical, -cale [trɔpikal] *adj, mpl* **-caux** [-ko] : tropical
tropique [trɔpik] *nm* **1** : tropic <tropique du Cancer : tropic of Cancer> **2 tropiques** *nmpl* : tropics
trop–plein [trɔplɛ̃] *nm, pl* **trop–pleins** **1** : overflow **2** SURPLUS : excess, surplus
troquer [trɔke] *vt* : to swap, to trade
trot [tro] *nm* : trot
trotte [trɔt] *nf fam* : good distance <ça fait une trotte : it's a good walk>
trotter [trɔte] *vi* **1** : to trot **2** : to scamper, to run along **3 trotter dans la tête** : to keep running through one's mind
trotteuse [trɔtøz] *nf* : second hand (of a watch)
trottiner [trɔtine] *vi* : to scurry along
trottinette [trɔtinɛt] *nf* PATINETTE : scooter
trottoir [trɔtwar] *nm* **1** : sidewalk **2 trottoir roulant** : moving walkway
trou [tru] *nm* **1** : hole **2** TERRIER : burrow **3** : eye (of a needle) **4** DÉCHIRURE : tear, rip, hole **5** : gap (of time) <avoir une heure de trou : to have an hour's free time> <trou de mémoire : blank, memory lapse> **6** *fam* : little place, hole-in-the-wall **7 trou d'homme** : manhole **8 trou noir** : black hole **9 trou de serrure** : keyhole
troubadour [trubadur] *nm* : troubadour
troublant, -blante [trublɑ̃, -blɑ̃t] *adj* : disturbing, unsettling
trouble[1] [trubl] *adj* **1** : cloudy, dim **2** FLOU : blurred **3** : confused, unclear
trouble[2] *nm* **1** : distress, confusion, embarrassment **2** : trouble, discord <semer le trouble : to sow discord> **3** : disorder (in medicine) <trouble respiratoire : respiratory disorder> **4 troubles** *nmpl* : unrest <troubles politiques : political unrest>
troubler [truble] *vt* **1** : to disturb, to trouble **2** : to disrupt **3** BROUILLER : to blur, to cloud **4** : to confuse, to disconcert — **se troubler** *vr* **1** : to become cloudy **2** : to get confused
trouée [true] *nf* : gap, breach
trouer [true] *vt* : to make a hole in, to pierce
trouillard, -larde [trujar, -jard] *n fam* : chicken, coward

trouille [truj] *nf fam* : fear, fright <avoir la trouille : to be scared stiff>
troupe [trup] *nf* **1** : troop **2** : troupe **3** : herd (of horses, elephants, etc.) **4 la troupe** : the army
troupeau [trupo] *nm, pl* **troupeaux** : herd, flock
trousse [trus] *nf* **1** : kit, case <trousse de secours : first-aid kit> **2 aux trousses de** : on the heels of <la police est à mes trousses : the police are after me>
trousseau [truso] *nm, pl* **trousseaux 1** : trousseau **2 trousseau de clefs** : bunch of keys
trousser [truse] *vt* : to truss (a fowl)
trouvaille [truvaj] *nf* **1** DÉCOUVERTE : find **2** : inspiration, brainstorm
trouver [truve] *vt* **1** DÉCOUVRIR : to find, to discover **2** SE PROCURER : to find, to obtain, to get **3** IMAGINER : to find, to think up **4** ESTIMER : to think, to consider <je trouve que c'est incroyable : I think it's incredible> — **se trouver** *vr* **1** : to be (found) <ça se trouve un peu partout : it's found almost anywhere> **2** : to find oneself <je me suis trouvé incapable de répondre : I found myself unable to answer> **3** : to feel <il se trouve mieux : he feels better> — *v impers* **il se trouve que** : it turns out that
truand [tryɑ̃] *nm* : gangster, crook
truc [tryk] *nm* **1** ASTUCE : trick <trucs du métier : tricks of the trade> **2** *fam* MACHIN : thingamajig, contraption, thing
trucage [trykaʒ] *nm* : special effect (in movies)
truchement [tryʃmɑ̃] *nm* **par le truchement de** : through, with the help of, by means of
truculent, -lente [trykylɑ̃, -lɑ̃t] *adj* : earthy, racy, colorful
truelle [tryɛl] *nf* : trowel
truffe [tryf] *nf* **1** : truffle **2** : nose (of a dog)
truffer [tryfe] *vt* : to fill with, to pepper with, to riddle with
truie [trɥi] *nf* : sow (pig)
truisme [tryism] *nm* : truism
truite [trɥit] *nf* : trout
truquage [trykaʒ] *nm* → **trucage**
truquer [tryke] *vt* **1** : to fix, to rig (an election, etc.) **2** : to use special effects in
trust [trœst] *nm* : trust, cartel
tsar [tsar, dzar] *nm* : czar
tsarine [tsarin, dzarin] *nf* : czarina
t–shirt [tiʃœrt] *nm* → **tee–shirt**
tu[1] [ty] *pp* → **taire**
tu[2] [ty] *pron* : you
tuant, tuante [tɥɑ̃, tɥɑ̃t] *adj fam* **1** : exhausting **2** : exasperating
tuba [tyba] *nm* **1** : tuba **2** : snorkel
tube [tyb] *nm* **1** : tube, pipe **2** : tube (of toothpaste, etc.) **3 tube digestif** : digestive tract, alimentary canal
tubercule [tybɛrkyl] *nm* : tuber
tuberculeux, -leuse [tybɛrkylø, -løz] *adj* : tubercular, tuberculous
tuberculose [tybɛrkyloz] *nf* : tuberculosis
tubulaire [tybylɛr] *adj* : tubular
tubulure [tybylyr] *nf* : manifold (of an automobile)
tue–mouches[1] [tymuʃ] *adj* **papier tue–mouches** : flypaper
tue–mouches[2] *nms & pl Can* : flyswatter
tuer [tɥe] *vt* **1** : to kill **2** ÉPUISER : to wear out, to exhaust **3 tuer le temps** : to kill time — **se tuer** *vr* **1** : to be killed, to die **2** : to kill oneself
tuerie [tyri] *nf* CARNAGE : slaughter, carnage
tue–tête [tytɛt] **à ~** : at the top of one's lungs
tueur, tueuse [tɥœr, tɥøz] *n* MEURTRIER : killer, murderer
tuile [tɥil] *nf* **1** : tile **2** *fam* : bad luck
tulipe [tylip] *nf* : tulip
tuméfié, -fiée [tymefje] *adj* : swollen, puffed-up
tumeur [tymœr] *nf* : tumor, growth
tumulte [tymylt] *nm* **1** BROUHAHA : tumult, commotion, hubbub **2** : (emotional) turmoil
tumultueux, -tueuse [tymyltɥø, -tɥøz] *adj* : stormy, turbulent — **tumultueusement** [-tɥøzmɑ̃] *adv*
tungstène [tœ̃kstɛn] *nm* : tungsten
tunique [tynik] *nf* : tunic
tunisien, -sienne [tynizjɛ̃, -zjɛn] *adj* : Tunisian
Tunisien, -sienne *n* : Tunisian
tunnel [tynɛl] *nm* : tunnel
tuque [tyk] *nf Can* : stocking cap, tuque
turban [tyrbɑ̃] *nm* : turban
turbide [tyrbid] *adj* : turbid
turbine [tyrbin] *nf* : turbine
turbopropulseur [tyrbɔpropylsœr] *nm* : turboprop
turboréacteur [tyrbɔreaktœr] *nm* : turbojet
turbulence [tyrbylɑ̃s] *nf* : turbulence
turbulent, -lente [tyrbylɑ̃, -lɑ̃t] *adj* **1** : boisterous, unruly **2** : turbulent
turc[1], **turque** [tyrk] *adj* : Turkish
turc[2] *nm* : Turkish (language)
Turc, Turque *n* : Turk
turf [tœrf] *nm* **1** : racetrack **2** : horse racing
turquoise[1] [tyrkwaz] *adj* : turquoise
turquoise[2] *nf* : turquoise (stone)
turquoise[3] *nm* : turquoise (color)
tutelle [tytɛl] *nf* **1** : guardianship **2** : trusteeship **3** : care, protection (of the law, etc.)
tuteur[1], **-trice** [tytœr, -tris] *n* **1** : guardian **2** : tutor
tuteur[2] *nm* : stake, prop (for plants)
tutoiement [tytwamɑ̃] *nm* : use of the familiar "tu" form

tutoyer [tytwaje] {58} *vt* : to address someone as "tu"
tuyau [tɥijo] *nm, pl* **tuyaux 1** : pipe, tube, conduit <tuyau d'échappement : exhaust pipe> <tuyau d'arrosage : garden hose> **2** : quill **3** *fam* : tip, inside information
tuyauter [tɥijote] *vt* **1** : to flute, to pleat **2** *fam* : to give someone a tip
tuyauterie [tɥijotri] *nf* : piping, pipes *pl*, plumbing
tuyère [tyjɛr] *nf* : nozzle
TV [teve] *nf* : TV
tweed [twid] *nm* : tweed
tympan [tɛ̃pɑ̃] *nm* : eardrum
type [tip] *nm* **1** : type, kind **2** : example, model **3** : (physical) type **4** *fam* : guy, fellow
typé, -pée [tipe] *adj* : typical, distinctive (of features)
typhoïde [tifɔid] *adj & nf* : typhoid
typhon [tifɔ̃] *nm* : typhoon
typhus [tifys] *nms & pl* : typhus
typique [tipik] *adj* : typical — **typiquement** [-pikmɑ̃] *adv*
typographie [tipɔgrafi] *nf* : typography
typographique [tipɔgrafik] *adj* : typographic, typographical — **typographiquement** [-fikmɑ̃] *adv*
tyran [tirɑ̃] *nm* : tyrant
tyrannie [tirani] *nf* : tyranny
tyrannique [tiranik] *adj* : tyrannical — **tyranniquement** [-nikmɑ̃] *adv*
tyranniser [tiranize] *vt* : to tyrannize
tzar [tsar, dzar] → **tsar**
tzigane [dzigan] *adj & nmf* : gypsy

U

u [y] *nm* : u, the 21st letter of the alphabet
ubiquité [ybikɥite] *nf* : ubiquity
ukrainien¹, -nienne [ykrɛnjɛ̃, -njɛn] *adj* : Ukrainian
ukrainien² *nm* : Ukrainian (language)
Ukrainien, -nienne *n* : Ukrainian
ulcération [ylserasjɔ̃] *nf* : ulceration
ulcère [ylsɛr] *nm* : ulcer <ulcère à l'estomac : stomach ulcer>
ulcérer [ylsere] {87} *vt* **1** : to ulcerate **2** RÉVOLTER : to revolt, to appall
ulcéreux, -reuse [ylserø, -røz] *adj* **1** : ulcerous **2** : ulcerated
ultérieur, -rieure [ylterjœr] *adj* : later, subsequent
ultérieurement [ylterjœrmɑ̃] *adv* : at a later time, subsequently
ultimatum [yltimatɔm] *nm* : ultimatum
ultime [yltim] *adj* : ultimate, final
ultraviolet, -lette [yltravjolɛ, -lɛt] *adj* : ultraviolet
ululement, uluer [ylylmɑ̃] → **hululement, hululer**
un¹, une [œ̃ (œn *before a vowel or mute h*), yn] *adj* : a, an, one <rester une semaine : to stay a week, to stay one week> <il y a un seul problème : there's just one problem>
un², une *n* : one <les filles marchent une par une : the girls are walking one by one> <la page une : page one>
un³ *nm* : (number) one <huit et un font neuf : eight and one are nine>
un⁴, une *pron, pl* **uns, unes** : one <un de ces jours : one of these days> <l'une de mes amies : one of my friends>
un⁵, une *art, pl* **des 1** (*used in the singular*) : a, an <un exemple : an example> <une nouvelle maison : a new house> **2** (*used in the plural*) : some <voici des bonbons : here are some candies> <des gens sont déjà arrivés : some people have already arrived> **3** (*used for emphasis*) <il a attendu des heures : he waited for hours> <il y a une pluie! : there's so much rain!>
unanime [ynanim] *adj* : unanimous — **unanimement** [-nimmɑ̃] *adv*
unanimité [ynanimite] *nf* : unanimity
une [yn] *nf* **faire la une** : to be on the front page
uni, -nie [yni] *adj* **1** : united <les États-Unis : the United States> **2** LISSE : smooth, even **3** : plain-colored, solid **4** : close-knit
unième [ynjɛm] *adj* : first <trente et unième : thirty-first>
unificateur, -trice [ynifikatœr, -tris] *adj* : unifying
unification [ynifikasjɔ̃] *nf* : unification
unifier [ynifje] {96} *vt* **1** UNIR : to unite, to unify **2** NORMALISER : to standardize — **s'unifier** *vr* : to unite
uniforme¹ [ynifɔrm] *adj* **1** RÉGULIER : uniform, even **2** : unchanging
uniforme² *nm* : uniform
uniformément [ynifɔrmemɑ̃] *adv* : uniformly
uniformiser *vt* **1** : to make uniform **2** STANDARDISER : to standardize
uniformité [ynifɔrmite] *nf* : uniformity, evenness
unilatéral, -rale [ynilateral] *adj, pl* **-raux** [-ro] : unilateral — **unilatéralement** [-ralmɑ̃] *adv*
unilingue [ynilɛ̃g] *adj* : monolingual
union [ynjɔ̃] *nf* **1** : union <union conjugale : marriage> <Union soviétique : Soviet Union> **2** ASSOCIATION : association
unique [ynik] *adj* **1** SEUL : only <mon unique espoir : my only hope> **2** EXCEPTIONNEL : unique, exceptional **3** → **enfant**

uniquement [ynikmɑ̃] *adv* **1** EXCLUSIVEMENT : exclusively **2** SEULEMENT : only, solely
unir [ynir] *vt* **1** : to unite, to bring together **2** : to combine — **s'unir** *vr* **1** : to unite **2** : to be joined in marriage
unisson [ynisɔ̃] *nm* : unison
unitaire [ynitɛr] *adj* **1** : unitary **2 prix unitaire** : unit price
unité [ynite] *nf* **1** : unity **2** : unit
univers [ynivɛr] *nm* : universe
universel, -selle [ynivɛrsɛl] *adj* : universal — **universellement** [-sɛlmɑ̃] *adv*
universitaire[1] [ynivɛrsitɛr] *adj* : university, academic
universitaire[2] *nmf* : academic
université [ynivɛrsite] *nf* : university
univoque [ynivɔk] *adj* : unambiguous, certain
uranium [yranjɔm] *nm* : uranium
Uranus [yranys] *nm* : Uranus
urbain, -baine [yrbɛ̃, -bɛn] *adj* : urban, city
urbanisme [yrbanism] *nm* : city planning
urbanité [yrbanite] *nf* : urbanity
urètre [yrɛtr] *nm* : urethra
urgence [yrʒɑ̃s] *nf* **1** : urgency **2** : emergency **3 d'urgence** : immediately, without delay
urgent, -gente [yrʒɑ̃, -ʒɑ̃t] *adj* : urgent
urinaire [yrinɛr] *adj* : urinary
urinal [yrinal] *nm, pl* **-naux** [-no] : urinal, bedpan
urine [yrin] *nf* : urine
uriner [yrine] *vi* : to urinate — **urination** [yrinasjɔ̃] *nf*
urinoir [yrinwar] *nm* : (public) urinal
urne [yrn] *nf* **1** : urn **2** : ballot box
urticaire [yrtikɛr] *nf* : hives
uruguayen, -guayenne [yrygwejɛ̃, -jɛn] *adj* : Uruguayan
Uruguayen, -guayenne *n* : Uruguayan
us [ys] *nmpl* **les us et coutumes** : habits and customs
usage [yzaʒ] *nm* **1** : use <à usage thérapeutique : for therapeutic use> <perdre l'usage d'un bras : to lose the use of an arm> **2** : usage (of a word or expression) **3** COUTUME : usage, custom <c'est l'usage : it's customary> **4** POLITESSE : (good) manners
usagé, -gée [yzaʒe] *adj* **1** : worn **2** : used, secondhand
usager [yzaʒe] *nm* : user
usé, -sée [yze] *adj* **1** : worn (down), worn-out **2** : hackneyed, trite
user [yze] *vt* **1** CONSOMMER : to use, to consume **2** : to wear out, to use up — *vi* **1 ~ de** : to exercise (one's rights) **2 ~ de** : to make use of — **s'user** *vr* **1** : to wear out, to get used up **2** : to wear oneself out
usine [yzin] *nf* : factory
usiner [yzine] *vt* **1** : to machine **2** : to manufacture
usité, -tée [yzite] *adj* : common, commonly used <prénom peu usité : uncommon name>
ustensile [ystɑ̃sil] *nm* : utensil, implement
usuel, -suelle [yzɥɛl] *adj* **1** : common, everyday **2** : usual <dans l'ordre usuel : in the usual order>
usuellement [yzɥɛlmɑ̃] *adv* : usually, ordinarily
usure [yzyr] *nf* **1** : wear (and tear) **2** : wearing down, erosion **3** : usury
usurpateur, -trice [yzyrpatœr, -tris] *n* : usurper
usurper [yzyrpe] *vt* : to usurp
utérin, -rine [yterɛ̃, -rin] *adj* : uterine
utérus [yterus] *nms & pl* : uterus
utile [ytil] *adj* : useful — **utilement** [ytilmɑ̃] *adv*
utilisable [ytilizabl] *adj* : usable
utilisateur, -trice [ytilizatœr, -tris] *n* : user
utilisation [ytilizasjɔ̃] *nf* : utilization, use
utiliser [ytilize] *vt* : to utilize, to use
utilitaire [ytilitɛr] *adj* : utilitarian
utilité [ytilite] *nf* : utility, usefulness
utopie [ytɔpi] *nf* : utopia
utopique [ytɔpik] *adj* : utopian

V

v [ve] *nm* : v, the 22d letter of the alphabet
va [va], *etc.* → **aller**
vacance [vakɑ̃s] *nf* **1** : vacancy, opening **2 vacances** *nfpl* : vacation, holiday *Brit* <en vacances : on vacation>
vacancier, -cière [vakɑ̃sje, -sjɛr] *n* : vacationer
vacant, -cante [vakɑ̃, -kɑ̃t] *adj* : vacant <poste vacant : vacant position>
vacarme [vakarm] *nm* : racket, din
vacataire [vakatɛr] *nmf France* : temporary worker, substitute
vaccin [vaksɛ̃] *nm* : vaccine
vacciner [vaksine] *vt* : to vaccinate — **vaccination** [vaksinasjɔ̃] *nf*
vache[1] [vaʃ] *adj fam* : mean, nasty
vache[2] *nf* **1** : cow <vache laitière : dairy cow> **2** : cowhide **3** *fam* : nasty person, swine
vachement [vaʃmɑ̃] *adv fam* JOLIMENT : really, very <cela m'aide vachement! : that's a big help!>
vacher, -chère [vaʃe, -ʃɛr] *n* : cowherd, cowboy *m,* cowgirl *f*

vacherie [vaʃri] *nf fam* **1** : nastiness, meanness **2** : dirty trick
vacillant, -lante [vasijɑ̃, -jɑ̃t] *adj* **1** : unsteady, shaky **2** : flickering **3** : failing, faltering (of memory, etc.)
vacillement [vasijmɑ̃] *nm* **1** : flickering **2** : wavering, faltering
vaciller [vasije] *vi* **1** : to stagger, to totter **2** : to flicker, to wobble, to sway **3** : to waver, to falter, to be failing
vacuité [vakɥite] *nf* : vacuity, emptiness
vadrouille [vadruj] *nf* **1** *Can* : long-handled mop for cleaning or dusting floors **2 en ∼** *fam* : wandering
vadrouiller [vadruje] *vi fam* : to wander about, to ramble
va–et–vient [vaevjɛ̃] *nms & pl* **1** : comings and goings **2** : to-and-fro motion **3** : two-way switch
vagabond[1], **-bonde** [vagabɔ̃, -bɔ̃d] *adj* : wandering, roving
vagabond[2], **-bonde** *n* : vagrant, tramp, vagabond
vagabondage [vagabɔ̃daʒ] *nm* **1** : vagrancy **2** : wandering <vagabondage de l'esprit : wandering(s) of the mind>
vagabonder [vagabɔ̃de] *vi* **1** : to wander **2** : to stray (of thoughts, etc.)
vagin [vaʒɛ̃] *nm* : vagina
vaginal, -nale [vaʒinal] *adj, mpl* **-naux** [-no] : vaginal
vague[1] [vag] *adj* **1** IMPRÉCIS : vague **2** : vacant, abstracted **3** : loose-fitting, ample
vague[2] *nf* : wave
vague[3] *nm* **1** : vagueness <rester dans le vague : to remain vague> **2 regarder dans le vague** : to stare into space
vaguement [vagmɑ̃] *adv* : vaguely
vaillamment [vajamɑ̃] *adv* : bravely, courageously
vaillance [vajɑ̃s] *nf* : valor, courage
vaillant, -lante [vajɑ̃, -jɑ̃t] *adj* **1** COURAGEUX : valiant, courageous **2** : strong, robust
vaille [vaj], *etc.* → **valoir**
vain, vaine [vɛ̃, vɛn] *adj* **1** FUTILE : vain, futile <en vain : in vain> **2** VANITEUX : vain — **vainement** [vɛnmɑ̃] *adv*
vaincre [vɛ̃kr] {94} *vt* **1** BATTRE : to defeat **2** SURMONTER : to overcome, to master
vaincu[1], **-cue** [vɛ̃ky] *adj* : defeated
vaincu[2], **-cue** *n* : loser
vainquais [vɛ̃kɛ], **vainquions** [vɛ̃kjɔ̃], *etc.* → **vaincre**
vainque [vɛ̃k], *etc.* → **vaincre**
vainqueur [vɛ̃kœr] *nm* : victor, winner
vairon [vɛrɔ̃] *nm* : minnow
vaisseau [vɛso] *nm, pl* **vaisseaux 1** : vessel <vaisseau sanguin : blood vessel> **2** : vessel, ship <vaisseau spatial : spaceship> **3** : nave
vaisselle [vɛsɛl] *nf* : crockery, dishes *pl*
val [val] *nm, pl* **vals** *or* **vaux** : valley
valable [valabl] *adj* **1** VALIDE : valid **2** BON : good, worthwhile
valablement [valabləmɑ̃] *adv* : validly, legitimately
valentin [valɑ̃tɛ̃] *nm Can* : valentine
valet [valɛ] *nm* **1** : valet, manservant <valet de pied : footman> **2** : jack (in playing cards)
valeur [valœr] *nf* **1** : value, worth, merit <objets de valeur : valuables> <valeur nominale : face value> **2** VALIDITÉ : validity **3** : (moral) value <valeurs familiales : family values> **4 valeurs** *nfpl* : stocks, securities **5 c'est de valeur** *Can fam* : that's a pity, that's too bad **6 mettre en valeur** : to develop (land)
valeureux, -reuse [valœrø, -røz] *adj* : courageous, valiant
valide [valid] *adj* **1** : valid **2** : fit, able-bodied
valider [valide] *vt* : to validate
validité [validite] *nf* : validity
valise [valiz] *nf* : suitcase <faire ses valises : to pack one's bags>
vallée [vale] *nf* : valley
vallon [valɔ̃] *nm* : small valley, dale
vallonné, -née [valɔne] *adj* : undulating, hilly
valoir [valwar] {95} *vi* **1** : to have a (certain) cost <valoir très cher : to be very expensive> **2** : to have value <il sait ce qu'il vaut : he knows what he's worth> <valoir rien : to be worthless> **3** : to apply, to be valid <cela vaut pour tous les employés : that holds for all employees> **4 faire valoir** : to put forth, to point out, to assert <faire valoir ses droits : to assert one's rights> — *vt* **1** PROCURER : to provide, to bring (to) **2** : to be equivalent to <un dollar vaut 100 cents : one dollar equals 100 cents> **3** : to be worth <valoir la peine : to be worth the trouble> — *v impers* **valoir mieux** : to be better <il vaut mieux rester ici : it would be better to stay here> — **se valoir** *vr* : to be the same (thing)
valoriser [valɔrize] *vt* : to increase the value of, to develop, to enhance
valse [vals] *nf* : waltz
valser [valse] *vi* : to waltz
valve [valv] *nf* : valve
vampire [vɑ̃pir] *nm* : vampire
vandale [vɑ̃dal] *nmf* : vandal
vandalisme [vɑ̃dalism] *nm* : vandalism
vanille [vanij] *nf* : vanilla
vanité [vanite] *nf* : vanity
vaniteux, -teuse [vanitø, -tøz] *adj* : vain, conceited — **vaniteusement** [-tøzmɑ̃] *adv*
vanne [van] *nf* **1** : sluice, sluiceway **2** *fam* : dig, gibe
vanner [vane] *vt* : to winnow, to husk

vannerie [vanri] *nf* : wickerwork

vantail [vɑ̃taj] *nm, pl* **-taux** [-to] : leaf, casement <portes à deux vantaux : double doors>

vantard[1], **-tarde** [vɑ̃tar, -tard] *adj* : boastful, bragging

vantard[2], **-tarde** *n* : braggart

vantardise [vɑ̃tardiz] *nf* **1** : boastfulness **2** : boast, brag

vanter [vɑ̃te] *vt* : to vaunt — **se vanter** *vr* **1** : to boast, to brag **2 ~ de** : to pride oneself on

va–nu–pieds [vanypje] *nmfs & pl* : beggar, tramp, ragamuffin

vapeur[1] [vapœr] *nf* **1** : steam **2** : vapor, fume <vapeurs d'essence : gas fumes>

vapeur[2] *nm* : steamship, steamboat

vaporeux, -reuse [vaporø, -røz] *adj* **1** : misty, hazy **2** : filmy, diaphanous

vaporisateur [vaporizatœr] *nm* ATOMISEUR : spray, atomizer

vaporiser [vaporize] *vt* **1** : to spray **2** : to vaporize

vaquer [vake] *vi* **~ à** : to attend to, to see to

varappe [varap] *nf* : rock climbing

varech [varɛk] *nm* : kelp, seaweed

vareuse [varøz] *nf* **1** : loose-fitting jacket, tunic **2** : pea jacket

variable[1] [varjabl] *adj* CHANGEANT : variable, changeable

variable[2] *nf* : variable

variante [varjɑ̃t] *nf* : variant

variation [varjasjɔ̃] *nf* : variation

varice [varis] *nf* : varicose vein

varicelle [varisɛl] *nf* : chicken pox

varié, -riée [varje] *adj* **1** : varied, varying **2** : various

varier [varje] {96} *v* : to vary

variété [varjete] *nf* : variety

variole [varjol] *nf* : smallpox

vasculaire [vaskylɛr] *adj* : vascular

vase[1] [vaz] *nf* BOUE : mud, silt

vase[2] *nm* **1** : vase (for flowers) **2** : vessel, container <vase à bec : beaker>

vaseux, -seuse [vazø, -zøz] *adj* **1** BOUEUX : muddy **2** *fam* : sickly, under the weather **3** : hazy, woolly (of thinking, etc.)

vasistas [vazistas] *nms & pl* : fanlight, transom

vasque [vask] *nf* **1** : basin (of a fountain) **2** : bowl **3 vasque pour les oiseaux** : birdbath

vaste [vast] *adj* **1** IMMENSE : huge, immense **2** ÉTENDU : extensive, wide

va–tout [vatu] *nms & pl* **jouer son va–tout** : to risk one's all

vaudeville [vodvil] *nm* : vaudeville

vaudou [vodu] *nm* : voodoo

vaudra [vodra], *etc.* → **valoir**

vau–l'eau [volo] *adv* **aller à vau–l'eau** : to be ruined, to be going down the drain

vaurien, -rienne [vorjɛ̃, -rjɛn] *n* : good-for-nothing, scoundrel, rogue

vaut [vo], *etc.* → **valoir**

vautour [votur] *nm* : vulture

vautrer [votre] *v* **se vautrer** *vr* **1** : to sprawl **2** : to wallow

va–vite [vavit] **à la va–vite** : quickly, hurriedly

veau [vo] *nm, pl* **veaux 1** : calf **2** : veal **3** : calfskin

vecteur [vɛktœr] *nm* **1** : vector **2** : carrier (of disease)

vécu[1] [veky] *pp* → **vivre**

vécu[2], **-cue** [veky] *adj* : real, real-life

vedette [vədɛt] *nf* **1** STAR : star (in movies, etc.), celebrity <avoir la vedette : to be in the limelight> <mettre en vedette : to put the spotlight on> **2** : patrol boat, launch

végétal[1], **-tale** [veʒetal] *adj, mpl* **-taux** : vegetable, plant <le règne végétal : the plant kingdom>

végétal[2] *nm* : vegetable, plant

végétarien, -rienne [veʒetarjɛ̃, -rjɛn] *adj & n* : vegetarian

végétarisme [veʒetarism] *nm* : vegetarianism

végétatif, -tive [veʒetatif, -tiv] *adj* : vegetative

végétation [veʒetasjɔ̃] *nf* **1** : vegetation **2 végétations** *nfpl* : adenoids

végéter [veʒete] {87} *vi* : to vegetate

véhémence [veemɑ̃s] *nf* : vehemence <avec véhémence : vehemently>

véhément, -mente [veemɑ̃, -mɑ̃t] *adj* : vehement

véhicule [veikyl] *nm* **1** : vehicle **2 véhicule utilitaire sport** *Can* : sport-utility vehicle

véhiculer [veikyle] *vt* : to convey

veille [vɛj] *nf* **1** : day before, eve <la veille de Noël : Christmas Eve> **2** : watch, vigil **3** : wakefulness

veillée [veje] *nf* **1** SOIRÉE : evening **2 veillée funèbre** : wake

veiller [veje] *vt* : to sit up with, to watch over — *vi* **1** : to stay awake **2** : to keep watch **3** : to be vigilant **4 ~ à** : to watch over, to look after

veilleur, -leuse [vejœr, -jøz] *n* **1** : lookout, sentry **2 veilleur de nuit** : night watchman

veilleuse *nf* **1** : night-light **2** : pilot light **3 mettre en veilleuse** : to put on hold, to set aside **4 mettre en veilleuse** : to dim (a light)

veine [vɛn] *nf* **1** : vein (in anatomy and botany) **2** : vein, lode (of a mineral) **3** : (artistic) inspiration **4** *fam* : luck <coup de veine : fluke> **5 en veine de** : in the mood for

veiné, -née [vene] *adj* : veined, grained

velléitaire [veleitɛr] *adj* : indecisive

velléité [veleite] *nf* : vague impulse, whim

vélo [velo] *nm* : bike, bicycle <faire du vélo : to ride a bike>

véloce [velɔs] *adj* : swift

vélocité [velɔsite] *nf* **1** : swiftness **2** : velocity

velours [vəlur] *nm* **1 :** velvet, velour **2 velours côtelé :** corduroy
velouté[1], **-tée** [vəlute] *adj* **:** velvety, smooth
velouté[2] *nm* **:** softness, smoothness
velu, -lue [vəly] *adj* POILU **:** hairy
venaison [vənɛzɔ̃] *nf* **:** venison
vénal, -nale [venal] *adj* **:** venal
vendable [vɑ̃dabl] *adj* **:** marketable
vendange [vɑ̃dɑ̃ʒ] *nf* **:** grape harvest
vendanger [vɑ̃dɑ̃ʒe] {17} *vi* **:** to harvest (the) grapes — *vt* **:** to harvest (grapes)
vendetta [vɑ̃deta] *nf* **:** vendetta
vendeur, -deuse [vɑ̃dœr, -døz] *n* **1 :** salesperson, salesman *m,* saleswoman *f* **2 :** seller, vendor
vendre [vɑ̃dr] {63} *vt* **1 :** to sell **2 à ~ :** for sale — **se vendre** *vr* **1 :** to be sold **2 :** to sell <ça se vend bien : it's selling well>
vendredi [vɑ̃drədi] *nm* **:** Friday <vendredi saint : Good Friday>
vénéneux, -neuse [venenø, -nøz] *adj* **:** poisonous
vénérable [venerabl] *adj* **:** venerable, revered
vénérer [venere] {87} *vt* RÉVÉRER **:** to venerate — **vénération** [-rasjɔ̃] *nf*
vénérien, -rienne [venerjɛ̃, -rjɛn] *adj* **:** venereal <maladie vénérienne : venereal disease>
vénézuélien, -lienne [venezɥeljɛ̃, -ljɛn] *adj* **:** Venezuelan
Vénézuélien, -lienne *n* **:** Venezuelan
vengeance [vɑ̃ʒɑ̃s] *nf* **:** vengeance, revenge
venger [vɑ̃ʒe] {17} *vt* **:** to avenge — **se venger** *vr* **:** to take revenge, to avenge oneself
vengeur[1], **-geresse** [vɑ̃ʒœr, -ʒrɛs] *adj* **:** vengeful
vengeur[2], **-geresse** *n* **:** avenger
véniel, -nielle [venjɛl] *adj* **:** venial
venimeux, -meuse [vənimø, -møz] *adj* **1 :** venomous, poisonous **2 :** spiteful
venin [vənɛ̃] *nm* **1 :** venom, poison **2 :** ill will, malice
venir [vənir] {92} *vi* **1 :** to come **2 en venir à :** to come to <en venir aux coups : to come to blows> <j'en suis venu à une conclusion : I've reached a conclusion> **3 faire venir :** to send for **4 ~ de :** to come from — *v aux* **1 :** to come and, to come to <viens la voir : come and see her> **2 ~ de :** to have just <je viens de nager : I've just been swimming>
vent [vɑ̃] *nm* **1 :** wind <il y a du vent : it's windy> <le vent du changement : the winds of change> **2 avoir vent de :** to get wind of
vente [vɑ̃t] *nf* **:** sale, selling <en vente : for sale>
venteux, -teuse [vɑ̃tø, -tøz] *adj* **:** windy
ventilateur [vɑ̃tilatœr] *nm* **:** (electric) fan, ventilator
ventilation [vɑ̃tilasjɔ̃] *nf* **1 :** ventilation **2 :** breakdown (in finance)
ventiler [vɑ̃tile] *vt* **1** AÉRER **:** to ventilate **2 :** to break down <ventiler les dépenses : to break down expenses>
ventouse [vɑ̃tuz] *nf* **1 :** suction cup **2 :** plunger **3 :** sucker (in zoology)
ventre [vɑ̃tr] *nm* **1 :** stomach, belly <avoir mal au ventre : to have a stomachache> **2 :** womb **3 avoir qqch dans le ventre** *fam* **:** to have guts
ventricule [vɑ̃trikyl] *nm* **:** ventricle
ventriloque [vɑ̃trilɔk] *nmf* **:** ventriloquist
ventriloquie [vɑ̃trilɔki] *nf* **:** ventriloquism
ventru, -true [vɑ̃try] *adj* **1** PANSU **:** potbellied **2** RENFLÉ **:** bulging, swelling
venu[1] [vəny] *pp* → **venir**
venu[2], **-nue** [vəny] *adj* **1 bien venu :** timely, welcome **2 mal venu :** ill-advised, unwelcome **3 nouveau venu :** newcomer **4 premier venu :** just anyone
venue *nf* AVÈNEMENT **:** coming, advent
Vénus [venys] *nf* **:** Venus (planet)
vêpres [vɛpr] *nfpl* **:** vespers
ver [vɛr] *nm* **:** worm <vers blanc : grub> <ver luisant : glowworm> <ver à soie : silkworm> <ver de terre : earthworm> <ver solitaire : tapeworm>
véracité [verasite] *nf* **:** veracity, truthfulness
véranda [verɑ̃da] *nf* **:** veranda, porch
verbal, -bale [vɛrbal] *adj, mpl* **verbaux** [-bo] **:** verbal — **verbalement** [-balmɑ̃] *adv*
verbaliser [vɛrbalize] *vt* **:** to verbalize
verbe [vɛrb] *nm* **1 :** verb <verbe pronominal : reflexive verb> **2 :** language, words <la magie du verbe : the magic of words> **3 :** tone of voice
verbeux, -beuse [vɛrbø, -bøz] *adj* **:** wordy, verbose
verbiage [vɛrbjaʒ] *nm* **:** verbiage
verdâtre [vɛrdatr] *adj* **:** greenish
verdeur [vɛrdœr] *nf* **1** ACIDITÉ **:** tartness, acidity **2** VIGUEUR **:** vigor, vitality **3** GROSSIÈRETÉ **:** crudeness
verdict [vɛrdikt] *nm* **:** verdict
verdir [vɛrdir] *v* **:** to turn green
verdoyant, verdoyante [vɛrdwajɑ̃, -jɑ̃t] *adj* **:** green, verdant
véreux, -reuse [verø, -røz] *adj* **1 :** wormy **2** LOUCHE **:** shady, suspect
verge [vɛrʒ] *nf* **1** BAGUETTE **:** rod, stick **2** *Can* **:** yard (measure) **3** PÉNIS **:** penis **4 verge d'or :** goldenrod
verger [vɛrʒe] *nm* **:** orchard
verglacé, -cée [vɛrglase] *adj* **:** icy
verglas [vɛrgla] *nm* **:** black ice
vergogne [vɛrgɔɲ] *nf* **sans ~ :** shamelessly
vergue [vɛrg] *nf* **:** yard (of a ship)
véridique [veridik] *adj* **:** truthful
vérifiable [verifjabl] *adj* **:** verifiable

vérificateur, -trice [verifikatœr, -tris] *n* **1** : controller, inspector **2 vérificateur de comptes** : (financial) auditor
vérification [verifikasjɔ̃] *nf* : check, verification
vérifier [verifje] {96} *vt* CONFIRMER : to verify, to check
vérin [verɛ̃] *nm* : jack <vérin hydraulique : hydraulic jack>
véritable [veritabl] *adj* **1** RÉEL : true, actual, real <mon véritable nom : my real name> **2** AUTHENTIQUE : genuine, authentic **3** (*used as an intensive*) : real <c'est un véritable cauchemar! : it's a real nightmare!>
véritablement [-tabləmɑ̃] *adv* **1** : actually, really **2** (*used as an intensive*) : absolutely
vérité [verite] *nf* **1** : truth <dire la vérité : to tell the truth> **2** : fact, truth <une vérité éternelle : an eternal truth> **3** : sincerity, truthfulness
vermeil, -meille [vɛrmɛj] *adj* : vermilion
vermicelle [vɛrmisɛl] *nm* : vermicelli
vermine [vɛrmin] *nf* : vermin
vermoulu, -lue [vɛrmuly] *adj* : worm-eaten, dilapidated
vermouth *or* **vermout** [vɛrmut] *nm* : vermouth
vernir [vɛrnir] *vt* : to varnish
vernis [vɛrni] *nms & pl* **1** LAQUE : varnish, lacquer **2** APPARENCE : veneer, facade **3 vernis à ongles** : nail polish
vernissage [vɛrnisaʒ] *nm* **1** : varnishing **2** : opening (of an art exhibition)
vernisser [vɛrnise] *vt* : to glaze
vérole [verɔl] *nf* **1** *fam* : syphilis **2** → **petit**[2]
verra [vera], *etc.* → **voir**
verrat [vera] *nm* : male pig, boar
verre [vɛr] *nm* **1** : glass **2** : (drinking) glass <verre à vin : wineglass> <verre à pied : goblet> **3** : glassful <prendre un verre : to have a drink> **4 verres** *nmpl* : eyeglasses, lenses <verres de contact : contact lenses> <verres à double foyer : bifocals>
verrerie [vɛrri] *nf* **1** : glassware **2** : glassmaking **3** : glass factory
verrière [vɛrjɛr] *nf* **1** : glass roof **2** : stained-glass window
verrou [vɛru] *nm* : bolt <sous les verrous : locked up>
verrouiller [vɛruje] *vt* : to bolt, to lock
verrue [vɛry] *nf* : wart
vers[1] [vɛr] *nms & pl* **1** : line, verse (of poetry) **2** : verse <vers libre : free verse>
vers[2] *prep* **1** : toward, towards <vers le nord : toward the north> **2** : about, around, near <vers treize heures : around one o'clock>
versant [vɛrsɑ̃] *nm* : slope, side (of a hill, etc.)
versatile [vɛrsatil] *adj* : fickle
verse [vɛrs] *nf* **pleuvoir à verse** : to pour (rain)
versé, -sée [vɛrse] *adj* **~ dans** : (well) versed in
Verseau [vɛrso] *nm* : Aquarius
versement [vɛrsəmɑ̃] *nm* **1** : payment **2** : installing, installment
verser [vɛrse] *vt* **1** : to pour **2** PAYER : to pay **3** RÉPANDRE : to shed (tears, blood etc.) — *vi* **1** : to overturn **2 ~ dans** : to lapse into
verset [vɛrsɛ] *nm* : verse (of the Bible, etc.)
version [vɛrsjɔ̃] *nf* **1** : version **2** : translation (into one's native language)
verso [vɛrso] *nm* : verso, back (of a page)
vert[1], **verte** [vɛr, vɛrt] *adj* **1** : green **2** : unripe, sour **3** GAILLARD : vigorous, sprightly **4** CRU : crude, forthright **5** SÉVÈRE : harsh, severe
vert[2] *nm* : green
vertébral, -brale [vɛrtebral] *adj, mpl* **-braux** [-bro] : vertebral, back
vertèbre [vɛrtɛbr] *nf* : vertebra
vertébré[1], **-brée** [vɛrtebre] *adj* : vertebrate
vertébré[2] *nm* : vertebrate
vertement [vɛrtəmɑ̃] *adv* : sharply, severely
vertical, -cale [vɛrtikal] *adj, mpl* **-caux** [-ko] : vertical — **verticalement** [-kalmɑ̃] *adv*
verticale *nf* : vertical
verticille [vɛrtisil] *nf* : whorl (of petals, leaves etc.)
vertige [vɛrtiʒ] *nm* : vertigo, dizziness
vertigineux, -neuse [vɛrtiʒinø, -nøz] *adj* **1** : dizzy, giddy <hauteurs vertigineuses : dizzying heights> **2** : breathtaking
vertu [vɛrty] *nf* **1** : virtue **2** : power, property **3 en vertu de** : by virtue of, according to
vertueux, -tueuse [vɛrtɥø, -tɥøz] *adj* : virtuous — **vertueusement** [-tɥøzmɑ̃] *adv*
verve [vɛrv] *nf* BRIO : verve, panache
vésicule [vezikyl] *nf* **1** : vesicle **2 vésicule biliaire** : gallbladder
vessie [vesi] *nf* : bladder
veste [vɛst] *nf* **1** : jacket **2** *Can* : vest
vestiaire [vɛstjɛr] *nm* **1** : cloakroom **2** : locker room **3** : locker
vestibule [vɛstibyl] *nm* : vestibule, hall
vestige [vɛstiʒ] *nm* **1** RESTE : vestige, trace **2** : relic, remains *pl*
vestimentaire [vɛstimɑ̃tɛr] *adj* : clothing, sartorial
veston [vɛstɔ̃] *nm* : (man's) jacket
vêtement [vɛtmɑ̃] *nm* **1** : garment, article of clothing **2 vêtements** *nmpl* : clothes, clothing **3 vêtement sacerdotal** : vestment (in religion)
vétéran [veterɑ̃] *nm* : veteran
vétérinaire[1] [veterinɛr] *adj* : veterinary
vétérinaire[2] *nmf* : veterinarian
vétille [vetij] *nf* BAGATELLE : trifle

vêtir |vetir| {97} *vt* HABILLER : to dress — **se vêtir** *vr*

veto |veto| *nms & pl* : veto

vêtu, -tue |vɛty| *adj* : dressed <bien vêtu : well-dressed>

vétuste |vetyst| *adj* : dilapidated

veuf[1], veuve |vœf, vœv| *adj* : widowed

veuf[2], veuve *n* : widower *m,* widow *f*

veuille |vœj|, *etc.* → **vouloir**

veule |vœl| *adj* : weak, spineless

veut |vœ|, *etc.* → **vouloir**

veuvage |vœvaʒ| *nm* : widowhood

veuve → **veuf**

vexant, vexante |vɛksɑ̃, -ksɑ̃t| *adj* **1** : hurtful (of a remark, etc.) **2** : vexing, annoying

vexation |vɛksasjɔ̃| *nf* : humiliation

vexer |vɛkse| *vt* : to vex, to upset — **se vexer** *vr* : to be upset, to take offense

via |vja| *prep* : via

viabilité |vjabilite| *nf* **1** : viability **2** : practicality

viable |vjabl| *adj* **1** : viable **2** : practical, feasible

viaduc |vjadyk| *nm* : viaduct

viager, -gère |vjaʒe, -ʒɛr| *adj or* **rente viagère** : life annuity

viande |vjɑ̃d| *nf* : meat <viande de bœuf : beef> <viande hachée : hamburger>

vibrant, -brante |vibrɑ̃, -brɑ̃t| *adj* **1** : vibrating **2** : vibrant, stirring

vibration |vibrasjɔ̃| *nf* : vibration

vibrer |vibre| *vi* **1** : to vibrate **2** : to stir, to thrill

vicaire |vikɛr| *nm* : vicar, curate

vice |vis| *nm* **1** DÉBAUCHE : vice **2** DÉFAUT : defect, fault, flaw

vice-amiral |visamiral| *nm, pl* **-raux** |-ro| : vice admiral

vice-président, -dente |visprezidɑ̃, -dɑ̃t| *n, pl* **-dents, -dentes** : vice president

vice-roi |visrwa| *nm, pl* **vice-rois** : viceroy

vice versa *or* **vice-versa** |vis(e)vɛrsa| *adv* : vice versa

vichy |viʃi| *nm* **1** : gingham **2** : Vichy water

vicier |visje| {96} *vt* **1** : to pollute, to taint **2** : to invalidate (in law)

vicieusement |visjøzmɑ̃| *nm* : viciously

vicieux, -cieuse |visjø, -sjøz| *adj* **1** : vicious (of an animal) **2** : devious, sly **3** PERVERS : perverse, depraved **4** FAUTIF : incorrect, faulty **5 cercle vicieux** : vicious circle

vicissitudes |visisityd| *nfpl* : vicissitudes, trials and tribulations

vicomte |vikɔ̃t| *nm* : viscount

vicomtesse |vikɔ̃tɛs| *nf* : viscountess

victime |viktim| *nf* : victim

victoire |viktwar| *nf* : victory

victorien, -rienne |viktɔrjɛ̃, -rjɛn| *adj* : Victorian

victorieux, -rieuse |viktɔrjø, -rjøz| *adj* : victorious <l'équipe victorieuse : the winning team> — **victorieusement** |-rjøzmɑ̃| *adv*

victuailles |viktɥaj| *nfpl* : victuals, provisions

vidange |vidɑ̃ʒ| *nf* **1** : emptying, draining **2** : oil change <faire la vidange : to change the oil> **3 vidanges** *nfpl* : sewage **4 vidanges** *nfpl Can* : garbage collection

vidanger |vidɑ̃ʒe| {17} *vt* : to empty, to drain

vide[1] |vid| *adj* **1** : empty <les mains vides : empty-handed> **2** : blank

vide[2] *nm* **1** : emptiness, void, space **2** : vacuum **3** : gap <combler le vide : to fill the gap>

vidéo[1] |video| *adj s & pl* : video

vidéo[2] *nf* : video

vidéocassette |videɔkasɛt| *nf* : videocassette, videotape

vider |vide| *vt* **1** : to empty **2** : to empty out (a place) **3** VIDANGER : to drain **4** : to core (fruit), to clean (a fowl), to gut (a fish) **5** *fam* : to kick out, to throw out

vie |vi| *nf* **1** : life <être en vie : to be alive> **2** : lifetime, life <à vie : for life> <jamais de la vie! : never!> **3** : living, livelihood

vieil → **vieux**

vieillard |vjɛjar| *nm* : old man

vieille → **vieux**

vieillesse |vjɛjɛs| *nf* : old age

vieilli, -lie |vjeji| *adj* **1** : aged, old-looking **2** DÉMODÉ : old-fashioned, dated

vieillir |vjejir| *vt* : to make (someone) look older — *vi* **1** : to grow old, to age **2** : to become outdated — **se vieillir** *vr* : to make oneself seem older

vieillissant, -sante |vjejisɑ̃, -sɑ̃t| *adj* : aging, ageing

vieillissement |vjejismɑ̃| *nm* : aging, growing old

vieillot, -lotte |vjejo, -jɔt| *adj* : quaint, antiquated

viendra |vjɛ̃dra|, *etc.* → **venir**

vienne |vjɛn|, *etc.* → **venir**

vient |vjɛ̃|, *etc.* → **venir**

vierge[1] |vjɛrʒ| *adj* **1** : virgin **2** : blank, empty <cassette vierge : blank tape> **3** : fresh, unspoiled

vierge[2] *nf* : virgin <la Sainte Vierge : the Blessed Virgin>

Vierge *nf* : Virgo

vietnamien[1], -mienne |vjɛtnamjɛ̃, -mjɛn| *adj* : Vietnamese

vietnamien[2] *nm* : Vietnamese (language)

Vietnamien, -mienne *n* : Vietnamese

vieux[1] |vjø| **(vieil** |vjɛj| *before a vowel or mute h*), **vieille** |vjɛj| *adj, mpl* **vieux 1** : old **2 vieille fille** : old maid **3 vieux jeu** : old-fashioned, old hat

vieux[2], vieille *n* : old man *m,* old woman *f*

vif[1], vive |vif, viv| *adj* **1** VIVANT : living, live <de vive voix : in person> **2**

ANIMÉ : lively, vivacious **3** AIGU : sharp, keen **4** EMPORTÉ : brusque, quick-tempered **5** : bright, vivid **6** : brisk, bracing **7** → **mémoire**

vif[2] *nm* **1 à ~** : open, raw, exposed **2 entrer dans le vif du sujet** : to get to the heart of the matter **3 piqué au vif** : cut to the quick **4 sur le vif** : on the spot, live

vif–argent [vifarʒɑ̃] *nm, pl* **vifs–argents** : quicksilver

vigie [viʒi] *nf* **1** : lookout **2** : crow's nest, lookout (post)

vigilant, -lante [viʒilɑ̃, -lɑ̃t] *adj* : vigilant — **vigilance** [viʒilɑ̃s] *nf*

vigile[1] [viʒil] *nf* : vigil (in religion)

vigile[2] *nm* : security guard

vigne [viɲ] *nf* **1** : grapevine **2** VIGNOBLE : vineyard

vigneron, -ronne [viɲrɔ̃, -rɔn] *n* : winegrower

vignette [viɲɛt] *nf* **1** : label **2** : vignette

vignoble [viɲɔbl] *nm* : vineyard

vigoureux, -reuse [vigurø, -røz] *adj* **1** : vigorous, sturdy **2** : lively, energetic — **vigoureusement** [-røzmɑ̃] *adv*

vigueur [vigœr] *nf* **1** : vigor **2 en ~** : in force, in effect

VIH [veiaʃ] *nm* : HIV

Viking [vikiŋ] *nmf* : Viking

vil, vile [vil] *adj* **1** MÉPRISABLE : vile, despicable **2 à vil prix** : very cheap

vilain, -laine [vilɛ̃, -lɛn] *adj* **1** MÉCHANT : naughty **2** LAID : ugly **3** : nasty, disagreeable

vilebrequin [vilbrəkɛ̃] *nm* **1** : brace (for a bit) **2** : crankshaft

vilement [vilmɑ̃] *adv* : vilely, basely

vilenie [vileni] *nf* **1** : vileness, baseness **2** : base deed

vilipender [vilipɑ̃de] *vt* : to revile

villa [vila] *nf* : villa

village [vilaʒ] *nm* : village

villageois, -geoise [vilaʒwa, -ʒwaz] *n* : villager

ville [vil] *nf* : city, town <aller en ville : to go into town, to go downtown>

villégiature [vileʒjatyr] *nf* **1** : vacation **2** *or* **lieu de villégiature** : resort

vin [vɛ̃] *nm* : wine

vinaigre [vinɛgr] *nm* : vinegar <vinaigre balsamique : balsamic vinegar>

vinaigrette [vinɛgrɛt] *nf* : vinaigrette

vinaigrier [vinɛgrije] *nm* : vinegar cruet

vindicatif, -tive [vɛ̃dikatif, -tiv] *adj* : vindictive

vingt[1] [vɛ̃ (vɛ̃t *before a vowel, mute h, and the numbers 22-29*)] *adj* **1** : twenty **2** : twentieth <le vingt avril : April twentieth>

vingt[2] *nms & pl* : twenty

vingtaine [vɛ̃tɛn] *nf* : about twenty, group of twenty

vingtième [vɛ̃tjɛm] *adj & nmf & nm* : twentieth

vinicole [vinikɔl] *adj* VITICOLE : wine, wine-growing

vinyle [vinil] *nm* : vinyl

viol [vjɔl] *nm* **1** : rape **2** PROFANATION : violation, desecration

violacé, -cée [vjɔlase] *adj* : purplish

violateur, -trice [vjɔlatœr] *n* : violator

violation [vjɔlasjɔ̃] *nf* : violation

violemment [vjɔlamɑ̃] *adv* : violently

violent, -lente [vjɔlɑ̃, -lɑ̃t] *adj* : violent — **violence** [vjɔlɑ̃s] *nf*

violenter [vjɔlɑ̃te] *vt* **1** : to do violence to **2** VIOLER : to rape

violer [vjɔle] *vt* **1** : to rape **2** : to desecrate **3** : to violate, to break (a law, promise, etc.)

violet[1], **-lette** [vjɔlɛ, -lɛt] *adj* : purple, violet

violet[2] *nm* : purple, violet

violette *nf* : violet (flower)

violeur [vjɔlœr] *nm* : rapist

violon [vjɔlɔ̃] *nm* : violin, fiddle

violoncelle [vjɔlɔ̃sɛl] *nm* : cello

violoncelliste [vjɔlɔ̃selist] *nmf* : cellist

violoniste [vjɔlɔnist] *nmf* : violinist, fiddler

vipère [vipɛr] *nf* : adder, viper

virage [viraʒ] *nm* **1** COURBE : bend, turn, curve **2** : change, shift (in orientation) **3** : change in color

viral, -rale [viral] *adj, mpl* **viraux** [viro] : viral <infection virale : viral infection>

virée [vire] *nf fam* : outing, trip <faire une virée : to go for a spin>

virement [virmɑ̃] *nm* : transfer (in finance) <virement bancaire : bank transfer>

virer [vire] *vt* **1** : to transfer (funds) **2** : to tone (a photograph) **3** *fam* : to fire, to expel, to throw out — *vi* **1** : to veer, to turn **2** : to change color **3 ~ à** : to turn (to), to change to <virer au vert : to turn green>

virevolte [virvɔlt] *nf* **1** : twirl **2** VOLTE-FACE : about-face

virevolter [virvɔlte] *vi* : to twirl

virginité [virʒinite] *nf* : virginity

virgule [virgyl] *nf* **1** : comma **2** : point, decimal point <5 virgule 7 milliards : 5 point 7 billion>

viril, -rile [viril] *adj* : virile, manly

virilité [virilite] *nf* : virility, manliness

virtuel, -tuelle [virtɥɛl] *adj* **1** : virtual (in science) **2** POTENTIEL : potential

virtuose [virtɥoz] *nmf* : virtuoso

virtuosité [virtɥozite] *nf* : virtuosity

virulent, -lente [virylɑ̃, -lɑ̃t] *adj* : virulent — **virulence** [virylɑ̃s] *nf*

virus [virys] *nms & pl* : virus

vis [vi] *nfs & pl* : screw

visa [viza] *nm* **1** : visa **2** : stamp, seal

visage [vizaʒ] *nm* **1** : face <un visage familier : a familiar face> <à visage découvert : openly> **2** : aspect, nature

visagiste [vizaʒist] *nmf* ESTHÉTICIEN : beautician

vis–à–vis[1] |vizavi| *adv* **1 ~ de** : opposite, facing **2 ~ de** : towards, with respect to
vis–à–vis[2] *nms & pl* **1** : person opposite **2** : building opposite
viscéral, -rale |viseral| *adj, mpl* **-raux** |-ro| : visceral
viscères |visɛr| *nmpl* : viscera, innards
viscosité |viskozite| *nf* : viscosity
visée |vize| *nf* **1** : aim, design **2** : sighting, aiming
viser |vize| *vt* **1** : to aim for, to aim at **2** : to stamp (a document) — *vi* **1** : to aim, to take aim **2 ~ à** : to aim at, to intend
viseur |vizœr| *nm* **1** : viewfinder **2** : sight (of a firearm)
visibilité |vizibilite| *nf* : visibility
visible |vizibl| *adj* **1** : visible **2** : obvious — **visiblement** |-zibləmɑ̃| *adv*
visière |vizjɛr| *nf* : visor (of a cap, etc.)
vision |vizjɔ̃| *nf* **1** : vision, eyesight **2** : view, outlook **3** : vision, apparition
visionnaire |vizjɔnɛr| *adj & nmf* : visionary
visionner |vizjɔne| *vt* : to view
visionneuse |vizjɔnøz| *nf* : viewer (for slides)
visite |vizit| *nf* **1** : visit <rendre visite à : to visit> <heures de visite : visiting hours> **2** VISITEUR : visitor <avoir une visite : to have a visitor> **3** : examination, inspection <visite de douane : customs inspection>
visiter |vizite| *vt* **1** : to visit **2** EXAMINER : to inspect, to examine
visiteur, -teuse |vizitœr, -tøz| *n* **1** : visitor **2** : inspector
vison |vizɔ̃| *nm* : mink
visqueux, -queuse |viskø, -køz| *adj* **1** : viscous **2** : slimy, gooey
visser |vise| *vt* : to screw, to screw on — **se visser** *vr* : to screw together
visualiser |vizɥalize| *vt* : to visualize — **visualisation** |-zɥalizasjɔ̃| *nf*
visuel, -suelle |vizɥɛl| *adj* : visual — **visuellement** |-zɥɛlmɑ̃| *adv*
vital, -tale |vital| *adj, mpl* **vitaux** |vito| : vital
vitalité |vitalite| *nf* : vitality
vitamine |vitamin| *nf* : vitamin
vite |vit| *adv* **1** RAPIDEMENT : fast, quickly <fais vite! : hurry up!> **2** TÔT : soon <au plus vite : as soon as possible>
vitesse |vitɛs| *nf* **1** : speed <à toute vitesse : at full speed> **2** : gear <en première vitesse : in first gear> **3 boîte de vitesses** : transmission **4** → **limite**
viticole |vitikɔl| *adj* VINICOLE : wine, wine-growing
viticulture |vitikyltyr| *nf* : wine growing
vitrail |vitraj| *nm, pl* **vitraux** |vitro| : stained-glass window
vitre |vitr| *nf* **1** : pane, windowpane **2** : window (of a car, train, etc.) <vitre arrière : rear window>
vitré, -trée |vitre| *adj* **1** : glass, glazed **2** → **baie**
vitreux, -treuse |vitrø, -trøz| *adj* **1** : vitreous **2** : glassy <les yeux vitreux : glassy eyes>
vitrier |vitrije| *nm* : glazier
vitrine |vitrin| *nf* **1** : shop window **2** : showcase, display case
vitupération |vityperasjɔ̃| *nf* : vituperation
vitupérer |vitypere| {87} *vt* : to vituperate, to berate — *vi* **~ contre** : to rant and rave against
vivable |vivabl| *adj* SUPPORTABLE : bearable
vivace |vivas| *adj* **1** : hardy <plante vivace : perennial plant> **2** DURABLE : enduring
vivacité |vivasite| *nf* **1** : vivacity, liveliness **2** : brusqueness, quickness **3** : vividness, intensity
vivant[1], **-vante** |vivɑ̃, -vɑ̃t| *adj* **1** VIF : living, live **2** ANIMÉ : lively, vivacious, peppy **3** → **langue**
vivant[2] *nm* **1** : living being **2 du vivant de** : during the lifetime of
vivats |viva| *nmpl* : cheers
vive |viva| *interj* : long live, three cheers for <vive le roi! : long live the king!>
vivement |vivmɑ̃| *adv* **1** RAPIDEMENT : quickly **2** FORTEMENT : strongly, sharply, hotly
vivier |vivje| *nm* **1** : fishpond, fish tank **2** : breeding ground
vivifiant, -fiante |vivifjɑ̃, -fjɑ̃t| *adj* : bracing, invigorating
vivifier |vivifje| {96} *vt* REVIGORER : to invigorate
vivisection |viviseksjɔ̃| *nf* : vivisection
vivoter |vivɔte| *vi* : to get by, to subsist
vivre |vivr| {98} *vt* : to live through, to experience — *vi* **1** : to live **2 faire vivre** : to support **3 ~ de** : to live on, to live by
vivres |vivr| *nmpl* PROVISIONS : food, provisions
vocable |vɔkabl| *nm* MOT : term, word
vocabulaire |vɔkabylɛr| *nm* : vocabulary
vocal, -cale |vɔkal| *adj, mpl* **vocaux** |vɔko| : vocal — **vocalement** |-kalmɑ̃| *adv*
vocaliser |vɔkalize| *v* : to vocalize
vocation |vɔkasjɔ̃| *nf* : vocation, calling
vociférer |vɔsifere| {87} *v* : to shout, to scream
vodka |vɔdka| *nf* : vodka
vœu |vø| *nm, pl* **vœux 1** SOUHAIT : wish <faire un vœu : to make a wish> <mes meilleurs vœux : my best wishes> **2** SERMENT : vow
vogue |vɔg| *nf* : vogue, fashion

voguer |vɔge| *vi* : to sail, to navigate
voici |vwasi| *prep* **1** : here is, here are <me voici : here I am> <la voici qui vient : here she comes> **2** : this is, these are <voici pourquoi : this is why> **3** (*indicating a period of time*) <il est parti voici trois jours : he left three days ago> <voici un mois que je ne les vois plus : it's a month since I've seen them>
voie |vwa| *nf* **1** : road, route, way <voie express : expressway> <voie à sens unique : one-way street> <voie navigable : waterway> **2** : lane <route à deux voies : two-lane road> **3** *or* **voie ferrée** : railroad track **4** : way, course <montrer la voie : to show the way> <une voie médiane : a middle course> **5** : means *pl,* channels *pl* **6** : passage, duct (in physiology) **7 en voie de** : on the way to, in the process of **8 voie d'eau** : leak (of a boat) **9 la Voie lactée** : the Milky Way
voilà |vwala| *prep* **1** : there is, there are <les voilà! : there they are!> **2** : that is, those are <voilà tout! : that's all!> **3** VOICI : here is, here are **4** (*indicating a period of time*) <voilà un an : a year ago> <voilà quatre jours qu'il neige : it's been snowing for four days>
voile[1] |vwal| *nf* **1** : sail **2** : sailing
voile[2] *nm* **1** : veil **2** : voile (fabric) **3** : veil, covering <lever le voile : to reveal, to bring to the open> **4** : mist (of tears, fog, etc.)
voiler |vwale| *vt* **1** : to veil, to cover **2** : to conceal **3** : to mist (up), to cloud **4** : to warp — **se voiler** *vr*
voilier |vwalje| *nm* : sailboat
voilure |vwalyr| *nf* : sails *pl*
voir |vwar| {99} *v* **1** : to see **2** : to view, to imagine **3** : to look at, to consider **4** : to discover <c'est à voir : that remains to be seen> **5** : to visit, to call on **6 faire voir** *or* **laisser voir** : to show **7 n'avoir rien à voir avec** : to have nothing to do with — *vi* **1** : to see <voir double : to see double> **2** : to find out, to understand <il faut voir : we must wait and see> **3** : to take a look <voyons : well, let's see> **4 ~ à** : to see to, to make sure that <voyez à la prévenir : be sure to warn her> — **se voir** *vr* **1** : to see oneself **2** : to see each other **3** : to be visible, to show <ça se voit : that's obvious, it shows>
voire |vwar| *adv* : indeed, or even
voirie |vwari| *nf* **1** : highway department **2** *France* : garbage collection
voisin[1], -sine |vwazɛ̃, -zin| *adj* **1** : adjoining, neighboring **2** : similar, closely related <voisin de : akin to, resembling>
voisin[2], -sine *n* : neighbor
voisinage |vwazinaʒ| *nm* **1** : neighborhood **2** : proximity, closeness **3** : neighbors *pl*
voisiner |vwazine| *vi* **1** : to visit one's neighbors **2 ~ avec** : to be side by side with
voiture |vwatyr| *nf* **1** AUTOMOBILE : car, automobile <voiture de course : racing car> **2** WAGON : (railroad) car, coach **3** : carriage, cart <voiture d'enfant : baby carriage>
voix |vwa| *nfs & pl* **1** : voice <à haute voix : out loud, aloud> <voix traînante : drawl> **2** : voice, counsel <la voix de la raison : the voice of reason> **3** VOTE : vote <mettre aux voix : to put to the vote>
vol |vɔl| *nm* **1** : flight <prendre son vol : to take flight> <vols internationaux : international flights> **2** : theft, robbery <vol à main armée : armed robbery> <vol à la tire : pickpocketing> **3** VOLÉE : flock **4 au vol** : in midair
volage |vɔlaʒ| *adj* INCONSTANT : fickle, flighty
volaille |vɔlaj| *nf* **1** : poultry **2** : fowl, bird
volant[1], -lante |vɔlɑ̃, -lɑ̃t| *adj* : flying
volant[2] *nm* **1** : steering wheel **2** : shuttlecock **3** : flounce (of a skirt, etc.)
volatil, -tile |vɔlatil| *adj* : volatile
volatile *nm* : fowl, chicken, bird
volatiliser |vɔlatilize| *v* **se volatiliser** *vr* **1** : to volatilize **2** : to disappear, to vanish into thin air
volcan |vɔlkɑ̃| *nm* **1** : volcano **2** : hothead
volcanique |vɔlkanik| *adj* : volcanic
volée |vɔle| *nf* **1** : volley **2** VOL : flock, flight
voler |vɔle| *vt* **1** : to steal **2** : to rob, to cheat **3 voler à l'étalage** : to shoplift — *vi* **1** : to fly **2 voler en éclats** : to smash to bits, to shatter
volet |vɔlɛ| *nm* **1** : shutter **2** : flap (of an airplane, etc.) **3** : section (of a document) **4** : constituent, part, facet
voleter |vɔlte| {8} *vi* : to flutter, to flit
voleur[1], -leuse |vɔlœr, -løz| *adj* : thieving, dishonest
voleur[2], -leuse *n* **1** : thief, robber **2 voleur à la tire** : pickpocket **3 voleur à l'étalage** : shoplifter
volière |vɔljɛr| *nf* : aviary
volley |vɔlɛ| *or* **volley-ball** |vɔlɛbol| *nm* : volleyball
volontaire[1] |vɔlɔ̃tɛr| *adj* **1** : voluntary **2** : willful, deliberate **3** : headstrong
volontaire[2] *nmf* : volunteer
volontairement |vɔlɔ̃tɛrmɑ̃| *adv* : voluntarily, deliberately
volonté |vɔlɔ̃te| *nf* **1** : will <bonne volonté : willingness, goodwill> **2** : willpower **3 à ~** : at will
volontiers |vɔlɔ̃tje| *adv* : willingly, gladly
volt |vɔlt| *nm* : volt
voltage |vɔltaʒ| *nm* : voltage

volte–face [vɔltəfas] *nfs & pl* : about-face

voltige [vɔltiʒ] *nf* : acrobatics

voltiger [vɔltiʒe] {17} *vi* **1** : to do acrobatics **2** : to flutter about, to flit

voltigeur, -geuse [vɔltiʒœr, -ʒøz] *n Can* : outfielder

volubile [vɔlybil] *adj* : voluble

volume [vɔlym] *nm* : volume

volumineux, -neuse [vɔlyminø, -nøz] *adj* : voluminous

volupté [vɔlypte] *nf* : sensual pleasure, voluptuousness

voluptueux, -tueuse [vɔlyptɥø, -tɥøz] *adj* : voluptuous — **voluptueusement** [-tɥøzmɑ̃] *adv*

volute [vɔlyt] *nf* : curl, coil (of smoke, etc.)

vomi [vɔmi] *nm* : vomit

vomir [vɔmir] *vt* **1** : to vomit, to bring up **2** : to spew out — *vi* : to vomit

vomissement [vɔmismɑ̃] *nm* : vomiting

vorace [vɔras] *adj* : voracious — **voracement** [-rasmɑ̃] *adv*

voracité [vɔrasite] *nf* : voracity

votant, -tante [vɔtɑ̃, -tɑ̃t] *n* : voter

vote [vɔt] *nm* : vote

voter [vɔte] *vi* : to vote — *vt* : to vote for

votre [vɔtr] *adj, pl* **vos** [vo] : your

vôtre[1] [votr] *adj* : yours <ce livre est vôtre : this book is yours>

vôtre[2] *pron* **le vôtre, la vôtre, les vôtres** : yours, your own <c'est le vôtre : it's yours> <mes amitiés à vous et les vôtres : my regards to you and yours>

voudra [vudra], *etc.* → **vouloir**

vouer [vwe] *vt* **1** PROMETTRE : to vow, to pledge **2** CONSACRER : to dedicate, to consecrate <vouer sa vie : to devote one's life> **3** DESTINER : to destine, to doom <voué à l'échec : doomed to failure>

voulait [vulɛ], **voulions** [vuljɔ̃], *etc.* → **vouloir**

vouloir[1] [vulwar] {100} *vt* **1** : to want, to wish for <veux-tu du vin? : do you want some wine?> <je voudrais y aller : I would like to go> **2** ACCEPTER : to agree to, to be willing to <veuillez patienter : please wait> <voudriez-vous ouvrir la porte? : would you mind opening the door?> **3** : to expect, to intend <je ne leur veux aucun mal : I mean them no harm> <sans le vouloir : unintentionally> **4 en vouloir à** : to bear a grudge against **5 vouloir dire** : to mean <qu'est-ce que ça veut dire? : what does that mean?> — **se vouloir** *vr* **1** : to think of oneself as **2** : to try to be **3 s'en vouloir** : to be annoyed with oneself

vouloir[2] *nm* : will <bon vouloir : goodwill>

voulu, -lue [vuly] *adj* **1** DÉLIBÉRÉ : intentional, deliberate **2** REQUIS : required

vous [vu] *pron* **1** (*as subject or direct object*) : you <vous êtes mon ami : you're my friend> <elle vous aime : she loves you> **2** (*as indirect object*) : you, to you <il vous a écrit une lettre : he wrote you a letter> **3** : yourself <servez-vous : help yourself> <pensez à vous : think about yourselves> **4 à ~** : yours <est-ce que cette maison est à vous? : is this house yours?, is this your house?>

vous–même [vumɛm], *pl* **vous–mêmes** *pron* : yourself

voûte [vut] *nf* **1** : vault, arch **2 voûte du palais** : roof of the mouth

voûter [vute] *vt* : to vault, to arch — **se voûter** *vr* : to become stooped

vouvoyer [vuvwaje] {58} *vt* : to address as *vous*

voyage [vwajaʒ] *nm* **1** : voyage, trip **2 avoir son voyage** *Can fam* : to be fed up

voyager [vwajaʒe] {17} *vi* : to travel

voyageur, -geuse [vwajaʒœr, -ʒøz] *n* **1** : traveler **2** PASSAGER : passenger

voyait [vwajɛ], **voyions** [vwajɔ̃], *etc.* → **voir**

voyance [vwajɑ̃s] *nf* : clairvoyance

voyant[1], **voyante** [vwajɑ̃, -jɑ̃t] *adj* : loud, gaudy, garish

voyant[2], **voyante** *n* : seer, clairvoyant

voyant[3] *nm* : warning light, indicator light

voyelle [vwajɛl] *nf* : vowel

voyeur, voyeuse [vwajœr, -jøz] *n* : voyeur

voyou [vwaju] *nm* : thug, hoodlum

vrac [vrak] *adv* **1 en ~** : loose, in bulk **2 en ~** : jumbled, disorganized

vrai[1], **vraie** [vrɛ] *adj* **1** : true **2** : real

vrai[2] *nm* : truth <à vrai dire : to tell the truth>

vraiment [vrɛmɑ̃] *adv* : really

vraisemblable [vrɛzɑ̃blabl] *adj* : likely, probable — **vraisemblablement** [-blabləmɑ̃] *adv*

vraisemblance [vrɛzɑ̃blɑ̃s] *nf* **1** : likelihood, probability **2** : verisimilitude

vrille [vrij] *nf* **1** : gimlet (tool), auger **2** : spiral, tailspin **3** : tendril

vriller [vrije] *vt* : to bore into, to pierce

vrombir [vrɔ̃bir] *vi* **1** : to hum, to buzz **2** : to roar (of an engine)

vrombissement [vrɔ̃bismɑ̃] *nm* : humming, buzzing, roaring

vu[1] [vy] *pp* → **voir**

vu[2], **vue** [vy] *adj* : seen, regarded <bien vu : well thought of>

vu[3] *prep* : in view of, considering <vu sa timidité, c'est un homme brave : considering his timidity, he's a brave man>

vue *nf* **1** : sight <à première vue : at first sight> **2** : eyesight **3** : view, vista <vue d'ensemble : overall view> **4** : opinion, view **5 vues** *nfpl* : plans, designs **6 vues** *nfpl Can* : <aller aux vues : to go to the movies>

vulcaniser [vylkanize] *vt* : to vulcanize
vulgaire [vylgɛr] *adj* **1** GROSSIER : vulgar, coarse **2** ORDINAIRE : common, ordinary
vulgairement [vylgɛrmɑ̃] *adv* : vulgarly
vulgariser [vylgarize] *vt* : to popularize — **vulgarisation** [vylgarizasjɔ̃] *nf*
vulgarité [vylgarite] *nf* : vulgarity
vulnérabilité [vylnerabilite] *nf* : vulnerability
vulnérable [vylnerabl] *adj* : vulnerable
vulve [vylv] *nf* : vulva

W

w [dubləve] *nm* : w, the 23rd letter of the alphabet
wagon [vagɔ̃] *nm* **1** : car (of a train) **2** : carload, truckload, wagonload
wagon–citerne [vagɔ̃sitɛrn] *nm, pl* **wagons–citernes** : tanker
wagon–lit [vagɔ̃li] *nm, pl* **wagons–lits** : sleeping car, Pullman
wagonnet [vagɔnɛ] *nm* : small transport car (on a train)
wagon–restaurant [vagɔ̃rɛstɔrɑ̃] *nm, pl* **wagons–restaurants** : dining car
wallaby [walabi] *nm, pl* **wallabies** : wallaby
wallon[1], -lonne [walɔ̃, -lɔn] *adj* : Walloon
wallon[2] *nm* : Walloon (language)
Wallon, -lonne *n* : Walloon
wampum [wampum] *nm* : wampum
wapiti [wapiti] *nm* : wapiti
water–polo [watɛrpɔlo] *nm* : water polo
watt [wat] *nm* : watt
Web [wɛb] *nm* TOILE : World Wide Web, Web
week–end [wikɛnd] *nm, pl* **week–ends** : weekend
western [wɛstɛrn] *nm* : western (movie)
wharf [warf] *nm* : wharf
whippet [wipɛt] *nm* : whippet
whisky [wiski] *nm, pl* **whiskies** : whiskey
wigwam [wigwam] *nm* : wigwam
wolfram [vɔlfram] *nm* : wolfram

X

x [iks] *nm* : x, the 24th letter of the alphabet
X [iks] *nm* (*used to designate an unknown*) <monsieur X : Mr. X>
xénon [gzenɔ̃] *nm* : xenon
xénophile [gzenɔfil] *adj & nmf* : xenophile
xénophobe[1] [gzenɔfɔb] *adj* : xenophobic
xénophobe[2] *nmf* : xenophobe
xénophobie [gzenɔfɔbi] *nf* : xenophobia
xérès [gzerɛs, kserɛs] *nm* : sherry
xylophone [ksilɔfɔn] *nm* : xylophone

y [igrɛk] *nm* : y, the 25th letter of the alphabet
y[1] [i] *adv* **1** : there <il n'y était pas : he was not there> **2 ça y est !** : finally!, there you have it!
y[2] *pron* : it, for it, about it <nous n'y pouvons rien : we can't do anything about it> <pensons-y : let's think about it> <j'y suis! : I've got it!>
yacht [jɔt] *nm* : yacht
yachting [jɔtiŋ] *nm* : yachting
yack *or* **yak** [jak] *nm* : yak
yankee[1] [jɑ̃ki] *adj* : yankee
Yankee[2] *nmf* : Yankee
yaourt [jaurt] *nm* : yogurt
yéménite [jemenit] *adj* : Yemeni
Yéménite *nmf* : Yemeni
yeux [jø] → **œil**
yoga [jɔga] *nm* : yoga
yogourt *or* **yoghourt** [jɔgurt] → **yaourt**
Yom Kippour [jɔmkipur] *nm* : Yom Kippur
yougoslave [jugɔslav] *adj* : Yugoslav, Yugoslavian
Yougoslave *nmf* : Yugoslav, Yugoslavian
yo–yo *or* **yoyo** [jojo] *nm* : yo-yo
yucca [juka] *nm* : yucca

Z

z [zɛd] *nm* : z, the 26th letter of the alphabet
zaïrois, -roise [zairwa, -rwaz] *adj* : Zairian
Zaïrois, -roise *n* : Zairian
zambien, -bienne [zɑ̃bjɛ̃, -bjɛn] *adj* : Zambian
Zambien, -bienne *n* : Zambian
zèbre [zɛbr] *nm* : zebra
zébré, -brée [zebre] *adj* RAYÉ : striped, streaked
zébrure [zebryr] *nf* **1** RAYURE : stripe **2** : wheal, welt (on the skin) **3** : streak (of lightning)
zélateur, -trice [zelatœr, -tris] *n* : zealot, partisan
zèle [zɛl] *nm* : zeal
zélé, -lée [zele] *adj* : zealous
zénith [zenit] *nm* : zenith
zéphyr [zefir] *nm* : zephyr
zeppelin [zɛplɛ̃] *nm* : zeppelin
zéro[1] [zero] *adj* **1** : zero **2** : nil, worthless
zéro[2] *nm* : zero, nought
zeste [zɛst] *nm* : zest, peel (of a lemon, etc.)
zézaiement [zezɛmɑ̃] *nm* : lisp
zézayer [zezeje] {11} *vi* : to lisp
zibeline [ziblin] *nf* : sable
zieuter [zjøte] *vt fam* RELUQUER : to ogle, to eye
zig *or* **zigue** [zig] *nm fam* : guy, fellow
zigzag [zigzag] *nm* : zigzag
zigzaguer [zigzage] *vi* : to zigzag
zimbabwéen, -wéenne [zimbabweɛ̃, -weɛn] *adj* : Zimbabwean
Zimbabwéen, -wéenne *n* : Zimbabwean
zinc [zɛ̃g] *nm* : zinc
zinnia [zinja] *nm* : zinnia
zip [zip] *nm* : zipper
zipper [zipe] *vt* : to zip (up)
zircon [zirkɔ̃] *nm* : zircon
zirconium [zirkɔnjɔm] *nm* : zirconium
zizanie [zizani] *nf* DISCORDE : discord, conflict
zodiaque [zɔdjak] *nm* : zodiac
zombie [zɔ̃bi] *nm* : zombie
zona [zona] *nm* : shingles
zonage [zonaʒ] *nm* : zoning
zone [zon] *nf* : zone, area
zoo [zo(o)] *nm* : zoo
zoologie [zɔɔlɔʒi] *nf* : zoology
zoologique [zɔɔlɔʒik] *adj* : zoological
zoologiste [zɔɔlɔʒist] *nmf* : zoologist
zoom [zum] *nm* **1** : zoom lens **2 faire un zoom** : to zoom in (in photography)
zozo [zozo] *nm fam* : nitwit
zozoter [zɔzɔte] *vi* : to lisp
zut [zyt] *interj fam* : darn!, damn it!
zygote [zigɔt] *nm* : zygote

English–French Dictionary

A

a[1] ['eɪ] *n, pl* **a's** or **as** ['eɪz] : a *m,* première lettre de l'alphabet

a[2] [ə, 'eɪ] *art* (**an** [ən, 'æn] *before a vowel or silent h*) **1** : un *m,* une *f* <a book : un livre> <half an hour : une demi-heure> **2** PER : par <twice a month : deux fois par mois>

aardvark ['ɑrd,vɑrk] *n* : oryctérope *m*

aback [ə'bæk] *adv* **taken aback** : déconcerté, décontenancé

abacus ['æbəkəs] *n, pl* **abaci** ['æbə,saɪ, -kɪ:] or **abacuses** : boulier *m*

abaft [ə'bæft] *adv* : en poupe, sur l'arrière

abalone [,æbə'lo:ni] *n* : ormeau *m*

abandon[1] [ə'bændən] *vt* **1** DESERT, FORSAKE : abandonner, délaisser **2** LEAVE : abandonner, quitter (un lieu) <abandon ship! : abandonnez le navire!> **3** GIVE UP, SUSPEND : renoncer à, laisser tomber <she abandoned her studies : elle a laissé tomber ses études> **4 to abandon oneself to** : se livrer à, s'abandonner à

abandon[2] *n* : abandon *m,* désinvolture *m*

abandoned [ə'bændənd] *adj* **1** DESERTED : abandonné, délaissé **2** UNRESTRAINED : sans retenue

abandonment [ə'bændənmənt] *n* : abandon *m*

abase [ə'beɪs] *vt* **abased; abasing** : abaisser, humilier

abasement [ə'beɪsmənt] *n* : abaissement *f,* humiliation *f*

abash [ə'bæʃ] *vt* : décontenancer, confondre

abashed [ə'bæʃt] *adj* : décontenancé, confondu

abate [ə'beɪt] *v* **abated; abating** *vt* REDUCE : baisser, réduire, diminuer — *vi* DECREASE : s'apaiser, se calmer, diminuer <the fever abated : la fièvre s'est calmée>

abatement [ə'beɪtmənt] *n* : apaisement *m,* diminution *f*

abattoir ['æbə,twɑr] *n* : abattoir *m*

abbess ['æbɪs, -,bɛs, -bəs] *n* : abbesse *f*

abbey ['æbi] *n, pl* **-beys** : abbaye *f*

abbot ['æbət] *n* : abbé *m*

abbreviate [ə'bri:vi,eɪt] *vt* **-ated; -ating** : abréger

abbreviation [ə,bri:vi'eɪʃən] *n* : abréviation *f*

abdicate ['æbdɪ,keɪt] *v* **-cated; -cating** : abdiquer

abdication [,æbdɪ'keɪʃən] *n* : abdication *f*

abdomen ['æbdəmən, æb'do:mən] *n* : abdomen *m*

abdominal [æb'dɑmənəl] *adj* : abdominal

abduct [æb'dʌkt] *vt* : enlever

abduction [æb'dʌkʃən] *n* : enlèvement *m*

abductor [æb'dʌktər] *n* : ravisseur *m,* -seuse *f*

abed [ə'bɛd] *adv & adj* : au lit, dans le lit

aberrant [æ'bɛrənt, 'æbərənt] *adj* : aberrant

aberration [,æbə'reɪʃən] *n* : aberration *f*

abet [ə'bɛt] *vt* **abetted; abetting 1** ENCOURAGE : encourager, soutenir **2 to aid and abet** : être complice de

abettor *or* **abetter** [ə'bɛtər] *n* : complice *mf*

abeyance [ə'beɪənts] *n* **1** SUSPENSION : suspension *f,* interruption *f* **2 in ~** : en suspens

abhor [əb'hɔr, æb-] *vt* **-horred; -horring** : abhorrer, détester

abhorrence [əb'hɔrənts, æb-] *n* : horreur *f*

abhorrent [əb'hɔrənt, æb-] *adj* : odieux, détestable

abide [ə'baɪd] *v* **abode** [ə'bo:d] *or* **abided; abiding** *vt* STAND, TOLERATE : endurer, supporter — *vi* **1** LAST : continuer, durer **2** RESIDE : demeurer, habiter **3 to abide by** : respecter, se conformer à

ability [ə'bɪləṭi] *n, pl* **-ties 1** CAPABILITY : capacité *f,* aptitude *f* **2** SKILL : habileté *f,* talent *m*

abject ['æb,dʒɛkt, æb'-] *adj* **1** WRETCHED : abject, misérable **2** SERVILE : servile, obséquieux — **abjectly** *adv*

ablaze [ə'bleɪz] *adj* **1** BURNING : en flammes, en feu **2** RADIANT : brillant, resplendissant

able ['eɪbəl] *adj* **abler; ablest 1** CAPABLE : capable **2** SKILLED : compétent, habile

able-bodied [,eɪbəl'bɑdid] *n* : robuste, vigoureux

ably ['eɪbəli] *adv* : habilement

abnormal [æb'nɔrmel] *adj* : anormal — **abnormally** *adv*

abnormality [,æbnər'mæləṭi, -nɔr-] *n, pl* **-ties** : anormalité *f* (état), anomalie *f* (trait)

aboard[1] [ə'bord] *adv* : à bord

aboard[2] *prep* : à bord de, dans <aboard the train : dans le train>

abode [ə'bo:d] *n* : demeure *f,* domicile *m*

abolish [ə'bɑlɪʃ] *vt* : supprimer, abolir

abolition [,æbə'lɪʃən] *n* : abolition *f,* suppression *f*

abominable [ə'bɑmənəbəl] *adj* : abominable

abominate [ə,bɑmə'neɪʃən] *vt* **-nated; -nating** : abhorrer, abominer

abomination [ə'bɑməneɪt] *n* : abomination *f*

aboriginal [,æbə'rɪdʒənəl] *adj* : aborigène, indigène

aborigine [,æbə'rɪdʒəni] *n* : aborigène *mf*

abort [ə'bɔrt] *vt* **1** TERMINATE : faire avorter **2** SUSPEND : abandonner, interrompre — *vi* : avorter
abortion [ə'bɔrʃən] *n* : avortement *m*
abortive [ə'bɔrtɪv] *adj* **1** : avorté, manqué <abortive efforts : efforts avortés> **2** : abortif <abortive agent : agent abortif>
abound [ə'baʊnd] *vi* : abonder
about[1] [ə'baʊt] *adv* **1** APPROXIMATELY : vers, environ, à peu près **2** AROUND : autour, à la ronde <he looked all about : il regardait tout autour> **3** NEARBY : près, par ici, par là **4** : de tous côtés, ça et là, ici et là <books lying all about : des livres de tous côtés> **5** ALMOST : tout juste, à peu près, presque **6 to be about to** : être sur le point de
about[2] *prep* **1** AROUND : autour de, par, dans <to walk about the city : se promener dans la ville> **2** CONCERNING : sur, de, concernant <a book about jazz : un livre sur le jazz> <he's talking about me : il parle de moi> <what's it about? : de quoi s'agit-il?>
above[1] [ə'bʌv] *adv* **1** OVERHEAD : au-dessus, en haut **2** : ci-dessus, plus haut <as mentioned above : comme cité ci-dessus>
above[2] *prep* **1** OVER : au-dessus de, en haut de **2** EXCEEDING : plus de, au-dessus de <above one hundred applicants : plus de cent candidats> **3** BEYOND : au-delà de <above the call of duty : au-delà du strict devoir>
aboveboard[1] [ə'bʌv'bord, -ˌbord] *adv* : ouvertement, franchement
aboveboard[2] *adj* : ouvert, franc
abrade [ə'breɪd] *vt* **abraded; abrading** **1** SCRAPE : érafler (la peau), user en frottant **2** IRRITATE : agacer, irriter
abrasion [ə'breɪʒən] *n* **1** ABRADING : abrasion *f* **2** SCRATCH : écorchure *f*, éraflure *f*
abrasive[1] [ə'breɪsɪv] *adj* : abrasif
abrasive[2] *n* : abrasif *m*
abreast [ə'brɛst] *adv* **1** : de front, côte à côte <two abreast : à deux de front> **2 to keep abreast of** : se tenir au courant de
abridge [ə'brɪdʒ] *vt* **abridged; abridging** : abréger
abridgment *or* **abridgement** [ə'brɪdʒmənt] *n* **1** ABRIDGING : abrégement *m* **2** SUMMARY : abrégé *m*, résumé *m*
abroad [ə'brɔd] *adv* **1** WIDELY : au loin, de tous côtés <to spread abroad : circuler de tous côtés> **2** OVERSEAS : à l'étranger
abrupt [ə'brʌpt] *adj* **1** SUDDEN : soudain, précipité **2** CURT : abrupt, brusque **3** STEEP : escarpé, abrupt
abruptly [ə'brʌptli] *adv* : brusquement, tout d'un coup
abscess ['æbˌsɛs] *n* : abcès *m*
abscond [æb'skɑnd] *vi* : s'enfuir
absence ['æbsənts] *n* **1** : absence *f* (d'une personne) **2** LACK : manque *m*
absent[1] [æb'sɛnt] *vt* **to absent oneself** : s'absenter
absent[2] ['æbsənt] *adj* : absent
absentee [ˌæbsən'ti:] *n* : absent *m*, -sente *f*
absentminded [ˌæbsənt'maɪndəd] *adj* : distrait, préoccupé
absentmindedly [ˌæbsənt'maɪndədli] *adv* : d'un air distrait, distraitement
absentmindedness [ˌæbsənt'maɪndədnəs] *n* : distraction *f*
absolute ['æbsəˌlu:t, ˌæbsə'lu:t] *adj* **1** COMPLETE, PERFECT : absolu, total, parfait **2** UNCONDITIONAL : absolu, inconditionnel **3** DEFINITE : formel, définitif
absolutely ['æbsəˌlu:tli, ˌæbsə'lu:tli] *adv* **1** : absolument, tout à fait **2 absolutely not** : pas du tout
absolution [ˌæbsə'lu:ʃən] *n* : absolution *f*
absolve [əb'zɑlv, æb-, -'sɑlv] *vt* **-solved; -solving** : absoudre
absorb [əb'zɔrb, æb-, -'sɔrb] *vt* **1** : absorber (des liquides), amortir (des chocs, des sons, etc.), assimiler (personnes) **2 to become absorbed in** : s'absorber dans
absorbency [əb'zɔrbəntsi, æb-, -'sɔr-] *n, pl* **-cies** : pouvoir *m* absorbant
absorbent [əb'zɔrbənt, æb-, -'sɔr-] *adj* : absorbant
absorbing [əb'zɔrbɪŋ, æb-, -'sɔr-] *adj* : absorbant, fascinant
absorption [əb'zɔrpʃən, æb-, -'sɔrp-] *n* **1** : absorption *f* (des liquides), amortissement *m* (d'un choc, etc.) **2** CONCENTRATION : concentration *f* (d'esprit)
abstain [əb'steɪn, æb-] *vi* : s'abstenir
abstemious [æb'sti:miəs] *adj* : sobre, frugal — **abstemiously** *adv*
abstemiousness [æb'sti:miəsnəs] *n* : sobriété *f*, tempérence *f*
abstention [əb'stɛntʃən, æb-] *n* : abstention *f*
abstinence ['æbstənənts] *n* : abstinence *f*
abstinent ['æbstənənt] *adj* : sobre, frugal, modéré
abstract[1] [æb'strækt, 'æbˌ-] *vt* **1** REMOVE : extraire, retirer **2** SUMMARIZE : résumer
abstract[2] *adj* : abstrait — **abstractly** [æb'stræktli, 'æbˌ-] *adv*
abstract[3] ['æbˌstrækt] *n* **1** SUMMARY : résumé *m* **2** : abstrait *m* <in the abstract : dans l'abstrait>
abstraction [æb'strækʃən] *n* **1** : abstraction *f*, idée *f* abstraite **2** REMOVAL : extraction *f* **3** PREOCCUPATION : préoccupation *f*, distraction *f*
abstruse [əb'stru:s, æb-] *adj* : abstrus
absurd [əb'sərd, -'zərd] *adj* : absurde, ridicule, insensé

absurdity [əb'sərdəṭi, -'zər-] *n, pl* **-ties** : absurdité *f,* ridicule *m*
absurdly [əb'sərdli, -'zərd-] *adv* : ridiculement, de manière insensée
abundance [ə'bʌndənts] *n* : abondance *f,* profusion *f*
abundant [ə'bʌndənt] *adj* : abondant
abundantly [ə'bʌndəntli] *adv* : abondamment, en profusion
abuse[1] [ə'bju:z] *vt* **abused; abusing 1** MISUSE : abuser de **2** MISTREAT : maltraiter **3** INSULT : injurier, insulter
abuse[2] [ə'bju:s] *n* **1** MISUSE : abus *m* **2** MISTREATMENT : abus *m,* mauvais traitement *m* **3** INSULTS : insultes *fpl,* injures *fpl*
abusive [ə'bju:sɪv] *adj* **1** IMPROPER : abusif **2** HURTFUL : injurieux, brutal **3** OFFENSIVE : grossier — **abusively** *adv*
abut [ə'bʌt] *v* **abutted; abutting** *vt* : juxtaposer — *vi* **to abut on** : être contigu à
abutment [ə'bʌtmənt] *n* : contrefort *m,* butée *f*
abysmal [ə'bɪzməl] *adj* **1** DEEP : abyssal, insondable **2** WRETCHED : épouvantable
abysmally [ə'bɪzməli] *adv* : atrocement, abominablement
abyss [ə'bɪs, 'æbɪs] *n* : abîme *m,* gouffre *m*
acacia [ə'keɪʃə] *n* : acacia *m*
academic[1] [ˌækə'dɛmɪk] *adj* **1** SCHOLASTIC : académique, scolaire <the academic year : l'année scolaire> **2** THEORETICAL : théorique
academic[2] *n* : universitaire *mf*
academically [ˌækə'dɛmɪkli] *adv* : sur le plan intellectuel, intellectuellement
academy [ə'kædəmi] *n, pl* **-mies 1** SCHOOL : école *f,* collège *m* **2** SOCIETY : académie *f,* société *f* <the French Academy : l'Académie française>
acanthus [ə'kæntθəs] *ns & pl* : acanthe *f*
accede [æk'si:d] *vi* **-ceded; -ceding 1** : monter <to accede to the throne : monter sur le trône> **2 to accede to** : agréer, accepter <she acceded to his request : elle a agréé sa demande>
accelerate [ɪk'sɛləˌreɪt, æk-] *v* **-ated; -ating** : accélérer
acceleration [ɪkˌsɛlə'reɪʃən, æk-] *n* : accélération *f*
accelerator [ɪk'sɛləˌreɪṭər, æk-] *n* : accélérateur *m*
accent[1] ['ækˌsɛnt, æk'sɛnt] *vt* : accentuer
accent[2] ['ækˌsɛnt, -sənt] *n* : accent *m* <a Russian accent : un accent russe> <to put the accent on : mettre l'accent sur>
accentuate [ɪk'sɛntʃʊˌeɪt, æk-] *vt* **-ated; -ating** : accentuer, souligner
accept [ɪk'sɛpt, æk-] *vt* **1** : accepter <to accept a present : accepter un cadeau> **2** ACKNOWLEDGE : accepter, admettre
acceptability [ɪkˌsɛptə'bɪləṭi, æk-] *n* : acceptabilité *f*
acceptable [ɪk'sɛptəbəl, æk-] *adj* : acceptable
acceptably [ɪk'sɛptəbli] *adv* : passablement, suffisamment
acceptance [ɪk'sɛptənts, æk-] *n* **1** ACCEPTING : acceptation *f* **2** APPROVAL : approbation *f*
access[1] ['ækˌsɛs] *vt* : accéder à
access[2] *n* : accès *m* <no access : accès interdit>
accessibility [ɪkˌsɛsə'bɪləṭi] *n* : accessibilité *f*
accessible [ɪk'sɛsəbəl, æk-] *adj* : accessible
accession [ɪk'sɛʃən, æk-] *n* **1** : accession *f* <accession to the throne : accession au trône> **2** INCREASE : augmentation *f* **3** ACQUISITION : acquisition *f*
accessory[1] [ɪk'sɛsəri, æk-] *adj* : accessoire, auxiliaire
accessory[2] *n, pl* **-ries 1** ACCOMPLICE : complice *mf* **2** ADJUNCT : accessoire *m*
accident ['æksədənt] *n* **1** MISHAP : accident *m* **2** CHANCE : hasard *m,* chance *f* <by accident : par hasard>
accidental [ˌæksə'dɛntəl] *adj* : accidentel, fortuit
accidentally [ˌæksə'dɛntəli, -'dɛntli] *adv* : accidentellement, par hasard
acclaim[1] [ə'kleɪm] *vt* **1** PRAISE : acclamer **2** DECLARE, PROCLAIM : proclamer
acclaim[2] *n* : acclamation *f,* louange *f*
acclamation [ˌæklə'meɪʃən] *n* : acclamation *f* <elected by acclamation : élu par acclamation>
acclimate ['ækləˌmeɪt, ə'klaɪmət] → **acclimatize**
acclimatize [ə'klaɪməˌtaɪz] *vt* **-tized; -tizing 1** : acclimater **2 to acclimatize oneself** : s'acclimater
accolade ['ækəˌleɪd, -ˌlɑd] *n* : acclamation *f,* accolade *f*
accommodate [ə'kɑməˌdeɪt] *vt* **-dated; -dating 1** ADAPT : accommoder, adapter **2** RECONCILE : concilier **3** SATISFY : satisfaire, répondre aux besoins de **4** HOLD : contenir, avoir une capacité de
accommodation [əˌkɑmə'deɪʃən] *n* **1** ADJUSTMENT : accommodation *f,* adaptation *f* **2 accomodations** *npl* LODGING : logement *m,* hébergement *m*
accompaniment [ə'kʌmpənəmənt, -'kɑm-] *n* : accompagnement *m*
accompanist [ə'kʌmpənɪst, -'kɑm-] *n* : accompagnateur *m,* -trice *f*
accompany [ə'kʌmpəni, -'kɑm-] *vt* **-nied; -nying** : accompagner
accomplice [ə'kɑmpləs, -'kʌm-] *n* : complice *mf*

accomplish [ə'kɑmplɪʃ, -'kʌm-] *vt* : accomplir, réaliser
accomplished [ə'kɑmplɪʃt, -'kʌm-] *adj* : accompli <an accomplished pianist : un pianiste accompli>
accomplishment [ə'kɑmplɪʃmənt, -'kʌm-] *n* **1** COMPLETION : réalisation *f*, accomplissement *m* **2** ACHIEVEMENT : œuvre *f* accomplie, réussite *f* **3** SKILL : talent *m*
accord[1] [ə'kɔrd] *vt* CONCEDE, GRANT : accorder, concéder — *vi* AGREE : s'accorder, concorder
accord[2] *n* **1** AGREEMENT : accord *m* **2 of one's own accord** : de son plein gré, de soi-même
accordance [ə'kɔrdənts] *n* **1** ACCORD : accord *m*, conformité *f* **2 in accordance with** : conformément à, suivant
accordingly [ə'kɔrdɪŋli] *adv* **1** CORRESPONDINGLY : en conséquence <to act accordingly : agir en conséquence> **2** CONSEQUENTLY, THEREFORE : donc, par conséquent
according to [ə'kɔrdɪŋ] *prep* **1** : conformément à, selon, suivant <according to plan : conformément au plan prévu> **2** : selon, d'après <according to them : d'après eux>
accordion [ə'kɔrdiən] *n* : accordéon *m*
accordionist [ə'kɔrdiənɪst] *n* : accordéoniste *mf*
accost [ə'kɔst] *vt* : accoster, aborder
account[1] [ə'kaʊnt] *vt* CONSIDER : estimer, juger — *vi* **1 to account for** EXPLAIN : justifier, expliquer **2 to account for** REPRESENT : représenter
account[2] *n* **1** : compte *m* <bank account : compte bancaire> **2** REPORT : compte *m* rendu, exposé *m* **3** WORTH : importance *f* <to be of little account : avoir peu d'importance> **4 on account of** BECAUSE OF : à cause de **5 on no account** : en aucun cas, sous aucun prétexte **6 on one's account** : à cause de soi, à son sujet <don't worry on my account : ne t'inquiète pas à mon sujet> **7 to take into account** : tenir compte de
accountability [ə,kaʊntə'bɪləṭi] *n* : responsabilité *f*
accountable [ə'kaʊntəbəl] *adj* : responsable
accountant [ə'kaʊntənt] *n* : comptable *mf*
accounting [ə'kaʊntɪŋ] *n* : comptabilité *f*
accoutrements *or* **accouterments** [ə'ku:trəmənts, -'ku:ṭər-] *npl* **1** EQUIPMENT : équipement *m* **2** ACCESSORIES : accessoires *mpl* **3** TRAPPINGS : attributs *mpl* (du pouvoir, etc.)
accredit [ə'krɛdət] *vt* : accréditer
accreditation [ə,krɛdə'teɪʃən] *n* : accréditation *f*
accrual [ə'kru:əl] *n* : accumulation *f*
accrue [ə'kru:] *vi* **-crued; -cruing 1** : s'accumuler **2 to accrue to** : revenir à
accumulate [ə'kju:mjə,leɪt] *v* **-lated; -lating** *vt* : accumuler — *vi* s'accumuler
accumulation [ə,kju:mjə'leɪʃən] *n* : accumulation *f*
accuracy ['ækjərəsi] *n, pl* **-cies** : exactitude *f*, précision *f*
accurate ['ækjərət] *adj* : exact, précis, juste — **accurately** *adv*
accusation [,ækjə'zeɪʃən] *n* : accusation *f*
accuse [ə'kju:z] *vt* **-cused; -cusing** : accuser
accused [ə'kju:zd] *ns & pl* : accusé *m*, -sée *f*; inculpé *m*, -pée *f*
accuser [ə'kju:zər] *n* : accusateur *m*, -trice *f*
accustom [ə'kʌstəm] *vt* **1** : habituer, accoutumer **2 to get accustomed to** : s'habituer à, s'accoutumer à
accustomed [ə'kʌstəmd] *adj* **1** USED : habitué, accoutumé **2** USUAL : habituel, familier
ace ['eɪs] *n* : as *m*
acerbic [ə'sərbɪk, æ-] *adj* : acerbe
acetate ['æsə,teɪt] *n* : acétate *m*
acetylene [ə'sɛṭələn, -ṭə,li:n] *n* : acétylène *m*
ache[1] [eɪk] *vi* **ached; aching 1** HURT : avoir mal, faire mal <he aches all over : il a mal partout> <my leg aches : ma jambe me fait mal> **2 to ache for** : avoir très envie de
ache[2] *n* : douleur *f*, mal *m*
achieve [ə'tʃi:v] *vt* **achieved; achieving** : accomplir, atteindre
achievement [ə'tʃi:vmənt] *n* : accomplissement *m*, réussite *f*
acid[1] ['æsəd] *adj* : acide
acid[2] *n* : acide *m*
acidic [ə'sɪdɪk, æ-] *adj* : acide
acidity [ə'sɪdəṭi, æ-] *n, pl* **-ties** : acidité *f*
acknowledge [ɪk'nɑlɪdʒ, æk-] *vt* **-edged; -edging 1** ADMIT : admettre, reconnaître **2** RECOGNIZE : reconnaître **3** : remercier de, manifester sa gratitude pour **4 to acknowledge receipt of** : accuser réception de
acknowledgment [ɪk'nɑlɪdʒmənt, æk-] *n* **1** RECOGNITION : reconnaissance *f* **2** THANKS : remerciement *m* **3 acknowledgment of receipt** : accusé *m* de réception
acme ['ækmi] *n* : point *m* culminant, apogée *m*
acne ['ækni] *n* : acné *f*
acorn ['eɪ,kɔrn, -kərn] *n* : gland *m*
acoustic [ə'ku:stɪk] *or* **acoustical** [ə'ku:stɪkəl] *adj* : acoustique — **acoustically** *adv*
acoustics [ə'ku:stɪks] *ns & pl* : acoustique *f*
acquaint [ə'kweɪnt] *vt* **1** INFORM : informer, aviser, renseigner **2 to be ac-**

quainted with : connaître (une personne, un lieu, etc.), être au courant de (un fait, une situation, etc.)
acquaintance [ə'kweɪntənts] *n* **1** KNOWLEDGE : connaissance *f* **2** : relation *f*, connaissance *f* <friends and acquaintances : amis et relations>
acquiesce [ˌækwi'ɛs] *vi* **-esced; -escing** : acquiescer
acquiescence [ˌækwi'ɛsənts] *n* : acquiescement *m*
acquire [ə'kwaɪr] *vt* **-quired; -quiring** : acquérir
acquisition [ˌækwə'zɪʃən] *n* : acquisition *f*
acquisitive [ə'kwɪzəṭɪv] *adj* : âpre au gain, avide
acquit [ə'kwɪt] *vt* **-quitted; -quitting 1** : acquitter <to be acquitted of a crime : être disculpé d'un délit> **2 to acquit oneself** : se conduire, s'en tirer
acquittal [ə'kwɪṭəl] *n* : acquittement *m*
acre ['eɪkər] *n* : acre *m*
acreage ['eɪkərɪdʒ] *n* : superficie *f*
acrid ['ækrəd] *adj* **1** PUNGENT : âcre **2** CAUSTIC : caustique, acerbe
acrimonious [ˌækrə'mo:niəs] *adj* : acrimonieux — **acrimoniously** *adv*
acrimony ['ækrəˌmo:ni] *n, pl* **-nies** : acrimonie *f*
acrobat ['ækrəˌbæt] *n* : acrobate *mf* — **acrobatic** [ˌækrə'bæṭɪk] *adj*
acrobatics [ˌækrə'bæṭɪks] *ns & pl* : acrobatie *f*
across[1] [ə'krɔs] *adv* **1** : de large <40 feet across : 40 pieds de large> **2 ~ from** : en face de **3 to get one's point across** : se faire comprendre
across[2] *prep* **1** : de l'autre côté de <the house across the street : la maison de l'autre côté de la rue> <to go across the mountain : traverser la montagne> **2** : en travers de <a tree (lying) across the stream : un arbre en travers du ruisseau>
acrylic [ə'krɪlɪk] *n* : acrylique *m*
act[1] ['ækt] *vt* PERFORM : jouer (un rôle) — *vi* **1** : agir <we must act quickly : il faut agir rapidement> **2** PERFORM : jouer, faire du théâtre **3** BEHAVE : agir, se comporter **4** : agir (en médecine) **5 to act as** : servir de, faire office de **6 to act on** : suivre (de l'avis, etc.)
act[2] *n* **1** DEED : action *f*, acte *m* **2** DECREE : loi *f* **3** : acte *m* <a three-act play : une pièce en trois actes> **4** PRETENSE : comédie *f* <to put on an act : jouer la comédie>
action ['ækʃən] *n* **1** ACT, DEED : action *f*, acte *m*, fait *m* **2** LAWSUIT : procès *m*, action *f* <to take legal action : poursuivre en justice> **3** COMBAT : combat *m* **4** PLOT : intrigue *f* **5** MOVEMENT : mouvement *m* **6** MECHANISM : mécanisme *m* **7 actions** *npl* CONDUCT : conduite *f*, actes *mpl*
activate ['æktəˌveɪt] *vt* **-vated; -vating** : activer
active ['æktɪv] *adj* : actif
actively ['æktɪvli] *adv* : activement
activity [æk'tɪvəṭi] *n, pl* **-ties** : activité *f*
actor ['æktər] *n* : acteur *m*, -trice *f*; comédien *m*, -dienne *f*
actress ['æktrəs] *n* : actrice *f*, comédienne *f*
actual ['æktʃʊəl] *adj* **1** REAL : réel, véritable **2** VERY : même <the actual house where he was born : la maison même où il est né>
actuality [ˌæktʃʊ'æləti] *n, pl* **-ties** : réalité *f*
actually ['æktʃʊəli, -ʃəli] *adv* : vraiment, en fait, en réalité
actuary ['æktʃʊˌɛri] *n, pl* **-aries** : actuaire *mf*
acumen [ə'kju:mən] *n* : perspicacité *f*, finesse *f* <business acumen : sens des affaires>
acupuncture ['ækjʊˌpʌŋktʃər] *n* : acupuncture *f*
acute [ə'kju:t] *adj* **acuter; acutest 1** KEEN : fin <an acute sense of hearing : une ouïe fine> **2** PERCEPTIVE : perspicace, pénétrant **3** SEVERE : aigu, grave <an acute illness : une maladie grave> **4 acute accent** : accent *m* aigu **5 acute angle** : angle *m* aigu
acuteness [ə'kju:tnəs] *n* **1** SEVERITY : violence *f* (d'une maladie) **2** : finesse *f* (d'un sens) **3** PERSPICACITY : perspicacité *f*, finesse *f*
ad ['æd] *n* **1** → **advertisement 2 classified ad** *or* **want ad** : petite annonce *f*
adage ['ædɪdʒ] *n* : adage *m*
adamant ['ædəmənt, -ˌmænt] *adj* : inflexible, résolu — **adamantly** *adv*
adapt [ə'dæpt] *vt* : adapter — *vi* : s'adapter
adaptability [əˌdæptə'bɪləṭi] *n* : adaptabilité *f*
adaptable [əˌdæptəbəl] *adj* : adaptable
adaptation [ˌæˌdæp'teɪʃən, -dəp-] *n* : adaptation *f*
adapter [ə'dæptər] *n* : adapteur *m*
add ['æd] *vt* **1** : ajouter <I have nothing to add : je n'ai rien à ajouter> **2 to add up** TOTAL : additionner, totaliser — *vi* **1** : faire des additions **2 that doesn't add up** : cela ne s'accorde pas
adder ['ædər] *n* : vipère *f*
addict[1] [ə'dɪkt] *vt* **to be addicted to** : s'adonner à, avoir une dépendance à
addict[2] ['ædɪkt] *n* **1** DEVOTEE : fanatique *mf* **2** *or* **drug addict** : toxicomane *mf*; drogué *m*, -guée *f*
addiction [ə'dɪkʃən] *n* **1** : dépendance *f* **2 drug addiction** : toxicomanie *f*
addictive [ə'dɪktɪv] *adj* : qui crée une dépendance
addition [ə'dɪʃən] *n* **1** : ajout *m*, adjonction *f* (à une maison, une liste,

etc.) **2** : addition *f* (en mathématiques) **3 in ~** : en plus
additional [ə'dɪʃənəl] *adj* : additionnel, supplémentaire
additionally [ə'dɪʃənəli] *adv* : en plus, en outre
additive ['ædət̬ɪv] *n* : additif *m*
addle ['ædəl] *vt* **-dled; -dling** : embrouiller
address[1] [ə'drɛs] *vt* **1** : adresser, mettre l'adresse sur (une lettre, etc.) **2** : s'adresser à <to address the chair : s'adresser au président> **3** TACKLE : aborder (un problème, etc.)
address[2] [ə'drɛs, 'æ,drɛs] *n* **1** : adresse *f* <change of address : changement d'adresse> **2** SPEECH : discours *m*
addressee [,æ,drɛ'si, ə,drɛ'si] *n* : destinataire *mf*
adduce [ə'du:s, -'dju:s] *vt* **-duced; -ducing** : citer, alléguer
adenoids ['æd,nɔɪdz, -dən,ɔɪdz] *npl* : végétations *fpl* (adénoïdes)
adept [ə'dɛpt] *adj* : expert, adroit, habile — **adeptly** *adv*
adequate ['ædɪkwət] *adj* : adéquat, suffisant
adequately ['ædɪkwətli] *adv* : suffisamment
adhere [æd'hir, əd-] *vi* **-hered; -hering** **1** STICK : adhérer, coller **2 to adhere to** : adhérer à (un conviction, etc.), observer (une règle, etc.)
adherence [æd'hɪrənts, əd-] *n* : adhésion *f*
adherent [æd'hɪrənt, əd-] *n* FOLLOWER : partisan *m*, -sane *f*; adhérent *m*, -rente *f*
adhesion [æd'hiʒən, əd-] *n* : adhésion *f*, adhérence *f*
adhesive[1] [æd'hi:sɪv, əd-, -zɪv] *adj* : adhésif
adhesive[2] *n* : adhésif *m*
adjacent [ə'dʒeɪsənt] *adj* : contigu, voisin, adjacent
adjectival [,ædʒɪk'taɪvəl] *adj* : adjectif, adjectival
adjective ['ædʒɪktɪv] *n* : adjectif *m*
adjoin [ə'dʒɔɪn] *vt* : avoisiner, être contigu à, toucher à — *vi* : être contigu, se toucher
adjoining [ə'dʒɔɪnɪŋ] *adj* : attenant, contigu
adjourn [ə'dʒərn] *vt* SUSPEND : ajourner, lever <to adjourn the meeting : lever la séance> — *vi* **1** : suspendre la séance, lever la séance **2** : se retirer, passer <they adjourned to another room : ils sont passés dans une autre pièce>
adjournment [ə'dʒərnmənt] *n* : ajournement *m*, suspension *f*
adjudicate [ə'dʒu:dɪ,keɪt] *vt* **-cated; -cating** : juger, décider, régler
adjunct ['æ,dʒʌŋkt] *n* **1** ASSISTANT : adjoint *m*, -jointe *f* **2** ACCESSORY : accessoire *m*
adjust [ə'dʒʌst] *vt* : régler, ajuster — *vi* ADAPT : s'adapter
adjustable [ə'dʒʌstəbəl] *adj* : réglable, ajustable
adjustment [ə'dʒʌstmənt] *n* : ajustement *m*, réglage *m*
adjutant ['ædʒətənt] *n* : adjudant *m* (dans les forces armées)
ad–lib[1] ['æd'lɪb] *vt* **ad–libbed; ad–libbing** : improviser
ad–lib[2] *adj* : improvisé, spontané
ad–lib[3] *n* : improvisation *f*
administer [æd'mɪnəstər, əd-] *vt* : administrer, diriger, gérer
administration [æd,mɪnə'streɪʃən, əd-] *n* **1** MANAGING : administration *f*, gestion *f* **2** GOVERNMENT, MANAGEMENT : gouvernement *m*, direction *f*
administrative [æd'mɪnə,streɪt̬ɪv, əd-] *adj* : administratif — **administratively** *adv*
administrator [æd'mɪnə,streɪt̬ər, əd-] *n* : administrateur *m*, -trice *f*
admirable ['ædmərəbəl] *adj* : admirable — **admirably** *adv*
admiral ['ædmərəl] *n* : amiral *m*
admiration [,ædmə'reɪʃən] *n* : admiration *f*
admire [æd'maɪr] *vt* **-mired; -miring** : admirer
admirer [æd'maɪrər] *n* : admirateur *m*, -trice *f*
admiring [æd'maɪrɪŋ] *adj* : admiratif
admiringly [æd'maɪrɪŋli] *adv* : avec admiration, admirativement
admissible [æd'mɪsəbəl] *adj* : admissible
admission [æd'mɪʃən] *n* **1** ADMITTANCE : admission *f*, entrée *f*, accès *m* <no admission : accès interdit> <admission is free : l'entrée est gratuite> **2** CONFESSION : aveu *m* <by her own admission : de son propre aveu>
admit [æd'mɪt, əd-] *vt* **-mitted; -mitting** **1** ACKNOWLEDGE : admettre, reconnaître, avouer <he admits his guilt : il reconnaît sa culpabilité> **2** : laisser entrer, laisser passer, admettre <to admit light : laisser entrer la lumière> <admitted to the hospital : admis à l'hôpital> <the ticket admits one : le billet est valable pour une personne>
admittance [æd'mɪtənts, əd-] *n* : entrée *f*, admission *f*, accès *m*
admittedly [æd'mɪt̬ədli, əd-] *adv* : il faut en convenir, c'est vrai
admonish [æd'mɑnɪʃ, əd-] *vt* **1** REPRIMAND : admonester, réprimander **2** ADVISE, EXHORT : conseiller, exhorter
admonition [,ædmə'nɪʃən] *n* **1** REPROOF : réprimande *f*, admonition *f* **2** WARNING : avertissement *m*
ado [ə'du:] *n* **1** FUSS : agitation *f* **2 without further ado** : sans plus de cérémonie
adobe [ə'do:bi] *n* : adobe *m*

adolescence [ˌædəlˈɛsənts] *n* : adolescence *f*
adolescent[1] [ˌædəlˈɛsənt] *adj* : adolescent, de l'adolescence
adolescent[2] *n* : adolescent *m,* -cente *f*
adopt [əˈdɑpt] *vt* : adopter
adoption [əˈdɑpʃən] *n* : adoption *f*
adorable [əˈdorəbəl] *adj* : adorable — **adorably** [-rəbli] *adv*
adoration [ˌædəˈreɪʃən] *n* : adoration *f*
adore [əˈdor] *vt* **adored; adoring** : adorer
adorn [əˈdɔrn] *vt* **1** DECORATE : orner, parer **2 to adorn oneself** : se parer
adornment [əˈdɔrnmənt] *n* : ornement *m,* décoration *f*
adrift [əˈdrɪft] *adv & adj* : à la dérive
adroit [əˈdrɔɪt] *adj* : adroit, habile — **adroitly** *adv*
adroitness [əˈdrɔɪtnəs] *n* : adresse *f,* habileté *f*
adult[1] [əˈdʌlt, ˈæˌdʌlt] *adj* : adulte
adult[2] *n* : adulte *mf*
adulterate [əˈdʌltəˌreɪt] *vt* **-ated; -ating** : frelater, falsifier
adulterer [əˈdʌltərər] *n* : adultère *m*
adulteress [əˈdʌltərəs] *n* : adultère *f*
adulterous [əˈdʌltərəs] *adj* : adultère
adultery [əˈdʌltəri] *n, pl* **-teries** : adultère *m*
adulthood [əˈdʌltˌhʊd] *n* : âge *m* adulte
advance[1] [ædˈvænts, əd-] *v* **-vanced; -vancing** *vt* **1** : avancer, faire avancer <to advance the troops : avancer les troupes> **2** PROMOTE : promouvoir, servir (une cause, etc.) **3** PROPOSE : avancer (une théorie, etc.) **4** : avancer, faire une avance de (une somme d'argent) — *vi* **1** PROCEED : avancer **2** PROGRESS : progresser
advance[2] *adj* : fait à l'avance
advance[3] *n* **1** PROGRESSION : avance *f* **2** PROGRESS : progrès *m* <advances in medicine : des progrès en médecine> **3** INCREASE : hausse *f,* augmentation *f* **4 in ~** : à l'avance, d'avance **5 in advance of** : avant, en avance sur
advanced [ædˈvæntst, əd-] *adj* **1** : avancé <the advanced stages : les étapes avancées> **2** SUPERIOR : supérieur, avancé <advanced technology : technologie de pointe>
advancement [ædˈvæntsmənt, əd-] *n* : avancement *m*
advantage [ədˈvæntɪdʒ, æd-] *n* **1** : avantage *m* **2 to take advantage of** : profiter de
advantageous [ˌædˌvænˈteɪdʒəs, -vən-] *adj* : avantageux — **advantageously** *adv*
advent [ˈædˌvɛnt] *n* **1** : avènement *m,* venue *f,* arrivée *f* <the advent of spring : la venue du printemps> **2 Advent** : l'avent *m*
adventure [ædˈvɛntʃər, əd-] *n* : aventure *f*
adventurer [ædˈvɛntʃərər, əd-] *n* : aventurier *m,* -rière *f*
adventuresome [ædˈvɛntʃərsəm, əd-] *adj* : téméraire, aventureux
adventurous [ædˈvɛntʃərəs, əd-] *adj* **1** : aventureux <adventurous explorers : explorateurs aventureux> **2** RISKY : hasardeux, dangereux <an adventurous voyage : un voyage hasardeux>
adverb [ˈædˌvərb] *n* : adverbe *m* — **adverbial** [ædˈvɛrbiəl] *adj*
adversary [ˈædvərˌsɛri] *n, pl* **-saries** : adversaire *mf*
adverse [ædˈvɛrs, ˈædˌ-] *adj* : adverse, défavorable <in adverse circumstances : dans l'adversité>
adversity [ædˈvərsət̬i, əd-] *n, pl* **-ties** : adversité *f*
advertise [ˈædvərˌtaɪz] *v* **-tised; -tising** *vt* **1** : faire de la publicité pour (un produit) **2** : mettre une annonce pour (un poste, etc.) **3** PUBLICIZE : afficher, signaler — *vi* **1** : faire de la publicité (en commerce) **2** : passer une annonce <to advertise on television : passer une annonce à la télévision>
advertisement [ˈædvərˌtaɪzmənt; ædˈvərt̬əzmənt] *n* **1** : publicité *f,* annonce *f* (publicitaire), réclame *f* **2** → **ad**
advertiser [ˈædvərˌtaɪzər] *n* : annonceur *m* (publicitaire)
advertising [ˈædvərˌtaɪzɪŋ] *n* : publicité *f,* réclame *f*
advice [ædˈvaɪs] *n* **1** COUNSEL : conseils *mpl,* avis *m* **2** NOTICE : avis *m,* annonce *f*
advisability [ædˌvaɪzəˈbɪlət̬i, əd-] *n* : opportunité *f*
advisable [ædˈvaɪzəbəl, əd-] *adj* : recommandé, prudent
advise [ædˈvaɪz, əd-] *v* **-vised; -vising** *vt* **1** COUNSEL : conseiller, donner des conseils à **2** RECOMMEND : recommander <they advised caution : ils ont recommandé la prudence> **3** INFORM : aviser — *vi* **to advise on** : conseiller sur
adviser [ædˈvaɪzər, əd-] *or* **advisor** *n* : conseiller *m,* -lère *f*
advisory [ædˈvaɪzəri, əd-] *adj* : consultatif <in an advisory capacity : à titre consultatif>
advocate[1] [ˈædvəˌkeɪt] *vt* **-cated; -cating** : recommander, préconiser
advocate[2] [ˈædvəkət] *n* **1** SUPPORTER : défenseur *m;* avocat *m,* -cate *f;* partisan *m,* -sane *f* **2** ATTORNEY : avocat *m,* -cate *f*
adze [ˈædz] *n* : herminette *f*
aegis [ˈiːdʒəs] *n* : égide *f*
aeon [ˈiːən, ˈiːˌɑn] *n* : éternité *f*
aerate [ˈærˌeɪt] *vt* **-ated; -ating** : aérer
aeration [ˌærˈeɪʃən] *n* : aération *f*
aerial[1] [ˈæriəl] *adj* : aérien
aerial[2] *n* : antenne *f*
aerie [ˈæri, ˈɪri, ˈeɪəri] *n* : aire *f* (d'aigle)

aerobic [ˌærˈoːbɪk] *adj* : aérobie, aérobique *Can*

aerobics [ˌærˈoːbɪks] *ns & pl* : aérobic *m*

aerodynamic [ˌæroːdaɪˈnæmɪk] *adj* : aérodynamique — **aerodynamically** *adv*

aerodynamics [ˌæroːdaɪˈnæmɪks] *ns & pl* : aérodynamique *f*

aeronautical [ˌærəˈnɔt̬ɪkəl] *adj* : aéronautique

aeronautics [ˌærəˈnɔt̬ɪks] *n* : aéronautique *f*

aerosol [ˈærəˌsɔl] *n* : aérosol *m*

aerospace [ˈæroˌspeɪs] *adj* : aérospatial <the aerospace industry : l'industrie aérospatiale>

aesthetic [ɛsˈθɛt̬ɪk] *adj* : esthétique — **aesthetically** [-t̬ɪkli] *adv*

aesthetics [ɛsˈθɛt̬ɪks] *ns & pl* : esthétique *f*

afar [əˈfɑr] *adv* **1** : au loin, à distance **2 from ~** : de loin

affability [ˌæfəˈbɪlət̬i] *n* : affabilité *f*

affable [ˈæfəbəl] *adj* : affable — **affably** *adv*

affair [əˈfær] *n* **1** : affaire *f* <their affairs are in order : leurs affaires sont réglées> <a grand affair : une affaire prestigieuse> **2** *or* **love affair** : liaison *f*, affaire *f* de cœur

affect [əˈfɛkt, æ-] *vt* **1** INFLUENCE : affecter, influencer **2** FEIGN : affecter, feindre **3** MOVE : émouvoir, toucher

affectation [ˌæˌfɛkˈteɪʃən] *n* : affectation *f*

affected [əˈfɛktəd, æ-] *adj* **1** MANNERED : affecté, maniéré **2** MOVED : ému, touché

affectedly [əˈfɛktədli] *adv* : avec affectation

affecting [əˈfɛktɪŋ, æ-] *adj* MOVING : touchant, émouvant

affection [əˈfɛkʃən] *n* : affection *f*

affectionate [əˈfɛkʃənət] *adj* : affectueux — **affectionately** *adv*

affidavit [ˌæfəˈdeɪvət, ˈæfəˌ-] *n* : déclaration *f* (écrite) sous serment

affiliate[1] [əˈfɪliˌeɪt] *vt* **-ated; -ating** : affilier

affiliate[2] [əˈfɪliət] *n* : filiale *f* (organisation); affilié *m*, -liée *f* (personne)

affiliation [əˌfɪliˈeɪʃən] *n* : affiliation *f*

affinity [əˈfɪnət̬i] *n, pl* **-ties** : affinité *f*

affirm [əˈfərm] *vt* : affirmer, soutenir

affirmation [ˌæfərˈmeɪʃən] *n* : affirmation *f*

affirmative[1] [əˈfərmət̬ɪv] *adj* : affirmatif — **affirmatively** *adv*

affirmative[2] *n* **1** : affirmatif *m* (en grammaire) **2** : affirmative *f* <to answer in the affirmative : répondre par l'affirmative, répondre affirmativement>

affix [əˈfɪks] *vt* : apposer (une signature), coller (un timbre)

afflict [əˈflɪkt] *vt* **1** : affliger **2 to be afflicted with** : souffrir de, être touché de

affliction [əˈflɪkʃən] *n* : affliction *f*

affluence [ˈæˌfluːən*t*s; æˈfluː-, ə-] *n* **1** WEALTH : richesse *f* **2** PROFUSION : abondance *f*

affluent [ˈæˌfluːənt; æˈfluː-, ə-] *adj* **1** WEALTHY : riche, aisé **2** ABUNDANT, PROFUSE : abondant

afford [əˈford] *vt* **1** : avoir les moyens de <he can't afford to buy a car : il n'a pas les moyens d'acheter une voiture> **2** PROVIDE : fournir, offrir **3** : se permettre <I can't afford to wait : je ne peux pas me permettre d'attendre>

affront[1] [əˈfrʌnt] *vt* : offenser, insulter

affront[2] *n* : affront *m*, insulte *f*

afghan [ˈæfˌgæn, -gən] *n* : couverture *f* en lainage

Afghan[1] *adj* : afghan

Afghan[2] *n* : Afghan *m*, -ghane *f*

afire[1] [əˈfaɪr] *adv* **1** : en feu **2 to set afire** : mettre le feu à, embraser

afire[2] *adj* : en feu, embrasé

aflame [əˈfleɪm] *adj & adv* : en flammes

afloat [əˈfloːt] *adj & adv* : à flot

afoot [əˈfʊt] *adv & adj* **1** WALKING : à pied **2** UNDER WAY : en train

aforesaid [əˈforˌsɛd] *adj* : susmentionné

afraid [əˈfreɪd] *adj* **1 to be afraid of** FEAR : avoir peur de, craindre <he's afraid of falling : il a peur de tomber> **2** (*indicating regret*) <I'm afraid I can't come : je regrette de ne pas pouvoir venir> <I'm afraid not : hélas, non>

afresh [əˈfrɛʃ] *adv* **1** ANEW : de nouveau **2 to start afresh** : recommencer

African[1] [ˈæfrɪkən] *adj* : africain

African[2] *n* : Africain *m*, -caine *f*

aft [ˈæft] **adv** : l'arrière

after[1] [ˈæftər] *adv* **1** AFTERWARD : après, ensuite **2** BEHIND : en arrière

after[2] *adj* (*indicating a later time*) <in after years : plus tard dans la vie>

after[3] *conj* : après que <after he leaves : après qu'il part>

after[4] *prep* **1** FOLLOWING : après <after lunch : après le déjeuner> <day after day : tous les jours> <after four o'clock : après quatre heures> **2** BEHIND : derrière, après <close the door after me : fermez la porte derrière moi> **3** (*indicating pursuit*) <he was running after the cat : il courait après le chat> <the police are after me : je suis recherché par la police> **4 after all** : après tout

aftereffect [ˈæftərɪˌfɛkt] *n* : répercussion *f*, séquelle *f* (en médecine)

afterlife [ˈæftərˌlaɪf] *n* : vie *f* future, vie *f* après la mort

aftermath [ˈæftərˌmæθ] *n* CONSEQUENCES : suites *fpl*

afternoon [ˌæftərˈnuːn] *n* : après-midi *mf*

afterthought [ˈæftərˌθɔt] *n* : pensée *f* après coup

afterward [ˈæftərwərd] *or* **afterwards** [-wərdz] *adv* : après, ensuite <soon afterward : peu après>

again [əˈgɛn, -gɪn] *adv* **1** : encore (une fois), de nouveau <say it again : dites-le encore> <again and again : maintes et maintes fois> **2** BESIDES : en plus, d'ailleurs **3 then again** : d'autre part

against [əˈgɛntst, -ˈgɪntst] *prep* **1** : contre <against the wall : contre le mur> <a war against drugs : une guerre contre les drogues> **2** : sur <red flowers against the blue sky : des fleurs rouges sur un ciel bleu> **3 to go against** : aller à l'encontre

agape [əˈgeɪp] *adj* : bouche bée

agate [ˈægət] *n* : agate *f*

age[1] [ˈeɪdʒ] *v* : vieillir

age[2] *n* **1** : âge *m* <what age is she? : quel âge a-t-elle?> <she's 16 years of age : elle a 16 ans> **2** ERA : ère *f*, époque *f* **3 for ages** : depuis longtemps **4 to come of age** : atteindre la majorité **5 old age** : vieillesse *f*

aged [ˈeɪdʒəd, ˈeɪdʒd] *adj* **1** : âgé de <a man aged 40 years : un homme âgé de 40 ans> **2** : âgé, vieux (se dit du vin, du fromage, etc.) **3** [ˈeɪdʒd] OLD : vieux, âgé <my aged mother : ma vieille mère>

ageless [ˈeɪdʒləs] *adj* **1** : sans âge, toujours jeune **2** TIMELESS : éternel

agency [ˈeɪdʒəntsi] *n, pl* **-cies 1** : agence *f*, bureau *m* <travel agency : agence de voyages> **2 through the agency of** : par l'entremise de

agenda [əˈdʒɛndə] *n* : ordre *m* du jour, programme *m*

agent [ˈeɪdʒənt] *n* : agent *m*

aggravate [ˈægrəˌveɪt] *vt* **-vated; -vating 1** WORSEN : aggraver, empirer **2** IRRITATE : agacer, énerver

aggravation [ˌægrəˈveɪʃən] *n* **1** WORSENING : aggravation *f* **2** IRRITATION : agacement *m*, irritation *f*

aggregate[1] [ˈægrɪˌgeɪt] *vt* **-gated; -gating** : agréger, rassembler — *vi* : s'agréger

aggregate[2] [ˈægrɪgət] *adj* : total, global

aggregate[3] [ˈægrɪgət] *n* **1** TOTAL : ensemble *m*, total *m* **2** MASS : agrégat *m* (en géologie, etc.)

aggression [əˈgrɛʃən] *n* : agression *f*

aggressive [əˈgrɛsɪv] *adj* : agressif — **aggressively** *adv*

aggressiveness [əˈgrɛsɪvnəs] *n* : agressivité *f*

aggressor [əˈgrɛsər] *n* : agresseur *m*

aggrieved [əˈgriːvd] *adj* **1** DISTRESSED : affligé, peiné **2 the aggrieved party** : la partie lésée

aghast [əˈgæst] *adj* : horrifié, atterré

agile [ˈædʒəl] *adj* : agile, leste

agility [əˈdʒɪləṭi] *n, pl* **-ties** : agilité *f*

agitate [ˈædʒəˌteɪt] *v* **-tated; -tating** *vt* **1** SHAKE : agiter, secouer **2** TROUBLE : agiter, troubler — *vi* **to agitate against** : faire campagne contre

agitation [ˌædʒəˈteɪʃən] *n* : agitation *f*

agnostic[1] [ægˈnɑstɪk] *adj* : agnostique

agnostic[2] *n* : agnostique *mf*

ago [əˈgoː] *adv* : il y a <a week ago : il y a une semaine> <not long ago : il y a peu de temps>

agog [əˈgɑg] *adj* : en émoi

agonize [ˈægəˌnaɪz] *vi* **-nized; -nizing** : se tourmenter

agonizing [ˈægəˌnaɪzɪŋ] *adj* PAINFUL : douloureux, déchirant

agony [ˈægəni] *n, pl* **-nies 1** : angoisse *f*, douleur *f* atroce **2 death agony** : agonie *f*

agrarian [əˈgrɛriən] *adj* : agraire

agree [əˈgriː] *v* **agreed; agreeing** *vt* **1** ACKNOWLEDGE, ADMIT : convenir, reconnaître <I agree that you should go : je reconnais que vous devriez y aller> **2** CONSENT : accepter, consentir — *vi* **1** CONCUR : être d'accord **2** CONSENT : consentir **3** CORRESPOND, TALLY : correspondre, concorder **4 to agree with** : réussir à, convenir (bien) à <spicy food doesn't agree with me : la nourriture épicée ne me réussit pas>

agreeable [əˈgriːəbəl] *adj* **1** PLEASING : agréable **2** WILLING : consentant <to be agreeable to : être d'accord pour> **3** ACCEPTABLE : acceptable, satisfaisant

agreeably [əˈgriːəbli] *adv* : agréablement

agreement [əˈgriːmənt] *n* : accord *m* <to be in agreement : être d'accord> <international agreement : accord international>

agricultural [ˌægrɪˈkʌltʃərəl] *adj* : agricole

agriculture [ˈægrɪˌkʌltʃər] *n* : agriculture *f*

aground[1] [əˈgraʊnd] *adv* **to run aground** : s'échouer

aground[2] *adj* : échoué

ahead [əˈhɛd] *adv* **1** FORWARD : en avant, devant <he walked ahead : il marchait en avant> **2** BEFOREHAND : à l'avance **3** LEADING : de tête, en avance **4 go ahead!** : allez-y! **5 to get ahead** : prendre de l'avance

ahead of *prep* **1** : devant, d'avance sur <go ahead of me : mettez-vous devant moi> **2** : avant, en avance sur <to be ahead of one's time : être en avance sur son temps>

ahoy [əˈhɔɪ] *interj* **ship ahoy!** : ohé du navire!

aid[1] [ˈeɪd] *vt* **1** HELP : aider **2 to aid and abet** : être complice de

aid[2] *n* **1** HELP : aide *f*, secours *m* **2** ASSISTANT : aide *mf*; assistant *m*, -tante *f* **3** DEVICE : appareil *m* <hearing aid : appareil auditif>

aide ['eɪd] *n* : aide *mf;* assistant *m*, -tante *f*
AIDS ['eɪdz] *n* : sida *m*, SIDA *m*
ail ['eɪl] *vt* TROUBLE : affliger <what ails you? : qu'avez-vous?> — *vi* : être souffrant
aileron ['eɪlə,rɑn] *n* : aileron *m*
ailment ['eɪlmənt] *n* : maladie *f*, affection *f*
aim[1] ['eɪm] *vt* **1** : braquer (une arme à feu), diriger (une remarque, etc.) **2** INTEND : avoir l'intention de — *vi* **to aim at** *or* **to aim for** : viser
aim[2] *n* **1** GOAL : but *m*, objectif *m* **2 to take aim at** : viser
aimless ['eɪmləs] *adj* : sans but, sans objet
aimlessly ['eɪmləsli] *adv* : sans but
air[1] ['ær] *vt* **1** VENTILATE : aérer, ventiler **2** EXPRESS : exprimer, faire connaître **3** BROADCAST : diffuser
air[2] *n* **1** : air *m* **2** MELODY : air *m* **3** APPEARANCE : air *m*, aspect *m* <an air of mystery : un air mystérieux> **4 to be on the air** : être à l'antenne **5 to go by air** : voyager par avion **6 to put on airs** : se donner de grands airs
airborne ['ær,born] *adj* **1** : aéroporté (se dit des troupes, etc.) **2 to become airborne** : décoller
air–conditioned [,ærkən'dɪʃənd] *adj* : climatisé
air conditioner [,ærkən'dɪʃənər] *n* : climatiseur *m*
air–conditioning [,ærkən'dɪʃənɪŋ] *n* : climatisation *f*
aircraft ['ær,kræft] *ns & pl* : avion *m*, aéronef *m*
aircraft carrier *n* : porte-avions *m*
airfield ['ær,fi:ld] *n* : aérodrome *m*, terrain *m* d'aviation
air force *n* : armée *f* de l'air
airlift ['ær,lɪft] *n* : pont *m* aérien
airline ['ær,laɪn] *n* : ligne *f* (aérienne), compagnie *f* d'aviation
airliner ['ær,laɪnər] *n* : avion *m* de ligne
airmail ['ær,meɪl] *n* **1** : poste *f* aérienne **2 by ~** : par avion
airman ['ærmən] *n, pl* **-men** [-mən, -,mɛn] **1** AVIATOR : aviateur *m* **2** : soldat *m* de l'armée de l'air
airplane ['ær,pleɪn] *n* : avion *m*
airport ['ær,port] *n* : aéroport *m*
airship ['ær,ʃɪp] *n* : dirigeable *m*
airstrip ['ær,ʃtrɪp] *n* : piste *f* (d'atterrissage)
airtight ['ær'taɪt] *adj* : hermétique, étanche (à l'air)
airwaves ['ær,weɪvz] *npl* : ondes *fpl*
airy ['æri] *adj* **airier; -est 1** VENTILATED : aéré **2** DELICATE, LIGHT : léger **3** LOFTY : en l'air
aisle ['aɪl] *n* : nef *f* latérale (d'une église), allée *f* (d'un théâtre ou d'un magasin), couloir *m* (d'un avion, d'un train, etc.)
ajar [ə'dʒɑr] *adj & adv* : entrouvert
akimbo [ə'kɪmbo] *adj & adv* **with arms akimbo** : les poings sur les hanches
akin [ə'kɪn] *adj* **1** RELATED : apparenté **2 ~ to** : semblable à, qui ressemble à
alabaster ['ælə,bæstər] *n* : albâtre *m*
alacrity [ə'lækrəṭi] *n* : empressement *m*
alarm[1] [ə'lɑrm] *vt* **1** WARN : alerter **2** FRIGHTEN : alarmer, faire peur à
alarm[2] *n* **1** WARNING : alarme *f*, alerte *f* **2** FEAR : inquiétude *f*, alarme *f*
alarm clock *n* : réveil *m*, réveille-matin *m*, cadran *m Can fam*
alas [ə'læs] *interj* : hélas!
Albanian[1] [æl'beɪniən] *adj* : albanais
Albanian[2] *n* **1** : Albanais *m*, -naise *f*
albatross ['ælbə,trɔs] *n, pl* **-tross** *or* **-trosses** : albatros *m*
albeit [ɔl'bi:ət, æl-] *conj* : bien que, quoique
albino [æl'baɪno] *n, pl* **-nos** : albinos *mf*
album ['ælbəm] *n* : album *m*
albumen [æl'bju:mən] *n* **1** : albumen *m*, blanc *m* d'œuf **2** → **albumin**
albumin [æl'bju:mən] *n* : albumine *f*
alchemy ['ælkəmi] *n* : alchimie *f*
alcohol ['ælkə,hɔl] *n* **1** : alcool *m* **2** DRINK : boisson *f* alcoolisée, verre *m*
alcoholic[1] [,ælkə'hɔlɪk] *adj* : alcoolisé, alcoolique
alcoholic[2] *n* : alcoolique *mf*
alcoholism ['ælkəhɔ,lɪzəm] *n* : alcoolisme *m*
alcove ['æl,ko:v] *n* **1** : alcôve *f* (d'une salle) **2** RECESS : renfoncement *m*, niche *f*
alderman ['ɔldərmən] *n, pl* **-men** [-mən, -,mɛn] : conseiller *m* municipal, conseillère *f* municipale
ale ['eɪl] *n* : bière *f*
alert[1] [ə'lərt] *vt* : alerter, donner l'alerte à
alert[2] *adj* **1** WATCHFUL : vigilant **2** LIVELY : alerte, vif, éveillé
alert[3] *n* : alerte *f* <on the alert : en état d'alerte>
alertness [ə'lərtnəs] *n* **1** VIGILANCE : vigilance *f* **2** LIVELINESS : vivacité *f*
alfalfa [æl'fælfə] *n* : luzerne *f*
alga ['ælgə] *n, pl* **-gae** ['æl,dʒi:] : algue *f*
algebra ['ældʒəbrə] *n* : algèbre *f*
algebraic [,ældʒə'breɪɪk] *adj* : algébrique — **algebraically** *adv*
Algerian[1] [æl'dʒɪriən] *adj* : algérien
Algerian[2] *n* : Algérien *m*, -rienne *f*
alias[1] ['eɪliəs] *adv* : alias
alias[2] *n* : nom *m* d'emprunt, faux nom *m*
alibi ['ælə,baɪ] *n* : alibi *m*
alien[1] ['eɪliən] *adj* **1** FOREIGN : étranger **2** EXTRATERRESTRIAL : extraterrestre
alien[2] *n* **1** FOREIGNER : étranger *m*, -gère *f* **2** EXTRATERRESTRIAL : extraterrestre *mf*
alienate ['eɪliə,neɪt] *vt* **-ated; -ating** : aliéner
alienation [,eɪliə'neɪʃən] *n* : aliénation *f*

alight [ə'laɪt] *vi* **1** : descendre (se dit des personnes), se poser (se dit des oiseaux)

align [ə'laɪn] *vt* : aligner

alignment [ə'laɪnmənt] *n* **1** : alignement *m* <to be out of alignment : être désaligné> **2** *or* **wheel alignment** : parallélisme *m* des roues

alike[1] [ə'laɪk] *adv* : de la même façon

alike[2] *adj* **1** : semblable, pareil **2 to be alike** : se ressembler

alimentary [ˌælə'mɛntəri] *adj* **1** : alimentaire **2 alimentary canal** : tube *m* digestif

alimony ['æləˌmo:ni] *n, pl* **-nies** : pension *f* alimentaire

alive [ə'laɪv] *adj* **1** LIVING : vivant, en vie **2** LIVELY : vif, animé **3** AWARE : conscient, sensible <they are alive to the danger : ils sont conscients du danger>

alkali ['ælkəlaɪ] *n, pl* **-lies** *or* **-lis** : alcali *m*

alkaline ['ælkələn, -ˌlaɪn] *adj* : alcalin

all[1] ['ɔl] *adv* **1** COMPLETELY : tout, complètement <all alone : tout seul> **2** : partout <the score is six all : le score est de six partout> **3 all at once** : tout d'un coup **4 all the better** : tant mieux

all[2] *adj* : tout <in all probability : en toute probabilité> <all those people : tous ces gens>

all[3] *pron* **1** EVERYTHING : tout <is that all? : c'est tout?> **2** EVERYONE : tous, toutes <all have left the premises : tous sont partis des lieux> <they've all left : elles sont toutes parties> **3 all in all** : tout compte fait

Allah ['ɑlɑ, ɑ'lɑ] *n* : Allah *m*

all–around [ˌɔlə'raʊnd] *adj* **1** GENERAL : général **2** VERSATILE : complet, polyvalent <an all-around athlete : un athlète polyvalent>

allay [ə'leɪ] *vt* : soulager, apaiser

allegation [ˌælɪ'geɪʃən] *n* : allégation *f*

allege [ə'lɛdʒ] *vt* **-leged; -leging** : alléguer, prétendre

alleged [ə'lɛdʒd, ə'lɛdʒəd] *adj* : présumé, prétendu, allégué

allegedly [ə'lɛdʒədli] *adv* : prétendument

allegiance [ə'li:dʒən*t*s] *n* : allégeance *f*

allegorical [ˌælə'gɔrɪkəl] *adj* : allégorique

allegory ['æləˌgori] *n, pl* **-ries** : allégorie *f*

alleluia [ˌɑlə'lu:jə, ˌæ-] → **hallelujah**

allergic [ə'lərdʒɪk] *adj* : allergique

allergy ['ælərdʒi] *n, pl* **-gies** : allergie *f*

alleviate [ə'li:viˌeɪt] *vt* **-ated; -ating** : soulager, alléger, apaiser

alleviation [əˌli:vi'eɪʃən] *n* : soulagement *m,* allègement *m*

alley ['æli] *n, pl* **-leys 1** : ruelle *f,* allée *f* (dans un jardin, etc.) **2 bowling alley** : bowling *m*

alliance [ə'laɪən*t*s] *n* : alliance *f*

alligator ['æləˌgeɪt̬ər] *n* : alligator *m*

alliteration [əˌlɪt̬ə'reɪʃən] *n* : allitération *f*

allocate ['æləˌkeɪt] *vt* **-cated; -cating** : allouer, assigner

allocation ['ælə'keɪʃən] *n* : allocation *f,* affectation *f*

allot [ə'lɑt] *vt* **allotted; allotting 1** ASSIGN : attribuer, assigner **2** DISTRIBUTE : répartir, distribuer

allotment [ə'lɑtmənt] *n* : répartition *f,* allocation *f*

allow [ə'laʊ] *vt* **1** PERMIT : permettre **2** CONCEDE : admettre, reconnaître **3** GRANT : accorder, allouer — *vi* **to allow for** : tenir compte de

allowable [ə'laʊəbəl] *adj* **1** PERMISSIBLE : permis, admissible **2** DEDUCTIBLE : déductible

allowance [ə'laʊən*t*s] *n* **1** : allocation *f* (pour les dépenses), argent *m* de poche (pour les enfants) **2 to make allowances for** : tenir compte de

alloy ['æˌlɔɪ] *n* : alliage *m*

all right[1] *adv* **1** YES : d'accord **2** WELL : bien <she's doing all right : elle va bien> **3** CERTAINLY : bien, sans doute <it's hot all right : il fait bien chaud>

all right[2] *adj* : pas mal, bien <I'm all right, thanks : je vais bien, merci>

all–round [ˌɔl'raʊnd] → **all–around**

allspice ['ɔlspaɪs] *n* : piment *m* de la Jamaïque

allude [ə'lu:d] *vi* **-luded; -luding** : faire allusion (à)

allure[1] [ə'lʊr] *vt* **-lured; -luring** : séduire, attirer

allure[2] *n* : attrait *m,* charme *m*

allusion [ə'lu:ʒən] *n* : allusion *f*

ally[1] [ə'laɪ, 'æˌlaɪ] *vt* **-lied; -lying 1** : allier **2 to ally oneself with** : s'allier avec

ally[2] ['æˌlaɪ, ə'laɪ] *n, pl* **allies** : allié *m,* -liée *f*

almanac ['ɔlməˌnæk, 'æl-] *n* : almanach *m*

almighty [ɔl'maɪt̬i] *adj* : tout puissant, formidable

almond ['ɑmənd, 'ɑl-, 'æ-, 'æl-] *n* : amande *f*

almost ['ɔlˌmo:st, ɔl'mo:st] *adv* : presque <almost everyone : presque tout le monde> <she almost died : elle a failli mourir>

alms ['ɑmz, 'ɑlmz, 'ælmz] *ns & pl* : aumône *f*

aloft [ə'lɔft] *adv* : en haut, en l'air

alone[1] [ə'lo:n] *adv* **1** : seul <il travaille seul : he works alone> <she alone can do it : elle seule peut le faire> **2 to leave alone** : laisser tranquille, laisser en paix

alone[2] *adj* : seul <I'm all alone : je suis tout seul>

along[1] [ə'lɔŋ] *adv* **1** FORWARD : en avant <to step along : faire un pas en avant, avancer> <further along : plus avancé> **2** (*often not translated*) <to

bring along : apporter> <to run along : courir> <to pull along : tirer avec soi> **3 ~ with** : avec, accompagné de
along[2] *prep* **1** : le long de <along the coast : le long de la côte> **2** ON : sur <along the way : sur le chemin>
alongside[1] |əˌlɔŋ'saɪd| *adv* **1** : à côté **2 to come alongside** : accoster
alongside[2] *or* **alongside of** *prep* BESIDE : à côté de
aloof |ə'lu:f| *adj* : distant <to stand aloof from : se tenir à l'écart de>
aloofness |ə'lu:fnəs| *n* : réserve *f*
aloud |ə'laʊd| *adv* : à haute voix
alpaca |æl'pækə| *n* : alpaga *m*
alphabet |'ælfəˌbɛt| *n* : alphabet *m*
alphabetic |ˌælfə'bɛtɪk| *or* **alphabetical** |-tɪkəl| *adj* : alphabétique — **alphabetically** |-tɪkli| *adv*
alphabetize |'ælfəbəˌtaɪz| *vt* **-ized; -izing** : alphabétiser, classer par ordre alphabétique
already |ɔl'rɛdi| *adv* : déjà
also |'ɔlˌso:| *adv* **1** TOO : aussi, également **2** FURTHERMORE : de plus, en outre
altar |'ɔltər| *n* : autel *m*
alter |'ɔltər| *vt* **1** CHANGE : changer, modifier **2** : retoucher (un vêtement)
alteration |ˌɔltə'reɪʃən| *n* **1** : changement *m*, modification *f* **2 alterations** *npl* : retouches *fpl*
altercation |ˌɔltər'keɪʃən| *n* : altercation *f*
alternate[1] |'ɔltərˌneɪt| *v* **-nated; -nating** *vt* : faire alterner — *vi* : alterner, se relayer
alternate[2] |'ɔltərnət| *adj* : alternatif — **alternately** *adv*
alternate[3] |'ɔltərnət| *n* : remplaçant *m*, -çante *f*
alternating current |'ɔltərˌneɪṯɪŋ| *n* : courant *m* alternatif
alternation |ˌɔltər'neɪʃən| *n* : alternance *f*
alternative[1] |ɔl'tərnəṯɪv| *adj* : alternatif
alternative[2] *n* **1** : alternative *f* **2 to have no alternative** : ne pas avoir le choix
alternator |'ɔltərˌneɪṯər| *n* : alternateur *m*
although |ɔl'ðo:| *conj* : bien que, quoique
altitude |'æltəˌtu:d, -ˌtju:d| *n* : altitude *f*
alto |'ælˌto:| *n, pl* **-tos** : contralto *m* (voix), alto *m* (instrument)
altogether |ˌɔltə'gɛðər| *adv* **1** COMPLETELY : complètement, tout à fait **2** ON THE WHOLE : dans l'ensemble **3** : en tout <how much altogether? : combien en tout?>
altruism |'æltrʊˌɪzəm| *n* : altruisme *m*
altruist |'æltrʊɪst| *n* : altruiste *mf*
altruistic |ˌæltrʊ'ɪstɪk| *adj* : altruiste
alum |'æləm| *n* : alun *m*
aluminum |ə'lu:mənəm| *n* : aluminium *m*
alumna |ə'lʌmnə| *n, pl* **-nae** |-ˌni:| : ancienne élève *f*
alumnus |ə'lʌmnəs| *n, pl* **-ni** |-ˌnaɪ| : ancien élève *m*
always |'ɔlwiz, -ˌweɪz| *adv* **1** INVARIABLY : toujours **2** FOREVER : pour toujours
am → **be**
amalgam |ə'mælgəm| *n* : amalgame *m*
amalgamate |ə'mælgəˌmeɪt| *v* **-ated; -ating** *vt* : amalgamer, fusionner — *vi* : s'amalgamer, fusionner
amalgamation |əˌmælgə'meɪʃən| *n* : fusion *f*, amalgamation *f*
amaryllis |ˌæmə'rɪləs| *n* : amaryllis *f*
amass |ə'mæs| *vt* : amasser, accumuler
amateur[1] |'æmətʃər, -tər, -ˌtʊr, -ˌtjʊr| *adj* : amateur
amateur[2] *n* : amateur *m*
amateurish |'æməˌtʃərɪʃ, -ˌtər-, -ˌtʊr-, -ˌtjʊr-| *adj* : d'amateur
amaze |ə'meɪz| *vt* **amazed; amazing** : étonner, stupéfier
amazement |ə'meɪzmənt| *n* : stupéfaction *f*, étonnement *m*
amazing |ə'meɪzɪŋ| *adj* : étonnant, stupéfiant
amazingly |ə'meɪzɪŋli| *adv* : étonnamment, incroyablement
ambassador |æm'bæsəˌdər| *n* : ambassadeur *m*, -drice *f*
amber |'æmbər| *n* : ambre *m*
ambergris |'æmbərˌgrɪs, -gri:s| *n* : ambre *m* gris
ambidextrous |ˌæmbɪ'dɛkstrəs| *adj* : ambidextre
ambience *or* **ambiance** |'æmbiənts, 'ɑmbiˌɑnts| *n* : ambiance *f*
ambiguity |ˌæmbə'gju:əṯi| *n, pl* **-ties** : ambiguïté *f*
ambiguous |æm'bɪgjʊəs| *adj* : ambigu
ambition |æm'bɪʃən| *n* : ambition *f*
ambitious |æm'bɪʃəs| *adj* : ambitieux — **ambitiously** *adv*
ambivalence |æm'bɪvələnts| *n* : ambivalence *f*
ambivalent |æm'bɪvələnt| *adj* : ambivalent
amble[1] |'æmbəl| *vi* **-bled; -bling** : marcher d'un pas tranquille, aller l'amble (se dit d'un cheval)
amble[2] *n* : pas *m* tranquille, amble *m* (de cheval)
ambulance |'æmbjələnts| *n* : ambulance *f*
ambulatory |'æmbjələˌto:ri| *adj* : ambulatoire
ambush[1] |'æmbʊʃ| *vt* **1** : tendre une embuscade à **2** WAYLAY : attirer dans une embuscade
ambush[2] *n* : embuscade *f*
ameba, amebic → **amoeba, amoebic**
ameliorate |ə'mi:ljəˌreɪt| *v* **-rated; -rating** *vt* : améliorer — *vi* : s'améliorer
amelioration |əˌmi:ljə'reɪʃən| *n* : amélioration *f*
amen |'eɪ'mɛn, 'ɑ-| *interj* : amen, ainsi soit-il

amenable [ə'mi:nəbəl, -'mɛ-] *adj* : accommodant <to be amenable to : être disposé à>

amend [ə'mɛnd] *vt* : amender

amendment [ə'mɛndmənt] *n* : amendement *m*

amends [ə'mɛndz] *ns & pl* **1 to make amends** : se racheter, réparer ses torts **2 to make amends for** : dédommager de, réparer

amenity [ə'mɛnəṭi, -'mi:-] *n, pl* **-ties 1** PLEASANTNESS : agrément *m* **2 amenities** *npl* : équipements *mpl*, aménagements *mpl*

American[1] [ə'mɛrɪkən] *adj* : américain

American[2] *n* : Américain *m*, -caine *f*

American Indian *n* : indien *m*, -dienne *f* d'Amérique

amethyst ['æməθəst] *n* : améthyste *f*

amiability [ˌeɪmi:ə'bɪləṭi] *n* : amabilité *f*

amiable ['eɪmi:əbəl] *adj* : aimable — **amiably** *adv*

amicable ['æmɪkəbəl] *adj* : amical — **amicably** *adv*

amid [ə'mɪd] *or* **amidst** [ə'mɪdst] *prep* : au milieu de, parmi

amino acid [ə'mi:no] *n* : acide *m* aminé

amiss[1] [ə'mɪs] *adv* **1** WRONGLY : incorrectement, mal **2 to take sth amiss** : prendre qqch de travers

amiss[2] *adj* **1** WRONG : incorrect, mal à propos **2 something is amiss** : quelque chose ne va pas

ammeter ['æˌmi:ṭər] *n* : ampèremètre *m*

ammonia [ə'mo:njə] *n* **1** : ammoniac *m* (gaz) **2** : ammoniaque *f* (liquide)

ammunition [ˌæmjə'nɪʃən] *n* : munitions *fpl*

amnesia [æm'ni:ʒə] *n* : amnésie *f*

amnesiac[1] [æm'ni:ʒiˌæk, -zi-] *or* **amnesic** [æm'ni:ʒɪk, -sɪk] *adj* : amnésique

amnesiac[2] *or* **amnesic** *n* : amnésique *mf*

amnesty ['æmnəsti] *n, pl* **-ties** : amnistie *f*

amoeba [ə'mi:bə] *n, pl* **-bas** *or* **-bae** [-bi:] : amibe *f*

amoebic [ə'mi:bɪk] *adj* : amibien

amok [ə'mʌk, -'mɑk] *adv* **to run amok** : être pris d'un accès de folie furieuse

among [e'mʌŋ] *prep* : parmi, entre <among others : entre autres> <among young people : chez les jeunes>

amoral [eɪ'mɔrəl] *adj* : amoral

amorous ['æmərəs] *adj* : amoureux — **amorously** *adv*

amorphous [ə'mɔrfəs] *adj* : informe, amorphe (en science)

amortize ['æmərˌtaɪz, ə'mɔr-] *vt* **-tized; -tizing** : amortir

amount[1] [ə'maʊnt] *vi* **to amount to 1** TOTAL : se monter à, s'élever à **2** : équivaloir à, revenir à <that amounts to the same thing : cela revient au même>

amount[2] *n* **1** QUANTITY : quantité *f* **2** SUM : somme *f*, montant *m*

ampere ['æmˌpɪr] *n* : ampère *m*

ampersand ['æmpərˌsænd] *n* : esperluette *f*

amphibian [æm'fɪbiən] *n* : amphibien *m*

amphibious [æm'fɪbiəs] *adj* : amphibie

amphitheater ['æmfəˌθi:əṭər] *n* : amphithéâtre *m*

ample ['æmpəl] *adj* **-pler; -plest 1** LARGE, SPACIOUS : ample, grand, vaste **2** PLENTIFUL : largement suffisant, abondant

amplification [ˌæmpləfə'keɪʃən] *n* : amplification *f*

amplifier ['æmpləˌfaɪər] *n* : amplificateur *m*

amplify ['æmpləˌfaɪ] *vt* **-fied; -fying** : amplifier

amply ['æmpli] *adv* : largement, amplement

amputate ['æmpjəˌteɪt] *v* **-tated; -tating** : amputer

amputation [ˌæmpjə'teɪʃən] *n* : amputation *f*

amuck [ə'mʌk] → **amok**

amulet ['æmjələt] *n* : amulette *f*

amuse [ə'mju:z] *vt* **amused; amusing 1** ENTERTAIN : distraire, divertir **2** : amuser, faire rire <the joke amused me : la plaisanterie m'a fait rire>

amusement [ə'mju:zmənt] *n* **1** ENTERTAINMENT : distraction *f*, divertissement *m* **2** ENJOYMENT, MIRTH : amusement *m*

an → **a**[2]

anachronism [ə'nækrəˌnɪzəm] *n* : anachronisme *m*

anachronistic [əˌnækrə'nɪstɪk] *adj* : anachronique

anaconda [ˌænə'kɑndə] *n* : anaconda *m*

anagram ['ænəˌgræm] *n* : anagramme *f*

anal ['eɪnəl] *adj* : anal

analgesic[1] [ˌænəl'dʒi:zɪk, -sɪk] *adj* : analgésique

analgesic[2] *n* : analgésique *m*

analog ['ænəˌlɔg, -ˌlɑg] *adj* : analogique

analogous [ə'næləgəs] *adj* : analogue

analogy [ə'nælədʒi] *n, pl* **-gies** : analogie *f*

analyse *Brit* → **analyze**

analysis [ə'næləsəs] *n, pl* **-yses** [-ˌsi:z] **1** : analyse *f* **2** → **psychoanalysis**

analyst ['ænəlɪst] *n* **1** : analyste *mf* **2** → **psychoanalyst**

analytic [ˌænə'lɪtɪk] *or* **analytical** [-ṭɪkəl] *adj* : analytique — **analytically** [-ṭɪkli] *adv*

analyze *or Brit* **analyse** ['ænəˌlaɪz] *vt* **-lyzed** *or Brit* **-lysed; -lyzing** *or Brit* **-lysing** : analyser

anarchist ['ænərkɪst, -ˌnɑr-] *n* : anarchiste *mf*

anarchy ['ænərki, -ˌnɑr-] *n* : anarchie *f*

anathema [ə'næθəmə] *n* : anathème *m*

anatomic [ˌænə'tɑmɪk] *or* **anatomical** [-mɪkəl] *adj* : anatomique — **anatomically** [-mɪkli] *adv*

anatomy [ə'næṭəmi] *n, pl* **-mies** : anatomie *f*
ancestor ['æn,sɛstər] *n* : ancêtre *mf*
ancestral [æn'sɛstrəl] *adj* : ancestral
ancestry ['æn,sɛstri] *n* **1** LINEAGE : ascendance *f* **2** ANCESTORS : ancêtres *mpl*
anchor[1] ['æŋkər] *vt* **1** MOOR : ancrer, mettre à l'ancre **2** SECURE : fixer, ancrer **3** : présenter (un programme de télévision) — *vi* : jeter l'ancre, mouiller l'ancre
anchor[2] *n* **1** : ancre *f* **2** : présentateur *m*, -trice *f* (à la télévision)
anchorage ['æŋkərɪdʒ] *n* : mouillage *m*
anchovy ['æn,tʃo:vi, æn'tʃo:-] *n, pl* **-vies** *or* **-vy** : anchois *m*
ancient ['eɪntʃənt] *adj* **1** : ancien <ancient history : histoire ancienne> **2** OLD : très vieux
ancients ['eɪntʃənts] *npl* : les anciens
and ['ænd] *conj* **1** : et **2** (*used with numbers*) <three hundred and two : trois cent deux> **3** (*used between two verbs*) <come and see : venez voir> **4** (*used between two adjectives*) <better and better : de mieux en mieux> <more and more : de plus en plus>
andiron ['æn,daɪərn] *n* : chenet *m*
Andorran[1] [æn'dorən] *adj* : andorran
Andorran[2] *n* : Andorran *m*, -rane *f*
androgynous [æn'drɑdʒənəs] *adj* : androgyne
anecdotal [,ænɪk'do:ṭəl] *adj* : anecdotique
anecdote ['ænɪk,do:t] *n* : anecdote *f*
anemia [ə'ni:miə] *n* : anémie *f*
anemic [ə'ni:mɪk] *adj* **1** : anémique **2** INSIPID : fade
anemone [ə'nɛməni] *n* : anémone *f*
anesthesia [,ænəs'θi:ʒə] *n* : anesthésie *f*
anesthetic[1] ['ænəs'θɛṭɪk] *adj* : anesthésique
anesthetic[2] *n* : anesthésique *m*
anesthetist [ə'nɛsθətɪst] *n* : anesthésiste *mf*
anesthetize [ə'nɛsθətaɪz] *vt* **-tized; -tizing** : anesthésier
anew [ə'nu:, -'nju:] *adv* : encore, de nouveau
angel ['eɪndʒəl] *n* : ange *m*
angelic [æn'dʒɛlɪk] *or* **angelical** [-lɪkəl] *adj* : angélique — **angelically** [-lɪkli] *adv*
anger[1] ['æŋgər] *vt* : fâcher, mettre en colère — *vi* : se fâcher, se mettre en colère
anger[2] *n* : colère *f*
angina [æn'dʒaɪnə] *n or* **angina pectoris** : angine *f* de poitrine
angle[1] ['æŋgəl] *v* **-gled; -gling** *vt* : orienter, incliner — *vi* FISH : pêcher à la ligne
angle[2] *n* **1** : angle *m* <at an angle : de biais> **2** POINT OF VIEW : point *m* de vue
angler ['æŋglər] *n* : pêcheur *m*, -cheuse *f* à la ligne
angling ['æŋglɪŋ] *n* : pêche *f* (à la ligne)
Anglo–Saxon[1] [,æŋglo'sæksən] *adj* : anglo-saxon
Anglo–Saxon[2] *n* **1** : Anglo-Saxon *m*, -Saxonne *f* (personne) **2** : anglo-saxon *m* (langue)
Angolan[1] [æŋ'go:lən, æn-] *adj* : angolais
Angolan[2] *n* : Angolais *m*, -laise *f*
angora [æŋ'gorə, æn-] *n* : angora *m*
angrily ['æŋgrəlɪ] *adv* : avec colère
angry ['æŋgri] *adj* **-grier; -est** : fâché, en colère, furieux
anguish ['æŋgwɪʃ] *n* : angoisse *f*, douleur *f*
anguished ['æŋgwɪʃt] *adj* : angoissé, tourmenté
angular ['æŋgjələr] *adj* : anguleux (se dit du visage), angulaire (se dit des objets)
animal ['ænəməl] *n* : animal *m*
animate[1] ['ænə,meɪt] *vt* **-mated; -mating** : animer, stimuler
animate[2] ['ænəmət] *adj* **1** ALIVE : vivant **2** ANIMATED : animé
animated ['ænə,meɪṭəd] *adj* **1** LIVELY : animé **2 animated cartoon** : dessin *m* animé
animation [,ænə'meɪʃən] *n* : animation *f*
animosity [,ænə'mɑsəṭi] *n, pl* **-ties** : animosité *f*
anise ['ænəs] *n* : anis *m*
ankle ['æŋkəl] *n* : cheville *f*
annals ['ænəlz] *npl* : annales *fpl*
anneal [ə'ni:l] *vt* : recuire
annex[1] [ə'nɛks, 'æ,nɛks] *vt* : annexer
annex[2] ['æ,nɛks, -nɪks] *n* : annexe *f*
annexation [,æ,nɛk'seɪʃən] *n* : annexion *f*
annihilate [ə'naɪə,leɪt] *vt* **-lated; -lating** : anéantir, annihiler
annihilation [ə,naɪə'leɪʃən] *n* : anéantissement *m*
anniversary [,ænə'vərsəri] *n, pl* **-ries** : anniversaire *m*
annotate ['ænə,teɪt] *vt* **-tated; -tating** : annoter
annotation [,ænə'teɪʃən] *n* : annotation *f*
announce [ə'naʊnts] *vt* **-nounced; -nouncing** : annoncer
announcement [ə'naʊntsmənt] *n* **1** DECLARATION : annonce *f* **2** NOTIFICATION : avis *m*, faire-part *m*
announcer [ə'naʊntsər] *n* : présentateur *m*, -trice *f*; annonceur *m*, -ceuse *f*; speaker *m*, -kerine *f France*
annoy [ə'nɔɪ] *vt* : agacer, gêner, ennuyer, achaler *Can fam*
annoyance [ə'nɔɪənts] *n* : agacement *m*, contrariété *f*
annoying [ə'nɔɪɪŋ] *adj* : agaçant, gênant, ennuyant *Can*
annual[1] ['ænjʊəl] *adj* : annuel — **annually** *adv*

annual[2] *n* **1** YEARBOOK : annuaire *m* **2** *or* **annual plant** : plante *f* annuelle

annuity [ə'nu:əṭi] *n, pl* **-ties** : rente *f*

annul [ə'nʌl] *vt* **anulled; anulling** : annuler

annulment [ə'nʌlmənt] *n* : annulation *f*

anode ['æ,no:d] *n* : anode *f*

anoint [ə'nɔɪnt] *vt* : oindre

anomalous [ə'nɑmələs] *adj* ABNORMAL : anormal

anomaly [ə'nɑməli] *n, pl* **-lies** : anomalie *f*

anonymity [,ænə'nɪməṭi] *n* : anonymat *m*

anonymous [ə'nɑnəməs] *adj* : anonyme — **anonymously** *adv*

anorexia [,ænə'rɛksiə] *n* : anorexie *f* — **anorexic** *adj*

another[1] [ə'nʌðər] *adj* : un autre, encore un <another girl : une autre fille> <another beer : encore une bière> <without another word : sans rien dire de plus> <in another three years : dans trois ans>

another[2] *pron* **1** : un autre *m*, une autre *f* **2 many another** : beaucoup d'autres **3 one after another** : l'un après l'autre

answer[1] ['æn*t*sər] *vt* **1** : répondre à **2 to answer the door** : aller ouvrir la porte — *vi* **1** : répondre, donner une réponse **2 to answer for** : répondre de

answer[2] *n* **1** REPLY : réponse *f* <in answer to : en réponse à> **2** SOLUTION : solution *f*

answerable ['æn*t*sərəbəl] *adj* : responsable

ant ['ænt] *n* : fourmi *f*

antagonism [æn'tægə,nɪzəm] *n* : antagonisme *m*

antagonist [æn'tægə,nɪst] *n* : antagoniste *mf*

antagonistic [æn,tægə'nɪstɪk] *adj* : antagoniste

antagonize [æn'tægə,naɪz] *vt* **-nized; -nizing** : éveiller l'hostilité de, contrarier

antarctic [ænt'ɑrktɪk, -'ɑrṭɪk] *adj* : antarctique <antarctic circle : cercle polaire antarctique>

anteater ['ænt,iṭər] *n* : fourmilier *m*

antecedent[1] [,æntə'si:dənt] *adj* : antérieur, précédent

antecedent[2] *n* : antécédent *m*

antelope ['æntəl,o:p] *n, pl* **-lope** *or* **-lopes** : antilope *f*

antenna [æn'tɛnə] *n, pl* **-nae** *or* **-nas** : antenne *f*

anterior [æn'tɪriər] *adj* : antérieur

anteroom ['ænti,ru:m] *n* : antichambre *f*

anthem ['ænθəm] *n* : hymne *m* <national anthem : hymne national>

anther ['ænθər] *n* : anthère *f*

anthill ['ænt,hɪl] *n* : fourmilière *f*

anthology [æn'θɑlədʒi] *n, pl* **-gies** : anthologie *f*

anthracite ['ænθrə,saɪt] *n* : anthracite *m*

anthropoid[1] ['ænθrə,pɔɪd] *adj* : anthropoïde

anthropoid[2] *n* : anthropoïde *m*

anthropological [,ænθrəpə'lɑdʒɪkəl] *adj* : anthropologique

anthropologist [,ænθrə'pɑlədʒɪst] *n* : anthropologue *mf*, anthropologiste *mf*

anthropology [,ænθrə'pɑlədʒi] *n* : anthropologie *f*

antiaircraft [,ænti'ær,kræft, ,æn,taɪ-] *adj* : antiaérien

antibiotic[1] [,æntibaɪ'ɑṭɪk, ,æn,taɪ-, -bi-] *adj* : antibiotique

antibiotic[2] *n* : antibiotique *m*

antibody ['ænti,bɑdi] *n, pl* **-bodies** : anticorps *m*

anticipate [æn'tɪsə,peɪt] *vt* **-pated; -pating** **1** FORESEE : anticiper, prévoir **2** EXPECT : s'attendre à **3** FORESTALL : devancer

anticipation [æn,tɪsə'peɪʃən] *n* : anticipation *f*

anticipatory [æn'tɪsəpə,tori] *adj* : d'anticipation

anticlerical [,ænti'klɛrɪkəl, ,æn,taɪ-] *adj* : anticlérical

anticlimax [,ænti'klaɪ,mæks] *n* : déception *f*

anticommunist[1] [,ænti'kɑmjənɪst, ,æn,taɪ-] *adj* : anticommuniste

anticommunist[2] *n* : anticommuniste *mf*

antics ['æntɪks] *npl* : bouffonnerie *f*

anticyclone [,ænti'saɪ,klon] *n* : anticyclone *m*

antidemocratic [,ænti'dɛmə'kræṭɪk, ,æn,taɪ-] *adj* : antidémocratique

antidepressant[1] [,æntɪdɪ'prɛsənt, ,æn,taɪ] *adj* : antidépresseur

antidepressant[2] *n* : antidépresseur *m*

antidote ['æntɪ,do:t] *n* : antidote *m*

antifreeze ['æntɪ,fri:z] *n* : antigel *m*

antihistamine [,æntɪ'hɪstə,min, ,æn,taɪ-, -mən] *n* : antihistaminique *m*

anti–inflammatory [,æntɪn'flæmə,tori] *adj* : anti-inflammatoire

antilock ['ænti,lɑk, 'æn,taɪ-] *adj* **antilock brakes** : freins *mpl* antiblocage

antimony ['æntə,mo:ni] *n* : antimoine *m*

antioxidant[1] [,ænti'ɑksədənt, ,æn,taɪ-] *adj* : antioxydant

antioxidant[2] *n* : antioxydant *m*

antipathy [æn'tɪpəθi] *n, pl* **-thies** : antipathie *f*

antiperspirant [,ænti'pərspərənt, ,æn,taɪ-] *n* : déodorant *m*

antiquated ['æntə,kweɪṭəd] *adj* **1** OUTMODED : vieillot, dépassé **2** ANCIENT : très vieux

antique[1] [æn'ti:k] *adj* : ancien, antique

antique[2] *n* : objet *m* ancien, antiquité *f*

antiquity [æn'tɪkwəṭi] *n, pl* **-ties** : antiquité *f*

anti–Semitic [,æntisə'mɪṭɪk, ,æn,taɪ-] *adj* : antisémite

anti–Semitism [,ænti'sɛmə,tɪzəm, ,æn,taɪ-] *n* : antisémitisme *m*

antiseptic[1] [ˌæntəˈsɛptɪk] *adj* : antiseptique
antiseptic[2] *n* : antiseptique *m*
antismoking [ˌæntiˈsmoːkɪŋ, ˌænˌtaɪ-] *n* : antitabac
antisocial [ˌæntiˈsoːʃəl, ˌænˌtaɪ-] *adj* **1** : antisocial <antisocial behavior : comportement antisocial> **2** UNSOCIABLE : peu sociable
antitheft [ˌæntiˈθɛft, ˌænˌtaɪ-] *adj* : antivol
antithesis [ænˈtɪθəsɪs] *n, pl* **-eses** [-ˌsiːz] : antithèse *f*
antitoxin [ˌæntiˈtɑksən, ˌænˌtaɪ-] *n* : antitoxine *f*
antitrust [ˌæntiˈtrʌst, ˌænˌtaɪ-] *adj* : antitrust
antlers [ˈæntlərz] *npl* : bois *mpl*, ramure *f*
antonym [ˈæntəˌnɪm] *n* : antonyme *m*
anus [ˈeɪnəs] *n* : anus *m*
anvil [ˈænvəl, -vɪl] *n* : enclume *f*
anxiety [æŋˈkzaɪəṯi] *n, pl* **-ties 1** APPREHENSION, UNEASINESS : anxiété *f*, appréhension *f* **2** CONCERN : souci *m* <he's a great anxiety to me : il me donne énormément de soucis> **3** EAGERNESS : désir *m* ardent
anxious [ˈæŋkʃəs] *adj* **1** WORRIED : inquiet, anxieux **2** EAGER : impatient, anxieux
anxiously [ˈæŋkʃəsli] *adv* **1** UNEASILY : avec inquiétude, anxieusement **2** EAGERLY : avec impatience
any[1] [ˈɛni] *adv* **1** (*used in questions and conditional clauses*) : un peu <can they work any faster? : peuvent-ils travailler un peu plus vite?> <do you want any more coffee? : voulez-vous encore du café?> **2** (*used in negative constructions*) <I don't smoke any longer : je ne fume plus> <she doesn't know any more than that : c'est tout ce qu'elle sait> **3** AT ALL : du tout <that didn't help any : cela n'a pas aidé du tout>
any[2] *adj* **1** (*used in questions*) : de, de la, du, des <do you have any advice? : avez-vous des conseils?> **2** (*used in negative constructions*) <we don't have any money : nous n'avons pas d'argent> <without any problem : sans le moindre problème> <he hasn't any idea : il n'a aucune idée> **3** WHICHEVER : quelconque, n'importe quel, tout <take any book : prenez n'importe quel livre> <at any moment : à tout moment>
any[3] *pron* **1** : en <if you have any : si tu en as> <I don't like any of them : je n'en aime aucun d'entre eux> **2** : n'importe lequel <take any you want : prenez n'importe lequel>
anybody [ˈɛniˌbʌdi, -ˌbɑ-] → **anyone**
anyhow [ˈɛniˌhaʊ] *adv* **1** IN ANY CASE : de toute façon, en tout cas **2** HAPHAZARDLY : n'importe comment
anymore [ˌɛniˈmor] *adv* : plus <I don't dance anymore : je ne danse plus>
anyone [ˈɛniˌwʌn] *pron* **1** (*in questions or conditional clauses*) : quelqu'un <is anyone home? : est-ce qu'il y a quelqu'un à la maison?> **2** (*in negative constructions*) : personne <you didn't see anyone? : tu n'as vu personne?> **3** : tout le monde <anyone can play : tout le monde peut jouer>
anyplace [ˈɛniˌpleɪs] → **anywhere**
anything [ˈɛniˌθɪŋ] *pron* **1** : tout, n'importe quoi <he eats anything : il mange n'importe quoi> **2** SOMETHING : quelque chose <can anything be done? : peut-on faire quelque chose?> **3** : rien <hardly anything : presque rien> **4 anything but** : tout sauf
anytime [ˈɛniˌtaɪm] *adv* : n'importe quand <call me anytime : appelez-moi n'importe quand>
anyway [ˈɛniˌweɪ] → **anyhow**
anywhere [ˈɛniˌhwɛr] *adv* **1** : n'importe où, partout <sit down anywhere : asseyez-vous n'importe où> <anywhere else : partout ailleurs> **2** (*in questions*) : quelque part <do you have some glue anywhere? : avez-vous de la colle quelque part?> **3** (*in negative constructions*) : nulle part <she doesn't go anywhere : elle ne va nulle part>
aorta [eɪˈɔrṯə] *n, pl* **-tas** *or* **-tae** : aorte *f*
apart [əˈpɑrt] *adv* **1** : l'un de l'autre, d'intervalle <far apart : éloigné l'un de l'autre> <shots five minutes apart : des coups de feu à cinq minutes d'intervalle> **2** ASIDE : à part, à l'écart <apart from : en dehors de> **3** SEPARATELY : séparément **4 to fall apart** : s'en aller en morceaux, se défaire **5 to take apart** : démonter **6 to tell apart** : distinguer
apartheid [əˈpɑrˌteɪt, -ˌtaɪt] *n* : apartheid *m*
apartment [əˈpɑrtmənt] *n* **1** : appartement *m* **2** *or* **apartment house** : immeuble *m*
apathetic [ˌæpəˈθɛṯɪk] *adj* : apathique
apathetically [ˌæpəˈθɛṯɪkli] *adv* : avec apathie
apathy [ˈæpəθi] *n* : apathie *f*
ape[1] [ˈeɪp] *vt* **aped; aping** : singer
ape[2] *n* : grand singe *m*
aperture [ˈæpərtʃər, -ˌtʃʊr] *n* : ouverture *f*
apex [ˈeɪˌpɛks] *n, pl* **apexes** *or* **apices** [ˈeɪpəˌsiːz, ˈæ-] : sommet *m*, point *m* culminant
aphid [ˈeɪfɪd, ˈæ-] *n* : puceron *m*
aphorism [ˈæfəˌrɪzəm] *n* : aphorisme *m*
aphrodisiac [ˈæfrəˈdiːziˌæk, -ˈdɪ-] *n* : aphrodisiaque *m*
apiary [ˈeɪpiˌɛri] *n, pl* **-aries** : rucher *m*
apiece [əˈpiːs] *adv* **1** : par personne, chacun <two candies apiece : deux bon-

bons par personne> **2** : la pièce, chacun <they cost two dollars apiece : ils coûtent deux dollars la pièce>

aplenty [əˈplɛnti] *adv* : en abondance

aplomb [əˈplɑm, -ˈplʌm] *n* : aplomb *m*

apocalypse [əˈpɑkəˌlɪps] *n* : apocalypse *f*

apocalyptic [əˌpɑkəˈlɪptɪk] *adj* : apocalyptique

apocrypha [əˈpɑkrəfə] *n* **the Apocrypha** : les Apocryphes

apologetic [əˈpɑləˈdʒɛt̬ɪk] *adj* **1** : d'excuse <in an apologetic tone : d'un ton contrit> **2 to be apologetic** : s'excuser

apologetically [əˈpɑləˈdʒɛt̬ɪkli] *adv* : en s'excusant, d'un air contrit

apologize [əˈpɑləˌdʒaɪz] *vi* **-gized; -gizing** : s'excuser, faire des excuses

apology [əˈpɑlədʒi] *n, pl* **-gies** : excuses *fpl*

apoplectic [ˌæpəˈplɛktɪk] *adj* : apoplectique

apoplexy [ˈæpəˌplɛksi] *n* : apoplexie *f*

apostle [əˈpɑsəl] *n* : apôtre *m*

apostolic [ˌæpəˈstɑlɪk] *adj* : apostolique

apostrophe [əˈpɑstrəˌfiː] *n* : apostrophe *f*

apothecary [əˈpɑθəˌkɛri] *n, pl* **-caries** : pharmacien *m*, -cienne *f*

appall *or Brit* **appal** [əˈpɔl] *vt* **-palled; -palling** : épouvanter, horrifier

appalling [əˈpɔlɪŋ] *adj* : épouvantable, effroyable <appalling ignorance : ignorance consternante>

apparatus [ˌæpəˈræt̬əs, -ˈreɪ-] *n, pl* **-tuses** *or* **-tus** : appareil *m*, équipement *m*, agrès *mpl* (de gymnastique)

apparel [əˈpærəl] *n* : habillement *m*, vêtements *mpl*

apparent [əˈpærənt] *adj* **1** VISIBLE : visible **2** OBVIOUS : évident **3** SEEMING : apparent

apparently [əˈpærəntli] *adv* : apparemment

apparition [ˌæpəˈrɪʃən] *n* : apparition *f*

appeal[1] [əˈpiːl] *vt* : faire appel contre, en appeler de (un jugement) — *vi* **1** : interjeter appel (en droit) **2 to appeal for** : lancer un appel à **3 to appeal to** ATTRACT : attirer, plaire **4 to appeal to** INVOKE : faire appel à

appeal[2] *n* **1** CALL : appel *m* **2** ENTREATY : supplication *f* **3** ATTRACTION : attrait *m*

appear [əˈpɪr] *vi* **1** : apparaître, arriver <to appear on the scene : arriver sur place> **2** SEEM : sembler, paraître **3** COME OUT : sortir, paraître, être publié **4 to appear in court** : comparaître (devant le tribunal)

appearance [əˈpɪrənts] *n* **1** APPEARING : apparition *f*, arrivée *f*, comparution *f* (devant le tribunal) **2** LOOK : apparence *f*, semblant *m* **3 appearances** *npl* : apparences *fpl* <to keep up appearances : sauver les apparences>

appease [əˈpiːz] *vt* **-peased; -peasing** : apaiser

appeasement [əˈpiːzmənt] *n* : apaisement *m*

append [əˈpɛnd] *vt* : ajouter

appendage [əˈpɛndɪdʒ] *n* : appendice *m*

appendectomy [ˌæpənˈdɛktəmi] *n, pl* **-mies** : appendicectomie *f*

appendicitis [əˌpɛndəˈsaɪt̬əs] *n* : appendicite *f*

appendix [əˈpɛndɪks] *n, pl* **-dixes** *or* **-dices** [-dəˌsiːz] : appendice *m*

appetite [ˈæpəˌtaɪt] *n* : appétit *m*

appetizer [ˈæpəˌtaɪzər] *n* : amuse-gueule *m*

appetizing [ˈæpəˌtaɪzɪŋ] *adj* : appétissant

applaud [əˈplɔd] *v* : applaudir

applause [əˈplɔz] *n* : applaudissements *mpl*

apple [ˈæpəl] *n* : pomme *f*

appliance [əˈplaɪənts] *n* : appareil *m*

applicable [ˈæplɪkəbəl, əˈplɪkə-] *adj* : applicable

applicant [ˈæplɪkənt] *n* : candidat *m*, -date *f*

application [ˌæpləˈkeɪʃən] *n* **1** USE : application *f* **2** REQUEST : demande *f* <application form : formulaire de demande> **3** DILIGENCE : assiduité *f*, zèle *m*

applicator [ˈæpləˌkeɪt̬ər] *n* : applicateur *m*

appliqué[1] [ˌæpləˈkeɪ] *vt* **-quéd; -quéing** : orner d'appliques

appliqué[2] *n* : applique *f*

apply [əˈplaɪ] *v* **-plied; -plying** *vt* **1** : appliquer, mettre <to apply varnish : appliquer du vernis> **2** EXERT : exercer <apply pressure : exercez une pression> **3 to apply oneself** : s'appliquer — *vi* **1** : s'appliquer <the law applies to everyone : la loi s'applique à tous> **2 to apply for** : poser sa candidature pour, faire une demande de

appoint [əˈpɔɪnt] *vt* **1** DESIGNATE, SET : désigner, fixer **2** NAME : nommer **3** EQUIP : équiper <a well-appointed office : un bureau bien aménagé>

appointee [əˌpɔɪnˈtiː, æ-] *n* : candidat *m* retenu, candidate *f* retenue

appointment [əˈpɔɪntmənt] *n* **1** NOMINATION : nomination *f*, désignation *f* **2** MEETING : rendez-vous *m* **3** POSITION : poste *m*

apportion [əˈporʃən] *vt* ALLOT : répartir, distribuer

apportionment [əˈporʃənmənt] *n* : répartition *f*

apposite [ˈæpəzət] *adj* PERTINENT : pertinent, juste

appraisal [əˈpreɪzəl] *n* : évaluation *f*, appréciation *f*

appraise [əˈpreɪz] *vt* **-praised; -praising** : évaluer, estimer, apprécier

appreciable [əˈpriːʃəbəl, -ˈprɪʃiə-] *adj* : appréciable, sensible

appreciably [ə'pri:ʃəbli, -'prɪʃiə-] *adv* : sensiblement

appreciate [ə'pri:ʃi,eɪt, -'prɪ-] *v* **-ated; -ating** *vt* **1** VALUE : apprécier **2** REALIZE, UNDERSTAND : comprendre, se rendre compte de **3** : être sensible à, être reconnaissant de <I appreciate your kindness : je vous suis reconnaissant de votre gentillesse> — *vi* : s'apprécier

appreciation [ə,pri:ʃi'eɪʃən, -,prɪ-] *n* **1** EVALUATION : appréciation *f,* estimation *f* **2** GRATITUDE : reconnaissance *f* **3** UNDERSTANDING : compréhension *f* **4** INCREASE : hausse *f* (de valeur)

appreciative [ə'pri:ʃət̬ɪv, -'prɪ-; ə'pri:ʃi,eɪ-] *adj* **1** GRATEFUL : reconnaissant **2** ADMIRING : admiratif, élogieux

apprehend [,æprɪ'hɛnd] *vt* **1** ARREST : arrêter, appréhender **2** UNDERSTAND : comprendre **3** DREAD : appréhender, redouter

apprehensive [,æprɪ'hɛntsɪv] *adj* : inquiet

apprehensively [,æprɪ'hɛntsɪvli] *adv* : avec inquiétude

apprentice[1] [ə'prɛntɪs] *vt* **-ticed; -ticing** : mettre en apprentissage

apprentice[2] *n* : apprenti *m,* -tie *f*

apprenticeship [ə'prɛntɪs,ʃɪp] *n* : apprentissage *m*

apprise [ə'praɪz] *vt* **-prised; -prising** : informer, prévenir

approach[1] [ə'pro:tʃ] *vt* **1** NEAR : s'approcher de, s'avancer vers **2** : s'adresser à, aborder <he approached me : il m'a abordé> **3** CONSIDER : aborder (un problème, etc.) — *vi* NEAR : s'approcher

approach[2] *n* **1** NEARING : approche *f,* arrivée *f* <the approach of winter : la venue de l'hiver> **2** HANDLING : façon *f* (de faire), approche *f* **3** ACCESS : accès *m,* voie *f* d'accès

approachable [ə'pro:tʃəbəl] *adj* : abordable, d'un abord facile, accessible

approbation [,æprə'beɪʃən] *n* : approbation *f*

appropriate[1] [ə'pro:pri,eɪt] *vt* **-ated; -ating** **1** SEIZE, TAKE : s'approprier **2** ALLOCATE, ASSIGN : affecter, consacrer

appropriate[2] [ə'pro:priət] *adj* : approprié, convenable, qui convient

appropriately [ə'pro:priətli] *adv* : convenablement, avec à-propos

appropriateness [ə'pro:priətnəs] *n* : convenance *f,* à-propos *m*

appropriation [ə,pro:pri'eɪʃən] *n* **1** SEIZURE : appropriation *f* **2** ALLOCATION : affectation *f,* allocation *f*

approval [ə'pru:vəl] *n* **1** : approbation *f* **2 on ~** : à l'essai

approve [ə'pru:v] *v* **-proved; -proving** *vt* : approuver — *vi* **to approve of** : apprécier, être d'accord avec

approximate[1] [ə'prɑksə,meɪt] *vt* **-mated; -mating** : se rapprocher de

approximate[2] [ə'prɑksəmət] *adj* : approximatif

approximately [ə'prɑksəmətli] *adv* : à peu près, environ

approximation [ə,prɑksə'meɪʃən] *n* : approximation *f*

appurtenance [ə'pərtənənts] *n* : accessoire *m*

apricot ['æprə,kɑt, 'eɪ-] *n* : abricot *m*

April ['eɪprəl] *n* : avril *m*

apron ['eɪprən] *n* : tablier *m*

apropos[1] [,æprə'po:, 'æprə,po:] *adv* : à propos

apropos[2] *adj* : opportun, à propos

apropos of *prep* CONCERNING : quant à, à propos de

apt ['æpt] *adj* **1** SUITABLE : convenable, approprié **2** CLEVER : doué **3 to be apt to** : avoir tendance à <she's apt to forget : elle oublie facilement>

aptitude ['æptə,tu:d, -,tju:d] *n* : aptitude *f*

aptly ['æptli] *adv* : avec justesse, bien <aptly chosen : bien choisi>

aqua ['ækwə, 'ɑ-] *adj* : bleu-vert

aquarium [ə'kwæriəm] *n, pl* **-iums** *or* **-ia** [-iə] : aquarium *m*

Aquarius [ə'kwæriəm] *n* : Verseau *m*

aquatic [ə'kwɑt̬ɪk, -'kwæ-] *adj* : aquatique (se dit des plantes et des animaux), nautique (se dit des sports)

aqueduct ['ækwə,dʌkt] *n* : aqueduc *m*

aquiline ['ækwə,laɪn, -lən] *adj* : aquilin

Arab[1] ['ærəb] *adj* : arabe

Arab[2] *n* : Arabe *mf*

arabesque [,ærə'bɛsk] *n* : arabesque *f*

Arabian[1] [ə'reɪbiən] *adj* : arabe

Arabian[2] *n* → **Arab**[2]

Arabic[1] ['ærəbɪk] *adj* : arabe

Arabic[2] *n* : arabe *m* (langue)

arable ['ærəbəl] *adj* : arable

arbiter ['ɑrbət̬ər] *n* : arbitre *m*

arbitrary ['ɑrbə,trɛri] *adj* : arbitraire — **arbitrarily** [,ɑrbə'trɛrəli] *adv*

arbitrate ['ɑrbə,treɪt] *v* **-trated; -trating** *vt* : arbitrer, juger — *vi* : arbitrer

arbitration [,ɑrbə'treɪʃən] *n* : arbitrage *m*

arbitrator ['ɑrbə,treɪt̬ər] *n* : médiateur *m,* -trice *f;* arbitre *m*

arbor *or Brit* **arbour** ['ɑrbər] *n* : tonnelle *f*

arboreal [ɑr'boriəl] *adj* : arboricole

arbour *Brit* → **arbor**

arc[1] ['ɑrk] *vi* **arced; arcing** : décrire un arc

arc[2] *n* : arc *m*

arcade [ɑr'keɪd] *n* **1** ARCHES : arcade *f* **2 shopping arcade** : galerie *f* marchande

arcane [ɑr'keɪn] *adj* : mystérieux, obscur

arch[1] ['ɑrtʃ] *vt* **1** BEND : arquer, courber **2** VAULT : voûter — *vi* : former une voûte

arch[2] *adj* **1** CHIEF : principal <your arch opponent : ton principal adversaire> **2** MISCHIEVOUS : espiègle, malicieux

arch[3] *n* **1** : voûte *f*, arc *m*, arche *f* **2** ARCHING : courbe *f* (des sourcils, etc.)

archaeological [ˌarkiəˈladʒɪkəl] *adj* : archéologique

archaeologist [ˌarkiˈalədʒɪst] *n* : archéologue *mf*

archaeology *or* **archeology** [ˌarkiˈalədʒi] *n* : archéologie *f*

archaic [arˈkeɪɪk] *adj* : archaïque

archangel [ˈarkˌeɪndʒəl] *n* : archange *m*

archbishop [artʃˈbɪʃəp] *n* : archevêque *m*

archdiocese [artʃˈdaɪəsəs, -ˌsi:z, -ˌsi:s] *n* : archidiocèse *m*

archer [ˈartʃər] *n* : archer *m*

archery [ˈartʃəri] *n* : tir *m* à l'arc

archetype [ˈarkɪˌtaɪp] *n* : archétype *m*

archipelago [ˌarkəˈpɛləˌgo:, ˌartʃə-] *n, pl* **-goes** *or* **-gos** [-go:z] : archipel *m*

architect [ˈarkəˌtɛkt] *n* : architecte *mf*

architectural [ˌarkəˈtɛktʃərəl] *adj* : architectural

architecturally [ˌarkəˈtɛktʃərəli] *adv* : du point de vue architectural

architecture [ˈarkəˌtɛktʃər] *n* : architecture *f*

archives [ˈarˌkaɪvz] *npl* : archives *fpl*

archivist [ˈarkəvɪst, -ˌkaɪ-] *n* : archiviste *mf*

archway [ˈartʃˌweɪ] *n* : voûte *f*, arcade *f*

arctic [ˈarktɪk, ˈart-] *adj* **1** : arctique **2** FRIGID : glacial

arctic circle *n* : cercle *m* polaire arctique

ardent [ˈardənt] *adj* : ardent

ardently [ˈardəntli] *adv* : ardemment, passionnément

ardor *or Brit* **ardour** [ˈardər] *n* : ardeur *f*

arduous [ˈardʒʊəs] *adj* : ardu, pénible

arduously [ˈardʒʊəsli] *adv* : péniblement

arduousness [ˈardʒʊəsnəs] *n* : difficulté *f*, dureté *f*

area [ˈæriə] *n* **1** REGION : région *f*, zone *f*, quartier *m* **2** SURFACE : aire *f*, superficie *f* <the area of a circle : l'aire d'un cercle> **3** FIELD : domaine *m* <area of expertise : domaine d'expertise>

area code *n* : indicatif *m* de zone, indicatif *m* régional *Can*

arena [əˈri:nə] *n* : arène *f*, aréna *m Can*

aren't [ˈarnt, ˈarənt] (*contraction of* **are** *and* **not**) → **be**

Aries [ˈɛri:z, -iˌi:z] *n* : Bélier *m*

Argentine[1] [ˈardʒənˌtaɪn, -ˌti:n] *or* **Argentinean** *or* **Argentinian** [ˌardʒənˈtɪniən] *adj* : argentin

Argentine[2] *or* **Argentinean** *or* **Argentinian** *n* : Argentin *m*, -tine *f*

argon [ˈarˌgan] *n* : argon *m*

argot [ˈargət, -ˌgo:] *n* : argot *m*

arguable [ˈargjʊəbəl] *adj* : discutable

argue [ˈarˌgju:] *v* **-gued; -guing** *vt* **1** DEBATE, DISCUSS : discuter **2** PLEAD : plaider <to argue a case : plaider une cause> **3** MAINTAIN : soutenir **4** PERSUADE : persuader — *vi* **1** QUARREL : se disputer **2** DEBATE : argumenter

argument [ˈargjəmənt] *n* **1** QUARREL : dispute *f* **2** DEBATE : discussion *f*, débat *m* **3** REASONING : argument *m*, raisonnement *m* <his argument is that : il soutient que>

argumentative [ˌargjəˈmɛntət̬ɪv] *adj* : querelleur, ergoteur

argyle [ˈarˌgaɪl] *adj* : à motifs de losanges

aria [ˈariə] *n* : aria *f*

arid [ˈærəd] *adj* : aride

aridity [əˈrɪdət̬i, æ-] *n* : aridité *f*

arise [əˈraɪz] *vi* **arose** [əˈro:z]; **arisen** [əˈrɪzən]; **arising 1** RISE : se lever **2** APPEAR, OCCUR : se présenter, survenir <if the occasion arises : si l'occasion se présente> **3 to arise from** : provenir de, résulter de

aristocracy [ˌærəˈstakrəsi] *n, pl* **-cies** : aristocratie *f*

aristocrat [əˈrɪstəˌkræt] *n* : aristocrate *mf*

aristocratic [əˌrɪstəˈkræt̬ɪk] *adj* : aristocratique

arithmetic[1] [ˌærɪθˈmɛt̬ɪk] *or* **arithmetical** [-t̬ɪkəl] *adj* : arithmétique

arithmetic[2] [əˈrɪθməˌtɪk] *n* : arithmétique *f*

ark [ˈark] *n* : arche *f*

arm[1] [ˈarm] *vt* : armer

arm[2] *n* **1** : bras *m* (du corps ou d'une machine), accoudoir *m* (d'une chaise), manche *f* (d'un vêtement) **2** WEAPON : arme *f* <to take up arms : prendre les armes> **3** BRANCH : branche *f*, section *f* **4** → **coat of arms**

armada [arˈmadə, -ˈmeɪ-] *n* : armada *f*

armadillo [ˌarməˈdɪlo] *n, pl* **-los** : tatou *m*

armament [ˈarməmənt] *n* : armement *m*

armchair [ˈarmˌtʃɛr] *n* : fauteuil *m*

armed [ˈarmd] *adj* : armé <armed robbery : vol à main armée>

armed forces *npl* : forces *fpl* armées

Armenian[1] [arˈmi:niən] *adj* : arménien

Armenian[2] *n* **1** : Arménien *m*, -nienne *f* **2** : arménien *m* (langue)

armistice [ˈarməstɪs] *n* : armistice *m*

armor *or Brit* **armour** [ˈarmər] *n* **1** : armure *f* <a suit of armor : une armure complète> **2** *or* **armor plating** : blindage *m*

armored *or Brit* **armoured** [ˈarmərd] *adj* : blindé

armory *or Brit* **armoury** [ˈarməri] *n, pl* **-mories** *or Brit* **-mouries** : arsenal *m* (dépôt d'armes), fabrique *f* d'armes

armpit [ˈarmˌpɪt] *n* : aisselle *f*

army ['ɑrmi] *n, pl* **-mies** : armée *f*
aroma [ə'ro:mə] *n* : arôme *m*
aromatic [ˌærə'mæt̬ɪk] *adj* : aromatique
around[1] [ə'raʊnd] *adv* **1** : de circonférence <a tree two meters around : un arbre deux mètres de circonférence> **2** : autour, de tous côtés <all around : tout autour> <for miles around : sur un rayon de plusieurs milles> **3** NEARBY : pas loin, là, dans les parages <will he be around tonight? : il sera là ce soir?> **4** APPROXIMATELY : environ, à peu près <it costs around five dollars : ça coûte environ cinq dollars>
around[2] *prep* **1** SURROUNDING : autour de <the trees around the house : les arbres autour de la maison> **2** THROUGHOUT : à travers de <she traveled around the country : elle a voyagé partout dans le pays> <somewhere around the house : quelque part dans la maison> **3** AT : vers <come around noon : viens vers midi> **4 around here** : par ici **5 to go around the corner** : tourner le coin
arousal [ə'raʊzəl] *n* : excitation *f*
arouse [ə'raʊz] *vt* **aroused; arousing 1** AWAKEN : réveiller **2** STIMULATE : exciter, éveiller
arraign [ə'reɪn] *vt* : accuser, traduire en justice
arraignment [ə'reɪnmənt] *n* : lecture *f* de l'acte d'accusation
arrange [ə'reɪndʒ] *v* **-ranged; -ranging** *vt* : arranger — *vi* **to arrange for** : s'arranger pour, prendre des dispositions pour
arrangement [ə'reɪndʒmənt] *n* **1** LAYOUT : arrangement *m*, disposition *f* **2** AGREEMENT : arrangement *m*, accord *m* <under the present arrangement : selon l'accord actuel> **3 arrangements** *npl* PLANS : mesures *fpl*, dispositions *fpl*
array[1] [ə'reɪ] *vt* **1** ARRANGE : arranger, disposer, déployer (des troupes) **2** ADORN : parer <to array oneself : se parer>
array[2] *n* **1** ARRANGEMENT : arrangement *m*, ordre *m*, déploiement *m* (de troupes) **2** FINERY : parure *f*, habits *mpl* d'apparat **3** RANGE, SELECTION : panoplie *f*, sélection *f*
arrears [ə'rɪrz] *npl* **1** : arriéré *m* <rent arrears : arriéré de loyer> **2 to be in arrears** : avoir du retard
arrest[1] [ə'rɛst] *vt* : arrêter
arrest[2] *n* **1** : arrêt *m* <cardiac arrest : arrêt du cœur> **2** : arrestation *f* <under arrest : en état d'arrestation>
arrival [ə'raɪvəl] *n* : arrivée *f* (de personnes, d'avions, etc.), arrivage *m* (de marchandises)
arrive [ə'raɪv] *vi* **-rived; -riving 1** : arriver **2 to arrive at** : parvenir à (une résolution, etc.), atteindre (un état)
arrogance ['ærəgənts] *n* : arrogance *f*
arrogant ['ærəgənt] *adj* : arrogant, insolent
arrogantly ['ærəgəntli] *adv* : avec arrogance
arrow ['æro] *n* : flèche *f*
arrowhead ['æroˌhɛd] *n* : pointe *f* de flèche
arsenal ['ɑrsənəl] *n* : arsenal *m*
arsenic ['ɑrsənɪk] *n* : arsenic *m*
arson ['ɑrsən] *n* : incendie *m* criminel
arsonist ['ɑrsənɪst] *n* : incendiaire *mf*
art ['ɑrt] *n* **1** : art *m* **2** SKILL : art *m*, habileté *f*
artefact *Brit* → **artifact**
arterial [ɑr'tɪriəl] *adj* : artériel
arteriosclerosis [ɑrˌtɪriosklə'ro:sɪs] *n* : artériosclérose *f*
artery ['ɑrt̬əri] *n, pl* **-teries** : artère *f*
artful ['ɑrtfəl] *adj* **1** CLEVER, INGENIOUS : astucieux, ingénieux **2** CRAFTY : rusé, malin
arthritic [ɑr'θrɪt̬ɪk] *adj* : arthritique
arthritis [ɑr'θraɪt̬əs] *n, pl* **-thritides** [-'θrɪt̬əˌdi:z] : arthrite *f*
arthropod ['ɑrθrəˌpɑd] *n* : arthropode *m*
artichoke ['ɑrt̬əˌtʃo:k] *n* : artichaut *m*
article ['ɑrtɪkəl] *n* **1** THING : objet *m* <articles of clothing : vêtements> **2** : article *m* (dans une publication ou dans un acte judiciaire) **3** : article *m* <definite article : article défini>
articulate[1] [ɑr'tɪkjəˌleɪt] *vt* **-lated; -lating** : articuler
articulate[2] [ɑr'tɪkjələt] *adj* **1** INTELLIGIBLE : distinct, intelligible **2** WELL-SPOKEN : qui s'exprime bien **3** JOINTED : articulé
articulately [ɑr'tɪkjələtli] *adv* : clairement, distinctement
articulation [ɑrˌtɪkjə'leɪʃən] *n* : articulation *f*
artifact *or Brit* **artefact** ['ɑrt̬əˌfækt] *n* : objet *m* fabriqué
artifice ['ɑrt̬əfəs] *n* : artifice *m*
artificial [ˌɑrt̬ə'fɪʃəl] *adj* : artificiel — **artificially** *adv*
artificial respiration *n* : respiration *f* artificielle
artillery [ɑr'tɪləri] *n, pl* **-leries** : artillerie *f*
artisan ['ɑrt̬əzən, -sən] *n* : artisan *m*, -sane *f*
artist ['ɑrt̬ɪst] *n* : artiste *mf*
artistic [ɑr'tɪstɪk] *adj* : artistique — **artistically** [-tɪkli] *adv*
artistry ['ɑrt̬əstri] *n* : art *m*
artless ['ɑrtləs] *adj* **1** NATURAL : naturel **2** NAIVE : naïf, ingénu
arty ['ɑrt̬i] *adj* **artier; -est** : prétentieusement artistique
arugula [ə'ru:gələ] *n* : roquette *f*
as[1] ['æz] *adv* **1** EQUALLY : aussi <as green as grass : aussi vert que l'herbe> **2** : par exemple <some trees, as oak or pine : des arbres, par exemple le chêne ou le pin>
as[2] *conj* **1** LIKE : comme <white as snow : blanc comme la neige> **2**

WHEN, WHILE : tandis que, alors que, comme <he spoke to me as I was leaving : il m'a parlé tandis que je partais> **3** SINCE : puisque, comme <she stayed home as she has no car : elle est restée chez elle puisqu'elle n'a pas de voiture> **4** : que <so guilty as to leave no doubt : si coupable qu'il n'y a aucun doute> **5 as is** : tel quel

as[3] *prep* **1** LIKE : comme <to behave as a child : se comporter comme un enfant> **2** : en tant que <she works as an editor : elle travaille en tant qu'éditeur> **3** : en <he dressed as a clown : il s'est habillé en clown>

as[4] *pron* **1** : que <the same price as before : le même prix qu'avant> **2** : comme <she's rich, as you know : elle est riche, comme vous savez>

asbestos |æz'bɛstəs, æs-| *n* : amiante *m*

ascend |ə'sɛnd| *vt* : monter, monter à, gravir <to ascend the staircase : monter l'escalier> <to ascend to the throne : monter sur le trône> — *vi* : monter

ascendancy |ə'sɛndəntsi| *n* : ascendant *m*

ascendant[1] |ə'sɛndənt| *adj* : dominant

ascendant[2] *n* **to be in the ascendant** : être à l'ascendant

ascension |ə'sɛntʃən| *n* : ascension *f*

ascent |ə'sɛnt| *n* **1** RISING : ascension *f* **2** INCLINE : montée *f*, pente *f*

ascertain |ˌæsər'teɪn| *vt* : vérifier, établir, constater

ascertainable |ˌæsər'teɪnəbəl| *adj* : vérifiable

ascetic[1] |ə'sɛţɪk| *adj* : ascétique

ascetic[2] *n* : ascète *mf*

asceticism |ə'sɛţəˌsɪzəm| *n* : ascétisme *m*

ascribable |ə'skraɪbəbəl| *adj* : attribuable

ascribe |ə'skraɪb| *vt* **-cribed; -cribing** : attribuer

aseptic |eɪ'sɛptɪk| *adj* : aseptique

as for *prep* CONCERNING : quant à

ash |'æʃ| *n* **1** : cendre *f* <to reduce to ashes : réduire en cendres> **2** : frêne *m* (arbre)

ashamed |ə'ʃeɪmd| *adj* **1** : honteux **2 to be ashamed** : avoir honte

ashen |'æʃən| *adj* : cendreux, blême

ashore |ə'ʃor| *adv* **1** : à terre **2 to go ashore** : débarquer

ashtray |'æʃˌtreɪ| *n* : cendrier *m*

Asian[1] |'eɪʒən, -ʃən| *adj* : asiatique

Asian[2] *n* : Asiatique *mf*

aside[1] |ə'saɪd| *adv* **1** : de côté <let's put it aside : mettons-le de côté> **2** APART : à part, à l'écart

aside[2] *n* : aparté *m*

aside from *prep* **1** BESIDES : à part, en plus de **2** EXCEPT : sauf

as if *conj* : comme si

asinine |'æsənˌaɪn| *adj* : sot

ask |'æsk| *vt* **1** : poser, demander <to ask a question : poser une question> <to ask directions : demander son chemin> **2** REQUEST : demander <that's asking a lot! : c'est beaucoup en demander!> **3** INVITE : inviter <to ask s.o. in : inviter qqn à entrer> **4 to ask oneself** : se demander — *vi* : demander

askance |ə'skænts| *adv* **to look askance at** : regarder de travers, regarder d'un air méfiant

askew |ə'skju:| *adv & adj* : de travers

asleep |ə'sli:p| *adj* **1** : endormi **2 to fall asleep** : s'endormir

as of *prep* : dès, à partir de

asparagus |ə'spærəgəs| *ns & pl* : asperge *f* <do you have any asparagus? : avez-vous des asperges?>

aspect |'æˌspɛkt| *n* **1** SIDE : aspect *m* <to study the question from every aspect : étudier la question sous tous ses aspects> **2** ORIENTATION : orientation *f*, exposition *f* **3** APPEARANCE : aspect *m*, air *m*, mine *f*

aspen |'æspən| *n* : tremble *m*

asperity |æ'spɛrəţi, ə-| *n, pl* **-ties** : aspérité *f*

aspersion |ə'spərʒən| *n* **1** : calomnie *f* **2 to cast aspersions on** : dénigrer

asphalt |'æsˌfɔlt| *n* : asphalte *m*

asphyxiate |æ'sfɪksiˌeɪt| *vt* **-ated; -ating** : asphyxier

asphyxiation |æˌsfɪksi'eɪʃən| *n* : asphyxie *f*

aspic |'æspɪk| *n* : aspic *m*

aspirant |'æspərənt, ə'spaɪrənt| *n* : aspirant *m*, -rante *f*

aspiration |ˌæspə'reɪʃən| *n* : aspiration *f*

aspire |ə'spaɪr| *vi* **-pired; -piring** : aspirer

aspirin |'æsprən, 'æspə-| *n, pl* **aspirin** *or* **aspirins** : aspirine *f*

ass |'æs| *n* **1** : âne *m* **2** FOOL : idiot *m*, -diote *f*

assail |ə'seɪl| *vt* : assaillir, attaquer

assailant |ə'seɪlənt| *n* : agresseur *m*; assaillant *m*, -lante *f*

assassin |ə'sæsən| *n* : assassin *m*

assassinate |ə'sæsənˌeɪt| *vt* **-nated; -nating** : assassiner

assassination |əˌsæsən'eɪʃən| *n* : assassinat *m*

assault[1] |ə'sɔlt| *vt* : agresser, attaquer

assault[2] *n* : agression *f*, assaut *m* (militaire) <sexual assault : agression sexuelle> <assault and battery : coups et blessures>

assay[1] |æ'seɪ, 'æˌseɪ| *vt* : essayer

assay[2] |'æˌseɪ, æ'seɪ| *n* ANALYSIS : analyse *f*

assemble |ə'sɛmbəl| *v* **-bled; -bling** *vt* **1** CONSTRUCT : assembler **2** GATHER : rassembler — *vi* CONVENE : se rassembler, se réunir

assembly |ə'sɛmbli| *n, pl* **-blies 1** MEETING : assemblée *f*, réunion *f* **2** ASSEMBLING : assemblage *m*, montage *m* <assembly line : chaîne de montage>

assent[1] [ə'sɛnt] *vi* : consentir, donner son assentiment

assent[2] *n* : assentiment *m*

assert [ə'sərt] *vt* **1** DECLARE : affirmer, déclarer **2** DEMAND : revendiquer (ses droits, etc.) **3 to assert oneself** : s'affirmer, s'imposer

assertion [ə'sərʃən] *n* **1** DECLARATION : affirmation *f,* assertion *f* **2** CLAIM : revendication *f*

assertive [ə'sərt̬ɪv] *adj* : assuré

assertiveness [ə'sərt̬ɪvnəs] *n* : manière *f* assurée

assess [ə'sɛs] *vt* **1** EVALUATE : évaluer, estimer **2** IMPOSE : imposer (un impôt, etc.)

assessment [ə'sɛsmənt] *n* : évaluation *f,* estimation *f*

assessor [ə'sɛsər] *n* : expert *m;* contrôleur *m,* -leuse *f* (des impôts)

asset ['æˌsɛt] *n* **1** ADVANTAGE : avantage *m,* atout *m* **2 assets** *npl* : biens *mpl,* actif *m,* capital *m* <assets and liabilities : l'actif et le passif>

assiduity [ˌæsə'du:əti, -'dju:-] *n, pl* **-ities** : assiduité *f*

assiduous [ə'sɪdʒʊəs] *adj* : assidu

assiduously [ə'sɪdʒʊəsli] *adv* : assidûment

assign [ə'saɪn] *vt* **1** ALLOT : assigner **2** FIX, SPECIFY : fixer **3** APPOINT : nommer **4** ATTRIBUTE : attribuer

assignment [ə'saɪnmənt] *n* **1** TASK : tâche *f,* mission *f* **2** HOMEWORK : devoir *m* **3** ALLOCATION : allocation *f,* affectation *f*

assimilate [ə'sɪməˌleɪt] *v* **-lated; -lating** *vt* : assimiler — *vi* : s'assimiler

assimilation [əˌsɪmə'leɪʃən] *n* : assimilation *f*

assist [ə'sɪst] *vt* : aider, assister

assistance [ə'sɪstənts] *n* : aide *f,* assistance *f*

assistant [ə'sɪstənt] *n* : assistant *m,* -tante *f;* adjoint *m,* -jointe *f*

associate[1] [ə'so:ʃiˌeɪt, -si-] *v* **-ated; -ating** *vt* **1** : associer **2 to be associated with** : être associé à, faire partie de — *vi* **to associate with** : fréquenter

associate[2] [ə'so:ʃiət, -siət] *n* : associé *m,* -ciée *f*

association [əˌso:ʃi'eɪʃən, -si-] *n* : association *f*

as soon as *conj* : aussitôt que

assorted [ə'sɔrt̬əd] *adj* : assorti

assortment [ə'sɔrtmənt] *n* : assortiment *m*

assuage [ə'sweɪdʒ] *vt* **-suaged; -suaging** **1** CALM, EASE : apaiser, calmer **2** SATISFY : assouvir (la faim, etc.)

assume [ə'su:m] *vt* **-sumed; -suming** **1** TAKE ON : prendre, assumer **2** ADOPT, FEIGN : adopter, affecter **3** SUPPOSE : supposer, présumer

assumption [ə'sʌmpʃən] *n* **1** SUPPOSITION : supposition *f* **2** APPROPRIATION : appropriation *f,* prise *f* (de pouvoir, etc.)

assurance [ə'ʃʊrənts] *n* : assurance *f*

assure [ə'ʃʊr] *vt* **-sured; -suring** : assurer

assured [ə'ʃʊrd] *adj* **1** CERTAIN : assuré **2** CONFIDENT : assuré, plein d'assurance

assuredly [ə'ʃʊrədli] *adv* : assurément

aster ['æstər] *n* : aster *m*

asterisk ['æstəˌrɪsk] *n* : astérisque *m*

astern [ə'stərn] *adv* : à l'arrière

asteroid ['æstəˌrɔɪd] *n* : astéroïde *m*

asthma ['æzmə] *n* : asthme *m*

asthmatic [æz'mæt̬ɪk] *adj* : asthmatique

as though → **as if**

astigmatism [ə'stɪgməˌtɪzəm] *n* : astigmatisme *m*

astir [ə'stər] *adj* **1** UP : debout **2** ACTIVE, MOVING : en mouvement, animé

as to *prep* **1** ABOUT : sur, concernant **2** → **according to**

astonish [ə'stɑnɪʃ] *vt* : étonner, ahurir

astonishing [ə'stɑnɪʃɪŋ] *adj* : étonnant

astonishingly [ə'stɑnɪʃɪŋli] *adv* : incroyablement

astonishment [ə'stɑnɪʃmənt] *n* : étonnement *m,* stupéfaction *f*

astound [ə'staʊnd] *vt* : stupéfier

astounding [ə'staʊndɪŋ] *adj* : stupéfiant, ahurissant

astraddle [ə'strædəl] → **astride**

astral ['æstrəl] *adj* : astral

astray [ə'streɪ] *adv* **1 to go astray** : s'égarer **2 to lead s.o. astray** : égarer qqn, détourner qqn du droit chemin

astride [ə'straɪd] *adv* : à califourchon

astringent [ə'strɪndʒənt] *adj* : astringent

astrologer [ə'strɑlədʒər] *n* : astrologue *mf*

astrological [ˌæstrə'lɑdʒɪkəl] *adj* : astrologique

astrology [ə'strɑlədʒi] *n* : astrologie *f*

astronaut ['æstrəˌnɔt] *n* : astronaute *mf*

astronautics [ˌæstrə'nɔt̬ɪks] *ns & pl* : astronautique *f*

astronomer [ə'strɑnəmər] *n* : astronome *mf*

astronomical [ˌæstrə'nɑmɪkəl] *adj* : astronomique

astronomy [ə'strɑnəmi] *n, pl* **-mies** : astronomie *f*

astute [ə'stu:t, -'stju:t] *adj* : astucieux — **astutely** *adv*

astuteness [ə'stu:tnəs, -'stju:t-] *n* : astuce *f*

asunder [ə'sʌndər] *adv* : en morceaux

as well as[1] *conj* AND : en plus de

as well as[2] *prep* : ainsi que, à part

asylum [ə'saɪləm] *n* : asile *m*

asymmetrical [ˌeɪsə'mɛtrɪkəl] *or* **asymmetric** [ˌeɪsə'mɛtrɪk] *adj* : asymétrique

asymmetry [ˌeɪ'sɪmətri] *n* : asymétrie *f*

asymptomatic [ˌeɪˌsɪmptə'mæt̬ɪk] *adj* : asymptomatique

at ['æt] *prep* **1** : à <at the end : à la fin> <be here at 3 o'clock : soyez là à trois

heures> <at his age : à son âge> **2** : chez <at the dentist's : chez le dentiste> **3** : en <at war : en guerre> <to be good at : être bon en> **4** : de <to laugh at : rire de> **5** : sur <to shoot at : tirer sur> **6** : contre <to be angry at : être fâché contre>

at all *adv* : du tout

ate [ˈeɪt] → **eat**

atheism [ˈeɪθiˌɪzəm] *n* : athéisme *m*

atheist [ˈeɪθiɪst] *n* : athée *mf*

atheistic [ˌeɪθiˈɪstɪk] *adj* : athée

athlete [ˈæθˌliːt] *n* : athlète *mf*

athletic [æθˈlɛt̬ɪk] *adj* : athlétique

athletics [æθˈlɛt̬ɪks] *ns & pl* : athlétisme *m*

atlas [ˈætləs] *n* : atlas *m*

atmosphere [ˈætməˌsfɪr] *n* : atmosphère *f*

atmospheric [ˌætməˈsfɪrɪk, -ˈsfɛr-] *adj* : atmosphérique

atoll [ˈæˌtɔl, ˈeɪ-, -ˌtɑl] *n* : atoll *m*

atom [ˈæt̬əm] *n* : atome *m*

atomic [əˈtɑmɪk] *adj* : atomique

atomic bomb *n* : bombe *f* atomique

atomizer [ˈæt̬əˌmaɪzər] *n* : atomiseur *m*

atone [əˈtoːn] *v* **atoned; atoning** *vt* EXPIATE : expier — *vi* **to atone for** : expier

atonement [əˈtoːnmənt] *n* : expiation *f*

atop[1] [əˈtɑp] *adv & adj* : en haut

atop[2] *prep* : sur, en haut de

atrocious [əˈtroːʃəs] *adj* : atroce — **atrociously** *adv*

atrocity [əˈtrɑsət̬i] *n, pl* **-ties** : atrocité *f*

atrophy[1] [ˈætrəfi] *v* **-phied; phying** *vt* : atrophier — *vi* : s'atrophier

atrophy[2] *n, pl* **-phies** : atrophie *f*

attach [əˈtætʃ] *vt* **1** FASTEN, JOIN : attacher, fixer, joindre **2** ATTRIBUTE : attribuer, attacher <she attached little importance to the message : elle a attaché peu d'importance au message> **3** SEIZE : saisir (des biens) **4 to become attached to** : s'attacher à — *vi* ADHERE : s'attacher

attaché [ˌæt̬əˈʃeɪ, ˌæˌtæ-, əˌtæ-] *n* : attaché *m*, -chée *f*

attaché case *n* : attaché-case *m*

attachment [əˈtætʃmənt] *n* **1** AFFECTION, CLOSENESS : attachement *m*, affection *f* **2** ACCESSORY : accessoire *m* **3** SEIZURE : saisie *f* (de biens) **4** FASTENING : fixation *f*

attack[1] [əˈtæk] *vt* **1** ASSAULT : attaquer, agresser **2** TACKLE : s'attaquer à <he attacked the problem aggressively : il s'est attaqué au problème agressivement>

attack[2] *n* **1** ASSAULT : attaque *f*, assaut *m* **2** : crise *f*, accès *m* <heart attack : crise cardiaque> <an attack of fever : un accès de fièvre>

attain [əˈteɪn] *vt* : atteindre

attainable [əˈteɪnəbəl] *adj* : réalisable

attainment [əˈteɪnmənt] *n* **1** ACHIEVING : réalisation *f* **2** ACCOMPLISHMENT : réussite *f*, résultat *m* obtenu

attempt[1] [əˈtɛmpt] *vt* : tenter

attempt[2] *n* : tentative *f*, effort *m*, essai *m*

attend [əˈtɛnd] *vt* **1** : assister à (une réunion, etc.), aller à (l'église, etc.) **2** LOOK AFTER : soigner, servir **3** ACCOMPANY : accompagner — *vi* **1 to attend to** : s'occuper de (affaires, etc.), s'appliquer à (travaux) **2 to attend to** HEED : prêter attention à

attendance [əˈtɛndənts] *n* **1** PRESENCE : présence *f* **2** TURNOUT : assistance *f*

attendant[1] [əˈtɛndənt] *adj* : concomitant

attendant[2] *n* **1** : gardien *m*, -dienne *f* (à un musée, etc.) **2 service station attendant** : pompiste *mf*

attention [əˈtɛntʃən] *n* **1** : attention *f* **2 to stand at attention** : se mettre au garde-à-vous **3** → **pay**

attentive [əˈtɛntɪv] *adj* : attentif — **attentively** *adv*

attentiveness [əˈtɛntɪvnəs] *n* **1** CONCENTRATION : attention *f* **2** SOLICITUDE : prévenance *f*, égard *m*

attenuate [əˈtɛnjəˌweɪt] *vt* **-ated; -ating** : atténuer

attest [əˈtɛst] *vt* **1** AFFIRM : attester **2** PROVE, SHOW : démontrer, témoigner de — *vi* TESTIFY : témoigner

attestation [ˌæˌtɛsˈteɪʃən] *n* : attestation *f*

attic [ˈætɪk] *n* : grenier *m*

attire[1] [əˈtaɪr] *vt* **-tired; -tiring** : vêtir

attire[2] *n* : vêtements *mpl*

attitude [ˈætəˌtuːd, -ˌtjuːd] *n* **1** : attitude *f* <a negative attitude : une attitude négative> **2** POSTURE : position *f*, attitude *f* <to strike an attitude : prendre une pose affectée>

attorney [əˈtərni] *n, pl* **-neys** : avocat *m*, -cate *f*

attract [əˈtrækt] *vt* : attirer

attraction [əˈtrækʃən] *n* : attraction *f*

attractive [əˈtræktɪv] *adj* : séduisant, attrayant, attirant

attractively [əˈtræktɪvli] *adv* : de manière attrayante

attractiveness [əˈtræktɪvnəs] *n* : attrait *m*, charme *m*

attributable [əˈtrɪbjʊt̬əbəl] *adj* : attribuable

attribute[1] [əˈtrɪˌbjuːt] *vt* **-uted; -uting** : attribuer

attribute[2] [ˈætrəˌbjuːt] *n* : attribut *m*

attribution [ˌætrəˈbjuːʃən] *n* : attribution *f*

attune [əˈtuːn, -ˈtjuːn] *vt* : accorder <to be attuned to : être en accord avec>

auburn [ˈɔbərn] *adj* : auburn

auction[1] [ˈɔkʃən] *vt* : vendre aux enchères, encanter *Can*

auction[2] *n* : vente *f* aux enchères

auctioneer [ˌɔkʃəˈnɪr] *n* : commissaire-priseur *m*, encanteur *m Can*
audacious [ɔˈdeɪʃəs] *adj* : audacieux — **audaciously** *adv*
audacity [ɔˈdæsət̬i] *n, pl* **-ties** : audace *f*
audible [ˈɔdəbəl] *adj* : audible
audibly [ˈɔdəbli] *adv* : distinctement
audience [ˈɔdiənts] *n* **1** PUBLIC : assistance *f*, public *m* **2** HEARING, INTERVIEW : audience *f*
audio[1] [ˈɔdiˌoː] *adj* : audio
audio[2] *n* : son *m*, acoustique *f*
audiovisual [ˌɔdioˈvɪʒuəl] *adj* : audiovisuel
audit[1] [ˈɔdət] *vt* **1** : vérifier (des comptes, etc.) **2 to audit a course** : suivre un cours en auditeur libre
audit[2] *n* : audit *m*
audition[1] [ɔˈdɪʃən] *v* : auditionner
audition[2] *n* : audition *f*
auditor [ˈɔdət̬ər] *n* **1** : vérificateur *m*, -trice *f* (de comptes) **2** : auditeur *m*, -trice *f* (d'un cours)
auditorium [ˌɔdəˈtoriəm] *n, pl* **-riums** *or* **-ria** [-riə] : salle *f*, amphithéâtre *m*
auditory [ˈɔdəˌtori] *adj* : auditif
auger [ˈɔgər] *n* : vrille *f*
augment [ɔgˈmɛnt] *vt* : augmenter
augmentation [ˌɔgmənˈteɪʃən] *n* : augmentation *f*
augur[1] [ˈɔgər] *vt* : présager — *vi* **to augur well** : être de bon augure
augur[2] *n* : augure *m*
augury [ˈɔgjʊri, -gər-] *n, pl* **-ries** : augure *m*, présage *m*
august [ɔˈgʌst] *adj* : auguste
August [ˈɔgəst] *n* : août *m*
auk [ˈɔk] *n* **great auk** : grand pingouin *m*
aunt [ˈænt, ˈant] *n* : tante *f*
aura [ˈɔrə] *n* : aura *f*, atmosphère *f*
aural [ˈɔrəl] *adj* : auditif
auricle [ˈɔrɪkəl] *n* : oreillette *f* (du cœur)
aurora borealis [əˈrorəˌboriˈæləs] *n* : aurore *f* boréale
auspices [ˈɔspəsəz, -ˌsiːz] *npl* : auspices *mpl*
auspicious [ɔˈspɪʃəs] *adj* : favorable, propice, prometteur
austere [ɔˈstɪr] *adj* : austère — **austerely** *adv*
austerity [ɔˈstɛrət̬i] *n, pl* **-ties** : austérité *f*
Australian[1] [ɔˈstreɪljən] *adj* : australien
Australian[2] *n* : Australien *m*, -lienne *f*
Austrian[1] [ˈɔstriən] *adj* : autrichien
Austrian[2] *n* : Autrichien *m*, -chienne *f*
authentic [əˈθɛntɪk, ɔ-] *adj* : authentique — **authentically** [-tɪkli] *adv*
authenticate [əˈθɛntɪˌkeɪt, ɔ-] *vt* **-cated; -cating** : authentifier
authenticity [ɔˌθɛnˈtɪsət̬i] *n* : authenticité *f*
author [ˈɔθər] *n* : auteur *m*, auteure *f Can*
authoritarian [ɔˌθɔrəˈtɛriən, ə-] *adj* : autoritaire
authoritative [əˈθɔrəˌteɪt̬ɪv, ɔ-] *adj* **1** DICTATORIAL : autoritaire **2** DEFINITIVE : qui fait autorité
authoritatively [əˈθɔrəˌteɪt̬ɪvli, ɔ-] *adv* : de manière autoritaire, avec autorité
authority [əˈθɔrət̬i, ɔ-] *n, pl* **-ties 1** AUTHORIZATION : autorisation *f*, droit *m* **2** POWER : autorité *f*, pouvoir *m* **3** FORCEFULNESS : autorité *f*, assurance *f* <to speak with authority : parler avec autorité> **4 authorities** *npl* : autorités *fpl*, administration *f*
authorization [ˌɔθərəˈzeɪʃən] *n* : autorisation *f*
authorize [ˈɔθəˌraɪz] *vt* **-rized; -rizing** : autoriser
authorship [ˈɔθərˌʃɪp] *n* : paternité *f*
auto [ˈɔto] *n, pl* **autos** : auto *f*, voiture *f*
autobiographical [ˌɔt̬obaɪəˈgræfɪkəl] *adj* : autobiographique
autobiography [ˌɔt̬oˌbaɪˈagrəfi] *n, pl* **-phies** : autobiographie *f*
autocracy [ɔˈtakrəsi] *n, pl* **-cies** : autocratie *f*
autocrat [ˈɔtoˌkræt] *n* : autocrate *mf*
autocratic [ˌɔtəˈkræt̬ɪk] *adj* : autocratique
autograph[1] [ˈɔtəˌgræf] *vt* : dédicacer (un livre, etc.), signer
autograph[2] *n* : autographe *m*
automate [ˈɔtəˌmeɪt] *v* **-mated; -mating** : automatiser
automatic [ˌɔtəˈmæt̬ɪk] *adj* : automatique — **automatically** [-t̬ɪkli] *adv*
automation [ˌɔt̬əˈmeɪʃən] *n* : automatisation *f*
automaton [ɔˈtaməˌtan] *n, pl* **-atons** *or* **-ata** [-t̬ə, -ta] : automate *m*
automobile [ˌɔt̬əmoˈbiːl, -ˈmoːˌbiːl] *n* : automobile *f*, voiture *f*
automotive [ˌɔt̬əˈmoːt̬ɪv] *adj* : automobile
autonomous [ɔˈtanəməs] *adj* : autonome
autonomy [ɔˈtanəmi] *n, pl* **-mies** : autonomie *f*
autopsy [ˈɔˌtapsi, -təp-] *n, pl* **-sies** : autopsie *f*
autumn [ˈɔt̬əm] *n* : automne *m*
autumnal [ɔˈtʌmnəl] *adj* : automnal, d'automne
auxiliary[1] [ɔgˈzɪljəri, -ˈzɪləri] *adj* : auxiliaire
auxiliary[2] *n, pl* **-ries 1** : auxiliaire *mf* **2** *or* **auxiliary verb** : auxiliaire *m*
avail[1] [əˈveɪl] *vt* **to avail oneself of** : profiter de, se servir de
avail[2] *n* **1 to be of no avail** : être inutile, n'avoir aucun effet **2 to no avail** : en vain, sans résultat
availability [əˌveɪləˈbɪlət̬i] *n, pl* **-ties** : disponibilité *f*

available [ə'veɪləbəl] *adj* : disponible
avalanche ['ævə,læntʃ] *n* : avalanche *f*
avarice ['ævərəs] *n* : avarice *f*, avidité *f*, cupidité *f*
avaricious [,ævə'rɪʃəs] *adj* : avare, cupide, pingre
avenge [ə'vɛndʒ] *vt* **avenged; avenging** : venger
avenger [ə'vɛndʒər] *n* : vengeur *m*, -geresse *f*
avenue ['ævə,nu:, -,nju:] *n* **1** STREET : avenue *f* **2** MEANS, WAY : voie *f*, route *f*
average[1] ['ævrɪdʒ, 'ævə-] *vt* **-aged; -aging 1** : faire en moyenne <she averaged two goals per game : elle a fait en moyenne deux buts par jeu> **2** : faire la moyenne de (en mathématiques)
average[2] *adj* : moyen
average[3] *n* : moyenne *f*
averse [ə'vərs] *adj* **1** : opposé **2 to be averse to** : répugner à
aversion [ə'vərʒən] *n* : aversion *f*
avert [ə'vərt] *vt* **1** : détourner <to avert one's eyes : détourner les yeux> **2** AVOID : éviter, prévenir
aviary ['eɪvi,ɛri] *n, pl* **-aries** : volière *f*
aviation [,eɪvi'eɪʃən] *n* : aviation *f*
aviator ['eɪvi,eɪt̬ər] *n* : aviateur *m*, -trice *f*
avid ['ævɪd] *adj* **1** GREEDY : avide <to be avid for : être avide de> **2** ENTHUSIASTIC : passionné, fervent
avidly ['ævɪdli] *adv* : avidement, avec ferveur
avocado [,ævə'kɑdo, ,ɑvə-] *n, pl* **-dos** : avocat *m*
avocation [,ævə'keɪʃən] *n* HOBBY : passe-temps *m*
avoid [ə'vɔɪd] *vt* : éviter, prévenir
avoidable [ə'vɔɪdəbəl] *adj* : évitable
avoidance [ə'vɔɪdənts] *n* : action *f* d'éviter
avoirdupois [,ævərdə'pɔɪz] *n* : avoirdupois *m*
avow [ə'vaʊ] *vt* **1** DECLARE : affirmer, déclarer **2** ADMIT : avouer, reconnaître
avowal [ə'vaʊəl] *n* **1** DECLARATION : affirmation *f* **2** ADMISSION : aveu *m*
await [ə'weɪt] *vt* : attendre
awake[1] [ə'weɪk] *v* **awoke** [ə'wo:k]; **awoken** [ə'wo:kən] *or* **awaked** [ə'weɪkt]; **awaking** *vt* AROUSE : réveiller, éveiller — *vi* WAKE UP : se réveiller, s'éveiller
awake[2] *adj* : éveillé, réveillé
awaken [ə'weɪkən] **awakened; awakening** → **awake**[1]
award[1] [ə'wɔrd] *vt* **1** GRANT : accorder **2** CONFER : décerner
award[2] *n* **1** PRIZE : prix *m*, distinction *f* honorifique **2** GRANT : bourse *f*
aware [ə'wær] *adj* **1** CONSCIOUS : conscient **2** INFORMED : au courant
awareness [ə'wærnəs] *n* : conscience *f*
awash [ə'wɔʃ] *adj* : inondé
away[1] [ə'weɪ] *adv* **1** (*indicating movement*) <to get away early : partir en avance> <go away! : hors d'ici!, allez-vous en!> **2** (*indicating the opposite direction*) <to look away : détourner les yeux> **3** (*indicating an ending*) <the wind died away : le vent s'est arrêté> **4** (*indicating the end of possession*) <she gave away her money : elle a donné son argent> **5** NONSTOP : sans arrêt <to chatter away : bavarder sans arrêt> **6** (*indicating distance in space or time*) <away back in 1850 : en 1850>
away[2] *adj* **1** ABSENT : absent **2** : de distance <10 kilometers away : à 10 kilomètres de distance> **3** : à l'extérieur (aux sports) <an away game : un match à l'extérieur>
awe[1] ['ɔ] *vt* **awed; awing** : impressionner, intimider
awe[2] *n* : crainte *f* mêlée de respect, crainte *f* révérentielle
awesome ['ɔsəm] *adj* : impressionnant, imposant
awestruck ['ɔ,strʌk] *adj* : impressionné
awful ['ɔfəl] *adj* **1** TERRIBLE : affreux, terrible **2 an awful lot of** : énormément de
awfully ['ɔfəli] *adv* EXTREMELY : extrémement, terriblement, très
awhile [ə'hwaɪl] *adv* : un moment
awkward ['ɔkwərd] *adj* **1** CLUMSY : gauche, maladroit **2** EMBARRASSING : embarrassant, gênant **3** DIFFICULT : difficile, incommode
awkwardly ['ɔkwərdli] *adv* **1** CLUMSILY : maladroitement, avec maladresse **2** EMBARRASSEDLY : d'un ton embarrassé **3** INCONVENIENTLY : de façon malcommode
awkwardness ['ɔkwərdnəs] *n* **1** CLUMSINESS : gaucherie *f*, maladresse *f* **2** EMBARRASSMENT : embarras *m*, gêne *f*
awl ['ɔl] *n* : poinçon *m*, alène *f* (pour le cuir)
awning ['ɔnɪŋ] *n* : auvent *m*
awoke, awoken → **awake**[1]
awry [ə'raɪ] *adv & adj* **1** : de travers **2 to go awry** : mal tourner
ax *or* **axe** ['æks] *n* : hache *f*
axiom ['æksiəm] *n* : axiome *m*
axiomatic ['æksiəmæt̬ɪk] *adj* : axiomatique
axis ['æksɪs] *n, pl* **axes** [-si:z] : axe *m*
axle ['æksəl] *n* : essieu *m*
aye[1] ['aɪ] *adv* : oui <to vote aye : voter oui>
aye[2] *n* : oui *m*
azalea [ə'zeɪljə] *n* : azalée *f*
azimuth ['æzəməθ] *n* : azimut *m*
azure[1] ['æʒər] *adj* : d'azur
azure[2] *n* : azur *m*

B

b [ˈbiː] *n, pl* **b's** *or* **bs** biːz] : b *m,* deuxième lettre de l'alphabet

babble[1] [ˈbæbəl] *v* **-bled; -bling** *vt* : bafouiller <babbling an excuse : bafouillant une excuse> — *vi* **1** PRATTLE : babiller **2** CHATTER : bavarder **3** : gazouiller <a babbling brook : un ruisseau gazouillant>

babble[2] *n* : babillage *m* (d'un enfant), bavardage *m* (d'un adulte), rumeur *f* (de voix), gazouillement *m* (d'un ruisseau, etc.)

babe [ˈbeɪb] → **baby**[2]

babel [ˈbeɪbəl, ˈbæ-] *n* HUBBUB : brouhaha *m*

baboon [bæˈbuːn] *n* : babouin *m*

baby[1] [ˈbeɪbi] *vt* **-bied; -bying** : dorloter

baby[2] *n, pl* **-bies** : bébé *m*

baby carriage *n* : voiture *f* d'enfant, landau *m France*

babyhood [ˈbeɪbi,hʊd] *n* : petite enfance *f*

babyish [ˈbeɪbiɪʃ] *adj* : enfantin, puéril

baby–sit [ˈbeɪbi,sɪt] *vi* **-sat** [-,sæt]; **-sitting** : garder des enfants, faire du baby-sitting *France*

baby–sitter [ˈbeɪbi,sɪṭər] *n* : gardienne *f* d'enfants, baby-sitter *mf France*

baccalaureate [ˈbækəˈlɔriət] *n* : licence *f*

bachelor [ˈbætʃələr] *n* **1** : célibataire *m* **2** GRADUATE : licencié *m,* -ciée *f* <bachelor of science : licencié de sciences>

bacillus [bəˈsɪləs] *n, pl* **-li** [-,laɪ] : bacille *m*

back[1] [ˈbæk] *vt* **1** *or* **to back up** SUPPORT : soutenir, appuyer **2** FINANCE : financer **3** *or* **to back up** : reculer (un véhicule), mettre en marche arrière — *vi* **1 to back up** : reculer, faire marche arrière **2 to back out of** : se soustraire à, se dégager de **3 to back down** : céder, se résigner

back[2] *adv* **1** BACKWARD : en arrière, vers l'arrière **2** AGO : antérieurement **3 to come back** : être de retour **4 to give back** : rendre **5 to go back** : retourner **6 to walk back and forth** : marcher de long en large

back[3] *adj* **1** REAR : arrière, de derrière <the back door : la porte arrière> **2** OVERDUE : arriéré, impayé <back pay : rappel de salaire> **3 back street** : petite rue *f*

back[4] *n* **1** : dos *m* (du corps) <back to back : dos à dos> **2** REAR : derrière *m,* arrière *m,* fond *m* **3** : dossier *m* (d'un siège) **4** : arrière *m* (aux sports)

backache [ˈbæk,eɪk] *n* : mal *m* de dos

backbite [ˈbæk,baɪt] *vt* **-bit** [-,bɪt]; **-bitten** [-,bɪtən]; **-biting** : médire de, dénigrer

backbone [ˈbæk,boːn] *n* **1** : colonne *f* vertébrale **2** FORTITUDE : fermeté *f,* caractère *m*

backdrop [ˈbæk,drɑp] *n* : toile *f* de fond

backer [ˈbækər] *n* SUPPORTER : partisan *m,* -sane *f;* allié *m,* -liée *f*

backfire[1] [ˈbæk,faɪr] *vi* **-fired; -firing 1** : pétarader (se dit d'une voiture) **2** FAIL : échouer, tourner mal

backfire[2] *n* : pétarade *f* (d'une voiture)

background [ˈbæk,graʊnd] *n* **1** : arrière-plan *m,* fond *m* (d'un tableau) **2** EXPERIENCE, EDUCATION : expérience *f,* formation *f*

backhand[1] [ˈbæk,hænd] *adj & adv* : en revers

backhand[2] *n* : revers *m* (au tennis)

backhanded [ˈbæk,hændəd] *adj* **1** : en revers, de revers **2** INDIRECT, DEVIOUS : équivoque, sournois

backing [ˈbækɪŋ] *n* **1** SUPPORT : soutien *m,* appui *m* **2** REINFORCEMENT : renfort *m,* renforcement *m*

backlash [ˈbæk,læʃ] *n* : contrecoup *m,* répercussion *f*

backlog [ˈbæk,lɔg] *n* : arriéré *m,* accumulation *f*

backpack[1] [ˈbæk,pæk] *vi* : faire de la randonnée

backpack[2] *n* : sac *m* à dos

backrest [ˈbæk,rɛst] *n* : dossier *m*

backslide [ˈbæk,slaɪd] *vi* **-slid** [-,slɪd]; **-slid** *or* **-slidden** [-,slɪdən]; **-sliding** : retomber, récidiver

backstage [,bækˈsteɪdʒ, ˈbæk,-] *adv* : dans les coulisses, derrière la scène

backtrack [ˈbæk,træk] *vi* **1** : revenir sur ses pas **2** : faire marche arrière, revenir <she backtracked on her commitment : elle est revenue sur son engagement>

backup [ˈbæk,ʌp] *n* **1** SUPPORT : soutien *m,* appui *m* **2** SUBSTITUTE : réserve *f,* remplaçant *m* **3** : sauvegarde *f* (en informatique)

backward[1] [ˈbækwərd] *or* **backwards** [-wərdz] *adv* **1** BACK : en arrière **2** : à la renverse <to fall over backward : tomber à la renverse> **3** : à l'envers <say it backwards : dis-le à l'envers>

backward[2] *adj* **1** : en arrière, rétrograde <a backward glance : un regard en arrière> <backward motion : mouvement rétrograde> **2** RETARDED, SLOW : arriéré, peu avancé **3** UNDERDEVELOPED : sous-développé, arriéré <backward countries : pays arriérés> **4** BASHFUL, HESITANT : timide, peu disposé

backwardness [ˈbækwərdnəs] *n* **1** : retard *m* mental (d'une personne), sous-développement *m* (d'un pays) **2** BASHFULNESS : timidité *f*

backwoods [,bækˈwʊdz] *ns & pl* : région *f* forestière peu peuplée, forêts *fpl* de l'intérieur

bacon |beɪkən| *n* : lard *m,* bacon *m*
bacterial |bæk'tɪriəl| *adj* : bactérien
bacteriologist |bæk,tɪri'ɑlədʒɪst| *n* : bactériologiste *mf*
bacteriology |bæk,tɪri'ɑlədʒi| *n* : bactériologie *f*
bacterium |bæk'tɪriəm| *n, pl* **-ria** |-riə| : bactérie *f*
bad[1] |'bæd| *adv* → **badly**
bad[2] *adj* **worse; worst 1** POOR : mauvais <bad weather : mauvais temps> <bad breath : mauvaise haleine> **2** ROTTEN : pourri **3** SERIOUS, SEVERE : grave (se dit d'un accident, etc.), aigu (se dit d'une douleur) **4** DEFECTIVE : défectueux, de mauvaise qualité **5** WICKED : méchant, mauvais **6** UNWELL : malade, mal <to feel bad : se sentir mal> **7** HARMFUL : néfaste, nuisible **8** : sans provision <a bad check : un chèque sans provision> **9** NAUGHTY : méchant **10 from bad to worse** : de mal en pis
bad[3] *n* : mauvais *m* <to take the good with the bad : prendre le bon avec le mauvais>
bade → **bid**
badge |'bædʒ| *n* : insigne *m,* plaque *f* (d'un agent de police)
badger[1] |'bædʒər| *vt* : harceler, importuner
badger[2] *n* : blaireau *m*
badly |'bædli| *adv* **1** : mal <badly dressed : mal habillé> **2** SEVERELY : gravement, grièvement <badly injured : grièvement blessé> **3** URGENTLY : énormément, avec grand besoin <to want sth badly : avoir très envie de qqch>
badminton |'bæd,mɪntən, -,mɪt-| *n* : badminton *m*
badness |bædnəs| *n* : méchanceté *f*
baffle |'bæfəl| *vt* **-fled; -fling** : déconcerter, confondre
bafflement |'bæfəlmənt| *n* : confusion *f,* perplexité *f*
bag[1] |'bæg| *v* **bagged; bagging** *vt* **1** : mettre en sac, ensacher (des marchandises) **2** KILL : tuer (du gibier) — *vi* SAG : pocher, faire des poches
bag[2] *n* **1** : sac *m* <plastic bag : sac en plastique> **2** POCKETBOOK : sac *m* à main **3** SUITCASE : valise *f,* mallette *f*
bagatelle |,bægə'tɛl| *n* : bagatelle *f*
bagel |'beɪgəl| *n* : petit pain *m* en couronne, bagel *m Can*
baggage |'bægɪdʒ| *n* : bagages *mpl*
baggy |'bægi| *adj* **baggier; -est** : ample, qui fait des poches
bagpipes |'bæg,paɪps| *npl* : cornemuse *f*
Bahamian[1] |bə'heɪmiən, -'hɔ-| *adj* : des Bahamas
Bahamian[2] *n* : habitant *m,* -tante *f* des Bahamas
Bahraini[1] |bɑ:'reɪni| *adj* : bahreïni
Bahraini[2] *n* : Bahreïni *m,* -nie *f*
bail[1] |,beɪl| *vt* **1** : vider (l'eau d'un bateau), écoper (un bateau) **2 to bail out** RELEASE : mettre en liberté sous caution **3 to bail out** EXTRICATE : tirer d'affaire — *vi* **to bail out** : sauter en parachute
bail[2] *n* **1** SECURITY : caution *f* **2 to release on bail** : mettre en liberté sous caution
bailiff |'beɪlif| *n* : huissier *m*
bailiwick |'beɪli,wɪk| *n* : domaine *m*
bait[1] |'beɪt| *vt* **1** : appâter, amorcer (un hameçon, etc.) **2** HARASS : harceler, tourmenter
bait[2] *n* : appât *m,* amorce *f*
bake |'beɪk| *v* **baked; baking** *vt* : faire cuire au four — *vi* : cuire au four
baker |'beɪkər| *n* : boulanger *m,* -gère *f*
bakery |'beɪkəri| *n, pl* **-ries** : boulangerie *f*
bakeshop |'beɪk,ʃɑp| → **bakery**
baking powder *n* : levure *f* chimique, poudre *f* à pâte *Can*
baking soda *n* : bicarbonate *m* de soude
balance[1] |'bæləntsl| *v* **-anced; -ancing** *vt* **1** ADJUST : équilibrer (un budget, des roues, etc.) **2** WEIGH : peser <to balance the pros and cons : peser le pour et le contre> **3** : mettre en équilibre, poser en équilibre <he balanced the book on his head : il a posé le livre en équilibre sur sa tête> **4** OFFSET : compenser, contrebalancer — *vi* : être en équilibre, s'équilibrer
balance[2] *n* **1** SCALES : balance *f* <to hang in the balance : être en jeu> **2** EQUILIBRIUM : équilibre *m* **3** REMAINDER : solde *m* (en finances), restant *m* **4** COUNTERBALANCE, WEIGHT : contrepoids *m*
balcony |'bælkəni| *n, pl* **-nies** : balcon *m*
bald |'bɔld| *adj* **1** HAIRLESS : chauve **2** BARREN : pelé <a bald mountain : une montagne pelée> **3** PLAIN : pur, simple <the bald truth : la vérité pure et simple>
bald eagle *n* : aigle *m* d'Amérique, aigle *m* à tête blanche
balding |'bɔldɪŋ| *adj* : qui devient chauve
baldly |'bɔldli| *adv* : franchement, sans détours
baldness |'bɔldnəs| *n* : calvitie *f*
bale[1] |'beɪl| *vt* **baled; baling** : mettre en balles, emballer
bale[2] *n* : balle *f*
baleful |'beɪlfəl| *adj* OMINOUS : menaçant, sinistre
balk[1] |'bɔk| *vt* THWART : contrecarrer, frustrer — *vi* **to balk at** : reculer devant, rechigner à
balk[2] *n* HINDRANCE : obstacle *m*
balky |'bɔki| **balkier; -est** *adj* : contrariant, entêté

ball[1] ['bɔl] *vt* : mettre en boule, pelotonner — *vi or* **to ball up** : s'agglomérer

ball[2] *n* **1** : balle *f,* ballon *m,* boule *f* <to play ball : jouer au ballon> **2** : pelote *f* (de ficelle, etc.) **3** DANCE : bal *m* **4 ball of the foot** : plante *f* du pied

ballad ['bæləd] *n* **1** : ballade *f*

ballast[1] ['bæləst] *vt* : lester

ballast[2] *n* : lest *m,* ballast *m*

ball bearing *n* : roulement *m* à billes

ballerina [ˌbælə'ri:nə] *n* : ballerine *f*

ballet [bæ'leɪ, 'bæˌleɪ] *n* : ballet *m*

ballistic [bə'lɪstɪk] *adj* : balistique <ballistic missile : engin balistique>

ballistics [bə'lɪstɪks] *ns & pl* : balistique *f*

balloon[1] [bə'lu:n] *vi* **1** : faire une ascension en ballon **2** SWELL : gonfler **3** INCREASE : augmenter (rapidement)

balloon[2] *n* **1** : ballon *m,* balloune *f Can* **2** *or* **hot–air balloon** : montgolfière *f*

ballot[1] ['bælət] *vt* : sonder par vote — *vi* : voter au scrutin

ballot[2] *n* **1** VOTE : vote *m* **2** VOTING : scrutin *m*

ballroom ['bɔlˌru:m, -ˌrʊm] *n* : salle *f* de danse, salle *f* de bal

balm ['bɑm, 'bɑlm] *n* : baume *m*

balmy ['bɑmi, 'bɑl-] *adj* **balmier; -est 1** MILD : doux <a balmy climate : un climat doux> **2** CRAZY : toqué *fam,* timbré *fam*

baloney [bə'lo:ni] *n* NONSENSE : balivernes *fpl*

balsa ['bɔlsə] *n* : balsa *m*

balsam ['bɔlsəm] *n* **1** : baume *m* **2** *or* **balsam fir** : balsamine *f*

balsamic vinegar [bɔl'sæmɪk-] *n* : vinaigre *m* balsamique

baluster ['bæləstər] *n* : balustre *m*

balustrade ['bæləˌstreɪd] *n* : balustrade *f*

bamboo [bæm'bu:] *n, pl* **-boos** : bambou *m*

bamboozle [bæm'bu:zəl] *vt* **-zled; -zling** : embobiner *fam,* faire emplir *Can*

ban[1] ['bæn] *vt* **banned; banning** : interdire, défendre

ban[2] *n* : interdiction *f*

banal [bə'nɑl, -'næl, 'beɪnəl] *adj* : banal

banality [bə'næləṭi] *n* : banalité *f*

banana [bə'nænə] *n* : banane *f*

band[1] ['bænd] *vt* **1** BIND : lier, attacher **2** *or* **to band together** UNITE : unir, réunir — *vi* **to band together** : se réunir, se grouper

band[2] *n* **1** STRIP : bande *f,* bandelette *f* **2** GROUP : groupe *m,* troupe *f* **3** : ruban *m* (d'un chapeau) **4** : bande *f* (de transmission) **5** : orchestre *m* **6** → **rubber band**

bandage[1] ['bændɪdʒ] *vt* : bander, mettre un pansement sur

bandage[2] *n* : pansement *m,* bandage *m*

bandanna *or* **bandana** [bæn'dænə] *n* : foulard *m*

bandit ['bændət] *n* : bandit *m*

banditry ['bændətri] *n* : banditisme *m*

bandstand ['bændˌstænd] *n* : kiosque *m* à musique

bandwagon ['bændˌwægən] *n* **to jump on the bandwagon** : suivre le mouvement, prendre le train en marche

bandy[1] ['bændi] *vt* **-died; -dying 1** EXCHANGE : échanger **2 to bandy about** : faire circuler, avancer (des idées)

bandy[2] *adj* : arqué <bandy legs : jambes arquées>

bane [beɪn] *n* **1** POISON : poison *m* **2** : fléau *m* <the bane of one's existence : le fléau de son existence>

bang[1] ['bæŋ] *vt* **1** SLAM : claquer **2** HIT, STRIKE : se cogner, se frapper <to bang one's head : se cogner la tête> <he banged his fists on the table : il a frappé ses poings sur la table>

bang[2] *adv* : exactement, en plein <bang in the middle : en plein milieu>

bang[3] *n* **1** : claquement *m* (d'une porte, etc.) **2** : détonation *f* (d'un fusil) **3** BLOW : coup *m* **4 bangs** *npl* : frange *f* (de cheveux)

Bangladeshi[1] [ˌbɑŋglə'dɛʃi, ˌbæŋ-, ˌbʌŋ-, -deɪ-] *adj* : bangladais

Bangladeshi[2] *n* : Bangladais *m,* -daise *f*

bangle ['bæŋgəl] *n* : bracelet *m*

banish ['bænɪʃ] *vt* **1** EXILE : exiler, bannir **2** EXPEL : expulser

banishment ['bænɪʃmənt] *n* **1** EXILE : exile *m,* bannissement *m* **2** EXPULSION : expulsion *f*

banister ['bænəstər] *n* **1** BALUSTER : balustre *m* **2** HANDRAIL : rampe *f* (d'escalier)

banjo ['bænˌdʒo:] *n, pl* **-jos** : banjo *m*

bank[1] ['bæŋk] *vt* **1** : déposer (de l'argent, des chèques) à la banque **2** *or* **to bank up** : relever (un virage) **3** : couvrir (un feu) — *vi* **1** : avoir un compte en banque **2** PILE UP : s'entasser, s'amonceler **3** TILT : s'incliner sur l'aile (se dit d'un avion) **4 to bank on** : compter sur

bank[2] *n* **1** EMBANKMENT : talus *m* **2** : bord *m,* rive *f* <left bank : rive gauche> <the bank of a road : le bord d'une rue> **3** SHOAL : banc *m* <sand bank : banc de sable> **4** : banque *f,* institution *f* bancaire **5 data bank** : banque *f* de données

bankbook ['bæŋkˌbʊk] *n* : carnet *m* de banque, livret *m* bancaire

banker ['bæŋkər] *n* : banquier *m*

banking ['bæŋkɪŋ] *n* **1** : opérations *fpl* bancaires **2** : profession *f* de banquier

banknote ['bæŋkˌno:t] *n* : billet *m* (de banque)

bankrupt[1] ['bæŋˌkrʌpt] *vt* : mettre en faillite, ruiner

bankrupt[2] *adj* **1** : failli **2** LACKING : dépourvu, dénué <bankrupt of ideas : dénué d'idées>
bankrupt[3] *n* : failli *m,* -lie *f*
bankruptcy ['bæŋ,krʌptsi] *n, pl* **-cies** : faillite *f*
banner[1] ['bænər] *adj* : record, excellent <a banner year : une année record>
banner[2] *n* : bannière *f,* étendard *m*
banns ['bænz] *npl* : bans *mpl* (de mariage)
banquet ['bæŋkwət] *n* : banquet *m,* festin *m*
bantam ['bæntəm] *n* : coq *m* nain, poule *f* naine
banter[1] ['bæntər] *vi* : badiner, plaisanter
banter[2] *n* : badinage *m,* plaisanterie *f*
baptism ['bæp,tɪzəm] *n* : baptême *m*
baptismal [bæp'tɪzməl] *adj* : de baptême, baptismal
baptize [bæp'taɪz, 'bæp,taɪz] *vt* **-tized; -tizing** : baptiser
bar[1] ['bar] *vt* **barred; barring 1** OBSTRUCT : barrer, bloquer **2** EXCLUDE : exclure **3** BAN, PROHIBIT : défendre, interdire **4** : mettre la barre à (une porte, etc.)
bar[2] *n* **1** ROD, STRIP : barre *f* (de métal), barreau *m* (d'une fenêtre) **2** : barre *f,* tablette *f* (de chocolat, etc.) **3** OBSTRUCTION : obstacle *m,* barrière *f* **4** : barreau *m* <to be admitted to the bar : s'inscrire au barreau> **5** BAND, STREAK : raie *f* (de lumière), bande *f* (de couleur) **6** COUNTER : comptoir *m* **7** CAFÉ, TAVERN : bar *m,* café *m* **8 behind bars** : sous les verrous
bar[3] *prep* **1** : excepté, sauf **2 bar none** : sans exception
barb ['barb] *n* **1** POINT : ardillon *m* (d'hameçon), barbe *f* (d'une plume) **2** GIBE : moquerie *f,* raillerie *f*
barbarian[1] [bar'bæriən] *adj* : barbare, de barbare
barbarian[2] *n* : barbare *mf*
barbaric [bar'bærɪk] *adj* : barbare
barbarism ['barbə,rɪzəm] *n* : barbarie *f*
barbarity [bar'bærəṭi] *n, pl* **-ties** : barbarie *f,* cruauté *f*
barbarous ['barbərəs] *adj* : barbare, cruel
barbarously ['barbərəsli] *adv* : d'une façon barbare, cruellement
barbecue[1] ['barbɪ,kju:] *vt* **-cued; -cuing** : griller au charbon de bois
barbecue[2] *n* : barbecue *m*
barbed [barbd] *adj* : barbelé <a barbed-wire fence : une haie barbelée>
barber ['barbər] *n* : coiffeur *m,* -feuse *f;* barbier *m*
barbiturate [bar'bɪtʃərət] *n* : barbiturique *m*
bard ['bard] *n* : barde *m,* poète *m*
bare[1] ['bær] *vt* **bared; baring 1** UNCOVER : mettre à nu, se découvrir (la tête) **2 to bare one's teeth** : montrer les dents
bare[2] *adj* **barer; barest 1** NAKED : nu **2** EXPOSED : découvert, nu **3** EMPTY : vide <the cupboard was bare : l'armoire était vide> **4** PLAIN, STRICT : strict <the bare minimum : le strict minimum> **5** MERE : simple <the bare statement of facts : le simple énoncé des faits>
bareback ['bær,bæk] *or* **barebacked** [-,bækt] *adv & adj* : à cru
barefaced ['bær,feɪst] *adj* : éhonté <barefaced lie : mensonge éhonté>
barefoot[1] ['bær,fʊt] *or* **barefooted** [-,fʊṭəd] *adv* : nu-pieds, pieds nus
barefoot[2] *or* **barefooted** *adj* : aux pieds nus, nu-pieds
bareheaded[1] ['bær,hɛdəd] *adv* : nu-tête, (la) tête nue
bareheaded[2] *adj* : à la tête nue
barely ['bærli] *adv* : à peine, tout juste
bareness ['bærnəs] *n* **1** NUDITY : nudité *f* **2** AUSTERITY : dépouillement *m*
bargain[1] ['bargən] *vi* **1** NEGOTIATE : négocier **2** HAGGLE : marchander
bargain[2] *n* **1** : occasion *f,* (bonne) affaire *f* <that's a real bargain : c'est une véritable occasion> **2** AGREEMENT : marché *m* <to strike a bargain : conclure un marché>
barge[1] ['bardʒ] *vi* **barged; barging 1** : se bousculer <they were barging through the crowd : ils se bousculaient à travers la foule> **2 to barge into** : faire irruption dans (une pièce, etc.), interrompre (une conversation)
barge[2] *n* : chaland *m,* péniche *f*
bar graph *n* : histogramme *m*
baritone ['bærə,to:n] *n* : baryton *m*
barium ['bæriəm] *n* : baryum *m*
bark[1] ['bark] *vi* **1** : aboyer (se dit d'un chien) **2** SHOUT : crier, gueuler *fam* — *vt or* **to bark out** : aboyer
bark[2] *n* **1** : écorce *f* (d'un arbre) **2** : aboiement *m* (d'un chien) **3** BOAT : barque *f*
barker ['barkər] *n* : bonimenteur *m* (à une foire)
barley ['barli] *n* : orge *f* (plante), orge *m* (grain)
barn ['barn] *n* : grange *f,* écurie *f* (de chevaux), étable *f* (de bovins)
barnacle ['barnɪkəl] *n* : anatife *m*
barnyard ['barn,jard] *n* : basse-cour *f*
barometer [bə'ramət̬ər] *n* : baromètre *m*
barometric ['bærə'mɛtrɪk] *adj* : barométrique
baron ['bærən] *n* : baron *m*
baroness ['bærənɪs, -nəs, -'nɛs] *n* : baronne *f*
baronet [,bærə'nɛt, 'bærənət] *n* : baronnet *m*
baronial [bə'ro:niəl] *adj* **1** : de baron **2** STATELY : imposant

baroque [bəˈroːk, -ˈrɑk] *adj* : baroque
barracks [ˈbærəks] *ns & pl* : caserne *f*
barracuda [ˌbærəˈkuːdə] *n, pl* **-da** *or* **-das** : barracuda *m*
barrage [bəˈrɑʒ, -ˈrɑdʒ] *n* **1** : tir *m* de barrage (en artillerie) **2** DELUGE : pluie *f*, déluge *m* (de questions, etc.)
barrel[1] [ˈbærəl] *v* **-reled** *or* **-relled; -reling** *or* **-relling** *vt* : mettre en tonneau — *vi or* **to barrel along** : foncer *fam*
barrel[2] *n* **1** : tonneau *m*, fût *m*, baril *m* **2** : canon *m* (d'une arme à feu)
barren [ˈbærən] *adj* **1** STERILE : stérile, infertile <barren plants : plantes stériles> **2** BARE, DESOLATE : désertique, aride **3** UNPRODUCTIVE : aride, stérile
barrenness [ˈbærənnəs] *n* : aridité *f*, stérilité *f*
barrette [bɑˈrɛt, bə-] *n* : barrette *f*
barricade[1] *vt* [ˈbærəˌkeɪd, ˌbærəˈ-] **-caded; -cading** : barricader
barricade[2] *n* : barricade *f*
barrier [ˈbæriər] *n* : barrière *f*
barring [ˈbɑrɪŋ] *prep* : excepté, sauf, à moins de
barroom [ˈbɑrˌruːm, -rʊm] *n* : bar *m*
barrow [ˈbærˌoː] → **wheelbarrow**
bartender [ˈbɑrˌtendər] *n* : barman *m*
barter[1] [ˈbɑrtər] *vt* : échanger, troquer — *vi* : faire un échange, faire un troc
barter[2] *n* : échange *m*, troc *m*
basalt [bəˈsɔlt, ˈbeɪˌ-] *n* : basalte *m*
base[1] [ˈbeɪs] *vt* **based; basing 1** FOUND : baser, fonder (une opinion, un calcul, etc.) **2** LOCATE : baser
base[2] *adj* **baser; basest 1** CONTEMPTIBLE : bas, vil **2 base metal** : métal *m* non précieux
base[3] *n, pl* **bases 1** BOTTOM : base *f*, pied *m* **2** BASIS : fondement *m*, base *f*, point *m* de départ **3** *or* **army base** : base *f* militaire **4** : but *m Can* (au baseball)
baseness [ˈbeɪsnəs] *n* : bassesse *f*, vilenie *f*
baseball [ˈbeɪsˌbɔl] *n* : baseball *m*, baseball *m*
baseless [ˈbeɪsləs] *adj* : sans fondement
basely [ˈbeɪsli] *adv* : bassement, vilement
basement [ˈbeɪsmənt] *n* : sous-sol *m*
bash[1] [ˈbæʃ] *vt* **1** HIT : cogner, frapper **2 to bash in** SMASH : enfoncer, défoncer
bash[2] *n* **1** BLOW : coup *m* **2** PARTY : fête *f*
bashful [ˈbæʃfəl] *adj* SHY : timide, gêné *Can*
bashfulness [ˈbæʃfəlnəs] *n* : timidité *f*
basic [ˈbeɪsɪk] *adj* **1** : fondamental, de base <basic principle : principe fondamental> **2** : basique <basic salt : sel basique>
basically [ˈbeɪsɪkli] *adv* : au fond, fondamentalement
basil [ˈbeɪzel, ˈbæzəl] *n* : basilic *m*
basilica [bəˈsɪlɪkə] *n* : basilique *f*
basin [ˈbeɪsən] *n* **1** WASHBOWL : cuvette *f*, lavabo *m* **2** : bassin *m* (d'un fleuve)
basis [ˈbeɪsəs] *n, pl* **bases 1** BASE : base *f*, fondement *m* **2** PRINCIPLE : condition *f*, terme *m* <on that basis : dans ces conditions> **3 on a weekly basis** : à la semaine
bask [ˈbæsk] *vi* **1** : se prélasser (au soleil, etc.) **2** REVEL : se délecter
basket [ˈbæskət] *n* : corbeille *f*, panier *m*
basketball [ˈbæskətˌbɔl] *n* **1** : basket *m*, basket-ball *m*, basketball *m*, ballon-panier *m Can* (jeu) **2** : ballon *m* de basket <lancer un ballon de basket : to throw a basketball>
bas–relief [ˌbɑrɪˈliːf] *n* : bas-relief *m*
bass[1] [ˈbæs] *n, pl* **bass** *or* **basses 1** : perche *f*, bar *m* (pêche) **2** *or* **black bass** : achigan *m Can*
bass[2] [ˈbeɪs] *n* : basse *f* (voix, instrument)
basset hound [ˈbæsətˌhaʊnd] *n* : basset *m*
bassinet [ˌbæsəˈnɛt] *n* : berceau *m*, bercelonnette *f*
bassoon [bəˈsuːn, bæ-] *n* : basson *m*
bastard[1] [ˈbæstərd] *adj* : bâtard
bastard[2] *n* **1** : bâtard *m*, -tarde *f* **2** JERK : salaud *m*
bastardize [ˈbæstərˌdaɪz] *vt* **-ized; -izing** DEBASE : corrompre, abâtardir
baste [ˈbeɪst] *vt* **basted; basting 1** : faufiler, bâtir (en couture) **2** : arroser (un rôti, etc.)
bastion [ˈbæstʃən] *n* : bastion *m*
bat[1] [ˈbæt] *v* **batted; batting** *vt* **1** HIT : frapper (une balle) **2 without batting an eye** : sans sourciller — *vi* : manier la batte (au cricket)
bat[2] *n* **1** : batte *f*, bâton *m Can* <baseball bat : batte de baseball> **2** STROKE : coup *m* (au cricket) **3** : chauve-souris *f* (animal)
batch [ˈbætʃ] *n* **1** : fournée *f* <a batch of bread : une fournée de pain> **2** QUANTITY : liasse *f* (de papiers, etc.), lot *m* (de marchandises)
bate [ˈbeɪt] *vt* **bated; bating 1** REDUCE : réduire, diminuer **2 with bated breath** : en retenant son souffle
bath [ˈbæθ, ˈbaθ] *n, pl* **baths 1** : bain *m* <to take a bath : prendre un bain> **2** BATHROOM : salle *f* de bains **3** LOSS : perte *f* <he took a bath in the market : il a subi des pertes sur le marché>
bathe [ˈbeɪð] *v* **bathed; bathing** *vt* : baigner, laver — *vi* : se baigner, prendre un bain
bather [ˈbeɪðər] *n* : baigneur *m*, -gneuse *f*
bathrobe [ˈbæθˌroːb] *n* : peignoir *m* (de bain), robe *f* de chambre

bathroom ['bæθ,ru:m, -,rʊm] *n* **1** : salle *f* de bains **2 to go to the bathroom** : aller aux toilettes

bathtub ['bæθ,tʌb] *n* : baignoire *f*

batiste [bə'ti:st] *n* : batiste *f*

baton [bə'tɑn] *n* : bâton *m*

battalion [bə'tæljən] *n* : bataillon *m*

batten ['bætən] *vt* **to batten down the hatches** : fermer les écoutilles

batter[1] ['bæţər] *vt* BEAT : battre, frapper

batter[2] *n* **1** : pâte *f* <pancake batter : pâte à crêpes> **2** : batteur *m* (au baseball)

battered ['bæţərd] *adj* : cabossé <a battered old hat : un vieux chapeau cabossé>

battering ram *n* : bélier *m*

battery ['bæţəri] *n, pl* **-teries 1** : pile *f* (d'une radio, etc.), batterie *f* (d'un véhicule) **2** : batterie *f* (d'artillerie) **3** SERIES : série *f*, batterie *f* <a battery of tests : une batterie d'examens> **4** → **assault**

batting ['bæţɪŋ] *n* **1** *or* **cotton batting** : ouate *f*, bourre *f* **2** : maniement *m* de la batte (aux sports)

battle[1] ['bæţəl] *v* **-tled; -tling** *vi* : lutter, se battre — *vt* : lutter contre

battle[2] *n* **1** FIGHT : bataille *f*, combat *m* **2** STRUGGLE : lutte *f*

battle–ax ['bæţəl,æks] *n* : hache *f* d'armes

battlefield ['bæţəl,fi:ld] *n* : champ *m* de bataille

battlement ['bæţəlmənt] *n* : rempart *m*, créneau *m*

battleship ['bæţəl,ʃɪp] *n* : cuirassé *m*

batty ['bæţi] *adj* **battier; battiest** : toqué *fam*, fou

bauble ['bɔbəl] *n* : babiole *f*

bawdiness ['bɔdinəs] *n* : paillardise *f*

bawdy ['bɔdi] *adj* **bawdier; -est** : paillard, grivois

bawl ['bɔl] *vi* : brailler *fam*

bawl out *vt* : engueuler *fam*

bay[1] ['beɪ] *vi* : aboyer

bay[2] *adj* : bai (se dit d'un cheval)

bay[3] *n* **1** INLET : baie *f*, golfe *m* **2** *or* **bay horse** : cheval *m* bai **3** LAUREL : laurier *m* **4** BAYING : aboiement *m* (d'un chien, etc.) **5** AREA : aire *f* <cargo bay : aire de chargement> **6 to be at bay** : être aux abois

bayberry ['beɪ,bɛri] *n, pl* **-ries** : baie *f* de laurier

bayonet[1] [,beɪə'nɛt, 'beɪə,nɛt] *vt* **-neted; -neting** : passer à la baïonnette

bayonet[2] *n* : baïonnette *f*

bayou ['baɪ,u:, -,o] *n* : bayou *m*

bay window *n* : fenêtre *m* en saillie

bazaar [bə'zɑr] *n* **1** : bazar *m* **2** SALE : vente *f* (de charité)

bazooka [bə'zu:kə] *n* : bazooka *m*

BB ['bi:bi:] *n* **1** : plomb *m* **2 BB gun** : carabine *f* à air comprimé

be ['bi:] *v* **was** ['wəz, 'wɑz], **were** ['wər]; **been** ['bɪn]; **being; am** ['æm], **is** ['ɪz], **are** ['ɑr] *vi* **1** (*expressing an attribute*) : être <the sky is blue : le ciel est bleu> **2** (*expressing a state*) : être, avoir <he is healthy : il est en bonne santé> <I'm hot : j'ai chaud> **3** (*expressing age*) : avoir <how old is he? : quel âge a-t-il?> **4** (*expressing origin*) : être <she is from Canada : elle est canadienne> **5** LIVE : être, exister <I think, therefore I am : je pense, donc je suis> **6** (*expressing location*) : être, se trouver <the cottage is on a lake : la villa se trouve au bord d'un lac> **7** (*expressing equality*) : faire, égaler <two and two are four : deux et deux font quatre> **8** (*expressing health or well-being*) : aller, se porter <how are you? : comment allez-vous?> **9** (*expressing cost*) : coûter <meat is very expensive : la viande coûte très cher> — *v aux* **1** : être en train de <he is reading : il lit, il est en train de lire> **2** (*indicating obligation*) : devoir <you are to come when called : tu dois venir quand on t'appelle> **3** (*used in passive constructions*) : être <the doors had been locked : les portes avaient été barrées> — *v impers* **1** (*indicating weather*) : faire <it's nice out : il fait beau> **2** (*indicating time*) : être <it's ten o'clock : il est dix heures> <it's late : il est tard>

beach[1] ['bi:tʃ] *vt* : échouer (un bateau)

beach[2] *n* : plage *f*, grève *f*

beachhead ['bi:tʃ,hɛd] *n* : tête *f* de pont

beacon ['bi:kən] *n* : phare *m*, signal *m* lumineux

bead[1] ['bi:d] *vt* STRING : enfiler — *vi* : perler (se dit d'un liquide)

bead[2] *n* **1** : perle *f*, grain *m* <rosary beads : grains d'un chapelet> **2** DROP : goutte *f*, perle *f* **3 beads** *npl* NECKLACE : collier *m*

beady ['bi:di] *adj* **beadier; -est** : perçant, brillant

beagle ['bi:gəl] *n* : beagle *m*

beak ['bi:k] *n* : bec *m*

beaker ['bi:kər] *n* **1** CUP : gobelet *m* **2** : vase *f* à bec (en chimie)

beam[1] ['bi:m] *vt* : transmettre, diffuser (une émission) — *vi* **1** SHINE : rayonner **2** SMILE : sourire d'un air radieux

beam[2] *n* **1** : poutre *f* (de bois) **2** RAY : rayon *m* **3** *or* **radio beam** : faisceau *m* de guidage **4** SMILE : grand sourire *m*

bean ['bi:n] *n* **1** : haricot *m* <green bean : haricot vert> **2** : grain *m* (de café) **3** → **broad bean**

bear[1] ['bær] *v* **bore** ['bor]; **borne** ['bɔrn]; **bearing** *vt* **1** CARRY : porter, transporter **2** PRODUCE : produire, porter <a fruit-bearing tree : un arbre qui

produit des fruits> **3** : donner naissance *f* à (un enfant) **4** ENDURE : supporter, tolérer <he doesn't bear pain well : il ne supporte pas bien la douleur> — *vi* **1** : diriger, prendre <bear right : prenez à droite> **2 to bear down on** : exercer une pression sur **3 to bear with** : patienter **4 to bear in mind** : ne pas oublier

bear[2] *n, pl* **bears** *or* **bear** : ours *m*, ourse *f*

bearable [ˈbærəbəl] *adj* : supportable, tolérable

beard[1] [ˈbɪrd] *vt* DEFY : affronter, braver

beard[2] *n* **1** : barbe *f* (d'un homme), barbiche *f* (d'une chèvre) **2** TUFT : barbe *f* (d'une plante)

bearded [ˈbɪrdəd] *adj* : barbu, à barbe

bearer [ˈbærər] *n* **1** : porteur *m*, -teuse *f* **2** : titulaire *mf* (d'un passeport)

bearing [ˈbærɪŋ] *n* **1** MANNER : allure *f*, maintien *m* **2** SIGNIFICANCE : relation *f*, rapport *m* <to have no bearing : n'avoir aucun rapport> **3** COURSE, DIRECTION : orientation *f*, direction *f* <I've lost my bearings : je suis désorienté> **4** → **ball bearing**

bearish [ˈbærɪʃ] *adj* : rude, bourru

beast [ˈbi:st] *n* **1** : bête *f*, animal *m* **2** BRUTE : brute *f* (personne)

beastly [ˈbi:stli] *adj* **beastlier; -est 1** BRUTAL : bestial, brutal **2** NASTY : sale <what beastly weather! : quel sale temps!>

beat[1] [ˈbi:t] *v* **beat; beaten** [ˈbi:tən] *or* **beat; beating** *vt* **1** STRIKE : battre, frapper **2** DEFEAT : vaincre, battre <to beat one's competitors : devancer la compétition> <to beat s.o. up the hill : arriver au sommet avant qqn> <it beats me! : ça me dépasse!> **3** AVOID : éviter <to beat the crowds : éviter la foule> **4** MASH, WHIP : battre (des œufs, des pommes de terre, etc.) — *vi* THROB : battre, palpiter <with beating heart : le cœur battant>

beat[2] *adj* EXHAUSTED : éreinté, crevé *fam*

beat[3] *n* **1** BEATING : battement *m* <the beat of a drum : le battement d'un tambour> **2** RHYTHM : rythme *m*, temps *m*

beater [ˈbi:t̬ər] → **eggbeater**

beatific [ˌbi:əˈtɪfɪk] *adj* : béatifique

beating [ˈbitɪŋ] *n* **1** : battement *m* (de cœur, d'un tambour, etc.) **2** THRASHING : correction *f*, raclée *f fam* **3** DEFEAT : défaite *f*

beatitude [biˈæt̬əˌtu:d] *n* **1** : béatitude *f* **2 the Beatitudes** : les béatitudes

beau [ˈbo] *n, pl* **beaux** *or* **beaus** : galant *m*

beauteous [ˈbju:t̬iəs] → **beautiful**

beautician [bju:ˈtɪʃən] *n* : esthéticien *m*, -cienne *f*

beautiful [ˈbju:t̬ɪfəl] *adj* **1** : beau <a beautiful woman : une belle femme> **2** SPLENDID : magnifique, merveilleux

beautifully [ˈbju:t̬ɪfəli] *adv* **1** ATTRACTIVELY : admirablement, à la perfection **2** SPLENDIDLY : parfaitement, merveilleusement <that will do beautifully : cela convient parfaitement>

beautify [ˈbju:t̬ɪˌfaɪ] *vt* **-fied; -fying** : embellir, orner

beauty [ˈbju:t̬i] *n, pl* **-ties** : beauté *f*

beauty shop *n or* **beauty salon** : salon *m* de beauté

beaver [ˈbi:vər] *n* : castor *m*

because [biˈkʌz, -ˈkɔz] *conj* : parce que

because of *prep* : à cause de

beck [ˈbɛk] *n* **to be at the beck and call of** : obéir au doigt et à l'œil à

beckon [ˈbɛkən] *vt* : faire signe à, attirer — *vi* : faire signe

become [biˈkʌm] *v* **-came** [-ˈkeɪm]; **-come; -coming** *vt* SUIT : aller à, convenir à <the moustache doesn't become him : la moustache ne lui va pas> — *vi* : devenir <what's become of him? : qu'est-ce qu'il est devenu?> <they became friends : elles sont devenues amies>

becoming [biˈkʌmɪŋ] *adj* **1** SUITABLE : convenable, correct <becoming modesty : modestie convenable> **2** FLATTERING : seyant <a becoming hat : un chapeau seyant>

bed[1] [ˈbɛd] *vt* **bedded; bedding 1** : coucher **2** *or* **to bed out** : repiquer (des plantes)

bed[2] *n* **1** : lit *m* <to go to bed : se coucher, se mettre au lit> <to get out of bed : se lever> **2** LAYER : couche *f*, gisement *m* **3** BOTTOM : fond *m* (de la mer), lit *m* (d'un fleuve)

bedbug [ˈbɛdˌbʌg] *n* : punaise *f* de lit

bedclothes [ˈbɛdˌklo:ðz, -ˌklo:z] *npl* : draps *mpl* et couvertures *fpl*

bedding [ˈbɛdɪŋ] *n* **1** → **bedclothes 2** : litière *f* (pour les animaux)

bedeck [bɪˈdɛk] *vt* : parer, orner

bedevil [bɪˈdɛvəl] *vt* **-iled** *or* **-illed; -iling** *or* **-illing 1** PLAGUE : tourmenter, harceler **2** BEWILDER : déconcerter, embrouiller

bedlam [ˈbɛdləm] *n* UPROAR : chahut *m*, charivari *m*

bedraggled [bɪˈdrægəld] *adj* : débraillé, désordonné

bedridden [ˈbɛdˌrɪdən] *adj* : alité, cloué au lit

bedrock [ˈbɛdˌrɑk] *n* **1** : soubassement *m* (en géologie) **2** BASIS : base *f*, fondation *f*

bedroom [ˈbɛdˌru:m, -ˌrʊm] *n* : chambre *f* (à coucher)

bedsheet → **sheet**

bedspread [ˈbɛdˌsprɛd] *n* : couvre-lit *m*

bee [ˈbi:] *n* **1** : abeille *f* **2** GATHERING : groupe *m*, club *m* <sewing bee : groupe de couture>

beech |ˈbiːtʃ| *n, pl* **beeches** *or* **beech** : hêtre *m*

beechnut |ˈbiːtʃˌnʌt| *n* : faine *f*

beef[1] |ˈbiːf| *vt or* **to beef up** : renforcer, étoffer (un discours, etc.) — *vi* COMPLAIN : se plaindre, rouspéter *fam*

beef[2] *n* **1** : bœuf *m* <roast beef : rôti de bœuf> **2** *pl* **beefs** |ˈbiːfs| *or* **beeves** |ˈbiːvz| STEER : bœuf *m*

beefsteak |ˈbifˌsteɪk| *n* : bifteck *m*

beehive |ˈbiːˌhaɪv| *n* : ruche *f*

beekeeper |ˈbiːˌkiːpər| *n* : apiculteur *m*, -trice *f*

beeline |ˈbiːˌlaɪn| *n* : ligne *f* droite <to make a beeline for : se diriger tout droit vers>

been → **be**

beep[1] |ˈbiːp| *vi* : klaxonner (se dit d'une voiture), faire bip (se dit d'un appareil électronique)

beep[2] *n* : coup *m* de klaxon, bip *m*

beeper |ˈbiːpər| *n* : récepteur *m* de radiomessagerie *f*, téléavertisseur *m Can*

beer |ˈbɪr| *n* : bière *f*

beeswax |ˈbiːzˌwæks| *n* : cire *f* d'abeille

beet |ˈbiːt| *n* : betterave *f*

beetle |ˈbiːt̬əl| *n* : scarabée *m*

befall |bɪˈfɔl| *v* **-fell** |-ˈfɛl| ; **-fallen** |-ˈfɔlən| *vt* : arriver à <a misfortune befell her : il lui arriva un malheur> — *vi* HAPPEN : arriver, advenir

befit |bɪˈfɪt| *vt* **-fitted; -fitting** : convenir à

before[1] |bɪˈfor| *adv* **1** AHEAD : devant, en avant <marching on before : marchant devant> **2** PREVIOUSLY : avant <before and after : avant et après> <long before : bien avant> **3** EARLIER : en avance, avant <come at six o'clock, not before : viens à six heures, pas avant>

before[2] *prep* **1** : devant, en présence de <before the court : devant le tribunal> **2** : avant <before long : avant longtemps> **3** ABOVE : avant, plutôt que <he puts quantity before quality : il préfère la quantité plutôt que la qualité> **4 before my eyes** : sous mes yeux

before[3] *conj* **1** : avant de, avant que <before going : avant de partir> <before you go : avant que tu partes> **2** : plutôt que de <he would die before surrendering : il mourrait plutôt que de se rendre>

beforehand |bɪˈforˌhænd| *adv* : d'avance, à l'avance, au préalable

befriend |bɪˈfrɛnd| *vt* : se lier d'amitié avec

befuddle |bɪˈfʌdəl| *vt* **-dled; -dling** : brouiller les idées de, embrouiller

beg |ˈbɛg| *v* **begged; begging** *vt* **1** : mendier (la charité, la nourriture) **2** REQUEST, SOLICIT : demander, solliciter **3** ENTREAT : supplier, prier <I beg your mercy : je vous prie grâce> — *vi* **1** : mendier **2** : faire le beau (se dit d'un chien)

beget |bɪˈgɛt| *vt* **-got** |-gɑt|; **-gotten** |-gɑtən| *or* **-got; -getting** : engendrer

beggar |ˈbɛgər| *n* : mendiant *m*, -diante *f;* quêteux *m*, -teuse *f*

begin |bɪˈgɪn| *v* **-gan** |-ˈgæn|; **-gun** |-ˈgʌn|; **-ginning** *vt* **1** START : commencer, débuter **2** FOUND : inaugurer, fonder — *vi* **1** START : commencer **2** ORIGINATE : débuter, être fondé **3 to begin with** FIRST : d'abord

beginner |bɪˈgɪnər| *n* : débutant *m*, -tante *f*

beginning |bɪˈgɪnɪŋ| *n* : début *m*, commencement *m*

begone |biˈgɔn| *interj* : va-t-en!

begonia |bɪˈgoːnjə| *n* : bégonia *m*

begrudge |bɪˈgrʌdʒ| *vt* **-grudged; -grudging 1** : en vouloir à, accorder à regret **2** ENVY : envier

beguile |bɪˈgaɪl| *vt* **-guiled; -guiling 1** DECEIVE : tromper, duper **2** CHARM : séduire **3 to beguile (away) the time** : faire passer le temps agréablement

behalf |bɪˈhæf, -ˈhaf| *n* **1** INTEREST : défense *f*, sujet *m* <he argued in our behalf : il a argumenté pour notre défense> <in my behalf : à mon sujet> **2 on behalf of** : de la part de, au nom de

behave |bɪˈheɪv| *vi* **-haved; -having** : se conduire, se comporter

behavior *or Brit* **behaviour** |bɪˈheɪvjər| *n* : conduite *f*, comportement *m*

behead |bɪˈhɛd| *vt* : décapiter

behest |bɪˈhɛst| *n* **1** : demande *f*, instance *f* **2 at the behest of** : sur l'ordre de

behind[1] |bɪˈhaɪnd| *adv* **1** BACK : derrière, en arrière <I looked behind : j'ai regardé en arrière> <from behind : par derrière> **2** LATE : en retard <she's behind in her work : elle est en retard dans son travail>

behind[2] *prep* **1** : derrière, en arrière de <behind the building : derrière l'édifice> **2** : en retard sur <behind the times : en retard sur son temps> **3** SUPPORTING : soutenant <to be behind s.o. : soutenir qqn>

behold |bɪˈhoːld| *vt* **-held; -holding** : voir, apercevoir

beholder |bɪˈhoːldər| *n* : spectateur *m*, -trice *f*

behoove |bɪˈhuːv| *vt* **-hooved; -hooving** : incomber à, être de l'intérêt de

beige[1] |ˈbeɪʒ| *adj* : beige

beige[2] *n* : beige *m*

being |ˈbiːɪŋ| *n* **1** : être *m*, créature *f* **2** EXISTENCE : existence *f*

belabor *or Brit* **belabour** |bɪˈleɪbər| *vt* **to belabor the point** : insister sur le point

belated |bɪˈleɪt̬əd| *adj* : tardif

belch[1] |ˈbɛltʃ| *vi* BURP : faire un renvoi, roter *fam* — *vt* : vomir, cracher <to

belch (out) smoke : cracher de la fumée>
belch[2] *n* : renvoi *m*, rot *m fam*
beleaguer |bɪ'li:gər| *vt* **1** BESIEGE : assiéger **2** HARASS : harceler, assaillir
belfry |'bɛlfri| *n, pl* **-fries** : beffroi *m*, clocher *m*
Belgian[1] |'bɛldʒən| *adj* : belge
Belgian[2] *n* : Belge *mf*
belie |bɪ'laɪ| *vt* **-lied; -lying 1** MISREPRESENT : donner une fausse idée de **2** CONTRADICT : démentir, contredire
belief |bə'li:f| *n* **1** OPINION : croyance *f*, conviction *f* **2** TRUST : confiance *f* **3** FAITH : foi *f*, confession *f*
believe |bə'li:v| *v* **-lieved; -lieving** *vt* **1** : croire <she believes the reports : elle croit les reportages> **2** SUPPOSE : croire, estimer, penser <I believe it will rain : je crois qu'il va pleuvoir> — *vi* : croire <he believes in God : il croit en Dieu>
believable |bə'li:vəbəl| *adj* : croyable, crédible
believer |bə'li:vər| *n* **1** : croyant *m*, croyante *f* (en religion) **2** SUPPORTER : partisan *m*, -sane *f*; adepte *mf*
belittle |bɪ'lɪṭəl| *vt* **-littled; -littling** : déprécier, rabaisser
Belizean[1] |bə'li:ziən| *adj* : bélizien
Belizean[2] *n* : Bélizien *m*, -zienne *f*
bell |'bɛl| *n* **1** : cloche *f*, clochette *f* **2** : sonnette *f* (d'une porte, etc.)
belladonna |,bɛlə'dɑnə| *n* : belladone *f*
belle |'bɛl| *n* : beauté *f*, belle *f* <the belle of the ball : la reine du bal>
bellhop |'bɛl,hɑp| *n* : chasseur *m*
bellicose |'bɛlɪ,ko:s| *adj* : belliqueux, guerrier
belligerence |bə'lɪdʒərənts| *or* **belligerency** |bə'lɪdʒərəntsi| *n* : belligérance *f*
belligerent |bə'lɪdʒərənt| *adj* : belligérant
bellow[1] |'bɛ,lo:| *vt* : brailler *fam* — *vi* **1** : beugler, mugir **2** HOWL, SHOUT : brailler *fam*, hurler
bellow[2] *n* **1** : beuglement *m*, mugissement *m* **2** HOWL : hurlement *m*
bellows |'bɛ,lo:z| *ns & pl* : soufflet *m*
bellwether |'bɛl,wɛðər| *n* LEADER : dirigeant *m*, -geante *f*; chef *m*
belly[1] |'bɛli| *vi* **-lied; -lying** SWELL, BULGE : se gonfler, bomber
belly[2] *n, pl* **-lies** : ventre *m*
belong |bɪ'lɔŋ| *vi* **1 to belong to** : appartenir à, être à <it belongs to me : c'est à moi> **2** : être à sa place, aller <put it back where it belongs : remets-le à sa place> <where does it belong? : où va-t-il?> **3** : être membre, faire partie <he belongs to the athletic club : il fait partie du cercle sportif>
belongings |bɪ'lɔŋɪŋz| *npl* : affaires *fpl*, possessions *fpl*, effets *mpl* <personal belongings : effets personnels>
beloved[1] |bɪ'lʌvəd, -'lʌvd| *adj* : bienaimé, chéri
beloved[2] *n* : bien-aimé *m*, -mée *f*; chéri *m*, -rie *f*
below[1] |bɪ'lo:| *adv* : en dessous, en bas, plus bas
below[2] *prep* **1** : sous, au-dessous de, en dessous de <below the surface : sous la surface> <below average : au-dessous de la moyenne **2** : au-dessous de, inférieur à <temperatures below normal : températures inférieures à la normale>
belt[1] |'bɛlt| *vt* **1** : mettre une ceinture à (des pantalons, etc.) **2** THRASH : donner un coup à
belt[2] *n* **1** : ceinture *f* <safety belt : ceinture de sécurité> **2** : courroie *f* (d'une machine) <courroie de ventilateur : fan belt> **3** AREA : zone *f*, région *f*
bemoan |bɪ'mo:n| *vt* : déplorer, se lamenter sur
bemuse |bɪ'mju:z| *vt* **-mused; -musing 1** BEWILDER : déconcerter, rendre perplexe **2** ENGROSS : absorber
bench |'bɛntʃ| *n* **1** : banc *m*, banquette *f* **2** : cour *f*, tribunal *m* <to appear before the bench : comparaître devant le tribunal> **3** → **workbench**
bend[1] |'bɛnd| *v* **bent** |'bɛnt|; **bending** *vt* **1** : plier, courber, fléchir <to bend one's arm : plier le bras> <bend your head : baissez ta tête> **2** DIRECT : diriger <to bend one's step toward : se diriger vers> **3** DISTORT, TWIST : tordre, crochir *Can*, travestir (la vérité) <to bend the rules : contourner les règlements> — *vi* **1** : se courber, se pencher, plier **2** TURN : tourner, faire un coude
bend[2] *n* **1** BENDING : pli *m*, flexion *f* **2** CURVE, TURN : tournant *m*, virage *m*, coude *m* **3 bends** *npl* : maladie *f* des caissons
beneath[1] |bɪ'ni:θ| *adv* : au-dessous, dessous, en bas
beneath[2] *prep* **1** UNDER : sous, en dessous de <beneath the bed : sous le lit> **2** : indigne de <the work is beneath him : le travail est indigne de lui>
benediction |,bɛnə'dɪkʃən| *n* : bénédiction *f*
benefactor |'bɛnə,fæktər| *n* : bienfaiteur *m*, -trice *f*
beneficence |bə'nɛfəsənts| *n* : bienfaisance *f*
beneficent |bə'nɛfəsənt| *adj* : bienfaisant, généreux
beneficial |,bɛnə'fɪʃəl| *adj* : avantageux, salutaire, favorable
beneficially |,bɛnə'fɪʃəli| *adv* : avantageusement
beneficiary |,bɛnə'fɪʃi,ɛri, -'fɪʃəri| *n, pl* **-ries** : bénéficiaire *mf*
benefit[1] |'bɛnəfɪt| *vt* : faire du bien à, profiter à, être avantageux pour — *vi* : profiter, faire du bien, tirer avantage

benefit[2] *n* **1** : avantage *m* <it's to your benefit : c'est à votre avantage> <fringe benefits : avantages sociaux> **2** : allocation *f* <unemployment benefit : allocation de chômage>
benevolence |bəˈnɛvələnts| *n* : bienveillance *f*, charité *f*
benevolent |bəˈnɛvələnt| *adj* : bienveillant
benevolently |bəˈnɛvələntli| *adv* : avec bienveillance
Bengali[1] |bɛnˈgɔli, bɛŋ-| *adj* : bengali
Bengali[2] *n* **1** : bengali *m* (langue) **2** : Bengali *mf*
benign |bɪˈnaɪn| *adj* **1** KINDLY : bienveillant, affable, gentil **2** : bénin (en médecine) **3** MILD : doux
Beninese[1] |bəˌnɪˈniːz, -ˌniː-, -ˈniːs; ˌbɛnɪ-| *adj* : béninois
Beninese[2] *n* : Béninois *m*, -noise *f*
bent[1] |ˈbɛnt| *adj* **1** CURVED : tordu, courbé **2 to be bent on doing** : être décidé à faire
bent[2] *n* : aptitude *f*, dispositions *fpl*, penchant *m*
benumb |bɪˈnʌm| *vt* : engourdir, endormir
benzene |ˈbɛnˌziːn| *n* : benzène *m*
bequeath |bɪˈkwiːθ, -kwiːð| *vt* : léguer
bequest |bɪˈkwɛst| *n* : legs *m*
berate |bɪˈreɪt| *vt* **-rated; -rating** : réprimander
bereaved[1] |bɪˈriːvd| *adj* : endeuillé, attristé
bereaved[2] *ns & pl* **the bereaved** : la famille du défunt
bereavement |bɪˈriːvmənt| *n* : deuil *m*
bereft |bɪˈrɛft| *adj* : privé, dénué <bereft of hope : désespérée>
beret |bəˈreɪ| *n* : béret *m*
beriberi |ˌbɛriˈbɛri| *n* : béribéri *m*
berry |ˈbɛri| *n, pl* **-ries** : baie *f*
berserk |bərˈsərk, -ˈzərk| *adj* **1** : fou, enragé **2 to go berserk** : être pris de folie furieuse
berth[1] |ˈbərθ| *vt* : amarrer, donner un poste d'amarrage à — *vi* : mouiller l'ancre, s'amarrer
berth[2] *n* **1** ANCHORAGE : mouillage *m*, poste *m* d'amarrage **2** BUNK : couchette *f* **3 to give s.o. a wide berth** : éviter qqn
beryl |ˈbɛrəl| *n* : béryl *m*
beseech |bɪˈsiːtʃ| *vt* **-seeched** *or* **-sought** |-ˈsɔt|; **-seeching** : supplier, implorer
beset |bɪˈsɛt| *vt* **-set; -setting 1** ASSAIL, HARASS : assaillir, harceler <beset with doubts : assailli de doutes> **2** SURROUND : encercler
beside |bɪˈsaɪd| *prep* **1** : à côté de, près de **2 to be beside oneself** : être hors de soi
besides[1] |bɪˈsaɪdz| *adv* **1** : de plus, en outre <nothing besides : rien de plus> **2** MOREOVER : d'ailleurs, du reste <besides, I like him : d'ailleurs, je l'aime>
besides[2] *prep* **1** : en plus de, outre <besides being rich, he's handsome : outre qu'il est riche, il est beau> **2** EXCEPT : sauf, hormis <no one besides me : personne hormis moi>
besiege |bɪˈsiːdʒ| *vt* **-sieged; -sieging** : assiéger, encercler
besmirch |bɪˈsmərtʃ| *vt* : souiller, entacher
besought → **beseech**
best[1] |ˈbɛst| *vt* OUTDO : l'emporter sur, vaincre
best[2] *adv* (*superlative of* **well**) : le mieux, le plus <the best dressed man : l'homme le mieux habillé> <the best known actress : l'actrice la plus connue>
best[3] *adj* (*superlative of* **good**) **1** : meilleur <the best student : le meilleur élève> **2** : plus beau <her best dress : sa plus belle robe>
best[4] *n* **1** : meilleur *m*, -leure *f* <she's the best : elle est la meilleure> **2** : mieux *m* <all for the best : tout pour le mieux> **3 to do one's best** : faire tout son possible
bestial |ˈbɛstʃəl, ˈbiːs-| *adj* : bestial
bestir |biˈstər| *vt* **-stirred; -stirring 1** : activer, pousser à agir **2 to bestir oneself** : s'activer, s'agiter
best man *n* : garçon *m* d'honneur, témoin *m*
bestow |bɪˈstoː| *vt* : accorder, conférer
bet[1] |ˈbɛt| *v* **bet; betting** *vt* : parier, miser, gager *Can* — *vi* **to bet on** : parier sur
bet[2] *n* : pari *m*, gageure *f Can*
betoken |bɪˈtoːkən| *vt* : présager, annoncer, être l'indice de
betray |bɪˈtreɪ| *vt* **1** DECEIVE : trahir, tromper **2** REVEAL : révéler, laisser voir, divulguer (un secret, etc.)
betrayal |bɪˈtreɪəl| *n* **1** : trahison *f* **2 betrayal of trust** : abus *m* de confiance
betrothal |bɪˈtroːðəl, -ˈtrɔ-| *n* : fiançailles *fpl*
betrothed |bɪˈtroːðd, -trɔθt| *n* : fiancé *m*, -cée *f*
better[1] |ˈbɛt̬ər| *vt* **1** IMPROVE : améliorer <to better oneself : améliorer sa condition> **2** SURPASS : dépasser, surpasser
better[2] *adv* (*comparative of* **well**) **1** : mieux <he plays better than you : il joue mieux que toi> **2 all the better** : tant mieux
better[3] *adj* (*comparative of* **good**) **1** : meilleur <this store is better than that one : ce magasin est meilleur que celui-là> **2** MORE : plus <better than nine miles : plus de neuf milles> **3 to get better** : s'améliorer, se remettre
better[4] *n* **1** : meilleur *m* <the better of the two : le meilleur des deux> **2 change for the better** : amélioration *f*, changement *m* en mieux **3 to get the better of** : l'emporter sur

betterment [ˈbɛt̬ərmənt] *n* : amélioration *f*
bettor *or* **better** [ˈbɛt̬ər] *n* : parieur *m*, -rieuse *f*
between[1] [bɪˈtwiːn] *adv* **1** : au milieu, dans l'intervalle **2 in ~** : entre les deux
between[2] *prep* : entre <between five and ten : entre cinq et dix> <between you and me : entre nous>
bevel[1] [ˈbɛvəl] *vt* **-eled** *or* **-elled; -eling** *or* **-elling** : biseauter, tailler en biseau
bevel[2] *n* **1** : surface *f* oblique **2** *or* **bevel edge** : biseau *m*
beverage [ˈbɛvrɪdʒ, ˈbɛvə-] *n* : boisson *f*
bevy [ˈbɛvi] *n, pl* **bevies** : groupe *m* (de personnes), volée *f* (d'oiseaux)
bewail [bɪˈweɪl] *vt* : se lamenter sur, pleurer
beware [bɪˈwær] *vi* **to beware of** : se méfier de, prendre garde à
bewilder [bɪˈwɪldər] *vt* : dérouter, rendre perplexe, déconcerter
bewilderment [bɪˈwɪldərmənt] *n* : perplexité *f*, confusion *f*
bewitch [bɪˈwɪtʃ] *vt* **1** : ensorceler **2** CHARM : enchanter, captiver
beyond[1] [biˈjɑnd] *adv* : au-delà, plus loin, au loin <the mountains beyond : les montagnes au loin> <2000 and beyond : 2000 et au-delà>
beyond[2] *prep* **1** : au-delà de <beyond the sea : au-delà de la mer> **2** : au-dessus de, hors de <beyond doubt : hors de doute> **3** : plus de <he won't stay beyond a week : il ne restera pas plus d'une semaine> **4 it's beyond me** : ça me dépasse
biannual [ˌbaɪˈænjʊəl] *adj* : bisannuel, semestriel — **biannually** *adv*
bias[1] [ˈbaɪəs] *vt* **-ased** *or* **-assed; -asing** *or* **-assing** : influencer, prévenir (contre)
bias[2] *n* **1** : biais *m* <cut on the bias : coupé en biais> **2** PREJUDICE : préjugé *m*, parti *m* pris **3** TENDENCY : penchant *m*, tendance *f*
biased [ˈbaɪəst] *adj* : partial
bib [ˈbɪb] *n* : bavoir *m* (d'un bébé), bavette *f* (sur un vêtement)
Bible [ˈbaɪbəl] *n* : Bible *f*
biblical [ˈbɪblɪkəl] *adj* : biblique
bibliographer [ˌbɪbliˈɑgrəfər] *n* : bibliographe *mf*
bibliography [ˌbɪbliˈɑgrəfi] *n, pl* **-phies** : bibliographie *f* — **bibliographic** [-bliəˈgræfɪk] *adj*
bicameral [ˌbaɪˈkæmərəl] *adj* : bicaméral
bicarbonate [ˌbaɪˈkɑrbənət, -ˌneɪt] *n* : bicarbonate *m*
bicentennial [ˌbaɪsɛnˈtɛniəl] *n* : bicentenaire *m*
biceps [ˈbaɪˌsɛps] *ns & pl* : biceps *m*
bicker [ˈbɪkər] *vi* : se chamailler
bicuspid [baɪˈkʌspɪd] *n* : prémolaire *f*
bicycle[1] [ˈbaɪsɪkəl, -ˌsɪ-] *vi* **-cled; -cling** : faire de la bicyclette, faire du vélo
bicycle[2] *n* : bicyclette *f*, vélo *m*
bicyclist [ˈbaɪsɪkəlɪst] *n* : cycliste *mf*
bid[1] [ˈbɪd] *v* **bade** [ˈbæd, ˈbeɪd] *or* **bid** [ˈbɪd]; **bidden** [ˈbɪdən] *or* **bid; bidding** *vt* **1** ORDER : demander, ordonner **2** SAY : dire, souhaiter <to bid s.o. goodbye : dire au revoir à qqn> **3** INVITE : inviter <I bid him to come in : je l'ai invité à rentrer> **4** OFFER : offrir, faire une offre de <she bid five dollars : elle a fait une offre de cinq dollars> — *vi* : offrir, faire une offre
bid[2] *n* **1** OFFER : offre *f*, enchère *f* **2** INVITATION : invitation *f* **3** ATTEMPT : essai *m*, tentative *f*
bidder [ˈbɪdər] *n* : offrant *m;* enchérisseur *m*, -seuse *f* <to the highest bidder : au plus offrant>
bide [ˈbaɪd] *vt* **bode** [ˈboːd] *or* **bided; biding** : attendre <to bide one's time : attendre le bon moment>
biennial [baɪˈɛniəl] *adj* : biennal — **biennially** *adv*
bier [ˈbɪr] *n* **1** STAND : catafalque *m* **2** COFFIN : bière *f*
bifocals [baɪˌfoːkəlz] *npl* : lunettes *fpl* bifocales, verres *mpl* à double foyer
big [ˈbɪg] *adj* **bigger; biggest 1** LARGE : grand, gros **2** OLDER : grand, aîné <his big brother : son frère aîné> **3** IMPORTANT : important, grand <a big difference : une grande différence> <a big mistake : une grave erreur> **4** POPULAR : à la mode **5 to have a big heart** : avoir grand cœur
bigamist [ˈbɪgəmɪst] *n* : bigame *mf*
bigamous [ˈbɪgəməs] *adj* : bigame
bigamy [ˈbɪgəmi] *n* : bigamie *f*
Big Dipper → **dipper**
bighorn sheep [ˈbɪgˌhɔrn] *n* : mouton *m* sauvage à grandes cornes
bight [ˈbaɪt] *n* **1** COIL, LOOP : boucle *f* **2** BAY : baie *f*, anse *f*
bigot [ˈbɪgət] *n* : fanatique *mf;* bigot *m*, -gote *f* (en religion)
bigoted [ˈbɪgət̬əd] *adj* : fanatique, intolérant
bigotry [ˈbɪgətri] *n, pl* **-tries** : fanatisme *m*, intolérance *f*
big shot *n* : grosse légume *f fam*, gros bonnet *m fam*
bigwig [ˈbɪgˌwɪg] → **big shot**
bike [ˈbaɪk] *n* **1** : vélo *m* **2** MOTORBIKE, MOTORCYCLE : moto *f*, motocyclette *f*
bikini [bəˈkiːni] *n* : bikini *m*
bilateral [baɪˈlæt̬ərəl] *adj* : bilatéral — **bilaterally** *adv*
bile [ˈbaɪl] *n* **1** : bile *f* **2** IRRITABILITY : mauvaise humeur *f*
bilingual [baɪˈlɪŋgwəl] *adj* : bilingue
bilious [ˈbɪliəs] *adj* : bilieux
bilk [ˈbɪlk] *vt* : escroquer, frauder
bill[1] [ˈbɪl] *vt* **1** : facturer, envoyer la facture à **2** ADVERTISE : annoncer, mettre à l'affiche — *vi* **to bill and coo** : roucouler

bill[2] *n* **1** : bec *m* (d'un oiseau) **2** INVOICE : facture *f*, note *f*, addition *f* (au restaurant) **3** : projet *m* de loi <to pass a bill : voter un projet de loi> **4** POSTER : affiche *f* **5** BANKNOTE : billet *m* (de banque)

billboard [ˈbɪlˌbɔrd] *n* : panneau *m* publicitaire

billet[1] [ˈbɪlət] *vt* : cantonner, loger

billet[2] *n* : cantonnement *m*

billfold [ˈbɪlˌfoːld] *n* : portefeuille *m*

billiards [ˈbɪljərdz] *n* : billard *m*

billion [ˈbɪljən] *n* : milliard *m*

billow[1] [ˈbɪlo] *vi* **1** RISE, ROLL : se soulever (se dit de la mer) **2** SWELL : se gonfler (se dit d'une voile), onduler (se dit d'un drapeau)

billow[2] *n* **1** WAVE : vague *f* **2** CLOUD : nuage *m* <a billow of smoke : un nuage de fumée>

billowy [ˈbɪlowi] *adj* : houleux (se dit de la mer), ondoyant (se dit des nuages, de la fumée, etc.)

billy goat [ˈbɪliˌgoːt] *n* : bouc *m*

bin [ˈbɪn] *n* : coffre *m*, boîte *f*

binary [ˈbaɪnəri, -ˌnɛri] *adj* : binaire

bind [ˈbaɪnd] *vt* **bound** [ˈbaʊnd]; **binding** **1** TIE : lier, attacher, ligoter **2** OBLIGATE : obliger, contraindre **3** ENCIRCLE, GIRD : entourer, ceindre **4** BANDAGE : bander, panser (une blessure) **5** : relier (un livre)

binder [ˈbaɪndər] *n* **1** : relieur *m*, -lieuse *f* (de livres) **2** FOLDER : classeur *m*

binding [ˈbaɪndɪŋ] *n* : reliure *f* (d'un livre)

binge [ˈbɪndʒ] *n* : bringue *f fam* <to go on a binge : faire la bringue>

bingo [ˈbɪŋˌgoː] *n, pl* **-gos** : bingo *m*

binocular [baɪˈnɑkjələr, bə-] *adj* : binoculaire

binoculars [bəˈnɑkjələrz, baɪ-] *npl* : jumelles *fpl*

biochemical [baɪoˈkɛmɪkəl] *adj* : biochimique

biochemist [ˌbaɪoˈkɛmɪst] *n* : biochimiste *mf*

biochemistry [ˌbaɪoˈkɛməstri] *n* : biochimie *f*

biodegradable [ˌbaɪodɪˈgreɪdəbəl] *adj* : biodégradable

biographer [baɪˈɑgrəfər] *n* : biographe *mf*

biographical [ˌbaɪəˈgræfɪkəl] *adj* : biographique

biography [baɪˈɑgrəfi, biː-] *n, pl* **-phies** : biographie *f*

biological [-dʒɪkəl] *adj* : biologique

biologist [baɪˈɑlədʒɪst] *n* : biologiste *mf*

biology [baɪˈɑlədʒi] *n* : biologie *f*

biophysicist [ˌbaɪoˈfɪzəsɪst] *n* : biophysicien *m*, -cienne *f*

biophysics [ˌbaɪoˈfɪzɪks] *ns & pl* : biophysique *f*

biopsy [ˈbaɪˌɑpsi] *n, pl* **-sies** : biopsie *f*

biotechnology [ˌbaɪotɛkˈnɑlədʒi] *n* : biotechnologie *f*

bipartisan [baɪˈpɑrt̬əzən, -sən] *adj* : bipartite

biped [ˈbaɪˌpɛd] *n* : bipède *m*

birch [ˈbərtʃ] *n* : bouleau *m*

bird [ˈbərd] *n* **1** : oiseau *m* **2** FOWL : volaille *f*

birdbath [ˈbərdˌbæθ, -bɑθ] *n* : vasque *f* pour les oiseaux

bird dog *n* : chien *m* d'arrêt

birdhouse [ˈbərdˌhaʊs] *n* : volière *f*

bird of prey *n* : oiseau *m* de proie, rapace *m*

birdseed [ˈbərdˌsiːd] *n* : graines *fpl* pour les oiseaux

bird's–eye view [ˈbərdzˌaɪ] *n* : vue *f* panoramique, vue *f* d'ensemble

birth [ˈbərθ] *n* **1** : naissance *f*, accouchement *m* <to give birth : accoucher> **2** ORIGIN : naissance *f*, début *m* **3** LINEAGE : descendance *f*, lignée *f*

birthday [ˈbərθˌdeɪ] *n* : anniversaire *m* <happy birthday! : joyeux anniversaire!>

birthmark [ˈbərθˌmɑrk] *n* : tache *f* de vin

birthplace [ˈbərθˌpleɪs] *n* : lieu *m* de naissance

birthrate [ˈbərθˌreɪt] *n* : natalité *f*

birthright [ˈbərθˌraɪt] *n* : droit *m* (acquis à la naissance)

biscuit [ˈbɪskət] *n* : petit pain *m* au lait

bisect [ˈbaɪˌsɛkt, ˌbaɪˈ-] *vt* : couper en deux, diviser — *vi* INTERSECT : se couper, se croiser

bisexual [ˌbaɪˈsɛkʃəwəl, -ˈsɛkʃəl] *adj* : bisexuel

bishop [ˈbɪʃəp] *n* **1** : évêque *m* **2** : fou *m* (aux échecs)

bishopric [ˈbɪʃəˌprɪk] *n* : évêché *m*

bismuth [ˈbɪzməθ] *n* : bismuth *m*

bison [baɪzən, -sən] *ns & pl* **-son** : bison *m*

bistro [ˈbiːstro, ˈbɪs-] *n, pl* **-tros** : bistro *m*, bistrot *m*

bit [ˈbɪt] *n* **1** : mors *m* (d'un cheval) **2** PIECE : morceau *m*, bout *m*, petit peu *m* <a bit of paper : un bout de papier> **3** : bit *m* (en informatique) **4** **a bit** RATHER, SOMEWHAT : un peu *m*, un petit peu *m*

bitch[1] [ˈbitʃ] *vi* COMPLAIN : râler *fam*, rouspéter *fam*

bitch[2] *n* : chienne *f*

bite[1] [ˈbaɪt] *v* **bit** [ˈbɪt]; **bitten** [ˈbɪtən]; **biting** *vt* **1** : mordre **2** STING : piquer — *vi* : mordre

bite[2] *n* **1** : morsure *f* (de chien, etc.) **2** STING : piqûre *f* **3** MOUTHFUL : bouchée *f* **4** SNACK : morceau *m* <let's grab a bite : mangeons un morceau> **5** : touche *f* (de pêche)

biting *adj* **1** PENETRATING : pénétrant, cinglant **2** CAUSTIC : mordant, caustique

bitter [ˈbɪt̬ər] *adj* **1** ACRID : amer, âpre <a bitter taste : un goût amer> **2** PENETRATING : pénétrant, cinglant <bitter cold : froid glacial> **3** HARSH : acerbe, dur <to the bitter end

: jusqu'au bout> **4** FIERCE, RELENTLESS : acharné, féroce, violent <a bitter hatred : une haine profonde>
bitterly ['bɪt̬ərli] *adv* : amèrement
bittern ['bɪt̬ərn] *n* : butor *m*
bitterness ['bɪt̬ərnəs] *n* : amertume *f,* âpreté *f*
bituminous [bə'tu:mənəs, -'tju:-] *adj* **1** : bitumineux **2 bituminous coal** : huile *f* grasse
bivalve ['baɪ,vælv] *n* : bivalve *m*
bivouac[1] ['bɪvə,wæk, 'bɪv,wæk] *vi* **-ouacked; -ouacking** : bivouaquer
bivouac[2] *n* : bivouac *m*
bizarre [bə'zɑr] *adj* : bizarre — **bizarrely** *adv*
blab ['blæb] *vi* **blabbed; blabbing** CHATTER : jaser, jacasser, babiller
black[1] ['blæk] *vt* : noircir
black[2] *adj* **1** : noir (se dit de la couleur ou de la race) **2** DARK : obscur, sans lumière **3** WICKED : noir, mauvais **4** DIRTY : sale, noir **5** GLOOMY : noir, sombre
black[3] *n* **1** : noir *m* (couleur) **2** : Noir *m,* Noire *f* (personne) **3** DARKNESS : obscurité *f,* ténèbres *fpl* **4 to be in the black** : être créditeur
black–and–blue [,blækən'blu:] *adj* : couvert de bleus
blackball[1] ['blæk,bɔl] *vt* : blackbouler *fam*
blackball[2] *n* : vote *m* contraire
blackberry ['blæk,bɛri] *n, pl* **-ries** : mûre *f*
blackbird ['blæk,bərd] *n* : merle *m*
blackboard ['blæk,bɔrd] *n* : tableau *m* (noir)
blacken ['blækən] *vt* **1** BLACK : noircir **2** DEFAME : ternir, souiller, noircir
blackhead ['blæk,hɛd] *n* : point *m* noir
black hole *n* : trou *m* noir
blackish [blækɪʃ] *adj* : noirâtre
blackjack ['blæk,jæk] *n* **1** : assommoir *m* (arme) **2** : vingt-et-un *m* (jeu de cartes)
blacklist[1] ['blæk,lɪst] *vt* : mettre sur la liste noire
blacklist[2] *n* : liste *f* noire
blackmail[1] ['blæk,meɪl] *vi* : faire chanter
blackmail[2] *n* : chantage *m*
blackmailer ['blæk,meɪlər] *n* : maître-chanteur *m*
blackness ['blæk,nəs] *n* **1** : noirceur *f* **2** DARKNESS : obscurité *f*
blackout ['blæk,aʊt] *n* **1** : panne *f* d'électricité **2** FAINT : évanouissement *m*
black out *vi* **1** : avoir une panne d'électricité **2** FAINT : s'évanouir
blacksmith ['blæk,smɪθ] *n* : forgeron *m*
blacktop ['blæk,tɑp] *n* : asphalte *m*
bladder ['blædər] *n* : vessie *f*
blade ['bleɪd] *n* **1** : brin *m* (d'herbe) **2** : lame *f* (de couteau) **3** : pale *f* (d'hélice, de rame, etc.)
blame[1] ['bleɪm] *vt* **blamed; blaming** : blâmer, reprocher
blame[2] *n* **1** CONDEMNATION : blâme *m,* reproches *mpl* **2** RESPONSIBILITY : faute *f,* responsabilité *f*
blameless ['bleɪmləs] *adj* : irréprochable
blameworthy ['bleɪm,wərði] *adj* : blâmable, coupable
blanch ['blæntʃ] *vt* WHITEN : blanchir — *vi* PALE : pâlir
bland ['blænd] *adj* **1** SUAVE : affable, aimable **2** SOOTHING : apaisant, calmant **3** DULL, INSIPID : fade, insipide
blandly ['blændli] *adv* : avec affabilité, affablement
blandness ['blændnəs] *n* **1** SUAVENESS : affabilité *f* **2** TASTELESSNESS : fadeur *f*
blandishment ['blændɪʃmənt] *n* : flatterie *f,* cajoleries *fpl*
blank[1] ['blæŋk] *adj* **1** EXPRESSIONLESS : sans expression **2** DAZED, DISCONCERTED : déconcerté, dérouté **3** : blanc, vierge <a blank sheet : une feuille blanche> **4** EMPTY : vide <a blank wall : un mur vide> **5** DOWNRIGHT : catégorique, absolu <a blank refusal : un refus catégorique>
blank[2] *n* **1** GAP, SPACE : blanc *m,* vide *m,* trou *m* (de mémoire, etc.) **2** FORM : formulaire *m* à remplir, fiche *f* vierge **3** CARTRIDGE : cartouche *f* à blanc
blanket[1] ['blæŋkət] *vt* : couvrir, recouvrir
blanket[2] *adj* : général, global <blanket agreement : accord général>
blanket[3] *n* **1** : couverture *f* (d'un lit) **2** : couche *f,* manteau *f* <a blanket of snow : une couche de neige>
blankly ['blænkli] *adv* : sans expression, d'un air ébahi
blare[1] ['blær] *vi* **blared; blaring** : beugler, jouer à plein volume
blare[2] *n* : beuglement *m* (d'une radio, etc.), sonnerie *f* (d'une trompette)
blarney ['blɑrni] *n* : boniment *m,* baratin *m*
blasé [blɑ'zeɪ] *adj* : blasé
blaspheme [blæs'fi:m, 'blæs,-] *v* **-phemed; -pheming** : blasphémer
blasphemous ['blæsfəməs] *adj* : blasphématoire
blasphemy ['blæsfəmi] *n, pl* **-mies** : blasphème *m*
blast[1] ['blæst] *vt* **1** BLOW UP : faire sauter, dynamiter **2** ATTACK, CRITICIZE : attaquer violemment **3** BLIGHT : flétrir, détruire (des cultures) — *vi* **1** BLARE : beugler, retentir **2 to blast off** : décoller
blast[2] *n* **1** GUST : coup *m* de vent, rafale *f* **2** EXPLOSION : explosion *f* **3 at full blast** : à plein volume
blatant ['bleɪtənt] *adj* : flagrant, criant
blatantly ['bleɪtəntli] *adv* : d'une manière flagrante

blaze[1] [ˈbleɪz] *v* **blazed; blazing** *vt* MARK : griffer, marquer (un arbre), frayer <to blaze a trail : frayer un chemin> — *vi* **1** BURN, FLAME : flamber **2** SHINE : flamboyer, resplendir <the blazing sun : le soleil flamboyant>
blaze[2] *n* **1** : marque *f,* encoche *f* (sur un arbre) **2** FLAME : flamme *f,* feu *m* **3** BURST : éclat *m* (de couleur), torrent *m* (de lumière), explosion *f* (de colère)
blazer [ˈbleɪzər] *n* : blazer *m*
bleach[1] [ˈbliːtʃ] *vt* : blanchir, décolorer
bleach[2] *n* : décolorant *m,* eau *f* de Javel
bleachers [ˈbliːtʃərz] *npl* : gradins *mpl*
bleak [ˈbliːk] *adj* **1** GLOOMY : sombre, morne, lugubre <bleak thoughts : de sombres réflections> **2** DESOLATE : désolé <a bleak landscape : un terrain désolé>
bleakly [ˈbliːkli] *adv* : sombrement, lugubrement
bleakness [ˈbliːknəs] *n* **1** GLOOMINESS : caractère *m* sombre, monotonie *f* **2** BARRENNESS : désolation *f* (d'un paysage)
bleary [ˈblɪri] *adj* : trouble, voilé <bleary-eyed : aux yeux troubles>
bleat[1] [ˈbliːt] *vi* : bêler
bleat[2] *n* : bêlement *m*
bleed [ˈbliːd] *v* **bled** [ˈblɛd]; **bleeding** *vt* **1** : saigner **2** DRAIN : purger (des freins, etc.) **3 to bleed s.o. dry** : tirer de l'argent à qqn — *vi* **1** : saigner, perdre du sang **2 my heart bleeds for you** : tu me fends le cœur
blemish[1] [ˈblɛmɪʃ] *vt* : tacher, ternir
blemish[2] *n* : tache *f,* défaut *m,* imperfection *f*
blend[1] [ˈblɛnd] *vt* : mélanger, mêler, marier (des couleurs) — *vi* : se mélanger, se mêler
blend[2] *n* : mélange *m,* alliance *f*
blender [ˈblɛndər] *n* : mixer *m,* mélangeur *m Can*
bless [ˈblɛs] *vt* **blessed** [ˈblɛst]; **blessing** **1** GLORIFY : bénir, glorifier <bless the Lord : béni soit le Seigneur> **2** CONSECRATE : bénir, sanctifier **3** ENDOW : doter <to be blessed with : avoir le bonheur de, être doué de> **4 bless you!** : à vos souhaits! (lorsqu'on éternue) **5 to bless oneself** : se signer
blessed [ˈblɛsəd] *or* **blest** [ˈblɛst] *adj* **1** HOLY : bénit, saint **2** HAPPY : bienheureux, heureux
blessing [ˈblɛsɪŋ] *n* **1** : bénédiction *f* (en religion) **2** BENEFIT : avantage *m,* bienfait *m* <a blessing in disguise : un bienfait inattendu> **3** APPROVAL : bénédiction *f,* approbation *f*
blew → **blow**
blight[1] [ˈblaɪt] *vt* : détruire, flétrir
blight[2] *n* **1** : rouille *f* (des plantes) **2** SCOURGE : fléau *m* <urban blight : dégradation urbaine>
blimp [ˈblɪmp] *n* : dirigeable *m*
blind[1] [ˈblaɪnd] *adv* : sans visibilité <to fly blind : voler aux instruments>
blind[2] *vt* **1** : aveugler, rendre aveugle **2** DAZZLE : éblouir
blind[3] *adj* **1** SIGHTLESS : aveugle **2** UNQUESTIONING : aveugle, absolu, ignorant <blind faith : foi absolue> **3** CLOSED : sans issue <a blind alley : une voie sans issue>
blind[4] *n* **1** : store *m* <venetian blind : store vénitien> **2** COVER : affût *m* (en chasse) **3 the blind** : les non-voyants
blindfold[1] [ˈblaɪnd,foːld] *vt* : bander les yeux à
blindfold[2] *n* : bandeau *m*
blindly [ˈblaɪndli] *adv* : aveuglément, à l'aveuglette
blindness [ˈblaɪndnəs] *n* **1** : cécité *f* <snow blindness : cécité des neiges> **2** : aveuglement *m* <blindness to the truth : aveuglement devant la verité>
blink[1] [ˈblɪŋk] *vt* : cligner (des yeux) — *vi* **1** : cligner des yeux **2** FLICKER : clignoter, vaciller
blink[2] *n* : battement *m* des paupières
blinker [ˈblɪŋkər] *n* : clignotant *m*
bliss [ˈblɪs] *n* **1** HAPPINESS : félicité *f,* bonheur *m* absolu **2** HEAVEN : paradis *m*
blissful [ˈblɪsfəl] *adj* : heureux, bienheureux — **blissfully** *adv*
blister[1] [ˈblɪstər] *vi* **1** : se couvrir d'ampoules, cloquer (se dit de la peau) **2** : se boursoufler (se dit de la peinture, etc.)
blister[2] *n* **1** : ampoule *f,* cloque *f* (sur la peau) **2** : boursouflure *f* (sur une surface peinte)
blithe [ˈblaɪθ, ˈblaɪð] *adj* **blither; blithest** CHEERFUL : joyeux, gai — **blithely** *adv*
blitz[1] [ˈblɪts] *vt* : bombarder
blitz[2] *n* : bombardement *m,* raid *m* aérien
blizzard [ˈblɪzərd] *n* : tempête *f* de neige
bloat [ˈbloːt] *vi* SWELL : se gonfler, enfler
bloated [ˈbloːtəd] *adj* : boursouflé, gonflé
blob [ˈblɑb] *n* : tache *f,* (grosse) goutte *f*
bloc [ˈblɑk] *n* : bloc *m*
block[1] [ˈblɑk] *vt* **1** OBSTRUCT : bloquer, barrer **2** IMPEDE : bloquer, gêner, faire opposition à (un adversaire, un projet de loi, etc.) **3 to block out** HIDE : cacher, empêcher d'entrer **4 to block out** OUTLINE : ébaucher
block[2] *n* **1** : bloc *m,* billot *m* <a block of ice : un bloc de glace> <butcher's block : billot de boucherie> **2** OBSTRUCTION : obstacle *m,* obstruction *f* **3** : pâté *m* de maisons, bloc *m Can* <to walk around the block : faire le tour du pâté de maisons> <two blocks away : à deux rues d'ici> **4**

BUILDING : immeuble *m* <office block : immeuble de bureaux> **5** GROUP : groupe *m,* série *f* (de billets, etc.) **6 block and tackle** HOIST : palan *m*
blockade[1] [blɑˈkeɪd] *vt* **-aded; -ading 1** OBSTRUCT : bloquer **2** : faire le blocus de (un port)
blockade[2] *n* : blocus *m*
blockage [ˈblɑkɪdʒ] *n* : obstruction *f,* blocage *m*
blockhead [ˈblɑkˌhɛd] *n* : imbécile *mf fam*
bloke [ˈbloːk] *n Brit* : type *m*
blond[1] *or* **blonde** [ˈblɑnd] *adj* : blond
blond[2] *or* **blonde** *n* : blond *m,* blonde *f*
blood [ˈblʌd] *n* **1** : sang *m* **2** LINEAGE : lignée *f,* descendance *f*
blood bank *n* : banque *f* du sang
bloodcurdling [ˈblʌdˌkərdəlɪŋ] *adj* : à vous figer le sang
bloodhound [ˈblʌdˌhaʊnd] *n* : limier *m*
bloodless [ˈblʌdləs] *adj* **1** : sans effusion de sang **2** SPIRITLESS : apathique, sans vie
bloodmobile [ˈblʌdmoˌbiːl] *n* : centre *m* mobile de collecte du sang
blood pressure *n* : tension *f* artérielle
bloodshed [ˈblʌdˌʃɛd] *n* : effusion *f* de sang, carnage *m*
bloodshot [ˈblʌdˌʃɑt] *adj* : injecté de sang
bloodstain [ˈblʌdˌsteɪn] *n* : tache *f* de sang
bloodstream [ˈblʌdˌstriːm] *n* : sang *m,* système *m* sanguin
bloodsucker [ˈblʌdˌsʌkər] *n* : sangsue *f*
bloodthirsty [ˈblʌdˌθərsti] *adj* : sanguinaire, assoiffé de sang
blood vessel *n* : vaisseau *m* sanguin
bloody [ˈblʌdi] *adj* **bloodier; -est 1** : sanglant <a bloody battle : un combat sanglant> **2** : ensanglanté <bloody hands : mains ensanglantées>
bloom[1] [ˈbluːm] *vi* **1** FLOWER : fleurir, éclore **2** FLOURISH : s'épanouir
bloom[2] *n* **1** FLOWER : fleur *f* **2** BLOOMING : floraison *f,* épanouissement *m* **3 in bloom** *or* **in full bloom** : en fleurs, en pleine floraison
blooper [ˈbluːpər] *n* : gaffe *f fam*
blossom[1] [ˈblɑsəm] *vi* **1** : fleurir, être en fleurs **2** MATURE : s'épanouir, se développer **3 to blossom into** : devenir
blossom[2] *n* : fleur *f*
blot[1] [ˈblɑt] *vt* **blotted; blotting 1** STAIN : tacher, souiller **2** DRY : sécher (encre, etc.) **3 to blot out** : rayer, effacer
blot[2] *n* **1** SPOT : tache *f* **2** *or* **inkblot** : pâté *m* **3** BLEMISH : souillure *f,* tare *f*
blotch[1] [ˈblɑtʃ] *vt* : tacher, marbrer
blotch[2] *n* : tache *f,* marbrure *f* (sur la peau)
blotchy [ˈblɑtʃi] *adj* **blotchier; -est 1** : couvert de taches, marbré <blotchy complexion : teint marbré> **2** SMEARED : barbouillé <blotchy drawing : dessin barbouillé>
blotter [ˈblɑt̬ər] *n* : buvard *m*
blouse [ˈblaʊs, ˈblaʊz] *n* : chemisier *m,* corsage *m*
blow[1] [bloː] *v* **blew** [ˈbluː]; **blown** [ˈbloːn]; **blowing** *vt* **1** : souffler, pousser (un navire), chasser (des feuilles, etc.) <to blow sth away : faire voler qqch> <to blow one's nose : se moucher> **2** SOUND : jouer de (une trompette, etc.), donner (un coup de sifflet) **3** SHAPE : souffler, donner une forme à (le verre) **4** BUNGLE : rater, manquer <I blew it! : j'ai tout raté!> **5 to blow out** : souffler sur (une chandelle, etc.) — *vi* **1** : souffler **2** *or* **to blow away** : s'envoler **3** SOUND : sonner (se dit d'une trompette, etc.) **4 to blow down** FALL : se renverser, tomber **5 to blow out** : éclater (se dit d'un pneu), s'éteindre (se dit d'une bougie)
blow[2] *n* **1** GALE : coup *m* de vent **2** HIT, STROKE : coup *m,* coup *m* de poing **3** MISFORTUNE : coup *m,* malheur *m* **4 to come to blows** : en venir aux mains
blowout [ˈbloːˌaʊt] *n* : éclatement *m* (d'un pneu)
blowtorch [ˈbloˌtɔrtʃ] *n* : lampe *f* à souder, chalumeau *m*
blow up *vt* **1** EXPLODE : faire sauter, faire exploser **2** INFLATE : gonfler — *vi* : exploser, sauter
blubber[1] [ˈblʌbər] *vi* : pleurer (comme un veau)
blubber[2] *n* : graisse *f* de baleine
bludgeon[1] [ˈblʌdʒən] *vt* : matraquer
bludgeon[2] *n* : gourdin *m,* matraque *f*
blue[1] [ˈbluː] *adj* **bluer; bluest 1** : bleu <blue with cold : bleu de froid> **2** MELANCHOLY : triste
blue[2] *n* **1** : bleu *m,* azur *m* **2 out of the blue** : de façon imprévue
bluebell [ˈbluːˌbɛl] *n* : jacinthe *f* des bois
blueberry [ˈbluːˌbɛri] *n, pl* **-ries** : myrtille *f France,* bleuet *m Can*
bluebird [ˈbluːˌbərd] *n* : oiseau *m* bleu
blue cheese *n* : (fromage *m*) bleu *m*
bluefish [ˈbluːˌfɪʃ] *n, pl* **-fish** *or* **-fishes** : poisson *m* bleu de la côte atlantique
blue jay *n* : geai *m* bleu
blueprint [ˈbluːˌprɪnt] *n* **1** : bleu *m* **2** PROGRAM : plan *m* (de travail), projet *m*
blues [ˈbluːz] *npl* **1** DEPRESSION : cafard *m,* mélancolie *f* **2** : blues *m* (en musique)
bluff[1] [ˈblʌf] *v* : bluffer
bluff[2] *adj* **1** STEEP : escarpé, à pic **2** FRANK : carré, direct
bluff[3] *n* **1** CLIFF : falaise *f,* escarpement *m* **2** DECEPTION, RUSE : bluff *m*
bluing *or* **blueing** [ˈbluːɪŋ] *n* : produit *m* blanchissant

blunder[1] |ˈblʌndər| *vi* **1** *or* **to blunder along** : avancer à l'aveuglette, avancer à tâtons **2** ERR : faire une bévue, faire une gaffe
blunder[2] *n* MISTAKE : bévue *f,* gaffe *f fam,* impair *m*
blunderbuss |ˈblʌndər,bʌs| *n* : tromblon *m*
blunt[1] |ˈblʌnt| *vt* : émousser (des couteaux, des ciseaux, etc.), épointer (des crayons), couper (l'appétit)
blunt[2] *adj* **1** DULL : émoussé, épointé **2** ABRUPT, DIRECT : brusque, abrupt, carré
bluntly |ˈblʌntli| *adv* : franchement, carrément
bluntness *n* **1** DULLNESS : manque *m* de tranchant **2** ABRUPTNESS, FRANKNESS : brusquerie *f,* franc-parler *m*
blur[1] |ˈblər| *v* **blurred; blurring** *vt* : troubler, brouiller, rendre flou <eyes blurred with tears : yeux brouillés de larmes> — *vi* : se brouiller
blur[2] *n* **1** : image *f* floue, contour *m* imprécis **2** SMEAR : tache *f*
blurb |ˈblərb| *n* : notice *f* publicitaire
blurry |ˈbləri| *adj* **blurrier; -est** : flou, troublé <blurry vision : vision troublée>
blurt |ˈblərt| *vt or* **to blurt out** : laisser échapper
blush[1] |ˈblʌʃ| *vi* : rougir
blush[2] *n* : rougeur *f*
bluster[1] |ˈblʌstər| *vi* **1** BLOW, STORM : souffler violemment **2** BOAST : fanfaronner
bluster[2] *n* **1** : hurlement *m* (du vent) **2** BOASTING : fanfaronnade *f*
blustery |ˈblʌstəri| *adj* : violent, orageux
boa |ˈbo:ə| *n* : boa *m*
boar |ˈbor| *n* **1** PIG : verrat *m* **2** → **wild boar**
board[1] |ˈbord| *vt* **1** : monter à bord de (un avion, un navire), monter dans (un train) **2** LODGE : prendre en pension **3 to board up** : couvrir de planches
board[2] *n* **1** PLANK : planche *f* **2** : pension *f* <room and board : pension complète> **3** COMMITTEE, COUNCIL : conseil *m,* commission *f* <board meeting : réunion du conseil> **4** : tableau *m* (d'un jeu) **5 to go on board** : monter à bord
boarder |ˈbordər| *n* : pensionnaire *mf*
boardinghouse |ˈbordɪŋ,haʊs| *n* : pension *f*
boarding school *n* : pensionnat *m*
boardwalk |ˈbord,wɔk| *n* : promenade *f* (en planches)
boast[1] |ˈbo:st| *vt* : se glorifier de, être fier de posséder <the town boasts five churches : la ville est fière de posséder cinq églises> — *vi* : se vanter, fanfaronner
boast[2] *n* : vantardise *f,* fanfaronnade *f*
boaster |ˈbo:stər| *n* : vantard *m,* -tarde *f;* fanfaron *m,* -ronne *f*
boastful |ˈbo:stfəl| *adj* : vantard, fanfaron
boastfully |ˈbo:stfəli| *adv* : en se vantant, en fanfaronnant
boat[1] |ˈbo:t| *vt* : transporter en bateau — *vi* : aller en bateau
boat[2] *n* **1** : bateau *m* <to go by boat : prendre le bateau> <to be in the same boat : être tous dans la même galère> **2** → **rowboat, ship, sailboat**
boatswain |ˈbo:sən| *n* : maître *m* d'équipage
bob[1] |ˈbab| *v* **bobbed; bobbing** *vt* : couper court (les cheveux) — *vi* **1** : monter et descendre <to bob in the water : danser sur l'eau> **2 to bob up** APPEAR : apparaître, surgir
bob[2] *n* **1** : coupe *f* au carré (des cheveux) **2** FLOAT : bouchon *m* (de pêche) **3** NOD : hochement *m* de tête
bobbin |ˈbabən| *n* : bobine *f*
bobby pin |ˈbabi,pɪn| *n* : pince *f* à cheveux
bobcat |ˈbab,kæt| *n* : lynx *m* (roux)
bobolink |ˈbabə,lɪŋk| *n* : oiseau *m* chanteur de l'Amérique du Nord, goglu *m Can*
bobsled |ˈbab,slɛd| *n* : bob *m,* bobsleigh *m*
bobwhite |ˈbabˈhwaɪt| *n* : caille *f* de l'Amérique du Nord
bode[1] |bo:d| *vt* **boded; boding** : présager, augurer <to bode well for : être de bon augure pour>
bode[2] → **bide**
bodice |ˈbadəs| *n* : corsage *m* (d'une robe)
bodily[1] |ˈbadəli| *adv* **1** PHYSICALLY : physiquement, à bras-le-corps **2** ENTIRELY : tout entier
bodily[2] *adj* PHYSICAL : physique, corporel <bodily contact : contact physique>
body |ˈbadi| *n, pl* **bodies 1** : corps *m* **2** CORPSE : cadavre *m* **3** PERSON : personne *f,* être *m* humain **4** COLLECTION, MASS : masse *f,* ensemble *m* <in a body : en masse> <a body of evidence : un ensemble de preuves> **5** SUBSTANCE : corps *m,* fond *m* <the body of a letter : le corps d'une lettre> **6** : carrosserie *f* (d'une voiture), fuselage *m* (d'un avion)
bodyguard |ˈbadi,gard| *n* : garde *m* du corps
bog[1] |ˈbag, ˈbɔg| *vi* **bogged; bogging** *or* **to bog down** : s'embourber, s'enliser, s'empêtrer (dans un discours)
bog[2] *n* **1** MARSH : marais *m,* marécage *m* **2** *or* **peat bog** : tourbière *f*
bogey |ˌbugi, ˈbo:-| *n, pl* **-geys 1** GHOST : fantôme *m,* spectre *m* **2** *or* **bogeyman** : croque-mitaine *m,* épouvantail *m*
boggle |ˈbagəl| *v* **-gled; -gling** *vt* **to boggle the mind** : dépasser l'imagination

— *vi* **the mind boggles** : ça laisse perplexe, on a du mal à imaginer ça
boggy |'bɑgi, 'bɔ-| *adj* **boggier; -est** : marécageux
bogus |'bo:gəs| *adj* SHAM : faux, bidon *fam*
bohemian[1] |bo:'hi:miən| *adj* : bohème
bohemian[2] *n* : bohème *mf*
boil[1] |'bɔɪl| *vt* : faire bouillir — *vi* **1** : bouillir **2** SEETHE : bouillir, bouillonner
boil[2] *n* **1** : ébullition *f* <to bring to a boil : amener à ébullition> **2** : furoncle *m* (en médecine)
boiler |'bɔɪlər| *n* : chaudière *f*
boisterous |'bɔɪstərəs| *adj* **1** NOISY, ROWDY : bruyant, tapageur **2** STORMY : houleux, tumultueux
boisterously |'bɔɪstərəsli| *adv* : bruyamment, tumultueusement
bold |'bo:ld| *adj* **1** COURAGEOUS, DARING : hardi, audacieux **2** IMPUDENT : insolent, effronté — **boldly** *adv*
boldface |'bo:ld,feɪs| *n or* **boldface type** : caractères *mpl* gras
boldness |'bo:ldnəs| *n* : hardiesse *f*, audace *f*
bolero |bə'lɛro| *n, pl* **-ros** : boléro *m*
Bolivian[1] |bə'lɪviən| *adj* : bolivien
Bolivian[2] *n* : Bolivien *m*, -vienne *f*
boll weevil |'bo:l,wi:vəl| *n* : charançon *m* (du cotonnier)
bologna |bə'lo:ni| *n* : gros saucisson *m*
bolster[1] |'bo:lstər| *vt* **-stered; -stering** : soutenir, renforcer <to bolster morale : remonter le moral>
bolster[2] *n* : traversin *m*
bolt[1] |'bo:lt| *vt* **1** LOCK : verrouiller, fermer au verrou **2** *or* **to bolt down** : engloutir (de la nourriture) — *vi* **1** : s'emballer (se dit d'un cheval) **2** DASH : se précipiter, se lancer
bolt[2] *n* **1** THUNDERBOLT : éclair *m*, coup *m* de foudre **2** LOCK : verrou *m* **3** : rouleau *m* (de tissu) **4** : boulon *m* <nuts and bolts : écrous et boulons>
bomb[1] |'bɑm| *vt* : bombarder
bomb[2] *n* : bombe *f*
bombard |bɑm'bɑrd, bəm-| *vt* : bombarder
bombardier |,bɑmbə'dɪr| *n* : bombardier *m*
bombardment |bɑm,bɑrdmənt| *n* : bombardement *m*
bombast |'bɑm,bæst| *n* : grandiloquence *f*
bombastic |bɑm'bæstɪk| *adj* : grandiloquent, ampoulé
bomber |'bɑmər| *n* : bombardier *m* (avion)
bombshell |'bɑm,ʃɛl| *n* : bombe *f*
bona fide |'bo:nə,faɪd, 'bɑ-; ,bo:nə'faɪdi| *adj* **1** : de bonne foi **2** GENUINE : authentique, véritable
bonanza |bə'nænzə| *n* : filon *m*, aubaine *f*
bonbon |'bɑn,bɑn| *n* : bonbon *m*
bond[1] |'bɑnd| *vt* **1** : entreposer (des marchandises) **2** *or* **to bond together** STICK : coller, faire adhérer — *vi* **1** STICK : adhérer **2 to bond with** : s'attacher à
bond[2] *n* **1** TIE : lien *m*, attache *f* <the bonds of marriage : les liens conjugaux> **2** AGREEMENT : contrat *m*, engagement *m*, caution *f* (en droit) **3** ADHESION : adhérence *f* **4** SECURITY : bon *m* <savings bond : bon d'épargne> **5 bonds** *npl* FETTERS : fers *mpl*, chaînes *fpl*
bondage |'bɑndɪdʒ| *n* : esclavage *m*
bondholder |'bɑnd,ho:ldər| *n* : porteur *m* de bons
bondsman |'bɑndzmən| *n* **1** SLAVE : esclave *m*, serf *m* **2** SURETY : garant *m*, -rante *f*
bone[1] |'bo:n| *vt* **boned; boning** : désosser (de la viande), ôter les arêtes de (un poisson)
bone[2] *n* : os *m*, arête *f* (de poisson)
boneless |'bo:nləs| *adj* : sans os, sans arêtes
boner |'bo:nər| *n* BLUNDER : gaffe *f*, bourde *f*
bonfire |'bɑn,faɪr| *n* : feu *m* de joie
bonito |bə'ni:to| *n, pl* **-tos** *or* **-to** : bonite *f*
bonnet |'bɑnət| *n* : bonnet *m*, chapeau *m*
bonny |bɑni| *adj* **bonnier; -est** *Brit* : joli, beau
bonus |'bo:nəs| *n* : gratification *f*, prime *f*
boo[1] |'bu:| *vt* : huer, siffler
boo[2] *n, pl* **boos** : huée *f*
booby |'bu:bi| *n, pl* **-bies** DOPE : nigaud *m*, -gaude *f*
book[1] |'bʊk| *vt* : réserver, retenir <to book a room : réserver une chambre>
book[2] *n* **1** : livre *m*, bouquin *m fam* **2** : carnet *m*, pochette *f* <a book of stamps : un carnet de timbres> <a book of matches : une pochette d'allumettes> **3** STANDARD : règlement *m* <to go by the book : suivre le règlement> **4** LIBRETTO : livret *m* **5 books** *npl* RECORDS : registre *m* **6 books** *npl* ACCOUNTS : comptes *mpl*
bookcase |'bʊk,keɪs| *n* : bibliothèque *f*
bookend |'bʊk,ɛnd| *n* : serre-livres *m*, appui-livres *m Can*
bookie |'bʊki| → **bookmaker**
bookish |'bʊkɪʃ| *adj* : studieux
bookkeeper |'bʊk,ki:pər| *n* : comptable *mf*
bookkeeping |'bʊk,ki:pɪŋ| *n* : comptabilité *f*
booklet |'bʊklət| *n* : brochure *f*
bookmaker |'bʊk,meɪkər| *n* : bookmaker *m*
bookmark |'bʊk,mɑrk| *n* : signet *m*
bookseller |'bʊk,sɛlər| *n* : libraire *mf*
bookshelf |'bʊk,ʃɛlf| *n, pl* **-shelves** : rayon *m*, étagère *f*

bookstore [ˈbʊkˌstor] *n* : librairie *f*
bookworm [ˈbʊkˌwərm] *n* : rat *m* de bibliothèque
boom[1] [ˈbuːm] *vi* **1** RESOUND : gronder, mugir (se dit de la mer), retentir (se dit de la voix) **2** FLOURISH, PROSPER : être en expansion, être en plein essor
boom[2] *n* **1** BOOMING : grondement *m*, mugissement *m*, retentissement *m* **2** : gui *m* (d'un bateau) **3** FLOURISHING : essor *m*, boom *m* (en commerce)
boomerang [ˈbuːməˌræŋ] *n* : boomerang *m*
boon[1] [ˈbuːn] *adj* **boon companion** : gai compagnon *m*, bon compère *m*
boon[2] *n* : bienfait *m*, bénédiction *f*, aubaine *f*
boondocks [ˈbuːnˌdɑks] *npl* : bled *m fam*
boor [ˈbʊr] *n* : rustre *m*; malotru *m*, -true *f*
boorish [ˈbʊrɪʃ] *adj* : rustre, grossier
boost[1] [ˈbuːst] *vt* **1** : soulever (une personne) **2** INCREASE, RAISE : augmenter, faire monter (des prix, etc.) <to boost morale : remonter le moral> **3** : survolter (un circuit électrique)
boost[2] *n* **1** INCREASE : hausse *f*, augmentation *f* **2** STIMULATION : encouragement *m*, stimulation *f* **3 to give s.o. a boost** : soulever qqn
booster [ˈbuːstər] *n* **1** SUPPORTER : partisan *m*, -sane *f*; supporter *m* **2** : survolteur *m* (en électricité) **3** *or* **booster rocket** : fusée *f* d'appoint **4** *or* **booster shot** : vaccin *m* de rappel
boot[1] [ˈbuːt] *vt* **1** KICK : donner un coup de pied à **2** : amorcer (en informatique) **3 to boot out** FIRE : mettre à la porte, congédier
boot[2] *n* **1** : botte *f*, bottine *f* **2** KICK : coup *m* de pied
bootee *or* **bootie** [ˈbuːt̬i] *n* : petit chausson *m* (de bébé), pichou *m Can fam*
booth [ˈbuːθ] *n, pl* **booths** [ˈbuːðz, ˈbuːθs] : baraque *f* (d'un marché), cabine *f* (téléphonique), guichet *m* (pour acheter des billets)
booty [ˈbuːt̬i] *n, pl* **-ties** : butin *m*
booze [ˈbuːz] *n* : alcool *m*, boissons *fpl* alcoolisées
borax [ˈbɔrˌæks] *n* : borax *m*
border[1] [ˈbɔrdər] *vt* **1** EDGE, SURROUND : border, entourer <bordered with flowers : entouré de fleurs> **2** BOUND : toucher, avoir une frontière commune avec — *vi* **to border on** : friser, frôler <it borders on insanity : cela frôle la folie>
border[2] *n* **1** EDGE : bord *m*, lisière *f* <the border of a lake : le bord d'un lac> **2** BOUNDARY : frontière *f* (d'un pays, etc.) **3** EDGING, STRIP : bordure *f* <a cement border : une bordure en ciment>
bore[1] [ˈbor] *vt* **bored; boring 1** DRILL, PIERCE : percer, creuser (un trou), forer (un puits) **2** TIRE : ennuyer, embêter
bore[2] *n* **1** DIAMETER : calibre *m* (d'un fusil) **2** : barbe *f fam*, corvée *f* <what a bore! : quelle barbe!> **3** : raseur *m*, -seuse *f fam*; casse-pieds *mf fam* (personne)
bore[3] → **bear**[1]
boredom [ˈbordəm] *n* : ennui *m*
boring [ˈborɪŋ] *adj* : ennuyeux, sans intérêt, ennuyant *Can*, plat *Can*
born [ˈbɔrn] *adj* **1** : né <born in Paris : né à Paris> **2** INNATE : né, parfait <he's a born dancer : il est né danseur> <a born fool : un parfait idiot>
borne → **bear**[1]
boron [ˈborˌɑn] *n* : bore *m*
borough [ˈbəro] *n* : arrondissement *m* urbain
borrow [ˈbɑro] *vt* : emprunter, s'approprier <I borrowed his pen : j'ai emprunté son stylo> <to borrow an idea : s'approprier une idée>
Bosnian[1] [ˈbɑzniən, bɔz-] *adj* : bosniaque
Bosnian[2] *n* : Bosniaque *mf*
bosom[1] [ˈbʊzəm, ˈbuː-] *adj* : intime <bosom friend : ami intime>
bosom[2] *n* **1** CHEST : poitrine *f* **2** BREASTS : seins *mpl*, poitrine *f* <a big bosom : une grosse poitrine> **3** : sein *m*, milieu *m* <in the bosom of her family : au sein de sa famille>
boss[1] [ˈbɔs] *vt* **1** SUPERVISE : diriger **2 to boss around** : mener à la baguette
boss[2] *n* : patron *m*, -tronne *f*; chef *m*
bossy [ˈbɔsi] *adj* **bossier; -est** : autoritaire, dictatorial
botanical [bəˈtænɪkəl] *adj* : botanique
botanist [ˈbɑtənɪst] *n* : botaniste *mf*
botany [ˈbɑtəni] *n* : botanique *f*
botch [ˈbɑtʃ] *vt* : bousiller *fam*, saboter, estropier
both[1] [ˈboːθ] *adj* : les deux <I like both dresses : j'aime les deux robes>
both[2] *conj* : et . . . et, à la fois <both his brother and his sister : et son frère et sa sœur> <she's both beautiful and intelligent : elle est à la fois belle et intelligente>
both[3] *pron* : tous les deux, l'un et l'autre <they were both there : elles étaient là toutes les deux>
bother[1] [ˈbɑðər] *vt* **1** ANNOY, IRK : agacer, ennuyer, embêter **2** PESTER : harceler **3** WORRY : inquiéter, préoccuper — *vi* : s'en faire, se déranger <don't bother : ne te dérange pas>
bother[2] *n* **1** ANNOYANCE : ennui *m* <what a bother! : quel ennui!> **2** TROUBLE : peine *f* <it's not worth the bother : ça ne vaut pas la peine>
bothersome [ˈbɑðərsəm] *adj* : ennuyeux, gênant
bottle[1] [ˈbɑtəl] *vt* **bottled; bottling** : mettre en bouteille

bottle[2] *n* **1** : bouteille *f* **2** : biberon *m* (d'un bébé) **3** FLASK : flacon *m* <a bottle of perfume : un flacon de parfum> **4 bottle opener** : ouvre-bouteilles *m*

bottleneck |ˈbɑtəlˌnɛk| *n* **1** NARROWING : rétrécissement *m* (de la chaussée) **2** CONGESTION : embouteillage *m* (de la circulation) **3** HOLDUP : goulot *m* d'étranglement

bottom[1] |ˈbɑt̬əm| *adj* **1** : du bas, inférieur <bottom lip : lèvre inférieure> **2** : premier <the bottom step : la première marche>

bottom[2] *n* **1** : bas *m*, pied *m* (d'un escalier, d'une page, etc.), fond *m* (de la mer) **2** : dernière place *f;* bas *m* <at the bottom of her class : dernière de classe> **3** ORIGIN, ROOT : origine *f*, fond *m* <to get to the bottom of sth : découvrir le fin fond de qqch> **4** BUTTOCKS : fesses *fpl*, derrière *m fam*

bottomless |ˈbɑt̬əmləs| *adj* : sans fond, insondable

botulism |ˈbɑtʃəˌlɪzəm| *n* : botulisme *m*

bough |ˈbaʊ| *n* : branche *f*, rameau *m*

bought → **buy**[1]

bouillon |ˈbuːˌjɑn; ˈbʊlˌjɑn, -jən| *n* : bouillon *m*

boulder |ˈboːldər| *n* : rocher *m*

boulevard |ˈbʊləˌvɑrd, ˈbuː-| *n* : boulevard *m*

bounce[1] |ˈbaʊnts| *v* **bounced; bouncing** *vt* : faire rebondir (une balle) — *vi* **1** : rebondir, faire des bonds <the ball bounced into the air : la balle a rebondi dans l'espace> **2** : être sans provision (se dit d'un chèque)

bounce[2] *n* **1** : bond *m* (d'une balle) **2** LIVELINESS : vitalité *f*

bound[1] |ˈbaʊnd| *vt* CONFINE : limiter, borner — *vi* LEAP : bondir, sauter

bound[2] *adj* **1** TIED : lié, attaché <bound hand and foot : pieds et poings liés> **2** OBLIGED : obligé, tenu **3** CERTAIN : sûr, certain <it's bound to rain : il est sûr de pleuvoir> **4** : relié (se dit d'un livre) **5 bound for** : à destination de, en route pour

bound[3] *n* **1** LEAP : bond *m*, saut *m* **2 bounds** *npl* LIMIT : limite *f*, bornes *fpl*

boundary |ˈbaʊndri, -dəri| *n, pl* **-aries 1** : limite *f*, frontière *f* **2** *or* **boundary line** : limites *fpl* du terrain

boundless |ˈbaʊndləs| *adj* : sans limites, sans bornes

bounteous |ˈbaʊntiəs| *adj* **1** GENEROUS : généreux **2** ABUNDANT : abondant <a bounteous harvest : une bonne récolte>

bountiful |ˈbaʊntɪfəl| *adj* **1** GENEROUS : généreux, libéral **2** PLENTIFUL : abondant, copieux

bounty |ˈbaʊnti| *n, pl* **-ties 1** : générosité *f*, libéralité *f* **2** REWARD : prime *f*

bouquet |boːˈkeɪ, buː-| *n* **1** : bouquet *m* (de fleurs) **2** : arôme *m*, bouquet *m* (de vin, etc.)

bourbon |ˈbərbən, ˈbʊr-| *n* : bourbon *m*

bourgeois[1] |ˈbʊrʒˌwɑ, bʊrʒˈwɑ| *adj* : bourgeois

bourgeois[2] *n* : bourgeois *m*, -geoise *f*

bourgeoisie |ˌbʊrʒˌwɑˈzi| *n* : bourgeoisie *f*

bout |ˈbaʊt| *n* **1** CONTEST : combat *m*, match *m* **2** ATTACK : accès *m*, crise *f* <a bout of fever : un accès de fièvre> **3** PERIOD : période *f* (de travail, etc.) <a drinking bout : une beuverie>

boutique |buːˈtiːk| *n* : boutique *f*

bovine |ˈboːˌvaɪn, -ˌviːn| *adj* : bovin

bow[1] |ˈbaʊ| *vi* **1** : s'incliner, saluer de la tête <to bow to the audience : saluer le public> **2** BEND : se courber **3** YIELD : s'incliner, se soumettre — *vt* : incliner, courber <to bow one's head : baisser la tête>

bow[2] |ˈbaʊː| *n* **1** BOWING : révérence *f*, salut *m* **2** : proue *f*, avant *m* (d'un navire)

bow[3] |ˈboː| *n* **1** ARCH, BEND : arche *f*, arc *m*, courbe *f* **2** : arc *m* <bows and arrows : des arcs et des flèches> **3** : nœud *m* <bow tie : nœud papillon> **4** : archet *m* (de violon)

bowels |ˈbaʊəlz| *npl* **1** INTESTINES : intestins *mpl* **2** DEPTHS : entrailles *fpl*, profondeurs *fpl* <the bowels of the earth : les entrailles de la terre>

bower |ˈbaʊər| *n* : tonnelle *f*, berceau *m* de verdure

bowl[1] |ˈboːl| *vt* **1** : faire rouler (une boule) **2 to bowl over** OVERWHELM : bouleverser, renverser — *vi* : jouer au bowling

bowl[2] *n* : bol *m*, bassin *m*, cuvette *f*

bowling |ˈboːlɪŋ| *n* : bowling *m*

bowling alley *n* : bowling *m*, allée *f* de quilles *Can*

box[1] |ˈbɑks| *vt* **1** : mettre en boîte **2** SLAP : gifler, claquer (les oreilles, etc.) — *vi* : boxer, faire de la boxe

box[2] *n* **1** : boîte *f*, caisse *f*, coffre *m* <a box of chocolates : une boîte de chocolats> **2** : loge *f* (de théâtre), barre *f* (de témoin) **3** SLAP : gifle *f*, claque *f* **4** *pl* **box** *or* **boxes** : buis *m* (plante)

boxcar |ˈbɑksˌkɑr| *n* : wagon *m* de marchandises

boxer |ˈbɑksər| *n* **1** FIGHTER : boxeur *m* **2** : boxer *m* (chien)

boxing |ˈbɑksɪŋ| *n* : boxe *f*

box office *n* : guichet *m*, billetterie *f*

boxwood |ˈbɑksˌwʊd| *n* : buis *m*

boy |ˈbɔɪ| *n* : garçon *m*

boycott[1] |ˈbɔɪˌkɑt| *vt* : boycotter

boycott[2] *n* : boycott *m*, boycottage *m*

boyfriend |ˈbɔɪˌfrɛnd| *n* : petit ami *m*, chum *m Can fam*

boyhood |ˈbɔɪˌhʊd| *n* : enfance *f*

boyish |ˈbɔɪɪʃ| *adj* : de garçon, d'enfant

bra |ˈbrɑ| → **brassiere**

brace[1] |ˈbreɪs| *vt* **braced; bracing 1** STRENGTHEN : soutenir, renforcer **2**

INVIGORATE : revigorer **3 to brace oneself** : rassembler ses forces

brace[2] *n* **1** PAIR : paire *f* <a brace of quail : une paire de cailles> **2** SUPPORT : attache *f*, support *m* **3** *or* **brace and bit** : vilbrequin *m* **4** : appareil *m* orthopédique, appareil *m* orthodontique (en médecine) **5** BRACKET : accolade *f*

bracelet ['breɪslət] *n* : bracelet *m*

bracken ['brækən] *n* : fougère *f*

bracket[1] ['brækət] *vt* **1** : mettre entre parenthèses, mettre entre crochets **2** GROUP : regrouper, mettre dans le même groupe

bracket[2] *n* **1** SUPPORT : support *m*, tasseau *m* **2** : parenthèse *f*, crochet *m* <in square brackets : entre crochets> **3** CATEGORY : catégorie *f*, tranche *f* <the lower income bracket : la tranche des petits revenus>

brackish ['brækɪʃ] *adj* : saumâtre

brad ['bræd] *n* : semence *f*, clou *m* (sans tête)

brag[1] ['bræg] *vi* **bragged**; **bragging** : se vanter

brag[2] *n* : vantardise *f*, fanfaronnades *fpl*

braggart ['brægərt] *n* : vantard *m*, -tarde *f*

braid[1] ['breɪd] *vt* **1** INTERWEAVE : entrelacer **2** : tresser (les cheveux)

braid[2] *n* **1** TRIMMING : galon *m*, ganse *f* **2** : tresse *f*, natte *f* (de cheveux)

braille ['breɪl] *n* : braille *m*

brain[1] ['breɪn] *vt* KNOCK OUT : assommer

brain[2] *n* **1** : cerveau *m*, cervelle *f* **2** : intelligence *f* <to have brains : être intelligent>

brainless ['breɪnləs] *adj* : stupide, idiot

brainstorm ['breɪn,stɔrm] *n* : idée *f* de génie, inspiration *f*

brainy ['breɪni] *adj* **brainier**; **-est** : intelligent, calé *fam*

braise ['breɪz] *vt* **braised**; **braising** : braiser

brake[1] ['breɪk] *vi* **braked**; **braking** : freiner

brake[2] *n* : frein *m*

bramble ['bræmbəl] *n* : ronce *f*

bran ['bræn] *n* : son *m*

branch[1] ['bræntʃ] *vi* **1** : se ramifier (se dit d'une plante) **2** *or* **to branch off** DIVERGE : bifurquer

branch[2] *n* **1** : branche *f* (d'une plante) **2** : embranchement *m* (d'une route) **3** DIVISION : succursale *f*, agence *f*, section *f* <branch manager : directeur de succursale>

brand[1] ['brænd] *vt* **1** : marquer (au fer rouge) **2** LABEL, STIGMATIZE : flétrir, étiqueter, stigmatiser

brand[2] *n* **1** : marque *f* (sur des animaux) **2** STIGMA : marque *f*, stigmate *m* **3** MAKE : marque *f* (de fabrique)

brandish ['brændɪʃ] *vt* : brandir

brand–new ['brænd'nu:, -'nju:] *adj* : tout neuf

brandy ['brændi] *n, pl* **-dies** : cognac *m*, eau-de-vie *f*

brash ['bræʃ] *adj* **1** IMPULSIVE, RASH : impétueux, irréfléchi **2** IMPUDENT : impertinent, effronté

brass ['bræs] *n* **1** : cuivre *m* (jaune), laiton *m* **2** : cuivres *mpl* (d'un orchestre) **3** GALL, NERVE : impudence *f*, toupet *m fam* **4** OFFICERS : officiers *mpl* (militaires)

brassiere [brə'zɪr, brɑ-] *n* : soutien-gorge *m*, brassière *f Can*

brassy ['bræsi] *adj* **brassier**; **-est 1** : cuivré **2** IMPUDENT : effronté, impertinent

brat ['bræt] *n* : môme *mf France fam;* gosse *mf France fam;* polisson *m*, -sonne *f*

bravado [brə'vɑdo] *n, pl* **-does** *or* **-dos** : bravade *f*

brave[1] ['breɪv] *vt* **braved**; **braving** : braver, défier

brave[2] *adj* **braver**; **bravest** : courageux, brave — **bravely** *adv*

brave[3] *n* : guerrier *m* indien

bravery ['breɪvəri] *n, pl* **-eries** : courage *m*, bravoure *f*

bravo ['brɑ,vo:] *n, pl* **-vos** : bravo *m*

brawl[1] ['brɔl] *vi* : se bagarrer

brawl[2] *n* : bagarre *f*, rixe *f*

brawn ['brɔn] *n* : muscles *mpl*

brawny ['brɔni] *adj* **brawnier**; **-est** : musclé

bray[1] ['breɪ] *vi* : braire

bray[2] *n* : braiment *m*

brazen ['breɪzən] *adj* **1** COPPER : de cuivre **2** IMPUDENT : effronté, impudent <a brazen lie : un mensonge effronté>

brazenly ['breɪzənli] *adv* : effrontément

brazier ['breɪʒər] *n* : brasero *m*

Brazilian[1] [brə'zɪljən] *adj* : brésilien

Brazilian[2] *n* : Brésilien *m*, -lienne *f*

breach[1] [bri:tʃ] *vt* **1** BREAK, VIOLATE : enfreindre, transgresser **2** PENETRATE : ouvrir une brèche dans (un mur, etc.)

breach[2] *n* **1** VIOLATION : infraction *f*, violation *f* **2** : abus *m* <breach of faith : abus de confiance> **3** : rupture *f*, annulation *f* <breach of contract : rupture de contrat> **4** GAP : brèche *f*, ouverture *f*

bread[1] ['brɛd] *vt* : paner, couvrir de chapelure

bread[2] *n* : pain *m*

breadth ['brɛtθ] *n* : largeur *f*

breadwinner ['brɛd,wɪnər] *n* : soutien *m* de famille

break[1] ['breɪk] *v* **broke** ['bro:k]; **broken** ['bro:kən]; **breaking** *vt* **1** : casser, briser **2** VIOLATE : violer, transgresser **3** TELL : annoncer, faire part de <to break the news : annoncer la nouvelle> **4** SOFTEN : amortir, adoucir (une chute) **5** INTERRUPT : interrompre <to break the silence : percer le silence> **6** SURPASS : battre (un record, etc.) **7 to break down** : abattre, enfoncer <she broke down the door : elle a enfoncé la porte> — *vi* **1** : se casser, se briser **2** : se lever, se montrer <day is breaking : le jour se lève> **3** *or* **to break out** ESCAPE : s'évader, se libérer **4** HALT : prendre une pause, arrêter **5 to break down** FAIL : tomber en panne **6 to break down** COLLAPSE : s'effondrer, s'écrouler **7 to break in** : entrer par effraction (dans une maison) **8 to break up** SEPARATE : rompre, se quitter

break[2] *n* **1** : cassure *f,* rupture *f* **2** GAP : trouée *f,* brèche *f* **3** REST : pause *f,* récréation *f,* break *m Can* <to take a break : faire une pause> **4** CHANCE : chance *f,* veine *f fam* <I had a lucky break : j'ai eu de la chance> **5** : interruption *f* (d'une émission)

breakage |'breɪkɪdʒ| *n* : casse *f,* bris *m*

breakdown |'breɪk,daʊn| *n* **1** : rupture *f* <breakdown in negotiations : rupture des négociations> **2** FAILURE : panne *f* (d'une machine) **3** *or* **nervous breakdown** : dépression *f* nerveuse

breaker |breɪkər| *n* **1** WAVE : brisant *m* **2** → **circuit breaker**

breakfast |'brɛkfəst| *n* : petit déjeuner *m France,* déjeuner *m Can*

breakwater |'brek,wɔt̬ər, -,wɑ-| *n* : jetée *f,* brise-lames *m*

breast |'brɛst| *n* **1** : sein *m* (d'une femme) **2** CHEST : poitrine *f*

breastbone |'brɛst,bo:n| *n* : sternum *m*

breast–feed |'brɛst,fi:d| *vt* **-fed** |-,fɛd|; **-feeding** : allaiter

breath |'brɛθ| *n* **1** : souffle *m,* haleine *f* <out of breath : à bout de souffle> <bad breath : mauvaise haleine> **2** GUST : souffle *m* <a breath of air : un souffle d'air>

breathe |'bri:ð| *v* **breathed; breathing** *vt* **1** : respirer **2** : pousser, laisser échapper <I breathed a sigh of relief : j'ai poussé un soupir de soulagement> **3** UTTER : souffler <don't breathe a word about it : n'en souffle pas mot> — *vi* **1** : respirer **2** LIVE : vivre, être en vie

breathless |'brɛθləs| *adj* : à bout de souffle, haletant

breathlessly |'brɛθləsli| *adv* : en haletant

breathtaking |'brɛθ,teɪkɪŋ| *adj* : à vous couper le souffle, stupéfiant

breeches |'brɪtʃəz, bri:-| *npl* PANTS : culotte *f,* pantalon *m*

breed[1] |'bri:d| *v* **bred** |'brɛd|; **breeding** *vt* **1** RAISE : élever, faire l'élevage de **2** CAUSE, PRODUCE : faire naître, engendrer — *vi* : se reproduire, se multiplier

breed[2] *n* **1** : race *f,* espèce *f* **2** KIND : espèce *f,* sorte *f*

breeze[1] |'bri:z| *vi* **breezed; breezing 1** : aller vite <to breeze in : entrer en coup de vent> **2 to breeze through** : réussir facilement (un examen, etc.)

breeze[2] *n* **1** : brise *f* **2 it's a breeze!** : c'est du gâteau!, c'est facile comme tout!

breezy |'bri:zi| *adj* **breezier; -est 1** AIRY, WINDY : venteux, éventé **2** NONCHALANT : désinvolte, léger

brevity |'brɛvət̬i| *n, pl* **-ties** : brièveté *f*

brew[1] |'bru:| *vt* **1** : brasser (de la bière) **2** : préparer, faire infuser (du thé) — *vi* **1** : fermenter (se dit de la bière), infuser (se dit du thé, etc.) **2** : se préparer <there's a storm brewing : un orage se prépare, il y a de l'orage dans l'air>

brew[2] *n* **1** BEER : bière *f* **2** INFUSION : infusion *f* (de thé, etc.)

brewery |'bru:əri, 'brʊri| *n, pl* **-ries** : brasserie *f*

briar → **brier**

bribe[1] |'braɪb| *vt* **bribed; bribing** : soudoyer, acheter, suborner (un témoin)

bribe[2] *n* : pot-de-vin *m*

bribery |'braɪbəri| *n, pl* **-eries** : corruption *f*

bric–a–brac |'brɪkə,bræk| *ns & pl* : bric-à-brac *m*

brick[1] |'brɪk| *vt* **to brick up** : murer

brick[2] *n* : brique *f*

bricklayer |'brɪk,leɪər| *n* : maçon *m*

bricklaying |'brɪk,leɪɪŋ| *n* : maçonnerie *f*

bridal |'braɪdəl| *adj* : nuptial, de mariée, de noce

bride |'braɪd| *n* : mariée *f*

bridegroom |'braɪd,gru:m| *n* : marié *m*

bridesmaid |'braɪdz,meɪd| *n* : demoiselle *f* d'honneur

bridge[1] |'brɪdʒ| *vt* **1** : construire un pont sur **2 to bridge a gap** : combler une lacune, établir un rapprochement

bridge[2] *n* **1** : pont *m* **2** : arête *f* (du nez) **3** : passerelle *f* (d'un navire) **4** DENTURE : bridge *m* (dentaire) **5** : bridge *m* (jeu de cartes)

bridle[1] |'braɪdəl| *v* **-dled; -dling** *vt* **1** : brider (un cheval) **2** RESTRAIN : refréner, brider <to bridle one's tongue : tenir sa langue> — *vi* **to bridle at** : se cabrer contre

bridle[2] *n* : bride *f* (d'un cheval)

brief[1] |'bri:f| *vt* : donner des instructions à, mettre au courant

brief[2] *adj* : bref, court, concis

brief[3] *n* **1** SYNOPSIS : résumé *m* **2** : cause *f* à plaider, dossier *m* (en droit) **3 briefs** *npl* UNDERPANTS : slip *m*

briefcase |'bri:f,keɪs| *n* : serviette *f,* porte-documents *m*

briefly |'bri:fli| *adv* **1** CONCISELY : brièvement, de façon concise **2** IN SHORT : en bref

brier |'braɪər| *n* **1** BRAMBLE : ronce *f* **2** HEATH : bruyère *f*

brig ['brɪg] *n* **1** : brick *m* (navire) **2** : cellule *f* à bord d'un navire
brigade [brɪ'geɪd] *n* : brigade *f*
brigadier general [ˌbrɪgə'dɪr] *n* : général *m* de brigade
brigand ['brɪgənd] *n* : brigand *m*, bandit *m*
bright ['braɪt] *adj* **1** BRILLIANT, SHINING : brillant, éclatant **2** CLEVER : intelligent **3** VIVID : vif <bright colors : couleurs vives> **4** CHEERFUL : joyeux, animé, gai
brighten ['braɪtən] *vt* **1** : faire briller **2** ENLIVEN : égayer, animer — *vi* : s'éclaircir (se dit du temps)
brightly ['braɪtli] *adv* **1** INTENSELY : brillamment, intensément **2** CHEERFULLY : joyeusement, gaiement
brilliance ['brɪljənts] *n* **1** RADIANCE : éclat *m* (d'une lumière) **2** SPLENDOR : splendeur *f*, éclat *m* **3** : grande intelligence *f*
brilliant ['brɪljənt] *adj* **1** BRIGHT : éclatant **2** SPLENDID : brillant, génial <a brilliant idea : une idée géniale> **3** GIFTED : très intelligent, doué
brilliantly ['brɪljəntli] *adv* **1** RADIANTLY : avec éclat **2** EXCELLENTLY : brillamment **3** PARTICULARLY : extrêmement
brim[1] ['brɪm] *vi* **brimmed; brimming 1** *or* **to brim over** : être plein jusqu'à déborder **2 to brim with tears** : se remplir de larmes
brim[2] *n* : bord *m* <full to the brim : plein à ras bord>
brimful ['brɪm'fʊl] *adj* : plein à déborder
brimstone ['brɪmˌsto:n] *n* : soufre *m*
brindled ['brɪndəld] *adj* : moucheté, tacheté
brine ['braɪn] *n* **1** : eau *f* salée, saumure *f* **2** OCEAN : mer *f*, océan *m*
bring ['brɪŋ] *vt* **brought** ['brɔt]; **bringing 1** CARRY, CONVEY : amener (une personne ou un animal), apporter (une chose) **2** *or* **to bring about** PRODUCE : provoquer, causer, entraîner **3** INDUCE, PERSUADE : amener, pousser, persuader **4** LEAD : amener, mener, conduire **5** YIELD : rapporter (en finance) **6 to bring to light** : mettre en lumière **7 to bring sth to an end** : mettre fin à qqch
bring around *vt* **1** PERSUADE : convaincre, convertir **2** → **bring to**
bring out *vt* : sortir (un produit, un livre, etc.)
bring to *vt* REVIVE : ranimer
bring up *vt* **1** REAR : élever **2** MENTION : mentionner, signaler, aborder
brink ['brɪŋk] *n* : bord *m* <on the brink of war : au bord de la guerre> <on the brink of doing : sur le point de faire>
briny ['braɪni] *adj* **brinier; -est** : saumâtre, salé
brisk ['brɪsk] *adj* **1** LIVELY : vif, animé **2** INVIGORATING : vivifiant, frais **3** QUICK : vif, rapide
bristle[1] ['brɪsəl] *vi* **-tled; -tling 1** : se hérisser (se dit des cheveux, etc.) **2** : s'irriter, se hérisser <she's bristling with anger : elle se hérisse de colère>
bristle[2] *n* **1** : soie *f* (d'un animal) **2** : poil *m* (d'une brosse)
bristly ['brɪsəli] *adj* **bristlier; -est 1** PRICKLY : qui pique **2** : hérissé (se dit des cheveux, etc.)
British[1] ['brɪt̬ɪʃ] *adj* : britannique
British[2] *npl* **the British** : les Britanniques
brittle ['brɪtəl] *adj* **-tler; -tlest** : fragile, cassant
broach ['bro:tʃ] *vt* BRING UP : aborder, entamer <to broach a subject : aborder un sujet>
broad ['brɔd] *adj* **1** WIDE : large **2** SPACIOUS : vaste, immense **3** GENERAL : grand, général <broad outlines : grandes lignes> **4** OBVIOUS : transparent <a broad hint : une allusion transparente> **5** LIBERAL : large, libéral <broad ideas : idées larges> **6** CRUDE : gros, vulgaire **7 in broad daylight** : en plein jour
broad bean *n* : fève *f*
broadcast[1] ['brɔdˌkæst] *v* **-cast; -casting** *vt* **1** SCATTER : semer (des graines, etc.) **2** TRANSMIT : diffuser, téléviser **3** SPREAD : répandre — *vi* : émettre, faire des émissions
broadcast[2] *n* **1** BROADCASTING : transmission *f*, diffusion *f* **2** PROGRAM : émission *f* <news broadcast : bulletin d'informations>
broadcaster ['brɔdˌkæstər] *n* : personnalité *f*, journaliste *mf* (de la radio, de la télévision)
broadcloth ['brɔdklɔθ] *n* : drap *m* fin
broaden ['brɔdən] *vt* : élargir <to broaden one's outlook : élargir ses horizons> — *vi* EXPAND, WIDEN : s'élargir
broadloom ['brɔdˌlu:m] *adj* : en grande largeur
broadly ['brɔdli] *adv* **1** WIDELY : largement **2** GENERALLY : en gros, en général
broad-minded ['brɔd'maɪndəd] *adj* : tolérant, large d'esprit
broad-mindedness [brɔd'maɪndədnəs] *n* : largeur *f* d'esprit
broadside[1] ['brɔdˌsaɪd] *adv* : par le travers
broadside[2] *n* **1** VOLLEY : bordée *f* **2** TIRADE : invective *f*, attaque *f* cinglante
brocade [bro'keɪd] *n* : brocart *m*
broccoli ['brɑkəli] *n* : brocoli *m*
brochure [bro'ʃʊr] *n* : brochure *f*, dépliant *m*
brogue ['bro:g] *n* : accent *m* irlandais
broil ['brɔɪl] *v* : griller
broiler ['brɔɪlər] *n* **1** GRILL : gril *m* **2** : poulet *m* à rôtir

broke[1] ['bro:k] → **break**[1]
broke[2] *adj* : fauché *fam,* à sec *fam,* cassé *Can fam* <to go broke : faire faillite>
broken ['bro:kən] *adj* **1** DAMAGED, SHATTERED : cassé, brisé **2** IRREGULAR, UNEVEN : brisé, découpé, accidenté <a broken line : une ligne brisée> <broken coastlines : littoraux découpés> **3** VIOLATED : rompu, manqué <a broken promise : une promesse manquée> **4** IMPERFECT : mauvais, imparfait <in broken French : en mauvais français> **5** CRUSHED : brisé, abattu <he's a broken man : il a le cœur brisé>
brokenhearted [ˌbro:kən'hɑrt̬əd] *adj* : au cœur brisé
broker ['bro:kər] *n* **1** : courtier *m,* -tière *f;* agent *m* **2** → **stockbroker**
brokerage ['bro:kərɪdʒ] *n* : courtage *m*
bromine ['bro:ˌmi:n] *n* : brome *m*
bronchial tubes ['brɑnkiəl] *npl* : bronches *fpl*
bronchitis [brɑŋ'kaɪt̬əs, brɑn-] *n* : bronchite *f*
bronze[1] ['brɑnz] *vt* **bronzed; bronzing** : bronzer
bronze[2] *n* : bronze *m*
brooch ['bro:tʃ, 'bru:tʃ] *n* : broche *f,* épinglette *f Can*
brood[1] ['bru:d] *vi* **1** : couver (se dit d'un oiseau) **2** PONDER : broyer du noir, ruminer
brood[2] *n* : couvée *f,* nichée *f*
brook[1] ['brʊk] *vt* TOLERATE : accepter, tolérer
brook[2] *n* : ruisseau *m*
broom ['bru:m, 'brʊm] *n* **1** : genêt *m* (plante) **2** : balai *m* (pour balayer)
broomstick ['bru:mˌstɪk, 'brʊm-] *n* : manche *m* à balai
broth ['brɔθ] *n, pl* **broths** ['brɔθs, 'brɔðz] : bouillon *m*
brothel ['brɑθəl, 'brɔ-] *n* : maison *f* close, bordel *m fam*
brother ['brʌðər] *n* : frère *m*
brotherhood ['brʌðərˌhʊd] *n* **1** : fraternité *f* **2** ASSOCIATION : confrérie *f*
brother-in-law ['brʌðərɪnˌlɔ] *n, pl* **brothers-in-law** : beau-frère *m*
brotherly ['brʌðərli] *adj* : fraternel <brotherly love : amour fraternel>
brought → **bring**
brow ['braʊ] *n* **1** EYEBROW : sourcil *m* **2** FOREHEAD : front *m* **3** : sommet *m* <the brow of a hill : le sommet d'une colline>
browbeat ['braʊˌbi:t] *vt* **-beat; -beaten** [-ˌbi:t̬ən] *or* **-beat; -beating** : intimider
brown[1] [ˌbraʊn] *vt* **1** : faire dorer (en cuisine) **2** TAN : bronzer, brunir — *vi* : dorer (en cuisine)
brown[2] *adj* **1** : brun, marron **2** TANNED : bronzé, bruni
brown[3] *n* : brun *m,* marron *m*
brownish [ˌbraʊnɪʃ] *adj* : brunâtre
browse ['braʊz] *vi* **browsed; browsing 1** GRAZE : brouter, paître **2** LOOK : regarder
browser ['braʊzer] *n* : navigateur *m* (en informatique)
bruin ['bru:ɪn] *n* BEAR : ours *m*
bruise[1] ['bru:z] *v* **bruised; bruising** *vt* **1** : faire un bleu à, contusionner **2** : taler (un fruit) — *vi* : se faire des bleus (se dit d'une personne), se taler (se dit d'un fruit)
bruise[2] *n* : bleu *m,* contusion *f,* meurtrissure *f,* prune *f Can*
brunch ['brʌntʃ] *n* : brunch *m*
brunet[1] [bru:'nɛt] *or* **brunette** *adj* : châtain, brun (se dit des cheveux)
brunet[2] *or* **brunette** *n* : brun *m,* brune *f*
brunt ['brʌnt] *n* BURDEN : poids *m* <to bear the brunt of : subir tout le poids de, porter le plus gros de>
brush[1] ['brʌʃ] *vt* **1** : brosser, se brosser <I brushed my hair : je me suis brossé les cheveux> **2** GRAZE : frôler, effleurer **3** *or* **to brush up** SWEEP : balayer, ramasser **4 to brush off** DISMISS : écarter, repousser — *vi* **to brush up on** : se remettre à, réviser
brush[2] *n* **1** : brosse *f* (à cheveux), pinceau *m* (de peintre) **2** SCRUB, UNDERBRUSH : brousse *f,* broussailles *fpl,* fardoches *fpl Can* **3** TOUCH : effleurement *m* **4** SKIRMISH : accrochage *m,* escarmouche *f* <to have a brush with the law : avoir des démêlés avec la justice>
brush-off ['brʌʃˌɔf] *n* **to give s.o. the brush-off** : envoyer promener qqn
brusque ['brʌsk] *adj* : brusque
brusquely ['brʌskli] *adv* : brusquement, avec brusquerie
brutal ['bru:t̬əl] *adj* : brutal, cruel — **brutally** *adv*
brutality [bru:'tæləti] *n, pl* **-ties** : brutalité *f*
brutalize ['bru:t̬əlˌaɪz] *vt* **-ized; -izing** : brutaliser
brute[1] ['bru:t] *adj* **1** : bestial, animal **2** SHEER : brutal, vif, simple <brute force : force brutale>
brute[2] *n* **1** BEAST : brute *f,* bête *f* **2** : brute *f* (personne)
brutish ['bru:t̬ɪʃ] *adj* **1** : de brute, bestial **2** CRUEL : brutal, cruel **3** STUPID : bête, stupide
bubble[1] ['bʌbəl] *vi* **-bled; -bling 1** : bouillonner, pétiller **2 to bubble over** : déborder
bubble[2] *n* : bulle *f*
bubbly ['bʌbəli] *adj* **bubblier; -est 1** BUBBLING : plein de bulles, pétillant **2** LIVELY : plein d'entrain
bubonic plague [bu:'bɑnɪk, 'bju:-] *n* : peste *f* bubonique
buccaneer [ˌbʌkə'nɪr] *n* : boucanier *m*
buck[1] ['bʌk] *vi* **1** : lancer une ruade (se dit d'un cheval) **2 to buck up** : se secouer — *vt* OPPOSE : résister, s'op-

poser à <to buck the system : lutter contre le système>

buck[2] *n, pl* **bucks 1** *or pl* **buck** : mâle *m* (d'un animal) **2** DOLLAR : dollar *m,* piastre *f Can fam* **3** MONEY : fric *m fam* <to make a buck : se faire du fric> **4 to pass the buck** : refiler la responsabilité aux autres

bucket [ˈbʌkət] *n* : seau *m*

buckle[1] [ˈbʌkəl] *v* **-led; -ling** *vt* **1** FASTEN : boucler **2** DISTORT, WARP : gauchir, déformer — *vi* **1** BEND, WARP : se courber, se voiler **2 to buckle down** : s'atteler, s'appliquer

buckle[2] *n* **1** CLASP : boucle *f* **2** WARPING : gauchissement *m*

buckshot [ˈbʌkˌʃɑt] *n* : chevrotine *f*

buckskin [ˈbʌkˌskɪn] *n* : peau *f* de daim

bucktooth [ˈbʌkˌtu:θ] *n, pl* **-teeth** : dent *f* saillante <to have buckteeth : avoir des dents de lapin>

buckwheat [ˈbʌkˌ*h*wi:t] *n* : sarrasin *m,* blé *m* noir

bucolic [bju:ˈkɑlɪk] *adj* : bucolique

bud[1] [ˈbʌd] *vi* **budded; budding** : bourgeonner, former des boutons

bud[2] *n* : bourgeon *m* (d'une feuille), bouton *m* (d'une fleur)

Buddhism [ˈbu:ˌdɪzəm, ˈbʊ-] *n* : bouddhisme *m*

Buddhist[1] [ˈbu:ˌdɪst, ˈbʊ-] *adj* : bouddhiste

Buddhist[2] *n* : bouddhiste *mf*

buddy [ˈbʌdi] *n, pl* **-dies** : copain *m,* -pine *f*

budge [ˈbʌdʒ] *vi* **budged; budging 1** MOVE : bouger, se déplacer **2** YIELD : changer d'avis, céder

budget[1] [ˈbʌdʒət] *vt* : budgétiser — *vi* : dresser un budget

budget[2] *n* : budget *m*

budgetary [ˈbʌdʒəˌtɛri] *adj* : budgétaire

buff[1] [ˈbʌf] *vt* POLISH : polir, lustrer

buff[2] *adj* : chamois, beige

buff[3] *n* **1** : chamois *m* (couleur) **2** ENTHUSIAST : mordu *m,* -due *f fam;* fanatique *mf*

buffalo [ˈbʌfəˌlo:] *n, pl* **-lo** *or* **-loes** : buffle *m,* bison *m* (d'Amérique)

buffer [ˈbʌfər] *n* **1** : tampon *m* <buffer zone : région tampon> **2 nail buffer** : polissoir à ongles

buffet[1] [ˈbʌfət] *vt* BATTER : frapper, battre

buffet[2] *n* BLOW : coup *m*

buffet[3] [ˌbʌˈfeɪ, ˌbu:-] *n* **1** : buffet *m* (repas) **2** SIDEBOARD : buffet *m*

buffoon [ˌbʌˈfu:n] *n* : bouffon *m,* clown *m*

buffoonery [ˌbʌˈfu:nəri] *n, pl* **-eries** : bouffonnerie *f*

bug[1] [ˈbʌg] *vt* **bugged; bugging 1** : installer un microphone dans **2** BOTHER : embêter

bug[2] *n* **1** INSECT : insecte *m,* bestiole *f,* bébite *f Can fam* **2** FLAW : défaut *m,* erreur *f* (en informatique, etc.) **3** GERM : microbe *m,* virus *m* **4** MICROPHONE : microphone *m*

bugaboo [ˈbʌgəˌbu:] *n, pl* **-boos** → **bugbear**

bugbear [ˈbʌgˌbær] *n* BOGEY : épouvantail *m,* croque-mitaine *m*

buggy [ˈbʌgi] *n, pl* **-gies 1** CARRIAGE : buggy *m,* boghei *m,* calèche *f* **2** BABY CARRIAGE : voiture *f* d'enfant, landau *m France*

bugle [ˈbju:gəl] *n* : clairon *m*

bugler [ˈbju:gələr] *n* : clairon *m*

build[1] [ˈbɪld] *v* **built** [ˈbɪlt]; **building** *vt* **1** CONSTRUCT : construire, bâtir **2** DEVELOP, ESTABLISH : bâtir, établir, fonder **3** INCREASE : augmenter — *vi* INTENSIFY : augmenter

build[2] *n* PHYSIQUE : carrure *f,* charpente *f*

building [ˈbɪldɪŋ] *n* **1** EDIFICE : bâtiment *m,* immeuble *m* **2** CONSTRUCTION : construction *f*

built–in [ˈbɪltˈɪn] *adj* : encastré

bulb [ˈbʌlb] *n* **1** : bulbe *m* (d'une plante), réservoir *m* (d'un thermomètre) **2** LIGHTBULB : ampoule *f*

bulbous [ˈbʌlbəs] *adj* : bulbeux

Bulgarian[1] [bʌlˈgæriən, bʊl-] *adj* : bulgare

Bulgarian[2] *n* **1** : Bulgare *mf* **2** : bulgare *m* (langue)

bulge[1] [ˈbʌldʒ] *vi* **bulged; bulging 1** SWELL : bomber, être gonflé **2** : sortir de la tête (se dit des yeux)

bulge[2] *n* : renflement *m*

bulk [ˈbʌlk] *n* **1** MAGNITUDE : masse *f,* volume *m* **2** FIBER : fibre *m* (alimentaire) **3 in ~** : en gros **4 the bulk of** : la majeure partie de, le plus gros de

bulkhead [ˈbʌlkˌhɛd] *n* : cloison *f*

bulky [ˈbʌlki] *adj* **bulkier; -est** : volumineux, encombrant

bull [ˈbʊl] *n* **1** : taureau *m* **2** MALE : mâle *m* (de l'orignal, de la baleine, etc.) **3** *or* **papal bull** : bulle *f* (papale) **4** DECREE : décret *m,* règlement *m*

bulldog [ˈbʊlˌdɔg] *n* : bouledogue *m*

bulldoze [ˈbʊlˌdo:z] *vt* **-dozed; -dozing 1** : démolir au bulldozer, raser au bulldozer **2** FORCE : forcer <to bulldoze one's way : se frayer un chemin>

bulldozer [ˈbʊlˌdo:zər] *n* : bulldozer *m*

bullet [ˈbʊlət] *n* : balle *f* (d'un fusil)

bulletin [ˈbʊlətən, -lətən] *n* **1** NOTICE : bulletin *m,* communiqué *m* <news bulletin : bulletin d'informations> **2** NEWSLETTER : bulletin *m*

bulletin board *n* : tableau *m* d'affichage, babillard *m Can*

bulletproof [ˈbʊlətˌpru:f] *adj* : pare-balles (se dit des vêtements), blindé (se dit d'une voiture)

bullfight [ˈbʊlˌfaɪt] *n* : corrida *f*

bullfighter [ˈbʊlˌfaɪtər] *n* : matador *m,* torero *m*

bullfrog [ˈbʊlˌfrɔg] *n* : grenouille *f* taureau

bullheaded [ˈbʊl,hɛdəd] *adj* : entêté, têtu
bullion [ˈbʊljən] *n* : or *m* en lingots, argent *m* en lingots
bullock [ˈbʊlək] *n* **1** : bouvillon *m* **2** STEER : bœuf *m*
bull's–eye [ˈbʊlz,aɪ] *n, pl* **bull's–eyes** : centre *m* (de la cible), mille *m*
bully[1] [ˈbʊli] *vt* **-lied; -lying** : intimider, malmener, tyranniser
bully[2] *n, pl* **-lies** : tyran *m*, petite brute *f*
bulrush [ˈbʊl,rʌʃ] *n* : jonc *m*
bulwark [ˈbʊl,wərk, -,wɔrk; ˈbʌl,wərk] *n* : rempart *m*, fortification *f*
bum[1] [ˈbʌm] *v* **bummed; bumming** *vt* : taper qqn de *fam*, quémander <to bum money : quémander de l'argent> — *vi* **to bum around** LOAF : fainéanter, paresser
bum[2] *adj* BAD : minable, faux, mauvais <a bum rap : une accusation mensongère>
bum[3] *n* **1** HOBO, TRAMP : clochard *m*, -charde *f* **2** LOAFER : fainéant *m*, fainéante *f*
bumblebee [ˈbʌmbəl,bi:] *n* : bourdon *m*
bump[1] [ˈbʌmp] *vt* HIT : heurter, cogner <to bump one's head : se cogner la tête> — *vi* **to bump into** MEET : tomber sur, rencontrer par hasard
bump[2] *n* **1** JOLT : secousse *f* **2** COLLISION, IMPACT : choc *m*, heurt *m* **3** LUMP : bosse *f*, poque *f Can fam*
bumper[1] [ˈbʌmpər] *adj* : exceptionnel, record
bumper[2] *n* : pare-chocs *m*
bumpkin [ˈbʌmpkən] *n* : péquenaud *m*, -naude *f France fam;* rustre *mf*
bumpy [ˈbʌmpi] *adj* **bumpier; -est 1** ROUGH, UNEVEN : cahoteux, bosselé **2** : agité <a bumpy crossing : une traversée agitée>
bun [ˈbʌn] *n* : petit pain *m* (au lait)
bunch[1] [ˈbʌntʃ] *vt* : mettre ensemble, mettre en bottes — *vi* **to bunch up** : se serrer (se dit des personnes), être retroussé (se dit des vêtements)
bunch[2] *n* **1** : bouquet *m* (de fleurs), grappe *f* (de raisins), botte *f* (de légumes, etc.) **2** GROUP : groupe *m*
bundle[1] [ˈbʌndəl] *v* **-dled; -dling** *vt* **1** PACKAGE : mettre en paquet, empaqueter **2 to bundle up** : emmitoufler (un enfant, etc.) — *vi* **to bundle up** : s'emmitoufler
bundle[2] *n* **1** PACKAGE : paquet *m*, ballot *m* **2** : liasse *f* (de papiers, etc.), botte *f* (de foin, de légumes) **3** LOT : grande quantité *f*, tas *m* (d'argent, etc.)
bungalow [ˈbʌŋgə,lo:] *n* : maison *f* sans étage
bungle [ˈbʌŋgəl] *vt* **-gled; -gling** BOTCH : gâcher, bousiller *fam*
bungler [ˈbʌŋgələr] *n* : bousilleur *m*, -leuse *f*
bunion [ˈbʌnjən] *n* : oignon *m*
bunk[1] [ˈbʌŋk] *vi* : coucher
bunk[2] *n* **1** BERTH : couchette *f* **2** NONSENSE : balivernes *fpl*, sottises *fpl* **3** *or* **bunk bed** : lits *mpl* superposés
bunker [ˈbʌŋkər] *n* **1** : coffre *m*, soute *f* (d'un navire) <coal bunker : soute à charbon> **2** : blockhaus *m* (militaire)
bunny [ˈbʌni] *n, pl* **-nies → rabbit**
bunt [ˈbʌnt] *n* : amorti *m Can* (au baseball)
bunting [ˈbʌntɪŋ] *n* **1** : bruant *m* (oiseau) **2** : étamine *f*, étoffe *f* (pour les drapeaux)
buoy[1] [ˈbu:i, ˈbɔɪ] *vt* **1** : faire flotter **2** *or* **to buoy up** CHEER, HEARTEN : revigorer, soutenir
buoy[2] *n* : bouée *f*, balise *f* (flottante)
buoyancy [ˈbɔɪəntsi, ˈbu:jən-] *n* : flottabilité *f*
buoyant [ˈbɔɪənt, ˈbu:jənt] *adj* **1** : flottable **2** LIGHTHEARTED : gai, enjoué
bur *or* **burr** [ˈbər] *n* : bardane *f*
burden[1] [ˈbərdən] *vt* : charger, accabler
burden[2] *n* : charge *f*, fardeau *m*
burdensome [ˈbərdənsəm] *adj* : lourd, pesant
burdock [ˈbər,dɑk] *n* : bardane *f*
bureau [ˈbjʊro] *n* **1** CHEST OF DRAWERS : commode *f* **2** DEPARTMENT : service *m* (gouvernemental) **3** AGENCY : agence *f*, bureau *m* <credit bureau : agence de recouvrement>
bureaucracy [bjʊˈrɑkrəsi] *n, pl* **-cies** : bureaucratie *f*
bureaucrat [ˈbjʊrə,kræt] *n* : bureaucrate *mf* — **bureaucratic** [,bjʊrəˈkrætɪk] *adj*
burgeon [ˈbərdʒən] *vi* **1** BLOOM : éclore, bourgeonner **2** FLOURISH : fleurir, croître
burglar [ˈbərglər] *n* : cambrioleur *m*, -leuse *f*
burglarize [ˈbərglə,raɪz] *vt* **-ized; -izing** : cambrioler, dévaliser
burglary [ˈbərgləri] *n, pl* **-glaries** : cambriolage *m*
burgundy [ˈbərgəndi] *n, pl* **-dies** : bourgogne *m* (vin)
burial [ˈbɛriəl] *n* : enterrement *m*, inhumation *f*
burlap [ˈbər,læp] *n* : toile *f* à sac
burlesque[1] [bərˈlɛsk] *vt* **-lesqued; -lesquing** : tourner en ridicule, parodier
burlesque[2] *n* **1** PARODY : burlesque *m*, parodie *f* **2** *or* **burlesqe show** : revue *f* déshabillée
burly [ˈbərli] *adj* **burlier; -est** : de forte carrure, costaud *fam*
burn[1] [ˈbərn] *v* **burned** [ˈbərnd, ˈbərnt] *or* **burnt** [ˈbərnt]; **burning** *vi* **1** : brûler <to burn down : brûler complètement> <burning with desire : brûlant de désir> <she burns easily : elle brûle facilement> **2** : être allumé (se dit d'une lumière) — *vt* **1** : brûler, incendier **2** CONSUME : consommer, brûler (de l'essence, des calories, etc.)

burn[2] *n* : brûlure *f*
burner |ˈbərnər| *n* : brûleur *m* (d'une cuisinière), rond *m Can*
burnish |ˈbərnɪʃ| *vt* : brunir, polir
burp[1] |ˈbərp| *vi* : avoir des renvois, roter *fam*
burp[2] *n* : renvoi *m*, rot *m fam*
burro |ˈbəro, ˈbʊr-| *n, pl* **burros** : (petit) âne *m*
burrow[1] |ˈbəro| *vt* : creuser — *vi* **1** : creuser un terrier **2 to burrow into** SEARCH : fouiller dans
burrow[2] *n* : terrier *m*
bursar |ˈbərsər| *n* : économe *mf*
burst[1] |ˈbərst| *v* **burst** *or* **bursted; bursting** *vt* : crever, faire éclater — *vi* **1** : crever, éclater (se dit d'un obus, d'une bombe, etc.) **2** OVERFLOW : déborder, être rempli <bursting with energy : débordant d'énergie> **3 to burst in** : entrer en coup de vent **4 to burst into tears** : fondre en larmes **5 to burst out laughing** : éclater de rire
burst[2] *n* **1** EXPLOSION : éclatement *m*, explosion *f* **2** OUTBURST : élan *m* (d'enthousiasme), éclat *m* (de rire)
Burundian[1] |bʊˈruːndiən, -ˈrʊn-| *adj* : burundais
Burundian[2] *n* : Burundais *m*, -daise *f*
bury |ˈbɛri| *vt* **buried; burying 1** INTER : enterrer, ensevelir **2** CONCEAL : enfouir, cacher **3** IMMERSE : plonger, immerger
bus[1] |ˈbʌs| *v* **bused** *or* **bussed** |ˈbʌst|; **busing** *or* **bussing** |ˈbʌsɪŋ| *vt* : transporter en autobus — *vi* : voyager en autobus
bus[2] *n, pl* **buses** *or* **busses** : bus *m*, autobus *m*
bush |ˈbʊʃ| *n* **1** SHRUB : buisson *m*, arbuste *m* **2** THICKET : fourré *m* **3 the bush** WILDERNESS : la brousse
bushel |ˈbʊʃəl| *n* : boisseau *m*
bushy |ˈbʊʃi| *adj* **bushier; -est** : touffu, broussailleux
busily |ˈbɪzəli| *adv* : activement
business |ˈbɪznəs, -nəz| *n* **1** OCCUPATION : occupation *f*, profession *f* <he's in the restaurant business : il est restaurateur de profession> **2** COMMERCE, TRADE : affaires *fpl*, commerce *m* **3** FIRM : entreprise *f*, firme *f*, affaire *f* **4** AFFAIR, CONCERN : affaire *f*, question *f* <that's none of your business : ce n'est pas de vos affaires>
businessman |ˈbɪznəsˌmæn, -nəz-| *n, pl* **-men** : homme *m* d'affaires
businesswoman |ˈbɪznəsˌwʊmən, -nəz-| *n, pl* **-women** : femme *f* d'affaires
bust[1] |ˈbʌst| *vt* **1** BREAK, SMASH : casser, briser **2** TAME : dresser (un cheval sauvage, etc.)
bust[2] *n* **1** : buste *m* (en sculpture) **2** BREASTS : seins *mpl*, poitrine *f*
bustle[1] |ˈbʌsəl| *vi* **-tled; -tling** : s'affairer, s'agiter
bustle[2] *n or* **hustle and bustle** : agitation *f*, activité *f*
busy[1] |ˈbɪzi| *vt* **busied; busying 1** : occuper **2 to busy oneself** : s'occuper
busy[2] *adj* **busier; -est 1** : occupé, affairé <to look busy : avoir l'air occupé> **2** : occupé, engagé *Can fam* (se dit d'une ligne téléphonique) **3** BUSTLING : animé, actif (se dit d'une rue, d'une ville, etc.)
busybody |ˈbɪziˌbɑdi| *n* **to be a busybody** : faire la mouche du coche
but[1] |ˈbʌt| *conj* **1** EXCEPT : mais <I would like to stay but I can't : j'aimerais rester mais je ne peux pas> **2** THAT : que <there is no doubt but he will win : il n'y a pas de doute qu'il gagnera> **3** YET : mais <poor but proud : pauvre mais fière>
but[2] *prep* EXCEPT : sauf, excepté <everyone but Anne : tout le monde sauf Anne> <it's nothing but an insult : ça n'est qu'une insulte>
butcher[1] |ˈbʊtʃər| *vt* **1** SLAUGHTER : abattre, tuer (un animal) **2** KILL : massacrer (une personne) **3** BOTCH : bousiller *fam*
butcher[2] *n* : boucher *m*, -chère *f*
butler |ˈbʌtlər| *n* : maître *m* d'hôtel
butt[1] |ˈbʌt| *vt* **1** : donner un coup de tête à, donner un coup de corne à **2** ABUT : être contigu à — *vi* **to butt in** : interrompre, se mêler
butt[2] *n* **1** BUTTING : coup *m* de tête, coup *m* de corne **2** TARGET : cible *f*, victime *f* <the butt of a practical joke : la victime d'une farce> **3** END : crosse *f* (d'un rifle), mégot *m fam* (de cigarette)
butte |ˈbjuːt| *n* : butte *f*, tertre *m*
butter[1] |ˈbʌt̬ər| *vt* : beurrer
butter[2] *n* : beurre *m*
buttercup |ˈbʌt̬ərˌkʌp| *n* : bouton-d'or *m*
butterfat |ˈbʌt̬ərˌfæt| *n* : matière *f* grasse
butterfly |ˈbʌt̬ərˌflaɪ| *n, pl* **-flies** : papillon *m*
buttermilk |ˈbʌt̬ərˌmɪlk| *n* : babeurre *m*
butterscotch |ˈbʌt̬ərˌskɑtʃ| *n* : caramel *m* dur au beurre
buttocks |ˈbʌt̬əks, -ˌtɑks| *npl* : fesses *fpl*
button[1] |ˈbʌtən| *vt* : boutonner (une blouse, etc.) — *vi* : se boutonner
button[2] *n* **1** : bouton *m* (de vêtements) **2** SWITCH : bouton *m*, piton *m Can fam*
buttonhole[1] |ˈbʌtənˌhoːl| *vt* **-holed; -holing** : accrocher, retenir (une personne)
buttonhole[2] *n* : boutonnière *f*
buttress[1] |ˈbʌtrəs| *vt* : étayer
buttress[2] *n* **1** : contrefort *m* (en architecture) **2** SUPPORT : pilier *m*, soutien *m*
buxom |ˈbʌksəm| *adj* : plantureux, bien en chair
buy[1] |ˈbaɪ| *vt* **bought** |ˈbɔt|; **buying** : acheter

buy[2] *n* **1** BARGAIN : affaire *f* <a good buy : une bonne affaire> **2** PURCHASE : acquisition *f*
buyer [ˈbaɪər] *n* : acheteur *m*, -teuse *f*
buzz[1] [ˈbʌz] *vi* : bourdonner, vrombrir
buzz[2] *n* **1** : bourdonnement *m* (des insectes) **2** MURMUR : brouhaha *m* (de voix), murmure *m* **3** : coup *m* de fil *fam* <I gave him a buzz : je lui ai passé un coup de fil>
buzzard [ˈbʌzərd] *n* : buse *f*
buzzer [ˈbʌzər] *n* : sonnette *f*
buzzword [ˈbʌz,wərd] *n* : mot *m* à la mode
by[1] [ˈbaɪ] *adv* **1** NEAR : près <close by : tout près> **2 to go by** : passer <he walked straight by : il est passé tout droit> <in times gone by : il y a bien longtemps> **3 to stop by** : s'arrêter en passant
by[2] *prep* **1** NEAR : près de, à côté de <he's sitting by the window : il est assis près de la fenêtre> **2** VIA : par, en <by car : en voiture> <by airmail : par avion> **3** PAST : devant, à côté de <she went by the house : elle est passée devant la maison> **4** DURING : pendant <he studied by night : il étudiait pendant la nuit> **5** BEFORE : avant, pas plus tard que <he'll be home by ten : il sera rentré avant dix heures> **6** ACCORDING TO : d'après, selon <by what she says : d'après ce qu'elle dit> **7** (*indicating cause or agent*) : par <she was sent by me : elle était envoyée par moi> <to divide by 4 : diviser par 4>
by and by *adv* : bientôt
by and large *adv* : en général
bygone[1] [ˈbaɪ,gɔn] *adj* : passé, d'autrefois <in bygone days : jadis>
bygone[2] *n* **let bygones be bygones** : oublions le passé
bylaw *or* **byelaw** [ˈbaɪ,lɔ] *n* : statut *m* (d'une organisation), arrêté *m* (municipal)
by–line [ˈbaɪ,laɪn] *n* : signature *f* de journaliste
bypass[1] [ˈbaɪ,pæs] *vt* CIRCUMVENT : contourner, éviter
bypass[2] *n* **1** : route *f* de contournement, déviation *f* **2** : pontage *m* (en médecine)
by–product [ˈbaɪ,prɑdəkt] *n* : sous-produit *m*, dérivé *m*
bystander [ˈbaɪ,stændər] *n* : spectateur *m*, -trice *f*
byway [ˈbaɪ,weɪ] *n* : route *f* secondaire
byword [ˈbaɪ,wərd] *n* : proverbe *m*

C

c [ˈsiː] *n, pl* **c's** *or* **cs** : c *m*, troisième lettre de l'alphabet
cab [ˈkæb] *n* **1** TAXICAB : taxi *m* **2** : cabine *f* (d'un camion, d'une locomotive, etc.) **3** CARRIAGE : fiacre *m*
cabal [kəˈbɑl, -ˈbæl] *n* : cabale *f*
cabana [kəˈbænjə, -ˈbænə] *n* : cabine *f* de plage, tente *f* de plage
cabaret [,kæbəˈreɪ] *n* : cabaret *m*
cabbage [ˈkæbɪdʒ] *n* : chou *m*
cabdriver [ˈkæb,draɪvər] *n* : chauffeur *m* de taxi
cabin [ˈkæbən] *n* **1** : cabine *f* (d'un navire, d'un avion, etc.) **2** HUT : cabane *f*
cabinet [ˈkæbnət, ˈkæbə-] *n* **1** : meuble *m* de rangement, vitrine *f* **2** : cabinet *m* (du gouvernement) **3** *or* **filing cabinet** : classeur *m* **4** *or* **medicine cabinet** : armoire *f* à pharmacie
cabinetmaker [ˈkæbnət,meɪkər ˈkæbə-] *n* : ébéniste *mf*
cabinetmaking [ˈkæbnət,meɪkɪŋ ˈkæbə-] *n* : ébénisterie *f*
cable[1] [ˈkeɪbəl] *vt* **-bled; -bling** : câbler
cable[2] *n* **1** ROPE, WIRE : câble *m* **2** → **cablegram**
cablegram [ˈkeɪbəl,græm] *n* : câblogramme *m*, câble *m*
caboose [kə,buːs] *n* : fourgon *m* de queue
cabstand [ˈkæb,stænd] *n* : station *f* de taxis
cacao [kəˈkaʊ, -ˈkeɪo] *n, pl* **cacaos** : cacao *m*
cache [ˈkæʃ] *n* : cache *f* (de provisions), cachette *f*
cachet [kæˈʃeɪ] *n* : cachet *m*
cackle[1] [ˈkækəl] *vi* **-led; -ling** : caqueter, glousser
cackle[2] *n* : caquet *m*, gloussement *m*
cacophony [kəˈkɑfəni, -kɔ-] *n, pl* **-nies** : cacophonie *f*
cactus [ˈkæktəs] *n, pl* **cacti** [-,taɪ] *or* **-tuses** : cactus *m*
cadaver [kəˈdævər] *n* : cadavre *m*
caddie *or* **caddy** [ˈkædi] *n, pl* **-dies** : caddie *m*
caddy [ˈkædi] *n, pl* **-dies** : boîte *f* à thé
cadence [ˈkeɪdənts] *n* : cadence *f*, rythme *m*
cadet [kəˈdɛt] *n* : élève *mf* officier, élève *mf* agent de police
cadge [ˈkædʒ] *vt* **cadged; cadging** : quémander, se procurer en quémandant
cadmium [ˈkædmiəm] *n* : cadmium *m*
cadre [ˈkæ,dreɪ, ˈkɑ-, -driː] *n* : cadre *m*
caesarean [sɪˈzæriən, -zɛr-] → **cesarean**
caesium *Brit* → **cesium**
café [kæˈfeɪ] *n* : café *m*
cafeteria [,kæfəˈtɪriə] *n* : cafétéria *f*, restaurant *m* libre-service, cantine *f* (dans une école)
caffeine [kæˈfiːn, kə-] *n* : caféine *f*
cage[1] [ˈkeɪdʒ] *vt* **caged; caging** : mettre en cage

cage[2] *n* : cage *f*
cagey ['keɪdʒi] *adj* **cagier; -est 1** CAUTIOUS : prudent, réticent **2** SHREWD : perspicace, astucieux
caisson ['keɪˌsɑn, -sən] *n* : caisson *m*
cajole [kə'dʒo:l] *vt* **-joled; -joling** : cajoler, enjôler
Cajun[1] ['keɪdʒən] *adj* : acadien, cajun
Cajun[2] *n* : Acadien *m*, -dienne *f*; Cajun *mf*
cake[1] ['keɪk] *v* **caked; caking** *vt* ENCRUST : former une croûte sur <caked with mud : couvert de boue séchée> — *vi* HARDEN : durcir, faire croûte
cake[2] *n* **1** : gâteau *m* **2** BAR : pain *m* (de savon)
calabash ['kæləˌbæʃ] *n* : calebasse *f*
calamine ['kæləˌmaɪn] *n* : calamine *f*
calamitous [kə'læmət̬əs] *adj* : catastrophique, désastreux — **calamitously** *adv*
calamity [kə'læmət̬i] *n, pl* **-ties** : calamité *f*
calcium ['kælsiəm] *n* : calcium *m*
calculate ['kælkjəˌleɪt] *v* **-lated; -lating** *vt* **1** COMPUTE : calculer **2** ESTIMATE : calculer, évaluer, estimer — *vi* **1** : calculer, faire des calculs **2** COUNT, RELY : compter <he had calculated on winning : il avait compté sur une victoire>
calculating ['kælkjəˌleɪt̬ɪŋ] *adj* : calculateur, astucieux
calculation [ˌkælkjə'leɪʃən] *n* : calcul *m*
calculator ['kælkjəˌleɪt̬ər] *n* : calculatrice *f*
calculus ['kælkjələs] *n, pl* **-li** [-ˌlaɪ] : calcul *m*
caldron ['kɔldrən] → **cauldron**
calendar ['kæləndər] *n* **1** : calendrier *m* **2** SCHEDULE : programme *m*, agenda *m*
calf ['kæf, 'kaf] *n, pl* **calves** ['kævz, 'kavz] **1** : veau *m* (de bovin) **2** : mollet *m* (de la jambe)
calfskin ['kæfskɪn] *n* : veau *m*
caliber *or* **calibre** ['kæləbər] *n* **1** : calibre *m* <a .38 caliber revolver : un revolver de calibre 38> **2** QUALITY, STATURE : qualité *f*, calibre *m*
calibrate ['kæləbreɪt] *vt* **-brated; -brating** : calibrer (une arme, etc.), étalonner (une balance)
calibration ['kæləˌbreɪʃən] *n* : calibrage *m*, étalonnage *m*
calico ['kælɪˌko:] *n, pl* **-coes** *or* **-cos 1** : calicot *m* **2** *or* **calico cat** : chat *m* tigré
calipers *or Brit* **callipers** ['kæləpərz] *n* : compas *m* (à calibrer)
caliph *or* **calif** ['keɪləf, 'kæ-] *n* : calife *m*
calisthenics [ˌkæləs'θɛnɪks] *ns & pl* : gymnastique *f* suédoise
calk ['kɔk] → **caulk**
call[1] ['kɔl] *vi* **1** CRY, SHOUT : crier **2 to call for** REQUIRE : exiger, demander **3** VISIT : rendre visite, passer — *vt* **1** *or* **to call out** : appeler (un nom, etc.), crier (un ordre), annoncer (des résultats) **2** SUMMON : appeler, faire venir, convoquer **3** TELEPHONE : téléphoner à, appeler (au téléphone) **4** NAME : appeler, nommer **5** WAKEN : réveiller **6 to call back** : rappeler **7 to call off** CANCEL : annuler
call[2] *n* **1** CRY, SHOUT : appel *m*, cri *m* (d'un animal) **2** *or* **telephone call** : appel *m* <to give a call to : appeler, téléphoner à> **3** SUMMONS : appel *m* **4** DEMAND, NEED : demande *f* <a call for improvement : une demande d'amélioration> <there's no call to worry : il n'y a aucune raison de s'inquiéter> **5** VISIT : visite *f* <to pay a call : rendre visite>
caller ['kɔlər] *n* **1** VISITOR : visiteur *m*, -teuse *f* **2** : personne *f* qui appelle (au téléphone)
calling ['kɔlɪŋ] *n* : vocation *f*, profession *f*
calliope [kə'laɪəˌpi:, 'kæliˌo:p] *n* : orgue *m* à vapeur
callipers *Brit* → **calipers**
callous[1] ['kæləs] *vt* : rendre calleux
callous[2] *adj* **1** : calleux <callous skin : peau calleuse> **2** UNFEELING : insensible, sans cœur
callously ['kæləsli] *adv* : insensiblement, impitoyablement
callousness ['kæləsnəs] *n* : insensibilité *f*, dureté *f*
callow ['kælo] *adj* : sans expérience, gauche
callus ['kæləs] *n* : cal *m*
calm[1] ['kɑm, 'kɑlm] *v* **calmed; calming** *vt* : calmer, apaiser — *vi* : se calmer <calm down! : calmez-vous!>
calm[2] *adj* : calme, tranquille — **calmly** *adv*
calm[3] *n* **1** QUIETNESS : calme *m*, tranquillité *f* **2** COMPOSURE : sang-froid *m*
caloric [kə'lɔrɪk] *adj* : calorique
calorie ['kæləri] *n* : calorie *f*
calve ['kæv, 'kav] *vi* **calved; calving** : vêler (se dit de la vache)
calves → **calf**
calypso [kə'lɪpˌso:] *n, pl* **-sos** : calypso *m*
calyx ['keɪlɪks, 'kæ-] *n, pl* **-lyxes** *or* **-lyces** [-ləˌsi:z] : calice *m*
cam ['kæm] *n* : came *f*
camaraderie [ˌkɑm'rɑdəri, ˌkæm-; ˌkɑmə'rɑ-] *n* : camaraderie *f*
Cambodian[1] [kæm'bo:diən] *adj* : cambodgien
Cambodian[2] *n* : Cambodgien *m*, -gienne *f*
came → **come**
camel ['kæməl] *n* : chameau *m*
camellia [kə'mi:ljə] *n* : camélia *f*
cameo ['kæmiˌo:] *n, pl* **-eos** : camée
camera ['kæmrə, 'kæmərə] *n* : appareil *m* photo, caméra *f*

Cameroonian[1] [ˌkæməˈruːniən] *adj* : camerounais
Cameroonian[2] *n* : Camerounais *m*, -naise *f*
camouflage[1] [ˈkæməˌflɑʒ, -ˌflɑdʒ] *vt* **-flaged; -flaging** : camoufler
camouflage[2] *n* : camouflage *m*
camp[1] [ˈkæmp] *vi* : camper, faire du camping
camp[2] *n* **1** : camp *m* <to pitch camp : planter son camp> **2** FACTION, GROUP : camp *m*, parti *m* <in the same camp : du même côté>
campaign[1] [kæmˈpeɪn] *vi* : faire campagne
campaign[2] *n* : campagne *f*
campground [ˈkæmpˌgraʊnd] *n* : camping *m*, terrain *m* de camping
camphor [ˈkæmpfər] *n* : camphre *m*
campus [ˈkæmpəs] *n* : campus *m*, cité *f* universitaire *Can*
can[1] [ˈkæn] *v aux, past* **could** [ˈkʊd]; *present s & pl* **can 1** (*expressing possibility*) : pouvoir <he couldn't go : il ne pouvait pas aller> <how can we know? : comment peut-on savoir?> **2** (*expressing knowledge or ability*) : savoir <I can speak three languages : je sais parler trois langues> <her son can't drive : son fils ne sait pas conduire> **3** (*expressing permission*) <can they stay? : peuvent-ils rester?> <you can't smoke here : vous n'avez pas le droit de fumer ici> **4** (*with verbs of sense perception*) <he can see the mountain : il voit la montagne> <I can taste garlic : je goûte l'ail> **5** (*in emphatic expressions*) <that cannot be! : cela n'est pas possible!>
can[2] *vt* **canned; canning** : mettre en boîte, conserver, canner *Can*
can[3] *n* : boîte *f* (d'aliments), canette *f* (de boissons), bidon *m* (d'essence, etc.)
Canada goose *n* : outarde *f Can*
Canadian[1] [kəˈneɪdiən] *adj* : canadien
Canadian[2] *n* : Canadien *m*, -dienne *f*
canal [kəˈnæl] *n* **1** : canal *m* <Panama Canal : Canal de Panama> **2** : conduit *m*, canal *m* (en anatomie)
canapé [ˈkænəpi, -ˌpeɪ] *n* : canapé *m*
canary [kəˈnɛri] *n, pl* **-naries** : canari *m*, serin *m*
cancel [ˈkæntsəl] *vt* **-celed** *or* **-celled; -celing** *or* **-celling** : annuler
cancellation [ˌkæntsəˈleɪʃən] *n* : annulation *f*
cancer [ˈkæntsər] *n* : cancer *m* — **cancerous** *adj*
Cancer *n* : Cancer *m*
cancerous [ˈkæntsərəs] *adj* : cancéreux
candelabra [ˌkændəˈlɑbrə, -læ-] *n* : candélabre *m*
candelabrum [ˌkændəˈlɑbrəm, -læ-] *n, pl* **-bra** → **candelabra**
candid [ˈkændɪd] *adj* **1** : franc, sincère **2** : instantané (se dit d'une photo)
candidacy [ˈkændədəsi] *n, pl* **-cies** : candidature *f*
candidate [ˈkændəˌdeɪt, -dət] *n* : candidat *m*, -date *f*
candidly [ˈkændɪdli] *adv* : franchement, sincèrement
candidness [ˈkændɪdnəs] *n* : franchise *f*
candle [ˈkændəl] *n* : bougie *f*, chandelle *f*, cierge *m* (à l'église)
candlestick [ˈkændəlˌstɪk] *n* : chandelier *m*, bougeoir *m*
candor *or Brit* **candour** [ˈkændər] *n* : franchise *f*
candy[1] [ˈkændi] *vt* **-died; -dying** : confire
candy[2] *n, pl* **-dies 1** : bonbon *m* **2 candies** *pl* : confiserie *f*
cane[1] [ˈkeɪn] *vt* **caned; caning 1** FLOG : donner des coups de badine à (un élève, etc.) **2** : canner (une chaise, etc.)
cane[2] *n* **1** : canne *f* (d'une plante) **2** STICK : canne *f* (pour marcher), badine *f* (pour punir) **3** RATTAN, RUSH : rotin *m*, jonc *m*
canine[1] [ˈkeɪˌnaɪn] *adj* : canin
canine[2] *n* **1** *or* **canine tooth** : canine *f* **2** DOG : canidé *m*
canister [ˈkænəstər] *n* : boîte *f* (métallique)
canker [ˈkæŋkər] *n* : ulcère *f* buccale
cannery [ˈkænəri] *n, pl* **-ries** : conserverie *f*
cannibal [ˈkænəbəl] *n* : cannibale *mf*, anthropophage *mf*
cannibalism [ˈkænəbəˌlɪzəm] *n* : cannibalisme *m*, anthropophagie *f*
cannon [ˈkænən] *n, pl* **-nons** *or* **-non** : canon *m*
cannonball [ˈkænənˌbɔl] *n* : boulet *m* de canon
cannot (can not) [ˈkænˌɑt, kəˈnɑt] → **can**[1]
canny [ˈkæni] *adj* **cannier; -est** SHREWD : prudent, astucieux
canoe [kəˈnuː] *n* : canoë *m*, canot *m Can*
canon [ˈkænən] *n* **1** : canon *m* <canon law : droit canon> **2** WORKS : œuvres *fpl* (littéraires) **3** RULE : canon *m*, règle *f* <the canons of good taste : les règles du bon goût> **4** : chanoine *m* (ecclésiastique)
canonize [ˈkænəˌnaɪz] *vt* **-ized; -izing** : canoniser
canopy [ˈkænəpi] *n, pl* **-pies** : auvent *m*, baldaquin *m*
cant[1] [ˈkænt] *v* **canted; canting** *vt* TILT : incliner, pencher — *vi* LEAN, TIP : s'incliner, se pencher
cant[2] *n* **1** SLANT : pente *f*, inclinaison *f* **2** JARGON : jargon *m* **3** : paroles *fpl* hypocrites
can't [ˈkænt, ˈkant] (*contraction of* **can not**) → **can**[1]
cantaloupe [ˈkæntəlˌoːp] *n* : cantaloup *m*
cantankerous [kænˈtæŋkərəs] *adj* : acariâtre, grincheux, malcommode *Can*

cantata [kən'tɑt̬ə] *n* : cantate *f*

canteen [kæn'ti:n] *n* **1** CAFETERIA : cantine *f* **2** FLASK : flasque *f*, gourde *f*

canter[1] ['kæntər] *vi* : aller au petit galop

canter[2] *n* : petit galop *m*

cantilever[1] ['kæntə,li:vər, -lɛvər] *adj* : cantilever <cantilever bridge : pont cantilever>

cantilever[2] *n* : cantilever *m*

canto ['kæn,to:] *n, pl* **-tos** : chant *m* (d'un poème)

cantor ['kæntər] *n* : chantre *m*

canvas ['kænvəs] *n* **1** : toile *f*, canevas *m* **2** SAIL : voile *f* **3** PAINTING : toile *f*

canvass[1] ['kænvəs] *vt* **-vassed; -vassing 1** POLL : sonder (des opinions) **2** SOLICIT : faire du démarchage électoral auprès

canvass[2] *n* **1** SURVEY : sondage *m* **2** : démarchage *m* électoral

canyon ['kænjən] *n* : canyon *m*

cap[1] ['kæp] *vt* **capped; capping 1** COVER : couvrir **2** CROWN : couronner (une dent) **3** OUTDO : surpasser **4** LIMIT : restreindre, limiter

cap[2] *n* **1** : casquette *f*, bonnet *m*, calotte *f Can* <baseball cap : casquette de baseball> **2** COVER, TOP : capsule *f* (d'une bouteille), capuchon *m* (d'un stylo), couronne *f* (d'une dent) **3** LIMIT : plafond *m*, limite *f*

capability [,keɪpə'bɪlət̬i] *n, pl* **-ties** : aptitude *f*, capacité *f*

capable ['keɪpəbəl] *adj* : compétent, capable

capably ['keɪpəbli] *adv* : avec compétence

capacious [kə'peɪʃəs] *adj* : de grande capacité

capacity[1] [kə'pæsət̬i] *adj* FILLED, PACKED : comble

capacity[2] *n, pl* **-ties 1** ROOM, SPACE : capacité *f*, contenance *f* **2** ABILITY : aptitude *f*, capacité *f* **3** FUNCTION, ROLE : qualité *f*, fonction *f* <in his capacity as supervisor : en qualité de superviseur>

cape ['keɪp] *n* **1** CLOAK : cape *f*, pèlerine *f* **2** : cap *m* <Cape of Good Hope : le cap de Bonne Espérance>

caper[1] ['keɪpər] *vi* GAMBOL : gambader, cabrioler

caper[2] *n* **1** : câpre *f* (assaisonnement) **2** LEAP : gambade *f*, cabriole *f* **3** PRANK : farce *f*

Cape Verdean[1] ['keɪp'vərdiən] *adj* : capverdien

Cape Verdean[2] *n* : Cap-Verdien *m*, -dienne *f*

capillary[1] ['kæpə,lɛri] *adj* : capillaire

capillary[2] *n, pl* **-laries** : capillaire *m*

capital[1] ['kæpət̬əl] *adj* **1** : capital <capital punishment : peine capitale> **2** UPPERCASE : majuscule <capital A : A majuscule> **3** : de capital, des capitaux <capital gain : revenu des capitaux> **4** FIRST-RATE : excellent <a capital idea : une idée excellente>

capital[2] *n* **1** *or* **capital letter** : majuscule *f* **2** *or* **capital city** : capitale *f* **3** WEALTH : capital *m*, fonds *mpl* **4** : chapiteau *m* (d'une colonne)

capitalism ['kæpət̬əl,ɪzəm] *n* : capitalisme *m*

capitalist[1] ['kæpət̬əlɪst] *or* **capitalistic** ['kæpət̬əl,ɪstɪk] *adj* : capitaliste

capitalist[2] *n* : capitaliste *mf*

capitalization [,kæpət̬ələ'zeɪʃən] *n* **1** : capitalisation *f* (en finance) **2** : emploi *m* de lettres majuscules

capitalize ['kæpət̬əl,aɪz] *v* **-ized; -izing** *vt* **1** : capitaliser (en finance) **2** : écrire en majuscules — *vi* **to capitalize on** : tirer profit de, tirer parti de

capitol ['kæpət̬əl] *n* : capitole *m*

capitulate [kə'pɪtʃə,leɪt] *vi* **-lated; -lating** : capituler

capitulation [kə,pɪtʃə'leɪʃən] *n* : capitulation *f*

capon ['keɪ,pɑn, -pən] *n* : chapon *m*

caprice [kə'pri:s] *n* : caprice *m*

capricious [kə'prɪʃəs, -'pri:-] *adj* : capricieux — **capriciously** *adv*

Capricorn ['kæprɪ,kɔrn] *n* : Capricorne *m*

capsize ['kæp,saɪz, kæp'saɪz] *v* **-sized; -sizing** *vt* : faire chavirer — *vi* : chavirer

capstan ['kæpstən, -,stæn] *n* : cabestan *m*

capsule ['kæpsəl, -,su:l] *n* : capsule *f*

captain[1] ['kæptən] *vt* : être le capitaine de

captain[2] *n* : capitaine *m*

caption[1] ['kæpʃən] *vt* : mettre une légende à (une illustration), sous-titrer (un film)

caption[2] *n* **1** HEADING, TITLE : titre *m* **2** : légende *f* (d'une illustration) **3** SUBTITLE : sous-titre *m*

captivate ['kæptə,veɪt] *vt* **-vated; -vating** : captiver, fasciner

captive[1] ['kæptɪv] *adj* : captif

captive[2] *n* : captif *m*, -tive *f*

captivity [kæp'tɪvət̬i] *n* : captivité *f*

captor ['kæptər] *n* : personne *f* qui capture

capture[1] ['kæpʃər] *vt* **-tured; -turing 1** SEIZE : capturer, prendre **2** : rendre (une ressemblance), gagner (l'intérêt), captiver (l'imagination)

capture[2] *n* : capture *f*, prise *f*

car ['kɑr] *n* **1** AUTOMOBILE : voiture *f*, automobile *f* **2** *or* **railroad car** : wagon *m* **3** *or* **elevator car** : cabine *f* (d'ascenseur)

carafe [kə'ræf, -'rɑf] *n* : carafe *f*

caramel ['kɑrməl; 'kærəməl, -,mɛl] *n* : caramel *m*

carat ['kærət] *n* : carat *m*

caravan ['kærə,væn] *n* : caravane *f*

caraway ['kærə,weɪ] *n* : carvi *m*

carbine ['kɑr,baɪn, -,bi:n] *n* : carabine *f*

carbohydrate [ˌkɑrboˈhaɪˌdreɪt, -drət] *n* : hydrate *m* de carbone
carbon [ˈkɑrbən] *n* : carbone *m*
carbonated [ˈkɑrbəˌneɪt̬əd] *adj* : gazéifié
carbon copy *n* **1** : copie *f* carbone **2** REPLICA : réplique *f*
carbon paper *n* : carbone *m*, papier *m* carbone
carbuncle [ˈkɑrˌbʌŋkəl] *n* : furoncle *m*
carburetor [ˈkɑrbəˌreɪt̬ər, -bjə-] *n* : carburateur *m*
carcass [ˈkɑrkəs] *n* : carcasse *f*
carcinogen [kɑrˈsɪnədʒən, ˈkɑrsənəˌdʒɛn] *n* : carcinogène *m*, cancérogène *m*
carcinogenic [ˌkɑrsənoˈdʒɛnɪk] *adj* : carcinogène, cancérogène
card[1] [ˈkɑrd] *vt* **carded; carding** : carder (des fibres textiles)
card[2] *n* **1** : carte *f* <library card : carte de bibliothèque> <Christmas card : carte de Noël> **2** : carde *f* (pour carder fibres) **3** → **playing card**
cardboard [ˈkɑrdˌbord] *n* : carton *m*
cardiac [ˈkɑrdiˌæk] *adj* : cardiaque
cardigan [ˈkɑrdɪgən] *n* : cardigan *m*
cardinal[1] [ˈkɑrdənəl] *adj* CHIEF : cardinal
cardinal[2] *n* : cardinal *m*
cardinal number *n* : nombre *m* cardinal
cardinal point *n* : point *m* cardinal
cardiologist [ˌkɑrdiˈɑlədʒɪst] *n* : cardiologue *mf*
cardiology [ˌkɑrdiˈɑlədʒi] *n* : cardiologie *f*
cardiovascular [ˌkɑrdioˈvæskjələr] *adj* : cardio-vasculaire
care[1] [ˈkær] *v* **cared; caring** *vi* **1** : se soucier, s'intéresser <she cares about the poor : elle se soucie des pauvres> <I don't care : ça m'est égal> **2 to care for** LIKE : aimer **3 to care for** LOOK AFTER : s'occuper de, soigner <to care for the sick : soigner les malades> — *vt* WISH : vouloir, désirer <would you care to come in? : voulez-vous entrer?>
care[2] *n* **1** ANXIETY : souci *m*, ennui *m* **2** TREATMENT : soins *mpl*, traitement *m* <medical care : soins médicaux> **3** MAINTENANCE, UPKEEP : entretien *m* **4** ATTENTION : soin *m*, attention *f* <take care not to fall : faites attention de ne pas tomber>
careen [kəˈriːn] *vi* **-reened; -reening 1** LURCH : tanguer **2** → **career**[1]
career[1] [kəˈrɪr] *vi* : aller à toute vitesse
career[2] *n* : carrière *f*, profession *f*
carefree [ˈkærˌfriː, ˌkærˈ-] *adj* : insouciant
careful [ˈkærfəl] *adj* **1** CAUTIOUS : prudent <be careful! : soyez prudent!> <be careful of the ice : fais attention à la glace> **2** THOROUGH : soigneux, approfondi
carefully [ˈkærfəli] *adv* : prudemment, avec soin
careless [ˈkærləs] *adj* : négligent
carelessly [ˈkærləsli] *adv* : négligemment, sans faire attention
carelessness [ˈkærləsnəs] *n* : négligence *f*, étourderie *f*, inattention *f*
caress[1] [kəˈrɛs] *vt* : caresser, minoucher *Can fam*
caress[2] *n* : caresse *f*
caret [ˈkærət] *n* : signe *m* d'insertion
caretaker [ˈkɛrˌteɪkər] *n* : gardien *m*, -dienne *f*; concierge *mf* (d'un immeuble, etc.)
cargo [ˈkɑrˌgoː] *n, pl* **-goes** *or* **-gos** : chargement *m*, cargaison *f*
caribou [ˈkærəˌbuː] *n, pl* **-bou** *or* **-bous** : caribou *m*
caricature[1] [ˈkærɪkəˌtʃʊr] *vt* **-tured; -turing** : caricaturer
caricature[2] *n* : caricature *f*
caricaturist [ˈkærɪkəˌtʃʊrɪst] *n* : caricaturiste *mf*
caries [ˈkærˌiːz] *ns & pl* : carie *f*
carillon [ˈkærəˌlɑn] *n* : carillon *m*
carmine [ˈkɑrmən, -ˌmaɪn] *n* : carmin *m*
carnage [ˈkɑrnɪdʒ] *n* : carnage *m*, boucherie *f*
carnal [ˈkɑrnəl] *adj* : charnel
carnation [kɑrˈneɪʃən] *n* : œillet *m*
carnival [ˈkɑrnəvəl] *n* : carnaval *m*, fête *f* foraine
carnivore [ˈkɑrnəˌvor] *n* : carnivore *m*, carnassier *m*
carnivorous [kɑrˈnɪvərəs] *adj* : carnivore, carnassier
carol[1] [ˈkærəl] *vi* **-oled** *or* **-olled; -oling** *or* **-olling** : chanter des chants de Noël
carol[2] *n* : chant *m* de Noël
carom[1] [ˈkærəm] *vi* **1** : caramboler (au billiard) **2** REBOUND : rebondir
carom[2] *n* : carambolage *m*
carouse [kəˈraʊz] *vi* **-roused; -rousing** : faire la bombe *fam*
carousel [ˌkærəˈsɛl, ˈkærəˌ-] *n* **1** MERRY-GO-ROUND : manège *m* **2** : carrousel *m* (pour les bagages, les diapositives, etc.)
carp[1] [ˈkɑrp] *vi* **1** COMPLAIN : se plaindre **2 to carp at** : critiquer
carp[2] *n, pl* **carp** *or* **carps** : carpe *f*
carpel [ˈkɑrpəl] *n* : carpelle *m*
carpenter [ˈkɑrpəntər] *n* : charpentier *m*, menuisier *m*
carpentry [ˈkɑrpəntri] *n* : charpenterie *f*, menuiserie *f*
carpet[1] [ˈkɑrpət] *vt* **1** : recouvrir d'un tapis, recouvrir d'une moquette **2** COVER : tapisser <carpeted with leaves : tapissé de feuilles>
carpet[2] *n* : tapis *m*, moquette *f*
carpeting [ˈkɑrpət̬ɪŋ] *n* : moquette *f*
carport [ˈkɑrˌpɔrt] *n* : abri *m* d'auto, auvent *m* pour voiture
carriage [ˈkærɪdʒ] *n* **1** TRANSPORT : transport *m* **2** BEARING : maintien *m*, port *m* **3** *or* **horse–drawn carriage** : calèche *f*, fiacre *m*, carrosse *m* **4** → **baby carriage**

carrier ['kæriər] *n* **1** TRANSPORTER : transporteur *m* **2** : porteur *m*, -teuse *f* (d'une maladie) **3** → **aircraft carrier**

carrion ['kærien] *n* : charogne *f*

carrot ['kærət] *n* : carotte *f*

carrousel → **carousel**

carry ['kæri] *v* **-ried; -rying** *vt* **1** TRANSPORT : transporter, porter, emporter **2** BEAR : porter, supporter **3** STOCK : vendre, tenir en magasin **4** WIN : remporter, emporter, gagner <the motion was carried by 10 votes : la motion l'a emporté par 10 votes> **5** ENTAIL : comporter, entraîner **6 to carry oneself** : se présenter, se comporter — *vi* : porter <her voice carries well : sa voix porte bien>

carryall ['kæri,ɔl] *n* : fourre-tout *m*

carry away *vt* **to get carried away** : se laisser emporter, s'emballer

carry on *vt* CONDUCT : conduire (des affaires), entretenir (une correspondence, etc.) — *vi* **1** : se conduire, faire des histoires <he's always carrying on over nothing : il fait toujours des histoires pour des riens> **2** CONTINUE : continuer

carry out *vt* ACCOMPLISH, EXECUTE : réaliser, effectuer, accomplir, mettre à l'exécution

cart[1] ['kɑrt] *vt* **1** CONVEY : charrier **2** HAUL : trimbaler *fam*

cart[2] *n* : charette *f* (de foin, etc.), chariot *m* <shopping cart : chariot de supermarché>

cartel [kɑr'tɛl] *n* : cartel *m*

cartilage ['kɑrṭəlɪdʒ] *n* : cartilage *m*

cartilaginous [,kɑrṭəl'ædʒənəs] *adj* : cartilagineux

cartographer [kɑr'tɑgrəfər] *n* : cartographe *mf*

cartography [kɑr'tɑgrəfi] *n* : cartographie *f*

carton ['kɑrtən] *n* **1** : carton *m*, boîte *f* de carton **2** : cartouche *f* (de cigarettes)

cartoon [kɑr'tu:n] *n* **1** : dessin *m* humoristique, caricature *f* **2** COMIC STRIP : bande *f* dessinée **3** *or* **animated cartoon** : dessin *m* animé

cartoonist [kɑr'tu:nɪst] *n* : dessinateur *m*, -trice *f* (humoristique); caricaturiste *mf*

cartridge ['kɑrtrɪdʒ] *n* : cartouche *f*

carve ['kɑrv] *vt* **carved; carving 1** : tailler (la pierre, le bois, etc.) **2** INSCRIBE : graver **3** SLICE : couper <to carve a turkey : couper une dinde>

cascade[1] [kæs'keɪd] *vi* **-caded; -cading** : tomber en cascade

cascade[2] *n* : cascade *f*

case[1] ['keɪs] *vt* **cased; casing 1** BOX, PACK : emballer, empaqueter **2** INSPECT : surveiller (un lieu)

case[2] *n* **1** BOX, CRATE : boîte *f*, caisse *f* **2** CONTAINER : étui *m* (à lunettes, etc.), écrin *m*, coffre *m*, boîte *f* <a display case : une vitrine> **3** INSTANCE : cas *m*, exemple *m* <a case of the flu : un cas de grippe> **4** : cas *m* (en grammaire) **5** : affaire *f*, procès *m* (en droit) **6 in any case** : en tout cas **7 in case** : au cas où **8 in case of** : en cas de

casement ['keɪsmənt] *n or* **casement window** : fenêtre *f* à battants

cash[1] ['kæʃ] *vt* **1** : encaisser (un chèque) **2 to cash in** : se faire rembourser, réaliser (un bon, etc.)

cash[2] *n* : espèces *fpl*, argent *m* liquide

cashew ['kæ,ʃu:, kə'ʃu:] *n or* **cashew nut** : noix *f* de cajou

cashier[1] [kæ'ʃɪr] *vt* DISMISS : renvoyer, congédier

cashier[2] *n* : caissier *m*, -sière *f*

cashmere ['kæʒ,mɪr, 'kæʃ-] *n* : cachemire *m*

cash register *n* : caisse *f* (enregistreuse)

casino [kə'si:,no:] *n*, *pl* **-nos** : casino *m*

cask ['kæsk] *n* : fût *m*, tonneau *f*

casket ['kæskət] *n* : cercueil *m*

casserole ['kæsə,ro:l] *n* **1** *or* **casserole dish** : cocotte *f*, marmite *f* **2** : ragoût *m* (cuit au four)

cassette [kə'sɛt, kæ-] *n* : cassette *f*

cassock ['kæsək] *n* : soutane *f*

cast[1] ['kæst] *vt* **cast; casting 1** THROW : jeter, lancer <to cast dice : jeter les dés> <to cast an eye on : jeter un coup d'œil sur> <to cast aside : mettre de côté> **2** : déposer (un vote) <to cast a vote for : voter pour> **3** : distribuer les rôles de (une pièce de théâtre, un film, etc.) <he was cast in the leading role : on lui a donné le rôle principal> **4** MOLD : mouler, couler, fondre <to cast metal : faire fondre du métal>

cast[2] *n* **1** : lancer *m* (d'une ligne de pêche) **2** : distribution *f* (d'acteurs) **3** MOLD : moulage *m* **4** *or* **plaster cast** : plâtre *m* **5** APPEARANCE : aspect *f*, forme *f* <the delicate cast of her features : la finesse de ses traits>

castanets [,kæstə'nɛts] *npl* : castagnettes *fpl*

castaway[1] ['kæstə,weɪ] *adj* : naufragé

castaway[2] *n* : naufragé *m*, -gée *f*

caste ['kæst] *n* : caste *f*

caster ['kæstər] *n* : roulette *f* (d'un meuble)

castigate ['kæstə,geɪt] *vt* **-gated; -gating 1** PUNISH : punir, châtier **2** CRITICIZE : critiquer sévèrement

castigation ['kæstə,geɪʃən] *n* **1** PUNISHMENT : punition *f*, châtiment *m* **2** CRITICISM : critique *f* sévère, condamnation *f*

cast iron *n* : fonte *f*

castle ['kæsəl] *n* **1** : château *m* **2** : tour *f* (aux échecs)

cast–off ['kæst,ɔf] *adj* : dont on ne veut, mis au rebut

castoff ['kæst,ɔf] *n*, *pl* **castoffs** : vêtement *m* dont on ne veut

castrate [ˈkæsˌtreɪt] *vt* **-trated; -trating** : castrer, châtrer
castration [kæˈstreɪʃən] *n* : castration *f*
casual [ˈkæʒʊəl] *adj* **1** CHANCE : fortuit, de hasard **2** OCCASIONAL : intermittent, de passage **3** NONCHALANT : désinvolte, nonchalant **4** INFORMAL : simple, détendu <casual clothes : vêtements sport>
casually [ˈkæʒʊəli, ˈkæʒəli] *adv* **1** FORTUITOUSLY : par hasard, accidentellement **2** NONCHALANTLY : nonchalamment **3** INFORMALLY : simplement
casualty [ˈkæʒʊəlti, ˈkæʒəl-] *n, pl* **-ties 1** ACCIDENT : accident *m* grave, désastre *m* **2** VICTIM : blessé *m*, -sée *f*; accidenté *m*, -tée *f*; mort *m*, morte *f* <casualties of battle : pertes de bataille>
cat [ˈkæt] *n* **1** : chat *m*, chatte *f* **2** FELINE : félin *m* <the big cats : les grands félins>
cataclysm [ˈkæt̬əˌklɪzəm] *n* : cataclysme *m*
catacombs [ˈkæt̬əˌko:mz] *npl* : catacombes *fpl*
catalog[1] *or* **catalogue** [ˈkæt̬əˌlɔg] *vt* **-loged** *or* **-logued; -loging** *or* **-loguing** : cataloguer, dresser un catalogue de
catalog[2] *or* **catalogue** *n* : catalogue *m*
catalpa [kəˈtælpə, -ˈtɔl-] *n* : catalpa *m*
catalyst [ˈkætələst] *n* : catalyseur *m*
catalytic [ˌkæt̬əlˈɪtɪk] *adj* : catalytique
catamaran [ˌkæt̬əməˈræn, ˈkæt̬əməˌræn] *n* : catamaran *m*
catapult[1] [ˈkæt̬əˌpʌlt, -ˌpʊlt] *vt* : catapulter
catapult[2] *n* : catapulte *f*
cataract [ˈkæt̬əˌrækt] *n* : cataracte *f*
catarrh [kəˈtɑr] *n* : catarrhe *m*
catastrophe [kəˈtæstrəˌfi:] *n* : catastrophe *f* — **catastrophic** [ˌkæt̬əˈstrɑfɪk] *adj* : catastrophique
catcalls [ˈkætˌkɔlz] *npl* : huées *fpl*, sifflets *mpl*
catch[1] [ˈkætʃ, ˈkɛtʃ] *v* **caught** [ˈkɔt]; **catching** *vt* **1** CAPTURE, TRAP : attraper, piéger **2** CONTRACT : attraper, prendre <to catch a cold : attraper un rhume> **3** SURPRISE : surprendre, prendre <I caught him red-handed : je l'ai pris en flagrant délit> **4** GRASP, SEIZE : attraper, saisir **5** SNAG : accrocher **6** PERCEIVE : discerner, remarquer (une expression, une odeur, etc.) <to catch sight of : apercevoir> **7** : attraper, prendre (un train, etc.) **8 to catch one's breath** : reprendre son souffle — *vi* **1** START : démarrer (se dit d'un moteur), prendre (se dit du feu) **2** HOOK, SNAG : s'accrocher, se prendre <her fingers caught in a drawer : ses doigts se sont pris dans un tiroir>
catch[2] *n* **1** CATCHING : prise *f* **2** : prise *f*, pêche *f* (de poissons) **3** LATCH : loquet *m* **4** PITFALL, SNAG : piège *f*
catcher [ˈkætʃər, ˈkɛ-] *n* : receveur *m* *Can* (au baseball)
catching [ˈkætʃɪŋ, ˈkɛ-] *adj* : contagieux
catch on *vi* **1** UNDERSTAND : comprendre, saisir **2** : devenir populaire, devenir célèbre <the song caught on : la chanson est devenue populaire>
catchup [ˈkætʃəp, ˈkɛ-] → **ketchup**
catch up *vi* **to catch up with** : rattraper
catchword [ˈkætʃˌwərd, ˈkɛtʃ-] *n* : slogan *m*, mot *m* d'ordre
catchy [ˈkætʃi, ˈkɛ-] *adj* **catchier; -est** : entraînant <a catchy tune : un air entraînant>
catechism [ˈkæt̬əˌkɪzəm] *n* : catéchisme *m*
categorical [ˌkæt̬əˈgɔrɪkəl] *adj* : catégorique, absolu, indiscutable — **categorically** [-rəkli] *adv*
categorize [ˈkæt̬ɪgəraɪz] *vt* **-ized; -izing** : classer (par catégories)
category [ˈkæt̬əˌgori] *n, pl* **-ries** : catégorie *f*, classe *f*
cater [ˈkeɪt̬ər] *vi* **1** : fournir des repas (pour les fêtes, les noces, etc.) **2 to cater to** : pourvoir à <she caters to his every need : elle pourvoit à tous ses besoins>
catercorner[1] [ˈkæt̬iˌkɔrnər, ˈkæt̬ə-, ˈkɪt̬i-] *adv* : diagonalement
catercorner[2] *adj* : diagonal
caterer [ˈkeɪt̬ərər] *n* : traiteur *m*
caterpillar [ˈkæt̬ərˌpɪlər] *n* : chenille *f*
catfish [ˈkætˌfɪʃ] *n* : poisson-chat *m*
catgut [ˈkætˌgʌt] *n* : boyau *m* (de chat)
catharsis [kəˈθɑrsɪs] *n, pl* **catharses** [-ˌsi:z] : catharsis *f*
cathartic [kəˈθɑrt̬ɪk] *adj* : cathartique
cathedral [kəˈθi:drəl] *n* : cathédrale *f*
catheter [ˈkæθət̬ər] *n* : cathéter *m*, sonde *f*
cathode [ˈkæˌθo:d] *n* : cathode *f*
catholic [ˈkæθəlɪk] *adj* UNIVERSAL : universel
Catholic[1] *adj* : catholique <the Catholic Church : l'Église catholique>
Catholic[2] *n* : catholique *mf*
Catholicism [kəˈθɑləˌsɪzəm] *n* : catholicisme *m*
catkin [ˈkætkɪn] *n* : chaton *m*
catnap[1] [ˈkætˌnæp] *vi* **-napped; -napping** : faire un somme
catnap[2] *n* : somme *m*
catnip [ˈkætˌnɪp] *n* : herbe *f* aux chats
catsup [ˈkɛtʃəp, ˈkætsəp] → **ketchup**
cattail [ˈkætˌteɪl] *n* : massette *f*, quenouille *f* *Can*
cattiness [ˈkæt̬inəs] *n* : méchanceté *f*, malveillance *f*
cattle [ˈkæt̬əl] *npl* : bétail *m*, bovins *mpl*
cattleman [ˈkæt̬əlmən, -ˌmæn] *n* : bouvier *m*, -vière *f*; vacher *m*, -chère *f*
catty [ˈkæt̬i] *adj* **cattier; -est** : méchant, malveillant
catwalk [ˈkætˌwɔk] *n* : passerelle *f*
Caucasian[1] [kɔˈkeɪʒən] *adj* : caucasien
Caucasian[2] *n* : Caucasien *m*, -sienne *f*

caucus ['kɔkəs] *n* : comité *m* électoral
caught → **catch**[1]
cauldron ['kɔldrən] *n* : chaudron *m*
cauliflower ['kɑlɪˌflaʊər, 'kɔ-] *n* : chou-fleur *m*
caulk[1] ['kɔk] *vt* : calfater (un bateau), mastiquer (une fenêtre, etc.)
caulk[2] *n* : mastic *m*
causal ['kɔzəl] *adj* : causal
cause[1] ['kɔz] *vt* **caused; causing** : causer, occasionner
cause[2] *n* **1** ORIGIN : cause *f* **2** MOTIVE, REASON : raison *f,* motif *m* <with good cause : à juste titre> **3** GROUNDS : cause *f* (en droit) **4** MOVEMENT : cause *f,* mouvement *m*
causeway ['kɔzˌweɪ] *n* : chaussée *f*
caustic ['kɔstɪk] *adj* **1** CORROSIVE : caustique, corrosif **2** BITING : mordant, sarcastique
cauterize ['kɔt̬əˌraɪz] *vt* **-ized; -izing** : cautériser
caution[1] ['kɔʃən] *vt* WARN : avertir, mettre en garde
caution[2] *n* **1** WARNING : avertissement *m* **2** CARE : prudence *f,* précaution *f*
cautious ['kɔʃəs] *adj* : prudent, avisé, circonspect
cautiously ['kɔʃəsli] *adv* : prudemment, avec prudence
cavalcade [ˌkævəl'keɪd, 'kævəl-] *n* **1** : cavalcade *f* **2** SERIES : série *f*
cavalier[1] [ˌkævə'lɪr] *adj* OFFHAND : cavalier, désinvolte
cavalier[2] *n* : cavalier *m*
cavalierly [ˌkævə'lɪrli] *adv* : de façon cavalière
cavalry ['kævəlri] *n, pl* **-ries** : cavalerie *f*
cavalryman ['kævəlrimən] *n, pl* **-men** [-mən, -ˌmɛn] : cavalier *m*
cave[1] ['keɪv] *vi* **caved; caving** *or* **to cave in** : s'affaisser, s'effondrer
cave[2] *n* : grotte *f,* caverne *f*
cavern ['kævərn] *n* : caverne *f*
cavernous ['kævərnəs] *adj* : caverneux
caviar *or* **caviare** ['kæviˌɑr, 'kɑ-] *n* : caviar *m*
cavity ['kævət̬i] *n, pl* **-ties 1** HOLE : cavité *f* **2** CARIES : carie *f* (dentaire), cavité *f*
cavort [kə'vɔrt] *vi* CAPER : gambader, faire des cabrioles
caw[1] ['kɔ] *vi* : croasser
caw[2] *n* : croassement *m*
cayenne pepper [ˌkaɪ'ɛn, ˌkeɪ-] *n* : poivre *m* de cayenne
CD [ˌsiː'diː] *n* : CD *m,* disque *m* compact
cease ['siːs] *v* **ceased; ceasing** : cesser
ceaseless ['siːsləs] *adj* : incessant, continuel
cedar ['siːdər] *n* : cèdre *m*
cede ['siːd] *vt* **ceded; ceding** : céder
cedilla [sɪ'dɪlə] *n* : cédille *nf*
ceiling ['siːlɪŋ] *n* **1** : plafond *m* **2** LIMIT : plafond *m,* limite *f*
celebrate ['sɛləˌbreɪt] *vt* **-brated; -brating** *vt* **1** FETE : fêter, célébrer **2** : célébrer <to celebrate Mass : célébrer la messe> **3** EXTOL : louer, glorifier
celebration [ˌsɛlə'breɪʃən] *n* **1** : célébration *f,* fête *f* **2** PRAISE : louange *f*
celebrated ['sɛləˌbreɪt̬əd] *adj* FAMOUS : célèbre, réputé
celebrity [sə'lɛbrət̬i] *n, pl* **-ties 1** FAME : célébrité *f,* renommée *f* **2** PERSONALITY : célébrité *f,* vedette *f*
celery ['sɛləri] *n, pl* **-eries** : céleri *m*
celestial [sə'lɛstʃəl, -'lɛstiəl] *adj* : céleste
celibacy ['sɛləbəsi] *n* : célibat *m*
celibate[1] ['sɛləbət] *adj* **1** CHASTE : chaste **2** UNMARRIED : célibataire
celibate[2] *n* : célibataire *mf*
cell ['sɛl] *n* **1** : cellule *f* (d'un organisme, d'une prison, etc.) **2** : élément *m* (d'une pile)
cellar ['sɛlər] *n* : cave *f* <wine cellar : cave à vin>
cellist ['tʃɛlɪst] *n* : violoncelliste *mf*
cello ['tʃɛˌloː] *n, pl* **-los** : violoncelle *m*
cellophane ['sɛləˌfeɪn] *n* : cellophane *f*
cell phone *n US* : téléphone *m* portable, portable *m*
cellular ['sɛljələr] *adj* : cellulaire
cellulose ['sɛljəˌloːs] *n* : cellulose *f*
Celsius ['sɛlsiəs] *adj* : Celsius, centigrade
Celt ['kɛlt, 'sɛlt] *n* : Celte *mf*
Celtic ['kɛltɪk, 'sɛl-] *adj* : celte, celtique
cement[1] [sɪ'mɛnt] *vt* : cimenter
cement[2] *n* **1** : ciment *m* **2** GLUE : colle *f*
cemetery ['sɛməˌtɛri] *n, pl* **-teries** : cimetière *m*
censer ['sɛntsər] *n* : encensoir *m*
censor[1] ['sɛntsər] *vt* : censurer
censor[2] *n* : censeur *m*
censorship ['sɛntsərˌʃɪp] *n* : censure *f*
censure[1] ['sɛntʃər] *vt* **-sured; -suring** : critiquer, blâmer
censure[2] *n* : censure *f*
census ['sɛntsəs] *n* : recensement *m*
cent ['sɛnt] *n* : cent *m*
centaur ['sɛnˌtɔr] *n* : centaure *m*
centennial [sɛn'tɛniəl] *n* : centenaire *m*
center[1] *or Brit* **centre** ['sɛntər] *vt* **centered** *or Brit* **centred; centering** *or Brit* **centring 1** : centrer **2** CONCENTRATE, FOCUS : concentrer, fixer — *vi* **to center around** : se concentrer sur, tourner autour de
center[2] *or Brit* **centre** *n* **1** : centre *m* <center of attention : centre d'attention> **2** SEAT : siège (du gouvernement, etc.) **3** : centre *m* (aux sports)
centigrade ['sɛntəˌgreɪd, 'sɑn-] *adj* : centigrade
centigram ['sɛntəˌgræm, 'sɑn-] *n* : centigramme *m*
centimeter ['sɛntəˌmiːt̬ər, 'sɑn-] *n* : centimètre *m*
centipede ['sɛntəˌpiːd] *n* : mille-pattes *m*
central ['sɛntrəl] *adj* **1** : central <in a central location : au centre-ville> **2**

MAIN, PRINCIPAL : fundamental, principal
Central American[1] *adj* : centraméricain
Central American[2] *n* : Centraméricain *m*, -caine *f*
centralization [ˌsɛntrələˈzeɪʃən] *n* : centralisation *f*
centralize [ˈsɛntrəˌlaɪz] *vt* **-ized; -izing** : centraliser
central nervous system *n* : système *m* nerveux central
centre [ˈsɛntər] *Brit* → **center**
centrifugal force [sɛnˈtrɪfjəgəl, -ˈtrɪfɪgəl] *n* : force *f* centrifuge
century [ˈsɛntʃəri] *n, pl* **-ries** : siècle *m*
ceramic [səˈræmɪk] *adj* : céramique <ceramic tiles : carreaux en céramique>
ceramics [səˈræmɪks] *npl* : céramique *f*
cereal[1] [ˈsɪriəl] *adj* : céréalier
cereal[2] *n* : céréale *f*
cerebellum [ˌsɛrəˈbɛləm] *n, pl* **-bellums** *or* **-bella** [-ˈbɛlə] : cervelet *m*
cerebral [səˈri:brəl, ˈsɛrə-] *adj* : cérébral
cerebral palsy *n* : paralysie *f* cérébrale
cerebrum [səˈri:brəm, ˈsɛrə-] *n, pl* **-brums** *or* **-bra** [-brə] : cerveau *m*
ceremonial[1] [ˌsɛrəˈmo:niəl] *adj* : cérémoniel, de cérémonie
ceremonial[2] *n* : cérémonial *m*
ceremonious [ˌsɛrəˈmo:niəs] *adj* **1** FORMAL : cérémonieux **2** CEREMONIAL : cérémonial
ceremony [ˈsɛrəˌmo:ni] *n, pl* **-nies** : cérémonie *f*
cerise [səˈri:s] *n* : cerise *f*
certain[1] [ˈsərtən] *adj* **1** FIXED : certain, déterminé <a certain percentage : un pourcentage déterminé> **2** SURE : certain, convaincu <I'm certain that he got lost : je suis convaincu qu'il s'est perdu> **3** : certain, quelconque <a certain charm : un certain charme> **4** : sûr, assuré <she is certain to win : elle est assurée de gagner> **5** INEVITABLE : certain <a certain death : une mort certaine>
certain[2] *pron* : certains, certaines *pl* <certain of my friends : certains de mes amis>
certainly [ˈsərtənli] *adv* **1** DEFINITELY : certainement, assurément **2** OF COURSE : bien sûr
certainty [ˈsərtənti] *n, pl* **-ties** : certitude *f*
certificate [sərˈtɪfɪkət] *n* : certificat *m*, acte *m*, extrait *m* <birth certificate : extrait de naissance>
certification [ˌsərţəfəˈkeɪʃən] *n* : certification *f*, attestation *f*
certify [ˈsərţəˌfaɪ] *vt* **-fied; -fying 1** CONFIRM : certifier **2** GUARANTEE : certifier (un chèque), garantir (des marchandises, etc.)
certitude [ˈsərţəˌtu:d, -ˌtju:d] *n* : certitude *f*
cervical [ˈsərvɪkəl] *adj* : cervical
cervix [ˈsərvɪks] *n, pl* **-vices** [-vəˌsi:z] *or* **-vixes** : col *m* de l'utérus
cesarean section [sɪˈzæriən] *n* : césarienne *f*
cesium *or Brit* **caesium** [ˈsi:ziəm] *n* : césium *m*
cessation [sɛˈseɪʃən] *n* : cessation *f*
cesspool [ˈsɛsˌpu:l] *n* : fosse *f* d'aisances
Chadian[1] [ˈtʃædiən] *adj* : tchadien
Chadian[2] *n* : Tchadien *m*, -dienne *f*
chafe [ˈtʃeɪf] *v* **chafed; chafing** *vt* IRRITATE : irriter — *vi* **1** RUB : frotter **2** : s'irriter, s'impatienter <to chafe at : s'irriter de>
chaff [ˈtʃæf] *n* : balle *f* (en agriculture)
chafing dish [ˈtʃeɪfɪŋˌdɪʃ] *n* : réchaud *m* de table
chagrin[1] [ʃəˈgrɪn] *vt* VEX : contrarier, décevoir
chagrin[2] *n* : dépit *m*, déception *f*
chain[1] [ˈtʃeɪn] *vt* : enchaîner
chain[2] *n* **1** : chaîne *f* **2** SEQUENCE, SERIES : série *f*, suite *f* <a chain of events : une série d'événements> **3 chains** *npl* FETTERS : entraves *fpl*
chair[1] [ˈtʃɛr] *vt* : présider
chair[2] *n* **1** : chaise *f* **2** : chaire *f* (dans une université) **3** CHAIRMAN, CHAIRWOMAN : président *m*, -dente *f*
chairman [ˈtʃɛrmən] *n, pl* **-men** [-mən, -ˌmɛn] : président *m*
chairmanship [ˈtʃɛrmənˌʃɪp] : présidence *f*
chairwoman [ˈtʃɛrˌwʊmən] *n, pl* **-women** [-ˌwɪmən] : présidente *f*
chaise longue [ˈʃeɪzˈlɔŋ] *n, pl* **chaise longues** [-ˈlɔŋ, -ˈlɔŋz] : chaise *f* longue
chalet [ʃæˈleɪ] *n* : chalet *m*
chalice [ˈtʃælɪs] *n* : calice *m*
chalk[1] [ˈtʃɔk] *vt* **1** : écrire avec de la craie **2 to chalk up** CREDIT : attribuer, mettre <chalk it up to experience : mets-le au compte de l'expérience> **3 to chalk up** ACHIEVE, ATTAIN : marquer (des points), remporter (une victoire)
chalk[2] *n* **1** LIMESTONE : calcaire *m* **2** : craie *f* (pour écrire)
chalkboard [ˈtʃɔkˌbɔrd] → **blackboard**
chalky [ˈtʃɔki] *adj* **chalkier; -est** : calcaire (se dit de l'eau, du sol, etc.), couvert de craie (se dit des mains), crayeux (se dit du teint)
challenge[1] [ˈtʃælɪndʒ] *vt* **-lenged; -lenging 1** DISPUTE : contester, remettre en question **2** DARE, DEFY : défier
challenge[2] *n* : défi *m* <to meet the challenge : relever le défi>
challenger [ˈtʃælɪndʒər] *n* : challenger *m* (aux sports, en politique)
challenging [ˈtʃælɪndʒɪŋ] *adj* : stimulant, provocateur
chamber [ˈtʃeɪmbər] *n* **1** ROOM : chambre *f*, salle *f* **2** BODY : chambre *f* <chamber of commerce : chambre de commerce> **3** : chambre *f* (d'une

arme à feu) **4** CAVITY : cavité *f* (du cœur) **5 chambers** *npl* : cabinet *m* (d'un juge)
chambermaid ['tʃeɪmbər,meɪd] *n* : femme *f* de chambre
chamber music *n* : musique *f* de chambre
chameleon [kə'mi:ljən, -liən] *n* : caméléon *m*
chamois ['ʃæmi] *n, pl* **chamois** [-mi, -miz] : chamois *m*
champ[1] ['tʃæmp, 'tʃɑmp] *vi* **1** CHEW : mâchonner **2 to champ at the bit** : ronger son frein
champ[2] ['tʃæmp] → **champion**[1]
champagne [ʃæm'peɪn] *n* : champagne *m*
champion[1] ['tʃæmpiən] *vt* : défendre, soutenir <to champion a cause : se faire le champion d'un mouvement>
champion[2] *n* : champion *m*, -pionne *f*
championship ['tʃæmpiən,ʃɪp] *n* : championnat *m*
chance[1] ['tʃænts] *v* **chanced; chancing** *vi* **1** HAPPEN : arriver (par hasard) **2 to chance upon** : rencontrer par hasard — *vt* RISK : hasarder, courir le risque de
chance[2] *adj* : fortuit, accidentel
chance[3] *n* **1** LUCK : hasard *m* **2** OPPORTUNITY : occasion *f* **3** PROBABILITY : chances *fpl* **4** RISK : risque *m* **5** : billet *m* (de loterie) **6 by chance** : par hasard
chancellor ['tʃæntsələr] *n* **1** : chancelier *m* **2** : président *m*, -dente *f* (d'une université)
chancre ['ʃæŋkər] *n* : chancre *m*
chandelier [,ʃændə'lɪr] *n* : lustre *m*
change[1] ['tʃeɪndʒ] *v* **changed; changing** *vt* **1** ALTER : changer, modifier **2** EXCHANGE : changer de <to change places : changer de place> — *vi* **1** : changer <times change : les temps changent> **2** *or* **to change clothes** : se changer **3** : muer (se dit de la voix)
change[2] *n* **1** : changement *m*, modification *f* **2** COINS : monnaie *f*
changeable ['tʃeɪndʒəbəl] *adj* : changeant, variable
changeless ['tʃeɪndʒləs] *adj* UNCHANGING : inaltérable, immuable
channel[1] ['tʃænəl] *vt* **-neled** *or* **-nelled; -neling** *or* **-nelling** : canaliser, creuser
channel[2] *n* **1** PASSAGE : voie *f*, canal *m* **2** : chenal *m* (dans un fleuve, un port, etc.) **3** STRAIT : détroit *m* **4** : chaîne *f* (de télévision)
chant[1] ['tʃænt] *vt* **1** : psalmodier, chanter **2** : scander (un slogan, etc.) — *vi* : psalmodier
chant[2] *n* : chant *m*, psalmodie *f* (en religion), chant *m* scandé (d'un slogan, etc.)
chantey *or* **chanty** ['ʃænti, 'tʃæn-] *n, pl* **-teys** *or* **-ties** : chanson *f* de marin
Chanukah ['xɑnəkə, 'hɑ-] → **Hanukkah**
chaos ['keɪ,ɑs] *n* : chaos *m*
chaotic [keɪ'ɑṭɪk] *adj* : chaotique
chap[1] ['tʃæp] *v* **chapped; chapping** *vt* : gercer — *vi* : se gercer
chap[2] *n* : type *m fam*, bonhomme *m fam*
chapel ['tʃæpəl] *n* : chapelle *f*
chaperon[1] *or* **chaperone** ['ʃæpə,ro:n] *vt* **-oned; -oning** : chaperonner
chaperon[2] *or* **chaperone** *n* : chaperon *m*
chaplain ['tʃæplɪn] *n* : aumônier *m*
chapter ['tʃæptər] *n* **1** : châpitre *m* (d'un livre, etc.) **2** BRANCH : section *f*, division *f* (d'un groupe)
char ['tʃɑr] *vt* **charred; charring 1** BURN : carboniser, réduire en charbon **2** SCORCH : brûler légèrement
character ['kærɪktər] *n* **1** LETTER, SYMBOL : caractère *m* **2** CHARACTERISTIC : caractère *m* **3** NATURE, PERSONALITY : caractère *m*, personnalité *f* **4** PERSON : individu *m* <he's quite a character : c'est un drôle de type> **5** : personnage *m* (d'un roman, d'un film, etc.)
characteristic[1] [,kærɪktə'rɪstɪk] *adj* : caractéristique, distinctif
characteristic[2] *n* : caractéristique *f*
characteristically [,kærɪktə'rɪstɪkli] *adv* : typiquement, comme d'habitude
characterization [,kærɪktərə'zeɪʃən] *n* : caractérisation *f*
characterize ['kærɪktə,raɪz] *vt* : caractériser
charade [ʃə'reɪd] *n* **1** PRETENSE : feinte *f*, comédie **2 charades** *npl* : charades *fpl* (jeu)
charcoal ['tʃɑr,ko:l] *n* **1** : charbon *m* de bois **2** : fusain *m* <charcoal drawing : portrait au fusain>
chard ['tʃɑrd] → **Swiss chard**
charge[1] ['tʃɑrdʒ] *v* **charged; charging** *vt* **1** : charger <to charge a battery : charger une batterie> **2** ENTRUST : charger, confier **3** COMMAND : ordonner **4** ACCUSE : inculper **5** ATTACK : donner l'assaut à, charger **6** : porter à un compte, payer par carte de crédit — *vi* **1** ATTACK : charger, donner l'assaut **2** RUSH : se précipiter, foncer, se précipiter **3** ASK : demander, faire payer <they charge too much : ils font payer de trop>
charge[2] *n* **1** : charge *f* (éléctrique) **2** RESPONSIBILITY : charge *f*, responsabilité *f* <to be in charge : être responsable> **3** COST : frais *mpl*, charge *f* <free of charge : gratuit> **4** ACCUSATION : inculpation *f*, accusation *f* **5** ATTACK : charge *f*, attaque *f* <charge! : à l'assaut!>
charge card → **credit card**
charger ['tʃɑrdʒər] *n* : cheval *m* de bataille
chariot ['tʃæriət] *n* : char *m*
charisma [kə'rɪzmə] *n* : charisme *m*
charismatic [,kærəz'mæṭɪk] *adj* : charismatique

charitable [ˈtʃærət̬əbəl] *adj* : charitable, caritatif <a charitable organization : une organisation caritative>
charitably [ˈtʃærət̬əbli] *adv* : charitablement
charity [ˈtʃærət̬i] *n, pl* **-ties 1** GOODWILL : charité *f* **2** GENEROSITY : charité *f,* générosité *f* **3** ALMS : aumônes *fpl* **4** : organisation *f* caritative
charlatan [ˈʃɑrlətən] *n* : charlatan *m*
charley horse [ˈtʃɑrli,hɔrs] *n* : courbature *f* (de jambe)
charm[1] [ˈtʃɑrm] *vt* : charmer, enchanter
charm[2] *n* **1** SPELL : charme *m,* sortilège *m* **2** AMULET : amulette *f* <a lucky charm : un porte-bonheur> **3** APPEAL : charme *m* **4** : breloque *f* <a charm bracelet : un bracelet à breloques>
charming [ˈtʃɑrmɪŋ] *adj* : charmant, engageant
charmingly [ˈtʃɑrmɪŋli] *adv* : de façon charmante
chart[1] [ˈtʃɑrt] *vt* **1** MAP : porter (une route) sur la carte **2** GRAPH : faire la courbe de **3** *or* **to chart out** : tracer (un plan, etc.)
chart[2] *n* **1** MAP : carte *f* (marine) **2** GRAPH, DIAGRAM : courbe *f,* graphique *m,* tableau *m*
charter[1] [ˈtʃɑrt̬ər] *vt* **1** : accorder une charte à (une organisation) **2** HIRE : affréter, noliser <chartered flights : vols affrétés>
charter[2] *n* **1** STATUTES : charte *f,* statuts *mpl* **2** LEASE : affrètement *m*
chartreuse [ʃɑrˈtru:z, -ˈtru:s] *n* : couleur *f* vert-jaune intense
chary [ˈtʃæri] *adj* **charier; -est** : prudent, méfiant, circonspect
chase[1] [ˈtʃeɪs] *v* **chased; chasing** *vt* **1** PURSUE : poursuivre, courir après **2** *or* **to chase away** : chasser <he chased the dog from the garden : il a chassé le chien du jardin> **3** : ciseler (des métaux)
chase[2] *n* **1** PURSUIT : poursuite *f* **2 the chase** HUNTING : la chasse
chasm [ˈkæzəm] *n* : gouffre *m,* abîme *m*
chassis [ˈtʃæsi, ˈʃæsi] *ns & pl* : châssis *m*
chaste [ˈtʃeɪst] *adj* **chaster; chastest 1** MODEST : chaste, pure **2** AUSTERE : austère, sévère
chastely [ˈtʃeɪstli] *adv* : chastement
chasten [ˈtʃeɪsən] *vt* DISCIPLINE : châtier
chastise [ˈtʃæs,taɪz, tʃæsˈ-] *vt* **-tised; -tising 1** PUNISH : châtier, punir **2** CASTIGATE : fustiger, critiquer
chastisement [ˈtʃæs,taɪzmənt, tʃæsˈtaɪz-, ˈtʃæstəz-] *n* : châtiment *m,* admonition *f*
chastity [ˈtʃæstət̬i] *n* : chasteté *f*
chat[1] [ˈtʃæt] *vi* **chatted; chatting** : bavarder, causer, placoter *Can fam*
chat[2] *n* : causerie *f,* causette *f fam*
château [ʃæˈto:] *n, pl* **-teaus** [-ˈto:z] *or* **-teaux** [-ˈto:, -ˈto:z] : château *m*
chattel [ˈtʃæt̬əl] *n* : bien *m* meuble <goods and chattels : biens et effets>
chatter[1] [ˈtʃæt̬ər] *vi* **1** : claquer (se dit des dents) **2** GAB : bavarder, papoter, jacasser
chatter[2] *n* **1** : claquement *m* (de dents) **2** GABBING : bavardage *m,* papotage *m*
chatterbox [ˈtʃæt̬ər,bɑks] *n* : moulin *m* à paroles *fam*
chatterer [ˈtʃæt̬ərər] *n* : bavard *m,* -varde *f*
chatty [ˈtʃæt̬i] *adj* **chattier; -est** : bavard
chauffeur[1] [ˈʃo:fər, ʃoˈfər] *vi* : travailler comme chauffeur — *vt* : conduire
chauffeur[2] *n* : chauffeur *m*
chauvinism [ˈʃo:və,nɪzəm] *n* : chauvinisme *m*
chauvinist[1] [ˈʃo:vənɪst] *or* **chauvinistic** [,ʃo:vəˈnɪstɪk] *adj* : chauvin
chauvinist[2] *n* : chauvin *m,* -vine *f*
cheap[1] [ˈtʃi:p] *adv* : à bon marché, au rabais
cheap[2] *adj* **1** INEXPENSIVE : bon marché **2** SHODDY : de mauvaise qualité **3** STINGY : mesquin
cheapen [ˈtʃi:pən] *vt* **1** : baisser le prix de **2** DEGRADE, LOWER : rabaisser, abaisser
cheaply [ˈtʃi:pli] *adv* : à bon marché, à bon compte
cheapskate [ˈtʃi:p,skeɪt] *n* : radin *m,* -dine *f fam*
cheat[1] [ˈtʃi:t] *vt* : frauder, tromper, duper — *vi* **to cheat on** : tricher à (un examen, etc.), tromper (un époux)
cheat[2] *n* **1** DECEPTION : déception *f,* fraude *f* **2** → **cheater**
cheater [ˈtʃi:t̬ər] *n* : tricheur *m,* -cheuse *f;* fraudeur *m,* -deuse *f*
check[1] [ˈtʃɛk] *vt* **1** HALT : freiner, arrêter **2** RESTRAIN : retenir, contenir **3** VERIFY : vérifier **4** INSPECT : inspecter, contrôler **5** MARK : cocher **6** : enregistrer (ses bagages), mettre au vestiaire (un manteau, un chapeau) **7** CHECKER : faire des carreaux — *vi* **1** STOP : s'arrêter **2** CONFIRM : vérifier
check[2] *n* **1** HALT : arrêt *m,* pause *f* **2** RESTRAINT : limite *f,* frein *m* **3** INSPECTION : contrôle *m,* vérification *f* **4** *or Brit* **cheque** : chèque *m* <to pay by check : payer par chèque> **5** : ticket *m* <baggage check : ticket de bagages> **6** BILL : addition *f,* note *f* **7** SQUARE : carreau *m* **8** MARK, TICK : croix *f* **9** : échec *m* au roi (aux échecs)
checker[1] [ˈtʃɛkər] *vt* : marquer avec des carreaux
checker[2] *n* **1** : pièce *f* (de jeu de dames) **2** CASHIER : caissier *m,* -sière *f* **3** SQUARE : carreau *m* **4** : personne *f* qui vérifie qqch

checkerboard [ˈtʃɛkərˌbɔrd] *n* : damier *m*
checkers [ˈtʃɛkərz] *n* : jeu *m* de dames
check in *vi* : s'inscrire (à l'hôtel), enregistrer
checkmate[1] [ˈtʃɛkˌmeɪt] *vt* **1** THWART : contrecarrer **2** : faire échec et mat à (aux échecs)
checkmate[2] *n* : échec *m* et mat
check out *vt* INVESTIGATE : enquêter sur, vérifier — *vi* : régler sa note (à l'hôtel)
checkpoint [ˈtʃɛkˌpɔɪnt] *n* : poste *m* de contrôle
checkup [ˈtʃɛkˌʌp] *n* : examen *m* médical, bilan *m* de santé
cheddar [ˈtʃɛdər] *n* : cheddar *m*
cheek [ˈtʃik] *n* **1** : joue *f* **2** IMPUDENCE : culot *m fam*, toupet *m fam*
cheeky [ˈtʃi:ki] *adj* **cheekier; -est** : effronté, culotté *fam*
cheep[1] [ˈtʃi:p] *vi* : piauler
cheep[2] *n* : piaulement *m*
cheer[1] [ˈtʃɪr] *vt* **1** COMFORT : encourager, réconforter <his card cheered me up : sa carte m'a remonté le moral> **2** GLADDEN : réjouir **3** ACCLAIM : applaudir, acclamer
cheer[2] *n* **1** GLADNESS : bonne humeur *f*, gaieté *f* **2** APPLAUSE : acclamation *f*, bravos *mpl* **3 cheers!** : à votre santé!, à la vôtre!
cheerful [ˈtʃɪrfəl] *adj* : de bonne humeur, joyeux, gaie
cheerfully [ˈtʃɪrfəli] *adv* : joyeusement, gaiement
cheerfulness [ˈtʃɪrfəlnəs] *n* : gaieté *f*
cheerily [ˈtʃɪrəli] *adv* : joyeusement
cheerleader [ˈtʃɪrˌli:dər] *n* : meneuse *f* de claque *Can*
cheerless [ˈtʃɪrləs] *adj* : sombre, triste, morne
cheery [ˈtʃɪri] *adj* **cheerier; -est** : gai, joyeux
cheese [ˈtʃi:z] *n* : fromage *m*
cheesecloth [ˈtʃi:zˌklɔθ] *n* : étamine *f*
cheesy [ˈtʃi:zi] *adj* **cheesier; -est 1** : qui a le goût de fromage, qui sent le fromage **2** CHEAP, TACKY : de mauvaise qualité, minable
cheetah [ˈtʃi:t̬ə] *n* : guépard *m*
chef [ˈʃɛf] *n* : cuisinier *m*, -nière *f*; chef *m* cuisinier
chemical[1] [ˈkɛmɪkəl] *adj* : chimique — **chemically** [-mɪkli] *adv*
chemical[2] *n* : produit *m* chimique
chemise [ʃəˈmi:z] *n* **1** : chemise *f* (de femme) **2** *or* **chemise dress** : robe-chemisier *f*
chemist [ˈkɛmɪst] *n* : chimiste *mf*
chemistry [ˈkɛmɪstri] *n, pl* **-tries** : chimie *f*
chemotherapy [ˌki:moˈθɛrəpi, ˌkɛmo-] *n, pl* **-pies** : chimiothérapie *f*
chenille [ʃəˈni:l] *n* : chenille *f*
cheque *Brit* → **check**[2] **4**
cherish [ˈtʃɛrɪʃ] *vt* **1** LOVE : chérir, aimer **2** HARBOR, ENTERTAIN : caresser, tenir à (des espoirs, etc.)
cherry [ˈtʃɛri] *n, pl* **cherries** : cerise *f* (fruit), cerisier *m* (arbre)
cherub [ˈtʃɛrəb] *n* **1** *pl* **cherubim** [ˈtʃɛrəˌbɪm, ˈtʃɛrjə-] ANGEL : chérubin *m*, ange *m* **2** *pl* **cherubs** : angelot *m*, enfant *m* au visage angélique
cherubic [tʃɛˈru:bɪk] *adj* : de chérubin, angélique
chess [ˈtʃɛs] *n* : échecs *mpl*
chest [ˈtʃɛst] *n* **1** BOX : coffre *m*, caisse *f* **2** : poitrine *f* <chest pain : douleur à la poitrine>
chestnut[1] [ˈtʃɛsṭˌnʌt] *adj* : châtain (couleur)
chestnut[2] *n* **1** : marron *m*, châtaigne *f* (fruit) **2** : marronier *m*, châtaignier *m* (arbre)
chest of drawers *n* : commode *f*
chevron [ˈʃɛvrən] *n* : chevron *m*
chew[1] [ˈtʃu:] *vt* **1** : mâcher, mastiquer **2** : chiquer (du tabac)
chew[2] *n* : chique *f* (de tabac)
chewing gum *n* : chewing-gum *m France*, gomme *f* à mâcher
chic[1] [ˈʃi:k] *adj* : chic, élégant, à la mode
chic[2] *n* : chic *m*, élégance *f*
chick [ˈtʃɪk] *n* **1** : poussin *m* (de poulet) **2** FLEDGLING : oisillon *m*
chickadee [ˈtʃɪkədi] *n* : mésange *f* à tête noire
chicken [ˈtʃɪkən] *n* **1** : poulet *m* **2** COWARD : poltron *m*, -tronne *f*; poule *f* mouillée *fam*
chickenhearted [ˈtʃɪkənˌhɑrt̬əd] *adj* : poltron, peureux
chicken pox *n* : varicelle *f*
chicle [ˈtʃɪkəl] *n* : chiclé *m*
chicory [ˈtʃɪkəri] *n, pl* **-ries 1** : endive *f* (pour les salades) **2** : chicorée *f* (additif de café)
chide [ˈtʃaɪd] *vt* **chid** [ˈtʃɪd] *or* **chided; chid** *or* **chidden** [ˈtʃɪdən] *or* **chided; chiding** [ˈtʃaɪdɪŋ] : gronder, réprimander
chief[1] [ˈtʃi:f] *adj* : principal, en chef <chief editor : rédacteur en chef>
chief[2] *n* : chef *m*
chiefly [ˈtʃi:fli] *adv* : principalement, surtout
chieftain [ˈtʃi:ftən] *n* : chef *m* (d'une tribu)
chiffon [ʃɪˈfɑn, ˈʃɪˌ-] *n* : mousseline *f* (de soie)
chigger [ˈtʃɪgər] *n* : aoûtat *m*
chignon [ˈʃi:nˌjɑn, -jɔn] *n* : chignon *m*
chilblain [ˈtʃɪlˌbleɪn] *n* : engelure *f*
child [ˈtʃaɪld] *n, pl* **children** [ˈtʃɪldrən] **1** YOUNGSTER : enfant *mf* **2** OFFSPRING : fils *m*, fille *f*
childbirth [ˈtʃaɪldˌbərθ] *n* : accouchement *m*
childhood [ˈtʃaɪldˌhʊd] *n* : enfance *f*
childish [ˈtʃaɪldɪʃ] *adj* : puéril, enfantin
childishly [ˈtʃaɪldɪʃli] *adv* : puérilement

childishness ['tʃaɪldɪʃnəs] *n* : puérilité *f,* enfantillage *m*

childless ['tʃaɪldləs] *adj* : sans enfants

childlike ['tʃaɪld,laɪk] *adj* : enfantin, d'enfant <a childlike voice : une voix d'enfant>

childproof ['tʃaɪld,pru:f] *adj* : de sécurité pour enfants

Chilean[1] ['tʃɪliən, tʃɪ'leɪən] *adj* : chilien

Chiliean[2] *n* : Chilien *m,* -lienne *f*

chili *or* **chile** *or* **chilli** ['tʃɪli] *n, pl* **chilies** *or* **chiles** *or* **chillies** **1** *or* **chili pepper** : piment *m* fort **2** : chili *m* con carne

chill[1] ['tʃɪl] *vt* : refroidir, réfrigérer, mettre au frais — *vi* : se refroidir

chill[2] *adj* : frais <a chill wind : un vent frais>

chill[3] *n* **1** CHILLINESS : fraîcheur *f,* froideur *f* **2** SHIVER : frisson *m* <it sent a chill down my spine : ça m'a donné des frissons> **3 to catch a chill** : attraper un coup de froid

chilliness ['tʃɪlinəs] *n* : fraîcheur *f,* froideur *f*

chilly ['tʃɪli] *adj* **chillier; -est** : frais, froid

chime[1] ['tʃaɪm] *v* **chimed; chiming** *vt* : sonner <to chime the hour : sonner l'heure> — *vi* : carillonner, sonner

chime[2] *n* : carillon *m*

chime in *vi* : interrompre

chimera *or* **chimaera** [kaɪ'mɪrə, kə-] *n* : chimère *f*

chimney ['tʃɪmni] *n, pl* **-neys** **1** : cheminée *f* **2** : verre *m* (d'une lampe)

chimney sweep *n* : ramoneur *m*

chimp ['tʃɪmp, 'ʃɪmp] → **chimpanzee**

chimpanzee [,tʃɪm,pæn'zi:, ,ʃɪm-; tʃɪm'pænzi, ʃɪm-] *n* : chimpanzé *m*

chin *n* : menton *m*

china ['tʃaɪnə] *n* **1** PORCELAIN : porcelaine *f* **2** TABLEWARE : vaisselle *f*

chinchilla [tʃɪn'tʃɪlə] *n* : chinchilla *m*

Chinese[1] ['tʃaɪ'ni:z, -ni:s] *adj* : chinois

Chinese[2] *n* **1** : Chinois *m,* -noise *f* **2** : chinois *m* (langue)

chink ['tʃɪŋk] *n* : fente *f,* fissure *f*

chintz ['tʃɪnts] *n* : chintz *m*

chip[1] ['tʃɪp] *v* **chipped; chipping** *vt* : ébrécher, éborgner *Can* (de la vaisselle, etc.), écorner (des meubles), écailler (de la peinture) — *vi* **1** : s'ébrécher, s'écorner, s'écailler **2 to chip in** CONTRIBUTE : contribuer

chip[2] *n* **1** PIECE : éclat *m* (de verre, etc.), copeau *m* (de bois ou de métal), fragment *m* <he's a chip off the old block : il est bien le fils de son père> **2** COUNTER : jeton *m* (de poker, etc.) **3** NICK : ébréchure *f* **4** *or* **computer chip** : puce *f* **5** → **potato chips**

chipmunk ['tʃɪp,mʌŋk] *n* : tamia *m,* suisse *m Can*

chipper ['tʃɪpər] *adj* : vif, en pleine forme

chiropodist [kə'rɑpədɪst, ʃə-] *n* PODIATRIST : pédicure *mf,* podologue *mf*

chiropody [kə'rɑpədi, ʃe-] *n* PODIATRY : podologie *f*

chiropractic ['kaɪrə,præktɪk] *n* : chiropraxie *f,* chiropractie *f,* chiropractique *f Can*

chiropractor ['kaɪrə,præktər] *n* : chiropraticien *m,* -cienne *f*

chirp[1] ['tʃərp] *vi* : pépier (se dit des oiseaux), chanter (se dit des insectes)

chirp[2] *n* : pépiement *m,* chant *m*

chisel[1] ['tʃɪzəl] *vt* **-eled** *or* **-elled; -eling** *or* **-elling 1** : ciseler, tailler au ciseau **2** CHEAT : carotter *fam*

chisel[2] *n* : ciseau *m*

chit ['tʃɪt] *n* VOUCHER : bon *m,* note *f*

chitchat ['tʃɪt,tʃæt] *n* : bavardage *m*

chivalric [ʃə'vælrɪk] → **chivalrous**

chivalrous ['ʃɪvəlrəs] *adj* **1** KNIGHTLY : chevaleresque **2** GENTLEMANLY : galant, courtois

chivalry ['ʃɪvəlri] *n, pl* **-ries 1** : chevalerie *f* **2** COURTESY : courtoisie *f,* galanterie *f*

chive ['tʃaɪv] *n* : ciboulette *f*

chloride ['klo,raɪd] *n* : chlorure *m*

chlorinate ['klorə,neɪt] *vt* **-nated; -nating** : javelliser

chlorination [,klorə'neɪʃən] *n* : javellisation *f*

chlorine ['klor,i:n] *n* : chlore *m*

chloroform[1] ['klorə,fɔrm] *vt* : chloroformer

chloroform[2] *n* : chloroforme *m*

chlorophyll ['klorə,fɪl] *n* : chlorophylle *f*

chock–full ['tʃɑk'fʊl, 'tʃʌk-] *adj* : bondé, plein à craquer

chocolate ['tʃɑkələt, 'tʃɔk-] *n* : chocolat *m*

choice[1] ['tʃɔɪs] *adj* **choicer; choicest** EXCELLENT, SELECT : de choix, de première qualité

choice[2] *n* : choix *m*

choir ['kwaɪr] *n* : chœur *m*

choke[1] ['tʃo:k] *v* **choked; choking** *vt* **1** STRANGLE : étrangler, asphyxier, étouffer **2** BLOCK : boucher, embouteiller, obstruer — *vi* : s'étouffer, s'étrangler <to choke to death : mourir étouffé>

choke[2] *n* **1** CHOKING : étouffement *m* **2** : starter *m* (d'une voiture)

choker ['tʃo:kər] *n* : collier *m* court

cholera ['kɑlərə] *n* : choléra *m*

cholesterol [kə'lɛstə,rɔl] *n* : cholestérol *m*

choose ['tʃu:z] *v* **chose** ['tʃo:z]; **chosen** ['tʃo:zən]; **choosing** *vt* **1** SELECT : choisir, élire <to choose sides : choisir son camp> **2** DECIDE : décider **3** PREFER : préférer, aimer mieux — *vi* : choisir

choosy *or* **choosey** ['tʃu:zi] *adj* **choosier; -est** : difficile, exigeant

chop[1] ['tʃɑp] *vt* **chopped; chopping 1** : couper <to chop wood : couper du bois> **2** MINCE : hacher (des légumes, etc.) **3 to chop down** : abattre **4 to chop off** : trancher, couper

chop[2] *n* **1** BLOW, CUT : coup *m* **2** : côtelette *f* <pork chops : côtelettes de porc> **3 chops** *npl* : joue *f* (d'une personne), bajoues *fpl* (d'un animal) <to lick one's chops : se lécher les babines>

chopper ['tʃɑpər] → **helicopter**

choppy ['tʃɑpi] *adj* **choppier; -est 1** : agité <a choppy sea : une mer agitée> **2** DISCONNECTED, JERKY : saccadé, discontinu, irrégulier

chopsticks ['tʃɑp,stɪks] *npl* : baguettes *fpl*

choral ['korəl] *adj* : choral

chorale [kə'ræl, -'rɑl] *n* **1** : choral *m*, chant *m* religieux **2** CHOIR, CHORUS : chorale *f*

chord ['kɔrd] *n* **1** : accord *m* (en musique) **2** : corde *f* (géométrique)

chore ['tʃor] *n* **1** TASK : besogne *f*, travail *m* de routine <household chores : travaux ménagers> **2** BURDEN : corvée *f*

choreograph ['koriə,græf] *vt* : chorégraphier

choreographer [,kori'ɑgrəfər] *n* : chorégraphe *mf*

choreography [,kori'ɑgrəfi] *n, pl* **-phies** : chorégraphie *f* — **choreographic** [-ə'græfɪk] *adj*

chorister ['korɪstər] *n* : choriste *mf*

chortle[1] ['tʃɔrt̬əl] *vi* **-tled; -tling** : glousser

chortle[2] *n* : gloussement *m*, petit rire *m*

chorus[1] ['korəs] *vt* : chanter en chœur

chorus[2] *n* **1** : chœur *m* (de chanteurs), troupe *f* (de danseurs) **2** REFRAIN : refrain *m* **3** SONG : chœur *m*, choral *m* **4** : concert *m* <a chorus of cries : un concert de cris>

chose → **choose**

chosen ['tʃo:zən] *adj* : choisi, privilégié <the chosen few : les privilégiés>

chow ['tʃaʊ] *n* **1** FOOD, GRUB : bouffe *f fam* **2** → **chow chow**

chow chow ['tʃaʊ,tʃaʊ] *n* : chow-chow *m* (chien)

chowder ['tʃaʊdər] *n* : soupe *f* au poisson, soupe *f* aux fruits de mer

christen ['krɪsən] *vt* **1** BAPTIZE : baptiser **2** NAME : appeler, nommer

Christendom ['krɪsəndəm] *n* : chrétienté *f*

christening ['krɪsənɪŋ] *n* : baptême *m*

Christian[1] ['krɪstʃən] *adj* : chrétien

Christian[2] *n* : chrétien *m*, -tienne *f*

Christianity [,krɪstʃi'ænət̬i, ,krɪs'tʃæ-] *n* : christianisme *m*

Christian name *n* : nom *m* de baptême, prénom *m*

Christmas ['krɪsməs] *n* : Noël *m* <the Christmas season : la période de Noël>

chromatic [kro:'mæt̬ɪk] *adj* : chromatique

chrome ['kro:m] *n* : chrome *m*

chromium ['kro:miəm] *n* : chrome *m*

chromosome ['kro:mə,so:m, -,zo:m] *n* : chromosome *m*

chronic ['krɑnɪk] *adj* : chronique — **chronically** [-nɪkli] *adv*

chronicle[1] ['krɑnɪkəl] *vt* **-cled; -cling** : faire la chronique de, écrire une chronique de

chronicle[2] *n* : chronique *f*

chronicler ['krɑnɪklər] *n* : chroniqueur *m*, -queuse *f*

chronological [,krɑnəl'ɑdʒɪkəl] *adj* : chronologique — **chronologically** [-kli] *adv*

chronology [krə'nɑlədʒi] *n, pl* **-gies** : chronologie *f*

chronometer [krə'nɑmət̬ər] *n* : chronomètre *m*

chrysalis ['krɪsələs] *n, pl* **chrysalides** [krɪ'sælə,di:z] *or* **chrysalises**: chrysalide *f*

chrysanthemum [krɪ'sæntθəməm] *n* : chrysanthème *m*

chubby ['tʃʌbi] *adj* **chubbier; -est** : dodu, potelé, grassouillet

chuck[1] ['tʃʌk] *vt* **1** PAT, TAP : tapoter <to chuck s.o. under the chin : tapoter le menton de qqn> **2** TOSS : tirer, lancer **3** GIVE UP : renoncer à, laisser tomber (une activité)

chuck[2] *n* **1** PAT, TAP : tapotement *m* **2** TOSS : lancer *m* **3** *or* **chuck steak** : paleron *m* de bœuf

chuckle[1] ['tʃʌkəl] *vi* **-led; -ling** : glousser, rire tout bas

chuckle[2] *n* : gloussement *m*, petit rire *m*

chug ['tʃʌg] *vi* **chugged; chugging** PUFF : haleter (se dit d'un moteur)

chum[1] ['tʃʌm] *vi* **chummed; chumming** : être copain, être copine <to chum around with : être copain avec>

chum[2] *n* : copain *m*, -pine *f;* camarade *mf*

chummy ['tʃʌmi] **chummier; -est** : familier, amical, sociable

chump ['tʃʌmp] *n* : gourde *f fam;* idiot *m*, -diote *f*

chunk ['tʃʌŋk] *n* **1** PIECE : morceau *m* **2** : grande quantité *f* (d'argent, etc.)

chunky ['tʃʌŋki] *adj* **chunkier; -est 1** STOCKY : trapu **2** : qui contient des morceaux

church ['tʃərtʃ] *n* **1** : église *f* **2** : Église *f* <Church and State : l'Église et l'État> **3** DENOMINATION : culte *m*, confession *f* **4** CONGREGATION : assemblée *f* de fidèles

churchgoer ['tʃərtʃ,go:ər] *n* : pratiquant *m*, -quante *f*

churchyard ['tʃərtʃ,jard] *n* : cimetière *m* (autour d'une église)

churn[1] ['tʃərn] *vt* **1** : battre (du beurre), baratter (de la crème) **2** STIR : agiter, remuer — *vi* : bouillonner

churn[2] *n* : baratte *f*

chute [ˈʃuːt] *n* **1** : glissière *f* (de paquets, etc.) **2** : piste *f* de toboggan (aux sports) **3** → **parachute**
chutney [ˈtʃʌtni] *n, pl* **-neys** : chutney *m*
chutzpah [ˈhʊtspə, ˈxʊt-, -ˌspɑ] *n* GALL, NERVE : culot *m fam,* toupet *m fam*
cicada [səˈkeɪdə, -ˈkɑ-] *n* : cigale *f*
cider [ˈsaɪdər] *n* : cidre *m*
cigar [sɪˈgɑr] *n* : cigare *m*
cigarette [ˌsɪgəˈrɛt, ˈsɪgəˌrɛt] *n* : cigarette *f*
cinch¹ [ˈsɪntʃ] *vt* **1** : sangler (un cheval) **2** : attacher (une selle) par une sangle
cinch² *n* **1** : sangle *f* (de selle) **2** : quelque chose facile ou sûr <it's a cinch : c'est du gateau>
cincture [ˈsɪŋktʃər] *n* : ceinture *f* (d'un religieux)
cinder [ˈsɪndər] *n* **1** EMBER : morceau *m* de braise **2 cinders** *npl* ASHES : cendres *fpl*
cinema [ˈsɪnəmə] *n* : cinéma *m*
cinematic [ˌsɪnəˈmæt̬ɪk] *adj* : cinématographique
cinnamon [ˈsɪnəmən] *n* : cannelle *f*
cipher [ˈsaɪfər] *n* **1** ZERO : zéro *m* **2** CODE : chiffre *m,* code *m* secret
circa [ˈsərkə] *prep* : environ, vers <born circa 1700 : né au début du 18e siècle>
circle¹ [ˈsərkəl] *v* **-cled; -cling** *vt* **1** SURROUND : entourer, encercler **2** : tourner autour de, faire le tour de <the earth circles the sun : la terre tourne autour du soleil> — *vi* : faire des cercles
circle² *n* **1** : cercle *m* **2** CYCLE : cycle *m* <to come full circle : boucler la boucle> **3** GROUP : cercle *m,* milieu *m* (social)
circuit [ˈsərkət] *n* **1** BOUNDARY : limite *f,* frontière *f* **2** TOUR : circuit *m,* tour *m* **3** : circuit *m* (électrique)
circuit breaker *n* : disjoncteur *m*
circuitous [ˌsərˈkjuːət̬əs] *adj* **1** : détourné, indirect <a circuitous route : un chemin détourné> **2** : contourné, compliqué <circuitous reasoning : raisonnement contourné>
circuitry [ˈsərkətri] *n, pl* **-ries** : système *m* de circuits
circular¹ [ˈsərkjələr] *adj* ROUND : circulaire, rond
circular² *n* **1** LEAFLET : circulaire *f* **2** ADVERTISEMENT : prospectus *m*
circulate [ˈsərkjəˌleɪt] *v* **-lated; -lating** *vt* : faire circuler, propager <to circulate a rumor : propager une rumeur> — *vi* : circuler
circulation [ˌsərkjəˈleɪʃən] *n* **1** FLOW : circulation *f* **2** : tirage *m* (d'un journal)
circulatory [ˈsərkjələˌtori] *adj* : circulatoire
circumcise [ˈsərkəmˌsaɪz] *vt* **-cised; -cising** : circoncire
circumcision [ˌsərkəmˈsɪʒən, ˈsərkəmˌ-] *n* : circoncision *f*
circumference [sərˈkʌmpfrənts] *n* : circonférence *f*
circumflex [ˈsərkəmˌflɛks] *n* : accent *m* circonflexe
circumlocution [ˌsərkəmloˈkjuːʃən] *n* : circonlocution *f*
circumnavigate [ˌsərkəmˈnævəˌgeɪt] *vt* **-gated; -gating** : faire le tour de, contourner
circumscribe [ˈsərkəmˌskraɪb] *vt* **1** : circonscrire (en géométrie) **2** LIMIT : circonscrire, limiter
circumspect [ˈsərkəmˌspɛkt] *adj* : circonspect, prudent
circumspection [ˌsərkəmˈspɛkʃən] *n* : circonspection *f,* prudence *f*
circumstance [ˈsərkəmˌstænts] *n* **1** EVENT, FACT : circonstance *f,* événement *m* **2 circonstances** *npl* CONDITIONS : circonstances *fpl,* situation *f* <financial circumstances : situation financière> <under no circumstances : en aucun cas>
circumstantial [ˌsərkəmˈstæntʃəl] *adj* **1** INCIDENTAL : accidentel, fortuit <circumstantial evidence : preuves indirectes> **2** DETAILED : détaillé, circonstancié
circumvent [ˌsərkəmˈvɛnt] *vt* : contourner, circonvenir <to circumvent the law : contourner la loi>
circus [ˈsərkəs] *n* : cirque *m*
cirrhosis [səˈroːsɪs] *n, pl* **-rhoses** [-ˌsiːz] : cirrhose *f*
cirrus [ˈsɪrəs] *n, pl* **-ri** [ˈsɪrˌaɪ] : cirrus *m*
cistern [ˈsɪstərn] *n* TANK : citerne *f*
citadel [ˈsɪt̬ədəl, -ˌdɛl] *n* : citadelle *f*
citation [saɪˈteɪʃən] *n* : citation *f*
cite [ˈsaɪt] *vt* **cited; citing 1** SUMMON : citer, appeler (en justice) **2** QUOTE : citer **3** COMMEND : citer
citizen [ˈsɪt̬əzən] *n* : citoyen *m,* -toyenne *f*
citizenry [ˈsɪtəzənri] *n, pl* **-ries** : ensemble *m* des citoyens
citizenship [ˈsɪt̬əzənˌʃɪp] *n* : citoyenneté *f*
citron [ˈsɪtrən] *n* : cédrat *m*
citrus [ˈsɪtrəs] *n, pl* **citrus** *or* **citruses** *or* **citrus fruit** : agrume *m*
city [ˈsɪt̬i] *n, pl* **cities** : ville *f*
city hall *n* : hôtel *m* de ville
civic [ˈsɪvɪk] *adj* : civique
civics [ˈsɪvɪks] *ns & pl* : instruction *f* civique
civil [ˈsɪvəl] *adj* **1** : civil <civil engineering : génie civil> **2** POLITE : courtois, civil
civilian [səˈvɪljən] *n* : civil *m,* -vile *f*
civility [səˈvɪlət̬i] *n, pl* **-ties** POLITENESS : civilité *f,* courtoisie *f*
civilization [ˌsɪvələˈzeɪʃən] *n* : civilisation *f*
civilize [ˈsɪvəˌlaɪz] *vt* **-lized; -lizing** : civiliser

civilly [ˈsɪvəli] *adj* : poliment

civil rights *npl* : droits *mpl* civiques, droits *mpl* civils

civil service *n* : fonction *f* publique

civil war *n* : guerre *f* civile

clack[1] [ˈklæk] *vi* : cliqueter

clack[2] *n* : cliquetis *m*

clad [ˈklæd] *adj* **1** CLOTHED : vêtu, habillé **2** COVERED : couvert

claim[1] [ˈkleɪm] *vt* **1** DEMAND : revendiquer, réclamer <to claim one's rights : réclamer ses droits> **2** MAINTAIN : déclarer, prétendre <he claims to know you : il prétend vous connaître> **3 to claim a life** : faire un mort, faire une victime

claim[2] *n* **1** DEMAND : revendication *f*, demande *f* **2** ASSERTION : déclaration *f*, affirmation *f* **3** *or* **land claim** : concession *f* (de terrain)

clairvoyance [klærˈvɔɪənts] *n* : voyance *f*, don *m* de seconde vue

clairvoyant[1] [klærˈvɔɪənt] *adj* : doué de seconde vue

clairvoyant[2] *n* : voyant *m*, -voyante *f*

clam [ˈklæm] *n* : palourde *f*

clamber [ˈklæmbər] *vi* : grimper, se hisser (avec difficulté)

clammy [ˈklæmi] *adj* **clammier; -est** : moite, humide et froid

clamor[1] *or Brit* **clamour** [ˈklæmər] *vi* **1** : vociférer, crier **2 to clamor for** : demander, réclamer

clamor[2] *or Brit* **clamour** *n* **1** UPROAR : clameur *f*, vociférations *fpl* **2** DEMAND : réclamations *fpl* **3** PROTEST : protestation *f*

clamorous [ˈklæmərəs] *adj* : bruyant, vociférant

clamour *Brit* → **clamor**

clamp[1] [ˈklæmp] *vt* **1** CLENCH : serrer <she clamped her mouth shut : elle serrait les mâchoires> **2** ATTACH : cramponner, fixer

clamp[2] *n* : crampon *m*, pince *f*

clan [ˈklæn] *n* : clan *m*

clandestine [klænˈdɛstɪn] *adj* : clandestin, secret

clang[1] [ˈklæŋ] *vi* : résonner, retentir

clang[2] *n* : bruit *m* métallique

clangor *or Brit* **clangour** [ˈklæŋər, -gər] *n* : suite *f* de bruits métalliques

clank[1] [ˈklæŋk] *vi* : résonner, cliqueter

clank[2] *n* : cliquetis *m*

clannish [ˈklænɪʃ] *adj* : exclusif, fermé

clap[1] [ˈklæp] *vt* **clapped; clapping 1** STRIKE : frapper bruyamment **2** APPLAUD : applaudir — *vi* APPLAUD : applaudir

clap[2] *n* **1** NOISE : retentissement *m*, coup *m* <a clap of thunder : un grondement de tonnerre> **2** PAT, SLAP : claque *f*, petite tape *f* **3** APPLAUDING : applaudissement *m*

clapboard [ˈklæbərd, ˈklæpˌbord] *n* : bardeau *m* (en bois)

clapper [ˈklæpər] *n* : battant *m* (d'une cloche)

claret [ˈklærət] *n* : bordeaux *m* (vin)

clarification [ˌklærəfəˈkeɪʃən] *n* : clarification *f*

clarify [ˈklærəˌfaɪ] *vt* **-fied; -fying** : clarifier, éclaircir

clarinet [ˌklærəˈnɛt] *n* : clarinette *f*

clarinetist *or* **clarinettist** [ˌklærəˈnɛt̬ɪst] *n* : clarinettiste *mf*

clarion [ˈklæriən] *adj* : claironnant, sonore

clarity [ˈklærət̬i] *n* : clarté *f*

clash[1] [ˈklæʃ] *vi* **1** : produire un bruit métallique, résonner **2** CONFLICT, COLLIDE : s'opposer, se heurter

clash[2] *n* **1** : bruit *m* métallique, retentissement *m* **2** CONFLICT : conflit *m*, incompatibilité *f* **3** : discordance *f* (se dit des couleurs)

clasp[1] [ˈklæsp] *vt* **1** FASTEN : attacher **2** EMBRACE, GRASP : étreindre, embrasser, serrer

clasp[2] *n* **1** FASTENER : attache *f*, fermoir *m* **2** EMBRACE, HOLD : étreinte *f*, prise *f*

class[1] [ˈklæs] *vt* : classer, classifier

class[2] *n* **1** TYPE, KIND : classe *f*, division *f*, catégorie *f* **2** *or* **social class** : classe *f*, rang *m* social **3** COURSE : cours *m* <night classes : cours du soir> **4** : classe *f* (d'élèves)

classic[1] [ˈklæsɪk] *adj* : classique

classic[2] *n* : classique *m*

classical [ˈklæsɪkəl] *adj* : classique

classically [ˈklæsɪkli] *adv* : de façon classique, dans un style classique

classicism [ˈklæsəˌsɪzəm] *n* : classicisme *m*

classification [ˌklæsəfəˈkeɪʃən] *n* : classification *f*

classified [ˈklæsəˌfaɪd] *adj* **1** : classifié <classified ads : des petites annonces> **2** SECRET : secret, confidentiel

classify [ˈklæsəˌfaɪ] *vt* **-fied; -fying** : classer, classifier

classmate [ˈklæsˌmeɪt] *n* : compagnon *m* de classe, compagne *f* de classe

classroom [ˈklæsˌruːm] *n* : salle *f* de classe

clatter[1] [ˈklæt̬ər] *vi* : faire du bruit, s'entrechoquer

clatter[2] *n* : bruit *m*, cliquetis *m*

clause [ˈklɔz] *n* **1** : clause *f* (dans les actes judiciares, etc.) **2** : proposition *f* (en grammaire)

claustrophobia [ˌklɔstrəˈfoːbiə] *n* : claustrophobie *f* — **claustrophobic** [-ˈfoːbɪk] *adj*

clavicle [ˈklævɪkəl] *n* : clavicule *f*

claw[1] [ˈklɔ] *vt* : griffer

claw[2] *n* : griffe *f* (d'un chat, etc.), pince *f* (des crustacés)

clay [ˈkleɪ] *n* : argile *f*

clayey [ˈkleɪi] *adj* : argileux

clean[1] [ˈkliːn] *vt* : nettoyer, laver

clean[2] *adv* **1** FAIRLY, PROPERLY : de façon propre, sans faute (en sports) **2** COMPLETELY : complètement **3 to**

come clean about : tout dire sur, révéler
clean[3] *adj* **1** : propre **2** UNADULTERATED : pur **3** DECENT, UNSULLIED : honorable, sans tache **4** COMPLETE : définitif
cleanliness [ˈklɛnlinəs] *n* : propreté *f*
cleanly[1] [ˈkli:nli] *adv* : proprement, nettement
cleanly[2] [ˈklɛnli] *adj* **cleanlier; -est** : propre
cleanness [ˈkli:nnəs] *n* : propreté *f*
cleanse [ˈklɛnz] *vt* **cleansed; cleansing** : nettoyer, purifier
clear[1] [ˈkli:r] *vt* **1** CLARIFY : clarifier **2** *or* **to clear away** : débarrasser, déblayer, déboucher (un tuyau, etc.), dégager (une voie) <to clear the table : débarrasser la table> **3** VINDICATE : innocenter, disculper <to clear one's name : blanchir son nom, se disculper> **4** LIQUIDATE : liquider (un compte, etc.) **5** NET : réaliser, rapporter <to clear a profit : réaliser un profit> **6** : franchir, éviter <to clear a hurdle : franchir une haie> **7 to clear up** RESOLVE : résoudre (un problème) — *vi* **1** *or* **to clear up** : s'éclaircir, se lever (se dit du temps) **2** *or* **to clear up** VANISH : disparaître <the symptoms cleared up : les symptômes ont disparu> **3** : être compensé (se dit d'un chèque)
clear[2] *adv* **1** DISTINCTLY : distinctement, nettement **2** COMPLETELY : complètement **3 to get clear of** : se débarrasser de
clear[3] *adj* **1** BRIGHT : éclatant, lumineux **2** FAIR : clair, beau (se dit du temps) <a clear sky : un ciel sans nuages> **3** TRANSPARENT : transparent, clair, limpide **4** EXPLICIT, STRAIGHTFORWARD : clair, explicite, intelligible **5** FREE, UNBLOCKED : libre, dégagé
clear[4] *n* **in the clear** : libre de tout soupçon
clearance [ˈklɪrənts] *n* **1** : déblaiement *m*, dégagement *m* **2** SPACE : espace *m* libre **3** AUTHORIZATION : autorisation *f* (d'une chèque)
clearing [ˈklɪrɪŋ] *n* : clairière *f* (dans un bois)
clearly [ˈklɪrli] *adv* **1** DISTINCTLY : clairement, distinctement **2** EVIDENTLY : évidemment, manifestement
cleat [ˈkli:t] *n* **1** : taquet *m* (d'un navire) **2 cleats** *mpl* : chaussures *fpl* à crampons
cleavage [ˈkli:vɪdʒ] *n* **1** CLEAVING, SPLIT : clivage *m* **2** : décolleté *m* <a dress showing cleavage : une robe décolletée>
cleave[1] [ˈkli:v] *vi* **cleaved** [ˈkli:vd] *or* **clove** [ˈklo:v]; **cleaving** CLING : adhérer, coller
cleave[2] *vt* **cleaved; cleaving** SPLIT : diviser, fendre
cleaver [ˈkli:vər] *n* : couperet *m*
clef [ˈklɛf] *n* : clé *f*, clef *f* (en musique)
cleft [ˈklɛft] *n* : crevasse *f*, fissure *f*
clemency [ˈklɛməntsi] *n, pl* **-cies** : clémence *f*
clement [ˈklɛmənt] *adj* **1** LENIENT, MERCIFUL : clément, indulgent **2** MILD : doux, clément (se dit de la température)
clench [ˈklɛntʃ] *vt* : serrer <to clench one's fist : serrer le poing> <to clench one's teeth : serrer les dents>
clergy [ˈklərdʒi] *n, pl* **-gies** : clergé *m*
clergyman [ˈklərdʒimən] *n, pl* **-men** [-mən, -ˌmɛn] : ecclésiastique *m*
cleric [ˈklɛrɪk] *n* : ecclésiastique *m*
clerical [ˈklɛrɪkəl] *adj* **1** : clérical, du clergé **2** : de bureau <clerical work : travail de bureau>
clerk [ˈklərk, *Brit* ˈklɑrk] *n* **1** : commis *mf* (de bureau); employé *m*, -ployée *f* de bureau **2** SALESPERSON : vendeur *m*, -deuse *f*
clever [ˈklɛvər] *adj* **1** SKILLFUL : habile, adroit **2** WITTY : ingénieux, astucieux
cleverly [ˈklɛvərli] *adv* **1** SKILLFULLY : habilement **2** INTELLIGENTLY : astucieusement, intelligemment
cleverness [ˈklɛvərnəs] *n* **1** SKILL : habileté *f* **2** INTELLIGENCE : intelligence *f*
clew [ˈklu:] → **clue**
cliché [kliˈʃeɪ] *n* : cliché *m*
click[1] [ˈklɪk] *vt* : faire claquer — *vi* **1** : faire un déclic **2** AGREE, GET ALONG : bien fonctionner ensemble, bien s'entendre **3** SUCCEED : bien marcher **4** : cliquer (en informatique)
click[2] *n* : clic *m*, déclic *m*
client [ˈklaɪənt] *n* : client *m*, cliente *f*
clientele [ˌklaɪənˈtɛl, ˌkli:-] *n* : clientèle *f*
cliff [ˈklɪf] *n* : falaise *f*, escarpement *m*
climate [ˈklaɪmət] *n* : climat *m*
climax[1] [ˈklaɪˌmæks] *vi* : atteindre un point culminant
climax[2] *n* : point *m* culminant, apogée *m*
climb[1] [ˈklaɪm] *vt* : monter, gravir, escalader <to climb a mountain : gravir une montagne> — *vi* RISE, ASCEND : monter, augmenter <prices are climbing : les prix augmentent>
climb[2] *n* : montée *f*, ascension *f*
clinch[1] [ˈklɪntʃ] *vt* **1** FASTEN, SECURE : river (un clou), attacher **2** SETTLE : résoudre, conclure <to clinch the deal : conclure l'affaire>
clinch[2] *n* EMBRACE : étreinte *f*, corps à corps *m* (en boxe)
cling [ˈklɪŋ] *vi* **clung** [ˈklʌŋ]; **clinging 1** STICK : adhérer, coller **2** : se cramponner, s'agripper <he was clinging to the railing : il se cramponnait à la balustrade>

clinic ['klɪnɪk] *n* : clinique *f*
clinical ['klɪnɪkəl] *adj* : clinique — **clinically** [-kli] *adv*
clink[1] ['klɪŋk] *vi* : tinter
clink[2] *n* : tintement *m*
clinker ['klɪŋkər] *n* : mâchefer *m*, scories *fpl*
clip[1] ['klɪp] *vt* **clipped; clipping 1** CUT : couper, tailler **2** HIT : frapper, donner un coup de poing à **3** FASTEN : attacher (avec un trombone)
clip[2] *n* **1** → **clippers 2** BLOW : coup *m*, taloche *f fam* **3** PACE : pas *m* rapide <at a good clip : à vive allure> **4** FASTENER : attache *f*, pince *f* **5** → **paper clip**
clipper ['klɪpər] *n* **1** *or* **clipper ship** : clipper *m* **2 clippers** *npl or* **nail clippers** : coupe-ongles *m* **3 clippers** *npl* SHEARS : tondeuse *f*
clique ['kli:k, 'klɪk] *n* : clique *m*, coterie *f*
clitoris ['klɪtərəs, klɪ'tɔrəs] *n, pl* **clitorides** [-'tɔrə,di:z] : clitoris *m*
cloak[1] ['klo:k] *vt* : cacher, camoufler <cloaked in secrecy : empreint de secret>
cloak[2] *n* **1** CAPE : cape *f* **2** PRETENSE, DISGUISE : masque *m*, voile *m*
clobber ['klɑbər] *vt* : tabasser *fam*
clock[1] ['klɑk] *vi* : chronométrer (un coureur, etc.)
clock[2] *n* **1** : horloge *f*, chronomètre *m* (aux sports) **2 to work around the clock** : travailler 24 heures d'affilée
clockwise ['klɑkwaɪz] *adv & adj* : dans le sens des aiguilles d'une montre
clod ['klɑd] *n* **1** : motte *f* (de terre) **2** OAF : rustre *m*; lourdaud *m*, -daude *f*
clog[1] ['klɑg] *v* **clogged; clogging** *vt* **1** HINDER : entraver, gêner **2** OBSTRUCT : boucher, bloquer, obstruer — *vi or* **to clog up** : se boucher
clog[2] *n* **1** HINDRANCE : entrave *f* **2** : sabot *m* (chaussure)
cloister[1] ['klɔɪstər] *vt* : cloîtrer
cloister[2] *n* : cloître *m*
clone ['klo:n] *n* : clone *m*
close[1] ['klo:z] *v* **closed; closing** *vt* **1** SHUT : fermer **2** STOP, END : terminer, clore, conclure **3** REDUCE : réduire, diminuer <to close a gap : réduire un espace> — *vi* **1** : fermer, se fermer **2** TERMINATE : prendre fin, se terminer **3 to close in** APPROACH : se rapprocher
close[2] ['klo:s] *adv* **1** NEARBY : tout près **2** SOON : dans peu de temps **3 to hold s.o. close** : serrer qqn dans ses bras
close[3] *adj* **closer; closest 1** CONFINING : étroit, limité <to live in close quarters : vivre à l'étroit> **2** SECRETIVE : peu communicatif, réservé **3** STRICT : rigoureux, étroit <a close watch : une surveillance étroite> **4** STUFFY : mal aéré (se dit d'une salle, etc.), lourd (se dit du temps) **5** TIGHT : serré <it's a close fit : il est très serré> **6** INTIMATE : intime, proche <close friends : amies intimes> **7** ACCURATE : précis, exact <a close translation : une traduction très exacte> **8** : serré (se dit d'une concurrence) <a close contest : une lutte serrée>
close[4] ['klo:z] *n* CONCLUSION, END : fin *f*, conclusion *f*
closely ['klo:sli] *adv* **1** NEAR : de près **2** ATTENTIVELY : attentivement
closeness ['klo:snəs] *n* : proximité *f*
closet[1] ['klɑzət] *vt* : enfermer <to be closeted with s.o. : être tête à tête avec qqn>
closet[2] *n* : placard *m*, garde-robe *f*, penderie *f*
closure ['klo:ʒər] *n* : fermeture *f*, clôture *f*
clot[1] ['klɑt] *vi* **clotted; clotting** : former des caillots, se coaguler
clot[2] *n* : caillot *m*
cloth ['klɔθ] *n, pl* **cloths** ['klɔðz, 'klɔθs] **1** FABRIC : tissu *m*, étoffe *f* **2** RAG : chiffon *m* **3** TABLECLOTH : nappe *f*
clothe ['klo:ð] *vt* **clothed** *or* **clad** ['klæd]; **clothing** : habiller, vêtir
clothes ['klo:z, 'klo:ðz] *npl* **1** → **clothing 2** → **bedclothes**
clothespin ['klo:z,pɪn, 'klo:ðz-] *n*: pince *f* (à linge)
clothier ['klo:ðjər, 'klo:ðiər] *n* : marchand *m* de vêtements
clothing ['klo:ðɪŋ] *n* : vêtements *mpl*
cloud[1] ['klaʊd] *vt* : embuer, obscurcir — *vi or* **to cloud over** : se couvrir de nuages
cloud[2] *n* **1** : nuage *m* **2** SWARM : essaim *m*, nuée *f* (d'insectes)
cloudburst ['klaʊd,bərst] *n* : trombes *fpl* d'eau, grosse averse *f*
cloudy ['klaʊdi] *adj* **cloudier; -est** : nuageux, couvert
clout[1] ['klaʊt] *vt* : donner un coup (de poing) à
clout[2] *n* **1** BLOW : coup *m*, taloche *f fam* **2** INFLUENCE, PULL : influence *m*, pouvoir *m*
clove[1] ['klo:v] *n* **1** : clou *m* de girofle **2** *or* **garlic clove** : gousse *f* d'ail
clove[2] → **cleave**
clover ['klo:vər] *n* : trêfle *m*
cloverleaf ['klo:vər,li:f] *n, pl* **-leafs** *or* **-leaves** [-,li:vz] : croisement *m* en trêfle
clown[1] ['klaʊn] *vi or* **to clown around** : faire le clown
clown[2] *n* : clown *m*
cloying ['klɔɪɪŋ] *adj* **1** DISGUSTING : écœurant **2** MAWKISH : mièvre
club[1] ['klʌb] *vt* **clubbed; clubbing** : frapper
club[2] *n* **1** BLUDGEON : massue *f*, matraque *f* **2** : club *m* (aux sports) **3** : trêfle *m* (aux cartes) **4** ASSOCIATION : club *m*, groupe *m*, association *f*
clubfoot ['klʌb,fʊt] *n, pl* **-feet** : pied *m* bot

clubhouse ['klʌb,haʊs] *n* : club *m,* maison *f* de club
cluck[1] ['klʌk] *vi* : glousser
cluck[2] *n* : gloussement *m*
clue[1] ['klu:] *vt* **clued; clueing** *or* **cluing** INFORM : mettre au courant, informer
clue[2] *n* : indice *m,* indication *f* <I haven't got a clue : je n'ai aucune idée>
clump[1] ['klʌmp] *vi* : marcher lourdement
clump[2] *n* **1** : massif *m* (d'arbres), touffe *f* (d'herbe) **2** : pas *m* lourd
clumsiness ['klʌmzinəs] *n* **1** AWKWARDNESS : gaucherie *f* **2** TACTLESSNESS : manque *m* de tact
clumsy ['klʌmzi] *adj* **clumsier; -est 1** AWKWARD : maladroit, gauche **2** TACTLESS : sans tact, malhabile, gauche — **clumsily** *adv*
clung → **cling**
cluster[1] ['klʌstər] *vt* : rassembler — *vi* : se rassembler, se grouper
cluster[2] *n* : groupe *m* (de personnes), grappe *f* (de raisins, etc.), ensemble *m* (de maisons, d'idées, etc.)
clutch[1] ['klʌtʃ] *vt* GRASP : saisir, étreindre — *vi* **to clutch at** : s'agripper à, se cramponner à
clutch[2] *n* **1** GRASP, GRIP : prise *f,* étreinte *f* <to fall into s.o.'s clutches : tomber dans les griffes de qqn> **2** : embrayage *m* (d'une voiture) **3** *or* **clutch pedal** : pédale *f* d'embrayage
clutter[1] ['klʌt̬ər] *vt* : encombrer, mettre en désordre
clutter[2] *n* : désordre *m,* fouillis *m*
coach[1] ['ko:tʃ] *vt* **1** : entraîner (une équipe sportive) **2** TUTOR : donner des leçons à
coach[2] *n* **1** CARRIAGE : carrosse *m* **2** : voiture *f,* wagon *m* (d'un train) **3** BUS : autocar *m,* autobus *m* **4** : deuxième classe *f* (en avion) **5** TRAINER : entraîneur *m,* -neuse *f*
coagulate [ko'ægjə,leɪt] *v* **-lated; -lating** *vt* CLOT : coaguler — *vi* : se coaguler
coagulation [ko,ægjə'leɪʃən] *n* : coagulation *f*
coal ['ko:l] *n* **1** : charbon *m,* houille *f* **2 coals** *npl* : EMBERS : braise *f*
coalesce [,ko:ə'lɛs] *vi* **-alesced; -alescing** : s'unir
coalition [,ko:ə'lɪʃən] *n* : coalition *f*
coarse [,kors] *adj* **coarser; coarsest 1** : gros (se dit du sable, du sel, etc.), grossier (se dit des textiles), épais (se dit des cheveux, etc.) **2** CRUDE : grossier, vulgaire
coarsely [,korsli] *adv* : grossièrement
coarsen ['korsən] *vt* : rendre rude, rendre grossier — *vi* : devenir rude, devenir grossier
coarseness ['korsnəs] *n* **1** ROUGHNESS : rudesse *f* **2** CRUDENESS : grossièreté *f,* vulgarité *f*
coast[1] ['ko:st] *vi* : avancer en roue libre
coast[2] *n* : côte *f,* littoral *m*
coastal ['ko:stəl] *adj* : côtier, littoral
coaster ['ko:stər] *n* : dessous-de-verre *m,* sous-verre *m Can*
coast guard *n* : gendarmerie *f* maritime *France,* garde *f* côtière *Can*
coastline ['ko:st,laɪn] *n* : littoral *m*
coat[1] ['ko:t] *vt* : couvrir (d'une couche), enduire
coat[2] *n* **1** : manteau *m* (vêtement) **2** FUR : fourrure *f,* pelage *m,* poil *m* **3** LAYER : couche *f* <a coat of paint : une couche de peinture>
coat hanger → **hanger**
coating ['ko:t̬ɪŋ] *n* : couche *f,* revêtement *m*
coat of arms *n* : blason *m,* armoiries *fpl*
coatrack ['ko:t,ræk] *n* : portemanteau *m*
coax ['ko:ks] *vt* : amadouer, cajoler, enjoler
cob ['kɑb] → **corncob**
cobalt ['ko:,bɔlt] *n* : cobalt *m*
cobble ['kɑbəl] *vt* **-bled; -bling** *or* **to cobble together** : concocter (à la hâte), bricoler
cobbled ['kɑbəld] *adj* : pavé
cobbler ['kɑblər] *n* **1** SHOEMAKER : cordonnier *m,* -nière *f* **2** *or* **fruit cobbler** : tarte *f* aux fruits
cobblestone ['kɑbəl,sto:n] *n* : pavé *m*
cobra ['ko:brə] *n* : cobra *m*
cobweb ['kɑb,wɛb] *n* : toile *f* d'araignée
cocaine [ko'keɪn, 'ko:,keɪn] *n* : cocaïne *f*
cock[1] ['kɑk] *vt* **1** : armer (un fusil) **2** TILT : pencher (la tête, etc.) **3 to cock one's ears** : dresser les oreilles
cock[2] *n* **1** ROOSTER : coq *m* **2** FAUCET : robinet *m* **3** : chien *m* (de fusil)
cockatoo ['kɑkə,tu:] *n, pl* **-toos** : cacatoès *m*
cockeyed ['kɑk,aɪd] *adj* **1** ASKEW : de travers **2** ABSURD : absurde, insensé
cockiness ['kɑkinəs] *n* : impertinence *f,* impudence *f*
cockle ['kɑkəl] *n* : coque *f*
cockpit ['kɑk,pɪt] *n* : cockpit *m,* poste *m* de pilotage
cockroach ['kɑk,ro:tʃ] *n* : cafard *m,* blatte *f France,* coquerelle *f Can*
cocktail ['kɑk,teɪl] *n* : cocktail *m*
cocky ['kɑki] *adj* **cockier; -est** : impudent, suffisant
cocoa ['ko:,ko:] *n* : cacao *m*
coconut ['ko:kə,nʌt] *n* : noix *f* de coco
coconut palm *n* : cocotier *m*
cocoon [kə'ku:n] *n* : cocon *m*
cod ['kɑd] *ns & pl* : morue *f*
coddle ['kɑdəl] *vt* **-dled; -dling** : dorloter
code ['ko:d] *n* **1** CIPHER : code *m,* chiffre *m* **2** RULES : code *m,* règlement *m* <penal code : code pénal>
codeine ['ko:,di:n] *n* : codéine *f*
codger ['kɑdʒər] *n* : vieux bonhomme *m,* vieillard *m*

codicil ['kadəsəl, -ˌsɪl] *n* : codicille *m*
codify ['kadəˌfaɪ, 'ko:-] *vt* **-fied; -fying** : codifier
coeducation [ˌko:ˌɛdʒə'keɪʃən] *n* : éducation *f* mixte
coeducational [ˌko:ˌɛdʒə'keɪʃənəl] *adj* : mixte
coefficient [ˌko:ə'fɪʃənt] *n* : coefficient *m*
coerce [ko'ərs] *vt* **-erced; -ercing** : obliger, contraindre
coercion [ko'ərʒən, -ʃən] *n* : contrainte *f,* coercition *f*
coercive [ko'ərsɪv] *adj* : coercitif
coexist [ˌko:ɪg'zɪst] *vi* : coexister
coexistence [ˌko:ɪg'zɪstən*t*s] *n* : coexistence *f*
coffee ['kɔfi] *n* : café *m*
coffeepot ['kɔfiˌpat] *n* : cafetière *f*
coffer ['kɔfər] *n* : coffre *m,* caisse *f*
coffin ['kɔfən] *n* : cercueil *m,* bière *f*
cog ['kag] *n* : dent *f* (d'une roue)
cogent ['ko:dʒənt] *adj* : convaincant, persuasif
cogitate ['kadʒəˌteɪt] *vi* **-tated; -tating** : réfléchir, méditer
cogitation [ˌkadʒə'teɪʃən] *n* : réflexion *f,* méditation *f*
cognac ['ko:nˌjæk] *n* : cognac *m*
cognate[1] ['kagˌneɪt] *adj* : apparenté
cognate[2] *n* : mot *m* apparenté
cognizant ['kagnəzənt] *adj* : conscient
cogwheel ['kagˌ*h*wi:l] *n* : roue *f* dentée, pignon *m*
cohabit [ˌko:'hæbət] *vi* : cohabiter
cohere [ko'hɪr] *vi* **-hered; -hering 1** ADHERE : adhérer **2** : être cohérent, être logique
coherence [ko'hɪrən*t*s] *n* : cohérence *f*
coherent [ko'hɪrənt] *adj* : cohérent, logique — **coherently** *adv*
cohesion [ko'hi:ʒən] *n* : cohésion *f*
cohort ['ko:ˌhɔrt] *n* **1** : cohorte *f* (militaire) **2** COMPANION : compagnon *m,* compagne *f,* collègue *mf*
coiffure [kwa'fjʊr] *n* : coiffure *f*
coil[1] ['kɔɪl] *vt* : enrouler — *vi* : s'enrouler
coil[2] *n* : rouleau *m,* bobine *f,* boucle *f* (de cheveux), volute *f* (de fumée)
coin[1] ['kɔɪn] *vt* **1** MINT : frapper (de la monnaie) **2** INVENT : forger, inventer (un mot, un terme) <to coin a phrase : comme on dit>
coin[2] *n* : pièce *f* de monnaie
coincide [ˌko:ɪn'saɪd, 'ko:ɪnˌsaɪd] *vi* **-cided; -ciding** : coïncider
coincidence [ko'ɪn*t*sədən*t*s] *n* : coïncidence *f*
coincidental [koˌɪn*t*sə'dɛntəl] *adj* : fortuit, de coïncidence
coincidentally [koˌɪn*t*sə'dɛntəli] *adv* : par hasard
coitus ['ko:əṭəs] *n* : coït *m*
coke ['ko:k] *n* : coke *m* <coke stove : four à coke>
colander ['kaləndər, 'kʌ-] *n* : passoire *f*
cold[1] ['ko:ld] *adj* : froid <it's cold out : il fait froid> <my feet are cold : j'ai froid aux pieds> <to be cold toward s.o. : être froid avec qqn> <a cold heart : un cœur de pierre>
cold[2] *n* **1** : froid *m* **2** : rhume *m* (en médecine) <to have a cold : être enrhumé>
cold–blooded ['ko:ld'blʌdəd] *adj* **1** : à sang froid (se dit des animaux) **2** CRUEL : cruel, sans pitié
coldly ['ko:ldli] *adv* : avec froideur, froidement
coldness ['ko:ldnəs] *n* : froideur *f*
coleslaw ['ko:lˌslɔ] *n* : salade *f* de chou cru
colic ['kalik] *n* : coliques *fpl*
coliseum [ˌkalə'si:əm] *n* : stade *m,* arène *f*
collaborate [kə'læbəˌreɪt] *vi* **-rated; -rating** : collaborer, coopérer
collaboration [kəˌlæbə'reɪʃən] *n* : collaboration *f*
collaborator [kə'læbəˌreɪṭər] *n* : collaborateur *m,* -trice *f*
collapse[1] [kə'læps] *vi* **-lapsed; -lapsing 1** : s'effondrer, s'écrouler **2** FOLD : se plier
collapse[2] *n* : effondrement *m,* écroulement *m*
collapsible [kə'læpsəbəl] *adj* : pliant <collapsible chair : chaise pliante>
collar[1] ['kalər] *vt* : saisir au collet, arrêter (un criminel)
collar[2] *n* : col *m*
collarbone ['kalərˌbo:n] *n* : clavicule *f*
collate [kə'leɪt; 'kaˌleɪt; 'ko:-] *vt* **-lated; -lating 1** COMPARE : comparer **2** ASSEMBLE : collationner (les feuilles d'un livre)
collateral[1] [kə'læṭərəl] *adj* **1** SECONDARY : secondaire, subsidiaire **2** PARALLEL : parallèle, concomitant
collateral[2] *n* : nantissement *m*
colleague ['kaˌli:g] *n* : confrère *m,* consœur *f,* collègue *mf*
collect[1] [kə'lɛkt] *vt* **1** GATHER : ramasser, recueillir **2** : percevoir, encaisser (une somme d'argent) **3** : collectionner (des objets) — *vi* **1** CONGREGATE : se regrouper, se rejoindre **2** ACCUMULATE : s'accumuler
collect[2] *adv* **to call collect** : téléphoner en PCV *France,* téléphoner à frais virés *Can*
collection [kə'lɛkʃən] *n* **1** COLLECTING : ramassage *m* (d'objets), recouvrement *m* (de dettes, etc.), rassemblement *m* (d'information), accumulation *f* (de richesses) **2** : collection *f* <book collection : collection de livres>
collective[1] [kə'lɛktɪv] *adj* : collectif
collective[2] *n* : coopérative *f,* entreprise *f* collective
college ['kalɪdʒ] *n* **1** : établissement *m* d'enseignement supérieur **2** GROUP

: association *f* (de professionels, etc.), collège *m* (électoral)
collegiate [kəˈliːdʒət] *adj* : universitaire
collide [kəˈlaɪd] *vi* **-lided; -liding** : se heurter, entrer en collision
collie [ˈkɑli] *n* : colley *m*
collision [kəˈlɪʒən] *n* : collision *f*
colloquial [kəˈloːkwiəl] *adj* : familier
colloquialism [kəˈloːkwiə,lɪzəm] *n* : expression *f* familière
collusion [kəˈluːʒən] *n* : collusion *f*
cologne [kəˈloːn] *n* : eau *f* de Cologne
Colombian[1] [kəˈlʌmbiən] *adj* : colombien
Colombian[2] *n* : Colombien *m*, -bienne *f*
colon[1] [ˈkoːlən] *n, pl* **colons** *or* **cola** [-lə] : côlon *m* (en anatomie)
colon[2] *n, pl* **colons** : deux-points *m* (signe orthographique)
colonel [ˈkərnəl] *n* : colonel *m*
colonial[1] [kəˈloːniəl] *adj* : colonial
colonial[2] *n* : colonial *m*, -niale *f*
colonist [ˈkɑlənɪst] *n* : colon *m*
colonization [,kɑlənəˈzeɪʃən] *n* : colonisation *f*
colonize [ˈkɑlə,naɪz] *vt* **-nized; -nizing** : établir une colonie en, coloniser
colonnade [,kɑləˈneɪd] *n* : colonnade *f*
colony [ˈkɑləni] *n, pl* **-nies** : colonie *f*
color[1] *or Brit* **colour** [ˈkʌlər] *vt* **1** : colorer **2** INFLUENCE : influer sur, influencer — *vi* BLUSH : rougir
color[2] *or Brit* **colour** *n* **1** : couleur *f* <bright colors : couleurs vives> **2** INTEREST, VIVIDNESS : couleur *f* <local color : couleur locale> **3 colors** *npl* FLAG : couleurs *fpl*
color–blind *or Brit* **colour–blind** [ˈkʌlər,blaɪnd] *adj* : daltonien
colored *or Brit* **coloured** [ˈkʌlərd] *adj* **1** : coloré **2** : de couleur (se dit des personnes)
colorfast *or Brit* **colourfast** [ˈkʌlər,fæst] *adj* : grand teint, bon teint
colorful *or Brit* **colourful** [ˈkʌlərfəl] *adj* **1** : coloré **2** PICTURESQUE, STRIKING : pittoresque, frappant, original
colorless *or Brit* **colourless** [ˈkʌlərləs] *adj* **1** : incolore **2** DULL : terne, fade
colossal [kəˈlɑsəl] *adj* : colossal
colossus [kəˈlɑsəs] *n, pl* **-si** [-,saɪ] : colosse *m*
colour *Brit* → **color**
colt [ˈkoːlt] *n* : poulain *m*
column [ˈkɑləm] *n* **1** : colonne *f* (en architecture) **2** : colonne *f* (en imprimerie), rubrique *f* (dans la presse), chronique *f* (dans un journal)
columnist [ˈkɑləmnɪst, -ləmɪst] *n* : chroniqueur *m*, -queuse *f*
coma [ˈkoːmə] *n* : coma *m*
comatose [ˈkoːmə,toːs, ˈkɑ-] *adj* : comateux, dans le coma
comb[1] [ˈkoːm] *vt* **1** : peigner <to comb one's hair : se peigner> **2** *or* **to comb out** : démêler (les cheveux) **3** SEARCH : ratisser, passer (un lieu) au peigne fin
comb[2] *n* **1** : peigne *m* **2** : crête *f* (d'un coq)
combat[1] [kəmˈbæt, ˈkɑm,bæt] *vt* **-bated** *or* **-batted; -bating** *or* **-batting** : combattre, lutter contre
combat[2] [ˈkɑm,bæt] *n* : combat *m*
combatant [kəmˈbætənt] *n* : combattant *m*, -tante *f*
combative [kəmˈbæt̬ɪv] *adj* : combatif, belliqueux
combination [,kɑmbəˈneɪʃən] *n* : combinaison *f*
combine[1] [kəmˈbaɪn] *v* **-bined; -bining** *vt* : combiner, joindre, unir — *vi* : se combiner, s'associer, s'unir
combine[2] [ˈkɑm,baɪn] *n* **1** ASSOCIATION : association *f*, cartel *m* (en finances) **2** HARVESTER : moisonneuse-batteuse *f*
combustible [kəmˈbʌstəbəl] *adj* : combustible, inflammable
combustion [kəmˈbʌstʃən] *n* : combustion *f*
come [ˈkʌm] *vi* **came; come; coming 1** APPROACH : venir, s'approcher <come here! : viens ici!> <he came running : il est venu en courant> **2** ARRIVE : arriver <they came last night : ils sont arrivés hier soir> **3** ORIGINATE : venir, provenir <this cheese comes from Provence : ce fromage provient de Provence> **4** AMOUNT : monter, s'élever <the charge comes to $200 : les frais s'élèvent à $200> **5 to come clean** : décharger sa conscience **6 to come into** GAIN : acquérir, gagner <to come into a fortune : hériter d'une fortune> **7 to come off** SUCCEED : réussir **8 to come out** : paraître, sortir (se dit d'une publication, d'un produit commercial, etc.) **9 to come to** REVIVE : revenir à soi, reprendre conscience **10 to come to pass** HAPPEN : arriver, se produire <how come? : comment ça se fait?> **11 to come to terms** : parvenir à une entente
comeback [ˈkʌm,bæk] *n* **1** RETORT : réplique *f* **2** RETURN : retour *f*, rentrée *f* <to make a comeback : faire une rentrée>
come back *vi* **1** RETORT : répliquer, rétorquer **2** RETURN : revenir <I came back with him : je suis revenu avec lui> <this hairdo is coming back : cette coiffure revient à la mode>
comedian [kəˈmiːdiən] *n* : comédien *m*, -dienne *f*; comique *mf*
comedienne [kə,miːdiˈɛn] *n* : comédienne *f*
comedy [ˈkɑmədi] *n, pl* **-dies** : comédie *f*
comely [ˈkʌmli] *adj* **comelier; -est** : beau, gracieux
comet [ˈkɑmət] *n* : comète *f*

comfort[1] [ˈkʌmpfərt] *vt* **1** CONSOLE : consoler **2** CHEER : encourager, réconforter

comfort[2] *n* **1** SOLACE : consolation *f* **2** WELL-BEING : confort *m*, bien-être *m* **3** CONVENIENCE : commodité *f*, confort *m* <the comforts of home : le confort du foyer>

comfortable [ˈkʌmpfərṭəbəl, ˈkʌmpftə-] *adj* : confortable, agréable — **comfortably** *adv*

comforter [ˈkʌmpfərṭər] *n* **1** : consolateur *m*, -trice *f* **2** QUILT : édredon *m*, douillette *f Can*

comic[1] [ˈkɑmɪk] *adj* **1** : comique, qui appartient à la comédie **2** COMICAL : drôle, amusant

comic[2] *n* **1** COMEDIAN : comédien *m*, -dienne *f*; comique *mf* **2** *or* **comic book** : magazine *m* de bandes dessinées

comical [ˈkɑmɪkəl] *adj* : drôle, amusant

comic strip *n* : bande *f* dessinée

coming [ˈkʌmɪŋ] *adj* : suivante <during the coming week : pendant la semaine suivante>

comma [ˈkɑmə] *n* : virgule *f*

command[1] [kəˈmænd] *vt* **1** ORDER : ordonner, mandater **2** CONTROL : diriger, commander **3** DEMAND : demander, exiger <he commands a high price : il exige un prix élevé> — *vi* **1** ORDER : donner des ordres **2** GOVERN : diriger, gouverner

command[2] *n* **1** ORDER : ordre *m*, commande *f* (en informatique) **2** : commandement *m* (dans les forces armées) **3** MASTERY : maîtrise *f*

commandant [ˈkɑmənˌdɑnt, -ˌdænt] *n* : commandant *m*

commandeer [ˌkɑmənˈdɪr] *vt* : réquisitionner

commander [kəˈmændər] *n* : commandant *m*

commandment [kəˈmændmənt] *n* : commandement *m* <the Ten Commandments : les dix commandements>

commemorate [kəˈmɛməˌreɪt] *vt* **-rated; -rating** : commémorer

commemoration [kəˌmɛməˈreɪʃən] *n* : commémoration *f*

commemorative [kəˈmɛmrəṭɪv, -ˈmɛməˌreɪṭɪv] *adj* : commémoratif

commence [kəˈmɛnts] *v* **-menced; -mencing** *vt* : commencer <to commence working : commencer à travailler> — *vi* : commencer

commencement [kəˈmɛntsmənt] *n* **1** BEGINNING : commencement *m*, début *m* **2** : remise *f* des diplômes

commend [kəˈmɛnd] *vt* **1** ENTRUST : confier **2** RECOMMEND : recommander, préconiser **3** PRAISE : louer

commendable [kəˈmɛndəbəl] *adj* : louable

commendation [ˌkɑmənˈdeɪʃən] *n* : louange *f*, éloge *m*

commensurate [kəˈmɛntsərət, -ˈmɛntʃʊrət] *adj* **to be commensurate with** : être proportionné à

comment[1] [ˈkɑˌmɛnt] *vi* : faire des commentaires, faire une remarque

comment[2] *n* : commentaire *m*, remarque *f*

commentary [ˈkɑmənˌtɛri] *n, pl* **-taries** : commentaire *m*

commentator [ˈkɑmənˌteɪṭər] *n* : commentateur *m*, -trice *f*

commerce [ˈkɑmərs] *n* : commerce *m*

commercial[1] [kəˈmɛrʃəl] *adj* : commercial

commercial[2] *n* : annonce *f* publicitaire

commercialize [kəˈmərʃəˌlaɪz] *vt* **-ized; -izing** : commercialiser

commiserate [kəˈmɪzəˌreɪt] *vi* **-ated; -ating** : éprouver de la sympathie, compatir

commiseration [kəˌmɪzəˈreɪʃən] *n* : commisération *f*

commission[1] [kəˈmɪʃən] *vt* **1** APPOINT : nommer (un officier) **2** : commander <to commission a portrait : commander un portrait>

commission[2] *n* **1** : brevet *m* (militaire) **2** COMMITTEE : commission *f*, comité *m* **3** COMMITTING : perpétration *f*, commission *f* **4** FEE, PERCENTAGE : commission *f*

commissioned officer *n* : officier *m*

commissioner [kəˈmɪʃənər] *n* : commissaire *m*

commit [kəˈmɪt] *vt* **committed; committing 1** ENTRUST : confier **2** CONFINE : interner (dans un hôpital) **3** PERPETRATE : commettre <to commit a crime : commettre un crime> **4 to commit oneself** : s'engager

commitment [kəˈmɪtmənt] *n* **1** ENGAGEMENT, PROMISE : engagement *m* **2** OBLIGATION : obligation *f*, responsabilité *f*

committee [kəˈmɪṭi] *n* : comité *m*

commodious [kəˈmoːdiəs] *adj* : spacieux, ample, vaste

commodity [kəˈmɑdəṭi] *n, pl* **-ties** : produit *m*, denrée *f* (alimentaire), marchandise *f*

commodore [ˈkɑməˌdor] *n* : commodore *m*

common[1] [ˈkɑmən] *adj* **1** PUBLIC : commun, public <for the common good : pour le bien commun> **2** GENERAL : universel, général, public <it's common knowledge : c'est de notoriété publique> **3** ORDINARY : commun, ordinaire <the common man : l'homme du peuple> **4** SHARED : commun, semblable <common tastes : goûts semblables>

common[2] *n* **1** : terre *f* commune **2 in common** : en commun

common cold *n* : rhume *m*

common denominator *n* : dénominateur *m* commun

commoner ['kamənər] *n* : roturier *m*, -rière *f*

commonly ['kamənli] *adv* : communément, généralement

commonplace[1] ['kamən,pleɪs] *adj* : commun, banal, ordinaire

commonplace[2] *n* : lieu *m* commun, banalité *f*

common sense *n* : bon sens *m*, sens *m* commun

commonwealth ['kamən,wɛlθ] *n* : corps *m* politique <the British Commonwealth : le Commonwealth>

commotion [kə'mo:ʃən] *n* **1** AGITATION : agitation *f*, émoi *m* **2** RUCKUS, TUMULT : vacarme *m*, brouhaha *m*

communal [kə'mju:nəl] *adj* : communautaire

commune[1] [kə'mju:n] *vi* **-muned; -muning** : communier <to commune with nature : communier avec la nature>

commune[2] ['ka,mju:n, kə'mju:n] *n* : communauté *f*

communicable [kə'mju:nɪkəbəl] *adj* CONTAGIOUS : contagieux, transmissible

communicate [kə'mju:nə,keɪt] *v* **-cated; -cating** *vt* **1** CONVEY : communiquer, transmettre **2** TRANSMIT : transmettre (une maladie) — *vi* : communiquer

communication [kə,mju:nə'keɪʃən] *n* : communication *f*

communicative [kə'mju:nɪ,keɪt̬ɪv, -kət̬ɪv] *adj* : communicatif

communion [kə'mju:njən] *n* **1** SHARING : communion *f* **2 Communion** : Communion *f*

communiqué [kə'mju:nə,keɪ, -,mju:nə'keɪ] *n* : communiqué *m*

communism *or* **Communism** ['kamjə,nɪzəm] *n* : communisme *m*

communist[1] *or* **Communist** ['kamjə,nɪst] *adj* : communiste

communist[2] *or* **Communist** *n* : communiste *mf*

communistic *or* **Communistic** *adj* : communiste

community [kə'mju:nət̬i] *n, pl* **-ties** : communauté *f*

commute[1] [kə'mju:t] *v* **-muted; -muting** *vt* REDUCE : commuer (une peine) — *vi* : faire la navette, faire un trajet journalier (à son travail)

commute[2] *n* : trajet *m* journalier

compact[1] [kəm'pækt, 'kam,pækt] *vt* PACK : comprimer, tasser

compact[2] [kəm'pækt, 'kam,pækt] *adj* **1** DENSE, SOLID : compact, dense **2** CONCISE : concis, bref

compact[3] ['kam,pækt] *n* **1** AGREEMENT : entente *f*, accord *m* **2** *or* **powder compact** : poudrier *m* **3** *or* **compact car** : voiture *f* compacte

compact disc ['kam,pækt'dɪsk] *n* : disque *m* compact, compact *m*

companion [kəm'pænjən] *n* **1** FRIEND : compagnon *m*, compagne *f* **2** COUNTERPART : pendant *m*

companionable [kəm'pænjənəbəl] *adj* : sociable

companionship [kəm'pænjən,ʃɪp] *n* : compagnie *f*

company ['kʌmpəni] *n, pl* **-nies 1** FIRM : compagnie *f*, société *f* **2** GROUP : compagnie *f* (militaire), troupe *f* (de théâtre) **3** VISITORS : invités *mpl*

comparable ['kampərəbəl] *adj* : comparable

comparative[1] [kəm'pærət̬ɪv] *adj* : comparatif — **comparatively** *adv*

comparative[2] *n* : comparatif *m*

compare [kəm'pær] *v* **-pared; -paring** *vt* : comparer — *vi* : être comparable

comparison [kəm'pærəsən] *n* : comparaison *f*

compartment [kəm'partmənt] *n* : compartiment *m*

compass ['kʌmpəs, 'kam-] *n* **1** : boussole *f* <the points of the compass : les points cardinaux> **2** : compas *m* (en géométrie) **3** RANGE, SCOPE : étendue *f*, portée *f*

compassion [kəm'pæʃən] *n* : compassion *f*, sympathie *f*

compassionate [kəm'pæʃənət] *adj* : compatissant

compatibility [kəm,pæt̬ə'bɪlət̬i] *n* : compatibilité *f*

compatible [kəm'pæt̬əbəl] *adj* : compatible

compatriot [kəm'peɪtriət, -'pæ-] *n* : compatriote *mf*

compel [kəm'pɛl] *vt* **-pelled; -pelling** : contraindre, obliger

compelling [kəm'pɛlɪŋ] *adj* : irrésistible, convaincant

compendium [kəm'pendiəm] *n, pl* **-diums** *or* **-dia** [-diə] : abrégé *m*

compensate ['kampən,seɪt] *v* **-sated; -sating** *vt* : compenser, indemniser — *vi* **to compensate for** : compenser

compensation [,kampən'seɪʃən] *n* : compensation *f*, indemnisation *f*

compensatory [kəm'pɛn*t*sə,tori] *adj* : compensatoire

compete [kəm'pi:t] *vi* **-peted; -peting** : faire concurrence, rivaliser

competence ['kampətən*t*s] *n* : compétence *f*, capacité *f*, aptitude *f*

competency ['kampətən*t*si] *n, pl* **-cies** → **competence**

competent ['kampətənt] *adj* : compétent, qualifié, capable

competition [,kampə'tɪʃən] *n* : compétition *f*, concurrence *f*

competitive [kəm'pɛt̬ət̬ɪv] *adj* : compétitif, concurrentiel

competitiveness [kəm'pɛt̬ət̬ɪvnəs] *n* : compétitivité *f*

competitor [kəm'pɛt̬ət̬ər] *n* : concurrent *m*, -rente *f*

compilation ['kampɪ'leɪʃən] *n* : compilation *f*

compile [kəm'paɪl] *vt* **-piled; -piling** : compiler, dresser (une liste, etc.)
compiler [kəm'paɪlər] *n* : compilateur *m*, -trice *f*
complacency [kəm'pleɪsəntsi] *n, pl* **-cies** : satisfaction *f* de soi, suffisance *f*
complacent [kəm'pleɪsənt] *adj* : satisfait de soi, suffisant
complain [kəm'pleɪn] *vi* **1** GRIPE, GRUMBLE : se plaindre **2** PROTEST : faire une réclamation, se plaindre
complaint [kəm'pleɪnt] *n* **1** GRIPE : plainte *f* **2** AILMENT : maladie *f*, affection *f* **3** ACCUSATION, PROTEST : réclamation *f* <to lodge a complaint : se plaindre>
complement[1] ['kɑmplə,mɛnt] *vt* : compléter
complement[2] ['kɑmpləmənt] *n* **1** : complément *m* (en mathématiques, en grammaire, etc.) **2** QUOTA : effectif *m* (complet)
complementary [,kɑmplə'mɛntəri] *adj* : complémentaire
complete[1] [kəm'pli:t] *vt* **-pleted; -pleting** **1** FINISH : terminer, achever **2** : compléter <this piece completes the puzzle : cette pièce complète le puzzle>
complete[2] *adj* **-pleter; -est** **1** WHOLE : complet, intégral <a complete set : un jeu complet> **2** FINISHED : terminé, achevé **3** THOROUGH : complet, total, absolu
completely [kəm'pli:tli] *adv* : complètement, totalement
completion [kəm'pli:ʃən] *n* : achèvement *m*
complex[1] [kɑm'plɛks, kəm-; 'kɑm,plɛks] *adj* INTRICATE : complexe
complex[2] ['kɑm,plɛks] *n* **1** : complexe *m* (psychologique) **2** GROUP : complexe *m*, ensemble *m* <housing complex : complexe résidentiel
complexion [kəm'plɛkʃən] *n* : teint *m* <a fair complexion : un teint clair>
complexity [kəm'plɛksəṭi, kɑm-] *n, pl* **-ties** : complexité *f*
compliance [kəm'plaɪənts] *n* **1** : conformité *f* **2 in compliance with** : conformément à
compliant [kəm'plaɪənt] *n* : docile, accommodant
complicate ['kɑmplə,keɪt] *vt* **-cated; -cating** : compliquer
complicated ['kɑmplə,keɪṭəd] *adj* : compliqué, complexe
complication [,kɑmplə'keɪʃən] *n* : complication *f*, difficulté *f*
complicity [kəm'plɪsəṭi] *n, pl* **-ties** : complicité *f*
compliment[1] ['kɑmplə,mɛnt] *vt* : complimenter
compliment[2] ['kɑmpləmənt] *n* **1** : compliment *m* **2 compliments** *npl* : compliments *mpl*, respects *mpl* <to pay one's compliments to s.o. : faire ses compliments à qqn>
complimentary [,kɑmplə'mɛntəri] *adj* **1** FLATTERING : flatteur **2** FREE : gratuit, (à titre) gracieux <complimentary ticket : billet de faveur>
comply [kəm'plaɪ] *vi* **-plied; -plying** **1** : se soumettre, obéir **2 to comply with** : respecter, observer
component[1] [kəm'po:nənt, 'kɑm,po:-] *adj* : composant, constituant
component[2] *n* : composant *m*, composante *f* (en mathématiques), pièce *f*
compose [kəm'po:z] *vt* **-posed; -posing** **1** FORM : former, composer **2** : composer (un texte, une chanson, etc.) **3 to compose oneself** : retrouver son calme
composer [kəm'po:zər] *n* : compositeur *m*, -trice *f*
composite[1] [kɑm'pɑzət, kəm-; 'kɑmpəzət] *adj* : composite
composite[2] *n* : composite *m*
composition [,kɑmpə'zɪʃən] *n* **1** CREATION : composition *f*, création *f* **2** WORK : œuvre *m*, composition *f*, dissertation *f* (à l'école)
compost ['kɑm,po:st] *n* : compost *m*
composure [kəm'po:ʒər] *n* : calme *m*, sang-froid *m*, sérénité *f*
compound[1] [kɑm'paʊnd, kəm-; 'kɑm,paʊnd] *vt* **1** COMBINE : combiner, mélanger **2** AUGMENT : augmenter, aggraver <to compound a problem : aggraver un problème>
compound[2] ['kɑm,paʊnd; kɑm'paʊnd, kəm-] *adj* : composé <compound interest : intérêt composé>
compound[3] ['kɑm,paʊnd] *n* **1** *or* **compound word** : mot *m* composé **2** ENCLOSURE : enceinte *f*, enclos *m* **3** : composé *m* (en chimie)
comprehend [,kɑmprɪ'hɛnd] *vt* **1** UNDERSTAND : comprendre, saisir **2** INCLUDE : comprendre, comporter
comprehensible [,kɑmprɪ'hɛntsɪbəl] *adj* : compréhensible, clair
comprehension [,kɑmprɪ'hɛntʃən] *n* : compréhension *f*
comprehensive [,kɑmprɪ'hɛntsɪv] *adj* : compréhensif, complet, détaillé
compress[1] [kəm'prɛs] *vt* : comprimer
compress[2] ['kɑm,prɛs] *n* : compresse *f*
compression [kəm'prɛʃən] *n* : compression *f*
comprise [kəm'praɪz] *vt* **-prised; -prising** **1** INCLUDE : comprendre, inclure, consister en **2** MAKE UP : constituer, composer <girls comprise half of the students : les filles constituent une moitié des étudiants>
compromise[1] ['kɑmprə,maɪz] *v* **-mised; -mising** *vi* : faire un compromis — *vt* JEOPARDIZE : compromettre, mettre en péril
compromise[2] *n* : compromis *m*
comptroller [kən'tro:lər, 'kɑmp,tro:-] *n* : contrôleur *m*, -leuse *f* (de finances)

compulsion [kəm'pʌlʃən] *n* **1** COERCION : coercition *f*, contrainte *f* **2** IMPULSE : compulsion *f* (en psychologie)

compulsive [kəm'pʌlsɪv] *adj* : compulsif

compulsory [kəm'pʌlsəri] *adj* : obligatoire

compunction [kəm'pʌŋkʃən] *n* **1** QUALM : scruple *m* **2** REMORSE : remords *m*

computation [kɑmpjʊ'teɪʃən] *n* : calcul *m*

compute [kəm'pju:t] *vt* **-puted; -puting** : calculer

computer [kəm'pju:t̬ər] *n* : ordinateur *m*

computerize [kəm'pju:t̬əˌraɪz] *vt* **-ized; -izing** : informatiser, mettre sur ordinateur

comrade ['kɑmˌræd] *n* : camarade *mf*, compagnon *m*, compagne *f*

comradeship ['kɑmrædˌʃɪp] *n* : camaraderie *f*

con[1] ['kɑn] *vt* **conned; conning** SWINDLE : duper, escroquer

con[2] *adv* : contre

con[3] *n* **1** DISADVANTAGE : désavantage *m*, inconvénient *m* <the pros and cons : le pour et le contre> **2** SWINDLE : escroquerie *f*

concave [kɑn'keɪv, 'kɑnˌkeɪv] *adj* : concave

conceal [kən'si:l] *vt* : dissimuler, cacher

concealment [kən'si:lmənt] *n* : dissimulation *f*

concede [kən'si:d] *v* **-ceded; -ceding** *vt* GRANT : accorder, concéder — *vi* YIELD : céder

conceit [kən'si:t] *n* : suffisance *f*, vanité *f*

conceited [kən'si:təd] *adj* : suffisant, vaniteux

conceive [kən'si:v] *v* **-ceived; -ceiving** *vt* **1** : concevoir (un enfant) **2** IMAGINE : imaginer, concevoir — *vi* **1** : devenir enceinte **2 to conceive of** : concevoir

concentrate[1] ['kɑntsənˌtreɪt] *v* **-trated; -trating** *vt* : concentrer — *vi* : se concentrer

concentrate[2] *n* : concentré *m* <orange juice concentrate : concentré du jus d'orange>

concentration [ˌkɑntsən'treɪʃən] *n* : concentration *f*

concentric [kən'sentrɪk] *adj* : concentrique

concept ['kɑnˌsɛpt] *n* : concept *m*

conception [kən'sɛpʃən] *n* **1** : conception *f* (en médecine) **2** IDEA : idée *f*, concept *m*

concern[1] [kən'sərn] *vt* **1** AFFECT : concerner, intéresser **2** INVOLVE : concerner <as far as I'm concerned : en ce qui me concerne> **3** : traiter de, parler de <the novel concerns the war : le roman traite de la guerre> **4** WORRY : inquiéter <that concerns me very much : ça m'inquiète beaucoup>

concern[2] *n* **1** AFFAIR : affaire *f* <it's not my concern : ce n'est pas de mes affaires> **2** WORRY : inquiétude *f* **3** BUSINESS : firme *f*, société *f* <a banking concern : une firme bancaire>

concerned [kən'sərnd] *adj* **1** ANXIOUS : préoccupé, inquiet **2** INTERESTED : intéressé **3** IMPLICATED : impliqué

concerning [kən'sərnɪŋ] *prep* REGARDING : concernant, touchant

concert ['kɑnˌsərt] *n* **1** : concert *m*, récital *m* (musical) **2** AGREEMENT, UNISON : concert *m* <to work in concert : travailler de concert>

concerted [kən'sərt̬əd] *adj* : concerté

concertina [ˌkɑntsər'ti:nə] *n* : concertina *m*

concerto [kən'tʃɛrt̬o:] *n, pl* **-ti** [-t̬i, -ˌti:] *or* **-tos** : concerto *m* <piano concerto : concerto pour piano>

concession [kən'sɛʃən] *n* : concession *f*

conch ['kɑŋk, 'kɑntʃ] *n, pl* **conchs** ['kɑŋks] *or* **conches** ['kɑntʃəz] : conque *f*

conciliatory [kən'sɪliəˌtori] *adj* : conciliateur, conciliant

concise [kən'saɪs] *adj* : concis, bref, succinct

concisely [kən'saɪsli] *adv* : avec concision

conciseness [kən'saɪsnəs] *n* : concision *f*

conclave ['kɑnˌkleɪv] *n* : conclave *m*

conclude [kən'klu:d] *v* **-cluded; -cluding** *vt* **1** END : terminer, conclure **2** DECIDE : décider **3** INFER : inférer, déduire — *vi* END : s'achever, se terminer

conclusion [kən'klu:ʒən] *n* : conclusion *f*

conclusive [kən'klu:sɪv] *adj* : concluant, définitif

conclusively [kən'klu:sɪvli] *adv* : définitivement, de façon concluant

concoct [kən'kɑkt, kɑn-] *vt* **1** PREPARE : préparer, confectionner **2** DEVISE : fabriquer, concocter (une excuse, etc.)

concoction [kən'kɑkʃən] *n* **1** PREPARATION : élaboration *f* **2** MIXTURE : mélange *m*

concord ['kɑnˌkɔrd, 'kɑŋ-] *n* : concorde *f*, harmonie *f*

concordance [kən'kɔrdənts] *n* **1** AGREEMENT : accord *m* **2** INDEX : concordance *f*, index *f*

concourse ['kɔnˌkors] *n* **1** GATHERING : rassemblement *m*, assemblée *f* **2** HALL : hall *m*, lieu *m* de rassemblement

concrete[1] [kɑn'kri:t, 'kɑnˌkri:t] *adj* **1** REAL : concret, réel **2** : de béton <concrete walls : murs de béton>

concrete[2] ['kɑnˌkri:t, kɑn'kri:t] *n* : béton *m*

concur [kən'kər] *vi* **-curred, -curring 1** AGREE : être d'accord **2** TALLY : coïncider, concorder

concurrent [kən'kərənt] *adj* : simultané, concomitant

concussion [kən'kʌʃən] *n* : commotion *f* cérébrale
condemn [kən'dɛm] *vt* **1** CENSURE : condamner, censurer **2** CONVICT : condamner <condemned to death : condamné à mort> **3** : déclarer inhabitable (se dit d'un bâtiment)
condemnation [ˌkɑnˌdɛm'neɪʃən] *n* : condamnation *f*
condensation [ˌkɑnˌdɛn'seɪʃən] *n* : condensation *f*
condense [kən'dɛnts] *vt* **-densed; -densing 1** COMPRESS : condenser, comprimer **2** ABRIDGE : abréger, condenser
condescend [ˌkɑndɪ'sɛnd] *vt* **1 to condescend to do** : daigner faire, condescendre à faire **2 to condescend to s.o.** : être condescendant envers qqn
condescension [ˌkɑndɪ'sɛntʃən] *n* : condescendance *f*
condiment ['kɑndəmənt] *n* : condiment *m*
condition[1] [kən'dɪʃən] *vt* **1** TRAIN : conditionner **2** : mettre en forme (le corps, etc.), traiter (les cheveux)
condition[2] *n* **1** STIPULATION : condition *f*, stipulation *f* <on the condition that : à condition que> **2** STATE : état *m*, condition *f* **3 conditions** *npl* : circonstances *fpl*, conditions *fpl* <living conditions : conditions de vie>
conditional [kən'dɪʃənəl] *adj* : conditionnel — **conditionally** *adv*
condolence [kən'doːlənts] *n* : condoléance *f*
condom ['kɑndəm] *n* : condom *m*, préservatif *m*
condominium [ˌkɑndə'mɪniəm] *n, pl* **-ums** : condominium *m*
condone [kən'doːn] *vt* **-doned; -doning** : fermer les yeux sur, pardonner
condor ['kɑndər, -ˌdɔr] *n* : condor *m*
conducive [kən'duːsɪv, -'djuː-] *adj* : favorable
conduct[1] [kən'dʌkt] *vt* **1** GUIDE : conduire, guider <a conducted tour : une visite guidée> **2** DIRECT : diriger (un orchestre) **3** CARRY ON : mener, conduire <to conduct an investigation : conduire une enquête> **4** TRANSMIT : conduire (l'électricité, etc.) **5 to conduct oneself** : se comporter
conduct[2] ['kɑnˌdʌkt] *n* **1** BEHAVIOR : comportement *m*, conduite *f* **2** MANAGEMENT : conduite *f* (des affaires, etc.)
conduction [kən'dʌkʃən] *n* : conduction *f*
conductivity [ˌkɑnˌdʌk'tɪvət̬i] *n, pl* **-ties** : conductivité *f*
conductor [kən'dʌktər] *n* **1** : conducteur *m* (d'électricité) **2** : chef *m* d'orchestre **3** : contrôleur *m* (de train)
conduit ['kɑnˌduːət, -djuː-] *n* : conduit *m*, tuyau *m*
cone ['koːn] *n* **1** : cône *m* (fruit du pin) **2** : cône *m* (en géométrie) **3** *or* **ice-cream cone** : cornet *m* (de crème glacée)
confection [kən'fɛkʃən] *n* : confiserie *f*, friandise *f*, bonbon *m*
confectioner [kən'fɛkʃənər] *n* : confiseur *m*, -seuse *f*
confederacy [kən'fɛdərəsi] *n, pl* **-cies** : confédération *f*
confederate[1] [kən'fɛdəˌreɪt] *v* **-ated; -ating** *vt* : confédérer — *vi* : se confédérer
confederate[2] [kən'fɛdəˌrət] *adj* : confédéré
confederate[3] *n* : allié *m*, -liée *f*; complice *mf*
confederation [kənˌfɛdə'reɪʃən] *n* : confédération *f*
confer [kən'fɛr] *v* **-ferred; -ferring** *vt* BESTOW : conférer, accorder — *vi* CONSULT : conférer, parler
conference ['kɑnfrənts, -fərənts] *n* : conférence *f*
confess [kən'fɛs] *vt* : confesser, avouer — *vi* **1** : avouer, faire des aveux <the prisoner confessed : le prisonnier a fait des aveux> **2** : se confesser (en religion)
confession [kən'fɛʃən] *n* : confession *f*
confessional [kən'fɛʃənəl] *n* : confessionnal *m*
confetti [kən'fɛt̬i] *n* : confettis *mpl*
confidant ['kɑnfəˌdɑnt, -ˌdænt] *n* : confident *m*
confidante ['kɑnfəˌdɑnt, -ˌdænt] *n* : confidente *f*
confide [kən'faɪd] *v* **-fided; -fiding** *vt* ENTRUST : confier — *vi* : se confier <to confide in s.o. : se confier à qqn>
confidence ['kɑnfədənts] *n* **1** TRUST : confiance *f* **2** SELF-CONFIDENCE : confiance *f*, assurance *f* **3** SECRET : confidence *f*
confident ['kɑnfədənt] *adj* **1** TRUSTFUL : confiant, ouvert **2** SELF-CONFIDENT : confiant, sûr de soi
confidential [ˌkɑnfə'dɛntʃəl] *adj* : confidentiel — **confidentially** *adv*
configuration [kənˌfɪgjə'reɪʃən] *n* : configuration *f*
configure [kən'fɪgjər] *vt* : configurer
confine [kən'faɪn] *vt* **-fined; -fining 1** LIMIT : confiner, limiter **2** IMPRISON : emprisonner, enfermer
confines ['kɑnˌfaɪnz] *npl* BOUNDS : confins *mpl*, limites *fpl*
confirm [kən'fərm] *vt* **1** : confirmer, fortifier <to confirm one's faith : confirmer sa foi> **2** RATIFY : approuver, sanctionner **3** VERIFY : démontrer, corroborer **4** : confirmer (en religion)
confirmation [ˌkɑnfər'meɪʃən] *n* : confirmation *f*
confiscate ['kɑnfəˌskeɪt] *vt* **-cated; -cating** : confisquer
confiscation [ˌkɑnfə'skeɪʃən] *n* : confiscation *f*

conflagration [ˌkɑnflə'greɪʃən] *n* : conflagration *f,* incendie *f*

conflict[1] [kən'flɪkt] *vi* : être en conflit, s'opposer

conflict[2] ['kɑnˌflɪkt] *n* : conflit *m*

conform [kən'fɔrm] *vi* **to conform with** : se conformer à, être conforme à

conformity [kən'fɔrmət̬i] *n, pl* **-ties** : conformité *f*

confound [kən'faʊnd, kɑn-] *vt* : confondre, déconcerter

confront [kən'frʌnt] *vt* : confronter, affronter, faire face à

confrontation [ˌkɑnfrən'teɪʃən] *n* : confrontation *f*

confuse [kən'fju:z] *vt* **-fused; -fusing 1** PERPLEX : confondre, déconcerter **2** JUMBLE : embrouiller, brouiller

confusing [kən'fju:zɪŋ] *adj* : déroutant, embrouillé, mêlant *Can*

confusion [kən'fju:ʒən] *n* **1** PERPLEXITY : confusion *f,* embarras *m* **2** MESS, TURMOIL : désordre *m,* confusion *f*

congeal [kən'dʒi:l] *vt* **1** FREEZE : congeler **2** COAGULATE : figer, coaguler — *vi* : se figer, se coaguler

congenial [kən'dʒi:niəl] *adj* : agréable, sympathique

congenital [kən'dʒɛnət̬əl] *adj* : congénital

congest [kən'dʒɛst] *vt* **1** : congestionner (en médecine) **2** CLOG, OBSTRUCT : embouteiller, encombrer

congestion [kən'dʒɛstʃən] *n* : congestion *f*

conglomerate[1] [kən'glɑmərət] *adj* : congloméré

conglomerate[2] *n* : conglomérat *m*

conglomeration [kənˌglɑmə'reɪʃən] *n* : conglomérat *m,* agglomération *f*

Congolese[1] [ˌkɑŋgə'li:z, -'li:s] *adj* : congolais

Congolese[2] *n* : Congolais *m,* -laise *f*

congratulate [kən'grædʒəˌleɪt, -'grætʃə-] *vt* **-lated; -lating** : féliciter

congratulations [kənˌgrædʒə'leɪʃənz, -ˌgrætʃə-] *npl* : félicitations *fpl*

congregate ['kɑŋgrɪˌgeɪt] *v* **-gated; -gating** *vt* ASSEMBLE : rassembler, réunir — *vi* GATHER : se réunir

congregation [ˌkɑŋgrɪ'geɪʃən] *n* **1** GATHERING : assemblée *f,* rassemblement *m* **2** CHURCHGOERS : assemblée *f* des fidèles

congress ['kɑŋgrəs] *n* : congrès *m*

congressional [kən'grɛʃənəl, kɑn-] *adj* : d'un congrès

congressman ['kɑŋgrəsmən] *n, pl* **-men** [-mən, -mɛn] : membre *m* du Congrès

congresswoman ['kɑŋgrəsˌwʊmən] *n, pl* **-women** [-ˌwɪmən] : membre *m* du Congrès

congruent [kən'gru:ənt, 'kɑngrʊənt] *adj* : congru <congruent triangles : triangles congrus>

conic ['kɑnɪk] → **conical**

conical ['kɑnɪkəl] *adj* : conique

conifer ['kɑnəfər, 'ko:-] *n* : conifère *m*

coniferous [ko:'nɪfərəs, kə-] *adj* : conifère

conjecture[1] [kən'dʒɛktʃər] *vt* : conjecturer, présumer

conjecture[2] *n* : conjecture *f,* supposition *f*

conjugal ['kɑndʒɪgəl, kən'dʒu:-] *adj* : conjugal

conjugate ['kɑndʒəˌgeɪt] *vt* **-gated; -gating** : conjuguer

conjugation [ˌkɑndʒə'geɪʃən] *n* : conjugaison *f*

conjunction [kən'dʒʌŋkʃən] *n* **1** UNION : conjonction *f,* union *f* **2** : conjonction *f* (en astronomie, en grammaire) **3 in conjunction with** : conjointement avec

conjure ['kɑndʒər, 'kʌn-] *v* **-jured; -juring** *vt* **1** ENTREAT : implorer, supplier **2 to conjure up** : invoquer (des esprits), évoquer (une image) — *vi* : faire des tours de magie

connect [kə'nɛkt] *vt* **1** JOIN, LINK : joindre, relier **2** ASSOCIATE : associer, lier — *vi* : assurer la correspondance (se dit des trains, des avions, etc.)

connection [kə'nɛkʃən] *n* **1** LINK : lien *m,* rapport *m* **2** RELATIONSHIP : lien *m,* relation *f* <business connections : relations d'affaires> **3** : correspondance *f* <train connection : correspondance de train>

connective [kə'nɛktɪv] *adj* : conjonctif <connective tissue : tissu conjonctif>

connivance [kə'naɪvənts] *n* : connivence *f,* complicité *f*

connive [kə'naɪv] *vi* **-nived; -niving** : être de connivence

connoisseur [ˌkɑnə'sər] *n* : connaisseur *m,* -seuse *f*

connotation [ˌkɑnə'teɪʃən] *n* : connotation *f*

connote [kə'no:t] *vt* **-noted; -noting 1** CONVEY : évoquer **2** IMPLY : indiquer

conquer ['kɑŋkər] *vt* : conquérir, vaincre

conqueror ['kɑŋkərər] *n* : conquérant *m,* -rante *f*

conquest ['kɑnˌkwɛst, 'kɑŋ-] *n* : conquête *f*

conscience ['kɑntʃənts] *n* : conscience *f* <to have a clear conscience : avoir la conscience tranquille>

conscientious [ˌkɑntʃi'ɛntʃəs] *adj* : consciencieux — **conscientiously** *adv*

conscious ['kɑntʃəs] *adj* **1** AWARE : conscient <to become conscious of : prendre conscience de> **2** ALERT, AWAKE : conscient, lucide **3** INTENTIONAL : délibéré, intentionnel

consciously ['kɑntʃəsli] *adv* : consciemment

consciousness ['kɑntʃəsnəs] *n* **1** AWARENESS : conscience *f* **2** : connaissance *f* <to lose consciousness : perdre connaissance>

conscription [kən'skrɪpʃən] *n* : conscription *f*

consecrate ['kantsə,kreɪt] *vt* **-crated; -crating** : consacrer
consecration [,kantsə'kreɪʃən] *n* : consécration *f*
consecutive [kən'sɛkjəṭɪv] *adj* : consécutif — **consecutively** *adv*
consensus [kən'sɛntsəs] *n* : consensus *m*
consent[1] [kən'sɛnt] *vi* : consentir
consent[2] *n* : consentement *m*, accord *m*
consequence ['kantsə,kwɛnts, -kwənts] *n* **1** RESULT : conséquence *f*, effet *m*, suite *f* **2** IMPORTANCE : importance *f*, conséquence *f* <a person of consequence : une personne importante>
consequential [,kantsə'kwɛntʃəl] *adj* : important, conséquent
consequently ['kantsəkwəntli, -,kwɛnt-] *adv* : par conséquent
conservation [,kantsər'veɪʃən] *n* : conservation *f*, préservation *f*
conservatism [kən'sɛrvə,tɪzəm] *n* : conservatisme *m*
conservative[1] [kən'sərvəṭɪv] *adj* **1** : conservateur **2** CAUTIOUS : prudent, modéré <a conservative estimate : une estimation prudente>
conservative[2] *n* : conservateur *m*, -trice *f*
conservatory [kən'sərvə,tori] *n, pl* **-ries** : conservatoire *m*
conserve[1] [kən'sərv] *vt* **-served; -serving** : conserver, préserver
conserve[2] *n* PRESERVE : confiture *f*
consider [kən'sɪdər] *vt* **1** STUDY, WEIGH : considérer, étudier **2** REGARD : tenir compte de <he doesn't consider my feelings : il ne tient pas compte de mes sentiments> **3** BELIEVE : croire, penser, considérer <he considers this essential : il considère que c'est essentiel>
considerable [kən'sɪdərəbəl] *adj* : considérable — **considerably** *adv*
considerate [kən'sɪdərət] *adj* THOUGHTFUL : attentionné, prévenant
consideration [kən,sɪdə'reɪʃən] *n* **1** DELIBERATION : considération *f*, réflexion *f* **2** THOUGHTFULNESS : attention *f*, considération *f* **3** PAYMENT : rémunération *f*, paiement *m*
considering [kən'sɪdərɪŋ] *prep* : étant donné, vu <considering the circumstances, it's better to stay here : vu les circonstances, il vaut mieux rester ici>
consign [kən'saɪn] *vt* **1** ENTRUST : confier **2** SEND : expédier, envoyer (des marchandises)
consignment [kən'saɪnmənt] *n* : expédition *f*, envoi *m*
consist [kən'sɪst] *vi* **1** LIE, RESIDE : consister <charity consists in good deeds : la charité consiste à faire de bonnes actions> **2 to consist of** : se composer de, consister en
consistency [kən'sɪstəntsi] *n, pl* **-cies 1** TEXTURE : consistance *f* **2** UNIFORMITY : cohérence *f*, uniformité *f*
consistent [kən'sɪstənt] *adj* **1** REGULAR, STEADY : constant, régulier <consistent behavior : comportement constant> **2 consistent with** : selon <consistent with our records : selon nos dossiers>
consistently [kən'sɪstəntli] *adv* : constamment, régulièrement
consolation [,kantsə'leɪʃən] *n* : consolation *f*
console[1] [kən'so:l] *vt* **-soled; -soling** : consoler, réconforter
console[2] ['kan,so:l] *n* : console *f*
consolidate [kən'salə,deɪt] *vt* **-dated; -dating** : consolider
consolidation [kən,salə'deɪʃən] *n* : consolidation *f*
consommé [,kantsə'meɪ] *n* : consommé *m*
consonant ['kantsənənt] *n* : consonne *f*
consort[1] [kən'sɔrt] *vi* **to consort with** : fréquenter
consort[2] ['kan,sɔrt] *n* : époux *m*, épouse *f* (d'un roi ou d'une reine)
conspicuous [kən'spɪkjuəs] *adj* **1** OBVIOUS : évident, visible **2** STRIKING : remarquable, voyant
conspicuously [kən'spɪkjuəsli] *adv* **1** NOTICEABLY : bien en évidence **2** STRIKINGLY : de façon voyante, remarquablement
conspiracy [kən'spɪrəsi] *n, pl* **-cies** : conspiration *f*, complot *m*
conspirator [kən'spɪrəṭər] *n* : conspirateur *m*, -trice *f*
conspire [kən'spaɪr] *vi* **-spired; -spiring** : conspirer, comploter — **conspiratorial** [kən,spɪrə'toriel] *adj*
constable ['kantstəbəl] *n* : gendarme *m*, agent *m* de police
constancy ['kantstəntsi] *n, pl* **-cies 1** STEADFASTNESS : constance *f* **2** LOYALTY : fidélité *f*, loyauté *f*
constant[1] ['kantstənt] *adj* **1** STEADFAST : constant **2** UNCHANGING : constant, régulier **3** CONTINUAL : continuel, constant
constant[2] *n* : constante *f*
constantly ['kantstəntli] *adv* : constamment, continuellement
constellation [,kantstə'leɪʃən] *n* : constellation *f*
consternation [,kantstər'neɪʃən] *n* : consternation *f*
constipate ['kantstə,peɪt] *vt* **-pated; -pating** : constiper
constipation [,kantstə'peɪʃən] *n* : constipation *f*
constituent[1] [kən'stɪtʃuənt] *adj* **1** COMPONENT : composant, constituant **2** : constituant, constitutif <constituent assembly : assemblée constituante>

constituent[2] *n* **1** ELEMENT : élément *m* constitutif, composant *m* **2** VOTER : électeur *m* , -trice *f*
constitute [ˈkɑnʈstəˌtuːt, -tjuːt] *vt* **-tuted; -tuting 1** ESTABLISH : constituer, créer **2** FORM : composer, former
constitution [ˌkɑnʈstəˈtuːʃən, -ˈtjuː-] *n* **1** COMPOSITION : constitution *f*, composition *f* **2** : constitution *f* (d'un pays)
constitutional[1] [ˌkɑnʈstəˈtuːʃənəl, -ˈtjuː-] *adj* : constitutionnel
constitutional[2] *n* WALK : promenade *f*, petit tour *m*
constrain [kənˈstreɪn] *vt* **1** COMPEL, FORCE : contraindre, obliger **2** CONFINE : restreindre, limiter
constraint [kənˈstreɪnt] *n* : contrainte *f*
constrict [kənˈstrɪkt] *vt* : resserrer, serrer
constriction [kənˈstrɪkʃən] *n* : constriction *f*, resserrement *m*
construct [kənˈstrʌkt] *vt* : construire, bâtir
construction [kənˈstrʌkʃən] *n* : construction *f*
constructive [kənˈstrʌktɪv] *adj* : constructif
construe [kənˈstruː] *vt* **-strued; -struing** : interpréter, expliquer
consul [ˈkɑnʈsəl] *n* : consul *m* — **consular** [ˈkɑnʈsələr] *adj*
consulate [ˈkɑnʈsələt] *n* : consulat *m*
consult [kənˈsʌlt] *vt* : consulter — *vi* : se consulter <to consult with : entrer en consultation avec>
consultant [kənˈsʌltənt] *n* : consultant *m*, -tante *f*
consultation [ˌkɑnʈsəlˈteɪʃən] *n* : consultation *f*
consume [kənˈsuːm] *vt* **-sumed; -suming 1** DESTROY : détruire <consumed by fire : détruit par le feu> **2** USE UP : utiliser, consommer **3** INGEST : consommer (de la nourriture ou de la boisson)
consumer [kənˈsuːmər] *n* : consommateur *m*, -trice *f*
consummate[1] [ˈkɑnʈsəˌmeɪt] *vt* **-mated; -mating** : consommer (un mariage, etc.)
consummate[2] [kənˈsʌmət, ˈkɑnʈsəmət] *adj* : consommé, accompli, parfait <a consummate liar : un menteur accompli>
consummation [ˌkɑnʈsəˈmeɪʃən] *n* : consommation *f*
consumption [kənˈsʌmpʃən] *n* **1** : consommation *f* <oil consumption : consommation d'huile> **2** TUBERCULOSIS : tuberculose *f*
contact[1] [ˈkɑnˌtækt, kən'-] *vt* : contacter, se mettre en contact avec
contact[2] [ˈkɑnˌtækt] *n* **1** TOUCHING : contact *m* **2** CONNECTION : contact *m* <business contacts : contacts professionnels> **3** COMMUNICATION : contact *m*, communication *f* <to be in contact with : être en rapport avec>
contact lens [ˈkɑnˌtæktˈlɛnz] *n* : verre *m* de contact, lentille *f* de contact
contagion [kənˈteɪdʒən] *n* : contagion *f*
contagious [kənˈteɪdʒəs] *adj* : contagieux
contain [kənˈteɪn] *vt* **1** HOLD : contenir, renfermer **2** INCLUDE : contenir, inclure **3** RESTRAIN : contenir, maîtriser <to contain oneself : se contenir>
container [kənˈteɪnər] *n* : récipient *m*, conteneur *m* (de transport)
contaminate [kənˈtæməˌneɪt] *vt* **-nated; -nating** : contaminer
contamination [kənˌtæməˈneɪʃən] *n* : contamination *f*
contemplate [ˈkɑntəmˌpleɪt] *vt* **-plated; -plating 1** VIEW : contempler **2** PONDER : réfléchir sur **3** CONSIDER, PLAN : envisager, considérer
contemplation [ˌkɑntəmˈpleɪʃən] *n* : contemplation *f*, réflexion *f*
contemplative [kənˈtɛmplətɪv, ˈkɑntəmˌpleɪt̬ɪv] *adj* : contemplatif
contemporaneous [kənˌtɛmpəˈreɪniəs] *adj* → **contemporary**[1]
contemporary[1] [kənˈtɛmpəˌrɛri] *adj* : contemporain, moderne
contemporary[2] *n* : contemporain *m*, -raine *f*
contempt [kənˈtɛmpt] *n* **1** SCORN : mépris, dédain **2** *or* **contempt of court** : outrage *m* à magistrat *France*, outrage *m* au tribunal *Can*
contemptible [kənˈtɛmptəbəl] *adj* DESPICABLE : méprisable
contemptuous [kənˈtɛmptʃuəs] *adj* : méprisant — **contemptuously** *adv*
contend [kənˈtɛnd] *vt* ARGUE, MAINTAIN : soutenir, maintenir — *vi* **1** COMPETE : rivaliser <to contend for first prize : rivaliser pour le premier prix> **2 to contend with** : affronter, faire face à <problems to contend with : problèmes à affronter>
contender [kənˈtɛndər] *n* : concurrent *m*, -rente *f* (aux sports); candidat *m*, -date *f* (en politique)
content[1] [kənˈtɛnt] *vt* : contenter, satisfaire
content[2] *adj* : content, satisfait
content[3] *n* → **contentment**
content[4] [ˈkɑnˌtɛnt] *n* **1** GIST : contenu *m*, signification *f* **2** : teneur *f* <high fiber content : haute teneur en fibres> **3 contents** *npl* : contenu *m* **4 table of contents** : table *f* des matières
contented [kənˈtɛntəd] *adj* : satisfait, content
contention [kənˈtɛnʈʃən] *n* **1** ARGUMENT : dispute *f*, discussion *f* **2** RIVALRY : compétition *f*, rivalité *f* **3** OPINION : assertion *f*, affirmation *f*
contentious [kənˈtɛnʈʃəs] *adj* **1** : litigieux **2** BELLIGERENT : bel-

liqueux, combatif — **contentiously** *adv*

contentment [kən'tɛntmənt] *n* : contentement *m,* satisfaction *f*

contest[1] [kən'tɛst] *vt* : contester, disputer

contest[2] ['kɑn,tɛst] *n* **1** STRUGGLE : lutte *f* **2** GAME : concours *m,* compétition *f*

contestant [kən'tɛstənt] *n* : concurrent *m,* -rente *f;* adversaire *mf*

context ['kɑn,tɛkst] *n* : contexte *m*

contiguous [kən'tɪgjʊəs] *adj* : contigu

continence ['kɑntənənts] *n* : continence *f*

continent[1] ['kɑntənənt] *adj* : continent

continent[2] *n* : continent *m* — **continental** [,kɑntən'ɛntəl] *adj*

contingency [kən'tɪndʒəntsi] *n, pl* **-cies** : éventualité *f,* contingence *f*

contingent[1] [kən'tɪndʒənt] *adj* **1** : contingent **2 to be contingent on** : dépendre de

contingent[2] *n* : contingent *m*

continual [kə'tɪnjʊəl] *adj* : continuel — **continually** [-'tɪnjʊəli, -'tɪnjəli] *adv*

continuance [kə'tɪnjʊənts] *n* **1** CONTINUATION : continuation *f* **2** DURATION : durée *f* **3** : ajournement *m* (d'un procès)

continuation [kən,tɪnjʊ'eɪʃən] *n* : continuation *f*

continue [kən'tɪnju:] *v* **-tinued; -tinuing** *vt* **1** KEEP UP : continuer <to continue writing : continuer à écrire> **2** RESUME : continuer, reprendre **3** EXTEND : continuer, prolonger — *vi* **1** CARRY ON : continuer **2** LAST : durer, se perpétuer <his good luck seems to continue : sa bonne fortune semble durer>

continuity [,kɑntən'u:əṭi, -'ju:-] *n, pl* **-ties** : continuité *f*

continuous [kən'tɪnjʊəs] *adj* : continu

continuously [kən'tɪnjʊəsli] *adv* : continuellement, constamment

contort [kən'tɔrt] *vt* : tordre

contortion [kən'tɔrʃən] *n* : contorsion *f*

contour ['kɑn,tʊr] *n* **1** OUTLINE : contour *m* **2 contours** *npl* SHAPE : contours *fpl*, forme *f*

contraband ['kɑntrə,bænd] *n* : contrebande *f*

contraception [,kɑntrə'sɛpʃən] *n* : contraception *f*

contraceptive[1] [,kɑntrə'sɛptɪv] *adj* : contraceptif

contraceptive[2] *n* : contraceptif *m*

contract[1] [kən'trækt, *vt and vi usu* 'kɑn,trækt] *vt* **1** INCUR : contracter (des dettes, etc.) **2** ARRANGE : contracter (un mariage, etc.) **3** CATCH : contracter, attraper (un virus) **4** TIGHTEN : contracter (un muscle) **5** SHORTEN : contracter (un mot) — *vi* : se contracter

contract[2] ['kɑn,trækt] *n* AGREEMENT : contrat *m*

contraction [kən'trækʃən] *n* : contraction *f*

contractor ['kɑn,træktər, kən'træk-] *n* : entrepreneur *m,* -neuse *f;* contracteur *m,* -teuse *f Can*

contractual [kən'træktʃʊəl] *adj* : contractuel — **contractually** *adv*

contradict [,kɑntrə'dɪkt] *vt* : contredire

contradiction [,kɑntrə'dɪkʃən] *n* : contradiction *f*

contradictory [,kɑntrə'dɪktəri] *adj* : contradictoire

contralto [kən'træl,to:] *n, pl* **-tos** : contralto *m* (voix), contralto *mf* (chanteur)

contraption [kən'træpʃən] *n* : truc *m fam*, machin *m fam*

contrary[1] ['kɑn,trɛri *often* kən'trɛri] *adj* **1** OPPOSITE : contraire **2** CONFLICTING : contradictoire <contrary evidence : preuves contradictoires> **3** BALKY, STUBBORN : têtu, opiniâtre **4 contrary to** : contrairement à

contrary[2] *n, pl* **-traries** : contraire *m* <on the contrary : au contraire>

contrast[1] [kən'træst] *vt* : mettre en contraste — *vi* : contraster

contrast[2] *n* : contraste *m*

contribute [kən'trɪbjət] *v* **-uted; -uting** *vi* : contribuer — *vt* GIVE, SUPPLY : donner, apporter

contribution [,kɑntrə'bju:ʃən] *n* : contribution *f*

contrite ['kɑn,traɪt, kən'traɪt] *adj* : contrit, pénitent

contrition [kən'trɪʃən] *n* : contrition *f,* pénitence *f*

contrivance [kən'traɪvənts] *n* **1** DEVICE : appareil *m,* dispositif *m* **2** SCHEME : machination *f,* manigance *f*

contrive [kən'traɪv] *v* **-trived; -triving** *vt* DEVISE : concevoir, inventer — *vi* **to contrive to** : parvenir à, réussir à, trouver le moyen de <she contrived to extricate herself from the situation : elle a trouvé le moyen de s'en sortir>

control[1] [kən'tro:l] *vt* **-trolled; -trolling** **1** REGULATE : contrôler **2** RULE : diriger, dominer **3** RESTRAIN : maîtriser (des émotions, etc.)

control[2] *n* **1** AUTHORITY : contrôle *m,* autorité *f* **2** RESTRAINT : maîtrise *f* **3** REGULATION : régulation *f,* contrôle *m* <price control : régulation des prix> **4** DEVICE : bouton *m,* commande *f* <remote control : commande à distance>

controller [kən'tro:lər, 'kɑn,-] *n* : contrôleur *m,* -leuse *f* <air traffic controller : contrôleur du trafic aérien>

controversial [,kɑntrə'vərʃəl, -siəl] *adj* : controversé, contesté

controversy ['kɑntrə,vərsi] *n, pl* **-sies** : controverse *f*

contusion [kən'tu:ʒən, -tju:-] *n* : contusion *f,* ecchymose *f*

conundrum [kə'nʌndrəm] *n* : énigme *f*
convalesce [,kɑnvə'lɛs] *vi* **-lesced; -lescing** : se remettre, être en convalescence
convalescence [,kɑnvə'lɛsənts] *n* : convalescence *f*
convalescent¹ [,kɑnvə'lɛsənt] *adj* : convalescent
convalescent² *n* : convalescent *m*, -cente *f*
convection [kən'vɛkʃən] *n* : convection *f*
convene [kən'vi:n] *v* **-vened; -vening** *vt* : convoquer — *vi* MEET : se réunir, s'assembler
convenience [kən'vi:njənts] *n* **1** AMENITY : commodité *f*, confort *m* <modern conveniences : commodités modernes> **2 at your convenience** : quand cela vous conviendra **3 at your earliest convenience** : dans les meilleurs délais, dès que cela vous sera possible
convenient [kən'vi:njənt] *adj* : commode, qui convient
conveniently [kən'vi:njəntli] *adv* : commodément
convent ['kɑnvənt, -,vɛnt] *n* : couvent *m*
convention [kən'vɛntʃən] *n* **1** AGREEMENT : convention *f* **2** ASSEMBLY, MEETING : conférence *f*, congrès *m* **3** CUSTOM : convention *f*, usage *m*
conventional [kən'vɛntʃənəl] *adj* : conventionnel — **conventionally** *adv*
converge [kən'vərdʒ] *vi* **-verged; -verging** : converger
conversant [kən'vərsənt] *adj* **to be conversant with** : connaître, être versé dans
conversation [,kɑnvər'seɪʃən] *n* : conversation *f*
conversational [,kɑnvər'seɪʃənəl] *adj* : familier <conversational style : style familier>
converse¹ [kən'vɛrs] *vi* **-versed; -versing** : converser
converse² [kən'vərs, 'kɑn,vɛrs] *adj* : contraire, inverse (en mathématiques, etc.)
conversely [kən'vərsli, 'kɑn,vɛrs-] *adv* : inversement
conversion [kən'vərʒən] *n* **1** : conversion *f* (en religion) **2** CHANGE : transformation *f*, changement *m*
convert¹ [kən'vɛrt] *vt* **1** : convertir (en religion) **2** CHANGE : transformer, changer — *vi* : se convertir
convert² ['kɑn,vərt] *n* : converti *m*, -tie *f*
converter *or* **convertor** [kən'vərṭər] *n* : convertisseur *m*
convertible¹ [kən'vərṭəbəl] *adj* : convertible
convertible² *n* : décapotable *f* (voiture)
convex [kɑn'vɛks, 'kɑn,-, kən'-] *adj* : convexe
convey [kən'veɪ] *vt* **-veyed; -veying 1** TRANSPORT : transporter **2** COMMUNICATE, TRANSMIT : transmettre, exprimer, communiquer
conveyance [kən'veɪənts] *n* **1** TRANSPORT : transport *m* **2** COMMUNICATION : transmission *f*, communication *f*
convict¹ [kən'vɪkt] *vt* : déclarer coupable, condamner
convict² ['kɑn,vɪkt] *n* : détenu *m*, -nue *f*
conviction [kən'vɪkʃən] *n* **1** : condamnation *f* (en droit) **2** BELIEF : conviction *f*, certitude *f* <personal convictions : convictions personnelles>
convince [kən'vɪnts] *vt* **-vinced; -vincing** : convaincre, persuader
convincing [kən'vɪntsɪŋ] *adj* : convaincant, persuasif
convivial [kən'vɪvjəl, -'vɪviəl] *adj* : convivial, jovial
conviviality [kən,vɪvi'æləṭi] *n, pl* **-ties** : convivialité *f*, gaieté *f*
convocation [,kɑnvə'keɪʃən] *n* : convocation *f*
convoke [kən'vo:k] *vt* **-voked; -voking** : convoquer
convoluted ['kɑnvə,lu:ṭəd] *adj* **1** TWISTED : convoluté **2** INTRICATE : alambiqué, compliqué <convoluted reasoning : raisonnement alambiqué>
convoy ['kɑn,vɔɪ] *n* : convoi *m*
convulse [kən'vʌls] *v* **-vulsed; -vulsing** *vt* : convulser <convulsed with pain : convulsé par la douleur> <to be convulsed with laughter : se tordre de rire> — *vi* : se convulser, souffrir de convulsions
convulsion [kən'vʌlʃən] *n* : convulsion *f*
convulsive [kən'vʌlsɪv] *adj* : convulsif
coo¹ ['ku:] *vi* : roucouler
coo² *n* : roucoulement *m*
cook¹ ['kʊk] *vi* **1** : cuire (se dit des aliments) **2**: cuisiner, faire la cuisine (se dit d'une personne) — *vt* **1** : cuisiner, cuire **2** *or* **to cook up** CONCOCT : inventer, mijoter
cook² *n* : cuisinier *m*, -nière *f*
cookbook ['kʊk,bʊk] *n* : livre *m* de recettes, livre *m* de cuisine
cookery ['kʊkəri] *n, pl* **-eries** : cuisine *f*
cookie *or* **cooky** ['kʊki] *n, pl* **-ies** : biscuit *m*, gâteau *m* sec
cool¹ ['ku:l] *vt* : refroidir — *vi* **1** *or* **to cool down** : se refroidir **2** : se dissiper <his anger cooled : sa colère s'est dissipée>
cool² *adj* **1** : frais <a cool breeze : une brise fraîche> **2** CALM : calme **3** UNFRIENDLY : indifférent, froid
cool³ *n* **1** COOLNESS : fraîcheur *m* **2** COMPOSURE : calme *m*, sang-froid *m* <to lose one's cool : perdre son sang-froid>
coolant ['ku:lənt] *n* : liquide *m* de refroidissement
cooler ['ku:lər] *n* : glacière *f*
coolie ['ku:li] *n* : coolie *m*

coolly ['ku:li] *adv* : froidement
coolness ['ku:lnəs] *n* **1** : fraîcheur *f* <the coolness of the evening : la fraîcheur du soir> **2** COLDNESS, INDIFFERENCE : froideur *m*, indifférence *f* **3** COMPOSURE : calme *m*, sang-froid *m*
coop[1] ['ku:p, 'kʊp] *vt or* **to coop up** : enfermer <cooped up in his apartment : enfermé dans son appartement>
coop[2] *n* : poulailler *m*
co–op ['ko:ˌɑp] → **cooperative**[2]
cooperate [ko'ɑpəˌreɪt] *vi* **-ated; -ating** : coopérer, collaborer
cooperation [koˌɑpə'reɪʃən] *n* : coopération *f*, collaboration *f*
cooperative[1] [ko'ɑpərət̬ɪv] *adj* : coopératif
cooperative[2] *n* : coopérative *f*
co–opt [ko'ɑpt] *vt* : coopter
coordinate[1] [ko'ɔrdənˌeɪt] *v* **-nated; -nating** *vt* : coordonner — *vi* : agir en coordination
coordinate[2] [ko'ɔrdənət] *adj* : coordonné <coordinate clause : proposition coordonnée>
coordinate[3] [ko'ɔrdənət] *n* : coordonnée *f*
coordination [koˌɔrdən'eɪʃən] *n* : coordination *f*
coordinator [ko'ɔrdənˌeɪt̬ər] *n* : coordinateur *m*, -trice *f*
cop ['kɑp] *n* : flic *m fam*
cope ['ko:p] *vi* **coped; coping 1** MANAGE : se débrouiller, s'en sortir **2 to cope with** DEAL, FACE : faire face à, affronter <I can't cope with all that : je ne peux pas supporter tout cela>
copier ['kɑpiər] *n* **1** : copieur *m*, -pieuse *f* (personne) **2** PHOTOCOPIER : photocopieur *m*, machine à photocopier
copilot ['ko:ˌpaɪlət] *n* : copilote *mf*
copious ['ko:piəs] *adj* : copieux, abondant
copiously ['ko:piəsli] *adv* : copieusement, abondamment
copper ['kɑpər] *n* : cuivre *m*
copperhead ['kɑpərˌhɛd] *n* : vipère *f* cuivrée
coppery ['kɑpəri] *adj* : cuivré
coppice ['kɑpəs] *n* THICKET : taillis *m*
copra ['ko:prə, 'kɑ-] *n* : copra *m*
copse ['kɑps] → **coppice**
copulate ['kɑpjəˌleɪt] *vi* **-lated; -lating** : copuler
copulation [ˌkɑpjə'leɪʃən] *n* : copulation *f*
copy[1] ['kɑpi] *v* **copied; copying** : copier
copy[2] *n, pl* **copies 1** IMITATION, REPRODUCTION : copie *f*, reproduction *f* **2** : exemplaire *m* (d'un livre, etc.), numéro *m* (d'une revue)
copyright[1] ['kɑpiˌraɪt] *vt* : protéger les droits d'auteur de
copyright[2] *n* : droits *mpl* d'auteur, copyright *m*
coquette [ko:'kɛt] *n* : coquette *f*
coral ['kɔrəl] *n* **1** : corail *m* <coral reef : récif de corail> **2** : couleur *f* de corail
coral snake *n* : serpent *m* corail
cord ['kɔrd] *n* **1** ROPE, STRING : corde *f*, cordon *m* **2** : cordon *m* (ombilical) **3** *or* **electrical cord** : fil *m* (électrique) **4** : corde *f* (de bois)
cordial[1] ['kɔrdʒəl] *adj* : cordial, amical — **cordially** *adv*
cordial[2] *n* LIQUEUR : cordial *m*
cordon ['kɔrdən] *n* : cordon *m* (d'agents de police)
corduroy ['kɔrdəˌrɔɪ] *n* **1** : velours *m* côtelé **2 corduroys** *npl* : pantalon *m* en velours côtelé
core[1] ['kor] *vt* **cored; coring** : enlever le cœur de (un fruit)
core[2] *n* **1** : cœur *m*, trognon *m* (d'un fruit) **2** CENTER : cœur *m*, noyau *m* <the core of the problem : le cœur du problème> **3 to the core** : jusqu'à l'os <honest to the core : honnête jusqu'à l'os>
cork[1] ['kɔrk] *vt* : boucher (avec un bouchon)
cork[2] *n* **1** : liège *m* **2** : bouchon *m* (d'une bouteille)
corkscrew ['kɔrkˌskru:] *n* : tire-bouchon *m*
cormorant ['kɔrmərənt, -ˌrænt] *n* : cormoran *m*
corn ['kɔrn] *n* **1** GRAIN : grain *m* (de blé, etc.) **2** → **Indian corn 3** : cor *m* (sur le pied)
corncob ['kɔrnˌkɑb] *n* : épi *m* de maïs
cornea ['kɔrniə] *n* : cornée *f*
corned beef *n* : corned-beef *m*
corner[1] ['kɔrnər] *vt* **1** TRAP : acculer (un animal, etc.) **2** MONOPOLIZE : accaparer <to corner the market : accaparer le marché> — *vi* TURN : prendre un virage (se dit d'une voiture)
corner[2] *n* **1** : coin *m*, angle *m*, encoignure *f* <the corner of a room : le coin d'une chambre> **2** INTERSECTION : coin *m*, intersection *f* <to turn the corner : tourner au coin de la rue> <around the corner : à deux pas d'ici> **3** PLACE : coin *m*, endroit *m* <a quiet corner : un endroit tranquille> **4** MONOPOLY : monopole *m*
cornerstone ['kɔrnərˌsto:n] *n* : pierre *f* angulaire
cornet [kɔr'nɛt] *n* : cornet *m* à pistons
cornice ['kɔrnɪs] *n* : corniche *f*
cornmeal ['kɔrnˌmi:l] *n* : farine *f* de maïs
cornstalk ['kɔrnˌstɔk] *n* : tige *f* de maïs
cornstarch ['kɔrnˌstɑrtʃ] *n* : fécule *f* de maïs
cornucopia [ˌkɔrnə'ko:piə, -njə-] *n* : corne *f* d'abondance
corny ['kɔrni] *adj* **cornier; -est** : bateau, banal, quétaine *Can fam* <corny novels : des romans à l'eau de rose>
corolla [kə'rɑlə] *n* : corolle *f*

corollary ['kɔrə,lɛri] *n, pl* **-laries** : corollaire *m*
corona [kə'ro:nə] *n* : couronne *f* (en astronomie)
coronary[1] ['kɔrə,nɛri] *adj* : coronaire
coronary[2] *n, pl* **-naries** HEART ATTACK : infarctus *m* myocarde, crise *f* cardiaque
coronation [,kɔrə'neɪʃən] *n* : couronnement *m*
coroner ['kɔrənər] *n* : coroner *m*
corporal[1] ['kɔrpərəl] *adj* : corporel <corporal punishment : châtiment corporel>
corporal[2] *n* : caporal-chef *m*
corporate ['kɔrpərət] *adj* **1** : de la société, d'entreprise **2** COLLECTIVE : collectif, commun
corporation [,kɔrpə'reɪʃən] *n* : compagnie *f* commerciale, société *f*
corporeal [kɔr'poriəl] *adj* **1** PHYSICAL : physique, corporel **2** MATERIAL : matériel
corps ['kor] *ns & pl* **1** : corps *m* (militaire) **2** BODY, GROUP : corps *m* <diplomatic corps : corps diplomatique>
corpse ['kɔrps] *n* : cadavre *m*
corpulence ['kɔrpjələnts] *n* : corpulence *f*, embonpoint *m*
corpulent ['kɔrpjələnt] *adj* : corpulent, gras
corpus ['kɔrpəs] *n, pl* **-pora** [-pərə] : recueil *m* (d'œuvres écrits)
corpuscle ['kɔr,pʌsəl] *n* **1** : corpuscule *m* (en physiologie) **2 red blood corpuscles** : globules *m* rouges
corral[1] [kə'ræl] *vt* **-ralled; -ralling** : enfermer dans un corral (se dit du bétail)
corral[2] *n* : corral *m*
correct[1] [kə'rɛkt] *vt* **1** RECTIFY : corriger (un texte, etc.), rectifier (une situation, etc.) **2** : corriger (un examen, une erreur), reprendre (à une personne) <to correct s.o.'s French : corriger le français de qqn>
correct[2] *adj* **1** RIGHT : exact, correct, juste <that's correct : c'est exact> **2** APPROPRIATE : correct, convenable
correction [kə'rɛkʃən] *n* : correction *f*
corrective [kə'rɛktɪv] *adj* : correctif
correctly [kə'rɛktli] *adv* : correctement
correlate ['kɔrə,leɪt] *vt* **-lated; -lating** : mettre en corrélation
correlation [,kɔrə'leɪʃən] *n* : corrélation *f*
correspond [,kɔrə'spɑnd] *vi* **1** MATCH, TALLY : correspondre, concorder **2** WRITE : correspondre, s'écrire
correspondence [,kɔrə'spɑndənts] *n* : correspondance *f*
correspondent [,kɔrə'spɑndənt] *n* **1** : correspondant *m*, -dante *f* **2** REPORTER : journaliste *mf;* correspondant *m*, -dante *f*
corridor ['kɔrədər, -,dɔr] *n* : corridor *m*, passage *m*, couloir *m*
corroborate [kə'rɑbə,reɪt] *vt* **-rated; -rating** : corroborer, confirmer
corroboration [kə,rɑbə'reɪʃən] *n* : confirmation *f*, corroboration *f*
corrode [kə'ro:d] *v* **-roded; -roding** *vt* : corroder — *vi* : se corroder
corrosion [kə'ro:ʒən] *n* : corrosion *f*
corrosive [kə'ro:sɪv] *adj* : corrosif
corrugated ['kɔrə,geɪtəd] *adj* : ondulé <corrugated cardboard : carton ondulé>
corrupt[1] [kə'rʌpt] *vt* **1** DEBASE, PERVERT : corrompre, pervertir **2** BRIBE : corrompre, soudoyer **3** ALTER : altérer (un texte)
corrupt[2] *adj* **1** IMMORAL : corrumpu, dépravé **2** ALTERED : altéré
corruption [kə'rʌpʃən] *n* : corruption *f*
corsage [kɔr'sɑʒ, -'sɑdʒ] *n* : petit bouquet *m* de fleurs (porté au corsage d'une robe, etc.)
corset ['kɔrsət] *n* : corset *m*
Corsican[1] ['kɔrsɪkən] *adj* : corse
Corsican[2] *n* : Corse *mf*
cortege [kɔr'tɛʒ] *n* : cortège *m*
cortex ['kɔr,tɛks] *n, pl* **-tices** ['kɔrt̬ə,si:z] *or* **-texes** : cortex *m*
cortisone ['kɔrt̬ə,so:n, -zo:n] *n* : cortisone *f*
cosmetic[1] [kɑz'mɛt̬ɪk] *adj* : cosmétique, esthétique <cosmetic surgery : chirurgie esthétique>
cosmetic[2] *n* : cosmétique *f*
cosmic ['kɑzmɪk] *adj* **1** : cosmique <cosmic ray : rayon cosmique> **2** VAST : vaste, gigantesque
cosmonaut ['kɑzmə,nɔt] *n* : cosmonaute *mf*
cosmopolitan [,kɑzmə'pɑlətən] *adj* : cosmopolite
cosmos ['kɑzməs, -,mo:s, -,mɑs] *n* : cosmos *m*, univers *m*
cost[1] ['kɔst] *v* **cost; costing** *vt* : coûter <how much does it cost? : combien ça coûte?> <it cost him his job : ça lui a coûté son emploi> — *vi* : coûter <this one costs less : celui-ci coûte moins cher>
cost[2] *n* **1** PRICE : coût *m*, prix *m* <the cost of living : le coût de la vie> <victory at any cost : la victoire à tout prix> <at cost : à prix coûtant> **2 costs** *npl* : frais *mpl*, dépenses *fpl* <traveling costs : frais de voyagement>
Costa Rican[1] [,kɔstə'ri:kən] *adj* : costaricain
Costa Rican[2] *n* : Costaricain *m*, -caine *f*
costly ['kɔstli] *adj* **costlier; -est** : coûteux, cher
costume ['kɑs,tu:m, -,tju:m] *n* **1** : costume *m* <national costume : costume national> <Halloween costume : costume d'Halloween> **2** OUTFIT : costume *m* (d'une femme)
cosy ['ko:zi] → **cozy**
cot ['kɑt] *n* : lit *m* de camp

cottage ['kɑtɪdʒ] *n* : petite maison *f,* chalet *m Can*
cottage cheese *n* : fromage *m* blanc, fromage *m* cottage
cotton ['kɑtən] *n* : coton *m*
cottonwood ['kɑtən,wʊd] *n* : liard *m Can*
couch[1] ['kaʊtʃ] *vt* : formuler, exprimer <couched in diplomatic language : formulé en langage diplomatique>
couch[2] *n* SOFA : canapé *m,* sofa *m,* divan *m*
cougar ['ku:gər] *n* : puma *m,* couguar *m*
cough[1] ['kɔf] *vi* : tousser
cough[2] *n* : toux *f*
could ['kʊd] → **can**[1]
council ['kaʊntsəl] *n* : conseil *m,* assemblée *f* <city council : conseil municipal>
councillor *or* **councilor** ['kaʊntsələr] *n* : conseiller *m,* -lère *f*
counsel[1] ['kaʊntsəl] *v* **-seled** *or* **-selled; -seling** *or* **-selling** *vt* ADVISE : conseiller, guider — *vi* CONSULT : consulter
counsel[2] *n* **1** ADVICE : conseil *m* **2** CONSULTATION : consultation *f,* délibération *f* **3** LAWYER : avocat *m,* -cate *f*
counselor *or* **counsellor** ['kaʊntsələr] *n* **1** : conseiller *m,* -lère *f* <guidance counselor : conseiller d'orientation> **2** LAWYER : avocat *m,* -cate *f* **3** *or* **camp counselor** : moniteur *m,* -trice *f*
count[1] ['kaʊnt] *vt* ENUMERATE : dénombrer, compter — *vi* **1** : compter <to count to ten : compter jusqu'à dix> **2** MATTER : compter, importer **3 to count on** : compter sur
count[2] *n* **1** COMPUTATION : compte *m,* décompte *m* **2** CHARGE : chef *m* d'accusation <convicted on two counts : condamné pour deux chefs d'accusation> **3** : comte *m* (noble)
countable ['kaʊntəbəl] *adj* : nombrable, dénombrable
countenance[1] ['kaʊntənənts] *vt* **-nanced; -nancing** : approuver, sanctionner
countenance[2] *n* FACE : visage *m,* expression *f*
counter[1] ['kaʊntər] *vt* OPPOSE : s'opposer à, contrecarrer — *vi* RETALIATE : contre-attaquer, riposter
counter[2] *adv* **counter to** : à l'encontre de <to act counter to his advice : agir à l'encontre de ses conseils>
counter[3] *adj* : contraire, opposé
counter[4] *n* **1** PIECE : jeton *m* (d'un jeu de société) **2** : comptoir *m,* guichet *m* <post office counter : guichet de la poste> **3** : compteur *m* (dispositif) <Geiger counter : compteur Geiger>
counteract [,kaʊntər'ækt] *vt* : contrebalancer, neutraliser
counterattack[1] ['kaʊntərə,tæk] *vi* : contre-attaquer
counterattack[2] *n* : contre-attaque *f*
counterbalance[1] [,kaʊntər'bæləntsl] *vt* : contrebalancer, faire contrepoids à
counterbalance[2] *n* : contrepoids *m*
counterclockwise [,kaʊntər'klɑk,waɪz] *adv & adj* : dans le sens contraire des aiguilles d'une montre
counterfeit[1] ['kaʊntər,fɪt] *vt* **1** : contrefaire, falsifier (une monnaie, etc.) **2** FEIGN : feindre (une émotion)
counterfeit[2] *adj* : faux <counterfeit money : fausse monnaie>
counterfeit[3] *n* : contrefaçon *f,* faux *m*
counterfeiter ['kaʊntər,fɪtər] *n* : faussaire *mf,* faux-monnayeur *m*
countermand ['kaʊntər,mænd] *vt* : annuler (un ordre)
counterpart ['kaʊntər,pɑrt] *n* : homologue *mf* (d'une personne), équivalent *m* (d'une chose)
counterpoint ['kaʊntər,pɔɪnt] *n* : contrepoint *m*
counterrevolution [,kaʊntər,rɛvə'lu:ʃən] *n* : contre-révolution *f*
counterrevolutionary[1] [,kaʊntər,rɛvə'lu:ʃən,ɛri] *adj* : contre-révolutionnaire
counterrevolutionary[2] *n, pl* **-aries** : contre-révolutionnaire *mf*
countersign ['kaʊntər,saɪn] *vt* : contresigner
countess ['kaʊntɪs] *n* : comtesse *f*
countless ['kaʊntləs] *adj* : innombrable, incalculable
country[1] ['kʌntri] *adj* RURAL : champêtre, rural
country[2] *n, pl* **-tries 1** NATION : pays *m,* patrie *f,* nation *f* <neighboring countries : pays voisins> <love of one's country : amour de la patrie> **2** : campagne *f* <she lives in the country : elle demeure à la campagne>
countryman ['kʌntrimən] *n, pl* **-men** [-mən, -,mɛn] **1** COMPATRIOT : compatriote *mf* **2** RUSTIC : campagnard *m,* -gnarde *f;* habitant *m,* -tante *f* de la campagne
countryside ['kʌntri,saɪd] *n* : campagne *f*
county ['kaʊnti] *n, pl* **-ties** : comté *m*
coup ['ku:] *n, pl* **coups 1** ACT, FEAT : (beau) coup *m* **2** *or* **coup d'état** : coup *m* d'état
coupé [ku:'peɪ] *or* **coupe** ['ku:p] *n* : coupé *m*
couple[1] ['kʌpəl] *v* **-pled; -pling** *vt* : accoupler — *vi* : s'accoupler
couple[2] *n* **1** : couple *m* <a happy couple : un couple heureux> **2 a couple of** : deux <a couple of days ago : il y a deux ou trois jours>
coupling ['kʌplɪŋ] *n* : couplage *m* (en électricité, etc.)
coupon ['ku:,pɑn, 'kju:-] *n* : coupon *m*
courage ['kərɪdʒ] *n* : courage *m*
courageous [kə'reɪdʒəs] *adj* : courageux — **courageously** *adv*
courier ['kʊriər, 'kəriər] *n* MESSENGER : messager *m,* -gère *f*

course[1] [ˈkors] *vi* **coursed; coursing** FLOW : couler, ruisseler <blood was coursing through his veins : le sang coulait dans ses veines>

course[2] *n* **1** PROGRESS : cours *m* <in the course of : au cours de> **2** DIRECTION, PATH : cours *m* (d'un fleuve, etc.), direction *f,* ligne *f* <to change course : changer de direction> <course of action : ligne de conduite> **3** : parcours *m,* terrain *m* (aux sports) <golf course : terrain de golf> **4** : service *m,* plat *m* <seven-course meal : repas de sept services> **5** : cours *m* (universitaire) **6 of course** : évidemment, bien sûr

court[1] [ˈkort] *vt* : courtiser, faire la cour à

court[2] *n* **1** : cour *f* (d'un souverain) **2** COURTYARD : cour *f* **3** : court *m,* terrain *m* (aux sports) **4** TRIBUNAL : cour *f,* tribunal *m* <to appear in court : comparaître au tribunal>

courteous [ˈkərt̬iəs] *adj* : courtois, poli — **courteously** *adv*

courtesan [ˈkort̬əzən, ˈkər-] *n* : courtisane *f*

courtesy [ˈkərt̬əsi] *n, pl* **-sies** : courtoisie *f*

courthouse [ˈkortˌhaʊs] *n* : palais *m* de justice

courtier [ˈkort̬iər, ˈkortjər] *n* : courtisan *m*

courtly [ˈkortli] *adj* **courtlier; -est** : poli, élégant

court–martial [ˈkortˌmɑrʃəl] *n, pl* **courts–martial** [ˈkortsˌmɑrʃəl] : cour *f* martiale

courtroom [ˈkortˌru:m] *n* : salle *f* d'audience

courtship [ˈkortˌʃɪp] *n* : cour *f*

courtyard [ˈkortˌjɑrd] *n* : cour *f,* patio *m*

cousin [ˈkʌzən] *n* : cousin *m,* -sine *f*

cove [ˈko:v] *n* : anse *f,* crique *f*

coven [ˈkəvən, ˈko:-] *n* : groupe *m* de sorcières

covenant [ˈkʌvənənt] *n* : contrat *m,* pacte *m*

cover[1] [ˈkʌvər] *vt* **1** : couvrir, recouvrir **2** PROTECT : couvrir, protéger **3** HIDE : cacher, dissimuler **4** INCLUDE, TREAT : inclure, comprendre **5** : faire un reportage sur <she covered the story : elle a fait un reportage sur l'affaire> **6** INSURE : assurer, couvrir

cover[2] *n* **1** SHELTER : abri *m,* refuge *m* <to take cover : se mettre à l'abri> **2** LID : couvercle *m* **3** : couverture *f* (d'un livre), pochette *f* (d'un disque) **4** → **slipcover 5 covers** *npl* BEDCLOTHES : couvertures *fpl*

coverage [ˈkʌvərɪdʒ] *n* **1** COVERING : couverture *f* **2** REPORTING : reportage *m,* couverture *f* **3** *or* **insurance coverage** : couverture *f* d'assurance

coverlet [ˈkʌvərlət] *n* BEDSPREAD : couvre-lit *m*

covert[1] [ˈko:ˌvərt, ˈkʌvərt] *adj* : voilé, secret

covert[2] [ˈkʌvərt, ˈko:-] *n* THICKET : fourré *m*

cover-up [ˈkʌvərˌʌp] *n* : opération *f* de camouflage

covet [ˈkʌvət] *vt* : convoiter

covetous [ˈkʌvət̬əs] *adj* : avide, cupide

covey [ˈkʌvi] *n, pl* **-eys 1** : compagnie *f* (d'oiseaux) **2** GROUP : groupe *m*

cow[1] [ˈkaʊ] *vt* : intimider, effrayer

cow[2] *n* : vache *f*

coward [ˈkaʊərd] *n* : lâche *mf;* poltron *m,* -tronne *f*

cowardice [ˈkaʊərdɪs] *n* : lâcheté *f*

cowardly [ˈkaʊərdli] *adj* : lâche

cowboy [ˈkaʊˌbɔɪ] *n* : cow-boy *m,* vacher *m*

cower [ˈkaʊər] *vi* : se tapir (se dit d'un animal), trembler (de peur)

cowgirl [ˈkaʊˌgərl] *n* : vachère *f*

cowhide [ˈkaʊˌhaɪd] *n* : peau *f* de vache

cowl [ˈkaʊl] *n* : capuchon *m*

cowlick [ˈkaʊˌlɪk] *n* : mèche *f* rebelle

cowpuncher [ˈkaʊˌpʌntʃər] → **cowboy**

cowslip [ˈkaʊˌslɪp] *n* : primevère *f* sauvage, coucou *m*

coxswain [ˈkɑksən, -ˌsweɪn] *n* : patron *m* (d'un bateau)

coy [ˈkɔɪ] *adj* **1** SHY : (faussement) timide **2** COQUETTISH : coquet

coyote [kaɪˈo:t̬i, ˈkaɪˌo:t] *n, pl* **coyotes** *or* **coyote** : coyote *m*

cozen [ˈkʌzən] *vt* : décevoir

cozy [ˈko:zi] *adj* **cozier; -est** : douillet, confortable

crab [ˈkræb] *n* : crabe *m*

crabby [ˈkræbi] *adj* **crabbier; -est** : revêche, acariâtre, grognon

crack[1] [ˈkræk] *vt* **1** SPLIT : fêler, fendre **2** BREAK : casser (un œuf, etc.) **3** : faire claquer (un fouet), faire craquer (les jointures) **4 to crack jokes** : faire des blagues — *vi* **1** SPLIT : se fêler, se fendre **2** : craquer, claquer <the whip cracked : le fouet a claqué> **3** BREAK : se casser, muer (se dit de la voix) **4** : craquer, s'effondrer <he cracked under the strain : il s'est effondré faute d'un trop grand effort>

crack[2] *adj* FIRST-RATE : de première classe, d'élite

crack[3] *n* **1** SNAP : craquement *m,* bruit *m* sec **2** SPLIT : crevasse *f,* fissure *f,* craque *f Can* **3** JOKE : plaisanterie *f,* blague *f* **4** ATTEMPT : essai *m,* tentative *f* <to have a crack at : essayer (un coup)>

crackdown [ˈkrækˌdaʊn] *n* : mesures *fpl* énergiques

crack down *vi* : prendre des mesures énergiques

cracker [ˈkrækər] *n* : biscuit *m* salé

crackle[1] [ˈkrækəl] *vi* **-led; -ling** : crépiter, pétiller <a crackling fire : un feu qui crépite>

crackle[2] *n* : crépitement *m*

crackpot [ˈkræk͵pɑt] *n* : excentrique *mf,* personne *f* originale

crack–up [ˈkræk͵ʌp] *n* **1** CRASH : accident *m,* collision *f* **2** BREAKDOWN : dépression *f* nerveuse

crack up *vi* **1** CRASH : s'écraser **2** LAUGH : rire **3** BREAK DOWN : s'effondrer

cradle[1] [ˈkreɪdəl] *vt* **-dled; -dling** : tenir délicatement, bercer (un enfant)

cradle[2] *n* : berceau *m*

craft [ˈkræft] *n* **1** SKILL, TRADE : métier *m,* art *m* **2** CRAFTINESS : astuce *f,* ruse *f* **3** *pl usu* **craft** BOAT : bateau *m,* embarcation *f* **4** *pl usu* **craft** AIRCRAFT : avion *m,* aéronef *m*

craftiness [ˈkræftinəs] *n* : astuce *f,* ruse *f*

craftsman [ˈkræftsmən] *n, pl* **-men** [-mən, -͵mɛn] : artisan *m,* -sane *f*

crafty [ˈkræfti] *adj* **craftier; -est** : astucieux, rusé, ratourneur *Can*

crag [ˈkræg] *n* : rocher *m* escarpé

craggy [ˈkrægi] *adj* **craggier; -est** : escarpé et rocheux

cram [ˈkræm] *v* **crammed; cramming** *vt* JAM, PACK : fourrer, bourrer, entasser — *vi* : étudier (à la dernière minute)

cramp[1] [ˈkræmp] *vt* HAMPER : entraver, gêner <to cramp s.o.'s style : priver qqn de ses moyens> — *vi* : avoir une crampe

cramp[2] *n* : crampe *f* (musculaire)

cranberry [ˈkræn͵bɛri] *n, pl* **-berries** : canneberge *f,* atoca(s) *m Can*

crane[1] [ˈkreɪn] *vt* **craned; craning** STRETCH : tendre <to crane one's neck : tendre le cou>

crane[2] *n* : grue *f* (oiseau ou machine)

cranial [ˈkreɪniəl] *adj* : crânien

cranium [ˈkreɪniəm] *n, pl* **-niums** *or* **-nia** : crâne *m,* boîte *f* crânienne

crank[1] [ˈkræŋk] *vt or* **to crank up** : démarrer (un moteur) à la manivelle

crank[2] *n* **1** : manivelle *f* **2** ECCENTRIC : excentrique *mf*

cranky [ˈkræŋki] *adj* **crankier; -est** : de mauvaise humeur, irritable

cranny [ˈkræni] *n, pl* **-nies 1** CREVICE : (petite) fente *f* **2** NOOK : coin *m,* recoin *m* <every nook and cranny : tous les coins et recoins>

crash[1] [ˈkræʃ] *vt* **to crash one's car** : avoir un accident de voiture — *vi* **1** SMASH : se fracasser, s'écraser <to crash to the ground : s'écraser au sol> **2** RESOUND : retentir **3** : faire faillite (se dit des banques, etc.), s'effondrer (se dit des prix à la Bourse)

crash[2] *n* **1** DIN : fracas *m,* bruit *m* sourd <a crash of thunder : un coup de tonnerre> **2** COLLISION : accident *m,* collision *f* **3** FAILURE : effondrement *m,* krach *m* (boursier)

crass [ˈkræs] *adj* : crasse, grossier

crate[1] [ˈkreɪt] *vt* **crated; crating** : mettre en cageot, mettre en caisse

crate[2] *n* : cageot *m,* caisse *f*

crater [ˈkreɪṭər] *n* : cratère *m*

cravat [krəˈvæt] *n* **1** SCARF : foulard *m* **2** NECKTIE : cravate *f*

crave [ˈkreɪv] *vt* **craved; craving** : désirer, avoir très envie de

craven [ˈkreɪvən] *adj* : lâche, poltron

craving [ˈkreɪvɪŋ] *n* : envie *f* (incontrôlable), soif *f*

crawfish [ˈkrɔ͵fɪʃ] → **crayfish**

crawl[1] [ˈkrɔl] *vi* **1** : ramper, se traîner, marcher à quatre pattes (se dit d'un bébé) **2** SWARM : fourmiller, grouiller <to be crawling with : grouiller de>

crawl[2] *n* **1** : pas *m* de tortue <to move at a crawl : avancer à un pas de tortue> **2** : crawl *m* (en natation)

crayfish [ˈkreɪ͵fɪʃ] *n* **1** : écrevisse *f* (d'eau douce) **2** : langouste *f* (de mer)

crayon [ˈkreɪ͵ɑn, -ən] *n* : crayon *m* de cire

craze [ˈkreɪz] *n* FAD : mode *f,* vogue *f*

crazily [ˈkreɪzəli] *adv* : comme un fou, d'une manière insensée

craziness [ˈkreɪzinəs] *n* : folie *f*

crazy [ˈkreɪzi] *adj* **crazier; -est 1** INSANE : fou, dément **2** FOOLISH : fou, insensé **3 to be crazy about** : être fou de

creak[1] [ˈkri:k] *vi* : grincer, craquer

creak[2] *n* : grincement *m,* craquement *m*

creaky [ˈkri:ki] *adj* **creakier; -est** : grinçant, qui craque

cream[1] [ˈkri:m] *vt* **1** BEAT, BLEND : battre en crème, travailler <to cream butter and sugar together : travailler le beurre et le sucre> **2** : préparer (des légumes, etc.) à la béchamel

cream[2] *n* **1** : crème *f* (de lait) **2** LOTION : crème *f,* lotion *f* **3** ELITE : crème *f,* élite *f* <the cream of society : la crème de la société>

creamery [ˈkri:məri] *n, pl* **-eries** DAIRY : laiterie *f*

creamy [ˈkri:mi] *adj* **creamier; -est 1** : crémeux **2** : laiteux <creamy skin : peau laiteuse>

crease[1] [ˈkri:s] *v* **creased; creasing** *vt* **1** : faire les plis de (pantalons, etc.) **2** CRUMPLE : froisser — *vi* : se froisser

crease[2] *n* : pli *m,* faux pli *m*

create [kriˈeɪt] *vt* **-ated; -ating 1** MAKE : créer, faire **2** CAUSE : créer, provoquer

creation [kriˈeɪʃən] *n* : création *f*

creative [kriˈeɪṭɪv] *adj* : créatif, créateur

creatively [kriˈeɪṭɪvli] *adv* : de manière créative

creativity [͵kri:eɪˈtɪvəṭi] *n* : créativité *f*

creator [kriˈeɪṭər] *n* **1** : créateur *m,* -trice *f* **2 the Creator** : le Créateur

creature [ˈkri:tʃər] *n* **1** : créature *f* **2** ANIMAL : animal *m,* bête *f*

credence [ˈkri:dənts] *n* : crédit *m*

credentials [krɪˈdɛntʃəlz] *n* : références *fpl,* lettres *fpl* de créance

credibility [ˌkrɛdəˈbɪlət̬i] *n* : crédibilité *f*
credible [ˈkrɛdəbəl] *adj* : credible
credit[1] [ˈkrɛdɪt] *vt* **1** BELIEVE : croire, ajouter foi à (une histoire, etc.) **2** ATTRIBUTE : attribuer <they credit him with the new idea : on lui attribue la nouvelle idée> **3** : créditer (un compte de banque)
credit[2] *n* **1** *or* **credit balance** : solde *m* créditeur (d'un compte) **2** : crédit *m* <to buy on credit : acheter à crédit> **3** CREDENCE : crédit *m*, croyance *f* <to lose credit in s.o.'s eyes : perdre de son crédit aux yeux de qqn> **4** HONOR : honneur *m*, mérite *m* <it's to his credit : c'est à son honneur> <to be a credit to : faire honneur à>
creditable [ˈkrɛdɪt̬əbəl] *adj* : honorable <a creditable attempt : une tentative honorable> — **creditably** [-bli] *adv*
credit card *n* : carte *f* de crédit
creditor [ˈkrɛdɪt̬ər] *n* : créancier *m*, -cière *f*
credulity [krɪˈduːlət̬i, -ˈdjuː-] *n* : crédulité *f*
credulous [ˈkrɛdʒələs] *adj* : crédule
creed [ˈkriːd] *n* : crédo *m*, croyance *f*
creek [ˈkriːk, ˈkrɪk] *n* **1** STREAM : ruisseau *m*, crique *m Can* **2** *Brit* COVE, INLET : crique *f*, anse *f*
creel [ˈkriːl] *n* : panier *m* de pêche
creep[1] [ˈkriːp] *vi* **crept; creeping 1** CRAWL : ramper, se glisser, marcher à quatre pattes (se dit des enfants) **2** : avancer lentement, marcher sans bruit <to creep out of the house : partir de la maison sans aucun bruit> **3** SPREAD : ramper, grimper (se dit des plantes) **4 to creep up on** : s'approcher furtivement
creep[2] *n* **1** CRAWL : pas *m* de tortue, ralenti *m* <traffic's moving at a creep : la circulation avance au ralenti> **2 creeps** *npl* : frissons *mpl* <to give s.o. the creeps : donner froid dans le dos à qqn>
cremate [ˈkriːˌmeɪt] *vt* **-mated; -mating** : incinérer
cremation [krɪˈmeɪʃən] *n* : incinération *f*
creole [ˈkriːˌoːl] *adj* : créole
Creole *n* **1** : créole *m* (langue) **2** : Créole *mf* (personne)
creosote [ˈkriːəˌsoːt] *n* : créosote *f*
crepe *or* **crêpe** [ˈkreɪp] *n* **1** : crêpe *m* (tissu) **2** PANCAKE : crêpe *f*
crescendo [krɪˈʃɛnˌdoː] *n, pl* **-dos** *or* **-does** : crescendo *m*
crescent [ˈkrɛsənt] *n* : croissant *m*
cress [ˈkrɛs] *n* : cresson *m*
crest [ˈkrɛst] *n* **1** : crête *f* (d'un oiseau) **2** PEAK : crête *f*, sommet *m* (d'une montagne) **3** COAT OF ARMS : armoiries *fpl* **4** : timbre *m* (au-dessus des armoiries)
crestfallen [ˈkrɛstˌfɔlən] *adj* : déconfit, abattu
cretin [ˈkriːtən] *n* : crétin *m*, -tine *f*
crevasse [krɪˈvæs] *n* : crevasse *f*
crevice [ˈkrɛvəs] *n* : fissure *f*, fente *f*
crew[1] *Brit* → **crow**[1]
crew[2] [ˈkruː] *n* **1** : équipage *m* (d'un navire) **2** TEAM : équipe *f* (d'ouvriers ou d'athlètes)
crib [ˈkrɪb] *n* **1** MANGER : mangeoire *f* **2** : lit *m* d'enfant
crick [ˈkrɪk] *n* SPASM : crampe *f* <to have a crick in one's neck : avoir un torticolis>
cricket [ˈkrɪkət] *n* **1** : grillon *m* (insecte), criquet *m Can* **2** : cricket *m* (jeu)
crier [ˈkraɪər] *n* : crieur *m* <the town crier : le crieur public>
crime [ˈkraɪm] *n* : crime *m*, délit *m*
criminal[1] [ˈkrɪmənəl] *adj* : criminel
criminal[2] *n* : criminel *m*, -nelle *f*
crimp [ˈkrɪmp] *vt* : onduler, friser <to crimp one's hair : friser ses cheveux>
crimson [ˈkrɪmzən] *n* : cramoisi *m*
cringe [ˈkrɪndʒ] *vi* **cringed; cringing** : avoir un mouvement de recul
crinkle [ˈkrɪŋkəl] *v* **-kled; -kling** *vt* : froisser, gaufrer, chiffonner — *vi* : se froisser, se chiffonner
crinkly [ˈkrɪŋkəli] *adj* **crinklier; -est** : gaufré
cripple[1] [ˈkrɪpəl] *vt* **-pled; -pling 1** DISABLE : estropier **2** INCAPACITATE : mettre hors d'usage, paralyser <crippled by fear : paralysé par la peur>
cripple[2] *n, sometimes taken to be offensive* : infirme *mf;* handicapé *m*, -pée *f*
crisis [ˈkraɪsɪs] *n, pl* **crises** [-ˌsiːz] : crise *f*
crisp [ˈkrɪsp] *adj* **1** CRUNCHY : croustillant, croquant <crisp cereal : céréale croustillante> <crisp celery : céleri croquant> **2** SHARP : sec, brusque <a crisp comment : un commentaire sec> **3** INVIGORATING : frais, rafraîchissant <the air was crisp : l'air était rafraîchissant> **4** CLEAR : net, clair <a crisp illustration : une illustration nette>
crisply [ˈkrɪspli] *adv* SHARPLY : d'un ton acerbe, brusquement
crispy [ˈkrɪspi] *adj* **crispier; -est** : croustillant, croquant
crisscross [ˈkrɪsˌkrɔs] *vt* : entrecroiser
criterion [kraɪˈtɪriən] *n, pl* **-ria** [-riə] : critère *m*
critic [ˈkrɪt̬ɪk] *n* **1** : critique *mf* <movie critic : critique de cinéma> **2** FAULTFINDER : critiqueur *m*, -queuse *f;* détracteur *m*, -trice *f*
critical [ˈkrɪt̬ɪkəl] *adj* **1** DISAPPROVING : critique **2** ANALYTICAL : critique <critical analysis : analyse critique> **3** CRUCIAL : critique, décisif <critical stage : étape critique>
criticism [ˈkrɪt̬əˌsɪzəm] *n* : critique *f*
criticize [ˈkrɪt̬əˌsaɪz] *vt* **-cized; -cizing** : critiquer

critique |krɪ'ti:k| *n* : critique *f*
croak[1] |'kro:k| *vi* : coasser (se dit d'une grenouille)
croak[2] *n* : coassement *m*
Croatian[1] |kro'eɪʃən| *adj* : croate
Croatian[2] *n or* **Croat** |'kro,æt| : Croate *mf*
crochet[1] |kro:'ʃeɪ| *vt* : faire (qqch) au crochet — *vi* : faire du crochet
crochet[2] *n* : crochet *m*
crock |'krɑk| *n* : pot *m* (en terre cuite)
crockery |'krɑkəri| *n* EARTHENWARE : faïence *f*
crocodile |'krɑkə,daɪl| *n* : crocodile *m*
crocus |'kro:kəs| *n, pl* **-cuses** : crocus *m*
crone |'kro:n| *n* : vieille *f* bique, vieille *f* taupe
crony |'kro:ni| *n, pl* **-nies** : copain *m*, -pine *f*
crook[1] |'krʊk| *vt* : recourber (le doigt), plier (le coude)
crook[2] *n* **1** : houlette *f* (d'un berger), crosse *f* (d'un évêque) **2** CRIMINEL : escroc *m* **3** BEND, CURVE : courbe *f*, coude *m*
crooked |'krʊkəd| *adj* **1** BENT : crochu, croche *Can* <nez crochu : crooked nose> **2** DISHONEST : malhonnête
croon |'kru:n| *v* : chantonner, chanter doucement
crop[1] |'krɑp| *v* **cropped**; **cropping** *vt* TRIM : tailler, couper court — *vi* **to crop up** : surgir, se présenter
crop[2] *n* **1** : jabot *m* (d'un oiseau) **2** WHIP : cravache *f* **3** PRODUCE : culture *f* <food crops : cultures vivières> **4** : HARVEST : récolte *f*, moisson *f*
croquet |,kro:'keɪ| *n* : croquet *m*
croquette |,kro:'kɛt| *n* : croquette *f*
crosier |'kro:ʒər| *n* : crosse *f* (d'évêque)
cross[1] |'krɔs| *vt* **1** TRAVERSE : traverser <to cross the road : traverser la rue> **2** *or* **to cross out** CANCEL : rayer, biffer <to cross out a word : rayer un mot> **3** CROSSBREED : croiser (deux espèces) **4** OPPOSE : aller à l'encontre de **5** : se croiser (les bras, les jambes, etc.) — *vi* INTERSECT : se croiser
cross[2] *adj* **1** : transversal <cross street : rue transversale> **2** CONTRARY : contraire, opposé <at cross purposes : ayant des buts contraires> **3** ANGRY : fâché, contrarié
cross[3] *n* **1** : croix *f* **2** HYBRID : croisement *m*, hybride *m*
crossbones |'krɔs,bo:nz| *npl* **1** : os *mpl* en croix **2** → **skull**
crossbow |'krɔs,bo:| *n* : arbalète *f*
crossbreed |'krɔs,bri:d| *vt* **-bred** |-,brɛd, -'brɛd|; **-breeding** : croiser (deux espèces)
cross–examination |,krɔsɪg,zæmə'neɪʃən| *nm* : contre-interrogatoire *m*
cross–examine |,krɔsɪg'zæmən| *vt* **-ined**; **-ining** : faire subir un contre-interrogatoire à, interroger
cross–eyed |'krɔs,aɪd| *adj* : qui louche, coq-d'œil *Can*
crossing |'krɔsɪŋ| *n* **1** INTERSECTION : croisement *m* **2** VOYAGE : traversée *f* (de la mer) **3** → **crosswalk**
cross–reference |,krɔs'rɛfrənts, -'rɛfərənts| *n* : renvoi *m*
crossroads |'krɔs,ro:dz| *ns & pl* : carrefour *m*
cross section *n* **1** SECTION : coupe *f* transversale **2** SAMPLE : échantillon *m* <a cross section of the population : un échantillon de la population>
crosswalk |'krɔs,wɔk| *n* : passage *m* pour piétons
crossways |'krɔs,weɪz| → **crosswise**
crosswise[1] |'krɔs,waɪz| *adv* : transversalement
crosswise[2] *adj* : en travers
crossword puzzle |'krɔs,wərd| *n* : mots *mpl* croisés
crotch |'krɑtʃ| *n* : entre-jambes *m* (d'un vêtement), fourche *f* (d'un arbre)
crotchety |'krɑtʃəṭi| *adj* : grincheux, grognon
crouch |'kraʊtʃ| *vi* : s'accroupir
croup |'kru:p| *n* : croup *m*
crouton |'kru:,tɑn| *n* : croûton *m*
crow[1] |'kro:| *vi* **crowed** *or in sense 1 Brit* **crew**; **crowing 1** : chanter (se dit du coq) **2** EXULT : exulter **3** BOAST : se vanter
crow[2] *n* **1** : corbeau *m* (oiseau) **2** : chant *m* (du coq)
crowbar |'kro:,bɑr| *n* : (pince à) levier *m*
crowd[1] |'kraʊd| *vt* CRAM, PACK : entasser, serrer — *vi* : se presser, s'entasser
crowd[2] *n* **1** THRONG : foule *f* **2** GROUP : bande *f* <to stand out from the crowd : se distinguer de la masse>
crown[1] |'kraʊn| *vt* : couronner
crown[2] *n* **1** : couronne *f* **2** SUMMIT : sommet *m*, cime *f* **3** : fond *m* (d'une casquette)
crow's nest *n* : nid *m* de pie
crucial |'kru:ʃəl| *adj* : crucial
crucible |'kru:səbəl| *n* : creuset *m*
crucifix |'kru:sə,fɪks| *n* : crucifix *m*
crucifixion |,kru:sə'fɪkʃən| *n* : crucifixion *f*
crucify |'kru:sə,faɪ| *vt* **-fied**; **-fying** : crucifier
crude |'kru:d| *adj* **cruder**; **-est 1** RAW, UNREFINED : brut <crude sugar : sucre brut> **2** VULGAR : grossier, fruste **3** ROUGH : grossier, rudimentaire <a crude shelter : un abri rudimentaire>
crudely |'kru:dli| *adv* : grossièrement
cruel |'kru:əl| *adj* **-eler** *or* **-eller**; **-elest** *or* **-ellest** : cruel — **cruelly** *adv*
cruelty |'kru:əlti| *n, pl* **-ties** : cruauté *f*
cruet |'kru:ɪt| *n* **1** : burette *f* (en religion) **2** : huilier *m*, vinaigrier *m* (pour la table)
cruise[1] |'kru:z| *vi* **cruised**; **cruising 1** : faire une croisière, croiser (se dit

d'un bateau) **2** : rouler à sa vitesse de croisière (se dit d'une voiture), voler à sa vitesse de croisière (se dit d'un avion)
cruise[2] *n* : croisière *f*
cruiser [ˈkru:zər] *n* **1** WARSHIP : croiseur *m* **2** *or* **police cruiser** : véhicule *m* de police
crumb [ˈkrʌm] *n* : miette *f*
crumble [ˈkrʌmbəl] *v* **-bled; -bling** *vt* : émietter — *vi* : s'émietter, s'effriter
crumbly [ˈkrʌmbli] *adj* **crumblier; -est** : friable
crumple [ˈkrʌmpəl] *v* **-pled; -pling** *vt* : froisser, chiffonner — *vi* **1** *or* **to crumple up** : se froisser **2** COLLAPSE : s'effondrer
crunch[1] [ˈkrʌntʃ] *vt* **1** CHEW : croquer **2** CRUSH : faire crisser — *vi* : craquer, crisser <the snow was crunching underfoot : la neige craquait sous nos pas>
crunch[2] *n* : craquement *m*, crissement *m*
crunchy [ˈkrʌntʃi] *adj* **crunchier; -est** : croquant
crusade [kru:ˈseɪd] *n* **1** CAMPAIGN : croisade *f*, campagne *f* **2 the Crusades** : les croisades *f*
crusader [kru:ˈseɪdər] *n* **1** : croisé *m* (militaire) **2** ACTIVIST : militant *m*, -tante *f*
crush[1] [ˈkrʌʃ] *vt* **1** SQUASH : écraser, aplatir, écrapoutir *Can* **2** GRIND : broyer, concasser **3** OVERWHELM : écraser
crush[2] *n* **1** CROWD, MOB : bousculade *f*, cohue *f* **2** INFATUATION : tocade *f fam*, béguin *m*
crust [ˈkrʌst] *n* **1** : croûte *f* (de pain) **2** LAYER : couche *f* <a crust of snow : une couche de neige>
crustacean [ˌkrʌsˈteɪʃən] *n* : crustacé *m*
crusty [ˈkrʌsti] *adj* **crustier; -est 1** : croustillant **2** CROSS, GRUMPY : grincheux, hargneux <a crusty reply : une brusque réplique>
crutch [ˈkrʌtʃ] *n* : béquille *f*
crux [ˈkrʌks, ˈkrʊks] *n, pl* **cruxes** : point *m* crucial, cœur *m*, noyau *m* <the crux of the matter : le cœur de l'affaire>
cry[1] [ˈkraɪ] *v* **cried; crying** *vi* **1** SHOUT : crier, pousser un cri **2** WEEP : pleurer — *vt* SHOUT : crier
cry[2] *n, pl* **cries** : cri *m*
crypt [ˈkrɪpt] *n* : crypte *f*
cryptic [ˈkrɪptɪk] *adj* : énigmatique, secret
crystal [ˈkrɪstəl] *n* : cristal *m*
crystalline [ˈkrɪstəlɪn] *adj* : cristallin
crystallize [ˈkrɪstəˌlaɪz] *v* **-lized; -lizing** *vt* : cristalliser — *vi* : se cristalliser
cub [ˈkʌb] *n* : petit *m* (d'un animal)
Cuban[1] [ˈkju:bən] *adj* : cubain
Cuban[2] *n* : Cubain *m*, -baine *f*
cubbyhole [ˈkʌbiˌho:l] *n* : réduit *m*
cube[1] [ˈkju:b] *vt* **cubed; cubing 1** : élever (un nombre) au cube **2** DICE : couper en cubes
cube[2] *n* : cube *m*
cubic [ˈkju:bɪk] *adj* : cubique
cubicle [ˈkju:bɪkəl] *n* : box *m*
Cub Scout *n* : louveteau *m*
cuckoo[1] [ˈku:ˌku:, ˈkʊ-] *adj* : toqué *fam*, cinglé *fam*
cuckoo[2] *n, pl* **-oos** : coucou *m* (oiseau)
cucumber [ˈkju:ˌkʌmbər] *n* : concombre *m*
cud [ˈkʌd] *n* **to chew the cud** : ruminer
cuddle [ˈkʌdəl] *v* **-dled; -dling** *vt* : caresser, câliner — *vi* : se câliner
cudgel[1] [ˈkʌdʒəl] *vt* **-geled** *or* **-gelled; -geling** *or* **-gelling** : battre (à coups de gourdin), matraquer
cudgel[2] *n* : gourdin *m*, trique *f*
cue [ˈkju:] *n* **1** SIGNAL : signal *m*, réplique *f* (au théâtre) **2** *or* **cue stick** : queue *f* de billard
cuff[1] [ˈkʌf] *vt* SLAP : gifler, claquer
cuff[2] *n* **1** : poignet *m* (de chemise), revers *m* (de pantalon) **2** SLAP : gifle *f*, claque *f* **3 cuffs** *npl* → **handcuffs**
cuisine [kwɪˈzi:n] *n* : cuisine *f*
culinary [ˈkʌləˌnɛri, ˈkju:lə-] *adj* : culinaire
cull [ˈkʌl] *vt* CHOOSE : choisir, sélectionner
culminate [ˈkʌlməˌneɪt] *vi* **-nated; -nating** : culminer, plafonner
culmination [ˌkʌlməˈneɪʃən] *n* : point *m* culminant
culpable [ˈkʌlpəbəl] *adj* BLAMEWORTHY : répréhensible, condamnable
culprit [ˈkʌlprɪt] *n* : coupable *mf*
cult [ˈkʌlt] *n* : culte *m*
cultivate [ˈkʌltəˌveɪt] *vt* **-vated; -vating 1** : cultiver (la terre) **2** FOSTER : promouvoir, encourager **3** IMPROVE, REFINE : cultiver, perfectionner <to cultivate one's mind : se cultiver l'esprit>
cultivation [ˌkʌltəˈveɪʃən] *n* **1** : culture *f* <under cultivation : en culture> **2** REFINEMENT : raffinement *m*, perfectionnement *m*
cultural [ˈkʌltʃərəl] *adj* : culturel — **culturally** *adv*
culture [ˈkʌltʃər] *n* **1** CULTIVATION : culture *f* **2** REFINEMENT : culture *f*, savoir *m* **3** CIVILIZATION : culture *f*, civilisation *f*
culvert [ˈkʌlvərt] *n* : passage *m* hydraulique
cumbersome [ˈkʌmbərsəm] *adj* : encombrant, embarrassant, lourd
cumulative [ˈkju:mjələtɪv, -ˌleɪtɪv] *adj* : cumulatif
cumulus [ˈkju:mjələs] *n, pl* **-li** [-laɪ, -li:] : cumulus
cunning[1] [ˈkʌnɪŋ] *adj* **1** CRAFTY : astucieux **2** CLEVER : ingénieux, habile **3**

CUTE : joli, mignon <a cunning baby : un joli petit bébé>
cunning[2] *n* **1** CRAFTINESS : astuce *f,* ruse *f* **2** SKILL : ingéniosité *f,* habileté *f*
cup[1] [ˈkʌp] *vt* **cupped; cupping** : faire prendre la forme d'une tasse <to cup one's hands around sth : mettre les mains autour de qqch>
cup[2] *n* **1** : tasse *f* <a cup of tea : une tasse de thé> <a cup of flour : une tasse *f* de farine> **2** TROPHY : coupe *f*
cupboard [ˈkʌbərd] *n* : placard *m,* armoire *f*
cupcake [ˈkʌpˌkeɪk] *n* : petit gateau *m*
cupful [ˈkʌpˌfʊl] *n* : tasse *f*
cupidity [kjuːˈpɪdəti] *n, pl* **-ties** GREED : cupidité *f*
cupola [ˈkjuːpələ, -ˌloː] *n* : coupole *f*
cur [ˈkər] *n* : chien *m* métis, sale chien *m*
curate [ˈkjʊrət] *n* : vicaire *m*
curator [ˈkjʊrˌeɪtər, kjʊˈreɪtər] *n* : conservateur *m,* -trice *f* (d'un musée)
curb[1] [ˈkərb] *vt* : refréner, mettre un frein à
curb[2] *n* **1** CHECK : contrainte *f,* frein *m* **2** : bord *m* du trottoir <to step off the curb : descendre du trottoir>
curdle [ˈkərdəl] *v* **-dled; -dling** *vt* : cailler — *vi* : se cailler, se figer
curds [ˈkərdz] *npl* : lait *m* caillé
cure[1] [ˈkjʊr] *vt* **cured; curing 1** HEAL, REMEDY : guérir **2** : fumer, saler <to cure meat : fumer de la viande>
cure[2] *n* **1** RECOVERY : rétablissement *m,* guérison *f* **2** REMEDY : remède *m*
curfew [ˈkərˌfjuː] *n* : couvre-feu *m*
curio [ˈkjʊriˌoː] *n, pl* **-rios** : curiosité *f,* babiole *f*
curiosity [ˌkjʊriˈɑsəṭi] *n, pl* **-ties 1** INQUISITIVENESS : curiosité *f* **2** → **curio**
curious [ˈkjʊriəs] *adj* **1** INQUISITIVE : curieux **2** ODD : étrange, curieux
curl[1] [ˈkərl] *vt* **1** : friser (les cheveux) **2** COIL : enrouler **3 to curl one's lip** : faire une moue (de mépris) — *vi* : se friser, boucler
curl[2] *n* **1** RINGLET : boucle *f* (de cheveux) **2** SPIRAL : spirale *f* <curl of smoke : spirale de fumée>
curler [ˈkərlər] *n* : bigoudi *m,* rouleau *m*
curlew [ˈkərˌluː, ˈkərlˌjuː] *n, pl* **-lews** *or* **-lew** : courlis *m*
curly [ˈkərli] *adj* **curlier; -est** : frisé
currant [ˈkərənt] *n* **1** : groseille *f,* gadelle *f Can* **2** RAISIN : raisin *m* de Corinthe
currency [ˈkərəntsi] *n, pl* **-cies 1** MONEY : monnaie *f,* devise *f* <foreign currency : devises étrangères> **2** PREVALENCE : cours *m,* acceptation *f*
current[1] [ˈkərənt] *adj* **1** PRESENT : actuel, en cours <the current week : la semaine en cours> **2** PREVALENT : courant, commun <current customs : coutumes usuelles>
current[2] *n* **1** FLOW : courant *m,* cours *m* <the current of a river : le cours d'un fleuve> **2** TREND : tendance *f,* penchant *m* **3** : courant *m* (électrique)
curriculum [kəˈrɪkjələm] *n, pl* **-la** [-lə] : programme *m* (scolaire)
curry[1] [ˈkəri] *vt* **-ried; -rying 1** : étriller (un cheval) **2** : faire un curry de (en cuisine) **3 to curry favor with** : chercher à gagner la faveur de
curry[2] *n, pl* **-ries** : curry *m*
curse[1] [ˈkərs] *v* **cursed; cursing** *vt* **1** : maudire <the gods cursed him : les dieux l'ont maudit> **2** AFFLICT : affliger — *vi* SWEAR : sacrer, jurer
curse[2] *n* **1** : malédiction *f* <to put a curse on : appeler une malédiction sur> **2** CALAMITY : fléau *m,* calamité *f* **3** OATH, SWEARWORD : juron *m*
cursor [ˈkərsər] *n* : curseur *m* (en informatique)
cursory [ˈkərsəri] *adj* : superficiel, hâtif
curt [ˈkərt] *adj* : brusque, sec
curtail [kərˈteɪl] *vt* : réduire, diminuer <to curtail expenses : réduire les dépenses>
curtailment [kərˈteɪlmənt] *n* : réduction *f,* diminution *f*
curtain [ˈkərtən] *n* : rideau *m*
curtly [ˈkərtli] *adv* : brusquement, sèchement
curtsy[1] *or* **curtsey** [ˈkərtsi] *vi* **-sied** *or* **-seyed; -sying** *or* **-seying** : faire une révérence
curtsy[2] *or* **curtsey** *n, pl* **-sies** *or* **-seys** : révérence *f*
curvature [ˈkərvəˌtʃʊr] *n* : courbure *f*
curve[1] [ˈkərv] *v* **curved; curving** *vt* : courber — *vi* : se courber
curve[2] *n* : courbe *f*
cushion[1] [ˈkʊʃən] *vt* **1** : mettre des coussins à **2** LESSEN : amortir, réduire <to cushion the blow : amortir le choc>
cushion[2] *n* : coussin *m*
cusp [ˈkʌsp] *n* : cuspide *f* (d'une dent, etc.)
cuspid [ˈkʌspɪd] *n* : canine *f* (dent)
custard [ˈkʌstərd] *n* : flan *m*
custody [ˈkʌstədi] *n, pl* **-dies 1** CARE : garde *f* <in the custody of : sous la garde de> **2** DETENTION : détention *f,* emprisonnement *m*
custom[1] [ˈkʌstəm] *adj* : fait sur commande
custom[2] *n* **1** CONVENTION, TRADITION : coutume *f,* tradition *f,* usage *m* **2 customs** *npl* : douane *f*
customarily [ˌkʌstəˈmɛrəli] *adv* : habituellement, normalement
customary [ˈkʌstəˌmɛri] *adj* : habituel, coutumier
customer [ˈkʌstəmər] *n* : client *m,* cliente *f*

cut[1] ['kʌt] *v* **cut; cutting** *vt* **1** : couper <to cut paper : couper du papier> **2** SLICE : découper (du gâteau, des viandes, etc.) **3** SLASH : se couper <I cut my finger : je me suis coupé le doigt> **4** TRIM : couper (les ongles), tailler (une barbe, des cheveux, etc.) **5** INTERSECT : croiser **6** SHORTEN : couper (un texte, etc.) **7** REDUCE : réduire, diminuer <to cut costs : réduire les coûts> **8 to cut a tooth** : faire une dent — *vi* **1** : couper **2 to cut in** : interrompre, s'interposer, s'immiscer

cut[2] *n* **1** : coupure *f* **2** REDUCTION : réduction *f*, diminution *f* <a cut in pay : une réduction de salaire>

cute ['kju:t] *adj* **cuter; -est** : mignon, joli

cuticle ['kju:tɪkəl] *n* : petites peaux *fpl* (de l'ongle)

cutlass ['kʌtləs] *n* : coutelas *m*

cutlery ['kʌtləri] *n* **1** KNIVES : coutellerie *f* **2** FLATWARE : couverts *mpl*

cutlet ['kʌtlət] *n* : escalope *f*

cutter ['kʌt̬ər] *n* **1** : coupoir *m* (outil) **2** : cotre *m* (bateau)

cutthroat[1] ['kʌt,θro:t] *adj* : acharné, féroce <cutthroat competition : compétition acharnée>

cutthroat[2] *n* : meurtrier *m*, -trière *f*; assassin *m*

cutting ['kʌt̬ɪŋ] *adj* **1** SHARP : aigu, cinglant <a cutting wind : un vent cinglant> **2** CURT, SCATHING : mordant, tranchant

cyanide ['saɪə,naɪd, -nɪd] *n* : cyanure *m*

cyberspace ['saɪbər,speɪs] *n* : cyberespace *m*

cycle[1] ['saɪkəl] *vi* **-cled; -cling** : faire de la bicyclette

cycle[2] *n* **1** : cycle *m* <life cycle : cycle de vie> **2** BICYCLE : bicyclette *f*, vélo *m* **3** MOTORCYCLE : motocyclette *f*

cyclic ['saɪklɪk, sɪ-] *or* **cyclical** [-klɪkəl] *adj* : cyclique, périodique

cyclist ['saɪklɪst] *n* : cycliste *mf*

cyclone ['saɪ,klo:n] *n* **1** : cyclône *m* **2** TORNADO : tornade *f*

cyclopedia *or* **cyclopaedia** [,saɪklə'pi:diə] → **encyclopedia**

cylinder ['sɪləndər] *n* : cylindre *m*

cylindrical [sə'lɪndrɪkəl] *adj* : cylindrique

cymbal ['sɪmbəl] *n* : cymbale *f*

cynic ['sɪnɪk] *n* : cynique *mf*

cynical ['sɪnɪkəl] *adj* : cynique

cynicism ['sɪnəsɪzəm] *n* : cynisme *m*

cypress ['saɪprəs] *n* : cyprès *m*

Cypriot[1] *or* **Cypriote** ['sɪpriət, -,ɑt] *adj* : chypriote, cypriote

Cypriot[2] *or* **Cypriote** *n* : Chypriote *mf*, Cypriote *mf*

cyst ['sɪst] *n* : kyste *m*

cytoplasm ['saɪt̬o,plæzəm] *n* : cytoplasme *m*

czar ['zɑr, 'sɑr] *n* : tsar *m*

czarina [zɑ'ri:nə, sɑ-] *n* : tsarine *f*

Czech[1] ['tʃɛk] *adj* : tchèque

Czech[2] *n* **1** : Tchèque *mf* **2** : tchèque *m* (langue)

Czechoslovak[1] [,tʃɛko'slo:,vɑk, -,væk] *or* **Czechoslovakian** [-slo'vɑkiən, -'væ-] *adj* : tchécoslovaque

Czechoslovak[2] *or* **Czechoslovakian** *n* : Tchécoslovaque *mf*

D

d ['di:] *n, pl* **d's** *or* **ds** ['di:z] : d *m*, quatrième lettre de l'alphabet

dab[1] ['dæb] *vt* **dabbed; dabbing 1** PAT : tamponner **2** APPLY : appliquer (par petites touches)

dab[2] *n* BIT, TOUCH : touche *f*, petite quantité *f*

dabble ['dæbəl] *v* **-bled; -bling** *vt* SPATTER : éclabousser — *vi* **1** SPLASH : faire des éclaboussures (dans l'eau) **2** : s'intéresser brièvement <to dabble in art : faire un peu d'art>

dabbler ['dæbələr] *n* : dilettante *mf*, amateur *m*

dachshund ['dɑks,hʊnt, -hʊnd; 'dɑksənt, -sənd] *n* : teckel *m*

dad ['dæd] *n* : papa *m fam*

daddy ['dædi] *n, pl* **-dies** : papa *m fam*

daffodil ['dæfə,dɪl] *n* : jonquille *f*

daft ['dæft] *adj* : idiot, bête

dagger ['dægər] *n* : dague *f*, poignard *m*

dahlia ['dæljə, 'dɑl-, 'deɪl-] *n* : dahlia *m*

daily[1] ['deɪli] *adv* : quotidiennement

daily[2] *adj* : quotidien, journalier

daily[3] *n, pl* **-lies** *or* **daily newspaper** : quotidien *m*

daintily ['deɪntəli] *adv* : délicatement

daintiness ['deɪntinəs] *n* : délicatesse *f*

dainty[1] ['deɪnti] *adj* **daintier; -est 1** DELICATE : délicat, mignon **2** TASTY : de choix <dainty food : nourriture de choix> **3** FINICKY : difficile (sur la nourriture)

dainty[2] *n, pl* **-ties** DELICACY : mets *m* délicat

dairy ['dæri] *n, pl* **-ies** : laiterie *f*, crémerie *f France*

dairymaid ['dæri,meɪd] *n* : fille *f* de laiterie

dairyman ['dærimən, -mæn] *n, pl* **-men** [-mən, -,mɛn] : employé *m* de laiterie

dais ['deɪəs] *n* : estrade *f*

daisy ['deɪzi] *n, pl* **-sies** : marguerite *f*

dale ['deɪl] *n* : vallée *f*, val *m*

dally ['dæli] *vi* **-lied; -lying 1** TRIFLE : jouer, badiner **2** DAWDLE : traîner, lambiner *fam*

dalmatian [dæl'meɪʃən, dɔl-] *n* : dalmatien *m*
dam[1] ['dæm] *vt* **dammed; damming** : construire un barrage sur
dam[2] *n* **1** : barrage *m* **2** : mère *f* (d'un animal domestique)
damage[1] ['dæmɪdʒ] *vt* **-aged; -aging** : endommager (des objets), abîmer (sa santé), nuire à (une réputation, etc.)
damage[2] *n* **1** : dégâts *mpl* **2 damages** *npl* : dommages *mpl* et intérêts *mpl*
damask ['dæməsk] *n* : damas *m*
dame ['deɪm] *n* LADY : dame *f*
damn[1] ['dæm] *vt* **1** CONDEMN : condamner **2** CURSE : maudire
damn[2] *n* **1 not to give a damn** : s'en ficher *fam* **2 it's not worth a damn** : ça ne vaut pas un clou
damnable ['dæmnəbəl] *adj* **1** REPREHENSIBLE : condamnable **2** DETESTABLE : fichu *fam* <this damnable weather! : ce fichu temps!>
damnation [dæm'neɪʃən] *n* : damnation *f*
damned ['dæmd] *adj* DAMNABLE : sacré *fam,* fichu *fam*
damp[1] ['dæmp] → **dampen**
damp[2] *adj* : humide, moite
damp[3] *n* : humidité *f*
dampen ['dæmpən] *vt* **1** MOISTEN : humecter **2** COOL, DEADEN : refroidir <to dampen s.o.'s spirits : décourager qqn>
damper ['dæmpər] *n* **1** : registre *m* (d'une cheminée) **2 to put a damper on** : jeter un froid sur, décourager
dampness ['dæmpnəs] *n* : humidité *f*
damsel ['dæmzəl] *n* : demoiselle *f*
dance[1] ['dænts] *v* **danced; dancing** : danser
dance[2] *n* **1** : danse *f* **2** : soirée *f* dansante
dancer ['dæntsər] *n* : danseur *m,* -seuse *f*
dandelion ['dændəˌlaɪən] *n* : pissenlit *m*
dander ['dændər] *n* TEMPER : colère *f,* rogne *f* <don't get your dander up : ne te mets pas en colère>
dandruff ['dændrəf] *n* : pellicules *fpl*
dandy[1] ['dændi] *adj* **dandier; -est** : chouette *fam,* épatant *fam*
dandy[2] *n, pl* **-dies** : dandy *m*
Dane ['deɪn] *n* : danois *m,* -noise *f*
danger ['deɪndʒər] *n* : danger *m*
dangerous ['deɪndʒərəs] *adj* : dangereux
dangle ['dæŋgəl] *v* **-gled; -gling** *vi* HANG : se balancer, pendre — *vt* **1** SWING : balancer, laisser pendre **2** : faire miroiter <they dangled the prospect of a promotion before him : on lui a fait miroiter une promotion>
Danish[1] ['deɪnɪʃ] *adj* : danois
Danish[2] *nm* **1** : danois *m* (langue) **2 the Danish** : les Danois *mpl*
Danish[3] *n* **the Danish** : les Danois
dank ['dæŋk] *adj* : froid et humide
dapper ['dæpər] *adj* : soigné
dappled ['dæpəld] *adj* : tacheté, pommelé
dare[1] ['dær] *v* **dared; daring** *vt* CHALLENGE : lancer un défi à, défier — *vi* VENTURE : oser
dare[2] *n* CHALLENGE : défi *m*
daredevil ['dærˌdɛvəl] *n* : casse-cou *mf*
daring[1] ['deɪrɪŋ] *adj* BOLD : audacieux, hardi
daring[2] *n* : audace *f,* hardiesse *f*
dark[1] ['dɑrk] *adj* **1** : noir, sombre, foncé <dark clothes : vêtements foncés> <to get dark : faire nuit> **2** GLOOMY : lugubre, sombre
dark[2] *n* **1** NIGHT : tombée *f* du jour **2** DARKNESS : noir *m,* obscurité *f*
darken ['dɑrkən] *vt* : obscurcir, assombrir — *vi* : s'obscurcir, s'assombrir
darkly ['dɑrkli] *adv* **1** DIMLY : sombrement **2** GLOOMILY : d'un air lugubre **3** MYSTERIOUSLY : énigmatiquement, mystérieusement
darkness ['dɑrknəs] *n* : obscurité *f,* ténèbres *fpl,* noirceur *f Can*
darling[1] ['dɑrlɪŋ] *adj* **1** BELOVED : bien-aimé, chéri **2** CHARMING : adorable <a darling puppy : un chiot adorable>
darling[2] *n* **1** BELOVED : chéri *m,* -rie *f* **2** FAVORITE : chouchou *m,* -choute *f fam;* coqueluche *f fam*
darn[1] ['dɑrn] *vt* : repriser (en couture)
darn[2] *n* **1** : reprise *f* **2** → **damn**[2]
dart[1] ['dɑrt] *vi* : se précipiter, s'élancer <he darted out : il est sorti comme une flèche>
dart[2] *n* **1** : flèche *f* (courte), fléchette *f,* dard *m Can* **2 darts** *npl* : fléchettes *fpl* (jeu) **3** : pince *f* (en couture)
dash[1] ['dæʃ] *vt* **1** SMASH : briser, fracasser **2** HURL : lancer violemment **3** SPLASH : éclabousser **4** RUIN : détruire, anéantir <to dash s.o.'s hopes : anéantir les espoirs de qqn> **5** *or* **to dash off** : terminer à la hâte — *vi* : se précipiter, se ruer
dash[2] *n* **1** BURST, SPLASH : éclat *m,* plouf *m* **2** : tiret *m* (signe de ponctuation) **3** DROP, PINCH : pincée *f,* soupçon *m* <a dash of pepper : une pincée de poivre> **4** VERVE : brio *m,* panache *m* **5** RUSH : mouvement *m* précipité, course *f* folle **6** : sprint *m* (aux sports) **7** → **dashboard**
dashboard ['dæʃˌbord] *n* : tableau *m* de bord
dashing ['dæʃɪŋ] *adj* : fringant, élégant
data ['deɪtə, 'dæ-, 'dɑ-] *ns & pl* : données *fpl*
database ['deɪtəˌbeɪs, 'dæ-, 'dɑ-] *n* : base *f* de données
date[1] ['deɪt] *v* **dated; dating** *vt* **1** : dater (un chèque, un objet, etc.) **2** : sortir avec — *vi* **1** : sortir avec quelqu'un, se fréquenter **2** ORIGINATE : remonter <a friendship dating from high school : une amitié qui remonte au lycée>

date[2] *n* **1** : date *f* <date of birth : date de naissance> **2** PERIOD : date *f,* période *f* (historique) **3** APPOINTMENT : rendez-vous *m* **4** : datte *f* (fruit) **5 to ~** : à ce jour, jusqu'à maintenant

dated ['deɪt̬əd] *adj* OLD-FASHIONED : vieilli, démodé

datum ['deɪt̬əm, 'dæ-, 'dɑ-] *n, pl* **-ta** [-tə] *or* **-tums** : donnée *f*

daub[1] ['dɔb] *vt* **1** COVER : couvrir <daubed with mud : couvert de boue> **2** SMEAR : barbouiller

daub[2] *n* : barbouillage *m*

daughter ['dɔt̬ər] *n* : fille *f*

daughter-in-law ['dɔt̬ərɪn,lɔ] *n, pl* **daughters-in-law** : belle-fille *f,* bru *f*

daunt ['dɔnt] *vt* : décourager, intimider

dauntless ['dɔntləs] *adj* : intrépide, hardi

davenport ['dævən,port] *n* : canapé *m*

dawdle ['dɔdəl] *vi* **-dled; -dling 1** DALLY : traîner, lambiner *fam,* farfiner *Can fam* **2** LOITER : flâner

dawn[1] ['dɔn] *vi* **1** : se lever (se dit du jour) **2 to dawn on** : venir à <it dawned on him that it was late : il s'est aperçu qu'il était tard>

dawn[2] *n* **1** : aube *f* **2** BEGINNING : aube *f,* début *m* <the dawn of the space age : le début de l'ère spatiale>

day ['deɪ] *n* **1** : jour *m* <every day : tous les jours> <day by day : jour après jour> **2** : journée *f* <have a good day! : bonne journée!> <an eight-hour day : une journée de huit heures> **3** AGE, TIME : époque *f,* temps *m* <in my day : à mon époque> <in this day and age : par les temps qui courent> **4** → **weekday, workday**

daybreak ['deɪ,breɪk] *n* : aube *f,* point *m* du jour, lever *m* du jour

day care *n* : service *m* de garderie

daydream[1] ['deɪ,dri:m] *vi* : rêver, rêvasser

daydream[2] *n* : rêve *m,* rêverie *f*

daylight ['deɪ,laɪt] *n* **1** : lumière *f* du jour <in broad daylight : en plein jour> **2** → **daybreak 3** → **daytime**

daylight saving time *n* : heure *f* d'été, heure *f* avancée (de l'Est) *Can*

daytime ['deɪ,taɪm] *n* : jour *m,* journée *f* <in the daytime : pendant le jour>

daze[1] ['deɪz] *vt* **dazed; dazing 1** STUN : étourdir, abasourdir **2** DAZZLE : éblouir

daze[2] *n* : ahurissement *m,* étourdissement *m*

dazzle ['dæzəl] *vt* **-zled; -zling 1** BLIND : éblouir, aveugler **2** IMPRESS : impressionner, épater *fam*

DDT [,di:,di:'ti:] *n* : DDT *m*

deacon ['di:kən] *n* : diacre *m*

dead[1] ['dɛd] *adv* **1** ABSOLUTELY : absolument <dead certain : absolument sûr> **2** SUDDENLY : soudainement <to stop dead : s'arrêter net> **3** DIRECTLY : directement, droit <dead ahead : droit devant, tout droit>

dead[2] *adj* **1** LIFELESS : mort **2** NUMB : engourdi **3** EXTINCT, INACTIVE : inactif, éteint, mort **4** : coupé (se dit d'une ligne téléphonique), à plat (se dit d'une batterie) **5** EXHAUSTED : éreinté, crevé *fam* **6** OBSOLETE : mort, désuet <dead language : langue morte> **7** EXACT : exact, précis <at the dead center : exactement au centre> **8** COMPLETE : absolu, total <dead silence : silence absolu>

dead[3] *ns & pl* **1** DEPTHS : milieu *m,* profondeur *f* <in the dead of night : au plus profond de la nuit> <in the dead of winter : en plein hiver> **2 the dead** : les morts

deadbeat ['dɛd,bi:t] *n* : bon à rien *m,* bonne à rien *f*

deaden ['dɛdən] *vt* **1** ALLAY : calmer, endormir (des douleurs) **2** CUSHION, SOFTEN : assourdir (des sons), amortir (un coup, etc.)

dead-end ['dɛd'ɛnd] *adj* : sans issue (se dit d'une rue), sans perspectives (se dit d'un travail)

dead end *n* : cul-de-sac *m,* impasse *f*

dead heat *n* TIE : match *m* nul

deadline *n* ['dɛd,laɪn] : date *f* limite, délai *m*

deadlock[1] ['dɛd,lɑk] *vt* : mettre dans une impasse

deadlock[2] *n* : impasse *f*

deadly[1] ['dɛdli] *adv* : extrêmement, très <deadly serious : très sérieux>

deadly[2] *adj* **deadlier; -est 1** LETHAL : mortel **2** ACCURATE : précis, juste <deadly accuracy : une extrême précision> **3** : capital <the seven deadly sins : les sept péchés capitaux> **4** EXTREME : extrême, absolu

deadpan ['dɛd,pæn] *adj* : impassible, pince-sans-rire

deaf ['dɛf] *adj* : sourd

deafen ['dɛfən] *vt* : assourdir

deaf-mute ['dɛf'mju:t] *n* : sourd-muet *m,* sourde-muette *f*

deafness ['dɛfnəs] *n* : surdité *f*

deal[1] ['di:l] *v* **dealt; dealing** *vt* **1** APPORTION : rendre <to deal (out) justice : rendre la justice> **2** DISTRIBUTE : donner, distribuer (des cartes à jouer) **3** DELIVER : administrer, assener (un coup) **4** SELL : revendre (des drogues) — *vi* **1** : distribuer les cartes **2 to deal in** SELL : être dans le commerce de **3 to deal with** CONCERN, TREAT : traiter de **4 to deal with** FACE : accepter, faire face à

deal[2] *n* **1** : donne *f* (aux cartes) **2** AGREEMENT, TRANSACTION : accord *m,* affaire *f,* marché *m* **3** TREATMENT : traitement *m* <to get a bad deal : être mal traité> **4** BARGAIN : bonne affaire *f* **5 a good deal** LOTS : beaucoup

dealer [ˈdiːlər] *n* : marchand *m*, -chande *f*; négociant *m*, -ciante *f*

dealings [ˈdiːlɪŋz] *npl* **1** : relations *fpl* (personnelles) **2** TRANSACTIONS : transactions *fpl*, affaires *fpl*

dean [ˈdiːn] *n* : doyen *m*, doyenne *f*

dear[1] [ˈdɪr] *adj* **1** ESTEEMED, LOVED : cher <a dear friend : un ami très cher> **2** (*used in correspondence*) : cher <Dear Anne : Chère Anne> **3** COSTLY : cher, coûteux **4** EARNEST : cher, sincère <my dearest wish : mon vœu le plus cher>

dear[2] *n* : chéri *m*, -rie *f*

dearly [ˈdɪrli] *adv* **1 to love dearly** : aimer tendrement, aimer beaucoup **2 to pay dearly** : payer cher

dearness [ˈdɪrnəs] *n* **1** FONDNESS : affection *f*, amitié *f* **2** COSTLINESS : cherté *f*

dearth [ˈdərθ] *n* : pénurie *f*, manque *m*

death [ˈdɛθ] *n* **1** : mort *f*, décès *m* **2** DESTRUCTION, END : disparition *f* <the death of all hope : la disparition de tout espoir> <he'll be the death of me : il me fera mourir>

deathless [ˈdɛθləs] *adj* : immortel

deathly[1] [ˈdɛθli] *adv* : de mort, comme la mort <deathly pale : pâle comme la mort>

deathly[2] *adj* **1** FATAL : mortel **2** : cadavérique <deathly pallor : pâleur cadavérique>

debacle [dɪˈbɑkəl, -ˈbæ-] *n* : débâcle *f*, désastre *m*, fiasco *m*

debar [diˈbɑr] *vt* **-barred; -barring** : exclure, interdire à

debark [diˈbɑrk] → **disembark**

debase [diˈbeɪs] *vt* **-based; -basing** : avilir, abaisser, dégrader

debasement [diˈbeɪsmənt] *n* : avilissement *m*, abaissement *m*, dégradation *f*

debatable [dɪˈbeɪţəbəl] *adj* : discutable

debate[1] [dɪˈbeɪt] *v* **-bated; -bating** *vt* : débattre, discuter — *vi* : discuter

debate[2] *n* : débat *m*, discussion *f*

debauch [dɪˈbɔtʃ] *vt* : débaucher

debauchery [dɪˈbɔtʃəri] *n, pl* **-eries** : débauche *f*

debilitate [dɪˈbɪləˌteɪt] *vt* **-tated; -tating** : débiliter, affaiblir

debility [dɪˈbɪləţi] *n, pl* **-ties** : débilité *f*

debit[1] [ˈdɛbɪt] *vt* : débiter (un compte bancaire, etc.)

debit[2] *n* : débit

debonair [ˌdɛbəˈnær] *adj* : élégant, raffiné

debris [dəˈbriː, deɪ-; ˈdeɪˌbriː] *n, pl* **-bris** [-ˈbriːz, -ˌbriːz] **1** RUBBLE : décombres *mpl*, débris *mpl* **2** RUBBISH : déchets *mpl*

debt [ˈdɛt] *n* : dette *f*, créance *f*

debtor [ˈdɛţər] *n* : débiteur *m*, -trice *f*

debug [diˈbʌg] *vt* **-bugged; -bugging** : déboguer

debunk [diˈbʌŋk] *vt* : discréditer, démentir

debut[1] [deɪˈbjuː, ˈdeɪˌbjuː] *vi* : débuter

debut[2] *n* **1** : débuts *mpl* <my acting debut : mes débuts sur la scène> **2** : entrée *f* dans le monde

debutante [ˈdɛbjʊˌtɑnt] *n* : débutante *f*

decade [ˈdɛˌkeɪd, dɛˈkeɪd] *n* : décennie *f*

decadence [ˈdɛkədənts] *n* : décadence *f*

decadent [ˈdɛkədənt] *adj* : décadent

decal [ˈdiːˌkæl, diˈkæl] *n* : décalcomanie *f*

decamp [diˈkæmp] *vi* : décamper, déguerpir

decant [diˈkænt] *vt* : transvaser (un liquide), décanter (du vin)

decanter [diˈkæntər] *n* : carafe *f*

decapitate [diˈkæpəˌteɪt] *vt* **-tated; -tating** : décapiter

decay[1] [diˈkeɪ] *vi* **1** DETERIORATE : se détériorer, se délabrer (se dit d'un édifice) **2** DECOMPOSE, ROT : se décomposer, se putréfier **3** : se carier (se dit d'une dent)

decay[2] *n* **1** DETERIORATION : délabrement *f*, pourrissement *m* **2** DECOMPOSITION, ROTTING : décomposition *f* **3** *or* **tooth decay** : carie *f* (dentaire)

decease[1] [diˈsiːs] *vi* **-ceased; -ceasing** : décéder

decease[2] *n* DEATH : décès *m*

deceit [dɪˈsiːt] *n* **1** DUPLICITY : duplicité *f*, fausseté *f* **2** TRICK : tromperie *f*

deceitful [dɪˈsiːtfəl] *adj* **1** MISLEADING : trompeur **2** DISHONEST : malhonnête

deceitfully [dɪˈsiːtfəli] *adv* : de façon malhonnête, trompeusement

deceive [dɪˈsiːv] *v* **-ceived; -ceiving** *vt* : tromper, leurrer — *vi* : donner une fausse impression

deceiver [dɪˈsiːvər] *n* : trompeur *m*, -peuse *f*

decelerate [diˈsɛləˌreɪt] *v* **-ated; -ating** : ralentir

December [diˈsɛmbər] *n* : décembre *m*

decency [ˈdisəntsi] *n, pl* **-cies** : décence *f*, bienséance f

decent [ˈdiːsənt] *adj* **1** PROPER, SUITABLE : décent, convenable, approprié **2** CLOTHED : habillé **3** ADEQUATE : acceptable, suffisant **4** KIND : gentil, sympathique

decently [ˈdiːsəntli] *adv* **1** PROPERLY : décemment, convenablement **2** ADEQUATELY : acceptablement

deception [dɪˈsɛpʃən] *n* **1** : tromperie *f*, duperie *f* **2** FRAUD : fraude *f*

deceptive [dɪˈsɛptɪv] *adj* : trompeur

deceptively [dɪˈsɛptɪvli] *adv* : trompeusement <it's deceptively small : c'est plus grand qu'il n'y paraît>

decibel [ˈdɛsəbəl, -ˌbɛl] *n* : décibel *m*

decide [dɪˈsaɪd] *v* **-cided; -ciding** *vt* **1** : décider <I decided to buy a hat : j'ai décidé d'acheter un chapeau> **2** DETERMINE, SETTLE : décider de, trancher **3** PERSUADE : décider — *vi* : se décider

decided [dɪ'saɪdəd] *adj* **1** RESOLUTE : décidé, ferme **2** UNQUESTIONABLE : incontestable, certain

decidedly [dɪ'saɪdədli] *adv* **1** RESOLUTELY : résolument **2** UNQUESTIONABLY : vraiment, décidément

deciduous [dɪ'sɪdʒuəs] *adj* : caduc <deciduous tree : arbre à feuilles caduques>

decimal[1] ['dɛsəməl] *adj* : décimal

decimal[2] *n* : décimale *f*

decimal point *n* : virgule *f*

decipher [di'saɪfər] *vt* : déchiffrer

decision [dɪ'sɪʒən] *n* : décision *f*

decisive [dɪ'saɪsɪv] *adj* **1** DECIDING : décisif <the decisive vote : le vote décisif> **2** RESOLUTE : résolu, déterminé **3** CONCLUSIVE : définitif, décisif

deck[1] ['dɛk] *vt* **1** FLOOR : envoyer par terre **2 to deck out** : orner, décorer, parer (une personne)

deck[2] *n* **1** : pont *m* (d'un navire) **2** *or* **deck of cards** : jeu *m* de cartes **3** TERRACE : terrasse *f* (d'une maison, etc.)

declaim [di'kleɪm] *v* : déclamer

declaration [ˌdɛklə'reɪʃən] *n* : déclaration *f*

declarative [dɪ'klærət̬ɪv, -klɛr-] *adj* : déclaratif

declare [dɪ'klær] *vt* **-clared; -claring** **1** ANNOUNCE : déclarer, annoncer <to declare war : déclarer la guerre> **2** AFFIRM : déclarer, maintenir

declension [dɪ'klɛntʃən] *n* : déclinaison *f* (en grammaire)

decline[1] [dɪ'klaɪn] *v* **-clined; -clining** *vt* **1** REFUSE : décliner, refuser **2** : décliner (un nom) — *vi* **1** DESCEND, DROP : descendre, baisser **2** WANE : être sur le déclin **3** DETERIORATE, WEAKEN : s'affaiblir, dépérir **4** REFUSE : refuser

decline[2] *n* **1** DETERIORATION : déclin *m* **2** LOWERING : baisse *f*, chute *f* (des prix) **3** SLOPE : pente *f*, descente *f*

decode [di'ko:d] *vt* **-coded; -coding** : décoder, déchiffrer

decompose [ˌdi:kəm'po:z] *vt* **-posed; -posing** : décomposer — *vi* : se décomposer

decomposition [ˌdi:ˌkɑmpə'zɪʃən] *n* : décomposition *f*

decongestant [ˌdi:kən'dʒɛstənt] *n* : décongestif *m*, décongestionnant *m*

decor *or* **décor** [deɪ'kɔr, 'deɪˌkɔr] *n* : décor *m*

decorate ['dɛkəˌreɪt] *vt* **-rated; -rating** **1** ADORN : décorer, embellir **2** : décorer <decorated for bravery : décoré pour son courage>

decoration [ˌdɛkə'reɪʃən] *n* : décoration *f*

decorative ['dɛkərət̬ɪv, -ˌreɪ-] *adj* : décoratif, ornemental

decorator ['dɛkəˌreɪt̬ər] *n* : décorateur *m*, -trice *f*

decorum [dɪ'ko:rəm, -kɔr-] *n* : bienséance *f*, décorum *m*

decoy[1] ['diˌkɔɪ] *vt* : attirer avec un appeau

decoy[2] *n* : appeau *m*, leurre *m*

decrease[1] [di'kri:s] *v* **-creased; -creasing** *vi* : diminuer, décroître — *vt* REDUCE : diminuer, réduire

decrease[2] ['diˌkris, di'-] *n* : diminution *f*, baisse *f*

decree[1] [di'kri:] *vt* **-creed; -creeing** : décréter

decree[2] *n* : décret *m*

decrepit [dɪ'krɛpɪt] *adj* **1** FEEBLE : décrépit **2** DILAPIDATED : délabré, en ruine

decry [dɪ'kraɪ] *vt* **-cried; -crying** : décrier, dénigrer

dedicate ['dɛdɪˌkeɪt] *vt* **-cated; -cating** **1** DEVOTE : dédier, consacrer **2** : dédier <she dedicated the book to her daughter : elle a dédié le livre à sa fille>

dedication [dɛdɪ'keɪʃən] *n* **1** DEVOTION : dévouement *m* **2** INSCRIPTION : dédicace *f* **3** CONSECRATION : consécration *f* (d'une église, etc.)

deduce [dɪ'du:s, -'dju:s] *vt* **-duced; -ducing** : déduire, inférer

deduct [dɪ'dʌkt] *vt* : déduire, prélever

deductible [dɪ'dʌktəbəl] *adj* : déductible

deduction [dɪ'dʌkʃən] *n* **1** SUBTRACTION : déduction *f* **2** CONCLUSION : déduction *f*, raisonnement *m* déductif

deed[1] ['di:d] *vt* : transférer (par acte notarié)

deed[2] *n* **1** ACT : action *f* **2** FEAT : exploit *m* **3** : acte *m* notarié, titre *m* de propriété

deem ['di:m] *vt* CONSIDER : juger, estimer, considérer

deep[1] ['di:p] *adj* **1** : profond <a deep well : un puits profond> **2** WIDE : large, profond **3** ENGROSSED : préoccupé, absorbé <deep in thought : préoccupé par ses pensées> **4** LOW : grave, profond <a deep voice : une voix profonde> **5** DARK : intense <a deep blue : un bleu intense> **6** INTENSE, PROFOUND : profond <a deep insight : un aperçu profond>

deep[2] *n* **1** : cœur *m*, profondeur *f* <in the deep of winter : au plus profond de l'hiver, au cœur de l'hiver> **2 the deep** : l'océan *m*

deepen ['di:pən] *vt* **1** : approfondir **2** INTENSIFY : intensifier, augmenter — *vi* **1** : devenir plus profond **2** INTENSIFY : augmenter, s'intensifier

deeply ['di:pli] *adv* : profondément

deep–seated ['dip'sit̬əd] *adj* : fermement établi, profondément enraciné

deer ['dɪr] *ns & pl* : cerf *m*, chevreuil *m*, biche *f*

deerskin ['dɪrˌskɪn] *n* : peau *f* de daim

deface [dɪ'feɪs] *vt* **-faced; -facing** : abîmer, dégrader, défigurer

defamation [ˌdɛfəˈmeɪʃən] *n* : diffamation *f*
defamatory [dɪˈfæməˌtori] *adj* : diffamatoire
defame [dɪˈfeɪm] *vt* **-famed; -faming** : diffamer
default[1] [dɪˈfɔlt, ˈdiːˌfɔlt] *vi* **1** : ne pas s'acquitter (se dit d'une dette), ne pas régler (se dit d'un compte) **2** : manquer de comparaître (devant le tribunal)
default[2] *n* **1** : non-paiement *m* (d'une dette) **2** : non-comparution *f* (en cour) **3 by ~** : par forfait
defeat[1] [dɪˈfiːt] *vt* **1** BEAT : battre, vaincre **2** FRUSTRATE : faire échouer, mettre fin à (un plan, une ambition)
defeat[2] *n* : défaite *f*, échec *m*
defecate [ˈdɛfɪˌkeɪt] *vi* **-cated; -cating** : déféquer
defect[1] [dɪˈfɛkt] *vi* : faire défection, s'enfuir
defect[2] [ˈdiːˌfɛkt, diˈfɛkt] *n* : défaut *m*
defection [dɪˈfɛkʃən] *n* : défection *f*
defective [dɪˈfɛktɪv] *adj* **1** FAULTY : défectueux **2** DEFICIENT : déficient <defective eyesight : yeux déficients>
defector [dɪˈfɛktər] *n* : transfuge *mf*
defence *Brit* → **defense**
defend [dɪˈfɛnd] *vt* : défendre
defendant [dɪˈfɛndənt] *n* : défendeur *m*, -deresse *f;* intimé *m*, -mée *f* (en appel)
defender [dɪˈfɛndər] *n* **1** ADVOCATE : défenseur *m*, avocat *m* **2** : défenseur *m* (aux sports)
defense *or Brit* **defence** [dɪˈfɛnts, ˈdiːˌfɛnts] *n* : défense *f*
defenseless *or Brit* **defenceless** [dɪˈfɛntsləs] *adj* : sans défense
defensive[1] [dɪˈfɛntsɪv] *adj* : défensif
defensive[2] *n* : défensive *f* <to be on the defensive : se tenir sur la défensive>
defer [dɪˈfər] *v* **-ferred; -ferring** *vt* POSTPONE : remettre, reporter — *vi* **to defer to** : s'en remettre à, déférer à
deference [ˈdɛfərənts] *n* : déférence *f*, égard *m* <in deference to his family : par égard pour sa famille>
deferential [ˌdɛfəˈrɛntʃəl] *adj* : déférent, respectueux
deferment [dɪˈfərmənt] *n* : report *m*, renvoi *m*
defiance [dɪˈfaɪənts] *n* **1** : défi *m* **2 in defiance of** : au mépris de
defiant [dɪˈfaɪənt] *adj* : provocant, de défi
deficiency [dɪˈfɪʃəntsi] *n, pl* **-cies 1** INADEQUACY : manque *m*, insuffisance *f* **2** FLAW : faille *f*, faiblesse *f*
deficient [dɪˈfɪʃənt] *adj* **1** INADEQUATE : insuffisant **2** FAULTY : défectueux
deficit [ˈdɛfəsɪt] *n* : déficit *m*
defile [dɪˈfaɪl] *vt* **-filed; -filing 1** SULLY : souiller **2** PROFANE : profaner, déshonorer
defilement [dɪˈfaɪlmənt] *n* **1** DEBASEMENT : souillure *f* **2** DESECRATION : profanation *f*
define [dɪˈfaɪn] *vt* **-fined; -fining 1** BOUND : définir, délimiter **2** CLARIFY : clarifier, définir <the issues are not well defined : les problèmes ne sont pas clairs> **3** : définir (un mot)
definite [ˈdɛfənɪt] *adj* **1** CLEAR, DISTINCT : précis, déterminé, net **2** CERTAIN : certain, sûr <is that definite? : c'est sûr?> **3** : défini (en grammaire) <definite article : article défini>
definitely [ˈdɛfənɪtli] *adv* **1** CERTAINLY : certainement, sans aucun doute **2** APPRECIABLY : sensiblement, nettement **3** CATEGORICALLY : absolument, catégoriquement <definitely! : bien sûr!>
definition [ˌdɛfəˈnɪʃən] *n* : définition *f*
definitive [dəˈfɪnət̬ɪv] *adj* **1** CONCLUSIVE : définitif, décisif **2** AUTHORITATIVE : qui fait autorité
deflate [dɪˈfleɪt] *v* **-flated; -flating** *vt* **1** : dégonfler (un ballon, etc.) **2** REDUCE : saper, miner (l'égo, la confiance) — *vi* : se dégonfler
deflation [dɪˈfleɪʃən] *n* **1** : dégonflement *m* (d'un ballon, etc.) **2** : déflation *f* (économique)
deflect [dɪˈflɛkt] *vt* : faire dévier, détourner — *vi* DEVIATE : dévier
deforest [diˈfɔrəst] *vt* : déboiser
deform [diˈfɔrm] *vt* : déformer
deformity [diˈfɔrmət̬i] *n, pl* **-ties** : difformité *f*
defraud [diˈfrɔd] *vt* : frauder, escroquer
defray [diˈfreɪ] *vt* : rembourser, couvrir (des coûts)
defrost [diˈfrɔst] *vt* **1** THAW : décongeler (des aliments) **2** : dégivrer (un réfrigérateur, etc.)
deft [ˈdɛft] *adj* : adroit, habile — **deftly** *adv*
defunct [dɪˈfʌŋkt] *adj* : défunt
defy [dɪˈfaɪ] *vt* **-fied; -fying 1** CHALLENGE : défier, braver **2** RESIST : résister à, s'opposer à <to defy all one's efforts : résister à tous les efforts>
degenerate[1] [dɪˈdʒɛnəˌreɪt] *vi* **-ated; -ating** : dégénérer, s'abâtardir
degenerate[2] [dɪˈdʒɛnərət] *adj* : dégénéré
degeneration [didʒɛnəˈreɪʃən] *n* : dégénérescence *f*
degradation [ˌdɛgrəˈdeɪʃən] *n* : dégradation *f*
degrade [dɪˈgreɪd] *vt* **-graded; -grading 1** : dégrader **2 to degrade oneself** : s'abaisser
degree [dɪˈgriː] *n* **1** AMOUNT, EXTENT : degré *m*, point *m*, mesure *f* <to a certain degree : à un certain degré, jusqu'à un certain point> **2** : diplôme *m* <college degree : diplôme universitaire> **3** : degré *m* (en physique, en mathématiques, etc.) **4 by degrees** : par degrés, petit à petit

dehydrate [di'haɪˌdreɪt] *v* **-drated; -drating** *vt* : déshydrater — *vi* : se déshydrater

dehydration [ˌdi:haɪ'dreɪʃən] *n* : déshydratation *f*

deice [ˌdi:'aɪs] *vt* **-iced; -icing** : dégivrer

deify ['di:əˌfaɪ, 'deɪ-] *vt* **-fied; -fying** : déifier

deign ['deɪn] *vt* : daigner, condescendre à

deity ['di:əṭi, 'deɪ-] *n, pl* **-ties 1** GOD, GODDESS : dieu *m*, déesse *f* **2 the Deity** : Dieu *m*

dejected [dɪ'dʒɛktəd] *adj* : découragé, abattu

dejection [dɪ'dʒɛkʃən] *n* : découragement *m*, abattement *m*

delay[1] [dɪ'leɪ] *vt* **1** POSTPONE : reporter, différer **2** HOLD UP : retarder, retenir <he delayed me for no reason : il m'a retenu sans raison>

delay[2] *n* **1** POSTPONEMENT : report *m* **2** HOLDUP : délai *m* <without further delay : sans plus tarder>

delectable [dɪ'lɛktəbəl] *adj* : délicieux

delegate[1] ['dɛlɪˌgeɪt] *vt* **-gated; -gating** : déléguer

delegate[2] ['dɛlɪgət, -ˌgeɪt] *n* : délégué *m*, -guée *f*

delegation [ˌdɛlə'geɪʃən] *n* : délégation *f*

delete [dɪ'li:t] *vt* **-leted; -leting** : supprimer, effacer

deletion [dɪ'li:ʃən] *n* : suppression *f*

deliberate[1] [dɪ'lɪbəˌreɪt] *v* **-ated; -ating** *vt* : délibérer sur, réfléchir sur — *vi* : délibérer, considérer

deliberate[2] [dɪ'lɪbərət] *adj* **1** CONSIDERED : délibéré, réfléchi **2** INTENTIONAL : délibéré, intentionnel **3** UNHURRIED : mesuré, posé

deliberately [dɪ'lɪbərətli] *adv* **1** INTENTIONALLY : délibérément, à dessein, exprès **2** STEADILY : de façon mesurée

deliberation [dɪˌlɪbə'reɪʃən] *n* **1** CONSIDERATION : délibération *f*, réflexion *f* **2** DISCUSSION : délibérations *fpl*, débats *mpl* **3** RESTRAINT : mesure *f*, manière *f* posée

delicacy ['dɛlɪkəsi] *n, pl* **-cies 1** : mets *m* délicat **2** FINENESS : délicatesse *f*, finesse *f* **3** FRAILTY : délicatesse *f*, fragilité *f*

delicate ['dɛlɪkət] *adj* **1** SUBTLE : délicat <a delicate fragrance : un parfum délicat> **2** DAINTY, FINE : délicat, fin **3** FRAGILE : fragile **4** SENSITIVE : délicat, sensible <a delicate situation : une question délicate>

delicately ['dɛlɪkətli] *adv* : délicatement, avec délicatesse

delicatessen [ˌdɛlɪkə'tɛsən] *n* : charcuterie *f*

delicious [dɪ'lɪʃəs] *adj* : délicieux

delight[1] [dɪ'laɪt] *vt* : réjouir, enchanter — *vi* **to delight in** : prendre plaisir à

delight[2] *n* **1** PLEASURE : plaisir *m*, joie *f* **2** : délice *m*, merveille *f* <my new car is a delight : ma nouvelle voiture est une merveille>

delightful [dɪ'laɪtfəl] *adj* : charmant, merveilleux, ravissant

delightfully [dɪ'laɪtfəli] *adv* : de façon charmante, merveilleusement

delineate [dɪ'lɪniˌeɪt] *vt* **-eated; -eating 1** SKETCH : tracer **2** PORTRAY : décrire, dépeindre

delinquency [dɪ'lɪŋkwəntsi] *n, pl* **-cies** : délinquance *f*

delinquent[1] [dɪ'lɪŋkwənt] *adj* **1** : délinquant <delinquent children : enfants délinquants> **2** OVERDUE : arriéré

delinquent[2] *n* : délinquant *m*, -quante *f*

delirious [dɪ'lɪriəs] *adj* : délirant, en délire

delirium [dɪ'lɪriəm] *n* : délire *m*

deliver [dɪ'lɪvər] *vt* **1** FREE : délivrer <deliver us from evil : délivre-nous de tout mal> **2** DISTRIBUTE : livrer **3** : mettre au monde (un enfant) **4** : faire, prononcer <to deliver a speech : prononcer un discours> **5** DEAL : porter, asséner <to deliver a blow : porter un coup>

deliverance [dɪ'lɪvərənts] *n* : délivrance *f*

delivery [dɪ'lɪvəri] *n, pl* **-eries 1** LIBERATION : délivrance *f* **2** DISTRIBUTION : livraison *f*, distribution *f* **3** CHILDBIRTH : accouchement *m* **4** SPEECH : élocution *f*, débit *m*

dell ['dɛl] *n* : vallon *m* (boisé)

delta ['dɛltə] *n* : delta *m*

delude [dɪ'lu:d] *vt* **-luded; -luding 1** : tromper, duper **2 to delude oneself** : se leurrer, se faire des illusions

deluge[1] ['dɛlˌju:dʒ, -ju:ʒ] *vt* **-uged; -uging 1** FLOOD : inonder **2** SWAMP : inonder, submerger <deluged with calls : inondé d'appels>

deluge[2] *n* : inondation *f*, déluge *m*

delusion [dɪ'lu:ʒən] *n* **1** : illusion *f* **2 delusions of grandeur** : la folie des grandeurs

deluxe [dɪ'lʌks, -lʊks] *adj* : de luxe, luxueux

delve ['dɛlv] *vi* **delved; delving 1** DIG : creuser **2 to delve into** : fouiller dans

demand[1] [dɪ'mænd] *vt* : exiger, réclamer

demand[2] *n* **1** REQUIREMENT : exigence *f* **2** CLAIM : réclamation *f*, revendication *f* **3** : demande *f* (en commerce) **4** → **supply**

demarcation [ˌdi:ˌmɑr'keɪʃən] *n* : démarcation *f*

demean [dɪ'mi:n] *vt* **1** : abaisser, rabaisser **2 to demean oneself** : s'abaisser

demeanor *or Brit* **demeanour** [dɪ'mi:nər] *n* **1** BEHAVIOR : comportement *m* **2** MANNER : air *m*, allure *f*, mine *f*

demented [dɪ'mɛntəd] *adj* : dément, fou

demerit [dɪ'mɛrət] *n* : démérite *m*

demigod ['dɛmi,gɑd, -,gɔd] *n* : demi-dieu *m*

demise [dɪ'maɪz] *n* **1** DEATH : mort *f*, décès *m* **2** END : fin *f*, mort *f* (d'une institution, etc.)

demitasse ['dɛmi,tæs, -,tɑs] *n* : tasse *f* de café noir

demobilize [di'mo:bə,laɪz-] *vt* **-lized; -lizing** : démobiliser

democracy [dɪ'mɑkrəsi] *n, pl* **-cies** : démocratie *f*

democrat ['dɛmə,kræt] *n* : démocrate *mf*

democratic [,dɛmə'kræṭɪk] *adj* : démocratique — **democratically** *adv*

demolish [di'mɑlɪʃ] *vt* **1** RAZE : démolir, raser **2** DESTROY : détruire, démolir (une théorie, etc.)

demolition [,dɛmə'lɪʃən, ,di:-] *n* : démolition *f*

demon ['di:mən] *n* : démon *m*

demonic [dɪ'mɑnɪk, di-] *adj* : diabolique

demonstrably [də'mɑn*t*strəbli] *adv* : manifestement

demonstrate ['dɛmən,streɪt] *v* **-strated; -strating** *vt* **1** SHOW : manifester, démontrer **2** EXPLAIN, PROVE : démontrer, établir **3** : faire une démonstration de — *vi* **1** : faire une démonstration **2** PROTEST : manifester, protester

demonstration [dɛmən'streɪʃən] *n* **1** : démonstration *f* **2** PROTEST : manifestation *f*

demonstrative [dɪ'mɑn*t*strəṭɪv] *adj* : démonstratif

demonstrator ['dɛmən,streɪṭər] *n* **1** : démonstrateur *m*, -trice *f* **2** PROTESTOR : manifestant *m*, -tante *f*

demoralize [dɪ'mɔrə,laɪz] *vt* **-ized; -izing** : démoraliser

demote [di'mo:t] *vt* **-moted; -moting** : rétrograder

demur [dɪ'mər] *vi* **-murred; -murring** : élever des objections, s'opposer

demure [dɪ'mjʊr] *adj* : modeste, réservé

den ['dɛn] *n* **1** LAIR : antre *m*, tanière *f* **2** HIDEOUT : repaire *m* <a den of iniquity : un lieu de perdition> **3** STUDY : petit salon *m*, petit bureau *m* de travail

denature [di'neɪtʃər] *vt* **-tured; -turing** : dénaturer

denial [di'naɪəl] *n* **1** DENYING : démenti *m*, dénégation *f* **2** REFUSAL : refus *m*, rejet *m* **3** DISAVOWAL : reniement *m*

denigrate ['dɛnɪ,greɪt] *vt* **-grated; -grating** : dénigrer

denim ['dɛnəm] *n* **1** : jean *m* **2 denims** *npl* JEANS : jean *m*, blue-jean *m*

denizen ['dɛnəzən] *n* : habitant *m*, -tante *f*

denomination [dɪ,nɑmə'neɪʃən] *n* **1** : confession *f* (religieuse) **2** DESIGNATION : dénomination *f* **3** VALUE : valeur *f* (de monnaie)

denominator [dɪ'nɑmə,neɪṭər] *n* : dénominateur *m*

denote [di'no:t] *vt* **-noted; -noting 1** INDICATE : dénoter **2** MEAN : signifier

denouement [,deɪ,nu:'mɑ:] *n* : dénouement *m*

denounce [dɪ'naʊn*t*s] *vt* **-nounced; -nouncing 1** CENSURE : dénoncer **2** ACCUSE : accuser

dense ['dɛn*t*s] *adj* **denser; -est 1** THICK : dense **2** STUPID : bête, obtus

densely ['dɛn*t*sli] *adv* : densément

density ['dɛn*t*səṭi] *n, pl* **-ties** : densité *f*

dent[1] ['dɛnt] *vt* : bosseler, poquer *Can fam* (une voiture), cabosser (un chapeau, etc.)

dent[2] *n* : bosse *f* (en métal), creux *m*

dental ['dɛntəl] *adj* : dentaire

dental floss *n* : fil *m* dentaire

dentifrice ['dɛntəfrɪs] *n* : dentifrice *m*, pâte *f* dentifrice

dentist ['dɛntɪst] *n* : dentiste *mf*

dentistry ['dɛntɪstri] *n* : dentisterie *f*

dentures ['dɛntʃərz] *npl* : dentier *m*

denude [di'nu:d, -'nju:d] *vt* **-nuded; -nuding** : dénuder

denunciation [dɪ,nʌn*t*si'eɪʃən] *n* : dénonciation *f*

deny [dɪ'naɪ] *vt* **-nied; -nying 1** REFUTE : démentir, nier <he denied the charges : il a démenti les accusations> **2** REPUDIATE : renier <to deny one's religion : renier sa religion> **3** REFUSE : refuser **4 to deny oneself** : se priver

deodorant [di'o:dərənt] *n* **1** : déodorant *m* **2** *or* **room deodorant** : désodorisant *m*

deodorize [di'o:də,raɪz] *vt* **-ized; -izing** : désodoriser

depart [dɪ'pɑrt] *vt* : quitter <to depart this life : quitter ce monde> — *vi* LEAVE : partir

department [dɪ'pɑrtmənt] *n* **1** DIVISION : ministère *m* (gouvernemental), service *m* (d'un hôpital, etc.), rayon *m* (d'un magasin) **2** FIELD : champ *m*, domaine *m* <it's not my department : ce n'est pas mon champ d'expertise>

departmental [dɪ,pɑrt'mɛntəl, ,di:-] *adj* : de service, de département

department store *n* : grand magasin *m*

departure [dɪ'pɑrtʃər] *n* **1** LEAVING : départ *m* **2** DEVIATION : écart *m*, déviation *f*, entorse *f* <a departure from procedure : un écart à la procédure>

depend [dɪ'pɛnd] *vi* **1** RELY : compter, se fier <depend on me! : comptez sur moi!> **2 to depend on** : dépendre de <success depends on hard work : le succès est le résultat d'un travail acharné> **3 depending on** : selon, dépendamment de *Can* <depending

on what happens : selon ce qui se passera>

dependable |dɪ'pɛndəbəl| *adj* : fiable, sûr

dependent[1] |dɪ'pɛndənt| *adj* : dépendant

dependent[2] *n* : personne *f* à charge

depict |dɪ'pɪkt| *vt* : dépeindre, décrire

deplete |dɪ'pli:t| *vt* **-pleted; -pleting** : épuiser, réduire

depletion |dɪ'pli:ʃən| *n* : diminution *f*, réduction *f*

deplorable |dɪ'plorəbəl| *adj* : déplorable, lamentable

deplore |dɪ'plor| *vt* **-plored; -ploring** : déplorer, regretter

deploy |dɪ'plɔɪ| *vt* : déployer

deployment |dɪ'plɔɪmənt| *n* : déploiement *m*

deport |dɪ'port| *vt* **1** EXPEL : déporter, expulser (d'un pays) **2 to deport oneself** BEHAVE : se comporter

deportment |dɪ'portmənt| *n* BEHAVIOR : comportement *m*

depose |dɪ'po:z| *vt* **-posed; -posing** : déposer (un souverain, etc.)

deposit[1] |dɪ'pazət| *vt* **-ited; -iting** : déposer

deposit[2] *n* **1** : dépôt *m* <a $500 deposit : un dépôt de 500$> **2** DOWN PAYMENT : acompte *m*, arrhes *fpl France* **3** : dépôt *m* (en géologie)

depositor |dɪ'pazət̬ər| *n* : déposant *m*, -sante *f*

depository |dɪ'pazə,tori| *n, pl* **-ries** : dépôt *m*, lieu *m* sûr

depot |*1 usu* 'dɛ,po:, *2 usu* 'di:-| *n* **1** WAREHOUSE : dépôt *m*, entrepôt *m* **2** STATION : gare *f* (ferroviaire), gare *f* d'autobus

deprave |dɪ'preɪv| *vt* **-praved; -praving** : dépraver, corrompre

depravity |dɪ'prævət̬i| *n, pl* **-ties** : dépravation *f*

depreciate |dɪ'pri:ʃi,eɪt| *v* **-ated; -ating** *vt* **1** DEVALUE : dévaluer **2** DISPARAGE : déprécier, dénigrer — *vi* : se déprécier (se dit d'une valeur)

depreciation |dɪ,priʃi'eɪʃən| *n* : dépréciation *f*

depress |dɪ'prɛs| *vt* **1** PRESS : appuyer sur **2** REDUCE : réduire, faire baisser (les ventes, les prix, etc.) **3** DISCOURAGE, SADDEN : déprimer, attrister **4** DEVALUE : dévaluer

depressant |dɪ'prɛsənt| *n* : dépresseur *m*

depressed |dɪ'prɛst| *adj* : déprimé, abattu

depressing |dɪ'prɛsɪŋ| *adj* : déprimant, décourageant

depression |dɪ'prɛʃən| *n* **1** : dépression *f* (en médecine) **2** : récession *f*, crise *f* <economic depression : crise économique> **3** HOLLOW : creux *m*, dépression *f*

deprivation |,dɛprə'veɪʃən| *n* : privation *f*

deprive |dɪ'praɪv| *vt* **-prived; -priving** : priver

depth |'dɛpθ| *n, pl* **depths 1** : profondeur *f* <the depth of a cupboard : la profondeur d'une armoire> **2** EXTENT : étendue *f* <the depth of his knowledge : l'étendue de ses connaissances> **3** INTENSITY : intensité *f* (de couleurs) **4 in the depths of** : au milieu de, au cœur de

deputize |'dɛpjʊ,taɪz| *vt* **-tized; -tizing** : députer

deputy |'dɛpjʊt̬i| *n, pl* **-ties** : député *m*, -tée *f*

derail |di'reɪl| *vt* : faire dérailler — *vi* : dérailler

derailment |di'reɪlmənt| *n* : déraillement *m*

derange |dɪ'reɪndʒ| *vt* **-ranged; -ranging 1** DISARRANGE : déranger, déplacer **2** CRAZE : rendre fou

derangement |dɪ'reɪndʒmənt| *n* **1** DISARRAY : confusion *f*, désordre *m* **2** INSANITY : aliénation *f* mentale

derby |'dərbi| *n, pl* **-bies 1** : derby *m* (course de chevaux) **2** *or* **derby hat** : chapeau *m* melon

deregulate |di'rɛgjʊ,leɪt| *vt* **-lated; -lating** : déréglementer

deregulation |di,rɛgjʊ'leɪʃən| *n* : déréglementation *f*

derelict[1] |'dɛrə,lɪkt| *adj* **1** ABANDONED : abandonné **2** NEGLIGENT : négligent, insouciant

derelict[2] *n* **1** : propriété *f* abandonnée, navire *m* abandonné **2** VAGRANT : vagabond *m*, -bonde *f*; clochard *m*, -charde *f*

deride |dɪ'raɪd| *vt* **-rided; -riding** : railler, tourner en dérision

derision |dɪ'rɪʒən| *n* : dérision *f*

derisive |dɪ'raɪsɪv| *adj* : moqueur, railleur

derivation |,dɛrə'veɪʃən| *n* : dérivation *f*

derivative[1] |dɪ'rɪvət̬ɪv| *adj* : dérivé

derivative[2] *n* : dérivé *m*

derive |dɪ'raɪv| *v* **-rived; -riving** *vt* **1** OBTAIN : tirer, trouver **2** DEDUCE : déduire, dériver de — *vi* **to derive from** : découler de, provenir de

dermatologist |,dərmə'talədʒɪst| *n* : dermatologue *mf*

dermatology |,dərmə'talədʒi| *n* : dermatologie *f*

derogatory |dɪ'ragə,tori| *adj* : désobligeant

derrick |'dɛrɪk| *n* **1** CRANE : grue *f* **2** : tour *f* de forage (pour le pétrole)

descend |dɪ'sɛnd| *vt* : descendre — *vi* **1** : descendre <she descended from the train : elle est descendue du train> **2** DERIVE : dériver, provenir <to be descended from : descendre de> **3** INCLINE : descendre **4** STOOP : s'abaisser, descendre (au niveau de qqn) **5 to descend upon** : se précipiter sur, s'élancer vers

descendant[1] *or* **descendent** |dɪ'sɛndənt| *adj* : descendant
descendant[2] *or* **descendent** *n* : descendant *m*, -dante *f*
descent |dɪ'sɛnt| *n* **1** : descente *f* <the descent of the airplane : la descente de l'avion> **2** LINEAGE : origine *f*, descendance *f* **3** DECLINE, SLOPE : descente *f* **4** ATTACK, INRUSH : descente *f*, irruption *f*
describe |dɪ'skraɪb| *vt* **-scribed; -scribing** : décrire
description |dɪ'skrɪpʃən| *n* : description *f*
descriptive |dɪ'skrɪptɪv| *adj* : descriptif
desecrate |'dɛsɪˌkreɪt| *vt* **-crated; -crating** : profaner
desecration |ˌdɛsɪ'kreɪʃən| *n* : profanation *f*
desegregate |di'sɛgrəˌgeɪt| *vt* **-gated; -gating** : éliminer la ségrégation raciale dans
desegregation |diˌsɛgrə'geɪʃən| *n* : déségrégation *f*
desert[1] |dɪ'zərt| *vt* : abandonner (une personne ou un lieu), déserter (une cause) — *vi* : déserter
desert[2] |'dɛzərt| *adj* : désert <a desert isle : une île déserte>
desert[3] *n* **1** |'dɛzərt| : désert *m* **2** |dɪ'zərt| → **deserts**
deserter |dɪ'zərṭər| *n* : déserteur *m*
desertion |dɪ'zərʃən| *n* : désertion *f*
deserts |dɪ'zərts| *npl* **to get one's just deserts** : avoir ce que l'on mérite
deserve |dɪ'zərv| *vt* **-served; -serving** : mériter
desiccate |'dɛsɪˌkeɪt| *vt* **-cated; -cating** : sécher, dessécher
design[1] |dɪ'zaɪn| *vt* **1** DEVISE : concevoir, élaborer **2** DRAW, SKETCH : dessiner **3** INTEND : concevoir, destiner <a book designed for students : un livre destiné pour les étudiants>
design[2] *n* **1** CONCEPTION : conception *f*, élaboration *f* **2** PLAN : plan *m*, projet *m* **3** PURPOSE : dessein *m*, intention *f* <by design : à dessein, exprès> **4** SKETCH : dessin *m*, croquis *m* **5** PATTERN : motif *m*
designate |'dɛzɪgˌneɪt| *vt* **-nated; -nating 1** INDICATE : indiquer, montrer **2** APPOINT : nommer, désigner
designation |ˌdɛzɪg'neɪʃən| *n* **1** APPOINTMENT : nomination *f*, désignation *f* **2** NAME : désignation *f*, dénomination *f*
designer |də'zaɪnər| *n* **1** : concepteur *m*, -trice *f*; dessinateur *m*, -trice *f* **2** *or* **fashion designer** : designer *m*, couturier *m*
desirable |dɪ'zaɪrəbəl| *adj* **1** ATTRACTIVE : désirable, enviable **2** ADVISABLE : désirable, souhaitable
desire[1] |dɪ'zaɪr| *vt* **-sired; -siring 1** WANT : désirer, avoir envie de **2** REQUEST : demander
desire[2] *n* **1** LONGING : désir *m*, envie *f* **2** REQUEST : demande *f*, requête *f*
desist |dɪ'sɪst| *vi* : cesser, s'arrêter
desk |'dɛsk| *n* : bureau *m*, pupitre *m* (d'un élève)
desolate[1] |'dɛsəˌleɪt, -zə-| *vt* **-lated; -lating** RAVAGE : dévaster, ravager
desolate[2] |'dɛsələt, -zə-| *adj* **1** BARREN : désolé, désert <a desolate landscape : un paysage désert> **2** GLOOMY : morne, sombre
desolation |'dɛsə'leɪʃən, -zə-| *n* **1** BARRENNESS : désolation *f* **2** GRIEF : affliction *f*, chagrin *m*
despair[1] |dɪ'spær| *vi* : désespérer, perdre espoir
despair[2] *n* : désespoir *m*
desperate |'dɛspərət| *adj* : désespéré — **desperately** *adv*
desperation |ˌdɛspə'reɪʃən| *n* : désespoir *m*
despicable |dɪ'spɪkəbəl, 'dɛspɪ-| *adj* : ignoble, méprisable
despise |dɪ'spaɪz| *vt* **-spised; -spising** : mépriser, détester
despite |də'spaɪt| *prep* : malgré, en dépit de
despoil |də'spɔɪl| *vt* : dépouiller, spolier
despondency |dɪ'spɑndəntsi| *n* : abattement *m*, découragement *m*
despondent |dɪ'spɑndənt| *adj* : abattu, découragé
despot |'dɛspət, -ˌpɑt| *n* : despote *m*
despotic |dəs'pɑṭɪk| *adj* : despotique, tyrannique
despotism |'dɛspə'tɪzəm| *n* : despotisme *m*
dessert |dɪ'zərt| *n* : dessert *m*
destination |ˌdɛstɪ'neɪʃən| *n* : destination *f*
destined |'dɛstənd| *adj* **1** FATED : prédestiné **2** BOUND : destiné, en route <destined for Quebec : à destination de Québec>
destiny |'dɛstəni| *n, pl* **-nies** : destin *m*, destinée *f*
destitute |'dɛstəˌtu:t| *adj* **1** LACKING : dépourvu, dénué <a lake destitute of fish : un lac dépourvu de poissons> **2** POOR : sans ressources, indigent
destitution |'dɛstə'tu:ʃən, -'tju:-| *n* : misère *f*, indigence *f*
destroy |dɪ'strɔɪ| *vt* **1** RUIN : détruire **2** KILL : détruire, anéantir
destroyer |dɪ'strɔɪər| *n* **1** : destructeur *m*, -trice *f* **2** WARSHIP : contre-torpilleur *m*
destructible |dɪ'strʌktəbəl| *adj* : destructible
destruction |dɪ'strʌkʃən| *n* : destruction *f*
destructive |dɪ'strʌktɪv| *adj* : destructeur, destructif
desultory |'dɛsəlˌtori| *adj* : décousu, sans suite

detach [dɪ'tætʃ] *vt* **1** SEPARATE : détacher, séparer **2 to detach oneself** : se détacher
detached [dɪ'tætʃt] *adj* **1** SEPARATE : détaché, séparé **2** ALOOF : distant, indifférent **3** IMPARTIAL : objectif, désintéressé
detachment [dɪ'tætʃmənt] *n* **1** SEPARATION : séparation *f* **2** ALOOFNESS : détachement *m*, indifférence *f* **3** IMPARTIALITY : impartialité *f* **4** : détachement *m* (militaire)
detail[1] [dɪ'teɪl, 'di:ˌteɪl] *vt* : détailler, énumérer
detail[2] *n* **1** : détail *m* <to go into details : rentrer dans les détails> **2** : détachement *m* (militaire)
detain [dɪ'teɪn] *vt* **1** : détenir (un prisonnier) **2** DELAY : retenir, retarder
detect [dɪ'tɛkt] *vt* : détecter, déceler, découvrir
detection [dɪ'tɛkʃən] *n* : détection *f*, découverte *f*
detective [dɪ'tɛktɪv] *n* : détective *mf* <private detective : détective privé>
detector [dɪ'tɛktər] *n* : détecteur *m*
detention [dɪ'tɛntʃən] *n* : détention *f*
deter [dɪ'tər] *vt* **-terred; -terring** : dissuader, décourager
detergent [dɪ'tərdʒənt] *n* : détergent *m*
deteriorate [dɪ'tɪriəˌreɪt] *vi* **-rated; -rating** : se détériorer, se dégrader
deterioration [diˌtɪriə'reɪʃən] *n* : détérioration *f*
determination [dɪˌtərmə'neɪʃən] *n* **1** DECISION : décision *f*, jugement *m* **2** RESOLVE : détermination *f*, résolution *f*
determine [dɪ'tərmən] *vt* **-mined; -mining 1** FIND OUT : déterminer, découvrir **2** FIX, SETTLE : fixer, déterminer **3** RESOLVE : décider **4** CAUSE, GOVERN : décider de, déterminer
determined [di'tərmənd] *adj* RESOLUTE : déterminé, résolu
deterrence [dɪ'tərənts, -'tɛr-] *n* : dissuasion *f*
deterrent[1] [dɪ'tərənt] *adj* : dissuasif
deterrent[2] *n* : moyen *m* de dissuasion
detest [dɪ'tɛst] *vt* : détester, haïr
detestable [dɪ'tɛstəbəl] *adj* : détestable
dethrone [di'θro:n] *vt* **-throned; -throning** : détrôner
detonate ['dɛtənˌeɪt] *v* **-nated; -nating** *vt* : faire détoner — *vi* EXPLODE : détoner
detonation [ˌdɛtən'eɪʃən, 'dɛtən-] *n* : détonation *f*, explosion *f*
detour[1] ['di:ˌtʊr, di'tʊr] *vt* DIVERT : détourner, dévier — *vi* : faire un détour
detour[2] *n* : détour *m*
detract [dɪ'trækt] *vt* : détourner <to detract attention : détourner l'attention> — *vi* **to detract from** : diminuer, porter atteinte à
detriment ['dɛtrəmənt] *n* : détriment *m*, préjudice *m*
detrimental [ˌdɛtrə'mɛntəl] *adj* : nuisible, préjudiciable
devaluation [diˌvæljʊ'eɪʃən] *n* : dévaluation *f*
devalue [di'vælˌju:] *vt* : dévaluer
devastate ['dɛvəˌsteɪt] *vt* **-tated; -tating** : dévaster, ravager
devastation [ˌdɛvə'steɪʃən] *n* : dévastation *f*
develop [dɪ'vɛləp] *vt* **1** FOSTER, PERFECT : mettre au point, développer, cultiver **2** EXPLOIT : développer, exploiter, mettre en valeur (des terres, etc.) **3** : développer (un film) **4** CONTRACT : contracter (une maladie) **5** ACQUIRE : développer, acquérir <he acquired a taste for olives : il a développé un goût pour les olives> — *vi* **1** GROW : se développer, grandir **2** HAPPEN : se produire, se manifester **3** UNFOLD : se développer, se dérouler
developing [dɪ'vɛləpɪŋ] *adj* : en expansion <developing countries : pays en expansion>
development [dɪ'vɛləpmənt] *n* **1** FORMATION, GROWTH : développement *m*, formation *f*, expansion *f* **2** : exploitation *f*, mise *f* en valeur (de ressources) **3** INCIDENT : événement *m*, fait *m* nouveau **4** *or* **housing development** : ensemble *m* résidentiel
deviant ['di:viənt] *adj* : déviant
deviate ['di:viˌeɪt] *vi* **-ated; -ating** : dévier, s'écarter
deviation [ˌdi:vi'eɪʃən] *n* : déviation *f*
device [dɪ'vaɪs] *n* **1** MECHANISM : appareil *m*, dispositif *m*, mécanisme *m* **2** SCHEME : ruse *f*, stratagème *m* **3 to leave s.o. to their own devices** : laisser qqn se débrouiller tout seul
devil[1] ['dɛvəl] *vt* **-iled** *or* **-illed; -iling** *or* **-illing 1** : assaisonner avec des épices fortes <deviled eggs : œufs à la diable> **2** PESTER : ennuyer, agacer
devil[2] *n* **1** DEMON : diable *m*, démon *m* **2 the Devil** : le Démon *m*, Satan *m* **3** : monstre *m*, démon *m* <what a little devil! : quel petit monstre!>
devilish ['dɛvəlɪʃ] *adj* : diabolique
devious ['di:viəs] *adj* **1** CUNNING : sournois, astucieux **2** WINDING : tortueux, sinueux
devise [dɪ'vaɪz] *vt* **-vised; -vising 1** INVENT : inventer, concevoir **2** PLOT : manigancer
devoid [dɪ'vɔɪd] *adj* **~ of** : dépourvu de, dénué de
devote [dɪ'vo:t] *vt* **-voted; -voting 1** DEDICATE : consacrer, vouer **2 to devote oneself to** : se consacrer à
devoted [dɪ'vo:təd] *adj* **1** FAITHFUL : dévoué, fidèle **2 to be devoted to** : être très attaché à
devotee [ˌdɛvə'ti:, -'teɪ] *n* **1** ENTHUSIAST : passionné *m*, -née *f* (d'un sport, etc.) **2** FOLLOWER : adepte *mf*; partisan *m*, -sane *f*

devotion [dɪ'vo:ʃən] *n* **1** DEDICATION : dévouement *m* **2** PIETY : dévotion *f,* piété *f* **3 devotions** *npl* PRAYER : dévotions *fpl,* prières *fpl*

devour [dɪ'vaʊər] *vt* : dévorer

devout [dɪ'vaʊt] *adj* **1** PIOUS : dévot, pieux **2** EARNEST : fervent, ardent

devoutness [dɪ'vaʊtnəs] *n* : dévotion *f,* piété *f*

dew ['du:, 'dju:] *n* : rosée *f*

dewdrop ['du:ˌdrɑp, 'dju:-] *n* : goutte *f* de rosée

dewlap ['duˌlæp, 'dju-] *n* : fanon *m*

dexterity [dɛk'stɛrəṭi] *n, pl* **-ties** : dextérité *f,* adresse *f*

dexterous ['dɛkstrəs] *adj* : adroit, habile, agile

dextrose ['dɛkˌstro:s] *n* : dextrose *m*

diabetes [ˌdaɪə'bi:ṭiz] *n* : diabète *m*

diabetic[1] [ˌdaɪə'bɛṭɪk] *adj* : diabétique

diabetic[2] *n* : diabétique *mf*

diabolic [ˌdaɪə'bɑlɪk] *or* **diabolical** [-lɪkəl] *adj* : diabolique

diacritic [ˌdaɪə'krɪṭɪk] *n or* **diacritical mark** [ˌdaɪə'krɪṭɪkəl] : signe *m* diacritique

diadem ['daɪəˌdɛm, -dəm] *n* : diadème *m*

diagnose ['daɪɪgˌno:s, ˌdaɪɪg'no:s] *vt* **-nosed; -nosing** : diagnostiquer

diagnosis [ˌdaɪɪg'no:sɪs] *n, pl* **-noses** [-'no:ˌsi:z] : diagnostic *m*

diagnostic [ˌdaɪɪg'nɑstɪk] *adj* : diagnostique

diagonal[1] [daɪ'ægənəl] *adj* : diagonal

diagonal[2] *n* : diagonale *f*

diagram[1] ['daɪəˌgræm] *vt* **-grammed** *or* **-gramed; -gramming** *or* **-graming** : donner une représentation graphique de

diagram[2] *n* : diagramme *m,* schéma *m*

dial[1] ['daɪl] *vt* **-aled** *or* **-alled; -aling** *or* **-alling** : faire, composer (un numéro de téléphone)

dial[2] *n* : cadran *m* (d'une horloge, d'un téléphone), bouton *m* (d'une radio, etc.)

dialect ['daɪəˌlɛkt] *n* : dialecte *m*

dialogue ['daɪəˌlɔg] *n* : dialogue *m*

diameter [daɪ'æməṭər] *n* : diamètre *m*

diametric [ˌdaɪə'mɛtrɪk] *or* **diametrical** [-trɪkəl] *adj* : diamétral — **diametrically** [-trɪkəli] *adv*

diamond ['daɪmənd, 'daɪə-] *n* **1** : diamant *m* (pierre précieuse) **2** : losange *m* (forme géométrique) **3** : carreau *m* (aux cartes) **4** INFIELD : terrain *m* de baseball, losange *m Can*

diaper ['daɪpər, 'daɪə-] *n* : couche *f* (de bébé)

diaphragm ['daɪəˌfræm] *n* : diaphragme *m*

diarrhea *or Brit* **diarrhoea** [ˌdaɪə'ri:ə] *n* : diarrhée *f*

diary ['daɪəri:] *n, pl* **-ries** : journal *m* intime

diatribe ['daɪəˌtraɪb] *n* : diatribe *f*

dice[1] ['daɪs] *vt* **diced; dicing** CUBE : couper en dés

dice[2] *ns & pl* **1** → **die[2]** **2** : dé *m* (jeu) <to play dice : jouer aux dés>

dicker ['dɪkər] *vi* : marchander

dictate[1] ['dɪkˌteɪt] *vt* **-tated; -tating** : dicter

dictate[2] *n* : précepte *m,* ordre *m* <the dictates of conscience : la voix de la conscience>

dictation [dɪk'teɪʃən] *n* : dictée *f*

dictator ['dɪkˌteɪṭər] *n* : dictateur *m*

dictatorship [dɪk'teɪṭərˌʃɪp, 'dɪk,-] *n* : dictature *f*

diction ['dɪkʃən] *n* **1** WORDING : langage *m,* style *m* **2** ENUNCIATION : diction *f,* élocution *f*

dictionary ['dɪkʃəˌnɛri] *n, pl* **-naries** : dictionnaire *m*

did → **do**

didactic [daɪ'dæktɪk] *adj* : didactique

die[1] ['daɪ] *vi* **died** ['daɪd]; **dying** ['daɪɪŋ] **1** : mourir, décéder **2** *or* **to die down** SUBSIDE : tomber (se dit du vent, de la colère, etc.) **3** STOP : s'arrêter <the motor died : le moteur s'est arrêté> **4** LONG : mourir d'envie <I'm dying to go : je meurs d'envie d'y aller>

die[2] ['daɪ] *n, pl* **dice** ['daɪs] : dé *m* (à jouer)

die[3] *n, pl* **dies** ['daɪz] MOLD, STAMP : étampe *f,* matrice *f*

diesel ['di:zəl, -səl] *n* : diesel *m*

diet[1] ['daɪət] *vi* : suivre un régime

diet[2] *n* **1** NOURISHMENT : alimentation *f,* nourriture *f* <a balanced diet : une alimentation équilibrée> **2** : régime *m* <to be on a diet : être au régime>

dietary ['daɪəˌtɛri] *adj* : alimentaire, diététique

dietitian *or* **dietician** [daɪə'tɪʃən] *n* : diététicien *m,* -cienne *f*

differ ['dɪfər] *vi* **1** : différer, être différent **2** VARY : varier **3** DISAGREE : être en désaccord

difference ['dɪfrənts, 'dɪfərənts] *n* : différence *f*

different ['dɪfrənt, 'dɪfərənt] *adj* **1** DISSIMILAR : différent **2** OTHER : autre <that's different : c'est autre chose> **3** VARIOUS : divers, différent, plusieurs

differentiate [dɪfə'rɛntʃiˌeɪt] *v* **-ated; -ating** *vt* : différencier, distinguer — *vi* **to differentiate between** : faire la différence entre

differently ['dɪfrəntli, 'dɪfərəntli] *adv* : différemment, autrement

difficult ['dɪfɪˌkʌlt] *adj* : difficile

difficulty ['dɪfɪˌkʌlti] *n, pl* **-ties** : difficulté *f*

diffidence ['dɪfədənts] *n* **1** SHYNESS : timidité *f,* manque *m* d'assurance **2** RETICENCE : réserve *f,* réticence *f*

diffident ['dɪfədənt] *adj* **1** SHY : qui manque d'assurance, timide **2** RESERVED : réservé

diffuse[1] [dɪ'fju:z] *v* **-fused; -fusing** *vt* : diffuser — *vi* : se diffuser

diffuse[2] |dɪ'fju:s| *adj* **1** WORDY : verbeux, diffus **2** : diffus, non concentré (se dit de la lumière, etc.)

diffusion |dɪ'fju:ʒən| *n* : diffusion *f*

dig[1] |'dɪg| *v* **dug** |'dʌg|; **digging** *vt* **1** : creuser (un trou), bêcher (la terre) **2** *or* **to dig up** EXTRACT : arracher, extraire **3** POKE, THRUST : enfoncer <to dig s.o. in the ribs : donner un coup de coude dans les côtes de qqn> **4 to dig up** UNEARTH : déterrer — *vi* **1** EXCAVATE : creuser **2 to dig in** : se retrancher

dig[2] *n* **1** POKE : coup *m* de coude **2** GIBE : pointe *f*, remarque *f* blessante

digest[1] |'daɪ,dʒɛst, dɪ-| *vt* **1** : digérer (de la nourriture) **2** ASSIMILATE : assimiler, digérer **3** SUMMARIZE : résumer

digest[2] |'daɪ,dʒɛst| *n* : résumé *m*

digestible |daɪ'dʒɛstəbəl, dɪ-| *adj* : digestible

digestion |daɪ'dʒɛstʃən| *n* : digestion *f*

digestive |daɪ'dʒɛstʃən, dɪ-| *adj* : digestif <the digestive system : l'appareil digestif>

digit |'dɪdʒət| *n* **1** NUMERAL : chiffre *m* **2** FINGER : doigt *m* **3** TOE : orteil *m*

digital |'dɪdʒət̬əl| *adj* : digital

dignified |'dɪgnə,faɪd| *adj* : digne, plein de dignité

dignify |'dɪgnə,faɪ| *vt* **-fied; -fying** : donner de la dignité à

dignitary |'dɪgnə'tɛri| *n, pl* **-taries** : dignitaire *m*

dignity |'dɪgnət̬i| *n, pl* **-ties** : dignité *f*

digress |daɪ'grɛs, də-| *vi* : faire une digression, s'écarter

digression |daɪ'grɛʃən, də-| *n* : digression *f*

dike |'daɪk| *n* : digue *f*

dilapidated |də'læpə,deɪt̬əd| *adj* : délabré

dilapidation |də,læpə'deɪʃən| *n* : délabrement *m*

dilate |daɪ'leɪt, 'daɪ,leɪt| *v* **-lated; -lating** *vt* : dilater — *vi* : se dilater

dilemma |dɪ'lɛmə| *n* : dilemme *m*

dilettante |'dɪlə,tɑnt, -,tænt| *n, pl* **-tantes** *or* **-tanti** |-tɑnts, -tænts| : dilettante *mf*

diligence |'dɪlədʒən*t*s| *n* : assiduité *f*, application *f*

diligent |'dɪlədʒənt| *adj* : assidu, appliqué

diligently |'dɪlədʒəntli| *adv* : assidûment, avec zèle

dill |'dɪl| *n* : aneth *m*

dillydally |'dɪli,dæli| *vi* **-lied; -lying** : traîner, lambiner *fam*, farfiner *Can fam*, niaiser *Can fam*

dilute |daɪ'lu:t, də-| *vt* **-luted; -luting** : diluer

dilution |daɪ'lu:ʃən, də-| *n* : dilution *f*

dim[1] |'dɪm| *v* **dimmed; dimming** *vt* : baisser (les lumières), ternir (des couleurs, etc.), affaiblir (des sons), effacer (des souvenirs) — *vi* : baisser, se ternir, s'effacer, s'affaiblir

dim[2] *adj* **dimmer; dimmest 1** DARK : sombre **2** FAINT : faible (se dit de la lumière), terne (se dit des couleurs, etc.), vague (se dit des sons, des formes, de la mémoire)

dime |'daɪm| *n* : pièce *f* de dix cents

dimension |də'mɛntʃən, daɪ-| *n* **1** : dimension *f* **2 dimensions** *npl* SCOPE : étendue *f*, ampleur *f*

diminish |də'mɪnɪʃ| *vt* REDUCE : diminuer, réduire, amoindrir — *vi* DWINDLE : diminuer, se réduire

diminutive |də'mɪnjət̬ɪv| *adj* : minuscule

dimly |'dɪmli| *adv* **1** : sombrement <dimly lit : sombrement éclairé> **2** FAINTLY : vaguement, indistinctement

dimmer |'dɪmər| *n* : rhéostat *m* (d'une lumière)

dimple |'dɪmpəl| *n* : fossette *f*

din |'dɪn| *n* : vacarme *m*, tapage *m*

dine |'daɪn| *vi* **dined; dining** : dîner

diner |'daɪnər| *n* **1** : dîneur *m*, -neuse *f* **2** : wagon-restaurant *m* (d'un train) **3** : petit restaurant *m*

dinghy |'dɪŋi, 'dɪŋgi, 'dɪŋki| *n, pl* **-ghies** : petit canot *m*

dingy |'dɪndʒi| *adj* **dingier; -est 1** DIRTY : malpropre, sale **2** SHABBY : minable, miteux

dinner |'dɪnər| *n* : dîner *m*

dinosaur |'daɪnə,sɔr| *n* : dinosaure *m*

dint |'dɪnt| *n* **by dint of** : à force de

diocese |'daɪəsəs, -,si:z, -,si:s| *n, pl* **-ceses** |'daɪəsəzəz| : diocèse *m*

dip[1] |'dɪp| *v* **dipped; dipping** *vt* **1** PLUNGE : plonger, tremper **2** LADLE : servir avec une louche — *vi* **1** DESCEND, DROP : baisser, diminuer <prices dipped : les prix ont baissé> <to dip below the horizon : disparaître derrière l'horizon> **2** INCLINE : descendre, s'incliner

dip[2] *n* **1** SWIM : petite baignade *f* <to go for a dip : aller faire trempette> **2** DROP : baisse *f*, diminution *f* **3** INCLINE : inclinaison *f*, pente *f* **4** SAUCE : trempette *f Can*, sauce *f*

diphtheria |dɪf'θɪriə| *n* : diphtérie *f*

diphthong |'dɪf,θɔŋ| *n* : diphtongue *f*

diploma |də'plo:mə| *n* : diplôme *m*

diplomacy |də'plo:məsi| *n* : diplomatie *f*

diplomat |'dɪplə,mæt| *n* : diplomate *mf*

diplomatic |,dɪplə'mæt̬ɪk| *adj* **1** : diplomatique <diplomatic relations : relations diplomatiques> **2** TACTFUL : diplomate, plein de tact

dipper |'dɪpər| *n* **1** LADLE : louche *f* **2 Big Dipper** : Grande Ourse *f* **3 Little Dipper** : Petite Ourse *f*

dire |'daɪr| *adj* **direr; -est 1** HORRIBLE : affreux, terrible **2** EXTREME : extrême, absolu <dire poverty : misère noire> <dire necessity : nécessité absolue>

direct[1] [də'rɛkt, daɪ-] *vt* **1** ADDRESS : adresser, diriger **2** AIM : destiner <directed to the public : destiné au grand public> **3** GUIDE : diriger, indiquer le chemin à **4** CONTROL : diriger, gérer, être en charge de **5** ORDER : ordonner

direct[2] *adv* : directement

direct[3] *adj* **1** : direct <a direct flight : un vol direct> **2** FRANK : direct, franc

direct current *n* : courant *m* continu

direction [də'rɛkʃən, daɪ-] *n* **1** SUPERVISION : direction *f* **2** ORDER : instruction *f*, ordre *m* **3** COURSE : direction *f*, sens *m* <in the right direction : dans le bon sens> **4** TENDENCY, TREND : direction *f*, tendence *f* **5 directions** *npl* INSTRUCTIONS : indications *fpl*

directly [də'rɛktli, daɪ-] *adv* **1** STRAIGHT : directement **2** FRANKLY : franchement **3** EXACTLY : juste, exactement <directly opposite my house : juste en face de ma maison> **4** IMMEDIATELY : immédiatement, tout de suite

directness [də'rɛktnəs, daɪ-] *n* FRANKNESS : franchise *f*

director [də'rɛktər, daɪ-] *n* **1** HEAD, MANAGER : directeur *m*, -trice *f* **2** : réalisateur *m*, -trice *f* (d'un film ou d'une pièce de théatre); metteur *m* en scène (d'une pièce de théâtre)

directory [də'rɛktəri, daɪ-] *n*, *pl* **-ries** : répertoire *m* (d'adresses), annuaire *m* (téléphonique)

dirge ['dərdʒ] *n* : hymne *m* funèbre

dirigible ['dɪrədʒəbəl, də'rɪdʒə-] *n* : dirigeable *m*

dirt ['dərt] *n* **1** FILTH : saleté *f*, crasse *f* **2** SOIL : terre *f*

dirtiness ['dərt̬inəs] *n* : saleté *f*

dirty[1] ['dərt̬i] *vt* **dirtied; dirtying** : salir

dirty[2] *adj* **dirtier; -est 1** SOILED : sale, malpropre **2** DISHONEST, UNFAIR : sale, malhonnête <a dirty trick : un sale tour> **3** INDECENT : obscène, cochon *fam*

disability [ˌdɪsə'bɪlət̬i] *n*, *pl* **-ties** : infirmité *f*, incapacité *f*, handicap *m*

disable [dɪs'eɪbəl] *vt* **-abled; -abling 1** : rendre infirme, handicaper (une personne) **2** : immobiliser (une machine), mettre hors d'action (un navire, etc.)

disabled [dɪs'eɪbəld] *adj* : handicapé

disabuse [ˌdɪsə'bju:z] *vt* **-bused; -busing** : détromper

disadvantage [ˌdɪsəd'væntɪdʒ] *n* : désavantage *m*

disadvantageous [ˌdɪsˌædˌvæn'teɪdʒəs] *adj* : défavorable, désavantageux

disagree [ˌdɪsə'gri:] *vi* **1** DIFFER : ne pas concorder, différer **2** DISSENT : être en désaccord, s'opposer **3** : ne pas convenir <fried foods disagree with me : les aliments frits ne me conviennent pas>

disagreeable [ˌdɪsə'gri:əbəl] *adj* : désagréable, déplaisant, malavenant *Can*

disagreement [ˌdɪsə'gri:mənt] *n* **1** DISAGREEING : désaccord *m* **2** DISCREPANCY : différence *f* **3** ARGUMENT : différend *m*

disappear [ˌdɪsə'pɪr] *vi* : disparaître

disappearance [ˌdɪsə'pi:rənts] *n* : disparition *f*

disappoint [ˌdɪsə'pɔɪnt] *vt* : désappointer, décevoir

disappointment [ˌdɪsə'pɔɪntmənt] *n* : désappointement *m*, déception *f*

disapproval [ˌdɪsə'pru:vəl] *n* : désapprobation *f*

disapprove [ˌdɪsə'pru:v] *vi* **-proved; -proving 1** : ne pas être d'accord **2 to disapprove of** : désapprouver

disarm [dɪs'ɑrm] *v* : désarmer

disarmament [dɪs'ɑrməmənt] *n* : désarmement *m*

disarming [dɪs'ɑrmɪŋ] *adj* : désarmant

disarrange [ˌdɪsə'reɪndʒ] *vt* **-ranged; -ranging** : mettre en désordre, déranger

disarray [dɪsə'reɪ] *n* **1** DISORDER, MESS : désordre *m* **2** CONFUSION : désarroi *m*, confusion *f*

disassemble [dɪsə'sɛmbəl] *vt* **-bled; -bling** : démonter

disaster [dɪ'zæstər] *n* : désastre *m*, catastrophe *f*

disastrous [dɪ'zæstrəs] *adj* : désastreux

disband [dɪs'bænd] *vi* DISPERSE : se disperser — *vt* DISSOLVE : dissoudre

disbar [dɪs'bɑr] *vt* **-barred; -barring** : radier (un avocat)

disbelief [ˌdɪsbɪ'li:f] *n* : incrédulité *f*

disbelieve [ˌdɪsbɪ'li:v] *vt* **-lieved; -lieving** : ne pas croire

disburse [dɪs'bərs] *vt* **-bursed; -bursing** : débourser

disbursement [dɪsˌbərsmənt] *n* : débours *m*

disc ['dɪsk] → **disk**

discard [dɪs'kɑrd, 'dɪsˌkɑrd] *vt* **1** THROW AWAY : se débarrasser de, jeter **2** : se défausser de (une carte à jouer)

discern [dɪ'sərn, -'zərn] *vt* : discerner, percevoir

discernible [dɪ'sərnəbəl, -'zərn-] *adj* : perceptible, visible

discernment [dɪ'sərnmənt, -zərn-] *n* : discernement *m*

discharge[1] [dɪs'tʃɑrdʒ, 'dɪs-] *vt* **-charged; -charging 1** UNLOAD : décharger (un chargement), débarquer (des passagers) **2** SHOOT : décharger (un fusil) **3** DISMISS : renvoyer (un salarié) **4** RELEASE : décharger, libérer (un soldat) **5** EMIT : émettre (un gaz, un courant d'électricité) **6** PERFORM : remplir, s'acquitter de (un devoir)

discharge[2] ['dɪsˌtʃɑrdʒ, dɪs'-] *n* **1** FIRING : décharge *f* (d'un fusil) **2** FLOW : écoulement *m* <discharge of blood : écoulement de sang> **3** DISMISSAL

: renvoi *m* **4** RELEASE : libération *f* (d'un soldat)
disciple [dɪ'saɪpəl] *n* : disciple *mf*
disciplinary ['dɪsəpəˌnɛri] *adj* : disciplinaire
discipline[1] ['dɪsəplən] *vt* **-plined; -plining 1** PUNISH : punir **2** CONTROL, TRAIN : discipliner, former **3 to discipline oneself** : se discipliner
discipline[2] *n* **1** FIELD : discipline *f*, matière *f* **2** TRAINING : discipline *f* **3** PUNISHMENT : punition *f* **4** CONTROL : discipline *f*, maîtrise *f*
disc jockey *n* : disc-jockey *mf*
disclaim [dɪs'kleɪm] *vt* DENY : démentir, nier
disclose [dɪs'klo:z] *vt* **-closed; -closing** : divulguer, révéler
disclosure [dɪs'klo:ʒər] *n* : divulgation *f*, révélation *f*
discolor [dɪs'kʌlər] *vt* **1** FADE : décolorer **2** YELLOW : jaunir — *vi* : se décolorer
discoloration [dɪs'kʌlə'reɪʃən] *n* : décoloration *f*
discomfit [dɪs'kəmpfət] *vt* : déconcerter
discomfort [dɪs'kʌmfərt] *n* : malaise *m*
disconcert [ˌdɪskən'sərt] *vt* : déconcerter, dérouter
disconnect [ˌdɪskə'nɛkt] *vt* : débrancher (un appareil électrique), couper (l'électricité, etc.)
disconsolate [dɪs'kɑntsələt] *adj* : inconsolable, triste
discontent [ˌdɪskən'tɛnt] *n* : mécontentement *m*
discontented [ˌdɪskən'tɛntəd] *adj* : mécontent
discontinue [ˌdɪskən'tɪnˌju:] *vt* **-tinued; -tinuing** : cesser, interrompre
discord ['dɪsˌkɔrd] *n* **1** STRIFE : discorde *m*, dissensions *fpl* **2** : dissonance *f* (en musique)
discordant [dɪs'kɔrdənt] *adj* : discordant
discount[1] ['dɪsˌkaʊnt, dɪs'-] *vt* **1** : faire une remise de, escompter (de l'argent) **2** DISREGARD : ne pas tenir compte de
discount[2] ['dɪsˌkaʊnt] *n* : rabais *m*, remise *f*
discourage [dɪs'kərɪdʒ] *vt* **-aged; -aging 1** DISHEARTEN : décourager, abattre **2** DISSUADE : décourager, détourner, dissuader
discouragement [dɪs'kərɪdʒmənt] *n* : découragement *m*
discourse[1] [dɪs'kors] *vi* **-coursed; -coursing** : discourir
discourse[2] ['dɪsˌkors] *n* **1** CONVERSATION : conversation *f* **2** SPEECH : discours *m*
discourteous [dɪs'kərt̬iəs] *adj* : impoli, peu courtois
discourtesy [dɪs'kərt̬əsi] *n, pl* **-sies** : manque *m* de courtoisie
discover [dɪs'kʌvər] *vt* : découvrir
discoverer *n* [dɪs'kʌvərər] : découvreur *m* (d'une terre), personne *f* qui a découvert qqch
discovery [dɪs'kʌvəri] *n, pl* **-eries** : découverte *f*
discredit[1] [dɪs'krɛdət] *vt* **1** DISBELIEVE : ne pas croire **2** QUESTION : discréditer, mettre en doute
discredit[2] *n* : discrédit *m*
discreet [dɪ'skri:t] *adj* : discret
discreetly [dɪs'kri:tli] *adv* : discrètement
discrepancy [dɪs'krɛpəntsi] *n, pl* **-cies** : divergence *f*, désaccord *m*
discrete [dɪs'kri:t] *adj* : distinct
discretion [dɪs'krɛʃən] *n* : discrétion *f*
discriminate [dɪs'krɪməˌneɪt] *v* **-nated; -nating** *vt* DIFFERENTIATE : distinguer, différencier — *vi* **1** DISTINGUISH : distinguer, faire une distinction **2 to discriminate against** : établir une discrimination contre
discrimination [dɪsˌkrɪmə'neɪʃən] *n* **1** DISCERNMENT : discernement *m* **2** PREJUDICE : discrimination *f*, préjugés *mpl*
discriminatory [dɪs'krɪmənəˌtori] *adj* : discriminatoire
discus ['dɪskəs] *n, pl* **-cuses** [-kəsəz] : disque *m* <discus thrower : lanceur de disque>
discuss [dɪs'kʌs] *vt* : discuter de, parler de
discussion [dɪs'kʌʃən] *n* : discussion *f*, conversation *f*, débat *m*
disdain[1] [dɪs'deɪn] *vt* : dédaigner <he disdained to answer : il a dédaigné de répondre>
disdain[2] *n* : dédain *m*
disdainful [dɪs'deɪnfəl] *adj* : dédaigneux — **disdainfully** *adv*
disease [dɪ'zi:z] *n* : maladie *f*
diseased [dɪ'zi:zd] *adj* : malade
disembark [ˌdɪsɪm'bɑrk] *v* : débarquer
disembarkation [dɪsˌɛmˌbɑr'keɪʃən] *n* : débarquement *m*
disembodied [ˌdɪsɪm'bɑdid] *adj* : désincarné
disenchant [ˌdɪsɪn'tʃænt] *vt* : désenchanter
disenchantment [ˌdɪsɪn'tʃæntmənt] *n* : désenchantement *m*
disengage [ˌdɪsɪn'geɪdʒ] *vt* **-gaged; -gaging 1** RELEASE : dégager **2 to disengage the clutch** : débrayer
disentangle [ˌdɪsɪn'tæŋgəl] *vt* **-gled; -gling** : démêler
disfavor [dɪs'feɪvər] *n* : défaveur *f*, désapprobation *f*
disfigure [dɪs'fɪgjər] *vt* **-ured; -uring** : défigurer
disfigurement [dɪs'fɪgjərmənt] *n* : défigurement *m*
disfranchise [dɪs'frænˌtʃaɪz] *vt* **-chised; -chising** : priver du droit électoral
disgrace[1] [dɪ'skreɪs] *vt* **-graced; -gracing** : déshonorer, faire honte à

disgrace[2] *n* **1** DISFAVOR : disgrâce *f,* défaveur *f* <fallen into disgrace : tombé en disgrâce> **2** SHAME : honte *f,* déshonneur *f*

disgraceful [dɪ'skreɪsfəl] *adj* : honteux, scandaleux — **disgracefully** *adv*

disgruntled [dɪs'grʌntəld] *adj* : mécontent

disguise[1] [dɪ'skaɪz] *vt* **-guised; -guising 1** : déguiser <to be disguised as : être déguisé en> **2** CONCEAL : camoufler, dissimuler

disguise[2] *n* : déguisement *m*

disgust[1] [dɪ'skʌst] *vt* : dégoûter, écœurer

disgust[2] *n* : dégoût *m,* aversion *f,* répugnance *f*

disgusting [dɪ'skʌstɪŋ] *adj* : dégoûtant

dish[1] ['dɪʃ] *vt or* **to dish up** : servir (de la nourriture)

dish[2] *n* **1** PLATE : assiette *f* **2** : mets *m,* plat *m* <a Mexican dish : un mets mexicain> **3** SERVING : plat *m* <a dish of strawberries : un plat de fraises> **4 dishes** *npl* : vaisselle *f* <to wash the dishes : faire la vaisselle>

dishcloth ['dɪʃ,klɔθ] *n* : torchon *m* (à vaisselle), linge à vaisselle

dishearten [dɪs'hɑrṭən] *vt* : décourager, abattre

disheveled *or* **dishevelled** [dɪ'ʃɛvəld] *adj* : en désordre (se dit des vêtements, etc.), échevelé (se dit des cheveux)

dishonest [dɪ'sɑnəst] *adj* : malhonnête — **dishonestly** *adv*

dishonesty [dɪ'sɑnəsti] *n* : malhonnêteté *f*

dishonor[1] [dɪ'sɑnər] *vt* : déshonorer

dishonor[2] *n* : déshonneur *m*

dishonorable [dɪ'sɑnərəbəl] *adj* : déshonorant

dishonorably [dɪ'sɑnərəbli] *adv* : de façon déshonorante

dishrag ['dɪʃ,ræg] → **dishcloth**

dishwasher ['dɪʃ,wɔʃər] *n* : lave-vaisselle *m*

disillusion [dɪsə'lu:ʒən] *vt* : désillusionner

disillusionment [,dɪsə'lu:ʒənmənt] *n* : désillusion *f*

disinclination [dɪs,ɪnklə'neɪʃən, -ɪŋ-] *n* : manque *m* d'enthousiasme

disinclined [,dɪsɪn'klaɪnd] *adj* : peu disposé

disinfect [,dɪsɪn'fɛkt] *vt* : désinfecter

disinfectant[1] [,dɪsɪn'fɛktənt] *adj* : désinfectant

disinfectant[2] *n* : désinfectant *m*

disinherit [,dɪsɪn'hɛrət] *vt* : déshériter

disintegrate [dɪs'ɪntə,greɪt] *v* **-grated; -grating** *vt* : désintégrer, désagréger — *vi* : se désintégrer, se désagréger

disintegration [dɪs'ɪntə'greɪʃən] *n* : désintégration *f,* désagrégation *f*

disinterested [dɪs'ɪntərəstəd, -,rɛs-] *adj* **1** INDIFFERENT : indifférent **2** UNBIASED : désintéressé

disjointed [dɪs'dʒɔɪntəd] *adj* : décousu, incohérent <disjointed speech : discours décousu>

disk *or* **disc** ['dɪsk] *n* : disque *m*

diskette [,dɪs'kɛt] → **floppy disk**

dislike[1] [dɪs'laɪk] *vt* **-liked; -liking** : ne pas aimer

dislike[2] *n* : aversion *f,* antipathie *f*

dislocate ['dɪslo,keɪt, dɪs'lo:-] *vt* **-cated; -cating** : luxer, déboîter, démettre <to dislocate one's knee : se luxer le genou>

dislocation [,dɪslo'keɪʃən] *n* : luxation *f,* déboîtement *m*

dislodge [dɪs'lɑdʒ] *vt* **-lodged; -lodging** : déplacer, dégager, déloger

disloyal [dɪs'lɔɪəl] *adj* : déloyal

disloyalty [dɪs'lɔɪəlti] *n* : déloyauté *f*

dismal ['dɪzməl] *adj* : sombre, lugubre, triste

dismantle [dɪs'mæntəl] *vt* **-tled; -tling** : démanteler, démonter

dismay[1] [dɪs'meɪ] *vt* : consterner

dismay[2] *n* : consternation *f,* désarroi *m*

dismember [dɪs'mɛmbər] *vt* : démembrer

dismiss [dɪs'mɪs] *vt* **1** : laisser sortir <class dismissed! : vous pouvez sortir!> **2** DISCHARGE : démettre (de ses fonctions), renvoyer, congédier **3** REJECT : ne pas tenir compte de, écarter

dismissal [dɪs'mɪsəl] *n* **1** : permission *f* de partir **2** DISCHARGE, LAYOFF : licenciement *m,* renvoi *m* **3** : rejet *m* (devant les tribunaux)

dismount [dɪs'maʊnt] *vt* DISASSEMBLE : démonter — *vi* **to dismount from** : descendre de

disobedience [,dɪsə'bi:diənts] *n* : désobéissance *f*

disobedient [dɪsə'bi:diənt] *adj* : désobéissant

disobey [,dɪsə'beɪ] *vt* : désobéir à — *vi* : désobéir

disorder[1] [dɪs'ɔrdər] *vt* : mettre en désordre

disorder[2] *n* **1** UNTIDINESS : désordre *m,* fouillis *m* **2** CONFUSION : désordre *m,* confusion *f* **3** RIOTING, UNREST : troubles *mpl,* émeutes *fpl* **4** AILMENT : troubles *mpl,* maladie *f* <digestive disorder : troubles digestifs>

disorderly [dɪs'ɔrdərli] *adj* **1** UNTIDY : désordonné **2** UNRULY : turbulent, incontrôlé, désordonné <disorderly conduct : conduite désordonnée>

disorganization [dɪs,ɔrgənə'zeɪʃən] *n* : désorganisation *f*

disorganize [dɪs'ɔrgə,naɪz] *vt* **-nized; -nizing** : désorganiser

disown [dɪs'o:n] *vt* : désavouer, renier

disparage [dɪs'pærɪdʒ] *vt* **-aged; -aging** : dénigrer, déprécier

disparagement [dɪs'pærɪdʒmənt] *n* : dénigrement *m*

disparate [ˈdɪspərət, dɪsˈpærət] *adj* : disparate

disparity [dɪsˈpærət̬i] *n, pl* **-ties** : disparité *f*

dispassionate [dɪsˈpæʃənət] *adj* : impartial, objectif

dispatch[1] [dɪsˈpætʃ] *vt* **1** SEND : envoyer, expédier **2** KILL : tuer **3** HANDLE : expédier (une tâche, etc.)

dispatch[2] *n* **1** SHIPMENT : envoi *m*, expédition *f* **2** PROMPTNESS : promptitude *f* **3** *or* **news dispatch** : dépêche *f*

dispel [dɪsˈpɛl] *vt* **-pelled; -pelling** : chasser, dissiper

dispensation [ˌdɪspɛnˈseɪʃən] *n* : dispense *f*

dispense [dɪsˈpɛnts] *v* **-pensed; -pensing** *vt* **1** DISTRIBUTE : dispenser, distribuer **2** ADMINISTER : exercer, administrer (la justice, etc.) **3** : préparer (une prescription) — *vi* **to dispense with** : se passer de

dispenser [dɪsˈpɛntsər] *n* : distributeur *m*

dispersal [dɪsˈpərsəl] *n* : dispersion *f*

disperse [dɪsˈpərs] *v* **-persed; -persing** *vt* **1** SCATTER : disperser, disséminer **2** DISSIPATE : disperser, dissiper — *vi* : se disperser

displace [dɪsˈpleɪs] *vt* **-placed; -placing** **1** EXPEL : expulser, déplacer <displaced persons : personnes déplacées> **2** REPLACE : supplanter, remplacer **3** : déplacer (un liquide, etc.)

displacement [dɪsˈpleɪsmənt] *n* : déplacement *m*, remplacement *m*

display[1] [dɪsˈpleɪ] *vt* **1** PRESENT : exposer, étaler **2** SHOW : faire preuve de, montrer <he displayed great talent : il a montré beaucoup de talent>

display[2] *n* **1** PRESENTATION : exposition *f*, étalage *m* **2** MANIFESTATION : démonstration *f*, manifestation *f*

displease [dɪsˈpliːz] *vt* **-pleased; -pleasing** : déplaire à, mécontenter

displeasure [dɪsˈplɛʒər] *n* : déplaisir *m*, mécontentement *m*

disposable [dɪsˈpoːzəbəl] *adj* **1** : jetable <disposable diapers : couches jetables> **2** AVAILABLE : disponible <disposable income : revenu disponible>

disposal [dɪsˈpoːzəl] *n* **1** ARRANGEMENT : disposition *f*, ordre *m* **2** AVAILABILITY : disposition *f* <to have at one's disposal : avoir à sa disposition> **3** : élimination *f* (des déchets)

dispose [dɪsˈpoːz] *v* **-posed; -posing** *vt* **1** ARRANGE : disposer, arranger **2** INCLINE : disposer <disposed to help : prêt à aider> — *vi* **1 to dispose of** HANDLE : expédier **2 to dispose of** DISCARD : se débarrasser de

disposition [ˌdɪspəˈzɪʃən] *n* **1** ARRANGEMENT : disposition *f*, arrangement *m* **2** TEMPERAMENT : tempérament *m*, caractère *m* **3** TENDENCY : inclination *f*, penchant *m*

dispossess [ˌdɪspəˈzɛs] *vt* : déposséder, dépouiller

disproportion [ˌdɪsprəˈporʃən] *n* : disproportion *f*

disproportionate [ˌdɪsprəˈporʃənət] *adj* : disproportionné

disprove [dɪsˈpruːv] *vt* **-proved; -proving** : réfuter

disputable [dɪsˈpjuːt̬əbəl, ˈdɪspjʊt̬əbəl] *adj* : discutable, contestable

dispute[1] [dɪsˈpjuːt] *v* **-puted; -puting** *vt* **1** QUESTION : contester, mettre en doute **2** CONTEST : disputer — *vi* ARGUE, DEBATE : se disputer, débattre

dispute[2] *n* **1** DEBATE : débat *m* <beyond dispute : incontestable> **2** QUARREL : dispute *f*, conflit *m*

disqualification [dɪsˌkwɑləfəˈkeɪʃən] *n* : exclusion *f*, disqualification *f*

disqualify [dɪsˈkwɑləˌfaɪ] *vt* **-fied; -fying** : disqualifier

disquiet[1] [dɪsˈkwaɪət̬] *vt* : inquiéter, troubler

disquiet[2] *n* ANXIETY : inquiétude *f*

disregard[1] [ˌdɪsrɪˈgɑrd] *vt* : ne tenir aucun compte de, ne pas s'occuper de

disregard[2] *n* : indifférence *f*, négligence *f*, mépris *m* (du danger)

disrepair [ˌdɪsrɪˈpær] *n* : délabrement *m*

disreputable [dɪsˈrɛpjʊt̬əbəl] *adj* : peu recommandable, mal famé

disrepute [ˌdɪsrɪˈpjuːt] *n* : discrédit *m*, déconsidération *f*

disrespect [ˌdɪsrɪˈspɛkt] *n* : irrespect *m*, manque *m* de respect

disrespectful [ˌdɪsrɪˈspɛktfəl] *adj* : irrespectueux

disrobe [dɪsˈroːb] *vi* **-robed; -robing** UNDRESS : se déshabiller

disrupt [dɪsˈrʌpt] *vt* : perturber, déranger

disruption [dɪsˈrʌpʃən] *n* : perturbation *f*, bouleversement *m*

disruptive [dɪsˈrʌptɪv] *adj* : perturbateur

dissatisfaction [dɪsˌsæt̬əsˈfækʃən] *n* : insatisfaction *f*, mécontentement *m*

dissatisfied [dɪsˈsæt̬əsˌfaɪd] *adj* : mécontent

dissatisfy [dɪsˈsæt̬əsˌfaɪ] *vt* **-fied; -fying** : ne pas satisfaire

dissect [dɪˈsɛkt] *vt* : disséquer

dissection [dɪˈsɛkʃən] *n* : dissection *f*

dissemble [dɪˈsɛmbəl] *v* **-bled; -bling** : dissimuler

disseminate [dɪˈsɛməˌneɪt] *vt* **-nated; -nating** : disséminer, propager

dissemination [dɪˌsɛməˈneɪʃən] *n* : dissémination *f*

dissension [dɪˈsɛntʃən] *n* : dissension *f*

dissent[1] [dɪˈsɛnt] *vi* : différer, être en désaccord

dissent[2] *n* : dissentiment *m*

dissertation [ˌdɪsərˈteɪʃən] *n* **1** TREATISE : traité *m* **2** THESIS : thèse *f*

disservice [dɪsˈsərvɪs] *n* : mauvais service *m*
dissident[1] [ˈdɪsədənt] *adj* : dissident
dissident[2] *n* : dissident *m*, -dente *f*
dissimilar [dɪˈsɪmələr] *adj* : dissemblable, différent
dissimilarity [dɪˌsɪməˈlærət̬i] *n, pl* **-ties** : dissemblance *f*
dissipate [ˈdɪsəˌpeɪt] *v* **-pated; -pating** *vt* **1** DISPERSE : dissiper, disperser **2** SQUANDER : gaspiller — *vi* : se dissiper
dissipation [ˌdɪsəˈpeɪʃən] *n* : dissipation *f*
dissolute [ˈdɪsəˌluːt] *adj* : dissolu, corrompu
dissolution [ˌdɪsəˈluːʃən] *n* : dissolution *f*
dissolve [dɪˈzɑlv] *v* **-solved; -solving** *vt* : dissoudre — *vi* : se dissoudre <to dissolve into tears : fondre en larmes>
dissonance [ˈdɪsənən*t*s] *n* : dissonance *f*
dissonant [ˈdɪsənənt] *adj* : dissonant
dissuade [dɪˈsweɪd] *vt* **-suaded; -suading** : dissuader
distance [ˈdɪstən*t*s] *n* **1** : distance *f* <at a distance of nine miles : à une distance de neuf milles> <in the distance : au loin> **2** RESERVE : distance *f*, réserve *f* <to keep one's distance : garder ses distances>
distant [ˈdɪstənt] *adj* **1** (*indicating separation*) <five miles distant from here : à cinq milles d'ici> **2** FARAWAY, REMOTE : lointain, éloigné **3** COLD : distant, réservé
distantly [ˈdɪstəntli] *adv* **1** : vaguement, un peu <distantly related : d'une parenté éloignée> **2** COLDLY : froidement, d'un air distant
distaste [dɪsˈteɪst] *n* : aversion *f*, répugnance *f*
distasteful [dɪsˈteɪstfəl] *adj* : déplaisant, répugnant
distemper [dɪsˈtɛmpər] *n* : maladie *f* de Carré
distend [dɪsˈtɛnd] *vt* : gonfler — *vi* : se gonfler, se distendre
distill *or Brit* **distil** [dɪˈstɪl] *vt* **-tilled; -tilling** : distiller
distillation [ˌdɪstəˈleɪʃən] *n* : distillation *f*
distillery [dɪˈstɪləri, -ˈstɪlri] *n, pl* **-ries** : distillerie *f*
distinct [dɪˈstɪŋkt] *adj* **1** DIFFERENT : distinct, différent **2** CLEAR : distinct, net <a distinct impression : une nette impression>
distinction [dɪˈstɪŋkʃən] *n* : distinction *f*
distinctive [dɪˈstɪŋktɪv] *adj* : distinctif
distinctively [dɪˈstɪŋktɪvli] *adv* : de manière distinctive
distinctly [dɪˈstɪŋktli] *adv* : distinctement, clairement
distinguish [dɪˈstɪŋgwɪʃ] *vt* **1** DIFFERENTIATE : distinguer, différencier **2** DISCERN : distinguer, discerner **3 to distinguish oneself** : se distinguer, s'illustrer — *vi* DISCRIMINATE : faire une distinction
distinguished [dɪˈstɪŋgwɪʃt] *adj* : distingué <distinguished-looking : à l'allure distinguée>
distort [dɪˈstɔrt] *vt* **1** DEFORM : déformer, distordre <a face distorted by pain : un visage déformé par la douleur> **2** MISREPRESENT : déformer, dénaturer
distortion [dɪˈstɔrʃən] *n* : déformation *f*
distract [dɪˈstrækt] *vt* : distraire <to distract s.o.'s attention : détourner l'attention de qqn>
distraction [dɪˈstrækʃən] *n* **1** INTERRUPTION : distraction *f*, interruption *f* **2** INATTENTION : inattention *f* **3** CONFUSION, MADNESS : folie *f* <to drive to distraction : rendre fou> **4** AMUSEMENT : distraction *f*, divertissement *m*
distraught [dɪˈstrɔt] *adj* : bouleversé, éperdu
distress[1] [dɪˈstrɛs] *vt* : affliger, peiner
distress[2] *n* **1** SUFFERING : douleur *f*, souffrance *f*, affliction *f* **2** MISFORTUNE : détresse *f*, adversité *f* **3** DANGER : détresse *f* <a ship in distress : un navire en détresse>
distressful [dɪˈstrɛsfəl] *adj* : pénible, affligeant
distribute [dɪˈstrɪˌbjuːt, -bjʊt] *vt* **-uted; -uting** : distribuer, répartir
distribution [ˌdɪstrəˈbjuːʃən] *n* : distribution *f*, répartition *f*
distributor [dɪˈstrɪbjʊt̬ər] *n* **1** : distributeur *m*, -trice *f* (personne) **2** : distributeur *m* (d'une voiture)
district [ˈdɪsˌtrɪkt] *n* **1** AREA : région *f* **2** : quartier *m* <residential district : quartier résidentiel> **3** : district *m* (administratif), circonscription *f* (électorale)
distrust[1] [dɪsˈtrʌst] *vt* : se méfier de
distrust[2] *n* : méfiance *f*
distrustful [dɪsˈtrʌstfəl] *adj* : méfiant
disturb [dɪˈstərb] *vt* **1** BOTHER : déranger, interrompre **2** DISARRANGE : déplacer, déranger **3** WORRY : troubler, inquiéter **4 to disturb the peace** : troubler l'ordre public
disturbance [dɪˈstərbən*t*s] *n* **1** INTERRUPTION : dérangement *m*, interruption *f* **2** COMMOTION : troubles *mpl*, émeute *f*, tapage *m* <to cause a disturbance : faire du tapage>
disuse [dɪsˈjuːs] *n* : désuétude *f*
ditch[1] [ˈdɪtʃ] *vt* **1** : creuser un fossé dans **2** DISCARD : se débarrasser de
ditch[2] *n* : fossé *m*
dither [ˈdɪðər] *n* **to be in a dither** : être dans tous ses états
ditto [ˈdɪt̬oː] *adv* : idem
ditty [ˈdɪt̬i] *n, pl* **-ties** : chansonnette *f*

diurnal [daɪ'ərnəl] *adj* **1** DAILY : quotidien **2** : diurne (se dit des animaux et des plantes)

divan ['daɪˌvæn, dɪ'-] *n* : divan *m*

dive[1] ['daɪv] *vi* **dived** *or* **dove** ['do:v]; **dived; diving 1** : plonger <to dive into the water : plonger dans l'eau> **2** SUBMERGE : s'immerger **3** DESCEND : descendre en piqué, piquer (se dit d'un avion, etc.)

dive[2] *n* **1** : plongeon *m* (dans l'eau) **2** DESCENT, NOSEDIVE : piqué *m*

diver ['daɪvər] *n* : plongeur *m*, -geuse *f*

diverge [də'vərdʒ, daɪ-] *vi* **-verged; -verging 1** SEPARATE : diverger, s'écarter **2** DIFFER : diverger, différer

divergence [də'vərdʒənts, daɪ-] *n* : divergence *f* — **divergent** [-dʒənt] *adj*

diverse [daɪ'vərs, də-, 'daɪˌvərs] *adj* : divers, varié

diversification [dəˌvərsəfə'keɪʃən] *n* : diversification *f*

diversify [daɪ'vərsəˌfaɪ, də-] *v* **-fied; -fying** *vt* : diversifier — *vi* : se diversifier

diversion [daɪ'vərʒən, də-] *n* **1** DEVIATION : déviation *f* **2** AMUSEMENT : distraction *f*, divertissement *m*

diversity [daɪ'vərsət̬i, də-] *n, pl* **-ties** : diversité *f*

divert [də'vərt, daɪ-] *vt* **1** DEFLECT : détourner, dévier **2** DISTRACT : distraire **3** AMUSE : divertir

divest [daɪ'vɛst, də-] *vt* **1** DISPOSSESS : dépouiller **2 to divest oneself of** : se débarrasser de, se défaire de

divide [də'vaɪd] *v* **-vided; -viding** *vt* **1** SEPARATE : diviser, séparer, désunir **2** SHARE : diviser, partager **3** : diviser <twelve divided by three is four : douze divisé par trois égale quatre> — *vi* : se diviser, se séparer

dividend ['dɪvɪˌdɛnd, -dənd] *n* **1** : dividende *m* (en finance et en mathématiques) **2** BONUS : prime *f*

divider [dɪ'vaɪdər] *n* **1** *or* **file divider** : intercalaire *m*, fiche *f* intercalaire **2** *or* **room divider** : cloison *f*, meuble *m* de séparation

divine[1] [də'vaɪn] *adj* **diviner; -est 1** : divin **2** SUPERB : divin, sublime

divine[2] *n* CLERGYMAN : ecclésiastique *m*

divinely [də'vaɪnli] *adv* : divinement

divinity [də'vɪnət̬i] *n, pl* **-ties** : divinité *f*

divisible [dɪ'vɪzəbəl] *adj* : divisible

division [dɪ'vɪʒən] *n* : division *f*

divisor [dɪ'vaɪzər] *n* : diviseur *m*

divorce[1] [də'vors] *v* **-vorced; -vorcing** *vi* : divorcer — *vt* : divorcer de, divorcer avec

divorce[2] *n* : divorce *m*

divorcé [dɪˌvor'seɪ, -'si:; -'vorˌ-] *n* : divorcé *m*

divorcée [dɪˌvor'seɪ, -'si:; -'vorˌ-] *n* : divorcée *f*

divulge [də'vʌldʒ, daɪ-] *vt* **-vulged; -vulging** : divulguer, révéler, placoter *Can fam*

dizziness *n* ['dɪzinəs] : vertige *m*, étourdissement *m*

dizzy ['dɪzi] *adj* **dizzier; -est 1** GIDDY, UNSTEADY : pris de vertiges **2** : vertigineux <dizzy heights : des hauteurs vertigineuses>

DNA [ˌdi:ˌɛn'eɪ] *n* : ADN *m*

do ['du:]; **did** ['dɪd]; **done** ['dʌn]; **doing; does** ['dʌz] *vt* **1** CARRY OUT, PERFORM : faire, accomplir (une action, une tâche) <do your best : fais de ton mieux> **2** PRACTICE : faire, entreprendre <what does he do for a living? : que fait-il comme métier?> **3** ARRANGE : arranger <to do one's hair : se coiffer> **4** PREPARE : faire, préparer <do your homework : fais tes devoirs> — *vi* **1** ACT, BEHAVE : faire <do as I say : faites ce que je dis> **2** FARE : réussir <he does well in school : il réussit bien à l'école> **3** SUFFICE : suffire, faire l'affaire <that will do : ça suffit> **4 to do away with** DESTROY, KILL : tuer, détruire **5 to do away with** ELIMINATE : éliminer, abolir — *v aux* **1** (*in interrogative sentences*) <does he work? : travaille-t-il?> **2** (*in negative sentences*) <I don't know : je ne sais pas> <don't go : n'y va pas> **3** (*for emphasis*) <do be careful : fais attention, je t'en prie> **4** (*as a substitute for a preceding predicate*) <he succeeds better than I do : il réussit mieux que moi>

docile ['dɑsəl] *adj* : docile

dock[1] ['dɑk] *vt* **1** SHORTEN : couper la queue à (un chien) **2** DEDUCT : faire une retenue sur <they docked $10 from his paycheck : ils ont retenu 10 $ sur son chèque de paie> — *vi* : se mettre à quai (se dit d'un bateau)

dock[2] *n* **1** BERTH : dock *m* **2** WHARF : embarcadère *m*, quai *m* **3** : banc *m* des accusés (dans un tribunal)

doctor[1] ['dɑktər] *vt* **1** TREAT : soigner (un patient) **2** ALTER : altérer, falsifier

doctor[2] *n* **1** : docteur *m* <Doctor of Law : docteur en droit> **2** PHYSICIAN : médecin *m*; docteur *m*

doctrine ['dɑktrɪn] *n* : doctrine *f*

document[1] ['dɑkjʊˌmɛnt] *vt* : documenter

document[2] ['dɑkjʊmənt] *n* : document *m*

documentary[1] [ˌdɑkjʊ'mɛntəri] *adj* : documentaire

documentary[2] *n, pl* **-ries** : documentaire *m*

documentation [ˌdɑkjʊmən'teɪʃən] *n* : documentation *f*

dodge[1] ['dɑdʒ] *v* **dodged; dodging** *vt* : esquiver, éviter, échapper à — *vi* : faire un saut de côté, faire une esquive

dodge[2] *n* **1** : mouvement *m* de côté, esquive *f* (aux sports) **2** RUSE, TRICK : ruse *f*, truc *m*

dodo [ˈdːˌdoː] *n, pl* **-does** *or* **-dos** : dodo *m*

doe [ˈdoː] *n, pl* **does** *or* **doe** : biche *f*

doer [ˈduːər] *n* : personne *f* qui préfère l'action, personne *f* efficace

does → **do**

doff [ˈdɑf, ˈdɔf] *vt* : ôter, enlever (son chapeau, etc.)

dog[1] [ˈdɔg, ˈdɑg] *vt* **dogged; dogging 1** FOLLOW : talonner, suivre de près <he's dogging my footsteps : il marche sur mes talons> **2** HOUND : poursuivre, être en proie à <dogged by financial worries : en proie à des difficultés financières>

dog[2] *n* : chien *m*

dog–eared [ˈdɔgˌɪrd] *adj* : écorné

dogged [ˈdɔgəd] *adj* : tenace, persévérant

doghouse [ˈdɔgˌhaʊs] *n* : niche *f* (à chien)

dogma [ˈdɔgmə] *n* : dogme *m*

dogmatic [dɔgˈmæt̬ɪk] *adj* : dogmatique

dogmatism [ˈdɔgməˈtɪzəm] *n* : dogmatisme *m*

dogwood [ˈdɔgˌwʊd] *n* : cornouiller *m*

doily [ˈdɔɪli] *n, pl* **-lies** : napperon *m*

doings [ˈduːɪŋz] *npl* GOINGS-ON : événements *mpl*, faits *mpl* et gestes *mpl*

doldrums [ˈdoːldrəmz, ˈdɑl-] *npl* **1** : zone *f* des calmes (équatoriaux) **2** BLUES : cafard *m*, mélancolie *f* **3** STAGNATION : marasme *m* <economic doldrums : marasme économique>

dole [ˈdoːl] *n* : allocation *f* de chômage, indemnité *f* de chômage

doleful [ˈdoːlfəl] *adj* : dolent, triste

dolefully [ˈdoːlfəli] *adv* : d'un air triste

dole out *vt* **doled out; doling out** : distribuer, donner

doll [ˈdɑl, ˈdɔl] *n* : poupée *f*

dollar [ˈdɑlər] *n* : dollar *m*, piastre *f Can fam*

dolly [ˈdɑli] *n, pl* **-lies 1** → **doll 2** CART, PLATFORM : chariot *m*, plate-forme *f*

dolphin [ˈdɑlfən, ˈdɔl-] *n* : dauphin *m*

dolt [ˈdoːlt] *n* : balourd *m*, -lourde *f*

domain [doˈmeɪn, də-] *n* **1** TERRITORY : domaine *m*, territoire *m* **2** SPHERE : domaine *m* <the domain of art : le domaine de l'art>

dome [ˈdoːm] *n* : dôme *m*, coupole *f*

domestic[1] [dəˈmɛstɪk] *adj* **1** HOUSEHOLD : domestique **2** : intérieur, national <domestic affairs : affaires intérieures> **3** TAME : domestique

domestic[2] *n* SERVANT : domestique *mf*

domesticate [dəˈmɛstɪˌkeɪt] *vt* **-cated; -cating** : domestiquer, apprivoiser

domicile [ˈdɑməˌsaɪl, ˈdoː-; ˈdɑməsɪl] *n* : domicile *m*

dominance [ˈdɑmənənts] *n* : dominance *f*, prédominance *f*

dominant [ˈdɑmənənt] *adj* : dominant

dominate [ˈdɑməˌneɪt] *v* **-nated; -nating** : dominer

domination [ˌdɑməˈneɪʃən] *n* : domination *f*

domineer [ˌdɑməˈnɪr] *vi* : agir en maître, se montrer autoritaire

Dominican[1] [dəˈmɪnɪkən] *adj* : dominicain

Dominican[2] *n* : Dominicain *m*, -caine *f*

dominion [dəˈmɪnjən] *n* **1** SUPREMACY : domination *f* **2** TERRITORY : territoire *m*, domaine *m*

domino [ˈdɑməˌnoː] *n, pl* **-noes** *or* **-nos** : domino *m*

don [ˈdɑn] *vt* **donned; donning** : mettre (des vêtements)

donate [ˈdoːˌneɪt, doːˈ-] *v* **-nated; -nating** *vt* : faire (un) don de — *vi* : faire un don

donation [doːˈneɪʃən] *n* : don *m*, donation *f*

done[1] [ˈdʌn] → **do**

done[2] *adj* **1** FINISHED : fini, terminé **2** WELL-DONE : bien cuit

donkey [ˈdɑŋki, ˈdʌŋ] *n, pl* **-keys** : âne *m*

donor [ˈdoːnər] *n* : donateur *m*, -trice *f*; donneur *m*, -neuse *f* <blood donor : donneur de sang>

doodle[1] [ˈduːdəl] *v* **-dled; -dling** : gribouiller

doodle[2] *n* : gribouillage *m*

doom[1] [ˈduːm] *vt* **1** CONDEMN : condamner **2** DESTINE : vouer <doomed to failure : voué à l'échec>

doom[2] *n* **1** JUDGMENT : jugement *m*, sentence *f* **2** DESTINY : destin *m*, sort *m* **3** RUIN : perte *f*, ruine *f*

door [ˈdor] *n* **1** : porte *f*, portière *f* (d'une voiture) **2** ENTRANCE : entrée *f* <pay at the door : payez à l'entrée>

doorbell [ˈdorˌbɛl] *n* : sonnette *f*

doorknob [ˈdorˌnɑb] *n* : poignée *f* de porte, bouton *m* de porte

doorman [ˈdormən] *n, pl* **-men** : portier *m*

doormat [ˈdorˌmæt] *n* : paillasson *m*

doorstep [ˈdorˌstɛp] *n* : seuil *m* (de porte), pas *m* de la porte

doorway [ˈdorˌweɪ] *n* : embrasure *f* (de la porte)

dope[1] [ˈdoːp] *vt* **doped; doping** : droguer (une personne), doper (un animal, un athlète)

dope[2] *n* **1** DRUG : narcotique *m*, stupéfiant *m* **2** IDIOT : cornichon *m fam*, imbécile *mf* **3** INFORMATION, TIP : tuyau *m fam*, renseignement *m*

dormant [ˈdormənt] *adj* : qui sommeille, latent, dormant (en botanique)

dormer [ˈdɔrmər] *n* : lucarne *f*

dormitory [ˈdɔrməˌtori] *n, pl* **-ries** : dortoir *m*, résidence *f* universitaire

dormouse [ˈdɔrˌmaʊs] *n, pl* **-mice** : loir *m*

dorsal ['dɔrsəl] *adj* : dorsal
dory ['dori] *n, pl* **-ries** : doris *m*
dosage ['do:sɪdʒ] *n* : posologie *f*
dose[1] ['do:s] *vt* **dosed; dosing** : doser, administrer un médicament à
dose[2] *n* : dose *f*
dot[1] ['dɑt] *vt* **dotted; dotting** : mettre un point sur (un *i,* etc.)
dot[2] *n* **1** POINT, SPECK : point *m* **2 on the dot** : à l'heure pile *fam*
dote ['do:t] *vi* **doted; doting** : raffoler, adorer <to dote on s.o. : aimer qqn à la folie, raffoler de qqn>
double[1] ['dʌbəl] *v* **-bled; -bling** *vt* **1** : doubler (une quantité) **2** BEND, FOLD : plier (en deux) **3 to double one's fists** : serrer les poings — *vi* **1** : doubler **2 to double up in pain** : se plier en deux par la douleur
double[2] *adv* **1** TWICE : deux fois <she's double your age : elle est deux fois plus âgé que toi> **2** : double <to see double : voir double>
double[3] *adj* : double
double[4] *n* : double *m*
double bass *n* : contrebasse *f*
double–cross [ˌdʌbəl'krɔs] *vt* : trahir, doubler *fam*
double–jointed [ˌdʌbəl'dʒɔɪntəd] *adj* : désarticulé
double–talk ['dʌbəlˌtɔk] *n* : paroles *fpl* trompeuses, paroles *fpl* ambiguës
doubly ['dʌbli] *adv* : doublement, deux fois plus
doubt[1] ['daʊt] *vt* **1** : douter <I doubt that he'll accept : je doute qu'il accepte> **2** DISTRUST : douter de <I doubt it very much : j'en doute beaucoup>
doubt[2] *n* **1** UNCERTAINTY : doute *m,* incertitude *f* **2** DISTRUST : doute *m,* méfiance *f* **3** SKEPTICISM : doute *m,* scepticisme *m*
doubtful ['daʊtfəl] *adj* **1** UNCERTAIN : douteux, incertain **2** QUESTIONABLE : douteux, discutable
doubtless ['daʊtləs] *adv* : sans aucun doute, sûrement
douche ['du:ʃ] *n* : douche *f* (en médecine)
dough ['do:] *n* : pâte *f* (en cuisine)
doughnut ['do:ˌnʌt] *n* : beignet *m,* beigne *m Can*
doughty ['daʊt̬i] *adj* **doughtier; -est** : vaillant
dour ['daʊər, 'dʊr] *adj* **1** STERN : austère, dur **2** SULLEN : maussade, renfrogné
douse ['daʊs, 'daʊz] *vt* **doused; dousing** **1** DRENCH : inonder, tremper **2** EXTINGUISH : éteindre
dove[1] ['do:v] → **dive**[1]
dove[2] ['dʌv] *n* : colombe *f*
dovetail ['dʌvˌteɪl] *vt* **1** : assembler à queue d'aronde (en charpenterie) **2** : faire concorder (des plans, etc.) — *vi* AGREE : concorder, bien cadrer
dowdy ['daʊdi] *adj* **dowdier; -est** : sans chic
dowel ['daʊəl] *n* : goujon *m*
down[1] ['daʊn] *vt* **1** KNOCK DOWN : terrasser, abattre **2** DEFEAT : vaincre
down[2] *adv* **1** DOWNWARD : en bas, vers le bas **2 down to** : jusqu'à <down to the present : jusqu'à nos jours> **3 to lie down** : se coucher, s'allonger **4 to put down** PAY : payer, verser **5 to put down** WRITE : écrire **6 to sit down** : s'asseoir
down[3] *adj* **1** : qui descend <the down escalator : l'escalier mécanique qui descend> **2** LOWER : qui diminue, qui baisse <sales were down : les ventes avaient diminué> **3** DOWNCAST : déprimé, abattu
down[4] *n* : duvet *m*
down[5] *prep* **1** : en bas de, dans <he fell down the stairs : il est tombé dans l'escalier> **2** ALONG : le long de <to walk down the road : marcher le long de la rue> **3** THROUGH : au cours de, à travers de <down through the ages : à travers les siècles>
downcast ['daʊnˌkæst] *adj* **1** SAD : abattu, découragé **2** LOWERED : baissé <with a downcast glance : avec les yeux baissés>
downfall ['daʊnˌfɔl] *n* : chute *f,* renversement *m*
downgrade[1] ['daʊnˌgreɪd] *vt* **-graded; -grading** : déclasser (un poste, etc.), rétrograder (une personne)
downgrade[2] *n* : descente *f,* pente *f*
downhearted ['daʊnˌhɑrt̬əd] *adj* : abattu, découragé
downhill[1] ['daʊn'hɪl] *adv* **to go downhill** : descendre
downhill[2] *adj* : en pente, qui descend
download[1] ['daʊnˌlo:d] *vt* : télécharger (en informatique)
download[2] *n* : téléchargement *m*
down payment *n* : acompte *m,* arrhes *fpl France*
downpour ['daʊnˌpor] *n* : déluge *m,* averse *f*
downright[1] ['daʊnˌraɪt] *adv* THOROUGHLY : carrément, tout à fait
downright[2] *adj* ABSOLUTE : véritable, catégorique
downstairs[1] [*adv* 'daʊn'stærz, *adj* 'daʊnˌstærz] *adv & adj* : en bas
downstairs[2] ['daʊn'stærz, -ˌstærz] *n* : rez-de-chaussé *m*
downstream ['daʊn'stri:m] *adv* : en aval
down–to–earth [ˌdaʊntu'ərθ] *adj* : terre à terre, avec les pieds sur terre
downtown[1] [ˌdaʊn'taʊn] *adv* : en ville
downtown[2] *adj* : du centre-ville
downtown[3] [ˌdaʊn'taʊn, 'daʊnˌtaʊn] *n* : centre-ville *m*
downtrodden ['daʊnˌtrɑdən] *adj* : opprimé
downward[1] ['daʊnwərd] *or* **downwards** [-wərdz] *adv* : en bas, vers le bas <to look downward : regarder en bas> <the prophets from Elijah downward : les prophètes depuis Élie>

downward[2] *adj* : vers le bas <a downward movement : un mouvement vers le bas> <a downward trend : une tendance à la baisse>

downwind ['daʊn'wɪnd] *adv & adj* : dans le sens du vent

downy ['daʊni] *adj* **downier; -est** : duveteux

dowry ['daʊri] *n, pl* **-ries** : dot *f*

doze[1] ['do:z] *vi* **dozed; dozing** : sommeiller, somnoler

doze[2] *n* : somme *m*, sieste *f*

dozen ['dʌzən] *n, pl* **-ens** *or* **-en** : douzaine *f*

drab ['dræb] *adj* **drabber; drabbest** : terne, fade

draft[1] ['dræft, 'drɑft] *vt* **1** : appeler (des soldats) sous les drapeaux **2** OUTLINE : faire le brouillon de **3** COMPOSE : rédiger

draft[2] *adj* : en fût, à la pression <draft beer : bière en fût>

draft[3] *n* **1** HAULAGE : tirage *m*, traction *f* **2** DRINK, GULP : trait *m*, gorgée *f* **3** OUTLINE : brouillon *m*, avant-projet *m* **4** CONSCRIPTION : service *m* militaire, conscription *f* **5** : courant *m* d'air **6** *or* **bank draft** : traite *f* bancaire

draftsman ['dræftsmən] *n, pl* **-men** [-mən, -ˌmɛn] : dessinateur *m*, -trice *f*

drafty ['dræfti] *adj* **draftier; -est** : plein de courants d'air

drag[1] ['dræg] *v* **dragged; dragging** *vt* **1** HAUL : tirer, traîner **2** TRAIL : traîner <to drag one's feet : traîner les pieds> **3** DREDGE : draguer **4** : glisser (en informatique) — *vi* TRAIL : traîner

drag[2] *n* **1** RESISTANCE : résistance *f*, traînée *f* **2** DREDGE : drague *f* **3** SLEDGE : traîneau *m* **4** : barbe *f fam* <what a drag! : quelle barbe!> **5** PUFF : bouffée *f* (de cigarette)

dragnet ['drægˌnɛt] *n* **1** TRAWL : drège *f* **2** : rafle *f*, descente *f* (policière)

dragon ['drægən] *n* : dragon *m*

dragonfly ['drægənˌflaɪ] *n, pl* **-flies** : libellule *f*

drain[1] ['dreɪn] *vt* **1** EMPTY : vider, drainer **2** DEPLETE, EXHAUST : fatiguer, épuiser — *vi* : s'écouler (se dit d'un cours d'eau), s'égoutter (se dit de la vaisselle)

drain[2] *n* **1** : tuyau *m* d'écoulement **2** SEWER : égout *m* **3** DEPLETION : épuisement *m*, perte *f*

drainage ['dreɪnɪdʒ] *n* : drainage *m*

drainpipe ['dreɪnˌpaɪp] *n* : tuyau *m* d'évacuation, drain *m*

drake ['dreɪk] *n* : canard *m* (mâle)

drama ['drɑmə, 'dræ-] *n* **1** : art *m* dramatique, théâtre *m* **2** PLAY : drame *m*, pièce *f* de théâtre

dramatic [drə'mæṭɪk] *adj* : dramatique

dramatically [drə'mæṭɪkli] *adv* : d'une manière dramatique

dramatist ['dræməṭɪst, 'drɑ-] *n* : dramaturge *mf*

dramatization [ˌdræməṭə'zeɪʃən] *n* **1** : adaptation *f* pour la scène **2** DRAMATIZING : dramatisation *f*

dramatize ['dræməˌtaɪz, 'drɑ-] *vt* **-tized; -tizing** : dramatiser

drank → **drink**[1]

drape[1] ['dreɪp] *v* **draped; draping** *vt* : draper — *vi* : tomber <silk drapes beautifully : la soie tombe à merveille>

drape[2] *n* **1** HANG : drapé *m* (d'une étoffe) **2** **drapes** *npl* CURTAINS : rideaux *mpl*

drapery ['dreɪpəri] *n, pl* **-eries** **1** HANGINGS : tentures *fpl* **2** CURTAINS : rideaux *mpl*

drastic ['dræstɪk] *adj* **1** : drastique <a drastic purgative : un purgatif drastique> **2** SEVERE : rigoureux, énergique <drastic measures : mesures énergiques>

draught ['dræft, 'draft] → **draft**[3]

draughty ['drafti] → **drafty**

draw[1] ['drɔ] *v* **drew** ['dru:]; **drawn** ['draʊn]; **drawing** ['drɔɪŋ] *vt* **1** PULL : tirer **2** ATTRACT : attirer **3** PROVOKE : provoquer, susciter **4** INHALE : aspirer, respirer **5** EXTRACT : extraire, retirer **6** TAKE : prendre <to draw a number : prendre un numéro> **7** COLLECT : toucher (un salaire) **8** BEND : bander <to draw a bow : bander un arc> **9** TIE : faire match de (aux sports) **10** SKETCH : dessiner, tracer **11** MAKE : faire (une distinction, une comparaison, etc.) **12** *or* **to draw up** DRAFT, FORMULATE : dresser (une liste, etc.), rédiger (un plan) — *vi* **1** SKETCH : dessiner **2** (*indicating movement*) <to draw near : approcher> <to draw to an end : tirer à sa fin> **3** : tirer (se dit d'une cheminée, d'une pipe, etc.)

draw[2] *n* **1** DRAWING : tirage *m* (au sort) **2** TIE : match *m* nul (aux sports) **3** ATTRACTION : attraction *f* **4** PUFF : bouffée *f* (de cigarette, etc.)

drawback ['drɔˌbæk] *n* : désavantage *m*, inconvénient *m*

drawbridge ['drɔˌbrɪdʒ] *n* : pont-levis *m*

drawer ['drɔr, 'drɔər] *n* **1** ILLUSTRATOR : dessinateur *m*, -trice *f* **2** : tiroir *m* (d'un meuble) **3** **drawers** *npl* UNDERPANTS : caleçon *m* (d'homme), culotte *f* (de femme)

drawing ['drɔɪŋ] *n* **1** LOTTERY : tirage *m* (au sort), loterie *f* **2** SKETCH : dessin *m*

drawl[1] ['drɔl] *vt* : dire d'une voix traînante — *vi* : parler d'une voix traînante

drawl[2] *n* : voix *f* traînante

draw out *vt* : faire parler (une personne)

draw up *vt* **1** FORMULATE : dresser, rédiger **2** APPROACH : approcher **3** *or* **to draw oneself up** : se redresser — *vi* STOP : s'arrêter

dread[1] [ˈdrɛd] *vt* : redouter, craindre

dread[2] *adj* : redoutable, terrible

dread[3] *n* : crainte *f*, terreur *f*

dreadful [ˈdrɛdfəl] *adj* **1** HORRIBLE : affreux, épouvantable **2** TERRIBLE, UNPLEASANT : terrible <a dreadful cold : un rhume terrible>

dream[1] [ˈdri:m] *v* **dreamed** [ˈdrɛmpt, ˈdri:md] *or* **dreamt** [ˈdrɛmpt]; **dreaming** *vi* **1** : rêver <to dream about : rêver de> **2** DAYDREAM : rêvasser, songer — *vt* **1** : rêver <to dream a dream : faire un rêve> **2** IMAGINE : imaginer, penser, songer

dream[2] *n* **1** : rêve *m* **2** DAYDREAM : rêverie *f* **3** : merveille *f*, bijou *m* <my new car is a dream : ma nouvelle voiture est une merveille> **4** IDEAL : idéal *m*

dreamer [ˈdri:mər] **1** : rêveur *m*, -veuse *f* **2** IDEALIST : idéaliste *mf*

dreamless [ˈdri:mləs] *adj* : sans rêves

dreamlike [ˈdri:m,laɪk] *adj* : irréel

dreamy [ˈdri:mi] *adj* **dreamier; -est 1** : rêveur <a dreamy child : un enfant rêveur> **2** SOOTHING : apaisant, reposant **3** DELIGHTFUL : ravissant, superbe

drearily [ˈdrɪrəli] *adv* : tristement, sombrement

dreary [ˈdrɪri] *adj* **drearier; -est** : morne, sombre

dredge[1] [ˈdrɛdʒ] *vt* **dredged; dredging 1** : draguer **2** COAT : saupoudrer, paner (en cuisine)

dredge[2] *n* : drague *f*

dregs [ˈdrɛgz] *npl* : lie *f* <the dregs of society : la lie de la société>

drench [ˈdrɛntʃ] *vt* : tremper, mouiller

dress[1] [ˈdrɛs] *vt* **1** CLOTHE : habiller, vêtir **2** DECORATE : décorer <to dress a shop window : faire une vitrine> **3** : préparer, parer (une dinde, etc.), assaisonner (une salade) **4** BANDAGE : panser (une blessure) **5** FERTILIZE : fertiliser (la terre) — *vi* **1** : s'habiller **2** *or* **to dress up** : se mettre en grande toilette

dress[2] *n* **1** CLOTHING : habillement *m*, tenue *f* **2** : robe *f* (de femme) <a silk dress : une robe de soie>

dresser [ˈdrɛsər] *n* : commode *f* à miroir

dressing [ˈdrɛsɪŋ] *n* **1** CLOTHING : habillement *m* **2** SAUCE : sauce *f*, vinaigrette *f* **3** BANDAGE : pansement *m* **4** FERTILIZER : engrais *m*

dressmaker [ˈdrɛs,meɪkər] *n* : couturière *f*

dressmaking [ˈdrɛs,meɪkɪŋ] *n* : couture *f*

dressy [ˈdrɛsi] *adj* **dressier; -est** : habillé, élégant

drew → **draw**[1]

dribble[1] [ˈdrɪbəl] *vi* **-bled; -bling 1** TRICKLE : dégoutter, tomber goutte à goutte **2** DROOL : baver **3** : dribbler (au basketball)

dribble[2] *n* **1** TRICKLE : filet *m* (d'eau) **2** DROOL : bave *f* **3** : dribble *m* (au basketball)

drier, driest → **dry**[2]

drift[1] [ˈdrɪft] *vi* **1** : dériver (sur l'eau), être emporté (par le vent) **2** ACCUMULATE : s'amonceler, former des bancs *Can*, poudrer *Can* (se dit de la neige) **3 to drift along** : flâner, errer <she drifted through life : elle a passé sa vie à errer> **4 to drift away** : s'éloigner

drift[2] *n* **1** COURSE : mouvement *m*, courant *m* **2** HEAP, MASS : amoncellement *m*, entassement *m*, banc *m* (de neige) *Can* **3** MEANING : sens *m*, portée *f*

drill[1] [ˈdrɪl] *vt* **1** BORE : percer, forer **2** TRAIN : faire faire des exercices à, entraîner — *vi* **1** BORE : forer, percer un trou **2** PRACTICE, TRAIN : faire de l'exercice

drill[2] *n* **1** : perceuse *f* (outil) **2** EXERCISE, PRACTICE : exercice *m* **3** : semoir *m* (en agriculture)

drily → **dryly**

drink[1] [ˈdrɪŋk] *v* **drank** [ˈdræŋk]; **drunk** [ˈdrʌŋk] *or* **drank; drinking** *vt* **1** : boire **2 to drink up** ABSORB : boire, s'imbiber — *vi* : boire

drink[2] *n* **1** BEVERAGE : boisson *f* **2** : boisson *f* alcoolisée

drip[1] [ˈdrɪp] *v* **dripped; dripping** *vt* : laisser tomber goutte à goutte — *vi* : tomber goutte à goutte, dégoutter

drip[2] *n* **1** DROP : goutte *f* **2** : bruit *m* de goutte

drive[1] [ˈdraɪv] *v* **drove** [ˈdro:v]; **driven** [ˈdrɪvən]; **driving** *vt* **1** : mener, conduire (un troupeau) **2** : conduire, piloter (un véhicule) **3** COMPEL : inciter **4** PUSH : conduire, amener <hunger drove him to steal : la faim l'a amené à voler> **5** PROPEL : envoyer (une balle) — *vi* : conduire, rouler <I was driving at 65 mph : je roulais à 65 milles à l'heure>

drive[2] *n* **1** : promenade *f* (en voiture) **2** CAMPAIGN : campagne *f* **3** VIGOR : énergie *f*, initiative *f* **4** NEED : besoin *m* fondamental

drivel [ˈdrɪvəl] *n* : bêtises *fpl*

driver [ˈdraɪvər] *n* **1** : conducteur *m*, -trice *f* **2** CHAUFFEUR : chauffeur *m*

driveway [ˈdraɪv,weɪ] *n* : allée *f*, entrée *f* (de garage)

drizzle[1] [ˈdrɪzəl] *vi* **-zled; -zling** : bruiner, crachiner

drizzle[2] *n* : bruine *f*, crachin *m*

droll [ˈdro:l] *adj* **1** COMICAL : drôle, comique **2** ODD : curieux, bizarre

dromedary [ˈdrɑmə,dɛri] *n, pl* **-daries** : dromadaire *m*

drone[1] [ˈdro:n] *vi* **droned; droning 1** BUZZ, HUM : bourdonner (se dit d'un insecte), ronronner (se dit d'un moteur) **2** *or* **to drone on** : parler d'un ton monotone

drone[2] *n* **1** BEE : abeille *f* mâle **2** HUM : bourdonnement *m* (d'un insecte), ronronnement *m* (d'un moteur)
drool[1] ['dru:l] *vi* : baver
drool[2] *n* : bave *f*
droop[1] ['dru:p] *vi* **1** HANG, SAG : pencher (se dit de la tête), tomber (se dit des épaules ou des paupières), se faner (se dit des fleurs) **2** FLAG : baisser <her spirits were drooping : elle était démoralisée>
droop[2] *n* : abaissement *m*, affaissement *m*, attitude *f* penchée
drop[1] ['drɑp] *v* **dropped; dropping** *vt* **1** : laisser tomber <he dropped the book : il a laissé tomber le livre> **2** LOWER : baisser <to drop one's voice : baisser la voix> **3** SEND : envoyer <drop me a line : écris-moi un mot> **4** ABANDON : abandonner (une conversation, une matière, etc.) **5** OMIT : omettre, supprimer **6 to drop a hint about** : faire allusion à, suggérer **7 to drop off** LEAVE : déposer, laisser — *vi* **1** DRIP : tomber goutte à goutte **2** FALL : tomber **3** DECREASE : se calmer (se dit du vent), baisser (se dit des prix) **4 to drop back** *or* **to drop behind** : rester en arrière, prendre du retard **5 to drop by** VISIT : passer, entrer en passant
drop[2] *n* **1** : goutte *f* (de liquide) **2** DECLINE, FALL : réduction *f*, diminution *f* **3** DESCENT : hauteur *f* de chute, descente *f* <a 10-foot drop : une hauteur de 10 pieds> **4** : pastille *f*, bonbon *f* <cough drops : pastilles contre la toux>
droplet ['drɑplət] *n* : gouttelette *f*
dropper ['drɑpər] *n* : compte-gouttes *m*
dross ['drɑs, 'drɔs] *n* **1** : crasse *f*, scories *fpl* (de métaux) **2** WASTE : déchets *mpl*
drought ['draʊt] *n* : sécheresse *f*
drove[1] ['dro:v] → **drive**[1]
drove[2] *n* **1** HERD : troupeau *m* **2** CROWD : foule *f* <people came in droves : il y avait une foule de gens>
drown ['draʊn] *vt* **1** : noyer **2** *or* **to drown out** : noyer, couvrir (un son, une voix) — *vi* : se noyer
drowse[1] ['draʊz] *vi* **drowsed; drowsing** : somnoler, sommeiller
drowse[2] *n* DOZE : somme *m*, sieste *f*
drowsiness ['draʊzinəs] *n* : somnolence *f*
drowsy ['draʊzi] *adj* **drowsier; -est** : somnolent, qui a envie de dormir
drub ['drʌb] *vt* **drubbed; drubbing 1** BEAT : battre, maltraiter **2** DEFEAT : vaincre
drudge[1] ['drʌdʒ] *vi* **drudged; drudging** : besogner, trimer *fam*
drudge[2] *n* : bête *f* de somme, gratte-papier *m*
drudgery ['drʌdʒəri] *n, pl* **-eries** : corvée *f*, (grosse) besogne *f*
drug[1] ['drʌg] *vt* **drugged; drugging** : droguer
drug[2] *n* **1** MEDICATION : médicament *m* **2** NARCOTIC : drogue *f*, stupéfiant *m*
druggist ['drʌgɪst] *n* : pharmacien *m*, -cienne *f*
drugstore ['drʌg,stor] *n* : pharmacie *f*
drum[1] ['drʌm] *v* **drummed; drumming** *vi* : jouer du tambour — *vt* **1** TAP : tambouriner (les doigts, les pieds, etc.) **2** DRIVE, PUSH : enfoncer, fourrer <he drummed it into my head : il me l'a enfoncé dans la tête>
drum[2] *n* **1** : tambour *m* **2** *or* **oil drum** : bidon *m*
drumbeat ['drʌm,bi:t] *n* : roulement *m* de tambour
drumstick ['drʌm,stɪk] *n* **1** : baguette *f* de tambour **2** : cuisse *f* (de poulet)
drunk[1] → **drink**[1]
drunk[2] ['drʌŋk] *adj* : ivre, soûl *fam*, en boisson *Can* <drunk driving : conduite en état d'ébriété>
drunk[3] *n* : ivrogne *m*, ivrognesse *f*
drunkard ['drʌŋkərd] *n* : ivrogne *m*, ivrognesse *f*
drunken ['drʌŋkən] *adj* : ivre, en état d'ébriété
drunkenly ['drʌŋkənli] *adv* : comme un ivrogne
drunkenness ['drʌŋkənli] *n* : ivresse *f*, ébriété
dry[1] ['draɪ] *v* **dried; drying** *vt* **1** : sécher **2** WIPE : essuyer — *vi* : sécher
dry[2] *adj* **drier; driest 1** : sec <a dry climate : un climat sec> **2** THIRSTY : assoiffé **3** : qui interdit la vente d'alcool <a dry town : une ville où on ne vend pas d'alcool> **4** UNINTERESTING : plate, aride **5** BITING, KEEN : mordant, caustique <to have a dry wit : être pince-sans-rire> **6** : sec (se dit du vin), brut (se dit du champagne) **7 on dry land** : sur la terre ferme
dry–clean ['draɪ,kli:n] *vt* : nettoyer à sec
dry cleaner *n* : teinturerie *f* (service)
dry cleaning *n* : nettoyage *m* à sec
dryer ['draɪər] *n* : séchoir *m*
dry goods *npl* : tissus *mpl*, étoffes *fpl*
dry ice *n* : neige *f* carbonique
dryly ['draɪli] *adv* : sèchement
dryness ['draɪnəs] *n* : sécheresse *f*
dual ['du:əl, 'dju:-] *adj* : double
dub ['dʌb] *vt* **dubbed; dubbing 1** NAME, NICKNAME : surnommer **2** : doubler (un film, etc.)
dubious ['du:biəs, 'dju:-] *adj* **1** DOUBTFUL : dubitatif **2** QUESTIONABLE : louche, suspect
dubiously ['du:biəsli, 'dju:-] *adv* : d'un air incertain, avec doute
duchess ['dʌtʃəs] *n* : duchesse *f*
duck[1] ['dʌk] *vt* **1** PLUNGE : plonger (dans l'eau) **2** LOWER : baisser <to duck one's head : baisser la tête> **3** AVOID, DODGE : éviter, esquiver — *vi* : se baisser vivement, esquiver un coup (en boxe)
duck[2] *n, pl* **ducks** *or* **duck** : canard *m*

duckling ['dʌklɪŋ] *n* : caneton *m*, canette *f*
duct ['dʌkt] *n* **1** PIPE : conduite *f* (d'eau, etc.) **2** CHANNEL, TUBE : conduit *m*, canal *m* <tear duct : canal lacrymal>
dude ['du:d, 'dju:d] *n* **1** DANDY : dandy *m* **2** GUY : gars *m fam*, mec *m fam*
due[1] ['du:, 'dju:] *adv* DIRECTLY : plein, droit vers <due north : plein nord>
due[2] *adj* **1** OWING : dû, payable **2** APPROPRIATE : qui convient, dû <after due consideration : après mûre réflexion> **3** EXPECTED : attendu <the plane is due at midnight : l'avion doit arriver à minuit>
due[3] *n* **1 to give s.o. his (her) due** : rendre justice à qqn **2 dues** *npl* FEE : cotisation *f*
duel[1] ['du:əl, 'dju:-] *vi* **duelled; duelling** : se battre en duel
duel[2] *n* : duel *m*
duet [du'ɛt, dju:-] *n* : duo *m*
due to *prep* : en raison de, à cause de
dug → **dig**[1]
dugout ['dʌg,aʊt] *n* **1** CANOE : pirogue *f* **2** SHELTER : tranchée-abri *f*
duke ['du:k, 'dju:k] *n* : duc *m*
dull[1] ['dʌl] *vt* **1** BLUNT : émousser, épointer **2** DIM, TARNISH : ternir (des couleurs, des métaux, etc.)
dull[2] *adj* **1** STUPID : stupide, lent **2** BLUNT : émoussé <a dull knife : un couteau émoussé> **3** BORING : ennuyeux, ennuyant *Can* **4** LACKLUSTER : terne, fade <a dull red : un rouge fade>
dullness ['dʌlnəs] *n* **1** STUPIDITY : stupidité *f*, lenteur *f* **2** BLUNTNESS : manque *m* de tranchant **3** TEDIUM : monotonie *f*
duly ['du:li] *adv* **1** PROPERLY : dûment, de façon convenable <duly recorded : dûment enregistré> **2** EXPECTEDLY : comme prévu
dumb ['dʌm] *adj* **1** MUTE : muet **2** STUPID : bête
dumbbell ['dʌm,bɛl] *n* **1** WEIGHT : haltère *m* **2** DOPE : idiot *m*, -diote *f*; gourde *f fam*
dumbfound *or* **dumfound** [,dʌm'faʊnd] *vt* AMAZE : abasourdir, sidérer *fam*
dummy ['dʌmi] *n, pl* **-mies 1** DOPE, FOOL : imbécile *mf*, ballot *m fam* **2** MANNEQUIN : mannequin *m*
dump[1] ['dʌmp] *vt* : déposer, jeter, déverser
dump[2] *n* **1** : tas *m* d'ordures **2 to be down in the dumps** : avoir le cafard
dumpling ['dʌmplɪŋ] *n* : boulette *f* de pâte
dumpy ['dʌmpi] *adj* **dumpier; -est** CHUBBY : boulot, rondelet *fam*
dun[1] ['dʌn] *vt* **dunned; dunning** : harceler (afin d'obtenir un paiement)
dun[2] *adj* : brun gris
dunce [dʌn*t*s] *n* : cancre *m fam*
dune ['du:n, 'dju:n] *n* : dune *f*
dung ['dʌŋ] *n* : excréments *mpl*, fumier *m*, bouse *f* (de vache), crottin *m* (de cheval)
dungaree [,dʌŋgə'ri:] *n* **1** DENIM : jean *m* **2 dungarees** *npl* JEANS : jean *m*, blue-jean *m*
dungeon ['dʌndʒən] *n* : cachot *m* (souterrain)
dunghill ['dʌŋ,hɪl] *n* : tas *m* de fumier
dunk ['dʌŋk] *vt* : tremper
duo ['du:o:, 'dju:-] *n, pl* **duos** : duo *m*
dupe[1] ['du:p, 'dju:p] *vt* **duped; duping** : duper, tromper
dupe[2] *n* : dupe *f*
duplex[1] ['du:,plɛks, 'dju:-] *adj* : double
duplex[2] *n* : duplex *m*, maison *f* jumelée
duplicate[1] ['du:plɪ,keɪt, 'dju:-] *vt* **-cated; -cating 1** COPY : faire un double de, copier **2** REPEAT : répéter, refaire
duplicate[2] ['du:plɪkət, 'dju:-] *adj* : en double
duplicate[3] ['du:plɪkət, 'dju:-] *n* : double *m*, copie *f* exacte
duplication [,du:plɪ'keɪʃən, ,dju:-] *n* **1** DUPLICATING : action *f* de copier, reproduction *f* **2** REPETITION : répétition *f*
duplicity [dʊ'plɪsəṭi, ,dju:-] *n, pl* **-ties** : duplicité *f*
durability [,dʊrə'bɪləṭi, ,djʊr-] *n* : durabilité *f*, résistance *f*
durable ['dʊrəbəl, 'djʊr-] *adj* : durable, résistant
duration [dʊ'reɪʃən, djʊ-] *n* : durée *f*
duress [dʊ'rɛs, djʊ-] *n* : contrainte *f*
during ['dʊrɪŋ, 'djʊr-] *prep* : durant, pendant
dusk ['dʌsk] *n* : crépuscule *m*, nuit *f* tombante, brunante *f Can*
dusky ['dʌski] *adj* **duskier; -est** : sombre, obscur (se dit des couleurs)
dust[1] ['dʌst] *vt* **1** : épousseter **2** SPRINKLE : saupoudrer
dust[2] *n* : poussière *f*
duster ['dʌstər] *n* **1** *or* **dust cloth** : chiffon *m* à poussière **2** *or* **feather duster** : plumeau *m* **3** HOUSECOAT : blouse *f*, sarrau *m*
dustpan ['dʌst,pæn] *n* : pelle *f* à poussière, porte-poussière *m Can*
dusty ['dʌsti] *adj* **dustier; -est** : poussiéreux
Dutch[1] ['dʌtʃ] *adj* : néerlandais, hollandais
Dutch[2] *n* **1** : néerlandais *m*, hollandais *m* (langue) **2 the Dutch** *npl* : les Néerlandais, les Hollandais
Dutch treat *n* : sortie *f* où chacun paie sa part
dutiful ['du:ṭɪfəl, 'dju:-] *adj* : obéissant, respectueux, consciencieux
duty ['du:ṭi, ,dju:-] *n, pl* **-ties 1** TASK : fonction *f* <to perform one's duties : remplir ses fonctions> **2** OBLIGATION : devoir *m* **3** TAX : taxe *f*, droit *m* **4 to be on duty** : être de garde
DVD [,di:,vi:'di:] *n* : DVD *m*
dwarf[1] ['dwɔrf] *vt* **1** STUNT : rabougrir (un arbre) **2** : faire paraître tout petit

dwarf[2] *n* : nain *m,* naine *f*
dwell [ˈdwɛl] *vi* **dwelled** *or* **dwelt** [ˈdwɛlt]; **dwelling 1** RESIDE : résider, demeurer **2 to dwell on** : penser sans cesse à, ruminer
dweller [ˈdwɛlər] *n* : habitant *m,* -tante *f*
dwelling [ˈdwɛlɪŋ] *n* : demeure *f,* résidence *f*
dwindle [ˈdwɪndəl] *vi* **-dled; -dling** : diminuer
dye[1] [ˈdaɪ] *vt* **dyed; dyeing** : teindre <to dye one's hair : se teindre les cheveux>
dye[2] *n* : teinture *f*
dying → **die**[1]
dyke → **dike**
dynamic [daɪˈnæmɪk] *adj* : dynamique
dynamite[1] [ˈdaɪnəˌmaɪt] *vt* **-mited; -miting** : dynamiter
dynamite[2] *n* : dynamite *f*
dynamo [ˈdaɪnəˌmoː] *n, pl* **-mos** : dynamo *f*
dynasty [ˈdaɪnəsti, -næs-] *n, pl* **-ties** : dynastie *f*
dysentery [ˈdɪsənˌtɛri] *n, pl* **-teries** : dysenterie *f*
dyslexia [dɪsˈlɛksiə] *n* : dyslexie *f* — **dyslexic** [-ˈlɛksɪk] *adj*
dystrophy [ˈdɪstrəfi] *n, pl* **-phies 1** : dystrophie *f* **2** → **muscular dystrophy**

E

e [ˈiː] *n, pl* **e's** *or* **es** [ˈiːz] : e *m,* cinquième lettre de l'alphabet
each[1] [ˈiːtʃ] *adv* APIECE : chacun, la pièce <one dollar each : un dollar la pièce>
each[2] *adj* : chaque <each week : chaque semaine>
each[3] *pron* **1** : chacun *m,* -cune *f* <each of the girls : chacune des filles> <each and every one : chacun sans exception> **2 each other** : l'un l'autre <they love each other : ils s'aiment (l'un l'autre)> **3 to each his own** : chacun son goût
eager [ˈiːgər] *adj* **1** ENTHUSIASTIC : désireux, avide **2** ANXIOUS, IMPATIENT : impatient, pressé
eagerly [ˈiːgərli] *adv* : avidement, avec empressement
eagerness [ˈiːgərnəs] *n* : avidité *f,* empressement *m*
eagle [ˈiːgəl] *n* : aigle *m*
ear [ˈɪr] *n* **1** : oreille *f* (en anatomie) **2** : épi *m* (de maïs, etc.)
earache [ˈɪrˌeɪk] *n* : mal *m* d'oreille
eardrum [ˈɪrˌdrʌm] *n* : tympan *m*
earl [ˈərl] *n* : comte *m*
earlobe [ˈɪrˌloːb] *n* : lobe *m* de l'oreille
early[1] [ˈərli] *adv* **earlier; -est 1** : tôt, de bonne heure <to go to bed early : se coucher de bonne heure> <as early as possible : le plus tôt possible> **2** : en avance <five minutes early : en avance de cinq minutes>
early[2] *adj* **earlier; -est 1** FIRST : premier <his early novels : ses premiers romans> **2** (*referring to a designated time*) <to be early : arriver de bonne heure> <early fruits : fruits précoces> <an early death : une mort prématurée> **3** (*referring to a beginning*) <in the early afternoon : au commencement de l'après-midi> <in early December : début décembre> **4** ANCIENT : ancien, primitif <early man : l'homme primitif>
earmark [ˈɪrˌmɑrk] *vt* : réserver, désigner
earn [ˈərn] *vt* **1** : gagner <to earn one's living : gagner sa vie> **2** DESERVE : mériter
earnest[1] [ˈərnəst] *adj* **1** SERIOUS : sérieux **2** SINCERE : sincère — **earnestly** *adv*
earnest[2] *n* **in ~** : sérieusement
earnestness [ˈərnəstnəs] *n* : sérieux *m,* gravité *f*
earnings [ˈərnɪŋz] *npl* **1** WAGES : salaire *m* **2** PROFITS : bénéfices *mpl,* profits *mpl*
earphone [ˈɪrˌfoːn] *n* : écouteur *m*
earring [ˈɪrˌrɪŋ] *n* : boucle *f* d'oreille
earshot [ˈɪrˌʃɑt] *n* : portée *f* de voix
earth [ˈərθ] *n* **1** GROUND, SOIL : terre *f,* sol *m* **2 the Earth** : la Terre
earthen [ˈərθən, -ðən] *adj* : en terre
earthenware [ˈərθənˌwær, -ðən-] *n* : faïence *f*
earthly [ˈərθli] *adj* **1** : terrestre <earthly pleasures : joies terrestres> **2** (*indicating possibility*) <of no earthly use : d'aucune utilité>
earthquake [ˈərθˌkweɪk] *n* : tremblement *m* de terre
earthworm [ˈərθˌwərm] *n* : ver *m* de terre, lombric *m France*
earthy [ˈərθi] *adj* **earthier; -est 1** : terreux <earthy colors : couleurs de terre> **2** DOWN-TO-EARTH : pratique, terre à terre **3** COARSE, CRUDE : truculent, grossier
earwax [ˈɪrˌwæks] *n* : cérumen *m*
earwig [ˈɪrˌwɪg] *n* : perce-oreille *m*
ease[1] [ˈiːz] *v* **eased; easing** *vt* **1** FACILITATE : faciliter **2** ALLEVIATE, LESSEN : soulager, atténuer, calmer (l'inquiétude) **3 to ease oneself into** : se laisser glisser dans — *vi or* **to ease up** : s'atténuer, se détendre
ease[2] *n* **1** : aise *f* <to put s.o. at ease : mettre qqn à son aise> **2** FACILITY : facilité *f* **3** COMFORT : bien-être *m,*

tranquillité *f* 4 AFFLUENCE : aisance *f* 5 **at ease!** : repos! 6 **with ∼** : aisément, facilement

easel [ˈi:zəl] *n* : chevalet *m*

easily [ˈi:zəli] *adv* 1 : facilement, aisément 2 UNQUESTIONABLY : sans doute, de loin

easiness [ˈi:zinəs] *n* : facilité *f*

east[1] [ˈi:st] *adv* : vers l'est, à l'est

east[2] *adj* : est <the east coast : la côte est> <the east wind : le vent d'est>

east[3] *n* 1 : est *m* 2 **the East** : l'Est *m*, l'Orient *m*

Easter [ˈi:stər] *n* : Pâques *m*, Pâques *fpl*

easterly[1] [ˈi:stərli] *adv* : vers l'est

easterly[2] *adj* : d'est, de l'est <in an easterly direction : en direction de l'est>

eastern [ˈi:stərn] *adj* 1 : est, de l'est 2 **Eastern** : de l'Est, d'Orient

easy[1] [ˈi:zi] *adv* **easier; -est** : doucement <to go easy on : aller doucement avec> <easy does it! : doucement!>

easy[2] *adj* **easier; -est** 1 : facile, aisé 2 RELAXED : décontracté <an easy manner : une attitude pleine d'aisance> 3 LENIENT : indulgent, clément

easygoing [ˌi:ziˈgo:ɪŋ] *adj* : accommodant, complaisant

eat [ˈi:t] *v* **ate** [ˈeɪt]; **eaten** [ˈi:tən]; **eating** *vt* 1 : manger, prendre (un repas) 2 CONSUME : manger, consommer (des ressources, des bénéfices, etc.) 3 CORRODE : ronger, corroder — *vi* : manger

eatable [ˈi:t̬əbəl] *adj* : mangeable, bon à manger

eaves [ˈi:vz] *npl* : avant-toit *m*

eavesdrop [ˈi:vzˌdrɑp] *vi* **-dropped; -dropping** : écouter aux portes

ebb[1] [ˈɛb] *vi* 1 : refluer, descendre (se dit de la mer) 2 DECLINE : décliner, baisser

ebb[2] *n* 1 : reflux *m* (de la mer) 2 DECLIN : déclin *m*, baisse *f*

ebony[1] [ˈɛbəni] *adj* 1 : d'ébène 2 BLACK : d'un noir d'ébène

ebony[2] *n, pl* **-nies** : ébène *f*

ebullience [ɪˈbʊljənts, -ˈbʌl-] *n* : exubérance *f*

ebullient [ɪˈbʊljənt, -ˈbʌl-] *adj* : exubérant

eccentric[1] [ɪkˈsɛntrɪk] *adj* : excentrique — **eccentrically** [-trɪkli] *adv*

eccentric[2] *n* : excentrique *mf*

eccentricity [ˌɛkˌsɛnˈtrɪsət̬i] *n, pl* **-ties** : excentricité *f*

ecclesiastic [ɪˌkli:ziˈæstɪk] *n* : ecclésiastique *mf*

ecclesiastical [ɪˌkli:ziˈæstɪkəl] *or* **ecclesiastic** *adj* : ecclésiastique

echelon [ˈɛʃəˌlɑn] *n* : échelon *m*

echo[1] [ˈɛˌko:] *v* **echoed; echoing** *vt* : répercuter (un son), répéter (des mots) — *vi* : se répercuter, résonner

echo[2] *n, pl* **echoes** : écho *m*

éclair [eɪˈklær, i-] *n* : éclair *m*

eclectic [ɛˈklɛktɪk, ɪ-] *adj* : éclectique

eclipse[1] [ɪˈklɪps] *vt* **eclipsed; eclipsing** : éclipser

eclipse[2] *n* : éclipse *f*

ecological [ˌi:kəˈlɑdʒɪkəl, ˌɛkə-] *adj* : écologique — **ecologically** *adv*

ecologist [iˈkɑlədʒɪst, ɛ-] *n* : écologiste *mf*

ecology [iˈkɑlədʒi, ɛ-] *n, pl* **-gies** : écologie *f*

economic [ˌi:kəˈnɑmɪk, ˌɛkə-] *adj* : économique

economical [ˌi:kəˈnɑmɪkəl, ˌɛkə-] *adj* THRIFTY : économe

economically [ˌi:kəˈnɑmɪkli, ˌɛkə-] *adv* : économiquement, de façon économique

economics [ˌi:kəˈnɑmɪks, ˌɛkə-] *ns & pl* : sciences *fpl* économiques, économie *f*

economist [iˈkɑnəmɪst] *n* : économiste *mf*

economize [iˈkɑnəˌmaɪz] *v* **-mized; -mizing** : économiser

economy [iˈkɑnəmi] *n, pl* **-mies** : économie *f*

ecosystem [ˈi:koˌsɪstəm] *n* : écosystème *m*

ecru [ˈɛˌkru:, ˈeɪ-] *n* : écru *m*

ecstasy [ˈɛkstəsi] *n, pl* **-sies** : extase *f*

ecstatic [ɛkˈstæt̬ɪk, ɪk-] *adj* : extatique, ravi, en extase

ecstatically [ɛkˈstæt̬ɪkli, ɪk-] *adv* : avec extase

Ecuadoran[1] [ˌɛkwəˈdorən] *or* **Ecuadorean** *or* **Ecuadorian** [-ˈdoriən] *adj* : équatorien

Ecuadoran[2] *or* **Ecuadorean** *or* **Ecuadorian** *n* : Équatorien *m*, -rienne *f*

ecumenical [ˌɛkjʊˈmɛnɪkəl] *adj* : œcuménique

eczema [ɪgˈzi:mə, ˈɛgzəmə, ˈɛksə-] *n* : eczéma *m*

eddy[1] [ˈɛdi] *vi* **eddied; eddying** : tourbillonner

eddy[2] *n, pl* **-dies** : tourbillon *m*

edema [ɪˈdi:mə] *n* : œdème *m*

edge[1] [ˈɛdʒ] *vt* **edged; edging** 1 BORDER : border 2 SHARPEN : aiguiser, affiler 3 **to edge one's way** : avancer lentement 4 **to edge out** : pousser (qqn) doucement vers la sortie, évincer en douceur — *vi* ADVANCE : avancer (doucement)

edge[2] *n* 1 BORDER, MARGIN : bord *m* 2 : tranchant *m*, fil *m* (d'un couteau, etc.) 3 ADVANTAGE : avantage *m*

edgewise [ˈɛdʒˌwaɪz] *adv* 1 → **sideways** 2 **to get a word in edgewise** : placer un mot

edginess [ˈɛdʒinəs] *n* : nervosité *f*

edging [ˈɛdʒɪŋ] *n* : bordure *f*

edgy [ˈɛdʒi] *adj* **edgier; -est** : énervé

edible [ˈɛdəbəl] *adj* : comestible

edict [ˈi:ˌdɪkt] *n* : édit *m*, décret *m*

edification [ˌɛdəfəˈkeɪʃən] *n* : édification *f*

edifice [ˈɛdəˈfɪs] *n* : édifice *m*
edify [ˈɛdəˈfaɪ] *vt* **-fied; -fying** : édifier
edit [ˈɛdɪt] *vt* **1** : réviser, corriger, diriger la rédaction de **2 to edit out** : couper, supprimer
edition [ɪˈdɪʃən] *n* : édition *f* <limited edition : édition à tirage limité>
editor [ˈɛdɪt̬ər] *n* : rédacteur *m*, -trice *f* (d'un journal); éditeur *m*, -trice *f* (d'un livre); monteur *m*, -teuse *f* (d'un film)
editorial[1] [ˌɛdɪˈtoriəl] *adj* **1** : de la rédaction <editorial staff : personnel de rédaction> **2** : éditorial <an editorial comment : un commentaire éditorial>
editorial[2] *n* : éditorial *m*
educate [ˈɛdʒəˌkeɪt] *vt* **-cated; -cating 1** INSTRUCT, TEACH : instruire, donner l'instruction à (des élèves) **2** DEVELOP, REFINE : éduquer <to educate s.o.'s taste : éduquer le goût de qqn>
education [ˌɛdʒəˈkeɪʃən] *n* **1** : éducation *f*, études *fpl* <university education : études supérieures> **2** TEACHING : enseignement *m*, instruction *f*
educational [ˌɛdʒəˈkeɪʃənəl] *adj* **1** INSTRUCTIVE : éducatif **2** TEACHING : d'enseignement, pédagogique
educator [ˈɛdʒəˌkeɪt̬ər] *n* : éducateur *m*, -trice *f*
eel [ˈiːl] *n* : anguille *f*
eerie [ˈɪri] *adj* **eerier; -est** : sinistre, étrange
eerily [ˈɪrəli] *adv* : d'une manière sinistre
efface [ɪˈfeɪs, ɛ-] *vt* **-faced; -facing** : effacer
effect[1] [ɪˈfɛkt] *vt* : effectuer, réaliser
effect[2] *n* **1** RESULT : effet *m*, conséquence *f* **2** MEANING : sens *m* <something to that effect : quelque chose dans ce sens> **3** EFFECTIVENESS : efficacité *f* <to little effect : sans grand résultat> **4 effects** *npl* BELONGINGS : effets *mpl* (personnels) **5 to go into effect** : entrer en vigueur **6 in ~** REALLY : en fait, en réalité
effective [ɪˈfɛktɪv] *adj* **1** EFFECTUAL : efficace **2** ACTUAL : effectif **3** OPERATIVE : en vigueur
effectively [ɪˈfɛktɪvli] *adv* **1** EFFICIENTLY : efficacement **2** ACTUALLY, REALLY : effectivement
effectiveness [ɪˈfɛktɪvnəs] *n* : efficacité *f*
effectual [ɪˈfɛktʃʊəl] *adj* : efficace — **effectually** *adv*
effeminate [əˈfɛmənət] *adj* : efféminé
effervesce [ˌɛfərˈvɛs] *vi* **-vesced; -vescing 1** FIZZ : pétiller **2** : être exubérant (se dit des personnes)
effervescence [ˌɛfərˈvɛsənts] *n* : effervescence *f*
effervescent [ˌɛfərˈvɛsənt] *adj* : effervescent
effete [ɛˈfiːt, ɪ-] *adj* **1** DECADENT, WEAKENED : veule, affaibli, décadent **2** EFFEMINATE : efféminé
efficacious [ˌɛfəˈkeɪʃəs] *adj* : efficace
efficacy [ˈɛfɪkəsi] *n, pl* **-cies** : efficacité *f*
efficiency [ˈɪfɪʃəntsi] *n pl* **-cies** : efficacité *f*, efficience *f*
efficient [ɪˈfɪʃənt] *adj* : efficace, efficient
efficiently [ɪˈfɪʃəntli] *adv* : efficacement <to work efficiently : fonctionner à bon rendement>
effigy [ˈɛfədʒi] *n, pl* **-gies** : effigie *f*
effort [ˈɛfərt] *n* **1** EXERTION : effort *m* <to be worth the effort : en valoir la peine> **2** ATTEMPT : essai *m*, tentative *f*
effortless [ˈɛfərtləs] *adj* : facile, aisé — **effortlessly** *adv*
effrontery [ɪˈfrʌntəri] *n, pl* **-teries** : effronterie *f*
effusion [ɪˈfjuːʒən, ɛ-] *n* : effusion *f*
effusive [ɪˈfjuːsɪv, ɛ-] *adj* : expansif, démonstratif <an effusive welcome : un accueil chaleureux>
effusively [ɪˈfjuːsɪvli, ɛ-] *adv* : avec effusion
egg[1] [ˈɛg] *vt* **to egg on** : inciter, pousser
egg[2] *n* : œuf *m*
eggbeater [ˈɛgˌbiːt̬ər] *n* : batteur *m* (à œufs)
eggnog [ˈɛgˌnɑg] *n* : lait *m* de poule
eggplant [ˈɛgˌplænt] *n* : aubergine *f*
eggshell [ˈɛgˌʃɛl] *n* : coquille *f* d'œuf
ego [ˈiːˌgoː] *n, pl* **egos 1** SELF : ego *m*, moi *m* **2** SELF-ESTEEM : amour-propre *m*
egocentric [iːgoˈsɛntrɪk] *adj* : égocentrique
egoism [ˈiːgoˌwɪzəm] *m* : égoïsme *m*
egoist [ˈiːgowɪst] *n* : égoïste *mf*
egoistic [ˌiːgoˈwɪstɪk] *adj* : égoïste
egotism [ˈiːgəˈtɪzəm] *n* : égotisme *m*
egotist [ˈiːgətɪst] *n* : égotiste *mf*
egotistic [ˌiːgəˈtɪstɪk] *or* **egotistical** [-ˈtɪstɪkəl] *adj* : égotiste
egregious [ɪˈgriːdʒəs] *adj* : flagrant <an egregious error : une erreur énorme>
egress [ˈiːˌgrɛs] *n* : sortie *f*, issue *f*
egret [ˈiːgrət, -ˌgrɛt] *n* : aigrette *f*
Egyptian[1] [iˈdʒɪpʃən] *adj* : égyptien
Egyptian[2] *n* : Égyptien *m*, -tienne *f*
eider [ˈaɪdər] *n* : eider *m*, moyac *m* Can
eiderdown [ˈaɪdərˌdaʊn] *n* **1** DOWN : duvet *m* **2** COMFORTER : édredon *m*
eight[1] [ˈeɪt] *adj* : huit
eight[2] *n* : huit *m*
eighteen[1] [eɪtˈtiːn] *adj* : dix-huit
eighteen[2] *n* : dix-huit *m*
eighteenth[1] [eɪtˈtiːnθ] *adj* : dix-huitième
eighteenth[2] *n* **1** : dix-huitième *mf* (dans une série) **2** : dix-huitième *m* (en mathématiques) **3** (*used for dates*) <the eighteenth of May : le dix-huit mai>

eighth[1] ['eɪtθ] *adj* : huitième
eighth[2] *n* **1** : huitième *mf* (dans une série) **2** : huitième *m* (en mathématiques) **3** (*used in dates*) <the eighth of June : le huit juin>
eightieth[1] ['eɪt̬iəθ] *adj* : quatre-vingtième
eightieth[2] *n* **1** : quatre-vingtième *mf* (dans une série) **2** : quatre-vingtième *m* (en mathématiques)
eighty[1] ['eɪt̬i] *adj* : quatre-vingts
eighty[2] *n, pl* **eighties** : quatre-vingts *m* <in the late eighties : vers la fin des années quatre-vingts>
either[1] ['i:ðər, 'aɪ-] *adj* **1** EACH : chaque <there are trees on either side : il y a des arbres de chaque côté> **2** (*referring to one or the other*) <take either road : prenez l'une ou l'autre des deux routes> <he doesn't like either restaurant : il n'aime ni l'un ni l'autre de ces restaurants> <give me either book : donnez-moi n'importe quel livre>
either[2] *pron* : l'un ou l'autre, n'importe lequel <take either one : prenez l'un ou l'autre> <I don't believe either of them : je ne les crois ni l'un ni l'autre>
either[3] *conj* **either . . . or** : ou . . . ou, ou bien . . . ou bien, soit . . . soit <you either love him or hate him : soit on l'adore, soit on le déteste>
ejaculate [i'dʒækjə,leɪt] *vi* **-lated; -lating 1** : éjaculer (en physiologie) **2** EXCLAIM : s'exclamer, s'écrier
ejaculation [i,dʒækjə'leɪʃən] *n* **1** : éjaculation *f* (en physiologie) **2** EXCLAMATION : exclamation *f*, cri *m*
eject [i'dʒɛkt] *vt* : éjecter, expulser
ejection [i'dʒɛkʃən] *n* : éjection *f*, expulsion *f*
eke [i:k] *vt* **eked; eking** *or* **to eke out 1** SUPPLEMENT : augmenter **2** : gagner difficilement <she eked out a living : elle a gagné tout juste sa vie>
elaborate[1] [i'læbə,reɪt] *v* **-rated; -rating** *vt* : élaborer (un plan, etc.) — *vi* **to elaborate on** : donner des détails sur, développer
elaborate[2] [i'læbərət] *adj* **1** DETAILED : minutieux **2** ORNATE : orné, travaillé **3** COMPLEX : compliqué, complexe
elapse [i'læps] *vi* **elapsed; elapsing** : s'écouler, passer
elastic[1] [i'læstɪk] *adj* : élastique
elastic[2] *n* : élastique *m*
elasticity [i,læs'tɪsət̬i, ,i:,læs-] *n, pl* **-ties** : élasticité *f*
elate [i'leɪt] *vt* **elated; elating** : ravir, transporter de joie
elation [i'leɪʃən] *n* : exultation *f*, joie *f*
elbow[1] ['ɛl,bo:] *vt* : donner un coup de coude à
elbow[2] *n* : coude *m* <to be at s.o.'s elbow : être à portée de main>
elder[1] ['ɛldər] *adj* : aîné, plus âgé <an elder sister : une sœur aînée>
elder[2] *n* **1** : aîné *m*, aînée *f* **2** : ancien *m* (d'une église ou d'un village)
elderberry ['ɛldər,bɛri] *n, pl* **-ries 1** : sureau *m* (arbre) **2** : baie *f* de sureau (fruit)
elderly ['ɛldərli] *adj* : âgé
eldest ['ɛldəst] *adj* : aîné <his eldest son : son fils aîné>
elect[1] [i'lɛkt] *vt* : élire, choisir
elect[2] *adj* : élu, futur <the president elect : le futur president>
elect[3] *npl* **the elect** : les élus
election [i'lɛkʃən] *n* : élection *f*
elective[1] [i'lɛktɪv] *adj* **1** : électif **2** OPTIONAL : facultatif
elective[2] *n* : cours *m* facultatif
electoral [i'lɛktərəl] *adj* : électoral
electorate [i'lɛktərət] *n* : électorat *m*
electric [i'lɛktrɪk] *or* **electrical** [-trɪkəl] *adj* : électrique — **electrically** [-trɪkəli] *adv*
electrician [i,lɛk'trɪʃən] *n* : électricien *m*, -cienne *f*
electricity [i,lɛk'trɪsət̬i] *n, pl* **-ties 1** : électricité *f* **2** CURRENT : courant *m* électrique
electrification [i,lɛktrəfə'keɪʃən] *n* : électrification *f*
electrify [i'lɛktrə,faɪ] *vt* **-fied; -fying 1** : électrifier, électriser **2** THRILL : électriser
electrocardiogram [i,lɛktro'kɑrdiə,græm] *n* : électrocardiogramme *m*
electrocardiograph [i,lɛktro'kɑrdiə,græf] *n* : électrocardiographe *m*
electrocute [i'lɛktrə,kju:t] *vt* **-cuted; -cuting** : électrocuter
electrocution [i,lɛktrə'kju:ʃən] *n* : électrocution *f*
electrode [i'lɛk,tro:d] *n* : électrode *f*
electrolysis [i,lɛk'trɑləsɪs] *n* : électrolyse *f*
electrolyte [i'lɛktrə,laɪt] *n* : électrolyte *m*
electromagnet [i,lɛktro'mægnət] *n* : électroaimant *m*
electromagnetic [i,lɛktromæg'nɛt̬ɪk] *adj* : électromagnétique
electromagnetism [i,lɛktro'mægnə,tɪzəm] *n* : électromagnétisme *m*
electron [i'lɛk,trɑn] *n* : électron *m*
electronic [i,lɛk'trɑnɪk] *adj* : électronique — **electronically** [-nɪkli] *adv*
electronic mail → **e-mail**
electronics [i,lɛk'trɑnɪks] *n* : électronique *f*
elegance ['ɛlɪgənts] *n* : élégance *f*
elegant ['ɛlɪgənt] *adj* : élégant
elegantly ['ɛlɪgəntli] *adv* : élégamment
elegiac [,ɛlə'dʒaɪək] *adj* : élégiaque
elegy ['ɛlədʒi] *n, pl* **-gies** : élégie *f*
element ['ɛləmənt] *n* **1** : élément *m* (en science) **2** COMPONENT : élément *m*, part *f*, facteur *m* <an element of truth : une part de vérité> <the element of chance : le facteur chance> **3 elements** *npl* RUDIMENTS : éléments

mpl, rudiments *mpl* **4 the elements** WEATHER : les éléments
elemental [ˌɛlə'mɛntəl] *adj* : élémentaire
elementary [ˌɛlə'mɛntri] *adj* **1** SIMPLE : élémentaire **2** : de l'enseignement primaire
elementary school *n* : école *f* primaire
elephant ['ɛləfənt] *n* : éléphant *m*
elevate ['ɛləˌveɪt] *vt* **-vated; -vating** : élever
elevation [ˌɛlə'veɪʃən] *n* **1** ELEVATING : élévation *f* **2** ALTITUDE : altitude *f*, hauteur *f*
elevator ['ɛləˌveɪt̬ər] *n* **1** : ascenseur *m* (dans un bâtiment) **2** *or* **grain elevator** : élévateur *m*
eleven[1] [ɪ'lɛvən] *adj* : onze
eleven[2] *n* : onze *m*
eleventh[1] [ɪ'lɛvəntθ] *adj* : onzième
eleventh[2] *n* **1** : onzième *mf* (dans une série) **2** : onzième *m* (en mathématiques) **3** (*used in dates*) <the eleventh of February : le onze février>
elf ['ɛlf] *n, pl* **elves** ['ɛlvz] : elfe *m*, lutin *m*
elfin ['ɛlfən] *adj* **1** : d'elfe, de lutin **2** ENCHANTING, MAGICAL : féerique
elicit [ɪ'lɪsət] *vt* : tirer, arracher, provoquer
eligibility [ˌɛlədʒəˌbɪlət̬i] *n, pl* **-ties** : éligibilité *f*, admissibilité *f*
eligible ['ɛlədʒəbəl] *adj* : éligible, admissible <eligible for a job : admissible à un poste> <to be eligible for a pension : avoir droit à une retraite>
eliminate [ɪ'lɪməˌneɪt] *vt* **-nated; -nating** : éliminer
elimination [ɪˌlɪmə'neɪʃən] *n* : élimination *f* <by process of elimination : en procédant par élimination>
elite [eɪ'li:t, i-] *n* : élite *f*
elixir [i'lɪksər] *n* : élixir *m*
elk ['ɛlk] *n* : élan *m* (d'Europe), wapiti *m* (d'Amérique)
ellipse [ɪ'lɪps, ɛ-] *n* : ellipse *f*
ellipsis [ɪ'lɪpsəs, ɛ-] *n, pl* **-lipses 1** : ellipse *f* **2** : points *mpl* de suspension (en ponctuation)
elliptical [ɪ'lɪptɪkəl, ɛ-] *or* **elliptic** [-tɪk] *adj* : elliptique
elm ['ɛlm] *n* : orme *m*
elocution [ˌɛlə'kju:ʃən] *n* : élocution *f*
elongate [i'lɔŋˌgeɪt] *vt* **-gated; -gating** : allonger
elongation [ˌi:ˌlɔŋ'geɪʃən] *n* : allongement *m*
elope [i'lo:p] *vi* **eloped; eloping** : s'enfuir (pour se marier)
elopement [i'lo:pmənt] *n* : fugue *f* amoureuse
eloquence ['ɛləkwənts] *n* : éloquence *f*
eloquent ['ɛləˌkwənt] *adj* : éloquent
eloquently ['ɛləˌkwəntli] *adv* : éloquemment
El Salvadoran[1] [ɛlˌsælvə'dɔrən] *adj* : salvadorien
El Salvadoran[2] *n* : Salvadorien *m*, -rienne *f*
else[1] ['ɛls] *adv* **1** DIFFERENTLY : d'autre, de plus <what else could I do? : que pouvais-je faire d'autre?> **2** ELSEWHERE : ailleurs, autre part <everywhere else : partout ailleurs> **3 or else** : autrement, sinon, ou bien <leave now or else you'll be late : partez vite, autrement vous serez en retard>
else[2] *adj* **1** OTHER : d'autre <somebody else : quelqu'un d'autre> <everyone else : tous les autres> **2** MORE : de plus, d'autre <nothing else : rien d'autre> <what else? : quoi d'autre?> <what else did he say? : que disait-il de plus?>
elsewhere ['ɛlsˌhwɛr] *adv* : ailleurs, autre part <my thoughts were elsewhere : j'avais l'esprit ailleurs>
elucidate [i'lu:səˌdeɪt] *vt* **-dated; -dating** : élucider, expliquer
elucidation [iˌlu:sə'deɪʃən] *n* : élucidation *f*, explication *f*
elude [i'lu:d] *vt* **eluded; eluding** : éluder, échapper à
elusive [i'lu:sɪv] *adj* : élusif, évasif, insaisissable
elusively [i'lu:sɪvli] *adv* : de façon élusive
elves → **elf**
emaciated [i'meɪʃiˌeɪt̬əd] *adj* : émacié, décharné
emaciation [i'meɪsiˌeɪʃən, -ʃi-] *n* : émaciation *f*, amaigrissement *m*
e-mail ['i:ˌmeɪl] *n* : e-mail *m*, courriel *m*, courrier *m* électronique, mél *m*
emanate ['ɛməˌneɪt] *v* **-nated; -nating** *vi* : émaner — *vt* : exsuder, rayonner de
emanation [ˌɛmə'neɪʃən] *n* : émanation *f*
emancipate [i'mæntsəˌpeɪt] *vt* **-pated; -pating** : émanciper, affranchir (un esclave)
emancipation [iˌmæntsə'peɪʃən] *n* : émancipation *f*, affranchissement *m* (d'un esclave)
emasculate [iˌmæskjə'leɪt] *vt* **-lated; -lating** : émasculer
embalm [ɪm'bɑm, ɛm-, -bɑlm] *vt* : embaumer
embankment [ɪm'bæŋkmənt, ɛm-] *n* **1** : digue *f* (d'une rivière) **2** : remblai *m*, talus *m* (d'une route)
embargo[1] [ɪm'bɑrgo, ɛm-] *vt* **-goed; -going** : mettre l'embargo sur
embargo[2] *n, pl* **-goes** : embargo *m*
embark [ɪm'bɑrk, ɛm-] *vt* : embarquer — *vi* **1** : s'embarquer **2 to embark upon** : entreprendre, s'embarquer dans
embarkation [ˌɛmˌbɑr'keɪʃən] *n* : embarquement *m*
embarrass [ɪm'bærəs, ɛm-] *vt* : gêner, embarrasser
embarrassment [ɪm'bærəsmənt, ɛm-] *n* : gêne *f*, embarras *m*

embassy [ˈɛmbəsi] *n, pl* **-sies** : ambassade *f*
embed [ɪmˈbɛd, ɛm-] *vt* **-bedded; -bedding** : enfoncer, enchâsser <embedded in one's memory : gravé dans sa mémoire>
embellish [ɪmˈbɛlɪʃ, ɛm-] *vt* : embellir, orner, décorer
embellishment [ɪmˈbɛlɪʃmənt, ɛm-] *n* : embellissement *m*, ornement *m*
ember [ˈɛmbər] *n* **1** : charbon *m* ardent, morceau *m* de braise **2 embers** *npl* : braise *f*
embezzle [ɪmˈbɛzəl, ɛm-] *vt* **-zled; -zling** : détourner
embezzlement [ɪmˈbɛzəlmənt, ɛm-] *n* : détournement *m* de fonds
embitter [ɪmˈbɪt̬ər, ɛm-] *vt* : aigrir, remplir d'amertume
emblem [ˈɛmbləm] *n* : emblème *m*
emblematic [ˌɛmbləˈmæt̬ɪk] *adj* : emblématique
embodiment [ɪmˈbɑdɪmənt, ɛm-] *n* : incarnation *f*, personnification *f*
embody [ɪmˈbɑdi, ɛm-] *vt* **-bodied; -bodying 1** INCARNATE : incarner, personnifier **2** INCLUDE : incorporer, inclure
emboss [ɪmˈbɑs, ɛm-, -ˈbɔs] *vt* : emboutir, estamper (un métal), gaufrer (des étoffes, du cuir, du papier)
embrace[1] [ɪmˈbreɪs, ɛm-] *vt* **-braced; -bracing 1** HUG : embrasser, étreindre **2** ADOPT, TAKE ON : embrasser, adopter, épouser **3** INCLUDE : comprendre, inclure
embrace[2] *n* : étreinte *f*, enlacement *m*
embroider [ɪmˈbrɔɪdər, ɛm-] *vt* : broder
embroidery [ɪmˈbrɔɪdəri, ɛm-] *n, pl* **-deries** : broderie *f*
embroil [ɪmˈbrɔɪl, ɛm-] *vt* : entraîner, mêler <to become embroiled in : se laisser entraîner dans>
embryo [ˈɛmbriˌo:] *n* : embryon *m*
embryonic [ˌɛmbriˈɑnɪk] *adj* : embryonnaire
emend [iˈmɛnd] *vt* : corriger
emendation [ˌi:mɛnˈdeɪʃən] *n* : correction *f*
emerald[1] [ˈɛmrəld, ˈɛmə-] *adj* : émeraude, en émeraude
emerald[2] *n* : émeraude *f* (pierre précieuse), émeraude *m* (couleur)
emerge [iˈmərdʒ] *vi* **emerged; emerging 1** APPEAR : apparaître, surgir **2 to emerge from** : émerger de
emergence [iˈmərdʒənts] *n* : apparition *f*, émergence *f*
emergency [iˈmərdʒəntsi] *n, pl* **-cies 1** : cas *m* d'urgence *f* <in case of emergency : en cas d'urgence> **2 emergency exit** : sortie *f* de secours **3 emergency room** : salle *f* des urgences **4 state of emergency** : état *m* d'urgence
emergent [iˈmərdʒənt] *adj* : qui émerge, naissant <emergent nations : pays en voie de développement>
emery [ˈɛməri] *n, pl* **-eries** : émeri *m*
emery board *n* : lime *f* à ongles
emetic[1] [iˈmɛt̬ɪk] *adj* : émétique
emetic[2] *n* : émétique *m*
emigrant [ˈɛmɪgrənt] *n* : émigrant *m*, -grante *f*
emigrate [ˈɛməˌgreɪt] *vi* **-grated; -grating** : émigrer
emigration [ˌɛməˈgreɪʃən] *n* : émigration *f*
eminence [ˈɛmənənts] *n* **1** DISTINCTION, PROMINENCE : distinction *f*, rang *m* éminent **2** ELEVATION : éminence *f*, hauteur *f* **3 Your Eminence** : Votre Éminence
eminent [ˈɛmənənt] *adj* : éminent
eminently [ˈɛmənəntli] *adv* : éminemment, hautement
emissary [ˈɛməˌsɛri] *n, pl* **-saries** : émissaire *m*
emission [iˈmɪʃən] *n* : émission *f*
emit [iˈmɪt] *vt* **emitted; emitting** : émettre, dégager
emote [iˈmo:t] *vi* **emoted; emoting** : donner dans les émotions (exalté)
emotion [iˈmo:ʃən] *n* : émotion *f*
emotional [iˈmo:ʃənəl] *adj* **1** : émotionnel, émotif <emotional reactions : réactions émotives> **2** MOVING : émouvant
emotionally [iˈmo:ʃənəli] *adv* : avec émotion <to be emotionally disturbed : avoir des troubles émotifs>
emperor [ˈɛmpərər] *n* : empereur *m*
emphasis [ˈɛmfəsɪs] *n, pl* **-phases** [-ˌsi:z] : accent *m*
emphasize [ˈɛmfəˌsaɪz] *vt* **-sized; -sizing** : insister sur, mettre l'accent sur
emphatic [ɪmˈfæt̬ɪk, ɛm-] *adj* : énergique, catégorique <an emphatic refusal : un refus catégorique> — **emphatically** [-ɪkli] *adv*
empire [ˈɛmˌpaɪr] *n* : empire *m*
empirical [ɪmˈpɪrɪkəl, ɛm-] *adj* : empirique — **empirically** [-ɪkli] *adv*
employ[1] [ɪmˈplɔɪ, ɛm-] *vt* : employer
employ[2] [ɪmˈplɔɪ, ɛm-; ˈɪmˌ-, ˈɛmˌ-] *n* **to be in the employ of** : être employé par
employee *or* **employe** [ɪmˌplɔɪˈi:, ɛm-, -ˈplɔɪˌi:] *n* : employé *m*, -ployée *f*; salarié *m*, -riée *f*
employer [ɪmˈplɔiər, ɛm-] *n* : employeur *m*, -ployeuse *f*
employment [ɪmˈplɔɪmənt, ɛm-] *n* : emploi *m*, travail *m*
empower [ɪmˈpaʊər, ɛm-] *vt* : autoriser, habiliter
empowerment [ɪmˈpaʊərmənt, ɛm-] *n* : autorisation *f*
empress [ˈɛmprəs] *n* : impératrice *f*
emptiness [ˈɛmptinəs] *n* : vide *m*
empty[1] [ˈɛmpti] *v* **-tied; -tying** *vt* : vider — *vi* **1** : se vider **2** : se jeter <the river empties into the ocean : la rivière se jette dans l'océan>
empty[2] *adj* **emptier; -est 1** : vide **2** VACANT : inocupé, vacant, désert **3**

MEANINGLESS : creux (se dit d'un discours), vain (se dit d'une menace, d'une promesse, etc.)
empty–handed [ˌɛmptiˈhændəd] *adj* : les mains vides
empty–headed [ˌɛmptiˈhɛdəd] *adj* : écervelé
emu [ˈiːˌmjuː] *n* : émeu *m*
emulate [ˈɛmjəˌleɪt] *vt* **-lated; -lating** : imiter
emulation [ˌɛmjəˈleɪʃən] *n* : émulation *f*, imitation *f*
emulsify [ɪˈmʌlsəˌfaɪ] *vt* **-fied; -fying** : émulsionner
emulsion [ɪˈmʌlʃən] *n* : émulsion *f*
enable [ɪˈneɪbəl, ɛ-] *vt* **-abled; -abling 1** EMPOWER : habiliter **2** PERMIT : permettre <it enabled him to swim : ça lui permettait de nager>
enact [ɪˈnækt, ɛ-] *vt* **1** : promulguer (une loi, etc.) **2** PERFORM : jouer, représenter (une scène, un rôle, etc.)
enactment [ɪˈnæktmənt, ɛ-] *n* **1** : promulgation *f* (d'une loi) **2** PERFORMANCE : représentation *f*
enamel[1] [ɪˈnæməl] *vt* **-eled** *or* **-elled; -eling** *or* **-elling** : émailler
enamel[2] *n* : émail *m*
enamor *or Brit* **enamour** [ɪˈnæmər] *vt* **to be enamored of** : être épris de (une personne), être enchanté de (une chose)
encamp [ɪnˈkæmp, ɛn-] *vi* : camper
encampment [ɪnˈkæmpmənt, ɛn-] *n* : campement *m*
encase [ɪnˈkeɪs, ɛn-] *vt* **-cased; -casing 1** CONTAIN : enfermer **2** COVER : recouvrir, entourer
enchant [ɪnˈtʃænt, ɛn-] *vt* : enchanter
enchanting [ɪnˈtʃæntɪŋ, ɛn-] *adj* : charmant, enchanteur, ravissant
enchantment [ɪnˈtʃæntmənt, ɛn-] *n* : enchantement *m*
enchantress [ɪnˈtʃæntrəs, ɛn-] *n* : enchanteresse *f*
encircle [ɪnˈsərkəl, ɛn-] *vt* **-cled; -cling** : entourer, encercler
enclose [ɪnˈkloːz, ɛn-] *vt* **-closed; -closing 1** SURROUND : entourer, clôturer **2** INCLUDE : joindre (à une lettre) <enclosed please find : veuillez trouver ci-joint>
enclosure [ɪnˈkloːʒər, ɛn-] *n* **1** ENCLOSING : clôture *f* **2** AREA, SPACE : enclos *m*, enceinte *f* **3** : pièce *f* jointe (à une lettre)
encompass [ɪnˈkʌmpəs, ɛn-, -ˈkɑm-] *vt* **1** ENCIRCLE : entourer **2** INCLUDE : inclure, comprendre
encore [ˈɑnˌkor] *n* **1** : bis *m* **2 to call for an encore** : bisser
encounter[1] [ɪnˈkaʊntər, ɛn-] *vt* : rencontrer
encounter[2] *n* : rencontre *f*
encourage [ɪnˈkərɪdʒ, ɛn-] *vt* **-aged; -aging 1** HEARTEN : encourager **2** FOSTER, STIMULATE : stimuler, favoriser
encouragement [ɪnˈkərɪdʒmənt, ɛn-] *n* : encouragement *m*
encroach [ɪnˈkroːtʃ, ɛn-] *vi* **to encroach upon** : empiéter sur
encrust [ɪnˈkrʌst, ɛn-] *vt* : incruster
encumber [ɪnˈkʌmbər, ɛn-] *vt* : encombrer, grever <encumbered by debts : grevé de dettes>
encumbrance [ɪnˈkʌmbrənts, ɛn-] *n* **1** BURDEN : charge *f*, fardeau *m* **2** HINDRANCE : gêne *f*, entrave *f*
encyclopedia [ɪnˌsaɪkləˈpiːdiə, ɛn-] *n* : encyclopédie *f* — **encyclopedic** [-dɪk] *adj*
end[1] [ˈɛnd] *vt* **1** STOP : finir, achever, terminer **2** CONCLUDE : conclure — *vi* **1** : finir, s'achever, se terminer **2 to end up** : finir **3 to end up with** : finir par
end[2] *n* **1** : fin *f* **2** EXTREMITY : bout *m*, extrémité *f* **3** PURPOSE : but *m*, fin *f*, dessein *m* <to this end : dans ce but>
endanger [ɪnˈdeɪndʒər, ɛn-] *vt* : mettre en danger
endear [ɪnˈdɪr, ɛn-] *vt* : faire aimer <to endear oneself to s.o. : se faire aimer de qqn>
endearment [ɪnˈdɪrmənt, ɛn-] *n* : tendresse *f* <terms of endearment : mots tendres>
endeavor[1] *or Brit* **endeavour** [ɪnˈdɛvər, ɛn-] *vt* : s'efforcer, essayer <to endeavor to understand : s'efforcer de comprendre>
endeavor[2] *or Brit* **endeavour** *n* : effort *m*, tentative *f*
ending [ˈɛndɪŋ] *n* **1** CONCLUSION : fin *f*, dénouement *m* <a happy ending : un dénouement heureux> **2** SUFFIX : terminaison *f*
endive [ˈɛnˌdaɪv, ˌɑnˈdiːv] *n* : endive *f*
endless [ˈɛndləs] *adj* **1** INTERMINABLE : sans fin, interminable **2** INNUMERABLE : innombrable, sans nombre **3** INEXHAUSTIBLE : inépuisable, infini
endlessly [ˈɛndləsli] *adv* : interminablement, continuellement, sans fin
endocrine [ˈɛndəkrən, -ˌkraɪn, -ˌkriːn] *adj* : endocrine
endorse [ɪnˈdɔrs, ɛn-] *vt* **-dorsed; -dorsing 1** SIGN : endosser **2** SUPPORT : avaliser **3** APPROVE : approuver
endorsement [ɪnˈdɔrsmənt, ɛn-] *n* **1** SIGNATURE : endossement *m* **2** SUPPORT : aval *m* **3** APPROVAL : approbation *f*
endow [ɪnˈdaʊ, ɛn-] *vt* : doter
endowment [ɪnˈdaʊmənt, ɛn-] *n* : dotation *f*
endurable [ɪnˈdʊrəbəl, ɛn-, -ˈdjʊr-] *adj* : supportable, endurable
endurance [ɪnˈdʊrənts, ɛn-, -ˈdjʊr-] *n* : endurance *f*
endure [ɪnˈdʊr, ɛn-, -ˈdjʊr-] *v* **-dured; -during** *vt* BEAR, TOLERATE : supporter, endurer — *vi* LAST : durer
enema [ˈɛnəmə] *n* : lavement *m*

enemy [ˈɛnəmi] *n, pl* **-mies** : ennemi *m*, -mie *f*

energetic [ˌɛnərˈdʒɛt̬ɪk] *adj* : énergique — **energetically** [-t̬ɪkli] *adv*

energize [ˈɛnərˌdʒaɪz] *vt* **-gized; -gizing** : donner de l'énergie à, stimuler

energy [ˈɛnərdʒi] *n, pl* **-gies** : énergie *f*

enervate [ˈɛnərˌveɪt] *vt* **-vated; -vating** : affaiblir, débiliter

enfold [ɪnˈfoːld, ɛn-] *vt* : envelopper, étreindre

enforce [ɪnˈfors, ɛn-] *vt* **-forced; -forcing** : appliquer, imposer (la discipline, etc.), faire respecter (une loi) <to enforce obedience : se faire obéir>

enforcement [ɪnˈforsmənt, ɛn-] *n* : exécution *f*, application *f*

enfranchise [ɪnˈfrænˌtʃaɪz, ɛn-] *vt* **-chised; -chising** : accorder le droit de vote à

enfranchisement [ɪnˈfrænˌtʃaɪzmənt, ɛn-] *n* : admission *f* au suffrage

engage [ɪnˈgeɪdʒ, ɛn-] *v* **-gaged; -gaging** *vt* **1** INVOLVE : engager <to engage s.o. in conversation : engager la conversation avec qqn> **2** EMPLOY : embaucher, engager **3** ATTRACT, DRAW : attirer, éveiller <to engage s.o.'s attention : éveiller l'attention de qqn> **4 to engage the clutch** : embrayer — *vi* **1 to engage in** : se lancer dans, prendre part à **2 to engage in combat** : engager l'ennemi

engaged [ɪnˈgeɪdʒd, ɛn-] *adj* : fiancé <to get engaged to : se fiancer à>

engagement [ɪnˈgeɪdʒmənt, ɛn-] *n* **1** APPOINTMENT : rendez-vous *m* **2** : engagement *m* (d'un acteur, etc.) **3** BETROTHAL : fiançailles *fpl*

engaging [ɪnˈgeɪdʒɪŋ, ɛn-] *adj* : engageant, attirant

engender [ɪnˈdʒɛndər, ɛn-] *vt* **-dered; -dering** : engendrer

engine [ˈɛndʒən] *n* **1** MOTOR : moteur *m* (d'une voiture) **2** LOCOMOTIVE : locomotive *f*

engineer[1] [ˌɛndʒəˈnɪr] *vt* **1** CONSTRUCT : construire **2** CONTRIVE, PLOT : manigancer

engineer[2] *n* **1** : ingénieur *m*, -nieure *f* <civil engineer : ingénieur civil> **2** : mécanicien *m*, -cienne *f* (d'une locomotive)

engineering [ˌɛndʒəˈnɪrɪŋ] *n* : ingénierie *f*, génie *m* <chemical engineering : génie chimique>

English[1] [ˈɪŋglɪʃ, ˈɪŋlɪʃ] *adj* : anglais

English[2] *n* **1** : anglais *m* (langue) **2 the English** : les Anglais

Englishman [ˈɪŋglɪʃmən, ˈɪŋlɪʃ-] *n* : Anglais *m*

Englishwoman [ˈɪŋglɪʃˌwʊmən, ˈɪŋlɪʃ-] *n* : Anglaise *f*

engrave [ɪnˈgreɪv, ɛn-] *vt* **-graved; -graving** : graver

engraver [ɪnˈgreɪvər, ɛn-] *n* : graveur *m*, -veuse *f*

engraving [ɪnˈgreɪvɪŋ, ɛn-] *n* : gravure *f*

engross [ɪnˈgroːs, ɛn-] *vt* : absorber, occuper

engulf [ɪnˈgʌlf, ɛn-] *vt* : engouffrer, engloutir

enhance [ɪnˈhæn*t*s, ɛn-] *vt* **-hanced; -hancing** : améliorer, augmenter, rehausser

enhancement [ɪnˈhæn*t*smənt, ɛn-] *n* : amélioration *f*, augmentation *f*, majoration *f*

enigma [ɪˈnɪgmə] *n* : énigme *f*

enigmatic [ˌɛnɪgˈmæt̬ɪk, ˌiːnɪg-] *adj* : énigmatique — **enigmatically** [-t̬ɪkli] *adv*

enjoin [ɪnˈdʒɔɪn, ɛn-] *vt* **1** COMMAND : enjoindre, ordonner **2** FORBID : interdire

enjoy [ɪnˈdʒɔɪ, ɛn-] *vt* **1** : aimer, prendre plaisir à <I enjoy reading : je prends plaisir à lire> **2** : jouir de <she enjoys good health : elle jouit d'une bonne santé> **3 to enjoy oneself** : s'amuser

enjoyable [ɪnˈdʒɔɪəbəl, ɛn-] *adj* : agréable

enjoyment [ɪnˈdʒɔɪmənt, ɛn-] *n* : plaisir *m*, jouissance *f*

enlarge [ɪnˈlɑrdʒ, ɛn-] *v* **-larged; -larging** *vt* : agrandir, élargir — *vi* **1** : s'agrandir **2 to enlarge upon** : s'étendre sur, développer

enlargement [ɪnˈlɑrdʒmənt, ɛn-] *n* : agrandissement *m*, élargissement *m*

enlighten [ɪnˈlaɪtən, ɛn-] *vt* : éclairer

enlightenment [ɪnˈlaɪtənmənt, ɛn-] *n* **1** CLARIFICATION : éclaircissements *mpl* **2** EDIFICATION : édification *f*, instruction *f* **3 the Enlightenment** : le Siècle des lumières

enlist [ɪnˈlɪst, ɛn-] *vt* **1** ENROLL : enrôler, recruter **2** OBTAIN : obtenir, mobiliser (du soutien, etc.) — *vi* : s'engager, s'enrôler <he enlisted in the army : il s'est engagé dans l'armée>

enlistment [ɪnˈlɪstmənt, ɛn-] *n* : engagement *m*, recrutement *m*, enrôlement *m*

enliven [ɪnˈlaɪvən, ɛn-] *vt* : animer, égayer

enmity [ˈɛnmət̬i] *n, pl* **-ties** : inimitié *f*, hostilité *f*

ennoble [ɪˈnoːbəl, ɛ-] *vt* **-bled; -bling** : ennoblir, élever

ennui [ˌɑnˈwiː] *n* : ennui *m*

enormity [ɪˈnɔrmət̬i] *n, pl* **-ties 1** ATROCITY : atrocité *f* **2** IMMENSITY : énormité *f*

enormous [ɪˈnɔrməs] *adj* : énorme, immense

enormously [ɪˈnɔrməsli] *adv* EXTREMELY : énormément, extrêmement

enough[1] [iˈnʌf] *adv* : assez, suffisamment <he's old enough : il est suffisamment grand> <she writes well enough : elle écrit assez bien>

enough[2] *adj* **1** : assez de, suffisant **2 more than enough** : plus qu'il n'en faut

enough[3] *pron* (*representing a sufficient number, quantity, or amount*) <to have eaten enough : avoir assez mangé> <I've had enough of his foolishness : j'en ai assez de ses bêtises>

enquire |ɪn'kwaɪr, ɛn-|, **enquiry** |'ɪn,kwaɪri, 'ɛn-, -kwəri; ɪn'kwaɪri, ɛn-| → **inquire, inquiry**

enrage |ɪn'reɪdʒ, ɛn-| *vt* **-raged; -raging** : rendre furieux, mettre en rage

enrich |ɪn'rɪtʃ, ɛn-| *vt* : enrichir

enrichment |ɪn'rɪtʃmənt, ɛn-| *n* : enrichissement *m*

enroll *or* **enrol** |ɪn'ro:l, ɛn-| *v* **-rolled; -rolling** *vt* **1** : inscrire (à l'école, etc.) **2** ENLIST : enrôler — *vi* : s'inscrire, s'enrôler

enrollment |ɪn'ro:lmənt, ɛn-| *n* **1** REGISTRATION : inscription *f* **2** ENLISTMENT : enrôlement *m*

en route |ɑn'ru:t, ɛn'raʊt| *adv* : en route

ensconce |ɪn'skɑnts, ɛn-| *vt* **-sconced; -sconcing 1** INSTALL, SETTLE : installer, placer **2 to ensconce oneself** : bien s'installer

ensemble |ɑn'sɑmbəl| *n* : ensemble *m*

enshrine |ɪn'ʃraɪn, ɛn-| *vt* **-shrined; -shrining** : conserver pieusement

ensign |'ɛntsən, 'ɛn,saɪn| *n* **1** FLAG : drapeau *m*, pavillon *m* **2** : enseigne *m* (de vaisseau)

enslave |ɪn'sleɪv, ɛn-| *vt* **-slaved; -slaving** : asservir

ensnare |ɪn'snær, ɛn-| *vt* **-snared; -snaring** : prendre au piège, attraper

ensue |ɪn'su:, ɛn-| *vi* **-sued; -suing** : s'ensuivre

ensure |ɪn'ʃʊr, ɛn-| *vt* **-sured; -suring** : assurer, garantir

entail |ɪn'teɪl, ɛn-| *vt* : entraîner, occasionner

entangle |ɪn'tæŋgəl, ɛn-| *vt* **-gled; -gling** : emmêler, enchevêtrer

entanglement |ɪn'tæŋgəlmənt, ɛn-| *n* : enchevêtrement *m*

enter |'ɛntər| *vt* **1** : entrer dans, entrer à **2** RECORD : inscrire, noter **3** INSERT : entrer des données (en informatique) **4** BEGIN : entrer dans, entamer **5 to enter one's mind** : venir à l'esprit — *vi* **1** : entrer **2 to enter into** : entamer, entrer en

enterprise |'ɛntər,praɪz| *n* **1** UNDERTAKING : entreprise *f* **2** BUSINESS : affaire *f* commerciale **3** INITIATIVE : initiative *f*

enterprising |'ɛntər,praɪzɪŋ| *adj* : entreprenant

entertain |,ɛntər'teɪn| *vt* **1** AMUSE : amuser, divertir **2** : recevoir <to entertain guests : recevoir des invités> **3** CONSIDER : penser à, considérer (une idée, etc.)

entertainment |,ɛntər'teɪnmənt| *n* **1** AMUSEMENT : amusement *m*, divertissement *m* **2** PERFORMANCE : spectacle *m*

enthrall *or* **enthral** |ɪn'θrɔl, ɛn-| *vt* **-thralled; -thralling** : captiver, passionner

enthusiasm |ɪn'θu:zi,æzəm, ɛn-, -'θju:-| *n* : enthousiasme *m*

enthusiast |ɪn'θu:zi,æst, ɛn-, -'θju:-, -əst| *n* : enthousiaste *mf;* passionné *m*, -née *f* <a soccer enthusiast : un passionné de football>

enthusiastic |ɪn,θu:zi'æstɪk, ɛn-, -'θju:-| *adj* : enthousiaste

enthusiastically |ɪn,θu:zi'æstɪkli, ɛn-, -'θju:-| *adv* : avec enthousiasme

entice |ɪn'taɪs, ɛn-| *vt* **-ticed; -ticing** : attirer, allécher <to entice s.o. away from : entraîner qqn à l'écart de>

enticement |ɪn'taɪsmənt, ɛn-| *n* : attrait *m*

entire |ɪn'taɪr, ɛn-| *adj* : entier, complet <my entire life : toute ma vie>

entirely |ɪn'taɪrli, ɛn-| *adv* : entièrement, totalement

entirety |ɪn'taɪrt̬i, ɛn-, -taɪrət̬i| *n, pl* **-ties 1** : totalité *f* **2 in its entirety** : en son entier, dans son ensemble

entitle |ɪn'taɪt̬əl, ɛn-| *vt* **-tled; -tling 1** NAME : intituler **2** AUTHORIZE : autoriser, donner droit à **3 to be entitled to** : avoir le droit de

entitlement |ɪn'taɪt̬əlmənt, ɛn-| *n* : droit *m*

entity |'ɛntət̬i| *n, pl* **-ties** : entité *f*

entomologist |,ɛntə'mɑlədʒɪst| *n* : entomologiste *mf*

entomology |,ɛntə'mɑlədʒi| *n* : entomologie *f*

entourage |,ɑntʊ'rɑʒ| *n* : entourage *m*

entrails |'ɛn,treɪlz, -trəlz| *npl* : entrailles *fpl*

entrance[1] |ɪn'træn*t*s, ɛn-| *vt* **-tranced; -trancing** : transporter, ravir

entrance[2] |'ɛntrən*t*s| *n* : entrée *f* <main entrance : entrée principale> <to make an entrance : faire son entrée>

entrant |'ɛntrənt| *n* : concurrent *m*, -rente *f* (dans une course); candidat *m*, -date *f;* participant *m*, -pante *f*

entrap |ɪn'træp, ɛn-| *vt* **-trapped; -trapping** : prendre au piège

entreat |ɪn'tri:t, ɛn-| *vt* : implorer, supplier

entreaty |ɪn'tri:t̬i, ɛn-| *n, pl* **-ties** : supplication *f*, prière *f*

entrée *or* **entree** |'ɑn,treɪ, ,ɑn'-| *n* : entrée *f*, plat *m* principal

entrench |ɪn'trɛntʃ, ɛn-| *vt* : retrancher

entrenched |ɪn'trɛntʃt, ɛn-| *adj* **1** UNWAVERING : inébranlable, ferme **2** ESTABLISHED : implanté, bien établi

entrepreneur |,ɑntrəprə'nər, -'njʊr| *n* : entrepreneur *m*, -neuse *f*

entrust |ɪn'trʌst, ɛn-| *vt* : confier <to entrust s.o. with a mission : confier une mission à qqn>

entry |'ɛntri| *n, pl* **-tries 1** ENTRANCE : entrée *f* **2** : inscription *f* (sur une liste), entrée *f*

entwine [ɪn'twaɪn, ɛn-] *vt* **-twined; -twining** : entrelacer, enlacer
enumerate [ɪ'nu:məˌreɪt, ɛ-, -'nju:-] *vt* **-ated; -ating 1** LIST : énumérer **2** COUNT : dénombrer
enumeration [ɪˌnu:mə'reɪʃən, ɛ-, -ˌnju:-] *n* : énumération *f*, dénombrement *m*
enunciate [i'nʌntsiˌeɪt, ɛ-] *vt* **-ated; -ating 1** STATE : énoncer, exprimer **2** PRONOUNCE : articuler, prononcer
enunciation [iˌnʌntsi'eɪʃən, ɛ-] *n* **1** STATEMENT : énonciation *f*, exposition *f* **2** PRONUNCIATION : articulation *f*
envelop [ɪn'vɛləp, ɛn-] *vt* : envelopper
envelope ['ɛnvəˌlo:p, 'ɑn-] *n* : enveloppe *f*
enviable ['ɛnviəbəl] *adj* : enviable
envious ['ɛnviəs] *adj* : envieux, jaloux
enviously ['ɛnviəsli] *adv* : avec envie
environment [ɪn'vaɪrənmənt, ɛn-, -vaɪərn-] *n* : environnement *m*, milieu *m*
environmental [ɪnˌvaɪrən'mɛntəl, ɛn-, -ˌvaɪərn-] *adj* : du milieu, écologique <environmental studies : études de l'environnement>
environmentalist [ɪnˌvaɪrən'məntəlɪst, ɛn-, -ˌvaɪərn] *n* : écologiste *mf*
environs [ɪn'vaɪrənz, ɛn-, -'vaɪərnz] *npl* : environs *mpl*, alentours *mpl*
envisage [ɪn'vɪzɪdʒ, ɛn-] *vt* **-aged; -aging 1** IMAGINE : envisager **2** FORESEE : prévoir
envision [ɪn'vɪʒən, ɛn-] *vt* : envisager
envoy ['ɛnˌvɔɪ, 'ɑn-] *n* : envoyé *m*, -voyée *f*
envy[1] ['ɛnvi] *vt* **-vied; -vying** : envier
envy[2] *n* : envie *f*, jalousie *f*
enzyme ['ɛnˌzaɪm] *n* : enzyme *f*
eon ['i:ən, i:ˌɑn] → **aeon**
epaulet [ˌɛpə'lɛt] *n* : épaulette *f*
ephemeral [ɪ'fɛmərəl, -'fi:-] *adj* : éphémère
epic[1] ['ɛpɪk] *adj* : épique
epic[2] *n* : épopée *f*
epicure ['ɛpɪˌkjʊr] *n* : gourmet *m*, gastronome *mf*
epicurean [ˌɛpɪkjʊ'ri:ən, -'kjʊriən] *adj* : épicurien
epidemic[1] [ˌɛpə'dɛmɪk] *adj* : épidémique
epidemic[2] *n* : épidémie *f*
epidermis [ˌɛpə'dərməs] *n* : épiderme *m*
epigram ['ɛpəˌgræm] *n* : épigramme *f*
epilepsy ['ɛpəˌlɛpsi] *n, pl* **-sies** : épilepsie *f*
epileptic[1] [ˌɛpə'lɛptɪk] *adj* : épileptique <epileptic fit : crise d'épilepsie>
epileptic[2] *n* : épileptique *mf*
episcopal [ɪ'pɪskəpəl] *adj* : épiscopal <the Episcopal Church : l'Église épiscopale>
episode ['ɛpəˌso:d] *n* : épisode *m*
episodic [ˌɛpə'sɑdɪk] *adj* : épisodique
epistle [ɪ'pɪsəl] *n* : épître *f*
epitaph ['ɛpəˌtæf] *n* : épitaphe *f*
epithet ['ɛpəˌθɛt, -θət] *n* : épithète *f*
epitome [ɪ'pɪt̬əmi] *n* **1** SUMMARY : abrégé *m*, résumé *m* **2** EMBODIMENT : exemple *m* même, modèle *m*
epitomize [ɪ'pɪt̬əˌmaɪz] *vt* **-mized; -mizing 1** SUMMARIZE : abréger **2** EMBODY : incarner, personnifier
epoch ['ɛpək, 'ɛˌpɑk, 'i:ˌpɑk] *n* : époque *f*
equable ['ɛkwəbəl, 'i:-] *adj* : égal, constant (se dit du climat), placide (se dit des personnes)
equal[1] ['i:kwəl] *vt* **equaled** *or* **equalled; equaling** *or* **equalling** : égaler
equal[2] *adj* **1** SAME : égal, même <equal pay : salaire égal> <of equal value : de même valeur> **2 to be equal to** : être à la hauteur de <I didn't feel equal to going : je ne me sentais pas capable de sortir>
equal[3] *n* : égal *m*, -gale *f*
equality [ɪ'kwɑlət̬i] *n, pl* **-ties** : égalité *f*
equalize ['i:kwəˌlaɪz] *vt* **-ized; -izing** : égaliser
equally ['i:kwəli] *adv* : également <to divide sth equally : diviser qqch en parts égales>
equanimity [ˌi:kwə'nɪmət̬i, ˌɛ-] *n, pl* **-ties** : égalité *f* d'humeur, sérénité *f*, équanimité *f*
equate [ɪ'kweɪt] *vt* **equated; equating 1** LIKEN, COMPARE : mettre sur le même pied, assimiler **2** EQUALIZE : égaliser **3 to equate with** : mettre en équation avec (en mathématiques)
equation [ɪ'kweɪʒən] *n* : équation *f*
equator [ɪ'kweɪt̬ər] *n* : équateur *m*
equatorial [ˌi:kwə'toriəl, ˌɛ-] *adj* : équatorial
equestrian[1] [ɪ'kwɛstriən, ɛ-] *adj* : équestre
equestrian[2] *n* : cavalier *m*, -lière *f*
equilateral [ˌi:kwə'læt̬ərəl, ˌɛ-] *adj* : équilatéral
equilibrium [ˌi:kwə'lɪbriəm, ˌɛ-] *n, pl* **-riums** *or* **-ria** : équilibre *m*
equine ['i:ˌkwaɪn, 'ɛ-] *adj* : chevalin
equinox ['i:kwəˌnɑks, 'ɛ-] *n* : équinoxe *m*
equip [ɪ'kwɪp] *vt* **equipped; equipping 1** FURNISH, SUPPLY : équiper, outiller, munir **2** PREPARE : préparer
equipment [ɪ'kwɪpmənt] *n* : équipement *m*, matériel *m*
equitable ['ɛkwət̬əbəl] *adj* : équitable, juste
equity ['ɛkwət̬i] *n, pl* **-ties 1** FAIRNESS : équité *f* **2 equities** *npl* SECURITIES : actions *fpl* ordinaires
equivalence [ɪ'kwɪvələnts] *n* : équivalence *f*
equivalent[1] [ɪ'kwɪvələnt] *adj* : équivalent
equivalent[2] *n* : équivalent *m*
equivocal [ɪ'kwɪvəkəl] *adj* : équivoque
equivocate [ɪ'kwɪvəˌkeɪt] *vi* **-cated; -cating** : user d'équivoques
equivocation [ɪˌkwɪvə'keɪʃən] *n* : paroles *fpl* équivoques

era ['ırə, 'ɛrə, 'i:rə] *n* : ère *f*, époque *f*
eradicate [ı'rædəˌkeıt] *vt* **-cated; -cating** : éradiquer
erase [ı'reıs] *vt* **erased; erasing** : effacer, gommer
eraser [ı'reısər] *n* : gomme *f*, efface *f Can*
erasure [ı'reıʃər] *n* : effacement *m*
ere[1] ['ɛr] *conj* : avant que
ere[2] *prep* **1** BEFORE : avant **2 ere long** : sous peu, bientôt
erect[1] [ı'rɛkt] *vt* **1** BUILD : bâtir, construire **2** RAISE : ériger, élever (une statue, un édifice, etc.) **3** ESTABLISH : ériger, établir
erect[2] *adj* : droit <to stand erect : se tenir droit>
erection [ı'rɛkʃən] *n* **1** CONSTRUCTION : construction *f* **2** : érection *f* (en physiologie)
ergonomic [ˌərgə'namık] *adj* : ergonomique
Eritrean[1] [ˌɛrə'tri:ən, -'treıən] *adj* : erythréen
Eritrean[2] *n* : Erythréen *m*, -thréenne *f*
ermine ['ərmən] *n* : hermine *f*
erode [ı'ro:d] *v* **eroded; eroding** *vt* : éroder, ronger — *vi* : s'éroder
erosion [ı'ro:ʒən] *n* : érosion *f*
erotic [ı'raṭık] *adj* : érotique — **erotically** [-ṭıkli] *adv*
eroticism [ı'raṭəˌsızəm] *n* : érotisme *m*
err ['ɛr, 'ər] *vi* : se tromper <to err on the side of caution : pécher par excès de prudence>
errand ['ɛrənd] *n* : course *f*, commission *f*
errant ['ɛrənt] *adj* **1** WANDERING : errant **2** MISBEHAVING : dévoyé
erratic [ı'ræṭık] *adj* **1** IRREGULAR, UNPREDICTABLE : irrégulier, imprévisible **2** : erratique (en géologie, en médecine)
erratically [ı'ræṭıkli] *adv* : irregulièrement, de manière capricieuse
erroneous [ı'ro:niəs, ɛ-] *adj* : erroné, faux
erroneously [ı'ro:niəsli, ɛ-] *adv* : à tort, erronément
error ['ɛrər] *n* : erreur *f*, faute *f* <to see the error of one's ways : revenir de ses erreurs>
erstwhile ['ərstˌ*h*waıl] *adj* FORMER : d'autrefois, ancien
erudite ['ɛrəˌdaıt, 'ɛrjʊ-] *adj* : érudit, savant
erudition [ˌɛrə'dıʃən, ˌɛrjʊ-] *n* : érudition *f*
erupt [ı'rʌpt] *vi* **1** : entrer en éruption (se dit d'un volcan) **2** : éclater (se dit de la guerre, d'un rire, etc.)
eruption [ı'rʌpʃən] *n* : éruption *f*
escalate ['ɛskəˌleıt] *v* **-lated; -lating** *vt* **1** INTENSIFY : intensifier, aggraver **2** INCREASE : augmenter — *vi* **1** INTENSIFY : s'intensifier, s'aggraver **2** INCREASE : monter en flèche (se dit des prix, etc.)
escalation [ˌɛskə'leıʃən] *n* **1** INTENSIFICATION : intensification *f* **2** INCREASE : montée *f* en flèche
escalator ['ɛskəˌleıtər] *n* : escalier *m* mécanique
escapade ['ɛskəˌpeıd] *n* : équipée *f*, frasque *f*
escape[1] [ı'skeıp, ɛ-] *v* **-caped; -caping** *vt* **1** AVOID : échapper à, éviter **2** ELUDE : échapper à <his name escapes me : son nom m'échappe> **3 to escape notice** : passer inaperçu — *vi* **1** : s'échapper, s'évader **2 to escape from reality** : fuir la réalité
escape[2] *n* **1** FLIGHT : fuite *f*, évasion *f* **2** LEAKAGE : fuite *f* (d'un liquide ou d'un gaz), échappement *m* (de vapeurs)
escapee [ıˌskeı'pi:, ˌɛ-] *n* : évadé *m*, -dée *f*
escarole ['ɛskəˌro:l] *n* : scarole *f*
escarpment [ıs'karpmənt, ɛs-] *n* : escarpement *m*
eschew [ɛ'ʃu:, ıs'tʃu:] *vt* : éviter, s'abstenir de
escort[1] [ı'skɔrt, ɛ-] *vt* : escorter, accompagner
escort[2] ['ɛsˌkɔrt] *n* **1** : escorte *f* <under police escort : sous escorte policière> **2** COMPANION : compagnon *m*, compagne *f*
escrow ['ɛsˌkro:] *n* : séquestre *m* <in escrow : en séquestre>
esophagus [ı'safəgəs, i:-] *n, pl* **-gi** [-ˌgaı, -ˌdʒaı] : œsophage *m*
esoteric [ˌɛsə'tɛrık] *adj* : ésotérique
especially [ı'spɛʃəli] *adv* **1** PARTICULARLY : particulièrement, surtout **2** EXPRESSLY : exprès <he came especially to see you : il est venu exprès pour vous voir> **3 especially as** : d'autant plus que
espionage ['ɛspiəˌnaʒ, -ˌnadʒ] *n* : espionnage *m*
espouse [ı'spaʊz, ɛ-] *vt* **espoused; espousing** : épouser
espresso [ɛ'sprɛˌso:] *n, pl* **-sos** : express *m*, café *m* express
essay[1] [ɛ'seı, 'ɛˌseı] *vt* ATTEMPT : essayer, tenter
essay[2] ['ɛˌseı] *n* **1** ATTEMPT : essai *m*, tentative *f* **2** COMPOSITION : essai *m* (littéraire), dissertation *f* académique
essayist ['ɛˌseııst] *n* : essayiste *mf*
essence ['ɛsən*t*s] *n* **1** CORE : essence *f* <in essence : par essence, essentiellement> **2** EXTRACT : essence *f*, extrait *m* <essence of violets : essence de violette> <essence of vanilla : extrait de vanille>
essential[1] [ı'sɛntʃəl] *adj* : essentiel — **essentially** *adv*
essential[2] *n* **1** : objet *m* essentiel **2 the essentials** : l'essentiel *m*
establish [ı'stæblıʃ, ɛ-] *vt* **1** PROVE : établir, démontrer **2** FOUND : établir, fonder, créer

establishment [ɪ'stæblɪʃmənt, ɛ-] *n* **1** ESTABLISHING : fondation *f*, création *f*, établissement *m* **2** INSTITUTION : établissement *m* **3 the Establishment** : les pouvoirs établis
estate [ɪ'steɪt, ɛ-] *n* **1** POSSESSIONS : biens *mpl*, fortune *f* **2** LAND, PROPERTY : propriété *f*, domaine *m*
esteem[1] [ɪ'sti:m, ɛ-] *vt* : estimer
esteem[2] *n* : estime *f* <in high esteem : en haute estime>
ester ['ɛstər] *n* : ester *m*
esthetic [ɛs'θɛt̬ɪk] → **aesthetic**
estimable ['ɛstəməbəl] *adj* : estimable
estimate[1] ['ɛstə,meɪt] *vt* **-mated; -mating** : estimer, évaluer
estimate[2] ['ɛstəmət] *n* : estimation *f*, évaluation *f*, devis *m*
estimation [,ɛstə'meɪʃən] *n* **1** JUDGMENT : jugement *m* <in my estimation : à mon avis> **2** ESTIMATE : estimation *f* **3** ESTEEM : estime *f*, considération *f*
Estonian[1] [ɛ'sto:niən] *adj* : estonien
Estonian[2] *n* **1** : Estonien *m*, -nienne *f* **2** : estonien *m* (langue)
estrange [ɪ'streɪndʒ, ɛ-] *vt* **-tranged; -tranging** : brouiller, éloigner
estrangement [ɪ'streɪndʒmənt, ɛ-] *n* : éloignement *m*, brouille *f* (avec un ami), séparation *f* (d'un époux)
estrogen ['ɛstrədʒən] *n* : estrogène *m*
estuary ['ɛstʃʊ,wɛri] *n, pl* **-aries** : estuaire *m*
et cetera [ɛt'sɛt̬ərə, -'sɛtrə] : et cætera, et cetera
etch ['ɛtʃ] *vt* : graver à l'eau-forte <etched in her memory : gravé dans sa mémoire>
etching ['ɛtʃɪŋ] *n* : eau-forte *f* (dessin), gravure *f* à l'eau-forte (technique)
eternal [ɪ'tərnəl, i:-] *adj* : éternel — **eternally** *adv*
eternity [ɪ'tərnət̬i, i:-] *n, pl* **-ties** : éternité *f*
ethane ['ɛ,θeɪn] *n* : éthane *m*
ether ['i:θər] *n* : éther *m*
ethereal [ɪ'θɪriəl, i:-] *adj* : éthéré
ethical ['ɛθɪkəl] *adj* : éthique, moral
ethically ['ɛθɪkəli] *adv* : moralement
ethics ['ɛθɪks] *ns & pl* : éthique *f*, morale *f*
Ethiopian[1] [,i:θi'o:piən] *adj* : éthiopien
Ethiopian[2] *n* : Éthiopien *m*, -pienne *f*
ethnic ['ɛθnɪk] *adj* : ethnique
ethnologist [ɛθ'nɑlədʒɪst] *n* : ethnologue *mf*
ethnology [ɛθ'nɑlədʒi] *n* : ethnologie *f*
etiquette ['ɛt̬ɪkət, -,kɛt] *n* : étiquette *f*, convenances *fpl*, bienséance *f*
etymological [,ɛt̬əmə'lɑdʒɪkəl] *adj* : étymologique
etymology [,ɛt̬ə'mɑlədʒi] *n, pl* **-gies** : étymologie *f*
eucalyptus [,ju:kə'lɪptəs] *n, pl* **-ti** [-,taɪ] *or* **-tuses** [-təsəz] : eucalyptus *m*
Eucharist ['ju:kərɪst] *n* : Eucharistie *f*
eulogize ['ju:lə,dʒaɪz] *vt* **-gized; -gizing** : faire l'éloge de, faire le panégyrique de
eulogy ['ju:lədʒi] *n, pl* **-gies** : éloge *m*, panégyrique *m*
eunuch ['ju:nək] *n* : eunuque *m*
euphemism ['ju:fə,mɪzəm] *n* : euphémisme *m*
euphemistic [,ju:fə'mɪstɪk] *adj* : euphémique
euphony ['ju:fəni] *n, pl* **-nies** : euphonie *f*
euphoria [jʊ'foriə] *n* : euphorie *f*
euphoric [jʊ'forɪk] *adj* : euphorique
European[1] [,ju:rə'pi:ən, -pi:n] *adj* : européen
European[2] *n* : Européen *m*, -péenne *f*
euthanasia [,ju:θə'neɪʒə, -ʒiə] *n* : euthanasie *f*
evacuate [ɪ'vækjʊ,eɪt] *vt* **-ated; -ating** : évacuer
evacuation [ɪ,vækjʊ'eɪʃən] *n* : évacuation *f*
evade [ɪ'veɪd] *vt* **evaded; evading** : éviter, esquiver, échapper à
evaluate [ɪ'væljʊ,eɪt] *vt* **-ated; -ating** : évaluer
evaluation [ɪ'væljʊ'eɪʃən] *n* : évaluation *f*
evangelical [,i:,væn'dʒɛlɪkəl, ,ɛvən-] *adj* : évangélique
evangelist [ɪ'vændʒəlɪst] *n* : évangéliste *m*
evaporate [ɪ'væpə,reɪt] *v* **-rated; -rating** *vi* **1** VAPORIZE : s'évaporer **2** DISAPPEAR : s'envoler, s'évaporer *fam* — *vt* : faire évaporer
evaporation [ɪ,væpə'reɪʃən] *n* : évaporation *f*
evasion [ɪ'veɪʒən] *n* : évasion *f*
evasive [ɪ'veɪsɪv] *adj* : évasif
eve ['i:v] *n* : veille *f* <Christmas Eve : la veille de Noël>
even[1] ['i:vən] *vt* : égaliser — *vi or* **to even out** : s'égaliser
even[2] *adv* **1** : même <even a child can do it : même un enfant peut le faire> <he didn't even try : il n'a même pas essayé> **2** (*in comparisons*) : encore <even better : encore mieux> **3 even as** : au moment même où **4 even if** : même si **5 even so** : quand même **6 even then** : même alors
even[3] *adj* **1** REGULAR, STEADY : régulier, égal, constant <an even temperature : une température constante> **2** FLAT, SMOOTH : uni, plat **3** EQUAL : égal, équitable <an even trade : un échange équitable> <to get even : se venger> <we're even! : nous sommes quittes!> **4** : pair <an even number : un nombre pair>
evening ['i:vnɪŋ] *n* **1** : soir *m* <he's going out this evening : il sort ce soir> <good evening! : bon soir!> <every evening : tous les soirs> **2** (*emphasizing duration*) : soirée *f* <the whole

evening : toute la soirée> <have a nice evening! : bonne soirée!>

event |ɪ'vɛnt| *n* **1** OCCURRENCE : événement *m* **2** CONTINGENCY : cas *m* <in any event : en tout cas> <in the event that : au cas où> **3** : épreuve *f* (aux sports)

eventful |ɪ'vɛntfəl| *adj* **1** : mouvementé <an eventful week : une semaine mouvementée> **2** MOMENTOUS : mémorable

eventual |ɪ'vɛntʃʊəl| *adj* : final, qui s'ensuit <his eventual ruin : sa ruine finale>

eventuality |ɪˌvɛntʃʊ'æləṭi| *n, pl* **-ties** : éventualité *f*

eventually |ɪ'vɛntʃʊəli| *adv* : finalement

ever |'ɛvər| *adv* **1** ALWAYS : toujours <he's the same as ever : il est toujours le même> **2** : jamais <more beautiful than ever : plus belle que jamais> <nothing ever happens : il ne se passe jamais rien> **3 ever since** : depuis (lors)

evergreen[1] |'ɛvərˌgri:n| *adj* : à feuilles persistantes

evergreen[2] *n* : plante *f* à feuilles persistantes

everlasting |ˌɛvər'læstɪŋ| *adj* : éternel

every |'ɛvri| *adj* **1** EACH : chaque, tout, tous les <every morning : chaque matin> <every moment : à tout moment> <every store in town : tous les magasins de la ville> **2** ALL : tous <every kind of : toutes sortes de> **3** COMPLETE : plein, entier <to have every confidence in : avoir pleine confiance en> **4 every other** : tous les deux <every other day : tous les deux jours>

everybody |'ɛvriˌbʌdi, -ˌbɑ-| *pron* : tout le monde, chacun

everyday |ˌɛvri'deɪ, 'ɛvriˌ-| *adj* : quotidien, de tous les jours <everyday clothes : vêtements de tous les jours> <in everyday use : d'usage courant>

everyone |'ɛvriˌwʌn| → **everybody**

everything |'ɛvriˌθɪŋ| *pron* : tout

everywhere |'ɛvriˌhwɛr| *adv* : partout <everywhere in the world : partout dans le monde>

evict |ɪ'vɪkt| *vt* : expulser

eviction |ɪ'vɪkʃən| *n* : expulsion *f*

evidence |'ɛvədənts| *n* **1** INDICATION : signe *m*, marque *f* <to be in evidence : être (très) en vue> **2** PROOF : témoignage *m*, évidence *f* **3** TESTIMONY : témoignage *m*, déposition *f* <to give evidence : témoigner>

evident |'ɛvɪdənt| *adj* : évident, manifeste

evidently |'ɛvɪdəntli, ˌɛvɪ'dɛntli| *adv* **1** OBVIOUSLY : évidemment, manifestement **2** APPARENTLY : apparemment

evil[1] |'i:vəl, -vɪl| *adj* **eviler** *or* **eviller**; **evilest** *or* **evillest** : mauvais, méchant

evil[2] *n* : mal *m* <good and evil : le bien et le mal>

evildoer |ˌi:vəl'du:ər, ˌi:vɪl-| *n* : malfaiteur *m*; scélérat *m*, -rate *f*

evince |ɪ'vɪnts| *vt* **evinced; evincing** : manifester, faire preuve de

eviscerate |ɪ'vɪsəˌreɪt| *vt* **-ated; -ating** : éventrer, étriper

evocation |ˌi:vo'keɪʃən, ˌɛ-| *n* : évocation *f*

evocative |i'vɑkəṭɪv| *adj* : évocateur

evoke |i'vo:k| *vt* **evoked; evoking** : évoquer

evolution |ˌɛvə'lu:ʃən, ˌi:-| *n* : évolution *f*

evolve |i'vɑlv| *v* **evolved; evolving** *vt* : développer, élaborer — *vi* : évoluer

ewe |'ju:| *n* : brebis *f*

exact[1] |ɪg'zækt, ɛ-| *vt* : exiger

exact[2] *adj* : exact, précis, juste <to have the exact time : avoir l'heure juste> <can you be more exact? : pouvez-vous préciser un peu?>

exacting |ɪ'zæktɪŋ, ɛg-| *adj* : exigeant, astreignant

exactitude |ɪg'zæktəˌtu:d, ɛg-, -ˌtju:d| *n* : exactitude *f*

exactly |ɪg'zæktli, ɛg-| *adv* : exactement, juste <that's exactly what I thought : c'est exactement ce que je pensais> <it's exactly four o'clock : il est quatre heures juste>

exaggerate |ɪg'zædʒəˌreɪt, ɛg-| *v* **-ated; -ating** : exagérer

exaggeration |ɪg'zædʒə'reɪʃən, ɛg-| *n* : exagération *f*

exalt |ɪg'zɔlt, ɛg-| *vt* : exalter, glorifier

exaltation |ˌɛgˌzɔl'teɪʃən, ɛkˌsɔl-| *n* : exaltation *f*

exam |ɪg'zæm, ɛg-| → **examination**

examination |ɪgˌzæmə'neɪʃən, ɛg-| *n* **1** TEST : examen *m* **2** INSPECTION : inspection *f*, examen *m* **3** INTERROGATION : interrogatoire *m*

examine |ɪg'zæmən, ɛg-| *vt* **-ined; -ining 1** TEST : examiner **2** INSPECT : examiner, inspecter, étudier **3** QUESTION : interroger <to examine a witness : interroger un témoin>

example |ɪg'zæmpəl, ɛg-| *n* : exemple *m* <for example : par exemple> <to set an example : donner l'exemple>

exasperate |ɪg'zæspəˌreɪt, ɛg-| *vt* **-ated; -ating 1** : exaspérer **2 to become exasperated** : s'exaspérer

exasperation |ɪgˌzæspə'reɪʃən, ɛg-| *n* : exaspération *f*

excavate |'ɛkskəˌveɪt| *v* **-vated; -vating** *vt* **1** DIG : creuser, excaver **2** UNEARTH : fouiller, déterrer — *vi* : faire des fouilles (en archéologie)

excavation |ˌɛkskə'veɪʃən| *n* **1** DIGGING : excavation *f*, creusement *m* **2** : fouilles *nfpl* (en archéologie)

exceed |ɪk'si:d, ɛk-| *vt* **1** SURPASS : excéder, dépasser **2** OVERSTEP : excéder, outrepasser <to exceed one's authority : outrepasser ses pouvoirs>

exceedingly [ɪk'si:dɪŋli, ɛk-] *adv* : extrêmement

excel [ɪk'sɛl, ɛk-] *v* **-celled; -celling** *vt* : surpasser — *vi* : exceller

excellence ['ɛksələnts] *n* : excellence *f*

excellency ['ɛksələntsi] *n, pl* **-cies** : excellence *f* <Your Excellency : Votre Excellence>

excellent ['ɛksələnt] *adj* : excellent

excellently *adv* : admirablement, de façon excellente

except[1] [ɪk'sɛpt] *vt* : excepter, exclure

except[2] *conj* : sauf que, mais <I'd go except it's too far : j'irais mais c'est trop loin>

except[3] *prep* **1** : sauf, excepté <everyone except me : tout le monde sauf moi> **2** (*in questions and negative constructions*) : sinon, sauf <what can one do except wait? : que peut-on faire sinon attendre?> **3 except for** : à part, à l'exception de

exception [ɪk'sɛpʃən] *n* **1** : exception *f* <to make an exception for : faire une exception pour> **2 to take exception to** : s'offenser de

exceptional [ɪk'sɛpʃənəl] *adj* : exceptionnel — **exceptionally** *adv*

excerpt[1] [ɛk'sərpt, ɛg'zərpt, 'ɛk,-, 'ɛg,-] *vt* : extraire

excerpt[2] [ɛk'sərpt, 'ɛg,zərpt] *n* : extrait *m*

excess[1] ['ɛk,sɛs, ɪk'sɛs] *adj* : excédentaire, en trop <excess baggage : un excédent de bagages>

excess[2] [ɪk'sɛs, 'ɛk,sɛs] *n* **1** : excès *m* <to drink to excess : boire à l'excès> **2** SURPLUS : surplus *m,* excédent *m* **3 in excess of** : en plus de, dépassant

excessive [ɪk'sɛsɪv, ɛk-] *adj* : excessif — **excessively** *adv*

exchange[1] [ɪks'tʃeɪndʒ, ɛks-; 'ɛks,tʃeɪndʒ] *vt* **-changed; -changing** : échanger

exchange[2] *n* **1** : échange *m* <in exchange for : en échange de> <exchange of ideas : échange d'idées> **2** : change *m* (en finances) <rate of exchange : taux de change>

excise[1] [ɪk'saɪz, ɛk-] *vt* **-cised; -cising** : exciser

excise[2] ['ɛk,saɪz] *n or* **excise tax** : taxe *f*

excision [ɪk'sɪʒən, ɛk-] *n* : excision *f*

excitable [ɪk'saɪt̬əbəl, ɛk-] *adj* : excitable, nerveux (se dit d'une personne)

excite [ɪk'saɪt, ɛk-] *vt* **-cited; -citing 1** STIMULATE : exciter <to excite enthusiasm : enthousiasmer> **2** AROUSE : exciter, éveiller, piquer (l'intérêt, la curiosité, etc.)

excited [ɪk'saɪt̬əd, ɛk-] *adj* **1** : excité, énervé, agité **2 to get excited** : s'exciter

excitedly [ɪk'saɪt̬ədli, ɛk-] *adv* : avec agitation <to speak excitedly : parler sur un ton animé>

excitement [ɪk'saɪtmənt, ɛk-] *n* : excitation *f,* agitation *f*

exciting [ɪk'saɪtɪŋ, ɛk-] *adj* : passionnant, excitant

exclaim [ɪks'kleɪm, ɛk-] *vt* : s'écrier — *vi* : s'exclamer

exclamation [,ɛksklə'meɪʃən] *n* : exclamation *f*

exclamation point *n* : point *m* d'exclamation

exclamatory [ɪks'klæmə,tori, ɛks-] *adj* : exclamatif

exclude [ɪks'klu:d, ɛks-] *vt* **-cluded; -cluding** : exclure

excluding [ɪks'klu:dɪŋ, ɛks-] *prep* : à part, à l'exclusion de

exclusion [ɪks'klu:ʒən, ɛks-] *n* : exclusion *f*

exclusive [ɪks'klu:sɪv, ɛks-] *adj* : exclusif — **exclusively** *adv*

excommunicate [ɛkskə'mju:nə,keɪt] *vt* **-cated; -cating** : excommunier

excommunication [,ɛkskə,mju:nə'keɪʃən] *n* : excommunication *f*

excrement ['ɛkskrəmənt] *n* : excréments *mpl*

excrete [ɪk'skri:t, ɛk-] *vt* **-creted; -creting** : excréter

excretion [ɪk'skri:ʃən, ɛk-] *n* : excrétion *f*

excruciating [ɪk'skru:ʃi,eɪt̬ɪŋ, ɛk-] *adj* : atroce, insupportable — **excruciatingly** *adv*

exculpate ['ɛkskəl,peɪt] *vt* **-pated; -pating** : disculper

excursion [ɪk'skərʒən, ɛk-] *n* **1** OUTING : excursion *f,* sortie *f* **2** DIGRESSION : digression *f*

excuse[1] [ɪk'skju:z, ɛk-] *vt* **-cused; -cusing 1** PARDON : excuser, pardonner **2** EXEMPT : exempter, dispenser **3** JUSTIFY : excuser, justifier **4 to excuse oneself** : s'excuser (de la table, etc.)

excuse[2] [ɪk'skju:s, ɛk-] *n* **1** JUSTIFICATION : excuse *f* **2** PRETEXT : prétexte *m,* excuse *f* **3 to make one's excuses** : présenter ses excuses

execute ['ɛksɪ,kju:t] *vt* **-cuted; -cuting** : exécuter

execution [,ɛksɪ'kju:ʃən] *n* : exécution *f*

executioner [,ɛksɪ'kju:ʃənər] *n* : bourreau *m*

executive[1] [ɪg'zɛkjət̬ɪv, ɛg-] *adj* : exécutif

executive[2] *n* **1** MANAGER : cadre *m;* dirigeant *m,* -geante *f* **2** *or* **executive branch** : pouvoir *m* exécutif

executor [ɪg'zɛkjət̬ər, ɛg-] *n* : exécuteur *m* testamentaire

executrix [ɪg'zɛkjə,trɪks, ɛg-] *n, pl* **executrices** [-zɛkjə'traɪ,si:z] *or* **executrixes** [-'zɛkjə,trɪksəz] : exécutrice *f* testamentaire

exemplary [ɪg'zɛmpləri, ɛg-] *adj* : exemplaire

exemplify [ɪg'zɛmplə,faɪ, ɛg-] *vt* **-fied; -fying** : exemplifier, illustrer

exempt[1] [ɪg'zɛmpt, ɛg-] *vt* : exempter, dispenser

exempt[2] *adj* : exempt

exemption [ɪg'zɛmpʃən, ɛg-] *n* : exemption *f*

exercise[1] ['ɛksər,saɪz] *v* **-cised; -cising** *vt* **1** : exercer (le corps) **2** APPLY : exercer, user de, faire valoir — *vi* : faire de l'exercice

exercise[2] *n* **1** : exercice *m* **2 exercises** *npl* CEREMONY : cérémonie *f*

exert [ɪg'zərt, ɛg-] *vt* **1** APPLY, WIELD : exercer, employer **2 to exert oneself** : se dépenser, s'appliquer, se donner de la peine

exertion [ɪg'zərʃən, ɛg-] *n* **1** EFFORT : effort *m* **2** USE : exercice *m*, emploi *m* (de la force, etc.)

exhalation [,ɛksə'leɪʃən, ,ɛkshə-] *n* : expiration *f*, exhalation *f*

exhale [ɛks'heɪl] *v* **-haled; -haling** *vt* **1** : expirer, exhaler **2** EMIT : exhaler (une odeur) — *vi* : expirer

exhaust[1] [ɪg'zɔst, ɛg-] *vt* **1** : épuiser **2 to exhaust oneself** : s'épuiser, se morfondre *Can*

exhaust[2] *n* **1** *or* **exhaust fumes** : gaz *m* d'échappement **2** *or* **exhaust pipe** : tuyau *m* d'échappement

exhaustion [ɪg'zɔstʃən, ɛg-] *n* : épuisement *m*

exhaustive [ɪg'zɔstɪv, ɛg-] *adj* : exhaustif

exhibit[1] [ɪg'zɪbət, ɛg-] *vt* **1** DISPLAY : exposer (des œuvres d'art, etc.), étaler (des marchandises) **2** PRESENT : montrer, présenter (un document, etc.) **3** MANIFEST : manifester, montrer

exhibit[2] *n* **1** : objet *m* exposé, œuvre *f* exposée **2** EXHIBITION : exposition *f* **3** : pièce *f* à conviction (dans les poursuites judiciaires)

exhibition [,ɛksə'bɪʃən] *n* **1** EXHIBIT : exposition *f* **2 to make an exhibition of oneself** : se donner en spectacle

exhibitor [ɪg'zɪbət̬ər] *n* : exposant *m*, -sante *f*

exhilarate [ɪg'zɪlə,reɪt, ɛg-] *vt* **-rated; -rating** : griser, vivifier

exhilaration [ɪg'zɪlə'reɪʃən, ɛg-] *n* : joie *f*, griserie *f*

exhort [ɪg'zɔrt, ɛg-] *vt* : exhorter

exhortation [,ɛk,sɔr'teɪʃən, -sər-; ,ɛg,zɔr-] *n* : exhortation *f*

exhume [ɪg'zu:m, -'zju:m; ɪks'ju:m, -'hju:m] *vt* **-humed; -huming** : exhumer

exigencies ['ɛksɪdʒəntsiz, ɪg'zɪdʒənt,si:z] *npl* : exigences *fpl*

exile[1] ['ɛg,zaɪl, 'ɛk,saɪl] *vt* **exiled; exiling** : exiler

exile[2] *n* **1** BANISHMENT : exil *m* **2** OUTCAST : exilé *m*, -lée *f*

exist [ɪg'zɪst, ɛg-] *vi* **1** BE : exister **2** LIVE, SURVIVE : vivre, survivre

existence [ɪg'zɪstənts, ɛg-] *n* : existence *f*

exit[1] ['ɛgzət, 'ɛksət] *vi* : sortir — *vt* LEAVE : sortir de, quitter

exit[2] *n* : sortie *f*

exodus ['ɛksədəs] *n* : exode *m*

exonerate [ɪg'zɑnə,reɪt, ɛg-] *vt* **-ated; -ating** : disculper, innocenter

exoneration [ɪg,zɑnə'reɪʃən, ɛg-] *n* : disculpation *f*

exorbitant [ɪg'zɔrbətənt, ɛg-] *adj* : exorbitant, excessif

exorcise ['ɛk,sɔr,saɪz, -sər-] *vt* **-cised; -cising** : exorciser

exorcism ['ɛksər,sɪzəm] *n* : exorcisme *m*

exotic [ɪg'zɑtɪk, ɛg-] *adj* : exotique

expand [ɪk'spænd, ɛk-] *vt* **1** ENLARGE, EXTEND : étendre, élargir **2** DEVELOP : développer — *vi* **1** GROW, SPREAD : s'étendre, s'agrandir, se dilater (se dit des métaux) **2** DEVELOP : se développer

expanse [ɪk'spænts, ɛk-] *n* : étendue *f*

expansion [ɪk'spæntʃən, ɛk-] *n* : expansion *f*, élargissement *m*, développement *m*

expansive [ɪk'spæntsɪv, ɛk-] *adj* **1** OUTGOING : expansif, démonstratif **2** AMPLE : large, vaste

expansively [ɪk'spæntsɪvli, ɛk-] *adv* : de manière expansive

expansiveness [ɪk'spæntsɪvnəs, ɛk-] *n* : expansivité *f*

expatriate[1] [,ɛks'peɪtri,eɪt] *vt* **-ated; -ating** : expatrier

expatriate[2] [ɛks'peɪtriət, -,eɪt] *adj* : expatrié

expatriate[3] [ɛks'peɪtriət, -,eɪt] *n* : expatrié *m*, -triée *f*

expect [ɪk'spɛkt, ɛk-] *vt* **1** ANTICIPATE : s'attendre à <expect the worst : attendez-vous au pire> **2** AWAIT : attendre **3** REQUIRE : exiger, demander — *vi* **to be expecting** : attendre un bébé, être enceinte

expectancy [ɪk'spɛktəntsi, ɛk-] *n, pl* **-cies** : attente *f*, espérance *f* <life expectancy : espérance de vie>

expectant [ɪk'spɛktənt, ɛk-] *adj* **1** ANTICIPATING : qui attend **2** EXPECTING : futur <an expectant mother : une future mère>

expectation [,ɛk,spɛk'teɪʃən] *n* : attente *f*

expedient[1] [ɪk'spi:diənt] *adj* : opportun, indiqué, convenable

expedient[2] *n* : expédient *m*

expedite ['ɛkspə,daɪt] *vt* **-dited; -diting** : expédier, accélerer, hâter

expedition [,ɛkspə'dɪʃən] *n* : expédition *f*

expeditious [,ɛkspə'dɪʃəs] *adj* : expéditif, rapide

expel [ɪk'spɛl, ɛk-] *vt* **-pelled; -pelling** : expulser, renvoyer (un élève)

expend [ɪk'spɛnd, ɛk-] *vt* **1** SPEND : dépenser (de l'argent) **2** UTILIZE : utiliser, employer, consacrer (de l'énergie, du temps, etc.) **3** EXHAUST : épuiser

expendable [ɪk'spɛndəbəl, ɛk-] *adj* : remplaçable
expenditure [ɪk'spɛndɪtʃər, ɛk-, -ˌtʃʊr] *n* : dépense *f*
expense [ɪk'spɛnts, ɛk-] *n* **1** COST : coût *m,* dépense *f* **2 expenses** *npl* : frais *mpl* **3 at the expense of** : aux dépens de
expensive [ɪk'spɛntsɪv, ɛk-] *adj* : cher, coûteux
expensively [ɪk'spɛntsɪvli, ɛk-] *adv* : à grands frais
experience[1] [ɪk'spɪriənts, ɛk-] *vt* **-enced; -encing** : éprouver, faire l'expérience de, connaître <to experience difficulties : rencontrer des difficultés>
experience[2] *n* : expérience *f*
experienced [ɪk'spɪriəntst, ɛk-] *adj* : expérimenté
experiment[1] [ɪk'spɛrəmənt, ɛk-, -'spɪr-] *vi* : expérimenter, faire des expériences
experiment[2] *n* : expérience *f*
experimental [ɪkˌspɛrə'mɛntəl, ɛk-, -ˌspɪr-] *adj* : expérimental
experimentation [ɪkˌspɛrəmən'teɪʃən, ɛk-, -ˌspɪr-] *n* : expérimentation *f*
expert[1] ['ɛkˌspərt, ɪk'spərt] *adj* : expert <expert testimony : témoignage d'expert>
expert[2] ['ɛkˌspərt] *n* : expert *m,* -perte *f;* spécialiste *mf*
expertise [ˌɛkspər'ti:z] *n* : compétence *f,* expertise *f*
expertly ['ɛkˌspərtli] *adv* : de manière experte
expiate ['ɛkspiˌeɪt] *vt* **-ated; -ating** : expier
expiation [ˌɛkspi'eɪʃən] *n* : expiation *f*
expiration [ˌɛkspə'reɪʃən] *n* : expiration *f*
expire [ɪk'spaɪr, ɛk-] *vi* **-pired; -piring 1** EXHALE : expirer **2** END : expirer, arriver à terme **3** DIE : mourir
explain [ɪk'spleɪn, ɛk-] *vt* **1** : expliquer **2 to explain oneself** : s'expliquer
explanation [ˌɛksplə'neɪʃən] *n* : explication *f*
explanatory [ɪk'splænəˌtori, ɛk-] *adj* : explicatif
expletive ['ɛksplət̬ɪv] *n* SWEARWORD : juron *m*
explicable [ɛk'splɪkəbəl, 'ɛksplɪ-] *adj* : explicable
explicit [ɪk'splɪsət, ɛk-] *adj* : explicite — **explicitly** *adv*
explode [ɪk'splo:d, ɛk-] *v* **-ploded; -ploding** *vt* **1** BURST : faire exploser **2** DISCREDIT : discréditer — *vi* **1** : exploser **2 to explode with laughter** : éclater de rire
exploit[1] [ɪk'splɔɪt, ɛk-] *vt* : exploiter
exploit[2] ['ɛkˌsplɔɪt] *n* : exploit *m*
exploitation [ˌɛkˌsplɔɪ'teɪʃən] *n* : exploitation *f*
exploration [ˌɛksplə'reɪʃən] *n* : exploration *f*
exploratory [ɪk'splorəˌtori, ɛk-] *adj* : exploratoire
explore [ɪk'splor, ɛk-] *v* **-plored; -ploring** : explorer
explorer [ɪk'splorər, ɛk-] *n* : explorateur *m,* -trice *f*
explosion [ɪk'splo:ʒən, ɛk-] *n* : explosion *f*
explosive[1] [ɪk'splo:sɪv, ɛk-] *adj* : explosif
explosive[2] *n* : explosif *m*
exponent [ɪk'spo:nənt, 'ɛkˌspo:-] *n* **1** : exposant *m* (en mathématiques) **2** ADVOCATE : partisan *m,* -sane *f;* avocat *m,* -cate *f*
export[1] [ɛk'sport, 'ɛkˌsport] *v* : exporter
export[2] ['ɛkˌsport] *n* : exportation *f*
expose [ɪk'spo:z, ɛk-] *vt* **-posed; -posing 1** DISPLAY : exposer **2** DISCLOSE : révéler, démasquer **3 to expose oneself to** : s'exposer à
exposé [ˌɛkspo'zeɪ] *n* : exposé *m,* révélation *f*
exposition [ˌɛkspə'zɪʃən] *n* : exposition *f*
exposure [ɪk'spo:ʒər, ɛk-] *n* **1** : exposition *f* (au danger, etc.) <to die of exposure : mourir de froid> **2** DISCLOSURE : révélation *f,* divulgation *f* **3** : pose *f* (en photographie) **4** ORIENTATION : exposition *f* <to have a southern exposure : être exposé au sud>
expound [ɪk'spaʊnd, ɛk-] *vt* : exposer, expliquer — *vi* **to expound on** : disserter sur
express[1] [ɪk'sprɛs, ɛk-] *vt* **1** CONVEY : exprimer, énoncer **2** SQUEEZE : exprimer, extraire (du jus, etc.)
express[2] *adv* : en exprès <to send express : envoyer en exprès>
express[3] *adj* **1** EXPLICIT, SPECIFIC : exprès, explicite, formel <with the express purpose of : dans le seul but de> **2** FAST : rapide, express <an express bus : un autobus express>
express[4] *n* **1** *or* **express train** : rapide *m,* express *m* **2 to send by express** : envoyer par transport rapide
expression [ɪk'sprɛʃən, ɛk-] *n* : expression *f*
expressionless [ɪk'sprɛʃənləs, ɛk-] *adj* : inexpressif, sans expression
expressive [ɪk'sprɛsɪv, ɛk-] *adj* : expressif
expressiveness [ɪk'sprɛsɪvnəs, ɛk-] *n* : expressivité *f*
expressly [ɪk'sprɛsli, ɛk-] *adv* : expressément
expressway [ɪk'sprɛsˌweɪ, ɛk-] *n* : autoroute *f*
expulsion [ɪk'spʌlʃən, ɛk-] *n* : expulsion *f,* renvoi *m* (d'un élève)
expurgate ['ɛkspərˌgeɪt] *vt* **-gated; -gating** : expurger
exquisite [ɛk'skwɪzət, 'ɛkˌskwɪ-] *adj* **1** FINE : exquis, raffiné **2** INTENSE : vif (se dit des plaisirs, etc.), aigu (se dit d'une douleur)
extant ['ɛkstənt, ɛk'stænt] *adj* : existant

extemporaneous [ɛk,stɛmpəˈreɪniəs] *adj* : improvisé, impromptu
extend [ɪkˈstɛnd, ɛk-] *vt* **1** STRETCH : étendre **2** PROLONG : prolonger **3** ENLARGE : agrandir **4 to extend one's hand** : tendre la main — *vi* **1** STRETCH : s'étendre **2** LAST : se prolonger
extension [ɪkˈstɛntʃən, ɛk-] *n* **1** EXTENDING : extension *f* **2** PROLONGATION : prolongation *f,* délai *m* **3** ADDITION, ANNEX : agrandissement *m* (d'une maison), prolongement *m* (d'une route, etc.) **4** : poste *m* (de téléphone) **5 extension cord** : rallonge *f*
extensive [ɪkˈstɛntsɪv, ɛk-] *adj* : étendu, vaste
extensively [ɪkˈstɛntsɪvli, ɛk-] *adv* : considérablement, abondamment
extent [ɪkˈstɛnt, ɛk-] *n* **1** SIZE : étendue *f* **2** SCOPE : importance *f,* ampleur *f* **3** DEGREE : mesure *f,* degré *m* <to a certain extent : dans une certaine mesure, jusqu'à un certain point>
extenuating [ɪkˈstɛnjə,weɪtɪŋ, ɛk-] *adj* : atténuant
exterior[1] [ɛkˈstɪriər] *adj* : extérieur
exterior[2] *n* : extérieur *m*
exterminate [ɪkˈstərmə,neɪt, ɛk-] *vt* **-nated; -nating** : exterminer
extermination [ɪk,stərməˈneɪʃən, ɛk-] *n* : extermination *f*
external [ɪkˈstərnəl, ɛk-] *adj* : externe <for external use only : à usage externe>
externally [ɪkˈstərnəli, ɛk-] *adv* : extérieurement
extinct [ɪkˈstɪŋkt, ɛk-] *adj* : éteint (se dit d'un volcan, d'un feu, etc.), disparu (se dit d'une espèce)
extinction [ɪkˈstɪŋkʃən, ɛk-] *n* : extinction *f,* disparition *f*
extinguish [ɪkˈstɪŋgwɪʃ, ɛk-] *vt* : éteindre
extinguisher [ɪkˈstɪŋgwɪʃər, ɛk-] *n* : extincteur *m*
extirpate [ˈɛkstər,peɪt] *vt* **-pated; -pating** : extirper
extol [ɪkˈstoːl, ɛk-] *vt* **-tolled; -tolling** : louer
extort [ɪkˈstɔrt, ɛk-] *vt* : extorquer
extortion [ɪkˈstɔrʃən, ɛk-] *n* : extorsion *f*
extra[1] [ˈɛkstrə] *adv* **1** ESPECIALLY : plus que d'habitude, particulièrement <extra nice : plus gentil que d'habitude> **2 to pay extra** : payer un supplément **3 to cost extra** : coûter plus cher
extra[2] *adj* **1** ADDITIONAL : supplémentaire, en supplément <extra hours : heures supplémentaires> <the wine is extra : le vin est en plus> **2** SPARE : en trop, de trop <an extra chair : une chaise en trop> **3** SUPERIOR : supérieur <extra quality : de qualité supérieure>
extra[3] *n* **1** ADDITION : supplément *m* **2** : édition *f* spéciale (d'un journal) **3** : figurant *m,* -rante *f* (au cinéma)
extract[1] [ɪkˈstrækt, ɛk-] *vt* : extraire, arracher (une dent, un aveu, etc.)
extract[2] [ˈɛk,strækt] *n* : extrait *m*
extraction [ɪkˈstrækʃən, ɛk-] *n* **1** REMOVAL : extraction *f* **2** ORIGIN : origine *f* <of French extraction : d'origine française>
extracurricular [,ɛkstrəkəˈrɪkjələr] *adj* : parascolaire
extradite [ˈɛkstrə,daɪt] *vt* **-dited; -diting** : extrader
extradition [,ɛkstrəˈdɪʃən] *n* : extradition *f*
extramarital [,ɛkstrəˈmærəṭəl] *adj* : extraconjugal
extraneous [ɛkˈstreɪniəs] *adj* **1** OUTSIDE : extérieur, étranger **2** SUPERFLUOUS : superflu
extraordinary [ɪkˈstrɔrdən,ɛri, ,ɛkstrəˈɔrd-] *adj* : extraordinaire — **extraordinarily** [ɪk,strɔrdənˈɛrəli, ,ɛkstrə,ɔrd-] *adv*
extrasensory [,ɛkstrəˈsɛntsəri] *adj* : extrasensoriel
extraterrestrial[1] [,ɛkstrətəˈrɛstriəl] *adj* : extraterrestre
extraterrestrial[2] *n* : extraterrestre *mf*
extravagance [ɪkˈstrævɪgənts, ɛk-] *n* **1** EXCESS : extravagance *f* **2** WASTEFULNESS : prodigalité *f* **3** LUXURY : luxe *m*
extravagant [ɪkˈstrævɪgənt, ɛk-] *adj* **1** EXCESSIVE : extravagant, excessif **2** WASTEFUL : prodigue **3** LUXURIOUS : luxueux
extravagantly [ɪkˈstrævɪgəntli, ɛk-] *adv* **1** LAVISHLY : avec prodigalité, luxueusement **2** EXCESSIVELY : d'une manière extravagante, à outrance
extravaganza [ɪk,strævəˈgænzə, ɛk-] *n* : œuvre *f* à grand spectacle, spectacle *m* somptueux
extreme[1] [ɪkˈstriːm, ɛk-] *adj* : extrême — **extremely** *adv*
extreme[2] *n* **1** : extrême *m* **2 to go to extremes** : pousser (les choses) à l'extrême
extremity [ɪkˈstrɛməṭi, ɛk-] *n, pl* **-ties** : extrémité *f*
extricate [ˈɛkstrə,keɪt] *vt* **-cated; -cating** **1** : dégager, extirper **2 to extricate oneself from** : se dégager de, se sortir de
extrovert [ˈɛkstrə,vərt] *n* : extraverti *m,* -tie *f*
extroverted [ˈɛkstrə,vərṭəd] *adj* : extraverti
extrude [ɪkˈstruːd, ɛk-] *vt* **-truded; -truding** : extruder, faire sortir
exuberance [ɪgˈzuːbərənts, ɛg-] *n* : exubérance *f*
exuberant [ɪgˈzuːbərənt, ɛg-] *adj* : exubérant
exuberantly [ɪgˈzuːbərəntli, ɛg-] *adv* : avec exubérance

exude |ɪg'zu:d, ɛg-| *v* **-uded; -uding** *vt* **1** : exsuder (un liquide) **2 to exude confidence** : respirer la confiance en soi — *vi* : exsuder

exult |ɪg'zʌlt, ɛg-| *vi* : exulter, se réjouir

exultant |ɪg'zʌltənt, ɛg-| *adj* : triomphant, jubilant

exultation |ˌɛksəl'teɪʃən, ˌɛgzəl-| *n* : exultation *f*

eye[1] |'aɪ| *vt* **eyed; eyeing** *or* **eying** : regarder, lorgner

eye[2] *n* **1** : œil *m* <to have brown eyes : avoir les yeux bruns> <the eye of the storm : l'œil de la tempête> **2** VISION : vision *f* **3** GLANCE : regard *m* <her eyes fell on the letter : son regard est tombé sur la lettre> **4** POINT OF VIEW : point *m* de vue <in the eyes of the law : selon la loi> **5 eye of a needle** : chas *m*

eyeball |'aɪˌbɔl| *n* : globe *m* oculaire

eyebrow |'aɪˌbraʊ| *n* : sourcil *m*

eyedropper |'aɪˌdrɑpər| → **dropper**

eyeglasses |'aɪˌglæsəz| *npl* : lunettes *fpl*

eyelash |'aɪˌlæʃ| *n* : cil *m*

eyelet |'aɪlət| *n* : œillet *m*

eyelid |aɪˌlɪd| *n* : paupière *f*

eye–opener |'aɪˌo:pənər| *n* : révélation *f*

eyepiece |'aɪˌpics| *n* : oculaire *m*

eyesight |'aɪˌsaɪt| *n* : vue *f*, vision *f* <to lose one's eyesight : perdre la vue>

eyesore |'aɪˌsor| *n* : horreur *f* <to be an eyesore : choquer la vue>

eyestrain |'aɪˌstreɪn| *n* : fatigue *f* des yeux

eyetooth |'aɪˌtu:θ| *n, pl* **-teeth** |-ˌti:θ| : dent *f* canine

eyewitness |'aɪ'wɪtnəs| *n* : témoin *m* oculaire

eyrie |'aɪri| → **aerie**

F

f |'ɛf| *n, pl* **f's** *or* **fs** |'ɛfs| : f *m*, sixième lettre de l'alphabet

fable |'feɪbəl| *n* : fable *f*, légende *f*

fabled |'feɪbəld| *adj* : légendaire, fabuleux

fabric |'fæbrɪk| *n* **1** CLOTH : tissu *m*, étoffe *f* **2** STRUCTURE : structure *f* <the fabric of society : la structure de la société>

fabricate |'fæbrɪˌkeɪt| *vt* **-cated; -cating 1** CONSTRUCT : fabriquer (un objet) **2** INVENT : fabriquer, inventer (une histoire, etc.)

fabrication |ˌfæbrɪ'keɪʃən| *n* **1** CONSTRUCTION : fabrication *f* **2** FALSEHOOD : mensonge *m*

fabulous |'fæbjələs| *adj* **1** LEGENDARY : fabuleux, légendaire **2** INCREDIBLE : incroyable **3** MARVELOUS : fabuleux, formidable

fabulously |'fæbjələsli| *adv* : fabuleusement

facade |fə'sɑd| *n* : façade *f*

face[1] |'feɪs| *vt* **faced; facing 1** CONFRONT : faire face à, affronter <to be faced with : se trouver confronté à> **2** COVER : revêtir (un mur, etc.) **3** : faire face à <to face the sun : faire face au soleil> **4** FRONT, OVERLOOK : être en face de, donner sur

face[2] *n* **1** : visage *m*, figure *f* **2** EXPRESSION : mine *f*, air *m* <he put on a sad face : il faisait triste mine> **3** : grimace *f* <to make a face : faire la grimace> **4** APPEARANCE : aspect *m*, visage *m*, apparence *f* (de la société, etc.) **5** PRESENCE : présence *f* <in the face of the enemy : face à l'ennemi> **6** SURFACE : face *f* (d'une monnaie), façade *f* (d'un bâtiment) **7** DIGNITY : face *f* <to lose face : perdre la face> **8 in the face of** DESPITE : en dépit de

facedown |'feɪsˌdaʊn| *adv* : face contre terre <to lie facedown : être étendu à plat ventre>

faceless |'feɪsləs| *adj* ANONYMOUS : anonyme

face–lift |'feɪsˌlɪft| *n* **1** : lifting *m* **2** RENOVATION : ravalement *m* (d'une façade), restauration *f*

facet |'fæsət| *n* **1** : facette *f* (d'une pierre précieuse) **2** ASPECT : aspect *m*, facette *f*

facetious |fə'si:ʃəs| *adj* : facétieux — **facetiously** *adv*

facetiousness |fə'si:ʃəsnəs| *n* : caractère *m* facétieux

face–to–face *adv* : face à face, en personne

faceup |'feɪs'ʌp| *adv* : face en dessus <to lie faceup : être étendu sur le dos>

face value *n* : valeur *f* nominale

facial[1] |'feɪʃəl| *adj* : facial, du visage

facial[2] *n* : soin *m* du visage

facile |'fæsəl| *adj* **1** EASY : facile **2** SUPERFICIAL : superficiel, creux **3** FLUENT : coulant, aisé

facilitate |fə'sɪləˌteɪt| *vt* **-tated; -tating** : faciliter

facility |fə'sɪləṭi| *n, pl* **-ties 1** EASE : facilité *f*, aisance *f* **2** APTITUDE : facilité *f*, aptitude *f* **3** CENTER, COMPLEX : complexe *m* <hospital facility : complexe hospitalier> **4 facilities** *npl* : installations *fpl*, équipements *mpl* <sports facilities : équipements sportifs>

facing |'feɪsɪŋ| *n* **1** : revers *m* (en couture) **2** : revêtement *m* (d'un bâtiment)

facsimile |fæk'sɪməli| *n* **1** REPRODUCTION : fac-similé *m* **2** FAX : fac-similé *m*, télécopie *f*

fact |ˈfækt| *n* **1** DATA, INFORMATION : fait *m* **2** REALITY : faits *mpl,* réalité *f* **3 in ~** : en fait, effectivement

faction |ˈfækʃən| *n* : faction *f*

factitious |fækˈtɪʃəs| *adj* : factice, artificiel

factor |ˈfæktər| *n* : facteur *m*

factory |ˈfæktəri| *n, pl* **-ries** : usine *f,* fabrique *f*

factual |ˈfæktʃuəl| *adj* : factuel, basé sur les faits

factually |ˈfæktʃuəli| *adv* : en se tenant aux faits

faculty |ˈfækəlti| *n, pl* **-ties 1** : faculté *f* <the faculty of hearing : la faculté de l'ouïe> **2** APTITUDE : aptitude *f,* faculté *f* **3** TEACHERS : faculté *f* (dans une université), corps *m* enseignant

fad |ˈfæd| *n* : mode *f* passagère, marotte *f*

fade |ˈfeɪd| *v* **faded; fading** *vt* : décolorer — *vi* **1** WITHER : se flétrir, se faner **2** DISCOLOR : se décolorer **3** DIM : s'affaiblir, diminuer (se dit de la lumière) **4** VANISH : disparaître <to fade from sight : disparaître aux regards>

faded |ˈfeɪdəd| *adj* : décoloré, délavé

fag |ˈfæg| *vt* **fagged; fagging** EXHAUST : épuiser, fatiguer

fagot *or* **faggot** |ˈfægət| *n* : fagot *m*

Fahrenheit |ˈfærən,haɪt| *adj* : Fahrenheit

fail[1] |ˈfeɪl| *vi* **1** WEAKEN : faiblir, baisser <my eyes are failing : ma vue faiblit> **2** BREAK DOWN : tomber en panne, lâcher (se dit des freins) <her heart failed : son cœur s'est arrêté> **3** (*indicating a lack of success*) : échouer, ne pas réussir, faire faillite <the business is failing : l'entreprise fait faillite> **4 to fail in** : manquer à, faire défaut à <I failed in my duty : j'ai manqué à mon devoir> — *vt* **1** DISAPPOINT, LET DOWN : décevoir, laisser tomber, faire défaut **2** NEGLECT : manquer à, négliger <to fail to keep one's word : manquer à sa parole> **3** : échouer à, ne pas réussir à <to fail an exam : échouer à un examen>

fail[2] *n* **1** FAILURE : échec *m* **2 without ~** : à coup sûr, sans faute

failing[1] |ˈfeɪlɪŋ| *n* : défaut *m*

failing[2] *prep* : à défaut de

failure |ˈfeɪljər| *n* **1** : échec *m,* insuccès *m,* faillite *f* (en finances) <a complete failure : un échec total> **2** LACK, OMISSION : manque *m,* manquement *m,* défaut *m* **3** BREAKDOWN, LOSS : panne *f,* défaillance *f* (en médecine) <power failure : panne de courant> <crop failure : perte des récoltes> **4 to be a failure** : être nul, ne pas être doué

faint[1] |ˈfeɪnt| *vi* : s'évanouir

faint[2] *adj* **1** COWARDLY : lâche, peureux **2** WEAK : défaillant, faible <to feel faint : se sentir mal> **3** FEEBLE, SLIGHT : faible, léger **4** INDISTINCT : vague, flou

faint[3] *n* : évanouissement *m*

fainthearted |ˈfeɪntˈhɑrṭəd| *adj* : timide, timoré

faintly |ˈfeɪntli| *adv* **1** SLIGHTLY : faiblement **2** INDISTINCTLY : vaguement

faintness |ˈfeɪntnəs| *n* **1** INDISTINCTNESS : faiblesse *f,* légèreté *f* **2** DIZZINESS : vertige *m*

fair[1] |ˈfær| *adv* → **fairly**

fair[2] *adj* **1** BEAUTIFUL : beau **2** FINE : beau (se dit du temps), favorable (se dit du vent) **3** HONEST, JUST : juste, équitable <it's not fair : ce n'est pas juste> <fair play : franc jeu> **4** BLOND, LIGHT : blond (se dit des cheveux), clair (se dit de la peau) **5** ADEQUATE : assez bon, passable **6** LARGE : considérable, important

fair[3] *n* : foire *f,* fête *f* foraine

fairground |ˈfær,graʊnd| *n* : champ *m* de foire

fairly |ˈfærli| *adv* **1** HONESTLY, JUSTLY : équitablement, impartialement, honnêtement **2** QUITE, RATHER : assez, passablement **3** POSITIVELY : vraiment <fairly bursting with pride : vraiment fier de soi>

fairness |ˈfærnəs| *n* **1** IMPARTIALITY : équité *f,* impartialité *f,* justice *f* <in all fairness : en toute justice> **2** LIGHTNESS : blondeur *f* (des cheveux), blancheur *f* (de la peau)

fairy |ˈfæri| *n, pl* **fairies** : fée *f*

fairyland |ˈfæri,lænd| *n* : royaume *m* des fées, féerie *f*

fairy tale *n* : conte *m* de fées

faith |ˈfeɪθ| *n, pl* **faiths** |ˈfeɪθs, ˈfeɪðz| **1** LOYALTY : loyauté *f,* foi *f* **2** BELIEF : foi *f,* croyance *f* (en Dieu) **3** CONFIDENCE, TRUST : confiance *f,* foi *f* <to have faith in : avoir confiance en> <in good faith : en toute bonne foi> **4** RELIGION : foi *f,* religion *f*

faithful |ˈfeɪθfəl| *adj* **1** RELIABLE : fidèle, loyal **2** ACCURATE : fidèle, exact — **faithfully** *adv*

faithfulness |ˈfeɪθfəlnəs| *n* : fidélité *f*

faithless |ˈfeɪθləs| *adj* : déloyal, infidèle — **faithlessly** *adv*

faithlessness |ˈfeɪθləsnəs| *n* : déloyauté *f,* infidélité *f*

fake[1] |ˈfeɪk| *v* **faked; faking** *vt* **1** COUNTERFEIT, FALSIFY : falsifier, contrefaire **2** FEIGN : simuler, feindre — *vi* **1** PRETEND : faire semblant **2** : feinter (aux sports)

fake[2] *adj* : faux, falsifié

fake[3] *n* **1** : article *m* truqué, faux *m* (œuvre d'art) **2** : imposteur *m* (personne) **3** : feinte *f* (aux sports)

fakir |fəˈkɪr, ˈfeɪkər| *n* : fakir *m*

falcon |ˈfælkən, ˈfɔl-| *n* : faucon *m*

falconry |ˈfælkənri, ˈfɔl-| *n* : fauconnerie *f*

fall[1] |ˈfɔl| *vi* **fell** |ˈfɛl|; **fallen** |ˈfɔlən|; **falling 1** : tomber <to fall off a roof : tomber d'un toit> <the snow was falling : la neige tombait> **2** DROP : baisser, tomber, diminuer **3** HANG : tomber (se dit des cheveux), descendre (se dit des rideaux, etc.) **4** : tomber, être renversé <the government has fallen : le gouvernement a été renversé> **5** SIN : tomber, pécher **6** OCCUR : tomber, arriver <Christmas falls on a Wednesday : Noël tombe un mercredi> **7 to fall asleep** : s'endormir **8 to fall behind** : prendre du retard **9 to fall in love** : tomber amoureux

fall[2] *n* **1** : chute *f* <to have a fall : faire une chute, tomber> <a heavy fall of snow : une forte chute de neige> **2** DECREASE : baisse *f*, chute *f* (des prix, de la température, etc.), dépréciation *f* (de la monnaie) **3** COLLAPSE : effondrement *m* (d'un édifice), chute *f*, renversement *m* (d'un régime, etc.) **4** AUTUMN : automne *m* **5 falls** → **waterfall**

fallacious |fəˈleɪʃəs| *adj* : fallacieux

fallacy |ˈfæləsi| *n, pl* **-cies** : erreur *f*, faux raisonnement *m*

fall back *vi* **1** RETREAT : reculer, se retirer **2 to fall back on** : avoir recours à

fallible |ˈfæləbəl| *adj* : faillible

fallout |ˈfɔlˌaʊt| *n* **1** : retombées *fpl* (radioactives) **2** CONSEQUENCES : répercussions *fpl*

fall out *vi* QUARREL : se disputer, se quereller

fallow[1] |ˈfælo| *vt* : labourer une terre en vue des récoltes à venir

fallow[2] *adj* **1** : en jachère (se dit d'une terre) **2** DORMANT : inactif

false |ˈfɔls| *adj* **falser**; **falsest 1** UNTRUE : faux, erroné **2** FAKE : faux, artificiel **3** DECEPTIVE : faux, mensonger **4** DISLOYAL : faux, déloyal

falsehood |ˈfɔlsˌhʊd| *n* **1** LIE : mensonge *m* **2** LYING : fausseté *f*

falsely |ˈfɔlsli| *adv* : faussement

falseness |ˈfɔlsnəs| *n* : fausseté *f*

falsetto |fɔlˈsɛt̬oː| *n, pl* **-tos** : fausset *m*

falsification |ˌfɔlsəfəˈkeɪʃən| *n* : falsification *f*

falsify |ˈfɔlsəˌfaɪ| *vt* **-fied**; **-fying** : falsifier

falsity |ˈfɔlsət̬i| *n, pl* **-ties** : fausseté *f*

falter |ˈfɔltər| *vi* **1** STUMBLE : chanceler, trébucher **2** STAMMER : bredouiller **3** WAVER : hésiter, vaciller, chanceler

fame |ˈfeɪm| *n* : célébrité *f*, renommée *f*

famed |ˈfeɪmd| *adj* : célèbre, renommé

familial |fəˈmɪljəl, -liəl| *adj* : familial

familiar |fəˈmɪljər| *adj* **1** KNOWN : familier, (bien) connu <to be on familiar ground : être en terrain connu> <to be familiar with sth : bien connaître qqch> **2** INFORMAL, INTIMATE : familier, intime **3** FORWARD : entreprenant, effronté

familiarity |fəˌmɪliˈærət̬i, -ˌmɪlˈjær-| *n, pl* **-ties 1** ACQUAINTANCE, KNOWLEDGE : connaissance *f*, caractère *m* familier **2** INFORMALITY, INTIMACY : familiarité *f*, intimité *f* **3** FORWARDNESS : familiarités *fpl*, privautés *fpl*

familiarize |fəˈmɪljəˌraɪz| *vt* **-ized**; **-izing 1** : familiariser **2 to familiarize oneself with** : se familiariser avec

family |ˈfæmli, ˈfæmə-| *n, pl* **-lies** : famille *f*

family name → **surname**

family tree *n* : arbre *m* généalogique

famine |ˈfæmən| *n* : famine *f*

famished |ˈfæmɪʃt| *adj* : affamé <I'm famished! : je meurs de faim!>

famous |ˈfeɪməs| *adj* : célèbre, renommé

famously |ˈfeɪməsli| *adv* : à merveille, rudement bien *fam*

fan[1] |ˈfæn| *vt* **fanned**; **fanning 1** : éventer (le visage, etc.), attiser (un feu) **2** STIMULATE : attiser, aviver

fan[2] *n* **1** : éventail *m*, ventilateur *m* (électrique) **2** ADMIRER, ENTHUSIAST : admirateur *m*, -trice *f*; enthousiaste *mf*; fan *mf* (d'une vedette)

fanatic[1] |fəˈnæt̬ɪk| *or* **fanatical** |-t̬ɪkəl| *adj* : fanatique

fanatic[2] *n* : fanatique *mf*

fanaticism |fəˈnæt̬əˌsɪzəm| *n* : fanatisme *m*

fanciful |ˈfæntsɪfəl| *adj* **1** IMAGINATIVE : imaginatif **2** CAPRICIOUS, WHIMSICAL : fantasque, bizarre, capricieux

fancy[1] |ˈfæntsi| *vt* **-cied**; **-cying 1** IMAGINE : s'imaginer, se figurer, croire **2** LIKE, WANT : avoir envie de, aimer

fancy[2] *adj* **fancier**; **-est 1** ELABORATE : élaboré, extravagant **2** LUXURIOUS : de luxe

fancy[3] *n, pl* **-cies 1** LIKING : goût *m*, envie *f* <to take a fancy to s.o. : se prendre d'affection pour qqn> **2** WHIM : caprice *m*, fantaisie *f* **3** IMAGINATION : imagination *f*, fantaisie *f*

fanfare |ˈfænˌfær| *n* : fanfare *f*

fang |ˈfæŋ| *n* : croc *m* (d'un animal), crochet *m* (d'un serpent)

fanlight |ˈfænˌlaɪt| *n* : imposte *f*

fantasia |fænˈteɪʒə, -ziə; ˌfæntəˈziːə| *n* : fantaisie *f*

fantasize |ˈfæntəˌsaɪz| *vi* **-sized**; **-sizing** : fantasmer

fantastic |fænˈtæstɪk| *adj* **1** FANCIFUL, STRANGE : fantasque, bizarre **2** INCREDIBLE : incroyable, fabuleux, inouï **3** WONDERFUL : superbe, sensationnel

fantastically |fænˈtæstɪkli| *adv* : fantastiquement, incroyablement

fantasy |ˈfæntəsi| *n, pl* **-sies 1** IMAGINATION : imagination *f*, fantaisie *f* **2** FANTASIZING : fantasme *m*, rêverie *f*

far[1] |ˈfɑr| *adv* **farther** |ˈfɑrðər| *or* **further** |ˈfər-|; **farthest** *or* **furthest** |-ðəst| **1** : loin <is it far? : est-ce loin?> <far away : au loin, dans le lointain> <far and wide : de tous côtés> **2** MUCH : beaucoup, bien <far worse : bien pire> <far too short : beaucoup trop court> **3** (*expressing degree or extent*) <as far as possible : autant que possible> <as far as the city : jusqu'à la ville> <as far as that goes : pour ce qui est de cela> **4** (*expressing progress*) : loin <she'll go far : elle ira loin> **5 by ~** : de loin **6 far from it!** : pas du tout! **7 so far** : jusqu'ici, jusqu'à maintenant

far[2] *adj* **farther** *or* **further**; **farthest** *or* **furthest 1** REMOTE : éloigné, lointain <a far country : un pays lointain> **2** LONG : long <a far journey : un long voyage> **3** OTHER : autre <the far side of the lake : l'autre côté du lac> **4** EXTREME : extrême <the far right : l'extrême droite>

faraway |ˈfɑrəˌweɪ| *adj* : éloigné, lointain

farce |ˈfɑrs| *n* : farce *f*

farcical |ˈfɑrsɪkəl| *adj* : risible, grotesque

fare[1] |ˈfær| *vi* **fared; faring** : aller, se passer

fare[2] *n* **1** : tarif *m*, prix *m* du billet <full fare : plein tarif> **2** FOOD : nourriture *f*

farewell[1] |færˈwɛl| *adj* : d'adieu <a farewell speech : un discours d'adieu>

farewell[2] *n* : adieu *m* <to say one's farewells : faire ses adieux>

far–fetched |ˈfɑrˈfɛtʃt| *adj* : improbable, bizarre

farm[1] |ˈfɑrm| *vt* : cultiver, exploiter (une terre) — *vi* : être fermier

farm[2] *n* : ferme *f*, exploitation *f* agricole

farmer |ˈfɑrmər| *n* : fermier *m*, -mière *f;* agriculteur *m*, -trice *f;* habitant *m Can*

farmhand |ˈfɑrmˌhænd| *n* : ouvrier *m*, -vrière *f* agricole

farmhouse |ˈfɑrmˌhaʊs| *n* : ferme *f*

farming |ˈfɑrmɪŋ| *n* : agriculture *f*, élevage *m* (de bovins, etc.)

farmland |ˈfɑrmˌlænd| *n* : terres *fpl* arables, terres *fpl* cultivées

farmyard |ˈfɑrmˌjɑrd| *n* : cour *f* de ferme

far–off |ˈfɑrˌɔf, -ˈɔf| *adj* : lointain

far–reaching |ˈfɑrˈriːtʃɪŋ| *adj* : considérable, d'une grande portée

farsighted |ˈfɑrˌsaɪṭəd| *adj* **1** : hypermétrope, presbyte **2** SHREWD : clairvoyant, perspicace

farsightedness |ˈfɑrˌsaɪṭədnəs| *n* **1** : hypermétropie *f*, presbytie *f* **2** SHREWDNESS : clairvoyance *f*, perspicacité *f*

farther[1] |ˈfɑrðər| *adv* **1** : plus loin <nothing could be farther from the truth : rien n'est plus loin de la vérité> <farther ahead : loin devant> **2** MORE : encore plus, davantage

farther[2] *adj* : plus éloigné, plus lointain <the farther side of the house : l'autre côté de la maison>

farthest[1] |ˈfɑrðəst| *adv* **1** : le plus loin **2** MOST : le plus

farthest[2] *adj* : le plus éloigné, le plus lointain

fascicle |ˈfæsɪkəl| *n* : fascicule *m*

fascinate |ˈfæsənˌeɪt| *vt* **-nated; -nating** : fasciner, captiver

fascination |ˌfæsənˈeɪʃən| *n* : fascination *f*

fascism |ˈfæʃˌɪzəm| *n* : fascisme *m*

fascist[1] |ˈfæʃɪst| *adj* : fasciste

fascist[2] *n* : fasciste *mf*

fashion[1] |ˈfæʃən| *vt* : façonner, fabriquer

fashion[2] *n* **1** MANNER : façon *f*, manière *f* **2** STYLE : mode *f*, vogue *f* <the latest fashion : la dernière mode> <to be out of fashion : être démodé>

fashionable |ˈfæʃənəbəl| *adj* : à la mode, en vogue

fashionably |ˈfæʃənəbli| *adv* : à la mode, élégamment

fast[1] |ˈfæst| *vi* : jeûner

fast[2] *adv* **1** SECURELY : solidement, ferme **2** DEEPLY : profondément <fast asleep : profondément endormi> **3** SWIFTLY : rapidement, vite

fast[3] *adj* **1** SECURE : solide, ferme <to make fast : amarrer (un bateau)> **2** LOYAL : fidèle, sûr <fast friends : amis fidèles> **3** SWIFT : rapide, vite **4** DEEP : profond <a fast sleep : un sommeil profond> **5** COLORFAST : grand teint **6** : en avance (se dit d'une montre) <my watch is fast : ma montre avance>

fast[4] *n* : jeûne *m*

fasten |ˈfæsən| *vt* **1** ATTACH, SECURE : attacher, fermer **2** FIX, FOCUS : fixer — *vi* : s'attacher, se fermer

fastener |ˈfæsənər| *n* **1** HOOK, SNAP : attache *f*, bouton-pression *m* **2** LATCH : fermeture *f* (d'une porte) **3** CLASP : fermoir *m* (d'un bracelet, d'un sac, etc.)

fastening |ˈfæsənɪŋ| → **fastener**

fastidious |fæsˈtɪdiəs| *adj* **1** FUSSY : exigeant, difficile à contenter **2** METICULOUS : méticuleux

fastidiously |fæsˈtɪdiəsli| *n* : méticuleusement

fat[1] |ˈfæt| *adj* **fatter; fattest 1** OBESE : gros, gras, corpulent **2** THICK : gros, épais **3** PROFITABLE : gros, lucratif <a fat contract : un gros contrat>

fat[2] *n* **1** : gras *m* (de la viande), graisse *f* (du corps) **2** : matières *fpl* grasses <fat content : teneur en matières grasses>

fatal [ˈfeɪtəl] *adj* **1** DEADLY : mortel **2** FATEFUL : fatidique **3** DISASTROUS : fatal
fatalism [ˈfeɪtəlˌɪzəm] *n* : fatalisme *m*
fatalist [ˈfeɪtəlɪst] *n* : fataliste *mf*
fatalistic [ˌfeɪtəlˈɪstɪk] *adj* : fataliste
fatality [feɪˈtæləṭi, fə-] *n, pl* **-ties** : accident *m* mortel, mort *m*
fatally [ˈfeɪtəli] *adv* : mortellement
fate [ˈfeɪt] *n* **1** DESTINY : destin *m*, sort *m* **2** OUTCOME : sort *m* <a fate worse than death : un sort pire que la mort>
fated [ˈfeɪṭəd] *adj* : destiné
fateful [ˈfeɪtfəl] *adj* : fatidique
father[1] [ˈfɑðər] *vt* **1** BEGET : engendrer **2** : créer, inventer (un projet, etc.)
father[2] *n* **1** PARENT : père *m* **2** ANCESTOR : père *m*, ancêtre *m* **3** FOUNDER : père *m*, fondateur *m* **4** PRIEST : père *m* <Father Brown : le père Brown> **5 Father** GOD : Père *m*, Dieu *m*
fatherhood [ˈfɑðərˌhʊd] *n* : paternité *f*
father-in-law [ˈfɑðərɪnˌlɔ] *n, pl* **fathers-in-law** : beau-père *m*
fatherland [ˈfɑðərˌlænd] *n* : patrie *f*
fatherless [ˈfɑðərləs] *adj* : sans père
fatherly [ˈfɑðərli] *adj* : paternel
fathom[1] [ˈfæðəm] *vt* **1** SOUND : sonder **2** PENETRATE, UNDERSTAND : sonder, pénétrer, comprendre
fathom[2] *n* : brasse *f*
fatigue[1] [fəˈtiːg] *vt* **-tigued; -tiguing** : fatiguer, épuiser
fatigue[2] *n* : fatigue *f*, épuisement *m*
fatness [ˈfætnəs] *n* : corpulence *f*, embonpoint *m*
fatten [ˈfætən] *vt* : engraisser (un animal)
fatty [ˈfæti] *adj* **fattier; -est** : gras (se dit de la viande, etc.), graisseux (se dit d'un tissu)
fatuous [ˈfætʃʊəs] *adj* : imbécile, stupide, niais
fatuously [ˈfætʃʊəsli] *adv* : niaisement, bêtement
faucet [ˈfɔsət] *n* : robinet *m*, champlure *f Can*
fault[1] [ˈfɔlt] *vt* : trouver des défauts à, critiquer
fault[2] *n* **1** FLAW : défaut *m*, imperfection *f* **2** SHORTCOMING : défaut *m*, faiblesse *f* **3** RESPONSIBILITY : faute *f* <it's my fault : c'est de ma faute> **4** MISTAKE : erreur *f* **5** : faille *f* (géologique)
faultfinder [ˈfɔltˌfaɪndər] *n* : critiqueur *m*, -queuse *f*
faultfinding [ˈfɔltˌfaɪndɪŋ] *n* : critiques *fpl*
faultless [ˈfɔltləs] *adj* : irréprochable, impeccable
faultlessly [ˈfɔltləsli] *adv* : parfaitement, impeccablement
faulty [ˈfɔlti] *adj* **faultier; -est** : fautif, défectueux
fauna [ˈfɔnə] *n* : faune *f*
faux pas [ˌfoːˈpɑ] *ns & pl* : faux pas *m*, gaffe *f*
favor[1] *or Brit* **favour** [ˈfeɪvər] *vt* **1** SUPPORT : favoriser, être partisan de, appuyer **2** OBLIGE : rendre un service à **3** PREFER : favoriser, préférer **4** RESEMBLE : ressembler à
favor[2] *or Brit* **favour** *n* **1** APPROVAL : faveur *f*, approbation *f* **2** PARTIALITY : faveur *f*, partialité *f* **3** : service *m*, faveur *f* <can you do me a favor? : peux-tu me rendre un service?> **4 to be in favor of** : être pour
favorable *or Brit* **favourable** [ˈfeɪvərəbəl] *adj* : favorable — **favorably** *or Brit* **favourably** [-rəbli] *adv*
favorite[1] *or Brit* **favourite** [ˈfeɪvərət] *adj* : favori, préféré
favorite[2] *or Brit* **favourite** *n* : favori *m*, -rite *f*; préféré *m*, -rée *f*
favoritism *or Brit* **favouritism** [ˈfeɪvərəˌtɪzəm] *n* : favoritisme *m*
favour *Brit* → **favor**
favourite *Brit* → **favorite**
fawn[1] [ˈfɔn] *vi* **to fawn upon** : flatter servilement, faire fête à (se dit d'un chien)
fawn[2] *n* : faon *m*
fax[1] [ˈfæks] *vt* : faxer, envoyer par télécopie
fax[2] *n* : fax *m*, télécopie *f*
faze [ˈfeɪz] *vt* **fazed; fazing** : déconcerter
fear[1] [ˈfɪr] *vt* : craindre, avoir peur de <I fear he won't come : j'ai peur qu'il ne vienne pas> — *vi* **1** : avoir peur **2 to fear for** : craindre pour
fear[2] *n* : crainte *f*, peur *f*
fearful [ˈfɪrfəl] *adj* **1** DREADFUL : affreux **2** AFRAID : craintif, peureux
fearfully [ˈfɪrfəli] *adv* : craintivement, peureusement
fearless [ˈfɪrləs] *adj* : intrépide, sans peur
fearlessly [ˈfɪrləsli] *adv* : avec intrépidité
fearlessness [ˈfɪrləsnəs] *n* : intrépidité *f*
fearsome [ˈfɪrsəm] *adj* **1** FRIGHTENING : effrayant **2** FORMIDABLE : redoutable
feasibility [ˈfiːzəˈbɪləṭi] *n* : faisabilité *f*, possibilité *f*
feasible [ˌfiːzəbəl] *adj* : faisable, possible, réalisable
feast[1] [ˈfiːst] *vt* **1** : donner un banquet en l'honneur de **2 to feast one's eyes on** : se délecter à regarder — *vi* **1** : festoyer **2 to feast on** : se régaler de
feast[2] *n* **1** BANQUET : banquet *m*, festin *m* **2** FESTIVAL : fête *f* religieuse
feat [ˈfiːt] *n* : exploit *m*, prouesse *f*
feather[1] [ˈfɛðər] *vt* **1** : empenner, couvrir de plumes **2 to feather one's nest** : s'enrichir
feather[2] *n* : plume *f* (d'oiseau), penne *f* (de flèche)
feathered [ˈfɛðərd] *adj* : à plumes

feathery [ˈfɛðəri] *adj* : duveteux, doux et léger comme la plume

feature[1] [ˈfiːtʃər] *vt* : mettre en vedette (une personne), faire figurer (des nouvelles, etc.) — *vi* : figurer

feature[2] *n* **1** : trait *m* (du visage) **2** CHARACTERISTIC : caractéristique *f*, trait *m*, particularité *f* **3** : article *m* de fond (en journalisme) **4** *or* **feature film** : long métrage *m*

February [ˈfɛbjʊˌɛri, ˈfɛbʊ-, ˈfɛbrʊ-] *n* : février *m*

fecal [ˈfiːkəl] *adj* : fécal

feces [ˈfiːˌsiːz] *npl* : fèces *fpl*

feckless [ˈfɛkləs] *adj* **1** IRRESPONSIBLE : irresponsable **2** INEFFECTUAL : inepte, incapable

fecund [ˈfɛkənd, ˈfiː-] *adj* : fécond

fecundity [fɪˈkʌndəṭi, fɛ-] *n* : fécondité *f*

federal [ˈfɛdrəl, -dərəl] *adj* : fédéral

federalism [ˈfɛdrəˌlɪzəm, -dərə-] *n* : fédéralisme *m*

federalist[1] [ˈfɛdrəlɪst, -dərə-] *adj* : fédéraliste

federalist[2] *n* : fédéraliste *mf*

federate [ˈfɛdəˌreɪt] *vt* **-ated; -ating** : fédérer

federation [ˌfɛdəˈreɪʃən] *n* : fédération *f*

fed up *adj* **to be fed up** : en avoir assez, en avoir marre *fam*

fee [ˈfiː] *n* **1** : frais *mpl* (de scolarité), honoraires *mpl* (médicaux), cachet *m* (d'un artiste, etc.) **2** *or* **entrance fee** : droit *m* d'entrée

feeble [ˈfiːbəl] *adj* **-bler; -blest 1** FRAIL : faible, frêle **2** INADEQUATE, POOR : pauvre, piètre <a feeble excuse : une piètre excuse>

feebleminded [ˌfiːbəlˈmaɪndəd] *adj* : faible d'esprit

feeblemindedness [ˌfiːbəlˈmaɪndədnəs] *n* : faiblesse *f* d'esprit

feebleness [ˈfiːbəlnəs] *n* : faiblesse *f*

feebly [ˈfiːbli] *adv* **1** WEAKLY : faiblement **2** : sans grande conviction

feed[1] [ˈfiːd] *v* **fed** [ˈfɛd]; **feeding** *vt* **1** : nourrir, donner à manger à <to feed a child : nourrir un enfant> **2** : alimenter (une machine, un feu, etc.) — *vi* EAT : manger, se nourrir

feed[2] *n* **1** NOURISHMENT : nourriture *f* **2** FODDER : fourrage *m*

feel[1] [ˈfiːl] *v* **felt** [ˈfɛlt]; **feeling** *vt* **1** TOUCH : toucher, tâter, palper **2** SENSE : sentir **3** EXPERIENCE : éprouver, ressentir (un sentiment) **4** BELIEVE : avoir l'impression que, estimer que **5 to feel out** : sonder (une personne) — *vi* **1** : se sentir <I feel much better : je me sens beaucoup mieux> **2** SEEM : sembler, donner l'impression **3 to feel like** : avoir envie de

feel[2] *n* **1** TOUCH : toucher *m* <soft to the feel : doux au toucher> **2** FEELING, SENSATION : sensation *f* **3** KNACK : facilité *f* <a feel for learning : une facilité d'apprentissage>

feeler [ˈfiːlər] *n* : antenne *f* (d'un insecte)

feeling [ˈfiːlɪŋ] *n* **1** TOUCH : toucher *m* **2** SENSATION : sensation *f* **3** SENSE : sentiment *m*, impression *f* **4** BELIEF : opinion *f*, sentiment *m* **5 feelings** *npl* : sentiments *mpl*, sensibilité *f* <to hurt s.o.'s feelings : blesser qqn, faire de la peine à qqn>

feet → **foot**

feign [ˈfeɪn] *vt* : feindre, simuler

feint[1] [ˈfeɪnt] *vi* : feinter

feint[2] *n* : feinte *f*

felicitate [fɪˈlɪsəˌteɪt] *vt* **-tated; -tating** : féliciter, congratuler

felicitation [fɪˌlɪsəˈteɪʃən] *n* : félicitation *f*

felicitous [fɪˈlɪsəṭəs] *adj* : heureux

felicity [fɪˈlɪsəṭi] *n, pl* **-ties 1** HAPPINESS : félicité *f* **2** APPROPRIATENESS : justesse *f* (d'une expression, etc.)

feline[1] [ˈfiːˌlaɪn] *adj* : félin

feline[2] *n* : félin *m*

fell[1] [ˈfɛl] *vt* **1** : abattre, bûcher *Can* (des arbres) **2** : assommer (des personnes)

fell[2] → **fall**[1]

fellow [ˈfɛˌloː] *n* **1** COMPANION : camarade *mf;* compagnon *m*, compagne *f* **2** EQUAL, PEER : semblable *m*, pair *m* **3** COLLEAGUE : confrère *m* **4** BOY, MAN : gars *m fam*, type *m fam*

fellowman [ˌfɛloˈmæn] *n, pl* **-men** [-mən, -ˌmɛn] : prochain *m*

fellowship [ˈfɛloˌʃɪp] *n* **1** COMPANIONSHIP : camaraderie *f* **2** ASSOCIATION : association *f* **3** GRANT : bourse *f* universitaire

felon [ˈfɛlən] *n* : criminel *m*, -nelle *f*

felonious [fəˈloːniəs] *adj* : criminel

felony [ˈfɛləni] *n, pl* **-nies** : crime *m*

felt[1] [ˈfɛlt] *n* : feutre *m*

felt[2] → **feel**[1]

female[1] [ˈfiːˌmeɪl] *adj* : femelle (se dit des animaux et des plantes), féminin (se dit des personnes)

female[2] *n* **1** : femelle *f* (animal ou plante) **2** GIRL, WOMAN : femme *f*, fille *f*

feminine [ˈfɛmənən] *adj* : féminin

femininity [ˌfɛməˈnɪnəṭi] *n* : féminité *f*

feminism [ˈfɛməˌnɪzəm] *n* : féminisme *m*

feminist[1] [ˈfɛmənɪst] *adj* : féministe

feminist[2] *n* : féministe *mf*

femoral [ˈfɛmərəl] *adj* : fémoral

femur [ˈfiːmər] *n, pl* **femurs** *or* **femora** [ˈfɛmərə] : fémur *m*

fence[1] [ˈfɛnts] *v* **fenced; fencing** *vt* ENCLOSE : clôturer, entourer d'une clôture — *vi* : faire de l'escrime (aux sports)

fence[2] *n* : clôture *f*, barrière *f*

fencer [ˈfɛntsər] *n* : escrimeur *m*, -meuse *f*

fencing |ˈfɛntsɪŋ| *n* **1** : escrime *f* (sport) **2** : matériaux *mpl* pour clôture **3** FENCES : clôture *f*, barrière *f*

fend |ˈfɛnd| *vt or* **to fend off** : parer (un coup), détourner (une attaque), éluder (une question) — *vi* **to fend for oneself** : se débrouiller tout seul

fender |ˈfɛndər| *n* : aile *f* (d'une voiture)

fennel |ˈfɛnəl| *n* : fenouil *m*

ferment[1] |fɛrˈmɛnt| *vi* : fermenter

ferment[2] |ˈfər͵mɛnt| *n* **1** : ferment *m* (en chimie) **2** TURMOIL : agitation *f*, effervescence *f*

fermentation |͵fərmənˈteɪʃən, -͵mɛn-| *n* : fermentation *f*

fern |ˈfərn| *n* : fougère *f*

ferocious |fəˈroːʃəs| *adj* : féroce — **ferociously** *adv*

ferociousness |fəˈroːʃəsnəs| *n* : férocité *f*

ferocity |fəˈrɑsət̬i| *n* : férocité *f*

ferret[1] |ˈfɛrət| *vt* **to ferret out** : découvrir, dénicher — *vi* DELVE, RUMMAGE : fureter, fouiller

ferret[2] *n* : furet *m*

ferric |ˈfɛrɪk| *or* **ferrous** |ˈfɛrəs| *adj* : ferrique, ferreux

Ferris wheel |ˈfɛrɪs| *n* : grande roue *f*

ferry[1] |ˈfɛri| *vt* **-ried; -rying** : transporter, faire passer (en bac, par avion, etc.)

ferry[2] *n, pl* **-ries** : bac *m*, ferry-boat *m*, traversier *m Can*

ferryboat |ˈfɛri͵boːt| → **ferry**[2]

fertile |ˈfərt̬əl| *adj* : fertile, fécond

fertility |fərˈtɪlət̬i| *n* : fertilité *f*, fécondité *f*

fertilization |͵fərt̬ələˈzeɪʃən| *n* : fertilisation *f*, fécondation *f*

fertilize |ˈfərt̬əl͵aɪz| *vt* **-ized; -izing** : fertiliser (une terre), féconder (un œuf, etc.)

fertilizer |ˈfərt̬əl͵aɪzər| *n* : engrais *m*

fervent |ˈfərvənt| *adj* : fervent, ardent

fervently |ˈfərvəntli| *adv* : avec ferveur

fervid |ˈfərvɪd| *adj* IMPASSIONED : passionné

fervor *or Brit* **fervour** |ˈfərvər| *n* : ferveur *f*, ardeur *f*

fester |ˈfɛstər| *vi* : suppurer

festival |ˈfɛstəvəl| *n* **1** FEAST : fête *f* (religieuse) **2** : festival *m* <a dance festival : un festival de danse>

festive |ˈfɛstɪv| *adj* : joyeux, de fête

festivity |fɛsˈtɪvət̬i| *n, pl* **-ties 1** MERRIMENT : réjouissance *f* **2 festivities** *npl* : réjouissances *fpl*, festivités *fpl*

festoon[1] |fɛsˈtuːn| *vt* : festonner, orner de festons

festoon[2] *n* : feston *m*, guirlande *f*

fetal |ˈfiːt̬əl| *adj* : fœtal

fetch |ˈfɛtʃ| *vt* **1** BRING : aller chercher, apporter **2** REALIZE : rapporter (de l'argent), atteindre (un prix)

fetching |ˈfɛtʃɪŋ| *adj* : attrayant, charmant

fete[1] *or* **fête** |ˈfeɪt, ˈfɛt| *vt* **feted** *or* **fêted; feting** *or* **fêting** : fêter

fete[2] *or* **fête** *n* : fête *f*

fetid |ˈfɛt̬əd| *adj* : fétide

fetish |ˈfɛt̬ɪʃ| *n* : fétiche *m*

fetlock |ˈfɛt͵lɑk| *n* : boulet *m* (d'un cheval)

fetter |ˈfɛt̬ər| *vt* **1** SHACKLE : enchaîner, entraver (un animal) **2** HAMPER : entraver

fetters |ˈfɛt̬ərz| *npl* : fers *mpl*, chaînes *fpl*, entraves *fpl* (d'un animal)

fettle |ˈfɛt̬əl| *n* **in fine fettle** : en pleine forme, en bonne condition

fetus |ˈfiːt̬əs| *n* : fœtus *m*

feud[1] |ˈfjuːd| *vi* : se quereller, se disputer

feud[2] *n* : querelle *f*, vendetta *f* <a family feud : une querelle familiale>

feudal |ˈfjuːdəl| *adj* : féodal

feudalism |ˈfjuːdəl͵ɪzəm| *n* : féodalisme *m*

fever |ˈfiːvər| *n* : fièvre *f*, température *f*

feverish |ˈfiːvərɪʃ| *adj* : fiévreux, fébrile — **feverishly** *adv*

few[1] |ˈfjuː| *adj* **1** : peu de <we have few friends : nous avons peu d'amis> **2 a few** : quelques <in a few minutes : dans quelques minutes>

few[2] *pron* : peu, quelques-uns, quelques-unes <few remember him : peu se souviennent de lui> <a few of them : quelques-unes d'entre elles> <quite a few : un assez grand nombre de>

fewer[1] |ˈfjuːər| *adj* : moins de <no fewer than : pas moins de>

fewer[2] *pron* : moins <the fewer the better : le moins possible>

fez |ˈfɛz| *n, pl* **fezzes** : fez *m*

fiancé |͵fiː͵ɑnˈseɪ, ͵fiːˈɑn͵seɪ| *n* : fiancé *m*

fiancée |͵fiː͵ɑnˈseɪ, ͵fiːˈɑn͵seɪ| *n* : fiancée *f*

fiasco |fiˈæs͵koː| *n, pl* **-coes** : fiasco *m*

fiat |ˈfiː͵ɑt, -͵æt, -ət; ˈfaɪət, -͵æt| *n* : décret *m*

fib[1] |ˈfɪb| *vi* **fibbed; fibbing** : blaguer *fam*, raconter des histoires

fib[2] *n* : blague *f fam*, bobard *m fam*, menterie *f Can fam*

fibber |ˈfɪbər| *n* : blagueur *m*, -gueuse *f fam*

fiber *or* **fibre** |ˈfaɪbər| *n* : fibre *f*

fiberboard |ˈfaɪbər͵bord| *n* : panneau *m* fibreux

fiberglass |ˈfaɪbər͵glæs| *n* : fibre *f* de verre

fibrillation |͵fɪbrəˈleɪʃən| *n* : fibrillation *f*

fibrous |ˈfaɪbrəs| *adj* : fibreux

fibula |ˈfɪbjələ| *n, pl* **-lae** |-͵liː, -͵laɪ| *or* **-las** : péroné *m*

fickle |ˈfɪkəl| *adj* : volage, inconstant

fickleness |ˈfɪkəlnəs| *n* : inconstance *f*

fiction |ˈfɪkʃən| *n* **1** : fiction *f*, invention *f* <truth is stranger than fiction : la réalité dépasse la fiction> **2** *or* **works of fiction** : romans *mpl*, œuvres *fpl* de fiction

fictional |ˈfɪkʃənəl| *adj* : fictif — **fictionally** *adv*

fictitious |fɪk'tɪʃəs| *adj* : fictif, imaginaire

fiddle[1] |'fɪdəl| *vi* **-dled; -dling 1** : jouer du violon **2 to fiddle with** : tripoter, bricoler, jouer avec

fiddle[2] *n* : violon *m*

fiddler |'fɪdlər, 'fɪdələr| *n* : joueur *m* de violon, joueuse *f* de violon

fiddlesticks |'fɪdəl,stɪks| *interj* : flûte alors!, quelle blague!

fidelity |fə'dɛləṭi, faɪ-| *n, pl* **-ties 1** LOYALTY : fidélité *f,* loyauté *f* **2** ACCURACY : exactitude *f,* fidélité *f*

fidget[1] |'fɪdʒət| *vi* : remuer, s'agiter, gigoter *fam*

fidget[2] *n* **to have the fidgets** : ne pas tenir en place

fidgety |'fɪdʒəti| *adj* : remuant, agité

fiduciary[1] |fə'du:ʃi,ɛri, -'dju:-, -ʃəri| *adj* : fiduciaire

fiduciary[2] *n, pl* **-ries** : fiduciaire *mf*

field[1] |'fi:ld| *vt* **1** : attraper (une balle), faire jouer (une équipe) **2** : répondre à (des questions, etc.)

field[2] *adj* : de campagne <field artillery : artillerie de campagne>

field[3] /'fild/ *n* **1** : champ *m* (de cultures, de bataille) **2** : domaine *m,* sphère *f* <the field of science : le domaine de la science> **3** : terrain *m* (de sport) **4** : champ *m* <magnetic field : champ magnétique> <field of vision : champ de vision>

field day *n* **1** : grande occasion *f* **2 to have a field day** : s'en donner à cœur joie

fielder |'fi:ldər| *n* : joueur *m* de champ (au baseball)

field glasses *npl* : jumelles *fpl*

field goal *n* : placement *m*

field hockey *n* : hockey *m* sur gazon

field test : essai *m* sur le terrain

field trip : sortie *f* éducative

fiend |'fi:nd| *n* **1** DEMON, DEVIL : diable *m,* démon *m* **2** EVILDOER : monstre *m* **3** FANATIC : mordu *m,* -due *f fam* **4** ADDICT : toxicomane *mf*

fiendish |'fi:ndɪʃ| *adj* : diabolique — **fiendishly** *adv*

fierce |'fɪrs| *adj* **fiercer; -est 1** FEROCIOUS : féroce, sauvage **2** HEATED : virulent **3** INTENSE : intense, acharné, violent

fiercely |'fɪrsli| *adv* : férocement, violemment, avec acharnement

fierceness |'fɪrsnəs| *n* **1** : férocité *f* (d'un animal) **2** INTENSITY : fureur *f* (d'un orage), violence *f* (d'un combat, etc.)

fieriness |'faɪərinəs| *n* : ardeur *f,* fougue *f*

fiery |'faɪəri| *adj* **fierier; -est 1** BURNING : brûlant, ardent **2** RED : rougeoyant **3** ARDENT, SPIRITED : fougueux, ardent

fiesta |fi'ɛstə| *n* : fête *f*

fife |'faɪf| *n* : fifre *m*

fifteen[1] |fɪf'ti:n| *adj* : quinze

fifteen[2] *n* : quinze *m*

fifteenth[1] |fɪf'ti:nθ| *adj* : quinzième

fifteenth[2] *n* **1** : quinzième *mf* (dans une série) **2** : quinzième *m* (en mathématiques) **3** (*used in dates*) <the fifteenth of August : le quinze août>

fifth[1] |'fɪfθ| *adj* : cinquième

fifth[2] *n* **1** : cinquième *mf* (dans une série) **2** : cinquième *m* (en mathématiques) **3** (*used in dates*) <the fifth of September : le cinq septembre>

fiftieth[1] |'fɪftiəθ| *adj* : cinquantième

fiftieth[2] *n* **1** : cinquantième *mf* (dans une série) **2** : cinquantième *m* (en mathématiques)

fifty[1] |'fɪfti| *adj* : cinquante

fifty[2] *n, pl* **-ties 1** : cinquante *m* **2 fifties** *npl* : cinquantaine *f* <she's in her fifties : elle est dans la cinquantaine>

fifty–fifty[1] |,fɪfti'fɪfti| *adv* : moitié-moitié <to go fifty-fifty : faire moitié-moitié>

fifty–fifty[2] *adj* **to have a fifty–fifty chance** : avoir une chance sur deux

fig |'fɪg| *n* : figue *f*

fight[1] |'faɪt| *v* **fought** |'fɔt|; **fighting** *vt* **1** : se battre avec, combattre (un ennemi) **2** : lutter contre, combattre (une maladie, un incendie, etc.) — *vi* **1** : combattre **2** QUARREL : se quereller, se disputer

fight[2] *n* **1** BATTLE, BRAWL : combat *m,* bataille *f,* bagarre *f* **2** MATCH : combat *m* (de boxe) **3** STRUGGLE : lutte *f* <the fight against cancer : la lutte contre le cancer> **4** QUARREL : querelle *f,* dispute *f* <to pick a fight with : chercher querelle à>

fighter |'faɪṭər| *n* **1** COMBATANT : combattant *m,* -tante *f;* lutteur *m,* -teuse *f* **2** BOXER : boxeur *m* **3** *or* **fighter plane** : avion *m* de chasse

figment |'fɪgmənt| *n* **figment of the imagination** : produit *m* de l'imagination

figurative |'fɪgjərəṭɪv, -gə-| *adj* : figuré, métaphorique

figuratively |'fɪgjərəṭɪvli, -gə-| *adv* : au sens figuré

figure[1] |'fɪgjər, -gər| *v* **-ured; -uring** *vt* **1** REPRESENT : représenter, illustrer **2** CONCLUDE, THINK : penser, supposer **3** CALCULATE, COMPUTE : calculer — *vi* **1** APPEAR : figurer **2 that figures!** : ça se comprend!, ça se tient!

figure[2] *n* **1** NUMERAL : chiffre *m* **2** PRICE : prix *m* **3** FORM, OUTLINE : forme *f,* silhouette *f* **4** : ligne *f* <to watch one's figure : surveiller sa ligne> **5** ILLUSTRATION : figure *f,* image *f* **6** PATTERN : motif *m* **7** PERSONAGE : figure *f,* personnage *m* **8 figures** *npl* : calcul *m* <he's good at figures : il est bon en calcul>

figurehead |'fɪgjər,hɛd, -gər-| *n* **1** : homme *m* de paille **2** : figure *f* de proue (d'un navire)

figure of speech *n* : figure *f* de rhétorique, façon *f* de parler

figure out *vt* **1** UNDERSTAND : arriver à comprendre **2** SOLVE : calculer (une somme), résoudre (un problème)

figurine [ˌfɪgjəˈriːn] *n* : figurine *f*

Fijian[1] [ˈfiːdʒiən, fɪˈjiːən] *adj* : fidjien

Fijian[2] *n* **1** : Fidjien *m*, -jienne *f* **2** : fidjien *m* (langue)

filament [ˈfɪləmənt] *n* : filament *m*

filbert [ˈfɪlbərt] *n* : aveline *f*

filch [ˈfɪltʃ] *vt* : chiper *fam*, piquer *fam*, voler

file[1] [ˈfaɪl] *v* **filed; filing** *vt* **1** CLASSIFY : classer, ranger **2** : déposer (une plainte), intenter (un procès) **3** : limer (ses ongles, etc.) — *vi* **1** : marcher en file <to file past : défiler devant> **2 to file for** : demander (un divorce, etc.)

file[2] *n* **1** : lime *f* (outil) **2** FOLDER : dossier *m* **3** *or* **file cabinet** : classeur *m* **4** RECORD : dossier *m* **5** : fichier *m* (en informatique) **6** LINE : file *f* <in single file : en file>

filial [ˈfɪliəl, ˈfɪljəl] *adj* : filial

filibuster[1] [ˈfɪləˌbʌstər] *vi* : faire de l'obstruction parlementaire

filibuster[2] *n* : obstruction *f* parlementaire

filigree [ˈfɪləˌgriː] *n* : filigrane *m*

Filipino[1] [ˌfɪləˈpiːnoː] *adj* : philippin

Filipino[2] *n* : Philippin *m*, -pine *f*

fill[1] [ˈfɪl] *vt* **1** : remplir <to fill a cup : remplir une tasse> <tears filled her eyes : ses yeux se remplissaient de larmes> **2** PLUG : boucher (un trou), plomber (une dent) **3** SATIATE : rassasier **4** *or* **to fill out** COMPLETE : remplir <to fill out a form : remplir un formulaire> **5** HOLD : prendre, occuper (un poste) **6** SATISFY : remplir, pourvoir à — *vi* : se remplir

fill[2] *n* **1** FILLING : remplissage *m* **2 to eat one's fill** : se rassasier **3 to have had one's fill of** : en avoir assez de

filler [ˈfɪlər] *n* : remplissage *m*

fillet[1] [fɪˈleɪ, ˈfɪˌleɪ, ˈfɪlət] *vt* : découper en filets

fillet[2] *n* : filet *m*

fill in *vt* INFORM : mettre au courant — *vi* **to fill in for** : remplacer

filling [ˈfɪlɪŋ] *n* **1** : plombage *m* (d'une dent), obturation *f* dentaire **2** : garniture *f* (d'une tarte, etc.)

filling station → **service station**

filly [ˈfɪli] *n, pl* **-lies** : pouliche *f*

film[1] [ˈfɪlm] *vt* : filmer, tourner (une scène) — *vi* **1** FILM : tourner **2** *or* **to film over** : s'embuer, se voiler

film[2] *n* **1** : pellicule *f* (en photographie) **2** COATING : couche *f*, pellicule *f* **3** MOTION PICTURE : film *m*

filmstrip [ˈfɪlmˌstrɪp] *n* : film *m* fixe

filmy [ˈfɪlmi] *adj* **filmier; -est 1** HAZY : embué, voilé **2** GAUZY : léger, transparent

filter[1] [ˈfɪltər] *v* : filtrer

filter[2] *n* : filtre *m*

filth [ˈfɪlθ] *n* **1** DIRT : saleté *f*, crasse *f* **2** OBSCENITY : obscénités *fpl*

filthiness [ˈfɪlθinəs] *n* : saleté *f*

filthy [ˈfɪlθi] *adj* **filthier; -est 1** DIRTY : sale, crasseux **2** VILE : dégoûtant **3** OBSCENE : obscène, ordurier

filtration [fɪlˈtreɪʃən] *n* : filtration *f*

fin [ˈfɪn] *n* **1** : nageoire *f* (d'un poisson), aileron *m* (d'un requin) **2** : aileron *m*, empennage *m* (d'un avion)

finagle [fəˈneɪgəl] *vt* **-gled; -gling** : obtenir par des moyens subreptices, se débrouiller pour obtenir

final[1] [ˈfaɪnəl] *adj* **1** CONCLUSIVE : définitif, irrévocable **2** LAST : dernier **3** ULTIMATE : ultime, final <our final goal : notre but ultime>

final[2] *n* **1** : finale *f* (d'une compétition) **2 finals** *npl* : examens *mpl* de fin de semestre

finale [fɪˈnæli, -ˈnɑ-] *n* **1** : finale *m* **2 grand finale** : apothéose *f*

finalist [ˈfaɪnəlɪst] *n* : finaliste *mf*

finality [faɪˈnæləṭi, fə-] *n, pl* **-ties** : irrévocabilité *f*

finalize [ˈfaɪnəlˌaɪz] *vt* **-ized; -izing** : mettre au point

finally [ˈfaɪnəli] *adv* : enfin, finalement

finance[1] [fəˈnænts, ˈfaɪˌnænts] *vt* **-nanced; -nancing** : financer

finance[2] *n* **1** : finance *f* <high finance : la haute finance> **2 finances** *npl* RESOURCES : finances *fpl*

financial [fəˈnæntʃəl, faɪ-] *adj* : financier

financially [fəˈnæntʃəli, faɪ-] *adv* : financièrement

financier [ˌfɪnənˈsɪr, ˌfaɪˌnæn-] *n* : financier *m*

finch [ˈfɪntʃ] *n* : fringillidé *m*

find[1] [ˈfaɪnd] *v* **found** [ˈfaʊnd]; **finding** *vt* **1** LOCATE : trouver, rencontrer, retrouver <I can't find it : je ne peux pas le trouver> <to find one's voice : retrouver sa voix> <to find its mark : atteindre sa cible> **2** DISCOVER, REALIZE : trouver, découvrir, s'apercevoir <I find it difficult : je trouve que c'est difficile> **3** DECLARE : déclarer, prononcer <to find s.o. guilty : prononcer qqn coupable> — *vi* : prononcer <to find for the accused : prononcer en faveur de l'accusé>

find[2] *n* : découverte *f*, trouvaille *f*

finder [ˈfaɪndər] *n* **1** : celui *m*, celle *f* qui trouve **2** : chercheur *m* (de télescope, etc.)

finding [ˈfaɪndɪŋ] *n* **1** FIND : découverte *f* **2** VERDICT : verdict *m* (en droit) **3 findings** *npl* : conclusions *fpl*

find out *vt* DISCOVER : découvrir — *vi* **to find out about** : se renseigner sur

fine[1] [ˈfaɪn] *vt* **fined; fining** : infliger une amende à, condamner à une amende

fine[2] *adv* **1** ALL RIGHT : très bien <I'm doing fine : je vais très bien> **2** FINELY : fin

fine[3] *adj* **finer; -est 1** PURE : pur (se dit de l'or, etc.) **2** DELICATE, THIN : fin <fine hair : cheveux fins> **3** : fin <fine sand : sable fin> **4** SUBTLE : subtil, sensible **5** EXCELLENT : beau, excellent <she did a fine job : elle a fait un beau travail> **6** FAIR : beau <the weather is fine : il fait beau> **7 to be fine** : aller bien <everyone's fine : tout le monde va bien> <that's fine with me : ça me va>

fine[4] *n* : amende *f*, contravention *f*

fine art *n* : beaux-arts *mpl*

finely [ˈfaɪnli] *adv* **1** : finement, fin <to chop finely : hacher finement, hacher menu> **2** EXCELLENTLY : admirablement **3** PRECISELY : avec précision **4** ELEGANTLY : élégamment

fineness [ˈfaɪnnəs] *n* **1** DELICACY : finesse *f* (d'un tissu, etc.) **2** EXCELLENCE : pureté *f* (d'un métal), excellence *f* **3** SUBTLETY : subtilité *f*, délicatesse *f*

finery [ˈfaɪnəri] *n, pl* **-eries** : parure *f*

finesse[1] [fəˈnɛs] *vt* **-nessed; -nessing** : manipuler adroitement

finesse[2] *n* : finesse *f*

finger[1] [ˈfɪŋgər] *vt* HANDLE : toucher, palper, tâter

finger[2] *n* : doigt *m*

fingerling [ˈfɪŋgərlɪŋ] *n* : petit poisson *m*

fingernail [ˈfɪŋgər,neɪl] *n* : ongle *m*

fingerprint[1] [ˈfɪŋgər,prɪnt] *vt* : prendre les empreintes digitales de

fingerprint[2] *n* : empreinte *f* digitale

fingertip [ˈfɪŋgər,tɪp] *n* : bout *m* du doigt

finicky [ˈfɪnɪki] *adj* : tatillon, pointilleux

finish[1] [ˈfɪnɪʃ] *vt* **1** COMPLETE, TERMINATE : terminer, finir, achever **2** : mettre une finition sur (un meuble, un parquet, etc.) — *vi* : finir, se terminer

finish[2] *n* **1** END : fin *f* **2** *or* **finish line** : arrivée *f* **3** : finition *f*, fini *m Can* <a glossy finish : une finition brillante>

finite [ˈfaɪ,naɪt] *adj* : fini, limité

Finn [ˈfɪn] *n* : Finlandais *m*, -daise *f*

Finnish[1] [ˈfɪnɪʃ] *adj* : finlandais

Finnish[2] *n* : finnois *m* (langue)

fiord [fiˈɔrd] → **fjord**

fir [ˈfər] *n* : sapin *m*

fire[1] [ˈfaɪr] *vt* **fired; firing 1** IGNITE : incendier **2** STIR : exciter, enflammer (l'imagination) **3** DISMISS : renvoyer, congédier (un employé) **4** SHOOT : tirer, décharger <to fire a gun : tirer un coup de fusil> **5** : cuire (de la poterie)

fire[2] *n* **1** : feu *m* **2** BURNING : feu *m*, incendie *m* <forest fire : incendie de forêt> **3** ENTHUSIASM : enthousiasme *m*, ardeur *f* **4** SHOOTING : feu *m*, tir *m* <to open fire : ouvrir le feu>

fire alarm *n* : avertisseur *m* d'incendie

firearm [ˈfaɪr,ɑrm] *n* : arme *f* à feu

fireball [ˈfaɪr,bɔl] *n* **1** : boule *f* de feu **2** METEORITE : bolide *m*

firebreak [ˈfaɪr,breɪk] *n* : pare-feu *m*, coupe-feu *m*

firebug [ˈfaɪr,bʌg] *n* : incendiaire *mf*, pyromane *mf*

firecracker [ˈfaɪr,krækər] *n* : pétard *m*

fire escape *n* : escalier *m* de secours

fire extinguisher *n* : extincteur *m*

firefighter [ˈfaɪr,faɪṭər] *n* : pompier *m*, sapeur-pompier *m France*

firefly [ˈfaɪr,flaɪ] *n, pl* **-flies** : luciole *f*

fire hall *Brit* → **fire station**

fireman [ˈfaɪrmən] *n, pl* **-men** [-mən, -,mɛn] **1** → **firefighter 2** STOKER : chauffeur *m*

fireplace [ˈfaɪr,pleɪs] *n* : cheminée *f*, foyer *m*

fireplug [ˈfaɪr,plʌg] → **hydrant**

fireproof[1] [ˈfaɪr,pruːf] *vt* : ignifuger

fireproof[2] *adj* : ignifuge, à l'épreuve du feu

fireside[1] [ˈfaɪr,saɪd] *adj* : familier, informel

fireside[2] *n* : coin *m* du feu

fire station *n* : caserne *f* de pompiers *France*, poste *m* de pompiers *Can*

firewood [ˈfaɪr,wʊd] *n* : bois *m* de chauffage

fireworks [ˈfaɪr,wərk] *n* : feux *mpl* d'artifice

firm[1] [ˈfərm] *vt or* **to firm up** : raffermir (des muscles), confirmer (des plans, etc.)

firm[2] *adj* **1** STRONG : ferme <to have a firm grip on : tenir fermement> **2** HARD, SOLID : ferme <on firm ground : sur la terre ferme> **3** STEADY : solide, stable **4** DEFINITE : solide, déterminé **5** RESOLUTE : ferme, résolu **6** STEADFAST : solide, ferme <a firm friendship : une amitié solide>

firm[3] *n* : entreprise *f*, firme *f*

firmament [ˈfərməmənt] *n* : firmament *m*

firmly [ˈfərmli] *adv* : fermement

firmness [ˈfərmnəs] *n* : fermeté *f*, solidité *f*

first[1] [ˈfərst] *adv* **1** : en premier, d'abord <first of all : tout d'abord> **2** : pour la première fois <when I first visited France : la première fois que je suis allé en France> **3** RATHER : plutôt <I'd die first : plutôt mourir>

first[2] *adj* : premier <at first sight : à première vue> <I don't know the first thing about physics : je ne connais absolument rien à la physique>

first[3] *n* **1** : premier *m*, -mière *f* (dans une série) **2** (*used in dates*) : premier *m* <the first of July : le premier juillet> **3** *or* **first gear** : première *f* **4 at ～** : au début

first aid *n* : premiers secours *mpl*, premiers soins *mpl*

first–class[1] [ˈfərstˈklæs] *adv* : en première <to travel first-class : voyager en première>

first–class[2] *adj* **1** EXCELLENT : excellent, de première qualité **2** : de première classe (se dit d'une place dans un avion, etc.), à tarif normal (se dit d'une lettre, etc.)

first class *n* : première classe *f*

first lieutenant *n* : lieutenant *m*

firstly [ˈfərstli] *adv* : premièrement

first–rate[1] [ˈfərstˈreɪt] *adv* : très bien

first–rate[2] *adj* : excellent, de premier ordre

fiscal [ˈfɪskəl] *adj* : fiscal — **fiscally** *adv*

fish[1] [ˈfɪʃ] *vi* **1** : pêcher **2 to fish for** SEEK : chercher

fish[2] *n, pl* **fish** *or* **fishes** : poisson *m*

fisherman [ˈfɪʃərmən] *n, pl* **-men** [-mən, -mɛn] : pêcheur *m*, -cheuse *f*

fishery [ˈfɪʃəri] *n, pl* **-eries 1** → **fishing 2** : pêcherie *f*, zone *f* de pêche

fishhook [ˈfɪʃˌhʊk] *n* : hameçon *m*

fishing [ˈfɪʃɪŋ] *n* : pêche *f*

fishy [ˈfɪʃi] *adj* **fishier; -est 1** : de poisson <a fishy taste : un goût de poisson> **2** QUESTIONABLE : douteux, louche

fission [ˈfɪʃən, -ʒən] *n* : fission *f*

fissure [ˈfɪʃər] *n* : fissure *f*

fist [ˈfɪst] *n* : poing *m* <to clench one's fists : serrer les poings>

fistfight [ˈfɪstˌfaɪt] *n* : coups *mpl* de poing, bagarre *f*

fit[1] [ˈfɪt] *v* **fitted; fitting** *vt* **1** : aller à <this suit fits you well : ce complet vous va bien> **2** MATCH : répondre à, correspondre à <to fit one's mood : correspondre à son humeur> **3** INSTALL : installer, mettre en place **4** EQUIP : équiper **5 to fit s.o. for** : prendre les mesures de qqn pour (un vêtement) — *vi* **1** : aller, être de la bonne taille <this dress doesn't fit : cette robe n'est pas à ma taille> **2** *or* **to fit in** BELONG : s'intégrer

fit[2] *adj* **fitter; fittest 1** APPROPRIATE, SUITED : convenable, qui convient <to see fit to : trouver bon de> **2** COMPETENT, QUALIFIED : capable, digne **3** HEALTHY : en bonne santé, en (pleine) forme

fit[3] *n* **1** : coupe *f* (d'un vêtement) <it's a tight fit : c'est trop juste> **2** : crise *f*, accès *m* <a fit of anger : un accès de colère>

fitful [ˈfɪtfəl] *adj* : agité, intermittent

fitfully [ˈfɪtfəli] *adv* : de manière intermittente

fitness [ˈfɪtnəs] *n* **1** HEALTH : santé *f*, forme *f* physique **2** SUITABILITY : aptitude *f*, compétences *fpl* (d'une personne), justesse *f* (d'une remarque)

fitting[1] [ˈfɪṭɪŋ] *adj* SUITABLE : approprié, convenable

fitting[2] *n* **1** : essayage *m* (de vêtements) **2** : installation *f* (électrique)

five[1] [ˈfaɪv] *adj* : cinq

five[2] *n* : cinq *m*

fix[1] [ˈfɪks] *vt* **1** ATTACH, SECURE : fixer, attacher **2** ESTABLISH : fixer <to fix a date : fixer un rendez-vous> **3** FOCUS : fixer **4** REPAIR : réparer **5** PREPARE : préparer **6** : truquer, arranger <to fix a race : truquer une course>

fix[2] *n* **1** PREDICAMENT : pétrin *m fam* **2** : position *f* <to get a fix on : déterminer la position de>

fixate [ˈfɪkˌseɪt] *vi* **-ated; -ating** : faire une fixation <to be fixated on : être fixé sur>

fixation [fɪkˈseɪʃən] *n* : fixation *f*

fixed [ˈfɪkst] *adj* **1** STATIONARY : fixe, immobile **2** INTENT : fixe <a fixed stare : un regard fixe> **3** SET : constant, fixe <fixed income : revenu fixe> <a fixed idea : une idée arrêtée>

fixedly [ˈfɪksədli] *adv* : fixement

fixture [ˈfɪkstʃər] *n* : installation *f* <bathroom fixtures : installations sanitaires>

fizz[1] [ˈfɪz] *vi* EFFERVESCE : pétiller

fizz[2] *n* : pétillement *m*

fizzle[1] [ˈfɪzəl] *vi* **-zled; -zling 1** FIZZ : pétiller **2** *or* **to fizzle out** FAIL : échouer, ne rien donner

fizzle[2] *n* FAILURE : échec *m*, fiasco *m*

fjord [fiˈɔrd] *n* : fjord *m*

flabbergast [ˈflæbərˌgæst] *vt* : sidérer *fam*, stupéfier

flabbiness [ˈflæbinəs] *n* : flaccidité *f*

flabby [ˈflæbi] *adj* **flabbier; -est** : flasque

flaccid [ˈflæksəd, ˈflæsəd] *adj* : flasque, mou

flag[1] [ˈflæg] *v* **flagged; flagging** *vt* SIGNAL : faire signe à (un taxi, etc.) — *vi* DECLINE, WEAKEN : dépérir, languir, faiblir

flag[2] *n* **1** : drapeau *m*, pavillon *m* (d'un navire) **2** *or* **flagstone** : dalle *f*

flagon [ˈflægən] *n* : cruche *f*, grosse bouteille *f*

flagpole [ˌflægˌpoːl] *n* : mât *m* (de drapeau)

flagrant [ˈfleɪgrənt] *adj* : flagrant

flagrantly [ˈfleɪgrəntli] *adv* : d'une manière flagrante

flagship [ˈflægˌʃɪp] *n* : navire *m* amiral

flagstaff [ˈflægˌstæf] → **flagpole**

flagstone [ˈflægˌstoːn] → **flag**[2]

flail[1] [ˈfleɪl] *vt* **1** : battre (des grains) au fléau **2** : agiter (les bras, etc.)

flail[2] *n* : fléau *m*

flair [ˈflær] *n* **1** TALENT : aptitude *f*, don *m* **2** STYLE : classe *f*, style *m*

flak [ˈflæk] *ns & pl* **1** : tir *m* antiaérien **2** CRITICISM : critiques *fpl*

flake[1] [ˈfleɪk] *v* **flaked; flaking** *vi or* **to flake off** : s'écailler, s'effriter — *vt* : émietter (un poisson, etc.)

flake[2] *n* : flocon *m* (de neige), paillette *f* (de métal, de savon, etc.), écaille *f* (de peinture)
flamboyance [flæm'bɔɪən*t*s] *n* : extravagance *f*
flamboyant [flæm'bɔɪənt] *adj* : extravagant, éclatant
flame[1] ['fleɪm] *vi* **flamed; flaming 1** BURN : flamber, brûler **2** BLAZE, GLOW : flamboyer
flame[2] *n* **1** : flamme *f* <to burst into flames : s'embraser> <to go up in flames : s'enflammer> **2** ARDOR : flamme *f*, feu *m*
flamethrower ['fleɪm,θro:ər] *n* : lance-flammes *m*
flaming ['fleɪmɪŋ] *adj* **1** : flamboyant <flaming red hair : cheveux rouges flamboyants> **2** PASSIONATE : ardent
flamingo [flə'mɪŋgo] *n, pl* **-gos** : flamant *m*
flammable ['flæməbəl] *adj* : inflammable
flange ['flændʒ] *n* : bride *f* (d'une pipe), boudin *m* (d'une roue)
flank[1] ['flæŋk] *vt* **1** : flanquer (dans l'armée) **2** BORDER : border, entourer
flank[2] *n* : flanc *m*
flannel ['flænəl] *n* : flanelle *f*
flap[1] ['flæp] *v* **flapped; flapping** *vt* : battre (des ailes) — *vi* : battre, claquer <to flap in the wind : battre au vent>
flap[2] *n* **1** : battement *m* (d'ailes), claquement *m* (d'une voile) **2** : rabat *m* (d'une enveloppe, d'un vêtement, etc.), abattant *m* (d'une table)
flapjack ['flæp,dʒæk] → **pancake**
flare[1] ['flær] *vi* **flared; flaring 1** FLAME : flamboyer, s'enflammer **2** WIDEN : s'évaser **3 to flare up** : s'emporter, fulminer (contre une personne) **4 to flare up** BREAK OUT, INTENSIFY : s'intensifier, éclater
flare[2] *n* **1** BLAZE : flamboiement *m* **2** SIGNAL : signal *m* lumineux **3** ROCKET : fusée *f* éclairante
flash[1] ['flæʃ] *vt* **1** PROJECT : projeter, diriger <he flashed the light in my eyes : il a dirigé la lumière dans mes yeux> **2** TRANSMIT : transmettre (un message, etc.) **3** SHOW : faire apparaître soudainement **4** : lancer (un sourire), jeter (un regard) — *vi* **1** GLEAM, SPARKLE : étinceler, briller **2** BLINK : clignoter (se dit d'une lumière, d'un signal lumineux) **3 to flash past** : passer comme un éclair
flash[2] *adj* : subit <flash flood : crue subite>
flash[3] *n* **1** : éclair *m* (de génie), éclat *m* (d'un diamant), lueur *f* (d'espoir) **2** INSTANT : minute *f*, instant *m* <I'll be back in a flash : je serai de retour dans un instant> **3** : flash *m* (d'un appareil photographique) **4 flash of lightning** : éclair *m*
flashiness ['flæʃinəs] *n* : tape-à-l'œil *m*
flashlight ['flæʃ,laɪt] *n* : lampe *f* de poche
flashy ['flæʃi] *adj* **flashier; -est** : tape-à-l'œil, tapageur, criard
flask ['flæsk] *n* : flacon *m*, flasque *f*
flat[1] ['flæt] *adv* **1** : à plat, planche *Can* <to lay (down) flat : mettre à plat> <to fall flat : tomber de tout son long> **2** EXACTLY : pile *fam* <in one hour flat : dans une heure pile> **3** : faux, en dessous du ton (en musique) **4 to be flat broke** : être complètement fauché
flat[2] *adj* **flatter; flattest 1** : plat (se dit d'une surface) **2** DOWNRIGHT : net, catégorique <a flat refusal : un refus catégorique> **3** FIXED : fixe <a flat rate : un taux fixe> **4** MONOTONOUS : plat, monotone **5** : éventé (se dit des boissons gazeuses) **6** DEFLATED : crevé, dégonflé **7** : faux (se dit d'une voix), bémol (se dit d'une note)
flat[3] *n* **1** PLAIN : plaine *f* **2** : plat *m* (de la main) **3** : bémol *m* (en musique) **4** *Brit* APARTMENT : appartement *m* **5** *or* **flat tire** : crevaison *f*
flatcar ['flæt,kɑr] *n* : wagon *m* plat
flatfish ['flæt,fɪʃ] *n* : poisson *m* plat
flatly ['flætli] *adv* CATEGORICALLY : carrément, catégoriquement
flatness ['flætnəs] *n* **1** EVENNESS : égalité *f* **2** DULLNESS : monotonie *f*
flat–out ['flæt'aʊt] *adj* OUT-AND-OUT : complet, total, absolu
flatten ['flætən] *vt* : aplatir, aplanir — *vi or* **to flatten out** : s'aplanir
flatter ['flæt̬ər] *vt* **1** PRAISE : flatter, louer **2** : flatter, avantager <this portrait flatters me : ce portrait me flatte>
flatterer ['flæt̬ərər] *n* : flatteur *m*, -teuse *f*
flattering ['flæt̬ərɪŋ] *adj* : flatteur
flattery ['flæt̬əri] *n, pl* **-ries** : flatterie *f*
flatulence ['flætʃələn*t*s] *n* : flatulence *f*
flatulent ['flætʃələnt] *adj* : flatulent
flatware ['flæt,wær] *n* : couverts *mpl*
flaunt ['flɔnt] *vt* : faire étalage de, étaler
flavor[1] *or Brit* **flavour** ['fleɪvər] *vt* : assaisonner, relever le goût de
flavor[2] *or Brit* **flavour** *n* **1** : saveur *f*, goût *m* **2** FLAVORING : assaisonnement *m*, arôme *m*, parfum *m* <artificial flavors : arômes artificiels>
flavorful *or Brit* **flavourful** ['fleɪvərfəl] *adj* : savoureux, délectable
flavoring *or Brit* **flavouring** ['fleɪvərɪŋ] *n* : assaisonnement *m*, arôme *m*, parfum *m*
flavorless *or Brit* **flavourless** ['fleɪvərləs] *adj* : sans saveur
flavour *Brit* → **flavor**
flaw ['flɔ] *n* : défaut *m*, imperfection *f*
flawless ['flɔləs] *adj* : sans défaut, parfait
flawlessly ['flɔləsli] *adv* : parfaitement
flax ['flæks] *n* : lin *m*

flaxen ['flæksən] *adj* : de lin
flay ['fleɪ] *vt* **1** SKIN : écorcher (un animal) **2** CRITICIZE : éreinter
flea ['fli:] *n* : puce *f*
fleck[1] ['flɛk] *vt* : tacheter, moucheter
fleck[2] *n* : petite tache *f,* moucheture *f*
fledgling ['flɛdʒlɪŋ] *n* : oisillon *m*
flee ['fli:] *v* **fled** ['flɛd]; **fleeing** *vt* : s'enfuir de, fuir — *vi* : s'enfuir, fuir
fleece[1] ['fli:s] *vt* **fleeced; fleecing 1** SHEAR : tondre **2** SWINDLE : escroquer
fleece[2] *n* : toison *f*
fleecy ['fli:si] *adj* **fleecier; -est** : laineux (se dit d'un tissu), cotonneux (se dit des nuages, etc.)
fleet[1] ['fli:t] *vi* : s'enfuir
fleet[2] *adj* : rapide
fleet[3] *n* : flotte *f* (de navires), parc *m* (de taxis, etc.)
fleet admiral *n* : amiral *m*
fleeting ['fli:t̬ɪŋ] *adj* : bref, éphémère, fugace
Flemish[1] ['flɛmɪʃ] *adj* : flamand
Flemish[2] *n* **1** : flamand *m* (langue) **2 the Flemish** : les Flamands
flesh ['flɛʃ] *n* **1** : chair *f* (d'un animal) **2** : chair *f,* pulpe *f* (d'un fruit)
flesh out *vt* : étoffer, enrichir
fleshly ['flɛʃli] *adj* **1** BODILY : corporel **2** CARNAL : charnel, sensuel
fleshy ['flɛʃi] *adj* **fleshier; -est** : charnu (se dit des fruits, etc.), bien en chair (se dit des personnes)
flew → **fly**[1]
flex ['flɛks] *vt* : faire jouer (des muscles), fléchir (un bras, une jambe, etc.)
flexibility [ˌflɛksə'bɪlət̬i] *n* : flexibilité *f*
flexible ['flɛksəbəl] *adj* : flexible, souple — **flexibly** [-bli] *adv*
flick[1] ['flɪk] *vt* **1** STRIKE : donner un petit coup à, donner une chiquenaude à **2 to flick a switch** : appuyer sur un bouton — *vi* **to flick through** : feuilleter (un livre, etc.)
flick[2] *n* : petit coup *m,* chiquenaude *f*
flicker[1] ['flɪkər] *vi* **1** FLUTTER : cligner, battre **2** : vaciller, trembloter <a flickering flame : une flamme qui vacille>
flicker[2] *n* **1** : clignement *m,* battement *m* (d'une paupière) **2** GLIMMER : lueur *f* <a flicker of hope : une lueur d'espoir> **3** : vacillement *m* (d'une flamme)
flier ['flaɪər] *n* **1** PILOT : aviateur *m,* -trice *f* **2** *or* **flyer** LEAFLET : prospectus *m*
flight ['flaɪt] *n* **1** FLYING : vol *m* (d'un oiseau, d'un avion), trajectoire *f* (d'un projectile) **2** GROUP : volée *f* (d'oiseaux), escadrille *f* (d'avions) **3** ESCAPE : fuite *f* **4 flight of fancy** : élan *m* de l'imagination **5 flight of stairs** : escalier *m*
flightless ['flaɪtləs] *adj* : coureur <flightless birds : oiseaux coureux>
flighty ['flaɪti] *adj* **flightier; -est** : volage, inconstant
flimsiness ['flɪmzinəs] *n* : fragilité *f,* construction *f* peu solide
flimsy ['flɪmzi] *adj* **flimsier; -est 1** LIGHT, THIN : fin, léger **2** WEAK : fragile, peu solide **3** IMPLAUSIBLE : pauvre, mince <a flimsy excuse : une pauvre excuse>
flinch ['flɪntʃ] *vi* **1** WINCE : tressaillir **2** RECOIL : reculer, fuir
fling[1] ['flɪŋ] *vt* **flung** ['flʌŋ]; **flinging 1** THROW : jeter, lancer, flanquer *fam* **2 to fling oneself** : se lancer, se jeter
fling[2] *n* **1** THROW : jet *m,* lancer *m* **2** ATTEMPT : essai *m* <to have a fling at sth : essayer de faire qqch> **3** AFFAIR : aventure *f*
flint ['flɪnt] *n* : silex *m*
flinty ['flɪnti] *adj* **flintier; -est 1** : à silex **2** STERN, UNYIELDING : dur, de pierre
flip[1] ['flɪp] *v* **flipped; flipping** *vt* **1** TOSS : lancer **2** FLICK : appuyer sur (un bouton) **3 to flip a coin** : jouer à pile ou face — *vi* **1** *or* **to flip over** : se retourner **2 to flip through** : feuilleter (un livre, etc.)
flip[2] *adj* : désinvolte, impertinent
flip[3] *n* **1** FLICK : petit coup *m* **2** SOMERSAULT : saut *m* périlleux
flippancy ['flɪpəntsi] *n, pl* **-cies** : désinvolture *f,* impertinence *f*
flippant ['flɪpənt] *adj* : désinvolte
flipper ['flɪpər] *n* : nageoire *f*
flirt[1] ['flərt] *vi* : flirter
flirt[2] *n* : charmeur *m,* -meuse *f;* personne *f* qui flirte
flirtation [ˌflər'teɪʃən] *n* : flirt *m*
flirtatious [ˌflər'teɪʃəs] *adj* : charmeur, séducteur
flit ['flɪt] *vi* **flitted; flitting 1** : voleter, voltiger **2 to flit about** : passer rapidement
float[1] ['flo:t] *vt* **1** : faire flotter **2** ISSUE : émettre, lancer (en finances) <to float a loan : émettre un emprunt> — *vi* : flotter
float[2] *n* **1** RAFT : radeau *m* **2** CORK : flotteur *m,* bouchon *m* **3** : char *m* (de carnaval)
flock[1] ['flɑk] *vi* : affluer, se rassembler
flock[2] *n* **1** : volée *f* (d'oiseaux), troupeau *m* (de moutons) **2** CROWD : foule *f* **3** : ouailles *fpl* (en religion)
floe ['flo:] *n or* **ice floe** : banquise *f*
flog ['flɑg] *vt* **flogged; flogging** : flageller, fouetter
flood[1] ['flʌd] *vt* : inonder, noyer — *vi* : déborder (se dit d'une rivière)
flood[2] *n* **1** : inondation *f,* crue *f* <spring flood : crue du printemps> **2** TORRENT : déluge *m,* torrent *m* <a flood of words : un déluge de paroles>
floodlight ['flʌdˌlaɪt] *n* : projecteur *m*
floodwaters ['flʌdˌwɔt̬ərz] *npl* : eaux *fpl* de crue

floor[1] |ˈflor| *vt* **1** : faire le sol de, parqueter (une maison, une salle) **2** KNOCK DOWN : terrasser (un adversaire) **3** NONPLUS : dérouter

floor[2] *n* **1** : plancher *m*, parquet *m* (d'une salle, etc.) <dance floor : piste de danse> **2** BOTTOM, GROUND : sol *m*, fond *m* (de la mer) **3** STORY : étage *m* <a 10-floor building : un édifice de 10 étages> <on the ground floor : au rez-de-chaussée>

floorboard |ˈflor,bord| *n* : planche *f*, latte *f*

flooring |ˈflorɪŋ| *n* **1** : revêtement *m* de sol **2** FLOOR : plancher *m*, parquet *m*

flop[1] |ˈflɑp| *vi* **flopped; flopping 1** FLAP : s'agiter mollement **2** *or* **to flop down** : s'affaler **3** FAIL : échouer, faire un four *fam*

flop[2] *n* FAILURE : fiasco *m*, four *m fam*

floppy |ˈflɑpi| *adj* **floppier; -est** : mou, pendant

floppy disk *n* : disquette *f*

flora |ˈflorə| *n* : flore *f*

floral |ˈflorəl| *adj* : floral

florid |ˈflorɪd| *adj* **1** ORNATE : fleuri **2** RUDDY : rougeaud

florist |ˈflorɪst| *n* : fleuriste *mf*

floss[1] |ˈflɔs| *vt* : utiliser du fil dentaire

floss[2] *n* **1** *or* **embroidery floss** : soie *f* à broder **2** → **dental floss**

flotation |floˈteɪʃən| *n* : mise *f* à flot

flotilla |floˈtɪlə| *n* : flottille *f*

flotsam |ˈflɑtsəm| *n* : épave *f* flottante

flounce[1] |ˈflaʊnts| *vi* **flounced; flouncing** : passer brusquement <to flounce in : entrer dans un mouvement d'humeur>

flounce[2] *n* : volant *m* (d'une jupe, etc.)

flounder[1] |ˈflaʊndər| *vi* **1** THRASH : patauger, se débattre **2** BOG DOWN, FALTER : s'empêtrer (dans un discours), piétiner (dans une carrière)

flounder[2] *n, pl* **flounder** *or* **flounders** : flet *m*, poisson *m* plat

flour[1] |ˈflaʊər| *vt* : fariner, enrober de farine

flour[2] *n* : farine *f*

flourish[1] |ˈflərɪʃ| *vt* BRANDISH : brandir — *vi* **1** PROSPER : prospérer **2** THRIVE : fleurir, s'épanouir

flourish[2] *n* **1** : fioriture *f* (en musique), paraphe *f* (d'une signature) **2** FANFARE : fanfare *f* **3** WAVING : grand geste *m* (de la main), moulinet *m* (d'une épée, etc.)

flourishing |ˈflərɪʃɪŋ| *adj* : florissant, prospère

flout |ˈflaʊt| *vt* : se moquer de, passer outre à

flow[1] |ˈflo:| *vi* **1** COURSE, RUN : couler, s'écouler <to flow past : passer devant> **2** CIRCULATE : circuler (se dit du sang, du trafic, etc.) **3** BILLOW, HANG : flotter, onduler

flow[2] *n* **1** STREAM : écoulement *m* **2** CIRCULATION : circulation *f* <blood flow : circulation du sang>

flower[1] |ˈflaʊər| *vi* **1** : fleurir **2** DEVELOP, FLOURISH : s'épanouir, se développer

flower[2] *n* **1** : fleur *f* **2** BLOOM : épanouissement *m* <in full flower : en plein épanouissement>

floweriness |ˈflaʊərinəs| *n* : ornementation *f*, fioritures *fpl*

flowering |ˈflaʊərɪŋ| *n* : floraison *f*

flowerpot |ˈflaʊər,pɑt| *n* : pot *m* de fleurs

flowery |ˈflaʊəri| *adj* : fleuri

flown → **fly**[1]

flu |ˈflu:| *n* : grippe *f*

flub |ˈflʌb| *vt* **flubbed; flubbing** : louper *fam*, rater

fluctuate |ˈflʌktʃʊ,eɪt| *vi* **-ated; -ating** : fluctuer

fluctuation |,flʌktʃʊˈeɪʃən| *n* : fluctuation *f*

flue |ˈflu:| *n* : conduit *m* (de cheminée)

fluency |ˈflu:əntsi| *n* : aisance *f*, facilité *f*

fluent |ˈflu:ənt| *adj* : coulant, aisé <she speaks fluent French : elle parle couramment le français>

fluently |ˈflu:əntli| *adv* : couramment

fluff[1] |ˈflʌf| *vt* **1** *or* **to fluff up** : faire bouffer **2** BOTCH : louper *fam*, rater

fluff[2] *n* **1** DOWN : duvet *m* **2** FUZZ : peluches *fpl*

fluffy |ˈflʌfi| *adj* **fluffier; -est 1** DOWNY, FUZZY : duveteux, pelucheux **2** LIGHT : léger, moelleux

fluid[1] |ˈflu:ɪd| *adj* : fluide

fluid[2] *n* : fluide *m*, liquide *m*

fluidity |flu:ˈɪdəṭi| *n* : fluidité *f*

fluid ounce *n* : once *f* liquide

fluke |ˈflu:k| *n* : coup *m* de chance, coup *m* de veine *fam*

flung → **fling**[1]

flunk |ˈflʌŋk| *vt* FAIL : rater

fluorescence |,flʊrˈɛsənts, ,flɔr-| *n* : fluorescence *f*

fluorescent |,flʊrˈɛsənt, ,flɔr-| *adj* : fluorescent

fluoridate |ˈflɔrə,deɪt, ˈflʊr-| *vt* **-dated; -dating** : ajouter du fluor à

fluoridation |,flɔrəˈdeɪʃən, ,flʊr-| *n* : traitement *m* au fluor, fluoration *f*

fluoride |ˈflɔr,aɪd, ˈflʊr-| *n* : fluorure *m*

fluorine |ˈflʊr,i:n| *n* : fluor *m*

flurry[1] |ˈfləri| *vt* **flurried; flurrying** FLUSTER : agiter, énerver

flurry[2] *n, pl* **-ries 1** GUST : rafale *f*, poudrerie *f Can* <snow flurries : rafales de neige> **2** BUSTLE : tourbillon *m* **3** BARRAGE : déluge *m* (de questions, etc.)

flush[1] |ˈflʌʃ| *vt* **1** REDDEN : empourprer, rougir (les joues) **2** *or* **to flush out** : lever, faire s'envoler (du gibier) **3 to flush the toilet** : tirer la chasse d'eau — *vi* BLUSH : rougir

flush[2] *adv* : de niveau, à ras

flush[3] *adj* **1** FILLED : plein à déborder **2** RUDDY : rouge, coloré **3** LEVEL : au même niveau **4** AFFLUENT : en fonds

flush[4] *n* **1** FLUSHING : chasse *f* (d'eau) **2** SURGE : élan *m*, accès *m* <a flush of anger : un accès de colère> **3** BLUSH : rougeur *f*
fluster[1] [ˈflʌstər] *vt* : énerver, troubler
fluster[2] *n* : trouble *m*, agitation *f*
flute [ˈfluːt] *n* : flûte *f*
fluted [ˈfluːt̬əd] *adj* GROOVED : cannelé
flutist [ˈfluːt̬ɪst] *n* : flûtiste *mf*
flutter[1] [ˈflʌt̬ər] *vi* **1** FLAP : battre (se dit des ailes) **2** BEAT : palpiter (se dit du cœur) **3** DRIFT, FLY : flotter <a sail fluttering in the wind : une voile qui flotte au vent> **4 to flutter about** : s'agiter, s'affairer
flutter[2] *n* **1** FLAPPING : battement *m* (d'ailes) **2** STIR : agitation *f*, émoi *m*
flux [ˈflʌks] *n* **1** : flux *m* (en médecine et en physique) **2** CHANGE : changement *m* <in a state of flux : dans un état de perpétuel changement>
fly[1] [ˈflaɪ] *v* **flew** [ˈfluː]; **flown** [ˈfloːn]; **flying** *vt* : faire voler — *vi* **1** : voler (se dit d'un oiseau, d'un avion, etc.) **2** TRAVEL : prendre l'avion **3** FLOAT : flotter, onduler **4** FLEE : fuir, s'enfuir **5** PASS : passer vite, filer *fam* <time was flying by : le temps filait>
fly[2] *n, pl* **flies 1** : mouche *f* (insecte) **2** : braguette *f* (d'un pantalon)
flyer → **flier**
flying saucer *n* : soucoupe *f* volante
flypaper [ˈflaɪˌpeɪpər] *n* : papier *m* tue-mouches
flyspeck [ˈflaɪˌspɛk] *n* **1** : chiure *f* de mouche **2** SPECK : petite tache *f*
flyswatter [ˈflaɪˌswɑt̬ər] *n* : tapette *f* à mouches, tue-mouches *m Can*
foal[1] [ˈfoːl] *vi* : pouliner, mettre bas
foal[2] *n* : poulain *m*
foam[1] [ˈfoːm] *vi* : mousser, écumer
foam[2] *n* : mousse *f*, écume *f*
foamy [ˈfoːmi] *adj* **foamier; -est** : mousseux, écumeux
focal [ˈfoːkəl] *adj* : focal
fo'c'sle [ˈfoːksəl] → **forecastle**
focus[1] [ˈfoːkəs] *vt* **1** : mettre au point (un instrument), fixer (les yeux) **2** CONCENTRATE : concentrer, faire converger — *vi* : converger, se concentrer
focus[2] *n, pl* **foci** [ˈfoːˌsaɪ, -ˌkaɪ] **1** : foyer *m* <to be in focus : être au point> <to bring into focus : mettre au point> **2** CENTER : centre *m* <the focus of attention : le centre d'attention, le point de mire>
fodder [ˈfɑdər] *n* : fourrage *m*
foe [ˈfoː] *n* : ennemi *m*, -mie *f*; adversaire *mf*
fog[1] [ˈfɔg, ˈfɑg] *v* **fogged; fogging** *vt* : embuer, brouiller — *vi or* **to fog up** : s'embuer, se couvrir de buée
fog[2] *n* **1** : brouillard *m*, brume *f* **2** CONFUSION : brouillard *m*, confusion *f*
foggy [ˈfɔgi, ˈfɑ-] *adj* **foggier; -est 1** : brumeux <a foggy night : une nuit brumeuse> **2** CONFUSED : confus <I haven't the foggiest notion : je n'en ai pas la moindre idée>
foghorn [ˈfɔgˌhɔrn, ˈfɑg-] *n* : corne *f* de brume
fogy [ˈfoːgi] *n, pl* **-gies** : vieille baderne *f fam*
foible [ˈfɔɪbəl] *n* : petit défaut *m*, petite manie *f*
foil[1] [ˈfɔɪl] *vt* THWART : déjouer, contrecarrer
foil[2] *n* **1** SWORD : fleuret *m* **2** : feuille *f* <aluminum foil : feuille d'aluminium> **3** COMPLEMENT, CONTRAST : repoussoir *m*
foist [ˈfɔɪst] *vt* **1 to foist sth off on** : refiler qqch à **2 to foist oneself on** : s'imposer à
fold[1] [ˈfoːld] *vt* **1** : plier <to fold a blanket : plier une couverture> **2** CLASP : croiser (les bras), joindre (les mains) **3** EMBRACE : serrer, enlacer — *vi* FAIL : échouer, s'écrouler
fold[2] *n* **1** CREASE, PLEAT : pli *m* **2** SHEEPFOLD : parc *m* à moutons **3** GROUP : bercail *m*, sein *m* <to return to the fold : rentrer au bercail>
folder [ˈfoːldər] *n* **1** FILE : chemise *f*, dossier *m* **2** CIRCULAR : dépliant *m*
foliage [ˈfoːliɪdʒ, -lɪdʒ] *n* : feuillage *m*
folio [ˈfoːliˌoː] *n, pl* **-lios** : folio *m*
folk[1] [ˈfoːk] *adj* : populaire, folklorique
folk[2] *n, pl* **folk** *or* **folks 1** PEOPLE : gens *mfpl* <plain folks : des gens ordinaires> **2 folks** *npl* PARENTS : famille *f*, parents *mpl*
folklore [ˈfoːkˌlor] *n* : folklore *m*
folk music *n* : musique *f* folklorique, folk *m*
folksy [ˈfoːksi] *adj* **folksier; -est** : populaire, sympa *fam*
follicle [ˈfɑlɪkəl] *n* : follicule *m*
follow [ˈfɑlo] *vt* **1** : suivre <follow the guide : suivez le guide> <they followed the road : ils ont longé la route> **2** PURSUE : exercer, poursuivre (une carrière, etc.) **3** OBEY : suivre, se soumettre à, se conformer à **4** UNDERSTAND : suivre, comprendre — *vi* **1** : suivre <in the days that followed : dans les jours qui ont suivi> **2** ENSUE : s'ensuivre, résulter **3** UNDERSTAND : suivre
follower [ˈfɑloər] *n* : partisan *m*, -sane *f*; disciple *mf*
following[1] [ˈfɑloɪŋ] *adj* : suivant
following[2] *n* : partisans *mpl*
following[3] *prep* : après
follow through *vi* **to follow through on** : suivre (jusqu'au bout)
follow up *vt* : donner suite à, confirmer
folly [ˈfɑli] *n, pl* **-lies** : folie *f*, absurdité *f*
foment [foˈmɛnt] *vt* : fomenter
fond [ˈfɑnd] *adj* **1** LOVING : affectueux, tendre **2** FERVENT : cher, fervent <my fondest hope : mon espoir le plus cher> **3 to be fond of** : aimer beaucoup

fondle |'fandəl| *vt* **-dled; -dling** : caresser

fondly |'fandli| *adv* **1** AFFECTIONATELY : affectueusement **2** DEARLY : chèrement

fondness |'fandnəs| *n* **1** AFFECTION : affection *f,* tendresse *f* **2** PARTIALITY : prédilection *f,* penchant *m*

fondue |fan'du:, -'dju:| *n* : fondue *f*

font |'fant| *n* **1** *or* **baptismal font** : fonts *mpl* baptismaux **2** SOURCE : source *f,* fontaine *f* **3** : police *f* (de caractères typographiques)

food |'fu:d| *n* **1** : nourriture *f,* aliments *mpl* **2** : cuisine *f,* mets *m* <Chinese food : mets chinois> **3 food for thought** : matière *f* à réflexion

food chain *n* : chaîne *f* alimentaire

food poisoning : intoxication *f* alimentaire

foodstuffs |'fu:d,stʌfs| *npl* : aliments *mpl,* denrées *fpl* alimentaires

fool[1] |'fu:l| *vt* DECEIVE : duper, berner — *vi* **1** JOKE : plaisanter <I was just fooling : je plaisantais> **2 to fool around** : perdre son temps **3 to fool with** : jouer avec

fool[2] *n* **1** : imbécile *mf;* idiot *m,* -diote *f;* nono *m,* -note *f Can fam* <don't be a fool! : ne fais pas l'idiot!> **2** JESTER : fou *m*

foolhardiness |'fu:l,hardinəs| *n* : témérité *f*

foolhardy |'fu:l,hardi| *adj* RASH : téméraire

foolish |'fu:lɪʃ| *adj* **1** STUPID : bête, idiot **2** RIDICULOUS : absurde, ridicule

foolishly |'fu:lɪʃli| *adv* : bêtement, sottement

foolishness |'fu:lɪʃnəs| *n* **1** STUPIDITY : bêtise *f,* sottise *f* **2** FOLLY : folie *f,* absurdité *f*

foolproof |'fu:l,pru:f| *adj* : infaillible

foot |'fʊt| *n, pl* **feet** |'fi:t| **1** : pied *m* **2** : bas *m* <at the foot of the page : au bas de la page>

footage |'fʊtɪdʒ| *n* **1** : longueur *f* en pieds **2** : métrage *m* (d'un film)

football |'fʊt,bɔl| *n* : football *m* américain, football *m Can*

footbridge |'fʊt,brɪdʒ| *n* : passerelle *f*

foothills |'fʊt,hɪlz| *npl* : contreforts *mpl*

foothold |'fʊt,ho:ld| *n* **1** : prise *f* de pied **2 to gain a foothold in** : prendre pied sur

footing |'fʊtɪŋ| *n* **1** FOOTHOLD : prise *f* de pied <to keep one's footing : conserver l'équilibre> **2** STATUS : position *f,* niveau *m* <on the same footing : sur le même pied d'égalité>

footlights |'fʊt,laɪts| *npl* : rampe *f*

footloose |'fʊt,lu:s| *adj* : libre de toute attache

footman |'fʊtmən| *n, pl* **-men** |-mən, -,mɛn| : valet *m* de pied

footnote |'fʊt,no:t| *n* : note *f* en bas de la page

footpath |'fʊt,pæθ| *n* : sentier *m*

footprint |'fʊt,prɪnt| *n* : empreinte *f* (de pied), trace *f* (de pas)

footrest |'fʊt,rɛst| *n* : repose-pied *m*

footstep |'fʊt,stɛp| *n* : pas *m*

footstool |'fʊt,stu:l| *n* : tabouret *m*

footwear |'fʊt,wær| *n* : chaussures *fpl*

footwork |'fʊt,wərk| *n* : jeu *m* de jambes

fop |'fap| *n* : dandy *m*

for[1] |'fɔr| *conj* BECAUSE : car

for[2] *prep* **1** (*indicating a purpose*) : pour <to get ready for a trip : se préparer pour un voyage> <what's it for? : c'est pour quoi faire?> **2** BECAUSE OF : de, à cause de <to cry for joy : pleurer de joie> **3** (*indicating a recipient*) : pour <gifts for her sister : des cadeaux pour sa sœur> **4** (*indicating support*) : pour <to fight for one's country : se battre pour sa patrie> <he speaks for the poor : il parle au nom des pauvres> **5** (*indicating a goal or remedy*) : contre, pour <a cure for cancer : un remède contre le cancer> <it's for your own good : c'est pour ton bien> **6** (*indicating equivalence or exchange*) : pour <I bought it for $10 : je l'ai acheté pour 10 $> **7** (*indicating duration*) : pour, pendant, depuis <he's here for three days : il est là pour trois jours> <we talked for hours : on a parlé pendant des heures> <I've lived here for two years : j'habite ici depuis deux ans> **8** (*indicating destination*) : pour, à destination de <to leave for New York : partir pour New York> <a train for Paris : un train à destination de Paris> **9** → **as for**

forage[1] |'fɔrɪdʒ| *vi* **-aged; -aging** : fourrager, fouiller

forage[2] *n* : fourrage *m*

foray |'fɔr,eɪ| *n* : incursion *f*

forbear[1] |fɔr'bær| *vi* **-bore** |-'bor|; **-borne** |-'born|; **-bearing 1** ABSTAIN : s'abstenir **2** : être patient

forbear[2] → **forebear**

forbearance |fɔr'bærənts| *n* **1** RESTRAINT : abstention *f* **2** PATIENCE : patience *f*

forbid |fər'bɪd| *vt* **-bade** |-'bæd, -'beɪd| *or* **-bad** |-'bæd|; **-bidden** |-'bɪdən|; **-bidding 1** PROHIBIT : interdire, défendre **2** PREVENT : empêcher

forbidding |fər'bɪdɪŋ| *adj* **1** DISAGREEABLE : rebutant, déplaisant **2** MENACING : menaçant

force[1] |'fors| *vt* **forced; forcing 1** COMPEL : forcer, contraindre, obliger **2** *or* **to force open** : forcer **3** PRESS, PUSH : forcer <I forced my way through : je me suis frayé un passage> **4 to force a smile** : se forcer à sourire

force[2] *n* **1** POWER, STRENGTH : force *f* **2** *or* **forces** *npl* : forces *fpl,* troupes *fpl* <ground forces : forces terrestres> <the police force : les forces de po-

lice> **3** : force *f* (en physique) <the force of gravity : la pesanteur> **4 in ~** : en grand nombre, en force **5 in ~** : en vigueur (se dit d'une loi, etc.)
forceful ['forsfəl] *adj* : puissant, énergique, vigoureux
forcefully ['forsfəli] *adv* : avec force, avec vigueur
forceps ['fɔrsəps, -ˌsɛps] *ns & pl* : forceps *m*
forcible ['forsəbəl] *adj* **1** FORCED : de force **2** POWERFUL : énergique, vigoureux
forcibly ['forsəbli] *adv* **1** : de force **2** VIGOROUSLY : avec vigueur, énergiquement
ford[1] ['ford] *vt* : passer à gué
ford[2] *n* : gué *m*
fore[1] ['for] *adv* : à l'avant
fore[2] *adj* : à l'avant, antérieur
fore[3] *n* **1** : avant *m* (d'un navire) **2 to come to the fore** : se faire remarquer, se mettre en évidence
fore–and–aft ['forən'æft, -ənd-] *adj* : aurique <fore-and-aft sail : voile aurique>
forearm ['forˌɑrm] *n* : avant-bras *m*
forebear ['forˌbær] *n* : ancêtre *mf*
foreboding [for'bo:dɪŋ] *n* : (mauvais) pressentiment *m*, prémonition *f*
forecast[1] ['forˌkæst] *vt* **-cast; -casting** : prévoir
forecast[2] *n* **1** PREDICTION : prévision *f* **2** *or* **weather forecast** : prévisions *fpl* météorologiques, météo *f Can fam*
forecastle ['fo:ksəl] *n* : gaillard *m* d'avant
foreclose [for'klo:z] *vt* **-closed; -closing** : saisir (un bien hypothéqué)
foreclosure [for'klo:ʒər] *n* : forclusion *f*
forefathers ['forˌfɑðərz] *npl* : ancêtres *mfpl*, aïeux *mpl*
forefinger ['forˌfɪŋgər] *n* : index *m*
forefoot ['forˌfʊt] *n, pl* **-feet** [ˌfi:t] : pied *m* antérieur
forefront ['forˌfrʌnt] *n* : premier rang *m*
forego[1] [for'go:] *vt* **-went; -gone; -going** PRECEDE : précéder
forego[2] → **forgo**
foregoing [for'go:ɪŋ] *adj* : précédent
foregone [for'gɔn] *adj* **it's a foregone conclusion** : c'est gagné d'avance
foreground ['forˌgraʊnd] *n* : premier plan *m*
forehand[1] ['forˌhænd] *adj* : de coup droit
forehand[2] *n* : coup *m* droit
forehead ['fɔrəd, 'forˌhɛd] *n* : front *m*
foreign ['fɔrən] *adj* **1** : étranger <a foreign language : une langue étrangère> **2** : extérieur <foreign trade : commerce extérieur> **3** ALIEN : étranger <foreign bodies : corps étrangers>
foreigner ['fɔrənər] *n* : étranger *m*, -gère *f*
foreknowledge [for'nɑlɪdʒ] *n* : connaissance *f* anticipée, prescience *f*
foreleg ['forˌlɛg] *n* : jambe *f* antérieure, patte *f* de devant
foreman ['formən] *n, pl* **-men** [-mən, -ˌmɛn] **1** : président *m* du jury **2** SUPERVISOR : contremaître *m*
foremost[1] ['forˌmo:st] *adv* **first and foremost** : tout d'abord, avant tout
foremost[2] *adj* : principal, le plus en vue
forenoon ['forˌnu:n] *n* : matinée *f*
forensic [fə'rɛntsɪk] *adj* : légal, médico-légal
foreordain [ˌfɔrɔr'deɪn] *vt* : prédestiner, prédéterminer
forequarter ['forˌkwɔrt̬ər] *n* : quartier *m* de devant
forerunner ['forˌrʌnər] *n* : précurseur *m*
foresee [for'si:] *vt* **-saw; -seen; -seeing** : prévoir, anticiper
foreseeable [for'si:əbəl] *adj* : prévisible
foreshadow [for'ʃædo:] *vt* : présager, annoncer
foresight ['forˌsaɪt] *n* **1** PRESCIENCE : prévision *f* **2** PRUDENCE : prévoyance *f*, prudence *f*
foresighted ['forˌsaɪt̬əd] *adj* : prévoyant, prudent
forest ['fɔrəst] *n* : forêt *f*
forestall [for'stɔl] *vt* **1** PREVENT : empêcher, prévenir **2** ANTICIPATE : anticiper, devancer
forested ['fɔrəstəd] *adj* : boisé, forestier
forester ['fɔrəstər] *n* : forestier *m*, -tière *f*
forestry ['fɔrəstri] *n* : sylviculture *f*, foresterie *f*
foreswear → **forswear**
foretaste ['forˌteɪst] *n* : avant-goût *m*
foretell [for'tɛl] *vt* **-told; -telling** : prédire
forethought ['forˌθɔt] *n* **1** PREMEDITATION : préméditation *f* **2** FORESIGHT : prévoyance *f*
forever [fɔr'ɛvər] *adv* **1** ETERNALLY : toujours, éternellement **2** CONTINUALLY : toujours, sans cesse
forevermore [fɔrˌɛvər'mor] *adv* : (pour) toujours
forewarn [for'wɔrn] *vt* : avertir, prévenir
foreword ['forwərd] *n* : avant-propos *m*
forfeit[1] ['fɔrfət] *vt* : perdre, renoncer à (ses droits, etc.)
forfeit[2] *n* **1** PENALTY : prix *m*, peine *f* **2** : gage *m* <to pay a forfeit : avoir un gage>
forge[1] ['fordʒ] *v* **forged; forging** *vt* **1** : forger (un métal, un plan, etc.) **2** COUNTERFEIT : contrefaire, falsifier — *vi* **to forge ahead** : prendre de l'avance, avancer
forge[2] *n* : forge *f*
forger ['fordʒər] *n* : faussaire *mf*, faux-monnayeur *m*
forgery ['fordʒəri] *n, pl* **-eries** : contrefaçon *f*, falsification *f*

forget [fər'gɛt] *v* **-got** [-'gɑt]; **-gotten** [-'gɑtən] *or* **-got; -getting** *vt* **1** : oublier <I've forgotten your name : j'ai oublié votre nom> **2** NEGLECT : négliger, oublier **3 forget it!** : n'en parlons plus! — *vi* : oublier

forgetful [fər'gɛtfəl] *adj* **1** ABSENTMINDED : distrait **2** NEGLECTFUL : oublieux, négligent

forgetfulness [fər'gɛtfəlnəs] *n* **1** ABSENTMINDEDNESS : distraction *f* **2** CARELESSNESS : étourderie *f*, négligence *f*

forget–me–not [fər'gɛtmi,nɑt] *n* : myosotis *m*

forgettable [fər'gɛt̬əbəl] *adj* : peu mémorable

forgivable [fər'gɪvəbəl] *adj* : pardonnable

forgive [fər'gɪv] *vt* **-gave** [-'geɪv]; **-given** [-'gɪvən]; **-giving** : pardonner

forgiveness [fər'gɪvnəs] *n* : pardon *m*, indulgence *f*

forgiving [fər'gɪvɪŋ] *adj* : indulgent, clément

forgo *or* **forego** [for'go:] *vt* **-went; -gone; -going** : renoncer à, se priver de

fork[1] ['fɔrk] *vt* **1** : fourcher <to fork (up) the earth : fourcher la terre> **2** *or* **to fork over** : allonger *fam* — *vi* : bifurquer, fourcher <the road forks : la route bifurque>

fork[2] *n* **1** : fourchette *f* <dessert fork : fourchette à dessert> **2** PITCHFORK : fourche *f* (à foin) **3** JUNCTION : bifurcation *f* (d'une route), embranchement *m* (d'une voie ferrée)

forked ['forkt, 'forkəd] *adj* : fourchu

forklift ['fɔrk,lɪft] *n* : chariot *m* élévateur

forlorn [fɔr'lɔrn] *adj* **1** DESOLATE : abandonné, désolé **2** SAD : triste, misérable **3** DESPERATE : désespéré

forlornly [fɔr'lɔrnli] *adv* : d'un air triste

form[1] ['fɔrm] *vt* **1** FASHION, SHAPE : former, façonner **2** ARRANGE : se mettre en <to form a line : se mettre en ligne> **3** ACQUIRE, DEVELOP : se former, se faire (une idée, etc.), contracter (une habitude) **4** INSTRUCT, TRAIN : former **5** CONSTITUTE : constituer, former — *vi* : se former, prendre forme

form[2] *n* **1** SHAPE : forme *f* **2** FIGURE : forme *f*, corps *m* <the human form : la forme humaine> **3** DOCUMENT : formulaire *m* <to fill out a form : remplir un formulaire> **4** KIND : forme *f*, genre *m* **5** CONDITION : forme *f*, condition *f* <to be in good form : être en pleine forme>

formal[1] ['fɔrməl] *adj* **1** : officiel <a formal reception : une réception officielle> <a formal contract : un contrat en bonne et due forme> **2** ELEVATED : soigné, soutenu <formal language : langage soutenu>

formal[2] *n* **1** *or* **formal dance** : bal *m* **2** *or* **formal dress** : tenue *f* de soirée

formaldehyde [fɔr'mældə,haɪd] *n* : formaldéhyde *m*

formality [fɔr'mælət̬i] *n, pl* **-ties** : formalité *f*

formalize ['fɔrmə,laɪz] *vt* **-ized; -izing** : formaliser

formally ['fɔrməli] *adv* **1** OFFICIALLY : officiellement **2** CEREMONIOUSLY : cérémonieusement, solennellement

format[1] ['fɔr,mæt] *vt* **-matted; -matting** **1** : concevoir le format de **2** : formater (une diskette)

format[2] *n* : format *m*

formation [fɔr'meɪʃən] *n* **1** FORMING : formation *f*, établissement *m* **2** ARRANGEMENT, SHAPE : formation *f*

formative ['fɔrmət̬ɪv] *adj* : formateur

former ['fɔrmər] *adj* **1** PREVIOUS : ancien, précédent <a former president : un ancien président> **2** : premier (de deux choses)

formerly ['fɔrmərli] *adv* : autrefois, jadis

formidable ['fɔrmədəbəl, fɔr'mɪdə-] *adj* **1** : redoutable, terrible <a formidable foe : un ennemi redoutable> **2** OUTSTANDING : impressionnant, remarquable

formless ['fɔrmləs] *adj* : informe

formula ['fɔrmjələ] *n, pl* **-las** or **-lae** [-,li:, -,laɪ] **1** : formule *f* **2** *or* **baby formula** : lait *m* en poudre (pour biberon)

formulate ['fɔrmjə,leɪt] *vt* **-lated; -lating** : formuler

formulation [,fɔrmjə'leɪʃən] *n* : formulation *f*

fornicate ['fɔrnə,keɪt] *vi* **-cated; -cating** : forniquer

fornication [,fɔrnə'keɪʃən] *n* : fornication *f*

forsake [fər'seɪk] *vt* **-sook** [-'sʊk]; **-saken** [-'seɪkən]; **-saking** : abandonner, délaisser

forswear [fɔr'swær] *v* **-swore; -sworn; -swearing** *vt* RENOUNCE : abjurer, renoncer à — *vi* : commettre un parjure

forsythia [fər'sɪθiə] *n* : forsythia *m*

fort ['fɔrt] *n* : fort *m*

forte ['fort, 'for,teɪ] *n* : fort *m*

forth ['forθ] *adv* **1** FORWARD : en avant <from this day forth : dorénavant, à partir d'aujourd'hui> **2 and so forth** : et ainsi de suite

forthcoming [forθ'kʌmɪŋ, 'forθ-] *adj* **1** COMING : prochain, à venir, à paraître **2** COMMUNICATIVE, OPEN : ouvert, communicatif

forthright ['forθ,raɪt] *adj* : franc, direct

forthrightly ['forθ,raɪtli] *adv* : franchement, directement

forthrightness ['forθ,raɪtnəs] *n* : franchise *f*

forthwith [forθ'wɪθ, -'wɪð] *adv* : sur-le-champ, aussitôt

fortieth[1] [ˈfɔrt̬iəθ] *adj* : quarantième
fortieth[2] *n* **1** : quarantième *mf* (dans une série) **2** : quarantième *m* (en mathématiques)
fortification [ˌfɔrt̬əfəˈkeɪʃən] *n* : fortification *f*
fortify [ˈfɔrt̬əˌfaɪ] *vt* **-fied; -fying 1** STRENGTHEN, SECURE : fortifier (une ville, etc.) **2** ENCOURAGE, INVIGORATE : remonter, réconforter
fortitude [ˈfɔrt̬əˌtu:d, -ˌtju:d] *n* : force *f* d'âme, courage *m*
fortnight [ˈfortˌnaɪt] *n* : quinzaine *f*, quinze jours *mpl*
fortnightly[1] [ˈfortˌnaɪtli] *adv* : tous les quinze jours
fortnightly[2] *adj* : bimensuel
fortress [ˈfɔrtrəs] *n* : forteresse *f*
fortuitous [fɔrˈtu:ət̬əs, -ˈtju:-] *adj* : fortuit, imprévu
fortunate [ˈfɔrtʃənət] *adj* **1** AUSPICIOUS : propice, prometteur **2** LUCKY : heureux, chanceux
fortunately [ˈfɔrtʃənətli] *adv* : heureusement
fortune [ˈfɔrtʃən] *n* **1** CHANCE, LUCK : chance *f*, fortune *f*, hasard *m* **2** DESTINY : destin *m*, sort *m* **3** WEALTH : fortune *f* <to make a fortune : faire fortune>
fortune–teller [ˈfɔrtʃənˌtɛlər] *n* : diseur *m*, -seuse *f* de bonne aventure; voyant *m*, voyante *f*
fortune–telling [ˈfɔrtʃənˌtɛlɪŋ] *n* : pratique *f* de dire la bonne aventure, divination *f*
forty[1] [ˈfɔrt̬i] *adj* : quarante
forty[2] *n, pl* **forties** : quarante *m*
forum [ˈforəm] *n, pl* **-rums** : forum *m*
forward[1] [ˈfɔrwərd] *vt* **1** PROMOTE : avancer, favoriser **2** SEND : expédier (des marchandises), faire suivre (du courrier)
forward[2] *adv* **1** : en avant, vers l'avant **2 from that day forward** : à partir de ce jour-là
forward[3] *adj* **1** : avant, en avant **2** BRASH : effronté, impertinent
forward[4] *n* : avant *m* (aux sports)
forwarder [ˈfɔrwərdər] *n* : expéditeur *m*, -trice *f*
forwardness [ˈfɔrwərdnəs] *n* : effronterie *f*, impertinence *f*
forwards [ˈfɔrwərdz] → **forward**[2]
fossil[1] [ˈfɑsəl] *adj* : fossile
fossil[2] *n* : fossile *m*
fossilize [ˈfɑsəˌlaɪz] *v* **-ized; -izing** *vt* : fossiliser — *vi* : se fossiliser
foster[1] [ˈfɔstər] *vt* **1** NURTURE : élever, placer (un enfant) **2** CHERISH : entretenir, nourrir (un espoir, etc.) **3** ENCOURAGE : favoriser, encourager
foster[2] *adj* : adoptif, d'accueil <foster parents : parents adoptifs> <foster home : famille d'accueil>
fought → **fight**[1]
foul[1] [ˈfaʊl] *vt* **1** DIRTY, POLLUTE : salir, souiller, polluer **2** CLOG : encrasser, obstruer **3** TANGLE : emmêler
foul[2] *adj* **1** REPULSIVE : infect, fétide **2** POLLUTED : pollué, vicié **3** DETESTABLE : horrible, atroce **4** OBSCENE : grossier, ordurier **5** NASTY : sale, infect <what foul weather! : quel sale temps!> **6** : déloyal, irrégulier (aux sports) <a foul play : un jeu irrégulier>
foul[3] *n* : coup *m* irrégulier, faute *f* (aux sports)
foully [ˈfaʊli] *adv* : de façon grossière
foulmouthed [ˈfaʊlˌmæu:ðd, -ˌmæʊθt] *adj* : grossier
foulness [ˈfaʊlnəs] *n* : grossièreté *f*
foul play *n* : violence *f*, meurtre *m*
foul–up [ˈfaʊlˌʌp] *n* : cafouillage *m fam*, confusion *f*
foul up *vt* **1** CONTAMINATE : polluer **2** CLOG : obstruer
found[1] → **find**[1]
found[2] [ˈfaʊnd] *vt* **1** ESTABLISH : fonder, établir **2** BASE : fonder, baser <founded on facts : basé sur des faits>
foundation [faʊnˈdeɪʃən] *n* **1** FOUNDING : fondation *f*, établissement *m* **2** BASIS : base *f*, fondement *m* **3** ENDOWMENT : fondation *f*, institution *f* dotée **4** : fondations *fpl* (d'un édifice), solage *m Can*
founder[1] [ˈfaʊndər] *vi* COLLAPSE, SINK : sombrer, s'effondrer
founder[2] *n* : fondateur *m*, -trice *f*
foundling [ˈfaʊndlɪŋ] *n* : enfant *m* trouvé, enfant *f* trouvée
foundry [ˈfaʊndri] *n, pl* **-dries** : fonderie *f*
fount [ˈfaʊnt] *n* : source *f*
fountain [ˈfaʊntən] *n* **1** : fontaine *f*, jet *m* d'eau <drinking fountain : jet d'eau potable> **2** SOURCE : fontaine *f*, source *f* **3** SPRING : source *f*
four[1] [ˈfor] *adj* : quatre
four[2] *n* : quatre *m*
fourfold [ˈforˌfo:ld, -ˈfo:ld] *adj* : quadruple
fourscore [ˈforˈskor] *adj* EIGHTY : quatre-vingts
fourteen[1] [forˈti:n] *adj* : quatorze
fourteen[2] *n* : quatorze *m*
fourteenth[1] [forˈti:nθ] *adj* : quatorzième
fourteenth[2] *n* **1** : quatorzième *mf* (dans une série) **2** : quatorzième *m* (en mathématiques) **3** (*used in dates*) <the fourteenth of June : le quatorze juin>
fourth[1] [ˈforθ] *adj* : quatrième
fourth[2] *n* **1** : quatrième *mf* (dans une série) **2** : quart *m* (en mathématiques) **3** (*used in dates*) <the Fourth of July : le quatre juillet>
fowl [ˈfaʊl] *n, pl* **fowl** *or* **fowls 1** BIRD : oiseau *m* **2** CHICKEN : poulet *m* **3** POULTRY : volaille *f*

fox[1] [ˈfɑks] *vt* TRICK : tromper, berner
fox[2] *n, pl* **foxes** : renard *m*
foxglove [ˈfɑksˌglʌv] *n* : digitale *f* (pourprée)
foxhole [ˈfɑksˌhoːl] *n* : gourbi *m*
foxy [ˈfɑksi] *adj* **foxier; -est** SLY : rusé, malin
foyer [ˈfɔɪər, ˈfɔɪˌjeɪ] *n* : vestibule *m*, entrée *f*
fracas [ˈfreɪkəs, ˈfræ-] *n, pl* **-cases** [-kəsəz] : bagarre *f*, rixe *f*
fraction [ˈfrækʃən] *n* **1** : fraction *f* (en mathématiques) **2** PORTION : fraction *f*, (petite) partie *f*
fractional [ˈfrækʃənəl] *adj* **1** : fractionnaire **2** INCONSIDERABLE : infime, tout petit
fractious [ˈfrækʃəs] adj **1** UNRULY : indiscipliné, difficile **2** IRRITABLE : revêche
fracture[1] [ˈfræktʃər] *vt* **-tured; -turing** : fracturer
fracture[2] *n* : fracture *f*
fragile [ˈfrædʒəl, -ˌdʒaɪl] *adj* : fragile
fragility [frəˈdʒɪləṭi] *n* : fragilité *f*
fragment[1] [ˈfrægˌmɛnt] *vt* : fragmenter
fragment[2] [ˈfrægmənt] *n* : fragment *m*, morceau *m*
fragmentary [ˈfrægmənˌtɛri] *adj* : fragmentaire
fragmentation [ˌfrægmənˈteɪʃən, -ˌmɛn-] *n* : fragmentation *f*
fragrance [ˈfreɪgrən*t*s] *n* : parfum *m*, fragrance *f*
fragrant [ˈfreɪgrənt] *adj* : parfumé, odorant
frail [ˈfreɪl] *adj* : frêle, fragile
frailty [ˈfreɪlti] *n, pl* **-ties** : fragilité *f*
frame[1] [ˈfreɪm] *vt* **framed; framing 1** FORMULATE : formuler, élaborer **2** BORDER, ENCLOSE : encadrer **3** INCRIMINATE : monter un coup contre
frame[2] *n* **1** PHYSIQUE : charpente *f*, ossature *f* **2** STRUCTURE : charpente *f* (d'un édifice), châssis *m* (d'une voiture), cadre *m* (d'une bicyclette, etc.) **3** BORDER : cadre *m* (d'un tableau, d'une fenêtre, etc.) **4 frames** *npl* : monture *f* (de lunettes) **5 frame of mind** : état *m* d'esprit
framework [ˈfreɪmˌwərk] *n* **1** STRUCTURE : charpente *f*, squelette *f* **2** BASIS : cadre *m*
franc [ˈfræŋk] *n* : franc *m*
franchise [ˈfrænˌtʃaɪz] *n* **1** : franchise *f* (en commerce) **2** SUFFRAGE : droit *m* de vote, suffrage *m*
frank[1] [ˈfræŋk] *vt* POSTMARK : affranchir
frank[2] *adj* CANDID : franc
frankfurter [ˈfræŋkfərṭər, -ˌfər-] *or* **frankfurt** [-fərt] *n* : saucisse *f* de Francfort, saucisse *f* à hot-dog *Can*
frankincense [ˈfræŋkənˌsɛn*t*s] *n* : encens *m*
frankly [ˈfræŋkli] *adv* : franchement
frankness [ˈfræŋknəs] *n* : franchise *f*
frantic [ˈfræntɪk] *adj* : frénétique, effréné
frantically [ˈfræntɪkli] *adv* : frénétiquement
fraternal [frəˈtərnəl] *adj* : fraternel — **fraternally** *adv*
fraternity [frəˈtərnəṭi] *n, pl* **-ties 1** BROTHERHOOD : fraternité *f* **2** : confrérie *f* d'étudiants <fraternity pin : insigne de confrérie>
fraternization [ˌfræṭərnəˈzeɪʃən] *n* : fraternisation *f*
fraternize [ˈfræṭərˌnaɪz] *vi* **-nized; -nizing** : fraterniser
fratricide [ˈfrætrəˌsaɪd] *n* : fratricide *m*
fraud [ˈfrɔd] *n* **1** DECEPTION, SWINDLE : fraude *f*, tromperie *f* **2** IMPOSTOR : imposteur *m*
fraudulent [ˈfrɔdʒələnt] *adj* : frauduleux — **fraudulently** *adv*
fraught [ˈfrɔt] *adj* : rempli, plein, chargé <fraught with danger : rempli de dangers>
fray[1] [ˈfreɪ] *vt* **1** : effilocher, effiler (des tissus, etc.) **2** IRRITATE : mettre (les nerfs) à vif — *vi* : s'effilocher
fray[2] *n* BRAWL, FIGHT : bagarre *f*, rixe *f* <to join the fray : se jeter dans la mêlée>
frazzle[1] [ˈfræzəl] *vt* **-zled; -zling 1** FRAY : effiler, effranger **2** EXHAUST : épuiser, éreinter
frazzle[2] *n* **worn to a frazzle** : éreinté, crevé *fam*
freak [ˈfriːk] *n* **1** ODDITY : phénomène *m*, monstre *m* <a freak of nature : un caprice de la nature> **2** ENTHUSIAST : fana *mf fam*
freakish [ˈfriːkɪʃ] *adj* : anormal, bizarre
freckle[1] [ˈfrɛkəl] *vi* **-led; -ling** : se couvrir de taches de rousseur, rousseler *Can*
freckle[2] *n* : tache *f* de rousseur
free[1] [ˈfriː] *vt* **freed; freeing 1** LIBERATE : libérer, relâcher **2** RELIEVE, RID : libérer, dégager **3** RELEASE, UNTIE : détacher, dégager **4** CLEAR, UNBLOCK : déboucher
free[2] *adv* **1** FREELY : en toute liberté, librement **2** : gratuitement <children admitted free : entrée gratuite pour les enfants>
free[3] *adj* **freer; freest 1** : libre <a free country : un pays libre> **2** : exempt <free from taxes : exempt d'impôt> **3** : gratuit <free admission : entrée gratuite> **4** VACANT : libre <is this seat free? : est-ce que la place est libre?> **5** OPEN : ouvert, franc **6** CLEAR : libre, dégagé
freebooter [ˈfriːˌbuːṭər] *n* : pirate *m*
freeborn [ˈfriːˈbɔrn] *adj* : né libre
freedom [ˈfriːdəm] *n* : liberté *f*
free–for–all [ˈfriːfərˌɔl] *n* : mêlée *f* générale
freelance [ˈfriːˌlæn*t*s] *adj* : indépendant

freelancer [ˈfriːˌlæntsər] *n* : travailleur *m* indépendant, travailleuse *f* indépendante; pigiste *mf*

freeload [ˈfriːˌloːd] *vi* : vivre en pique-assiette

freeloader [ˈfriːˌloːdər] *n* : pique-assiette *mf*

freely [ˈfriːli] *adv* **1** FRANKLY, OPENLY : librement **2** LAVISHLY : largement

Freemason [friːˈmeɪsən] *n* : franc-maçon *m*

Freemasonry [friːˈmeɪsənri] *n* : franc-maçonnerie *f*

freestanding [ˈfriːˈstændɪŋ] *adj* : non-encastré, sur pied

freeway [ˈfriːˌweɪ] *n* : autoroute *f*

freewill [ˈfriːˌwɪl] *adj* : volontaire

free will *n* : libre arbitre *m*

freeze[1] [ˈfriːz] *v* **froze** [ˈfroːz]; **frozen** [ˈfroːzən]; **freezing** *vt* **1** : geler (de l'eau), congeler (de l'eau, des aliments, etc.) **2** : geler, bloquer (des prix, etc.) — *vi* **1** : geler <the lake has frozen over : le lac a gelé> **2** : se congeler, se surgeler <bread freezes well : le pain se congèle bien> **3 to be frozen in one's tracks** : rester cloué sur place **4 it's freezing!** : on caille! *France fam*, on gèle **5 to freeze to death** : mourir de froid

freeze[2] *n* **1** FREEZING, FROST : gel *m* **2** : gel *m*, blocage *m* <salary freeze : gel des salaires>

freeze-dry [ˈfriːzˈdraɪ] *vt* **-dried; -drying** : lyophiliser

freezer [ˈfriːzər] *n* : congélateur *m*

freezing point *n* : point *m* de congélation

freight[1] [ˈfreɪt] *vt* : transporter (des marchandises)

freight[2] *n* **1** SHIPPING : transport *m* **2** GOODS : fret *m*, marchandises *fpl*

freighter [ˈfreɪt̬ər] *n* : cargo *m* (navire), avion-cargo *m*

French[1] [ˈfrɛntʃ] *adj* : français

French[2] *n* **1** : français *m* (langue) **2 the French** : les Français

French Canadian[1] *adj* : canadien français

French Canadian[2] *n* : Canadien *m* français, Canadienne *f* française

french fries [ˈfrɛntʃˌfraɪz] *npl* : frites *fpl*

Frenchman [ˈfrɛntʃmən] *n, pl* **-men** [-mən, -ˌmɛn] : Français *m*

Frenchwoman [ˈfrɛntʃˌwʊmən] *n, pl* **-women** [-ˌwɪmən] : Française *f*

frenetic [frɪˈnɛt̬ɪk] *adj* : frénétique — **frenetically** [-t̬ɪkli] *adv*

frenzied [ˈfrɛnzid] *adj* : frénétique, agité

frenzy [ˈfrɛnzi] *n, pl* **-zies** : frénésie *f*

frequency [ˈfriːkwəntsi] *n, pl* **-cies** : fréquence *f*

frequent[1] [friˈkwɛnt, ˈfriːkwənt] *vt* : fréquenter

frequent[2] [ˈfriːkwənt] *adj* : fréquent

frequently [ˈfriːkwəntli] *adv* : fréquemment

fresco [ˈfrɛsˌkoː] *n, pl* **-coes** : fresque *f*

fresh [ˈfrɛʃ] *adj* **1** : frais <fresh bread : du pain frais> **2** : frais, récent <fresh paint : peinture fraîche> **3** : doux <fresh water : eau douce> **4** PURE : frais, pur <fresh air : air pur> **5** NEW : nouveau <a fresh start : un nouveau départ> **6** BRISK : frais <a fresh wind : un vent frais> **7** IMPUDENT : insolent

freshen [ˈfrɛʃən] *vt* : se rafraîchir (la mémoire) — *vi* **1** : fraîchir <the wind has freshened : le vent a fraîchi> **2 to freshen up** : se rafraîchir

freshet [ˈfrɛʃət] *n* : crue *f* soudaine

freshly [ˈfrɛʃli] *adv* RECENTLY : fraîchement, récemment

freshman [ˈfrɛʃmən] *n, pl* **-men** [-mən, -ˌmɛn] : étudiant *m*, -diante *f* de première année (à l'université)

freshness [ˈfrɛʃnəs] *n* : fraîcheur *f*

freshwater [ˈfrɛʃˌwɔt̬ər] *adj* : d'eau douce

fret[1] [ˈfrɛt] *vi* **fretted; fretting** : se tracasser, s'en faire

fret[2] *n* **1** IRRITATION, WORRY : irritation *f*, inquiétude *f* **2** : frette *f* (d'une guitare)

fretful [ˈfrɛtfəl] *adj* : irritable, agité, énervé

fretfully [ˈfrɛtfəli] *adj* : avec inquiétude, avec énervement

friar [ˈfraɪər] *n* : frère *m*, moine *m*

fricassee[1] [ˈfrɪkəˌsiː, ˌfrɪkəˈsiː] *vt* **-seed; -seeing** : fricasser

fricassee[2] *n* : fricassée *f*

friction [ˈfrɪkʃən] *n* **1** RUBBING : friction *f*, frottement *m* **2** DISAGREEMENT : friction *f*, désaccord *m*

Friday [ˈfraɪˌdeɪ, -di] *n* : vendredi *m*

friend [ˈfrɛnd] *n* : ami *m*, amie *f*

friendless [ˈfrɛndləs] *adj* : sans amis

friendliness [ˈfrɛndlinəs] *n* : gentillesse *f*, attitude *f* amicale

friendly [ˈfrɛndli] *adj* **friendlier; -est** : gentil, amical

friendship [ˈfrɛndˌʃɪp] *n* : amitié *f*

frieze [ˈfriːz] *n* : frise *f*

frigate [ˈfrɪgət] *n* : frégate *f*

fright [ˈfraɪt] *n* : peur *f*, frayeur *f*

frighten [ˈfraɪtən] *vt* : faire peur à, effrayer

frightful [ˈfraɪtfəl] *adj* **1** TERRIFYING : terrible, épouvantable **2** SHOCKING, STARTLING : effrayant, effarant <frightful costs : coûts effarants> **3** EXTREME : terrible <a frightful thirst : une soif terrible>

frightfully [ˈfraɪtfəli] *adv* : terriblement, affreusement

frightfulness [ˈfraɪtfəlnəs] *n* : horreur *f*

frigid [ˈfrɪdʒɪd] *adj* : glacial

frigidity [frɪˈdʒɪdət̬i] *n* **1** : frigidité *f* (en médecine) **2** COLDNESS : froideur *f*

frill [ˈfrɪl] *n* **1** RUFFLE : jabot *m* (d'une chemise), volant *m* (d'une jupe) **2** EMBELLISHMENT : fioriture *f*

frilly [ˈfrɪli] *adj* **frillier; -est 1 :** à jabot, à volant **2 :** à fioritures (se dit du style, etc.)
fringe[1] [ˈfrɪndʒ] *vt* **fringed; fringing :** franger, border
fringe[2] *n* **1 :** frange *f* **2** EDGE **:** bordure *f*, bord *m* **3 fringe benefits :** avantages *mpl* sociaux, avantages *mpl* en nature
frisk [ˈfrɪsk] *vt* SEARCH **:** fouiller (un suspect) — *vi* FROLIC **:** gambader, folâtrer
friskiness [ˈfrɪskinəs] *n* **:** vivacité *f*
frisky [ˈfrɪski] *adj* **friskier; -est 1** SPIRITED **:** fringant (se dit d'un cheval) **2** PLAYFUL **:** vif, folâtre
fritter[1] [ˈfrɪtər] *vt or* **to fritter away :** gaspiller
fritter[2] *n* **:** beignet *m*
frivolity [frɪˈvɑləṭi] *n, pl* **-ties :** frivolité *f*
frivolous [ˈfrɪvələs] *adj* **:** frivole — **frivolously** *adv*
frizz[1] [ˈfrɪz] *vt* **:** friser (ses cheveux)
frizz[2] *n* **:** cheveux *mpl* frisés
frizzy [ˈfrɪzi] *adj* **frizzier; -est :** frisé, bouclé
fro [ˈfro:] *adv* **to and fro :** de long en large
frock [ˈfrɑk] *n* DRESS **:** robe *f*
frog [ˈfrɔg, ˈfrɑg] *n* **1 :** grenouille *f* **2** LOOP **:** brandebourg *m* **3 to have a frog in one's throat :** avoir un chat dans la gorge
frogman [ˈfrɔg,mæn, ˈfrɑg-, -mən] *n, pl* **-men** [-mən, -ˌmɛn] **:** homme-grenouille *m*
frolic[1] [ˈfrɑlɪk] *vi* **-icked; -icking :** gambader, folâtrer
frolic[2] *n* **:** gambades *fpl*, ébats *mpl*
frolicsome [ˈfrɑlɪksəm] *adj* **:** folâtre
from [ˈfrʌm, ˈfrɑm] *prep* **1** (*indicating a starting point*) **:** de, à partir de <they're coming from Boston : ils arrivent de Boston> <from that day on : à partir de ce jour-là> **2** (*indicating removal or separation*) **:** contre <protection from the sun : protection contre le soleil> **3** (*indicating a source or cause*) **:** de, par, à <he's suffering from a cold : il souffre d'un rhume> <to work from necessity : travailler par nécessité> <to borrow money from a friend : emprunter de l'argent à un ami>
frond [ˈfrɑnd] *n* **:** fronde *f* (d'une fougère), feuille *f* (d'un palmier)
front[1] [ˈfrʌnt] *vi* **1** FACE **:** faire face <the building fronts south : l'édifice fait face au sud> **2 to front for :** servir de couverture à (qqn) **3 to front on :** donner sur — *vt* FACE **:** donner sur
front[2] *adj* **:** de devant, premier, (en) avant <the front row : le premier rang>
front[3] *n* **1 :** avant *m*, devant *m* (d'une voiture, etc.), façade *f* (d'un bâtiment) **2** APPEARANCE **:** air *m*, contenance *f* <a bold front : une contenance assurée> **3 :** front *m* (en météorologie) **4** VANGUARD **:** front *m* <the western front : le front ouest>
frontage [ˈfrʌntɪdʒ] *n* **:** façade *f*, devanture *f*
frontal [ˈfrʌntəl] *adj* **:** frontal, de front
frontier [ˌfrʌnˈtɪr] *n* **:** frontière *f*
frontiersman [ˌfrʌnˈtɪrzmən] *n, pl* **-men** [-mən, -ˌmɛn] **:** homme *m* de la frontière
frontispiece [ˈfrʌntəs,pi:s] *n* **:** frontispice *m*
frost[1] [ˈfrɔst] *vt* **1** FREEZE **:** geler, givrer **2** ICE **:** glacer (un gâteau)
frost[2] *n* **1 :** givre *m* **2** FREEZING **:** gel *m*, gelée *f*
frostbite [ˈfrɔst,baɪt] *n* **:** gelure *f*
frostbitten [ˈfrɔst,bɪtən] *adj* **:** gelé
frosting [ˈfrɔstɪŋ] *n* ICING **:** glaçage *m* (d'un gâteau)
frosty [ˈfrɔsti] *adj* **frostier; -est 1 :** givré, couvert de givre <frosty windows : vitres givrées> **2** FRIGID **:** glacial
froth [ˈfrɔθ] *n, pl* **froths** [ˈfrɔθs, ˈfrɔðz] **:** écume *f*, mousse *f*, broue *f Can*
frothy [ˈfrɔθi, -ði] *adj* **frothier; -est :** écumeux, mousseux
frown[1] [ˈfraʊn] *vi* **:** froncer les sourcils
frown[2] *n* **:** froncement *m* de sourcils
frowsy *or* **frowzy** [ˈfraʊzi] *adj* **frowsier** *or* **frowzier; -est :** négligé, peu soigné
froze, frozen → **freeze**[1]
frugal [ˈfru:gəl] *adj* **:** économe, frugal
frugality [fru:ˈgæləṭi] *n* **:** frugalité *f*
frugally [ˈfru:gəli] *adv* **:** simplement, frugalement
fruit[1] [ˈfru:t] *vi* **:** donner des fruits
fruit[2] *n* **1 :** fruit *m* **2 fruits** *npl* RESULTS **:** fruits *mpl* <the fruits of one's labors : les fruits de son travail>
fruitcake [ˈfru:t,keɪk] *n* **:** cake *m*
fruitful [ˈfru:tfəl] *adj* **:** fécond, fructueux
fruitfulness [ˈfru:tfəlnəs] *n* **:** fécondité *f*
fruition [fru:ˈɪʃən] *n* **:** réalisation *f* <to come to fruition : se réaliser>
fruitless [ˈfru:tləs] *adj* **:** stérile <a fruitless discussion : une discussion sans résultat>
fruitlessly [ˈfru:tləsli] *adv* **:** en vain
fruity [ˈfru:ṭi] *adj* **fruitier; -est :** fruité, de fruit
frumpy [ˈfrʌmpi] *adj* **frumpier; -est :** mal fagoté
frustrate [ˈfrʌs,treɪt] *vt* **-trated; -trating 1** DISAPPOINT, DISCOURAGE **:** frustrer, décevoir **2** THWART **:** contrecarrer, faire échouer
frustrating [ˈfrʌs,treɪṭɪŋ] *adj* **:** frustrant
frustration [ˌfrʌsˈtreɪʃən] *n* **:** frustration *f*
fry[1] [ˈfraɪ] *v* **fried; frying :** frire
fry[2] *n, pl* **fries 1** FRYING **:** friture *f* **2 fries** *npl* FRENCH FRIES **:** frites *fpl* **3** *pl* **fry :** fretin *m* (poisson) **4 small fry :** menu fretin *m*
frying pan *n* **:** poêle *f*, poêlon *m Can*

fuddle [ˈfʌdəl] *vt* **-dled; -dling** : brouiller, embrouiller
fudge[1] [ˈfʌdʒ] *v* **fudged; fudging** *vt* **1** FALSIFY : truquer **2** DODGE : esquiver — *vi* HEDGE : esquiver le problème
fudge[2] *n* : caramel *m* mou
fuel[1] [ˈfjuːəl] *vt* **-eled** *or* **-elled; -eling** *or* **-elling 1** : alimenter en combustible (un fourneau), ravitailler en carburant (un navire, etc.) **2** STIMULATE : aviver (des soupçons, etc.)
fuel[2] *n* : combustible *m*, carburant *m*
fugitive[1] [ˈfjuːdʒəṭɪv] *adj* **1** RUNAWAY : fugitif **2** ELUSIVE : fugace, éphémère
fugitive[2] *n* : fugitif *m*, -tive *f*
fulcrum [ˈfʊlkrəm, ˈfʌl-] *n, pl* **-crums** *or* **-cra** [-krə] : point *m* d'appui
fulfill *or* **fulfil** [fʊlˈfɪl] *vt* **-filled; -filling 1** EXECUTE : accomplir, réaliser **2** FILL, MEET : remplir, satisfaire à, répondre à
fulfillment [fʊlˈfɪlmənt] *n* **1** ACCOMPLISHMENT : accomplissement *m*, réalisation *f* **2** SATISFACTION : satisfaction *f*, contentement *m*
full[1] [ˈfʊl, ˈfʌl] *adv* **1** VERY : très, fort <you knew full well : tu le savais très bien> **2** ENTIRELY : entièrement <to turn full around : faire volte-face> **3** DIRECTLY : carrément <he hit me full in the face : il m'a frappé en plein visage>
full[2] *adj* **1** FILLED : plein, rempli, complet <the hotel is full : l'hôtel est complet> **2** COMPLETE, ENTIRE : entier, total <a full year : une année entière> **3** PLUMP : plein, rond <a full face : un visage rond> **4** AMPLE : ample **5** SATIATED : repu, rassasié <I'm full : j'ai assez mangé>
full[3] *n* **1 in ~** : en détail, intégralement **2 to the full** : au plus haut degré
full–fledged [ˈfʊlˈflɛdʒd] *adj* : à part entière
fullness [ˈfʊlnəs] *n* **1** ABUNDANCE : abondance *f* **2** : rondeur *f* (d'une silhouette), ampleur *f* (d'un vêtement)
fully [ˈfʊli] *adv* **1** COMPLETELY : tout à fait, complètement **2** : au moins <fully nine tenths of us : au moins neuf dixièmes d'entre nous>
fulsome [ˈfʊlsəm] *adj* : excessif, exagéré
fumble[1] [ˈfʌmbəl] *v* **-bled; -bling** *vt* : manier maladroitement, mal attraper (aux sports) — *vi* : tâtonner, fouiller
fumble[2] *n* : tâtonnement *m*
fume[1] [ˈfjuːm] *vi* **fumed; fuming 1** SMOKE : émettre des vapeurs, fumer **2** RAGE : fulminer, bouillonner
fume[2] *n* : émanation *f*, gaz *m* d'échappement (d'une voiture)
fumigate [ˈfjuːməˌgeɪt] *vt* **-gated; -gating** : désinfecter par fumigation
fumigation [ˌfjuːməˈgeɪʃən] *n* : fumigation *f*
fun[1] [ˈfʌn] *adj* : amusant, marrant *fam*
fun[2] *n* **1** ENJOYMENT : amusement *m*, plaisir *m*, fun *m Can fam* <to have fun : s'amuser> **2 for ~** : pour rire **3 to make fun of** : se moquer de
function[1] [ˈfʌŋkʃən] *vi* **1** WORK : fonctionner, marcher **2 to function as** : faire fonction de, servir de
function[2] *n* **1** OCCUPATION : fonction *f*, charge *f* **2** PURPOSE : fonction *f*, rôle *m* **3** CEREMONY : réception *f*, cérémonie *f*
functional [ˈfʌŋkʃənəl] *adj* : fonctionnel — **functionally** *adv*
functionary [ˈfʌŋkʃəˌnɛri] *n, pl* **-aries** : fonctionnaire *mf*
fund[1] [ˈfʌnd] *vt* : financer, fournir des fonds à
fund[2] *n* **1** SUPPLY : fond *m*, réserve *f* <a fund of jokes : un répertoire de plaisanteries> **2** : caisse *f*, fonds *mpl* <relief fund : caisse de secours> **3 funds** *npl* RESOURCES : fonds *mpl*, capitaux *mpl*
fundamental[1] [ˌfʌndəˈmɛntəl] *adj* **1** BASIC : fondamental, essentiel **2** PRINCIPAL : principal — **fundamentally** *adv*
fundamental[2] *n* : principe *m* essentiel
funeral[1] [ˈfjuːnərəl] *adj* : funèbre, funéraire
funeral[2] *n* : enterrement *m*, funérailles *fpl*
funeral home *or* **funeral parlor** *n* : entreprise *f* de pompes funèbres, salon *m* funéraire *Can*, salon *m* mortuaire *Can*
funereal [fjuːˈnɪriəl] *adj* : funèbre
fungal [ˈfʌŋgəl] *adj* : fongique
fungicide [ˈfʌndʒəˌsaɪd, ˈfʌŋgə-] *n* : fongicide *m*
fungicidal [ˌfʌndʒəˈsaɪdəl, ˌfʌŋgə-] *adj* : fongicide
fungous [ˈfʌŋgəs] → **fungal**
fungus [ˈfʌŋgəs] *n, pl* **fungi** [ˈfʌnˌdʒaɪ, ˈfʌŋˌgaɪ] **1** MUSHROOM : champignon *m* **2** MOLD : moisissure *f*
funnel[1] [ˈfʌnəl] *vt* **-neled; -neling 1** : faire passer dans un entonnoir **2** CHANNEL : canaliser
funnel[2] *n* **1** : entonnoir *m* **2** SMOKESTACK : cheminée *f*
funnies [ˈfʌniz] *npl* : bandes *fpl* dessinées
funny [ˈfʌni] *adj* **funnier; -est 1** AMUSING : drôle, amusant, rigolo *fam* **2** PECULIAR : bizarre, curieux, drôle
fur[1] [ˈfər] *adj* : de fourrure
fur[2] *n* **1** : fourrure *f*, pelage *m* (d'un animal) **2** : fourrure *f* <fake fur : fausse fourrure>
furbish [ˈfərbɪʃ] *vt* **1** POLISH : fourbir, polir **2** RENOVATE : remettre à neuf
furious [ˈfjʊriəs] *adj* **1** ANGRY : furieux **2** FIERCE, VIOLENT : acharné, déchaîné <a furious storm : un orage déchaîné>

furiously [ˈfjʊriəsli] *adv* **1** ANGRILY : furieusement **2** FRANTICALLY : frénétiquement

furlong [ˈfər,lɔŋ] *n* : furlong *m* (201,17 mètres)

furlough[1] [ˈfər,lo:] *vt* : accorder une permission à

furlough[2] *n* : congé *m*, permission *f*

furnace [ˈfərnəs] *n* : fourneau *m*, fournaise *f Can*

furnish [ˈfərnɪʃ] *vt* **1** SUPPLY : fournir, donner **2** : meubler <a furnished apartment : un appartement meublé>

furnishings [ˈfərnɪʃɪŋz] *npl* : ameublement *m*, meubles *mpl*

furniture [ˈfərnɪtʃər] *n* : meubles *mpl*

furor [ˈfjʊr,ɔr, -ər] *n* **1** RAGE : fureur *f* **2** UPROAR : scandale *m*, tumulte *m*

furrier [ˈfəriər] *n* : fourreur *m*, -reuse *f*

furrow[1] [ˈfəro:] *vt* **1** : sillonner (la terre) **2 to furrow one's brow** : plisser son front

furrow[2] *n* **1** : sillon *m* **2** WRINKLE : ride *f*

furry [ˈfəri] *adj* **furrier; -est** : au poil touffu (se dit d'un animal), en peluche (se dit d'un jouet, etc.)

further[1] [ˈfərðər] *vt* PROMOTE : promouvoir, avancer

further[2] *adv* **1** FARTHER : plus loin **2** MORE : davantage, plus **3** MOREOVER : en outre

further[3] *adj* **1** FARTHER : plus éloigné **2** ADDITIONAL : nouveau, supplémentaire <until further notice : jusqu'à nouvel ordre>

furtherance [ˈfərðərənts] *n* : avancement *m*

furthermore [ˈfərðər,mor] *adv* : en outre, de plus

furthermost [ˈfərðər,mo:st] *adj* : le plus lointain

furthest [ˈfərðəst] *adv & adj* → **farthest**

furtive [ˈfərṭɪv] *adj* : furtif — **furtively** *adv*

furtiveness [ˈfərṭɪvnəs] *n* : caractère *m* furtif

fury [ˈfjʊri] *n, pl* **-ries 1** RAGE : furie *f*, fureur *f* **2** VIOLENCE : fureur *f*, violence *f* **3** FRENZY : frénésie *f*

fuse[1] *or* **fuze** [ˈfju:z] *vt* **fused** *or* **fuzed; fusing** *or* **fuzing** : munir d'un fusible

fuse[2] *v* **fused; fusing** *vt* **1** MELT : fondre (des métaux) **2** BLEND, UNITE : fusionner, unifier — *vi* : fusionner

fuse[3] *n* **1** : mèche *f* (d'un explosif) **2** : fusible *m*, plomb *m* <to blow a fuse : faire sauter un plomb> **3** *usu* **fuze** : détonateur *m*

fuselage [ˈfju:sə,lɑʒ, -zə-] *n* : fuselage *m*

fusillade [ˈfju:sə,lɑd, -,leɪd, ,fju:səˈ-, -zə-] *n* : fusillade *f*

fusion [ˈfju:ʒən] *n* : fusion *f*

fuss[1] [ˈfʌs] *vi* **1** : s'affairer <fussing over the children : s'affairant autour des enfants> **2** WORRY : s'inquiéter, se tracasser

fuss[2] *n* **1** AGITATION, COMMOTION : agitation *f*, remue-ménage *m* **2** PROTEST : histoires *fpl* <to make a fuss : faire des histoires>

fussbudget [ˈfʌs,bʌdʒət] *n* : tatillon *m*, -lonne *f*

fussiness [ˈfʌsinəs] *n* : façon *f* tatillonne

fussy [ˈfʌsi] *adj* **fussier; -est 1** IRRITABLE : irritable **2** FINICKY : tatillon, pointilleux, difficile <he's a fussy eater : il est difficile pour la nourriture> **3** OVERELABORATE : tarabiscoté

futile [ˈfju:ṭəl, ˈfju:,taɪl] *adj* : futile, vain

futility [fju:ˈtɪləṭi] *n* : futilité *f*

future[1] [ˈfju:tʃər] *adj* : futur

future[2] *n* **1** : avenir *m*, futur *m* <in the near future : dans un proche avenir> **2** *or* **future tense** : futur *m*

futuristic [,fju:tʃəˈrɪstɪk] *adj* : futuriste

fuze → **fuse**

fuzz [ˈfʌz] *n* **1** DOWN : duvet *m* **2** FLUFF : peluches *fpl*

fuzziness [ˈfʌzinəs] *n* **1** : caractère *m* duveteux **2** : flou *m* (en photographie)

fuzzy [ˈfʌzi] *adj* **fuzzier; -est 1** DOWNY : duveteux **2** INDISTINCT : flou

G

g [ˈdʒi:] *n, pl* **g's** *or* **gs** [ˈdʒi:z] : g *m*, septième lettre de l'alphabet

gab[1] [ˈgæb] *vi* **gabbed; gabbing** : bavarder, jacasser, papoter

gab[2] *n* CHATTER : bavardage *m*, papotage *m*

gabardine [ˈgæbər,di:n] *n* : gabardine *f*

gabby [ˈgæbi] *adj* **gabbier; -est** : bavard

gable [ˈgeɪbəl] *n* : pignon *m*

Gabonese[1] [,gæbɔˈni:z] *adj* : gabonais

Gabonese[2] *n* : Gabonais *m*, -naise *f*

gad [ˈgæd] *vi* **gadded; gadding** *or* **to gad about** : se balader, vadrouiller *fam*

gadfly [ˈgæd,flaɪ] *n, pl* **-flies 1** : taon *m* (insecte) **2** FAULTFINDER : critiqueur *m*, -queuse *f*; casse-pieds *mf fam*

gadget [ˈgædʒət] *n* : gadget *m*, bebelle *f Can fam*

gadgetry [ˈgædʒətri] *n* : gadgets *mpl*

gaff [ˈgæf] *n* HOOK : gaffe *f*

gaffe [ˈgæf] *n* : gaffe *f*

gag[1] [ˈgæg] *v* **gagged; gagging** *vt* : bâillonner — *vi* **1** CHOKE : s'étrangler **2** RETCH : avoir des haut-le-coeur

gag[2] *n* **1** : bâillon *m* **2** JOKE : blague *f*

gage → **gauge**

gaggle [ˈgægəl] *n* : troupeau *m* (d'oies, etc.)

gaiety [ˈgeɪət̬i] *n, pl* **-eties** : gaieté *f*

gaily [ˈgeɪli] *adv* : gaiement, de bonne humeur

gain[1] [ˈgeɪn] *vt* **1** ACQUIRE : acquérir, gagner, obtenir <to gain ground : gagner du terrain> <to gain experience : acquérir de l'expérience> **2** REACH : arriver, atteindre <to gain the shore : atteindre la rive> **3** INCREASE : prendre <to gain weight : prendre du poids> — *vi* **1** PROFIT : gagner, profiter **2** ADVANCE : avancer (se dit d'une horloge) **3 to gain on** : rattraper

gain[2] *n* **1** PROFIT : profit *m*, bénéfice *m* <gains and losses : profits et pertes> **2** INCREASE : augmentation *f*

gainful [ˈgeɪnfəl] *adj* : rémunéré

gait [ˈgeɪt] *n* : démarche *f*

gal [ˈgæl] *n* : jeune fille *f*

gala[1] [ˈgeɪlə, ˈgæ-, ˈgɑ-] *adj* : de gala

gala[2] *n* : gala *m*

galactic [gəˈlæktɪk] *adj* : galactique

galaxy [ˈgæləksi] *n, pl* **-axies** : galaxie *f*

gale [ˈgeɪl] *n* **1** WIND : vent *m* fort **2** OUTBURST : éclat *m* <gales of laughter : éclats de rire>

gall[1] [ˈgɔl] *vt* **1** CHAFE : écorcher, excorier **2** IRRITATE : irriter, exaspérer

gall[2] *n* **1** BILE : bile *f* **2** IMPUDENCE : impudence *f* **3** SORE : écorchure *f* **4** : galle *f* (d'une plante)

gallant [ˈgælənt] *adj* **1** BRAVE : vaillant, courageux **2** CHIVALROUS : galant, courtois

gallantly [ˈgæləntli] *adv* **1** BRAVELY : vaillamment **2** CHIVALROUSLY : galamment

gallantry [ˈgæləntri] *n, pl* **-ries** : galanterie *f*

gallbladder [ˈgɔlˌblædər] *n* : vesicule *f* biliaire

galleon [ˈgæljən] *n* : galion *m*

gallery [ˈgæləri] *n, pl* **-leries 1** BALCONY : galerie *f*, tribune *f* <press gallery : tribune de la presse> **2** ARCADE, CORRIDOR : galerie *f* **3** *or* **art gallery** : musée *m* des beaux-arts, galerie *f*

galley [ˈgæli] *n, pl* **-leys 1** SHIP : galère *f* **2** KITCHEN : coquerie *f* (d'un navire)

gallium [ˈgæliəm] *n* : gallium *m*

gallivant [ˈgæləˌvænt] *vi* : se balader, courir la galipote *Can*

gallon [ˈgælən] *n* : gallon *m*

gallop[1] [ˈgæləp] *vi* : galoper

gallop[2] *n* : galop *m*

gallows [ˈgæˌloːz] *n, pl* **-lows** *or* **-lowses** [-ˌloːzəz] : gibet *m*, potence *f*

gallstone [ˈgɔlˌstoːn] *n* : calcul *m* biliaire

galore [gəˈlor] *adj* : en abondance

galoshes [gəˈlɑʃəz] *npl* : caoutchoucs *mpl*, claques *fpl Can*

galvanize [ˈgælvənˌaɪz] *vt* **-nized; -nizing** : galvaniser

Gambian[1] [ˈgæmbiən] *adj* : gambien

Gambian[2] *n* : Gambien *m*, -bienne *f*

gambit [ˈgæmbɪt] *n* **1** : gambit *m* (aux échecs) **2** STRATAGEM : stratagème *m*, manœuvre *f*

gamble[1] [ˈgæmbəl] *v* **-bled; -bling** *vi* : jouer — *vt* WAGER : parier

gamble[2] *n* **1** BET : pari *m* **2** RISK : entreprise *f* risquée

gambler [ˈgæmbələr] *n* : joueur *m*, joueuse *f*

gambol [ˈgæmbəl] *vi* **-boled** *or* **-bolled; -boling** *or* **-bolling** : gambader

game[1] [ˈgeɪm] *adj* **1** PLUCKY : courageux **2** READY : partant <to be game for anything : être toujours partant> **3** LAME : estropié

game[2] *n* **1** : jeu *m* <game of chance : jeu de hasard> **2** MATCH : match *m*, partie *f* **3** : gibier *m* <big game : gros gibier>

gamekeeper [ˈgeɪmˌkiːpər] *n* : garde-chasse *m*

gamely [ˈgeɪmli] *adv* : courageusement

gamete [ˈgæˌmiːt, gəˈmiːt] *n* : gamète *m*

gamma ray [ˈgæmə] *n* : rayon *m* gamma

gamut [ˈgæmət] *n* : gamme *f* <the whole gamut : toute la gamme>

gamy *or* **gamey** [ˈgeɪmi] *adj* **gamier; -est** : faisandé

gander [ˈgændər] *n* **1** : jars *m* (oiseau) **2** GLANCE : coup *m* d'oeil

gang[1] [ˈgæŋ] *vi* **to gang up on** : se liguer contre

gang[2] *n* : bande *f*, gang *f Can fam*, gang *m France* (de criminels)

gangling [ˈgæŋglɪŋ] *adj* LANKY : dégingandé

ganglion [ˈgæŋgliən] *n, pl* **-glia** /-gliə/ : ganglion *m*

gangplank [ˈgæŋˌplæŋk] *n* : passerelle *f*

gangrene [ˈgæŋˌgriːn, ˈgæn-; gæŋˈ-, gænˈ-] *n* : gangrène *f*

gangrenous [ˈgæŋgrənəs] *adj* : gangreneux

gangster [ˈgæŋstər] *n* : gangster *m*

gangway [ˈgæŋˌweɪ] *n* **1** PASSAGEWAY : passage *m* **2** GANGPLANK : passerelle *f* **3 gangway!** : dégagez le passage!

gannet [ˈgænət] *n* : fou *m* de Bassan

gap [ˈgæp] *n* **1** OPENING : trou *m*, vide *m*, brèche *f* **2** INTERVAL : intervalle *m*, période *f* **3** DISPARITY : gouffre *m*, écart *m* **4** LACUNA : lacune *f* <a gap in one's knowledge : une lacune dans sa connaissance> **5** GORGE : gorge *f*, col *m*

gape[1] [ˈgeɪp] *vi* **gaped; gaping 1** OPEN : bâiller, s'ouvrir **2** STARE : rester bouche bée

gape[2] *n* **1** CHASM, OPENING : trou *m* béant **2** STARE : regard *m* ébahi, regard *m* bouche bée

garage[1] [gəˈrɑʒ, -ˈrɑdʒ] *vt* **-raged; -raging** : mettre au garage

garage[2] *n* : garage *m*

garb[1] [ˈgarb] *vt* : vêtir
garb[2] *n* : costume *m*, mise *f*
garbage [ˈgarbɪdʒ] *n* : ordures *fpl*
garbage can *n* : poubelle *f*
garbageman [ˈgarbɪdʒmən] *n, pl* **-men** [-mən, -ˌmɛn] : éboueur *m*
garble [ˈgarbəl] *vt* **-bled; -bling** : raconter de travers, déformer, embrouiller
garbled [ˈgarbəld] *adj* : confus, embrouillé, déformé
garden[1] [ˈgardən] *vi* : jardiner
garden[2] *n* : jardin *m*
gardener [ˈgardənər] *n* : jardinier *m*, -nière *f*
gardenia [garˈdi:njə] *n* : gardénia *m*
gargantuan [garˈgæntʃuən] *adj* : gargantuesque
gargle[1] [ˈgargəl] *vi* **-gled; -gling** : se gargariser
gargle[2] *n* : gargarisme *m* (acte et produit)
gargoyle [ˈgarˌgɔɪl] *n* : gargouille *f*
garish [ˈgærɪʃ] *adj* : criard, voyant
garland[1] [ˈgarlənd] *vt* : enguirlander (de fleurs, etc.)
garland[2] *n* : guirlande *f*
garlic [ˈgarlɪk] *n* : ail *m*
garment [ˈgarmənt] *n* : vêtement *m*
garner [ˈgarnər] *vt* : accumuler, recueillir, engranger (des récoltes)
garnet [ˈgarnət] *n* : grenat *m*
garnish[1] [ˈgarnɪʃ] *vt* : garnir
garnish[2] *n* : garniture *f*
garret [ˈgærət] *n* : mansarde *f*
garrison[1] [ˈgærəsən] *vt* **1** QUARTER : mettre (des troupes) en garnison **2** OCCUPY : placer une garnison dans (une ville, etc.)
garrison[2] *n* : garnison *f*
garrulous [ˈgærələs] *adj* : loquace, bavard
garrulousness [ˈgærələsnəs] *n* : loquacité *f*
garter [ˈgarṭər] *n* : jarretière *f*
gas[1] [ˈgæs] *v* **gassed; gassing** *vt* : gazer — *vi* **to gas up** : faire le plein d'essence
gas[2] *n, pl* **gases 1** : gaz *m* <to cook with gas : cuisiner au gaz> **2** GASOLINE : essence *f*
gaseous [ˈgæʃəs, ˈgæsiəs] *adj* : gazeux
gash[1] [ˈgæʃ] *vt* : entailler
gash[2] *n* : entaille *f*
gasket [ˈgæskət] *n* : joint *m*
gasoline [ˈgæsəˌli:n, ˌgæsəˈ-] *n* : essence *f*, gaz *m Can fam*
gasp[1] [ˈgæsp] *vi* **1** : avoir le souffle coupé (par la surprise, etc.) **2** PANT : haleter — *vt* : dire en haletant
gasp[2] *n* : halètement *m* <to the last gasp : jusqu'au dernier souffle>
gastric [ˈgæstrɪk] *adj* : gastrique
gastronomy [gæsˈtrɑnəmi] *n* : gastronomie *f* — **gastronomic** [ˌgæstrəˈnɑmɪk] *adj*
gate [ˈgeɪt] *n* **1** DOOR : porte *f* **2** BARRIER : barrière *f*, grille *f*
gatekeeper [ˈgeɪtˌki:pər] *n* : gardien *m*, -dienne *f*; portier *m*, -tière *f*
gateway [ˈgeɪtˌweɪ] *n* : porte *f*, portail *m*
gather[1] [ˈgæðər] *vt* **1** ASSEMBLE : rassembler **2** COLLECT : recueillir, ramasser **3** DEDUCE : déduire **4** : froncer (une étoffe) **5 to gather speed** : prendre de la vitesse — *vi* ASSEMBLE : se rassembler, se réunir
gather[2] *n* : fronce *f* (d'une étoffe)
gathering [ˈgæðərɪŋ] *n* : rassemblement *m*
gauche [ˈgo:ʃ] *adj* : gauche
gaudy [ˈgɔdi] *adj* **gaudier; -est** : criard, tape-à-l'oeil
gauge[1] [ˈgeɪdʒ] *vt* **gauged; gauging 1** MEASURE : jauger, mesurer **2** ESTIMATE : évaluer, calculer
gauge[2] *n* **1** INDICATOR : jauge *f*, indicateur *m* **2** CALIBER : calibre *m* **3** INDICATION : moyen *m* de jauger, test *m* (de caractère, etc.)
gaunt [ˈgɔnt] *adj* : décharné, émacié
gauntlet [ˈgɔntlət] *n* : gant *m* (à crispin) <to throw down the gauntlet : jeter le gant>
gauze [ˈgɔz] *n* : gaze *f*
gauzy [ˈgɔzi] *adj* **gauzier; -est** : transparent, diaphane
gave → **give**[1]
gavel [ˈgævəl] *n* : marteau *m* (de magistrat, etc.)
gawk [ˈgɔk] *vi* **to gawk at** : regarder bouche bée, être bouche bée devant
gawky [ˈgɔki] *adj* **gawkier; -est** : gauche, malhabile, emprunté
gay [ˈgeɪ] *adj* **1** MERRY : gai, joyeux **2** BRIGHT, COLORFUL : vif, éclatant **3** HOMOSEXUAL : gai, gay
gaze[1] [ˈgeɪz] *vi* **gazed; gazing** : regarder (fixement)
gaze[2] *n* : regard *m*
gazelle [gəˈzɛl] *n* : gazelle *f*
gazette [gəˈzɛt] *n* **1** NEWSPAPER : journal *m* **2** : journal *m* officiel
gazetteer [ˌgæzəˈtɪr] *n* : dictionnaire *m* géographique, index *m* géographique
gear[1] [ˈgɪr] *vt* ADAPT, ORIENT : adapter <a book geared to children : un livre adapté aux enfants> — *vi* **to gear up** : se préparer, être fin prêt
gear[2] *n* **1** EQUIPMENT : équipement *m*, matériel *m* <fishing gear : matériel de pêche> **2** BELONGINGS : effets *mpl* personnels **3** SPEED : vitesse *f* <to change gear : changer de vitesse> <to be in first gear : être en première> **4** COGWHEEL : roue *f* dentée, pignon *m*
gearshift [ˈgɪrˌʃɪft] *n* : levier *m* de vitesses
geese → **goose**
Geiger counter [ˈgaɪgərˌkaʊntər] *n* : compteur *m* Geiger
gelatin [ˈdʒɛlətən] *n* : gélatine *f*
gem [ˈdʒɛm] *n* **1** : pierre *f* précieuse, gemme *f* **2** JEWEL : joyau *m* <the gem

of my collection : le joyau de ma collection>
Gemini |ˈdʒɛməˌnaɪ| *n* : Gémeaux *mpl*
gemstone |ˈdʒɛmˌsto:n| *n* : pierre *f* précieuse
gender |ˈdʒɛndər| *n* **1** : genre *m* (en grammaire) **2** SEX : sexe *m*
gene |ˈdʒi:n| *n* : gène *m*
genealogical |ˌdʒi:niəˈlɑdʒɪkəl| *adj* : généalogique
genealogy |ˌdʒi:niˈɑlədʒi, ˌdʒɛ-, -ˈæ-| *n, pl* **-gies** : généalogie *f*
genera → **genus**
general[1] |ˈdʒɛnrəl, ˈdʒɛnə-| *adj* : général <as a general rule : en règle générale>
general[2] *n* **1** : général *m* (militaire) **2 in ~** : en général
generality |ˌdʒɛnəˈrælət̬i| *n, pl* **-ties** : généralité *f*
generalization |ˌdʒɛnrələˈzeɪʃən, ˌdʒɛnərə-| *n* : généralisation *f*
generalize |ˈdʒɛnrəˌlaɪz, ˈdʒɛnərə-| *vi* **-ized; -izing** : généraliser
generally |ˈdʒɛnrəli, ˈdʒɛnərə-| *adv* **1** USUALLY : généralement, en général **2** OVERALL, WIDELY : dans l'ensemble, en général
generate |ˈdʒɛnəˌreɪt| *vt* **-ated; -ating** : générer
generation |ˌdʒɛnəˈreɪʃən| *n* : génération *f*
generator |ˈdʒɛnəˌreɪt̬ər| *n* **1** PRODUCER : générateur *m* **2** : génératrice *f* (d'énergie électrique)
generic |dʒəˈnɛrɪk| *adj* : générique
generosity |ˌdʒɛnəˈrɑsət̬i| *n, pl* **-ties** : générosité *f*
generous |ˈdʒɛnərəs| *adj* **1** OPENHANDED : généreux **2** ABUNDANT, COPIOUS : abondant, copieux — **generously** *adv*
genetic |dʒəˈnɛt̬ɪk| *adj* : génétique — **genetically** *adv*
geneticist |dʒəˈnɛt̬ɪsəst| *n* : généticien *m*, -cienne *f*
genetics |dʒəˈnɛt̬ɪks| *n* : génétique *f*
genial |ˈdʒi:niəl| *adj* : affable, cordial, aimable — **genially** *adv*
geniality |ˌdʒi:niˈælət̬i| *n* : cordialité *f*
genie |ˈdʒi:ni| *n* : génie *m*
genital |ˈdʒɛnət̬əl| *adj* : génital
genitals |ˈdʒɛnət̬əlz| *npl* : organes *mpl* génitaux
genius |ˈdʒi:njəs| *n* : génie *m*
genocide |ˈdʒɛnəˌsaɪd| *n* : génocide *m*
genre |ˈʒɑnrə, ˈʒɑr| *n* : genre *m*
genteel |dʒɛnˈti:l| *adj* : distingué
gentile |ˈdʒɛnˌtaɪl| *n* : gentil *m*
gentility |ˌdʒɛnˈtɪlət̬i| *n, pl* **-ties 1** GENTRY : petite noblesse *f* **2** COURTESY : politesse *f*
gentle |ˈdʒɛntəl| *adj* **-tler; -tlest 1** NOBLE : noble, de bonne famille **2** DOCILE, MILD : doux **3** LIGHT : léger <a gentle blow : un coup bien léger> **4** GRADUAL : doux, sans heurts <a gentle slope : une pente douce> <to come to a gentle stop : s'arrêter doucement>
gentleman |ˈdʒɛntəlmən| *n, pl* **-men** |-mən, -ˌmɛn| **1** MAN : monsieur *m* **2** : gentleman *m* <to act like a gentleman : agir en gentleman>
gentlemanly |ˈdʒɛntəlmənli| *adj* : courtois, distingué
gentleness |ˈdʒɛntəlnəs| *n* : douceur *f*
gentlewoman |ˈdʒɛntəlˌwʊmən| *n, pl* **-women** |-ˌwɪmən| : dame *f* (bien née)
gentry |ˈdʒɛntri| *n, pl* **-tries** : petite noblesse *f*
genuflect |ˈdʒɛnjʊˌflɛkt| *vi* : faire une génuflexion
genuflection |ˌdʒɛnjʊˈflɛkʃən| *n* : génuflexion *f*
genuine |ˌdʒɛnjʊwən| *adj* **1** AUTHENTIC, REAL : authentique, vrai, véritable **2** SINCERE : sincère — **genuinely** *adv*
genus |ˈdʒi:nəs| *n, pl* **genera** |ˈdʒɛnərə| : genre *m*
geochemistry |ˌdʒi:oˈkɛməstri| *n* : géochimie *f*
geodesic |ˌdʒi:əˈdɛsɪk, -ˈdi:-, -zɪk| *adj* : géodésique
geographer |dʒiˈɑgrəfər| *n* : géographe *mf*
geographic |ˌdʒi:əˈgræfɪk| *or* **geographical** |-fɪkəl| *adj* : géographique — **geographically** |-fɪkli| *adv*
geography |dʒiˈɑgrəfi| *n, pl* **-phies** : géographie *f*
geologic |ˌdʒi:əˈlɑdʒɪk| *or* **geological** |-dʒɪkəl| *adj* : géologique — **geologically** |-dʒɪkli| *adv*
geologist |dʒiˈɑlədʒɪst| *n* : géologue *mf*
geology |dʒiˈɑlədʒi| *n, pl* **-gies** : géologie *f*
geomagnetic |dʒi:omægˈnɛt̬ɪk| *adj* : géomagnétique
geometric |ˌdʒi:əˈmɛtrɪk| *or* **geometrical** |-ˈmɛtrɪkəl| *adj* : géométrique
geometry |dʒiˈɑmətri| *n, pl* **-tries** : géométrie *f*
geranium |dʒəˈreɪniəm| *n* : géranium *m*
gerbil |ˈdʒərbəl| *n* : gerbille *f*
geriatric |ˌdʒɛriˈætrɪk| *adj* : gériatrique
geriatrics |ˌdʒɛriˈætrɪks| *n* : gériatrie *f*
germ |ˈdʒərm| *n* **1** MICROBE : microbe *m*, germe *m* **2** : germe *m* (en biologie) **3** RUDIMENTS : germe *m* (d'une idée, etc.)
German[1] |ˈdʒərmən| *adj* : allemand
German[2] *n* **1** : Allemand *m*, -mande *f* **2** : allemand *m* (langue)
germane |dʒərˈmeɪn| *adj* : pertinent
germanium |dʒərˈmeɪniəm| *n* : germanium *m*
German measles *n* : rubéole *f*
German shepherd *n* : berger *m* allemand
germ cell *n* : gamète *m*, cellule *f* germinale
germicide |ˈdʒərməˌsaɪd| *n* : germicide *m*

germinate [ˈdʒərməˌneɪt] *v* **-nated; -nating** *vi* : germer — *vt* : faire germer

germination [ˌdʒərməˈneɪʃən] *n* : germination *f*

gerund [ˈdʒɛrənd] *n* : gérondif *m*

gestation [dʒɛˈsteɪʃən] *n* : gestation *f*

gesture[1] [ˈdʒɛstʃər] *vi* **-tured; -turing 1** : gesticuler, faire des gestes **2 to gesture to** : faire signe à

gesture[2] *n* : geste *m*

get [ˈgɛt] *v* **got** [ˈgɑt]; **got** *or* **gotten** [ˈgɑtən]; **getting** *vt* **1** OBTAIN : obtenir, trouver, se procurer **2** RECEIVE : recevoir, avoir <the garden gets a lot of sun : le jardin reçoit beaucoup de soleil> **3** EARN : gagner, mériter **4** FETCH : chercher (un objet), aller chercher (une personne) **5** CATCH : prendre (un train, etc.), attraper (une balle, un rhume), saisir (une personne) **6** PUT, TAKE : faire parvenir <to get sth to s.o. : faire parvenir qqch à qqn> <we can get the car through here : nous pouvons faire passer la voiture par ici> **7** UNDERSTAND : comprendre, piger *fam* <now I get it! : je pige!> **8** PREPARE : préparer <to get dinner : préparer le dîner> **9** PERSUADE : persuader, convaincre <I got her to agree : j'ai réussi à obtenir son accord> **10** (*to cause to be*) <to get one's hair cut : se faire couper les cheveux> **11 to have got** : avoir <I've got a headache : j'ai mal à la tête> **12 to have got to** : devoir — *vi* **1** BECOME : devenir <she's getting impatient : elle devient impatiente> <it's getting late : il se fait tard> **2** GO, MOVE : aller, arriver, se rendre <to get to the top of : arriver au sommet> <where did he get to? : où en est-il allé?> **3** PROGRESS : avancer <she got to be a director : elle a avancé à la position de directeur> **4 to get ahead** : progresser, prendre de l'avance **5 to get around** EVADE : contourner **6 to get at** REACH : atteindre **7 to get at** INSINUATE, MEAN : vouloir dire <what are you getting at? : où voulez-vous en venir?> **8 to get at** ASCERTAIN : découvrir, parvenir à **9 to get away with** : échapper à, s'en tirer à **10 to get back at** : se venger de **11 to get over** : se remettre de (une maladie, etc.) **12 to get together** MEET : se réunir

get along *vi* **1** PROGRESS : avancer, progresser **2** MANAGE : aller <how are you getting along? : comment vas-tu?> **3 to get along with** : bien s'entendre avec

getaway [ˈgɛt̬əˌweɪ] *n* : fuite *f* <to make one's getaway : s'enfuir>

get off *vi* **1** START : partir **2** : tirer d'affaire, s'en tirer <to get off lightly : s'en tirer à bon compte>

get out *vi* **1** ESCAPE : sortir **2** : être révélé <our secret got out : notre secret est révélé>

get–together [ˈgɛttəˌgɛðər] *n* : réunion *f*, petite fête *f*

get up *vi* ARISE : se lever — *vt* **1** PREPARE, ORGANIZE : former, organiser **2** DRESS : habiller

geyser [ˈgaɪzər] *n* : geyser *m*

Ghanian[1] [ˈgɑniən, ˈgæ-] *adj* : ghanéen

Ghanian[2] *n* : Ghanéen *m*, -néenne *f*

ghastly [ˈgæstli] *adj* **ghastlier; -est 1** HORRIBLE : horrible, épouvantable **2** PALE : blème, blafard

gherkin [ˈgərkən] *n* : cornichon *m*

ghetto [ˈgɛt̬oː] *n, pl* **-tos** *or* **-toes** : ghetto *m*

ghost [ˈgoːst] *n* : fantôme *m*, spectre *m*

ghostly [ˈgoːstli] *adj* **ghostlier; -est** : spectral

ghost town *n* : ville *f* morte

ghoul [ˈguːl] *n* : goule *f*

ghoulish [ˈguːlɪʃ] *adj* : macabre

GI [ˌdʒiːˈaɪ] *n, pl* **GI's** *or* **GIs** : soldat *m* américain

giant[1] [ˈdʒaɪənt] *adj* : géant, gigantesque

giant[2] *n* : géant *m*, géante *f*

gibberish [ˈdʒɪbərɪʃ] *n* : charabia *m fam*, baragouin *m*

gibbon [ˈgɪbən] *n* : gibbon *m*

gibe[1] [ˈdʒaɪb] *vi* **gibed; gibing** : se moquer <to gibe at s.o. : railler qqn, se moquer de qqn>

gibe[2] *n* : raillerie *f*, moquerie *f*

giblets [ˈdʒɪbləts] *npl* : abats *mpl* (de volaille)

giddiness [ˈgɪdinəs] *n* **1** DIZZINESS : vertiges *mpl*, étourdissements *mpl* **2** SILLINESS : légèreté *f*, étourderie *f*

giddy [ˈgɪdi] *adj* **giddier; -est 1** DIZZY : vertigineux **2** FRIVOLOUS, SILLY : frivole, écervelé, étourdi

gift [ˈgɪft] *n* **1** PRESENT : cadeau *m* **2** TALENT : don *m*

gifted [ˈgɪftəd] *adj* TALENTED : doué

gigantic [dʒaɪˈgæntɪk] *adj* : gigantesque

giggle[1] [ˈgɪgəl] *vi* **-gled; -gling** : rire bêtement

giggle[2] *n* : fou rire *m*, petit rire *m* sot

Gila monster [ˈhiːlə] *n* : monstre *m* de Gila

gild [ˈgɪld] *vt* **gilded** [ˈgɪldəd] *or* **gilt** [ˈgɪlt]; **gilding** : dorer

gill [ˈgɪl] *n* : branchie *f*, ouïe *f*

gilt[1] [ˈgɪlt] *adj* : doré

gilt[2] *n* : dorure *f*

gimlet [ˈgɪmlət] *n* : vrille *f* (outil)

gimmick [ˈgɪmɪk] *n* : truc *m*, gadget *m* <publicity gimmick : truc publicitaire>

gin [ˈdʒɪn] *n* **1** *or* **cotton gin** : égreneuse *f* (de coton) **2** : gin *m* (boisson)

ginger [ˈdʒɪndʒər] *n* : gingembre *m*

ginger ale *n* : boisson *f* gazeuse au gingembre

gingerbread [ˈdʒɪndʒərˌbrɛd] *n* : pain *m* d'épice

gingerly ['dʒɪndʒərli] *adv* : précautionneusement, avec circonspection
gingham ['gɪŋəm] *n* : vichy *m*
ginseng ['dʒɪn,sɪŋ] *n* : ginseng *m*
giraffe [dʒə'ræf] *n* : girafe *f*
gird ['gərd] *vt* **girded** ['gərdəd] *or* **girt** ['gərt]; **girding 1** PUT ON : ceindre **2 to gird oneself** : se préparer
girder ['gərdər] *n* : poutre *f*
girdle[1] ['gərdəl] *vt* **-dled; -dling** : encercler
girdle[2] *n* CORSET : gaine *f*
girl ['gərl] *n* **1** : fille *f*, jeune fille *f* **2** SWEETHEART : petite amie *f* **3** DAUGHTER : fille *f*
girlfriend ['gərl,frɛnd] *n* : copine *f*, petite amie *f*, blonde *f Can fam*
girlhood ['gərl,hʊd] *n* : jeunesse *f*
girlish ['gərlɪʃ] *adj* : de jeune fille
girth [gərθ] *n* **1** CIRCUMFERENCE : circonférence *f* (d'un arbre, etc.), tour *m* de taille (d'une personne) **2** : sangle *f* (d'une selle de cheval)
gist ['dʒɪst] *n* : essentiel *m*
give[1] ['gɪv] *v* **gave** ['geɪv]; **given** ['gɪvən]; **giving** *vt* **1** : donner, faire don à, conférer (un honneur, etc.) **2** PAY : payer **3** CAUSE : faire, causer <to give s.o. to understand : faire entendre à qqn> — *vi* **1** : donner **2** YIELD : céder **3 to give in** *or* **to give up** : se rendre **4 to give out** DISTRIBUTE : distribuer **5 to give out** COLLAPSE : s'épuiser
give[2] *n* : élasticité *f*, souplesse *f*
giveaway ['gɪvə,weɪ] *n* **1** : révélation *f* (involontaire) **2** GIFT : prime *f*, cadeau *m*
given ['gɪvən] *adj* **1** SPECIFIED : donné, déterminé **2** INCLINED : enclin <given to violence : enclin à la violence>
given name *n* : prénom *m*
gizzard ['gɪzərd] *n* : gésier *m*
glacial ['gleɪʃəl] *adj* **1** FRIGID : glacial **2** : glaciaire (en géologie)
glacier ['gleɪʃər] *n* : glacier *m*
glad ['glæd] *adj* **gladder; gladdest 1** HAPPY, PLEASED : content, heureux **2** JOYFUL, PLEASANT : joyeux, heureux <glad tidings : bonnes nouvelles> **3 to be glad to** : être heureux de <I'll be glad to do it! : avec plaisir!>
gladden ['glædən] *vt* : réjouir
glade ['gleɪd] *n* : clairière *f*
gladiator ['glædi,eɪtər] *n* : gladiateur *m*
gladiolus [,glædi'o:ləs] *n, pl* **-li** [-li, -,laɪ] : glaïeul *m*
gladly ['glædli] *adv* : avec plaisir, de bon coeur, volontiers
gladness ['glædnəs] *n* : joie *f*, contentement *m*
glamor *or* **glamour** ['glæmər] *n* **1** ALLURE : fascination *f*, charme *m* **2** ELEGANCE : élégance *f*, chic *m*
glamorize ['glæmə,raɪz] *vt* **-ized; -izing** : idéaliser, présenter sous des couleurs séduisantes
glamorous ['glæmərəs] *adj* **1** ALLURING : séduisant, fascinant **2** ELEGANT, EXCITING : élégant, brillant
glance[1] ['glænts] *vi* **glanced; glancing 1 to glance at** : jeter un coup d'œil à **2 to glance off** : ricocher sur (un mur, etc.)
glance[2] *n* : coup *m* d'œil
gland ['glænd] *n* : glande *f*
glandular ['glændʒʊlər] *adj* : glandulaire
glare[1] ['glær] *vi* **glared; glaring 1** SHINE : briller d'un éclat éblouissant **2 to glare at** : lancer un regard furieux à, regarder avec colère
glare[2] *n* **1** BRIGHTNESS : lumière *f* éblouissante **2** STARE : regard *m* furieux
glaring ['glærɪŋ] *adj* **1** BRIGHT : éblouissant **2** FLAGRANT : flagrant, qui saute aux yeux **3** FIERCE : furieux
glass[1] ['glæs] *vt or* **to glass in** : vitrer
glass[2] *adj* : en verre
glass[3] *n* **1** : verre *m* <broken glass : éclats de verre> <a glass of wine : un verre de vin> **2 glasses** *npl* SPECTACLES : lunettes *fpl*
glassblowing ['glæs,blo:ɪŋ] *n* : soufflage *m* du verre
glassful ['glæs,fʊl] *n* : verre *m*
glassware ['glæs,wær] *n* : verrerie *f*
glassy ['glæsi] *adj* **glassier; -est 1** VITREOUS : vitreux **2** SMOOTH : lisse **3 glassy eyes** : yeux *mpl* vitreux
glaucoma [glaʊ'ko:mə, glɔ-] *n* : glaucome *m*
glaze[1] ['gleɪz] *vt* **glazed; glazing 1** : vitrer (une fenêtre, etc.) **2** : vernisser (des céramiques), vitrifier (des carreaux, etc.) **3** ICE : glacer (des pâtisseries)
glaze[2] *n* **1** GLAZING : glaçage *m* **2** : vernis *m* (de céramiques), glacé *m* (d'étoffes, de photos, etc.)
glazier ['gleɪʒər] *n* : vitrier *m*
gleam[1] ['gli:m] *vi* : luire, reluire
gleam[2] *n* : lueur *f* <the first gleam of dawn : les premières lueurs de l'aube> <a gleam of hope : une lueur d'espoir>
glean ['gli:n] *vt* : glaner
glee ['gli:] *n* : joie *f*, allégresse *f*
gleeful ['gli:fəl] *adj* : joyeux — **gleefully** *adv*
glen ['glɛn] *n* : vallon *m*, vallée *f* encaissée
glib ['glɪb] *adj* **glibber; glibbest** : facile, désinvolte
glibly ['glɪbli] *adv*: avec désinvolture
glide[1] ['glaɪd] *vi* **glided; gliding** : glisser (sur une surface), planer (en l'air)
glide[2] *n* : glissement *m*
glider ['glaɪdər] *n* **1** : planeur *m* (en aéronautique) **2** SWING : balançoire *f*
glimmer[1] ['glɪmər] *vi* : jeter une faible lueur
glimmer[2] *n* GLEAM : lueur *f*

glimpse[1] ['glɪmps] *vt* **glimpsed; glimpsing** : entrevoir
glimpse[2] *n* : aperçu *m*
glint[1] ['glɪnt] *vi* : étinceler, miroiter (sur l'eau, etc.)
glint[2] *n* : reflet *m*, miroitement *m*
glisten ['glɪsən] *vi* : briller, miroiter, luire
glitter[1] ['glɪt̬ər] *vi* : scintiller, étinceler
glitter[2] *n* : scintillement *m*
gloat ['glo:t] *vi* : jubiler <to gloat over : se réjouir de>
glob ['glɑb] *n* : globule *m*, petite boule *f*
global ['glo:bəl] *adj* : mondial — **globally** *adv*
globe ['glo:b] *n* : globe *m*
globe–trotter ['glo:bˌtrɑt̬ər] *n* : globe-trotter *m*
globular ['glɑbjʊlər] *adj* : globulaire
globule ['glɑbju:l] *n* : gouttelette *f*
glockenspiel ['glɑkənˌspi:l, -ʃpi:l] *n* : glockenspiel *m*
gloom ['glu:m] *n* **1** DARKNESS : obscurité *f*, ténèbres *fpl* **2** SADNESS : tristesse *f*, mélancolie *f*
gloomily ['glu:məli] *adv* : sombrement, tristement
gloomy ['glu:mi] *adj* **gloomier; -est 1** DARK : obscur, sombre **2** MELANCHOLY : mélancolique, lugubre **3** PESSIMISTIC : sombre, triste **4** DEPRESSING : déprimant, morne
glorification [ˌglorəfə'keɪʃən] *n* : glorification *f*
glorify ['glorəˌfaɪ] *vt* **-fied; -fying** : glorifier
glorious ['gloriəs] *adj* : glorieux — **gloriously** *adv*
glory[1] ['glori] *vi* **-ried; -rying** : se glorifier <to glory in : se glorifier de>
glory[2] *n, pl* **-ries 1** : gloire *f* **2 in all one's glory** : dans toute sa splendeur
gloss[1] ['glɔs, 'glɑs] *vt* **1** EXPLAIN, DEFINE : gloser **2** POLISH : faire briller, lustrer **3 to gloss over** : glisser sur, atténuer, dissimuler (la vérité, etc.)
gloss[2] *n* **1** SHINE : brillant *m*, lustre *m* **2** EXPLANATION : glose *f*
glossary ['glɔsəri, 'glɑ-] *n, pl* **-ries** : glossaire *m*
glossy ['glɔsi, 'glɑ-] *adj* **glossier; -est** : brillant, luisant, glacé (se dit du papier)
glove ['glʌv] *n* : gant *m*
glow[1] ['glo:] *vi* **1** SHINE : rougeoyer, luire **2** : rayonner <to glow with health : rayonner de santé>
glow[2] *n* : rougeoiement *m*, lueur *f*
glower ['glaʊər] *vi* : lancer des regards furieux
glowworm ['glo:ˌwərm] *n* : ver *m* luisant
glucose ['glu:ˌko:s] *n* : glucose *m*
glue[1] ['glu:] *vt* **glued; gluing 1** : coller **2 to glue one's eyes on** : garder les yeux rivés sur
glue[2] *n* : colle *f*
gluey ['glu:i] *adj* **gluier; -est** : gluant, collant
glum ['glʌm] *adj* **glummer; glummest** : morne, triste, morose
glut[1] ['glʌt] *vt* **glutted; glutting** SATURATE : inonder, saturer
glut[2] *n* : surabondance *f*, excès *m*
glutinous ['glu:tənəs] *adj* : gluant
glutton ['glʌtən] *n* : glouton *m*, -tonne *f*; gourmand *m*, -mande *f*
gluttonous ['glʌtənəs] *adj* : glouton
gluttony ['glʌtəni] *n, pl* **-tonies** : gloutonnerie *f*
gnarled ['nɑrld] *adj* : noueux
gnash ['næʃ] *vt* **to gnash one's teeth** : grincer des dents
gnat ['næt] *n* : moucheron *m*, brulôt *m Can*
gnaw ['nɔ] *vt* : ronger
gnome ['no:m] *n* : gnome *m*
gnu ['nu:, 'nju:] *n, pl* **gnu** *or* **gnus** : gnou *m*
go[1] ['go:] *v* **went** ['wɛnt]; **gone** ['gɔn]; **going** ['go:ɪŋ]; **goes** ['go:z] *vi* **1** : aller **2** LEAVE : partir, s'en aller <I have to go : il faut que je m'en aille> **3** EXTEND : s'étendre <this road goes to the river : cette rue s'étend jusqu'au fleuve> **4** SELL : se vendre <it goes for $15 : cela se vend pour 15 $> **5** BECOME : devenir <he's going crazy : il devient fou> **6** FUNCTION : marcher <to get it going : le mettre en marche> **7** DISAPPEAR : disparaître <my pen is gone! : mon stylo a disparu!> **8 to go back on** BETRAY : trahir **9 to go for** FAVOR : aimer **10 to go off** EXPLODE : exploser **11 to go off** RING : sonner **12 to go out** LEAVE : sortir **13 to go out** : s'éteindre <the fire went out : le feu s'est éteint> **14 to go over** CHECK : vérifier — *vt* **to go it alone** : le faire tout seul — *v aux* **to be going to** : aller <I'm going to talk to you (about it) : je vais t'en parler>
go[2] *n, pl* **goes 1** ATTEMPT : essai *m*, tentative *f* <to have a go at sth : essayer de faire qqch> **2** SUCCESS : réussite *f* <to make a go of sth : réussir qqch> **3 to be always on the go** : ne s'arrêter jamais
goad[1] ['go:d] *vt* : aiguillonner (un animal), provoquer (une personne)
goad[2] *n* : aiguillon *m*
goal ['go:l] *n* : but *m*
goalie ['go:li] → **goalkeeper**
goalkeeper ['go:lˌki:pər] *n* : gardien *m* de but, cerbère *m Can*
goat ['go:t] *n* **1** : chèvre *f* **2** *or* **billie goat** : bouc *m*
goatee [go:'ti:] *n* : barbiche *f*
goatskin ['go:tˌskɪn] *n* : cuir *m* de chèvre
gob ['gɑb] *n* **1** LUMP : boule *f* **2 gobs of** : beaucoup de
gobble ['gɑbəl] *v* **-bled; -bling** *vt or* **to gobble up** DEVOUR : engloutir — *vi* : glouglouter (se dit d'un dindon)

gobbledygook [ˈgabəldi,guk, -,gu:k] *n* : charabia *m fam*
go–between [ˈgo:bɪ,twi:n] *n* : intermédiaire *mf*
goblet [ˈgablət] *n* : verre *m* à pied
goblin [ˈgablən] *n* : lutin *m*
god [ˈgad, ˈgɔd] *n* **1** : dieu *m* **2 God** : Dieu *m*
godchild [ˈgad,tʃaɪld, ˈgɔd-] *n, pl* **-children** : filleul *m*, -leule *f*
goddess [ˈgadəs, ˈgɔ-] *n* : déesse *f*
godfather [ˈgad,faðər, ˈgɔd-] *n* : parrain *m*
godless [ˈgadləs, ˈgɔd-] *adj* : impie
godlike [ˈgad,laɪk, ˈgɔd-] *adj* : divin
godly [ˈgadli, ˈgɔd-] *adj* **godlier; est 1** DIVINE : divin **2** DEVOUT, PIOUS : dévot, pieux
godmother [ˈgad,mʌðər, ˈgɔd-] *n* : marraine *f*
godparent [ˈgad,pærənt, ˈgɔd-] *n* : parrain *m*, marraine *f*
godsend [ˈgad,sɛnd, ˈgɔd-] *n* : aubaine *f*, bénédiction *f*, don *m* (du ciel)
goes → **go**[1]
go–getter [ˈgo:,gɛtər] *n* : battant *m*, -tante *f;* fonceur *m*, -ceuse *f fam*
goggle [ˈgagəl] *vi* **-gled; -gling** : ouvrir de grands yeux, regarder avec des yeux ronds
goggles [ˈgagəlz] *npl* : lunettes *fpl* (protectrices)
goings–on [,go:ɪŋˈzan, -ˈɔn] *npl* : événements *mpl*, activités *fpl*, conduite *f*
goiter *or Brit* **goitre** [ˈgɔɪtər] *n* : goitre *m*
gold [ˈgo:ld] *n* : or *m*
golden [ˈgo:ldən] *adj* **1** : en or, d'or **2** : doré, (couleur) d'or <golden hair : cheveux dorés> **3** FAVORABLE : idyllique, en or <a golden opportunity : une occasion magnifique, une occasion en or>
golden mean *n* : juste milieu *m*
goldenrod [ˈgo:ldən,rad] *n* : verge *f* d'or
golden rule *n* : règle *f* d'or
goldfinch [ˈgo:ld,fɪntʃ] *n* : chardonneret *m*
goldfish [ˈgo:ld,fɪʃ] *ns & pl* : poisson *m* rouge
goldsmith [ˈgo:ld,smɪθ] *n* : orfèvre *m*
golf[1] [ˈgalf, ˈgɔlf] *vi* : jouer au golf
golf[2] *n* : golf *m*
golfer [ˈgalfər, ˈgɔl-] *n* : golfeur *m*, -feuse *f;* joueur *m*, joueuse *f* de golf
gondola [ˈgandələ, ganˈdo:lə] *n* : gondole *f*
gone [ˈgɔn] *adj* **1** LOST : perdu **2** PAST : passé <gone is the time when . . . : le temps n'est plus où . . . > **3** DEAD : mort **4** WORN : usé **5 to be far gone** : être bien faible
goner [ˈgɔnər] *n* **to be a goner** : être fichu *fam*
gong [ˈgɔŋ, ˈgaŋ] *n* : gong *m*
gonorrhea [,ganəˈri:ə] *n* : blennorragie *f*
good[1] [ˈgʊd] *adv* **1** (*used as an intensifier*) : bien, bon <a good strong rope : une corde bien forte> <a good long walk : une bonne promenade> **2 to make good** : réussir
good[2] *adj* **better** [ˈbɛtər]; **best** [ˈbɛst] **1** : bon <good news : bonnes nouvelles> <a good salary : un bon salaire> <good evening : bonsoir> <good morning : bonjour> **2** KIND : bon, aimable <a good deed : une bonne action> **3** FULL : bon <she waited for a good hour : elle attendu pendant une bonne heure> **4** SKILLED : bon, habile <to be good at : être bon en (des études), être bon à (un jeu)> **5** OBEDIENT : sage <be good! : sois sage!> **6** : beau <good weather : beau temps>
good[3] *n* **1** RIGHT : bien *m* <good and evil : le bien et le mal> **2** GOODNESS : bonté *f* **3** BENEFIT : bien *m* <for your own good : pour votre bien> **4 goods** *npl* PROPERTY : biens *mpl* **5 goods** *npl* WARES : marchandises *fpl* **6 for ~** : pour de bon **7 the good** : les bons *mpl*
good–bye *or* **good–by** [gʊdˈbaɪ] *n* : au revoir *m*
good–for–nothing [ˈgʊdfər,nʌθɪŋ] *adj* : bon à rien
Good Friday *n* : le Vendredi saint
good–hearted [ˈgʊdˈhartəd] *adj* : généreux, qui a bon coeur
good–looking [ˈgʊdˈlʊkɪŋ] *adj* : beau
goodly [ˈgʊdli] *adj* **goodlier; -est** : grand, ample <a goodly sum : une somme considérable>
good–natured [ˈgʊdˈneɪtʃərd] *adj* : aimable, qui a un bon naturel
goodness [ˈgʊdnəs] *n* **1** : bonté *f* **2 goodness me!** *or* **my goodness!** : mon Dieu!
good–tempered [ˈgʊdˈtɛmpərd] *adj* : de bon caractère
goodwill [,gʊdˈwɪl] *n* : bienveillance *f*
goody [ˈgʊdi] *n, pl* **goodies 1** : bon *m* **2 goody!** : chouette! *f fam* **3 goodies** *npl* : friandises *fpl*
gooey [ˈgu:i] *adj* **gooier; gooiest** : gluant
goof[1] [ˈgu:f] *vi* **1** *or* **to goof up** : gaffer *fam*, faire une gaffe **2 to goof around** : faire l'imbécile
goof[2] *n* : gaffe *f fam*
goofy [ˈgu:fi] *adj* **goofier; -est** : dingue *fam*
goose [ˈgu:s] *n, pl* **geese** [ˈgi:s] : oie *f*
gooseberry [ˈgu:s,bɛri:, ˈgu:z-] *n, pl* **-berries** : groseille *f* à maquereau
goose bumps *npl* : chair *f* de poule
gooseflesh [ˈgu:s,flɛʃ] → **goose bumps**
goose pimples → **goose bumps**
gopher [ˈgo:fər] *n* : gaufre *m Can*
gore[1] [ˈgor] *vt* **gored; goring** : encorner
gore[2] *n* BLOOD : sang *m*

gorge[1] ['gɔrdʒ] *vt* **gorged; gorging 1** SATIATE : rassasier **2 to gorge oneself** : se gorger

gorge[2] *n* RAVINE : gorge *f,* défilé *m*

gorgeous ['gɔrdʒəs] *adj* : magnifique, splendide

gorilla [gə'rɪlə] *n* : gorille *m*

gory ['gori] *adj* **gorier; -est** : sanglant

gosling ['gɑzlɪŋ, 'gɔz-] *n* : oison *m*

gospel ['gɑspəl] *n* **1 the Gospel** : l'Évangile *m* **2 the gospel truth** : la vérité vraie

gossamer ['gɑsəmər, 'gɑzə-] *n* **1** COBWEB : fils *mpl* de la Vierge **2** : étoffe *f* très légère

gossip[1] ['gɑsɪp] *vi* : bavarder, faire des commérages, mémérer *Can fam*

gossip[2] *n* **1** : commère *f fam* (personne) **2** RUMOR : racontars *mpl,* commérages *mpl fam,* cancans *mpl,* ragots *mpl fam,* mémérage *m Can*

gossipy ['gɑsɪpi] *adj* : bavard, cancanier

got → **get**

Gothic ['gɑθɪk] *adj* : gothique

gotten → **get**

gouge[1] ['gaʊdʒ] *vt* **gouged; gouging 1** : creuser, tailler à la gouge **2** SWINDLE : estamper

gouge[2] *n* **1** CHISEL : gouge *f* **2** GROOVE : rainure *f*

goulash ['gu:ˌlɑʃ, -ˌlæʃ] *n* : goulasch *mf,* goulache *mf*

gourd ['gord, 'gʊrd] *n* : gourde *f*

gourmand ['gʊrˌmɑnd] *n* : gourmand *m,* -mande *f*

gourmet ['gʊrˌmeɪ, gʊr'meɪ] *n* : gourmet *m*

gout ['gaʊt] *n* : goutte *f*

govern ['gʌvərn] *vt* **1** RULE : gouverner **2** CONTROL, DETERMINE : régir **3** RESTRAIN : maîtriser, dominer (les émotions, etc.) — *vi* : gouverner

governess ['gʌvərnəs] *n* : gouvernante *f*

government ['gʌvərmənt] *n* : gouvernement *m* — **governmental** [ˌgʌvər'mɛntəl] *adj*

governor ['gʌvənər, 'gʌvərnər] *n* **1** : gouverneur *m* **2** : régulateur *m* (d'une machine)

governorship ['gʌvənərˌʃɪp, 'gʌvərnər-] *n* : fonctions *fpl* de gouverneur

gown ['gaʊn] *n* **1** : robe *f* <evening gown : robe du soir> **2** : toge *f* (de juge, etc.)

grab[1] ['græb] *v* **grabbed; grabbing** *vt* SEIZE : saisir, empoigner — *vi* CLING : s'agripper

grab[2] *n* **1 to make a grab for** : essayer d'attraper **2 to be up for grabs** : être disponible, être à prendre

grace[1] ['greɪs] *vt* **graced; gracing 1** HONOR : honorer **2** ADORN : orner, embellir

grace[2] *n* **1** : grâce *f* <by the grace of God : par la grâce de Dieu> **2** PRAYER : bénédicité *m* <to say grace : dire le bénédicité> **3** RESPITE : grâce *f,* répit *m* <a grace period : un délai> **4** GRACIOUSNESS : bienveillance *f,* gentillesse *f* **5** ELEGANCE : élégance *f,* charme *m,* grâce *f* **6 to be in the good graces of** : être dans les bonnes grâces de

graceful ['greɪsfəl] *adj* : gracieux — **gracefully** *adv*

gracefulness ['greɪsfəlnəs] *n* : grâce *f*

graceless ['greɪsləs] *adj* : inélégant, gauche

grace note *n* : note *f* d'agrément

gracious ['greɪʃəs] *adj* : courtois, gracieux — **graciously** *adv*

graciousness ['greɪʃəsnəs] *n* : bienveillance *f,* gentillesse *f,* courtoisie *f*

grackle ['grækəl] *n* : quiscale *m*

gradation [greɪ'deɪʃən, grə-] *n* : gradation *f*

grade[1] ['greɪd] *vt* **graded; grading 1** CLASSIFY : classer **2** LEVEL : niveler **3** MARK : noter (à l'école)

grade[2] *n* **1** CLASS, QUALITY : catégorie *f,* calibre *m,* qualité *f* **2** RANK : rang *m,* grade *m* **3** YEAR : classe *f* (à l'école) **4** MARK : note *f* **5** SLOPE : pente *f*

grade school → **elementary school**

gradual ['grædʒʊəl] *adj* : graduel, progressif — **gradually** *adv*

graduate[1] ['grædʒʊˌeɪt] *v* **-ated; -ating** *vi* : recevoir son diplôme — *vt* : graduer <a graduated thermometer : un thermomètre gradué>

graduate[2] ['grædʒʊət] *n* : diplômé *m,* -mée *f*

graduation [ˌgrædʒʊ'eɪʃən] *n* **1** : remise *f* des diplômes (à l'université) **2** CALIBRATION : graduation *f*

graffiti [grə'fi:ṭi, græ-] *npl* : graffiti *mpl*

graft[1] ['græft] *vt* : greffer

graft[2] *n* **1** : greffe *f* **2** CORRUPTION : magouille *f*

grain ['greɪn] *n* **1** : grain *m* <a grain of sand : un grain de sable> **2** CEREALS : céréales *fpl* **3** : fibre *f* (de bois, de cuir, etc.), fil *m* (de fibres) **4 to go against one's grain** : n'être pas dans sa nature

gram ['græm] *n* : gramme *m* (unité de mesure et de masse)

grammar ['græmər] *n* : grammaire *f*

grammar school → **elementary school**

grammatical [grə'mæṭɪkəl] *adj* : grammatical — **grammatically** [-kli] *adv*

granary ['greɪnəri, 'græ-] *n, pl* **-ries** : grenier *m* à blé

grand ['grænd] *adj* **1** FOREMOST : plus grand, principal <the grand prize : le grand prix> **2** IMPRESSIVE : grand, magnifique, grandiose <in a grand manner : dans un style de grand seigneur> **3** DIGNIFIED, MAJESTIC : digne, majestueux **4** PRETENTIOUS : prétentieux, suffisant **5** GREAT, WONDERFUL : formidable *fam* **6**

grand total : somme *f* globale, résultat *m* final

grandaunt ['græn'dænt, -'dant] *n* : grand-tante *f*

grandchild ['grænd,tʃaɪld] *n, pl* **-children** [-,tʃɪldrən] : petit-fils *m*, petite-fille *f*

granddaughter ['grænd,dɔt̬ər] *n* : petite-fille *f*

grandeur ['grændʒər] *n* : grandeur *f*, splendeur *f*, magnificence *f*

grandfather ['grænd,fɑðər] *n* : grand-père *m*

grandiose ['grændi,o:s, ,grændi'-] *adj* : grandiose

grandma ['grænd,ma, -mɔ] *n* : mémé *f France fam*, mémère *f fam*

grandmother ['grænd,mʌðər] *n* : grand-mère *f*

grandparents ['grænd,pærənts] *npl* : grands-parents *mpl*

grand piano *n* : piano *m* à queue

grandson ['grænd,sʌn] *n* : petit-fils *m*

grandstand ['grænd,stænd] *n* : tribune *f*

granduncle ['græn'dəŋkəl] *n* : grand-oncle *m*

granite ['grænɪt] *n* : granit *m*, granite *m*

grant[1] ['grænt] *vt* **1** ALLOW, BESTOW : accorder, octroyer **2** ADMIT : admettre, reconnaître **3 to take for granted** : prendre pour acquis

grant[2] *n* **1** CONCESSION : concession *f* **2** SUBSIDY : subvention *f* **3** SCHOLARSHIP : bourse *f*

granular ['grænjʊlər] *adj* : granuleux

grape ['greɪp] *n* : raisin *m* <a bunch of grapes : une grappe de raisins>

grapefruit ['greɪp,fru:t] *n* : pamplemousse *mf*

grapevine ['greɪp,vaɪn] *n* **1** : vigne *f* **2 to hear through the grapevine** : entendre dire, apprendre à travers les branches

graph ['græf] *n* : graphique *m*

graphic ['græfɪk] *adj* **1** : graphique <graphic art : l'art graphique> **2** VIVID : vivant — **graphically** [-ɪkli] *adv*

graphite ['græ,faɪt] *n* : graphite *m*

grapnel ['græpnəl] *n* : grappin *m*

grapple ['græpəl] *v* **-pled; -pling** *vt* : saisir avec un grappin — *vi* STRUGGLE : lutter, se colleter

grasp[1] ['græsp] *vt* **1** GRIP, SEIZE : saisir **2** UNDERSTAND : comprendre, saisir

grasp[2] *n* **1** GRIP : prise *f*, poigne *f* **2** COMPREHENSION : compréhension *f* **3** REACH : portée *f* <within the grasp of : à la portée de>

grass ['græs] *n* **1** : herbe *f* (plante) **2** LAWN : gazon *m*, pelouse *f*

grasshopper ['græs,hɑpər] *n* : sauterelle *f*

grassland ['græs,lænd] *n* : prairie *f*

grassy ['græsi] *adj* **grassier; -est** : herbeux

grate[1] ['greɪt] *v* **grated; -ing** *vt* **1** : râper <to grate cheese : râper du fromage> **2 to grate one's teeth** : grincer des dents — *vi* **1** CREAK, RASP : grincer **2** IRRITATE : agacer <to grate on the nerves of : taper sur les nerfs de>

grate[2] *n* **1** : grille *f* de foyer (de cuisine) **2** GRATING : grille *f*

grateful ['greɪtfəl] *adj* : reconnaissant

gratefully ['greɪtfəli] *adv* : avec reconnaissance

gratefulness ['greɪtfəlnəs] *n* : gratitude *f*, reconnaissance *f*

grater ['greɪt̬ər] *n* : râpe *f*

gratification [,græt̬əfə'keɪʃən] *n* : satisfaction *f*, plaisir *m*

gratify ['græt̬ə,faɪ] *vt* **-fied; -fying 1** PLEASE : faire plaisir à **2** SATISFY : satisfaire

grating ['greɪt̬ɪŋ] *n* : grille *f*

gratis[1] ['græt̬əs, 'greɪ-] *adv* : gratis, gratuitement

gratis[2] *adj* : gratis, gratuit

gratitude ['græt̬ə,tu:d, -,tju:d] *n* : gratitude *f*, reconnaissance *f*

gratuitous [grə'tu:ət̬əs] *adj* : gratuit

gratuity [grə'tu:ət̬i] *n, pl* **-ities** TIP : pourboire *m*

grave[1] ['greɪv] *adj* **graver; -est** : grave

grave[2] *n* : tombe *f*

gravel ['grævəl] *n* : gravier *m*, gravillon *m*

gravelly ['grævəli] *adj* **1** : graveleux **2** HARSH, GRATING : râpeux <a gravelly voice : une voix râpeuse>

gravely ['greɪvli] *adv* : gravement

gravestone ['greɪv,sto:n] *n* : pierre *f* tombale

graveyard ['greɪv,jɑrd] *n* : cimetière *m*

gravitate ['grævə,teɪt] *vi* **-tated; -tating** : graviter

gravitation [,grævə'teɪʃən] *n* : gravitation *f*

gravity ['grævət̬i] *n, pl* **-ties 1** SERIOUSNESS : gravité *f* **2** GRAVITATION : gravitation *f*, pesanteur *f* <the law of gravity : la loi de la pesanteur>

gravy ['greɪvi] *n, pl* **-vies** : sauce *f* (au jus de viande)

gray[1] ['greɪ] *vi or* **to turn gray** : grisonner

gray[2] *adj* **1** : gris <gray hair : cheveux gris> **2** GLOOMY : morne **3** DREARY, DULL : terne

gray[3] *n* : gris *m*

grayish ['greɪɪʃ] *adj* : grisâtre

graze ['greɪz] *v* **grazed; grazing** *vi* : paître, brouter — *vt* **1** PASTURE : faire paître (des animaux) **2** SCRAPE : écorcher, érafler **3** BRUSH, TOUCH : frôler

grease[1] ['gri:s] *vt* **greased; greasing** : graisser, lubrifier (une voiture)

grease[2] *n* : graisse *f*, lubrifiant *m* (pour une voiture)

greasy ['gri:si] *adj* **greasier; -est 1** : graisseux **2** OILY : gras

great [ˈgreɪt] *adj* **1** LARGE : grand <a great mountain : une grande montagne> **2** INTENSE : grand <to be in great pain : souffrir beaucoup> **3** EMINENT : grand, éminent <a great man : un grand homme> **4** FANTASTIC : génial *fam*, formidable *fam* <to have a great time : s'amuser follement>

great-aunt [ˌgreɪtˈænt, -ˈant] → **grand-aunt**

great-grandchild [ˌgreɪtˈgrændˌtʃaɪld] *n, pl* **-children** [-ˌtʃɪldrən] : arrière-petit-enfant *m*, arrière-petite-enfant *f*

great-grandfather [ˌgreɪtˈgrændˌfɑðər] *n* : arrière-grand-père *m*

great-grandmother [ˌgreɪtˈgrændˌmʌðər] *n* : arrière-grand-mère *f*

greatly [ˈgreɪtli] *adv* **1** MUCH : beaucoup <greatly improved : beaucoup amélioré> **2** VERY : très, énormément <greatly surprised : très surpris>

greatness [ˈgreɪtnəs] *n* : grandeur *f*

great-uncle [ˌgreɪtˈʌŋkəl] → **grand-uncle**

grebe [ˈgri:b] *n* : grèbe *m*

greed [ˈgri:d] *n* **1** AVARICE : avidité *f*, cupidité *f*, avarice *f* **2** GLUTTONY : gloutonnerie *f*

greedily [ˈgri:dəli] *adv* : avidement

greediness [ˈgri:dinəs] → **greed**

greedy [ˈgri:di] *adj* **greedier; -est 1** AVARICIOUS : avare, cupide, pingre **2** GLUTTONOUS : glouton

Greek[1] [ˈgri:k] *adj* : grec

Greek[2] *n* **1** : Grec *m*, Grecque *f* **2** : grec *m* (langue)

green[1] [ˈgri:n] *adj* **1** : vert **2** INEXPERIENCED : inexpérimenté, naïf

green[2] *n* **1** : vert *m* (couleur) **2 greens** *npl* : légumes *mpl* verts

greenery [ˈgri:nəri] *n, pl* **-eries** : verdure *f*

greenhorn [ˈgri:nˌhɔrn] *n* : novice *mf*

greenhouse [ˈgri:nˌhaʊs] *n* : serre *f*

greenhouse effect *n* : effet *m* de serre

greenish [ˈgri:nɪʃ] *adj* : verdâtre

green onion → **chive, scallion**

green pepper *n* : poivron *m* vert

green thumb *n* **to have a green thumb** : avoir la main verte

greet [ˈgri:t] *vt* **1** WELCOME : saluer, accueillir **2 to be greeted with** : provoquer <to greet with laughter : provoquer des rires>

greeting [ˈgri:t̬ɪŋ] *n* **1** : salutation *f* **2 greetings** *npl* REGARDS : voeux *mpl* <Christmas greetings : voeux de Noël>

gregarious [grɪˈgæriəs] *adj* : grégaire (se dit des animaux), sociable (se dit des personnes)

gregariousness [grɪˈgæriəsnəs] *n* : sociabilité *f*

gremlin [ˈgrɛmlən] *n* : lutin *m*, diablotin *m*

grenade [grəˈneɪd] *n* : grenade *f*

Grenadian[1] [grəˈneɪdiən] *adj* : grenadin

Grenadian[2] *n* : Grenadin *m*, -dine *f*

grew → **grow**

grey → **gray**

greyhound [ˈgreɪˌhaʊnd] *n* : lévrier *m*

grid [grɪd] *n* **1** GRATING : grille *f* **2** NETWORK : réseau *m* (électrique) **3** : quadrillage *m* (d'une carte routière)

griddle [ˈgrɪdəl] *n* : plaque *f* chauffante

griddle cake → **pancake**

gridiron [ˈgrɪdˌaɪərn] *n* **1** GRILL : gril *m* **2** : terrain *m* de football américain

grief [ˈgri:f] *n* **1** SORROW : chagrin *m*, douleur *f* **2 to come to grief** : avoir des ennuis **3 good grief!** : mon Dieu!

grievance [ˈgri:vənts] *n* : grief *m*

grieve [ˈgri:v] *v* **grieved; grieving** *vt* DISTRESS : peiner, chagriner, affliger — *vi* **1** : avoir de la peine, s'affliger **2 to grieve for** : pleurer

grievous [ˈgri:vəs] *adj* **1** GRAVE, SERIOUS : grave, sérieux <a grievous injury : une blessure sérieuse> **2** CRUEL, ONEROUS : cruel, atroce <a grievous offense : un délit atroce>

grill[1] [ˈgrɪl] *vt* **1** : griller, faire griller (en cuisine) **2** INTERROGATE : cuisiner *fam*

grill[2] *n* **1** : gril *m* (de cuisine) **2** RESTAURANT : grill *m*

grille *or* **grill** [ˈgrɪl] *n* GRATING : grille *f*

grim [ˈgrɪm] *adj* **grimmer; grimmest 1** STERN : sévère <with grim determination : avec une volonté inflexible> **2** GLOOMY : lugubre, sinistre **3** UNPLEASANT : désagréable, (très) mauvais, pas bien

grimace[1] [ˈgrɪməs, grɪˈmeɪs] *vi* **-maced; -macing** : grimacer

grimace[2] *n* : grimace *f*

grime [ˈgraɪm] *n* : saleté *f*, crasse *f*

grimly [ˈgrɪmli] *adv* **1** SEVERELY : sévèrement, durement **2** RESOLUTELY : d'un air résolu, fermement

grimy [ˈgraɪmi] *adj* **grimier; -est** : sale, crasseux

grin[1] [ˈgrɪn] *vi* **grinned; grinning** : sourire

grin[2] *n* : (grand) sourire *m*

grind[1] [ˈgraɪnd] *v* **ground** [ˈgraʊnd]; **grinding** *vt* **1** CRUSH : moudre, pulvériser **2** POLISH, SHARPEN : aiguiser, affûter, polir **3 to grind down** OPPRESS : opprimer **4 to grind one's teeth** : grincer des dents, gricher des dents *Can* — *vi* : grincer

grind[2] *n* CHORE : corvée *f*

grinder [ˈgraɪndər] *n* : moulin *m* <coffee grinder : moulin à café>

grindstone [ˈgraɪndˌsto:n] *n* : meule *f*

grip[1] [ˈgrɪp] *vt* **gripped; gripping 1** SEIZE : serrer **2** CAPTIVATE : empoigner, captiver **3 to grip the road** : adhérer à la route

grip[2] *n* **1** GRASP : étreinte *f*, prise *f* **2** CONTROL : contrôle *m* <to get a grip on oneself : se ressaisir> **3** UNDERSTANDING : compréhension *f* **4** TRAC-

TION : adhérence *f* **5** HANDLE : poignée *f*

gripe[1] |ˈgraɪp| *vi* **griped; griping** : rouspéter *fam,* ronchonner *fam*

gripe[2] *n* : plainte *f,* rouspétance *f fam*

grippe |ˈgrɪp| *n* : grippe *f*

grisly |ˈgrɪzli| *adj* **grislier; -est** : horrible, macabre

grist |ˈgrɪst| *n* **1** : blé *m* (à moudre) **2 it's all grist for his mill** : ça apporte de l'eau à son moulin

gristle |ˈgrɪsəl| *n* : cartilage *m*

gristly |ˈgrɪsli| *adj* **gristlier; -est** : cartilagineux

grit[1] |ˈgrɪt| *vt* **gritted; gritting** : serrer <to grit one's teeth : serrer les dents>

grit[2] *n* **1** GRAVEL, SAND : sable *m,* gravillon *m* **2** PLUCK : cran *m fam,* courage *m* **3 grits** *npl* : gruau *m* de maïs

gritty |ˈgrɪṭi| *adj* **grittier; -est 1** : sablonneux, graveleux **2** PLUCKY : courageux

grizzled |ˈgrɪzəld| *adj* : grisonnant

groan[1] |ˈgro:n| *vi* : gémir

groan[2] *n* : gémissement *m*

grocer |ˈgro:sər| *n* : épicier *m,* -cière *f*

grocery |ˈgro:səri, -ʃəri| *n, pl* **-ceries 1** *or* **grocery store** : épicerie *f* **2 groceries** *npl* : épiceries *fpl,* provisions *fpl*

groggy |ˈgrɑgi| *adj* **groggier; -est** : chancelant, sonné *fam*

groin |ˈgrɔɪn| *n* : aine *f*

grommet |ˈgrɑmət, ˈgrʌ-| *n* : œillet *m*

groom[1] |ˈgru:m, ˈgrʊm| *vt* **1** : panser (un animal) **2** PREPARE : préparer, former

groom[2] *n* **1** : palefrenier *m,* -nière *f* **2** BRIDEGROOM : marié *m*

groove[1] |ˈgru:v| *vt* **grooved; grooving** : rainer, canneler

groove[2] *n* **1** FURROW, SLOT : rainure *f,* sillon *m* **2** ROUTINE, RUT : routine *f*

grope |ˈgro:p| *v* **groped; groping** *vi* **1** : tâtonner **2 to grope for** : chercher à tâtons — *vt* **1** PAW : peloter **2 to grope one's way** : avancer à tâtons

gross[1] |ˈgro:s| *vt* : gagner brut, produire brut

gross[2] *adj* **1** FLAGRANT : flagrant, crasse **2** OBESE : gros, obèse **3** TOTAL : brut <gross domestic product : produit intérieur brut> **4** VULGAR : grossier

gross[3] *n* **1** *pl* **gross** : grosse *f* (12 douzaines) **2** *or* **gross income** : recettes *fpl* brutes

grossly |ˈgro:sli| *adv* **1** EXTREMELY : extrêmement **2** CRUDELY : grossièrement

grotesque |gro:ˈtɛsk| *adj* : grotesque

grotesquely |gro:ˈtɛskli| *adv* : de façon grotesque

grotto |ˈgrɑṭo:| *n, pl* **-toes** : grotte *f*

grouch[1] |ˈgraʊtʃ| *vi* : grogner, rouspéter *fam,* ronchonner *fam*

grouch[2] *n* **1** GRUMBLER : rouspéteur *m,* -teuse *f fam;* plaignard *m,* -gnarde *f Can* **2** COMPLAINT : grognement *m*

grouchy |ˈgraʊtʃi| *adj* **grouchier; -est** : grognon, grincheux

ground[1] |ˈgraʊnd| *vt* **1** BASE : baser, fonder **2** INSTRUCT : former <to be well grounded in : avoir une bonne formation en> **3** : mettre à la terre (un appareil électrique) **4** : faire échouer (un navire) **5** : interdire de voler à (un avion ou un pilote)

ground[2] *n* **1** EARTH, SOIL : sol *m,* terre *f* <on the ground : par terre> **2** LAND, TERRAIN : terrain *m* <on hilly ground : sur un terrain vallonné> **3** BASIS, REASON : motif *m,* raison *f* <grounds for complaint : motifs de se plaindre> **4** : terre *f* (pour l'électricité) **5 grounds** *npl* PREMISES : parc *m* **6 grounds** *npl* : marc *m* (de café)

ground[3] → **grind**[1]

groundhog |ˈgraʊnd,hɔg| *n* : marmotte *f* d'Amérique

groundless |ˈgraʊndləs| *adj* : sans fondement

groundwork |ˈgraʊnd,wərk| *n* : travail *m* préparatoire

group[1] |ˈgru:p| *vt* : grouper, réunir — *vi* **to group together** : se grouper

group[2] *n* : groupe *m*

grouper |ˈgru:pər| *n* : mérou *m*

grouse[1] |ˈgraʊs| *vi* **groused; grousing** COMPLAIN : rouspéter *fam,* râler *fam*

grouse[2] *n, pl* **grouse** *or* **grouses** : grouse *f*

grove |ˈgro:v| *n* : bosquet *m*

grovel |ˈgrɑvəl, ˈgrʌ-| *vi* **-eled** *or* **-elled; -eling** *or* **-elling** : ramper

grow |ˈgro:| *v* **grew** |ˈgru:|; **grown** |ˈgro:n|; **growing** *vi* **1** : pousser (se dit des plantes, des cheveux, etc.), grandir (se dit des personnes) **2** INCREASE : croître, augmenter **3** BECOME : devenir <she's growing old : elle devient vieille> — *vt* **1** CULTIVATE : cultiver, faire pousser **2** : laisser pousser <he grew a beard : il a laissé pousser la barbe>

grower |ˈgro:ər| *n* : cultivateur *m,* -trice *f*

growl[1] |ˈgraʊl| *vi* : grogner, gronder

growl[2] *n* : grognement *m,* grondement *m*

grown–up[1] |ˈgro:n,əp| *adj* : adulte

grown–up[2] *n* : adulte *mf,* grande personne *f*

growth |ˈgro:θ| *n* **1** : croissance *f,* développement *m* <to stunt one's growth : retarder sa croissance> **2** INCREASE : croissance *f,* augmentation *f* **3** GROWING : pousse *f* (des plantes) **4** LUMP, TUMOR : grosseur *f,* tumeur *f*

grub[1] |ˈgrʌb| *vi* **grubbed; grubbing 1** DIG : fouir **2** RUMMAGE : fouiller **3** DRUDGE : besogner

grub[2] *n* **1** LARVA : larve *f* **2** FOOD : bouffe *f fam*

grubby |ˈgrʌbi| *adj* **grubbier; -est** : sale

grudge[1] ['grʌdʒ] *vt* **grudged; grudging** : donner à contrecœur <to grudge s.o. their success : en vouloir à qqn de sa réussite>
grudge[2] *n* : rancune *f* <to hold a grudge against : garder rancune à, avoir de la rancune contre>
gruel ['gru:əl] *n* : bouillie *f* (d'avoine)
grueling *or* **gruelling** ['gru:lɪŋ, gruə-] *adj* : exténuant, épuisant <a grueling experience : une expérience très dure>
gruesome ['gru:səm] *adj* : horrible, épouvantable
gruff ['grʌf] *adj* : bourru, brusque, malendurant *Can*
gruffly ['grʌfli] *adv* : d'un ton bourru, avec brusquerie
grumble[1] ['grʌmbəl] *vi* **-bled; -bling 1** COMPLAIN, GROUSE : grommeler, ronchonner *fam* **2** RUMBLE : gronder
grumble[2] *n* **1** GROUSING : ronchonnement *m fam* **2** RUMBLE : grondement *m*
grumpy ['grʌmpi] *adj* **grumpier; -est** : grincheux, grognon
grunt[1] ['grʌnt] *vi* : grogner
grunt[2] *n* : grognement *m*
guarantee[1] [,gærən'ti:] *vt* **-teed; -teeing** : garantir
guarantee[2] *n* : garantie *f*
guarantor [,gærən'tɔr] *n* : garant *m*, -rante *f*
guaranty [,gærən'ti:] → **guarantee**
guard[1] ['gɑrd] *vt* **1** DEFEND : garder, défendre **2** WATCH : surveiller, garder — *vi* **to guard against** : se garder de
guard[2] *n* **1** SENTRY, WARDEN : garde *m* **2** GUARDIAN, OVERSEER : gardien *m*, -dienne *f*; surveillant *m*, -lante *f* **3** PROTECTION : garde *f*, protection *f* **4** READINESS : garde *f* <to be on one's guard : être sur ses gardes> **5** SAFEGUARD : sauvegarde *f*, dispositif *m* de sûreté
guardhouse ['gɑrd,haʊs] *n* **1** : guérite *f* (pour des sentinelles) **2** PRISON : salle *f* de garde (militaire)
guardian ['gɑrdiən] *n* : gardien *m*, -dienne *f*
guardianship ['gɑrdiən,ʃɪp] *n* : tutelle *f*
Guatemalan[1] [,gwɑṭə'mɑlən] *adj* : guatémaltèque
Guatemalan[2] *n* : Guatémaltèque *mf*
guava ['gwɑvə] *n* : goyave *f*
gubernatorial [,gu:bənə'tori:əl, ,gju:-] *adj* : du gouverneur
guerrilla *or* **guerilla** [gə'rɪlə] *n* **1** : guérillero *m* **2 guerrillas** *npl* : guérilla *f* (combattants) **3 guerrilla warfare** : guérilla *f*
guess[1] ['gɛs] *vt* **1** CONJECTURE : deviner <guess who! : devine qui c'est!> <to guess s.o.'s age : deviner l'âge de qqn> **2** SUPPOSE : penser, croire <I guess so : je pense que oui> — *vi* : deviner
guess[2] *n* : conjecture *f*, supposition *f* <he made a good guess : il a deviné juste>
guesswork ['gɛs,wərk] *n* : hypothèse *f*, supposition *f*
guest ['gɛst] *n* **1** VISITOR : invité *m*, -tée *f*; hôte *mf* **2** PATRON : client *m*, cliente *f*; hôte *mf* (d'un hôtel, etc.)
guffaw[1] [gə'fɔ] *vi* : s'esclaffer
guffaw[2] [gə'fɔ, 'gʌ,fɔ] *n* : gros éclat *m* de rire
guidance ['gaɪdənts] *n* : conseils *mpl*, direction *f*
guide[1] ['gaɪd] *vt* **guided; guiding 1** DIRECT : guider, diriger **2** ADVISE, COUNSEL : conseiller, guider
guide[2] *n* : guide *m*
guidebook ['gaɪd,bʊk] *n* : guide *m*
guideline ['gaɪd,laɪn] *n* : ligne *f* directrice
guidepost ['gaɪd,po:st] *n* : poteau *m* indicateur
guild ['gɪld] *n* : association *f*
guile ['gaɪl] *n* : ruse *f*, astuce *f*
guileful ['gaɪlfəl] *adj* : rusé
guileless ['gaɪlləs] *adj* : candide, sans astuce
guillotine[1] ['gɪlə,ti:n, ,gi:jə'-] *vt* **-tined; -tining** : guillotiner
guillotine[2] *n* : guillotine *f*
guilt ['gɪlt] *n* : culpabilité *f*
guilty ['gɪlti] *adj* **guiltier; -est** : coupable
guinea fowl ['gɪni] *n* : pintade *f*
guinea pig *n* : cobaye *m*
Guinean[1] ['gɪnɪən] *adj* : guinéen
Guinean[2] *n* : Guinéen *m*, -néenne *f*
guise ['gaɪz] *n* : apparence *f* <under the guise of : sous l'apparence de>
guitar [gə'tɑr, gɪ-] *n* : guitare *f*
gulch ['gʌltʃ] *n* : ravin *m*
gulf ['gʌlf] *n* **1** : golfe *m* <the gulf of California : le golfe de la Californie> **2** ABYSS : gouffre *m*, abîme *m*
gull ['gʌl] *n* : mouette *f*
gullet ['gʌlət] *n* **1** THROAT : gosier *m* **2** ESOPHAGUS : œsophage *m*
gullible ['gʌlɪbəl] *adj* : crédule
gully ['gʌli] *n, pl* **-lies 1** GULCH : ravin *m* **2** TRENCH : rigole *f*
gulp[1] ['gʌlp] *vt or* **to gulp down 1** SWALLOW : avaler (à grosses bouchées), caler *Can* **2** SUPPRESS : ravaler <to gulp down tears : ravaler des larmes> — *vi* : avoir la gorge serrée
gulp[2] *n* : gorgée *f*, bouchée *f*
gum ['gʌm] *n* **1** CHEWING GUM : chewing-gum *m France*, gomme *f* à mâcher **2 gums** *npl* : gencives *fpl*
gumbo ['gʌm,bo:] *n* : gombo *m*
gumdrop ['gʌm,drɑp] *n* : boule *f* de gomme
gummy ['gʌmi] *adj* **gummier; -est** : gluant
gumption ['gʌmpʃən] *n* : initiative *f*, cran *m fam*

gun[1] [ˈgʌn] *vt* **gunned; gunning 1** *or* **to gun down** : abattre **2 to gun the engine** : accélérer le moteur

gun[2] *n* **1** FIREARM : arme *f* à feu, fusil *m* **2** CANNON : canon *m* **3** → **spray gun 4 to jump the gun** : brûler le feu

gunboat [ˈgʌn,boːt] *n* : canonnière *f*

gunfight [ˈgʌn,faɪt] *n* : combat *m* avec armes à feu

gunfire [ˈgʌn,faɪr] *n* : fusillade *f*, coups *mpl* de feu

gunman [ˈgʌnmən] *n, pl* **-men** [-mən, -,mɛn] : bandit *m* armé

gunner [ˈgʌnər] *n* : artilleur *m*

gunnery [ˈgʌnəri] *n* : artillerie *f*

gunpowder [ˈgʌn,paʊdər] *n* : poudre *f* (à canon)

gunshot [ˈgʌn,ʃɑt] *n* : coup *m* de feu

gunwale [ˈgʌnəl] *n* : plat-bord *m*

guppy [ˈgʌpi] *n, pl* **-pies** : guppy *m*

gurgle[1] [ˈgərgəl] *vi* **-gled; -gling 1** : murmurer, glouglouter *fam* <a gurgling stream : un ruisseau murmurant> **2** : gazouiller (se dit d'un bébé)

gurgle[2] *n* **1** : glouglou *m fam* (d'un liquide) **2** : gazouillement *m* (d'un enfant)

gush [ˈgʌʃ] *vi* **1** SPOUT : jaillir **2 to gush over** : s'extasier devant

gust [ˈgʌst] *n* : rafale *f*, bourrasque *f* <a gust of wind : un coup de vent>

gusto [ˈgʌs,toː] *n, pl* **-toes** : enthousiasme *m*, entrain *m*

gusty [ˈgʌsti] *adj* **gustier; -est** : venteux <gusty wind : rafales de vent>

gut[1] [ˈgʌt] *vt* **gutted; gutting 1** EVISCERATE : vider **2** DESTROY : ravager

gut[2] *n* **1** INTESTINE : intestin *m*, boyau *m* **2 guts** *npl* INNARDS : entrailles *fpl*, tripes *fpl fam* **3 guts** *npl* COURAGE : cran *m fam*

gutter [ˈgʌtər] *n* **1** : gouttière *f* (d'un toit) **2** : caniveau *m* (de la rue)

guttural [ˈgʌtərəl] *adj* : guttural

guy [ˈgaɪ] *n* **1** *or* **guyline** : corde *f* de tente **2** FELLOW : type *m fam*, mec *m fam*, gars *m fam*

Guyanese[1] [,gaɪəˈniːz] *adj* : guyanais

Guyanese[2] *n* : Guyanais *m*, -naise *f*

guzzle [ˈgʌzəl] *vt* **-zled; -zling** : bâfrer *fam*, engloutir

gym [ˈdʒɪm] → **gymnasium**

gymnasium [dʒɪmˈneɪziəm, -ʒəm] *n, pl* **-siums** *or* **-sia** [-ziːə, -ʒə] : gymnase *m*

gymnast [ˈdʒɪmnəst, -,næst] *n* : gymnaste *mf*

gymnastic [dʒɪmˈnæstɪk] *adj* : gymnastique

gymnastics [dʒɪmˈnæstɪks] *n* : gymnastique *f*

gynecologic [,gaɪnɪkəˈlɑdʒɪk] *or* **gynecological** [-ˈlɑdʒɪkəl] *adj* : gynécologique

gynecologist [,gaɪnəˈkɑlədʒɪst] *n* : gynécologue *mf*

gynecology [,gaɪnəˈkɑlədʒi] *n* : gynécologie *f*

gyp[1] [ˈdʒɪp] *vt* **gypped; gypping** : escroquer, arnaquer *fam*

gyp[2] *n* **1** CHEAT, SWINDLER : escroc *m*; arnaqueur *m*, -queuse *f fam* **2** FRAUD, SWINDLE : escroquerie *f*, arnaque *f fam*

gypsum [ˈdʒɪpsəm] *n* : gypse *m*

Gypsy [ˈdʒɪpsi] *n, pl* **-sies** : gitan *m*, -tane *f*

gyrate [ˈdʒaɪ,reɪt] *vi* **-rated; -rating** : tournoyer

gyroscope [ˈdʒaɪrə,skoːp] *n* : gyroscope *m*

H

h [ˈeɪtʃ] *n, pl* **h's** *or* **hs** [ˈeɪtʃəz] : h *m*, huitième lettre de l'alphabet

haberdashery [ˈhæbər,dæʃəri] *n, pl* **-eries** : magasin *m* de vêtements pour hommes

habit [ˈhæbɪt] *n* **1** : habit *m* (religieux) **2** CUSTOM : habitude *f*, coutume *f* **3** ADDICTION : accoutumance *f*, dépendance *f*

habitable [ˈhæbɪtəbəl] *adj* : habitable

habitat [ˈhæbɪ,tæt] *n* : habitat *m*

habitation [,hæbɪˈteɪʃən] *n* **1** OCCUPANCY : habitation *f* **2** RESIDENCE : habitation *f*, domicile *m*, résidence *f*

habit-forming [ˈhæbɪt,fɔrmɪŋ] *adj* ADDICTIVE : qui crée une accoutumance

habitual [həˈbɪtʃʊəl] *adj* **1** CUSTOMARY : habituel **2** INVETERATE : invétéré <a habitual drunkard : un ivrogne invétéré>

habitually [həˈbɪtʃʊəli] *adv* : habituellement

habituate [həˈbɪtʃʊ,eɪt] *vt* **-ated; -ating 1** : habituer **2 to habituate oneself to** : s'habituer à, s'accoutumer à

hack[1] [ˈhæk] *vt* : tailler, taillader <to hack one's way through sth : tailler un passage à travers qqch> — *vi* **1** CHOP : donner des coups de couteau **2** COUGH : tousser (d'une toux sèche) **3 to hack into** : s'introduire dans, entrer dans (en informatique)

hack[2] *n* **1** : entaille *f* **2** BLOW : coup *m* violent **3** HORSE : cheval *m* de louage **4** *or* **hack writer** : écrivaillon *m*, plumitif *m* **5** COUGH : toux *f* sèche

hackle [ˈhækəl] *n* **1** : plume *f* du cou (d'un oiseau) **2 hackles** *npl* : poils *mpl* hérissés (d'un chien, etc.) <don't get your hackles up : ne t'énerve pas>

hackney [ˈhækni] *n, pl* **-neys** : fiacre *m*

hackneyed [ˈhæknid] *adj* TRITE : banal, rebattu

hacksaw [ˈhæk,sɔ] *n* : scie *f* à métaux

had → have

haddock [ˈhædək] *ns & pl* : églefin *m*

hadn't [ˈhædənt] (*contraction of* **had not**) **→ have**

haft [ˈhæft] *n* : manche *m* (d'un outil), poignée *f* (d'une dague)

hag [ˈhæg] *n* **1** WITCH : sorcière *f* **2** CRONE : vieille *f* bique, grébiche *f Can*

haggard [ˈhægərd] *adj* : hâve, exténué

haggle [ˈhægəl] *vi* **-gled; -gling** : marchander

ha–ha [,hɑˈhɑ, ˈhɑˈhɑ] *interj* : ha ha

hail[1] [ˈheɪl] *vi* : grêler (en météorologie) — *vt* **1** GREET : saluer, acclamer **2** : héler (un taxi)

hail[2] *n* **1** : grêle *f* (en météorologie) **2** GREETING : salutation *f*

hailstone [ˈheɪl,sto:n] *n* : grêlon *m*

hailstorm [ˈheɪl,stɔrm] *n* : averse *f* de grêle

hair [ˈhær] *n* **1** : cheveux *mpl* <to have short hair : avoir les cheveux courts> **2** : poil *m* <to have hair on one's legs : avoir du poil sur les jambes> <dog hair : poils de chien>

hairbreadth [ˈhær,brɛdθ] *or* **hairsbreadth** [ˈhærz-] *n* **by a hairbreadth** : d'un poil, de justesse

hairbrush [ˈhær,brʌʃ] *n* : brosse *f* à cheveux

haircut [ˈhær,kʌt] *n* : coupe *f* de cheveux

hairdo [ˈhær,du:] *n, pl* **-dos** : coiffure *f*, peignure *f Can fam*

hairdresser [ˈhær,drɛsər] *n* : coiffeur *m*, -feuse *f*

hairiness [ˈhærinəs] *n* : pilosité *f*

hairless [ˈhærləs] *adj* : sans cheveux, glabre (se dit du corps), sans poils (se dit des animaux)

hairline [ˈhær,laɪn] *n* **1** : ligne *f* très mince **2** : naissance *f* des cheveux <to have a receding hairline : avoir un front qui se dégarnit>

hairpin [ˈhær,pɪn] *n* : épingle *f* à cheveux

hair–raising [ˈhær,reɪzɪŋ] *adj* : à faire dresser les cheveux sur la tête, horrifique

hairy [ˈhæri] *adj* **hairier; -est** : poilu, velu

Haitian[1] [ˈheɪʃən, ˈheɪţiən] *adj* : haïtien

Haitian[2] *n* : Haïtien *m*, -tienne *f*

hake [ˈheɪk] *n* : merlu *m* (vivant), colin *m* (en cuisine)

hale[1] [ˈheɪl] *vt* **haled; haling** HAUL : haler, tirer <to hale into court : traîner devant le tribunal>

hale[2] *adj* : vigoureux <hale and hearty : en pleine forme>

half[1] [ˈhæf, ˈhaf] *adv* : à demi, à moitié <to be half full : être à demi rempli>

half[2] *adj* **1** : demi <a half sheet of paper : une demi-feuille de papier> <two hours and a half : deux heures et demie> **2** PARTIAL : demi <a half smile : un demi sourire>

half[3] *n, pl* **halves** [ˈhævz, ˈhavz] **1** : demi *m* <two halves : deux demis> **2** : moitié *f* <half of the profits : la moitié des profits> **3** *or* **halftime** : mi-temps *f* (aux sports)

half brother *n* : demi-frère *m*

halfhearted [ˈhæfˈharţəd] *adj* : qui manque d'enthousiasme

halfheartedly [ˈhæfˈharţədli] *adv* : sans enthousiasme, sans conviction

half–life [ˈhæf,laɪf] *n* : demi-vie *f*

half sister *n* : demi-soeur *f*

halfway [ˈhæfˈweɪ] *adv & adj* : à mi-chemin

half–wit [ˈhæf,wɪt] *n* : imbécile *mf;* idiot *m*, idiote *f*

half–witted [ˈhæf,wɪţəd] *adj* : bête, stupide

halibut [ˈhælɪbət] *ns & pl* : flétan *m*

halitosis [,hæləˈtosəs] *n* : mauvaise haleine *f*

hall [ˈhɔl] *n* **1** AUDITORIUM : salle *f* (de concert, etc.) **2** LOBBY : entrée *f*, vestibule *m*, hall *m* (d'entrée), portique *m Can fam* **3** DORMITORY : résidence *f* universitaire **4 → city hall**

hallelujah [,hæləˈlu:jə, ,hɑ,lo:d] *interj* : alléluia

hallmark [ˈhɔl,mark] *n* : caractéristique *f*, sceau *m*

hallow [ˈhæ,lo:] *vt* : sanctifier, consacrer

hallowed [ˈhæ,lo:d, ˈhæ,lo:əd, ˈhɑ-] *adj* : sanctifié, saint

Halloween [,hæləˈwi:n, ,hɑ-] *n* : Halloween *f*

hallucinate [həˈlu:sən,eɪt] *vi* **-nated; -nating** : avoir des hallucinations

hallucination [hə,lu:sənˈeɪʃən] *n* : hallucination *f*

hallucinogen [həˈlu:sənədʒən] *n* : hallucinogène *m*

hallucinogenic [hə,lu:sənəˈdʒɛnɪk] *adj* : hallucinogène

hallway [ˈhɔl,weɪ] *n* **1** ENTRANCE : entrée *f*, vestibule *m* **2** CORRIDOR : corridor *m*, couloir *m*

halo [ˈheɪ,lo:] *n, pl* **-los** *or* **-loes** : auréole *f*

halt[1] [ˈhɔlt] *vi* : s'arrêter — *vt* **1** STOP : arrêter (une personne) **2** : interrompre <the strike halted buses : la grève a interrompu le service d'autobus>

halt[2] *n* : halte *f*, arrêt *m* <to come to a halt : s'interrompre>

halter [ˈhɔltər] *n* **1** : licou *m* (d'un animal) **2** *or* **halter top** : chemisier *m* à dos nu

halting [ˈhɔltɪŋ] *adj* HESITANT : hésitant

halve [ˈhæv, ˈhav] *vt* **halved; halving 1** DIVIDE : couper en deux **2** REDUCE : réduire de moitié

halves → half[3]

ham [ˈhæm] *n* **1** : jambon *m* **2** *or* **ham actor** : cabotin *m*, -tine *f* **3 hams** *npl*

BUTTOCKS, THIGHS : cuisses *fpl*, fesses *fpl* **4** *or* **ham radio operator** : radioamateur *m*

hamburger [ˈhæm,bərgər] *or* **hamburg** [-,bərg] *n* **1** : hamburger *m* (cuit) **2** : viande *f* hachée <a pound of hamburger : une livre de viande hachée>

hamlet [ˈhæmlət] *n* : hameau *m*

hammer[1] [ˈhæmər] *vt* : marteler, enfoncer (à coups de marteau) — *vi* : frapper à coups de marteau

hammer[2] *n* **1** : marteau *m* **2** : chien *m* (d'une arme à feu)

hammock [ˈhæmək] *n* : hamac *m*

hamper[1] [ˈhæmpər] *vt* : entraver, gêner

hamper[2] *n* : panier *m* <clothes hamper : panier à linge sale>

hamster [ˈhæmpstər] *n* : hamster *m*

hamstring[1] [ˈhæm,strɪŋ] *vt* **-strung** [-ˈstrʌŋ]; **-stringing** [-strɪŋɪŋ] **1** : couper le jarret à (un animal) **2** INCAPACITATE : paralyser <hamstrung by guilt : paralysé par les remords>

hamstring[2] *n* : jarret *m* (d'un animal), tendon *m* (d'une personne)

hand[1] [ˈhænd] *vt* : donner, passer

hand[2] *n* **1** : main *f* <good with one's hands : adroit de ses mains> <to lend a hand : prêter une main> **2** POINTER : aiguille *f* (d'une montre, etc.) **3** SIDE : côté *m* <on the other hand : par contre, d'un autre côté> **4** HANDWRITING : écriture *f* **5** HELP : aide *f* <to give s.o. a hand : donner un coup de main à qqn> **6** APPLAUSE : applaudissements *mpl* **7** : main *f*, jeu *m* (aux cartes) **8** WORKER : ouvrier *m*, -vrière *f* **9 to ask for s.o.'s hand (in marriage)** : demander qqn en mariage **10 to try one's hand at** : s'essayer à

handbag [ˈhænd,bæg] *n* : sac *m* à main

handball [ˈhænd,bɔl] *n* : handball *m*

handbill [ˈhænd,bɪl] *n* : prospectus *m*

handbook [ˈhænd,bʊk] *n* : manuel *m*, guide *m*

handcuff [ˈhænd,kʌf] *vt* : passer les menottes à

handcuffs [ˈhænd,kʌfs] *npl* : menottes *fpl*

handful [ˈhænd,fʊl] *n* : poignée *f*

handgun [ˈhænd,gʌn] *n* : pistolet *m*, revolver *m*

handicap[1] [ˈhændi,kæp] *vt* **-capped**; **-capping** : handicaper

handicap[2] *n* **1** DISABILITY : handicap *m* **2** DISADVANTAGE : désavantage *m*, handicap *m*

handicapped [ˈhændi,kæpt] *adj* : handicapé

handicraft [ˈhændi,kræft] *n* **1** : travail *m* artisanal **2 handicrafts** *npl* : objets *mpl* artisanaux

handily [ˈhændəli] *adv* EASILY : haut la main

handiwork [ˈhændi,wərk] *n* **1** WORK : travail *m* manuel **2** ARTICLES, CRAFTS : objets *mpl* artisanaux

handkerchief [ˈhæŋkərtʃəf, -,tʃi:f] *n, pl* **-chiefs** : mouchoir *m*

handle[1] [ˈhændəl] *vt* **-dled**; **-dling** **1** TOUCH : toucher à, manipuler **2** STAND : supporter <I can't handle the heat : je ne peux pas supporter la chaleur> **3** MANAGE : manier, gérer

handle[2] *n* : manche *m* (d'un ustensile), poignée *f* (de porte), anse *f* (de panier)

handlebars [ˈhændəl,bɑrz] *npl* : guidon *m*

handmade [ˈhænd,meɪd] *adj* : fait à la main

hand–me–downs [ˈhændmi,daʊnz] *npl* : vêtements *mpl* de seconde main

handout [ˈhænd,aʊt] *n* **1** CHARITY : aumône *f*, don *m* **2** LEAFLET : prospectus *m*

handpick [ˈhændˈpɪk] *vt* : sélectionner avec soin

handrail [ˈhænd,reɪl] *n* **1** : rampe *f*, main *f* courante (d'un escalier) **2** : garde-fou *m* (d'un pont)

handsaw [ˈhænd,sɔ] *n* : scie *f* à main

hands down *adv* EASILY, UNQUESTIONABLY : sans aucun doute

handshake [ˈhænd,ʃeɪk] *n* : poignée *f* de main

handsome [ˈhæntsəm] *adj* **handsomer**; **-est** **1** CONSIDERABLE : important, considérable **2** GENEROUS : généreux **3** GOOD-LOOKING : beau

handsomely [ˈhæntsəmli] *adv* **1** ELEGANTLY : élégamment **2** GENEROUSLY : avec générosité

handspring [ˈhænd,sprɪŋ] *n* : saut *m* de mains

handstand [ˈhænd,stænd] *n* : équilibre *m* sur les mains

hand–to–hand [ˈhændtəˈhænd] *adj* : (au) corps à corps

handwriting [ˈhænd,raɪt̬ɪŋ] *n* : écriture *f*

handwritten [ˈhænd,rɪtən] *adj* : écrit à la main

handy [ˈhændi] *adj* **handier**; **-est** **1** NEARBY : à portée de la main, proche **2** CONVENIENT, USEFUL : utile, pratique **3** CLEVER : adroit, habile

handyman [ˈhændimən] *n, pl* **-men** [-mən, -,mɛn] : bricoleur *m*, homme *m* à tout faire

hang[1] [ˈhæŋ] *v* **hung** [ˈhʌŋ]; **hanging** *vt* **1** SUSPEND : suspendre, accrocher **2** (*past tense often* **hanged**) : pendre (un criminel) **3** : poser (une porte, etc.) **4 to hang one's head** : baisser la tête de honte — *vi* **1** DANGLE : être accroché, être suspendu **2** FALL : être accroché, être suspendu (se dit des vêtements, des rideaux, etc.) **3** HOVER : flotter, être suspendu (en l'air) **4** DROOP : pencher, tomber

hang[2] *n* **1** : drapé *m* (d'un rideau, etc.) **2 to get the hang of doing sth** : prendre le coup pour faire qqch <I can't get the hang of it! : je ne pige pas!>

hangar [ˈhæŋər, ˈhæŋgər] *n* : hangar *m*

hanger [ˈhæŋər] *n or* **coat hanger** : cintre *m*

hangman [ˈhæŋmən] *n, pl* **-men** [-mən, -ˌmɛn] : bourreau *m*

hangnail [ˈhæŋˌneɪl] *n* : envie *f*

hangout [ˈhæŋˌaʊt] *n* : endroit *m* préféré (pour flâner)

hangover [ˈhæŋˌo:vər] *n* : gueule *f* de bois

hank [ˈhæŋk] *n* : écheveau *m*

hanker [ˈhæŋkər] *vi* **to hanker for** : désirer, avoir envie de

hankering [ˈhæŋkərɪŋ] *n* : désir *m,* envie *f*

hansom [ˈhæntsəm] *n* : cabriolet *m*

Hanukkah [ˈxɑnəkə, ˈhɑ-] *n* : Hanukkah *m*

haphazard [hæpˈhæzərd] *adj* : fortuit, mal organisé <in a haphazard way : de façon peu méthodique>

haphazardly [hæpˈhæzərdli] *adv* : n'importe comment, sans organisation

hapless [ˈhæpləs] *adj* : infortuné, malchanceux

happen [ˈhæpən] *vi* **1** OCCUR : arriver, se passer <what's happening? : qu'est-ce qui se passe?> **2** CHANCE : arriver par hasard <I happened to overhear her plans : j'ai entendu ses plans par hasard> **3** : se trouver <it so happens that I was right : il se trouve que j'avais raison> **4** BEFALL : arriver <what happened to you? : qu'est-ce qui t'est arrivé?>

happening [ˈhæpənɪŋ] *n* : incident *m,* événement *m*

happily [ˈhæpəli] *adv* : heureusement

happiness [ˈhæpinəs] *n* : bonheur *m*

happy [ˈhæpi] *adj* **happier; -est 1** FORTUNATE : heureux, favorable **2** CHEERFUL : heureux **3** PLEASED : content, satisfait **4** (*expressing willingness*) <to be happy to do sth : être heureux de faire qqch> <I'm happy to help you : je suis ravi de vous aider>

happy–go–lucky [ˈhæpigo:ˈlʌki] *adj* : insouciant

harangue[1] [həˈræŋ] *vt* **-rangued; -ranguing** : haranguer

harangue[2] *n* : harangue *f*

harass [həˈræs, ˈhærəs] *vt* **1** TORMENT, WORRY : tourmenter, harceler **2** ANNOY, PESTER : harceler

harassment [həˈræsmənt, ˈhærəsmənt] *n* : harcèlement *m*

harbinger [ˈhɑrbɪndʒər] *n* **1** PRECURSOR : signe *m* avant-coureur, précurseur *m* **2** OMEN : présage *m* <a harbinger of doom : un mauvais présage>

harbor[1] *or Brit* **harbour** [ˈhɑrbər] *vt* **1** SHELTER : héberger (une personne), receler (un criminel) **2** HOLD, KEEP : nourrir (un espoir, etc.), entretenir (de doutes)

harbor[2] *or Brit* **harbour** *n* PORT : port *m*

hard[1] [ˈhɑrd] *adv* **1** FORCEFULLY, STRENUOUSLY : dur, fort <to work hard : travailler dur> <to snow hard : neiger fort> **2 to take sth hard** : mal prendre qqch

hard[2] *adj* **1** FIRM : dur, solide **2** : calcaire <hard water : eau calcaire> **3** DEFINITE : définitif **4** SEARCHING : pénétrant <a hard look : un regard pénétrant> **5** UNFEELING : dur, insensible **6** TROUBLESOME : difficile, pénible **7** INTENSE : dur, ferme <hard blows : coups durs> **8** DILIGENT : consciencieux

harden [ˈhɑrdən] *vt* : durcir, endurcir <to harden one's heart : endurcir son coeur> — *vi* : s'endurcir

hardheaded [ˈhɑrdˈhɛdəd] *adj* **1** STUBBORN : têtu, obstiné **2** REALISTIC : réaliste, pratique

hard–hearted [ˈhɑrdˈhɑrṭəd] *adj* : dur, insensible

hardly [ˈhɑrdli] *adv* **1** BARELY : à peine, ne . . . guère **2** NOT : ne . . . pas, presque jamais <it's hardly surprising : ce n'est pas surprenant>

hardness [ˈhɑrdnəs] *n* **1** FIRMNESS : dureté *f* **2** DIFFICULTY : difficulté *f,* dureté *f* **3** SEVERITY : sévérité *f,* dureté *f*

hardship [ˈhɑrdˌʃɪp] *n* **1** DIFFICULTY : détresse *f* **2** DISTRESS, SUFFERING : épreuves *fpl,* privations *fpl*

hardware [ˈhɑrdˌwær] *n* **1** : quincaillerie *f* **2** : matériel *m* (en informatique)

hardwood [ˈhɑrdˌwʊd] *n* : bois *m* dur, bois *m* franc *Can*

hardworking [ˈhɑrdˈwərkɪŋ] *adj* : travailleur, travaillant *Can*

hardy [ˈhɑrdi] *adj* **hardier; -est 1** BOLD : hardi, intrépide **2** ROBUST : résistant, robuste

hare [ˈhær] *n, pl* **hare** *or* **hares** : lièvre *m*

harebrained [ˈhærˌbreɪnd] *adj* : écervelé, insensé

harelip [ˈhærˈlɪp] *n* : bec-de-lièvre *m*

harem [ˈhærəm] *n* : harem *m*

hark [ˈhɑrk] *vi* **1** LISTEN : prêter l'oreille, ouïr **2 to hark back to** : revenir à

harlequin [ˈhɑrlɪkən, -kwən] *n* : arlequin *m*

harm[1] [ˈhɑrm] *vt* : faire du mal à, nuire à

harm[2] *n* : mal *m,* dommage *m,* tort *m*

harmful [ˈhɑrmfəl] *adj* : nuisible, nocif

harmfully [ˈhɑrmfəli] *adv* : de façon nuisible

harmless [ˈhɑrmləs] *adj* : inoffensif, anodin

harmlessly [ˈhɑrmləsli] *adv* : sans faire de mal

harmonic [hɑrˈmɑnɪk] *adj* : harmonique — **harmonically** [-nɪkli] *adv*

harmonica [hɑrˈmɑnɪkə] *n* : harmonica *m*

harmonious [hɑrˈmo:niəs] *adj* : harmonieux — **harmoniously** *adv*

harmonize [ˈhɑrməˌnaɪz] *v* **-nized; -nizing** *vt* : harmoniser — *vi* : s'harmoniser

harmony [ˈhɑrməni] *n, pl* **-nies** : harmonie *f*

harness[1] [ˈhɑrnəs] *vt* **1** : harnacher (un cheval) **2** UTILIZE : exploiter (de l'énergie, etc.)

harness[2] *n* : harnais *m,* harnachement *m*

harp[1] [ˈhɑrp] *vi* **to harp on** : rabâcher, répéter continuellement

harp[2] *n* : harpe *f*

harpist [ˈhɑrpɪst] *n* : harpiste *mf*

harpoon[1] [hɑrˈpuːn] *vt* : harponner

harpoon[2] *n* : harpon *m*

harpsichord [ˈhɑrpsɪˌkɔrd] *n* : clavecin *m*

harrow[1] [ˈhærˌoː] *vt* **1** : herser (la terre) **2** TORMENT, VEX : torturer, tourmenter

harrow[2] *n* : herse *f*

harry [ˈhæri] *vt* **-ried; -rying** HARASS : harceler

harsh [ˈhɑrʃ] *adj* **1** ROUGH : rude <a harsh surface : une surface rude> **2** SEVERE : dur, sévère **3** DIFFICULT, RIGOROUS : rigoureux

harshly [ˈhɑrʃli] *adv* : sévèrement, durement

harshness [ˈhɑrʃnəs] *n* : sévérité *f*

hart [ˈhɑrt] *n Brit* STAG : cerf *m*

harvest[1] [ˈhɑrvəst] *vt* : moissonner, récolter

harvest[2] *n* : moisson *f,* récolte *f*

harvester [ˈhɑrvəstər] *n* **1** : moissonneur *m,* -neuse *f* (personne) **2** : moissonneuse *f* (machine)

has → **have**

hash[1] [ˈhæʃ] *vt* **1** CHOP : hacher **2 to hash over** DISCUSS : parler de, discuter

hash[2] *n* **1** : hachis *m* **2** JUMBLE, MESS : gâchis *m*

hasn't [ˈhæzənt] (*contraction of* **has not**) → **have**

hasp [ˈhæsp] *n* : moraillon *m,* loquet *m*

hassle[1] [ˈhæsəl] *v* **-sled; -sling** *vi* ARGUE : se chamailler, se disputer — *vt* ANNOY, HARASS : tracasser, harceler

hassle[2] *n* **1** QUARREL : chicane *f,* dispute *f* **2** BOTHER, TROUBLE : embêtements *mpl,* ennuis *mpl*

hassock [ˈhæsək] *n* **1** CUSHION : coussin *m* (d'agenouilloir) **2** FOOTSTOOL : pouf *m,* tabouret *m*

haste [ˈheɪst] *n* : hâte *f,* précipitation *f* <to make haste : se hâter>

hasten [ˈheɪsən] *vt* : hâter, précipiter — *vi* HURRY : se hâter, se dépêcher

hastily [ˈheɪstəli] *adv* : à la hâte

hasty [ˈheɪsti] *adj* **hastier; -est 1** HURRIED : précipité, à la hâte **2** RASH : hâtif, irréfléchi

hat [ˈhæt] *n* : chapeau *m*

hatch[1] [ˈhætʃ] *vt* **1** INCUBATE : couver, faire éclore **2** CONCOCT : ourdir (un complot) — *vi* : éclore

hatch[2] *n* **1** : écoutille *f* (d'un navire) **2** BROOD : couvée *f,* éclosion *f*

hatchery [ˈhætʃəri] *n, pl* **-ries 1** : couvoir *m* (de poules) **2** *or* **fish hatchery** : station *f* d'alevinage

hatchet [ˈhætʃət] *n* : hachette *f*

hatchway [ˈhætʃˌweɪ] *n* HATCH : écoutille *f* (d'un navire)

hate[1] [ˈheɪt] *vt* **hated; hating** : détester, haïr, avoir horreur de

hate[2] *n* : haine *f*

hateful [ˈheɪtfəl] *adj* : odieux, détestable — **hatefully** *adv*

hatred [ˈheɪtrəd] *n* : haine *f*

hatter [ˈhæt̬ər] *n* : chapelier *m,* -lière *f*

haughtily [ˈhɔt̬əli] *adv* : de façon hautaine

haughty [ˈhɔt̬i] *adj* **haughtier; -est** : hautain, arrogant

haul[1] [ˈhɔl] *vt* **1** DRAG, PULL : tirer **2** TRANSPORT : transporter, camionner

haul[2] *n* **1** PULL, TUG : coup *m* **2** CATCH : prise *f* (de poissons) **3** LOOT : butin *m* **4** JOURNEY : chemin *m,* route *f,* voyage *m* <it's a long haul : la route est longue>

hauler [ˈhɔlər] *n* DRIVER, TRUCKER : routier *m;* camionneur *m,* -neuse *f*

haunch [ˈhɔntʃ] *n* **1** HIP : hanche *f* **2 haunches** *npl* HINDQUARTERS : arrière-train *m,* derrière *m* (d'un animal)

haunt[1] [ˈhɔnt] *vt* **1** : hanter <a haunted house : une maison hantée> **2** PREOCCUPY : hanter, obséder **3** FREQUENT : fréquenter, hanter

haunt[2] *n* : lieu *m* fréquenté

haunting [ˈhɔntɪŋ] *adj* : obsédant

have [ˈhæv, *in senses 3 and 4 as an auxiliary verb usu* ˈhæf] *v* **had** [ˈhæd]; **having; has** [ˈhæz, *in senses 3 and 4 as an auxiliary verb usu* ˈhæs] *vt* **1** POSSESS : avoir <do you have change? : avez-vous de la monnaie?> <April has 30 days : il y a 30 jours en avril> **2** EXPERIENCE, UNDERGO : avoir <I have a cold : j'ai un rhume> **3** (*indicating consumption*) <to have a sandwich : manger un sandwich> <to have a cigarette : fumer une cigarette> **4** RECEIVE : recevoir, avoir <to have permission : avoir la permission> <I have a letter from Anne : j'ai reçu une lettre d'Anne> **5** WANT : vouloir, prendre <I'll have coffee : je voudrais du café> **6** ALLOW : permettre, tolérer <I won't have it! : je ne le tolérerai pas!> **7** HOLD : tenir, faire <he had me by the arm : il me tenait par le bras> <to have a party : faire une fête> **8** BEAR : avoir (un enfant) **9** (*indicating causation*) <she had a dress made : elle s'est fait faire une robe> — *v aux* **1** : avoir, être <he had seen me : il m'avait vu> <she has left : elle est partie> **2** (*used in tags*) <you have finished, haven't you? : vous avez fini, n'est-ce pas?> **3 to have to**

: devoir <we have to meet the deadline : nous devons rencontrer la date d'échéance> **4 to have to do with** : concerner

haven [ˈheɪvən] *n* : refuge *m,* havre *m*

havoc [ˈhævək] *n* **1** DEVASTATION : destruction *f,* dévastation *f* **2** CHAOS : désordre *m,* chaos *m*

Hawaiian[1] [həˈwaɪən] *adj* : hawaïen

Hawaiian[2] *n* **1** : Hawaïen *m,* -waïenne *f* **2** : hawaïen *m* (langue)

hawk[1] [ˈhɔk] *vt* : colporter, vendre (à la criée)

hawk[2] *n* : faucon *m* (oiseau)

hawker [ˈhɔkər] *n* PEDDLER : colporteur *m,* -teuse *f*

hawthorn [ˈhɔˌθɔrn] *n* : aubépine *f,* cenellier *m Can*

hay [ˈheɪ] *n* : foin *m*

hay fever *n* : rhume *m* des foins

hayloft [ˈheɪˌlɔft] *n* : grenier *m* à foin

haystack [ˈheɪˌstæk] *n* : meule *f* de foin

haywire [ˈheɪˌwaɪr] *adj* : détraqué <to go haywire : se détraquer>

hazard[1] [ˈhæzərd] *vt* : hasarder, risquer

hazard[2] *n* **1** PERIL : danger *m,* risque *m* **2** CHANCE : chance *f,* hasard *m*

hazardous [ˈhæzərdəs] *adj* : dangereux, risqué

haze[1] [ˈheɪz] *vi* **hazed; hazing** *or* **to haze over** : devenir brumeux

haze[2] *n* : brume *f*

hazel [ˈheɪzəl] *n* **1** : noisetier *m* (arbre) **2** : noisette *f* (couleur)

hazelnut [ˈheɪzəlˌnʌt] *n* : noisette *f*

haziness [ˈheɪzinəs] *n* **1** MISTINESS : état *m* brumeux **2** VAGUENESS : flou *m*

hazy [ˈheɪzi] *adj* **hazier; -est 1** : brumeux <hazy sky : ciel brumeux> **2** VAGUE : vague, flou

he [ˈhiː] *pron* **1** : il <he spoke to me : il m'a parlé> **2** : lui <she's younger than he (is) : elle est plus jeune que lui>

head[1] [ˈhɛd] *vt* **1** LEAD : être en tête de **2** DIRECT : diriger **3** TITLE : intituler — *vi* **1** : former une tête (se dit d'un chou, etc.) **2** : se diriger, aller <where are you headed? : où vas-tu?>

head[2] *adj* CHIEF : en chef

head[3] *n* **1** : tête *f* <from head to toe : de la tête aux pieds> **2** MIND : tête *f,* esprit *m* **3** END : bout *m* (d'une table), chevet *m* (d'un lit) **4** DIRECTOR : chef *m;* directeur *m,* -trice *f* **5** : personne *f* <$8.00 per head : 8,00 $ par personne> **6 at the head of** : à la tête de (une classe, etc.) **7 to come to a head** : arriver au point critique

headache [ˈhɛdˌeɪk] *n* : mal *m* de tête

headband [ˈhɛdˌbænd] *n* : bandeau *m*

headdress [ˈhɛdˌdrɛs] *n* : coiffe *f*

headfirst [ˈhɛdˈfərst] *adv* : la tête la première

headgear [ˈhɛdˌgɪr] *n* : couvre-chef *m,* coiffure *f*

heading [ˈhɛdɪŋ] *n* **1** DIRECTION : cap *m* (d'un navire) **2** : titre *m* (d'un article), rubrique *f* (d'un sujet) **3** LETTERHEAD : en-tête *m*

headland [ˈhɛdlənd, -ˌlænd] *n* : promontoire *m*

headlight [ˈhɛdˌlaɪt] *n* : phare *m*

headline [ˈhɛdˌlaɪn] *n* : manchette *f,* (gros) titre *m*

headlong[1] [ˈhɛdˈlɔŋ] *adv* **1** HEADFIRST : la tête la première **2** HASTILY, RECKLESSLY : à toute allure, à toute vitesse

headlong[2] [ˈhɛdˌlɔŋ] *adj* : précipité

headmaster [ˈhɛdˌmæstər] *n* : directeur *m* (d'école)

headmistress [ˈhɛdˌmɪstrəs, -ˈmɪs-] *n* : directrice *f* (d'école)

head–on [ˈhɛdˈɑn, -ˈɔn] *adv & adj* : de front, face-à-face

headphones [ˈhɛdˌfoːnz] *npl* : écouteurs *mpl,* casque *m*

headquarters [ˈhɛdˌkwɔrt̬ərz] *ns & pl* **1** : siège *m* social (d'une compagnie) **2** : quartier *m* général (dans l'armée, etc.)

headrest [ˈhɛdˌrɛst] *n* : appui-tête *m*

head start *n* : avance *f,* longueur *f* d'avance

headstone [ˈhɛdˌstoːn] *n* : pierre *f* tombale

headstrong [ˈhɛdˌstrɔŋ] *adj* : têtu, obstiné

headwaiter [ˈhɛdˈweɪt̬ər] *n* : maître *m* d'hôtel

headwaters [ˈhɛdˌwɔt̬ərz, -ˌwɑ-] *npl* : sources *fpl*

headway [ˈhɛdˌweɪ] *n* **1** PROGRESS : progrès *m* **2 to make headway** : avancer, progresser

heady [ˈhɛdi] *adj* **headier; -est 1** INTOXICATING : qui monte à la tête **2** EXCITING, STIMULATING : passionnant, excitant

heal [ˈhiːl] *vt* : guérir, cicatriser — *vi* : guérir, se cicatriser

healer [ˈhiːlər] *n* : guérisseur *m,* -seuse *f*

health [ˈhɛlθ] *n* : santé *f*

healthful [ˈhɛlθfəl] *adj* : bon pour la santé, sain

healthily [ˈhɛlθəli] *adv* : sainement

health maintenance organization → **HMO**

healthy [ˈhɛlθi] *adj* **healthier; -est 1** WELL : en bonne santé **2** PROSPEROUS : prospère, florissant

heap[1] [ˈhiːp] *vt* : entasser, amasser

heap[2] *n* PILE : amas *m,* tas *m*

hear [ˈhɪr] *v* **heard** [ˈhərd]; **hearing** *vt* **1** : entendre <I can't hear you : je ne t'entends pas> **2** HEED : écouter **3** LEARN : apprendre, entendre <I heard the news : j'ai appris la nouvelle> — *vi* **1** : entendre <she doesn't hear very well : elle n'entends pas très bien> **2 to hear from** : avoir des nouvelles de

hearing [ˈhɪrɪŋ] *n* **1** : ouïe *f,* audition *f* **2** : audience *f* (d'un tribunal) **3 within hearing** : à portée de voix

hearing aid *n* : appareil *m* auditif

hearken [ˈhɑrkən] *vi* **to hearken to** : écouter

hearsay [ˈhɪrˌseɪ] *n* : ouï-dire *m,* rumeur *f*

hearse [ˈhərs] *n* : corbillard *m*

heart [ˈhɑrt] *n* **1** : cœur *m* **2** AFFECTION, LOVE : cœur *m,* amour *m* **3** COURAGE : courage *m,* ardeur *f* <to lose heart : perdre courage> **4** CENTER : cœur *m,* centre *m* <the heart of the matter : le fond du problème> **5** : cœur *m* (aux cartes) **6 at ~** : au fond **7 by ~** : par cœur

heartache [ˈhɑrt̬ˌeɪk] *n* : chagrin *m,* peine *f*

heart attack *n* : crise *f* cardiaque

heartbeat [ˈhɑrtˌbi:t] *n* : battement *m* de cœur

heartbreak [ˈhɑrtˌbreɪk] *n* : déchirement *m,* douleur *f,* chagrin *m*

heartbreaking [ˈhɑrtˌbreɪkɪŋ] *adj* : déchirant, qui fend le cœur

heartbroken [ˈhɑrtˌbro:kən] *adj* **to be heartbroken** : avoir le cœur brisé

heartburn [ˈhɑrtˌbərn] *n* : brûlures *fpl* d'estomac

hearten [ˈhɑrtən] *vt* : encourager

hearth [ˈhɑrθ] *n* : foyer *m,* âtre *m*

heartily [ˈhɑrt̬əli] *adv* **1** ENTHUSIASTICALLY : de tout son cœur <to laugh heartily : rire de bon cœur> **2** TOTALLY : tout à fait <I agree heartily : je suis tout à fait d'accord>

heartless [ˈhɑrtləs] *adj* : sans cœur, cruel

heartsick [ˈhɑrtˌsɪk] *adj* : déprimé <to be heartsick : avoir la mort dans l'âme>

heartstrings [ˈhɑrtˌstrɪŋz] *npl* : corde *f* sensible

heartwarming [ˈhɑrtˌwɔrmɪŋ] *adj* CHEERING : réconfortant

heartwood [ˈhɑrtˌwʊd] *n* : cœur *m* du bois

hearty [ˈhɑrt̬i] *adj* **heartier; -est 1** JOVIAL : jovial, enjoué **2** VIGOROUS : vigoureux, robuste **3** CORDIAL, WARM : cordial, chaleureux **4** AMPLE : copieux

heat[1] [ˈhi:t] *v* : chauffer

heat[2] *n* **1** WARMTH : chaleur *f* **2** TEMPERATURE : température *f,* chaleur *f* **3** HEATING : chauffage *m* **4** PASSION : feu *m,* intensité *f* <in the heat of the moment : dans l'excitation du moment>

heated [ˈhi:t̬əd] *adj* **1** WARMED : chauffé **2** IMPASSIONED : animé, passionné

heatedly [ˈhi:t̬ədli] *adv* : avec fougue

heater [ˈhi:t̬ər] *n* : radiateur *m,* appareil *m* de chauffage

heath [ˈhi:θ] *n* **1** HEATHER : bruyère *f* **2** MOOR : lande *f*

heathen[1] [hi:ðən] *adj* : païen

heathen[2] *n, pl* **-thens** *or* **-then** : païen *m,* païenne *f*

heather [ˈhɛðər] *n* : bruyère *f*

heave[1] [ˈhi:v] *v* **heaved** *or* **hove** [ˈho:v]; **heaving** *vt* **1** LIFT : lever, soulever (avec effort) **2** HURL : lancer, jeter **3 to heave a sigh** : pousser un soupir — *vi* **1** : se soulever et s'abaisser (se dit de la poitrine) **2 to heave up** RISE : se soulever

heave[2] *n* **1** EFFORT : effort *m* **2** THROW : lancement *m* (avec force)

heaven [ˈhɛvən] *n* **1** : ciel *m* <heaven and hell : le ciel et l'enfer> <for heaven's sake! : pour l'amour du ciel!> **2 heavens** *npl* SKY : ciel *m*

heavenly [ˈhɛvənli] *adj* : céleste, divin

heavily [ˈhɛvəli] *adv* **1** : lourdement, pesamment <to walk heavily : marcher lourdement> **2** LABORIOUSLY : péniblement **3** MUCH : beaucoup

heaviness [ˈhɛvinəs] *n* : lourdeur *f,* pesanteur *f*

heavy [ˈhɛvi] *adj* **heavier; -est 1** WEIGHTY : lourd, pesant **2** BURDENSOME : lourd, gros <a heavy sorrow : un lourd chagrin> **3** DENSE, THICK : dense, abondant **4** DEEP : profond <heavy sleep : sommeil profond> **5** STOUT : gros, corpulent **6** IMMODERATE : gros <a heavy smoker : un gros fumeur>

heavy–duty [ˈhɛviˈdu:t̬i, -ˈdju:-] *adj* : à haute résistance, à usage industriel

heavyweight [ˈhɛviˌweɪt] *n* : poids *m* lourd (aux sports)

Hebrew[1] [ˈhi:ˌbru:] *adj* : hébreu, hébraïque

Hebrew[2] *n* **1** : Hébreu *m,* Israélite *mf* **2** : hébreu *m* (langue)

heckle [ˈhɛkəl] *vt* **-led; -ling** : interrompre bruyamment

hectic [ˈhɛktɪk] *adj* : mouvementé, agité

hedge[1] [ˈhɛdʒ] *v* **hedged; hedging** *vt* **1** *or* **to hedge in** ENCIRCLE : entourer, encercler **2 to hedge one's bets** : se couvrir — *vi* : chercher des échappatoires, patiner *Can*

hedge[2] *n* **1** : haie *f* **2** SAFEGUARD : sauvegarde *f,* protection *f*

hedgehog [ˈhɛdʒˌhɔg, -ˌhɑg] *n* : hérisson *m*

heed[1] [ˈhi:d] *vt* : faire attention à, écouter

heed[2] *n* : attention *f* <to take heed of : tenir compte de>

heedful [ˈhi:dfəl] *adj* : attentif — **heedfully** *adv*

heedless [ˈhi:dləs] *adj* : sans prêter attention, irréfléchi, insouciant

heedlessly [ˈhi:dləsli] *adv* : avec insouciance

heel[1] [ˈhi:l] *vi* : gîter (se dit d'un bateau)

heel[2] *n* : talon *m*

heft [ˈhɛft] *vt* : hisser, soulever

hefty [ˈhɛfti] *adj* **heftier; -est** : pesant, lourd

heifer [ˈhɛfər] *n* : génisse *f*

height [ˈhaɪt] *n* **1** PEAK : comble *m,* point *m* culminant **2** TALLNESS : taille *f,* hauteur *f* <what is your height? : combien mesures-tu?> **3** ALTITUDE : altitude *f,* élévation *f*

heighten [ˈhaɪtən] *vt* **1** RAISE : rehausser, élever **2** INTENSIFY : augmenter, intensifier

heinous [ˈheɪnəs] *adj* : odieux, exécrable, atroce

heir [ˈær] *n* : héritier *m,* -tière *f*

heiress [ˈærəs] *n* : héritière *f*

heirloom [ˈærˌluːm] *n* : objet *m* de famille

held → **hold**[1]

helicopter [ˈhɛləˌkɑptər] *n* : hélicoptère *m*

helium [ˈhiːliəm] *n* : hélium *m*

helix [ˈhiːlɪks] *n, pl* **-lices** [-ləˌsiːz] : hélice *f*

hell [ˈhɛl] *n* : enfer *m*

he'll [ˈhiːl] (*contraction of* **he shall** *or* **he will**) → **shall, will**

hellish [ˈhɛlɪʃ] *adj* : infernal, diabolique

hello [həˈloː, hɛ-] *or Brit* **hullo** [hʌˈleʊ] *interj* : bonjour!, allô! (au téléphone)

helm [ˈhɛlm] *n* : barre *f,* gouvernail *m* <to take the helm : prendre la barre>

helmet [ˈhɛlmət] *n* : casque *m*

help[1] [ˈhɛlp] *vt* **1** AID, ASSIST : aider, venir à l'aide de **2** ALLEVIATE : aider, améliorer **3** PREVENT : empêcher <they couldn't help the accident : ils n'ont pas pu empêcher l'accident> **4** SERVE : se servir <help yourself! : servez-vous!>

help[2] *n* **1** ASSISTANCE : aide *f,* secours *m* **2** STAFF : personnel *m;* employés *mpl,* -ployées *fpl*

helper [ˈhɛlpər] *n* : aide *mf;* assistant *m,* -tante *f*

helpful [ˈhɛlpfəl] *adj* **1** USEFUL : utile **2** OBLIGING : serviable, obligeant

helpfully [ˈhɛlpfəli] *adv* : avec obligeance

helpfulness [ˈhɛlpfəlnəs] *n* **1** KINDNESS : obligeance *f* **2** USEFULNESS : utilité *f*

helping [ˈhɛlpɪŋ] *n* SERVING : portion *f*

helpless [ˈhɛlpləs] *adj* **1** DEFENSELESS : sans défense, désarmé **2** POWERLESS : impuissant

helplessly [ˈhɛlpləsli] *adv* : en vain, désespérément

helplessness [ˈhɛlpləsnəs] *n* : impuissance *f,* impotence *f*

helter-skelter [ˌhɛltərˈskɛltər] *adv* : à la débandade

hem[1] [ˈhɛm] *vt* **hemmed; hemming 1** : ourler, faire un ourlet à (une jupe, etc.) **2 to hem in** SURROUND : entourer

hem[2] *n* : ourlet *m*

hemisphere [ˈhɛməˌsfɪr] *n* : hémisphère *m*

hemispheric [ˌhɛməˈsfɪrɪk, -ˈsfɛr-] *or* **hemispherical** [-ɪkəl] *adj* : hémisphérique

hemlock [ˈhɛmˌlɑk] *n* **1** : ciguë *f* (plante) **2** : tsuga *m* du Canada, pruche *f Can* (arbre)

hemoglobin [ˈhiːməˌgloːbən] *n* : hémoglobine *f*

hemophilia [ˌhiːməˈfɪliə] *n* : hémophilie *f*

hemophiliac[1] [ˌhiːməˈfɪliˌæk] *adj* : hémophile

hemophiliac[2] *n* : hémophile *mf*

hemorrhage[1] [ˈhɛmərɪdʒ] *vi* **-rhaged; -rhaging** : faire une hémorragie

hemorrhage[2] *n* : hémorragie *f*

hemorrhoids [ˈhɛməˌrɔɪdz, ˈhɛmˌrɔɪdz] *npl* : hémorroïdes *fpl*

hemp [ˈhɛmp] *n* : chanvre *m*

hen [ˈhɛn] *n* : poule *f*

hence [ˈhɛnts] *adv* **1** THEREFORE : d'où, donc **2** : d'ici <ten years hence : d'ici dix ans>

henceforth [ˈhɛntsˌforθ, ˌhɛntsˈ-] *adv* : dorénavant, désormais

henchman [ˈhɛntʃmən] *n, pl* **-men** [-mən, -ˌmɛn] : partisan *m,* adepte *m*

henna [ˈhɛnə] *n* : henné *m*

henpeck [ˈhɛnˌpɛk] *vt* : mener par le bout du nez

hepatitis [ˌhɛpəˈtaɪtəs] *n, pl* **-titides** [-ˈtɪtəˌdiːz] : hépatite *f*

her[1] [ˈhər] *adj* : son, sa, ses

her[2] [ˈhər, ər] *pron* **1** (*used as a direct object*) : la, l' <I can see her : je la vois> **2** (*used as an indirect object*) : lui <tell her that I want to go home : dis-lui que je veux rentrer> **3** (*used as object of a preposition*) : elle <he's thinking of her : il pense à elle>

herald[1] [ˈhɛrəld] *vt* ANNOUNCE : annoncer, proclamer

herald[2] *n* **1** MESSENGER : héraut *m* **2** HARBINGER : signe *m* avant-coureur

heraldic [hɛˈrældɪk, hə-] *adj* : héraldique

heraldry [ˈhɛrəldri] *n, pl* **-ries** : héraldique *f*

herb [ˈərb, ˈhərb] *n* : herbe *f*

herbicide [ˈərbəˌsaɪd, ˈhər-] *n* : herbicide *m*

herbivore [ˈərbəˌvor, ˈhər-] *n* : herbivore *m*

herbivorous [ˌərˈbɪvərəs, ˌhər-] *adj* : herbivore

herculean [ˌhərkjəˈliːən, ˌhərˈkjuːliən] *adj* : herculéen

herd[1] [ˈhərd] *vt* : rassembler en troupeau — *vi or* **to herd together** : s'assembler

herd[2] *n* : troupeau *m* (de bétail), troupe *f* (de chevaux, d'éléphants, etc.)

herder [ˈhərdər] → **herdsman**

herdsman [ˈhərdzmən] *n, pl* **-men** [-mən, -ˌmɛn] : gardien *m* de troupeau

here [ˈhɪr] *adv* **1** : ici, là <turn here : tournez ici> <he's not here today : il n'est pas là aujourd'hui> **2** NOW : alors, à ce moment-là **3 here!** : tenez!, écoutez!

hereabouts [ˈhɪrəˌbaʊts] *or* **hereabout** [-ˌbaʊt] *adv* : par ici, près d'ici, dans les environs

hereafter[1] [hɪrˈæftər] *adv* **1** HENCEFORTH : désormais, à l'avenir **2** : ci-après (en droit)

hereafter[2] *n* **the hereafter** : l'au-delà *m*

hereby [hɪrˈbaɪ] *adv* : par la présente

hereditary [həˈrɛdəˌtɛri] *adj* : héréditaire

heredity [həˈrɛdət̬i] *n* : hérédité *f*

herein [hɪrˈɪn] *adv* : ci-après

hereof [hɪrˈʌv] *adv* : des présentes (en droit)

hereon [hɪrˈɑn, -ˈɔn] *adv* : sur ce

heresy [ˈhɛrəsi] *n, pl* **-sies** : hérésie *f*

heretic [ˈhɛrəˌtɪk] *n* : hérétique *mf*

heretical [həˈrɛt̬ɪkəl] *adj* : hérétique

hereto [hɪrˈtuː] *adv* : à ceci, à cela

heretofore [ˈhɪrt̬əˌfor] *adv* : jusqu'ici

hereunder [hɪrˈʌndər] *adv* : ci-après

hereupon [ˈhɪrəˌpɑn, -ˌpɔn] *adv* : sur ce, à ce moment

herewith [hɪrˈwɪθ] *adv* **1** : ci-joint **2** HEREBY : par la présente

heritage [ˈhɛrət̬ɪdʒ] *n* : héritage *m*, patrimoine *m*

hermaphrodite [hərˈmæfrəˌdaɪt] *n* : hermaphrodite *mf*

hermetic [hərˈmɛt̬ɪk] *adj* : hermétique — **hermetically** [-t̬ɪkli] *adv*

hermit [ˈhərmət] *n* : ermite *m*

hernia [ˈhərniə] *n, pl* **-nias** *or* **-niae** [-niˌiː, -niˌaɪ] : hernie *f*

hero [ˈhiːˌroː, ˈhɪrˌoː] *n, pl* **-roes** : héros *m*

heroic [hɪˈroːɪk] *adj* : héroïque — **heroically** [-ɪkli] *adv*

heroics [hɪˈroːɪks] *npl* : mélodrame *m*

heroin [ˈhɛroən] *n* : héroïne *f*

heroine [ˈhɛroən] *n* : héroïne *f*

heroism [ˈhɛroˌɪzəm] *n* : héroïsme *m*

heron [ˈhɛrən] *n* : héron *m*

herpes [ˈhərˌpiːz] *n* : herpès *m*

herring [ˈhɛrɪŋ] *n, pl* **-ring** *or* **-rings** : hareng *m*

hers [ˈhərz] *pron* **1** : le sien, la sienne, les siens, les siennes <my suggestion is good, but hers is better : ma suggestion est bonne, mais la sienne est meilleure> **2** (*used after a preposition*) <some friends of hers : des amis à elle>

herself [hərˈsɛlf] *pron* **1** (*used reflexively*) : se, s' <she hurt herself : elle s'est blessée> **2** (*used emphatically*) <she did it herself : elle l'a fait elle-même>

hertz [ˈhərts, ˈhɛrts] *ns & pl* : hertz *m*

he's [ˈhiːz] (*contraction of* **he is** *or* **he has**) → **be, have**

hesitancy [ˈhɛzət̬əntsi] *n, pl* **-cies** : hésitation *f*, indécision *f*

hesitant [ˈhɛzət̬ənt] *adj* : hésitant, indécis

hesitantly [ˈhɛzət̬əntli] *adv* : avec hésitation

hesitate [ˈhɛzəˌteɪt] *vi* **-tated; -tating** **1** : hésiter **2** PAUSE : faire une pause

hesitation [ˌhɛzəˈteɪʃən] *n* : hésitation *f*

heterogeneous [ˌhɛt̬ərəˈdʒiːniəs, -njəs] *adj* : hétérogène

heterosexual[1] [ˌhɛt̬əroˈsɛkʃʊəl] *adj* : hétérosexuel

heterosexual[2] *n* : hétérosexuel *m*, -sexuelle *f*

heterosexuality [ˌhɛt̬əroˌsɛkʃʊˈælət̬i] *n* : hétérosexualité *f*

hew [ˈhjuː] *v* **hewed; hewed** *or* **hewn** [ˈhjuːn]; **hewing** *vt* **1** CUT, SHAPE : tailler, couper **2** FELL : abattre (un arbre) — *vi* ADHERE : se conformer

hex[1] [ˈhɛks] *vt* : jeter un sort à

hex[2] *n* : sort *m*, sortilège *m*

hexagon [ˈhɛksəˌgɑn] *n* : hexagone *m* — **hexagonal** [hɛkˈsægənəl] *adj*

hey [ˈheɪ] *interj* : hé!, ohé!

heyday [ˈheɪˌdeɪ] *n* : sommet *m*, apogée *f* <in the heyday of his power : au sommet de son pouvoir>

hi [ˈhaɪ] *interj* : hé!, ohé!, salut!

hiatus [haɪˈeɪt̬əs] *n* **1** GAP : hiatus *m*, lacune *f* **2** PAUSE : pause *f*

hibernate [ˈhaɪbərˌneɪt] *vi* **-nated; -nating** : hiberner

hibernation [ˌhaɪbərˈneɪʃən] *n* : hibernation *f*

hiccup[1] [ˈhɪkəp] *vi* **-cuped; -cuping** : hoqueter

hiccup[2] *n* : hoquet *m* <to have the hiccups : avoir le hoquet>

hick [ˈhɪk] *n* BUMPKIN : rustre *mf*, plouc *mf France fam*

hickory [ˈhɪkəri] *n, pl* **-ries** : hickory *m*, noyer *m* blanc d'Amérique

hide[1] [ˈhaɪd] *v* **hid** [ˈhɪd]; **hidden** [ˈhɪdən] *or* **hid; hiding** *vt* **1** CONCEAL : cacher **2** : dissimuler, occulter <to hide one's motives : occulter ses motifs> **3** SHIELD : voiler <the clouds were hiding the sun : les nuages voilaient le soleil> — *vi* : se cacher

hide[2] *n* : peau *f* d'animal

hide-and-seek [ˈhaɪdəndˌsiːk] *n* : cache-cache *m*, cachette *f Can*

hidebound [ˈhaɪdˌbaʊnd] *adj* : à l'esprit étroit, borné

hideous [ˈhɪdiəs] *adj* : hideux, affreux — **hideously** *adv*

hideout [ˈhaɪdˌaʊt] *n* : cachette *f*

hierarchical [ˌhaɪəˈrɑrkɪkəl] *adj* : hiérarchique

hierarchy [ˈhaɪəˌrɑrki] *n, pl* **-chies** : hiérarchie *f*

hieroglyphic [ˌhaɪəˌrəˈglɪfɪk] *n* : hiéroglyphe *m*

high[1] [ˈhaɪ] *adv* : haut

high[2] *adj* **1** TALL : haut <how high is the table? : quelle est la hauteur de la table?> **2** : haut, élevé <high prices : prix élevés> **3** : aigu, haut (en musique) **4** GREAT, IMPORTANT : haut, éminent <high society : haute société> **5** INTOXICATED : parti *fam*, drogué

high[3] *n* **1** RECORD : record *m,* niveau *m* élevé <to reach an all-time high : réaliser un niveau élevé> **2** : zone *f* de haute pression (en météorologie) **3** *or* **high gear** : quatrième vitesse *f* **4 on ~** : dans le ciel

highbrow [ˈhaɪˌbraʊ] *n* : intellectuel *m,* -tuelle *f*

higher [ˈhaɪər] *adj* **1** : plus haut **2** ADVANCED : supérieur

high fidelity *n* : haute-fidélité *f*

high–flown [ˈhaɪˈflo:n] *adj* : ampoulé

high–handed [ˈhaɪˈhændəd] *adj* : despotique, autoritaire

highland [ˈhaɪlənd] *n* : région *f* montagneuse

highlander [ˈhaɪləndər] *n* : montagnard *m,* -narde *f*

highlight[1] [ˈhaɪˌlaɪt] *vt* **1** EMPHASIZE : souligner **2** : être le point culminant de (une cérémonie, etc.) **3** : rehausser (en photographie, etc.)

highlight[2] *n* : clou *m,* point *m* culminant

highly [ˈhaɪli] *adv* **1** VERY : très, extrêmement **2** FAVORABLY : bien <to think very highly of : penser beaucoup de bien de>

highness [ˈhaɪnəs] *n* **1** HEIGHT : hauteur *f* **2** (*used as a title*) <His/Her Highness : son Altesse>

high–rise [ˈhaɪˌraɪz] *adj* : dans une tour

high school *n* : lycée *m France,* école *f* secondaire *Can,* polyvalente *f Can*

high seas *npl* : haute mer *f*

high–spirited [ˈhaɪˈspɪrət̬əd] *adj* : plein d'entrain

high–strung [ˈhaɪˈstrʌŋ] *adj* : nerveux, très tendu

highway [ˈhaɪˌweɪ] *n* **1** : route *f* **2** → **interstate**

highwayman [ˈhaɪˌweɪmən] *n, pl* **-men** [-mən, -ˌmɛn] : bandit *m* de grand chemin

hijack [ˈhaɪˌdʒæk] *vt* : détourner (un avion), saisir de force (une voiture)

hijacker [ˈhaɪˌdʒækər] *n* : pirate *m* de l'air

hike[1] [ˈhaɪk] *v* **hiked; hiking** *vi* : faire une randonnée — *vt or* **to hike up** RAISE : augmenter

hike[2] *n* **1** WALK : randonnée *f* **2** INCREASE : hausse *f*

hiker [ˈhaɪkər] *n* : randonneur *m,* -neuse *f*

hilarious [hɪˈlæriəs, haɪ-] *adj* : désopilant, hilarant

hilarity [hɪˈlærət̬i, haɪ-] *n* : hilarité *f*

hill [ˈhɪl] *n* : colline *f*

hillbilly [ˈhɪlˌbɪli] *n, pl* **-lies** : montagnard *m,* -narde *f*

hillock [ˈhɪlək] *n* : petite colline *f,* butte *f*

hillside [ˈhɪlˌsaɪd] *n* : coteau *m*

hilltop [ˈhɪlˌtɑp] *n* : sommet *m* d'une colline

hilly [ˈhɪli] *adj* **hillier; -est** : vallonné, côteux *Can*

hilt [ˈhɪlt] *n* : poignée *f* (d'une épée), manche *m* (d'un poignard)

him [ˈhɪm, əm] *pron* **1** (*used as a direct object*) : le, l' <I met him at the restaurant : je l'ai rencontré au restaurant> **2** (*used as an indirect object*) : lui <tell him that I am delighted : dis-lui que je suis ravi> **3** (*used as object of a preposition*) : lui <richer than him : plus riche que lui>

himself [hɪmˈsɛlf] *pron* **1** (*used reflexively*) : se, s' <he washed himself : il s'est lavé> **2** (*used emphatically*) : lui-même <he did it himself : il l'a fait lui-même> **3** (*used after a preposition*) : lui, lui-même <by himself : par lui-même, tout seul>

hind[1] [ˈhaɪnd] *adj* REAR : de derrière

hind[2] *n* : biche *f*

hinder [ˈhɪndər] *vt* : empêcher, entraver

hindquarters [ˈhaɪndˌkwɔrt̬ərz] *npl* : arrière-train *m*

hindrance [ˈhɪndrənts] *n* : entrave *f,* obstacle *m*

hindsight [ˈhaɪndˌsaɪt] *n* **in ~** : avec du recul

Hindu[1] [ˈhɪnˌdu:] *adj* : hindou

Hindu[2] *n* : Hindou *m,* -doue *f*

Hinduism [ˈhɪndu:ˌɪzəm] *n* : hindouisme *m*

hinge[1] [ˈhɪndʒ] *v* **hinged; hinging** *vi* **to hinge on** : dépendre de — *vt* : mettre une charnière à

hinge[2] *n* : charnière *f,* gond *m*

hint[1] [ˈhɪnt] *vt* : insinuer — *vi* **to hint at** : faire une allusion à

hint[2] *n* **1** SUGGESTION : allusion *f,* insinuation *f* **2** CLUE : indice *m,* idée *f* **3** TRACE : soupçon *m,* trace *f* <a hint of perfume : un soupçon de parfum>

hinterland [ˈhɪntərˌlænd, -lənd] *n* : arrière-pays *m*

hip [ˈhɪp] *n* : hanche *f*

hippie *or* **hippy** [ˈhɪpi] *n, pl* **hippies** : hippie *mf,* hippy *mf*

hippopotamus [ˌhɪpəˈpɑt̬əməs] *n, pl* **-muses** *or* **-mi** [-ˌmaɪ] : hippopotame *m*

hire[1] [ˈhaɪr] *vt* **hired; hiring 1** EMPLOY : engager, embaucher **2** RENT : louer

hire[2] *n* **1** WAGES : gages *mpl* **2** RENTAL : location *f* <for hire : à louer> **3** EMPLOYEE : employé *m,* -ployée *f*

his[1] [ˈhɪz, ɪz] *adj* : son, sa, ses <his house : sa maison> <it's his : c'est à lui>

his[2] *pron* **1** : le sien, la sienne, les siens, les siennes **2** (*used after a preposition*) <a friend of his : un ami à lui, un de ses amis>

Hispanic[1] [hɪˈspænɪk] *adj* : hispanique

Hispanic[2] *n* : Hispano-Américain *m,* Hispano-Américaine *f*

hiss[1] [ˈhɪs] *vi* : siffler, chuinter

hiss[2] *n* : sifflement *m*

historian [hɪˈstɔriən] *n* : historien *m,* -rienne *f*

historic [hɪ'stɔrɪk] *or* **historical** [-ɪkəl] *adj* : historique — **historically** [-ɪkli] *adv*

history ['hɪstəri] *n, pl* **-ries 1** : histoire *f* **2** RECORD : antécédents *mpl* <medical history : antécédents médicaux>

histrionics [,hɪstri'ɑnɪks] *ns & pl* : airs *mpl* dramatiques

hit[1] ['hɪt] *v* **hit; hitting** *vt* **1** STRIKE : frapper **2** : heurter, percuter <the car hit a tree : la voiture a heurté un arbre> **3** AFFECT : affecter, toucher <the loss hit him hard : la perte l'a beaucoup affecté> **4** REACH : atteindre, arriver à — *vi* **1** : frapper, cogner **2** OCCUR : arriver, se produire <the storm hit without warning : la tempête est arrivée par surprise>

hit[2] *n* **1** BLOW : coup *m* **2** SUCCESS : succès *m*

hitch[1] ['hɪtʃ] *vt* **1** FASTEN, HARNESS : accrocher, atteler **2** → **hitchhike 3 to hitch up** : remonter (ses pantalons, etc.)

hitch[2] *n* **1** JERK : saccade *f*, secousse *f* **2** OBSTACLE : problème *m*, pépin *m*

hitchhike ['hɪtʃ,haɪk] *vi* **-hiked; -hiking** : faire de l'auto-stop, faire du pouce *Can*

hitchhiker ['hɪtʃ,haɪkər] *n* : auto-stoppeur *m*, -peuse *f*

hither ['hɪðər] *adv* : ici <come hither : venez çà>

hitherto ['hɪðər,tu:, ,hɪðər'-] *adv* : jusqu'ici, jusqu'à présent

hitter ['hɪt̬ər] *n* BATTER : batteur *m*

HIV [,eɪtʃ,aɪ'vi:] *n* : VIH *m*

hive ['haɪv] *n* **1** *or* **beehive** : ruche *f* **2** SWARM : essaim *m* **3 a hive of activity** : une vraie ruche

hives ['haɪvz] *ns & pl* : urticaire *f*

HMO [,eɪtʃ,ɛm'o:] *n* : centre *m* de santé financé par sa clientèle

hoard[1] ['hord] *vt* : accumuler, amasser, faire des réserves de — *vi* : faire des réserves

hoard[2] *n* : réserve *f*, provisions *fpl*

hoarfrost ['hor,frɔst] *n* : gelée *f* blanche, givre *m*

hoarse ['hors] *adj* **hoarser; -est 1** GRATING : discordant **2** : rauque, enroué <a hoarse cough : une toux rauque>

hoarsely ['horsli] *adv* : d'une voix rauque

hoary ['hori] *adj* **hoarier; -est** : aux cheveux blancs, chenu

hoax[1] ['ho:ks] *vt* : faire un canular à

hoax[2] *n* : canular *m*, farce *f*

hobble[1] ['hɑbəl] *v* **-bled; -bling** *vi* LIMP : boitiller — *vt* FETTER : entraver (un animal)

hobble[2] *n* **1** LIMP : boitillement *m* **2** : entrave *f* (d'un animal)

hobby ['hɑbi] *n, pl* **-bies** : passe-temps *m*

hobgoblin ['hɑb,gɑblən] *n* **1** GOBLIN : lutin *m* **2** BOGEY : épouvantail *m*

hobnail ['hɑb,neɪl] *n* : caboche *f*

hobnailed ['hɑb,neɪld] *adj* : ferré

hobnob ['hɑb,nɑb] *vi* **-nobbed; -nobbing** : frayer <to hobnob with : fréquenter, frayer avec>

hobo ['ho:,bo:] *n, pl* **-boes** : vagabond *m*, -bonde *f*; clochard *m*, -charde *f*

hock[1] ['hɑk] *vt* : mettre au clou, mettre en gage

hock[2] *n* **in ~** : au clou

hockey ['hɑki] *n* : hockey *m*

hod ['hɑd] *n* : oiseau *m*, auge *f* (de maçon)

hodgepodge ['hɑdʒ,pɑdʒ] *n* JUMBLE : méli-mélo *m*, salmigondis *m*

hoe[1] ['ho:] *vi* **hoed; hoeing** : sarcler, biner

hoe[2] *n* : houe *f*, binette *f*

hog[1] ['hɔg, 'hɑg] *vt* **hogged; hogging** : monopoliser

hog[2] *n* **1** : porc *m*, cochon *m* **2** GLUTTON : glouton *m*, -tonne *f*

hoggish ['hɔgɪʃ, 'hɑg-] *adj* : glouton, goulu

hogshead ['hɔgz,hɛd, 'hɑgz-] *n* CASK : barrique *f*

hoist[1] ['hɔɪst] *vt* : hisser

hoist[2] *n* : palan *m*, monte-charge *m*

hold[1] ['ho:ld] *v* **held** ['hɛld]; **holding** *vt* **1** POSSESS : posséder **2** RESTRAIN : tenir <hold the dog! : tiens le chien!> **3** GRASP : tenir **4** SUPPORT : soutenir, supporter (un poids) **5** CONTAIN : contenir **6** REGARD : avoir, tenir <I hold him in high esteem : j'ai beaucoup d'estime pour lui > **7** CONDUCT : organiser (un colloque, etc.) **8** : avoir, occuper (un poste) **9** : détenir (un prisonnier) **10** : avoir, maintenir (une opinion) — *vi* **1** LAST : durer, continuer **2** APPLY : tenir, être en vigueur <the rule still holds : le règlement est encore en vigueur> **3 to hold forth** : pérorer **4 to hold to** : s'en tenir à **5 to hold with** : être d'accord avec

hold[2] *n* **1** GRIP : prise *f* **2** INFLUENCE : emprise *f* **3** : cale *f* (d'un navire)

holder ['ho:ldər] *n* : détenteur *m*, -trice *f*; titulaire *mf*

holdings ['ho:ldɪŋz] *npl* PROPERTY : propriétés *fpl*

holdup ['ho:ld,ʌp] *n* **1** ROBBERY : vol *m* à main armée **2** DELAY : retard *m*

hold up *vt* **1** ROB : faire un vol à main armée **2** DELAY : retarder

hole ['ho:l] *n* : trou *m*

holiday ['hɑlə,deɪ] *n* **1** : jour *m* férié **2** *Brit* VACATION : vacances *fpl*

holiness ['ho:linəs] *n* **1** : sainteté *f* **2** (*used as a title*) <His Holiness : Sa Sainteté>

holistic [ho:'lɪstɪk] *adj* : holistique

holler[1] ['hɑlər] *vi* : gueuler *fam*, hurler

holler[2] *n* : hurlement *m*

hollow[1] ['hɑ,lo:] *vt or* **to hollow out** : creuser

hollow[2] *adj* **hollower; -est 1** : creux **2** MUFFLED : caverneux <a hollow laugh : un rire forcé> **3** MEANING-

LESS : faux <hollow promises : fausses promesses>
hollow[3] *n* **1** CAVITY : creux *m*, dépression *f*, cavité *f* **2** VALLEY : vallon *m*
hollowness [ˈhɑˌloːnəs] *n* **1** HOLLOW : creux *m*, cavité *f* **2** FALSENESS : fausseté *f* **3** EMPTINESS : vide *m*
holly [ˈhɑli] *n, pl* **-lies** : houx *m*
hollyhock [ˈhɑliˌhɑk] *n* : rose *f* trémière
holocaust [ˈhɑləˌkɔst, ˈhoː-, ˈhɔ-] *n* : holocauste *m*
holster [ˈhoːlstər] *n* : étui *m* de revolver
holy [ˈhoːli] *adj* **holier; -est 1** SAINTLY : saint **2** SACRED : bénit <holy water : eau bénite>
Holy Ghost → Holy Spirit
Holy Spirit *n* : Saint-Esprit *m*
homage [ˈɑmɪdʒ, ˈhɑ-] *n* : hommage *m*
home[1] [ˈhoːm] *adv* **1** : à la maison, chez soi **2** DEEPLY : à fond <to hammer a nail home : enfoncer un clou jusqu'au bout>
home[2] *n* **1** RESIDENCE : maison *f* **2** : foyer *m*, chez-soi *m* <home is where the heart is : où le coeur aime, là est le foyer> **3** HABITAT : habitat *m* **4 → funeral home, nursing home**
homecoming [ˈhoːmˌkʌmɪŋ] *n* : retour *m* au foyer
homegrown [ˈhoːmˈgroːn] *adj* : du pays, du jardin
homeland [ˈhoːmˌlænd] *n* : pays *m* natal, patrie *f*
homeless [ˈhoːmləs] *adj* : sans foyer
homely [ˈhoːmli] *adj* **homelier; -est 1** SIMPLE : simple, sans prétentions **2** UNATTRACTIVE : sans attraits
homemade [ˈhoːmˈmeɪd] *adj* : fait à la maison <homemade cookies : biscuits maison>
homemaker [ˈhoːmˌmeɪkər] *n* : femme *f* au foyer
home run *n* : coup *m* de circuit *Can*
homesick [ˈhoːmˌsɪk] *adj* : nostalgique <to be homesick : avoir le mal du pays>
homesickness [ˈhoːmˌsɪknəs] *n* : nostalgie *f*, mal *m* du pays
homespun [ˈhoːmˌspʌn] *adj* : simple, naturel
homestead [ˈhoːmˌstɛd] *n* : propriété *f*, terres *fpl*
homeward[1] [ˈhoːmwərd] *or* **homewards** [-wərdz] *adv* : vers la maison, vers la patrie <homeward bound : sur le chemin du retour>
homeward[2] *adj* : de retour
homework [ˈhoːmˌwərk] *n* : devoirs *mpl*
homey [ˈhoːmi] *adj* **homier; -est** : accueillant
homicidal [ˌhɑməˈsaɪdəl, ˌhoː-] *adj* : homicide
homicide [ˈhɑməˌsaɪd, ˈhoː-] *n* : homicide *m*
hominy [ˈhɑməni] *n* : bouillie *f* de semoule de maïs
homogeneity [ˌhoːmədʒəˈniːəti, -ˈneɪ] *n* : homogénéité *f*
homogeneous [ˌhoːməˈdʒiːniəs, -njəs] *adj* : homogène
homogenize [hoːˈmɑdʒəˌnaɪz, hə-] *vt* **-nized; -nizing** : homogénéiser
homograph [ˈhɑməˌgræf, ˈhoː-] *n* : homographe *m*
homonym [ˈhɑməˌnɪm, ˈhoː-] *n* : homonyme *m*
homophone [ˈhɑməˌfoːn, ˈhoː-] *n* : homophone *m*
homosexual[1] [ˌhoːməˈsɛkʃuəl] *adj* : homosexuel
homosexual[2] *n* : homosexuel *m*, -sexuelle *f*
homosexuality [ˌhoːməˌsɛkʃʊˈæləṭi] *n* : homosexualité *f*
Honduran[1] [hɑnˈdʊrən, -ˈdjʊr-] *adj* : hondurien
Honduran[2] *n* : Hondurien *m* -rienne *f*
hone [ˈhoːn] *vt* **honed; honing** : aiguiser, affûter
honest [ˈɑnəst] *adj* **1** STRAIGHTFORWARD, TRUTHFUL : honnête, franc **2** CREDITABLE : bon, honorable <an honest day's work : une bonne journée de travail>
honestly [ˈɑnəstli] *adv* : honnêtement
honesty [ˈɑnəsti] *n* : honnêteté *f*
honey [ˈhʌni] *n, pl* **-eys** : miel *m*
honeybee [ˈhʌniˌbiː] *n* : abeille *f*
honeycomb[1] [ˈhʌniˌkoːm] *vi* : cribler (de petits trous)
honeycomb[2] *n* : rayon *m* de miel
honeymoon[1] [ˈhʌniˌmuːn] *vi* : passer sa lune de miel
honeymoon[2] *n* : lune *f* de miel
honeysuckle [ˈhʌniˌsʌkəl] *n* : chèvrefeuille *m*
honk[1] [ˈhɑŋk, ˈhɔŋk] *vi* : cacarder (se dit d'une oie), klaxonner (se dit d'une voiture)
honk[2] *n* : cri *m* (de l'oie), coup *m* de klaxon (d'une voiture)
honor[1] *or Brit* **honour** [ˈɑnər] *vt* **1** : honorer <honor your parents : honore tes parents> **2** : honorer (un chèque, etc.), remplir (un engagement)
honor[2] *or Brit* **honour** *n* **1** RECOGNITION, RESPECT : honneur *m* <in honor of : en l'honneur de> **2 honors** *npl* AWARDS : distinctions *fpl* honorifiques **3 Your Honor** : Votre Honneur
honorable *or Brit* **honourable** [ˈɑnərəbəl] *adj* : honorable — **honorably** *or Brit* **honourably** [-bli] *adv*
honorary [ˈɑnəˌrɛri] *adj* : honoraire, honorifique <an honorary member : un membre honoraire> <an honorary title : un titre honorifique>
honour *Brit* **→ honor**
hood [ˈhʊd] *n* **1** : capuchon *m* (d'un vêtement) **2** : capot *m* (d'une voiture)
hooded [ˈhʊdəd] *adj* : à capuchon
hoodlum [ˈhʊdləm, ˈhuːd-] *n* : voyou *m*, truand *m*
hoodwink [ˈhʊdˌwɪŋk] *vt* : tromper, duper

hoof [ˈhʊf, ˈhu:f] *n, pl* **hooves** [ˈhʊvz, ˈhu:vz] *or* **hoofs** : sabot *m* (d'un animal)

hoofed [ˈhʊft, ˈhu:ft] *adj* : à sabots

hook[1] [ˈhʊk] *vt* : accrocher

hook[2] *n* **1** : crochet *m* **2** FASTENER : agrafe *f* **3** → **fishhook**

hookworm [ˈhʊk,wərm] *n* : ankylostome *m*

hooligan [ˈhu:lɪgən] *n* : vandale *m*, voyou *m*

hoop [ˈhu:p] *n* : cerceau *m*

hoorah [hʊˈra], **hooray** [hʊˈreɪ] → **hurrah**

hoot[1] [ˈhu:t] *vi* **1** SHOUT : huer, hurler <to hoot with laughter : pouffer de rire> **2** : hululer (se dit d'un hibou), siffler (se dit d'un train), klaxonner (se dit d'une voiture)

hoot[2] *n* **1** : hululement *m* (d'un hibou), sifflement *m* (d'un train) **2 hoots** *npl* BOOS : huées *fpl* **3 I don't give a hoot** : je m'en fiche

hop[1] [ˈhap] *v* **hopped**; **hopping** *vi* : sauter, sautiller — *vt or* **to hop over** : sauter, franchir

hop[2] *n* **1** LEAP : saut *m*, sautillement *m* **2** : houblon *m* (plante) **3** FLIGHT : court vol *m* en avion

hope[1] [ˈho:p] *v* **hoped**; **hoping** : espérer

hope[2] *n* : espoir *m*, espérance *f*

hopeful [ˈho:pfəl] *adj* **1** : plein d'espoir, optimiste **2** PROMISING : prometteur

hopefully [ˈho:pfəli] *adv* **1** OPTIMISTICALLY : avec optimisme, avec espoir **2** : avec un peu de chance <hopefully, he will come : on espère qu'il viendra>

hopefulness [ˈho:pfəlnəs] *n* : espoir *m*

hopeless [ˈho:pləs] *adj* : désespéré

hopelessly [ˈho:pləsli] *adv* : éperdument

hopelessness [ˈho:pləsnəs] *n* : désespoir *m*

hopper [ˈhapər] *n* : trémie *f*

hopscotch [ˈhap,skatʃ] *n* : marelle *f*

horde [ˈhord] *n* : horde *f*, foule *f*, essaim *m*

horizon [həˈraɪzən] *n* : horizon *m*

horizontal [,hɔrəˈzantəl] *adj* : horizontal — **horizontally** *adv*

hormone [ˈhɔr,mo:n] *n* : hormone *f* — **hormonal** [hɔrˈmo:nəl] *adj*

horn [ˈhɔrn] *n* **1** : corne *f* (d'un animal) **2** : cor *m* (instrument de musique) **3** : klaxon *m* (d'un véhicule)

horned [ˈhɔrnd] *adj* : cornu

hornless [ˈhɔrnləs] *adj* : sans cornes

hornet [ˈhɔrnət] *n* : frelon *m*

horn of plenty → **cornucopia**

horny [ˈhɔrni] *adj* **hornier**; **-est** : calleux

horoscope [ˈhɔrə,sko:p] *n* : horoscope *m*

horrendous [həˈrɛndəs] *adj* : épouvantable, effroyable

horrible [ˈhɔrəbəl] *adj* : horrible, affreux, détestable — **horribly** [-bli] *adv*

horrid [ˈhɔrɪd] *adj* **1** HIDEOUS : horrible, hideux **2** DISGUSTING : repoussant

horrify [ˈhɔrə,faɪ] *vt* **-fied**; **-fying** : horrifier, remplir d'horreur

horror [ˈhɔrər] *n* : horreur *f*

hors d'oeuvre [ɔrˈdərv] *n, pl* **hors d'oeuvres** [-ˈdərvz] : hors-d'œuvre *m*

horse [ˈhɔrs] *n* : cheval *m*

horseback [ˈhɔrs,bæk] *n* **on ~** : à cheval

horse chestnut *n* : marronnier *m* (arbre), marron *m* (noix)

horsefly [ˈhɔrs,flaɪ] *n, pl* **-flies** : taon *m*

horsehair [ˈhɔrs,hær] *n* : crin *m* (de cheval)

horseman [ˈhɔrsmən] *n, pl* **-men** [-mən, -,mɛn] : cavalier *m*

horsemanship [ˈhɔrsmən,ʃɪp] *n* : équitation *f*

horseplay [ˈhɔrs,pleɪ] *n* : jeux *mpl* de mains

horsepower [ˈhɔrs,paʊər] *n* : cheval-vapeur *m*

horseradish [ˈhɔrs,rædɪʃ] *n* : raifort *m*

horseshoe [ˈhɔrs,ʃu:] *n* : fer *m* à cheval

horsewhip [ˈhɔrs,*h*wɪp] *vt* **-whipped**; **-whipping** : cravacher

horsewoman [ˈhɔrs,wʊmən] *n, pl* **-women** [-,wɪmən] : cavalière *f*

horsey *or* **horsy** [ˈhɔrsi] *adj* **horsier**; **-est** : chevalin

horticultural [,hɔrṭəˈkʌltʃərəl] *adj* : horticole

horticulture [ˈhɔrṭə,kʌltʃər] *n* : horticulture *f*

hosanna [ho:ˈzænə, -za-] *interj* : hosanna!

hose[1] [ˈho:z] *vt* **hosed**; **hosing** : arroser

hose[2] *n* **1** *pl* **hoses** : tuyau *m* <garden hose : tuyau d'arrosage> <fire hose : tuyau d'incendie> **2** *pl* **hose** STOCKINGS : bas *mpl*, collants *mpl*

hosiery [ˈho:ʒəri, ˈho:zə-] *n* : bas *mpl*, collants *mpl*

hospice [ˈhaspəs] *n* : hospice *m*

hospitable [hasˈpɪṭəbəl, ˈha,spɪ-] *adj* : hospitalier, accueillant, invitant *Can*, recevant *Can*

hospitably [hasˈpɪṭəbli, ˈha,spɪ-] *adv* : avec hospitalité

hospital [ˈhas,pɪṭəl] *n* : hôpital *m*

hospitality [,haspəˈtæləṭi] *n, pl* **-ties** : hospitalité *f*

hospitalization [,has,pɪṭələˈzeɪʃən] *n* : hospitalisation *f*

hospitalize [ˈhas,pɪṭə,laɪz] *vt* **-ized**; **-izing** : hospitaliser

host[1] [ˈho:st] *vt* **1** : être l'hôte de <to host a dinner : recevoir à dîner> **2** : animer (une émission de télévision, etc.)

host[2] *n* **1** ARMY : armée *f* **2** MULTITUDE : foule *f* **3** : hôte *mf* (à la maison, etc.) **4** EUCHARIST : hostie *f*, Eucharistie *f* **5** : animateur *m*, -trice *f* <radio host : animateur de radio> **6** : hôte *m* (en biologie)

hostage [ˈhastɪdʒ] *n* : otage *m*

hostel [ˈhɑstəl] *n* : auberge *f* <youth hostel : auberge de jeunesse>
hostess [ˈho:stəs] *n* : hôtesse *f*
hostile [ˈhɑstəl, -ˌtaɪl] *adj* : hostile — **hostilely** *adv*
hostility [hɑsˈtɪləṭi] *n, pl* **-ties** : hostilité *f*
hot [ˈhɑt] *adj* **hotter; hottest 1** : chaud <a hot stove : une cuisinière chaude> <it's hot today : il fait chaud aujourd'hui> **2** ARDENT, FIERY : coléreux <to have a hot temper : s'emporter facilement> **3** SPICY : fort, épicé **4** EAGER : empressé, passionné **5** LATEST : dernier <hot news : les dernières nouvelles> **6** RADIOACTIVE : radioactif **7** STOLEN : volé
hot air *n* : paroles *fpl* en l'air
hotbed [ˈhɑtˌbɛd] *n* **1** : couche *f* chaude, pépinière *f* (en botanique) **2** CENTER, SOURCE : foyer *m* <a hotbed of dissent : un foyer de conflit>
hot dog *n* : hot-dog *m*
hotel [ho:ˈtɛl] *n* : hôtel *m*
hothead [ˈhɑtˌhɛd] *n* : tête *f* brûlée
hotheaded [ˈhɑtˈhɛdəd] *adj* : impétueux, exalté
hothouse [ˈhɑtˌhaʊs] *n* : serre *f*
hotly [ˈhɑtli] *adv* : vivement, passionnément
hound[1] [ˈhaʊnd] *vt* : traquer, poursuivre
hound[2] *n* : chien *m* de meute
hour [ˈaʊər] *n* : heure *f*
hourglass [ˈaʊərˌglæs] *n* : sablier *m*
hourly [ˈaʊərli] *adv & adj* : toutes les heures
house[1] [ˈhaʊz] *vt* **housed; housing** : loger, héberger
house[2] [ˈhaʊs] *n, pl* **houses** [ˈhaʊzəz, -səz] **1** HOME, RESIDENCE : maison *f* **2** : chambre *f* (en politique) **3** COMPANY, FIRM : maison *f*, compagnie *f* **4** AUDIENCE : assistance *f*, auditoire *m*
houseboat [ˈhaʊsˌbo:t] *n* : péniche *f* aménagée
housebroken [ˈhaʊsˌbro:kən] *adj* : propre
housefly [ˈhaʊsˌflaɪ] *n, pl* **-flies** : mouche *f*
household[1] [ˈhaʊsˌho:ld] *adj* **1** DOMESTIC : ménager **2** COMMON, FAMILIAR : commun
household[2] *n* : maison *f*, ménage *m*
householder [ˈhaʊsˌho:ldər] *n* : propriétaire *mf*, chef *m* de famille
housekeeper [ˈhaʊsˌki:pər] *n* : ménagère *f*, gouvernante *f*
housekeeping [ˈhaʊsˌki:pɪŋ] *n* : ménage *m*
housemaid [ˈhaʊsˌmeɪd] *n* : bonne *f*, femme *f* de chambre
housewarming [ˈhaʊsˌwɔrmɪŋ] *n* : pendaison *f* de crémaillère
housewife [ˈhaʊsˌwaɪf] *n, pl* **-wives** : femme *f* au foyer, ménagère *f*
housework [ˈhaʊsˌwərk] *n* : travaux *mpl* ménagers
housing [ˈhaʊzɪŋ] *n* **1** LODGING : logement *m* **2** CASING : boîtier *m*
hove → **heave**[1]
hovel [ˈhʌvəl, ˈhɑ-] *n* : bicoque *f*, baraque *f*, masure *f*, taudis *m*
hover [ˈhʌvər] *vi* **1** : planer, voltiger **2** *or* **to hover about** : rôder
how[1] [ˈhaʊ] *adv* **1** : comment <how are you? : comment allez-vous?> <how do you spell it? : comment ça s'écrit?> <I know how to do it : je sais comment faire> **2** (*referring to degree or extent*) <how old are you? : quel âge as-tu?> <how tall is he? : combien mesure-t-il?> **3** (*used in exclamations*) : comme, que <how beautiful it is! : comme c'est beau!> **4 how about . . . ?** : que dirais-tu de . . . ? **5 how come** WHY : comment, pourquoi
how[2] *conj* : comment <I asked them how they were : je leur ai demandé comment ils allaient>
however[1] [haʊˈɛvər] *adv* **1** : cependant, toutefois, pourtant **2** : comme <however you want : comme tu veux> **3** : si . . . que, quelque . . . que <however important it is : si important que ce soit>
however[2] *conj* : de quelque manière que <I will help you however I can : je vais t'aider de quelque manière que ce soit>
howl[1] [ˈhaʊl] *vi* : hurler
howl[2] *n* : hurlement *m*
hub [ˈhʌb] *n* **1** CENTER : centre *m*, pivot *m* **2** : moyeu *m* (d'une roue)
hubbub [ˈhʌˌbʌb] *n* : vacarme *m*, brouhaha *m*
hubcap [ˈhʌbˌkæp] *n* : enjoliveur *m*
huckleberry [ˈhʌkəlˈbɛri] *n, pl* **-ries** : myrtille *f France*, bleuet *m Can*
huckster [ˈhʌkstər] *n* PEDDLER : camelot *m;* colporteur *m*, -teuse *f*
huddle[1] [ˈhʌdəl] *vi* **-dled; -dling 1** : se blottir **2** *or* **to huddle together** : se serrer, se blottir les uns contre les autres
huddle[2] *n* : (petit) groupe *m* <to go into a huddle : se réunir en petit comité>
hue [ˈhju:] *n* : couleur *f*, teinte *f*
huff [ˈhʌf] *n* **to be in a huff** : être fâché, être vexé
huffy [ˈhʌfi] *adj* **huffier; -est 1** IRRITATED : fâché, vexé **2** TOUCHY : susceptible
hug[1] [ˈhʌg] *vt* **hugged; hugging 1** EMBRACE : serrer dans ses bras, étreindre **2** : serrer, longer <the ship was hugging the coast : le navire serrait la côte>
hug[2] *n* : étreinte *f*
huge [ˈhju:dʒ] *adj* **huger; hugest** : énorme, immense — **hugely** *adv*
hulk [ˈhʌlk] *n* **1** : mastodonte *m* (homme) **2** : épave *f* (d'un navire)

hulking [ˈhʌlkɪŋ] *adj* : énorme, massif
hull[1] [ˈhʌl] *vt* SHELL, SHUCK : écosser (des pois), écaler (des noix), décortiquer (du grain, des noix, etc.)
hull[2] *n* **1** : cosse *f* (de pois), écale *f* (d'une noix) **2** : coque *f* (d'un navire ou d'un avion)
hullabaloo [ˈhʌləbəˌlu:] *n, pl* **-loos** : raffut *m fam,* boucan *m fam*
hullo *Brit* → **hello**
hum[1] [ˈhʌm] *v* **hummed; humming** *vi* **1** BUZZ, DRONE : bourdonner **2** BUSTLE : grouiller — *vt* : fredonner, chantonner
hum[2] *n* : bourdonnement *m*
human[1] [ˈhju:mən, ˈju:-] *adj* **1** : humain <the human race : le genre humain> **2** : de la personne <human rights : droits de la personne>
human[2] *n* : humain *m,* être *m* humain
humane [hju:ˈmeɪn, ju:-] *adj* : humain — **humanely** *adv*
humanism [ˈhju:məˌnɪzəm, ˈju:-] *n* : humanisme *m*
humanist[1] [ˈhju:mənɪst, ˈju:-] *or* **humanistic** [ˌhju:məˈnɪstɪk, ˈju:-] *adj* : humaniste
humanist[2] *n* : humaniste *mf*
humanitarian[1] [hju:ˌmænəˈtɛriən, ju:-] *adj* : humanitaire
humanitarian[2] *n* : humaniste *m*
humanity [hju:ˈmænət̬i, ju:-] *n, pl* **-ties** : humanité *f*
humankind [ˈhju:mənˈkaɪnd, ˈju:-] *n* : humanité *f,* le genre humain
humanly [ˈhju:mənli, ˈju:-] *adv* : humainement
humble[1] [ˈhʌmbəl] *vt* **-bled; -bling 1** : humilier **2 to humble oneself** : s'humilier
humble[2] *adj* **humbler; -blest** : humble, modeste <of humble origin : d'origine modeste> — **humbly** [ˈhʌmbli] *adv*
humbug [ˈhʌmˌbʌg] *n* **1** : charlatan *m* (personne) **2** NONSENSE : balivernes *fpl*
humdrum [ˈhʌmˌdrʌm] *adj* : monotone, banal
humid [ˈhju:məd, ˈju:-] *adj* : humide
humidifier [hju:ˈmɪdəˌfaɪər, ju:-] *n* : humidificateur *m*
humidify [hju:ˈmɪdəˌfaɪ, ju:-] *vt* **-fied; -fying** : humidifier
humidity [hju:ˈmɪdət̬i, ju:-] *n, pl* **-ties** : humidité *f*
humiliate [hju:ˈmɪliˌeɪt, ju:-] *vt* **-ated; -ating** : humilier
humiliating [hju:ˈmɪliˌeɪtɪŋ, ju:-] *adj* : humiliant
humiliation [hju:ˌmɪliˈeɪʃən, ju:-] *n* : humiliation *f*
humility [hju:ˈmɪlət̬i, ju:-] *n* : humilité *f*
hummingbird [ˈhʌmɪŋˌbərd] *n* : oiseau-mouche *m*
hummock [ˈhʌmək] *n* : monticule *m*
humor[1] *or Brit* **humour** [ˈhju:mər, ˈju:-] *vt* : faire plaisir à, ménager
humor[2] *or Brit* **humour** *n* **1** MOOD : humeur *f* **2** WIT : humour *m*
humorist [ˈhju:mərɪst, ˈju:-] *n* : humoriste *mf*
humorless *or Brit* **humourless** [ˈhju:mərləs, ˈju:-] *adj* : qui manque d'humour
humorous [ˈhju:mərəs, ˈju:-] *adj* : plein d'humour, drôle
humorously [ˈhju:mərəsli, ˈju:-] *adv* : avec humour
humour *Brit* → **humor**
hump [ˈhʌmp] *n* : bosse *f*
humpback [ˈhʌmpˌbæk] *n* : bosse *f*
humpbacked [ˈhʌmpˌbækt] *adj* : bossu
humus [ˈhju:məs, ˈju:-] *n* : humus *m*
hunch[1] [ˈhʌntʃ] *vt* **to hunch one's shoulders** : rentrer les épaules — *vi or* **to hunch over** : se pencher
hunch[2] *n* : pressentiment *m,* intuition *f*
hunchback [ˈhʌntʃˌbæk] *n* **1** : bosse *f* (sur le dos d'une personne) **2** : bossu *m,* -sue *f* (personne)
hunchbacked [ˈhʌntʃˌbækt] *adj* : bossu
hundred[1] [ˈhʌndrəd] *adj* : cent
hundred[2] *n, pl* **-dreds** *or* **-dred** : cent *m*
hundredth[1] [ˈhʌndrədθ] *adj* : centième
hundredth[2] *n* **1** : centième *mf* (dans une série) **2** : centième *m* (en mathématiques)
hung → **hang**[1]
Hungarian[1] [hʌŋˈgæriən] *adj* : hongrois
Hungarian[2] *n* **1** : Hongrois *m,* -groise *f* **2** : hongrois *m* (langue)
hunger[1] [ˈhʌŋgər] *vi* : avoir faim <to hunger for : avoir faim de, avoir envie de>
hunger[2] *n* **1** : faim *f* **2** CRAVING : désir *m,* envie *f*
hungrily [ˈhʌŋgrəli] *adv* : avidement, voracement
hungry [ˈhʌŋgri] *adj* **hungrier; -est 1** : avide <hungry for affection : avide d'affection> **2 to be hungry** : avoir faim
hunk [ˈhʌŋk] *n* : gros morceau *m*
hunt[1] [ˈhʌnt] *vt* **1** : chasser <to hunt buffalo : chasser le bison> **2** *or* **to hunt for** PURSUE, SEEK : rechercher, chercher, poursuivre
hunt[2] *n* **1** : chasse *f* (sport) **2** SEARCH : recherche *f*
hunter [ˈhʌntər] *n* : chasseur *m,* -seuse *f*
hurdle[1] [ˈhərdəl] *vt* **-dled; -dling** : franchir, sauter
hurdle[2] *n* **1** : haie *f* (aux sports) **2** OBSTACLE : obstacle *m*
hurl [ˈhərl] *vt* : lancer, jeter
hurrah [hʊˈrɑ, -ˈrɔ] *interj* : hourra!
hurricane [ˈhərəˌkeɪn] *n* : ouragan *m*
hurriedly [ˈhərədli] *adv* : à la hâte, précipitamment
hurry[1] [ˈhəri] *v* **-ried; -rying** *vt* : presser, bousculer, brusquer — *vi* : se presser, se dépêcher, se hâter <hurry up! : dépêche-toi!>

hurry[2] *n* : hâte *f*, empressement *m*
hurt[1] [ˈhərt] *v* **hurt; hurting** *vt* **1** INJURE : faire mal à, blesser <I hurt my thumb : je me suis fait mal au pouce> **2** OFFEND : blesser, offenser — *vi* : faire mal <my foot hurts : mon pied me fait mal> <my throat hurts : j'ai mal à la gorge>
hurt[2] *n* **1** INJURY, PAIN : blessure *f*, mal *m* **2** DISTRESS : peine *f*
hurtful [ˈhərtfəl] *adj* : blessant, pénible
hurtle [ˈhərtəl] *vi* **-tled; -tling** : aller à toute vitesse
husband[1] [ˈhʌzbənd] *vt* : ménager, économiser
husband[2] *n* : mari *m*, époux *m*
husbandry [ˈhʌzbəndri] *n* **1** THRIFT : économie *f* **2** AGRICULTURE : agriculture *f* <animal husbandry : l'élevage>
hush[1] [ˈhʌʃ] *vt* **1** *or* **to hush up** : faire taire **2** CALM, SOOTHE : calmer, apaiser <to hush a baby : appaiser un bébé> — *vi* **1** : se taire **2 hush!** : chut!
hush[2] *n* SILENCE : silence *m*
husk[1] [ˈhʌsk] *vt* : écaler (des noix), éplucher (des légumes), vanner (du blé)
husk[2] *n* : écale *f* (de noix), cosse *f* (de pois, etc.), enveloppe *f* (de maïs)
huskily [ˈhʌskəli] *adv* : d'une voix enrouée
husky[1] [ˈhʌski] *adj* **huskier; -est 1** HOARSE : enroué **2** BURLY : costaud *fam*
husky[2] *n, pl* **-kies** : chien *m* esquimau
hustle[1] [ˈhəsəl] *v* **-tled; -tling** *vt* : presser, pousser, bousculer — *vi* HURRY : se dépêcher, se presser
hustle[2] *n* BUSTLE : grande activité *f*
hut [ˈhʌt] *n* : hutte *f*, cabane *f*, bicoque *f*
hutch [ˈhʌtʃ] *n* **1** CUPBOARD : dressoir *m* **2** : cage *f* <rabbit hutch : cage à lapin>
hyacinth [ˈhaɪəˌsɪnθ] *n* : jacinthe *f*
hybrid[1] [ˈhaɪbrɪd] *adj* : hybride
hybrid[2] *n* : hybride *m*
hydrant [ˈhaɪdrənt] *n* **1** : prise *f* d'eau **2** *or* **fire hydrant** : bouche *f* d'incendie, borne-fontaine *f Can*
hydraulic [haɪˈdrɔlɪk] *adj* : hydraulique — **hydraulically** [-lɪkli] *adv*
hydrocarbon [ˌhaɪdroˈkɑrbən] *n* : hydrocarbure *m*
hydrochloric acid [ˌhaɪdroˈklorɪk] *n* : acide *m* chlorhydrique
hydroelectric [ˌhaɪdroɪˈlɛktrɪk] *adj* : hydroélectrique
hydrogen [ˈhaɪdrədʒən] *n* : hydrogène *m*
hydrogen bomb *n* : bombe *f* à hydrogène
hydrogen peroxide *n* : eau *f* oxygénée
hydrophobia [ˌhaɪdrəˈfo:biə] *n* : hydrophobie *f*
hydroplane [ˈhaɪdrəˌpleɪn] *n* : hydroglisseur *m*
hyena [haɪˈi:nə] *n* : hyène *f*
hygiene [ˈhaɪˌdʒi:n] *n* : hygiène *f*
hygienic [haɪˈdʒɛnɪk, -ˈdʒi:-; ˌhaɪdʒi:ˈɛnɪk] *adj* : hygiénique — **hygienically** [-nɪkli] *adv*
hygienist [haɪˈdʒi:nɪst, -ˈdʒɛ:-, ˈhaɪˌdʒi:-] *n* : hygiéniste *mf*
hygrometer [haɪˈgrɑmət̬ər] *n* : hygromètre *m*
hymn [ˈhɪm] *n* : hymne *m*, cantique *m*
hymnal [ˈhɪmnəl] *n* : livre *m* d'hymnes
hype [ˈhaɪp] *n* : battage *m* publicitaire
hyperactive [ˌhaɪpərˈæktɪv] *adj* : hyperactif
hyperbole [haɪˈpərbəli] *n* : hyperbole *f*
hypercritical [ˌhaɪpərˈkrɪt̬əkəl] *adj* : excessivement critique
hypersensitive [ˌhaɪpərˈsɛnt̬sətɪv] *adj* : hypersensible
hypertension [ˌhaɪpərˈtɛntʃən] *n* : hypertension *f*
hypertext [ˈhaɪpərˌtɛkst] *n* : hypertexte *m*
hyphen [ˈhaɪfən] *n* : trait *m* d'union
hyphenate [ˈhaɪfənˌeɪt] *vt* **-ated; -ating** : mettre un trait d'union à
hypnosis [hɪpˈno:sɪs] *n, pl* **-noses** [-ˌsi:z] : hypnose *f*
hypnotic [hɪpˈnɑt̬ɪk] *adj* : hypnotique
hypnotism [ˈhɪpnəˌtɪzəm] *n* : hypnotisme *m*
hypnotize [ˈhɪpnəˌtaɪz] *vt* **-tized; -tizing** : hypnotiser
hypochondria [ˌhaɪpəˈkɑndriə] *n* : hypocondrie *f*
hypochondriac [ˌhaɪpəˈkɑndriˌæk] *n* : hypocondriaque *mf*
hypocrisy [hɪˈpɑkrəsi] *n, pl* **-sies** : hypocrisie *f*
hypocrite [ˈhɪpəˌkrɪt] *n* : hypocrite *mf*
hypocritical [ˌhɪpəˈkrɪt̬ɪkəl] *adj* : hypocrite — **hypocritically** [-t̬ɪkli] *adv*
hypodermic[1] [ˌhaɪpəˈdərmɪk] *adj* : hypodermique
hypodermic[2] *n* : piqûre *f* hypodermique
hypotenuse [haɪˈpɑtənˌu:s, -ˌu:z, -ˌju:s, -ˌju:z] *n* : hypoténuse *f*
hypothesis [haɪˈpɑθəsɪs] *n, pl* **-eses** [-ˌsi:z] : hypothèse *f*
hypothetical [ˌhaɪpəˈθɛt̬ɪkəl] *adj* : hypothétique — **hypothetically** [-t̬ɪkli] *adv*
hysterectomy [ˌhɪstəˈrɛktəmi] *n, pl* **-mies** : hystérectomie *f*
hysteria [hɪsˈtɛriə, -ˈtɪr-] *n* : hystérie *f*
hysterical [hɪsˈtɛrɪkəl] *adj* : hystérique — **hysterically** [-ɪkli] *adv*
hysterics [hɪsˈtɛrɪks] *ns & pl* : crise *f* (de nerfs, de rire, etc.)

I

i [ˈaɪ] *n, pl* **i's** *or* **is** [ˈaɪz] : i *m*, neuvième lettre de l'alphabet

I [ˈaɪ] *pron* : je

ibis [ˈaɪbəs] *n, pl* **ibis** *or* **ibises** : ibis *m*

ice[1] [ˈaɪs] *v* **iced; icing** *vt* **1** FREEZE : glacer **2** CHILL : rafraîchir **3** FROST : glacer (un gâteau, etc.) — *vi or* **to ice up** : se givrer

ice[2] *n* **1** : glace *f* **2** SHERBET : sorbet *m*

ice age *n* : période *f* glacière

iceberg [ˈaɪsˌbərg] *n* : iceberg *m*

icebox [ˈaɪsˌbɑks] → **refrigerator**

icebreaker [ˈaɪsˌbreɪkər] *n* : brise-glace *m*

ice cap *n* : calotte *f* glacière

ice-cold [ˈaɪsˈkoːld] *adj* : glacé

ice cream *n* : glace *f France*, crème *f* glacée *Can*

ice floe → **floe**

Icelander [ˈaɪsˌlændər, -lən-] *n* : Islandais *m*, -daise *f*

Icelandic[1] [aɪsˈlændɪk] *adj* : islandais

Icelandic[2] *n* : islandais *m* (langue)

ice-skate [ˈaɪsˌskeɪt] *vi* **-skated; -skating** : patiner

ice skater *n* : patineur *m*, -neuse *f*

ichthyology [ˌɪkθiˈɑlədʒi] *n* : ichtyologie *f*

icicle [ˈaɪˌsɪkəl] *n* : glaçon *m*

icily [ˈaɪsəli] *adv* : d'un ton glacial, d'un air glacial

icing [ˈaɪsɪŋ] *n* : glaçage *m*, crémage *m Can*

icon [ˈaɪˌkɑn, -kən] *n* : icône *f*

iconoclasm [aɪˈkɑnəˌklæzəm] *n* : iconoclasme *m*

iconoclast [aɪˈkɑnəˌklæst] *n* : iconoclaste *mf*

icy [ˈaɪsi] *adj* **icier; -est 1** FREEZING : glacial, glacé **2** : verglacé <an icy road : une route verglacée> **3** FROSTY : glacial <an icy smile : un sourire glacial>

id [ˈɪd] *n* : ça *m*

I'd [ˈaɪd] (*contraction of* **I should** *or* **I would**) → **should, would**

idea [aɪˈdiːə] *n* : idée *f*

ideal[1] [aɪˈdiːəl] *adj* : idéal

ideal[2] *n* : idéal *m*

idealism [aɪˈdiːəˌlɪzəm] *n* : idéalisme *m*

idealist [aɪˈdiːəˌlɪst] *n* : idéaliste *mf*

idealistic [aɪˌdiːəˈlɪstɪk] *adj* : idéaliste

idealization [aɪˌdiːələˈzeɪʃən] *n* : idéalisation *f*

idealize [aɪˈdiːəˌlaɪz] *vt* **-ized; -izing** : idéaliser

ideally [aɪˈdiːəli] *adv* : idéalement

identical [aɪˈdɛntɪkəl] *adj* : identique — **identically** [-tɪkli] *adv*

identifiable [aɪˌdɛntəˈfaɪəbəl] *adj* : identifiable

identification [aɪˌdɛntəfəˈkeɪʃən] *n* **1** : identification *f* **2** *or* **identification card** : carte *f* d'identité

identify [aɪˈdɛntəˌfaɪ] *v* **-fied; -fying** *vt* : identifier — *vi* **to identify with** : s'identifier à

identity [aɪˈdɛntət̬i] *n, pl* **-ties** : identité *f*

ideological [ˌaɪdiəˈlɑdʒɪkəl, ˌɪ-] *adj* : idéologique

ideologically [ˌaɪdiəˈlɑdʒɪkli, ˌɪ-] *adv* : du point de vue idéologique

ideology [ˌaɪdiˈɑlədʒi, ˌɪ-] *n, pl* **-gies** : idéologie *f*

idiocy [ˈɪdiəsi] *n, pl* **-cies 1** : idiotie *f* (en médecine) **2** NONSENSE : idiotie *f*, stupidité *f*

idiom [ˈɪdiəm] *n* **1** LANGUAGE : idiome *m*, langue *f* **2** EXPRESSION : idiotisme *m*, expression *f* idiomatique

idiomatic [ˌɪdiəˈmæt̬ɪk] *adj* : idiomatique

idiosyncrasy [ˌɪdioˈsɪŋkrəsi] *n, pl* **-sies** : particularité *f*, idiosyncrasie *f*

idiosyncratic [ˌɪdiosɪnˈkræt̬ɪk] *adj* : particulier, caractéristique

idiot [ˈɪdiət] *n* : idiot *m*, -diote *f*

idiotic [ˌɪdiˈɑt̬ɪk] *adj* : idiot — **idiotically** [-t̬ɪkli] *adv*

idle[1] [ˈaɪdəl] *v* **idled; idling** *vi* **1** *or* **to idle about** : fainéanter, traîner **2** : tourner au ralenti (se dit d'un moteur) — *vt or* **to idle away** : gaspiller (son temps)

idle[2] *adj* **idler; idlest 1** VAIN : vain, inutile <idle curiosity : pure curiosité> **2** INACTIVE : oisif, désœuvré **3** LAZY : paresseux

idleness [ˈaɪdəlnəs] *n* : oisiveté *f*, désœuvrement *m*

idler [ˈaɪdələr] *n* : paresseux *m*, -seuse *f*

idly [ˈadəli] *adv* **1** LAZILY : paresseusement **2** ABSENTMINDEDLY : d'un air distrait

idol [ˈaɪdəl] *n* : idole *f*

idolatry [aɪˈdɑlətri] *n, pl* **-tries** : idolâtrie *f*

idolization [ˌaɪdələˈzeɪʃən] *n* : idolâtrie *f*

idolize [ˈaɪdəlˌaɪz] *vt* **-ized; izing** : idolâtrer

idyll [ˈaɪdəl] *n* : idylle *f*

idyllic [aɪˈdɪlɪk] *adj* : idyllique

if [ˈɪf] *conj* **1** : si <I would do it if I could : je le ferais si je pouvais> <as if : comme si> <if I were you : si j'étais vous> **2** WHETHER : si <do you know if they are here? : savez-vous s'ils sont ici?> **3** THOUGH : bien que, même que <it's pretty, if somewhat old-fashioned : c'est joli, bien qu'un peu démodé>

igloo [ˈɪˌgluː] *n, pl* **-loos** : igloo *m*

ignite [ɪgˈnaɪt] *v* **-nited; -niting** *vt* : mettre le feu à, enflammer — *vi* : prendre feu, s'enflammer

ignition [ɪgˈnɪʃən] *n* **1** : allumage *m* **2** *or* **ignition switch** : contact *m*

ignoble [ɪg'no:bəl] *adj* : infâme
ignominious [ˌɪgnə'mɪniəs] *adj* : ignominieux — **ignominiously** *adv*
ignominy ['ɪgnəˌmɪni] *n, pl* **-nies** : ignominie *f*
ignoramus [ˌɪgnə'reɪməs] *n* : ignare *mf*
ignorance ['ɪgnərənts] *n* : ignorance *f*
ignorant ['ɪgnərənt] *adj* : ignorant
ignorantly ['ɪgnərəntli] *adv* : d'une manière grossière <to speak ignorantly : parler par ignorance>
ignore [ɪg'nor] *vt* **-nored; -noring** : ignorer, ne pas tenir compte de, ne pas faire attention à
iguana [ɪ'gwɑnə] *n* : iguane *m*
ilk ['ɪlk] *n* : espèce *f*, acabit *m*
ill[1] ['ɪl] *adv* **worse** ['wərs]; **worst** ['wərst] : mal <ill prepared : mal préparé> <to speak ill of : dire du mal de>
ill[2] *adj* **worse; worst 1** SICK : malade <to be taken ill : tomber malade> **2** BAD : mauvais <ill humor : mauvaise humeur>
ill[3] *n* : mal *m*
I'll ['aɪl] (*contraction of* **I shall** *or* **I will**) → **shall, will**
illegal [ɪl'li:gəl] *adj* : illégal — **illegally** *adv*
illegality [ɪli'gæləṭi] *n* : illégalité *f*
illegible [ɪl'lɛdʒəbəl] *adj* : illisible — **illegibly** [-bli] *adv*
illegitimacy [ˌɪlɪ'dʒɪṭəməsi] *n* : illégitimité *f*
illegitimate [ˌɪlɪ'dʒɪṭəmət] *adj* : illégitime — **illegitimately** *adv*
illicit [ɪl'lɪsət] *adj* : illicite — **illicitly** *adv*
illimitable [ɪl'lɪməṭəbəl] *adj* : illimité
illiteracy [ɪl'lɪṭərəsi] *n, pl* **-cies** : analphabétisme *m*
illiterate[1] [ɪl'lɪṭərət] *adj* **1** : analphabète, illettré **2** IGNORANT : ignorant, sans éducation
illiterate[2] *n* : analphabète *mf*
ill–mannered [ˌɪl'mænərd] *adj* : impoli, grossier
ill–natured [ˌɪl'neɪtʃərd] *adj* : désagréable — **ill–naturedly** *adv*
illness ['ɪlnəs] *n* : maladie *f*
illogical [ɪl'lɑdʒɪkəl] *adj* : illogique — **illogically** [-kli] *adv*
ill–tempered [ˌɪl'tɛmpərd] → **ill–natured**
ill–treat [ˌɪl'tri:t] *vt* : maltraiter
ill–treatment [ˌɪl'tri:tmənt] *n* : mauvais traitement *m*
illuminate [ɪ'lu:məˌneɪt] *vt* **-nated; -nating** : éclairer, illuminer
illumination [ɪˌlu:mə'neɪʃən] *n* : éclairage *m*, illumination *f*
ill–use ['ɪl'ju:z] → **ill–treat**
illusion [ɪ'lu:ʒən] *n* : illusion *f*
illusory [ɪ'lu:səri, -zəri] *adj* : illusoire
illustrate ['ɪləsˌtreɪt] *v* **-trated; -trating** : illustrer
illustration [ˌɪləs'treɪʃən] *n* : illustration *f*
illustrative [ɪ'lʌstrəṭɪv, 'ɪləˌstreɪṭɪv] *adj* : explicatif
illustrator ['ɪləˌstreɪṭər] *n* : illustrateur *m*, -trice *f*
illustrious [ɪ'lʌstriəs] *adj* RENOWNED : illustre
illustriousness [ɪ'lʌstriəsnəs] *n* RENOWN : renommée *f*
ill will *n* : malveillance *f*, rancune *f*
I'm ['aɪm] (*contraction of* **I am**) → **be**
image ['ɪmɪdʒ] *n* : image *f*
imagery ['ɪmɪdʒri] *n, pl* **-eries 1** : images *fpl* (en litérature, etc.) **2** PICTURES : imagerie *f*
imaginable [ɪ'mædʒənəbəl] *adj* : imaginable
imaginary [ɪ'mædʒəˌnɛri] *adj* : imaginaire
imagination [ɪ'mædʒə'neɪʃən] *n* : imagination *f*
imaginative [ɪ'mædʒɪnəṭɪv] *adj* : imaginatif, plein d'imagination
imaginatively [ɪ'mædʒɪnəṭɪvli] *adv* : avec imagination
imagine [ɪ'mædʒən] *vt* **-ined; -ining 1** : imaginer, se représenter (une scène, etc.) **2** SUPPOSE : s'imaginer, supposer
imbalance [ɪm'bælənts] *n* : déséquilibre *m*
imbecile[1] ['ɪmbəsəl, -ˌsɪl] *or* **imbecilic** [ˌɪmbə'sɪlɪk] *adj* : imbécile
imbecile[2] *n* : imbécile *mf*
imbecility [ˌɪmbə'sɪləṭi] *n, pl* **-ties** : imbécillité *f*
imbibe [ɪm'baɪb] *v* **-bibed; -bibing** *vt* ABSORB : assimiler, absorber — *vi* DRINK : boire
imbue [ɪm'bju:] *vt* **-bued; -buing 1** : imprégner **2 to be imbued with** : être imbu de
imitate ['ɪməˌteɪt] *vt* **-tated; -tating** : imiter
imitation[1] [ˌɪmə'teɪʃən] *adj* : artificiel, faux
imitation[2] *n* : imitation *f*
imitative ['ɪməˌteɪṭɪv] *adj* : imitatif, imitateur
imitator ['ɪməˌteɪṭər] *n* : imitateur *m*, -trice *f*
immaculate [ɪ'mækjələt] *adj* **1** PURE : immaculé **2** CLEAN, IMPECCABLE : impeccable
immaculately [ɪ'mækjələtli] *adv* : impeccablement
immaterial [ˌɪmə'tɪriəl] *adj* : sans importance
immature [ˌɪmə'tʃʊr, -'tjʊr, -'tʊr] *adj* : immature
immaturity [ˌɪmə'tʃʊrəṭi, -'tjʊr-, -'tʊr-] *n, pl* **-ties** : immaturité *f*
immeasurable [ɪ'mɛʒərəbəl] *adj* : incommensurable — **immeasurably** [-bli] *adv*
immediate [ɪ'mi:diət] *adj* **1** INSTANT, URGENT : immédiat, urgent **2** NEARBY : proche, immédiat <our immediate neighbors : nos voisins

immédiats> 3 DIRECT : direct, immédiat <the immediate cause of her death : la cause immédiate de sa mort>

immediately [ɪ'mi:diətli] *adv* **1** INSTANTLY : immédiatement **2** DIRECTLY, JUST : juste <immediately after : juste après>

immemorial [,ɪmə'moriəl] *adj* : immémorial

immense [ɪ'mɛnts] *adj* : immense

immensely [ɪ'mɛntsli] *adv* : immensément, énormément

immensity [ɪ'mɛntsəṭi] *n, pl* **-ties** : immensité *f*

immerse [ɪ'mərs] *vt* **-mersed; -mersing** **1** : plonger, immerger **2 to immerse oneself in** : se plonger dans

immersion [ɪ'mərʒən] *n* : immersion *f*

immigrant ['ɪmɪgrənt] *n* : immigrant *m*, -grante *f*

immigrate ['ɪmə,greɪt] *vi* **-grated; -grating** : immigrer

immigration [,ɪmə'greɪʃən] *n* : immigration *f*

imminence ['ɪmənənts] *n* : imminence *f*

imminent ['ɪmənənt] *adj* : imminent

immobile [ɪ'mo:bəl] *adj* **1** FIXED, IMMOVABLE : fixe, impossible à déplacer **2** MOTIONLESS : immobile

immobility [,ɪmo'bɪləṭi] *n* : immobilité *f*

immobilize [ɪ'mo:bə,laɪz] *vt* **-ized; -izing** : immobiliser

immoderate [ɪ'mɑdərət] *adj* : immodéré, excessif — **immoderately** *adv*

immodest [ɪ'mɑdəst] *adj* **1** VAIN : vaniteux **2** INDECENT : impudique, indécent

immodestly [ɪ'mɑdəstli] *adv* : sans modestie, impudiquement

immodesty [ɪ'mɑdəsti] *n* **1** VANITY : vanité *f* **2** INDECENCY : indécence *f*, impudeur *f*

immoral [ɪ'mɔrəl] *adj* : immoral — **immorally** *adv*

immorality [,ɪmɔ'ræləṭi, ,ɪmə-] *n* : immoralité *f*

immortal[1] [ɪ'mɔrṭəl] *adj* : immortel

immortal[2] *n* : immortel *m*, -telle *f*

immortality [,ɪ,mɔr'tæləṭi] *n* : immortalité *f*

immortalize [ɪ'mɔrṭəl,aɪz] *vt* **-ized; -izing** : immortaliser

immovable [ɪ'mu:vəbəl] *adj* **1** STATIONARY : fixe **2** UNYIELDING : inébranlable

immune [ɪ'mju:n] *adj* **1** : immunisé <immune against measles : immunisé contre la rougeole> **2** EXEMPT : exempt

immune system *n* : système *m* immunitaire

immunity [ɪ'mju:nəṭi] *n, pl* **-ties** : immunité *f*

immunization [,ɪmjʊnə'zeɪʃən] *n* : immunisation *f*

immunize ['ɪmjʊ,naɪz] *vt* **-nized; -nizing** : immuniser

immunology [,ɪmjʊ'nɑlədʒi] *n* : immunologie *f*

immutable [ɪ'mju:ṭəbəl] *adj* : immuable — **immutably** [-bli] *adv*

imp ['ɪmp] *n* **1** DEMON : lutin *m*, diablotin *m* **2** RASCAL : polisson *m*, -sonne *f*

impact[1] [ɪm'pækt] *vt* **1** STRIKE : frapper, percuter **2** AFFECT : avoir un impact sur, affecter — *vi* **to impact on** : avoir un impact sur

impact[2] ['ɪm,pækt] *n* : impact *m*

impacted [ɪm'pæktəd] *adj* : inclus <impacted tooth : dent incluse>

impair [ɪm'pær] *vt* **1** DIMINISH, WEAKEN : diminuer, affaiblir, affecter **2** DAMAGE : détériorer (la santé, etc.)

impairment [ɪm'pærmənt] *n* : affaiblissement *m*, diminution *f* <visual impairment : troubles visuels>

impala [ɪm'pɑlə, -'pæ-] *n, pl* **impalas** *or* **impala** : impala *m*

impale [ɪm'peɪl] *vt* **-paled; -paling** : empaler

impanel [ɪm'pænəl] *vt* **-eled** *or* **-elled; -eling** *or* **-elling** : constituer (un jury, etc.)

impart [ɪm'pɑrt] *vt* **1** COMMUNICATE : communiquer **2** BESTOW, CONVEY : donner, transmettre

impartial [ɪm'pɑrʃəl] *adj* : impartial — **impartially** *adv*

impartiality [ɪm,pɑrʃi'æləṭi] *n* : impartialité *f*

impassable [ɪm'pæsəbəl] *adj* : impraticable, infranchissable

impasse ['ɪm,pæs] *n* : impasse *f*

impassioned [ɪm'pæʃənd] *adj* : passionné

impassive [ɪm'pæsɪv] *adj* : impassible — **impassively** *adv*

impatience [ɪm'peɪʃənts] *n* : impatience *f*

impatient [ɪm'peɪʃənt] *adj* : impatient

impatiently [ɪm'peɪʃəntli] *adv* : impatiemment

impeach [ɪm'pi:tʃ] *vt* : destituer (un fonctionnaire du gouvernement)

impeachment [ɪm'pi:tʃmənt] *n* : destitution *f* (d'un fonctionnaire du gouvernement)

impeccable [ɪm'pɛkəbəl] *adj* : impeccable — **impeccably** [-bli] *adv*

impecunious [,ɪmpɪ'kju:niəs] *adj* : impécunieux

impede [ɪm'pi:d] *vt* **-peded; -peding** : entraver, gêner

impediment [ɪm'pɛdəmənt] *n* **1** HINDRANCE : entrave *f*, obstacle *m* **2** *or* **speech impediment** : défaut *m* de l'élocution

impel [ɪm'pɛl] *vt* **-pelled; -pelling** **1** URGE : inciter **2** DRIVE : pousser

impend [ɪm'pɛnd] *vi* : être imminent

impending [ɪm'pɛndɪŋ] *adj* : imminent

impenetrable [ɪm'pɛnətrəbəl] *adj* : impénétrable
impenitent [ɪm'pɛnətənt] *adj* : impénitent
imperative[1] [ɪm'pɛrəṭɪv] *adj* **1** AUTHORITATIVE : autoritaire **2** URGENT : impérieux, urgent — **imperatively** *adv*
imperative[2] *n* : impératif *m*
imperceptible [ˌɪmpər'sɛptəbəl] *adj* : imperceptible — **imperceptibly** [-bli] *adv*
imperfect[1] [ɪm'pərfɪkt] *adj* : imparfait — **imperfectly** *adv*
imperfect[2] *n or* **imperfect tense** : imparfait *m*
imperfection [ɪmˌpər'fɛkʃən] *n* : imperfection *f*
imperial [ɪm'pɪriəl] *adj* **1** SOVEREIGN : impérial **2** IMPERIOUS : impérieux
imperialism [ɪm'pɪriəˌlɪzəm] *n* : impérialisme *m*
imperialist[1] [ɪm'pɪriəlɪst] *or* **imperialistic** [ɪmˌpɪri:ə'lɪstɪk] *adj* : impérialiste
imperialist[2] *n* : impérialiste *mf*
imperil [ɪm'pɛrəl] *vt* **-iled** *or* **-illed; -iling** *or* **-illing** : mettre en péril
imperious [ɪm'pɪriəs] *adj* : impérieux — **imperiously** *adv*
imperishable [ɪm'pɛrɪʃəbəl] *adj* : impérissable
impermanent [ɪm'pərmənənt] *adj* : éphémère, fugace
impermeable [ɪm'pərmiəbəl] *adj* : imperméable
impersonal [ɪm'pərsənəl] *adj* : impersonnel — **impersonally** *adv*
impersonate [ɪm'pərsənˌeɪt] *vt* **-ated; -ating** : se faire passer pour
impersonation [ɪmˌpərsən'eɪʃən] *n* : imitation *f*
impersonator [ɪm'pərsənˌeɪṭər] *n* : imitateur *m*, -trice *f*
impertinence [ɪm'pərtənən*t*s] *n* : impertinence *f*
impertinent [ɪm'pərtənənt] *adj* : impertinent
impertinently [ɪm'pərtənəntli] *adv* : avec impertinence
imperturbable [ˌɪmpər'tərbəbəl] *adj* : imperturbable
impervious [ɪm'pərviəs] *adj* **1** IMPENETRABLE : imperméable **2** UNAFFECTED : indifférent
impetuosity [ɪmˌpɛtʃʊ'ɑsəṭi] *n, pl* **-ties** : impétuosité *f*
impetuous [ɪm'pɛtʃʊəs] *adj* : impétueux — **impetuously** *adv*
impetus ['ɪmpəṭəs] *n* : impulsion *f*
impiety [ɪm'paɪəṭi] *n, pl* **-ties** : impiété *f*
impinge [ɪm'pɪndʒ] *vi* **-pinged; -pinging** **1 to impinge on** AFFECT : affecter **2 to impinge on** VIOLATE : empiéter sur
impious ['ɪmpiəs, ɪm'paɪəs] *adj* : impie
impish ['ɪmpɪʃ] *adj* : espiègle
impishly ['ɪmpɪʃli] *adv* : en espiègle
impishness ['ɪmpɪʃnəs] *n* : espièglerie *f*
implacable [ɪm'plækəbəl] *adj* : implacable — **implacably** [-bli] *adv*
implant[1] [ɪm'plænt] *vt* **1** INSERT : implanter **2** INSTILL : inculquer
implant[2] ['ɪmˌplænt] *n* : implant *m*
implantation [ˌɪmˌplæn'teɪʃən] *n* : implantation *f*
implausibility [ɪmˌplɔzə'bɪləṭi] *n, pl* **-ties** : invraisemblance *f*
implausible [ɪm'plɔzəbəl] *adj* : peu plausible, invraisemblable
implement[1] ['ɪmpləˌmɛnt] *vt* : mettre en œuvre, exécuter
implement[2] ['ɪmpləmənt] *n* : outil *m*, instrument *m*
implementation [ˌɪmpləmən'teɪʃən] *n* : mise *f* en œuvre, exécution *f*
implicate ['ɪmpləˌkeɪt] *vt* **-cated; -cating** : impliquer
implication [ˌɪmplə'keɪʃən] *n* **1** CONSEQUENCE : implication *f* **2** INFERENCE : insinuation *f*
implicit [ɪm'plɪsət] *adj* **1** IMPLIED, POTENTIAL : implicite **2** UNQUESTIONING : absolu, total
implicitly [ɪm'plɪsətli] *adv* **1** TACITLY : implicitement **2** ABSOLUTELY : absolument
implode [ɪm'plo:d] *vi* **-ploded; -ploding** : imploser
implosion [ɪm'plo:ʒən] *n* : implosion *f*
implore [ɪm'plor] *vt* **-plored; -ploring** : implorer, supplier
imply [ɪm'plaɪ] *vt* **-plied; -plying** **1** MEAN : impliquer, laisser entendre **2** INDICATE : suggérer, impliquer <her answer implies a true understanding : sa réponse suggère une vraie compréhension>
impolite [ˌɪmpə'laɪt] *adj* : impoli — **impolitely** *adv*
impoliteness [ˌɪmpə'laɪtnəs] *n* : impolitesse *f*
impolitic [ɪm'pɑləˌtɪk] *adj* : peu politique, mal avisé
imponderable [ɪm'pɑndərəbəl] *adj* : impondérable
import[1] [ɪm'port] *vt* **1** : importer (des marchandises) **2** SIGNIFY : signifier
import[2] ['ɪmˌport] *n* **1** IMPORTANCE, MEANING : signification *f*, importance *f* **2** IMPORTATION : importation *f*
importance [ɪm'pɔrtən*t*s] *n* : importance *f*
important [ɪm'pɔrtənt] *adj* : important
importantly [ɪm'pɔrtəntli] *adv* **1** : avec importance **2 more importantly** : ce qui est plus important
importation [ˌɪmˌpɔr'teɪʃən] *n* : importation *f*
importer [ɪm'porṭər] *n* : importateur *m*, -trice *f*
importunate [ɪm'pɔrtʃənət] *adj* : importun
importune [ˌɪmpər'tu:n, -'tju:n; ɪm'pɔrtʃən] *vt* **-tuned; -tuning** : importuner, harceler

impose [ɪm'po:z] *v* **-posed; -posing** *vt* : imposer, infliger <to impose a penalty : infliger une peine> — *vi* : s'imposer
imposing [ɪm'po:zɪŋ] *adj* : imposant, impressionnant
imposition [ˌɪmpə'zɪʃən] *n* : imposition *f*
impossibility [ɪmˌpɑsə'bɪləṭi] *n, pl* **-ties** : impossibilité *f*
impossible [ɪm'pɑsəbəl] *adj* : impossible
impossibly [ɪm'pɑsəbli] *adv* **1** : de façon impossible **2** UNBELIEVABLY : incroyablement, extrêmement
impostor *or* **imposter** [ɪm'pɑstər] *n* : imposteur *m*
imposture [ɪm'pɑstʃər] *n* : imposture *f*
impotence ['ɪmpətənts] *n* : impuissance *f*
impotency ['ɪmpətəntsi] → **impotence**
impotent ['ɪmpətənt] *adj* : impuissant
impound [ɪm'paʊnd] *vt* : saisir, confisquer
impoverish [ɪm'pɑvərɪʃ] *vt* : appauvrir
impoverishment [ɪm'pɑvərɪʃmənt] *n* : appauvrissement *m*
impracticable [ɪm'præktɪkəbəl] *adj* : impraticable, irréalisable
impractical [ɪm'præktɪkəl] *adj* : peu pratique, peu réaliste
imprecise [ˌɪmprɪ'saɪs] *adj* : imprécis
imprecisely [ˌɪmprɪ'saɪsli] *adv* : de manière imprécise
imprecision [ˌɪmprɪ'sɪʒən] *n* : imprécision *f*
impregnable [ɪm'prɛgnəbəl] *adj* : imprenable
impregnate [ɪm'prɛgˌneɪt] *vt* **-nated; -nating 1** FERTILIZE : féconder **2** SATURATE : imprégner
impregnation [ˌɪmˌprɛg'neɪʃən] *n* **1** FERTILIZATION : fécondation *f* **2** SATURATION : imprégnation *f*
impresario [ˌɪmprə'sɑriˌo, -'sær-] *n, pl* **-rios** : impresario *m*
impress [ɪm'prɛs] *vt* **1** IMPRINT : imprimer **2** AFFECT, INFLUENCE : faire impression sur, impressionner <he didn't impress me : il ne m'a pas impressionné> **3 to impress upon s.o.** : faire bien comprendre à qqn
impression [ɪm'prɛʃən] *n* **1** IMPRINT : marque *f*, empreinte *f*, impression *f* **2** IDEA, NOTION : idée *f*, impression *f* **3** PRINTING : tirage *m*
impressionable [ɪm'prɛʃənəbəl] *adj* : impressionnable
impressive [ɪm'prɛsɪv] *adj* : impressionnant
impressively [ɪm'prɛsɪvli] *adv* : remarquablement, de manière impressionnante
imprint[1] [ɪm'prɪnt, 'ɪmˌ-] *vt* : imprimer
imprint[2] ['ɪmˌprɪnt] *n* : empreinte *f*, marque *f*
imprison [ɪm'prɪzən] *vt* : emprisonner, mettre en prison
imprisonment [ɪm'prɪzənmənt] *n* : emprisonnement *m*
improbability [ɪmˌprɑbə'bɪləṭi] *n, pl* **-ties** : improbabilité *f*, invraisemblance *f*
improbable [ɪm'prɑbəbəl] *adj* : improbable, invraisemblable
impromptu[1] [ɪm'prɑmpˌtu:, -ˌtju:] *adv* : à l'impromptu
impromptu[2] *adj* : impromptu
improper [ɪm'prɑpər] *adj* **1** UNSEEMLY : malséant, inconvenant **2** INCORRECT : incorrect, erroné **3** INDECENT : indécent
improperly [ɪm'prɑpərli] *adv* **1** INCORRECTLY : incorrectement **2** INDECENTLY : indécemment
impropriety [ˌɪmprə'praɪəṭi] *n, pl* **-ties** : inconvenance *f*
improve [ɪm'pru:v] *v* **-proved; -proving** *vt* : améliorer, perfectionner — *vi* : s'améliorer, se perfectionner
improvement [ɪm'pru:vmənt] *n* : amélioration *f*
improvidence [ɪm'prɑvədənts] *n* : imprévoyance *f*
improvident [ɪm'prɑvədənt] *adj* : imprévoyant
improvisation [ɪmˌprɑvə'zeɪʃən, ˌɪmprəvə-] *n* : improvisation *f*
improvise ['ɪmprəˌvaɪz] *v* **-vised; -vising** : improviser
imprudence [ɪm'pru:dənts] *n* : imprudence *f*
imprudent [ɪm'pru:dənt] *adj* : imprudent
impudence ['ɪmpjədənts] *n* : impudence *f*, insolence *f*, effronterie *f*
impudent ['ɪmpjədənt] *adj* : insolent, impudent
impugn [ɪm'pju:n] *vt* : contester
impulse ['ɪmˌpʌls] *n* **1** : impulsion *f* **2 on ~** : sans réfléchir
impulsive [ɪm'pʌlsɪv] *adj* : impulsif — **impulsively** *adv*
impulsiveness [ɪm'pʌlsɪvnəs] *n* : impulsivité *f*
impunity [ɪm'pju:nəṭi] *n* **1** : impunité *f* **2 with ~** : impunément
impure [ɪm'pjʊr] *adj* : impur
impurity [ɪm'pjʊrəṭi] *n, pl* **-ties** : impureté *f*
impute [ɪm'pju:t] *vt* **-puted; -puting** ATTRIBUTE : imputer, attribuer
in[1] ['ɪn] *adv* **1** INSIDE : dedans, à l'intérieur <to come in : entrer> **2 to be in** : être là, être chez soi <is she in today? : est-elle là aujourd'hui?> **3 to be in** : être au pouvoir <the democrats are in : les démocrates sont au pouvoir> **4 to be in for** : aller avoir **5 to be in on** : être dans le coup
in[2] *adj* **1** INSIDE : intérieur <the in part : la partie intérieure> **2** FASHIONABLE : à la mode
in[3] *prep* **1** (*indicating location or position*) <in France : en France> <in Canada : au Canada> <in Montreal : à Montréal> <in the hospital : à

l'hôpital> <in my house : chez moi> **2** (*indicating time or season*) <in 1938 : en 1938> <in the spring : au printemps> <in the summer : en été> <in the past : dans le passé> **3** (*indicating manner*) <in French : en français> <written in pencil : écrit en crayon> <in this way : de cette manière> **4** (*indicating states or circumstances*) <to be in luck : avoir de la chance> <to be in love : être amoureux> <to be in a hurry : être pressé> **5** (*indicating purpose*) <in response : en réponse> **6** INSIDE, WITHIN : dans <in this book : dans ce livre> <I'll be back in a week : je serai de retour dans une semaine> **7** INTO : dans, en <she went in the house : elle est entrée dans la maison> <he broke it in pieces : il l'a cassé en morceaux> **8** DURING : pendant, dans <in the afternoon : pendant l'après-midi, dans l'après-midi>

inability |ˌɪnəˈbɪləṭi| *n, pl* **-ties** : incapacité *f*

inaccessibility |ˌɪnɪkˌsɛsəˈbɪləṭi| *n, pl* **-ties** : inaccessibilité *f*

inaccessible |ˌɪnɪkˈsɛsəbəl| *adj* : inaccessible

inaccuracy |ɪnˈækjərəsi| *n, pl* **-cies** : inexactitude *f*

inaccurate |ɪnˈækjərət| *adj* : inexact — **inaccurately** *adv*

inaction |ɪnˈækʃən| *n* : inaction *f*

inactive |ɪnˈæktɪv| *adj* : inactif

inactivity |ˌɪnˌækˈtɪvəṭi| *n, pl* **-ties** : inactivité *f*, inaction *f*

inadequacy |ɪˈnædɪkwəsi| *n, pl* **-cies 1** INSUFFICIENCY : insuffisance *f* **2** DEFICIENCY : défauts *mpl*, incompétence *f*

inadequate |ɪˈnædɪkwət| *adj* : insuffisant

inadmissible |ˌɪnædˈmɪsəbəl| *adj* : inadmissible

inadvertence |ˌɪnədˈvərtənts| *n* : inadvertance *f*

inadvertent |ˌɪnədˈvərtənt| *adj* : commis par inadvertance, involontaire

inadvertently |ˌɪnədˈvərtəntli| *adv* : par inadvertance

inadvisable |ˌɪnædˈvaɪzəbəl| *adj* : déconseillé

inalienable |ɪnˈeɪljənəbəl, -ˈeɪliən-| *adj* : inaliénable

inane |ɪˈneɪn| *adj* **inaner; -est** : inepte, stupide

inanimate |ɪˈnænəmət| *adj* : inanimé

inanity |ɪˈnænəṭi| *n, pl* **-ties 1** STUPIDITY : stupidité *f* **2** NONSENSE : ineptie *f*

inapplicable |ɪˈnæplɪkəbəl, ˌɪnəˈplɪkəbəl| *adj* : inapplicable

inappreciable |ˌɪnəˈpriːʃəbəl| *adj* : inappréciable, imperceptible

inappropriate |ˌɪnəˈproːpriət| *adj* : inapproprié, inopportun

inappropriately |ˌɪnəˈproːpriətli| *adv* : mal à propos, inopportunément

inapt |ɪnˈæpt| *adj* : inapte

inarticulate |ˌɪnɑrˈtɪkjələt| *adj* **1** INCOHERENT : incohérent, incapable de s'exprimer **2** INEXPRESSIBLE : inexprimable **3** : inarticulé (en physiologie)

inasmuch as |ˌɪnæzˈmʌtʃæz| *conj* : attendu que, vu que, dans la mesure où

inattention |ˌɪnəˈtɛntʃən| *n* : inattention *f*

inattentive |ˌɪnəˈtɛntɪv| *adj* : inattentif

inattentively |ˌɪnəˈtɛntɪvli| *adv* : distraitement, sans prêter attention

inaudible |ɪnˈɔdəbəl| *adj* : inaudible

inaudibly |ɪnˈɔdəbli| *adv* : de manière inaudible, indistinctement

inaugural[1] |ɪˈnɔgjərəl, -gərəl| *adj* : inaugural

inaugural[2] *n* **1** *or* **inaugural address** : discours *m* d'inauguration **2** INAUGURATION : investiture *f*, installation *f*

inaugurate |ɪˈnɔgjəˌreɪt, -gə-| *vt* **-rated; -rating 1** BEGIN : inaugurer **2** INDUCT : investir, installer

inauguration |ɪˌnɔgjəˈreɪʃən, -gə-| *n* **1** BEGINNING : inauguration *f* **2** INDUCTION : investiture *f*, installation *f*

inauspicious |ˌɪnɔˈspɪʃəs| *adj* : peu propice, défavorable

inborn |ˈɪnˌbɔrn| *adj* : inné, congénital

inbred |ˈɪnˌbrɛd| *adj* **1** : consanguin **2** INNATE : inné

inbreed |ˈɪnˌbriːd| *vt* **-bred; -breeding** : croiser (des animaux de même souche)

incalculable |ɪnˈkælkjələbəl| *adj* : incalculable

incandescence |ˌɪnkənˈdɛsənts| *n* : incandescence *f*

incandescent |ˌɪnkənˈdɛsənt| *adj* : incandescent

incantation |ˌɪnˌkænˈteɪʃən| *n* : incantation *f*

incapable |ɪnˈkeɪpəbəl| *adj* : incapable

incapacitate |ˌɪnkəˈpæsəˌteɪt| *vt* **-tated; -tating** : rendre incapable

incapacity |ˌɪnkəˈpæsəṭi| *n, pl* **-ties** : incapacité *f*

incarcerate |ɪnˈkɑrsəˌreɪt| *vt* **-ated; -ating** : incarcérer

incarceration |ɪnˌkɑrsəˈreɪʃən| *n* : incarcération *f*

incarnate[1] |ɪnˈkɑrˌneɪt| *vt* **-ated; -ating** : incarner

incarnate[2] |ɪnˈkɑrnət, -ˌneɪt| *adj* : incarné

incarnation |ˌɪnˌkɑrˈneɪʃən| *n* : incarnation *f*

incendiary[1] |ɪnˈsɛndiˌɛri| *adj* : incendiaire

incendiary[2] *n, pl* **-aries** ARSONIST : incendiaire *mf*

incense[1] |ɪnˈsɛnts| *vt* **-censed; -censing** : mettre en colère, rendre furieux

incense[2] [ˈɪnsɛnts] *n* : encens *m*
incentive [ɪnˈsɛntɪv] *n* : motivation *f*
inception [ɪnˈsɛpʃən] *n* : début *m*, commencement *m*
incessant [ɪnˈsɛsənt] *adj* : incessant — **incessantly** *adv*
incest [ˈɪn,sɛst] *n* : inceste *m*
incestuous [ɪnˈsɛstʃʊəs] *adj* : incestueux
inch[1] [ˈɪntʃ] *v* : avancer petit à petit
inch[2] *n* : pouce *m*
incidence [ˈɪntsədənts] *n* : fréquence *f*, taux *m*
incident [ˈɪntsədənt] *n* : incident *m*
incidental[1] [,ɪntsəˈdɛntəl] *adj* **1** ACCESSORY : secondaire, accessoire **2** FORTUITOUS : fortuit
incidental[2] *n* **1** : détail *m* secondaire **2** **incidentals** *npl* EXPENSES : (faux) frais *mpl*
incidentally [,ɪntsəˈdɛntəli, -ˈdɛntli] *adv* : à propos
incinerate [ɪnˈsɪnə,reɪt] *vt* **-ated; -ating** : incinérer
incinerator [ɪnˈsɪnə,reɪt̬ər] *n* : incinérateur *m*
incipient [ɪnˈsɪpiənt] *adj* : naissant
incise [ɪnˈsaɪz] *vt* **-cised; -cising 1** CUT : inciser **2** ENGRAVE : graver
incision [ɪnˈsɪʒən] *n* : incision *f*
incisive [ɪnˈsaɪsɪv] *adj* : incisif
incisively [ɪnˈsaɪsɪvli] *adv* : d'une manière incisive
incisor [ɪnˈsaɪzər] *n* : incisive *f*
incite [ɪnˈsaɪt] *vt* **-cited; -citing** : inciter
incitement [ɪnˈsaɪtmənt] *n* : incitation *f*
inclemency [ɪnˈklɛməntsi] *n* : inclémence *f* (du temps)
inclement [ɪnˈklɛmənt] *adj* : inclément
inclination [,ɪnkləˈneɪʃən] *n* **1** PROPENSITY : tendance *f* **2** DESIRE : envie *f*, désir *m* **3** BOW, NOD : inclination *f*
incline[1] [ɪnˈklaɪn] *v* **-clined; -clining** *vi* **1** SLOPE : s'incliner **2** TEND : avoir tendance, tendre — *vt* **1** DISPOSE, PROMPT : incliner, disposer **2** BEND : pencher, incliner
incline[2] [ˈɪn,klaɪn] *n* : inclinaison *f*
inclined *adj* **1** SLOPING : incliné **2** **to be inclined to** : avoir tendance à
inclose, inclosure → **enclose, enclosure**
include [ɪnˈklu:d] *vt* **-cluded; -cluding** : inclure, comprendre
inclusion [ɪnˈklu:ʒən] *n* : inclusion *f*
inclusive [ɪnˈklu:sɪv] *adj* : inclus, compris
incognito [,ɪn,kɑgˈni:t̬o, ɪnˈkɑgnə,to:] *adv & adj* : incognito
incoherence [,ɪnkoˈhɪrənts, -ˈhɛr-] *n* : incohérence *f*
incoherent [,ɪnkoˈhɪrənt, -ˈhɛr-] *adj* : incohérent
incoherently [,ɪnkoˈhɪrəntli, -ˈhɛr-] *adv* : de manière incohérente
incombustible [,ɪnkəmˈbʌstəbəl] *adj* : incombustible
income [ˈɪn,kʌm] *n* : revenu *m*
income tax *n* : impôt *m* sur le revenu
incoming [ˈɪn,kʌmɪŋ] *adj* **1** ARRIVING : entrant, qui arrive **2** NEW : nouveau
incommunicado [,ɪnkə,mju:nəˈkɑdo] *adj* : tenu au secret, sans contact avec l'extérieur
incomparable [ɪnˈkɑmpərəbəl] *adj* : incomparable — **incomparably** [-bli] *adv*
incompatibility [,ɪnkəm,pæt̬əˈbɪlət̬i] *n* : incompatibilité *f*
incompatible [,ɪnkəmˈpæt̬əbəl] *adj* : incompatible
incompetence [ɪnˈkɑmpət̬ənts] *n* : incompétence *f*
incompetent [ɪnˈkɑmpət̬ənt] *adj* : incompétent
incomplete [,ɪnkəmˈpli:t] *adj* : incomplet, inachevé
incompletely [,ɪnkəmˈpli:tli] *adv* : incomplètement
incomprehensible [,ɪn,kɑmpriˈhɛntsəbəl] *adj* : incompréhensible
inconceivable [,ɪnkənˈsi:vəbəl] *adj* : inconcevable
inconceivably [,ɪnkənˈsi:vəbli] *adv* : incroyablement
inconclusive [,ɪnkənˈklu:sɪv] *adj* : peu concluant
incongruity [,ɪnkənˈgru:ət̬i, -,kɑn-] *n, pl* **-ties** : incongruité *f*
incongruous [ɪnˈkɑŋgrʊəs] *adj* : incongru, déplacé
incongruously [ɪnˈkɑŋgrʊəsli] *adv* : de façon incongrue
inconsequential [,ɪn,kɑnsəˈkwɛntʃəl] *adj* : sans importance
inconsiderable [,ɪnkənˈsɪdərəbəl] *adj* : insignifiant, négligeable
inconsiderate [,ɪnkənˈsɪdərət] *adj* : qui manque de considération, irréfléchi
inconsiderately [,ɪnkənˈsɪdərətli] *adv* : sans aucune considération
inconsistency [,ɪnkənˈsɪstəntsi] *n, pl* **-cies** : incohérence *f*, contradiction *f*
inconsistent [,ɪnkənˈsɪstənt] *adj* **1** CHANGEABLE, ERRATIC : inégal, changeant **2** CONTRADICTORY : contradictoire
inconsolable [,ɪnkənˈso:ləbəl] *adj* : inconsolable
inconsolably [,ɪnkənˈso:ləbli] *adv* : de façon inconsolable
inconspicuous [,ɪnkənˈspɪkjʊəs] *adj* : peu apparent, qui passe inaperçu
inconspicuously [,ɪnkənˈspɪkjʊəsli] *adv* : discrètement
incontestable [,ɪnkənˈtɛstəbəl] *adj* : incontestable — **incontestably** [-bli] *adv*
incontinent [ɪnˈkɑntənənt] *adj* : incontinent
inconvenience[1] [,ɪnkənˈvi:njənts] *vt* **-nienced; -niencing** : déranger
inconvenience[2] *n* **1** BOTHER : dérangement *m* **2** DISADVANTAGE : inconvénient *m*

inconvenient [ˌɪnkənˈviːnjənt] *adj* : incommode, inopportun
inconveniently [ˌɪnkənˈviːnjəntli] *adv* **1** INOPPORTUNELY : inopportunément **2** : de façon peu practique <inconveniently located : mal placé>
incorporate [ɪnˈkɔrpəˌreɪt] *v* **-rated; -rating** *vt* INCLUDE : incorporer — *vi* : se constituer en société commerciale
incorporated [ɪnˈkɔrpəˌreɪt̬əd] *adj* : constitué en société commerciale
incorporation [ɪnˌkɔrpəˈreɪʃən] *n* **1** INCLUSION, INTEGRATION : incorporation *f*, intégration *f* **2** *Can* : incorporation *f* (d'une société)
incorporeal [ˌɪnˌkɔrˈpɔriəl] *adj* : incorporel
incorrect [ˌɪnkəˈrɛkt] *adj* **1** WRONG : erroné **2** IMPROPER : incorrect
incorrectly [ˌɪnkəˈrɛktli] *adv* : inexactement, incorrectement
incorrigible [ɪnˈkɔrədʒəbəl] *adj* : incorrigible
incorruptible [ɪnkəˈrʌptəbəl] *adj* : incorruptible
increase[1] [ɪnˈkriːs, ˈɪnˌkriːs] *v* **-creased; -creasing** : augmenter
increase[2] [ˈɪnˌkriːs, ɪnˈkriːs] *n* **1** : augmentation *f* **2 on the increase** : en hausse, à la hausse
increasingly [ɪnˈkriːsɪŋli] *adv* : de plus en plus
incredible [ɪnˈkrɛdəbəl] *adj* : incroyable — **incredibly** [-bli] *adv*
incredulity [ˌɪnkrɪˈduːlət̬i, -ˈdjuː-] *n* : incrédulité *f*
incredulous [ɪnˈkrɛdʒələs] *adj* : incrédule
incredulously [ɪnˈkrɛdʒələsli] *adv* : avec incrédulité
increment [ˈɪnkrəmənt, ˈɪn-] *n* : augmentation *f*
incremental [ˌɪŋkrəˈməntəl, ˈɪn-] *adj* : progressif, par augmentation
incriminate [ɪnˈkrɪməˌneɪt] *vt* **-nated; -nating** : incriminer
incrimination [ɪnˌkrɪməˈneɪʃən] *n* : incrimination *f*
incriminatory [ɪnˈkrɪmənəˌtɔri] *adj* : compromettant
incubate [ˈɪŋkjʊˌbeɪt, ˈɪn-] *v* **-bated; -bating** *vt* : incuber — *vi* : être en incubation
incubation [ˌɪŋkjʊˈbeɪʃən, ˌɪn-] *n* : incubation *f*
incubator [ˈɪŋkjʊˈbeɪt̬ər, -ˈɪn-] *n* : incubateur *m*, couveuse *f* (pour enfants)
inculcate [ɪnˈkʌlˌkeɪt, ˈɪnˌkʌl-] *vt* **-cated; -cating** : inculquer
incumbency [ɪnˈkʌmbəntsi] *n, pl* **-cies** : office *m*, période *f* de fonction
incumbent[1] [ɪnˈkʌmbənt] *adj* : obligatoire <to be incumbent upon : incomber à>
incumbent[2] *n* OFFICEHOLDER : titulaire *mf*
incur [ɪnˈkər] *vt* **-curred; -curring** : encourir <to incur expenses : encourir des dépenses>
incurable [ɪnˈkjʊrəbəl] *adj* : incurable
incursion [ɪnˈkərʒən] *n* : incursion *f*
indebted [ɪnˈdɛt̬əd] *adj* **1** : endetté **2 to be indebted to** : être redevable à
indebtedness [ɪnˈdɛt̬ədnəs] *n* : dette *f*, endettement *m*
indecency [ɪnˈdiːsəntsi] *n, pl* **-cies** : indécence *f*
indecent [ɪnˈdiːsənt] *adj* : indécent
indecently [ɪnˈdiːsəntli] *adv* : indécemment
indecipherable [ˌɪndɪˈsaɪfərəbəl] *adj* : indéchiffrable
indecision [ˌɪndɪˈsɪʒən] *n* : indécision *f*
indecisive [ˌɪndɪˈsaɪsɪv] *adj* : indécis
indecisively [ˌɪndɪˈsaɪsɪvli] *adv* : de manière indécise
indecorous [ɪnˈdɛkərəs, ˌɪndɪˈkorəsli] *adj* : inconvenant
indecorously [ɪnˈdɛkərəsli] *adv* : de manière inconvenante
indecorousness [ɪnˈdɛkərəsnəs, ˌɪndɪˈkorəs-] *n* : inconvenance *f*
indeed [ɪnˈdiːd] *adv* **1** TRULY : vraiment, en effet, comme de fait *Can* **2** (*used as an intensifier*) <it's very big indeed : c'est vraiment très grand> **3** OF COURSE : bien sûr
indefatigable [ˌɪndɪˈfæt̬ɪgəbəl] *adj* : infatigable, inlassable
indefensible [ˌɪndɪˈfɛntsəbəl] *adj* : inexcusable, injustifiable
indefinable [ɪndɪˈfaɪnəbəl] *adj* : indéfinissable
indefinite [ɪnˈdɛfənət] *adj* **1** : indéfini <an indefinite period : une période indéfinie> **2** VAGUE : imprécis
indefinite article *n* : article *m* indéfini
indefinitely [ɪnˈdɛfənətli] *adv* : indéfiniment
indelible [ɪnˈdɛləbəl] *adj* : indélébile
indelibly [ɪnˈdɛləbli] *adv* : de manière indélébile
indelicacy [ɪnˈdɛləkəsi] *n* : indélicatesse *f*
indelicate [ɪnˈdɛlɪkət] *adj* : indélicat
indemnify [ɪnˈdɛmnəˌfaɪ] *vt* **-fied; -fying** **1** INSURE : assurer **2** COMPENSATE : indemniser
indemnity [ɪnˈdɛmnət̬i] *n, pl* **-ties** : indemnité *f*
indent [ɪnˈdɛnt] *vt* **1** : renfoncer, mettre en alinéa <indent 4 spaces : renfoncez de 4 espaces> **2** DENT : bosseler
indentation [ˌɪnˌdɛnˈteɪʃən] *n* **1** DENT : creux *m*, bosse *f* **2** SPACE : alinéa *m* (en typographie)
indenture[1] [ɪnˈdɛntʃər] *vt* **-tured; -turing** : engager sous contrat
indenture[2] *n* : contrat *m* d'apprentissage
independence [ˌɪndəˈpɛndənts] *n* : indépendance *f*

Independence Day *n* : fête *f* de l'Indépendance américaine (le 4 juillet)

independent[1] [ˌɪndəˈpɛndənt] *adj* : indépendant

independent[2] *n* : indépendant *m*, -dante *f*

independently [ˌɪndəˈpɛndəntli] *adv* : de façon indépendante, indépendamment

indescribable [ˌɪndɪˈskraɪbəbəl] *adj* : indescriptible

indescribably [ˌɪndɪˈskraɪbəbli] *adv* : incroyablement

indestructibility [ˌɪndɪˌstrʌktəˈbɪləṭi] *n* : indestructibilité *f*

indestructible [ˌɪndɪˈstrʌktəbəl] *adj* : indestructible

indeterminate [ˌɪndɪˈtərmənət] *adj* : indéterminé

index[1] [ˈɪnˌdɛks] *vt* **1** : mettre un index à (un livre, etc.) **2** CATALOG : classer, cataloguer

index[2] *n, pl* **-dexes** *or* **-dices** [ˈɪndəˌsiːz] **1** LIST : index *m* **2** INDICATION : indice *m* <cost of living index : indice du coût de la vie>

index finger *n* : index *m*

Indian[1] [ˈɪndiən] *adj* : indien

Indian[2] *n* : Indien *m*, -dienne *f*

Indian corn *n* : maïs *m*, blé *m* d'Inde *Can*

indicate [ˈɪndəˌkeɪt] *vt* **-cated; -cating** : indiquer

indication [ˌɪndəˈkeɪʃən] *n* : indice *m*, indication *f*

indicative [ɪnˈdɪkəṭɪv] *adj* : indicatif

indicator [ˈɪndəˌkeɪṭər] *n* : indicateur *m*

indict [ɪnˈdaɪt] *vt* : inculper

indictment [ɪnˈdaɪtmənt] *n* : inculpation *f*

indifference [ɪnˈdɪfrənts, -ˈdɪfə-] *n* : indifférence *f*

indifferent [ɪnˈdɪfrənt, -ˈdɪfə-] *adj* **1** UNCONCERNED : indifférent **2** MEDIOCRE : médiocre, quelconque

indifferently [ɪnˈdɪfrəntli, -ˈdɪfə-] *adv* **1** UNCONCERNEDLY : avec indifférence **2** SO-SO : médiocrement

indigence [ˈɪndɪdʒənts] *n* : indigence *f*

indigenous [ɪnˈdɪdʒənəs] *adj* : indigène

indigent [ˈɪndɪdʒənt] *adj* : indigent

indigestible [ˌɪndaɪˈdʒɛstəbəl, -dɪ-] *adj* : indigeste

indigestion [ˌɪndaɪˈdʒɛstʃən, -dɪ-] *n* : indigestion *f*

indignant [ɪnˈdɪgnənt] *adj* : indigné, outré

indignantly [ɪnˈdɪgnəntli] *adv* : avec indignation

indignation [ˌɪndɪgˈneɪʃən] *n* : indignation *f*

indignity [ɪnˈdɪgnəṭi] *n, pl* **-ties** : indignité *f*

indigo [ˈɪndɪˌgoː] *n, pl* **-gos** *or* **-goes** : indigo *m*

indirect [ˌɪndəˈrɛkt, -daɪ-] *adj* : indirect — **indirectly** *adv*

indiscernible [ˌɪndɪˈsərnəbəl, -ˈzər-] *adj* : indiscernable, imperceptible

indiscreet [ˌɪndɪˈskriːt] *adj* : indiscret

indiscreetly [ˌɪndɪˈskriːtli] *adv* : indiscrètement

indiscretion [ˌɪndɪˈskrɛʃən] *n* : indiscrétion *f*

indiscriminate [ˌɪndɪˈskrɪmənət] *adj* **1** : qui manque de discernement **2** HAPHAZARD : fait au hasard

indiscriminately [ˌɪndɪˈskrɪmənətli] *adv* **1** : sans discernement **2** RANDOMLY : au hasard

indispensable [ˌɪndɪˈspɛntsəbəl] *adj* : indispensable

indisposed [ˌɪndɪˈspoːzd] *adj* **1** ILL : indisposé **2** DISINCLINED : peu disposé, peu enclin

indisposition [ˌɪnˌdɪspəˈzɪʃən] *n* : indisposition *f*

indisputable [ˌɪndɪˈspjuːṭəbəl] *adj* : incontestable — **indisputably** [-bli] *adv*

indistinct [ˌɪndɪˈstɪŋkt] *adj* : indistinct — **indistinctly** *adv*

individual[1] [ˌɪndəˈvɪdʒʊəl] *adj* **1** SEPARATE : individuel **2** DISTINCTIVE, PERSONAL : particulier, personnel, original

individual[2] *n* : individu *m*

individualist [ˌɪndəˈvɪdʒʊəlɪst] *n* : individualiste *mf*

individuality [ˌɪndəˌvɪdʒʊˈæləṭi] *n, pl* **-ties** : individualité *f*

individually [ˌɪndəˈvɪdʒʊəli, -dʒəli] *adv* **1** SEPARATELY : individuellement **2** DISTINCTIVELY : de façon distinctive

indivisible [ˌɪndɪˈvɪzəbəl] *adj* : indivisible

indoctrinate [ɪnˈdɑktrəˌneɪt] *vt* **-nated; -nating** : endoctriner

indoctrination [ɪnˌdɑktrəˈneɪʃən] *n* : endoctrinement *m*

indolence [ˈɪndələnts] *n* : indolence *f*

indolent [ˈɪndələnt] *adj* : indolent

indomitable [ɪnˈdɑməṭəbəl] *adj* : indomptable, invincible, irréductible

indomitably [ɪnˈdɑməṭəbli] *adv* : de façon indomptable

Indonesian[1] [ˌɪndoˈniːʒən, -ʃən] *adj* : indonésien

Indonesian[2] *n* **1** : Indonésien *m*, -sienne *f* **2** : indonésien *m* (langue)

indoor [ˈɪnˈdor] *adj* **1** : d'intérieur, à l'intérieur **2** : couvert <indoor swimming pool : piscine couverte>

indoors [ˈɪnˈdorz] *adv* : à l'intérieur

indubitable [ɪnˈduːbəṭəbəl, -ˈdjuː-] *adj* : indubitable — **indubitably** [-bli] *adv*

induce [ɪnˈduːs, -ˈdjuːs] *vt* **-duced; -ducing 1** PERSUADE : persuader **2** CAUSE : provoquer, déclencher <to induce labor : déclencher l'accouchement>

inducement [ɪnˈduːsmənt, -ˈdjuːs-] *n* **1** INCENTIVE : motivation *f* **2** REWARD : récompense *f*

induct [ɪnˈdʌkt] *vt* **1** INSTALL : installer (qqn dans ses fonctions) **2** DRAFT, RECRUIT : incorporer

inductee [ˌɪnˌdʌk'ti:] *n* DRAFTEE : appelé *m*, conscrit *m*

induction [ɪn'dʌktʃən] *n* **1** INSTALLATION : installation *f*, incorporation *f* **2** : induction *f* (en logique, en électricité)

inductive [ɪn'dʌktɪv] *adj* : inductif

indulge [ɪn'dʌldʒ] *v* **-dulged; -dulging** *vt* **1** GRATIFY : céder à, satisfaire **2** PAMPER, SPOIL : gâter — *vi* **to indulge in** : se livrer à, se permettre

indulgence [ɪn'dʌldʒən*t*s] *n* **1** TOLERANCE : complaisance *f*, indulgence *f* **2** GRATIFICATION : satisfaction *f*, gratification *f* **3** : indulgence *f* (en religion)

indulgent [ɪn'dʌldʒənt] *adj* : indulgent

indulgently [ɪn'dʌldʒəntli] *adv* : avec indulgence

industrial [ɪn'dʌstriəl] *adj* : industriel

industrialist [ɪn'dʌstriəlɪst] *n* : industriel *m*, -trielle *f*

industrialization [ɪnˌdʌstriələ'zeɪʃən] *n* : industrialisation *f*

industrialize [ɪn'dʌstriəˌlaɪz] *vt* **-ized; -izing** : industrialiser

industrious [ɪn'dʌstriəs] *adj* : industrieux, travailleur, travaillant *Can*

industriously [ɪn'dʌstriəsli] *adv* : avec diligence

industriousness [ɪn'dʌstriəsnəs] *n* : assiduité *f*, application *f*

industry ['ɪndəstri] *n, pl* **-tries 1** : industrie *f* <the steel industry : l'industrie sidérurgique> **2** DILIGENCE : assiduité *f*

inebriated [ɪ'ni:briˌeɪṭəd] *adj* : ivre

inebriation [ɪˌni:bri'eɪʃən] *n* : ivresse *f*

inedible [ɪ'nɛdəbəl] *adj* : non comestible (se dit d'une plante, etc.), immangeable (se dit d'un plat)

ineffable [ɪn'ɛfəbəl] *adj* : ineffable — **ineffably** [-bli] *adv*

ineffective [ˌɪnɪ'fɛktɪv] *adj* **1** INEFFECTUAL : inefficace **2** INCAPABLE : incapable

ineffectively [ˌɪnɪ'fɛktɪvli] *adv* : sans effet, en vain

ineffectual [ˌɪnɪ'fɛk*t*ʃʊəl], **ineffectually** [ˌɪnɪ'fɛk*t*ʃʊəli] → **ineffective, ineffectively**

inefficiency [ˌɪnɪ'fɪʃən*t*si] *n, pl* **-cies** : inefficacité *f*

inefficient [ˌɪnɪ'fɪʃənt] *adj* **1** : inefficace (se dit d'une machine, etc.) **2** INCOMPETENT : incompétent, mal organisé

inefficiently [ˌɪnɪ'fɪʃəntli] *adv* : inefficacement

inelegance [ɪn'ɛləgən*t*s] *n* : inélégance *f*

inelegant [ɪn'ɛləgənt] *adj* : inélégant

ineligibility [ɪnˌɛlədʒə'bɪləṭi] *n* : inéligibilité *f*

ineligible [ɪn'ɛlədʒəbəl] *adj* : inéligible

inept [ɪ'nɛpt] *adj* **1** INCOMPETENT : inepte **2** INAPPROPRIATE : inapproprié

ineptitude [ɪ'nɛptəˌtu:d, -ˌtju:d] *n* : ineptie *f*

inequality [ˌɪnɪ'kwɑləṭi] *n, pl* **-ties** : inégalité *f*

inert [ɪ'nərt] *adj* : inerte

inertia [ɪ'nərʃə] *n* : inertie *f*

inescapable [ˌɪnɪ'skeɪpəbəl] *adj* : inéluctable, indéniable — **inescapably** [-bli] *adv*

inessential [ˌɪnɪ'sɛn*t*ʃəl] *adj* : non essentiel, superflu

inestimable [ɪn'ɛstəməbəl] *adj* : inestimable

inevitability [ɪnˌɛvəṭə'bɪləṭi] *n, pl* **-ties** : inévitabilité *f*

inevitable [ɪn'ɛvəṭəbəl] *adj* : inévitable — **inevitably** [-bli] *adv*

inexact [ˌɪnɪg'zækt] *adj* : inexact

inexactly [ˌɪnɪg'zæktli] *adv* : inexactement, incorrectement

inexcusable [ˌɪnɪk'skju:zəbəl] *adj* : inexcusable

inexcusably [ˌɪnɪk'skju:zəbli] *adv* : de façon inexcusable

inexhaustible [ˌɪnɪg'zɔstəbəl] *adj* **1** LIMITLESS : inépuisable **2** INDEFATIGABLE : infatigable

inexorable [ɪn'ɛksərəbəl] *adj* : inexorable — **inexorably** [-bli] *adv*

inexpedient [ˌɪnɪk'spi:diənt] *adj* : inopportun, malavisé

inexpensive [ˌɪnɪk'spɛn*t*sɪv] *adj* : pas cher, bon marché

inexperience [ˌɪnɪk'spɪriən*t*s] *n* : inexpérience *f*

inexperienced [ˌɪnɪk'spɪriən*t*st] *adj* : inexpérimenté

inexplicable [ˌɪnɪk'splɪkəbəl] *adj* : inexplicable — **inexplicably** [-bli] *adv*

inexpressible [ˌɪnɪk'sprɛsəbəl] *adj* : inexprimable

inextricable [ˌɪnɪk'strɪkəbəl, ɪ'nɛkˌstrɪ-] *adj* : inextricable — **inextricably** [-bli] *adv*

infallibility [ɪnˌfælə'bɪləṭi] *n* : infaillibilité *f*

infallible [ɪn'fæləbəl] *adj* : infaillible — **infallibly** [-bli] *adv*

infamous ['ɪnfəməs] *adj* : infâme, notoire

infamy ['ɪnfəmi] *n, pl* **-mies** : infamie *f*

infancy ['ɪnfən*t*si] *n, pl* **-cies 1** : petite enfance *f* **2 in its infancy** : à ses débuts

infant ['ɪnfənt] *n* : petit enfant *m*, petite enfant *f*; bébé *m*; nourrisson *m*

infantile ['ɪnfənˌtaɪl, -təl, -ˌti:l] *adj* : infantile

infantile paralysis → **poliomyelitis**

infantry ['ɪnfəntri] *n, pl* **-tries** : infanterie *f*

infatuated [ɪn'fætʃʊˌeɪṭəd] *adj* **to be infatuated with** : être entiché de

infatuation [ɪnˌfætʃʊ'eɪʃən] *n* : engouement *m*

infect [ɪn'fɛkt] *vt* : infecter

infection [ɪn'fɛkʃən] *n* : infection *f*

infectious [ɪn'fɛkʃəs] *adj* **1** : infectieux, contagieux <une maladie infectieuse : an infectious disease> **2** : con-

tagieux, communicatif <rythme communicatif : infectious rhythm>
infer [ɪn'fər] *vt* **-ferred; -ferring** : déduire, inférer
inference ['ɪnfərənts] *n* : déduction *f*, inférence *f*
inferior[1] [ɪn'fɪriər] *adj* : inférieur
inferior[2] *n* : inférieur *m*, -rieure *f*
inferiority [ɪn,fɪri'ɔrəṭi] *n, pl* **-ties** : infériorité *f*
infernal [ɪn'fərnəl] *adj* : infernal
infernally [ɪn'fərnəli] *adv* TERRIBLY : terriblement, abominablement
inferno [ɪn'fər,no:] *n, pl* **-nos 1** BLAZE, FIRE : brasier *m* **2** HELL : enfer *m*
infertile [ɪn'fɛrṭəl, -,taɪl] *adj* : infertile, stérile
infertility [,ɪnfər'tɪləṭi] *n* : infertilité *f*
infest [ɪn'fɛst] *vt* : infester
infidel ['ɪnfədəl, -,dɛl] *n* : infidèle *mf*
infidelity [,ɪnfə'dɛləṭi, -faɪ-] *n, pl* **-ties** : infidélité *f*
infield ['ɪn,fi:ld] *n* : petit champ *m*
infiltrate [ɪn'fɪl,treɪt, 'ɪnfɪl-] *v* **-trated; -trating** *vt* : infiltrer — *vi* : s'infiltrer
infiltration [,ɪnfɪl'treɪʃən] *n* : infiltration *f*
infinite ['ɪnfənət] *adj* **1** LIMITLESS : infini **2** VAST : sans bornes, incalculable, infini
infinitely ['ɪnfənətli] *adv* : infiniment
infinitesimal [,ɪn,fɪnə'tɛsəməl] *adj* : infinitésimal — **infinitesimally** *adv*
infinitive [ɪn'fɪnəṭɪv] *n* : infinitif *m*
infinity [ɪn'fɪnəṭi] *n, pl* **-ties 1** : infinité *f* **2** : infini *m* (en mathématiques)
infirm [ɪn'fərm] *adj* : infirme
infirmary [ɪn'fərməri] *n, pl* **-ries** : infirmerie *f*
infirmity [ɪn'fərməṭi] *n, pl* **-ties** : infirmité *f*
inflame [ɪn'fleɪm] *v* **-flamed; -flaming** *vt* **1** IGNITE : enflammer, mettre le feu à **2** : enflammer (en médecine) **3** EXCITE, STIR UP : exciter, enflammer — *vi* : s'enflammer
inflammable [ɪn'flæməbəl] *adj* : inflammable, flammable
inflammation [,ɪnflə'meɪʃən] *n* : inflammation *f*
inflammatory [ɪn'flæmə,tori] *adj* **1** : incendiaire <inflammatory remarks : propos incendiaires> **2** : inflammatoire (en médecine)
inflatable [ɪn'fleɪṭəbəl] *adj* : gonflable
inflate [ɪn'fleɪt] *v* **-flated; -flating** *vt* : gonfler — *vi* : se gonfler
inflation [ɪn'fleɪʃən] *n* : inflation *f*
inflationary [ɪn'fleɪʃə,nɛri] *adj* : inflationniste
inflect [ɪn'flɛkt] *vt* **1** CURVE : infléchir **2** MODULATE : moduler (la voix) **3** CONJUGATE : conjuger (un verbe) **4** DECLINE : décliner (un adjectif, etc.)
inflection [ɪn,flɛkʃən] *n* **1** : inflexion *f*, modulation *f* (de la voix) **2** : flexion *f* (en linguistique) **3** : inflexion *f* (en mathématiques)
inflexibility [ɪn'flɛksə'bɪləṭi] *n, pl* **-ties** : inflexibilité *f*
inflexible [ɪn'flɛksɪbəl] *adj* : inflexible
inflict [ɪn'flɪkt] *vt* : infliger
influence[1] ['ɪn,flu:ənts, ɪn'flu:ənts] *vt* **-enced; -encing** : influencer, influer sur
influence[2] *n* **1** : influence *f* **2 under the influence of** : sous l'effet de
influential [,ɪnflu'ɛntʃəl] *adj* : influent
influenza [,ɪnflu'ɛnzə] *n* : grippe *f*
influx ['ɪn,flʌks] *n* : afflux *m*
inform [ɪn'fɔrm] *vt* : informer, renseigner — *vi* **to inform on** : dénoncer
informal [ɪn'fɔrməl] *adj* **1** UNCEREMONIOUS : sans cérémonie **2** CASUAL : familier (se dit du langage) **3** UNOFFICIAL : officieux, non officiel
informality [,ɪnfɔr'mæləṭi, -fər-] *n* **1** : simplicité *f*, absence *f* de cérémonie **2** : style *m* familier (de langage)
informally [ɪn'fɔrməli] *adv* **1** CASUALLY : sans cérémonie, simplement **2** UNOFFICIALLY : officieusement **3** COLLOQUIALLY : familièrement
informant [ɪn'fɔrmənt] *n* : informateur *m*, -trice *f*
information [,ɪnfər'meɪʃən] *n* **1** : renseignements *mpl*, information *f* **2 for your information** : à titre d'information
informative [ɪn'fɔrməṭɪv] *adj* : informatif
informer [ɪn'fɔrmər] *n* : informateur *m*, -trice *f*
infraction [ɪn'frækʃən] *n* : infraction *f*
infrared [,ɪnfrə'rɛd] *adj* : infrarouge
infrastructure ['ɪnfrə,strʌktʃər] *n* : infrastructure *f*
infrequent [ɪn'fri:kwənt] *adj* : rare, peu fréquent
infrequently [ɪn'fri:kwəntli] *adv* : rarement
infringe [ɪn'frɪndʒ] *v* **-fringed; -fringing** *vt* : enfreindre — *vi* **to infringe on** : empiéter sur
infringement [ɪn'frɪndʒmənt] *n* : infraction *f* (à la loi)
infuriate [ɪn'fjʊri,eɪt] *vt* **-ated; -ating** : rendre furieux
infuse [ɪn'fju:z] *vt* **-fused; -fusing 1** IMBUE, INSPIRE : insuffler, inspirer **2** STEEP : infuser
infusion [ɪn'fju:ʒən] *n* : infusion *f*
ingenious [ɪn'dʒi:njəs] *adj* : ingénieux — **ingeniously** *adv*
ingenue *or* **ingénue** ['ɑndʒə,nu:, 'æn-; 'æʒə-, 'ɑ-] *n* : ingénue *f*
ingenuity [,ɪndʒə'nu:əṭi, -'nju:-] *n, pl* **-ties** : ingéniosité *f*
ingenuous [ɪn'dʒɛnjʊəs] *adj* **1** FRANK : candide, franc **2** NAIVE : naïf — **ingenuously** *adv*
ingenuousness [ɪn'dʒɛnjʊəsnəs] *n* **1** FRANKNESS : franchise *f* **2** NAÏVETÉ : naïveté *f*

ingest [ɪn'dʒɛst] *vt* : ingérer
ingot ['ɪŋgət] *n* : lingot *m*
ingrained [ɪn'greɪnd] *adj* : enraciné, invétéré
ingrate ['ɪn,greɪt] *n* : ingrat *m*, -grate *f*
ingratiate [ɪn'greɪʃi,eɪt] *vt* **-ated; -ating** : trouver grâce aux yeux de (qqn) <to ingratiate oneself with : s'insinuer dans les bonnes grâces de>
ingratiating [ɪn'greɪʃi,eɪṭɪŋ] *adj* : insinuant
ingratitude [ɪn'græṭə'tu:d, -'tju:d] *n* : ingratitude *f*
ingredient [ɪn'gri:diənt] *n* : ingrédient *m*
ingrown ['ɪn,gro:n] *adj* : incarné <ingrown nail : ongle incarné>
inhabit [ɪn'hæbət] *vt* : habiter
inhabitable [ɪn'hæbəṭəbəl] *adj* : habitable
inhabitant [ɪn'hæbəṭənt] *n* : habitant *m*, -tante *f*
inhalant [ɪn'heɪlənt] *n* : inhalant *m*
inhale [ɪn'heɪl] *v* **-haled; -haling** *vt* : inhaler, aspirer — *vi* : inspirer
inhaler [ɪn'heɪlər] *n* : inhalateur *m*
inhere [ɪn'hɪr] *vi* **-hered; -hering** : être inhérent
inherent [ɪn'hɪrənt, -'hɛr-] *adj* : inhérent
inherently [ɪn'hɪrəntli, -'hɛr-] *adv* : fondamentalement, naturellement
inherit [ɪn'hɛrət] *v* : hériter
inheritance [ɪn'hɛrəṭən*t*s] *n* : héritage *m*
inheritor [ɪn'hɛrəṭər] *n* : héritier *m*, -tière *f*
inhibit [ɪn'hɪbət] *vt* IMPEDE : entraver, gêner
inhibition [,ɪnhə'bɪʃən, ,ɪnə-] *n* : inhibition *f*
inhuman [ɪn'hju:mən, -'ju:-] *adj* : inhumain — **inhumanly** *adv*
inhumane [,ɪnhju'meɪn, -ju-] *adj* : inhumain, cruel
inhumanity [,ɪnhju'mænəṭi, -ju-] *n, pl* **-ties** : inhumanité *f*
inimical [ɪ'nɪmɪkəl] *adj* **1** UNFAVORABLE : peu favorable **2** HOSTILE : inamical, hostile
inimitable [ɪ'nɪməṭəbəl] *adj* : inimitable
iniquitous [ɪ'nɪkwəṭəs] *adj* : inique
iniquity [ɪ'nɪkwəṭi] *n, pl* **-ties** : iniquité *f*
initial[1] [ɪ'nɪʃəl] *vt* **-tialed** *or* **-tialled; -tialing** *or* **-tialling** : parapher
initial[2] *adj* **1** INCIPIENT : initial **2** FIRST : premier
initially [ɪ'nɪʃəli] *adv* : à l'origine, au départ
initial[3] *n* : initiale *f*
initiate[1] [ɪ'nɪʃi,eɪt] *vt* **-ated; -ating 1** BEGIN : commencer, entreprendre **2** INDUCT : initier, admettre (à un club, etc.) **3** INTRODUCE : initier (qqn au rudiments de qqch)
initiate[2] [ɪ'nɪʃiət] *n* : initié *m*, -tiée *f*
initiation [ɪ,nɪʃi'eɪʃən] *n* : initiation *f*
initiative [ɪ'nɪʃəṭɪv] *n* : initiative *f*
inject [ɪn'dʒɛkt] *vt* : injecter
injection [ɪn'dʒɛkʃən] *n* : injection *f*
injudicious [,ɪndʒʊ'dɪʃəs] *adj* : peu judicieux
injunction [ɪn'dʒʌŋkʃən] *n* : injonction *f*
injure ['ɪndʒər] *vt* **-jured; -juring 1** WOUND : blesser **2** HARM : nuire à, faire du tort à **3 to injure oneself** : se blesser
injurious [ɪn'dʒʊriəs] *adj* : nuisible, préjudiciable <injurious to one's health : nuisible à la santé>
injury ['ɪndʒəri] *n, pl* **-ries 1** WOUND : blessure *f* **2** WRONG : tort *m*, dommage *m*
injustice [ɪn'dʒʌstəs] *n* : injustice *f*
ink[1] ['ɪŋk] *vt* : encrer
ink[2] *n* : encre *f*
inkling ['ɪŋklɪŋ] *n* : petite idée *f*
inkwell ['ɪŋk,wɛl] *n* : encrier *m*
inky ['ɪŋki] *adj* **inkier; -est 1** : taché d'encre **2** DARK : noir comme de l'encre
inland[1] ['ɪn,lænd, -lənd] *adv* : à l'intérieur, vers l'intérieur
inland[2] *adj* : intérieur
inland[3] *n* : intérieur *m*
in–law ['ɪn,lɔ] *n* **1** : parent *m* par alliance **2 in–laws** *npl* : beaux-parents *mpl*
inlay[1] [ɪn'leɪ, 'ɪn,leɪ] *vt* **-laid** [-'leɪd, -,leɪd]; **-laying** : incruster
inlay[2] ['ɪn,leɪ] *n* : incrustation *f*
inlet ['ɪn,lɛt, -lət] *n* : crique *f*, bras *m* de mer
inmate ['ɪn,meɪt] *n* **1** PRISONER : détenu *m*, -nue *f* **2** PATIENT : malade *mf*
in memoriam [,ɪnmə'moriəm] *prep* : en mémoire de
inmost ['ɪn,mo:st] *adj* INNERMOST : le plus profond, le plus intime
inn ['ɪn] *n* **1** HOTEL : auberge *f* **2** TAVERN : taverne *f*
innards ['ɪnərdz] *npl* : entrailles *fpl*
innate [ɪ'neɪt] *adj* **1** INBORN : inné **2** INHERENT : inhérent
inner ['ɪnər] *adj* : intérieur, interne
innermost ['ɪnər,mo:st] *adj* INMOST : le plus profond, le plus intime
innersole ['ɪnər'so:l] → **insole**
inning ['ɪnɪŋ] *n* : tour *m* de batte, manche *f Can* (au baseball)
innkeeper ['ɪn,ki:pər] *n* : aubergiste *mf*
innocence ['ɪnəsən*t*s] *n* : innocence *f*
innocent[1] ['ɪnəsənt] *adj* : innocent
innocent[2] *n* : innocent *m*, -cente *f*
innocently ['ɪnəsəntli] *adv* : innocemment
innocuous [ɪ'nɑkjəwəs] *adj* : inoffensif
innovate ['ɪnə,veɪt] *v* **-vated; -vating** : innover
innovation [,ɪnə'veɪʃən] *n* : innovation *f*
innovative ['ɪnə,veɪṭɪv] *adj* : innovateur, novateur
innovator ['ɪnə,veɪṭər] *n* : innovateur *m*, -trice *f*; novateur *m*, -trice *f*

innuendo [ˌɪnjʊ'ɛndo] *n, pl* **-dos** *or* **-does** : insinuation *f*, allusion *f* (malveillante)
innumerable [ɪ'nu:mərəbəl, -'nju:-] *adj* : innombrable, sans nombre
inoculate [ɪ'nɑkjəˌleɪt] *vt* **-lated; -lating** : inoculer, vacciner
inoculation [ɪˌnɑkjə'leɪʃən] *n* : inoculation *f*
inoffensive [ˌɪnə'fɛntsɪv] *adj* : inoffensif
inoperable [ɪn'ɑpərəbəl] *adj* : inopérable
inoperative [ɪn'ɑpərəţɪv, -ˌreɪ-] *adj* : inopérant
inopportune [ɪnˌɑpər'tu:n, -'tju:n] *adj* : inopportun
inopportunely [ɪnˌɑpər'tu:nli, -'tju:n-] *adv* : inopportunément
inordinate [ɪn'ɔrdənət] *adj* : excessif, démesuré — **inordinately** *adv*
inorganic [ˌɪnɔr'gænɪk] *adj* : inorganique
inpatient ['ɪnˌpeɪʃənt] *n* : malade *m* hospitalisé, malade *f* hospitalisée
input[1] ['ɪnˌpʊt] *vt* **inputted** *or* **input; inputting** : entrer (des données)
input[2] *n* **1** CONTRIBUTION : contribution *f*, concours *m* **2** ENTRY : entrée *f* (de données) **3** ADVICE, OPINION : conseils *mpl*
inquest ['ɪnˌkwɛst] *n* : enquête *f*
inquire [ɪn'kwaɪr] *v* **-quired; -quiring** *vt* : demander — *vi* **1 to inquire about** : se renseigner sur, s'informer de **2 to inquire into** INVESTIGATE : enquêter sur
inquirer [ɪn'kwaɪrər] *n* : investigateur *m*, -trice *f*
inquiringly [ɪn'kwaɪrɪŋli] *adv* : d'un air interrogateur
inquiry [ɪn'kwaɪri, 'ɪnˌkwaɪri, 'ɪnkwəri] *n, pl* **-ries 1** QUESTION : demande *f* **2** INVESTIGATION : enquête *f*
inquisition [ˌɪnkwə'zɪʃən, ˌɪŋ-] *n* **1** : inquisition *f* **2 the Inquisition** : l'Inquisition *f*
inquisitive [ɪn'kwɪzəţɪv] *adj* : inquisiteur, curieux
inquisitively [ɪn'kwɪzəţɪvli] *adv* : avec curiosité
inquisitiveness [ɪn'kwɪzəţɪvnəs] *n* : curiosité *f*
inroad ['ɪnˌro:d] *n* **1** ENCROACHMENT : incursion *f* **2 to make inroads into** : entamer
inrush ['ɪnˌrʌʃ] *n* : irruption *f*
insane [ɪn'seɪn] *adj* **1** MAD : fou **2** ABSURD : insensé, démentiel
insanely [ɪn'seɪnli] *adv* : follement, comme un fou
insanity [ɪn'sænəţi] *n, pl* **-ties** : folie *f*, démence *f*
insatiable [ɪn'seɪʃəbəl] *adj* : insatiable
inscribe [ɪn'skraɪb] *vt* **-scribed; -scribing 1** ENGRAVE : graver **2** ENROLL : inscrire **3** DEDICATE : dédicacer (un livre, etc.)
inscription [ɪn'skrɪpʃən] *n* : inscription *f*
inscrutable [ɪn'skru:ţəbəl] *adj* : impénétrable, énigmatique
inseam ['ɪnˌsi:m] *n* : longueur *f* d'un pantalon
insect ['ɪnˌsɛkt] *n* : insecte *m*
insecticide [ɪn'sɛktəˌsaɪd] *n* : insecticide *m*
insecure [ˌɪnsɪ'kjʊr] *adj* **1** UNCERTAIN : incertain **2** UNSAFE : peu sûr **3** FEARFUL : anxieux
insecurity [ˌɪnsɪ'kjʊrəţi] *n, pl* **-ties** : insécurité *f*, manque *m* d'assurance
inseminate [ɪn'sɛməˌneɪt] *vt* **-nated; -nating** : inséminer
insemination [ɪnˌsɛmə'neɪʃən] *n* : insémination *f*
insensibility [ɪnˌsɛntsə'bɪləţi] *n, pl* **-ties** : insensibilité *f*
insensible [ɪn'sɛntsəbəl] *adj* **1** NUMB : insensible **2** UNCONSCIOUS : inconscient **3** UNAWARE : inconscient
insensitive [ɪn'sɛntsəţɪv] *adj* : insensible
insensitivity [ɪnˌsɛntsə'tɪvəţi] *n* : insensibilité *f*
inseparable [ɪn'sɛpərəbəl] *adj* : inséparable
insert[1] [ɪn'sɛrt] *vt* : insérer, introduire
insert[2] ['ɪnˌsərt] *n* : insertion *f*, encart *m* (dans un texte)
insertion [ɪn'sərʃən] *n* : insertion *f*
inset ['ɪnˌsɛt] *n* **1** INSERTION : insertion *f* **2** : encart *m* (dans un livre), entredeux *m* (dans un vêtement), insert *m* (dans une carte)
inshore[1] ['ɪn'ʃor] *adv* : vers la côte, près de la côte
inshore[2] *adj* : côtier
inside[1] [ɪn'saɪd, 'ɪnˌsaɪd] *adv* : à l'intérieur
inside[2] *adj* : intérieur <the inside pages : les pages intérieures> <to get inside information : obtenir des renseignements à la source>
inside[3] *n* **1** : intérieur *m* **2 insides** *npl* GUTS : entrailles *fpl*, tripes *fpl fam*
inside[4] *prep* : à l'intérieur de
inside of *prep* INSIDE : à l'intérieur de, dans
inside out *adv* : à l'envers
insider [ɪn'saɪdər] *n* : initié *m*, -tiée *f*
insidious [ɪn'sɪdiəs] *adj* : insidieux — **insidiously** *adv*
insight ['ɪnˌsaɪt] *n* **1** PERSPICACITY : perspicacité *f* **2** UNDERSTANDING : aperçu *m*
insightful [ɪn'saɪtfəl] *adj* : perspicace
insignia [ɪn'sɪgniə] *or* **insigne** [-ˌni:] *n, pl* **-nia** *or* **-nias** : insigne *m*
insignificance [ˌɪnsɪg'nɪfɪkənts] *n* : insignifiance *f*
insignificant [ˌɪnsɪg'nɪfɪkənt] *adj* : insignifiant
insincere [ˌɪnsɪn'sɪr] *adj* : pas sincère
insincerely [ˌɪnsɪn'sɪrli] *adv* : de manière peu sincère

insincerity [ˌɪnsɪnˈsɛrət̬i, -ˈsɪr-] *n, pl* **-ties** : manque *m* de sincérité

insinuate [ɪnˈsɪnjʊˌeɪt] *vt* **-ated; -ating** : insinuer

insinuation [ɪnˌsɪnjʊˈeɪʃən] *n* : insinuation *f*

insipid [ɪnˈsɪpəd] *adj* : fade, insipide

insist [ɪnˈsɪst] *vi* : insister — *vt* AFFIRM, MAINTAIN : affirmer, insister

insistence [ɪnˈsɪstənts] *n* : insistance *f*

insistent [ɪnˈsɪstənt] *adj* PERSISTENT : insistant **2** COMPELLING : pressant

insistently [ɪnˈsɪstəntli] *adv* : avec insistance

insofar as [ˌɪnsoˈfɑræz] *conj* : dans la mesure où

insole [ˈɪnˌso:l] *n* : semelle *f* (intérieure)

insolence [ˈɪntsələnts] *n* : insolence *f*

insolent [ˈɪntsələnt] *adj* : insolent

insolubility [ɪnˌsɑljʊˈbɪlət̬i] *n* : insolubilité *f*

insoluble [ɪnˈsɑljʊbəl] *adj* : insoluble

insolvency [ɪnˈsɑlvəntsi] *n, pl* **-cies** : insolvabilité *f*

insolvent [ɪnˈsɑlvənt] *adj* : insolvable

insomnia [ɪnˈsɑmniə] *n* : insomnie *f*

insomuch as [ˌɪnsoˈmʌtʃæz] → **inasmuch as**

insomuch that *conj* SO : à tel point que

inspect [ɪnˈspɛkt] *vt* **1** EXAMINE : examiner, inspecter **2** REVIEW : passer en revue (des troupes)

inspection [ɪnˈspɛkʃən] *n* **1** : inspection *f* **2** : revue *f* (des troupes)

inspector [ɪnˈspɛktər] *n* : inspecteur *m*, -trice *f*

inspiration [ˌɪntspəˈreɪʃən] *n* : inspiration *f*

inspirational [ˌɪntspəˈreɪʃənəl] *adj* : inspirant

inspire [ɪnˈspaɪr] *v* **-spired; -spiring** *vt* **1** INHALE : inspirer, aspirer **2** INCITE : stimuler, inciter **3** IMPEL, MOTIVATE : inspirer, motiver — *vi* INHALE : inspirer

instability [ˌɪntstəˈbɪlət̬i] *n* : instabilité *f*

install [ɪnˈstɔl] *vt* **-stalled; -stalling 1** : installer <to install a fan : installer un ventilateur> <to install a new president : installer un nouveau président> **2 to install oneself** SETTLE : s'installer

installation [ˌɪntstəˈleɪʃən] *n* : installation *f*

installment [ɪnˈstɔlmənt] *n* **1** PAYMENT : versement *m*, acompte *m* **2** CHAPTER, EPISODE : épisode *m*

instance [ˈɪntstənts] *n* **1** CIRCUMSTANCE : cas *m*, circonstance *f* <in the first instance : en premier lieu> **2** EXAMPLE : exemple *m* <for instance : par exemple>

instant[1] [ˈɪntstənt] *adj* **1** IMMEDIATE : instantané, immédiat **2** : instantané, soluble <instant coffee : café instantané>

instant[2] *n* MOMENT : instant *m*, moment *m*

instantaneous [ˌɪntstənˈteɪniəs] *adj* : instantané — **instantaneously** *adv*

instantly [ˈɪntstəntli] *adv* : instantanément, immédiatement, sur-le-champ

instead [ɪnˈstɛd] *adv* : plutôt, au lieu de cela <she couldn't go, so I went instead : elle n'a pas pu y aller, donc j'y suis allé à sa place>

instead of *prep* : au lieu de, à la place de

instep [ˈɪnˌstɛp] *n* : cou-de-pied *m*

instigate [ˈɪntstəˌgeɪt] *vt* **-gated; -gating** : inciter, engager

instigation [ˌɪntstəˈgeɪʃən] *n* : instigation *f*, incitation *f*

instigator [ˈɪntstəˌgeɪt̬ər] *n* : instigateur *m*, -trice *f*

instill *or Brit* **instil** [ɪnˈstɪl] *vt* **-stilled; -stilling** : instiller, inculquer

instinct [ˈɪnˌstɪŋkt] *n* : instinct *m*

instinctive [ɪnˈstɪŋktɪv] *adj* : instinctif — **instinctively** *adv*

instinctual [ɪnˈstɪŋktʃʊəl] *adj* : instinctif

institute[1] [ˈɪnstəˌtu:t, -ˌtju:t] *vt* **-tuted; -tuting** : instituer

institute[2] *n* : institut *m*

institution [ˌɪnstəˈtu:ʃən, -ˈtju:-] *n* : institution *f*, établissement *m*

institutional [ˌɪnstəˈtu:ʃənəl, -ˈtju:-] *adj* : institutionnel

institutionalize [ˌɪnstəˈtu:ʃənəˌlaɪz, -ˈtju:-] *vt* **-ized; -izing 1** ESTABLISH : institutionnaliser **2** INTERN : interner, placer dans un établissement spécialisé

instruct [ɪnˈstrʌkt] *vt* **1** TEACH : instruire, former, enseigner **2** COMMAND : charger

instruction [ɪnˈstrʌkʃən] *n* : instruction *f*

instructional [ɪnˈstrʌkʃənəl] *adj* : instructif, éducatif

instructive [ɪnˈstrʌktɪv] *adj* : instructif

instructor [ɪnˈstrʌktər] *n* : instructeur *m*, -trice *f*; éducateur *m*, -trice *f*

instrument [ˈɪntstrəmənt] *n* : instrument *m*

instrumental [ˌɪntstrəˈmɛntəl] *adj* **1** : instrumental **2 to be instrumental in** : contribuer à

instrumentalist [ˌɪntstrəˈmɛntəlɪst] *n* : instrumentaliste *mf*

insubordinate [ˌɪnsəˈbɔrdənət] *adj* : insubordonné

insubordination [ˌɪnsəˌbɔrdənˈeɪʃən] *n* : insubordination *f*

insubstantial [ˌɪnsəbˈstæntʃəl] *adj* **1** : peu substantiel, peu solide **2** IMAGINARY : imaginaire, irréel

insufferable [ɪnˈsʌfərəbəl] *adj* : intolérable, insupportable — **insufferably** [-bli] *adv*

insufficiency [ˌɪnsəˈfɪʃəntsi] *n, pl* **-cies** : insuffisance *f*

insufficient [ˌɪnsəˈfɪʃənt] *adj* : insuffisant — **insufficiently** *adv*

insular [ˈɪntsʊlər, -sjʊ-] *adj* **1** : insulaire **2** NARROW-MINDED : borné, étroit d'esprit

insularity [ˌɪntsʊˈlærəṭi, -sjʊ-] *n* : insularité *f*

insulate [ˈɪntsəˌleɪt] *vt* **-lated; -lating** : isoler

insulation [ˌɪntsəˈleɪʃən] *n* **1** : isolation *f* <thermal insulation : isolation thermique> **2** (*referring to material*) : isolant *m* <fiberglass insulation : isolant en fibre de verre>

insulator [ˈɪntsəˌleɪṭər] *n* : isolateur *m*

insulin [ˈɪntsələn] *n* : insuline *f*

insult[1] [ɪnˈsʌlt] *vt* : insulter, injurier

insult[2] [ˈɪnˌsʌlt] *n* : insulte *f*, injure *f*

insulting [ɪnˈsʌltɪŋ] *adj* : insultant, injurieux

insultingly [ɪnˈsʌltɪŋli] *adv* : de façon insultante

insurance [ɪnˈʃʊrənts] *n* : assurance *f* <fire insurance : assurance contre l'incendie>

insure [ɪnˈʃʊr] *vt* **-sured; -suring 1** UNDERWRITE : assurer **2** ENSURE : assurer, garantir

insured [ɪnˈʃʊrd] *n* : assuré *m*, -rée *f*

insurer [ɪnˈʃʊrər] *n* : assureur *m*

insurgence [ɪnˈsərdʒənts] *n* : insurrection *f*

insurgency [ɪnˈsərdʒəntsi] *n, pl* **-cies** → **insurgence**

insurgent[1] [ɪnˈsərdʒənt] *adj* : insurgé

insurgent[2] *n* : insurgé *m*, -gée *f*

insurmountable [ˌɪnsərˈmaʊntəbəl] *adj* : insurmontable

insurrection [ˌɪnsəˈrɛkʃən] *n* : insurrection *f*

intact [ɪnˈtækt] *adj* : intact

intake [ˈɪnˌteɪk] *n* **1** OPENING : prise *f*, arrivée *f* <intake valve : soupape d'admission> **2** ADMISSION : admission *f* **3** CONSUMPTION : consommation *f*

intangible [ɪnˈtændʒəbəl] *adj* : intangible

integer [ˈɪntɪdʒər] *n* : nombre *m* entier

integral [ˈɪntɪgrəl] *adj* **1** ENTIRE, WHOLE : intégral, complet **2** CONSTITUENT : intégrant <to be an integral part of : faire partie intégrante de>

integrate [ˈɪntəˌgreɪt] *v* **-grated; -grating** *vt* : intégrer — *vi* : s'intégrer

integration [ˌɪntəˈgreɪʃən] *n* : intégration *f*

integrity [ɪnˈtɛgrəṭi] *n* : intégrité *f*

intellect [ˈɪntəlˌɛkt] *n* : intelligence *f*, esprit *m*

intellectual[1] [ˌɪntəˈlɛktʃʊəl] *adj* : intellectuel — **intellectually** *adv*

intellectual[2] *n* : intellectuel *m*, -tuelle *f*

intellectualism [ˌɪntəˈlɛktʃʊəˌlɪzəm] *n* : intellectualisme *m*

intelligence [ɪnˈtɛlədʒənts] *n* **1** : intelligence *f* **2** INFORMATION : renseignements *mpl*

intelligent [ɪnˈtɛlədʒənt] *adj* : intelligent

intelligently [ɪnˈtɛlədʒəntli] *adv* : intelligemment

intelligibility [ɪnˌtɛlədʒəˈbɪləṭi] *n* : intelligibilité *f*

intelligible [ɪnˈtɛlədʒəbəl] *adj* : intelligible — **intelligibly** [-bli] *adv*

intemperance [ɪnˈtɛmpərənts] *n* : intempérance *f*, manque *m* de modération

intemperate [ɪnˈtɛmpərət] *adj* : intempérant, incontrôlé

intend [ɪnˈtɛnd] *vt* **1** DESTINE : destiner <a movie intended for children : un film destiné aux enfants> **2 to intend to** : avoir en tête de, avoir l'intention de <I intend to go : j'ai l'intention d'y aller, je pense y aller>

intended[1] [ɪnˈtɛndəd] *adj* **1** PLANNED : projeté, voulu **2** INTENTIONAL : intentionnel

intended[2] *n* BETROTHED : fiancé *m*, -cée *f*

intense [ɪnˈtɛnts] *adj* : intense, vif <intense pain : douleur intense>

intensely [ɪnˈtɛntsli] *adv* **1** : intensément, avec intensité **2** EXTREMELY : extrêmement, profondément

intensification [ɪnˌtɛntsəfəˈkeɪʃən] *n* : intensification *f*

intensify [ɪnˈtɛntsəˌfaɪ] *v* **-fied; -fying** *vt* : intensifier, renforcer — *vi* : s'intensifier

intensity [ɪnˈtɛntsəṭi] *n, pl* **-ties** : intensité *f*

intensive [ɪnˈtɛntsɪv] *adj* : intensif — **intensively** [ɪnˈtɛntsɪvli] *adv*

intent[1] [ɪnˈtɛnt] *adj* **1** CONCENTRATED : absorbé, fixe <an intent stare : un regard fixe> **2 intent on** *or* **intent upon** : résolu à

intent[2] *n* **1** PURPOSE : intention *f* **2 for all intents and purposes** : à toutes fins utiles

intention [ɪnˈtɛntʃən] *n* : intention *f*

intentional [ɪnˈtɛntʃənəl] *adj* : intentionnel, voulu

intentionally [ɪnˈtɛntʃənəli] *adv* : intentionnellement

intently [ɪnˈtɛntli] *adv* : attentivement

inter [ɪnˈtər] *vt* **-terred; -terring** : enterrer

interact [ˌɪntərˈækt] *vi* **1** : agir l'un sur l'autre <we interact well : le courant passe bien entre nous> **2** (*referring to chemical reactions*) : agir réciproquement

interaction [ˌɪntərˈækʃən] *n* : interaction *f*

interactive [ˌɪntərˈækṭɪv] *adj* : interactif

interbreed [ˌɪntərˈbriːd] *v* **-bred** [-ˈbrɛd]; **-breeding** *vt* : croiser — *vi* : se croiser

intercede [ˌɪntərˈsiːd] *vi* **-ceded; -ceding** : intercéder

intercept [ˌɪntərˈsɛpt] *vt* : intercepter

interception [ˌɪntərˈsɛpʃən] *n* : interception *f*

intercession [ˌɪntərˈsɛʃən] *n* : intercession *f*

interchange[1] [ˌɪntərˈtʃeɪndʒ] *vt* **-changed; -changing** EXCHANGE : échanger

interchange[2] *n* [ˈɪntərˌtʃeɪndʒ] **1** EXCHANGE : échange *m* **2** JUNCTION : échangeur *m*

interchangeable [ˌɪntərˈtʃeɪndʒəbəl] *adj* : interchangeable

intercity [ˈɪntərˈsɪṭi] *adj* : interurbain

intercollegiate [ˌɪntərkəˈliːdʒət, -dʒiət] *adj* : interuniversitaire

intercontinental [ˌɪntərˌkɑntənˈɛntəl] *adj* : intercontinental

intercourse [ˈɪntərˌkors] *n* **1** RELATIONS : relations *fpl*, rapports *mpl* **2** COPULATION : rapports *mpl* sexuels

interdenominational [ˌɪntərdɪˌnɑməˈneɪʃənəl] *adj* : interconfessionnel

interdepartmental [ˌɪntərdɪˌpɑrtˈmɛntəl, -ˌdiː-] *adj* : interdépartemental

interdependence [ˌɪntərdɪˈpɛndənts] *n* : interdépendance *f*

interdependent [ˌɪntərdɪˈpɛndənt] *adj* : interdépendant

interdict [ˌɪntərˈdɪkt] *vt* PROHIBIT : interdire

interest[1] [ˈɪntrəst, -təˌrɛst] *vt* : intéresser

interest[2] *n* **1** CURIOSITY : intérêt *m* **2** BENEFIT : avantage *m*, intérêt *m* <the public interest : l'intérêt public> **3** CHARGE : intérêt *m*, intérêts *mpl* <compound interest : intérêts composés> <interest rate : taux d'intérêt> **4** SHARE, STAKE : intérêts *mpl* **5** PURSUIT : centre *m* d'intérêt

interesting [ˈɪntrəstɪŋli, -təˌrɛstɪŋli] *adj* : intéressant

interestingly [ˈɪntrəstɪŋ, -təˌrɛstɪŋ] *adv* : de façon intéressante

interface [ˈɪntərˌfeɪs] *n* : interface *f*

interfere [ˌɪntərˈfɪr] *vi* **-fered; -fering 1** INTERVENE : intervenir, s'interposer **2** MEDDLE : s'immiscer, s'ingérer **3 to interfere with** DISRUPT : perturber, déranger **4 to interfere with** TOUCH : toucher à <who interfered with my work? : qui est-ce qui a touché à mon travail?>

interference [ˌɪntərˈfɪrənts] *n* **1** INTERVENTION : intervention *f*, ingérence *f* **2** : interférence *f* (en physique, de radio, etc.)

intergalactic [ˌɪntərgəˈlæktɪk] *adj* : intergalactique

intergovernmental [ˌɪntərˌgʌvərˈmɛntəl, -vərn-] *adj* : intergouvernemental

interim[1] [ˌɪntərəm] *adj* : provisoire, intérimaire <interim government : gouvernement provisoire>

interim[2] *n* **1** : intérim *m* **2 in the interim** : entre-temps

interior[1] [ɪnˈtɪriər] *adj* : intérieur

interior[2] *n* : intérieur *m*

interject [ˌɪntərˈdʒɛkt] *vt* : placer, lancer (un mot)

interjection [ˌɪntərˈdʒɛkʃən] *n* **1** : interjection *f* (en linguistique) **2** INTERRUPTION : interruption *f*

interlace [ˌɪntərˈleɪs] *vt* **-laced; -lacing** : entrelacer, entrecroiser

interlock [ˌɪntərˈlɑk] *vt* **1** INTERTWINE : entrelacer **2** ENGAGE, MESH : enclencher — *vi* : s'enclencher

interloper [ˌɪntərˈloːpər] *n* INTRUDER : intrus *m*, -truse *f*

interlude [ˈɪntərˌluːd] *n* **1** INTERVAL : intervalle *m* **2** : intermède *m* (au théâtre) **3** : interlude *m* (en musique)

intermarriage [ˌɪntərˈmærɪdʒ] *n* : mariage *m* mixte

intermarry [ˌɪntərˈmæri] *vi* **-married; -marrying 1** : se marier (entre membres d'autres groupes) **2** : se marier entre soi (entre membres du même groupe)

intermediary[1] [ˌɪntərˈmiːdiˌɛri] *adj* : intermédiaire

intermediary[2] *n, pl* **-aries** : intermédiaire *mf*

intermediate[1] [ˌɪntərˈmiːdiət] *adj* : intermédiaire

intermediate[2] *n* : intermédiaire *mf*

interment [ɪnˈtərmənt] *n* : enterrement *m*, inhumation *f*

interminable [ɪnˈtərmənəbəl] *adj* : interminable — **interminably** [-bli] *adv*

intermingle [ˌɪntərˈmɪŋgəl] *v* **-mingled; -mingling** *vt* : entremêler — *vi* : se mélanger, s'entremêler

intermission [ˌɪntərˈmɪʃən] *n* **1** BREAK, PAUSE : interruption *f*, pause *f* **2** : entracte *m* (au théâtre)

intermittent [ˌɪntərˈmɪtənt] *adj* : intermittent

intermittently [ˌɪntərˈmɪtəntli] *adv* : par intermittence

intern[1] [ˈɪnˌtərn, ɪnˈtərn] *vt* : interner — *vi* : faire un stage, faire son internat (en médecine)

intern[2] [ˈɪnˌtərn] *n* **1** : interne *mf* (à l'hôpital) **2** : stagiaire *mf* (en entreprise)

internal [ɪnˈtərnəl] *adj* **1** : interne <internal investigation : enquête interne> <internal bleeding : hémorragie interne> <internal combustion engine : moteur à combustion interne> **2** : intérieur <internal affairs : affaires intérieures>

internally [ɪnˈtərnəli] *adv* : intérieurement

international [ˌɪntərˈnæʃənəl] *adj* : international — **internationally** *adv*

internationalize [ˌɪntərˈnæʃənəˌlaɪz] *vt* **-ized; -izing** : internationaliser

internee [ˌɪnˌtərˈniː] *n* : interné *m*, -née *f*

Internet [ˈɪntərˌnɛt] *n* : Internet *m*

internist [ˈɪnˌtərnɪst] *n* : interniste *mf*

internment [ɪnˈtərnmənt, ˈɪn-] *n* : internement *m*

internship |ˈɪn,tɛrn,ʃɪp| *n* : stage *m* (en entreprise), internat *m* (en médecine)

interpersonal |,ɪntərˈpərsənəl| *adj* : interpersonnel

interplay |ˈɪntər,pleɪ| *n* : interaction *f*

interpolate |ɪnˈtərpə,leɪt| *vt* **-lated; -lating** : interpoler

interpose |,ɪntərˈpoːz| *v* **-posed; -posing** *vt* : interposer — *vi* : s'interposer, intervenir

interposition |,ɪntərpəˈzɪʃən| *n* : interposition *f*

interpret |ɪnˈtərprət| *vt* : interpréter

interpretation |ɪn,tərprəˈteɪʃən| *n* : interprétation *f*

interpretative |ɪnˈtərprə,teɪţɪv| *adj* : interprétatif

interpreter |ɪnˈtərprəţər| *n* : interprète *mf*

interpretive |ɪnˈtərprəţɪv| → **interpretative**

interracial |,ɪntərˈreɪʃəl| *adj* : interracial

interrelate |,ɪntərɪˈleɪt| *v* **-lated; -lating** *vt* : mettre en corrélation — *vi* : être en corrélation

interrelationship |,ɪntərɪˈleɪʃən,ʃɪp| *n* : interrelation *f*, corrélation *f*

interrogate |ɪnˈtɛrə,geɪt| *vt* **-gated; -gating** : interroger

interrogation |ɪn,tɛrəˈgeɪʃən| *n* : interrogation *f*

interrogative[1] |,ɪntəˈrɑgəţɪv| *adj* : interrogatif, interrogateur

interrogative[2] *n* : interrogatif *m* (en linguistique)

interrogator |ɪnˈtɛrə,geɪţər| *n* : interrogateur *m*, -trice *f*

interrogatory |,ɪntəˈrɑgə,tɔri| → **interrogative**[1]

interrupt |,ɪntəˈrʌpt| *v* : interrompre

interruption |,ɪntəˈrʌpʃən| *n* : interruption *f*

intersect |,ɪntərˈsɛkt| *vt* : croiser, couper — *vi* : se croiser, se couper

intersection |,ɪntərˈsɛkʃən| *n* **1** JUNCTION : croisement *m*, carrefour *m* **2** : intersection *f* (en géométrie)

intersperse |,ɪntərˈspɛrs| *vt* **-spersed; -spersing** : parsemer, entremêler

interstate |ˈɪntər,steɪt| *n or* **interstate highway** : autoroute *f*

interstellar |,ɪntərˈstɛlər| *adj* : interstellaire

interstice |ɪnˈtərstəs| *n, pl* **-stices** |-stə,siːz, -stəsəz| : interstice *m*

intertwine |,ɪntərˈtwaɪn| *v* **-twined; -twining** *vt* : entrelacer — *vi* : s'entrelacer

interval |ˈɪntərvəl| *n* : intervalle *m*

intervene |,ɪntərˈviːn| *vi* **-vened; -vening** **1** ELAPSE : s'écouler **2** INTERCEDE : intervenir, s'interposer

intervention |,ɪntərˈvɛntʃən| *n* : intervention *f*

interview[1] |ˈɪntər,vjuː| *vt* **1** : faire passer un entretien, faire passer une entrevue **2** : interviewer (à la télévision, etc.)

interview[2] *n* **1** : entretien *m*, entrevue *f* **2** : interview *f* (à la télévision, etc.)

interviewer |ˈɪntər,vjuːər| *n* **1** : personne *f* qui fait passer des entretiens **2** : intervieweur *m*, -vieweuse *f* (à la télévision)

interweave |,ɪntərˈwiːv| *v* **-wove** |-ˈwoːv|; **-woven** |-ˈwoːvən|; **-weaving** *vt* : entremêler, entrelacer — *vi* : s'entremêler, s'entrelacer

intestate |ɪnˈtɛs,teɪt, -tət| *adj* : intestat

intestinal |ɪnˈtɛstənəl| *adj* : intestinal

intestine |ɪnˈtɛstən| *n* : intestin *m* <large intestine : gros intestin> <small intestine : intestin grêle>

intimacy |ˈɪntəməsi| *n, pl* **-cies** : intimité *f*

intimate[1] |ˈɪntə,məɪt| *vt* **-mated; -mating** : laisser entendre, insinuer

intimate[2] |ˈɪntəmət| *adj* : intime — **intimately** *adv*

intimate[3] *n* : intime *mf*

intimation |,ɪntəˈmeɪʃən| *n* : indication *f*, pressentiment *m*

intimidate |ɪnˈtɪmə,deɪt| *vt* **-dated; -dating** : intimider

intimidation |ɪn,tɪməˈdeɪʃən| *n* : intimidation *f*

into |ˈɪn,tuː| *prep* **1** (*indicating motion*) : dans, en <to go into the house : entrer dans la maison> <to go into town : aller en ville> <to put into a drawer : mettre dans un tiroir> **2** (*indicating state or condition*) : en <to burst into tears : fondre en larmes> <to translate into English : traduire en anglais> **3** AGAINST : contre <to crash into a wall : s'écraser contre un mur> **4** (*used in mathematics*) <3 into 12 is 4 : 12 divisé par 3 fait 4>

intolerable |ɪnˈtɑlərəbəl| *adj* : intolérable — **intolerably** |-bli| *adv*

intolerance |ɪnˈtɑlərən*t*s| *n* : intolérance *f*

intolerant |ɪnˈtɑlərənt| *adj* : intolérant

intonation |,ɪntəˈneɪʃən| *n* : intonation *f*

intoxicate |ɪnˈtɑksə,keɪt| *vt* **-cated; -cating** : enivrer

intoxicated |ɪnˈtɑksə,keɪţəd| *adj* : ivre

intoxicating |ɪnˈtɑksə,keɪţɪŋ| *adj* : enivrant, excitant

intoxication |ɪn,tɑksəˈkeɪʃən| *n* : ivresse *f*

intractable |ɪnˈtræktəbəl| *adj* : intraitable, inflexible

intramural |,ɪntrəˈmjʊrəl| *adj* : interne, entre élèves de la même université

intransigence |ɪnˈtræn*t*sədʒən*t*s, -ˈtrænzə-| *n* : intransigeance *f*

intransigent |ɪnˈtræn*t*sədʒənt, -ˈtrænzə-| *adj* : intransigeant

intravenous |,ɪntrəˈviːnəs| *adj* : intraveineux

intrepid |ɪnˈtrɛpəd| *adj* : intrépide

intricacy |ˈɪntrɪkəsi| *n, pl* **-cies** : complexité *f*

intricate |ˈɪntrɪkət| *adj* : compliqué, complexe

intricately [ˈɪntrɪkətli] *adv* : de façon complexe
intrigue[1] [ɪnˈtriːg] *v* **-trigued; -triguing** : intriguer
intrigue[2] [ˈɪnˌtriːg, ɪnˈtriːg] *n* : intrigue *f*
intriguing [ɪnˈtriːgɪŋ] *adj* : fascinant
intrinsic [ɪnˈtrɪnzɪk, -ˈtrɪntsɪk] *adj* : intrinsèque — **intrinsically** [-zɪkli, -sɪ-] *adv*
introduce [ˌɪntrəˈduːs, -ˈdjuːs] *vt* **-duced; -ducing 1** : introduire (une idée, un nouveau produit, etc.) **2** PRESENT : présenter <let me introduce my father : permettez-moi de présenter mon père>
introduction [ˌɪntrəˈdʌkʃən] *n* **1** : introduction *f* (d'une idée, d'un produit, etc.) **2** PRESENTATION : présentation *f*
introductory [ˌɪntrəˈdʌktəri] *adj* : d'introduction, préliminaire
introspection [ˌɪntrəˈspɛkʃən] *n* : introspection *f*
introspective [ˌɪntrəˈspɛktɪv] *adj* : introspectif — **introspectively** *adv*
introvert [ˈɪntrəˌvərt] *n* : introverti *m*, -tie *f*
introverted [ˈɪntrəˌvərt̬əd] *adj* : introverti
intrude [ɪnˈtruːd] *vi* **-truded; -truding 1** INTERRUPT : s'imposer <I don't wish to intrude : je ne veux pas vous déranger> **2** INTERFERE : s'ingérer, s'immiscer <to intrude on s.o.'s private life : s'immiscer dans la vie privée de qqn>
intruder [ɪnˈtruːdər] *n* : intrus *m*, -truse *f*
intrusion [ɪnˈtruːʒən] *n* : intrusion *f*
intrusive [ɪnˈtruːsɪv] *adj* : importun, gênant
intuit [ɪnˈtuːɪt, -ˈtjuː-] *vt* : savoir intuitivement
intuition [ˌɪntʊˈɪʃən, -tjʊ-] *n* : intuition *f*
intuitive [ɪnˈtuːət̬ɪv, -ˈtjuː-] *adj* : intuitif — **intuitively** *adv*
Inuit[1] [ˈɪnʊwət, -njʊ-] *adj* : inuit
Inuit[2] *n* : Inuit *m*, Inuite *f*
inundate [ˈɪnənˌdeɪt] *vt* **-dated; -dating** : inonder
inundation [ˌɪnənˈdeɪʃən] *n* : inondation *f*
inure [ɪˈnʊr, -ˈnjʊr] *vt* **-ured; -uring** : endurcir <to be inured to hardship : être habitué aux épreuves>
invade [ɪnˈveɪd] *vt* **-vaded; -vading** : envahir
invader [ɪnˈveɪdər] *n* : envahisseur *m*, -seuse *f*
invalid[1] [ɪnˈvæləd] *adj* NULL : invalide
invalid[2] [ˈɪnvələd] *adj* ILL : malade, infirme
invalid[3] [ˈɪnvələd] *n* : invalide *mf*
invalidate [ɪnˈvæləˌdeɪt] *vt* **-dated; -dating** : invalider
invalidity [ˌɪnvəˈlɪdət̬i] *n, pl* **-ties** : invalidité *f*
invaluable [ɪnˈvæljəbəl, -ˈvæljʊə-] *adj* : inestimable, précieux
invariable [ɪnˈværiəbəl] *adj* : invariable — **invariably** [-bli] *adv*
invasion [ɪnˈveɪʒən] *n* : invasion *f*
invasive [ɪnˈveɪsɪv] *adj* : invasif
invective [ɪnˈvɛktɪv] *n* : invective *f*
inveigh [ɪnˈveɪ] *vi* **to inveigh against** : invectiver contre
inveigle [ɪnˈveɪgəl, -ˈviː-] *vt* **-gled; -gling** : enjôler, manipuler
invent [ɪnˈvɛnt] *vt* : inventer
invention [ɪnˈvɛntʃən] *n* : invention *f*
inventive [ɪnˈvɛntɪv] *adj* : inventif
inventiveness [ɪnˈvɛntɪvnəs] *n* : esprit *m* d'invention
inventor [ɪnˈvɛntər] *n* : inventeur *m*, -trice *f*
inventory[1] [ˈɪnvənˌtɔri] *vt* **-ried; -rying** : inventorier
inventory[2] *n, pl* **-ries 1** LIST : inventaire *m* **2** STOCK : stock *m*
inverse[1] [ɪnˈvərs, ˈɪnˌvərs] *adj* : inverse — **inversely** *adv*
inverse[2] *n* : inverse *m*
inversion [ɪnˈvərʒən] *n* : inversion *f*
invert [ɪnˈvərt] *vt* : inverser, renverser
invertebrate[1] [ɪnˈvərt̬əbrət, -ˌbreɪt] *adj* : invertébré
invertebrate[2] *n* : invertébré *m*
invest [ɪnˈvɛst] *vt* **1** AUTHORIZE, EMPOWER : investir **2** CONFER, ENDOW : investir, revêtir **3** : investir (de l'argent, du temps, etc.) — *vi* : investir <to invest in stocks : investir en actions>
investigate [ɪnˈvɛstəˌgeɪt] *v* **-gated; -gating** *vt* : enquêter sur, examiner — *vi* : enquêter
investigation [ɪnˌvɛstəˈgeɪʃən] *n* : investigation *f*, enquête *f*
investigative [ɪnˈvɛstəˌgeɪt̬ɪv] *adj* : d'investigation <investigative reporter : journaliste d'investigation>
investigator [ɪnˈvɛstəˌgeɪt̬ər] *n* : investigateur *m*, -trice *f*
investiture [ɪnˈvɛstəˌtʃʊr, -tʃər] *n* : investiture *f*
investment [ɪnˈvɛstmənt] *n* : investissement *m*, placement *m*
investor [ɪnˈvɛstər] *n* : investisseur *m*, -seuse *f*; actionnaire *mf*
inveterate [ɪnˈvɛt̬ərət] *adj* : invétéré
invidious [ɪnˈvɪdiəs] *adj* **1** OBNOXIOUS : odieux **2** UNJUST : injuste
invigorate [ɪnˈvɪgəˌreɪt] *vt* **-rated; -rating** : revigorer
invigorating [ɪnˈvɪgəˌreɪt̬ɪŋ] *adj* : revigorant
invigoration [ɪnˌvɪgəˈreɪʃən] *n* : revigoration *f*
invincibility [ɪnˌvɪntsəˈbɪlət̬i] *n* : invincibilité *f*
invincible [ɪnˈvɪntsəbəl] *adj* : invincible
inviolable [ɪnˈvaɪələbəl] *adj* : inviolable
inviolate [ɪnˈvaɪələt] *adj* : inviolé
invisibility [ɪnˌvɪzəˈbɪlət̬i] *n* : invisibilité *f*

invisible |ɪn'vɪzəbəl| *adj* : invisible — **invisibly** |-bli| *adv*
invitation |ˌɪnvə'teɪʃən| *n* : invitation *f*
invite |ɪn'vaɪt| *vt* **-vited; -viting 1** ASK : inviter <we invited them for dinner : nous les avons invités à dîner> **2** PROVOKE : provoquer, chercher <to invite trouble : chercher des ennuis> **3** REQUEST, SOLICIT : solliciter (des questions, des observations, etc.)
inviting |ɪn'vaɪt̬ɪŋ| *adj* : attrayant, engageant
invocation |ˌɪnvə'keɪʃən| *n* : invocation *f*
invoice[1] |'ɪnˌvɔɪs| *vt* **-voiced; -voicing** : facturer
invoice[2] *n* : facture *f*
invoke |ɪn'vo:k| *vt* **-voked; -voking 1** : invoquer, demander (de l'aide, etc.) **2** CITE : invoquer **3** CONJURE UP : évoquer, invoquer (des esprits, etc.)
involuntary |ɪn'vɑlənˌtɛri| *adj* : involontaire — **involuntarily** |ɪnˌvɑlən'tɛrəli| *adv*
involve |ɪn'vɑlv| *vt* **-volved; -volving 1** ENGAGE : engager **2** IMPLICATE : impliquer <to be involved in a crime : être impliqué dans un crime> **3** ENTAIL : entraîner, impliquer, occasionner
involved |ɪn'vɑlvd| *adj* INTRICATE : compliqué
involvement |ɪn'vɑlvmənt| *n* **1** PARTICIPATION : participation *f* **2** RELATIONSHIP : relation *f*, rapport *m*
invulnerable |ɪn'vʌlnərəbəl| *adj* : invulnérable
inward[1] |'ɪnwərd| *or* **inwards** |'ɪnwərdz| *adv* : vers l'intérieur
inward[2] *adj* INSIDE : intérieur
inwardly |'ɪnwərdli| *adv* **1** INTERNALLY : intérieurement **2** PRIVATELY : secrètement, en son for intérieur
iodide |'aɪəˌdaɪd| *n* : iodure *m*
iodine |'aɪəˌdaɪn| *n* : iode *m*, teinture *f* d'iode
iodized |'aɪəˌdaɪzd| *adj* : iodé
ion |'aɪən, 'aɪˌɑn| *n* : ion *m*
ionize |'aɪəˌnaɪz| *v* **-ized; -izing** : ioniser
ionosphere |aɪ'ɑnəˌsfɪr| *n* : ionosphère *f*
iota |aɪ'o:t̬ə| *n* : iota *m*, brin *m*
IOU |ˌaɪˌo'ju:| *n* : reconnaissance *f* de dette
Iranian[1] |ɪ'reɪniən, -'ræ-, -'rɑ-; aɪ'-| *adj* : iranien
Iranian[2] *n* : Iranien *m*, -nienne *f*
Iraqi[1] |ɪ'raki, -'ræ-| *adj* : irakien
Iraqi[2] *n* : Irakien *m*, -kienne *f*
irascible |ɪ'ræsəbəl| *adj* : irascible
irate |aɪ'reɪt| *adj* : furieux — **irately** *adv*
ire |'aɪr| *n* : courroux *m*, colère *f*
iridescence |ˌɪrə'dɛsənts| *n* : irisation *f*
iridescent |ˌɪrə'dɛsənt| *adj* : irisé
iris |'aɪrəs| *n, pl* **irises** *or* **irides** |'aɪrəˌdi:z, 'ɪr-| **1** : iris *m* (de l'œil) **2** *pl* **irises** : iris *m* (plante)
Irish[1] |'aɪrɪʃ| *adj* : irlandais
Irish[2] *n* **1** : irlandais *m* (langue) **2 the Irish** : les Irlandais
Irishman |'aɪrɪʃmən| *n* : Irlandais *m*
Irishwoman |'aɪrɪʃˌwʊmən| *n* : Irlandaise *f*
irk |'ərk| *vt* : ennuyer, irriter, agacer
irksome |'ərksəm| *adj* : ennuyeux, irritant, agaçant
iron[1] |'aɪərn| *vt* **1** : repasser (des vêtements) **2 to iron out** : aplanir (un problème) — *vi* : se repasser
iron[2] *n* **1** : fer *m* (métal) **2** : fer *m* à repasser
ironclad |'aɪərn'klæd| *adj* **1** : cuirassé (se dit d'un navire) **2** STRICT : rigoureux, strict
ironic |aɪ'rɑnɪk| *or* **ironical** |-nɪkəl| *adj* : ironique — **ironically** |-kli| *adv*
ironing |'aɪərnɪŋ| *n* : repassage *m*
ironwork |'aɪərnˌwərk| *n* **1** : ferronnerie *f* **2 ironworks** *npl* : usine *f* sidérurgique
irony |'aɪrəni| *n, pl* **-nies** : ironie *f*
irradiate |ɪ'reɪdiˌeɪt| *vt* **-ated; -ating** : irradier
irradiation |ɪˌreɪdi'eɪʃən| *n* : irradiation *f*
irrational |ɪ'ræʃənəl| *adj* : irrationnel — **irrationally** *adv*
irrationality |ɪˌræʃə'nælət̬i| *n* : irrationalité *f*
irreconcilable |ɪˌrɛkən'saɪləbəl| *adj* : irréconciliable, inconciliable
irrecoverable |ˌɪrɪ'kʌvərəbəl| *adj* : irrécupérable
irredeemable |ˌɪrɪ'di:məbəl| *adj* **1** HOPELESS : irrémédiable **2** : non remboursable (se dit d'un bon, etc.)
irreducible |ˌɪrɪ'du:səbəl, -'dju:-| *adj* : irréductible — **irreducibly** |-bli| *adv*
irrefutable |ˌɪrɪ'fju:t̬əbəl, ɪr'rɛfjə-| *adj* : irréfutable — **irrefutably** |-bli| *adv*
irregular |ɪ'rɛgjələr| *adj* : irrégulier
irregularity |ɪˌrɛgjə'lærət̬i| *n, pl* **-ties** : irrégularité *f*
irregularly |ɪ'rɛgjələrli| *adv* : irrégulièrement
irrelevance |ɪ'rɛləvənts| *n* : manque *m* de rapport
irrelevant |ɪ'rɛləvənt| *adj* : sans rapport, non pertinent
irreligious |ˌɪrɪ'lɪdʒəs| *adj* : irréligieux
irreparable |ɪ'rɛpərəbəl| *adj* : irréparable
irreplaceable |ˌɪrɪ'pleɪsəbəl| *adj* : irremplaçable
irrepressible |ˌɪrɪ'prɛsəbəl| *adj* : irrépressible
irreproachable |ˌɪrɪ'pro:tʃəbəl| *adj* : irréprochable
irresistible |ˌɪrɪ'zɪstəbəl| *adj* : irrésistible — **irresistibly** |-bli| *adv*
irresolute |ɪ'rɛzəˌlu:t| *adj* : irrésolu, indécis
irresolutely |ɪ'rɛzəˌlu:tli, -ˌrɛzə'lu:t-| *adv* : d'un air indécis

irrespective of [ˌɪrɪ'spɛktɪvəv] *prep* : sans tenir compte de
irresponsibility [ˌɪrɪˌspɑnʦə'bɪləṯi] *n* : irresponsabilité *f*
irresponsible [ˌɪrɪ'spɑnʦəbəl] *adj* : irresponsable
irresponsibly [ˌɪrɪ'spɑnʦəbli] *adv* : de façon irresponsable
irretrievable [ˌɪrɪ'tri:vəbəl] *adj* **1** LOST : introuvable **2** IRREPARABLE : irréparable, irrémédiable
irreverence [ɪ'rɛvərənʦ] *n* : irrévérence
irreverent [ɪ'rɛvərənt] *adj* : irrévérencieux
irreversible [ˌɪrɪ'vərsəbəl] *adj* : irréversible
irrevocable [ɪ'rɛvəkəbəl] *adj* : irrévocable — **irrevocably** [-bli] *adv*
irrigate ['ɪrəˌgeɪt] *vt* **-gated; -gating** : irriguer
irrigation [ˌɪrə'geɪʃən] *n* : irrigation *f*
irritability [ˌɪrəṯə'bɪləṯi] *n* : irritabilité *f*
irritable ['ɪrəṯəbəl] *adj* : irritable
irritably ['ɪrəṯəbli] *adv* : avec irritation
irritant[1] ['ɪrətənt] *adj* : irritant
irritant[2] *n* : irritant *m*
irritate ['ɪrəˌteɪt] *vt* **-tated; -tating 1** ANNOY : irriter, agacer **2** INFLAME : irriter
irritating ['ɪrəˌteɪṯɪŋ] *adj* : irritant, agaçant
irritatingly ['ɪrəˌteɪṯɪŋli] *adv* : de façon irritante
irritation [ˌɪrə'teɪʃən] *n* : irritation *f*
is → **be**
Islam [ɪs'lɑm, ɪz-, -'læm; 'ɪsˌlɑm] *n* : islam *m* — **Islamic** [-mɪk] *adj*
island ['aɪlənd] *n* : île *f*
islander ['aɪləndər] *n* : insulaire *mf*
isle ['aɪl] *n* : île *f*, îlot *m*
islet ['aɪlət] *n* : îlot *m*
isolate ['aɪsəˌleɪt] *vt* **-lated; -lating** : isoler
isolation [ˌaɪsə'leɪʃən] *n* : isolement *m* <to be in isolation : être isolé>
isometric [ˌaɪsə'mɛtrɪk] *adj* : isométrique
isometrics [ˌaɪsə'mɛtrɪks] *ns & pl* : exercices *mpl* isométriques
isosceles [aɪ'sɑsəˌli:z] *adj* : isocèle
isotope ['aɪsəˌto:p] *n* : isotope *m*
Israeli[1] [ɪz'reɪli] *adj* : israélien
Israeli[2] *n* : Israélien *m*, -lienne *f*
issue[1] ['ɪˌʃu:] *v* **-sued; -suing** *vi* **1** EMERGE : s'écouler, sortir, déboucher **2** EMANATE, RESULT : provenir, résulter — *vt* **1** EMIT : émaner, émettre **2** DISTRIBUTE : distribuer **3** PUBLISH : publier, sortir **4** GIVE : donner, émettre <to issue orders : donner des ordres> <to issue a permit : émettre un permis>
issue[2] *n* **1** EGRESS : sortie *f*, issue *f* **2** OFFSPRING : descendance *f*, progéniture *f* **3** RESULT : résultat *m* **4** MATTER, QUESTION : question *f*, problème *m* **5** PUBLICATION : publication *f*, émission *f* **6** : numéro *m* <the latest issue of the magazine : le dernier numéro de la revue>
isthmus ['ɪsməs] *n* : isthme *m*
it ['ɪt] *pron* **1** (*as subject*) : il, elle **2** (*as direct object*) : le, la l' <give it to me : donne-le moi> **3** (*as indirect object*) : lui <I'll give it some water : je lui donnerai de l'eau> **4** (*as a nonspecific subject*) : ce, cela, ça <it's me : c'est moi> <what does it mean? : qu'est-ce que cela veut dire?> <that's it : c'est ça> **5** (*as subject of an impersonal verb*) <it's snowing : il neige> <it doesn't matter : cela ne fait rien>
Italian[1] [ɪ'tæliən, aɪ-] *adj* : italien
Italian[2] *n* **1** : Italien *m*, -lienne *f* **2** : italien *m* (langue)
italic[1] [ɪ'tælɪk, aɪ-] *adj* : italique
italic[2] *n* : italique *m* <in italics : en italique>
italicize [ɪ'tæləˌsaɪz, aɪ-] *vt* **-cized; -cizing** : mettre en italique
itch[1] ['ɪʧ] *vi* **1** : avoir des démangeaisons **2** DESIRE : avoir très envie
itch[2] *n* **1** IRRITATION : démangeaison *f* **2** URGE : envie *f*, démangeaison *f*
itchy ['ɪʧi] *adj* **itchier; -est** : qui démange
item ['aɪṯəm] *n* **1** OBJECT : article *m* **2** POINT, ISSUE : point *m* **3** *or* **news item** ARTICLE : article *m*
itemize ['aɪṯəˌmaɪz] *vt* **-ized; -izing** : détailler
itinerant [aɪ'tɪnərənt] *adj* : itinérant, ambulant
itinerary [aɪ'tɪnəˌrɛri] *n, pl* **-aries** : itinéraire *m*
its ["Its] *adj* : son, sa, ses <she liked its smell : elle aimait son odeur>
it's ["Its] (*contraction of* **it is** *or* **it has**) → **be, have**
itself [ɪt'sɛlf] *pron* **1** (*used reflexively*) : se <the cat hurt itself : le chat s'est fait mal> **2** (*for emphasis*) : lui-même, elle-même, soi-même <the car itself was not damaged : la voiture elle-même n'était pas endommagée>
I've ['aɪv] (*contraction of* **I have**) → **have**
ivory ['aɪvəri] *n, pl* **-ries** : ivoire *m*
ivy ['aɪvi] *n, pl* **ivies 1** : lierre *m* **2** → **poison ivy**

J

j ['dʒeɪ] *n, pl* **j's** *or* **js** ['dʒeɪz] : j *m,* dixième lettre de l'alphabet

jab[1] ['dʒæb] *v* **jabbed; jabbing** *vt* **1** PIERCE : piquer **2** THRUST : enfoncer, planter — *vi* **to jab at** : donner un coup à, envoyer un direct à (un boxeur)

jab[2] *n* : petit coup *m,* direct *m* (en boxe)

jabber[1] ['dʒæbər] *vi* : jacasser, bavarder

jabber[2] *n* **1** CHATTER : bavardage *m,* papotage *m* **2** GIBBERISH : baragouin *m*

jack[1] ['dʒæk] *vt or* **to jack up 1** : soulever avec un cric **2** INCREASE : faire monter (des prix, etc.)

jack[2] *n* **1** : cric *m,* vérin *m* <hydraulic jack : vérin hydraulique> **2** FLAG : pavillon *m* **3** SOCKET : jack *m* **4** : valet *m* (aux cartes) **5 jacks** *npl* : osselets *mpl* (jeu)

jackal ['dʒækəl] *n* : chacal *m*

jackass ['dʒæk,æs] *n* **1** DONKEY : âne *m,* baudet *m fam* **2** FOOL : idiot *m,* -diote *f*

jacket ['dʒækət] *n* **1** : veste *f,* veston *m* **2** : jaquette *f* (d'un livre), pochette *f* (d'un disque)

jackhammer ['dʒæk,hæmər] *n* : marteau-piqueur *m*

jack–in–the–box ['dʒækɪnðə,bɑks] *n, pl* **jack–in–the–boxes** *or* **jacks–in–the–box** : diable *m* à ressort

jackknife[1] ['dʒæk,naɪf] *vi* **-knifed; -knifing** : se mettre en travers de la route (se dit d'un camion)

jackknife[2] *n, pl* **-knives**: couteau *m* de poche

jack–of–all–trades *n, pl* **jacks–of–all–trades** : homme *m* à tout faire

jack–o'–lantern ['dʒækə,læntərn] *n* : citrouille *f* taillée en forme de visage

jackpot ['dʒæk,pɑt] *n* : gros lot *m*

jackrabbit ['dʒæk,ræbət] *n* : gros lièvre *m* d'Amérique

jade ['dʒeɪd] *n* : jade *m*

jaded ['dʒeɪdəd] *adj* **1** EXHAUSTED : fatigué **2** BORED : blasé

jagged ['dʒægəd] *adj* : dentelé, irrégulier

jaguar ['dʒæg,wɑr, 'dʒægjʊ,wɑr] *n* : jaguar *m*

jail[1] ['dʒeɪl] *vt* : emprisonner, incarcérer

jail[2] *n* : prison *f*

jailbreak ['dʒeɪl,breɪk] *n* : évasion *f* de prison

jailer *or* **jailor** ['dʒeɪlər] *n* : geôlier *m,* -lière *f*

jalopy [dʒə'lɑpi] *n, pl* **-lopies** : tacot *m fam,* guimbarde *f fam,* bazou *m Can fam*

jam[1] ['dʒæm] *v* **jammed; jamming** *vt* **1** CRAM : entasser **2** : bloquer, coincer <the computer keys are jammed : les touches de l'ordinateur sont coincées> **3** CONGEST, OBSTRUCT : bloquer, boucher — *vi* **1** : se bloquer, se coincer **2** PACK : s'entasser, s'empiler

jam[2] *n* **1** CONGESTION : encombrement *m,* embouteillage *m* **2** PRESERVE : confiture *f* **3** FIX, PREDICAMENT : pétrin *m fam*

Jamaican[1] [dʒə'meɪkən] *adj* : jamaïquain

Jamaican[2] *n* : Jamaïquain *m,* -quaine *f*

jamb ['dʒæm] *n* : jambage *m*

jamboree [,dʒæmbə'ri:] *n* : grande fête *f*

jangle[1] ['dʒæŋgəl] *v* **-gled; -gling** *vi* : cliqueter — *vt* : faire cliqueter

jangle[2] *n* : cliquetis *m*

janitor ['dʒænəṭər] *n* : gardien *m,* -dienne *f;* concierge *mf*

January ['dʒænjʊ,ɛri] *n* : janvier *m*

Japanese[1] [,dʒæpə'ni:z, -'ni:s] *adj* : japonais

Japanese[2] *n* **1** : Japonais *m,* -naise *f* **2** : japonais *m* (langue)

jar[1] ['dʒɑr] *v* **jarred; jarring** *vi* **1** GRATE : grincer, crisser **2** CLASH : jurer **3 to jar on** : heurter <to jar on s.o.'s feelings : heurter la sensibilité de qqn> — *vt* **1** UNSETTLE : perturber **2** JOLT, SHAKE : ébranler, secouer

jar[2] *n* **1** JOLT, SHOCK : secousse *f,* choc *m* **2** : bocal *m,* pot *m* <a jar of honey : un bocal de miel>

jargon ['dʒɑrgən] *n* : jargon *m*

jasmine ['dʒæzmən] *n* : jasmin *m*

jasper ['dʒæspər] *n* : jaspe *m*

jaundice ['dʒɔndɪs] *n* : jaunisse *f*

jaundiced ['dʒɔndɪst] *adj* **1** : qui a la jaunisse **2** EMBITTERED : aigri, cynique, négatif <with a jaundiced eye : d'un mauvais œil>

jaunt ['dʒɔnt] *n* : balade *f,* excursion *f*

jauntily ['dʒɔntəli] *adv* : d'un air vif, joyeusement

jauntiness ['dʒɔntinəs] *n* : vivacité *f,* animation *f*

jaunty ['dʒɔnti] *adj* **jauntier; -est** : joyeux, guilleret

Javanese[1] [,dʒævə'ni:z, ,dʒavə-; -'ni:s] *adj* : javanais

Javanese[2] *n* : Javanais *m,* -naise *f*

javelin ['dʒævələn] *n* : javelot *m*

jaw[1] ['dʒɔ] *vi* GAB : papoter, bavarder

jaw[2] *n* **1** : mâchoire *f* (d'un animal, d'un outil) **2 the jaws of death** : les griffes de la mort

jawbone ['dʒɔ,bo:n] *n* : maxillaire *m*

jay ['dʒeɪ] *n* : geai *m*

jaybird ['dʒeɪ,bərd] → **jay**

jaywalk ['dʒeɪ,wɔk] *vi* : traverser la rue en dehors des passages pour piétons

jaywalker ['dʒeɪ,wɔkər] *n* : piéton *m* qui traverse la rue en dehors des passages pour piétons

jazz[1] ['dʒæz] *vt or* **to jazz up** ENLIVEN : égayer, animer

jazz[2] *n* : jazz *m*

jazzy [ˈdʒæzi] *adj* **jazzier; -est 1** : de jazz **2** FLASHY, SHOWY : tapageur, voyant

jealous [ˈdʒɛləs] *adj* : jaloux — **jealously** *adv*

jealousy [ˈdʒɛləsi] *n, pl* **-sies** : jalousie *f*

jeans [ˈdʒi:nz] *npl* : jean *m*, blue-jean *m*

jeep [ˈdʒi:p] *n* : jeep *f*

jeer[1] [ˈdʒɪr] *vi* SCOFF : se moquer, se railler — *vt* **1** BOO : huer **2** TAUNT : railler

jeer[2] *n* TAUNT : raillerie *f*

Jehovah [dʒɪˈho:və] *n* : Jéhovah *m*

jell [ˈdʒɛl] *vi* **1** CONGEAL, SET : prendre (en gelée), se gélifier **2** CRYSTALLIZE : prendre forme

jelly[1] [ˈdʒɛli] *v* **jellied; jellying** *vi* JELL : se gélifier — *vt* : gélifier

jelly[2] *n, pl* **-lies** : gelée *f*

jellyfish [ˈdʒɛli,fɪʃ] *n* : méduse *f*

jeopardize [ˈdʒɛpər,daɪz] *vt* **-dized; -dizing** : mettre en danger, compromettre

jeopardy [ˈdʒɛpərdi] *n* : danger *m*, péril *m*

jerk[1] [ˈdʒərk] *vt* **1** TUG, YANK : tirer brusquement **2** JOLT : secouer — *vi or* **to jerk about** : cahoter

jerk[2] *n* **1** JOLT : saccade *f*, secousse *f* **2** : mouvement *m* brusque <he got up with a jerk : il s'est levé brusquement> **3** FOOL : idiot *m*, -diote *f*

jerkily [ˈdʒərkəli] *adv* : d'une manière saccadée, par à-coups

jerkin [ˈdʒərkən] *n* : gilet *m*

jerky [ˈdʒərki] *adj* **jerkier; -est** : saccadé

jerry–built [ˈdʒɛri,bɪlt] *adj* : peu solide, construit en carton-pâte

jersey [ˈdʒərzi] *n, pl* **-seys 1** : jersey *m* (tissu) **2** : tricot *m* (vêtement)

jest[1] [ˈdʒɛst] *vi* : plaisanter

jest[2] *n* : plaisanterie *f*

jester [ˈdʒɛstər] *n* : bouffon *m*

Jesus [ˈdʒi:zəs, -zəz] *n* : Jésus *m*

jet[1] [ˈdʒɛt] *vi* **jetted; jetting 1** SPURT : gicler, jaillir **2** : voyager en avion

jet[2] *n* **1** : jais *m* (minéral) **2** SPURT : jet *m* **3** *or* **jet airplane** : jet *m*, avion *m* à réaction

jet engine *n* : moteur *m* à réaction, réacteur *m*

jet–propelled *adj* : à réaction

jetsam [ˈdʒɛtsəm] *n* : épave *f* flottante <flotsam and jetsam : épaves flottantes>

jettison [ˈdʒɛt̬əsən] *vt* **1** : jeter par-dessus bord **2** DISCARD : se débarrasser de

jetty [ˈdʒɛt̬i] *n, pl* **-ties 1** PIER, WHARF : embarcadère *m* **2** BREAKWATER : jetée *f*, brise-lames *m*

Jew [ˈdʒu:] *n* : Juif *m*, Juive *f*

jewel [ˈdʒu:əl] *n* **1** : bijou *m* **2** GEM : pierre *f* précieuse **3** : rubis *m* (d'une montre) **4** TREASURE : perle *f* (personne)

jeweler *or* **jeweller** [ˈdʒu:ələr] *n* : bijoutier *m*, -tière *f*; joaillier *m*, -lière *f*

jewelry *or Brit* **jewellery** [ˈdʒu:əlri] *n* : bijoux *mpl*

Jewish [ˈdʒu:ɪʃ] *adj* : juif

jib [ˈdʒɪb] *n* : foc *m*

jibe [ˈdʒaɪb] *vi* **jibed; jibing** AGREE : concorder

jiffy [ˈdʒɪfi] *n, pl* **-fies** : seconde *f*, instant *m* <in a jiffy : en un rien de temps>

jig[1] [ˈdʒɪg] *vi* **jigged; jigging** : danser la gigue

jig[2] *n* : gigue *f* (danse)

jigger [ˈdʒɪgər] *n* : mesure *f* qui contient une ou deux onces

jiggle[1] [ˈdʒɪgəl] *v* **-gled; -gling** *vt* : secouer, agiter — *vi* : se trémousser

jiggle[2] *n* : secousse *f*

jigsaw [ˈdʒɪg,sɔ] *n* : scie *f* sauteuse

jigsaw puzzle *n* : puzzle *m*

jilt [ˈdʒɪlt] *vt* : abandonner, plaquer *fam*

jimmy[1] [ˈdʒɪmi] *vt* **-mied; -mying** : forcer à la pince-monseigneur

jimmy[2] *n, pl* **-mies** : pince-monseigneur *m*

jingle[1] [ˈdʒɪŋgəl] *v* **-gled; -gling** *vt* : faire tinter — *vi* : tinter

jingle[2] *n* **1** TINKLE : tintement *m* **2** : jingle *m*, refrain *m* publicitaire

jinx[1] [ˈdʒɪŋks] *vt* : porter la poisse à *fam*, porter la guigne à *fam*

jinx[2] *n* : guigne *f fam*, poisse *f fam*

jitters [ˈdʒɪt̬ərz] *npl* : frousse *f* <to have the jitters : être nerveux>

jittery [ˈdʒɪt̬əri] *adj* : nerveux

job [ˈdʒɑb] *n* **1** EMPLOYMENT : emploi *m*, travail *m* <to have a good job : avoir une belle situation> **2** TASK, WORK : travail *m*, tâche *f*

jobber [ˈdʒɑbər] *n* : grossiste *mf*

jobless [ˈdʒɑbləs] *adj* : sans emploi

jockey[1] [ˈdʒɑki] *v* **-eyed; -eying** *vt* MANIPULATE : manoeuvrer, manipuler — *vi* **to jockey for position** : essayer de se placer

jockey[2] *n, pl* **-eys** : jockey *m*

jocose [dʒoˈko:s] *adj* **1** MERRY : jovial, joyeux **2** HUMOROUS : facétieux

jocular [ˈdʒɑkjʊlər] *adj* : badin, jovial

jocularity [,dʒɑkjʊˈlærət̬i] *n* : jovialité *f*

jocularly [ˈdʒɑkjʊlərli] *adv* : jovialement

jodhpurs [ˈdʒɑdpərz] *npl* : jodhpurs *mpl*

jog[1] [ˈdʒɑg] *v* **jogged; jogging** *vt* **1** NUDGE : donner un petit coup à **2 to jog s.o.'s memory** : rafraîchir la mémoire à qqn — *vi* : faire du jogging

jog[2] *n* **1** PUSH, SHAKE : coup *m*, petite secousse *f* **2** : jogging *m* (aux sports), petit trot *m* (d'un cheval) **3** BEND : coude *m*, tournant *m* (d'une route)

jogger [ˈdʒɑgər] *n* : joggeur *m*, -geuse *f*

join [ˈdʒɔɪn] *vt* **1** UNITE : relier, unir <to be joined in marriage : être uni par les liens du mariage> **2** ADJOIN : avoisiner, être contigu à **3** MEET : rejoindre, retrouver **4** : se joindre à, devenir membre (d'un club, etc.) — *vi* **1** MEET : se rejoindre **2** : devenir membre (d'un club, etc.) **3 to join together** : s'unir, se rejoindre

joiner [ˈdʒɔɪnər] *n* CARPENTER : menuisier *m*

joint[1] [dʒɔɪnt] *adj* : commun, conjugué

joint[2] *n* **1** : articulation *f* <knee joint : articulation du genou> <to put one's shoulder out of joint : se déboîter l'épaule> **2** JUNCTURE : joint *m*, raccord *m* (en menuiserie)

jointed [dʒɔɪntəd] *adj* : articulé

jointly [ˈdʒɔɪntli] *adv* : conjointement

joist [ˈdʒɔɪst] *n* : solive *f*

joke[1] [ˈdʒo:k] *vi* **joked; joking** : plaisanter

joke[2] *n* : plaisanterie *f*, blague *f*

joker [ˈdʒo:kər] *n* **1** WAG : farceur *m*, -ceuse *f*; blagueur *m*, -gueuse *f* **2** : joker *m* (aux cartes)

jokingly [ˈdʒo:kɪŋli] *adv* : en plaisantant

jollity [ˈdʒɑləṭi] *n, pl* **-ties** : gaieté *f*

jolly [ˈdʒɑli] *adj* **jollier; -est** : joyeux, gai

jolt[1] [ˈdʒo:lt] *vt* : secouer — *vi or* **to jolt along** : cahoter

jolt[2] *n* **1** BLOW, JAR : secousse *f*, coup *m* **2** SHOCK : choc *m* <the defeat was quite a jolt : la défaite nous a fait tout un choc>

jonquil [ˈdʒɑnkwɪl] *n* : jonquille *f*

Jordanian[1] [dʒɔrˈdeɪniən] *adj* : jordanien

Jordanian[2] *n* : Jordanien *m*, -nienne *f*

josh [ˈdʒɑʃ] *vt* TEASE : taquiner — *vi* JOKE : blaguer

jostle [ˈdʒɑsəl] *v* **-tled; -tling** *vt* : bousculer — *vi* : se bousculer

jot[1] [ˈdʒɑt] *vt* **jotted; jotting** : prendre note de <jot this down : prends ça en note>

jot[2] *n* BIT : iota *m* <it doesn't matter a jot : ça n'a pas la moindre importance>

jounce[1] [ˈdʒæunts] *vt* **jounced; jouncing** : secouer

jounce[2] *n* JOLT : secousse *f*

journal [ˈdʒərnəl] *n* **1** DIARY : journal *m* intime **2** PERIODICAL : revue *f* **3** NEWSPAPER : journal *m*, quotidien *m*

journalism [ˈdʒərnəlˌɪzəm] *n* : journalisme *m*

journalist ["dZ^ərn^əlIst] *n* : journaliste *mf*

journalistic [ˌdʒərnəlˈɪstɪk] *adj* : journalistique

journey[1] [ˈdʒərni] *vi* **-neyed; -neying** TRAVEL : voyager

journey[2] *n, pl* **-neys** : voyage *m*

journeyman [ˈdʒərnimən] *n, pl* **-men** [-mən, -ˌmɛn] : compagnon *m*

joust[1] [ˈdʒaust] *vi* : jouter

joust[2] *n* : joute *f*

jovial [ˈdʒo:viəl] *adj* : jovial — **jovially** *adv*

joviality [ˌdʒo:viˈæləṭi] *n* : jovialité *f*

jowl [ˈdʒæul] *n* **1** JAW : mâchoire *f* **2** CHEEK : bajoue *f*

joy [ˈdʒɔɪ] *n* **1** HAPPINESS : joie *f*, allégresse *f* **2** PLEASURE : joie *f*, plaisir *m* <she's the joy of my life : elle est la joie de ma vie>

joyful [ˈdʒɔɪfəl] *adj* : joyeux — **joyfully** *adv*

joyless [ˈdʒɔɪləs] *adj* : sans joie, triste

joyous [ˈdʒɔɪəs] *adj* JOYFUL : joyeux — **joyously** *adv*

joyride [ˈdʒɔɪˌraɪd] *n* : virée *f* dans une voiture volée

jubilant [ˈdʒu:bələnt] *adj* : exultant, débordant de joie

jubilation [ˌdʒu:bəˈleɪʃən] *n* : jubilation *f*

jubilee [ˈdʒu:bəˌli:] *n* : jubilé *m*

Judaic [dʒu:ˈdeɪɪk] *adj* : judaïque

Judaism [ˈdʒu:dəˌɪzəm, ˈdʒu:di-, ˈdʒu:ˌdeɪ-] *n* : judaïsme *m*

judge[1] [ˈdʒʌdʒ] *vt* **judged; judging 1** ASSESS : juger, évaluer **2** TRY : juger (une cause) **3** CONSIDER, DEEM : juger, estimer

judge[2] *n* **1** : juge *m* **2 to be a good judge of** : savoir juger de, être un bon juge en

judgment *or* **judgement** [ˈdʒʌdʒmənt] *n* **1** RULING : jugement *m*, verdict *m* **2** OPINION : avis *m*, opinion *f* **3** DISCERNMENT : jugement *m*, discernement *m*

judgmental [ˌdʒʌdʒˈmɛntəl] *adj* : enclin à juger <to be judgmental : s'ériger toujours en juge>

judicature [ˈdʒu:dɪkəˌtʃʊr] *n* : justice *f*

judicial [dʒʊˈdɪʃəl] *adj* : judiciaire — **judicially** *adv*

judiciary[1] [dʒʊˈdɪʃiˌɛri, -ˈdɪʃəri] *adj* : judiciaire

judiciary[2] *n* **1** → **judicature 2** : système *m* judiciaire

judicious [dʒʊˈdɪʃəs] *adj* : judicieux — **judiciously** *adv*

judo [ˈdʒu:ˌdo:] *n* : judo *m*

jug [ˈdʒʌg] *n* : cruche *f*, pichet *m*, carafe *f*

juggernaut [ˈdʒʌgərˌnɔt] *n* : force *f* irrésistible

juggle [ˈdʒʌgəl] *vi* **-gled; -gling 1** : jongler **2 to juggle with** MANIPULATE : jongler avec

juggler [ˈdʒʌgələr] *n* : jongleur *m*, -gleuse *f*

jugular vein [ˈdʒʌgjʊlər] *n* : jugulaire *f*

juice [ˈdʒu:s] *n* **1** : jus *m* <orange juice : jus d'orange> **2** ELECTRICITY : jus *m fam*, électricité *f*

juicer [ˈdʒu:sər] *n* : presse-fruits *m*

juiciness [ˈdʒu:sinəs] *n* : teneur *f* en jus

juicy [ˈdʒu:si] *adj* **juicier; -est 1** : juteux <a juicy fruit : un fruit juteux> **2** RACY : savoureux

jukebox [ˈdʒu:kˌbɑks] *n* : juke-box *m*

julep [ˈdʒu:ləp] *n* : cocktail *m* à la menthe

July [dʒʊ'laɪ] *n* : juillet *m*
jumble[1] ['dʒʌmbəl] *vt* **-bled; -bling** : brouiller, mélanger
jumble[2] *n* : fouillis *m*, désordre *m*
jumbo[1] ['dʒʌm,bo:] *adj* : énorme, géant
jumbo[2] *n, pl* **-bos** : quelque chose de très grand en son genre
jump[1] ['dʒʌmp] *vi* **1** LEAP : sauter, bondir **2** START : sursauter **3** MOVE : passer <she jumped from job to job : elle a passé d'un emploi à un autre> **4** RISE : monter en flèche (se dit des prix, etc) **5 to jump at** : saisir (une occasion, etc.) — *vt* : sauter, franchir <to jump a hurdle : franchir une haie>
jump[2] *n* **1** LEAP : saut *m*, bond *m* **2** INCREASE : bond *m*, hausse *f* **3** ADVANTAGE : avantage *m* <to get the jump on s.o. : devancer qqn>
jumper ['dʒʌmpər] *n* **1** : sauteur *m*, -teuse *f* (aux sports) **2** : robe-chasuble *f* (vêtement)
jumpy ['dʒʌmpi] *adj* **jumpier; -est** : nerveux
junction ['dʒʌŋkʃən] *n* **1** JOINING : jonction *f* **2** : carrefour *m*, embranchement *m* (de deux routes)
juncture ['dʒʌŋktʃər] *n* **1** JOINT : joint *m*, jointure *f* **2** POINT, SITUATION : conjoncture *f* <at this juncture : dans la conjoncture actuelle>
June ['dʒu:n] *n* : juin *m*
jungle ['dʒʌŋgəl] *n* : jungle *f*
junior[1] ['dʒu:njər] *adj* **1** YOUNGER : cadet, plus jeune **2** SUBORDINATE : subalterne
junior[2] *n* **1** : cadet *m*, -dette *f* <a man six years my junior : un homme de six ans mon cadet> **2** SUBORDINATE : subalterne *mf* **3** : élève *mf* de troisième année; étudiant *m*, -diante *f* de troisième année
juniper ['dʒu:nəpər] *n* : genévrier *m*
junk[1] ['dʒʌŋk] *vt* SCRAP : balancer *fam*, mettre au rancart *fam*
junk[2] *n* **1** RUBBISH : camelote *f fam*, pacotille *f* **2** STUFF : choses *fpl*, trucs *mpl fam* **3** : jonque *f* (bateau)
junket ['dʒʌŋkət] *n* : voyage *m* (aux frais de l'État)
junta ['hʊntə, 'dʒʌn-, 'hʌn-] *n* : junte *f*
Jupiter ['dʒu:pət̬ər] *n* : Jupiter *f* (planète)
jurisdiction [,dʒʊrəs'dɪkʃən] *n* : juridiction *f*
jurisprudence [,dʒʊrəs'pru:dənts] *n* : jurisprudence *f*
jurist ['dʒʊrɪst] *n* : juriste *mf*
juror ['dʒʊrər] *n* : juré *m*, -rée *f*
jury ["dZUri] *n, pl* **-ries** : jury *m*
just[1] ['dʒʌst] *adv* **1** EXACTLY : exactement <it's just right : c'est parfait> **2** : tout juste <the bell just rang : la cloche vient tout juste de sonner> **3** BARELY : à peine <he just made it : il est à peine arrivé à temps> **4** SIMPLY : simplement <just be yourself : sois toi-même, tout simplement> **5** QUITE : vraiment <just wonderful : vraiment merveilleux> **6** POSSIBLY : peut-être <it just might work : ça peut peut-être marcher> **7 just about** ALMOST : presque
just[2] *adj* **1** FAIR : juste, équitable **2** DESERVED : mérité
justice ['dʒʌstɪs] *n* **1** : justice *f*, équité *f* **2** JUDGE : juge *m*
justifiable [,dʒʌstə'faɪəbəl] *adj* : justifiable
justification [,dʒʌstəfə'keɪʃən] *n* : justification *f*
justify ['dʒʌstə,faɪ] *vt* **-fied; -fying** : justifier
justly ['dʒʌstli] *adv* : avec justice, justement
jut ['dʒʌt] *vi* **jutted; jutting** *or* **to jut out** : dépasser, s'avancer en saillie
jute ['dʒu:t] *n* : jute *m*
juvenile[1] ['dʒu:və,naɪl, -vənəl] *adj* **1** YOUNG : jeune <juvenile delinquent : jeune délinquant> **2** CHILDISH : puéril
juvenile[2] *n* : mineur *m*, -neure *f*; jeune *mf*
juxtapose ['dʒʌkstə,po:z] *vt* **-posed; -posing** : juxtaposer
juxtaposition [,dʒʌkstəpə'zɪʃən] *n* : juxtaposition *f*

K

k ['keɪ] *n, pl* **k's** *or* **ks** ['keɪz] : k *m*, onzième lettre de l'alphabet
kale ['keɪl] *n* : chou *m* frisé
kaleidoscope [kə'laɪdə,sko:p] *n* : kaléidoscope *m*
kangaroo [,kæŋgə'ru:] *n, pl* **-roos** : kangourou *m*
kaolin ['keɪələn] *n* : kaolin *m*
karat ['kærət] *n* : carat *m*
karate [kə'rɑt̬i] *n* : karaté *m*
katydid ['keɪt̬i,dɪd] *n* : sauterelle *f* d'Amérique du Nord
kayak ['kaɪ,æk] *n* : kayak *m*, kayac *m*
keel[1] ['ki:l] *vi* **to keel over** : chavirer (se dit d'un bateau), s'évanouir, tomber dans les pommes *fam* (se dit des personnes)
keel[2] *n* : quille *f*
keen ['ki:n] *adj* **1** SHARP : aiguisé, affilé **2** PENETRATING : vif, pénétrant **3** EA-

GER, ENTHUSIASTIC : enthousiaste 4 ACUTE : perçant <keen eyesight : vue perçante>

keenly ['ki:nli] *adv* : vivement, profondément

keep[1] ['ki:p] *v* **kept** ['kɛpt]; **keeping** *vt* **1** FULFILL : tenir (une promesse, etc.) **2** PROTECT : garder **3** MAINTAIN : tenir, garder <to keep a diary : tenir un journal> **4** DETAIN, RETAIN : garder, retenir **5** PRESERVE : garder (un secret) **6 to keep out** : empêcher d'entrer **7 to keep up** : continuer, maintenir — *vi* **1** : garder <keep to the right : gardez la droite> **2** REFRAIN : s'empêcher **3** : se conserver <food that keeps well : des aliments qui se conservent bien> **4 to keep on** : continuer <she kept on trying : elle continuait à essayer>

keep[2] *n* **1** : donjon *m* (d'un château fort) **2 to earn one's keep** : gagner de quoi vivre **3 for keeps** : pour de bon

keeper ['ki:pər] *n* : gardien *m*, -dienne *f*

keeping ['ki:pɪŋ] *n* **1** CARE : garde *f* <in the keeping of : à la garde de> **2 in keeping with** : en accord avec, conformément à

keepsake ['ki:p,seɪk] *n* : souvenir *m*

keg ['kɛg] *n* : baril *m*, tonnelet *m*

kelp ['kɛlp] *n* : varech *m*

ken ['kɛn] *n* **1** SIGHT : vision *f* **2** UNDERSTANDING : entendement *m* <it's beyond my ken : ça dépasse mon entendement>

kennel ['kɛnəl] *n* : chenil *m*

Kenyan[1] ['kɛnjən, 'ki:n-] *adj* : kenyan

Kenyan[2] *n* : Kenyan *m*, Kenyane *f*

kept → **keep**

kerchief ['kərtʃəf, -,tʃi:f] *n* : fichu *m*

kernel ['kərnəl] *n* **1** : amande *f* (d'un fruit ou d'une noix) **2** SEED : graine *f* (d'une céréale) **3** CORE : noyau *m*, cœur *m* <a kernel of truth : un fond de vérité>

kerosene *or* **kerosine** ['kɛrə,si:n, ,kɛrə'-] *n* : kérosène *m*, pétrole *m* lampant

ketchup ['kɛtʃəp, 'kæ-] *n* : ketchup *m*

kettle ['kɛtəl] *n* : bouilloire *f*

kettledrum ['kɛtəl,drʌm] *n* : timbale *f*

key[1] ['ki:] *vt* **1** ATTUNE : accorder **2 to be keyed up** : être tendu, être surexcité

key[2] *adj* : fondamental, clé, crucial

key[3] *n* **1** : clé *f*, clef *f* <car key : clé de voiture> **2** MEANS, SOLUTION : clé *f*, clef *f* **3** : légende *f* (sur une carte) **4** : touche *f* (d'un clavier) **5** PITCH : ton *m* <in a major key : en majeur> **6** REEF : récif *m*

keyboard[1] ['ki:,bord] *vt* : saisir

keyboard[2] *n* : clavier *m*

keyhole ['ki:,ho:l] *n* : trou *m* de serrure

keynote ['ki:,no:t] *n* **1** : tonique *f* (en musique) **2** : thème *m* principal, point *m* capital

keystone ['ki:,sto:n] *n* : clé *f* de voûte

khaki ['kæki, 'kɑ-] *n* : kaki *m*

khan ['kɑn, 'kæn] *n* : khan *m*

kibbutz [kə'bʊts, -'bu:ts] *n, pl* **-butzim** [-,bʊt'si:m, -,bu:t-] : kibboutz *m*

kibitz ['kɪbɪts] *vi* : se mêler des affaires d'autrui

kibitzer ['kɪbɪtsər, kɪ'bɪt-] *n* : personne *f* qui se mêle des affaires d'autrui

kick[1] ['kɪk] *vt* : donner un coup de pied à — *vi* **1** PROTEST : se plaindre **2** RECOIL : reculer (se dit d'un fusil)

kick[2] *n* **1** : coup *m* de pied **2** RECOIL : recul *m* (d'un fusil) **3** PLEASURE, THRILL : plaisir *m* <to get a kick out of : prendre plaisir à>

kicker ['kɪkər] *n* : botteur *m*, -teuse *f* (aux sports)

kid[1] ['kɪd] *v* **kidded; kidding** *vi* : blaguer, plaisanter <no kidding! : sans blague!> — *vt* TEASE : taquiner

kid[2] *n* **1** GOAT : chevreau *m*, -vrette *f* **2** CHILD : gosse *mf France fam;* gamin *m*, -mine *f fam;* flot *m Can*

kidder ['kɪdər] *n* : blagueur *m*, -gueuse *f fam*

kidnap ['kɪd,næp] *vt* **-napped** *or* **-naped** [-,næpt]; **-napping** *or* **-naping** [-,næpɪŋ] : kidnapper, enlever

kidnapper *or* **kidnaper** ['kɪd,næpər] *n* : ravisseur *m*, -seuse *f;* kidnappeur *m*, -peuse *f*

kidney ['kɪd,ni] *n, pl* **-neys** : rein *m*

kidney bean *n* : haricot *m* rouge

kill[1] ['kɪl] *vt* **1** : tuer **2** DEFEAT : mettre son véto à (une loi, etc.) **3 to kill time** : tuer le temps — *vi* : tuer

kill[2] *n* **1** KILLING : mise *f* à mort **2** PREY : proie *f*

killer ['kɪlər] *n* : meurtrier *m*, -trière *f;* tueur *m*, tueuse *f*

killjoy ['kɪl,dʒɔɪ] *n* : rabat-joie *mf*

kiln ['kɪl, 'kɪln] *n* : four *m* (à céramique)

kilo ['ki:,lo:] *n, pl* **-los** : kilo *m*

kilogram ['kɪlə,græm, 'ki:-] *n* : kilogramme *m*

kilohertz ['kɪlə,hərts] *ns & pl* : kilohertz *m*

kilometer [kɪ'lɑmət̬ər] *n* : kilomètre *m*

kilowatt ['kɪlə,wɑt] *n* : kilowatt *m*

kilt ['kɪlt] *n* : kilt *m*

kilter ['kɪltər] *n* **out of kilter** : en panne, détraqué, en dérangement

kimono [kə'mo:no, -nə] *n, pl* **-nos** : kimono *m*

kin ['kɪn] *n* : parents *mpl*, famille *f*

kind[1] ['kaɪnd] *adj* : gentil, bienveillant, aimable

kind[2] *n* **1** ESSENCE : nature *f*, essence *f* <in degree, not in kind : en degré, pas en nature> **2** TYPE : genre *m*, sorte *f*, type *m* **3** CATEGORY : classe *f*

kindergarten ['kɪndər,gɑrtən, -dən] *n* : jardin *m* d'enfants *France*, maternelle *f*, école *f* maternelle

kindhearted ['kaɪnd'hɑrt̬əd] *adj* : bon, qui a bon cœur

kindle |'kɪndəl| *vt* **-dled; -dling 1** LIGHT : allumer, enflammer **2** AROUSE : susciter, éveiller — *vi* : s'enflammer

kindliness |'kaɪndlinəs| *n* : gentillesse *f*, amabilité *f*

kindling |'kɪndlɪŋ, kɪndlən| *n* : petit bois *m*

kindly[1] |'kaɪndli| *adv* **1** AMIABLY, WARMLY : chaleureusement, affablement **2** COURTEOUSLY : gentiment, aimablement **3** PLEASE : s'il vous plaît <would you kindly pass the salad : pouvez-vous me passer la salade, s'il vous plaît> **4 to look kindly on sth** : voir qqch d'un bon œil

kindly[2] *adj* **kindlier; -est** : aimable, bienveillant

kindness |'kaɪndnəs| *n* : gentillesse *f*, bonté *f*

kind of *adv* SOMEWHAT : quelque peu

kindred[1] |'kɪndrəd| *adj* : apparenté, semblable <kindred spirits : âmes sœurs>

kindred[2] *n* : parents *mpl*, famille *f*

kinfolk |'kɪn,fo:k| *or* **kinfolks** *npl* → **kin**

king |'kɪŋ| *n* : roi *m*

kingdom |'kɪŋdəm| *n* : royaume *m*

kingfisher |'kɪŋ,fɪʃər| *n* : martin-pêcheur *m*

kingly |'kɪŋli| *adj* : royal, majestueux

king–size |'kɪŋ,saɪz| *or* **king–sized** |-,saɪzd| *adj* : (très) grand, géant

kink[1] |'kɪŋk| *vt* : entortiller — *vi* : s'entortiller

kink[2] *n* **1** TWIST : nœud *m* **2** CRAMP : crampe *f* <a kink in one's back : une crampe dans le dos> **3** IMPERFECTION : défaut *m*

kinky |'kɪŋki| *adj* **kinkier; -est** : excentrique, bizarre

kinship |'kɪn,ʃɪp| *n* : parenté *f*

kinsman |'kɪnzmən| *n, pl* **-men** |-mən, -,mɛn| : parent *m*

kinswoman |'kɪnz,wʊmən| *n, pl* **-women** |-,wɪmən| : parente *f*

kipper |'kɪpər| *n* : kipper *m*, hareng *m* saur

kiss[1] |'kɪs| *vt* : embrasser, donner un baiser à — *vi* : s'embrasser

kiss[2] *n* : baiser *m*, bec *m Can fam*

kit |'kɪt| *n* **1** : trousse *f* <first-aid kit : trousse de secours> **2 the whole kit and caboodle** : tout le bataclan *fam*

kitchen |'kɪtʃən| *n* : cuisine *f*

kite |'kaɪt| *n* **1** : milan *m* (oiseau) **2** : cerf-volant *m* <to fly a kite : faire voler un cerf-volant>

kith |'kɪθ| *n* **kith and kin** : amis *mpl* et parents *mpl*

kitten |'kɪtən| *n* : chaton *m*

kitty |'kɪt̬i| *n, pl* **-ties 1** KITTEN : chaton *m* **2** FUND : cagnotte *f*

kitty–corner |'kɪt̬i,kɔrnər| *or* **kitty–cornered** |-nərd| → **catercorner**

kiwi |'ki:,wi:| *n* : kiwi *m*

kleptomania |,klɛptə'meɪniə| *n* : kleptomanie *f*

kleptomaniac |,klɛptə'meɪni,æk| *n* : kleptomane *mf*

knack |'næk| *n* : don *m* <to have a knack for : avoir le don de>

knapsack |'næp,sæk| *n* : sac *m* à dos

knave |'neɪv| *n* **1** → **rascal 2** JACK : valet *m* (aux cartes)

knead |'ni:d| *vt* **1** : pétrir (de la pâte) **2** MASSAGE : masser

knee |'ni:| *n* : genou *m*

kneecap |'ni:,kæp| *n* : rotule *f*

kneel |'ni:l| *vi* **knelt** |'nɛlt| *or* **kneeled** |'ni:ld|; **kneeling** : s'agenouiller

knell |'nɛl| *n* : glas *m*

knew → **know**

knickers |'nɪkərz| *npl* : knickers *mpl*, pantalons *mpl* de golf

knickknack |'nɪk,næk| *n* : bibelot *m*, babiole *f*

knife[1] |naɪf| *vt* **knifed** |naɪft|; **knifing** : donner un coup de couteau à

knife[2] *n, pl* **knives** |'naɪvz| : couteau *m*

knight[1] |'naɪt| *vt* : faire chevalier

knight[2] *n* **1** : chevalier *m* **2** : cavalier *m* (aux échecs)

knighthood |'naɪt,hu:d| *n* : chevalerie *f*

knightly |'naɪtli| *adv* : chevaleresque

knit[1] |'nɪt| *v* **knit** *or* **knitted; knitting** *vt* **1** UNITE : joindre **2** : tricoter <to knit a sweater : tricoter un chandail> **3 to knit one's brows** : froncer les sourcils — *vi* : tricoter

knit[2] *n* : tricot *m*

knitter |'nɪtər| *n* : tricoteur *m*, -teuse *f*

knob |'nɑb| *n* : poignée *f*, bouton *m*

knobby |'nɑbi| *adj* **knobbier; -est** : noueux

knock[1] |'nɑk| *vt* **1** HIT : cogner, frapper **2** DRIVE : enfoncer (un clou) **3** CRITICIZE : critiquer, dénigrer <don't knock it! : arrête de critiquer!> **4 to knock out** : assommer <the drug knocked him out : le médicament l'a assommé> **5 to knock out** DESTROY : mettre hors service — *vi* **1** : cogner <the engine is knocking : le moteur cogne> **2** COLLIDE : heurter

knock[2] *n* : coup *m*

knock down *vt* : renverser, envoyer par terre

knocker |'nɑkər| *n* : heurtoir *m* (d'une porte)

knock–kneed |'nɑk'ni:d| *adj* : cagneux

knoll |'no:l| *n* : butte *f*, tertre *m*

knot[1] |'nɑt| *v* **knotted; knotting** *vt* : nouer, faire un nœud dans (une cravate, etc.) — *vi* : se nouer

knot[2] *n* **1** : nœud *m* (dans une corde, dans un tronc d'arbre) **2** CLUSTER : petit groupe *m* **3** : nœud *m*, mille *m* marin (en navigation) **4 to tie the knot** : se marier

knotty |'nɑt̬i| *adj* **knottier; -est 1** GNARLED : noueux **2** INTRICATE : compliqué, complexe

know |'no:| *v* **knew** |'nu:, 'nju:|; **known** |'no:n|; **knowing** *vt* **1** : connaître (une personne, un lieu) <he knows me well

: il me connaît bien> <to be known to : être connu de> **2** : savoir <she knows everything : elle sait tout> <he knows how to write : il sait écrire> **3** UNDERSTAND : comprendre <they know English : ils comprennent l'anglais> **4** RECOGNIZE : reconnaître **5** DISCERN, DISTINGUISH : discerner, distinguir **6 to know how to** : savoir <I don't know how to swim : je ne sais pas nager> — *vi* **1** : savoir <not that I know : pas que je sache> **2 to know about** : être au courant de (des nouvelles, etc.), s'y connaître en (un sujet)

knowable [ˈnoːəbəl] *adj* : connaissable

knowing [ˈnoːɪŋ] *adj* : entendu <a knowing look : un regard entendu>

knowingly [ˈnoːɪŋli] *adv* : d'un air entendu

know–it–all [ˈnoːɪṭˌɔl] *n* : je-sais-tout *mf*

knowledge [ˈnɑlɪdʒ] *n* **1** LEARNING : connaissances *fpl,* savoir *m* **2** UNDERSTANDING : connaissance *f* <to the best of my knowledge : au meilleur de ma connaissance>

knowledgeable [ˈnɑlɪdʒəbəl] *adj* : bien informé

knuckle [ˈnʌkəl] *n* : jointure *f* du doigt, articulation *f* du doigt

koala [koˈwɑlə] *n* : koala *m*

kohlrabi [ˌkoːlˈrɑbi, -ˈræ-] *n, pl* **-bies** : chou-rave *m*

Koran [kəˈrɑn, -ˈræn] *n* **the Koran** : le Coran

Korean[1] [kəˈriːən] *adj* : coréen

Korean[2] *n* **1** : Coréen *m,* -réenne *f* **2** : coréen *m* (langue)

kosher [ˈkoːʃər] *adj* : kascher, casher

kowtow [ˌkaʊˈtaʊ, ˈkaʊˌtaʊ] *vi* **to kowtow to** : faire des courbettes à

krypton [ˈkrɪpˌtɑn] *n* : krypton *m*

kudos [ˈkjuːˌdɑs, ˈkuː-, -ˌdoːz] *n* : prestige *m*

kumquat [ˈkʌmˌkwɑt] *n* : kumquat *m*

Kuwaiti[1] [kʊˈweɪṭi] *adj* : koweïtien

Kuwaiti[2] *n* : Koweïtien *m,* -tienne *f*

L

l [ˈɛl] *n, pl* **l's** *or* **ls** [ˈɛlz] : l *m,* douzième lettre de l'alphabet

lab [ˈlæb] → **laboratory**

label[1] [ˈleɪbəl] *vt* **-beled** *or* **-belled; -beling** *or* **-belling 1** : étiqueter <to label a jar : étiqueter un bocal> **2** BRAND, CATEGORIZE : classer, étiqueter

label[2] *n* **1** TAG : étiquette *f* **2** BRAND : marque *f*

labial [ˈleɪbiəl] *adj* : labial

labor[1] *or Brit* **labour** [ˈleɪbər] *vi* **1** TOIL : travailler **2** STRUGGLE : gravir, aller péniblement <the truck was laboring up the hill : le camion montait péniblement la côte> — *vt* BELABOR : insister sur (un point)

labor[2] *or Brit* **labour** *n* **1** WORK : travail *m,* labeur *m* **2** : travail *m,* accouchement *m* (en médecine) <to be in labor : être en travail> **3** TASK : tâche *f* **4** WORKERS : main-d'œuvre *f*

laboratory [ˈlæbrəˌtori, ləˈbɔrə-] *n, pl* **-ries** : laboratoire *m*

Labor Day *or Brit* **Labour Day** *n* : fête *f* du Travail

laborer *or Brit* **labourer** [ˈleɪbərər] *n* : ouvrier *m,* -vrière *f*

laborious [ləˈboriəs] *adj* : laborieux, pénible — **laboriously** [-riəsli] *adv*

labor union *or Brit* **labour union** → **union**

labyrinth [ˈlæbəˌrɪnθ] *n* : labyrinthe *m*

lace[1] [ˈleɪs] *vt* **laced; lacing 1** TIE : lacer (ses souliers) **2** : orner (une robe, etc.) de dentelle **3 to be laced with** : être mêlé de

lace[2] *n* **1** SHOELACE : lacet *m* **2** : dentelle *f* <lace doilies : napperons en dentelle>

lacerate [ˈlæsəˌreɪt] *vt* **-ated; -ating** : lacérer

laceration [ˌlæsəˈreɪʃən] *n* : lacération *f*

lack[1] [ˈlæk] *vt* : manquer de <he lacks strength : il manque de force> — *vi or* **to be lacking** : manquer

lack[2] *n* : manque *m,* faute *f*

lackadaisical [ˌlækəˈdeɪzɪkəl] *adj* : apathique, amorphe, indolent

lackey [ˈlæki] *n, pl* **-eys 1** SERVANT : laquais *m* **2** TOADY : larbin *m fam*

lackluster [ˈlækˌlʌstər] *adj* : terne

laconic [ləˈkɑnɪk] *adj* : laconique — **laconically** [-nɪkli] *adv*

lacquer[1] [ˈlækər] *vt* : laquer, vernir

lacquer[2] *n* : laque *m*

lacrosse [ləˈkrɔs] *n* : crosse *f*

lactate [ˈlækˌteɪt] *vi* **-tated; -tating** : sécréter du lait

lactation [lækˈteɪʃən] *n* : lactation *f*

lactic [ˈlæktɪk] *adj* : lactique

lacuna [ləˈkuːnə, -ˈkjuː-] *n, pl* **-nae** [-ˌniː, -ˌnaɪ] *or* **-nas** : lacune *f*

lacy [ˈleɪsi] *adj* **lacier; -est** : de dentelle

lad [ˈlæd] *n* : garçon *m*

ladder [ˈlædər] *n* : échelle *f*

laden [ˈleɪdən] *adj* : chargé

ladle[1] [ˈleɪdəl] *vt* **-dled; -dling** : servir à la louche

ladle[2] *n* : louche *f*

lady [ˈleɪdi] *n, pl* **-dies 1** WOMAN : dame *f* **2** : madame *f* <ladies and gentlemen : mesdames et messieurs>

ladybird [ˈleɪdiˌbərd] → **ladybug**

ladybug [ˈleɪdiˌbʌg] *n* : coccinelle *f*

lag[1] |ˈlæg| *vi* **lagged; lagging** : traîner, rester en arrière <to lag behind : prendre du retard>
lag[2] *n* **1** DELAY : retard *m* **2** INTERVAL : intervalle *m*, décalage *m*
lager |ˈlɑgər| *n* : bière *f* blonde
laggard[1] |ˈlægərd| *adj* : tardif
laggard[2] *n* : traînard *m*, -narde *f fam*
lagoon |ləˈgu:n| *n* : lagune *f*
laid → **lay**[1]
lain → **lie**[1]
lair |ˈlær| *n* : tanière *f*, repaire *m*
laissez–faire *or Brit* **laisser–faire** |ˌlɛˌseɪˈfær, ˌleɪˌzeɪ-| *n* : laisser-faire *m*
laity |ˈleɪət̬i| *n* : laïcs *mpl*
lake |ˈleɪk| *n* : lac *m*
lama |ˈlɑmə| *n* : lama *m*
lamb |ˈlæm| *n* : agneau *m*
lambaste |læmˈbeɪst| *or* **lambast** |-ˈbæst| *vt* **-basted; -basting 1** BEAT, THRASH : battre, rosser **2** CENSURE : critiquer, réprimander
lame[1] |ˈleɪm| *vt* **lamed; laming** : estropier
lame[2] *adj* **lamer; lamest 1** : boiteux **2** WEAK : pauvre, piètre <a lame excuse : une piètre excuse>
lamé |lɑˈmeɪ, læ-| *n* : lamé *m*
lamely |ˈleɪmli| *adv* : de façon peu convaincante
lameness |ˈleɪmnəs| *n* **1** : claudication (en médecine) **2** : faiblesse *f* (d'une excuse, etc.)
lament[1] |ləˈmɛnt| *vt* **1** MOURN : pleurer **2** DEPLORE : déplorer, regretter
lament[2] *n* : lamentation *f*
lamentable |ˈlæməntəbəl, ləˈmɛntə-| *adj* : lamentable, déplorable — **lamentably** |-bli| *adv*
lamentation |ˌlæmənˈteɪʃən| *n* : lamentation *f*
laminate |ˈlæməˌneɪt| *vt* **-nated; -nating** : laminer
laminated |ˈlæməˌneɪt̬əd| *adj* : stratifié (se dit du bois), feuilleté (se dit du verre)
lamp |ˈlæmp| *n* : lampe *f*
lampoon[1] |læmˈpu:n| *vt* : railler, ridiculiser
lampoon[2] *n* : satire *f*
lamprey |ˈlæmpri| *n, pl* **-preys** : lamproie *f*
lance[1] |ˈlænts| *vt* **lanced; lancing** : inciser, percer (en médecine)
lance[2] *n* SPEAR : lance *f*
lance corporal *n* : soldat *m* de première classe
lancet |ˈlæntsət| *n* : lancette *f*, bistouri *m*
land[1] |ˈlænd| *vt* **1** DISEMBARK : débarquer (des passagers) **2** CATCH : attraper (un poisson) **3** GAIN, SECURE : décrocher (un emploi, etc.) **4** : flanquer *fam* <to land a punch : flanquer un coup de poing> — *vi* **1** : atterrir (se dit d'un avion), accoster (se dit d'un navire) **2** ALIGHT : tomber, retomber <to land on one's feet : retomber sur ses pieds> **3** END UP : finir, atterrir <he landed in jail : il s'est retrouvé en prison>
land[2] *n* **1** : terre *f* <on dry land : sur la terre ferme> **2** COUNTRY : pays *m* **3** PROPERTY : terrain *m* <land for sale : terrain à vendre>
landfill |ˈlændˌfɪl| *n* : enfouissement *m* de déchets
landing |ˈlændɪŋ| *n* **1** : atterrissage *m* (d'un avion) **2** : débarquement *m* (d'un navire) **3** : palier *m* (d'un escalier)
landing strip → **airstrip**
landlady |ˈlændˌleɪdi| *n, pl* **-dies** : propriétaire *f*
landless |ˈlændləs| *adj* : sans terre
landlocked |ˈlændˌlɑkt| *adj* : sans accès à la mer
landlord |ˈlændˌlɔrd| *n* : propriétaire *m*
landlubber |ˈlændˌlʌbər| *n* : marin *m* d'eau douce
landmark |ˈlændˌmɑrk| *n* **1** : point *m* de repère **2** MILESTONE : étape *f* décisive, étape *f* importante (dans la vie de qqn) **3** MONUMENT : monument *m* (historique)
landowner |ˈlændˌo:nər| *n* : propriétaire *m* foncier, propriétaire *f* foncière
landscape[1] |ˈlændˌskeɪp| *vt* **-scaped; -scaping** : aménager (un terrain)
landscape[2] *n* : paysage *m*
landslide |ˈlændˌslaɪd| *n* **1** : glissement *m* de terrain **2** *or* **landslide victory** : victoire *f* écrasante
landward |ˈlændwərd| *adv & adj* : vers la terre, en direction de la terre
lane |ˈleɪn| *n* : voie *f* (d'une autoroute), chemin *m* (de campagne)
language |ˈlæŋgwɪdʒ| *n* **1** : langue *f* <she speaks three languages : elle parle trois langues> **2** : langage *m* <computer language : langage informatique>
languid |ˈlæŋgwɪd| *adj* : languissant
languidly |ˈlæŋgwɪdli| *adv* : langoureusement
languish |ˈlæŋgwɪʃ| *vi* **1** WEAKEN, WITHER : dépérir **2** PINE : croupir
languor |ˈlæŋgər| *n* : langueur *f*
languorous |ˈlæŋgərəs| *adj* : langoureux — **languorously** *adv*
lank |ˈlæŋk| *adj* **1** THIN : maigre **2** LIMP : plat
lanky |ˈlæŋki| *adj* **lankier; -est** : grand et maigre, dégingandé
lanolin |ˈlænəlɪn| *n* : lanoline *f*
lantern |ˈlæntərn| *n* : lanterne *f*
Laotian[1] |leɪˈo:ʃən, ˈlɑuʃən| *adj* : laotien
Laotian[2] *n* : Laotien *m*, -tienne *f*
lap[1] |ˈlæp| *v* **lapped; lapping** *vt* **1** *or* **to lap up** : laper (du lait, etc.) **2** SWALLOW : gober *fam*, avaler <the crowd lapped up every word he said : la foule gobait tout ce qu'il disait> **3** OVERLAP : chevaucher — *vi* SPLASH : clapoter (se dit des vagues)

lap[2] *n* **1** : genoux *mpl,* giron *m* <to sit on s.o.'s lap : s'asseoir sur les genoux de qqn> **2** : tour *m* de piste, tour *m* de circuit (aux sports) **3** : étape *f* (d'un voyage)

lapdog [ˈlæpˌdɔg] *n* : chien *m* de manchon, petit chien *m* d'appartement

lapel [ləˈpɛl] *n* : revers *m*

Lapp [ˈlæp] *n* **1** : Lapon *m,* -ponne *f* **2** : lapon *m* (langue)

Lappish[1] [ˈlæpɪʃ] *adj* : lapon

Lappish[2] *n* : lapon *m* (langue)

lapse[1] [ˈlæps] *vi* **lapsed; lapsing 1** CEASE, EXPIRE : expirer, cesser d'être en vigueur **2** ELAPSE : s'écouler, passer **3 to lapse into** : tomber dans <they lapsed into silence : ils se sont tus> <to lapse into unconsciousness : perdre connaissance>

lapse[2] *n* **1** : trou *m* (de mémoire, etc.) **2** EXPIRATION : expiration *f,* échéance *f* **3** INTERVAL : intervalle *m,* laps *m* (de temps)

laptop [ˈlæpˌtɑp] *adj* : portable <laptop computer : ordinateur portable>

larboard [ˈlɑrbərd] *n* : bâbord *m*

larceny [ˈlɑrsəni] *n, pl* **-nies** : vol *m*

larch [ˈlɑrtʃ] *n* : mélèze *m*

lard [ˈlɑrd] *n* : saindoux *m*

larder [ˈlɑrdər] *n* PANTRY : garde-manger *m*

large [ˈlɑrdʒ] *adj* **larger; largest 1** BIG : grand, gros **2 at ~** FREE : en liberté **3 at ~** : en général <the public at large : le grand public>

largely [ˈlɑrdʒli] *adv* **1** : en grande partie, en grande mesure **2** MOSTLY : principalement

largeness [ˈlɑrdʒnəs] *n* : grandeur *f*

largesse *or* **largess** [lɑrˈʒɛs, -ˈdʒɛs] *n* : largesse *f,* générosité *f*

lariat [ˈlæriət] *n* : lasso *m*

lark [ˈlɑrk] *n* **1** : alouette *f* (oiseau) **2** JOKE, PRANK : rigolade *f*

larva [ˈlɑrvə] *n, pl* **-vae** [-ˌviː, -ˌvaɪ] : larve *f*

larval [ˈlɑrvəl] *adj* : larvaire

laryngitis [ˌlærənˈdʒaɪtəs] *n* : laryngite *f*

larynx [ˈlærɪŋks] *n, pl* **-rynges** [ləˈrɪnˌdʒiːz] *or* **-ynxes** [ˈlærɪŋksəz] : larynx *m*

lasagna [ləˈzɑnjə] *n* : lasagnes *fpl*

lascivious [ləˈsɪviəs] *adj* : lascif

lasciviousness [ləˈsɪviəsnəs] *n* : lascivité *f*

laser [ˈleɪzər] *n* : laser *m*

lash[1] [ˈlæʃ] *vt* **1** WHIP : fouetter **2** BIND : attacher, lier — *vi* **1** BEAT : battre <the rain lashed at the windowpanes : la pluie battait contre les vitres> **2 to lash out at** : invectiver contre

lash[2] *n* **1** WHIP : fouet *m* **2** BLOW, STRIKE : coup *m* de fouet **3** EYELASH : cil *m*

lass [ˈlæs] *or* **lassie** [ˈlæsi] *n* : fille *f*

lassitude [ˈlæsəˌtuːd, -ˌtjuːd] *n* : lassitude *f*

lasso[1] [ˈlæˌsoː, læˈsuː] *vt* : prendre au lasso

lasso[2] *n, pl* **-sos** *or* **-soes** : lasso *m*

last[1] [ˈlæst] *vi* **1** CONTINUE, ENDURE : durer **2** : se conserver (se dit des aliments), faire de l'usage (se dit des tissus), durer — *vt* **1** : faire <it lasted me three days : ça m'a fait trois jours> <they will last you a lifetime : vous en aurez pour la vie> **2 to last out** : tenir jusqu'à la fin de

last[2] *adv* **1** : en dernier <he came last : il est arrivé en dernier> **2** RECENTLY : dernièrement **3** FINALLY : enfin, en conclusion

last[3] *adj* : dernier

last[4] *n* **1** : dernier *m,* -nière *f* **2** : forme *f* (pour les souliers) **3 at ~** FINALLY : enfin, finalement

lastly [ˈlæstli] *adv* : enfin, en dernier lieu

latch[1] [ˈlætʃ] *vt* : fermer au loquet, clencher *Can* — *vi* **to latch onto** : s'accrocher à

latch[2] *n* : loquet *m*

late[1] [ˈleɪt] *adv* **later; latest** : en retard

late[2] *adj* **later; latest 1** : en retard <he's always late : il est toujours en retard> **2** : tardif <a late spring : un printemps tardif> **3** DECEASED : défunt, feu <his late son : son défunt fils> <the late queen : feu la reine> **4** RECENT : dernier, récent

latecomer [ˈleɪtˌkʌmər] *n* : retardataire *mf*

lately [ˈleɪtli] *adv* : récemment, dernièrement

lateness [ˈleɪtnəs] *n* : retard *m*

latent [ˈleɪtənt] *adj* : latent

later [ˈleɪtər] *adv* : plus tard, tantôt *Can*

lateral [ˈlæt̬ərəl] *adj* : latéral — **laterally** *adv*

latex [ˈleɪˌtɛks] *n, pl* **-tices** [ˈleɪt̬əˌsiːz, ˈlætə-] *or* **-texes** : latex *m*

lath [ˈlæθ, ˈlæð] *n, pl* **laths** *or* **lath** : latte *f*

lathe [ˈleɪð] *n* : tour *m*

lather[1] [ˈlæðər] *vt* : savonner — *vi* : mousser

lather[2] *n* : mousse *f* (à savon), écume *f* (sur un cheval)

Latin[1] [ˈlætən] *adj* : latin

Latin[2] *n* **1** : latin *m* (langue) **2** → **Latin American**

Latin–American [ˈlætənəˈmɛrɪkən] *adj* : latino-américain

Latin American *n* : Latino-américain *m,* -caine *f*

latitude [ˈlæt̬əˌtuːd, -ˌtjuːd] *n* : latitude *f*

latrine [ləˈtriːn] *n* : latrines *fpl,* toilette *f*

latter[1] [ˈlæt̬ər] *adj* LAST, SECOND : dernier, second

latter[2] *pron* **the latter** : le dernier, le second

lattice [ˈlæt̬əs] *n* : treillis *m,* treillage *m*

Latvian[1] [ˈlætviən] *adj* : letton

Latvian[2] *n* **1** : Letton *m,* -tonne *f* **2** : letton *m* (langue)

laud[1] ['lɔd] *vt* : louer
laud[2] *n* : louanges *fpl*
laugh[1] ['læf] *vi* : rire
laugh[2] *n* : rire *m*
laughable ['læfəbəl] *adj* : risible
laughingly ['læfıŋli] *adv* : en riant
laughingstock ['læfıŋˌstɑk] *n* : risée *f*, objet *m* de risée
laughter ['læftər] *n* : rire *m*, rires *mpl*
launch[1] ['lɔntʃ] *vt* **1** HURL : lancer **2** : mettre à l'eau (un bateau) **3** START : lancer (un programme, une campagne, etc.)
launch[2] *n* : vedette *f*, bateau *m* de plaisance
launder ['lɔndər] *vt* : laver (du linge)
launderer ['lɔndərər] *n* : blanchisseur *m*, -seuse *f*; buandier *m*, -dière *f Can*
laundress ['lɔndrəs] *n* : blanchisseuse *f*, buandière *f Can*
laundry ['lɔndri] *n, pl* **-dries 1** : lavage *m*, linge *m* <to do the laundry : faire la lessive> **2** : blanchisserie *f* (commerciale)
laureate ['lɔriət] *n* : lauréat *m*, -réate *f*
laurel ['lɔrəl] *n* **1** : laurier *m* (arbre) **2 laurels** *npl* : lauriers *mpl* <to rest on one's laurels : reposer sur ses lauriers>
lava ['lɑvə, 'læ-] *n* : lave *f*
lavatory ['lævəˌtori] *n, pl* **-ries** : toilettes *fpl*
lavender ['lævəndər] *n* : lavande *f*
lavish[1] ['lævıʃ] *vt* : prodiguer
lavish[2] *adj* **1** EXTRAVAGANT : prodigue **2** ABUNDANT : abondant, copieux **3** LUXURIOUS : somptueux, fastueux
lavishly ['lævıʃli] *adv* : généreusement, luxueusement
law ['lɔ] *n* **1** : loi *f* <to break the law : enfreindre la loi> **2** : droit *m* <to study law : faire son droit> <civil law : droit civil> **3** LEGISLATION : loi *f*, législation *f* <the law of the land : la législation du pays> **4** PRINCIPLE : loi *f*, principe *m* <the law of gravity : la loi de la pesanteur>
law–abiding ['lɔəˌbaıdıŋ] *adj* : respectueux des lois
lawbreaker ['lɔˌbreıkər] *n* : personne *f* qui enfreint la loi
lawful ['lɔfəl] *adj* : légal, légitime — **lawfully** *adv*
lawgiver ['lɔˌgıvər] → **legislator**
lawless ['lɔləs] *adj* : anarchique <a lawless person : une personne sans foi ni loi>
lawmaker ['lɔˌmeıkər] *n* : législateur *m*, -trice *f*
lawman ['lɔmən] *n, pl* **-men** [-mən, -ˌmɛn] : policier *m*
lawn ['lɔn] *n* : pelouse *f*
lawn mower *n* : tondeuse *f*
lawsuit ['lɔˌsu:t] *n* : procès *m*
lawyer ['lɔıər, 'lɔjər] *n* : avocat *m*, -cate *f*
lax ['læks] *adj* **1** LOOSE, SLACK : lâche, relâché **2** NEGLIGENT : négligent
laxative ['læksət̬ıv] *n* : laxatif *m*
laxity ['læksət̬i] *n* : laxisme *m*
lay[1] ['leı] *vt* **laid** ['leıd]; **laying 1** PLACE : mettre, poser, déposer **2** : pondre (des œufs) **3** IMPOSE : imposer (une taxe) **4 to lay a bet** : parier **5 to lay out** ARRANGE, DISPLAY : étaler, disposer **6 to lay out** DESIGN : concevoir
lay[2] → **lie**[1]
lay[3] *adj* **1** SECULAR : laïc **2** NONPROFESSIONAL : profane
lay[4] *n* **1** : emplacement *m*, position *f* <the lay of the land : l'emplacement du terrain> **2** BALLAD : lai *m*
layer ['leıər] *n* **1** : pondeuse *f* (poule) **2** : couche *f* (de peinture), strate *f* (en géologie)
layman ['leımən] *n, pl* **-men** [-mən, -ˌmɛn] : profane *mf*, laïque *mf* (en religion)
layoff ['leıˌɔf] *n* : licenciement *m*, renvoi *m*
lay off *vt* : licencier, congédier (un employé)
layout ['leıˌaʊt] *n* **1** ARRANGEMENT : disposition *f*, arrangement *m* **2** : mise *f* en page (en informatique), plan *m* (d'une ville)
layperson ['leıˌpərsən] *n* : profane *mf*
lay up *vt* **1** STORE : mettre de côté **2 to be laid up** : être alité
laywoman ['leıˌwʊmən] *n, pl* **-women** [-ˌwımən] : laïque *f*
lazily ['leızəli] *adv* : paresseusement
laziness ['leızinəs] *n* : paresse *f*
lazy ['leızi] *adj* **lazier; -est** : paresseux
leach ['li:tʃ] *vt* : lessiver
lead[1] ['li:d] *v* **led** ['lɛd]; **leading** *vt* **1** GUIDE : mener, conduire **2** DIRECT : diriger (un orchestre, etc.) **3** HEAD : être à la tête de **4** CONDUCT : mener <he leads a quiet life : il mène une vie tranquille> — *vi* : mener
lead[2] *n* INITIATIVE : initiative *f*
lead[3] ['lɛd] *n* **1** : plomb *m* (métal) **2** GRAPHITE : mine *f* <pencil lead : mine de crayon>
leaden ['lɛdən] *adj* **1** : de plomb **2** HEAVY : lourd <with leaden steps : d'un pas lourd>
leader ['li:dər] *n* : chef *m*; dirigeant *m*, -geante *f*
leadership ['li:dərˌʃıp] *n* : direction *f*
leaf[1] ['li:f] *vi* **1** : se feuiller (se dit d'un arbre) **2 to leaf through** : feuilleter (un livre, etc.)
leaf[2] *n, pl* **leaves** ['li:vz] **1** : feuille *f* <maple leaves : feuilles d'érable> **2** : page *f* (d'un livre) **3** : rallonge *f* (de table)
leafless ['li:fləs] *adj* : sans feuilles
leaflet ['li:flət] *n* : dépliant *m*, prospectus *m*
leafy ['li:fi] *adj* **leafier; -est** : feuillu
league[1] ['li:g] *v* **leagued; leaguing** *vt* : allier — *vi* : se liguer
league[2] *n* **1** : lieue *f* <three leagues from here : à trois lieues d'ici> **2** ASSOCIA-

TION : ligue *f* **3** CLASS : classe *f,* niveau *m*

leak[1] ['li:k] *vt* **1** : faire couler (un liquide) **2** : répandre (une nouvelle), divulguer (un secret) — *vi* **1** : fuir (se dit d'un liquide ou d'un gaz) **2** : faire eau (se dit d'un bateau) **3** *or* **to leak out** : filtrer, être divulgué (se dit de l'information)

leak[2] *n* : fuite *f,* voie *f* d'eau

leakage ['li:kɪdʒ] *n* : fuite *f* (d'eau)

leaky ['li:ki] *adj* **leakier; -est** : qui prend l'eau

lean[1] ['li:n] *v* **leaned** *or Brit* **leant** ['lɛnt]; **leaning** *vi* **1** BEND : se pencher, s'incliner **2** RECLINE : s'appuyer **3** TILT : pencher **4 to lean on** DEPEND ON : se fier sur, compter sur, dépendre de **5 to lean toward** : pencher pour, pencher vers — *vt* **1** PROP, REST : appuyer **2** INCLINE : incliner, pencher

lean[2] *adj* **1** THIN : mince, maigre **2** : maigre <lean meat : viande maigre> **3** : difficile <lean years : années difficiles>

leaning ['li:nɪŋ] *n* INCLINATION : tendance *f*

leanness ['li:nnəs] *n* : minceur *f,* maigreur *f*

leant *Brit* → **lean**[1]

leap[1] ['li:p] *vi* **leaped** *or* **leapt** ['li:pt, 'lɛpt]; **leaping** : sauter, bondir

leap[2] *n* : saut *m,* bond *m*

leap year *n* : année *f* bissextile

learn ['lərn] *v* **learned** ['lərnd, 'lərnt] *or Brit* **learnt** ['lərnt]; **learning** *vt* **1** : apprendre <to learn a language : apprendre une langue> **2** MEMORIZE : mémoriser **3** HEAR : apprendre <I just learned the news : je viens d'apprendre la nouvelle> — *vi* : apprendre

learned ['lərnəd] *adj* : savant, érudit

learner ['lərnər] *n* : débutant *m,* -tante *f*

learning ['lərnɪŋ] *n* **1** KNOWLEDGE : savoir *m,* érudition *f* **2** : apprentissage *m* <the learning of a trade : l'apprentissage d'un métier>

learnt *Brit* → **learn**

lease[1] ['li:s] *vt* **leased; leasing** : louer à bail

lease[2] *n* : bail *m*

leash[1] ['li:ʃ] *vt* : tenir (un animal) en laisse

leash[2] *n* : laisse *f* (d'un animal)

least[1] ['li:st] *adv* : (le) moins <to be least interesting : être le moins intéressant>

least[2] *adj* **1** : moins <the least money : le moins d'argent> **2** SLIGHTEST : moindre <the least noise startles her : le moindre bruit la surprend>

least[3] *n* **1** : moins *m* <you have the least : c'est vous qui en avez le moins> **2 at ~** : au moins **3 to say the least** : c'est le moins qu'on puisse dire

leather ['lɛðər] *n* : cuir *m*

leathery ['lɛðəri] *adj* : tanné

leave[1] ['li:v] *v* **left** ['lɛft]; **leaving** *vt* **1** BEQUEATH : léguer **2** : partir de, quitter <to leave the house : partir de la maison> <she left her husband : elle a quitté son mari> **3** FORGET : laisser <I left my books at home : j'ai laissé mes livres à la maison> **4** EQUAL : égaler <4 from 7 leaves 3 : 7 moins 4 égale 3> **5** LET : laisser <leave her alone : laisse-la tranquille> <leave the door open : laissez la porte ouverte> **6 to be left** : rester <there's no money left : il ne reste plus d'argent> **7 to leave out** : omettre — *vi* DEPART : partir

leave[2] *n* **1** PERMISSION : permission *f* **2** *or* **leave of absence** : congé *m* **3 to take one's leave** : prendre son congé

leaved ['li:vd] *adj* : qui a des feuilles

leaven ['lɛvən] *n* : levain *m*

leaves → **leaf**

leavings ['li:vɪŋz] *npl* : restes *mpl*

Lebanese[1] [ˌlɛbə'ni:z, -'ni:s] *adj* : libanais

Lebanese[2] *n* : Libanais *m,* -naise *f*

lecherous ['lɛtʃərəs] *adj* : lubrique, lascif

lechery ['lɛtʃəri] *n* : lubricité *f,* lascivité *f*

lecture[1] ['lɛktʃər] *v* **-tured; -turing** *vt* : faire la morale à, sermonner — *vi* : faire une conférence

lecture[2] *n* **1** TALK : conférence *f* **2** : cours *m* magistral (à l'université) **3** REPRIMAND : sermon *m*

lecturer ['lɛktʃərər] *n* : conférencier *m,* -cière *f*

led → **lead**[1]

ledge ['lɛdʒ] *n* : rebord *m* (d'une fenêtre, etc.), saillie *f* (d'une montagne)

ledger ['lɛdʒər] *n* : grand livre *m* (en comptabilité)

lee[1] ['li:] *adj* : sous le vent

lee[2] *n* : côté *m* sous le vent

leech ['li:tʃ] *n* : sangsue *f*

leek ['li:k] *n* : poireau *m*

leer[1] ['lɪr] *vi* **to leer at** : lorgner

leer[2] *n* : regard *m* malveillant, regard *m* lubrique

leery ['lɪri] *adj* : méfiant, soupçonneux <to be leery of : se méfier de>

lees ['li:z] *npl* DREGS : lie *f*

leeward[1] ['li:wərd, 'lu:ərd] *adj* : sous le vent

leeward[2] *n* : côté *m* sous le vent

leeway ['li:ˌweɪ] *n* : marge *f* de manœuvre

left[1] → **leave**[1]

left[2] ['lɛft] *adv* : à gauche

left[3] *adj* : gauche

left[4] *n* : gauche *f* <it's on your left : c'est à votre gauche>

leg ['lɛg] *n* **1** : patte *f* (d'un animal), jambe *f* (d'une personne ou d'un pantalon) **2** : pied *m* (d'une table, etc.) **3** STAGE : étape *f* (d'un voyage)

legacy ['lɛgəsi] *n, pl* **-cies** : legs *m,* héritage *m*

legal [ˈliːgəl] *adj* **1** LAWFUL : légal, légitime **2** JUDICIAL : juridique, judiciaire <legal adviser : conseiller juridique> <legal aid : aide judiciaire>

legality [liˈgæləṭi] *n, pl* **-ties** : légalité *f*

legalize [ˈliːgəˌlaɪz] *vt* **-ized; -izing** : légaliser

legally [ˈliːgəli] *adv* : légalement

legate [ˈlɛgət] *n* : légat *m*

legation [lɪˈgeɪʃən] *n* : légation *f*

legend [ˈlɛdʒənd] *n* : légende *f*

legendary [ˈlɛdʒənˌdɛri] *adj* : légendaire

legerdemain [ˌlɛdʒərdəˈmeɪn] → **sleight of hand**

leggings [ˈlɛgɪŋz, ˈlɛgənz] *npl* : caleçon *m* (porté comme pantalon)

legibility [ˌlɛdʒəˈbɪləṭi] *n* : lisibilité *f*

legible [ˈlɛdʒəbəl] *adj* : lisible — **legibly** [-bli] *adv*

legion [ˈliːdʒən] *n* : légion *f*

legionary [ˈliːdʒənəri] → **legionnaire**

legionnaire [ˌliːdʒəˈnær] *n* : légionnaire *m*

legislate [ˈlɛdʒəsˌleɪt] *vi* **-lated; -lating** : légiférer

legislation [ˌlɛdʒəsˈleɪʃən] *n* : législation *f*

legislative [ˈlɛdʒəsˌleɪṭɪv] *adj* : législatif

legislator [ˈlɛdʒəsˌleɪṭər] *n* : législateur *m*, -trice *f*

legislature [ˈlɛdʒəsˌleɪtʃər] *n* : législatif *m*, corps *m* législatif

legitimacy [lɪˈdʒɪṭəməsi] *n* : légitimité *f*

legitimate [lɪˈdʒɪṭəmət] *adj* **1** LAWFUL : légitime **2** VALID : légitime, admissible

legitimately [lɪˈdʒɪṭəmətli] *adv* : légitimement

legitimize [lɪˈdʒɪṭəˌmaɪz] *vt* **-mized; -mizing** : légitimer

legless [ˈlɛgləs] *adj* : sans jambes

legume [ˈlɛˌgjuːm, lɪˈgjuːm] *n* : légumineuse *f*

leisure [ˈliːʒər, ˈlɛ-] *n* **1** : loisir *m* <leisure time : les loisirs> **2 at your leisure** : à votre convenance

leisurely[1] [ˈliːʒərli, ˈlɛ-] *adv* : sans hâte, sans se presser

leisurely[2] *adj* : tranquille, paisible <a leisurely stroll : une balade faite sans se presser>

lemming [ˈlɛmɪŋ] *n* : lemming *m*

lemon [ˈlɛmən] *n* : citron *m*

lemonade [ˌlɛməˈneɪd] *n* : limonade *f*

lemony [ˈlɛməni] *adj* : citronné

lend [ˈlɛnd] *vt* **lent** [ˈlɛnt]; **lending 1** : prêter <to lend money : prêter de l'argent> **2** GIVE, SUPPORT : conférer, apporter <to lend a hand : prêter une main> **3 to lend itself to** : se prêter à

lender [ˈlɛndər] *n* : prêteur *m*, -teuse *f*

length [ˈlɛŋkθ] *n* **1** : longueur *f* <10 meters in length : 10 mètres de longueur> **2** DURATION : durée *f* **3** PIECE, SECTION : bout *m*, morceau *m* <a length of pipe : un bout de tuyau> **4 at ~** : longuement, en détail **5 to go to great lengths** : se donner beaucoup de mal

lengthen [ˈlɛŋkθən] *vt* **1** : rallonger (une jupe, etc.) **2** PROLONG : prolonger — *vi* : s'allonger, se prolonger

lengthways [ˈlɛŋkθˌweɪz] → **lengthwise**

lengthwise [ˈlɛŋkθˌwaɪz] *adv & adj* : dans le sens de la longueur

lengthy [ˈlɛŋkθi] *adj* **lengthier; -est** : long, interminable

leniency [ˈliːniəntsi] *n* : indulgence *f*, clémence *f*

lenient [ˈliːniənt] *adj* : indulgent, clément

leniently [ˈliːniəntli] *adv* : avec indulgence, avec clémence

lens [ˈlɛnz] *n* **1** : lentille *f*, objectif *m* (d'un instrument) **2** : cristallin *m* (de l'œil) **3** : verre *m* (d'une paire de lunettes) **4** → **contact lens**

Lent [ˈlɛnt] *n* : carême *m*

Lenten [ˈlɛntən] *adj* : de carême

lentil [ˈlɛntəl] *n* : lentille *f*

Leo [ˈliːoː] *n* : Lion *m*

leopard [ˈlɛpərd] *n* : léopard *m*

leotard [ˈliːəˌtɑrd] *n* : justaucorps *m*

leper [ˈlɛpər] *n* : lépreux *m*, -preuse *f*

leprechaun [ˈlɛprəˌkɑn] *n* : lutin *m*

leprosy [ˈlɛprəsi] *n* : lèpre *f*

lesbian[1] [ˈlɛzbiən] *adj* : lesbien

lesbian[2] *n* : lesbienne *f*

lesbianism [ˈlɛzbiəˌnɪzəm] *n* : lesbianisme *m*

lesion [ˈliːʒən] *n* : lésion *f*

less[1] [ˈlɛs] (*comparative of* **little**[1]) *adv* **1** : moins <much less important : beaucoup moins important> **2 less and less** : de moins en moins

less[2] (*comparative of* **little**[2]) *adj* **1** : moins <less money : moins d'argent> **2** : moindre <of less importance : de moindre importance>

less[3] *prep* MINUS : moins <the regular price less a discount : le prix régulier moins un escompte>

less[4] *pron* : moins <I cannot do less : je ne peux pas en faire moins>

lessen [ˈlɛsən] *vi* DECREASE : diminuer — *vt* REDUCE : amoindrir, diminuer

lesser[1] [ˈlɛsər] *adv* LESS : moins <lesser-known writers : des écrivains moins connus>

lesser[2] *adj* : moindre <to a lesser degree : à un moindre degré>

lesson [ˈlɛsən] *n* : leçon *f*

lest [ˈlɛst] *conj* : de peur que, de crainte que

let [ˈlɛt] *vt* **let; letting 1** MAKE : laisser <let me know : laisse-moi savoir> **2** RENT : louer <rooms to let : chambres à louer> **3** ALLOW, PERMIT : laisser <let them through : laissez-les passer> **4** (*used in commands*) <let him try : qu'il essaie> **5 to let go** RELEASE : lâcher

letdown [ˈlɛtˌdaʊn] *n* DISAPPOINTMENT : déception *f*

let down *vt* DISAPPOINT : décevoir

lethal [ˈliːθəl] *adj* : mortel, létal
lethargic [lɪˈθɑrdʒɪk] *adj* : léthargique
lethargy [ˈlɛθərdʒi] *n* : léthargie *f*
let on *vi* ADMIT : admettre, révéler
let's [ˈlɛts] (*contraction of* **let us**) → **let**
letter[1] [ˈlɛt̬ər] *vt* : inscrire des lettres sur
letter[2] *n* **1** : lettre *f* (de l'alphabet) **2** : lettre *f* <a letter to my mother : une lettre à ma mère> **3 letters** *npl* CORRESPONDENCE : courrier *m* <letters to the editor : courrier des lecteurs> **4 letters** *npl* : belles-lettres *fpl*, littérature *f* **5 the letter of the law** : la lettre de la loi
letterhead [ˈlɛt̬ərˌhɛd] *n* : en-tête *m*
lettuce [ˈlɛt̬əs] *n* : laitue *f*
let up *vi* ABATE : diminuer, se calmer
leukemia [luːˈkiːmiə] *n* : leucémie *f*
levee [ˈlɛvi] *n* : digue *f*
level[1] [ˈlɛvəl] *vt* **-eled** *or* **-elled; -eling** *or* **-elling 1** FLATTEN : niveler, aplanir **2** AIM, DIRECT : lancer (une accusation), braquer (une arme) **3** RAZE : raser (un immeuble)
level[2] *adj* **1** FLAT : plat **2** HORIZONTAL : horizontal <in a level position : à l'horizontale> **3** EVEN : à égalité <to draw level : se trouver à égalité> **4** CALM, STEADY : calme, mesuré <to keep a level head : garder son sang-froid>
level[3] *n* : niveau *m*
levelheaded [ˈlɛvəlˈhɛdəd] *adj* : pondéré, équilibré
lever [ˈlɛvər, ˈliː-] *n* : levier *m*
leverage [ˈlɛvərɪdʒ, ˈliː-] *n* **1** : force *f* de levier (en physique) **2** INFLUENCE : influence *f*, moyen *m* de pression
leviathan [lɪˈvaɪəθən] *n* : chose *f* énorme et redoutable
levity [ˈlɛvət̬i] *n* : légèreté *f*, manque *m* de sérieux
levy[1] [ˈlɛvi] *vt* **levied; levying 1** IMPOSE : imposer, prélever (des impôts) **2** COLLECT : lever, percevoir (des impôts) **3** ENLIST : lever (des troupes)
levy[2] *n, pl* **levies 1** : impôt *m*, taxe *f* **2** : levée *f* (militaire)
lewd [ˈluːd] *adj* : luxurieux, lubrique
lewdly [ˈluːdli] *adv* : de façon obscène
lewdness [ˈluːdnəs] *n* : lubricité *f*
lexicographer [ˌlɛksəˈkɑgrəfər] *n* : lexicographe *mf*
lexicographical [ˌlɛksəkoˈgræfɪkəl] *or* **lexicographic** [-ˈgræfɪk] *adj* : lexicographique
lexicography [ˌlɛksəˈkɑgrəfi] *n* : lexicographie *f*
lexicon [ˈlɛksɪˌkɑn] *n, pl* **-ica** [-kə] *or* **-icons** : lexique *m*
liability [ˌlaɪəˈbɪlət̬i] *n, pl* **-ties 1** RESPONSIBILITY : responsabilité *f* **2** DRAWBACK : désavantage *m*, handicap *m* **3 liabilities** *npl* : passif *m*, dettes *fpl* <assets and liabilities : l'actif et le passif>
liable [ˈlaɪəbəl] *adj* **1** : responsable <liable for damages : responsable pour les dommages> **2** LIKELY : probable <it's liable to rain : il se peut qu'il pleuve> **3** SUSCEPTIBLE : sujet, susceptible <he's liable to fall : il est sujet aux chutes>
liaison [ˈliːəˌzɑn, liˈeɪ-] *n* : liaison *f*
liar [ˈlaɪər] *n* : menteur *m*, -teuse *f*
libel[1] [ˈlaɪbəl] *vt* **-beled** *or* **-belled; -beling** *or* **-belling** : diffamer, calomnier
libel[2] *n* : diffamation *f*, calomnie *f*
libelous *or* **libellous** [ˈlaɪbələs] *adj* : diffamatoire
liberal[1] [ˈlɪbrəl, ˈlɪbərəl] *adj* **1** ABUNDANT, GENEROUS : libéral, prodigue **2** TOLERANT : libéral, tolérant
liberal[2] *n* : libéral *m*, -rale *f*
liberal arts *n* : arts *mpl* et sciences *fpl* humaines
liberalism [ˈlɪbrəˌlɪzəm, ˈlɪbərə-] *n* : libéralisme *m*
liberality [ˌlɪbəˈrælət̬i] *n, pl* **-ties** : libéralité *f*
liberalize [ˈlɪbrəˌlaɪz, ˈlɪbərə-] *vt* **-ized; -izing** : libéraliser
liberally [ˈlɪbrəli, ˈlɪbərə-] *adv* : libéralement
liberate [ˈlɪbəˌreɪt] *vt* **-ated; -ating** : libérer
liberation [ˌlɪbəˈreɪʃən] *n* : libération *f*
liberator [ˈlɪbəˌreɪt̬ər] *n* : libérateur *m*, -trice *f*
Liberian[1] [laɪˈbɪriən] *adj* : libérien
Liberian[2] *n* : Libérien *m*, -rienne *f*
libertine [ˈlɪbərˌtiːn] *n* : libertin *m*, -tine *f*
liberty [ˈlɪbərt̬i] *n, pl* **-ties 1** FREEDOM : liberté *f* **2** CHANCE, RISK : risque *m* <he's taking liberties with his health : il prend des risques avec sa santé> **3 liberties** *npl* FAMILIARITY : libertés *fpl*
libido [ləˈbiːdoː, -ˈbaɪ-] *n, pl* **-dos** : libido *f*
Libra [ˈliːbrə] *n* : Balance *f*
librarian [laɪˈbrɛriən] *n* : bibliothécaire *mf*
library [ˈlaɪˌbrɛri] *n, pl* **-braries** : bibliothèque *f*
libretto [lɪˈbrɛt̬o] *n, pl* **-tos** *or* **-ti** [-t̬iː] : livret *m*
Libyan[1] [ˈlɪbiən] *adj* : libyen
Libyan[2] *n* : Libyen *m*, Libyenne *f*
lice → **louse**
license[1] [ˈlaɪsənts] *vt* **-censed; -censing 1** : accorder une licence à **2** AUTHORIZE : autoriser
license[2] *or* **licence** *n* **1** PERMIT : permis *m*, licence *f* <driver's license : permis de conduire> **2** FREEDOM : licence *f*, liberté *f* **3** AUTHORIZATION : licence *f*, autorisation *f*
licentious [laɪˈsɛntʃəs] *adj* : licencieux — **licentiously** *adv*
lichen [ˈlaɪkən] *n* : lichen *m*
licit [ˈlɪsət] *adj* LAWFUL : licite
lick[1] [ˈlɪk] *vt* **1** : lécher **2** BEAT : battre à plate couture, écraser

lick[2] *n* **1** : coup *m* de langue **2** BIT : brin *m* <a lick and a promise : un brin de toilette>

licorice *or Brit* **liquorice** [ˈlɪkərɪʃ, -rəs] *n* : réglisse *f*

lid [ˈlɪd] *n* **1** COVER : couvercle *m* **2** EYELID : paupière *f*

lie[1] [ˈlaɪ] *vi* **lay** [ˈleɪ]; **lain** [ˈleɪn]; **lying** [ˈlaɪɪŋ] **1** *or* **to lie down** : se coucher, s'allonger <to lie on the grass : s'allonger sur l'herbe> <to lie motionless : rester immobile> **2** : se trouver, être <the book is lying on the table : le livre se trouve sur la table> **3** EXTEND, STRETCH : s'étendre <the route lay to the west : la route s'étendait vers l'ouest> **4** REMAIN : être, rester <to lie idle : être arrêté> **5 to lie in** : résider en

lie[2] *vi* **lied; lying** [ˈlaɪɪŋ] : mentir

lie[3] *n* **1** : mensonge *m* **2** : position *f* (au golf), configuration *f* (de la terre)

liege [ˈliːdʒ] *n* : suzerain *m*, seigneur *m*

lien [ˈliːn] *n* : droit *m* de rétention

lieutenant [luːˈtɛnənt] *n* : lieutenant *m*

lieutenant colonel *n* : lieutenant-colonel *m*

lieutenant commander *n* : capitaine *m* de corvette

lieutenant general *n* : général *m* de corps d'armée

life [ˈlaɪf] *n, pl* **lives** [ˈlaɪvz] **1** EXISTENCE : vie *f*, existence *f* **2** : vie *f* <his adult life : sa vie adulte> <plant life : la flore> <way of life : mode de vie> **3** BIOGRAPHY : biographie *f* **4** DURATION : durée *f* (d'une machine, etc.) **5** LIVELINESS : vie *f*, animation *f*

lifeblood [ˈlaɪfˌblʌd] *n* : force *f* vitale

lifeboat [ˈlaɪfˌboːt] *n* : canot *m* de sauvetage

lifeguard [ˈlaɪfˌgɑrd] *n* : surveillant *m*, -lante *f* de baignade

lifeless [ˈlaɪfləs] *adj* : inanimé, sans vie

lifelike [ˈlaɪfˌlaɪk] *adj* : ressemblant

lifelong [ˈlaɪfˈlɔŋ] *adj* : de toute la vie

life preserver *n* : gilet *m* de sauvetage

lifesaver [ˈlaɪfˌseɪvər] *n* **1** → **lifeguard 2 to be a lifesaver** : sauver la vie à qqn

lifesaving [ˈlaɪfˌseɪvɪŋ] *n* : sauvetage *m*

lifestyle [ˈlaɪfˌstaɪl] *n* : mode *m* de vie

lifetime [ˈlaɪfˌtaɪm] *n* : vie *f* <a lifetime of regrets : toute une vie de regrets>

lift[1] [ˈlɪft] *vt* **1** RAISE : lever, soulever **2** END : lever <to lift a ban : lever une interdiction> **3** BOOST : remonter — *vi* **1** CLEAR UP : se dissiper <the fog has lifted : la brume s'est dissipée> **2** *or* **to lift off** : décoller (se dit d'un avion, etc.)

lift[2] *n* **1** LIFTING : soulèvement *m* **2** BOOST : encouragement *m*, stimulation *f* <to give s.o.'s spirits a lift : remonter le moral à qqn> **3** *Brit* → **elevator 4 to give s.o. a lift** : emmener qqn en voiture

liftoff [ˈlɪftˌɔf] *n* : lancement *m* (en aéronautique)

ligament [ˈlɪgəmənt] *n* : ligament *m*

ligature [ˈlɪgəˌtʃʊr, -tʃər] *n* : ligature *f*

light[1] [ˈlaɪt] *v* **lit** [ˈlɪt] *or* **lighted; lighting** *vt* **1** : allumer (un feu) **2** GUIDE : éclairer, illuminer <to light the way : éclairer le chemin> — *vi* **1** BRIGHTEN : s'éclairer, s'illuminer **2** ALIGHT : se poser **3** DISMOUNT : descendre

light[2] *adv* : légèrement <to travel light : voyager avec peu de bagages>

light[3] *adj* **1** BRIGHT : clair **2** PALE : pâle <light blue : bleu pâle> **3** LIGHTWEIGHT : léger **4** GENTLE : léger <a light breeze : une brise légère> <a light rain : une pluie fine> **5** EASY : léger, facile <light reading : quelque chose de facile à lire> <light work : des travaux peu fatigants>

light[4] *n* **1** : lumière *f* <ray of light : rayon de lumière> **2** DAYLIGHT : lumière *f* du jour **3** LAMP : lumière *f* **4** ASPECT : jour *m*, lumière *f* <in a different light : sous un autre jour> <in the light of recent developments : à la lumière des derniers événements> **5** FLAME : feu *m* <do you have a light? : as-tu du feu?> **6** → **traffic light 7 lights** *npl* : phares *mpl* (d'une voiture)

lightbulb [ˈlaɪtˌbʌlb] *n* : ampoule *f*

lighten [ˈlaɪtən] *vt* **1** BRIGHTEN : éclairer (les esprits, une salle, les cheveux) **2** ALLEVIATE, RELIEVE : alléger, soulager — *vi* : s'éclairer

lighter [ˈlaɪtər] *n* : briquet *m*

lighthearted [ˈlaɪtˌhɑrṭəd] *adj* : allègre, joyeux — **lightheartedly** *adv*

lighthouse [ˈlaɪtˌhaʊs] *n* : phare *m*

lightly [ˈlaɪtli] *adv* **1** GENTLY : légèrement **2** FRIVOLOUSLY : à la légère, légèrement **3 to get off lightly** : s'en tirer à bon compte

lightness [ˈlaɪtnəs] *n* **1** : légèreté *f* **2** BRIGHTNESS : clarté *f*

lightning [ˈlaɪtnɪŋ] *n* : éclairs *mpl*, foudre *f*

lightning bug → **firefly**

lightproof [ˈlaɪtˌpruːf] *adj* : à l'épreuve de la lumière

lightweight [ˈlaɪtˌweɪt] *adj* : léger <lightweight fabric : tissu léger>

light–year [ˈlaɪtˌjɪr] *n* : année-lumière *f*

lignite [ˈlɪgˌnaɪt] *n* : lignite *m*

likable *or* **likeable** [ˈlaɪkəbəl] *adj* : agréable, sympathique

like[1] [ˈlaɪk] *v* **liked; liking** *vt* **1** ENJOY : aimer <he likes tennis : il aime le tennis> **2** WANT : aimer, vouloir <I would like a drink of water : j'aimerais un verre d'eau> — *vi* CHOOSE, PREFER : vouloir, plaire <if you like : si vous voulez>

like[2] *adj* SIMILAR : pareil, semblable

like[3] *n* **1** LIKING, PREFERENCE : goût *m* <our likes and dislikes : ce que nous aimons et ce que nous n'aimons pas> **2 the like** : une chose pareille <I've never seen the like : je n'ai jamais rien vu de pareil> <cats, dogs,

and the like : des chats, des chiens et d'autres animaux de ce genre>

like[4] *conj* **1** AS : comme <she talks exactly like I do : elle parle exactement comme moi> **2** AS IF : comme si <he acted like he was cold : il s'est conduit comme s'il avait froid> <it looks like it might rain : on dirait qu'il va pleuvoir>

like[5] *prep* **1** : comme <you're not like the rest of them : tu n'es pas comme les autres> <it's just like her to be late : c'est bien son genre d'être en retard> **2** SUCH AS : comme, tel que <a city like Chicago : une ville telle que Chicago>

likelihood ['laɪkli,hʊd] *n* : probabilité *f*

likely[1] ['laɪkli] *adv* : probablement <most likely : très probablement>

likely[2] *adj* **likelier; -est 1** PROBABLE : probable **2** BELIEVABLE : plausible, vraisemblable <a likely excuse! : une belle excuse!> **3** PROMISING : prometteur

liken ['laɪkən] *vt* : comparer

likeness ['laɪknəs] *n* **1** SIMILARITY : ressemblance *f* **2** PORTRAIT : portrait *m*

likewise ['laɪk,waɪz] *adv* **1** SIMILARLY : de même <do likewise : fais de même> **2** ALSO : de plus, aussi

liking ['laɪkɪŋ] *n* **1** LEANING, TASTE : goût *m,* penchant *m* **2** FONDNESS : affection *f* <to take a liking to : se prendre d'affection pour>

lilac ['laɪlək, -læk, -lɑk] *n* : lilas *m*

lilt ['lɪlt] *n* : rythme *m,* cadence *f* (en musique), intonation *f* (de la voix)

lily ['lɪli] *n, pl* **lilies** : lis *m,* lys *m*

lima bean ['laɪmə] *n* : haricot *m* de Lima

limb ['lɪm] *n* **1** : membre *m* (en anatomie) **2** BRANCH : branche *f* (d'un arbre)

limber[1] ['lɪmbər] *vt or* **to limber up** : assouplir — *vi* **to limber up** : s'échauffer

limber[2] *adj* : souple, agile

limbo ['lɪm,bo:] *n, pl* **-bos 1** : limbes *mpl* (en religion) **2** UNCERTAINTY : incertitude *f,* état *m* d'incertitude

lime ['laɪm] *n* **1** : chaux *m* (en agriculture) **2** : citron *m* vert (fruit)

limelight ['laɪm,laɪt] *n* **to be in the limelight** : être en vedette, avoir la vedette

limerick ['lɪmərɪk] *n* : petit poème *m* humoristique

limestone ['laɪm,sto:n] *n* : calcaire *m*

limit[1] ['lɪmət] *vt* : limiter

limit[2] *n* **1** BOUNDARY : limite *f* **2** RESTRICTION : limitation *f*

limitation [,lɪmə'teɪʃən] *n* : limitation *f,* restriction *f*

limitless ['lɪmətləs] *adj* : illimité

limousine ['lɪmə,zi:n, ,lɪmə'-] *n* : limousine *f*

limp[1] ['lɪmp] *vi* : boiter

limp[2] *adj* : mou, flasque

limp[3] *n* : boiterie *f,* claudication *f*

limpid ['lɪmpəd] *adj* : limpide, transparent

limply ['lɪmpli] *adv* : mollement

limpness ['lɪmpnəs] *n* : mollesse *f*

linden ['lɪndən] *n* : tilleul *m*

line[1] ['laɪn] *v* **lined; lining** *vt* **1** : ligner <lined paper : papier ligné> **2** BORDER : border <lined with trees : bordé d'arbres> **3** : doubler (un vêtement) **4** ALIGN : aligner, mettre en ligne — *vi* **to line up** : se mettre en ligne, faire la queue

line[2] *n* **1** ROPE : cordage *m,* corde *f* **2** CABLE, WIRE : ligne *f* <power line : ligne à haute tension> **3** *or* **telephone line** : ligne *f* de téléphone <the line has gone dead : il n'y a plus de tonalité> **4** ROW : rangée *f* **5** QUEUE : file *f,* queue *f,* filée *f Can fam* **6** NOTE : mot *m* <drop me a line : écris-moi un mot> **7** ORIENTATION, OUTLOOK : ligne *f* **8** AGREEMENT : accord *m* <to be in line with s.o. : être conforme à qqn> **9** JOB, OCCUPATION : métier *m* **10** LINEAGE : lignée *f,* descendance *f* **11** ROUTE : ligne *f* <bus line : ligne d'autobus> **12** WRINKLE : ride *f* **13** RANGE : gamme *f* (de produits) **14** MARK : ligne *f* <dotted line : ligne pointillée> **15** *or* **dividing line** LIMIT : limite *f* **16** → **online**

lineage ['lɪniɪdʒ] *n* : lignée *f,* descendance *f*

lineal ['lɪniəl] *adj* : en ligne directe

lineaments ['lɪniəmənts] *npl* : linéaments *mpl,* traits *mpl*

linear ['lɪniər] *adj* : linéaire

linen ['lɪnən] *n* : lin *m*

liner ['laɪnər] *n* **1** LINING : doublure *f* **2** : paquebot *m* (navire), gros-porteur *m* (avion)

lineup ['laɪn,əp] *n* **1** : séance *f* d'identification de suspects **2** : équipe *f* (aux sports) **3** : composition *f* (d'un programme, etc.)

linger ['lɪŋgər] *vi* **1** TARRY : s'attarder **2** PERSIST : persister, persévérer

lingerie [,lɑndʒə'reɪ, ,lænʒə'ri:] *n* : lingerie *f*

lingo ['lɪŋgo] *n, pl* **-goes 1** LANGUAGE : langue *f* (du pays) **2** JARGON : jargon *m*

linguist ['lɪŋgwɪst] *n* : linguiste *mf*

linguistic [lɪŋ'gwɪstɪk] *adj* : linguistique

linguistics [lɪŋ'gwɪstɪks] *n* : linguistique *f*

liniment ['lɪnəmənt] *n* : liniment *m,* onguent *m*

lining ['laɪnɪŋ] *n* : doublure *f*

link[1] ['lɪŋk] *vt* : relier, lier — *vi or* **to link up** : s'associer, se rejoindre

link[2] *n* **1** : maillon *m* (d'une chaîne) **2** BOND : lien *m,* rapport *m* **3** : liaison *f* <satellite link : liaison satellite>

linkage [ˈlɪŋkɪdʒ] *n* LINK : lien *m,* rapport *m*
linoleum [ləˈnoːliəm] *n* : linoléum *m,* prélart *m Can*
linseed oil [ˈlɪnˌsiːd] *n* : huile *f* de lin
lint [ˈlɪnt] *n* : peluches *fpl*
lintel [ˈlɪntəl] *n* : linteau *m*
lion [ˈlaɪən] *n* : lion *m*
lioness [ˈlaɪənɪs] *n* : lionne *f*
lionize [ˈlaɪəˌnaɪz] *vt* **-ized; -izing** : aduler, fêter comme une célébrité
lip [ˈlɪp] *n* **1** : lèvre *f* <the upper lip : la lèvre supérieure> **2** EDGE, RIM : bord *m,* rebord *m*
lipreading [ˈlɪpˌriːdɪŋ] *n* : lecture *f* sur les lèvres
lipstick [ˈlɪpˌstɪk] *n* : rouge *m* à lèvres
liquefy [ˈlɪkwəˌfaɪ] *v* **-fied; -fying** *vt* : liquéfier — *vi* : se liquéfier
liqueur [lɪˈkər, -ˈkʊr, -ˈkjʊr] *n* : liqueur *f*
liquid[1] [ˈlɪkwəd] *adj* : liquide
liquid[2] *n* : liquide *m*
liquidate [ˈlɪkwəˌdeɪt] *vt* **-dated; -dating** : liquider
liquidation [ˌlɪkwəˈdeɪʃən] *n* : liquidation *f*
liquidity [lɪkˈwɪdət̬i] *n* : liquidité *f*
liquor [ˈlɪkər] *n* : alcool *m,* boissons *fpl* alcoolisées
liquorice *Brit* → **licorice**
lisp[1] [ˈlɪsp] *vi* : zézayer
lisp[2] *n* : zézaiement *m*
lissome [ˈlɪsəm] *adj* : souple, agile
list[1] [ˈlɪst] *vt* **1** ENUMERATE : énumérer **2** : mettre sur une liste — *vi* TILT : donner de la bande, gîter (se dit d'un bateau)
list[2] *n* **1** : liste *f* **2** SLANT : gîte *f,* bande *f* (d'un bateau)
listen [ˈlɪsən] *vi* **1 to listen to** HEAR : écouter <listen to the rain : écoutez la pluie> **2 to listen to** HEED : tenir compte de, écouter
listener [ˈlɪsənər] *n* : personne *f* qui écoute <he's a good listener : il sait écouter les autres>
listless [ˈlɪstləs] *adj* : apathique, amorphe
listlessly [ˈlɪstləsli] *adv* : avec apathie, sans énergie
listlessness [ˈlɪstləsnəs] *n* : apathie *f,* manque *m* d'énergie
lit [ˈlɪt] → **light[1]**
litany [ˈlɪtəni] *n, pl* **-nies** : litanie *f*
liter [ˈliːt̬ər] *n* : litre *m*
literacy [ˈlɪt̬ərəsi] *n* **1** : capacité *f* de lire et d'écrire **2 literacy campaign** : campagne *f* d'alphabétisation
literal [ˈlɪt̬ərəl] *adj* : littéral — **literally** *adv*
literary [ˈlɪt̬əˌrɛri] *adj* : littéraire
literate [ˈlɪt̬ərət] *adj* : qui sait lire et écrire
literature [ˈlɪt̬ərəˌtʃʊr, -tʃər] *n* : littérature *f*
lithe [ˈlaɪð, ˈlaɪθ] *adj* : souple, agile
lithesome [ˈlaɪðsəm, ˈlaɪθ-] → **lissome**
lithium [ˈlɪθiəm] *n* : lithium *m*
lithograph [ˈlɪθəˌgræf] *n* : lithographie *f*
lithographer [lɪˈθɑgrəfər, ˈlɪθəˌgræfər] *n* : lithographe *mf*
lithography [lɪˈθɑgrəfi] *n* : lithographie *f* — **lithographic** [ˌlɪθəˈgræfɪk] *adj*
Lithuanian[1] [ˌlɪθəˈweɪniən, -njən] *adj* : lituanien
Lithuanian[2] *n* **1** : Lituanien *m,* -nienne *f* **2** : lituanien *m* (langue)
litigant [ˈlɪt̬ɪgənt] *n* : plaideur *m,* -deuse *f*
litigate [ˈlɪt̬əˌgeɪt] *v* **-gated; -gating** *vi* : plaider — *vt* : mettre en litige
litigation [ˌlɪt̬əˈgeɪʃən] *n* : litige *m*
litmus paper [ˈlɪtməs] *n* : papier *m* de tournesol
litre → **liter**
litter[1] [ˈlɪt̬ər] *vt* : mettre du désordre dans, laisser des détritus dans
litter[2] *n* **1** : portée *f* <a litter of puppies : une portée de chiots> **2** STRETCHER : brancard *m,* civière *f* **3** RUBBISH : détritus *mpl* **4** *or* **kitty litter** : litière *f* (de chat)
little[1] [ˈlɪt̬əl] *adv* **less** [ˈlɛs]; **least** [ˈliːst] **1** RARELY : peu <she sings very little these days : elle chante tres peu ces temps-ci> **2 little did I think that . . .** : jamais j'aurais cru que . . . **3 as little as possible** : le moins possible
little[2] *adj* **littler** *or* **less** [ˈlɛs] *or* **lesser** [ˈlɛsər]; **littlest** *or* **least** [ˈliːst] **1** SMALL : petit <little feet : petits pieds> **2** : peu de <very little money : bien peu d'argent> <little time : peu de temps> **3** YOUNG : petit, jeune <my little brother : mon petit frère> **4** TRIVIAL : insignifiant, sans importance
little[3] *n* **1** : peu *m* <I'm happy with little : je me contente de peu> **2 a little** SOMEWHAT : un peu
Little Dipper → **dipper**
liturgical [ləˈtərdʒɪkəl] *adj* : liturgique
liturgy [ˈlɪt̬ərdʒi] *n, pl* **-gies** : liturgie *f*
livable [ˈlɪvəbəl] *adj* **1** INHABITABLE : habitable **2** ENDURABLE : supportable
live[1] [ˈlɪv] *v* **lived; living** *vi* **1** : être vivant, vivre **2** DWELL : demeurer, habiter **3 to live on** : vivre de, se nourrir de **4 to live for** : vivre pour — *vt* : vivre <to live one's life : vivre sa vie>
live[2] [ˈlaɪv] *adj* **1** LIVING : vivant **2** BURNING : ardent <live coals : charbons ardents> **3** : sous tension <live circuits : circuits sous tension> **4** : non explosé <a live bomb : une bombe non explosée> **5** : d'actualité <live issues : sujets d'actualité> **6** : en direct <a live interview : une entrevue en direct>
livelihood [ˈlaɪvliˌhʊd] *n* : moyens *mpl* de subsistance
liveliness [ˈlaɪvlinəs] *n* : vivacité *f,* entrain *m*
livelong [ˈlɪvˈlɔŋ] *adj* **all the livelong day** : tout au long de la journée

lively [ˈlaɪvli] *adj* **livelier; -est** : vif, vivant, entraînant, enlevant *Can*

liven [ˈlaɪvən] *vt* ENLIVEN : animer, égayer — *vi* : s'animer, s'égayer

liver [ˈlɪvər] *n* : foie *m*

liveried [ˈlɪvəri:d, ˈlɪvri:d] *adj* : en livrée

livery [ˈlɪvəri] *n, pl* **-eries 1** UNIFORM : livrée *f* **2** : pension *f* (pour un cheval)

lives → **life**

livestock [ˈlaɪv,stɑk] *n* : bétail *m*

livid [ˈlɪvəd] *adj* **1** BLACK-AND-BLUE : couvert de bleus **2** PALE : livide, blême **3** ENRAGED : furibond, en rage

living[1] [ˈlɪvɪŋ] *adj* : vivant

living[2] *n* **to earn one's living** : gagner sa vie

living room *n* : salle *f* de séjour, salon *m*

lizard [ˈlɪzərd] *n* : lézard *m*

llama [ˈlɑmə, ˈjɑ-] *n* : lama *m*

load[1] [ˈlo:d] *vt* **1** : charger <to load a truck : charger un camion> **2** : charger (un fusil, un appareil photo, etc.) **3 to be loaded (down) with** : être chargé de, être plein de

load[2] *n* **1** CARGO : chargement *m*, cargaison *f* **2** WEIGHT : charge *f* **3** BURDEN : fardeau *m*, poids *m* **4 loads of** : beaucoup <loads of work : beaucoup de travail>

loaf[1] [ˈlo:f] *vi* : fainéanter, paresser

loaf[2] *n, pl* **loaves** [ˈlo:vz] : pain *m* <a loaf of bread : un pain>

loafer [ˈlo:fər] *n* : fainéant *m*, fainéante *f*

loam [ˈlo:m] *n* : terreau *m*

loan[1] [ˈlo:n] *vt* : prêter

loan[2] *n* : emprunt *m*, prêt *m*

loath [ˈlo:θ, ˈlo:ð] *adj* : peu enclin, peu disposé

loathe [ˈlo:ð] *vt* **loathed; loathing** : détester, haïr

loathing [ˈlo:ðɪŋ] *n* : aversion *f*, répugnance *f*

loathsome [ˈlo:θsəm, ˈlo:ð-] *adj* : répugnant, dégoûtant

lob[1] [ˈlɑb] *v* **lobbed; lobbing** : lober (aux sports)

lob[2] *n* : lob *m*

lobby[1] [ˈlɑbi] *v* **-bied; -bying** *vt* : faire des pressions sur (en politique) — *vi* : faire pression

lobby[2] *n, pl* **-bies 1** : hall *m*, vestibule *m* <hotel lobby : hall d'hôtel> **2** LOBBYISTS : groupe *m* de pression

lobbyist [ˈlɑbiɪst] *n* : membre *m* d'un groupe de pression

lobe [ˈlo:b] *n* : lobe *m*

lobster [ˈlɑbstər] *n* : homard *m*

local[1] [ˈlo:kəl] *adj* : local — **locally** *adv*

local[2] *n* **1** : omnibus *m* local, train *m* local **2 locals** *npl* : gens *mpl* du pays, personnes *fpl* du coin

locale [loˈkæl] *n* **1** PLACE : endroit *m*, lieu *m* **2** SETTING : scène *f*

locality [loˈkæləṭi] *n, pl* **-ties** : localité *f*

localization [ˌlo:kələˈzeɪʃən] *n* : localisation *f*

localize [ˈlo:kəˌlaɪz] *vt* **-ized; -izing** : localiser

locate [ˈlo:ˌkeɪt] *v* **-cated; -cating** *vi* SETTLE : s'établir — *vt* **1** POSITION, SITUATE : situer **2** FIND : trouver, localiser

location [loˈkeɪʃən] *n* **1** POSITION : emplacement *m*, site *m* **2** PLACE : endroit *m* **3 on ~** : en extérieur <filmed on location : tourné en extérieur>

lock[1] [ˈlɑk] *vt* **1** : fermer à clé, verrouiller, barrer *Can* <lock the door : verrouillez la porte> **2** CONFINE : enfermer **3** GRIP : bloquer (un mécanisme) **4** HOLD : serrer <to be locked in an embrace : être enlacé> — *vi* **1** : se fermer à clé **2** : se bloquer (se dit des freins, etc.)

lock[2] *n* **1** : mèche *f*, boucle *f* <a lock of hair : une mèche de cheveux> **2** : serrure *f* (d'une porte, etc.) **3** : écluse *f* (dans un canal)

locker [ˈlɑkər] *n* : vestiaire *m*

locket [ˈlɑkət] *n* : médaillon *m* (bijou)

lockjaw [ˈlɑkˌjɔ] *n* : tétanos *m*

lockout [ˈlɑkˌaʊt] *n* : lock-out *m*

locksmith [ˈlɑkˌsmɪθ] *n* : serrurier *m*

locomotion [ˌlo:kəˈmo:ʃən] *n* : locomotion *f*

locomotive[1] [ˌlo:kəˈmo:ṭɪv] *adj* : locomoteur

locomotive[2] *n* : locomotive *f*

locust [ˈlo:kəst] *n* **1** : criquet *m* migrateur (insecte) **2** *or* **locust tree** : caroubier *m*

locution [loˈkju:ʃən] *n* : locution *f*

lode [ˈlo:d] *n* : veine *f*, filon *m*

lodestone [ˈlo:dˌsto:n] *n* : magnétite *f*

lodge[1] [ˈlɑdʒ] *v* **lodged; lodging** *vt* **1** HOUSE : loger, héberger **2** FILE : déposer <to lodge a complaint : porter plainte> — *vi* : se loger <the bullet was lodged in a tree : la balle s'est logée dans un arbre>

lodge[2] *n* **1** : pavillon *m* <hunting lodge : pavillon de chasse> **2** : abri *m* (d'un animal) **3** : loge *f* (de francs-maçons)

lodger [ˈlɑdʒər] *n* : locataire *mf*, pensionnaire *mf*

lodging [ˈlɑdʒɪŋ] *n* **1** : hébergement *m* **2 lodgings** *npl* : logement *m*

loft [ˈlɔft] *n* **1** ATTIC : grenier *m* **2** *or* **hayloft** : grenier *m* à foin **3** GALLERY : tribune *f* <choir loft : tribune de la chorale>

lofty [ˈlɔfti] *adj* **loftier; -est 1** NOBLE : noble **2** HAUGHTY : fier, hautain **3** HIGH : haut, élevé

log[1] [ˈlɔg, ˈlɑg] *vt* **logged; logging 1** : abattre, tronçonner (des arbres) **2** RECORD : noter, consigner (des renseignements)

log[2] *n* **1** : rondin *m*, bûche *f*, billot *m* *Can* **2** RECORD : journal *m* de bord (d'un avion, d'un navire)

logarithm [ˈlɔgəˌrɪðəm, ˈlɑ-] *n* : logarithme *m*

logger [ˈlɔgər, ˈlɑ-] *n* : bûcheron *m*, -ronne *f*

loggerhead [ˈlɔgərˌhɛd, ˈlɑ-] *n* **to be at loggerheads** : être en désaccord

logic [ˈlɑdʒɪk] *n* : logique *f*

logical [ˈlɑdʒɪkəl] *adj* : logique — **logically** [-kli] *adv*

logician [loˈdʒɪʃən] *n* : logicien *m*, -cienne *f*

logistic [ləˈdʒɪstɪk, lo-] *adj* : logistique

logistics [ləˈdʒɪstɪks, lo-] *ns & pl* : logistique *f*

logo [ˈloːˌgoː] *n, pl* **logos** [-ˌgoːz] : logo *m*

loin [ˈlɔɪn] *n* **1** : longe *f* (de porc, etc.) **2 loins** *npl* : reins *mpl* (en anatomie)

loiter [ˈlɔɪt̬ər] *vi* : traîner, lambiner *fam*

loiterer [ˈlɔɪt̬ərər] *n* : flâneur *m*, -neuse *f*

loll [ˈlɑl] *vi* LOUNGE : se prélasser

lollipop *or* **lollypop** [ˈlɑliˌpɑp] *n* : sucette *f France*, suçon *m Can*

lone [ˈloːn] *adj* **1** SOLITARY : seul, solitaire **2** SOLE : seul, unique

loneliness [ˈloːnlinəs] *n* : solitude *f*

lonely [ˈloːnli] *adj* **lonelier; -est 1** SOLITARY : solitaire, isolé **2** LONESOME : seul

loner [ˈloːnər] *n* : solitaire *mf*

lonesome [ˈloːnsəm] *adj* : seul

long[1] [ˈlɔŋ] *vi* **to long for** : désirer, avoir envie de

long[2] *adv* **1** : longtemps <long ago : il y a longtemps> **2 all day long** : toute la journée **3 as long as** *or* **so long as** : aussi longtemps que **4 so long!** : à bientôt!

long[3] *adj* **longer** [ˈlɔŋgər]; **longest** [ˈlɔŋgəst] **1** (*indicating length*) : long <a long road : une route longue> <10 feet long : 10 pieds de long> **2** (*indicating time*) : long <a long silence : un long silence> <how long is the trip? : combien de temps durera le voyage?> **3 to be long on** : avoir beaucoup de

long[4] *n* **1 before long** : dans peu de temps **2 the long and short** : l'essentiel *m*

longevity [lɑnˈdʒɛvət̬i] *n* : longévité *f*

longhand [ˈlɔŋˌhænd] *n* : écriture *f* normale <written in longhand : écrit à la main>

longhorn [ˈlɔŋˌhɔrn] *n* : longhorn *mf*

longing [ˈlɔŋɪŋ] *n* : désir *m*, envie *f*

longingly [ˈlɔŋɪŋli] *adj* : avec désir, avec envie

longitude [ˈlɑndʒəˌtuːd, -ˌtjuːd] *n* : longitude *f*

longitudinal [ˌlɑndʒəˈtuːdənəl, -ˈtjuːd-] *adj* : longitudinal — **longitudinally** *adv*

longshoreman [ˈlɔŋˈʃormən] *n, pl* **-men** [-mən, -ˌmɛn] : débardeur *m*, docker *m*

look[1] [ˈlʊk] *vi* **1** SEE : regarder <look, here he comes! : regarde, le voici!> **2** SEEM : sembler <it looks unlikely : cela semble peu probable> **3** FACE : être exposé, être orienté <the house looks east : la maison est exposée à l'est> **4 to look after** : prendre soin de **5 to look for** EXPECT : attendre **6 to look for** SEEK : chercher **7 to look upon** CONSIDER : considérer, regarder — *vt* : regarder <to look s.o. in the eye : regarder qqn dans les yeux>

look[2] *n* **1** : coup *m* d'œil <to take a look around : jeter un coup d'œil> **2** EXPRESSION : apparence *f*, mine *f* **3** ASPECT : aspect *m*, air *m*

lookout [ˈlʊkˌaʊt] *n* **1** WATCHMAN : guetteur *m*, sentinelle *f* **2** WATCH : guet *m* <to be on the lookout : faire le guet>

loom[1] [ˈluːm] *vi* **1** APPEAR : surgir **2** APPROACH : être imminent **3 to loom large** : menacer

loom[2] *n* : métier *m* à tisser

loon [ˈluːn] *n* : plongeon *m*, huard *m Can*

loony *or* **looney** [ˈluːni] *adj* **loonier; -est** : dingue *fam*, fou

loop[1] [ˈluːp] *vt* : boucler — *vi* : faire une boucle

loop[2] *n* : boucle *f*

loophole [ˈluːpˌhoːl] *n* : échappatoire *m*, lacune *f*

loose[1] [ˈluːs] *v* **loosed; loosing** *vt* **1** RELEASE : libérer **2** UNTIE : défaire **3** UNLEASH : déchaîner (la colère, etc.)

loose[2] *adj* **looser; -est 1** : qui bouge, mal fixé <a loose tooth : une dent qui bouge> <a loose board : une planche mal fixée>**2** SLACK : lâche, mou, lousse *Can fam* **3** ROOMY : ample, flottant **4** APPROXIMATE : libre, peu exact **5** FREE : échappé, évadé <the horse is loose : le cheval s'est échappé> **6** FRIABLE : meuble <loose soil : terre meuble> **7** : mobile, volant <loose sheets of paper : feuilles mobiles> **8** : dissolu <loose conduct : conduite dissolue>

loosely [ˈluːsli] *adv* **1** : sans serrer **2** APPROXIMATELY : approximativement

loosen [ˈluːsən] *vt* : desserrer, relâcher

looseness [ˈluːsnəs] *n* : relâchement *m* (d'une corde), ampleur *f* (d'un vêtement)

loot[1] [ˈluːt] *vi* : piller

loot[2] *n* : butin *m*

looter [ˈluːt̬ər] *n* : pillard *m*, -larde *f*

lop [ˈlɑp] *vt* **lopped; lopping** PRUNE : élaguer, tailler

lope[1] [ˈloːp] *vi* **loped; loping 1** : courir en bondissant (se dit d'un animal) **2 to lope away** : partir à grandes foulées

lope[2] *n* : course *f* (d'un animal), pas *m* de course (d'une personne)

lopsided [ˈlɑpˌsaɪdəd] *adj* **1** CROOKED : de travers **2** ASYMMETRICAL : asymétrique

loquacious [loˈkweɪʃəs] *adj* : loquace, bavard

loquacity [lo'kwæsəṭi] *n* : loquacité *f*

lord ['lɔrd] *n* **1** : seigneur *m* <his lord and master : son seigneur et maître> **2** : lord *m* <Lord Carrington : Lord Carrington> **3 the Lord** : le Seigneur

lordly ['lɔrdli] *adj* **lordlier; -est** : hautain, altier

lordship ['lɔrd,ʃɪp] *n* **Your Lordship** : Monsieur le comte, Monsieur le juge, etc.

Lord's Supper *n* : Eucharistie *f*

lore ['lor] *n* : traditions *fpl*, coutumes *fpl*

lose ['lu:z] *v* **lost** ['lɔst]; **losing** ['lu:zɪŋ] *vt* **1** : perdre <I've lost my keys : j'ai perdu mes clés> <to lose weight : perdre du poids> <to lose one's way : perdre son chemin> **2** : faire perdre <the errors lost him his job : les erreurs lui ont fait perdre son emploi> **3** : retarder de <my watch loses three minutes a day : ma montre retarde de trois minutes par jour> — *vi* **1** : perdre **2** : retarder (se dit des horloges, etc.)

loser ['lu:zər] *n* : perdant *m*, -dante *f*

loss ['lɔs] *n* **1** : perte *f* <loss of sight : perte de vue> <it's no great loss : ce n'est pas une grosse perte> **2** : déperdition *f*, perte *f* <loss of heat : déperdition de chaleur> **3 losses** *npl* : pertes *fpl*, victimes *fpl* (de la guerre) **4 to be at a loss for words** : ne pas savoir quoi dire

lost ['lɔst] *adj* **1** MISSED : perdu, manqué <a lost opportunity : une occasion manquée> **2** : perdu, égaré <a lost child : un enfant perdu> <to get lost : se perdre> **3** BEWILDERED : perdu, désorienté **4 to be lost in thought** : être absorbé par ses pensées, être plongé dans la réflexion

lot ['lɑt] *n* **1** : tirage *m* <to draw lots : tirer au sort> **2** SHARE : part *m*, partage *m* **3** FATE : lot *m*, destin *m*, sort *m* **4** PLOT : lot *m*, parcelle *f* (de terrain) **5 a lot** : beaucoup <a lot of money : beaucoup d'argent> **6 a lot** OFTEN : souvent

loth ['lo:θ, 'lo:ð] → **loath**

lotion ['lo:ʃən] *n* : lotion *f*

lottery ['lɑṭəri] *n, pl* **-teries** : loterie *f*

lotus ['lo:ṭəs] *n* : lotus *m*

loud[1] ['laʊd] *adv* : fort <to think out loud : penser tout haut>

loud[2] *adj* **1** : fort, grand <loud music : musique forte> <a loud cry : un grand cri> **2** FLASHY : criard, voyant

loudly ['laʊdli] *adv* : bruyamment

loudness ['laʊdnəs] *n* : force *f*, intensité *f*

loudspeaker ['laʊd,spi:kər] *n* : haut-parleur *m*

lounge[1] ['laʊndʒ] *vi* **lounged; lounging** : flâner, paresser

lounge[2] *n* : salon *m*

louse ['laʊs] *n, pl* **lice** ['laɪs] : pou *m*

lousy ['laʊzi] *adj* **lousier; -est 1** : pouilleux, couvert de poux **2** POOR, SORRY : piètre, mauvais <lousy results : de piètres résultats>

lout ['laʊt] *n* : rustre *m*

louver *or* **louvre** ['lu:vər] *n* **1** SLAT : lame *f* **2** *or* **louver window** : persienne *f*, jalousie *f*

lovable ['lʌvəbəl] *adj* : adorable, charmant

love[1] ['lʌv] *v* **loved; loving** *vt* **1** CHERISH : aimer **2** LIKE : aimer, adorer *fam* <he loved to play the violin : il adorait jouer du violon> — *vi* : aimer

love[2] *n* **1** : amour *m* <to fall in love : être amoureux> **2** ENTHUSIASM, INTEREST : amour *m*, passion *f* **3** BELOVED : amour *m*

loveless ['lʌvləs] *adj* : sans amour

loveliness ['lʌvlinəs] *n* : beauté *f*, charme *f*

lovelorn ['lʌv,lɔrn] *adj* : malheureux en amour, privé d'amour

lovely ['lʌvli] *adj* **lovelier; -est 1** ATTRACTIVE : beau, joli **2** ENJOYABLE : agréable <we had a lovely time : ce fut très agréable>

lover ['lʌvər] *n* : amant *m*, -mante *f*

lovingly ['lʌvɪŋli] *adv* : affectueusement, tendrement

low[1] ['lo:] *vi* : meugler

low[2] *adv* : bas <aim low : visez bas>

low[3] *adj* **lower; lowest 1** : bas <a low wall : un mur bas> <low prices : des bas prix> **2** HUMBLE : modeste <of low birth : d'origine modeste> **3** DEPRESSED : démoralisé, déprimé **4** POOR, INFERIOR : faible <low income : faible revenu> **5** UNFAVORABLE : piètre

low[4] *n* **1** : bas *m* <to reach a low : atteindre un bas> **2** *or* **low gear** : première *f* **3** MOO : meuglement *m*

lowbrow ['lo:,braʊ] *n* : personne *f* peu intellectuelle

lower[1] ['laʊər, 'lo:ər] *vi* **1** SCOWL : se renfrogner **2** DARKEN : s'assombrir

lower[2] ['lo:ər] *vt* **1** : baisser <to lower one's eyes : baisser les yeux> **2** REDUCE : baisser, diminuer **3 to lower oneself** : s'abaisser, s'humilier — *vi* DROP, DIMINISH : baisser

lower[3] *adj* : inférieur, bas

lowland ['lo:lənd, -,lænd] *n* : plaine *f*, basse terre *f*

lowly ['lo:li] *adj* **lowlier; -est** : humble, modeste

loyal ['lɔɪəl] *adj* : loyal, fidèle — **loyally** *adv*

loyalist ['lɔɪəlɪst] *n* : loyaliste *mf*

loyalty ['lɔɪəlti] *n, pl* **-ties** : loyauté *f*

lozenge ['lɑzəndʒ] *n* : pastille *f*

LSD [,ɛl,ɛs'di:] *n* : LSD *m*

lubricant ['lu:brɪkənt] *n* : lubrifiant *m*

lubricate ['lu:brə,keɪt] *vt* **-cated; -cating** : lubrifier

lubrication [,lu:brə'keɪʃən] *n* : lubrification *f*

lucid [ˈluːsəd] *adj* : lucide, clair — **lucidly** *adv*

lucidity [luːˈsɪdət̬i] *n* : lucidité *f*

luck [ˈlʌk] *n* **1** FORTUNE : chance *f*, fortune *f* <good luck! : bonne chance!> **2** CHANCE, OPPORTUNITY : hasard *m*, chance *f* <a stroke of luck : un heureux hasard> <as luck would have it : par hasard> <to be out of luck : ne pas avoir de chance>

luckily [ˈlʌkəli] *adv* : heureusement, par bonheur

luckless [ˈlʌkləs] *adj* : malchanceux

lucky [ˈlʌki] *adj* **luckier; -est** **1** FORTUNATE : chanceux **2** FORTUITOUS : heureux, fortuné **3** : de chance, porte-bonheur <my lucky day : mon jour de chance>

lucrative [ˈluːkrət̬ɪv] *adj* : lucratif

ludicrous [ˈluːdəkrəs] *adj* : ridicule, insensé — **ludicrously** *adv*

lug [ˈlʌg] *vt* **lugged; lugging** : traîner, trimbaler *fam*

luggage [ˈlʌgɪdʒ] *n* : bagages *mpl*

lugubrious [lʊˈguːbriəs] *adj* : lugubre — **lugubriously** *adv*

lukewarm [ˈluːkˈwɔrm] *adj* **1** TEPID : tiède **2** HALFHEARTED : tiède, indifférent

lull[1] [ˈlʌl] *vt* **1** CALM : apaiser, calmer **2** **to lull to sleep** : endormir

lull[2] *n* : accalmie *f*

lullaby [ˈlʌləˌbaɪ] *n, pl* **-bies** : berceuse *f*

lumbago [lʌmˈbeɪgo] *n* : lumbago *m*

lumber[1] [ˈlʌmbər] *vt* : abattre les arbres — *vi* : marcher pesamment, avancer d'un pas lourd

lumber[2] *n* : bois *m*

lumberjack [ˈlʌmbərˌdʒæk] *n* : bûcheron *m*, -ronne *f*

lumberyard [ˈlʌmbərˌjɑrd] *n* : dépôt *m* de bois

luminary [ˈluːməˌnɛri] *n, pl* **-naries** : lumière *f*, sommité *f*

luminescence [ˌluːməˈnɛsənts] *n* : luminescence *f*

luminescent [luːməˈnɛsənt] *adj* : luminescent

luminosity [ˌluːməˈnɑsət̬i] *n, pl* **-ties** : luminosité *f*

luminous [ˈluːmənəs] *adj* : lumineux — **luminously** *adv*

lump[1] [ˈlʌmp] *vt or* **to lump together** : regrouper, rassembler

lump[2] *n* **1** CHUNK, PIECE : morceau *m*, motton *m Can* <a lump of butter : un morceau de beurre> **2** SWELLING : bosse *f*, grosseur *f* **3** : grumeau *m* (dans la sauce, etc.) **4** **to have a lump in one's throat** : avoir la gorge serrée

lumpy [ˈlʌmpi] *adj* **lumpier; -est** : grumeleux (se dit d'une sauce), plein de bosses (se dit d'un matelas)

lunacy [ˈluːnəsi] *n, pl* **-cies** : folie *f*, démence *f*

lunar [ˈluːnər] *adj* : lunaire

lunatic[1] [ˈluːnəˌtɪk] *adj* : fou, dément

lunatic[2] *n* : fou *m*, folle *f*; dément *m*, -mente *f*

lunch[1] [ˈlʌntʃ] *vi* : déjeuner, dîner *Can*

lunch[2] *n* : déjeuner *m*, dîner *m Can*, lunch *m Can*

luncheon [ˈlʌntʃən] *n* : déjeuner *m*

lung [ˈlʌŋ] *n* : poumon *m*

lunge[1] [ˈlʌndʒ] *vi* **lunged; lunging** **1** : se jeter en avant **2** **to lunge at** : porter une botte à (en escrime)

lunge[2] *n* **1** THRUST : botte *f*, coup *m* **2** **to lunge forward** : faire un mouvement vers l'avant

lurch[1] [ˈlərtʃ] *vi* **1** STAGGER : vaciller, tituber **2** : faire une embardée (se dit d'une voiture)

lurch[2] *n* : embardée *f* (d'une voiture), écart *m* (d'une personne)

lure[1] [ˈlʊr] *vt* **lured; luring** : attirer

lure[2] *n* **1** BAIT : leurre *m*, amorce *f* **2** ATTRACTION : attrait *m*

lurid [ˈlʊrəd] *adj* **1** GRUESOME : affreux, horrible **2** SENSATIONAL : à sensation **3** GAUDY : criard, voyant

lurk [ˈlərk] *vi* : se cacher, se tapir

luscious [ˈlʌʃəs] *adj* **1** DELICIOUS, DELIGHTFUL : succulent, délicieux **2** SEDUCTIVE : séduisant

lush [ˈlʌʃ] *adj* : luxuriant, riche

lust[1] [ˈlʌst] *vi* **to lust after** : désirer (une personne), convoiter (des richesses, etc.)

lust[2] *n* **1** DESIRE : désir *m* (charnel) **2** CRAVING : soif *f*, convoitise *f*

luster *or* **lustre** [ˈlʌstər] *n* **1** SHEEN : lustre *m* **2** SPLENDOR : éclat *m*

lusterless [ˈlʌstərləs] *adj* : sans éclat

lustful [ˈlʌstfəl] *adj* : concupiscent

lustily [ˈlʌstəli] *adv* : avec vigueur

lustrous [ˈlʌstrəs] *adj* : lustré, brillant

lusty [ˈlʌsti] *adj* **lustier; -est** : robuste, vigoureux

lute [ˈluːt] *n* : luth *m*

Luxembourger [ˈlʌksəmbərgər] *n* : Luxembourgeois *m*, -geoise *f*

Luxembourgian [ˌlʌksəmˈbərgiən] *adj* : luxembourgeois

luxuriance [ˌlʌgˈʒʊriənts, ˌlʌkˈʃʊr-] *n* : luxuriance *f*

luxuriant [ˌlʌgˈʒʊriənt, ˌlʌkˈʃʊr-] *adj* : luxuriant, abondant

luxuriate [ˌlʌgˈʒʊriˌeɪt, ˌlʌkˈʃʊr-] *vi* **-ated; -ating** **1** FLOURISH : pousser, proliférer **2** **to luxuriate in** : prendre plaisir à, s'abandonner à

luxurious [ˌlʌgˈʒʊriəs, ˌlʌkˈʃʊr-] *adj* : luxueux — **luxuriously** *adv*

luxury [ˈlʌkʃəri, ˈlʌgʒə-] *n, pl* **-ries** : luxe *m*

lye [ˈlaɪ] *n* : lessive *f*

lying → **lie**[1], **lie**[2]

lymph [ˈlɪmpf] *n* : lymphe *f*

lymphatic [lɪmˈfæt̬ɪk] *adj* : lymphatique

lynch ['lɪntʃ] *vt* : lyncher
lynx ['lɪŋks] *n, pl* **lynx** *or* **lynxes** : lynx *m,* loup-cervier *m*
lyre ['laɪr] *n* : lyre *f*
lyric[1] ['lɪrɪk] *adj* : lyrique
lyric[2] *n* **1** : poème *m* lyrique **2 lyrics** *npl* : paroles *fpl* (d'une chanson)
lyrical ['lɪrɪkəl] → **lyric**[1]

M

m ['ɛm] *n, pl* **m's** *or* **ms** ['ɛmz] : m *m,* treizième lettre de l'alphabet
ma'am ['mæm] → **madam**
macabre [mə'kɑb, -'kɑbər, -'kɑbrə] *adj* : macabre
macadam [mə'kædəm] *n* : macadam *m*
macaroni [ˌmækə'ro:ni] *n* : macaronis *mpl*
macaroon [ˌmækə'ru:n] *n* : macaron *m*
macaw [mə'kɔ] *n* : ara *m*
mace ['meɪs] *n* **1** : masse *f* (arme ou symbole) **2** : macis *m* (épice)
Macedonian[1] [ˌmæsə'do:njən, -niən] *adj* : macédonien
Macedonian[2] *n* : Macédonien *m,* -nienne *f*
machete [mə'ʃɛṭi] *n* : machette *f*
machination [ˌmækə'neɪʃən, ˌmæʃə-] *n* : machination *f,* complot *m*
machine[1] [mə'ʃi:n] *vt* **-chined; -chining** : fabriquer (à la machine), usiner
machine[2] *n* **1** VEHICLE : véhicule *m* **2** : machine *f* <sewing machine : machine à coudre>
machine gun *n* : mitrailleuse *f*
machine language *n* : langage *m* machine
machine–readable *adj* : exploitable par (une) machine
machinery [mə'ʃi:nəri] *n, pl* **-eries 1** MACHINES : machines *fpl* **2** MECHANISM : mécanisme *m* **3** SYSTEM : rouages *mpl* <the machinery of state : les rouages de l'état>
machinist [mə'ʃi:nɪst] *n* : opérateur *m,* -trice *f* (sur machine)
mackerel ['mækərəl] *n, pl* **-el** *or* **-els** : maquereau *m*
mackinaw ['mækəˌnɔ] *n* : grosse veste *f* de laine
mackintosh ['mækənˌtɑʃ] *n Brit* RAINCOAT : imperméable *m*
macramé ['mækrəˌmeɪ] *n* : macramé *m*
mad ['mæd] *adj* **madder; maddest 1** INSANE : fou **2** FOOLISH : insensé **3** ANGRY : furieux **4** ENTHUSIASTIC, CRAZY : fou <mad about her : fou d'elle> **5** RABID : enragé
Madagascan[1] [ˌmædə'gæskən] *adj* : malgache
Madagascan[2] *n* : Malgache *mf*
madam ['mædəm] *n, pl* **mesdames** [meɪ'dɑm, -'dæm] : madame *f*
madcap[1] ['mædˌkæp] *adj* : fou, écervelé, étourdi
madcap[2] *n* : fou *m,* folle *f*
madden ['mædən] *vt* **1** CRAZE : rendre fou, exaspérer **2** ENRAGE : mettre en rage, rendre furieux
maddeningly ['mædənɪŋli] *adv* : de façon exaspérante <maddeningly slow : d'une lenteur exaspérante>
made → **make**[1]
madhouse ['mædˌhaʊs] *n* : maison *f* de fous
madly ['mædli] *adv* : follement <to love s.o. madly : aimer qqn à la folie>
madman ['mædˌmæn, -mən] *n, pl* **-men** [-mən, -ˌmɛn] : fou *m,* aliéné *m*
madness ['mædnəs] *n* : folie *f,* démence *f*
madwoman ['mædˌwʊmən] *n, pl* **-women** [-ˌwɪmən] : folle *f,* aliénée *f*
maelstrom ['meɪlstrəm] *n* : maelström *m*
maestro ['maɪˌstro:] *n, pl* **-stros** *or* **-stri** [-ˌstri:] : maestro *m*
Mafia ['mɑfiə] *n* : mafia *f*
magazine ['mægəˌzi:n] *n* **1** STOREHOUSE : magasin *m* **2** PERIODICAL : magazine *m,* revue *f* **3** : chargeur *m* (d'une arme à feu)
magenta [mə'dʒɛntə] *n* : magenta *m*
maggot ['mægət] *n* : ver *m,* asticot *m*
magic[1] ['mædʒɪk] *or* **magical** ['mædʒɪkəl] *adj* : magique
magic[2] *n* : magie *f* <as if by magic : comme par enchantement>
magically ['mædʒɪkli] *adv* : magiquement, par magie
magician [mə'dʒɪʃən] *n* : magicien *m,* -cienne *f*
magistrate ['mædʒəˌstreɪt] *n* : magistrat *m*
magma ['mægmə] *n* : magma *m*
magnanimity [ˌmægnə'nɪməṭi] *n, pl* **-ties** : magnanimité *f*
magnanimous [mæg'nænəməs] *adj* : magnanime
magnanimously [mæg'nænəməsli] *adv* : avec magnanimité
magnesium [mæg'ni:ziəm, -ʒəm] *n* : magnésium *m*
magnet ['mægnət] *n* : aimant *m*
magnetic [mæg'nɛṭɪk] *adj* : magnétique — **magnetically** [-ṭɪkli] *adv*
magnetic field *n* : champ *m* magnétique
magnetic tape *n* : bande *f* magnétique
magnetism ['mægnəˌtɪzəm] *n* : magnétisme *m*
magnetize ['mægnəˌtaɪz] *vt* **-tized; -tizing 1** : aimanter **2** ATTRACT : magnétiser

magnification [ˌmægnəfəˈkeɪʃən] *n* : grossissement *m*

magnificence [mægˈnɪfəsənts] *n* : magnificence *f*

magnificent [mægˈnɪfəsənt] *adj* : magnifique — **magnificently** *adv*

magnify [ˈmægnəˌfaɪ] *vt* **-fied; -fying 1** ENLARGE : grossir **2** EXAGGERATE : exagérer

magnifying glass *n* : loupe *f*

magnitude [ˈmægnəˌtuːd, -ˌtjuːd] *n* **1** GREATNESS : ampleur *f*, grandeur *f* **2** QUANTITY : quantité *f* **3** IMPORTANCE : importance *f*, magnitude *f*

magnolia [mægˈnoːljə] *n* : magnolia *m*

magpie [ˈmægˌpaɪ] *n* : pie *f*

mahogany [məˈhɑgəni] *n, pl* **-nies** : acajou *m*

maid [ˈmeɪd] *n* **1** MAIDEN : demoiselle *f*, vierge *f* **2** *or* **maidservant** : bonne *f*, domestique *f*, femme *f* de chambre

maiden[1] [ˈmeɪdən] *adj* **1** UNMARRIED : célibataire **2** FIRST : premier, inaugural <maiden voyage : voyage inaugural>

maiden[2] *n* : demoiselle *f*, vierge *f*

maidenhood [ˈmeɪdənˌhʊd] *n* : virginité *f*

maiden name *n* : nom *m* de jeune fille

mail[1] [ˈmeɪl] *vt* : envoyer par la poste

mail[2] *n* **1** : poste *f* <to put in the mail : mettre à la poste> **2** LETTERS : courrier *m* **3** : mailles *fpl* <coat of mail : cotte de mailles>

mailbox [ˈmeɪlˌbɑks] *n* : boîte *f* aux lettres

mailman [ˈmeɪlˌmæn, -mən] *n, pl* **-men** [-mən, -ˌmɛn] : facteur *m*

maim [ˈmeɪm] *vt* : estropier, mutiler

main[1] [ˈmeɪn] *adj* : principal <the main course : le plat principal>

main[2] *n* **1** : canalisation *f* principale (d'eau, de gaz), conduite *f* principale (d'électricité) **2** HIGH SEAS : large *m*, haute mer *f*

mainframe [ˈmeɪnˌfreɪm] *n* : ordinateur *m* central

mainland [ˈmeɪnˌlænd, -lənd] *n* : continent *m*

mainly [ˈmeɪnli] *adv* : principalement, surtout

mainstay [ˈmeɪnˌsteɪ] *n* : pilier *m*, soutien *m* (principal)

mainstream[1] [ˈmeɪnˌstriːm] *adj* : dominant, traditionnel

mainstream[2] *n* : courant *m* dominant

maintain [meɪnˈteɪn] *vt* **1** SERVICE : entretenir (un véhicule, une route, etc.) **2** PRESERVE : maintenir <to maintain silence : garder le silence> **3** SUPPORT soutenir **4** ASSERT : affirmer

maintenance [ˈmeɪntənənts] *n* **1** UPKEEP : entretien *m* **2** UPHOLDING : maintien *m*

maize [ˈmeɪz] → **indian corn**

majestic [məˈdʒɛstɪk] *adj* : majestueux — **majestically** [-tɪkli] *adv*

majesty [ˈmædʒəsti] *n, pl* **-ties 1** : majesté *f* <Your Majesty : Votre Majesté> **2** GRANDEUR : grandeur *f*, majesté *f*

major[1] [ˈmeɪdʒər] *vi* **-jored; -joring** : se spécialiser

major[2] *adj* **1** MAIN : principal <the major part : la plus grande partie> **2** NOTEWORTHY : majeur, notable **3** SERIOUS : majeur <major surgery : une grosse opération> **4** : majeur (en musique)

major[3] *n* **1** : commandant *m* (de l'armée) **2** FIELD : spécialité *f* (universitaire)

major general *n* : général *m* de division

majority [məˈdʒɔrəṭi] *n, pl* **-ties** : majorité *f*

make[1] [ˈmeɪk] *v* **made** [ˈmeɪd]; **making** *vt* **1** CREATE : faire, créer <to make noise : faire du bruit> **2** MANUFACTURE : fabriquer, faire **3** CONSTITUTE : constituer <made of gold : en or> **4** PREPARE : préparer <to make a meal : préparer un repas> **5** RENDER : rendre <to make sick : rendre malade> **6** FORM : faire, former **7** COMPEL : faire, obliger <you make me laugh : tu me fais rire> **8** EARN : gagner <to make a living : gagner sa vie> **9** ATTAIN : atteindre, arriver jusqu'à (une position, etc.) — *vi* **1** HEAD : se diriger <she made for home : elle s'est dirigée vers la maison> **2 to make do** : se débrouiller **3 to make good** SUCCEED : réussir **4 to make of** : comprendre à **5 to make off with** : partir avec

make[2] *n* BRAND : marque *f*

make–believe[1] [ˌmeɪkbəˈliːv] *adj* : imaginaire

make–believe[2] *n* : fantaisie *f* <a world of make-believe : un monde d'illusions>

make out *vt* **1** WRITE : faire, écrire <to make out a cheque : faire un chèque> **2** DISCERN : discerner, distinguer **3** UNDERSTAND : comprendre — *vi* FARE : se débrouiller <how did you make out? : comment ça s'est passé?>

maker [ˈmeɪkər] *n* MANUFACTURER : fabricant *m*, -cante *f*

makeshift [ˈmeɪkˌʃɪft] *adj* : improvisé

makeup [ˈmeɪkˌʌp] *n* **1** COMPOSITION : composition *f* **2** COSMETICS : maquillage **3** CHARACTER : caractère *m*, nature *f*

make up *vt* **1** INVENT : inventer **2** : rattraper <to make up the time : rattraper le temps> — *vi* RECONCILE : se réconcilier

maladjusted [ˌmæləˈdʒʌstəd] *adj* : inadapté

maladjustment [ˌmæləˈdʒʌstmənt] *n* : inadaptation *f*

maladroit [ˌmælə'drɔɪt] *adj* : maladroit
malady ['mælədi] *n, pl* **-dies** : maladie *f,* mal *m*
Malagasy[1] [ˌmælə'gæsi; ˌmɑlə'gɑsi, -ʃi] *adj* : malgache
Malagasy[2] *n* **1** : Malgache *mf* **2** : malgache *m* (langue)
malaise [mə'leɪz] *n* : malaise *m*
malamute ['mæləˌmju:t, -ˌmu:t] *n* : malamute *m,* chien *m* malamute
malapropism ['mæləˌprɑˌpɪzəm] *n* : impropriété *f* de langage
malaria [mə'lɛriə] *n* : paludisme *m*
malarkey [mə'lɑrki] *n* : balivernes *fpl,* sottises *fpl*
Malawian[1] [mə'lɑwiən] *adj* : malawien
Malawian[2] *n* : Malawien *m,* -wienne *f*
Malay[1] [mə'leɪ, 'meɪˌleɪ] *or* **Malayan** [mə'leɪən, meɪ-; 'meɪˌleɪən] *adj* : malais
Malay[2] *n* **1** *or* **Malayan** : Malais *m,* -laise *f* **2** : malais *m* (langue)
Malaysian[1] [mə'leɪʒən] *adj* : malaisien
Malaysian[2] *n* : Malaisien *m,* -sienne *f*
male[1] ['meɪl] *adj* **1** : mâle **2** MASCULINE : masculin
male[2] *n* **1** : mâle *m* (en botanique ou en zoologie) **2** MAN : homme *m*
malefactor ['mæləˌfæktər] *n* : malfaiteur *m,* -trice *f*
maleness ['meɪlnəs] *n* : masculinité *f*
malevolence [mə'lɛvələnts] *n* : malveillance *f*
malevolent [mə'lɛvələnt] *adj* : malveillant
malformation [ˌmælfɔr'meɪʃən] *n* : malformation *f*
malformed [mæl'fɔrmd] *adj* : difforme
malfunction[1] [mæl'fʌŋkʃən] *vi* : mal fonctionner
malfunction[2] *n* : défaillance *f,* mauvais fonctionnement *m*
Malian[1] ['maliən] *adj* : malien
Malian[2] *n* : Malien *m,* -lienne *f*
malice ['mælɪs] *n* **1** : malveillance *f,* méchanceté *f* **2 with malice aforethought** : avec préméditation
malicious [mə'lɪʃəs] *adj* : malveillant, méchant
maliciously [mə'lɪʃəsli] *adv* : méchamment, avec méchanceté
malign[1] [mə'laɪn] *vt* : calomnier, diffamer
malign[2] *adj* : nuisible, pernicieux
malignancy [mə'lɪgnəntsi] *n, pl* **-cies** : malignité *f*
malignant [mə'lɪgnənt] *adj* : malin
malinger [mə'lɪŋgər] *vi* : faire le malade
mall ['mɔl] *n* **1** PROMENADE : mail *m,* allée *f* **2** *or* **shopping mall** : centre *m* commercial
mallard ['mælərd] *n, pl* **-lard** *or* **-lards** : colvert *m,* malard *m Can*
malleable ['mæliəbəl] *adj* : malléable
mallet ['mælət] *n* : maillet *m*
malnourished [mæl'nərɪʃt] *adj* : sous-alimenté
malnutrition [ˌmælnʊ'trɪʃən, -njʊ-] *n* : sous-alimentation *f,* malnutrition *f*
malodorous [mæl'o:dərəs] *adj* : malodorant
malpractice [ˌmæl'præktəs] *n* : faute *f* professionnelle
malt ['mɔlt] *n* : malt *m*
Maltese[1] [mɔl'ti:z, -'ti:s] *adj* : maltais
Maltese[2] *n* : Maltais *m,* -taise *f*
maltreat [mæl'tri:t] *vt* : maltraiter
mama *or* **mamma** ['mɑmə] *n* : maman *f*
mammal ['mæməl] *n* : mammifère *m*
mammary gland ['mæməri] *n* : glande *f* mammaire
mammogram ['mæməˌgræm] *n* : mammographie *f*
mammoth[1] ['mæməθ] *adj* : colossal, énorme
mammoth[2] *n* : mammouth *m*
man[1] ['mæn] *vt* **manned; manning** : équiper en personnel, assurer une permanence à
man[2] *n, pl* **men** ['mɛn] **1** PERSON : homme *m,* personne *f* **2** MALE : homme *m* **3** MANKIND : humanité *f*
manacles ['mænɪkəlz] *npl* **1** SHACKLES : chaînes *fpl* **2** HANDCUFFS : menottes *fpl*
manage ['mænɪdʒ] *v* **-aged; -aging** *vt* **1** HANDLE : manier **2** DIRECT : gérer, diriger **3** CONTRIVE : réussir, arriver — *vi* COPE : se débrouiller
manageable ['mænɪdʒəbəl] *adj* : maniable
management ['mænɪdʒmənt] *n* **1** DIRECTION : gestion *f,* direction *f* **2** MANAGERS : direction *f*
manager ['mænɪdʒər] *n* : directeur *m,* -trice *f;* gérant *m,* -rante *f;* manager *m* (aux sports)
managerial [ˌmænə'dʒɪriəl] *adj* : directorial
mandarin ['mændərən] *n* **1** : mandarin *m* **2** *or* **mandarin orange** : mandarine *f*
mandate ['mænˌdeɪt] *n* : mandat *m*
mandatory ['mændəˌtɔri] *adj* : obligatoire
mandible ['mændəbəl] *n* **1** JAW : mâchoire *f* inférieure **2** : mandibule *f* (d'un oiseau ou d'un insecte)
mandolin [ˌmændə'lɪn, 'mændələn] *n* : mandoline *f*
mane ['meɪn] *n* : crinière *f*
maneuver[1] *or Brit* **manoeuvre** [mə'nu:vər, -'nju:-] *v* **-vered** *or Brit* **-vred; -vering** *or Brit* **-vring** : manœuvrer
maneuver[2] *or Brit* **manoeuvre** *n* : manœuvre *f*
maneuverable [mə'nu:vərəbəl, -'nju:-] *adj* : manœuvrable
manfully ['mænfəli] *adv* : courageusement, vaillamment
manganese ['mæŋgəˌni:z, -ˌni:s] *n* : manganèse *m*
mange ['meɪndʒ] *n* : gale *f*
manger ['meɪndʒər] *n* : mangeoire *f*

mangle [ˈmæŋgəl] *vt* **-gled; -gling 1** MUTILATE : mutiler, déchirer **2** BOTCH : estropier (un texte, un discours, etc.)
mango [ˈmæŋˌgoː] *n, pl* **-goes** : mangue *f*
mangrove [ˈmænˌgroːv, ˈmæŋ-] *n* : manglier *m*
mangy [ˈmeɪndʒi] *adj* **mangier; -est 1** : galeux **2** SHABBY : minable, miteux, élimé
manhandle [ˈmænˌhændəl] *vt* **-dled; -dling** : malmener, maltraiter
manhole [ˈmænˌhoːl] *n* : trou *m* d'homme, bouche *f* d'égout
manhood [ˈmænˌhʊd] *n* **1** COURAGE, MANLINESS : courage *m*, virilité *f* **2** ADULTHOOD : âge *m* d'homme **3** MEN : hommes *mpl*
manhunt [ˈmænˌhʌnt] *n* : chasse *f* à l'homme
mania [ˈmeɪniə, -njə] *n* : manie *f*
maniac [ˈmeɪniˌæk] *n* : fou *m*, folle *f*; maniaque *mf*
maniacal [məˈnaɪəkəl] *adj* : maniaque
manicure[1] [ˈmænəˌkjʊr] *vt* **-cured; -curing 1** : manucurer, faire les ongles de **2** CUT, TRIM : tondre <a manicured lawn : une pelouse impeccable>
manicure[2] *n* : manucure *f*
manicurist [ˈmænəˌkjʊrɪst] *n* : manucure *mf*
manifest[1] [ˈmænəˌfɛst] *vt* : manifester
manifest[2] *adj* : manifeste, évident — **manifestly** *adv*
manifestation [ˌmænəfəˈsteɪʃən] *n* : manifestation *f*
manifesto [ˌmænəˈfɛsˌtoː] *n, pl* **-tos** *or* **-toes** : manifeste *m*
manifold[1] [ˈmænəˌfoːld] *adj* : multiple, nombreux
manifold[2] *n* : collecteur *m* (d'échappement), tubulure *f* (d'admission)
manipulate [məˈnɪpjəˌleɪt] *vt* **-lated; -lating** : manipuler
manipulation [məˌnɪpjəˈleɪʃən] *n* : manipulation *f*
mankind [ˈmænˈkaɪnd, -ˌkaɪnd] *n* : humanité *f*, le genre humain
manliness [ˈmænlinəs] *n* : virilité *f*
manly [ˈmænli] *adj* **manlier; -est** : viril
manna [ˈmænə] *n* : manne *f*
mannequin [ˈmænɪkən] *n* : mannequin *m*
manner [ˈmænər] *n* **1** KIND : sorte *f* **2** WAY, METHOD : manière *f*, façon *f* <a manner of speaking : une façon de parler> **3** BEARING : attitude *f*, maintien *m* **4 manners** *npl* ETIQUETTE : manières *fpl* **5 manners** *npl* CUSTOMS : mœurs *fpl*, usages *mpl*
mannered [ˈmænərd] *adj* **1** AFFECTED : maniéré, affecté **2 well-mannered** : bien élevé
mannerism [ˈmænəˌrɪzəm] *n* **1** HABIT : particularité *f*, manie *f*, tic *m* **2** AFFECTATION : maniérisme *m*
mannerly [ˈmænərli] *adj* : poli, bien élevé
mannish [ˈmænɪʃ] *adj* : masculin, hommasse
manoeuvre *Brit* → **maneuver**
man–of–war [ˌmænəˈwɔr, -əvˈwɔr] *n, pl* **men–of–war** [ˌmɛn-] : bâtiment *m* de guerre, navire *m* de guerre
manor [ˈmænər] *n* : manoir *m*
manpower [ˈmænˌpaʊər] *n* : main-d'œuvre *f*
mansion [ˈmæntʃən] *n* : château *m*, manoir *m*, hôtel *m* particulier
manslaughter [ˈmænˌslɔt̬ər] *n* : homicide *m* involontaire
mantel [ˈmæntəl] *or* **mantelpiece** [ˈmæntəlˌpiːs] *n* : cheminée *f*
mantis [ˈmæntɪs] *n, pl* **-tises** *or* **-tes** [ˈmænˌtiːz] : mante *f*
mantle [ˈmæntəl] *n* **1** CLOAK : manteau *m*, cape *f* **2** BLANKET, COVERING : manteau *f*, couche *f* <a mantle of fog : un manteau de brume>
manual[1] [ˈmænjʊəl] *adj* : manuel — **manually** *adv*
manual[2] *n* : manuel *m*
manufacture[1] [ˌmænjəˈfæktʃər] *vt* **-tured; -turing** : fabriquer, manufacturer, confectionner (des vêtements)
manufacture[2] *n* : fabrication *f*
manufacturer [ˌmænjəˈfæktʃərər] *n* : fabricant *m*, -cante *f*
manure [məˈnʊr, -ˈnjʊr] *n* **1** : fumier *m* (des animaux) **2** FERTILIZER : engrais *m*
manuscript [ˈmænjəˌskrɪpt] *n* : manuscrit *m*
many[1] [ˈmɛni] *adj* **more** [ˈmor]; **most** [ˈmoːst] **1** : beaucoup de, un grand nombre de **2 as many** : autant de **3 many a time** : maintes fois **4 so many** : tant de **5 too many** : trop de
many[2] *pron* : beaucoup, un grand nombre
map[1] [ˈmæp] *vt* **mapped; mapping 1** : faire la carte de **2** *or* **to map out** PLAN : tracer, organiser
map[2] *n* : carte *f*
maple [ˈmeɪpəl] *n* **1** : érable *m* **2 maple syrup** : sirop *m* d'érable
mar [ˈmɑr] *vt* **marred; marring** : gâter, gâcher
maraschino [ˌmærəˈskiːnoː, -ˈʃiː-] *n, pl* **-nos** : marasquin *m*
marathon [ˈmærəˌθɑn] *n* : marathon *m*
maraud [məˈrɔd] *vi* : marauder
marauder [məˈrɔdər] *n* : maradeur *m*, -deuse *f*
marble [ˈmɑrbəl] *n* **1** : marbre *m* **2** : bille *f* <to play marbles : jouer aux billes>
marbling [ˈmɑrblɪŋ] *n* : marbrure *f*
march[1] [ˈmɑrtʃ] *vi* **1** : marcher (au pas) **2** DEMONSTRATE : manifester (en signe de protestation) **3 to march (right) up to** : s'approcher (de qqn) d'un air décidé
march[2] *n* **1** MARCHING : marche *f* **2** DEMONSTRATION : manifestation *f* **3**

PROGRESS : avancée *f* <the march of time : la marche du temps> **4** : marche *f* (en musique)

March *n* : mars *m*

marchioness [ˈmarʃənɪs] *n* : marquise *f*

Mardi Gras [ˈmardiˌgra] *n* : mardi *m* gras

mare [ˈmær] *n* : jument *f*

margarine [ˈmardʒərən] *n* : margarine *f*

margin [ˈmardʒən] *n* **1** : marge *f* (du papier, etc.) **2** EDGE : bord *m*

marginal [ˈmardʒənəl] *adj* : marginal

marigold [ˈmærəˌgoːld] *n* : souci *m*

marijuana [ˌmærəˈhwanə] *n* : marijuana *f*

marina [məˈriːnə] *n* : marina *f*

marinate [ˈmærəˌneɪt] *v* **-nated**; **-nating** : mariner

marine[1] [məˈriːn] *adj* **1** UNDERWATER : marin <marine biology : biologie marine> **2** NAUTICAL : maritime <marine law : droit maritime>

marine[2] *n* **1** : fusilier *m* marin **2 merchant marine** : marine *f* marchande

mariner [ˈmærɪnər] *n* : marin *m*

marionette [ˌmæriəˈnɛt] *n* : marionnette *f* (à fils)

marital [ˈmærət̬əl] *adj* **1** : matrimonial, conjugal **2 marital status** : état *m* civil, situation *f* de famille

maritime [ˈmærəˌtaɪm] *adj* : maritime

marjoram [ˈmardʒərəm] *n* : marjolaine *f*

mark[1] [ˈmark] *vt* **1** : marquer **2** STAIN : tacher, marquer **3** CHARACTERIZE : caractériser **4** INDICATE : marquer, indiquer **5** GRADE : corriger (des examens, etc.) **6** : faire attention à <mark my words! : notez bien ce que je vous dis!> **7 to mark down** : noter, inscrire **8 to mark off** : délimiter

mark[2] *n* **1** TARGET : cible *f* **2** SIGN, SYMBOL : marque *f*, signe *m* **3** GRADE : note *f* **4** IMPRINT : empreinte *f*, marque *f* **5** BLEMISH : tache *f*, marque *f*

marked [ˈmarkt] *adj* NOTICEABLE : marqué

markedly [ˈmarkədli] *adv* : sensiblement, d'une façon marquée

marker [ˈmarkər] *n* **1** SIGN : marque *f*, repère *m* **2** *or* **marker pen** : marqueur *m*

market[1] [ˈmarkət] *vt* : vendre, commercialiser

market[2] *n* **1** MARKETPLACE : marché *m* <the black market : le marché noir> <wholesale market : marché en gros> **2** DEMAND : demande *f*, marché *m* **3** *or* **food market** : marché *m* (de vivres) <fish market : marché aux poissons> **4** → **stock market**

marketable [ˈmarkət̬əbəl] *adj* : vendable

marketplace [ˈmarkətˌpleɪs] *n* : marché *m*

marksman [ˈmarksmən] *n, pl* **-men** [-mən, -ˌmɛn] : tireur *m*, -reuse *f* d'élite

marksmanship [ˈmarksmənˌʃɪp] *n* : adresse *f* au tir, habileté *f* au tir

marlin [ˈmarlɪn] *n* : marlin *m*

marmalade [ˈmarməˌleɪd] *n* : marmelade *f*

marmoset [ˈmarməˌsɛt] *n* : ouistiti *m*

marmot [ˈmarmət] *n* : marmotte *f*

maroon[1] [məˈruːn] *vt* : abandonner

maroon[2] *n* : bordeaux *m* (couleur)

marquee [marˈkiː] *n* **1** CANOPY : marquise *f* **2** *Brit* TENT : grande tente *f*

marquess [ˈmarkwɪs] *or* **marquis** [ˈmarkwɪs, marˈkiː] *n, pl* **-quesses** *or* **-quises** [-ˈkiːz, -ˈkiːzəz] *or* **-quis** [-ˈkiː, -ˈkiːz] : marquis *m*

marquise [marˈkiːz] *nf* → **marchioness**

marriage [ˈmærɪdʒ] *n* **1** : mariage *m* <aunt by marriage : tante par alliance> **2** WEDDING : mariage *m*, noces *fpl*

marriageable [ˈmærɪdʒəbəl] *adj* : mariable <of marriageable age : en âge de se marier>

married [ˈmærid] *adj* **1** : marié <a married couple : un couple marié> <married life : la vie conjugale> **2 to get married** : se marier

marrow [ˈmæroː] *n* : moelle *f*

marry [ˈmæri] *v* **-ried; -rying** *vt* **1** WED : se marier avec, épouser, marier *Can* **2** : marier <the priest married them : le prêtre les a mariés> — *vi* : se marier

Mars [ˈmarz] *n* : Mars *f* (planète)

marsh [ˈmarʃ] *n* : marais *m*, marécage *m*

marshal[1] [ˈmarʃəl] *vt* **-shaled** *or* **-shalled; -shaling** *or* **-shalling** **1** ARRANGE, ASSEMBLE : assembler **2** USHER : conduire

marshal[2] *n* **1** : commisaire *m*, capitaine *m* <fire marshall : capitaine des pompiers> **2** : maréchal *m* (militaire) **3** : membre *m* du service d'ordre (d'un défilé, d'une cérémonie, etc.)

marshmallow [ˈmarʃˌmɛloː, -ˌmæloː] *n* : guimauve *f*

marshy [ˈmarʃi] *adj* **marshier; -est** : marécageux

marsupial [marˈsuːpiəl] *n* : marsupial *m*

mart [ˈmart] *n* MARKET : marché *m*

marten [ˈmartən] *n, pl* **-ten** *or* **-tens** : martre *f*

martial [ˈmarʃəl] *adj* : martial <martial law : la loi martiale>

martin [ˈmartən] *n* : martinet *m* (oiseau)

martyr[1] [ˈmart̬ər] *vt* : martyriser

martyr[2] *n* : martyr *m*, -tyre *f*

martyrdom [ˈmart̬ərdəm] *n* : martyre *m*

marvel[1] [ˈmarvəl] *vi* **-veled** *or* **-velled; -veling** *or* **-velling** : s'émerveiller

marvel[2] *n* : merveille *f*, miracle *m*

marvelous [ˈmarvələs] *or* **marvellous** *adj* : merveilleux — **marvelously** *adv*

Marxism [ˈmarkˌsɪzəm] *n* : marxisme *m*

Marxist[1] [ˈmarksɪst] *adj* : marxiste

Marxist[2] *n* : marxiste *mf*

mascara [mæs'kærə] *n* : mascara *m*

mascot ['mæs,kɑt, -kət] *n* : mascotte *f*

masculine ['mæskjələn] *adj* : masculin

masculinity [,mæskjə'lɪnət̬i] *n* : masculinité *f*

mash[1] ['mæʃ] *vt* **1** CRUSH : écraser **2** PUREE : faire une purée de, piler *Can*

mash[2] *n* **1** PUREE : purée *f* **2** FEED : pâtée *f* **3** MALT : moût *m*

mask[1] ['mæsk] *vt* **1** DISGUISE : masquer **2** COVER, HIDE : cacher (des émotions, etc.)

mask[2] *n* : masque *m*

masochism ['mæsə,kɪzəm, 'mæzə-] *n* : masochisme *m*

masochist ['mæsə,kɪst, 'mæzə-] *n* : masochiste *mf*

masochistic [,mæsə'kɪstɪk] *adj* : masochiste

mason ['meɪsən] *n* **1** : maçon *m* **2** → **Freemason**

masonry ['meɪsənri] *n, pl* **-ries 1** : maçonnerie *f* **2** → **Freemasonry**

masquerade[1] [,mæskə'reɪd] *vi* **-aded; -ading** : se déguiser, se faire passer

masquerade[2] *n* : mascarade *f*

mass[1] ['mæs] *vi* : se masser

mass[2] *n* **1** : masse *f* (en physique) **2** CLUSTER : masse *f*, ensemble *m* <a mass of houses : un ensemble de maisons> **3** QUANTITY : quantité *f*, masse *f* **4 the masses** : les masses *fpl*

Mass *n* : messe *f*

massacre[1] ['mæsɪkər] *vt* **-cred; -cring** : massacrer

massacre[2] *n* : massacre *m*

massage[1] [mə'sɑʒ] *vt* **-saged; -saging** : masser

massage[2] *n* : massage *m*

masseur [mæ'sər] *n* : masseur *m*

masseuse [mæ'søz, -'su:z] *n* : masseuse *f*

massive ['mæsɪv] *adj* **1** BULKY : massif **2** HUGE : énorme — **massively** *adv*

mass media → **media**

mast ['mæst] *n* **1** : mât *m* (d'un navire) **2** POLE, POST : pylône *m*

master[1] ['mæstər] *vt* **1** CONTROL, SUBDUE : dominer, dompter, maîtriser **2** LEARN : maîtriser

master[2] *n* **1** : maître *m* **2** *or* **master copy** : original *m* **3 master's degree** : maîtrise *f*

masterful ['mæstərfəl] *adj* **1** IMPERIOUS : autoritaire, impérieux, dominateur **2** SKILLFUL : magistral

masterfully ['mæstərfəli] *adv* : magistralement

masterly ['mæstərli] *adj* : magistral

masterpiece ['mæstər,pi:s] *n* : chef *m* d'œuvre

masterwork ['mæstər,wərk] → **masterpiece**

mastery ['mæstəri] *n* **1** CONTROL : domination *f*, maîtrise *f* **2** KNOWLEDGE, SKILL : maîtrise *f*

masticate ['mæstə,keɪt] *vt* **-cated; -cating** : mastiquer

mastiff ['mæstɪf] *n* : mastiff *m*

mastodon ['mæstə,dɑn] *n* : mastodonte *m*

masturbate ['mæstər,beɪt] *vi* **-bated; -bating** : se masturber

masturbation [,mæstər'beɪʃən] *n* : masturbation *f*

mat[1] ['mæt] *v* **matted; matting** *vt* TANGLE : emmêler — *vi* : s'emmêler

mat[2] *n* **1** DOORMAT : paillasson *m* **2** RUG : natte *f*, tapis *m* **3** TANGLE : enchevêtrement *m* **4** *or* **exercise mat** : tapis *m* (d'exercice) **5** *or* **matt** *or* **matte** FRAME : bord *m*, cadre *m*

mat[3] → **matte**

matador ['mætə,dɔr] *n* : matador *m*

match[1] ['mætʃ] *vt* **1** OPPOSE, PIT : opposer, rivaliser avec **2** EQUAL : égaler **3** : s'accorder avec, aller avec <her shoes match her dress : ses chaussures vont avec sa robe> — *vi* CORRESPOND : correspondre

match[2] *n* **1** EQUAL : égal *m*, égale *f* <to meet one's match : trouver à qui parler (avec qqn)> **2** : allumette *f* <to strike a match : gratter une allumette> **3** FIGHT, GAME : match *m* **4** MARRIAGE : mariage *m* <they're a good match : ils vont bien ensemble>

matchless ['mætʃləs] *adj* : sans pareil, incomparable

matchmaker ['mætʃ,meɪkər] *n* : marieur *m*, -rieuse *f*

mate[1] ['meɪt] *v* **mated; mating** *vi* **1** FIT : s'emboîter **2** COUPLE : s'accoupler **3** : s'accoupler (se dit des animaux) — *vt* : accoupler (des animaux)

mate[2] *n* **1** COMPANION : camarade *mf;* compagnon *m*, compagne *f* **2** : mâle *m*, femelle *f* (d'animaux) **3** *or* **first mate** : second *m*

material[1] [mə'tɪriəl] *adj* **1** PHYSICAL : matériel <the material world : le monde matériel> <material goods : biens matériels> **2** IMPORTANT : important, pertinent **3 material evidence** : preuve *f* matérielle

material[2] *n* **1** : matière *f*, substance *f* <raw materials : matières premières> **2** FABRIC : tissu *m*, étoffe *f*

materialism [mə'tɪriə,lɪzəm] *n* : matérialisme *m*

materialist [mə'tɪriəlɪst] *n* : matérialiste *mf*

materialistic [mə,tɪriə'lɪstɪk] *adj* : matérialiste

materialize [mə'tɪriə,laɪz] *v* **-ized; -izing** *vt* : matérialiser — *vi* : se matérialiser, se réaliser, prendre forme

materially [mə'tɪriəli] *adv* : matériellement

maternal [mə'tərnəl] *adj* : maternel — **maternally** *adv*

maternity[1] [mə'tərnət̬i] *adj* : de maternité <maternity leave : congé de maternité>

maternity[2] *n, pl* **-ties** : maternité *f*

math [ˈmæθ] → **mathematics**
mathematical [ˌmæθəˈmæt̬ɪkəl] *adj* : mathématique — **mathematically** *adv*
mathematician [ˌmæθəməˈtɪʃən] *n* : mathématicien *m*, -cienne *f*
mathematics [ˌmæθəˈmæt̬ɪks] *ns & pl* : mathématiques *fpl*
matinee *or* **matinée** [ˌmætənˈeɪ] *n* : matinée *f*
matriarch [ˈmeɪtriˌɑrk] *n* : matrone *f*, femme *f* chef de famille
matriarchy [ˈmeɪtriˌɑrki] *n, pl* **-chies** : matriarcat *m*
matriculate [məˈtrɪkjəˌleɪt] *vi* **-lated; -lating** ENROLL : s'inscrire
matriculation [məˌtrɪkjəˈleɪʃən] *n* : inscription *f*, immatriculation *f*
matrimonial [ˌmætrəˈmoːniəl] *adj* : matrimonial, conjugal
matrimony [ˈmætrəˌmoːni] *n* : mariage *m*
matrix [ˈmeɪtrɪks] *n, pl* **-trices** [ˈmeɪtrəˌsiːz, ˈmæ-] *or* **-trixes** [ˈmeɪtrɪksəz] : matrice *f*
matron [ˈmeɪtrən] *n* : matrone *f*
matronly [ˈmeɪtrənli] *adj* : de matrone
matte [ˈmæt] *adj* : mat <a photo with a matte finish : une photo mate>
matter[1] [ˈmæt̬ər] *vi* : importer, avoir de l'importance <it doesn't matter : cela ne fait rien, peu importe>
matter[2] *n* **1** SUBSTANCE : matière *f* **2** QUESTION : question *f* <a matter of taste : une question de goût> **3** AFFAIR : affaire *f*, cas *m*, sujet *m* **4** (*indicating a problem or trouble*) <what's the matter? : qu'est-ce qui se passe?> <what's the matter with your leg? : qu'est-ce que vous avez à la jambe?> **5 matters** *npl* CIRCUMSTANCES : choses *fpl*, circonstances *fpl* <to make matters worse : pour ne rien arranger> **6 as a matter of fact** : à vrai dire, en fait **7 for that matter** : d'ailleurs **8 no matter how** : peu importe comment **9 no matter when** : quelle que soit l'heure
mattress [ˈmætrəs] *n* : matelas *m*
mature[1] [məˈtʊr, -ˈtjʊr, -ˈtʃʊr] *vi* **-tured; -turing 1** : mûrir (se dit d'une personne) **2** : arriver à maturité (se dit du vin), se faire (se dit du fromage) **3** : échoir, arriver à échéance (se dit d'une dette, etc.)
mature[2] *adj* **-turer; -est 1** : mûr **2** DUE : échu
maturity [məˈtʊrət̬i, -ˈtjʊr-, -ˈtʃʊr-] *n* : maturité *f*
maudlin [ˈmɔdlɪn] *adj* : larmoyant
maul[1] [ˈmɔl] *vt* **1** MANGLE, MUTILATE : mutiler **2** MANHANDLE : malmener
maul[2] *n* MALLET : maillet *m*
Mauritanian[1] [ˌmɔrəˈteɪniən] *adj* : mauritanien
Mauritanian[2] *n* : Mauritanien *m*, -nienne *f*
Mauritian[1] [mɔˈriːʃən] *adj* : mauricien
Mauritian[2] *n* : Mauricien *m*, -cienne *f*
mausoleum [ˌmɔsəˈliːəm, ˌmɔzə-] *n, pl* **-leums** *or* **-lea** [-ˈliːə] : mausolée *m*
mauve [ˈmoːv, ˈmɔv] *n* : mauve *m*
maven *or* **mavin** [ˈmeɪvən] *n* EXPERT : expert *m*, -perte *f*
maverick [ˈmævrɪk, ˈmævə-] *n* **1** : veau *m* non marqué **2** NONCONFORMIST : non-conformiste *mf*
mawkish [ˈmɔkɪʃ] *adj* : mièvre
maxim [ˈmæksəm] *n* : maxime *f*, adage *m*
maximize [ˈmæksəˌmaɪz] *vt* **-mized; -mizing** : maximiser, porter au maximum
maximum[1] [ˈmæksəməm] *adj* : maximum
maximum[2] *n, pl* **-ma** [ˈmæksəmə] *or* **-mums** : maximum *m*
may [ˈmeɪ] *v aux, past* **might** [ˈmaɪt]; *present s & pl* **may 1** (*expressing permission*) : pouvoir <you may leave : vous pouvez partir> <may I? : puis-je?> **2** (*expressing possibility or probability*) : pouvoir <it may fall : il peut tomber> <you may be right : tu as peut-être raison> <it may rain : il se peut qu'il pleuve> **3** (*expressing desires, intentions, or contingencies*) <come what may : quoiqu'il arrive> <may the best man win! : que le meilleur gagne!>
May [ˈmeɪ] *n* : mai *m*
maybe [ˈmeɪbi] *adv* PERHAPS : peut-être
mayfly [ˈmeɪˌflaɪ] *n, pl* **-flies** : éphémère *m*
mayhem [ˈmeɪˌhɛm, ˈmeɪəm] *n* **1** MUTILATION : mutilation *f* **2** HAVOC : destruction *f*, désordre *m*
mayonnaise [ˈmeɪəˌneɪz] *n* : mayonnaise *f*
mayor [ˈmeɪər, ˈmɛr] *n* : maire *m*, mairesse *f*
mayoral [ˈmeɪərəl, ˈmɛrəl] *adj* : de maire
maze [ˈmeɪz] *n* : dédale *m*, labyrinthe *m*
me [ˈmiː] *pron* **1** : moi <give me the book : donne-moi le livre> <for me : pour moi> <it's me : c'est moi> <as big as me : aussi grand que moi> **2** : me, m' <she told me : elle m'a dit> <he's looking at me : il me regarde>
meadow [ˈmɛdoː] *n* : pré *m*, prairie *f*
meadowland [ˈmɛdoˌlænd] *n* : prairies *fpl*
meager *or* **meagre** [ˈmiːgər] *adj* : maigre — **meagerly** *adv*
meagerness [ˈmiːgərnəs] *n* : maigreur *f*
meal [ˈmiːl] *n* **1** : repas *m* <to have a meal : prendre un repas> **2** : farine *f* (de maïs, etc.)
mealtime [ˈmiːlˌtaɪm] *n* : heure *f* de repas
mealy [ˈmiːli] *adj* **mealier; -est** : farineux
mean[1] [ˈmiːn] *vt* **meant** [ˈmɛnt]; **meaning 1** INTEND : avoir l'intention de <I

mean to go : j'ai l'intention d'aller> <to be meant for : être destiné à> **2** SIGNIFY : signifier, vouloir dire <what do you mean? : qu'est-ce que tu veux dire?> **3** MATTER : compter, importer <it means a lot to me : ça compte beaucoup pour moi>

mean[2] *adj* **1** LOWLY : pauvre, misérable **2** AVERAGE : moyen **3** STINGY : avare, mesquin **4** MALICIOUS : méchant **5** **that's no mean feat** : ce n'est pas un mince exploit

mean[3] *n* **1** MIDPOINT : milieu *m* **2** AVERAGE : moyenne *f* **3** **means** *npl* WAY : moyen *m* **4** **means** *npl* RESOURCES : ressources *fpl,* moyens *mpl*

meander [mi'ændər] *vi* **1** WIND : serpenter, faire des méandres **2** WANDER : errer

meaning ['mi:nɪŋ] *n* **1** : sens *m,* signification *f* <double meaning : double sens> **2** INTENT : intention *f*

meaningful ['mi:nɪŋfəl] *adj* : significatif

meaningfully ['mi:nɪŋfəli] *adv* : de façon significative

meaningless ['mi:nɪŋləs] *adj* : sans signification, dénué de sens

meanness ['mi:nnəs] *n* **1** NASTINESS : méchanceté *f* **2** STINGINESS : avarice *f*

meantime[1] ['mi:n,taɪm] *adv* → **meanwhile**[1]

meantime[2] *n* **1** : intervalle *m* **2** **in the meantime** : en attendant, entretemps

meanwhile[1] ['mi:n,*h*waɪl] *adv* : entretemps

meanwhile[2] *n* → **meantime**[2]

measles ['mi:zəlz] *npl* : rougeole *f*

measly ['mi:zli] *adj* **measlier; -est** : misérable, minable *fam*

measurable ['mɛʒərəbəl, 'meɪ-] *adj* : mesurable

measure[1] ['mɛʒər, 'meɪ-] *v* **-sured; -suring** : mesurer

measure[2] *n* **1** AMOUNT : mesure *f,* dose *f* <in large measure : dans une large mesure> <a measure of success : un certain succès> **2** DIMENSIONS : mesure *f* **3** RULER : règle *f* **4** **measures** *npl* : mesures *fpl* <security measures : mesures de sécurité>

measureless ['mɛʒərləs, 'meɪ-] *adj* : infini, incommensurable

measurement ['mɛʒərmənt, 'meɪ-] *n* **1** MEASURING : mesurage *m* **2** DIMENSION : dimension *f,* mesure *f*

measure up *vi* **to measure up to** : être à la hauteur de

meat ['mi:t] *n* **1** : viande *f* **2** FOOD : aliments *mpl,* nourriture *f* **3** SUBSTANCE : substance *f*

meatball ['mi:t,bɔl] *n* : boulette *f* de viande

meaty ['mi:ṭi] *adj* **meatier; -est** **1** : de viande **2** SUBSTANTIAL : substantiel

mechanic [mɪ'kænɪk] *n* : mécanicien *m,* -cienne *f*

mechanical [mɪ'kænɪkəl] *adj* **1** : mécanique **2** AUTOMATIC : machinal, automatique — **mechanically** *adv*

mechanics [mɪ'kænɪks] *ns & pl* **1** : mécanique *f* **2** MECHANISMS, WORKINGS : mécanismes *mpl*

mechanism ['mɛkə,nɪzəm] *n* : mécanisme *m*

mechanization [,mɛkənə'zeɪʃən] *n* : mécanisation *f*

mechanize ['mɛkə,naɪz] *vt* **-nized; -nizing** : mécaniser

medal ['mɛdəl] *n* : médaille *f*

medalist *or* **medallist** ['mɛdəlɪst] *n* : médaillé *m,* -lée *f*

medallion [mə'dæljən] *n* : médaillon *m*

meddle ['mɛdəl] *vi* **-dled; -dling** : se mêler

meddlesome ['mɛdəlsəm] *adj* : qui se mêle de tout, indiscret

media ['mi:diə] *ns & pl* **the media** : les médias *mpl*

median[1] ['mi:diən] *adj* : médian

median[2] *n* : médiane *f* (en mathématiques)

mediate ['mi:di,eɪt] *vi* **-ated; -ating** : servir de médiateur, arbitrer

mediation [,mi:di'eɪʃən] *n* : médiation *f*

mediator ['mi:di,eɪṭər] *n* : médiateur *m,* -trice *f*

medical ['mɛdɪkəl] *adj* : médical — **medically** [-kli] *adv*

medicated ['mɛdə,keɪṭəd] *adj* : médical, traitant

medication [,mɛdə'keɪʃən] *n* **1** TREATMENT : médication *f,* soins *mpl* **2** MEDICINE : médicament *m*

medicinal [mə'dɪsənəl] *adj* : médicinal

medicine ['mɛdəsən] *n* **1** : médecine *f* <she's studying medicine : elle étudie la médecine> **2** MEDICATION : médicament *m*

medicine man *n* : sorcier *m*

medieval *or* **mediaeval** [mɪ'di:vəl, ,mi:-, ,mɛ-, -di'i:vəl] *adj* : médiéval

mediocre [,mi:di'o:kər] *adj* : médiocre

mediocrity [,mi:di'ɑkrəṭi] *n, pl* **-ties** : médiocrité *f*

meditate ['mɛdə,teɪt] *vi* **-tated; -tating** : méditer

meditation [,mɛdə'teɪʃən] *n* : méditation *f*

meditative ['mɛdə,teɪṭɪv] *adj* : méditatif

medium[1] ['mi:diəm] *adj* : moyen <of medium height : de taille moyenne>

medium[2] *n, pl* **-diums** *or* **-dia** ['mi:diə] **1** MEAN : milieu *m* <the happy medium : le juste milieu> **2** MEANS : moyen *m* (de communication) **3** SUBSTANCE : milieu *m,* véhicule *m* (en biologique ou en physique) **4** : moyen *m* (artistique) **5** *pl* **mediums** SPIRITUALIST : médium *m*

medley ['mɛdli] *n, pl* **-leys** **1** MIXTURE : mélange *m* **2** : pot-pourri *m* (de chansons)

meek ['mi:k] *adj* : doux, docile

meekly ['mi:kli] *adv* : doucement

meekness [ˈmiːknəs] *n* : douceur *f*
meet[1] [ˈmiːt] *v* **met** [ˈmɛt]; **meeting** *vt* **1** ENCOUNTER : rencontrer **2** : faire la connaissance de <I've never met her : je n'ai pas fait sa connaissance> **3** JOIN : rejoindre **4** CONFRONT : affronter <to meet the enemy : affronter l'ennemi> **5** SATISFY : satisfaire **6** AWAIT : attendre <I'll meet you at the station : je t'attendrai à la gare> — *vi* **1** : se rencontrer **2** : ASSEMBLE : se réunir
meet[2] *n* : rencontre *f* (aux sports)
meeting [ˈmiːt̬ɪŋ] *n* : réunion *f*
meetinghouse [ˈmiːt̬ɪŋˌhaʊs] *n* : temple *m*
megabyte [ˈmɛgəˌbaɪt] *n* : mégaoctet *m*
megahertz [ˈmɛgəˌhərts, -ˌhɛrts] *ns & pl* : mégahertz *m*
megaphone [ˈmɛgəˌfoːn] *n* : porte-voix *m*, mégaphone *m*
melancholy[1] [ˈmɛlənˌkɑli] *adj* : mélancolique
melancholy[2] *n, pl* **-cholies** : mélancolie *f*
melanoma [ˌmɛləˈnoːmə] *n, pl* **-mas** : mélanome *m*
melee [ˈmeɪˌleɪ, meɪˈleɪ] *n* : mêlée *f*
meliorate [ˈmiːljəˌreɪt, ˈmiːliə-] → **ameliorate**
mellow[1] [ˈmɛloː] *vt* : adoucir — *vi* **1** : s'adoucir **2** AGE : mûrir
mellow[2] *adj* **1** MILD : doux, moelleux **2** RIPE : mûr **3** RELAXED : détendu
mellowness [ˈmɛlonəs] *n* : douceur *f*, moelleux *m*
melodic [məˈlɑdɪk] *adj* : mélodique — **melodically** [-dɪkli] *adv*
melodious [məˈloːdiəs] *adj* : mélodieux — **melodiously** *adv*
melodrama [ˈmɛləˌdrɑmə, -ˌdræ-] *n* : mélodrame *m*
melodramatic [ˌmɛlədrəˈmæt̬ɪk] *adj* : mélodramatique
melodramatically [ˌmɛlədrəˈmæt̬ɪkli] *adv* : de façon mélodramatique
melody [ˈmɛlədi] *n, pl* **-dies** : mélodie *f*
melon [ˈmɛlən] *n* : melon *m*
melt [ˈmɛlt] *vi* **1** : fondre **2** SOFTEN : s'attendrir — *vt* **1** : fondre, faire fondre **2** SOFTEN : attendrir <to melt s.o.'s heart : attendrir le cœur de qqn>
melting point *n* : point *m* de fusion
member [ˈmɛmbər] *n* **1** : membre *m;* adhérent *m,* -rente *f* **2** LIMB : membre *m*
membership [ˈmɛmbərˌʃɪp] *n* **1** : adhésion *f* **2** MEMBERS : membres *mpl;* adhérents *mpl,* -rentes *fpl*
membrane [ˈmɛmˌbreɪn] *n* : membrane *f* — **membranous** [ˈmɛmbrənəs] *adj*
memento [mɪˈmɛnˌtoː] *n, pl* **-tos** *or* **-toes** : souvenir *m*
memo [ˈmɛmoː] *n, pl* **memos** : mémorandum *m*
memoirs [ˈmɛmˌwɑrz] *npl* : mémoires *mpl*
memorabilia [ˌmɛmərəˈbiliə, -ˈbɪljə] *npl* : souvenirs *mpl*
memorable [ˈmɛmərəbəl] *adj* : mémorable
memorably [ˈmɛmərəbli] *adv* : de façon mémorable
memorandum [ˌmɛməˈrændəm] *n, pl* **-dums** *or* **-da** [-də] : mémorandum *m*
memorial[1] [məˈmoriəl] *adj* : commémoratif
memorial[2] *n* : mémorial *m,* monument *m* (commémoratif)
Memorial Day *n* : le dernier lundi du mois de mai (férié aux États-Unis en commémoration des soldats morts à la guerre)
memorialize [məˈmoriəˌlaɪz] *vt* **-ized; -izing** COMMEMORATE : commémorer
memorize [ˈmɛməˌraɪz] *vt* **-rized; -rizing** : mémoriser
memory [ˈmɛmri, ˈmɛmə-] *n, pl* **-ries 1** : mémoire *f* <to have a good memory : avoir une bonne mémoire> **2** RECOLLECTION : souvenir *m*
men → **man**[2]
menace[1] [ˈmɛnəs] *vt* **-aced; -acing** : menacer
menace[2] *n* **1** THREAT : menace *f* **2** DANGER : danger *m*
menacing [ˈmɛnəsɪŋ] *adj* : menaçant
menagerie [məˈnædʒəri, -ˈnæʒəri] *n* : ménagerie *f*
mend[1] [ˈmɛnd] *vt* **1** IMPROVE : améliorer **2** REPAIR : réparer **3** DARN, SEW : repriser, raccommoder — *vi* HEAL : s'améliorer
mend[2] *n* : reprise *f*
mendicant [ˈmɛndɪkənt] *n* BEGGAR : mendiant *m,* -diante *f*
menial[1] [ˈmiːniəl] *adj* : servile <a menial position : un poste subalterne>
menial[2] *n* : domestique *mf*
meningitis [ˌmɛnənˈdʒaɪt̬əs] *n, pl* **-gitides** [-ˈdʒɪt̬əˌdiːz] : méningite *f*
menopause [ˈmɛnəˌpɔz] *n* : ménopause *f*
menorah [məˈnɔrə] *n* : candélabre *m* (employé dans des cérémonies religieuses juives)
menstrual [ˈmɛntstrʊəl] *adj* : menstruel
menstruate [ˈmɛntstrʊˌeɪt] *vi* **-ated; -ating** : avoir ses règles
menstruation [ˌmɛntstrʊˈeɪʃən] *n* : menstruation *f,* règles *fpl*
mental [ˈmɛntəl] *adj* : mental — **mentally** *adv*
mentality [mɛnˈtæləti] *n, pl* **-ties** : mentalité *f*
menthol [ˈmɛnˌθɔl, -ˌθoːl] *n* : menthol *m*
mentholated [ˈmɛntθəˌleɪt̬əd] *adj* : mentholé
mention[1] [ˈmɛntʃən] *vt* **1** : mentionner **2 don't mention it!** : il n'y a pas de quoi! **3 not to mention** : sans parler de
mention[2] *n* : mention *f*

mentor ['mɛn,tɔr, 'mɛntər] *n* : mentor *m*
menu ['mɛn,ju:] *n* : menu *m*
meow[1] [mi:'aʊ] *vi* : miauler
meow[2] *n* : miaou *m*
mercantile ['mɛrkən,ti:l, -,taɪl] *adj* : mercantile, commercial
mercenary[1] ['mərsən,ɛri] *adj* : mercenaire
mercenary[2] *n, pl* **-naries** : mercenaire *mf*
merchandise ['mərtʃən,daɪz, -,daɪs] *n* : marchandises *fpl*
merchant ['mərtʃənt] *n* : marchand *m*, -chande *f;* commerçant *m*, -çante *f;* négociant *m*, -ciante *f*
merchant marine *n* : marine *f* marchande
merciful ['mərsɪfəl] *adj* : miséricordieux
mercifully ['mərsɪfli] *adv* **1** COMPASSIONATELY : avec clémence **2** FORTUNATELY : par bonheur, heureusement
merciless ['mərsɪləs] *adj* : impitoyable — **mercilessly** *adv*
mercurial [mər'kjʊriəl] *adj* TEMPERAMENTAL : inconstant, d'humeur inégale
mercury ['mərkjəri] *n* : mercure *m*
Mercury ['mərkjəri] *n* : Mercure *f* (planète)
mercy ['mɛrsi] *n, pl* **-cies 1** CLEMENCY : clémence *f*, miséricorde *f* (en religion) **2** BLESSING, FORTUNE : chance *f*, bonheur *m*
mere ['mɪr] *adj, superlative* **merest** : simple, pur, seul <the mere sight of him : sa seule vue> <a mere ten percent : dix pour cent seulement>
merely ['mɪrli] *adv* : simplement, seulement
merge ['mərdʒ] *v* **merged; merging** *vi* **1** BLEND, COMBINE : se mêler, se joindre, se fondre **2** : fusionner (se dit des affaires) — *vt* : fusionner, joindre
merger ['mərdʒər] *n* : fusion *f*
meridian [mə'rɪdiən] *n* : méridien *m*
meringue [mə'ræŋ] *n* : meringue *f*
merino [mə'ri:no] *n, pl* **-nos** : mérinos *m*
merit[1] ['mɛrət] *vt* : mériter
merit[2] *n* : mérite *m*
meritorious [,mɛrə'toriəs] *adj* : méritoire (se dit d'une action, etc.), méritant (se dit d'une personne)
mermaid ['mər,meɪd] *n* : sirène *f*
merriment ['mɛrɪmənt] *n* : gaieté *f*, hilarité *f*
merry ['mɛri] *adj* **merrier; -est** : joyeux, gai <Merry Christmas! : Joyeux Noël!> — **merrily** *adv*
merry-go-round ['mɛrigo,raʊnd] *n* : manège *m* (de chevaux de bois)
merrymaker ['mɛri,meɪkər] *n* : fêtard *m*, -tarde *f*
merrymaking ['mɛri,meɪkɪŋ] *n* : réjouissances *fpl*
mesa ['meɪsə] *n* : mesa *f*
mesdames → **madam, Mrs.**
mesh[1] ['mɛʃ] *vi* **1** ENGAGE : s'engrener (en méchanique) **2** TANGLE : s'enchevêtrer **3** COINCIDE, TALLY : cadrer, concorder
mesh[2] *n* **1** NET : maille *f* **2** NETWORK : réseau *m* **3** MESHING : engrenure *f* (en technologie)
mesmerize ['mɛzmə,raɪz] *vt* **-ized; -izing 1** HYPNOTIZE : hypnotiser **2** FASCINATE : fasciner, captiver
mess[1] ['mɛs] *vt* **1** SOIL : salir **2 to mess up** DISARRANGE : mettre en désordre **3 to mess up** BUNGLE : gâcher — *vi* **1 to mess around** PUTTER : bricoler **2 to mess with** INTERFERE : s'immiscer
mess[2] *n* **1** : mess *m* <officer's mess : mess des officiers> **2** DISORDER : désordre *m*, gâchis *m* <your room is a mess : ta chambre est un désastre>
message ['mɛsɪdʒ] *n* : message *m*
messenger ['mɛsəndʒər] *n* : messager *m*, -gère *f*
Messiah [mə'saɪə] *n* **the Messiah** : le Messie *m*
Messrs. → **Mr.**
messy ['mɛsi] *adj* **messier; -est 1** DIRTY : sale **2** UNTIDY : désordonné, en désordre **3** AWKWARD, DIFFICULT : embrouillé, difficile
met → **meet**[1]
metabolic [,mɛt̬ə'bɑlɪk] *adj* : métabolique
metabolism [mə'tæbə,lɪzəm] *n* : métabolisme *m*
metabolize [mə'tæbə,laɪz] *vt* **-lized; -lizing** : métaboliser
metal ['mɛt̬əl] *n* : métal *m*
metallic [mə'tælɪk] *adj* : métallique
metallurgy ['mɛt̬əl,ərdʒi] *n* : métallurgie *f*
metalwork ['mɛt̬əl,wərk] *n* : ferronnerie *f*
metamorphosis [,mɛt̬ə'mɔrfəsɪs] *n, pl* **-phoses** [-'si:z] : métamorphose *f*
metaphor ['mɛt̬ə,fɔr, -fər] *n* : métaphore *f*
metaphoric [,mɛt̬ə'fɔrɪk] *or* **metaphorical** [-ɪkəl] *adj* : métaphorique
metaphysical [,mɛt̬ə'fɪzəkəl] *adj* : métaphysique
metaphysics [,mɛt̬ə'fɪzɪks] *n* : métaphysique *f*
mete ['mi:t] *vt* **meted; meting** : infliger, rendre <to mete out punishment : infliger un châtiment>
meteor ['mi:t̬iər, -t̬i,ɔr] *n* : météore *m*
meteoric [,mi:t̬i'ɔrɪk] *adj* : météorique
meteorite ['mi:t̬iə,raɪt] *n* : météorite *mf*
meteorologic [,mi:t̬i,ɔrə'lɑdʒɪk] *or* **meteorological** [-'lɑdʒɪkəl] *adj* : météorologique
meteorologist [,mi:t̬iə'rɑlədʒɪst] *n* : météorologue *mf*, météorologiste *mf*
meteorology [,mi:t̬iə'rɑlədʒi] *n* : météorologie *f*

meter *or Brit* **metre** [ˈmiːt̬ər] *n* **1** : mètre *m* <two meters high : deux mètres de hauteur> **2** : compteur *m* (d'électricité, etc.) **3** : mesure *f* (en poésie, en musique, etc.) **4** *or* **parking meter** : parcmètre *m France*, parcomètre *m Can*
methane [ˈmɛˌθeɪn] *n* : méthane *m*
method [ˈmɛθəd] *n* : méthode *f*
methodical [məˈθɑdɪkəl] *adj* : méthodique — **methodically** *adv*
meticulous [məˈtɪkjələs] *adj* : méticuleux — **meticulously** *adv*
metre *Brit* → **meter**
metric [ˈmɛtrɪk] *or* **metrical** [-trɪkəl] *adj* : métrique
metric system *n* : système *m* métrique
metronome [ˈmɛtrəˌnoːm] *n* : métronome *m*
metropolis [məˈtrɑpələs] *n* : métropole *f*
metropolitan [ˌmɛtrəˈpɑlətən] *adj* : métropolitain
mettle [ˈmɛt̬əl] *n* : courage *m*, ardeur *f* <to show one's mettle : montrer de quoi on est capable>
Mexican[1] [ˈmɛksɪkən] *adj* : mexicain
Mexican[2] *n* : Mexicain *m*, -caine *f*
mezzanine [ˈmɛzəˌniːn, ˌmɛzəˈniːn] *n* : mezzanine *f*
miasma [maɪˈæzmə] *n* : miasme *m*
mica [ˈmaɪkə] *n* : mica *m*
mice → **mouse**
microbe [ˈmaɪˌkroːb] *n* : microbe *m*
microbiology [ˌmaɪkrobaɪˈɑləd͡ʒi] *n* : microbiologie *f*
microcomputer [ˈmaɪkrokəmˌpjuːt̬ər] *n* : micro-ordinateur *m*
microcosm [ˈmaɪkroˌkɑzəm] *n* : microcosme *m*
microfilm [ˈmaɪkroˌfɪlm] *n* : microfilm *m*
micrometer *or Brit* **micrometre** [ˈmaɪkroˌmiːtər] *n* : micromètre *m* (unité de mesure)
micron [ˈmaɪˌkrɑn] → **micrometer**
microorganism [ˌmaɪkroˈɔrgəˌnɪzəm] *n* : micro-organisme *m*
microphone [ˈmaɪkrəˌfoːn] *n* : microphone *m*
microprocessor [ˌmaɪkroˈprɑˌsɛsər] *n* : microprocesseur *m*
microscope [ˈmaɪkrəˌskoːp] *n* : microscope *m*
microscopic [ˌmaɪkrəˈskɑpɪk] *adj* : microscopique
microscopy [maɪˈkrɑskəpi] *n* : microscopie *f*
microwave [ˈmaɪkrəˌweɪv] *n* **1** : micro-onde *f* **2** *or* **microwave oven** : four *m* à micro-ondes, micro-ondes *m*
mid [ˈmɪd] *adj* : mi <since mid-June : dès la mi-juin> <in the mid nineteenth century : au milieu du dix-neuvième siècle> <she's in her mid thirties : elle a dans les 35 ans>
midair [ˈmɪdˈær] *n* **in ~** : en plein ciel
midday [ˈmɪdˈdeɪ] *n* NOON : midi *m*
middle[1] [ˈmɪdəl] *adj* **1** CENTRAL : du milieu, central **2** INTERMEDIATE : moyen
middle[2] *n* **1** CENTER : centre *m*, milieu *m* **2 in the middle of** : au milieu de
middle age *n* : la cinquantaine, l'âge *m* mûr
Middle Ages *npl* : Moyen Âge *m*
middle class *n* : classe *f* moyenne
middleman [ˈmɪdəlˌmæn] *n, pl* **-men** [-mən, -ˌmɛn] : intermédiaire *mf*
middling [ˈmɪdlɪŋ, -lən] *adj* **1** AVERAGE : moyen **2** MEDIOCRE : médiocre
midge [ˈmɪd͡ʒ] *n* : moucheron *m*
midget [ˈmɪd͡ʒət] *n* : nain *m*, naine *f*
midland [ˈmɪdlənd, -ˌlænd] *n* : région *f* centrale (d'un pays)
midnight [ˈmɪdˌnaɪt] *n* : minuit *m*
midpoint [ˈmɪdˌpɔɪnt] *n* : milieu *m*
midriff [ˈmɪdˌrɪf] *n* : ventre *m*
midshipman [ˈmɪdˌʃɪpmən, ˌmɪdˈʃɪp-] *n, pl* **-men** [-mən, -ˌmɛn] : aspirant *m*
midst[1] [ˈmɪdst] *n* : milieu *m* <in the midst of : en plein milieu de> <in our midst : parmi nous>
midst[2] *prep* : parmi
midstream [ˈmɪdˈstriːm, -ˌstriːm] *n* **in ~** : au milieu du courant
midsummer [ˈmɪdˈsʌmər, -ˌsʌ-] *n* : milieu *m* de l'été
midway [ˈmɪdˌweɪ] *adv* : à mi-chemin
midweek [ˈmɪdˌwiːk] *n* : milieu *m* de la semaine
midwife [ˈmɪdˌwaɪf] *n, pl* **-wives** [-ˌwaɪvz] : sage-femme *f*
midwinter [ˈmɪdˈwɪntər, -ˌwɪn-] *n* : milieu *m* de l'hiver
midyear [ˈmɪdˌjɪr] *n* : milieu *m* de l'année
mien [ˈmiːn] *n* DEMEANOR : mine *f*
miff [ˈmɪf] *vt* : vexer
might[1] [ˈmaɪt] (*used to express permission or possibility or as a polite alternative to* **may**) → **may** <it might be true : il se peut que cela soit vrai> <might I speak with her? : puis-je lui parler?>
might[2] *n* **1** STRENGTH : force *f* **2** POWER : puissance *f*, pouvoir *m*
mightily [ˈmaɪt̬əli] *adv* **1** EXTREMELY : extrêmement **2** VIGOROUSLY : vigoureusement
mighty[1] [ˈmaɪt̬i] *adv* : très, rudement *fam* <that's mighty nice : c'est rudement gentil>
mighty[2] *adj* **mightier; -est 1** STRONG : puissant **2** GREAT : imposant, grand
migraine [ˈmaɪˌgreɪn] *n* : migraine *f*
migrant [ˈmaɪgrənt] *n* : migrant *m*, -grante *f*
migrate [ˈmaɪˌgreɪt] *vi* **-grated; -grating** : migrer
migration [maɪˈgreɪʃən] *n* : migration *f*
migratory [ˈmaɪgrəˌtori] *adj* : migrateur <migratory birds : oiseaux migrateurs>
mild [ˈmaɪld] *adj* **1** GENTLE : doux **2** LIGHT : léger **3** TEMPERATE : tempéré

<a mild climate : un climat tempéré> <it's a mild day : il fait doux>

mildew[1] |'mɪl,du:, -,dju:| *vi* : moisir

mildew[2] *n* : moisissure *f*

mildly |'maɪldli| *adv* **1** GENTLY : doucement, avec douceur **2** LIGHTLY, MODERATELY : légèrement, modérément

mildness |'maɪldnəs| *n* : douceur *f*

mile |'maɪl| *n* : mille *m*, mile *m*

mileage |'maɪlɪdʒ| *n* **1** *or* **mileage allowance** : indemnité *f* **2** CONSUMPTION : consommation *f* (de l'essence) <the car gets better mileage : la voiture consomme moins> **3** DISTANCE : distance *f*, nombre *m* de milles, millage *m Can*

milestone |'maɪl,sto:n| *n* **1** LANDMARK : borne *f* milliaire **2** : étape *f* importante, jalon *m* <an important milestone in science : un jalon important dans la science>

milieu |mi:l'ju:, -'jø| *n, pl* **-lieus** *or* **-lieux** |-'ju:z, -'jø| SURROUNDINGS : milieu *m*

militant[1] |'mɪlətənt| *adj* : militant

militant[2] *n* : militant *m*, -tante *f*

militarism |'mɪlət̬ə,rɪzəm| *n* : militarisme *m*

militaristic |,mɪlət̬ə'rɪstɪk| *adj* : militariste

military[1] |'mɪlə,tɛri| *adj* : militaire

military[2] *n* **the military** *n* : l'armée *f*

militia |mə'lɪʃə| *n* : milice *f*

milk[1] |'mɪlk| *vt* **1** : traire (une vache, etc.) **2** EXPLOIT : exploiter

milk[2] *n* : lait *m*

milkman |'mɪlk,mæn, -mən| *n, pl* **-men** |-mən, -,mɛn| : laitier *m*

milk shake *n* : milk-shake *m*

milkweed |'mɪlk,wi:d| *n* : laiteron *m*

milky |'mɪlki| *adj* **milkier; -est** : laiteux

Milky Way : la Voie lactée

mill[1] |'mɪl| *vt* **1** GRIND : moudre **2** GROOVE : créneler — *vi or* **to mill about** SWARM : fourmiller

mill[2] *n* **1** : moulin *m* **2** FACTORY : usine *f*, fabrique *f*

millennium |mə'lɛniəm| *n, pl* **-nia** |-niə| *or* **-niums** : millénaire *m*

miller |'mɪlər| *n* : meunier *m*, -nière *f*

millet |'mɪlət| *n* : millet *m*

milligram |'mɪlə,græm| *n* : milligramme *m*

milliliter |'mɪlə,li:t̬ər| *n* : millilitre *m*

millimeter *or Brit* **millimetre** |'mɪlə,mi:t̬ər| : millimètre *m*

milliner |'mɪlənər| *n* : modiste *mf*

million[1] |'mɪljən| *adj* **a million** : un million de

million[2] *n, pl* **millions** *or* **million 1** : million *m* **2 millions** *npl* MASSES : masses *fpl*

millionaire |,mɪljə'nær, 'mɪljə,nær| *n* : millionnaire *mf*

millionth[1] |'mɪljənθ| *adj* : millionième

millionth[2] *n* **1** : millionième *mf* (dans une série) **2** : millionième *m* (en mathématiques)

millipede |'mɪlə,pi:d| *n* : mille-pattes *m*

millstone |'mɪl,sto:n| *n* : meule *f*

mime[1] |'maɪm| *v* **mimed; miming** *vt* : mimer — *vi* : faire du mime

mime[2] *n* : mime *mf*

mimeograph[1] |'mɪmiə,græf| *vt* : polycopier

mimeograph[2] *n* : polycopie *f*

mimic[1] |'mɪmɪk| *vt* **-icked; -icking 1** IMITATE : imiter, mimer **2** APE : singer, parodier

mimic[2] *n* : imitateur *m*, -trice *f*

mimicry |'mɪmɪkri| *n, pl* **-ries** : imitation *f*

minaret |,mɪnə'rɛt| *n* : minaret *m*

mince |'mɪnts| *v* **minced; mincing** *vt* **1** CHOP : hacher **2 not to mince one's words** : ne pas mâcher ses mots — *vi* : marcher d'un air affecté

mind[1] |'maɪnd| *vt* **1** TEND : garder, surveiller **2** OBEY : obéir à **3** WATCH : faire attention à <mind your language! : surveille ton langage!> <mind the step! : attention à la marche!> **4** (*indicating dislike*) <I don't mind going : ça ne me dérange pas d'aller> <I wouldn't mind a drink : j'aimerais bien un verre> — *vi* **1** OBEY : obéir **2** (*indicating an objection*) <I don't mind : ça m'est égal> <do you mind if I take the car? : est-ce que cela vous ennuie que je prenne la voiture?>

mind[2] *n* **1** : esprit *m* <state of mind : état d'esprit> <it never entered my mind : cela ne m'est jamais venu à l'esprit> <mind over matter : l'esprit sur la matière> **2** INTELLIGENCE : intelligence *f* **3** OPINION : avis *m* <to change one's mind : changer d'avis> **4** MEMORY : mémoire *f* <to call to mind : se rappeler> **5** REASON : raison *f* <he's out of his mind : il est fou>

minded |'maɪndəd| *adj* **1** INCLINED : disposé **2** (*used in combination*) <narrow-minded : étroit d'esprit> <health-minded : soucieux de la santé>

mindful |'maɪndfəl| *adj* AWARE : attentif — **mindfully** *adv*

mindless |'maɪndləs| *adj* **1** SENSELESS : insensé, stupide **2** HEEDLESS : insouciant **3** BORING : machinal, ennuyeux <a mindless task : un travail machinal>

mindlessly |'maɪndləsli| *adv* **1** SENSELESSLY : stupidement **2** HEEDLESSLY : avec insouciance **3** AUTOMATICALLY : machinalement

mine[1] |'maɪn| *vt* **mined; mining 1** : extraire (du charbon, etc.) **2** : miner (avec des explosifs)

mine[2] *n* : mine *f*

mine[3] *pron* : le mien *m*, la mienne *f*, les miens *mpl*, les miennes *fpl* <not your car but mine : pas ta voiture mais la mienne> <her French is better than mine : son français est

supérieur au mien> <a friend of mine : un ami à moi>
minefield [ˈmaɪn,fi:ld] *n* : champ *m* de mines
miner [ˈmaɪnər] *n* : mineur *m*
mineral [ˈmɪnərəl] *n* : minéral *m* — **mineral** *adj*
mineralogical [,mɪnərəˈlɑdʒɪkəl] *adj* : minéralogique
mineralogy [,mɪnəˈrɑlədʒi] *n* : minéralogie *f*
mingle [ˈmɪŋgəl] *v* **-gled; -gling** *vt* : mêler, mélanger — *vi* : se mêler, se mélanger
miniature[1] [ˈmɪniə,tʃʊr, ˈmɪnɪ,tʃʊr, -tʃər] *adj* : en miniature
miniature[2] *n* : miniature *f*
minibus [ˈmɪni,bʌs] *n* : minibus *m*
minicomputer [ˈmɪnikəm,pju:t̬ər] *n* : mini-ordinateur *m*
minimal [ˈmɪnəməl] *adj* : minimal
minimally [ˈmɪnəmli] *adv* : à peine, très légèrement
minimize [ˈmɪnə,maɪz] *vt* **-mized; -mizing** : minimiser
minimum[1] [ˈmɪnəmem] *adj* : minimum, minimal
minimum[2] *n, pl* **-ma** [ˈmɪnəme] *or* **-mums** : minimum *m*
miniscule → **minuscule**
miniskirt [ˈmɪni,skərt] *n* : minijupe *f*
minister[1] [ˈmɪnəstər] *vi* **to minister to** : pourvoir à, donner des soins à
minister[2] *n* **1** : ministre *m* (en politique) **2** : pasteur *m* (d'une église)
ministerial [,mɪnəˈstɪriəl] *adj* : ministériel
ministry [ˈmɪnəstri] *n, pl* **-tries** : ministère *m*
minivan [ˈmɪni,væn] *n* : fourgonnette *f*
mink [ˈmɪŋk] *n, pl* **mink** *or* **minks** : vison *m*
minnow [ˈmɪno:] *n* : vairon *m*, mené *m* *Can*
minor[1] [ˈmaɪnər] *adj* **1** UNIMPORTANT : mineur **2** SECONDARY : secondaire <minor role : rôle secondaire>
minor[2] *n* : mineur *m*, -neure *f*
minority [məˈnɔrət̬i, maɪ-] *n, pl* **-ties** : minorité *f*
minstrel [ˈmɪn*t*strəl] *n* : ménestrel *m*
mint[1] [ˈmɪnt] *vt* : frapper
mint[2] *adj* **in mint condition** : à l'état neuf
mint[3] *n* **1** : menthe *f* (herbe) **2** : bonbon *m* à la menthe **3 the Mint** : l'Hôtel *m* de la Monnaie, la Monnaie **4 to be worth a mint** : valoir une fortune
minuet [,mɪnjoˈɛt] *n* : menuet *m*
minus[1] [ˈmaɪnəs] *n* **1** : quantité *f* négative **2** *or* **minus sign** : moins *m*
minus[2] *prep* **1** : moins <four minus two : quatre moins deux> **2** WITHOUT : sans <minus her gloves : sans ses gants>
minuscule *or* **miniscule** [ˈmɪnəs,kju:l, mɪˈnʌs-] *adj* : minuscule
minute[1] [maɪˈnu:t, mɪ-, -ˈnju:t] *adj* **minuter; -est 1** TINY : minuscule **2** DETAILED : minutieux
minute[2] [ˈmɪnət] *n* **1** : minute *f* <in ten minutes : dans dix minutes> **2** MOMENT : moment *m* **3 minutes** *npl* : procès-verbal *m* (d'une réunion)
minutely [maɪˈnu:tli, mɪ-, -ˈnju:t-] *adv* : minutieusement
miracle [ˈmɪrɪkəl] *n* : miracle *m*
miraculous [məˈrækjələs] *adj* : miraculeux — **miraculously** *adv*
mirage [mɪˈrɑʒ, *chiefly Brit* ˈmɪr,ɑʒ] *n* : mirage *m*
mire[1] [ˈmaɪr] *vt* **mired; miring** STICK : embourber <to get mired down in : s'embourber dans>
mire[2] *n* : boue *f*, fange *f*
mirror[1] [ˈmɪrər] *vt* : refléter, réfléchir
mirror[2] *n* : miroir *m*, glace *f*
mirth [ˈmərθ] *n* : gaité *f*, hilarité *f*
mirthful [ˈmərθfəl] *adj* : gai, joyeux
misanthrope [ˈmɪsən,θro:p] *n* : misanthrope *mf*
misanthropic [,mɪsənˈθrɑpɪk] *adj* : misanthrope
misanthropy [mɪˈsænθrəpi] *n* : misanthropie *f*
misapprehend [,mɪs,æprəˈhɛnd] *vt* : mal comprendre
misapprehension [,mɪs,æprəˈhɛntʃən] *n* : malentendu *m*, méprise *f*
misappropriate [,mɪsəˈpro:pri,eɪt] *vt* **-ated; -ating** : détourner
misbegotten [,mɪsbiˈgɑtən] *adj* **1** ILLEGITIMATE : illégitime **2** : mal conçu (se dit des plans, des lois, etc.)
misbehave [,mɪsbiˈheɪv] *vi* **-haved; -having** : se conduire mal
misbehavior [,mɪsbiˈheɪvjər] *n* : mauvaise conduite *f*
miscalculate [mɪsˈkælkjə,leɪt] *v* **-lated; -lating** *vt* : mal calculer — *vi* : se tromper
miscalculation [mɪs,kælkjəˈleɪʃən] *n* : erreur *f* de calcul, mauvais calcul *m*
miscarriage [,mɪsˈkærɪdʒ, ˈmɪs,kærɪdʒ] *n* **1** : fausse couche *f* **2** FAILURE : échec *m* <miscarriage of justice : erreur judiciaire>
miscarry [,mɪsˈkæri, ˈmɪs,kæri] *vi* **-ried; -rying 1** ABORT : faire une fausse couche **2** FAIL : échouer
miscellaneous [,mɪsəˈleɪniəs] *adj* : divers, varié
miscellany [ˈmɪsə,leɪni] *n, pl* **-nies** : mélange *m*, collection *f* disparate
mischance [mɪsˈtʃæn*t*s] *n* : malchance *f*
mischief [ˈmɪstʃəf] *n* : espièglerie *f*, malice *f*
mischievous [ˈmɪstʃəvəs] *adj* : espiègle, malicieux
mischievously [ˈmɪstʃəvəsli] *adv* : malicieusement
misconception [,mɪskənˈsɛpʃən] *n* : idée *f* fausse
misconduct [mɪsˈkɑndəkt] *n* : inconduite *f*, mauvaise conduite *f*

misconstrue [ˌmɪskən'stru:] *vt* **-strued; -struing** : mal interpréter

miscreant ['mɪskriənt] *n* VILLAIN : scélérat *m*, -rate *f*

misdeed [mɪs'di:d] *n* : méfait *m*

misdemeanor [ˌmɪsdɪ'mi:nər] *n* : méfait *m*, délit *m* (judiciaire)

miser ['maɪzər] *n* : avare *m*

miserable ['mɪzərəbəl] *adj* **1** UNHAPPY : triste, malheureux **2** WRETCHED : misérable, minable **3** AWFUL : affreux

miserably ['mɪzərəbli] *adv* **1** SADLY : tristement **2** WRETCHEDLY : misérablement, lamentablement

miserly ['maɪzərli] *adj* : avare, séraphin *Can*

misery ['mɪzəri] *n, pl* **-eries** : tristesse *f*, misère *f*

misfire [mɪs'faɪr] *vi* **-fired; -firing** : rater <the engine is misfiring : le moteur a des ratés> <the gun misfired : l'arme a fait long feu>

misfit ['mɪsˌfɪt] *n* : inadapté *m*, -tée *f*

misfortune [mɪs'fɔrtʃən] *n* : malchance *f*, infortune *f*

misgiving [mɪs'gɪvɪŋ] *n* : doute *m*, crainte *f*

misguided [mɪs'gaɪdəd] *adj* : malencontreux, fourvoyé, peu judicieux

mishap ['mɪsˌhæp] *n* : mésaventure *f*

misinform [ˌmɪsɪn'fɔrm] *vt* : mal renseigner

misinterpret [ˌmɪsɪn'tərprət] *vt* : mal interpréter

misinterpretation [ˌmɪsɪnˌtərprə'teɪʃən] *n* : interprétation *f* erronée

misjudge [mɪs'dʒʌdʒ] *vt* **-judged; -judging** : mal juger

mislay [mɪs'leɪ] *vt* **-laid** [-'leɪd]; **-laying** : égarer

mislead [mɪs'li:d] *vt* **-led** [-'lɛd]; **-leading** : tromper, induire en erreur

misleading [mɪs'li:dɪŋ] *adj* : trompeur

mismanage [mɪs'mænɪdʒ] *vt* **-aged; -aging** : mal gérer, mal administrer

mismanagement [mɪs'mænɪdʒmənt] *n* : mauvaise gestion *f*

misnomer [mɪs'no:mər] *n* : nom *m* inapproprié

misogynist [mɪ'sɑdʒənɪst] *n* : misogyne *mf*

misplace [mɪs'pleɪs] *vt* **-placed; -placing** : mal placer, égarer

misprint ['mɪsˌprɪnt, mɪs'-] *n* : faute *f* typographique, coquille *f*

mispronounce [ˌmɪsprə'naʊnts] *vt* **-nounced; -nouncing** : mal prononcer

mispronunciation [ˌmɪsprəˌnʌntsi'eɪʃən] *n* : faute *f* de prononciation

misquote [mɪs'kwo:t] *vt* **-quoted; -quoting** : citer inexactement

misread [mɪs'ri:d] *vt* **-read** [-'rɛd]; **-reading 1** : mal lire **2** MISUNDERSTAND : mal interpréter

misrepresent [ˌmɪsˌrɛprɪ'zɛnt] *vt* : dénaturer , déformer

misrule[1] [mɪs'ru:l] *vt* **-ruled; -ruling** : mal gouverner

misrule[2] *n* : mauvais gouvernement *m*

miss[1] ['mɪs] *vt* **1** : rater, manquer <to miss the target : manquer le but> <he missed his plane : il a raté son avion> **2** : regretter l'absence de <she misses her brother : son frère lui manque> **3** AVOID, ESCAPE : éviter, échapper <he just missed being caught : il a failli être pris> **4** OMIT : omettre, sauter — *vi* : rater son coup (aux sports)

miss[2] *n* **1** : coup *m* manqué **2** FAILURE : échec *m* **3** : mademoiselle *f* <Miss Jones : Mademoiselle Jones> <excuse me, miss : pardonnez-moi, mademoiselle>

missal ['mɪsəl] *n* : missel *m*

misshapen [mɪ'ʃeɪpən] *adj* : difforme (se dit d'une personne), déformé (se dit d'une chose)

missile ['mɪsəl] *n* **1** : missile *m* <guided missile : missile téléguidé> **2** PROJECTILE : projectile *m*

missing ['mɪsɪŋ] *adj* **1** ABSENT : absent **2** LOST : égaré, disparu <missing person : personne disparue>

mission ['mɪʃən] *n* : mission *f*

missionary[1] ['mɪʃəˌnɛri] *adj* : missionnaire

missionary[2] *n, pl* **-aries** : missionnaire *mf*

missive ['mɪsɪv] *n* : missive *f*

misspell [mɪs'spɛl] *vt* : mal orthographier, mal écrire

misspelling [mɪs'spɛlɪŋ] *n* : faute *f* d'orthographe

misstep ['mɪsˌstɛp] *n* : faux pas *m*

mist ['mɪst] *n* **1** FOG : brume *f* **2** CONDENSATION : buée *f*

mistake[1] [mɪ'steɪk] *vt* **-took** [-'stʊk]; **-taken** [-'steɪkən]; **-taking 1** MISINTERPRET : mal comprendre **2** CONFUSE : confondre <he mistook her for Nicole : il l'a prise pour Nicole>

mistake[2] *n* **1** ERROR : faute *f*, erreur *f* <by mistake : par erreur> <to make a mistake : se tromper> **2** MISUNDERSTANDING : méprise *f*, malentendu *m*

mistaken [mɪ'steɪkən] *adj* WRONG : erroné

mistakenly [mɪ'steɪkənli] *adv* : à tort, par erreur

mister ['mɪstər] *n* : monsieur *m* <watch out, mister! : attention, monsieur!>

mistletoe ['mɪsəlˌto:] *n* : gui *m*

mistreat [mɪs'tri:t] *vt* : maltraiter

mistreatment [mɪs'tri:tmənt] *n* : mauvais traitement *m*

mistress ['mɪstrəs] *n* : maîtresse *f*

mistrust[1] [mɪs'trʌst] *vt* : se méfier de, douter de

mistrust[2] *n* : méfiance *f*

mistrustful [mɪs'trʌstfəl] *adj* : méfiant

misty ['mɪsti] *adj* **mistier; -est 1** FOGGY : brumeux, embrumé **2** TEARFUL : embué

misunderstand [ˌmɪsˌʌndərˈstænd] *vt* **-stood** [-ˈstʊd]; **-standing** : mal comprendre

misunderstanding [ˌmɪsˌʌndərˈstændɪŋ] *n* : malentendu *m*

misuse[1] [mɪsˈjuːz] *vt* **-used; -using 1** : faire mauvais usage de **2** MISTREAT : maltraiter

misuse[2] [mɪsˈjuːs] *n* : abus *m,* mauvais usage *m*

mite [ˈmaɪt] *n* **1** : mite *f* (insecte) **2** BIT : brin *m,* grain *m*

miter *or* **mitre** [ˈmaɪt̬ər] *n* **1** : mitre *f* (d'un évêque, etc.) **2** *or* **miter joint** : assemblage *m* à onglet

mitigate [ˈmɪt̬əˌgeɪt] *vt* **-gated; -gating** : atténuer, réduire, adoucir

mitigation [ˌmɪt̬əˈgeɪʃən] *n* : atténuation *f,* adoucissement *m*

mitosis [maɪˈtoːsɪs] *n, pl* **-toses** [-ˌsiːz] : mitose *f*

mitt [ˈmɪt] *n* **1** → **mitten 2** : gant *m* (de baseball)

mitten [ˈmɪtən] *n* : moufle *f,* mitaine *f Can*

mix[1] [ˈmɪks] *vt* **1** COMBINE : mélanger, combiner **2** STIR : malaxer **3 to mix up** CONFUSE : confondre — *vi* : se mélanger, se mêler

mix[2] *n* : mélange *m*

mixer [ˈmɪksər] *n* **1** *or* **cake mixer** : batteur *m* (électrique), mixer *m,* malaxeur *m Can* **2** : malaxeur *m* (de ciment, etc.)

mixture [ˈmɪkstʃər] *n* : mélange *m*

mix–up [ˈmɪksˌʌp] *n* CONFUSION : confusion *f*

mnemonic [nɪˈmɑnɪk] *adj* : mnémotechnique

moan[1] [ˈmoːn] *vi* : gémir

moan[2] *n* : gémissement *m*

moat [ˈmoːt] *n* : douve *f*

mob[1] [ˈmɑb] *vt* **mobbed; mobbing 1** ATTACK : assaillir **2** CROWD : entourer

mob[2] *n* **1** THRONG : foule *f* **2** GANG : bande *f*

mobile[1] [ˈmoːbəl, -ˌbiːl, -ˌbaɪl] *adj* : mobile

mobile[2] [ˈmoːˌbiːl] *n* : mobile *m*

mobility [moˈbɪlət̬i] *n* : mobilité *f*

mobilization [ˌmoːbələˈzeɪʃən] *n* : mobilisation *f*

mobilize [ˈmoːbəˌlaɪz] *vt* **-lized; -lizing** : mobiliser

moccasin [ˈmɑkəsən] *n* **1** : mocassin *m* **2** *or* **water moccasin** : serpent *m* venimeux de l'Amérique du nord

mocha [ˈmoːkə] *n* : moka *m*

mock[1] [ˈmɑk, ˈmɔk] *vt* **1** RIDICULE : se moquer de **2** MIMIC : singer, parodier

mock[2] *adj* **1** SIMULATED : simulé **2** PHONY : faux

mockery [ˈmɑkəri, ˈmɔ-] *n, pl* **-eries** : moquerie *f*

mockingbird [ˈmɑkɪŋˌbərd, ˈmɔ-] *n* : oiseau *m* moqueur

mode [ˈmoːd] *n* **1** MANNER : mode *m,* manière *f,* façon *f* **2** FASHION : mode *m*

model[1] [ˈmɑdəl] *v* **-eled** *or* **-elled; -eling** *or* **-elling** *vt* **1** SHAPE : modeler **2** : présenter <to model a dress : présenter une robe> — *vi* : travailler comme mannequin

model[2] *adj* **1** EXEMPLARY : modèle <a model student : un élève modèle> **2** MINIATURE : en miniature

model[3] *n* **1** PATTERN : modèle *m* **2** MINIATURE : maquette *f,* modèle *m* réduit **3** MANNEQUIN : mannequin *m*

modem [ˈmoːdəm, -ˌdɛm] *n* : modem *m*

moderate[1] [ˈmɑdəˌreɪt] *v* **-ated; -ating** *vt* : modérer, tempérer — *vi* **1** CALM : se modérer **2** PRESIDE : présider

moderate[2] [ˈmɑdərət] *adj* : modéré, modique

moderate[3] *n* : modéré *m,* -rée *f*

moderately [ˈmɑdərətli] *adv* **1** FAIRLY : moyennement **2** REASONABLY : modérément, avec modération <moderately priced : d'un prix raisonnable>

moderation [ˌmɑdəˈreɪʃən] *n* : modération *f*

moderator [ˈmɑdəˌreɪt̬ər] *n* : animateur *m,* -trice *f;* président *m,* -dente *f*

modern [ˈmɑdərn] *adj* : moderne

modernity [məˈdərnət̬i] *n* : modernité *f*

modernization [ˌmɑdərnəˈzeɪʃən] *n* : modernisation *f*

modernize [ˈmɑdərˌnaɪz] *vt* **-nized; -nizing** : moderniser

modest [ˈmɑdəst] *adj* **1** HUMBLE : modeste **2** DEMURE : pudique, modeste **3** MODERATE : modique <a modest sum : une somme modique>

modestly [ˈmɑdəstli] *adv* **1** : modestement, avec modestie **2** DEMURELY : décemment, avec pudeur **3** SIMPLY : simplement, sans prétensions

modesty [ˈmɑdəsti] *n* : modestie *f*

modicum [ˈmɑdɪkəm] *n* : petite quantité *f*

modification [ˌmɑdəfəˈkeɪʃən] *n* : modification *f*

modifier [ˈmɑdəˌfaɪər] *n* : modificateur *m*

modify [ˈmɑdəˌfaɪ] *vt* **-fied; -fying** : modifier

modish [ˈmɑdɪʃ] *adj* STYLISH : à la mode

modular [ˈmɑdʒələr] *adj* : modulaire

modulate [ˈmɑdʒəˌleɪt] *vt* **-lated; -lating** : moduler

modulation [ˌmɑdʒəˈleɪʃən] *n* : modulation *f*

module [ˈmɑˌdʒuːl] *n* : module *m*

mogul [ˈmoːgəl] *n* : magnat *m*

mohair [ˈmoːˌhær] *n* : mohair *m*

moist [ˈmɔɪst] *adj* **1** DAMP : humide **2** : moelleux <gâteau moelleux : moist cake>

moisten [ˈmɔɪsən] *vt* : humecter

moistness [ˈmɔɪstnəs] *n* : humidité *f,* moiteur *f*

moisture ['mɔɪstʃər] *n* : humidité *f*
moisturize ['mɔɪstʃə,raɪz] *vt* **-ized; -izing** : hydrater
moisturizer ['mɔɪstʃə,raɪzər] *n* : crème *f* hydratante
molar ['mo:lər] *n* : molaire *f*
molasses [mə'læsəz] *n* : mélasse *f*
mold[1] ['mo:ld] *vt* **1** SHAPE : mouler, modeler **2** FASHION : façonner, former — *vi* : moisir <the bread will mold : le pain moisira>
mold[2] *n* **1** FORM : moule *m* **2** FUNGUS : moisissure *f*
Moldavian[1] [mal'deɪviən] *adj* : moldave
Moldavian[2] *n* : Moldave *mf*
molder ['mo:ldər] *vi* CRUMBLE : tomber en poussière, émietter
molding ['mo:ldɪŋ] *n* : moulure *f* (en architecture)
moldy ['mo:ldi] *adj* **moldier; -est** : moisi
mole ['mo:l] *n* **1** : grain *m* de beauté (sur la peau) **2** : taupe *f* (animal)
molecular [mə'lɛkjələr] *adj* : moléculaire
molecule ['malɪ,kju:l] *n* : molécule *f*
molehill ['mo:l,hɪl] *n* : taupinière *f*
molest [mə'lɛst] *vt* : molester
mollify ['malə,faɪ] *vt* **-fied; -fying** : apaiser
mollusk *or* **mollusc** ['maləsk] *n* : mollusque *m*
mollycoddle ['mali,kadəl] *vt* **-dled; -dling** PAMPER : dorloter
molt ['mo:lt] *vi* : muer
molten ['mo:ltən] *adj* : en fusion
mom ['mam] *n* : maman *f*
moment ['mo:mənt] *n* **1** INSTANT : instant *m*, moment *m* <a moment ago : il y a un instant> **2** TIME : moment *m* <at the moment : en ce moment> **3** IMPORTANCE : importance *f* <to be of great moment : être de grande importance>
momentarily [,mo:mən'tɛrəli] *adv* **1** : momentanément **2** SOON : dans un instant, immédiatement
momentary ['mo:mən,tɛri] *adj* : momentané
momentous [mo'mɛntəs] *adj* : important, capital
momentum [mo'mɛntəm] *n, pl* **-ta** [-tə] *or* **-tums 1** : moment *m* (en physique) **2** IMPETUS : élan *m*, vitesse *f*
monarch ['ma,nark, -nərk] *n* : monarque *m*
monarchism ['mɔ,nar,kɪzəm, -nər-] *n* : monarchisme *m*
monarchist ['ma,narkɪst, -nər-] *n* : monarchiste *mf*
monarchy ['ma,narki, -nər-] *n, pl* **-chies** : monarchie *f*
monastery ['manə,stɛri] *n, pl* **-teries** : monastère *m*
monastic [mə'næstɪk] *adj* : monastique
Monday ['mʌn,deɪ, -di] *n* : lundi *m*
monetary ['manə,tɛri, 'mʌnə-] *adj* : monétaire
money ['mʌni] *n, pl* **-eys** *or* **-ies** ['mʌniz] : argent *m*
moneyed ['mʌnid] *adj* : nanti, riche
moneylender ['mʌni,lɛndər] *n* : prêteur *m*, -teuse *f*
money order *n* : mandat-poste *m*, mandat *m* postal
Mongolian[1] [man'go:liən, maŋ-] *adj* : mongol
Mongolian[2] *n* **1** : Mongol *m*, -gole *f* **2** : mongol *m* (langue)
mongoose ['man,gu:s, 'maŋ-] *n, pl* **-gooses** : mangouste *f*
mongrel ['maŋgrəl, 'mʌŋ-] *n* : chien *m* bâtard
monitor[1] ['manətər] *vt* : surveiller
monitor[2] *n* : moniteur *m*
monk ['mʌŋk] *n* : moine *m*
monkey[1] ['mʌŋki] *vi* **-keyed; -keying 1 to monkey around** : s'amuser **2 to monkey with** : tripoter
monkey[2] *n, pl* **-keys** : singe *m*
monkey wrench *n* : clé *f* à molette
monkshood ['mʌŋks,hud] *n* : aconit *m*
monocle ['manɪkəl] *n* : monocle *m*
monogamous [mə'nagəməs] *adj* : monogame
monogamy [mə'nagəmi] *n* : monogamie *f*
monogram[1] ['manə,græm] *vt* **-grammed; -gramming** : marquer d'un monogramme
monogram[2] *n* : monogramme *m*
monograph ['manə,græf] *n* : monographie *f*
monolingual [,manə'lɪŋgwəl] *adj* : monolingue
monolith ['manə,lɪθ] *n* : monolithe *m* — **monolithic** [,manə'lɪθɪk] *adj*
monologue ['manə,lɔg] *n* : monologue *m*
monoplane ['manə,pleɪn] *n* : monoplan *m*
monopolize [mə'napə,laɪz] *vt* **-lized; -lizing** : monopoliser
monopoly [mə'napəli] *n, pl* **-lies** : monopole *m*
monosyllabic [,manəsə'læbɪk] *adj* : monosyllabique
monosyllable ['manə,sɪləbəl] *n* : monosyllabe *m*
monotheism ['manəθi:,ɪzəm] *n* : monothéisme *m*
monotheistic [,manəθi:'ɪstɪk] *adj* : monothéiste
monotone ['manə,to:n] *n* : voix *f* monotone
monotonous [mə'natənəs] *adj* : monotone
monotonously [mə'natənəsli] *adv* : de façon monotone
monotony [mə'natəni] *n* : monotonie *f*
monoxide [mə'nak,saɪd] *n* : monoxyde *m*
monsoon [man'su:n] *n* : mousson *f*
monster ['mantstər] *n* : monstre *m*
monstrosity [man'strasəṭi] *n, pl* **-ties** : monstruosité *f*

monstrous [ˈmɑntstrəs] *adj* : monstrueux — **monstrously** *adv*
montage [mɑnˈtɑʒ] *n* : montage *m*
month [ˈmʌnθ] *n* : mois *m*
monthly[1] [ˈmʌnθli] *adv* : mensuellement
monthly[2] *adj* : mensuel
monthly[3] *n, pl* **-lies** : mensuel *m*, publication *f* mensuelle
monument [ˈmɑnjəmənt] *n* : monument *m*
monumental [ˌmɑnjəˈmɛntəl] *adj* : monumental
moo[1] [ˈmu:] *vi* : meugler
moo[2] *n* : meuglement *m*
mood [ˈmu:d] *n* **1** : humeur *f* <to be in a good mood : être de bonne humeur> <I'm not in the mood : ça ne me dit rien> **2** ATMOSPHERE : ambiance *f*
moodily [ˈmu:dəli] *adv* : d'un air morose
moodiness [ˈmu:dinəs] *n* : humeur *f* changeante
moody [ˈmu:di] *adj* **moodier; -est 1** SAD : de mauvaise humeur **2** TEMPERAMENTAL : lunatique, d'humeur changeante
moon [ˈmu:n] *n* : lune *f*
moonbeam [ˈmu:nˌbi:m] *n* : rayon *m* de lune
moonlight[1] [ˈmu:nˌlaɪt] *vi* **-ed; -ing** : travailler au noir
moonlight[2] *n* : clair *m* de lune
moonlit [ˈmu:nˌlɪt] *adj* : éclairé par la lune
moonshine [ˈmu:nˌʃaɪn] *n* **1** MOONLIGHT : claire *m* de lune **2** NONSENSE : balivernes *fpl* **3** *or* **moonshine liquor** : alcool *m* de contrebande
moor[1] [ˈmʊr] *vt* : amarrer
moor[2] *n* : lande *f*
mooring [ˈmʊrɪŋ] *n* : mouillage *m*
moose [ˈmu:s] *ns & pl* : orignal *m*
moot [ˈmu:t] *adj* DEBATABLE : discutable
mop[1] [ˈmɑp] *vt* **mopped; mopping** : laver (à grande eau)
mop[2] *n* : balai *m* à franges, balai *m* éponge
mope [ˈmo:p] *vi* **moped; moping** : broyer du noir
moped [ˈmo:ˌpɛd] *n* : cyclomoteur *m*
moral[1] [ˈmɔrəl] *adj* : moral <moral support : soutien moral> — **morally** *adv*
moral[2] *n* **1** LESSON : morale *f* **2 morals** *npl* : mœurs *fpl*
morale [məˈræl] *n* SPIRITS : moral *m*
morality [məˈræləṭi] *n, pl* **-ties** : moralité *f*
morass [məˈræs] *n* **1** SWAMP : marais *m* **2** CONFUSION, MESS : fatras *m*, bourbier *m*
moratorium [ˌmɔrəˈtoriəm] *n, pl* **-riums** *or* **-ria** [-iə] : moratoire *m*
moray [ˈmɔrˌeɪ, məˈreɪ] *n or* **moray eel** : murène *f*
morbid [ˈmɔrbɪd] *adj* : morbide
morbidity [ˌmɔrˈbɪdəṭi] *n* : morbidité *f*
more[1] [ˈmor] *adv* : plus, davantage <more important : plus important> <the more you eat, the more you want : plus on mange, plus on veut> <once more : une fois de plus> <I don't remember more : je ne me souviens pas davantage>
more[2] *adj* : plus de <more work : plus de travail>
more and more *adv* : de plus en plus
morel [məˈrɛl, mɔ-] *n* : morille *f*
moreover [morˈo:vər] *adv* : de plus
mores [ˈmɔrˌeɪz, -i:z] *npl* CUSTOMS : mœurs *fpl*
morgue [ˈmɔrg] *n* : morgue *f*
moribund [ˈmɔrəˌbʌnd] *adj* : moribond
morning [ˈmɔrnɪŋ] *n* **1** : matin *m*, avant-midi *f Can* <tomorrow morning : demain matin> **2** (*indicating duration*) : matinée *f* <all morning long : pendant toute la matinée>
Moroccan[1] [məˈrɑkən] *adj* : marocain
Moroccan[2] *n* : Marocain *m*, -caine *f*
moron [ˈmorˌɑn] *n* : crétin *m*, -tine *f*
morose [məˈro:s] *adj* : morose
morosely [məˈro:sli] *adv* : avec morosité
moroseness [məˈro:snəs] *n* : morosité *f*
morphine [ˈmɔrˌfi:n] *n* : morphine *f*
morrow [ˈmɑro:] *n* : lendemain *m*
Morse code [ˈmɔrs] *n* : morse *m*
morsel [ˈmɔrsəl] *n* : morceau *m*, bouchée *f*
mortal[1] [ˈmɔrṭəl] *adj* : mortel — **mortally** *adv*
mortal[2] *n* : mortel *m*, -telle *f*
mortality [mɔrˈtæləṭi] *n* : mortalité *f*
mortar [ˈmɔrṭər] *n* : mortier *m*
mortgage[1] [ˈmɔrgɪdʒ] *vt* **-gaged; -gaging** : hypothéquer
mortgage[2] *n* : hypothèque *f*
mortification [ˌmɔrṭəfəˈkeɪʃən] *n* : mortification *f*
mortify [ˈmɔrṭəˌfaɪ] *vt* **-fied; -fying 1** : mortifier (en religion) **2** HUMILIATE : humilier
mortuary [ˈmɔrtʃəˌwɛri] *n, pl* **-aries** : morgue *f*
mosaic [moˈzeɪɪk] *n* : mosaïque *f*
Moslem [ˈmɑzləm] → **Muslim**
mosque [ˈmɑsk] *n* : mosquée *f*
mosquito [məˈski:ṭo] *n, pl* **-toes** : moustique *m*, cousin *m*, maringouin *m Can*
moss [ˈmɔs] *n* : mousse *f*
mossy [ˈmɔsi] *adj* **-mossier; -iest** : moussu
most[1] [ˈmo:st] *adv* : très, bien, fort <it's most interesting : c'est fort intéressant> <the most beautiful girl : la plus belle fille>
most[2] *adj* **1** : la plupart de <most people believe it : la plupart des gens y croient> **2** GREATEST : le plus de <the most money : le plus d'argent>

most[3] *n* : plus *m* <three weeks at the most : trois semaines au plus> <she had the most : elle en avait le plus>

most[4] *pron* : la plupart <most are discouraged : la plupart sont découragés>

mostly |'mo:stli| *adv* **1** MAINLY : principalement, surtout **2** USUALLY : la plupart du temps

mote |'mo:t| *n* SPECK : grain *m*

motel |mo'tɛl| *n* : motel *m*

moth |'mɔθ| *n* **1** : papillon *m* de nuit **2** : mite *f* (qui détruit des vêtements)

mother[1] |'mʌðər| *vt* **1** BEAR : donner naissance à **2** PAMPER, PROTECT : dorloter

mother[2] *n* : mère *f*

motherhood |'mʌðər,hʊd| *n* : maternité *f*

mother-in-law |'mʌðərın,lɔ| *n, pl* **mothers-in-law** : belle-mère *f*

motherland |'mʌðər,lænd| *n* : patrie *f*

motherly |'mʌðərli| *adj* : maternel

motif |mo'ti:f| *n* : motif *m*

motion[1] |'mo:ʃən| *vi* **to motion to** : faire signe à

motion[2] *n* **1** MOVEMENT : mouvement *m* <to set in motion : mettre en mouvement> **2** PROPOSAL : motion *f* <to second the motion : appuyer la motion>

motionless |'mo:ʃənləs| *adj* : immobile

motion picture *n* MOVIE : film *m*

motivate |'mo:t̬ə,veıt| *vt* **-vated; -vating** : motiver

motivation |,mo:t̬ə'veıʃən| *n* : motivation *f*

motive[1] |'mo:t̬ıv| *adj* : moteur <motive power : force motrice>

motive[2] *n* : motif *m*

motley |'mɑtli| *adj* **1** DIVERSE : divers, hétéroclite **2** MULTICOLORED : bigarré, bariolé

motor[1] |'mo:t̬ər| *vi* : voyager en voiture

motor[2] *n* : moteur *m*

motorbike |'mo:t̬ər,baık| *n* : moto *f*

motorboat |'mo:t̬ər,bo:t| *n* : canot *m* automobile

motorcar |'mo:t̬ər,kɑr| *n* : automobile *m*, voiture *f*

motorcycle |'mo:t̬ər,saıkəl| *n* : motocyclette *f*

motorcyclist |'mo:t̬ər,saıkəlıst| *n* : motocycliste *mf*

motorist |'mo:t̬ərıst| *n* : automobiliste *mf*

mottle |'mɑt̬əl| *vt* **-tled; -tling** : tacheter, moucheter

motto |'mɑt̬o:| *n, pl* **-toes** : devise *f*

mould |'mo:ld| → **mold**

mound |'maʊnd| *n* **1** PILE : monceau *m*, tas *m* **2** HILL : monticule *m*, tertre *m*

mount[1] |'maʊnt| *vt* : monter — *vi* INCREASE : augmenter, monter

mount[2] *n* **1** SUPPORT : support *m* **2** HORSE : monture *f* **3** MOUNTAIN : mont *m*

mountain |'maʊntən| *n* : montagne *f*

mountaineer |,maʊntən'ır| *n* : alpiniste *mf*

mountain goat *n* : chamois *m*

mountain lion → **cougar**

mountaintop |'maʊntən,tɑp| *n* : cime *f*, sommet *m*

mounting |'maʊntıŋ| *n* SUPPORT : support *m*

mourn |'morn| *v* : pleurer

mournful |'mornfəl| *adj* : triste, lugubre — **mournfully** *adv*

mourning |'mornıŋ| *n* : deuil *m* <to be in mourning : porter le deuil>

mouse |'maʊs| *n, pl* **mice** |'maıs| : souris *f*

mousetrap |'maʊs,træp| *n* : souricière *f*

mousse |'mu:s| *n* : mousse *f*

moustache |'mʌ,stæʃ, mə'stæʃ| → **mustache**

mouth[1] |'maʊð| *vt* **1** : débiter, dire sans conviction <to mouth platitudes : débiter des lieux communs> **2** : articuler silencieusement

mouth[2] |'maʊθ| *n* : bouche *f*

mouthful |'maʊθ,fʊl| *n* : bouchée *f*

mouthpiece |'maʊθ,pi:s| *n* : embouchure *f*, bec *m*

movable *or* **moveable** |'mu:vəbəl| *adj* : mobile

move[1] |'mu:v| *v* **moved; moving** *vi* **1** : bouger <don't move! : ne bougez pas!> **2** PROCEED : avancer **3** RELOCATE : déménager **4** ACT : agir **5** : jouer (aux échecs, etc.) **6** PROPOSE : proposer — *vt* **1** SHIFT : déplacer, bouger **2** PERSUADE : inciter, pousser **3** : émouvoir, toucher <she moved him to tears : elle l'a ému jusqu'aux larmes>

move[2] *n* **1** MOVEMENT : mouvement *m* **2** RELOCATION : déménagement *m* **3** STEP : coup *m*, tour *m* <his next move : son prochain coup> <it's her move : c'est à elle de jouer>

movement |'mu:vmənt| *n* : mouvement *m*

mover |'mu:vər| *n* : déménageur *m*, -geuse *f*

movie |'mu:vi| *n* **1** : film *m* **2 movies** *npl* : cinéma *m*, vues *fpl Can*

mow[1] |'mo:| *vt* **mowed; mowed** *or* **mown** |'mo:n|; **mowing** : tondre

mow[2] |'maʊ| *n* : meule *f*

mower |'mo:ər| → **lawn mower**

Mozambican[1] |,mo:zəm'bi:kən, -zam-| *adj* : mozambicain

Mozambican[2] *n* : Mozambicain *m*, -caine *f*

Mr. |'mıstər| *n, pl* **Messrs.** |'mɛsərz| : Monsieur *m*

Mrs. |'mısəz, -səs, *esp South* 'mızəz, -zəs| *n, pl* **Mesdames** |meı'dɑm, -'dæm| : Madame *f*

Ms. |'mız| *n, pl* **Mss.** *or* **Mses.** |'mızəz| : Madame *f*, Mademoiselle *f*

much[1] |'mʌtʃ| *adv* **more** |'mor|; **most** |'mo:st| **1** : beaucoup <much better : beaucoup mieux> **2 as much** : autant

much[2] *adj* **more; most** : beaucoup de <I don't have much money : je n'ai pas beaucoup d'argent>

much[3] *pron* : beaucoup <there is much to do : il y a beaucoup à faire>

mucilage |'mju:sǝlɪdʒ| *n* : mucilage *m*

muck |'mʌk| *n* **1** MANURE : fumier *m* **2** DIRT, FILTH : saleté *f* **3** MIRE, MUD : boue *f*, fange *f*

mucous |'mju:kǝs| *adj* : muqueux

mucus |'mju:kǝs| *n* : mucus *m*

mud |'mʌd| *n* : boue *f*, bouette *f Can fam*

muddle[1] |'mʌdǝl| *v* **muddled; muddling** *vt* : confondre, embrouiller — *vi* **to muddle through** : se tirer d'affaire

muddle[2] *n* : désordre *m*, fouillis *m*

muddleheaded |,mʌdǝl'hɛdǝd, 'mʌdǝl,-| *adj* : désordonné, confus

muddy[1] |'mʌdi| *vt* **muddied; muddying** : salir, couvrir de boue

muddy[2] *adj* **muddier; -est** : boueux

muff[1] |'mʌf| *vt* BUNGLE : rater, gâcher, louper *fam*

muff[2] *n* : manchon *m*

muffin |'mʌfǝn| *n* : muffin *m Can*

muffle |'mʌfǝl| *vt* **muffled; muffling 1** ENVELOP : envelopper **2** DEADEN : étouffer, assourdir (des sons)

muffler |'mʌflǝr| *n* **1** SCARF : écharpe *f*, cache-nez *m* **2** : silencieux *m* (d'un véhicule)

mug[1] |'mʌg| *v* **mugged; mugging** *vi* : faire des grimaces — *vt* ASSAULT : agresser

mug[2] *n* : tasse *f* (pour le café), chope *f* (pour la bière)

mugger |'mʌgǝr| *n* : agresseur *m*

muggy |'mʌgi| *adj* **muggier; -est** : lourd et humide

mulatto |mʊ'latˌo, -'læ-| *n, pl* **-toes** *or* **-tos** : mulâtre *m*, -tresse *f*

mulberry |'mʌl,bɛri| *n, pl* **-ries** : mûrier *m* (arbre), mûre *f* (fruit)

mulch[1] |'mʌltʃ| *vt* : pailler

mulch[2] *n* : paillis *m*

mule |'mju:l| *n* : mule *f*, mulet *m*

mulish |'mju:lɪʃ| *adj* : entêté, têtu

mull |'mʌl| *vt or* **to mull over** : ruminer, réfléchir sur

mullet |'mʌlǝt| *n, pl* **-let** *or* **-lets** : muge *m*, rouget *m*

multicolored |'mʌlti,kʌlǝrd, 'mʌl,taɪ-| *adj* : multicolore, bigarré, bariolé

multifaceted |,mʌlti'fæsǝtˌǝd, ,mʌl,taɪ-| *adj* : à multiples facettes

multifamily |'mʌlti,fæmli, ,mʌl,taɪ-| *adj* : pour plusieurs familles

multifarious |,mʌltǝ'færiǝs| *adj* : divers, très varié

multilateral |,mʌlti'lætˌǝrǝl, ,mʌl,taɪ-| *adj* : multilatéral

multimedia |,mʌlti'mi:diǝ, ,mʌl,taɪ-| *adj* : multimédia

multimillionaire |,mʌlti,mɪljǝ'nær, ,mʌl,taɪ-, -'mɪljǝ,nær| *n* : multimillionaire *mf*

multinational |,mʌlti'næʃǝnǝl, ,mʌl,taɪ-| *adj* : multinational

multiple[1] |'mʌltǝpǝl| *adj* : multiple

multiple[2] *n* : multiple *m*

multiple sclerosis |sklǝ'ro:sɪs| *n* : sclérose *f* en plaques

multiplication |,mʌltǝplǝ'keɪʃǝn| *n* : multiplication *f*

multiplicity |,mʌltǝ'plɪsǝtˌi| *n, pl* **-ties** : multiplicité *f*

multiply |'mʌltǝ,plaɪ| *v* **-plied; -plying** *vt* : multiplier — *vi* : se multiplier

multipurpose |,mʌlti'pǝrpǝs, ,mʌltaɪ-| *adj* : polyvalent, aux usages multiples

multitude |'mʌltǝ,tu:d, -,tju:d| *n* : multitude *f*

multitudinous |,mʌltǝ'tu:dnǝs, -'tju:d-, -'tu:dǝnǝs, -'tju:-| *adj* : innombrable

mum[1] |'mʌm| *adj* SILENT : silencieux <to keep mum : garder le silence>

mum[2] *n* **1** → **chrysanthemum 2** *Brit* → **mom**

mumble[1] |'mʌmbǝl| *v* **-bled; -bling** : marmonner

mumble[2] *n* : marmonnement *m*

mummy |'mʌmi| *n, pl* **-mies** : momie *f*

mumps |'mʌmps| *ns & pl* : oreillons *mpl*

munch |'mʌntʃ| *v* : croquer

mundane |,mʌn'deɪn, 'mʌn,-| *adj* **1** EARTHLY, WORLDLY : de ce monde, terrestre **2** COMMONPLACE : banal, ordinaire

municipal |mjʊ'nɪsǝpǝl| *adj* : municipal

municipality |mjʊ,nɪsǝ'pælǝtˌi| *n, pl* **-ties** : municipalité *f*

munificent |mjʊ'nɪfǝsǝnt| *adj* : munificent

munitions |mjʊ'nɪʃǝnz| *npl* : munitions *fpl*

mural[1] |'mjʊrǝl| *adj* : mural

mural[2] *n* : peinture *f* murale, murale *f*

murder[1] |'mǝrdǝr| *vt* : assassiner

murder[2] *n* : meurtre *m*

murderer |'mǝrdǝrǝr| *n* : meurtrier *m*, -trière *f;* assassin *m*

murderess |'mǝrdǝrɪs, -dǝ,rɛs, -dǝrǝs| *n* : meurtrière *f*

murderous |'mǝrdǝrǝs| *adj* : meurtrier

murk |'mǝrk| *n* DARKNESS : obscurité *f*

murkiness |'mǝrkinǝs| *n* : obscurité *f*

murky |'mǝrki| *adj* **murkier; -est** : obscur, sombre

murmur[1] |'mǝrmǝr| *v* : murmurer

murmur[2] *n* : murmure *m*

muscatel |,mǝskǝ'tɛl| *n* : muscat *m*

muscle[1] |'mʌsǝl| *vi* **-cled; -cling** *or* **to muscle in** INTERVENE : intervenir

muscle[2] *n* **1** : muscle *m* **2** BRAWN : force *f*, muscle *m* **3** POWER : puissance *f*, poids *m*

muscular |'mʌskjǝlǝr| *adj* **1** : musculaire <muscular tissue : tissu musculaire> **2** STRONG : musclé

muscular dystrophy *n* : dystrophie *f* musculaire
musculature [ˈmʌskjələˌtʃʊr, -tʃər] *n* : musculature *f*
muse[1] [ˈmju:z] *vi* **mused; musing** PONDER : méditer
muse[2] *n* : muse *f*
museum [mjʊˈzi:əm] *n* : musée *m*
mush [ˈmʌʃ] *n* **1** : bouillie *f* **2** SENTIMENTALITY : mièverie *f*
mushroom[1] [ˈmʌʃˌru:m, -ˌrʊm] *vi* GROW, MULTIPLY : proliférer, se multiplier
mushroom[2] *n* : champignon *m*
mushy [ˈmʌʃi] *adj* **mushier; -est 1** SOFT : en bouillie (se dit de la nourriture), bourbeux (se dit de la terre) **2** MAWKISH : mièvre
music [ˈmju:zɪk] *n* : musique *f*
musical[1] [ˈmju:zɪkəl] *adj* : musical <musical instruments : instruments de musique> — **musically** *adv*
musical[2] *n* : comédie *f* musicale
musician [mjʊˈzɪʃən] *n* : musicien *m*, -cienne *f*
musk [ˈmʌsk] *n* : musc *m*
musket [ˈmʌskət] *n* : mousquet *m*
musketeer [ˌmʌskəˈtɪr] *n* : mousquetaire *m*
muskrat [ˈmʌskˌræt] *n, pl* **-rat** *or* **-rats** : rat *m* musqué
Muslim[1] [ˈmʌzləm, ˈmʊs-, ˈmʊz-] *adj* : musulman
Muslim[2] *n* : Musulman *m*, -mane *f*
muslin [ˈmʌzlən] *n* : mousseline *f*
muss [ˈmʌs] *vt* : chiffonner, froisser, décoiffer (les cheveux de qqn)
mussel [ˈmʌsəl] *n* : moule *f*
must[1] [ˈmʌst] *v aux* **1** (*expressing obligation or necessity*) : falloir, devoir <you must go : il faut que tu y ailles> <we must obey : nous devons obéir> **2** (*expressing probability*) : devoir <you must be tired : vous devez être fatigué> <it must be late : il doit être tard>
must[2] *n* : nécessité *f* <exercise is a must : l'exercice est indispensable>
mustache [ˈmʌˌstæʃ, mʌˈstæʃ] *n* : moustache *f*
mustang [ˈmʌˌstæŋ] *n* : mustang *m*
mustard [ˈmʌstərd] *n* : moutarde *f*
muster[1] [ˈmʌstər] *vt* : rassembler, réunir
muster[2] *n* **1** : rassemblement *m* **2 to pass muster** : être acceptable
mustiness [ˈmʌstinəs] *n* : odeur *f* de moisi, odeur *f* de renfermé
musty [ˈmʌsti] *adj* **mustier; -est** : de moisi, de renfermé
mutable [ˈmju:t̬əbəl] *adj* : mutable
mutant[1] [ˈmju:tənt] *adj* : mutant
mutant[2] *n* : mutant *m*, -tante *f*
mutate [ˈmju:ˌteɪt] *vi* **-tated; -tating** : muter
mutation [mju:ˈteɪʃən] *n* : mutation *f*
mute[1] [ˈmju:t] *vt* **muted; muting** MUFFLE : étouffer, assourdir
mute[2] *adj* **muter; mutest** : muet
mute[3] *n* : muet *m*, muette *f*
mutilate [ˈmju:t̬əˌleɪt] *vt* **-lated; -lating** : mutiler
mutilation [ˌmju:t̬əˈleɪʃən] *n* : mutilation *f*
mutineer [ˌmju:tənˈɪr] *n* : mutiné *m*, -née *f*
mutinous [ˈmju:tənəs] *adj* : mutiné
mutiny[1] [ˈmju:təni] *vi* **-nied; -nying** : se mutiner
mutiny[2] *n, pl* **-nies** : mutinerie *f*
mutt [ˈmʌt] *n* MONGREL : chien *m* bâtard
mutter [ˈmʌt̬ər] *vi* **1** MUMBLE : marmonner **2** GRUMBLE : grommeler
mutton [ˈmʌtən] *n* : mouton *m*
mutual [ˈmju:tʃʊəl] *adj* **1** : mutuel, réciproque **2** COMMON : commun <a mutual friend : un ami commun>
mutually [ˈmju:tʃʊəli, -tʃəli] *adv* **1** : mutuellement, réciproquement **2** JOINTLY : conjointement
muzzle[1] [ˈmʌzəl] *vt* **-zled; -zling** : museler
muzzle[2] *n* **1** SNOUT : museau *m* **2** : muselière *f* (pour un chien, etc.) **3** : canon *m* (d'une arme à feu)
my[1] [ˈmaɪ] *adj* : mon, ma, mes <my parents : mes parents> <in my opinion : à mon avis>
my[2] *interj* **oh, my!** : eh, bien!, oh là là!, mon Dieu!
myopia [maɪˈo:piə] *n* : myopie *f*
myopic [maɪˈo:pɪk, -ˈɑ-] *adj* : myope
myriad[1] [ˈmɪriəd] *adj* : innombrable
myriad[2] *n* : myriade *f*
myrrh [ˈmər] *n* : myrrhe *f*
myrtle [ˈmərt̬əl] *n* : myrte *m*
myself [maɪˈsɛlf] *pron* **1** (*used reflexively*) : me <I hurt myself : je me suis fait mal> **2** (*used for emphasis*) : moi-même <I tried it myself : je l'ai essayé moi-même> **3 all by myself** : tout seul
mysterious [mɪˈstɪriəs] *adj* : mystérieux — **mysteriously** *adv*
mysteriousness [mɪˈstɪriəsnəs] *n* : mystère *m*, caractère *m* mystérieux
mystery [ˈmɪstəri] *n, pl* **-teries** : mystère *m*
mystic[1] [ˈmɪstɪk] *adj or* **mystical** [ˈmɪstɪkəl] : mystique — **mystically** [-kli] *adv*
mystic[2] *n* : mystique *mf*
mysticism [ˈmɪstəˌsɪzəm] *n* : mysticisme *m*
mystify [ˈmɪstəˌfaɪ] *vt* **-fied; -fying 1** PUZZLE : déconcerter **2** DECEIVE, DUPE : mystifier
mystique [mɪˈsti:k] *n* : mystique *f*
myth [ˈmɪθ] *n* : mythe *m*
mythical [ˈmɪθɪkəl] *adj* : mythique
mythological [ˌmɪθəˈlɑdʒɪkəl] *adj* : mythologique
mythology [mɪˈθɑlədʒi] *n, pl* **-gies** : mythologie *f*

N

n |'ɛn| *n, pl* **n's** *or* **ns** |'ɛnz| : n *m,* quatorzième lettre de l'alphabet

nab |'næb| *vt* **nabbed; nabbing 1** APPREHEND : arrêter, pincer *fam* **2** STEAL : piquer *fam,* voler

nadir |'neɪ,dɪr, 'neɪdər| *n* : nadir *m,* point *m* le plus bas

nag[1] |'næg| *v* **nagged; nagging** *vi* **1** COMPLAIN : se plaindre, maugréer **2** PERSIST : persister <a nagging toothache : un mal de dents qui persiste> — *vt* SCOLD : critiquer, enquiquiner *fam*

nag[2] *n* **1** HORSE : canasson *m fam* **2** GROUCH : rouspéteur *m,* -teuse *f fam*

naiad |'neɪəd, 'naɪ-, -,æd| *n, pl* **-iads** *or* **-iades** |-ə,diz| : naïade *f*

nail[1] |'neɪl| *vt* : clouer

nail[2] *n* **1** FINGERNAIL : ongle *m* <to bite one's nails : se ronger les ongles> **2** : clou *m* (en technologie) <to hit the nail on the head : mettre le doigt dessus>

naive *or* **naïve** |nɑ'i:v| *adj* **-iver; -est** : naïf

naïveté |,nɑ,i:və'teɪ, nɑ'i:və,-| *n* : naïveté *f*

naked |'neɪkəd| *adj* **1** NUDE : nu **2** UNADORNED : tout nu, brut <the naked truth : la vérité pure et simple> **3 to the naked eye** : à l'œil nu

nakedness |'neɪkədnəs| *n* : nudité *f*

name[1] |'neɪm| *vt* **named; naming 1** CALL : nommer, appeler <I named him "John" : je l'ai nommé «John»> **2** CITE : nommer, citer **3** APPOINT : nommer **4** SPECIFY : choisir, fixer <to name the date : choisir la date> <to name a price : fixer un prix>

name[2] *adj* : de marque <name brand : produit de marque>

name[3] *n* **1** : nom *m* <what is your name? : comment t'appelles-tu?, quel est ton nom?> **2** REPUTATION : nom *m,* réputation *f* <to make a name for oneself : se faire un nom> **3 to call someone names** : traiter quelqu'un de tous les noms

nameless |'neɪmləs| *adj* **1** : sans nom <a nameless grave : une tombe sans nom> **2** UNKNOWN : anonyme **3** INDEFINABLE : indéfinissable, inexplicable

namely |'neɪmli| *adv* : notamment, c'est-à-dire

namesake |'neɪm,seɪk| *n* : homonyme *m*

Namibian[1] |nə'mɪbiən| *adj* : namibien

Namibian[2] *n* : Namibien *m,* -bienne *f*

nap[1] |'næp| *vi* **napped; napping** : faire un somme, faire une sieste

nap[2] *n* **1** SNOOZE : somme *m,* sieste *f* **2** : poil *m* (d'un tissu)

nape |'neɪp, 'næp| *n* : nuque *f*

naphtha |'næfθə| *n* : naphte *m*

napkin |'næpkən| *n* **1** : serviette *f* (de table) **2** → **sanitary**

narcissism |'nɑrsə,sɪzəm| *n* : narcissisme *m*

narcissist |'nɑrsəsɪst| *n* : narcisse *m*

narcissistic |,nɑrsə'sɪstɪk| *adj* : narcissique

narcissus |nɑr'sɪsəs| *n, pl* **-cissi** *or* **-cissuses** *or* **-cissus** |-'sɪ,saɪ, -,si:| : narcisse *m* (fleur)

narcotic[1] |nɑr'kɑṭɪk| *adj* : narcotique

narcotic[2] *n* **1** : narcotique *m* (en pharmacie) **2** DRUG : stupéfiant *m*

narrate |'nær,eɪt| *vt* **narrated; narrating** : raconter, narrer

narration |næ'reɪʃən| *n* : narration *f,* récit *m*

narrative[1] |'nærəṭɪv| *adj* : narratif

narrative[2] *n* : récit *m,* histoire *f,* narration *f*

narrator |'nær,eɪṭər| *n* : narrateur *m,* -trice *f*

narrow[1] |'nær,o:| *vt* **1** LIMIT : limiter **2** REDUCE : réduire — *vi* : se rétrécir <the road narrows : la route se rétrécit>

narrow[2] *adj* **1** : étroit <a narrow passage : un passage étroit> **2** LIMITED : limité, restreint **3** BIGOTED : étroit, borné **4 by a narrow margin** : de justesse

narrowly |'næroli| *adv* : de justesse, de peu

narrow–minded |,næro'maɪndəd| *adj* : étroit d'esprit

narrowness |'nærонəs| *n* : étroitesse *f*

narrows |'næro:z| *npl* STRAIT : passages *mpl* étroits

narwhal |'nɑr,*h*wɑl, 'nɑrwəl| *n* : narval *m*

nasal |'neɪzəl| *adj* : nasal

nasally |'neɪzəli| *adv* : d'une voix nasale

nastily |'næstəli| *adv* : méchamment

nastiness |'næstinəs| *n* : méchanceté *f*

nasturtium |nə'stərʃəm, næ-| *n* : capucine *f*

nasty |'næsti| *adj* **nastier; -est 1** FILTHY : sale, crasseux **2** INDECENT : obscène **3** MALICIOUS : méchant <a nasty disposition : un air méchant> **4** UNPLEASANT : sale, vilain <nasty weather : sale temps> <a nasty trick : un vilain tour>

natal |'neɪṭəl| *adj* : natal

nation |'neɪʃən| *n* : pays *m,* nation *f*

national[1] |'næʃənəl| *adj* : national — **nationally** *adv*

national[2] *n* : ressortissant *m,* -sante *f*

nationalism |'næʃənə,lɪzəm| *n* : nationalisme *m*

nationalist |'næʃənəlɪst| *n* : nationaliste *mf*

nationalistic |,næʃənə'lɪstɪk| *adj* : nationaliste

nationality |,næʃə'næləṭi| *n, pl* **-ties** : nationalité *f*

nationalization |,næʃənələ'zeɪʃən| *n* : nationalisation *f*

nationalize [ˈnæʃənəˌlaɪz] *vt* **-ized; -izing** : nationaliser

nationwide [ˈneɪʃənˈwaɪd] *adj* : dans tout le pays

native[1] [ˈneɪt̬ɪv] *adj* **1** NATURAL : inné **2** : natal <in his native country : dans son pays natal> **3** : maternel <her native language : sa langue maternelle>

native[2] *n* **to be a native of** : être originaire de, être natif de

Native American → **American Indian**

nativity [nəˈtɪvət̬i, neɪ-] *n, pl* **-ties 1** : Nativité *f* (en religion) **2** BIRTH : naissance *f*

natty [ˈnæt̬i] *adj* **nattier; -est** : coquet, élégant

natural[1] [ˈnætʃərəl] *adj* **1** : à l'état naturel <natural woodlands : forêt à l'état naturel> **2** : naturel <natural causes : causes naturelles> **3** INBORN : né, inné <natural abilities : talents innés> **4** SIMPLE : naturel, simple

natural[2] *n* : quelqu'un qui a un talent inné

naturalism [ˈnætʃərəˌlɪzəm] *n* : naturalisme *m*

naturalist [ˈnætʃərəlɪst] *n* : naturaliste *mf*

naturalistic [ˌnæchərəˈlɪstɪk] *adj* : naturaliste

naturalization [ˌnætʃərələˈzeɪʃən] *n* : naturalisation *f*

naturalize [ˈnætʃərəˌlaɪz] *vt* **-ized; -izing** : naturaliser

naturally [ˈnætʃərəli] *adv* **1** : naturellement <naturally blonde : naturellement blonde> **2** OF COURSE : bien sûr, bien entendu, évidemment

naturalness [ˈnætʃərəlnəs] *n* : naturel *m*

nature [ˈneɪtʃər] *n* **1** ESSENCE : nature *f*, essence *f* **2** KIND : espèce *f*, genre *m* **3** DISPOSITION : nature *f*, tempérament *m* <a generous nature : une nature généreuse> **4** : nature *f* <the beauties of nature : les beautés de la nature>

naught [ˈnɔt] *n* **1** NOTHING : rien *m* <to come to naught : ne mener à rien> **2** ZERO : zéro *m*

naughtiness [ˈnɔt̬inəs] *n* : désobéissance *f*, mauvaise conduite *f*

naughty [ˈnɔti] *adj* **naughtier; -est 1** DISOBEDIENT, MISCHIEVOUS : méchant, vilain **2** RISQUÉ : osé, risqué

nausea [ˈnɔziə, ˈnɔʃə] *n* **1** : nausée *f* **2** DISGUST : nausée *f*, écœurement *m*

nauseate [ˈnɔziˌeɪt, -ʒi-, -si-, -ʃi-] *v* **-ated; -ating** *vi* : avoir la nausée — *vt* : donner la nausée à

nauseating [ˈnɔziˌeɪt̬ɪŋ] *adj* : écœurant

nauseatingly [ˈnɔziˌeɪt̬ɪŋli, -ʒi-, -si-, -ʃi-] *adv* : au point d'écœurer <nauseatingly sweet : d'une douceur écœurante>

nauseous [ˈnɔʃəs, -ziəs] *adj* **1** SICK : écœuré **2** REVOLTING : nauséabond

nautical [ˈnɔt̬ɪkəl] *adj* : nautique

nautilus [ˈnɔt̬ələs] *n, pl* **-luses** *or* **-li** [-ˌlaɪ, -ˌliː] : nautile *m*

naval [ˈneɪvəl] *adj* : naval

nave [ˈneɪv] *n* : nef *f* (d'une église)

navel [ˈneɪvəl] *n* : nombril *m*

navigable [ˈnævɪgəbəl] *adj* : navigable

navigability [ˌnævɪgəˈbɪlət̬i] *n* : navigabilité *f*

navigate [ˈnævəˌgeɪt] *v* **-gated; -gating** *vi* SAIL : naviguer, voguer — *vt* **1** SAIL : naviguer sur, traverser **2** STEER : diriger, gouverner (un bateau)

navigation [ˌnævəˈgeɪʃən] *n* : navigation *f*

navigator [ˈnævəˌgeɪt̬ər] *n* : navigateur *m*, -trice *f*

navy [ˈneɪvi] *n, pl* **-vies 1** FLEET : flotte *f* **2** : marine *f* (nationale) <the United States Navy : la Marine américaine> **3** *or* **navy blue** : marine *m*

nay[1] [ˈneɪ] *adv* EVEN : que dis-je, voire <a huge, nay, monstrous animal : un animal énorme, que dis-je, monstrueux>

nay[2] *n* : non *m*, vote *m* négatif <the nays outnumbered the ayes : les non l'ont emporté sur les oui>

Nazi[1] [ˈnɑtsi, ˈnæt-] *adj* : nazi

Nazi[2] *n* : nazi *m*, -zie *f*

Nazism [ˈnɑtˌsɪzəm, ˈnæt-] *or* **Naziism** [ˈnɑtsiˌɪzəm, ˈnæt-] *n* : nazisme *m*

near[1] [ˈnɪr] *vt* : approcher — *vi* : s'approcher

near[2] *adv* **1** : près <she lives very near : elle habite tout près> <to draw near : approcher> **2** ALMOST, NEARLY : presque <near dead : presque mort>

near[3] *adj* : proche <in the near future : dans un proche avenir> <to the nearest dollar : à un dollar près> <the nearest route : le chemin le plus court>

near[4] *prep* : à côté de, près de <the table near the window : la table à côté de la fenêtre>

nearby[1] [nɪrˈbaɪ, ˈnirˌbaɪ] *adv* CLOSE : tout près, à proximité

nearby[2] *adj* : voisin, proche <a nearby house : une maison voisine>

nearly [ˈnɪrli] *adv* : presque

nearness [ˈnɪrnəs] *n* : proximité *f*

nearsighted [ˈnɪrˌsaɪt̬əd] *adj* : myope

nearsightedness [ˈnɪrˌsaɪt̬ədnəs] *n* : myopie *f*

neat [ˈniːt] *adj* **1** UNDILUTED : sec, pur **2** PRETTY, SMART : joli, coquet **3** CLEAN, ORDERLY : propre, soigné **4** SKILLFUL : habile <a neat trick : un truc habile>

neatly [ˈniːtli] *adv* **1** TIDILY : proprement, soigneusement **2** CLEVERLY : habilement

neatness [ˈniːtnəs] *n* : ordre *m*, propreté *f*

nebula [ˈnɛbjələ] *n, pl* **-lae** [-ˌliː, -ˌlaɪ] : nébuleuse *f*

nebulous [ˈnɛbjələs] *adj* : nébuleux

necessarily [ˌnɛsəˈserəli] *adv* : nécessairement, forcément

necessary[1] [ˈnɛsəˌsɛri] *adj* **1** INEVITABLE : inévitable **2** COMPULSORY : obligatoire **3** ESSENTIAL : indispensable

necessary[2] *n, pl* **-saries** : nécessaire *m*

necessitate [nɪˈsɛsəˌteɪt] *vt* **-tated; -tating** : nécessiter, exiger

necessity [nɪˈsɛsəṭi] *n, pl* **-ties 1** NEED : nécessité *f*, besoin *m* **2** : quelque chose d'indispensable <eating is a necessity : il est indispensable de manger> **3** POVERTY : pauvreté *f* **4 necessities** *npl* : le nécessaire, les choses essentielles

neck[1] [ˈnɛk] *vi* : se peloter *fam*

neck[2] *n* **1** : cou *m* **2** COLLAR : col *m*, encolure *f* <a high neck : un col montant> **3** : col *m*, goulot *m* (d'une bouteille)

neckerchief [ˈnɛkərtʃəf, -ˌtʃi:f] *n, pl* **-chiefs** [-tʃəfs, -ˌtʃi:fs] : foulard *m*

necklace [ˈnɛkləs] *n* : collier *m*

necktie [ˈnɛkˌtaɪ] *n* : cravate *f*

nectar [ˈnɛktər] *n* : nectar *m*

nectarine [ˌnɛktəˈri:n] *n* : nectarine *f*

née *or* **nee** [ˈneɪ] *adj* : né

need[1] [ˈni:d] *vi* : avoir besoin, être dans le besoin — *vt* **1** : avoir besoin de <he needs a car : il a besoin d'une voiture> **2 to need to** : devoir <something needs to be done : on doit faire quelque chose> — *v aux* : avoir besoin de, devoir, être obligé de <you need not answer : vous n'êtes pas obligé de répondre> <need we go? : est-ce que nous devons vraiment y aller?>

need[2] *n* **1** OBLIGATION : besoin *m*, nécessité *f* **2** DISTRESS : difficulté *f* <in times of need : pendant les moments difficiles> **3** WANT : besoin *m* <to be in need : être dans le besoin> **4 if need be** : si nécessaire, s'il le faut

needful [ˈni:dfəl] *adj* : nécessaire

needle[1] [ˈni:dəl] *vt* **-dled; -dling** TEASE : taquiner

needle[2] *n* : aiguille *f*

needlepoint [ˈnidəlˌpɔɪnt] *n* **1** LACE : dentelle *f* à l'aiguille **2** EMBROIDERY : tapisserie *f* à l'aiguille

needless [ˈni:dləs] *adj* **1** UNNECESSARY : inutile **2 needless to say** : il va sans dire

needlessly [ˈni:dləsli] *adv* : inutilement

needlework [ˈni:dəlˌwərk] *n* : travaux *mpl* d'aiguille

needy [ˈni:di:] *adj* **needier; -est** : dans le besoin

nefarious [nɪˈfæriəs] *adj* : infâme, odieux

negate [nɪˈgeɪt] *vt* **-gated; -gating 1** DENY : nier, contredire **2** NULLIFY : abroger

negation [nɪˈgeɪʃən] *n* : négation *f*

negative[1] [ˈnɛgəṭɪv] *adj* : négatif

negative[2] *n* **1** *or* **negative number** : nombre *m* négatif **2** : négatif *m* (en photographie) **3** : négation *f* (en grammaire) **4 to answer in the negative** : répondre par la négative

negatively [ˈnɛgəṭɪvli] *adv* : négativement

negativity [ˌnɛgəˈtɪvəṭi] *n* : négativité *f*

neglect[1] [nɪˈglɛkt] *vt* **1** DISREGARD : négliger **2** : manquer à (son devoir, une promesse, etc.)

neglect[2] *n* **1** : négligence *f* <due to neglect : dû à la négligence> **2** : manque *m* de soins (envers une personne), manque *m* d'entretien (d'un bâtiment, etc.)

neglectful [nɪˈglɛktfəl] *adj* : négligent

negligee [ˌnɛgləˈʒeɪ] *n* : négligé *m*, déshabillé *m*

negligence [ˈnɛglɪdʒənts] *n* : négligence *f* <criminal negligence : négligence criminelle>

negligent [ˈnɛglɪdʒənt] *adj* : négligent — **negligently** *adv*

negligible [ˈnɛglɪdʒəbəl] *adj* : négligeable

negotiable [nɪˈgo:ʃəbəl, -ʃiə-] *adj* : négociable

negotiate [nɪˈgo:ʃiˌeɪt] *v* **-ated; -ating** *vi* : négocier — *vt* **1** : négocier (une entente, etc.) **2** : franchir, surmonter (une difficulté)

negotiation [nɪˌgoʃiˈeɪshən, -siˈeɪ-] *n* : négociation *f*

negotiator [nɪˈgo:ʃiˌeɪṭər, -siˌeɪ-] *n* : négociateur *m*, -trice *f*

Negro[1] [ˈni:ˌgro:] *adj* : noir, nègre

Negro[2] *n, pl* **-groes** *sometimes offensive* : nègre *m sometimes offensive*, négresse *f sometimes offensive*

neigh[1] [ˈneɪ] *vi* : hennir

neigh[2] *n* : hennissement *m*

neighbor[1] *or Brit* **neighbour** [ˈneɪbər] *vt* : avoisiner — *vi* **to neighbor on** : être voisin de

neighbor[2] *or Brit* **neighbour** *n* **1** : voisin *m*, -sine *f* **2** FELLOWMAN : prochain *m* <love thy neighbor : aime ton prochain>

neighborhood *or Brit* **neighbourhood** [ˈneɪbərˌhʊd] *n* **1** : voisinage *m* **2 in the neighborhood of** APPROXIMATELY : au voisinage de, environ

neighborly *or Brit* **neighbourly** [ˈneɪbərli] *adj* : amical, de bon voisin

neighbour *Brit* → **neighbor**

neither[1] [ˈni:ðər, ˈnaɪ-] *adj* : aucun (des deux) <neither girl : aucune des deux filles>

neither[2] *conj* **1** : non plus <he doesn't want to go, and neither do I : il ne veut pas y aller, et moi non plus> **2 neither . . . nor** : ni . . . ni <neither good nor bad : ni bon ni mauvais>

neither[3] *pron* : aucun <neither of the bottles is full : aucune des deux bouteilles n'est pleine>

nemesis ['nɛməsɪs] *n, pl* **-eses** [-ˌsiːz] **1** RIVAL : vieux rival *m* **2** RETRIBUTION : juste punition *f*

neologism [ni'ɑləˌdʒɪzəm] *n* : néologisme *m*

neon ['niːˌɑn] *n* : néon *m* <neon lighting : éclairage au néon>

neophyte ['niːəˌfaɪt] *n* : néophyte *mf*

Nepali[1] [nə'pɔliː, -'pɑ-, -'pæ-] *adj* : népalais

Nepali[2] *n* **1** : Népalais *m*, -laise *f* **2** : népalais *m* (langue)

nephew ['nɛˌfjuː, *chiefly Brit* 'nɛˌvjuː] *n* : neveu *m*

nepotism ['nɛpəˌtɪzəm] *n* : népotisme *m*

Neptune ['nɛpˌtuːn, -ˌtjuːn] *n* : Neptune *f* (planète)

nerd ['nərd] *n* : crétin *m*, -tine *f fam*

nerve ['nərv] *n* **1** : nerf *m* <sensory nerve : nerf sensoriel> **2** AUDACITY : culot *m fam*, toupet *m fam* <to have a lot of nerve : avoir du culot> **3** FORTITUDE : confiance *f*, assurance *f* **4** **nerves** *npl* JITTERS : nerfs *mpl* <to be all nerves : être sur les nerfs>

nervous ['nərvəs] *adj* **1** : nerveux <nervous system : système nerveux> **2** ANXIOUS : appréhensif, anxieux **3** TIMID : timide <a nervous smile : un sourire timide>

nervously ['nərvəsli] *adv* : nerveusement, avec inquiétude

nervousness ['nərvəsnəs] *n* : nervosité *f*

nervy ['nərvi] *adj* **nervier; -est** **1** BOLD : audacieux **2** INSOLENT : culotté *fam*, effronté **3** NERVOUS : nerveux

nest[1] ['nɛst] *vi* : se nicher, faire son nid

nest[2] *n* **1** : nid *m* **2** SET : ensemble *m* (de tables, etc.)

nestle ['nɛsəl] *vi* **-tled; -tling** : se blottir

net[1] ['nɛt] *vt* **netted; netting** **1** CATCH : prendre au filet (des poissons) **2** YIELD : rapporter (en finance)

net[2] *adj* : net <net salary : salaire net>

net[3] *n* : filet *m*

nether ['nɛðər] *adj* **1** LOWER : inférieur, bas **2** **the nether regions** : les enfers

nettle[1] ['nɛt̬əl] *vt* **-tled; -tling** : piquer au vif, irriter

nettle[2] *n* : ortie *f*

network ['nɛtˌwərk] *n* : réseau *m*

neural ['nʊrəl, 'njʊr-] *adj* : neural

neuralgia [nʊ'rældʒə, njʊ-] *n* : névralgie *f*

neuralgic [nʊ'rældʒɪk] *adj* : névralgique

neuritis [nʊ'raɪt̬əs, njʊ-] *n, pl* **-ritides** [-'rɪt̬əˌdiːz] *or* **-ritises** : névrite *f*

neurological [ˌnʊrə'lɑdʒɪkəl, ˌnjʊr-] *or* **neurologic** [ˌnʊrə'lɑdʒɪk, ˌnjʊ-] *adj* : neurologique

neurologist [nʊ'rɑlədʒɪst, njʊ-] *n* : neurologue *mf*

neurology [nʊ'rɑlədʒi, njʊ-] *n* : neurologie *f*

neurosis [nʊ'roːsɪs, njʊ-] *n, pl* **-roses** [-ˌsiːz] : névrose *f*

neurotic[1] [nʊ'rɑt̬ɪk, njʊ-] *adj* : névrosé

neurotic[2] *n* : névrosé *m*, -sée *f*

neuter[1] ['nuːt̬ər, 'njuː-] *vt* : châtrer

neuter[2] *adj* : neutre (en grammaire)

neutral[1] ['nuːtrəl, 'njuː-] *adj* **1** : neutre <neutral territory : territoire neutre> **2** IMPARTIAL : neutre, objectif **3** : neutre (se dit d'une couleur, d'une charge électrique)

neutral[2] *n or* **neutral gear** : point *m* mort, neutre *m Can*

neutralization [ˌnuːtrələ'zeɪʃən, ˌnjuː-] *n* : neutralisation *f*

neutralize ['nuːtrəˌlaɪz, 'njuː-] *vt* **-ized; -izing** : neutraliser

neutrality [nuː'trælət̬i, njuː-] *n* : neutralité *f*

neutron ['nuːˌtrɑn, 'njuː-] *n* : neutron *m*

never ['nɛvər] *adv* **1** : jamais <I never saw her : je ne l'ai jamais vue> **2** (*used for emphasis*) <never fear : ne crains pas> <I never said a word : je n'ai rien dit>

nevermore [ˌnɛvər'mor] *adv* : plus jamais, jamais plus

nevertheless [ˌnɛvərðə'lɛs] *adv* : néanmoins

new[1] ['nuː, 'njuː] *adv* NEWLY : fraîchement <a new-mown lawn : une pelouse fraîchement tondue>

new[2] *adj* **1** RECENT : nouveau, moderne <a new arrival : un nouveau arrivé> <what's new? : quoi de neuf?> **2** : neuf <we bought a new house : nous avons acheté une maison neuve> **3** DIFFERENT, NOVEL : nouveau, original <a new idea : une nouvelle idée> **4** **like new** : comme neuf

newborn[1] ['nuːˌbɔrn, 'njuː-] *adj* : nouveau-né

newborn[2] *n, pl* **-born** *or* **-borns** : nouveau-né *m*, nouveau-née *f*

newly ['nuːli, 'njuː-] *adv* : récemment, nouvellement <newly furnished : nouvellement meublé> <newly painted : fraîchement peint>

new moon *n* : nouvelle lune *f*

newness ['nuːnəs, 'njuː-] *n* : nouveauté *f*

news ['nuːz, 'njuːz] *n* : nouvelles *fpl*

newscast ['nuːzˌkæst, 'njuːz-] *n* : journal *m* télévisé

newscaster ['nuːzˌkæstər, 'njuːz-] *n* : présentateur *m*, -trice *f* (d'un journal télévisé)

newsgroup ['nuːzˌgruːp] *n* : forum *m*

newsletter ['nuːzˌlɛt̬ər, 'njuːz-] *n* : bulletin *m*

newsman ['nuːzmən, 'njuːz-, -ˌmæn] *n, pl* **-men** [-mən, -ˌmɛn] : journaliste *m*

newspaper ['nuːzˌpeɪpər, 'njuːz-] *n* : journal *m*

newspaperman ['nuːzˌpeɪpərˌmæn, 'njuːz-] *n, pl* **-men** [-mən, -ˌmɛn] : journaliste *m*

newsprint ['nuːzˌprɪnt, 'njuːz-] *n* : papier *m* journal

newsstand ['nuːzˌstænd, 'njuːz-] *n* : kiosque *m* à journaux

newswoman ['nu:z,wʊmən, 'nju:z-] *n, pl* **-women** [-,wɪmən] : journaliste *f*
newsworthy ['nu:z,wərði, 'nju:z-] *adj* : médiatique
newsy ['nu:zi:, 'nju:-] *adj* **newsier; -est** : plein de nouvelles
newt ['nu:t, 'nju:t] *n* : triton *m*
New Testament *n* : Nouveau Testament *m*
New Year *n* : Nouvel An *m*
New Year's Day *n* : jour *m* de l'An
New Zealander [nu:'zi:ləndər, nju:-] *n* : Néo-Zélandais *m*, -daise *f*
next[1] ['nɛkst] *adv* **1** AFTERWARD : ensuite, après <what happened next? : que s'est-il passé ensuite?> **2** NOW : maintenant <what is she doing next? : qu'est-ce qu'elle fait maintenant?> **3** : la prochaine fois <when next we meet : quand nous nous rencontrerons la prochaine fois>
next[2] *adj* **1** : prochain <the next time : la prochaine fois> **2** FOLLOWING : suivant <the next page : la page suivante>
next door *adv* : à côté (de chez nous)
next–door ['nɛkst'dor] *adj* : voisin, d'à côté
next to *prep* **1** : à côté de <next to the bank : à côté de la banque> **2** : à comparer à <next to you I'm wealthy : à comparer à toi je suis riche>
nib ['nɪb] *n* : bec *m* (d'un stylo)
nibble[1] ['nɪbəl] *v* **-bled; -bling** *vt* : grignoter, mordiller — *vi* : grignoter
nibble[2] *n* **1** NIBBLING : mordillement *m* **2** SNACK : collation *f*
Nicaraguan[1] [,nɪkə'rɑgwən] *adj* : nicaraguayen
Nicaraguan[2] *n* : Nicaraguayen *m*, -guayenne *f*
nice ['naɪs] *adj* **nicer; nicest 1** FINICKY : particulier <too nice a palate : un palais trop particulier> **2** PRECISE : subtil, fin **3** PLEASANT : bon <we had a nice time : nous avons eu du bon temps> **4** AGREEABLE : gentil, aimable **5** WELL-BRED : respectable
nicely ['naɪsli] *adv* **1** WELL : bien <he is doing nicely : il se porte bien> **2** KINDLY, POLITELY : gentiment **3** PRECISELY : avec précision
niceness ['naɪsnəs] *n* : gentillesse *f*
nicety ['naɪsət̬i] *n, pl* **-ties 1** SUBTLETY : subtilité *f* **2 niceties** *npl* : raffinements *mpl*
niche ['nɪtʃ] *n* **1** RECESS : niche *f* **2** PLACE : place *f*, voie *f* <she found her niche : elle a trouvé sa place>
nick[1] ['nɪk] *vt* : faire une entaille dans, faire une encoche sur
nick[2] *n* **1** NOTCH : entaille *f*, encoche *f* **2 in the nick of time** : juste à temps
nickel ['nɪkəl] *n* **1** : nickel *m* (métal) **2** : pièce *f* de cinq cents
nickname[1] ['nɪk,neɪm] *vt* : surnommer
nickname[2] *n* : surnom *m*
nicotine ['nɪkə,ti:n] *n* : nicotine *f*
niece ['ni:s] *n* : nièce *f*
Nigerian[1] [naɪ'dʒɪriən] *adj* : nigérian
Nigerian[2] *n* : Nigérian *m*, -rianne *f*
niggardly ['nɪgərdli] *adj* : avare, mesquin
niggling ['nɪgəlɪŋ] *adj* **1** PETTY : insignifiant <niggling details : détails insignifiants> **2** PERSISTENT : persistant <a niggling doubt : un doute persistant>
nigh[1] ['naɪ] *adv* **1** NEARLY : presque **2 to draw nigh** : se rapprocher
nigh[2] *adj* CLOSE, NEAR : proche <the end is nigh : la fin est proche>
night[1] ['naɪt] *adj* : de nuit <night shift : équipe de nuit>
night[2] *n* **1** EVENING : nuit *f*, soir *m* <at night : le soir> <last night : hier soir> <night and day : nuit et jour> **2** : soir *m* <it's his night off : ce soir il est libre> **3** DARKNESS : nuit *f*
nightclothes ['naɪt,klo:ðz, -,klo:z] *npl* : vêtements *mpl* de nuit
nightclub ['naɪt,klʌb] *n* : boîte *f* de nuit
night crawler *n* → **earthworm**
nightfall ['naɪt,fɔl] *n* : tombée *f* de la nuit
nightgown ['naɪt,gaʊn] *n* : chemise *f* de nuit, robe *f* de nuit *Can*
nightingale ['naɪtən,geɪl, 'naɪt̬ɪŋ-] *n* : rossignol *m*
nightly[1] ['naɪtli] *adv* : tous les soirs
nightly[2] *adj* : de tous les soirs
nightmare ['naɪt,mær] *n* : cauchemar *m*
nightmarish ['naɪt,mærɪʃ] *adj* : cauchemardesque
nightshade ['naɪt,ʃeɪd] *n* : morelle *f*
nighttime ['naɪt,taɪm] *n* : nuit *f*
nil[1] ['nɪl] *adj* : nul <visibility is nil : la visibilité est nulle>
nil[2] *n* NOTHING, ZERO : zéro *m*
nimble ['nɪmbəl] *adj* **-bler; -blest 1** AGILE : agile, leste **2** CLEVER : vif, alerte
nimbleness ['nɪmbəlnəs] *n* : agilité *f*
nimbly ['nɪmbli] *adv* : agilement
nincompoop ['nɪnkəm,pu:p, 'nɪŋ-] *n* FOOL : imbécile *mf*; idiot *m*, -diote *f*
nine[1] ['naɪn] *adj* : neuf
nine[2] *n* : neuf *m*
ninepins ['naɪn,pɪnz] *n* : quilles *fpl*
nineteen[1] [naɪn'ti:n] *adj* : dix-neuf
nineteen[2] *n* : dix-neuf *m*
nineteenth[1] [naɪn'ti:nθ] *adj* : dix-neuvième
nineteenth[2] *n* **1** : dix-neuvième *mf* (dans une série) **2** : dix-neuvième *m* (en mathématiques) **3** (*used in dates*) <the nineteenth of May : le dix-neuf mai>
ninetieth[1] ['naɪnt̬iəθ] *adj* : quatre-vingt-dixième
ninetieth[2] *n* **1** : quatre-vingt-dixième *mf* (dans une série) **2** : quatre-vingt-dixième *m* (en mathématiques)
ninety[1] ['naɪnt̬i] *adj* : quatre-vingt-dix, nonante *Bel, Switz*

ninety[2] *n, pl* **-ties** : quatre-vingt-dix *m,* nonante *mf Bel, Switz*

ninny ['nɪni] *n, pl* **ninnies** NITWIT : cruche *f fam,* imbécile *mf*

ninth[1] ['naɪnθ] *adj* : neuvième

ninth[2] *n* **1** : neuvième *mf* (dans une série) **2** : neuvième *m* (en mathématiques) **3** (*used in dates*) <the ninth of September : le neuf septembre>

nip[1] ['nɪp] *vt* **nipped; nipping 1** BITE : mordre **2** PINCH : pincer **3 to nip in the bud** : tuer dans l'œuf

nip[2] *n* **1** BITE : morsure *f* (d'un animal) **2** PINCH : pincement *m* **3** TANG : piquant *m* **4** SWALLOW : goutte *f* (d'alcool, etc.) **5 there's a nip in the air** : il fait frisquet

nipple ['nɪpəl] *n* : mamelon *m*

nippy ['nɪpi] *adj* **nippier; -est 1** PUNGENT : piquant, fort **2** CHILLY : frisquet

nit ['nɪt] *n* : lente *f*

nitrate ['naɪ,treɪt] *n* : nitrate *m*

nitric acid ['naɪtrɪk] *n* : acide *m* nitrique

nitrite ['naɪ,traɪt] *n* : nitrite *m*

nitrogen ['naɪtrədʒən] *n* : azote *m*

nitroglycerin *or* **nitroglycerine** [,naɪtro'glɪsərən] *n* : nitroglycérine *f*

nitwit ['nɪt,wɪt] *n* : andouille *f fam,* imbécile *mf*

no[1] ['no:] *adv* **1** (*used to express the negative of an alternative choice*) : non <shall we go out or no? : allons-nous sortir ou non?> **2** : pas <he is no better than the others : il n'est pas mieux que les autres> **3** (*used to express negation, dissent, denial or refusal*) : non <no, I'm not going : non, je n'y vais pas> **4** (*used as an interjection of surprise or doubt*) : mais <no, you don't say! : mais, ce n'est pas possible!> **5** : plus <we can no longer pretend : nous ne pouvons plus faire semblant>

no[2] *adj* **1** : pas de, point de <he has no money : il n'a pas d'argent> **2** (*used to express an order or command*) <no parking : stationnement interdit> **3 to be no** : ne pas être <I'm no liar : je ne suis pas menteur>

no[3] *n, pl* **noes** *or* **nos** ['no:z] **1** REFUSAL : non *m* **2** : non *m,* vote *m* négatif <ayes and noes : les oui et les non>

nobility [no'bɪləṭi] *n* : noblesse *f*

noble ['nobəl] *adj* **-bler; -blest 1** EMINENT : noble, distingué **2** ARISTOCRATIC : noble, aristocratique **3** STATELY : majestueux <a noble building : un édifice majestueux>

nobleman ['no:bəlmən] *n* : noble *m,* aristocrate *m*

nobleness ['no:bəlnəs] *n* : noblesse *f*

noblewoman ['no:bəl,wʊmən] *n, pl* **-women** [-,wɪmən] : noble *f,* aristocrate *f*

nobody[1] ['no:bədi, -,bɑdi] *n, pl* **-bodies** : moins que rien *mf,* zéro *m* <he's a nobody : il est complètement insignifiant>

nobody[2] *pron* : personne <nobody waited for me : personne ne m'a attendu>

nocturnal [nɑk'tərnəl] *adj* : nocturne

nocturne ['nɑk,tərn] *n* : nocturne *m*

nod[1] ['nɑd] *v* **nodded; nodding** *vt* : incliner (la tête), faire un signe de la tête <we nodded in agreement : nous avons fait un signe d'assentiment> — *vi* **to nod off** : s'endormir

nod[2] *n* : signe *m* de la tête, hochement *m* de la tête

node ['no:d] *n* : nœud *m* (d'une plante)

nodule ['nɑ,dʒu:l] *n* : nodule *m*

noel [no'ɛl] *n* **1** CAROL : chant *m* de Noël **2 Noel** CHRISTMAS : Noël *m*

noes → **no**

noise[1] ['nɔɪz] *vt* **noised; noising** : ébruiter

noise[2] *n* : bruit *m,* son *m*

noiseless ['nɔɪzləs] *adj* : silencieux — **noiselessly** *adv*

noisemaker ['nɔɪz,meɪkər] *n* : crécelle *f*

noisily ['nɔɪzəli] *adv* : bruyamment

noisiness ['nɔɪzinəs] *n* : bruit *m*

noisome ['nɔɪsəm] *adj* **1** NOXIOUS : nocif **2** OFFENSIVE : nauséabond <a noisome stench : une odeur nauséabonde>

noisy ['nɔɪzi] *adj* **noisier; -est** : bruyant

nomad[1] ['no:,mæd] *adj* → **nomadic**

nomad[2] *n* : nomade *mf*

nomadic [no'mædɪk] *adj* : nomade

nomenclature ['no:mən,kleɪtʃər] *n* : nomenclature *f*

nominal ['nɑmənəl] *adj* **1** : de nom <the nominal president : président que de nom> **2** TRIFLING : insignifiant

nominally ['nɑmənəli] *adv* : nominalement

nominate ['nɑmə,neɪt] *vt* **-nated; -nating 1** PROPOSE : proposer (comme candidat) **2** APPOINT : nommer, désigner

nomination [,nɑmə'neɪʃən] *n* : nomination *f*

nominative[1] ['nɑmənəṭɪv] *adj* : nominatif

nominative[2] *n or* **nominative case** : nominatif *m*

nominee [,nɑmə'ni:] *n* : candidat *m,* -date *f*

nonaddictive [,nɑnə'dɪktɪv] *adj* : qui ne crée pas de dépendance

nonalcoholic [,nɑn,ælkə'hɔlɪk] *adj* : non alcoolisé

nonaligned [,nɑnə'laɪnd] *adj* : non aligné

nonbeliever [,nɑnbə'li:vər] *n* : noncroyant *m,* -croyante *f*

nonbreakable [,nɑn'breɪkəbəl] *adj* : incassable

nonce ['nɑnts] *n* **for the nonce** : pour l'instant

nonchalance [,nɑnʃə'lɑnts] *n* : nonchalance *f*

nonchalant [ˌnɑnʃəˈlɑnt] *adj* : nonchalant

nonchalantly [ˌnɑnʃəˈlɑntli] *adv* : nonchalamment

noncombatant *n* : non-combattant *m*, -tante *f*

noncombustible *adj* : incombustible

noncommissioned officer [ˌnɑnkəˈmɪʃənd] *n* : sous-officier *m*

noncommittal [ˌnɑnkəˈmɪt̬əl] *adj* : évasif

nonconductor [ˌnɑnkənˈdʌktər] *n* : mauvais conducteur *m*

nonconformist [ˌnɑnkənˈfɔrmɪst] *n* : non-conformiste *mf*

nonconformity [ˌnɑnkənˈfɔrmət̬i] *n* : non-conformité *f*

nondenominational [ˌnɑndɪˌnɑməˈneɪʃənəl] *adj* : œcuménique

nondescript [ˌnɑndɪˈskrɪpt] *adj* : indéfinissable, quelconque

none[1] [ˈnʌn] *adv* **1 none too** : loin de <it's none too clear : c'est loin d'être clair> <they arrived none too soon : ils sont arrivés juste à temps> **2 to be none the worse** : n'en être pas plus mal

none[2] *pron* : aucun, aucune <none of them went : aucun d'entre eux n'y est allé>

nonentity [ˌnɑnˈɛntət̬i] *n, pl* **-ties** : être *m* insignifiant, nullité *f*

nonessential [ˌnɑnɪˈsɛntʃəl] *adj* : accessoire, non essentiel

nonetheless [ˌnʌnðəˈlɛs] *adv* NEVERTHELESS : néanmoins

nonexistence [ˌnɑnɪgˈzɪstənts] *n* : non-existence *f* — **nonexistent** [-stənt] *adj*

nonfat [ˌnɑnˈfæt] *adj* : sans matières grasses

nonfiction [ˌnɑnˈfɪkʃən] *n* : œuvres *fpl* non fictionnelles

nonflammable [ˌnɑnˈflæməbəl] *adj* : ininflammable

nonpareil[1] [ˌnɑnpəˈrɛl] *adj* : inégalé, sans égal

nonpareil[2] *n* **1** : personne *f* sans égale **2** : petit disque *m* en chocolat recouvert de sucre

nonpartisan [ˌnɑnˈpɑrt̬əzən, -sən] *adj* : impartial, neutre

nonperson [ˌnɑnˈpərsən] *n* : personne *f* non reconnue

nonplus [ˌnɑnˈplʌs] *vt* **-plussed; -plussing** DISCONCERT : déconcerter, dérouter

nonproductive [ˌnɑnprəˈdʌktɪv] *adj* : improductif

nonprofit [ˌnɑnˈprɑfət] *adj* : à but non lucratif

nonproliferation [ˌnɑnprəˌlɪfəˈreɪʃən] *n* : non-prolifération *f*

nonrefundable [ˌnɑnriˈfəndəbəl] *adj* : non remboursable

nonrenewable [ˌnɑnriˈnuːəbəl, -ˈnjuː-] *adj* : non renouvelable

nonresident [ˌnɑnˈrɛzədənt, -ˌdɛnt] *n* : non-résident *m*, -dente *f*

nonscheduled [ˌnɑnˈskɛˌdʒuːld] *adj* : irrégulier <nonscheduled flights : vols irréguliers>

nonsectarian [ˌnɑnˌsɛkˈtæriən] *adj* : non sectaire

nonsense [ˈnɑnˌsɛnts, -sənts] *n* : absurdités *fpl*, sottises *fpl*

nonsensical [nɑnˈsɛntsɪkəl] *adj* : absurde, insensé — **nonsensically** [-kli] *adv*

nonsmoker [ˌnɑnˈsmoːkər] *n* : non-fumeur *m*, -meuse *f*

nonstandard [ˌnɑnˈstændərd] *adj* : non standard

nonstick [ˌnɑnˈstɪk] *adj* : antiadhésif <nonstick pan : poêle antiadhésive>

nonstop [ˌnɑnˈstɑp] *adj* **1** : sans arrêt <to drive nonstop : rouler sans arrêt> **2** : direct, sans escale <nonstop flight : vol direct>

nonsupport [ˌnɑnsəˈpɔrt] *n* : défaut *m* de versement de pension alimentaire

nontaxable [ˌnɑnˈtæksəbəl] *adj* : non imposable

nonviolence [ˌnɑnˈvaɪlənts, -ˈvaɪə-] *n* : non-violence *f*

nonviolent [ˌnɑnˈvaɪlənt, -ˈvaɪə-] *adj* : non violent

noodle [ˈnuːdəl] *n* : nouille *f*

nook [ˈnʊk] *n* : coin *m*, recoin *m* <every nook and cranny : tous les coins et les recoins>

noon[1] [ˈnuːn] *adj* : de midi

noon[2] *n* : midi *m*

noonday [ˈnuːnˌdeɪ] → **midday, noon**

no one *pron* : personne *f*

noontime [ˈnuːnˌtaɪm] → **noon**

noose [ˈnuːs] *n* : nœud *m* coulant

nor [ˈnɔr] *conj* : ni <neither young nor old : ni jeune ni vieux> <he can't swim, nor can I : il ne sait pas nager, moi non plus>

norm [ˈnɔrm] *n* : norme *f*

normal [ˈnɔrməl] *adj* : normal — **normally** *adv*

normalcy [ˈnɔrməlsi] → **normality**

normality [nɔrˈmælət̬i] *n* : normalité *f*

normalization [ˌnɔrmələˈzeʃən] *n* : normalisation *f*

normalize [ˈnɔrməˌlaɪz] *vt* **-ized; -izing** : normaliser

north[1] [ˈnɔrθ] *adv* : au nord, vers le nord

north[2] *adj* : nord <the north coast : la côte nord>

north[3] *n* **1** : nord *m* **2 the North** : le Nord

North American[1] *adj* : nord-américain

North American[2] *n* : Nord-Américain *m*, -caine *f*

northbound [ˈnɔrθˌbaʊnd] *adj* : en direction du nord

northeast[1] [nɔrθˈiːst] *adv* : au nord-est, vers le nord-est

northeast[2] *adj* : de nord-est <northeast winds : vents de nord-est>

northeast[3] *n* : nord-est *m*

northeasterly[1] [nɔrθ'iːstərli] *adv* : vers le nord-est

northeasterly[2] *adj* : du nord-est

northeastern [nɔrθ'iːstərn] *adj* : nord-est, du nord-est

northerly[1] ['nɔrðərli] *adv* : vers le nord

northerly[2] *adj* : du nord

northern ['nɔrðərn] *adj* : nord, du nord <northern Canada : le nord du Canada>

Northerner ['nɔrðərnər] *n* : natif *m* du Nord, native *f* du Nord

northern lights → **aurora borealis**

North Pole *n* : pôle *m* Nord

North Star *n* : étoile *f* polaire

northward[1] ['nɔrθwərd] *adv* : vers le nord

northward[2] *adj* : du côté nord

northwest[1] [nɔrθ'wɛst] *adv* : au nord-ouest, vers le nord-ouest

northwest[2] *adj* : de nord-ouest <northwest winds : vents de nord-ouest>

northwest[3] *n* : nord-ouest *m*

northwesterly[1] [nɔrθ'wɛstərli] *adv* : vers le nord-ouest

northwesterly[2] *adj* : du nord-ouest

northwestern [nɔrθ'wɛstərn] *adj* : nord-ouest, du nord-ouest

Norwegian[1] [nɔr'wiːdʒən] *adj* : norvégien

Norwegian[2] *n* **1** : Norvégien *m*, -gienne *f* **2** : norvégien *m* (langue)

nose[1] ['noːz] *v* **nosed; nosing** *vt* **1** SMELL : flairer, sentir **2** : pousser avec le museau <the dog nosed the door open : le chien a ouvert la porte avec son museau> **3 to nose in** : avancer avec précaution <the ship nosed into its berth : le bateau avançait prudemment dans son emplacement> — *vi* PRY : fouiner *fam* <stop nosing in my business! : arrête de fouiner dans mes affaires!>

nose[2] *n* **1** : nez *m* (d'une personne), museau *m* (d'un animal) **2** : flair *m*, odorat *m* <a dog with a good nose : un chien avec du flair> **3** FRONT : devant *m*, nez *m* (d'un avion, etc.) **4** INSTINCT : flair *m*, instinct *m* <to have a keen nose for politics : avoir du flair politique> **5 to blow one's nose** : se moucher

nosebleed ['noːz,bliːd] *n* : saignement *m* de nez

nosedive ['noːz,daɪv] *n* **1** : piqué *m* (d'un avion) **2** DROP : chute *f* (des prix, etc.)

nose–dive *vi* **-dived; -diving 1** : piquer (se dit d'un avion) **2** : chuter *fam* (se dit des prix, etc.)

nostalgia [nɑ'stældʒə, nə-] *n* : nostalgie *f* — **nostalgic** [-dʒɪk] *adj*

nostril ['nɑstrəl] *n* : narine *f* (d'une personne), naseau *m* (d'un animal)

nostrum ['nɑstrəm] *n* : panacée *f*

nosy *or* **nosey** ['noːzi] *adj* **nosier; -est** : fureteur

not ['nɑt] *adv* **1** (*used to form a negative*) : ne . . . pas <the boys are not here : les garçons ne sont pas ici> **2** (*used to replace a negative clause*) : pas <I don't see why not : je ne vois pas pourquoi> **3** : non <I hope not : j'espère que non>

notable[1] ['noːt̬əbəl] *adj* **1** NOTEWORTHY : notable, remarquable **2** PROMINENT : notable, important

notable[2] *n* : notable *m*

notably ['noːt̬əbli] *adv* **1** VERY : très <notably impressed : très impressionné> **2** ESPECIALLY : notamment

notarize ['noːt̬ə,raɪz] *vt* **-rized; -rizing** : certifier

notary public ['noːt̬əri] *n*, *pl* **notaries public** *or* **notary publics** : notaire *m*

notation [no'teɪʃən] *n* **1** NOTE : note *f*, notation *f* **2** : notation *f* (en musique)

notch[1] ['nɑtʃ] *vt* : entailler, encocher

notch[2] *n* : entaille *f*, encoche *f*, coche *f*

note[1] ['noːt] *vt* **noted; noting 1** NOTICE : noter, remarquer, observer **2** *or* **to note down** : noter, inscrire

note[2] *n* **1** : note *f* (de musique) **2** REMINDER : note *f*, avis *m* **3** LETTER : billet *m*, mot *m* **4** DISTINCTION : renom *m* <an artist of note : un artiste de renom> **5 to take note of** : prendre note de

notebook ['noːt,bʊk] *n* : carnet *m*, calepin *m*

noted ['noːt̬əd] *adj* FAMOUS : éminent, célèbre

notepad ['noːt,pæd] *n* : bloc-notes *m*, tablette *f* *Can*

noteworthy ['noːt,wərði] *adj* : notable, remarquable

nothing[1] ['nʌθɪŋ] *adv* **1 nothing daunted** : pas le moindrement découragé **2 nothing like** : pas du tout

nothing[2] *n* **1** TRIFLE : rien *m* **2** ZERO : zéro *m* **3** : nullité *f*, zéro *m* <he feels like a nothing : il se sent comme un zéro> **4** NOTHINGNESS : néant *m*

nothing[3] *pron* : rien <there's nothing in the box : il n'y a rien dans la boîte> <it means nothing to me : ça m'est égal>

nothingness ['nʌθɪŋnəs] *n* : néant *m*

notice[1] *vt* **-ticed; -ticing 1** OBSERVE : s'apercevoir de, remarquer **2 to take notice of** : faire attention à

notice[2] ['noːt̬ɪs] *n* **1** ANNOUNCEMENT : avis *m*, annonce *f* **2** DISMISSAL : congé *m* **3** RESIGNATION : démission *f* **4 to give notice** : donner un préavis

noticeable ['noːt̬ɪsəbəl] *adj* : visible, perceptible

notification [,noːt̬əfə'keɪʃən] *n* : avis *m*, notification *f*

notify ['noːt̬ə,faɪ] *vt* **-fied; -fying** : notifier, aviser, avertir

notion ['noːʃən] *n* **1** IDEA : notion *f*, concept *m* **2** WHIM : envie *f*, idée *f* <a sudden notion : une envie soudaine> **3 notions** *npl* : mercerie *f*

notoriety [,noːt̬ə'raɪət̬i] *n*, *pl* **-ties** : notoriété *f*

notorious [no'to:riəs] *adj* : notoire — **notoriously** *adv*

notwithstanding[1] [ˌnɑtwɪθ'stændɪŋ, -wɪð-] *adv* NEVERTHELESS : nonobstant, néanmoins

notwithstanding[2] *conj* : quoique

notwithstanding[3] *prep* : en dépit de, malgré

nougat ['nu:gət] *n* : nougat *m*

nought ['nɔt, 'nɑt] → **naught**

noun ['naʊn] *n* : nom *m,* substantif *m*

nourish ['nərɪʃ] *vt* : nourrir

nourishing ['nərɪʃɪŋ] *adj* : nourrissant

nourishment ['nərɪʃmənt] *n* : nourriture *f,* alimentation *f*

novel[1] ['nɑvəl] *adj* : nouveau, original

novel[2] *n* : roman *m*

novelist ['nɑvəlɪst] *n* : romancier *m,* -cière *f*

novelty ['nɑvəlt̬i] *n, pl* **-ties 1** : nouveauté *f* **2 novelties** *npl* TRINKETS : bibelots *mpl,* babioles *fpl*

November [no'vɛmbər] *n* : novembre *m*

novice ['nɑvɪs] *n* : novice *mf;* débutant *m,* -tante *f*

now[1] ['naʊ] *adv* **1** : maintenant, à présent <now what are we going to do? : qu'allons-nous faire maintenant?> **2** PRESENTLY : en ce moment, présentement <he is busy now : il est occupé en ce moment> **3** FORTHWITH : maintenant <you can come in now : vous pouvez rentrer maintenant> **4** (*used to express a command, a request, or an admonition*) <now, hear this : écoutez bien> **5** (*used to indicate a transition*) : or <now, his point of view seems illogical : or, son point de vue semble illogique> **6** SOMETIMES : tantôt <now one and now another : tantôt l'un et tantôt l'autre> **7 now and then** : de temps en temps

now[2] *n* **1** (*indicating the present time*) <up until now : jusqu'à maintenant, jusqu'à présent> **2 the now** : le présent

now[3] *conj* **now that** : maintenant que <now that you're here we can begin : maintenant que tu es ici, nous pouvons commencer>

nowadays ['naʊəˌdeɪz] *adv* : de nos jours

nowhere ['no:ˌhwɛr] *adv* : nulle part

noxious ['nɑkʃəs] *adj* : nocif

nozzle ['nɑzəl] *n* : ajutage *m* (d'un tuyau d'arrosage), lance *f* (à eau)

nuance ['nu:ˌɑnts, 'nju:-] *n* : nuance *f*

nub ['nʌb] *n* **1** KNOB, LUMP : protubérance *f* **2** GIST : cœur *m,* fond *m*

nubile ['nu:ˌbaɪl, 'nju:-, -bəl] *adj* : nubile

nuclear ['nu:kliər, 'nju:-] *adj* : nucléaire

nucleus ['nu:kliəs, 'nju:-] *n, pl* **-clei** [-kliˌaɪ] : noyau *m*

nude[1] ['nu:d, 'nju:d] *adj* **nuder; nudest** NAKED : nu

nude[2] *n* : nu *m*

nudge[1] ['nʌdʒ] *vt* **nudged; nudging** : donner un coup de coude à

nudge[2] *n* : coup *m* de coude

nudism ['nu:ˌdɪzəm, 'nju:-] *n* : nudisme *m*

nudist ['nu:dɪst, 'nju:-] *n* : nudiste *mf*

nudity ['nu:dət̬i, 'nju:-] *n* : nudité *f*

nugget ['nʌgət] *n* : pépite *f* (d'or, etc.)

nuisance ['nu:sənts, 'nju:-] *n* **1** ANNOYANCE : embêtement *m,* désagrément *m* **2** : casse-pieds *mf fam,* peste *f* <he's a real nuisance : il est vraiment casse-pieds>

null ['nʌl] *adj* : nul <null and void : nul et non avenu>

nullify ['nʌləˌfaɪ] *vt* **-fied; -fying** : annuler, invalider

numb[1] ['nʌm] *vt* : engourdir, transir (par le froid)

numb[2] *adj* : engourdi, transi, paralysé <numb with cold : transi par le froid> <numb with fear : paralysé par la peur>

number[1] ['nʌmbər] *vt* **1** COUNT : compter, énumérer **2** : numéroter (des pages) **3** TOTAL : compter **4 to number among** INCLUDE : compter parmi

number[2] *n* **1** : nombre *m,* numéro *m* <the number 35 : le nombre 35> **2** : chiffre *m* <add the numbers : additionne les chiffres> **3 a number of** : un certain nombre de, plusieurs, divers

numberless ['nʌmbərləs] *adj* : innombrable

numbness ['nʌmnəs] *n* : engourdissement *m*

numeral ['nu:mərəl, 'nju:-] *n* : nombre *m,* chiffre *m* <Roman numeral : chiffre romain>

numerator ['numəˌreɪt̬ər, 'nju:-] *n* : numérateur *m*

numerical [nʊ'mɛrɪkəl, nyʊ-] *or* **numeric** [-'mɛrɪk] *adj* : numérique — **numerically** [-kli] *adv*

numerous ['nu:mərəs, 'nju:-] *adj* : nombreux

numismatics [ˌnu:məz'mæt̬ɪks, ˌnju:-] *n* : numismatique *f*

numskull ['nʌmˌskʌl] *n* : cruche *f fam,* imbécile *mf*

nun ['nʌn] *n* : religieuse *f*

nuptial ['nʌpʃəl] *adj* : nuptial

nuptials ['nʌpʃəlz] *npl* WEDDING : noces *fpl*

nurse[1] ['nərs] *v* **nursed; nursing** *vt* **1** BREAST-FEED : allaiter **2** : soigner (un malade) **3 to nurse a grudge** : entretenir une rancune — *vi* SUCKLE : téter

nurse[2] *n* : infirmier *m,* -mière *f;* garde-malade *mf*

nursery ['nərsəri] *n, pl* **-eries 1** : crèche *f France,* garderie *f Can* **2** : pépinière *f* (pour les plantes)

nursing home *n* : maison *f* de retraite, centre *m* d'accueil *Can*

nurture[1] ['nərtʃər] *vt* **-tured; -turing 1** FEED : nourrir **2** EDUCATE : élever, éduquer **3** FOSTER : nourrir, entretenir (des espoirs, des plans, etc.)
nurture[2] *n* **1** UPBRINGING : éducation *f* **2** NOURISHMENT : nourriture *f*
nut ['nʌt] *n* **1** : noix *f* <Brazil nut : noix du Brésil> **2** : écrou *m* <nuts and bolts : des écrous et des boulons> **3** LUNATIC : fou *m,* folle *f;* cinglé *mf fam* **4** ENTHUSIAST : mordu *m,* -due *f fam;* passionné *m,* -née *f* <a golf nut : un mordu du golf>
nutcracker ['nʌt,krækər] *n* : casse-noix *m,* casse-noisettes *m*
nuthatch ['nʌt,hætʃ] *n* : sittelle *f*
nutmeg ['nʌt,mɛg] *n* : muscade *f*
nutrient ['nu:triənt, 'nju:-] *n* : substance *f* nutritive
nutriment ['nu:trəmənt, 'nju:-] *n* : nourriture *f*
nutrition [nʊ'trɪʃən, njʊ-] *n* : nutrition *f,* alimentation *f*
nutritional [nʊ'trɪʃənəl, njʊ-] *adj* : nutritif
nutritious [nʊ'trɪʃəs, njʊ-] *adj* : nourrissant, nutritif
nuts ['nʌts] *adj* **1** FANATICAL : fanatique **2** CRAZY : fou, cinglé *fam*
nutshell ['nʌt,ʃɛl] *n* : coquille *f* de noix
nutty ['nʌt̬i] *adj* **nuttier; -est** : timbré *fam,* toqué *fam*
nuzzle ['nʌzəl] *v* **-zled; -zling** *vt* : frotter son nez contre — *vi* NESTLE : se blottir
nylon ['naɪ,lɑn] *n* **1** : nylon *m* **2 nylons** *npl* : bas *mpl* de nylon
nymph ['nɪmpf] *n* : nymphe *f*

O

o ['o:] *n, pl* **o's** *or* **os** ['o:z] **1** : o *m,* quinzième lettre de l'alphabet **2** ZERO : zéro *m*
O ['o:] → **oh**
oaf ['o:f] *n* : balourd *m,* -lourde *f*
oafish ['o:fɪʃ] *adj* : balourd, lourdaud
oak ['o:k] *n, pl* **oaks** *or* **oak** : chêne *m*
oaken ['o:kən] *adj* : de chêne, en chêne
oar ['or] *n* : rame *f,* aviron *m*
oarlock ['or,lɑk] *n* : tolet *m*
oasis [o'eɪsɪs] *n, pl* **oases** [-,si:z] : oasis *f*
oat ['o:t] *n* : avoine *f*
oath ['o:θ] *n, pl* **oaths** ['o:ðz, 'o:θs] **1** : serment *m* <to take the oath : prêter serment> **2** SWEARWORD : juron *m*
oatmeal ['o:t,mi:l] *n* : farine *f* d'avoine, gruau *m Can*
obdurate ['ɑbdʊrət, -djʊ-] *adj* : opiniâtre
obedience [o'bi:diənts] *n* : obéissance *f*
obedient [o'bi:diənt] *adj* : obéissant
obediently [o'bi:diəntli] *adv* : avec obéissance, docilement
obelisk ['ɑbə,lɪsk] *n* : obélisque *m*
obese [o'bi:s] *adj* : obèse
obesity [o'bi:sət̬i] *n* : obésité *f*
obey [o'beɪ] *v* **obeyed; obeying** *vt* : obéir à <to obey the law : obéir à la loi> — *vi* : obéir
obfuscate ['ɑbfə,skeɪt] *vt* **-cated; -cating** : obscurcir
obituary [ə'bɪtʃʊ,ɛri] *n, pl* **-aries** : nécrologie *f*
object[1] [əb'dʒɛkt] *vt* : objecter — *vi* : protester, s'opposer, soulever des objections
object[2] ['ɑbdʒɪkt] *n* **1** : objet *m* **2** OBJECTIVE, PURPOSE : objectif *m,* but *m* **3** : complément *m* d'objet (en grammaire) <direct object : complément d'objet direct>
objection [əb'dʒɛkʃən] *n* : objection *f*
objectionable [əb'dʒɛkʃənəbəl] *adj* : désagréable, offensif — **objectionably** [-bli] *adv*
objective[1] [əb'dʒɛktɪv] *adj* : objectif
objective[2] *n* **1** AIM : objectif *m,* but *m* **2** *or* **objective case** : accusatif *m*
objectively [əb'dʒɛktɪvli] *adv* : objectivement
objectivity [,ɑb,dʒɛk'tɪvət̬i] *n, pl* **-ties** : objectivité *f*
obligate ['ɑblə,geɪt] *vt* **-gated; -gating** : contraindre, obliger
obligation [,ɑblə'geɪʃən] *n* : obligation *f*
obligatory [ə'blɪgə,tori] *adj* : obligatoire
oblige [ə'blaɪdʒ] *vt* **obliged; obliging 1** COMPEL : obliger **2 to oblige s.o.** : rendre service à qqn **3 to be obliged to s.o.** : savoir gré à qqn
obliging [ə'blaɪdʒɪŋ] *adj* : obligeant — **obligingly** *adv*
oblique [o'bli:k] *adj* **1** SLANTING : oblique **2** INDIRECT : indirect — **obliquely** *adv*
obliterate [ə'blɪt̬ə,reɪt] *vt* **-ated; -ating** : effacer, détruire
obliteration [ə,blɪt̬ə'reɪʃən] *n* : effacement *m*
oblivion [ə'blɪviən] *n* : oubli *m*
oblivious [ə'blɪviəs] *adj* : inconscient — **obliviously** *adv*
oblong[1] ['ɑ,blɔŋ] *adj* : oblong
oblong[2] *n* : rectangle *m*
obnoxious [ɑb'nɑkʃəs, əb-] *adj* : odieux, exécrable — **obnoxiously** *adv*
oboe ['o:,bo:] *n* : hautbois *m*
oboist ['o,boɪst] *n* : hautboïste *mf*
obscene [ɑb'si:n, əb-] *adj* : obscène
obscenely [ɑb'si:nli, əb-] *adv* : d'une manière obscène
obscenity [ɑb'sɛnət̬i, əb-] *n, pl* **-ties** : obscénité *f*

obscure[1] [ɑb'skjʊr, əb-] *vt* **-scured; -scuring 1** CLOUD, DIM : obscurcir **2** HIDE : cacher

obscure[2] *adj* **1** DIM : obscur **2** UNKNOWN : inconnu **3** VAGUE : vague

obscurely [ɑb'skjʊrli, əb-] *adv* : obscurément

obscurity [ɑb'skjʊrət̬i, əb-] *n, pl* **-ties** : obscurité *f*

obsequious [əb'si:kwiəs] *adj* : obséquieux — **obsequiously** *adv*

observable [əb'zərvəbəl] *adj* : visible, perceptible

observance [əb'zərvən*t*s] *n* **1** OBSERVATION : observance *f*, observation *f* **2** PRACTICE : observance *f* (en religion, etc.)

observant [əb'zərvənt] *adj* : observateur

observation [ˌɑbsər'veɪʃən, -zər-] *n* : observation *f*

observatory [əb'zərvəˌtori] *n, pl* **-ries** : observatoire *m*

observe [əb'zərv] *v* **-served; -serving** *vt* **1** OBEY : respecter, observer <observe the rules : observez les règles> **2** CELEBRATE : observer <to observe the sabbath : observer le sabbat> **3** NOTICE : observer, remarquer **4** REMARK : dire, faire remarquer — *vi* LOOK : regarder

obsess [əb'sɛs] *vt* : obséder

obsession [ɑb'sɛʃən, əb-] *n* : obsession *f*

obsessive [ɑb'sɛsɪv, əb-] *adj* **1** : obsessionnel <obsessive-compulsive disorder : trouble obsessionnel compulsif> **2** HAUNTING : obsédant

obsessively [ɑb'sɛsɪvli, əb-] *adv* : d'une manière obsessionnelle

obsolescence [ˌɑbsə'lɛsən*t*s] *n* : obsolescence *f* — **obsolescent** [-'lɛsənt] *adj*

obsolete [ˌɑbsə'li:t, 'ɑbsəˌ-] *adj* : obsolète, démodé

obstacle ['ɑbstɪkəl] *n* : obstacle *m*

obstetric [əb'stɛtrɪk] *or* **obstetrical** [-trɪkəl] *adj* : obstétrical

obstetrician [ˌɑbstə'trɪʃən] *n* : obstétricien *m*, -cienne *f*

obstetrics [əb'stɛtrɪks] *ns & pl* : obstétrique *f*

obstinacy ['ɑbstənəsi] *n, pl* **-cies** : obstination *f*, entêtement *m*

obstinate ['ɑbstənət] *adj* : obstiné, entêté

obstinately ['ɑbstənətli] *adv* : obstinément, avec acharnement

obstreperous [əb'strɛpərəs] *adj* : tapageur, turbulent

obstruct [əb'strʌkt] *vt* : obstruer, bloquer

obstruction [əb'strʌkʃən] *n* : obstruction *f*, obstacle *m*

obstructive [əb'strəktɪv] *adj* : obstructionniste

obtain [əb'teɪn] *vt* : obtenir, se procurer — *vi* PREVAIL : régner, avoir cours

obtainable [əb'teɪnəbəl] *adj* : qu'on peut obtenir, disponible

obtrude [əb'tru:d] *v* **-truded; -truding** *vt* **1** EXTRUDE : extruder, faire sortir **2** IMPOSE : imposer — *vi* INTRUDE : s'imposer

obtrusive [əb'tru:sɪv] *adj* **1** BOTHERSOME, MEDDLESOME : importun **2** PROTRUDING : protubérant

obtuse [ɑb'tu:s, əb-, -'tju:s] *adj* **1** DULL, STUPID : obtus **2** INDISTINCT : vague, indistinct **3 obtuse angle** : angle *m* obtus

obviate ['ɑbviˌeɪt] *vt* **-ated; -ating** : obvier à, eviter

obvious ['ɑbviəs] *adj* : évident

obviously ['ɑbviəsli] *adv* **1** CLEARLY : manifestement **2** OF COURSE : évidemment, bien sûr

occasion[1] [ə'keɪʒən] *vt* : occasionner, provoquer, entraîner

occasion[2] *n* **1** INSTANCE : occasion *f* <on one occasion : une fois> **2** OPPORTUNITY : occasion *f* <should the occasion arise : si l'occasion se présente> **3** CAUSE : raison *f*, motif *m* **4** EVENT : événement *m* **5 on ~** : de temps en temps

occasional [ə'keɪʒənəl] *adj* : occasionnel — **occasionally** *adv*

occidental [ˌɑksə'dɛntəl] *adj* : occidental

occult[1] [ə'kʌlt, 'ɑˌkʌlt] *adj* : occulte

occult[2] *n* : sciences *fpl* occultes

occupancy ['ɑkjəpən*t*si] *n, pl* **-cies** : occupation *f*

occupant ['ɑkjəpənt] *n* **1** : occupant *m*, -pante *f*; habitant *m*, -tante *f* **2** TENANT : locataire *mf*

occupation [ˌɑkjə'peɪʃən] *n* **1** OCCUPYING : occupation *f* **2** VOCATION : profession *f*, métier *m*

occupational [ˌɑkjə'peɪʃənəl] *adj* : professionnel, du métier <occupational hazard : risque du métier>

occupy ['ɑkjəˌpaɪ] *vt* **-pied; -pying 1** : occuper **2 to occupy oneself with** : s'occuper de

occur [ə'kər] *vi* **occurred; occurring 1** HAPPEN : avoir lieu, se produire, arriver **2** APPEAR, EXIST : se trouver, se présenter **3** : venir à l'esprit <it occurred to him that . . . : il lui est venu à l'esprit que . . . >

occurrence [ə'kərən*t*s] *n* **1** EVENT : événement *m*, occurrence *f* **2** INSTANCE, PRESENCE : cas *m*, apparition *f* (d'une maladie, etc.)

ocean ['o:ʃən] *n* : océan *m*

oceanic [ˌo:ʃi'ænɪk] *adj* : océanique

oceanography [ˌo:ʃə'nɑgrəfi] *n* : océanographie *f* — **oceanographic** [-nə'græfɪk] *adj*

ocelot ['ɑsəˌlɑt, 'o:-] *n* : ocelot *m*

ocher *or* **ochre** ['o:kər] *n* : ocre *mf*

o'clock [ə'klɑk] *adv* (*used in telling time*) <it's ten o'clock : il est dix heures> <at six o'clock : à six heures>

octagon [ˈɑktəˌgɑn] *n* : octogone *m* — **octagonal** [ɑkˈtægənəl] *adj*
octave [ˈɑktɪv] *n* : octave *f*
October [ɑkˈtoːbər] *n* : octobre *m*
octopus [ˈɑktəˌpʊs, -pəs] *n, pl* **-puses** *or* **-pi** [-ˌpaɪ] : pieuvre *f,* poulpe *m*
ocular [ˈɑkjələr] *adj* : oculaire
oculist [ˈɑkjəlɪst] *n* **1** OPHTHALMOLOGIST : ophtalmologiste *mf,* oculiste *mf* **2** OPTOMETRIST : optométriste *mf*
odd [ˈɑd] *adj* **1** : seul, dépareillé <an odd sock : une chaussette dépareillée> **2** UNEVEN : impair <odd numbers : nombres impairs> **3** : et quelques <a hundred odd dollars : cent dollars et quelques> <forty odd years ago : il y a une quarantaine d'années> **4** STRANGE : étrange, bizarre **5** OCCASIONAL : divers <odd jobs : petits boulots>
oddity [ˈɑdəṭi] *n, pl* **-ties** : étrangeté *f,* bizarrerie *f*
oddly [ˈɑdli] *adv* : étrangement
oddness [ˈɑdnəs] *n* : étrangeté *f*
odds [ˈɑdz] *npl* **1** CHANCES : chances *fpl* **2** RATIO : cote *f* <the odds are eight to five against : la cote est de huit contre cinq> **3 to be at odds** : être en conflit
ode [ˈoːd] *n* : ode *f*
odious [ˈoːdiəs] *adj* : odieux — **odiously** *adv*
odor *or Brit* **odour** [ˈoːdər] *n* : odeur *f*
odorless *or Brit* **odourless** [ˈoːdərləs] *adj* : inodore
odorous [ˈoːdərəs] *adj* : odorant
odour *Brit* → **odor**
odyssey [ˈɑdəsi] *n, pl* **-seys** : odyssée *f*
o'er [ˈor] → **over**
of [ˈʌv, ˈɑv] *prep* **1** FROM : de <a man of the city : un homme de la ville> **2** (*indicating a characteristic quality or possession*) : de <a woman of great ability : une femme de grand talent> **3** (*indicating cause*) : de <he died of the flu : il est mort de la grippe> **4** BY : de <the works of Shakespeare : les œuvres de Shakespeare> **5** (*indicating parts, contents, or material*) : de, en <a glass of water : un verre d'eau> <a house of wood : une maison en bois> **6** (*indicating quantity or amount*) : de <thousands of dollars : des milliers de dollars> **7** (*indicating belonging or connection*) : de <the front of the house : le devant de la maison> **8** ABOUT : sur, de <tales of the West : contes de l'Ouest> **9** (*indicating a particular example*) : de <the city of Chicago : la ville de Chicago> **10** FOR : pour, de <love of country : amour de la patrie> **11** (*indicating time or date*) <five minutes of ten : dix heures moins cinq> <the eighth of April : le huit avril>
off[1] [ˈɔf] *adv* **1** (*indicating change of position or state*) <to march off : s'en aller> <he dozed off : il s'est endormi> **2** (*indicating distance in space or time*) <far off : éloigné> <some miles off : à quelques kilomètres de distance> <the holiday is three weeks off : la fête est en trois semaines> **3** (*indicating removal*) <this paint comes off : cette peinture s'enlève> <to cut off : couper> **4** (*indicating termination*) <to finish off : terminer> <shut the television off : éteins la télévision> <shut the engine off : coupez le contact> **5** (*indicating suspension of work*) <to take a day off : prendre un jour de congé> **6 off and on** : par périodes, par intervalles
off[2] *adj* **1** OUT : éteint, fermé <the light is off : la lumière est éteinte> **2** STARTED : démarré <to be off on a spree : démarrer une partie de plaisir> **3** FREE : libre, de congé <his day off : son jour de congé> **4** CANCELED : annulé **5** DOWN : en baisse <stocks were off : les actions étaient en baisse> **6 on an off chance** : pour le cas où cela pourrait servir
off[3] *prep* **1** (*indicating physical separation*) : de <she took it off the table : elle l'a pris de la table> <a shop off the main street : un magasin prêt de la rue principale> **2** : aux frais de <he lives off his sister : il vit aux frais de sa sœur> **3** (*indicating the suspension of an activity*) <to be off duty : être libre> <she's off meat : elle ne mange plus de viande> **4 to be off one's game, to be off one's stride** : ne pas être à son meilleur
offal [ˈɔfəl] *n* : abats *mpl*
offend [əˈfɛnd] *vt* **1** HURT : offenser, blesser <to be easily offended : être très susceptible> **2** OUTRAGE, SHOCK : choquer, outrager
offender [əˈfɛndər] *n* : délinquant *m,* -quante *f;* contrevenant *m,* -nante *f*
offense *or* **offence** [əˈfɛnts, ˈɔˌfɛnts] *n* **1** INSULT : offense *f* <to take offense : s'offenser> **2** CRIME : délit *m,* infraction *f* **3** : attaque *f* (aux sports)
offensive[1] [əˈfɛntsɪv, ˈɔˌfɛnt-] *adj* : offensif — **offensively** *adv*
offensive[2] *n* : offensive *f,* attaque *f* <to go on the offensive : passer à l'offensive>
offer[1] [ˈɔfər] *vt* **1** : offrir, présenter <they offered him the job : ils lui ont offert le poste> **2** PROPOSE : proposer, suggérer **3** PROVIDE : donner, offrir <to offer no resistance : ne donner aucune résistance>
offer[2] *n* : proposition *f,* offre *f*
offering [ˈɔfərɪŋ] *n* : offre *f,* offrande *f* (en réligion)
offhand[1] [ˈɔfˈhænd] *adv* : spontanément, sur-le-champ
offhand[2] *adj* : désinvolte, impromptu
office [ˈɔfəs] *n* **1** : bureau *m,* cabinet *m* (d'un médecin, d'un avocat) **2** POSITION : fonction *f,* charge *f,* poste *m*

<a person in high office : une personne haut placée>

officeholder [ˈɔfəsˌhoːldər] *n* : fonctionnaire *mf*

officer [ˈɔfəsər] *n* **1** *or* **police officer** : policier *m,* -cière *f;* agent *m* de police **2** OFFICIAL : fonctionnaire *mf* **3** → **commissioned officer**

official[1] [əˈfɪʃəl] *adj* : officiel — **officially** *adv*

official[2] *n* : officiel *m,* -cielle *f*

officiate [əˈfɪʃiˌeɪt] *vi* **-ated; -ating 1** PRESIDE : officier, présider **2** : arbitrer (aux sports)

officious [əˈfɪʃəs] *adj* : importun, trop empressé

offing [ˈɔfɪŋ] *n* **in the offing** : en perspective, en vue

offset [ˈɔfˌsɛt] *vt* **-set; -setting** : compenser, contrebalancer

offshoot [ˈɔfˌʃuːt] *n* **1** : ramification *f,* conséquence *f* (d'une idée, etc.) **2** : rejeton *m* (en botanie)

offshore[1] [ˈɔfˈʃor] *adv* : en mer

offshore[2] *adj* : côtier, marin <offshore drilling : forage marin>

offspring [ˈɔfˌsprɪŋ] *ns & pl* PROGENY : progéniture *f*

often [ˈɔfən, ˈɔftən] *adv* : souvent, fréquemment

oftentimes [ˈɔfənˌtaɪmz, ˈɔftən-] *or* **ofttimes** [ˈɔftˌtaɪmz] → **often**

ogle [ˈoːgəl] *vt* **ogled; ogling** : lorgner, reluquer *fam*

ogre [ˈoːgər] *n* : ogre *m,* ogresse *f*

oh [ˈoː] *interj* : oh! <oh, really? : vraiment?> <oh dear! : oh la la!>

ohm [ˈoːm] *n* : ohm *m*

oil[1] [ˈɔɪl] *vt* : huiler, lubrifier, graisser

oil[2] *n* **1** : huile *f* <oil painting : peinture à l'huile> <olive oil : huile d'olive> **2** PETROLEUM : pétrole *m* **3** *or* **heating oil** : mazout *m*

oilcloth [ˈɔɪlˌklɔθ] *n* : toile *f* cirée

oiliness [ˈɔɪlinəs] *n* : nature *f* huileuse

oilskin [ˈɔɪlˌskɪn] *n* **1** OILCLOTH : toile *f* cirée **2** *or* **oilskins** *npl* : ciré *m*

oily [ˈɔɪli] **oilier; -est** *adj* : huileux

ointment [ˈɔɪntmənt] *n* : pommade *f*

OK[1] *or* **okay** [ˌoːˈkeɪ] *vt* **OK'd** *or* **okayed; OK'ing** *or* **okaying** APPROVE, AUTHORIZE : approuver

OK[2] *or* **okay** *adv* **1** WELL : bien <everything's going OK : tout va bien> **2** YES : oui

OK[3] *adj* : bien <I'm OK : je vais bien> <it's OK with me : je suis d'accord>

OK[4] *n* APPROVAL *n* : accord *m,* approbation *f*

okra [ˈoːkrə, *south also* -kri] *n* : gombo *m*

old[1] [ˈoːld] *adj* **1** : vieux <an old man : un vieil homme> **2** ANCIENT : ancien, antique **3** (*indicating a certain age*) <he's ten years old : il a dix ans> <she's not old enough : elle n'est pas encore en âge> **4** FORMER : ancien <her old neighborhood : son ancien voisinage> **5** WORN-OUT : usé **6 any old** : n'importe quel **7 old age** : vieillesse *f*

old[2] *n* **1 the old** : les vieux **2 in the days of old** : d'antan, d'autrefois

olden [ˈoːldən] *adj* : vieux, d'autrefois, d'antan <in olden days : autrefois, jadis>

old–fashioned [ˈoːldˈfæʃənd] *adj* : démodé, suranné <old-fashioned charm : charme suranné>

old maid *n* **1** SPINSTER : vieille fille *f* **2** FUSSBUDGET : tatillon *m,* -lonne *f*

Old Testament *n* : Ancien Testament *m*

old–timer [ˈoːldˈtaɪmər] *n* : vieillard *m;* ancien *m,* -cienne *f*

old–world [ˈoːldˈwərld] *adj* : d'autrefois, pittoresque

oleander [ˈoːliˌændər] *n* : laurier-rose *m*

oleomargarine [ˌoːlioˈmɑrdʒərən] → **margarine**

olfactory [ɑlˈfæktəri, ol-] *adj* : olfactif

oligarchy [ˈɑləˌgɑrki, ˈoːlə-] *n, pl* **-chies** : oligarchie *f*

olive [ˈɑlɪv, -ləv] *n* **1** : olive *f* (fruit) **2** : olivier *m* (arbre) **3** *or* **olive green** : vert *m* olive

Olympic Games [oˈlɪmpɪk] *or* **Olympics** [-pɪks] *npl* : jeux *mpl* Olympiques

Omani[1] [oˈmɑni] *adj* : omanais

Omani[2] *n* : Omanais *m,* -naise *f*

ombudsman [ˈɑmˌbʊdzmən, ɑmˈbʊdz-] *n, pl* **-men** [-mən, -ˌmɛn] : médiateur *m,* -trice *f France;* protecteur *m* du citoyen *Can*

omelet *or* **omelette** [ˈɑmlət, ˈɑmə-] *n* : omelette *f*

omen [ˈoːmən] *n* : augure *m,* présage *m*

ominous [ˈɑmənəs] *adj* : inquiétant, menaçant

ominously [ˈɑmənəsli] *adv* : de manière inquiétante

omission [oˈmɪʃən] *n* : omission *f*

omit [oˈmɪt] *vt* **omitted; omitting** : omettre <to omit to do sth : omettre de faire qqch>

omnipotence [ɑmˈnɪpət̬ənts] *n* : omnipotence *f* — **omnipotent** [-t̬ənt] *adj*

omnipresent [ˌɑmnɪˈprɛzənt] *adj* : omniprésent

omniscient [ɑmˈnɪʃənt] *adj* : omniscient

omnivorous [ɑmˈnɪvərəs] *adj* **1** : omnivore **2** AVID : avide

on[1] [ˈɑn, ˈɔn] *adv* **1** (*indicating contact with a surface*) <put the top on : mets le couvercle> <he has a hat on : il porte un chapeau> **2** (*indicating forward movement*) <from that moment on : à partir de ce moment-là> <farther on : un peu plus loin> **3** (*indicating operation or operating position*) <turn the light on : allumez la lumière>

on[2] *adj* **1** (*being in operation*) <the radio is on : la radio est allumée> <the faucet is on : le robinet est ouvert> <the engine is on : le moteur est en

marche> **2** (*taking place*) <the game is on : le match aura lieu> **3 to be on** : être mis <the lid is on : le couvercle est mis>

on[3] *prep* **1** (*indicating position*) : sur, à, de <on the table : sur la table> <on horseback : à cheval> <on page two : à la page deux> **2** AT, TO : à <on the right : à droite> **3** ABOARD, IN : en, dans <on the plane : dans l'avion> **4** (*indicating time*) <she worked on Saturdays : elle travaillait le samedi> <every hour on the hour : à toutes les heures justes> <on Tuesday : mardi> **5** (*indicating means or agency*) <to talk on the telephone : parler au téléphone> <he cut himself on a tin can : il s'est coupé avec une boîte de conserve> **6** (*indicating a state or process*) : en, à <on fire : en feu> <to be on the increase : aller en augmentant> <on foot : à pied> <on a diet : au régime> **7** (*indicating connection or membership*) <she's on a committee : elle fait partie d'un comité> **8** (*indicating an activity*) <on vacation : en vacances> **9** ABOUT, CONCERNING : sur <a book on insects : un livre sur les insectes> <reflect on that : réfléchissez-y>

once[1] ['wʌnts] *adv* **1** : une fois <once a month : une fois par mois> <once and for all : une fois pour toutes> **2** EVER : jamais <if you hesitate once, all will be lost : si jamais tu hésites, tout sera perdu> **3** FORMERLY : autrefois

once[2] *adj* FORMER : ancien, précédent

once[3] *n* **1** : une fois <for once : pour une fois> **2 at ~** SIMULTANEOUSLY : en même temps, simultanément **3 at ~** IMMEDIATELY : tout de suite, immédiatement

once[4] *conj* : dès que, une fois que

once–over [ˌwʌnts'oːvər, 'wʌntsˌ-] *n* : coup *m* d'œil <to give something the once-over : jeter un coup d'œil sur>

oncoming ['ɑnˌkʌmɪŋ, 'ɔn-] *adj* : approchant, qui approche <oncoming traffic : circulation venant en sens inverse>

one[1] ['wʌn] *adj* **1** (*being a single unit*) : un, une <he only wants one apple : il ne veut qu'une pomme> <with one motion : d'un seul mouvement> **2** (*being a particular one*) : un, une <he arrived early one morning : il est arrivé tôt un matin> **3** (*being the same*) : même <one and the same thing : la même chose> **4** SOME : un, une <one day we'll come : un jour nous viendrons> **5** ONLY : seul, unique <her one day off : son unique jour de congé>

one[2] *n* **1** : un *m* (numéro) **2** (*indicating the first of a set or series*) <from day one : depuis le premier jour> <one o'clock : une heure> **3** (*indicating a single person or thing*) <the one (girl) on the left : celle à gauche> <you can't have one without the other : l'un ne va pas sans l'autre>

one[3] *pron* **1** : un, une <one of his friends : un de ses amis> <one never knows : l'on ne sait jamais> **2 one and all** : tous, tout le monde **3 one another** : l'un l'autre **4 this one, that one** : celui-là, celle-là **5 which one?** : lequel?, laquelle?

oneness ['wʌnnəs] *n* **1** SINGLENESS : unité *f* **2** AGREEMENT : accord *m* **3** SAMENESS : identité *f*

onerous ['ɑnərəs, 'oːnə-] *adj* : pénible

oneself [ˌwən'sɛlf] *pron* **1** (*used reflexively*) : se <to control oneself : se contrôler> **2** (*used for emphasis*) : soi-même <to do it oneself : le faire soi-même> **3** (*used after prepositions*) : soi <sure of oneself : sûr de soi> **4 by ~** : seul

one–sided ['wʌn'saɪdəd] *adj* **1** UNEQUAL : inégal **2** PARTIAL : partial **3** UNILATERAL : unilatéral

onetime ['wʌn'taɪm] *adj* FORMER : ancien

one–way ['wʌn'weɪ] *adj* **1** : à sens unique (se dit d'une route) **2** : simple <a one-way ticket : un aller simple, un billet simple>

ongoing ['ɑnˌgoːɪŋ] *adj* : continu, en cours

onion ['ʌnjən] *n* : oignon *m*

online ['ɑn'laɪn, 'ɔn-] *adj* : en ligne

only[1] ['oːnli] *adv* **1** MERELY : seulement, ne...que <he's only five : il n'a que cinq ans> <this will only take a moment : ceci ne prendra qu'un moment> <only once : seulement une fois> **2** EXCLUSIVELY : seulement, uniquement <only in the morning : le matin seulement> <I'll tell it only to you : je le dirai seulement à toi> <only he knows it : lui seul le sait> **3** (*indicating a result*) <you know only too well : vous ne savez que trop bien> **4 if only** : si, si seulement <if he could only dance : si seulement il pouvait danser>

only[2] *adj* : seul, unique <an only child : un enfant unique> <the only chance : la seule chance> <we're the only ones : nous sommes les seuls>

only[3] *conj* BUT : mais <I would go, only I'm sick : j'irais mais je suis malade>

onset ['ɑnˌsɛt] *n* : début *m*, commencement *m*

onslaught ['ɑnˌslɔt, 'ɔn-] *n* : assaut *m*, attaque *f*

onto ['ɑnˌtuː, 'ɔn-] *prep* : sur

onus ['oːnəs] *n* : responsabilité *f*, charge *f*

onward[1] ['ɑnwərd, 'ɔn-] *adv* **1** FORWARD : en avant <to go onward : avancer> **2** (*used to express continuance from a point*) <from today onward : à partir d'aujourd'hui>

onward[2] *adj* : progressif <the onward march of time : la fuite du temps>
onyx [ˈɑnɪks] *n* : onyx *m*
ooze[1] [ˈuːz] *v* **oozed; oozing** *vi* : suinter — *vt* EXUDE : respirer <to ooze confidence : respirer la confiance>
ooze[2] *n* SLIME : vase *f*, boue *f*
opacity [oˈpæsət̬i] *n, pl* **-ties** : opacité *f*
opal [ˈoːpəl] *n* : opale *f*
opaque [oˈpeɪk] *adj* : opaque
open[1] [ˈoːpən] *vt* **1** : ouvrir **2** START : commencer, entamer (une négociation, etc.) **3** INAUGURATE : inaugurer, ouvrir (une entreprise, etc.) **4** CLEAR : ouvrir, dégager (la voie) — *vi* **1** : s'ouvrir **2** BEGIN : débuter, sortir <the film opens tomorrow : le film sort demain> **3 to open on to** : donner sur
open[2] *adj* **1** : ouvert <an open window : une fenêtre ouverte> <the store is open : le magasin est ouvert> **2** FRANK : franc **3** CLEAR : dégagé **4** DEBATABLE : discutable **5** VACANT : vacant **6** UNCOVERED : découvert
open[3] *n* **in the open 1** OUTDOORS : à la belle étoile, au grand air **2** KNOWN : connu
open–air [ˈoːpənˈær] *adj* OUTDOOR : en plein air
open–and–shut [ˈoːpənəndˈʃʌt] *adj* : clair, évident
opener [ˈoːpənər] *n* **1** : ouvreur *m*, -vreuse *f* (aux jeux, etc.) **2** : outil *m* servant à ouvrir <a can opener : un ouvre-boîtes>
openhanded [ˌoːpənˈhændəd] *adj* GENEROUS : généreux
openhearted [ˌoːpənˈhɑrt̬əd] *adj* **1** FRANK : franc, sincère **2** GENEROUS, KIND : généreux, qui a bon cœur
opening [ˈoːpənɪŋ] *n* **1** BEGINNING : commencement *m* **2** APERTURE : ouverture *f* **3** OPPORTUNITY : occasion *f*, chance *f* **4** : vernissage *m* (d'une exposition)
opera[1] → **opus**
opera[2] [ˈɑprə, ˈɑpərə] *n* : opéra *m*
opera glasses *n* : jumelles *fpl* de théâtre
operate [ˈɑpəˌreɪt] *v* **-ated; -ating** *vi* **1** FUNCTION : fonctionner, marcher **2 to operate on s.o.** : opérer qqn — *vt* **1** WORK : faire fonctionner **2** MANAGE : effectuer, gérer
operatic [ˌɑpəˈræt̬ɪk] *adj* : d'opéra
operation [ˌɑpəˈreɪʃən] *n* **1** FUNCTIONING : fonctionnement *m* **2** SURGERY : opération *f*, intervention *f* chirurgicale <to have an operation : se faire opérer> **3** DEALING, TRANSACTION : opération *f*
operational [ˌɑpəˈreɪʃənəl] *adj* : opérationnel
operative [ˈɑpərət̬ɪv, -ˌreɪ-] *adj* **1** OPERATING : en vigueur **2** OPERATIONAL, WORKING : opérationnel **3** SURGICAL : opératoire
operator [ˈɑpəˌreɪt̬ər] *n* **1** : opérateur *m*, -trice *f* (d'une machine, etc.) **2** *or* **switchboard operator** : standardiste *mf*
operetta [ˌɑpəˈrɛt̬ə] *n* : opérette *f*
ophthalmologist [ˌɑfˌθælˈmɑlədʒɪst, -θəˈmɑ-] *n* : ophtalmologiste *mf*
ophthalmology [ˌɑfˌθælˈmɑlədʒi, -θəˈmɑ-] *n* : ophtalmologie *f*
opiate [ˈoːpiət, -piˌeɪt] *n* : opiacé *m*
opinion [əˈpɪnjən] *n* : opinion *f*, avis *m*
opinionated [əˈpɪnjəˌneɪt̬əd] *adj* : opiniâtre
opium [ˈoːpiəm] *n* : opium *m*
opossum [əˈpɑsəm] *n* : opossum *m*
opponent [əˈpoːnənt] *n* : adversaire *mf*
opportune [ˌɑpərˈtuːn, -ˈtjuːn] *adj* : opportun — **opportunely** *adv*
opportunism [ˌɑpərˈtuːˌnɪzəm, -ˈtjuː-] *n* : opportunisme *m*
opportunist [ˌɑpərˈtuːnɪst, -ˈtjuː-] *n* : opportuniste *mf*
opportunistic [ˌɑpərtuːˈnɪstɪk, -tjuː-] *adj* : opportuniste
opportunity [ˌɑpərˈtuːnət̬i, -ˈtjuː-] *n, pl* **-ties** : occasion *f*
oppose [əˈpoːz] *vt* **-posed; -posing 1** CONTRAST : opposer **2** RESIST : s'opposer à, combattre
opposite[1] [ˈɑpəzət] *adv* : en face
opposite[2] *adj* **1** FACING : d'en face <the opposite side : le côté d'en face> **2** CONTRARY : opposé, inverse, contraire <in the opposite direction : en sens inverse> <the opposite sex : le sexe opposé>
opposite[3] *n* : contraire *m*
opposite[4] *prep* : en face de
opposition [ˌɑpəˈzɪʃən] *n* : opposition *f*, résistance *f*
oppress [əˈprɛs] *vt* **1** PERSECUTE : opprimer **2** BURDEN : oppresser
oppression [əˈprɛʃən] *n* : oppression *f*
oppressive [əˈprɛsɪv] *adj* : oppressif
oppressor [əˈprɛsər] *n* : oppresseur *m*
opprobrium [əˈproːbriəm] *n* : opprobre *m*
opt [ˈɑpt] *vi* : opter
optic [ˈɑptɪk] *adj* : optique <the optic nerve : le nerf optique>
optical [ˈɑptɪkəl] → **optic**
optician [ɑpˈtɪʃən] *n* : opticien *m*, -cienne *f*
optics [ˈɑptɪks] *n* : optique *f*
optimal [ˈɑptəməl] *adj* : optimal
optimism [ˈɑptəˌmɪzəm] *n* : optimisme *m*
optimist [ˈɑptəmɪst] *n* : optimiste *mf*
optimistic [ˌɑptəˈmɪstɪk] *adj* : optimiste
optimistically [ˌɑptəˈmɪstɪkli] *adv* : avec optimisme
optimum[1] [ˈɑptəməm] *adj* : optimum
optimum[2] *n, pl* **-ma** [ˈɑptəmə] : optimum *m*
option [ˈɑpʃən] *n* : option *f*
optional [ˈɑpʃənəl] *adj* : facultatif, optionnel

optometrist [ɑp'tɑmətrɪst] *n* : optométriste *mf*
optometry [ɑp'tɑmətri] *n* : optométrie *f*
opulence ['ɑpjələnts] *n* : opulence *f* — **opulent** [-lənt] *adj*
opus ['o:pəs] *n, pl* **opera** ['o:pərə, 'ɑpə-] : opus *m*
or ['ɔr] *conj* **1** (*indicating an alternative*) : ou <one or the other : l'un ou l'autre> **2** (*following a negative*) : ni <he didn't have his keys or his wallet : il n'avait eu ni ses clés ni son portefeuille> **3** OTHERWISE : sinon <do what I tell you, or you'll be sorry : faites ce que je dis, sinon vous le regretterez>
oracle ['ɔrəkəl] *n* : oracle *m*
oral ['orəl] *adj* : oral — **orally** *adv*
orange ['ɔrɪndʒ] *n* **1** : orange *f* (fruit) **2** : orange *m* (couleur)
orangeade [,ɔrɪndʒ'eɪd] *n* : orangeade *f*
orangutan [ə'ræŋə,tæŋ, -'ræŋgə-, -,tæn] *n* : orang-outan *m*
oration [ə'reɪʃən] *n* : discours *m* (solennel), allocution *f*
orator ['ɔrət̬ər] *n* : orateur *m*, -trice *f*
oratorical [,ɔrə'tɔrɪkəl] *adj* : oratoire
oratorio [,ɔrə'tori,o:] *n, pl* **-rios** : oratorio *m*
oratory ['ɔrə,tori] *n, pl* **-ries** : éloquence *f*, art *m* oratoire
orb ['ɔrb] *n* : orbe *m*
orbit[1] ['ɔrbət] *vt* : graviter autour de — *vi* : décrire une orbite
orbit[2] *n* : orbite *f*
orbital ['ɔrbət̬əl] *adj* : orbital
orchard ['ɔrtʃərd] *n* : verger *m*
orchestra ['ɔrkəstrə] *n* : orchestre *m* — **orchestral** [ɔr'kɛstrəl] *adj*
orchestrate ['ɔrkə,streɪt] *vt* **-trated; -trating** : orchestrer
orchestration [,ɔrkə'streɪʃən] *n* : orchestration *f*
orchid ['ɔrkɪd] *n* : orchidée *f*
ordain [ɔr'deɪn] *vt* **1** : ordonner (en religion) **2** DECREE : décréter, ordonner
ordeal [ɔr'di:l, 'ɔr,di:l] *n* : épreuve *f*, calvaire *m*
order[1] ['ɔrdər] *vt* **1** ORGANIZE : arranger, ranger **2** COMMAND : ordonner **3** REQUEST : commander (un repas, etc.) — *vi* : commander
order[2] *n* **1** : ordre *m* <religious order : ordre religieux> **2** COMMAND : commande *f*, ordre *m* <to give orders : donner des ordres> **3** REQUEST : commande *f*, bon *m* <purchase order : bon de commande> **4** DISCIPLINE : order *m* <law and order : l'ordre public> **5** CONDITION : état *m* <in working order : en bon état> **6** ARRANGEMENT : ordre *m* <in alphabetical order : en ordre alphabétique> **7 in order to** : afin de **8 orders** *npl or* **holy orders** : ordres *mpl* **9 out of order** : en panne
orderliness ['ɔrdərlinəs] *n* : ordre *m*
orderly[1] ['ɔrdərli] *adj* **1** TIDY : en ordre, ordonné **2** DISCIPLINED : discipliné, réglé
orderly[2] *n, pl* **-lies 1** : planton *m* (dans l'armée) **2** : aide-infirmier *m* (dans un hôpital)
ordinal ['ɔrdənəl] *n or* **ordinal number** : ordinal *m*
ordinance ['ɔrdənənts] *n* : ordonnance *f*
ordinarily [,ɔrdən'ɛrəli] *adv* : d'ordinaire, d'habitude
ordinary ['ɔrdən,ɛri] *adj* **1** NORMAL, USUAL : normal, habituel **2** AVERAGE : ordinaire **3** COMMONPLACE : quelconque
ordination [,ɔrdən'eɪʃən] *n* : ordination *f*
ordnance ['ɔrdnənts] *n* **1** SUPPLIES : équipement *m* militaire **2** ARTILLERY : artillerie *f*
ore ['or] *n* : minerai *m*
oregano [ə'rɛgə,no:] *n* : origan *m*
organ ['ɔrgən] *n* **1** : orgue *m* (instrument de musique) **2** : organe *m* (du corps) **3** PERIODICAL : périodique *m*
organic [ɔr'gænɪk] *adj* : organique — **organically** *adv*
organism ['ɔrgə,nɪzəm] *n* : organisme *m*
organist ['ɔrgənɪst] *n* : organiste *mf*
organization [,ɔrgənə'zeɪʃən] *n* **1** ORGANIZING : organisation *f* **2** BODY : organisme *m*
organizational [,ɔrgənə'zeɪʃənəl] *adj* : organisationnel, d'organisation
organize ['ɔrgə,naɪz] *vt* **-nized; -nizing 1** : organiser, mettre à l'ordre **2 to get organized** : s'organiser
organizer ['ɔrgə,naɪzər] *n* : organisateur *m*, -trice *f*
orgasm ['ɔr,gæzəm] *n* : orgasme *m*
orgy ['ɔrdʒi] *n, pl* **-gies** : orgie *f*
orient ['ori,ɛnt] *vt* : orienter
Orient *n* **the Orient** : l'Orient *m*
oriental [,ori'ɛntəl] *adj* : oriental, d'Orient
Oriental *n* : Oriental *m*, -tale *f*
orientation [,oriən'teɪʃən] *n* : orientation *f*
orifice ['ɔrəfəs] *n* : orifice *m*
origin ['ɔrədʒən] *n* **1** ANCESTRY : origine *f* <of Canadian origin : d'origine canadienne> **2** SOURCE : source *f*, provenance *f*
original[1] [ə'rɪdʒənəl] *adj* : original
original[2] *n* : original *m*
originality [ə,rɪdʒə'nælət̬i] *n* : originalité *f*
originally [ə'rɪdʒənəli] *adv* **1** AT FIRST : à l'origine, initialement, au début **2** INVENTIVELY : originalement, d'une manière originale
originate [ə'rɪdʒə,neɪt] *v* **-nated; -nating** *vt* : créer, donner naissance à — *vi* : provenir, prendre naissance <the

fire originated in the basement : le feu a pris naissance au sous-sol>

originator [ə'rɪdʒəˌneɪt̬ər] *n* : créateur *m*, -trice *f;* auteur *m*

oriole ['oriˌo:l, -iəl] *n* : loriot *m*

ornament[1] ['ɔrnəmənt] *vt* : orner

ornament[2] *n* : ornement *m* — **ornamental** [ˌɔrnə'mɛntəl] *adj*

ornamentation [ˌɔrnəmən'teɪʃən] *n* : ornementation *f*

ornate [ɔr'neɪt] *adj* : orné

ornery ['ɔrnəri, 'ɑrnəri] *adj* **ornerier; -est** : méchant, acariâtre, malcommode *Can*

ornithologist [ˌɔrnə'θɑlədʒɪst] *n* : ornithologiste *mf*, ornithologue *mf*

ornithology [ˌɔrnə'θɑlədʒi] *n, pl* **-gies** : ornithologie *f*

orphan[1] ['ɔrfən] *vt* : rendre orphelin

orphan[2] *n* : orphelin *m*, -line *f*

orphanage ['ɔrfənɪdʒ] *n* : orphelinat *m*

orthodontics [ˌɔrθə'dɑntɪks] *n* : orthodontie *f*

orthodontist [ˌɔrθə'dɑntɪst] *n* : orthodontiste *mf*

orthodox ['ɔrθəˌdɑks] *adj* : orthodoxe

orthodoxy ['ɔrθəˌdɑksi] *n, pl* **-doxies** : orthodoxie *f*

orthographic [ˌɔrθə'græfɪk] *adj* : orthographique

orthography [ɔr'θɑgrəfi] *n* : orthographie *f*

orthopedic [ˌɔrθə'pi:dɪk] *adj* : orthopédique

orthopedics [ˌɔrθə'pi:dɪks] *ns & pl* : orthopédie *f*

orthopedist [ˌɔrθə'pi:dɪst] *n* : orthopédiste *mf*

oscillate ['ɑsəˌleɪt] *vi* **-lated; -lating** : osciller

oscillation [ˌɑsə'leɪʃən] *n* : oscillation *f*

osmosis [ɑz'mo:səs, ɑs-] *n* : osmose *f*

osprey ['ɑspri, -ˌpreɪ] *n, pl* **-preys** : balbuzard *m* (pêcheur)

ostensible [ɑ'stɛntsəbəl] *adj* : ostensible — **ostensibly** [-bli] *adv*

ostentation [ˌɑstən'teɪʃən] *n* : ostentation *f*

ostentatious [ˌɑstən'teɪʃəs] *adj* : ostentatoire — **ostentatiously** *adv*

osteopath ['ɑstiəˌpæθ] *n* : ostéopathe *mf*

osteopathy [ˌɑsti'ɑpəθi] *n* : ostéopathie *f*

osteoporosis [ˌɑstiopə'rosɪs] *n, pl* **-roses** [-ˌsi:z] : ostéoporose *f*

ostracism ['ɑstrəˌsɪzəm] *n* : ostracisme *m*

ostracize ['ɑstrəˌsaɪz] *vt* **-cized; -cizing** : frapper d'ostracisme, mettre au ban de la société

ostrich ['ɑstrɪtʃ, 'ɔs-] *n* : autruche *f*

other[1] ['ʌðər] *adv* **other than** : autrement que, à part

other[2] *adj* : autre <the other boys : les autres garçons> <on the other hand : d'autre part, par contre> <every other day : tous les deux jours>

other[3] *pron* : autre <one in front of the other : l'un devant l'autre>

otherwise[1] ['ʌðərˌwaɪz] *adv* **1** DIFFERENTLY : autrement <he could not act otherwise : il n'a pas pu agir autrement> **2** : à part cela <I'm dizzy, but otherwise I'm fine : j'ai la tête qui tourne, mais à part cela je vais bien> **3** OR ELSE : sinon <do what I tell you, otherwise you'll be sorry : fais comme je dis, sinon tu le regretteras>

otherwise[2] *adj* : autre <the facts are otherwise : les faits sont autres>

otter ['ɑt̬ər] *n* : loutre *f*

ouch ['aʊtʃ] *interj* : aïe!, ayoye! *Can*

ought ['ɔt] *v aux* : devoir <you ought to take care of the children : vous devriez vous occuper des enfants>

oughtn't ['ɔtənt] (*contraction of* **ought not**) → **ought**

ounce ['aʊnts] *n* : once *f*

our ['ɑr, 'aʊr] *adj* : notre, nos <our house : notre maison> <our children : nos enfants>

ours ['aʊrz, 'ɑrz] *pron* : le nôtre, la nôtre <the car is ours : la voiture est la nôtre> <a cousin of ours : un de nos cousins> <that's ours : c'est à nous>

ourselves [ɑr'sɛlvz, aʊr-] *pron* **1** (*used reflexively*) : nous <we amused ourselves : nous nous sommes divertis> **2** (*used for emphasis*) : nous-mêmes <we did it ourselves : nous l'avons fait nous-mêmes>

oust ['aʊst] *vt* : évincer

ouster ['aʊstər] *n* : expulsion *f* (d'un pays, etc.), renvoi *m* (d'un poste)

out[1] ['aʊt] *vi* : se savoir <the truth will out : la vérité se saura>

out[2] *adv* **1** (*indicating direction or movement*) : dehors, à l'extérieur <let's go out tonight : sortons ce soir> <she opened the door and looked out : elle a ouvert la porte et regardait à l'extérieur> **2** (*indicating a location away from home or work*) <to eat out : aller au restaurant, dîner en ville> **3** (*indicating completion or discontinuance*) <his money ran out : il s'est trouvé à court d'argent> <to turn out the light : éteindre la lumière> **4** (*indicating possession or control*) <to lend out money : prêter de l'argent> <they let the secret out : ils ont laissé échapper le secret> **5** OUTSIDE : dehors <put the cat out : mettez le chat dehors> <the sun came out : il faisait soleil>

out[3] *adj* **1** OUTER : extérieur **2** ABSENT : absent **3** UNFASHIONABLE : démodé **4** EXTINGUISHED : éteint

out[4] *prep* **1** (*used to indicate an outward movement*) : par <I looked out the window : je regardais par la fenêtre> **2** → **out of**

out–and–out ['aʊtən'aʊt] *adj* UTTER : total, absolu

outboard motor ['aʊt,bord] *n* : hors-bord *m*

outbound ['aʊt,baʊnd] *adj* : en partance

outbreak ['aʊt,breɪk] *n* : début *m*, déclenchement *m* (de la guerre, etc.), éruption *f* (de violence, d'une maladie, etc.)

outbuilding ['aʊt,bɪldɪŋ] *n* : dépendance *f*

outburst ['aʊt,bərst] *n* : accès *m* (de colère, etc.), explosion *f*

outcast ['aʊt,kæst] *n* : proscrit *m*, -crite *f;* banni *m*, -nie *f*

outcome ['aʊt,kʌm] *n* : résultat *m*

outcrop ['aʊt,krɑp] *n* : affleurement *m*

outcry ['aʊt,kraɪ] *n, pl* **-cries** : tollé *m*

outdated [,aʊt'deɪṭəd] *adj* : démodé

outdistance [,aʊt'dɪstənts] *vt* **-tanced; -tancing** : distancer

outdo [,aʊt'du:] *vt* **-did** [-'dɪd]; **-done** [-'dʌn]; **-doing** [-'du:ɪŋ]; **-does** [-'dʌz] : surpasser

outdoor ['aʊt'dor] *adj* : en plein air, de plein air, d'extérieur <outdoor activities : activités en plein air> <outdoor sports : sports de plein air> <outdoor clothes : vêtements d'extérieur>

outdoors[1] ['aʊt'dorz] *adv* : à la belle étoile, au grand air, en plein air

outdoors[2] *n* **the great outdoors** : les grands espaces naturels, la pleine nature

outer ['aʊṭər] *adj* : externe, extérieur

outermost ['aʊṭər,mo:st] *adj* : le plus extérieur

outer space *n* : espace *m* intersidéral

outfield ['aʊt,fi:ld] *n* : champ *m* extérieur

outfielder ['aʊt,fi:ldər] *n Can* : voltigeur *m*, -geuse *f*

outfit[1] ['aʊt,fɪt] *vt* **-fitted; -fitting** EQUIP : équiper

outfit[2] *n* **1** EQUIPMENT : équipement *m*, attirail *m* **2** COSTUME : tenue *f* **3** GROUP : équipe *f*, bande *f*

outgoing ['aʊt,go:ɪŋ] *adj* **1** OUTBOUND : en partance **2** DEPARTING : sortant <the outgoing president : le président sortant> **3** EXTROVERTED : extraverti

outgrow [,aʊt'gro:] *vt* **-grew** [-'gru:]; **-grown** [-'gro:n]; **-growing** : devenir trop grand pour

outgrowth ['aʊt,gro:θ] *n* : excroissance *f*

outing ['aʊṭɪŋ] *n* : excursion *f*, sortie *f*

outlandish [aʊt'lændɪʃ] *adj* : bizarre, excentrique

outlast [,aʊt'læst] *vt* : durer plus longtemps que

outlaw[1] ['aʊt,lɔ] *vt* : proscrire, rendre illégal

outlaw[2] *n* : hors-la-loi *m*

outlay ['aʊt,leɪ] *n* : débours *m*, dépense *f*, mise *f* de fonds

outlet ['aʊt,lɛt, -lət] *n* **1** EXIT : sortie *f*, issue *f* **2** RELEASE : exutoire *m* **3** MARKET : débouché *m*, point *m* de vente **4** *or* **electrical outlet** : prise *f* de courant

outline[1] ['aʊt,laɪn] *vt* **-lined; -lining 1** SKETCH : esquisser, tracer **2** SUMMARIZE : résumer

outline[2] *n* **1** CONTOUR : contour *m* **2** SKETCH : ébauche *f* **3** SUMMARY : esquisse *f*

outlive [,aʊt'lɪv] *vt* **-lived; -living** : survivre à

outlook ['aʊt,lʊk] *n* **1** VIEW : vue *f* **2** POINT OF VIEW : perspective *f* **3** PROSPECTS : perspectives *fpl*

out loud *adv* ALOUD : à haute voix

outlying ['aʊt,laɪɪŋ] *adj* : isolé, périphérique <outlying areas : régions périphériques>

outmoded [,aʊt'mo:dəd] *adj* : démodé

outnumber [,aʊt'nʌmbər] *vt* : être plus nombreux que, surpasser en nombre

out of *prep* **1** (*indicating direction or movement from within*) : de, par <to look out of the window : regarder par la fenêtre> <we ran out of the house : nous sommes sortis de la maison en courant> **2** (*being beyond the limits of*) <out of control : hors de contrôle> **3** OF : sur <one out of four : un sur quatre> **4** (*indicating absence or loss*) : sans <out of money : sans argent> <we're out of matches : nous n'avons plus d'allumettes> **5** BECAUSE OF : par <out of curiosity : par curiosité> **6** FROM : en <made out of plastic : fait en plastique>

out–of–date [,aʊṭəv'deɪt] *adj* **1** OUTMODED : démodé **2** EXPIRED : périmé

out–of–door [,aʊṭəv'dor] *or* **out–of–doors** [-'dorz] → **outdoor**

out–of–doors → **outdoors**

outpatient ['aʊt,peɪʃənt] *n* : malade *mf* en consultation externe

outpost ['aʊt,po:st] *n* : avant-poste *m*

output[1] ['aʊt,pʊt] *vt* **-putted** *or* **-put; -putting** : sortir (en informatique)

output[2] *n* : rendement *m*, production *f*, productivité *f*

outrage[1] ['aʊt,reɪdʒ] *vt* **-raged; -raging** : outrager

outrage[2] *n* **1** AFFRONT, SCANDAL : outrage *m*, affront *m*, scandale *m* **2** ATROCITY : atrocité *f* **3** ANGER : indignation *f*

outrageous [,aʊt'reɪdʒəs] *adj* **1** SCANDALOUS : scandaleux **2** BIZARRE, UNCONVENTIONAL : extravagant, bizarre

outright[1] ['aʊt,raɪt] *adv* **1** COMPLETELY : complètement **2** INSTANTLY : sur le coup **3** FRANKLY : franchement, carrément

outright[2] *adj* **1** COMPLETE, UTTER : total, absolu <an outright lie : un mensonge absolu> **2** : sans réserve <an outright gift : un cadeau pur et simple, un cadeau sans réserve>

outset ['aʊt,sɛt] *n* : début *m*, commencement *m*

outshine [ˌaʊtˈʃaɪn] *vt* **-shone** [-ˈʃo:n, -ˈʃɒn] *or* **-shined; shining** : éclipser, surpasser

outside[1] [ˌaʊtˈsaɪd, ˈaʊtˌ-] *adv* : à l'extérieur, dehors

outside[2] *adj* **1** OUTER : extérieur <the outside edge : le bord extérieur> **2** OUTDOOR : extérieur, à l'extérieur **3** POOR, REMOTE : faible <an outside chance : une faible chance>

outside[3] *n* **1** EXTERIOR : extérieur *m*, dehors *m* **2** MOST : maximum *m*, plus *m* <three weeks at the outside : trois semaines au plus>

outside[4] *prep* : en dehors de, à l'extérieur de

outside of *prep* **1** → **outside[4]** **2** → **besides[2]**

outsider [ˌaʊtˈsaɪdər] *n* : étranger *m*, -gère *f*

outskirts [ˈaʊtˌskərts] *npl* : banlieue *f*, périphérie *f*

outsmart [ˌaʊtˈsmɑrt] → **outwit**

outspoken [ˌaʊtˈspo:kən] *adj* : franc, carré

outstanding [ˌaʊtˈstændɪŋ] *adj* **1** UNPAID : impayé, dû **2** NOTABLE : exceptionnel

outstandingly [ˌaʊtˈstændɪŋli] *adv* : exceptionnellement

outstrip [ˌaʊtˈstrɪp] *vt* **-stripped; -stripping 1** PASS : dépasser, devancer **2** SURPASS : surpasser

outward[1] [ˈaʊtwərd] *or* **outwards** [-wərdz] *adv* : au dehors <outward bound : en partance>

outward[2] *adj* **1** : vers l'extérieur <an outward flow : un écoulement vers l'extérieur> **2** EXTERIOR : extérieur, externe <an outward calm : un calme apparent>

outwardly [ˈaʊtwərdli] *adv* **1** EXTERNALLY : à l'extérieur **2** APPARENTLY : en apparence

outwit [ˌaʊtˈwɪt] *vt* **-witted; -witting** : se montrer plus futé que, duper

ova → **ovum**

oval[1] [ˈo:vəl] *adj* : ovale

oval[2] *n* : ovale *m*

ovary [ˈo:vəri] *n, pl* **-ries** : ovaire *m*

ovation [oˈveɪʃən] *n* : ovation *f*

oven [ˈʌvən] *n* : four *m*

over[1] [ˈo:vər] *adv* **1** (*indicating movement across*) <he flew over to London : il est venu à Londres en avion> <come on over! : venez donc!> **2** (*indicating an additional amount*) <the show ran 10 minutes over : le spectacle a duré 10 minutes de trop> <over twenty dollars : plus de vingt dollars> **3** ABOVE, OVERHEAD : au-dessus **4** AGAIN : encore, de nouveau <over and over : à plusieurs reprises> <to start over : commencer de nouveau> **5 all over** EVERYWHERE : partout

over[2] *adj* **1** HIGHER, UPPER : supérieur **2** REMAINING : en plus **3** ENDED : terminé, fini <the job is finally over : enfin le travail est fini>

over[3] *prep* **1** ABOVE : au-dessus de, par-dessus <over the fireplace : au-dessus de la cheminée> <the hawk flew over the hills : le faucon a volé par-dessus les collines> **2** : plus de <over $50 : plus de 50 $> **3** ALONG : sur <to glide over the ice : glisser sur la glace> **4** (*indicating movement across*) <he jumped over the ditch : il a franchi le fossé d'un bond> **5** DURING : pendant, au cours de <over the last few years : au cours des dernières années> **6** (*referring to a means of communication*) <to speak over the telephone : parler au téléphone> **7** BECAUSE OF : à cause de, au sujet de

overabundance [ˌo:vərəˈbʌndənts] *n* : surabondance *f* — **overabundant** [-dənt] *adj*

overactive [ˌo:vərˈæktɪv] *adj* : trop actif

overall[1] [ˌo:vərˈɔl] *adv* **1** : d'un bout à l'autre, en tout **2** GENERALLY : en général

overall[2] *adj* : d'ensemble, total, global <an overall view : une vue d'ensemble>

overalls [ˈo:vərˌɔlz] *npl* : salopette *f*

overawe [ˌo:vərˈɔ] *vt* **-awed; -awing** : impressionner, intimider

overbearing [ˌo:vərˈbærɪŋ] *adj* : impérieux, autoritaire

overboard [ˈo:vərˌbord] *adv* : par-dessus bord

overburden [ˌo:vərˈbərdən] *vt* : surcharger

overcast [ˈo:vərˌkæst] *adj* CLOUDY : couvert

overcharge [ˌo:vərˈtʃɑrdʒ] *v* **-charged; -charging** *vt* : faire payer trop cher à — *vi* : demander un prix excessif

overcoat [ˈo:vərˌko:t] *n* : pardessus *m*

overcome [ˌo:vərˈkʌm] *v* **-came** [-ˈkeɪm]; **-come; -coming** *vt* **1** CONQUER : vaincre, surmonter **2** OVERWHELM : accabler, écraser — *vi* : vaincre

overconfidence [ˌo:vərˈkɑnfədənts] *n* : confiance *f* excessive

overconfident [ˌo:vərˈkɑnfədənt] *adj* : trop confiant

overcook [ˌo:vərˈkʊk] *vt* : faire trop cuire

overdo [ˌo:vərˈdu:] *vt* **-did** [-ˈdɪd]; **-done** [-ˈdʌn]; **-doing; -does** [-ˈdʌz] **1** : exagérer **2** → **overcook**

overdose [ˈo:vərˌdo:s] *n* : overdose *f*, surdose *f*

overdraft [ˈo:vərˌdræft] *n* : découvert *m*

overdraw [ˌo:vərˈdrɔ] *vt* **-drew** [-ˈdru:]; **-drawn** [-ˈdrɔn]; **-drawing** : mettre à découvert

overdue [ˌo:vərˈdu:] *adj* **1** UNPAID : arriéré **2** TARDY : en retard

overeat [ˌo:vərˈi:t] *vt* **-ate** [-ˈeɪt]; **-eating** : trop manger

overelaborate [ˌo:vərɪˈlæbərət] *adj* : trop recherché

overestimate [ˌo:vərˈɛstəˌmeɪt] *vt* **-mated; -mating** : surestimer
overexcited [ˌo:vərɪkˈsaɪṭəd] *adj* : surexcité
overexpose [ˌo:vərɪkˈspo:z] *vt* **-posed; posing** : surexposer
overfeed [ˌo:vərˈfi:d] *vt* **-fed** [-ˈfɛd]; **-feeding** : suralimenter
overflow[1] [ˌo:vərˈflo:] *v* : déborder
overflow[2] [ˈo:vərˌflo:] *n* **1** : trop-plein *m*, débordement *m* (d'une rivière, etc.) **2** SURPLUS : surplus *m*, excédent *m*
overfly [ˌo:vərˈflaɪ] *vt* **-flew** [-ˈflu:]; **-flown** [-ˈflo:n]; **-flying** : survoler
overgrown [ˌo:vərˈgro:n] *adj* **1** EXCESSIVE, HUGE : démesuré **2** : couvert, envahi <overgrown with weeds : couvert de mauvaises herbes>
overhand[1] [ˈo:vərˌhænd] *adv* : pardessus la tête
overhand[2] *adj* : par le haut
overhang[1] [ˌo:vərˈhæŋ] *vt* **-hung** [-ˈhʌŋ]; **-hanging** : surplomber
overhang[2] [ˈo:vərˌhæŋ] *n* : surplomb *m*
overhaul [ˌo:vərˈhɔl] *vt* **1** : réviser (un moteur, etc.) **2** OVERTAKE : dépasser
overhead[1] [ˌo:vərˈhɛd] *adv* : au-dessus
overhead[2] [ˈo:vərˌhɛd] *adj* : au-dessus de la tête, aérien <overhead lighting : éclairage au plafond>
overhead[3] [ˈo:vərˌhɛd] *n or* **overhead expenses** : frais *mpl* généraux
overhear [ˌo:vərˈhɪr] *vt* **-heard** [-ˈhərd]; **-hearing** : entendre par hasard
overheat [ˌo:vərˈhi:t] *vt* : surchauffer
overjoyed [ˌo:vərˈdʒɔɪd] *adj* : ravi, rempli de joie
overkill [ˈo:vərˌkɪl] *n* : excès *m*
overland[1] [ˈo:vərˌlænd, -lənd] *adv* : par voie de terre
overland[2] *adj* : par (la) route
overlap[1] [ˌo:vərˈlæp] *v* **-lapped; -lapping** *vt* : chevaucher — *vi* : chevaucher, se recouvrir
overlap[2] [ˈo:vərˌlæp] *n* : chevauchement *m*
overlay[1] [ˌo:vərˈleɪ] *vt* **-laid** [-ˈleɪd]; **-laying** : recouvrir
overlay[2] [ˈo:vərˌleɪ] *n* : revêtement *m*, recouvrement *m*
overload [ˌo:vərˈlo:d] *vt* : surcharger
overlong [ˌo:vərˈlɔŋ] *adj* : trop long
overlook [ˌo:vərˈlʊk] *vt* **1** INSPECT : inspecter **2** : donner sur <the house overlooks the beach : la maison donne sur la plage> **3** MISS : manquer **4** IGNORE : laisser passer **5** SUPERVISE : surveiller
overly [ˈo:vərli] *adv* : trop
overnight[1] [ˌo:vərˈnaɪt] *adv* **1** : pendant la nuit **2** SUDDENLY : du jour au lendemain
overnight[2] [ˈo:vərˌnaɪt] *adj* **1** : de nuit, d'une nuit <an overnight stay : une visite d'une nuit> **2** SUDDEN : soudain, subit
overpass [ˈo:vərˌpæs] *n* : voie *f* surélevée
overpopulated [ˌo:vərˈpɑpjəˌleɪṭəd] *adj* : surpeuplé
overpower [ˌo:vərˈpaʊər] *vt* **1** CONQUER : vaincre **2** OVERWHELM : accabler
overrate [ˌo:vərˈreɪt] *vt* **-rated; -rating** : surestimer
override [ˌo:vərˈraɪd] *vt* **-rode** [-ˈro:d]; **-ridden** [-ˈrɪdən]; **-riding** : passer outre à, outrepasser
overrule [ˌo:vərˈru:l] *vt* **-ruled; -ruling** : rejeter
overrun [ˌo:vərˈrʌn] *v* **-ran** [-ˈræn]; **-running** *vt* **1** INVADE : envahir **2** INFEST : infester **3** EXCEED : dépasser — *vi* : dépasser le temps prévu
overseas[1] [ˌo:vərˈsi:z] *adv* : à l'étranger, outre-mer
overseas[2] [ˈo:vərˌsi:z] *adj* : à l'étranger, extérieur, d'outre-mer
oversee [ˌo:vərˈsi:] *vt* **-saw** [-ˈsɔ]; **-seen** [-ˈsi:n]; **-seeing** SUPERVISE : surveiller
overseer [ˈo:vərˌsi:ər] *n* : surveillant *m*, -lante *f*; contremaître *m*, -tresse *f*
overshadow [ˌo:vərˈʃæˌdo:] *vt* **1** DARKEN : ombrager **2** ECLIPSE, OUTSHINE : éclipser, surpasser
overshoe [ˈo:vərˌʃu:] *n* **1** : galoche *f* **2 overshoes** *npl* GALOSHES : caoutchoucs *mpl*, bottes *fpl* de caoutchouc
overshoot [ˌo:vərˈʃu:t] *vt* **-shot** [-ˈʃɑt]; **-shooting** : dépasser
oversight [ˈo:vərˌsaɪt] *n* **1** ERROR, OMISSION : oubli *m*, omission *f* **2** SUPERVISION : surveillance *f*
oversleep [ˌo:vərˈsli:p] *vi* **-slept** [-ˈslɛpt]; **-sleeping** : dormir trop longtemps
overstate [ˌo:vərˈsteɪt] *vt* **-stated; -stating** EXAGGERATE : exagérer
overstatement [ˌo:vərˈsteɪtmənt] *n* : exagération *f*
overstep [ˌo:vərˈstɛp] *vt* **-stepped; -stepping** : dépasser, outrepasser
overt [oˈvərt, ˈo:ˌvərt] *adj* : évident, manifeste
overtake [ˌo:vərˈteɪk] *vt* **-took** [-ˈtʊk]; **-taken** [-ˈteɪkən]; **-taking** : dépasser, doubler, devancer
overthrow[1] [ˌo:vərˈθro:] *vt* **-threw** [-ˈθru:]; **-thrown** [-ˈθro:n]; **-throwing 1** OVERTURN : renverser **2** DEFEAT : vaincre
overthrow[2] [ˈo:vərˌθro:] *n* : renversement *m*, défaite *f*
overtime [ˈo:vərˌtaɪm] *n* **1** : heures *fpl* supplémentaires (de travail) **2** : prolongations *fpl* (aux sports)
overtone [ˈo:vərˌto:n] *n* : son *m* harmonique
overture [ˈo:vərˌtʃʊr, -tʃər] *n* **1** : ouverture *f* (en musique) **2** PROPOSAL : proposition *f*
overturn [ˌo:vərˈtərn] *vt* **1** : renverser **2** NULLIFY : annuler — *vi* : se renverser
overuse [ˌo:vərˈju:z] *vt* **-used; -using** : abuser de, trop employer
overview [ˈo:vərˌvju:] *n* : vue *f* d'ensemble

overweening [ˌo:vərˈwi:nɪŋ] *adj* **1** ARROGANT : outrecuidant, arrogant **2** EXCESSIVE : démesuré
overweight [ˌo:vərˈweɪt] *adj* : trop gros, obèse
overwhelm [ˌo:vərˈ*h*wɛlm] *vt* : écraser, accabler
overwhelmingly [ˌo:vərˈ*h*wɛlmɪŋ] *adj* : accablant, écrasant
overwork [ˌo:vərˈwerk] *vt* **1** : surmener (une personne) **2** OVERUSE : abuser de — *vi* : se surmener
overwrought [ˌo:vərˈrɔt] *adj* : à bout de nerfs
ovoid [ˈoˌvɔɪd] *or* **ovoidal** [o:ˈvɔɪdəl] *adj* : ovoïde
ovulate [ˈɑvjəˌleɪt, ˈo:-] *vi* **-lated; -lating** : ovuler
ovulation [ˌɑvjəˈleɪʃən, ˌo:-] *n* : ovulation *f*
ovum [ˈo:vəm] *n, pl* **ova** [-və] : ovule *m*
owe [ˈo:] *vt* **owed; owing** : devoir <you owe me $10 : tu me dois 10 $> <he owes his wealth to his father : il doit sa fortune à son père>
owing to *prep* : pour cause de
owl [ˈaʊl] *n* : hibou *m*
own[1] [ˈo:n] *vt* **1** POSSESS : posséder **2** ADMIT : reconnaître, admettre — *vi* **to own up** : avouer
own[2] *adj* : propre <his own car : sa propre voiture>
own[3] *pron* **my (your, his/her, our, their) own** : le mien, la mienne; le tien, la tienne; le vôtre, la vôtre; le sien, la sienne; le nôtre, la nôtre; le leur, la leur <it's my own : c'est le mien> <to each his own : chacun son goût> <to be on one's own : être tout seul>
owner [ˈo:nər] *n* : propriétaire *mf*
ownership [ˈo:nərˌʃɪp] *n* : possession *f*
ox [ˈɑks] *n, pl* **oxen** [ˈɑksən] : bœuf *m*
oxide [ˈɑkˌsaɪd] *n* : oxyde *m*
oxidize [ˈɑksəˌdaɪz] *vt* **-dized; -dizing** : oxyder
oxygen [ˈɑksɪdʒən] *n* : oxygène *m*
oyster [ˈɔɪstər] *n* : huître *f*
ozone [ˈo:ˌzo:n] *n* : ozone *m*

P

p [ˈpi:] *n, pl* **p's** *or* **ps** [ˈpi:z] : p *m*, seizième lettre de l'alphabet
pace[1] [ˈpeɪs] *v* **paced; pacing** *vt* **1** : arpenter <to pace the room : arpenter la chambre> **2 to pace off** : mesurer en pas — *vi* **to pace to and fro** : faire les cent pas
pace[2] *n* **1** STEP : pas *m* **2** SPEED : allure *f*, vitesse *f* <to walk at a good pace : marcher à vive allure>
pacemaker [ˈpeɪsˌmeɪkər] *n* : stimulateur *m* cardiaque
pachyderm [ˈpækɪˌdərm] *n* : pachyderme *m*
pacific [pəˈsɪfɪk] *adj* : pacifique
pacifier [ˈpæsəˌfaɪər] *n* : tétine *f*, sucette *f*
pacifism [ˈpæsəˌfɪzəm] *n* : pacifisme *m*
pacifist[1] [ˈpæsəfɪst] *or* **pacifistic** [ˌpæsəˈfɪstɪk] *adj* : pacifiste
pacifist[2] *n* : pacifiste *mf*
pacify [ˈpæsəˌfaɪ] *vt* **-fied; -fying** : pacifier, apaiser
pack[1] [ˈpæk] *vt* **1** PACKAGE : empaqueter, emballer **2** CRAM, FILL : entasser, empiler, remplir **3** : faire (sa valise, ses bagages) **4 to pack off** SEND : envoyer
pack[2] *n* **1** PACKAGE : paquet *m*, colis *m* **2** BUNDLE : balle *f*, baluchon *m* **3** BACKPACK : sac *m* à dos **4** GROUP : meute *f* (de chiens), bande *f* (de loups, etc.)
package[1] [ˈpækɪdʒ] *vt* **-aged; -aging** : empaqueter
package[2] *n* : paquet *m*, colis *m*
packet [ˈpækət] *n* : (petit) paquet *m*
pact [ˈpækt] *n* : pacte *m*
pad[1] [ˈpæd] *v* **padded; padding** *vt* **1** STUFF : rembourrer, matelasser **2** EXPAND : étoffer (une note de frais), délayer (un discours) — *vi* : marcher à pas feutrés
pad[2] *n* **1** CUSHION : coussin *m*, protection *f* (aux sports) <a shoulder pad : une épaulette> **2** TABLET : bloc *m* (de papier) **3** *or* **lily pad** : feuille *f* (de nénuphar) **4 ink pad** : tampon *m* encreur **5 launching pad** : rampe *m* de lancement
padding [ˈpædɪŋ] *n* **1** FILLING, STUFFING : rembourrage *m* **2** : remplissage *m*, délayage *m* (d'un discours)
paddle[1] [ˈpædəl] *v* **-dled; -dling** *vt* **1** : pagayer **2** SPANK : donner une fessée à — *vi* WADE : patauger, barboter
paddle[2] *n* : pagaie *f*, aube *f*, aviron *m* *Can*
paddock [ˈpædək] *n* : paddock *m*, enclos *m*
paddy [ˈpædi] *n, pl* **-dies** : rizière *f*
padlock[1] [ˈpædˌlɑk] *vt* : cadenasser
padlock[2] *n* : cadenas *m*
pagan[1] [ˈpeɪgən] *adj* : païen
pagan[2] *n* : païen *m*, païenne *f*
paganism [ˈpeɪgənˌɪzəm] *n* : paganisme *m*
page[1] [ˈpeɪdʒ] *v* **paged; paging** *vt* : appeler, demander — *vi* **to page through** : feuilleter
page[2] *n* **1** ATTENDANT, BELLHOP : chasseur *m* **2** : page *f* (d'un livre)
pageant [ˈpædʒənt] *n* **1** : reconstitution *f* historique (comme de Noël) **2**

SHOW, SPECTACLE : spectacle *m* fastueux
pageantry ['pædʒəntri] *n* : apparat *m*, pompe *f*
pagoda [pə'go:də] *n* : pagode *f*
paid → **pay**
pail ['peɪl] *n* : seau *m*
pain[1] ['peɪn] *vt* : peiner, faire souffrir
pain[2] *n* **1** : mal *m*, douleur *f* <back pains : maux de dos> **2** GRIEF : peine *f*, souffrance *f* **3 pains** *npl* : peine *f*, mal *m* <to take great pains : se donner beaucoup de mal>
painful ['peɪnfəl] *adj* : douloureux — **painfully** *adv*
painkiller ['peɪn,kɪlər] *n* : analgésique *m*
painkilling ['peɪn,kɪlɪŋ] *adj* : analgésique
painless ['peɪnləs] *adj* : indolore, sans douleur
painlessly ['peɪnləsli] *adv* : sans douleur, sans mal
painstaking ['peɪn,steɪkɪŋ] *adj* : soigneux, méticuleux — **painstakingly** *adv*
paint[1] ['peɪnt] *v* : peindre, peinturer *Can*
paint[2] *n* : peinture *f*
paintbrush ['peɪnt,brʌʃ] *n* : pinceau *m*, brosse *f*
painter ['peɪntər] *n* : peintre *m*
painting ['peɪntɪŋ] *n* : peinture *f*
pair[1] ['pær] *vi* **1** MATCH : apparier **2 to pair off** : se mettre par deux
pair[2] *n* **1** : paire *f* <a pair of gloves : une paire de gants> <a pair of pliers : une pince> **2** COUPLE : couple *m* (de personnes ou d'animaux)
pajamas *or Brit* **pyjamas** [pə'dʒɑməz, -'dʒæ-] *npl* : pyjama *m*
Pakistani[1] [,pækɪ'stæni, ,pɑki'stɑni] *adj* : pakistanais
Pakistani[2] *n* : Pakistanais *m*, -naise *f*
pal ['pæl] *n* : copain *m*, -pine *f*
palace ['pæləs] *n* : palais *m*
palatable ['pælət̬əbəl] *adj* : savoureux
palate ['pælət] *n* : palais *m*
palatial [pə'leɪʃəl] *adj* : magnifique, somptueux
palaver[1] [pə'lævər, -'lɑ-] *vi* : palabrer, discuter
palaver[2] *n* : histoires *fpl*, palabres *fpl*
pale[1] ['peɪl] *vi* **paled; paling** : pâlir
pale[2] *adj* **paler; palest 1** PALLID : pâle, blême <to turn pale : pâlir> **2** : clair, pâle <pale bleu : bleu clair>
pale[3] *n* STAKE : pieu *m*
paleness ['peɪlnəs] *n* : pâleur *f*
Palestinian[1] [,pælə'stɪniən] *adj* : palestinien
Palestinian[2] *n* : Palestinien *m*, -nienne *f*
palette ['pælət] *n* : palette *f*
palisade [,pælə'seɪd] *n* **1** FENCE : palissade *f* **2** CLIFFS : ligne *f* de falaises
pall[1] ['pɔl] *vi* : perdre son charme, devenir ennuyeux
pall[2] *n* **1** : drap *m* mortuaire **2** CLOUD : voile *m* <a pall of smoke : un voile de fumée> <a pall of silence : un silence profond>
pallbearer ['pɔl,bɛrər] *n* : porteur *m*, -teuse *f* de cercueil
pallet ['pælət] *n* **1** BED : grabat *m* **2** PLATFORM : palette *f*, plateau *m* de chargement
palliative ['pæli,eɪt̬ɪv, 'pæljət̬ɪv] *adj* : palliatif
pallid ['pæləd] *adj* : pâle, blême
pallor ['pælər] *n* : pâleur *f*
palm[1] ['pɑm, 'pɑlm] *vt* **1** CONCEAL : escamoter (une carte, etc.) **2** *or* **to palm off** : refiler *fam*
palm[2] *n* **1** *or* **palm tree** : palmier *m* **2** : paume *f* (de la main)
Palm Sunday *n* : dimanche *m* des Rameaux
palomino [,pælə'mi:,no:] *n, pl* **-nos** : palomino *m*
palpable ['pælpəbəl] *adj* : palpable
palpitate ['pælpə,teɪt] *vi* **-tated; -tating** : palpiter
palpitation [,pælpə'teɪʃən] *n* : palpitation *f*
palsy ['pɔlzi] *n, pl* **-sies 1** : paralysie *f* **2** → **cerebral palsy**
paltry ['pɔltri] *adj* **paltrier; -est** : dérisoire, piètre
pamper ['pæmpər] *vt* : choyer, dorloter
pamphlet ['pæmpflət] *n* : dépliant *m*, brochure *f*
pan[1] ['pæn] *vt* **panned; panning 1** *or* **to pan for** : chercher (de l'or, etc.) **2** CRITICIZE : éreinter (un spectacle)
pan[2] *n* **1** SAUCEPAN : casserole *f* **2** FRYING PAN : poêle *f*
panacea [,pænə'si:ə] *n* : panacée *f*
Panamanian[1] [,pænə'meɪniən] *adj* : panaméen
Panamanian[2] *n* : Panaméen *m*, -méenne *f*
pancake ['pæn,keɪk] *n* : crêpe *f*
pancreas ['pæŋkriəs, 'pæn-] *n* : pancréas *m*
panda ['pændə] *n* : panda *m*
pandemonium [,pændə'mo:niəm] *n* : brouhaha *m*, tumulte *m*
pander ['pændər] *vi* : flatter (bassement)
pane ['peɪn] *n* : vitre *f*, carreau *m*
panel[1] ['pænəl] *vt* **-eled** *or* **-elled; -eling** *or* **-elling** : recouvrir de panneaux
panel[2] *n* **1** : liste *f* (des jurés) **2** : panneau *m* <plywood panels : panneaux en contreplaqué> **3** COMMITTEE, GROUP : comité *m*, commission *f* **4** *or* **control panel** : tableau *m* (de bord)
paneling ['pænəlɪŋ] *n* : panneaux *mpl*
pang ['pæŋ] *n* **1** : tiraillement *m*, crampe *f* <hunger pangs : tiraillements d'estomac> **2** : serrement *m* de cœur <pangs of conscience : remords de conscience>

panic[1] [ˈpænɪk] *v* **-icked; -icking** *vt* : paniquer *fam* — *vi* : paniquer *fam*, s'affoler
panic[2] *n* : panique *f*, affolement *m*
panicky [ˈpænɪki] *adj* : pris de panique
panorama [ˌpænəˈræmə, -ˈrɑ-] *n* : panorama *m*
panoramic [ˌpænəˈræmɪk, -ˈrɑ-] *adj* : panoramique
pansy [ˈpænzi] *n, pl* **-sies** : pensée *f*
pant[1] [ˈpænt] *vi* : haleter, souffler
pant[2] *n* : halètement *m*
pantaloons [ˌpæntəˈlu:nz] → **pants**
panther [ˈpænθər] *n* **1** LEOPARD : panthère *f* **2** COUGAR, PUMA : puma *m*
panties [ˈpæntiz] *npl* : (petite) culotte *f*, slip *m France*
pantomime[1] [ˈpæntəˌmaɪm] *vt* **-mimed; -miming** : représenter par une pantomime
pantomime[2] *n* : pantomime *f*
pantry [ˈpæntri] *n, pl* **-tries** : garde-manger *m*
pants [ˈpænts] *npl* **1** : pantalon *m* **2** → **panties**
panty hose [ˈpæntiˌho:z] *npl* : collant *m*
pap [ˈpæp] *n* GRUEL : bouillie *f*
papal [ˈpeɪpəl] *adj* : papal
papaya [pəˈpaɪə] *n* : papaye *f*
paper[1] [ˈpeɪpər] *vt* WALLPAPER : tapisser
paper[2] *adj* : de papier, en papier
paper[3] *n* **1** : papier *m* <a sheet of paper : une feuille de papier> **2** DOCUMENT : document *m* **3** NEWSPAPER : journal *m* **4** WALLPAPER : papier *m* peint **5** : travail *m* (scolaire)
paperback [ˈpeɪpərˌbæk] *n* : livre *m* de poche
paper clip *n* : trombone *m*
paperweight [ˈpeɪpərˌweɪt] *n* : presse-papiers *m*
papery [ˈpeɪpəri] *adj* : comme du papier
papier–mâché [ˌpeɪpərməˈʃeɪ, ˌpæˌpjeɪmæˈʃeɪ] *n* : papier *m* mâché
papoose [pæˈpu:s, pə-] *n* : enfant *mf* des Indiens nord-américains
paprika [pəˈpri:kə, pæ-] *n* : paprika *m*
papyrus [pəˈpaɪrəs] *n, pl* **-ruses** *or* **-ri** [-ˌri, -ˌraɪ] : papyrus *m*
par [ˈpɑr] *n* **1** : pair *m* (en finances) <at par value : à la valeur au pair> **2** EQUALITY : égalité *f* <to be on a par with : être l'égal de> **3** : par *m* (au golf)
parable [ˈpærəbəl] *n* : parabole *f*
parachute[1] [ˈpærəˌʃu:t] *v* **-chuted; -chuting** *vt* : parachuter — *vi* : sauter en parachute
parachute[2] *n* : parachute *m*
parachutist [ˈpærəˌʃu:t̬ɪst] *n* : parachutiste *mf*
parade[1] [pəˈreɪd] *vi* **-raded; -rading 1** MARCH : défiler **2** SHOW OFF : parader, faire étalage
parade[2] *n* **1** : parade *f*, défilé *m* <circus parade : parade de cirque> **2** DISPLAY : étalage *m*
paradigm [ˈpærəˌdaɪm] *n* : paradigme *m*
paradise [ˈpærəˌdaɪs, -ˌdaɪz] *n* : paradis *m*
paradox [ˈpærəˌdɑks] *n* : paradoxe *m*
paradoxical [ˌpærəˈdɑksɪkəl] *adj* : paradoxal — **paradoxically** [-kli] *adv*
paraffin [ˈpærəfən] *n* : paraffine *f*
paragon [ˈpærəˌgɑn, -gən] *n* : parangon *m*, modèle *m*
paragraph[1] [ˈpærəˌgræf] *vt* : diviser en paragraphes
paragraph[2] *n* : paragraphe *m*
Paraguayan[1] [ˌpærəˈgwaɪən, -ˈgweɪ-] *adj* : paraguayen
Paraguayan[2] *n* : Paraguayen *m*, -guayenne *f*
parakeet [ˈpærəˌki:t] *n* : perruche *f*
parallel[1] [ˈpærəˌlɛl, -ləl] *vt* **1** EQUAL, MATCH : égaler, être équivalent à **2** : longer, être parallèle à <the road parallels the river : la route longe la rivière>
parallel[2] *adj* : parallèle
parallel[3] *n* **1** *or* **parallel line** : ligne *f* parallèle **2** : parallèle *m* (en géographie) **3** SIMILARITY : parallèle *m*, comparaison *f* <to be on a parallel with : être comparable à>
parallelogram [ˌpærəˈlɛləˌgræm] *n* : parallélogramme *m*
paralyse *Brit* → **paralyze**
paralysis [pəˈræləsɪs] *n, pl* **-yses** [-ˌsi:z] : paralysie *f*
paralyze *or Brit* **paralyse** [ˈpærəˌlaɪz] *vt* **-lyzed** *or Brit* **-lysed; -lyzing** *or Brit* **-lysing** : paralyser
parameter [pəˈræmət̬ər] *n* : paramètre *m*
parametric [ˌpærəˈmɛtrɪk] *adj* : paramétrique
paramount [ˈpærəˌmaʊnt] *adj* : suprême <of paramount importance : de la plus grande importance>
paranoia [ˌpærəˈnɔɪə] *n* : paranoïa *f*
paranoid [ˈpærəˌnɔɪd] *adj* : paranoïaque
parapet [ˈpærəpət, -ˌpɛt] *n* : parapet *m*
paraphernalia [ˌpærəfəˈneɪljə, -fər-] *ns & pl* : équipement *m*, attirail *m fam*
paraphrase[1] [ˈpærəˌfreɪz] *vt* **-phrased; -phrasing** : paraphraser
paraphrase[2] *n* : paraphrase *f*
paraplegic[1] [ˌpærəˈpli:dʒɪk] *adj* : paraplégique
paraplegic[2] *n* : paraplégique *mf*
parasite [ˈpærəˌsaɪt] *n* : parasite *m*
parasitic [ˌpærəˈsɪtɪk] *adj* : parasite, parasitaire
parasol [ˈpærəˌsɔl] *n* : ombrelle *f*, parasol *m*
paratrooper [ˈpærəˌtru:pər] *n* : parachutiste *m* (militaire)
parboil [ˈpɑrˌbɔɪl] *vt* : blanchir (des légumes)

parcel[1] [ˈpɑrsəl] *vt* **-celed** *or* **-celled; -celing** *or* **-celling** *or* **to parcel out** : diviser, répartir

parcel[2] *n* **1** PLOT : parcelle *f* (de terrain) **2** PACKAGE : paquet *m,* colis *m* **3 a parcel of lies** : un tissu de mensonges

parch [ˈpɑrtʃ] *vt* : dessécher

parchment [ˈpɑrtʃmənt] *n* : parchemin *m*

pardon[1] [ˈpɑrdən] *vt* **1** EXCUSE, FORGIVE : pardonner <pardon me : pardonnez-moi> **2** ABSOLVE : grâcier (en droit)

pardon[2] *n* **1** FORGIVENESS : pardon *m* <I beg your pardon : je vous demande pardon> **2** : pardon *m,* grâce *f* (en droit)

pardonable [ˈpɑrdənəbəl] *adj* : pardonnable

pare [ˈpær] *vt* **pared; paring 1** : peler (un fruit), éplucher (une pomme de terre), ronger (ses ongles) **2** REDUCE : réduire <to pare expenses : réduire les dépenses>

paregoric [ˌpærəˈgɔrɪk] *n* : parégorique *m*

parent [ˈpærənt] *n* **1** : mère *f,* père *m* **2 parents** *npl* : parents *mpl*

parentage [ˈpærəntɪdʒ] *n* : ascendance *f,* origine *f*

parental [pəˈrɛntəl] *adj* : parental

parenthesis [pəˈrɛnθəsəs] *n, pl* **-theses** [-ˌsiːz] : parenthèse *f*

parenthetical [ˌpærənˈθɛt̬ɪkəl] *adj* : entre parenthèses

parenthetically [ˌpærənˈθɛt̬ɪkli] *adv* : entre parenthèses

parenthood [ˈpærəntˌhʊd] *n* : maternité *f,* paternité *f*

parfait [pɑrˈfeɪ] *n* : parfait *m*

pariah [pəˈraɪə] *n* : paria *m*

parish [ˈpærɪʃ] *n* : paroisse *f*

parishioner [pəˈrɪʃənər] *n* : paroissien *m,* -sienne *f*

Parisian[1] [pəˈrɪʒən, -ˈri-] *adj* : parisien

Parisian[2] *n* : Parisien *m,* -sienne *f*

parity [ˈpærət̬i] *n, pl* **-ties** EQUALITY : parité *f*

park[1] [ˈpɑrk] *vt* : garer, stationner <to park a car : garer une voiture> — *vi* : se garer, se stationner

park[2] *n* : parc *m,* jardin *m* public

parka [ˈpɑrkə] *n* : parka *m*

parkway [ˈpɑrkˌweɪ] *n* : route *f* à paysage

parley[1] [ˈpɑrli] *vi* **-leyed; -leying** : parlementer

parley[2] *n, pl* **-leys** : pourparlers *mpl*

parliament [ˈpɑrləmənt] *n* : parlement *m*

parliamentarian [ˌpɑrləˌmɛnˈtɛriən, -mən-] *n* : parlementaire *mf*

parliamentary [ˌpɑrləˈmɛntəri] *adj* : parlementaire

parlor *or Brit* **parlour** [ˈpɑrlər] *n* **1** : petit salon *m* (pour recevoir des invités) **2** : salon *m* <beauty parlor : salon de beauté> **3 funeral parlor** → **funeral home**

parochial [pəˈroːkiəl] *adj* **1** : paroissial **2** PROVINCIAL : de clocher, provincial

parody[1] [ˈpærədi] *vt* **-died; -dying** : parodier

parody[2] *n, pl* **-dies** : parodie *f*

parole[1] [pəˈroːl] *vt* **-roled; -roling** : mettre en liberté conditionnelle

parole[2] *n* : liberté *f* conditionnelle

parolee [pəˌroˈli, -ˈroːˌli] *n* : détenu *m* libéré sur parole

paroxysm [ˈpærəkˌsɪzəm, pəˈrɑk-] *n* : quinte *f,* crise *f* <a paroxysm of coughing : une quinte de toux>

parquet [ˈpɑrˌkeɪ, pɑrˈkeɪ] *n* : parquet *m*

parrakeet → **parakeet**

parrot [ˈpærət] *n* : perroquet *m*

parry[1] [ˈpæri] *vt* **-ried; -rying 1** WARD OFF : esquiver, parer (un coup) **2** EVADE : éluder (une question)

parry[2] *n, pl* **-ries** : parade *f* (aux sports)

parse [ˈpɑrs] *vt* **parsed; parsing** : faire l'analyse grammaticale de

parsimonious [ˌpɑrsəˈmoːniəs] *adj* : parcimonieux — **parsimoniously** *adv*

parsley [ˈpɑrsli] *n* : persil *m*

parsnip [ˈpɑrsnɪp] *n* : panais *m*

parson [ˈpɑrsən] *n* : pasteur *m,* ecclésiastique *m*

part[1] [ˈpɑrt] *vi* **1** *or* **to part company** : se séparer, se quitter **2** BREAK : se rompre **3 to part with** : se défaire de — *vt* **1** SEPARATE : séparer **2 to part one's hair** : se faire une raie

part[2] *n* **1** : partie *f* <the best part : la meilleure partie> **2** DUTY : rôle *m,* fonction *f* **3** ROLE : rôle *m* (dans une pièce de théâtre) **4** : voix *f* <four-part harmony : harmonie à quatre voix> **5** SHARE : part *f* **6** SIDE : parti *m* <to take s.o.'s part : prendre le parti de qqn>

partake [pɑrˈteɪk, pər-] *vi* **-took** [-ˈtʊk]; **-taken** [-ˈteɪkən]; **-taking 1 to partake in** : prendre part à, participer à (une activité) **2 to partake of** CONSUME : prendre, manger

partial [ˈpɑrʃəl] *adj* **1** : partiel <a partial solution : une solution partielle> **2** BIASED : partial — **partially** [ˈpɑrʃəli] *adv*

partiality [ˌpɑrʃiˈælət̬i] *n, pl* **-ties** : partialité *f*

participant [pərˈtɪsəpənt, pɑr-] *n* : participant *m,* -pante *f*

participate [pərˈtɪsəˌpeɪt, pɑr-] *vi* **-pated; -pating** : participer

participation [pərˌtɪsəˈpeɪʃən, pɑr-] *n* : participation *f*

participial [ˌpɑrtəˈsɪpiəl] *adj* : participial

participle [ˈpɑrt̬əˌsɪpəl] *n* : participe *m* <past participle : participe passé>

particle [ˈpɑrt̬ɪkəl] *n* : particule *f*

particular[1] [pɑr'tɪkjələr] *adj* **1** SPECIFIC : particulier, en particulier <one particular person : une personne en particulier> **2** SPECIAL : particulier <with particular care : avec un soin tout particulier> **3** FUSSY : tatillon, difficile

particular[2] *n* **1** : détail *m*, point *m* **2 in ~** : en particulier

particularly [pɑr'tɪkjələrli] *adv* : particulièrement, spécialement

partisan[1] ['pɑrṭəzən, -sən] *adj* : partisan

partisan[2] *n* SUPPORTER : partisan *m*, -sane *f*

partition[1] [pər'tɪʃən, pɑr-] *vt* : morceler (un domaine), diviser, cloisonner (une pièce)

partition[2] *n* **1** DISTRIBUTION : division *f*, répartition *f* **2** DIVIDER : cloison *f* (d'une pièce, etc.)

partly ['pɑrtli] *adv* : en partie

partner ['pɑrtnər] *n* **1** ASSOCIATE : associé *m*, -ciée *f*; partenaire *mf* (en commerce) **2** : partenaire *mf* (aux sports, en danse) **3** COMPANION : compagnon *m*, compagne *f* **4** SPOUSE : époux *m*, épouse *f*

partnership ['pɑrtnər,ʃɪp] *n* : association *f*

part of speech *n* : partie *f* du discours

partridge ['pɑrtrɪdʒ] *n, pl* **-tridge** *or* **-tridges** : perdrix *f*

party ['pɑrti] *n, pl* **-ties 1** : parti *m* (politique) **2** PARTICIPANT : partie *f* **3** GROUP : groupe *m* <a mountain-climbing party : un groupe d'alpinisme> **4** GATHERING : fête *f*, party *m Can fam*

parvenu ['pɑrvə,nu:, -,nju:] *n* : parvenu *m*, -nue *f*

pass[1] ['pæs] *vi* **1** MOVE, PROCEED : passer **2** *or* **to pass away** DIE : mourir **3** : ne pas tenir compte de <I let his remark pass : je n'ai pas tenu compte de son commentaire> **4** TRANSFER : changer **5** OCCUR : se passer, avoir lieu **6** : passer (aux cartes) **7 to pass for** : se prendre pour — *vt* **1** : passer (une loi) **2** : dépasser (une voiture, etc.) **3** : passer (un examen) **4** : passer <pass the salt, please : passez-moi le sel, s'il vous plaît>

pass[2] *n* **1** CROSSING, GAP : col *m* **2** : mention *f* passable (à un examen) **3** PERMISSION, PERMIT : permis *m* **4** : laissez-passer *m* <season pass : laissez-passer saisonnier> **5** : passe *f* (aux sports)

passable ['pæsəbəl] *adj* **1** ACCEPTABLE : passable, acceptable **2** NEGOTIABLE : praticable, passable *Can* <passable roads : chemins praticables>

passably ['pæsəbli] *adv* : passablement

passage ['pæsɪdʒ] *n* **1** PASSAGEWAY : passage *m*, corridor *m*, couloir *m* **2** ENACTMENT : adoption *f* (d'une loi) **3** VOYAGE : voyage *m* **4** : passage *m*, extrait *m* (d'un livre)

passageway ['pæsɪdʒ,weɪ] *n* : passage *m*, corridor *m*, couloir *m*

passbook ['pæs,bʊk] → **bankbook**

passé [pæ'seɪ] *adj* OUT-OF-DATE : dépassé, démodé

passenger ['pæsəndʒər] *n* : passager *m*, -gère *f*

passerby [,pæsər'baɪ, 'pæsər,-] *n, pl* **passersby** : passant *m*, -sante *f*

passing ['pæsɪŋ] *n* DEATH : disparition *f*, mort *f*

passion ['pæʃən] *n* **1** LOVE : passion *f*, ardeur *f* **2** EMOTION : émotion *f* forte, passion *f* **3** ANGER : (accès *m* de) colère *f*

passionate ['pæʃənət] *adj* : passionné — **passionately** *adv*

passive[1] ['pæsɪv] *adj* : passif — **passively** *adv*

passive[2] *n or* **passive case** : passif *m* (en grammaire)

Passover ['pæs,o:vər] *n* : Pâque *f* (juive)

passport ['pæs,port] *n* : passeport *m*

password ['pæs,wərd] *n* : mot *m* de passe

past[1] ['pæst] *adv* : devant <to run past : passer en courant>

past[2] *adj* **1** : dernier, passé <the past month : le mois dernier> **2** FORMER : ancien <a past president : un ancien président>

past[3] *n* **1** : passé *m* **2 in the past** : dans le passé, autrefois

past[4] *prep* **1** BEYOND : au-delà de <just past the corner : juste au-delà du coin> **2** (*in expressions of time*) <half past four : quatre heures et demie> **3 to go past** : passer

pasta ['pɑstə, 'pæs-] *n* : pâtes *fpl* (alimentaires)

paste[1] ['peɪst] *vt* **pasted; pasting** : coller

paste[2] *n* **1** : purée *f* <tomato paste : purée de tomates> **2** GLUE : colle *f*

pasteboard ['peɪst,bord] → **cardboard**

pastel[1] [pæ'stɛl] *adj* : pastel

pastel[2] *n* : pastel *m*

pasteurization [,pæstʃərə'zeɪʃən, ,pæstjə-] *n* : pasteurisation *f*

pasteurize ['pæstʃə,raɪz, 'pæstjə-] *vt* **-ized; -izing** : pasteuriser

pastime ['pæs,taɪm] *n* : passe-temps *m*

pastor ['pæstər] *n* : pasteur *m*

pastoral ['pæstərəl] *adj* : pastoral

pastry ['peɪstri] *n, pl* **-ries** : pâtisserie *f*

pasture[1] ['pæstʃər] *vt* **-tured; -turing** : faire paître

pasture[2] *n* : pâturage *m*

pasty ['peɪsti] *adj* **pastier; -est 1** : pâteux <a pasty consistency : une consistance pâteuse> **2** PALLID : terreux (se dit du teint)

pat[1] ['pæt] *vt* **patted; patting** : tapoter

pat[2] *adv* : parfaitement <to have sth down pat : connaître par cœur qqch>

pat[3] *adj* **1** APT : convenable, approprié **2** GLIB : tout prêt

pat[4] *n* **1** TAP : (petite) tape *f* **2** : noix *f* (de beurre, etc.)

patch[1] [ˈpætʃ] *vt* **1** MEND, REPAIR : rapiécer, réparer **2 to patch up** : résoudre (des difficultés, etc.) <they patched things up : ils se sont réconciliés>

patch[2] *n* **1** : pièce *f* (d'étoffe) **2** : parcelle *f* (de terre) **3** : tache *f* <a patch of white : une tache blanche> **4** : plaque *f* <patches of ice : plaques de glace>

patchwork [ˈpætʃˌwərk] *n* : patchwork *m*

patchy [ˈpætʃi] *adj* **patchier; -est 1** : inégal, irrégulier **2** INCOMPLETE : incomplet

patent[1] [ˈpætənt] *vt* : breveter

patent[2] [ˈpætənt] *adj* **1** *or* **patented** [-təd] : breveté **2** [ˈpætənt, ˈpeɪt-] OBVIOUS : patent, évident

patent[3] [ˈpætənt] *n* : brevet *m*

paternal [pəˈtərnəl] *adj* : paternel — **paternally** *adv*

paternity [pəˈtərnət̬i] *n* : paternité *f*

path [ˈpæθ, ˈpaθ] *n* **1** : allée *f* (dans un jardin) **2** TRACK, TRAIL : chemin *m*, sentier *m* **3** COURSE, TRAJECTORY : trajectoire *f*

pathetic [pəˈθɛt̬ɪk] *adj* **1** PITIFUL : pitoyable **2** DEPLORABLE : minable *fam*, déplorable

pathological [ˌpæθəˈlɑdʒɪkəl] *adj* : pathologique

pathologist [pəˈθɑlədʒɪst] *n* : pathologiste *mf*

pathology [pəˈθɑlədʒi] *n, pl* **-gies** : pathologie *f*

pathos [ˈpeɪˌθɑs, ˈpæ-, -ˌθɔs] *n* : pathos *m*

pathway [ˈpæθˌweɪ] *n* : sentier *m*, chemin *m*

patience [ˈpeɪʃənts] *n* : patience *f*

patient[1] [ˈpeɪʃənt] *adj* : patient

patient[2] *n* : patient *m*, -tiente *f*; malade *mf*

patiently [ˈpeɪʃəntli] *adv* : patiemment

patina [pəˈtiːnə, ˈpætənə] *n, pl* **-nas** [-nəz] *or* **-nae** [-ˌni, -ˌnaɪ] : patine *f*

patio [ˈpæt̬iˌoː, ˈpɑt-] *n, pl* **-tios** : patio *m*

patriarch [ˈpeɪtriˌɑrk] *n* : patriarche *m*

patrimony [ˈpætrəˌmoːni] *n* : patrimoine *m*

patriot [ˈpeɪtriət, -ˌɑt] *n* : patriote *mf*

patriotic [ˌpeɪtriˈɑt̬ɪk] *adj* : patriote

patriotically [ˌpeɪtriˈɑt̬ɪkli] *adv* : patriotiquement

patriotism [ˈpeɪtriəˌtɪzəm] *n* : patriotisme *m*

patrol[1] [pəˈtroːl] *vi* **-trolled; -trolling** : patrouiller

patrol[2] *n* : patrouille *f*

patrolman [pəˈtroːlmən] *n, pl* **-men** [-mən, -ˌmɛn] : agent *m* de police

patron [ˈpeɪtrən] *n* **1** SPONSOR, SUPPORTER : mécène *m* **2** CUSTOMER : client *m*, cliente *f*

patronage [ˈpeɪtrənɪdʒ, ˈpæ-] *n* **1** SPONSORSHIP : patronage *m* **2** CLIENTELE : clientèle *f* **3** : pouvoir *m* de nomination (en politique)

patronize [ˈpeɪtrəˌnaɪz, ˈpæ-] *vt* **-ized; -izing 1** SUPPORT : patronner, parrainer **2** : être un client de, fréquenter (un marché) **3** : traiter avec condescendance

patter[1] [ˈpæt̬ər] *vi* **1** TAP : tapoter **2** *or* **to patter about** : trottiner

patter[2] *n* **1** TALK : baratin *m* (d'un vendeur) **2** PAT, TAP : tapotement *m*

pattern[1] [ˈpætərn] *vt* : faire selon un motif, modeler

pattern[2] *n* **1** EXAMPLE, MODEL : modèle *m* **2** DESIGN : dessin *m*, motif *m* **3** NORM, STANDARD : mode *m*, norme *f*

patty [ˈpæt̬i] *n, pl* **-ties 1** : petit pâté *m* **2** *or* **hamburger patty** : steak *m* haché

paucity [ˈpɔsət̬i] *n* : manque *m*, pénurie *f*

paunch [ˈpɔntʃ] *n* : ventre *m*, bedaine *f*

pauper [ˈpɔpər] *n* : pauvre *m*; indigent *m*, -gente *f*

pause[1] [ˈpɔz] *vi* **paused; pausing** : faire une pause

pause[2] *n* : pause *f*, arrêt *m*

pave [ˈpeɪv] *vt* **paved; paving** : paver, revêtir (d'asphalte, etc.)

pavement [ˈpeɪvmənt] *n* : revêtement *m* de la chaussée

pavilion [pəˈvɪljən] *n* : pavillon *m*

paving [ˈpeɪvɪŋ] → **pavement**

paw[1] [ˈpɔ] *vt* **1** TOUCH : tripoter, taponner *Can fam* **2** : donner un coup de patte à <the dog was pawing at my hand : le chien me donnait des coups de patte sur la main>

paw[2] *n* : patte *f* (d'un animal)

pawn[1] [ˈpɔn] *vt* : mettre en gage

pawn[2] *n* : gage *m*

pawnbroker [ˈpɔnˌbroːkər] *n* : prêteur *m*, -teuse *f* sur gages

pawnshop [ˈpɔnˌʃɑp] *n* : mont-de-piété *m France*

pay[1] [ˈpeɪ] *v* **paid** [ˈpeɪd]; **paying** *vt* **1** : payer (un compte, etc.) **2 to pay attention to** : prêter attention à **3 to pay back** : rembourser, s'acquitter de (une dette) **4 to pay one's respects to** : présenter ses respects à **5 to pay s.o. a visit** : aller voir qqn, rendre visite à qqn — *vi* : payer <crime doesn't pay : le crime ne paie pas>

pay[2] *n* : paie *f*, salaire *m*

payable [ˈpeɪebel] *adj* : payable

paycheck [ˈpeɪˌtʃɛk] *n* : chèque *m* de paie

payee [peɪˈiː] *n* : bénéficiaire *mf*

payment [ˈpeɪmənt] *n* : paiement *m*

PC [ˌpiːˈsiː] *n, pl* **PCs** *or* **PC's** : PC *m*, micro-ordinateur *m*

pea [ˈpiː] *n* : pois *m*

peace [ˈpiːs] *n* : paix *f*

peaceable [ˈpiːsəbəl] *adj* : paisible — **peaceably** [-bli] *adv*

peaceful ['pi:sfəl] *adj* **1** PEACEABLE : de paix, paisible <peaceful times : temps de paix> **2** CALM : paisible, calme
peacefully ['pi:sfəli] *adv* : paisiblement, calmement
peacekeeper ['pi:s,ki:pər] *n* : soldat *m* de la paix
peacekeeping ['pi:s,ki:pɪŋ] *n* : maintien *m* de la paix
peacemaker ['pi:s,meɪkər] *n* : pacificateur *m*, -trice *f;* conciliateur *m*, -trice *f*
peach ['pi:tʃ] *n* : pêche *f*
peacock ['pi:,kɑk] *n* : paon *m*
peak[1] ['pi:k] *vi* : culminer, atteindre un sommet
peak[2] *adj* : maximal <peak performance : performance maximale>
peak[3] *n* **1** CREST : sommet *m* (d'une colline) **2** *or* **mountain peak** : pic *m* **3** APEX : apogée *f* <at the peak of his glory : à l'apogée de sa gloire>
peaked ['pi:kəd] *adj* SICKLY : pâlot, malade
peal[1] ['pi:l] *vi* RESOUND : résonner
peal[2] *n* : carillonnement *m* (des cloches)
peanut ['pi:,nʌt] *n* **1** : cacahouète *f*, pinotte *f Can fam* (noix) **2** : arachide *f* (plante)
pear ['pær] *n* : poire *f*
pearl ['pərl] *n* : perle *f*
pearly ['pərli] *adj* **pearlier; -est** : nacré, perlé
peasant ['pɛzənt] *n* : paysan *m*, -sanne *f*
peat ['pi:t] *n* **1** : tourbe *f* **2 peat bog** → **bog**
pebble ['pɛbəl] *n* : caillou *m*
pecan [pɪ'kɑn, -'kæn, 'pi:,kæn] *n* : noix *f* de pécan *France*, noix *f* de pacane *Can*
peccadillo [,pɛkə'dɪlo] *n, pl* **-loes** *or* **-los** : peccadille *f*
peck[1] ['pɛk] *vt* : picorer, becqueter — *vi* **to peck at one's food** : manger du bout des dents
peck[2] *n* **1** : picotin *m* (mesure) **2** : coup *m* de bec (d'un oiseau) **3** KISS : bécot *m France fam*, bec *m Can fam*
pectoral ['pɛktərəl] *adj* : pectoral
peculiar [pɪ'kju:ljər] *adj* **1** DISTINCTIVE : particulier **2** STRANGE : étrange, bizarre
peculiarity [pɪ,kju:l'jærəṭi, -,kju:li'ær-] *n, pl* **-ties 1** DISTINCTIVENESS : particularité *f* **2** STRANGENESS : étrangeté *f*, bizarrerie *f*
peculiarly [pɪ'kju:ljərli] *adv* **1** PARTICULARLY : particulièrement **2** STRANGELY : de manière étrange, bizarrement
pecuniary [pɪ'kju:ni,ɛri] *adj* : pécuniaire
pedagogical [,pɛdə'gɑdʒɪkəl, -'go:-] *adj* : pédagogique
pedagogy ['pɛdə,go:dʒi, -,gɑ-] *n* : pédagogie *f*
pedal[1] ['pɛdəl] *vt* **-aled** *or* **-alled; -aling** *or* **-alling** : pédaler
pedal[2] *n* : pédale *f*
pedant ['pɛdənt] *n* : pédant *m*, -dante *f*
pedantic [pɪ'dæntɪk] *adj* : pédant
pedantry ['pɛdəntri] *n, pl* **-ries** : pédantisme *m*
peddle ['pɛdəl] *v* **-dled; -dling** *vt* : colporter — *vi* : faire du colportage
peddler ['pɛdlər] *n* : colporteur *m*, -teuse *f*
pedestal ['pɛdəstəl] *n* : piédestal *m*
pedestrian[1] [pə'dɛstriən] *adj* **1** COMMONPLACE : prosaïque, commun **2** : piétonnier <pedestrian zone : zone piétonnière> <pedestrian crossing : passage pour piétons>
pedestrian[2] *n* : piéton *m*
pediatric [,pi:di'ætrɪk] *adj* : pédiatrique
pediatrician [,pi:diə'trɪʃən] *n* : pédiatre *mf*
pediatrics [,pi:di'ætrɪks] *ns & pl* : pédiatrie *f*
pedigree ['pɛdə,gri:] *n* **1** FAMILY TREE : arbre *m* généalogique **2** LINEAGE : pedigree *m* (d'un animal), lignée *f* (d'une personne)
pediment ['pɛdəmənt] *n* : fronton *m*
peek[1] ['pi:k] *vi* **1** PEEP : regarder furtivement **2** GLANCE : jeter un coup d'œil
peek[2] *n* : coup *m* d'œil furtif
peel[1] ['pi:l] *vt* **1** : peler (un fruit), éplucher (un oignon, etc.) **2** *or* **to peel off** : enlever (une étiquette, etc.) — *vi* **1** : peler, pleumer *Can fam* (se dit de la peau) **2** : s'écailler (se dit de la peinture)
peel[2] *n* : pelure *f* (d'une pomme), écorce *f* (d'une orange), épluchure *f* (de pommes de terre)
peeling → **peel**[2]
peep[1] ['pi:p] *vi* **1** : pépier, piauler (se dit d'un oiseau) **2** *or* **to peep through** EMERGE : apparaître, se montrer **3 to peep at** : jeter un coup d'œil à
peep[2] *n* **1** : pépiement *m* (d'un oiseau) **2** : coup *m* d'œil
peer[1] ['pɪr] *vi* : regarder attentivement
peer[2] *n* **1** EQUAL : pair *m*, égal *m* **2** NOBLEMAN : noble *m*, pair *m*
peerage ['pɪrɪdʒ] *n* : pairie *f*
peerless ['pɪrləs] *adj* : hors pair, sans égal
peeve[1] ['pi:v] *vt* **peeved; peeving** : mettre en rogne, irriter
peeve[2] *n or* **pet peeve** : bête *f* noire
peevish ['pi:vɪʃ] *adj* : grincheux, grognon
peg[1] ['pɛg] *vt* **pegged; pegging** ATTACH, FASTEN : accrocher, attacher
peg[2] *n* **1** HOOK : patère *f* (de bois), fiche *f* (de métal) **2** STAKE : piquet *m* (de tente)
peignoir [peɪn'wɑr, pɛn-] *n* : peignoir *m*, négligé *m*
pejorative [pɪ'dʒɔrəṭɪv] *adj* : péjoratif — **pejoratively** *adv*
pelican ['pɛlɪkən] *n* : pélican *m*
pellagra [pə'lægrə, -'leɪ-] *n* : pellagre *f*

pellet ['pɛlət] *n* **1** BALL : boulette *f* (de papier, etc.) **2** SHOT : plomb *m*

pell–mell ['pɛl'mɛl] *adv* : pêle-mêle

pelt[1] ['pɛlt] *vt* : cribler, bombarder <they pelted her with accusations : ils l'ont criblée d'accusations> <to pelt s.o. with stones : lancer des pierres à qqn>

pelt[2] *n* : peau *f* (d'un animal)

pelvic ['pɛlvɪk] *adj* : pelvien

pelvis ['pɛlvɪs] *n, pl* **-vises** [-vɪsəz] *or* **-ves** [-ˌvi:z] : bassin *m*, pelvis *m*

pen[1] ['pɛn] *vt* **penned; penning 1** : enfermer dans un abri ou un enclos **2** WRITE : écrire

pen[2] *n* **1** : enclos *m*, parc *m* (d'animaux) **2** : stylo *m* <ballpoint pen : stylo à bille>

penal ['pi:nəl] *adj* **1** : pénal <a penal offense : une offense pénale> **2** : pénitentiaire <a penal colony : une colonie pénitentiaire>

penalize ['pi:nəlˌaɪz, 'pɛn-] *vt* **-ized; -izing** : pénaliser, punir *Can* (aux sports)

penalty ['pɛnəlti] *n, pl* **-ties 1** : peine *f* (en droit) **2** : pénalité *f*, pénalisation *f*, punition *f Can* (aux sports)

penance ['pɛnən*t*s] *n* : pénitence *f*

pence ['pɛn*t*s] → **penny**

penchant ['pɛntʃənt] *n* : penchant *m*

pencil[1] ['pɛn*t*səl] *vt* **-ciled** *or* **-cilled; -ciling** *or* **-cilling** : écrire ou dessiner au crayon

pencil[2] *n* : crayon *m*

pencil sharpener *n* : taille-crayon *m*, aiguise-crayon *m Can*

pendant ['pɛndənt] *n* : pendentif *m*

pending[1] ['pɛndɪŋ] *adj* UNDECIDED : en instance

pending[2] *prep* **1** DURING : pendant **2** AWAITING : en attendant

pendulum ['pɛndʒələm, -djʊləm] *n* : pendule *m*

penetrate ['pɛnəˌtreɪt] *v* **-trated; -trating** *vt* : pénétrer — *vi* : pénétrer, s'infiltrer

penetration [ˌpɛnə'treɪʃən] *n* : pénétration *f*

penguin ['pɛŋgwɪn, 'pɛn-] *n* : manchot *m*

penicillin [ˌpɛnə'sɪlən] *n* : pénicilline *f*

peninsula [pə'nɪn*t*sələ, -'nɪntʃʊlə] *n* : péninsule *f*

penis ['pi:nəs] *n, pl* **-nes** [-ˌni:z] *or* **-nises** : pénis *m*

penitence ['pɛnət̬ən*t*s] *n* : pénitence *f*

penitent[1] ['pɛnət̬ənt] *adj* : pénitent, repentant

penitent[2] *n* : pénitent *m*, -tente *f*

penitential [ˌpɛnə'tɛntʃəl] *adj* : pénitentiel

penitentiary [ˌpɛnə'tɛntʃəri] *n, pl* **-ries** : pénitencier *m*, prison *f*

penmanship ['pɛnmənˌʃɪp] *n* : écriture *f*, calligraphie *f*

pen name *n* : nom *m* de plume, pseudonyme *m*

pennant ['pɛnənt] *n* : fanion *m*, flamme *f* (d'un navire)

penniless ['pɛnɪləs] *adj* : sans le sou

penny ['pɛni] *n, pl* **-nies** : centime *m*, cent *m*, sou *m Can*

pension[1] ['pɛntʃən] *vt* **1** : verser une pension à **2 to pension off** : mettre à la retraite

pension[2] *n* : pension *f*, retraite *f*

pensive ['pɛn*t*sɪv] *adj* : pensif, songeur — **pensively** *adv*

pent ['pɛnt] *adj* : réprimé <pent-up feelings : sentiments réprimés>

pentagon ['pɛntəˌgɑn] *n* : pentagone *m*

pentagonal [pɛn'tægənəl] *adj* : pentagonal

penthouse ['pɛntˌhaʊs] *n* : appartement *m* construit sur le toit d'un immeuble

penury ['pɛnjəri] *n* : indigence *f*

peon ['pi:ˌɑn, -ən] *n, pl* **-ons** *or* **-ones** [peɪ'o:ni:z] : péon *m*

peony ['pi:əni] *n, pl* **-nies** : pivoine *f*

people[1] ['pi:pəl] *vt* **-pled; -pling** : peupler

people[2] *ns & pl* **1 people** *npl* : personnes *fpl*, gens *mfpl* <we met several people : nous avons rencontré plusieurs personnes> <old people : vieilles gens> **2** *pl* **peoples** : peuple *m* <the peoples of Africa : les peuples d'Afrique>

pep[1] ['pɛp] *vt* **pepped; pepping** *or* **to pep up** : remonter le moral à

pep[2] *n* : dynamisme *m*, entrain *m*

pepper[1] ['pɛpər] *vt* **1** : poivrer (en cuisine) **2** RIDDLE : cribler (de balles, etc.) **3** SPRINKLE : émailler <peppered with quotations : émaillé de citations>

pepper[2] *n* **1** : poivre *m* (condiment) **2** : poivron *m* <green pepper : poivron vert> **3** → **chili**

peppermint ['pɛpərˌmɪnt] *n* : menthe *f* poivrée

peppery ['pɛpəri] *adj* : poivré

peppy ['pɛpi] *adj* **peppier; -est** : plein d'énergie, vivant

peptic ['pɛptɪk] *adj* **peptic ulcer** : ulcère *m* de l'estomac

per ['pər] *prep* **1** : par <ten dollars per day : dix dollars par jour> **2** ACCORDING TO : selon, conformément à <per instructions : selon les directives>

per annum [pər'ænəm] *adv* : par an, annuellement

percale [ˌpər'keɪl, 'pər-ˌ; ˌpər'kæl] *n* : percale *f*

perceive [pər'si:v] *vt* **-ceived; -ceiving** : percevoir

percent[1] [pər'sɛnt] *adv* : pour cent

percent[2] *n, pl* **-cent** *or* **-cents 1** : pour cent *m* <ten percent of the time : dix pour cent du temps> **2** PERCENTAGE : pourcentage *m* <a percent of his income : un pourcentage de son revenu>

percentage [pər'sɛntɪdʒ] *n* : pourcentage *m*
perceptible [pər'sɛptəbəl] *adj* : perceptible
perceptibly [pər'sɛptəbli] *adv* : de manière perceptible
perception [pər'sɛpʃən] *n* : perception *f*
perceptive [pər'sɛptɪv] *adj* : perspicace
perceptively [pər'sɛptɪvli] *adv* : avec perspicacité
perceptiveness [pər'sɛptɪvnəs] *n* : perspicacité *f*
perch[1] ['pərtʃ] *vt* : percher — *vi* : se percher
perch[2] *n* **1** ROOST : perchoir *m* **2** *pl* **perch** *or* **perches** : perche *f* (poisson)
percolate ['pərkə,leɪt] *v* **-lated; -lating** *vi* SEEP : filtrer, passer — *vt* : faire (du café) dans une cafetière
percolator ['pərkə,leɪt̬ər] *n* : cafetière *f* à pression
percussion [pər'kʌʃən] *n* : percussion *f*
peremptory [pə'rɛmptəri] *adj* : péremptoire
perennial[1] [pə'rɛniəl] *adj* **1** : vivace <perennial flowers : fleurs vivaces> **2** RECURRING : perpétuel
perennial[2] *n* : plante *f* vivace
perennially [pə'rɛniəli] *adv* : perpétuellement
perfect[1] [pər'fɛkt] *vt* : perfectionner
perfect[2] ['pərfɪkt] *adj* : parfait — **perfectly** *adv*
perfectible [pər'fɛktəbəl] *adj* : perfectible
perfection [pər'fɛkʃən] *n* : perfection *f*
perfectionist[1] [pər'fɛkʃənɪst] *or* **perfectionistic** [pər,fɛkʃə'nɪstɪk] *adj* : perfectionniste
perfectionist[2] *n* : perfectionniste *mf*
perfidious [pər'fɪdiəs] *adj* : perfide
perforate ['pərfə,reɪt] *vt* **-rated; -rating** : perforer
perforation [,pərfə'reɪʃən] *n* : perforation *f*
perform [pər'fɔrm] *vt* **1** CARRY OUT : réaliser, effectuer, accomplir **2** PRESENT : jouer, donner (une pièce de théâtre, etc.) — *vi* ACT : jouer (dans une pièce de théâtre, etc.)
performance [pər'fɔr,mənts] *n* **1** EXECUTION : rendement *m* **2** : interprétation *f* (d'un acteur, d'un comédien), performance *f* (d'une équipe) **3** PRESENTATION, SHOW : spectacle *m*
performer [pər'fɔrmər] *n* : interprète *mf*
perfume[1] [pər'fju:m, 'pər,-] *vt* **-fumed; -fuming** : parfumer
perfume[2] ['pər,fju:m, pər'-] *n* : parfum *m*
perfunctory [pər'fʌŋktəri] *adj* : mécanique, sommaire
perhaps [pər'hæps] *adv* : peut-être
peril ['pɛrəl] *n* : péril *m*, danger *m*
perilous ['pɛrələs] *adj* : périlleux, dangereux — **perilously** *adv*
perimeter [pə'rɪmət̬ər] *n* : périmètre *m*
period ['pɪriəd] *n* **1** : point *m* (signe de ponctuation) **2** INTERVAL, TIME : période *f* **3** EPOCH, ERA : ère *f*, période *f*, époque *f* **4** *or* **menstrual period** : règles *fpl*
periodic [,pɪri'ɑdɪk] *adj* : périodique — **periodically** [-dɪkli] *adv*
periodical [,pɪri'ɑdɪkəl] *n* : périodique *m*, journal *m*
peripheral [pə'rɪfərəl] *adj* : périphérique
periphery [pə'rɪfəri] *n, pl* **-eries** : périphérie *f*
periscope ['pɛrə,sko:p] *n* : périscope *m*
perish ['pɛrɪʃ] *vi* DIE : périr
perishable ['pɛrɪʃəbəl] *adj* : périssable
perishables ['pɛrɪʃəbəlz] *npl* : denrées *fpl* périssables
perjure ['pərdʒər] *vt* **-jured; -juring** *or* **to perjure onself** : se parjurer
perjurer ['pərdʒərər] *n* : parjure *mf*
perjury ['pərdʒəri] *n* : faux témoignage *m*
perk[1] ['pərk] *vi* **to perk up** : se ragaillardir — *vt* **1** ENLIVEN, STIMULATE : revigorer **2** FRESHEN : égayer **3** **to perk up one's ears** : dresser les oreilles
perk[2] *n* : avantage *m*, privilège *m* (d'un emploi)
perky ['pərki] *adj* **perkier; -est** : guilleret, fringant
permanence ['pərmənənts] *n* : permanence *f*
permanent[1] ['pərmənənt] *adj* : permanent
permanent[2] *n* : permanente *f*
permanently ['pərmənəntli] *adv* : de façon permanente, en permanence
permeable ['pərmiəbəl] *adj* : perméable
permeate ['pərmi,eɪt] *v* **-ated; -ating** *vi* : se diffuser, se répandre — *vt* **1** IMPREGNATE : impregner <permeated with smoke : impregné de fumée> **2** PERVADE : s'infiltrer dans, se répandre dans
permissible [pər'mɪsəbəl] *adj* : permis, admissible
permission [pər'mɪʃən] *n* : permission *f*, autorisation *f*
permissive [pər'mɪsɪv] *adj* : permissif — **permissively** *adv*
permit[1] [pər'mɪt] *v* **-mitted; -mitting** *vt* : permettre, autoriser — *vi* ALLOW : permettre <if time permits : si le temps le permet>
permit[2] ['pər,mɪt, pər'-] *n* : permis *m*, licence *f*
pernicious [pər'nɪʃəs] *adj* : pernicieux — **perniciously** *adv*
peroxide [pə'rɑk,saɪd] *n* : peroxyde *m*
perpendicular [,pərpən'dɪkjələr] *adj* : perpendiculaire — **perpendicularly** *adv*
perpetrate ['pərpə,treɪt] *vt* **-trated; -trating** : perpétrer
perpetration [,pərpə'treɪʃən] *n* : perpétration *f*
perpetrator ['pərpə,treɪt̬ər] *n* : auteur *m* (d'un délit)

perpetual [pər'pɛtʃʊəl] *adj* : éternel, perpétuel
perpetually [pər'pɛtʃʊəli, -tʃəli] *adv* : perpétuellement
perpetuate [pər'pɛtʃʊ,eɪt] *vt* **-ated; -ating** : perpétuer
perpetuation [pər,pɛtʃə'weɪʃən] *n* : perpétuation *f*
perplex [pər'plɛks] *vt* : laisser perplexe
perplexity [pər'plɛksəti] *n, pl* **-ties** : perplexité *f*
persecute ['pərsɪ,kju:t] *vt* **-cuted; -cuting** : persécuter
persecution [,pərsɪ'kju:ʃən] *n* : persécution *f*
persecutor ['pərsɪ,kju:ţər] *n* : persécuteur *m*, -trice *f*
perseverance [,pərsə'vɪrənts] *n* : persévérance *f*
persevere [,pərsə'vɪr] *vi* **-vered; -vering** : persévérer
Persian[1] ['pərʒən] *adj* : persan
Persian[2] *n* **1** : Persan *m*, -sane *f* **2** : persan *m* (langue)
persist [pər'sɪst] *vi* : persister
persistence [pər'sɪstənts] *n* : persistance *f*, persévérance *f*
persistent [pər'sɪstənt] *adj* : persistant
persistently [pər'sɪstəntli] *adv* : sans cesse, continuellement
person ['pərsən] *n* **1** INDIVIDUAL : personne *f*, individu *m* **2** : personne *f* (en grammaire) **3 in ~** : en personne
personable ['pərsənəbəl] *adj* : agréable, aimable
personage ['pərsənɪdʒ] *n* : personnage *m*, personne *f* haut placée
personal ['pərsənəl] *adj* **1** PRIVATE : personnel, privé <personal property : biens mobiliers personnels> <personal hygiene : hygiène personnelle> **2** : en personne <a personal visit : une visite en personne> **3** INTIMATE : personnel <a personal conversation : une conversation personnelle>
personality [,pərsən'æləţi] *n, pl* **-ties 1** CHARACTER, TEMPERAMENT : personnalité *f* **2** CELEBRITY : vedette *f*
personalize ['pərsənə,laɪz] *vt* **-ized; -izing** : personnaliser
personally ['pərsənəli] *adv* **1** : personnellement <I'll attend to the matter personally : je vais y voir personnellement> **2** DIRECTLY : en personne **3** INDIVIDUALLY : personnellement <not you personally : pas toi personnellement>
personification [pər,sɑnəfə'keɪʃən] *n* : personnification *f*
personify [pər'sɑnə,faɪ] *vt* **-fied; -fying** : personnifier
personnel [,pərsən'ɛl] *n* : personnel *m*
perspective [pər'spɛktɪv] *n* : perspective *f*
perspicacious [,pərspə'keɪʃəs] *adj* : perspicace
perspicacity [,pərspə'kæsəti] *n* : perspicacité *f*
perspiration [,pərspə'reɪʃən] *n* : transpiration *f*, sueur *f*
perspire [pər'spaɪr] *vi* **-spired; -spiring** : transpirer, suer
persuade [pər'sweɪd] *vt* **-suaded; -suading** : persuader, convaincre
persuasion [pər'sweɪʒən] *n* **1** : persuasion *f* <the power of persuasion : le pouvoir de persuasion> **2** BELIEF : conviction *f*
persuasive [pər'sweɪsɪv, -zɪv] *adj* : persuasif, convaincant
persuasively [pər'sweɪsɪvli, -zɪv-] *adv* : persuasivement
persuasiveness [pər'sweɪsɪvnəs, -zɪv-] *n* : force *f* de persuasion
pert ['pərt] *adj* **1** FLIPPANT : effronté, insolent **2** JAUNTY : coquet
pertain [pər'teɪn] *vi* **1** BELONG : se rapporter <duties pertaining to the office : des fonctions qui se rapportent au bureau> **2** RELATE : traiter, avoir rapport <books pertaining to birds : livres sur les oiseaux>
pertinence ['pərtənənts] *n* : pertinence *f*
pertinent ['pərtənənt] *adj* : pertinent
perturb [pər'tərb] *vt* : troubler, inquiéter
perusal [pə'ru:zəl] *n* : lecture *f* attentive
peruse [pə'ru:z] *vt* **-rused; -rusing** : lire attentivement
Peruvian[1] [pə'ru:viən] *adj* : péruvien
Peruvian[2] *n* : Péruvien *m*, -vienne *f*
pervade [pər'veɪd] *vt* **-vaded; -vading** : s'infiltrer à, se répandre dans
pervasive [pər'veɪsɪv, -zɪv] *adj* : envahissant, pénétrant
perverse [pər'vərs] *adj* **1** CORRUPT : pervers, vicieux **2** STUBBORN : obstiné, entêté
perversely [pər'vərsli] *adv* **1** VICIOUSLY : avec un malin plaisir **2** STUBBORNLY : obstinément
perversion [pər'vərʒən] *n* : perversion *f*
perversity [pər'vərsəţi] *n, pl* **-ties** : perversité *f*
pervert[1] [pər'vərt] *vt* **1** CORRUPT : pervertir, corrompre **2** DISTORT : déformer
pervert[2] ['pər,vərt] *n* : pervers *m*, -verse *f*
peso ['peɪ,so:] *n, pl* **-sos** : peso *m*
pessimism ['pɛsə,mɪzəm] *n* : pessimisme *m*
pessimist ['pɛsəmɪst] *n* : pessimiste *mf*
pessimistic [,pɛsə'mɪstɪk] *adj* : pessimiste
pest ['pɛst] *n* **1** NUISANCE : peste *f*, plaie *f fam* **2** : plante *f* ou animal *m* nuisible
pester ['pɛstər] *vt* **-tered; -tering** : importuner, harceler
pesticide ['pɛstə,saɪd] *n* : pesticide *m*
pestilence ['pɛstələnts] *n* : peste *f*, pestilence *f*
pestle ['pɛsəl, 'pɛstəl] *n* : pilon *m*
pet[1] ['pɛt] *vt* **petted; petting** : caresser

pet[2] *n* **1** : animal *m* domestique **2** FAVORITE : chouchou *m fam*
petal ['pɛt̬əl] *n* : pétale *m*
petite [pə'ti:t] *adj* : menue, petite
petition[1] [pə'tɪʃən] *vi* : faire une pétition — *vt* : adresser une pétition à
petition[2] *n* : pétition *f*
petitioner [pə'tɪʃənər] *n* : pétitionnaire *mf*
petrify ['pɛtrə,faɪ] *vt* **-fied; -fying** : pétrifier
petroleum [pə'tro:liəm] *n* : pétrole *m*
petticoat ['pɛt̬i,ko:t] *n* : jupon *m*
pettiness ['pɛt̬inəs] *n* **1** INSIGNIFICANCE : insignifiance *f* **2** MEANNESS : mesquinerie *f*
petty ['pɛt̬i] *adj* **pettier; -est 1** MINOR : petit <petty cash : petite monnaie> **2** INSIGNIFICANT : sans importance, insignifiant **3** MEAN : mesquin
petty officer *n* : maître *m*
petulance ['pɛtʃələn*t*s] *n* : irritabilité *f*, irascibilité *f*
petulant ['pɛtʃələnt] *adj* : irritable, irascible
petunia [pɪ'tu:njə, -'tju:-] *n* : pétunia *m*
pew ['pju:] *n* : banc *m* d'église
pewter ['pju:t̬ər] *n* : étain *m*
pH [,pi:'eɪtʃ] *n* : pH *m*
phallic ['fælɪk] *adj* : phallique
phallus ['fæləs] *n, pl* **-li** ['fæ,laɪ] *or* **-luses** : phallus *m*
phantasy ['fæntəsi] → **fantasy**
phantom ['fæntəm] *n* : fantôme *m*
pharaoh ['fɛr,o:, 'feɪ,ro:] *n* : pharaon *m*
pharmaceutical [,fɑrmə'su:t̬ɪkəl] *adj* : pharmaceutique
pharmacist ['fɑrməsɪst] *n* : pharmacien *m*, -cienne *f*
pharmacology [,fɑrmə'kɑlədʒi] *n* : pharmacologie *f*
pharmacy ['fɑrməsi] *n, pl* **-cies** : pharmacie *f*
pharynx ['færɪŋks] *n, pl* **pharynges** [fə'rɪn,dʒi:z] : pharynx *m*
phase[1] ['feɪz] *vt* **phased; phasing 1** SYNCHRONIZE : synchroniser **2 to phase in** : introduire graduellement **3 to phase out** : discontinuer progressivement
phase[2] *n* **1** : phase *f* (de la lune) **2** STAGE : phase *f*, stade *m*
pheasant ['fɛzənt] *n, pl* **-ant** *or* **-ants** : faisan *m*, -sane *f*
phenomenal [fɪ'nɑmənəl] *adj* : phénoménal — **phenomenally** *adv*
phenomenon [fɪ'nɑmə,nɑn, -nən] *n, pl* **-na** [-nə] *or* **-nons 1** EVENT, FACT : phénomène *m* **2** *pl* **-nons** PRODIGY : phénomène *m*
philanthropic [,fɪlən'θrɑpɪk] *adj* : philanthropique
philanthropist [fə'læn*t*θrəpɪst] *n* : philanthrope *mf*
philanthropy [fə'læn*t*θrəpi] *n, pl* **-pies** : philanthropie *f*
philately [fə'lætəli] *n* : philatélie *f*
philodendron [,fɪlə'dɛndrən] *n, pl* **-drons** *or* **-dra** [-drə] : philodendron *m*
philosopher [fə'lɑsəfər] *n* : philosophe *mf*
philosophical [,fɪlə'sɑfɪkəl] *adj* : philosophique — **philosophically** [-kli] *adv*
philosophize [fə'lɑsə,faɪz] *vt* **-phized; -phizing** : philosopher
philosophy [fə'lɑsəfi] *n, pl* **-phies** : philosophie *f*
phlebitis [flɪ'baɪt̬əs] *n* : phlébite *f*
phlegm ['flɛm] *n* : mucosité *f*
phlox ['flɑks] *n, pl* **phlox** *or* **phloxes** : phlox *m*
phobia ['fo:biə] *n* : phobie *f*
phoenix ['fi:nɪks] *n* : phénix *m*
phone[1] ['fo:n] *v* → **telephone**[1]
phone[2] *n* → **telephone**[2]
phoneme ['fo:,ni:m] *n* : phonème *m*
phonetic [fə'nɛt̬ɪk] *adj* : phonétique
phonetics [fə'nɛt̬ɪks] *n* : phonétique *f*
phonics ['fɑnɪks] *n* : méthode *f* d'enseignement de la lecture par la phonétique
phonograph ['fo:nə,græf] *n* : phonographe *m*
phony[1] *or* **phoney** ['fo:ni] *adj* **phonier; -est** : faux
phony[2] *or* **phoney** *n, pl* **-nies** : charlatan *m*
phosphate ['fɑs,feɪt] *n* : phosphate *m*
phosphorescence [,fɑsfə'rɛsən*t*s] *n* : phosphorescence *f*
phosphorescent [,fɑsfə'rɛsənt] *adj* : phosphorescent
phosphorus ['fɑsfərəs] *n* : phosphore *m*
photo ['fo:t̬o:] *n, pl* **-tos** : photo *f*
photocopy[1] ['fo:t̬o,kɑpi] *vt* **-copied; -copying** : photocopier
photocopy[2] *n, pl* **-pies** : photocopie *f*
photoelectric [,fo:t̬oɪ'lɛktrɪk] *adj* : photoélectrique
photogenic [,fo:t̬ə'dʒɛnɪk] *adj* : photogénique
photograph[1] ['fo:t̬ə,græf] *vt* : photographier
photograph[2] *n* : photo *f*, photographie *f*
photographer [fə'tɑgrəfər] *n* : photographe *mf*
photographic [,fo:t̬ə'græfɪk] *adj* : photographique — **photographically** [-fɪkli] *adv*
photography [fə'tɑgrəfi] *n* : photographie *f*
photosynthesis [,fo:t̬o'sɪn*t*θəsəs] *n* : photosynthèse *f*
photosynthetic [,fo:t̬osɪn'θɛt̬ɪk] *adj* : photosynthétique
phrase[1] ['freɪz] *vt* **phrased; phrasing** : formuler, exprimer
phrase[2] *n* **1** : expression *f*, locution *f* **2** : syntagme *m* (en grammaire)
phraseology [,freɪzi'ɑlədʒi] *n, pl* **-gies** : phraséologie *f*
phylum ['faɪləm] *n, pl* **-la** : phylum *m*

physical[1] [ˈfɪzɪkəl] *adj* : physique — **physically** [-kli] *adv*
physical[2] *n* : examen *m* médical
physician [fəˈzɪʃən] *n* : médecin *mf*
physicist [ˈfɪzəsɪst] *n* : physicien *m*, -cienne *f*
physics [ˈfɪzɪks] *ns & pl* : physique *f*
physiognomy [ˌfɪziˈɑgnəmi] *n, pl* **-mies** : physionomie *f*
physiological [ˌfɪziəˈlɑdʒɪkəl] *or* **physiologic** [-dʒɪk] *adj* : physiologique
physiologist [ˌfɪziˈɑlədʒɪst] *n* : physiologiste *mf*
physiology [ˌfɪziˈɑlədʒi] *n* : physiologie *f*
physique [fəˈziːk] *n* : physique *m*
pi [ˈpaɪ] *n, pl* **pis** [ˈpaɪz] : pi *m*
pianist [piˈænɪst, ˈpiːənɪst] *n* : pianiste *mf*
piano [piˈænoː] *n, pl* **-anos** : piano *m*
piazza [piˈæzə, -ˈɑtsə] *n, pl* **-zas** *or* **-ze** [-ˈɑtˌseɪ] : piazza *f*
picayune [ˌpɪkiˈjuːn] *adj* : insignifiant, sans valeur
piccolo [ˈpɪkəˌloː] *n, pl* **-los** : piccolo *m*, picolo *m*
pick[1] [ˈpɪk] *vt* **1** : casser, percer (une surface) **2** : enlever <to pick meat from bones : enlever la viande des os> **3** : cueillir (des fleurs) **4** *or* **to pick out** SELECT : choisir **5 to pick a fight** : chercher la chicane **6 to pick a lock** : crocheter une serrure **7 to pick one's teeth** : se curer les dents **8 to pick pockets** : voler à la tire — *vi* **1 to pick at** NAG : critiquer **2 to pick at one's food** : manger du bout des doigts **3 to pick and choose** : faire le difficile
pick[2] *n* **1** : choix *m* <take your pick : faites votre choix> **2** : meilleur *m* <the pick of the herd : le meilleur du lot> **3** : pic *m* (outil)
pickax [ˈpɪkˌæks] *n* : pic *m*
pickerel [ˈpɪkərəl] *n, pl* **-el** *or* **-els** : espèce *f* de petit brochet
picket[1] [ˈpɪkət] *vi* : faire un piquet de grève, piqueter *Can*
picket[2] *n* **1** STAKE : piquet *m* (de clôture) **2** *or* **picket line** : piquet *m* de grève
pickle[1] [ˈpɪkəl] *vt* **-led; -ling** : conserver dans la saumure
pickle[2] *n* **1** BRINE : saumure *f* **2** GHERKIN : cornichon *m* **3** FIX, JAM : pétrin *m fam* <to be in a pickle : être dans le pétrin>
pickpocket [ˈpɪkˌpɑkət] *n* : voleur *m*, -leuse *f* à la tire
pickup [ˈpɪkˌəp] *n* **1** IMPROVEMENT : amélioration *f* **2** *or* **pickup truck** : pick-up *m*, camionnette *f*
pick up *vt* **1** GATHER, LIFT : ramasser, soulever, décrocher (le téléphone) <to pick oneself up : se relever> **2** CATCH, LEARN : saisir, comprendre (des renseignements) **3** RESUME : reprendre (une conversation, etc.) **4** TIDY : mettre en ordre **5 to pick up speed** : prendre de la vitesse — *vi* **1** IMPROVE : s'améliorer, remonter **2 to pick up after oneself** : se ramasser *Can*
picnic[1] [ˈpɪkˌnɪk] *vi* **-nicked; -nicking** : pique-niquer
picnic[2] *n* : pique-nique *m*
pictorial [pɪkˈtoriəl] *adj* : illustré, pictural
picture[1] [ˈpɪktʃər] *vt* **-tured; -turing 1** DEPICT : dépeindre, décrire **2** IMAGINE : se représenter, s'imaginer
picture[2] *n* **1** : tableau *m*, image *f*, dessin *m* **2** DESCRIPTION : description *f* **3** IMAGE : image *f* <he's the picture of his father : il est l'image de son père> **4** MOVIE : film *m*
picturesque [ˌpɪktʃəˈrɛsk] *adj* : pittoresque
pie [ˈpaɪ] *n* **1** : tarte *f* <apple pie : tarte aux pommes> **2** : pâté *m*, tourte *f France* <meat pie : pâté à la viande>
piebald [ˈpaɪˌbɔld] *adj* : pie (se dit d'un animal)
piece[1] [ˈpiːs] *vt* **pieced; piecing** *or* **to piece together** : rassembler, constituer
piece[2] *n* **1** FRAGMENT : bout *m*, morceau *m* <a piece of string : un bout de corde> **2** : pièce *f* (dans un jeu de société) **3** UNIT : objet *m*, chose *f*, pièce *f* <a piece of fruit : un fruit> <a piece of mail : du courrier> <a fifty-cent piece : une pièce de cinquante cents> **4** WORK : œuvre *f*, morceau *m* (de musique) **5** COMPONENT : pièce *f* <a three-piece suit : un costume de trois pièces>
piecemeal[1] [ˈpiːsˌmiːl] *adv* : graduellement
piecemeal[2] *adj* : fragmentaire <piecemeal reforms : réformes fragmentaires>
pied [ˈpaɪd] *adj* : pie (se dit d'un cheval, etc.)
pier [ˈpɪr] *n* **1** JETTY : jetée *f* **2** : pile *f* (d'un pont) **3** COLUMN : pilier *m*
pierce [ˈpɪrs] *vt* **pierced; piercing 1** STAB : donner un coup de couteau à **2** PERFORATE : percer, transpercer **3** PENETRATE : pénétrer **4** DISCERN : comprendre, discerner
piety [ˈpaɪət̬i] *n, pl* **-eties** : piété *f*
pig [ˈpɪg] *n* **1** : porc *m*, cochon *m* (animal) **2** SLOB : cochon *m*, -chonne *f fam* **3** CASTING : moulage *m* en fer
pigeon [ˈpɪdʒən] *n* : pigeon *m*
pigeonhole [ˈpɪdʒənˌhoːl] *n* : casier *m*
piggish [ˈpɪgɪʃ] *adj* **1** GREEDY : goinfre, glouton **2** DIRTY : sale, cochon
piggyback [ˈpɪgiˌbæk] *adv & adj* : sur le dos
pigheaded [ˈpɪgˌhɛdəd] *adj* STUBBORN : têtu, obstiné
piglet [ˈpɪglət] *n* : porcelet *m*
pigment [ˈpɪgmənt] *n* : pigment *m*
pigmentation [ˌpɪgmənˈteɪʃən] *n* : pigmentation *f*

pigmy → **pygmy**

pigpen ['pɪg,pɛn] *n* : porcherie *f*, soue *f* *Can*

pigsty ['pɪg,staɪ] *n, pl* **-sties** → **pigpen**

pigtail ['pɪg,teɪl] *n* : natte *f*

pike ['paɪk] *n* **1** WEAPON : pique *f* **2** → **turnpike** **3** *pl* **pike** *or* **pikes** : brochet *m* (poisson)

pilaf *or* **pilaff** [pɪ'lɑf, 'pi,lɑf] *or* **pilau** [pɪ'lo:, -'lɔ; 'pilo, -lɔ] *n* : pilaf *m*

pile[1] ['paɪəl] *v* **piled; piling** *vt* **1** STACK : empiler **2** LOAD : remplir <he piled potatoes on his plate : il a rempli son assiette de pommes de terre> — *vi* **1** *or* **to pile up** : s'accumuler **2** CROWD : s'empiler <they piled into the car : ils se sont empilés dans la voiture>

pile[2] *n* **1** PILING, POST : pilotis *m*, pieu *m* **2** HEAP : pile *f*, tas *m* **3** NAP : poil *m* (d'un tapis, etc.)

piles ['paɪls] *npl* : hémorroïdes *fpl*

pilfer ['pɪlfər] *vt* : chaparder *fam*, dérober

pilgrim ['pɪlgrəm] *n* : pèlerin *m*, -rine *f*

pilgrimage ['pɪlgrəmɪdʒ] *n* : pèlerinage *m*

pill ['pɪl] *n* : pilule *f*, cachet *m*

pillage[1] ['pɪlɪdʒ] *vt* **-laged; -laging** : piller

pillage[2] *n* : pillage *m*

pillar ['pɪlər] *n* : pilier *m*, colonne *f*

pillbox ['pɪl,bɑks] *n* : boîte *f* à pilules

pillory[1] ['pɪləri] *vt* **-ried; -rying** : mettre au pilori

pillory[2] *n, pl* **-ries** : pilori *m*

pillow ['pɪ,lo:] *n* : oreiller *m*

pillowcase ['pɪlo,keɪs] *n* : taie *f* d'oreiller

pilot[1] ['paɪlət] *vt* : piloter (un avion, un navire)

pilot[2] *n* : pilote *m*

pimento [pə'mɛn,to:] *n, pl* **-tos** *or* **-to** **1** → **allspice** **2** → **pimiento**

pimiento [pə'mɛn,to:, -'mjɛn-] *n, pl* **-tos** : piment *m* doux

pimp ['pɪmp] *n* : entremetteur *m*, souteneur *m*

pimple ['pɪmpəl] *n* : bouton *m*

pimply ['pɪmpəli] *adj* **pimplier; -est** : boutonneux

pin[1] ['pɪn] *vt* **pinned; pinning** **1** FASTEN : épingler **2** HOLD, IMMOBILIZE : fixer, immobiliser **3** **to pin down** DEFINE, DETERMINE : définir, déterminer, cerner **4** **to pin one's hopes on** : mettre tout son espoir dans

pin[2] *n* **1** : épingle *f* <safety pin : épingle de sûreté> **2** BROOCH : broche *f*, épinglette *f* *Can* **3** BADGE, INSIGNIA : insigne *m*, épinglette *f* **4** *or* **bowling pin** : quille *f*

pinafore ['pɪnə,for] *n* **1** APRON : tablier *m* **2** *or* **pinafore dress** : chasuble *f*

pincer ['pɪntsər] *n* **1** : pince *f* (d'un homard) **2** **pincers** *npl* : tenailles *fpl*, pinces *fpl*

pinch[1] ['pɪntʃ] *vt* **1** : pincer <to pinch oneself : se pincer> **2** STEAL : faucher *fam*, voler — *vi* : serrer, être étroit (se dit des chaussures)

pinch[2] *n* **1** SQUEEZE : pincement *m* **2** : pincée *f* <a pinch of salt : une pincée de sel> **3** **in a pinch** : à la rigueur

pincushion ['pɪn,kʊʃən] *n* : pelote *f* (à épingles)

pine[1] ['paɪn] *vi* **pined; pining** **1** **to pine away** LANGUISH : languir **2** **to pine for** : désirer ardemment

pine[2] *n* : pin *m*

pineapple ['paɪn,æpəl] *n* : ananas *m*

pinecone ['paɪn,ko:n] *n* : pomme *f* de pin, cocotte *f* *Can*

pinion ['pɪnjən] *n* **1** : aileron *m* (d'un oiseau) **2** COGWHEEL : pignon *m*

pink[1] ['pɪŋk] *adj* : rose

pink[2] *n* **1** : œillet *m* (fleur) **2** : rose *m* (couleur) **3** **to be in the pink** : être en pleine forme

pinkeye ['pɪŋk,aɪ] *n* : conjonctivite *f*

pinkish ['pɪŋkɪʃ] *adj* : rosé

pinnacle ['pɪnɪkəl] *n* **1** : pinacle *m* (en architecture) **2** PEAK : sommet *m*, pic *m* **3** ACME : sommet *m*, comble *m* (d'une carrière, etc.)

pinpoint ['pɪn,pɔɪnt] *vt* : indiquer, localiser avec précision

pint ['paɪnt] *n* : pinte *f*

pinto ['pɪn,to:] *n, pl* **pintos** : cheval *m* pie

pinworm ['pɪn,wərm] *n* : oxyure *m*

pioneer[1] [,paɪə'nɪr] *vt* : être un innovateur de, mettre au point (des recherches, etc.)

pioneer[2] *n* : pionnier *m*, -nière *f*

pious ['paɪəs] *adj* : pieux, religieux

piously ['paɪəsli] *adv* : pieusement

pipe[1] ['paɪp] *v* **piped; piping** *vi* **1** : jouer de la cornemuse ou du pipeau **2** *or* **to pipe up** : se faire entendre, parler fort — *vt* *or* **to pipe in** : amener ou alimenter par tuyau (de l'eau, du pétrole, etc.)

pipe[2] *n* **1** FLUTE : pipeau *m* **2** BAGPIPE : cornemuse *f* **3** : tuyau *m*, conduit *m* (pour transporter un liquide, un gaz, etc.) **4** : pipe *f* (pour fumer du tabac) **5** : tuyau *m* (d'un orgue)

pipeline ['paɪp,laɪn] *n* **1** : pipeline *m* **2** CONDUIT : voie *f*, canal *m* <a pipeline for data : une voie de transmission pour les données>

piper ['paɪpər] *n* : joueur *m*, joueuse *f* (de cornemuse)

piping ['paɪpɪŋ] *n* **1** : musique *f* de cornemuse **2** TRIM : passepoil *m* (en couture)

piquancy ['pi:kəntsi, 'pɪkwəntsi] *n* SPICINESS : piquant *m*

piquant ['pi:kənt, 'pɪkwənt] *adj* : piquant

pique[1] ['pi:k] *vt* **piqued; piquing** **1** IRRITATE : froisser, irriter **2** AROUSE : éveiller, susciter <to pique s.o.'s curiosity : éveiller la curiosité de qqn>

pique[2] *n* : ressentiment *m*, dépit *m*

piqué *or* **pique** [pɪ'keɪ, 'pi:,-] *n* : piqué *m*

piracy [ˈpaɪrəsi] *n, pl* **-cies 1** : piraterie *f* (sur un navire) **2** : piratage *m* <software piracy : piratage de logiciels>
piranha [pəˈrɑnə, -ˈrɑnjə, -ˈrænjə] *n* : piranha *m*
pirate[1] [ˈpaɪrət] *vt* **-rated; -rating** : pirater
pirate[2] *n* : pirate *m*
pirouette *n* : pirouette *f*
pis → **pi**
Pisces [ˈpaɪˌsiːz] *n* : Poissons *mpl*
pistachio [pəˈstæʃiˌoː, -ˈstɑ-] *n, pl* **-chios** : pistache *f* (noix)
pistil [ˈpɪstəl] *n* : pistil *m*
pistol [ˈpɪstəl] *n* : pistolet *m*
piston [ˈpɪstən] *n* : piston *m*
pit[1] [ˈpɪt] *vt* **pitted; pitting 1** : dénoyauter (un fruit) **2** RIDDLE : cribler <pitted by explosions : criblé par les explosions> **3** : marquer <a face pitted from smallpox : un visage marqué par la variole>
pit[2] *n* **1** HOLE : trou *m,* fosse *f* **2** MINE, SHAFT : mine *f,* puits *m* **3** : creux *m* (de l'estomac) **4** POCKMARK : marque *f* (sur la peau) **5** : noyau *m* (d'un fruit) **6** : fosse *f* <orchestra pit : fosse d'orchestre>
pitch[1] [ˈpɪtʃ] *vt* **1** ERECT : monter, dresser (une tente, etc.) **2** : jeter, fourcher <to pitch hay : fourcher du foin> **3** : lancer (une balle) **4** : donner le ton de (en musique) — *vi* **1** *or* **to pitch forward** : tomber **2** LURCH : tanguer (se dit d'un navire, etc.) **3** SLOPE : être incliné
pitch[2] *n* **1** THROWING : lancer *m,* lancement *m* **2** DEGREE, LEVEL : degré *m* (d'une pente), niveau *m* (d'enthousiasme, etc.) **3** TONE : ton *m* (en musique) **4** TAR : poix *f* **5** *or* **sales pitch** : boniment *m* de vente
pitcher [ˈpɪtʃər] *n* **1** JUG : cruche *f,* pichet *m* **2** : lanceur *m,* -ceuse *f;* artilleur *m Can* (au baseball)
pitchfork [ˈpɪtʃˌfɔrk] *n* : fourche *f*
pitfall [ˈpɪtˌfɔl] *n* : piège *m,* trappe *f*
pith [ˈpɪθ] *n* **1** : moelle *f* (d'une plante) **2** CORE : essence *f,* signification *f*
pithy [ˈpɪθi] *adj* **pithier; -est** : bref, incisif, concis
pitiable [ˈpɪţiəbəl] → **pitiful**
pitiful [ˈpɪţɪfəl] *adj* **1** : pitoyable <a pitiful cry : un cri pitoyable> **2** DEPLORABLE : lamentable, piteux <pitiful wages : salaires minables>
pitifully [ˈpɪţɪfli] *adv* : pitoyablement
pitiless [ˈpɪţɪləs] *adj* : impitoyable — **pitilessly** *adv*
pittance [ˈpɪtənts] *n* : somme *f* dérisoire
pituitary [pəˈtuːəˌteri, -ˈtjuː-] *adj* : pituitaire
pity[1] [ˈpɪţi] *vt* **pitied; pitying** : avoir pitié de
pity[2] *n, pl* **pities** : pitié *f* <to feel pity for : avoir pitié de> <what a pity! : quel dommage!>
pivot[1] [ˈpɪvət] *vi* : pivoter, tourner
pivot[2] *n* : pivot *m*
pivotal [ˈpɪvəţəl] *adj* : crucial, essentiel
pixie *or* **pixy** [ˈpɪksi] *n, pl* **pixies** : lutin *m*
pizza [ˈpiːtsə] *n* : pizza *f*
pizzazz *or* **pizazz** [pəˈzæz] *n* : panache *m*
placard [ˈplækərd, -ˌkɑrd] *n* POSTER : affiche *f,* placard *m*
placate [ˈpleɪˌkeɪt, ˈplæ-] *vt* **-cated; -cating** : apaiser, calmer
place[1] [ˈpleɪs] *v* **placed; placing** *vt* **1** PUT, SET : placer, mettre **2** APPOINT : placer (un employé) **3** RECOGNIZE : se rappeler de, remettre <I couldn't quite place her face : je n'arrivais pas à me rappeler d'elle> **4 to place an order** : passer une commande — *vi* RANK : se placer, se classer <he placed second : il est arrivé deuxième>
place[2] *n* **1** SPACE : place *f* <is this place taken? : cette place est-elle prise?> **2** LOCATION, SPOT : endroit *m,* lieu *m* **3** POSITION : place *f,* position *f* **4** RANK : place *f* <to take first place : prendre la première place> **5** SEAT : place *f,* siège *f* (au théâtre) **6** JOB : poste *m,* emploi *m* **7 in the first place** : tout d'abord **8 to take place** : avoir lieu
placebo [pləˈsiːˌboː] *n, pl* **-bos** : placebo *m*
placement [ˈpleɪsmənt] *n* : placement *m*
placenta [pləˈsɛntə] *n, pl* **-tas** *or* **-tae** [-ti, -ˌtaɪ] : placenta *m*
placid [ˈplæsəd] *adj* : placide, paisible — **placidly** *adv*
plagiarism [ˈpleɪdʒəˌrɪzəm] *n* : plagiat *m*
plagiarist [ˈpleɪdʒərɪst] *n* : plagiaire *mf*
plagiarize [ˈpleɪdʒəˌraɪz] *vt* **-rized; -rizing** : plagier
plague[1] [ˈpleɪg] *vt* **plagued; plaguing 1** AFFLICT : tourmenter **2** HARASS : harceler
plague[2] *n* **1** PESTILENCE : peste *f* **2** CALAMITY : fléau *m,* cataclysme *m*
plaid[1] [ˈplæd] *adj* : écossais
plaid[2] *n* : tissu *m* écossais
plain[1] [ˈpleɪn] *adj* **1** SIMPLE, UNADORNED : simple **2** CLEAR : clair, évident **3** FRANK : franc <plain speaking : le franc-parler> **4** HOMELY : sans attraits, ordinaire
plain[2] *n* : plaine *f*
plainly [ˈpleɪnli] *adv* **1** SIMPLY : simplement **2** CLEARLY : clairement, évidemment **3** FRANKLY : franchement
plaintiff [ˈpleɪntɪf] *n* : demandeur *m,* -deresse *f;* plaignant *m,* -nante *f*
plaintive [ˈpleɪntɪv] *adj* : plaintif — **plaintively** *adv*
plait[1] [ˈpleɪt, ˈplæt] *vt* : natter, tresser
plait[2] *n* **1** PLEAT : pli *m* **2** BRAID : natte *f,* tresse *f*
plan[1] [ˈplæn] *v* **planned; planning** *vt* **1** : faire des plans pour, concevoir (un

édifice) **2** : organiser, planifier <to plan an outing : organiser une sortie> **3** INTEND : penser <I was planning to go : je pensais y aller> — *vi* : faire des projets

plan[2] *n* **1** DIAGRAM : plan *m*, dessin *m* **2** PROCEDURE : plan *m* <a plan of action : un plan d'action> **3** : régime *m*, plan *m* <pension plan : régime de retraite>

plane[1] [ˈpleɪn] *v* **planed; planing** *vt* : raboter, aplanir (une surface) — *vi* GLIDE : planer

plane[2] *adj* FLAT : plat

plane[3] *n* **1** : rabot *m* (outil) **2** SURFACE : plan *m* <horizontal plane : plan horizontal> **3** LEVEL : plan *m* **4** → **airplane**

planet [ˈplænət] *n* : planète *f*

planetarium [ˌplænəˈtɛriəm] *n, pl* **-iums** *or* **-ia** [-iə] : planétarium *m*

planetary [ˈplænəˌtɛri] *adj* : planétaire

plank [ˈplæŋk] *n* **1** : planche *f* (de bois) **2** : article *m* d'une plateforme électorale

plankton [ˈplæŋktən] *n* : plancton *m*

plant[1] [ˈplænt] *vt* **1** : planter (des graines, des fleurs, etc.) **2** AFFIX : planter, enfoncer

plant[2] *n* **1** : plante *f* <indoor plants : plantes d'intérieur> **2** FACTORY : usine *f* <an electric power plant : une centrale hydroélectrique> **3** EQUIPMENT : machinerie *f*, installations *fpl*

plantain [ˈplæntən] *n* : plantain *m* (arbre et fruit)

plantation [plænˈteɪʃən] *n* : plantation *f*

planter [ˈplæntər] *n* **1** : planteur *m*, -teuse *f* **2** : cache-pot *m* (pour des pots de fleurs)

plaque [ˈplæk] *n* **1** : plaque *f* <commemorative plaque : plaque commémorative> **2** : plaque *f* (dentaire)

plasma [ˈplæzmə] *n* : plasma *m*

plaster[1] [ˈplæstər] *vt* **1** : enduire (de plâtre) **2** COVER : couvrir <plastered with posters : couvert d'affiches>

plaster[2] *n* : plâtre *m*

plasterer [ˈplæstərər] *n* : plâtrier *m*

plastic[1] [ˈplæstɪk] *adj* **1** : de plastique, en plastique **2** FLEXIBLE : plastique, malléable

plastic[2] *n* : plastique *m*

plastic surgery *n* : chirurgie *f* plastique

plate[1] [ˈpleɪt] *vt* **plated; plating** : plaquer (avec un métal)

plate[2] *n* **1** SHEET : plaque *f* <steel plate : plaque d'acier> **2** DISH : assiette *f* **3** DENTURES : dentier *m* **4** ILLUSTRATION : planche *f* **5** *or* **license plate** : plaque *f* d'immatriculation

plateau [plæˈtoː] *n, pl* **-teaus** *or* **-teaux** [-ˈtoːz] : plateau *m*

platform [ˈplætˌfɔrm] *n* **1** STAGE : tribune *f*, estrade *f* **2** : quai *m* (d'un chemin de fer) **3** *or* **political platform** : plate-forme *f* (électorale)

plating [ˈpleɪt̬ɪŋ] *n* : placage *m*

platinum [ˈplætənəm] *n* : platine *m*

platitude [ˈplæt̬əˌtuːd, -ˌtjuːd] *n* : platitude *f*, lieu *m* commun

platoon [pləˈtuːn] *n* : section *f* (dans l'armée)

platter [ˈplæt̬ər] *n* : plateau *m* de service

platypus [ˈplæt̬ɪpəs, -ˌpʊs] *n* : ornithorynque *m*

plaudits [ˈplɔdəts] *npl* : applaudissements *mpl*

plausibility [ˌplɔzəˈbɪlət̬i] *n, pl* **-ties** : plausibilité *f*

plausible [ˈplɔzəbəl] *adj* : plausible, vraisemblable

plausibly [ˈplɔzəbli] *adv* : de façon convaincante, avec vraisemblance

play[1] [ˈpleɪ] *vi* **1** : s'amuser, jouer <come out to play : viens jouer> **2** : jouer (se dit d'un orchestre, etc.), se jouer (se dit d'une pièce de théâtre) **3** FIDDLE, TOY : jouer (avec qqch) **4 to play fair** : jouer franc jeu — *vt* **1** : jouer à (un jeu, un sport) **2** : jouer de (un instrument de musique) **3** PERFORM : jouer (une œuvre, un rôle) **4 to play a trick on** : jouer un tour à **5 to play up** EMPHASIZE : souligner, mettre en valeur

play[2] *n* **1** : jeu *m* (aux sports) **2** : jeu *m*, activité *f* <children at play : des enfants qui jouent> **3** : jeu *m* (de couleurs), mouvement *m* léger (du vent) **4** TURN : tour *m* <it's your play : c'est à ton tour> **5** : pièce *f* de théâtre

playacting [ˈpleɪˌæktɪŋ] *n* : comédie *f*, affectation *f*

player [ˈpleɪər] *n* : joueur *m*, joueuse *f*

playful [ˈpleɪfəl] *adj* : enjoué, gai

playfully [ˈpleɪfəli] *adv* : de façon enjouée

playfulness [ˈpleɪfəlnəs] *n* : enjouement *m*

playground [ˈpleɪˌgraʊnd] *n* : cour *f* de récréation

playhouse [ˈpleɪˌhaʊs] *n* **1** THEATER : théâtre *m* **2** : maison *f* de jeu pour les enfants

playing card *n* : carte *f* à jouer

playmate [ˈpleɪˌmeɪt] *n* : camarade *mf* de jeu

play–off [ˈpleɪˌɔf] *n* : finale *f* (de coupe), match *m* crucial

playpen [ˈpleɪˌpɛn] *n* : parc *m* (pour bébés)

plaything [ˈpleɪˌθɪŋ] *n* : jouet *m*

playwright [ˈpleɪˌraɪt] *n* : dramaturge *mf*, auteur *m* dramatique

plaza [ˈplæzə, ˈplɑ-] *n* **1** : place *f* (publique) **2** *or* **shopping plaza** : centre *m* commercial

plea [ˈpliː] *n* **1** : défense *f* (en droit) **2** REQUEST : appel *m*, requête *f* <a plea for mercy : un appel à la clémence>

plead [ˈpli:d] *v* **pleaded** *or* **pled** [ˈplɛd]; **pleading** *vt* **1** : plaider (une cause) **2** (*used to introduce an excuse*) <I pleaded ignorance : j'ai prétendu que je ne savais rien> — *vi* **1** : plaider <to plead guilty : plaider coupable> **2** BEG : supplier, implorer
pleasant [ˈplɛzənt] *adj* : agréable, plaisant
pleasantly [ˈplɛzəntli] *adv* : agréablement, aimablement
pleasantness [ˈplɛzəntnəs] *n* : aimabilité *f,* agrément *m*
pleasantries [ˈplɛzəntriz] *npl* : plaisanteries *fpl,* civilités *fpl*
please[1] [ˈpli:z] *v* **pleased; pleasing** *vt* **1** GRATIFY : plaire à, faire plaisir à <to please everybody : faire plaisir à tout le monde> **2** SATISFY : contenter — *vi* **1** : plaire, faire plaisir <to be anxious to please : chercher à faire plaisir> **2** (*indicating choice*) <do as you please : fais comme il te plaît>
please[2] *adv* : s'il vous plaît, je vous en prie <please come in : rentrez, s'il vous plaît>
pleasing [ˈpli:zɪŋ] *adj* : agréable, plaisant — **pleasingly** *adv*
pleasurable [ˈplɛʒərəbəl] *adj* : agréable, plaisant
pleasure [ˈplɛʒər] *n* **1** DESIRE : gré *m,* guise *f* <at your pleasure : à votre guise> **2** ENJOYMENT : plaisir *m* **3** DELIGHT : plaisir *m,* bonheur *m* <it was a pleasure to see you again! : quel plaisir de vous revoir!>
pleat[1] [ˈpli:t] *vt* : plisser
pleat[2] *n* : pli *m*
plebeian [plɪˈbiən] *adj* : plébéien
pledge[1] [ˈplɛdʒ] *vt* **pledged; pledging 1** PAWN : mettre en gage **2** PROMISE : promettre
pledge[2] *n* **1** SECURITY : gage *m,* nantissement *m* **2** VOW : promesse *f* **3** TOKEN : gage *m* <a pledge of our love : un gage de notre amour>
plenteous [ˈplɛntiəs] → **plentiful**
plentiful [ˈplɛntɪfəl] *adj* : abondant — **plentifully** *adv*
plenty [ˈplɛnti] *n* **1** ABUNDANCE : abondance *f* **2** ∼ **of** : beaucoup de <plenty of time : beaucoup de temps>
plethora [ˈplɛθərə] *n* : pléthore *f*
pleurisy [ˈplʊrəsi] *n* : pleurésie *f*
pliable [ˈplaɪəbəl] *adj* : flexible, malléable
pliancy [ˈplaɪəntsi] *n* : flexibilité *f*
pliant [ˈplaɪənt] → **pliable**
pliers [ˈplaɪərz] *npl* : pinces *fpl*
plight [ˈplaɪt] *n* : situation *f* difficile
plod [ˈplɑd] *vi* **plodded; plodding 1** : marcher lourdement **2** DRUDGE : travailler laborieusement
plot[1] [ˈplɑt] *v* **plotted; plotting** *vt* : faire un plan de — *vi* CONSPIRE : comploter
plot[2] *n* **1** : lot *m,* parcelle *f* (de terre) **2** : plan *m* (d'un édifice) **3** : intrigue *f* (dans un livre, etc.) **4** CONSPIRACY : complot *m,* conspiration *f*
plotter [ˈplɑt̬ər] *n* : conspirateur *m,* -trice *f;* comploteur *m,* -teuse *f*
plover [ˈplʌvər, ˈplo:vər] *n, pl* **-ver** *or* **-vers** : pluvier *m*
plow[1] *or* **plough** [ˈplaʊ] *vt* **1** : labourer (la terre), creuser (un sillon) **2** : déneiger, déblayer <to plow the streets : déneiger les rues> — *vi* **1 to plow into** : percuter, heurter <the car plowed into the fence : la voiture a percuté la clôture> **2 to plow through** : avancer péniblement dans, éplucher <he plowed through a stack of letters : il a épluché une pile de lettres>
plow[2] *or* **plough** *n* : charrue *f*
plowshare [ˈplaʊˌʃɛr] *n* : soc *m* (de charrue)
ploy [ˈplɔɪ] *n* : manigance *f,* truc *m*
pluck[1] [ˈplʌk] *vt* **1** : cueillir <to pluck grapes : cueillir des raisins> **2** : plumer (un poulet), arracher (des plumes à) **3** : pincer les cordes de (un instrument de musique) **4 to pluck one's eyebrows** : s'épiler les sourcis
pluck[2] *n* COURAGE : courage *m,* audace *m*
plucky [ˈplʌki] *adj* **pluckier; -est** : courageux, fougeux
plug[1] [ˈplʌg] *v* **plugged; plugging** *vt* **1** BLOCK : boucher, obstruer **2** ADVERTISE : faire de la publicité pour **3 to plug in** : brancher <to plug in a lamp : brancher une lampe> — *vi or* **to plug away** : s'acharner
plug[2] *n* **1** STOPPER : bouchon *m,* tampon *m* **2** PUBLICITY : annonce *f* publicitaire **3** : fiche *f,* prise *f* (électrique) <telephone plug : prise téléphonique>
plum [ˈplʌm] *n* **1** : prune *f,* pruneau *m Can* (fruit) **2** PRIZE, REWARD : prix *m,* récompense *f*
plumage [ˈplu:mɪdʒ] *n* : plumage *m*
plumb[1] [ˈplʌm] *vt* SOUND : sonder
plumb[2] *adv* **1** VERTICALLY : d'aplomb **2** ABSOLUTELY : complètement <plumb crazy : complètement cinglé>
plumb[3] *adj* : vertical, droit
plumber [ˈplʌmər] *n* : plombier *m*
plumbing [ˈplʌmɪŋ] *n* **1** : plomberie *f* (travail de plombier) **2** PIPES : tuyauterie *f*
plumb line *n* : fil *m* à plomb
plume [ˈplu:m] *n* **1** FEATHER : plume *f* **2** : plumet *m* (sur un chapeau)
plumed [ˈplu:md] *adj* : aux plumes
plummet [ˈplʌmət] *vi* : descendre brusquement, tomber à pic (se dit d'un oiseau)
plump[1] [ˈplʌmp] *vi or* **to plump down** : s'affaler
plump[2] *adv* DIRECTLY : en plein, directement <he ran plump into the

wall : il a heurté le mur de plein fouet>

plump[3] *adj* : grassouillet, dodu

plumpness ['plʌmpnəs] *n* : embonpoint *m*, grosseur *f*

plunder[1] ['plʌndər] *vt* : piller

plunder[2] *n* : pillage *m*

plunderer ['plʌndərər] *n* : pillard *m*, -larde *f*

plunge[1] ['plʌndʒ] *v* **plunged; plunging** *vt* SUBMERGE : plonger, immerger — *vi* **1** DIVE : plonger **2** DESCEND : dévaler **3** RUSH : se précipiter, se lancer

plunge[2] *n* DIVE : plongeon *m*

plunger ['plʌndʒər] *n* : ventouse *f*

plural[1] ['plʊrəl] *adj* : pluriel

plural[2] *n* : pluriel *m*

plurality [plʊ'rælət̬i] *n, pl* **-ties** : pluralité *f*

pluralize ['plʊrə,laɪz] *vi* **-ized; -izing** : prendre le pluriel

plus[1] ['plʌs] *adj* : positif <a plus factor : un facteur positif>

plus[2] *n* **1** *or* **plus sign** : plus *m* **2** ADVANTAGE : plus *m*, avantage *m*

plus[3] *conj* AND : et

plus[4] *prep* : plus <six boys plus a girl : six garçons plus une fille> <4 plus 5 : 4 plus 5>

plush[1] ['plʌʃ] *adj* : luxueux, somptueux

plush[2] *n* : peluche *f*

plushy ['plʌʃi] *adj* **plushier; -est** : luxueux

Pluto ['plu:t̬o:] *n* : Pluton *f* (planète)

plutocracy [plu:'tɑkrəsi] *n, pl* **-cies** : ploutocratie *f*

plutonium [plu:'to:niəm] *n* : plutonium *m*

ply[1] ['plaɪ] *vt* **plied; plying 1** USE, WIELD : manier (un outil) **2** PRACTICE : pratiquer, exercer <to ply a trade : pratiquer un métier> **3 to ply s.o. with** : assaillir qqn de (questions, etc.)

ply[2] *n, pl* **plies 1** THICKNESS : épaisseur *f* **2** LAYER : pli *m* **3** STRAND : brin *m* (de laine)

plywood ['plaɪ,wʊd] *n* : contre-plaqué *m*

pneumatic [nʊ'mæt̬ɪk, njʊ-] *adj* : pneumatique

pneumonia [nʊ'mo:njə, njʊ-] *n* : pneumonie *f*

poach ['po:tʃ] *vt* **1** : pocher (des œufs) **2 to poach game** : braconner le gibier

poacher ['po:tʃər] *n* : braconnier *m*, -nière *f*

pock ['pɑk] *n* **1** PUSTULE : pustule *f* **2** → **pockmark**

pocket[1] ['pɑkət] *vt* **1** STEAL : empocher **2** : mettre dans sa poche <to pocket the change : mettre la monnaie dans sa poche>

pocket[2] *n* **1** : poche *f* (dans un vêtement) **2** : blouse *f* (au billard), poche *f* (marsupiale), poche *f* (d'or, d'eau, de gaz) **3** AREA : poche *f*, secteur *m* <pockets of unemployment : poches de chômage> **4** *or* **air pocket** : trou *m* d'air

pocketbook ['pɑkət,bʊk] *n* **1** WALLET : portefeuille *m* **2** PURSE : sac *m* à main, sacoche *f Can* **3** INCOME : revenu *m*, ressources *fpl* financières

pocketknife ['pɑkət,naɪf] *n* : canif *m*

pockmark ['pɑk,mɑrk] *n* : cicatrice *f*

pod ['pɑd] *n* : cosse *f* <pea pod : cosse de pois>

podiatrist [pə'daɪətrɪst, po-] *n* : podologue *mf*

podiatry [pə'daɪətri, po-] *n* : podologie *f*

podium ['po:diəm] *n, pl* **-diums** *or* **-dia** [-iə] : podium *m*

poem ['po:əm] *n* : poème *m*

poet ['po:ət] *n* : poète *mf*

poetic [po'ɛt̬ɪk,] *or* **poetical** [-t̬ɪkəl] *adj* : poétique

poetry ['po:ətri] *n* : poésie *f*

pogrom ['po:grəm, pə'grɑm, 'pɑgrəm] *n* : pogrom *m*

poignancy ['pɔɪnjəntsi] *n, pl* **-cies** : caractère *m* poignant

poignant ['pɔɪnjənt] *adj* : poignant

poinsettia [pɔɪn'sɛt̬iə, -'sɛt̬ə] *n* : poinsettia *m*

point[1] ['pɔɪnt] *vt* **1** SHARPEN : aiguiser (un crayon, etc.) **2** AIM : pointer, montrer, braquer <to point one's finger at s.o. : montrer qqn du doigt> <to point a gun : braquer un fusil> **3** INDICATE : montrer, indiquer <to point the way : montrer la voie> **4 to point out** : signaler, remarquer — *vi* : tomber en arrêt (se dit d'un chien)

point[2] *n* **1** ITEM : point *m*, question *f* <the main points : les points principaux> **2** QUALITY : point *m*, force *f* <one of his strong points : un de ses points forts> **3** PURPOSE : utilité *f*, but *m* <there's no point in trying : il est inutile d'essayer> <what's the point? : où veux-tu en venir?> **4** PLACE : point *m*, endroit *m* <a distant point : un point distant> **5** MOMENT : moment *m*, instant *m* <at this point : à ce moment-là> **6** DEGREE, STAGE : point *m* <boiling point : point d'ébullition> **7** END, TIP : pointe *f* (d'un crayon, d'une épée) **8** VERGE : point *m* <at the point of death : au bord de la tombe> **9** HEADLAND : cap *m*, promontoire *m* **10** DOT, PERIOD : point *m* (signe de ponctuation) **11** : point *m* (aux sports) **12** → **decimal point**

point–blank[1] ['pɔɪnt'blæŋk] *adv* **1** : à bout portant <to shoot point-blank : tirer à bout portant> **2** ABSOLUTELY, BLUNTLY : catégoriquement

point–blank[2] *adj* **1** : à bout portant <point-blank shot : tir à bout portant> **2** BLUNT : catégorique <a point-blank refusal : un refus catégorique>

pointedly ['pɔɪntədli] *adv* : ostensiblement, de façon marquée

pointer [ˈpɔɪntər] *n* **1** ROD : baguette *f* **2** : chien *m* d'arrêt **3** TIP : conseil *m*, suggestion *f*
pointless [ˈpɔɪntləs] *adj* **1** SENSELESS : absurde **2** USELESS : inutile, futile <pointless attempts : tentatives inutiles>
point of view *n* : point *m* de vue
poise[1] [ˈpɔɪz] *vt* **poised; poising** BALANCE : tenir en équilibre
poise[2] *n* **1** EQUILIBRIUM : équilibre *m* **2** COMPOSURE : calme *m*, assurance *f*
poison[1] [ˈpɔɪzən] *vt* **1** : empoisonner <poisoned arrows : flèches empoisonnées> **2** CORRUPT : pervertir, corrompre <to poison s.o.'s mind : pervertir l'esprit de qqn>
poison[2] *n* : poison *m*
poison ivy *n* : sumac *m* vénéneux, herbe *f* à (la) puce *Can*
poisonous [ˈpɔɪzənəs] *adj* **1** : vénéneux (se dit d'une plante), vénimeux (se dit d'un serpent ou d'un insecte), toxique (se dit d'une émanation, d'une plante, etc.) **2** HARMFUL : destructeur, pernicieux
poke[1] [ˈpoːk] *v* **poked; poking** *vt* **1** JAB : donner un coup de coude à (les côtes, etc.) **2** PROD : donner des petits coups à **3** THRUST : fourrer *fam*, passer <I poked my head out of the window : j'ai passé ma tête par la fenêtre> — *vi or* **to poke around** : fureter, fouiner *fam*
poke[2] *n* JAB : coup *m*
poker [ˈpoːkər] *n* **1** : tisonnier *m* (pour le feu) **2** : poker *m* (jeu de cartes)
polar [ˈpoːlər] *adj* : polaire
polar bear *n* : ours *m* polaire, ours *m* blanc
Polaris [poˈlærɪs, -ˈlɑr-] → **North Star**
polarize [ˈpoːlə,raɪz] *vt* **-ized; -izing** : polariser
pole [ˈpoːl] *n* **1** ROD, STICK : perche *f* <a telephone pole : un poteau> <ski pole : bâton de ski> **2** : pôle *m* <the South Pole : le pôle Sud> **3** : pôle *m* (électrique)
Pole [ˈpoːl] *n* : Polonais *m*, -naise *f*
polecat [ˈpoːl,kæt] *n, pl* **polecats** *or* **polecat 1** FERRET : putois *m* **2** SKUNK : mouffette *f*
polemical [pəˈlɛmɪkəl] *adj* : polémique
polemics [pəˈlɛmɪks] *ns & pl* : polémique *f*
police[1] [pəˈliːs] *vt* **-liced; -licing** : surveiller, maintenir l'ordre et la paix de
police[2] *ns & pl* **1** *or* **police force** : police *f*, gendarmerie *f* **2** POLICE OFFICERS : policiers *mpl*
policeman [pəˈliːsmən] *n, pl* **-men** [-mən, -,mɛn] : policier *m*
police officer *n* : policier *m*, agent *m* de police
policewoman [pəˈliːs,wʊmən] *n, pl* **-women** [-,wɪmən] : femme *f* policier
policy [ˈpɑləsi] *n, pl* **-cies 1** : politique *f* <foreign policy : politique étrangère> **2** *or* **insurance policy** : police *f* d'assurance
policyholder [ˈpɑləsi,hoːldər] *n* : assuré *m*, -rée *f*
polio [ˈpoːli,oː] → **poliomyelitis**
poliomyelitis [,poːli,oː,maɪəˈlaɪṭəs] *n* : poliomyélite *f*
polish[1] [ˈpɑlɪʃ] *vt* **1** : polir (une surface) **2** REFINE : parfaire, peaufiner
polish[2] *n* **1** LUSTER : poli *m*, éclat *m* **2** WAX : cire *f* (pour les meubles, etc.), cirage *m* (pour les chaussures) **3** REFINEMENT : perfection *f*, raffinement *m* **4 nail polish** : vernis *m* à ongles
Polish[1] [ˈpoːlɪʃ] *adj* : polonais
Polish[2] *n* : polonais *m* (langue)
polite [pəˈlaɪt] *adj* **politer; -est** : poli, courtois
politely [pəˈlaɪtli] *adv* : poliment
politeness [pəˈlaɪtnəs] *n* : politesse *f*
politic [ˈpɑlə,tɪk] *adj* : habile, diplomate
political [pəˈlɪṭɪkəl] *adj* : politique — **politically** [-ṭɪkli] *adv*
politician [,pɑləˈtɪʃən] *n* : politicien *m*, -cienne *f*
politics [ˈpɑlə,tɪks] *ns & pl* : politique *f*
polka [ˈpoːlkə, ˈpoːkə] *n* : polka *f*
polka dot *n* : pois *m*, picot *m Can*
poll[1] [ˈpoːl] *vt* **1** : obtenir, recueillir (des voix) **2** CANVASS : sonder — *vi* : voter
poll[2] *n* **1** SURVEY : sondage *m*, enquête *f* **2 polls** *npl* : urnes *fpl* <to go to the polls : aller aux urnes>
pollen [ˈpɑlən] *n* : pollen *m*
pollinate [ˈpɑlə,neɪt] *vt* **-nated; -nating** : polliniser
pollination [,pɑləˈneɪʃən] *n* : pollinisation *f*
pollster [ˈpoːlstər] *n* : sondeur *m*, -deuse *f*; enquêteur *m*, -teuse *f*
pollutant [pəˈluːtənt] *n* : polluant *m*
pollute [pəˈluːt] *vt* **-luted; -luting** : polluer
pollution [pəˈluːʃən] *n* : pollution *f*
pollywog *or* **polliwog** [ˈpɑli,wɔg] *n* TADPOLE : têtard *m*
polo [ˈpoː,loː] *n* : polo *m*
poltergeist [ˈpoːlṭər,gaɪst] *n* : esprit *m* frappeur
polyester [ˈpɑli,ɛstər, ,pɑliˈ-] *n* : polyester *m*
polygamist [pəˈlɪgəmɪst] *n* : polygame *mf*
polygamous [pəˈlɪgəməs] *adj* : polygame
polygamy [pəˈlɪgəmi] *n* : polygamie *f*
polygon [ˈpɑlɪ,gɑn] *n* : polygone *m*
polymer [ˈpɑləmər] *n* : polymère *m*
Polynesian[1] [,pɑləˈniːʒən, -ʃən] *adj* : polynésien
Polynesian[2] *n* **1** : Polynésien *m*, -sienne *f* **2** : polynésien *m* (langue)
polyp [ˈpɑləp] *n* : polype *m*
polytheism [ˈpɑli,θi,ɪzəm] *n* : polythéisme *m*
polyunsaturated [,pɑli,ʌnˈsætʃə,reɪṭəd] *adj* : polyinsaturé

pomegranate [ˈpɑməˌgrænət, ˈpɑmˌgræ-] *n* : grenade *f* (fruit)

pommel[1] [ˈpʌməl] *vt* → **pummel**

pommel[2] [ˈpʌməl, ˈpɑ-] *n* : pommeau *m* (sur une épée, d'une selle)

pomp [ˈpɑmp] *n* **1** SPLENDOR : pompe *f*, faste *m* **2** OSTENTATION : apparat *m*, ostentation *f*

pompous [ˈpɑmpəs] *adj* : pompeux — **pompously** *adv*

poncho [ˈpɑnˌtʃoː] *n, pl* **-chos** : poncho *m*

pond [ˈpɑnd] *n* : étang *m*, mare *f*

ponder [ˈpɑndər] *vt* : évaluer, estimer — *vi* **to ponder over** : réfléchir à, méditer sur

ponderous [ˈpɑndərəs] *adj* : pesant, lourd

pontiff [ˈpɑntɪf] *n* : pontife *m*

pontifical [pɑnˈtɪfɪkəl] *adj* : pontifical

pontificate [pɑnˈtɪfəˌkeɪt] *vi* **-cated; -cating** : pontifier

pontoon [pɑnˈtuːn] *n* : ponton *m*

pony [ˈpoːni] *n, pl* **-nies** : poney *m*

ponytail [ˈpoːniˌteɪl] *n* : queue *f* de cheval

poodle [ˈpuːdəl] *n* : caniche *m*

pool[1] [ˈpuːl] *vt* : mettre en commun <to pool resources : mettre en commun des ressources>

pool[2] *n* **1** PUDDLE : flaque *f* (d'eau), mare *f* (de sang) **2** RESERVE : fonds *m* commun **3** BILLIARDS : billard *m* américain **4** *or* **swimming pool** : piscine *f*

poor [ˈpʊr, ˈpor] *adj* **1** : pauvre <poor people : gens pauvres> **2** : mauvais, piètre <a poor crop : une mauvaise récolte> <poor results : piètres résultats> <poor health : santé précaire> **3** BARREN : stérile, improductif <poor soil : terre stérile> **4** : pauvre <you poor thing! : pauvre de toi!> **5** UNFAVORABLE : défavorable

poorly [ˈpʊrli, ˈpor-] *adv* BADLY : mal

pop[1] [ˈpɑp] *v* **popped; popping** *vt* **1** BURST : faire éclater **2** PUT : mettre <he popped it into his mouth : il l'a mis dans sa bouche> — *vi* **1** BURST : éclater, exploser **2** *or* **to pop out** : sortir <his eyes were popping : les yeux lui sortaient de la tête> **3 to pop in** : faire une petite visite

pop[2] *adj* : pop <pop music : musique pop>

pop[3] *n* **1** : bruit *m* sec **2** SODA : boisson *f* gazeuse, liqueur *f Can*

popcorn [ˈpɑpˌkɔrn] *n* : maïs *m* explosé, pop-corn *m*

pope [ˈpoːp] *n* : pape *m* <Pope Pius XII : le pape Pie XII>

poplar [ˈpɑplər] *n* : peuplier *m*

poplin [ˈpɑplɪn] *n* : popeline *f*

poppy [ˈpɑpi] *n, pl* **-pies** : coquelicot *m*

populace [ˈpɑpjələs] *n* **1** MASSES : masses *fpl*, peuple *m* **2** POPULATION : population *f*

popular [ˈpɑpjələr] *adj* **1** : populaire <popular government : gouvernement populaire> **2** PREVALENT, WIDESPREAD : répandu **3** : aimé, prisé, populaire <a popular destination : une destination prisée>

popularity [ˌpɑpjəˈlærət̬i] *n* : popularité *f*

popularize [ˈpɑpjələˌraɪz] *vt* **-ized; -izing** : populariser

popularly [ˈpɑpjələrli] *adv* : communément, généralement

populate [ˈpɑpjəˌleɪt] *vt* **-lated; -lating** : peupler

population [ˌpɑpjəˈleɪʃən] *n* : population *f*

populous [ˈpɑpjələs] *adj* : populeux

porcelain [ˈporsələn] *n* : porcelaine *f*

porch [ˈportʃ] *n* : véranda *f*, porche *m*, galerie *f Can*, perron *m Can*

porcupine [ˈpɔrkjəˌpaɪn] *n* : porc-épic *m*

pore[1] [ˈpor] *vi* **pored; poring** : lire attentivement, étudier de près

pore[2] *n* : pore *m* (de la peau)

pork [ˈpork] *n* : porc *m*

pornographic [ˌpɔrnəˈgræfɪk] *adj* : pornographique

pornography [pɔrˈnɑgrəfi] *n* : pornographie *f*

porous [ˈporəs] *adj* : poreux

porpoise [ˈpɔrpəs] *n* : marsouin *m*

porridge [ˈpɔrɪdʒ] *n* : porridge *m France*, gruau *m Can*

port[1] [ˈport] *adj* : portuaire

port[2] *n* **1** HARBOR : port *m*, ville *f* portuaire **2** ORIFICE : orifice *m* **3** PORTHOLE : hublot *m* **4** *or* **port side** : bâbord *m* (d'un navire) **5** *or* **port wine** : porto *m* **6** : port *m* (d'un ordinateur)

portable [ˈport̬əbəl] *adj* : portatif, portable <portable computer : ordinateur portable>

portal [ˈport̬əl] *n* : portail *m*

portend [pɔrˈtɛnd] *vt* : présager, annoncer

portent [ˈpɔrˌtɛnt] *n* : présage *m*, prédiction *f*

portentous [pɔrˈtɛntəs] *adj* **1** : de mauvais augure **2** MARVELOUS : extraordinaire, prodigieux **3** GRAVE : grave, sérieux <portentous decisions : de graves décisions>

porter [ˈport̬ər] *n* : porteur *m*, -teuse *f*

portfolio [portˈfoːliˌo] *n, pl* **-lios 1** BRIEFCASE, FOLDER : porte-documents *m* **2** : dossier *m* (diplomatique) **3** *or* **investment portfolio** : portefeuille *m*

porthole [ˈportˌhoːl] *n* : hublot *m*

portico [ˈport̬ɪˌko] *n, pl* **-coes** *or* **-cos** : portique *m*

portion[1] [ˈporʃən] *vt* : distribuer, diviser

portion[2] *n* PART, SHARE : portion *f*, part *m*

portly [ˈportli] *adj* **portlier; -est** : corpulent

portrait [ˈportrət, -ˌtreɪt] *n* : portrait *m*

portray [porˈtreɪ] *vt* **1** DEPICT : représenter (par le dessin) **2** DESCRIBE : dépeindre (par la parole) **3** ENACT : jouer, interpréter (un rôle)

portrayal [porˈtreɪəl] *n* **1** REPRESENTATION : représentation *f* **2** PORTRAIT : portrait *m*

Portuguese[1] [ˈportʃəˌgi:z, -ˌgi:s] *adj* : portugais

Portuguese[2] *n* **1** : Portugais *m*, -gaise *f* **2** : portugais *m* (langue)

pose[1] [ˈpo:z] *v* **posed; posing** *vt* : poser (une question, etc.) — *vi* **1** : poser (se dit d'un modèle) **2 to pose as** : se faire passer pour

pose[2] *n* **1** : pose *f* <to strike a pose : adapter une pose> **2** PRETENSE : affectation *f*, faux-semblant *m*

posh [ˈpɑʃ] *adj* : chic, élégant

position[1] [pəˈzɪʃən] *vt* : positionner

position[2] *n* **1** STANCE : position *f*, perspective *f* **2** LOCATION : position *f*, emplacement *m* **3** STATUS : position *f*, rang *m* **4** JOB : poste *m*

positive [ˈpɑzəṭɪv] *adj* **1** DEFINITE : catégorique <a positive no : un non catégorique> **2** CONFIDENT : certain, convaincu **3** : positif (en grammaire, en mathématiques, en physique, etc.) **4** AFFIRMATIVE : positif

positively [ˈpɑzəṭɪvli] *adv* **1** CERTAINLY : sans aucun doute, incontestablement **2** (*used for emphasis*) : réellement <positively surprised : réellement surpris>

possess [pəˈzɛs] *vt* : posséder, détenir

possession [pəˈzɛʃən] *n* **1** OWNERSHIP : possession *f* **2** PROPERTY : possession *f*, jouissance *f* (en droit) **3 possessions** *npl* BELONGINGS : biens *mpl*

possessive[1] [pəˈzɛsɪv] *adj* **1** JEALOUS : possessif, jaloux **2** : possessif (en grammaire)

possessive[2] *n or* **possessive case** : possessif *m*

possessor [pəˈzɛsər] *n* : possesseur *m*

possibility [ˌpɑsəˈbɪləṭi] *n, pl* **-ties** : possibilité *f*

possible [ˈpɑsəbəl] *adj* : possible

possibly [ˈpɑsəbli] *adv* : peut-être, possiblement *Can*

possum [ˈpɑsəm] → **opossum**

post[1] [ˈpo:st] *vt* **1** MAIL : poster (une lettre) **2** INFORM : tenir au courant, tenir informé <I'll keep you posted : je te tiendrai au courant> **3** STATION : poster <to post guards : poster des gardiens> **4** AFFIX : afficher, placarder

post[2] *n* **1** OFFICE, POSITION : poste *m* **2** POLE : poteau *m* **3** *Brit* → **mail**[2] **1, 2; postal service**

postage [ˈpo:stɪdʒ] *n* : affranchissement *m*, tarifs *mpl* postaux

postal [ˈpostəl] *adj* : postal

postal service *n* : courrier *m*, poste *f*

postcard [ˈpo:stˌkɑrd] *n* : carte *f* postale

poster [ˈpo:stər] *n* : poster *m*, affiche *f*

posterior[1] [pɑˈstɪriər, po-] *adj* : postérieur

posterior[2] *n* BUTTOCKS : postérieur *m fam*, derrière *m fam*

posterity [pɑˈstɛrəṭi] *n* : postérité *f*

postgraduate [ˌpo:stˈgrædʒuət] *n* : étudiant *m*, -diante *f* de troisième cycle

posthaste [ˈpo:stˈheɪst] *adv* : en toute vitesse, en toute hâte

posthumous [ˈpɑstʃəməs] *adj* : posthume

posthumously [ˈpɑstʃəməsli] *adv* : après la mort

postman [ˈpo:stmən, -ˌmæn] *n, pl* **-men** [-mən, -ˌmɛn] → **mailman**

postmark[1] [ˈpo:stˌmɑrk] *vt* : oblitérer (un timbre)

postmark[2] *n* : cachet *m* de la poste

postmaster [ˈpo:stˌmæstər] *n* : receveur *m* des Postes

postmortem [ˌpo:stˈmɔrṭəm] *n* : autopsie *f*

postnatal [ˌpo:stˈneɪṭəl] *adj* : postnatal

post office *n* : bureau *m* de poste

postoperative [ˌpo:stˈɑpərəṭɪv, -ˌreɪ-] *adj* : postopératoire

postpaid [ˌpo:stˈpeɪd] *adj* : franco de port, port payé

postpone [ˌpo:stˈpo:n] *vt* **-poned; -poning** : reporter, remettre

postponement [ˌpo:stˈpo:nmənt] *n* : renvoi *m*, remise *f*

postscript [ˈpo:stˌskrɪpt] *n* : post-scriptum *m*

postulate [ˈpɑstʃəˌleɪt] *vt* **-lated; -lating** : poser comme postulat

posture[1] [ˈpɑstʃər] *vi* **-tured; -turing** : poser, prendre des airs

posture[2] *n* : posture *f*

postwar [ˌpo:stˈwɔr] *adj* : d'après-guerre

posy [ˈpo:zi] *n, pl* **-sies 1** FLOWER : fleur *f* **2** BOUQUET : (petit) bouquet *m* de fleurs

pot[1] [ˈpɑt] *vt* **potted; potting** : empoter (une plante)

pot[2] *n* **1** POTFUL : pot *m* <a pot of soup : un pot de soupe> **2** *or* **cooking pot** : marmite *f*, casserole *f*

potable [ˈpo:ṭəbəl] *adj* : potable

potash [ˈpɑtˌæʃ] *n* : potasse *f*

potassium [pəˈtæsiəm] *n* : potassium *m*

potato [pəˈteɪṭo] *n, pl* **-toes** : pomme *f* de terre, patate *f fam*

potbellied [ˈpɑtˌbɛlid] *adj* : bedonnant

potbelly [ˈpɑtˌbɛli] *n, pl* **-lies** : bedaine *f*

potency [ˈpo:tənᵗsi] *n, pl* **-cies 1** POWER : puissance *f*, force *f* **2** EFFECTIVENESS : efficacité *f*

potent [ˈpo:tənt] *adj* **1** POWERFUL : puissant **2** EFFECTIVE : efficace

potential[1] [pəˈtɛntʃəl] *adj* : potentiel — **potentially** *adv*

potential[2] *n* : potentiel *m*

potful [ˈpɑtˌfʊl] *n* : pot *m*, contenu *m* d'un pot

pothole [ˈpɑtˌho:l] *n* : nid-de-poule *m*
potion [ˈpo:ʃən] *n* : potion *f*
potluck [ˈpɑtˌlʌk] *n or* **potluck supper** : souper *m* communautaire
potpourri [ˌpo:pʊˈri:] *n* **1** : pot-pourri *m*, fleurs *fpl* séchées **2** COLLECTION : pot-pourri *m*, mélange *m*
potshot [ˈpɑtˌʃɑt] *n* **1** CRITICISM : commentaire *m* désobligeant **2 to take a potshot at** : tirer à vue sur
potter [ˈpɑt̬ər] *n* : potier *m*, -tière *f*
pottery [ˈpɑt̬əri] *n, pl* **-teries** : poterie *f*
pouch [ˈpaʊtʃ] *n* **1** BAG : petit sac *m* **2** : poche *f* (des marsupiaux)
poultice [ˈpo:lt̬əs] *n* : cataplasme *m*
poultry [ˈpo:ltri] *n* : volaille *f*
pounce [ˈpaʊnts] *vi* **pounced; pouncing** **1** : sauter, bondir **2 to pounce upon** : attaquer, assaillir
pound[1] [ˈpaʊnd] *vt* **1** CRUSH : broyer, écraser **2** HAMMER : marteler **3** BEAT : battre, frapper <to pound one's chest : frapper la poitrine> **4 to pound the pavement** : battre le pavé — *vi* **1** BEAT : palpiter, battre <my heart was pounding : mon cœur battait la chamade> **2 to pound away at** : travailler avec acharnement à
pound[2] *n* **1** : livre *f* (unité de mesure) **2** : livre *f* sterling **3** SHELTER : fourrière *f* (pour des animaux)
pour [ˈpor] *vt* **1** : verser (des boissons) **2 to pour all one's energy into** : mettre toute son énergie dans — *vi* **1** FLOW : couler **2** RAIN : pleuvoir à verse
pout[1] [ˈpaʊt] *vi* : faire la moue
pout[2] *n* : moue *f*
poverty [ˈpɑvərt̬i] *n* : pauvreté *f*
powder[1] [ˈpaʊdər] *vt* **1** : poudrer <to powder one's nose : se poudrer le nez> **2** CRUSH : pulvériser
powder[2] *n* : poudre *f*
powdery [ˈpaʊdəri] *adj* : poudreux
power[1] [ˈpaʊər] *vt* : faire fonctionner, faire marcher
power[2] *n* **1** AUTHORITY : pouvoir *m*, autorité *f* **2** ABILITY : capacité *f* **3** : puissance *f* <foreign power : puissance extérieure> **4** STRENGTH : force *f* (d'une personne), puissance *f* (d'une machine) **5** : énergie *f* (électrique)
powerful [ˈpaʊərfəl] *adj* : puissant, fort
powerfully [ˈpaʊərfəli] *adv* : puissamment, fortement
powerhouse [ˈpaʊərˌhaʊs] *n* : personne *f* très énergique
powerless [ˈpaʊərləs] *adj* : impuissant
powwow [ˈpaʊˌwaʊ] *n* : pow-wow *m* *Can*, assemblée *f* d'Amérindiens
pox [ˈpɑks] *n, pl* **pox** *or* **poxes** **1** → **chicken pox** **2** → **syphilis**
practicable [ˈpræktɪkəbəl] *adj* : praticable, réalisable
practical [ˈpræktɪkəl] *adj* : pratique
practically [ˈpræktɪkli] *adv* **1** : pratiquement, d'une façon pratique **2** ALMOST, NEARLY : presque, pratiquement
practice[1] *or* **practise** [ˈpræktəs] *v* **-ticed** *or* **-tised; -ticing** *or* **-tising** *vt* **1** : pratiquer (un sport, un métier) **2** CARRY OUT : pratiquer, mettre en application **3** OBSERVE : observer <to practice politeness : observer les règles de politesse> — *vi* : s'exercer, s'entraîner
practice[2] *n* **1** USE : pratique *f* <to put into practice : mettre en pratique> **2** CUSTOM, HABIT : coutume *f*, pratique *f* **3** : exercice *m* (d'une profession)
practitioner [prækˈtɪʃənər] *n* : praticien *m*, -cienne *f*
pragmatic [prægˈmæt̬ɪk] *adj* : pragmatique
pragmatism [ˈprægməˌtɪzəm] *n* : pragmatisme *m*
prairie [ˈprɛri] *n* : prairie *f*
praise[1] [ˈpreɪz] *vt* **praised; praising** **1** COMMEND : louer, faire l'éloge de **2** GLORIFY : louer, glorifier
praise[2] *n* : louange *f*
praiseworthy [ˈpreɪzˌwərði] *adj* : louable, digne d'éloges
pram [ˈpræm] *n Brit* : voiture *f* d'enfant, landau *m France*
prance[1] [ˈprænts] *vt* **pranced; prancing** : caracoler (se dit d'un cheval), cabrioler (se dit d'une personne)
prance[2] *n* : cabriole *f*
prank [ˈpræŋk] *n* : farce *f*, tour *m*
prankster [ˈpræŋkstər] *n* : farceur *m*, -ceuse *f*
prattle[1] [ˈprætəl] *vi* **-tled; -tling** BABBLE : babiller, bavarder
prattle[2] *n* : bavardage *m*
prawn [ˈprɔn] *n* : crevette *f* (rose)
pray [ˈpreɪ] *vt* ENTREAT : supplier, implorer <pray be careful : je te prie de faire attention> — *vi* : prier (à Dieu)
prayer [ˈprɛr] *n* **1** : prière *f* <to say one's prayers : faire sa prière> <the Lord's Prayer : le Notre Père> <to kneel in prayer : prier à genoux> **2** WISH : désir *m*, souhait *m*
praying mantis → **mantis**
preach [ˈpri:tʃ] *vt* **1** : prêcher <to preach the gospel : prêcher l'Évangile> **2** ADVOCATE : prêcher, prôner <to preach patience : prôner la patience> — *vi* : prêcher
preacher [ˈpri:tʃər] *n* MINISTER : pasteur *m*
preamble [ˈpri:ˌæmbəl] *n* : préambule *m*, introduction *f*
precarious [prɪˈkæriəs] *adj* : précaire — **precariously** *adv*
precariousness [prɪˈkæriəsnəs] *n* : précarité *f*
precaution [prɪˈkɔʃən] *n* : précaution *f*
precautionary [prɪˈkɔʃəˌnɛri] *adj* : de précaution, préventif
precede [prɪˈsi:d] *vt* **-ceded; -ceding** : précéder

precedence ['prɛsədən*t*s, prɪ'si:dən*t*s] *n* **1** : préséance *f* <in order of precedence : par ordre de préséance> **2** PRIORITY : priorité *f* <to take precedence over : avoir la priorité sur>

precedent ['prɛsədənt] *n* : précédent *m*

precept ['pri:ˌsɛpt] *n* : précepte *m*, principe *m*

precinct ['pri:ˌsɪŋkt] *n* **1** DISTRICT : arrondissement *m* (en France), circonscription *f* (au Canada) **2 precincts** *npl* : alentours *mpl*, environs *mpl*

precious ['prɛʃəs] *adj* **1** : précieux <precious stones : pierres précieuses> **2** CHERISHED, DEAR : cher **3** AFFECTED : affecté, forcé

precipice ['prɛsəpəs] *n* : précipice *m*

precipitate[1] [pri'sɪpəˌteɪt] *v* **-tated; -tating** *vt* **1** PROVOKE : provoquer **2** : condenser (un liquide) — *vi* : précipiter (en chimie)

precipitate[2] [pri'sɪpətət] *adj* **1** PRECIPITOUS : escarpé, à pic **2** RASH : précipité, prématuré

precipitate[3] [pri'sɪpətət, -ˌteɪt] *n* : précipité *m*

precipitation [priˌsɪpə'teɪʃən] *n* **1** HASTE : précipitation *f*, hâte *f* **2** : précipitations *fpl* (en météorologie)

precipitous [pri'sɪpət̬əs] *adj* STEEP : à pic, abrupt

précis [preɪ'si:] *n, pl* **précis** [-'si:z] : précis *m*, résumé *m*

precise [pri'saɪs] *adj* : précis — **precisely** *adv*

preciseness [pri'saɪsnəs] *n* : précision *f*

precision [pri'sɪʒən] *n* : précision *f*

preclude [pri'klu:d] *vt* **-cluded; -cluding** : empêcher, prévenir

precocious [pri'ko:ʃəs] *adj* : précoce — **precociously** *adv*

precocity [pri'kɑsət̬i] *n* : précocité *f*

preconceived [ˌpri:kən'si:vd] *adj* : préconçu

precondition [ˌpri:kən'dɪʃən] *n* : condition *f* préalable

precook [ˌpri:'kʊk] *vt* : précuire

precursor [prɪ'kərsər] *n* : précurseur *m*

predator ['prɛdət̬ər] *n* : prédateur *m*

predatory ['prɛdəˌtori] *adj* : prédateur

predecessor ['prɛdəˌsɛsər, 'pri:-] *n* : prédécesseur *m*

predestination [priˌdɛstə'neɪʃən] *n* : prédestination *f*

predestine [pri'dɛstən] *vt* **-tined; -tining** : prédestiner

predetermine [ˌpri:dɪ'tərmən] *vt* **-mined; mining** : prédéterminer

predicament [pri'dɪkəmənt] *n* : situation *f* difficile

predicate[1] ['prɛdəˌkeɪt] *vt* **-cated; -cating 1** AFFIRM : affirmer, déclarer **2** BASE : fonder

predicate[2] ['prɛdɪkət] *n* : prédicat *m*

predict [pri'dɪkt] *vt* : prédire

predictability [priˌdɪktə'bɪlət̬i] *n* : prévisibilité *f*

predictable [pri'dɪktəbəl] *adj* : prévisible

predictably [pri'dɪktəbli] *adv* : comme prévu

prediction [pri'dɪkʃən] *n* : prédiction *f*

predilection [ˌprɛdəl'ɛkʃən, ˌpri:-] *n* : prédilection *f*

predispose [ˌpri:dɪ'spo:z] *vt* : prédisposer

predisposition [ˌpri:ˌdɪspə'zɪʃən] *n* : prédisposition *f*

predominance [pri'dɑmənən*t*s] *n* : prédominance *f*

predominant [pri'dɑmənənt] *adj* : prédominant

predominantly [pri'dɑmənəntli] *adv* MAINLY : principalement

predominate [pri'dɑməˌneɪt] *vt* **-nated; -nating** : prédominer

preeminence [pri'ɛmənən*t*s] *n* : prééminence *f*

preeminent [pri'ɛmənənt] *adj* : prééminent

preeminently [pri'ɛmənəntli] *adv* : surtout, avant tout

preempt [pri'ɛmpt] *vt* **1** : préempter (un terrain) **2** APPROPRIATE : s'approprier, s'attribuer

preen ['pri:n] *vt* **1** : lisser (ses plumes) **2 to preen oneself** : se bichonner, se pomponner

prefabricated [ˌpri:'fæbrəˌkeɪt̬əd] *adj* : préfabriqué

preface[1] ['prɛfəs] *vt* **-aced; -acing** : préfacer (un livre), faire précéder (un discours, etc.)

preface[2] *n* : préface *f*

prefatory ['prɛfəˌtori] *adj* : préliminaire

prefect ['priˌfɛkt] *n* : préfet *m*

prefer [pri'fər] *vt* **-ferred; -ferring 1** : préférer <he prefers sports to reading : il préfère les sports à la lecture> **2 to prefer charges** : porter plainte

preferable ['prɛfərəbəl] *adj* : préférable — **preferably** [-bli] *adv*

preference ['prɛfrən*t*s, 'prɛfər-] *n* : préférence *f*, choix *m*

preferential [ˌprɛfə'rɛntʃəl] *adj* : préférentiel

prefigure [pri'fɪgjər] *vt* **-ured; -uring** : préfigurer, annoncer

prefix[1] ['pri:ˌfɪks, pri:'-] *vt* : préfixer (en linguistique)

prefix[2] ['pri:ˌfɪks] *n* : préfixe *m*

pregnancy ['prɛgnən*t*si] *n, pl* **-cies** : grossesse *f*

pregnant ['prɛgnənt] *adj* **1** : enceinte, grosse **2** MEANINGFUL : profond, chargé de sens

preheat [ˌpri:'hi:t] *vt* : préchauffer

prehensile [pri'hɛn*t*səl, -'hɛnˌsaɪl] *adj* : préhensile

prehistoric [ˌpri:hɪs'tɔrɪk] *or* **prehistorical** [-ɪkəl] *adj* : préhistorique

prejudge [ˌpri:'dʒʌdʒ] *vt* **-judged; -judging** : préjuger

prejudice[1] ['prɛdʒədəs] *vt* **-diced; -dicing 1** : porter préjudice à (en droit) **2 to be prejudiced against** : avoir des préjugés contre

prejudice[2] *n* **1** DAMAGES : préjudice *m*, dommage *m* **2** BIAS : préjugés *mpl*

prelate [ˈprɛlət] *n* : prélat *m*

preliminary[1] [priˈlɪməˌnɛri] *adj* : préliminaire

preliminary[2] *n, pl* **-naries** : préliminaire *m*

prelude [ˈprɛˌluːd, ˈprɛlˌjuːd; ˈpreɪˌluːd, ˈpriː-] *n* : prélude *m*

premarital [ˌpriːˈmærəṭəl] *adj* : avant le mariage, prénuptial

premature [ˌpriːməˈtʊr, -ˈtjʊr, -ˈtʃʊr] *adj* : prématuré — **prematurely** *adv*

premeditate [priˈmɛdəˌteɪt] *vt* **-tated; -tating** : préméditer

premeditation [priˌmɛdəˈteɪʃən] *n* : préméditation *f*

premenstrual [priˈmɛnᵗstruəl] *adj* : prémenstruel

premier[1] [priˈmɪr, -ˈmjɪr; ˈpriːmiər] *adj* : premier

premier[2] → **prime minister**

premiere[1] [prɪˈmjɛr, -ˈmɪr] *vi* **-miered; -miering** : se donner en première

premiere[2] *n* : première *f* (d'un spectacle)

premise [ˈprɛmɪs] *n* **1** : prémisse *f* (d'un raisonnement) **2 premises** *npl* : lieux *mpl* <on the premises : sur les lieux>

premium [ˈpriːmiəm] *n* **1** BONUS : prime *f*, supplément *m* **2** *or* **insurance premium** : prime *f* d'assurance **3 to put a premium on** : mettre au premier plan **4 to sell at a premium** : vendre au-dessus du pair

premonition [ˌpriːməˈnɪʃən, ˌprɛmə-] *n* : prémonition *f*, pressentiment *m*

prenatal [ˌpriːˈneɪṭəl] *adj* : prénatal

preoccupation [priˌɑkjəˈpeɪʃən] *n* : préoccupation *f*

preoccupied [priˈɑkjəˌpaɪd] *adj* : préoccupé, distrait

preoccupy [priˈɑkjəˌpaɪ] *vt* **-pied; -pying** : préoccuper

preparation [ˌprɛpəˈreɪʃən] *n* **1** PREPARING : préparation *f* <the preparation of meals : la préparation des repas> **2 preparations** *npl* : préparatifs *mpl*

preparatory [priˈpærəˌtori] *adj* : préparatoire

prepare [prɪˈpær] *v* **-pared; -paring** *vt* : préparer — *vi* : se préparer

prepay [ˌpriːˈpeɪ] *vt* **-paid; -paying** : payer d'avance

preponderance [prɪˈpɑndərənᵗs] *n* : prépondérance *f*

preponderant [prɪˈpɑndərənt] *adj* : prépondérant

preponderantly [prɪˈpɑndərəntli] *adv* : de façon prépondérante

preposition [ˌprɛpəˈzɪʃən] *n* : préposition *f*

prepositional [ˌprɛpəˈzɪʃənəl] *adj* : prépositionnel

prepossessing [ˌpriːpəˈzɛsɪŋ] *adj* : attrayant, avenant

preposterous [priˈpɑstərəs] *adj* : absurde, insensé

prerecorded [priːrɪˈkɔrdəd] *adj* : en différé

prerequisite[1] [priˈrɛkwəzət] *adj* : nécessaire au préalable

prerequisite[2] *n* : préalable *m*, préreequis *m Can*

prerogative [prɪˈrɑgəṭɪv] *n* : prérogative *f*

presage[1] [ˈprɛsɪdʒ, prɪˈseɪdʒ] *vt* **-saged; -saging** : présager

presage[2] [ˈprɛsɪdʒ] *n* : présage *m*

preschool [ˈpriːˌskuːl] *adj* : préscolaire

prescribe [priˈskraɪb] *vt* **-scribed; -scribing 1** RECOMMEND : préconiser, recommander **2** : prescrire (en médecine)

prescription [priˈskrɪpʃən] *n* : prescription *f*

presence [ˈprɛzənᵗs] *n* : présence *f*

present[1] [prɪˈzɛnt] *vt* **1** INTRODUCE : présenter **2** SHOW : présenter, donner, montrer <to present a play : présenter une pièce> **3** GIVE : offrir, présenter <the winner was presented with a medal : on a présenté une médaille au gagnant>

present[2] [ˈprɛzənt] *adj* **1** CURRENT : actuel <present conditions : conditions actuelles> **2** ATTENDING : présent

present[3] [ˈprɛzənt] *n* **1** GIFT : cadeau *m* **2** *or* **present time** : présent *m* <at present : actuellement>

presentation [ˌpriːˌzɛnˈteɪʃən, ˌprɛzən-] *n* : présentation *f*

presentiment [priˈzɛntəmənt] *n* : pressentiment *m*, prémonition *f*

presently [ˈprɛzəntli] *adv* **1** SOON : bientôt **2** NOW : à présent, en ce moment

present participle *n* : participe *m* présent

preservation [ˌprɛzərˈveɪʃən] *n* : préservation *f*, maintien *m*

preservative [priˈzərvəṭɪv] *n* : agent *m* de conservation

preserve[1] [priˈzərv] *vt* **-served; -serving 1** PROTECT : préserver, protéger **2** MAINTAIN : garder, conserver <to preserve silence : garder le silence>

preserve[2] *n* **1** : chasse *f* réservée, réserve *f* <game preserve : chasse gardée> **2 preserves** *npl* : confitures *fpl*

preside [priˈzaɪd] *vi* **-sided; -siding 1 to preside over** : présider <to preside over a meeting : présider une réunion> **2 to preside over** OVERSEE : présider à

presidency [ˈprɛzədənᵗsi] *n, pl* **-cies** : présidence *f*

president [ˈprɛzədənt] *n* : président *m*

presidential [ˌprɛzəˈdɛntʃəl] *adj* : présidentiel

press[1] [ˈprɛs] *vt* **1** PUSH : presser, appuyer sur **2** IRON : repasser **3** SQUEEZE : presser **4** URGE : presser, inciter — *vi* **1** PUSH : appuyer (sur un bouton, etc.) **2** CROWD : se presser **3 to press through** : se frayer un chemin dans

press[2] *n* **1** CROWD : foule *f* **2** *or* **printing press** : presse *f* <to go to press : mettre sous presse> **3** URGENCY : urgence *f* **4** : presse *f* <the story is getting good press : l'article a bonne presse> **5** PUBLISHER : maison *f* d'édition, presses *fpl* **6** PRINTER : imprimerie *f*

pressing [ˈprɛsɪŋ] *adj* : pressant, urgent

pressure[1] [ˈprɛʃər] *vt* **-sured; -suring** : pousser, faire pression sur

pressure[2] *n* **1** : pression *f* <to be under pressure : être sous pression> **2** → **blood pressure**

pressurize [ˈprɛʃəˌraɪz] *vt* **-ized; -izing** : pressuriser

prestidigitation [ˌprɛstəˌdɪdʒəˈteɪʃən] *n* SLEIGHT OF HAND : prestidigitation *f*

prestige [prɛˈstiʒ, -ˈstiːdʒ] *n* : prestige *m*

prestigious [prɛˈstɪdʒəs, -ˈsti-, prə-] *adj* : prestigieux

presto [ˈprɛsˌtoː] *adv & interj* : presto!, tout de suite

presumably [priˈzuːməbli] adv : vraisemblablement, apparemment, présumément *Can*

presume [priˈzuːm] *vt* **-sumed; -suming** **1** DARE : se permettre <he presumed to contradict him : il s'est permis de le contredire> **2** ASSUME : présumer, supposer <to be presumed innocent : être présumé innocent> **3** IMPLY : présupposer, laisser supposer

presumption [prɪˈzʌmpʃən] *n* **1** EFFRONTERY : présomption *f*, arrogance *f* **2** ASSUMPTION : présomption *f*, supposition *f*

presumptuous [prɪˈzʌmptʃʊəs] *adj* : présomptueux, prétentieux

presuppose [ˌpriːsəˈpoːz] *vt* **-posed; -posing** : présupposer

presupposition [ˌpriːˌsəpəˈzɪʃən] *n* : présupposition *f*

pretend [priˈtɛnd] *vt* **1** PROFESS : prétendre <he doesn't pretend to be a psychiatrist : il ne prétend pas être psychiatre> **2** FEIGN : feindre, simuler <to pretend friendship : feindre l'amitié> — *vi* : faire semblant

pretense *or* **pretence** [ˈpriːˌtɛnts, priˈtɛnts] *n* **1** CLAIM : prétention *f* **2** : semblant *m*, simulacre *m* <to make a pretense of : faire semblant de> **3** SIMULATION : faux-semblant *m*

pretension [priˈtɛntʃən] *n* **1** CLAIM : prétention *f*, revendication *f* **2** PRETENTIOUSNESS : prétention *f* **3** ASPIRATION : ambition *f*, aspiration *f*

pretentious [priˈtɛntʃəs] *adj* : prétentieux — **pretentiously** *adv*

pretentiousness [priˈtɛntʃəsnəs] *n* : prétention *f*

pretext [ˈpriːˌtɛkst] *n* : prétexte *m*, excuse *f*

prettily [ˈprɪtəli] *adv* : joliment

prettiness [ˈprɪtinəs] *n* : beauté *f*

pretty[1] [ˈprɪti] *vt* **-tied; -tying** *or* **to pretty up** : enjoliver

pretty[2] *adv* FAIRLY : assez

pretty[3] *adj* **prettier; -est** : joli, beau <pretty flowers : de jolies fleurs> <it's not a pretty sight : ce n'est pas beau à voir>

pretzel [ˈprɛtsəl] *n* : bretzel *m*

prevail [priˈveɪl] *vi* **1** TRIUMPH : prévaloir, l'emporter **2** PREDOMINATE : prévaloir, prédominer **3 to prevail upon** : persuader

prevalence [ˈprɛvələnts] *n* : fréquence *f*, prédominance *f*, prévalence *f* (d'une maladie)

prevalent [ˈprɛvələnt] *adj* : répandu, commun

prevaricate [priˈværəˌkeɪt] *vi* **-cated; -cating** : tergiverser, user de détours

prevarication [priˌværəˈkeɪʃən] *n* : tergiversation *f*, faux-fuyant *m*

prevent [priˈvɛnt] *vt* **1** AVOID : prévenir, éviter **2** STOP : empêcher <bad weather prevented us from leaving : le mauvais temps nous a empêchés de partir>

preventable [priˈvɛntəbəl] *adj* : évitable

preventative [priˈvɛntətɪv] → **preventive**

prevention [priˈvɛntʃən] *n* : prévention *f*

preventive [priˈvɛntɪv] *adj* : préventif

preview [ˈpriːˌvju] *n* : avant-première *f*

previous [ˈpriːviəs] *adj* : antérieur, précédent, initial <his previous position : sa position initiale> <a previous era : une époque antérieure> <the previous paragraph : le paragraphe précédent>

previously [ˈpriːviəsli] *adv* : antérieurement, auparavant

prewar [ˌpriːˈwɔr] *adj* : d'avant-guerre

prey[1] [ˈpreɪ] *vi* **1 to prey on** : faire sa proie de **2 to prey on s.o.'s mind** : ronger l'esprit à qqn

prey[2] *ns & pl* : proie *f*

price[1] [ˈpraɪs] *vt* **priced; pricing** : fixer un prix sur

price[2] *n* : prix *m*

priceless [ˈpraɪsləs] *adj* : inestimable

prick[1] [ˈprɪk] *vt* **1** PIERCE : piquer, percer **2** GOAD : aiguillonner, piquer <guilt was pricking (at) his conscience : les remords aiguillonnaient sa conscience> **3 to prick up one's ears** : dresser l'oreille

prick[2] *n* : piqûre *f*

pricker [ˈprɪkər] *n* THORN : épine *f*

prickle[1] [ˈprɪkəl] *vt* **-led; -ling** : picoter

prickle[2] *n* **1** THORN : épine *f* (d'un rosier, etc.) **2** STING : picotement *m*

prickly [ˈprɪkəli] *adj* **pricklier; -est** **1** STINGING : épineux, piquant <a prickly sensation : une sensation de

picotement> **2** THORNY : épineux <prickly issues : questions épineuses>

pride[1] ['praɪd] *vt* **prided; priding** *or* **to pride oneself** : être fier

pride[2] *n* : fierté *f*, orgueil *m*

prideful ['praɪdfəl] *adj* : hautain, arrogant

priest ['pri:st] *n* : prêtre *m*

priestess ['pri:stɪs] *n* : prêtresse *f*

priesthood ['pri:st,hʊd] *n* : prêtrise *f*

priestly ['pri:stli] *adj* : sacerdotal

prim ['prɪm] *adj* **primmer; primmest** : collet monté, guindé

primarily [praɪ'mɛrəli] *adv* **1** ORIGINALLY : d'abord, à l'origine **2** PRINCIPALLY : essentiellement, principalement

primary[1] ['praɪ,mɛri, 'praɪməri] *adj* **1** FIRST : primaire <primary education : enseignement primaire> **2** PRINCIPAL : principal **3** BASIC : fondamental, de base

primary[2] *n, pl* **-ries** : élection *f* primaire

primary school → **elementary school**

primate ['praɪ,meɪt, -mət] *n* : primate *m*

prime[1] ['praɪm] *vt* **primed; priming 1** FILL, LOAD : remplir, charger **2** PREPARE : apprêter (une surface, un mur) **3** COACH : préparer <to prime a witness : préparer un témoin>

prime[2] *adj* : de première qualité, de premier choix

prime[3] *n* **in the prime of one's life** : dans la force de l'âge

prime minister *n* : Premier ministre *m*

primer[1] ['prɪmər] *n* : premier livre *m* de lecture, abécédaire *m*

primer[2] ['praɪmər] *n* **1** : amorce *f* (d'un explosif) **2** *or* **prime coat** : apprêt *m*

primeval [praɪ'mi:vəl] *adj* : primitif

primitive ['prɪmət̬ɪv] *adj* : primitif

primly ['prɪmli] *adv* : d'une façon guindée

primness ['prɪmnəs] *n* : air *m* collet monté

primordial [praɪ'mɔrdiəl] *adj* : primordial

primp ['prɪmp] *vt* : se pomponner, se bichonner

primrose ['prɪm,ro:z] *n* : primevère *f*

prince ['prɪnts] *n* : prince *m*

princely ['prɪntsli] *adj* : princier

princess ['prɪntsəs, 'prɪn,sɛs] *n* : princesse *f*

principal[1] ['prɪntsəpəl] *adj* : principal — **principally** *adv*

principal[2] *n* **1** : directeur *m*, -trice *f* <school principal : directeur d'école> **2** : principal *m* (d'une dette), capital *m* (d'une somme)

principality [,prɪntsə'pæləṭi] *n, pl* **-ties** : principauté *f*

principle ['prɪntsəpəl] *n* : principe *m*

print[1] ['prɪnt] *vt* : imprimer (un texte, etc.) — *vi* : écrire en lettres moulées

print[2] *n* **1** IMPRESSION, MARK : empreinte *f* **2** LETTER : caractère *m* <in fine print : en petits caractères> **3** ENGRAVING : gravure *f* **4** : imprimé *m* (d'un tissu) **5** : épreuve *f* (en photographie) **6 in ~** : disponible

printer ['prɪnt̬ər] *n* **1** : imprimeur *m* (personne) **2** : imprimante *f* (machine) <laser printer : imprimante laser>

printing ['prɪntɪŋ] *n* **1** : imprimerie *f* (technique) **2** IMPRESSION : impression *f* <the second printing : le second tirage> **3** LETTERING : écriture *f* en lettres moulées

printout ['prɪnt,aʊt] *n* : sortie *f* sur imprimante

print out *vt* : faire une sortie sur imprimante

prior ['praɪər] *adj* **1** PREVIOUS : antérieur, précédent **2** : qui prévaut, prioritaire <a prior claim : un droit de priorité>

priority [praɪ'ɔrəṭi] *n, pl* **-ties** : priorité *f*

priory ['praɪəri] *n, pl* **-ries** : prieuré *m*

prism ['prɪzəm] *n* : prisme *m*

prison ['prɪzən] *n* : prison *f*

prisoner ['prɪzənər] *n* : prisonnier *m*, -nière *f*

prissy ['prɪsi] *adj* **prissier; -est** : collet monté

pristine ['prɪs,ti:n, prɪs'-] *adj* : pur, immaculé

privacy ['praɪvəsi] *n, pl* **-cies 1** SECLUSION, SOLITUDE : intimité *f*, solitude *f* **2** : vie *f* privée <the right to privacy : le droit à la vie privée>

private[1] ['praɪvət] *adj* **1** : privé <private property : propriété privée> **2** PERSONAL : personnel, privé

private[2] *n* : soldat *m* de deuxième classe

privateer [,praɪvə'tɪr] *n* : corsaire *m*

privately ['praɪvətli] *adv* **1** SECRETLY : en privé **2 privately owned** : privé

privation [praɪ'veɪʃən] *n* : privation *f*

privilege ['prɪvlɪdʒ, 'prɪvə-] *n* : privilège *m*

privileged ['prɪvlɪdʒd, 'prɪvə-] *adj* : privilégié

privy ['prɪvi] *adj* **to be privy to** : être au courant de

prize[1] ['praɪz] *vt* **prized; prizing** : priser, chérir

prize[2] *adj* **1** PRIZEWINNING : primé **2** OUTSTANDING : remarquable, exceptionnel

prize[3] *n* : prix *m*

prizefight ['praɪz,faɪt] *n* : combat *m* de boxe

prizefighter ['praɪz,faɪṭər] *n* : boxeur *m* professionnel

prizefighting ['praɪz,faɪṭɪŋ] *n* : boxe *f* professionnelle

prizewinner ['praɪz,wɪnər] *n* : gagnant *m*, -gnante *f*

prizewinning [ˈpraɪzˌwɪnɪŋ] *adj* : primé, qui remporte le prix

pro[1] [ˈproː] *adv* **to argue pro** : argumenter en faveur

pro[2] *adj* → **professional**

pro[3] *n* **1** → **professional 2 the pros and cons** : le pour et le contre

probability [ˌprɑbəˈbɪləṭi] *n, pl* **-ties** : probabilité *f*

probable [ˈprɑbəbəl] *adj* : probable — **probably** [-bli] *adv*

probate[1] [ˈproːˌbeɪt] *vt* **-bated; -bating** : homologuer (un testament)

probate[2] *n* : homologation *f*

probation [proˈbeɪʃən] *n* **1** *or* **probation period** : mise *f* à l'essai, probation *f* **2 on ~** : en sursis avec mise à l'épreuve (en droit)

probationary [proˈbeɪʃəˌnɛri] *adj* **1** : d'essai <probationary period : période d'essai> **2** : de sursis, de probation (en droit)

probe[1] [ˈproːb] *vt* **probed; probing 1** EXAMINE : sonder **2** INVESTIGATE : enquêter sur

probe[2] *n* **1** : sonde *f* (en médecine) **2** INVESTIGATION : enquête *f*, investigation *f*

probity [ˈproːbəṭi] *n* : probité *f*

problem[1] [ˈprɑbləm] *adj* : difficile <a problem child : un enfant difficile>

problem[2] *n* : problème *m*

problematic [ˌprɑbləˈmæṭɪk] *or* **problematical** [-ṭɪkəl] *adj* : problématique

proboscis [prəˈbɑsɪs] *n, pl* **-cises** : trompe *f*

procedural [prəˈsiːdʒərəl] *adj* : de procédure

procedure [prəˈsiːdʒər] *n* : procédure *f*

proceed [proˈsiːd] *vi* **1** ADVANCE : avancer, aller **2** ACT : procéder **3** CONTINUE : continuer, poursuivre **4 to proceed from** : provenir de

proceeding [proˈsiːdɪŋ] *n* **1** : procédure *f* <a divorce proceeding : une procédure de divorce> **2** *or* **legal proceeding** : poursuite *f* judiciaire

proceeds [ˈproːˌsiːdz] *npl* : recette *f*, argent *m* recueilli

process[1] [ˈprɑˌsɛs, ˈproː-] *vt* **1** : traiter <to process one's request : traiter sa demande> **2** : traiter, transformer <processed cheese : fromage en tranches>

process[2] *n, pl* **-cesses** [ˈprɑˌsɛsəz, ˈproː-, -səsəz, -səˌsiːz] **1** : processus *m* <the process of growth : le processus de croissance> **2** METHOD : procédé *m* <a manufacturing process : un procédé de fabrication> **3** : procès *m* (en droit) **4** SUMMONS : citation *f* **5** PROJECTION : excroissance *f* (en biologie) **6 in the process of** : en train de

procession [prəˈsɛʃən] *n* : procession *f*

processional [prəˈsɛʃənəl] *n* : musique *f* processionnelle

processor [ˈprɑˌsɛsər, ˈproː-, -səsər] *n* : processeur *m* (en informatique)

proclaim [proˈkleɪm] *vt* : proclamer

proclamation [ˌprɑkləˈmeɪʃən] *n* : proclamation *f*

proclivity [proˈklɪvəṭi] *n, pl* **-ties** : propension *f*, tendance *f*, inclination *f*

procrastinate [prəˈkræstəˌneɪt] *vi* **-nated; -nating** : remettre à plus tard, remettre au lendemain

procrastination [prəˌkræstəˈneɪʃən] *n* : tendance *f* à tout remettre à plus tard

procreate [ˈproːkriˌeɪt] *v* **-ated; -ating** *vt* : procréer — *vi* REPRODUCE : se reproduire

procreation [ˌproːkriˈeɪʃən] *n* : procréation *f*

proctor[1] [ˈprɑktər] *vt* : surveiller (un examen)

proctor[2] *n* : surveillant *m*, -lante *f* (à un examen)

procurable [prəˈkjʊrəbəl] *adj* : que l'on peut se procurer

procure [prəˈkjʊr] *vt* **-cured; -curing** : obtenir, se procurer

procurement [prəˈkjʊrmənt] *n* : achat *m*, acquisition *f*

prod[1] [ˈprɑd] *vt* **prodded; prodding 1** POKE : pousser doucement, donner des petits coups à **2** GOAD, URGE : inciter

prod[2] *n* **1** POKE : petit coup *m*, poussée *f* **2** GOAD : aiguillon *m* <cattle prod : aiguillon pour le bétail>

prodigal[1] [ˈprɑdɪgəl] *adj* : prodigue

prodigal[2] *n* : prodigue *mf*

prodigality [ˌprɑdəˈgæləṭi] *n* : prodigalité *f*

prodigious [prəˈdɪdʒəs] *adj* **1** EXTRAORDINARY : prodigieux, extraordinaire **2** HUGE : énorme, monstre — **prodigiously** *adv*

prodigy [ˈprɑdədʒi] *n, pl* **-gies** : prodige *m*

produce[1] [prəˈduːs, -ˈdjuːs] *vt* **-duced; -ducing 1** : donner naissance à, engendrer (un enfant), produire (une œuvre), causer (un problème, etc.) **2** MAKE, MANUFACTURE : faire, produire, fabriquer **3** YIELD : produire, rapporter **4** EXHIBIT : présenter <to produce evidence : fournir des preuves> **5** STAGE : présenter, mettre en scène

produce[2] [ˈprɑˌduːs, ˈproː-, -ˌdjuːs] *n* : produits *mpl* agricoles

producer [prəˈduːsər, -ˈdjuː-] *n* : producteur *m*, -trice *f*

product [ˈprɑˌdʌkt] *n* : produit *m*

production [prəˈdʌkʃən] *n* : production *f*

productive [prəˈdʌktɪv] *adj* : productif

productivity [ˌproːˌdʌkˈtɪvəṭi, ˌprɑ-] *n* : productivité *f*

profane[1] [proˈfeɪn] *vt* **-faned; -faning** : profaner

profane[2] *adj* **1** SECULAR : profane **2** IRREVERENT : sacrilège, blasphématoire
profanity [pro'fænəṭi] *n, pl* **-ties 1** IRREVERENCE : impiété *f* **2** BLASPHEMY : blasphème *m,* juron *m*
profess [prə'fɛs] *vt* **1** DECLARE : professer, affirmer **2** : professer (sa foi)
professedly [prə'fɛsədli] *adv* **1** AVOWEDLY : de son propre aveu **2** ALLEGEDLY, SUPPOSEDLY : soi-disant, prétendument
profession [prə'fɛʃən] *n* **1** DECLARATION : profession *f* (de foi, etc.) **2** OCCUPATION : profession *f,* occupation *f*
professional[1] [prə'fɛʃənəl] *adj* : professionnel — **professionally** *adv*
professional[2] *n* : professionnel *m,* -nelle *f*
professionalism [prə'fɛʃənə,lɪzəm] *n* : professionnalisme *m*
professor [prə'fɛsər] *n* : professeur *m* (de faculté)
proffer ['prɑfər] *vt* **-fered; -fering** : tendre, offrir
proficiency [prə'fɪʃəntsi] *n, pl* **-cies** : compétence *f,* capacité *f*
proficient [prə'fɪʃənt] *adj* : compétent, capable — **proficiently** *adv*
profile[1] ['pro:,faɪl] *vt* **-filed; -filing** : profiler
profile[2] *n* : profil *m*
profit[1] ['prɑfət] *vi* **to profit from** : tirer profit de — *vt* BENEFIT : profiter à
profit[2] *n* **1** GAIN : profit *m,* bénéfice *m* <to make a profit : faire un bénéfice> <profit and loss : pertes et profits> **2** ADVANTAGE : avantage *m,* profit *m*
profitable ['prɑfətəbəl] *adj* : profitable — **profitably** [-bli] *adv*
profitless ['prɑfətləs] *adj* : qui ne rapporte pas de profits, sans profits
profligate ['prɑflɪgət, -,geɪt] *adj* **1** IMMORAL : licentieux, débauché **2** EXTRAVAGANT : prodigue, dépensier
profound [prə'faʊnd] *adj* : profond
profoundly [prə'faʊndli] *adv* : profondément
profundity [prə'fʌndəṭi] *n, pl* **-ties** : profondeur *f*
profuse [prə'fju:s] *adj* **1** BOUNTIFUL : abondant **2** LAVISH : prodigue <they were profuse in their thanks : ils se confondaient en remerciements>
profusely [prə'fju:sli] *adv* : abondamment
profusion [prə'fju:ʒən] *n* : profusion *f,* abondance *f*
progeny ['prɑdʒəni] *n, pl* **-nies** : progéniture *f,* descendance *f*
progesterone [pro'dʒɛstə,ro:n] *n* : progestérone *f*
prognosis [prɑg'no:sɪs] *n, pl* **-noses** [-,si:z] : pronostic *m*
program[1] *or Brit* **programme** ['pro:,græm, -grəm] *vt* **-grammed** *or* **-gramed; -gramming** *or* **-graming** : programmer
program[2] *or Brit* **programme** *n* **1** : programme *m* (d'un concert, etc.) **2** PLAN : programme *m,* plan *m* **3** : programme *m* (d'un ordinateur) **4** SHOW : émission *f* <television program : émission de télévision>
programmable ['pro:,græməbəl] *adj* : programmable
programme *Brit* → **program**
programmer ['pro:,græmər] *n* : programmeur *m,* -meuse *f*
progress[1] [prə'grɛs] *vi* **1** PROCEED : progresser, avancer **2** IMPROVE : progresser, s'améliorer
progress[2] ['prɑgrəs, -,grɛs] *n* : progrès *m*
progression [prə'grɛʃən] *n* **1** ADVANCE : progression *f,* avancement *m* **2** SERIES : progression *f,* suite *f*
progressive [prə'grɛsɪv] *adj* **1** : progressiste (en politique, etc.) **2** : progressif <a progressive city : une ville progressive> **3** GRADUAL : progressif, graduel
progressively [prə'grɛsɪvli] *adv* : progressivement
prohibit [pro'hɪbət] *vt* **1** FORBID : interdire, défendre **2** PREVENT : empêcher, rendre impossible
prohibition [,pro:ə'bɪʃən, ,pro:hə-] *n* **1** : interdiction *f,* défense *f* **2** : prohibition *f* (de l'alcool)
prohibitive [pro'hɪbəṭɪv] *adj* : prohibitif
project[1] [prə'dʒɛkt] *vt* **1** DESIGN, PLAN : faire un plan de **2** HURL, THRUST : projeter, lancer — *vi* PROTRUDE : faire saillie
project[2] ['prɑ,dʒɛkt, -dʒɪkt] *n* **1** PLAN : projet *m,* plan *m* **2** *or* **research project** : étude *f* **3** *or* **school project** : travail *m* pratique
projectile [prə'dʒɛktəl, -,taɪl] *n* : projectile *m*
projection [prə'dʒɛkʃən] *n* **1** PROTRUSION : saillie *f* **2** : projection *f* (d'une image) **3** ESTIMATE : projection *f,* prévision *f*
projector [prə'dʒɛktər] *n* : projecteur *m*
proletarian[1] [,pro:lə'tɛriən] *adj* : prolétaire, prolétarien
proletarian[2] *n* : prolétaire *mf*
proletariat [,pro:lə'tɛriət] *n* : prolétariat *m*
proliferate [prə'lɪfə,reɪt] *vi* **-ated; -ating** : proliférer
proliferation [prə,lɪfə'reɪʃən] *n* : prolifération *f*
prolific [prə'lɪfɪk] *adj* : prolifique, fécond — **prolifically** [-fɪkli] *adv*
prologue ['pro:,lɔg, -,lɑg] *n* : prologue *m,* préface *f*
prolong [prə'lɔŋ] *vt* : prolonger
prolongation [,pro:,lɔŋ'geɪʃən] *n* : prolongation *f*
prom ['prɑm] *n* : bal *m* d'étudiants
promenade[1] [,prɑmə'neɪd, -'nɑd] *vi* **-naded; -nading** : se promener

promenade[2] *n* : promenade *f*
prominence [ˈprɑmənənts] *n* **1** PROTUBERANCE : proéminence *f* **2** EMINENCE : distinction *f*
prominent [ˈprɑmənənt] *adj* **1** PROTRUDING : proéminent **2** CONSPICUOUS : bien en vue **3** LEADING : de premier plan **4** WELL-KNOWN : connu, célèbre
prominently [ˈprɑmənəntli] *adv* : bien en vue, en évidence
promiscuity [ˌprɑmɪsˈkjuːət̬i] *n, pl* **-ties** : promiscuité *f* sexuelle
promiscuous [prəˈmɪskjʊəs] *adj* : de mœurs légères
promise[1] [ˈprɑməs] *v* **-mised; -mising** : promettre
promise[2] *n* : promesse *f*
promising [ˈprɑməsɪŋ] *adj* : prometteur
promissory [ˈprɑməˌsori] *adj* : à ordre <a promissory note : un billet à ordre>
promontory [ˈprɑmənˌtori] *n, pl* **-ries** : promontoire *m*
promote [prəˈmoːt] *vt* **-moted; -moting 1** ADVANCE : promouvoir (un employé) **2** ADVERTISE : faire la promotion de **3** FURTHER : promouvoir, contribuer à
promoter [prəˈmoːt̬ər] *n* : promoteur *m*, -trice *f*
promotion [prəˈmoːʃən] *n* : promotion *f*
promotional [prəˈmoːʃənəl] *adj* : promotionnel
prompt[1] [ˈprɑmpt] *vt* **1** INCITE, INDUCE : inciter, pousser **2** CUE : souffler son rôle à (un acteur)
prompt[2] *adj* **1** PUNCTUAL : ponctuel **2** QUICK : prompt <to be prompt to answer : avoir la repartie prompte>
prompter [ˈprɑmptər] *n* : souffleur *m*, -fleuse *f* (au théâtre)
promptly [ˈprɑmptli] *adv* QUICKLY : immédiatement, sans délai
promptness [ˈprɑmptnəs] *n* : promptitude *f*
prone [ˈproːn] *adj* **1** APT : sujet, enclin <she's prone to forget names : elle a tendance à oublier les noms> <accident-prone : sujet aux accidents> **2** FLAT : à plat ventre <to lie prone : être allongé sur le ventre>
prong [ˈprɔŋ] *n* : dent *f*
pronged [ˈprɔŋd] *adj* : à dents
pronoun [ˈproːˌnaʊn] *n* : pronom *m*
pronounce [prəˈnaʊnts] *vt* **-nounced; -nouncing 1** : prononcer, rendre (un jugement) **2** SAY : prononcer (un mot) **3** DECLARE : déclarer, prononcer
pronounced [prəˈnaʊntst] *adj* DECIDED : prononcé, marqué
pronouncement [prəˈnaʊntsmənt] *n* : déclaration *f*
pronunciation [prəˌnʌntsiˈeɪʃən] *n* : prononciation *f*
proof[1] [ˈpruːf] *adj* : à l'épreuve <proof against tampering : à l'épreuve de l'altération>
proof[2] *n* **1** EVIDENCE : preuve *f* <proof of purchase : preuve d'achat> **2** PRINT : épreuve *f* (en photographie) **3 proofs** *npl* : épreuves *fpl* (d'un manuscrit)
proofread [ˈpruːfˌriːd] *vt* **-read** [-ˌrɛd]; **-reading** : corriger les épreuves de
proofreader [ˈpruːfˌriːdər] *n* : correcteur *m*, -trice *f* d'épreuves
prop[1] [ˈprɑp] *vt* **propped; propping 1** LEAN : appuyer **2 to prop up** SUPPORT, SUSTAIN : étayer, soutenir
prop[2] *n* **1** SUPPORT : étai *m* **2 props** *npl* : accessoires *mpl* (au théâtre)
propaganda [ˌprɑpəˈgændə, ˌproː-] *n* : propagande *f*
propagandize [ˌprɑpəˈgænˌdaɪz, ˌproː-] *vi* **-dized; -dizing** : faire de la propagande
propagate [ˈprɑpəˌgeɪt] *v* **-gated; -gating** *vt* : propager — *vi* : se propager
propagation [ˌprɑpəˈgeɪʃən] *n* : propagation *f*
propane [ˈproːˌpeɪn] *n* : propane *m*
propel [prəˈpɛl] *vt* **-pelled; -pelling** : propulser
propellant[1] [prəˈpɛlənt] *adj* : propulsif
propellant[2] *n* : propergol *m* (pour les roquettes), gaz *m* propulseur
propeller [prəˈpɛlər] *n* : hélice *f*
propensity [prəˈpɛntsət̬i] *n, pl* **-ties** : propension *f*, tendance *f*
proper [ˈprɑpər] *adj* **1** FIT : juste, approprié **2** : même, proprement dit <the city proper : la ville même> **3** CORRECT : correct, convenable
properly [ˈprɑpərli] *adv* **1** WELL : correctement, convenablement, comme du monde *Can* **2 properly speaking** : à proprement parler
property [ˈprɑpərt̬i] *n, pl* **-ties 1** QUALITY : propriété *f*, qualité *f* **2** POSSESSIONS : biens *mpl* **3** REAL ESTATE : biens *mpl* immobiliers
prophecy [ˈprɑfəsi] *n, pl* **-cies** : prophétie *f*, prédiction *f*
prophesy [ˈprɑfəˌsaɪ] *vt* **-sied; -sying** : prophétiser, prédire
prophet [ˈprɑfət] *n* : prophète *m*, prophétesse *f*
prophetic [prəˈfɛt̬ɪk] *adj* : prophétique — **prophetically** [-t̬ɪkli] *adv*
propitiate [proˈpɪʃiˌeɪt] *vt* **-ated; -ating** : se concilier, apaiser
propitious [prəˈpɪʃəs] *adj* : propice
proponent [prəˈpoːnənt] *n* : partisan *m*, -sane *f*
proportion[1] [prəˈporʃən] *vt* : proportionner
proportion[2] *n* **1** RATIO : proportion *f*, rapport *m* **2** SYMMETRY : proportion *f*, équilibre *m* <to be out of proportion : être disproportionné> **3** SHARE

: part *f* **4 proportions** *npl* SIZE : dimensions *fpl*

proportional [prəˈporʃənəl] *adj* : proportionnel — **proportionally** *adv*

proportionate [prəˈporʃənət] *adj* : proportionnel — **proportionately** *adv*

proposal [prəˈpo:zəl] *n* : proposition *f*

propose [prəˈpo:z] *v* **-posed; -posing** *vt* **1** SUGGEST : proposer, suggérer **2** INTEND : (se) proposer, penser **3** NOMINATE : proposer, présenter — *vi* : faire une demande en mariage

proposition [ˌprɑpəˈzɪʃən] *n* **1** PROPOSAL : proposition *f* **2** AFFAIR, BUSINESS : affaire *f*, situation *f* <it's not a paying proposition : ce n'est pas une affaire payante>

propound [prəˈpaʊnd] *vt* : avancer, proposer

proprietary [prəˈpraɪəˌtɛri] *adj* **1** : du propriétaire **2 proprietary brand** : marque *f* déposée

proprietor [prəˈpraɪət̬ər] *n* : propriétaire *mf*

propriety [prəˈpraɪət̬i] *n, pl* **-eties 1** APPROPRIATENESS : convenance *f* **2 proprieties** *npl* : bienséances *fpl*, convenances *fpl*

propulsion [prəˈpʌlʃən] *n* : propulsion *f*

propulsive [prəˈpʌlsɪv] *adj* : propulsif

prosaic [proˈzeɪɪk] *adj* : prosaïque

proscribe [proˈskraɪb] *vt* **-scribed; -scribing** : proscrire

proscription [proˈskrɪpʃən] *n* : proscription *f*

prose [ˈpro:z] *n* : prose *f*

prosecute [ˈprɑsɪˌkju:t] *v* **-cuted; -cuting** *vt* **1** CARRY OUT, PURSUE : poursuivre **2** : poursuivre en justice (en droit) — *vi* : engager des poursuites judiciaires

prosecution [ˌprɑsɪˈkju:ʃən] *n* **1** : poursuites *fpl* judiciaires **2** PROSECUTOR : avocat *m* de la partie civile, procureur *m*

prosecutor [ˈprɑsɪˌkju:t̬ər] *n* : procureur *m*

prospect[1] [ˈprɑˌspɛkt] *vt* : prospecter

prospect[2] *n* **1** VIEW : vue *f* **2** POSSIBILITY : chance *f*, perspective *f* **3** BUYER : client *m* éventuel

prospective [prəˈspɛktɪv, ˈprɑˌspɛk-] *adj* **1** : éventuel, potentiel <a prospective buyer : un acheteur éventuel> **2** : futur <a prospective mother : une future mère>

prospector [ˈprɑˌspɛktər, prɑˈspɛk-] *n* : prospecteur *m*, -trice *f*

prospectus [prəˈspɛktəs] *n* : prospectus *m* (d'une entreprise)

prosper [ˈprɑspər] *vt* **1** SUCCEED : prospérer, réussir **2** THRIVE : prospérer

prosperity [prɑˈspɛrət̬i] *n* : prospérité *f*

prosperous [ˈprɑspərəs] *adj* : prospère

prostate [ˈprɑˌsteɪt] *n or* **prostate gland** : prostate *f*

prosthesis [prɑsˈθi:sɪs, ˈprɑsθə-] *n, pl* **-theses** [-ˌsi:z] : prothèse *f*

prostitute[1] [ˈprɑstəˌtu:t, -ˌtju:t] *vt* **-tuted; -tuting 1** DEBASE : prostituer, dégrader **2 to prostitute oneself** : se prostituer

prostitute[2] *n* : prostituée *f*

prostitution [ˌprɑstəˈtu:ʃən, -ˈtju:-] *n* : prostitution *f*

prostrate[1] [ˈprɑˌstreɪt] *vt* **-trated; -trating 1** OVERWHELM : abattre, accabler <prostrated with grief : accablé de chagrin> **2 to prostrate oneself** : se prosterner

prostrate[2] *adj* **1** : allongé à plat ventre **2** : accablé, prostré <prostrate from the heat : accablé par la chaleur>

prostration [prɑsˈtreɪʃən] *n* : prostration *f*

protagonist [proˈtægənɪst] *n* : protagoniste *mf*

protect [prəˈtɛkt] *vt* : protéger

protection [prəˈtɛkʃən] *n* : protection *f*

protective [prəˈtɛktɪv] *adj* : protecteur

protector [prəˈtɛktər] *n* **1** : protecteur *m*, -trice *f* **2** : dispositif *m* de protection (d'une machine)

protectorate [prəˈtɛktərət] *n* : protectorat *m*

protégé [ˈpro:t̬əˌʒeɪ] *n* : protégé *m*, -gée *f*

protein [ˈpro:ˌti:n] *n* : protéine *f*

protest[1] [proˈtɛst] *vt* **1** : protester de <to protest one's innocence : protester de son innocence> **2** *or* **to protest against** : protester contre — *vi* COMPLAIN : protester

protest[2] [ˈpro:ˌtɛst] *n* **1** DEMONSTRATION : manifestation *f* **2** OBJECTION : protestation *f*, plainte *f*

Protestant [ˈprɑt̬əstənt] *n* : protestant *m*, -tante *f*

Protestantism [ˈprɑt̬əstənˌtɪzəm] *n* : protestantisme *m*

protestation [ˌprɑt̬əsˈteɪʃən, ˌpro:-, -ˌtɛs-] *n* : protestation *f*

protester *or* **protestor** [ˈpro:ˌtɛstər, prə'-] *n* : manifestant *m*, -tante *f*

protocol [ˈpro:t̬əˌkɔl] *n* : protocole *m*

proton [ˈproˌtɑn] *n* : proton *m*

protoplasm [ˈpro:t̬əˌplæzəm] *n* : protoplasme *m*

prototype [ˈpro:t̬əˌtaɪp] *n* : prototype *m*

protozoan [ˌpro:t̬əˈzo:ən] *n* : protozoaire *m*

protozoon [ˌpro:t̬əˈzo:ˌɑn] *n, pl* **-zoa** [-ˈzoə] → **protozoan**

protract [proˈtrækt] *vt* : prolonger

protractor [proˈtræktər] *n* : rapporteur *m* (en géométrie)

protrude [proˈtru:d] *vi* **-truded; -truding** : dépasser, faire saillie

protrusion [proˈtru:ʒən] *n* : saillie *f*

protuberance [proˈtu:bərənts, -ˈtju:-] *n* : protubérance *f*

protuberant [proˈtu:bərənt, -ˈtju:-] *adj* : protubérant, saillant

proud ['praʊd] *adj* **1** HAUGHTY : fier, arrogant **2** PRIDEFUL : fier, orgueilleux <too proud to ask for help : trop fier pour demander de l'aide> **3** GLORIOUS : glorieux <the proudest moment in her life : le moment le plus glorieux de sa vie>

proudly ['praʊdli] *adv* : fièrement, orgueilleusement

prove ['pru:v] *v* **proved; proved** *or* **proven** ['pru:vən]; **proving** *vt* **1** TEST : confirmer, prouver <the exception proves the rule : l'exception confirme la règle> **2** ESTABLISH : prouver, établir — *vi* : s'avérer, se montrer

proverb ['prɑ,vərb] *n* : proverbe *m*, adage *m*

proverbial [prə'vərbiəl] *adj* : proverbial — **proverbially** *adv*

provide [prə'vaɪd] *v* **-vided; -viding** *vt* **1** SUPPLY : fournir, donner **2** STIPULATE : prévoir — *vi* **1 to provide against** : parer à **2 to provide for one's family** : subvenir aux besoins de sa famille

provided [prə'vaɪdəd] *conj* : pourvu que, à condition que <provided (that) you agree : à condition que tu sois d'accord>

providence ['prɑvədənts] *n* **1** FORESIGHT : prévoyance *f* **2** *or* **Providence** : providence *f* <divine providence : la divine providence> **3 Providence** GOD : Providence *f*

provident ['prɑvədənt] *adj* **1** PRUDENT : prévoyant **2** THRIFTY : économe

providential [,prɑvə'dɛntʃəl] *adj* : providentiel

provider [prə'vaɪdər] *n* BREADWINNER : soutien *m* de famille

providing → **provided**

province ['prɑvɪnts] *n* **1** : province *f* <the province of Quebec : la province de Québec> <to live in the provinces : vivre dans les provinces> **2** SPHERE : domaine *m*, sphère *f* <the province of science : le domaine des sciences>

provincial [prə'vɪntʃəl] *adj* **1** RURAL : provincial **2** NARROW : provincial, peu raffiné **3** : provincial *Can* <the provincial government : le gouvernement provincial>

provincialism [prə'vɪntʃəl,ɪzəm] *n* : provincialisme *m*

provision[1] [prə'vɪʒən] *vt* : approvisionner, ravitailler

provision[2] *n* **1** SUPPLYING : approvisionnement *m*, ravitaillement *m* **2** PREPARATION : dispositions *fpl* <to make provision for : prendre des dispositions pour> **3** PROVISO : stipulation *f* **4 provisions** *npl* : provisions *fpl*, vivres *mpl*

provisional [prə'vɪʒənəl] *adj* : provisoire, temporaire — **provisionally** *adv*

proviso [prə'vaɪ,zo:] *n, pl* **-sos** *or* **-soes** : stipulation *f*, clause *f*

provocation [,prɑvə'keɪʃən] *n* : provocation *f*

provocative [prə'vɑkət̬ɪv] *adj* : provocant, provocateur

provoke [prə'vo:k] *vt* **-voked; -voking** : provoquer

prow ['praʊ] *n* : proue *f*

prowess ['praʊəs] *n* **1** VALOR : bravoure *f*, vaillance *f* **2** SKILL : habileté *f*, prouesses *fpl*

prowl[1] ['praʊl] *vi* : rôder, errer

prowl[2] *n* **to be on the prowl** : rôder

prowler ['praʊlər] *n* : rôdeur *m*, -deuse *f*

proximate ['prɑksəmət] *adj* : direct

proximity [prɑk'sɪmət̬i] *n* : proximité *f*

proxy ['prɑksi] *n, pl* **proxies** : procuration *f* <to vote by proxy : voter par procuration>

prude ['pru:d] *n* : prude *f*

prudence ['pru:dənts] *n* : prudence *f*

prudent ['pru:dənt] *adj* **1** SHREWD : astucieux **2** CAUTIOUS : prudent, avisé **3** THRIFTY : économe

prudential [pru:'dɛntʃəl] *adj* : prudent

prudently [pru:dəntli] *adv* : prudemment

prudery ['pru:dəri] *n, pl* **-eries** : pruderie *f*

prudish ['pru:dɪʃ] *adj* : pudibond, prude

prune[1] ['pru:n] *vt* **pruned; pruning 1** : élaguer, tailler (un arbre, etc.) **2** : élaguer (un texte)

prune[2] *n* : pruneau *m*

prurient ['prʊriənt] *adj* : lubrique, luxurieux

pry ['praɪ] *v* **pried; prying** *vi* **to pry into** : mettre son nez dans — *vt* **1** *or* **to pry up** RAISE : forcer avec un levier **2 to pry sth out of s.o.** : soutirer qqch à qqn

psalm ['sɑm, 'sɑlm] *n* : psaume *m*

pseudonym ['su:də,nɪm] *n* : pseudonyme *m*

pseudonymous [su:'dɑnəməs] *adj* : pseudonyme

psoriasis [sə'raɪəsəs] *n* : psoriasis *m*

psyche ['saɪki] *n* : psychisme *m*, psyché *f*

psychiatric [,saɪki'ætrɪk] *adj* : psychiatrique

psychiatrist [sə'kaɪətrɪst, saɪ-] *n* : psychiatre *mf*

psychiatry [sə'kaɪətri, saɪ-] *n* : psychiatrie *f*

psychic ['saɪkɪk] *adj* : psychique

psychoanalysis [,saɪkoə'næləsɪs] *n* : psychanalyse *f*

psychoanalyst [,saɪko'ænəlɪst] *n* : psychanalyste *mf*

psychoanalytic [,saɪko,ænəl'ɪt̬ɪk] *adj* : psychanalytique

psychoanalyze [,saɪko'ænəl,aɪz] *vt* **-lyzed; -lyzing** : psychanalyser

psychological [,saɪkə'lɑdʒɪkəl] *adj* : psychologique — **psychologically** *adv*

psychologist [saɪ'kɑlədʒɪst] *n* : psychologue *mf*

psychology [saɪˈkɑlədʒi] *n, pl* **-gies** : psychologie *f*

psychopath [ˈsaɪkəˌpæθ] *n* : psychopathe *mf*

psychopathic [ˌsaɪkəˈpæθɪk] *adj* : psychopathe

psychosis [saɪˈkoːsɪs] *n, pl* **-choses** [-ˈkoːˌsiz] : psychose *f*

psychosomatic [ˌsaɪkəsəˈmæt̬ɪk] *adj* : psychosomatique

psychotherapist [ˌsaɪkoˈθɛrəpɪst] *n* : psychothérapeute *mf*

psychotherapy [ˌsaɪkoˈθɛrəpi] *n* : psychothérapie *f*

psychotic[1] [saɪˈkɑt̬ɪk] *adj* : psychotique

psychotic[2] *n* : psychotique *mf*

pub [ˈpʌb] *n Brit* : pub *m*

puberty [ˈpjuːbərt̬i] *n* : puberté *f*

pubic [ˈpjuːbɪk] *adj* : pubien

public[1] [ˈpʌblɪk] *adj* : public

public[2] *n* : public *m*

publication [ˌpʌbləˈkeɪʃən] *n* : publication *f*

publicist [ˈpʌbləsɪst] *n* : agent *m* publicitaire

publicity [pəˈblɪsət̬i] *n* : publicité *f*

publicize [ˈpʌbləˌsaɪz] *vt* **-cized; -cizing** : rendre public, faire connaître

publicly [ˈpʌblɪkli] *adv* : publiquement

publish [ˈpʌblɪʃ] *vt* **1** ANNOUNCE : faire connaître, déclarer **2** : publier (un livre)

publisher [ˈpʌblɪʃər] *n* **1** : éditeur *m*, -trice *f* **2** : maison *f* d'édition (entreprise)

puck [ˈpʌk] *n* : palet *m*, rondelle *f Can* (au hockey)

pucker[1] [ˈpʌkər] *vt* : plisser — *vi* : se plisser

pucker[2] *n* : pli *m*

pudding [ˈpʊdɪŋ] *n* : pudding *m*, pouding *m*

puddle [ˈpʌdəl] *n* : flaque *f* (d'eau)

pudgy [ˈpʌdʒi] *adj* **pudgier; -est** : grassouillet, potelé

puerile [ˈpjʊrəl, -ˌaɪl] *adj* : puéril

Puerto Rican[1] [ˌpwɛrt̬əˈriːkən, ˌpɔrt̬ə-] *adj* : portoricain

Puerto Rican[2] *n* : Portoricain *m*, -caine *f*

puff[1] [ˈpʌf] *vi* **1** BLOW : souffler **2** PANT : haleter **3 to puff up** SWELL : enfler, bouffir — *vt* **1** *or* **to puff out** : envoyer des bouffées de (la fumée, etc.) **2** *or* **to puff up** INFLATE : gonfler

puff[2] *n* **1** : bouffée *f* <a puff of air : une bouffée d'air> <to take a puff : tirer une bouffée> **2** SWELLING : bouffissure *f* **3 cream puff** : feuilleté *m* à la crème **4** *or* **powder puff** : houppette *f*

puffy [ˈpʌfi] *adj* **puffier; -est** : enflé, bouffi

pug [ˈpʌg] *n* : carlin *m*

pugilism [ˈpjuːdʒəˌlɪzəm] *n* : pugilat *m*

pugnacious [ˌpʌgˈneɪʃəs] *adj* : combatif, pugnace

puke [ˈpjuːk] *vt* **puked; puking** : vomir, renvoyer *Can fam*

pull[1] [ˈpʊl, ˈpʌl] *vt* **1** : tirer <to pull a rope : tirer une corde> **2** STRAIN : se froisser (un muscle, etc.) **3** EXTRACT : arracher, extraire **4** DRAW : sortir <to pull a gun : sortir un fusil> **5** COMMIT : perpétrer (un crime) **6 to pull off** : enlever **7 to pull oneself together** : se ressaisir, se reprendre **8 to pull up** : remonter — *vi* **1 to pull away** WITHDRAW : se retirer **2 to pull out of** : quitter <the train was pulling out of the station : le train quittait la gare> **3 to pull through** : s'en tirer **4 to pull together** COOPERATE : agir en concert

pull[2] *n* **1** TUG : (petit) coup *m* **2** CLOUT : influence *f*, pouvoir *m* **3** EFFORT : effort *m* <a long uphill pull : une montée pénible> **4** ATTRACTION : force *f*, attrait *m* <the pull of gravity : la force gravitationnelle>

pullet [ˈpʊlət] *n* : poulette *f*

pulley [ˈpʊli] *n, pl* **-leys** : poulie *f*

pullover [ˈpʊlˌoːvər] *n* : chandail *m*, pullover *m France*

pulmonary [ˈpʊlməˌnɛri, ˈpʌl-] *adj* : pulmonaire

pulp [ˈpʌlp] *n* **1** : pulpe *f*, chair *f* (d'un fruit, etc.) **2** *or* **paper pulp** : pâte *f* à papier

pulpit [ˈpʊlˌpɪt] *n* : chaire *f*

pulsate [ˈpʌlˌseɪt] *vi* **-sated; -sating 1** BEAT : battre, palpiter **2** VIBRATE : vibrer

pulsation [ˌpʌlˈseɪʃən] *n* : battement *m*, pulsation *f*

pulse [ˈpʌls] *n* : pouls *m* <to take s.o.'s pulse : tâter le pouls de qqn>

pulverize [ˈpʌlvəˌraɪz] *vt* **-ized; -izing** : pulvériser

puma [ˈpuːmə, ˈpjuː-] *n* : puma *m*, cougar *m*

pumice [ˈpʌməs] *n or* **pumice stone** : pierre *f* ponce

pummel [ˈpʌməl] *vt* **-meled; -meling** : battre, rouer de coups

pump[1] [ˈpʌmp] *vt* **1** : pomper (de l'eau) **2 to pump through** : faire circuler (un gaz, un liquide, du sang) **3 to pump up** : gonfler (un pneu)

pump[2] *n* **1** : pompe *f* <bicycle pump : pompe à bicyclette> **2** : escarpin *m* (chaussure)

pumpernickel [ˈpʌmpərˌnɪkəl] *n* : pain *m* noir

pumpkin [ˈpʌmpkɪn, ˈpʌŋkən] *n* : citrouille *f*, potiron *m France*

pun[1] [ˈpʌn] *vi* **punned; punning** : faire des jeux de mots

pun[2] *n* : jeu *m* de mots, calembour *m*

punch[1] [ˈpʌntʃ] *vt* **1** : donner un coup de poing à **2** PERFORATE : poinçonner, perforer

punch[2] *n* **1** BLOW : coup *m* de poing **2** *or* **hole punch** : poinçonneuse *f* **3**

: punch *m* <fruit punch : punch aux fruits>

punctilious [pəŋk'tɪliəs] *adj* : pointilleux, méticuleux

punctual ['pʌŋktʃʊəl] *adj* : ponctuel — **punctually** *adv*

punctuality [ˌpʌŋktʃʊ'æləṯi] *n* : ponctualité *f*

punctuate ['pʌŋktʃʊˌeɪt] *vt* **-ated; -ating** : ponctuer

punctuation [ˌpʌŋktʃʊ'eɪʃən] *n* : ponctuation *f*

puncture[1] ['pʌŋktʃər] *vt* **-tured; -turing** **1** PIERCE : perforer **2** : crever (un ballon, un pneu, etc.)

puncture[2] *n* **1** HOLE : perforation *f* **2** PRICK : piqûre *f*

pundit ['pʌndɪt] *n* EXPERT : critique *mf;* expert *m,* -perte *f*

pungency ['pʌndʒəntsi] *n* : piquant *m,* âpreté *f*

pungent ['pʌndʒənt] *adj* **1** BITING, SHARP : âcre, piquant **2** CAUSTIC : mordant

punish ['pʌnɪʃ] *vt* : punir

punishable ['pʌnɪʃəbəl] *adj* : punissable

punishment ['pʌnɪʃmənt] *n* : punition *f*

punitive ['pju:nəṯɪv] *adj* : punitif

punt[1] ['pʌnt] *vt* : faire avancer (une barque) à la perche — *vi* KICK : envoyer d'un coup de volée

punt[2] *n* **1** : barque *f* (à fond plat) **2** KICK : coup *m* de volée

puny ['pju:ni] *adj* **punier; -est** : malingre, chétif

pup ['pʌp] *n* : chiot *m,* jeune animal *m*

pupa ['pju:pə] *n, pl* **-pae** [-pi, -ˌpaɪ] *or* **-pas** : pupe *f,* chrysalide *f*

pupil ['pju:pəl] *n* **1** : élève *mf* (à l'école) **2** : pupille *f* (de l'œil)

puppet ['pʌpət] *n* : marionnette *f*

puppeteer [ˌpʌpə'tɪr] *n* : marionnettiste *mf*

puppy ['pʌpi] *n, pl* **-pies** : chiot *m*

purchase[1] ['pərtʃəs] *vt* **-chased; -chasing** : acheter, acquérir

purchase[2] *n* **1** : achat *m,* acquisition *f* **2** GRASP : prise *f*

purchase order *n* : ordre *m* d'achat

purchaser ['pərtʃəsər] *n* : acheteur *m,* -teuse *f*

pure ['pjʊr] *adj* **purer; purest** : pur

puree[1] [pjʊ'reɪ, -'ri:] *vt* **-reed; -reeing** : réduire en purée

puree[2] *n* : purée *f*

purely ['pjʊrli] *adv* : purement

purgative[1] ['pərgəṯɪv] *adj* : purgatif

purgative[2] *n* LAXATIVE : purgatif *m*

purgatory ['pərgəˌtori] *n, pl* **-ries** : purgatoire *m*

purge[1] ['pərdʒ] *vt* **purged; purging** : purger

purge[2] *n* : purge *f* (des intestins), épuration *f* (en politique)

purification [ˌpjʊrəfə'keɪʃən] *n* : purification *f*

purifier ['pjʊrəˌfaɪər] *n* : purificateur *m* <air purifier : purificateur d'air>

purify ['pjʊrəˌfaɪ] *vt* **-fied; -fying** : purifier

puritan ['pju:rətən] *n* : puritain *m,* -taine *f*

puritanical [ˌpju:rə'tænɪkəl] *adj* : puritain

purity ['pjʊrəṯi] *n* : pureté *f*

purl[1] ['pərl] *vt* : tricoter à l'envers

purl[2] *n* : maille *f* à l'envers

purloin [pər'lɔɪn, 'pərˌlɔɪn] *vt* : dérober, voler

purple ['pərpəl] *n* : violet *m,* pourpre *m*

purplish ['pərpəlɪʃ] *adj* : violacé

purport [pər'port] *vt* : prétendre <to purport to be : prétendre être, se faire passer pour>

purportedly [pər'portədli] *adv* : prétendument

purpose ['pərpəs] *n* **1** AIM : intention *f,* but *m* **2** DETERMINATION : résolution *f* <to have a sense of purpose : être résolu> **3 for this purpose** : à cet effet, à cette fin **4 on ~** : exprès

purposeful ['pərpəsfəl] *adj* **1** MEANINGFUL : significatif **2** INTENTIONAL : prémédité, réfléchi **3** DETERMINED : résolu, décidé

purposefully ['pərpəsfəli] *adv* : résolument

purposeless ['pərpəsləs] *adj* MEANINGLESS : vide de sens

purposely ['pərpəsli] *adv* : délibérément, intentionnellement

purr[1] ['pər] *vi* : ronronner

purr[2] *n* : ronronnement *m*

purse[1] ['pərs] *vt* **pursed; pursing** : pincer, serrer <to purse one's lips : pincer les lèvres>

purse[2] *n* **1** *or* **change purse** : portemonnaie *m* **2** HANDBAG : sac *m* à main, sacoche *f Can* **3** FUNDS, RESOURCES : moyens *mpl* **4** PRIZE : prix *m,* récompense *f*

pursue [pər'su:] *vt* **-sued; -suing** **1** CHASE : poursuivre, pourchasser **2** SEEK : poursuivre <to pursue a goal : poursuivre un but> **3** CARRY ON : poursuivre, continuer, conduire <to pursue a career : faire carrière>

pursuer [pər'su:ər] *n* : poursuivant *m,* -vante *f*

pursuit [pər'su:t] *n* **1** CHASE : poursuite *f* **2** ACTIVITY, OCCUPATION : activité *f,* occupation *f* **3** SEARCH : poursuite *f,* recherche *f* <the pursuit of happiness : la recherche du bonheur>

purvey [pər'veɪ] *vt* **-veyed; -veying** : fournir (des provisions, etc.)

purveyor [pər'veɪər] *n* : fournisseur *m,* -seuse *f*

pus ['pʌs] *n* : pus *m*

push[1] ['pʊʃ] *vt* **1** : pousser <to push a cart : pousser un chariot> <to push the door open : ouvrir la porte> **2** THRUST : enfoncer **3** *or* **to push up** RAISE : augmenter **4** URGE : pousser, inciter **5** APPROACH : approcher, friser <she must be pushing sixty

: elle doit approcher de la soixantaine> **6 to push away** : repousser — *vi* **1 to push for** : demander, réclamer **2 to push on** : continuer, persévérer **3 to push (oneself)** : s'exercer

push[2] *n* **1** SHOVE : poussée *f* <I gave him a push : je l'ai poussé> **2** DRIVE : effort *m* **3** IMPETUS : poussée *f*, impulsion *f*

pushcart ['pʊʃ,kɑrt] *n* : charrette *f* à bras

pushy ['pʊʃi] *adj* **pushier; -est** : arriviste

pussy ['pʊsi] *n, pl* **pussies** : minet *m*, minou *m fam*

pustule ['pʌs,tʃu:l] *n* : pustule *f*

put ['pʊt] *vt* **put; putting 1** PLACE : mettre <put it on the table : mets-le sur la table> **2** INSERT : insérer, introduire **3** (*indicating causation of a state or feeling*) : mettre <it puts her in a good mood : ça la met de bonne humeur> **4** IMPOSE : infliger, imposer (une taxe, etc.) **5** SUBJECT : mettre <to put to the test : mettre à l'épreuve> <to put to death : mettre à mort> **6** EXPRESS : exprimer, dire <to put it mildly : c'est peu dire> **7** APPLY : mettre, appliquer <if you put your minds to it : si vous vous y mettez> **8** SET : mettre <to put to work : employer, mettre au travail> **9** ATTACH : attribuer, attacher <to put great value on : attacher beaucoup d'importance à> **10** PRESENT : soumettre, présenter <they put their case well : ils ont bien présenté leur cas> **11 to put forward** PROPOSE : avancer, proposer — *vi* **1 to put to sea** : lever l'ancre **2 to put up with** TOLERATE : supporter

put away *vt* **1** STORE : ranger **2** DISCARD, RENOUNCE : renoncer à (des idées, des émotions, etc.) **3** CONSUME : avaler, engloutir (de la nourriture) **4** CONFINE : enfermer, mettre sous les verrous

put by *vt* SAVE : économiser, mettre de côté

put down *vt* **1** SUPPRESS : réprimer **2** WRITE : écrire, mettre (par écrit) **3** ASCRIBE : mettre sur le compte <I put it down to luck : je l'ai mis sur le compte de la chance>

put off *vt* POSTPONE : remettre à plus tard, retarder

put on *vt* **1** ASSUME : prendre, assumer **2** PRESENT : monter (un spectacle, etc.) **3** WEAR : mettre (des vêtements)

put out *vt* **1** EXTINGUISH, TURN OFF : éteindre **2** INCONVENIENCE : déranger, importuner **3** ANNOY : contrarier, fâcher

putrefaction [,pju:trə'fækʃən] *n* : putréfaction *f*

putrefy ['pju:trə,faɪ] *v* **-fied; -fying** *vt* : putréfier — *vi* : se putréfier

putrid ['pju:trɪd] *adj* : putride

putty[1] ['pʌt̬i] *vt* **-tied; -tying** : mastiquer

putty[2] *n, pl* **-ties** : mastic *m*

put up *vt* **1** ACCOMMODATE, LODGE : loger, héberger **2** BUILD : construire, ériger **3** NOMINATE : proposer (un candidat) **4** CONTRIBUTE : contribuer

puzzle[1] ['pʌzəl] *vt* **-zled; -zling 1** CONFUSE : intriguer, laisser perplexe **2 to puzzle out** SOLVE : résoudre, deviner

puzzle[2] *n* **1** : casse-tête *m* **2** *or* **jigsaw puzzle** : puzzle *m* **3** MYSTERY : énigme *f*, mystère *m*

puzzlement ['pʌzəlmənt] *n* : perplexité *f*

pygmy[1] ['pɪgmi] *adj* : pygmée

pygmy[2] *n, pl* **-mies 1** DWARF : pygmée *m* **2 Pygmy** : Pygmée *mf*

pyjamas *Brit* → **pajamas**

pylon ['paɪ,lɑn, -lən] *n* : pylône *m*

pyramid ['pɪrə,mɪd] *n* : pyramide *f*

pyre ['paɪr] *n* : bûcher *m*

pyromania [,paɪro'meɪniə] *n* : pyromanie *f*

pyromaniac [,paɪro'meɪni,æk] *n* : pyromane *mf*

pyrotechnics [,paɪrə'tɛknɪks] *npl* : pyrotechnie *f*

python ['paɪ,θɑn, -θən] *n* : python *m*

Q

q ['kju:] *n, pl* **q's** *or* **qs** ['kju:z] : q *m*, dix-septième lettre de l'alphabet

quack[1] ['kwæk] *vi* : faire des coin-coin, cancaner

quack[2] *n* **1** : coin-coin *m* (d'un canard) **2** CHARLATAN : charlatan *m*

quadrangle ['kwɑ,dræŋgəl] *n* **1** COURTYARD : cour *f* (rectangulaire), patio *m* **2** → **quadrilateral**

quadrant ['kwɑdrənt] *n* : quadrant *m*

quadrilateral [,kwɑdrə'læt̬ərəl] *n* : quadrilatère *m*

quadruped ['kwɑdrə,pɛd] *n* : quadrupède *m*

quadruple[1] [kwɑ'dru:pəl, -'drʌ-; 'kwɑdrə-] *vt* **-pled; -pling** : quadrupler

quadruple[2] *adj* : quadruple

quadruplet [kwɑ'dru:plət, -'drʌ-; 'kwɑdrə-] *n* : quadruplé *m*, -plée *f*

quagmire ['kwæg,maɪr, 'kwɑg-] *n* : bourbier *m*

quail[1] ['kweɪl] *vi* : trembler <to quail before : perdre courage devant>

quail[2] *n, pl* **quail** *or* **quails** : caille *f*

quaint ['kweɪnt] *adj* **1** ODD : étrange, bizarre **2** PICTURESQUE : pittoresque
quaintly ['kweɪntli] *adv* **1** : étrangement, bizarrement **2** : de façon pittoresque
quake[1] ['kweɪk] *vi* **quaked; quaking** : frémir, trembler
quake[2] *n* EARTHQUAKE : tremblement *m* de terre
qualification [ˌkwɑləfə'keɪʃən] *n* **1** QUALIFYING : qualification *f* **2** LIMITATION : réserve *f*, restriction *f* <without qualification : sans réserve> **3** SKILL : compétence *f*, aptitude *f*
qualified ['kwɑləˌfaɪd] *adj* : qualifié, compétent
qualify ['kwɑləˌfaɪ] *v* **-fied; -fying** *vt* **1** LIMIT, MODIFY : nuancer, préciser, poser des conditions sur **2** : qualifier, rendre compétent <to be qualified for : être habilité à> **3** MODERATE : adoucir, mitiger — *vi* : se qualifier, remplir les conditions requises
quality ['kwɑləṭi] *n, pl* **-ties** **1** GRADE : qualité *f*, excellence *f* **2** CHARACTERISTIC : qualité *f*, attribut *m*, propriété *f*
qualm ['kwɑm, 'kwɑlm, 'kwɔm] *n* : scrupule *m*, doute *m* <to have no qualms about : ne pas avoir le moindre scrupule à>
quandary ['kwɑndri] *n, pl* **-ries** : doute *m*, confusion *f* <to be in a quandary : ne pas savoir que faire>
quantity ['kwɑntəṭi] *n, pl* **-ties** : quantité *f*
quantum theory ['kwɑntəm] *n* : théorie *f* des quanta
quarantine[1] ['kwɔrənˌti:n] *vt* **-tined; -tining** : mettre en quarantaine
quarantine[2] *n* : quarantaine *f*
quarrel[1] ['kwɔrəl] *vi* **-reled** *or* **-relled; -reling** *or* **-relling** : se quereller, se disputer
quarrel[2] *n* : dispute *f*, querelle *f*
quarrelsome ['kwɔrəlsəm] *adj* : querelleur
quarry[1] ['kwɔri] *vt* **quarried; quarrying** **1** EXTRACT : extraire <to quarry marble : extraire du marbre> **2** EXCAVATE : excaver
quarry[2] *n, pl* **quarries** **1** PREY : proie *f* **2** EXCAVATION : carrière *f*
quart ['kwɔrt] *n* : quart *m* de gallon
quarter[1] ['kwɔrṭər] *vt* : diviser en quatre
quarter[2] *n* **1** : quart *m* **2** (*used in expressions of time*) <a quarter after three : trois heures et quart> **3** : (pièce de) vingt-cinq cents *m*, trente-sous *m Can fam* **4** DISTRICT : quartier *m* (d'une ville) **5** : trimestre *m* (de l'année fiscale) **6 quarters** *npl* LODGINGS : logement *m*
quarterly[1] ['kwɔrṭərli] *adv* : tous les trois mois, trimestriellement
quarterly[2] *adj* : trimestriel
quarterly[3] *n, pl* **-lies** : publication *f* trimestrielle
quartermaster ['kwɔrṭərˌmæstər] *n* : intendant *m* militaire
quartet [kwɔr'tɛt] *n* : quatuor *m* <string quartet : quatuor à cordes>
quartz ['kwɔrts] *n* : quartz *m*
quash ['kwɑʃ, 'kwɔʃ] *vt* **1** : annuler (un jugement) **2** SUPPRESS : étouffer, refouler (ses émotions)
quaver[1] ['kweɪvər] *vi* : trembloter, chevroter (se dit de la voix)
quaver[2] *n* : tremblement *m*, chevrotement *m*
quay ['ki:, 'keɪ, 'kweɪ] *n* WHARF : quai *m*
queasiness ['kwi:zinəs] *n* : nausée *f*
queasy ['kwi:zi] *adj* **queasier; -est** : nauséeux <to feel queasy : avoir mal au cœur>
Quebecer *or* **Quebecker** [kwɪ'bɛkər] *n* : Québécois *m*, -coise *f*
Quebecois *or* **Québécois** [kebe'kwɑ:] *n* : Québécois *m*, -coise *f*
queen ['kwi:n] *n* : reine *f*
queenly ['kwi:nli] *adj* : de reine
queer ['kwɪr] *adj* : étrange, bizarre — **queerly** *adv*
quell ['kwɛl] *vt* : réprimer, étouffer
quench ['kwɛntʃ] *vt* **1** EXTINGUISH : éteindre (un feu) **2** SATISFY : apaiser, étancher (la soif)
querulous ['kwɛrələs, -jələs] *adj* : plaintif, grincheux
querulously ['kwɛrələsli, -jələs-] *adv* : plaintivement
query[1] ['kwɪri, 'kwɛr-] *vt* **-ried; -rying** **1** ASK : poser une question à **2** QUESTION : mettre en doute, poser des questions sur
query[2] *n, pl* **-ries** : question *f*
quest[1] ['kwɛst] *vi* **to quest for** : être en quête de, être à la recherche de
quest[2] *n* : quête *f*, recherche *f*
question[1] ['kwɛstʃən] *vt* **1** INTERROGATE : questionner, interroger **2** DISPUTE : mettre en doute
question[2] *n* **1** : question *f*, interrogation *f* **2** MATTER : question *f*, problème *m* **3 without ~** : sans l'ombre d'un doute
questionable ['kwɛstʃənəbəl] *adj* DUBIOUS : contestable, discutable, douteux
questioner ['kwɛstʃənər] *n* : interrogateur *m*, -trice *f*
question mark *n* : point *m* d'interrogation
questionnaire [ˌkwɛstʃə'nær] *n* : questionnaire *m*
queue[1] ['kju:] *vi* **queued; queuing** *or* **queueing** : faire la queue
queue[2] *n* **1** PIGTAIL : tresse *f* (de cheveux) **2** LINE : queue *f*, file *f* (d'attente)
quibble[1] ['kwɪbəl] *vi* **-bled; -bling** : chicaner
quibble[2] *n* : chicane *f*

quick[1] ['kwɪk] *adv* : rapidement
quick[2] *adj* **1** FAST : rapide **2** ALERT : vif, éveillé **3 to have a quick temper** : s'emporter facilement
quick[3] *n* **1** : chair *f* vive <his nails were bitten to the quick : il se rongeait les ongles jusqu'au sang> **2 to cut to the quick** : piquer au vif
quicken ['kwɪkən] *vt* **1** HASTEN : accélérer **2** AROUSE : stimuler
quickly ['kwɪkli] *adv* : rapidement, vite
quickness ['kwɪknəs] *n* : rapidité *f*, vitesse *f*
quicksand ['kwɪk,sænd] *n* : sables *mpl* mouvants
quicksilver ['kwɪk,sɪlvər] *n* : mercure *m*, vif-argent *m*
quick–tempered ['kwɪk'tɛmpərd] *adj* : coléreux, irascible
quick–witted ['kwɪk'wɪṭəd] *adj* : à l'esprit vif
quiet[1] ['kwaɪət] *vt* : calmer <to quiet the crowd : calmer la foule> — *vi* **to quiet down** : se calmer
quiet[2] *adj* **1** CALM : tranquille **2** EASYGOING : doux **3** STILL : tranquille, silencieux **4** : sobre, simple <quiet clothes : vêtements sobres> **5** SECLUDED : tranquille, retiré <a quiet nook : un coin tranquille>
quiet[3] *n* : tranquillité *f*, calme *m* <the quiet before the storm : le calme avant la tempête>
quietly ['kwaɪətli] *adv* **1** : sans bruit **2** CALMLY : tranquillement, paisiblement
quietness ['kwaɪətnəs] *n* : tranquillité *f*, silence *f*
quietude ['kwaɪə,tu:d, -,tju:d] *n* : quiétude *f*
quill ['kwɪl] *n* **1** : piquant *m* (d'un porc-épic, etc.) **2** *or* **quill pen** : penne *f*, plume *f* d'oie
quilt[1] ['kwɪlt] *vt* : matelasser, piquer
quilt[2] *n* : courtepointe *f*, édredon *m* (piqué)
quince ['kwɪnts] *n* : coing *m* (fruit), cognassier *m* (arbre)
quinine ['kwaɪ,naɪn] *n* : quinine *f*
quintessence [kwɪn'tɛsənts] *n* : quintessence *f*
quintet [kwɪn'tɛt] *n* : quintette *m*
quintuple [kwɪn'tu:pəl, -'tju:-, -'tʌ-; 'kwɪntə-] *adj* : quintuple
quintuplet [kwɪn'tʌplət, -'tu:-, -'tju:-; 'kwɪntə-] *n* : quintuplé *m*, -plée *f*
quip[1] ['kwɪp] *vi* **quipped; quipping** : lancer des mots piquants
quip[2] *n* : mot *m* piquant, trait *m* d'esprit
quirk ['kwərk] *n* : excentricité *f*, bizarrerie *f*
quirky ['kwərki] *adj* **quirkier; -iest** : excentrique
quit ['kwɪt] *v* **quit; quitting** *vt* **1** STOP : arrêter <quit fooling around : arrête de faire l'imbécile> **2** LEAVE : quitter, cesser <to quit school : quitter l'école> — *vi* **1** GIVE UP : abandonner, renoncer **2** RESIGN : démissionner
quite ['kwaɪt] *adv* **1** COMPLETELY : tout à fait **2** RATHER : assez <quite near : assez proche> **3** POSITIVELY : vraiment <I'm quite sure : je suis vraiment certaine>
quits ['kwɪts] *adj* : quitte <to be quits with s.o. : être quitte envers qqn> <let's call it quits! : restons-en là!>
quitter ['kwɪṭər] *n* : personne *f* qui abandonne facilement
quiver[1] ['kwɪvər] *vi* : trembler, frémir
quiver[2] *n* **1** : carquois *m* (pour des flèches) **2** TREMOR : tremblement *m*
quixotic [kwɪk'sɑṭɪk] *adj* : chimérique, utopique
quiz[1] ['kwɪz] *vt* **quizzed; quizzing** : questionner, interroger
quiz[2] *n, pl* **quizzes** : petit examen *m*, épreuve *f*
quizzical ['kwɪzɪkəl] *adj* **1** TEASING : moqueur, taquin, ironique **2** PUZZLED : perplexe
quorum ['kworəm] *n* : quorum *m*
quota ['kwo:ṭə] *n* : quota *m*
quotable ['kwo:ṭəbəl] *adj* : qui peut être cité
quotation [kwo'teɪʃən] *n* **1** CITATION : citation *f* **2** ESTIMATE : devis *m* **3** : cote *f*, cotation *f* (à la Bourse)
quotation marks *npl* : guillemets *mpl*
quote[1] ['kwo:t] *vt* **quoted; quoting 1** : citer <to quote a poem : citer un poème> **2** STATE : donner, soumettre (un prix) **3** : coter (un prix à la Bourse)
quote[2] *n* **1** → **quotation 2 quotes** *npl* → **quotation marks**
quotient ['kwo:ʃənt] *n* : quotient *m*

R

r ['ɑr] *n, pl* **r's** *or* **rs** ['ɑrz] : r *m*, dix-huitième lettre de l'alphabet
rabbi ['ræ,baɪ] *n* : rabbin *m*
rabbit ['ræbət] *n, pl* **-bit** *or* **-bits** : lapin *m*, -pine *f*
rabble ['ræbəl] *n* **1** CROWD, MOB : cohue *f*, foule *f* **2** MASSES : populace *f*, masses *fpl*
rabid ['ræbɪd] *adj* **1** FURIOUS : furieux **2** FANATICAL : zélé, fanatique **3** : enragé (se dit d'un chien)
rabies ['reɪbi:z] *ns & pl* : rage *f*
raccoon [ræ'ku:n] *n, pl* **-coon** *or* **-coons** : raton *m* laveur, chat *m* sauvage *Can*
race[1] ['reɪs] *vi* **raced; racing 1** : faire une course **2** RUSH : courir, se hâter

race[2] *n* **1** CURRENT : courant *m,* cours *m* (d'eau) **2** : course *f* <horse race : course de chevaux> <presidential race : course à la présidence> **3** : race *f* <the white race : la race blanche>

racecourse [ˈreɪsˌkors] *n* : champ *m* de courses

racehorse [ˈreɪsˌhors] *n* : cheval *m* de course

racer [ˈreɪsər] *n* : coureur *m,* -reuse *f*

racetrack [ˈreɪsˌtræk] *n* : champ *m* de courses

racial [ˈreɪʃəl] *adj* : racial — **racially** *adv*

racism [ˈreɪˌsɪzəm] *n* : racisme *m*

racist [ˈreɪsɪst] *n* : raciste *mf*

rack[1] [ˈræk] *vt* : torturer <to be racked with pain : être torturé par la douleur> <to rack one's brains : se creuser la tête>

rack[2] *n* **1** SHELF : étagère *f* <a luggage rack : un porte-bagages> <a roof rack : une galerie> <a clothes rack : un portemanteau> **2** : chevalet *m* (instrument de torture)

racket [ˈrækət] *n* **1** : raquette *f* <tennis racket : raquette de tennis> **2** CLAMOR : vacarme *m* **3** FRAUD : escroquerie *f,* racket *m*

racketeer [ˌrækəˈtɪr] *n* : racketteur *m*

racketeering [ˌrækəˈtɪrɪŋ] *n* : racket *m*

raconteur [ˌræˌkɑnˈtər] *n* STORYTELLER : raconteur *m,* -teuse *f*

racy [ˈreɪsi] *adj* **racier; -est 1** LIVELY : plein de verve **2** RISQUÉ : osé

radar [ˈreɪˌdɑr] *n* : radar *m*

radial [ˈreɪdiəl] *adj* : radial

radiance [ˈreɪdiənts] *n* : éclat *m,* rayonnement *m*

radiant [ˈreɪdiənt] *adj* **1** GLOWING : éclatant, brillant **2** : radieux, rayonnant <a radiant smile : un sourire radieux> **3** : radiant (en physique)

radiantly [ˈreɪdiəntli] *adv* : d'un air radieux

radiate [ˈreɪdiˌeɪt] *v* **-ated; -ating** *vi* SHINE : briller, rayonner — *vt* **1** IRRADIATE : irradier **2** EMIT : dégager, émettre <to radiate heat : dégager de la chaleur>

radiation [ˌreɪdiˈeɪʃən] *n* : rayonnement *m,* radiation *f*

radiator [ˈreɪdiˌeɪtər] *n* : radiateur *m,* calorifère *m Can*

radical[1] [ˈrædɪkəl] *adj* : radical — **radically** [ˈrædɪkli] *adv*

radical[2] *n* : radical *m,* -cale *f*

radii → **radius**

radio[1] [ˈreɪdiˌoː] *vt* : envoyer (un message) par radio

radio[2] *n, pl* **-dios** : radio *f*

radioactive [ˌreɪdioˈæktɪv] *adj* : radioactif

radioactivity [ˌreɪdioˌækˈtɪvət̬i] *n* : radioactivité *f*

radiologist [ˌreɪdiˈɑlədʒɪst] *n* : radiologiste *mf,* radiologue *mf*

radiology [ˌreɪdiˈɑlədʒi] *n* : radiologie *f*

radish [ˈrædɪʃ] *n* : radis *m*

radium [ˈreɪdiəm] *n* : radium *m*

radius [ˈreɪdiəs] *n, pl* **-dii** [-diˌaɪ] : rayon *m*

radon [ˈreɪˌdɑn] *n* : radon *m*

raffle[1] [ˈræfəl] *vt* **-fled; -fling** : mettre en tombola

raffle[2] *n* : tombola *f*

raft[1] [ˈræft] *vt* : transporter par radeau

raft[2] *n* **1** : radeau *m* **2** SLEW : tas *m,* multitude *f* <a raft of errors : un tas d'erreurs>

rafter [ˈræftər] *n* : chevron *m*

rag [ˈræg] *n* **1** : chiffon *m,* guenille *f Can* **2 rags** *npl* : haillons *mpl,* guenilles *fpl* <clothed in rags : vêtu de haillons> **3** → **ragtime**

ragamuffin [ˈrægəˌmʌfən] *n* : va-nu-pieds *m*

rage[1] [ˈreɪdʒ] *vi* **raged; raging 1** : être enragé (se dit d'une personne) **2** : faire rage <the fire raged for hours : le feu a fait rage pendant des heures>

rage[2] *n* **1** FURY : rage *f* **2 to be all the rage** : faire fureur

ragged [ˈrægəd] *adj* **1** : inégal <ragged cliffs : falaises inégales> **2** TATTERED : en loques, en lambeaux **3** DISCONNECTED, DISJOINTED : décousu

ragout [ræˈguː] *n* : ragoût *m*

ragtime [ˈrægˌtaɪm] *n* : ragtime *m*

ragweed [ˈrægˌwiːd] *n* : ambroisie *f*

raid[1] [ˈreɪd] *vt* : faire un raid (militaire) sur, faire une descente (policière) dans

raid[2] *n* **1** INCURSION : raid *m* (militaire) **2** *or* **police raid** : descente *f,* rafle *f*

raider [ˈreɪdər] *n* **1** : membre *m* d'un commando **2** LOOTER, MARAUDER : pillard *m,* -larde *f*

rail[1] [ˈreɪl] *vi* **to rail at** : invectiver contre

rail[2] *n* **1** RAILING : rampe *f* (d'un escalier), balustrade *f* (d'un balcon) **2** TRACK : rail *m* (d'une voie ferrée) **3** RAILROAD : train *m,* chemin *m* de fer <by rail : par train>

railing [ˈreɪlɪŋ] *n* : rampe *f,* balustrade *f*

raillery [ˈreɪləri] *n, pl* **-leries** : raillerie *f*

railroad [ˈreɪlˌroːd] *n* : chemin *m* de fer

railway [ˈreɪlˌweɪ] → **railroad**

raiment [ˈreɪmənt] *n* : habits *mpl,* vêtements *mpl*

rain[1] [ˈreɪn] *vi* : pleuvoir

rain[2] *n* : pluie *f*

rainbow [ˈreɪnˌboː] *n* : arc-en-ciel *m*

raincoat [ˈreɪnˌkoːt] *n* : imperméable *m*

raindrop [ˈreɪnˌdrɑp] *n* : goutte *f* de pluie

rainfall [ˈreɪnˌfɔl] *n* : précipitations *fpl*

rainstorm [ˈreɪnˌstɔrm] *n* : pluie *f* torrentielle

rainwater [ˈreɪnˌwɔt̬ər] *n* : eau *f* de pluie

rainy ['reɪni] *adj* **rainier; -est** : pluvieux

raise[1] ['reɪz] *vt* **raised; raising 1** LIFT : lever **2** AWAKEN : ressusciter **3** BUILD : ériger **4** COLLECT : collecter (des fonds) **5** GROW : cultiver (des produits agricoles) **6** REAR : élever **7** BRING UP : soulever (une question, etc.) **8** INCREASE : augmenter **9** PROVOKE : susciter, provoquer <to raise a commotion : susciter un émoi>

raise[2] *n* : augmentation *f* (de salaire)

raisin ['reɪzən] *n* : raisin *m* sec

raja *or* **rajah** ['rɑdʒə, -ˌdʒɑ, -ˌʒɑ] *n* : rajah *m*

rake[1] ['reɪk] *vt* **raked; raking 1** : ratisser, râteler (des feuilles) **2 to rake with gunfire** : balayer avec une mitrailleuse

rake[2] *n* **1** : râteau *m* **2** LIBERTINE : débauché *m*

rakish ['reɪkɪʃ] *adj* **1** JAUNTY : gaillard **2** WILD : libertin, dissolu

rally[1] ['ræli] *v* **-lied; -lying** *vt* MOBILIZE : rallier, rassembler — *vi* **1** : se rallier **2** RECOVER : retrouver ses forces, se remettre

rally[2] *n,pl* **-lies** : ralliement *m*, rassemblement *m*

ram[1] ['ræm] *vt* **rammed; ramming 1** HIT : heurter, percuter **2** CRAM : fourrer, entasser **3 to ram home** : forcer l'acceptation de (une idée, un projet de loi, etc.)

ram[2] *n* **1** : bélier *m* (mouton) **2** → **battering ram**

RAM ['ræm] *n* : RAM *f*, mémoire *f* vive

ramble[1] ['ræmbəl] *vi* **-bled; -ling 1** ROAM : flâner, se balader **2** *or* **to ramble on** : discourir, pérorer

ramble[2] *n* : randonnée *f*, balade *f*

rambler ['ræmblər] *n* WALKER : randonneur *m*, -neuse *f*

rambunctious [ræm'bʌŋkʃəs] *adj* : exubérant, turbulent

ramification [ˌræməfə'keɪʃən] *n* : ramification *f*

ramify ['ræməˌfaɪ] *vi* **-fied; -fying** : se ramifier

ramp ['ræmp] *n* **1** : rampe *f* **2** : passerelle *f* (pour accéder à un avion)

rampage[1] ['ræmˌpeɪdʒ, ræm'peɪdʒ] *vi* **-paged; -paging** : se déchaîner, donner libre cours à

rampage[2] ['ræmˌpeɪdʒ] *n* **to go on a rampage** : se livrer à des actes de destruction

rampant ['ræmpənt] *adj* WIDESPREAD : endémique, qui sévit

rampart ['ræmˌpɑrt] *n* : rempart *m*

ramrod ['ræmˌrɑd] *n* : baguette *f* (d'une arme à feu)

ramshackle ['ræmˌʃækəl] *adj* : délabré, en mauvais état

ran → **run**[1]

ranch[1] ['ræntʃ] *vi* : exploiter un ranch

ranch[2] *n* : ranch *m*

rancher ['ræntʃər] *n* : propriétaire *mf* de ranch

rancid ['ræntsɪd] *adj* : rance

rancor *or Brit* **rancour** ['ræŋkər] *n* : rancœur *f*, rancune *f*

random ['rændəm] *adj* **1** : aléatoire <random process : processus aléatoire> **2 at ~** : au hasard

randomly ['rændəmli] *adv* : au hasard

rang → **ring**[1]

range[1] ['reɪndʒ] *v* **ranged; ranging** *vt* ARRANGE : classer, ranger — *vi* **1** WANDER : vagabonder, errer **2 to range from** : varier entre, aller de

range[2] *n* **1** ROW : rangée *f* **2** PRAIRIE : prairie *f* **3** : chaîne *f* (de montagnes) **4** STOVE : cuisinière *f* **5** SERIES, SPREAD : éventail *m*, gamme *f* **6** *or* **shooting range** : champ *m* de tir **7** SCOPE : champ *m*, étendue *f* **8** VARIETY : variété *f* (de couleurs, de motifs)

ranger ['reɪndʒər] *n or* **forest ranger** : garde *m* forestier

rangy ['reɪndʒi] *adj* **rangier; -est** : élancé

rank[1] ['ræŋk] *vt* **1** ARRANGE : placer, ranger **2** CLASSIFY : classer — *vi* : se classer, compter <he ranks among the best in his class : il se classe parmi les meilleurs de sa classe>

rank[2] *adj* **1** : luxuriant (se dit de la végétation), envahissant (se dit des mauvais herbes) **2** MALODOROUS : fétide, nauséabond **3** FLAGRANT : complet, flagrant <rank disloyalty : déloyauté flagrante>

rank[3] *n* **1** LINE, ROW : rang *m* <to close ranks : serrer les rangs> **2** GRADE, POSITION : rang *m*, grade *m* <to pull rank : abuser de son rang> **3** CLASS : rang *m*, condition *f* (sociale) **4 ranks** *npl* : rangs *mpl* (militaires), échelons *mpl*

rank and file *n* **1** : hommes *mpl* du rang (dans les forces armées) **2** : base *f* (politique)

rankle ['ræŋkəl] *vi* **-kled; -kling** : rester sur le cœur, laisser une rancœur

ransack ['rænˌsæk] *vt* **1** SEARCH : fouiller **2** PLUNDER : saccager, piller

ransom[1] ['ræntsəm] *vt* : payer une rançon pour, rançonner

ransom[2] *n* : rançon *f*

rant ['rænt] *vi or* **to rant and rave** : tempêter, fulminer

rap[1] ['ræp] *v* **rapped; rapping** *vt* **1** STRIKE : frapper, taper **2** CRITICIZE : critiquer, réprimander — *vi* **1** KNOCK : frapper **2** CHAT : causer, bavarder

rap[2] *n* **1** BLOW, TAP : coup *m* sec, tape *f* **2** CHAT : causerie *f*, bavardage *m* **3** *or* **rap music** : rap *m* **4 to beat the rap** : échapper à la justice

rapacious [rə'peɪʃəs] *adj* **1** GREEDY : rapace, avide **2** RAVENOUS : rapace, vorace

rape[1] ['reɪp] *vt* **raped; raping** : violer
rape[2] *n* **1** : viol *m* **2** : colza *m* (plante)
rapid ['ræpɪd] *adj* : rapide
rapidity [rə'pɪdət̬i] *n* : rapidité *f*
rapids ['ræpɪdz] *ns & pl* : rapides *mpl*
rapier ['reɪpiər] *n* : rapière *f*
rapist ['reɪpɪst] *n* : violeur *m*
rapport [ræ'pɔr] *n* : rapport *m*, relation *f*
rapt ['ræpt] *adj* : captivé, transporté
rapture ['ræptʃər] *n* : extase *f*, ravissement *m*
rapturous ['ræptʃərəs] *adj* : extasié, extatique
rare ['rær] *adj* **rarer; rarest 1** RAREFIED : raréfié (se dit de l'air) **2** DISTINCTIVE, FINE : extraordinaire, exceptionnel <a rare June day : une de ces journées extraordinaires du mois de juin> **3** UNCOMMON : rare **4** : saignant (se dit de la viande)
rarefy ['rærə,faɪ] *v* **-fied; -fying** *vt* : raréfier — *vi* : se raréfier
rarely ['rærli] *adv* SELDOM : rarement
raring ['rærən, -ɪŋ] *adj* : impatient <raring to go : impatient de partir>
rarity ['rærət̬i] *n, pl* **-ties** : rareté *f*
rascal ['ræskəl] *n* **1** : polisson *m*, -sonne *f* **2** ROGUE : scélérat *m*, -rate *f*
rash[1] ['ræʃ] *adj* : irréfléchi, téméraire
rash[2] *n* : rougeurs *fpl*
rashly ['ræʃli] *adv* : sans réfléchir, imprudemment
rasp[1] ['ræsp] *vt* **1** SCRAPE : râper **2** IRRITATE : irriter **3 to rasp out** : dire d'une voix rauque
rasp[2] *n* : râpe *f*
raspberry ['ræz,bɛri] *n, pl* **-ries** : framboise *f*
rat ['ræt] *n* : rat *m*
ratchet ['rætʃət] *n or* **ratchet wheel** : roue *f* à rochet
rate[1] ['reɪt] *vt* **rated; rating 1** APPRAISE : estimer, évaluer **2** REGARD : considérer, estimer <she is rated an excellent pianist : on la considère comme une excellente pianiste> **3** DESERVE : mériter
rate[2] *n* **1** : taux *m* <interest rate : taux d'intérêt> **2** PRICE : tarif *m* <hotel rates : tarifs hôteliers> **3** PACE : rythme *m*, train *m* <at a rate of 40 miles per hour : à un rythme de 40 milles à l'heure> **4 at any rate** : en tous cas
rather ['ræðər, 'rʌ-, 'rɑ-] *adv* **1** PREFERABLY : mieux <I'd rather not go : j'aimerais mieux ne pas y aller> **2** : plutôt <my father, or rather my stepfather : mon père, ou plutôt mon beau-père> **3** SOMEWHAT : assez, plutôt
ratification [,ræt̬əfə'keɪʃən] *n* : ratification *f*
ratify ['ræt̬ə,faɪ] *vt* **-fied; -fying** : ratifier
rating ['reɪtɪŋ] *n* **1** STANDING : classement *m*, cote *f* **2 ratings** *npl* : indice *m* d'écoute
ratio ['reɪʃio] *n, pl* **-tios** : rapport *m*, proportion *f*
ration[1] ['ræʃən, 'reɪʃən] *vt* **rationed; rationing** : rationner
ration[2] *n* **1** : ration *f* **2 rations** *npl* PROVISIONS : rations *fpl*, provisions *fpl*
rational ['ræʃənəl] *adj* : raisonnable, sensé, logique
rationale [,ræʃə'næl] *n* **1** EXPLANATION : raisons *fpl*, logique *f* **2** BASIS : justification *f*, raison *f* d'être
rationalization [,ræʃənələ'zeɪʃən] *n* : justification *f*, rationalisation *f*
rationalize ['ræʃənə,laɪz] *vt* **-ized; -izing** : justifier, rationaliser
rationally ['ræʃənəli] *adv* : rationnellement
rattle[1] ['ræt̬əl] *v* **-tled; -tling** *vi* : faire du bruit, vibrer — *vt* **1** UPSET : ébranler, secouer **2 to rattle off** : débiter à toute vitesse
rattle[2] *n* **1** : cliquetis *m*, bruit *m* **2** *or* **baby's rattle** : hochet *m* **3** : grelot *m* (d'un serpent à sonnettes)
rattler ['ræt̬ələr] → **rattlesnake**
rattlesnake ['ræt̬əl,sneɪk] *n* : serpent *m* à sonnettes, crotale *m*
ratty ['ræt̬i] *adj* **rattier; -est** : miteux, misérable
raucous ['rɔkəs] *adj* **1** HARSH : rauque (se dit de la voix) **2** BOISTEROUS : bruyant — **raucously** *adv*
ravage ['rævɪdʒ] *vt* **-aged; -aging** : ravager
ravages ['rævɪdʒəz] *npl* : ravages *mpl*
rave ['reɪv] *vi* **raved; raving 1** : délirer (se dit d'un malade) **2 to rave about** : s'extasier sur, s'emballer au sujet de
ravel[1] ['rævəl] *v* **-eled** *or* **-elled; -eling** *or* **-elling** *vt* UNRAVEL : défaire (un tricot) — *vi* FRAY : s'effilocher
ravel[2] *n* : effiloche *f*
raven ['reɪvən] *n* : grand corbeau *m*
ravenous ['rævənəs] *adj* **1** HUNGRY : affamé <to be ravenous : avoir une faim de loup> **2** RAPACIOUS : vorace
ravenously ['rævənəsli] *adv* : voracement
ravine [rə'viːn] *n* : ravin *m*, coulée *f Can*
ravish ['rævɪʃ] *vt* **1** SEIZE : ravir, emporter de force **2** DELIGHT : ravir, enchanter **3** RAPE : violer
raw ['rɔ] *adj* **rawer; rawest 1** UNCOOKED : cru **2** UNTREATED : brut, écru (se dit des étoffes) <raw silk : soie grège> **3** INEXPERIENCED : inexpérimenté **4** OPEN : à vif, ouvert <a raw wound : une plaie ouverte> **5** : froid et humide, cru <a raw day : une journée crue> **6** COARSE, VULGAR : grossier, obscène **7 raw material** : matière *f* première **8 to get a raw deal** : être traité injustement
rawhide ['rɔ,haɪd] *n* : cuir *m* brut

ray ['reɪ] *n* **1** : rayon *m* (de lumière) **2** BIT, GLIMMER : lueur *f* <a ray of hope : une lueur d'espoir>
rayon ['reɪˌɑn] *n* : rayonne *f*
raze ['reɪz] *vt* **razed; razing** : raser, détruire
razor ['reɪzər] *n* : rasoir *m*
reach[1] ['ri:tʃ] *vt* **1** EXTEND : tendre, étendre <to reach out one's hand : tendre la main> **2** GRASP, TOUCH : atteindre **3** : arriver à, aller jusqu'à <his shadow reached the wall : son ombre arrivait jusqu'au mur> **4** : parvenir à <to reach an agreement : parvenir à une entente> **5** CONTACT : rejoindre — *vi* EXTEND : s'étendre
reach[2] *n* : portée *f* <within reach : à portée de la main>
react [ri'ækt] *vi* : réagir
reaction [ri'ækʃən] *n* : réaction *f*
reactionary[1] [ri'ækʃəˌnɛri] *adj* : réactionnaire
reactionary[2] *n, pl* **-ries** : réactionnaire *mf*
reactor [ri'æktər] *n* : réacteur *m* <nuclear reactor : réacteur nucléaire>
read[1] ['ri:d] *v* **read** ['rɛd]; **reading** *vt* **1** : lire <to read a book : lire un livre> **2** INTERPRET : interpréter, reconnaître <to read nature's signs : interpréter les signes de la nature> **3** UNDERSTAND : connaître, comprendre <she reads him like a book : elle connaît ses moindres réactions> **4** STUDY : faire, étudier <she reads law : elle fait son droit> **5** INDICATE : indiquer, montrer <the thermometer reads 10° : le thermomètre indique 10°> — *vi* : se lire <this book reads smoothly : ce livre se lit facilement>
read[2] ['rɛd] *adj* **well read** : instruit, informé
readable ['ri:dəbəl] *adj* : lisible
reader ['ri:dər] *n* : lecteur *m*, -trice *f*
readily ['rɛdəli] *adv* **1** WILLINGLY : avec empressement, volontiers **2** EASILY : facilement
readiness ['rɛdinəs] *n* **1** ALACRITY : empressement *m* **2** EASE : facilité *f*, aisance *f*
reading ['ri:dɪŋ] *n* **1** : lecture *f* (d'un livre) **2** : indication *f* (d'un instrument), relevé *m* (d'un compteur) <to take a reading : faire un relevé>
readjust [ˌri:ə'dʒʌst] *vt* : rajuster, réajuster — *vi* : se réadapter
readjustment [ˌri:ə'dʒʌstmənt] *n* : réajustement *m*
ready[1] ['rɛdi] *vt* **readied; readying** : préparer
ready[2] *adj* **readier; -est 1** : prêt <dinner is ready : le dîner est prêt> <ready to cry : au bord des larmes> **2** WILLING : prêt <always ready to help : toujours prêt à aider> **3 to have a ready wit** : avoir la repartie facile **4 ready money** : argent *m* liquide
ready-made [ˌrɛdi'meɪd] *adj* : de prêt-à-porter (se dit des vêtements)
reaffirm [ˌri:ə'fərm] *vt* : réaffirmer
real[1] ['ri:l] *adv* VERY : vraiment
real[2] *adj* **1** : réel <real income : revenu réel> **2** GENUINE : vrai, véritable **3** ACTUAL : réel, vrai <in real life : en réalité> **4 for ~** : pour de vrai
real estate *n* : biens *mpl* immobiliers
realism ['ri:əˌlɪzəm] *n* : réalisme *m*
realist ['ri:əlɪst] *n* : réaliste *mf*
realistic [ˌri:ə'lɪstɪk] *adj* : réaliste
realistically [ˌri:ə'lɪstɪkli] *adv* : de façon réaliste
reality [ri'æləṭi] *n, pl* **-ties** : réalité *f*
realization [ˌri:ələ'zeɪʃən] *n* : réalisation *f*
realize ['ri:əˌlaɪz] *vt* **-ized; -izing 1** ACCOMPLISH : réaliser **2** GAIN, OBTAIN : réaliser (un profit) **3** UNDERSTAND : se rendre compte de, comprendre
really ['rɪli, 'rɪ:-] *adv* **1** ACTUALLY : vraiment <I didn't really mean it : je n'étais pas vraiment sérieux> **2** TRULY : incontestablement, vraiment **3** (*used as an intensifier*) <really, you're being ridiculous : vraiment, tu es ridicule>
realm ['rɛlm] *n* **1** KINGDOM : royaume *m* **2** SPHERE : domaine *m*
ream[1] ['ri:m] *vt* : fraiser
ream[2] *n* : rame *f* (de papier)
reap ['ri:p] *vt* **1** : moissonner, faucher (des récoltes) **2** HARVEST : récolter <he reaped a rich reward : il a récolté une riche récompense>
reaper ['ri:pər] *n* : moissonneuse *f* (machine)
reappear [ˌri:ə'pɪr] *vi* : réapparaître, reparaître
rear[1] ['rɪr] *vt* **1** RAISE : lever, relever **2** BREED, BRING UP : élever (des animaux ou des enfants) — *vi* : se cabrer (se dit d'un cheval)
rear[2] *adj* : derrière
rear[3] *n* **1** BACK : derrière *m* **2** BUTTOCKS : derrière *m fam*, arrière-train *m fam*
rear admiral *n* : contre-amiral *m*
rearrange [ˌri:ə'reɪndʒ] *vt* **-ranged; -ranging** : réarranger
reason[1] ['ri:zən] *vi* : raisonner
reason[2] *n* **1** EXPLANATION : raison *f* **2** BASIS : motif *m*, raisons *fpl* **3** CAUSE : cause *f*, raison *f* **4** COMMON SENSE : raison *f*, bon sens *m*
reasonable ['ri:zənəbəl] *adj* **1** : raisonnable, sensé **2** AFFORDABLE : raisonnable, abordable
reasonably ['ri:zənəbli] *adv* : raisonnablement
reasoning ['ri:zənɪŋ] *n* : raisonnement *m*
reassess [ˌri:ə'sɛs] *vt* : réexaminer
reassurance [ˌri:ə'ʃʊrənts] *n* **1** ASSURANCE : assurance *f* **2** COMFORTING : réconfort *m*
reassure [ˌri:ə'ʃʊr] *vt* **-sured; -suring** : rassurer

reawaken [ˌriːəˈweɪkən] *vt* : réveiller
rebate[1] [ˈriːˌbeɪt] *vt* **-bated; -bating** : donner une ristourne à
rebate[2] *n* : ristourne *f*
rebel[1] [rɪˈbɛl] *vi* **-belled; -belling** : se rebeller, se révolter
rebel[2] [ˈrɛbəl] *adj* : rebelle
rebel[3] [ˈrɛbəl] *n* : rebelle *mf*
rebellion [rɪˈbɛljən] *n* : rébellion *f*, révolte *f*
rebellious [rɪˈbɛljəs] *adj* : rebelle
rebirth [ˌriːˈbərθ] *n* : renaissance *f*
reboot [ˌriːˈbuːt] *v* : redémarrer
rebound[1] [ˈriːˌbaʊnd, rɪˈbaʊnd] *vi* **1** : rebondir (se dit d'un ballon) **2** RECOVER : rebondir, repartir à zéro
rebound[2] [ˈriːˌbaʊnd] *n* : rebond *m*
rebuff[1] [rɪˈbʌf] *vt* : mal accueillir
rebuff[2] *n* : rebuffade *f*
rebuild [ˌriːˈbɪld] *vt* **-built** [-ˈbɪlt]; **-building** : reconstruire
rebuke[1] [rɪˈbjuːk] *vt* **-buked; -buking** : reprocher, réprimander
rebuke[2] *n* : reproche *m*, réprimande *f*
rebut [rɪˈbʌt] *vt* **-butted; -butting** : réfuter
rebuttal [rɪˈbʌtəl] *n* : réfutation *f*
recalcitrant [rɪˈkælsətrənt] *adj* : récalcitrant
recall[1] [rɪˈkɔl] *vt* **1** : rappeler <to be recalled to duty : être rappelé au devoir> **2** REMEMBER : se rappeler, se souvenir de **3** CANCEL, REVOKE : révoquer, annuler
recall[2] [rɪˈkɔl, ˈriːˌkɔl] *n* **1** : rappel *m* (de personnes ou de marchandises) **2** MEMORY : mémoire *f* **3** REVOCATION : révocation *f*, annulation *f*
recant [rɪˈkænt] *vt* : rétracter (une opinion) — *vi* : abjurer
recapitulate [ˌriːkəˈpɪtʃəˌleɪt] *vt* **-lated; -lating** : récapituler, résumer
recapitulation [ˌriːkəˌpɪtʃəˈleɪʃən] *n* : récapitulation *f*
recapture [ˌriːˈkæptʃər] *vt* **-tured; -turing 1** : reprendre (une ville, etc.) **2** RECOVER : recréer <to recapture the past : recréer le passé>
recede [rɪˈsiːd] *vi* **-ceded; -ceding 1** WITHDRAW : s'éloigner, redescendre (se dit de la marée), refluer (se dit des eaux) **2** DIMINISH : diminuer, baisser <to recede into the distance : disparaître dans le lointain>
receipt [rɪˈsiːt] *n* **1** : reçu *m*, récépissé *m* **2 receipts** *npl* : recettes *fpl*
receivable [rɪˈsiːvəbəl] *adj* : à recevoir <accounts receivable : comptes clients>
receive [rɪˈsiːv] *vt* **-ceived; -ceiving 1** GET : recevoir <to receive a gift : recevoir un cadeau> **2** GREET : accueillir (des visiteurs) **3** : recevoir, capter (des ondes radio)
receiver [rɪˈsiːvər] *n* **1** : receveur *m*, -veuse *f* (personne) **2** : récepteur *m* (de radio), combiné *m* (téléphonique)
recent [ˈriːsənt] *adj* : récent
recently [ˈriːsəntli] *adv* : récemment
receptacle [rɪˈsɛptɪkəl] *n* : récipient *m*
reception [rɪˈsɛpʃən] *n* : réception *f*
receptionist [rɪˈsɛpʃənɪst] *n* : réceptionniste *mf*
receptive [rɪˈsɛptɪv] *adj* : réceptif
receptivity [ˌriːˌsɛpˈtɪvəṭi] *n* : réceptivité *f*
recess[1] [ˈriːˌsɛs, rɪˈsɛs] *vt* : encastrer <recessed lighting : éclairage encastré> — *vi* : suspendre les séances
recess[2] *n* **1** ALCOVE : recoin *m*, alcôve *f* **2** BREAK : récréation *f* (scolaire)
recession [rɪˈsɛʃən] *n* : récession *f*
recharge [ˌriːˈtʃɑrdʒ] *vt* **-charged; -charging** : recharger
rechargeable [ˌriːˈtʃɑrdʒəbəl] *adj* : rechargeable
recipe [ˈrɛsəˌpiː] *n* : recette *f*
recipient [rɪˈsɪpiənt] *n* : destinataire *mf* (d'une lettre), récipiendaire *m* (d'un prix, d'un diplôme, etc.)
reciprocal [rɪˈsɪprəkəl] *adj* : réciproque — **reciprocally** *adv*
reciprocate [rɪˈsɪprəˌkeɪt] *v* **-cated; -cating** *vt* : retourner (un service) — *vi* : rendre la pareille, en faire autant
reciprocity [ˌrɛsəˈprɑsəṭi] *n, pl* **-ties** : réciprocité *f*
recital [rɪˈsaɪṭəl] *n* **1** NARRATIVE : narration *f*, énumération *f* **2** : récital *m* <dance recital : récital de danse>
recitation [ˌrɛsəˈteɪʃən] *n* : récitation *f*
recite [rɪˈsaɪt] *vt* **-cited; -citing 1** : réciter (un poème, etc.) **2** RECOUNT : relater, raconter
reckless [ˈrɛkləs] *adj* : imprudent, irréfléchi, téméraire
recklessly [ˈrɛkləsli] *adv* : imprudemment, sans réfléchir
recklessness [ˈrɛkləsnəs] *n* : imprudence *f*, témérité *f*
reckon [ˈrɛkən] *vt* **1** CALCULATE, COUNT : compter **2** CONSIDER : estimer, considérer
reckoning [ˈrɛkənɪŋ] *n* **1** CALCULATION : compte *m*, calcul *m* **2** ESTIMATION : estimation *f*, calculs *mpl* <according to his reckoning : selon ses calculs>
reclaim [rɪˈkleɪm] *vt* **1** : mettre en valeur (un terrain) **2** RECYCLE : recycler **3** RECOVER : récupérer
recline [rɪˈklaɪn] *vi* **-clined; -clining 1** LIE : être couché, être allongé **2** : s'incliner (se dit d'un siège)
recluse [ˈrɛˌkluːs, rɪˈkluːs] *n* : reclus *m*, -cluse *f*
recognition [ˌrɛkɪgˈnɪʃən] *n* : reconnaissance *f*
recognizable [ˈrɛkəgˌnaɪzəbəl] *adj* : reconnaissable
recognizably [ˈrɛkəgˌnaɪzəbli] *adv* : manifestement, d'une façon reconnaissable
recognize [ˈrɛkɪgˌnaɪz] *vt* **-nized; -nizing** : reconnaître

recoil[1] [rɪ'kɔɪl] *vi* : reculer
recoil[2] ['ri:,kɔɪl, rɪ'-] *n* : recul *m*, mouvement *m* de recul
recollect [,rɛkə'lɛkt] *vt* : se souvenir de, se rappeler — *vi* : se souvenir
recollection [,rɛkə'lɛkʃən] *n* : souvenir *m*
recommend [,rɛkə'mɛnd] *vt* : recommander
recommendation [,rɛkəmən'deɪʃən] *n* : recommandation *f*
recompense[1] ['rɛkəm,pɛnts] *vt* **-pensed; -pensing 1** REWARD : récompenser **2** COMPENSATE : dédommager, compenser
recompense[2] *n* **1** REWARD : récompense *f* **2** COMPENSATION : dédommagement *m*
reconcile ['rɛkən,saɪl] *v* **-ciled; -ciling** *vt* **1** : réconcilier **2 to reconcile oneself to** : se résigner à — *vi* MAKE UP : se réconcilier
reconciliation [,rɛkən,sɪli'eɪʃən] *n* : réconciliation *f*
recondite ['rɛkən,daɪt, rɪ'kɑn-] *adj* : abstrus, obscur
recondition [,ri:kən,dɪʃən] *vt* : remettre à neuf
reconnaissance [rɪ'kɑnəzənts, -sənts] *n* : reconnaissance *f*
reconnoiter *or* **reconnoitre** [,ri:kə'nɔɪʇər, ,rɛkə-] *v* **-tered** *or* **-tred; -tering** *or* **-tring** *vt* : reconnaître — *vi* : faire une reconnaissance
reconsider [,ri:kən'sɪdər] *vt* : réexaminer (un plan, une décision) — *vi* : repenser <I asked him to reconsider : je lui ai demandé d'y repenser>
reconsideration [,ri:kən,sɪdə'reɪʃən] *n* : révision *f*, réexamen *m*
reconstruct [,ri:kən'strʌkt] *vt* : reconstruire
record[1] [rɪ'kɔrd] *vt* **1** WRITE DOWN : noter, enregistrer **2** REGISTER : enregistrer **3** INDICATE : indiquer (la température, etc.) **4** TAPE : enregistrer (une émission)
record[2] ['rɛkərd] *n* **1** DOCUMENT : document *m*, écrit *m* **2** HISTORY, REPORT : compte rendu *m*, récit *m* (des événements, etc.) **3** : record *m* <the world record : le record mondial> **4** : disque *m* (de musique) **5** *or* **school record** : dossier *m* (scolaire) **6** *or* **police record** : casier *m* judiciaire
recorder [rɪ'kɔrdər] *n* **1** *or* **tape recorder** : magnétophone *m* **2** : flûte *f* à bec (instrument de musique)
recount [rɪ'kaʊnt] *vt* **1** NARRATE : raconter, conter **2** [,ri:'-] : recompter (des votes, etc.), compter de nouveau
recoup [rɪ'ku:p] *vt* : recouvrer, récupérer
recourse ['ri:,kors, rɪ'-] *n* : recours *m*
recover [rɪ'kʌvər] *vt* **1** REGAIN : retrouver, récupérer **2** RECOUP : recouvrer — *vi* RECUPERATE : se remettre, se rétablir
recovery [rɪ'kʌvəri] *n, pl* **-ries** : rétablissement *m*
re–create [,ri:kri'eɪt] *vt* **-ated; -ating** : recréer
recreation [,rɛkri'eɪʃən] *n* : loisirs *mpl*, récréation *f*
recreational [,rɛkri'eɪʃənəl] *adj* : récréatif
recriminate [rɪ'krɪmə,neɪt] *vi* **-nated; -nating** : récriminer <to recriminate against : récriminer contre>
recrimination [rɪ,krɪmə'neɪʃən] *n* : récrimination *f*
recruit[1] [rɪ'kru:t] *vt* : recruter
recruit[2] *n* : recrue *f*
recruitment [rɪ'kru:tmənt] *n* : recrutement *m*
rectal ['rɛktəl] *adj* : rectal
rectangle ['rɛk,tæŋgəl] *n* : rectangle *m*
rectangular [rɛk'tæŋgjələr] *adj* : rectangulaire
rectify ['rɛktə,faɪ] *vt* **-fied; -fying** : rectifier
rectitude ['rɛktə,tu:d, -,tju:d] *n* : rectitude *f*
rector ['rɛktər] *n* : pasteur *m*
rectory ['rɛktəri] *n, pl* **-ries** : presbytère *m*
rectum ['rɛktəm] *n, pl* **-tums** *or* **-ta** [-tə] : rectum *m*
recumbent [rɪ'kəmbənt] *adj* : couché, étendu
recuperate [rɪ'ku:pə,reɪt, -'kju:-] *v* **-ated; -ating** *vi* : se rétablir, se remettre — *vt* REGAIN : retrouver (ses forces), récupérer (ses débours)
recuperation [rɪ,ku:pə'reɪʃən, -,kju:-] *n* : rétablissement *m* (de la santé), recouvrement *m* (d'une dette, etc.)
recur [rɪ'kər] *vi* **-curred; -curring** : réapparaître
recurrence [rɪ'kərənts] *n* : réapparition *f*, retour *m*
recurrent [rɪ'kərənt] *adj* : récurrent, fréquent
recyclable [rɪ'saɪkələbəl] *adj* : recyclable
recycle [rɪ'saɪkəl] *vt* **-cled; -cling** : recycler
red[1] ['rɛd] *adj* : rouge
red[2] *n* **1** : rouge *m* **2 Red** : communiste *mf*, rouge *mf* **3 in the red** : dans le rouge, en déficit
red blood cell *n* : globule *m* rouge
red–blooded ['rɛd'blʌdəd] *adj* : vigoureux
redcap ['rɛd,kæp] → **porter**
redden ['rɛdən] *vt* : rougir — *vi* BLUSH : rougir
reddish ['rɛdɪʃ] *adj* : rougeâtre
redecorate [,ri:'dɛkə,reɪt] *vt* **-rated; -rating** : repeindre et retapisser
redeem [ri'di:m] *vt* **1** RESCUE, SAVE : racheter, sauver <to redeem oneself : se racheter> **2** REPAY, REPURCHASE : rembourser (une dette), racheter (une propriété chez un prêteur sur gages) **3** EXCHANGE : échanger <to

redeem savings bonds : échanger des bons d'épargne> **4** : racheter (en religion)

redeemer [rɪ'di:mər] *n* : rédempteur *m*

redemption [rɪ'dɛmpʃən] *n* : rédemption *f*

red–handed ['rɛd'hændəd] *adv* : la main dans le sac

redhead ['rɛd,hɛd] *n* : roux *m*, rousse *f*

rediscover [,ri:di'skʌvər] *vt* : redécouvrir

redistribute [,ri:di'strɪ,bju:t] *vt* **-uted; -uting** : redistribuer

redness ['rɛdnəs] *n* : rougeur *f*

redo [,ri:'du:] *vt* **-did** [-dɪd]; **-done** [-'dʌn]; **-doing 1** : refaire **2** → **redecorate**

redolence ['rɛdələnts] *n* : arôme *m*, parfum *m*

redolent ['rɛdələnt] *adj* **1** FRAGRANT : aromatique, parfumé **2** SUGGESTIVE : évocateur **3 ~ of** *or* **~ with** : qui sent de, qui dégage (une odeur)

redouble [rɪ'dʌbəl] *vt* **-bled; -bling** : redoubler

redoubtable [rɪ'daʊṭəbəl] *adj* : redoutable, formidable

redress [rɪ'drɛs] *vt* : redresser, réparer

red tape *n* : lenteurs *fpl* bureaucratiques, paperasserie *f*

reduce [rɪ'du:s, -'dju:s] *v* **-duced; -ducing** *vt* **1** LESSEN : réduire, diminuer **2** LOWER : baisser (des prix, etc.) **3** DEMOTE : rétrograder **4 to reduce to tears** : faire pleurer — *vi* : maigrir, perdre du poids

reduction [rɪ'dʌkʃən] *n* : réduction *f*, diminution *f*

redundant [rɪ'dʌndənt] *adj* : superflu, redondant

redwood ['rɛd,wʊd] *n* : séquoia *m*

reed ['ri:d] *n* **1** : roseau *m* **2** : anche *f* (d'un instrument de musique)

reef ['ri:f] *n* : récif *m*, écueil *m*

reek[1] ['ri:k] *vi* : empester, puer

reek[2] *n* : puanteur *f*

reel[1] ['ri:l] *vt* **1 to reel in** : enrouler (une ligne de pêche, etc.), ramener (un poisson) **2 to reel off** : débiter (un discours, etc.) — *vi* **1** SPIN, WHIRL : tournoyer <her head was reeling : elle avait la tête qui tournait> **2** STAGGER : chanceler, tituber

reel[2] *n* **1** : bobine *f*, rouleau *m*, moulinet *m* (de pêche) **2** : quadrille *m* écossais (danse)

reelect [,ri:ɪ'lɛkt] *vt* : réélire

reenact [,ri:ɪ'nækt] *vt* : reconstituer, reproduire

reenter [,ri:'ɛntər] *vt* : entrer à nouveau

reestablish [,ri:ɪ'stæblɪʃ] *vt* : rétablir

reevaluate [,ri:ɪ'væljʊ,eɪt] *vt* **-ated; -ating** : réévaluer

reexamine [,ri:ɪg'zæmən] *vt* **-ined; -ining** : réexaminer

refer [ri'fər] *v* **-ferred; -ferring** *vt* **1** DIRECT : envoyer, diriger <to refer a patient to a specialist : diriger un patient à un spécialiste> **2** SUBMIT : soumettre, présenter <to refer a proposal to a committee : soumettre un plan à un comité> — *vi* **to refer to** MENTION : faire allusion à, mentionner

referee[1] [,rɛfə'ri:] *v* **-eed; -eeing** : arbitrer

referee[2] *n* : arbitre *m*

reference ['rɛfərənts] *n* **1** *or* **reference book** : ouvrage *m* de référence **2** ALLUSION : allusion *f* **3** RECOMMENDATION : référence *f* **4 in reference to** : en ce qui concerne

referendum [,rɛfə'rɛndəm] *n, pl* **-da** [-də] *or* **-dums** : référendum *m*

refill[1] [,ri:'fɪl] *vt* : remplir à nouveau

refill[2] ['ri:,fɪl] *n* : recharge *f* (de stylo), cartouche *f* (d'encre)

refine [rɪ'faɪn] *vt* **-fined; -fining 1** : raffiner (le sucre, le pétrole, etc.) **2** IMPROVE, PERFECT : peaufiner, perfectionner

refinement [rɪ'faɪnmənt] *n* **1** : raffinage *m* (du pétrole, du sucre, etc.) **2** CULTIVATION, ELEGANCE : raffinement *m* **3** IMPROVEMENT : amélioration *f*, perfectionnement *m*

refinery [rɪ'faɪnəri] *n, pl* **-eries** : raffinerie *f*

reflect [rɪ'flɛkt] *vt* **1** : réfléchir (la lumière), renvoyer (des sons, de la chaleur, etc.) **2** : refléter (une image, des idées, des émotions, etc.) <art reflects life : l'art reflète la vie> — *vi* **1** PONDER : réfléchir **2 to reflect badly on** : faire du tort à **3 to reflect well on** : faire honneur à

reflection [rɪ'flɛkʃən] *n* **1** : réflexion *f* (de la lumière, des sons, etc.) **2** IMAGE : reflet *m*, image *f* **3** THOUGHT : réflexion *f*, pensée *f*

reflective [rɪ'flɛktɪv] *adj* **1** : réfléchissant (en physique) **2** THOUGHTFUL : pensif, songeur

reflector [rɪ'flɛktər] *n* : réflecteur *m*

reflex[1] ['ri:,flɛks] *adj* : réflexe

reflex[2] *n* : réflexe *m*

reflexive[1] [rɪ'flɛksɪv] *adj* : réfléchi <reflexive pronoun : pronom réfléchi>

reflexive[2] *n or* **reflexive verb** : verbe *m* réfléchi

reform[1] [rɪ'fɔrm] *vt* : réformer — *vi* : se réformer

reform[2] *n* : réforme *f* — **reformable** *adj*

reformation [,rɛfər'meɪʃən] *n* **1** : réforme *f* **2 the Reformation** : la Réforme

reformatory [rɪ'fɔrmə,tori] *n, pl* **-ries** : maison *f* de correction

reformer [rɪ'fɔrmər] *n* : réformateur *m*, -trice *f*

refract [rɪ'frækt] *vt* : réfracter — *vi* : se réfracter

refraction [rɪ'frækʃən] *n* : réfraction *f*

refractory [rɪ'fræktəri] *adj* : réfractaire

refrain[1] [rɪ'freɪn] *vi* **to refrain from** : se retenir de, s'empêcher de

refrain[2] *n* : refrain *m* (en musique)
refresh [rɪˈfrɛʃ] *vt* **1** RESTORE, REVIVE : rafraîchir <to refresh oneself : se rafraîchir> **2 to refresh s.o.'s memory** : rafraîchir la mémoire de qqn
refreshment [rɪˈfrɛʃmənt] *n* **1** REST : repos *m* **2 refreshments** *npl* : rafraîchissements *mpl*
refrigerate [rɪˈfrɪdʒəˌreɪt] *vt* **-ated; -ating** : réfrigérer, frigorifier
refrigeration [rɪˌfrɪdʒəˈreɪʃən] *n* : réfrigération *f*
refrigerator [rɪˈfrɪdʒəˌreɪt̬ər] *n* : réfrigérateur *m*
refuel [riːˈfjuːəl] *v* **-eled** *or* **-elled; -eling** *or* **-elling** *vt* : ravitailler — *vi* : se ravitailler
refuge [ˈrɛˌfjuːdʒ] *n* : refuge *m*, abri *m*
refugee [ˌrɛfjʊˈdʒiː] *n* : réfugié *m*, -giée *f*
refund[1] [rɪˈfʌnd, ˈriːˌfʌnd] *vt* : rembourser (de l'argent)
refund[2] [ˈriːˌfʌnd] *n* : remboursement *m*, ristourne *f*
refundable [rɪˈfʌndəbəl] *adj* : remboursable
refurbish [rɪˈfərbɪʃ] *vt* : remettre à neuf, réaménager
refusal [rɪˈfjuːzəl] *n* : refus *m*
refuse[1] [rɪˈfjuːz] *vt* **-fused; -fusing 1** REJECT : refuser **2** DENY : refuser <they were refused admittance : on leur a refusé l'entrée> **3 to refuse to do sth** : se refuser à faire qqch
refuse[2] [ˈrɛˌfjuːs, -ˌfjuːz] *n* : ordures *fpl*, déchets *mpl*
refutation [ˌrɛfjʊˈteɪʃən] *n* : réfutation *f*
refute [rɪˈfjuːt] *vt* **-futed; -futing** : réfuter
regal [ˈriːgəl] *adj* : royal, majestueux
regale [rɪˈgeɪl] *vt* **-galed; -galing** : régaler
regalia [rɪˈgeɪljə] *npl* **1** INSIGNIA : insignes *mpl* **2** FINERY : atours *mpl*, accoutrement *m*
regard[1] [rɪˈgɑrd] *vt* **1** CONSIDER : considérer <I regard her as my sister : je la considère comme une sœur> **2** HEED : tenir compte de **3** OBSERVE : observer, considérer avec attention **4** RESPECT : respecter <highly regarded : très estimé>
regard[2] *n* **1** CONSIDERATION : égard *m*, considération *f* <without regard for : sans égard pour> **2** ESTEEM : respect *m*, estime *f* **3 regards** *npl* : amitiés *fpl* <send him my regards : transmettez-lui mes amitiés> **4 as regards** *or* **with regard to** : en ce qui concerne
regarding [rɪˈgɑrdɪŋ] *prep* : concernant
regardless [rɪˈgɑrdləs] *adv* : malgré tout, quand même
regardless of *prep* : sans tenir compte de
regenerate [rɪˈdʒɛnəˌreɪt] *v* **-ated; -ating** *vt* : régénérer — *vi* : se régénérer
regeneration [rɪˌdʒɛnəˈreɪʃən] *n* : régénération *f*
regent [ˈriːdʒənt] *n* : régent *m*, -gente *f*
regime [reɪˈʒiːm, rɪ-] *n* : régime *m*
regimen [ˈrɛdʒəmən] *n* : régime *m*
regiment[1] [ˈrɛdʒəˌmɛnt] *vt* : enrégimenter
regiment[2] [ˈrɛdʒəmənt] *n* : régiment *m*
region [ˈriːdʒən] *n* : région *f*
regional [ˈriːdʒənəl] *adj* : régional — **regionally** *adv*
register[1] [ˈrɛdʒəstər] *vt* **1** RECORD : inscrire, enregistrer **2** : immatriculer (un véhicule) **3** : enregistrer (une lettre) **4** SHOW : exprimer <to register surprise : exprimer la surprise> **5** : indiquer (la température, etc.) — *vi* ENROLL : s'inscrire
register[2] *n* **1** RECORD : registre *m* <a register of births : un registre des naissances> **2** RANGE : registre *m* (de la voix) **3** → **cash register**
registrar [ˈrɛdʒəˌstrɑr] *n* : chef *m* de la division des inscriptions (dans une université)
registration [ˌrɛdʒəˈstreɪʃən] *n* **1** : enregistrement *m* (de bagages), immatriculation *f* (d'un véhicule) **2** ENROLLMENT : inscription *f*
registry [ˈrɛdʒəstri] *n, pl* **-tries 1** REGISTRATION : enregistrement *m* **2** : bureau *m* d'enregistrement
regress [rɪˈgrɛs] *vi* : régresser
regression [rɪˈgrɛʃən] *n* : régression *f*
regressive [rɪˈgrɛsɪv] *adj* : régressif
regret[1] [rɪˈgrɛt] *vt* **-gretted; -gretting** : regretter
regret[2] *n* **1** SORROW : regret *m* **2** REMORSE : remords *mpl*, regrets *mpl* **3 regrets** *npl* : excuses *fpl* <to send one's regrets to s.o. : s'excuser auprès de qqn>
regretful [rɪˈgrɛtfəl] *adj* : plein de regrets
regretfully [rɪˈgrɛtfəli] *adv* : avec regret
regrettable [rɪˈgrɛt̬əbəl] *adj* : regrettable
regrettably [rɪˈgrɛt̬əbli] *adv* : malheureusement
regular[1] [ˈrɛgjələr] *adj* **1** SYMMETRICAL : régulier **2** NORMAL : régulier, normal **3** STEADY : régulier, égal <a regular pace : un pas régulier> **4** ORDERLY : fixe <regular habits : habitudes fixes>
regular[2] *n* : habitué *m*, -tuée *f*
regularity [ˌrɛgjəˈlærət̬i] *n, pl* **-ties** : régularité *f*
regularly [ˈrɛgjələrli] *adv* : régulièrement
regulate [ˈrɛgjəˌleɪt] *vt* **-lated; -lating** : régler
regulation [ˌrɛgjəˈleɪʃən] *n* **1** RULE : règlement *m*, règle *f* <safety regulations : règlements de sécurité> **2** CONTROL : réglementation *f*
regurgitate [rɪˈgərdʒəˌteɪt] *vt* **-tated; -tating** : régurgiter
rehabilitate [ˌriːhəˈbɪləˌteɪt] *vt* **-tated; -tating 1** REINSTATE : réhabiliter **2**

RESTORE : rénover, réhabiliter (un quartier) **3** : rééduquer (un patient), réhabiliter (un détenu, un toxicomane, etc.)

rehabilitation [ˌriːhəˌbɪləˈteɪʃən] *n* : réhabilitation *f*

rehearsal [rɪˈhərsəl] *n* : répétition *f* (au théâtre)

rehearse [rɪˈhərs] *vt* **-hearsed; -hearsing** : répéter, réciter

reheat [riːˈhiːt] *vt* : réchauffer

reign[1] [ˈreɪn] *vi* **1** RULE : régner **2** PREVAIL : régner, prédominer

reign[2] *n* : règne *m*

reimburse [ˌriːəmˈbərs] *vt* **-bursed; -bursing** : rembourser

reimbursement [ˌriːəmˈbərsmənt] *n* : remboursement *m*

rein[1] [ˈreɪn] *vt* **1** : serrer la bride à (un cheval) **2 to rein in** CHECK : contenir, maîtriser (des émotions, etc.)

rein[2] *n* **1** : rêne *f*, bride *f* (d'un cheval) **2 to give full rein to** : donner libre cours à **3 to keep a tight rein on** : tenir la bride serrée à

reincarnate [ˌriːɪnˈkɑrˌneɪt] *vt* **-nated; -nating** : réincarner

reincarnation [ˌriːɪnˌkɑrˈneɪʃən] *n* : réincarnation *f*

reindeer [ˈreɪnˌdɪr] *n* : renne *f*

reinforce [ˌriːənˈfors] *vt* **-forced; -forcing** : renforcer

reinforcement [ˌriːənˈforsmənt] *n* : renforcement *m*

reinstate [ˌriːənˈsteɪt] *vt* **-stated; -stating** : réintégrer, rétablir

reinstatement [ˌriːənˈsteɪtmənt] *n* : réintégration *f*, rétablissement *m*

reiterate [riːˈɪt̬əˌreɪt] *vt* **-ated; -ating** : réitérer, répéter

reiteration [riːˌɪt̬əˈreɪʃən] *n* : réitération *f*, répétition *f*

reject[1] [rɪˈdʒɛkt] *vt* : rejeter

reject[2] [ˈriːˌdʒɛkt] *n* **1** : marchandise *f* de second choix **2** : personne *f* méprisée

rejection [rɪˈdʒɛkʃən] *n* : rejet *m*

rejoice [rɪˈdʒɔɪs] *vi* **-joiced; -joicing** : se réjouir

rejoin *vt* **1** [ˌriːˈdʒɔɪn] : rejoindre <he rejoined the company : il a rejoint la compagnie> **2** [rɪ-] RETORT : répliquer, rétorquer

rejoinder [rɪˈdʒɔɪndər] *n* : réplique *f*

rejuvenate [riˈdʒuːvəˌneɪt] *vt* **-nated; -nating** : rajeunir

rejuvenation [riˌdʒuːvəˈneɪʃən] *n* : rajeunissement *m*

rekindle [ˌriːˈkɪndəl] *vt* **-dled; -dling** : raviver, ranimer (un feu, l'espoir etc.)

relapse[1] [riˈlæps] *vi* **-lapsed; -lapsing** : retomber, rechuter

relapse[2] [ˈriːˌlæps, riˈlæps] *n* : rechute *f* (en médecine)

relate [rɪˈleɪt] *v* **-lated; -lating** *vt* **1** TELL : raconter **2** ASSOCIATE : établir un lien entre, relier <to relate crime to poverty : relier le crime à la pauvreté> — *vi* **1** CONNECT : se rapporter **2** INTERACT : communiquer (avec) **3 to relate to** APPRECIATE, UNDERSTAND : apprécier

related [rɪˈleɪt̬əd] *adj* : apparenté

relation [rɪˈleɪʃən] *n* **1** NARRATION : récit *m* **2** CONNECTION, RELATIONSHIP : rapport *m* <in relation to : par rapport à> **3** RELATIVE : parent *m*, -rente *f* **4 relations** *npl* : rapports *mpl*, relations *fpl* <sexual relations : relations sexuelles> <foreign relations : affaires étrangères>

relationship [rɪˈleɪʃənˌʃɪp] *n* **1** CONNECTION : rapport *m*, relations *fpl* **2** KINSHIP : liens *mpl* de parenté

relative[1] [ˈrɛlət̬ɪv] *adj* : relatif — **relatively** *adv*

relative[2] *n* : parent *m*, -rente *f*

relativity [ˌrɛləˈtɪvət̬i] *n* : relativité *f*

relax [rɪˈlæks] *vt* **1** SLACKEN : relâcher, desserrer **2** MODIFY : assouplir <to relax immigration laws : assouplir les lois d'immigration> — *vi* REST : se détendre, se reposer

relaxation [ˌriːˌlækˈseɪʃən] *n* **1** RELAXING : relâchement *m*, desserrement *m* **2** DIVERSION : détente *f*

relay[1] [ˈriːˌleɪ, riˈleɪ] *vt* **-layed; -laying** : relayer

relay[2] [ˈriːˌleɪ] *n or* **relay race** : course *f* de relais

release[1] [riˈliːs] *vt* **-leased; -leasing 1** FREE : libérer **2** RELINQUISH : renoncer à (une réclamation, etc.) **3** RELIEVE : dégager <she was released from her promise : elle s'est dégagée de sa promesse> **4** : publier (un livre), sortir (un nouveau film), rendre public (un document, etc.) **5** LET GO, LOOSEN : desserrer, déclencher <to release the clutch : débrayer>

release[2] *n* **1** RELIEF : soulagement *m* (à la douleur) **2** LIBERATION : libération *f*, mise *f* en liberté **3** ISSUE : sortie *f* (d'un film), parution *f* (d'un livre) **4** : déclenchement *m* (d'un mécanisme) **5** *or* **news release** : communiqué *m*

relegate [ˈrɛləˌgeɪt] *vt* **-gated; -gating** : reléguer

relent [rɪˈlɛnt] *vi* **1** GIVE IN : se rendre **2** ABATE : se calmer

relentless [rɪˈlɛntləs] *adj* : implacable, impitoyable — **relentlessly** *adv*

relevance [ˈrɛləvənts] *n* : pertinence *f*

relevant [ˈrɛləvənt] *adj* : pertinent

relevantly [ˈrɛləvəntli] *adv* : pertinemment

reliability [rɪˌlaɪəˈbɪlət̬i] *n*, *pl* **-ties 1** : sérieux *m*, intégrité *f* (d'une personne) **2** : fiabilité *f* (d'information, d'une machine, etc.)

reliable [rɪˈlaɪəbəl] *adj* : fiable, sûr

reliance [rɪˈlaɪənts] *n* **1** DEPENDENCE : dépendance *f* **2** TRUST : confiance *f*

reliant [rɪˈlaɪənt] *adj* **1** DEPENDENT : dépendant **2** TRUSTING : confiant

relic [ˈrɛlɪk] *n* **1** : relique *f* **2 relics** *mpl* : vestiges *mpl* (du passé)

relief [rɪˈli:f] *n* **1** : soulagement *m* <much to my relief : à mon grand soulagement> **2** AID, WELFARE : aide *f* (sociale) **3** : relief *m* <a relief map : une carte en relief> **4** REPLACEMENT : relève *f,* équipe *f* de relève

relieve [rɪˈli:v] *vt* **-lieved; -lieving 1** MITIGATE : soulager, alléger **2** UNBURDEN : libérer, débarrasser <to relieve s.o. of his suitcase : débarrasser qqn de ses valises> <to be relieved of a command : être relevé d'une fonction> **3** AID : secourir, venir en aide à **4** ALLEVIATE : briser (la monotonie), dissiper (la mélancolie), égayer (la noirceur d'un vêtement, etc.)

religion [rɪˈlɪdʒən] *n* : religion *f*

religious [rɪˈlɪdʒəs] *adj* : religieux — **religiously** *adv*

relinquish [rɪˈlɪŋkwɪʃ, -ˈlɪn-] *vt* **1** GIVE UP : renoncer à, abandonner **2** RELEASE : relâcher

relish¹ [ˈrɛlɪʃ] *vt* **1** : savourer (le boire et le manger) **2** ENJOY : se réjouir de, savourer (une idée, etc.)

relish² *n* **1** ENJOYMENT : plaisir *m,* délectation *f* **2** : condiment *m* à base de cornichons et de vinaigre, relish *f Can*

relive [ˌri:ˈlɪv] *vi* **-lived; -living** : revivre

relocate [ˌri:ˈlo:ˌkeɪt, ˌri:loˈkeɪt] *v* **-cated; -cating** *vt* : muter, transférer <to relocate an employee : muter un employé> — *vi* : déménager, s'établir ailleurs

relocation [ˌri:loˈkeɪʃən] *n* **1** : mutation *f,* transfert *m* (d'un employé) **2** : déménagement *m* (d'une firme, etc.)

reluctance [rɪˈlʌktənts] *n* : réticence *f,* répugnance *f*

reluctant [rɪˈlʌktənt] *adj* **to be reluctant to** : être peu enclin à, être peu disposé à

reluctantly [rɪˈlʌktəntli] *adv* : à contrecœur

rely [rɪˈlaɪ] *vi* **-lied**; **-lying 1** DEPEND : compter (sur), dépendre (de) **2** TRUST : se fier (à)

remain [rɪˈmeɪn] *vi* **1** : rester <only ruins remain : il ne reste que des ruines> **2** STAY : rester, demeurer **3 it remains to be seen** : il reste à voir **4 the fact remains that** : toujours est-il que

remainder [rɪˈmeɪndər] *n* : reste *m,* restant *m*

remains [rɪˈmeɪnz] *npl* **1** : restes *mpl* <the remains of a meal : les restes d'un repas> **2** *or* **last remains** : restes *mpl,* dépouille *f* mortelle

remark¹ [rɪˈmɑrk] *vt* **1** NOTICE : remarquer, constater **2** SAY : remarquer, mentionner — *vi* **to remark on** : faire des remarques sur

remark² *n* : remarque *f,* observation *f*

remarkable [rɪˈmɑrkəbəl] *adj* : remarquable, extraordinaire — **remarkably** [-bli] *adv*

remedial [rɪˈmi:diəl] *adj* : de rattrapage

remedy¹ [ˈrɛmədi] *vt* **-died; -dying** : remédier à

remedy² *n, pl* **-dies** : remède *m* (en médecine)

remember [rɪˈmɛmbər] *vt* **1** RECOLLECT : se rappeler, se souvenir de **2** : penser à, ne pas oublier de <remember to open the window : pensez à ouvrir la fenêtre, n'oubliez pas d'ouvrir la fenêtre> **3** COMMEMORATE : commémorer **4 remember me to your sister** : rappelez-moi au bon souvenir de votre sœur

remembrance [rɪˈmɛmbrənts] *n* **1** RECOLLECTION : mémoire *f,* souvenir *m* **2** KEEPSAKE : souvenir *m*

remind [rɪˈmaɪnd] *vt* : rappeler <remind me to do it : rappelle-moi de le faire>

reminder [rɪˈmaɪndər] *n* : rappel *m*

reminisce [ˌrɛməˈnɪs] *vi* : évoquer ses souvenirs

reminiscence [ˌrɛməˈnɪsənts] *n* **1** MEMORY : souvenir *m* **2** RECALLING : réminiscence *f*

reminiscent [ˌrɛməˈnɪsənt] *adj* **1** NOSTALGIC : nostalgique **2 ~ of** : qui rappelle, qui fait penser à

remiss [rɪˈmɪs] *adj* : négligent, inattentif

remission [rɪˈmɪʃən] *n* : rémission *f*

remit [rɪˈmɪt] *vt* **-mitted; -mitting 1** PARDON : remettre <to remit s.o.'s debt : remettre la dette de qqn> **2** SEND : envoyer (de l'argent)

remittance [rɪˈmɪtənts] *n* : paiement *m,* envoi *m*

remnant [ˈrɛmnənt] *n* : reste *m,* restant *m*

remodel [rɪˈmɑdəl] *vt* **-eled** *or* **-elled; -eling** *or* **-elling** : remodeler

remonstrate [ˈrɛmənˌstreɪt, rɪˈmɑn-] *vi* **-strated; -strating** : protester <to remonstrate with : faire des remontrances à>

remorse [rɪˈmɔrs] *n* : remords *m*

remorseful [rɪˈmɔrsfəl] *adj* : plein de remords, contrit

remorseless [rɪˈmɔrsləs] *adj* **1** MERCILESS : sans remords, sans pitié **2** RELENTLESS : impitoyable, implacable

remote [rɪˈmo:t] *adj* **remoter; -est 1** : lointain, éloigné <the remote past : le passé lointain> **2** SECLUDED : retiré, isolé **3** : à distance <remote control : commande à distance> **4** SLIGHT : petit, faible <there's a remote chance : c'est très peu probable> **5** ALOOF : indifférent

remotely [rɪˈmo:tli] *adv* SLIGHTLY : faiblement, vaguement

remoteness [rɪˈmo:tnəs] *n* : isolement *m,* éloignement *m*

removable [rɪˈmu:vəbəl] *adj* : amovible

removal [rɪ'mu:vəl] *n* **1** ELIMINATION : suppression *f* (d'abus, etc.), enlèvement *m* (de tâches) **2** : ablation *f* (en médecine) **3** : renvoi (d'un employé), révocation *f* (d'un fonctionnaire)

remove [rɪ'mu:v] *vt* **-moved; -moving 1** : enlever, ôter <remove the lid : enlevez le couvercle> <to remove one's coat : ôter son manteau> **2** DISMISS : renvoyer (un employé), démettre (un fonctionnaire) **3** ELIMINATE : supprimer (une menace), écarter (un obstacle), dissiper (la peur)

remunerate [rɪ'mju:nə,reɪt] *vt* **-ated; -ating** : rémunérer

remuneration [rɪ,mju:nə'reɪʃən] *n* : rémunération *f*

remunerative [rɪ'mju:nərət̬ɪv, -,reɪ-] *adj* : rémunérateur, lucratif

renaissance [,rɛnə'sɑnts, -'zɑnts; 'rɛnə,-] *n* **1** : renaissance *f* **2 the Renaissance** : la Renaissance

renal ['ri:nəl] *adj* : rénal

rename [,ri:'neɪm] *vt* **-named; -naming** : rebaptiser

rend ['rɛnd] *vt* **rent** ['rɛnt]; **rending** : déchirer

render ['rɛndər] *vt* **1** EXTRACT : fondre (de la graisse) **2** GIVE UP : rendre, retourner **3** : rendre (un service), prêter (de l'aide) **4** MAKE : laisser, rendre <she was rendered helpless by the blow : le coup l'a laissée complètement impuissante> **5** PERFORM : interpréter (une chanson, etc.)

rendezvous ['rɑndɪ,vu:, -deɪ-] *ns & pl* : rendez-vous *m*

rendition [rɛn'dɪʃən] *n* : interprétation *f*

renegade ['rɛnɪ,geɪd] *n* : renégat *m*, -gate *f*

renege [rɪ'nɪg, -'nɛg] *vi* **-neged; -neging** : revenir (sur une promesse, etc.)

renew [rɪ'nu:, -'nju:] *vt* **1** REVIVE : raviver (la force, le courage, etc.) **2** RESUME : renouveler, reprendre <to renew one's efforts : renouveler ses efforts> **3** EXTEND : renouveler (un passeport, un abonnement, etc.)

renewable [rɪ'nu:əbəl, -'nju:-] *adj* : renouvelable

renewal [rɪ'nu:əl, -'nju:-] *n* : renouvellement *m*

renounce [rɪ'naʊnts] *vt* **-nounced; -nouncing 1** : renoncer à, abandonner <to renounce the throne : renoncer au trône> **2** REPUDIATE : renier, rejeter

renovate ['rɛnə,veɪt] *vt* **-vated; -vating** : rénover

renovation [,rɛnə'veɪʃən] *n* : rénovation *f*, restoration *f*

renown [rɪ'naʊn] *n* : renommée *f*, renom *m*

renowned [rɪ'naʊnd] *adj* : renommé, célèbre

rent[1] ['rɛnt] *vt* : louer

rent[2] *n* **1** : loyer *m* (somme d'argent) **2** TEAR : déchirure *f* **3 for ~** : à louer

rental[1] ['rɛntəl] *adj* : de location <rental car : voiture de location>

rental[2] *n* **1** : location *f* <film rentals : location de films> **2** RENT : loyer *m*

renter ['rɛntər] *n* : locataire *mf*

renunciation [rɪ,nʌntsi'eɪʃən] *n* : renonciation *f*

repair[1] [rɪ'pær] *vt* : réparer

repair[2] *n* **1** : réparation *f* <car repair : réparation de voiture> **2** CONDITION : état *m*, condition *f* <in bad repair : en mauvais état>

reparations [,rɛpə'reɪʃənz] *npl* DAMAGES : réparations *fpl*

repartee [,rɛpər'ti:, -,pɑr-, -'teɪ] *n* : repartie *f*, réplique *f*

repast [rɪ'pæst, 'ri:,pæst] *n* : repas *m*

repatriate [rɪ'peɪtri,eɪt] *vt* **-ated; -ating** : rapatrier

repay [rɪ'peɪ] *vt* **-paid; -paying** : rembourser (un emprunt), rendre (une faveur, etc.)

repeal[1] [rɪ'pi:l] *vt* : abroger

repeal[2] *n* : abrogation *f*

repeat[1] [rɪ'pi:t] *vt* : répéter — *vi* : se répéter

repeat[2] *n* **1** REPETITION : répétition *f* **2** : rediffusion *f*, reprise *f* <the show is a repeat : l'émission est en rediffusion>

repeatedly [rɪ'pi:t̬ədli] *adv* : à plusieurs reprises

repel [rɪ'pɛl] *vt* **-pelled; -pelling 1** : repousser (l'ennemi, etc.) **2** REJECT : rejeter **3** RESIST : résister à **4** DISGUST : repousser, répugner

repellent[1] [rɪ'pɛlənt] *adj* : repoussant, répugnant

repellent[2] *n or* **insect repellent** : insectifuge *m*

repent [rɪ'pɛnt] *vi* : se repentir

repentance [rɪ'pɛntənts] *n* : repentir *m*

repentant [rɪ'pɛntənt] *adj* : repentant

repercussion [,ri:pər'kʌʃən, ,rɛpər-] *n* : répercussion *f*

repertoire ['rɛpər,twɑr] *n* : répertoire *m*

repertory ['rɛpər,tori] *n, pl* **-ries 1 → repertoire 2** *or* **repertory theater** : théâtre *m* de répertoire

repetition [,rɛpə'tɪʃən] *n* : répétition *f*

repetitious [,rɛpə'tɪʃəs] *adj* : répétitif

repetitive [rɪ'pɛt̬ət̬ɪv] *adj* : répétitif

repetitively [rɪ'pɛt̬ət̬ɪvli] *adv* : de façon répétitive

replace [rɪ'pleɪs] *vt* **-placed; -placing 1** RESTORE : remettre **2** SUBSTITUTE : remplacer, substituer

replaceable [rɪ'pleɪsəbəl] *adj* : remplaçable

replacement [rɪ'pleɪsmənt] *n* **1** REPLACING : remplacement *m* **2** SUBSTITUTE : remplaçant *m*, -çante *f*

replenish [rɪ'plɛnɪʃ] *vt* : remplir (de nouveau)

replenishment [rɪ'plɛnɪʃmənt] *n* : remplissage *m*
replete [rɪ'pli:t] *adj* **1** FULL : rempli <replete with details : rempli de détails> **2** SATIATED : rassasié
replica ['rɛplɪkə] *n* : copie *f* exacte, réplique *f*
replicate ['rɛplə,keɪt] *vt* **-cated; -cating** : reproduire, faire un double de
reply[1] [rɪ'plaɪ] *vi* **-plied; -plying** : répondre, répliquer
reply[2] *n, pl* **-plies** : réponse *f*, réplique *f*
report[1] [rɪ'port] *vt* **1** RELATE : raconter, faire le compte rendu de **2** : faire un reportage sur (en journalisme) **3** : signaler (un feu, un crime, etc.), dénoncer (un malfaiteur) — *vi* **1** : faire un rapport **2** : se présenter <to report for duty : se présenter au travail>
report[2] *n* **1** RUMOR : rumeur *f* **2** REPUTE : réputation *f* <of good report : de bonne réputation> **3** ACCOUNT : rapport *m*, compte rendu *m* **4** : détonation *f* (d'un fusil) **5** : bulletin *m* <weather report : bulletin météorologique> **6** *or* **news report** : reportage *m*
report card *n* : bulletin *m* scolaire
reportedly [rɪ'portədli] *adv* : à ce que l'on dit
reporter [rɪ'portər] *n* : journaliste *mf*, reporter *m*
repose[1] [rɪ'po:z] *vi* **-posed; -posing** : se reposer, relaxer
repose[2] *n* **1** REST : repos *m* **2** PEACE : tranquillité *f*, calme *f*
repository [rɪ'pɑzə,tori] *n, pl* **-ries** : dépôt *m*, entrepôt *m*
repossess [,ri:pə'zɛs] *vt* : reprendre possession de, saisir
repossession [,ri:pə'zɛʃən] *n* : reprise *f* de possession
reprehend [,rɛpri'hɛnd] *vt* : réprimander, critiquer
reprehensible [,rɛpri'hɛntsəbəl] *adj* : répréhensible
reprehensibly [,rɛpri'hɛntsəbli] *adv* : de façon répréhensible
represent [,rɛprɪ'zɛnt] *vt* **1** PORTRAY : représenter, dépeindre **2** SYMBOLIZE : représenter <the flag represents our country : le drapeau représente notre pays> **3** : représenter <an attorney who represents his client : un avocat qui représente son client>
representation [,rɛprɪ,zɛn'teɪʃən, -zən-] *n* : représentation *f*
representative[1] [,rɛprɪ'zɛntətɪv] *adj* : représentatif
representative[2] *n* : représentant *m*, -tante *f*
repress [rɪ'prɛs] *vt* : réprimer
repression [rɪ'prɛʃən] *n* : répression *f*
repressive [rɪ'prɛsɪv] *adj* : répressif
reprieve[1] [rɪ'pri:v] *vt* **-prievd; -prieving** : accorder un sursis à
reprieve[2] *n* **1** : remise *f* de peine (en droit) **2** RESPITE : délai *m*, sursis *m*, répit *m*
reprimand[1] ['rɛprə,mænd] *vt* : réprimander
reprimand[2] *n* : réprimande *f*
reprint[1] [ri'prɪnt] *vt* : réimprimer
reprint[2] ['ri:,prɪnt, ri'prɪnt] *n* : réimpression *f*
reprisal [rɪ'praɪzəl] *n* : représailles *fpl*
reproach[1] [rɪ'pro:tʃ] *vt* : reprocher à, faire des reproches à
reproach[2] *n* **1** REBUKE : reproche *m* **2 beyond ~** : irréprochable, au-dessus de tout reproche
reproachful [rɪ'pro:tʃfəl] *adj* : de reproche, réprobateur
reproachfully [rɪ'pro:tʃfəli] *adv* : d'un ton réprobateur
reproduce [,ri:prə'du:s, -'dju:s] *v* **-duced; -ducing** *vt* : reproduire — *vi* : se reproduire
reproduction [,ri:prə'dʌkʃən] *n* : reproduction *f*
reproductive [,ri:prə'dʌktɪv] *adj* : reproducteur
reproof [rɪ'pru:f] *n* : réprimande *f*
reprove [rɪ'pru:v] *vt* **-proved; -proving** : réprimander, réprouver
reptile ['rɛp,taɪl] *n* : reptile *m*
republic [rɪ'pʌblɪk] *n* : république *f*
republican[1] [rɪ'pʌblɪkən] *adj* : républicain
republican[2] *n* : républicain *m*, -caine *f*
repudiate [rɪ'pju:di,eɪt] *vt* **-ated; -ating 1** DISOWN : répudier, rejeter **2** : refuser d'honorer (une dette, etc.)
repudiation [rɪ,pju:di'eɪʃən] *n* **1** : répudiation *f*, désaveu *m* **2** : refus *m* d'honerer (une dette)
repugnance [rɪ'pʌgnənts] *n* : répugnance *f*, aversion *f*
repugnant [rɪ'pʌgnənt] *adj* : répugnant
repulse[1] [rɪ'pʌls] *vt* **-pulsed; -pulsing 1** REBUFF, REPEL : repousser **2** DISGUST : repousser, dégoûter
repulse[2] *n* REBUFF : rejet *m*, rebuffade *f*
repulsive [rɪ'pʌlsɪv] *adj* : repoussant, répugnant
repulsively [rɪ'pʌlsɪvli] *adv* : de façon répugnante
reputable ['rɛpjət̬əbəl] *adj* : de bonne réputation
reputation [,rɛpjə'teɪʃən] *n* : réputation *f*
repute [rɪ'pju:t] *n* **1** : réputation *f* **2 to hold s.o. in high repute** : tenir qqn en haute estime
reputed [rɪ'pju:t̬əd] *adj* **1** CONSIDERED : réputé **2 to be reputed to be** : avoir la réputation d'être
reputedly [rɪ'pju:t̬ədli] *adv* : d'après ce que l'on dit
request[1] [rɪ'kwɛst] *vt* ASK : demander
request[2] *n* : demande *f*, requête *f*
requiem ['rɛkwiəm, 'reɪ-] *n* : requiem *m*

require [rɪ'kwaɪr] *vt* **-quired; -quiring 1** CALL FOR : demander, exiger **2** NEED : avoir besoin de
requirement [rɪ'kwaɪrmənt] *n* **1** NEED : besoin *m* **2** CONDITION : exigence *f*, condition *f*
requisite[1] ['rɛkwəzɪt] *adj* : nécessaire, essentiel
requisite[2] *n* : nécessité *f*
requisition[1] [ˌrɛkwə'zɪʃən] *vt* : réquisitionner
requisition[2] *n* : réquisition *f*
reread [ˌriː'riːd] *vt* **-read** [-'rɛd]; **-reading** : relire
reroute [ˌriː'ruːt, -'raʊt] *vt* **-routed; -routing** : dérouter, changer l'itinéraire de
resale ['riːˌseɪl, ˌriː'seɪl] *n* : revente *f*
reschedule [riː'skɛˌdʒuːl, -dʒəl] *vt* **-uled; -uling** : changer l'heure ou la date de
rescind [rɪ'sɪnd] *vt* : annuler (une commande), résilier (un contrat)
rescue[1] ['rɛsˌkjuː] *vt* **-cued; -cuing** : sauver, secourir
rescue[2] *n* : sauvetage *m*
rescuer ['rɛsˌkjuːər] *n* : sauveteur *m*, secouriste *mf*
research[1] [rɪ'sɔrtʃ, 'riːˌsɔrtʃ] *vt* : faire des recherches sur
research[2] *n* : recherches *fpl*
researcher [rɪ'sɔrtʃər, 'riːˌ-] *n* : chercheur *m*, -cheuse *f*
resemblance [rɪ'zɛmblən*t*s] *n* : ressemblance *f*
resemble [rɪ'zɛmbəl] *vt* **-sembled; -sembling** : ressembler à
resent [rɪ'zɛnt] *vt* : en vouloir à, éprouver de l'amertume envers
resentful [rɪ'zɛntfəl] *adj* : plein de ressentiment
resentfully [rɪ'zɛntfəli] *adv* : avec ressentiment
resentment [rɪ'zɛntmənt] *n* : ressentiment *m*
reservation [ˌrɛzər'veɪʃən] *n* **1** RESERVING : réservation *f* **2** : réserve *f* <Indian reservation : réserve indienne> **3 without ~** : sans réserve
reserve[1] [rɪ'zərv] *vt* **-served; -serving** : réserver
reserve[2] *n* **1** SUPPLY : réserve *f*, provision *f* **2** : réserve *f* (dans les forces armées) **3** RESTRAINT : réserve *f*, discrétion *f*
reserved [rɪ'zərvd] *adj* : réservé, discret
reservoir ['rɛzərˌvwɑr, -ˌvwɔr, -ˌvɔr] *n* : réservoir *m*
reset [ˌriː'sɛt] *vt* **-set; -setting** : remettre à l'heure (une montre), remettre à zéro (un compteur)
reside [rɪ'zaɪd] *vi* **-sided; -siding 1** DWELL : résider **2 to reside in** : résider dans
residence ['rɛzədən*t*s] *n* **1** DWELLING : résidence *f*, demeure *f* **2** *or* **residence hall** : résidence *f* (universitaire)
resident[1] ['rɛzədənt] *adj* **1** RESIDING : résidant **2** : à demeure <resident doctors : médecins à demeure>
resident[2] *n* : résident *m*, -dente *f*
residential [ˌrɛzə'dɛntʃəl] *adj* : résidentiel
residual [rɪ'zɪdʒʊəl] *adj* : résiduel
residue ['rɛzəˌduː, -ˌdjuː] *n* : résidu *m*, reste *m*
resign [rɪ'zaɪn] *vi* QUIT : démissionner — *vt* **to resign oneself to** : se résigner à
resignation [ˌrɛzɪg'neɪʃən] *n* **1** RESIGNING : démission *f*, résignation *f* **2** ACCEPTANCE : résignation *f*
resignedly [rɪ'zaɪnədli] *adv* : avec résignation
resilience [rɪ'zɪljən*t*s] *n* : élasticité *f*, résistance *f*
resilient [rɪ'zɪljənt] *adj* **1** STRONG : résistant, fort **2** ELASTIC : élastique
resin ['rɛzən] *n* : résine *f*
resinous ['rɛzənəs] *adj* : résineux
resist [rɪ'zɪst] *vt* **1** WITHSTAND : résister à <to resist disease : résister à la maladie> **2** OPPOSE : s'opposer à, résister à
resistance [rɪ'zɪstən*t*s] *n* : résistance *f*
resistant [rɪ'zɪstənt] *adj* : résistant <fire-resistant : qui résiste au feu>
resolute ['rɛzəˌluːt] *adj* : résolu, décidé — **resolutely** *adv*
resolution [ˌrɛzə'luːʃən] *n* **1** SOLUTION : résolution *f* <conflict resolution : résolution de conflits> **2** RESOLVE : détermination *f*, résolution *f* **3** DECISION, PROMISE : résolution *f* <New Year's resolutions : résolutions du nouvel an> **4** MOTION, PROPOSAL : motion *f*, résolution *f* (legislative)
resolve[1] [rɪ'zɑlv] *v* **-solved; -solving** *vt* **1** SOLVE : résoudre (un problème) **2** DECIDE : (se) résoudre, décider — *vi* : se résoudre
resolve[2] *n* : résolution *f*, détermination *f*
resonance ['rɛzənən*t*s] *n* : résonance *f*
resonant ['rɛzənənt] *adj* **1** : résonant (en physique) **2** : sonore (se dit des sons, des voix, etc.)
resort[1] [rɪ'zɔrt] *vi* **to resort to** : recourir à, avoir recours à
resort[2] *n* **1** RESOURCE : recours *m* <as a last resort : en dernier recours> **2** HAUNT : endroit *m* préféré, repaire *m* **3** : station *f* <ski resort : station de ski> <vacation resorts : lieux de villégiature>
resound [rɪ'zaʊnd] *vi* : résonner, retentir
resounding [rɪ'zaʊndɪŋ] *adj* : retentissant, éclatant <a resounding success : un succès retentissant>
resource ['riːˌsɔrs, rɪ'sɔrs] *n* : ressource *f* <natural resources : ressources naturelles> <to be left to one's own resources : être livré à soi-même>

resourceful [rɪ'sorsfəl, -'zors-] *adj* : ingénieux, plein de ressources

resourcefulness [rɪ'sorsfəlnəs, -'zors-] *n* : ingéniosité *f*

respect[1] [rɪ'spɛkt] *vt* : respecter

respect[2] *n* **1** ESTEEM : respect *m*, estime *f* **2** CONSIDERATION : considération *f*, respect *m* **3** DETAIL : respect *m*, égard *m* <in some respects : à certains égards> **4 respects** *npl* : respects *mpl*, hommages *mpl* <to pay one's respects to s.o. : présenter ses respects à qqn> **5 in respect to** : en ce qui concerne

respectability [rɪˌspɛktə'bɪləṭi] *n* : respectabilité *f*

respectable [ri'spɛktəbəl] *adj* **1** PROPER : respectable, correct <respectable people : gens respectables> **2** CONSIDERABLE : respectable, considérable, assez bon <a respectable amount : une somme respectable>

respectably [rɪ'spɛktəbli] *adv* : respectablement, convenablement

respectful [rɪ'spɛktfəl] *adj* : respectueux — **respectfully** *adv*

respective [rɪ'spɛktɪv] *adj* : respectif — **respectively** *adv*

respiration [ˌrɛspə'reɪʃən] *n* : respiration *f*

respirator ['rɛspəˌreɪṭər] *n* : respirateur *m*

respiratory ['rɛspərəˌtori, rɪ'spaɪrə-] *adj* : respiratoire

respite ['rɛspət] *n* : répit *m*, sursis *m*

resplendent [rɪ'splɛndənt] *adj* : resplendissant

respond [rɪ'spɑnd] *vi* **1** ANSWER : répondre **2** REACT : réagir <I didn't respond well to the surgery : j'ai mal réagi à la chirurgie> <to respond to pressure : céder aux pressions>

response [rɪ'spɑnts] *n* **1** ANSWER : réponse *f* **2** REACTION : réaction *f*, réponse *f*

responsibility [rɪˌspɑntsə'bɪləṭi] *n, pl* **-ties** : responsabilité *f*

responsible [rɪ'spɑntsəbəl] *adj* : responsable

responsibly [rɪ'spɑntsəbli] *adv* : de manière responsable

responsive [rɪ'spɑntsɪv] *adj* : sensible, réceptif

rest[1] ['rɛst] *vi* **1** RELAX, REPOSE : se reposer <to rest easy : être tranquille> **2** DEPEND : reposer, dépendre <the decision rests with me : la décision dépend de moi> **3 to rest on** *or* **to rest against** : reposer sur, être appuyé sur — *vt* **1** : reposer <rest your eyes now and then : reposez-vous la vue de temps à autre> **2** PLACE : placer, mettre <I rest all my hopes in him : je place tous mes espoirs en lui>

rest[2] *n* **1** REPOSE : repos *m* **2** BREAK : repos *m*, pause *f* **3** SUPPORT : appui *m*, support *m* **4** REMAINDER : reste *m* **5** : pause *f* (en musique) **6 rest area** : aire *f* de repos, halte *f* routière *Can*

restart [riː'stɑrt] *vt* : remettre en marche (un moteur)

restaurant ['rɛstəˌrɑnt, -rənt] *n* : restaurant *m*

restful ['rɛstfəl] *adj* : reposant

restitution [ˌrɛstə'tuːʃən, -'tjuː-] *n* : restitution *f*

restive ['rɛstɪv] *adj* : agité, nerveux

restless ['rɛstləs] *adj* : agité, nerveux, impatient <a restless night : une nuit agitée>

restlessly ['rɛstləsli] *adv* : nerveusement, avec impatience

restlessness ['rɛstləsnəs] *n* : nervosité *f*, agitation *f*

restoration [ˌrɛstə'reɪʃən] *n* **1** : restitution *f*, rétablissement *m* (de la paix, de l'ordre, etc.) **2** : restauration *f* (d'une peinture, d'un édifice, etc.)

restore [rɪ'stor] *vt* **-stored; -storing 1** RETURN : rendre, restituer **2** RENOVATE : restaurer, rénover **3** REESTABLISH : rétablir, retrouver <to restore peace : rétablir la paix> <to be restored to health : être rétabli> <to have one's sight restored : recouvrer la vue>

restrain [rɪ'streɪn] *vt* **1** PREVENT : empêcher, retenir **2** CURB : contenir, refréner

restrained [rɪ'streɪnd] *adj* **1** : sobre <restrained style : style sobre> **2** RESERVED : réservé, contenu

restraining order *n* : injonction *f*

restraint [rɪ'streɪnt] *n* **1** RESTRICTION : restriction *f*, contrainte *f* **2** RESERVE, SELF-CONTROL : retenue *f*, mesure *f*

restrict [rɪ'strɪkt] *vt* : restreindre, limiter

restricted [rɪ'strɪktəd] *adj* **1** LIMITED : restreint, limité **2** CLASSIFIED : secret, confidentiel

restriction [rɪ'strɪkʃən] *n* : restriction *f*, limitation *f*

restrictive [rɪ'strɪktɪv] *adj* : restrictif

restructure [riː'strʌktʃər] *vt* **-tured; -turing** : restructurer

result[1] [rɪ'zʌlt] *vi* **1 to result from** : résulter de, provenir de **2 to result in** : avoir pour résultat, aboutir à

result[2] *n* : résultat *m*, conséquence *f*

resultant [rɪ'zʌltənt] *adj* : résultant

resume [rɪ'zuːm] *v* **-sumed; -suming** *vt* : reprendre — *vi* : reprendre, recommencer, continuer

résumé *or* **resume** *or* **resumé** ['rɛzəˌmeɪ, ˌrɛzə'-] *n* **1** SUMMARY : résumé *m* **2** : curriculum *m* vitæ

resumption [rɪ'zʌmpʃən] *n* : reprise *f*

resurface [ˌriː'sərfəs] *vt* **-faced; -facing** : refaire le revêtement de (une route)

resurgence [rɪ'sərdʒənts] *n* : résurgence *f*, réapparition *f*

resurgent [rɪ'sərdʒənt] *adj* : renaissant

resurrect [ˌrɛzəˈrɛkt] *vt* : ressusciter

resurrection [ˌrɛzəˈrɛkʃən] *n* : résurrection *f*

resuscitate [rɪˈsʌsəˌteɪt] *vt* **-tated; -tating** : réanimer

resuscitation [rɪˌsʌsəˈteɪʃən, ˌri-] *n* : réanimation *f*

retail[1] [ˈriːˌteɪl] *vt* : vendre au détail

retail[2] *adv* : au détail

retail[3] *adj* : de détail <retail store : magasin de détail>

retail[4] *n* : vente *f* au détail

retailer [ˈriːˌteɪlər] *n* : détaillant *m*, -lante *f*

retain [rɪˈteɪn] *vt* **1** KEEP : garder, retenir **2** HOLD : retenir, conserver <lead retains heat : le plomb conserve la chaleur> **3** ENGAGE : engager (les services de qqn)

retainer [rɪˈteɪnər] *n* **1** SERVANT : domestique *mf* **2** ADVANCE : provision *f*

retaliate [rɪˈtæliˌeɪt] *vi* **-ated; -ating** : riposter, se venger <to retaliate against : user de représailles envers>

retaliation [rɪˌtæliˈeɪʃən] *n* : riposte *f*, représailles *fpl*

retard [rɪˈtɑrd] *vt* : retarder

retarded [rɪˈtɑrdəd] *adj* : arriéré

retch [ˈrɛtʃ] *vi* : avoir des haut-le-cœur

retention [rɪˈtɛntʃən] *n* : rétention *f*

retentive [rɪˈtɛntɪv] *adj* : qui retient bien <a retentive memory : une mémoire fidèle>

reticence [ˈrɛt̬əsənts] *n* : réticence *f*, hésitation *f*

reticent [ˈrɛt̬əsənt] *adj* : réticent, hésitant

reticently [ˈrɛt̬əsəntli] *adv* : avec réticence

retina [ˈrɛtənə] *n, pl* **-nas** *or* **-nae** [-ənˌiː, -ənˌaɪ] : rétine *f*

retinue [ˈrɛtənˌuː, -juː] *n* : suite *f*, escorte *f*

retire [rɪˈtaɪr] *vi* **-tired; -tiring 1** WITHDRAW : se retirer, partir **2** : prendre sa retraite <he retired at 65 : il a pris sa retraite à 65 ans> **3** : aller se coucher

retiree [rɪˌtaɪˈriː] *n* : retraité *m*, -tée *f*

retirement [rɪˈtaɪrmənt] *n* : retraite *f*

retiring [rɪˈtaɪrɪŋ] *adj* : réservé, timide

retort[1] [rɪˈtɔrt] *vt* : rétorquer, riposter

retort[2] *n* : réplique *f*, riposte *f*

retrace [ˌriːˈtreɪs] *vt* **-traced; -tracing** : reconstituer <to retrace one's steps : revenir sur ses pas>

retract [rɪˈtrækt] *vt* **1** : rétracter (ses griffes, ses cornes etc.) **2** WITHDRAW : rétracter, retirer — *vi* : se rétracter

retractable [rɪˈtræktəbəl] *adj* : escamotable

retrain [ˌriːˈtreɪn] *vt* : recycler

retreat[1] [rɪˈtriːt] *vi* : se retirer, reculer

retreat[2] *n* **1** WITHDRAWAL : retraite *f*, recul *m* **2** REFUGE : retraite *f*, abri *m*

retrench [rɪˈtrɛntʃ] *vt* : réduire, restreindre (les dépenses) — *vi* : faire des économies

retribution [ˌrɛtrəˈbjuːʃən] *n* : châtiment *m*, punition *f*

retrieval [rɪˈtriːvəl] *n* : récupération *f* <text retrieval : récupération d'un texte> <beyond retrieval : irrécupérable>

retrieve [rɪˈtriːv] *vt* **-trieved; -trieving 1** : rapporter <to retrieve game : rapporter du gibier> **2** RECOVER : récupérer

retriever [rɪˈtriːvər] *n* : chien *m* d'arrêt

retroactive [ˌrɛtroˈæktɪv] *adj* : rétroactif — **retroactively** *adv*

retrograde [ˈrɛtrəˌgreɪd] *adj* : rétrograde

retrospect [ˈrɛtrəˌspɛkt] *n* **in ~** : rétrospectivement

retrospective [ˌrɛtrəˈspɛktɪv] *adj* : rétrospectif — **retrospectively** *adv*

return[1] [rɪˈtərn] *vi* **1** : retourner, rentrer <to return home : retourner à la maison> **2 to return to** : reprendre, revenir à <she returned to her old habits : elle a repris ses vieilles habitudes> — *vt* **1** RESTORE : rapporter, rendre <to return a book to the library : retourner un livre à la bibliothèque> **2** REPLACE : remettre **3** ANSWER : répondre, répliquer **4** YIELD : rapporter, produire **5** REPAY : retourner, rendre <to return the compliment : retourner le compliment> <to return a favor : en faire autant> **6** : rendre, prononcer <to return a verdict : rendre un verdict>

return[2] *adj* : aller et retour <a return ticket : un billet aller et retour>

return[3] *n* **1** : retour *m* <on their return : à leur retour> **2** YIELD : rapport *m*, rendement *m* **3** RETURNING : renvoi *m*, retour *m* (de marchandise) **4** *or* **income tax return** : déclaration *f* de revenus **5 returns** *npl* : résultats *mpl* (d'une élection)

reunion [riˈjuːnjən] *n* : réunion *f* <family reunion : réunion familiale>

reuse [riˈjuːz] *vt* **-used; -using** : réutiliser

revamp [ˌriːˈvæmp] *vt* : retaper (une maison), réviser (un texte)

reveal [rɪˈviːl] *vt* **1** DIVULGE : révéler, dévoiler (un secret) **2** SHOW : révéler, laisser voir

reveille [ˈrɛvəli] *n* : réveil *m* (dans les forces armées)

revel[1] [ˈrɛvəl] *vi* **-eled** *or* **-elled; -eling** *or* **-elling 1** : faire la fête **2 to revel in** : se délecter de

revel[2] *n* : festivités *fpl*

revelation [ˌrɛvəˈleɪʃən] *n* : révélation *f*

reveler *or* **reveller** [ˈrɛvələr] *n* : fêtard *m*, -tarde *f fam*

revelry [ˈrɛvəlri] *n* : festivités *fpl*, réjouissances *fpl*

revenge[1] [rɪ'vɛndʒ] *vt* **-venged; -venging** : venger <to revenge oneself on : se venger sur>

revenge[2] *n* : vengeance *f*

revenue ['rɛvəˌnu:, -ˌnju:] *n* : revenu *m*

reverberate [rɪ'vərbəˌreɪt] *vi* **-ated; -ating** : retentir, résonner

reverberation [rɪˌvərbə'reɪʃən] *n* : réverbération *f*, retentissement *m*

revere [rɪ'vɪr] *vt* **-vered; -vering** : révérer, vénérer

reverence ['rɛvərənts] *n* : révérence *f*, vénération *f*

reverend ['rɛvərənd] *adj* **1** REVERED : vénérable **2** : révérend (en religion) <the Reverend Richard Parker : le révérend Richard Parker>

reverent ['rɛvərənt] *adj* : respectueux — **reverently** *adv*

reverie ['rɛvəri] *n, pl* **-eries** : rêverie *f*

reversal [rɪ'vərsəl] *n* : revirement *m* (d'opinion), renversement *m* (d'une situation)

reverse[1] [rɪ'vərs] *v* **-versed; -versing** *vt* **1** INVERT : inverser **2** CHANGE : renverser, retourner **3** ANNUL : annuler — *vi* : faire marche arrière (se dit d'une voiture)

reverse[2] *adj* : inverse, opposé <in reverse order : en ordre inverse>

reverse[3] *n* **1** OPPOSITE : contraire *m* **2** SETBACK : revers *m*, épreuve *f* **3** BACK : envers *m* **4** *or* **reverse gear** : marche *f* arrière

reversible [rɪ'vərsəbəl] *adj* : réversible

reversion [rɪ'vərʒən] *n* **1** : retour *m* <a reversion to paganism : un retour au paganisme> **2** : réversion *f* (en biologie)

revert [rɪ'vərt] *vi* **to revert to** : revenir à, retourner à

review[1] [rɪ'vju:] *vt* **1** REEXAMINE : revoir, réviser **2** CRITICIZE : faire la critique de (un roman, etc.) **3** ASSESS, EXAMINE : examiner, faire le bilan de **4 to review the troops** : passer les troupes en revue

review[2] *n* **1** REAPPRAISAL : révision *f* **2** INSPECTION : revue *f* (militaire) **3** ANALYSIS, OVERVIEW : bilan *m*, examen *m* <to pass one's life in review : faire le bilan de sa vie> **4** EVALUATION : critique *f* **5** → **revue**

reviewer [rɪ'vju:ər] *n* : critique *mf* <book reviewer : critique littéraire>

revile [rɪ'vaɪl] *vt* **-viled; -viling** : injurier, vilipender

revise [rɪ'vaɪz] *vt* **-vised; -vising 1** CORRECT : réviser, revoir (un manuscrit, etc.) **2** UPDATE : réviser, mettre à jour **3** ALTER : réviser (une idée, une politique, etc.)

reviser *or* **revisor** [rɪ'vaɪzər] *n* : réviseur *m*; correcteur *m*, -trice *f*

revision [rɪ'vɪʒən] *n* : révision *f*

revival [rɪ'vaɪvəl] *n* **1** : renouveau *m*, renaissance *f* (d'intérêt, d'idées, etc.) **2** : rétablissement *m* (des coutumes) **3** : reprise *f* (en médecine) **4** *or* **revival meeting** : réunion *f* pour le renouveau de la foi

revive [rɪ'vaɪv] *v* **-vived; -viving** *vt* **1** REESTABLISH : rétablir (une tradition, etc.) **2** REAWAKEN : ranimer, raviver — *vi* **1** COME TO : reprendre connaissance **2** : renaître, se réveiller <hope revived in him : l'espoir renaissait en lui>

revoke [rɪ'vo:k] *vt* **-voked; -voking** : révoquer, annuler

revolt[1] [ri'vo:lt] *vt* DISGUST : révolter, dégoûter — *vi* **to revolt against** : se révolter contre

revolt[2] *n* : révolte *f*, insurrection *f*

revolting [rɪ'vo:ltɪŋ] *adj* : révoltant, dégoûtant

revolution [ˌrɛvə'lu:ʃən] *n* **1** ROTATION : révolution *f*, tour *m* **2** : révolution *f* <the French Revolution : la Révolution française> <a technological revolution : une révolution technologique>

revolutionary[1] [ˌrɛvə'lu:ʃənˌeri] *adj* : révolutionnaire

revolutionary[2] *n* : révolutionnaire *mf*

revolutionize [ˌrɛvə'lu:ʃənˌaɪz] *vt* **-ized; -izing** : révolutionner

revolve [rɪ'vɑlv] *v* **-volved; -volving** *vt* ROTATE : faire tourner — *vi* **1** TURN : tourner <to revolve around : tourner autour> **2 to revolve around s.o.** : dépendre de qqn **3 to revolve in one's mind** : tourner et retourner dans son esprit

revolver [rɪ'vɑlvər] *n* : revolver *m*

revue [rɪ'vju:] *n* : revue *f* (au théâtre)

revulsion [rɪ'vʌlʃən] *n* REPUGNANCE : répulsion *f*, répugnance *f*

reward[1] [rɪ'wɔrd] *vt* : récompenser

reward[2] *n* : récompense *f*

rewind [ˌri:'waɪnd] *vt* **-wound** [-'waʊnd]; **-winding** : rembobiner

rewrite [ˌri:'raɪt] *vt* **-wrote** [-'ro:t]; **-written** [-'rɪtən]; **-writing** : récrire

rhapsody ['ræpsədi] *n, pl* **-dies 1** : rhapsodie *f* (en musique, en poésie) **2** RAPTURE : extase *f*

rhetoric ['rɛt̮ərɪk] *n* : rhétorique *f*

rhetorical [rɪ'tɔrɪkəl] *adj* : rhétorique

rheumatic [rʊ'mæt̮ɪk] *adj* : rhumatismal

rheumatism ['ru:məˌtɪzəm, 'rʊ-] *n* : rhumatisme *m*

rhinestone ['raɪnˌsto:n] *n* : faux diamant *m*

rhino ['raɪˌno:] *n, pl* **rhino** *or* **rhinos** → **rhinoceros**

rhinoceros [raɪ'nɑsərəs] *n, pl* **-eroses** *or* **-eros** *or* **-eri** [-ˌraɪ] : rhinocéros *m*

rhododendron [ˌro:də'dɛndrən] *n* : rhododendron *m*

rhombus ['rɑmbəs] *n, pl* **-buses** *or* **-bi** [-ˌbaɪ, -bi] : losange *m*

rhubarb ['ru:ˌbɑrb] *n* : rhubarbe *f*

rhyme[1] ['raɪm] *v* **rhymed; rhyming** *vt* : faire rimer — *vi* : rimer

rhyme[2] *n* **1** : rime *m* **2** VERSE : vers *m* (en poésie)

rhythm [ˈrɪðəm] *n* : rythme *m*

rhythmic [ˈrɪðmɪk] *or* **rhythmical** [-mɪkəl] *adj* : rythmique — **rythmically** [-mɪkli] *adv*

rib[1] [ˈrɪb] *vt* **ribbed; ribbing 1** : faire aux côtes <ribbed fabric : tissu à côtes> **2** TEASE : taquiner

rib[2] *n* **1** : côte *f* (en anatomie) **2** : baleine *f* (d'un parapluie), nervure *f* (d'une feuille, en architecture, etc.), côte *f* (d'un tricot)

ribald [ˈrɪbəld] *adj* : grivois, paillard

ribbon [ˈrɪbən] *n* **1** : ruban *m* <silk ribbon : ruban de soie> <typewriter ribbon : ruban d'une machine à écrire> **2 in ribbons** : en lambeaux

rice [ˈraɪs] *n* : riz *m*

rich [ˈrɪtʃ] *adj* **1** WEALTHY : riche, aisé **2** SUMPTUOUS : somptueux, riche **3** : riche <rich food : aliments riches> **4** ABUNDANT : abondant **5** FERTILE : fertile, riche

riches [ˈrɪtʃəz] *npl* : richesses *fpl*

richly [ˈrɪtʃli] *adv* : richement, somptueusement

richness [ˈrɪtʃnəs] *n* : richesse *f*

rickets [ˈrɪkəts] *n* : rachitisme *m*

rickety [ˈrɪkət̬i] *adj* : branlant

ricksha *or* **rickshaw** [ˈrɪkˌʃɔ] *n* : pousse-pousse *m*

ricochet[1] [ˈrikəˌsheɪ] *vi* **-cheted** [-ˌʃeɪd] *or* **-chetted** [-ˌʃɛt̬əd]; **-cheting** [-ˌʃeɪɪŋ] *or* **-chetting** [-ˌʃɛt̬ɪŋ] : ricocher

ricochet[2] *n* : ricochet *m*

rid [ˈrɪd] *vt* **rid; ridding 1** : débarrasser <to rid a dog of fleas : débarrasser un chien de ses puces> **2 to rid oneself of** : se débarrasser de

riddance [ˈrɪdənts] *n* : débarras *m* <good riddance! : bon débarras!>

riddle[1] [ˈrɪdəl] *vt* **-dled; -dling** : cribler <to riddle with bullets : cribler de balles> <riddled with errors : plein de fautes>

riddle[2] *n* : énigme *f*, devinette *f*

ride[1] [ˈraɪd] *v* **rode** [ˈroːd]; **ridden** [ˈrɪdən]; **riding** *vt* **1** : monter à (un cheval), monter sur (une bicyclette), prendre (le bus, un taxi, etc.) **2** TRAVERSE : parcourir <he rode the countryside : il a parcouru tout le pays> **3** TEASE : taquiner **4** *or* **to ride out** WEATHER : réchapper à, surmonter **5 to ride the waves** : voguer sur les vagues (se dit d'une navire) — *vi* **1** : monter à cheval, aller à bicyclette **2** TRAVEL : aller <to ride in a bus : aller en autobus> **3 to ride at anchor** : être ancré **4 to let things ride** : laisser courir

ride[2] *n* **1** : tour *m*, promenade *f* <to go for a ride : aller faire un tour> **2** : manège *m* (à la foire) **3 to give s.o. a ride** : conduire qqn en voiture

rider [ˈraɪdər] *n* **1** HORSEMAN : cavalier *m*, -lière *f* **2** CYCLIST : cycliste *mf*, motocycliste *mf* **3** ANNEX : annexe *f* (en droit)

ridge [ˈrɪdʒ] *n* : chaîne *f* (de montagnes), crête *f* (d'un toit), billon *m* (dans un champ)

ridicule[1] [ˈrɪdəˌkjuːl] *vt* **-culed; -culing** : ridiculiser, tourner en ridicule

ridicule[2] *n* : moquerie *f*, dérision *f*

ridiculous [rəˈdɪkjələs] *adj* : ridicule, absurde — **ridiculously** *adv*

rife [ˈraɪf] *adj* : abondant, répandu <to be rife with : être abondant en> <rumor was rife : les rumeurs allaient bon train>

riffraff [ˈrɪfˌræf] *n* : racaille *f*, canaille *f*

rifle[1] [ˈraɪfəl] *v* **-fled; -fling** *vt* RANSACK : fouiller — *vi* **to rifle through** : fouiller dans

rifle[2] *n* : carabine *f*, fusil *m*

rift [ˈrɪft] *n* **1** FISSURE : fente *f*, fissure *f* **2** BREACH : désaccord *m*, rupture *f* (entre personnes)

rig[1] [ˈrɪg] *vt* **rigged; rigging 1** : gréer (un navire) **2** CLOTHE, DRESS : habiller **3** FIX : truquer (les élections, etc.) **4** *or* **to rig up** : bricoler, monter <to rig up a shelter : bricoler un abri> **5 to rig out** EQUIP : équiper

rig[2] *n* **1** RIGGING : gréement *m* (d'un navire) **2** *or* **oil rig** : plate-forme *f* pétrolière

rigging [ˈrɪgɪŋ, -gən] *n* : gréement *m*

right[1] [ˈraɪt] *vt* **1** RESTORE : redresser <to right the economy : redresser l'économie> **2** REDRESS : réparer <to right a wrong : réparer un tort>

right[2] *adv* **1** CORRECTLY : bien, comme il faut <to answer right : bien répondre> <you're not doing it right : tu ne le fais pas comme il faut> **2** EXACTLY : exactement, précisément <the book is right where you left it : le livre est juste là, où tu l'as laissé> <right here : ici même> **3** DIRECTLY : directement <he went right home : il est rentré directement chez lui> **4** IMMEDIATELY : tout de suite <right after lunch : tout de suite après le déjeuner> **5** COMPLETELY : tout à fait, complètement <he felt right at home : il se sentait tout à fait à l'aise> <right to the end : jusqu'au bout> **6** : à droite <turn right : tournez à droite>

right[3] *adj* **1** JUST, PROPER : juste, bien <it's not right : ce n'est pas bien> **2** CORRECT : bon, juste <the right answer : la bonne réponse> **3** SUITABLE : approprié, convenable <the right person for the job : la personne qui convient le mieux pour l'emploi> **4** STRAIGHT : droit <a right line : une ligne droite> **5** HEALTHY, SOUND : bien <she's not in her right mind : elle n'a pas toute sa raison> <the patient didn't look right : le patient n'avait pas l'air bien> **6** : droit <the right side : le côté droit>

right[4] *n* **1** GOOD : bien *m* <right against wrong : le bien contre le mal> **2** : droite *f* <to be on the right : être à droite> **3** ENTITLEMENT : droit *m* <to exercise a right : exercer un droit> <women's rights : les droits de la femme> **4 rights** *npl* : droits *mpl* <film rights : droits d'adaptation cinématographique> <all rights reserved : tous droits réservés>

right angle *n* : angle *m* droit

right–angled [ˈraɪtˈæŋgəld] *or* **right–angle** [-gəl] *adj* : à angle droit

righteous [ˈraɪtʃəs] *adj* : juste, vertueux — **righteously** *adv*

righteousness [ˈraɪtʃəsnəs] *n* : droiture *f*

rightful [ˈraɪtfəl] *adj* LAWFUL : légitime, véritable

rightfully [ˈraɪtfəli] *adv* : à juste titre, légitimement

right–hand [ˈraɪtˈhænd] *adj* **1** : du côté droit **2** RIGHT-HANDED : de la main droite **3 right–hand man** : bras *m* droit

right–handed [ˈraɪtˈhændəd] *adj* **1** : droitier <a right-handed pitcher : un lanceur droitier> **2** : de la main droite <a right-handed glove : un gant de la main droite>

rightly [ˈraɪtli] *adv* **1** FAIRLY : à juste titre **2** FITTINGLY : de façon appropriée **3** CORRECTLY : exactement, au juste

right–of–way [ˌraɪtəˈweɪ, -əv-] *n, pl* **rights–of–way** : priorité *f* (sur la route), droit *m* de passage (sur un terrain)

rightward [ˈraɪtwərd] *adv* : vers la droite

right–wing [ˈraɪtˈwɪŋ] *adj* : de droite (en politique)

right wing *n* **the right wing** : la droite

right–winger [ˈraɪtˈwɪŋər] *n* : personne *f* de droite

rigid [ˈrɪdʒɪd] *adj* **1** STIFF : rigide, raide **2** STRICT : rigide, sévère

rigidity [rɪˈdʒɪdəti] *n, pl* **-ties 1** STIFFNESS : rigidité *f* **2** STRICTNESS : rigidité *f*, inflexibilité *f*

rigmarole [ˈrɪgməˌro:l, ˈrɪgə-] *n* **1** NONSENSE : galimatias *m* **2** PROCEDURE : procédure *f* compliquée

rigor *or Brit* **rigour** [ˈrɪgər] *n* **1** SEVERITY : rigueur *f*, sévérité *f* **2** EXACTNESS : rigueur *f*, précision *f* **3 rigors** *npl* HARSHNESS : rigueurs *fpl*, intempéries *fpl* <the rigors of winter : les rigueurs de l'hiver>

rigorous [ˈrɪgərəs] *adj* **1** STRICT : rigoureux, sévère **2** HARSH : rigoureux, rude

rigorously [ˈrɪgərəsli] *adv* : rigoureusement, sévèrement

rile [ˈraɪl] *vt* **riled; riling** : énerver, mettre en colère

rill [ˈrɪl] *n* : ruisselet *m*

rim[1] [ˈrɪm] *vt* **rimmed; rimming** BORDER : border, entourer

rim[2] *n* **1** : bord *m* <the rim of a cup : le bord d'une tasse> **2** : jante *f* (d'une roue)

rime [ˈraɪm] *n* : givre *m*

rind [ˈraɪnd] *n* : écorce *f*

ring[1] [ˈrɪŋ] *vt* **ringed; ringing** SURROUND : encercler

ring[2] *v* **rang** [ˈræŋ]; **rung** [ˈrʌŋ]; **ringing** *vi* **1** : sonner <the doorbell rang : on a sonné à la porte> **2** RESOUND : résonner **3 to ring true** : sonner vrai — *vt* : sonner <to ring the alarm : sonner l'alarme>

ring[3] *n* **1** : bague *f*, anneau *m* <engagement ring : bague de fiançailles> **2** : rond *m* <smoke rings : ronds de fumée> **3** ARENA : ring *m* (de boxe), piste *f* (d'un cirque) **4** GANG : cercle *m*, gang *m* **5** SOUND : son *m*, tintement *m* **6** RINGING : sonnerie *f* (du téléphone, etc.) **7** CALL : coup *m* de téléphone <give me a ring in the morning : appelle-moi dans la matinée>

ringer [ˈrɪŋər] *n* **to be a dead ringer for** : être le sosie de

ringleader [ˈrɪŋˌli:dər] *n* : meneur *m*, -neuse *f*

ringlet [ˈrɪŋlət] *n* : boucle *f* (de cheveux)

ringworm [ˈrɪŋˌwərm] *n* : teigne *f*

rink [ˈrɪŋk] *n* : patinoire *f*

rinse[1] [ˈrɪnts] *vt* **rinsed; rinsing 1** : rincer <to rinse the dishes : rincer la vaisselle> **2** : se rincer <to rinse one's mouth : se rincer la bouche>

rinse[2] *n* : rinçage *m*

riot[1] [ˈraɪət] *vi* : faire une émeute, manifester avec violence

riot[2] *n* : émeute *f*

rioter [ˈraɪətər] *n* : émeutier *m*, -tière *f*

riotous [ˈraɪətəs] *adj* **1** NOISY, ROWDY : tapageur, bruyant **2** ABUNDANT : abondant, exubérant

rip[1] [ˈrɪp] *v* **ripped; ripping** *vt* : déchirer — *vi* : se déchirer

rip[2] *n* : déchirure *f*

ripe [ˈraɪp] *adj* **riper; ripest 1** MATURE : mûr <a ripe pear : une poire mûre> **2** READY : prêt

ripen [ˈraɪpən] *v* : mûrir

ripeness [ˈraɪpnəs] *n* : maturité *f*

rip–off [ˈrɪpˌɔf] *n* SWINDLE, THEFT : escroquerie *f*, vol *m*, arnaque *f fam*

rip off *vt* : escroquer, arnaquer *fam*

ripple[1] [ˈrɪpəl] *v* **-pled; -pling** *vi* : onduler, se rider — *vt* : rider

ripple[2] *n* **1** : ondulation *f*, ride *f* **2** EFFECT, REPERCUSSION : répercussion *f* **3 a ripple of laughter** : une cascade de rires

rise[1] [ˈraɪz] *vi* **rose** [ˈro:z]; **risen** [ˈrɪzən]; **rising 1** ARISE : se lever <to rise to one's feet : se lever, se mettre debout> <to rise from the dead : ressusciter (des morts)> **2** : s'élever, se dresser <mountains rising in the distance : des montagnes qui s'élèvent au loin> **3** : se lever (se dit du soleil, de la lune) **4** : monter <smoke rises : la fumée monte> **5** INCREASE : augmenter, monter **6** ORIGINATE : prendre sa source (dans) **7 to rise from the ranks** : sortir du rang **8 to rise to the occasion** : se montrer à la hauteur de la situation **9 to rise up** REBEL : se soulever (contre), se révolter

rise[2] *n* **1** ASCENT : lever *m* (du soleil), montée *f*, ascension *f* **2** ORIGIN : début *m*, source *f* **3** ELEVATION : élévation *f* <the rise of a step : l'élévation d'une marche> **4** INCREASE : augmentation *f*, hausse *f* **5** INCLINE : montée *f*, pente *f*

riser ['raɪzər] *n* **1** : contremarche *f* (d'un escalier) **2 early riser** : lève-tôt *mf* **3 late riser** : lève-tard *mf*

risk[1] ['rɪsk] *vt* : risquer

risk[2] *n* : risque *m*, danger *m*

riskiness ['rɪskinəs] *n* : risques *mpl*

risky ['rɪski] *adj* **riskier; -est** : risqué, hasardeux

risqué [rɪ'skeɪ] *adj* : risqué, osé

rite ['raɪt] *n* : rite *m*

ritual[1] ['rɪtʃʊəl] *adj* : rituel

ritual[2] *n* : rituel *m*

rival[1] ['raɪvəl] *vt* **-valed** *or* **-valled; -valing** *or* **-valling** : rivaliser avec

rival[2] *adj* : rival <rival factions : factions rivales>

rival[3] *n* : rival *m*, -vale *f*; compétiteur *m*, -trice *f*

rivalry ['raɪvəlri] *n, pl* **-ries** : rivalité *f*

river ['rɪvər] *n* : rivière *f*, fleuve *m*

riverbank ['rɪvər,bæŋk] *n* : rive *f*, berge *f*

riverbed ['rɪvər,bɛd] *n* : lit *m* de rivière

riverside ['rɪvər,saɪd] *n* : rive *f*, bord *m* d'une rivière

rivet[1] ['rɪvət] *vt* **1** : riveter, river **2 to be riveted to the spot** : être cloué sur place

rivet[2] *n* : rivet *m*

rivulet ['rɪvjələt] *n* : ruisselet *m*

roach ['ro:tʃ] → **cockroach**

road ['ro:d] *n* **1** : route *f*, rue *f* **2** PATH, WAY : chemin *m*, voie *f* <on the road to success : sur le chemin de la réussite>

roadblock ['ro:d,blɑk] *n* : barrage *m* routier

roadrunner ['ro:d,rʌnər] *n* : coucou *m* terrestre

roadside ['ro:d,saɪd] *n* : bord *m* de la route

roadway ['ro:d,weɪ] *n* : chaussée *f*

roam ['ro:m] *vi* WANDER : errer, rôder

roan[1] ['ro:n] *adj* : rouan

roan[2] *n* : rouan *m*, rouanne *f*

roar[1] ['ror] *vi* **1** : rugir (se dit d'un lion), mugir (se dit du vent, de la mer, etc.), gronder (se dit d'un moteur, du tonnerre, etc.) **2** : éclater, hurler <to roar with laughter : hurler de rire> — *vt* : hurler, vociférer <he roared approval : il a hurlé son approbation>

roar[2] *n* **1** : rugissement *m* (d'un lion) **2** : hurlement *m*, cri *m* <a roar of pain : un hurlement de douleur> **3** : vrombissement *m* (d'un moteur), grondement *m* (du tonnerre)

roast[1] ['ro:st] *vt* : rôtir (de la viande, etc.), griller (des noix), torréfier (du café)

roast[2] *adj* : rôti <roast beef : rôti de bœuf>

roast[3] *n* : rôti *m*

rob ['rɑb] *vt* **robbed; robbing 1** : dévaliser (une banque, etc.), cambrioler (une maison) **2** STEAL : voler <to rob jewelry : voler des bijoux>

robber ['rɑbər] *n* : voleur *m*, -leuse *f*

robbery ['rɑbəri] *n, pl* **-beries** : vol *m* <armed robbery : vol à main armé>

robe[1] ['ro:b] *vt* **robed; robing** : vêtir, habiller

robe[2] *n* **1** : toge *f* (d'un juge) **2** → **bathrobe**

robin ['rɑbən] *n* : rouge-gorge *m*

robot ['ro:,bɑt, -bət] *n* : robot *m*

robust [ro'bʌst, 'ro:,bʌst] *adj* : robuste, vigoureux — **robustly** *adv*

rock[1] ['rɑk] *vt* **1** : balancer (un berceau), bercer (un enfant) **2** SHAKE : ébranler, secouer — *vi* SWAY : se balancer

rock[2] *n* **1** STONE : roche *f*, roc *m* **2** BOULDER : rocher *m* **3** ROCKING : mouvement *m* de va-et-vient **4** : rock *m* (musique)

rocker ['rɑkər] *n* **1** : bascule *f* (d'un fauteuil) **2** → **rocking chair**

rocket[1] ['rɑkət] *vi* : monter en flèche

rocket[2] *n* : fusée *f*

rocking chair *n* : fauteuil *m* à bascule, chaise *f* berçante *Can*

rocking horse *n* : cheval *m* à bascule

rock salt *n* : sel *m* gemme

rocky ['rɑki] *adj* **rockier; -est** : rocheux

rod ['rɑd] *n* **1** STICK : baguette *f* **2** : tige *f*, tringle *f* <iron rod : tige de fer> **3** : unité *f* de mesure qui équivaut à 16,5 pieds **4** *or* **fishing rod** : canne *f* à pêche

rode → **ride**[1]

rodent ['ro:dənt] *n* : rongeur *m*

rodeo ['ro:di,o:, ro'deɪ,o:] *n, pl* **-deos** : rodéo *m*

roe ['ro:] *n* : œufs *mpl* de poisson

roe deer *n* : chevreuil *m*

rogue ['ro:g] *n* SCOUNDREL : escroc *m*, fripouille *f fam*

roguish ['ro:gɪʃ] *adj* : espiègle, coquin

role ['ro:l] *n* **1** PART : rôle *m* (dans une pièce de théâtre) **2** FUNCTION : rôle *m*, fonction *f*

roll[1] ['ro:l] *vt* **1** : rouler <to roll a barrel : rouler un tonneau> <to roll cigarettes : rouler des cigarettes> **2** FLATTEN : étendre (de la pâte) **3** : faire tourner <to roll the cameras : faire tourner les caméras> **4 to roll out** : dérouler (un tapis) **5 to roll up one's sleeves** : retrousser ses manches — *vi* **1** : se rouler <the children were rolling in the grass : les enfants se roulaient dans l'herbe> **2** : tanguer, faire du roulis (se dit d'un bateau) **3 to roll in** : affluer <money was rolling in : l'argent affluait> **4 to roll on** ELAPSE : passer **5 to roll over** : se retourner

roll[2] *n* **1** LIST : liste *f* <class roll : liste des élèves> <to call the roll : faire l'appel> **2** : rouleau *m* (de papier, etc.), liasse *f* (d'argent) **3** BUN : petit pain *m* **4** RUMBLE : roulement *m* (de tambour), grondement *m* (du tonnerre) **5** ROLLING : roulis *m* (d'un navire), lancement *m* (de dés), balancement *m* (des hanches, etc.)

roller ['ro:lər] *n* : rouleau *m*

roller coaster ['ro:lər,ko:stər] *n* : montagnes *fpl* russes

roller–skate ['ro:lər,skeɪt] *vi* **-skated; -skating** : faire du patin à roulettes

roller skate *n* : patin *m* à roulettes

rollicking ['rɑlɪkɪŋ] *adj* : joyeux, exubérant

rolling pin *n* : rouleau *m* à pâtisserie

Roman[1] ['ro:mən] *adj* : romain

Roman[2] *n* : Romain *m*, -maine *f*

Roman Catholic[1] *adj* : catholique

Roman Catholic[2] *n* : catholique *mf*

romance[1] [ro'mænts, 'ro:,mænts] *vi* **-manced; -mancing** : exagérer, fabuler

romance[2] *n* **1** : roman *m* du Moyen Âge **2** : histoire *f* d'amour **3** AFFAIR : liaison *f* amoureuse **4** APPEAL : charme *m*, attrait *m* <the romance of the sea : l'attrait de la mer>

Romanian[1] [rʊ'meɪniən, ro-] *adj* : roumain

Romanian[2] *n* **1** : Roumain *m*, -maine *f* **2** : roumain *m* (langue)

romantic [ro'mæntɪk] *adj* : romantique

romantically [ro'mæntɪkli] *adv* : de façon romantique

romp[1] ['rɑmp] *vi* : s'ébattre, folâtrer

romp[2] *n* : ébats *mpl*, jeux *mpl* folâtres

roof[1] ['ru:f, 'rʊf] *vt* : couvrir d'un toit

roof[2] *n, pl* **roofs** ['ru:fs, 'rʊfs; 'ru:vz, 'rʊvz] : toit *m*

roofing ['ru:fɪŋ, 'rʊfɪŋ] *n* : toiture *f*, couverture *f*

rooftop ['ru:f,tɑp, 'rʊf-] *n* ROOF : toit *m*

rook[1] ['rʊk] *vt* CHEAT : frauder, escroquer

rook[2] *n* **1** : freux *m*, corbeau *m* (oiseau) **2** : tour *f* (en échecs)

rookie ['rʊki] *n* : novice *mf*

room[1] ['ru:m, 'rʊm] *vi* : loger <to room with s.o. : partager un logement avec qqn>

room[2] *n* **1** SPACE : espace *m*, place *f* <there's not enough room : il manque d'espace> **2** : chambre *f* (d'hôtel), pièce *f* (d'une maison), salle *f* (de conférence) **3** OPPORTUNITY : chance *f*, possibilité *f* <there was no room for doubt : il n'y avait aucun doute possible>

roomer ['ru:mər, 'rʊmər] *n* : pensionnaire *mf*; chambreur *m*, -breuse *f Can*

rooming house *n* : immeuble *m* locatif

roommate ['ru:m,meɪt, 'rʊm-] *n* : camarade *mf* de chambre, colocataire *mf Can*

roomy ['ru:mi, 'rʊmi] *adj* **roomier; -est** : spacieux, vaste

roost[1] ['ru:st] *vi* : se percher

roost[2] *n* : perchoir *m*

rooster ['ru:stər, 'rʊs-] *n* : coq *m*

root[1] ['ru:t, 'rʊt] *vi* **1** : s'enraciner (se dit d'une plante) **2** : fouiller (se dit des cochons) **3 to root for** CHEER : encourager, applaudir — *vt* **1 to root out** UNCOVER : découvrir, déterrer **2 to root out** ERADICATE : extirper

root[2] *n* **1** : racine *f* (d'une plante) **2** : racine *f*, base *f* (d'une dent) **3** SOURCE : origine *f*, source *f* <the root of evil : l'origine du mal> **4** CORE : fond *m*, cœur *m* <let's get to the root of the matter : allons au fond des choses>

rootless ['ru:tləs, 'rʊt-] *adj* : sans racines

rope[1] ['ro:p] *vt* **roped; roping 1** TIE : attacher (avec une corde) **2** LASSO : prendre au lasso **3 to rope off** : interdire l'accès à, délimiter par une corde

rope[2] *n* : corde *f*

rosary ['ro:zəri] *n, pl* **-ries** : chapelet *m*

rose[1] → **rise**[1]

rose[2] ['ro:z] *adj* : (de couleur) rose

rose[3] *n* : rose *f* (fleur), rose *m* (couleur)

rosebud ['ro:z,bʌd] *n* : bouton *m* de rose

rosebush ['ro:z,bʊʃ] *n* : rosier *m*

rosemary ['ro:z,mɛri] *n, pl* **-maries** : romarin *m*

rosette [ro'zɛt] *n* : rosette *f* (fait de rubans), rosace *f* (en architecture)

Rosh Hashanah [,rɑʃhɑ'ʃɑnə, ,ro:ʃ-] *n* : Rosh Hashana *m*, fête *f* du nouvel an juif

rosin ['rɑzən] *n* : colophane *f*

roster ['rɑstər] *n* : tableau *m*, liste *f* <roster of duties : tableau de services>

rostrum ['rɑstrəm] *n, pl* **-trums** *or* **-tra** [-trə] : tribune *f*, estrade *f*

rosy ['ro:zi] *adj* **rosier; -est 1** : rose, rosé <rosy cheeks : joues rosées> **2** HOPEFUL : prometteur

rot[1] ['rɑt] *v* **rotted; rotting** *vt* : pourrir — *vi* : pourrir, se décomposer

rot[2] *n* : pourriture *f*

rotary[1] ['ro:ţəri] *adj* : rotatif

rotary[2] *n* : rond-point *m*

rotate ['ro:,teɪt] *v* **-tated; -tating** *vi* REVOLVE : tourner — *vt* **1** TURN : faire tourner **2** ALTERNATE : alterner (des cultures agricoles)

rotation [ro'teɪʃən] *n* : rotation *f*

rote ['ro:t] *n* **by ~** : par cœur, machinalement

rotor ['ro:tər] *n* : rotor *m*

rotten ['rɑtən] *adj* **1** : pourri <rotten wood : bois pourri> **2** CORRUPT : pourri, corrompu (se dit d'une personne) **3** BAD : pourri, mauvais <rotten weather : temps pourri>

rottenness [ˈrɑtənnəs] *n* : pourriture *f*

rotund [roˈtʌnd] *adj* : rondelet, potelé

rotunda [roˈtʌndə] *n* : rotonde *f*

rouge [ˈruːʒ] *n* : rouge *m* à joues

rough[1] [ˈrʌf] *vt* **1** → **roughen 2** *or* **to rough out** : ébaucher, esquisser **3** *or* **to rough up** MANHANDLE : tabasser *fam*, battre

rough[2] *adj* **1** : rugueux, rude <a rough surface : une surface rugueuse> **2** : inégal, accidenté <rough terrain : terrain inégal> **3** TURBULENT : agité **4** HARSH : rude, violent **5** UNCOUTH : rude, fruste **6** APPROXIMATE : approximatif, sommaire <a rough estimate : une estimation approximative>

rough[3] *n* : rough *m* (au golf)

roughage [ˈrʌfɪdʒ] *n* : fibres *mpl* alimentaires

roughen [ˈrʌfən] *vt* : rendre rude, rendre rugueux

roughly [ˈrʌfli] *adv* **1** HARSHLY : rudement, brutalement **2** IMPERFECTLY : grossièrement **3** NEARLY : à peu près, environ <roughly 20 percent : environ 20 pour cent>

roughneck [ˈrʌf,nɛk] *n* : dur *m fam*

roughness [ˈrʌfnəs] *n* : rudesse *f*, rugosité *f*

roulette [,ruːˈlɛt] *n* : roulette *f* (au casino)

round[1] [ˈraʊnd] *vt* **1** : arrondir <to round the lips : arrondir les lèvres> **2** TURN : tourner <she rounded the corner : elle a tourné au coin> **3** **to round off** : arrondir (un chiffre) **4** **to round out** COMPLETE : compléter **5** **to round up** GATHER : rassembler

round[2] *adv* → **around**[1]

round[3] *adj* **1** : rond <a round face : un visage rond> <to have round shoulders : avoir le dos voûté> **2** COMPLETE, FULL : exact, tout rond <a round dozen : une douzaine tout rond>

round[4] *n* **1** CIRCLE : rond *m*, cercle *m* **2** : série *f* <a round of talks : une série de négociations> <the daily round : la routine quotidienne> **3** : manche *f* (d'un match), partie *f* (de golf) **4** : cartouche *f* (d'une arme à feu) **5** **round of applause** : salve *f* d'applaudissements **6** **round of drinks** : tournée *f fam* **7** **rounds** *npl* : tournée *f* (de ses amis), ronde *f* (d'un lieu), visites *fpl* (d'un médecin)

round[5] *prep* → **around**[2]

roundabout [ˈraʊndə,baʊt] *adj* : détourné, indirect

roundness [ˈraʊndnəs] *n* : rondeur *f*

round–trip [ˈraʊndˌtrɪp] *n* : voyage *m* aller et retour

roundup [ˈraʊnd,ʌp] *n* **1** : rassemblement *m* (de bétail, de personnes, etc.) **2** SUMMARY : rappel *m*, résumé *m*

round up *vt* GATHER : rassembler, regrouper

roundworm [ˈraʊnd,wərm] *n* : ascaride *m*

rouse [ˈraʊz] *v* **roused; rousing** *vt* **1** : réveiller **2** EXCITE : éveiller, susciter <to rouse s.o. to fury : éveiller la furie en qqn> — *vi* AWAKEN : se réveiller

rout[1] [ˈraʊt] *vt* **1** : mettre en déroute **2** **to rout out** : expulser, déloger

rout[2] *n* : déroute *f*, débâcle *f*

route[1] [ˈruːt, ˈraʊt] *vt* **routed; routing** DIRECT : fixer l'itinéraire de, diriger

route[2] *n* **1** HIGHWAY : route *f* **2** LINE : parcours *m*, trajet *m* <bus route : parcours d'autobus> **3** : chemin *m*, itinéraire *m* <the best route : le meilleur chemin> **4** **newspaper route** : tournée *f* de livraison

routine[1] [ruːˈtiːn] *adj* : routinier

routine[2] *n* : routine *f*

routinely [ruːˈtiːnli] *adv* : systématiquement

rove [ˈroːv] *v* **roved; roving** *vi* ROAM : errer, vagabonder — *vt* : rôder dans, parcourir

rover [ˈroːvər] *n* : vagabond *m*, -bonde *f*

row[1] [ˈroː] *vi* : ramer — *vt* : transporter par canot

row[2] [ˈroː] *n* **1** LINE, RANK : rang *m*, rangée *f* <a row of houses : une rangée de maisons> <to stand in a row : être debout en rang> **2** : excursion *f* en bateau **3** SUCCESSION : série *f* <twice in a row : deux fois de suite> **4** [ˈraʊ] QUARREL : altercation *f*, dispute *f*

rowboat [ˈroː,boːt] *n* : bateau *m* à rames

rowdiness [ˈraʊdinəs] *n* : tapage *m*, vacarme *m*

rowdy[1] [ˈraʊdi] *adj* **rowdier; -est** : tapageur, bruyant

rowdy[2] *n, pl* **-dies** : voyou *m*

royal[1] [ˈrɔɪəl] *adj* : royal — **royally** *adv*

royal[2] *n* : membre *m* d'une famille royale

royalty [ˈrɔɪəlti] *n, pl* **-ties** **1** : membres *m* d'une famille royale **2** : royauté *f* (position) **3** **royalties** *npl* : droits *mpl* d'auteur

rub[1] [ˈrʌb] *v* **rubbed; rubbing** *vt* **1** : frotter, se frotter <to rub one's hands together : se frotter les mains> **2** MASSAGE : frictionner **3** CHAFE : frotter contre, blesser **4** POLISH : frotter, polir **5** **to rub shoulders with s.o.** : coudoyer qqn **6** **to rub s.o. the wrong way** : prendre qqn à rebrousse-poil — *vi* : frotter

rub[2] *n* **1** : friction *f*, frottement *m* <an alcohol rub : une friction à l'alcool> **2** OBSTACLE : obstacle *m*, difficulté *f*

rubber[1] [ˈrʌbər] *adj* : en caoutchouc

rubber[2] *n* **1** : caoutchouc *m* **2** **rubbers** *npl* : caoutchoucs *mpl*, claques *fpl Can*, pardessus *m Can*

rubber band *n* : élastique *m*

rubber–stamp [ˈrʌbərˈstæmp] *vt* : tamponner
rubber stamp *n* : tampon *m* (de caoutchouc)
rubbery [ˈrʌbəri] *adj* : caoutchouteux
rubbish [ˈrʌbɪʃ] *n* : ordures *fpl,* déchets *mpl*
rubble [ˈrʌbəl] *n* : décombres *mpl*
ruble [ˈru:bəl] *n* : rouble *m*
ruby[1] [ˈru:bi] *adj* : vermeil (couleur)
ruby[2] *n, pl* **-bies 1** : rubis *m* **2** : couleur *f* rubis, couleur *f* vermeille
rudder [ˈrʌdər] *n* : gouvernail *m*
ruddy [ˈrʌdi] *adj* **ruddier; -est** : rougeâtre, rougeaud
rude [ˈru:d] *adj* **ruder; rudest 1** CRUDE : grossier, rudimentaire **2** UNDEVELOPED : primitif, rude **3** IMPOLITE : grossier, insolent
rudely [ˈru:dli] *adv* : impoliment, grossièrement
rudeness [ˈru:dnəs] *n* : impolitesse *f,* grossièreté *f*
rudiment [ˈru:dəmənt] *n* : rudiment *m*
rudimentary [ˌru:dəˈmɛntəri] *adj* : rudimentaire
rue [ˈru:] *vt* **rued; ruing** : regretter
rueful [ˈru:fəl] *adj* : triste, chagrin, attristé
ruffian [ˈrʌfiən] *n* : voyou *m*
ruffle[1] [ˈrʌfəl] *vt* **-fled; -fling 1** : hérisser (ses plumes), ébouriffer (ses cheveux) **2** TROUBLE, VEX : décontenancer, troubler, énerver
ruffle[2] *n* : ruche *f*
rug [ˈrʌg] *n* : tapis *m,* carpette *f*
rugged [ˈrʌgəd] *adj* **1** : accidenté <rugged landscape : paysage accidenté> **2** JAGGED : en dents de scie (se dit des montagnes) **3** HARSH : sévère, exigeant **4** STURDY : robuste, fort
ruin[1] [ˈru:ən] *vt* **1** DESTROY : ruiner, anéantir **2** DAMAGE : abîmer **3** BANKRUPT : ruiner
ruin[2] *n* : ruine *f* <to be in ruins : être en ruines>
ruinous [ˈru:ənəs] *adj* : ruineux
rule[1] [ˈru:l] *v* **ruled; ruling** *vt* **1** GOVERN : régner sur, gouverner (un pays, etc.) **2** DOMINATE : dominer, maîtriser (les émotions, etc.) **3** DRAW : tirer (à la règle) **4** DECREE, JUDGE : décréter, décider, juger — *vi* : régner
rule[2] *n* **1** : règle *f,* règlement *m* <as a rule : en règle générale> **2** CUSTOM : coutume *f,* habitude *f* **3** DOMINION : autorité *f,* gouvernement *m* **4** → **ruler**
ruler [ˈru:lər] *n* : règle *f* (pour mesurer)
rum [ˈrʌm] *n* : rhum *m*
Rumanian [rʊˈmeɪniən] → **Romanian**
rumble[1] [ˈrʌmbəl] *vi* **-bled; -bling 1** ROAR : gronder (se dit du tonnerre, etc.) **2** : gargouiller (se dit de l'estomac)
rumble[2] *n* : grondement *m* (du tonnerre, etc.), gargouillement *m* (de l'estomac)
ruminant[1] [ˈru:mənənt] *adj* : ruminant
ruminant[2] *n* : ruminant *m*
ruminate [ˈru:məˌneɪt] *vi* **-nated; -nating 1** : ruminer (se dit d'une vâche) **2** MUSE : ruminer, réfléchir
rummage [ˈrʌmɪdʒ] *vi* **-maged; -maging** : fouiller, fourrager
rummy [ˈrʌmi] *n* : rami *m* (jeu de cartes)
rumor[1] *or Brit* **rumour** [ˈru:mər] *vt* **it is rumored that** : le bruit court que, il paraît que
rumor[2] *or Brit* **rumour** *n* : rumeur *f,* bruit *m*
rump [ˈrʌmp] *n* **1** : croupe *f* (d'un animal) **2** *or* **rump steak** : romsteck *m*
rumple [ˈrʌmpəl] *vt* **-pled; -pling 1** TOUSLE : ébouriffer **2** WRINKLE : froisser, friper
rumpus [ˈrʌmpəs] *n* : vacarme *m,* boucan *m*
run[1] [ˈrʌn] *v* **ran** [ˈræn]; **run; running** *vi* **1** : courir <he ran home : il est rentré chez lui en courant> **2** : être candidat <to run for the presidency : être candidat à la présidence> **3** FLOW : couler **4** FUNCTION, OPERATE : tourner <the engine was running : le moteur tournait> **5** BE : être <profits were running high : les profits étaient élevés> <I was running late : j'étais en retard> **6** : faire le service, circuler <the train runs between Washington and New York : le train fait le service entre Washington et New York> **7** OCCUR : être courant <it runs in our family : c'est courant dans notre famille> **8** : déteindre (se dit des couleurs) **9** EXTEND : passer **10 to run away** : s'enfuir, se sauver **11 to run out** EXPIRE : expirer **12 to run out of** : manquer — *vt* **1** : courir <to run the marathon : courir le marathon> **2** : faire, effectuer <to run errands : faire des courses> **3** OPERATE : faire marcher **4** INCUR : courir <to run a risk : courir un risque> **5** MANAGE : gérer, diriger **6** CHASE : chasser <we ran the thieves out of town : les bandits ont été chassés de la ville> **7 to run a fever** : faire de la température **8 to run a red light** : brûler un feu rouge **9 to run one's car off the road** : perdre la maîtrise de son véhicule
run[2] *n* **1** : course *f* <a three-mile run : une course de trois milles> <to break into a run : se mettre à courir> **2** SERIES : succession *f,* série *f* <a run of cloudy days : une succession de journées nuageuses> **3** RIDE : tour *m,* promenade *f* <a run in the car : un tour en voiture> **4** TRIP : trajet *m,* parcours *m* <the New York run : le trajet jusqu'à New York> **5** : maille *f* filée, échelle *f* (dans les bas) **6** SLOPE : pente *f* <ski run : pente de ski> **7** DEMAND, RUSH : ruée *f* (sur la

banque, etc.) **8** : point *m* (aux sports) **9** : enclos *m* (pour des animaux) **10** : tirage *m* (en imprimerie) **11 to have the run of the house** : avoir la maison à sa disposition **12 on the run** : en fuite, en cavale

runaway[1] [ˈrʌnəˌweɪ] *adj* : fugueur (se dit d'un enfant), emballé (se dit d'un cheval), incontrôlé (se dit d'un véhicule)

runaway[2] *n* : fugitif *m*, -tive *f*; fugeur *m*, -geuse *f*

run–down [ˈrʌnˈdaʊn] *adj* **1** DILAPIDATED : délabré **2** EXHAUSTED, WORN-OUT : fatigué, éreinté

rung[1] → **ring**[2]

rung[2] [ˈrʌŋ] *n* : barreau *m* (d'une échelle, d'une chaise, etc.)

runner [ˈrʌnər] *n* **1** RACER : coureur *m*, -reuse *f* **2** BLADE : lame *f* (d'un patin) **3** TRACK : glissière *f* (d'une porte, etc.), coulisse *f* **4** : coulant *m*, stolon *m* (d'une plante) **5** MESSENGER : coursier *m*, -sière *f*

runner–up [ˌrʌnərˈʌp] *n, pl* **runners–up** : second *m*, -conde *f*

running [ˈrʌnɪŋ] *adj* **1** FLOWING : courant <running water : eau courante> **2** CONTINUOUS : continuel <a running battle : une bataille continuelle> **3** CONSECUTIVE : de suite <three days running : trois jours consécutifs>

runt [ˈrʌnt] *n* : avorton *m*

runway [ˈrʌnˌweɪ] *n* : piste *f* d'envol, piste *f* d'atterrissage

rupee [ruːˈpiː, ˈruːˌ-] *n* : roupie *f*

rupture[1] [ˈrʌptʃər] *v* **-tured; -turing** *vt* BREAK, BURST : rompre — *vi* : se rompre

rupture[2] *n* **1** BREACH, BREAK : rupture *f* **2** HERNIA : hernie *f*

rural [ˈrʊrəl] *adj* : rural

ruse [ˈruːs, ˈruːz] *n* : ruse *f*, stratagème *m*

rush[1] [rʌʃ] *vi* HURRY : se précipiter, se dépêcher <to rush toward s.o. : se précipiter vers qqn> — *vt* **1** HURRY, PRESS : presser, bousculer **2** *or* **to rush through** : expédier <to rush one's work : expédier son travail> **3** ATTACK : attaquer, agresser **4** TRANSPORT : transporter d'urgence (à l'hôpital, etc.)

rush[2] *adj* : urgent <a rush order : une commande urgente>

rush[3] *n* **1** : jonc *m* (plante) **2** : ruée *f* <a rush towards the exit : une ruée vers la sortie> **3** HASTE : hâte *f*, empressement *m*

rush hour *n* : heure *f* de pointe

russet[1] [ˈrʌsət] *adj* : roussâtre, roux

russet[2] *n* : roux *m* (couleur)

Russian[1] [ˈrʌʃən] *adj* : russe

Russian[2] *n* **1** : Russe *mf* **2** : russe *m* (langue)

rust[1] [ˈrʌst] *vt* : rouiller — *vi* : se rouiller

rust[2] *n* **1** : rouille *f* (sur métal) **2** : couleur *f* rouille

rustic[1] [ˈrʌstɪk] *adj* : rustique, champêtre

rustic[2] *n* : campagnard *m*, -gnarde *f*

rustle[1] [ˈrʌsəl] *v* **-tled; -tling** *vi* : bruire <the pine needles rustled : on entendait bruire les aiguilles de pin> — *vt* STEAL : voler (du bétail)

rustle[2] *n* : bruissement *m*, froissement

rusty [ˈrʌsti] *adj* **rustier; -est 1** : rouillé <a rusty nail : un clou rouillé> **2** SLOW : rouillé, peu agile

rut [ˈrʌt] *n* **1** TRACK : ornière *f* **2 to be in a rut** : s'enliser dans une routine

ruthless [ˈruːθləs] *adj* : impitoyable, cruel — **ruthlessly** *adv*

ruthlessness [ˈruːθləsnəs] *n* : caractère *m* impitoyable

Rwandan[1] [rʊˈɑndən] *adj* : rwandais

Rwandan[2] *n* : Rwandais *m*, -daise *f*

rye [ˈraɪ] *n* **1** : seigle *m* <rye bread : pain de seigle> **2** *or* **rye whiskey** : whisky *m* (de seigle)

S

s [ˈɛs] *n, pl* **s's** *or* **ss** [ˈɛsəz] : s *m*, dix-neuvième lettre de l'alphabet

Sabbath [ˈsæbəθ] *n* : sabbat *m* (en judaïsme), dimanche *m* (en christianisme)

saber [ˈseɪbər] *n* : sabre *m*

sable [ˈseɪbəl] *n* **1** BLACK : noir *m* **2** : zibeline *f* (animal)

sabotage[1] [ˈsæbəˌtɑʒ] *vt* **-taged; -taging** : saboter

sabotage[2] *n* : sabotage *m*

saboteur [ˌsæbəˈtər, -ˈtʊr, -ˈtjʊr] *n* : saboteur *m*, -teuse *f*

sac [ˈsæk] *n* : sac *m*

saccharin [ˈsækərən] *n* : saccharine *f*

saccharine [ˈsækərən, -ˌriːn, -ˌraɪn] *adj* : mielleux, doucereux (se dit d'un sourire, etc.)

sachet [sæˈʃeɪ] *n* : sachet *m*

sack[1] [ˈsæk] *vt* **1** PLUNDER : mettre à sac **2** DISMISS, FIRE : virer, congédier

sack[2] *n* BAG : sac *m*

sacrament [ˈsækrəmənt] *n* : sacrement *m*

sacramental [ˌsækrəˈmɛntəl] *adj* : sacramentel

sacred [ˈseɪkrəd] *adj* : sacré

sacrifice[1] [ˈsækrəˌfaɪs] *vt* **-ficed; -ficing 1** : sacrifier **2 to sacrifice oneself** : se sacrifier

sacrifice[2] *n* : sacrifice *m*

sacrificial [ˌsækrəˈfɪʃəl] *adj* : sacrificiel
sacrilege [ˈsækrəlɪdʒ] *n* : sacrilège *m*
sacrilegious [ˌsækrəˈlɪdʒəs, -ˈli:-] *adj* : sacrilège
sacrosanct [ˈsækroˌsæŋkt] *adj* : sacro-saint
sad [ˈsæd] *adj* **sadder; saddest** : triste
sadden [ˈsædən] *vt* : attrister
saddle[1] [ˈsædəl] *vt* **-dled; -dling** : seller
saddle[2] *n* : selle *f* <in the saddle : en selle>
sadism [ˈseɪˌdɪzəm, ˈsæ-] *n* : sadisme *m*
sadist [ˈseɪdɪst, ˈsæ-] *n* : sadiste *mf*
sadistic [səˈdɪstɪk] *adj* : sadique — **sadistically** [-tɪkli] *adv*
sadly [ˈsædli] *adv* **1** SORROWFULLY : tristement **2** UNFORTUNATELY : malheureusement **3** (*used for emphasis*) <you are sadly mistaken : vous vous trompez fort>
sadness [ˈsædnəs] *n* : tristesse *f*
safari [səˈfɑri, -ˈfær-] *n* : safari *m*
safe[1] [ˈseɪf] *adj* **safer; safest 1** PROTECTED : en sécurité, à l'abri <safe and sound : sain et sauf> **2** SECURE : sûr **3 to play it safe** : ne prendre aucun risque
safe[2] *n* : coffre-fort *m*
safeguard[1] [ˈseɪfˌgɑrd] *vt* : sauvegarder
safeguard[2] *n* : sauvegarde *f*
safekeeping [ˈseɪfˈki:pɪŋ] *n* : bonne garde *f*
safely [ˈseɪfli] *adv* **1** : sans incident, sûrement <the plane landed safely : l'avion a atterri sans incident> <to arrive safely : bien arriver> **2** SECURELY : en sécurité, à l'abri **3** CAREFULLY : prudemment
safety [ˈseɪfti] *n, pl* **-ties** : sécurité *f*
safety belt *n* : ceinture *f* de sécurité
safety pin *n* : épingle *f* de sûreté
saffron [ˈsæfrən] *n* : safran *m*
sag[1] [ˈsæg] *vi* **sagged; sagging** : s'affaisser
sag[2] *n* : affaissement *m*
saga [ˈsɑgə, ˈsæ-] *n* : saga *f*
sagacious [səˈgeɪʃəs] *adj* : sagace
sage[1] [ˈseɪdʒ] *adj* **sager; -est** : sage, avisé
sage[2] *n* **1** : sage *m* (personne) **2** : sauge *f* (plante)
sagebrush [ˈseɪdʒˌbrʌʃ] *n* : armoise *f*
sagely [ˈseɪdʒli] *adv* : avec sagesse
Sagittarius [ˌsædʒəˈtɛriəs] *n* : Sagittaire *m*
said → **say**[1]
sail[1] [ˈseɪl] *vi* **1** : voyager en bateau **2** *or* **to go sailing** : faire de la voile **3** : aller facilement <we sailed right in : nous sommes entrés sans problème> — *vt* **1** : naviguer, manœuvrer (un bateau) **2** CROSS : traverser, parcourir <to sail the seas : parcourir les mers>
sail[2] *n* **1** : voile *f* (d'un bateau) **2** : promenade *f* en bateau **3 to set sail** : appareiller, prendre la mer
sailboat [ˈseɪlˌbo:t] *n* : bateau *m* à voiles, voilier *m*
sailor [ˈseɪlər] *n* : marin *m*, matelot *m*
saint [ˈseɪnt, *before a name* ˌseɪnt *or* sənt] *n* : saint *m*, sainte *f*
saintliness [ˈseɪntlinəs] *n* : sainteté *f*
saintly [ˈseɪntli] *adj* **saintlier; -est** : saint
sake [ˈseɪk] *n* **1** BENEFIT : bien *m* <for the children's sake : pour le bien des enfants> **2** (*indicating an end or purpose*) <art for art's sake : l'art pour l'art> <for the sake of money : pour l'argent> **3 for goodness' sake!** : pour l'amour de Dieu!
salacious [səˈleɪʃəs] *adj* : salace
salad [ˈsæləd] *n* : salade *f*
salamander [ˈsæləˌmændər] *n* : salamandre *f*
salami [səˈlɑmi] *n* : salami *m*, saucisson *m* sec
salary [ˈsæləri] *n, pl* **-ries** : salaire *m*
sale [ˈseɪl] *n* **1** SELLING : vente *f* <for sale : à vendre> **2** : solde *m* <on sale : en solde> **3 sales** *npl or* **sales department** : service *m* des ventes
salesman [ˈseɪlzmən] *n, pl* **-men** [-mən, -ˌmɛn] **1** : vendeur *m* **2 traveling salesman** : représentant *m* (de commerce)
salesperson [ˈseɪlzˌpərsən] *n* : vendeur *m*, -deuse *f*; représentant *m*, -tante *f* des ventes
saleswoman [ˈseɪlzˌwʊmən] *n, pl* **-women** [-ˌwɪmən] **1** : vendeuse *f* **2 traveling saleswoman** : représentante *f* (de commerce)
salient [ˈseɪljənt] *adj* : saillant
saline [ˈseɪˌli:n, -ˌlaɪn] *adj* : salin
saliva [səˈlaɪvə] *n* : salive *f*
salivary [ˈsæləˌvɛri] *adj* : salivaire
salivate [ˈsæləˌveɪt] *vi* **-vated; -vating** : saliver
sallow [ˈsælo:] *adj* : jaunâtre
sally[1] [ˈsæli] *vi* **-lied; -lying** SET OUT : sortir
sally[2] *n, pl* **-lies 1** : sortie *f* (militaire) **2** EXCURSION : sortie *f* **3** QUIP : saillie *f*
salmon [ˈsæmən] *ns & pl* : saumon *m*
salon [səˈlɑn, ˈsæˌlɑn, sæˈlɔ̃] *n* : salon *m* <beauty salon : salon de beauté>
saloon [səˈlu:n] *n* **1** : salon *m* (dans un navire) **2** BARROOM : bar *m*
salsa [ˈsɔlsə, ˈsɑl-] *n* **1** : sauce *f* pimentée **2** : salsa *f* (musique)
salt[1] [ˈsɔlt] *vt* : saler
salt[2] *adj* : salé
salt[3] *n* : sel *m*
saltshaker [ˈsɔltˌʃeɪkər] *n* : salière *f*
saltwater [ˈsɔltˌwɔt̬ər, -ˌwɑ-] *adj* : de mer
salty [ˈsɔlti] *adj* **saltier; -est** : salé
salubrious [səˈlu:briəs] *adj* : salubre
salutary [ˈsæljəˌtɛri] *adj* : salutaire
salutation [ˌsæljəˈteɪʃən] *n* : salutation *f*
salute[1] [səˈlu:t] *v* **-luted; -luting** *vt* : saluer — *vi* : faire un salut
salute[2] *n* **1** : salut *m* (avec la main), salve *f* (de canon) <twenty-one gun

salute : salve de vingt et un coups> **2** TRIBUTE : hommage *m*

salvage[1] ['sælvɪdʒ] *vt* **-vaged; -vaging** : sauver, récupérer

salvage[2] *n* : sauvetage *m*

salvation [sæl'veɪʃən] *n* : salut *m*

salve[1] ['sæv, 'sav] *vt* **salved; salving** : adoucir, apaiser, soulager

salve[2] *n* : onguent *m*, pommade *f*

salvo ['sæl,vo:] *n, pl* **-vos** *or* **-voes** : salve *f*

same[1] ['seɪm] *adj* : même <he's reading the same book : il lit le même livre> <same time, same place : à la même heure, au même endroit>

same[2] *pron* : même <she's never been the same since : elle n'est plus la même depuis> <I'll have the same : je prends la même chose>

sameness ['seɪmnəs] *n* **1** SIMILARITY : similitude *f* **2** MONOTONY : monotonie *f*

sample[1] ['sæmpəl] *vt* **-pled; -pling** : goûter (des mets, etc.), essayer (des produits)

sample[2] *n* : échantillon *m*

sampler ['sæmplər] *n* : modèle *m* de broderie

sanatorium [,sænə'toriəm] *n, pl* **-riums** *or* **-ria** [-iə] : sanatorium *m*

sanctify ['sæŋktə,faɪ] *vt* **-fied; -fying** : sanctifier

sanctimonious [,sæŋktə'mo:niəs] *adj* : moralisateur

sanction[1] ['sæŋkʃən] *vt* : sanctionner, approuver

sanction[2] *n* **1** APPROVAL : sanction *f* **2 sanctions** *npl* : sanctions *fpl* <to impose sanctions on : prendre des sanctions à l'encontre de>

sanctity ['sæŋktət̬i] *n, pl* **-ties** : sainteté *f*

sanctuary ['sæŋktʃʊ,ɛri] *n, pl* **-aries 1** : sanctuaire *m* (d'une église) **2** REFUGE : refuge *m*

sand[1] ['sænd] *vt* **1** : sabler <to sand the driveway : sabler la voie> **2** SMOOTH : poncer

sand[2] *n* : sable *m*

sandal ['sændəl] *n* : sandale *f*

sandbank ['sænd,bæŋk] *n* : banc *m* de sable

sandbar ['sænd,bɑr] *n* : barre *f*, batture *f Can*

sandpaper[1] ['sænd,peɪpər] *vt* : poncer (au papier de verre)

sandpaper[2] *n* : papier *m* de verre, papier *m* sablé *Can*

sandpiper ['sænd,paɪpər] *n* : bécasseau *m*

sandstone ['sænd,sto:n] *n* : grès *m*

sandstorm ['sænd,stɔrm] *n* : tempête *f* de sable

sandwich[1] ['sænd,wɪtʃ] *vt* WEDGE : prendre en sandwich, coincer

sandwich[2] *n* : sandwich *m*

sandy ['sændi] *adj* **sandier; -est** : sableux, sablonneux

sane ['seɪn] *adj* **saner; sanest 1** : sain d'esprit **2** SENSIBLE : raisonnable, sensé

sang → **sing**

sanguine ['sæŋgwən] *adj* **1** RUDDY : rubicond, sanguin **2** HOPEFUL : optimiste, confiant

sanitarium [,sænə'tɛriəm] *n, pl* **-iums** *or* **-ia** [-iə] → **sanatorium**

sanitary ['sænətɛri] *adj* **1** : sanitaire <sanitary conditions : conditions sanitaires> **2** HYGIENIC : hygiénique

sanitary napkin *n* : serviette *f* hygiénique

sanitation [,sænə'teɪʃən] *n* : hygiène *f* publique

sanity ['sænət̬i] *n* : santé *f* mentale

sank → **sink**[1]

sap[1] ['sæp] *vt* **sapped; sapping** UNDERMINE : saper, miner

sap[2] *n* **1** : sève *f* (d'un arbre) **2** FOOL : nigaud *m*, -gaude *f*; andouille *f fam*

sapling ['sæplɪŋ] *n* : jeune arbre *m*

sapphire ['sæ,faɪr] *n* : saphir *m*

sarcasm ['sɑr,kæzəm] *n* : sarcasme *m*

sarcastic [sɑr'kæstɪk] *adj* : sarcastique — **sarcastically** [-tɪkli] *adv*

sarcophagus [sɑr'kɑfəgəs] *n, pl* **-gi** [-,gaɪ, -,dʒaɪ] : sarcophage *m*

sardine [sɑr'di:n] *n* : sardine *f*

sardonic [sɑr'dɑnɪk] *adj* : sardonique — **sardonically** [-nɪkli] *adv*

sarsaparilla [,sæspə'rɪlə, ,sɑrs-] *n* : salsepareille *f*

sartorial [sɑr'toriəl, sər-, -'tɔr-] *adj* : vestimentaire

sash ['sæʃ] *n* **1** : large ceinture *f* (d'une robe), écharpe *f* (insigne) **2** *pl* **sash** : châssis *m* (d'une fenêtre)

sassafras ['sæsə,fræs] *n* : sassafras *m*

sassy ['sæsi] *adj* **sassier; -est** → **saucy**

sat → **sit**

Satan ['seɪtən] *n* : Satan *m*

satanic [sə'tænɪk, seɪ-] *adj* : satanique — **satanically** [-nɪkli] *adv*

satchel ['sætʃəl] *n* : sacoche *f*

sate ['seɪt] *vt* **sated; sating** : rassasier, assouvir

satellite ['sæt̬ə,laɪt] *n* : satellite *m*

satiate ['seɪʃi,eɪt] *vt* **-ated; -ating** : rassasier, assouvir

satin ['sætən] *n* : satin *m*

satire ['sæ,taɪr] *n* : satire *f*

satiric [sə'tɪrɪk] *or* **satirical** [-ɪkəl] *adj* : satirique

satirize ['sæt̬ə,raɪz] *vt* **-rized; -rizing** : satiriser

satisfaction [,sæt̬əs'fækʃən] *n* : satisfaction *f*

satisfactorily [,sæt̬əs'fæktərəli] *adv* : de façon satisfaisante

satisfactory [,sæt̬əs'fæktəri] *adj* : satisfaisant

satisfy ['sæt̬əs,faɪ] *v* **-fied; -fying** *vt* **1** PLEASE : satisfaire, contenter **2** CONVINCE : convaincre, persuader **3** FULFILL : satisfaire à, répondre à, remplir <to satisfy the demand for

: répondre à la demande de> <to satisfy our needs : satisfaire à nos besoins> — *vi* SUFFICE : suffir

satisfying ['sæṭəs,faɪɪŋ] *adj* : satisfaisant

saturate ['sætʃə,reɪt] *vt* **-rated; -rating** : saturer

saturation [,sætʃə'reɪʃən] *n* : saturation *f*

Saturday ['sæṭər,deɪ, -di] *n* : samedi *m*

Saturn ['sæṭərn] *n* : Saturne *f* (planète)

satyr ['seɪṭər, 'sæ-] *n* : satyre *m*

sauce ['sɔs] *n* : sauce *f*

saucepan ['sɔs,pæn] *n* : casserole *f*

saucer ['sɔsər] *n* : soucoupe *f*

saucily ['sɔsəli] *adv* : avec impertinence

sauciness ['sɔsinəs] *n* : impertinence *f*

saucy ['sɔsi] *adj* **saucier; -est** : impertinent

Saudi[1] ['saʊdɪ] *or* **Saudi Arabian** ['saʊdɪə'reɪbɪən] *adj* : saoudien

Saudi[2] *or* **Saudi Arabian** *n* : Saoudien *m*, -dienne *f*

sauerkraut ['saʊər,kraʊt] *n* : choucroute *f*

sauna ['sɔnə, 'saʊnə] *n* : sauna *m*

saunter ['sɔntər, 'sɑn-] *vi* : flâner, marcher d'un pas nonchalant

sausage ['sɔsɪdʒ] *n* : saucisse *f* (crue), saucisson *m* (cuit)

sauté [sɔ'teɪ, so-] *vt* **-téed** *or* **-téd; -téing** : faire sauter

savage[1] ['sævɪdʒ] *adj* : féroce, sauvage, brutal — **savagely** *adv*

savage[2] *n* : sauvage *mf*

savagery ['sævɪdʒri] *n, pl* **-ries** : sauvagerie *f*

save[1] ['seɪv] *v* **saved; saving** *vt* **1** RESCUE : sauver **2** KEEP, RESERVE : mettre de côté, garder (des biens, une place, etc.), économiser (de l'argent) **3** SPARE : épargner <she saved me an unnecessary trip : elle m'a épargné un déplacement inutile> **4** : sauvegarder (en informatique) — *vi* : économiser

save[2] *n* : arrêt *m* (aux sports)

save[3] *prep* EXCEPT : sauf, excepté

savior ['seɪvjər] *n* : sauveur *m*

savor[1] ['seɪvər] *vt* : savourer

savor[2] *n* : saveur *f*

savory ['seɪvəri] *adj* : savoureux

saw[1] → **see**[1]

saw[2] ['sɔ] *vt* **sawed; sawed** *or* **sawn** ['sɔn]; **sawing** : scier

saw[3] *n* : scie *f*

sawdust ['sɔ,dʌst] *n* : sciure *f*

sawhorse ['sɔ,hɔrs] *n* : chevalet *m*

sawmill *n* ['sɔ,mɪl] : scierie *f*

saxophone ['sæksə,foːn] *n* : saxophone *m*

say[1] ['seɪ] *v* **said** ['sɛd]; **saying; says** ['sɛz] *vt* **1** SPEAK, UTTER : dire <to say no : dire non> <it goes without saying that . . . : il va sans dire que . . .> <say your prayers : fais tes prières> **2** EXPRESS, INDICATE : exprimer, indiquer, dire <my watch says three o'clock : ma montre indique trois heures> **3** ALLEGE : dire <it's said that she's pretty : l'on dit qu'elle est belle> — *vi* : dire <I'd rather not say : je préfère ne pas le dire> <that is to say : c'est-à-dire>

say[2] *n, pl* **says** ['seɪz] : mot *m*, voix *f* <to have no say : ne pas avoir voix au chapitre> <to have one's say : dire son mot, dire ce qu'on a à dire>

saying ['seɪɪŋ] *n* : dicton *m*, proverbe *m*

scab ['skæb] *n* **1** : croûte *f*, gale *f Can* **2** STRIKEBREAKER : jaune *mf*

scabbard ['skæbərd] *n* : fourreau *m*

scabby ['skæbi] *adj* **scabbier; -est** : croûteux

scaffold ['skæfəld, -,foːld] *n* **1** *or* **scaffolding** : échafaudage *m* **2** : échafaud *m* (pour exécutions)

scald ['skɔld] *vt* **1** BURN : ébouillanter **2** HEAT : échauder

scale[1] ['skeɪl] *v* **scaled; scaling** *vt* **1** : écailler (un poisson) **2** CLIMB : escalader **3 to scale down** : réduire — *vi* WEIGH : peser <he scaled in at 200 pounds : il pesait 200 livres>

scale[2] *n* **1** *or* **scales** : pèse-personne *m*, balance *f* **2** : écaille *f* (d'un poisson) **3** EXTENT : étendue *f*, échelle *f* <on a large scale : sur une grande échelle> **4** : échelle *f* <drawn to scale : dessiné à l'échelle> **5** : gamme *f* (en musique)

scallion ['skæljən] *n* : ciboule *f*, échalote *f*

scallop ['skɑləp, 'skæ-] *n* **1** : coquille *f* Saint-Jacques **2** : feston *m* (en couture)

scalp[1] ['skælp] *vt* : scalper

scalp[2] *n* : cuir *m* chevelu

scalpel ['skælpəl] *n* : scalpel *m*

scaly ['skeɪli] *adj* **scalier; -est** : écailleux

scamp ['skæmp] *n* : polisson *m*, -sonne *f*; galopin *m*

scamper ['skæmpər] *vi* : gambader, galoper

scan[1] ['skæn] *v* **scanned; scanning** *vt* **1** : scander (un vers) **2** SCRUTINIZE : scruter <to scan the horizon : scruter l'horizon> **3** PERUSE : parcourir rapidement (un texte), feuilleter (une revue) **4** : examiner au scanner (en médecine) **5** : balayer (en électronique) — *vi* : se scander (se dit d'un vers)

scan[2] *n* **1** : balayage *m* (électronique) **2** : scanographie *f*, échographie *f* (ultrasonore) **3** : scansion *f* (littéraire)

scandal ['skændəl] *n* **1** DISGRACE : scandale *m* **2** GOSSIP : médisance *f*

scandalize ['skændəl,aɪz] *vt* **-ized; -izing** : scandaliser

scandalous ['skændələs] *adj* : scandaleux

Scandinavian[1] [,skændə'neɪviən] *adj* : scandinave

Scandinavian[2] *n* : Scandinave *mf*
scanner ['skænər] *n* : scanner *m*
scant ['skænt] *adj* : maigre, insuffisant
scanty ['skænti] *adj* **scantier; -est 1** : maigre, insuffisant <a scanty meal : un repas insuffisant> **2** BRIEF : léger (se dit des vêtements)
scapegoat ['skeɪp,go:t] *n* : bouc *m* émissaire
scapula ['skæpjələ] *n, pl* **-lae** [-,li:, -,laɪ] *or* **-las** : omoplate *f*
scar[1] ['skɑr] *v* **scarred; scarring** *vt* : marquer d'une cicatrice — *vi* : se cicatriser
scar[2] *n* : cicatrice *f*
scarab ['skærəb] *n* : scarabée *m*
scarce ['skɛrs] *adj* **scarcer; -est** : rare
scarcely ['skɛrsli] *adv* **1** BARELY : à peine <he can scarcely read : il sait à peine lire> **2** HARDLY : difficilement <I can scarcely blame him : je peux difficilement le reprocher>
scarcity ['skɛrsəṭi] *n, pl* **-ties** : rareté *f*, manque *m*
scare[1] ['skɛr] *vt* **scared; scaring** : faire peur à, effrayer
scare[2] *n* **1** FRIGHT : peur *f* **2** ALARM : alerte *f*
scarecrow ['skɛr,kro:] *n* : épouvantail *m*
scarf ['skɑrf] *n, pl* **scarves** ['skɑrvz] *or* **scarfs** : écharpe *f* (longue), foulard *m* (carré)
scarlet[1] ['skɑrlət] *adj* : écarlate
scarlet[2] *n* : écarlate *f*
scarlet fever *n* : scarlatine *f*
scary ['skɛri] *adj* **scarier, -est** : qui fait peur, effrayant, épeurant *Can*
scathing ['skeɪðɪŋ] *adj* : cinglant, mordant
scatter ['skæṭər] *vt* : disperser, éparpiller — *vi* DISPERSE : se disperser
scavenge ['skævəndʒ] *v* **-venged; -venging** *vt* : récupérer — *vi* : fouiller
scavenger ['skævəndʒər] *n* : charognard *m* (animal), pilleur *m* de poubelles (personne)
scenario [sə'næri,o:, -'nɑr-] *n, pl* **-ios** : scénario *m*
scene ['si:n] *n* **1** : scène *f* <the political scene : la scène politique> **2** SCENERY, SET : décor *m* **3** VIEW : vue *f* **4** LOCATION : lieu *m* <the scene of the crime : le lieu du crime>
scenery ['si:nəri] *n, pl* **-eries 1** : décor *m* **2** LANDSCAPE : paysages *mpl*
scenic ['si:nɪk] *adj* : pittoresque
scent[1] ['sɛnt] *vt* **1** SMELL : flairer (le gibier, le danger, etc.) **2** PERFUME : parfumer
scent[2] *n* **1** ODOR : odeur *f*, senteur *f* **2** NOSE, SMELLING : odorat *m*, flair *m* <a dog with a keen scent : un chien qui a du flair> **3** PERFUME : parfum *m*
scented ['sɛntəd] *adj* : parfumé
scepter ['sɛptər] *n* : sceptre *m*
sceptic ['skɛptɪk] → **skeptic**
schedule[1] ['skɛ,dʒu:l, -dʒəl *esp Brit* ʃɛdju:l] *vt* **-uled; -uling** : prévoir, programmer
schedule[2] *n* **1** LIST : liste *f* **2** TIMETABLE : horaire *m* **3** PLAN : programme *m*, plan *m*
schematic [ski'mæṭɪk] *adj* : schématique
scheme[1] ['ski:m] *vi* **schemed; scheming** : intriguer, comploter
scheme[2] *n* **1** PLAN : projet *m*, plan *m* **2** PLOT : complot *m*, intrigue *f* **3** SYSTEM : système *m*
schemer ['ski:mər] *n* : intrigant *m*, -gante *f*
schism ['sɪzəm, 'skɪ-] *n* : schisme *m*
schizophrenia [,skɪtsə'fri:niə, ,skɪzə-, -'frɛ-] *n* : schizophrénie *f*
schizophrenic [,skɪtsə'frɛnɪk, ,skɪzə-] *adj* : schizophrène
scholar ['skɑlər] *n* **1** STUDENT : étudiant *m*, -diante *f*; élève *mf* **2** EXPERT : spécialiste *mf*; savant *m*, -vante *f*; érudit *m*, -dite *f*
scholarly ['skɑlərli] *adj* : savant, érudit
scholarship ['skɑlər,ʃɪp] *n* **1** LEARNING : érudition *f* **2** GRANT : bourse *f*
scholastic [skə'læstɪk] *adj* : scolaire
school[1] ['sku:l] *vt* : instruire, entraîner
school[2] *n* **1** : école *f* (institution) <elementary school : école primaire> **2** : école *f* (en peinture, etc.) <the Flemish school : l'école flamande> **3** COLLEGE : faculté *f* <medical school : faculté de médecine> **4** *or* **school of fish** : banc *m*
schoolboy ['sku:l,bɔɪ] *n* : écolier *m*
schoolgirl ['sku:l,gərl] *n* : écolière *f*
schoolhouse ['sku:l,haʊs] *n* : école *f*
schoolmate ['sku:l,meɪt] *n* : camarade *mf* de classe
schoolroom ['sku:l,ru:m] *n* : salle *f* de classe
schoolteacher ['sku:l,ti:tʃər] *n* : instituteur *m*, -trice *f*; enseignant *m*, -gnante *f*
schooner ['sku:nər] *n* : schooner *m*, goélette *f*
science ['saɪənts] *n* : science *f*
scientific [,saɪən'tɪfɪk] *adj* : scientifique — **scientifically** [-fɪkli] *adv*
scientist ['saɪəntɪst] *n* : scientifique *mf*
scintillate ['sɪntəl,eɪt] *vi* **-lated; -lating** : scintiller
scintillating ['sɪntəl,eɪtɪŋ] *adj* : scintillant
scissors ['sɪzərz] *ns & pl* : ciseaux *mpl*
scoff ['skɑf] *vi* **to scoff at** : se moquer de
scold ['sko:ld] *vt* : gronder, réprimander
scoop[1] ['sku:p] *vt* **1 to scoop out** : évider, creuser **2 to scoop up** : prendre, ramasser (à la pelle)
scoop[2] *n* **1** SHOVEL : pelle *f* **2** *or* **ice cream scoop** : cuillère *f* à glace **3** : exclusivité *f* (en journalisme)
scoot ['sku:t] *vi* : filer *fam*

scooter ['sku:t̬ər] *n* **1** : trottinette *f* **2** *or* **motor scooter** : scooter *m*
scope ['sko:p] *n* **1** EXTENT : étendue *f*, limites *fpl* **2** OPPORTUNITY : possibilité *f*, occasion *f*
scorch ['skɔrtʃ] *vt* : roussir
score[1] ['skor] *v* **scored; scoring** *vt* **1** RECORD : enregistrer **2** MARK, SCRATCH : marquer, rayer **3** : marquer (aux sports) **4** GRADE : noter **5** ORCHESTRATE : orchestrer, arranger — *vi* **1** : marquer des points (aux sports) **2** : obtenir une note (sur un examen)
score[2] *n, pl* **scores 1** *or pl* **score** TWENTY : vingt *m*, vingtaine *f* **2** : score *m*, marque *f*, pointage *m* *Can* (aux sports) **3** LINE, SCRATCH : rayure *f*, entaille *f* **4** ACCOUNT : compte *m*, point *m* <to settle a score : régler un compte> <on that score : sur ce point> **5** : partition *f* (en musique)
scorekeeper ['skor,ki:pər] *n* : marqueur *m*, -queuse *f*; pointeur *m*, -teuse *f* *Can*
scorn[1] ['skɔrn] *vt* : mépriser
scorn[2] *n* : mépris *m*, dédain *m*
scornful ['skɔrnfəl] *adj* : méprisant — **scornfully** *adv*
Scorpio ['skɔrpi,o:] *n* : Scorpion *m*
scorpion ['skɔrpiən] *n* : scorpion *m*
Scot ['skɑt] *n* : Écossais *m*, -saise *f*
Scotch[1] ['skɑtʃ] *adj* → **Scottish**[1]
Scotch[2] *n* **1** *or* **Scotch whiskey** : scotch *m* **2 the Scotch** : les Écossais
scot–free ['skɑt'fri:] *adj* **to get off scot–free** : s'en tirer sans être puni
Scots ['skɑts] *n* : écossais *m* (langue)
Scottish[1] ['skɑt̬ɪʃ] *adj* : écossais
Scottish[2] *n* → **Scots**
scoundrel ['skaʊndrəl] *n* : scélérat *m*, vaurien *m*
scour ['skaʊər] *vt* : récurer
scourge[1] ['skərdʒ] *vt* **scourged; scourging 1** WHIP : fouetter **2** PUNISH : châtier
scourge[2] *n* **1** WHIP : fouet *m* **2** BANE : fléau *m*
scout[1] ['skaʊt] *vi* **1** RECONNOITER : aller en reconnaissance **2 to scout around for** : aller à la recherche de
scout[2] *n* **1** : éclaireur *m*, -reuse *f*; scout *m*, scoute *f* **2** *or* **talent scout** : découvreur *m*, -vreuse *f* de nouveaux talents
scow ['skaʊ] *n* : chaland *m*
scowl[1] ['skaʊl] *vi* : se renfrogner, faire la grimace
scowl[2] *n* : mine *f* renfrognée
scraggly ['skrægli] *adj* UNKEMPT : en bataille (se dit d'une barbe, etc.)
scram ['skræm] *vi* **scrammed; scramming** : filer *fam*
scramble[1] ['skræmbəl] *v* **-bled; -bling** *vi* **1** CLAMBER : grimper <to scramble over : escalader> **2 to scramble for** : se bousculer pour, se disputer — *vt* : brouiller <to scramble eggs : faire des œufs brouillés>
scramble[2] *n* : bousculade *f*
scrap[1] ['skræp] *v* **scrapped; scrapping** *vt* DISCARD : mettre au rebut <we scrapped that idea : nous avons laissé tomber cette idée-là> — *vi* FIGHT : se battre
scrap[2] *n* **1** FRAGMENT : bout *m*, fragment *m* **2** FIGHT : bagarre *f* **3** *or* **scrap metal** : ferraille *f* **4 scraps** *npl* LEFTOVERS : restes *mpl*
scrapbook ['skræp,bʊk] *n* : album *m*
scrape[1] ['skreɪp] *v* **scraped; scraping** *vt* **1** SCRATCH : écorcher, érafler <to scrape one's knees : s'écorcher les genoux> **2** CLEAN : gratter <to scrape mud off : décrotter> **3 to scrape up** *or* **to scrape together** : réunir, rassembler — *vi* **1** RUB : frotter **2 to scrape by** : se débrouiller
scrape[2] *n* **1** SCRAPING : grattement *m* **2** SCRATCH : éraflure *f* **3** PREDICAMENT : embarras *m*
scraper ['skreɪpər] *n* : grattoir *m*
scratch[1] ['skrætʃ] *vt* **1** : gratter <to scratch one's head : se gratter la tête> **2** MARK : rayer **3** DELETE : supprimer **4** WOUND : écorcher, griffer, grafigner *Can* — *vi* **1** : se gratter <stop scratching! : arrête de te gratter!> **2** : griffer (se dit d'un chat)
scratch[2] *n* **1** SCRAPE : éraflure *f*, égratignure *f*, grafignure *f* *Can* **2** SCRATCHING : grattement *m*
scratchy ['skrætʃi] *adj* **scratchier; -est** : rêche <a scratchy sweater : un pull qui gratte>
scrawl[1] ['skrɔl] *v* : griffonner, gribouiller
scrawl[2] *n* : griffonnage *m*, gribouillage *m*
scrawny ['skrɔni] *adj* **scrawnier; -est** : maigre, décharné
scream[1] ['skri:m] *v* : hurler, crier
scream[2] *n* : hurlement *m*, cri *m* perçant
screech[1] ['skri:tʃ] *vi* **1** CRY, SCREAM : crier, hurler **2** : crisser (se dit des pneus, etc.)
screech[2] *n* **1** : cri *m* **2** : crissement *m* <the screech of tires : le crissement des pneus>
screen[1] ['skri:n] *vt* **1** SHIELD : protéger **2** CONCEAL : cacher **3** EXAMINE : trier, passer au crible **4** PROJECT : projeter, passer (un film)
screen[2] *n* **1** : écran *m* <smoke screen : écran de fumée> **2** PARTITION : paravent *m* **3** SIEVE : crible *m* **4** MOVIES : cinéma *m* **5** *or* **window screen** : moustiquaire *f*
screening ['skri:nɪŋ] *n* **1** SHOWING : projection *f* **2** SELECTION : sélection *f* **3** TEST : (test *m* de) dépistage *m* <cancer screening : dépistage du cancer>
screenplay ['skri:n,pleɪ] *n* : scénario *m*
screw[1] ['skru:] *vt* **1** : visser **2 to screw together** : se visser l'un à l'autre

screw[2] *n* **1** : vis *f* **2** PROPELLER : hélice *f*
screwdriver [ˈskruːˌdraɪvər] *n* : tourne-vis *m*
scribble[1] [ˈskrɪbəl] *v* **-bled; -bling** : gribouiller, griffonner
scribble[2] *n* : gribouillage *m*, griffonnage *m*
scribe [ˈskraɪb] *n* : scribe *m*
scrimp [ˈskrɪmp] *vi* : économiser, faire des économies
script [ˈskrɪpt] *n* **1** HANDWRITING : écriture *f* **2** TEXT : scénario *m*, script *m*
scriptural [ˈskrɪptʃərəl] *adj* : biblique
scripture [ˈskrɪptʃər] *n* **1** : texte *m* sacré **2 the Holy Scripture(s)** : l'Écriture *f* sainte, les Saintes Écritures
scroll[1] [ˈskroːl] *vi* : défiler (en informatique)
scroll[2] *n* : rouleau *m*
scrotum [ˈskroːtəm] *n, pl* **scrota** [-tə] *or* **scrotums** : scrotum *m*
scrounge [ˈskraʊndʒ] *v* **scrounged; scrounging** *vt* **1** CADGE : quémander **2** BORROW : emprunter — *vi* **1 to scrounge around for** : chercher **2 to scrounge off s.o.** : vivre aux crochets de qqn
scrub[1] [ˈskrʌb] *vt* **scrubbed; scrubbing 1** CLEAN : frotter, nettoyer à la brosse **2** SCRAP : laisser tomber, annuler
scrub[2] *n* **1** UNDERBRUSH : broussailles *fpl* **2** CLEANING : nettoyage *m*
scrubby [ˈskrʌbi] *adj* **scrubbier; -est 1** STUNTED : rabougri **2** OVERGROWN : broussailleux
scruff [ˈskrʌf] *n* **by the scruff of the neck** : par la peau du cou
scrumptious [ˈskrəmpʃəs] *adj* : délicieux
scruple [ˈskruːpəl] *n* : scrupule *m*
scrupulous [ˈskruːpjələs] *adj* : scrupuleux — **scrupulously** *adv*
scrutinize [ˈskruːtənˌaɪz] *vt* **-nized; -nizing** : scruter
scrutiny [ˈskruːtəni] *n, pl* **-nies** : examen *m* (approfondi)
scuff [ˈskʌf] *vt* **1** SCRAPE : érafler **2 to scuff one's feet** : traîner les pieds
scuffle[1] [ˈskʌfəl] *vi* **-fled; -fling** TUSSLE : se bagarrer
scuffle[2] *n* : bagarre *f*
scull[1] [ˈskʌl] *vi* : godiller, ramer
scull[2] *n* PADDLE : godille *f*
sculpt [ˈskʌlpt] *vt* : sculpter
sculptor [ˈskʌlptər] *n* : sculpteur *m*
sculpture[1] [ˈskəlptʃər] *vt* **-tured; -turing** : sculpter
sculpture[2] *n* : sculpture *f*
scum [ˈskʌm] *n* FROTH : écume *f*
scurrilous [ˈskərələs] *adj* : calomnieux
scurry [ˈskəri] *vi* **-ried; -rying** : se précipiter
scurvy [ˈskərvi] *n* : scorbut *m*
scuttle[1] [ˈskʌtəl] *v* **-tled; -tling** *vt* : saborder (un navire) — *vi* : courir à toute vitesse, se précipiter
scuttle[2] *n or* **coal scuttle** : seau *m* à charbon
scythe [ˈsaɪð] *n* : faux *f*
sea[1] [ˈsiː] *adj* : de mer
sea[2] *n* **1** OCEAN : mer *f* **2** MASS : multitude *f*
seabird [ˈsiːˌbərd] *n* : oiseau *m* de mer
seaboard [ˈsiːˌbɔrd] *n* : littoral *m*
seacoast [ˈsiːˌkoːst] *n* : côte *f* (de la mer)
seafarer [ˈsiːˌfærər] *n* : marin *m*
seafaring[1] [ˈsiːˌfærɪŋ] *adj* : maritime
seafaring[2] *n* : navigation *f*
seafood [ˈsiːˌfuːd] *n* : fruits *mpl* de mer
seagull [ˈsiːˌgʌl] *n* : mouette *f*
sea horse [ˈsiːˌhɔrs] *n* : hippocampe *m*
seal[1] [ˈsiːl] *vt* : sceller
seal[2] *n* **1** STAMP : sceau *m*, cachet *m* **2** CLOSURE : fermeture *f* **3** GASKET : joint *m* étanche **4** : phoque *m*, loup-marin *m Can* (animal)
sea level *n* : niveau *m* de la mer
sea lion *n* : otarie *f*
sealskin [ˈsiːlˌskɪn] *n* : peau *f* de phoque
seam[1] [ˈsiːm] *vt* **1** STITCH : coudre **2** MARK : marquer <a face seamed with wrinkles : un visage marqué de rides>
seam[2] *n* **1** STITCHING : couture *f* **2** VEIN, LODE : veine *f*, filon *m*
seaman [ˈsiːmən] *n, pl* **-men** [-mən, -ˌmɛn] : marin *m*
seamless [ˈsiːmləs] *adj* : sans couture
seamstress [ˈsiːmpstrəs] *n* : couturière *f*
seamy [ˈsiːmi] *adj* **seamier; -est** : sordide
séance [ˈseɪˌɑnts] *n* : séance *f* de spiritisme
seaplane [ˈsiːˌpleɪn] *n* : hydravion *m*
seaport [ˈsiːˌport] *n* : port *m* maritime
sear [ˈsɪr] *vt* **1** PARCH, WITHER : dessécher, flétrir **2** BURN, SCORCH : calciner, brûler
search[1] [ˈsərtʃ] *vt* **1** : chercher dans, fouiller (dans) <I searched the house : j'ai cherché dans la maison> <to search a suspect : fouiller un suspect> **2** : rechercher dans (en informatique) — *vi* **to search for** : chercher
search[2] *n* **1** EXAMINATION : fouille *f* **2** QUEST : recherche *f*
searcher [ˈsərtʃər] *n* : chercheur *m*, -cheuse *f*
searchlight [ˈsərtʃˌlaɪt] *n* : projecteur *m*
seashell [ˈsiːˌʃɛl] *n* : coquillage *m*
seashore [ˈsiːˌʃor] *n* : bord *m* de la mer
seasick [ˈsiːˌsɪk] *adj* **to be seasick** : avoir le mal de mer
seasickness [ˈsiːˌsɪknəs] *n* : mal *m* de mer
seaside [ˈsiːˌsaɪd] → **seacoast**
season[1] [ˈsiːzən] *vt* **1** FLAVOR, SPICE : assaisonner, épicer **2** CURE : sécher (du bois)
season[2] *n* : saison *f*
seasonable [ˈsiːzənəbəl] *adj* : de saison
seasonal [ˈsiːzənəl] *adj* : saisonnier

seasonally [ˈsiːzənəli] *adj* : de façon saisonnière
seasoned [ˈsiːzənd] *adj* **1** SPICED : assaisonné **2** EXPERIENCED : expérimenté, éprouvé **3** : desséché (se dit du bois)
seasoning [ˈsiːzənɪŋ] *n* : assaisonnement *m*
seat[1] [ˈsiːt] *vt* **1** SIT : faire asseoir <please be seated : veuillez vous asseoir> **2** ACCOMMODATE, HOLD : avoir des places assises pour, tenir <this car seats five : on tient à cinq dans cette voiture>
seat[2] *n* **1** CHAIR : siège *m* **2** ACCOMMODATION, PLACE : place *f* **3** : fond *m* (de pantalon) **4** CENTER : centre *m*, siège *m* (du gouvernement, etc.)
seat belt *n* : ceinture *f* de sécurité
sea urchin *n* : oursin *m*
seawall [ˈsiːˌwɑl] *n* : digue *f*
seawater *n* [ˈsiːˌwɔt̬ər, -ˌwɑ-] : eau *f* de mer
seaweed *n* [ˈsiːˌwiːd] : algue *f*
seaworthy [ˈsiːˌwərði] *adj* : en état de naviguer
secede [sɪˈsiːd] *vi* **-ceded; -ceding** : se séparer, faire sécession
seclude [sɪˈkluːd] *vt* **-cluded; -cluding** : isoler
secluded *adj* : isolé, retiré, à l'écart
seclusion [sɪˈkluːʒən] *n* : isolement *m*, solitude *f*
second[1] [ˈsɛkənd] *vt* : affirmer, appuyer (une motion)
second[2] *or* **secondly** [ˈsɛkəndli] *adv* : deuxièmement, en second lieu
second[3] *adj* : second, deuxième <in the second place : en deuxième lieu> <a second chance : une seconde chance>
second[4] *n* **1** MOMENT : seconde *f* **2** : deuxième *mf;* second *m*, -conde *f* <the second of June : le deux juin> **3** : soigneur *m* (à la boxe), témoin *m* (dans un duel) **4** *or* **factory second** : articles *mpl* de second choix
secondary [ˈsɛkənˌdɛri] *adj* : secondaire
secondhand [ˈsɛkəndˈhænd] *adj* : d'occasion
second lieutenant *n* : sous-lieutenant *m*
secrecy [ˈsiːkrəsi] *n, pl* **-cies** : secret *m* <to swear to secrecy : faire jurer le secret>
secret[1] [ˈsiːkrət] *adj* : secret
secret[2] *n* : secret *m*
secretarial [ˌsɛkrəˈtɛriəl] *adj* : de secrétaire
secretariat [ˌsɛkrəˈtɛriət] *n* : secrétariat *m*
secretary [ˈsɛkrəˌtɛri] *n, pl* **-taries** : secrétaire *mf*
secrete [sɪˈkriːt] *vt* **-creted; -creting 1** EXUDE : sécréter **2** HIDE : cacher
secretion [sɪˈkriːʃən] *n* : sécrétion *f*
secretive [ˈsiːkrət̬ɪv, sɪˈkriːt̬ɪv] *adj* : cachottier, secret
secretly [ˈsiːkrətli] *adv* : secrètement
sect [ˈsɛkt] *n* : secte *f*
sectarian [sɛkˈtɛriən] *adj* : sectaire
section [ˈsɛkʃən] *n* : section *f*, partie *f*
sectional [ˈsɛkʃənəl] *adj* **1** : en coupe, en profil <a sectional diagram : un schéma en coupe> **2** FACTIONAL : d'un groupe **3** MODULAR : à éléments
sector [ˈsɛktər] *n* : secteur *m*
secular [ˈsɛkjələr] *adj* **1** : séculaire, laïque **2** : profane (se dit de la musique, etc.)
secure[1] [sɪˈkjʊr] *vt* **-cured; -curing 1** FASTEN : fixer **2** OBTAIN : procurer **3** GUARANTEE : assurer
secure[2] *adj* **securer; -est** : sûr, en sécurité
securely [sɪˈkjʊrli] *adv* **1** FIRMLY : fermement, solidement, bien **2** SAFELY : en sécurité
security [sɪˈkjʊrət̬i] *n, pl* **-ties 1** SAFETY : sécurité *f* **2** GUARANTEE : garantie *f* **3 securities** *npl* : titres *mpl*, valeurs *fpl*, actions *fpl*
sedan [sɪˈdæn] *n* : berline *f*
sedate[1] [sɪˈdeɪt] *vt* **-dated; -dating** : tranquilliser, mettre sous calmants
sedate[2] *adj* : posé, calme — **sedately** *adv*
sedation [sɪˈdeɪʃən] *n* : sédation *f*
sedative[1] [ˈsɛdət̬ɪv] *adj* : sédatif
sedative[2] *n* : calmant *m*, sédatif *m*
sedentary [ˈsɛdənˌtɛri] *adj* : sédentaire
sedge [ˈsɛdʒ] *n* : laîche *f*
sediment [ˈsɛdəmənt] *n* : sédiment *m*
sedimentary [ˌsɛdəˈmɛntəri] *adj* : sédimentaire
sedition [sɪˈdɪʃən] *n* : sédition *f*
seditious [sɪˈdɪʃəs] *adj* : séditieux
seduce [sɪˈduːs, -ˈdjuːs] *vt* **-duced; -ducing** : séduire
seduction [sɪˈdʌkʃən] *n* : séduction *f*
seductive [sɪˈdʌktɪv] *adj* : séduisant
see[1] [ˈsiː] *v* **saw** [ˈsɔ]; **seen** [ˈsiːn]; **seeing** *vt* **1** : voir <I saw a dog : j'ai vu un chien> <see you later! : au revoir!> **2** EXPERIENCE : connaître, voir **3** UNDERSTAND : voir, comprendre **4** *or* **to see that** ENSURE : s'assurer, veiller à **5** ACCOMPANY : accompagner <he'll see me home : il me raccompagnera chez moi> — *vi* **1** : voir <seeing is believing : voir c'est croire> **2** UNDERSTAND : comprendre, voir **3** CONSIDER : voir <let's see : voyons> **4 to see to** : s'occuper de
see[2] *n* : évêché *m*
seed[1] [ˈsiːd] *vt* **1** SOW : semer **2** : épépiner, enlever la graine de <to seed grapes : épépiner des raisins>
seed[2] *n, pl* **seed** *or* **seeds 1** : graine *f* **2** SOURCE : germe *m*
seedless [ˈsiːdləs] *adj* : sans pépins
seedling [ˈsiːdlɪŋ] *n* : semis *m*, jeune plant *m*

seedy ['si:di] *adj* **seedier; -est** **1** : plein de graines **2** SHABBY : miteux
seek ['si:k] *v* **sought** ['sɔt]; **seeking** *vt* **1** : chercher **2** REQUEST : demander — *vi* **to seek after** : rechercher, chercher
seem ['si:m] *vi* : paraître, sembler, avoir l'air <she seems tired : elle a l'air fatiguée> <it would seem not : il paraît que non>
seemingly ['si:mɪŋli] *adv* : apparemment
seemly ['si:mli] *adj* **seemlier; -est** : convenable
seep ['si:p] *vi* : suinter
seepage ['si:pɪdʒ] *n* : suintement *m*
seer ['si:ər] *n* : voyant *m*, voyante *f*
seesaw[1] ['si:,sɔ] *vi* **1** : jouer à la bascule **2** VACILLATE : balancer, osciller
seesaw[2] *n* : balançoire *f*, bascule *f*
seethe ['si:ð] *vi* **seethed; seething** : bouillonner
segment ['sɛgmənt] *n* : segment *m*
segmented ['sɛg,mɛntəd, sɛg'mɛn-] *adj* : segmentaire
segregate ['sɛgrɪ,geɪt] *vt* **-gated; -gating** : séparer, isoler
segregation [,sɛgrɪ'geɪʃən] *n* : ségrégation *f*
seismic ['saɪzmɪk, 'saɪs-] *adj* : sismique
seize ['si:z] *v* **seized; seizing** *vt* **1** CAPTURE : se saisir de, capturer, appréhender **2** GRASP : saisir, s'emparer de — *vi or* **to seize up** : se gripper
seizure ['si:ʒər] *n* **1** CAPTURE : prise *f*, saisie *f* **2** ARREST : arrestation *f* **3** ATTACK : attaque *f*, crise *f* <epileptic seizure : crise d'épilepsie>
seldom ['sɛldəm] *adv* : rarement
select[1] [sə'lɛkt] *vt* : choisir, sélectionner
select[2] *adj* : privilégié, sélect *fam*, choisi <a select few : seulement quelques privilégiés>
selection [sə'lɛkʃən] *n* : sélection *f*
selective [sə'lɛktɪv] *adj* : sélectif
self ['sɛlf] *n, pl* **selves** ['sɛlvz] **1** : moi *m*, être *m* <with his whole self : avec tout son être> <the self : le moi> **2** SIDE : côté *m* <his better self : son meilleur côté>
self-addressed envelope [,sɛlfə'drɛst] *n* : enveloppe *f* à mon (son) nom et adresse
self-appointed [,sɛlfə'pɔɪntəd] *adj* : qui s'est nommé
self-assurance [,sɛlfə'ʃʊrənts] *n* : assurance *f*, confiance *f* en soi
self-assured [,sɛlfə'ʃʊrd] *adj* : sûr de soi
self-centered [,sɛlf'sɛntərd] *adj* : égocentrique
self-confidence [,sɛlf'kɑnfədənts] *n* : confiance *f* en soi
self-confident [,sɛlf'kɑnfədənt] *adj* : sûr de soi
self-conscious [,sɛlf'kɑntʃəs] *adj* **1** EMBARRASSED : timide, gêné **2** DELIBERATE : appuyé
self-consciously [,sɛlf'kɑntʃəsli] *adv* : timidement
self-consciousness [,sɛlf'kɑntʃəsnəs] *n* : timidité *f*, gêne *f*
self-contained [,sɛlfkən'teɪnd] *adj* : indépendant
self-control [,sɛlfkən'tro:l] *n* : maîtrise *f* de soi
self-defense [,sɛlfdɪ'fɛnts] *n* : légitime défense *f*
self-denial [,sɛlfdɪ'naɪəl] *n* : abnégation *f*
self-destructive [,sɛlfdɪ'strʌktɪv] *adj* : autodestructeur
self-determination [,sɛlfdɪ,tərmə'neɪʃən] *n* : autodétermination *f*
self-discipline [,sɛlf'dɪsəplən] *n* : autodiscipline *f*
self-employed [,sɛlfɪm'plɔɪd] *adj* : indépendant <she's self-employed : elle travaille à son compte>
self-esteem [,sɛlfɪ'sti:m] *n* : respect *m* de soi, amour-propre *m*
self-evident [,sɛlf'ɛvədənt] *adj* : évident
self-explanatory [,sɛlfɪk'splænə,tori] *adj* : évident, explicite
self-expression [,sɛlfɪk'sprɛʃən] *n* : expression *f* libre
self-government [,sɛlf'gʌvərmənt, -vərn-] *n* : autonomie *f*
self-help [,sɛlf'hɛlp] *n* : initiative *f* personnelle <self-help group : groupe d'entraide>
self-important [,sɛlfɪm'pɔrtənt] *adj* : vaniteux, suffisant
self-indulgent [,sɛlfɪn'dʌldʒənt] *adj* : complaisant, qui ne se refuse rien
self-inflicted [,sɛlfɪn'flɪktəd] *adj* : autoinfligé
self-interest [,sɛlf'ɪntrəst, -tə,rɛst] *n* : intérêt *m* personnel
selfish ['sɛlfɪʃ] *adj* : égoïste
selfishly ['sɛlfɪʃli] *adv* : égoïstement
selfishness ['sɛlfɪʃnəs] *n* : égoïsme *m*
selfless ['sɛlfləs] *adj* UNSELFISH : désintéressé, altruiste
self-made [,sɛlf'meɪd] *adj* : qui a réussi tout seul <a self-made man : un self-made-man>
self-pity [,sɛlf'pɪṭi] *n, pl* **-ties** : apitoiement *m* sur soi-même
self-portrait [,sɛlf'pɔrtrət] *n* : autoportrait *m*
self-propelled [,sɛlfpro'pɛld] *adj* : autopropulsé
self-reliance [,sɛlfrɪ'laɪənts] *n* : autosuffisance *f*
self-respect [,sɛlfrɪ'spɛkt] *n* : respect *m* de soi
self-restraint [,sɛlfrɪ'streɪnt] *n* : retenue *f*
self-righteous [,sɛlf'raɪtʃəs] *adj* : suffisant
self-sacrifice [,sɛlf'sækrə,faɪs] *n* : abnégation *f*
selfsame ['sɛlf,seɪm] *adj* : même

self–service [ˌsɛlfˈsɛrvəs] *n* : libre-service *m*
self–sufficiency [ˌsɛlfsəˈfɪʃəntsi] *n* : autosuffisance *f,* indépendance *f*
self–sufficient [ˌsɛlfsəˈfɪʃənt] *adj* : autosuffisant, indépendant
self–taught [ˌsɛlfˈtɔt] *adj* : autodidacte
sell [ˈsɛl] *v* **sold** [ˈsoːld]; **selling** *vt* : vendre — *vi* : se vendre
seller [ˈsɛlər] *n* : vendeur *m,* -deuse *f*
selves → **self**
semantic [sɪˈmæntɪk] *adj* : sémantique
semantics [sɪˈmæntɪks] *ns & pl* : sémantique *f*
semaphore [ˈsɛməˌfor] *n* : sémaphore *m*
semblance [ˈsɛmblənts] *n* : semblant *m,* apparence *f*
semen [ˈsiːmən] *n* : sperme *m*
semester [səˈmɛstər] *n* : semestre *m*
semicolon [ˈsɛmiˌkoːlən, ˈsɛˌmaɪ-] *n* : point-virgule *m*
semiconductor [ˈsɛmikənˌdʌktər, ˈsɛˌmaɪ-] *n* : semiconducteur *m*
semifinal [ˈsɛmiˌfaɪnəl, ˈsɛˌmaɪ-] *n* : demi-finale *f*
seminal [ˈsɛmənəl] *adj* : séminal
seminar [ˈsɛməˌnɑr] *n* : séminaire *m*
seminary [ˈsɛməˌnɛri] *n, pl* **-naries** : séminaire *m*
senate [ˈsɛnət] *n* : sénat *m*
senator [ˈsɛnət̬ər] *n* **1** : sénateur *m* **2** : sénateur *m,* -trice *f Can*
send [ˈsɛnd] *vt* **sent** [ˈsɛnt]; **sending 1** : envoyer, expédier <he was sent to prison : on l'a envoyé en prison> <to send a letter : expédier une lettre> <to send word : faire dire> **2** PROPEL : pousser, envoyer **3 to send away for** : se faire envoyer, commander par correspondance **4 to send for** : appeler, faire venir
sender [ˈsɛndər] *n* : expéditeur *m,* -trice *f*
Senegalese[1] [ˌsɛnəgəˈliːz, -ˈliːs] *adj* : sénégalais
Senegalese[2] *n* : Sénégalais *m,* -laise *f*
senile [ˈsiːˌnaɪl] *adj* : sénile
senility [sɪˈnɪlət̬i] *n* : sénilité *f*
senior[1] [ˈsiːnjər] *adj* **1** ELDER : aîné, plus âgé <John Durant, Senior : John Durant, père> **2** : supérieur <a senior official : un officiel supérieur, un haut fonctionnaire>
senior[2] *n* **1** : aîné *m,* aînée *f* **2** *or* **high school senior** : élève *mf* de terminale **3** *or* **college senior** : étudiant *m,* -diante *f* de licence **4 to be s.o.'s senior** : être plus âgé que qqn <he is six years my senior : il a six ans de plus que moi>
seniority [ˌsiːˈnjɔrət̬i] *n* : ancienneté *f,* priorité *f* d'âge
sensation [sɛnˈseɪʃən] *n* : sensation *f*
sensational [sɛnˈseɪʃənəl] *adj* : sensationnel
sense[1] [ˈsɛnts] *vt* **sensed; sensing** : sentir <he sensed danger : il a senti le danger>
sense[2] *n* **1** FACULTY : sens *m* <sense of touch : sens du toucher> **2** MEANING : sens *m,* signification *f* **3** SENSATION : sensation *f,* sentiment *m* <a sense of guilt : un sentiment de culpabilité> **4** WISDOM : sens *m* <common sense : bon sens> **5 to make sense** : avoir du sens
senseless [ˈsɛntsləs] *adj* **1** MEANINGLESS : insensé **2** UNCONSCIOUS : sans connaissance
senselessly [ˈsɛntsləsli] *adv* : stupidement, de manière insensée
sensibility [ˌsɛntsəˈbɪlət̬i] *n, pl* **-ties** : sensibilité *f*
sensible [ˈsɛntsəbəl] *adj* **1** PERCEPTIBLE : sensible **2** AWARE : conscient **3** REASONABLE : raisonnable
sensibly [ˈsɛntsəbli] *adv* **1** PERCEPTIBLY : sensiblement, perceptiblement **2** REASONABLY : raisonnablement, de façon raisonnable
sensitive [ˈsɛntsət̬ɪv] *adj* **1** : sensible <sensitive skin : peau sensible> **2** DELICATE : délicat **3** AWARE : conscient, sensibilisé
sensitiveness [ˈsɛntsət̬ɪvnəs] → **sensitivity**
sensitivity [ˌsɛntsəˈtɪvət̬i] *n, pl* **-ties** : sensibilité *f*
sensitize [ˈsɛntsəˌtaɪz] *vt* **-tized; -tizing** : sensibiliser
sensor [ˈsɛnˌsɔr, ˈsɛntsər] *n* : détecteur *m*
sensory [ˈsɛntsəri] *adj* : sensoriel
sensual [ˈsɛntʃuəl] *adj* : sensuel — **sensually** *adv*
sensuality [ˌsɛnʃəˈwælət̬i] *n* : sensualité *f*
sensuous [ˈsɛnʃuəs] *adj* : sensuel
sent → **send**
sentence[1] [ˈsɛntənts, -ənz] *vt* **-tenced; -tencing** : condamner
sentence[2] *n* **1** : phrase *f* (en grammaire) **2** JUDGMENT : sentence *f,* condamnation *f*
sentiment [ˈsɛntəmənt] *n* **1** BELIEF : avis *m* **2** FEELING : sentiment *m* **3** → **sentimentality**
sentimental [ˌsɛntəˈmɛntəl] *adj* : sentimental
sentimentality [ˌsɛntəˌmɛnˈtælət̬i] *n, pl* **-ties** : sentimentalité *f,* sensiblerie *f*
sentinel [ˈsɛntənəl] *n* : sentinelle *f,* factionnaire *m*
sentry [ˈsɛntri] *n, pl* **-tries** : sentinelle *f,* factionnaire *m*
separate[1] [ˈsɛpəˌreɪt] *v* **-rated; -rating** *vt* **1** DETACH, SEVER : séparer, détacher **2** DISTINGUISH : distinguer — *vi* : se séparer
separate[2] [ˈsɛpərət] *adj* **1** INDIVIDUAL : séparé **2** DISTINCT : distinct
separately [ˈsɛpərətli] *adv* : séparément
separation [ˌsɛpəˈreɪʃən] *n* : séparation *f*
sepia [ˈsiːpiə] *n* : sépia *f*

September [sɛp'tɛmbər] *n* : septembre *m*
sepulchre ['sɛpəlkər] *n* : sépulcre *m*
sequel ['si:kwəl] *n* **1** CONSEQUENCE : conséquence *f* **2** CONTINUATION : suite *f* (d'un roman, d'un film, etc.)
sequence ['si:kwənts] *n* **1** SERIES : série *f*, succession *f* **2** ORDER : ordre *m*, suite *f*
sequential [sɪ'kwɛntʃəl] *adj* : séquentiel
sequester [sɪ'kwɛstər] *vt* : séquestrer
sequin ['si:kwən] *n* : paillette *f*, sequin *m*
sequoia [sɪ'kwɔɪə] *n* : séquoia *m*
sera → **serum**
Serb[1] ['sərb] *adj* : serbe
Serb[2] *n* **1** : Serbe *mf* **2** → **Serbian**
Serbian ['sərbiən] *n* **1** : serbe *m* (langue) **2** → **Serb**[2]
Serbo–Croatian[1] [,sərbokro'eɪʃən] *adj* : serbo-croate
Serbo–Croatian[2] *n* : serbo-croate *m* (langue)
serenade[1] [,sɛrə'neɪd] *vt* **-naded; -nading** : donner une sérénade à
serenade[2] *n* : sérénade *f*
serene [sə'ri:n] *adj* : serein — **serenely** *adv*
serenity [sə'rɛnət̬i] *n* : sérénité *f*
serf ['sərf] *n* : serf *m*, serve *f*
serge ['sərdʒ] *n* : serge *f*
sergeant ['sɑrdʒənt] *n* : sergent *m*
serial[1] ['sɪriəl] *adj* : en série, d'une série <serial number : numéro de série>
serial[2] *n* **1** : feuilleton *m* (histoire) **2** PERIODICAL : périodique *m*
serially ['sɪriəli] *adv* : en série
series ['sɪr,i:z] *ns & pl* : série *f*
serious ['sɪriəs] *adj* **1** SOBER : sérieux **2** DEDICATED, EARNEST : sérieux, dédié **3** SIGNIFICANT : important, considérable <serious damage : dommages importants> **4** GRAVE : grave, sérieux
seriously ['sɪriəsli] *adv* **1** : sérieusement <to take oneself too seriously : se prendre trop au sérieux> **2** GRAVELY : gravement
seriousness ['sɪriəsnəs] *n* : sérieux *m*
sermon ['sərmən] *n* : sermon *m*
serpent ['sərpənt] *n* : serpent *m*
serum ['sɪrəm] *n, pl* **serums** *or* **sera** ['sɪrə] : sérum *m*
servant ['sərvənt] *n* : domestique *mf*
serve[1] ['sərv] *v* **served; serving** *vi* **1** : servir <to serve in the navy : servir dans la marine> <to serve on a committee : être membre d'un comité> **2 to serve as** : servir de **3 to serve to** : servir à — *vt* **1** : servir <to serve one's country : servir son pays> **2** : desservir <a train serving the public : un train qui dessert le public> **3** PROVIDE, SUPPLY : alimenter (des services publiques) **4 to serve a sentence** : purger une peine **5 to serve a summons to** : remettre une assignation à
serve[2] *n* : service *m* (aux sports)
server ['sərvər] *n* **1** WAITER : serveur *m*, -veuse *f* **2** : serveur *m* (en informatique)
service[1] ['sərvəs] *vt* **-viced; -vicing 1** MAINTAIN : réviser, entretenir <to service a car : réviser une voiture> **2** REPAIR : réparer
service[2] *n* **1** : service *m* <to do s.o. a service : rendre un service à qqn> **2** CEREMONY : office *m* (en religion) **3** FACILITY : service *m* <social services : services sociaux> <train service : service de train> **4** SET : service *m* <tea service : service à thé> **5** MAINTENANCE : entretien *m*, révision *f* (d'une voiture, etc.) **6 services** *npl or* **armed services** : forces *fpl* armées
serviceable ['sərvəsəbəl] *adj* USABLE : utilisable
serviceman ['sərvəs,mæn, -mən] *n, pl* **-men** [-mən, -,mɛn] : militaire *m*
service station *n* : station-service *f*, poste *m* d'essence
servicewoman ['sərvəs,wʊmən] *n, pl* **-women** [-,wɪmən] : femme *f* soldat
servile ['sərvəl, -,vaɪl] *adj* : servile
serving ['sərvɪŋ] *n* HELPING : portion *f*
servitude ['sərvə,tu:d, -,tju:d] *n* : servitude *f*
sesame ['sɛsəmi] *n* : sésame *m*
session ['sɛʃən] *n* : séance *f*, session *f*
set[1] ['sɛt] *v* **set; setting** *vt* **1** *or* **to set down** PLACE : placer, mettre, poser **2** SITUATE : disposer, situer <she set the story in France : elle a situé l'histoire en France> **3** PREPARE : mettre, tendre, dresser <to set the table : mettre la table> <to set a trap : tendre un piège> **4** FIX, ESTABLISH : fixer, établir <to set a time : fixer l'heure> <to set prices : fixer les prix> <to set a record : établir un record> **5** (*indicating the cause of a certain condition*) <to set fire to : mettre le feu à> <he set it free : il l'a libéré> **6** SOLIDIFY : faire prendre — *vi* **1** SOLIDIFY : durcir, prendre **2** : se coucher (se dit du soleil et de la lune)
set[2] *adj* **1** ESTABLISHED, SETTLED : fixe, établi **2** READY : prêt, préparé **3** DETERMINED : résolu, déterminé
set[3] *n* **1** COLLECTION : ensemble *m*, série *f* <chess set : jeu d'échecs> **2** GROUP : cercle *m*, milieu *m* (social) **3** *or* **stage set** : scène *f*, plateau *m*, décor *m* **4** APPARATUS : appareil *m*, poste *m* <television set : poste de télévision> **5** SERVICE : service *m* (à thé, à café, etc.) **6** : set *m* (aux sports) **7** : ensemble *m* (en mathématiques)
setback ['sɛt,bæk] *n* : revers *m*
set off *vt* **1** PROVOKE : déclencher, provoquer **2** EXPLODE : faire exploser **3** HIGHLIGHT : mettre en valeur — *vi or* **to set forth** : se mettre en route

set out *vt* **1** ARRANGE : disposer, étaler (des marchandises, etc.) **2** PRESENT : présenter, exposer (des idées) — *vi* **1** LEAVE : se mettre en route **2 to set out to do** : avoir pour but de faire

settee [sɛ'ti:] *n* : canapé *m*

setter ['sɛtər] *n* : setter *m* <Irish setter : setter irlandais>

setting ['sɛţıŋ] *n* **1** SURROUNDINGS : cadre *m*, décor *m* **2** MOUNTING : monture *f* (d'un bijou) **3** : réglage *m* (d'une machine) **4** : coucher *m* (du soleil)

settle ['sɛţəl] *v* **settled; settling** *vi* **1** LAND : poser (se dit des oiseaux), laisser tomber (se dit de la poussière) **2** SINK : s'effondrer (se dit des bâtiments) **3** : s'installer (dans une maison, dans un fauteuil), se fixer (dans une région, dans un pays, etc.) **4 to settle down** : se calmer **5 to settle for** : accepter, se contenter de **6 to settle over** : descendre sur — *vt* **1** ARRANGE, RESOLVE : résoudre, régler **2** DETERMINE : décider, fixer **3** CALM : calmer, apaiser **4** PAY : payer, régler (une dette) **5** COLONIZE : coloniser

settlement ['sɛţəlmənt] *n* **1** PAYMENT : règlement *m* **2** COLONY : colonie *f* **3** RESOLUTION : résolution *f*, accord *m*

settler ['sɛţələr] *n* : colonisateur *m*, -trice *f*; colon *m*

set up *vt* **1** ASSEMBLE : installer **2** ERECT : monter **3** ESTABLISH : établir

seven[1] ['sɛvən] *adj* : sept

seven[2] *n* : sept *m*

seventeen[1] [ˌsɛvən'ti:n] *adj* : dix-sept

seventeen[2] *n* : dix-sept *m*

seventeenth[1] [ˌsɛvən'ti:nθ] *adj* : dix-septième

seventeenth[2] *n* **1** : dix-septième *mf* (dans une série) **2** : dix-septième *m* (en mathématiques) **3** (*used in dates*) <the seventeenth of January : le dix-sept janvier>

seventh[1] [ˌsɛvənθ] *adj* : septième

seventh[2] *n* **1** : septième *mf* (dans une série) **2** : septième *m* (en mathématiques) **3** (*used in dates*) <the seventh of March : le sept Mars>

seventieth[1] ['sɛvəntiəθ] *adj* : soixante-dixième, septantième *Bel, Switz*

seventieth[2] *n* **1** : soixante-dixième *mf*, septantième *mf Bel, Switz* (dans une série) **2** : soixante-dixième *m* (en mathématiques)

seventy[1] ['sɛvənti] *adj* : soixante-dix, septante *Bel, Switz*

seventy[2] *n, pl* **-ties** : soixante-dix *m*, septante *mf Bel, Switz*

sever ['sɛvər] *vt* **-ered; -ering** **1** CUT : couper **2** BREAK : rompre, cesser <to sever ties with : rompre les liens avec>

several[1] ['sɛvrəl, 'sɛvə-] *adj* : plusieurs

several[2] *pron* : plusieurs

severance ['sɛvrənts, 'sɛvə-] *n* **1** : rupture *f* **2 severance pay** : indemnité *f* de départ

severe [sə'vır] *adj* **severer; -est** **1** STRICT : sévère **2** AUSTERE : austère, sévère **3** SERIOUS : grave **4** DIFFICULT : dur, rigoureux

severely [sə'vırli] *adv* **1** HARSHLY : durement, sévèrement **2** SERIOUSLY : gravement, sérieusement **3** AUSTERELY : d'une façon austère

severity [sə'vɛrəţi] *n* **1** HARSHNESS : sévérité *f* **2** SERIOUSNESS : gravité *f*

sew ['so:] *v* **sewed; sewn** ['so:n] *or* **sewed; sewing** : coudre

sewage ['su:ıdʒ] *n* : eaux *fpl* d'égout

sewer[1] ['so:ər] *n* : couseur *m*, -seuse *f*

sewer[2] ['su:ər] *n* : égout *m*

sewing ['so:ıŋ] *n* : couture *f*

sex ['sɛks] *n* **1** GENDER : sexe *m* **2** COPULATION : rapports *mpl* sexuels

sexism ['sɛkˌsızəm] *n* : sexisme *m*

sexist[1] ['sɛksıst] *adj* : sexiste

sexist[2] *n* : sexiste *mf*

sextant ['sɛkstənt] *n* : sextant *m*

sextet [sɛk'stɛt] *n* : sextuor *m*

sexton ['sɛkstən] *n* : sacristain *m*

sexual ['sɛkʃuəl] *adj* : sexuel — **sexually** *adv*

sexuality [ˌsɛkʃu'ælətˌi] *n* : sexualité *f*

sexy ['sɛksi] *adj* **sexier; -est** : sexy

shabbily ['ʃæbəli] *adv* **1** POORLY : pauvrement **2** MEANLY : mesquinement

shabbiness ['ʃæbinəs] *n* **1** : pauvreté *f*, délabrement *m* **2** MEANNESS : mesquinerie *f*

shabby ['ʃæbi] *adj* **shabbier; -est** **1** WORN : usé, miteux **2** MEAN : vilain, mesquin

shack ['ʃæk] *n* : cabane *f*, hutte *f*

shackle ['ʃækəl] *vt* **-led; -ling** **1** BIND : enchaîner, mettre aux fers **2** HAMPER : entraver

shackles ['ʃækəlz] *npl* : chaînes *fpl*, fers *mpl*

shad ['ʃæd] *n* : alose *f*

shade[1] ['ʃeıd] *v* **shaded; shading** *vt* **1** : ombrager <the trees shade the courtyard : les arbres ombragent la cour> **2** SCREEN : abriter, donner de l'ombre à, protéger <to shade one's eyes : s'abriter les yeux> **3** *or* **to shade in** : hachurer — *vi* **to shade into** : se fondre en

shade[2] *n* **1** : ombre *f* <in the shade : à l'ombre> **2** GRADATION : ton *m*, nuance *f* **3** BIT : peu *m* <a shade larger : un peu plus grand>

shadow[1] ['ʃædo:] *vt* **1** DARKEN : ombrager **2** FOLLOW : filer

shadow[2] *n* **1** : ombre *f* **2 to cast a shadow over** : projeter une ombre sur

shadowy ['ʃædowi] *adj* **1** DARK : sombre **2** INDISTINCT : vague **3** MYSTERIOUS : mystérieux

shady [ˈʃeɪdi] *adj* **shadier; -est 1** : ombragé **2** DISREPUTABLE : louche
shaft [ˈʃæft] *n* **1** : arbre *m* (d'un moteur) **2** *or* **mine shaft** : puits *m* **3** *or* **shaft of light** : rai *m* **4** HANDLE, STEM : manche *m* (d'un outil), tige *f* (d'une flèche) **5 elevator shaft** : cage *f*
shaggy [ˈʃægi] *adj* **shaggier; -est 1** HAIRY : poilu, broussailleux **2** UNKEMPT : débraillé
shake[1] [ˈʃeɪk] *v* **shook** [ˈʃʊk]; **shaken** [ˈʃeɪkən]; **shaking** *vt* **1** : secouer <he shook his head : il a secoué la tête> **2** UPSET : ébranler <shaken by the news : ébranlé par la nouvelle> **3 to shake hands with s.o.** : serrer la main à qqn — *vi* TREMBLE : trembler
shake[2] *n* : secousse *f,* ébranlement *m*
shaker [ˈʃeɪkər] *n* **1** → **saltshaker 2 pepper shaker** : poivrier *m* **3 cocktail shaker** : shaker *m*
shake–up [ˈʃeɪkˌʌp] *n* : réorganisation *f*
shake up *vt* : secouer, agiter
shakily [ˈʃeɪkəli] *adv* **1** : en tremblant **2** UNSTEADILY : à pas chancelants **3** WEAKLY : faiblement
shaky [ˈʃeɪki] *adj* **shakier; -est 1** TREMBLING : tremblant **2** UNSTEADY : branlant **3** UNCERTAIN : chancelant, incertain
shale [ˈʃeɪl] *n* : schiste *m* argileux
shall [ˈʃæl] *v aux, past* **should** [ˈʃʊd]; *pres sing & pl* **shall 1** (*used to express a command*) <you shall do as I say : vous ferez comme je vous dis> **2** (*used to express futurity*) <what shall we do? : que ferons-nous?> <I shall have finished it : je l'aurai fini> **3** (*used to express determination*) <you shall have the money : vous aurez l'argent>
shallow [ˈʃælo:] *adj* **1** : peu profond **2** SUPERFICIAL : superficiel
shallows [ˈʃælo:z] *npl* : haut-fond *m,* bas-fond *m*
sham[1] [ˈʃæm] *v* **shammed; shamming** *vt* : feindre, faire semblant de — *vi* : faire semblant
sham[2] *adj* : faux
sham[3] *n* **1** PRETENSE : faux-semblant *m,* comédie *f* **2** IMPOSTER : imposteur *m*
shamble [ˈʃæmbəl] *vi* **-bled; -bling** : marcher en traînant les pieds
shambles [ˈʃæmbəlz] *ns & pl* : désordre *m*
shame[1] [ˈʃeɪm] *vt* **shamed; shaming** : faire honte à
shame[2] *n* **1** : honte *f* **2** PITY : dommage *m* <what a shame! : quel dommage!>
shamefaced [ˈʃeɪmˌfeɪst] *adj* : penaud, honteux
shameful [ˈʃeɪmfəl] *adj* : honteux — **shamefully** *adv*
shameless [ˈʃeɪmləs] *adj* : éhonté
shamelessly [ˈʃeɪmləsli] *adv* : sans vergogne, sans honte
shampoo[1] [ʃæmˈpu:] *vt* : faire un shampooing à
shampoo[2] *n, pl* **-poos** : shampooing *m*
shamrock [ˈʃæmˌrɑk] *n* : trèfle *m*
shank [ˈʃæŋk] *n* **1** LEG : jambe *f,* canon *m* (d'un cheval) **2** SHAFT : tige *f*
shan't [ˈʃænt] (*contraction of* **shall not**) → **shall**
shanty [ˈʃænti] *n, pl* **-ties** : cabane *f*
shape[1] [ˈʃeɪp] *v* **shaped; shaping** *vt* **1** MOLD : façonner, modeler **2** DETERMINE : former — *vi or* **to shape up** : prendre forme
shape[2] *n* **1** : forme *f* <in the shape of a circle : en forme de cercle> **2** CONDITION : forme *f,* état *m* <to be in good shape : être en bonne forme>
shapeless [ˈʃeɪpləs] *adj* : informe, sans forme
shapely [ˈʃeɪpli] *adj* **shapelier; -est** : bien fait, bien tourné
shard [ˈʃɑrd] *n* : tesson *m*
share[1] [ˈʃɛr] *v* **shared; sharing** *vt* : partager <to share the work : partager le travail> <they share the responsibility : ils se partagent la responsabilité> — *vi* **to share in** : prendre part à
share[2] *n* **1** PORTION : portion *f,* part *f* **2** STOCK : action *f*
sharecropper [ˈʃɛrˌkrɑpər] *n* : métayer *m,* -tayère *f*
shareholder [ˈʃɛrˌho:ldər] *n* : actionnaire *mf*
shark [ˈʃɑrk] *n* : requin *m*
sharp[1] [ˈʃɑrp] *adv* **1** PRECISELY : précisément, pile <at five o'clock sharp : à cinq heures pile> **2** ABRUPTLY : brusquement
sharp[2] *adj* **1** : aigu, tranchant, affilé <a sharp knife : un couteau tranchant> **2** CLEVER : vif **3** POINTED : pointu **4** INTENSE : vif, fort <a sharp pain : une douleur vive> **5** SUDDEN : brusque **6** DISTINCT : net, distinct **7** : dièse (en musique) **8** STYLISH : chic **9** KEEN : perçant, fin
sharp[3] *n* : dièse *m* (en musique)
sharpen [ˈʃɑrpən] *vt* : aiguiser, affiler
sharpener [ˈʃɑrpənər] *n* **1** *or* **knife sharpener** : aiguisoir *m* **2** → **pencil sharpener**
sharply [ˈʃɑrpli] *adv* **1** ABRUPTLY : brusquement **2** DISTINCTLY : nettement, clairement **3** HARSHLY : sévèrement
sharpness [ˈʃɑrpnəs] *n* **1** : tranchant *m* (d'un couteau, etc.) **2** ACUTENESS : acuité *f* **3** ABRUPTNESS : brusquerie *f* **4** INTENSITY : intensité *f* **5** HARSHNESS : sévérité *f* **6** CLARITY : netteté *f*
sharpshooter [ˈʃɑrpˌʃu:t̬ər] *n* : tireur *m* d'élite
shatter [ˈʃæt̬ər] *vt* : briser, fracasser — *vi* : se briser, se fracasser

shave[1] [ˈʃeɪv] *v* **shaved; shaved** *or* **shaven** [ˈʃeɪvən]; **shaving** *vt* **1** : raser **2** PLANE : raboter, planer — *vi* : se raser

shave[2] *n* : rasage *m*

shaver [ˈʃeɪvər] *n or* **electric shaver** : rasoir *m* électrique

shawl [ˈʃɔl] *n* : châle *m*

she [ˈʃiː] *pron* : elle

sheaf [ˈʃiːf] *n, pl* **sheaves** [ˈʃiːvz] : gerbe *f* (de céréales), liasse *f* (de papier)

shear [ˈʃɪr] *vt* **sheared; sheared** *or* **shorn** [ˈʃorn]; **shearing** : tondre

shears [ˈʃɪrz] *npl* **1** SCISSORS : cisailles *fpl* **2** CLIPPERS : tondeuse *f*

sheath [ˈʃiːθ] *n, pl* **sheaths** [ˈʃiːðz, ˈʃiːθs] : fourreau *m* (d'épée), gaine *f* (de poignard, des plantes)

sheathe [ˈʃiːð] *vt* **sheathed; sheathing** : rengainer

shed[1] [ˈʃɛd] *v* **shed; shedding** *vt* **1** : verser (des larmes, du sang) **2** : perdre (des feuilles, du poids) **3 to shed light on** : éclairer, éclaircir — *vi* : perdre ses poils

shed[2] *n* : abri *m*, remise *f*

she'd [ˈʃiːd] (*contraction of* **she had** *or* **she would**) → **have, would**

sheen [ˈʃiːn] *n* : lustre *m*, éclat *m*

sheep [ˈʃiːp] *ns & pl* : mouton *m*

sheepfold [ˈʃiːpˌfoːld] *n* : parc *m* à moutons

sheepish [ˈʃiːpɪʃ] *adj* : penaud

sheepskin [ˈʃiːpˌskɪn] *n* **1** : peau *f* de mouton **2** DIPLOMA : diplôme *m*

sheer[1] [ˈʃɪr] *adv* : à pic, abruptement

sheer[2] *adj* **1** PURE : pur **2** STEEP : à pic, abrupt **3** TRANSPARENT : transparent, fin

sheet [ˈʃiːt] *n* **1** *or* **bedsheet** [ˈbɛdˌʃiːt] : drap *m* **2** : feuille *f* (de papier) **3** : plaque *f* <baking sheet : plaque de four>

sheikh *or* **sheik** [ˈʃiːk, ˈʃeɪk] *n* : cheikh *m*

shelf [ˈʃɛlf] *n, pl* **shelves** [ˈʃɛlvz] **1** : étagère *f*, rayon *m* **2** : rebord *m*, saillie *f* (en géologie) <continental shelf : plate-forme continentale>

shell[1] [ˈʃɛl] *vt* **1** : décortiquer (des noix), écosser (des pois) **2** BOMBARD : bombarder

shell[2] *n* **1** : coquille *f*, coque *f*, carapace *f* (de tortue, de homard) **2** SEASHELL : coquillage *m* **3** MISSILE : obus *m* **4** CARTRIDGE : cartouche *f* **5** *or* **racing shell** : canot *m*

she'll [ˈʃiːl, ʃɪl] (*contraction of* **she shall** *or* **she will**) → **shall, will**

shellac[1] [ʃəˈlæk] *vt* **-lacked; -lacking** **1** : laquer **2** DEFEAT : piler *fam*

shellac[2] *n* : laque *f*

shellfish [ˈʃɛlˌfɪʃ] *n* : crustacé *m*

shelter[1] [ˈʃɛltər] *vt* **1** PROTECT : abriter, protéger **2** HARBOR : donner asile à, recueillir

shelter[2] *n* : abri *m*

shelve [ˈʃɛlv] *vt* **shelved; shelving** **1** : mettre sur les rayons **2** DEFER : remettre

shenanigans [ʃəˈnænɪgənz] *npl* **1** TRICKERY : manigances *fpl* **2** MISCHIEF : espièglerie *f*

shepherd[1] [ˈʃɛpərd] *vt* **1** GUARD : surveiller, garder **2** GUIDE : guider, conduire

shepherd[2] *n* : berger *m*

shepherdess [ˈʃɛpərdəs] *n* : bergère *f*

sherbet [ˈʃərbət] *n* : sorbet *m*

sheriff [ˈʃɛrɪf] *n* : shérif *m*

sherry [ˈʃɛri] *n, pl* **-ries** : xérès *m*

she's [ˈʃiːz] (*contraction of* **she is** *or* **she has**) → **be, have**

shield[1] [ˈʃiːld] *vt* **1** PROTECT : protéger **2** CONCEAL : couvrir

shield[2] *n* **1** : bouclier *m* **2** PROTECTION : protection *f*

shier, shiest → **shy**

shift[1] [ˈʃɪft] *vt* **1** CHANGE : changer de <to shift gears : changer de vitesse> **2** MOVE : déplacer — *vi* **1** CHANGE : changer **2** MOVE : se déplacer, bouger

shift[2] *n* **1** CHANGE : changement *m* <a shift in priorities : un changement de priorités> **2** : poste *m*, équipe *f* <night shift : équipe de nuit> **3** *or* **shift dress** : robe *f* fourreau **4** → **gearshift**

shiftless [ˈʃɪftləs] *adj* : fainéant, paresseux

shifty [ˈʃɪfti] *adj* **shiftier; -est** : sournois, rusé

shilling [ˈʃɪlɪŋ] *n* : shilling *m*

shimmer [ˈʃɪmər] *vi* GLIMMER : chatoyer, miroiter

shin[1] [ˈʃɪn] *vi* **shinned; shinning** : grimper <she shinned up a tree : elle a grimpé à un arbre>

shin[2] *n* : tibia *m*

shine[1] [ˈʃaɪn] *v* **shone** [ˈʃoːn, *esp Brit and Can* ˈʃɒn] *or* **shined; shining** *vi* **1** : briller, luire **2** EXCEL : briller — *vt* **1** AIM : braquer, diriger <he shined the flashlight at the dog : il a braqué la lampe de poche sur le chien> **2** POLISH : astiquer, cirer (des chaussures)

shine[2] *n* : éclat *m*, lustre *m*

shingle[1] [ˈʃɪŋgəl] *vt* **-gled; -gling** : couvrir de bardeaux

shingle[2] *n* : bardeau *m*

shingles [ˈʃɪŋgəlz] *npl* : zona *m*

shinny [ˈʃɪni] *vi* **-nied; -nying** → **shin**[1]

shiny [ˈʃaɪni] *adj* **shinier; -est** : luisant, brillant

ship[1] [ˈʃɪp] *vt* **shipped; shipping** **1** LOAD : embarquer, mettre à bord **2** SEND : expédier (par bateau), transporter (par avion)

ship[2] *n* **1** : navire *m*, bateau *m* **2** → **spaceship**

shipboard [ˈʃɪpˌbord] *n* **on ~** : à bord

shipbuilder [ˈʃɪpˌbɪldər] *n* : constructeur *m*, -trice *f* de navires

shipment [ˈʃɪpmənt] *n* **1** SHIPPING : expédition *f,* transport *m* **2** CARGO : cargaison *f* (par mer), chargement *m* (terrestre)
shipping [ˈʃɪpɪŋ] *n* **1** SHIPS : navires *mpl* **2** TRANSPORT : transport *m* (maritime)
shipshape [ˈʃɪpˈʃeɪp] *adj* : en bon ordre
shipwreck[1] [ˈʃɪpˌrɛk] *vt* **to be shipwrecked** : faire naufrage
shipwreck[2] *n* : naufrage *m*
shipyard [ˈʃɪpˌjard] *n* : chantier *m* naval
shirk [ˈʃərk] *vt* : se dérober à, esquiver <to shirk one's duties : se dérober à ses responsabilités>
shirt [ˈʃərt] *n* : chemise *f*
shiver[1] [ˈʃɪvər] *vi* : frissonner
shiver[2] *n* : frisson *m*
shoal [ˈʃo:l] *n* **1** : banc *m* (de poissons) **2** SANDBANK : banc *m* de sable
shock[1] [ˈʃak] *vt* : choquer
shock[2] *n* **1** : choc *m* <in a state of shock : en état de choc> **2** *or* **electric shock** : décharge *f* (électrique) **3 shock of hair** : tignasse *f*
shock absorber *n* : amortisseur *m*
shoddy [ˈʃadi] *adj* **shoddier; -est** : de mauvaise qualité
shoe[1] [ˈʃu:] *vt* **shod** [ˈʃad]; **shoeing** : ferrer (un cheval)
shoe[2] *n* **1** : chaussure *f* **2** → **horseshoe 3 brake shoe** : sabot *m* (de frein)
shoelace [ˈʃu:ˌleɪs] *n* : lacet *m*
shoemaker [ˈʃu:ˌmeɪkər] *n* : cordonnier *m,* -nière *f*
shone → **shine**[1]
shook → **shake**[1]
shoot[1] [ˈʃu:t] *v* **shot** [ˈʃat]; **shooting** *vt* **1** FIRE : tirer (une balle ou une flèche), lancer (un missile) **2** : tirer sur (une personne) <to shoot s.o. dead : abattre qqn> **3** : jouer, marquer (aux sports) <to shoot a basket : marquer un panier> **4** FILM : tourner **5** PHOTOGRAPH : prendre (en photo) **6** DIRECT : décocher, lancer (un regard) — *vi* **1** : tirer <to shoot to kill : tirer pour tuer> **2** DART : se précipiter **3** FILM : tourner
shoot[2] *n* : rejeton *m,* pousse *f* (d'une plante)
shooter [ˈʃu:t̬ər] *n* : tireur *m,* -reuse *f*
shooting star *n* : étoile *f* filante
shop[1] [ˈʃap] *vi* **shopped; shopping** : faire des courses
shop[2] *n* **1** STORE : magasin *m,* boutique *f* **2** → **workshop**
shopkeeper [ˈʃapˌki:pər] *n* : commerçant *m,* -çante *f;* marchand *m,* -chande *f*
shoplift [ˈʃapˌlɪft] *vt* : voler à l'étalage
shoplifter [ˈʃapˌlɪftər] *n* : voleur *m,* -leuse *f* à l'étalage
shopper [ˈʃapər] *n* : personne *f* qui fait ses courses
shopping [ˈʃapɪŋ] *n* : courses *fpl,* magasinage *m Can* <to go shopping : faire des courses>
shopwindow [ˈʃapˌwɪndo:] *n* : vitrine *f,* devanture *f*
shore[1] [ˈʃor] *vt* **shored; shoring** *or* **to shore up** : étayer
shore[2] *n* **1** : rivage *m,* bord *m* <on shore : à terre> **2** PROP : étai *m*
shorebird [ˈʃorˌbərd] *n* : oiseau *m* des rivages
shoreline [ˈʃorˌlaɪn] *n* : côte *f,* littoral *m*
shorn → **shear**
short[1] [ˈʃort] *adv* : court, de court <to fall short of : ne pas répondre à, ne pas atteindre>
short[2] *adj* **1** : court <a short dress : une robe courte> **2** : petit, de petite taille (se dit d'une personne) **3** BRIEF : bref <for a short time : pendant peu de temps> **4** CURT : brusque **5** INSUFFICIENT : insuffisant
short[3] *n* **1** → **short circuit 2 shorts** *pl* : short *m* <tennis shorts : short de tennis> **3 in short** : en bref
shortage [ˈʃɔrtɪdʒ] *n* : manque *m,* insuffisance *f*
shortcake [ˈʃɔrtˌkeɪk] *n* : tarte *f* sablée
shortchange [ˈʃɔrtˈtʃeɪndʒ] *vt* **-changed; -changing 1** : ne pas rendre assez de monnaie à **2** SWINDLE : escroquer
short–circuit [ˈʃɔrtˈsərkət] *vt* : court-circuiter
short circuit *n* : court-circuit *m*
shortcoming [ˈʃɔrtˌkʌmɪŋ] *n* : défaut *m*
shortcut [ˈʃɔrtˌkʌt] *n* : raccourci *m*
shorten [ˈʃɔrtən] *vt* : raccourcir
shorthand [ˈʃɔrtˌhænd] *n* : sténographie *f*
short–lived [ˈʃɔrtˈlɪvd, -ˈlaɪvd] *adj* : éphémère
shortly [ˈʃɔrtli] *adv* **1** BRIEFLY : brièvement **2** SOON : bientôt
shortness [ˈʃɔrtnəs] *n* **1** : petite taille *f* **2** BREVITY : brièveté *f,* petite durée *f* **3** CURTNESS : brusquerie *f* **4 shortness of breath** : manque *m* de souffle
shortsighted [ˈʃɔrtˌsaɪt̬əd] → **nearsighted**
shortstop [ˈʃɔrtˌstap] *n* : arrêt-court *m Can*
shot[1] [ˈʃat] *n* **1** : tir *m,* coup *m* <to fire a shot : tirer un coup> **2** ATTEMPT : essai *m,* tentative *f* <to give it one's best shot : faire de son mieux> **3** PELLETS : plombs *mpl* **4** PHOTOGRAPH : photo *f* **5** INJECTION : piqûre *f* **6** MARKSMAN : tireur *m,* -reuse *f* **7** SCENE : plan *m* (au cinéma)
shot[2] → **shoot**[1]
shotgun [ˈʃatˌgʌn] *n* : fusil *m* de chasse
should [ˈʃʊd] *past of* **shall 1** (*used to express obligation*) : devoir <you should go : tu devrais y aller> **2** (*used to express probability*) <he should be here soon : il devrait être arrivé bientôt> **3** (*used in conditional sentences*) <if

he should die : s'il mourrait> <if you should change your mind : si vous changez d'avis>

shoulder[1] [ˈʃo:ldər] *vt* **1** PUSH : pousser **2 to shoulder the responsibility** : endosser

shoulder[2] *n* **1** : épaule *f* (d'une personne) **2** : accotement *m* (d'une chaussée) <soft shoulder : accotement non stabilisé>

shoulder blade *n* : omoplate *f*

shouldn't [ˈʃʊdənt] (*contraction of* **should not**) → **should**

shout[1] [ˈʃaʊt] *v* : crier, hurler

shout[2] *n* : cri *m*, hurlement *m*

shove[1] [ˈʃʌv] *v* **shoved; shoving** *vt* **1** PUSH : pousser **2** JOSTLE : bousculer — *vi* **to shove off** : s'en aller

shove[2] *n* : poussée *f*

shovel[1] [ˈʃʌvəl] *vt* **-veled** *or* **-velled; -veling** *or* **-velling** : pelleter, enlever à la pelle

shovel[2] *n* : pelle *f*

show[1] [ˈʃo:] *v* **showed; shown** [ˈʃo:n] *or* **showed; showing** *vt* **1** DISPLAY, PRESENT : montrer, présenter **2** REVEAL : révéler **3** DEMONSTRATE, TEACH : montrer, indiquer **4** PROVE : prouver, démontrer **5** CONDUCT : conduire <he showed her to the door : il l'a conduite à la porte> — *vi* : se voir

show[2] *n* **1** DEMONSTRATION : démonstration *f*, manifestation *f* <a show of strength : une manifestation de force> **2** EXHIBITION : exposition *f* **3** : spectacle *m* (de théâtre), émission *f* (de télévision, de radio, etc.), séance *f* (de cinéma)

showcase [ˈʃo:ˌkeɪs] *n* : vitrine *f*

showdown [ˈʃo:ˌdaʊn] *n* : confrontation *f*

shower[1] [ˈʃaʊər] *vt* **1** WET : doucher **2 to shower sth on** : faire pleuvoir qqch sur **3 to shower s.o. with** : couvrir qqn de <they showered him with gifts : ils l'ont couvert de cadeaux> — *vi* **1** BATHE : prendre une douche **2** RAIN : pleuvoir

shower[2] *n* **1** : averse *f* <snow showers : averses de neige> **2** : douche *f* <he's in the shower : il est sous la douche> **3** PARTY : fête *f* (donnée à l'occasion d'un mariage ou d'une naissance)

show off *vt* : faire valoir, faire parade de — *vi* : faire l'intéressant

show up *vi* **1** ARRIVE : arriver **2** APPEAR : ressortir, se voir — *vt* EXPOSE : démasquer

showy [ˈʃo:i] *adj* **showier; -est** : tapageur, voyant

shrapnel [ˈʃræpnəl] *ns & pl* : shrapnel *m*

shred[1] [ˈʃrɛd] *vt* **shredded; shredding** : déchirer, déchiqueter (le papier, le tissu), râper (les aliments)

shred[2] *n* **1** : lambeau *m* <to be in shreds : être en lambeaux> **2** BIT : brin *m*, parcelle *f* <not a shred of evidence : pas une parcelle d'évidence>

shrew [ˈʃru:] *n* **1** : musaraigne *f* (animal) **2** : mégère *f* (femme)

shrewd [ˈʃru:d] *adj* : habile, sagace

shrewdly [ˈʃru:dli] *adv* : avec perspicacité, avec sagacité

shrewdness [ˈʃru:dnəs] *n* : perspicacité *f*, astuce *f*, sagacité *f*

shriek[1] [ˈʃri:k] *vi* : hurler, crier, pousser un cri perçant

shriek[2] *n* : cri *m* perçant

shrill [ˈʃrɪl] *adj* : aigu, perçant, strident

shrilly [ˈʃrɪli] *adv* : d'un ton aigu

shrimp [ˈʃrɪmp] *n* : crevette *f*

shrine [ˈʃraɪn] *n* **1** TOMB : tombeau *m* (d'un saint) **2** SANCTUARY : sanctuaire *m*, lieu *m* saint

shrink [ˈʃrɪŋk] *v* **shrank** [ˈʃræŋk]; **shrunk** [ˈʃrʌŋk] *or* **shrunken** [ˈʃrʌŋkən]; **shrinking** *vi* **1** RECOIL : reculer **2** : rétrécir, fouler *Can* (se dit des vêtements) **3** DWINDLE : rétrécir, diminuer — *vt* : rétrécir

shrinkage [ˈʃrɪŋkɪdʒ] *n* : rétrécissement *m*

shrivel [ˈʃrɪvəl] *v* **-eled** *or* **-elled; -eling** *or* **-elling** *vt* : ratatiner, dessécher — *vi* : se ratatiner

shroud[1] [ˈʃraʊd] *vt* : envelopper, voiler

shroud[2] *n* **1** : linceul *m* **2** COVERING, VEIL : voile *m* <a shroud of mystery : un voile de mystère>

shrub [ˈʃrʌb] *n* : arbuste *m*, arbrisseau *m*

shrubbery [ˈʃrʌbəri] *n, pl* **-beries** : massif *m* d'arbustes, arbustes *mpl*

shrug[1] [ˈʃrʌg] *v* **shrugged; shrugging** *vt* : hausser (les épaules) — *vi* : hausser les épaules

shrug[2] *n* : haussement *m* d'épaules

shuck[1] [ˈʃʌk] *vt* : écosser (des légumes), écaler, décortiquer (des noix) <to shuck corn : enlever l'enveloppe de maïs>

shuck[2] *n* : cosse *f* (de légumes), écale *f* (de noix), enveloppe *f* (de maïs)

shudder[1] [ˈʃʌdər] *vi* : frissonner, frémir

shudder[2] *n* : frisson *m*, frémissement *m*

shuffle[1] [ˈʃʌfəl] *v* **-fled; -fling** *vt* MIX : mêler, battre (des cartes) — *vi* : marcher en traînant les pieds

shuffle[2] *n* **1** : pas *m* traînant **2** : battage *m* (des cartes) **3** JUMBLE : confusion *f*

shun [ˈʃʌn] *vt* **shunned; shunning** : éviter

shunt [ˈʃʌnt] *vt* : aiguiller, manœuvrer (un train)

shut[1] [ˈʃʌt] *v* **shut; shutting** *vt* **1** CLOSE : fermer **2 to shut in** *or* **to shut up** CONFINE : enfermer **3 to shut off** : couper **4 to shut out** EXCLUDE : exclure — *vi* **1** : (se) fermer <the door is shutting : la porte se ferme> **2** : fermer <the store shuts at noon : le magasin ferme à midi>

shut[2] *adj* : fermé

shut-in [ˈʃʌtˌɪn] *n* : invalide *mf*

shutout [ˈʃʌtˌaʊt] *n* : victoire *f* écrasante, blanchissage *m Can*

shutter [ˈʃʌt̬ər] *n* **1** : volet *m* (d'une fenêtre) **2** : obturateur *m* (d'un appareil photo)

shuttle[1] [ˈʃʌt̬əl] *v* **-tled; -tling** *vi* : faire la navette — *vt* : transporter

shuttle[2] *n* : navette *f*

shuttlecock [ˈʃʌt̬əlˌkɑk] *n* : volant *m*

shut up *vi* : se taire <shut up! : tais-toi!> — *vt* SILENCE : faire taire

shy[1] [ˈʃaɪ] *vi* **shied**; **shying** *or* **to shy away** : reculer

shy[2] *adj* **shier** *or* **shyer** [ˈʃaɪər]; **shiest** *or* **shyest** [ˈʃaɪəst] **1** TIMID : timide, gêné *Can* **2** WARY : peureux **3** (*indicating a lack*) <I'm two dollars shy of my goal : il me manque deux dollars pour atteindre mon objectif> <he's shy of ideas : il est à court d'idées>

shyly [ˈʃaɪli] *adv* : timidement

shyness [ˈʃaɪnəs] *n* : timidité *f*

sibling [ˈsɪblɪŋ] *n* : frère *m*, sœur *f*

sick [ˈsɪk] *adj* **1** ILL : malade **2** (*indicating nausea*) <to feel sick : avoir mal au cœur> <to get sick : vomir> **3 I'm sick of it** : j'en ai marre, j'en ai assez

sickbed [ˈsɪkˌbɛd] *n* : lit *m* de malade

sicken [ˈsɪkən] *vt* : rendre malade — *vi* : tomber malade

sickening [ˈsɪkənɪŋ] *adj* : écœurant, nauséabond

sickle [ˈsɪkəl] *n* : faucille *f*

sickly [ˈsɪkli] *adj* **sicklier**; **-est** : maladif

sickness [ˈsɪknəs] *n* : maladie *f*

side [ˈsaɪd] *n* **1** : côté *m* (d'une personne), flanc *m* (d'un animal) **2** EDGE : bord *m* **3** FACTION, GROUP : camp *m*, côté *m* <to take sides : prendre parti> **4** ASPECT : facette *f*, aspect *m*

sideboard [ˈsaɪdˌbord] *n* : buffet *m*

sideburns [ˈsaɪdˌbərnz] *npl* : favoris *mpl*

sided [ˈsaɪdəd] *adj* : à côtés <three-sided : à trois côtés>

side effect *n* : effet *m* secondaire

sideline [ˈsaɪdˌlaɪn] *n* **1** : activité *f* secondaire **2** : ligne *f* de côté, ligne *f* de touche (aux sports)

sidelong [ˈsaɪdˌlɔŋ] *adj* : de côté, oblique

sideshow [ˈsaɪdˌʃoː] *n* : attraction *f*

sidestep [ˈsaɪdˌstɛp] *v* **-stepped; -stepping** *vi* : faire un pas de côté — *vt* AVOID : éviter

sidetrack [ˈsaɪdˌtræk] *vt* : détourner l'attention de, faire dévier de son sujet

sidewalk [ˈsaɪdˌwɔk] *n* : trottoir *m*

sideways[1] [ˈsaɪdˌweɪz] *adv* : de côté, en travers, latéralement

sideways[2] *adj* : de côté, oblique, latéral

siding [ˈsaɪdɪŋ] *n* **1** : voie *f* de garage (pour trains) **2** : revêtement *m* extérieur (d'un édifice)

sidle [ˈsaɪdəl] *vi* **-dled; -dling** : avancer de biais, marcher de côté

siege [ˈsiːdʒ, ˈsiːʒ] *n* : siège *m*

siesta [siːˈɛstə] *n* : sieste *f*

sieve [ˈsɪv] *n* : tamis *m*, crible *m*

sift [ˈsɪft] *vt* **1** : tamiser, passer au tamis **2** *or* **to sift through** : passer au crible

sifter [ˈsɪftər] *n* : tamis *m*

sigh[1] [ˈsaɪ] *vi* : soupirer

sigh[2] *n* : soupir *m*

sight[1] [ˈsaɪt] *vt* : apercevoir

sight[2] *n* **1** : vue *f* <out of sight : hors de vue> <at first sight : à première vue> **2** SPECTACLE : spectacle *m* **3** : viseur *m* (d'une arme à feu)

sightless [ˈsaɪtləs] *adj* : aveugle

sightseer [ˈsaɪtˌsiːər] *n* : touriste *mf*

sign[1] [ˈsaɪn] *vt* **1** : signer <to sign a check : signer un chèque> **2** *or* **to sign on** HIRE : engager — *vi* **1** : signer **2** SIGNAL : faire signe **3** *or* **to sign on** JOIN : s'engager

sign[2] *n* **1** SYMBOL : signe *m* **2** GESTURE : geste *m*, signe *m* **3** : panneau *m*, enseigne *f* <traffic signs : panneaux de signalisation> <neon sign : enseigne au néon> **4** TRACE : trace *f*

signal[1] [ˈsɪgnəl] *v* **-naled** *or* **-nalled**; **-naling** *or* **-nalling** *vt* **1** INDICATE : signaler, indiquer **2** : envoyer un signal à <to signal s.o. : faire signe à qqn> — *vi* : donner un signal

signal[2] *adj* NOTABLE : insigne

signal[3] *n* : signal *m*

signature [ˈsɪgnəˌtʃʊr] *n* : signature *f*

signet [ˈsɪgnət] *n* : sceau *m*

significance [sɪgˈnɪfɪkənts] *n* **1** MEANING : signification *f*, sens *m* **2** IMPORTANCE : importance *f*, portée *f*

significant [sɪgˈnɪfɪkənt] *adj* **1** MEANINGFUL : significatif **2** IMPORTANT : important

significantly [sɪgˈnɪfɪkəntli] *adv* **1** CONSIDERABLY : considérablement, sensiblement **2** MEANINGFULLY : de façon significative

signify [ˈsɪgnəˌfaɪ] *vt* **-fied; -fying 1** INDICATE : signaler, indiquer **2** MEAN : signifier

sign language *n* : langage *m* des signes

signpost [ˈsaɪnˌpoːst] *n* **1** : poteau *m* indicateur **2** INDICATION : indication *f*, indice *m*

silence[1] [ˈsaɪlənts] *vt* **-lenced; -lencing** : faire taire, réduire au silence

silence[2] *n* : silence *m*

silent [ˈsaɪlənt] *adj* : silencieux — **silently** *adv*

silhouette[1] [ˌsɪləˈwɛt] *vt* **-etted; -etting** : silhouetter <to be silhouetted against : se découper contre, se profiler sur>

silhouette[2] *n* : silhouette *f*

silica [ˈsɪlɪkə] *n* : silice *f*

silicon [ˈsɪlɪkən, -ˌkɑn] *n* : silicium *m*

silk [ˈsɪlk] *n* : soie *f*

silken [ˈsɪlkən] *adj* **1** : de soie **2** SILKY : soyeux

silkworm ['sɪlk,wərm] *n* : ver *m* à soie
silky ['sɪlki] *adj* **silkier; -est** : soyeux
sill ['sɪl] *n* : rebord *m* (d'une fenêtre), seuil *m* (d'une porte)
silliness ['sɪlinəs] *n* : sottise *f*, stupidité *f*
silly ['sɪli] *adj* **sillier; -est 1** STUPID : sot, niais **2** RIDICULOUS : fou, ridicule
silo ['saɪ,lo:] *n, pl* **silos** : silo *m*
silt ['sɪlt] *n* : limon *m*
silver[1] ['sɪlvər] *adj* **1** : d'argent, en argent <a silver spoon : une cuillère d'argent> **2** → **silvery**
silver[2] *n* **1** : argent *m* **2** → **silverware 3** : couleur *f* argent
silverware ['sɪlvər,wær] *n* : argenterie *f*, coutellerie *f Can*
silvery ['sɪlvəri] *adj* : argenté
similar ['sɪmələr] *adj* : semblable, similaire
similarity [,sɪmə'lærəṭi] *n, pl* **-ties** : ressemblance *f*, similarité *f*
similarly ['sɪmələrli] *adv* : de la même façon
simile ['sɪmə,li:] *n* : comparaison *f*
simmer ['sɪmər] *vi* : cuire à feu doux, frémir — *vt* : faire cuire à feu doux, laisser frémir
simper[1] ['sɪmpər] *vi* : minauder
simper[2] *n* : sourire *m* affecté
simple ['sɪmpəl] *adj* **simpler; -plest** : simple
simpleton ['sɪmpəltən] *n* : nigaud *m*, -gaude *f*
simplicity [sɪm'plɪsəṭi] *n* : simplicité *f*
simplification [,sɪmpləfə'keɪʃən] *n* : simplification *f*
simplify ['sɪmplə,faɪ] *vt* **-fied; -fying** : simplifier
simply ['sɪmpli] *adv* : simplement
simulate ['sɪmjə,leɪt] *vt* **-lated; -lating** : simuler
simultaneous [,saɪməl'teɪniəs] *adj* : simultané — **simultaneously** *adv*
sin[1] ['sɪn] *vi* **sinned; sinning** : pécher
sin[2] *n* : péché *m*
since[1] ['sɪnts] *adv* **1** : depuis <they've been friends ever since : ils sont amis depuis> <she's since become mayor : elle est devenue maire depuis> **2 long since** : il y a longtemps **3 not long since** : il y a peu de temps
since[2] *conj* **1** : depuis que <since I've been here : depuis que je suis là> **2** BECAUSE, INASMUCH AS : puisque, comme
since[3] *prep* : depuis
sincere [sɪn'sɪr] *adj* **sincerer; -est** : sincère — **sincerely** *adv*
sincerity [sɪn'sɛrəṭi] *n* : sincérité *f*
sinew ['sɪn,ju:, 'sɪ,nu:] *n* **1** TENDON : tendon *m* **2** POWER : force *f*
sinewy ['sɪnjʊi, 'sɪnʊi] *adj* **1** : tendineux **2** MUSCLED : musclé
sinful ['sɪnfəl] *adj* : coupable, honteux
sing ['sɪŋ] *v* **sang** ['sæŋ] *or* **sung** ['sʌŋ]; **sung; singing** : chanter
Singaporean[1] [,sɪŋə'poriən, -'pɔr-] *adj* : singapourien
Singaporean[2] *n* : Singapourien *m*, -rienne *f*
singe ['sɪndʒ] *vt* **singed; singeing** : brûler légèrement, roussir
singer ['sɪŋər] *n* : chanteur *m*, -teuse *f*
single[1] ['sɪŋgəl] *vt* **-gled; -gling** *or* **to single out 1** SELECT : choisir, sélectionner **2** DISTINGUISH : distinguer
single[2] *adj* **1** SOLE : seul <not a single one : pas un seul> **2** UNMARRIED : célibataire
single[3] *n* **1** *or* **single room** : chambre *f* simple **2** : simple *m Can* (au baseball) **3 singles** *npl* : simple *m* (au tennis)
singly ['sɪŋgli] *adv* : séparément, individuellement
singular[1] ['sɪŋgjələr] *adj* **1** : singulier (en grammaire) **2** OUTSTANDING : remarquable **3** STRANGE : étrange
singular[2] *n* : singulier *m*
singularly ['sɪŋgjələrli] *adv* : singulièrement
sinister ['sɪnəstər] *adj* : sinistre
sink[1] ['sɪŋk] *v* **sank** ['sæŋk] *or* **sunk** ['sʌŋk]; **sunk; sinking** *vi* **1** : couler, sombrer <to sink into oblivion : sombrer dans l'oubli> **2** DROP, FALL : baisser **3** : s'enfoncer, s'affaisser <to sink into a chair : s'affaisser dans un fauteuil> — *vt* **1** : couler (un bateau, etc.) **2** LOWER : baisser **3** DRIVE, PLUNGE : enfoncer **4** EXCAVATE : creuser **5** INVEST : investir
sink[2] *n* **1 kitchen sink** : évier *m* **2 bathroom sink** : lavabo *m*
sinner ['sɪnər] *n* : pécheur *m*, -cheresse *f*
sinuous ['sɪnjʊəs] *adj* : sinueux
sinus ['saɪnəs] *n* : sinus *m*
sip[1] ['sɪp] *vt* **sipped; sipping** : boire à petites gorgées, siroter *fam*
sip[2] *n* : petite gorgée *f*
siphon[1] ['saɪfən] *vt* : siphonner
siphon[2] *n* : siphon *m*
sir ['sər] *n* **1** (*as a form of address*) : monsieur *m* <Dear Sir : Monsieur> <yes, sir! : oui, monsieur!> **2** (*in titles*) : sir *m*
sire[1] ['saɪr] *vt* **sired; siring** : engendrer
sire[2] *n* **1** : père *m* **2** (*as a form of address*) : sire *m*
siren ['saɪrən] *n* : sirène *f*
sirloin ['sər,lɔɪn] *n* : aloyau *m*
sirup → **syrup**
sisal ['saɪsəl, -zəl] *n* : sisal *m*
sissy ['sɪsi] *n, pl* **-sies** : poule *f* mouillée *fam*
sister ['sɪstər] *n* **1** : sœur *f* **2** *Brit* → **nurse**[2]
sisterhood ['sɪstər,hʊd] *n* **1** : communauté *f* de femmes (religieuses) **2** : solidarité *f* féminine
sister–in–law ['sɪstərɪn,lɔ] *n, pl* **sisters–in–law** : belle-sœur *f*
sisterly ['sɪstərli] *adj* : de sœur
sit ['sɪt] *v* **sat** ['sæt]; **sitting** *vi* **1** *or* **to sit down** : s'asseoir **2** ROOST : se percher

3 MEET : siéger, se réunir <the legislature is sitting : le corps législatif siège> 4 POSE : poser 5 REMAIN : rester <the mail sits unopened : le courrier reste fermé> 6 : se trouver, être <the house sits on a hill : la maison se trouve sur une colline> — *vt* 1 PLACE : placer, installer 2 SEAT : (faire) asseoir

site [ˈsaɪt] *n* : site *m*

sitter [ˈsɪt̬ər] → **baby–sitter**

sitting room → **living room**

situated [ˈsɪtʃʊˌeɪt̬əd] *adj* LOCATED : situé

situation [ˌsɪtʃʊˈeɪʃən] *n* 1 LOCATION : situation *f,* emplacement *m* 2 CIRCUMSTANCES : situation *f* 3 JOB : emploi *m,* situation *f*

six[1] [ˈsɪks] *adj* : six

six[2] *n* : six *m*

six–gun [ˈsɪksˌgʌn] *n* : revolver *m* (à six coups)

six–shooter [ˈsɪksˌʃu:t̬ər] → **six–gun**

sixteen[1] [sɪksˈti:n] *adj* : seize

sixteen[2] *n* : seize *m*

sixteenth[1] [sɪksˈti:nθ] *adj* : seizième

sixteenth[2] *n* 1 : seizième *mf* (dans une série) 2 : seizième *m* (en mathématiques) 3 (*used in dates*) <the sixteenth of May : le seize mai>

sixth[1] [ˈsɪksθ, ˈsɪkst] *adj* : sixième

sixth[2] *n* 1 : sixième *mf* (dans une série) 2 : sixième *m* (en mathématiques) 3 (*used in dates*) <the sixth of July : le six juillet>

sixtieth[1] [ˈsɪkst̬iəθ] *adj* : soixantième

sixtieth[2] *n* 1 : soixantième *mf* (dans une série) 2 : soixantième *m* (en mathématiques)

sixty[1] [ˈsɪkst̬i] *adj* : soixante

sixty[2] *n, pl* **-ties** : soixante *m*

sizable *or* **sizeable** [ˈsaɪzəbəl] *adj* : assez grand

size[1] [ˈsaɪz] *vt* **sized; sizing 1** : classer selon la grosseur **2 to size up** : jauger, évaluer

size[2] *n* 1 DIMENSIONS : grandeur *f,* taille *f* 2 : taille *f,* pointure *f* (de chaussures, de gants, etc.) <what is your size? : quelle est votre taille?> 3 MAGNITUDE : ampleur *f,* taille *f*

sizzle [ˈsɪzəl] *vi* **-zled; -zling** : grésiller

skate[1] [ˈskeɪt] *vi* **skated; skating** : patiner, faire du patin

skate[2] *n* 1 : patin *m* 2 : raie *f* (poisson)

skater [ˈskeɪt̬ər] *n* : patineur *m,* -neuse *f*

skein [ˈskeɪn] *n* : écheveau *m*

skeletal [ˈskɛlət̬əl] *adj* : squelettique

skeleton [ˈskɛlətən] *n* : squelette *m*

skeptic [ˈskɛptɪk] *n* : sceptique *mf*

skeptical [ˈskɛptɪkəl] *adj* : sceptique

skepticism [ˈskɛptəˌsɪzəm] *n* : scepticisme *m*

sketch[1] [ˈskɛtʃ] *vt* : esquisser — *vi* : faire des esquisses

sketch[2] *n* : esquisse *f,* croquis *m*

sketchy [ˈskɛtʃi] *adj* **sketchier; -est** : imprécis, vague

skewer[1] [ˈskju:ər] *vt* : embrocher

skewer[2] *n* : brochette *f*

ski[1] [ˈski:] *vi* **skied; skiing** : faire du ski

ski[2] *n, pl* **skis** : ski *m*

skid[1] [ˈskɪd] *vi* **skidded; skidding** : déraper

skid[2] *n* : dérapage *m*

skier [ˈski:ər] *n* : skieur *m,* skieuse *f*

skiff [ˈskɪf] *n* : skiff *m*

skilful *Brit* → **skillful**

skill [ˈskɪl] *n* 1 CAPABILITY : habileté *f,* adresse *f,* compétence *f* 2 TRADE : métier *m* 3 **skills** : capacités *fpl,* compétences *fpl*

skilled [ˈskɪld] *adj* : habile, expérimenté

skillet [ˈskɪlət] *n* : poêle *f* (à frire)

skillful *or Brit* **skilful** [ˈskɪlfəl] *adj* : habile, adroit

skim[1] [ˈskɪm] *vt* **skimmed; skimming 1** *or* **to skim off** : écumer, écrémer (le lait) 2 : parcourir (un livre, un journal, etc.) 3 : effleurer, raser (une surface)

skim[2] *adj* : écrémé <skim milk : lait écrémé>

skimp [ˈskɪmp] *vi* **to skimp on** : lésiner sur

skimpy [ˈskɪmpi] *adj* **skimpier; -est** : étriqué

skin[1] [ˈskɪn] *vt* **skinned; skinning 1** : écorcher, dépouiller 2 PEEL : peler, éplucher

skin[2] *n* 1 : peau *f* 2 RIND : pelure *f*

skin diving *n* : plongée *f* sous-marine

skinflint [ˈskɪnˌflɪnt] *n* : grippe-sou *m*

skinned [ˈskɪnd] *adj* 1 : à (la) peau <fair-skinned : à peau claire> 2 → **thick–skinned, thin–skinned**

skinny [ˈskɪni] *adj* **skinnier; -est** : maigre

skip[1] [ˈskɪp] *v* **skipped; skipping** *vi* : sautiller, gambader — *vt* MISS, OMIT : sauter

skip[2] *n* : petit saut *m,* petit bond *m*

skipper [ˈskɪpər] *n* : capitaine *m,* skipper *m*

skirmish[1] [ˈskərmɪʃ] *vi* : s'engager dans une escarmouche

skirmish[2] *n* : escarmouche *f*

skirt[1] [ˈskərt] *vt* : contourner

skirt[2] *n* : jupe *f*

skit [ˈskɪt] *n* : sketch *m* (satirique)

skittish [ˈskɪt̬ɪʃ] *adj* : ombrageux, difficile (se dit d'un cheval, etc.)

skulk [ˈskʌlk] *vi* : rôder

skull [ˈskʌl] *n* 1 : crâne *m* **2 skull and crossbones** : tête *f* de mort

skunk [ˈskʌŋk] *n* : mouffette *f*

sky [ˈskaɪ] *n, pl* **skies** : ciel *m*

skylark [ˈskaɪˌlɑrk] *n* : alouette *f* des champs

skylight [ˈskaɪˌlaɪt] *n* : lucarne *f*

skyline [ˈskaɪˌlaɪn] *n* : ligne *f* d'horizon

skyrocket [ˈskaɪˌrɑkət] *vi* : monter en flèche

skyscraper ['skaɪˌskreɪpər] *n* : gratte-ciel *m*
skyward ['skaɪwərd] *adv* : vers le ciel
slab ['slæb] *n* : dalle *f*, bloc *m*
slack[1] ['slæk] *adj* **1** CARELESS : négligent **2** LOOSE : mou, lâche **3** SLOW : calme, stagnant <business is slack : les affaires marchent au ralenti>
slack[2] *n* **1** LOOSENESS : mou *m* **2 slacks** *npl* : pantalon *m*
slacken ['slækən] *vt* : relâcher — *vi* : se relâcher, ralentir
slag ['slæg] *n* : scories *fpl*
slain → **slay**
slake ['sleɪk] *vt* **slaked; slaking** : étancher (la soif), assouvir (les désirs)
slam[1] ['slæm] *v* **slammed; slamming** *vt* **1** : claquer <he slammed the door : il a claqué la porte> **2** HIT : frapper — *vi* : claquer
slam[2] *n* : claquement *m*
slander[1] ['slændər] *vt* : calomnier, diffamer
slander[2] *n* : calomnie *f*, diffamation *f*
slanderous ['slændərəs] *adj* : calomnieux, diffamatoire
slang ['slæŋ] *n* : argot *m*
slant[1] ['slænt] *vi* : pencher, s'incliner — *vt* : faire pencher, incliner
slant[2] *n* **1** : pente *f*, inclinaison *f* **2** POINT OF VIEW : point *m* de vue, perspective *f*
slap[1] ['slæp] *vt* **slapped; slapping** : gifler, donner une claque à
slap[2] *n* : gifle *f*, claque *f*
slash[1] ['slæʃ] *vt* **1** CUT : entailler **2** REDUCE : réduire
slash[2] *n* GASH : entaille *f*
slat ['slæt] *n* : lame *f*, lamelle *f*
slate ['sleɪt] *n* **1** : ardoise *f* <a slate roof : un toit d'ardoise> **2** LIST : liste *f* (de candidats)
slaughter[1] ['slɔt̬ər] *vt* **1** : abattre (des animaux) **2** MASSACRE : massacrer (des personnes)
slaughter[2] *n* **1** : abattage *m* (d'animaux) **2** MASSACRE : massacre *m*
slaughterhouse ['slɔt̬ərˌhaʊs] *n* : abattoir *m*
Slav ['slɑv, 'slæv] *n* : Slave *mf*
slave[1] ['sleɪv] *vi* **slaved; slaving** : travailler comme un esclave, trimer *fam*
slave[2] *n* : esclave *mf*
slaver ['slævər, 'sleɪ-] *vi* : baver
slavery ['sleɪvəri] *n* : esclavage *m*
slavish ['sleɪvɪʃ] *adj* : servile
slay ['sleɪ] *vt* **slew** ['slu:]; **slain** ['sleɪn]; **slaying** : tuer
slayer ['sleɪər] *n* : tueur *m*, tueuse *f*
sleazy ['sli:zi] *adj* **sleazier; -est 1** SHODDY : de mauvaise qualité **2** SQUALID : miteux, sordide **3** DISREPUTABLE : mal famé
sled[1] ['slɛd] *vi* **sledded; sledding** : faire du traîneau, faire de la luge
sled[2] *n* : traîneau *m*, luge *f*
sledge ['slɛdʒ] *n* **1** : traîneau *m* **2** → **sledgehammer**
sledgehammer ['slɛdʒˌhæmər] *n* : masse *f*
sleek[1] ['sli:k] *vt or* **to sleek down** : se lisser (les cheveux, etc.)
sleek[2] *adj* : lisse
sleep[1] ['sli:p] *vi* **slept** ['slɛpt]; **sleeping** : dormir
sleep[2] *n* **1** : sommeil *m* **2 to go to sleep** : s'endormir
sleeper ['sli:pər] *n* : dormeur *m*, -meuse *f*
sleepily ['sli:pəli] *adv* : d'un air endormi
sleepiness ['sli:pinəs] *n* : somnolence *f*, torpeur *f*
sleepless ['sli:pləs] *adj* : sans sommeil
sleepwalker ['sli:pˌwɔkər] *n* : somnambule *mf*
sleepy ['sli:pi] *adj* **sleepier; -est 1** DROWSY : somnolent <to be sleepy : avoir sommeil> **2** QUIET : endormi, somnolent <a sleepy town : une ville somnolente>
sleet[1] ['sli:t] *vi* : grésiller
sleet[2] *n* : grésil *m*
sleeve ['sli:v] *n* : manche *f*
sleeveless ['sli:vləs] *adj* : sans manches
sleigh ['sleɪ] *n* : traîneau *m*, carriole *f* *Can*
sleight of hand ['slaɪt̬əv'hænd] *n* : tour *m* de passe-passe
slender ['slɛndər] *adj* **1** SLIM : mince **2** FEEBLE : faible <a slender hope : une faible espérance>
sleuth ['slu:θ] *n* : détective *m*, limier *m*
slew ['slu:] → **slay**
slice[1] ['slaɪs] *vt* **sliced; slicing** : trancher, découper en tranches
slice[2] *n* : tranche *f*, rondelle *f* (de saucisson)
slick[1] ['slɪk] *vt* : lisser
slick[2] *adj* **1** SLIPPERY : lisse **2** CRAFTY : habile
slicker ['slɪkər] *n* : imperméable *m*, ciré *m*
slide[1] ['slaɪd] *v* **slid** ['slɪd]; **sliding** ['slaɪdɪŋ] *vi* **1** : glisser **2** DECLINE : baisser <to let things slide : laisser aller> — *vt* : faire glisser
slide[2] *n* **1** SLIP : glissade *f* **2** : toboggan *m* (dans un terrain de jeu) **3** TRANSPARENCY : diapositive *f* **4** DECLINE : baisse *f*
slier, sliest → **sly**
slight[1] ['slaɪt] *vt* : offenser
slight[2] *adj* **1** SLENDER : mince **2** FRAIL : frêle **3** TRIFLING : léger <a slight injury : une légère blessure> **4** SMALL : menu <slight mishaps : menues méchancetés>
slight[3] *n* : affront *m*
slightly ['slaɪtli] *adv* **1** : légèrement, un peu, moindrement *Can* **2 slightly built** : mince

slim[1] [ˈslɪm] *v* **slimmed; slimming** *vi* : maigrir — *vt* : faire maigrir, amincir
slim[2] *adj* **slimmer; slimmest** **1** SLENDER : svelte, élancé, mince **2** FAINT, SLIGHT : faible, mince <she has only a slim chance : elle n'a que de faibles chances>
slime [ˈslaɪm] *n* **1** : bave *f* (sécrétée par un escargot) **2** MUD : vase *f,* boue *f*
slimy [ˈslaɪmi] *adj* **slimier; -est** : visqueux
sling[1] [ˈslɪŋ] *vt* **slung** [ˈslʌŋ]; **slinging** **1** THROW : lancer, jeter **2** HANG : suspendre
sling[2] *n* **1** : écharpe *f* <his arm is in a sling : son bras est en écharpe> **2** STRAP : bretelle *f* **3** → **slingshot**
slingshot [ˈslɪŋˌʃɑt] *n* : fronde *f,* lance-pierres *m*
slink [ˈslɪŋk] *vi* **slunk** [ˈslʌŋk]; **slinking** **1** : entrer ou sortir furtivement **2 to slink away** : s'éclipser, s'éloigner furtivement
slip[1] [ˈslɪp] *v* **slipped; slipping** *vi* **1** SLIDE : glisser <he slipped on the sidewalk : il a glissé sur le trottoir> **2** DECLINE : décliner **3 to let slip** : laisser échapper **4 to slip away** : partir furtivement — *vt* **1** PASS : glisser <I slipped him ten dollars : j'ai glissé dix dollars dans sa main> **2** ESCAPE : échapper à **3 it slipped his mind** : ça lui est sorti de la tête, ça lui a échappé
slip[2] *n* **1** : glissade *f* **2** BERTH : slip *m* (de bateaux) **3** MISTAKE : erreur *f* <a slip of the tongue : un lapsus> **4** PETTICOAT : jupon *m* **5** CUTTING : bouture *f* (d'une plante)
slipcover [ˈslɪpˌkʌvər] *n* : housse *f*
slipper [ˈslɪpər] *n* : pantoufle *f*
slipperiness [ˈslɪpərinəs] *n* : état *m* glissant
slippery [ˈslɪpəri] *adj* **slipperier; -est** **1** : glissant **2** TRICKY : rusé **3** EVASIVE : fuyant
slipshod [ˈslɪpˌʃɑd] *adj* : négligent
slip up *vi* : faire une gaffe
slit[1] [ˈslɪt] *vt* **slit; slitting** **1** SPLIT : fendre **2** CUT : couper, inciser
slit[2] *n* **1** OPENING : fente *f* **2** CUT : coupure *f,* incision *f*
slither [ˈslɪðər] *vi* : ramper
sliver [ˈslɪvər] *n* **1** : éclat *m* (de bois) **2** SLICE : petite tranche *f,* petit morceau *m*
slob [ˈslɑb] *n* : personne *f* débraillée
slobber[1] [ˈslɑbər] *vi* : baver
slobber[2] *n* : bave *f*
slogan [ˈsloːgən] *n* : slogan *m*
sloop [ˈsluːp] *n* : sloop *m*
slop[1] [ˈslɑp] *v* **slopped; slopping** *vt* : renverser, répandre — *vi or* **to slop over** : se répandre, déborder
slop[2] *n* : pâtée *f*
slope[1] [ˈsloːp] *vi* **sloped; sloping** : pencher, être en pente
slope[2] *n* : pente *f*
sloppy [ˈslɑpi] *adj* **sloppier; -est** **1** MUDDY : boueux, mouillé **2** UNTIDY : négligé **3** CARELESS : bâclé
slot [ˈslɑt] *n* **1** : fente *f* **2** GROOVE : rainure *f* **3** *or* **time slot** : créneau *m,* tranche *f* horaire
sloth [ˈslɔθ, ˈsloːθ] *n,* **1** LAZINESS : paresse *f* **2** : paresseux *m* (animal)
slouch[1] [ˈslaʊtʃ] *vi* : être avachi, ne pas se tenir droit
slouch[2] *n* **1 to walk with a slouch** : marcher le dos voûté **2 he's no slouch** : il n'est pas empoté
slough[1] [ˈslʌf] *vt or* **to slough off** : se débarrasser de
slough[2] [ˈsluː, ˈslaʊ] *n* SWAMP : bourbier *m,* marécage *m*
Slovak [ˈsloːˌvɑk, -ˌvæk] *or* **Slovakian** [ˌsloːˈvɑkiən, -ˈvæ-] *adj* : slovaque
Slovakian *n* : Slovaque *mf*
Slovene [ˈsloːˌviːn] *or* **Slovenian** [sloːˈviːniən] *adj* : slovène
Slovenian *n* : Slovène *mf*
slovenly [ˈslɑvənli, ˈslʌv-] *adj* **1** : négligé, sale **2** CARELESS : bâclé
slow[1] [ˈsloː] *vt* **1** : ralentir **2** DELAY : retarder — *vi* : ralentir
slow[2] *adv* : lentement
slow[3] *adj* **1** : lent <a slow process : un processus lent> <my watch is five minutes slow : ma montre retarde de cinq minutes> **2** STUPID : peu intelligent, lent **3** SLACK : calme, stagnant <sales are slow : les ventes ne marchent pas fort> **4** SLUGGISH : léthargique, lent
slowly [ˈsloːli] *adv* : lentement
slowness [ˈsloːnəs] *n* : lenteur *f,* lourdeur *m*
slowpoke [ˈsloːˌpoːk] *n* : traînard *m,* -narde *f;* lambineux *m,* -neuse *f* *Can fam*
sludge [ˈslʌdʒ] *n* : boue *f,* vase *f*
slug[1] [ˈslʌg] *vt* **slugged; slugging** : assommer
slug[2] *n* **1** : limace *f* (mollusque) **2** BULLET : balle *f* **3** TOKEN : jeton *m* **4** BLOW : coup *m*
sluggish [ˈslʌgɪʃ] *adj* : léthargique, lent
sluice[1] [ˈsluːs] *vt* **sluiced; sluicing** *or* **to sluice down** : laver à grande eau
sluice[2] *n* : vanne *f*
slum [ˈslʌm] *n* : taudis *m,* quartier *m* pauvre
slumber[1] [ˈslʌmbər] *vi* : dormir, sommeiller
slumber[2] *n* : sommeil *m*
slump[1] [ˈslʌmp] *vi* **1** DECLINE, DROP : baisser **2** SLOUCH : être avachi
slump[2] *n* : baisse *f,* crise *f* (économique)
slung → **sling**[1]
slunk → **slink**
slur[1] [ˈslər] *vt* **slurred; slurring** **1** : mal articuler (les mots) **2** : lier (en musique)

slur[2] *n* : affront *m,* insulte *f* <racial slur : insulte raciste>
slurp [ˈslərp] *v* : boire avec bruit
slush [ˈslʌʃ] *n* : neige *f* fondue, sloche *f Can,* gadoue *f Can*
slut [ˈslʌt] *n* PROSTITUTE : prostituée *f*
sly [ˈslaɪ] *adj* **slier** [ˈslaɪər]; **sliest** [ˈslaɪəst] **1** CUNNING : rusé **2** UNDERHANDED : sournois
slyly [ˈslaɪli] *adv* **1** CUNNINGLY : de façon rusée **2** UNDERHANDEDLY : sournoisement
slyness [ˈslaɪnəs] *n* CUNNING : ruse *f*
smack[1] [ˈsmæk] *vi* **to smack of** : sentir — *vt* **1** KISS : donner un baiser à **2** SLAP : gifler, claquer **3 to smack one's lips** : se lécher les babines
smack[2] *adv* **smack in the middle** : en plein milieu
smack[3] *n* **1** TASTE, TRACE : soupçon *m* **2** KISS : gros baiser *m* **3** SLAP : gifle *f,* claque *f*
small [ˈsmɔl] *adj* **1** : petit <a small house : une petite maison> <small change : petite monnaie> **2** TRIVIAL : insignifiant, peu important
smallness [ˈsmɔlnəs] *n* : petitesse *f*
smallpox [ˈsmɔlˌpɑks] *n* : variole *f*
smart[1] [ˈsmɑrt] *vi* **1** STING : brûler, piquer **2** : être piqué au vif (par l'insulte)
smart[2] *adj* **1** INTELLIGENT : intelligent **2** STYLISH : chic
smart[3] *n* : douleur *f* cuisante
smartly [ˈsmɑrtli] *adv* **1** CLEVERLY : habilement, astucieusement **2** STYLISHLY : avec beaucoup de chic **3** QUICKLY : vivement
smartness [ˈsmɑrtnəs] *n* **1** INTELLIGENCE : intelligence *f* **2** ELEGANCE : élégance *f*
smash[1] [ˈsmæʃ] *vt* **1** BREAK : briser **2** CRASH : écraser **3** SHATTER : fracasser, briser — *vi* **1** SHATTER : se briser, se fracasser **2** COLLIDE, CRASH : s'écraser
smash[2] *n* **1** BLOW : coup *m,* gifle *f* **2** COLLISION : collision *f* **3** BANG, CRASH : fracas *m*
smattering [ˈsmæt̬ərɪŋ] *n* : notions *fpl* vagues, rudiments *mpl* <a smattering of French : quelques notions de français> <a smattering of spectators : quelques spectateurs>
smear[1] [ˈsmɪr] *vt* **1** SMUDGE : faire des taches sur, barbouiller **2** SLANDER : diffamer
smear[2] *n* **1** STAIN : tache *f* **2** SLANDER : diffamation *f*
smell[1] [ˈsmɛl] *v* **smelled** [ˈsmɛld] *or* **smelt** [ˈsmɛlt]; **smelling** *vt* : sentir <to smell danger : sentir le danger> — *vi* : sentir <to smell good : sentir bon>
smell[2] *n* **1** : odorat *m* (sens) **2** ODOR : odeur *f*
smelly [ˈsmɛli] *adj* **smellier; -est** : malodorant <it's smelly in here : ça sent mauvais ici>
smelt[1] [ˈsmɛlt] *vt* : fondre
smelt[2] *n, pl* **smelts** *or* **smelt** : éperlan *m* (poisson)
smile[1] [ˈsmaɪl] *vi* **smiled; smiling** : sourire
smile[2] *n* : sourire *m*
smirk[1] [ˈsmərk] *vi* : sourire d'un air satisfait
smirk[2] *n* : petit sourire *m* satisfait
smite [ˈsmaɪt] *vt* **smote** [ˈsmoːt]; **smitten** [ˈsmɪtən] *or* **smote; smiting 1** STRIKE : frapper **2 to be smitten with** : être pris de <smitten with remorse : accablé de remords>
smith [ˈsmɪθ] *n* : forgeron *m*
smithy [ˈsmɪθi] *n, pl* **smithies** : forge *f*
smock [ˈsmɑk] *n* : blouse *f,* sarrau *m*
smog [ˈsmɑg, ˈsmɔg] *n* : smog *m*
smoke[1] [ˈsmoːk] *v* **smoked; smoking** *vt* : fumer <to smoke a cigarette : fumer une cigarette> — *vi* : fumer
smoke[2] *n* : fumée *f,* boucane *f Can*
smoke detector *n* : détecteur *m* de fumée
smoker [ˈsmoːkər] *n* : fumeur *m,* -meuse *f*
smokestack [ˈsmoːkˌstæk] *n* : cheminée *f*
smoky [ˈsmoːki] *adj* **smokier; -est** : enfumé
smolder [ˈsmoːldər] *vi* : couver
smooth[1] [ˈsmuːð] *vt* : lisser
smooth[2] *adj* **1** : lisse <smooth skin : peau lisse> **2** CALM : calme <a smooth landing : un atterrissage en douceur> **3** MILD : doux **4** FLOWING : fluide <smooth writing : écriture fluide>
smoothly [ˈsmuːðli] *adv* **1** GENTLY, SOFTLY : doucement **2** EASILY : facilement
smoothness [ˈsmuːðnəs] *n* : douceur *f*
smother [ˈsmʌðər] *vt* **1** SUFFOCATE : étouffer **2** COVER : recouvrir (un feu) — *vi* : être étouffé
smudge[1] [ˈsmʌdʒ] *v* **smudged; smudging** *vt* : salir, faire des taches sur — *vi* : se salir, s'étaler
smudge[2] *n* : tache *f,* bavure *f*
smug [ˈsmʌg] *adj* **smugger; smuggest** : suffisant, content de soi
smuggle [ˈsmʌgəl] *v* **-gled; -gling** *vt* : faire passer en contrebande — *vi* : faire de la contrebande
smuggler [ˈsmʌgələr] *n* : contrebandier *m,* -dière *f*
smugly [ˈsmʌgli] *adv* : avec suffisance
smut [ˈsmʌt] *n* **1** SOOT : tache *f* de suie **2** OBSCENITY : cochonnerie *f* **3** FUNGUS : charbon *m* (du blé)
smutty [ˈsmʌti] *adj* **smuttier; -est 1** SOOTY : noirci, sali **2** OBSCENE : cochon, ordurier
snack [ˈsnæk] *n* : casse-croûte *m*
snag[1] [ˈsnæg] *v* **snagged; snagging** *vt* : accrocher — *vi* : s'accrocher
snag[2] *n* : accroc *m*

snail ['sneɪl] *n* : escargot *m*
snake ['sneɪk] *n* : serpent *m*
snakebite ['sneɪk,baɪt] *n* : morsure *f* de serpent
snap[1] ['snæp] *v* **snapped; snapping** *vi* **1** CLICK : claquer **2** : essayer de mordre (se dit d'un chien, etc.) **3** BREAK : se casser, se briser **4** : parler d'un ton brusque — *vt* **1** CLICK : faire claquer **2** BREAK : casser, briser **3 to snap up** : arracher, saisir
snap[2] *n* **1** CLICK : claquement *m* **2** BREAK : cassure *f* **3** FASTENER : bouton-pression *m* **4** CINCH : quelque chose *f* de facile <it's a snap! : c'est du gâteau!>
snapdragon ['snæp,drægən] *n* : gueule-de-loup *f*
snapper ['snæpər] *n* : lutjanidé *m* (poisson)
snappy ['snæpi] *adj* **snappier; -est 1** FAST : vite <make it snappy! : fais ça vite!> **2** LIVELY : vif **3** STYLISH : chic
snapshot ['snæp,ʃɑt] *n* : instantané *m*
snare[1] ['snær] *vt* **snared; snaring** : attraper, prendre au piège
snare[2] *n* : piège *m*, collet *m*
snare drum *n* : caisse *f* claire
snarl[1] ['snɑrl] *vi* **1** TANGLE : enchevêtrer **2** GROWL : grogner
snarl[2] *n* **1** TANGLE : enchevêtrement *m* **2** GROWL : grognement *m*
snatch[1] ['snætʃ] *vt* : saisir
snatch[2] *n* : fragment *m*, bribe *f* <snatches of conversation : bribes de conversation>
sneak[1] ['sni:k] *vi* : se glisser, se faufiler — *vt* : faire furtivement <to sneak a look : jeter un coup d'œil> <he sneaked a smoke : il a fumé en cachette>
sneak[2] *n* : sournois *m*, -noise *f;* cafard *m*, -farde *f France fam*
sneakers ['sni:kərz] *npl* : tennis *mpl France*, espadrilles *fpl Can*
sneaky ['sni:ki] *adj* **sneakier; -est** : sournois
sneer[1] ['snɪr] *vi* : ricaner, sourire d'un air méprisant
sneer[2] *n* : ricanement *m*
sneeze[1] ['sni:z] *vi* **sneezed; sneezing** : éternuer
sneeze[2] *n* : éternuement *m*
snicker[1] ['snɪkər] *vi* : rire doucement, rire dans sa barbe
snicker[2] *n* : rire *m* étouffé
snide ['snaɪd] *adj* : narquois
sniff[1] ['snɪf] *vi* **1** : renifler **2 to sniff at** : dédaigner, faire la grimace à — *vt* **1** SMELL : sentir, humer **2 to sniff out** : flairer
sniff[2] *n* : reniflement *m*
sniffle[1] ['snɪfəl] *vi* **-fled; -fling** : renifler
sniffle[2] *n* **1** SNIFF : reniflement *m* **2 sniffles** *npl* : petit rhume *m* <to have the sniffles : être enrhumé>
snip[1] ['snɪp] *vt* **snipped; snipping** : couper
snip[2] *n* **1** CUT : coupure *f* **2** FRAGMENT, PIECE : petit bout *m*
snipe[1] ['snaɪp] *vi* **sniped; sniping 1 to snipe at** SHOOT : tirer sur **2 to snipe at** CRITICIZE : critiquer par en-dessous
snipe[2] *n, pl* **snipes** *or* **snipe** : bécassine *f* (oiseau)
sniper ['snaɪpər] *n* : tireur *m* embusqué
snivel ['snɪvəl] *vi* **-eled** *or* **-elled; -eling** *or* **-elling 1** → **snuffle 2** WHINE : pleurnicher *fam*, chialer *fam*
snob ['snɑb] *n* : snob *mf*
snobbery ['snɑbəri] *n, pl* **-beries** : snobisme *m*
snobbish ['snɑbɪʃ] *adj* : snob
snobbishness ['snɑbɪʃnəs] *n* : snobisme *m*
snoop[1] ['snu:p] *vi* **1 to snoop around** : fouiner, fureter **2 to snoop on s.o.** : espionner qqn
snoop[2] *n* **1** : espion *m*, -pionne *f;* fouineur *m*, -neuse *f* **2 to have a snoop around** : fureter discrètement dans
snooze[1] ['snu:z] *vi* **snoozed; snoozing** : sommeiller
snooze[2] *n* : petit somme *m*
snore[1] ['snor] *vi* **snored; snoring** : ronfler
snore[2] *n* : ronflement *m*
snort[1] ['snɔrt] *vi* : grogner (se dit d'une personne ou d'un cochon), s'ébrouer (se dit d'un cheval)
snort[2] *n* : grognement *m*, ébrouement *m*
snout ['snaʊt] *n* : museau *m*, groin *m* (d'un porc)
snow[1] ['sno:] *vi* : neiger
snow[2] *n* : neige *f*
snowball ['sno:,bɔl] *n* : boule *f* de neige, pelote *f* de neige *Can*
snowbank ['sno:,bæŋk] *n* : congère *f France*, banc *m* de neige *Can*
snowblower ['sno:,blo:ər] *n* : souffleuse *f* (à neige) *Can*
snowdrift ['sno:,drɪft] *n* : congère *f France*, banc *m* de neige *Can*
snowfall ['sno:,fɔl] *n* : chute *f* de neige
snowplow ['sno:,plaʊ] *n* : chasse-neige *m*, gratte *f Can*
snowshoes ['sno:,ʃu:z] *npl* : raquettes *fpl*
snowstorm ['sno:,stɔrm] *n* : tempête *f* de neige, bordée *f* de neige *Can*
snowy ['sno:i] *adj* **snowier; -est** : neigeux
snub[1] ['snʌb] *vt* **snubbed; snubbing** : rabrouer
snub[2] *n* : rebuffade *f*
snub–nosed ['snʌb,no:zd] *adj* : au nez retroussé
snuff[1] ['snʌf] *vt* **1** EXTINGUISH : moucher **2** SNIFF : renifler
snuff[2] *n* : tabac *m* à priser
snuffle ['snʌfəl] *vi* **-fled; -fling** : renifler

snug [ˈsnʌg] *adj* **snugger; snuggest 1** COMFORTABLE : confortable **2** TIGHT : bien ajusté

snuggle [ˈsnʌgəl] *vi* **-gled; -gling** : se pelotonner

snugly [ˈsnʌgli] *adv* **1** COMFORTABLY : confortablement **2** WELL : bien <the dress fits snugly : la robe est parfaitement ajustée>

so[1] [ˈso:] *adv* **1** (*referring to something indicated or suggested*) <do you think so? : tu crois?> <so be it : ainsi soit-il> <I told her so : je le lui ai dit> **2** : si, tellement <it's so hot : il fait si chaud> <they were so late : ils ont été tellement en retard> **3** ALSO : aussi <so do I : moi aussi> **4** THUS : ainsi <it would seem so : il paraîtrait ainsi> <do it like so : fais-le ainsi> **5** AS : aussi <he'd never been so happy : il n'a jamais été aussi content> **6 is that so?** : c'est vrai?

so[2] *conj* **1** THEREFORE : donc, alors **2** *or* **so that** : afin de **3 so what?** : et alors?

soak[1] [ˈso:k] *vi* : tremper — *vt* **1** WET : tremper **2** IMMERSE : faire tremper (la lessive, etc.) **3 to soak up** ABSORB : absorber

soak[2] *n* : trempage *m*

soap[1] [ˈso:p] *vt* : savonner

soap[2] *n* : savon *m*

soapsuds [ˈso:pˌsʌdz] → **suds**

soapy [ˈso:pi] *adj* **soapier; -est** : savonneux

soar [ˈsor] *vi* **1** GLIDE : planer **2** TOWER : se dresser (vers le ciel), s'élever **3** RISE : monter (en flèche) <prices have soared : les prix ont monté> <my spirits soared : mon moral est remonté en flèche>

sob[1] [ˈsɑb] *vi* **sobbed; sobbing** : sangloter

sob[2] *n* : sanglot *m*

sober [ˈso:bər] *adj* **1** : sobre <he's perfectly sober : il est parfaitement sobre> **2** SERIOUS : sérieux

soberly [ˈso:bərli] *adv* **1** : avec sobriété, sobrement **2** SERIOUSLY : sérieusement

sobriety [səˈbraɪət̬i, so-] *n* : sobriété *f*

soccer [ˈsɑkər] *n* : football *m France,* soccer *m Can*

sociability [ˌso:ʃəˈbɪlət̬i] *n* : sociabilité *f*

sociable [ˈso:ʃəbəl] *adj* : sociable

social[1] [ˈso:ʃəl] *adj* : social — **socially** *adv*

social[2] *n* **1** PARTY : soirée *f* **2** GATHERING : réunion *f*

socialism [ˈso:ʃəˌlɪzəm] *n* : socialisme *m*

socialist[1] [ˈso:ʃəlɪst] *adj* : socialiste

socialist[2] *n* : socialiste *mf*

socialize [ˈso:ʃəˌlaɪz] *v* **-ized; -izing** *vt* : socialiser — *vi* : fréquenter des gens

social work *n* : travail *m* social

society [səˈsaɪət̬i] *n, pl* **-eties 1** COMPANIONSHIP : compagnie *f* **2** : société *f* <a democratic society : une société démocratique> <high society : haute société> **3** ASSOCIATION : association *f,* société *f*

sociological [ˌso:siəˈlɑdʒɪkəl] *adj* : sociologique

sociologist [ˌso:siˈɑlədʒɪst] *n* : sociologue *mf*

sociology [ˌso:siˈɑlədʒi] *n* : sociologie *f*

sock[1] [ˈsɑk] *vt* : donner un coup de poing à

sock[2] *n* **1** PUNCH : coup *m,* beigne *f fam* **2** *pl* **socks** *or* **sox** : chaussette *f*

socket [ˈsɑkət] *n* **1** : cavité *f* **2** *or* **electric socket** : prise *f* de courant **3 eye socket** : orbite *f*

sod[1] [ˈsɑd] *vt* **sodded; sodding** : gazonner

sod[2] *n* TURF : gazon *m,* motte *f* (de gazon)

soda [ˈso:də] *n* **1** *or* **soda pop** : boisson *f* gazeuse, soda *m France,* liqueur *f Can* **2** : soude *f* <baking soda : bicarbonate de soude>

sodden [ˈsɑdən] *adj* SOGGY : trempé, détrempé

sodium [ˈso:diəm] *n* : sodium *m*

sofa [ˈso:fə] *n* : canapé *m*

soft [ˈsɔft] *adj* **1** : mou <a soft pillow : un mol oreiller> **2** SMOOTH : doux <soft to the touch : doux au toucher> <a soft ride : un roulement doux>

softball [ˈsɔftˌbɔl] *n* : balle-molle *f Can,* softball *m Can*

soft drink *n* : boisson *f* non alcoolisée, boisson *f* gazeuse

soften [ˈsɔfən] *vt* : amollir, adoucir (la peau), ramollir (le beurre, etc.) — *vi* : s'adoucir, se ramollir

softly [ˈsɔftli] *adv* : doucement, mollement

softness [ˈsɔftnəs] *n* : douceur *f,* mollesse *f*

software [ˈsɔftˌwær] *n* : logiciel *m,* software *m*

soggy [ˈsɑgi] *adj* **soggier; -est** : détrempé, trempé

soil[1] [ˈsɔɪl] *vt* : salir, souiller <he soiled his hands : il s'est sali les mains> — *vi* : se salir

soil[2] *n* **1** DIRT, EARTH : sol *m,* terre *f* **2** COUNTRY : sol *m,* terre *f* <her native soil : sa terre natale>

sojourn[1] [ˈso:ˌdʒərn, so:ˈdʒərn] *vi* : séjourner

sojourn[2] *n* : séjour *m*

solace [ˈsɑləs] *n* : consolation *f*

solar [ˈso:lər] *adj* : solaire

sold → **sell**

solder[1] [ˈsɑdər, ˈsɔ-] *vt* : souder

solder[2] *n* : soudure *f*

soldier[1] [ˈso:ldʒər] *vi* **1** : être soldat **2 to soldier on** : persévérer

soldier[2] *n* : soldat *m,* femme soldat *f,* militaire *m*

sole[1] [ˈso:l] *adj* : seul

sole[2] *n* **1** : plante *f* (du pied) **2** : sole *f* (poisson)

solemn ['sɑləm] *adj* : solonnel — **solemnly** *adv*
solemnity [sə'lɛmnət̬i] *n, pl* **-ties** : solennité *f*
solicit [sə'lɪsət] *vt* : solliciter
solicitous [sə'lɪsət̬əs] *adj* : plein de sollicitude
solicitude [sə'lɪsə,tu:d, -,tju:d] *n* : sollicitude *f*
solid[1] ['sɑləd] *adj* **1** : solide <solid food : aliments solides> **2** : plein, massif <solid gold : or massif> <a solid rubber ball : un ballon plein en caoutchouc> **3** CONTINUOUS : de suite <two solid hours : deux heures de suite>
solid[2] *n* : solide *m*
solidarity [,sɑlə'dærət̬i] *n* : solidarité *f*
solidify [sə'lɪdə,faɪ] *v* **-fied; -fying** *vt* : solidifier — *vi* : se solidifier
solidity [sə'lɪdət̬i] *n, pl* **-ties** : solidité *f*
solidly ['sɑlədli] *adv* : solidement
soliloquy [sə'lɪləkwi] *n, pl* **-quies** : soliloque *m*
solitaire ['sɑlə,tɛr] *n* : solitaire *m*
solitary ['sɑlə,tɛri] *adj* **1** ALONE : solitaire **2** SINGLE : seul
solitude ['sɑlə,tu:d, -,tju:d] *n* : solitude *f*
solo[1] ['so:,lo:] *vi* : jouer en solo
solo[2] *adv* : en solo
solo[3] *adj* : solo
solo[4] *n, pl* **solos** : solo *m*
soloist ['so:,loɪst] *n* : soliste *mf*
solstice ['sɑlstɪs] *n* : solstice *m*
soluble ['sɑljəbəl] *adj* : soluble
solution [sə'lu:ʃən] *n* : solution *f*
solve ['sɑlv] *vt* **solved; solving** : résoudre, trouver la solution de
solvency ['sɑlvən*t*si] *n* : solvabilité *f*
solvent[1] ['sɑlvənt] *adj* : solvable
solvent[2] *n* : solvant *m,* dissolvant *m*
Somali[1] [so'mɑli, sə-] *adj* : somali
Somali[2] *n* : Somali *m,* -lie *f*
Somalian[1] [so'mɑliən, -ljən, sə-] *adj* : somalien
Somalian[2] *n* : Somalien *m,* -lienne *f*
somber ['sɑmbər] *adj* : sombre
sombrero [səm'brɛr,o:] *n, pl* **-ros** : sombrero *m*
some[1] ['sʌm] *adj* **1** (*being an amount*) : de <some water : de l'eau> <do you want some apples? : voulez-vous des pommes?> **2** (*being an unspecified or indefinite number*) : certains <he read some books : il a lu certains livres> **3** SEVERAL : quelques <some good candidates : quelques bons candidats> <some years ago : il y a quelques années> **4** (*being an unspecified individual or thing*) : un, une, quelque <some lady stopped me : une dame m'a arrêté> <some distant galaxy : quelque galaxie lointaine>
some[2] *pron* **1** : certains *mpl,* certaines *fpl,* quelques-uns *mpl,* quelques-unes *fpl* <some left, others stayed : certains sont partis, d'autres sont restés> **2** : un peu, en <there's some left : il en reste un peu> <do you want some? : en voulez-vous?>
somebody ['sʌmbədi, -,bɑdi] *pron* : quelqu'un, on
someday ['sʌm,deɪ] *adv* : un jour
somehow ['sʌm,haʊ] *adv* **1** : de quelque manière <somehow or other : d'une manière ou d'une autre> **2** : pour quelque raison <somehow I don't trust him : pour quelque raison je ne lui fais pas confiance>
someone ['sʌm,wʌn] *pron* : quelqu'un, on
somersault[1] ['sʌmər,sɔlt] *vi* : faire une culbute
somersault[2] *n* : culbute *f*
something ['sʌmθɪŋ] *pron* : quelque chose <something happened : quelque chose est arrivé> <something else : autre chose>
sometime ['sʌm,taɪm] *adv* **1** (*indicating a time in the future*) : un jour, un de ces jours <you should try it sometime : tu devrais l'essayer un jour> **2** (*indicating a time in the past*) <she called sometime last week : elle a téléphoné au cours de la semaine passée>
sometimes ['sʌm,taɪmz] *adv* : quelquefois, parfois
somewhat ['sʌm,hwʌt, -,hwɑt] *adv* : un peu, quelque peu, assez
somewhere ['sʌm,*h*wɛr] *adv* **1** : quelque part **2 somewhere else** : ailleurs, autre part
son ['sʌn] *n* : fils *m*
sonar ['so:,nɑr] *n* : sonar *m*
sonata [sə'nɑt̬ə] *n* : sonate *f*
song ['sɔŋ] *n* : chanson *f*
songbird ['sɔŋ,bərd] *n* : oiseau *m* chanteur
sonic ['sɑnɪk] *adj* : sonique
son–in–law ['sʌnɪn,lɔ] *n, pl* **sons–in–law** : gendre *m,* beau-fils *m*
sonnet ['sɑnət] *n* : sonnet *m*
sonorous ['sɑnərəs, sə'norəs] *adj* : sonore
soon ['su:n] *adv* **1** : bientôt <he'll arrive soon : il arrivera bientôt> <soon after : peu après> **2** QUICKLY : vite <as soon as possible : le plus tôt possible>
soot ['sʊt, 'su:t, 'sʌt] *n* : suie *f*
soothe ['su:ð] *v* **soothed; soothing 1** CALM : calmer, apaiser **2** RELIEVE : soulager
soothsayer ['su:θ,seɪər] *n* : devin *m,* -vineresse *f*
sooty ['sʊt̬i, 'su:-, 'sʌ-] *adj* **sootier; -est** : couvert de suie
sop[1] ['sɑp] *vt* **sopped; sopping 1** SOAK : tremper **2 to sop up** : éponger
sop[2] *n* : concession *f* (symbolique) <as a sop to his pride : pour flatter son orgueil>
sophisticated [sə'fɪstə,keɪt̬əd] *adj* **1** COMPLEX : compliqué **2** WORLDLY : raffiné, sophistiqué
sophistication [sə,fɪstə'keɪʃən] *n* **1** WORLDLINESS : sophistication *f* **2**

COMPLEXITY : sophistication *f,* perfectionnement *m* **3** REFINEMENT, URBANITY : raffinement *m*

sophomore ['sɑf,mor, 'sɑfə,mor] *n* : étudiant *m,* -diante *f* de seconde année

soporific [,sɑpə'rɪfɪk, ,so:-] *adj* : soporifique

soprano [sə'præ,no:] *n, pl* **-nos** : soprano *mf* (personne), soprano *m* (voix)

sorcerer ['sɔrsərər] *n* : sorcier *m*

sorceress ['sɔrsərəs] *n* : sorcière *f*

sorcery ['sɔrsəri] *n* : sorcellerie *f*

sordid ['sɔrdɪd] *adj* : sordide

sore[1] ['sor] *adj* **sorer; sorest 1** PAINFUL : douloureux **2** GREAT : grand <to be in sore need of : avoir grand besoin de> **3** ANGRY : fâché, vexé

sore[2] *n* : plaie *f*

sorely ['sorli] *adv* : gravement, grandement, extrêmement

soreness ['sornəs] *n* : douleur *f*

sorghum ['sɔrgəm] *n* : sorgho *m*

sorority [sə'rɔrəṭi] *n, pl* **-ties** : club *m* d'étudiantes

sorrel ['sɔrəl] *n* **1** : oseille *f* (plante) **2** : brun *m* roux (couleur)

sorrow ['sɑr,o:] *n* : chagrin *m,* peine *f,* tristesse *f*

sorrowful ['sɑrofəl] *adj* : triste

sorrowfully ['sɑrofəli] *adv* : tristement

sorry ['sɑri] *adj* **sorrier; -est 1** PITIFUL : piteux <in a sorry state : dans un piteux état> **2 to be sorry** : être désolé, regretter <I'm sorry : je suis désolé> **3 to feel sorry for** : plaindre <I don't feel sorry for him : je ne le plains pas>

sort[1] ['sɔrt] *vt* : trier

sort[2] *n* **1** KIND : genre *m,* sorte *f* **2 out of sorts** : de mauvaise humeur

sortie ['sɔrṭi, sɔr'ti:] *n* : sortie *f*

SOS [,ɛs,o:'ɛs] *n* : S.O.S. *m*

so–so[1] ['so:'so:] *adv* : comme ci comme ça

so–so[2] *adj* : moyen

soufflé [su:'fleɪ] *n* : soufflé *m*

sought → **seek**

soul ['so:l] *n* **1** SPIRIT : âme *f* **2** ESSENCE : essence *f* **3** PERSON : âme *f,* personne *f* <not a soul : pas âme qui vive>

soulful ['so:lfəl] *adj* : attendrissant, émouvant, sentimental

sound[1] ['saʊnd] *vt* **1** : sonner <to sound the alarm : sonner l'alarme> <to sound the horn : klaxonner> **2** *or* **to sound out** PROBE : sonder — *vi* **1** : sonner **2** SEEM : sembler, paraître

sound[2] *adj* **1** HEALTHY : sain <safe and sound : sain et sauf> **2** FIRM, SOLID : solide **3** SENSIBLE : raisonnable **4** DEEP : profond <a sound sleep : un sommeil profond>

sound[3] *n* **1** : son *m* **2** NOISE : bruit *m* **3** CHANNEL : détroit *m,* bras *m* de mer

soundless ['saʊndləs] *adj* : silencieux — **soundlessly** *adv*

soundly ['saʊndli] *adv* **1** SOLIDLY : solidement **2** SENSIBLY : judicieusement **3** DEEPLY : profondément <to sleep soundly : dormir profondément>

soundness ['saʊndnəs] *n* **1** SOLIDITY : solidité *f* **2** SENSE, WISDOM : sagesse *f,* bon sens *m,* justesse *f*

soundproof ['saʊnd,pru:f] *adj* : insonorisé

soup ['su:p] *n* : soupe *f* <vegetable soup : soupe aux légumes>

sour[1] ['saʊər] *v* : aigrir

sour[2] *adj* **1** ACID : aigre, sur **2** DISAGREEABLE : revêche, acerbe

source ['sors] *n* : source *f*

sourness ['saʊərnəs] *n* : aigreur *f*

south[1] ['saʊθ] *adv* : au sud, vers le sud <further south : plus au sud>

south[2] *adj* : sud, du sud <the south entrance : l'entrée sud> <South America : Amérique du Sud>

south[3] *n* : sud *m*

South African[1] *adj* : sud-africain

South African[2] *n* : Sud-Africain *m,* -caine *f*

South American[1] *adj* : sud-américain

South American[2] *n* : Sud-Américain *m,* -caine *f*

southbound ['saʊθ,baʊnd] *adj* : qui va vers le sud

southeast[1] [saʊ'θi:st, *as a nautical term often* saʊ'i:st] *adj* : sud-est

southeast[2] *n* : sud-est *m*

southeasterly[1] [saʊ'θi:stərli] *adv* : vers le sud-est

southeasterly[2] *adj* : du sud-est

southeastern [saʊ'θi:stərn] → **southeast**[1]

southerly[1] ['sʌðərli] *adv* : vers le sud

southerly[2] *adj* : du sud

southern ['sʌðərn] *adj* : du sud

Southerner ['sʌðərnər] *n* : habitant *m,* -tante *f* du Sud

south pole *n* : pôle *m* Sud

southward[1] ['saʊθwərd] *or* **southwards** [-wərdz] *adv* : vers le sud

southward[2] *or* **southwards** *adj* : au sud, du sud

southwest[1] [saʊθ'west, *as a nautical term often* saʊ'west] *adj* : sud-ouest

southwest[2] *n* : sud-ouest *m*

southwesterly[1] [saʊθ'westərli] *adv* : vers le sud-ouest

southwesterly[2] *adj* : du sud-ouest

southwestern [saʊθ'westərn] → **southwest**[1]

souvenir [,su:və'nɪr, 'su:və,-] *n* : souvenir *m*

sovereign[1] ['sɑvərən] *adj* : souverain

sovereign[2] *n* **1** MONARCH : souverain *m,* -raine *f* **2** : souverain *m* (pièce de monnaie)

sovereignty ['sɑvərənti] *n, pl* **-ties** : souveraineté *f*

Soviet ['so:vi,et, 'sɑ-, -viət] *adj* : soviétique

sow[1] [ˈsoː] *vt* **sowed; sown** [ˈsoːn] *or* **sowed; sowing** : semer
sow[2] [ˈsaʊ] *n* : truie *f*
sox → **sock**[2]
soybean [ˈsɔɪˌbiːn] *n* : graine *f* de soja
spa [ˈspɑ] *n* : station *f* thermale
space[1] [ˈspeɪs] *vt* **spaced; spacing** *or* **to space out** : espacer, étaler, échelonner
space[2] *n* **1** *or* **outer space** : espace *m* **2** INTERVAL : espace *m* <in the space of a few days : en l'espace de quelques jours> **3** ROOM : place *f* <there's no more space : il n'y a plus de place> **4** : espace *f* (typographique)
spacecraft [ˈspeɪsˌkræft] *n* : vaisseau *m* spatial
spaceflight [ˈspeɪsˌflaɪt] *n* : vol *m* spatial
spaceman [ˈspeɪsmən, -ˌmæn] *n, pl* **-men** [-mən, -ˌmɛn] : astronaute *mf*, cosmonaute *mf*
spaceship [ˈspeɪsˌʃɪp] *n* : vaisseau *m* spatial
space shuttle *n* : navette *f* spatiale
space suit *n* : combinaison *f* spatiale
spacious [ˈspeɪʃəs] *adj* : spacieux
spade[1] [ˈspeɪd] *vt* **spaded; spading** : bêcher, pelleter
spade[2] *n* **1** SHOVEL : bêche *f*, pelle *f* **2** : pique *f* (aux cartes)
spaghetti [spəˈgɛṭi] *n* : spaghetti *mpl*, spaghettis *mpl*
span[1] [ˈspæn] *vt* **spanned; spanning 1** CROSS : franchir, enjamber **2** ENCOMPASS : embrasser, comprendre
span[2] *n* **1** WIDTH : envergure *f*, portée *f*, travée *f* **2** DURATION : durée *f*
spangle [ˈspæŋgəl] *n* : paillette *f*
Spaniard [ˈspænjərd] *n* : Espagnol *m*, -gnole *f*
spaniel [ˈspænjəl] *n* : épagneul *m*
Spanish[1] [ˈspænɪʃ] *adj* : espagnol
Spanish[2] *n* **1** : espagnol *m* (langue) **2 the Spanish** : les Espagnols
spank [ˈspæŋk] *vt* : fesser
spanking[1] [ˈspæŋkɪŋ] *adj* BRISK : vif
spanking[2] *n* : fessée *f*
spanner [ˈspænər] *Brit* → **wrench**[2] **3**
spar[1] [ˈspɑr] *vi* **sparred; sparring** : s'entraîner à la boxe
spar[2] *n* : espar *m*, verge *f* *Can*
spare[1] [ˈspær] *vt* **spared; sparing 1** SAVE : épargner <to spare s.o.'s life : épargner la vie de qqn> <to spare oneself the trouble of : s'épargner l'ennui de> **2** DISPENSE WITH : se passer de <we can't spare him : nous ne pouvons pas nous passer de lui> <can you spare me $10? : est-ce que tu as 10 $ à me passer?> **3 to spare no effort** : faire tout son possible
spare[2] *adj* **1** : de réserve **2** EXTRA, SURPLUS : de trop <a spare moment : un moment de libre> **3** LEAN : maigre
spare[3] *n* **1** *or* **spare part** : pièce *f* de rechange **2** *or* **spare tire** : pneu *m* de rechange
sparing [ˈspærɪŋ] *adj* : économe
sparingly [ˈspærɪŋli] *adv* : avec modération, frugalement
spark[1] [ˈspɑrk] *vi* : émettre des étincelles — *vt* **1** PROVOKE : déclencher <to spark a dispute : déclencher une dispute> **2** AWAKEN : éveiller <to spark the curiosity of : éveiller la curiosité de>
spark[2] *n* : étincelle *f*
sparkle[1] [ˈspɑrkəl] *vi* **-kled; -kling 1** FLASH : étinceler, scintiller **2** EFFERVESCE : pétiller
sparkle[2] *n* : scintillement *m*, éclat *m*
sparkler [ˈspɑrklər] *n* : cierge *m* magique
spark plug *n* : bougie *f*
sparrow [ˈspæroː] *n* : moineau *m*
sparse [ˈspɑrs] *adj* **sparser; -est** : clairsemé, épars
sparsely [ˈspɑrsli] *adv* : peu <sparsely furnished : peu meublé>
spasm [ˈspæzəm] *n* **1** : spasme *m* **2** FIT : accès *m*
spasmodic [spæzˈmɑdɪk] *adj* **1** : spasmodique (se dit de la douleur, etc.) **2** SPORADIC : intermittent
spasmodically [spæzˈmɑdɪkli] *adv* : par à-coups
spastic [ˈspæstɪk] *adj* : spasmodique, handicapé moteur
spat[1] [ˈspæt] → **spit**[1]
spat[2] *n* **1** QUARREL : prise *f* de bec **2 spats** *npl* : guêtres *fpl*
spatial [ˈspeɪʃəl] *adj* : spatial
spatter[1] [ˈspæṭər] *vt* : éclabousser — *vi* : crépiter, gicler
spatter[2] *n* : éclaboussure *f*
spatula [ˈspætʃələ] *n* : spatule *f*
spawn[1] [ˈspɔn] *vi* : frayer — *vt* GENERATE : engendrer
spawn[2] *n* : frai *m*
spay [ˈspeɪ] *vt* : châtrer
speak [ˈspiːk] *v* **spoke** [ˈspoːk]; **spoken** [ˈspoːkən]; **speaking** *vi* **1** TALK : parler <to speak to s.o. : parler à qqn> <to speak well of : dire du bien de> <strictly speaking : à proprement parler> <so to speak : pour ainsi dire> **2 to speak out** : parler clairement **3 to speak out against** : s'élever contre **4 to speak up** : parler plus fort **5 to speak up for** : soutenir, défendre — *vt* **1** SAY : dire <she spoke her mind : elle a dit sa pensée> **2** : parler (une langue)
speaker [ˈspiːkər] *n* **1** : personne *f* qui parle **2** ORATOR : orateur *m*, -trice *f*; conférencier *m*, -cière *f* **3** LOUDSPEAKER : haut-parleur *m*, enceinte *f* acoustique (d'une chaîne stéréo)
spear[1] [ˈspɪr] *vt* : transpercer d'un coup de lance
spear[2] *n* : lance *f*
spearhead[1] [ˈspɪrˌhɛd] *vt* : être le fer de lance de, mener
spearhead[2] *n* : fer *m* de lance

spearmint [ˈspɪrˌmɪnt] *n* : menthe *f* verte

special [ˈspɛʃəl] *adj* : spécial, particulier <nothing special : rien de particulier>

specialist [ˈspɛʃəlɪst] *n* : spécialiste *mf*

specialization [ˌspɛʃələˈzeɪʃən] *n* : spécialisation *f*

specialize [ˈspɛʃəˌlaɪz] *vi* **-ized; -izing** : se spécialiser

specially [ˈspɛʃəli] *adv* **1** PARTICULARLY : spécialement, particulièrement **2** SPECIFICALLY : exprès, spécialement

specialty [ˈspɛʃəlti] *n, pl* **-ties** : spécialité *f*

species [ˈspiːˌʃiːz, -ˌsiːz] *ns & pl* : espèce *f*

specific [spɪˈsɪfɪk] *adj* **1** EXPLICIT : précis, explicite **2** : spécifique (en biologie, en médecine, etc.)

specifically [spɪˈsɪfɪkli] *adv* **1** EXPLICITLY : précisément, explicitement **2** PARTICULARLY : spécialement, en particulier

specification [ˌspɛsəfəˈkeɪʃən] *n* : spécification *f*

specify [ˈspɛsəˌfaɪ] *vt* **-fied; -fying** : spécifier

specimen [ˈspɛsəmən] *n* **1** SAMPLE : échantillon *m* **2** EXAMPLE : spécimen *m*, exemplaire *m*

speck [ˈspɛk] *n* **1** SPOT : tache *f* **2** BIT, TRACE : grain *m* <a speck of dust : un grain de poussière>

speckled [ˈspɛkəld] *adj* : tacheté, moucheté

spectacle [ˈspɛktɪkəl] *n* **1** : spectacle *m* **2 spectacles** *npl* GLASSES : lunettes *fpl*

spectacular [spɛkˈtækjələr] *adj* : spectaculaire

spectator [ˈspɛkˌteɪtər] *n* : spectateur *m*, -trice *f*

specter [ˈspɛktər] *n* : spectre *m*

spectrum [ˈspɛktrəm] *n, pl* **spectra** [-trə] *or* **spectrums 1** : spectre *m* <the visible spectrum : le spectre visible> **2** RANGE : gamme *f*

speculate [ˈspɛkjəˌleɪt] *vi* **-lated; -lating** : spéculer

speculation [ˌspɛkjəˈleɪʃən] *n* : conjectures *fpl*, spéculations *fpl*

speculative [ˈspɛkjəˌleɪtɪv] *adj* : spéculatif

speculator [ˈspɛkjəˌleɪtər] *n* : spéculateur *m*, -trice *f*

speech [ˈspiːtʃ] *n* **1** : parole *f* <to lose the power of speech : perdre la parole> **2** ADDRESS : discours *m*

speechless [ˈspiːtʃləs] *adj* : muet

speed[1] [ˈspiːd] *v* **sped** [ˈspɛd] *or* **speeded; speeding** *vi* **1** : aller à toute allure, aller à toute vitesse <he sped off : il est parti à toute allure> **2** : rouler trop vite (dans une voiture) <a ticket for speeding : une contravention pour excès de vitesse> — *vt or* **to speed up** : accélérer

speed[2] *n* **1** SWIFTNESS : vitesse *f* **2** VELOCITY : vélocité *f*

speedboat [ˈspiːdˌboːt] *n* : vedette *f* (rapide), hors-bord *m*

speed bump *n* : casse-vitesse *m*

speed limit *n* : limite *f* de vitesse

speedometer [spɪˈdɑmətər] *n* : compteur *m* de vitesse

speedup [ˈspiːdˌʌp] *n* : accélération *f*

speedy [ˈspiːdi] *adj* **speedier; -est** : rapide — **speedily** [-dəli] *adv*

spell[1] [ˈspɛl] *vt* **1** : écrire, orthographier <how do you spell it? : comment est-ce que ça s'écrit?> **2** MEAN : signifier <that could spell trouble : on pourrait avoir des ennuis> **3** RELIEVE : relayer, relever — *vi* : connaître l'orthographe

spell[2] *n* **1** TURN : tour *m* **2** PERIOD : période *f* **3** ENCHANTMENT : charme *m*, sortilège *m*

spellbound [ˈspɛlˌbaʊnd] *adj* : captivé

speller [ˈspɛlər] *n* **to be a good speller** : être forte en orthographe

spelling [ˈspɛlɪŋ] *n* : orthographe *f*

spell out *vt* **1** : épeler (les lettres d'un mot) **2** EXPLAIN : expliquer

spend [ˈspɛnd] *vt* **spent** [ˈspɛnt]; **spending 1** : dépenser (de l'argent) **2** PASS : passer <to spend time on : passer son temps à>

spendthrift [ˈspɛndˌθrɪft] *n* : dépensier *m*, -sière *f*

sperm [ˈspərm] *n, pl* **sperm** *or* **sperms** : sperme *m*

spew [ˈspjuː] *vt or* **to spew out** : vomir (de la fumée, de la lave, etc.) — *vi* : jaillir, gicler

sphere [ˈsfɪr] *n* : sphère *f*

spherical [ˈsfɪrɪkəl, ˈsfɛr-] *adj* : sphérique

spice[1] [ˈspaɪs] *vt* **spiced; spicing 1** SEASON : épicer **2** *or* **to spice up** : pimenter

spice[2] *n* **1** : épice *f* **2** EXCITEMENT, PIQUANCY : piquant *m*

spick–and–span [ˈspɪkəndˈspæn] *adj* : impeccable

spicy [ˈspaɪsi] *adj* **spicier; -est 1** SPICED : épicé **2** RACY : pimenté, piquant

spider [ˈspaɪdər] *n* : araignée *f*

spigot [ˈspɪgət, -kət] *n* : robinet *m*

spike[1] [ˈspaɪk] *vt* **spiked; spiking 1** FASTEN : clouer **2** PIERCE : transpercer **3** : corser (de l'alcool)

spike[2] *n* **1** NAIL : (gros) clou *m* **2** : pointe *f* (d'une chaussure), épi *m* (des cheveux), épine *f* (d'un cactus)

spill[1] [ˈspɪl] *vt* **1** : renverser, répandre <to spill blood : verser du sang> **2** DIVULGE : révéler — *vi* : se répandre

spill[2] *n* **1** SPILLING : renversement *m* **2** FALL : chute *f*, culbute *f*

spin[1] [ˈspɪn] *v* **spun** [ˈspʌn]; **spinning** *vi* **1** ROTATE : tourner, tournoyer <my head is spinning : j'ai la tête qui tourne> **2** : filer (avec un rouet) —

vt **1** : faire tourner **2** : filer <to spin wool : filer de la laine>
spin[2] *n* : tour *m* <to go for a spin : faire un petit tour>
spinach ['spɪnɪtʃ] *n* : épinards *mpl*
spinal column ['spaɪnəl] *adj* BACKBONE : colonne *f* vertébrale
spinal cord *n* : moelle *f* épinière
spindle ['spɪndəl] *n* **1** : fuseau *m*, broche *f* (pour filer) **2** AXLE : axe *m*
spindly ['spɪndli] *adj* : grêle (se dit des jambes), étiolé (se dit d'une plante)
spine ['spaɪn] *n* **1** BACKBONE : colonne *f* vertébrale **2** QUILL : piquant *m* (d'un animal) **3** THORN : épine *f* **4** : dos *m* (d'un livre)
spineless ['spaɪnləs] *adj* **1** : sans piquants, sans épines **2** INVERTEBRATE : invertébré **3** COWARDLY, WEAK : lâche, mou
spinet ['spɪnət] *n* : épinette *f*
spinster ['spɪn*t*stər] *n* : célibataire *f*, vieille fille *f*
spiny ['spaɪni] *adj* **spinier; -est** : couvert de piquants (se dit des animaux), épineux (se dit des plantes)
spiral[1] ['spaɪrəl] *vi* **-raled** *or* **-ralled; -raling** *or* **-ralling** : aller en spirale
spiral[2] *adj* : spirale, en spirale <spiral staircase : escalier en spirale>
spiral[3] *n* : spirale *f*
spire ['spaɪr] *n* : flèche *f*
spirit[1] ['spɪrət] *vt* **to spirit away** : faire disparaître
spirit[2] *n* **1** : esprit *m* <in the spirit of friendship : dans l'esprit de l'amitié> **2** GHOST : esprit *m*, spectre *m*, fantôme *m* **3** ENTHUSIASM, VIVACITY : entrain *m* **4 spirits** *npl* MOOD : humeur *f* <to be in good spirits : être de bonne humeur> **5 spirits** *npl* LIQUORS : spiritueux *mpl*
spirited ['spɪrəṭəd] *adj* : animé, vif
spiritless ['spɪrətləs] *adj* : sans vie, sans entrain
spiritual[1] ['spɪrɪtʃʊəl, -tʃəl] *adj* : spirituel — **spiritually** *adv*
spiritual[2] *n* : spiritual *m*
spiritualism ['spɪrɪtʃʊəˌlɪzəm, -tʃə-] *n* : spiritisme *m*
spirituality [ˌspɪrɪtʃʊ'æləṭi] *n* : spiritualité *f*
spit[1] ['spɪt] *v* **spit** *or* **spat** ['spæt]; **spitting** : cracher
spit[2] *n* **1** SALIVA : crachat *m*, salive *f* **2** ROTISSERIE : broche *f* **3** POINT : pointe *f* (de terre)
spite[1] ['spaɪt] *vt* **spited; spiting** : contrarier
spite[2] *n* **1** : dépit *m*, malveillance *f* **2 in spite of** : en dépit de, malgré
spiteful ['spaɪtfəl] *adj* : malveillant
spittle ['spɪṭəl] *n* : salive *f*
splash[1] ['splæʃ] *vt* : éclabousser — *vi* **1** *or* **to splash about** : barboter, patauger **2 to splash through** : traverser en faisant des éclaboussures
splash[2] *n* **1** SPLASHING : éclaboussement *m* **2** SQUIRT : goutte *f* **3** SPOT : tache *f*, éclaboussure *f* **4 to make a splash** : faire sensation
splatter ['splæṭər] → **spatter**
splay ['spleɪ] *vt* : écarter (des doigts, des jambes) — *vi* : s'écarter
spleen ['spli:n] *n* **1** : rate *f* (organe) **2** ANGER, SPITE : mauvaise humeur *f*
splendid ['splɛndəd] *adj* : splendide, superbe
splendidly ['splɛndədli] *adv* : superbement, magnifiquement
splendor *or Brit* **splendour** ['splɛndər] *n* : splendeur *f*
splice[1] ['splaɪs] *vt* **spliced; splicing** : épisser, coller
splice[2] *n* : épissure *f*
splint ['splɪnt] *n* : attelle *f*
splinter[1] ['splɪntər] *vt* : briser en éclats — *vi* : se briser en éclats
splinter[2] *n* : éclat *m*
split[1] ['splɪt] *v* **split; splitting** *vt* **1** CLEAVE : fendre, couper <to split wood : fendre du bois> **2** TEAR : déchirer **3** SHARE : partager **4** DIVIDE : diviser — *vi* **1** CRACK : se fendre **2** TEAR : se déchirer **3** DIVIDE, SEPARATE : se diviser
split[2] *n* **1** CRACK : fente *f* **2** TEAR : déchirure *f* **3** DIVISION : division *f*, scission *f*
splurge[1] ['splərdʒ] *v* **splurged; splurging** *vi* : faire des folles dépenses — *vt* : dépenser
splurge[2] *n* : folles dépenses *fpl*
spoil ['spɔɪl] *v* **spoiled** ['spɔɪld, 'spɔɪlt] *or* **spoilt** ['spɔɪlt]; **spoiling 1** PILLAGE : piller **2** RUIN : gâcher, abîmer **3** PAMPER : gâter — *vi* : se gâter, s'abîmer
spoils ['spɔɪlz] *npl* PLUNDER : butin *m*, dépouilles *fpl*
spoke[1] → **speak**
spoke[2] ['spo:k] *n* : rayon *m*
spoken → **speak**
spokesman ['spo:ksmən] *n, pl* **-men** [-mən, -ˌmɛn] : porte-parole *m*
spokeswoman ['spo:ksˌwʊmən] *n, pl* **-women** [-ˌwɪmən] : porte-parole *m*
sponge[1] ['spʌndʒ] *vt* **sponged; sponging** : éponger
sponge[2] *n* : éponge *f*
spongy ['spʌndʒi] *adj* **spongier; -est** : spongieux
sponsor[1] ['spɑn*t*sər] *vt* : patronner, sponsoriser
sponsor[2] *n* : sponsor *m*, commanditaire *m*, parrain *m*
sponsorship ['spɑn*t*sərˌʃɪp] *n* : parrainage *m*, patronage *m*
spontaneity [ˌspɑntə'ni:əṭi, -'neɪ-] *n* : spontanéité *f*
spontaneous [spɑn'teɪniəs] *adj* : spontané — **spontaneously** *adv*
spoof ['spu:f] *n* : parodie *f*
spook[1] ['spu:k] *vt* : faire peur à
spook[2] *n* : fantôme *m*

spooky [ˈspuːki] *adj* **spookier; -est** : sinistre, qui fait froid dans le dos

spool [ˈspuːl] *n* : bobine *f*

spoon[1] [ˈspuːn] *vt* : servir, verser (avec une cuillère)

spoon[2] *n* : cuillère *f*, cuiller *f*

spoonful [ˈspuːnˌfʊl] *n* : cuillerée *f*

spoor [ˈspʊr, ˈspor] *n* : piste *f*, trace *f*

sporadic [spəˈrædɪk] *adj* : sporadique — **sporadically** [-dɪkli] *adv*

spore [ˈspor] *n* : spore *f*

sport[1] [ˈsport] *vi* FROLIC : s'amuser — *vt* WEAR : arborer, porter

sport[2] *n* **1** : sport *m* **2** JEST : jeu *m* **3 to be a good sport** : être beau joueur

sportsman [ˈsportsmən] *n*, *pl* **-men** [-mən, -ˌmɛn] : sportif *m*

sportsmanship [ˈsportsmənˌʃɪp] *n* : sportivité *f*

sportswoman [ˈsportsˌwʊmən] *n*, *pl* **-women** [-ˌwɪmən] : sportive *f*

sporty [ˈsporti] *adj* **sportier; -est** : sportif

spot[1] [ˈspɑt] *v* **spotted; spotting** *vt* **1** STAIN : tacher **2** NOTICE : apercevoir, repérer <to spot an error : apercevoir une erreur> — *vi* : se tacher

spot[2] *adj* : fait au hasard <a spot check : un contrôle au hasard>

spot[3] *n* **1** STAIN : tache *f* **2** DOT : pois *m* **3** PREDICAMENT : situation *f* difficile **4** PLACE : endroit *m*, lieu *m*, <on the spot : sur place>

spotless [ˈspɑtləs] *adj* : sans tache

spotlessly [ˈspɑtləsli] *adv* **spotlessly clean** : impeccable, reluisant de propreté

spotlight[1] [ˈspɑtˌlaɪt] *vt* **-lighted** *or* **-lit** [-ˌlɪt]; **-lighting 1** LIGHT : diriger les projecteurs sur **2** HIGHLIGHT : mettre en lumière

spotlight[2] *n* **1** : projecteur *m*, spot *m* **2 to be in the spotlight** : être en vedette

spotty [ˈspɑti] *adj* **spottier; -est 1** SPOTTED : tacheté **2** UNEVEN : irrégulier

spouse [ˈspaʊs] *n* : époux *m*, épouse *f*

spout[1] [ˈspaʊt] *vt* **1** : faire jaillir **2** DECLAIM : déclamer — *vi* : jaillir

spout[2] *n* **1** : bec *m* verseur **2** STREAM : jet *m*

sprain[1] [ˈspreɪn] *vt* : faire une entorse à, fouler

sprain[2] *n* : entorse *f*, foulure *f*

sprawl[1] [ˈsprɔl] *vi* **1** : être affalé (se dit d'une personne) **2** SPREAD : s'étaler

sprawl[2] *n* **1** : position *f* affalée **2** EXTENT, SPREAD : étendue *f*

spray[1] [ˈspreɪ] *vt* : atomiser, vaporiser, arroser (un jardin)

spray[2] *n* **1** BOUQUET : bouquet *m* **2** MIST : gouttelettes *fpl* fines, embruns *mpl* (de la mer) **3** ATOMIZER : atomiseur *m*, vaporisateur *m*, bombe *f*

spray gun *n* : pistolet *m* (à peinture)

spread[1] [ˈsprɛd] *v* **spread; spreading** *vt* **1** *or* **to spread out** : étendre **2** : étaler, tartiner <to spread butter : étaler du beurre> **3** DISSEMINATE : répandre, propager — *vi* **1** EXTEND : s'étendre, s'étaler **2** : se répandre, se propager <the disease is spreading : la maladie se répand>

spread[2] *n* **1** EXTENT, RANGE : éventail *m*, envergure *f* **2** → **bedspread 3** PASTE : pâte *f* à tartiner <cheese spread : fromage à tartiner> **4** PROPAGATION : propagation *f*

spreadsheet [ˈsprɛdˌʃiːt] *n* : tableur *m*

spree [ˈspri] *n* : fête *f* <to go on a spending spree : faire de folles dépenses>

sprig [ˈsprɪg] *n* : brin *m*

sprightly [ˈspraɪtli] *adj* **sprightlier; -est** : vif, alerte

spring[1] [ˈsprɪŋ] *v* **sprang** [ˈspræŋ] *or* **sprung** [ˈsprʌŋ]; **sprung; springing** *vi* **1** LEAP : sauter, bondir **2** (*indicating rapid movement*) <to spring to s.o.'s aid : se précipiter pour aider qqn> <tears sprang to my eyes : les larmes me sont montées aux yeux> **3 to spring up** : surgir — *vt* **1** RELEASE : déclencher, faire jouer <to spring a trap : faire jouer un piège> **2** : annoncer (une nouvelle, etc.), poser (une question) <to spring the news on s.o. : surprendre qqn avec les nouvelles> **3 to spring a leak** : commencer à fuir

spring[2] *n* **1** SOURCE : source *f* **2** : printemps *m* (saison) <in the spring : au printemps> **3** COIL : ressort *m* **4** LEAP : bond *m*, saut *m* **5** RESILIENCE : élasticité *f*

springboard [ˈsprɪŋˌbord] *n* : tremplin *m*

springtime [ˈsprɪŋˌtaɪm] *n* : printemps *m*

springy [ˈsprɪŋi] *adj* **springier; -est 1** RESILIENT : élastique **2** LIVELY : énergique

sprinkle[1] [ˈsprɪŋkəl] *v* **-kled; -kling** *vt* **1** : saupoudrer <sprinkle with oregano : saupoudrez d'oregano> **2** : asperger, arroser <to sprinkle the lawn : arroser la pelouse> — *vi* : tomber des gouttes (se dit de la pluie)

sprinkle[2] *n* **1** PINCH : pincée *f*, petite quantité *f* **2** RAIN : petite pluie *f*

sprinkler [ˈsprɪŋkələr] *n* : arroseur *m*

sprint[1] [ˈsprɪnt] *vi* : sprinter

sprint[2] *n* : sprint *m*

sprite [ˈspraɪt] *n* **1** : lutin *m* **2** *or* **water sprite** : naïade *f*

sprocket [ˈsprɑkət] *n* : pignon *m*

sprout[1] [ˈspraʊt] *v* : pousser

sprout[2] *n* : pousse *f*

spruce[1] [ˈspruːs] *vt* **spruced; sprucing 1** *or* **to spruce up** : faire beau (un enfant, etc.), astiquer (une maison) **2 to spruce oneself up** : se faire beau

spruce[2] *adj* **sprucer; sprucest** : pimpant

spruce[3] *n* : sapinette *f*, épicéa *m France*, épinette *f Can*

spry [ˈspraɪ] *adj* **sprier** *or* **spryer** [ˈspraɪər]; **spriest** *or* **spryest** [ˈspraɪəst] : alerte, plein d'entrain

spun → **spin**[1]
spunk ['spʌŋk] *n* : courage *m,* cran *m fam*
spunky ['spʌŋki] *adj* **spunkier; -est** : courageux
spur[1] ['spər] *vt* **spurred; spurring** *or* **to spur on** : éperonner (un cheval), aiguillonner (une personne)
spur[2] *n* **1** : éperon *m* **2** STIMULUS : stimulant *m,* aiguillon *m* **3** RIDGE : éperon *m,* contrefort *m* **4 on the spur of the moment** : sur le coup, sur l'impulsion du moment
spurious ['spjʊriəs] *adj* : faux, fallacieux
spurn ['spərn] *vt* : rejeter
spurt[1] ['spərt] *vt* SQUIRT : faire gicler — *vi* : jaillir, gicler
spurt[2] *n* **1** BURST : sursaut *m,* bourrée *f Can* <a spurt of enthusiasm : un sursaut d'enthousiasme> **2** GUSH, JET : jaillissement *m*
sputter[1] ['spʌt̬ər] *vi* **1** JABBER, MUTTER : bredouiller **2** : grésiller, crépiter (se dit d'un feu), tousser (se dit d'un moteur)
sputter[2] *n* **1** JABBERING, MUTTERING : bredouillement *m* **2** : crépitement *m* (d'un feu), raté *m* (d'un moteur)
spy[1] ['spaɪ] *v* **spied; spying** *vt* SEE : apercevoir, discerner — *vi* **1** : faire de l'espionnage **2 to spy on s.o.** : espionner qqn
spy[2] *n* : espion *m*
squab ['skwɑb] *n, pl* **squabs** *or* **squab** : pigeonneau *m*
squabble[1] ['skwɑbəl] *vi* **-bled; -bling** : se disputer, se chamailler
squabble[2] *n* : dispute *f,* querelle *f*
squad ['skwɑd] *n* : équipe *f,* peloton *m* (militaire), brigade *f* (de police)
squadron ['skwɑdrən] *n* : escadron *m*
squalid ['skwɑlɪd] *adj* : sordide
squall ['skwɔl] *n* : bourrasque *f* <snow squall : bourrasque de neige>
squalor ['skwɑlər] *n* : conditions *fpl* sordides, misère *f*
squander ['skwɑndər] *vt* : gaspiller
square[1] ['skwær] *v* **squared; squaring** *vt* **1** : équarrir, carrer **2** : carrer (en mathématiques) **3** *or* **to square away** SETTLE : régler — *vi* **to square with** : cadrer avec, coïncider avec
square[2] *adj* **squarer; -est 1** : carré <a square house : une maison carrée> **2** RIGHT-ANGLED : à angle droit **3** : carré (en mathématiques) <a square meter : un mètre carré> **4** HONEST : honnête
square[3] *n* **1** : équerre *f* (instrument) **2** : carré *m* <to fold into squares : plier en forme de carré> **3** : place *f* (d'une ville) **4** : carré *m* (en mathématiques)
squarely ['skwærli] *adv* **1** EXACTLY : carrément **2** HONESTLY : honnêtement
square root *n* : racine *f* carrée
squash[1] ['skwɑʃ, 'skwɔʃ] *vt* **1** CRUSH : écraser, aplatir, écrapoutir *Can* **2** SUPPRESS : remettre à sa place (une personne), réduire à néant (des espoirs), réprimer (une révolte) — *vi* : s'écraser
squash[2] *n, pl* **squashes** *or* **squash 1** : courge *f* **2** *or* **squash rackets** : squash *m*
squat[1] ['skwɑt] *vi* **squatted; squatting 1** CROUCH : s'accroupir **2 to squat in** : squatter (un bâtiment, etc.)
squat[2] *adj* **squatter; squattest** : trapu
squat[3] *n* **1** : position *f* accroupie **2** : squat *m* (dans un bâtiment)
squaw ['skwɔ] *n* : squaw *f*
squawk[1] ['skwɔk] *vi* : criailler
squawk[2] *n* : criaillement *m* (d'un oiseau), cri *m* rauque (d'une personne)
squeak[1] ['skwi:k] *vi* : grincer, couiner
squeak[2] *n* : grincement *m,* couinement *m*
squeaky ['skwi:ki] *adj* **squeakier; -est** : grinçant, aigu <a squeaky voice : une voix aiguë> <squeaky shoes : des chaussures qui craquent>
squeal[1] ['skwi:l] *vi* **1** : pousser des cris aigus (se dit des personnes et des animaux), crisser (se dit des pneus), grincer (se dit des freins) **2 to squeal on** : dénoncer
squeal[2] *n* **1** : cri *m* aigu **2** SCREECH : crissement *m* (de pneus), grincement *m* (de freins)
squeamish ['skwi:mɪʃ] *adj* : délicat, sensible, facilement dégoûté
squeeze[1] ['skwi:z] *v* **squeezed; squeezing** *vt* **1** PRESS : presser, serrer **2** EXTRACT : exprimer **3** EXTORT : extorquer, soutirer — *vi* : se glisser <he squeezed into the room : il s'est glissé dans la salle>
squeeze[2] *n* : pression *f,* resserrement *m*
squelch ['skwɛltʃ] *vt* : écraser, étouffer, aplatir
squid ['skwɪd] *n, pl* **squid** *or* **squids** : calmar *m,* encornet *m*
squint[1] ['skwɪnt] *vi* : plisser les yeux, loucher
squint[2] *adj or* **squint–eyed** : qui louche
squint[3] *n* : strabisme *m*
squire ['skwaɪr] *n* **1** LANDOWNER : propriétaire *mf* **2** : écuyer *m* (d'un chevalier)
squirm ['skwərm] *vi* : se tortiller
squirrel ['skwərəl] *n* : écureuil *m*
squirt[1] ['skwərt] *vt* : faire gicler — *vi* : gicler
squirt[2] *n* : jet *m,* giclée *f*
Sri Lankan[1] [ˌsri:'læŋkən] *adj* : sri lankais
Sri Lankan[2] *n* : Sri Lankais *m,* -kaise *f*
stab[1] ['stæb] *vt* **stabbed; stabbing 1** KNIFE : poignarder **2** STICK : piquer
stab[2] *n* **1** : coup *m* de couteau **2 to take a stab at** : essayer, tenter

stability [stəˈbɪləţi] *n, pl* **-ties** : stabilité *f*

stabilize [ˈsteɪbəˌlaɪz] *v* **-lized; -lizing** *vt* : stabiliser — *vi* : se stabiliser

stable[1] [ˈsteɪbəl] *vt* **-bled; -bling** : mettre à l'écurie

stable[2] *adj* **-bler; -blest 1** FIXED, STEADY : stable, fixe **2** LASTING : stable, durable **3** : équilibré (en psychologie), stationnaire (en médicine)

stable[3] *n* : écurie *f*

staccato [stəˈkɑţoː] *adj* : staccato

stack[1] [ˈstæk] *vt* **1** PILE : entasser, empiler, mettre en meule (se dit du foin) **2** FILL : remplir <the table was stacked with books : la table était remplie de livres>

stack[2] *n* **1** PILE : tas *m,* pile *f* **2** → **smokestack**

stadium [ˈsteɪdiəm] *n, pl* **-dia** [-diə] *or* **-diums** : stade *m*

staff[1] [ˈstæf] *vt* : pourvoir en personnel

staff[2] *n, pl* **staffs** [ˈstæfs, ˈstævz] *or* **staves** [ˈstævz, ˈsteɪvz] **1** STICK : bâton *m* **2** *pl* **staffs** PERSONNEL : personnel *m* **3** : portée *f* (en musique)

stag[1] [ˈstæg] *adv* : seul <to go stag : aller sans compagne>

stag[2] *adj* : entre hommes

stag[3] *n, pl* **stags** *or* **stag** : cerf *m*

stage[1] [ˈsteɪdʒ] *vt* **staged; staging 1** ORGANIZE : organiser (une manifestation, etc.) **2** : monter, mettre en scène (une pièce de théâtre)

stage[2] *n* **1** PLATFORM : estrade *f,* scène *f* (au théâtre) **2** PHASE : stade *m,* phase *f,* étape *f* **3 the stage** : le théâtre

stagecoach [ˈsteɪdʒˌkoːtʃ] *n* : diligence *f*

stagger[1] [ˈstægər] *vi* TOTTER : tituber, chanceler — *vt* **1** SPACE OUT : échelonner, étaler **2** AMAZE : stupéfier

stagger[2] *n* : pas *m* chancelant

staggering [ˈstægərɪŋ] *adj* : stupéfiant

stagnant [ˈstægnənt] *adj* : stagnant

stagnate [ˈstægˌneɪt] *vi* **-nated; -nating** : stagner

stagnation [stægˈneɪʃən] *n* : stagnation *f*

staid [ˈsteɪd] *adj* : collet monté, guindé

stain[1] [ˈsteɪn] *vt* **1** DISCOLOR : tacher **2** DYE : teindre, teinter **3** SULLY : souiller — *vi* : se tacher

stain[2] *n* **1** SPOT : tache *f* **2** DYE : teinture *f* **3** BLEMISH : souillure *f*

stainless [ˈsteɪnləs] *adj* : inoxydable <stainless steel : acier inoxydable>

stair [ˈstær] *n* **1** STEP : marche *f* **2 stairs** *npl* : escalier *m*

staircase [ˈstærˌkeɪs] *n* : escalier *m*

stairway [ˈstærˌweɪ] *n* : escalier *m*

stairwell [ˈsteɪrˌwɛl] *n* : cage *f* d'escalier

stake[1] [ˈsteɪk] *vt* **staked; staking 1** *or* **to stake out** : jalonner, marquer (une ligne frontière), délimiter (un espace) **2** BET : miser, parier **3 to stake a claim to** : établir son droit à, revendiquer

stake[2] *n* **1** POST : poteau *m,* pieu *m,* piquet *m* **2** BET : enjeu *m* <to be at stake : être en jeu> **3** INTEREST, SHARE : intérêt *m,* part *f*

stalactite [stəˈlækˌtaɪt] *n* : stalactite *f*

stalagmite [stəˈlægˌmaɪt] *n* : stalagmite *f*

stale [ˈsteɪl] *adj* **staler; stalest** : vieux, rassis (se dit du pain), éventé (se dit d'une boisson)

stalemate [ˈsteɪlˌmeɪt] *n* : pat *m,* impasse *f*

stalk[1] [ˈstɔk] *vt* **1** TRACK : traquer **2** PROWL : rôder dans <to stalk the countryside : rôder dans les campagnes> — *vi* : marcher fièrement <to stalk out : sortir d'un air hautain>

stalk[2] *n* : tige *f* (d'une plante)

stall[1] [ˈstɔl] *vt* **1** : faire caler (un moteur) **2** DELAY : retarder, bloquer — *vi* **1** : caler (se dit d'un moteur) **2** *or* **to stall for time** : essayer de gagner du temps

stall[2] *n* **1** : stalle *f* (d'un cheval, etc.) **2** BOOTH : stand *m,* étal *m*

stallion [ˈstæljən] *n* : étalon *m*

stalwart [ˈstɔlwərt] *adj* **1** STRONG : robuste <a stalwart supporter : un supporter inconditionnel> **2** BRAVE : vaillant, brave

stamen [ˈsteɪmən] *n* : étamine *f*

stamina [ˈstæmənə] *n* : vigueur *f,* résistance *f*

stammer[1] [ˈstæmər] *v* : bégayer

stammer[2] *n* : bégaiement *m*

stamp[1] [ˈstæmp] *vt* **1** IMPRESS, IMPRINT : frapper, estamper (le métal, etc.) **2** : timbrer, affranchir (le courrier), viser (un passeport) **3 to stamp one's feet** : taper des pieds

stamp[2] *n* **1** IMPRESSION, MARK : cachet *m,* tampon *m* **2** *or* **postage stamp** : timbre *m* **3** → **rubber stamp 4** HALLMARK, TRAIT : empreinte *f,* marque *f* <to bear the stamp of s.o. : avoir la marque de qqn>

stampede[1] [stæmˈpiːd] *vi* **-peded; -peding** : s'enfuir à la débandade

stampede[2] *n* : débandade *f*

stance [ˈstænts] *n* : position *f*

stanch [ˈstɔntʃ, ˈstɑntʃ] *vt* : étancher

stand[1] [ˈstænd] *v* **stood** [ˈstʊd]; **standing** *vi* **1** : être debout **2** *or* **to stand up** : se mettre debout, se lever **3** (*indicating a specified position or location*) <the machines are standing idle : les machines restent inutilisées> **4** (*referring to an opinion*) <where does he stand on the matter? : quelle est sa position là-dessus?> **5** BE : être, se trouver <the house stands on a hill : la maison se trouve sur une colline> **6** CONTINUE : rester valable <the offer stands : l'offre reste valable> **7** REMAIN, REST : reposer <the statue stands on a pedestal : la statue repose sur un piédestal> — *vt* **1** PLACE, SET

: mettre 2 ENDURE, TOLERATE : supporter <I can't stand it any longer : je ne peux plus supporter ça>

stand[2] *n* 1 RESISTANCE : résistance *f* (militaire) 2 BOOTH, STALL : stand *m*, étal *m* 3 BASE : pied *m*, piédestal *m* 4 GROVE : bosquet *m* (d' arbres) 5 POSITION : position *f* 6 **stands** *npl* GRANDSTAND : tribune *f*

standard[1] ['stændərd] *adj* 1 ESTABLISHED : établi <standard English : l'anglais correct> 2 NORMAL : normal, standard 3 CLASSIC : classique <a standard work : une œuvre classique>

standard[2] *n* 1 BANNER : étendard *m* 2 CRITERION, NORM : critère *m*, norme *f*, étalon *m* <the gold standard : l'étalon-or> 3 LEVEL : niveau *m* <standard of living : niveau de vie> 4 SUPPORT : pied *m*, poteau *m*

standardize ['stændər,daɪz] *vt* **-ized; -izing** : standardiser

standard time *n* : heure *f* légale

stand by *vt* 1 SUPPORT : soutenir 2 MAINTAIN : tenir, s'en tenir à (une promesse, une opinion, etc.) — *vi* 1 : rester là <to stand by and do nothing : rester là sans rien faire> 2 : être prêt, se tenir prêt

stand for *vt* 1 REPRESENT : représenter 2 PERMIT, TOLERATE : supporter, tolérer

standing ['stændɪŋ] *n* 1 POSITION, RANK : position *f*, standing *m*, cote *f* 2 DURATION : durée *f* <of long standing : de longue date>

stand out *vi* 1 : ressortir, se détacher <she stands out from her colleagues : elle se détache de ses collègues> 2 **to stand out against** RESIST : s'opposer à

standpoint ['stænd,pɔɪnt] *n* : point *m* de vue

standstill ['stænd,stɪl] *n* 1 STOP : arrêt *m* <to come to a standstill : s'arrêter> 2 DEADLOCK : impasse *f*

stand up *vt* 1 : mettre debout 2 **to stand s.o. up** : poser un lapin à qqn *fam* — *vi* 1 ENDURE : tenir 2 **to stand up for** : défendre 3 **to stand up to** : résister à

stank → **stink**[1]

stanza ['stænzə] *n* : strophe *f*

staple[1] ['steɪpəl] *vt* **-pled; -pling** : agrafer

staple[2] *adj* : principal, de base <staple foods : denrées de base>

staple[3] *n* : agrafe *f*

stapler ['steɪplər] *n* : agrafeuse *f*

star[1] ['stɑr] *v* **starred; starring** *vt* 1 : marquer d'une étoile ou d'un astérisque 2 FEATURE : avoir pour vedette — *vi* : être la vedette

star[2] *n* 1 : étoile *f* 2 : vedette *f*, étoile *f*, star *f* <a movie star : une vedette de cinéma>

starboard ['stɑrbərd] *n* : tribord *m*

starch[1] ['stɑrtʃ] *vt* : amidonner

starch[2] *n* 1 : amidon *m* 2 **starches** *npl* : féculents *mpl* (aliments)

starchy ['stɑrtʃi] *adj* **starchier; -est** : féculent <a starchy diet : un régime riche en féculents>

stardom ['stɑrdəm] *n* : célébrité *f*

stare[1] ['stær] *vi* **stared; staring** : regarder fixement

stare[2] *n* : regard *m* fixe

starfish ['stɑr,fɪʃ] *n* : étoile *f* de mer

stark[1] ['stɑrk] *adv* : complètement <stark raving mad : complètement fou> <stark naked : tout nu>

stark[2] *adj* 1 ABSOLUTE : absolu, pur 2 BARREN, DESOLATE : désolé, dénudé 3 BLUNT, HARSH : cru, catégorique, dur <the stark realities : les dures réalités>

starlight ['stɑr,laɪt] *n* : lumière *f* des étoiles

starling ['stɑrlɪŋ] *n* : étourneau *m*

starry ['stɑri] *adj* **starrier; -est** : étoilé

start[1] ['stɑrt] *vi* 1 JUMP : sursauter 2 BEGIN : commencer 3 DEPART : partir (en voyage, etc.) 4 : démarrer (se dit d'un moteur) — *vt* 1 BEGIN : commencer, se mettre à 2 CAUSE : provoquer 3 ESTABLISH : établir, créer <to start a business : établir une entreprise> 4 : mettre en marche, démarrer <to start the car : démarrer la voiture>

start[2] *n* 1 JUMP : sursaut *m* 2 BEGINNING : commencement *m*, début *m* <to get an early start : commencer tôt>

starter ['stɑrtər] *n* 1 ENTRANT : partant *m*, -tante *f*; participant *m*, -pante *f* (aux sports) 2 APPETIZER : hors-d'œuvre *m*, entrée *f* 3 : démarreur *m* (d'un véhicule)

startle ['stɑrṭəl] *vt* **-tled; -tling** : surprendre, alarmer, faire tressaillir

starve ['stɑrv] *v* **starved; starving** *vi* : mourir de faim — *vt* : affamer, faire mourir de faim

stash ['stæʃ] *vt* : cacher, mettre de côté

state[1] ['steɪt] *vt* **stated; stating** 1 REPORT : exposer, déclarer 2 SPECIFY : spécifier, indiquer <as stated above : ainsi qu'il est indiqué plus haut>

state[2] *n* 1 CONDITION : état *m* 2 NATION : état *m*, nation *f* 3 : état *m* (d'un pays) 4 **the States** : les États-Unis

stateliness ['steɪtlinəs] *n* : majesté *f*, grandeur *f*

stately ['steɪtli] *adj* **statelier; -est** : majestueux, imposant

statement ['steɪtmənt] *n* 1 DECLARATION : déclaration *f* 2 *or* **bank statement** : relevé *m* de compte

stateroom ['steɪt,ru:m] *n* : cabine *f* de luxe

statesman ['steɪtsmən] *n, pl* **-men** [-mən, -,mɛn] : homme *m* d'État

static[1] ['stæṭɪk] *adj* : statique

static[2] *n* **1** : parasites *mpl* (de radio, de télévision) **2** *or* **static electricity** : électricité *f* statique
station[1] ['steɪʃən] *vt* : poster, placer
station[2] *n* **1** : gare *f* (de train), station *f* (de métro) **2** RANK, STANDING : rang *m* **3** : station *f* (de radio), chaîne *f* (de télévision) **4 police station** : poste *m* de police **5 fire station** : caserne *f* de pompiers **6** → **service station**
stationary ['steɪʃə,nɛri] *adj* **1** IMMOBILE : stationnaire, immobile **2** UNCHANGING : fixe
stationery ['steɪʃə,nɛri] *n* : papeterie *f*, papier *m* à lettres
station wagon *n* : familiale *f*
statistic [stə'tɪstɪk] *n* : statistique *f*
statistical [stə'tɪstɪkəl] *adj* : statistique, de statistique
statue ['stæ,tʃu:] *n* : statue *f*
statuesque [,stætʃʊ'ɛsk] *adj* : sculptural
statuette [,stætʃʊ'ɛt] *n* : statuette *f*
stature ['stætʃər] *n* **1** HEIGHT : stature *f*, taille *f* **2** CALIBRE, STATUS : stature *f*, envergure *f*, calibre *m*
status ['steɪṭəs, 'stæ-] *n* **1** : situation *f* (légale), statut *m* <marital status : situation de famille> **2** PRESTIGE : prestige *m*, standing *m* **3** POSITION : position *f*, rang *m* (social)
statute ['stæ,tʃu:t] *n* : loi *f*, règle *f*
staunch ['stɔntʃ] *adj* : dévoué, loyal <a staunch supporter : un fidèle>
staunchly ['stɔntʃli] *adv* : avec dévouement, loyalement
stave[1] ['steɪv] *vt* **staved** *or* **stove** ['stov]; **staving 1 to stave in** : enfoncer **2 to stave off** : écarter, tromper (la faim, etc.), éviter
stave[2] *n* : douve *f* (d'un tonneau)
staves → **staff**[2]
stay[1] ['steɪ] *vi* **1** REMAIN : rester, demeurer <to stay in : rester à la maison> <he stays in the city : il demeure en ville> **2** CONTINUE : rester <to stay awake : rester éveillé> **3** LODGE : loger — *vt* **1** HALT : arrêter, surseoir à (en droit) **2 to stay the course** : tenir jusqu'au bout
stay[2] *n* **1** SOJOURN : séjour *m* **2** SUPPORT : soutien *m*
stead ['stɛd] *n* **1** : place *f* <she went in his stead : elle est allée à sa place> **2 to stand s.o. in good stead** : être utile à qqn
steadfast ['stɛd,fæst] *adj* **1** IMMOVABLE : fixe **2** FIRM : ferme, résolu **3** LOYAL : dévoué <a steadfast friend : un fidèle ami>
steadily ['stɛdəli] *adv* **1** CONSTANTLY : régulièrement, sans arrêt **2** FIRMLY : fermement **3** FIXEDLY : fixement **4** GRADUALLY : progressivement
steady[1] ['stɛdi] *v* **steadied; steadying** *vt* : stabiliser <she steadied herself : elle a retrouvé son équilibre> — *vi* : se stabiliser
steady[2] *adj* **steadier; -est 1** FIRM, SURE : ferme, sûr **2** REGULAR, CONSTANT : régulier, constant **3** CALM : calme **4** STABLE : stable
steak ['steɪk] *n* : bifteck *m*, steak *m*
steal ['sti:l] *v* **stole** ['sto:l]; **stolen** ['stolən]; **stealing** *vt* : voler — *vi* **1** : voler <thou shalt not steal : tu ne voleras point> **2** CREEP, SLIP : se glisser **3 to steal away** : s'esquiver
stealth ['stɛlθ] *n* : discrétion *f* <by stealth : furtivement>
stealthily ['stɛlθəli] *adv* : furtivement
stealthy ['stɛlθi] *adj* **stealthier; -est** : furtif
steam[1] ['sti:m] *vi* **1** : fumer **2 to steam ahead** : avancer — *vt* **1** : cuire à la vapeur **2 to steam open** : décacheter à la vapeur
steam[2] *n* : vapeur *f*
steamboat ['sti:m,bo:t] → **steamship**
steam engine *n* : moteur *m* à vapeur
steamroller ['sti:m,ro:lər] *n* : rouleau *m* compresseur
steamship ['sti:m,ʃɪp] *n* : paquebot *m*, navire *m* à vapeur
steamy ['sti:mi] *adj* **steamier; -est 1** : plein de vapeur, embué **2** EROTIC : érotique
steed ['sti:d] *n* : coursier *m*
steel[1] ['sti:l] *vt* **1 to steel oneself** : s'armer de courage **2 to steel oneself against** : se cuirasser contre
steel[2] *adj* : en acier, d'acier
steel[3] *n* : acier *m*
steely ['sti:li] *adj* **steelier; -est** : d'acier <a steely gaze : un regard d'acier> <steely determination : une volonté de fer>
steep[1] ['sti:p] *vt* : tremper, faire tremper
steep[2] *adj* **1** : raide, à pic **2** SHARP : fort <a steep increase : une forte augmentation> **3** EXCESSIVE : excessif <steep prices : des prix exorbitants>
steeple ['sti:pəl] *n* : clocher *m*, flèche *f*
steeplechase ['sti:pəl,tʃeɪs] *n* : course *f* d'obstacles
steeply ['sti:pli] *adv* **1** : à pic, abruptement, en pente raide **2 to rise steeply** : monter en flèche (se dit des prix)
steer[1] ['stɪr] *vt* **1** : conduire (une voiture), gouverner (un navire) **2** GUIDE : diriger, guider
steer[2] *n* : bœuf *m*
steering wheel *n* : volant *m*
stein ['staɪn] *n* : chope *f*
stellar ['stɛlər] *adj* **1** : stellaire **2** SUPERB : superbe
stem[1] ['stɛm] *v* **stemmed; stemming** *vt* : arrêter, contenir, endiguer <to stem the tide : endiguer le flot> — *vi* **to stem from** : provenir de
stem[2] *n* : tige *f* (d'une plante)
stench ['stɛntʃ] *n* : puanteur *f*
stencil[1] ['stɛntsəl] *vt* **-ciled** *or* **-cilled; -ciling** *or* **-cilling** : dessiner au pochoir

stencil[2] *n* : pochoir *m*

stenographer [stə'nɑgrəfər] *n* : sténographe *mf*

stenographic [,stɛnə'græfɪk] *adj* : sténographique

stenography [stə'nɑgrəfi] *n* : sténographie *f*

step[1] ['stɛp] *vi* **stepped; stepping 1** : aller, marcher <step this way, please : par ici, s'il vous plaît> <he stepped outside : il est sorti> **2 to step on** : marcher sur

step[2] *n* **1** : pas *m* <step by step : pas à pas> <with a quick step : d'un pas rapide> **2** STAIR : marche *f* **3** RUNG : échelon *m*, barreau *m* **4** MEASURE : mesure *f*, disposition *f* <to take steps : prendre des mesures> **5** MOVE : pas *m* <a step in the right direction : un pas dans la bonne voie>

stepbrother ['stɛp,brʌðər] *n* : beau-frère *m*

stepdaughter ['stɛp,dɔt̬ər] *n* : belle-fille *f*

stepfather ['stɛp,fɑðər, -,fa-] *n* : beau-père *m*

stepladder ['stɛp,lædər] *n* : escabeau *m*

stepmother ['stɛp,mʌðər] *n* : belle-mère *f*

steppe ['stɛp] *n* : steppe *f*

stepson ['stɛp,sʌn] *n* : beau-fils *m*

step up *vt* INCREASE : intensifier

stereo[1] ['stɛri,o:, 'stɪr-] *adj* : stéréo

stereo[2] *n, pl* **stereos 1** : stéréo *f* <in stereo : en stéréo> **2** *or* **stereo system** : chaîne *f* stéréo

stereophonic [,stɛrio'fɑnɪk, ,stɪr-] *adj* : stéréophonique

stereotype[1] ['stɛrio,taɪp, 'stɪr-] *vt* **-typed; -typing** : stéréotyper

stereotype[2] *n* : stéréotype *m*

sterile ['stɛrəl] *adj* : stérile

sterility [stə'rɪlət̬i] *n* : stérilité *f*

sterilization [,stɛrələ'zeɪʃən] *n* : stérilisation *f*

sterilize ['stɛrə,laɪz] *vt* **-ized; -izing** : stériliser

sterling ['stərlɪŋ] *adj* **1** : fin (se dit de l'argent) **2** EXCELLENT : excellent, de premier ordre

stern[1] ['stərn] *adj* : sévère — **sternly** *adv*

stern[2] *n* : arrière *m*, poupe *f*

sternness ['stərnnəs] *n* : sévérité *f*

sternum ['stərnəm] *n, pl* **sternums** *or* **sterna** [-nə] : sternum *m*

stethoscope ['stɛθə,sko:p] *n* : stéthoscope *m*

stevedore ['sti:və,dor] *n* : docker *m*

stew[1] ['stu:, 'stju:] *vt* : cuire, faire cuire (en ragoût) — *vi* **1** : cuire (se dit des fruits), cuire en ragoût, mijoter (se dit de la viande) **2** FRET : être dans tous ses états

stew[2] *n* **1** : ragoût *m* **2 to be in a stew** : être dans tous ses états

steward ['stu:ərd, 'stju:-] *n* **1** MANAGER : régisseur *m* (d'un domaine) **2** : steward *m* (d'un avion, etc.)

stewardess ['stu:ərdəs, 'stju:-] *n* : hôtesse *f*

stick[1] ['stɪk] *v* **stuck** ['stʌk]; **sticking** *vt* **1** STAB : piquer, enfoncer **2** AFFIX : coller **3** PUT : mettre, insérer <to stick one's head out the window : passer la tête par la fenêtre> **4 to stick out** : sortir, tirer (la langue) **5 to stick up** ROB : dévaliser — *vi* **1** ADHERE : coller **2** : se planter, s'enfoncer <the nail stuck in my hand : je me suis planté le clou dans la main> **3** JAM : se coincer, se bloquer **4 to stick around** : attendre **5 to stick out** PROTRUDE : faire saillie, dépasser (d'une superficie), ressortir (d'un contexte) **6 to stick to** : ne pas abandonner <to stick to one's guns : ne pas en démordre> **7 to stick up** : se dresser (se dit des cheveux, etc.), dépasser, sortir **8 to stick with** : rester avec

stick[2] *n* **1** BRANCH : bâton *m* **2** : crosse *f* (aux sports) **3** → **walking stick**

sticker ['stɪkər] *n* : autocollant *m*, collant *m Can*

stickler ['stɪklər] *n* : personne *f* exigeante <to be a stickler for : être à cheval sur>

sticky ['stɪki] *adj* **stickier; -est 1** : collant **2** MUGGY : humide **3** DIFFICULT : difficile

stiff ['stɪf] *adj* **1** RIGID : rigide, raide <a stiff dough : une pâte ferme> **2** : ankylosé, courbaturé <stiff muscles : des muscles courbaturés> **3** FORMAL : guindé **4** STRONG : fort (se dit du vent, etc.) **5** DIFFICULT, SEVERE : sévère, difficile

stiffen ['stɪfən] *vt* **1** STRENGTHEN : renforcer **2** THICKEN : donner de la consistance à (des œufs, une sauce) **3** : courbaturer (les muscles) — *vi* **1** HARDEN : se durcir, se raidir **2** THICKEN : devenir ferme, épaisser **3** : s'ankyloser (se dit des articulations, etc.)

stiffly ['stɪfli] *adv* **1** RIGIDLY : avec raideur, rigidement **2** COLDLY : avec froideur

stiffness ['stɪfnəs] *n* **1** RIGIDITY : raideur *f*, rigidité *f* **2** COLDNESS : froideur *f* **3** SEVERITY : sévérité *f*

stifle ['staɪfəl] *vt* **-fled; -fling** SMOTHER, SUPPRESS : étouffer, réprimer, retenir <to stifle a yawn : retenir un bâillement>

stigma ['stɪgmə] *n, pl* **stigmata** [stɪg'mɑt̬ə, 'stɪgmət̬ə] *or* **stigmas** : stigmate *m*

stigmatize ['stɪgmə,taɪz] *vt* **-tized; -tizing** : stigmatiser

stile ['staɪl] *n* : échalier *m*

stiletto [stə'lɛt̬o:] *n, pl* **-tos** *or* **-toes 1** : stylet *m* **2** *or* **stiletto heel** : talon *m* aiguille

still[1] [ˈstɪl] *vt* CALM : calmer — *vi* : se calmer

still[2] *adv* **1** MOTIONLESSLY : sans bouger <sit still! : reste tranquille!> **2** : encore, toujours <she still lives there : elle y habite toujours> <it's still the same : c'est toujours pareille> **3** : quand même, tout de même <he still has doubts : il a quand même des doutes> <I still prefer that you stay : je préfère tout de même que tu restes>

still[3] *adj* **1** MOTIONLESS : immobile **2** CALM : tranquille **3** SILENT : silencieux

still[4] *n* **1** SILENCE : silence *m* **2** : alambic *m* (pour distiller l'alcool)

stillborn [ˈstɪl,bɔrn] *adj* : mort-né

stillness [ˈstɪlnəs] *n* : calme *m*, tranquillité *f*

stilt [ˈstɪlt] *n* : échasse *f*

stilted [ˈstɪltəd] *adj* : guindé

stimulant [ˈstɪmjələnt] *n* : stimulant *m*

stimulate [ˈstɪmjə,leɪt] *vt* **-lated; -lating** : stimuler

stimulation [,stɪmjəˈleɪʃən] *n* **1** STIMULATING : stimulation *f* **2** STIMULUS : stimulant *m*

stimulus [ˈstɪmjələs] *n, pl* **-li** [-,laɪ] **1** : stimulus *m* (en physiologie) **2** INCENTIVE : stimulant *m*

sting[1] [ˈstɪŋ] *v* **stung** [ˈstʌŋ]; **stinging** *vt* **1** : piquer <a bee stung him : une abeille l'a piqué> **2** HURT : blesser, piquer au vif

sting[2] *n* : piqûre *f*

stinger [ˈstɪŋər] *n* : dard *m*, aiguillon *m*

stinginess [ˈstɪndʒinəs] *n* : avarice *f*, pingrerie *f*

stingy [ˈstɪndʒi] *adj* **stingier; -est** : avare, pingre

stink[1] [ˈstɪŋk] *vi* **stank** [ˈstæŋk] *or* **stunk** [ˈstʌŋk]; **stunk; stinking** : puer

stink[2] *n* : puanteur *f*

stint[1] [ˈstɪnt] *vt* DEPRIVE : priver — *vi* **to stint on** : lésiner sur

stint[2] *n* : période *f* (de travail)

stipend [ˈstaɪ,pɛnd, -pənd] *n* : traitement *m*

stipulate [ˈstɪpjə,leɪt] *vt* **-lated; -lating** : stipuler

stipulation [,stɪpjəˈleɪʃən] *n* : stipulation *f*

stir[1] [ˈstər] *v* **stirred; stirring** *vt* **1** AGITATE : agiter **2** MIX : remuer **3** INCITE : inciter **4** MOVE : émouvoir (une personne), exciter (la curiosité, etc.) **5** *or* **to stir up** PROVOKE : susciter (un sentiment, etc.), provoquer (la colère, etc.) — *vi* : bouger

stir[2] *n* **1** MOTION : mouvement *m* **2** COMMOTION : agitation *f*

stirrup [ˈstərəp, ˈstɪr-] *n* : étrier *m*

stitch[1] [ˈstɪtʃ] *vt* : coudre, suturer (en médecine) — *vi* : coudre

stitch[2] *n* **1** : point *m* **2** TWINGE : point *m* (au côté)

stock[1] [ˈstɑk] *vt* **1** SUPPLY : approvisionner **2** SELL : avoir pour vendre — *vi* **to stock up** : s'approvisionner

stock[2] *n* **1** SUPPLY : réserve *f*, stock *m* <to be out of stock : être épuisé> **2** LIVESTOCK : bétail *m* **3** ANCESTRY : lignée *f*, souche *f* **4** BROTH : bouillon *m* **5** STANDING : cote *f* **6 stocks** *npl* SECURITIES : actions *fpl*, valeurs *fpl* **7 to take stock** : évaluer, faire le point

stockade [stɑˈkeɪd] *n* : palissade *f*

stockbroker [ˈstɑk,bro:kər] *n* : agent *m* de change

stockholder [ˈstɑk,ho:ldər] *n* : actionnaire *mf*

stocking [ˈstɑkɪŋ] *n* : bas *m* <a pair of stockings : une paire de bas>

stock market *n* : Bourse *f*

stockpile[1] [ˈstɑk,paɪl] *vt* **-piled; -piling** : stocker, amasser

stockpile[2] *n* : stock *m*, réserve *f*

stocky [ˈstɑki] *adj* **stockier; -est** : trapu

stockyard [ˈstɑk,jɑrd] *n* : parc *m* à bétail

stodgy [ˈstɑdʒi] *adj* **stodgier; -est 1** DULL : ennuyeux, lourd **2** HIDEBOUND : borné, rigide

stoic[1] [ˈsto:ɪk] *or* **stoical** [-ɪkəl] *adj* : stoïque — **stoically** [-ɪkli] *adv*

stoic[2] *n* : stoïque *mf*

stoicism [ˈsto:ə,sɪzəm] *n* : stoïcisme *m*

stoke [ˈsto:k] *vt* **stoked; stoking** : alimenter, entretenir

stole[1] → **steal**

stole[2] [ˈsto:l] *n* : étole *f*

stolen → **steal**

stolid [ˈstɑlɪd] *adj* : impassible — **stolidly** *adv*

stomach[1] [ˈstʌmɪk] *vt* : supporter, tolérer

stomach[2] *n* **1** : estomac *m* **2** BELLY : ventre *m* <to have a fat stomach : avoir du ventre> **3** DESIRE : envie *f* <to have no stomach for : n'avoir aucune envie de>

stomachache [ˈstʌmɪk,eɪk] *n* : mal *m* de ventre

stomp [ˈstɑmp, ˈstɔmp] *vt* : piétiner — *vi* : marcher d'un pas lourd

stone[1] [ˈsto:n] *vt* **stoned; stoning** : jeter des pierres sur

stone[2] *n* **1** : pierre *f* **2** PIT : noyau *m* (d'un fruit)

Stone Age *n* : âge *m* de pierre

stony [ˈsto:ni] *adj* **stonier; -est 1** ROCKY : pierreux **2** UNFEELING : insensible, glacial <a stony stare : un regard glacial>

stood → **stand**[1]

stool [ˈstu:l] *n* **1** SEAT : tabouret *m*, escabeau *m* **2** FOOTSTOOL : tabouret *m* **3** FECES : selle *f*

stoop[1] [ˈstu:p] *vi* **1** CROUCH : se baisser, se pencher **2 to stoop to** : s'abaisser à

stoop[2] *n* **1** : dos *m* voûté <to have a stoop : avoir le dos voûté> **2** PORCH, VERANDA : porche *m,* véranda *f*

stop[1] ['stɑp] *v* **stopped; stopping** *vt* **1** *or* **to stop up** PLUG : boucher **2** PREVENT : empêcher <she stopped me from leaving : elle m'a empêché de partir> **3** HALT : arrêter, stopper **4** CEASE : arrêter, cesser <he stopped talking : il a cessé de parler> — *vi* **1** HALT : s'arrêter, stopper **2** CEASE : cesser, s'arrêter <the rain won't stop : la pluie n'arrête pas> **3** STAY : rester **4 to stop by** : passer <stop by at my house : passe chez moi>

stop[2] *n* **1** STOPPER : bouchon *m* **2** HALT : arrêt *m,* halte *f* <to come to a stop : s'arrêter> <to put a stop to : mettre fin à> **3** : arrêt *m* <bus stop : arrêt de bus>

stopgap ['stɑp,gæp] *n* : bouche-trou *m*

stoplight ['stɑp,laɪt] *n* : feu *m* rouge

stoppage ['stɑpɪdʒ] *n* : arrêt *m,* suspension *f* <work stoppage : arrêt de travail>

stopper ['stɑpər] *n* : bouchon *m*

storage ['storɪdʒ] *n* **1** : emmagasinage *m,* entreposage *m* **2** : stockage *m* (des données)

storage battery *n* : accumulateur *m*

store[1] ['stor] *vt* **stored; storing** : emmagasiner, entreposer

store[2] *n* **1** RESERVE, SUPPLY : réserve *f,* provision *f* **2** SHOP : magasin *m* **3 to have in store** : avoir en réserve

storehouse ['stor,haʊs] *n* : entrepôt *m*

storekeeper ['stor,ki:pər] *n* : commerçant *m,* -çante *f*

storeroom ['stor,ru:m, -,rʊm] *n* : magasin *m,* réserve *f*

stork ['stɔrk] *n* : cigogne *f*

storm[1] ['stɔrm] *vi* **1** : faire rage (se dit d'une tempête) **2** RAGE : tempêter, fulminer <to storm out : sortir comme un ouragan, partir furieux> — *vt* ATTACK : prendre d'assaut

storm[2] *n* **1** : orage *m,* tempête *f* **2** UPROAR : tempête *f* <a storm of abuse : une tempête d'injures>

stormy ['stɔrmi] *adj* **stormier; -est** : orageux

story ['stori] *n, pl* **stories 1** NARRATIVE : histoire *f* **2** ACCOUNT : article *m* (en journalisme) **3** PLOT : intrigue *f,* scénario *m* **4** FLOOR : étage *m*

stout ['staʊt] *adj* **1** FIRM, RESOLUTE : ferme, résolu **2** STURDY : solide **3** FAT : corpulent, gros

stove[1] ['sto:v] *n* : poêle *m* (pour chauffer), cuisinière *f* (pour cuisiner)

stove[2] → **stave**[1]

stow ['sto:] *vt* **1** STORE : ranger, emmagasiner, arrimer (la cargaison) **2** LOAD : remplir — *vi* **to stow away** : s'embarquer clandestinement

straddle ['strædəl] *vt* **-dled; -dling 1** : enfourcher (un cheval, une bicyclette) **2** SPAN : enjamber

straggle ['strægəl] *vi* **-gled; -gling** : traîner

straggler ['strægələr] *n* : traînard *m,* -narde *f*

straight[1] ['streɪt] *adv* **1** : droit <go straight, then turn right : allez tout droit, puis tournez à droite> **2** HONESTLY : honnêtement <to go straight : vivre honnêtement> **3** CLEARLY : clairement **4** DIRECTLY : directement **5** FRANKLY : franchement

straight[2] *adj* **1** : droit, d'aplomb (se dit d'un objet vertical), raide (se dit des cheveux), sec (se dit d'une boisson alcoolisée) **2** HONEST, JUST : honnête, juste **3** NEAT, ORDERLY : en ordre **4** DIRECT : direct

straightaway [,streɪtə'weɪ] *adv* : immédiatement

straighten ['streɪtən] *vt* **1** : redresser, rendre droit **2** *or* **to straighten up** ORGANIZE : mettre en ordre, ranger

straightforward [streɪt'fɔrwərd] *adj* **1** FRANK : franc, honnête **2** CLEAR, PRECISE : clair, simple

strain[1] ['streɪn] *vt* **1** EXERT, STRETCH : tendre, forcer <to strain oneself : faire un grand effort> **2** FILTER : filtrer **3** INJURE : froisser, fatiguer <to strain a muscle : se froisser un muscle>

strain[2] *n* **1** LINEAGE : lignée *f* **2** EFFORT : effort *m* **3** VARIETY : variété *f* **4** STRESS : stress *m,* tension *f* **5** SPRAIN : foulure *f* **6 strains** *npl* TUNE : air *m,* accents *mpl*

strainer ['streɪnər] *n* : passoire *f*

strait ['streɪt] *n* **1** : détroit *m* **2 straits** *npl* DISTRESS : gêne *f* <in dire straits : aux abois>

straitened ['streɪtənd] *adj* **in straitened circumstances** : dans le besoin

strand[1] ['strænd] *vt* **1** : échouer **2 to be left stranded** : être abandonné

strand[2] *n* **1** : toron *m,* brin *m* <a strand of hair : un cheveu> **2** BEACH : plage *f*

strange ['streɪndʒ] *adj* **stranger; -est 1** QUEER, UNUSUAL : étrange, bizarre **2** UNFAMILIAR : inconnu

strangely ['streɪndʒli] *adv* : étrangement, bizarrement <to behave strangely : se comporter de façon étrange> <strangely, he didn't call : curieusement, il n'a pas téléphoné>

strangeness ['streɪndʒnəs] *n* : étrangeté *f*

stranger ['streɪndʒər] *n* : étranger *m,* -gère *f*

strangle ['stræŋgəl] *vt* **-gled; -gling** : étrangler

strangler ['stræŋglər] *n* : étrangleur *m,* -gleuse *f*

strap[1] ['stræp] *vt* **strapped; strapping 1** FASTEN : attacher **2** FLOG : fouetter

strap[2] *n* **1** : courroie *f,* sangle *f* **2 shoulder strap** : bretelle *f*

strapless [ˈstræpləs] *n* : sans bretelles

strapping [ˈstræpɪŋ] *adj* : robuste, costaud *fam*

stratagem [ˈstrætədʒəm, -ˌdʒɛm] *n* : stratagème *m*

strategic [strəˈtiːdʒɪk] *adj* : stratégique

strategy [ˈstrætədʒi] *n, pl* **-gies** : stratégie *f*

stratified [ˈstrætəˌfaɪd] *adj* : stratifié

stratosphere [ˈstrætəˌsfɪr] *n* : stratosphère *f*

stratum [ˈstreɪtəm, ˈstræ-] *n, pl* **strata** [-tə] : strate *f,* couche *f*

straw [ˈstrɔ] *n* : paille *f*

strawberry [ˈstrɔˌbɛri] *n, pl* **-ries** : fraise *f*

stray[1] [ˈstreɪ] *vi* **1** WANDER : errer, s'égarer <the cattle strayed away : les bœufs se sont égarés> **2** : errer, vagabonder (se dit des pensées, des yeux, etc.) <to stray from the point : s'éloigner du sujet>

stray[2] *adj* : errant, perdu

stray[3] *n* : animal *m* errant

streak[1] [ˈstriːk] *vt* : rayer <blue streaked with grey : bleu rayé de gris> — *vi* DASH, RUSH : s'élancer

streak[2] *n* **1** LINE : raie *f,* bande *f,* mèche *f* (dans les cheveux) **2** TENDENCY : tendance *f,* côté *m* <a stubborn streak : un côté obstiné> **3** TRACE : trace *f* **4** PERIOD : période *f,* passe *f* <a streak of luck : une bonne passe>

stream[1] [ˈstriːm] *vi* : couler, ruisseler <tears streamed from his eyes : des larmes ruisselaient de ses yeux> — *vt* : ruisseler de <to stream blood : ruisseler de sang>

stream[2] *n* **1** BROOK : ruisseau *m* **2** FLOW : courant *m,* flot *m*

streamer [ˈstriːmər] *n* **1** BANNER : banderole *f* **2** RIBBON : serpentin *m* (de papier)

streamlined [ˈstriːmˌlaɪnd] *adj* **1** : aérodynamique **2** EFFICIENT : rationalisé, dégraissé

street [ˈstriːt] *n* : rue *f*

streetcar [ˈstriːtˌkɑr] *n* : tramway *m*

strength [ˈstrɛŋkθ] *n* **1** POWER : force *f,* puissance *f* **2** SOLIDITY : solidité *f* **3** INTENSITY : intensité *f,* force *f* **4** NUMBERS : effectif *m* <we're at full strength : nos effectifs sont au complet> **5** : qualité *f* <strengths and weaknesses : qualités et faiblesses>

strengthen [ˈstrɛŋkθən] *vt* **1** : fortifier (les muscles, etc.), raffermir **2** REINFORCE : renforcer **3** INTENSIFY : intensifier

strenuous [ˈstrɛnjʊəs] *adj* **1** VIGOROUS : vigoureux, énergique **2** ARDUOUS : ardu, fatiguant

strenuously [ˈstrɛnjʊəsli] *adv* : vigoureusement

stress[1] [ˈstrɛs] *vt* **1** : charger, mettre sous tension **2** EMPHASIZE : mettre l'accent sur, souligner, accentuer (en prononciation) **3 to stress out** : stresser

stress[2] *n* **1** PRESSURE : contrainte *f,* effort *m* **2** EMPHASIS : accent *m,* insistance *f* **3** TENSION : tension *f,* stress *m*

stressful [ˈstrɛsfəl] *adj* : stressant

stretch[1] [ˈstrɛtʃ] *vt* **1** EXTEND : tendre, allonger **2** : distendre, étirer (les muscles) **3** PROLONG : prolonger, faire durer **4 to stretch the truth** : exagérer — *vi* : s'étirer

stretch[2] *n* **1** STRETCHING : extension *f,* étirement *m* (des muscles) **2** ELASTICITY : élasticité *f* **3** EXPANSE : étendue *f* <the home stretch : la ligne d'arrivée> **4** PERIOD : période *f* (de temps)

stretcher [ˈstrɛtʃər] *n* : civière *f,* brancard *m*

strew [ˈstruː] *vt* **strewed; strewed** *or* **strewn** [ˈstruːn]; **strewing 1** SCATTER : répandre **2 to be strewn with** : être jonché de

stricken [ˈstrɪkən] *adj* **stricken with** : affligé de (une émotion), atteint de (une maladie)

strict [ˈstrɪkt] *adj* : strict — **strictly** *adv*

strictness [ˈstrɪktlɪ] *n* **1** SEVERITY : sévérité *f* **2** RIGOR : rigueur *f*

stricture [ˈstrɪktʃər] *n* **1** NARROWING : rétrécissement *m* (en médecine) **2** CENSURE : critique *f* (sévère) **3** RESTRICTION : contrainte *f*

stride[1] [ˈstraɪd] *vi* **strode** [ˈstroːd]; **stridden** [ˈstrɪdən]; **striding** : marcher à grands pas, marcher à grandes enjambées

stride[2] *n* **1** : grand pas *m,* enjambée *f* **2 to make great strides** : faire de grands progrès

strident [ˈstraɪdənt] *adj* : strident

strife [ˈstraɪf] *n* : conflit *m,* lutte *f*

strike[1] [ˈstraɪk] *v* **struck** [ˈstrʌk]; **struck; striking** *vt* **1** HIT : frapper **2** DELETE : rayer **3** COIN, MINT : frapper **4** : sonner (l'heure) **5** AFFLICT : frapper <he was stricken with a fever : il a eu une poussée de fièvre> **6** IMPRESS : impressionner <her voice struck me : sa voix m'a impressionné> <it struck him as funny : ça lui a paru drôle> **7** : frotter (une allumette) **8** FIND : trouver, découvrir (de l'or, du pétrole) **9** ADOPT : adopter, prendre (une pose, une attitude) — *vi* **1** HIT : frapper **2** ATTACK : attaquer **3** *or* **to go on strike** : faire grève

strike[2] *n* **1** BLOW : coup *m* **2** : grève *f* <to be on strike : faire grève> **3** ATTACK : attaque *f* **4** : prise *f* *Can* (au baseball)

strikebreaker [ˈstraɪkˌbreɪkər] *n* : briseur *m,* -seuse *f* de grève, jaune *mf*

strike out *vi* **1** GO : aller, partir **2** : retirer *Can* (au baseball)

striker [ˈstraɪkər] *n* : gréviste *mf;* piqueteur *m,* -teuse *f*

strike up *vt* START : commencer

striking ['straɪkɪŋ] *adj* : frappant, saisissant <a striking beauty : une beauté frappante>

strikingly ['straɪkɪŋli] *adv* : de manière frappante, remarquablement

string[1] ['strɪŋ] *vt* **strung** ['strʌŋ]; **stringing 1** : mettre des cordes à, monter (une guitare, etc.) **2** : enfiler (des perles) **3** HANG : suspendre

string[2] *n* **1** CORD : ficelle *f*, cordon *m* **2** SERIES : suite *f* **3 strings** *npl* : cordes *fpl* (d'un orchestre)

string bean *n* : haricot *m* vert

stringent ['strɪndʒənt] *adj* : rigoureux, strict

stringy ['strɪŋi] *adj* **stringier; -est** : fibreux, filandreux (se dit des viandes, des légumes, etc.)

strip[1] ['strɪp] *v* **stripped; stripping** *vt* **1** REMOVE : enlever **2** UNDRESS : déshabiller — *vi* : se déshabiller

strip[2] *n* : bande *f* <a strip of land : une bande de terre>

stripe[1] ['straɪp] *vt* **striped** ['straɪpt]; **striping** : marquer avec rayures

stripe[2] *n* **1** : rayure *f*, bande *f* **2** CHEVRON : chevron *m*, galon *m*

striped ['straɪpt, 'straɪpəd] *adj* : rayé, à rayures

strive ['straɪv] *vi* **strove** ['stro:v]; **striven** ['strɪvən] *or* **strived; striving 1 to strive for** : lutter pour **2 to strive to** : s'efforcer de

strode → **stride**[1]

stroke[1] ['stro:k] *vt* **stroked; stroking** : caresser

stroke[2] *n* **1** MOVEMENT : coup *m* <stroke of luck : coup de chance> **2** *or* **brush stroke** : trait *m* (de pinceau) **3** : attaque *f* (en médecine)

stroll[1] ['stro:l] *vi* : se promener

stroll[2] *n* : promenade *f*, petit tour *m*

stroller ['stro:lər] *n* : poussette *f* (pour enfants), carrosse *m Can*

strong ['strɔŋ] *adj* **1** : fort **2** HEALTHY : robuste, en forme **3** ZEALOUS : acharné, fervent

stronghold ['strɔŋˌho:ld] *n* : forteresse *f*, bastion *m* <a cultural stronghold : un bastion de la culture>

strongly ['strɔŋli] *adv* **1** POWERFULLY : fortement **2** STURDILY : solidement **3** INTENSELY : intensément **4** WHOLEHEARTEDLY : vivement, fermement

struck → **strike**[1]

structural ['strʌktʃərəl] *adj* : structural, de construction

structure[1] ['strʌktʃər] *vt* **-tured; -turing** : structurer

structure[2] *n* **1** BUILDING : construction *f* **2** ARRANGEMENT, FRAMEWORK : structure *f*

struggle[1] ['strʌgəl] *vi* **-gled; -gling 1** CONTEND : lutter, se débattre **2** : faire avec difficulté <she struggled forward : elle s'est avancée avec difficulté>

struggle[2] *n* : lutte *f*

strum ['strʌm] *v* **strummed; strumming** *vt* : gratter de — *vi* **to strum on** : gratter sur

strung → **string**[1]

strut[1] ['strʌt] *vi* **strutted; strutting** : se pavaner

strut[2] *n* **1** SWAGGER : démarche *f* arrogante **2** SUPPORT : étai *m*, support *m*

strychnine ['strɪkˌnaɪn, -nən, -ˌni:n] *n* : strychnine *f*

stub[1] ['stʌb] *vt* **stubbed; stubbing 1 to stub one's toe** : se cogner le doigt de pied **2 to stub out** : écraser

stub[2] *n* : mégot *m* (de cigarette), bout *m* (de crayon, etc.), talon *m* (de chèque)

stubble ['stʌbəl] *n* **1** : chaume *m* (de plantes) **2** : barbe *f* de plusieurs jours

stubborn ['stʌbərn] *adj* **1** OBSTINATE : obstiné, têtu **2** PERSISTENT : tenace

stubbornly ['stʌbərnli] *adv* : obstinément, de façon têtue

stubbornness ['stʌbərnnəs] *n* : entêtement *m*

stubby ['stʌbi] **stubbier; -est** *adj* : gros et court, trapu (se dit d'une personne) <stubby fingers : doigts épais>

stucco ['stʌko:] *n, pl* **stuccos** *or* **stuccoes** : stuc *m*

stuck → **stick**[1]

stuck–up ['stʌk'ʌp] *adj* : bêcheur, prétentieux, snob

stud[1] ['stʌd] *vt* **studded; studding** : clouter

stud[2] *n* **1** *or* **stud horse** : étalon *m* **2** UPRIGHT : montant *m* **3** HOBNAIL : caboche *f* **4** *or* **collar stud** : bouton *m* de col

student ['stu:dənt, 'stju:-] *n* : étudiant *m*, -diante *f*

studied ['stʌdi:d] *adj* : étudié, calculé, recherché

studio ['stu:diˌo:, 'stju:-] *n, pl* **-dios** : studio *m*, atelier *m* (d'un artist, etc.)

studious ['stu:diəs, 'stju:-] *adj* **1** : studieux **2** DELIBERATE : étudié, délibéré

studiously ['stu:diəsli, 'stju:-] *adv* : délibérément

study[1] ['stʌdi] *v* **studied; studying** *vt* **1** : étudier, faire des études de **2** EXAMINE : examiner — *vi* : étudier, faire ses études

study[2] *n, pl* **studies 1** : étude *f* **2** OFFICE : bureau *m*, cabinet *m* de travail

stuff[1] ['stʌf] *vt* **1** FILL : rembourrer (un meuble, etc.), empailler (en taxidermie), farcir (en cuisine) **2** SHOVE : fourrer <I stuffed it in my pocket : je l'ai fourré dans ma poche>

stuff[2] *n* **1** POSSESSIONS : affaires *fpl*, choses *fpl* **2** ESSENCE : essence *f*, étoffe *f* **3** SUBSTANCE : substance *f*, matière *f* <some sticky stuff : une

substance collante> <she knows her stuff : elle s'y connaît>

stuffing [ˈstʌfɪŋ] *n* **1** FILLING, PADDING : rembourrage *m,* bourrure *f Can* **2** : farce *f* (en cuisine)

stuffy [ˈstʌfi] *adj* **stuffier; -est 1** CLOSE : mal aéré **2** BLOCKED : bouché (se dit du nez) **3** STODGY : ennuyeux

stumble[1] [ˈstʌmbəl] *vi* **-bled; -bling 1** TRIP : trébucher **2 to stumble across** *or* **to stumble upon** : tomber sur

stumble[2] *n* : trébuchement *m*

stump[1] [ˈstʌmp] *vt* BAFFLE : déconcerter, laisser perplexe

stump[2] *n* **1** : bout *m,* moignon *m* (d'un membre) **2** *or* **tree stump** : souche *f*

stun [ˈstʌn] *vt* **stunned; stunning 1** : assommer (avec un coup) **2** ASTONISH : étonner, stupéfier

stung → **sting[1]**

stunk → **stink[1]**

stunning [ˈstʌnɪŋ] *adj* **1** ASTONISHING : épatant **2** STRIKING : ravissant, sensationnel

stunt[1] [ˈstʌnt] *vt* : retarder <to stunt s.o.'s growth : retarder la croissance de qqn>

stunt[2] *n* **1** : cascade *f,* acrobatie *f* **2** *or* **publicity stunt** : coup *m* de publicité

stupefy [ˈstuːpəˌfaɪ, ˈstjuː-] *vt* **-fied; -fying 1** : abrutir (avec des drogues, etc.) **2** AMAZE : stupéfier, abasourdir

stupendous [stʊˈpɛndəs, stjʊ-] *adj* : prodigieux, extraordinaire — **stupendously** *adv*

stupid [ˈstuːpəd, ˈstjuː-] *adj* **1** IDIOTIC, SILLY : idiot, bête **2** DULL, OBTUSE : stupide, bête, nounoune *Can*

stupidity [stʊˈpɪdəṭi, stjʊ-] *n, pl* **-ties** : stupidité *f,* bêtise *f*

stupidly [ˈstuːpədli, ˈstjuː-] *adv* : stupidement

stupor [ˈstuːpər, ˈstjuː-] *n* : stupeur *f*

sturdily [ˈstərdəli] *adv* : solidement

sturdiness [ˈstərdinəs] *n* : solidité *f,* robustesse *f*

sturdy [ˈstərdi] *adj* **sturdier; -est** : solide, robuste

sturgeon [ˈstərdʒən] *n* : esturgeon *m*

stutter[1] [ˈstʌṭər] *v* : bégayer

stutter[2] *n* : bégaiement *m*

sty [ˈstaɪ] *n* **1** *pl* **sties** PIGPEN : porcherie *f,* soue *f Can* **2** *pl* **sties** *or* **styes** : orgelet *m* (dans l'œil)

style[1] [ˈstaɪl] *vt* **styled; styling 1** NAME : appeler, dénommer **2** DESIGN : dessiner, concevoir, créer <carefully styled prose : prose conçue avec soin> **3** : coiffer (les cheveux)

style[2] *n* **1** : style *m,* manière *f* <that's just his style : c'est bien son genre> **2** FASHION : mode *f* **3** ELEGANCE : élégance *f,* style *m* <to live in style : mener grand train, vivre dans le luxe>

stylish [ˈstaɪlɪʃ] *adj* : chic, élégant

stylishly [ˈstaɪlɪʃli] *adv* : avec chic, élégamment

stylishness [ˈstaɪlɪʃnəs] *n* : chic *m,* élégance *f*

stylize [ˈstaɪəˌlaɪz] *vt* **-lized; -lizing** : styliser

stylus [ˈstaɪləs] *n, pl* **styli** [ˈstaɪˌlaɪ] **1** PEN : style *m* **2** NEEDLE : saphir *m* (d'un tourne-disque)

stymie [ˈstaɪmi] *vt* **-mied; -mieing** : coincer

suave [ˈswɑv] *adj* : suave

sub[1] [ˈsʌb] *vi* **subbed; subbing** → **substitute[1]**

sub[2] *n* **1** → **substitute[2]** **2** → **submarine[2]**

subcommittee [ˈsʌbkəˌmɪṭi] *n* : sous-comité *m*

subconscious[1] [ˌsʌbˈkɑntʃəs] *adj* : subconscient

subconscious[2] *n* : subconscient *m*

subconsciously [ˌsʌbˈkɑntʃəsli] *adv* : inconsciemment, de façon subconsciente

subcontract [ˌsʌbˈkɑnˌtrækt] *vt* : sous-traiter

subdivide [ˌsʌbdəˈvaɪd, ˈsʌbdəˌ-] *vt* **-vided; -viding** : subdiviser

subdivision [ˈsʌbdəˌvɪʒən] *n* : subdivision *f*

subdue [səbˈduː, -ˈdjuː] *vt* **-dued; -duing 1** OVERCOME : subjuguer, soumettre **2** CONTROL : maîtriser, réprimer **3** SOFTEN : adoucir, atténuer

subhead [ˈsʌbˌhɛd] *or* **subheading** [-ˌhɛdɪŋ] *n* : sous-titre *m*

subject[1] [səbˈdʒɛkt] *vt* **1** CONTROL, DOMINATE : soumettre, assujettir **2 to subject to** : exposer à, soumettre à

subject[2] [ˈsʌbdʒɪkt] *adj* **1** : sujet, soumis **2** PRONE : sujet <subject to colds : sujet aux rhumes> **3 subject to** : à condition de, sous réserve de <subject to change : sous réserve de modification>

subject[3] *n* **1** : sujet *m,* -jette *f* **2** TOPIC : sujet *m* **3** : sujet *m* (en grammaire)

subjection [səbˈdʒɛkʃən] *n* : sujétion *f,* soumission *f*

subjective [səbˈdʒɛktɪv] *adj* : subjectif — **subjectively** *adv*

subjectivity [ˌsʌbˌdʒɛkˈtɪvəṭi] *n* : subjectivité *f*

subjugate [ˈsʌbdʒɪˌgeɪt] *vt* **-gated; -gating** : subjuguer, soumettre

subjunctive[1] [səbˈdʒʌnktɪv] *adj* : subjonctif

subjunctive[2] *n* : subjonctif *m*

sublet [ˈsʌbˌlɛt] *vt* **-let; -letting** : sous-louer

sublime [səˈblaɪm] *adj* : sublime

sublimely [səˈblaɪmli] *adv* **1** : de manière sublime **2** UTTERLY : suprêmement

submarine[1] [ˈsʌbməˌriːn, ˌsʌbməˈ-] *adj* : sous-marin

submarine[2] *n* : sous-marin *m*

submerge [səbˈmərdʒ] *v* **-merged; -merging** *vt* : submerger, immerger — *vi* : s'immerger

submission [səb'mɪʃən] *n* **1** OBEDIENCE : soumission *f* **2** PRESENTATION : présentation *f*, soumission *f*
submissive [səb'mɪsɪv] *adj* : soumis
submit [səb'mɪt] *v* **-mitted; -mitting** *vi* YIELD : se soumettre — *vt* PRESENT : présenter, soumettre
subnormal [ˌsʌb'nɔrməl] *adj* : au-dessous de la normale
subordinate[1] [sə'bɔrdənˌeɪt] *vt* **-nated; -nating** : subordonner
subordinate[2] [sə'bɔrdənət] *adj* : subalterne, inférieur
subordinate[3] *n* : subordonné *m*, -née *f*
subordination [səˌbɔrdən'eɪʃən] *n* : subordination *f*
subpoena[1] [sə'pi:nə] *vt* **-naed; -naing** : citer
subpoena[2] *n* : assignation *f*, citation *f*
subscribe [səb'skraɪb] *vi* **-scribed; -scribing 1** : s'abonner (à un magazine) **2 to subscribe to** : souscrire à, être d'accord avec (un point de vue, etc.)
subscriber [səb'skraɪbər] *n* : abonné *m*, -née *f*
subscription [səb'skrɪpʃən] *n* : abonnement *m*
subsequent ['sʌbsɪkwənt, -səˌkwɛnt] *adj* : subséquent, suivant
subsequently ['sʌbsɪˌkwɛntli, -ˌkwənt-] *adv* : par la suite, plus tard
subservient [səb'sərviənt] *adj* : servile
subside [səb'saɪd] *vi* **-sided; -siding 1** SINK : s'affaisser **2** ABATE : s'apaiser, se calmer
subsidiary[1] [səb'sɪdiˌɛri] *adj* : subsidiaire
subsidiary[2] *n, pl* **-ries** *or* **subsidiary company** : filiale *f*
subsidize ['sʌbsəˌdaɪz] *vt* **-dized; -dizing** : subventionner
subsidy ['sʌbsədi] *n, pl* **-dies** : subvention *f*
subsist [səb'sɪst] *vi* : subsister
subsistence [səb'sɪstən*t*s] *n* : subsistance *f*
substance ['sʌbstən*t*s] *n* **1** ESSENCE : substance *f*, essentiel *m* **2** MATERIAL : substance *f* **3** WEALTH : richesses *fpl* <a man of substance : un homme riche>
substandard [ˌsʌb'stændərd] *adj* : inférieur
substantial [səb'stæntʃəl] *adj* **1** ABUNDANT : substantiel, copieux **2** CONSIDERABLE : considérable, appréciable
substantially [səb'stæntʃəli] *adv* : considérablement
substantiate [səb'stæntʃiˌeɪt] *vt* **-ated; -ating** : confirmer
substitute[1] ['sʌbstəˌtu:t, -ˌtju:t] *v* **-tuted; -tuting** *vt* : substituer, remplacer — *vi* **to substitute for** : remplacer
substitute[2] *n* **1** ALTERNATE, STAND-IN : remplaçant *m*, -çante *f* **2** : produit *m* de remplacement, succédané *m* <sugar substitute : succédané de sucre>
substitute teacher *n* : suppléant *m*, -pléante *f*
substitution [ˌsʌbstə'tu:ʃən, -'tju:-] *n* : substitution *f*
subterfuge ['sʌbtərˌfju:dʒ] *n* : subterfuge *m*
subterranean [ˌsʌbtə'reɪniən] *adj* : souterrain
subtitle ['sʌbˌtaɪt̬əl] *n* : sous-titre *m*
subtle ['sʌt̬əl] *adj* **-tler; -tlest** : subtil
subtlety ['sʌt̬əlti] *n, pl* **-ties** : subtilité *f*
subtly ['sʌt̬əli] *adv* : subtilement
subtotal ['sʌbˌto:t̬əl] *n* : total *m* partiel
subtract [səb'trækt] *vt* : soustraire — *vi* : faire des soustractions
subtraction [səb'trækʃən] *n* : soustraction *f*
suburb ['sʌˌbərb] *n* : banlieue *f*
suburban [sə'bərbən] *adj* : de banlieue
subversion [səb'vərʒən] *n* : subversion *f*
subversive [səb'vərsɪv] *adj* : subversif
subway ['səbˌweɪ] *n* : métro *m*
succeed [sək'si:d] *vt* FOLLOW : succéder à — *vi* : réussir <she succeeded in finishing : elle a réussi à terminer>
success [sək'sɛs] *n* : réussite *f*, succès *m*
successful [sək'sɛsfəl] *adj* : réussi, courronné de succès
successfully [sək'sɛsfəli] *adv* : avec succès
succession [sək'sɛʃən] *n* : succession *f*
successive [sək'sɛsɪv] *adj* : successif — **successively** *adv*
successor [sək'sɛsər] *n* : successeur *m*
succinct [sək'sɪŋkt, sə'sɪŋkt] *adj* : succinct — **succinctly** *adv*
succor[1] *or Brit* **succour** ['sʌkər] *vt* : secourir, aider
succor[2] *or Brit* **succour** *n* : secours *m*, aide *f*
succotash ['sʌkəˌtæʃ] *n* : plat *m* de maïs et de fèves
succour *Brit* → **succor**
succulent[1] ['sʌkjələnt] *adj* : succulent
succulent[2] *n* : plante *f* grasse
succumb [sə'kʌm] *vi* : succomber
such[1] ['sʌtʃ] *adv* **1** SO : aussi <such tall buildings : des bâtiments aussi grands> **2** VERY : si, tellement <he's not in such good shape : il n'est pas en tellement bonne forme> **3** SUCH THAT : de telle manière que
such[2] *adj* : tel, pareil <there's no such thing : une telle chose n'existe pas> <in such a case : dans un cas pareil> <animals such as cows and sheep : des animaux tels que les moutons et les vaches>
such[3] *pron* **1** : tel <such is the result : tel est le résultat> <he's a child, and acts as such : c'est un enfant et il se comporte comme tel> **2** : choses *fpl* semblables <books, papers, and such

: des livres, des papiers, et autres choses de ce genre> **3 as such** : en soi, comme tel

suck[1] [ˈsʌk] *vt* **1** : sucer (par la bouche) **2** PULL : aspirer (avec une machine, etc.) **3 to get sucked into sth** : être entraîné dans qqch — *vi* : têter (se dit d'un enfant) <to suck at : sucer>

suck[2] *n* : action *f* de sucer

sucker [ˈsʌkər] *n* **1** : suçoir *m* (d'un insecte), drageon *m* (d'une plante) **2** → **lollipop 3** FOOL : poire *f fam*, gogo *m fam*

suckle [ˈsʌkəl] *v* **-led; -ling** *vt* : allaiter — *vi* : téter

suckling [ˈsʌklɪŋ] *n* : nourrisson *m*

sucrose [ˈsuːˌkroːs, -ˌkroːz] *n* : saccharose *f*

suction [ˈsʌkʃən] *n* : succion *f*

Sudanese[1] [ˌsuːdənˈiːz] *adj* : soudanais

Sudanese[2] *n* : Soudanais *m*, -naise *f*

sudden [ˈsʌdən] *adj* **1** : soudain, subit <all of a sudden : tout à coup> **2** UNEXPECTED : imprévu, inattendu **3** ABRUPT, HASTY : brusque

suddenly [ˈsʌdənli] *adv* **1** : soudainement, subitement, tout à coup **2** ABRUPTLY : brusquement

suddenness [ˈsʌdənnəs] *n* **1** : soudaineté *f* **2** ABRUPTNESS : brusquerie *f*

suds [ˈsʌdz] *npl* : mousse *f* (de savon)

sue [ˈsuː] *v* **sued; suing** *vt* : intenter un procès à, poursuivre en justice — *vi* **to sue for** : solliciter

suede [ˈsweɪd] *n* : daim *m*, suède *m*

suet [ˈsuːət] *n* : graisse *f* de rognon (de bœuf)

suffer [ˈsʌfər] *vi* : souffrir — *vt* **1** UNDERGO : souffrir, subir **2** PERMIT : permettre, souffrir **3** TOLERATE : tolérer, supporter

sufferer [ˈsʌfərər] *n* : victime *f*, malade *mf*

suffering [ˈsʌfərɪŋ] *n* : souffrance *f*

suffice [səˈfaɪs] *vi* **-ficed; -ficing** : être suffisant, suffir

sufficient [səˈfɪʃənt] *adj* : suffisant

sufficiently [səˈfɪʃəntli] *adv* : suffisamment

suffix [ˈsʌˌfɪks] *n* : suffixe *m*

suffocate [ˈsʌfəˌkeɪt] *v* **-cated; -cating** : suffoquer

suffocation [ˌsʌfəˈkeɪʃən] *n* : suffocation *f*

suffrage [ˈsʌfrɪdʒ] *n* : suffrage *m*

suffuse [səˈfjuːz] *vt* **-fused; -fusing** : se répandre sur, baigner

sugar[1] [ˈʃʊgər] *vt* : sucrer

sugar[2] *n* : sucre *m*

sugarcane [ˈʃʊgərˌkeɪn] *n* : canne *f* à sucre

sugarhouse [ˈʃʊgərˌhaʊs] *n* : cabane *f* (à sucre) *Can*

sugary [ˈʃʊgəri] *adj* : sucré

suggest [səgˈdʒɛst, sə-] *vt* **1** PROPOSE : proposer, suggérer **2** INDICATE : sembler indiquer, laisser supposer **3** EVOKE : évoquer, suggérer

suggestible [səgˈdʒɛstəbəl, sə-] *adj* : influençable, suggestible

suggestion [səgˈdʒɛstʃən, sə-] *n* **1** PROPOSAL : suggestion *f*, proposition *f* **2** INDICATION : indication *f* **3** HINT, TRACE : soupçon *m* **4 the power of suggestion** : la force de suggestion

suggestive [səgˈdʒɛstɪv, sə-] *adj* : suggestif

suggestively [səgˈdʒɛstɪvli, sə-] *adv* : de façon suggestive

suicidal [ˌsuːəˈsaɪdəl] *adj* : suicidaire

suicide [ˈsuːəˌsaɪd] *n* **1** : suicide *m* (acte) **2** : suicidé *m*, -dée *f* (personne)

suit[1] [ˈsuːt] *vt* **1** ADAPT : accommoder, adapter **2** BECOME, BEFIT : convenir à, aller à <the dress suits you : la robe te va bien> **3** PLEASE : convenir à, arranger <does Friday suit you? : est-ce que vendredi t'arrange?> <suit yourself! : faites comme vous voulez!>

suit[2] *n* **1** → **lawsuit 2** : costume *m*, complet *m* (d'homme), tailleur *m* (de femme) **3** : couleur *f* (aux cartes)

suitability [ˌsuːt̬əˈbɪlət̬i] *n* : caractère *m* convenable, pertinence *f*, aptitude *f* (d'une personne)

suitable [ˈsuːt̬əbəl] *adj* : convenable, approprié

suitably [ˈsuːt̬əbli] *adv* : convenablement

suitcase [ˈsuːtˌkeɪs] *n* : valise *f*

suite [ˈswiːt, *for 2 also* ˈsuːt] *n* **1** : suite *f* **2** : mobilier *m* <dining-room suite : mobilier de salle à manger>

suitor [ˈsuːt̬ər] *n* : prétendant *m*

sulfur *or Brit* **sulphur** [ˈsʌlfər] *n* : soufre *m*

sulfuric acid *or Brit* **sulphuric acid** [ˌsʌlˈfjʊrɪk] *adj* : acide *m* sulfurique

sulfurous *or Brit* **sulphurous** [ˌsʌlˈfjʊrəs, ˈsʌlfərəs, ˈsʌlfjə-] *adj* : sulfureux

sulk[1] [ˈsʌlk] *vi* : bouder

sulk[2] *n* : bouderie *f*

sulky [ˈsʌlki] *adj* **sulkier; -est** : boudeur

sullen [ˈsʌlən] *adj* **1** MOROSE : maussade, morose, renfrogné **2** GLOOMY : maussade, morne <sullen clouds : des nuages menaçants>

sullenly [ˈsʌlənli] *adv* : d'un air maussade, d'un air renfrogné

sully [ˈsʌli] *vt* **sullied; sullying** : souiller

sulphur *Brit* → **sulfur**

sultan [ˈsʌltən] *n* : sultan *m*

sultry [ˈsʌltri] *adj* **sultrier; -est 1** : étouffant <sultry weather : temps lourd> **2** SENSUAL : sensuel

sum[1] [ˈsʌm] *vt* **summed; summing 1** ADD : additionner **2** → **sum up**

sum[2] *n* **1** AMOUNT : somme *f* **2** TOTAL : total *m*, tout *m* **3** : calcul *m* (en mathématiques)

sumac [ˈʃuːˌmæk, ˈsuː-] *n* : sumac *m*

summarize [ˈsʌməˌraɪz] *v* **-rized; -rizing** *vt* : résumer — *vi* : se résumer

summary[1] [ˈsʌməri] *adj* : sommaire
summary[2] *n, pl* **-ries** : sommaire *m*
summer [ˈsʌmər] *n* : été *m*
summery [ˈsʌməri] *adj* : d'été
summit [ˈsʌmət] *n* **1** : sommet *m,* cime *f* **2** *or* **summit conference** : conférence *f* au sommet
summon [ˈsʌmən] *vt* **1** CALL : appeler, convoquer (une réunion, etc.) **2** : sommer de comparaître (en droit) **3 to summon up** : rassembler, faire appel à <to summon up one's strength : rassembler ses forces>
summons [ˈsʌmənz] *n, pl* **summonses 1** SUPOENA : assignation *f* **2** CALL : appel *m*
sumptuous [ˈsʌmptʃuəs] *adj* : somptueux
sum up *vt* **1** SUMMARIZE : résumer **2** ASSESS : apprécier, jauger
sun[1] [ˈsʌn] *vt* **sunned; sunning 1** : exposer au soleil **2 to sun oneself** : prendre le soleil
sun[2] *n* **1** : soleil *m* **2** → **sunshine**
sunbeam [ˈsʌn,bi:m] *n* : rayon *m* de soleil
sunblock [ˈsʌn,blɑk] *n* : écran *m* total
sunburn[1] [ˈsʌn,bərn] *vi* **-burned** *or* **-burnt** [-,bərnt]; **-burning** : prendre un coup de soleil
sunburn[2] *n* : coup *m* de soleil
sundae [ˈsʌndi] *n* : sundae *m Can*
Sunday [ˈsʌn,deɪ, -di] *n* : dimanche *m*
sundial [ˈsʌn,daɪəl] *n* : cadran *m* solaire
sundown [ˈsʌn,daʊn] → **sunset**
sundries [ˈsʌndriz] *npl* : articles *mpl* divers
sundry [ˈsʌndri] *adj* : divers
sunflower [ˈsʌn,flaʊər] *n* : tournesol *m*
sung → **sing**
sunglasses [ˈsʌn,glæsəz] *npl* : lunettes *fpl* de soleil
sunk → **sink**[1]
sunken [ˈsʌŋkən] *adj* **1** HOLLOW : creux **2** SUBMERGED : submergé
sunlight [ˈsʌn,laɪt] *n* : soleil *m,* lumière *f* du soleil
sunny [ˈsʌni] *adj* **sunnier; -est 1** : ensoleillé **2** CHEERFUL : heureux
sunrise [ˈsʌn,raɪz] *n* : lever *m* du soleil
sunset [ˈsʌn,sɛt] *n* : coucher *m* du soleil
sunshine [ˈsʌn,ʃaɪn] *n* : lumière *f* du soleil
sunspot [ˈsʌn,spɑt] *n* : tache *f* solaire
sunstroke [ˈsʌn,stro:k] *n* : insolation *f*
suntan [ˈsʌn,tæn] *n* : hâle *m,* bronzage *m*
super [ˈsu:pər] *adj* **1** GREAT, TERRIFIC : super *fam,* génial **2** SUPERIOR : supérieur
superabundance [,su:pərəˈbʌndən*t*s] *n* : surabondance *f*
superb [sʊˈpərb] *adj* : superbe — **superbly** *adv*
supercilious [,su:pərˈsɪliəs] *adj* : hautain, dédaigneux
superficial [,su:pərˈfɪʃəl] *adj* : superficiel — **superficially** *adv*
superfluous [sʊˈpərfluəs] *adj* : superflu
superhuman [,su:pərˈ*h*ju:mən] *adj* : surhumain
superimpose [,su:pərɪmˈpo:z] *vt* **-posed; -posing** : superposer
superintend [,su:pərɪnˈtɛnd] *vt* : surveiller
superintendent [,su:pərɪnˈtɛndənt] *n* **1** : directeur *m,* -trice *f* **2** : concierge *mf* (d'un immeuble) **3** : inspecteur *m,* -trice *f* (d'école)
superior[1] [sʊˈpɪriər] *adj* : supérieur
superior[2] *n* : supérieur *m,* -rieure *f*
superiority [sʊ,pɪriˈɔrət̬i] *n, pl* **-ties** : supériorité *f*
superlative[1] [sʊˈpərlət̬ɪv] *adj* **1** : superlatif (en grammaire) **2** SUPREME : suprême **3** EXCELLENT, OUTSTANDING : superbe, exceptionnel, sans pareil
superlative[2] *n* : superlatif *m*
supermarket [ˈsu:pər,mɑrkət] *n* : supermarché *m*
supernatural [,su:pərˈnætʃərəl] *adj* : surnaturel
supernaturally [,su:pərˈnætʃərəli] *adv* : de manière surnaturelle
superpower [ˈsu:pər,paʊər] *n* : superpuissance *f*
supersede [,su:pərˈsi:d] *vt* **-seded; -seding** : remplacer, supplanter
supersonic [,su:pərˈsɑnɪk] *adj* : supersonique
superstition [,su:pərˈstɪʃən] *n* : superstition *f*
superstitious [,su:pərˈstɪʃəs] *adj* : superstitieux
superstructure [ˈsu:pər,strʌktʃər] *n* : superstructure *f*
supervise [ˈsu:pər,vaɪz] *vt* **-vised; -vising** : surveiller, superviser
supervision [,su:pərˈvɪʒən] *n* : surveillance *f,* supervision *f*
supervisor [ˈsu:pər,vaɪzər] *n* : surveillant *m,* -lante *f*
supervisory [,su:pərˈvaɪzəri] *adj* : de surveillance
supine [sʊˈpaɪn] *adj* **1** : couché sur le dos **2** INDOLENT, SLACK : indolent, mou
supper [ˈsʌpər] *n* : dîner *m,* souper *m Can*
supplant [səˈplænt] *vt* : supplanter
supple [ˈsʌpəl] *adj* **-pler; -plest** : souple
supplement[1] [ˈsʌplə,mɛnt] *vt* : compléter, augmenter
supplement[2] *n* : supplément *m*
supplementary [,sʌpləˈmɛntəri] *adj* : supplémentaire
supplicate [ˈsʌplə,keɪt] *vt* **-cated; -cating** : supplier, implorer
supplier [səˈplaɪər] *n* : fournisseur *m,* -seuse *f*
supply[1] [səˈplaɪ] *vt* **-plied; -plying** : fournir, munir, approvisionner
supply[2] *n, pl* **-plies 1** PROVISION : fourniture *f,* approvisionnement *m* **2** STOCK : provision *f,* réserve *f* **3 sup-**

plies *npl* : provisions *fpl,* approvisionnements *mpl,* vivres *mpl*

support[1] [sə'port] *vt* **1** BACK : soutenir, appuyer **2** MAINTAIN : maintenir, entretenir **3** PROP UP : supporter, soutenir

support[2] *n* **1** BACKING : appui *m,* soutien *m* **2** PROP : support *m,* appui *m*

supporter [sə'portər] *n* **1** : partisan *m,* -sane *f* **2** FAN : supporter *m*

suppose [sə'po:z] *vt* **-posed; -posing 1** ASSUME : supposer **2** BELIEVE : croire **3 to be supposed to do sth** : être censé faire qqch

supposedly [sə'po:zədli] *adv* : censément

supposition [ˌsʌpə'zɪʃən] *n* : supposition *f*

suppository [sə'pɑzəˌtori] *n, pl* **-ries** : suppositoire *m*

suppress [sə'prɛs] *vt* **1** SUBDUE : maîtriser, réprimer (une révolte, etc.) **2** WITHHOLD : supprimer **3** REPRESS : étouffer, réprimer <to suppress a yawn : étouffer un bâillement>

suppression [sə'prɛʃən] *n* **1** SUBDUING : répression *f* **2** : suppression *f* (d'information) **3** REPRESSION : étouffement *m,* refoulement *m*

supremacy [sʊ'prɛməsi] *n, pl* **-cies** : suprématie *f*

supreme [sʊ'pri:m] *adj* : suprême — **supremely** *adv*

Supreme Being *n* GOD : Être *m* suprême

surcharge ['sərˌtʃɑrdʒ] *n* : surcharge *f*

sure[1] ['ʃʊr] *adv* **1** ALL RIGHT : bien sûr **2** (*used as an intensifier*) : vraiment, drôlement <it sure is hot! : il fait drôlement chaud!> <she sure is pretty! : qu'est-ce qu'elle est belle!>

sure[2] *adj* **surer; -est** : sûr <I'm sure of it : j'en suis sûr> <she's sure to succeed : elle va sûrement réussir> <for sure : pour sûr>

surely ['ʃʊrli] *adv* **1** CERTAINLY : sûrement **2** (*used as an intensifier*) <you surely don't mean that! : tu ne peux pas vouloir dire cela!>

sureness ['ʃʊrnəs] *n* : sûreté *f*

surety ['ʃʊrəṭi] *n, pl* **-ties 1** GUARANTOR : garant *m,* -rante *f* **2** COLLATERAL : sûreté *f,* caution *f*

surf ['sərf] *n* **1** WAVES : vagues *fpl* (déferlantes) **2** FOAM : écume *f*

surface[1] ['sərfəs] *v* **-faced; -facing** *vi* : faire surface, remonter à la surface — *vt* : revêtir (une chaussée)

surface[2] *n* : surface *f*

surfboard ['sərfˌbord] *n* : planche *f* de surf

surfeit ['sərfət] *n* : excès *m*

surfing ['sərfɪŋ] *n* : surf *m*

surge[1] ['sərdʒ] *vi* **surged; surging 1** SWELL : s'enfler, déferler (se dit de la mer) **2** INCREASE : monter **3** SWARM : se presser, déferler (se dit d'une foule, etc.)

surge[2] *n* **1** RUSH : brusque montée *f* (de la mer), ruée *f* (de personnes) **2** FLUSH : vague *f,* accès *m* (de colère, etc.) **3** INCREASE : augmentation *f,* surtension *f* (de l'électricité)

surgeon ['sərdʒən] *n* : chirurgien *m,* -gienne *f*

surgery ['sərdʒəri] *n, pl* **-geries** : chirurgie *f*

surgical ['sərdʒɪkəl] *adj* : chirurgical

surgically ['sərdʒɪkli] *adv* : par opération, par intervention chirurgicale

Surinamese[1] [ˌsʊrəna'mi:z, -'mi:s] *adj* : surinamien

Surinamese[2] *n* : Surinamien *m,* -mienne *f*

surly ['sərli] *adj* **surlier; -est** : revêche, bourru, hargneux

surmise[1] [sər'maɪz] *v* **-mised; -mising** : conjecturer, présumer

surmise[2] *n* : conjecture *f,* hypothèse *f*

surmount [sər'maʊnt] *vt* **1** OVERCOME : surmonter, vaincre **2** CAP, TOP : surmonter

surname ['sərˌneɪm] *n* : nom *m* de famille

surpass [sər'pæs] *vt* : surpasser, dépasser

surplus ['sərˌplʌs] *n* : excédent *m,* surplus *m*

surprise[1] [sə'praɪz, sər-] *vt* **-prised; -prising** : surprendre

surprise[2] *n* : surprise *f* <to take by surprise : prendre au dépourvu>

surprising [sə'praɪzɪŋ, sər-] *adj* : surprenant, étonnant

surprisingly [sə'praɪzɪŋli, sər-] *adv* : étonnamment, incroyablement

surrender[1] [sə'rɛndər] *vt* **1** : rendre, livrer, céder **2 to surrender oneself to** : se livrer à — *vi* : se rendre, capituler

surrender[2] *n* : capitulation *f,* reddition *f*

surreptitious [ˌsərəp'tɪʃəs] *adj* : subreptice, furtif — **surreptitiously** *adv*

surrogate ['sərəgət, -ˌgeɪt] *n* : substitut *m;* remplaçant *m,* -çante *f*

surround [sə'raʊnd] *vt* : entourer, cerner

surroundings [sə'raʊndɪŋz] *npl* : environs *mpl,* alentours *mpl*

surveillance [sər'veɪlənts, -'veɪljənts, -'veɪənts] *n* : surveillance *f*

survey[1] [sər'veɪ] *vt* **-veyed; -veying 1** : arpenter (un terrain) **2** EXAMINE : examiner, inspecter **3** POLL : sonder

survey[2] ['sərˌveɪ] *n, pl* **-veys 1** INSPECTION : inspection *f* **2** : arpentage *m* (d'un terrain) **3** POLL : sondage *m*

surveyor [sər'veɪər] *n* : arpenteur *m,* -teuse *f*

survival [sər'vaɪvəl] *n* **1** : survie *f* (d'une personne, d'un animal, d'une plante) **2** REMAINDER, VESTIGE : survivance *f,* vestige *m*

survive [sər'vaɪv] *v* **-vived; -viving** *vi* : survivre — *vt* OUTLIVE : survivre à

survivor [sər'vaɪvər] *n* : survivant *m*, -vante *f*
susceptibility [sə,sɛptə'bɪləṭi] *n, pl* **-ties** : susceptibilité *f*
susceptible [sə'sɛptəbəl] *adj* : sensible, susceptible
suspect¹ [sə'spɛkt] *vt* **1** DISTRUST : douter de, se méfier de **2** : soupçonner (d'un crime) **3** IMAGINE, THINK : imaginer, soupçonner
suspect² ['sʌs,pɛkt, sə'spɛkt] *adj* : suspect
suspect³ ['sʌs,pɛkt] *n* : suspect *m*, -pecte *f*
suspend [sə'spɛnd] *vt* : suspendre
suspenders [sə'spɛndərz] *npl* : bretelles *fpl*
suspense [sə'spɛnts] *n* : attente *f*, suspense *m* <to keep in suspense : laisser dans l'incertitude>
suspenseful [sə'spɛntsfəl] *adj* : plein de suspense
suspension [sə'spɛntʃən] *n* : suspension *f*
suspicion [sə'spɪʃən] *n* : soupçon *m*, méfiance *f*
suspicious [sə'spɪʃəs] *adj* **1** QUESTIONABLE : suspect **2** DISTRUSTFUL : méfiant, soupçonneux
suspiciously [sə'spɪʃəsli] *adv* **1** : d'une manière suspecte **2** WARILY : d'un air soupçonneux, avec méfiance
sustain [sə'steɪn] *vt* **1** NOURISH : nourrir **2** MAINTAIN : maintenir, entretenir **3** SUFFER : éprouver <to sustain an injury : recevoir une blessure> **4** SUPPORT : soutenir
sustenance ['sʌstənənts] *n* **1** NOURISHMENT : nourriture *f* **2** LIVELIHOOD, SUBSISTENCE : (moyens *mpl* de) subsistance *f*
svelte ['sfɛlt] *adj* : svelte
swab¹ ['swɑb] *vt* **swabbed; swabbing 1** CLEAN : nettoyer **2** *or* **to swab down** MOP : laver
swab² *n or* **cotton swab** : tampon *m*
swaddle ['swɑdəl] *vt* **-dled; -dling** [-dəlɪŋ] WRAP : emmitoufler, envelopper
swagger¹ ['swægər] *vi* **-gered; -gering** : se pavaner
swagger² *n* : démarche *f* arrogante
swallow¹ ['swɑlo:] *vt* **1** : avaler **2** *or* **to swallow up** ENGULF : engloutir **3** REPRESS : ravaler — *vi* : avaler, déglutir
swallow² *n* **1** GULP : gorgée *f* **2** : hirondelle *f* (oiseau)
swam → **swim¹**
swamp¹ ['swɑmp] *vi* : inonder
swamp² *n* : marais *m*, marécage *m*, savane *f Can*
swampy ['swɑmpi] *adj* **swampier; -est** : marécageux
swan ['swɑn] *n* : cygne *m*
swap¹ ['swɑp] *vt* **swapped; swapping** : échanger
swap² *n* : échange *m*
swarm¹ ['swɔrm] *vi* **1** : essaimer (se dit des abeilles) **2** TEEM, THRONG : grouiller, se presser <to be swarming with people : grouiller de gens>
swarm² *n* **1** : essaim *m* (d'abeilles) **2** : masse *f*, essaim *m* (de personnes)
swarthy ['swɔrði, -θi] *adj* **swarthier; -est** : basané
swashbuckling ['swɑʃ,bʌklɪŋ] *adj* : de cape et d'épée (se dit d'un film, etc.)
swat¹ ['swɑt] *vt* **swatted; swatting** : écraser (un insecte), frapper (une personne)
swat² *n* : tape *f*
swatch ['swɑtʃ] *n* : échantillon *m* (de tissu)
swath ['swɑθ, 'swɔθ,] *or* **swathe** ['swɑð, 'swɔð, 'sweɪð] *n* : andain *m* (en agriculture), bande *f* (de terre)
swathe ['swɑð, 'swɔð, 'sweɪð] *vt* **swathed; swathing** : emmailloter, envelopper
swatter ['swɑṭər] → **flyswatter**
sway¹ ['sweɪ] *vi* : se balancer — *vt* **1** INFLUENCE : influencer **2** ROCK : balancer
sway² *n* **1** SWINGING : balancement *m* **2** INFLUENCE : influence *f*
swear ['swær] *v* **swore** ['swor]; **sworn** ['sworn]; **swearing** *vi* **1** VOW : jurer <to swear on the Bible : jurer sur la Bible> **2** CURSE : jurer, injurier — *vt* : jurer <to swear allegiance : jurer allégeance> <to swear an oath : prêter serment>
swearword ['swær,wərd] *n* : juron *m*, grossièreté *f*
sweat¹ ['swɛt] *vi* **sweat** *or* **sweated; sweating 1** PERSPIRE : transpirer **2** OOZE : suinter, suer **3 to sweat over** : suer sur
sweat² *n* : sueur *f*, transpiration *f*
sweater ['swɛṭər] *n* : pull-over *m France*, chandail *m*
sweatshirt ['swɛt,ʃərt] *n* : sweat-shirt *m*
sweaty ['swɛṭi] *adj* **sweatier; -est** : couvert de sueur
Swede ['swi:d] *n* : Suédois *m*, -doise *f*
Swedish¹ ['swi:dɪʃ] *adj* : suédois
Swedish² *n* **1** : suédois *m* (langue) **2** **the Swedish** : les Suédois
sweep¹ ['swi:p] *v* **swept** ['swɛpt]; **sweeping** *vt* **1** : balayer **2** *or* **to sweep away** : emporter, entraîner **3** *or* **to sweep through** : gagner, s'emparer de <panic swept the city : la panique s'est emparée de la ville> — *vi* **1** : balayer **2** EXTEND : s'étendre, décrire (une courbe) <the sun swept across the sky : le soleil a décrit une courbe dans le ciel>
sweep² *n* **1** : coup *m* de balai **2** : mouvement *m* circulaire (de la main, etc.) **3** SCOPE : étendue *f*
sweeper ['swi:pər] *n* : balayeur *m*, balayeuse *f*
sweeping ['swi:pɪŋ] *adj* **1** WIDE : large **2** EXTENSIVE : considérable, radical **3**

INDISCRIMINATE : péremptoire, trop général
sweepstakes ['swi:pˌsteɪks] *ns & pl* : sweepstake *m*
sweet[1] ['swi:t] *adj* **1** : doux, sucré <sweet desserts : desserts sucrés> **2** FRESH : frais (se dit de l'eau, etc.) **3** : sans sel (se dit du beurre) **4** KIND, PLEASANT : agréable, gentil **5** CUTE, PRETTY : mignon, adorable
sweet[2] *n* : bonbon *m*, dessert *m*
sweeten ['swi:tən] *vt* : sucrer
sweetener ['swi:tənər] *n* : édulcorant *m*
sweetheart ['swi:tˌhɑrt] *n* **1** : petit ami *m*, petite amie *f* **2** (*used as a term of address*) : chéri *m*, chérie *f*
sweetly ['swi:tli] *adv* : doucement
sweetness ['swi:tnəs] *n* : douceur *f*
sweet potato *n* : patate *f* douce
swell[1] ['swɛl] *vi* **swelled; swelled** *or* **swollen** ['swo:lən]; **swelling 1** *or* **to swell up** : enfler, gonfler <her ankle swelled : sa cheville enflait> **2** INCREASE : augmenter, grossir
swell[2] *n* **1** : houle *f* (de la mer) **2** INCREASE : augmentation *f*
swelling ['swɛlɪŋ] *n* : enflure *f*, gonflement *m*
swelter ['swɛltər] *vi* : étouffer de chaleur
swept → sweep[1]
swerve[1] ['swərv] *vi* **swerved; swerving** : faire une embardée
swerve[2] *n* : embardée *f*
swift[1] ['swɪft] *adj* **1** FAST : rapide **2** PROMPT : prompt — **swiftly** *adv*
swift[2] *n* : martinet *m* (oiseau)
swiftness ['swɪftnəs] *n* **1** SPEED : rapidité *f* **2** PROMPTNESS : promptitude *f*
swig[1] ['swɪg] *vi* **swigged; swigging** : boire à grands traits, siffler *fam*
swig[2] *n* : lampée *f fam*, gorgée *f*
swill[1] ['swɪl] *vt or* **to swill down** : lamper, écluser *fam*
swill[2] *n* **1** SLOP : pâtée *f* **2** GARBAGE : ordures *fpl*
swim[1] ['swɪm] *vi* **swam** ['swæm]; **swum** ['swʌm]; **swimming 1** : nager, faire de la natation, se baigner **2** FLOAT : flotter **3** REEL : tourner <his head was swimming : il avait la tête qui tournait>
swim[2] *n* : baignade *f* <to go for a swim : aller se baigner>
swimmer ['swɪmər] *n* : nageur *m*, -geuse *f*
swindle[1] ['swɪndəl] *vt* **-dled; -dling** : escroquer
swindle[2] *n* : escroquerie *f*
swindler ['swɪndələr] *n* : escroc *m*
swine ['swaɪn] *ns & pl* : porc *m*
swing[1] ['swɪŋ] *v* **swung** ['swʌŋ]; **swinging** *vt* **1** : balancer (les bras, etc.), faire osciller **2** : décrire une courbe avec, brandir <he swung his ax : il a brandi sa hache> <to swing into the saddle : sauter en selle> **3** SUSPEND : suspendre — *vi* **1** SWAY : se balancer **2** CHANGE : virer, passer <to swing from enthusiasm to disappointment : passer de l'enthousiasme à la déception> **3** SWIVEL : tourner, pivoter <the door swung shut : la porte s'est refermée>
swing[2] *n* **1** SWINGING : balancement *m*, oscillation *f* **2** CHANGE, SHIFT : revirement *m* **3** : balançoire *f* (pour les enfants)
swipe[1] ['swaɪp] *v* **swiped; swiping** *vi* **to swipe at** : essayer de frapper, donner un coup pour frapper — *vt* STEAL : chiper *fam*, faucher *fam*
swipe[2] *n* : grand coup *m*
swirl[1] ['swərl] *vi* : tourbillonner
swirl[2] *n* : tourbillon *m*
swish[1] ['swɪʃ] *vi* : siffler (se dit d'un fouet, etc.), bruire (se dit de l'eau), froufrouter (se dit d'une étoffe)
swish[2] *n* : sifflement *m*, bruissement *m*, froufrou *m*
Swiss[1] ['swɪs] *adj* : suisse
Swiss[2] *ns & pl* : Suisse *m*, Suissesse *f*
switch[1] ['swɪtʃ] *vt* **1** LASH, WHIP : fouetter **2** CHANGE : changer de **3 to switch on** : ouvrir, allumer **4 to switch off** : couper, fermer, éteindre — *vi* **1** CHANGE : changer **2** SWAP : échanger
switch[2] *n* **1** CANE, STICK : badine *f* **2** CHANGE, SHIFT : changement *m* **3** : interrupteur *m* (d'électricité), bouton *m* (d'une radio ou d'une télévision)
switchboard ['swɪtʃˌbord] *n or* **telephone switchboard** : standard *m*
swivel[1] ['swɪvəl] *vi* **-eled** *or* **-elled; -eling** *or* **-elling** : pivoter
swivel[2] *n* : pivot *m*
swollen → swell[1]
swoon[1] ['swu:n] *vi* **1** FAINT : s'évanouir **2 to swoon over** : se pâmer devant
swoon[2] *n* **1** FAINT : évanouissement *m* **2** DAZE, RAPTURE : pâmoison *f*
swoop[1] ['swu:p] *vi* : fondre, piquer
swoop[2] *n* : descente *f* en piqué
sword ['sɔrd] *n* : épée *f*
swordfish ['sɔrdˌfɪʃ] *n* : espadon *m*
swore, sworn → swear
swum → swim[1]
swung → swing[1]
sycamore ['sɪkəˌmor] *n* : sycomore *m*
sycophant ['sɪkəfənt, -ˌfænt] *n* : flagorneur *m*, -neuse *f*
syllabic [sə'læbɪk] *adj* : syllabique
syllable ['sɪləbəl] *n* : syllabe *f*
syllabus ['sɪləbəs] *n, pl* **-bi** [-ˌbaɪ] *or* **-buses** : programme *m*
symbol ['sɪmbəl] *n* : symbole *m*
symbolic [sɪm'bɑlɪk] *adj* : symbolique — **symbolically** [-kli] *adv*
symbolism ['sɪmbəˌlɪzəm] *n* : symbolisme *m*
symbolize ['sɪmbəˌlaɪz] *vt* **-ized; -izing** : symboliser

symmetrical [sə'mɛtrɪkəl] *adj* : symétrique — **symmetrically** [-kli] *adv*
symmetry ['sɪmətri] *n, pl* **-tries** : symétrie *f*
sympathetic [ˌsɪmpə'θɛt̬ɪk] *adj* **1** PLEASING : agréable, sympathique **2** RECEPTIVE : bien disposé **3** COMPASSIONATE, UNDERSTANDING : compatissant, compréhensif
sympathetically [ˌsɪmpə'θɛt̬ɪkli] *adv* : avec compassion, avec compréhension
sympathize ['sɪmpəˌθaɪz] *vi* **-thized; -thizing 1** : compatir, comprendre <I sympathize with him : je le plains> **2 to sympathize with** SUPPORT : sympathiser avec
sympathizer ['sɪmpəˌθaɪzər] *n* : sympathisant *m*, -sante *f*
sympathy ['sɪmpəθi] *n, pl* **-thies 1** COMPASSION : compassion *f*, sympathie *f* **2** UNDERSTANDING : compréhension *f* **3** AGREEMENT : approbation *f*, sympathie *f*
symphonic [sɪm'fɑnɪk] *adj* : symphonique
symphony ['sɪmpfəni] *n, pl* **-nies** : symphonie *f*
symposium [sɪm'po:ziəm] *n, pl* **-sia** [-ziə] *or* **-siums** : symposium *m*
symptom ['sɪmptəm] *n* : symptôme *m*
symptomatic [ˌsɪmptə'mæt̬ɪk] *adj* : symptomatique
synagogue ['sɪnəˌgɑg, -ˌgɔg] *n* : synagogue *f*
synchronize ['sɪŋkrəˌnaɪz, 'sɪn-] *v* **-nized; -nizing** *vt* : synchroniser — *vi* : être synchrone
syndicate[1] ['sɪndɪˌkeɪt] *v* **-cated; -cating** *vi* UNITE : se syndiquer — *vt* : publier simultanément dans plusieurs journaux
syndicate[2] ['sɪndɪkət] *n* : syndicat *m*
syndrome ['sɪnˌdro:m] *n* : syndrome *m*
synonym ['sɪnəˌnɪm] *n* : synonyme *m*
synonymous [sə'nɑnəməs] *adj* : synonyme
synopsis [sə'nɑpsɪs] *n, pl* **-opses** [-ˌsi:z] : résumé *m*
syntax ['sɪnˌtæks] *n* : syntaxe *f*
synthesis ['sɪnθəsəs] *n, pl* **-theses** [-ˌsi:z] : synthèse *f*
synthesize ['sɪnθəˌsaɪz] *vt* **-sized; -sizing** : synthétiser
synthetic[1] [sɪn'θɛt̬ɪk] *adj* : synthétique — **synthetically** [-t̬ɪkli] *adv*
synthetic[2] *n* : produit *m* synthétique
syphilis ['sɪfələs] *n* : syphilis *f*
Syrian[1] ['sɪriən] *adj* : syrien
Syrian[2] *n* : Syrien *m*, -rienne *f*
syringe [sə'rɪndʒ, 'sɪrɪndʒ] *n* : seringue *f*
syrup ['sərəp, 'sɪrəp] *n* : sirop *m*
system ['sɪstəm] *n* **1** METHOD : système *m*, méthode *f* **2** STRUCTURE : système *m* <the solar system : le système solaire> **3** APPARATUS : appareil *m*, système *m* <digestive system : appareil digestif> **4** BODY : organisme *m* **5** NETWORK : réseau *m*
systematic [ˌsɪstə'mæt̬ɪk] *adj* : systématique — **systematically** [-t̬ɪkli] *adv*
systematize ['sɪstəməˌtaɪz] *vt* **-tized; -tizing** : systématiser
systemic [sɪs'tɛmɪk] *adj* : du système, systémique

T

t ['ti:] *n, pl* **t's** *or* **ts** ['ti:z] : t *m*, vingtième lettre de l'alphabet
tab ['tæb] *n* **1** FLAP : patte *f* **2** BILL, CHECK : note *f*, addition *f* **3** LOOP : attache *f* **4 to keep tabs on s.o.** : surveiller qqn, garder qqn à l'œil
tabby ['tæbi] *n, pl* **-bies** : chat *m* tigré, chatte *f* tigrée
tabernacle ['tæbərˌnækəl] *n* : tabernacle *m*
table ['teɪbəl] *n* **1** : table *f* <kitchen table : table de cuisine> **2** MEAL : table *f* <to serve a good table : servir une bonne table> **3** CHART : table *f*, tableau *m* **4 table of contents** : table *f* des matières
tableau [tæ'blo:, 'tæˌ-] *n, pl* **tableaux** [tæ'blo:z, 'tæˌblo:z] : tableau *m*
tablecloth ['teɪbəlˌklɔθ] *n* : nappe *f*
tablespoon ['teɪbəlˌspu:n] *n* : cuillère *f* à soupe
tablespoonful ['teɪbəlˌspu:nˌfʊl] *n* : cuillère *f* à soupe
tablet ['tæblət] *n* **1** PLAQUE : plaque *f*, tablette *f* (de pierre) **2** NOTEPAD : bloc-notes *m*, tablette *f Can* **3** PILL : comprimé *m* <aspirin tablet : comprimé d'aspirine>
table tennis *n* : tennis *m* de table
tabletop ['teɪbəlˌtɑp] *n* : dessus *m* de table
tableware ['teɪbəlˌweɪr] *n* : vaisselle *f*
tabloid ['tæˌblɔɪd] *n* : quotidien *m* populaire, tabloïde *m*
taboo[1] [tə'bu:, tæ-] *adj* : tabou, interdit
taboo[2] *n, pl* **taboos** : tabou *m*
tabular ['tæbjələr] *adj* : tabulaire
tabulate ['tæbjəˌleɪt] *vt* **-lated; -lating** : mettre sous forme de tableau
tabulator ['tæbjəˌleɪt̬ər] *n* : tabulateur *m*
tacit ['tæsɪt] *adj* : tacite, implicite — **tacitly** *adv*
taciturn ['tæsɪˌtərn] *adj* : taciturne
tack[1] ['tæk] *vt* **1** ATTACH : clouer, fixer <to tack down a carpet : clouer un

tapis> **2 to tack on** ADD : ajouter, rajouter — *vi* : faire une bordée (se dit d'un navire)

tack[2] *n* **1** BRAD : semence *f,* clou *m* **2** → **thumbtack 3** COURSE : voie *f,* tactique *f* <to change tack : changer de voie>

tackle[1] ['takəl] *vt* **-led; -ling 1** : plaquer (au football) **2** : s'attaquer à <to tackle a problem : s'attaquer à un problème>

tackle[2] *n* **1** GEAR : équipement *m,* matériel *m* <fishing tackle : matériel de pêche> **2** PULLEYS : appareil *m* de levage **3** : plaquage *m* (au football)

tacky ['tæki] *adj* **tackier; -est 1** STICKY : collant **2** SHABBY : moche, minable **3** TASTELESS : de mauvais goût

tact ['tækt] *n* : tact *m,* diplomatie *f*

tactful ['tæktfəl] *adj* : plein de tact

tactfully ['tæktfəli] *adv* : avec tact, avec diplomatie

tactic ['tæktɪk] *n* : tactique *f,* plan *m*

tactical ['tæktɪkəl] *adj* : tactique

tactics ['tæktɪks] *ns & pl* : tactique *f*

tactile ['tæktəl, -ˌtaɪl] *adj* : tactile

tactless ['tæktləs] *adj* : qui manque de tact

tactlessly ['tæktləsli] *adv* : sans tact

tadpole ['tædˌpoːl] *n* : têtard *m*

taffeta ['tæfət̬ə] *n* : taffetas *m*

taffy ['tæfi] *n, pl* **-fies** : bonbon *m* au caramel

tag[1] ['tæg] *v* **tagged; tagging** *vt* **1** LABEL : étiqueter **2** TOUCH : toucher (au jeu de chat, au baseball, etc.) — *vi* **to tag along behind** : suivre

tag[2] *n* **1** : jeu *m* de chat **2** *or* **price tag** : étiquette *f*

Tahitian[1] [tə'hiːʃən] *adj* : tahitien

Tahitian[2] *n* : Tahitien, -tienne *f*

tail[1] ['teɪl] *vt* FOLLOW : suivre de près

tail[2] *n* **1** : queue *f* (d'un animal) **2** : queue *f* (d'un avion, d'une comète, etc.) **3 tails** *npl* : pile *f* (d'une pièce de monnaie) <heads or tails? : pile ou face?>

tailgate[1] ['teɪlˌgeɪt] *vt* **-gated; -gating** : coller au pare-chocs de

tailgate[2] *n* : hayon *m*

taillight ['teɪlˌlaɪt] *n* : feu *m* arrière (d'un véhicule)

tailor[1] ['teɪlər] *vt* **1** : faire sur mesure, confectionner (un vêtement) **2** ADAPT : faire, concevoir, adapter

tailor[2] *n* : tailleur *m*

tailpipe ['teɪlˌpaɪp] *n* : tuyau *m* d'échappement

tailspin ['teɪlˌspɪn] *n* : vrille *f* (d'un avion)

taint[1] ['teɪnt] *vt* **1** SULLY : entacher, souiller (une reputation, etc.) **2** SPOIL : gâter (des aliments)

taint[2] *n* : souillure *f*

Taiwanese[1] [ˌtaɪwə'niːz, -'niːs] *adj* : taiwanais

Taiwanese[2] *n* : Taiwanais *m,* -naise *f*

take[1] ['teɪk] *v* **took** ['tʊk]; **taken** ['teɪkən]; **taking** *vt* **1** CAPTURE : prendre, retenir **2** GRASP : prendre, saisir **3** CAPTIVATE : éprendre **4** INGEST : prendre <take your medicine : prends tes medicaments> **5** ACCEPT : entrer, accepter, prendre <to take office : entrer en fonction> <to take a job : accepter un emploi> **6** ASSUME : prendre, s'attribuer <she took all the credit : elle s'est attribuée tout le mérite> **7** BRING : porter, apporter <he took his father some coffee : il a apporté du café à son père> **8** WIN : remporter **9** SELECT : prendre, choisir **10** : prendre <she takes the train : elle prend le train> <take a seat : asseyez-vous> **11** FOLLOW : prendre, emprunter <they took a different route : ils ont pris un autre chemin> **12** CONDUCT : mener, conduire, emmener <the bus will take you there : l'autobus vous y mènera> **13 to take apart** DISMANTLE : démonter, démancher *Can* **14 to take place** HAPPEN : avoir lieu **15 to take s.o.'s side** : prendre parti pour qqn — *vi* **1** : faire effet <the vaccination took : le vaccin a fait effet> **2** BECOME, FALL : tomber <he took ill : il est tombé malade>

take[2] *n* : prise *f*

take back *vt* : retirer

take in *vt* **1** : reprendre (un vêtement) **2** INCLUDE : inclure, couvrir **3** ATTEND : aller à <let's take in a movie : allons au cinéma> **4** UNDERSTAND : saisir, comprendre **5** DECEIVE : tromper, se faire avoir

takeoff ['teɪkˌɔf] *n* **1** : décollage *m* (d'un avion) **2** PARODY : parodie *f,* imitation *f*

take off *vt* **1** REMOVE : enlever, ôter <take your shoes off : enlevez vos chaussures> **2** DEDUCT : déduire, soustraire **3** TAKE : prendre <he took two weeks off : il a pris deux semaines de vacances> — *vi* **1** DEPART : s'en aller, décamper **2** : décoller (se dit d'un avion)

take on *vt* **1** ACCEPT : assumer, prendre, accepter (des responsabilités, etc.) **2** : jouer contre <he took on the champion : il a joué contre le champion> **3** ADOPT : arborer, prendre <the city took on a festive air : la ville arborait un air de fête> **4** HIRE : engager, embaucher

takeover ['teɪkˌoːvər] *n* : prise *f* de pouvoir

take over *vt* : prendre le pouvoir, prendre la relève

taker ['teɪkər] *n* : preneur *m,* -neuse *f*

take up *vt* **1** LIFT : enlever, prendre **2** BEGIN : faire <to take up painting : faire de la peinture> **3** RESUME

: reprendre **4** SHORTEN : raccourcir (une jupe, une robe etc.)
takings [ˈteɪkɪŋz] *npl Brit* : recette *f*
talc [ˈtælk] → **talcum powder**
talcum powder [ˈtælkəm] *n* : talc *m*
tale [ˈteɪl] *n* **1** STORY : conte *m*, récit *m* **2** FALSEHOOD : histoires *fpl*, mensonge *m*
talent [ˈtælənt] *n* : talent *m*
talented [ˈtæləntəd] *adj* : talentueux, doué
talisman [ˈtæləsmən, -ləz-] *n, pl* **-mans** : talisman *m*
talk[1] [ˈtɔk] *vt* **1** SPEAK : parler <to talk French : parler français> **2** DISCUSS : parler (de) <to talk business : parler affaires> **3 to talk s.o. into doing sth** : persuader qqn de faire qqch — *vi* **1** CHAT : parler, causer **2** LECTURE : parler, discourir **3** GOSSIP : cancaner, jaser
talk[2] *n* **1** TALKING : paroles *fpl*, propos *mpl* **2** CONVERSATION, DISCUSSION : entretien *m*, conversation *f* <I had a talk with him : j'ai discuté avec lui> **3** RUMOR : racontars *mpl*, commérage *m fam* <it's the talk of the town : on ne parle que de ça> **4** SPEECH : discours *m*, exposé *m*
talkative [ˈtɔkəṭɪv] *adj* : bavard, loquace
talker [ˈtɔkər] *n* **he's a talker** : il est bavard
tall [ˈtɔl] *adj* **1** : grand <she's six feet tall : elle mesure six pieds> **2** : haut, élevé <a building two meters tall : un édifice haut de deux mètres> **3 a tall tale** : une histoire invraisemblable
tallness [ˈtɔlnəs] *n* : hauteur *f* (d'un édifice, etc.), taille *f* (d'une personne)
tallow [ˈtæloː] *n* : suif *m*
tally[1] [ˈtæli] *v* **-lied; -lying** *vt* RECORD : tenir le compte de — *vi* MATCH : correspondre
tally[2] *n, pl* **-lies** : compte *m*, pointage *m*
talon [ˈtælən] *n* : serre *f* (d'aigle)
tambourine [ˌtæmbəˈriːn] *n* : tambourin *m*
tame[1] [ˈteɪm] *vt* **tamed; taming** : apprivoiser, domestiquer
tame[2] *adj* **tamer; tamest 1** DOMESTICATED : apprivoisé **2** SUBDUED : docile, soumis **3** DULL : fade, terne
tamely [ˈteɪmli] *adv* : docilement
tamer [ˈteɪmər] *n* : dompteur *m*, -teuse *f* (de lions, etc.)
tamp [ˈtæmp] *vt* **to tamp down** : damer, tasser
tamper [ˈtæmpər] *vi* **1 to tamper with** ALTER : altérer, falsifier **2 to tamper with** BRIBE : suborner <to tamper with a witness : suborner un témoin>
tampon [ˈtæmˌpɑn] *n* : tampon *m* (hygiénique)
tan[1] [ˈtæn] *v* **tanned; tanning** *vt* : tanner <to tan hides : tanner des peaux> — *vi* : bronzer
tan[2] *n* **1** SUNTAN : bronzage *m* <to get a tan : se faire bronzer> **2** : brun *m* clair (couleur)
tandem[1] [ˈtændəm] *adv* **to ride tandem** : se promener en tandem
tandem[2] *n* : tandem *m*
tang [ˈtæŋ] *n* : goût *m* piquant
tangent [ˈtændʒənt] *n* **1** : tangente *f* (en mathématiques) **2** DIGRESSION : digression *f* <to go off on a tangent : partir dans une digression>
tangerine [ˈtændʒəˌriːn, ˌtændʒəˈ-] *n* : mandarine *f*
tangible [ˈtændʒəbəl] *adj* : tangible, palpable
tangibly [ˈtændʒəbli] *adv* : manifestement, de manière tangible
tangle[1] [ˈtæŋgəl] *v* **-gled; -gling** *vt* : emmêler, enchevêtrer — *vi* : s'emmêler
tangle[2] *n* **1** : enchevêtrement *m* **2** MUDDLE : confusion *f*, fouillis *m*
tango[1] [ˈtæŋgoː] *vi* : danser le tango
tango[2] *n, pl* **-gos** : tango *m*
tangy [ˈtæŋi] *adj* **tangier; tangiest** : acidulé
tank [ˈtæŋk] *n* **1** : réservoir *m*, citerne *f*, cuve *f* <gas tank : réservoir à essence> **2** : char *m* (militaire)
tankard [ˈtæŋkərd] *n* : chope *f*
tanker [ˈtæŋkər] *n* **1** : navire-citern *m*, camion-citern *m* **2** *or* **oil tanker** : pétrolier *m*
tanner [ˈtænər] *n* : tanneur *m*
tannery [ˈtænəri] *n, pl* **-neries** : tannerie *f*
tannin [ˈtænən] *n* : tanin *m*
tantalize [ˈtæntəˌlaɪz] *vt* **-lized; -lizing** : tourmenter, allécher
tantalizing [ˈtæntəˌlaɪzɪŋ] *adj* : tentant, alléchant
tantamount [ˈtæntəˌmaʊnt] *adj* **~ to** : équivalent à
tantrum [ˈtæntrəm] *n* : accès *m* de colère, crise *f* <to throw a tantrum : piquer une crise>
Tanzanian[1] [ˌtænzəˈniːən] *adj* : tanzanien
Tanzanian[2] *n* : Tanzanien *m*, -nienne *f*
tap[1] [ˈtæp] *v* **tapped; tapping** *vt* **1** : percer (un tonneau), inciser (des arbres) **2** PAT, TOUCH : tapoter, taper <he tapped me on the shoulder : il me tapotait sur l'épaule> **3 to tap a phone** : mettre un téléphone sur écoute — *vi* : taper légèrement
tap[2] *n* **1** FAUCET : robinet *m* <beer on tap : bière en fût> **2** PAT, TOUCH : petit coup *m*, petite tape *f* <a sharp tap : un coup sec>
tape[1] [ˈteɪp] *vt* **taped; taping 1** : coller avec un ruban adhésif **2** RECORD : enregistrer (une cassette)
tape[2] *n* **1** STRIP : bande *f*, ruban *m* **2** *or* **adhesive tape** : ruban *m* adhésif **3** → **magnetic tape, tape measure**

tape measure *n* : mètre *m* ruban *France*, ruban *m* à mesurer *Can*
taper[1] ['teɪpər] *vt* : effiler, tailler en pointe — *vi* : s'effiler, se terminer en pointe
taper[2] *n* **1** CANDLE : cierge *m* **2** TAPERING : forme *f* effilée
tapestry ['tæpəstri] *n, pl* **-tries** : tapisserie *f*
tapeworm ['teɪp,wərm] *n* : ténia *m*, ver *m* solitaire
tapioca [,tæpi'o:kə] *n* : tapioca *m*
tar[1] ['tɑr] *vt* **tarred; tarring** : goudronner
tar[2] *n* : goudron *m*
tarantula [tə'ræntʃələ, -'ræntələ] *n* : tarentule *f*
tardily ['tɑrdəli] *adv* : tardivement
tardiness ['tɑrdinəs] *n* : retard *m*
tardy ['tɑrdi] *adj* **tardier; -est** : tardif, en retard
target[1] ['tɑrgət] *vt* : viser, cibler
target[2] *n* **1** : cible *f* **2** GOAL : objectif *m*, but *m*
tariff ['tærɪf] *n* : tarif *m* douanier
tarnish[1] ['tɑrnɪʃ] *vt* : ternir
tarnish[2] *n* : ternissure *f*
tarpaulin [tɑr'pɔlən, 'tɑrpə-] *n* : bâche *f*
tarry[1] ['tæri] *vi* **-ried; -rying** : tarder
tarry[2] ['tɑri] *adj* : goudronneux, couvert de goudron
tart[1] ['tɑrt] *adj* **1** SOUR : aigre, âpre **2** CAUSTIC : aigre, acrimonieux
tart[2] *n* : tartelette *f*
tartan ['tɑrtən] *n* : tartan *m*, tissu *m* écossais
tartar ['tɑrt̬ər] *n* **1** : tartre *m* (sur les dents) **2** **tartar sauce** : sauce *f* tartare
tartness ['tɑrtnəs] *n* **1** SOURNESS : aigreur *f*, acidité *f* **2** ACRIMONY : acrimonie *f*
task ['tæsk] *n* : tâche *f*
taskmaster ['tæsk,mæstər] *n* **to be a hard taskmaster** : être très exigeant
tassel ['tæsəl] *n* : gland *m* (ornement)
taste[1] ['teɪst] *v* **tasted; tasting** *vt* **1** : goûter (à) <taste the sauce : goûte la sauce> **2** : sentir le goût de <you can't taste the pepper : on ne sent pas le goût du poivre> — *vi* : goûter <to taste sour : goûter amère> <to taste good : avoir bon goût>
taste[2] *n* **1** : goût *m* (sens) **2** FLAVOR : goût *m*, saveur *f* **3** BIT, SAMPLE : aperçu *m* <a taste of high life : un aperçu de la grande vie> **4** INCLINATION : goût *m*, penchant *m*
taste bud *n* : papille *f* gustative
tasteful ['teɪstfəl] *adj* : de bon goût
tastefully ['teɪstfəli] *adv* : avec goût
tasteless ['teɪstləs] *adj* **1** FLAVORLESS : insipide, qui n'a aucun goût **2** : de mauvais goût <a tasteless joke : une blague de mauvais goût>
taster ['teɪstər] *n* : dégustateur *m*, -trice *f*
tastiness ['teɪstinəs] *n* : saveur *f* agréable, bon goût *m*
tasty ['teɪsti] *adj* **tastier; -est** : savoureux, délicieux
tattered ['tæt̬ərd] *adj* : en lambeaux, en loques
tatters ['tæt̬ərz] *npl* **to be in tatters** : être en loques
tattle ['tæt̬əl] *vi* **-tled; -tling 1** CHATTER : jaser **2** **to tattle on s.o.** : dénoncer qqn
tattletale ['tæt̬əl,teɪl] *n* : rapporteur *m*, -teuse *f*
tattoo[1] [tæ'tu:] *vt* : tatouer
tattoo[2] *n* **1** : tatouage *m* **2** **to beat a tattoo on** : tambouriner sur
taught → **teach**
taunt[1] ['tɔnt] *vt* : ridiculiser, railler
taunt[2] *n* : raillerie *f*, insulte *f*
Taurus [tɔrəs] *n* : Taureau *m*
taut ['tɔt] *adj* : tendu, raide
tautly ['tɔtli] *adv* : de façon tendue
tautness ['tɔtnəs] *n* : tension *f*, raideur *f*
tavern ['tævərn] *n* : taverne *f*
tawdry ['tɔdri] *adj* **tawdrier; -est** : tape-à-l'œil, criard, tapageur
tawny ['tɔni] *adj* **tawnier; -est** : fauve (couleur)
tax[1] ['tæks] *vt* **1** : imposer (une personne), taxer (des marchandises) **2** CHARGE : accuser <he taxed them with carelessness : il les a accusés d'être négligents> **3** TRY : mettre à l'épreuve <the job taxed her strength : l'emploi la fatiguait>
tax[2] *n* **1** : taxe *f* <sales tax : taxe à l'achat> **2** : impôt *m* <income tax : impôt sur le revenu> **3** STRAIN : fardeau *m*, poids *m*
taxable ['tæksəbəl] *adj* : imposable
taxation [tæk'seɪʃən] *n* : taxation *f*, imposition *f*
tax–exempt ['tæksɪg'zɛmpt, -ɛg-] *adj* : exempt d'impôts
taxi[1] ['tæksi] *vi* **taxied; taxiing** *or* **taxying; taxis** *or* **taxies 1** : transporter par taxi **2** : rouler au sol (se dit d'un avion)
taxi[2] *n, pl* **taxis** : taxi *m*
taxicab ['tæksi,kæb] → **taxi**[2]
taxidermist ['tæksə,dərmɪst] *n* : taxidermiste *mf*
taxidermy ['tæksə,dərmi] *n* : taxidermie *f*
taxpayer ['tæks,peɪər] *n* : contribuable *mf*
TB [,ti:'bi:] → **tuberculosis**
tea ['ti:] *n* : thé *m*
teach ['ti:tʃ] *v* **taught** ['tɔt]; **teaching** *vt* **1** : apprendre, montrer <he's teaching me to drive : il m'apprend à conduire> **2** : enseigner, faire cours à <she teaches French : elle enseigne le français> **3** **to teach s.o. a lesson** : servir de leçon à qqn — *vi* : enseigner
teacher ['ti:tʃər] *n* : enseignant *m*, -nante *f*; professeur *m*

teaching ['ti:tʃɪŋ] *n* : enseignement *m*
teacup ['ti:,kʌp] *n* : tasse *f* à thé
teak ['ti:k] *n* : teck *m*
teakettle ['ti:,kɛtəl] *n* : bouilloire *f*
teal ['ti:l] *n, pl* **teal** *or* **teals** : sarcelle *f* (canard)
team[1] ['ti:m] *vi* **to team up with** : faire équipe avec
team[2] *adj* : d'équipe <a team effort : un effort d'équipe>
team[3] *n* **1** : attelage *m* (d'animaux) **2** : équipe *f* (aux sports, etc.)
teammate ['ti:m,meɪt] *n* : coéquipier *m*, -pière *f*
teamster ['ti:mstər] *n* : camionneur *m*, -neuse *f*; routier *m*
teamwork ['ti:m,wərk] *n* : travail *m* d'équipe
teapot ['ti:,pɑt] *n* : théière *f*
tear[1] ['tær] *v* **tore** ['tor]; **torn** ['torn]; **tearing** *vt* **1** RIP : déchirer (un papier, etc.), se dechirer (un muscle) <to tear to shreds : mettre en lambeaux> **2** LACERATE : blesser (la peau) **3** REMOVE, SNATCH : arracher **4** *or* **to tear apart** DIVIDE : déchirer **5 to tear down** : démolir — *vi* **1** : se déchirer <this cloth tears easily : ce tissu se déchire facilement> **2** RUSH : se précipiter <he tore out of the house : il est sorti en trombe de la maison>
tear[2] *n* : déchirure *f*
tear[3] ['tɪr] *n* : larme *f* <to break into tears : fondre en larmes>
teardrop ['tɪr,drɑp] → **tear**[3]
tearful ['tɪrfəl] *adj* : larmoyant
tearfully ['tɪrfəli] *adv* : en pleurant, les larmes aux yeux
tease[1] ['ti:z] *vt* **teased; teasing** : taquiner
tease[2] *n* : taquin *m*, -quine *f*
teaspoon ['ti:,spu:n] *n* : petite cuillère *f*, cuillère *f* à café
teaspoonful ['ti:,spu:n,fʊl] *n* : cuillerée *f* à café
teat ['ti:t] *n* : tétine *f*
technical ['tɛknɪkəl] *adj* : technique — **technically** [-kli] *adv*
technicality [,tɛknə'kælət̬i] *n, pl* **-ties** : détail *m* technique
technician [tɛk'nɪʃən] *n* : technicien *m*, -cienne *f*
technique [tɛk'ni:k] *n* : technique *f*
technological [,tɛknə'lɑdʒɪkəl] *adj* : technologique
technology [tɛk'nɑlədʒi] *n, pl* **-gies** : technologie *f*
tedious ['ti:diəs] *adj* : fastidieux, ennuyeux
tediously ['ti:diəsli] *adv* : fastidieusement, de façon ennuyeuse
tediousness ['ti:diəsnəs] *n* : ennui *m*
tedium ['ti:diəm] → **tediousness**
tee ['ti:] *n* : tee *m* (au golf)
teem ['ti:m] *vi* **to teem with** : foisonner de, abonder en
teenage ['ti:n,eɪdʒ] *or* **teenaged** [-,eɪdʒd] *adj* : jeune, adolescent, d'adolescence
teenager ['ti:n,eɪdʒər] *n* : adolescent *m*, -cente *f*
teens ['ti:nz] *npl* : adolescence *f*
teepee → **tepee**
teeter[1] ['ti:t̬ər] *vi* **1** WAVER : vaciller, chanceler **2** SEESAW : balancer, basculer
teeter[2] *n or* **teeter–totter** ['ti:t̬ər-,tɑt̬ər] → **seesaw**
teeth → **tooth**
teethe ['ti:ð] *vi* **teethed; teething** : faire ses dents
telecast[1] ['tɛlə,kæst] *vt* **-cast; -casting** : téléviser, diffuser
telecast[2] *n* : émission *f* de télévision
telecommunication [,tɛləkə,mju:nə'keɪʃən] *n* : télécommunication *f*
telegram ['tɛlə,græm] *n* : télégramme *m*
telegraph[1] ['tɛlə,græf] *v* : télégraphier
telegraph[2] *n* : télégraphe *m*
telepathic [,tɛlə'pæθɪk] *adj* : télépathique
telepathy [tə'lɛpəθi] *n* : télépathie *f*
telephone[1] ['tɛlə,fo:n] *v* **-phoned; -phoning** *vt* : téléphoner à — *vi* : appeler, téléphoner
telephone[2] *n* : téléphone *m*
telescope[1] ['tɛlə,sko:p] *v* **-scoped; -scoping** *vi* : se télescoper — *vt* CONDENSE : comprimer, condenser
telescope[2] *n* : télescope *m*
telescopic [,tɛlə'skɑpɪk] *adj* : télescopique
televise ['tɛlə,vaɪz] *vt* **-vised; -vising** : téléviser
television ['tɛlə,vɪʒən] *n* **1** : télévision *f* **2** *or* **television set** : téléviseur *m*
tell ['tɛl] *v* **told** ['to:ld]; **telling** *vt* **1** COUNT : compter, être en tout <all told there were 27 of us : nous étions 27 en tout> **2** NARRATE : raconter, conter **3** REVEAL : divulguer, dévoiler **4** ORDER : dire à <they told me to wait : ils m'ont dit d'attendre> **5** RECOGNIZE : voir, lire <you can tell it's a masterpiece : on voit bien que c'est un chef-d'œuvre> <to tell time : lire l'heure> — *vi* **1** SAY : dire **2** KNOW : savoir <as far as I can tell : pour autant que je sache> **3** SHOW : se faire sentir <the tension began to tell : la tension a commencé à se faire sentir>
teller ['tɛlər] *n* **1** NARRATOR : conteur *m*, -teuse *f* **2** *or* **bank teller** : caissier *m*, -sière *f*
temerity [tə'mɛrət̬i] *n, pl* **-ties** : témérité *f*, audace *f*
temp ['tɛmp] *n* : intérimaire *mf*; occasionnel *m*, -nelle *f Can*
temper[1] ['tɛmpər] *vt* **1** MODERATE : tempérer **2** TOUGHEN : endurcir
temper[2] *n* **1** HARDNESS : trempe *f* (de métal) **2** DISPOSITION : tempérament

m, caractère *m* **3 to lose one's temper** : se mettre en colère, s'emporter

temperament [ˈtɛmpərmənt, -prə-, -pərə-] *n* : tempérament *m,* nature *f*

temperamental [ˌtɛmpərˈmɛntəl, -prə-, -pərə-] *adj* : capricieux

temperance [ˈtɛmprənts] *n* : tempérance *f,* modération *f*

temperate [ˈtɛmpərət] *adj* **1** MILD : tempéré <temperate climate : climat tempéré> **2** MODERATE : modéré <to be a temperate drinker : boire modérément>

temperature [ˈtɛmpərˌtʃʊr, -prə-, -tʃər] *n* **1** : température *f* **2** FEVER : température *f,* fièvre *f* <to run a temperature : faire de la température>

tempest [ˈtɛmpəst] *n* **1** STORM : tempête *f,* orage *m* **2** UPROAR : tumulte *m,* chahut *m*

tempestuous [tɛmˈpɛstʃʊəs] *adj* **1** STORMY : tempétueux **2** ARDENT, RAGING : impétueux, fougueux

temple [ˈtɛmpəl] *n* **1** : temple *m* (religieux) **2** : tempe *f* (en anatomie)

tempo [ˈtɛmˌpoː] *n, pl* **-pi** [-ˌpiː] *or* **-pos** : tempo *m*

temporal [ˈtɛmpərəl] *adj* : temporel

temporary [ˈtɛmpəˌrɛri] *adj* : temporaire — **temporarily** [ˌtɛmpəˈrɛrəli] *adv*

tempt [ˈtɛmpt] *vt* : tenter

temptation [tɛmpˈteɪʃən] *n* : tentation *f*

tempter [ˈtɛmptər] *n* : tentateur *m*

temptress [ˈtɛmptrəs] *n* : tentatrice *f*

ten[1] [ˈtɛn] *adj* : dix

ten[2] *n* **1** : dix *m* **2** : dizaine *f* <there were tens of them : il y en avait des dizaines>

tenable [ˈtɛnəbəl] *adj* : soutenable, défendable

tenacious [təˈneɪʃəs] *adj* : tenace

tenaciously [təˈneɪʃəsli] *adv* : avec ténacité

tenacity [təˈnæsəṭi] *n* : ténacité *f,* opiniâtreté *f*

tenancy [ˈtɛnəntsi] *n, pl* **-cies 1** : location *f* <terms of tenancy : conditions de location> **2** : période *f* d'occupation (d'un logement)

tenant [ˈtɛnənt] *n* : locataire *mf*

tend [ˈtɛnd] *vi* **1** : se diriger <we cannot tell where society is tending : on ne peut pas dire où notre société se dirige> **2 to tend to** : avoir tendance à, être enclin à <she tends to be pessimistic : elle a tendance à être pessimiste> — *vt* : surveiller, s'occuper de <to tend the plants : s'occuper des plantes>

tendency [ˈtɛndəntsi] *n, pl* **-cies** : tendance *f*

tender[1] [ˈtɛndər] *vt* OFFER : donner, offrir <I tendered my resignation : j'ai donné ma démission> <to tender thanks : offrir ses remerciements>

tender[2] *adj* **1** DELICATE : tendre, fragile **2** LOVING : tendre, affectueux **3** SORE : sensible **4** YOUNG : tendre <a tender age : un âge tendre> **5** SUCCULENT : tendre <a tender steak : un steak tendre>

tender[3] *n* **1** OFFER : soumission *f,* offre *f* **2 legal tender** : cours *m* légal

tenderize [ˈtɛndəˌraɪz] *vt* **-ized; -izing** : attendrir (de la viande)

tenderloin [ˈtɛndərˌlɔɪn] *n* : filet *m* (de bœuf, de porc, etc.)

tenderly [ˈtɛndərli] *adv* : tendrement, avec tendresse

tenderness [ˈtɛndərnəs] *n* : tendresse *f*

tendon [ˈtɛndən] *n* : tendon *m*

tendril [ˈtɛndrɪl] *n* : vrille *f* (d'une plante)

tenement [ˈtɛnəmənt] *n or* **tenement house** : immeuble *m*

tenet [ˈtɛnət] *n* : principe *m,* croyance *f*

tennis [ˈtɛnəs] *n* : tennis *m*

tenor [ˈtɛnər] *n* **1** DRIFT, GIST : contenu *m,* sens *m* général (d'une conversation, etc.) **2** : ténor *m* <tenor voice : voix de ténor>

tenpins [ˈtɛnˌpɪnz] *n* : bowling *m*

tense[1] [ˈtɛnts] *vi* **tensed; tensing** *or* **to tense up** : se raidir, se tendre

tense[2] *adj* **tenser; tensest 1** RIGID : tendu, raide **2** UPTIGHT : tendu, stressé

tense[3] *n* : temps *m* (en grammaire) <the past tense : le passé composé>

tensely [ˈtɛntsli] *adv* : de façon tendue

tenseness [ˈtɛntsnəs] *n* : tension *f*

tensile [ˈtɛntsəl, ˈtɛnˌsaɪl] *adj* : extensible

tension [ˈtɛntʃən] *n* **1** TAUTNESS : tension *f,* raideur *f* **2** STRESS : tension *f,* stress *m*

tent [ˈtɛnt] *n* : tente *f*

tentacle [ˈtɛntɪkəl] *n* : tentacule *m*

tentative [ˈtɛntəṭɪv] *adj* **1** : provisoire <tentative plans : plans provisoires> **2** HESITANT : hésitant, indécis <tentative steps : pas hésitants>

tentatively [ˈtɛntəṭɪvli] *adv* **1** : provisoirement **2** HESITANTLY : incertainement, timidement

tenth[1] [ˈtɛnθ] *adv & adj* : dixième

tenth[2] *n* **1** : dizième *mf* (dans une série) **2** : dizième *m* (en mathématiques) **3** (*used in dates*) <the tenth of May : le dix mai>

tenuous [ˈtɛnjʊəs] *adj* : précaire, ténu

tenuously [ˈtɛnjʊəsli] *adv* : de manière ténue

tenure [ˈtɛnjər] *n* : période *f* de jouissance (en droit), titularisation *f* (à un poste universitaire)

tenured [ˈtɛnjərd] *adj* : titulaire

tepee [ˈtiːˌpiː] *n* : tipi *m*

tepid [ˈtɛpɪd] *adj* : tiède

term[1] [ˈtərm] *vt* : appeler, nommer

term[2] *n* **1** PERIOD : terme *m* **2** : terme *m* (en mathématiques) **3** WORD : terme *m,* expression *f* **4 terms** *npl* CONDITIONS : termes *mpl,* conditions *fpl* **5 terms** *npl* RELATIONS : termes

mpl, rapports *mpl* <on good terms with : en bons termes avec>
terminal[1] [ˈtərmənəl] *adj* : terminal
terminal[2] *n* **1** : borne *f* (en électricité) **2** *or* **computer terminal** : terminal *m* **3** : terminus *m* (de train, de bus)
terminate [ˈtərməˌneɪt] *v* **-nated; -nating** *vt* : mettre fin à — *vi* : se terminer
termination [ˌtərməˈneɪʃən] *n* **1** END : fin *f* **2** ENDING : terminaison *f* (en grammaire)
terminology [ˌtərməˈnɑlədʒi] *n, pl* **-gies** : terminologie *f*
terminus [ˈtərmənəs] *n, pl* **-ni** [-ˌnaɪ] *or* **-nuses 1** END : bout *m,* fin *f* **2** TERMINAL : terminus *m*
termite [ˈtərˌmaɪt] *n* : termite *m*
tern [ˈtərn] *n* : hirondelle *f* de mer, sterne *f*
terrace[1] [ˈtɛrəs] *vt* **-raced; -racing** : aménager en terrasses
terrace[2] *n* **1** PATIO : terrasse *f* **2** EMBANKMENT : terre-plein *m* **3** : terrasse *f* (en agriculture) **4** *or* **terraced houses** : rangée *f* de maisons
terra–cotta [ˌtɛrəˈkɑṭə] *n* : terre *f* cuite
terrain [təˈreɪn] *n* : terrain *m*
terrapin [ˈtɛrəpɪn] *n* : tortue *f* d'eau douce
terrarium [təˈræriəm] *n, pl* **-ia** [-iə] *or* **-iums** : vivarium *m* (pour les animaux), serre *f* miniature (pour les plantes)
terrestrial [təˈrɛstriəl] *adj* : terrestre
terrible [ˈtɛrəbəl] *adj* : terrible, épouvantable
terribly [ˈtɛrəbli] *adv* **1** VERY : terriblement, vraiment <I'm terribly sorry : je suis vraiment désolée> **2** BADLY : terriblement, affreusement mal <terribly ill : terriblement malade>
terrier [ˈtɛriər] *n* : terrier *m*
terrific [təˈrɪfɪk] *adj* **1** FRIGHTFUL : terrible, terrifiant **2** EXTRAORDINARY : terrible, extrême <a terrific speed : une allure vertigineuse> **3** EXCELLENT : formidable, épatant *fam* <we had a terrific time : nous nous sommes vraiment amusés>
terrify [ˈtɛrəˌfaɪ] *vt* **-fied; -fying** : terrifier
terrifying [ˈtɛrəˌfaɪɪŋ] *adj* : terrifiant, effroyable
territorial [ˌtɛrəˈtoriəl] *adj* : territorial
territory [ˈtɛrəˌtori] *n, pl* **-ries** : territoire *m*
terror [ˈtɛrər] *n* : terreur *f*
terrorism [ˈtɛrərˌɪzəm] *n* : terrorisme *m*
terrorist[1] [ˈtɛrərɪst] *adj* : terroriste
terrorist[2] *n* : terroriste *mf*
terrorize [ˈtɛrərˌaɪz] *vt* **-ized; -izing** : terroriser
terry [ˈtɛri] *n, pl* **-ries** *or* **terry cloth** : tissu *m* éponge, ratine *f Can*
terse [ˈtərs] *adj* **terser; tersest** : concis, succinct
tersely [ˈtərsli] *adv* : succinctement, brièvement
tertiary [ˈtərʃiˌɛri] *adj* : tertiaire
test[1] [ˈtɛst] *vt* : examiner, tester — *vi* **to test for** : faire une recherche de
test[2] *n* **1** : examen *m* (scolaire), test *m* **2** TRIAL : épreuve *f* **3** : analyse *f,* examen *m* <blood test : analyse de sang>
testament [ˈtɛstəmənt] *n* **1** WILL : testament *m* **2** : Testament *m* <the New Testament : le Nouveau Testament>
testicle [ˈtɛstɪkəl] *n* : testicule *m*
testify [ˈtɛstəˌfaɪ] *v* **-fied; -fying** : témoigner
testimonial [ˌtɛstəˈmoːniəl] *n* **1** RECOMMENDATION : recommandation *f,* attestation *f* **2** TRIBUTE : témoignage *m*
testimony [ˈtɛstəˌmoːni] *n, pl* **-nies** : témoignage *m,* déposition *f*
testy [ˈtɛsti] *adj* **testier; -est** : irritable, irascible
tetanus [ˈtɛtənəs] *n* : tétanos *m*
tête–à–tête [ˌtɛṭəˈtɛt, ˌteɪṭəˈteɪt] *n* : tête-à-tête *m*
tether[1] [ˈtɛðər] *vt* : attacher (un animal)
tether[2] *n* **1** : longe *f* **2 at the end of one's tether** : à bout de patience
text [ˈtɛkst] *n* **1** : texte *m* **2** TOPIC : thème *m,* sujet *m* **3** → **textbook**
textbook [ˈtɛkstˌbʊk] *n* : manuel *m* scolaire
textile [ˈtɛkˌstaɪl, ˈtɛkstəl] *n* : textile *m*
textual [ˈtɛkstʃʊəl] *adj* : textuel
texture [ˈtɛkstʃər] *n* : texture *f*
Thai[1] [ˈtaɪ] *adj* : thaïlandais
Thai[2] *n* : Thaïlandais *m,* -daise *f*
than[1] [ˈðæn] *conj* : que <older than I am : plus âgé que moi> <nothing is worse than boredom : rien n'est pire que l'ennui> <he'd do anything rather than lie : il ferait tout plutôt que mentir>
than[2] *prep* : que, de <thinner than me : plus mince que moi> <fewer than 10 : moins de 10>
thank [ˈθæŋk] *vt* : remercier
thankful [ˈθæŋkfəl] *adj* : reconnaissant
thankfully [ˈθæŋkfəli] *adv* **1** GRATEFULLY : avec reconnaissance, avec gratitude **2** FORTUNATELY : heureusement
thankfulness [ˈθæŋkfəlnəs] *n* : reconnaissance *f,* gratitude *f*
thankless [ˈθæŋkləs] *adj* : ingrat
thanks [ˈθæŋks] *npl* **1** : remerciements *mpl* **2 ~ to** : grâce à
Thanksgiving [θæŋksˈgɪvɪŋ, ˈθæŋksˌ-] *n* : jour *m* d'Action de Grâces
that[1] [ˈðæt] *adv* **1** : comme ça <a nail about that long : un clou environ long comme ça> **2** VERY : tellement, très <he did not take his classes that seriously : il ne prenait pas ses cours tellement au sérieux>
that[2] *adj, pl* **those** : ce, cet, cette, ces <that girl : cette fille> <those people : ces gens-là>
that[3] *conj* **1** : que <she said that she was busy : elle a dit qu'elle était oc-

cupée> <it's unlikely that he'll be there : il y a peu de chances qu'il soit là> **2** SO : afin que <he shouted that all might hear : il a crié afin que tout le monde puisse entendre>

that[4] *pron, pl* **those** [ˈðo:z] **1** (*used to introduce relative clauses*) : que <the house that we built : la maison que nous avons construite> **2** WHO : qui <the person that won the race : la personne qui a gagné la course> **3** : celui-là, celle-là <do you prefer this or that? : préférez-vous celui-ci ou celui-là?> **4** : cela, ce, ça <is that you? : c'est toi?> <after that : après cela>

thatch[1] [ˈθætʃ] *vt* : couvrir (un toit) de chaume

thatch[2] *n* : chaume *m*

thaw[1] [ˈθɔ] *vt* : dégeler — *vi* : fondre

thaw[2] *n* : dégel *m*

the[1] [ðə, *before vowel sounds usu* ði:] *adv* : le <the sooner the better : le plus tôt sera le mieux>

the[2] *art* **1** : le, la, l', les <let the cat out : laisse le chat sortir> <the right answer : la bonne réponse> <the elite : l'élite> <the English : les Anglais> **2** EACH : le, la <forty cookies the box : quarante biscuits la boîte>

theater *or* **theatre** [ˈθi:əṭər] *n* **1** : théâtre *m* (édifice) **2** DRAMA : théâtre *m*, art *m* dramatique **3** : théâtre *m* (de la guerre, etc.)

theatrical [θiˈætrɪkəl] *adj* : théâtral

thee [ˈði:] *pron* : te, toi

theft [ˈθɛft] *n* : vol *m*

their [ˈðɛr] *adj* : leur <their notebooks : leurs cahiers>

theirs [ˈðɛrz] *pron* : le leur, la leur, les leurs <the red house is theirs : la maison rouge est la leur>

them [ˈðɛm] *pron* **1** (*as a direct object*) : les <in order to understand them : afin de les comprendre> **2** (*as an indirect object*) : leur <we sent them a present : nous leur avons envoyé un cadeau> **3** (*as the object of a preposition*) : eux, elles <he thought of them : il a pensé à eux> <some of them : quelques-unes d'entre elles>

theme [ˈθi:m] *n* **1** TOPIC : thème *m* **2** COMPOSITION : composition *f* **3** : thème *m* (musical)

themselves [ðəmˈsɛlvz, ðɛm-] *pron* **1** (*used reflexively*) : se <they hurt themselves : ils se sont blessés> **2** (*used for emphasis*) : eux-mêmes, elles-mêmes <they made the dresses themselves : elles ont fait les robes elles-mêmes> **3** (*used after a preposition*) : eux, elles, eux-mêmes, elles-mêmes <they talked among themselves : ils discutaient entre eux> **4 by themselves** : tous seuls, toutes seules

then[1] [ˈðɛn] *adv* **1** : alors, à ce moment-là <from then on : à partir de ce moment-là> **2** : ensuite, puis <he answered the questions and then he left : il a répondu aux questions, puis il est parti> **3** BESIDES : et puis <then there is the interest to be paid : et puis il y a l'intérêt à payer> **4** : donc, alors <take it, then, if you want it so much : prends-le, alors, si tu le veux tant> **5** CONSEQUENTLY : donc

then[2] *adj* : d'alors, de l'époque <the then treasurer : le trésorier d'alors>

then[3] *n* : ce temps-là <since then : depuis ce temps-là>

thence [ˈðɛnts, ˈθɛnts] *adv* : de là

theologian [ˌθi:əˈlo:dʒən] *n* : théologien *m*, -gienne *f*

theological [ˌθi:əˈlɑdʒɪkəl] *adj* : théologique

theology [θiˈɑlədʒi] *n, pl* **-gies** : théologie *f*

theorem [ˈθi:ərəm, ˈθɪrəm] *n* : théorème *m*

theoretical [ˌθi:əˈrɛtɪkəl] *adj* : théorique — **theoretically** *adv*

theorize [ˈθi:əˌraɪz] *vi* **-rized; -rizing** : théoriser

theory [ˈθi:əri, ˈθɪri] *n, pl* **-ries** : théorie *f*

therapeutic [ˌθɛrəˈpju:ṭɪk] *adj* : thérapeutique — **therapeutically** *adv*

therapist [ˈθɛrəpɪst] *n* : thérapeute *mf*

therapy [ˈθɛrəpi] *n, pl* **-pies** : thérapie *f*

there[1] [ˈðær] *adv* **1** : là, là-bas, y <stand over there : mettez-vous debout là-bas> <he went there after class : il s'y est rendu après ses cours> **2** (*used for emphasis*) : voilà <there's where I disagree : voilà où je ne suis pas d'accord> <there, I'm finished! : voilà, j'ai terminé!>

there[2] *pron* **1** (*used as a function word to introduce a sentence or clause*) <there shall come a time : le jour viendra> **2** (*used as an indefinite substitute for a name*) <hi there! : salut, toi!> **3 there is** : il y a <there's someone waiting for you : il y a quelqu'un qui t'attend>

thereabouts [ðærəˈbaʊts, ˈðærəˌ-] *or* **thereabout** [ðærəˈbaʊt, ˈðærəˌ-] *adv* **1** NEARBY : dans les environs, par là **2** : environ <a boy of 18 or thereabouts : un garçon d'environ 18 ans>

thereafter [ðærˈæftər] *adv* : par la suite

thereby [ðærˈbaɪ, ˈðærˌbaɪ] *adv* **1** THUS : ainsi <she thereby lost her chance to win : elle a ainsi perdu sa chance de gagner> **2 thereby hangs a tale** : c'est toute une histoire

therefore [ˈðærˌfor] *adv* : donc, par conséquent

therein [ðærˈɪn] *adv* **1** : dedans, à l'intérieur <the box and the jewels therein : la boîte et les bijoux qui étaient dedans> **2** : là <therein lies the problem : là réside le problème>

thereof [ðærˈʌv, -ˈɑv] *adv* : de cela, en

thereupon [ˈðærəˌpɑn, -ˌpɔn; ˌðærəˈpɑn, -ˈpɔn] *adv* : sur ce

therewith [ðær'wɪð, -'wɪθ] *adv* : avec cela
thermal ['θərməl] *adj* : thermal, thermique <thermal spring : source thermale> <thermal power station : centrale thermique>
thermodynamics [ˌθərmodaɪ'næmɪks] *ns & pl* : thermodynamique *f*
thermometer [θər'mɑmət̬ər] *n* : thermomètre *m*
thermos ['θərməs] *n* : thermos *mf*
thermostat ['θərməˌstæt] *n* : thermostat *m*
thesaurus [θɪ'sɔrəs] *n, pl* **-sauri** [-'sɔrˌaɪ] *or* **-sauruses** [-'sɔrəsəz] : dictionnaire *m* analogique, dictionnaire *m* des synonymes
these → **this[2]**, **this[3]**
thesis ['θi:sɪs] *n, pl* **theses** ['θiˌsi:z] : thèse *f*
they ['ðeɪ] *pron* **1** : ils, elles <they dance well : ils dansent bien> <there they are : les voici> **2** (*used for emphasis*) : eux, elles <*they* won't be coming : ils ne viennent pas, eux> **3** PEOPLE : on <they say she's pretty : on dit qu'elle est belle>
thiamine ['θaɪəmɪn, -ˌmi:n] *n* : thiamine *f*
thick[1] ['θɪk] *adj* **1** : épais <a thick plank : une planche épaisse> <two millimeters thick : deux millimètres d'épaisseur> **2** : dense, épais <thick fog : brume épaisse> **3** STUPID : bête, obtus **4 to be thick with** : être rempli de
thick[2] *n* **1 in the thick of** : au plus fort de (une bataille, etc.) **2 through thick and thin** : contre vents et marées
thicken ['θɪkən] *vi* : s'épaissir — *vt* : épaissir (une sauce, etc.)
thickener ['θɪkənər] *n* : épaississant *m*
thicket ['θɪkət] *n* : fourré *m,* hallier *m*
thickly ['θɪkli] *adv* **1** : en couche épaisse, en tranches épaisses **2** DENSELY : dru <snow was falling thickly : la neige tombait dru> <thickly wooded : très boisé>
thickness ['θɪknəs] *n* : épaisseur *f,* grosseur *f*
thick–skinned ['θɪk'skɪnd] *adj* : dur, insensible
thief ['θi:f] *n, pl* **thieves** ['θi:vz] : voleur *m,* -leuse *f*
thieve ['θi:v] *v* **thieved; thieving** : voler
thigh ['θaɪ] *n* : cuisse *f*
thighbone ['θaɪˌbo:n] *n* : fémur *m*
thimble ['θɪmbəl] *n* : dé *m* à coudre
thin[1] ['θɪn] *v* **thinned; thinning** *vt* : allonger, diluer (un liquide) — *vi* : se dissiper (se dit du brouillard, etc.), se disperser (se dit d'une foule) <his hair was thinning : il perdait ses cheveux>
thin[2] *adj* **thinner; thinnest 1** : fin, mince <thin paper : papier fin> **2** LEAN, SLIM : mince, maigre **3** SPARSE : clairsemé <thin hair : cheveux clairsemés> **4** : raréfié (de l'air), clair (d'un potage)
thing ['θɪŋ] *n* **1** OBJECT : chose *f,* objet *m,* truc *m fam* <a thing of beauty : une belle chose> **2** ACTIVITY, EVENT : chose *f* <the first thing to do : la première chose à faire> <it was a terrible thing : c'était une chose épouvantable> **3 things** *npl* BELONGINGS : affaires *fpl,* effets *mpl* personnels <to pack one's things : faire ses valises> <I don't have a thing to wear : je n'ai rien à me mettre>
think ['θɪŋk] *v* **thought** ['θɔt]; **thinking** *vt* **1** INTEND : penser <he thought to return early : il a pensé revenir tôt> **2** BELIEVE : penser, croire **3** PONDER : penser à, réfléchir à <to think things out : bien réfléchir> **4** REMEMBER : penser à, se rappeler <I didn't think to ask him : je n'ai pas pensé à lui demander> **5 to think up** : inventer — *vi* **1** REASON : penser, raisonner **2 to think of** CONSIDER : penser à, considérer <think of your family first : pense à ta famille en premier>
thinker ['θɪŋkər] *n* : penseur *m,* -seuse *f*
thinly ['θɪnli] *adv* **1** LIGHTLY : légèrement **2 to cut thinly** : couper en tranches minces **3 to spread thinly** : étaler en couche mince **4 thinly populated** : à la population éparse
thinness ['θɪnnəs] *n* : minceur *f*
thin–skinned ['θɪn'skɪnd] *adj* : susceptible, sensible
third[1] ['θərd] *or* **thirdly** [-li] *adv* : troisième, troisièmement, en troisième place
third[2] *adj* : troisième
third[3] *n* **1** : troisième *mf* (dans une série) **2** : tiers *m* (en mathématiques) **3** (*used in dates*) <the third of December : le trois décembre>
Third World *n* : le tiers-monde *m*
thirst[1] ['θərst] *vi* **to thirst for** : avoir soif de
thirst[2] *n* : soif *f*
thirsty ['θərsti] *adj* **thirstier; -est** : assoiffé
thirteen[1] [ˌθər'ti:n] *adj* : treize
thirteen[2] *n* : treize *m*
thirteenth[1] [ˌθər'ti:nθ] *adj* : treizième
thirteenth[2] *n* **1** : treizième *mf* (dans une série) **2** : treizième *m* (en mathématiques) **3** (*used in dates*) <the thirteenth of January : le treize janvier>
thirtieth[1] ['θərt̬iəθ] *adj* : trentième
thirtieth[2] *n* **1** : trentième *mf* (dans une série) **2** : trentième *m* (en mathématiques)
thirty[1] ['θərt̬i] *adj* : trente
thirty[2] *n, pl* **thirties** : trente *m*
this[1] ['ðɪs] *adv* : si, aussi <it was this big : c'était aussi grand que ça>

this[2] *adj, pl* **these** [ˈðiːz] **1** : ce, cet, cette, ces <this morning : ce matin> <all these years : toutes ces années> **2** : ce . . . -ci, cet . . . -ci, cette . . . -ci, ces . . . -ci <this car or that one : cette voiture-ci ou celle-là>

this[3] *pron, pl* **these 1** : voici <this is your book : voici ton livre> **2** : ce, ceci <who is this? : qui est-ce?> <after this, he left : après ceci, il est parti> <this is my sister : je vous présente ma sœur>

thistle [ˈθɪsəl] *n* : chardon *m*

thong [ˈθɔŋ] *n* : lanière *f* (de cuir, etc.)

thorax [ˈθorˌæks] *n, pl* **-raxes** *or* **-races** [ˈθorəˌsiːz] : thorax *m*

thorn [ˈθɔrn] *n* : épine *f*

thorny [ˈθɔrni] *adj* **thornier; -est** : épineux

thorough [ˈθəˌroː] *adj* **1** COMPLETE : approfondi **2** PAINSTAKING : consciencieux, minutieux

thoroughbred [ˈθəroˌbrɛd] *adj* : de pure race

Thoroughbred *n* : pur-sang *m*

thoroughfare [ˈθəroˌfær] *n* : voie *f* de communication, rue *f*

thoroughly [ˈθəroli] *adv* **1** METICULOUSLY : minutieusement, à fond **2** COMPLETELY : tout à fait, absolument

those → **that**[2], **that**[4]

thou [ˈðaʊ] *pron* : tu

though[1] [ˈðoː] *adv* HOWEVER : cependant, pourtant

though[2] *conj* : bien que, quoique

thought[1] [ˈθɔt] → **think**

thought[2] *n* **1** THINKING : pensée *f* <Western thought : la pensée de l'Ouest> **2** CONSIDERATION : réflexion *f* <after much thought : après mûre réflexion> **3** IDEA : pensée *f*, idée *f*

thoughtful [ˈθɔtfəl] *adj* **1** PENSIVE : pensif, songeur **2** CONSIDERATE : attentionné, prévenant **3** REASONED : réfléchi, sérieux <a thoughtful essay : une composition réfléchie>

thoughtfully [ˈθɔtfəli] *adv* **1** PENSIVELY : pensivement **2** CONSIDERATELY : avec prévenance **3** REFLECTIVELY : de façon réfléchie

thoughtfulness [ˈθɔtfəlnəs] *n* : considération *f*, attention *f*

thoughtless [ˈθɔtləs] *adj* **1** RASH : irréfléchi, hâtif **2** INCONSIDERATE : irréfléchi, inconsidéré

thoughtlessly [ˈθɔtləsli] *adv* : inconsidérément

thousand[1] [ˈθaʊzənd] *adj* : mille

thousand[2] *n, pl* **-sands** *or* **-sand** : mille *m* <two thousand : deux mille>

thousandth[1] [ˈθaʊzəntθ] *adj* : millième

thousandth[2] *n* **1** : millième *mf* (dans une série) **2** : millième *m* (en mathématiques)

thrash [ˈθræʃ] *vt* **1** THRESH : battre (le grain) **2** BEAT : battre — *vi or* **to thrash about** : se débattre

thread[1] *vt* **1** : enfiler (une aiguille, des perles) **2 to thread one's way through** : se faufiler entre

thread[2] [ˈθrɛd] *n* **1** : fil *m* (en couture) **2** : fil *m*, cours *m* <the thread of the story : le fil de l'histoire> **3** TRICKLE, WISP : filet *m* <a thread of smoke : un filet de fumée>

threadbare [ˈθrɛdˈbær] *adj* **1** WORN : usé jusqu'à la corde, élimé **2** TRITE : usé, banal

threat [ˈθrɛt] *n* : menace *f*

threaten [ˈθrɛtən] *v* : menacer

threateningly [ˈθrɛtənɪŋli] *adv* : de façon menaçante

three[1] [ˈθriː] *adj* : trois

three[2] *n* : trois *m*

threefold[1] [ˈθriːˌfoːld] *adv* : trois fois autant

threefold[2] *adj* : triple

threescore [ˈθriːˈskor] *adj* : soixante

thresh [ˈθrɛʃ] *vt* : battre (le grain)

thresher [ˈθrɛʃər] *n or* **threshing machine** : batteuse *f*

threshold [ˈθrɛʃˌhoːld, -ˌoːld] *n* : seuil *m*

threw → **throw**[1]

thrice [ˈθraɪs] *adv* : trois fois

thrift [ˈθrɪft] *n* : économie *f*

thriftless [ˈθrɪftləs] *adj* : dépensier

thrifty [ˈθrɪfti] *adj* **thriftier; -est** : économe

thrill[1] [ˈθrɪl] *vt* : électriser, transporter (d'émotion) — *vi* : frissonner

thrill[2] *n* : frisson *m*, émotion *f*

thriller [ˈθrɪlər] *n* : thriller *m*, roman *m* ou film *m* à suspense

thrive [ˈθraɪv] *vi* **throve** [ˈθroːv] *or* **thrived; thriven** [ˈθrɪvən] **1** FLOURISH : bien pousser, bien se porter **2** PROSPER : prospérer, réussir

throat [ˈθroːt] *n* : gorge *f* <sore throat : mal de gorge> <to clear one's throat : s'éclaircir la voix>

throaty [ˈθroːti] *adj* **throatier; -est** : rauque, guttural

throb[1] [ˈθrɑb] *vi* **throbbed; throbbing 1** PALPITATE : battre, palpiter (se dit du cœur) **2** : vibrer (se dit d'un moteur) **3 to throb with pain** : lanciner <my head was throbbing : j'avais mal à la tête>

throb[2] *n* **1** BEAT : battement *m*, pulsation *f* (cardiaque) **2** VIBRATION : vibration *f*, vrombissement *m* (d'un moteur, etc.) **3** : élancement *m* <a throb of pain : un élancement de douleur>

throe [ˈθroː] *n* **1** PANG : agonie *f* <the throes of childbirth : les douleurs de l'enfantement> **2 in the throes of** : en proie à

throne [ˈθroːn] *n* : trône *m*

throng[1] [ˈθrɔŋ] *vt* CROWD : se presser dans, remplir — *vi* : se presser

throng[2] *n* : foule *f*

throttle[1] ['θrɑtəl] *vt* **-tled; -tling 1** CHOKE : étrangler **2 to throttle down** : mettre au ralenti (un moteur)

throttle[2] *n* **1** : accélérateur *m* (d'une voiture) **2** *or* **throttle valve** : papillon *m* des gaz

through[1] ['θru:] *adv* **1** : à travers, d'un côte à l'autre <let me through : laissez-moi passer> **2** : d'un trait, jusqu'au bout <I read the book through : j'ai lu le livre d'un trait> **3** THOROUGHLY : complètement <soaked through : complètement mouillé>

through[2] *adj* **1** DIRECT : direct <a through road : une route directe> **2** : en transit <through traffic : trafic en transit> **3** FINISHED : fini, terminé <are you through? : as-tu fini?>

through[3] *prep* **1** (*indicating movement from one side to the other*) : à travers <the bullet went right through his arm : la balle lui a transpercé le bras> **2** (*indicating passage*) : par <he got in through the window : il est rentré par la fenêtre> <she went through a red light : elle a brûlé un feu rouge> **3** (*indicating a period of time*) <through the whole night : pendant toute la nuit> <from Monday through Friday : du lundi au vendredi)

throughout[1] [θru:'aʊt] *adv* **1** EVERYWHERE : partout <one color throughout : d'une seule couleur> **2** : toujours <he remained loyal throughout : il est toujours demeuré fidèle>

throughout[2] *prep* **1** : partout dans <he traveled throughout the country : il voyageait partout dans le pays> **2** : tout au long de <throughout her life : tout au long de sa vie>

throve → **thrive**

throw[1] ['θro:] *vt* **threw** ['θru:]; **thrown** ['θro:n]; **throwing 1** : lancer <to throw a ball : lancer une balle> **2** *or* **to throw down** : jeter à terre, envoyer au tapis **3** CAST : jeter, projeter <she threw her arms around him : elle s'est jetée à son cou> <to throw a shadow : projeter une ombre> **4 to throw a party** : organiser une fête **5 to throw a tantrum** : piquer une crise **6 to throw sth into confusion** : semer la confusion dans qqch **7 to throw away, to throw out** : jeter

throw[2] *n* TOSS : lancer *m*, jet *m*

thrower ['θro:ər] *n* : lanceur *m*, -ceuse *f*

throw up *vt* : vomir, renvoyer *Can fam*, restituer *Can fam*

thrush ['θrʌʃ] *n* : grive *f* (oiseau)

thrust[1] ['θrʌst] *vt* **thrust; thrusting 1** SHOVE : pousser violemment **2** PLUNGE, STAB : enfoncer, planter **3 to thrust upon** : imposer à

thrust[2] *n* **1** PUSH : poussée *f* **2** STAB : coup *m* (de couteau, d'épée, etc.) **3** AIM, POINT : portée *f*, sens *m* (d'un argument, etc.)

thud[1] ['θʌd] *vi* **thudded; thudding** : faire un bruit sourd

thud[2] *n* : bruit *m* sourd

thug ['θʌg] *n* : voyou *m*

thumb[1] ['θʌm] *vt or* **to thumb through** : feuilleter (un livre, etc.)

thumb[2] *n* : pouce *m*

thumbnail ['θʌm,neɪl] *n* : ongle *m* du pouce

thumbtack ['θʌm,tæk] *n* : punaise *f*

thump[1] ['θʌmp] *vt* POUND : cogner à, frapper sur — *vi* : battre fort (se dit du cœur)

thump[2] *n* **1** BLOW : coup *m* **2** THUD : bruit *m* sourd

thunder[1] ['θʌndər] *vi* **1** : tonner <it was thundering : il tonnait> **2** BOOM, RESOUND : gronder, retentir — *vt* ROAR : vociférer <they thundered their disapproval : ils ont vociféré leur désaccord>

thunder[2] *n* **1** : tonnerre *m* **2** RUMBLE : tonnerre *m*, bruit *m* assourdissant

thunderbolt ['θʌndər,bo:lt] *n* : foudre *f*

thunderclap ['θʌndər,klæp] *n* : coup *m* de tonnerre

thunderous ['θəndərəs] *adj* : étourdissant <thunderous applause : un tonnerre d'applaudissements>

thundershower ['θʌndər,ʃaʊər] → **thunderstorm**

thunderstorm ['θʌndər,storm] *n* : orage *m*

thunderstruck ['θʌndər,strʌk] *adj* : abasourdi, stupéfié

Thursday ['θərz,deɪ, -di] *n* : jeudi *m*

thus ['ðʌs] *adv* **1** SO : ainsi, donc, par conséquent **2 thus far** : jusqu'à présent, jusqu'ici

thwart ['θwɔrt] *vt* : contrecarrer, contrarier

thy ['ðaɪ] *adj* : ton, ta, tes

thyme ['taɪm, 'θaɪm] *n* : thym *m*

thyroid ['θaɪ,rɔɪd] *n or* **thyroid gland** : thyroïde *f*

thyself [ðaɪ'sɛlf] *pron* : toi-même

tiara [ti'ærə, -'ɑr-] *n* : diadème *m*

Tibetan[1] [tə'bɛtən] *adj* : tibétain

Tibetan[2] *n* **1** : Tibétain *m*, -taine *f* **2** : tibétain *m* (langue)

tibia ['tɪbiə] *n, pl* **-iae** [-bi,i:] : tibia *m*

tic ['tɪk] *n* : tic *m* (nerveux)

tick[1] ['tɪk] *vi* **1** : faire tic-tac (se dit d'une horloge) **2** OPERATE, RUN : tourner (se dit d'un moteur) — *vt or* **to tick off** CHECK : cocher, marquer

tick[2] *n* **1** : tique *f* (insecte) **2** : tic-tac *m* (d'une horloge) **3** CHECK : coche *f*

ticket[1] ['tɪkət] *vt* **1** LABEL : étiqueter **2** : donner une contravention à (un automobiliste)

ticket[2] *n* **1** TAG : étiquette *f* **2** : billet *m*, ticket *m* <bus ticket : billet d'autobus> **3** : contravention *f* <a speeding ticket : une contravention pour

excès de vitesse> **4** SLATE : liste *f* (électorale)
tickle[1] ['tɪkəl] *v* **-led; -ling** *vt* **1** : chatouiller <don't tickle my feet : ne me chatouillez pas les pieds> **2** PLEASE : chatouiller, émouvoir **3** AMUSE : amuser — *vi* : chatouiller, piquer
tickle[2] *n* : chatouillement *m*
ticklish ['tɪkəlɪʃ] *adj* **1** : chatouilleux **2** DELICATE, TRICKY : épineux, délicat
tidal ['taɪdəl] *adj* : des marées
tidal wave *n* : raz-de-marée *m*
tidbit ['tɪd,bɪt] *n* **1** : détail *m* intéressant **2** DELICACY : gâterie *f*
tide[1] ['taɪd] *vt* **tided; tiding** *or* **to tide over** : dépanner
tide[2] *n* : marée *f*
tidewater ['taɪd,wɔṭər, -,wɑ-] *n* : eaux *nfpl* de marée
tidiness ['taɪdinəs] *n* : ordre *m*, propreté *f*
tidings ['taɪdɪŋz] *npl* : nouvelles *fpl* <good tidings : de bonnes nouvelles>
tidy[1] ['taɪdi] *vt or* **to tidy up** : ranger — *vi or* **to tidy up** : tout ranger, faire du rangement
tidy[2] *adj* **tidier; -est 1** NEAT : bien rangé, propre **2** LARGE : joli *fam*, coquet *fam* <a tidy sum : une jolie somme>
tie[1] ['taɪ] *v* **tied; tying** *or* **tieing** *vt* **1** : attacher, nouer <tie your shoelaces : attache tes lacets> **2** CONNECT : unir, lier — *vi* **1** FASTEN : s'attacher, se nouer **2** : faire match nul, être ex æquo <to tie for third place : être troisième ex æquo>
tie[2] *n* **1** FASTENER : attache *f* **2** *or* **railroad tie** : traverse *f* **3** BOND : lien *m*, nœud *m* <family ties : liens familiaux> **4** : match *m* nul, égalité *f* (aux sports) **5** NECKTIE : cravate *f*
tier ['tɪr] *n* : étage *m* (d'un gâteau), gradin *m* (au théâtre)
tiff ['tɪf] *n* : chicane *f*, dispute *f*
tiger ['taɪgər] *n* : tigre *m*
tight[1] ['taɪt] *adv* **1** TIGHTLY : bien, fermement <is the door shut tight? : la porte est-elle bien fermée?> <hold on tight : tenez-vous bien> **2** DEEPLY : profondément <to sleep tight : dormir profondément>
tight[2] *adj* **1** : étanche, hermétique <a tight seal : une fermeture étanche> **2** SNUG : serré, étriqué **3** TAUT : tendu, raide **4** DIFFICULT : difficile <to be in a tight spot : être dans une situation difficile> **5** STINGY : avare **6** CLOSE : serré <a tight game : un match serré> **7** SCARCE : juste, serré <money is a bit tight : les finances sont un peu justes>
tighten ['taɪtən] *vt* : serrer, resserrer
tightly ['taɪtli] *adv* : fermement, bien
tightness ['taɪtnəs] *n* **1** : étroitesse *f* (d'un vêtement, etc.) **2** STRICTNESS : sévérité *f*, rigueur *f* **3** TAUTNESS : tension *f*, raideur *f*
tightrope ['taɪt,ro:p] *n* : corde *f* raide
tights ['taɪts] *npl* : collants *mpl*
tightwad ['taɪt,wɑd] *n* : grippe-sou *mf fam*
tigress ['taɪgrəs] *n* : tigresse *f*
tile[1] ['taɪl] *vt* **tiled; tiling** : poser des tuiles sur, carreler
tile[2] *n* : tuile *f*
till[1] ['tɪl] *vt* : labourer
till[2] *n* : tiroir-caisse *m*
till[3] *conj & prep* → **until**
tiller ['tɪlər] *n* **1** : cultivateur *m*, -trice *f* **2** : barre *f*, gouvernail *m* (d'un bateau)
tilt[1] ['tɪlt] *vt* SLANT : pencher, incliner — *vi* : se pencher, s'incliner
tilt[2] *n* **1** SLOPE : inclinaison *f* **2 at full tilt** : à toute vitesse
timber ['tɪmbər] *n* **1** : bois *m* de construction **2** BEAM : poutre *f*, madrier *m*
timberland ['tɪmbər,lænd] *n* : terrain *m* forestier (exploitable)
timbre ['tæmbər, 'tɪm-] *n* : timbre *m* (de la voix)
time[1] ['taɪm] *vt* **timed; timing 1** SCHEDULE : prévoir, fixer **2** : minuter, chronométrer <to time a race : chronométrer une course>
time[2] *n* **1** : temps *m* <it's a matter of time : c'est une question de temps> <to find time for : trouver du temps pour> <time flies : le temps passe vite> **2** OCCASION : fois *f* **3** AGE : époque *f*, temps *m* **4** TEMPO : mesure *f*, rythme *m* **5** : heure *f* <what time is it? : quelle heure est-il?> <she arrived on time : elle est arrivée à l'heure> <on company time : pendant les heures de travail> **6** : temps *m* (de l'année) <it's very hot for this time of year : il fait très chaud pour la saison> **7** PERIOD : moment *m*, période *f* <hard times : des moments difficiles> **8 times** *npl* : fois *f* <you've told me several times : tu me l'as dit plusieurs fois> **9 at times** : parfois **10 for the time being** : pour le moment **11 from time to time** : de temps à autre **12 time and time again** : maintes et maintes fois
timekeeper ['taɪm,ki:pər] *n* : chronométreur *m*, -treuse *f*
timeless ['taɪmləs] *adj* : éternel
timely ['taɪmli] *adj* **-lier; -est** : opportun, propice
timepiece ['taɪm,pi:s] *n* : montre *f*, horloge *f*
timer ['taɪmər] *n* **1** TIMEKEEPER : chronométreur *m*, -treuse *f* **2** STOPWATCH : chronomètre *m* **3** : minuteur *m* (en cuisine)
times ['taɪmz] *prep* : fois (en mathématiques) <seven times two is fourteen : sept fois deux font quatorze>
timetable ['taɪm,teɪbəl] *n* **1** : horaire *m* (de trains, d'autobus, etc.) **2** SCHEDULE : programme *m*, horaire *m*

timid [ˈtɪmɪd] *adj* : timide — **timidly** *adv*

timidity [təˈmɪdət̬i] *n* : timidité *f*

timorous [ˈtɪmərəs] *adj* FEARFUL : timoré

timpani [ˈtɪmpəni] *npl* : timbales *fpl*

tin [ˈtɪn] *n* **1** : étain *m* (métal) **2** *or* **tin can** : boîte *f* de conserve

tincture [ˈtɪŋktʃər] *n* : teinture *f*

tinder [ˈtɪndər] *n* : amadou *m*, petit bois *m*

tine [ˈtaɪn] *n* : dent *f* (d'une fourchette, etc.)

tinfoil [ˈtɪn͵fɔɪl] *n* : papier *m* d'aluminium

tinge[1] [ˈtɪndʒ] *vt* **tinged; tingeing** *or* **tinging** [ˈtɪndʒɪŋ] : teinter

tinge[2] *n* : teinte *f*, nuance *f*

tingle[1] [ˈtɪŋgəl] *vi* **-gled; -gling** : picoter, fourmiller

tingle[2] *n* : picotement *m*

tinker [ˈtɪŋkər] *vi* : bricoler

tinkle[1] [ˈtɪŋkəl] *v* **-kled; -kling** *vi* : tinter, sonner — *vt* : faire tinter

tinkle[2] *n* : tintement *m*

tinsel [ˈtɪntsəl] *n* : guirlandes *fpl* (de Noël)

tint[1] [ˈtɪnt] *vt* : teinter

tint[2] *n* : teinte *f*, nuance *f*

tiny [ˈtaɪni] *adj* **tinier; -est** : minuscule, tout petit

tip[1] [ˈtɪp] *v* **tipped; tipping** *vt* **1** : mettre un embout à (une canne, etc.) **2** OVERTURN : chavirer, renverser **3** TILT : pencher, incliner **4** : donner un pourboire à (un serveur) **5 to tip off** : donner un tuyau à, renseigner — *vi* TILT : pencher, basculer

tip[2] *n* **1** END : pointe *f*, bout *m* (d'un crayon) <the tip of the island : la pointe de l'île> **2** GRATUITY : pourboire *m* **3** INFORMATION : conseil *m*, tuyau *m fam*

tip–off [ˈtɪp͵ɔf] *n* : tuyau *m fam*

tipple [ˈtɪpəl] *vi* **-pled; -pling** : prendre un coup *fam*, picoler *fam*

tipsy [ˈtɪpsi] *adj* **tipsier; -est** : pompette *fam*, éméché *fam*

tiptoe[1] [ˈtɪp͵toː] *vi* **-toed; -toeing** : marcher sur la pointe des pieds

tiptoe[2] *n* **on ~** : sur la pointe des pieds

tip–top[1] [ˈtɪp͵toː] *adj* : excellent <in tiptop shape : en excellente forme>

tip–top[2] *n* : sommet *m*, haut *m*

tirade [ˈtaɪ͵reɪd] *n* : tirade *f*, diatribe *f*

tire[1] [ˈtaɪr] *v* **tired; tiring** *vt* **1** FATIGUE : fatiguer **2** BORE : fatiguer, lasser — *vi* : se fatiguer

tire[2] *n* : pneu *m*

tired [ˈtaɪrd] *adj* : fatigué, las

tireless [ˈtaɪrləs] *adj* : infatigable, inlassable

tirelessly [ˈtaɪrləsli] *adv* : infatigablement, sans relâche

tiresome [ˈtaɪrsəm] *adj* : ennuyeux, fastidieux, agaçant

tiresomely [ˈtaɪrsəmli] *adv* : fastidieusement, de façon agaçante

tissue [ˈtɪ͵ʃuː] *n* **1** : mouchoir *m* en papier, papier *m* mouchoir *Can* **2** : tissu *m* (en biologie)

titanic [taɪˈtænɪk, tə-] *adj* : titanesque, colossal

titanium [taɪˈteɪniəm, tə-] *n* : titane *m*

titillate [ˈtɪtəl͵eɪt] *vt* **-lated; -lating** : titiller

title[1] [ˈtaɪt̬əl] **-tled; -tling** *vt* : intituler

title[2] *n* : titre *m*

titter[1] [ˈtɪt̬ər] *vi* : rire nerveusement

titter[2] *n* : petit rire *m* nerveux

tizzy [ˈtɪzi] *n, pl* **tizzies** : panique *f*, agitation *f* <to be in a tizzy : être dans tous ses états>

TNT [͵tiː͵ɛnˈtiː] *n* : TNT *m*

to[1] [ˈtuː] *adv* **1 to come to** : reprendre connaissance **2 to run to and fro** : aller et venir

to[2] *prep* **1** (*indicating movement or direction*) : à, en <I walk to school : je vais à l'école à pied> <we drove to town : nous sommes allés en ville en voiture> **2** TOWARD : vers <his back was turned to the door : il avait le dos tourné vers la porte> **3** AGAINST, ON : sur <she put her hand to her heart : elle a placé sa main sur son cœur> **4** (*indicating intent*) : à <he came to our aid : il est venu à notre aide> **5** (*indicating a point or position*) : à, de <100 miles to the nearest town : à 100 milles de la ville la plus proche> <perpendicular to the floor : perpendiculaire au plancher> **6** (*in expressions of time*) : moins <five minutes to five : cinq heures moins cinq> **7** UNTIL : à, jusqu'à <from Monday to Friday : du lundi au vendredi> **8** FOR : de, pour <the key to the door : la clé de la porte> **9** (*indicating comparison or proportion*) : à <similar to that one : semblable à celui-là> <we won ten to six : nous avons gagné dix à six> **10** (*indicating agreement or conformity*) : à <add salt to taste : salez au goût> <to my knowledge : à ma connaissance> **11** (*used to form the infinitive*) <I like to swim : j'aime nager> <he wants to go there : il veut y aller>

toad [ˈtoːd] *n* : crapaud *m*

toadstool [ˈtoːd͵stuːl] *n* : champignon *m* vénéneux

toady [ˈtoːdi] *n, pl* **toadies** : flagorneur *m*, -neuse *f*; flatteur *m*, -teuse *f*

toast[1] [ˈtoːst] *vt* **1** : griller (du pain), toaster *Can* **2** : boire à la santé de (un invité) — *vi* WARM : chauffer <to toast oneself : se réchauffer>

toast[2] *n* **1** : toast *m*, pain *m* grillé, rôtie *f* **2** : toast *m* <to drink a toast to : porter un toast à>

toaster [ˈtoːstər] *n* : grille-pain *m*

tobacco [təˈbæ͵koː] *n, pl* **-cos** : tabac *m*

toboggan[1] [təˈbɑgən] *vi* : faire du toboggan

toboggan[2] *n* : toboggan *m*, traîne *f Can*

today[1] [tə'deɪ] *adv* **1** : aujourd'hui **2** NOWADAYS : de nos jours

today[2] *n* : aujourd'hui *m*

toddle ['tɑdəl] *vi* **-dled; -dling** : marcher d'un pas chancelant

toddler ['tɑdələr] *n* : bambin *m*, -bine *f*

to–do [tə'du:] *n, pl* **to–dos** [-'du:z] FUSS : agitation *f*, remue-ménage *m*

toe ['to:] *n* : orteil *m*, doigt *m* de pied

toenail ['to:ˌneɪl] *n* : ongle *m* d'orteil

toffee ['tɔfi, 'tɑ-] *n, pl* **toffees** : caramel *m*

toga ['to:gə] *n* : toge *f*

together [tə'gɛðər] *adv* **1** : ensemble <let's go together : allons-y ensemble> **2** SIMULTANEOUSLY : en même temps, simultanément **3 together with** : ainsi que, avec, en même temps que

togetherness [tə'gɛðərnəs] *n* : unité *f*, camaraderie *f*

Togolese[1] [ˌto:gə'li:z, -'li:s] *adj* : togolais

Togolese[2] *n* : Togolais *m*, -laise *f*

togs ['tɑgz, 'tɔgz] *npl* : fringues *fpl fam*

toil[1] ['tɔɪl] *vi* **1** : travailler dur, peiner **2** PLOD : marcher péniblement

toil[2] *n* : labeur *m*, dur travail *m*

toilet ['tɔɪlət] *n* **1** DRESSING, GROOMING : toilette *f* **2** BATHROOM : toilettes *fpl*, toilette *f Can* <to go to the toilet : aller aux toilettes>

toilet paper *n* : papier *m* hygiénique

token ['to:kən] *n* **1** SIGN, SYMBOL : signe *m*, marque *f*, témoignage *m* <as a token of our friendship : en signe de notre amitié> **2** : jeton *m* <subway token : jeton de métro>

told → **tell**

tolerable ['tɑlərəbəl] *adj* **1** : tolérable, supportable <tolerable pain : douleur tolérable> **2** PASSABLE : pas (trop) mal, acceptable

tolerably ['tɑlərəbli] *adv* : passablement, acceptablement

tolerance ['tɑlərən*t*s] *n* **1** ENDURANCE : tolérance *f* <to have a high tolerance for pain : tolérer bien la douleur> **2** OPEN-MINDEDNESS : tolérance *f*, indulgence *f*

tolerant ['tɑlərənt] *adj* : tolérant, libéral

tolerantly ['tɑlərəntli] *adv* : avec tolérance

tolerate ['tɑləˌreɪt] *vt* **-ated; -ating** : tolérer

toleration [ˌtɑlə'reɪʃən] *n* : tolérance *f*

toll[1] ['to:l] *vt* : sonner (une cloche) — *vi* : sonner

toll[2] *n* **1** : péage *m* (sur une autoroute) **2 death toll** : nombre *m* de victimes **3 to take its toll** : avoir des conséquences néfastes

tollbooth ['to:lˌbu:θ] *n* : poste *m* de péage

tollgate ['to:lˌgeɪt] *n* : barrière *f* de péage

tomahawk ['tɑməˌhɔk] *n* : tomahawk *m*

tomato [tə'meɪṭo, -'mɑ-] *n, pl* **-toes** : tomate *f*

tomb ['tu:m] *n* : tombeau *m*, tombe *f*

tomboy ['tɑmˌbɔɪ] *n* : garçon *m* manqué

tombstone ['tu:mˌsto:n] *n* : pierre *f* tombale

tomcat ['tɑmˌkæt] *n* : matou *m*

tome ['to:m] *n* : gros volume *m*

tomorrow[1] [tə'mɑro] *adv* : demain

tomorrow[2] *n* : demain *m*

tom–tom ['tɑmˌtɑm] *n* : tam-tam *m*

ton ['tən] *n* : tonne *f*

tonality [to'nælət̬i] *n* : tonalité *f*

tone[1] ['to:n] *vt* **toned; toning** *or* **to tone down** : atténuer

tone[2] *n* **1** : sonorité *f*, ton *m* (en musique) **2** : ton *m*, intonation *f* <in a friendly tone : d'un ton chaleureux> <to speak in low tones : parler d'une voix basse>

tongs ['tɑŋz, 'tɔŋz] *npl* : pinces *fpl*, pincettes *fpl*

tongue ['tʌŋ] *n* **1** : langue *f* (de la bouche) **2** LANGUAGE : langue *f* <mother tongue : langue maternelle> **3** FLAP : languette *f* (d'un soulier)

tongue–tied ['tʌŋˌtaɪd] *adj* **1** : muet **2 to get tongue–tied** : ne plus savoir que dire

tonic[1] ['tɑnɪk] *adj* : tonique

tonic[2] *n* : tonique *m*

tonight[1] [tə'naɪt] *adv* : ce soir

tonight[2] *n* : ce soir, cette nuit <tonight's party : la fête de ce soir>

tonsil ['tɑn*t*səl] *n* : amygdale *f*

tonsillitis [ˌtɑn*t*sə'laɪt̬əs] *n* : amygdalite *f*

too ['tu:] *adv* **1** ALSO, BESIDES : aussi **2** VERY : très <he didn't seem too interested : il ne semblait pas très intéressé> <not too bad : pas trop mal>

took → **take**[1]

tool[1] ['tu:l] *vt* : travailler, ouvrager

tool[2] *n* : outil *m*, instrument *m*

toolbar ['tu:lˌbɑr] *n* : barre *f* d'outils (en informatique)

toolbox ['tu:lˌbɑks] *n* : boîte *f* à outils

toot[1] ['tu:t] *vi* : klaxonner (se dit d'une voiture), siffler (se dit d'un train) — *vt* **to toot one's horn** : donner un coup de klaxon

toot[2] *n* : coup *m* de klaxon, coup *m* de sifflet

tooth ['tu:θ] *n, pl* **teeth** ['ti:θ] **1** : dent *f* <to brush one's teeth : se brosser les dents> **2** : dent *f* (d'un peigne, d'une roue, etc.)

toothache ['tu:θˌeɪk] *n* : mal *m* de dents

toothbrush ['tu:θˌbrʌʃ] *n* : brosse *f* à dents

toothless ['tu:θləs] *adj* : édenté

toothpaste ['tu:θˌpeɪst] *n* : dentifrice *m*

toothpick ['tu:θˌpɪk] *n* : cure-dents *m*

top[1] ['tɑp] *vt* **topped; topping 1** CAP, CROWN : couvrir, recouvrir **2** SURPASS : dépasser, surpasser **3** HEAD : être en tête de (une liste, etc.)

top[2] *adj* **1** : dernier <the top floor : le dernier étage> **2** CHIEF, LEADING : premier, prinicipal, de tête

top[3] *n* **1** SUMMIT : haut *m,* cime *f,* tête *f* <at the top of one's class : à la tête de sa classe> **2** : dessus *m* <the top of the table : le dessus de la table> **3** LID : couvercle *m* **4** : toupie *f* (jouet) **5 on top of** : sur

topaz [ˈtoːˌpæz] *n* : topaze *f*

topcoat [ˈtɑpˌkoːt] *n* : pardessus *m*

topic [ˈtɑpɪk] *n* : sujet *m,* thème *m*

topical [ˈtɑpɪkəl] *adj* **1** LOCAL : à usage local (en médecine) **2** CURRENT : d'actualité

topmost [ˈtɑpˌmoːst] *adj* : le plus haut

top–notch [ˈtɑpˈnɑtʃ] *adj* : excellent, de premier ordre

topographic [ˌtɑpəˈgræfɪk] *or* **topographical** [-fɪkəl] *adj* : topographique

topography [təˈpɑgrəfi] *n* : topographie *f*

topple [ˈtɑpəl] *v* **-pled; -pling** *vt* : renverser, faire tomber — *vi or* **to topple over** : basculer, se renverser

topsy–turvy [ˌtɑpsiˈtərvi] *adv & adj* : sens dessus dessous, à l'envers

torch [ˈtɔrtʃ] *n* : torche *f,* flambeau *m*

tore → **tear**[1]

torment[1] [ˈtɔrˌmɛnt, tɔrˈ-] *vt* : tourmenter, torturer

torment[2] [ˈtɔrˌmɛnt] *n* : tourment *m,* supplice *m*

tormentor [ˈtɔrˌmɛntər, tɔrˈ-] *n* : persécuteur *m,* -trice *f;* bourreau *m*

torn → **tear**[1]

tornado [tɔrˈneɪdo] *n, pl* **-does** *or* **-dos** : tornade *f*

torpedo[1] [tɔrˈpiːdo] *vt* : torpiller

torpedo[2] *n, pl* **-does** : torpille *f*

torpid [ˈtɔrpɪd] *adj* : léthargique, torpide, engourdi

torpor [ˈtɔrpər] *n* : torpeur *f,* léthargie *f*

torrent [ˈtɔrənt] *n* : torrent *m*

torrential [tɔˈrɛntʃəl, tə-] *adj* : torrentiel

torrid [ˈtɔrɪd] *adj* : torride

torso [ˈtɔrˌsoː] *n, pl* **-sos** *or* **-si** [-ˌsiː] : torse *m*

tortilla [tɔrˈtiːjə] *n* : tortilla *f*

tortoise [ˈtɔrt̬əs] *n* : tortue *f*

tortoiseshell [ˈtɔrt̬əsˌʃɛl] *n* : écaille *f*

tortuous [ˈtɔrtʃuəs] *adj* : tortueux

torture[1] [ˈtɔrtʃər] *vt* **-tured; -turing** : torturer

torture[2] *n* : torture *f*

torturer [ˈtɔrtʃərər] *n* : tortionnaire *mf*

toss[1] [ˈtɔs, ˈtɑs] *vt* **1** THROW : lancer, jeter **2** *or* **to toss about** AGITATE : ballotter, secouer **3 to toss a coin** : jouer à pile ou face — *vi* **to toss and turn** : s'agiter, se tourner et se retourner

toss[2] *n* THROW : lancer *m,* lancement *m*

toss–up [ˈtɔsˌʌp] *n* : chances *fpl* égales

tot [ˈtɑt] *n* : petit enfant *m*

total[1] [ˈtoːtəl] *vt* **-taled** *or* **-talled; -taling** *or* **-talling** : totaliser

total[2] *adj* : total

total[3] *n* : total *m*

totalitarian [ˌtoːˌtæləˈtɛriən] *adj* : totalitaire

totalitarianism [ˌtoːˌtæləˈtɛriəˌnɪzəm] *n* : totalitarisme *m*

totality [toˈtæləţi] *n, pl* **-ties** : totalité *f*

totally [ˈtoːtəli] *adv* : totalement, entièrement, complètement

tote [ˈtoːt] *vt* **toted; toting** : porter, transporter

totem [ˈtoːtəm] *n* : totem *m*

totter [ˈtɑtər] *vi* : chanceler, tituber

touch[1] [ˈtʌtʃ] *vt* **1** FEEL, HANDLE : toucher **2** : toucher à <he never touches alcohol : il ne touche jamais à l'alcool> **3** HARM : toucher **4** AFFECT, MOVE : émouvoir, toucher — *vi* : se toucher, être en contact

touch[2] *n* **1** : toucher *m* (sens) **2** FEEL : toucher *m* <soft to the touch : doux au toucher> **3** DETAIL : touche *f* <a touch of color : une touche de couleur> **4** HINT, TRACE : touche *f,* pointe *f* **5** CONTACT : contact *m* <to keep in touch with : rester en contact avec>

touchdown [ˈtʌtʃˌdaʊn] *n* **1** : atterrissage *m* (d'un avion) **2** : but *m* (au football américain)

touch up *vt* : faire des retouches à, retoucher

touchy [ˈtʌtʃi] *adj* **touchier; -est 1** : susceptible (se dit des personnes) **2** : délicat, épineux <a touchy subject : un sujet épineux>

tough[1] [ˈtʌf] *adj* **1** HARDY : robuste, résistant **2** : dur, coriace (se dit de la viande) **3** STRICT : strict, sévère **4** DIFFICULT : difficile, pénible **5** STUBBORN : inflexible, dur **6** ROUGH : dur <a tough neighbourhood : un quartier dur> **7 tough luck!** : tant pis pour toi!

tough[2] *n* : dur *m fam*

toughen [ˈtʌfən] *vt* : endurcir, rendre plus résistant — *vi* : s'endurcir

toughness [ˈtʌfnəs] *n* : résistance *f*

toupee [tuːˈpeɪ] *n* : postiche *m*

tour[1] [ˈtʊr] *vt* : visiter <we toured the city : nous avons visité la ville> — *vi* : faire du tourisme, voyager

tour[2] *n* **1** : tour *m* (d'une ville, etc.), visite *f* (d'un édifice) <a bus tour : une excursion en autobus> **2 to go on tour** : faire une tournée

tourist [ˈtʊrɪst, ˈtər-] *n* : touriste *mf*

tournament [ˈtərnəmənt, ˈtʊr-] *n* : tournoi *m*

tourniquet [ˈtərnɪkət, ˈtʊr-] *n* : garrot *m,* tourniquet *m*

tousle [ˈtaʊzəl] *vt* **-sled; -sling** : ébouriffer (les cheveux)

tout [ˈtaʊt] *vt* : vanter les mérites de

tow[1] [ˈtoː] *vt* : remorquer (une voiture)

tow[2] *n* : remorquage *m* <he gave me a tow : il m'a remorqué>

toward [ˈtord, təˈwɔrd] *or* **towards** [ˈtordz, təˈwɔrdz] *prep* **1** : vers, dans la direction de <toward the river : vers

la rivière> <their backs were toward me : ils étaient dos à moi> **2** : envers <his attitude toward life : son attitude envers la vie> **3** : pour <she put $100 toward a new car : elle a mis 100 $ de côté pour une nouvelle voiture> **4** NEAR : vers <toward the middle : vers le milieu>

towel [ˈtaʊəl] *n* : serviette *f*

tower[1] [ˈtaʊər] *vi* **to tower over** : dominer

tower[2] *n* : tour *f*

towering [ˈtaʊərɪŋ] *adj* **1** IMPOSING : imposant, très haut **2** EXCESSIVE : sans bornes, démesuré <towering ambition : ambition démesurée>

town [ˈtaʊn] *n* : ville *f* <to go to town : aller en ville> <to be out of town : être en déplacement>

township [ˈtaʊn,ʃɪp] *n* **1** : commune *f*, municipalité *f* **2** : canton *m Can* (division territoriale)

tow truck [ˈto:,trʌk] *n* : dépanneuse *f*, remorqueuse *f Can*

toxic [ˈtɑksɪk] *adj* : toxique

toxicity [tɑkˈsɪsət̬i] *n, pl* **-ties** : toxicité *f*

toxin [ˈtɑksɪn] *n* : toxine *f*

toy[1] [ˈtɔɪ] *vi* **to toy with** : jouer avec

toy[2] *adj* : de jeu <toy soldiers : soldats de plomb> <a toy house : une maison miniature>

toy[3] *n* : jouet *m*

trace[1] [ˈtreɪs] *vt* **traced; tracing 1** OUTLINE, SKETCH : tracer, dessiner **2** FOLLOW : suivre (la trace de) **3** LOCATE : retrouver, localiser

trace[2] *n* **1** TRACK : trace *f*, empreinte *f* **2** VESTIGE : trace *f* <traces of blood : traces de sang> **3** HINT : soupçon *m*, pointe *f* <a trace of a smile : un léger sourire> <without a trace of anger : sans la moindre colère> **4** : trait *m* (d'un harnais)

trachea [ˈtreɪkiə] *n, pl* **-cheae** [-ki,i:] : trachée *f*

track[1] [ˈtræk] *vt* : suivre la trace de, suivre la piste de

track[2] *n* **1** MARK, TRAIL : trace *f*, piste *f* <rabbit tracks : traces de lapin> **2** PATH, TRAJECTORY : piste *f*, trajectoire *f* **3** : piste *f* (aux sports) **4** → **racetrack 5** *or* **railroad track** : voie *f* ferrée **6 to keep track of** : faire attention à

track–and–field [,trækəndˈfi:ld] *adj* : d'athlétisme <track-and-field events : événements d'athlétisme>

tract [ˈtrækt] *n* **1** AREA : étendue *f* (de terre) **2** : appareil *m*, voie *f* (en physiologie) <respiratory tract : appareil respiratoire> **3** PAMPHLET : tract *m*, brochure *f*

tractable [ˈtræktəbəl] *adj* **1** DOCILE : docile (se dit d'un animal) **2** MALLEABLE : malléable

traction [ˈtrækʃən] *n* : traction *f*

tractor [ˈtræktər] *n* : tracteur *m*

trade[1] [ˈtreɪd] *v* **traded; trading** *vt* EXCHANGE : échanger, troquer — *vi* : faire du commerce

trade[2] *n* **1** : commerce *m*, industrie *f* <the tourist trade : l'industrie touristique> <foreign trade : commerce extérieur> **2** OCCUPATION : métier *m*, profession *f*

trade–in [ˈtreɪd,ɪn] *n* : reprise *f*

trade in *vt* : faire reprendre <to trade in a car : échanger une vieille voiture pour une neuve>

trademark[1] [ˈtreɪd,mɑrk] *vt* : déposer une marque sur

trademark[2] *n* : marque *f* de fabrique

tradesman [ˈtreɪdzmən] *n, pl* **-men** [-mən, -,mɛn] : commerçant *m*, -çante *f*

trade wind *n* : alizé *m*

tradition [trəˈdɪʃən] *n* : tradition *f*

traditional [trəˈdɪʃənəl] *adj* : traditionnel — **traditionally** *adv*

traffic[1] [ˈtræfɪk] *vi* **trafficked; trafficking** : trafiquer <to traffic in : faire le trafic de>

traffic[2] *n* **1** TRADE : commerce *m*, trafic *m* <the drug traffic : le trafic de drogue> **2** : circulation *f*, trafic *m* <road traffic : circulation routière> <air traffic : trafic aérien>

traffic circle *n* : rond-point *m*

trafficker [ˈtræfɪkər] *n* : trafiquant *m*, -quante *f*

traffic light *n* : feu *m* de signalisation

tragedy [ˈtrædʒədi] *n, pl* **-dies** : tragédie *f*

tragic [ˈtrædʒɪk] *adj* : tragique — **tragically** [-dʒɪkəli] *adv*

trail[1] [ˈtreɪl] *vi* **1** DRAG, HANG : traîner, pendre **2** *or* **to trail behind** LAG : traîner, être à la traîne **3 to trail away** *or* **to trail off** : s'estomper, diminuer <the sound trailed off : le bruit s'estompait> — *vt* **1** DRAG : traîner, tirer **2** FOLLOW : suivre, poursuivre

trail[2] *n* **1** PATH : chemin *m*, sentier *m*, piste *f* <ski trail : piste de ski> **2** TRACK : trace *f*, piste *f* <to be on one's trail : être sur sa trace> **3** MARK, TRACE : traînée *f*, trace *f* <a trail of smoke : une traînée de fumée>

trailer [ˈtreɪlər] *n* **1** : remorque *f* (de camion, etc.) **2** : caravane *f*, roulotte *f Can* <he toured the country in a trailer : il a fait le tour du pays en caravane>

train[1] [ˈtreɪn] *vt* **1** : palisser (une vigne, etc.), former, entraîner (du personnel) **2** AIM, DIRECT : pointer, diriger — *vi* : recevoir une formation, s'entraîner

train[2] *n* **1** : traîne *f* (d'une robe) **2** PROCESSION : cortège *m*, file *f* **3** SUCCESSION : suite *f*, série *f*, fil *m* <train of thought : fil des pensées> **4** : train *m* <train de banlieue : commuter train>

trainee [treɪ'ni:] *n* : apprenti *m*, -tie *f;* stagiaire *mf*
trainer ['treɪnər] *n* **1** : entraîneur *m*, -neuse *f* (aux sports) **2** : dresseur *m*, -seuse *f* (d'animaux)
traipse ['treɪps] *vi* **traipsed; traipsing** : traîner <to traipse in : entrer en traînassant>
trait ['treɪt] *n* : trait *m*, qualité *f*
traitor ['treɪt̬ər] *n* : traître *m*, -tresse *f*
traitorous ['treɪt̬ərəs] *adj* : traître
trajectory [trə'dʒɛktəri] *n, pl* **-ries** : trajectoire *f*
tram ['træm] *n Brit* : tramway *m*
tramp[1] ['træmp] *vi* : marcher d'un pas lourd — *vt* : parcourir à pied
tramp[2] *n* : clochard *m*, -charde *f;* vagabond *m*, -bonde *f*
trample ['træmpəl] *vt* **-pled; -pling** : fouler aux pieds, piétiner
trampoline [ˌtræmpə'li:n, 'træmpəˌ-] *n* : trampoline *m*
trance ['træn*t*s] *n* : transe *f*
tranquil ['træŋkwəl] *adj* : tranquille, paisible — **tranquilly** *adv*
tranquilize ['træŋkwəˌlaɪz] *vt* **-ized; -izing** : tranquilliser
tranquilizer ['træŋkwəˌlaɪzər] *n* : tranquillisant *m*
tranquillity *or* **tranquility** [træŋ'kwɪlət̬i] *n* : tranquillité *f*
transact [træn'zækt] *vt* : négocier, régler (des affaires)
transaction [træn'zækʃən] *n* **1** : transaction *f*, opération *f* <market transactions : opérations de la Bourse> **2** **transactions** *npl* : actes *mpl* (d'une société)
transcend [træn'sɛnd] *vt* : transcender
transcribe [træn'skraɪb] *vt* **-scribed; -scribing** : transcrire
transcript ['trænˌskrɪpt] *n* : transcription *f*
transcription [træn'skrɪpʃən] *n* : transcription *f*
transfer[1] [træn*t*s'fər, 'træn*t*sˌfər] *v* **-ferred; -ferring** *vt* **1** : transférer, transmettre <to transfer a title : transférer un titre> **2** : transférer, muter (un employé) **3** : transborder (des marchandises) — *vi* : être transféré, être muté
transfer[2] ['træn*t*sˌfər] *n* **1** : transfert *m*, mutation *f* (d'un employé), cession *f* (de propriété), virement *m* (de fonds) **2** TICKET : billet *m* de correspondance **3** DECAL : décalcomanie *f*
transferable [træn*t*s'fərəbəl] *adj* : transmissible
transference [træn*t*s'fərən*t*s] *n* : transfert *m*
transfiguration [ˌtræn*t*sˌfɪgjə'reɪʃən] *n* : transfiguration *f*
transfigure [træn*t*s'fɪgjər] *vt* **-ured; -uring** : transfigurer
transfix [træn*t*s'fɪks] *vt* **1** PIERCE : transpercer **2** IMMOBILIZE : paralyser, figer
transform [træn*t*s'fɔrm] *vt* : transformer
transformation [ˌtræn*t*sfər'meɪʃən] *n* : transformation *f*
transformer [træn*t*s'fɔrmər] *n* : transformateur *m*
transfusion [træn*t*s'fju:ʒən] *n* : transfusion *f*
transgress [træn*t*s'grɛs, trænz-] *vt* : transgresser
transgression [træn*t*s'grɛʃən, trænz-] *n* : transgression *f*
transient[1] ['træntʃənt, 'trænsiənt] *adj* : transitoire, passager
transient[2] *n* : personne *f* de passage
transistor [træn'zɪstər, -'sɪs-] *n* : transistor *m*
transit ['træn*t*sɪt, 'trænzɪt] *n* **1** : transit *m* <in transit : en transit> **2** TRANSPORTATION : transit *m*, transport *m* (de marchandises) **3** : théodolite *m* (instrument d'arpenteur)
transition [træn'sɪʃən, -'zɪʃ-] *n* : transition *f*
transitional [træn'sɪʃənəl, -'zɪʃ-] *adj* : transitoire, de transition
transitive ['træn*t*sət̬ɪv, 'trænzə-] *adj* : transitif
transitory ['træn*t*səˌtori, 'trænzə-] *adj* : transitoire, passager
translate [træn*t*s'leɪt, trænz-; 'træn*t*sˌ-, 'trænzˌ-] *v* **-lated; -lating** *vt* : traduire — *vi* : se traduire
translation [træn*t*s'leɪʃən, trænz-] *n* : traduction *f*
translator [træn*t*s'leɪtər, trænz-; 'træn*t*sˌ-, 'trænzˌ-] *n* : traducteur *m*, -trice *f*
translucent [træn*t*s'lu:sənt, trænz-] *adj* : translucide
transmissible [træn*t*s'mɪsəbəl, trænz-] *adj* : transmissible
transmission [træn*t*s'mɪʃən, trænz-] *n* **1** TRANSMITTING : transmission *f* (d'une maladie, etc.) **2** : transmission *f* (d'une voiture)
transmit [træn*t*s'mɪt, trænz-] *v* **-mitted; -mitting** *vt* : transmettre — *vi* : émettre, diffuser (se dit de la radio, de la télévision, etc.)
transmitter [træn*t*s'mɪt̬ər, trænz-; 'træn*t*sˌ-, 'trænzˌ-] *n* : émetteur *m*
transom ['træn*t*səm] *n* : traverse *f*
transparency [træn*t*s'pærən*t*si] *n, pl* **-cies 1** : transparence *f* **2** SLIDE : diapositive *f*, acétate *f Can*
transparent [træn*t*s'pærənt] *adj* : transparent
transpiration [ˌtræn*t*spə'reɪʃən] *n* : transpiration *f*
transpire [træn*t*s'paɪr] *v* **-spired; -spiring** *vt* : transpirer — *vi* OCCUR : arriver, se passer
transplant[1] [træn*t*s'plænt] *vt* : transplanter
transplant[2] ['træn*t*sˌplænt] *n* : transplantation *f*
transport[1] [træn*t*s'port, 'træn*t*sˌ-] *vt* : transporter

transport[2] ['træn*ts*ˌport] *n* **1** TRANSPORTATION : transport *m* <public transport : transports en commun> **2** *or* **transport ship** : navire *m* de transport **3 transports** *npl* : transports *mpl* (de joie), accès *mpl* (de colère, etc.)

transportation [ˌtræn*ts*pər'teɪʃən] *n* : transport *m*

transpose [træn*ts*'po:z] *vt* **-posed; -posing** : transposer

transposition [ˌtræn*ts*pə'zɪʃən] *n* : transposition *f*

transverse [træn*ts*'vərs, trænz-] *adj* : transversal — **transversely** *adv*

trap[1] ['træp] *vt* **trapped; trapping** : prendre au piège, attraper

trap[2] *n* **1** : piège *m* <to set a trap : tendre un piège> **2** : siphon *m* <the trap in a drainpipe : le siphon dans un tuyau d'écoulement>

trapdoor ['træp'dor] *n* : trappe *f*

trapeze [træ'pi:z] *n* : trapèze *m*

trapezoid ['træpəˌzɔɪd] *n* : trapèze *m*

trapper ['træpər] *n* : trappeur *m*

trappings ['træpɪŋz] *npl* **1** : caparaçon *m* (d'un cheval) **2** SIGNS : attributs *mpl* <the trappings of success : les signes extérieurs de la réussite>

trash ['træʃ] *n* : déchets *mpl*, ordures *fpl*

trauma ['trɔmə, 'traʊ-] *n* : traumatisme *m*

traumatic [trə'mæt̬ɪk, trɔ-, traʊ-] *adj* : traumatisant

traumatize ['trɔməˌtaɪz, traʊ-] *vt* : traumatiser

travel[1] ['trævəl] *v* **-eled** *or* **-elled; -eling** *or* **-elling** *vi* **1** JOURNEY : faire un voyage, voyager **2** SPREAD : circuler, se répandre <news traveled fast : les nouvelles circulaient vite> **3** GO, MOVE : aller, rouler <the train traveled at 60 miles per hour : le train roulait à 60 milles à l'heure> — *vt* : parcourir <to travel the countryside : parcourir la campagne>

travel[2] *n* : voyages *mpl*

traveler *or* **traveller** ['trævələr] *n* : voyageur *m*, -geuse *f*

traverse [trə'vərs, træ'vərs, 'trævərs] *vt* **-versed; -versing** : traverser, franchir

travesty ['trævəsti] *n, pl* **-ties** : parodie *f*

trawl[1] ['trɔl] *vi* : pêcher au chalut

trawl[2] *n* : chalut *m*

trawler ['trɔlər] *n* : chalutier *m*

tray ['treɪ] *n* : plateau *m*

treacherous ['trɛtʃərəs] *adj* **1** : traître, déloyal **2** UNRELIABLE : infidèle, incertain **3** DANGEROUS : dangereux, périlleux

treacherously ['trɛtʃərəsli] *adv* : traîtreusement

treachery ['trɛtʃəri] *n, pl* **-eries** : traîtrise *f*, déloyauté *f*

tread[1] ['trɛd] *v* **trod** ['trɑd]; **trodden** ['trɑdən] *or* **trod; treading** *vi* **1** WALK : marcher **2 to tread on** : marcher sur, piétiner — *vt* BEAT : tracer <to tread a path : tracer un chemin>

tread[2] *n* **1** FOOTSTEP : pas *m*, trace *f* de pas **2** : bande *f* de roulement (d'un pneu), semelle *f* (d'un soulier) **3** *or* **stair tread** : dessus *m* (d'une marche)

treadle ['trɛdəl] *n* : pédale *f*

treadmill ['trɛdˌmɪl] *n* **1** : exerciseur *m* **2** ROUTINE : engrenage *m*, train-train *m*

treason ['tri:zən] *n* : trahison *f*

treasure[1] ['trɛʒər, 'treɪ-] *vt* **-sured; -suring** CHERISH : tenir beaucoup à

treasure[2] *n* : trésor *m*

treasurer ['trɛʒərər, 'treɪ-] *n* : trésorier *m*, -rière *f*

treasury ['trɛʒəri, 'treɪ-] *n, pl* **-suries 1** : trésorerie *f* (édifice) **2 Treasury** : ministère *m* des Finances

treat[1] ['tri:t] *vi or* **to treat of** : traiter de, parler de <a book treating of animals : un livre qui traite des animaux> — *vt* **1** DEAL WITH, HANDLE : traiter <he treated him as inferior : il le traitait en inférieur> **2** PROCESS : traiter <to treat soil with lime : traiter le sol avec du chaux> **3** : traiter, soigner (en médecine) **4 to treat s.o. to sth** : payer qqch à qqn, offrir qqch à qqn

treat[2] *n* : cadeau *m* spécial, (petit) plaisir *m* <let's give him a treat : faisons-lui un plaisir> <it's my treat : c'est moi qui paie>

treatise ['tri:t̬əs] *n* : traité *m*

treatment ['tri:tmənt] *n* **1** HANDLING : traitement *m* **2** : soins *mpl*, traitement *m* (en médecine)

treaty ['tri:t̬i] *n, pl* **-ties** : traité *m*

treble[1] ['trɛbəl] *v* **-bled; -bling** : tripler

treble[2] *adj* **1** → **triple 2** : de soprano

treble[3] *n* : soprano *m*

treble clef *n* : clé *f* de sol

tree ['tri:] *n* : arbre *m*

treeless ['tri:ləs] *adj* : sans arbres, dénué d'arbres

trek[1] ['trɛk] *vi* **trekked; trekking** : faire une longue randonnée, avancer avec peine

trek[2] *n* : randonnée *f*, marche *f* pénible

trellis ['trɛlɪs] *n* : treillis *m*, treillage *m*

tremble ['trɛmbəl] *vi* **-bled; -bling 1** SHIVER : trembler, frissonner **2** VIBRATE : trembler, vibrer (se dit de la voix)

tremendous [trɪ'mɛndəs] *adj* : énorme, immense

tremendously [trɪ'mɛndəsli] *adv* : extrêmement, énormément

tremor ['trɛmər] *n* **1** TREMBLING : tremblement *m*, frisson *m* **2** : secousse *f* sismique (en géologie)

tremulous ['trɛmjələs] *adj* **1** : tremblant, frémissant **2** TIMID : timide

trench ['trɛntʃ] *n* : tranchée *f*

trenchant ['trɛntʃənt] *adj* : incisif, tranchant

trend [ˈtrɛnd] *n* : tendance *f,* mode *f* <to set a trend : lancer une mode> <a downward trend : une tendance à la baisse>

trendy [ˈtrɛndi] *adj* **trendier; -est** : branché *fam,* à la mode <a trendy spot : un endroit branché> <trendy clothes : vêtements dernier cri>

trepidation [ˌtrɛpəˈdeɪʃən] *n* : appréhension *f,* inquiétude *f*

trespass[1] [ˈtrɛspəs, -ˌpæs] *vi* **1** SIN : offenser **2** : s'introduire illégalement <no trespassing : défense d'entrer>

trespass[2] *n* **1** SIN : offense *f,* péché *m* **2** : entrée *f* non autorisée

tress [ˈtrɛs] *n* : mèche *f* de cheveux, boucle *f* de cheveux

trestle [ˈtrɛsəl] *n* **1** : tréteau *m,* chevalet *m* **2** *or* **trestle bridge** : pont *m* sur chevalets

triad [ˈtraɪˌæd] *n* : triade *f*

trial[1] [ˈtraɪəl] *adj* : d'essai <trial period : période d'essai>

trial[2] *n* **1** HEARING : procès *m* **2** TEST : essai *m* **3** ORDEAL : épreuve *f,* difficulté *f* <the trials of youth : les épreuves de la jeunesse>

triangle [ˈtraɪˌæŋgəl] *n* : triangle *m*

triangular [traɪˈæŋgjələr] *adj* : triangulaire

tribal [ˈtraɪbəl] *adj* : tribal

tribe [ˈtraɪb] *n* : tribu *f*

tribesman [ˈtraɪbzmən] *n, pl* **-men** [-mən, -ˌmɛn] : membre *m* d'une tribu

tribulation [ˌtrɪbjəˈleɪʃən] *n* : affliction *f,* tourment *m*

tribunal [traɪˈbjuːnəl, trɪ-] *n* : tribunal *m*

tributary [ˈtrɪbjəˌtɛri] *n, pl* **-taries** : affluent *m*

tribute [ˈtrɪbˌjuːt] *n* : tribut *m,* hommage *m* <to pay tribute to s.o. : rendre hommage à qqn>

trick[1] [ˈtrɪk] *vt* : attraper, rouler *fam* <to trick s.o. : jouer un tour à qqn>

trick[2] *n* **1** RUSE : tour *m,* artifice *m,* ruse *f* **2** PRANK : farce *f,* tour *m* <to play a trick on : jouer un tour à> **3** *or* **magic trick** : tour *m* **4** MANNERISM : manie *f,* habitude *f* **5** KNACK : don *m,* truc *m* **6** : pli *m,* levée *f* (de cartes) <to take a trick : faire un pli>

trickery [ˈtrɪkəri] *n* : supercherie *f,* tromperie *f*

trickle[1] [ˈtrɪkəl] *vi* **-led; -ling 1** DRIP : dégouliner, couler **2** *or* **to trickle away** : se dissiper petit à petit

trickle[2] *n* : filet *m* (d'eau), écoulement *m* (de sable, etc.)

trickster [ˈtrɪkstər] *n* : filou *m,* escroc *m*

tricky [ˈtrɪki] *adj* **trickier; -est 1** SLY : rusé, fourbe **2** DIFFICULT : difficile, délicat, épineux

tricycle [ˈtraɪəkəl, -ˌsɪkəl] *n* : tricycle *m*

trident [ˈtraɪdənt] *n* : trident *m*

triennial [ˌtraɪˈɛniəl] *adj* : triennal

trifle[1] [ˈtraɪfəl] *vi* **-fled; -fling 1** TOY : jouer **2 to trifle with** : jouer avec (les sentiments de qqn), traîter (une personne) à la légère

trifle[2] *n* : bagatelle *f,* rien *m* <it's a mere trifle : c'est peu de chose>

trifling [ˈtraɪflɪŋ] *adj* : insignifiant, peu important

trigger[1] [ˈtrɪgər] *vt* : déclencher

trigger[2] *n* : détente *f,* gâchette *f* <to pull the trigger : appuyer sur la détente>

trigonometry [ˌtrɪgəˈnɑmətri] *n* : trigonométrie *f*

trill[1] [ˈtrɪl] *vi* : triller (en musique) — *vt* : triller, rouler <to trill one's *r*'s : rouler les *r*>

trill[2] *n* **1** : trille *m* (en musique) **2** : consonne *f* roulée (en linguistique)

trillion [ˈtrɪljən] *n* : billion *m*

trilogy [ˈtrɪlədʒi] *n, pl* **-gies** : trilogie *f*

trim[1] [ˈtrɪm] *vt* **trimmed; trimming 1** DECORATE : décorer, orner **2** CUT : tailler, couper (une haie, une barbe, etc.) **3** REDUCE : limiter

trim[2] *adj* **trimmer; trimmest 1** NEAT : soigné, bien tenu **2** SLIM : svelte, mince

trim[3] *n* **1** CONDITION, FITNESS : forme *f* <to keep in good trim : se maintenir en bonne forme> **2** CUT : coupe *f* d'entretien (des cheveux) **3** TRIMMING : garniture *f*

trimming [ˈtrɪmɪŋ] *n* **1** : parement *m* (en couture), garniture *f* **2 trimmings** *npl* : garniture *f* (en cuisine) **3 trimmings** *npl* SCRAPS : rognures *fpl,* chutes *fpl*

Trinidadian[1] [ˌtrɪnəˈdædiən] *adj* : trinidadien

Trinidadian[2] *n* : Trinidadien *m,* -dienne *f*

Trinity [ˈtrɪnəṭi] *n* : Trinité *f*

trinket [ˈtrɪŋkət] *n* : babiole *f,* colifichet *m*

trio [ˈtriːˌoː] *n, pl* **trios** : trio *m*

trip[1] [ˈtrɪp] *v* **tripped; tripping** *vi* **1** : marcher d'un pas léger **2** STUMBLE : trébucher, s'enfarger *Can* **3** *or* **to trip up** ERR : trébucher, faire un faux pas — *vt* **1** : faire trébucher (une personne) **2** : déclencher (un mécanisme) **3 to trip up** DISCONCERT, TRAP : désarçonner

trip[2] *n* **1** JOURNEY : voyage *m,* excursion *f,* tour *m* **2** STUMBLE : trébuchement *m*

tripartite [traɪˈpɑrˌtaɪt] *adj* : tripartite

tripe [ˈtraɪp] *n* **1** : tripes *fpl* (d'un animal) **2** NONSENSE : bêtises *fpl*

triple[1] [ˈtrɪpəl] *v* **-pled; -pling** : tripler

triple[2] *adj* : triple

triple[3] *n* : triple *m*

triplet [ˈtrɪplət] *n* **1** : triolet *m* (en musique) **2 triplets** *npl* : triplés *mpl*

triplicate [ˈtrɪplɪkət] *n* **in ~** : en trois exemplaires

tripod [ˈtraɪˌpɑd] *n* : trépied *m*

trite [ˈtraɪt] *adj* **triter; tritest** : banal

triumph[1] [ˈtraɪəmpf] *vi* : triompher

triumph[2] *n* : triomphe *m*

triumphal [traɪˈʌmpfəl] *adj* : triomphal

triumphant [traɪˈʌmpfənt] *adj* : triomphant

triumphantly [traɪˈʌmpfəntli] *adv* : triomphalement, en triomphe

trivia [ˈtrɪviə] *ns & pl* : futilités *fpl,* bagatelles *fpl*

trivial [ˈtrɪviəl] *adj* : sans importance, insignifiant

triviality [ˌtrɪviˈæləṭi] *n, pl* **-ties** : banalité *f,* insignifiance *f*

trod, trodden → **tread**[1]

troll [ˈtro:l] *n* : troll *m*

trolley [ˈtrɑli] *n, pl* **trolleys** : tramway *m*

trombone [trɑmˈbo:n] *n* : trombone *m*

trombonist [trɑmˈbo:nɪst] *n* : tromboniste *mf*

troop[1] [ˈtru:p] *vi* : aller en bande <to troop by : passer en troupe>

troop[2] *n* **1** GROUP : bande *f,* groupe *m* **2 troops** *npl* : troupes *fpl,* soldats *mpl*

trooper [ˈtru:pər] *n* **1** : soldat *m* de cavalerie **2** *or* **state trooper** : gendarme *m France,* policier *m*

trophy [ˈtro:fi] *n, pl* **-phies** : trophée *m*

tropic[1] [ˈtrɑpɪk] *or* **tropical** [ˈtrɑpɪkəl] *adj* : tropical

tropic[2] *n* : tropique *m* <Tropic of Cancer : tropique du Cancer>

trot[1] [ˈtrɑt] *vi* **trotted; trotting** : trotter

trot[2] *n* : trot *m*

trouble[1] [ˈtrʌbəl] *vt* **-bled; -bling 1** UPSET, WORRY : troubler, inquiéter **2** AFFLICT : faire mal à <to be troubled by a headache : être incommodé par un mal de tête> **3** BOTHER : déranger <please don't trouble yourself : je vous en prie, ne vous dérangez pas>

trouble[2] *n* **1** PROBLEMS : ennuis *mpl,* difficultés *fpl* <to get into trouble : avoir des ennuis> <he has trouble reading : il a de la difficulté à lire> <back trouble : problèmes de dos> **2** EFFORT : mal *m,* peine *f* <to take the trouble : se donner la peine>

troublemaker [ˈtrʌbəlˌmeɪkər] *n* : fauteur *m,* -trice *f* de troubles; provocateur *m,* -trice *f*

troublesome [ˈtrʌbəlsəm] *adj* : difficile, gênant, pénible

trough [ˈtrɔf] *n, pl* **troughs** [ˈtrɔfs, ˈtrɔvz] **1** : abreuvoir *m* (pour les animaux) **2** CHANNEL, DEPRESSION : chenal *m,* creux *m*

trounce [ˈtraʊnts] *vt* **trounced; trouncing 1** THRASH : battre, rosser **2** DEFEAT : battre à plates coutures, écraser

troupe [ˈtru:p] *n* : troupe *f*

trousers [ˈtraʊzərz] *npl* : pantalon *m*

trout [ˈtraʊt] *ns & pl* : truite *f*

trowel [ˈtraʊəl] *n* **1** : truelle *f* (pour étendre le mortier) **2** : déplantoir *m* (pour le jardinage)

truant [ˈtru:ənt] *n* : élève *mf* absentéiste <to play truant : faire l'école buissonnière>

truce [ˈtru:s] *n* : trêve *f*

truck[1] [ˈtrʌk] *vt* : camionner

truck[2] *n* **1** : camion *m* **2** DEALINGS : association *f,* relations *fpl* <to have no truck with : ne rien avoir à faire avec>

trucker [ˈtrʌkər] *n* : camionneur *m,* -neuse *f;* routier *m*

truculent [ˈtrʌkjələnt] *adj* : agressif

trudge [ˈtrʌdʒ] *vi* **trudged; trudging** : marcher péniblement, marcher lourdement

true[1] [ˈtru:] *vt* **trued; trueing** : ajuster, aligner <to true up a board : aligner une planche>

true[2] *adv* **1** TRUTHFULLY : honnêtement **2** ACCURATELY : juste

true[3] *adj* **truer; truest 1** LOYAL : fidèle, sincère **2** ACCURATE : juste, vrai, exact **3** GENUINE : vrai, véritable <a true love : un véritable amour> **4** RIGHTFUL : légitime

true–blue [ˈtru:ˈblu:] *adj* : loyal, fidèle

truffle [ˈtrʌfəl] *n* : truffe *f*

truism [ˈtru:ˌɪzəm] *n* : truisme *m*

truly [ˈtru:li] *adv* **1** INDEED : vraiment, réellement **2 Yours truly** : Veuillez agréer l'expression de mes sentiments distingués

trump[1] [ˈtrʌmp] *vt* : couper (une carte), jouer atout sur

trump[2] *n* : atout *m*

trumped–up [ˈtrʌmptˈʌp] *adj* : inventé de toutes parts

trumpet[1] [ˈtrʌmpət] *vi* **1** : sonner de la trompette **2** : barrir (se dit d'un éléphant) — *vt* : claironner (des nouvelles, etc.)

trumpet[2] *n* : trompette *f*

trumpeter [ˈtrʌmpəṭər] *n* : trompettiste *mf*

truncate [ˈtrʌŋˌkeɪt, ˈtrʌn-] *vt* **-cated; -cating** : tronquer

trundle [ˈtrʌndəl] *v* **-dled; -dling** *vi* ROLL : rouler — *vt* WHEEL : pousser, faire rouler (bruyamment)

trunk [ˈtrʌŋk] *n* **1** : tronc *m* (du corps, d'un arbre, etc.) **2** : trompe *f* (d'un éléphant) **3** : coffre *m* (d'une voiture), malle *f* (pour voyager) **4 trunks** *npl or* **bathing trunks** : maillot *m* de bain

truss[1] [ˈtrʌs] *vt* **1** BIND : trousser (une volaille) **2** REINFORCE : armer

truss[2] *n* **1** : bandage *m* herniaire **2** FRAMEWORK : armature *f*

trust[1] [ˈtrʌst] *vi* **to trust in** : croire en (Dieu), faire confiance à (une personne) — *vt* **1** ENTRUST : confier **2** : avoir confiance en <I trust his judgment : j'ai confiance en son jugement>

trust[2] *n* **1** : confiance *f* <breach of trust : abus de confiance> **2** HOPE : espoir *m,* espérance *f* **3** CARTEL : trust *m* **4** : fidéicommis *m* <to hold sth in trust : tenir qqch par fidéicommis> **5** CARE, CUSTODY : charge *f*

trustee [ˌtrʌsˈtiː] *n* : fiduciaire *mf,* fidéicommissaire *mf*
trustful [ˈtrʌstfəl] *adj* : qui a confiance, confiant
trustfully [ˈtrʌstfəli] *adv* : avec confiance
trustworthiness [ˈtrʌstˌwərðinəs] *n* : loyauté *f,* fiabilité *f*
trustworthy [ˈtrʌstˌwərði] *adj* : digne de confiance, loyal
trusty [ˈtrəsti] *adj* **trustier; -est** : loyal, fidèle
truth [ˈtruːθ] *n, pl* **truths** [ˈtruːðz, ˈtruːθs] : vérité *f*
truthful [ˈtruːθfəl] *adj* **1** HONEST : honnête **2** ACCURATE : exact, vrai
truthfully [ˈtruːθfəli] *adv* : sans mentir, sincèrement
truthfulness [ˈtruːθfəlnəs] *n* : véracité *f,* honnêteté *f*
try[1] [ˈtraɪ] *v* **tried; trying** *vt* **1** : juger (un accusé) **2** ATTEMPT : essayer, tenter <try to understand : essayez de comprendre> <to try one's luck : tenter sa chance> **3** TEST : éprouver, mettre à l'épreuve <to try one's patience : mettre sa patience à l'épreuve> **4** SAMPLE : goûter à, essayer — *vi* : essayer
try[2] *n, pl* **tries** : essai *m,* tentative *f*
tryout [ˈtraɪˌaʊt] *n* : essai *m*
try out *vt* : essayer, faire l'essai de
tsar [ˈzɑr, ˈtsɑr, ˈsɑr] → **czar**
T-shirt [ˈtiːˌʃərt] *n* : tee-shirt *m,* t-shirt *m*
tub [ˈtʌb] *n* **1** VAT : cuve *f,* bac *m* **2** CONTAINER : contenant *m,* pot *m* <a tub of margarine : un contenant de margarine> **3** → **bathtub**
tuba [ˈtuːbə, ˈtjuː-] *n* : tuba *m*
tube [ˈtuːb, ˈtjuːb] *n* **1** CYLINDER : tube *m,* cylindre *m* **2** : tube *m* (de dentifrice, etc.) **3** *or* **inner tube** : chambre *f* à air **4** *or* **cathode-ray tube** : tube *m* (cathodique)
tuber [ˈtuːbər, ˈtjuː-] *n* : tubercule *m*
tubercular [tʊˈbərkjələr, tjʊ-] *adj* : tuberculeux
tuberculosis [tʊˌbərkjəˈloːsəs, tjʊ-] *n, pl* **-loses** [-ˌsiːz] : tuberculose *f*
tuberculous [tʊˈbərkjələs, tjʊ-] *adj* : tuberculeux
tubing [ˈtuːbɪŋ, ˈtjuː-] *n* : tubes *mpl*
tubular [ˈtubjələr, ˈtjuː-] *adj* : tubulaire
tuck[1] [ˈtʌk] *vt* **1** *or* **to tuck away** : cacher, ranger <to tuck away one's money : mettre son argent en sécurité> **2 to tuck in** : rentrer (sa chemise), border (un enfant) — *vi* **to tuck into** : manger ou boire avec appétit
tuck[2] *n* : pli *m*
tucker [ˈtʌkər] *vt or* **to tucker out** : fatiguer, épuiser
Tuesday [ˈtuːzˌdeɪ, ˈtjuːz-, -di] *n* : mardi *m*
tuft [ˈtʌft] *n* : touffe *f* (de cheveux, de plantes, etc.)
tug[1] [ˈtʌg] *v* **tugged; tugging** *vt* **1** TOW : remorquer **2** LUG : tirer, traîner — *vi* **to tug at** : tirer sur
tug[2] *n* **1** : petit coup *m* **2** → **tugboat**
tugboat [ˈtʌgˌboːt] *n* : remorqueur *m*
tug-of-war [ˌtʌgəˈwɔr] *n, pl* **tugs-of-war** : lutte *f* à la corde
tuition [tʊˈɪʃən, ˈtjuː-] *n* : frais *mpl* de scolarité
tulip [ˈtuːlɪp, ˈtjuː-] *n* : tulipe *f*
tumble[1] [ˈtəmbəl] *v* **-bled; -bling** *vi* **1** FALL : tomber, dégringoler **2** : faire des culbutes, culbuter (en gymnastique) **3** PLUMMET : chuter (se dit des prix, etc.) — *vt* **1** TOPPLE : faire tomber, renverser **2** *or* **to tumble together** : mélanger
tumble[2] *n* **1** : culbute *f* (en gymnastique) **2** FALL : chute *f*
tumbler [ˈtʌmblər] *n* **1** ACROBAT : acrobate *mf* **2** GLASS : verre *m* droit **3** : gorge *f* (de serrure)
tummy [ˈtʌmi] *n, pl* **-mies** : ventre *m*
tumor *or Brit* **tumour** [ˈtuːmər, ˈtjuː-] *n* : tumeur *f*
tumult [ˈtuːˌmʌlt ˈtjuː-] *n* **1** COMMOTION : tumulte *m,* vacarme *m* **2** CONFUSION : agitation *f,* tumulte *m*
tumultuous [tʊˈmʌltʃʊəs, tjuː-] *adj* : tumultueux
tuna [ˈtuːnə ˈtjuː-] *n, pl* **-na** *or* **-nas** : thon *m*
tundra [ˈtʌndrə] *n* : toundra *f*
tune[1] [ˈtuːn, ˈtjuːn] *v* **tuned; tuning** *vt* **1** : accorder (un instrument de musique) **2** *or* **to tune up** : régler, mettre au point (un moteur) — *vi* **to tune in to** : se mettre à l'écoute de
tune[2] *n* **1** MELODY : air *m,* mélodie *f* **2 to be in tune** : être accordé (se dit d'un instrument), chanter juste **3 to be out of tune** : être désaccordé (se dit d'un instrument), chanter faux **4 to be in tune with** : être en accord avec
tuneful [ˈtuːnfəl, ˈtjuːn-] *adj* : mélodieux, harmonieux
tuner [ˈtuːnər, ˈtjuː-] *n* **1** : accordeur *m* <piano tuner : accordeur de piano> **2** : tuner *m* (de radio, etc.)
tungsten [ˈtʌŋkstən] *n* : tungstène *m*
tunic [ˈtuːnɪk, ˈtjuː-] *n* : tunique *f*
tuning fork *n* : diapason *m*
Tunisian[1] [tuːˈniːʒən, tjuːˈnɪziən] *adj* : tunisien
Tunisian[2] *n* : Tunisien *m,* -sienne *f*
tunnel[1] [ˈtʌnəl] *vi* **-neled** *or* **-nelled; -neling** *or* **-nelling** : creuser un tunnel
tunnel[2] *n* : tunnel *m*
turban [ˈtərbən] *n* : turban *m*
turbid [ˈtərbɪd] *adj* : turbide, trouble
turbine [ˈtərbən, -ˌbaɪn] *n* : turbine *f*
turboprop [ˈtərboːˌprɑp] *n* : turbopropulseur *m* (moteur), avion *m* à turbopropulseur
turbulence [ˈtərbjələnts] *n* : turbulence *f*

turbulent ['tərbjələnt] *adj* : turbulent, agité

turbulently ['tərbjələntli] *adv* : avec turbulence

tureen [tə'ri:n, tjʊ-] *n* : soupière *f*

turf ['tərf] *n* : gazon *m*, motte *f* de gazon

turgid ['tərdʒəd] *adj* **1** SWOLLEN : enflé, gonflé **2** BOMBASTIC : pompeux

Turk ['tərk] *n* : Turc *m*, Turque *f*

turkey ['tərki] *n, pl* **-keys** : dinde *f*

Turkish[1] ['tərkɪʃ] *adj* : turc

Turkish[2] *n* : turc *m* (langue)

turmoil ['tər,mɔɪl] *n* : désarroi *m*, confusion *f*

turn[1] ['tərn] *vt* **1** : tourner <to turn a wheel : tourner une roue> <turn the doorknob : tourne la poignée> **2** TWIST : tordre <to turn one's ankle : se tordre la cheville> **3** : tourner, retourner, changer de direction <she turned her chair toward the fire : elle a tourné sa chaise pour faire face au feu> <I turned the child over in bed : j'ai retourné l'enfant dans son lit> **4 to turn one's stomach** : se soulever le cœur **5 to turn over** PONDER : réfléchir à, tourner et retourner (un problème, une question, etc.) — *vi* **1** SPOIL : tourner, cailler **2** CHANGE : se transformer **3** BECOME : devenir <his hair turned gray : ses cheveux sont devenus gris> **4** : se tourner <he turned to them for help : il s'est tourné vers eux en espérant obtenir de l'aide> **5** HEAD : se diriger <we turned toward home : nous nous sommes dirigés vers la maison>

turn[2] *n* **1** ROTATION : tour *m* **2** CHANGE : amélioration *f*, tournure *f* <to take a turn for the better : s'être amélioré> **3** BEND : virage *m*, tournant *m* <a sharp turn : un brusque virage> <to make a right turn : tourner à droite> **4** DEED : service *m* <to do a good turn to : rendre service à> **5** : tour *m* <wait your turn : attendez votre tour> **6** STROLL : tour *m*, promenade *f*

turn away *vt* **1** AVERT : détourner (les yeux) **2 to turn s.o. away** : renvoyer qqn, refuser qqn — *vi* : se détourner

turncoat ['tərn,ko:t] *n* : renégat *m*, -gate *f*

turn down *vt* **1** : retourner (une carte), rabattre (un collet) **2** LOWER : baisser (le volume) **3** REFUSE : refuser, décliner

turn in *vi* : se coucher <I turned in early : je me suis couché tôt> — *vt* **1** : rendre, remettre <she turned in her paper : elle a remis son devoir> **2** DELIVER : livrer <we turned him in to police : nous l'avons livré à la police>

turnip ['tərnəp] *n* : navet *m*

turn off : éteindre (la lumière), fermer (une radio, etc.), arrêter (un moteur)

turnout ['tərn,aʊt] *n* : participation *f*

turn out *vt* **1** EVICT : expulser, mettre à la porte **2** TURN OFF : éteindre — *vi* **1** COME : venir, se présenter <voters turned out in droves : les électeurs se sont présentés en grands nombres> **2 to turn out to be** : s'avérer, se révéler <the outing turned out to be a disaster : la sortie s'est révélée désastreuse>

turnover ['tərn,o:vər] *n* **1** REVERSAL : renversement *m* **2** : chausson *m* <apple turnover : chausson aux pommes> **3** : roulement *m* (du personnel)

turn over *vt* **1** TRANSFER : remettre, rendre **2** : tourner, retourner <to turn over a playing card : retourner une carte> — *vi* **1** : se retourner (se dit d'une personne) **2** : commencer à tourner (se dit d'un moteur)

turnpike ['tərn,paɪk] *n* : autoroute *f* à péage

turnstile ['tərn,staɪl] *n* : tourniquet *m*

turntable ['tərn,teɪbəl] *n* : platine *f* (d'un tourne-disque)

turn up *vt* **1** : mettre plus fort (la lumière, etc.), augmenter (le volume) **2** DISCOVER : découvrir **3** : retrousser (ses manches), relever (son collet) — *vi* **1** APPEAR, ARRIVE : arriver, apparaître **2** HAPPEN : survenir, se passer

turpentine ['tərpən,taɪn] *n* : térébenthine *f*

turquoise ['tər,kɔɪz, -,kwɔɪz] *n* : turquoise *f* (minéral), turquoise *m* (couleur)

turret ['tərət] *n* : tourelle *f*

turtle ['tərṭəl] *n* : tortue *f*

turtledove ['tərṭəl,dʌv] *n* : tourterelle *f*

turtleneck ['tərṭəl,nɛk] *n* : col *m* roulé, col *m* montant

tusk ['tʌsk] *n* : défense *f* (d'un animal)

tussle[1] ['tʌsəl] *vi* : se bagarrer, se battre

tussle[2] *n* : bagarre *f*, mêlée *f*

tutor[1] ['tu:ṭər, 'tju:-] *vt* : donner des cours particuliers à

tutor[2] *n* : précepteur *m*, -trice *f*; professeur *m* particulier

tuxedo [,tək'si:,do:] *n, pl* **-dos** *or* **-does** : smoking *m*

TV [,ti:'vi:, 'ti:,vi:] *n* : TV *m*

twain ['tweɪn] *n* : deux *m*

twang[1] ['twæŋ] *vt* : pincer les cordes de (un instrument) — *vi* : vibrer

twang[2] *n* **1** : ton *m* nasillard (de la voix) **2** : son *m* de corde pincée

tweak[1] ['twi:k] *vt* : tirer, tordre

tweak[2] *n* : petit coup *m* sec

tweed ['twi:d] *n* : tweed *m*

tweet[1] ['twi:t] *vi* : pépier, gazouiller

tweet[2] *n* : pépiement *m*

tweezers ['twi:zərz] *ns & pl* : pince *f* à épiler

twelfth[1] ['twɛlfθ] *adj* : douzième

twelfth[2] *n* **1** : douzième *mf* (dans une série) **2** : douzième *m* (en mathé-

matiques) **3** (*used in dates*) <the twelfth of June : le douze juin>
twelve[1] [ˈtwɛlv] *adj* : douze
twelve[2] *n* : douze *m*
twentieth[1] [ˈtwʌntiəθ, ˈtwɛn-] *adj* : vingtième
twentieth[2] *n* **1** : vingtième *mf* (dans une série) **2** : vingtième *m* (en mathématiques) **3** (*used in dates*) <the twentieth of June : le vingt juin>
twenty[1] [ˈtwʌnti, ˈtwɛn-] *adj* : vingt
twenty[2] *n, pl* **-ties** : vingt *m*
twenty–twenty *or* **20/20** *adj* **to have twenty–twenty vision** : avoir dix dixièmes à chaque œil
twice [ˈtwaɪs] *adv* : deux fois <twice as much : deux fois plus>
twig [ˈtwɪg] *n* : petite branche *f*, brindille *f*
twilight [ˈtwaɪˌlaɪt] *n* : crépuscule *m* (du soir), aube *f* (du matin)
twill [ˈtwɪl] *n* : sergé *m*
twin[1] [ˈtwɪn] *adj* : jumeau <twin sister : sœur jumelle>
twin[2] *n* : jumeau *m*, -melle *f*
twine[1] [ˈtwaɪn] *v* **twined; twining** *vt* : enrouler — *vi* : s'enrouler
twine[2] *n* : ficelle *f*
twinge [ˈtwɪndʒ] *n* : élancement *m* (de douleur)
twinkle[1] [ˈtwɪŋkəl] *vi* **-kled; -kling 1** : briller, scintiller (se dit des étoiles, etc.) **2** : pétiller (se dit des yeux)
twinkle[2] *n* : scintillement *m* (des étoiles), pétillement *m* (des yeux)
twirl[1] [ˈtwərl] *vi* : tournoyer — *vt* : faire tournoyer
twirl[2] *n* : tournoiement *m*
twist[1] [ˈtwɪst] *vt* **1** : tourner, tordre <to twist one's ankle : se tordre la cheville> **2** DISTORT : déformer, pervertir <to twist the facts : déformer les faits> — *vi* **1** : serpenter (se dit d'une route) **2** ENTWINE : s'enrouler **3 to twist and turn** : se tortiller
twist[2] *n* **1** TURN : tour *m*, torsion *f* **2** BEND : tournant *m* (d'une route, etc.) **3** COIL : tortillon *m*, rouleau *m* <a twist of lemon : un zeste de citron> **4** : rebondissement *m*, tournure *f* (des événements) <a twist of fate : un coup du sort>
twister [ˈtwɪstər] *n* **1** → **tornado 2** → **waterspout**
twitch[1] [ˈtwɪtʃ] *vi* **1** QUIVER : trembloter, avoir un mouvement convulsif **2** : se convulser, se contracter (se dit d'un muscle)
twitch[2] *n* **1** JERK : saccade *f*, coup *m* sec **2** SPASM : spasme *m* **3** *or* **nervous twitch** : tic *m* (nerveux)
twitter[1] [ˈtwɪt̬ər] *vi* **1** CHIRP : pépier, gazouiller **2** CHATTER : jacasser **3** *or* **to twitter about** : s'agiter (nerveusement)
twitter[2] *n* : pépiement *m*, gazouillement *m* (d'un oiseau)
two[1] [ˈtuː] *adj* : deux
two[2] *n, pl* **twos** : deux *m*
twofold[1] [ˈtuːˈfoːld] *adv* : doublement
twofold[2] *adj* : double
twosome [ˈtuːsəm] *n* : couple *m*
tycoon [taɪˈkuːn] *n* : magnat *m*
tying → **tie[1]**
type[1] [ˈtaɪp] *v* **typed; typing** *vt* **1** : taper (une lettre, etc.) **2** CATEGORIZE : classifier, déterminer le type de — *vi* : taper (à la machine)
type[2] *n* **1** KIND : genre *m*, sorte *f*, type *m* **2** *or* **printing type** : caractère *m* (d'imprimerie)
typewriter [ˈtaɪpˌraɪt̬ər] *n* : machine *f* à écrire, dactylo *f Can*
typhoid [ˈtaɪˌfɔɪd, taɪˈ-] *n or* **typhoid fever** : typhoïde *f*, fièvre *f* typhoïde
typhoon [taɪˈfuːn] *n* : typhon *m*
typhus [ˈtaɪfəs] *n* : typhus *m*
typical [ˈtɪpɪkəl] *adj* : typique, caractéristique
typically [ˈtɪpɪkli] *adv* **1** : typiquement <typically American : typiquement américain> **2** USUALLY : d'habitude
typify [ˈtɪpəˌfaɪ] *vt* **-fied; -fying** : représenter, être typique de
typist [ˈtaɪpɪst] *n* : dactylo *mf*
typographic [ˌtaɪpəˈgræfɪk] *or* **typographical** [-fɪkəl] *adj* : typographique — **typographically** [-fɪkli] *adv*
typography [taɪˈpɑgrəfi] *n* : typographie *f*
tyrannical [təˈrænɪkəl, taɪ-] *adj* : tyrannique — **tyrannically** [-nɪkli] *adv*
tyrannize [ˈtɪrəˌnaɪz] *vt* **-nized; -nizing** : tyranniser
tyranny [ˈtɪrəni] *n, pl* **-nies** : tyrannie *f*
tyrant [ˈtaɪrənt] *n* : tyran *m*
tzar [ˈzɑr, ˈtsɑr, ˈsɑr] → **czar**

U

u [ˈjuː] *n, pl* **u's** *or* **us** [ˈjuːz] : u *m*, vingt et unième lettre de l'alphabet
ubiquitous [juːˈbɪkwət̬əs] *adj* : omniprésent
ubiquity [juːˈbɪkwət̬i] *n* : omniprésence *f*, ubiquité *f*
udder [ˈʌdər] *n* : pis *m* (d'une vache)
Ugandan[1] [juːˈgændən, -ˈgɑn-; uːˈgɑn-] *adj* : ougandais
Ugandan[2] *n* : Ougandais *m*, -daise *f*
ugliness [ˈʌglinəs] *n* : laideur *f*
ugly [ˈʌgli] *adj* **uglier; -est 1** : laid <an ugly color : une couleur laide> **2** DISAGREEABLE, FOUL : mauvais,

désagréable, vilain <ugly weather : du temps vilain> 3 QUARRELSOME : agressif, querelleur <the crowd turned ugly : la foule est devenue agressive>

Ukrainian[1] [juːˈkreɪniən, -ˈkraɪ-] *adj* : ukrainien

Ukrainian[2] *n* **1** : Ukrainien *m*, -nienne *f* **2** : ukrainien *m* (langue)

ukulele [ˌjuːkəˈleɪli] *n* : guitare *f* hawaïenne

ulcer [ˈʌlsər] *n* : ulcère *f*

ulcerate [ˈʌlsəˌreɪt] *vt* **-ated; -ating** : ulcérer

ulceration [ˌʌlsəˈreɪʃən] *n* : ulcération *f*

ulcerous [ˌʌlsərəs] *adj* : ulcéreux

ulna [ˈʌlnə] *n* : cubitus *m*

ulterior [ˌʌlˈtɪriər] *adj* HIDDEN : secret, inavoué <to have ulterior motives : avoir des arrière-pensées>

ultimate[1] [ˈʌltəmət] *adj* **1** FINAL : ultime, final **2** SUPREME : suprême **3** FUNDAMENTAL : absolu, fondamental

ultimate[2] *n* : summum *m* <the ultimate in modernity : le summum de la modernité>

ultimately [ˈʌltəmətli] *adv* : en fin de compte, finalement

ultimatum [ˌʌltəˈmeɪṭəm, -ˈmɑ-] *n, pl* **-tums** *or* **-ta** [-ṭə] : ultimatum *m* <to deliver an ultimatum : adresser un ultimatum>

ultraviolet [ˌʌltrəˈvaɪələt] *adj* : ultraviolet

umbilical cord [ˌʌmˈbɪlɪkəl] : cordon *m* ombilical

umbrage [ˈʌmbrɪdʒ] *n* **to take umbrage at** : prendre ombrage de, s'offenser de

umbrella [ˌʌmˈbrɛlə] *n* : parapluie *m*

umpire[1] [ˈʌmˌpaɪr] *v* **-pired; -piring** *vt* : arbitrer (aux sports) — *vi* : servir d'arbitre

umpire[2] *n* : arbitre *m*

umpteen [ˈʌmpˌtiːn, ˌʌmp'-] *adj* : des tas de

umpteenth [ˈʌmpˌtinθ, ˌʌmp'-] *adj* : énième

unable [ˌʌnˈeɪbəl] *adj* **to be unable to** : ne pas pouvoir, être incapable de

unabridged [ˌʌnəˈbrɪdʒd] *adj* : intégral

unacceptable [ˌʌnɪkˈsɛptəbəl] *adj* : inacceptable, inadmissible

unaccompanied [ˌʌnəˈkʌmpənid] *adj* : non accompagné

unaccountable [ˌʌnəˈkaʊntəbəl] *adj* : inexplicable — **unaccountably** [-bli] *adv*

unaccounted [ˌʌnəˈkaʊntəd] *adj* **~ for** : introuvable (se dit des choses), pas retrouvé (se dit des personnes)

unaccustomed [ˌʌnəˈkʌstəmd] *adj* **1** UNCHARACTERISTIC : inaccoutumé, inhabituel **2 to be unaccustomed to** : ne pas avoir l'habitude de

unacquainted [ˌʌnəˈkweɪntəd] *adj* **to be unacquainted with** : ne pas connaître

unadorned [ˌʌnəˈdɔrnd] *adj* : sans ornement

unadulterated [ˌʌnəˈdʌltəˌreɪṭəd] *adj* **1** PURE : pur, naturel **2** : pur (et simple) <unadulterated nonsense : de la pure bêtise>

unaffected [ˌʌnəˈfɛktəd] *adj* **1** : qui n'est pas affecté <I was unaffected by his plea : sa demande m'a laissé indifférent> **2** NATURAL : naturel, sincère, sans affectation

unaffectedly [ˌʌnəˈfɛktədli] *adv* : sans affectation

unafraid [ˌʌnəˈfreɪd] *adj* : sans peur

unaided [ˌʌnˈeɪdəd] *adj* : sans aide, tout seul

unalike [ˌʌnəˈlaɪk] *adj* : peu ressemblant, différent

unambiguous [ˌʌnæmˈbɪgjʊəs] *adj* : non équivoque

unanimity [ˌjuːnəˈnɪməṭi] *n* : unanimité *f*

unanimous [jʊˈnænəməs] *adj* : unanime

unanimously [jʊˈnænəməsli] *adv* : à l'unanimité, unanimement

unannounced [ˌʌnəˈnaʊnst] *adj* : inattendu, sans se faire annoncer

unanswered [ˌʌnˈæntsərd] *adj* : qui reste sans réponse

unappealing [ˌʌnəˈpiːlɪŋ] *adj* : peu attirant

unappetizing [ˌʌnˈæpəˌtaɪzɪŋ] *adj* : peu appétissant

unarguable [ˌʌnˈɑrgjuəbəl] *adj* : incontestable

unarmed [ˌʌnˈɑrmd] *adj* : non armé, sans armes

unassuming [ˌʌnəˈsuːmɪŋ] *adj* : modeste, sans prétention

unattached [ˌʌnəˈtætʃt] *adj* **1** : détaché, indépendant <unattached buildings : bâtiments détachés> **2** : libre (se dit d'une personne célibataire)

unattractive [ˌʌnəˈtræktɪv] *adj* : peu attrayant

unauthorized [ˌʌnˈɔθəˌraɪzd] *adj* : non autorisé

unavailable [ˌʌnəˈveɪləbəl] *adj* : indisponible

unavoidable [ˌʌnəˈvɔɪdəbəl] *adj* : inévitable

unaware[1] [ˌʌnəˈwær] *adv* → **unawares**

unaware[2] *adj* : qui n'est pas conscient, qui ignore <unaware of the danger : inconscient du danger>

unawares [ˌʌnəˈwærz] *adv* **1** UNEXPECTEDLY : soudainement, à l'improviste <to take unawares : prendre au dépourvu> **2** UNINTENTIONALLY : par mégarde, inconsciemment

unbalanced [ˌʌnˈbælənst] *adj* **1** LOPSIDED : qui n'est pas équilibré **2** UNSTABLE : déséquilibré (se dit d'une personne)

unbearable [ˌʌnˈbærəbəl] *adj* : insupportable, insoutenable

unbeaten [ˌʌnˈbiːtən] *adj* : invaincu

unbecoming [ˌʌnbɪˈkʌmɪŋ] *adj* **1** UNFLATTERING : peu seyant, peu flatteur **2** UNSEEMLY : inconvenant

unbelievable [ˌʌnbəˈli:vəbəl] *adj* : incroyable — **unbelievably** [-bli] *adv*

unbend [ˌʌnˈbɛnd] *v* **-bent; -bending** *vt* : détordre (un fil, etc.) — *vi* RELAX : se détendre

unbending [ˌʌnˈbɛndɪŋ] *adj* : inflexible

unbiased [ˌʌnˈbaɪəst] *adj* : impartial

unbind [ˌʌnˈbaɪnd] *vt* **-bound; -binding** **1** UNTIE : délier, détacher **2** RELEASE : libérer

unbolt [ˌʌnˈbo:lt] *vt* : déverrouiller

unborn [ˌʌnˈbɔrn] *adj* : qui n'est pas encore né

unbosom [ˌʌnˈbʊzəm, -ˈbu:-] *vt* **to unbosom oneself to** : se confier à

unbreakable [ˌʌnˈbreɪkəbəl] *adj* : incassable

unbridled [ˌʌnˈbraɪdəld] *adj* UNRESTRAINED : débridé, déchaîné, non contenu

unbroken [ˌʌnˈbro:kən] *adj* **1** WHOLE : intact, qui n'est pas brisé **2** UNTAMED : indompté **3** UNINTERRUPTED : continu

unbuckle [ˌʌnˈbʌkəl] *vt* **-led; -ling** : déboucler

unburden [ˌʌnˈbərdən] *vt* **1** RELIEVE : décharger (d'un fardeau) **2 to unburden oneself** : se confier, s'épancher

unbutton [ˌʌnˈbʌtən] *vt* : déboutonner

uncalled–for [ˌʌnˈkɔldˌfɔr] *adj* : déplacé, injustifié

uncannily [ənˈkænəli] *adv* : étrangement

uncanny [ənˈkæni] *adj* **1** EERIE, STRANGE : mystérieux, troublant, étrange **2** REMARKABLE : extraordinaire

unceasing [ˌʌnˈsi:sɪŋ] *adj* : incessant, continu

unceasingly [ˌʌnˈsi:sɪŋli] *adv* : sans cesse

unceremonious [ˌʌnsɛrəˈmo:niəs] *adj* **1** INFORMAL : informel, sans façon **2** ABRUPT : précipité, brusque <an unceremonious dismissal : un licenciement précipité>

unceremoniously [ˌʌnsɛrəˈmo:niəsli] *adv* : sans façon, sans cérémonie

uncertain [ˌʌnˈsərtən] *adj* **1** INDEFINITE, UNKNOWN : incertain, inconnu **2** CHANGEABLE : incertain, variable <uncertain weather : du temps incertain> **3** UNSURE : incertain

uncertainly [ˌʌnˈsərtənli] *adv* : avec hésitation, d'un air hésitant

uncertainty [ˌʌnˈsərtənti] *n, pl* **-ties** : incertitude *f*, doute *m*

unchangeable [ˌʌnˈtʃeɪndʒəbəl] *adj* : immuable, invariable

unchanged [ˌʌnˈtʃeɪndʒd] *adj* : inchangé

unchanging [ˌʌnˈtʃeɪndʒɪŋ] *adj* : immuable

uncharacteristic [ˌʌnˌkærɪktəˈrɪstɪk] *adj* : peu habituel, peu typique

uncharged [ˌʌnˈtʃɑrdʒd] *adj* : qui n'a pas de charge électrique

uncivilized [ˌʌnˈsɪvəˌlaɪzd] *adj* **1** WILD : non civilisé (se dit d'un endroit) **2** BARBAROUS : barbare, sauvage

uncle [ˈʌŋkəl] *n* : oncle *m*

unclean [ˌʌnˈkli:n] *adj* **1** IMPURE : impur **2** DIRTY : malpropre, sale

uncleanliness [ˌʌnˈklɛnlinəs] *n* : malpropreté *f*, saleté *f*

unclear [ˌʌnˈklɪr] *adj* : peu clair, incertain

unclog [ˌʌnˈklɑg] *vt* **-clogged; -clogging** : déboucher (un évier, etc.)

unclothed [ˌʌnˈklo:ðd] *adj* : nu, dévêtu

unclouded [ˌʌnˈklaʊdəd] *adj* : limpide, sans nuages

uncomfortable [ˌʌnˈkʌmpfərṭəbəl] *adj* **1** : inconfortable (se dit d'une chaise, etc.) **2** UNEASY : mal à l'aise, gêné (se dit d'une personne)

uncomfortably [ˌʌnˈkʌmpfərṭəbli] *adv* **1** DISAGREEABLY : désagréablement, inconfortablement **2** UNEASILY : avec gêne, avec inquiétude

uncommitted [ˌʌnkəˈmɪṭəd] *adj* : non engagé

uncommon [ˌʌnˈkɑmən] *adj* **1** UNUSUAL : rare, peu commun **2** REMARKABLE : remarquable, extraordinaire

uncommonly [ˌʌnˈkɑmənli] *adv* : extraordinairement, exceptionnellement

uncompromising [ˌʌnˈkɑmprəˈmaɪzɪŋ] *adj* : intransigeant, inflexible

unconcerned [ˌʌnkənˈsərnd] *adj* **1** UNINTERESTED : indifférent **2** UNWORRIED : insouciant, imperturbable

unconditional [ˌʌnkənˈdɪʃənəl] *adj* : inconditionnel — **unconditionally** *adv*

unconscious[1] [ˌʌnˈkɑnʃəs] *adj* **1** UNAWARE : inconscient **2** INSENSIBLE : sans connaissance

unconscious[2] *n* : inconscient *m*

unconsciously [ˌʌnˈkɑnʃəsli] *adv* : inconsciemment

unconsciousness [ˌʌnˈkɑnʃəsnəs] *n* : inconscience *f*

unconstitutional [ˌʌnˈkɑntstəˈtu:ʃənəl, -ˈtju:-] *adj* : inconstitutionnel

uncontrollable [ˌʌnkənˈtro:ləbəl] *adj* : incontrôlable, irrésistible

uncontrollably [ˌʌnkənˈtro:ləbli] *adv* : irrésistiblement <to laugh uncontrollably : rire sans pouvoir se contrôler>

uncontrolled [ˌʌnkənˈtro:ld] *adj* : incontrôlé, non maîtrisé

unconventional [ˌʌnkənˈvɛntʃənəl] *adj* : peu conventionnel

unconvincing [ˌʌnkənˈvɪntsɪŋ] *adj* : peu convaincant

uncouth [ˌʌnˈku:θ] *adj* : grossier, fruste

uncover [ˌʌnˈkʌvər] *vt* : découvrir

uncultivated [ˌʌnˈkʌltəˌveɪṭəd] *adj* : inculte

unctuous [ˈʌŋktʃʊəs] *adj* : onctueux, mielleux

uncut [ˌʌnˈkʌt] *adj* **1** : non coupé (se dit des cheveux), non taillé (se dit d'une pierre précieuse) **2** UNABRIDGED : intégral

undaunted [ˌʌnˈdɔnt̬əd] *adj* : imperturbable

undecided [ˌʌndɪˈsaɪdəd] *adj* **1** IRRESOLUTE : indécis, incertain **2** UNRESOLVED : non résolu

undefeated [ˌʌndɪˈfiːt̬əd] *adj* : invaincu

undeniable [ˌʌndɪˈnaɪəbəl] *adj* : indéniable — **undeniably** [-bli] *adv*

under[1] [ˈʌndər] *adv* **1** : en dessous <the diver went under again : le plongeur est retourné sous l'eau> **2** LESS : moins <$10 or under : 10 $ ou moins> **3 to put under** : anesthésier, endormir

under[2] *adj* **1** LOWER : inférieur **2** SUBORDINATE : subordonné **3** INSUFFICIENT : insuffisant <an under dose of medicine : une dose insuffisante du médicament>

under[3] *prep* **1** BELOW, BENEATH : sous <under a tree : sous un arbre> <we walked under the ladder : nous avons passé sous l'échelle> <it's under there : c'est là-dessous> **2** UNDERNEATH : sous, en dessous de <I wore a sweater under my coat : je portais un chandail sous mon manteau> **3** (*indicating rank or authority*) : sous, sous la direction de <to serve under the general : servir sous le général> **4** : moins de <under two pounds : moins de deux livres> **5** ACCORDING TO : d'après, selon <under the terms of the contract : selon les modalités du contrat> **6 under lock and key** : sous clef

underage [ˌʌndərˈeɪdʒ] *adj* : mineur, sous l'âge réglementaire

underbrush [ˈʌndərˌbrəʃ] *n* : sous-bois *m,* broussailles *fpl*

undercarriage [ˈʌndərˌkærɪdʒ] *n* **1** : châssis *m* (d'une voiture) **2** *Brit* : train *m* d'atterrissage (d'un avion)

underclothes [ˈʌndərˌkloːz, -ˌkloːðz] *npl* → **underwear**

underclothing [ˈʌndərˌkloðɪŋ] → **underwear**

undercover [ˌʌndərˈkʌvər] *adj* : secret, clandestin <an undercover agent : un agent secret>

undercurrent [ˈʌndərˌkərənt] *n* **1** : courant *m* sous-marin **2** : sentiment *m* sous-jacent <an undercurrent of resentment : un ressentiment sous-jacent>

undercut [ˌʌndərˈkʌt] *vt* **-cut; -cutting 1** : vendre moins cher que **2** UNDERMINE : amoindrir, saper

underdeveloped [ˌʌndərdɪˈvɛləpt] *adj* : sous-développé

underdog [ˈʌndərˌdɔg] *n* **1** : celui *m* que l'on donne perdant **2** : opprimé *m,* -mée *f*

underdone [ˌʌndərˈdʌn] *adj* : pas assez cuit

underestimate [ˌʌndərˈɛstəˌmeɪt] *vt* **-mated; -mating** : sous-estimer

underexpose [ˌʌndərɪkˈspoːz] *vt* **-posed; -posing** : sous-exposer (une photo)

underexposure [ˌʌndərɪkˈspoːʒər] *n* : sous-exposition *f* (en photographie)

underfoot [ˌʌndərˈfʊt] *adv* **1** : sous les pieds <warm sand underfoot : du sable chaud sous les pieds> **2 to be underfoot** : être dans les jambes

undergarment [ˈʌndərˌgɑrmənt] *n* : sous-vêtement *m*

undergo [ˌʌndərˈgoː] *vt* **-went** [-ˈwɛnt]; **-gone** [-ˈgɔn]; **-going** : éprouver (des souffrances), subir (une opération, des examens, etc.)

undergraduate [ˌʌndərˈgrædʒʊət] *n* : étudiant *m,* -diante *f* de premier cycle; étudiant *m,* -diante *f* qui prépare une licence *France*

underground[1] [ˌʌndərˈgraʊnd] *adv* **1** : sous terre **2** SECRETLY : clandestinement, secrètement <to go underground : passer dans la clandestinité>

underground[2] [ˈʌndərˌgraʊnd] *adj* **1** SUBTERRANEAN : souterrain **2** SECRET : clandestin, secret

underground[3] [ˈʌndərˌgraʊnd] *n* **1** SUBWAY : métro *m* **2** : résistance *f* (en politique)

undergrowth [ˈʌndərˈgroːθ] *n* : sous-bois *m,* broussailles *fpl,* fardoches *fpl Can*

underhand[1] [ˈʌndərˌhænd] *adv* **1** SECRETLY, SLYLY : sournoisement, en sous-main **2** : par en dessous <to throw underhand : lancer par en dessous>

underhand[2] *adj* **1** SLY : sournois **2** : par en dessous <an underhand throw : un lancer par en dessous>

underhanded[1] [ˌʌndərˈhændəd] *adv* → **underhand**[1]

underhanded[2] *adj* SECRET : clandestin <underhanded dealings : transactions en sous-main>

underline [ˈʌndərˌlaɪn] *vt* **-lined; -lining 1** : souligner (un mot) **2** STRESS : souligner, mettre l'accent sur

underling [ˈʌndərlɪŋ] *n* : subordonné *m,* -née *f;* subalterne *mf*

underlying [ˌʌndərˈlaɪɪŋ] *adj* **1** : sous-jacent <underlying strata : strates sous-jacentes> **2** FUNDAMENTAL : fondamental, sous-jacent

undermine [ˌʌndərˈmaɪn] *vt* **-mined; -mining 1** : saper, miner (un escarpement, une construction, etc.) **2** SAP, WEAKEN : saper, amoindrir <to undermine one's confidence : saper sa confiance>

underneath[1] [ˌʌndərˈniːθ] *adv* : en dessous, dessous <the part underneath : la partie d'en dessous>

underneath[2] *prep* : sous, au-dessous de

undernourished [ˌʌndərˈnərɪʃt] *adj* : sous-alimenté

undernourishment [ˌʌndərˈnərɪʃmənt] *n* : sous-alimentation *f*
underpants [ˈʌndərˌpænts] *npl* : slip *m France,* caleçon *m,* petite culotte *f Can*
underpass [ˈʌndərˌpæs] *n* : voie *f* inférieure (de l'autoroute), passage *m* souterrain (pour les piétons)
underprivileged [ˌʌndərˈprɪvlɪdʒd] *adj* : défavorisé, déshérité
underrate [ˌʌndərˈreɪt] *vt* **-rated; -rating** : sous-estimer
underscore [ˈʌndərˌskor] *vt* **-scored -scoring** → **underline**
undersea[1] [ˌʌndərˈsiː] *or* **underseas** [-ˈsiːz] *adv* : sous la mer
undersea[2] *adj* : sous-marin
undersecretary [ˌʌndərˈsɛkrəˌteri] *n, pl* **-taries** : sous-secrétaire *mf*
undersell [ˌʌndərˈsɛl] *vt* **-sold** [-ˈsoːld]; **-selling** : vendre moins cher que
undershirt [ˈʌndərˌʃərt] *n* : maillot *m* de corps, camisole *f Can*
undershorts [ˈʌndərˌʃɔrts] *npl* : caleçon *m*
underside [ˈʌndərˌsaɪd, ˌʌndərˈsaɪd] *n* : dessous *m*
undersized [ˌʌndərˈsaɪzd] *adj* : trop petit
understand [ˌʌndərˈstænd] *v* **-stood** [-ˈstʊd]; **-standing** *vt* **1** COMPREHEND : comprendre <I don't understand : je ne comprends pas> <to make oneself understood : se faire comprendre> **2** BELIEVE : croire, comprendre <I understand that he is sick : je crois qu'il est malade> **3** INFER : entendre <to let it be understood that : laisser entendre que> — *vi* : comprendre
understandable [ˌʌndərˈstændəbəl] *adj* : compréhensible <that's understandable : ça se comprend>
understandably [ˌʌndərˈstændəbli] *adv* : naturellement
understanding[1] [ˌʌndərˈstændɪŋ] *adj* : compréhensif, bienveillant
understanding[2] *n* **1** GRASP : compréhension *f,* entendement *m,* intelligence *f* **2** AGREEMENT : entente *f,* accord *m* **3** INTERPRETATION : interprétation *f* <my understanding was that : j'ai compris que> **4** SYMPATHY : compréhension *f*
understate [ˌʌndərˈsteɪt] *vt* **-stated; -stating** : minimiser, réduire l'importance de
understatement [ˌʌndərˈsteɪtmənt] *n* : affirmation *f* en dessous de la vérité <that's an understatement! : c'est peu dire!>
understudy [ˈʌndərˌstʌdi] *n, pl* **-dies** : doublure *f* (au théâtre)
undertake [ˌʌndərˈteɪk] *vt* **-took** [-ˈtʊk]; **-taken** [-ˈteɪkən]; **-taking 1** : entreprendre (une tâche), assumer (une responsabilité) **2** GUARANTEE : s'engager à, promettre (de faire quelque chose)
undertaker [ˈʌndərˌteɪkər] *n* : entrepreneur *m* de pompes funèbres
undertaking [ˈʌndərˌteɪkɪŋ, ˌʌndərˈ-] *n* **1** ENTERPRISE, VENTURE : entreprise *f* **2** PLEDGE : promesse *f,* garantie *f*
undertone [ˈʌndərˌtoːn] *n* **1** : voix *f* basse <to speak in an undertone : parler à mi-voix, parler à voix basse> **2** HINT, UNDERCURRENT : pointe *f,* note *f*
undertow [ˈʌndərˌtoː] *n* : courant *m* sous-marin
undervalue [ˌʌndərˈvælˌjuː] *vt* **-ued; -uing** : sous-évaluer, sous-estimer
underwater[1] [ˌʌndərˈwɔt̬ər, -ˈwɑ-] *adv* : sous l'eau
underwater[2] *adj* : sous-marin <underwater plants : plantes sous-marines>
under way [ˌʌndərˈweɪ] *adv* : en cours, en route <to get under way : se mettre en route>
underwear [ˈʌndərˌwær] *n* : sous-vêtements *mpl*
underworld [ˈʌndərˌwərld] *n* **1** *or* **criminal underworld** : milieu *m,* pègre *f* **2 the underworld** HELL : les enfers
underwrite [ˈʌndərˌraɪt, ˌʌndərˈ-] *vt* **-wrote** [-ˌroːt, -ˈroːt]; **-written** [-ˌrɪtən, -ˈrɪtən]; **-writing 1** FINANCE : soutenir financièrement **2** INSURE : garantir, souscrire (une police d'assurance)
underwriter [ˈʌndərˌraɪt̬ər, ˌʌndərˈ-] *n* INSURER : assureur *m*
undeserving [ˌʌndɪˈzərvɪŋ] *adj* : peu méritant
undesirable [ˌʌndɪˈzaɪrəbəl] *adj* : indésirable
undeveloped [ˌʌndɪˈvɛləpt] *adj* : non développé, inexploité
undies [ˈʌndiːz] *npl* → **underwear**
undignified [ˌʌnˈdɪgnəfaɪd] *adj* : indigne, qui manque de dignité
undiluted [ˌʌndaɪˈluːt̬əd, -də-] *adj* : non dilué, sans mélange
undiscovered [ˌʌndɪˈskʌvərd] *adj* : non découvert
undisputed [ˌʌndɪˈspjuːt̬əd] *adj* : incontesté
undisturbed [ˌʌndɪˈstərbd] *adj* **1** PEACEFUL : tranquille **2** UNTOUCHED : intact, non dérangé
undivided [ˌʌndɪˈvaɪdəd] *adj* : entier <your undivided attention : toute votre attention>
undo [ˌʌnˈduː] *vt* **-did; -done; -doing 1** UNTIE : défaire **2** UNWRAP : déballer **3** REVERSE : retourner, réparer (les dommages) **4** RUIN : détruire
undoing [ˌʌnˈduːɪŋ] *n* RUIN : ruine *f,* perte *f*
undoubted [ˌʌnˈdaʊt̬əd] *adj* : indubitable, certain
undoubtedly [ˌʌnˈdaʊt̬ədli] *adv* : indubitablement, sans aucun doute
undress [ˌʌnˈdrɛs] *vt* : déshabiller, dévêtir — *vi* : se déshabiller, se dévêtir

undrinkable [ˌʌn'drɪŋkəbəl] *adj* : non potable

undue [ˌʌn'du:, -'dju:] *adj* : excessif, démesuré — **unduly** [ˌʌn'du:li] *adv*

undulate ['ʌndʒəˌleɪt] *vi* **-lated; -lating** : onduler

undulation [ˌʌndʒə'leɪʃən] *n* : ondulation *f*

undying [ˌʌn'daɪɪŋ] *adj* : éternel, perpétuel <undying love : amour éternel>

unearth [ˌʌn'ɛrθ] *vt* **1** EXHUME : déterrer, exhumer **2** DISCOVER : dénicher, découvrir

unearthly [ˌʌn'ɛrθli] *adj* **1** STRANGE, WEIRD : surnaturel, étrange **2** UNGODLY : indu <at an unearthly hour : à une heure indue>

uneasily [ˌʌn'i:zəli] *adv* **1** UNCOMFORTABLY : d'un air gêné **2** APPREHENSIVELY : avec inquiétude

uneasiness [ˌʌn'i:zinəs] *n* : inquiétude *f*, malaise *m*

uneasy [ˌʌn'i:zi] *adj* **1** AWKWARD, EMBARRASSED : mal à l'aise, gêné **2** RESTLESS : agité, inquiet **3** UNSTABLE : précaire <an uneasy truce : une trêve précaire>

uneducated [ˌʌn'ɛdʒəˌkeɪt̬əd] *adj* : sans éducation

unemployed [ˌʌnɪm'plɔɪd] *adj* : en chômage, sans travail

unemployment [ˌʌnɪm'plɔɪmənt] *n* : chômage *m*

unending [ˌʌn'ɛndɪŋ] *adj* : sans fin, interminable

unendurable [ˌʌnɪn'dʊrəbəl] *adj* : intolérable

unequal [ˌʌn'i:kwəl] *adj* **1** : inégal **2 to be unequal to a task** : ne pas être à la hauteur d'une tâche

unequaled *or* **unequalled** [ˌʌn'i:kwəld] *adj* : inégalé, sans égal

unequally [ˌʌn'i:kwəli] *adv* : de manière inégale

unequivocal [ˌʌnɪ'kwɪvəkəl] *adj* : explicite, sans équivoque, clair

unequivocally [ˌʌnɪ'kwɪvəkəli] *adv* : explicitement

unerring [ˌʌn'ɛrɪŋ, -'ər-] *adj* : infaillible

uneven [ˌʌn'i:vən] *adj* **1** ODD : impair <uneven numbers : chiffres impairs> **2** : inégal <uneven terrain : terrain inégal> <an uneven performance : une performance inégale> **3** IRREGULAR : inégal, irrégulier <uneven teeth : dentition irrégulière>

unevenly [ˌʌn'i:vənli] *adv* **1** : de façon inégale **2** IRREGULARLY : de façon irrégulière

unevenness [ˌʌn'i:vənnəs] *n* : inégalité *f*, irrégularité *f*

uneventful [ˌʌnɪ'vɛntfəl] *adj* : sans histoires, peu mouvementé

uneventfully [ˌʌnɪ'vɛntfəli] *adv* : sans incidents

unexpected [ˌʌnɪk'spɛktəd] *adj* : inattendu, imprévu

unexpectedly [ˌʌnɪk'spɛktədli] *adv* : à l'improviste, contre toute attente

unexplained [ˌʌnɪk'spleɪnd] *adj* : inexpliqué

unfailing [ˌʌn'feɪlɪŋ] *adj* **1** CONSTANT : inaltérable, invariable <unfailing courtesy : courtoisie inaltérable> **2** INEXHAUSTIBLE : inépuisable, infini **3** SURE : infaillible, sûr

unfailingly [ˌʌn'feɪlɪŋli] *adv* : invariablement, inlassablement

unfair [ˌʌn'fær] *adj* : injuste — **unfairly** *adj*

unfairness [ˌʌn'færnəs] *n* : injustice *f*

unfaithful [ˌʌn'feɪθfəl] *adj* : infidèle — **unfaithfully** *adv*

unfaithfulness [ˌʌn'feɪθfəlnəs] *n* : infidélité *f*

unfamiliar [ˌʌnfə'mɪljər] *adj* **1** : inconnu, peu familier **2 to be unfamiliar with sth** : mal connaître qqch

unfamiliarity [ˌʌnfəˌmɪli'ærət̬i] *n, pl* **-ties** : caractère *m* peu connu, connaissance *f* limitée

unfasten [ˌn'fæsən] *vt* : déboucler (une ceinture), défaire (un bouton)

unfavorable [ˌʌn'feɪvərəbəl] *adj* : défavorable — **unfavorably** [-bli] *adv*

unfeeling [ˌʌn'fi:lɪŋ] *adj* : insensible, froid

unfeelingly [ˌʌn'fi:lɪŋli] *adv* : froidement, sans pitié

unfinished [ˌʌn'fɪnɪʃd] *adj* : inachevé, en cours

unfit [ˌʌn'fɪt] *adj* **1** UNSUITABLE : inapte, impropre <unfit for consumption : impropre à la consommation> **2** UNSUITED : inapte, incapable **3** : qui n'est pas en forme <he's physically unfit : physiquement, il n'est pas en forme>

unflappable [ˌʌn'flæpəbəl] *adj* : imperturbable

unflattering [ˌʌn'flæt̬ərɪŋ] *adj* : peu flatteur

unfold [ˌʌn'fo:ld] *vt* **1** EXPAND : déplier <to unfold a map : déplier une carte> **2** REVEAL : exposer, dévoiler (un plan, etc.) — *vi* **1** DEVELOP : se dérouler, évoluer <the story unfolded : l'histoire s'est déroulée> **2** : se dévoiler, se manifester <a panorama unfolded before their eyes : un panorama se dévoilait devant leurs yeux>

unforeseeable [ˌʌnfor'siəbəl] *adj* : imprévisible

unforeseen [ˌʌnfor'si:n] *adj* : imprévu, inattendu

unforgettable [ˌʌnfər'gɛt̬əbəl] *adj* : inoubliable, mémorable — **unforgettably** [-bli] *adv*

unforgivable [ˌʌnfər'gɪvəbəl] *adj* : impardonnable, inexcusable

unfortunate[1] [ˌʌn'fɔrtʃənət] *adj* **1** UNLUCKY : malchanceux **2** REGRETTABLE : malheureux, fâcheux <how unfortunate! : quel dommage!>

unfortunate[2] *n* : malheureux *m*, -reuse *f*

unfortunately [ˌʌn'fɔrtʃənətli] *adv* : malheureusement

unfounded [ˌʌn'faʊndəd] *adj* : sans fondement

unfreeze [ˌʌn'fri:z] *vt* **-froze; -frozen; -freezing 1** THAW : dégeler **2** : débloquer <to unfreeze prices : débloquer les prix>

unfriendliness [ˌʌn'frɛndlinəs] *n* : froideur *f*

unfriendly [ˌʌn'frɛndli] *adj* : peu amical, peu sympathique, froid

unfurl [ˌʌn'fərl] *vt* : dérouler, déployer — *vi* : se déployer

unfurnished [ˌʌn'fərnɪʃt] *adj* : non meublé

ungainly [ˌʌn'geɪnli] *adj* AWKWARD, CLUMSY : gauche, maladroit

ungodly [ˌʌn'gɔdli, -'gɑd-] *adj* **1** IMPIOUS : impie (en religion) **2** WICKED : mauvais, honteux **3** OUTRAGEOUS : indu, impossible <at an ungodly hour : à une heure indue>

ungracious [ˌʌn'greɪʃəs] *adj* : désobligeant, désagréable

ungrateful [ˌʌn'greɪtfəl] *adj* : ingrat

ungratefully [ˌʌn'greɪtfəli] *adv* : avec ingratitude

ungratefulness [ˌʌn'greɪtfəlnəs] *n* : ingratitude *f*

unhappily [ˌʌn'hæpəli] *adv* **1** UNFORTUNATELY : malheureusement **2** SADLY : tristement

unhappiness [ˌʌn'hæpinəs] *n* : tristesse *f*, peine *f*

unhappy [ˌʌn'hæpi] *adj* **-happier; -est 1** UNFORTUNATE : malheureux, regrettable **2** SAD : malheureux, triste **3** DISSATISFIED : mécontent

unhealthy [ˌʌn'hɛlθi] *adj* **-healthier; -est 1** UNWHOLESOME : insalubre, malsain <an unhealthy climate : un climat malsain> **2** SICKLY : malade, maladif **3** MORBID : morbid, malsain (se dit de la curiosité, etc.)

unheard–of [ˌʌn'hərdəv] *adj* : sans précédent, inconnu

unhinge [ən'hɪndʒ] *vt* **-hinged; -hinging 1** : démonter, enlever de ses gonds (une porte, une fenêtre) **2** UNBALANCE, UNSETTLE : déstabiliser, déséquilibrer (une personne)

unhitch [ˌʌn'hɪtʃ] *vt* : détacher, décrocher

unholy [ˌʌn'ho:li] *adj* **-holier; -est 1** : impie (en religion) **2** OUTRAGEOUS, SHOCKING : scandaleux, épouvantable <an unholy hour : une heure indue>

unhook [ˌʌn'hʊk] *vt* : décrocher (un tableau, etc.), dégrafer (un vêtement)

unhurried [ˌʌn'hʌrid] *adj* : qui ne se presse pas, tranquille

unhurt [ˌʌn'hərt] *adj* : indemne

unicorn ['ju:nəˌkɔrn] *n* : licorne *f*

unidentified [ˌʌnaɪ'dɛntəˌfaɪd] *adj* : non identifié <unidentified flying object : objet volant non identifié>

unification [ˌju:nəfə'keɪʃən] *n* : unification *f*

uniform[1] ['ju:nəˌfɔrm] *adj* **1** CONSTANT, UNCHANGING : uniforme, constant **2** IDENTICAL : identique

uniform[2] *n* : uniforme *m* <military uniform : uniforme militaire>

uniformity [ˌju:nə'fɔrməṭi] *n, pl* **-ties** : uniformité *f*

uniformly ['ju:nəˌfɔrmli] *adv* : uniformément

unify ['ju:nəˌfaɪ] *vt* **-fied; -fying** : unifier

unilateral [ˌju:nə'læṭərəl] *adj* : unilatéral — **unilaterally** *adv*

unimaginable [ˌʌnɪ'mædʒənəbəl] *adj* : inconcevable, inimaginable

unimportant [ˌʌnɪm'pɔrtənt] *adj* : sans importance

uninhabited [ˌʌnɪn'hæbəṭəd] *adj* : inhabité

uninhibited [ˌʌnɪn'hɪbəṭəd] *adj* : sans inhibitions, sans complexes

uninstall [ˌʌnɪn'stɔl] *vt* : désinstaller

unintelligent [ˌʌnɪn'tɛledʒənt] *adj* : inintelligent

unintelligible [ˌʌnɪn'tɛledʒəbəl] *adj* : inintelligible

unintentional [ˌʌnɪn'tɛntʃənəl] *adj* : involontaire — **unintentionally** *adv*

uninterested [ˌʌn'ɪntəˌrɛstəd, -trəstəd] *adj* : indifférent

uninteresting [ˌʌn'ɪntəˌrɛstɪŋ, -trəstɪŋ] *adj* : inintéressant, sans intérêt

uninterrupted [ˌʌnˌɪntə'rʌptəd] *adj* : ininterrompu, continu

union ['ju:njən] *n* **1** : union *f* **2** *or* **labor union** : syndicat *m*

unionize ['ju:njəˌnaɪz] *v* **-ized; -izing** *vt* : syndiquer, syndicaliser — *vi* : se syndicaliser

unique [jʊ'ni:k] *adj* **1** SOLE : unique, seul <his unique concern : son seul souci> **2** UNUSUAL : unique, particulier **3** UNEQUALED : exceptionnel, sans égal

uniquely [jʊ'ni:kli] *adv* **1** EXCLUSIVELY : uniquement, exclusivement **2** EXCEPTIONALLY : exceptionnellement

uniqueness [jʊ'ni:knəs] *n* : originalité *f*, caractère *m* unique

unison ['ju:nəsən, -zən] *n* **1** : unisson *m* <to sing in unison : chanter à l'unisson> **2 to act in unison** : agir de concert

unit[1] ['ju:nɪt] *adj* : unitaire <unit price : prix unitaire>

unit[2] *n* **1** ONE : unité *f* **2** : unité *f* <unit of measurement : unité de mesure> **3** GROUP : groupe *m*, unité *f* <research unit : groupe de recherche> **4** PART : élément *m*

unite [jʊ'naɪt] *v* **united; uniting** *vt* **1** JOIN, LINK : unir **2** UNIFY : unifier — *vi* : s'unir

unity [ˈjuːnət̬i] *n, pl* **-ties 1** ONENESS : unité *f* **2** HARMONY : unité *f*, harmonie *f*

universal [ˌjuːnəˈvərsəl] *adj* **1** GENERAL : universel, général <universal rules : des règles universelles> **2** WORLDWIDE : universel, mondial

universally [ˌjuːnəˈvərsəli] *adv* : universellement

universe [ˈjuːnəˌvərs] *n* : univers *m*

university [ˌjuːnəˈvərsət̬i] *n, pl* **-ties** : université *f*

unjust [ˌʌnˈdʒʌst] *adj* : injuste — **unjustly** *adv*

unjustifiable [ˌʌnˌdʒʌstəˈfaɪəbəl] *adj* : injustifiable

unjustified [ˌʌnˈdʒʌstəˌfaɪd] *adj* : injustifié

unkempt [ˌʌnˈkɛmpt] *adj* : en désordre, négligé, ébouriffé (se dit des cheveux)

unkind [ˌʌnˈkaɪnd] *adj* : peu aimable, pas gentil

unkindly [ˌʌnˈkaɪndli] *adv* : méchamment

unkindness [ˌʌnˈkaɪndnəs] *n* : manque *m* de gentillesse, méchanceté *f*

unknowing [ˌʌnˈnoːɪŋ] *adj* : inconscient

unknowingly [ˌʌnˈnoːɪŋli] *adv* : sans le savoir

unknown [ˌʌnˈnoːn] *adj* : inconnu

unlawful [ˌʌnˈlɔfəl] *adj* : illégal, illicite — **unlawfully** *adv*

unleash [ˌʌnˈliːʃ] *vt* **1** RELEASE : libérer, lâcher **2** : déchaîner (des passions, de la furie, etc.)

unless [ənˈlɛs] *conj* : à moins que, à moins de

unlike[1] [ˌʌnˈlaɪk] *adj* **1** DIFFERENT : dissemblable, différent **2** UNEQUAL : inégal

unlike[2] *prep* **1** : différent de <he's very unlike his brother : il est très différent de son frère> **2** : contrairement à, à la différence de <unlike him, she enjoys her work : contrairement à lui, elle aime son travail> **3** (*indicating an uncharacteristic state or action*) <it's unlike them to be late : ça n'est pas dans leur habitude d'être en retard>

unlikelihood [ˌʌnˈlaɪkliˌhʊd] *n* : improbabilité *f*

unlikely [ˌʌnˈlaɪkli] *adj* **-likelier; -est 1** IMPROBABLE : improbable, peu probable **2** UNPROMISING : peu prometteur

unlimited [ˌʌnˈlɪmət̬əd] *adj* : illimité

unload [ˌʌnˈloːd] *vt* **1** : décharger (un bateau, un fusil, de la cargaison, etc.) **2** DISPOSE OF, DUMP : se débarrasser de, se défaire de — *vi* : être déchargé

unlock [ˌʌnˈlɑk] *vt* **1** : ouvrir, débarrer *Can* (une porte, etc.) **2** DISCLOSE, REVEAL : découvrir, révéler

unluckily [ˌʌnˈlʌkəli] *adv* : malheureusement

unlucky [ˌʌnˈlʌki] *adj* **-luckier; -est 1** : malchanceux <an unlucky year : une année malchanceuse> **2** INAUSPICIOUS : qui porte malheur **3** REGRETTABLE : malencontreux, regrettable

unmanageable [ˌʌnˈmænɪdʒəbəl] *adj* : difficile à manier, peu maniable

unmarried [ˌʌnˈmærid] *adj* : non marié, célibataire

unmask [ˌʌnˈmæsk] *vt* : démasquer

unmatched [ˌʌnˈmætʃt] *adj* : sans égal, incomparable

unmerciful [ˌʌnˈmərsɪfəl] *adj* : sans merci, impitoyable

unmercifully [ˌʌnˈmərsɪfəl] *adv* : impitoyablement

unmistakable [ˌʌnmɪˈsteɪkəbəl] *adj* : évident, indubitable

unmistakably [ˌʌnmɪˈsteɪkəbli] *adv* : indubitablement

unmoved [ˌʌnˈmuːvd] *adj* : indifférent, insensible

unnatural [ˌʌnˈnætʃərəl] *adj* **1** ABNORMAL, UNUSUAL : anormal, peu naturel **2** AFFECTED : artificiel, affecté **3** PERVERSE : pervers, contre nature

unnaturally [ˌʌnˈnætʃərəli] *adv* : anormalement, de façon peu naturelle

unnecessarily [ˌʌnˌnɛsəˈsɛrəli] *adv* : inutilement, sans raison

unnecessary [ˌʌnˈnɛsəˌsɛri] *adj* : inutile, superflu

unnerve [ˌʌnˈnərv] *vt* **-nerved; -nerving** : décontenancer, déconcerter, rendre nerveux

unnoticeable [ˌʌnˈnoːt̬əsəbəl] *adj* : imperceptible

unnoticed [ˌʌnˈnoːt̬əst] *adj* : inaperçu

unobstructed [ˌʌnəbˈstrʌktəd] *adj* : non obstrué, dégagé

unobtainable [ˌʌnəbˈteɪnəbəl] *adj* : introuvable, impossible à obtenir

unobtrusive [ˌʌnəbˈtruːsɪv] *adj* : discret, pas trop visible

unoccupied [ˌʌnˈɑkjəˌpaɪd] *adj* **1** IDLE : inoccupé, oisif **2** EMPTY : libre, vacant

unofficial [ˌʌnəˈfɪʃəl] *adj* : officieux, non officiel

unorganized [ˌʌnˈɔrgəˌnaɪzd] *adj* : mal organisé, inorganisé

unorthodox [ˌʌnˈɔrθəˌdɑks] *adj* : peu orthodoxe

unpack [ˌʌnˈpæk] *vt* : défaire, déballer <to unpack one's suitcase : défaire sa valise> — *vi* : défaire ses bagages

unpaid [ˌʌnˈpeɪd] *adj* **1** : impayé (se dit d'une facture), non acquitté (se dit d'une dette) **2** : bénévole, non rémunéré <unpaid assistants : assistants bénévoles>

unparalleled [ˌʌnˈpærəˌlɛld] *adj* : sans égal, sans pareil

unpatriotic [ˌʌnˌpeɪtriˈɑtɪk] *adj* : peu patriote

unpleasant [ˌʌnˈplɛzənt] *adj* : désagréable, déplaisant

unpleasantly [ˌʌnˈplɛzəntli] *adv* : désagréablement, de façon déplaisante
unplug [ˌʌnˈplʌg] *vt* **-plugged; -plugging 1** UNCLOG : déboucher **2** DISCONNECT : débrancher, déconnecter
unpopular [ˌʌnˈpɑpjələr] *adj* : impopulaire, peu populaire
unpopularity [ˌʌnˌpɑpjəˈlærət̬i] *n* : impopularité *f*
unprecedented [ˌʌnˈprɛsəˌdɛntəd] *adj* : sans précédent
unpredictable [ˌʌnprɪˈdɪktəbəl] *adj* : imprévisible
unprejudiced [ˌʌnˈprɛdʒədəst] *adj* : sans préjugés, sans parti pris, impartial
unprepared [ˌʌnpriˈpærd] *adj* : mal préparé
unpretentious [ˌʌnpriˈtɛntʃəs] *adj* : sans prétention
unprincipled [ˌʌnˈprɪntsəpəld] *adj* : sans scrupules
unproductive [ˌʌnprəˈdʌktɪv] *adj* : improductif
unprofitable [ˌʌnˈprɑfət̬əbəl] *adj* **1** : non rentable (se dit d'une entreprise, etc.) **2** VAIN : peu profitable, inutile
unpromising [ˌʌnˈprɑməsɪŋ] *adj* : peu prometteur
unprotected [ˌʌnprəˈtɛktəd] *adj* **1** : sans protection **2** EXPOSED : exposé
unprovoked [ˌʌnprəˈvoːkt] *adj* : sans provocation, délibéré
unpunished [ˌʌnˈpʌnɪʃt] *adj* : impuni <to go unpunished : rester impuni>
unqualified [ˌʌnˈkwɑləˌfaɪd] *adj* **1** UNFIT : non qualifié, incompétent **2** COMPLETE : sans réserve, inconditionnel <an unqualified denial : un démenti sans réserve>
unquestionable [ˌʌnˈkwɛstʃənəbəl] *adj* : incontestable, indéniable
unquestionably [ˌʌnˈkwɛstʃənəbli] *adv* : incontestablement, sans aucun doute
unquestioning [ˌʌnˈkwɛstʃənɪŋ] *adj* : inconditionnel, absolu
unravel [ˌʌnˈrævəl] *v* **-eled** *or* **-elled; -eling** *or* **elling** *vt* **1** DISENTANGLE : démêler **2** SOLVE : résoudre, éclaircir <to unravel a mystery : résoudre un mystère> — *vi* : se démêler
unreal [ˌʌnˈriːl] *adj* : irréel
unrealistic [ˌʌnˌriːəˈlɪstɪk] *adj* : peu réaliste, irréaliste
unreality [ˌʌnriˈælət̬i] *n* : irréalité *f*
unreasonable [ˌʌnˈriːzənəbel] *adj* **1** SENSELESS : déraisonnable **2** EXCESSIVE : excessif, démesuré
unreasonably [ˌʌnˈriːzənəbli] *adv* **1** SENSELESSLY : déraisonnablement **2** EXCESSIVELY : excessivement
unrelated [ˌʌnrɪˈleɪt̬əd] *adj* : sans rapport
unrelenting [ˌʌnrɪˈlɛntɪŋ] *adj* **1** STERN : dur, implacable **2** CONSTANT : continuel
unrelentingly [ˌʌnrɪˈlɛntɪŋli] *adv* : sans répit
unreliable [ˌʌnrɪˈlaɪəbəl] *adj* : peu fidèle, peu sûr
unrepentant [ˌʌnrɪˈpɛntənt] *adj* : impénitent
unresolved [ˌʌnriˈzɑlvd] *adj* : non résolu
unrest [ˌʌnˈrɛst] *n* : agitation *f*, troubles *mpl* <social unrest : malaise social>
unrestrained [ˌʌnrɪˈstreɪnd] *adj* : effréné, non contenu
unrestricted [ˌʌnrɪˈstrɪktəd] *adj* : libre, illimité <unrestricted access : libre accès>
unrewarding [ˌʌnrɪˈwɔrdɪŋ] *adj* THANKLESS : ingrat
unripe [ˌʌnˈraɪp] *adj* : pas mûr, vert
unrivaled *or* **unrivalled** [ˌʌnˈraɪvəld] *adj* : sans égal, incomparable
unroll [ˌʌnˈroːl] *vt* : dérouler — *vi* : se dérouler
unruffled [ˌʌnˈrʌfəld] *adj* **1** : imperturbable (se dit d'une personne) **2** SMOOTH : calme <unruffled waters : eaux calmes>
unruly [ˌʌnˈruːli] *adj* : indiscipliné
unsafe [ˌʌnˈseɪf] *adj* **1** DANGEROUS : dangereux **2 to feel unsafe** : ne pas se sentir en sécurité, se sentir en danger
unsaid [ˌʌnˈsɛd] *adj* : inexprimé, non dit <to leave unsaid : passer sous silence>
unsanitary [ˌʌnˈsænəˌtɛri] *adj* : peu hygiénique
unsatisfactory [ˌʌnˌsætəsˈfæktəri] *adj* : peu satisfaisant
unsatisfied [ˌʌnˈsætəsˌfaɪd] *adj* : peu satisfait, insatisfait
unsavory [ˌʌnˈseɪvəri] *adj* **1** TASTELESS : peu savoureux, insipide **2** DISTASTEFUL : désagréable
unscathed [ˌʌnˈskeɪðd] *adj* UNHARMED : indemne
unscheduled [ˌʌnˈskɛˌdʒuːld] *adj* : imprévu
unscientific [ˌʌnˌsaɪənˈtɪfɪk] *adj* : non scientifique
unscrew [ˌʌnˈskruː] *vt* : dévisser
unscrupulous [ˌʌnˈskruːpjələs] *adj* : sans scrupules, peu scrupuleux
unscrupulously [ˌʌnˈskruːpjələsli] *adv* : sans scrupules, peu scrupuleusement
unseal [ˌʌnˈsiːl] *vt* : décacheter (une enveloppe, etc.)
unseasonable [ˌʌnˈsiːzənəbəl] *adj* **1** UNTIMELY : inopportun, mal choisi **2** : hors de saison <unseasonable weather : température qui n'est pas de saison>
unseemly [ˌʌnˈsiːmli] *adj* **-seemlier; -est 1** UNBECOMING : inconvenant **2** INAPPROPRIATE : inapproprié
unseen [ˌʌnˈsiːn] *adj* : invisible, inaperçu
unselfish [ˌʌnˈsɛlfɪʃ] *adj* : désintéressé, généreux

unselfishly [ˌʌn'sɛlfɪʃli] *adv* : généreusement, de façon désintéressée

unselfishness [ˌʌn'sɛlfɪʃnəs] *n* : générosité *f*, désintéressement *m*

unsettle [ˌʌn'sɛṭəl] *vt* **-tled; -tling 1** UPSET : déranger (l'estomac) **2** DISTURB : perturber, troubler

unsettled [ˌʌn'sɛtəld] *adj* **1** DISTURBED : perturbé, troublé **2** VARIABLE : changeant, variable <unsettled weather : temps variable> **3** DOUBTFUL, UNDECIDED : incertain, non résolu **4** UNPAID : impayé, non réglé **5** UNINHABITED : inhabité

unsightly [ˌʌn'saɪtli] *adj* : laid, disgracieux

unskilled [ˌʌn'skɪld] *adj* : non qualifié, non spécialisé

unskillful [ˌʌn'skɪlfəl] *adj* : malhabile, inexpert

unsociable [ˌʌn'so:ʃəbəl] *adj* : peu sociable, insociable

unsolved [ˌʌn'sɔlvd] *adj* : non résolu

unsophisticated [ˌʌnsə'fɪstəˌkeɪṭəd] *adj* : peu sophistiqué, simple

unsound [ˌʌn'saʊnd] *adj* **1** : peu judicieux (se dit d'une idée), instable (se dit d'une structure) **2 to be of unsound mind** : ne pas avoir toute sa raison

unspeakable [ˌʌn'spi:kəbəl] *adj* **1** INEXPRESSIBLE : indescriptible, indicible **2** ATROCIOUS : innommable, atroce

unspeakably [ˌʌn'spi:kəbli] *adv* **1** INEXPRESSIBLY : indiciblement **2** ATROCIOUSLY : atrocement

unspecified [ˌʌn'spɛsəˌfaɪd] *adj* : non spécifié

unspoiled [ˌʌn'spɔɪld] *adj* **1** : qui n'a pas été gâté (se dit d'un enfant) **2** : intact, naturel, vierge <unspoiled scenery : paysage intact>

unstable [ˌʌn'steɪbəl] *adj* : instable

unsteadily [ˌʌn'stɛdəli] *adv* : d'un pas chancelant, d'une main tremblante, d'une voix mal assurée

unsteady [ˌʌn'stɛdi] *adj* **1** : instable, branlant (se dit d'une structure, etc.) **2** SHAKY : tremblant, chancelant, mal assuré **3** IRREGULAR : irrégulier

unstoppable [ˌʌn'stɑpəbəl] *adj* : irrésistible, qu'on ne peut pas arrêter

unsubstantiated [ˌʌnsəb'stæntʃiˌeɪṭəd] *adj* : non confirmé, non corroboré

unsuccessful [ˌʌnsək'sɛsfəl] *adj* : infructueux, qui n'a pas réussi

unsuitable [ˌʌn'su:ṭəbəl] *adj* : qui ne convient pas, inconvenant, inapproprié <an unsuitable time : un moment inopportun>

unsuited [ˌʌn'su:ṭəd] *adj* : inadapté, mal adapté, inapproprié

unsung [ˌʌn'sʌŋ] *adj* : méconnu

unsure [ˌʌn'ʃʊr] *adj* : incertain, pas sûr <to be unsure of oneself : manquer de confiance en soi>

unsurpassed [ˌʌnsər'pæst] *adj* : sans pareil, sans égal

unsuspecting [ˌʌnsə'spɛktɪŋ] *adj* : qui ne se doute de rien, sans méfiance

unsympathetic [ˌʌnˌsɪmpə'θɛṭɪk] *adj* : incompréhensif, peu compatissant

untangle [ˌʌn'tæŋgəl] *vt* **-gled; -gling 1** : démêler (des fils, etc.), débrouiller (un problème, un mystère)

unthinkable [ˌʌn'θɪŋkəbəl] *adj* : impensable, inconcevable

unthinking [ˌʌn'θɪŋkɪŋ] *adj* : irréfléchi, inconsidéré

unthinkingly [ˌʌn'θɪŋkɪŋli] *adv* : inconsidérément, sans réfléchir

untidy [ˌʌn'taɪdi] *adj* **-tidier; -est 1** : désordonné, débraillé (se dit d'une personne) **2** : en désordre <an untidy room : une chambre en désordre>

untie [ˌʌn'taɪ] *vt* **-tied; -tying** *or* **-tieing 1** : défaire, dénouer <to untie a knot : défaire un nœud> **2** : délier, détacher (des mains, un prisonnier, etc.)

until[1] [ˌʌn'tɪl] *conj* : jusqu'à ce que, avant que, avant de <boil the eggs until cooked : bouillez les œufs jusqu'à ce qu'ils soient cuits> <don't speak until I tell you to : ne parlez pas avant que je ne vous le dise> <until I saw him : avant de l'avoir vu> <wait until I call : attend que j'appelle>

until[2] *prep* **1** UP TO : jusqu'à <I worked until noon : j'ai travaillé jusqu'à midi> **2** BEFORE : avant <it won't be available until tomorrow : ça ne sera pas disponible avant demain> <we don't open until ten : nous ouvrons à dix heures seulement>

untimely [ˌʌn'taɪmli] *adj* **1** PREMATURE : précoce, prématuré <an untimely death : une mort prématurée> **2** INOPPORTUNE : inopportun, déplacé

untold [ˌʌn'to:ld] *adj* **1** : jamais raconté <untold stories : des histoires jamais racontées> **2** VAST : incalculable, indicible

untouched [ˌʌn'tʌtʃt] *adj* **1** INTACT : intact, qui n'a pas été touché **2** UNHARMED : indemne **3** UNAFFECTED : non affecté

untoward [ˌʌn'tɔrd, -'to:ərd, -tə'wɔrd] *adj* **1** UNFORTUNATE : fâcheux, malencontreux **2** UNSEEMLY : inconvenant

untrained [ˌʌn'treɪnd] *adj* **1** : sans formation **2 to the untrained eye** : pour un œil inexercé

untreated [ˌʌn'tri:ṭəd] *adj* : non traité

untroubled [ˌʌn'trʌbəld] *adj* **1** : paisible, tranquille <untroubled waters : eaux paisibles> **2 to be untroubled by** : ne pas être affecté par

untrue [ˌʌn'tru:] *adj* **1** DISLOYAL : infidèle, déloyal **2** FALSE : faux, erroné

untruth [ˌʌn'tru:θ, 'ʌn-] *n* **1** FALSITY : fausseté *f* **2** LIE : mensonge *m*

untruthful [ˌʌnˈtruːθfəl] *adj* **1** FALSE : faux, inexact **2** DISHONEST : malhonnête
unusable [ˌʌnˈjuːzəbəl] *adj* : inutilisable
unused *adj* [ˌʌnˈjuːzd, *in sense* **1** *usually* -ˈjuːst] **1** UNACCUSTOMED : pas habitué **2** NEW : neuf, nouveau **3** IDLE : inutilisé **4** ACCRUED : cumulé
unusual [ˌʌnˈjuːʒʊəl] *adj* : peu commun, rare
unusually [ˌʌnˈjuːʒʊəli] *adv* : exceptionnellement
unwanted [ˌʌnˈwɑntəd] *adj* : non désiré, superflu
unwarranted [ˌʌnˈwɔrəntəd] *adj* : injustifié
unwary [ˌʌnˈwæri] *adj* : qui ne se méfie pas, sans méfiance
unwavering [ˌʌnˈweɪvərɪŋ] *adj* : ferme, inébranlable <an unwavering gaze : un regard fixe>
unwelcome [ˌʌnˈwɛlkəm] *adj* : inopportun, fâcheux
unwell [ˌʌnˈwɛl] *adj* : souffrant, malade, mal-en-train *Can*
unwholesome [ˌʌnˈhoːlsəm] *adj* **1** UNHEALTHY : malsain, insalubre **2** PERNICIOUS : pernicieux, nocif
unwieldy [ˌʌnˈwiːldi] *adj* CUMBERSOME : difficile à manier, encombrant
unwilling [ˌʌnˈwɪlɪŋ] *adj* : réticent, peu disposé
unwillingly [ˌʌnˈwɪlɪŋli] *adv* : à contrecœur
unwind [ˌʌnˈwaɪnd] *v* **-wound; -winding** *vt* UNROLL : dérouler — *vi* **1** : se dérouler **2** RELAX : se détendre
unwise [ˌʌnˈwaɪz] *adj* : imprudent, peu judicieux
unwisely [ˌʌnˈwaɪzli] *adv* : imprudemment
unwitting [ˌʌnˈwɪt̬ɪŋ] *adj* **1** UNAWARE : inconscient **2** INADVERTENT : involontaire
unwittingly [ˌʌnˈwɪt̬ɪŋli] *adv* **1** UNCONSCIOUSLY : inconsciemment **2** INADVERTENTLY : involontairement
unworthiness [ˌʌnˈwərðinəs] *n* : indignité *f*
unworthy [ˌʌnˈwərði] *adj* **1** UNDESERVING : indigne **2** UNMERITED : peu méritant
unwrap [ˌʌnˈræp] *vt* **-wrapped; -wrapped** : déballer
unwritten [ˌʌnˈrɪtən] *adj* : tacite, non écrit
unyielding [ˌʌnˈjiːldɪŋ] *adj* **1** STIFF : dur, ferme **2** ADAMANT : qui ne cède pas, inflexible
unzip [ˌʌnˈzɪp] *vt* **-zipped; -zipping** : défaire la fermeture à glissière de
up[1] [ˈʌp] *v* **upped; upping** *vt* **1** INCREASE : augmenter <they upped the prices : ils ont augmenté les prix> — *vi* (*used with* and *and another verb to indicate surprising or abrupt action*) <she up and left : elle est partie sans mot dire> <he up and married her : il l'a épousée sur-le-champ>
up[2] *adv* **1** (*in or to a higher position or level*) <the oil shot up 200 feet : le pétrole jaillissait du sol et atteignait 200 pieds de hauteur> **2** (*from beneath a surface or level*) <the fish swam up : les poissons montaient à la surface de l'eau> **3** (*in or into an upright position*) <we stayed up all night : nous avons veillé toute la nuit> <get up! : levez-vous!> **4** (*with greater intensity*) <speak up! : parlez plus fort!> **5** (*in continuance from a point or to a point*) <from third grade up : à partir de la troisième année> <at prices of $10 and up : à des prix de 10 $ et plus> <up until now : jusqu'à maintenant> **6** (*into existence, evidence, prominence, or prevalence*) <they put up several new buildings : ils ont construit plusieurs nouveaux immeubles> **7** (*into consideration or attention*) <we brought the matter up : nous avons soulevé la question> **8** COMPLETELY, ENTIRELY : au complet <button up your coat : boutonne ton manteau jusqu'au cou> **9** (*used as an intensifier*) <we cleaned up the house : nous avons nettoyé la maison> **10** (*so as to arrive or approach*) <he walked up to me and said "hello" : il s'est approché de moi et m'a dit «bonjour»> **11** (*in or into parts*) <she tore up the paper : elle a déchiré le papier en petits morceaux> **12** (*to a stop*) <he pulled up to the curb : il s'est garé le long de la courbe> **13** (*for each side*) <the score was 15 up : le score était nul avec 15 points pour chaque équipe>
up[3] *adj* **1** RISEN : levé (se dit du soleil) **2** RISING : en crue (se dit d'une rivière) **3** AWAKE, STANDING : levé, debout <he's up at 6 o'clock : il se lève à 6h> **4** LIFTED : levé, ouvert <the windows were up : les fenêtres étaient ouvertes> **5** BUILT : construit <the houses are up : la construction des maisons est terminée> **6** : qui pousse <the corn was up : le maïs poussait> **7** : qui monte <the up escalator : l'escalier mécanique qui monte> **8** INCREASING : qui augmente <attendance is up at the meetings : le nombre de personnes qui assiste aux réunions a augmenté> <the wind is up : le vent s'est levé> **9** READY : prêt <the team was up for the game : l'équipe était prête pour le match> **10** : qui se passe <what's up? : qu'est-ce qui se passe?> **11** UP-TO-DATE : au courant, à jour <to be up on the news : être au courant des nouvelles> <he was up on his homework : il était à jour dans ses devoirs> **12** EXPIRED : expiré, terminé <the

contract was up in June : le contrat s'est terminé en juin>

up[4] *n* **1 to be on the up** : être en train d'augmenter **2 ups and downs** : fluctuations *fpl*

up[5] *prep* **1** (*to, toward, or at a higher point of*) <she went up the stairs : elle a monté l'escalier> **2** (*to or toward the source of*) <to sail up the river : remonter la rivière en bateau> **3** (*near or toward the end of*) <to walk up the street : monter la rue> <we live a few miles up the coast : nous demeurons à quelques milles de la côte> **4** → **up to**

upbraid [ˌʌpˈbreɪd] *vt* : reprocher, réprimander

upbringing [ˈʌpˌbrɪŋɪŋ] *n* : éducation *f*

upcoming [ˌʌpˈkʌmɪŋ] *adj* : prochain, à venir

update[1] [ˌʌpˈdeɪt] *vt* **-dated; -dating** : mettre à jour, actualiser

update[2] [ˈʌpˌdeɪt] *n* : mise *f* à jour

upend [ˌʌpˈɛnd] *vt* **1** : mettre debout **2** OVERTURN : retourner, renverser

upgrade[1] [ˈʌpˌgreɪd, ˌʌp'-] *vt* **-graded; -grading** : améliorer (un produit), promouvoir (un employé)

upgrade[2] [ˈʌpˌgreɪd] *n* **1** SLOPE : pente *f* ascendante, montée *f* **2 to be on the upgrade** : monter, être en hausse

upheaval [ˌʌpˈhiːvəl] *n* **1** : soulèvement *m* (de la croûte terrestre) **2** COMMOTION : bouleversement *m*, remue-ménage *m*

uphill[1] [ˌʌpˈhɪl] *adv* **to go uphill** : monter, aller en montant

uphill[2] [ˈʌpˌhɪl] *adj* **1** ASCENDING : montant, qui monte **2** DIFFICULT : pénible, difficile

uphold [ˌʌpˈhoːld] *vt* **-held; -holding 1** SUPPORT : soutenir, défendre **2** RAISE : soutenir, élever **3** CONFIRM : confirmer, maintenir (en droit)

upholster [ˌʌpˈhoːlstər] *vt* **1** STUFF : rembourrer **2** COVER : tapisser, recouvrir

upholsterer [ˌʌpˈhoːlstərər] *n* : tapissier *m*, -sière *f*

upholstery [ˌʌpˈhoːlstəri] *n, pl* **-steries 1** STUFFING : rembourrage *m* **2** COVERING : tissu *m* d'ameublement, revêtement *m*

upkeep [ˈʌpˌkiːp] *n* : entretien *m*

upland [ˈʌplənd, -ˈlænd] *n* **1** : plateau *m* **2 the uplands** : les hautes terres

uplift[1] [ˌʌpˈlɪft] *vt* **1** RAISE : soulever, élever **2** : remonter, encourager <to uplift s.o.'s spirits : remonter le moral de qqn>

uplift[2] [ˈʌpˌlɪft] *n* **1** : élévation *f*, soulèvement *m* **2** IMPROVEMENT : amélioration *f*

upon [əˈpɔn, əˈpɑn] *prep* : sur, à <upon the table : sur la table> <upon our departure : à notre départ> <questions upon questions : des questions et des questions>

upper[1] [ˈʌpər] *adj* **1** : supérieur <the upper lip : la lèvre supérieure> **2** : plus haut, plus élevé <the upper classes : l'aristocratie> **3** NORTHERN : haut (en géographie) <the upper Mississippi : la haute Mississippi>

upper[2] *n* : empeigne *f* (d'un soulier)

upper hand *n* **to have the upper hand** : avoir le dessus

uppermost [ˈʌpərˌmoːst] *adj* **1** HIGHEST : le plus haut, le plus élevé **2** : de la plus haute importance <it was uppermost in my mind : ça me préoccupait par-dessus tout>

upright[1] [ˈʌpˌraɪt] *adv* : droit <to stand upright : se tenir droit>

upright[2] *adj* **1** PERPENDICULAR : vertical **2** ERECT : debout, droit <an upright freezer : un congélateur armoire> **3** JUST : honnête, droit

upright[3] *n* **1** : montant *m* (en construction) **2** *or* **upright piano** : piano *m* droit

uprightly [ˈʌpˌraɪtli] *adv* : honnêtement

uprising [ˈʌpˌraɪzɪŋ] *n* : soulèvement *m*, révolte *f*

uproar [ˈʌpˌroːr] *n* : tumulte *m*, vacarme *m*

uproarious [ˌʌpˈroriəs] *adj* **1** NOISY : bruyant **2** HILARIOUS : désopilant, comique

uproariously [ˌʌpˈroriəsli] *adv* : aux éclats

uproot [ˌʌpˈruːt, -ˈrʊt] *vt* : déraciner

upset[1] [ˌʌpˈsɛt] *vt* **-set; -setting 1** OVERTURN : renverser **2** DISTURB, TROUBLE : déranger, perturber **3** SICKEN : rendre malade <the food upset my stomach : la nourriture m'a dérangé l'estomac> **4** DISRUPT : déranger, bouleverser (des plans, etc.)

upset[2] *adj* **1** DISTRESSED : attristé, peiné **2** ANNOYED : ennuyé, contrarié **3** : dérangé (se dit de l'estomac)

upset[3] [ˈʌpˌsɛt] *n* **1** OVERTURNING : renversement *m* **2** DISRUPTION : bouleversement *m* (des plans) **3** DEFEAT : revers *m* (aux sports)

upshot [ˈʌpˌʃɑt] *n* : résultat *m*

upside–down [ˌʌpˌsaɪdˈdaʊn] *adj* : à l'envers

upside down *adv* **1** : à l'envers <turn the card upside down : tournez la carte à l'envers> **2** : sens dessus dessous <she turned the room upside down : elle a mis la pièce sens dessus dessous>

upstairs[1] [ˌʌpˈstærz] *adv* : en haut

upstairs[2] [ˈʌpˌstærz, ˌʌp'-] *adj* : d'en haut, à l'étage

upstairs[3] [ˈʌpˌstærz, ˌʌp'-] *ns & pl* : étage *m* (du haut)

upstanding [ˌʌpˈstændɪŋ, ˈʌpˌ-] *adj* : honnête, intègre

upstart [ˈʌpˌstɑrt] *n* : parvenu *m*, -nue *f*; arriviste *mf*

upstream [ˈʌpˈstriːm] *adv* : en amont

upswing [ˈʌpˌswɪŋ] *n* **1** : mouvement *m* ascendant **2** IMPROVEMENT : amélioration *f* notable
uptight [ˌʌpˈtaɪt] *adj* **1** TENSE : tendu, crispé, pogné *Can* **2** INDIGNANT : indigné, outré **3** REPRESSED : coincé *fam*
up to *prep* **1** : jusqu'à <in water up to my ankles : dans l'eau jusqu'aux chevilles> <up to here : jusqu'ici> **2 to be up to** : être à <if it were up to me : si c'était à moi de décider> **3 to be up to** : être capable de <he's not up to studying : il n'est pas en état d'étudier>
up–to–date [ˌʌptəˈdeɪt] *adj* **1** CURRENT : à jour <up-to-date maps : des cartes à jour> <to stay up-to-date : se tenir au courant> **2** MODERN : moderne
uptown [ˈʌpˈtaʊn] *adv* : dans les quartiers résidentiels
upturn [ˈʌpˌtərn] *n* : amélioration *f*, reprise *f* (économique)
upward[1] [ˈʌpwərd] *or* **upwards** [-wərdz] *adv* **1** : vers le haut, en montant **2** (*used to express continuance from a point*) <from $ 5 upward : à partir de 5 $>
upward[2] *adj* ASCENDING : ascendant <upward mobility : ascension sociale>
upwardly [ˈʌpwərdli] *adv* : vers le haut
upwind[1] [ˌʌpˈwɪnd] *adv* : contre le vent
upwind[2] *adj* **to be upwind of** : être dans le vent par rapport à
uranium [jʊˈreɪniəm] *n* : uranium *m*
Uranus [jʊˈreɪnəs, ˈjʊrənəs] *n* : Uranus *f*
urban [ˈərbən] *adj* : urbain, de ville
urbane [ˌərˈbeɪn] *adj* : raffiné, courtois
urchin [ˈərtʃən] *n* : polisson *m*, -sonne *f*
urethra [jʊˈriːθrə] *n, pl* **-thras** *or* **-thrae** [-ˌθriː] : urètre *m*
urge[1] [ˈərdʒ] *vt* **urged; urging 1** PUSH : pousser <we urged him to tell the truth : nous l'avons poussé à dire la vérité> **2** ADVOCATE : conseiller, préconiser **3 to urge on** : presser, faire avancer
urge[2] *n* : désir *m*, (forte) envie *f*
urgency [ˈərdʒəntsi] *n, pl* **-cies** : urgence *f*
urgent [ˈərdʒənt] *adj* **1** PRESSING : urgent, pressant **2** INSISTENT : insistant
urgently [ˈərdʒəntli] *adv* : d'urgence
urinal [ˈjʊrənəl, *esp Brit* jʊˈraɪnəl] *n* : urinoir *m*
urinary [ˈjʊrəˌnɛri] *adj* : urinaire
urinate [ˈjʊrəˌneɪt] *vi* **-nated; -nating** : uriner
urination [ˌjʊrəˈneɪʃən] *n* : urination *f*
urine [ˈjʊrən] *n* : urine *f*
urn [ˈərn] *n* **1** VASE : urne *f* **2** : fontaine *f* (à café)
Uruguayan[1] [ˌʊrəˈgwaɪən, ˌjʊr-, -ˈgweɪ-] *adj* : uruguayen
Uruguayan[2] *n* : Uruguayen *m*, -guayenne *f*
us [ˈʌs] *pron* **1** (*used as a direct object of a verb*) <they were visiting us : ils nous rendaient visite> **2** (*used as an indirect object of a verb*) <give us some time : donnez-nous du temps> **3** (*used as the object of a preposition*) <in front of us : devant nous>
usable [ˈjuːzəbəl] *adj* : utilisable
usage [ˈjuːsɪdʒ, -zɪdʒ] *n* **1** HABIT, PRACTICE : usage *m*, coutume *f* **2** : usage *m* (en linguistique) **3** USE : utilisation *f*, consommation *f*
use[1] [ˈjuːz] *v* **used** [ˈjuːzd; *in phrase "used to" usually* ˈjuːstuː]; **using** *vt* **1** EMPLOY : utiliser, se servir de **2** CONSUME : consommer <use before April : à consommer avant avril> **3** TREAT : traiter <they used the prisoners cruelly : ils ont traité les prisonniers avec cruauté> **4** EXPLOIT : se servir de, profiter de <he used his friends to get ahead : il s'est servi de ses amis afin d'avancer> **5 to use up** : épuiser, consommer — *vi* (*used in the past tense with* to *to indicate a former fact or state*) <she didn't use to smoke : elle ne fumait pas avant>
use[2] [ˈjuːs] *n* **1** APPLICATION, EMPLOYMENT : utilisation *f* **2** : usage *m*, jouissance *f* (d'un bien) <to have use of the beach : avoir la jouissance de la plage> <to lose the use of a limb : perdre l'usage d'un membre> **3** USEFULNESS : utilité *f* <it's no use : c'est inutile, ça ne sert à rien> <what's the use of complaining : à quoi bon se plaindre> **4** NEED : usage *m*, besoin *m* <they didn't have use for it : ils n'en avaient pas besoin>
used [ˈjuːzd] *adj* **1** SECONDHAND : usagé, de seconde main **2** ACCUSTOMED : habitué <not used to all the attention : pas habitué à recevoir autant d'attention>
useful [ˈjuːsfəl] *adj* : utile, pratique
usefully [ˈjuːsfəli] *adv* : utilement
usefulness [ˈjuːsfəlnəs] *n* : utilité *f*
useless [ˈjuːsləs] *adj* : inutile — **uselessly** *adv*
uselessness [ˈjuːsləsnəs] *n* : inutilité *f*
user [ˈjuːzər] *n* : usager *m*; utilisateur *m*, -trice *f* (d'un ordinateur)
user–friendly [ˌjuːzərˈfrɛndli] *adj* : facile à utiliser, convivial (en informatique)
usher[1] [ˈʌʃər] *vt* **1** ESCORT : conduire, accompagner <to usher s.o. in : faire entrer qqn> **2 to usher in** : inaugurer
usher[2] *n* : huissier *m* (à un tribunal); placeur *m*, -ceuse *f* (au théâtre)
usherette [ˌʌʃəˈrɛt] *n* : ouvreuse *f*
usual [ˈjuːʒʊəl] *adj* : CUSTOMARY, NORMAL : habituel <our usual route : notre chemin habituel> <more than usual : plus que d'habitude> <as usual : comme d'habitude>

usually [ˈjuːʒʊəli] *adv* : habituellement, d'habitude, normalement
usurp [jʊˈsərp, -ˈzərp] *vt* : usurper
usurper [jʊˈsərpər, -ˈzər-] *n* : usurpateur *m*, -trice *f*
utensil [jʊˈtɛntsəl] *n* : ustensile *m* (de cuisine, de jardinage, etc.)
uterine [ˈjuːtəˌraɪn, -rən] *adj* : utérin
uterus [ˈjuːt̬ərəs] *n, pl* **uteri** [-ˌraɪ] : utérus *m*
utilitarian [juːˌtɪləˈtɛriən] *adj* : utilitaire
utility [juːˈtɪlət̬i] *n, pl* **-ties 1** USEFULNESS : utilité *f* **2** *or* **public utility** : service *m* public
utilization [ˌjuːt̬ələˈzeɪʃən] *n* : utilisation *f*
utilize [ˈjuːt̬əlˌaɪz] *vt* **-lized; -lizing** : utiliser
utmost[1] [ˈʌtˌmoːst] *adj* **1** EXTREME : extrême <the utmost point of the earth : le bout de la terre> **2** : capital, important <a matter of utmost concern : une question de la plus haute importance>
utmost[2] *n* **1** : plus haut degré *m*, plus haut point *m* <the utmost in reliability : ce qu'il y a de plus fiable> **2 to do one's utmost** : faire son possible
utopia [jʊˈtoːpiə] *n* : utopie *f*
utopian [jʊˈtoːpiən] *adj* : utopique
utter[1] [ˈʌtər] *vt* : exprimer, prononcer (un mot), pousser (un cri)
utter[2] *adj* : absolu, total, complet <utter darkness : obscurité totale>
utterly [ˈʌtərli] *adv* : complètement
utterance [ˈʌt̬ərənts] *n* : déclaration *f*, paroles *fpl*

V

v [ˈviː] *n, pl* **v's** *or* **vs** [ˈviːz] : v *m*, vingt-deuxième lettre de l'alphabet
vacancy [ˈveɪkəntsi] *n, pl* **-cies 1** : chambre *f* disponible (dans un hôtel) <no vacancies : complet> **2** : poste *m* vacant <to fill a vacancy : pourvoir un poste> **3** EMPTINESS : vide *m*
vacant [ˈveɪkənt] *adj* **1** EMPTY : vide, inoccupé **2** UNOCCUPIED : libre (se dit d'une chambre), vacant (se dit d'un poste) **3** DISTRACTED : distrait, absent <a vacant smile : un sourire absent>
vacate [ˈveɪˌkeɪt] *vt* **-cated; -cating** : quitter, libérer (une chambre) <to vacate the premises : vider les lieux>
vacation[1] [veɪˈkeɪʃən, və-] *vi* : prendre des vacances
vacation[2] *n* : vacances *fpl*, congé *m*
vacationer [veɪˈkeɪʃənər, və-] *n* : vacancier *m*, -cière *f*
vaccinate [ˈvæksəˌneɪt] *vt* **-nated; -nating** : vacciner
vaccination [ˌvæksəˈneɪʃən] *n* : vaccination *f*
vaccine [vækˈsiːn, ˈvækˌ-] *n* : vaccin *m*
vacillate [ˈvæsəˌleɪt] *vi* **-lated; -lating 1** SWAY : vaciller, perdre son équilibre **2** HESITATE : hésiter
vacillation [ˌvæsəˈleɪʃən] *n* : hésitation *f*, indécision *f*
vacuous [ˈvækjʊəs] *adj* **1** BLANK, EMPTY : vide **2** INANE : stupide, idiot
vacuum[1] [ˈvæˌkjuːm, -kjəm] *vt* : passer l'aspirateur dans (un tapis, etc.)
vacuum[2] *n, pl* **vacuums** *or* **vacua** [ˈvækjʊə] **1** VOID : vide *m* **2** → **vacuum cleaner**
vacuum cleaner *n* : aspirateur *m*, balayeuse *f Can*
vagabond[1] [ˈvægəˌbɑnd] *adj* : vagabond, errant
vagabond[2] *n* : vagabond *m*, -bonde *f*
vagary [ˈveɪgəri, vəˈgɛri] *n, pl* **-ries** : caprice *m*
vagina [vəˈdʒaɪnə] *n, pl* **-nae** [-ˌniː, -ˌnaɪ] *or* **-nas** : vagin *m*
vaginal [ˈvædʒənəl] *adj* : vaginal
vagrancy [ˈveɪgrəntsi] *n, pl* **-cies** : vagabondage *m*
vagrant[1] [ˈveɪgrənt] *adj* : vagabond
vagrant[2] *n* : clochard *m*, -charde *f*; itinérant *m*, -rante *f Can*
vague [ˈveɪg] *adj* **vaguer; vaguest 1** IMPRECISE : vague, imprécis **2** SLIGHT : moindre <I haven't the vaguest idea : je n'en ai pas la moindre idée> **3** INDISTINCT : vague, flou **4** ABSENT-MINDED : distrait
vaguely [ˈveɪgli] *adv* : vaguement
vain [ˈveɪn] *adj* **1** WORTHLESS : sans valeur **2** FUTILE : inutile, futile **3** CONCEITED : vaniteux **4 in ~** : en vain
vainglorious [ˌveɪnˈgloriəs] *adj* PROUD : orgueilleux, vaniteux
vainly [ˈveɪnli] *adv* **1** UNSUCCESSFULLY : vainement, inutilement **2** CONCEITEDLY : avec vanité, vaniteusement
valance [ˈvælənts, ˈveɪ-] *n* : lambrequin *m* (d'un lit), cantonnière *f* (pour des rideaux)
vale [ˈveɪl] *n* : val *m*, vallée *f*
valedictorian [ˌvæləˌdɪkˈtoriən] *n* : étudiant *m*, -diante *f* qui prononce un discours lors d'une cérémonie de graduation
valedictory[1] [ˌvæləˈdɪktəri] *adj* : d'adieu
valedictory[2] *n, pl* **-ries** : discours *m* d'adieu
valentine [ˈvælənˌtaɪn] *n* : carte *f* de Saint-Valentin, valentin *m Can*
valet [ˈvæˌleɪ, væˈleɪ, ˈvælət] *n* : valet *m* de chambre

valiant ['væljənt] *adj* : vaillant, courageux
valiantly ['væljəntli] *adv* : vaillamment, courageusement
valid ['væləd] *adj* **1** : valid <a valid contract : un contrat valide> **2** : bien fondé, valable <valid arguments : raisonnements bien fondés>
validate ['vælə,deɪt] *vt* **-dated; -dating** : valider (un document), confirmer (une théorie, etc.)
validation [,vælə'deɪʃən] *n* : validation *f*
validity [və'lɪdəṭi, væ-] *n* : validité *f*
valise [və'li:s] *n* : mallette *f*, sac *m* de voyage
valley ['væli] *n, pl* **-leys** : vallée *f*
valor *or Brit* **valour** ['vælər] *n* : bravoure *f*, héroïsme *m*
valorous ['vælərəs] *adj* : valeureux
valour *Brit* → **valor**
valuable ['væljuəbəl, -jəbəl] *adj* **1** EXPENSIVE : de valeur **2** WORTHWHILE : précieux <a valuable friendship : une amitié précieuse>
valuables ['væljuəbəlz, -jəbəlz] *npl* : objets *mpl* de valeur
valuation [,vælju'eɪʃən] *n* **1** APPRAISAL : évaluation *f*, estimation *f* **2** WORTH : valeur *f*, prix *m*
value[1] ['vælju:] *vt* **valued; valuing 1** APPRAISE : estimer, évaluer **2** APPRECIATE, ESTEEM : apprécier, estimer
value[2] *n* **1** : valeur *f* <of no value : sans valeur> <to be of great value : valoir cher> **2** IMPORTANCE, MERIT : valeur *f*, mérite *m* <to place a high value on : attacher beaucoup d'importance à> **3 values** *npl* : valeurs *fpl* <family values : valeurs familiales>
valueless ['vælju:ləs] *adj* : sans valeur
valve ['vælv] *n* **1** : valve *f*, soupape *f* (en mécanique) **2** : valvule *f* (en anatomie)
vampire ['væm,paɪr] *n* : vampire *m*
van ['væn] *n* **1** : camionnette *f*, fourgonnette *f* (voiture) **2** → **vanguard**
vanadium [və'neɪdiəm] *n* : vanadium *m*
vandal ['vændəl] *n* : vandale *mf*
vandalism ['vændəl,ɪzəm] *n* : vandalisme *m*
vandalize ['vændəl,aɪz] *vt* **-ized; -izing** : saccager
vane ['veɪn] *n or* **weather vane** : girouette *f*
vanguard ['væn,gɑrd] *n* : avant-garde *f*
vanilla [və'nɪlə, -'nɛ-] *n* : vanille *f*
vanish ['vænɪʃ] *vi* : disparaître
vanity ['vænəṭi] *n, pl* **-ties 1** FUTILITY : futilité *f* **2** CONCEIT : vanité *f*, orgueil *m* **3** *or* **vanity table** : coiffeuse *f*
vanquish ['væŋkwɪʃ, 'væn-] *vt* : vaincre
vantage point ['væntɪdʒ] *n* : point *m* de vue, perspective *f*
vapid ['væpəd, 'veɪ-] *adj* : insipide, fade
vapor ['veɪpər] *n* : vapeur *f*
vaporize ['veɪpə,raɪz] *vt* **-ized; -izing** : vaporiser
vaporizer ['veɪpə,raɪzər] *n* : vaporisateur *m*
variability [,vɛriə'bɪləṭi] *n, pl* **-ties** : variabilité *f*
variable[1] ['vɛriəbəl] *adj* : variable
variable[2] *n* : variable *f*
variance ['vɛriənts] *n* **1** DIFFERENCE : différence *f*, écart *m* **2** DISAGREEMENT : désaccord *m* <to be at variance with s.o. : être en désaccord avec qqn>
variant[1] ['vɛriənt] *adj* : différent
variant[2] *n* : variante *f*
variation [,vɛri'eɪʃən] *n* : variation *f*, différence *f*
varicose ['værə,ko:s] *adj* : variqueux
varicose veins *npl* : varices *fpl*
varied ['vɛrid] *adj* : varié, divers
variegated ['vɛriə,geɪṭəd] *adj* **1** MULTICOLORED : bigarré, bariolé **2** : panaché (en botanique)
variety [və'raɪəṭi] *n, pl* **-eties 1** DIVERSITY : variété *f*, diversité *f* **2** ASSORTMENT : variété *f*, quantité *f* <a wide variety of : un grand nombre de> **3** TYPE : espèce *f*, sorte *f* **4** : variété *f* (en botanique)
various ['vɛriəs] *adj* : divers, varié
varnish[1] ['vɑrnɪʃ] *vt* **1** : vernir (du bois) **2** GLOSS : voiler, embellir
varnish[2] *n* : vernis *m*
varsity ['vɑrsəṭi] *n, pl* **-ties** : équipe *f* universitaire
vary ['vɛri] *v* **varied; varying** *vi* **1** CHANGE : varier, changer, se modifier **2** DIFFER : varier — *vt* : varier, diversifier
vascular ['væskjələr] *adj* : vasculaire
vase ['veɪs, 'veɪz, 'vɑz] *n* : vase *m*
vast ['væst] *adj* : vaste, énorme
vastly ['væstli] *adv* : immensément, énormément
vastness ['væstnəs] *n* : immensité *f*, grandeur *f*
vat ['væt] *n* : cuve *f*, bac *m*
vaudeville ['vɔdvəl, -,vɪl; 'vɔdə,vɪl] *n* : vaudeville *m*
vault[1] ['vɔlt] *vt* : sauter par-dessus — *vi* : sauter
vault[2] *n* **1** JUMP : saut *m* **2** DOME : voûte *f* **3** : cave *f* (à vin), chambre *f* forte (d'une banque) **4** *or* **burial vault** : caveau *m*
vaulted ['vɔltəd] *adj* : voûté
vaunted ['vɔntəd] *adj* : vanté <her much-vaunted beauty : sa beauté tant vantée>
VCR [,vi:,si:'ɑr] *n* : magnétoscope *m*
veal ['vi:l] *n* : veau *m*
veer ['vɪr] *vi* : tourner, virer (se dit d'un bateau, du vent, etc.)
vegetable[1] ['vɛdʒtəbəl, 'vɛdʒəṭə-] *adj* **1** : végétal <vegetable oil : huile végétale> **2** : de légumes <vegetable broth : bouillon de légumes>
vegetable[2] *n* **1** : végétal *m* (en botanique) **2** : légume *m* <fruits and vegetables : les fruits et les légumes>

vegetarian[1] [ˌvɛdʒəˈtɛriən] *adj* : végétarien
vegetarian[2] *n* : végétarien *m*, -rienne *f*
vegetarianism [ˌvɛdʒəˈtɛriəˌnɪzəm] *n* : végétarisme *m*
vegetate [ˈvɛdʒəˌteɪt] *vi* **-tated; -tating** : végéter
vegetation [ˌvɛdʒəˈteɪʃən] *n* : végétation *f*
vegetative [ˈvɛdʒəˌteɪt̬ɪv] *adj* : végétatif
vehemence [ˈviːəmənts] *n* : véhémence *f*, intensité *f*
vehement [ˈviːəmənt] *adj* : ardent, véhément
vehemently [ˈviːəməntli] *adv* : avec véhémence
vehicle [ˈviəkəl, ˈviːˌhɪkəl] *n* **1** CARRIER, MEDIUM : véhicule *m* **2** *or* **motor vehicle** : véhicule *m* (routier)
vehicular [viˈhɪkjələr, və-] *adj* : de véhicules <vehicular accidents : accidents de la route>
veil[1] [ˈveɪl] *vt* **1** CONCEAL : voiler, masquer **2** : couvrir d'un voile <to veil one's face : se voiler>
veil[2] *n* : voile *m* <bridal veil : voile de mariée> <veil of secrecy : voile du secret>
vein [ˈveɪn] *n* **1** : veine *f* (en anatomie) **2** LODE : filon *m*, veine *f* **3** : nervure *f* (d'une feuille) **4** STYLE : veine *f*, esprit *m* <in the same vein : dans le même esprit>
veined [ˈveɪnd] *adj* : veiné (se dit des minéraux, etc.), nervuré (se dit d'une feuille)
velocity [vəˈlɑsət̬i] *n, pl* **-ties** : vélocité *f*, vitesse *f*
velour [vəˈlʊr] *or* **velours** [-ˈlʊrz] *n, pl* **velours** : velours *m*
velvet[1] [ˈvɛlvət] *adj* **1** : de velours **2** → **velvety**
velvet[2] *n* : velours *m*
velvety [ˈvɛlvət̬i] *adj* : velouté
venal [ˈviːnəl] *adj* : vénal
vend [ˈvɛnd] *vt* : vendre
vendetta [vɛnˈdɛt̬ə] *n* : vendetta *f*
vending machine *n* : distributeur *m* automatique
vendor [ˈvɛndər] *n* **1** : vendeur *m*, -deuse *f*; marchand *m*, -chande *f* **2** → **vending machine**
veneer[1] [vəˈnɪr] *vt* : plaquer
veneer[2] *n* **1** : placage *m* (du bois) **2** APPEARANCE, FACADE : vernis *m*, fausse *f* apparence
venerable [ˈvɛnərəbəl] *adj* : vénérable
venerate [ˈvɛnəˌreɪt] *vt* **-ated; -ating** : vénérer
veneration [ˌvɛnəˈreɪʃən] *n* : vénération *f*
venereal disease [vəˈnɪriəl] *n* : maladie *f* vénérienne
venetian blind [vəˈniːʃən] : store *m* vénitien
Venezuelan[1] [ˌvɛnəˈzweɪlən, -zʊˈeɪ-] *adj* : vénézuélien
Venezuelan[2] *n* : Vénézuélien *m*, -lienne *f*
vengeance [ˈvɛndʒənts] *n* : vengeance *f* <to take vengeance on s.o. : se venger sur qqn>
vengeful [ˈvɛndʒfəl] *adj* : vengeur, vindicatif
venial [ˈviːniəl] *adj* : véniel <venial sins : péchés véniels>
venison [ˈvɛnəsən, -zən] *n* : venaison *f*
venom [ˈvɛnəm] *n* **1** : venin *m* (de serpent) **2** ILL WILL : venin *m*, malveillance *f*
venomous [ˈvɛnəməs] *adj* **1** : venimeux (se dit d'un serpent) **2** SPITEFUL : venimeux, haineux
vent[1] [ˈvɛnt] *vt* **1** EXPEL : évacuer, laisser échapper (de la fumée, etc.) **2** : décharger, donner libre cours à (ses émotions)
vent[2] *n* **1** OUTLET : orifice *m*, conduit *m*, bouche *f* d'aération **2 to give vent to** : donner libre cours à
ventilate [ˈvɛntəlˌeɪt] *vt* **-lated; -lating** : ventiler, aérer
ventilation [ˌvɛntəlˈeɪʃən] *n* : ventilation *f*, aération *f*
ventilator [ˈvɛntəlˌeɪt̬ər] *n* : ventilateur *m*
ventricle [ˈvɛntrɪkəl] *n* : ventricule *m*
ventriloquism [vɛnˈtrɪləˌkwɪzəm] *n* : ventriloquie *f*
ventriloquist [vɛnˈtrɪləˌkwɪst] *n* : ventriloque *mf*
venture[1] [ˈvɛntʃər] *v* **-tured; -turing** *vt* **1** RISK : risquer, hasarder **2** OFFER : hasarder, avancer <to venture an opinion : hasarder une opinion> — *vi* : s'embarquer, s'aventurer
venture[2] *n* **1** UNDERTAKING : entreprise *f* risquée, affaire *f* **2** STAKE : enjeu *m*
venturesome [ˈvɛntʃərsəm] *adj* **1** HAZARDOUS : dangereux, périlleux **2** DARING : audacieux, brave
venue [ˈvɛnˌjuː] *n* : lieu *m* (de rencontre)
Venus [ˈviːnəs] *n* : Vénus *f* (planète)
veracity [vəˈræsət̬i] *n, pl* **-ties** : véracité *f*
veranda *or* **verandah** [vəˈrændə] *n* : véranda *f*
verb [ˈvərb] *n* : verbe *m*
verbal [ˈvərbəl] *adj* : verbal
verbalize [ˈvərbəˌlaɪz] *vt* **-ized; -izing** : rendre par des mots, verbaliser
verbally [ˈvərbəli] *adv* : verbalement
verbatim[1] [vərˈbeɪt̬əm] *adv* : textuellement
verbatim[2] *adj* : mot pour mot, textuel
verbose [vərˈboːs] *adj* : verbeux, prolixe
verdant [ˈvərdənt] *adj* : verdoyant
verdict [ˈvərdɪkt] *n* **1** : verdict *m* (en droit) **2** JUDGMENT, OPINION : opinion *f*, jugement *m*
verdure [ˈvərdʒər, -djər] *n* : verdure *f*

verge[1] ['vərdʒ] *vi* **verged; verging 1** : être au bord **2 to verge on** : s'approcher de, friser

verge[2] *n* **1** EDGE, RIM : bord *m* **2 to be on the verge of** : être sur le bord de, être sur le point de

verifiable [ˌvɛrə'faɪəbəl] *adj* : vérifiable

verification [ˌvɛrəfə'keɪʃən] *n* : vérification *f*

verify ['vɛrəˌfaɪ] *vt* **-fied; -fying** : vérifier

veritable ['vɛrət̬əbəl] *adj* : véritable — **veritably** [-bli] *adv*

vermicelli [ˌvərmə'tʃɛli, -'sɛli] *n* : vermicelle *m*

vermin ['vərmən] *ns & pl* : vermine *f*, animaux *mpl* nuisibles

vermouth [vər'mu:θ] *n* : vermouth *m*

vernacular[1] [vər'nækjələr] *adj* : vernaculaire, du pays

vernacular[2] *n* : langage *m* vernaculaire

versatile ['vərsət̬əl] *adj* **1** : aux talents divers (se dit d'une personne) **2** MULTIPURPOSE : polyvalent, aux usages multiples

versatility [ˌvərsə'tɪlət̬i] *n* : souplesse *f* (de l'esprit), polyvalence *f* (d'un outil, etc.)

verse ['vərs] *n* **1** STANZA : strophe *f* **2** POETRY : vers *mpl*, poésie *f* **3** : verset *m* (de la Bible)

versed ['vərst] *adj* **to be well versed in** : être très versé dans

version ['vərʒən] *n* : version *f*

versus ['vərsəs] *prep* : contre, par rapport à

vertebra ['vərtəbrə] *n, pl* **-brae** [-ˌbreɪ, -ˌbri:] *or* **-bras** : vertèbre *f*

vertebral [vər'tibrəl, 'vərtə-] *adj* : vertébral

vertebrate[1] ['vərtəbrət, -ˌbreɪt] *adj* : vertébré

vertebrate[2] *n* : vertébré *m*

vertex ['vərˌtɛks] *n, pl* **vertices** ['vərtəˌsi:z] **1** : vertex *m* (en anatomie), sommet *m* (d'un angle) **2** SUMMIT, TOP : sommet *m*

vertical[1] ['vərtɪkəl] *adj* : vertical — **vertically** *adv*

vertical[2] *n* : verticale *f*

vertigo ['vərtɪˌgo:] *n, pl* **-goes** *or* **-gos** : vertige *m*

verve ['vərv] *n* : verve *f*, brio *m*

very[1] ['vɛri] *adv* **1** TRULY : vraiment, exactement <the very same story : exactement la même histoire> <at the very least : tout au moins> **2** EXCEEDINGLY : très, vraiment, tellement <very hot : très chaud> <it didn't hurt very much : ça ne m'a pas fait tellement mal>

very[2] *adj* **1** EXACT : même, précis <the very heart of the city : le cœur même de la ville> **2** PERFECT : parfait <the very tool for the job : le parfait outil pour le travail> **3** BARE, MERE : seul <the very thought of leaving : la seule idée de partir> **4** SELFSAME : même, identique <he's the very man I saw : c'est justement l'homme que j'ai vu>

vesicle ['vɛsɪkəl] *n* : vésicule *f*

vespers ['vɛspərz] *npl* : vêpres *fpl*

vessel ['vɛsəl] *n* **1** CONTAINER : récipient *m*, contenant *m* **2** SHIP : vaisseau *m* **3** → **blood vessel**

vest[1] ['vɛst] *vt* **1** : investir <to vest a deputy with authority : investir un député d'autorité> **2** CLOTHE : vêtir

vest[2] *n* : gilet *m*, veste *f Can*

vestibule ['vɛstəˌbju:l] *n* : vestibule *m*

vestige ['vɛstɪdʒ] *n* : vestige *m*, trace *f*

vestment ['vɛstmənt] *n* : vêtement *m* sacerdotal

vestry ['vɛstri] *n, pl* **-tries** : sacristie *f*

veteran[1] ['vɛt̬ərən, 'vɛtrən] *adj* : chevronné

veteran[2] *n* : ancien combattant *m*, vétéran *m*

veterinarian [ˌvɛt̬ərə'nɛriən, ˌvɛt̬rə-] *n* : vétérinaire *mf*

veterinary ['vɛt̬ərəˌnɛri, 'vɛtrə-] *adj* : vétérinaire

veto[1] ['vi:t̬o] *vt* **1** PROHIBIT : interdire, défendre **2** : mettre son veto à, opposer son veto à (une loi)

veto[2] *n, pl* **-toes 1** PROHIBITION : interdiction *f*, prohibition *f* **2** : veto *m* <right of veto : droit de veto>

vex ['vɛks] *vt* **vexed; vexing 1** UPSET : vexer, froisser **2** ANNOY : contrarier, ennuyer

vexation [vɛk'seɪʃən] *n* IRRITATION : contrariété *f*, agacement *m*

via ['vaɪə, 'vi:ə] *prep* : via, par

viability [ˌvaɪə'bɪlət̬i] *n* : viabilité *f*

viable ['vaɪəbəl] *adj* : viable

viaduct ['vaɪəˌdʌkt] *n* : viaduc *m*

vial ['vaɪəl] *n* : fiole *f*

vibrant ['vaɪbrənt] *adj* **1** BRIGHT : vif <a vibrant red : un rouge vif> **2** RESONANT : vibrant, résonant **3** LIVELY : vivant, animé

vibrate ['vaɪˌbreɪt] *v* **-brated; -brating** *vt* : faire vibrer — *vi* **1** OSCILLATE : vibrer, osciller **2** QUIVER, THRILL : frémir, vibrer

vibration [vaɪ'breɪʃən] *n* : vibration *f*

vicar ['vɪkər] *n* : vicaire *m*

vicarious [vaɪ'kæriəs, vɪ-] *adj* **1** DELEGATED : délégué **2** INDIRECT : indirect <vicarious experiences : expériences vécues indirectement>

vicariously [vaɪ'kæriəsli, vɪ-] *adv* : indirectement

vice ['vaɪs] *n* **1** : vice *m* **2** *Brit* → **vise**

vice admiral *n* : vice-amiral *m*

vice president *n* : vice-président *m*, -dente *f*

viceroy ['vaɪsˌrɔɪ] *n* : vice-roi *m*

vice versa [ˌvaɪsɪ'vərsə, ˌvaɪs'vər-] *adv* : vice versa

vicinity [və'sɪnət̬i] *n, pl* **-ties 1** NEARNESS : proximité *f* **2** NEIGHBORHOOD

: quartier *m,* voisinage *m,* environs *mpl*

vicious [ˈvɪʃəs] *adj* **1** DEPRAVED : vicieux, corrompu **2** SAVAGE : méchant <a vicious dog : un chien méchant> **3** SPITEFUL : malveillant, méchant

viciously [ˈvɪʃəsli] *adv* **1** SAVAGELY : brutalement, violemment **2** SPITEFULLY : méchamment, cruellement

viciousness [ˈvɪʃəsnəs] *n* **1** : brutalité *f,* violence *f* **2** MEANNESS : méchanceté *f,* cruauté *f*

vicissitude [vəˈsɪsəˌtu:d, vaɪ-, -ˌtju:d] *n* : vicissitude *f*

victim [ˈvɪktəm] *n* : victime *f*

victimize [ˈvɪktəˌmaɪz] *vt* **-ized; -izing** : persécuter, faire une victime de

victor [ˈvɪktər] *n* : vainqueur *m*

Victorian [vɪkˈto:riən] *adj* : victorien

victorious [vɪkˈto:riəs] *adj* : victorieux — **victoriously** *adv*

victory [ˈvɪktəri] *n, pl* **-ries** : victoire *f*

victuals [ˈvɪt̬əlz] *npl* : victuailles *fpl*

video[1] [ˈvɪdiˌo:] *adj* : vidéo

video[2] *n* **1** : vidéo *f* **2** → **videotape[2]**

videocassette [ˌvɪdiokəˈsɛt] *n* : vidéocassette *f*

videotape[1] [ˈvɪdioˌteɪp] **-taped; -taping** *vt* : enregistrer (sur magnétoscope)

videotape[2] *n* : bande *f* vidéo

vie [ˈvaɪ] *vi* **vied; vying** [ˈvaɪɪŋ] : rivaliser, être en compétition

Vietnamese[1] [viˌɛtnəˈmi:z, -ˈmi:s] *adj* : vietnamien

Vietnamese[2] *n* **1** : Vietnamien *m*, -mienne *f* **2** : vietnamien *m* (langue)

view[1] [ˈvju:] *vt* **1** EXAMINE : examiner, inspecter **2** SEE, WATCH : regarder, voir (un film, etc.) **3** CONSIDER : étudier, peser <to view all sides of a question : étudier tous les aspects d'un problème>

view[2] *n* **1** SIGHT : vue *f* <to come into view : apparaître> **2** ATTITUDE, OPINION : opinion *f,* avis *m* <in my view : d'après moi, à mon avis> **3** PROSPECT : vue *f,* panorama *m* <a room with a view : une chambre avec vue> **4** INTENTION : intention *f,* vue *f* <with a view to : dans l'intention de, en vue de> **5 in view of** : vu, étant donné

viewer [ˈvju:ər] *n* **1** *or* **television viewer** : téléspectateur *m,* -trice *f* **2** : visionneuse *f* (en photographie)

viewpoint [ˈvju:ˌpɔɪnt] *n* : point *m* de vue

vigil [ˈvɪdʒəl] *n* **1** : vigile *f* (en religion) **2** WAKEFULNESS, WATCH : veille *f* <to keep a vigil : veiller>

vigilance [ˈvɪdʒələn*t*s] *n* : vigilance *f*

vigilant [ˈvɪdʒələnt] *adj* : vigilant, attentif

vigilante [ˌvɪdʒəˈlænˌti:] *n* : membre *m* d'un groupe qui lutte contre le crime

vigilantly [ˈvɪdʒələntli] *adv* : avec vigilance

vigor *or Brit* **vigour** [ˈvɪgər] *n* : vigueur *f,* énergie *f*

vigorous [ˈvɪgərəs] *adj* : vigoureux, énergique — **vigorously** *adv*

vigour *Brit* → **vigor**

Viking [ˈvaɪkɪŋ] *n* : Viking *mf*

vile [ˈvaɪl] *adj* **viler; vilest 1** BASE : vil, ignoble **2** REVOLTING : abominable, écœurant **3** AWFUL, FOUL : exécrable, massacrant <in a vile temper : d'une humeur massacrante> <vile weather : sale temps>

vilely [ˈvaɪəlli] *adv* : vilement, ignoblement

vileness [ˈvaɪlnəs] *n* : caractère *m* ignoble

vilification [ˌvɪləfəˈkeɪʃən] *n* : diffamation *f,* calomnie *f*

vilify [ˈvɪləˌfaɪ] *vt* **-fied; -fying** : diffamer, calomnier

villa [ˈvɪlə] *n* : villa *f*

village [ˈvɪlɪdʒ] *n* : village *m*

villager [ˈvɪlɪdʒər] *n* : villageois *m,* -geoise *f*

villain [ˈvɪlən] *n* : scélérat *m,* -rate *f;* méchant *m,* -chante *f* (dans un livre, un film, etc.)

villainous [ˈvɪlənəs] *adj* : vil, ignoble, infâme

villainy [ˈvɪləni] *n, pl* **-lainies** : vilenie *f,* infamie *f*

vim [ˈvɪm] *n* : énergie *f,* vitalité *f,* entrain *m*

vindicate [ˈvɪndəˌkeɪt] *vt* **-cated; -cating 1** EXONERATE : innocenter **2** JUSTIFY : justifier

vindication [ˌvɪndəˈkeɪʃən] *n* : justification *f*

vindictive [vɪnˈdɪktɪv] *adj* : vindicatif, rancunier

vindictiveness [vɪnˈdɪktɪvnəs] *n* : esprit *m* rancunier

vine [ˈvaɪn] *n* **1** GRAPEVINE : vigne *f* **2** : plante *f* grimpante

vinegar [ˈvɪnɪgər] *n* : vinaigre *m*

vineyard [ˈvɪnjərd] *n* : vignoble *m*

vintage[1] [ˈvɪntɪdʒ] *adj* **1** : millésimé (se dit du vin) **2** CLASSIC : d'époque **3** : à son meilleur <vintage Shaw : du Shaw à son meilleur>

vintage[2] *n* **1** HARVEST : vendange *f* (en viticulture) **2** PERIOD : époque *f* <a piano of 1845 vintage : un piano qui date de 1845> **3** *or* **vintage wine** : vin *m* de grand cru **4** *or* **vintage year** : millésime *m*

vinyl [ˈvaɪnəl] *n* : vinyle *m*

viola [viːˈo:lə] *n* : alto *m*

violate [ˈvaɪəˌleɪt] *vt* **-lated; -lating 1** BREAK : transgresser, enfreindre <to violate the law : enfreindre la loi> **2** RAPE : violer **3** DESECRATE : profaner

violation [ˌvaɪəˈleɪʃən] *n* **1** INFRINGEMENT : infraction *f,* transgression *f* <traffic violation : infraction au code de la route> **2** RAPE : viol *m* **3** DESECRATION : profanation *f,* viol *m*

violator [ˈvaɪəˌleɪtər] *n* : violateur *m,* -trice *f*

violence ['vaɪələnts] *n* : violence *f*
violent ['vaɪələnt] *adj* : violent
violently ['vaɪələntli] *adv* : violemment, avec violence
violet ['vaɪələt] *n* **1** : violette *f* (plante) **2** : violet *m* (couleur)
violin [ˌvaɪə'lɪn] *n* : violon *m*
violincello [ˌvaɪə'lən'tʃɛˌloː, ˌviː-] → **cello**
violinist [ˌvaɪə'lɪnɪst] *n* : violoniste *mf*
VIP [ˌviːˌaɪː'piː] *n, pl* **VIPs** [-'piːz] : V.I.P. *m fam,* personnalité *f* de marque
viper ['vaɪpər] *n* : vipère *f*
viral ['vaɪrəl] *adj* : viral
virgin[1] ['vərdʒən] *adj* **1** CHASTE : vierge **2** UNSPOILED : vierge, intact
virgin[2] *n* **1** : vierge *f* **2 the Virgin Mary** : la Vierge Marie
virginity [vər'dʒɪnət̬i] *n, pl* **-ties** : virginité *f*
Virgo ['vərˌgoː, 'vɪr-] *n* : Vierge *f*
virile ['vɪrəl, -ˌaɪl] *adj* : viril
virility [və'rɪlət̬i] *n* : virilité *f*
virtual ['vərtʃuəl] *adj* **1** : en pratique, de fait <a virtual leader : un chef de fait> **2** NEAR : quasi-total <a virtual impossibility : une quasi-impossibilité> <it's a virtual certainty : c'est presque certain> **3** : virtuel (en informatique)
virtually ['vərtʃuəli] *adv* : pratiquement, presque
virtue ['vərˌtʃuː] *n* **1** GOODNESS : vertu *f* **2** MERIT : avantage *m,* mérite *m* **3 by virtue of** : en raison de, en vertu de
virtuosity [ˌvərtʃʊ'ɑsət̬i] *n, pl* **-ties** : virtuosité *f*
virtuoso [ˌvərtʃʊ'oːˌsoː, -ˌzoː] *n, pl* **-sos** *or* **-si** [-ˌsiː, -ˌziː] : virtuose *mf*
virtuous ['vərtʃuəs] *adj* : vertueux — **virtuously** ['vərtʃuəsli] *adv*
virulence ['vɪrələnts, -jələnts] *n* : virulence *f*
virulent ['vɪrələnt, -jələnt] *adj* : virulent
virulently ['vɪrələntli, -jələnt-] *adv* : avec virulence
virus ['vaɪrəs] *n* : virus *m* (en médecine, en informatique, etc.)
visa ['viːzə, -sə] *n* : visa *m*
visage ['vɪzɪdʒ] *n* : physionomie *f*
vis-à-vis [ˌviːzə'viː, -sə-] *prep* : vis-a-vis de, par rapport à
viscera ['vɪsərə] *npl* : viscères *mpl*
visceral ['vɪsərəl] *adj* : viscéral
viscosity [vɪs'kɑsət̬i] *n, pl* **-ties** : viscosité *f*
viscount ['vaɪˌkaʊnt] *n* : vicomte *m*
viscountess ['vaɪˌkaʊntəs] *n* : vicomtesse *f*
viscous ['vɪskəs] *adj* : visqueux
vise *or Brit* **vice** ['vaɪs] *n* : étau *m*
visibility [ˌvɪzə'bɪlət̬i] *n, pl* **-ties** : visibilité *f*
visible ['vɪzəbəl] *adj* **1** : visible <visible stars : étoiles visibles> **2** OBVIOUS : visible, manifeste, apparent
visibly ['vɪzəbli] *adv* : visiblement
vision ['vɪʒən] *n* **1** EYESIGHT : vision *f,* vue *f* **2** APPARITION : apparition *f,* vision *f* **3** FORESIGHT : vision *f* (de l'avenir), prévoyance *f,* imagination *f* **4** IMAGE : image *f* <a vision of beauty : une image de la beauté>
visionary[1] ['vɪʒəˌnɛri] *adj* **1** FARSIGHTED : visionnaire **2** UTOPIAN : utopique, irréel
visionary[2] *n, pl* **-aries** : visionnaire *mf*
visit[1] ['vɪzət] *vt* **1** : rendre visite à, aller voir (une personne) **2** : visiter, faire visite à (un lieu) **3 to be visited by** : être éprouvé par (des difficultés, etc.)
visit[2] *n* : visite *f*
visitor ['vɪzət̬ər] *n* : visiteur *m,* -teuse *f*
visor ['vaɪzər] *n* **1** : visière *f* (d'un casque) **2** *or* **sun visor** : pare-soleil *m*
vista ['vɪstə] *n* : vue *f,* perspective *f*
visual ['vɪʒuəl] *adj* : visuel — **visually** *adv*
visualize ['vɪʒuəˌlaɪz] *vt* **-ized; -izing 1** IMAGINE : visualiser, s'imaginer **2** ENVISAGE : prévoir, envisager
vital ['vaɪt̬əl] *adj* **1** : vital <vital organs : organes vitaux> **2** LIVELY : vivant, dynamique **3** ESSENTIAL : vital, indispensable, essentiel <to be of vital importance : être indispensable>
vitality [vaɪ'tælət̬i] *n, pl* **-ties** : vitalité *f*
vitally ['vaɪt̬əli] *adv* : extrêmement, très
vital statistics *n* : statistiques *fpl* démographiques
vitamin ['vaɪt̬əmən] *n* : vitamine *f*
vitreous ['vɪtriəs] *adj* : vitreux
vitriolic [ˌvɪtri'ɑlɪk] *adj* : au vitriol, venimeux
vituperate [vaɪ'tuːpəˌreɪt, və-, -'tjuː-] *vt* **-ated; -ating** : vitupérer
vituperation [vaɪˌtuːpə'reɪʃən, və-, -ˌtjuː-] *n* : vitupération *f*
vivacious [və'veɪʃəs, vaɪ-] *adj* : vif, animé, plein d'entrain
vivaciously [və'veɪʃəsli, vaɪ-] *adv* : avec vivacité
vivacity [və'væsət̬i, vaɪ-] *n* : vivacité *f,* entrain *m*
vivid ['vɪvəd] *adj* **1** FRESH, LIVELY : vivant, vif <a vivid imagination : une vive imagination> **2** BRIGHT : vif, éclatant <a vivid blue : un bleu vif> **3** SHARP : vivant, frappant <a vivid description : une description vivante>
vividly ['vɪvədli] *adv* : de façon éclatante, de façon vivante
vividness ['vɪvədnəs] *n* **1** BRIGHTNESS : éclat *m* **2** CLARITY, SHARPNESS : clarté *f,* vivacité *f*
vivisection [ˌvɪvə'sɛkʃən, 'vɪvəˌ-] *n* : vivisection *f*
vixen ['vɪksən] *n* : renarde *f*
vocabulary [voː'kæbjəˌlɛri] *n, pl* **-laries 1** LEXICON : vocabulaire *m,* lexique *m* **2** : vocabulaire *m* (de la langue)

vocal ['vo:kəl] *adj* **1** : vocal **2** OUTSPOKEN : franc, qui se fait bien entendre
vocal cords *npl* : cordes *fpl* vocales
vocalist ['vo:kəlɪst] *n* : chanteur *m*, -teuse *f*
vocalize ['vo:kəl,aɪz] *v* **-ized; -izing** *vt* UTTER : exprimer — *vi* : vocaliser (en musique)
vocation [vo'keɪʃən] *n* **1** : vocation *f* (religieuse) **2** OCCUPATION : emploi *m*, profession *f*
vocational [vo'keɪʃənəl] *adj* : professionnel <vocational guidance : orientation professionnelle>
vociferous [vo'sɪfərəs] *adj* : véhément, bruyant
vociferously [vo'sɪfərəsli] *adv* : avec véhémence, bruyamment
vodka ['vɑdkə] *n* : vodka *m*
vogue ['vo:g] *n* : vogue *f*, mode *f* <to be in vogue : être à la mode>
voice[1] ['vɔɪs] *vt* **voiced; voicing** : exprimer, formuler
voice[2] *n* **1** : voix *f* <a booming voice : une voix retentissante> <fear took his voice away : la peur l'avait rendu muet> **2** : voix *f* (en grammaire)
voice box → **larynx**
voiced ['vɔɪst] *adj* : sonore
void[1] ['vɔɪd] *vt* **1** DISCHARGE : évacuer (en physiologie) **2** ANNUL : annuler
void[2] *adj* **1** EMPTY : vide <void of common sense : dépourvu de bon sens> **2** NULL : nul
void[3] *n* : vide *m*
volatile ['vɑləṭəl] *adj* : volatil, instable
volatility [,vɑlə'tɪləṭi] *n* : volatilité *f*, instabilité *f*
volcanic [vɑl'kænɪk, vɔl-] *adj* : volcanique
volcano [vɑl'keɪ,no:, vɔl-] *n, pl* **-noes** *or* **-nos** : volcan *m*
vole ['vo:l] *n* : campagnol *m*
volition [vo'lɪʃən] *n* : volonté *f* <of one's own volition : de son propre gré>
volley ['vɑli] *n, pl* **-leys 1** : volée *f* (de missiles), salve *f* (d'applaudissements) **2** : bordée *f* <a volley of insults : une bordée d'injures> **3** : volée *f* (aux sports)
volleyball ['vɑli,bɔl] *n* : volley *m*, volley-ball *m*
volt ['vo:lt] *n* : volt *m*
voltage ['vo:ltɪdʒ] *n* : voltage *m*, tension *f*
voluble ['vɑljəbəl] *adj* : volubile
volume ['vɑljəm, -ju:m] *n* **1** BOOK : volume *m* **2** CAPACITY : capacité *f*, volume *m* (cubique) **3** AMOUNT : volume *m*, quantité *f* <a high volume of traffic : beaucoup de circulation> **4** LOUDNESS : volume *m* **5 to speak volumes** : être révélateur, en dire long
voluminous [və'lu:mənəs] *adj* : volumineux
voluntarily [,vɑlən'tɛrəli] *adv* : volontairement
voluntary ['vɑlən,tɛri] *adj* : volontaire
volunteer[1] [,vɑlən'tɪr] *vt* : offrir, donner volontairement — *vi* : se porter volontaire
volunteer[2] *adj* : bénévole
volunteer[3] *n* : volontaire *mf*, bénévole *mf*
voluptuous [və'lʌptʃuəs] *adj* : voluptueux — **voluptuously** *adv*
voluptuousness [və'lʌptʃuəsnəs] *n* : volupté *f*
vomit[1] ['vɑmət] *v* : vomir
vomit[2] *n* : vomi *m*
voodoo ['vu:,du:] *n, pl* **voodoos** : vaudou *m*
voracious [vɔ'reɪʃəs, və-] *adj* : vorace, avide
voraciously [vɔ'reɪʃəsli, və-] *adv* : voracement, avec voracité
voracity [vɔ'ræsəṭi, və-] *n* : voracité *f*
vortex ['vɔr,tɛks] *n, pl* **vortices** ['vɔrtə,si:z] : tourbillon *m*
vote[1] ['vo:t] *v* **voted; voting** : voter
vote[2] *n* **1** : vote *m* **2** FRANCHISE : vote *m*, droit *m* de vote
voter ['vo:ṭər] *n* : électeur *m*, -trice *f*
voting ['vo:ṭɪŋ] *n* : scrutin *m*, vote *m*
vouch ['vaʊtʃ] *vi* **to vouch for** : répondre de, se porter garant de
voucher ['vaʊtʃər] *n* **1** RECEIPT : récépissé *m*, reçu *m* **2** *or* **credit voucher** : bon *m*
vouchsafe [vaʊtʃ'seɪf] *vt* **-safed; -safing 1** GRANT : octroyer, accorder **2 to vouchsafe to do** : s'engager à faire
vow[1] [vaʊ] *vt* : jurer, promettre
vow[2] *n* **1** : serment *m*, promesse *f* **2** : vœu *m* (en religion)
vowel ['vaʊəl] *n* : voyelle *f*
voyage[1] ['vɔɪɪdʒ] *vi* **-aged; -aging** : voyager
voyage[2] *n* : voyage *m*
voyager ['vɔɪɪdʒər] *n* : voyageur *m*, -geuse *f*
vulcanize ['vʌlkə,naɪz] *vt* **-nized; -nizing** : vulcaniser
vulgar ['vʌlgər] *adj* **1** COMMON, PLEBEIAN : vulgaire, commun **2** COARSE, CRUDE : vulgaire, grossier
vulgarity [,vʌl'gærəṭi] *n, pl* **-ties** : vulgarité *f*
vulgarly ['vʌlgərli] *adv* : vulgairement
vulnerability [,vʌlnərə'bɪləṭi] *n* : vulnérabilité *f*
vulnerable ['vʌlnərəbəl] *adj* : vulnérable
vulture ['vʌltʃər] *n* : vautour *m*
vulva ['vʌlvə] *n, pl* **-vae** [-,vi:, -,vaɪ] : vulve *f*
vying → **vie**

W

w [ˈdʌbəlˌjuː] *n, pl* **w's** *or* **ws** [-juːz] : w *m,* vingt-troisième lettre de l'alphabet

wad¹ [ˈwɑd] *vt* **wadded; wadding 1** : bourrer (un fusil) **2** *or* **to wad up** : faire un tampon de

wad² *n* **1** : tampon *m* (d'ouate, etc.), bourre *f* de fusil **2** BUNDLE : liasse *f,* paquet *m* <wad of money : liasse de billets>

waddle¹ [ˈwɑdəl] *vi* **-dled; -dling** : se dandiner

waddle² *n* : dandinement *m*

wade [ˈweɪd] *vi* **waded; wading 1** : patauger, avancer dans l'eau **2 to wade through** : accomplir péniblement <to wade through an assignment : faire un travail avec beaucoup de mal>

wading bird *n* : échassier *m*

wafer [ˈweɪfər] *n* : gaufrette *f*

waffle [ˈwɑfəl] *n* : gaufre *f*

waffle iron *n* : gaufrier *m*

waft [ˈwɑft, ˈwæft] *vi* : flotter <to waft through the air : flotter dans l'air> — *vt* CARRY : apporter, transporter

wag¹ [ˈwæg] *v* **wagged; wagging** *vt* : agiter, remuer (la queue) — *vi* : frétiller, remuer

wag² *n* **1** : frétillement *m* (de la queue) **2** JOKER, WIT : farceur *m,* -ceuse *f*

wage¹ [ˈweɪdʒ] *vt* **waged; waging** : faire (la guerre), mener (une campagne)

wage² *n* **1** PAY : salaire *m,* paie *f* <hourly wage : salaire horaire> **2 wages** *ns & pl* REWARD : récompense *f* <the wages of sin is death : la mort est le prix du péché>

wager¹ [ˈweɪdʒər] *v* : parier

wager² *n* : pari *m*

waggish [ˈwægɪʃ] *adj* : facétieux, humoristique

waggle [ˈwægəl] *vt* **-gled; -gling** WAG : remuer, agiter

wagon [ˈwægən] *n* **1** : chariot *m* (tiré par des chevaux) **2** CART : chariot *m* **3** → **station wagon**

waif [ˈweɪf] *n* : enfant *m* abandonné, enfant *f* abandonnée

wail¹ [ˈweɪl] *vi* **1** : gémir, pleurer (se dit d'une personne) **2** : gémir (se dit du vent), hurler (se dit d'une sirène)

wail² *n* : gémissement *m*

wainscot [ˈweɪnskət, -ˌskɑt, -ˌskoːt] *or* **wainscoting** [-skət̬ɪŋ, -ˌskɑ-, -ˌskoː-] *n* : lambris *m,* boiseries *fpl*

waist [ˈweɪst] *n* : taille *f*

waistline [ˈweɪstˌlaɪn] *n* : taille *f*

wait¹ [ˈweɪt] *vt* **1** AWAIT : attendre <wait your turn : attendez votre tour> **2** DELAY : retarder (le dîner, etc.) <don't wait lunch for me : ne m'attendez pas pour déjeuner> **3** SERVE : servir <to wait tables : servir à table> — *vi* : attendre

wait² *n* **1** : attente *f* **2 to lie in wait for** : guetter, attendre

waiter [ˈweɪt̬ər] *n* : serveur *m,* garçon *m*

waiting room *n* : salle *f* d'attente

waitress [ˈweɪtrəs] *n* : serveuse *f*

waive [ˈweɪv] *vt* **waived; waiving** : renoncer à (un droit), déroger à (une règle), supprimer (une condition)

waiver [ˈweɪvər] *n* : renonciation *f,* abandon *m*

wake¹ [ˈweɪk] *v* **woke** [ˈwoːk]; **woken** [ˈwoːkən] *or* **waked; waking** *vi or* **to wake up** : se réveiller — *vt* : réveiller <to wake s.o. up : réveiller qqn>

wake² *n* **1** WATCH : veillée *f* funèbre **2** : sillage *m* (laissé par un bateau) **3 in the wake of** : à la suite de

wakeful [ˈweɪkfəl] *adj* : éveillé, alerte

waken [ˈweɪkən] *vi* AWAKE : se réveiller

walk¹ [ˈwɔk] *vi* **1** : marcher <to walk back and forth : marcher de long en large> **2** : aller à pied, se promener <he walks to school : il se rend à l'école à pied> — *vt* **1** TRAVERSE : faire à pied, parcourir <we walked the streets : nous parcourions les rues> **2** ACCOMPANY : raccompagner <she walked him home : elle l'a raccompagné chez lui> **3** : faire marcher, promener <to walk the dog : promener le chien>

walk² *n* **1** : marche *f,* promenade *f* <to go for a short walk : se promener quelques minutes> **2** PATH : chemin *m,* allée *f,* promenade *f* **3** GAIT : démarche *f* (d'une personne), pas *m* (d'un animal) **4 from all walks of life** : de tous les milieux

walker [ˈwɔkər] *n* **1** : marcheur *m,* -cheuse *f;* promeneur *m,* -neuse *f* **2** *or* **baby walker** : trotteur *m*

walking stick *n* : canne *f*

walkout [ˈwɔkˌaʊt] *n* STRIKE : grève *f*

walk out *vi* **1** STRIKE : se mettre en grève **2** LEAVE : partir, sortir **3 to walk out on** ABANDON : quitter, abandonner

wall¹ [ˈwɔl] *vt* **1 to wall in** : entourer d'un mur **2 to wall off** : séparer par un mur **3 to wall up** : murer

wall² *n* **1** : mur *m* (d'un édifice, d'une pièce, etc.) <a wall of silence : un mur de silence> **2** SIDE : paroi *f* <the wall of a container : la paroi d'un récipient> <heart walls : parois du cœur> **3** : paroi *f,* face *f* (d'une montagne)

wallaby [ˈwɑləbi] *n, pl* **-bies** : wallaby *m*

wallet [ˈwɑlət] *n* : portefeuille *m*

wallflower [ˈwɔlˌflaʊər] *n* **1** : giroflée *f* **2 to be a wallflower** : faire tapisserie

Walloon¹ [wɑˈluːn] *adj* : wallon

Walloon² *n* **1** : Wallon *m,* -lonne *f* **2** : wallon *m* (langue)

wallop[1] [ˈwɑləp] *vt* **1** BEAT : donner une raclée à **2** DEFEAT : battre à plates coutures **3** HIT : taper sur (une balle, etc.)

wallop[2] *n* BLOW : coup *m* fort, raclée *f*

wallow[1] [ˈwɑˌloː] *vi* **1** : se vautrer, s'étaler (se dit d'un animal) **2** INDULGE : se vautrer <to wallow in self-pity : s'apitoyer sur son sort>

wallow[2] *n* : bauge *f* (pour des animaux)

wallpaper[1] [ˈwɔlˌpeɪpər] *vt* : tapisser

wallpaper[2] *n* : tapisserie *f*

walnut [ˈwɔlˌnʌt] *n* : noyer *m* (arbre et bois), noix *f* (fruit)

walrus [ˈwɔlrəs, ˈwɑl-] *n, pl* **-rus** *or* **-ruses** : morse *m*

waltz[1] [ˈwɔlts] *vi* **1** : valser **2 to waltz in** : entrer d'un pas désinvolte

waltz[2] *n* : valse *f*

wampum [ˈwɑmpəm] *n* : wampum *m*

wan [ˈwɑn] *adj* **wanner; wannest 1** PALLID : blême, pâle **2** DIM, FAINT : faible <a wan smile : un faible sourire>

wand [ˈwɑnd] *n* : baguette *f* (magique)

wander [ˈwɑndər] *vi* **1** RAMBLE : se promener, se balader **2** STRAY : errer, s'égarer **3** : vagabonder <his thoughts were wandering : ses pensées vagabondaient>

wanderer [ˈwɑndərər] *n* : vagabond *m*, -bonde *f*

wanderlust [ˈwɑndərˌlʌst] *n* : envie *f* de voyager

wane[1] [ˈweɪn] *vi* **waned; waning 1** : décroître (se dit de la lune) **2** DECLINE : décliner, diminuer

wane[2] *n* : déclin *m*, décroissance *f* <to be on the wane : décliner>

wangle [ˈwæŋgəl] *vt* **-gled; -gling** FINAGLE : se débrouiller pour obtenir

wanly [ˈwɑnli] *adv* : faiblement

want[1] [ˈwɑnt, ˈwɔnt] *vt* **1** DESIRE : vouloir, désirer **2** NEED, REQUIRE : avoir besoin de **3** REQUEST : demander <you're wanted on the phone : on vous demande au téléphone> **4** SEEK : rechercher <to be wanted for murder : être recherché pour meurtre> — *vi* **1 to want for** LACK : manquer de **2 to want in** : vouloir entrer

want[2] *n* **1** LACK : manque *m* **2** DESIRE, NEED : besoin *m* **3** POVERTY : misère *f*, indigence *f* <to be in want : être dans le besoin>

wanting[1] [ˈwɑntɪŋ, ˈwɔnt-] *adj* **1** ABSENT : absent **2 to be wanting in** : manquer de

wanting[2] *prep* **1** LESS : moins <a month wanting two days : un mois moins deux jours> **2** WITHOUT : sans <a book wanting a cover : un livre sans couverture>

wanton [ˈwɑntən, ˈwɔn-] *adj* **1** PLAYFUL : capricieux <a wanton breeze : une brise capricieuse> **2** LEWD : impudique, licencieux **3** MALICIOUS : cruel, injustifié

wapiti [ˈwɑpəṭi] *n, pl* **-ti** *or* **-tis** : wapiti *m*

war[1] [ˈwɔr] *vi* **warred; warring** : faire la guerre

war[2] *n* : guerre *f* <to go to war with : entrer en guerre avec>

warble[1] [ˈwɔrbəl] *vi* **-bled; -bling** : gazouiller

warble[2] *n* : gazouillis *m*

warbler [ˈwɔrblər] *n* : fauvette *f*

ward[1] [ˈwɔrd] *vt or* **to ward off** : parer, éviter

ward[2] *n* **1** *or* **ward of the court** : pupille *f* **2** : salle *f* (d'un hôpital), quartier *m* (d'une prison) **3** : circonscription *f* électorale (d'une ville)

warden [ˈwɔrdən] *n* **1** KEEPER : gardien *m*, -dienne *f* (de parcs, etc.) **2** *or* **prison warden** : directeur *m*, -trice *f* de prison

wardrobe [ˈwɔrdˌroːb] *n* **1** CLOSET : armoire *f*, penderie *f*, garde-robe *mf Can* **2** CLOTHES : garde-robe *f*

ware [ˈwær] *n* **1** POTTERY : poterie *f* **2 wares** *npl* GOODS : marchandises *fpl*

warehouse [ˈwærˌhaʊs] *n* : entrepôt *m*, magasin *m*

warfare [ˈwɔrˌfær] *n* **1** WAR : guerre *f* **2** STRUGGLE : lutte *f*, guerre *f* <class warfare : lutte de classes>

warhead [ˈwɔrˌhɛd] *n* : ogive *f*

warily [ˈwærəli] *adv* : avec prudence, avec précaution

wariness [ˈwærinəs] *n* : circonspection *f*, prudence *f*

warlike [ˈwɔrˌlaɪk] *adj* : guerrier, belliqueux

warm[1] [ˈwɔrm] *vi* **1** : chauffer **2 to warm to** : se montrer intéressé envers, être sympathique envers — *vt* **1** HEAT : chauffer, réchauffer **2 to warm oneself** : se réchauffer

warm[2] *adj* **1** LUKEWARM : tiède <warm milk : lait tiède> **2** : chaud <warm clothing : vêtements chauds> <it's warm today : il fait chaud aujourd'hui> **3** CORDIAL, ENTHUSIASTIC : chaleureux, amical <a warm welcome : un accueil chaleureux> **4** : chaud (se dit des couleurs) **5** FRESH : récent <a warm trail : une piste récente> **6** (*used in guessing games*) <you're getting warm! : tu chauffes!>

warm–blooded [ˈwɔrmˈblʌdəd] *adj* : à sang chaud

warmhearted [ˈwɔrmˈhɑrṭəd] *adj* : chaleureux, affectueux

warmly [ˈwɔrmli] *adv* **1** : chaudement <warmly dressed : habillé chaudement> **2** ENTHUSIASTICALLY : chaleureusement, amicalement

warmonger [ˈwɔrˌmɑŋgər, -ˌmʌŋ-] *n* : belliciste *mf*

warmth [ˈwɔrmpθ] *n* **1** : chaleur *f* <the warmth of the sun : la chaleur du

soleil> **2** ENTHUSIASM : chaleur *f,* enthousiasme *m,* cordialité *f*

warm–up [ˈwɔrm,ʌp] *n* : échauffement *m*

warm up *vi* : s'échauffer (aux sports) — *vt* **1** : réchauffer <to warm up the leftovers : réchauffer les restes> **2** : faire chauffer (le moteur)

warn [ˈwɔrn] *vt* **1** CAUTION : avertir, prévenir **2** INFORM : aviser

warning[1] [ˈwɔrnɪŋ] *adj* : d'alarme, d'alerte <a warning bell : une sonnette d'alarme>

warning[2] *n* **1** CAUTION : avertissement *m* <without warning : sans prévenir> **2** NOTICE : avis *m* <gale warning : avis de vents violents>

warp[1] [ˈwɔrp] *vt* **1** : voiler, gauchir (le bois, etc.) **2** DISTORT, PERVERT : pervertir, fausser — *vi* : gauchir, se voiler, coffrer *Can* (se dit du bois)

warp[2] *n* **1** : chaîne *f* (en tissage) **2** DISTORTION : déformation *f,* gauchissement *m* (du bois, du métal)

warrant[1] [ˈwɔrənt] *vt* **1** : être certain que, parier <I warrant he'll be here by noon : je suis certain qu'il sera ici à midi> **2** GUARANTEE : garantir **3** JUSTIFY, MERIT : mériter

warrant[2] *n* **1** JUSTIFICATION : justification *f,* droit *m* **2** AUTHORIZATION : mandat *m* <search warrant : mandat de perquisition>

warrant officer *n* : adjudant *m* (dans les forces armées)

warranty [ˈwɔrənti, ˌwɔrənˈti:] *n, pl* **-ties** : garantie *f*

warren [ˈwɔrən] *n* : garenne *f*

warrior [ˈwɔriər] *n* : guerrier *m,* -rière *f*

warship [ˈwɔr,ʃɪp] *n* : navire *m* de guerre

wart [ˈwɔrt] *n* : verrue *f*

wartime [ˈwɔr,taɪm] *n* : temps *m* de guerre

wary [ˈwæri] *adj* **warier; -est** : prudent, circonspect <to be wary of : se méfier de>

was → **be**

wash[1] [ˈwɔʃ, ˈwɑʃ] *vt* **1** CLEAN : laver <to wash clothes : laver des vêtements> <to wash one's hands : se laver les mains> **2** LAP : baigner <waves washing the shore : des vagues qui baignent la côte> **3** CARRY, DRAG : entraîner, emporter <to be washed out to sea : être entraîné par la mer> **4** **to wash away** : emporter (un pont, etc.) — *vi* **1** : se laver (se dit d'une personne ou des vêtements) **2** WORK : marcher <her story just doesn't wash : son histoire ne marche pas, son histoire ne tient pas debout>

wash[2] *n* **1** : lavage *m,* lessive *f* <the clothes are in the wash : le linge est au lavage> <to do the wash : faire la lessive> **2** CLEANING, WASHING : lavage *m,* nettoyage *m* <to give sth a wash : laver qqch> **3** : remous *m* (d'un bateau)

washable [ˈwɔʃəbəl, ˈwɑʃ-] *adj* : lavable

washboard [ˈwɔʃ,bord, ˈwɑʃ-] *n* : planche *f* à laver

washbowl [ˈwɔʃ,bo:l, ˈwɑʃ-] *n* : cuvette *f,* bassine *f*

washcloth [ˈwɔʃ,klɔθ, ˈwɑʃ-] *n* : gant *m* de toilette, débarbouillette *f Can*

washed–out [ˈwɔʃtˈaʊt, ˈwɑʃt-] *adj* **1** FADED : délavé, décoloré **2** EXHAUSTED : épuisé

washed–up [ˈwɔʃtˈʌp, ˈwɑʃt-] *adj* : fichu *fam,* ruiné

washer [ˈwɔʃər, ˈwɑ-] *n* **1** : rondelle *f,* joint *m* (en technologie) **2** → **washing machine**

washing [ˈwɔʃɪŋ, ˈwɑ-] *n* WASH : lavage *m,* lessive *f*

washing machine *n* : machine *f* à laver, laveuse *f Can*

washout [ˈwɔʃ,aʊt, ˈwɑʃ-] *n* **1** : érosion *f* (dû à la pluie) **2** FAILURE : fiasco *m,* échec *m*

washroom [ˈwɔʃ,ru:m, ˈwɑʃ-, -,rʊm] *n* : toilettes *fpl*

wasn't [ˈwʌzənt] (*contraction of* **was not**) → **be**

wasp [ˈwɑsp] *n* : guêpe *f*

waspish [ˈwɑspɪʃ] *adj* : irritable, qui a mauvais caractère

waste[1] *v* **wasted; wasting** [ˈweɪst] *vt* **1** DEVASTATE : dévaster, ravager **2** SQUANDER : gaspiller (de l'argent) <to waste one's time : perdre son temps> — *vi or* **to waste away** : dépérir

waste[2] *adj* **1** DESOLATE : désert, désolé **2** DISCARDED : de rebut, usé **3** *or* **waste material** : déchets *mpl*

waste[3] *n* **1** → **wasteland** **2** MISUSE : perte *f,* gaspillage *m* <a waste of time : une perte de temps> **3** REFUSE : déchets *mpl,* ordures *fpl* <nuclear waste : déchets nucléaires> <household wastes : ordures ménagères> **4** EXCREMENT : excrément *m*

wastebasket [ˈweɪst,bæskət] *n* : corbeille *f* à papier

wasteful [ˈweɪstfəl] *adj* : gaspilleur, dépensier

wastefulness [ˈweɪstfəlnəs] *n* : gaspillage *m*

wasteland [ˈweɪst,lænd, -lənd] *n* : terrain *m* vague, désert *m*

watch[1] [ˈwɑtʃ] *vi* **1** *or* **to keep watch** : veiller **2** LOOK : regarder **3** **to watch for** AWAIT : guetter, attendre **4** **to watch out** : faire attention — *vt* **1** OBSERVE : regarder, surveiller **2** *or* **to watch over** : veiller sur, garder **3** : faire attention à <watch what you are doing! : faites attention à ce que vous faites!>

watch[2] *n* **1** SURVEILLANCE : surveillance *f* <to keep a close watch on : surveiller de près> **2** LOOKOUT, SEN-

TRY : sentinelle *m*, homme *m* de quart (sur un navire) **3** TIMEPIECE : montre *f*
watchdog [ˈwɑtʃˌdɔg] *n* : chien *m* de garde, chienne *f* de garde
watcher [ˈwɑtʃər] *n* : spectateur *m*, -trice *f*; observateur *m*, -trice *f*
watchful [ˈwɑtʃfəl] *adj* : attentif, vigilant
watchfully [ˈwɑtʃfəli] *adv* : attentivement, de façon vigilante
watchman [ˈwɑtʃmən] *n, pl* **-men** [-mən, -ˌmɛn] : gardien *m*
watchword [ˈwɑtʃˌwərd] *n* **1** PASSWORD : mot *m* de passe **2** SLOGAN : mot *m* d'ordre, slogan *m*
water[1] [ˈwɔt̬ər, ˈwɑ-] *vt* **1** : arroser (un jardin, etc.) **2** : donner à boire à (des animaux) **3** *or* **to water down** DILUTE : couper (d'eau) — *vi* **1** : larmoyer (se dit des yeux) **2** : avoir l'eau à la bouche <to make one's mouth water : faire venir l'eau à la bouche>
water[2] *n* **1** : eau *f* <fresh water : eau douce> **2 waters** *npl* : eaux *fpl* <in Canadian waters : dans les eaux territoriales canadiennes>
water buffalo *n* : buffle *m*
watercolor [ˈwɔt̬ərˌkʌlər, ˈwɑ-] *n* **1** : couleur *f* pour aquarelle **2** *or* **watercolor painting** : aquarelle *f*
watercourse [ˈwɔt̬ərˌkors, ˈwɑ-] *n* : cours *m* d'eau
watercress [ˈwɔt̬ərˌkrɛs, ˈwɑ-] *n* : cresson *m*
waterfall [ˈwɔt̬ərˌfɔl, ˈwɑ-] *n* : chute *f* (d'eau), cascade *f*
waterfowl [ˈwɔt̬ərˌfaʊl, ˈwɑ-] *ns & pl* **1** : oiseau *m* aquatique **2 waterfowl** *npl* : gibier *m* d'eau
waterfront [ˈwɔt̬ərˌfrʌnt, ˈwɑ-] *n* : front *m* de mer
water lily *n* : nénuphar *m*
waterlogged [ˈwɔt̬ərˌlɔgd, -ˌlɑgd] *adj* : imprégné d'eau, détrempé (se dit de la terre)
watermark [ˈwɔt̬ərˌmɑrk, ˈwɑ-] *n* **1** : laisse *f* de haute mer (en navigation) **2** : filigrane *m* (du papier)
watermelon [ˈwɔt̬ərˌmɛlən, ˈwɑ-] *n* : pastèque *f*, melon *m* d'eau
water moccasin → **moccasin**
waterpower [ˈwɔt̬ərˌpaʊər, ˈwɑ-] *n* : énergie *f* hydraulique
waterproof[1] [ˈwɔt̬ərˌpruːf, ˈwɑ-] *vt* : imperméabiliser
waterproof[2] *adj* : imperméable
watershed [ˈwɔt̬ərˌʃɛd, ˈwɑ-] *n* : ligne *m* de partage des eaux
water–ski [ˈwɔt̬ərˌskiː, ˈwɑ-] *vi* : faire du ski nautique
water ski *n* : ski *m* nautique
waterskiing [ˈwɔt̬ərˌskiːɪŋ, ˈwɑ-] *n* : ski *m* nautique
waterspout [ˈwɔt̬ərˌspaʊt, ˈwɑ-] *n* **1** : gouttière *f*, tuyau *m* de descente **2** : trombe *f* (en météorologie)
watertight [ˈwɔt̬ərˌtaɪt, ˈwɑ-] *adj* **1** : étanche <a watertight joint : un raccord étanche> **2** : inattaquable, incontestable <a watertight argument : un argument inattaquable>
waterway [ˈwɔt̬ərˌweɪ, ˈwɑ-] *n* : cours *m* d'eau navigable
waterworks [ˈwɔt̬ərˌwərks, ˈwɑ-] *npl* : système *m* hydraulique
watery [ˈwɔt̬əri, ˈwɑ-] *adj* **1** : larmoyant (se dit des yeux) **2** THIN, WEAK : faible, liquide <watery soup : soupe trop liquide> **3** SOGGY : détrempé
watt [ˈwɑt] *n* : watt *m*
wattage [ˈwɑt̬ɪdʒ] *n* : consommation *f* en watts
wattle [ˈwɑt̬əl] *n* : caroncule *f* (d'un oiseau)
wave[1] [ˈweɪv] *v* **waved; waving** *vi* **1** FLUTTER : flotter, ondoyer **2** : faire un signe de la main <to wave goodbye : faire au revoir de la main> **3** UNDULATE : onduler — *vt* **1** SHAKE : agiter **2** BRANDISH : brandir **3** CURL : onduler (ses cheveux) **4** SIGNAL : faire signe à <I waved down the passing car : j'ai fait signe à la voiture d'arrêter>
wave[2] *n* **1** : vague *f* (d'eau) **2** CURL : ondulation *f* (des cheveux) **3** GREETING : geste *m* de la main **4** FLOW, GUSH : vague *f*, déferlement *m* <a wave of anger : une vague de colère> **5** : onde *f* (en physique)
wavelength [ˈweɪvˌlɛŋkθ] *n* : longueur *f* d'onde (en physique)
waver [ˈweɪvər] *vi* **1** VACILLATE : vaciller, hésiter **2** FLICKER : vaciller **3** FALTER : chanceler, trembloter (se dit de la voix)
wavy [ˈweɪvi] *adj* **wavier; -est** : ondulé
wax[1] [ˈwæks] *vt* : cirer (le plancher, etc.), farter (des skis) — *vi* **1** : croître (se dit de la lune) **2** BECOME : devenir, se montrer <to wax indignant : se montrer indigné>
wax[2] *n* **1** : cire *f* (pour les planchers, les meubles, etc.) **2** → **beeswax 3** → **earwax**
waxen [ˈwæksən] *adj* : cireux
waxy [ˈwæksi] *adj* **waxier; -est** : cireux
way [ˈweɪ] *n* **1** PATH, STREET : chemin *m* **2** ROUTE : chemin *m*, passage *m* <the way back : le chemin du retour> <it's the only way out : c'est la seule façon de s'en sortir> **3** MEANS, RESPECT : façon *f*, manière *f* <a new way of thinking : une nouvelle façon de penser> <in no way does he resemble his mother : il ne ressemble aucunement à sa mère> **4** FACILITY : talent *m*, habileté *f* <he has a way with children : il s'y prend bien avec les enfants> **5** MANNER, STYLE : façon *f* de vivre, manières *fpl* <it's just her way : c'est sa façon de vivre habituelle> **6** CONDITION, STATE : état *m*, situation *f* <it's the way

things are : c'est ainsi> 7 DISTANCE : distance *f* <we walked a long way : nous avons marché longtemps> 8 DIRECTION : direction *f,* sens *m* <he was looking my way : il regardait dans ma direction> <she's coming this way : elle vient par ici> 9 **by the way** : à propos 10 **by way of** VIA : par, via 11 **in a way** : dans un certain sens 12 **in the way of** : en fait de <he had little in the way of help : il n'était pas choyé en fait d'aide> 13 **out of the way** : éloigné, isolé 14 → **under way**

wayfarer ['weɪˌfærər] *n* : voyageur *m,* -geuse *f*

waylay ['weɪˌleɪ] *vt* **-laid** [-ˌleɪd]; **-laying** : attaquer, attirer dans une embuscade

wayside ['weɪˌsaɪd] *n* **1** : bord *m* de la route **2 to fall by the wayside** : tomber à l'eau, tomber en désuétude

wayward ['weɪwərd] *adj* **1** UNRULY : rebelle, capricieux **2** UNPREDICTABLE : imprévisible **3** UNTOWARD : malencontreux

we ['wi:] *pron* : nous <we're ready : nous sommes prêts> <as we say in Canada : comme on dit au Canada>

weak ['wi:k] *adj* **1** FEEBLE : faible, fragile (se dit des personnes) **2** : peu solide, fragile (se dit des structures, etc.) **3** UNCONVINCING : peu convaincant, faible <a weak argument : un argument réfutable> **4** DEFICIENT : faible **5** DILUTED : faible, léger, dilué **6** FAINT : faible (se dit des couleurs, des sons, de la lumière, etc.)

weaken ['wi:kən] *vt* : affaiblir — *vi* : s'affaiblir, faiblir

weakling ['wi:klɪŋ] *n* : gringalet *m*

weakly ['wi:kli] *adv* : faiblement

weakness ['wi:knəs] *n* **1** : faiblesse *f,* point *m* faible <in a moment of weakness : dans un moment de faiblesse> **2** FAULT : défaut *m* **3** PARTIALITY : faible *m,* penchant *m* <a weakness for luxury : un faible pour le luxe>

wealth ['wɛlθ] *n* **1** RICHES : richesse *f,* fortune *f* **2** PROFUSION : abondance *f,* profusion *f*

wealthy ['wɛlθi] *adj* **wealthier; -est** : riche

wean ['wi:n] *vt* **1** : sevrer (un bébé) **2 to wean s.o. away from** : détacher qqn de, détourner qqn de

weapon ['wɛpən] *n* : arme *f*

wear[1] ['wær] *v* **wore** ['wor]; **worn** ['worn]; **wearing** *vt* **1** : porter (des vêtements, des lunettes, etc.) **2** EXHIBIT, PRESENT : arborer <to wear a happy smile : arborer un large sourire> **3 to wear away** : ronger, éroder (des roches, etc.) **4** *or* **to wear out** : user **5** EXHAUST : épuiser — *vi* **1** LAST : durer **2** *or* **to wear out** : s'user, se détériorer **3 to wear off** : diminuer

wear[2] *n* **1** USE : port *m* <for everyday wear : de tous les jours> **2** CLOTHES : vêtements *mpl* **3** *or* **wear and tear** : usure *f*

wearable ['wærəbəl] *adj* : mettable, portable

wearily ['wɪrəli] *adv* : d'un air las

weariness ['wɪrinəs] *n* : lassitude *f*

wearisome ['wɪrisəm] *adj* : fastidieux, fatigant

weary[1] ['wɪri] *v* **-ried; -rying** *vt* : lasser, fatiguer — *vi* : se lasser

weary[2] *adj* **wearier; -est** : fatigué, las

weasel ['wi:zəl] *n* : belette *f*

weather[1] ['wɛðər] *vt* **1** : exposer (le bois, etc.) aux intempéries **2** ENDURE : se tirer de, surmonter — *vi* : s'éroder (se dit des roches)

weather[2] *n* : temps *m*

weather–beaten ['wɛðərˌbi:tən] *adj* **1** : battu, usé (par les intempéries) **2** : hâlé <a weather-beaten face : un visage hâlé>

weatherman ['wɛðərˌmæn] *n, pl* **-men** : météorologiste *mf*

weatherproof[1] ['wɛðərˌpru:f] *vt* : imperméabiliser

weatherproof[2] *adj* : imperméable, étanche

weather vane → **vane**

weave[1] ['wi:v] *v* **wove** ['wo:v] *or* **weaved; woven** ['wo:vən] *or* **weaved; weaving** *vt* **1** : tisser **2** INTERLACE : entrelacer, tresser **3 to weave a tale** : inventer une histoire **4 to weave one's way through** : se faufiler à travers — *vi* **1** : tisser **2** WIND : serpenter

weave[2] *n* : tissage *m*

weaver ['wi:vər] *n* : tisserand *m,* -rande *f*

web ['wɛb] *n* **1** COBWEB : toile *f* (d'araignée) **2** : palmure *f* (d'un oiseau) **3** ENTANGLEMENT : tissu *m,* réseau *m* <a web of lies : un tissu de mensonges> **4** NETWORK : réseau *m* **5 Web** → **World Wide Web**

webbed ['wɛbd] *adj* : palmé <webbed feet : pattes palmées>

webmaster ['wɛbˌmæstər] *n* : webmaster *m,* webmestre *m*

Web site *n* : site *m* Web

wed ['wɛd] *vt* **wedded; wedding 1** MARRY : se marier à, épouser **2** UNITE : allier

we'd ['wi:d] (*contraction of* **we had, we should,** *or* **we would**) → **have, should, would**

wedding ['wɛdɪŋ] *n* : mariage *m,* noces *fpl*

wedge[1] ['wɛdʒ] *vt* **wedged; wedging 1** : caler, fixer (avec une cale) **2** CRAM : enfoncer, coincer

wedge[2] *n* **1** : cale *f* (pour tenir ouverte une porte, etc.), coin *m* (pour enfoncer dans une bûche) **2** PIECE : morceau *m,* part *m* (de gâteau, etc.)

wedlock ['wɛdˌlɑk] *n* : mariage *m*

Wednesday ['wɛnzˌdeɪ, -di] *n* : mercredi *m*

wee ['wi:] *adj* : tout petit <in the wee hours of the morning : aux petites heures du matin>

weed[1] ['wi:d] *vi* : désherber, enlever les mauvaises herbes — *vt* **1** : désherber (un jardin) **2 to weed out** : se débarrasser de, éliminer

weed[2] *n* : mauvaise herbe *f*

weedy ['wi:di] *adj* **weedier; -est 1** : couvert de mauvaises herbes **2** LANKY, SCRAWNY : dégingandé, décharné

week ['wi:k] *n* : semaine *f*

weekday ['wi:k,deɪ] *n* : jour *m* de semaine

weekend ['wi:k,ɛnd] *n* : fin *f* de semaine, week-end *m*

weekly[1] ['wi:kli] *adv* : à la semaine, chaque semaine

weekly[2] *adj* : hebdomadaire

weekly[3] *n, pl* **-lies** : hebdomadaire *m*, journal *m* hebdomadaire

weep ['wi:p] *vi* **wept** ['wɛpt]; **weeping** : pleurer

weeping willow *n* : saule *m* pleureur

weepy ['wi:pi] *adj* **weepier; -est** : larmoyant, au bord des larmes

weevil ['wi:vəl] *n* : charançon *m*

weft ['wɛft] *n* : trame *f*

weigh ['weɪ] *vt* **1** : peser **2** CONSIDER : peser, considérer **3 to weigh anchor** : lever l'ancre **4 to weigh down** : surcharger (un véhicule, etc.), accabler (une personne) — *vi* **1** : peser <she weighs 100 pounds : elle pèse 100 livres> **2** COUNT : compter, avoir de l'importance <to weigh against : jouer contre> **3 to weigh on s.o.'s mind** : préoccuper qqn

weight[1] ['weɪt] *vt* **1** LOAD : charger, lester **2** *or* **to weight down** BURDEN : alourdir, charger

weight[2] *n* **1** HEAVINESS : poids *m* <to lose weight : perdre du poids> <to sell by weight : vendre au poids> **2** : poids *m* <weights and measures : poids et mesures> **3** : poids *m* <to lift weights : soulever des poids> **4** BURDEN : poids *m*, pesanteur *f* <it's a weight on my mind : cela me pèse beaucoup> **5** IMPORTANCE : influence *f*, importance *f* <to throw one's weight around : essayer de faire l'important>

weightlessness ['weɪtləsnəs] *n* : apesanteur *f*

weighty ['weɪt̬i] *adj* **weightier; -est 1** HEAVY : pesant, lourd **2** POWERFUL : important, de poids

weird ['wɪrd] *adj* **1** UNEARTHLY : surnaturel, mystérieux **2** STRANGE : étrange, bizarre

weirdly ['wɪrdli] *adv* **1** MYSTERIOUSLY : mystérieusement **2** STRANGELY : étrangement, bizarrement

welcome[1] ['wɛlkəm] *vt* **-comed; -coming 1** GREET : accueillir, souhaiter la bienvenue à **2** ACCEPT : accepter avec plaisir, être heureux de recevoir

welcome[2] *adj* **1** : bienvenu <they are always welcome : ils sont toujours les bienvenus> <you're welcome to come and go : vous pouvez aller et venir à votre guise> **2** PLEASING : bienvenu, agréable <a welcome relief : un vrai soulagement> **3 you're welcome** : de rien, je vous en prie

welcome[3] *n* : accueil *m*

weld[1] ['wɛld] *vi* : souder — *vt* **1** : souder **2** UNITE : unir

weld[2] *n* : soudure *f*

welder ['wɛldər] *n* : soudeur *m*, -deuse *f*

welfare ['wɛl,fær] *n* **1** WELL-BEING : bien-être *m* **2** AID : aide *f* sociale, assistance *f* publique

well[1] ['wɛl] *vi or* **to well up** : monter

well[2] *adv* **better** ['bɛt̬ər]; **best** ['bɛst] **1** : bien <he did well in his classes : il réussissait bien dans ses cours> **2** HIGHLY : bien <to speak well of s.o. : dire du bien de qqn> <to think well of : avoir de l'estime pour> **3** COMPLETELY, FULLY : tout à fait <to be well aware of : être tout à fait conscient de> <it's well worth the price : cela vaut bien le prix> **4** INTIMATELY : bien, intimement <I know him well : je le connais bien> **5** CONSIDERABLY, FAR : considérablement, bien <well over one million dollars : bien au-delà d'un million de dollars> **6** DEFINITELY, EXACTLY : clairement, bien <she remembered it well : elle s'en souvenait très clairement> **7 as well** ALSO : aussi **8** → **as well as 9 it may well be that** : il se pourrait bien que

well[3] *adj* **1** PLEASING, SATISFACTORY : bien <all's well that ends well : tout est bien qui finit bien> **2** DESIRABLE : désirable, souhaitable <it would be well for you to leave : il vaudrait mieux pour vous de partir> **3** HEALTHY : bien portant <she's not well : elle ne se porte pas bien>

well[4] *n* **1** : puits *m* (d'eau, de pétrole, etc.) **2** ORIGIN, SOURCE : source *f*, fontaine *f* **3** → **stairwell**

well[5] *interj* **1** (*used to express surprise or doubt*) : ça alors!, eh bien! **2** (*used to begin or resume a conversation*) : bon, bien, enfin

we'll ['wi:l, wɪl] (*contraction of* **we shall** *or* **we will**) → **shall, will**

well–adjusted [,wɛlə'dʒʌstəd] *adj* : équilibré, bien adapté

well–advised [,wɛləd'vaɪzd] *adj* : prudent, sage

well–being ['wɛl'bi:ɪŋ] *n* : bien-être *m*

well–bred ['wɛl'brɛd] *adj* : bien élevé, poli

well–done ['wɛl'dʌn] *adj* **1** : bien fait **2** : bien cuit (en cuisine)

well–known ['wɛl'no:n] *adj* : bien connu

well–meaning [ˈwɛlˈmiːnɪŋ] *adj* : bien intentionné

well–nigh [ˈwɛlˈnaɪ] *adv* : presque, quasi <well-nigh impossible : quasi impossible>

well–off [ˈwɛlˈɔf] → **well–to–do**

well–rounded [ˈwɛlˈraʊndəd] *adj* : complet

well–to–do [ˌwɛltəˈduː] *adj* : prospère, aisé, riche

Welsh[1] [ˈwɛlʃ, ˈwɛltʃ] *adj* : gallois

Welsh[2] *n* **1** : gallois *m* (langue) **2 the Welsh** : les Gallois *mpl*

welt [ˈwɛlt] *n* **1** : trépointe *f* (de chaussures) **2** : zébrure *f,* marque *f* (sur la peau)

welter[1] [ˈwɛltər] *vi* : se rouler, se vautrer

welter[2] *n* JUMBLE : fatras *m,* fouillis *m*

wend [ˈwɛnd] *vi* **to wend one's way towards** : s'acheminer vers, se diriger vers

went → **go**[1]

wept → **weep**

were → **be**

we're [ˈwɪr, ˈwər, ˈwiːər] (*contraction of* **we are**) → **be**

werewolf [ˈwɪrˌwʊlf, ˈwɛr-, ˈwər-, -ˌwʌlf] *n, pl* **-wolves** [-ˌwʊlvz, -ˌwʌlvz] : loup-garou *m*

west[1] [ˈwɛst] *adv* : à l'ouest, vers l'ouest

west[2] *adj* : ouest, d'ouest

west[3] *n* **1** : ouest *m* **2 the West** : l'Ouest *m,* l'Occident *m*

westerly[1] [ˈwɛstərli] *adv* : vers l'ouest

westerly[2] *adj* : à l'ouest, d'ouest

western [ˈwɛstərn] *adj* **1** : ouest, de l'ouest, occidental **2 Western** : de l'Ouest, occidental <Western Europe : l'Europe occidentale>

Westerner [ˈwɛstərnər] *n* : habitant *m,* -tante *f* de l'Ouest

West Indian[1] *adj* : antillais

West Indian[2] *n* : Antillais, -laise *f*

westward [ˈwɛstwərd] *adj & adv* : vers l'ouest

westwards [ˈwɛstwərdz] *adv* : vers l'ouest

wet[1] [ˈwɛt] *vt* **wet** *or* **wetted; wetting** : mouiller

wet[2] *adj* **wetter; wettest 1** : mouillé, humide <a wet cloth : un chiffon humide> **2** RAINY : pluvieux **3** : frais <wet paint : peinture fraîche>

wet[3] *n* **1** WATER : eau *f* **2** MOISTURE : humidité *f* **3** RAIN : pluie *f*

we've [ˈwiːv] (*contraction of* **we have**) → **have**

whack[1] [ˈhwæk] *vt* : donner une claque à, donner un grand coup à

whack[2] *n* **1** BLOW : coup *m,* claque *f* **2** TRY : essai *m* <to have a whack at sth : essayer (de faire) qqch>

whale[1] [ˈhweɪl] *v* **whaled; whaling** *vi* : pêcher la baleine

whale[2] *n, pl* **whales** *or* **whale** : baleine *f*

whaleboat [ˈhweɪlˌboːt] *n* : baleinière *f,* baleinier *m*

whalebone [ˈhweɪlˌboːn] *n* : fanon *m* de baleine

whaler [ˈhweɪlər] *n* **1** : baleinier *m* (personne) **2** → **whaleboat**

wharf [ˈhwɔrf] *n, pl* **wharves** [ˈhwɔrvz] : quai *m*

what[1] [ˈhwɑt, ˈhwʌt] *adv* **1** (*used in rhetorical questions*) <what does it matter : qu'est-ce que ça fait> **2** (*used to introduce prepositional phrases*) <what with one thing and another : avec ceci et cela>

what[2] *adj* **1** (*used in questions*) : quel <what book are you reading? : quel livre lisez-vous?> **2** (*used in exclamations*) <what an idea! : quelle idée!> <what fun we had! : le plaisir qu'on a eu ensemble!> **3** ANY, WHATEVER : le peu de, tout <what money he had : tout l'argent qu'il avait>

what[3] *pron* **1** : qu'est-ce que, qu'est-ce qui <what is this? : qu'est-ce que c'est?> <what's happening? : qu'est-ce qui se passe?> **2** : ce que, ce qui <I know what you want : je sais ce que vous voulez> **3** (*used in interrogative sentences or to express surprise*) : quoi <what's new? : quoi de neuf?> <what, no breakfast? : quoi, vous ne déjeunez pas?> **4** WHATEVER : (tout) ce que <say what you want : dites ce que vous voulez> **5 what for** WHY : pourquoi <what did you do that for? : pourquoi as-tu fait ça?> **6 what if** : et si <what if they find out? : et s'ils l'apprenaient?>

whatever[1] [hwɑtˈɛvər, ˌhwʌt-] *adj* **1** : n'importe quel, tout <take whatever seat : prenez n'importe quel siège> **2** (*in negative constructions*) <we had no food whatever : nous n'avions pas la moindre nourriture> <nothing whatever : rien du tout>

whatever[2] *pron* **1** ANYTHING : (tout) ce que <I'll do whatever you ask : je ferai tout ce que vous me demandez> **2** : quoi que <whatever it may be : quoi que ce soit> **3** WHAT : qu'est-ce que, qu'est-ce qui <whatever do you mean? : qu'est-ce que vous voulez dire?>

whatsoever [ˌhwɑtsoˈɛvər, ˌhwʌt-] *pron & adj* → **whatever**

wheal [ˈhwiːl] *n* : marque *f* (sur la peau)

wheat [ˈhwiːt] *n* : blé *m*

wheaten [ˈhwiːtən] *adj* : de blé

wheedle [ˈhwiːdəl] *vt* **-dled; -dling** : cajoler, enjôler <to wheedle money out of s.o. : soutirer de l'argent à qqn par des cajoleries>

wheel[1] [ˈhwiːl] *vi* **1** REVOLVE : tourner **2** *or* **to wheel around** TURN : faire demi-tour — *vt* : pousser <they wheeled in the patient : ils ont fait entrer le patient sur un lit roulant>

wheel[2] *n* **1** : roue *f* (d'un véhicule), roulette *f* (d'un meuble, etc.) **2** → **steering wheel 3 wheels** *npl* WORKINGS : rouages *mpl* <wheels of government : rouages du gouvernement>

wheelbarrow [ˈ*h*wiːlˌbærˌoː] *n* : brouette *f*

wheelchair [ˈ*h*wiːlˌtʃær] *n* : fauteuil *m* roulant

wheeze[1] [ˈ*h*wiːz] *vi* **wheezed; wheezing** : respirer péniblement et bruyamment

wheeze[2] *n* : respiration *f* sifflante

whelk [ˈ*h*wɛlk] *n* : buccin *m*

whelp[1] [ˈ*h*wɛlp] *v* : mettre bas

whelp[2] *n* : petit *m* (d'un animal)

when[1] [ˈ*h*wɛn] *adv* **1** (*used in direct and indirect questions*) : quand <when did you return? : quand êtes-vous revenu?> <he asked me when I did it : il m'a demandé quand je l'ai fait> **2** : où <at a time when things were better : à une époque où les choses allaient mieux>

when[2] *conj* **1** (*referring to a specified time*) : quand, lorsque <when he was a boy : quand il était garçon> <I smiled when he said it : j'ai souri lorsqu'il l'a dit> **2** IF, WHENEVER : quand, si <you're disqualified when you cheat : vous serez disqualifié si vous trichez> **3** ALTHOUGH : alors que, quand, si <why do you tease me, when you know it's wrong? : pourquoi me taquines-tu alors que tu sais que c'est mal?>

when[3] *pron* **1 by when** : avant quand **2 since when** : depuis quand

whence [ˈ*h*wɛnts] *adv & conj* : d'où

whenever[1] [*h*wɛnˈɛvər] *adv* : quand

whenever[2] *conj* : chaque fois que

where[1] [ˈ*h*wɛr] *adv* **1** (*at what place*) : où <where are they? : où sont-ils?> **2** (*at which part*) : où <where did I go wrong? : où est-ce que je me suis trompée?>

where[2] *conj* **1** : où <he knows where the house is : il sait où se trouve la maison> <stay where you are : restez où vous êtes> **2** WHEREVER : où que, partout où <she goes where he likes to go : elle va partout où il aime aller>

where[3] *pron* : où <the town where she was born : la ville où elle est née>

whereabouts[1] [ˈ*h*wɛrəˌbaʊts] *adv* : où <whereabouts is the house? : où est la maison?>

whereabouts[2] *ns & pl* **to know s.o.'s whereabouts** : savoir où se trouve qqn

whereas [*h*wɛrˈæz] *conj* **1** : alors que, tandis que <I like the sea whereas she likes the mountains : j'aime la mer alors qu'elle aime les montagnes> **2** SINCE : attendu que (en droit)

whereby [*h*wɛrˈbaɪ] *conj* : par lequel, selon lequel

wherefore[1] [ˈ*h*wɛrˌfor] *adv* **1** WHY : pourquoi **2** THEREFORE : donc

wherefore[2] *n* **the whys and wherefores** : le pourquoi et le comment

wherein [*h*wɛrˈɪn] *adv* : en quoi

whereof [*h*wɛrˈʌv, -ɑv] *conj* : de quoi

whereupon [ˈ*h*wɛrəˌpɑn, -ˌpɔn] *conj* : sur quoi, sur ce

wherever[1] [*h*wɛrˈɛvər] *adv* **1** (*used for emphasis*) : mais où, où donc <wherever did you get that tie? : mais où donc as-tu déniché cette cravate?> **2 or wherever** : Dieu sait où

wherever[2] *conj* : où que, partout où <wherever you go : où que tu ailles>

wherewithal [ˈ*h*wɛrwɪˌðɔl, -ˌθɔl] *n* : ressources *fpl,* moyens *mpl*

whet [ˈ*h*wɛt] *vt* **whetted; whetting 1** SHARPEN : affûter, aiguiser (un couteau) **2** STIMULATE : stimuler <to whet one's appetite : ouvrir l'appétit>

whether [ˈ*h*wɛðər] *conj* **1** IF : si <see whether they've left : vérifie s'ils sont partis> **2** (*used to introduce alternatives*) <the game will be played whether it rains or not : nous allons jouer la partie qu'il pleuve ou non> <whether before or after : soit avant soit après>

whetstone [ˈ*h*wɛtˌstoːn] *n* : pierre *f* à aiguiser

whey [ˈ*h*weɪ] *n* : petit-lait *m*

which[1] [ˈ*h*wɪtʃ] *adj* : quel <which shirt should I wear? : quelle chemise devrais-je porter?> <which ones? : lesquels?>

which[2] *pron* **1** : lequel, quel <which of the answers is right? : laquelle des réponses est la bonne?> <he wondered which would be better : il se demandait quel serait mieux> **2** (*used as a function word to introduce a relative clause*) : qui, que <the suggestion which you made : la suggestion que vous avez faite>

whichever[1] [*h*wɪtʃˈɛvər] *adj* : peu importe quel <whichever way you go : peu importe quel chemin vous empruntez>

whichever[2] *pron* : quel que <whichever you prefer : quelle que soit votre préférence>

whiff[1] [ˈ*h*wɪf] *vi* **1** PUFF : souffler **2** : respirer une odeur

whiff[2] *n* **1** GUST, PUFF : bouffée *f* **2** SMELL, TRACE : odeur *f* <to catch a whiff of : sentir l'odeur de>

while[1] [ˈ*h*waɪl] *vt* **whiled; whiling** : (faire) passer <to while away the time : passer le temps>

while[2] *n* **1** : temps *m,* moment *m* <after a while : au bout d'un moment> <once in a while : de temps en temps> <a long while ago : il y a longtemps> **2 to be worth one's while** : valoir la peine

while[3] *conj* **1** : pendant que <while you're at it : pendant que vous y êtes>

<while you were out : pendant votre absence> 2 ALTHOUGH : bien que <while respected, he is not liked : bien que respecté, il n'est pas aimé> 3 WHEREAS : tandis que, alors que

whim [ˈhwɪm] *n* : caprice *m*, lubie *f*

whimper[1] [ˈhwɪmpər] *vi* : gémir, pleurnicher *fam*

whimper[2] *n* : gémissement *m*

whimsical [ˈhwɪmzɪkəl] *adj* 1 CAPRICIOUS : capricieux, fantasque 2 ERRATIC : changeant, imprévisible

whimsically [ˈhwɪmzɪkəli] *adv* : curieusement, de façon saugrenue

whimsy [ˈhwɪmzi] *n, pl* 1 → **whim** 2 : fantaisie *f*, caractère *m* fantasque

whine[1] [ˈhwaɪn] *vi* **whined; whining** 1 WHIMPER : gémir, geindre 2 COMPLAIN : se plaindre, se lamenter

whine[2] *n* : gémissement *m*

whinny[1] [ˈhwɪni] *vi* **-nied; -nying** : hennir

whinny[2] *n* : hennissement *m*

whip[1] [ˈhwɪp] *v* **whipped; whipping** *vt* 1 SNATCH : tirer brusquement, arracher <she whipped off the tablecloth : elle a brusquement arraché la nappe> 2 LASH : fouetter 3 DEFEAT : vaincre, battre à plates coutures 4 BEAT : battre (des œufs, etc.) 5 **to whip up** INCITE : attiser (une émotion), susciter (de l'intérêt) — *vi* 1 LASH : battre <the rain whipped against the shutters : la pluie battait contre les volets> 2 : aller rapidement <to whip along : filer à toute allure>

whip[2] *n* 1 : fouet *m*, cravache *f* (d'équitation) 2 : député *m* d'un parti législatif qui réglemente la discipline et les votes de son parti 3 : mousse *f* <prune whip : mousse aux pruneaux>

whiplash [ˈhwɪp,læʃ] *n or* **whiplash injury** : coup *m* du lapin

whippet [ˈhwɪpət] *n* : whippet *m*

whippoorwill [ˈhwɪpər,wɪl] *n* : engoulevent *m* (de l'Amérique du Nord)

whir[1] [ˈhwər] *vi* **whirred; whirring** 1 : bruire (se dit des ailes) 2 : ronronner, vrombir (se dit d'un moteur, d'un ventilateur, etc.)

whir[2] *n* 1 : bruissement *m* (de feuilles, d'ailes) 2 : ronronnement *m*, vrombissement *m* <the whir of propellers : le vrombissement des hélices>

whirl[1] [ˈhwərl] *vi* 1 SPIN : tournoyer, tourbillonner 2 REEL : tourner <my head was whirling : la tête me tournait> 3 **to whirl around** : se retourner 4 **to whirl by** : aller à toute vitesse, filer à toute allure — *vi* : faire tournoyer, faire tourbillonner

whirl[2] *n* 1 WHIRLING : tournoiement *m* 2 BUSTLE : tourbillon *m* 3 **to give sth a whirl** : s'essayer à qqch

whirlpool [ˈhwərl,pu:l] *n* : tourbillon *m* (d'eau)

whirlwind [ˈhwərl,wɪnd] *n* : tourbillon *m* (de vent), trombe *f*

whisk[1] [ˈhwɪsk] *vt* 1 : faire rapidement <I whisked it out of my purse : je l'ai brusquement sorti de mon sac à main> 2 BEAT : battre (des œufs) 3 *or* **to whisk away** : enlever d'un geste rapide — *vi* : aller vite

whisk[2] *n* 1 WHISKING : coup *m* léger 2 : fouet *m* (en cuisine)

whisk broom *n* : époussette *f*

whisker [ˈhwɪskər] *n* 1 : poil *m* de barbe <to win by a whisker : gagner d'un poil> 2 **whiskers** *npl* : barbe *f* (d'un homme), moustaches *fpl* (d'un chat, etc.)

whiskey *or* **whisky** [ˈhwɪski] *n, pl* **-keys** *or* **-kies** : whisky *m*

whisper[1] [ˈhwɪspər] *vi* : chuchoter, parler à voix basse — *vt* : chuchoter, dire à voix basse

whisper[2] *n* 1 : chuchotement *m* <to speak in whispers : parler tout bas> 2 RUMOR : rumeur *f*, bruit *m* 3 HINT : soupçon *m*, trace *f*

whistle[1] [ˈhwɪsəl] *vi* **-tled; -tling** 1 : siffler 2 **to whistle by** : passer en sifflant — *vt* : siffler

whistle[2] *n* 1 WHISTLING : sifflement *m* 2 : sifflet *m* <to blow a whistle : donner un coup de sifflet>

whit [ˈhwɪt] *n* BIT : brin *m*, petit peu *m*

white[1] [ˈhwaɪt] *adj* **whiter; -est** : blanc

white[2] *n* 1 : blanc *m* (couleur) 2 *or* **egg white** : blanc *m* d'œuf 3 : Blanc *m*, Blanche *f* (personne)

white blood cell *n* : globule *m* blanc

whitecaps [ˈhwaɪt,kæps] *npl* : moutons *mpl*

white–collar [ˈhwaɪtˈkɑlər] *adj* : de bureau, de col blanc

whitefish [ˈhwaɪt,fɪʃ] *n* : corégone *m*

whiten [ˈhwaɪtən] *v* : blanchir

whiteness [ˈhwaɪtnəs] *n* : blancheur *f*

white–tailed deer [ˈhwaɪtˈteɪld] *n* : cerf *m* de Virginie, chevreuil *m Can*

whitewash[1] [ˈhwaɪt,wɔʃ] *vt* 1 : blanchir (une clôture, etc.) à la chaux 2 CONCEAL : camoufler, dissimuler

whitewash[2] *n* 1 : lait *m* de chaux 2 COVER-UP : dissimulation *f*, camouflage *m*

whither [ˈhwɪðər] *adv* : où

whiting [ˈhwaɪt̬ɪŋ] *n* : merlan *m* (poisson)

whitish [ˈhwaɪt̬ɪʃ] *adj* : blanchâtre

whittle [ˈhwɪt̬əl] *vt* **-tled; -tling** 1 : tailler au couteau, gosser *Can fam* 2 PARE, REDUCE : réduire, amoindrir

whiz[1] *or* **whizz** [ˈhwɪz] *vi* **whizzed; whizzing** 1 BUZZ, HISS : bourdonner, siffler 2 *or* **to whiz by** : passer à toute vitesse, passer en sifflant

whiz[2] *or* **whizz** *n* 1 BUZZ : bourdonnement *m*, sifflement *m* 2 : expert *m*, as *m* <a computer whiz : un expert en informatique>

who [ˈhuː] *pron* **1** (*used as an interrogative*) : qui <who was elected? : qui a été élu?> <do you know who the message was from? : savez-vous qui a écrit le message?> **2** WHOEVER : qui, qui que ce soit **3** (*used to introduce a relative clause*) : qui <my father, who was a lawyer : mon père, qui était avocat>

whodunit [huːˈdʌnɪt] *n* : roman *m* policier

whoever [huːˈɛvər] *pron* **1** : qui que ce soit, n'importe qui <whoever told you that, he's wrong : qui que ce soit qui te l'a dit il se trompe> **2** : celui qui, quiconque <whoever wants to participate : quiconque veut participer> **3** (*used to express astonishment or perplexity*) <whoever can that be? : qui est-ce que ça peut bien être?>

whole[1] [ˈhoːl] *adj* **1** : entier <whole milk : lait entier> **2** INTACT : complet, intact **3** COMPLETE, ENTIRE : au complet, tout <she owns the whole island : l'île au complet lui appartient> <his whole attention : toute son attention> **4 a whole lot** : beaucoup

whole[2] *n* **1** : tout *m*, ensemble *m* **2 as a whole** : dans son ensemble, entièrement **3 on the whole** : en général, dans l'ensemble

wholehearted [ˈhoːlˈhɑrt̬əd] *adj* : de bon cœur, sans réserve

whole number *n* : nombre *m* entier

wholesale[1] [ˈhoːlˌseɪl] *v* **-saled; -saling** *vt* : vendre au prix de gros — *vi* : se vendre au prix de gros

wholesale[2] *adv* : en gros

wholesale[3] *adj* **1** : de gros <wholesale prices : prix de gros> **2** : en masse <wholesale slaughter : massacre en masse>

wholesale[4] *n* : vente *f* en gros

wholesaler [ˈhoːlˌseɪlər] *n* : grossiste *mf*

wholesome [ˈhoːlsəm] *adj* **1** HEALTHY, SOUND : sain, en santé **2** HEALTHFUL : sain, salubre

whole wheat *adj* : de blé entier

wholly [ˈhoːli] *adv* **1** COMPLETELY : complètement, entièrement **2** SOLELY : exclusivement

whom [ˈhuːm] *pron* **1** (*used as an interrogative*) <whom did he fight? : avec qui s'est-il battu?> **2** (*used as a relative pronoun*) <two professors whom I met in Italy : deux professeurs que j'ai rencontrés en Italie> **3** (*used as the object of a preposition*) <the politician to whom you wrote : le politicien à qui vous avez écrit>

whomever [huːmˈɛvər] → **whoever**

whoop[1] [ˈhwuːp, ˈhwʊp] *vi* : pousser des cris

whoop[2] *n* : cri *m*

whooping cough *n* : coqueluche *f*

whopper [ˈhwɑpər] *n* **1** : chose *f* énorme **2** LIE : bobard *m fam*, gros mensonge *m*

whopping [ˈhwɑpɪŋ] *adj* : colossal, monstre

whore [ˈhor] *n* : prostituée *f*

whorl [ˈhwɔrl, ˈhwərl] *n* **1** : spire *f* (d'un coquillage), verticille *m* (de pétales), volute *f* (d'un doigt) **2** SWIRL : spirale *f*, volute *f* <a whorl of smoke : une spirale de fumée>

whose[1] [ˈhuːz] *adj* **1** (*used in questions*) : de qui, à qui <whose daughter is she? : de qui est-elle la fille?> <whose fault is it? : à qui la faute?> **2** (*used in relative clauses*) : dont <a friend whose husband works with me : une amie dont le mari travaille avec moi>

whose[2] *pron* : à qui <whose is this? : à qui est ceci?>

why[1] [ˈhwaɪ] *adv* : pourquoi <why did you do it? : pourquoi l'as-tu fait?>

why[2] *n, pl* **whys** : pourquoi *m*

why[3] *conj* **1** : pourquoi <I know why he did it : je sais pourquoi il l'a fait> **2** : pour lequel <the reason why he accepted : la raison pour laquelle il a accepté>

why[4] *interj* : mais!, tiens!

wick [ˈwɪk] *n* : mèche *f*

wicked [ˈwɪkəd] *adj* **1** EVIL : corrompu, méchant **2** MISCHIEVOUS : espiègle, malicieux **3** TERRIBLE : mauvais, épouvantable

wickedly [ˈwɪkədli] *adv* **1** : avec méchanceté **2** MISCHIEVOUSLY : malicieusement

wickedness [ˈwɪkədnəs] *n* : méchanceté *f*, vilenie *f*

wicker[1] [ˈwɪkər] *adj* : en osier

wicker[2] *n* **1** : osier *m* **2** → **wickerwork**

wickerwork [ˈwɪkərˌwərk] *n* : vannerie *f*

wicket [ˈwɪkət] *n* : guichet *m*

wide[1] [ˈwaɪd] *adv* **wider; widest 1** : partout <to search far and wide : chercher partout> **2** FULLY : complètement <she opened her eyes wide : elle a ouvert grand les yeux>

wide[2] *adj* **wider; widest 1** EXTENSIVE, VAST : vaste, étendu <a wide area : une vaste superficie> <to have wide experience : avoir une grande expérience> **2** : de large <3 feet wide : trois pieds de large> **3** BROAD : large **4 to be wide of the mark** : être loin de la vérité

wide–awake [ˈwaɪdəˈweɪk] *adj* : éveillé, alerte

wide–eyed [ˈwaɪdˈaɪd] *adj* **1** : aux yeux écarquillés **2** AMAZED : étonné, stupéfait **3** NAIVE : naïf, crédule

widely [ˈwaɪdli] *adv* **1** EXTENSIVELY : largement, beaucoup **2** SIGNIFICANTLY : considérablement

widen [ˈwaɪdən] *vt* : élargir — *vi* : s'élargir

widespread ['waɪd'sprɛd] *adj* **1** EXTENDED, SPREAD : déployé, étendu **2** EXTENSIVE : diffus, répandu

widow[1] ['wɪˌdo:] *vt* **to be widowed** : devenir veuf, devenir veuve

widow[2] *n* : veuve *f*

widower ['wɪdowər] *n* : veuf *m*

width ['wɪdθ] *n* : largeur *f*

wield ['wi:ld] *vt* **1** : brandir <to wield a broom : brandir un balai> **2** EXERT : exercer (de l'influence, etc.)

wiener ['wi:nər] → **frankfurter**

wife ['waɪf] *n, pl* **wives** ['waɪvz] : femme *f*, épouse *f*

wifely ['waɪfli] *adj* : d'épouse

wig ['wɪg] *n* : perruque *f*, postiche *m*

wiggle[1] ['wɪgəl] *v* **-gled; -gling** *vi* **1** JIGGLE : remuer (se dit des personnes), branler (se dit des choses) **2** WRIGGLE : se tortiller — *vt* : faire branler, faire bouger

wiggle[2] *n* : tortillement *m*

wiggly ['wɪgəli] *adj* **wigglier; -est 1** : qui se tortille **2** WAVY : ondulé, sinueux

wigwam ['wɪgˌwɑm] *n* : wigwam *m*

wild[1] ['waɪld] *adv* **1 to go wild** : devenir fou **2 to grow wild** : pousser à l'état sauvage **3 to run wild** : courir en liberté (se dit des animaux)

wild[2] *adj* **1** : sauvage <wild ducks : canards sauvages> **2** UNRULY : dissolu, indiscipliné **3** TURBULENT : violent, déchaîné **4** CRAZY : insensé, fou <wild ideas : idées insensées> **5** UNCIVILIZED : sauvage, fruste **6** ERRATIC : imprévisible, inattendu <to take a wild guess : deviner au hasard>

wild[3] *n* → **wilderness**

wild boar *n* : sanglier *m*

wildcat ['waɪldˌkæt] *n* **1** : chat *m* sauvage **2** BOBCAT : lynx *m*

wilderness ['wɪldərnəs] *n* : région *f* sauvage

wildfire ['waɪldˌfaɪr] *n* **1** : feu *m* de forêt incontrôlé **2 to spread like wildfire** : se répandre comme une traînée de poudre

wildflower ['waɪldˌflaʊər] *n* : fleur *f* des champs

wildfowl ['waɪldˌfaʊl] *ns & pl* : oiseaux *mpl* sauvages

wildlife ['waɪldˌlaɪf] *n* : faune *f*

wildly ['waɪldli] *adv* **1** FRANTICALLY : de façon agitée **2** EXTREMELY : extrêmement, immensément

wile[1] ['waɪl] *vt* **wiled; wiling** LURE : attirer

wile[2] *n* : ruse *f*, artifice *m*

will[1] ['wɪl] *v, past* **would** ['wʊd]; *pres sing & pl* **will** *vt* WISH : vouloir <say what you will : dis ce que tu veux> — *v aux* **1** (*used to express willingness*) <no one would take the job : personne ne voulait l'emploi> **2** (*used to express habitual action*) <he'll get angry over nothing : il se fâche pour des riens> **3** (*used to express futurity*) <tomorrow we will go swimming : demain nous irons nous baigner> **4** (*used to express capacity*) <the back seat will hold three people : le siège arrière peut accommoder trois personnes> **5** (*used to express probability*) <that will be the mailman : ça doit être le facteur> **6** (*used to express determination*) <I won't give in : je refuse d'abandonner> **7** (*used to express a command*) <you will do as I say : je t'ordonne de faire ce que je te dis>

will[2] *vt* **1** ORDAIN : vouloir <if the Lord willed it : si le Seigneur l'a voulu ainsi> **2** : vouloir très fort <to will s.o.'s success : souhaiter ardemment la réussite de qqn> **3** BEQUEATH : léguer

will[3] *n* **1** DESIRE, WISH : désir *m*, envie *f* **2** INCLINATION : volonté *f*, détermination *f* <where there's a will there's a way : quand on veut on peut> **3** VOLITION : gré *m*, volonté *f* <of her own free will : de son propre gré> **4** : volonté *f*, résolution *f* <an iron will : une volonté de fer> **5** : testament *m* <to make a will : faire un testament>

willful *or* **wilful** ['wɪlfəl] *adj* **1** STUBBORN : volontaire, obstiné **2** INTENTIONAL : délibéré, voulu

willfully ['wɪlfəli] *adv* **1** STUBBORNLY : obstinément **2** INTENTIONALLY : délibérément, intentionnellement

willing ['wɪlɪŋ] *adj* **1** INCLINED, READY : prêt, disposé <willing to help : prêt à aider> **2** EAGER : empressé, de bonne volonté <willing workers : travailleurs empressés> **3** VOLUNTARY : volontaire <a willing sacrifice : un sacrifice volontaire>

willingly ['wɪlɪŋli] *adv* **1** GLADLY : volontiers, de bon cœur **2** VOLUNTARILY : volontairement

willingness ['wɪlɪŋnəs] *n* **1** ENTHUSIASM : empressement *m*, bonne volonté *f* **2** READINESS : volonté *f*

willow ['wɪˌlo:] *n* : saule *m*

willowy ['wɪlowi] *adj* : svelte, élancé

willpower ['wɪlˌpaʊər] *n* : volonté *f*

willy–nilly [ˌwɪli'nɪli] *adv & adj* : bon gré mal gré

wilt ['wɪlt] *vi* **1** : se faner (se dit des fleurs) **2** LANGUISH : dépérir, languir

wily ['waɪli] *adj* **wilier; -est** : rusé, malin

win[1] ['wɪn] *v* **won** ['wʌn]; **winning** *vt* **1** : gagner, remporter <to win the war : gagner la guerre> <to win a prize : remporter un prix> **2** GAIN : obtenir, s'attirer **3 to win over** : convaincre, rallier — *vi* : gagner

win[2] *n* : victoire *f*

wince[1] ['wɪnts] *vi* **winced; wincing** : tressaillir

wince[2] *n* : tressaillement *m*

winch[1] ['wɪntʃ] *vt or* **to winch up** : hisser à l'aide d'un treuil

winch[2] *n* : treuil *m*

wind[1] [ˈwɪnd] *vt* : faire perdre le souffle à, couper la respiration à
wind[2] *n* **1** : vent *m* **2** BREATH : souffle *m* **3** FLATULENCE : gaz *mpl* intestinaux **4 to get wind of** : avoir vent de
wind[3] [ˈwaɪnd] *v* **wound** [ˈwaʊnd]; **winding** *vt* **1** COIL : enrouler **2** WRAP : envelopper **3** : remonter (une horloge) — *vi* MEANDER : serpenter
wind[4] [ˈwaɪnd] *n* BEND : tournant *m*, courbe *f*
windbreak [ˈwɪnd,breɪk] *n* : brise-vent *m*
windbreaker [ˈwɪnd,breɪkər] *n* : coupe-vent *m*
windfall [ˈwɪnd,fɔl] *n* **1** : fruits *mpl* tombés **2** BENEFIT, GAIN : aubaine *f*, chance *f*
wind instrument *n* : instrument *m* à vent
windlass [ˈwɪndləs] *n* : guindeau *m*
windmill [ˈwɪnd,mɪl] *n* : moulin *m* à vent
window [ˈwɪn,do:] *n* **1** : fenêtre *f* (d'une maison), vitre *f* (d'une voiture), guichet *m* (dans une banque, etc.) **2** GAP, INTERVAL : espace *m*, créneau *m* <a window of time : un espace de temps> **3** : fenêtre *f* (en informatique) **4** → **shopwindow, windowpane**
windowpane [ˈwɪn,do:,peɪn] *n* : vitre *f*, carreau *m*
window–shop [ˈwɪndo,ʃɑp] *vi* **-shopped; -shopping** : faire du lèche-vitrines
windpipe [ˈwɪnd,paɪp] *n* : trachée *f*
windshield [ˈwɪnd,ʃi:ld] *n* : pare-brise *m*
windshield wiper → **wiper**
windup [ˈwaɪnd,ʌp] *n* : fin *f*, conclusion *f*
wind up *vt* : terminer, conclure — *vi* : finir
windward[1] [ˈwɪndwərd] *adj* : contre le vent, au vent
windward[2] *n* : côté *m* du vent
windy [ˈwɪndi] *adj* **windier; -est 1** : venteux **2** BOMBASTIC : verbeux, grandiloquent
wine[1] [ˈwaɪn] *vt* **to wine and dine s.o.** : inviter qqn dans les bons restaurants
wine[2] *n* : vin *m*
wing[1] [ˈwɪŋ] *vt* **1** WOUND : blesser (un oiseau) **2 to wing it** : improviser — *vi* FLY : voler, s'envoler
wing[2] *n* **1** : aile *f* (d'un oiseau) **2** : aile *f* (d'un édifice), pavillon *m* (d'un hôpital) **3** FACTION : aile *f*, partie *f* **4** : ailier *m* (aux sports) **5 on the wing** : en vol **6 to take s.o. under one's wing** : prendre qqn sous son aile **7 wings** *npl* : coulisses *fpl* (au théâtre)
winged [ˈwɪŋd, ˈwɪŋəd] *adj* : ailé
wink[1] [ˈwɪŋk] *vi* **1** : faire un clin d'œil **2** BLINK : cligner des yeux **3** TWINKLE : clignoter, scintiller
wink[2] *n* **1** : clin *m* d'œil **2** NAP : sieste *f*, somme *m* <I didn't get a wink of sleep : je n'ai pas fermé l'œil> **3 quick as a wink** : en un clin d'œil
winner [ˈwɪnər] *n* : gagnant *m*, -gnante *f*
winning [ˈwɪnɪŋ] *adj* **1** VICTORIOUS : gagnant **2** CHARMING : séduisant, engageant
winnings [ˈwɪnɪŋz] *npl* : gains *mpl*
winnow [ˈwɪno] *vt* **1** : vanner (en agriculture) **2** SEPARATE : trier, passer au crible
winsome [ˈwɪnsəm] *adj* : charmant, engageant
winter[1] [ˈwɪntər] *adj* : d'hiver
winter[2] *n* : hiver *m*
wintergreen [ˈwɪntər,gri:n] *n* : gaulthérie *f*
wintertime [ˈwɪntər,taɪm] *n* : hiver *m*
wintry [ˈwɪntri] *adj* **wintrier; -est 1** : hivernal <wintry weather : temps hivernal> **2** COLD : froid, glacial <a wintry welcome : un accueil froid>
wipe[1] [ˈwaɪp] *vt* **wiped; wiping 1** : essuyer <to wipe the dishes : essuyer la vaisselle> **2** *or* **to wipe away** : essuyer (des larmes), effacer (un souvenir, etc.) **3 to wipe out** : détruire
wipe[2] *n* : coup *m* d'éponge, coup *m* de torchon
wiper [ˈwaɪpər] *n or* **windshield wiper** : essuie-glace *m*
wire[1] [ˈwaɪr] *vt* **wired; wiring 1** : faire l'installation électrique de **2** BIND, CONNECT : relier, attacher (avec du fil métallique) **3** TELEGRAPH : envoyer un télégramme à
wire[2] *n* **1** : fil *m* métallique, broche *f* *Can* <barbed wire : fil de fer barbelé> **2** TELEGRAM : télégramme *m*
wireless [ˈwaɪrləs] *adj* : sans fil
wiretapping [ˈwaɪr,tæpɪŋ] *n* : mise *f* sur écoute téléphonique
wiring [ˈwaɪrɪŋ] *n* : installation *f* électrique
wiry [ˈwaɪri] *adj* **wirier** [ˈwaɪriər]; **-est 1** : raide (se dit des cheveux, etc.) **2** SINEWY : mince et musclé
wisdom [ˈwɪzdəm] *n* **1** KNOWLEDGE : sagesse *f*, connaissances *fpl* **2** JUDGMENT : sagesse *f*, discernement *m*
wisdom tooth *n* : dent *f* de sagesse
wise[1] [ˈwaɪz] *adj* **wiser; wisest 1** LEARNED : sage **2** PRUDENT, SENSIBLE : sage, prudent, judicieux **3 to be wise to** : être au courant de
wise[2] *n* : manière *f*, façon *f* <in no wise : en aucune façon>
wisecrack [ˈwaɪz,kræk] *n* : blague *f*, vanne *f fam*
wisely [ˈwaɪzli] *adv* : sagement, avec sagesse
wish[1] [ˈwɪʃ] *vt* **1** WANT : souhaiter, désirer **2 to wish (something) for** : souhaiter <we wished her a happy birthday : nous lui avons souhaité bonne fête> <she wished me good night : elle m'a dit bonsoir> — *vi* : souhaiter, vouloir <as you wish : comme vous voulez>

wish[2] *n* **1** : souhait *m,* désir *m,* vœu *m* <make a wish : fais un vœu> **2 wishes** *npl* : vœux *mpl,* amitiés *fpl* <best wishes : meilleurs vœux>

wishbone [ˈwɪʃˌboːn] *n* : bréchet *m,* fourchette *f*

wishful [ˈwɪʃfəl] *adj* **1** HOPEFUL : désireux **2 it's wishful thinking** : c'est prendre ses désirs pour des réalités

wishy–washy [ˈwɪʃiˌwɔʃi, -ˌwɑʃi] *adj* **1** INEFFECTUAL : incapable, incompétent **2** WEAK : faible, insipide

wisp [ˈwɪsp] *n* **1** : mèche *f* (de cheveux), volute *f* (de fumée), brin *m* (de foin) **2** HINT : trace *f,* soupçon *m*

wispy [ˈwɪspi] *adj* **wispier; -est** : fin, épars

wisteria [wɪsˈtɪriə] *n* : glycine *f*

wistful [ˈwɪstfəl] *adj* : mélancolique, pensif — **wistfully** *adv*

wistfulness [ˈwɪstfəlnəs] *n* : mélancolie *f*

wit [ˈwɪt] *n* **1** MIND : esprit *m,* intelligence *f* **2** CLEVERNESS, HUMOR : esprit *m* <to have a quick wit : avoir l'esprit vif> **3** JOKER : farceur *m,* -ceuse *f* **4 wits** *npl* : sens *m,* raison *f* <to be at one's wits' end : ne plus savoir que faire> <you scared me out of my wits : tu m'as fait une de ces peurs>

witch [ˈwɪtʃ] *n* : sorcière *f*

witchcraft [ˈwɪtʃˌkræft] *n* : sorcellerie *f*

witch doctor *n* : sorcier *m,* -cière *f*

witchery [ˈwɪtʃəri] *n, pl* **-eries 1** → **witchcraft 2** CHARM : ensorcellement *m*

witch hazel [ˈwɪtʃˌheɪzəl] *n* : hamamélis *m*

witch–hunt [ˈwɪtʃˌhʌnt] *n* **1** : chasse *f* aux sorcières **2** : persécution *f* (politique)

with [ˈwɪð, ˈwɪθ] *prep* **1** (*indicating accompaniment*) : avec <I'm going with you : je vais avec vous> **2** AGAINST : avec, contre <he had a fight with his brother : il s'est chicané avec son frère> <to be angry with s.o. : être fâché contre qqn> **3** (*used in descriptions*) : à <the girl with red hair : la fille aux cheveux roux> **4** (*indicating manner, means, or cause*) : avec <to cut with a knife : couper avec un couteau> <with any luck : avec un peu de chance> **5** DESPITE : malgré <with all her faults, she's still my friend : malgré tous ses défauts, elle est quand même mon amie> <with all your money . . . : il a beau avoir de l'argent . . .> **6** REGARDING, TOWARD : avec <be patient with the children : soyez patient avec les enfants> <it's a habit with her : c'est une habitude chez elle> **7** ACCORDING TO : avec <it varies with the season : ça change avec la saison> **8** (*indicating support or understanding*) : avec <I'm with you all the way : je suis avec vous cent pour cent>

withdraw [wɪðˈdrɔ, wɪθ-] *v* **-drew** [-ˈdruː]; **-drawn** [-ˈdrɔn]; **-drawing** *vt* **1** REMOVE : retirer <to withdraw money : retirer de l'argent> **2** RETRACT : retirer, rétracter (une parole, etc.) — *vi* LEAVE, RETREAT : se retirer

withdrawal [wɪðˈdrɔəl, wɪθ-] *n* **1** : retrait *m* (de fonds, des troupes) **2** RETRACTION : rétraction *f* **3** *or* **withdrawal symptoms** : symptômes *mpl* de manque

withdrawn [wɪðˈdrɔn, wɪθ-] *adj* : renfermé, replié sur soi-même

wither [ˈwɪðər] *vi* **1** WILT : se faner, se flétrir **2 to wither away** : s'évanouir

withers [ˈwɪðərz] *npl* : garrot *m* (d'un cheval)

withhold [wɪθˈhoːld, wɪð-] *vt* **-held** [-ˈhɛld]; **-holding** : retenir (des fonds), refuser (la permission, etc.), cacher (des faits, la vérité)

within[1] [wɪðˈɪn, wɪθ-] *adv* : à l'intérieur

within[2] *prep* **1** INSIDE : dans, à l'intérieur de <within the building : à l'intérieur de l'édifice> **2** (*indicating limitation*) <to live within one's income : vivre selon ses moyens> <within reach : à (la) portée de la main> **3** (*indicating distance*) <within a mile of the city : à moins d'un mille de la ville> **4** (*indicating time*) <within a month : en moins d'un mois> <within the time limit : dans les temps impartis>

without[1] [wɪðˈaʊt, wɪθ-] *adv* **1** OUTSIDE : à l'extérieur, au dehors **2 to do without** : se passer de

without[2] *prep* **1** OUTSIDE : à l'extérieur de **2** : sans <I spoke without thinking : j'ai parlé sans réfléchir> <without a doubt : sans aucun doute>

withstand [wɪθˈstænd, wɪð-] *vt* **-stood** [-ˈstʊd]; **-standing 1** BEAR : supporter **2** RESIST : résister à

witless [ˈwɪtləs] *adj* : stupide, sans génie

witness[1] [ˈwɪtnəs] *vt* **1** SEE : être témoin de, assister à **2** : servir de témoin de (une signature) — *vi* TESTIFY : témoigner

witness[2] *n* **1** TESTIMONY : témoignage *m* <to bear false witness : donner un faux témoignage> **2** : témoin *m* <to call as a witness : citer comme témoin>

witticism [ˈwɪt̬əˌsɪzəm] *n* : bon mot *m,* mot *m* d'esprit

witty [ˈwɪt̬i] *adj* **wittier; -est** : humoristique, amusant

wives → **wife**

wizard [ˈwɪzərd] *n* **1** SORCERER : magicien *m,* sorcier *m* **2** : génie *m* <a math wizard : un génie des mathématiques>

wizardry [ˈwɪzərdri] *n* : sorcellerie *f*

wizened [ˈwɪzənd, ˈwiː-] *adj* : desséché, ratatiné

wobble[1] [ˈwɑbəl] *vi* **-bled; -bling** : branler, osciller, trembler

wobble[2] *n* : branlement *m*
wobbly ['wɑbəli] *adj* : vacillant, branlant
woe ['wo:] *n* **1** SORROW : chagrin *m* **2** **woes** *npl* MISFORTUNE : malheur *m*
woeful ['wo:fəl] *adj* **1** SORROWFUL : désolé, affligé, triste **2** DEPLORABLE, UNFORTUNATE : lamentable, malheureux
woefully ['wo:fəli] *adv* **1** SADLY : tristement **2** DEPLORABLY : lamentablement
woke, woken → **wake**[1]
wolf[1] ['wʊlf] *vt or* **to wolf down** : engloutir, engouffrer
wolf[2] *n, pl* **wolves** ['wʊlvz] : loup *m*, louve *f*
wolfish ['wʊlfɪʃ] *adj* : féroce
wolfram ['wʊlfrəm] → **tungsten**
wolverine [,wʊlvə'ri:n] *n, pl* **-ines** : glouton *m*
woman ['wʊmən] *n, pl* **women** ['wɪmən] : femme *f*
womanhood ['wʊmən,hʊd] *n* **1** : féminité *f* **2** WOMEN : femmes *fpl*
womanly ['wʊmənli] *adj* : féminin, de femme
womb ['wu:m] *n* : utérus *m*
won → **win**[1]
wonder[1] ['wʌndər] *vi* **1** MARVEL : s'émerveiller, s'étonner **2** SPECULATE : penser, songer — *vt* : se demander <I wondered why : je me suis demandé pourquoi>
wonder[2] *n* **1** MARVEL : merveille *f* <to work wonders : faire des merveilles> <it's a wonder that : c'est étonnant que> **2** ASTONISHMENT : émerveillement *m*
wonderful ['wʌndərfəl] *adj* : merveilleux, formidable
wonderfully ['wʌndərfəli] *adv* : merveilleusement, à merveille
wonderland ['wʌndər,lænd, -lənd] *n* : pays *m* des merveilles, pays *m* enchanté
wonderment ['wʌndərmənt] *n* : émerveillement *m*, étonnement *m*
wondrous ['wəndrəs] → **wonderful**
wont[1] ['wɔnt, 'wo:nt] *adj* : habitué <to be wont to do : avoir coutume de faire>
wont[2] *n* : habitude *f*, coutume *f*
won't ['wo:nt] (*contraction of* **will not**) → **will**[1]
woo ['wu:] *vt* **1** COURT : courtiser, faire la cour à **2** : rechercher les faveurs de (des clients, etc.)
wood[1] ['wʊd] *adj* : de bois, en bois
wood[2] *n* **1** : bois *m* <solid wood : bois massif> **2** *or* **woods** *npl* FOREST : bois *m*, boisé *m Can*
woodchuck ['wʊd,tʃʌk] *n* : marmotte *f* d'Amérique
woodcraft ['wʊd,kræft] *n* **1** : connaissance *f* des bois **2** : art *m* de travailler le bois
woodcut ['wʊd,kʌt] *n* : gravure *f* sur bois
woodcutter ['wʊd,kʌṭər] *n* : bûcheron *m*, -ronne *f*
wooded ['wʊdəd] *adj* : boisé
wooden ['wʊdən] *adj* **1** : en bois, de bois **2** STIFF : raide, qui manque de naturel
woodland ['wʊdlənd, -,lænd] *n* : région *f* boisée, bois *m*
woodpecker ['wʊd,pɛkər] *n* : pic *m*, pic-bois *m Can*
woodpile ['wʊd,paɪl] *n* : tas *m* de bois
woodshed ['wʊd,ʃɛd] *n* : bûcher *m*, remise *f* à bois
woodsman ['wʊdzmən] *n, pl* **-men** [-mən, -,mɛn] **1** → **woodcutter** **2** FORESTER : forestier *m*, -tière *f*
woodwind ['wʊd,wɪnd] *n* : bois *m* (en musique)
woodwork ['wʊd,wərk] *n* : boiseries *fpl* (dans une maison)
woodworking ['wʊd,wərkɪŋ] *n* CARPENTRY : menuiserie *f*, ébénisterie *f*
woody ['wʊdi] *adj* **woodier; -est** **1** WOODED : boisé **2** : ligneux (se dit des plantes)
woof ['wʊf] → **weft**
wool ['wʊl] *n* : laine *f*
woolen[1] *or* **woollen** ['wʊlən] *adj* : de laine, en laine
woolen[2] *n* **1** : tissu *m* en laine **2** **woolens** *npl* : vêtements *mpl* de laine
woolly ['wʊli] *adj* **woolier; -est** **1** : de laine, en laine **2** : laineux (se dit d'un animal) **3** CONFUSED, VAGUE : confus, flou
woozy ['wu:zi] *adj* **woozier; -est** : écœuré, qui a la tête qui tourne <to feel woozy : avoir mal au cœur>
word[1] ['wərd] *vt* : formuler, rédiger
word[2] *n* **1** : mot *m*, parole *f* <word for word : mot pour mot> <in a word, no : en un mot, non> <in word and deed : en paroles et en fait> <what is the word for . . . ? : comment dit-on . . . ?> **2** TALK : parole *f* <to have a word with s.o. : parler avec qqn> **3** COMMAND : ordre *m*, mot *m* d'ordre <to give the word : donner l'ordre> **4** MESSAGE, NEWS : nouvelles *fpl* <there's no word from Marie : on est sans nouvelles de Marie> <to send word : envoyer un mot> **5** PROMISE : parole *f* <to keep one's word : tenir (sa) parole> **6** **words** *npl* QUARREL : dispute *f* <to have words with : se disputer avec> **7** **words** *npl* : texte *m*, paroles *fpl* (en musique)
wordiness ['wərdinəs] *n* : verbosité *f*
wording ['wərdɪŋ] *n* : termes *mpl* (d'un document), formulation *f* (d'une invitation, etc.)
wordless ['wərdləs] *adj* : muet
word processing *n* : traitement *m* de texte
word processor *n* : machine *f* de traitement de textes

wore → **wear**[1]

work[1] ['wərk] *v* **worked** ['wərkt] *or* **wrought** ['rɔt]; **working** *vt* **1** EFFECT : faire <to work miracles : faire des miracles> **2** FORGE, SHAPE : travailler (le fer, l'acier, etc.) **3** OPERATE : faire marcher, activer **4** EXPLOIT : faire travailler **5** ARRANGE : arranger, organiser **6** EXCITE, PROVOKE : provoquer, exciter <I worked myself into a rage : la rage montait en moi> — *vi* **1** LABOR : travailler **2** SUCCEED : fonctionner, réussir

work[2] *adj* : de travail <work clothes : vêtements de travail>

work[3] *n* **1** LABOR : travail *m* **2** EMPLOYMENT : travail *m*, emploi *m* **3** TASK : travail *m*, ouvrage *m* **4** WORKMANSHIP : travail *m*, exécution *f* **5** : œuvre *f*, ouvrage *m* <a work of art : une œuvre d'art> **6 works** *npl* FACTORY : usine *f* **7 works** *npl* : travaux *mpl* <public works : travaux publics> **8 works** *npl* MECHANISM : rouages *mpl* (d'une horloge, etc.) **9 in the works** : en train de se faire

workable ['wərkəbəl] *adj* **1** : exploitable (se dit d'une mine, etc.) **2** PRACTICABLE : possible, réalisable

workaday ['wərkə,deɪ] *adj* : commun, ordinaire

workbench ['wərk,bɛntʃ] *n* : établi *m*

workday ['wərk,deɪ] *n* **1** : journée *f* de travail **2** *or* **working day** : jour *m* ouvrable

worker ['wərkər] *n* **1** : travailleur *m*, -leuse *f*; employé *m*, -ployée *f* <he's a hard worker : c'est un grand travailleur> <white-collar workers : employés de bureau> **2** LABORER : ouvrier *m*, -vrière *f*

working ['wərkɪŋ] *adj* **1** : qui travaille <working people : gens qui travaillent> **2** : de bureau, de travail <during working hours : pendant les heures de bureau> **3** FUNCTIONING : qui fonctionne, qui marche <in working order : en état de marche> **4** SUFFICIENT : suffisant <a working knowledge : une connaissance adéquate>

workingman ['wərkɪŋ,mæn] *n, pl* **-men** [-mən, -,mɛn] : ouvrier *m*

workman ['wərkmən] *n, pl* **-men** [-mən, -,mɛn] **1** → **workingman** **2** ARTISAN : artisan *m*

workmanlike ['wərkmən,laɪk] *adj* **1** : professionnel, consciencieux (se dit d'une personne) **2** : bien fait (se dit d'un objet)

workmanship ['wərkmən,ʃɪp] *n* **1** SKILL : habileté *f* **2** QUALITY : qualité *f*, exécution *f*

workout ['wərk,aut] *n* : séance *f* d'entraînement

work out *vt* **1** SOLVE : résoudre (un problème) **2** DEVELOP : développer, élaborer (un plan, etc.) — *vi* **1** SUCCEED, WORK : marcher, fonctionner, réussir **2** EXERCISE : s'entraîner, faire de l'exercice

workroom ['wərk,ru:m, -,rʊm] *n* : salle *f* de travail

workshop ['wərk,ʃɑp] *n* **1** SHOP : atelier *m* **2** SEMINAR : atelier *m*, groupe *m* de travail

world[1] ['wərld] *adj* : du monde, mondial

world[2] *n* **1** : monde *m* <around the world : autour du monde> <that makes a world of difference : cela fait un monde de différence> <to think the world of s.o. : penser le plus grand bien de qqn> **2** PEOPLE : monde *m*, société *f* <in the eyes of the world : aux yeux du monde> <the academic world : le monde académique>

worldly ['wərldli] *adj* **1** : matériel, de ce monde **2** → **worldly-wise**

worldly–wise ['wərldli,waɪz] *adj* : qui a l'expérience du monde

worldwide[1] ['wərld'waɪd] *adv* : dans le monde entier, partout dans le monde

worldwide[2] *adj* : mondial, universel

World Wide Web *n* WEB : Web *m*, Toile *f*

worm[1] ['wərm] *vt* **1** : débarrasser (un animal) de ses vers **2 to worm one's way into** : s'insinuer dans **3 to worm one's way through** : se faufiler à travers

worm[2] *n* **1** : ver *m* **2 worms** *npl* : vers *mpl* (intestinaux)

wormy ['wərmi] *adj* **wormier**; **-est** : véreux

worn ['worn] → **wear**[1]

worn–out ['worn'aut] *adj* **1** : usé, fini (se dit d'un objet) **2** EXHAUSTED : épuisé, éreinté (se dit d'une personne)

worried ['wəri:d] *adj* : inquiet, soucieux

worrier ['wəriər] *n* : personne *f* qui s'inquiète

worrisome ['wərisəm] *adj* : inquiétant, préoccupant

worry[1] ['wəri] *v* **-ried**; **-rying** *vt* : inquiéter, tracasser — *vi* FRET : s'inquiéter

worry[2] *n, pl* **-ries** **1** ANXIETY : inquiétude *f* **2** DIFFICULTY : problème *m*, ennui *m*

worse[1] ['wərs] *adv* (*comparative of* **bad** *or of* **ill**) : moins bien, plus mal <we sleep worse in the warm weather : nous dormons moins bien quand il fait chaud>

worse[2] *adj* (*comparative of* **bad** *or of* **ill**) **1** : pire <it's worse than ever : c'est pire que jamais, c'est pire qu'avant> **2** : plus mal, plus malade <to feel worse : se sentir encore plus mal>

worse[3] *n* : pire *m* <to take a turn for the worse : s'aggraver, empirer> <none the worse : pas plus mal>

worsen ['wərsən] *vi* : empirer, se détériorer, rempirer *Can fam* — *vt* : aggraver, rendre pire

worship[1] ['wərʃəp] *v* **-shiped** *or* **-shipped; -shiping** *or* **-shipping** *vt* : adorer, vénérer — *vi* : faire ses dévotions

worship[2] *n* **1** : culte *m* <a place of worship : un lieu consacré au culte> **2** REVERENCE : adoration *f,* vénération *f*

worshiper *or* **worshipper** ['wərʃəpər] *n* : adorateur *m,* -trice *f*

worst[1] ['wərst] *vt* DEFEAT : battre, vaincre

worst[2] *adv* (*superlative of* **bad** *or of* **ill**) : plus mal <the worst dressed : le plus mal habillé>

worst[3] *adj* (*superlative of* **bad** *or of* **ill**) : pire, plus mauvais <the worst fate : le pire sort>

worst[4] *n* : pire *m* <to fear the worst : craindre le pire>

worsted ['wʊstəd, 'wərstəd] *n* : laine *f* peignée

worth[1] ['wərθ] *n* **1** : valeur *f* (monétaire) <what is its worth? : quelle est sa valeur?> **2** EXCELLENCE : valeur *f,* mérite *m*

worth[2] *prep* **to be worth** : valoir <he's worth thousands : il vaut des milliers> <to be well worth the effort : valoir bien l'effort>

worthiness ['wərðinəs] *n* : dignité *f,* mérite *m*

worthless ['wərθləs] *adj* : sans valeur

worthwhile [wərθ'*h*waɪl] *adj* : qui en vaut la peine

worthy ['wərði] *adj* **worthier; -est** : digne, méritant

would ['wʊd] *past of* **will 1** (*used to express preference*) <I would rather stay here : je préférerais rester ici> **2** (*used to express a wish, desire, or intent*) <those who would forbid gambling : ceux qui interdiraient les jeux d'argent> **3** (*used to express a plan*) <I said we would go : j'ai dit que nous irions> **4** (*used to express consent or choice*) <she would put off her work if she could : elle remettrait son travail à plus tard si elle pouvait> **5** (*used to express contingency*) <if they were coming, they would be here by now : s'ils venaient, ils seraient déjà arrivés> **6** (*used in a noun clause*) <we wish that he would go : nous aimerions qu'il parte> **7** (*used to express probability*) <I would have won if I had not tripped : j'aurais gagné si je n'avais pas trébuché> **8** (*used to express a request*) <would you please help us? : pourriez-vous nous aider s'il vous plaît?>

would–be ['wʊd'bi:] *adj* : soi-disant, prétendu

wouldn't ['wʊdənt] (*contraction of* **would** *and* **not**) → **would**

wound[1] ['wu:nd] *vt* : blesser

wound[2] *n* : blessure *f*

wound[3] ['waʊnd] → **wind**[3]

wove, woven → **weave**[1]

wrangle[1] ['ræŋgəl] *vi* **-gled; -gling** : se quereller, se disputer <to wrangle over : se disputer à propos de>

wrangle[2] *n* : querelle *f,* dispute *f,* chicane *f*

wrap[1] ['ræp] *v* **wrapped; wrapping** *vt* **1** COVER : envelopper, emballer <to wrap a present : envelopper un cadeau> **2** SURROUND : envelopper, entourer <wrapped in mystery : entouré de mystère> **3** WIND : enrouler **4** *or* **to wrap up** SUMMARIZE : résumer — *vi* **to wrap up** DRESS : se couvrir, s'habiller

wrap[2] *n* **1** → **wrapper 2** SHAWL : châle *m*

wrapper ['ræpər] *n* **1** : papier *m,* emballage *m* <candy wrapper : papier de bonbon> **2** : jaquette *f* (de livre), bande *f* (de journal)

wrapping ['ræpɪŋ] *n* **1** : emballage *m* **2 wrapping paper** : papier d'emballage

wrath ['ræθ] *n* : furie *f,* colère *f*

wrathful ['ræθfəl] *adj* : courroucé, en colère

wreak ['ri:k] *vt* **1** INFLICT : infliger (une punition, etc.) **2 to wreak havoc** : faire des ravages, dévaster

wreath ['ri:θ] *n, pl* **wreaths** ['ri:ðz, 'ri:θs] : couronne *f* (de fleurs, etc.)

wreathe ['ri:ð] *vt* **wreathed; wreathing 1** ADORN : couronner, orner **2** ENVELOP : envelopper <wreathed in mist : enveloppé de brume>

wreck[1] ['rɛk] *vt* **1** : provoquer le naufrage de (un navire), faire dérailler (un train), détruire (une voiture) **2** DESTROY, RUIN : détruire, miner, briser (un mariage, etc.) <to wreck one's chances : anéantir ses chances>

wreck[2] *n* **1** WRECKAGE : épave *f* (d'un navire), voiture *f* accidentée **2** ACCIDENT : accident *m* (de voiture), écrasement *m* (d'avion) **3 to be a wreck** : être à bout, être une épave

wreckage ['rɛkɪdʒ] *n* **1** : épave *f* (d'un navire), voiture *f* accidentée **2** REMAINS : décombres *mpl,* débris *mpl*

wrecker ['rɛkər] *n* **1** : destructeur *m,* -trice *f* **2** TOW TRUCK : dépanneuse *f*

wren ['rɛn] *n* : roitelet *m*

wrench[1] ['rɛntʃ] *vt* **1** PULL : tirer brusquement sur <to wrench sth away from s.o. : arracher qqch des mains de qqn> **2** TWIST : tordre <to wrench one's ankle : se tordre la cheville> — *vi* **to wrench free** : se dégager

wrench[2] *n* **1** PULL : mouvement *m* violent, secousse *f* (de torsion) **2** SPRAIN : foulure *f,* entorse *f* **3** : clef *f* (outil)

wrest ['rɛst] *vt* : arracher

wrestle[1] ['rɛsəl] *v* **-tled; -tling** *vi* **1** : lutter, pratiquer la lutte (aux sports) **2**

STRUGGLE : lutter <to wrestle with one's conscience : se débattre avec sa conscience> — *vt* : lutter contre
wrestle[2] *n* STRUGGLE : lutte *f*
wrestler ['rɛsələr] *n* : lutteur *m*, -teuse *f*
wrestling ['rɛsəlɪŋ] *n* : lutte *f* (sport)
wretch ['rɛtʃ] *n* **1** : misérable *mf* <a poor wretch : un pauvre misérable> **2** ROGUE : scélérat *m*
wretched ['rɛtʃəd] *adj* **1** POOR : misérable <wretched slums : taudis misérables> **2** MISERABLE, UNHAPPY : misérable, malheureux <to feel wretched : se sentir très mal> **3** AWFUL : affreux, déplorable <wretched weather : temps affreux>
wretchedly ['rɛtʃədli] *adv* : misérablement
wretchedness ['rɛtʃədnəs] *n* : misère *f*
wriggle ['rɪgəl] *v* **-gled; -gling** *vt* **1** SQUIRM, WIGGLE : gigoter, remuer **2** **to wriggle one's way** : s'avancer en se tortillant — *vi* **to wriggle out of** : s'extirper de
wring ['rɪŋ] *vt* **wrung** ['rʌŋ]; **wringing 1** *or* **to wring out** : essorer, tordre (le linge) **2** TWIST : tordre <to wring s.o.'s neck : tordre le cou à qqn> <to wring one's hands : se tordre les mains> **3** EXTRACT : arracher (un aveu, etc.) **4** **to wring one's heart** : se fendre le cœur
wringer ['rɪŋər] *n* : essoreuse *f*
wrinkle[1] ['rɪŋkəl] *v* **-kled; -kling** *vi* : se rider (se dit de la peau), se froisser (se dit des vêtements) — *vt* **1** : rider (la peau) **2** : plisser, faire des plis dans (des vêtements) <to wrinkle one's brow : plisser le front>
wrinkle[2] *n* : pli *m* (de vêtements), ride *f* (sur la peau)
wrinkly ['rɪŋkəli] *adj* : ridé
wrist ['rɪst] *n* : poignet *m*
wristband ['rɪst,bænd] *n* **1** CUFF : poignet *m* (d'une chemise, etc.) **2** : bracelet *m* (d'une montre)
wristwatch ['rɪst,wɑtʃ] *n* : montre-bracelet *f*
writ ['rɪt] *n* : ordonnance *f* (en droit)
write ['raɪt] *v* **wrote** ['ro:t]; **written** ['rɪtən]; **writing** : écrire
write down *vt* : mettre par écrit, noter
write off *vt* CANCEL : annuler
writer ['raɪţər] *n* : écrivain *m*, écrivaine *f Can*
writhe ['raɪð] *vi* **writhed; writhing** : se tordre, se tortiller
writing ['raɪţɪŋ] *n* **1** : écriture *f* <to put in writing : mettre par écrit> **2** HANDWRITING : écriture *f* **3** **writings** *npl* : écrits *mpl*, œuvres *fpl*
wrong[1] ['rɔŋ] *vt* **wronged; wronging 1** HARM, INJURE : faire du tort à **2** CHEAT : frauder
wrong[2] *adv* **1** WRONGLY : à tort **2** INCORRECTLY : mal <I guessed wrong : j'ai mal deviné>
wrong[3] *adj* **wronger; wrongest 1** SINFUL : mal, immoral **2** UNSUITABLE : mal, peu convenable, inapproprié **3** INCORRECT : mauvais, erroné <the wrong answer : la mauvaise réponse> **4** **to be wrong** : se tromper, avoir tort
wrong[4] *n* **1** EVIL : mal *m* **2** INJUSTICE : tort *m*, injustice *f*
wrongdoer ['rɔŋ,du:ər] *n* : malfaiteur *m*
wrongdoing ['rɔŋ,du:ɪŋ] *n* : méfait *m*, mal *m*
wrongful ['rɔŋfəl] *adj* **1** UNJUST, WRONG : mal, injustifié **2** UNLAWFUL : illégal <wrongful arrest : arrestation arbitraire>
wrongfully ['rɔŋfəli] *adv* : injustement, à tort
wrongly ['rɔŋli] *adv* : à tort <wrongly accused : accusé à tort>
wrote → **write**
wrought[1] → **work**[1]
wrought[2] ['rɔt] *adj* **1** SHAPED, WORKED : travaillé, ouvré <wrought iron : fer forgé> **2** **to be wrought up** : être énervé, être très tendu
wrung → **wring**
wry ['raɪ] *adj* **wrier** ['raɪər]; **wriest** ['raɪəst] **1** : forcé <a wry smile : un sourire forcé> **2** TWISTED : tordu <to have a wry neck : avoir un torticolis> **3** SARDONIC : ironique, moqueur

X

x[1] ['ɛks] *n, pl* **x's** *or* **xs** ['ɛksəz] **1** : x *m*, vingt-quatrième lettre de l'alphabet **2** : x *m* (en mathématiques)
x[2] ['ɛks] *vt* **x–ed** ['ɛkst]; **x–ing** *or* **x'ing** ['ɛksɪŋ] DELETE: barrer, rayer
xenon ['zi:,nɑn, 'zɛ-] *n* : xénon *m*
xenophobia [,zɛnə'fo:biə, ,zi:-] *n* : xénophobie *f*
xenophobic [,zɛnə'fo:bɪk, 'zi:-] *adj* : xénophobe
xerography [zə'rɑgrəfi] *n* : photocopie *f*
xerox ['zɪrɑks] *vt* : photocopier
Xmas ['krɪsməs] → **Christmas**
x–ray ['ɛks,reɪ] *vt* : radiographier
X ray ['ɛks,reɪ] *n* **1** : rayon *m* X **2** *or* **X–ray photograph** : radiographie *f*
xylophone ['zaɪlə,fo:n] *n* : xylophone *m*
xylophonist ['zaɪlə,fo:nɪst] *n* : xylophoniste *mf*

Y

y [ˈwaɪ] *n, pl* **y's** *or* **ys** [ˈwaɪz] : y *m*, vingt-cinquième lettre de l'alphabet
yacht[1] [ˈjɑt] *vi* : faire du yachting
yacht[2] *n* : yacht *m*
yak [ˈjæk] *n* : yack *m*
yam [ˈjæm] *n* **1** : igname *f* (plante) **2** SWEET POTATO : patate *f* douce
yank[1] [ˈjæŋk] *vt* : tirer d'un coup sec
yank[2] *n* : coup *m* sec
Yankee [ˈjæŋki] *n* : Yankee *mf*
yap[1] [ˈjæp] *vi* **yapped; yapping 1** YELP : japper (se dit d'un chien) **2** CHATTER : jacasser
yap[2] *n* : jappement *m*
yard [ˈjɑrd] *n* **1** : yard *m*, verge *f Can* (unité de mesure) **2** SPAR : vergue *f* (d'un navire) **3** COURTYARD : cour *f* (d'immeuble) **4** : jardin *m* (d'une maison) **5** : chantier *m* (de construction), dépôt *m* (de marchandises)
yardage [ˈjɑrdɪdʒ] *n* : longueur *f* en yards, longueur *f* en verges *Can*
yardarm [ˈjɑrd,ɑrm] *n* : bout *m* de vergue
yardstick [ˈjɑrd,stɪk] *n* **1** : mètre *m* **2** : CRITERION : critère *m*, point *m* de référence
yarn [ˈjɑrn] *n* **1** : fil *m* (à tisser) **2** TALE : histoire *f* <to spin a yarn : raconter des histoires>
yawl [ˈjɔl] *n* : yawl *m*
yawn[1] [ˈjɔn] *vi* : bâiller
yawn[2] *n* : bâillement *m*
ye [ˈji:] *pron* : vous
yea[1] [ˈjeɪ] *adv* YES : oui
yea[2] *n* : vote *m* affirmatif, oui *m* <the yeas and the nays : les oui et les non>
year [ˈjɪr] *n* **1** : an *m*, année *f* <next year : l'an prochain> <the school year : l'année scolaire> **2** : an *m* <their son is seven years olds : leur fils a sept ans> **3 years** *npl* AGE : âge *m* <she's getting on in years : elle prend de l'âge>
yearbook [ˈjɪr,bʊk] *n* : recueil *m* annuel, annuaire *m*
yearling [ˈjɪrlɪŋ, ˈjərlən] *n* : animal *m* d'un an
yearly[1] [ˈjɪrli] *adv* : annuellement
yearly[2] *adj* : annuel
yearn [ˈjərn] *vi* **to yearn for** : désirer ardemment, aspirer à
yearning [ˈjərnɪŋ] *n* : désir *m* ardent
yeast [ˈji:st] *n* : levure *f*
yell[1] [ˈjɛl] *vi* : crier — *vt* SHOUT : crier, hurler
yell[2] *n* : cri *m*, hurlement *m*
yellow[1] [ˈjɛlo] *v* : jaunir
yellow[2] *adj* **1** : jaune **2** COWARDLY : lâche, peureux
yellow[3] *n* **1** : jaune *m* (couleur) **2** YOLK : jaune *m* d'œuf
yellow fever *n* : fièvre *f* jaune
yellowish [ˈjɛloɪʃ] *adj* : jaunâtre
yellow jacket *n* : guêpe *f*
yelp[1] [ˈjɛlp] *vi* : glapir
yelp[2] *n* : glapissement *m*
Yemeni[1] [ˈjɛməni] *adj* : yéménite
Yemeni[2] *n* : Yéménite *mf*
yen [ˈjɛn] *n* : désir *m*, envie *f*
yeoman [ˈjo:mən] *n, pl* **-men** [-mən, -,mɛn] : sous-officier *m* de la marine
yes[1] [ˈjɛs] *adv* **1** (*used in general statements*) : oui <are you ready? yes, I am : êtes-vous prêt? oui, je suis prêt> **2** (*used after a negative question*) : si <you're not ready, are you? yes, I am : vous n'êtes pas prêt? mais si, je le suis>
yes[2] *n* : oui *m*
yesterday[1] [ˈjɛstər,deɪ, -di] *adv* : hier
yesterday[2] *n* **1** : hier *m* **2 the day before yesterday** : avant-hier *m*
yet[1] [ˈjɛt] *adv* **1** BESIDES : de plus, encore <yet another excuse : encore une autre excuse> <yet again : encore une fois> **2** SO FAR : jusqu'à présent, jusqu'ici <the best yet : le mieux jusqu'ici> **3** (*used in negative phrases*) : encore <not yet : pas encore> **4** EVENTUALLY, STILL : encore <they may yet return : ils pourraient encore revenir> **5** NEVERTHELESS : néanmoins
yet[2] *conj* BUT : mais
yew [ˈju:] *n* : if *m*
yield[1] [ˈji:ld] *vt* **1** SURRENDER : rendre, céder <to yield the right of way : céder le passage> **2** PRODUCE : produire, donner, rapporter — *vi* **1** GIVE : céder, fléchir <to yield under pressure : céder sous la pression> **2** GIVE IN, SURRENDER : se rendre, céder
yield[2] *n* : rendement *m*, rapport *m*, récolte *f* (en agriculture)
yodel [ˈjo:dəl] *vi* **-deled** *or* **-delled; -deling** *or* **-delling** : iodler
yoga [ˈjo:gə] *n* : yoga *m*
yogurt [ˈjo:gərt] *n* : yaourt *m*, yogourt *m*
yoke[1] [ˈjo:k] *vt* **yoked; yoking 1** : atteler (des animaux) **2** JOIN : joindre
yoke[2] *n* **1** : joug *m* (d'animaux) **2** DOMINION : joug *m* <the yoke of slavery : le joug de l'esclavage> **3** TEAM : attelage *m* **4** : empiècement *m* (d'un vêtement)
yokel [ˈjo:kəl] *n* : rustre *mf;* plouc *mf France fam;* péquenaud *m*, -naude *f France fam*
yolk [ˈjo:k] *n* : jaune *m* d'œuf
Yom Kippur [jo:mkɪˈpʊr, jɑm-, -ˈkɪpər] *n* : Yom Kippour *m*
yonder [ˈjɑndər] *adv & adj* : là-bas
yore [ˈjo:r] *n* **of ~** : d'antan <in days of yore : au temps jadis>
you [ˈju:] *pron* **1** (*used as subject — singular*) : tu (familier), vous (forme polie) <you may sit in the armchair : tu peux t'asseoir dans le fauteuil> <you were right : vous aviez raison> **2** (*used as subject — plural*) : vous

<you are my friends : vous êtes mes amis> **3** (*used as the direct or indirect object of a verb*) : te (familier), vous (forme polie), vous (pluriel) <can I pour you a cup of tea? : puis-je vous verser une tasse de thé?> <I will help you : je t'aiderai> **4** (*used as the object of a preposition*) : toi (familier), vous (forme polie), vous (pluriel) <bring the children with you : amenez les enfants avec toi> **5** ONE : on <you never know what's going to happen : on ne sait jamais ce qui va arriver>

you'd [ˈjʊd] (*contraction of* **you had** *or* **you would) → have, would**

you'll [ˈjuːl, ˈjʊl] (*contraction of* **you shall** *or* **you will) → shall, will**

young[1] [ˈjʌŋ] *adj* **younger** [ˈjʌŋgər]; **youngest** [ˈjʌŋgəst] **1** : jeune <very young children : enfants tout jeunes> **2** NEW : jeune <a young industry : une industrie jeune> **3** YOUTHFUL : jeune, jeune de cœur <to look young : avoir l'air jeune>

young[2] *ns & pl* **the young** : les jeunes (personnes), les petits (animaux)

youngish [ˈjʌŋɪʃ] *adj* : assez jeune, plutôt jeune

youngster [ˈjʌŋkstər] *n* **1** : jeune *mf* **2** CHILD : enfant *mf*

your [ˈjʊr, ˈjoːr, jər] *adj* **1** (*familiar singular*) : ta, ton <your book : ton livre> **2** (*formal singular)* : votre <it's your money : c'est votre argent> **3** (*familiar and formal plural*) : tes, vos <your teeth : tes dents> <your contributions : vos contributions> **4** (*impersonal*) : votre, vos <the house is at your right : la maison est à votre droite> <it's good for your health : c'est bon pour la santé> **5** (*used as an equivalent to the definite article* the) <he's different from your average teacher : il se démarque des autres professeurs> **6** (*used before a title*) : Votre <Your Majesty : Votre Majesté>

yours [ˈjʊrz, ˈjoːrz] *pron* **1** (*familiar singular*) : le tien, la tienne <is it yours? : est-ce que c'est le tien?> <the bike is yours : la bicyclette est à toi> **2** (*formal singular*) : le vôtre, la vôtre <a friend of yours : un de vos amis> **3** (*familiar plural*) : les tiens, les tiennes **4** (*formal plural*) : les vôtres <ours are here; yours are there : les nôtres sont ici, les vôtres sont là>

yourself [jərˈsɛlf] *pron, pl* **yourselves** [jərˈsɛlvz] **1** (*used reflexively*) : tu (familier), vous (forme polie), vous (pluriel) <you'll hurt yourself if you're not careful : tu te feras mal si tu ne fais pas attention> <please help yourself : servez-vous s'il vous plaît> **2** (*used for emphasis*) : toi-même (familier), vous-même (forme polie), vous-mêmes (pluriel) <carry them yourselves : emportez-les vous-mêmes>

youth [ˈjuːθ] *n, pl* **youths** [ˈjuːðz, ˈjuːθs] **1** : jeunesse *f* <to regain one's youth : retrouver sa jeunesse> **2** ADOLESCENT : jeune homme *m* **3** : jeunes *mf,* jeunesse *f* <the youth of today : les jeunes d'aujourd'hui>

youthful [ˈjuːθfəl] *adj* **1** : de jeunesse **2** YOUNG : jeune <to look youthful : avoir l'air jeune> **3** JUVENILE : juvénile

youthfulness [ˈjuːθfəlnəs] *n* : jeunesse *f*

you've [ˈjuːv] (*contraction of* **you have) → have**

yowl[1] [ˈjæʊl] *vi* : miauler (se dit d'un chat), hurler (se dit d'un chien ou d'une personne)

yowl[2] *n* : miaulement *m* (d'un chat) hurlement *m* (d'un chien ou d'une personne)

yo-yo [ˈjoːˌjoː] *n, pl* **yo-yos** : yo-yo *m*

yucca [ˈjʌkə] *n* : yucca *m*

Yugoslav[1] [ˈjuːgoˌslɑv] *or* **Yugoslavian** [ˌjuːgoˈslɑviən] *adj* : yougoslave

Yugoslav[2] *or* **Yugoslavian** *n* : Yougoslave *mf*

yule [ˈjuːl] *n* : Noël *m*

yuletide [ˈjuːlˌtaɪd] *n* : époque *f* de Noël

Z

z [ˈziː] *n, pl* **z's** *or* **zs** : z *m,* vingt-sixième lettre de l'alphabet

Zairian[1] [zaˈɪriən] *adj* : zaïrois

Zairian[2] *n* : Zaïrois *m,* -roise *f*

Zambian[1] [ˈzæmbiən] *adj* : zambien

Zambian[2] *n* : Zambien *m,* -bienne *f*

zany[1] [ˈzeɪni] *adj* **zanier; -est** : farfelu *fam,* loufoque *fam*

zany[2] *n, pl* **-nies** BUFFOON : bouffon *m*

zeal [ˈziːl] *n* : zèle *m,* enthousiasme *m*

zealot [ˈzɛlət] *n* : fanatique *mf;* zélateur *m,* -trice *f*

zealous [ˈzɛləs] *adj* : zélé, dévoué

zealously [ˈzɛləsli] *adv* : avec zèle

zebra [ˈziːbrə] *n* : zèbre *m*

zed [ˈzɛd] *Brit* → **z**

zenith [ˈziːnəθ] *n* : zénith *m,* apogée *m*

zephyr [ˈzɛfər] *n* : zéphyr *m*

zeppelin [ˈzɛplən, -pəlɪn] *n* : zeppelin *m*

zero[1] [ˈziːro, ˈzɪro] *vi* **to zero in on** : se diriger droit sur, faire porter tous ses efforts sur

zero[2] *adj* : zéro, nul <zero growth : croissance zéro>

zero[3] *n, pl* **-ros** : zéro *m*

zest [ˈzɛst] *n* **1** GUSTO : enthousiasme

m, entrain *m* **2** FLAVOR, PIQUANCY : saveur *f,* piquant *m*

zestful ['zɛstfəl] *adj* : enthousiaste, passionné

zestfully ['zɛstfəli] *adv* : avec enthousiasme

zigzag[1] ['zɪg,zæg] *vi* **-zagged; -zagging** : zigzaguer

zigzag[2] *adj & adv* : en zigzag

zigzag[3] *n* : zigzag *m*

Zimbabwean[1] [zɪm'bɑbwiən, -bweɪ-] *adj* : zimbabwéen

Zimbabwean[2] *n* : Zimbabwéen *m,* -wéenne *f*

zinc ['zɪŋk] *n* : zinc *m*

zing ['zɪŋ] *n* **1** HISS, HUM : sifflement *m* **2** ZEST : entrain *m*

zinnia ['zɪniə, 'zi:-, -njə] *n* : zinnia *m*

zip[1] ['zɪp] *v* **zipped; zipping** *vt or* **to zip up** : fermer avec une fermeture à glissière — *vi* **1** DASH : filer à toute allure **2 to zip by** *or* **to zip past** : passer comme une flèche **3** : siffler (se dit d'une balle, etc.)

zip[2] *n* **1** ENERGY, VIM : vitalité *f,* entrain *m* **2** HISSING, HUMMING : sifflement *m*

zip code *n* : code *m* postal

zipper ['zɪpər] *n* : fermeture *f* à glissière

zippy ['zɪpi] *adj* **zippier; -est** LIVELY : vif, entraînant

zircon ['zər,kɑn] *n* : zircon *m*

zirconium [,zər'ko:niəm] *n* : zirconium *m*

zither ['zɪðər, -θər] *n* : cithare *f*

zodiac ['zo:di,æk] *n* : zodiaque *m*

zombie ['zɑmbi] *n* : zombie *m*

zone[1] ['zo:n] *vt* **zoned; zoning 1** : diviser en zones **2 to be zoned for business** : être réservé à l'entreprise

zone[2] *n* : zone *f*

zoo ['zu:] *n, pl* **zoos** : zoo *m*

zookeeper ['zu:,ki:pər] *n* : gardien *m,* -dienne *f* de zoo

zoological [,zo:ə'lɑdʒɪkəl, ,zu:ə-] *adj* : zoologique

zoologist [zo'ɑlədʒɪst, zu:-] *n* : zoologiste *mf*

zoology [zo'ɑlədʒi, zu:-] *n* : zoologie *f*

zoom[1] ['zu:m] *vi* **1** : aller à toute allure <to zoom past : passer comme une trombe> <the plane zoomed up : l'avion a monté en chandelle> **2 to zoom in** : faire un zoom (en photographie)

zoom[2] *n* **1** : bourdonnement *m* (d'un moteur) **2** *or* **zoom lens** : zoom *m*

zucchini [zʊ'ki:ni] *n, pl* **-ni** *or* **-nis** : courgette *f*

zwieback ['swi:,bɑk, 'swaɪ-, 'zwi:-, 'zwaɪ-] *n* : biscotte *f*

zygote ['zaɪ,go:t] *n* : zygote *m*

Common French Abbreviations

FRENCH ABBREVIATION AND EXPANSION		ENGLISH EQUIVALENT	
AB, Alb.	Alberta	**AB, Alta.**	Alberta
ALÉNA	Accord de libre-échange nord-américain	**NAFTA**	North American Free Trade Agreement
AP	assistance publique (France)	—	welfare services
ap. J.-C.	après Jésus-Christ	**AD**	anno Domini
a/s	aux soins de	**c/o**	care of
A.T.	Ancien Testament	**O.T.**	Old Testament
av.	avenue	**ave.**	avenue
av. J.-C.	avant Jésus-Christ	**BC**	before Christ
avr.	avril	**Apr.**	April
BC	Colombie-Britannique	**BC, B.C.**	British Columbia
bd	boulevard	**blvd.**	boulevard
BD	bande dessinée	—	comic strip
BN	Bibliothèque nationale	—	national library
BP	boîte postale	**P.O.B.**	post office box
B.S.	bien-être social (Canada)	—	welfare services
c	centime	**c, ct.**	cent
C	centigrade, Celsius	**C**	centigrade, Celsius
CA	comptable agréé (Canada)	**CPA**	certified public accountant
CA	courant alternatif	**AC**	alternating current
c.-à-d.	c'est-à-dire	**i.e.**	that is
Cap.	capitaine	**Capt.**	captain
C.-B.	Colombie-Britannique	**BC, B.C.**	British Columbia
CC	courant continu	**DC**	direct current
CE	Communauté européenne	**EC**	European Community
CEE	Communauté européenne économique	**EEC**	European Economic Community
cf.	confer	**cf.**	compare
cg	centigramme	**cg**	centigram
chap.	chapitre	**ch., chap.**	chapter
Cie	compagnie	**Co.**	company
cm	centimètre	**cm**	centimeter
col.	colonne	**col.**	column
Col.	colonel	**Col.**	colonel
C.P.	case postale (Canada)	**P.O.B**	post office box
CV	curriculum vitae	**CV**	curriculum vitae
déc.	décembre	**Dec.**	December
dép., dépt.	département	**dept.**	department
DG	directeur général	**CEO**	chief executive officer
dim.	dimanche	**Sun.**	Sunday
dir.	directeur	**dir.**	director

FRENCH ABBREVIATION AND EXPANSION		ENGLISH EQUIVALENT	
DOM	Département(s) d'outre-mer	**—**	French overseas department
dr.	droite	**rt.**	right
Dr	docteur	**Dr.**	doctor
E	Est, est	**E**	East, east
ECG	électrocardiogramme	**EKG**	electrocardiogram
éd.	édition	**ed.**	edition
EPS	éducation physique et sportive	**PE**	physical education
etc.	et caetera, et cetera	**etc.**	et cetera
É.-U.	États-Unis	**US**	United States
F	Fahrenheit	**F**	Fahrenheit
F	franc	**fr.**	franc
FAB	franco à bord	**FOB**	free on board
FB	franc belge	**—**	Belgian franc
févr.	février	**Feb.**	February
FF	franc français	**—**	French franc
FMI	Fonds monétaire international	**IMF**	International Monetary Fund
g	gauche	**l., L**	left
g	gramme	**g**	gram
Gén.	général	**Gen.**	general
h	heure(s)	**hr.**	hour
ha	hectare	**ha**	hectare
HS	hors service	**—**	out of order
i.e.	c'est-à-dire	**i.e.**	that is
IPC	indice des prix à la consommation	**CPI**	consumer price index
Î.P.-É	île-du-Prince-Édouard	**PE, P.E.I.**	Prince Edward Island
janv.	janvier	**Jan.**	January
jeu.	jeudi	**Thurs.**	Thursday
juill.	juillet	**Jul.**	July
kg	kilogramme	**kg**	kilogram
km	kilomètre	**km**	kilometer
l	litre	**l**	liter
lun.	lundi	**Mon.**	Monday
m	mètre	**m.**	meter
M.	monsieur	**—**	Mr., mister
mar.	mardi	**Tues.**	Tuesday
MB, Man.	Manitoba	**MB, Man.**	Manitoba
mer.	mercredi	**Wed.**	Wednesday
Mgr.	Monseigneur	**Mgr., Msgr.**	Monsignor, Monseigneur
min	minute	**min.**	minute
MLF	mouvement de libération des femmes	**—**	—
Mlle	Mademoiselle	**—**	Ms., Miss
Mme	Madame	**—**	Ms., Mrs.
MST	maladie sexuellement transmissible	**STD**	sexually transmitted disease

FRENCH ABBREVIATION AND EXPANSION		ENGLISH EQUIVALENT	
N	Nord, nord	**N**	North, north
N°, n°	numéro	**no.**	number
NB, N.-B.	Nouveau-Brunswick	**NB, N.B.**	New Brunswick
n.d.	non daté	**n.d.**	no date, not dated
n.d.	non disponible	**NA**	not available
NF	Terre-Neuve	**NF, Nfld.**	Newfoundland
nov.	novembre	**Nov.**	November
NS, N.-É.	Nouvelle-Écosse	**NS, N.S.**	Nova Scotia
N.T.	Nouveau Testament	**N.T.**	New Testament
NT	Territoires du Nord-Ouest	**NT, N.T.**	Northwest Territories
O	Ouest, ouest	**W**	West, west
oc	ondes courtes	**s-w**	short wave
oct.	octobre	**Oct.**	October
OIT	Organisation internationale du travail	**ILO**	International Labor Organization
OMS	Organisation mondiale de la santé	**WHO**	World Health Organization
ON	Ontario	**ON, Ont.**	Ontario
ONG	organisation non gouvernementale	**NGO**	nongovernmental organization
Ont.	Ontario	**ON**	Ontario
ONU	Organisation des Nations Unies	**UN**	United Nations
OTAN	Organisation du traité de l'Atlantique Nord	**NATO**	North Atlantic Treaty Organization
OVNI, ovni	objet volant non identifié	**UFO**	unidentified flying object
p.	page	**p.**	page
P.	Père	**Fr.**	Father
PCV	paiement contre vérification	—	collect call
PDG	président-directeur général	**CEO**	chief executive officer
p.-ê.	peut-être	—	maybe
PE	Île-du-Prince-Édouard	**PE, P.E.I.**	Prince Edward Island
p. ex.	par exemple	**e.g.**	for example
PIB	produit intérieur brut	**GDP**	gross domestic product
PNB	produit national brut	**GNP**	gross national product
P.-S.	post-scriptum	**P.S.**	postscript
QC	Québec	**QC, Que.**	Quebec
QG	quartier général	**HQ**	headquarters
QI	quotient intellectuel	**IQ**	intelligence quotient
R-D	recherche-développement	**R and D**	research and development
réf.	référence	**ref.**	reference
RF	République Française	—	France
RN	route nationale	—	interstate highway
RV	rendez-vous	**rdv., R.V.**	rendezvous

FRENCH ABBREVIATION AND EXPANSION		ENGLISH EQUIVALENT	
s.	siècle	**c., cent.**	century
S	Sud, sud	**S, so.**	South, south
SA	société anonyme	**Inc.**	incorporated (company)
sam.	samedi	**Sat.**	Saturday
SARL	société à responsabilité limitée	**Ltd.**	limited (corporation)
Sask.	Saskatchewan	**SK, Sask.**	Saskatchewan
SDF	sans domicile fixe	**—**	homeless (person)
sept.	septembre	**Sept.**	September
Sgt.	sergent	**Sgt.**	sergeant
SK	Saskatchewan	**SK, Sask.**	Saskatchewan
SM	Sa Majesté	**HM**	His Majesty, Her Majesty
SME	Système monétaire européen	**—**	European Monetary System
S.S.	Sa Sainteté	**H.H.**	His Holiness
St	saint	**St.**	Saint
Ste	sainte	**St.**	Saint
SVP	s'il vous plaît	**pls.**	please
t	tonne	**t., tn.**	ton
tél.	téléphone	**tel.**	telephone
T.-N.	Terre-Neuve	**NF, Nfld.**	Newfoundland
T.N.-O.	Territoires du Nord-Ouest	**NT, N.T.**	Northwest Territories
TVA	taxe à valeur ajoutée	**VAT**	value-added tax
UE	Union européenne	**EU**	European Union
univ.	université	**U., univ.**	university
V., v.	voir	**vid.**	see
ven.	vendredi	**Fri.**	Friday
vol.	volume	**vol.**	volume
VPC	vente par correspondance	**—**	mail-order selling
vs	versus	**v., vs.**	versus
W-C	water closet	**w.c.**	water closet
YT, Yuk.	Yukon	**YT, Y.T.**	Yukon Territory

French Numbers

Cardinal Numbers

1	un
2	deux
3	trois
4	quatre
5	cinq
6	six
7	sept
8	huit
9	neuf
10	dix
11	onze
12	douze
13	treize
14	quatorze
15	quinze
16	seize
17	dix-sept
18	dix-huit
19	dix-neuf
20	vingt
21	vingt et un
22	vingt-deux
23	vingt-trois
24	vingt-quatre
25	vingt-cinq
26	vingt-six
27	vingt-sept
28	vingt-huit
29	vingt-neuf
30	trente
31	trente et un
32	trente-deux
33	trente-trois
34	trente-quatre
35	trente-cinq
36	trente-six
37	trente-sept
38	trente-huit
39	trente-neuf
40	quarante
41	quarante et un
50	cinquante
60	soixante
70	soixante-dix
80	quatre-vingts
90	quatre-vingt-dix
100	cent
101	cent un
102	cent deux
200	deux cents
300	trois cents
400	quatre cents
500	cinq cents
600	six cents
700	sept cents
800	huit cents
900	neuf cents
1 000	mille
1 001	mille un
2 000	deux mille
100 000	cent mille
1 000 000	un million
1 000 000 000	un milliard

Ordinal Numbers

1st	premier, première	16th	seizième
2nd	deuxième *or* second	17th	dix-septième
3rd	troisième	18th	dix-huitième
4th	quatrième	19th	dix-neuvième
5th	cinquième	20th	vingtième
6th	sixième	21st	vingt et unième
7th	septième	22nd	vingt-deuxième
8th	huitième	30th	trentième
9th	neuvième	40th	quarantième
10th	dixième	50th	cinquantième
11th	onzième	60th	soixantième
12th	douzième	70th	soixante-dixième
13th	treizième	80th	quatre-vingtième
14th	quatorzième	90th	quatre-vingt-dixième
15th	quinzième	100th	centième